Welfare Benefits and Tax Credits Handbook

19th edition

Child Poverty Action Group

Child Poverty Action Group works on behalf of the one in four children in the UK growing up in poverty. It does not have to be like this. We use our understanding of what causes poverty and the impact it has on children's lives to campaign for policies that will prevent and solve poverty – for good. We provide training, advice and information to make sure hard-up families get the financial support they need. We also carry out high-profile legal work to establish and protect families' rights. If you are not already supporting us, please consider making a donation, or ask for details of our membership schemes, training courses and publications.

Published by Child Poverty Action Group
30 Micawber Street
London N1 7TB
Tel: 020 7837 7979
staff@cpag.org.uk
www.cpag.org.uk

A CIP record for this book is available from the British Library
ISBN: 978 1 910715 23 9

Child Poverty Action Group is a charity registered in England and Wales (registration number 294841) and in Scotland (registration number SC039339), and is a company limited by guarantee, registered in England (registration number 1993854). VAT number: 690 808117

Cover design by Colorido Studios
Typeset by David Lewis XML Associates Ltd
Content management system by Konnect Soft
Printed by CPI Group (UK) Ltd, Croydon CR0 4YY

The authors

Mark Brough is a freelance writer. He previously worked for many years as a welfare rights adviser for people with learning disabilities.

Barbara Donegan is a welfare rights worker at CPAG in Scotland.

Carolyn George is a freelance trainer and writer on welfare rights.

Alison Gillies is a welfare rights worker at CPAG in Scotland.

Daphne Hall is an editor for *Rightsnet*, and a freelance trainer and writer on welfare rights.

Gwyneth King is a welfare rights worker at CPAG in Scotland.

Henri Krishna is a welfare rights worker at CPAG in Scotland.

Susan Mitchell is a welfare rights adviser and freelance writer on welfare rights.

Paul Moorhouse has 30 years' experience of advice work in voluntary and statutory agencies. He works as a freelance author on welfare rights.

Daniel Norris is a welfare rights worker at CPAG.

Simon Osborne is a welfare rights worker at CPAG, based at CPAG in Scotland.

Judith Paterson is CPAG in Scotland's welfare rights co-ordinator.

Jon Shaw is a researcher at the Scottish Parliament Information Centre. He previously worked as a welfare rights worker at CPAG in Scotland.

David Simmons is a welfare rights worker at CPAG.

Angela Toal is a welfare rights worker at CPAG in Scotland.

Paul Treloar is Senior Technical Advice Support Officer with Age UK.

Nick Turnill is a freelance welfare rights worker at CPAG.

Rebecca Walker is a freelance trainer and writer on welfare rights.

Martin Williams is a welfare rights worker at CPAG.

Mark Willis is a welfare rights worker at CPAG in Scotland.

Acknowledgements

The authors would like to thank Barbara Gray, Will Hadwen, Arnie James, David Malcolm, Kelly Smith and Ros White for their invaluable contribution.

Our thanks are also due to Simon Osborne for acting as the book's content consultant.

We must acknowledge the efforts of the many authors of previous editions of the *National Welfare Benefits Handbook*, the *Rights Guide to Non-Means-Tested Benefits* and the *Jobseeker's Allowance Handbook*, on which this book is based.

Thanks are also due to Nicola Johnston and Alison Key for once again editing and managing the production of the book so efficiently, and to Kathleen Armstrong, Anne Ketley and Pauline Phillips, for proofreading the text. Particular thanks must go to Katherine Dawson and Anne Ketley for producing the index.

We would also like to thank staff at the Department for Work and Pensions, the Child Support Agency, HM Revenue and Customs, HM Courts and Tribunals Service and the Department for Education for their help and co-operation.

Thanks to the staff at KonnectSoft, David Lewis XML Associates and CPI William Clowes for keeping up with our schedules.

The law covered in this book was correct on 6 March 2017 and includes regulations laid up to this date.

Foreword

Welcome to the 2017/18 edition of the *Welfare Benefits and Tax Credits Handbook*. This *Handbook* remains indispensable for anyone undertaking welfare rights advice. It provides comprehensive information and, crucially, the relevant law to challenge decisions. With your support, the book evolves every year to better meet the needs of advisers and the families they help. Please do let me or colleagues here know your suggestions for future editions.

We have been talking about universal credit for some time now – it feels an age since the white paper proposing it was published in 2011. At one stage, the steady accumulation of delays, ministerial obfuscation and damning National Audit Office reports seemed to place its future in doubt. But that moment has passed.

Now, it feels like we may have passed a point of no return. Whatever we think of its strengths and weaknesses, universal credit is coming. The roll-out of the 'full service' appears to be happening on time, and it undoubtedly remains a key – if not *the* key – priority for the new Work and Pensions Secretary.

Building a dialogue with welfare rights advisers on what is working well and what aspects of the roll-out are causing problems should be a DWP priority. It is early days yet, but we are hopeful that the DWP will be more willing to listen and to take a pragmatic approach than it has done in the past.

CPAG's 'early warning system' project in Scotland is a fine example of how this can be done. Over 3,000 cases have been gathered from frontline workers, including welfare rights advisers, housing officers and support workers. These have informed our policy work, influencing local authorities and leading to a number of service development improvements. We are excited to say that in the coming year, thanks to funding from the Oak Foundation and the Barrow Cadbury Trust, we will continue to expand the project to the rest of the UK. This work will strengthen CPAG's evidence base and ensure our campaigning work continues to be informed not only by our in-depth knowledge of the social security system, but also by the realities on the ground – enabling us to put problems in their proper context and identify solutions that work.

I strongly encourage users of this *Handbook*, whether experienced welfare rights officers or people for whom advice is a small part of their job, to sign up to CPAG's 'early warning system' and submit examples of where the system is not working. You can go to the CPAG website for more details.

Of course, it is one thing to provide early warning of problems and propose solutions to fix them, but quite another for them to be acted on by policymakers. As I say, it is early days, but we are hopeful. I am sure that the DWP is as determined as we are to avoid a universal credit 'meltdown' – the fall-out for families (and politically) would be huge.

But there are some well-publicised problems with universal credit on which we, and others, have already provided early warning and have seen little action – most notably, its adequacy in helping families with their living costs. The 2015 summer Budget, on average, left people worse off on universal credit than tax credits. Cross-party concern led to the Chancellor acknowledging the problem, offering an improved taper rate for universal credit, but no real solution.

Not only are people worse off under universal credit than they were under tax credits, but they are also worse off on today's version of universal credit than the version originally introduced in 2013. New CPAG analysis, commissioned from the Institute for Public Policy Research, shows that while improvements in the taper rate and help for childcare have benefited families, for many these have been overwhelmed by a litany of other cuts, most notably a failure to uprate benefits with inflation and cuts to work allowances. Overall, families with children have been hit the hardest. Universal credit would have taken 350,000 children out of poverty in 2011. This had dropped to 150,000 in 2013, and it may come as no surprise to learn that the DWP is no longer willing to say whether its flagship poverty policy will lift any children out of poverty at all.

In this edition of the *Handbook*, we have made a special effort to incorporate as much as we know about the 'two-child limit', which comes into force in April 2017. A policy that says not all children are equal will undoubtedly drive up child poverty and implementing it will be an exercise in bureaucratic meddling in the most personal of family decisions.

Universal credit may be coming, but it is clear that it is hamstrung by severe funding, policy design and practical problems. Its revolutionary promises have long faded. We now face the very real prospect of a large, single – and flawed – means test bearing down on working-age families. We are running out of time to avert a crash landing.

CPAG's urgent role is to work with advisers around the country – in CABx and advice centres, in local government and in the voluntary sector – to secure improvements to protect families as much as we can. Just as this *Handbook* is indispensable, the welfare rights movement is too.

Alison Garnham
Chief Executive

Contents

Part 1   **Introduction**

Provides an overview of the benefits and tax credits system and explains how to use this book. Use this part to find out how to identify which benefits, tax credits or statutory payments you can get and the amount you should receive, and to understand how to use the book to find answers to specific questions about your entitlement.

Part 2   **Main means-tested benefits and tax credits**

Contains chapters on all the main means-tested benefits and tax credits. Use this part if you are on a low income to check whether you qualify for means-tested benefits or tax credits, and to understand how and when you might be affected by the introduction of universal credit.

Contents

Part 6   **Special benefit rules**

Explains how particular circumstances, such as going into hospital, affect your entitlement to benefits and statutory payments. Use this part if any of the circumstances apply to you.

Part 7   **Work and work-related rules**

Outlines the national insurance contribution conditions for contributory benefits and when you might qualify for national insurance credits, and explains the benefit rules on work and limited capability for work. Use this part to check whether you qualify for contributory benefits, to find out how work affects your benefit entitlement, what you may have do to prepare for and find work in order to get benefit, and what might happen if you do not do so.

Contents

Abbreviations

AA	attendance allowance	ICE	Independent Case Examiner
CA	carer's allowance	IIDB	industrial injuries disablement benefit
CAB	Citizens Advice Bureau	IS	income support
CCST	Communications and Customer Service Team	ISA	individual savings account
		JSA	jobseeker's allowance
CJEU	Court of Justice of the European Union	MA	maternity allowance
CMS	Child Maintenance Service	MS	Medical Service
CPI	Consumer Prices Index	NI	national insurance
CRU	Compensation Recovery Unit	NICO	National Insurance Contributions Office
CSA	Child Support Agency	PAYE	pay as you earn
CTB	council tax benefit	PC	pension credit
CTC	child tax credit	PIP	personal independence payment
DLA	disability living allowance	REA	reduced earnings allowance
DWP	Department for Work and Pensions	SAAS	Student Awards Agency for Scotland
EC	European Community	SAP	statutory adoption pay
ECtHR	European Court of Human Rights	SAYE	save as you earn
EEA	European Economic Area	SDA	severe disablement allowance
EO	employment officer	SMP	statutory maternity pay
ESA	employment and support allowance	SPP	statutory paternity pay
EU	European Union	SSP	statutory sick pay
EWC	expected week of childbirth	SSPP	statutory shared parental pay
HB	housing benefit	TCO	Tax Credit Office
HMCTS	HM Courts and Tribunals Service	UC	universal credit
HMRC	HM Revenue and Customs	UEST	Under Eighteens Support Team
IB	incapacity benefit	WTC	working tax credit

Means-tested benefit rates

Income support/income-based jobseeker's allowance

Personal allowances

		£pw
Single	Under 25	57.90
	25 or over	73.10
Lone parent	Under 18	57.90
	18 or over	73.10
Couple	Both under 18	57.90
	Both under 18, certain cases	87.50
	One under 18, one 18–24	57.90
	One under 18, one 25 or over	73.10
	One under 18, certain cases	114.85
	Both 18 or over	114.85

Premiums

Carer		34.95
Disability	Single	32.55
	Couple	46.40
Enhanced disability	Single	15.90
	Couple	22.85
Severe disability	One qualifies	62.45
	Two qualify	124.90
Pensioner	Single (jobseeker's allowance only)	86.25
	Couple	128.40

Children

(Pre-6 April 2004 claims with no child tax credit)

Child under 20 personal allowance	66.90
Family premium	17.45
Disabled child premium	60.90
Enhanced disability premium (child)	24.78

Capital limits

	Lower	Upper
Standard	6,000	16,000
Care homes	10,000	16,000

Tariff income: £1 per £250 between lower and upper limit

Income-related employment and support allowance

		Assessment phase	Main phase
Personal allowances			
Single	Under 25	57.90	73.10
	25 or over	73.10	73.10
Lone parent	Under 18	57.90	73.10
	18 or over	73.10	73.10
Couple	One or both under 18	57.90–114.85	73.10–114.85
	Both 18 or over	114.85	114.85

Components			
Work-related activity		–	29.05
Support		–	36.55

Premiums			
Carer		34.95	34.95
Severe disability (one qualifies)		62.45	62.45
Severe disability (two qualify)		124.90	124.90
Enhanced disability	Single	15.90	15.90
	Couple	22.85	22.85
Pensioner	Single, no component	86.25	–
	Couple, no component	128.40	–
	Single, work-related activity component	–	57.20
	Couple, work-related activity component	–	99.35
	Single, support component	–	49.70
	Couple, support component	–	91.85

Capital limits
As for income support

Pension credit
Guarantee credit

Standard minimum guarantee	Single	159.35
	Couple	243.25
Severe disability addition	One qualifies	62.45
	Two qualify	124.90
Carer addition		34.95

Savings credit

Threshold	Single	137.35
	Couple	218.42
Maximum	Single	13.20
	Couple	14.90

Capital disregard
Standard/care homes   10,000
No upper limit
Deemed income: £1 per £500 above disregard

Housing benefit
Personal allowances

Single	Under 25	57.90
	Under 25 (on main phase ESA)	73.10
	25 or over	73.10
Lone parent	Under 18	57.90
	Under 18 (on main phase ESA)	73.10
	18 or over	73.10
Couple	Both under 18	87.50
	Both under 18 (claimant on main phase ESA)	114.85
	One or both 18 or over	114.85
Dependent children	Under 20	66.90
Over qualifying age for pension credit	Single under 65	159.35
	Single 65 or over	172.55
	Couple both under 65	243.25
	Couple one or both 65 or over	258.15

Components

Work-related activity	–	29.05
Support	–	36.55

Premiums

Carer		34.95
Disability	Single	32.55
	Couple	46.40
Disabled child		60.90
Enhanced disability	Single	15.90
	Couple	22.85
	Child	24.78
Severe disability	One qualifies	62.45
	Two qualify	124.90
Family	Ordinary rate	17.45
	Some lone parents	22.20

Capital limits

	Lower	Upper
Standard	6,000	16,000
Care home or over pension credit qualifying age	10,000	16,000

Tariff income £1 per £250 between lower and upper limit
£1 per £500 for those over qualifying age for pension credit
No upper limit or tariff income for those on pension credit guarantee credit

Social fund payments

Maternity grant		500.00
Cold weather payment		25.00
Winter fuel payment	Under 80	200.00
(over qualifying age for pension	80 or over	300.00
credit)	Care home (under 80)	100.00
	Care home (80 or over)	150.00

Universal credit
Standard allowance

		£pm
Single	Under 25	251.77
	25 or over	317.82
Couple	Both under 25	395.20
	One or both 25 or over	498.89

Elements

First child		277.08
Second child and each subsequent child who qualifies		231.67
Disabled child addition	Lower rate	126.11
	Higher rate	372.30
Limited capability for work		126.11
Limited capability for work-related activity		318.76
Carer		151.89
Childcare costs	One child	up to 646.35
	Two or more children	up to 1,108.04
	Percentage covered	85%

Capital limits

	Lower	Upper
	6,000	16,000

Tariff income £4.35 per £250 between lower and upper limits

Non-means-tested benefit rates

	£pw
Attendance allowance	
Higher rate	83.10
Lower rate	55.65
Bereavement benefits	
Bereavement payment (lump sum)	2,000
Bereavement allowance/widow's pension	
45–54	34.11–105.74
55 or over	113.70
Widowed parent's allowance/widowed mother's allowance	113.70
Bereavement support payment	
Higher rate	
Lump sum	3,500
Monthly amount	350.00
Standard rate	
Lump sum	2,500
Monthly amount	100.00
Carer's allowance	62.70
Adult dependant (some existing claimants only)	36.90
Child benefit	
Only/eldest child	20.70
Other child(ren)	13.70
Increase for child	
(some existing claimants only)	
Only/eldest child	8.00
Other child(ren)	11.35
Partner's earnings limits	
Only/eldest child	230.00
Additional amount for each other child	30.00

Disability living allowance
Care component
Highest rate	83.10
Middle rate	55.65
Lowest rate	22.00

Mobility component
Higher rate	58.00
Lower rate	22.00

Contributory employment and support allowance
Assessment phase
Under 25	57.90
25 or over	73.10

Main phase
16 or over	73.10
Work-related activity component	29.05
Support component	36.55

Guardian's allowance | 16.70

Short-term incapacity benefit
Under pension age
Lower rate	80.25
Higher rate	95.00
Adult dependant	48.15

Over pension age
Lower rate	102.10
Higher rate	106.40
Adult dependant	59.50

Long-term incapacity benefit | 106.40
Age addition (under 35)	11.25
Age addition (35–44)	6.25
Adult dependant	61.80

Industrial injuries disablement benefit | 20%: £33.94 to 100%: £169.70

Contribution-based jobseeker's allowance
Under 25	57.90
25 or over	73.10

Maternity allowance
Standard rate	140.98

Personal independence payment
Daily living component

Standard rate	55.65
Enhanced rate	83.10

Mobility component

Standard rate	22.00
Enhanced rate	58.00

Retirement pensions

State pension (full rate)	159.55
Category A	122.30
Adult dependant (some existing claimants only)	66.35
Category B (widow(er)/surviving civil partner)	122.30
Category B (spouse/civil partner)	73.30
Category D	73.30

Severe disablement allowance

	75.40
Age addition (under 40)	11.25
Age addition (40–49)	6.25
Age addition (50–59)	6.25
Adult dependant	37.10

Statutory maternity, adoption, paternity and shared parental pay

Standard rate	140.98

Statutory sick pay

	89.35

National insurance contributions

Lower earnings limit	113.00
Primary threshold	157.00
Employee's class 1 rate	12% of £157 to £866
	2% above £866
Class 2 rate (self-employed)	2.85

Tax credit rates

	£ per day	£ per year
Child tax credit		
Family element	1.50	545
Child element	7.62	2,780
Disabled child element	8.70	3,175
Severely disabled child element	3.54	1,290
Working tax credit		
Basic element	5.37	1,960
Couple element	5.51	2,010
Lone parent element	5.51	2,010
30-hour element	2.22	810
Disabled worker element	8.22	3000
Severe disability element	3.54	1,290
Childcare element		
70% of eligible weekly childcare costs :		
One child		weekly maximum 175
Two or more children		weekly maximum 300
Thresholds		
Income threshold		
Working tax credit only or with child tax credit		6,420
Child tax credit only		16,105
Taper		41%
Income decrease disregard		2,500
Income increase disregard		2,500

Part 1

Introduction

Chapter 1

How to use this book

This chapter covers:
1. About this *Handbook* (below)
2. Using this *Handbook* (p4)
3. How this *Handbook* is organised (p5)
4. Finding out which benefits and tax credits you can get (p8)
5. Working out how much benefit you should receive (p14)
6. Finding information on challenging a decision (p15)

1. **About this** *Handbook*

This *Handbook* is the definitive guide to benefits, tax credits and statutory payments, condensing a huge and complex area of law into a comprehensive and user-friendly book. It contains everything you need to know in order to understand your entitlement to benefits, tax credits and statutory payments, and aims to answer any questions you may have about your entitlement. The book explains how you claim and how much money you should get, how decisions are made and how to get them changed. It provides examples to illustrate how the rules work in practice and tactics to help you deal with common problems.

The book also helps you find the specific legislation, caselaw or official guidance relevant to the information contained in the text, should you need it.

If you are an adviser, this *Handbook* is an essential tool, containing all you need to provide practical, effective and accurate advice.

Northern Ireland and Scotland
The information in this *Handbook* applies to Great Britain.
Northern Ireland has its own benefits and tax credits legislation. Although the rules are very similar to those in Great Britain, the administration and adjudicating bodies may have different names, and sometimes the law in Northern Ireland is different – eg, because a particular rule or benefit does not yet apply there.

1

The Scottish Parliament has the power to make its own rules on payments to meet the needs currently covered by discretionary housing payments and to change some limited aspects of universal credit in Scotland. It can also top up some benefits and payments and introduce certain kinds of new ones. In the future, it will be able to make its own rules on payments to meet the needs currently covered by social fund payments (except budgeting loans) and to meet the needs of carers and people with a disability or health condition, which are currently provided through personal independence payment, disability living allowance, attendance allowance, industrial injuries disablement benefit, severe disablement allowance and carer's allowance.

2. Using this *Handbook*

There is a large amount of information in this *Handbook*, but you do not need to read it from cover to cover to find out about your benefit entitlement. If you are unfamiliar with the benefits system, a good place to start is the section in this chapter called 'Finding out which benefits and tax credits you can get' (p8). This explains the best way to determine which benefits, tax credits or statutory payments you may qualify for and to establish how they interact with each other.

If you want to find the answer to a particular question, or to understand the rules for a specific benefit, it should be easy to locate the information you need by using the detailed index or by using the individual benefit, tax credit and statutory payment chapters as your starting point.

Using the index

A simple way to find specific information in this book is to use the index. The index is designed to be detailed and intuitive to ensure you can easily locate the information you need.
- Use the entries in bold type, arranged alphabetically, to help you to find general information on a subject.
- Use the sub-entries under these, also arranged alphabetically, to find more specific information relevant to the question you have.
- Use the list at the start of the index to understand the abbreviations used.

For example, if you want to find information on how to claim attendance allowance, you can locate this either by looking up 'claims' and finding the 'AA' sub-heading underneath, or by looking up 'attendance allowance' and finding the 'claims' sub-heading underneath.

Using the individual benefit chapters

Another good starting point for finding specific information in this book is the chapter on the particular benefit, tax credit or statutory payment to which your question relates. These chapters follow a common structure to help you find the information contained in them easily, and they refer you to other relevant information that is elsewhere in the book.

- Find the chapter about the particular benefit, tax credit or statutory payment by using the contents list on p7. Find the relevant part of the book and then locate the appropriate chapter in that part. To assist with this, tabs on the side of each page identify the number of the part you are in. The parts and chapters are also identified at the top of each page.
- Familiarise yourself with the standard way information is presented in these chapters (see p7). This will help you to locate information in the text easily. For example, if you want to know whether there are age limits for claiming a particular benefit, it is helpful to know that each chapter has a section called 'The rules about your age'.
- Alternatively, use the chapter contents to direct you to the likely section in the chapter to check. The section of each chapter is identified at the top of the left-hand pages of the book.
- Follow any cross references in the text to find any other relevant information contained in the book.

Finding the law

To help you trace the source of the information given in the text, this *Handbook* provides references to the law (both legislation and caselaw) and to guidance. It may be helpful to refer to these references, particularly if you are challenging a decision, as they provide the legal justification for the statements made in the text. For a useful introduction to legal sources, see pp1347–51.

- Find the information in the book relevant to the issue you want to check and find the note for that information.
- Check the relevant note at the end of the chapter for the legal reference.
- Check Appendix 13 for an explanation of the abbreviations used in the references.
- See Appendices 2 and 3 for where to find the law and guidance online and for other useful sources of information.

The law referred to in this *Handbook* only applies in Great Britain. For information on the law in Northern Ireland, see p3.

3. How this *Handbook* is organised

The book is split into parts, and related chapters are grouped under these parts. A description of the information covered in each part, together with a list of chapters it contains, is included in the table of contents on p7.

Part 1: Introduction
Chapter 1: How to use this book
3. How this *Handbook* is organised

By developing a basic understanding of the purpose of each part, you can immediately identify where certain information will be in the book. For example, once you know that Part 11 covers your benefit entitlement if you are a European Economic Area (EEA) national or a person subject to immigration control, or if you are going or coming from abroad, you know to use this part if you need to check whether your immigration status affects your right to a particular benefit.

Similarly, the common structure of many of the chapters is designed to make it easier to find information in them.

How the parts are organised

The parts of the *Handbook* are:
- **Part 1:** Introduction.
- **Part 2:** Main means-tested benefits and tax credits. This contains chapters on each of the main means-tested benefits and tax credits and a chapter explaining how and when the introduction of universal credit (UC) affects you.
- **Part 3:** General rules for means-tested benefits. This contains chapters explaining who is included in a claim for a means-tested benefit and how your needs, income and capital affect your entitlement and the amount you receive.
- **Part 4:** Paying for housing. This contains chapters explaining the rules about the help you can get with certain housing costs, including mortgage interest and rent, if you are on a low income, and the rules on discretionary housing payments.
- **Part 5:** Other benefits. This contains chapters on non-means-tested benefits, statutory payments and other help you may get, arranged in alphabetical order.
- **Part 6:** Special benefit rules. This contains chapters explaining the rules for particular groups of people, including students, people in hospital or care homes, prisoners and people leaving care.
- **Part 7:** Work and work-related rules. This contains chapters covering the national insurance (NI) contribution conditions for contributory benefits and the qualifying conditions for NI credits, how work affects your benefit entitlement, how your capacity for work is assessed, and the conditions you may have to meet to prepare for or find work, and what happens if you do not meet them.
- **Part 8:** Claiming benefits and getting paid. This contains chapters on claiming and backdating benefit, how and when you should be paid, whether you are entitled to hardship payments or affected by the benefit cap, and information on overpayments and penalties.
- **Part 9:** Getting a benefit decision changed. This contains chapters on challenging decisions and how to complain.
- **Part 10:** General rules for tax credits. This contains chapters on the general rules for tax credits, including how your entitlement is worked out, how to make a claim and how to challenge decisions.

- **Part 11:** Immigration and residence rules for benefits and tax credits. This contains chapters explaining your entitlement if you are an EEA national or a person subject to immigration control, and if you are going to, or coming from, abroad.
- **Appendices.** These contain further information, such as useful addresses, relevant dates and the legislation on particular assessments.

How the chapters are organised

To help you locate information easily, many of the *Handbook* chapters have a similar structure. Each chapter contains the following.
- **Chapter contents:** to help you find the section you need.
- **Key facts:** covering the key points about the information in the chapter. If the chapter is about a specific benefit, tax credit or statutory payment, these include certain standard information, such as how work affects your entitlement, whether the benefit is means tested, whether you must have paid NI contributions to qualify and who administers your claim.
- **Endnotes:** to the numbered references in the text. These are at the end of each chapter and, in most cases, cite the legal source of the information in the text.

The chapters on specific benefits, tax credits and statutory payments also follow a similar structure, with the information organised under the following headings.
- **Who can claim:** the qualifying rules for that benefit, tax credit or statutory payment.
- **The rules about your age:** any age limits that are relevant.
- **People included in the claim:** who you can claim for, or whether you have to make a joint claim with someone else.
- **The amount of benefit:** the rules about how much money you should receive, with cross references to rules that are common to more than one benefit or tax credit.
- **Special benefit rules:** to alert you to when there are additional rules that apply to people in particular circumstances – eg, people in hospital.
- **Claims and backdating:** how to claim, who should claim, the information you must provide to support your claim, the date your claim is treated as having been made, whether your claim can be backdated, whether a claim for one benefit can be treated as a claim for another, and when claims can be made in advance.
- **Getting paid:** how and when you are paid, and what to do if your circumstances change.
- **Tax, other benefits and the benefit cap:** whether the benefit, tax credit or statutory payment is taxable, how it interacts with other benefits or tax credits, and whether it is affected by rules on the benefit cap. Plus information on other help you may get.

Part 1: Introduction
Chapter 1: How to use this book
4. Finding out which benefits and tax credits you can get

1

The text under these headings refers you to any other information in the book that is relevant. This is to ensure that, not only is information easy to find within each chapter, but also that you can answer almost any question you have on your entitlement by using the individual benefit, tax credit or statutory payment chapter as a starting point.

4. Finding out which benefits and tax credits you can get

To find out about all the help you can get, it is important to check your entitlement in the following order.
- First check whether you qualify for any non-means-tested benefits or statutory payments.
- Next, check your entitlement to means-tested benefits.
- Finally, check whether there is any other help available to you.

Step one: do you qualify for any non-means-tested benefits or statutory payments?

What are non-means-tested benefits and statutory payments?
A non-means-tested benefit is a benefit for which it is not necessary to carry out a detailed assessment of your income or capital to work out your entitlement. You may need to meet national insurance contribution conditions to qualify for some non-means-tested benefits ('contributory benefits') and you may qualify for others just because of your circumstances. Certain non-means-tested benefits ('earnings-replacement benefits') are intended to compensate you for loss of earnings. Your entitlement to non-means-tested benefits is not affected by any savings that you have and your income only affects your entitlement to some earnings-replacement benefits.

Statutory payments are payments an employer may be required to pay you if you are an employee and are unfit for work or off work on maternity, paternity, adoption or shared parental leave. Your entitlement to statutory payments depends on the level of your past earnings (and, for statutory shared parental pay, the past earnings of your partner in the application), but it is not affected by any other income or savings you have.

Both jobseeker's allowance (JSA) and employment and support allowance (ESA) have a non-means-tested, contributory element (contribution-based JSA and contributory ESA) and a means-tested element (income-based JSA and income-related ESA). Depending on your circumstances, and on whether you come under the universal credit (UC) system, you may qualify for either or both elements. If you qualify for both, in effect, the means-tested element tops up the contributory element, so check your entitlement to the contributory element first. If you come under the UC system, you cannot qualify for income-based JSA or income-related ESA (see p20).

- Use the table below to see which non-means-tested benefits or statutory payments you might get. Check the benefits under all the circumstances that apply to you.
- Check which of these are 'earnings-replacement benefits' (these are marked with an * in the table).
- Turn to the chapter on the benefits you are interested in, looking at any earnings-replacement benefits or statutory payments first. The chapters are arranged in alphabetical order in Part 5.
- Check whether you meet the qualifying conditions for the benefit by looking at the section 'Who can claim'. Cross references take you to further details you may need to check.
- Look in the section 'Tax, other benefits and the benefits cap' for details of how the benefit might be affected by other benefits you already get or want to claim. Because of the 'overlapping benefit' rules, certain non-means-tested benefits cannot be paid in full at the same time.
- If you think you qualify, use the section 'How to claim' for further information on what to do next.

Your circumstances	Benefits you might get	Chapter
Bereaved	Bereavement support allowance* or	Chapter24
	Bereavement payment	Chapter 24
	Widowed parent's allowance*	Chapter 24
	Bereavement allowance*	Chapter 24
Carer	Carer's allowance*	Chapter 25
Pregnant or have recently given birth	Statutory maternity pay	Chapter 37
	Maternity allowance*	Chapter 33
	Statutory paternity pay	Chapter 37
	Statutory shared parental pay	Chapter 37
	Child benefit	Chapter 26
Recently adopted a child	Statutory adoption pay	Chapter 37
	Statutory paternity pay	Chapter 37
	Statutory shared parental pay	Chapter 37
	Child benefit	Chapter 26
Father of a baby or partner of someone who has recently given birth or adopted a child	Statutory paternity pay	Chapter 37
	Statutory shared parental pay	Chapter 37
Responsible for a child	Child benefit	Chapter 26
	Guardian's allowance	Chapter 26
Disabled (including a disabled child)	Disability living allowance	Chapter 27
	Personal independence payment	Chapter 34
	Attendance allowance	Chapter 23
	Industrial injuries benefits	Chapter 31

Part 1: Introduction
Chapter 1: How to use this book
4. Finding out which benefits and tax credits you can get

1

Unfit for work	Contributory employment and support allowance*	Chapter 28
	Statutory sick pay	Chapter 38
	Industrial injuries benefits	Chapter 31
Pensioner	State pension* or category A or B retirement pension*	Chapter 35
Unemployed and seeking work, or working part time and seeking more work	Contribution-based jobseeker's allowance*	Chapter 32

Step two: do you qualify for any means-tested benefits and tax credits?

What are means-tested benefits and tax credits?
A means-tested benefit is one for which an assessment of your needs, income and capital is necessary to work out your entitlement. You only qualify for means-tested benefits if your (and your partner's) income and capital are not too high. Entitlement to tax credits, which are also means tested, depends on your assessed needs and the level of your (and your partner's) income. The assessment of the amount you need to live on for means-tested benefits and tax credits may increase if you get certain non-means-tested benefits.

UC is gradually replacing most other means-tested benefits and tax credits. When you come under the UC system (see p20), you usually cannot make a new claim for income support, income-based JSA, income-related ESA, housing benefit (unless this is for specified accommodation), child tax credit (but see p24) or working tax credit. You are expected to claim UC instead. See Chapter 2 for details.

You may be entitled to a combination of non-means-tested benefits, a statutory payment, means-tested benefits and/or tax credits.

You may qualify for more than one means-tested benefit or tax credit, but you cannot get certain means-tested benefits at the same time.

- Use Chapter 2 to see whether you come under the UC system and how this affects the benefits you can claim.
- If you do not come under the UC system, use the table on p11 to see which of the main means-tested benefits and/or tax credits you might get. Check under all the circumstances that apply to you.
- Turn to the chapter(s) on the benefits you may qualify for.
- Follow the procedure explained for checking non-means-tested benefits, by looking at the sections 'Who can claim', 'Tax, other benefits and the benefit cap' and 'How to claim' in any relevant chapters.

Chapter 1

Your circumstances	Benefits and other help you might get	Chapter
Carer	Income support	Chapter 5
Pregnant or recently given birth	Income support	Chapter 5
	Income-related employment and support allowance	Chapter 3
	Child tax credit	Chapter 9
	Working tax credit (in limited circumstances)	Chapter 10
Recently adopted a child	Child tax credit	Chapter 9
	Working tax credit (in limited circumstances)	Chapter 10
	Income support (in some circumstances)	Chapter 5
Responsible for a child	Child tax credit	Chapter 9
	Income support (in some circumstances)	Chapter 5
Disabled or unfit for work	Income-related employment and support allowance	Chapter 3
	Income support (in limited circumstances)	Chapter 5
	Working tax credit (in limited circumstances)	Chapter 10
Pensioners or men nearing pension age	Pension credit	Chapter 7
Have a mortgage	Income support	Chapter 5
	Income-based jobseeker's allowance	Chapter 6
	Income-related employment and support allowance	Chapter 3
	Pension credit	Chapter 7
Tenant	Housing benefit	Chapter 4
Working	Working tax credit	Chapter 10
Unemployed and seeking work, or working part time and seeking more work	Income-based jobseeker's allowance	Chapter 6

Part 1: Introduction
Chapter 1: How to use this book
4. Finding out which benefits and tax credits you can get

1

Step three: can you get any other help?

What further help is there?

If you are entitled to certain benefits or tax credits, you may qualify for other benefits on that basis. These are called 'passported benefits'. Some of these passported benefits can also be awarded on the basis of your circumstances or age, or if you have a low income.

Other assistance may be available to people in certain circumstances and may be means tested – eg, council tax reduction.

Entitlement to some of these payments is discretionary.

- Use the tables below to see the other help you may be able to get in your circumstances and to see whether the benefits or tax credits you get help you qualify for any additional 'passported benefits'.
- Use the relevant chapters to check whether you qualify for such help and how to apply.
- Check whether you qualify for council tax reduction (see p854).
- Check Chapter 39 to see if there are any other payments or other kinds of help you might be able to get.

Your circumstances	Benefits and other help you might get	Chapter
Bereaved	Funeral expenses payment	Chapter 36
Pregnant or recently given birth	Sure Start maternity grant	Chapter 36
or a adopted a child	Health benefits	Chapter 29
	Healthy Start food and vitamins	Chapter 39
Responsible for a child	Sure Start maternity grant (if child is no more than 12 months old)	Chapter 37
	Free school lunches	Chapter 39
	Health benefits for child	Chapter 29
	Healthy Start food and vitamins	Chapter 39
Disabled or unfit for work	Cold weather payment	Chapter 36
Pensioners or men nearing	Winter fuel payment	Chapter 36
pension age	Cold weather payment	Chapter 36
	Health benefits	Chapter 29
Own a home	Council tax reduction	Chapter 39
	Discretionary reduction in council tax	Chapter 39
Tenant	Council tax reduction	Chapter 39
	Discretionary housing payment	Chapter 21
	Discretionary reduction in council tax	Chapter 39
Not enough money to meet	Budgeting loan	Chapter 36
certain needs	Budgeting advance of universal credit	Chapter 8
	Health benefits	Chapter 29

Council tax reduction   Chapter 39

Other payments   Chapter 39

Passported benefit	Passports

Passported benefit

Free school lunches (p860)*

Passports

Income support

Income-based jobseeker's allowance

Income-related employment and support allowance

Some people on child tax credit

Working tax credit 'run on' (in England and Wales)

Guarantee credit of pension credit

(England and Wales only)

Universal credit**

Health benefits (Chapter 29)

Income support

Income-based jobseeker's allowance

Income-related employment and support allowance

Some people on child tax credit

Some people on working tax credit

Guarantee credit of pension credit

Some people on universal credit

Note: some health benefits are free for everyone in Scotland and Wales.

Sure Start maternity grant (p789)

Income support

Income-based jobseeker's allowance

Income-related employment and support allowance

Some people on child tax credit

Some people on working tax credit

Pension credit (either or both credits)

Universal credit

Social fund funeral expenses payment (p791)

Income support

Income-based jobseeker's allowance

Income-related employment and support allowance

Housing benefit

Some people on child tax credit

Some people on working tax credit

Pension credit (either or both credits)

Universal credit

Social fund cold weather payment (p797)

Some people on income support

Some people on income-based jobseeker's allowance

Some people on income-related employment and support allowance

Pension credit (either or both credits)

Some people on universal credit

Part 1: Introduction
Chapter 1: How to use this book
5. Working out how much benefit you should receive

1

Social fund budgeting loan (p784)	Income support
	Income-based jobseeker's allowance
	Income-related employment and support allowance
	Pension credit (either or both credits)

*In England and Scotland, all children in certain year groups are entitled to free school lunches and, in Scotland, pre-school children of parents getting certain benefits may qualify. In Wales, children in local authority maintained primary schools are entitled to free school breakfasts. See p860 for further information.

** At the time of writing, entitlement to UC acts as a passport to free school lunches, but see p860 for details of possible future changes.

5. Working out how much benefit you should receive

How much benefit will you get?

The amount you get depends on which benefit you are claiming. Some non-means-tested benefits are paid at different rates depending on your circumstances. The amount of some contributory benefits may depend on your national insurance contribution record (or that of your spouse or civil partner), and some (but not all) non-means-tested earnings-replacement benefits are affected by certain types of income. The amount of means-tested benefits you get always depends on your circumstances and involves a detailed assessment of your needs, your income and your capital. Your entitlement to tax credits also depends on an assessment of your needs and income. Tables of benefit and tax credit rates for 2017/18 are on ppxiii–xx.

- Look at the chapters dealing with the benefit(s) you are interested in, checking the non-means-tested benefits and statutory payments chapters first. This is because any non-means-tested benefits you get may affect the amount of means-tested benefit to which you are entitled.
- If you are not already getting the benefit, check you meet the entitlement conditions and then look at the section 'The amount of benefit'. Follow any relevant cross references for more detailed information about different aspects of the calculation.
- Check the section 'Tax, other benefits and the benefit cap' for additional information on how the benefit or tax credit may be affected by other benefits or tax credits you receive.
- If in doubt, use Appendix 2 for details of where you can get further help.

6. Finding information on challenging a decision

Who makes decisions?

The Department for Work and Pensions (DWP) is responsible for administering most benefits. HM Revenue and Customs (HMRC) is responsible for administering tax credits, child benefit and guardian's allowance. HMRC also makes decisions on your national insurance (NI) contribution record and on your entitlement to statutory payments if you and your employer do not agree. Local authorities administer housing benefit, council tax reduction schemes, certain education benefits and help with community care and when you are in a crisis (under local welfare assistance schemes).

HM Courts and Tribunals Service, which is part of the Ministry of Justice, is responsible for administering benefit and tax credit appeals.

If you are unhappy with a decision that has been made on your claim, you can try to get it changed. The ways you can challenge a decision, and the procedures and time limits for doing so, depend on the benefit concerned and on whether the decision you want to challenge is an initial decision on your claim or a decision that has been made following a revision, supersession or appeal. Use the following steps if you are considering challenging a decision.

- First check whether the decision is correct. See p4 for how to find answers to specific questions.
- If you think it is not correct, use the chapters in Part 9, or in Chapter 64 for tax credits, to find information on how you may be able to challenge the decision. For decisions relating to NI contributions, see p957. Check the information at the start of the chapter to be sure it is relevant to the benefit to which your challenge relates.
- Alternatively, look up 'challenging a decision' in the index. The sub-entries under it may help you to find the page number for the type of decision you want to challenge.

Part 2

Main means-tested benefits and tax credits

Part 2

Main means-tested benefits and tax credits

Chapter 2

Introduction of universal credit

This chapter covers:
1. The introduction of the universal credit system (below)
2. When you come under the universal credit system (p20)
3. How your means-tested benefits and tax credits are affected (p25)
4. Change of circumstances (p27)

Key facts
- When you come under the universal credit (UC) system, UC replaces most means-tested benefits and tax credits.
- UC is being introduced gradually. It has been introduced nationwide for all new single, unemployed claimants without children and, in some cases, for other new claimants. UC is due to have been introduced for all new claims by September 2018.
- It is planned that existing claims of most means-tested benefits and tax credits will be transferred to UC from 2019.
- Official plans for the introduction of UC, including who can claim and when you can claim, are subject to change.

1. The introduction of the universal credit system

Universal credit (UC) is a new benefit that combines means-tested support for adults under the qualifying age for pension credit (PC) and children into one benefit.

Because UC is being introduced gradually, this *Handbook* refers to you as coming 'under the UC system' when UC rules can apply to you.

When you come under the UC system (see p20), UC replaces the following means-tested benefits and tax credits:
- income support (IS);
- income-based jobseeker's allowance (JSA);

Part 2: Main means-tested benefits and tax credits
Chapter 2: Introduction of universal credit
2. When you come under the universal credit system

- income-related employment and support allowance (ESA);
- housing benefit (HB), except for specified accommodation (see p45);
- child tax credit (CTC);
- working tax credit (WTC).

UC does not replace PC. However, if you or your partner are entitled to PC, you may come under the UC system in certain situations (see below).

Even if you come under the UC system, you can still claim non-means benefits. So, for example, you can still claim contribution-based JSA, contributory ESA, child benefit and carer's allowance, as well as UC.

Timetable

UC is being introduced gradually across Great Britain, initially only for new claimants.

UC has now been introduced throughout Great Britain for certain new claimants. In some areas, only new claimants who satisfy certain 'gateway' conditions can claim UC. In an increasing number of areas (known UC 'full service' areas), all new claimants can claim UC. For more information on the areas in which UC has been introduced, see p21, and for more information on who can claim UC, see below.

UC is due to be introduced for all new claimants, by expanding the full service areas, by September 2018 (see p22). Existing means-tested benefit and tax credit claims will be transferred to UC between 2019 and 2022.[1]

Note: the official plans for the introduction of UC are subject to change. See CPAG's online service and *Welfare Rights Bulletin* for updates.

---

2. **When you come under the universal credit system**

You come under the universal credit (UC) system if:[2]
- you make a new claim for UC; *and*
- you live in a UC 'gateway' area and meet certain gateway conditions (see p22), or you live in a UC 'full service' area (see p24).

Even if you do not make a new claim for UC, but you make a new claim for contribution-based or income-based jobseeker's allowance (JSA), or contributory or income-related employment and support allowance (ESA), you cannot get either income-based JSA or income-related ESA if you satisfy the conditions in the second bullet point above. This is because they are 'abolished' (ie, replaced by UC) for you. You may therefore need to claim UC instead and come under the UC system. You may still be able to get contribution-based JSA or contributory ESA (see p24).

If you get UC, you cannot get other means-tested benefits or tax credits. For more on how claiming UC (and making a new claim for JSA or ESA) affects your entitlement to other means-tested benefits and tax credits, see p25.

In addition, even if you do not make a new claim for UC, but you live in a UC full service area, you usually cannot make a new claim for any of the means-tested benefits and tax credits that UC replaces (see p26).

If you provide incorrect information and you are treated as coming under the UC system, but the DWP subsequently discovers that, in fact, this is not the case, you cannot get UC if you have not yet been paid. You may instead be entitled to have a claim for income support (IS), JSA, ESA, housing benefit (HB) or tax credits backdated to, or treated as having been made on, the date of your UC claim. See the individual benefit or tax credit chapter concerned for more details. However, if you were paid UC, your award of UC continues.[3]

If you come under the UC system, but your circumstances then change and you no longer satisfy the above conditions (eg, if you move to a different area), special rules apply to decide whether you still come under the UC system (see p27).

Transferring to universal credit

Currently, UC is only being introduced for new claimants. From September 2019, the DWP plans to start transferring people with existing means-tested benefits and tax credit awards to UC. The DWP calls this process 'managed migration'.

However, it is possible for you to transfer to UC before you are affected by this managed migration process, including during 2017. This is sometimes called 'natural migration'. This can happen if there is a change in your circumstances which means you make a claim for UC, or a new claim for JSA or ESA, and you come under the UC system. Transferring to UC in this way is possible in any UC area. In the UC 'gateway' areas, it will only happen if you also satisfy the gateway conditions (see p26 for some examples). Transferring to UC in this way is particularly likely in the 'full service' areas because there are no gateway conditions and because you cannot usually make a new claim for any means-tested benefit or tax credit other than UC (see p26 for some examples).

See *Ask CPAG Online* at www.cpag.org.uk/content/ask-cpag-online-universal-credit-natural-migration for more on transferring to UC under 'natural migration'.

The areas in which universal credit has been introduced

There are currently two types of UC area: 'gateway' areas, in which you must satisfy certain gateway conditions to come under the UC system, and 'full service' areas, in which there are no gateway conditions.

Part 2: Main means-tested benefits and tax credits
Chapter 2: Introduction of universal credit
2. When you come under the universal credit system

- By April 2016, UC had been introduced throughout Great Britain for all new claimants who satisfied gateway conditions.[4] In most of these areas, the gateway conditions require that you must be single and without children. Before February 2015, UC was introduced for new claimants who satisfed gateway conditions in the postcode areas of Bath, Hammersmith, Harrogate, Inverness, north west England and Shotton. In these areas, the gateway conditions allow couples and people with children to come under the UC system. A list of the relevant postcodes and the jobcentres involved in the UC gateway areas can be found at www.gov.uk/government/publications/universal-credit-national-expansion.
- UC has been introduced for all new claimants without any gateway conditions in full service areas. The full service is replacing the gateway areas, and is due to be nationwide for all new claimants by September 2018. See www.gov.uk/government/publications/universal-credit-transition-to-full-service for a list of areas in which the full service is due to be introduced.

The gateway areas

In the UC 'gateway' areas (sometimes called 'live service' areas), in order to come under the UC system you must meet certain gateway conditions. Once you have satisfied these conditions and become entitled to UC, you can remain entitled even if a change in your circumstances means you no longer satisfy them (see p27).

The UC gateway areas are gradually being replaced by UC 'full service' areas.

The gateway conditions

To meet the gateway conditions, the following must all apply. If you are a member of a couple and are not reclaiming after a change in circumstances, the following conditions must apply to both you and your partner.[5]

- You must not be entitled to IS, contribution-based or income-based JSA, contributory or income-related ESA, incapacity benefit, severe disablement allowance, disability living allowance (DLA) or personal independence payment (PIP).
- You must not be waiting for the outcome of a claim for IS, JSA, ESA, child tax credit (CTC), working tax credit (WTC) or HB, or for the outcome of an application for a revision of a decision that you are not entitled to IS, JSA or ESA or HB. You must not have an ongoing appeal for IS, JSA or ESA. If an appeal has been determined, there must be no possibility of a further appeal.

In addition, you (and, if claiming as a couple, your partner) must:[6]

- in most areas, be a single person. In some UC areas (the postcode areas of Bath, Hammersmith, Harrogate, Inverness, north west England and Shotton), you can be a member of a couple. See p28 if you become a member of a couple after you have claimed UC as a single person;

- be aged at least 18, but under 60 years and six months;
- be a British citizen who has resided in the UK throughout the two years before your UC claim without a continuous absence of four weeks or more during this time;
- have a national insurance number, and a bank, building society, Post Office or credit union account;
- be fit for work – ie, you must not be covered by a medical certificate or you must not have been found by the DWP to have limited capability for work;
- have less than £6,000 capital.

You (and, if claiming as a couple, your partner) must not:

- be pregnant or within 15 weeks of having given birth;
- be expecting to earn more than £338 in the month after you claim UC. This earnings limit also applies to your partner if you are making a joint claim, in which case your joint earnings must not be more than £541;
- be self-employed (ie, have earnings from self-employment), be expecting to do such work in the month after you claim UC, or be a company director or member of a limited liability partnership;
- be in education or training, or planning to be in education or training within one month;
- in most areas, have a child living with you. In some areas (the postcode areas of Bath, Hammersmith, Harrogate, Inverness, north west England and Shotton), you can have a child living with you, unless s/he is certified as severely sight impaired or blind by a consultant ophthalmologist, or s/he is entitled to DLA or PIP, or s/he is being looked after (see p936) by a local authority (except for respite breaks). **Note:** if you live in an area where you can have a child living with you, but you have three or more children, see the note on p24. It is expected that this will also apply in UC gateway areas;
- be liable to pay child support maintenance under the Child Support Act 1991;
- be adopting a child and the child has been placed with you in the 12 months immediately before the date of your claim, or s/he is expected to be placed with you within two months of that date;
- be a foster parent;
- be a carer (except if you are providing care as paid or voluntary employment);
- be homeless (as defined in the Housing Act 1996), or live in temporary or supported accommodation;
- be an owner-occupier (including part owning the property in which you live);
- live in the same household as a member of the armed forces who is absent from the household in connection with that role.

If your circumstances change so that you no longer meet the gateway conditions, see p27. If you claim UC and do not meet the gateway conditions, your claim for UC is not allowed. If you claim UC and give incorrect information about your

Part 2: Main means-tested benefits and tax credits
Chapter 2: Introduction of universal credit
2. When you come under the universal credit system

personal circumstances and you then claim one of the means-tested benefits or tax credits it replaces within one month, the date of claim is treated as the date you claimed UC, unless you have already been paid UC. In this case, your UC award continues.[7]

The full service areas

In the UC 'full service' areas (formerly known as 'digital service' areas), UC has the following features.

- There are no 'gateway' conditions, so all new claimants can come under the UC system. However, if you have three or more children, see the note below.
- Contact with the DWP about your UC claim is mainly by electronic means – ie, via your online UC account. The DWP does not send you letters.
- A few rules are different from those that apply in the UC gateway areas. In particular, there are slightly different rules on reporting childcare costs (see p264), assessment periods when a couple form or split up or when a new award is made within six months of a previous award ending (see p28), and on calculating unearned income (see p352).

Note: the government intends that between 6 April 2017 and November 2018, new claimants who have three or more children included in their claim (see p220) will not be able to claim UC for a time and will instead be directed to claim tax credits and the other means-tested benefits that UC replaces.[8] Claimants already on UC who have a third or subsequent child on or after 6 April 2017 will remain on UC, but will only be able to get child elements for two children, unless an exception applies (see p258). These rules had not been finalised at the time this *Handbook* was written. See CPAG's online service and *Welfare Rights Bulletin* for updates.

Contribution-based jobseeker's allowance and contributory employment and support allowance

If you make a new claim for contribution-based JSA or contributory ESA and either you live in a UC 'gateway' area and meet the gateway conditions or you live in a 'full service' area, you come under the UC system.[9] Contribution-based JSA and contributory ESA are not replaced by UC. Although they count as income for UC, you can get them at the same time as getting UC. When paid under the UC system, the DWP refers to contribution-based JSA and contributory ESA as 'new style' JSA and 'new style' ESA. The rules about getting paid these benefits (eg, the rules on overpayments, claimant responsibilities and sanctions) are those that apply in the UC system.

If you come under the UC system, you must claim UC if you need to 'top up' your contribution-based JSA or contributory ESA.

In practice, many people have experienced problems when claiming these benefits under the UC system – eg, because DWP staff have wrongly told them that they are replaced by UC. For some practical points about making a claim, see p709 for contribution-based JSA and p648 for contributory ESA.

3. How your means-tested benefits and tax credits are affected

Universal credit (UC) replaces means-tested benefits and tax credits, so the general rule is that if you are, or become, entitled to UC (or if you have claimed it and are waiting for a decision on whether you are entitled), you can no longer qualify for:[10]

- income support (IS). You cannot get IS, but you can still qualify for a past period if you notified your intention to claim IS before the date of your UC claim;
- income-based jobseeker's allowance (JSA). This is 'abolished' (replaced by UC) in your case, whether or not you are entitled to UC, if you come under the UC system and you make a new claim for income-based or contribution-based JSA, income-related or contributory employment and support allowance (ESA) or UC;[11]
- income-related ESA. This is 'abolished' (replaced by UC) in your case, whether or not you are entitled to UC, if you come under the UC system and you make a new claim for income-related or contributory ESA, income-based or contribution-based JSA, or UC;[12]
- housing benefit (HB), except for specified accommodation (see p45). However, you can still qualify for a past period if you notified your intention to claim HB before the date of your UC claim;
- child tax credit (CTC). You can still qualify for provisional payments of CTC before the date of your UC claim (see p1462);
- working tax credit (WTC). You can still qualify for provisional payments of WTC before the date of your UC claim (see p1462);
- pension credit (PC). Single people must be under the qualifying age for PC to get UC. Couples with one person who has reached the qualifying age for PC can come under the UC system and be entitled to UC instead of PC. However, if you live in a UC 'gateway' area, you only come under the UC system if you and your partner are *both* aged under 60 years and six months (see p22). In these areas, if you come under the UC system as a single person, but later become a member of a couple and your partner is entitled to PC, you no longer come under the UC system. In the UC 'full service' areas, there are no gateway conditions, so you can still come under the UC system in this situation and get UC instead of PC (see p28).

If you are already getting one or more of these benefits and tax credits and have not claimed UC, you can continue to do so for the time being. However, if you

Part 2: Main means-tested benefits and tax credits
Chapter 2: Introduction of universal credit
3. How your means-tested benefits and tax credits are affected

then become entitled to UC (eg, because you come under the UC system and decide to claim it, or your claim is transferred to a claim for UC by the DWP), your entitlement (to all of them) stops.[13]

If you live in a UC gateway area and you have claimed UC but have been refused because your earnings are too high, for the next six months you cannot get income-based JSA, income-related ESA, IS, HB, CTC or WTC, even if you would qualify for them.[14] If you live in a UC full service area, you usually cannot make a new claim for these benefits (see below).

If you live in a gateway area

Even if you are already getting one or more of the benefits and tax credits that UC replaces, you may transfer to UC – eg, after a change of circumstances that means you need to claim UC instead. If you get UC, your entitlement to your previous benefit or tax credit stops. If you live in a 'gateway' area, you can only transfer to UC if you make a new claim for UC, JSA or ESA and satisfy the gateway conditions.

Examples
Sue gets income-related ESA. When she fails a work capability assessment, she immediately claims income-based JSA instead. Sue satisfies the UC gateway conditions, so income-based JSA (and income-related ESA) for her is replaced by UC. She claims UC and is transferred to UC. Even if Sue then successfully challenges the decision about her failing the work capability assessment, she remains on UC.

Bob gets income-related ESA and fails a work capability assessment. Bob decides to challenge this by asking for a mandatory reconsideration (see p1311) before he claims income-based JSA. Because one of the gateway conditions is that you must not be waiting for the outcome of a revision or appeal of a decision about ESA, Bob does not satisfy the gateway conditions for UC. He cannot claim UC and gets income-based JSA. If his challenge about his failing the work capability assessment is successful, he can return to income-related ESA.

Raj gets WTC and HB. However, after losing his job, Raj is no longer entitled to WTC and so makes a new claim for income-based JSA. Because Raj satisfies the gateway conditions for UC, income-based JSA for him is replaced by UC. Raj claims UC instead and is transferred to UC. His award of HB is terminated.

If you live in a full service area

If you live in a full service area, there are no 'gateway' conditions for coming under the UC system, so becoming entitled to UC is simpler than in the UC gateway areas. Even if you are already getting one or more of the benefits and tax credits that UC replaces, you may transfer to UC – eg, after a change of circumstances that means you must claim UC instead. If you get UC, your entitlement to all these benefits and tax credits stops.

Even if you have not claimed UC, you cannot start to get income-based JSA or income-related ESA – this is because they are replaced by UC in your case if you try to make a new claim. Also, usually you cannot make a new claim for IS, HB (except for specified accommodation – see p45), CTC or WTC, unless (for HB, CTC or WTC) either you or your partner has reached the qualifying age for PC (p147).[15]

If you have three or more children, see the note on p24.

Examples

Jules is getting income-based JSA and HB when the area in which she lives becomes a UC full service area. This, in itself, does not mean her JSA and HB come to an end. However, she then has a baby (her first child). Because she is in a full service area, she cannot make a new claim for CTC. Instead, Jules claims and gets UC. Her entitlement to income-based JSA and HB comes to an end.

Steve is getting income-related ESA when the area in which he lives becomes a UC full service area. This, in itself, does not mean his income-related ESA comes to an end. However, Steve then fails the work capability assessment for ESA. He decides to claim income-based JSA while he is challenging this decision. Both income-based JSA and income-related ESA for him are now replaced by UC. So Steve must claim UC instead. Steve cannot go back to income-related ESA, even if his challenge to the work capability assessment decision is successful. Instead, his award of UC will reflect the fact that he now passes the assessment.

Asha is getting WTC and HB when the area in which she lives becomes a UC full service area. Asha then moves to a different flat. Because this is in the same local authority area, she does not need to make a new HB claim and both her HB and WTC continue. Asha moves again, this time to another UC full service area in a different local authority. Her current HB claim comes to an end. Because she is in a full service area, she cannot make a new claim for HB. Instead, Asha claims and gets UC. Her entitlement to WTC comes to an end.

4. **Change of circumstances**

Once you are entitled to universal credit (UC), you remain under the UC system. In particular if you are entitled to UC and continue to satisfy the general rules of entitlement (the basic conditions and the financial conditions – see p161), you continue to get UC, even if you live in an area where 'gateway 'conditions apply and you would now cease to satisfy them.[16] So, for example, if you (or your partner) have a child or become ill after getting UC, you remain entitled to UC.

Part 2: Main means-tested benefits and tax credits
Chapter 2: Introduction of universal credit
4. Change of circumstances

2

If you get contribution-based jobseeker's allowance (JSA) or contributory employment and support allowance (ESA) and you come under the UC system but are not entitled to UC (eg, because your income is too high), you no longer come under the UC system if you live in an area where gateway conditions apply and you would now cease to satisfy them.[17]

In the UC 'full service' areas (see p21), if you are entitled to UC and continue to satisfy the entitlement conditions, you continue to get UC even if you move to an area in which gateway conditions still apply.

Couples

In the UC 'gateway' areas, you still come under the UC system (and can remain entitled to UC) if you cease to satisfy the gateway conditions because you claimed UC as a single person, but you have now become part of a couple. In this situation, you can be entitled to UC with your partner, provided you satisfy the basic and financial rules of entitlement as a couple.[18] In the UC 'full service' areas (see p21), you can also stop being entitled as a single person, but become entitled again as a couple.

If your partner was not entitled to UC as a single person, any award s/he has of income support (IS), income-based JSA, income-related ESA, housing benefit (HB) (except for specified accommodation – see p45), working tax credit (WTC) or child tax credit (CTC) stops and you are treated as claiming UC as a couple.[19] If your partner was also entitled to UC as a single person, you are entitled to UC as a couple without having to make a claim.[20]

Example
Gareth has been entitled to UC as a single person since April 2015. He meets Jane and moves in with her in August 2017. Jane has a two-year-old son and has been getting IS as a lone parent, together with CTC and HB. Gareth and Jane now come under the UC system as a couple. They satisfy the basic rules of entitlement for UC as a couple, and are therefore entitled to UC.
Jane's awards of IS, CTC and HB are terminated.

In UC gateway areas, if your new partner is entitled to pension credit (PC), you no longer come under the UC system unless your partner stops claiming PC.[21] However, in UC full service areas, you are treated as making a joint claim for UC. If you continue to get UC, your new partner's PC award stops.

You cannot make a new claim for PC as a couple while you continue to claim UC.

In UC gateway areas, if you were entitled to UC as a couple but separate from your partner, you may still be entitled to UC as a single person (and so remain under the UC system), even if you do not meet the gateway conditions. Whichever one of you reports the change to the DWP (or who is the first to do so) must make a new claim for UC.[22] In the UC full service areas, neither you nor your ex-partner must make a new claim for UC (although you should still report the change), and you both keep your existing UC assessment period (see p164 for what this is).[23]

Example

Rose and Nelson were entitled to UC as joint claimants in a UC gateway area. They separate and Rose, who is pregnant, leaves the area. Nelson notifies the DWP of the fact that they are no longer a couple. Nelson comes under the UC system as a single person and makes a new claim for UC. Rose remains under the UC system and is entitled to UC as a single claimant without having to make a claim, even though she does not meet the gateway conditions.

If you are no longer entitled to universal credit

If you live in a UC 'gateway' area and the change in your circumstances means that you are no longer entitled to UC because your earnings are too high, you automatically still come under the UC system for six months. During this period, you cannot get income-based JSA, income-related ESA, IS, HB (except in 'specified accommodation' – see p45), CTC or WTC instead of UC. If within six months your earnings go down (or some other change has happened) so that you become entitled to UC again, you do not have to make a new claim (see p169), but you should inform the DWP of your change of circumstances.[24]

If your UC entitlement ended for a reason other than your earnings being too high, you still come under the UC system if you satisfy the 'gateway' conditions. You cannot get income-based JSA or income-related ESA. Unless you are waiting for a decision on whether you are entitled to UC again, you may still be able to get IS, HB, CTC or WTC if you satisfy the basic rules. You may be entitled to UC again in the future.[25]

If your UC entitlement ended for a reason other than your earnings being too high, and you no longer satisfy the gateway conditions, you no longer come under the UC system and you cannot make a claim for UC. Instead, you can claim income-based JSA, income-related ESA or IS, HB, CTC and WTC.[26]

If you still live in a UC 'full service' area, even if you are no longer entitled to UC, you cannot make a new claim for income-based JSA or income-related ESA. Also, you cannot make a new claim for IS, HB (except in 'specified accommodation'), CTC or WTC, unless either you or your partner has reached the qualifying age for PC (see p147).[27] If your UC ended but you may now be entitled again (including if your earnings were too high, but they have now gone down), you must reapply for UC in order to become entitled again.[28] If you have three or more children, see the note on p24.

Part 2: Main means-tested benefits and tax credits
Chapter 2: Introduction of universal credit
Notes

Notes

2

1. **The introduction of the universal credit system**
   1 Public Accounts Committee, *Oral Evidence: Universal Credit: recall*, HC 601, 7 December 2015; *Universal Credit and Local Authorities: written statement*, House of Commons, *Hansard,* 10 December 2015, col 63WS; timetable revised on 20 July 2016: *Welfare Reform: written statement*, HCWS96, House of Commons, *Hansard,* 20 July 2016

2. **When you come under the universal credit system**
   2 Art 3(3) and Sch 5 WRA(No.9)O, as applied in UC areas by subsequent commencement orders
   3 Art 3A WRA(No.9)O
   4 Under The Welfare Reform Act 2012 (Commencement No.24 and Transitional and Transitory Provisions and Commencement No.9 and Transitional and Transitory Provisions (Amendment) Order 2015, No.1537, any area in Great Britain not already a UC area on 25 April 2016 becomes a UC area on that date.
   5 Sch 5 para 3 WRA(No.9)O, as applied in UC areas by subsequent commencement orders
   6 Sch 5 WRA(No.9)O, as applied in UC areas by subsequent commencement orders
   7 Art 3A WRA(No.9)O, as applied in UC areas by subsequent commencement orders
   8 *Welfare Reform: written statement*, HCWS96, House of Commons, *Hansard*, 20 July 2016
   9 These benefits are not abolished under the UC system and can be claimed under the JSA Regs 2013 and the ESA Regs 2013.

3. **How your means-tested benefits and tax credits are affected**
   10 Regs 5, 6 and 8 UC(TP) Regs
   11 Art 4 WRA(No.9)O
   12 Art 4 WRA(No.9)O
   13 Reg 5 UC(TP) Regs

   14 Arts 3(3)(e) and 4(2)(e) WRA(No.9)O; reg 6 UC(TP) Regs
   15 For example, for select postcodes in Sutton, Croydon and Southwark, see Arts 3-7 The Welfare Reform Act 2012 (Commencement No.23 and Transitional and Transitory Provisions) Order 2015, No.634

4. **Change of circumstances**
   16 Art 3(3) WRA(No.9)O, as applied in UC gateway areas by subsequent commencement orders, only requires that you live in a UC area and satisfy the personal conditions at the time of the claim; HB Circular A13/2013
   17 Art 6 WRA(No.9)O, as applied in UC gateway areas by subsequent commencement orders; paras S8041 and V8041 ADM
   18 Art 3 WRA (No.9)O, as applied in UC gateway areas by subsequent commencement orders
   19 Art 4 WRA(No.9)O, as applied in UC gateway areas by subsequent commencement orders; regs 5, 7 and 12A UC(TP) Regs; reg 9(8) UC, PIP,JSA&ESA(C&P) Regs
   20 Reg 9(7) UC, PIP,JSA&ESA(C&P) Regs; paras M4051-60 ADM
   21 Art 3(3)(c) and (f) and (7) and (9) WRA(No.9)O, as applied in UC gateway areas by subsequent commencement orders; paras M3022 and M3041 ADM
   22 Art 3(3)(f) WRA(No.9)O, as applied in UC gateway areas by subsequent commencement orders; reg 9(6) UC,PIP,JSA&ESA(C&P) Regs; paras M1024-25 ADM
   23 Reg 3 Universal Credit (Digital Service) Amendment Regulations 2014, No.2887
   24 Arts 3(3)(e) and 4(2)(e) WRA(No.9)O; reg 6 UC(TP) Regs
   25 Art 4 WRA(No.9)O still applies so as to abolish income-based JSA and income-related ESA. In this situation, reg 6 UC(TP) Regs does not prevent a claim for IS, HB, CTC or WTC.

26 Art 4 WRA(No.9)O only applies so as to abolish income-based JSA and income-related ESA if the claimant is in a UC area and satisfies the gateway conditions, or is (or may be) still entitled to UC following a change of circumstances.

27 For example, for select postcodes in Sutton, Croydon and Southwark, see Arts 3-7 The Welfare Reform Act 2012 (Commencement No.23 and Transitional and Transitory Provisions) Order 2015, No.634.

28 Reg 3 Universal Credit (Digital Service) Amendment Regulations 2014, No.2887

Chapter 3

Income-related employment and support allowance

This chapter covers:
1. Who can claim employment and support allowance (p33)
2. The rules about your age (p34)
3. People included in the claim (p34)
4. The amount of benefit (p35)
5. Special benefit rules (p38)
6. Claims and backdating (p38)
7. Getting paid (p40)
8. Tax, other benefits and the benefit cap (p41)

Key facts

- Employment and support allowance (ESA) is a benefit for people who have 'limited capability for work' (ie, they are unable to work because of illness or disability) and who are not entitled to statutory sick pay.
- Entitlement to ESA is assessed by a test called the work capability assessment.
- There are two types of ESA: **contributory ESA**, which is not means tested, and **income-related ESA**, which is means tested.
- You do not have to have paid national insurance contributions to qualify for income-related ESA.
- You may qualify for income-related ESA even if you do not qualify for contributory ESA. You may be able to get your contributory ESA topped up with income-related ESA.
- ESA is administered and paid by the DWP.
- If you disagree with an ESA decision, you can apply for a revision or supersession, or appeal against it. You must apply for a mandatory reconsideration before you can appeal. All parts of the decision may be looked at.

Future changes

At some point between 2016 and 2018, depending on where you live, you will no longer be able to make a new claim for income-related ESA. From 2019, the DWP will begin to transfer existing income-related ESA claims to universal credit. See p20 for further information, and CPAG's online service and *Welfare Rights Bulletin* for updates.

1. Who can claim employment and support allowance

You qualify for income-related employment and support allowance (ESA) if you satisfy the following basic rules that apply to both income-related and contributory ESA *and* if you satisfy the extra rules for income-related ESA below.

You satisfy the basic rules for ESA if you:[1]

- have 'limited capability for work' (see p1003); *and*
- are aged 16 or over but under pension age (see p147); *and*
- are in Great Britain (see p38 if you go abroad); *and*
- are not entitled in your own right to statutory sick pay, income support (IS) or jobseeker's allowance (JSA), and are not in a couple entitled to joint-claim JSA (see p120); *and*
- are not doing any work (except work you can do while claiming – see p1021).

You are not usually entitled to ESA for the first seven days of your claim (see p1021). However, you may be able to get a short-term advance of ESA paid to you during this waiting period (p1177). You cannot get ESA and certain other benefits at the same time (see p41). Some claimants of ESA (but not those in the 'support group' – see p641) must take part in work-focused interviews and some of those can also be required to undertake 'work-related activity' (see Chapter 46). From summer 2017, it is expected that new claimants will have to accept a claimant commitment (see Chapter 47).

Extra rules for income-related employment and support allowance

You qualify for income-related ESA if, in addition to satisfying the basic rules of entitlement to ESA above:[2]

- your income (see Chapter 14) is less than your applicable amount (see Chapter 12); *and*
- your capital is not over £16,000 (see Chapter 17);[3] *and*
- you are not entitled to pension credit (PC); *and*
- your partner, if you are in a couple (see p215), is not engaged in full-time paid work (p989) or treated as being in full-time paid work (p996); *and*

Part 2: Main means-tested benefits and tax credits
Chapter 3: Income-related employment and support allowance
3. People included in the claim

- your partner is not entitled to income-related ESA, income-based JSA, IS or PC in her/his own right; *and*
- you are not 'receiving education', unless you are entitled to disability living allowance, personal independence payment or armed forces independence payment, in which case you can still qualify for income-related ESA;[4] *and*
- you satisfy the 'right to reside' and 'habitual residence' tests (see Chapter 66);[5] *and*
- you are not a 'person subject to immigration control' (see p1516).[6]

Education

You are in **'education'** if you are a 'qualifying young person' (eg, you are aged under 20 and in full-time non-advanced education or approved training – see p572) or if you are on a course that is classed as full time.[7] The rules are very similar to those that apply to the definition of full-time courses for IS (see p875). Get advice if you are unsure.

Note: if you come under the universal credit (UC) system (see p20), you cannot get income-related ESA and must claim UC instead. If you already get income-related ESA but become entitled to UC, your income-related ESA stops.

Disqualification from benefit

You can be disqualified from receiving ESA for up to six weeks (or have your benefit paid at a reduced rate if you are a 'person in hardship') in the circumstances described on p637. The rules are the same for both income-related ESA and contributory ESA.

However, the rules for income-related ESA are different from those for contributory ESA if you are:
- absent from Great Britain (see p1594); *or*
- a prisoner or detained in legal custody (see p928).

2. **The rules about your age**

To satisfy the basic rules for employment and support allowance, you must be aged at least 16 but under pension age (see p772).

3. **People included in the claim**

If you are single, you claim income-related employment and support allowance (ESA) for yourself.

If you are a member of a couple (see p215 for who counts), either you claim income-related ESA for both you and your partner or, if your partner meets the qualifying conditions for income-related ESA, s/he can claim for you both instead. The applicable amount that forms part of the calculation of your benefit includes a personal allowance for a couple and can include premiums based on both your and your partner's circumstances. When your benefit is worked out, your partner's income and capital are usually added to yours. Whichever one of you claims ESA, the other may qualify for national insurance (NI) credits in order to protect her/his NI record. See Chapter 42 for more details.

There are some situations in which you must show that you are 'responsible' for a child who is living in your household – eg:

- in order to take advantage of exemptions from compulsory work-focused interviews and work-related activity (see p1063 and p1068);
- for some of the rules on help with housing costs (see Chapter 20).

You can count as responsible for any child under 16 and for any qualifying young person (referred to as a 'child' in this *Handbook)*. You do not have to be the child's parent. For when you count as responsible for a child and when s/he counts as living in your household, see pp222– 24.

---

4. The amount of benefit

The amount of income-related employment and support allowance (ESA) you get depends on your needs (your 'applicable amount') and how much income and capital you have.

You are paid a limited amount of ESA during an initial **'assessment phase'**. See p639 for more information (the rules on when the assessment phase applies are the same as for contributory ESA). After this, there is a **'main phase'**. During the main phase you may get an additional component included in your applicable amount. For the calculation, see p36.

Note:

- You are not entitled during for the first seven 'waiting days' of your period of limited capability for work, unless an exception applies (see p638 – the rules are the same as for contributory ESA).
- If you are appealing against a decision that you do not have limited capability for work and you get ESA pending the outcome of your appeal (see p1017), you are only paid at the assessment phase rate – ie, you do not get an additional component.
- You are entitled to just one award of ESA, but this may be made up of both contributory ESA and income-related ESA.[8] If you are entitled to both types of ESA, the total amount of ESA payable is the same amount as your income-related ESA, but is made up of contributory ESA topped up with income-related ESA.

Part 2: Main means-tested benefits and tax credits
Chapter 3: Income-related employment and support allowance
4. The amount of benefit

Calculating income-related employment and support allowance

Income-related ESA is worked out as follows.

Step one: calculate your applicable amount

Your applicable amount consists of:

- in both the assessment phase (see p639) and the main phase:
  - **a personal allowance** (see p230). Your personal allowance is paid at a lower rate if you are under 25 or, in some cases, if you are under 18 and in the assessment phase (see p639);
  - **premiums** for any special needs (see p236);
  - **housing costs**, principally for mortgage interest payments (see Chapter 20). However, you may have an initial 'waiting period' when your housing costs are not paid (see p468);
- usually in the main phase only: a **support component** (see p641 – the rules are the same as for contributory ESA) or a **work-related activity component** (see p641 – the rules are the same as for contributory ESA). **Note:** the work-related activity component has been abolished for new claimants from April 2017. In some circumstances (eg, if you are terminally ill), you can be entitled to one of these components (if you satisfy the rules) during the assessment phase.
- a **'transitional addition'** if you have been transferred to income-related ESA from income support (IS) which was paid on the grounds of disability. See p672 for details of the transfer process and p37 for how the transitional addition is calculated.

For more details on applicable amounts, see Chapter 12.

Step two: calculate your income

This is the amount you have coming in each week from, for instance, other benefits, part-time earnings, working tax credit and maintenance (see Chapter 14). If you have capital over £6,000 (£10,000 if you live in a care home), it also includes your tariff income (see p293).

Step three: deduct income from applicable amount

If your income is less than your applicable amount, your income-related ESA equals the difference between the two. If your income is the same as or more than your applicable amount, you are not entitled to ESA.

Example
Terry is aged 35 when he claims ESA. He lives with his wife, Julie, and six-year-old son, Ray. They get child benefit and child tax credit (CTC). Julie works 10 hours a week and earns £80 a week. Terry is assessed as being in the support group. He has not paid enough national insurance contributions to get contributory ESA.

Assessment phase

Applicable amount = £114.85 (personal allowance for couple both aged 18 or over)

Income to be taken into account = £60 (child benefit and CTC are ignored; £20 earnings disregard applies)

Terry's income-related ESA during assessment phase is £114.85 *minus* £60 = £54.85

Main phase

Applicable amount = £151.40 (personal allowance of £114.85 for couple both aged 18 or over *plus* support component of £36.55)

Income to be taken into account (as above) = £60

Terry's income-related ESA during the main phase is £151.40 *minus* £60 = £91.40

Note:

- If you are not currently entitled to ESA because of the level of your income, but will be when a component is included in your applicable amount, you may be given an **'advance award'**. Under this, you are entitled from the point the additional component is awarded, provided you still satisfy the other conditions, without needing to claim again.[9]

- Earnings you receive for 'permitted work' (see p1021) are disregarded when calculating the amount of your income-related ESA.

Your ESA may be reduced if:

- you do not comply with a requirement to attend work-focused interviews and work-related activity (see p1063 and p1068). **Note:** these requirements do not apply if you are entitled to the support component; *or*

- you are disqualified from ESA but are a person in 'hardship' (see p637 – the rules are the same as for contributory ESA); *or*

- your ESA is sanctioned because you have committed a benefit offence (see p1265).

Transitional addition

If you have transferred to income-related ESA from IS on the grounds of disability, you may be entitled to a transitional addition in your ESA to top up the amount of your ESA to that of your IS.

When deciding whether you qualify for a transitional addition, the decision maker compares the following amounts:[10]

- the IS applicable amount to which you were entitled immediately before the 'effective date' (ie, the date on which your IS was converted to an award of ESA – see p672), minus any part of your applicable amount which was for a child or for housing costs;

- the income-related ESA applicable amount to which you are entitled on the effective date, minus any part of your applicable amount that is for housing costs. Either the work-related activity component or support component is included in the amount.

Part 2: Main means-tested benefits and tax credits
Chapter 3: Income-related employment and support allowance
6. Claims and backdating

If the ESA amount is less than the IS amount, you get the difference between the two amounts as a transitional addition to your income-related ESA.

For more details, see p93 of the 2013/14 edition of this *Handbook*.

5. Special benefit rules

Special rules may apply to:
- people subject to immigration control (see Chapter 65);
- people who have come from or are going abroad (see Chapters 66, 67 and 68);
- people who are living in a care home or other similar accommodation, or people in prison or detention (see Chapter 41).

6. Claims and backdating

The general rules about claims and backdating are covered in Chapter 49. Most of the specific rules about claiming employment and support allowance (ESA) are described in Chapter 28.

To be entitled to ESA, you must usually make a claim for it. However, if you are appealing against a decision that you do not have limited capability for work, you do not need to make a claim, although you must submit a medical certificate.[11] For when ESA can be paid pending an appeal, see p1017.

In most cases (unless you are recognised as exempt straight away), you are required to attend a medical examination to assess whether you have limited capability for work and limited capability for work-related activity. In addition, unless you are in the 'support group' (see p641), you are usually required to attend compulsory work-focused interviews and, in some cases, carry out work-related activity (see p1064).

Making a claim

For details of how to make a claim for ESA, see p647.

Income-related and contributory ESA are two types of the same benefit. When you claim ESA, in order for the DWP to assess your entitlement to both, it is important to answer all the relevant questions and provide all the necessary information.

Note: if you come under the universal credit (UC) system (see p20), you cannot make a new claim for income-related ESA.

Who should claim

Usually, you must claim ESA on your own behalf. If you are unable to manage your own affairs, another person can claim ESA for you as your 'appointee' (see p1149). If you are a member of a couple you should choose which of you claims income-related ESA for you both (bearing in mind that the claimant must satisfy the entitlement rules, including having limited capability for work). Whoever is the claimant can be switched later by the other member of the couple claiming income-related ESA and (if s/he is entitled) by both you and your partner confirming in writing that you want the claimant to be changed.[12]

If you are employed

If you are employed, see p648. You should normally be paid statutory sick pay (SSP – see Chapter 38) for the first 28 weeks of your limited capability for work.

Information to support your claim

For the general information requirements that apply to all benefits, see p1150.

It is important to provide any information required when you claim. Until you do, you may not count as having made a valid claim (see p1152). Correct any defects as soon as possible or your date of claim may be affected.

In addition to providing the required information, you may also be referred for a medical assessment. If you fail to attend the medical without good cause, your claim can be refused.[13]

For further details about information or evidence (including medical evidence) that you should provide, see p649. The rules described for contributory ESA also apply to income-related ESA.

Even if you have provided all that was required when you claimed, you may be asked to provide further evidence to support your claim (see p1154). You may also be asked to provide information after you are awarded ESA and if you fail to do so, your ESA could be suspended or even terminated (see p1185).

The date of your claim

The date of your claim is important as it determines when your entitlement to income-related ESA starts (subject to the rules on waiting days – see p639). This is not necessarily the date from when you are paid. For information about when payment of income-related ESA starts, see p40.

The **'date of your claim'** is usually the date of your telephone call starting the claim, or the date your claim form is received. However, there are exceptions (see p649).

Note: you must make sure your claim is valid. If it is 'defective', you are given a short time to correct the defects (see p1152). If you do, your claim is treated as having been made when you initially claimed.[14]

In some cases, you can claim in advance (see p40), and in some cases your claim can be backdated (see p40). If you want this to be done, make this clear when you claim or the DWP might not consider it. If you claimed maternity allowance (MA) or SSP when you should have claimed ESA, see p40.

Part 2: Main means-tested benefits and tax credits
Chapter 3: Income-related employment and support allowance
7. Getting paid

Backdating your claim

Your claim can be backdated for up to three months before the day you actually claim (see p650).

If you claim the wrong benefit

In some circumstances a claim for MA may be treated as a claim for ESA (or vice versa) or your ESA claim can be treated as having been made on the date you applied for SSP (see p650). If you claimed UC when you should have claimed ESA, see p649 to see whether your date of claim can be backdated. If you make a new claim for incapacity benefit, income support on the grounds of disability or severe disablement allowance, this is treated as a claim for ESA.[15]

Claiming in advance

You can claim ESA up to three months in advance if you are not entitled to it now, but will become entitled within 13 weeks of claiming, unless the reason you do not qualify straight away is because you fail the habitual residence test (see p1537).[16] The date of your claim is the date on which you qualify.[17]

Starting work when your claim ends

If you start work and later become sick again, you may be able to benefit from the rules on linking periods of limited capability for work (see p1021). If you have to claim ESA again within a 12-week linking period, you can return to the same level of ESA that you were previously receiving. **Note:** you may be able to benefit from a 104-week linking rule for housing costs (see p470).

7. Getting paid

As income-related and contributory employment and support allowance (ESA) are two types of the same benefit, the rules described on p650 on getting paid contributory ESA also apply to income-related ESA.

For details of when your income-related ESA might be paid at a reduced rate, see p36.

Change of circumstances

You must report changes in your circumstances that you have been told to report, as well as any that you might reasonably be expected to know might affect your right to, the amount of or the payment of your benefit. You should do this as soon as possible, preferably in writing. See p1184 for further information.

If you have a mortgage, the DWP can ask your lender about any changes in the amount you owe. If you have this information (eg, from an annual statement from your lender), you must also advise the DWP just in case your lender fails to do so. Make sure the DWP takes this information into account so you are not overpaid.

Note: if you become a member of a couple with someone entitled to universal credit, your entitlement to income-related ESA ends (see p28).

8. Tax, other benefits and the benefit cap

Tax

Income-related employment and support allowance (ESA) is not taxable.[18]

Means-tested benefits and tax credits

Income-related ESA is an automatic passport to maximum housing benefit (HB), but you must make a separate claim for HB. It is also an automatic passport to maximum working tax credit (WTC) and child tax credit (CTC).

You might be able to choose between claiming income-related ESA, income support (IS), income-based jobseeker's allowance (JSA) and pension credit. If you have a partner, s/he may be able to claim one of these benefits for you instead of your claiming income-related ESA. Get advice about this. You may need to work out how you would be better off financially and the sort of work-focused interviews you must attend or work-related activity you must undertake. See p142 for further information.

If your partner works at least 16 hours but less than 24 hours a week, you and your partner may be able to claim WTC. Before deciding whether to claim, get advice about how you would be better off financially.

If you or your partner have just stopped work or reduced your hours, you might get what is known as 'WTC run-on' for a four-week period (see p202).

WTC is taken into account as income when working out your IS, but CTC is not.

Non-means-tested benefits

You can be entitled to income-related ESA and contributory ESA at the same time.

While you are on income-related ESA, you get national insurance credits (see p965).

You are not entitled to ESA if you are entitled to statutory sick pay.[19]

Most non-means-tested benefits are taken into account as income when working out the amount of income-related ESA you get. Attendance allowance, disability living allowance, personal independence payment, guardian's allowance and child benefit are not taken into account. Even so, it can be worth claiming non-means-tested benefits. If you or your partner qualify for certain of these, you also qualify for certain premiums and, therefore, a higher rate of income-related ESA.

Part 2: Main means-tested benefits and tax credits
Chapter 3: Income-related employment and support allowance
Notes

You cannot claim ESA and JSA in your own right at the same time. If your partner is entitled to contribution-based JSA, you can claim ESA. Your partner's JSA is taken into account when assessing your income for income-related ESA.

The benefit cap

In some cases, there is a limit on the total amount of specified benefits you can receive (a 'benefit cap'). ESA is one of the specified benefits. However, the benefit cap does *not* apply if you or your partner receive ESA which includes a support component. In other cases, it only applies if you are getting HB or universal credit. See p1180 for further information.

Passports and other sources of help

If you are entitled to income-related ESA, you also qualify for health benefits such as free prescriptions (see Chapter 29) and education benefits such as free school lunches (see p860). You may also qualify for social fund payments (see Chapter 36). You may be entitled to a council tax reduction (see p854).

Financial help on starting work

If you stop getting income-related ESA because you or your partner start work, or your partner's earnings or hours in her/his existing job increase, you might be able to get mortgage interest run-on if you have a home loan (see p474), or extended payments of HB if you pay rent (see p86). Your local authority may also provide extended help with council tax. See p866 for information about other financial help you might get.

Notes

1. Who can claim employment and support allowance
1 ss1 and 20(1) WRA 2007; reg 40(1) ESA Regs
2 Sch 1 para 6 WRA 2007
3 Reg 110 ESA Regs
4 Reg 18 ESA Regs; Sch 1 para 2 and Sch 2 para 2 ESA(TP)(EA)(No.2) Regs
5 Reg 70 and Sch 5 para 11 ESA Regs
6 s115 IAA 1999
7 Regs 14-17 ESA Regs

4. The amount of benefit
8 s6 WRA 2007
9 s5 WRA 2007; reg 146 ESA Regs
10 Regs 9, 11, 12 and 13 ESA(TP)(EA)(No.2) Regs

6. Claims and backdating
11 Reg 3(j) SS(C&P) Regs
12 Reg 4I(1) and (2) SS(C&P) Regs
13 s19 SSA 1998; reg 23 ESA Regs
14 Regs 4G(5) and 4H(7) SS(C&P) Regs
15 Reg 2 ESA(TP) Regs

16 Reg 13(9) SS(C&P) Regs
17 Reg 13(1) SS(C&P) Regs

8. Tax, other benefits and the benefit cap
18 s677 IT(EP)A 2003
19 s20 WRA 2007

Chapter 4

Housing benefit

This chapter covers:
1. Who can claim housing benefit (p45)
2. The rules about your age (p58)
3. People included in the claim (p59)
4. The amount of benefit (p59)
5. Special benefit rules (p71)
6. Claims and backdating (p72)
7. Getting paid (p82)
8. Tax, other benefits and the benefit cap (p93)

Key facts
- Housing benefit (HB) is a benefit for people on a low income who pay rent.
- The amount of HB you get may be restricted and is not necessarily based on the full amount of rent you must pay.
- HB is a means-tested benefit.
- You do not have to have paid national insurance contributions to qualify.
- You can qualify for HB whether you are in or out of work.
- If you need extra financial assistance to meet the costs of your housing, you can claim discretionary housing payments to top up your HB.
- A 'benefit cap' may be applied if the total amount of certain benefits you receive exceeds a specified amount and your HB can be reduced.
- HB is administered and paid by local authorities, although it is a national scheme and the rules are mainly determined by DWP regulations.
- If you disagree with an HB decision, you can apply for a revision or a supersession, or appeal against it. You do *not* have to apply for a mandatory reconsideration before you can appeal.

Future changes

At some point between 2016 and 2018, depending on where you live, you will no longer be able to make a new claim for HB unless you or your partner are at least the qualifying age for pension credit (PC) or you live in 'specified accommodation'. From 2019, the DWP will begin to transfer existing HB claims to universal credit (or PC). See p20 for further information, and CPAG's online service and *Welfare Rights Bulletin* for updates.

1. Who can claim housing benefit

You qualify for housing benefit (HB) if:[1]
- your income is low enough (see p59 and Chapters 14 and 15);
- unless you or your partner are getting the guarantee credit of pension credit (PC), your savings and other capital are worth £16,000 or less (see Chapters 17 and 18);[2]
- the payments you make can be met by HB (see below);
- you or your partner count as liable to pay rent (see p47);
- the payments you make are for the home in which you normally live (see p51) or you are only temporarily absent from it;
- you satisfy the 'right to reside test' and the 'habitual residence test' (see Chapter 66); *and*
- you are not a 'person subject to immigration control' (see p1516). There are exceptions to this rule.

Note: you cannot usually make a new claim for HB in a number of situations if you come under the universal credit (UC) system, unless this is for 'specified accommodation' or you (or your partner) are at least the qualifying age for PC. See p25 for further details. If you live in 'specified accommodation', you can get HB for the rent you pay even if you are getting UC. If you are getting HB but become entitled to UC, your HB may stop unless it is for 'specified accommodation'.

Specified accommodation
'Specified accommodation' is:[3]
- accommodation provided by a relevant body to meet your need for, and where you get, care, support or supervision; *or*
- temporary accommodation provided by a local authority or a relevant body because you have left your home because of domestic violence – eg, a refuge. See p1035 for the meaning of domestic violence, which is the same as for jobseeker's allowance (JSA); *or*
- a local authority hostel for homeless people where you get care, support or supervision to assist you to be rehabilitated or resettled within the community; *or*
- 'exempt accommodation' (see p428 for the meaning).

For these purposes, a **'relevant body'** is a county council in England, housing association, registered charity or voluntary organisation.

Payments that can be met by housing benefit

HB can meet:[4]
- rent paid in respect of a tenancy. This can include rent or ground rent payable in respect of a lease of 21 years or less.[5] If your lease is for longer than 21 years,

Part 2: Main means-tested benefits and tax credits
Chapter 4: Housing benefit
1. Who can claim housing benefit

the rent or ground rent may be met as 'other housing costs' by income support (IS), income-based JSA, income-related employment and support allowance (ESA) or PC (see p452);

- payments in respect of a licence or other permission to occupy premises – eg, if you are a lodger or live in bed and breakfast accommodation;
- 'mesne profits' (in Scotland, 'violent profits'), including payments made if you remain in occupation when a tenancy has been ended;
- other payments for the use and occupation of premises (including boat licence and mooring permit fees if you live in a houseboat[6]);
- payments for eligible service charges (see p65);
- rent, including mooring charges, for a houseboat;
- site rent for a caravan or mobile home (but not a tent, although this might be met as 'other housing costs' by IS, income-based JSA, income-related ESA or PC – see p452);
- rent paid on a garage or land (unless used for business purposes). Either you must be making a reasonable effort to end your liability for it, or you must have been unable to rent your home without it;[7]
- contributions made by a resident of a charity's almshouse;
- payments made under a rental purchase agreement under which the purchase price is paid in more than one instalment and you do not finally own your home until all, or an agreed part of, the purchase price has been paid;
- in Scotland, payments in respect of croft land.

In this *Handbook*, we refer to any of these payments as 'rent'. The payment must be in return for your occupation of the home. This usually means that the payments must be made to the person who has the right to let you occupy it, or someone acting on her/his behalf, but payments to someone else might qualify for HB. This depends on, for example, whether you have a valid tenancy agreement with that person.[8]

Payments that cannot be met by housing benefit

HB cannot meet payments made:[9]
- by an owner or under a long tenancy (ie, you own your accommodation or have a lease of more than 21 years), unless you have a shared ownership tenancy (ie, you are buying part of your house or flat and renting the rest). In this case, you can get HB on the part you rent. You are treated as the owner of the property if you have the right to sell it, even though you may not be able to do so without the consent of other joint owners;[10]
- for a dwelling owned (or part owned) by your partner;
- by a Crown tenant;
- under a co-ownership scheme under which you receive a payment related to the value of the accommodation when you leave;

- under a hire purchase (eg, for the purchase of a mobile home), credit sale or a conditional sale agreement except to the extent that it is in respect of land.

In all of these cases (other than the second), the payments might be met by IS, income-based JSA, income-related ESA or PC instead. In the second case, the payments you make to your partner cannot be met by IS, income-based JSA, income-related ESA or PC, but certain loans and other housing costs you (or your partner) have might be met by those benefits. See Chapter 20 for further information.

In addition, HB cannot meet payments if you are getting IS, income-based JSA or income-related ESA for these.[11] However, if you are now getting your housing costs met through IS, income-based JSA or income-related ESA but were previously getting HB for the same accommodation, your HB continues for your first four weeks on IS, income-based JSA or income-related ESA.[12] Remember that, if you buy a home and immediately before that you were renting accommodation and getting HB, your full housing costs might not be met (see p451).

If you live in a care home, you cannot usually get HB for the rent you pay to the home (see p923).

Liability to pay rent

To qualify for HB you must count as liable to pay rent. You count as liable if either you or your partner are liable.[13] You can be treated as liable even if you are not (see p48). You can be treated as not liable even if you are (or can be treated as) liable (see p48). If you pay your rent in advance, you are still treated as liable to pay it, even if you paid it before claiming HB.[14]

For you to be **'liable'** to pay rent, your agreement must be legally enforceable.[15] It is not enough if you only have a moral obligation, such as a promise to pay something whenever you can afford to do so. You can count as liable to pay rent even if someone else has been paying it on your behalf, or if your landlord has failed to provide notice of an address so rent is treated as not being due.[16] You can be liable to pay rent by yourself or you can be jointly liable to do so (see p50).

Does your agreement have to be in writing?

If you have a written agreement with your landlord, this should establish that you are liable to pay rent, provided the liability is a genuine part of the agreement.[17]

Your agreement can be legally enforceable even if it is not in writing. The fact that you have made a firm promise to pay money to your landlord in return for your occupation of the property should be sufficient to show you are liable to pay rent and so allow you to claim HB.[18] If the local authority refuses to accept that you have a legal liability, apply for a revision or appeal.

Part 2: Main means-tested benefits and tax credits
Chapter 4: Housing benefit
1. Who can claim housing benefit

Note: even if the local authority accepts that your agreement is legally enforceable, it may still treat you as not liable to pay rent (see below).

People treated as liable to pay rent

You are treated as liable to pay rent if:[19]

- you have to pay rent in order to continue to live in your home because the liable person is not doing so; *and*
  - you are the former partner of the liable person; *or*
  - you are not the former partner of the liable person and it is reasonable to treat you as liable.[20] It must be reasonable in all of the circumstances, and in light of the overall purpose of the HB scheme.[21]
  It does not matter whether or not the landlord is prepared to transfer the tenancy to you or wants to evict you. If the local authority refuses your HB claim, point out that the eligibility rules for HB and for transferring tenancies are separate, and apply for a revision or appeal; *or*
- your landlord allows you a rent-free period as compensation for carrying out repairs or redecoration which s/he would otherwise have had to carry out (for a maximum of eight benefit weeks in a rent-free period). If you expect the work to last longer, arrange with your landlord to schedule the work in periods of eight weeks or less, separated by at least one complete benefit week in which you resume paying rent; *or*
- you are the partner of a full-time student who is treated as not liable to pay rent (see below). This means that you can qualify for HB even if your partner cannot.

Even if you fall into one of these categories, in certain circumstances you can still be treated as not liable to pay rent, and so not entitled to HB (see below).

People treated as not liable to pay rent

Even if you or your partner are liable to pay rent, you can be treated as though you are not liable to pay rent. In this case, you cannot qualify for HB. This applies if you are in any of the situations below.[22]

- You are a full-time student. This does not apply if you are in one of the categories of student who can qualify for HB (see p883), or if you are at least the qualifying age for PC (see p147).
- You do not satisfy the habitual residence test (see p1537).
- You are a member of, and are fully maintained by, a religious order.[23]
- You are living in a care home or an independent hospital (but see p923).[24]
- You pay rent to someone who also lives in the dwelling and who is your (or your partner's) close relative (see p50 for who counts).[25] Your landlord might be regarded as living in your dwelling if you share some accommodation with her/him, other than a bathroom, toilet or a hall or passageway.[26] It does not matter if you use the accommodation at different times or if you pay to use it.[27]

- Your agreement to pay rent is not on a commercial basis.[28] In deciding whether or not your agreement is commercial, the local authority must look at the whole agreement, taking all the circumstances into account. It must consider, among other things:[29]
  - whether your agreement includes terms that are not legally enforceable;
  - the rent you must pay under the agreement. It does not have to be a market rent. Paying a low rent does not necessarily mean your agreement is not commercial – eg, if you do chores in exchange for a lower rent. Your agreement can count as commercial even if your landlord is not collecting the full contractual rent from you – eg, if it is not being met by HB because of the rent restriction rules (see Chapter 19);
  - your relationship to your landlord. However, just because you are a relative of, or have a close friendship with, her/him, or s/he provides you with care and support, does not mean that your agreement is non-commercial.
- You are renting from:[30]
  - any ex-partner of yours and the home is your former joint home with that ex-partner; *or*
  - any ex-partner of your partner and the home is your partner's former joint home with that ex-partner.
- You or your partner are responsible for a child (under 16) of your landlord.[31] This only applies if the child is included in your HB claim (see p220).
- You, your partner, your ex-partner or your partner's ex-partner, or your or your partner's close relative who lives with you is either:[32]
  - a director or employee of a company which is your landlord; *or*
  - a trustee or beneficiary of a trust which is your landlord.
  This rule does not apply if you can show the arrangement was not intended to take advantage of the HB scheme (see p50).
- You are renting accommodation from a trustee of a trust, of which your (or your partner's) child (under 16) is a beneficiary.
- You were previously the non-dependant (see p67) of someone who lived, and continues to live, in the accommodation. This rule does not apply if you can show that the agreement was not created to take advantage of the HB scheme (see p50).[33]
- You or your current partner previously owned, or had a long tenancy in (ie, a lease of more than 21 years), the accommodation and less than five years have passed since you last owned it (or the tenancy ceased).[34]
  This rule does not apply if you can show that you could not have continued to occupy the accommodation without giving up ownership (or the tenancy) – eg, the lender was seeking possession of your home. Whether you were legally or practically compelled to give up ownership or the tenancy is relevant, but your motivation for doing so is not.[35] You may need to show that you have taken steps to explore alternatives.[36]

Part 2: Main means-tested benefits and tax credits
Chapter 4: Housing benefit
1. Who can claim housing benefit

2

- You or your partner are employed by your landlord and are occupying your accommodation as a condition of employment. This should not apply if you continue to live in the accommodation after ceasing employment.
- Where none of the above apply, the local authority considers that your liability to pay rent has been created to take advantage of the HB scheme (see below).

Close relatives

A **'close relative'** is a parent, parent-in-law (including a civil partner's parent), son, son-in-law (including a son's civil partner), daughter, daughter-in-law (including a daughter's civil partner), brother, sister, step-parent (including a parent's civil partner), stepson (including a civil partner's son), stepdaughter (including a civil partner's daughter), or the partners of any of these.[37] It also includes half-brothers and half-sisters.[38] Relations with in-laws or step-relatives are severed by divorce (or dissolution of a civil partnership) but arguably not by death – eg, a stepchild is still a stepchild after the death of her/his mother.[39]

Agreements taking advantage of the housing benefit scheme

For your agreement to count as 'taking advantage of the HB scheme', it must amount to an abuse of the scheme or to taking improper advantage of it. It must be shown that the main reason you entered into the agreement was to obtain HB.[40] All the circumstances should be taken into account, including what your landlord has to say.[41] An agreement can count as taking advantage of the HB scheme even if it was created from the best of motives.[42] Bear the following in mind.

- You should *not* be seen as taking advantage of the HB scheme just because:
  - your landlord is your parent;[43] *or*
  - you hope to be able to claim HB to help you with your rent – ie, if your main purpose is to get accommodation, not to obtain HB;[44] *or*
  - you seek to find out what rent can be covered by HB before moving in.
- Tenants of a landlord who deliberately charges high rents to try to get them paid by HB may be affected by this provision, even if they had no such intention themselves. However, the fact that a landlord sets a high rent does not in itself mean that the liability takes advantage of the HB scheme.[45]
- If your landlord is going to evict you if you cannot get HB, this suggests that the agreement does *not* take advantage of the HB scheme.[46]

Joint liability

If you are a member of a couple (see p215) and are jointly liable for the rent, only one of you can claim HB.[47]

The way a group of single people living together and paying rent to their landlord is treated depends on how many of you are liable under the agreement. If all, or some, of you have joint liability for the rent, you can each make a separate claim and be paid HB on your share (unless the local authority thinks the joint tenancy has been created to take advantage of the HB scheme – see p50).

If you share accommodation with people other than your partner and children included in your claim, and are jointly liable for the rent with them, see p63 for information about how your eligible rent is apportioned between you.

16/17-year-olds

People under 18 can be liable to pay rent and, therefore, entitled to HB, if there is an intention to create legal relations. If you are under 16, an adult or a social services department is generally responsible for the rent, but HB departments should not decide HB entitlement based on what they think the social services department ought to provide. However, if you are being, or have previously been, looked after by a local authority, you cannot usually qualify for HB (see p936).

Occupying accommodation as your home

HB is paid for the home in which you and your partner and any children included in your claim (see p220) normally live.[48] You cannot usually be paid for any other home. However, there are special rules if you:
- have just moved into your home (see below);
- are temporarily absent from home (see p53);
- are liable to pay rent on more than one home (see p57);
- are in certain other situations (see p57).

Note:
- If you occupy more than one property or room as your home (eg, because you have a large family and rent adjacent flats, or have a live-in carer and rent two adjacent rooms in shared accommodation), you can argue that both properties or rooms count as part of your home – ie, that you only have one home.[49]
- If you have to live in an approved bail or probation hostel or are a prisoner on temporary release, you are treated as not occupying the accommodation in which you are staying.[50] You cannot qualify for HB for any rent you pay for the hostel, but you may be able to qualify for HB for your normal home. See p53 for the rules on temporary absence from home.

Moving home

If you have just moved into your home but were liable to pay rent before moving in, you can get HB on your new home for up to four weeks before you moved in.[51] Before moving, you must either have claimed HB or have notified the local authority of the move to the new home. If you have given up your previous home and have no other home, you can argue that the date you move in is the date you move your furniture and belongings in.[52]

Part 2: Main means-tested benefits and tax credits
Chapter 4: Housing benefit
1. Who can claim housing benefit

You can only qualify if the delay in moving was reasonable, and:

- you were waiting for 'local welfare provision' (see below) or a social fund payment for a need connected with the move – eg, removal expenses or to help you set up home. This only applies if:
  – you have a child of five or under living with you; *or*
  – you are at least the qualifying age for PC (see p147) and neither you nor your partner are getting IS, income-based JSA or income-related ESA (or UC); *or*
  – you are under the qualifying age for PC (see p147), or you or your partner are getting IS, income-based JSA or income-related ESA (or UC), and you qualify for a disability, severe disability or disabled child premium, or a support or work-related activity component. **Note:** this rule was not amended when the work-related activity component was abolished for claims on or after 3 April 2017 (see p641); *or*
- you were waiting for adaptations to be finished to meet needs you, your partner or a child included in your claim (see p220) have because of a disability. The adaptations do not have to involve a change to the fabric or structure of the dwelling, but must be reasonably required and have a clear connection to the disability needs;[53] *or*
- you became liable to make payments on your new home while you were a hospital patient or in residential accommodation (see p55 for the meaning).

Local welfare provision

'Local welfare provision' means occasional financial or other assistance provided by a local authority, the Welsh Ministers or the Scottish Ministers, or people authorised by them (called local welfare assistance schemes in this *Handbook*).[54] The assistance must be:

– to meet, or to help to meet, an immediate short-term need due to exceptional circumstances or to avoid a risk to a person's wellbeing; *or*

– to enable someone to establish or maintain a settled home if s/he has been (or without assistance might be) in prison, hospital, residential care or another institution, or homeless or living an unsettled way of life.

Your HB is not paid until you move in. If an earlier claim for HB you made before you moved in was turned down, you must claim again within four weeks of moving to qualify.

If you are obliged to pay rent for your old home as well as your new accommodation, you can only get HB for one of these unless you are covered by the rules described on p57.[55]

If you move and are not liable to pay rent in your new accommodation (eg, if you are now in prison or hospital and you cannot get HB while temporarily absent from home), you can get HB for up to four weeks for your former home if you:[56]

- were liable for rent on it immediately before moving into your new accommodation and continue to be liable – eg, because you have to give notice to your landlord; *and*
- could not reasonably have avoided liability for rent on your former home.

Temporary absence from home

If you are temporarily absent from your normal home, your entitlement to HB can continue for a period if you have not rented out your home and you intend to return to it.[57] The length of time you can be away depends on the circumstances and on whether you are absent from home within or outside Great Britain. You can argue that you count as temporarily absent from your home even if you have not yet stayed there – eg, you move your furniture and belongings in, but then have to go into hospital.[58]

You can get HB while you are absent from your normal home for up to:

- **13 weeks**, whatever the reason for your absence (see p54);
- **52 weeks**, if you come within any of the situations on pp54–55.

The period can be shorter if you are, or have been, absent from Great Britain (see p55).

The number of weeks runs from the date you leave home.[59] The day you leave home is included, but not the day you return home.[60] If, for example, you have been away from home for 10 weeks and then have grounds to continue to get HB for 52 weeks, you only get HB for the balance: 42 weeks. However, a new period of absence starts if you return home for even a short stay. A stay of at least 24 hours may be enough.[61] This does not apply if you are a prisoner on temporary release.[62]

Note: if you have someone living with you who is temporarily absent from home (eg, s/he is a student who is away during term time), the local authority may use these rules to decide whether s/he is a non-dependant (see p67).[63] It may also use these rules to decide whether your partner, or a child or young person included in your claim, counts as occupying your home.

Will you be away from home temporarily?

1. Let the local authority know that you are going to be absent from your normal home and the reason for this, as well as if you will be absent from Great Britain, preferably before you go away. Make it clear that your absence will be temporary and that you are unlikely to be away for longer than the period allowed.

2. Your intention to return, and whether or not you are unlikely to be away for longer than the period allowed, should be based initially on the circumstances on the date you leave your home, unless you are in residential accommodation for a trial period.[64]

3. If at any time after the date you leave your home, you no longer intend to return or it becomes likely that you will be away from home (or absent from Great Britain) for longer than the period allowed, inform the local authority of this change in your circumstances to avoid an overpayment. In this case, the local authority can reconsider your entitlement.[65]

Part 2: Main means-tested benefits and tax credits
Chapter 4: Housing benefit
1. Who can claim housing benefit

Housing benefit for up to 13 weeks

You can get HB for up to 13 weeks while you are absent from your normal home within Great Britain.[66] It does not matter why you are away from home. You must be unlikely to be away for more than 13 weeks. Within the 13-week period, you can be absent from Great Britain for up to four weeks. The four-week period can be extended by up to another four weeks in limited cases. See p55 for further information.

Housing benefit for up to 52 weeks

You can get HB for up to 52 weeks while you are in residential accommodation (see p55) in Great Britain for a trial period to see if it suits your needs.[67] On the date you enter the accommodation, you must intend to return home if it is not suitable.[68] You can only get HB for up to 13 weeks. If the accommodation does not suit your needs, you can have further trial periods in other accommodation provided you are not away from home for more than 52 weeks in total.

You can get HB for up to 52 weeks if you are absent from your normal home within Great Britain if you are unlikely to be away for longer than this (or, in exceptional circumstances, unlikely to be away for substantially longer than this) in the following situations.[69] There must be some causal link between your absence from home and being in one of these situations.[70] **Note:** within the 52-week period, you can be absent from Great Britain for up to four or 26 weeks at a time as the case may be (see below). Also within this period, you can be absent from Great Britain for up to four weeks, whatever the reason. This four-week period can be extended by up to another four weeks in limited cases. See p55 for further information. You can be absent from Great Britain as a member of the armed forces posted overseas, a mariner or a continental shelf worker for up to 26 weeks (see p55).

You can get HB for up to 52 weeks if:[71]

- you are resident in a hospital or similar institution as a patient. You cannot get HB after you have been resident in hospital for 52 weeks, even if this is because you are seriously mentally ill. A new period of absence starts if you return home for even a short stay;[72]
- you, your partner or a 'dependent child' under 16 are undergoing medical treatment or medically approved convalescence, other than in residential accommodation (see p55 for the meaning). 'Dependent child' is not defined in the rules, so could include children who are not included in your claim;
- you are receiving 'medically approved' care (ie, certified by a medical practitioner), other than in residential accommodation (see p55 for the meaning);
- you are away from home because of a fear of violence. You need not have experienced actual violence, but you must be in fear of violence in your home or from a former partner, or a child or qualifying young person previously included in your claim. The first category includes violence by neighbours and

racial attacks on your home. See p57 if you need to claim for two homes and p57 if you do not intend to return to your former home.

In the same situations, and within the 52-week period, you can get HB while you are temporarily absent from Great Britain for up to 26 weeks (see below).
You can get HB for up to 52 weeks if:[73]

- you are a remand prisoner held in custody pending trial or sentence. Once you are sentenced, you no longer qualify for HB under this rule, but might still qualify under the 13-week rule on p54. The 13 weeks run from the date you were first in prison, so any time you spend in prison awaiting trial or sentence counts towards the 13 weeks. **Note:** you are treated as still in custody if you are a prisoner on temporary release;[74]

- you are required to live in an approved hostel or at an address away from your normal home as a condition of bail;

- you are providing 'medically approved' care – ie, certified by a medical practitioner;

- you are caring for a child under 16 whose parent or guardian is away from home receiving medically approved care or medical treatment;

- you are undertaking a training course (see below);

- you are a student. You must not come into the first category under 'Other situations' on p58, or be entitled to HB on two homes (see p57);

- you are in residential accommodation (see below) for short-term or respite care.

In the same situations, and within the 52-week period, you can get HB while you are temporarily absent from Great Britain for up to four weeks. See below for further information.

Definitions[75]

'Residential accommodation' means a care home, an independent hospital or an Abbeyfield home. It also means an establishment managed or provided by a body incorporated by Royal Charter or constituted by an Act of Parliament, other than a local social services authority.

A **'training course'** is a course of training or instruction provided by or on behalf of, or approved by, a government department, the Secretary of State, Skills Development Scotland, Scottish Enterprise or Highlands and Islands Enterprise.

Absence from Great Britain

You can get HB while you are temporarily absent from Great Britain for up to:

- **four weeks,** whatever the reason.[76] You must be unlikely to be away for longer than four weeks. The four weeks can be extended by up to another four weeks if you are temporarily absent from Great Britain in connection with the death

Part 2: Main means-tested benefits and tax credits
Chapter 4: Housing benefit
1. Who can claim housing benefit

of your partner or a child or young person included in your claim (see p220), or the death of your or your partner's or child's or young person's close relative and the local authority thinks it is unreasonable to expect you to return to Great Britain within the first four weeks;

- **four or 26 weeks**, in the situations in which you can get HB while absent from home for up to 52 weeks (see p54). You must be unlikely to be away for longer than this (or, in exceptional circumstances, unlikely to be away for substantially longer than this);[77]
- **26 weeks**, while you are absent from Great Britain as a member of the armed forces posted overseas, a mariner or a continental shelf worker. You must be unlikely to be away for longer than 26 weeks.[78]

The number of weeks runs from the first day of absence from Great Britain.[79] The 13 or 52 weeks you are allowed to be absent from home *in* Great Britain continue to run during any period you are absent from Great Britain.[80] When you return to Great Britain, if you are still away from your normal home, you can continue to get HB for the remainder (if any) of the 13- or 52-week period allowed. However, if your HB ceased because you were no longer treated as occupying your normal home (eg, because you had been absent from Great Britain too long), you cannot qualify for HB until you return home.[81] **Note:** if you have a European Economic Area (EEA) right to reside in the UK and go abroad to another EEA state, see p1595.

Examples

Paul visits his mother in London for a week before going on a three-week a holiday to France. He lets the local authority know this and also that he plans to visit his sister in Manchester for two weeks on the way home. He can be absent from home for up to 13 weeks and absent from Great Britain for up to four weeks within that period. He gets HB for 1 + 3 + 2 = 6 weeks while he is temporarily absent from home.

Sheila travels to Canada to visit her grandmother for two weeks. At the end of the second week, she notifies the local authority that she intends to stay a further three weeks. She is no longer treated as occupying her normal home because she is going to be absent from Great Britain for longer than four weeks. She therefore only gets HB for two weeks.

Mary leaves home to go on a training course in Birmingham. She notifies the local authority that she will be away from home for 20 weeks. During the 20-week course, she will be on a placement in France for two weeks. Mary therefore continues to get HB for the 20-week period she is away from home (18 weeks in Great Britain and two weeks outside Great Britain).

Note: the rules about temporary absence from home changed on 28 July 2016. If you were temporarily absent from Great Britain when the new rules came into force, the rules limiting the time you can be absent from home outside Great Britain do not apply until you return (unless you are a member of the armed forces posted overseas, a continental shelf worker or a mariner).[82] For the rules that applied before 28 July 2016, see pp46–49 of the 2015/16 edition of this *Handbook*.

Housing benefit for more than one home

You can usually only get HB for one home. **Note:** if you occupy more than one property as a home (eg, you rent adjacent flats because you have a large family or two adjacent rooms in shared accommodation because you have a live-in carer), you can argue that you only have one home.[83]

If you occupy two homes, you *can* get HB for both in the following situations. You can get HB:

- **for up to four weeks** for a new and an old home, if:[84]
  - you have moved into the new home and you could not reasonably avoid having to pay rent on your old home.[85] The local authority must consider the reasons why you had to move quickly. For example, if you were forced to move quickly to take advantage of better accommodation, you may not have been able to avoid leaving without giving notice; *or*
  - a move was delayed while you were adapting your new home to meet needs you, your partner or a child included in your claim have because of disability (see p52). You can get HB on both homes for the four weeks prior to the date you move. The adaptations do not have to involve a change to the fabric or structure of the dwelling, but must be reasonably required and have a clear connection to the disability needs;[86]
- **for up to 52 weeks** for a temporary home and your normal home, if you have left your home because of a fear of violence (see p54 for the meaning). You must intend to return to your normal home, and it must be reasonable for you to receive payments for both homes. The payments can be either HB or UC. For example, if your temporary home counts as 'specified accommodation' (see p45), you can get HB for it, and HB (or a UC housing costs element) for the rent you pay for your normal home;[87]
- **indefinitely** for two normal homes, if:[88]
  - you are a member of a couple and you or your partner are a student eligible for HB (see p883) or are on a training course (see p55 for the meaning), it is necessary for you to live apart and it is reasonable for you to receive HB for both homes; *or*
  - the local authority has housed you in more than one home because your family is large.

Other situations

If you have left your home because of a **fear of violence** (see p54 for the meaning) and you do not intend to return, you can get HB for four weeks for your former

Part 2: Main means-tested benefits and tax credits
Chapter 4: Housing benefit
2. The rules about your age

home.[89] This only applies if your liability to pay rent was unavoidable – eg, you should have given your landlord notice, but had to leave in a hurry.

If you have two homes, and you are only liable to pay for one of them, you are treated as occupying the home for which you pay and therefore get HB for that home, even when you are not there. This only applies if:[90]

- you are a single claimant or a lone parent, and you are either a student eligible for HB (see p883) or are on a training course (see p55), and you live in one home during periods of study or training and another home at other times – eg, for vacations; *or*
- you had to move into temporary accommodation because essential repairs are being carried out on your main home. 'Essential repairs' means basic works rather than luxuries, but they need not be crucial to making the house habitable.[91]

Note: you cannot get HB under this rule if you pay rent for both homes, or if you pay rent for one and a mortgage on the other.

2. The rules about your age

There are no lower or upper age limits for claiming housing benefit (HB). However, if you are:

- **under 16**, there may be a question about whether you have a legally enforceable liability for rent (see p51);
- **16 or 17** and are being, or have been, looked after by a local authority, you cannot usually claim HB. See p936 for further information;
- **18 to 21**, from April 2017 if you are out of work and live in a universal credit (UC) 'full service' area and make a new claim for UC, you no longer qualify for help with your rent automatically. It appears that this will *not* apply to HB. See CPAG's online service and *Welfare Rights Bulletin* for updates;
- **a single claimant under 35** and are living in private rented accommodation, the amount of your rent that can be met by HB is usually restricted to the 'single room rent' or the local housing allowance for one-bedroom shared accommodation (see Chapter 19);
- **at least the qualifying age for pension credit** (see p147) and neither you nor your partner are getting income support, income-based jobseeker's allowance, income-related employment and support allowance or UC, more generous rules apply. The different rules for income, capital and applicable amounts are covered in other chapters in this *Handbook*.

3. People included in the claim

You claim housing benefit (HB) for yourself. However, if you are a member of a couple, you or your partner must claim HB for you both. Your applicable amount includes a personal allowance for a couple and can include premiums based on both your and your partner's circumstances. When your benefit is worked out, your partner's income and capital are usually added to yours. See p215 for who counts as a couple.

There are some situations in which you must show that you are 'responsible' for a child who is living in your household – eg:

- so your applicable amount can include allowances and premiums for child(ren);
- to show you are a lone parent so you can benefit from a higher earnings disregard (see p279 and p321);
- to qualify for a disregard of earnings for childcare costs (see p281 and p323);
- for some of the rules about the size of accommodation or the number of bedrooms you are allowed that affect your maximum HB (see Chapter 19).

See p220 for who counts as a child (this includes some qualifying young people). You do not have to be the child's parent. For when you count as responsible for a child, and when s/he counts as living in your household, see pp222–25.

4. The amount of benefit

The amount of housing benefit (HB) you get depends on:

- your 'applicable amount' (see Chapter 12). This is made up of personal allowances, as well as premiums and components for any special needs. It may include a transitional addition if you or your partner were transferred to contributory employment and support allowance (ESA), or are appealing a decision not to transfer you to ESA (see p252);
- your '**maximum HB**'. This is your 'eligible rent' (see p62), calculated on a weekly basis, minus any deductions made for your non-dependants (see p67).[92] The amount depends on whether your 'eligible rent' is restricted (see Chapter 19); *and*
- how much income and capital you have (see Chapters 14 or 15 and 17 or 18).

Example

Mr and Mrs Feinstein and their adult son live together in a two-bedroom flat rented from the local authority. They are allowed two bedrooms under the social sector rules (known as the 'bedroom tax'). Mr Feinstein is the sole tenant. The rent is £100 a week. This does not include any service charges. Their son earns £150 a week gross.

Part 2: Main means-tested benefits and tax credits
Chapter 4: Housing benefit
4. The amount of benefit

Eligible rent is the contractual rent	£100
Minus non-dependant deduction (see p69)	£34
Maximum HB	**£66**

If you do not qualify for HB currently, you may qualify if:

- the benefit rates go up; *or*
- you or your partner reach:
  - the qualifying age for pension credit (PC – see p147). If neither you nor your partner are on income support (IS), income-based jobseeker's allowance (JSA) or income-related ESA (or universal credit – UC), your applicable amount is higher and the income and capital rules are also more generous; *or*
  - 65. Your personal allowance is increased by the equivalent of the amount of the maximum savings credit of PC, whether or not you receive this, if neither you nor your partner are on IS, income-based JSA or income-related ESA (or UC). **Note:** this applies even though savings credit is being phased out (see p147). This may change. See CPAG's online service and *Welfare Rights Bulletin* for updates.

If your income is too high for you to qualify for HB currently, you might qualify once you (or your partner or a child included in your claim) become entitled to another benefit (a 'qualifying benefit' – see p81).

Remember that if you (or your partner) need help with the costs of your housing in addition to your HB, you might qualify for discretionary housing payments (see Chapter 21).

Note: you might get a reduced amount of HB if:

- you are affected by the 'benefit cap' (see p1180); *or*
- your HB is restricted because of a benefit offence (see p1265).

If you are on a means-tested benefit

Being on **IS, income-based JSA, income-related ESA, the guarantee credit of PC** or **UC** is an automatic passport to maximum HB, once you have made a claim for HB. Therefore, you do not need to work out your applicable amount, income or capital.[93] Your HB is always your 'maximum HB' (see p59 for the meaning).

For these purposes, you are treated as being on:[94]

- income-based JSA when it is payable to you and also:
  - when you satisfy the conditions of entitlement but are not being paid it because of a sanction (see p1093);
  - on your waiting days (see p132); *and*
  - when it is not paid because of the benefit offence rules (see p1265);
- income-related ESA when it is payable to you and also:

– when you satisfy the conditions of entitlement but are not being paid it because you are disqualified for the reasons on p34;
– on your waiting days (see p639). The rules are the same as for contributory ESA;
- UC on any day you are entitled to it, whether or not it is being paid to you.

Example

Glen and his partner Craig are the joint housing association tenants of a two-bedroom flat. Glen's aunt lives with them. They pay rent of £150 a week. They receive income-based JSA while they are looking for work. Glen's aunt receives IS. Glen claims HB. They are allowed two bedrooms under the social sector rules (known as the 'bedroom tax' – see p418). Eligible rent and, therefore, maximum HB is £150 a week.

Glen's aunt counts as a non-dependant and so £14.80 a week is deducted.

Therefore, Glen's maximum HB is £135.20 a week (£150 – £14.80).

Because they receive income-based JSA, Glen's HB is £135.20 a week.

If you are not on a means-tested benefit

If you are **not on IS, income-based JSA, income-related ESA or the guarantee credit of PC (or UC),** follow the steps below to calculate your HB.[95]
- **Step one:** check that your capital is not too high (see Chapters 17 or 18).
- **Step two:** work out your maximum HB (see p59 for the meaning).
- **Step three:** work out your applicable amount (see Chapter 12).
- **Step four:** work out your income (see Chapters 14 or 15, but also p891 if you are a student and p316 if you are getting the savings credit of PC).
- **Step five:** calculate HB.
  – **If your income is less than or equal to your applicable amount,** HB equals maximum HB.
  – **If your income is greater than your applicable amount,** work out the difference. HB equals maximum HB minus 65 per cent of the difference between your income and your applicable amount.

Examples

Mr Jopling is aged 45. He is unemployed and gets contribution-based JSA of £73.10 a week. Mrs Jopling is aged 46. She works 21 hours a week. She is paid £201.75 a week after deductions of tax and national insurance (NI) contributions. The couple are joint private tenants who pay £160 rent a week. Mrs Jopling claims HB. Her eligible rent is £120 a week because rent restriction rules have been applied.

Mr and Mrs Jopling have no non-dependants. Therefore, her maximum HB is £120 a week. Mrs Jopling's applicable amount is £114.85 (the standard rate for a couple).

Part 2: Main means-tested benefits and tax credits
Chapter 4: Housing benefit
4. The amount of benefit

Income to be taken into account is Mr Jopling's JSA and Mrs Jopling's earnings of £191.75 a week (because £10 of her earnings are disregarded – see p280).

£73.10 + £191.75 = £264.85

The difference between her income and her applicable amount is £150 a week.

65% x £150 = £97.50 a week.

Mrs Jopling's HB is, therefore, £120 – £97.50 = £22.50 a week.

Mr Haralambous is 64 years old. He receives contributory ESA including a support component, totalling £109.65 a week. His weekly income from his private pension is £60. His total weekly income is therefore £169.65 (£109.65 + £60). He is a sole tenant of his one-bedroom council flat. His rent of £125 a week includes his heating and hot water. His eligible rent is £92.85 a week because £28.80 and £3.35 are deducted from his contractual rent for heating and hot water. This is also his maximum HB because he does not have any non-dependants.

His applicable amount is £159.35 (adult personal allowance for a single person at least the qualifying age for PC but under 65).

The difference between his income and his applicable amount is £10.35.

65% x £10.35 = £6.73 a week.

Mr Haralambous's HB is, therefore, £92.85 – £6.73 = £86.12 a week.

Calculating a weekly amount of housing benefit

HB is always paid for a specific benefit week – a period of seven consecutive days beginning with a Monday and ending on a Sunday.[96] If you pay rent at different intervals (eg, monthly or daily), the amount must be converted to a weekly figure before HB can be calculated.[97]

Rent-free periods

If you have a regular rent-free period (eg, you only pay rent 48 weeks a year), you get no HB during your rent-free period. Your applicable amount, weekly income, non-dependant deductions, the set deductions for meals and fuel charges and the minimum amount payable (but not your eligible rent) are adjusted.[98] This is to ensure that you do not lose or gain benefit by ignoring your circumstances in the weeks that you do not pay rent.

This does not apply if your landlord has temporarily waived the rent in return for your doing repairs (see p48).

Eligible rent

Your 'eligible rent' is the amount of your rent used to calculate your HB. It may be lower than the actual rent you pay. Unless any of the rent restriction rules apply, your eligible rent is your contractual rent, minus any ineligible charges (see p64).[99] If any of the rent restriction rules apply, your eligible rent is usually your 'maximum rent' as determined under those rules – ie, the amount to which your rent is restricted.

The four rent restriction schemes are the local housing allowance rules, the social sector rules (known as the 'bedroom tax'), the local reference rent rules and the pre-January 1996 rules. See Chapter 19 for details of all the schemes and how your maximum rent (and, therefore, your eligible rent) is worked out.

If none of the rent restriction rules apply, the local authority has general powers to decrease your eligible rent to an amount it considers appropriate (see p407).

Remember the following.

- If you are in shared accommodation, your eligible rent might be apportioned between you and the people with whom you share (see below).
- If the rent you pay covers both residential and other accommodation (eg, for business use), your HB only covers the rent you pay for the residential accommodation.[100]

If you live in shared accommodation

Unless the local housing allowance rules or social sector rules apply to you (see p407 and p415), if you share accommodation with people other than your partner and children included in your claim and are jointly liable for the rent with them (see p50), the local authority apportions the eligible rent between you. If the rent includes any ineligible service charges, these are apportioned between you on the same basis. If only one of you is liable for the rent, that person is treated as the tenant and the other(s) might count as a non-dependant(s) (see p67).

To work out how to apportion the eligible rent, the local authority considers:[101]

- the number of jointly liable people in the property (including any students who are treated as not liable to pay rent);[102] *and*
- the proportion of the rent actually paid by each liable person; *and*
- any other relevant circumstances, such as:
  - the number of rooms occupied by each jointly liable person;
  - whether any formal or informal agreement exists between you regarding the use and occupation of the home; *and*
  - if one of the jointly liable people has left the accommodation, the demands being made by the landlord on those who remain, or the possibility of finding other accommodation.

In some circumstances, it could be appropriate to apportion the whole of the rent to you, even if you are jointly liable.[103]

Example

Sarah and Maude are friends who rent a two-bedroom housing association flat. They are joint tenants and pay rent of £100 a week. Sarah claims HB. The eligible rent is apportioned between them and Sarah's HB is based on £50 (£100 divided by two).

Part 2: Main means-tested benefits and tax credits
Chapter 4: Housing benefit
4. The amount of benefit

2

Note: if the local housing allowance or social sector rules apply to you, it is not necessary to apportion the eligible rent if you are jointly liable for it, but the local authority *does* apportion your 'cap rent' (under the local housing allowance rules) or your maximum rent (under the social sector rules).[104] See Chapter 19 for details.

Ineligible charges

The local authority deducts ineligible charges when it works out your eligible rent. Note, however, that if the local reference rent rules or the local housing allowance rules apply, an adjustment on account of ineligible charges is instead generally made when the rent officer makes determinations.

Ineligible charges include:

- water charges for your personal use. Water charges in respect of communal areas (see p65) – eg, in supported or sheltered accommodation – are eligible;[105]
- most fuel charges (see below); *and*
- some service charges (see p66), including charges for meals.

Remember that, in addition, you cannot get HB for:

- payments for any part of your accommodation that is used exclusively for business purposes;[106] *or*
- rent supplements charged to clear your rent arrears.[107]

Fuel charges

Fuel charges are ineligible unless they are for communal areas (see p65).[108] If your fuel charge is:

- specified on your rent book or is readily identifiable from your agreement with your landlord, the full amount of the charge is ineligible.[109] However, if your fuel charge is considered to be unrealistically low, a flat-rate amount is ineligible instead (see below). This is also the case if your total fuel charge is specified but contains an unknown amount for communal areas;
- not readily identifiable, a flat-rate amount is ineligible. The amounts are:[110]

If you and your family occupy more than one room:	
For heating (other than hot water)	£28.80
For hot water	£3.35
For lighting	£2.30
For cooking	£3.35
If you and your family occupy one room only:	
For heating alone, or heating combined with either hot water or lighting or both	£17.23
For cooking	£3.35

The above amounts are added together if fuel is supplied for more than one purpose. If you are a joint tenant, all the amounts are apportioned according to your share of the rent (see p63).

Note: the local authority must notify you if flat-rate fuel amounts have been used in calculating your HB. It must explain that, if you can produce evidence from which the actual or approximate amount of your fuel charge can be estimated, the flat-rate amounts may be varied accordingly.

Do you occupy one room only?

The lower amounts apply if the accommodation you and your partner and children occupy consists of one room only. This is not defined, but the decision maker is likely to say this means that, if you only occupy one room but share the use of other rooms (such as a communal lounge), the higher amounts apply.[111] Argue that bathrooms, toilets and shared kitchens are not rooms you occupy. If you are forced to live in one room because the other room(s) in your accommodation are, in practice, unfit to live in (eg, because of severe mould or dampness), argue that the lower amounts apply.

Fuel for communal areas

If you pay a service charge for the use of fuel in communal areas, and that charge is separately identified from any other charge for fuel used within your accommodation, it may be included as part of your eligible rent.[112] If you pay a charge for the provision of a heating system (eg, regular boiler maintenance), this is also eligible if the amount is separately identified from any other fuel charge you pay.[113]

Communal areas

'**Communal areas**' include access areas like halls and passageways, but not rooms in common use, except those in sheltered accommodation – eg, a shared TV lounge or dining room.[114]

Service charges

Service charges are only covered by HB if payment is a condition of occupying the accommodation rather than an optional extra.[115] Eligible and ineligible service charges are listed below. If the local authority regards any of the eligible charges as excessive, it estimates a reasonable amount given the cost of comparable services.[116] If you are in supported accommodation, see p67.

Eligible services

The following services are eligible for HB:

- services for the provision of adequate accommodation, including some warden and caretaker services, water charges in respect of communal areas (see above) – eg, in supported or sheltered accommodation, gardens (including the upkeep of a communal garden), children's play areas, lifts, entry phones, communal

Part 2: Main means-tested benefits and tax credits
Chapter 4: Housing benefit
4. The amount of benefit

telephone costs, portering and rubbish removal.[117] TV and radio relay charges are covered – eg, satellite or cable, including free-to-view UK channels;[118]
- laundry facilities (eg, a laundry room in an apartment block), but not charges for the provision of personal laundry;[119]
- furniture and household equipment, but not if there is an agreement that the furniture will eventually become yours;[120]
- cleaning of the outside of windows if you or a member of your household cannot clean them yourself, and cleaning of rooms and windows in communal areas, unless your local authority or the Welsh Ministers pays for these.[121]

Ineligible services
The following services are not eligible for HB:[122]
- food, including prepared meals (see below);
- sports facilities;
- TV rental, licence and subscription fees (but see above);
- transport;
- personal laundry service;
- provision of an emergency alarm system;
- medical expenses;
- nursing and personal care;
- counselling and other support services;
- any other charge not connected with the provision of adequate accommodation and not specifically included in the list of eligible charges above.

The amount of the charge specified in your rent agreement is not eligible for HB, although local authorities can substitute their own estimate if they consider the amount to be unreasonably low.[123] If the amount is not specified in your rent agreement, the local authority estimates how much is fairly attributable to the service, given the cost of comparable services.[124]

If your housing costs include an amount for meals, set amounts are ineligible regardless of the actual cost.[125] These are:

If at least three meals a day are provided:	
For the claimant, partner and each child aged 16 or over included in the claim	£27.10
For each child aged under 16 included in the claim	£13.75
If breakfast only is provided:	
For the claimant, partner and each child included in the claim	£3.35
In all other cases (part board):	
For the claimant, partner and each child aged 16 or over included in the claim	£18.05
For each child aged under 16 included in the claim	£9.10

A child only counts as having reached the age of 16 on the first Monday in September following her/his 16th birthday.

The standard amounts are also ineligible for everyone who has meals paid for by you – eg, a non-dependant.[126]

Support services in supported accommodation

If you live in supported accommodation, HB can help with your rent. However, HB is not available for the support services provided with your accommodation. Instead, the local authority funds these (eg, via your landlord or a voluntary organisation) and you may be charged for them.

Deductions for non-dependants

If other people normally live with you in your home, other than your partner and children included in your claim (called 'non-dependants'), a set deduction is usually made from your HB.[127] This is because it is assumed the non-dependant makes a contribution towards your outgoings, whether or not s/he does so. Examples of non-dependants are adult sons or daughters, elderly relatives or friends who share your home.

Non-dependant deductions: checklist

1. Do you have a non-dependant – ie, someone who normally lives with you? If not, no deduction can be made.

2. Even if you have a non-dependant, must a deduction be made?

3. If a non-dependant deduction must be made, what is the correct amount of the deduction?

Who counts as a non-dependant

A person only counts as your non-dependant if s/he normally lives with you.[128] So, for example, if someone is only staying with you temporarily but has a home elsewhere, or is homeless and is only using your address as a postal address, s/he should not count as a non-dependant. If you think the local authority has wrongly assumed that a person is your non-dependant, ask for a revision or appeal. **Note:** some people do not count as non-dependants even if they normally live with you (see p68).

A person is only living with you if s/he has her/his home with you and shares some accommodation with you.[129] If s/he only shares a bathroom, lavatory or a communal area such as a hall, passageway or a room in common use in sheltered accommodation, s/he does not count as living with you. If other areas of the house are shared (including the kitchen, unless it is only used by someone else to prepare food for her/him[130]), the person counts as living with you. This is the case even if you only use them at different times, provided you have a shared right to

Part 2: Main means-tested benefits and tax credits
Chapter 4: Housing benefit
4. The amount of benefit

use them and are living in the same household (see p225 for the meaning of 'household').[131] A person who is separately liable to pay rent to your landlord does not count as living with you.

A person should only count as normally living with you if s/he has been there long enough to regard your home as her/his normal home.[132] Factors to be taken into account include:[133]

- the relationship between you;
- how much time s/he spends at your address;
- where s/he has her/his post sent;
- where s/he keeps her/his clothes and personal belongings;
- whether her/his stay or absence from your address is temporary or permanent. The temporary absence rules on p53 may be used to work this out;[134]
- whether s/he has another place that could be regarded as home and if, for instance, s/he pays rent or water charges there, or s/he just travels around.

People who do not count as non-dependants

The following people do *not* count as non-dependants, and no non-dependant deduction is made for them, even if they normally live with you:[135]

- your partner;
- a child or qualifying young person included in your claim;
- a child or qualifying young person living with you who does not count as a member of your household (see p224) – eg, a foster child;
- someone who is employed by a charitable or voluntary organisation as a resident carer for you or your partner and who you pay for the service or if a public body pays on your behalf;
- any person, or a member of her/his household, to whom you or your partner are liable to pay rent on a commercial basis – eg, a resident landlord;
- someone who jointly occupies your home and is either the joint owner with you or your partner or is liable with you or your partner to make payments in respect of occupying it. You do not jointly occupy the home with someone unless you made a joint agreement with your landlord to do so. The mere fact that you live in the same home does not make you joint occupiers;[136]
- someone who is liable to pay rent on a commercial basis to you or your partner – eg, your tenants or lodgers. However, although no non-dependant deduction can be made for her/him, the rent s/he pays can count as your income (see p291 and p326).

Note: if the person comes within the last three categories above, s/he *does* count as a non-dependant if s/he is treated as not liable for rent under the rules explained on pp48–50 (other than if s/he is a student or a person who has failed the 'habitual residence test').[137]

When a non-dependant deduction is not made

No non-dependant deduction is made for any of your non-dependants if either you or your partner:[138]

- are certified as severely sight-impaired or blind by a consultant ophthalmologist (or are within 28 weeks of ceasing to be certified); *or*
- receive attendance allowance (AA) (or equivalent benefits paid because of injury at work or a war injury), the care component of disability living allowance (DLA), the daily living component of personal independence payment (PIP) or armed forces independence payment.

In addition, no deduction is made in respect of a non-dependant:[139]

- who is staying with you temporarily, but whose normal home is elsewhere;
- who is receiving a training allowance in connection with youth training under specified provisions;[140]
- who is a full-time student during her/his period of study. This includes those getting JSA who count as full-time students while on a specified scheme for assisting people to obtain employment (see p1103). **Note:** no deduction is made during the summer vacation but, if you or your partner are under 65, only if the student is not in full-time work;
- who usually lives with you, is a member of the armed or reserved forces and is away on operations, irrespective of how long s/he has been away;
- who is in hospital for more than 52 weeks. Separate stays in hospital which are not more than 28 days apart are added together when calculating the 52 weeks;
- who is in prison;
- who is under 18 years old;[141]
- who is under 25 and:
  – on IS; *or*
  – on income-based JSA; *or*
  – on income-related ESA, unless s/he receives the support component or s/he has been placed in the work-related activity group, irrespective of whether s/he receives the work-related activity component (see pp641–42); *or*
  – entitled to UC, provided s/he does not have any earned income.
  S/he can be treated as on income-based JSA or income-related ESA for these purposes (see p60).
- who is on PC.

The amount of deductions

If you have a non-dependant living with you who is 18 or over, and for whom a deduction must be made, a fixed amount is deducted from your HB, whatever s/he pays you. A deduction is made for every non-dependant living in your household, except in the case of a non-dependant couple (see p70).

Part 2: Main means-tested benefits and tax credits
Chapter 4: Housing benefit
4. The amount of benefit

Unless your non-dependant is in full-time paid work, a £14.80 deduction is made each week. If your non-dependant is in full-time paid work, the amount of the deduction depends on her/his gross weekly income as follows.[142]

Circumstances	Deduction
Aged 18 or over and in full-time paid work with a weekly gross income of:	
£430 or more	£95.45
£346–£429.99	£86.95
£259–£345.99	£76.35
£200–£258.99	£46.65
£136–£199.99	£34.00
All others (for whom a deduction is made)	£14.80

The rules on full-time paid work are in Chapter 43. Remember the following.

- A non-dependant who is not in (or is treated as not being in) full-time paid work does not attract the higher levels of deduction even if her/his weekly gross income is £136 or more.
- If someone is on IS, or is on or treated as being on income-based JSA or income-related ESA (see p60) for more than three days in a benefit week, s/he does not count as being in full-time paid work in that week.[143] This means the lower deduction (£14.80) is made (or, in some cases, no deduction).

Gross income includes wages before tax and NI are deducted, plus any other income the non-dependant has (apart from AA (or equivalent benefits paid because of injury at work or a war injury), DLA, PIP, armed forces independence payment and payments from any of the Macfarlane Trusts and similar funds (see p290).[144]

Do you know your non-dependant's income?
If you do not know your non-dependant's income, ask the local authority to consider the circumstances – eg, if your non-dependant is doing a job which is normally very low paid. The local authority should not assume the worst – eg, that your non-dependant is earning the highest amount. It should assess the likely level of her/his income on the evidence available.[145]

Non-dependant couples
Only one deduction is made for a couple (or the members of a polygamous marriage) who are non-dependants. The deduction made is the highest that

would have been made if they were treated as individuals.[146] For the purpose of deciding which income band applies (see p69), their joint income counts, even if only one of them is in full-time work.[147]

Non-dependants of joint occupiers

If you share a non-dependant with any other joint occupiers, the deduction is divided between you, taking into account the proportion of housing costs paid by each of you.[148] If the person is a non-dependant of only one of you, the full deduction is made from that person's benefit. No apportionment is made between the members of a couple (or polygamous marriage).

If you or your partner are 65 or over

Unless you or your partner are getting IS, income-based JSA or income-related ESA (or UC), if you or your partner are aged 65 or over and a non-dependant moves in with you so a deduction should be made, or there has been a change of circumstances in respect of a non-dependant so a higher deduction should be made, the effect of this can be delayed for 26 weeks.[149]

Your non-dependant's income or capital is more than yours

Normally, the income and capital of any non-dependant is only relevant when deciding which non-dependant deduction applies. However, unless you are on IS, income-based JSA, income-related ESA or the guarantee credit of PC, your HB entitlement is assessed on the basis of your non-dependant's income and capital rather than your own if:[150]

- her/his income and capital are both greater than yours; *and*
- the local authority is satisfied you have made an arrangement with your non-dependant to take advantage of the HB scheme (see p50).

Any income and capital normally treated as belonging to you is completely ignored, but the rest of the calculation proceeds as normal.

5. Special benefit rules

Special rules may apply to:
- 16/17-year-olds previously looked after by a local authority (see p936);
- people subject to immigration control (see Chapter 65);
- people who have come from or are going abroad (see Chapters 66 and 67);
- people who are studying (see Chapter 40);
- people who are living in a care home or other similar accommodation, or people in prison (see Chapter 41).

Part 2: Main means-tested benefits and tax credits
Chapter 4: Housing benefit
6. Claims and backdating

6. **Claims and backdating**

To be entitled to housing benefit (HB), you must make a claim for it.[151] Claim HB as soon as you think you might be entitled to it or you may lose benefit. The rules about backdating are explained on p78.

If you want to claim discretionary housing payments, you must claim separately (see Chapter 21).

Making a claim

A claim for HB must normally be made **in writing** on a properly completed claim form.[152] See p74 for information about where to claim. Note that if you are claiming another benefit (ie, income support (IS), income-based jobseeker's allowance (JSA), employment and support allowance (ESA), incapacity benefit (IB) or pension credit (PC)), you can claim HB at the same time (see p73).

You may also be able to claim:

- **by telephone** if:
  - your local authority has published a number for this purpose.[153] If the local authority provides a written statement of your circumstances, you must approve this statement for your claim to be valid. **Note:** even if you cannot claim by telephone, if you telephone to ask to be sent a claim form and you return it within one month, your written claim is backdated to the date of your call (see p76); *or*
  - you are claiming IS, JSA, ESA, IB or PC by telephone;
- **by electronic communication** (eg, online or by email), if your local authority has authorised it (by a chief executive's direction).[154]

If you claim in writing, keep a copy in case queries arise. **Note:** the local authority can treat any written document (eg, a letter) as a claim for benefit, provided the written information and evidence you provide is sufficient.[155]

You must provide any information and evidence required (see p76). You can amend or withdraw your claim before a decision is made (see p74). Claim as soon as you can so you do not lose benefit. Ensure your claim is accepted as valid (see p73).

Forms

Claim forms are available from your local authority.[156] You can use your postcode to find out where to get one from your local authority at www.gov.uk/apply-housing-benefit-from-council.

Rapid reclaim

You may be able claim HB without having to give as much detail of your circumstances as is usually required (known as 'rapid reclaim') if your circumstances have not changed since the last time you were claiming HB, and you are reclaiming within:[157]

- 26 weeks and you are also reclaiming IS, JSA or IB and are entitled to IS, income-based JSA or IB; *or*
- 12 weeks and you are also reclaiming ESA.

You are given the shortened form by the Jobcentre Plus office but you must send your HB claim to the local authority, *not* to the DWP.

If you are claiming another benefit

If you are:

- claiming IS, JSA, ESA, IB or PC by telephone, your HB claim is usually completed at the same time.[158] The DWP takes your details and sends you a statement of your circumstances to check, sign and return to the Jobcentre Plus office, along with evidence to support your claim. It forwards your HB claim to the local authority. You can claim HB by telephone to the DWP (using the number specified for this purpose) at any time before a decision is made on your claim for IS, JSA, ESA, IB or PC. **Note:** if the local authority or DWP provides a written statement of your circumstances, you must approve this for your claim to be valid;
- claiming IS, income-based JSA or PC on a written claim form, you are given an HB claim form with the IS/JSA/PC form to complete and return to the local authority. If the local authority asks you to complete its own form, do this as soon as possible;
- providing evidence or information that is required or notifying a change of circumstances to the DWP in connection with your IS, JSA, ESA, IB or PC claim (eg, by telephone), you can claim HB in the same manner if the DWP agrees. You must claim HB before a decision is made on the award of benefit to which the evidence, information or change of circumstances relates.[159]

You might be asked for further information and evidence (see p76).

Making sure your claim is valid

Where possible, your claim for HB should be accompanied by all the information and evidence needed to assess it.[160] Your claim is 'defective' if you:

- do not complete your claim form properly or you claim in writing, but not on the claim form (eg, by letter or email), and do not provide sufficient information and evidence;
- claim by telephone and do not provide all the information required by the local authority or DWP during the telephone call.

It is very important that you provide any information or evidence required. Until you do, your claim may be defective and you may not count as having made a

Part 2: Main means-tested benefits and tax credits
Chapter 4: Housing benefit
6. Claims and backdating

valid claim. However, you should not delay your claim just because you do not have all the evidence ready to send.

If you have:[161]

- not completed the claim form properly, the local authority can return it to you to do so. However, if you sent or gave your claim form to the DWP, it can ask you to provide the local authority with information needed to complete the form; or
- claimed in writing, but not on the claim form (eg, by letter or email), the local authority can send you a claim form to complete properly; or
- claimed by telephone to the local authority, the local authority must give you an opportunity to provide the information required; or
- claimed by telephone to the DWP, the DWP can give you an opportunity to provide the information required. However, if the DWP does not do so, the local authority *must* give you an opportunity to provide the information, unless it thinks it already has sufficient information. If it does, your claim is treated as though it was received on the date of your original claim.

If you return the form completed properly or provide the information or evidence within one month of the last time you were told your claim is defective, your claim is treated as though it was received on the date of your original claim.[162] The local authority can allow you longer than one month if it thinks this reasonable.

Note: if you are told your claim is defective and it is not accepted as valid, you should be given a decision saying so. You can appeal against the decision.

Amending or withdrawing your claim

You may amend your claim (this includes asking for your claim to be backdated) at any time before a decision is made. You can do this by writing to the local authority, by telephone to the local authority or the DWP on the specified number or by any other manner the local authority or DWP decides or accepts.[163] Amendments are treated as though they were part of your original claim.

You may withdraw your claim at any time before a decision is made.[164] You must do this by writing to the local authority or, if you made your claim by telephone to the local authority, by telephone to the local authority. A notice to withdraw your claim takes effect from the day it is received.

Where to make your claim

If you claim in writing, you must usually send or give your HB claim to the local authority's designated office for the receipt of HB claims.[165] The address is usually on the claim form or a notice accompanying it. You can use your postcode to find out where to claim at www.gov.uk/apply-housing-benefit-from-council. You can also send or give your claim to:[166]

- if you or your partner are also claiming IS, JSA, ESA, IB or PC, either your DWP office or the local authority's designated office for HB claims. If you send your

HB claim to the DWP, the DWP must usually forward it to the local authority within two working days of receiving it, or as soon as practicable after.[167]

It may speed up your claim if you send your HB form directly to the local authority. The local authority then verifies your entitlement to IS, JSA, ESA or IB before assessing your HB; *or*

- a county council office, if your local authority has arranged for claims to be received there; *or*
- if you are at least the qualifying age for PC (see p147), any 'authorised office' – ie, an office nominated by the DWP and authorised by the local authority for receiving HB claims.

Keep a copy of your claim form wherever possible. Ask for confirmation that you have delivered it to the relevant office.

If your local authority has authorised it and you are claiming by electronic communication, check the correct address for this with your local authority.[168]

If you are allowed to claim by telephone, you must make your claim to the telephone number published or specified for this purpose.[169]

Who should claim

If you are a single person or a lone parent, you claim HB on your own behalf. If you are a member of a couple, you can decide between you who should claim. If you cannot agree who should claim, the local authority can decide for you.[170]

Who should you choose to make the claim?

If you are a member of a couple, the choice of claimant may affect the level of HB you receive – eg, if one of you is a full-time student and not eligible for HB (see p882) or if one of you is getting ESA and the other is getting disability living allowance (DLA). In addition, if you are considering changing the claim to your partner's name, check whether this could result in your becoming subject to harsher rent restriction rules (see Chapter 19) or losing entitlement to any premiums or components (see Chapter 12).

Appointees

If a person is either temporarily or permanently unable to manage her/his own affairs, the local authority must accept a claim made by someone formally appointed to act legally on her/his behalf.[171] If no one has been formally appointed to look after a claimant's affairs, the local authority can decide to make someone aged over 18 an appointee who can act on her/his behalf. For the purpose of the claim, an appointee has the responsibility of exercising all rights and duties as though s/he were the claimant.

You can write to ask to be an appointee, and can resign after giving four weeks' notice. The local authority may terminate any appointment at any time.[172] If

Part 2: Main means-tested benefits and tax credits
Chapter 4: Housing benefit
6. Claims and backdating

someone is given a formal legal appointment, that person automatically takes over from the person appointed by the local authority.[173]

Information to support your claim

When you claim HB, you must:
- satisfy the national insurance (NI) number requirement (see below), unless you are living in a hostel.[174] If you are a member of a couple, your partner must also usually satisfy this requirement;
- provide proof of your identity, if required; *and*
- ensure your claim is valid – ie, you must provide information and evidence required with the claim (see p73).

It is important that you provide any information or evidence required when you claim. Until you do, you may not count as having made a valid claim (see p73). Correct any defects as soon as possible or your date of claim may be affected.

If you or your partner are getting IS or JSA and have notified the DWP that you have started work, the DWP can ask you to provide the local authority with any information or evidence it needs to decide whether you continue to be entitled to HB.[175] This only applies if, as a result of the change, your entitlement to IS or JSA will end or, if you are getting contribution-based JSA, the amount will reduce.

The local authority may ask you to provide information after you are awarded HB. You must then supply this within one month, or longer if the local authority thinks this is reasonable.[176] If you fail to do so, your HB could be suspended or even terminated (see p1185). **Note:** you must actually have been notified; proof of posting to your last known address is not sufficient.[177]

The national insurance number requirement

For how you (and your partner) can satisfy the NI number requirement, and for when your partner is exempt, see p1150. The rules are the same as for other benefits. However, note the following.
- You do not have to satisfy the NI number requirement if you live in a hostel.[178]
- If you have claimed HB in association with a claim for IS, *income-based* JSA or PC and the DWP has accepted that you satisfy the NI number requirement, the local authority can accept that you also satisfy it for HB purposes.[179]

The date of your claim

The date of your claim is important because it determines when your entitlement to HB starts (see p85). This is not necessarily the date from when you are paid. For information about when payment of HB starts, see p82.

Your date of claim is not necessarily the date it is received by the local authority. It can be an earlier date.

Your **'date of claim'** is usually the earliest of:[180]

- the date you first notify a designated office, DWP office or authorised office (see p74) (or county council office, if the local authority has arranged for claims there) that you want to claim HB, provided a properly completed claim is received in one of those offices within one month. The one-month period can be extended if the local authority thinks it is reasonable; *or*
- the date your valid claim is received by the designated office, DWP office or authorised office (see p74) (or county council office, if the local authority has arranged for claims there).

There are **exceptions** to the above rules if:[181]
- you or your partner have successfully claimed IS, income-based JSA, income-related ESA or the guarantee credit of PC and your HB claim is made within one month of that claim being received by the DWP. Your claim is treated as made on the first day of entitlement to that benefit. For example, if your claim for IS is backdated, your date of claim for HB purposes is the date to which your IS claim is backdated. **Note:** for these purposes, you are treated as entitled to JSA or ESA on your 'waiting days';[182]
- you or your partner are on IS, income-based JSA, income-related ESA or the guarantee credit of PC (or universal credit – UC), have just become liable to pay rent for your home and your HB claim reaches the local authority's designated office or DWP office within one month of your becoming liable. Your claim is treated as made on the date that you first became liable to pay rent;
- you are awarded UC and you claim HB within one month of your UC claim or, if you are someone who does not have to make a claim for UC, within one month of being notified that you were awarded UC. Your HB claim is treated as made on the first day of entitlement to UC;
- you have separated from your partner or s/he has died and s/he was claiming HB for you on the date this happened and you claim within one month of this. Your claim is treated as made on the date you separated or your partner died.

Note: you must make sure your claim is valid. If it is 'defective', you are given a short time to correct the defects (see p73). If you do, your claim is treated as having been made when you initially claimed.

In some cases, you can claim in advance (see p80) and in some cases your claim can be backdated (see p78).

Note: there is an additional exception if you claim UC. If on the basis of information you provided, you are treated as living in an area where there are gateway conditions for a claim for UC, or as satisfying those conditions, but the DWP discovers that the information was incorrect, unless you have already been paid UC, you should be advised by the DWP that you are not entitled to claim UC. If you then claim HB within a month of being told that, and if (taking into account any backdating you have requested and been allowed) your claim is later than the date of your UC claim, your HB claim is treated as made on the date of

Part 2: Main means-tested benefits and tax credits
Chapter 4: Housing benefit
6. Claims and backdating

your UC claim, or a later date from the date on which you would have been entitled.[183]

Backdating your claim

It is very important to claim in time. Even if your claim is backdated, the arrears of HB you can get are limited. Your claim can be backdated:

- for up to three months if you are at least the qualifying age for PC and neither you nor your partner are on IS, income-based JSA or income-related ESA (or UC) (see below);
- for up to one month if you are not yet the qualifying age for PC or you or your partner are on IS, income-based JSA or income-related ESA (or UC). In this case, you must show good cause for your late claim (see p79).

For backdated HB to be considered, you must ask for HB for a past period. Do this as soon as possible, preferably at the same time as your claim for HB. Any backdated HB is calculated on the basis of your circumstances and the HB rules as they were over the backdating period.

If you would have been entitled to HB for an earlier period than the backdating rules allow, you could:

- ask for an 'any time' revision if there are grounds (see p1279);
- ask for compensation from the local authority if you were given wrong information or misled by it (see p1396);
- complain to the Ombudsman (see p1403).

If you only qualify for HB when a qualifying benefit is awarded, see p81.

Three months' backdating

If you are at least the qualifying age for PC (see p147) and neither you nor your partner are on IS, income-based JSA or income-related ESA (or UC), your claim for HB can be backdated for up to three months.[184] This applies whatever the reasons were for your delay in claiming and, even if you do not ask for HB for a past period, until some time after you make your claim for HB. You only need to show that you qualified for HB during that period.

You can get backdated HB for the three months before the date of your HB claim (see p76) – eg, the date your claim was received or the date you notified the local authority that you wanted to claim HB.[185] However, if you or your partner successfully claimed the guarantee credit of PC and your claim for HB is received within one month of your PC claim being received by the DWP, your entitlement to HB cannot begin earlier than three months before your claim for PC was made (or treated as made).

One month's backdating

Your claim for HB can be backdated for up to one month, if you are not yet the qualifying age for PC (see p147) or, if you are at least that age, you or your partner are on IS, income-based JSA or income-related ESA (or UC).[186]

You must show that you qualified for HB during the period *and* prove you had continuous 'good cause' for your failure to claim or to ask for backdated HB (see below). You can only get backdated HB from the latest of:[187]

- **date one:** the day from which you had continuous good cause for your late claim; *or*
- **date two:** the day one month before your date of claim. Your date of claim is not necessarily the date it is received by the local authority; it can be an earlier date (see p76); *or*
- **date three:** the day one month before you asked for backdated HB.

Example

Rose claimed HB on 8 May 2017. After getting advice, she asked for backdated HB on 20 May 2017.

The local authority accepts that she had continuous good cause for her late claim from 23 February 2017.

Date one = 23 February 2017.

Date two = 8 April 2017. This is the day one month before her date of claim for HB.

Date three = 20 April 2017. This is the day one month before she asked for backdated HB.

Rose gets backdated HB from 20 April 2017, the latest of the three relevant dates.

If you are claiming HB after a previous entitlement ended, as well as asking for backdated HB, you should see if you can challenge the local authority's decision to end your entitlement to HB (see Chapters 54 and 55).

You count as having **'good cause'** for your late claim if you can show there is something that would probably have caused a reasonable person of your age and experience to act (or fail to act) as you did, having regard to all the circumstances (including your state of health and the information which you received and which you might have obtained).[188] The more reasonable your behaviour in not claiming earlier given your circumstances, the more likely it is that you have good cause.[189] It is your mental age, not your chronological age, that is relevant.[190] If you have a mental health problem that makes you act unreasonably, that must be borne in mind.[191] If you have difficulty communicating in English or understanding documents, or have little knowledge of the benefits system, this should be taken into account, but these are not usually good cause in themselves.[192]

If you choose not to claim but later change your mind, you must still show that you have good cause for your late claim. The longer you have delayed in claiming, the harder this may be.[193] However, you may be able to show that you

Part 2: Main means-tested benefits and tax credits
Chapter 4: Housing benefit
6. Claims and backdating

have good cause – eg, if the reason you did not claim earlier was because you were making real efforts to find work to avoid relying on benefits, and you only chose not to claim for a limited period.

Examples

1. You sought advice about your rights, but were misled by someone on whom you were entitled to rely – eg, officers from the local authority or the DWP or independent advisers such as solicitors, Citizens Advice Bureaux, trade union officials or accountants.[194] Relying on the advice of work colleagues, friends, or even a doctor, is not enough.[195] The enquiries that you made need not have been specific, provided the situation is such that you ought to have been told about your possible entitlement.

2. You did not seek advice about your rights because you misunderstood them (eg, you believed that you did not need to make a claim), you mistakenly thought that you understood them or you mistakenly thought that you had no entitlement and there was nothing for you to enquire about.[196] Generally, you are expected to find out about your rights, but if it was reasonable for you to form one of these views, you can still have good cause.

3. The delay was due to something beyond your control (eg, the failure of the post or of someone you asked to help with your claim), provided you checked whether the claim arrived in good time.[197]

4. You were unable to claim because of physical or mental ill health.[198] However, you might reasonably be expected to seek the assistance of friends or relatives if available.

5. You only qualify for HB when a qualifying benefit is awarded (see p81).

If you claim the wrong benefit

If you claimed UC when you should have claimed HB, see p77 to see whether your date of claim can be treated as made on an earlier date.

Claiming in advance

You can claim HB in advance if:

- you become liable for rent for the first time but cannot move into your accommodation until after your liability begins. You must claim HB as soon as you are liable for rent. Once you move in, you may be able to receive HB for the four weeks before moving in (see p51);
- you are not entitled to HB now, but will become entitled within 13 weeks of claiming (17 weeks if you or your partner will be the qualifying age for PC (see p147) within 17 weeks), unless the reason you do not qualify straight away is because you fail the 'habitual residence test' (see p1537). The local authority can treat your claim as having been made in the benefit week immediately before you are first entitled.[199] If this happens, you do not need to make a further claim later.

Housing benefit after an award of a qualifying benefit

You might not be entitled to HB currently, but would be once you, your partner, or a child or qualifying young person included in your claim become entitled to another 'qualifying benefit' – eg, DLA, personal independence payment or carer's allowance. Alternatively, you might be entitled to a higher rate of benefit once the qualifying benefit is awarded. If you are already entitled to HB when the qualifying benefit is awarded, see p1282, p1290 and p1300.

Do you only qualify for housing benefit when a qualifying benefit is awarded?

If you only qualify for HB when a qualifying benefit is awarded, the rules operate in an unfair way so you should do the following.

1. Claim HB while waiting to hear about the claim for a qualifying benefit.

2. If you do not qualify for HB, ask the local authority to wait to make a decision on your claim until the award of the qualifying benefit is made (known as 'stockpiling' your claim). If the local authority refuses, argue that its failure to delay making a decision on your claim was an 'error of law' and that there are grounds for an 'any time' revision (see p1279).[200]

3. If you are refused HB but are then awarded a qualifying benefit, claim again and ask for your claim to be backdated. If you need to, argue that you have good cause for your late claim (see p79).

4. If you lose benefit because of the way the rules operate, ask your local authority for compensation to cover the period before your fresh HB claim.

Notice of the decision

Once the local authority has all the information and evidence required, it must make a decision on your claim for HB within 14 days or as soon as 'reasonably practicable'.[201] If you are a person affected by the decision, you must be notified of it by the local authority without delay or as soon as 'reasonably practicable'.[202] In all other cases (eg, if a decision is made following a change in your circumstances), you (and other people affected by the decision) must be notified within 14 days or as soon as 'reasonably practicable'. You can request reasons for a decision. Your request must be in writing and it must be signed by you.[203]

Person affected by a decision

You are a **'person affected by a decision'** if you are:[204]

– a claimant;

– someone acting for a claimant who is unable to act for her/himself – eg, an appointee;

– someone from whom the local authority decides to recover an overpayment (including a landlord); *or*

– a landlord or agent if the decision concerns whether or not to make a direct payment of HB to you.[205]

Information a decision notice should contain

If the decision is one you can appeal (see p1314), you must be informed of:[206]

- your right to appeal against the decision; *and*
- your right to a written statement of reasons for the decision (if this is not already included – see p1166. The rules are the same as for other benefits).

The information that must be provided varies with the particular circumstances of your case and includes the following.[207]

- The normal weekly amount of HB to which you are entitled, including the amount of any deductions for non-dependants and fuel. You must be told why fuel deductions have been made and that they can be varied if you provide evidence of the actual amount involved.
- Your weekly eligible rent (see p62).
- If you are a private tenant, the day your HB will be paid and whether payment will be made weekly or monthly.
- The date on which your entitlement starts.
- In some cases, how your applicable amount is calculated, how your income has been assessed and the amount of capital the local authority has taken into account. If the income and capital of a non-dependant has been used instead of yours to calculate your HB (see p71), you must be informed of this and the reasons why.
- If your claim was:
  - successful, your duty to notify the local authority of any change in circumstances which might affect your entitlement and the kinds of changes that should be reported;
  - unsuccessful, a statement explaining exactly why you are not entitled.
- If it has been decided to pay your HB direct to your landlord, information saying how much is to be paid to her/him and when payments will start.

---

7. Getting paid

How payment of housing benefit (HB) is made depends on whether you are the tenant of the housing authority responsible for paying HB (a local authority) or a private or housing association tenant. If you are unable to act for yourself, payment can be made to someone else on your behalf (see p84). In some circumstances, payment can be made to your landlord (see p84). No HB is payable if the amount would be less than 50 pence a week.[208]

When is housing benefit paid?

You are normally paid in arrears at intervals of a week, two weeks, four weeks or a month, depending on when your rent is usually due. HB can also be paid at longer intervals if you agree.[209] If you are a private or housing association tenant, the local authority can pay your HB weekly to avoid an overpayment or if you are liable to pay rent weekly and it is in your interests for HB to be paid weekly.

Different rules apply if HB is paid direct to your landlord.[210]

Note:

- Your HB might be paid at a reduced rate if you have been sanctioned for a benefit offence (see p1265).
- If payment of your HB is delayed, see p89. You might be able to get a 'payment on account'. If you wish to complain about how your claim has been dealt with or claim compensation, see Chapter 58.
- If payment of your HB is suspended, see p1185.
- If you are overpaid HB, you might have to repay it (see Chapter 52) and, in some circumstances, you may have to pay a penalty (see p1256). If you have been accused of fraud, see Chapter 53.

How your benefit is paid

If your landlord is the housing authority responsible for paying HB, your HB is paid in the form of a reduction in your rent. This is called a 'rent rebate'.[211]

If you are a private or housing association tenant, you receive HB in the form of a 'rent allowance'.[212] If you live in a caravan, mobile home or houseboat, this applies even if you are also liable to make payments to a local authority – eg, for site or mooring fees. HB is normally paid to you although, in some cases, it may be paid direct to your landlord or to someone acting on your behalf.

Note: if your rent allowance is:

- less than £1 a week, the local authority can pay your HB up to six months in arrears;[213]
- more than £2 a week, you can insist on two-weekly payments, unless HB is paid direct to your landlord.[214]

The local authority has the discretion to pay you by whatever method it chooses, but, in doing so, it must have regard to your 'reasonable needs and convenience'.[215] It should not insist on paying your HB into a bank account if you do not have one (but it may encourage you to open one), nor should it make you collect it if it is difficult to reach the office by public transport.[216] If it does, complain to your local councillor. If that has no effect, ask your MP to take up the matter (see p1401) and also complain to the Ombudsman (see p1403).

If the local authority refuses to replace a payment which has never arrived, you could threaten to sue in the county court (sheriff court in Scotland).

Payment to someone acting on your behalf

If an appointee or some other person legally empowered to act for you has claimed HB on your behalf, that person can also receive the HB payments.[217]

If you are able to claim HB for yourself, you can still nominate an agent to receive or collect it for you. To do this, you must make a written request to the local authority. Anyone you nominate must be aged 18 or over.[218]

If a claimant dies, any unpaid HB may be paid to her/his personal representative or, if there is none, to her/his next of kin aged 16 or over.[219] A written application must be received by the local authority within 12 months of the claimant's death. The local authority may allow longer. If HB was being paid to the landlord before the claimant's death, the local authority can pay any outstanding HB to her/him to clear remaining rent due.

Payment direct to a landlord

Your HB can be paid direct to your landlord (or the person to whom you pay rent) but only in specified circumstances. Your landlord could contact the local authority about this.[220] The local authority can suspend payment while it makes enquiries about who should be paid your HB.[221] If the local authority is suspicious of your landlord, see p85.

If you have just claimed HB or the local authority has done a supersession of your award, and the local authority thinks you have not already paid your rent and that it would be in the interests of the 'efficient administration' of HB, it can make the first payment to your landlord.[222]

Both you and your landlord should be notified if HB is to be paid to your landlord. If it is *not* in your interests to have HB paid direct to your landlord, it is worth trying to persuade the local authority to withhold it rather than paying it to your landlord. *Always* seek advice before you do so.

When payment must be made to your landlord

The local authority *must* pay your HB, including payments on account (see p89), direct to your landlord (or the person to whom you pay rent) if:[223]

- you or your partner are on income support (IS), jobseeker's allowance (JSA), employment and support allowance (ESA) or pension credit (PC) and the DWP has decided to pay part of that benefit to your landlord for arrears (see p1191). **Note:** this does not apply if you are on universal credit (UC); *or*
- you have rent arrears equivalent to eight weeks' rent or more, unless the local authority considers it to be in your overriding interest not to make direct payments. Once your arrears have been reduced to less than eight weeks' rent, compulsory direct payments stop. The local authority may then choose to continue direct payments on a discretionary basis (see below).

Payment to your landlord on a discretionary basis

The local authority may pay your HB direct to your landlord (or the person to whom you pay rent):

- if the local housing allowance rules do *not* apply to you (see p407):[224]
  - if you have requested or agreed to direct payments; *or*
  - without your agreement, if it decides that direct payments are in your or your family's best interests. You do not have to have any of your family living with you for payment to be made to your landlord under this rule.[225]
- if the local housing allowance rules apply to you (see p407), if the local authority:[226]
  - thinks you are likely to have difficulty managing your own financial affairs or that it is improbable that you will pay your rent. The local authority can make direct payments (for a maximum of eight weeks) while it considers the situation; *or*
  - thinks it will help you to secure or to keep accommodation. **Note:** the government's intention is that this should only apply if the rent is at a level you can afford; *or*
  - has already made direct payments during your current award of HB in any of the situations when direct payments must be made (see p84).
- whether or not the local housing allowance rules apply to you, without your agreement if you have left the address for which you were getting HB and there are rent arrears. In this case, direct payments of any unpaid HB due in respect of that accommodation can be made, up to the total of the outstanding arrears.[227]

When the local authority has concerns about a landlord

The local authority may refuse to make direct payments to your landlord if it 'is not satisfied that s/he is a fit and proper person'.[228] However, direct payments may still be made if the requirements for discretionary direct payments are met and the local authority is satisfied it is in your or your family's best interests.[229]

If the local authority decides not to make payments to your landlord, it can make payments to you (including sending you a cheque payable to the landlord, or paying you in the presence of your landlord) or to a trusted third party, such as a social worker or solicitor.[230]

When your entitlement starts

Your entitlement to HB starts:[231]

- if you became liable for rent for the first time, for a home you have moved into, in the week your claim is made or is treated as made, from the Monday of that week. This includes if you become liable for daily payments in a hostel or accommodation provided by the local authority on a short-term lease or because you are homeless. This means that your HB starts on the same day your liability actually begins;[232] *or*
- in all other cases, from the Monday following your date of claim, or following the date from when you are treated as claiming if your claim is backdated (see pp76–80).

Continuing payments

Your HB can continue to be paid at the same rate, even though your entitlement might otherwise have changed, if you stop claiming:

- IS, income-based JSA or income-related ESA because you or your partner are moving onto PC. You may be able to continue to receive HB at the same rate for four weeks (see below);
- IS, income-based JSA, income-related or contributory ESA, incapacity benefit (IB) or severe disablement allowance (SDA) because you or your partner start work or increase your hours or earnings. You may be entitled to extended payments of HB (see below).

Continuing payments on claiming pension credit

To avoid problems caused by delays in reassessing your HB when you move from IS, income-based JSA or income-related ESA onto PC, provided you otherwise continue to qualify for HB, you continue to receive it for a period, normally at the same rate as before. **Note:** your maximum HB (see p59 for the meaning) is recalculated if your rent increases or there is a change in the non-dependant deductions (see p67) that should be made.[233]

You qualify for continuing payments if:[234]

- your partner has claimed PC and the DWP has certified this; *or*
- your IS, income-based JSA or income-related ESA ceased because you reached the qualifying age for PC (see p147) or, if you were getting income-based JSA or income-related ESA beyond that age, this ceased because you turned 65. The DWP must certify this and that you are required to claim or have claimed PC (or are treated as having done so). **Note:** this does not apply if you are getting UC.

You get continuing payments for:[235]

- a period of four weeks from the day after your IS, income-based JSA or income-related ESA ceases; *or*
- if the four-week period ends other than on a Sunday, until the Sunday after the end of the four-week period.

Extended payments of housing benefit

If you or your partner are on IS, income-based JSA, income-related or contributory ESA, IB or SDA and your entitlement ends because you (or your partner) start work or increase your hours or pay, you may be entitled to continue to receive the same amount of HB as you did before your entitlement ended for up to four weeks. These are called extended payments of HB.

You do not have to make a claim for extended payments of HB; they should be paid automatically.[236] However, your local authority needs to know that your or your partner's entitlement to IS, income-based JSA, ESA, IB or SDA has ceased, so you must notify it.

If you want to get an extended payments decision changed, you can apply for a revision or supersession or appeal (see Chapters 54 and 55).

Who can claim extended payments

You qualify for extended payments of HB if you are getting HB, you (or your partner) started work (including self-employed work) or increased your hours or pay, and your (or your partner's) entitlement to:

- IS, income-based JSA or income-related ESA ended.[237] You (or your partner) must have been entitled to, and in receipt of, either IS, contribution-based, income-based or joint-claim JSA or income-related ESA, or a combination of these, for at least 26 weeks. **Note:** you cannot qualify if, immediately before your entitlement to IS ended, you were getting mortgage interest run-on (see p474); *or*
- contributory ESA, IB or SDA ended, and you (or your partner):[238]
  - are *not* entitled to PC; *and*
  - were not entitled to or in receipt of IS, income-based JSA or income-related ESA; *and*
  - had been continuously entitled to, and in receipt of, contributory ESA, IB or SDA, or a combination of these, for at least 26 weeks.

In all cases, the work, or increase in earnings or hours, must be expected to last at least five weeks.

Do you need to report the change in your circumstances?

1. If you are claiming IS, JSA, ESA, IB or SDA and you start work or your hours or pay change, you must report this to the DWP. The end of your entitlement to these benefits is a change in your circumstances that you must report to the local authority (see p90).

2. If you do not report the end of your entitlement to IS/JSA/ESA/IB/SDA to the local authority, your entitlement to extended payments of HB is not affected, but this could result in an overpayment of HB at the end of the extended payment period.

3. You could be entitled to a higher rate of HB than you were before your entitlement to IS/JSA/ESA/IB/SDA ended. Report the change as soon as possible so it can be taken into account.

Note: if you move home, you can still qualify for extended payments of HB, provided the day you moved was in the same week, or the week before, you or your partner started work or increased your hours or pay.[239] See below for how the amount of the extended payments can be affected.

The amount of the extended payments and how long they last

Extended payments of HB are paid for four weeks unless:[240]

- any of the weeks count as rent-free periods (see p62); *or*
- your liability to pay rent ceases altogether within the four weeks.

The weekly amount of your extended payments (unless you move into local authority accommodation in a different local authority area – see below) is the higher of the amount of HB:[241]

- you got in the last (non-rent-free) week before your entitlement to IS/JSA/ESA/IB/SDA ended; *or*
- to which you would be entitled based on your new circumstances; *or*
- to which your partner would be entitled if s/he claimed based on her/his circumstances.

However, if the benefit cap is, or was, applied (see p1180), it is the amount of HB you would have got – ie, the amount before any reduction.[242]

Always report any changes in your circumstances during the four-week period. This is because the weekly amount you get is then the highest of the above amounts.[243]

Example

Jill is a local authority tenant with a non-dependant. Her rent is £102 a week. She was getting HB of £68 in the week before her entitlement to IS ceased, because a non-dependant deduction of £34 was made. Her weekly HB entitlement based on her circumstances in work is £54.37. Her extended payments are therefore £68 a week. In the second week of the four-week period, Jill's non-dependant moves out. Her weekly entitlement based on her circumstances in work is now £88.37 (£54.37 + £34), because a non-dependant deduction is no longer made. Her extended payments are now £88.37 for the remainder of the four-week period. This is also Jill's HB entitlement from the end of the period.

You may qualify for extended payments of HB for two homes (see p57). However, if your liability to pay rent for either of these ceases within the four-week period, the amount of your extended payments is reduced by the amount of HB payable for that home.[244]

If you were being paid discretionary housing payments (see Chapter 21), ask for these to continue for the extended payment period.

If you move into local authority accommodation in a different local authority area, the weekly amount of your extended payments of HB is the amount of HB you got in the last (non-rent-free) week before your entitlement to IS/JSA/ESA/IB/SDA ended – ie, the amount you got at your old address.[245] The extended payments can be paid to you or to the new local authority landlord. If you or your partner claim HB at your new address, the amount you or your partner get is reduced by the weekly amount of the extended payments. The effect of this is that, if your new HB entitlement is higher, your extended payments are 'topped up'.

If you move house in any other circumstances (eg, to privately rented or housing association accommodation, or within the same local authority area), your extended payments are worked out under the normal rules. If you also claim HB at your new address, it does not appear that the local authority can reduce the amount of HB you get by the weekly amount of your extended payments.[246] It is not clear if this was the intention.

Ongoing entitlement to housing benefit

Your entitlement to HB continues until at least the end of the extended payment period.[247] It can continue after that if you qualify under the normal rules, but at the weekly rate based on your new circumstances. You do not have to make a fresh claim. Your HB entitlement is continuous. This means if you have a form of transitional protection that requires continuous entitlement, your transitional protection continues.

Note: unless you move to local authority accommodation in a different local authority area, if your partner claims HB, this cannot be paid to her/him while you are getting extended payments of HB.[248]

Delays and complaints

The local authority must make a decision on your claim, tell you in writing what the decision is, and pay you any HB to which you are entitled within 14 days or, if that is not reasonably practicable, as soon as possible after that.[249] If you consider a delay to be unreasonable, make a complaint (see p1399). In serious cases, you may want to seek advice on whether you have grounds for judicial review (see p1378).

Payments on account

If you are a private or housing association tenant and the local authority has not been able to assess your HB within the required period, the local authority must normally make a 'payment on account' (sometimes called an interim payment) while your claim is being sorted out.[250] The local authority should automatically do this. You do not have to request a payment on account.[251] Bear the following in mind.

- Payments on account are not discretionary. The local authority *must* pay you an amount that it considers reasonable, given what it knows about your circumstances.
- Payments on account can only be refused if it is clear that you will not be entitled to HB, or the reason for the delay is that you have been asked for information or evidence in support of your claim and you have failed, without good cause, to provide it (see p76).[252] If the delay has been caused by a third party (eg, the rent officer, your bank or employer), this does not affect your right to a payment on account.

- The local authority must notify you of the amount of a payment on account and that it can recover any overpayment which occurs if your actual HB entitlement is different from the payment.[253]
- If your payment on account is less than your actual entitlement, your future HB can be adjusted to take account of the underpayment.[254]
- If the local authority has not made a payment on account, complain.

Change of circumstances

It is your duty to report any change in your circumstances which you might reasonably be expected to know might affect your right to, the amount of or payment of your HB.[255] You should do this promptly to the office handling your claim. The local authority must tell you in writing about the changes you must report.[256] There may be a number of changes which the local authority requires you to report, depending on the particular circumstances of your case. **Note:** if you are getting PC, you only have to report specified changes (see p91).

If you do not report a change promptly, any resulting overpayment may be recoverable from you (see Chapter 52) and, in some circumstances, you may have to pay a penalty (see p1256). If you are considered to have acted knowingly or dishonestly, you may also be guilty of an offence (see Chapter 53). Remember:

- it is important to report changes to the right department. Your duty to notify changes is to the HB department, not to the local authority as a whole;[257]
- if your benefit is paid to someone else on your behalf, the duty to report any relevant changes also extends to her/him.[258]

If in doubt, always report changes in circumstances. If you think that the local authority might not have taken a change into account, you should check with it.

How to report a change of circumstances

You can report a change in your circumstances to the local authority:

- in writing; *or*
- by telephone (unless the local authority says you must report it in writing), but only if your local authority has published a telephone number for this purpose or allows you to claim HB by telephone (see p72);
- electronically (eg, by email), if your local authority authorises it.[259]

However, it is always best to report a change in writing (eg, in a letter) and keep a copy in case of a dispute in the future.

You may report a change in your circumstances to the DWP, instead of the local authority, if the DWP has provided a telephone number for this purpose and:[260]

- you or your partner are getting IS or JSA; *and*
- the change of circumstances is that you or your partner have started work; *and*

• as a result of the change, entitlement to IS or JSA will end or, if you or your partner are getting contribution-based JSA, the amount will reduce.

If the change is a birth or a death, there is a special rule (sometimes called 'Tell Us Once'). You can report such a change in person at a local authority (and, in England, a county council) office, if such an office has been specified.[261] If the change is a death, you can notify it to the DWP electronically, or by telephone if a number has been specified for that purpose. Check with your local authority (eg, at the registrar's office) to see if it provides this service.

If you get pension credit

If you get PC, the only changes you must report to the local authority are:[262]

• any change to your tenancy, apart from changes in your rent if you are a local authority tenant; *and*
• any changes affecting the residence or income of a non-dependant normally living with you or with whom you normally live; *and*
• any absence from your home which is, or is likely to be, for more than 13 weeks; *and*
• if you are only getting the savings credit of PC:[263]
  – changes affecting a child under 16 who lives with you that could affect how much HB you get. You need not report changes in the child's age;
  – any changes to your capital that do, or could, take it above £16,000;
  – any changes in the income or capital of a non-dependant of yours, if your HB has been assessed on the basis of this instead of your own (see p71), and whether s/he has stopped, or resumed, living with you;
  – any changes in the income or capital of your partner that have not been taken into account since the determination of your PC award, and whether your partner has stopped, or resumed, living with you.

Note: you *do* have to report other changes in connection with your PC claim to the DWP. Relevant changes in your circumstances should be passed to the local authority by the DWP.

If you do not get pension credit

The changes you must report if you are getting PC, listed on p91, are all changes that could affect your right to, the amount of or payment of your HB. So they are also changes you must report if you are *not* getting PC. Examples of other types of change you must report if you do not get PC include changes to:

• your family income or capital;
• the number of boarders you have or the payments made by them;
• your status – eg, marriage, civil partnership, cohabitation or separation.

However, you do *not* have to report:[264]
- any change in your age, or that of your partner or child(ren) or your non-dependant(s). **Note:** you *do* have to report any change that results in a child or young person no longer being included in your claim (see p220);
- if you are on IS, income-based JSA or income-related ESA, any changes that affect the amount of those benefits. **Note:** you *do* have to report entitlement to IS, income-based JSA or income-related ESA ending. Do not assume that the DWP does this on your behalf.

When changes in circumstances take effect

In most cases, a change takes effect from the Monday after it occurred.[265] This applies whether or not a decision is advantageous to you. However, if you are liable to pay rent on a daily basis (eg, in a hostel) and the change means you are no longer entitled to HB, it takes effect on the day it occurs.[266] **Note:**
- If you report a change in circumstances before the local authority has assessed your HB claim, your claim is assessed on the basis of the revised information you have provided.
- Special rules apply if two or more changes occurring in the same benefit week would normally take effect in different benefit weeks.[267]

Exceptions

There are a number of exceptions to the general rule described above, which include the following.
- If the change is one you are required to notify to the local authority (other than one relating to your having to take part in a work-focused interview or, if you are on PC, one of the additional exceptions to the rules described on p93), it is advantageous to you and you fail to notify the change within the one-month time limit (or any longer period allowed by the local authority – see p1296), the date of notification is treated as if this is the date the change occurred. This means you lose out if you reported the change late.
- If you or your partner are at least 65 and either a non-dependant comes to live with you or there is a change so that a higher non-dependant deduction should be made, the effect of this can be delayed for 26 weeks.[268] This does not apply if you or your partner are getting IS, income-based JSA or income-related ESA (or UC).
- If you are entitled to HB (but not UC) when you become a member of a couple with someone getting UC and s/he moves in with you, unless your HB is for 'specified accommodation' (see p45), your entitlement to HB ends on the day before the day you are jointly entitled to UC with your new partner, or the day before the day you would have been entitled had you met all the financial conditions for UC.[269] **Note:** if instead you move in with your new partner, your HB entitlement ends under the normal rules.[270]

There are additional exceptions to the rules described above.

- If you are on PC, the amount of this changes because of a change in your circumstances or a correction of an official error (see p1280), and thus the amount of HB you can be paid changes.[271]
- If there is a change in your rent, if you move to a new home or if you become (or cease to be) entitled to HB for more than one home, and if you or your partner become entitled to ESA which includes a work-related activity or support component.[272]

8. Tax, other benefits and the benefit cap

Tax

Housing benefit (HB) is not taxable.

Means-tested benefits and tax credits

Entitlement to income support (IS), income-based jobseeker's allowance (JSA), income-related employment and support allowance (ESA), the guarantee credit of pension credit (PC) or universal credit (UC) acts as an automatic passport to maximum HB (see p60) because all your income and capital are ignored.

Working tax credit counts as income when working out your HB. So does child tax credit, unless you are at least the qualifying age for PC (see p147) and neither you nor your partner are on IS, income-based JSA or income-related ESA (or UC).

Non-means-tested benefits

Most non-means-tested benefits are taken into account as income when working out the amount of HB you get. However, attendance allowance, disability living allowance, personal independence payment, guardian's allowance and child benefit are not taken into account. It can still be worth claiming non-means-tested benefits, even if they are taken into account. If you, your partner or your child(ren) qualify for certain of these, you also qualify for certain premiums and components (see Chapter 12) and, potentially, a higher rate of HB. If you think you might qualify, seek advice to see whether you would be better off.

You may only qualify for HB once you or your partner, or a child or qualifying young person included in your claim, are awarded another benefit (known as a 'qualifying benefit'). You may be entitled to a higher rate of HB once the qualifying benefit is awarded (see p81).

The benefit cap

In some cases, there is a limit on the total amount of specified benefits you can receive (a 'benefit cap'). HB is one of the specified benefits, but HB for specified accommodation is ignored. The benefit cap only applies if you are getting HB or UC. See p1180 for further information.

2 Passports and other sources of help

If you have been awarded HB, you may qualify for a social fund funeral expenses payment (see p791). You may be entitled to a council tax reduction (see p854).

Financial help on starting work

You may be entitled to extended payments of HB (see p86). You might also be able to get mortgage interest run-on if you have a home loan (see p474). Your local authority may also help with extended help with council tax. See p866 for information about other financial help you might get.

Notes

1. Who can claim housing benefit

1 s130 SSCBA 1992; s115 IAA 1999; reg 10 HB Regs; reg 10 HB(SPC) Regs
2 Reg 26 HB(SPC) Regs
3 Reg 2(1) UC(TP) Regs 2014; Sch 1 para 3A UC Regs
4 Regs 11(1) and 12(1) HB Regs; regs 11(1) and 12(1) HB(SPC) Regs
5 CH/3110/2003; R(H) 3/07
6 CH/844/2002; R(H) 9/08
7 Reg 2(4)(a) HB Regs; reg 2(4)(a) HB(SPC) Regs
8 *R v Cambridge CC ex parte Thomas,* 10 February 1995 (QBD); CH/2959/2006
9 Reg 12(2) HB Regs; reg 12(2) HB(SPC) Regs
10 Reg 2(1) HB Regs and reg 2(1) HB(SPC) Regs, definition of 'long tenancy' and 'owner'; CH/2258/2004; *Burton v New Forest District Council* [2004] EWCA Civ 1510, reported as R(H) 7/05; R(H) 3/07; CH/3586/2005; R(H) 8/07; *CR v Wycombe District Council* [2009] UKUT 19 (AAC); *Blackburn with Darwen BC v DA (HB)* [2014] UKUT 431 (AAC); *GN v Sevenoaks BC (HB)* [2016] UKUT 271 (AAC)
11 Reg 11(2) HB Regs

12 Reg 11(4) HB Regs
13 Reg 8(1)(a) and (b) HB Regs; reg 8(1)(a) and (b) HB(SPC) Regs
14 Reg 8(2) HB Regs; reg 8(2) HB(SPC) Regs
15 *R v Rugby BC HBRB ex parte Harrison* [1994] 28 HLR 36 (QBD); CH/2959/2006
16 s48 Landlord and Tenant Act 1987; CH/3579/2003; CH/257/2005
17 R(H) 3/03
18 *R v Poole BC ex parte Ross* [1995] 28 HLR 351 (QBD); *R v Warrington BC ex parte Williams* [1997] 29 HLR 872 (QBD)
19 Reg 8(1)(c)-(e) HB Regs; reg 8(1)(c)-(e) HB(SPC) Regs
20 CSHB/606/2005
21 *FK v Wandsworth BC (HB)* [2016] UKUT 570 (AAC); *Babergh DC v GW (HB)* [2017] UKUT 40 (AAC)
22 Regs 9, 10 and 56 HB Regs; regs 9 and 10 HB(SPC) Regs
23 *Scott v SSWP* [2011] EWCA Civ 103
24 Reg 9(4) HB Regs; reg 9(4) HB(SPC) Regs; CH/1326/2004; CH/1328/2004
25 CH/542/2006; R(H) 5/06 decided that the rule did not conflict with the Human Rights Act.

26 Reg 3(4) HB Regs; reg 3(4) HB(SPC)
   Regs; R(H) 5/06; CPC/1446/2008; *RK v
   SSWP* [2008] UKUT 34 (AAC)
27 *Thamesdown BC v Goonery* [1995] 1 CLY
   2600
28 R(H) 1/03; CH/1171/2002; CH/2899/
   2005
29 Reg 9(2) HB Regs; reg 9(2) HB(SPC)
   Regs; *R v Poole BC ex parte Ross* [1995]
   28 HLR 351 (QBD); CH/1076/2002;
   CH/296/2004; CH/1097/2004; paras
   A3/3.258-65 GM
30 *DH v Kirklees MBC and SSWP (HB)* [2011]
   UKUT 301 (AAC); [2012] AACR 16
31 *R (Tucker) v Secretary of State* [2001]
   EWCA Civ 1646, unreported. The court
   decided that the rule did not conflict
   with the Human Rights Act; para A3/
   3.269 GM
32 Reg 9(3) HB Regs; reg 9(3) HB(SPC)
   Regs; *SD v London Borough of Brent*
   [2009] UKUT 7 (AAC)
33 Reg 9(3) HB Regs; reg 9(3) HB(SPC)
   Regs
34 Reg 2(1) HB Regs and reg 2(1),
   definition of 'owner' and 'long tenancy'
   HB(SPC), Regs; CH/1278/2002; CH/
   0296/2003; *MH v Wirral MBC* [2009]
   UKUT 60 (AAC); *Bradford MDC v MRC
   (HB)* [2010] UKUT 315 (AAC);
   Nottingham CC v CJ (HB) [2011] UKUT
   392 (AAC); *GN v Sevenoaks BC (HB)*
   [2016] UKUT 271 (AAC)
35 CH/3853/2001; CH/396/2002; R(H) 6/
   07; *KH v Sheffield CC* [2008] UKUT 11
   (AAC)
36 *CH v Wakefield DC* [2009] UKUT 20
   (AAC)
37 Reg 2(1) HB Regs; reg 2(1) HB(SPC)
   Regs
38 R(SB) 22/87; *Bristol CC v JKT (HB)* [2016]
   UKUT 517 (AAC)
39 paras A3/3.243-45 GM
40 *R v Solihull MBC ex parte Simpson* [1995]
   1 FLR 140 (CA); CH/39/2007
41 *R (Mackay) v Barking and Dagenham
   HBRB* [2001] EWHC Admin 234
42 CH/2258/2004
43 *R (Mackay) v Barking and Dagenham
   HBRB* [2001] EWHC Admin 234
44 *R v Sutton LBC HBRB ex parte Keegan*
   [1992] 27 HLR 92 (QBD)
45 *R v Manchester CC ex parte Baragrove
   Properties Ltd* [1991] 23 HLR 337 (QBD);
   R v Gloucestershire CC ex parte Dadds
   [1997] 29 HLR 700 (QBD); CH/39/2007
46 *R v Poole BC ex parte Ross* [1995] 28 HLR
   351 (QBD)

47 s134(2) SSCBA 1992; reg 82(1) HB
   Regs; reg 63(1) HB(SPC) Regs
48 s130(1) SSCBA 1992; reg 7(1) and (2)
   HB Regs; reg 7(1) and (2) HB(SPC) Regs
49 R(H) 5/09; *Birmingham City Council v IB*
   [2009] UKUT 116 (AAC)
50 Reg 7(5), (14) and (15)(c) HB Regs; reg
   7(5), (14) and (15)(c) HB(SPC) Regs
51 Reg 7(8) HB Regs; reg 7(8) HB(SPC)
   Regs
52 R(H) 9/05
53 *Bury MBC v DC (HB)* [2011] UKUT 43
   (AAC); *R (Mahmoudi) v LB Lewisham and
   Another* [2014] EWCA Civ 284
54 Reg 2(1) HB Regs; reg 2(1) HB(SPC)
   Regs
55 CH/2201/2002
56 Reg 7(7) HB Regs; reg 7(7) HB(SPC)
   Regs; para A3/3.430 GM
57 Reg 7(11)(b) and (c), (13)(a) and (b),
   (13D)(a) and (b)(13G)(a) and (b),
   (16)(a) and (b)-(c) and (18) HB Regs; reg
   7(11)(b) and (c), (13)(a) and (b),
   (13D)(a) and (b), (13G)(a) and (b),
   (16)(a) and (b) and (18) HB(SPC) Regs
58 R(H) 9/05
59 Reg 7(13) and (17) HB Regs; reg 7(13)
   and (17) HB(SPC) Regs
60 *KdeS v Camden LB (HB)* [2011] UKUT 457
   (AAC)
61 *R v Penwith DC ex parte Burt* [1988] 22
   HLR 292 (QBD); para A3/3.460 GM
62 Reg 7(14) and (15)(a) HB Regs; reg
   7(14) and (15)(a) HB(SPC) Regs
63 R(H) 8/09; *SK v South Hams DC (HB)*
   [2010] UKUT 129 (AAC); [2010] AACR
   40
64 CH/1237/2004
65 CH/3893/2004
66 Reg 13 HB Regs; reg 13 HB(SPC) Regs
67 Reg 7(11) and (12) HB Regs; reg 7(11)
   and (12) HB(SPC) Regs
68 *SSWP v Selby DC and Bowman* [2006]
   EWCA Civ 271, reported as R(H) 4/06
69 Reg 7(16)(d)(i) and (17) HB Regs; reg
   7(16)(d)(i) and (17) HB(SPC) Regs
70 *Torbay BC v RF* [2010] UKUT 7 (AAC);
   [2010] AACR 26
71 Reg 7(16)(c)(ii), (iii), (vii) and (x) HB
   Regs; reg 7(16)(ii), (iii), (vii) and (x)
   HB(SPC) Regs
72 *Obrey and Others v SSWP* [2013] EWCA
   Civ 1584
73 Reg 7(16)(c)(i), (iv)-(vi), (viii)-(ix) and
   (16A) HB Regs; reg 7(16)(i), (iv)-(vi) and
   (viii)-(ix) and (16A) HB(SPC) Regs

74 Reg 7(14) and (15)(b) HB Regs; reg 7(14) and (15)(b) HB(SPC) Regs; CSH/499/2006
75 Reg 7(18) HB Regs; reg 7(18) HB(SPC) Regs
76 Reg 7 (13C)-(13E) HB Regs; reg 7 (13C)-(13E) HB(SPC) Regs
77 Reg 7(16)(d)(ii) and (iii), (17C) and (17D) HB Regs; reg 7(16)(d)(ii) and (iii), (17C) and (17D) HB(SPC) Regs
78 Reg 7(13F), (13G) and (18) HB Regs; reg 7(13F), (13G) and (18) HB(SPC) Regs
79 Reg 7(13D), (13G), (17C) and (17D) HB Regs; reg 7(13D), (13G), (17C) and (17D) HB(SPC) Regs
80 Reg 7(13A) and (17A) HB Regs; reg 7(13A) and (17A) HB(SPC) Regs
81 Reg 7(13B) and (17B) HB Regs; reg 7(13B) and (17B) HB(SPC) Regs
82 Reg 5 HB&SPC(TA)(A) Regs
83 R(H) 5/09; *Birmingham CC v IB* [2009] UKUT 116 (AAC)
84 Reg 7(6)(d) and (e) HB Regs; reg 7(6)(d) and (e) HB(SPC) Regs
85 CH/1911/2006
86 *R (Mahmoudi) v LB Lewisham and Another* [2014] EWCA Civ 284
87 Reg 7(6)(a) HB Regs; reg 7(6)(a) HB(SPC) Regs
88 Reg 7(6)(b) and (c) HB Regs; reg 7(6)(b) and (c) HB(SPC) Regs
89 Reg 7(10) HB Regs; reg 7(10) HB(SPC) Regs
90 Reg 7(3) and (4) HB Regs; reg 7(3) and (4) HB(SPC) Regs
91 R(SB) 10/81

4. The amount of benefit

92 Reg 70 HB Regs; reg 50 HB(SPC) Regs
93 s130(3) SSCBA 1992; Schs 4 para 12, Sch 5 para 4 and 6 para 5 HB Regs; reg 26 HB(SPC) Regs; *R v Penwith DC ex parte Menear* [1991] 24 HLR 120 (QBD); *R v South Ribble DC HBRB ex parte Hamilton* [2000] 33 HLR 104 (CA)
94 Reg 2(3), (3A) and (3B) HB Regs; reg 2(3) and (3A) HB(SPC) Regs; *SMcH v Perth and Kinross Council (HB)* [2015] UKUT 126 (AAC)
95 s130(3) SSCBA 1992; reg 71 HB Regs; reg 51 HB(SPC) Regs
96 Reg 2(1) HB Regs; reg 2(1) HB(SPC) Regs
97 Reg 80 HB Regs; reg 61 HB(SPC) Regs
98 Reg 81(3) and Sch 1 para 7(2) HB Regs; reg 62(3) and Sch 1 para 7(2) HB(SPC) Regs

99 Reg 12B(2) HB Regs; reg 12B(2) HB(SPC) Regs
100 Regs 12B(3) and 12C(2) HB Regs; regs 12B(3) and 12C(2) HB(SPC) Regs; reg 12(4) HB Regs and reg 12(4) HB(SPC) Regs as set out in Sch 3 para 5 HB&CTB(CP) Regs
101 Regs 12B(4) and 12C(2) HB Regs; regs 12B(4) and 12C(2) HB(SPC) Regs; reg 12(5) HB Regs and reg 12(5) HB(SPC) Regs as set out in Sch 3 para 5 HB&CTB(CP) Regs; CH/3376/2002
102 *R (Naghshbandi) v Camden LBC* [2002] EWCA Civ 1038, *The Times*, 5 August 2002, unreported
103 CH/3376/2002
104 Regs B13(2) and 13D(12) HB Regs; regs 13B(2) and 13D(12) HB(SPC) Regs
105 Reg 12B(2) HB Regs; reg 12B(2) HB(SPC) Regs; reg 12(3) HB Regs and reg 12(3) HB(SPC) Regs as set out in Sch 3 para 5 HB&CTB(CP) Regs; *R v Bristol City Council ex parte Jacobs* [1999] 32 HLR 82 (QBD); *Liverpool City Council v (1) NM, (2) WD (HB)* [2015] UKUT 532 (AAC); [2016] AACR 19
106 Regs 12B(3) and 12C(2) HB Regs; regs 12B(3) and 12C(2) HB(SPC) Regs; reg 12(4) HB Regs and reg 12(4) HB(SPC) Regs as set out in Sch 3 para 5 HB&CTB(CP) Regs
107 Reg 11(3) HB Regs; reg 11(2) HB(SPC) Regs
108 Sch 1 para 5 HB Regs; Sch 1 para 5 HB(SPC) Regs
109 Sch 1 para 6(1) HB Regs; Sch 1 para 6(1) HB(SPC) Regs
110 Sch 1 para 6(2) and (3) HB Regs; Sch 1 para 6(2) and (3) HB(SPC) Regs
111 paras A4/4.912-13 GM
112 Sch 1 paras 5 and 6(1)(b) HB Regs; Sch 1 paras 5 and 6(1)(b) HB(SPC) Regs
113 Sch 1 para 8 HB Regs; Sch 1 para 8 HB(SPC) Regs
114 Sch 1 para 8 HB Regs; Sch 1 para 8 HB(SPC) Regs. For the meaning of 'sheltered accommodation', see *Oxford CC v Basey* [2012] EWCA Civ 115; [2012] AACR 38.
115 Reg 12(1)(e) HB Regs; reg 12(1)(e) HB(SPC) Regs
116 Sch 1 para 4 HB Regs; Sch 1 para 4 HB(SPC) Regs
117 para A4/4.730 GM; *CP and Others v Aylesbury Vale DC v SSWP (HB)* [2011] UKUT 22 (AAC); *Liverpool City Council v (1) NM, (2) WD (HB)* [2015] UKUT 532 (AAC); [2016] AACR 19

118 Sch 1 para 1(a)(iii) HB Regs; Sch 1 para 1(a)(iii) HB(SPC) Regs
119 Sch 1 para 1(a)(ii) HB Regs; Sch 1 para 1(a)(ii) HB(SPC) Regs
120 Sch 1 para 1(b) HB Regs; Sch 1 para 1(b) HB(SPC) Regs
121 Sch 1 para 1(a)(iv) HB Regs; Sch 1 para 1(a)(iv) HB(SPC) Regs
122 Reg 12B(2)(b) and Sch 1 para 1 HB Regs; reg 12B(2)(b) and Sch 1 para 1 HB(SPC) Regs; reg 12(3)(b) HB Regs and reg 12(3)(b) HB(SPC) Regs as set out in Sch 3 para 5 HB&CTB(CP) Regs
123 Reg 12B(2)(c) and Sch 1 para 3(2) HB Regs; reg 12B(2)(c) and Sch 1 para 3(2) HB(SPC) Regs; reg 12(3)(c) HB Regs and reg 12(3)(c) HB(SPC) Regs as set out in Sch 3 para 5 HB&CTB(CP) Regs
124 Sch 1 para 3 HB Regs; Sch 1 para 3 HB(SPC) Regs
125 Sch 1 paras 1(a)(i) and 2(1) HB Regs; Sch 1 paras 1(a)(i) and 2(1) HB(SPC) Regs
126 Sch 1 para 2(6) and (7) HB Regs; Sch 1 para 2(6) and (7) HB(SPC) Regs
127 Reg 70 HB Regs; reg 50 HB(SPC) Regs
128 Reg 3(1) HB Regs; reg 3(1) HB(SPC) Regs
129 Reg 3(4) and Sch 1 para 8 HB Regs; reg 3(4) and Sch 1 para 8 HB(SPC) Regs; CPC/1446/2008; *AM v SSWP (IS)* [2011] UKUT 387 (AAC)
130 CSIS/185/1995
131 *Thamesdown BC v Goonery* [1995] 1 CLY 2600 (CA); *RK v SSWP* [2008] UKUT 34 (AAC)
132 CIS/14850/1996
133 para A5/5.521 GM
134 R(H) 8/09; *SK v South Hams DC (HB)* [2010] UKUT 129 (AAC); [2010] AACR 40
135 Reg 3(2) HB Regs; reg 3(2) HB(SPC) Regs
136 *R v Chesterfield BC ex parte Fullwood* [1993] 26 HLR 126
137 Reg 3(3) HB Regs; reg 3(3) HB(SPC) Regs
138 Regs 2(1), definition of 'attendance allowance', and 74(6) HB Regs; regs 2(1), definition of 'attendance allowance', and 55(6) HB(SPC) Regs
139 Reg 74(7) and (10) HB Regs; reg 55(7) and (9) HB(SPC) Regs
140 s2 ETA 1973; s2 Enterprise and New Towns (Scotland) Act 1990
141 Reg 74(1) HB Regs; reg 55(1) HB(SPC) Regs

142 Reg 74(1) and (2) HB Regs; reg 55(1) and (2) HB(SPC) Regs
143 Reg 6(6) HB Regs; reg 6(6) HB(SPC) Regs
144 Reg 74(9) HB Regs; reg 55(10) HB(SPC) Regs
145 CH/48/2006
146 Reg 74(3) HB Regs; reg 55(3) HB(SPC) Regs
147 Reg 74(4) HB Regs; reg 55(4) HB(SPC) Regs
148 Reg 74(5) HB Regs; reg 55(5) HB(SPC) Regs
149 Reg 59(10)-(13) HB(SPC) Regs
150 Reg 26 HB Regs; reg 24 HB(SPC) Regs

6. Claims and backdating
151 s1 SSAA 1992
152 Reg 83(1) and (9) HB Regs; reg 64(2) and (10) HB(SPC) Regs
153 Reg 83(4A) and (4B) HB Regs; reg 64(5A) and (5C) HB(SPC) Regs
154 Reg 83A and Sch 11 HB Regs; reg 64A and Sch 10 HB(SPC) Regs
155 Reg 83(1) HB Regs; reg 64(2) HB(SPC) Regs
156 Reg 83(2) HB Regs; reg 64(3) HB(SPC) Regs
157 paras A2/2.560-65 GM
158 Reg 83(4AA), (4AB) and (4BA) HB Regs; reg 64(5B), (5BA) and (5CA) HB(SPC) Regs
159 Reg 83(4AC)-(4AE) HB Regs; reg 64(5BB)-(5BD) HB(SPC) Regs; Explanatory Memorandum to SI 2008 No.299
160 Reg 83(1), (4C), (6) and (9) HB Regs; reg 64(2), (5D), (7) and (10) HB(SPC) Regs
161 Reg 83(4D), (4DA), (7) and (7A) HB Regs; reg 64(5E), (5EA), (8) and (8A) HB(SPC) Regs
162 Reg 83(4E), (4F), (8) and (8A) HB Regs; reg 64(5F), (5G), (9) and (9A) HB(SPC) Regs
163 Reg 87(1) and (3) HB Regs; reg 68(1) and (3) HB(SPC) Regs
164 Reg 87(4)-(6) HB Regs; reg 68(4)-(6) HB(SPC) Regs
165 Reg 83(4)(b) HB Regs; reg 64(5)(b) HB(SPC) Regs
166 Regs 2, definition of 'appropriate DWP office', and 83(4)(a), (f) and (g) and (13) HB Regs; regs 2, definition of 'appropriate DWP office', and 64(5)(a), (f) and (g) and (14) HB(SPC) Regs
167 Reg 83(4)(c) HB Regs; reg 64(5)(c) HB(SPC) Regs

168 Reg 83A and Sch 11 HB Regs; reg 64A and Sch 10 HB(SPC) Regs
169 Reg 83(4A) and (4AA) HB Regs; reg 64(5A) and (5B) HB(SPC) Regs
170 Reg 82(1) HB Regs; reg 63(1) HB(SPC) Regs; CH/2995/2006
171 Reg 82(2), (3), (5) and (6) HB Regs; reg 63(2), (3), (5) and (6) HB(SPC) Regs
172 Reg 82(4) HB Regs; reg 63(4) HB(SPC) Regs
173 Reg 82(4)(c) HB Regs; reg 63(4)(c) HB(SPC) Regs
174 s1(1A)-(1C) SSAA 1992
175 Reg 86(1A) HB Regs; reg 67(1A) HB(SPC) Regs
176 Reg 86(1) HB Regs; reg 67(1) HB(SPC) Regs
177 *AA v LB Hounslow* [2008] UKUT 13 (AAC)
178 Reg 4(1)(a) HB Regs; reg 4(1)(a) HB(SPC) Regs
179 para A1/1.300 GM
180 Regs 83(5)(d) and (e) and 85(1) HB Regs; regs 64(6)(d) and (e) and 66(1) HB(SPC) Regs
181 Reg 83(5)(a)-(c) and (5A) HB Regs; reg 64(6)(a)-(c) HB(SPC) Regs
182 *Leicester CC v LG* [2009] UKUT 155 (AAC)
183 Art 3A WRA(No.9)O
184 Reg 64(1) HB(SPC) Regs
185 Regs 57 and 64(1), (1A) and (6) HB(SPC) Regs; *Leicester CC v LG* [2009] UKUT 155 (AAC)
186 Reg 83(12) HB Regs
187 Reg 83(12A) HB Regs
188 R(S) 2/63 (T); CH/2659/2002; CH/474/2002; CH/393/2003; A2/Annex A GM
189 *UH v LB Islington (HB)* [2010] UKUT 64 (AAC)
190 CH/393/2003
191 CH/474/2002
192 R(G) 1/75
193 *FR v Broadband DC* [2012] UKUT 449 (AAC)
194 R(SB) 6/83; CS/50/1950; R(U) 9/74; CI/146/1991; CI/142/1993; FC/39/1993; *R v Canterbury CC ex parte Goodman,* 11 July 1995, unreported (QBD)
195 R(U) 5/56; R(S) 5/56
196 CI/37/1995
197 R(P) 2/85
198 R(S) 10/59; R(SB) 17/83
199 Reg 83(10) and (11) HB Regs; reg 64(11) and (12) HB(SPC) Regs
200 CG/1479/1999; CIS/217/1999
201 Reg 89 HB Regs; reg 70 HB(SPC) Regs
202 Reg 90 HB Regs; reg 71 HB(SPC) Regs; reg 10 HB&CTB(DA) Regs

203 Reg 90(2) HB Regs; reg 71(2) HB(SPC) Regs; reg 10 HB&CTB(DA) Regs
204 Reg 3 HB&CTB(DA) Regs
205 CH/180/2006
206 Reg 10(1) HB&CTB(DA) Regs
207 Sch 9 paras 9-15 HB Regs; Sch 8 paras 9-15 HB(SPC) Regs; reg 10(1) HB&CTB(DA) Regs

7. Getting paid

208 Reg 75 HB Regs; reg 56 HB(SPC) Regs
209 Reg 92(1) and (6) HB Regs; reg 73(1) and (6) HB(SPC) Regs
210 Reg 92(3) and (4) HB Regs; reg 73(3) and (4) HB(SPC) Regs
211 s134(1A) SSAA 1992
212 s134(1B) SSAA 1992; regs 91A and 94(1) HB Regs; regs 72A and 75(1) HB(SPC) Regs
213 Reg 91(2) HB Regs; reg 72(2) HB(SPC) Regs
214 Reg 92(5) HB Regs; reg 73(5) HB(SPC) Regs
215 Reg 91(1)(b) HB Regs; reg 72(1)(b) HB(SPC) Regs
216 para A6/6.120 GM
217 Reg 94(2) HB Regs; reg 75(2) HB(SPC) Regs
218 Reg 94(3) HB Regs; reg 75(3) HB(SPC) Regs
219 Reg 97 HB Regs; reg 78 HB(SPC) Regs
220 *R v Haringey LBC ex parte Azad Ayub* [1992] 25 HLR 566 (QBD)
221 R(H) 1/08
222 Reg 96(2) HB Regs; reg 77(2) HB(SPC) Regs
223 Reg 95 HB Regs; reg 76 HB(SPC) Regs; Sch 9 SS(C&P) Regs; *R v Haringey LBC ex parte Azad Ayub* [1992] 25 HLR 566 (QBD)
224 Reg 96(1)(a) and (b) and (3A)(a) HB Regs; reg 77(1)(a) and (b) and (3A)(a) HB(SPC) Regs
225 *DLT v Eastleigh BC (HB)* [2014] UKUT 242 (AAC)
226 Regs 95(2A) and 96(3A)(b) HB Regs; regs 76(2A) and 77(3A)(b) HB(SPC) Regs
227 Regs 95(2A) and 96(1)(c) HB Regs; regs 76(2A) and 77(1)(c) HB(SPC) Regs
228 Regs 95(3) and 96(3) HB Regs; reg 76(3) and 77(3) HB(SPC) Regs
229 Reg 96(3) HB Regs; reg 77(3) HB(SPC) Regs
230 para A6/6.212 GM
231 Reg 76 HB Regs; reg 57 HB(SPC) Regs; R(H) 9/07; *SL v Renfrewshire Council (HB)* [2014] UKUT 411 (AAC)

232 Regs 2(1), definition of 'benefit week', and 80(2), (3)(a), (4) and (8) HB Regs; regs 2(1), 'definition of 'benefit week', and 61(2), (3)(a), (4) and (8) HB(SPC) Regs

233 Reg 54(6) HB(SPC) Regs

234 Reg 54(1) and (2) HB(SPC) Regs

235 Regs 2(1), definition of 'benefit week', and 54(3)-(5) HB(SPC) Regs

236 s32(4) WRA 2007

237 Reg 72 HB Regs

238 Reg 73 HB Regs; reg 53 HB(SPC) Regs

239 Regs 72(4) and 73(2) HB Regs; reg 53(2) HB(SPC) Regs; CH/1762/2004

240 Regs 72A, 72B(6), 73A and 73B(6) HB Regs; regs 53A and 53B(6) HB(SPC) Regs

241 Regs 72B and 73B HB Regs; regs 52 and 53B HB(SPC) Regs

242 Regs 72E and 73E HB Regs

243 Regs 72D(2) and 73D(2) HB Regs; regs 52 and 53D(2) HB(SPC) Regs

244 Regs 72B(5) and 73B(5) HB Regs; reg 53B(5) HB(SPC) Regs

245 Regs 72C and 73C HB Regs; regs 52 and 53C HB(SPC) Regs

246 s34(3) WRA 2007; reg 2(1) HB Regs and reg 2(1), definitions of 'mover' and 'second authority', HB(SPC) Regs

247 s32(1), (2) and (13) WRA 2007; regs 72D and 73D HB Regs; reg 53D HB(SPC) Regs

248 Regs 72B(7) and 73B(7) HB Regs; regs 52(3) and 53B(7) HB(SPC) Regs

249 Regs 89(2), 90(1) and 91(3) HB Regs; regs 70(2), 71(1) and 72(3) HB(SPC) Regs

250 Reg 93(1) HB Regs; reg 74(1) HB(SPC) Regs

251 *R v Haringey LBC ex parte Azad Ayub* [1992] 25 HLR 566 (QBD)

252 Reg 93(1) HB Regs; reg 74(1) HB(SPC) Regs; *R v Haringey LBC ex parte Azad Ayub* [1992] 25 HLR 566 (QBD)

253 Reg 93(2) HB Regs; reg 74(2) HB(SPC) Regs

254 Reg 93(3) HB Regs; reg 74(3) HB(SPC) Regs

255 Reg 88(1) HB Regs; reg 69(1) HB(SPC) Regs; reg 4 SS(NCC) Regs

256 Regs 86(3) and 90 and Sch 9 paras 9(1)(g) and 10(a) HB Regs; regs 67(3) and 71 and Sch 8 paras 9(1)(g) and 10(a) HB(SPC) Regs

257 Regs 2(1), 86(3) and 88(1) HB Regs; regs 2(1), 67(3) and 69(1) HB(SPC) Regs

258 Reg 88(1) HB Regs; reg 69(1) HB(SPC) Regs

259 Reg 88A and Sch 11 HB Regs; reg 69A and Sch 10 HB(SPC) Regs

260 Reg 88(6) HB Regs; reg 69(9) HB(SPC) Regs

261 Reg 88ZA HB Regs; reg 69ZA HB(SPC) Regs

262 Reg 69(6)-(8) HB(SPC) Regs

263 Reg 69(7) HB(SPC) Regs

264 Reg 88(1), (3) and (4) HB Regs; reg 69(1), (3) and (4) HB(SPC) Regs

265 Regs 2(1), definition of 'benefit week', and 79(1) HB Regs; regs 2(1), definition of 'benefit week', and 59(1) HB(SPC) Regs; reg 8(2) HB&CTB(DA) Regs

266 Reg 79(8) HB Regs; reg 59(8) HB(SPC) Regs

267 Reg 79(4) and (8) HB Regs; reg 59(4) and (8) HB(SPC) Regs

268 Reg 59(10)-(13) HB(SPC) Regs

269 Regs 5(2)(a) and 7 UC(TP) Regs

270 Regs 5(2)(b)(ii) and 7(5)(b) UC(TP) Regs

271 Reg 60 HB(SPC) Regs

272 Regs 7(2)(o) and 8(14D) HB&CTB(DA) Regs; reg 79(2), (2A), (2B), (8) and (9) HB Regs; reg 59(2), (2A), (2B), (8) and (9) HB(SPC) Regs

Chapter 5

Income support

This chapter covers:
1. Who can claim income support (p101)
2. The rules about your age (p107)
3. People included in the claim (p107)
4. The amount of benefit (p108)
5. Special benefit rules (p109)
6. Claims and backdating (p109)
7. Getting paid (p113)
8. Tax, other benefits and the benefit cap (p115)

Key facts
- Income support (IS) is a benefit for people on a low income who are in one of the specific groups of people who can claim.
- IS is a means-tested benefit.
- You do not have to have paid national insurance contributions to qualify.
- You cannot qualify for IS if you (or your partner) count as in full-time paid work.
- IS is administered and paid by the DWP.
- If you disagree with an IS decision, you can apply for a revision or a supersession, or appeal against it. You must apply for a mandatory reconsideration before you can appeal.

Future changes

At some point between 2016 and 2018, depending on where you live, you will no longer be able to make a new claim for IS. From 2019, the DWP will begin to transfer existing IS claims to universal credit. See p20 for further information, and CPAG's online service and *Welfare Rights Bulletin* for updates.

At some point in the future, you may have to accept a 'claimant commitment' (see p1071) that records what your responsibilities are. There may be exceptions. See CPAG's online service and *Welfare Rights Bulletin* for updates.

Chapter 5

1. Who can claim income support

You qualify for income support (IS) if:[1]
- you are in one of the specific groups of people who can claim IS (see pp102–06). Broadly, these are:
  - sick and disabled people;
  - certain people looking after children and with other responsibilities;
  - carers;
  - certain pupils, students and people on training courses;
  - other groups – eg, people in custody pending trial or sentence, refugees learning English and some people involved in a trade dispute;
- neither you nor your partner count as being in full-time paid work (see p106 and Chapter 43);
- you are not studying full time. There are exceptions to this rule (see p877). See p878 if you are studying part time and p872 if you are at school or college in 'relevant education';
- you are not entitled to jobseeker's allowance (JSA) or employment and support allowance (ESA);
- your partner is not entitled to income-based JSA, joint-claim JSA, income-related ESA or pension credit (PC). **Note:** if you become a member of a couple and your partner is getting universal credit (UC), you no longer qualify for IS (see p28);
- you are at least 16 and are under the qualifying age for PC (see p147);
- your income is less than your applicable amount (see p108);
- your savings and other capital are worth £16,000 or less. Some capital (in particular, your home) is ignored (see Chapter 17);
- you satisfy the 'habitual residence test' and the 'right to reside test', and are present in Great Britain. To find out if you are exempt from the tests, see Chapter 66. To see if you can claim IS during a temporary absence abroad, see p1597; *and*
- you are not a 'person subject to immigration control' (see p1516). There are exceptions to this rule.

In some cases, in order to get IS, you (and your partner) may be required to attend a work-focused interview (see p1063). If the only reason you are claiming IS is because you are a lone parent and you do not have any children under the age of three, you may also be required to undertake work-related activity (see p1068).

Note: if you come under the UC system (see p20), usually you cannot make a new claim for IS. However, if you notify the DWP that you intend to claim IS before you claim UC, you can claim IS for a period before your UC entitlement starts.[2] If you already get IS but become entitled to UC, your IS may stop.

Part 2: Main means-tested benefits and tax credits
Chapter 5: Income support
1. Who can claim income support

Groups of people who can claim income support

You can claim IS if you satisfy the other rules for getting IS described above and you are in one of the groups of people who can claim.[3] If you come into one of the groups on any day in a benefit week (see p303), you count as doing so for the whole week.

Note:

- If your circumstances change and you no longer come into a particular group, check whether you are in any of the other groups of people who can claim. If so, your entitlement to IS continues.[4]
- If you are a member of a couple and you are not in one of the groups of people who can claim IS, but your partner is, s/he could be the claimant. Whichever one of you claims IS, the other may qualify for national insurance (NI) credits to protect her/his NI record (see Chapter 42).
- In the past, there were additional groups of people who could claim IS. If you are getting IS on the basis that you were in one of these groups (referred to as 'transitional groups' – see p105), you may continue to qualify on this basis.

People who are sick or disabled

You can qualify for IS if either of the following applies to you.[5]

- You are entitled to statutory sick pay.
- You are incapable of work, but are treated as capable of work because you are disqualified from receiving incapacity benefit because of misconduct or failure to accept treatment (see p271 of the 2008/09 edition of this *Handbook*). **Note:** this does not apply if you have been transferred to contributory ESA (see p672). In this case, you should claim income-related ESA or UC instead.

Looking after children and other responsibilities

You can qualify for IS if any of the following apply to you.[6]

- You are a lone parent aged 18 or over and have at least one child under five, or you are a lone parent under the age of 18 and have a child of any age. Your child must be included in your claim (see p220).[7] You do not have to be the child's parent – eg, you could be her/his grandparent or sister or brother.
- You are entitled to and are on 'parental leave' from work under specific provisions (this does *not* include shared parental leave) and:
  - during the period for which you are claiming IS, you are not entitled to a payment of any kind from your employer; *and*
  - you and your child(ren) live in the same household (see p223); *and*
  - you were entitled to working tax credit (WTC), child tax credit (CTC) payable at a higher rate than the family element or housing benefit (HB) on the day before your parental leave began. **Note:** the CTC family element has been abolished for claims that only include children born on or after 6 April 2017. At the time of writing, it is not clear how this may affect entitlement to IS. See CPAG's online service and *Welfare Rights Bulletin* for updates.

- You are entitled to and are on paternity leave[8] and:
  - you are not entitled to statutory paternity pay or to a payment of any kind from your employer during the period for which you are claiming IS; *or*
  - you were entitled to WTC, CTC payable at a higher rate than the family element or HB on the day before your paternity leave began. **Note:** the CTC family element has been abolished for claims that only include children born on or after 6 April 2017. At the time of writing, it is not clear how this may affect entitlement to IS. See CPAG's online service and *Welfare Rights Bulletin* for updates.
- You are a lone foster parent – ie, a child under 16 has been placed with you by a local authority or voluntary organisation, or because of an order or warrant under the Children's Hearings (Scotland) Act 2011, and you are not a member of a couple. The child must be living with you or accommodated by you.[9]
- A child has been placed with you for adoption by an adoption agency and you are not a member of a couple.
- You are pregnant and:
  - incapable of work because of your pregnancy;[10] *or*
  - there are 11 weeks or less before the week your baby is due.
- You were pregnant and your pregnancy ended not more than 15 weeks ago – ie, when your baby was born or you had a miscarriage.

What happens when you can no longer claim as a lone parent?

1. The age limit for a child has changed a number of times in the past. If you were entitled to IS as the lone parent of a child aged over the relevant limit before the date it changed, you might be able to continue to receive IS as a lone parent for a period. See p105 for further information.

2. Unless you are under 18, once your only or youngest child turns five, you cannot qualify for IS unless you fit into one of the other groups of people who can claim – eg, if you are a carer or a lone foster parent of a child under 16. You can continue to qualify for IS on that basis, even if you can no longer qualify as a lone parent.[11]

3. If you no longer qualify for IS, claim CTC for your children if you are not already getting it. You may qualify for JSA or ESA (or UC). If you claim JSA (or UC), there are special rules that help you satisfy the jobseeking conditions (or work-related requirements).

You can qualify for IS for a temporary period while any of the following apply to you.[12]

- You are looking after a child under 16 because her/his parent or the person who usually looks after her/him is temporarily ill or temporarily away.[13]
- A child under 16 is included in your claim (see p220) and your partner is temporarily out of the UK.
- You are looking after your partner, or a child (this includes a 'qualifying young person') who is included in your claim (see p220), who is temporarily ill.[14]

Part 2: Main means-tested benefits and tax credits
Chapter 5: Income support
1. Who can claim income support

Carers

You can qualify for IS if you are a carer and either of the following applies to you.[15]

- You receive carer's allowance (CA), or would receive it had you not been given a sanction for a benefit offence (see p1265).
- The person you care for:
  - receives attendance allowance (AA), the highest or middle rate care component of disability living allowance (DLA), the daily living component of personal independence payment (PIP), or armed forces independence payment; *or*
  - has been awarded AA, the highest or middle rate care component of DLA or either rate of the daily living component of PIP on an advance claim, but payments have not yet been made; *or*
  - has claimed AA, DLA, PIP or armed forces independence payment. You are entitled to IS for up to 26 weeks from the date of that claim or until the claim is decided, whichever comes first.

You must be 'regularly and substantially engaged' in providing care. If you do not receive CA, the decision maker must look at the quality and quantity of care you provide. This could be less than the 35 hours a week needed to qualify for CA.[16]

If you stop meeting these conditions or stop being a carer, you can continue to qualify for IS for a further eight weeks. After that, you cannot get IS unless you come into one of the other groups of people who can claim.

Pupils, students and people on training courses

You can qualify for IS if any of the following apply to you.[17]

- You are a person in 'relevant education' or are a full-time student who can qualify for IS while studying (see p872 or p877). **Note:** if you are a full-time student who only qualifies because you are a lone parent and you started your course before your child turned five, see p52 of the 2013/14 edition of this *Handbook*.
- You are on a course of full-time, non-advanced education (or were accepted or enrolled on it) and you are under 21, or you are 21 but turned 21 while on such a course. This only applies if:
  - you are an orphan and have no one acting as your parent; *or*
  - you have to live away from your parents and any person acting in their place because you are estranged from them, are in physical or moral danger or there is a serious risk to your physical or mental health; *or*
  - you live away from your parents and any person acting in their place, they are unable to support you financially and:
    - they are chronically sick, or are mentally or physically disabled – ie, they could get a disability or a higher pensioner premium, or they are entitled to ESA including a work-related activity or support component (or would be but for their one-year's entitlement to contributory ESA expiring), or

they are 'substantially and permanently disabled'. **Note:** it is not clear how entitlement to IS will be affected by the abolition of the work-related activity component from 3 April 2017. See CPAG's online service and *Welfare Rights Bulletin* for updates; *or*
 – they are detained in custody pending trial or sentence or under a sentence from a court; *or*
 – they are not allowed to come to Great Britain because they do not have leave to enter under the UK Immigration Rules.
- You are aged 16 to 24 and on a training course provided by the Secretary of State, the Welsh Ministers or, in Scotland, by a local enterprise company. This does not apply if you count as a child for child benefit purposes (see p572). Some participants on training schemes have the legal status of employees (and are normally given contracts of employment). You do not qualify for IS if you are in full-time paid work; you might qualify for WTC instead.
 If you receive a training allowance while on a course, your income may be too high for you to qualify for IS. However, you may qualify if, for example, you are on a lower rate of training allowance or you qualify for a disability premium (see p238).

Others

You can qualify for IS if any of the following apply to you.[18]
- You have to go to a court or tribunal as a JP, juror, witness or party to the proceedings.
- You have been remanded in custody, or committed in custody, but only until your trial or until you have been sentenced. You can only get IS for your housing costs – eg, for your mortgage or loan for repairs and improvements (see Chapter 20).
- You are a refugee who is learning English in order to obtain employment. You must be on a course for more than 15 hours a week and, at the time the course started, you must have been in Great Britain for a year or less. You can only get IS for up to nine months under this rule.
- You are not treated as in full-time work because you qualify for 'mortgage interest run-on' (see p474 and p997).
- You are involved in a trade dispute or have been back at work for 15 days or less following a trade dispute (see p940).

Transitional groups

In the past, there were additional groups of people who could qualify for IS. If you come into one of these 'transitional groups', you may continue to qualify for IS on this basis. You may be in one of these groups if you are claiming IS:
- 'on the grounds of disability'. See pp50–51 of the 2013/14 edition and p31 of the 2014/15 edition of this *Handbook*;
- as a disabled worker. See p51 of the 2013/14 edition of this *Handbook*;

Part 2: Main means-tested benefits and tax credits
Chapter 5: Income support
1. Who can claim income support

- as a full-time student or in 'relevant education'. The rules changed on 27 October 2008, 30 December 2009 and 25 January 2010. See p50 of the 2013/14 edition of this *Handbook;*
- as a lone parent of a child aged five or over. The age limit for the only or youngest child has changed a number of times in the past. See p297 of the 2009/10 edition, p307 of the 2010/11 edition, p315 of the 2011/12 edition and p51 of the 2013/14 edition of this *Handbook.*

Full-time paid work

You cannot usually qualify for IS if you or your partner are in full-time paid work. If you are the IS claimant, this means 16 hours or more each week. For your partner, this means 24 hours or more each week. If you and your partner work fewer hours than these limits, you may be able to get IS. See Chapter 43 for the rules on work.

In some situations you are treated as *not* in full-time work even if you work 16/24 hours or more (see p996). In others, you are treated as in full-time work when you are not (see p996). See p992 for how your hours are calculated and p991 for what counts as paid work.

Note: if you or your partner have just taken up full-time paid work, you may be able to qualify for IS for help with your housing costs for the first four weeks. This is known as 'mortgage interest run-on' (see p474).

Would you be better off claiming another benefit instead?
1. You and your partner might be able to qualify for both WTC and IS because the rules on full-time paid work for WTC and IS are different. This may apply, for example, if:
– you or your partner normally work 16/24 hours or more but are off sick or on maternity, adoption, paternity or shared parental leave; *or*
– you work less than 16 hours and your partner works at least 16 hours but less than 24 hours each week.
Get advice to see how you would be better off financially.
2. If your partner is at least the qualifying age for PC (see p147) and either of you are working 16/24 hours or more each week, your partner might be able to claim PC, or you and your partner may be able to claim WTC (or both if your income is low enough). There is no full-time paid work rule for PC, but earnings are taken into account when working out how much PC you can get.

If you are claiming IS because you are incapable of work, consult the DWP *before* you do any work. For work you may do while you are claiming, see p684 of the 2013/14 edition of this *Handbook.*

2. The rules about your age

You must be at least 16 to qualify for income support (IS). There are some special rules if you are 16 or 17 (see below).

You cannot claim IS if you are at least the qualifying age for pension credit (PC – see p147). Instead, you can claim PC.

16/17-year-olds

If you are 16 or 17, you are entitled to IS in your own right if you satisfy the normal rules of entitlement described in this chapter.[19] You should not have your claim refused or be turned away by the DWP simply because of your age or because you have been included in someone else's benefit or tax credit claim.

Note:

- If you have been, or are being, looked after by a local authority, you cannot usually claim IS. Instead, your local authority should support and accommodate you. See p937 for when you are not excluded.
- In certain circumstances, you may satisfy the rules for both IS and income-based jobseeker's allowance (JSA). It is usually better to claim IS because you do not have to be available for and actively seeking work and training (see Chapter 45) and therefore risk benefit sanctions. You can still look for work. If you claim IS rather than JSA, however, you might not receive national insurance credits (see Chapter 42).

3. People included in the claim

If you are single, you claim income support (IS) for yourself. If you are a member of a couple, either you can claim IS for both of you or, if your partner also satisfies the qualifying conditions for IS, s/he can claim for you both. Your applicable amount includes a personal allowance for a couple and can include premiums based on both your and your partner's circumstances. When your benefit is worked out, your partner's income and capital are usually added to yours.

There are some situations in which you must show that you are 'responsible' for a child who is living in your household – eg:

- in order to fit into one of the groups of people who can claim IS – eg, to show you are looking after your child who is temporarily ill or that you are a lone parent (see pp102–03);
- to show you are a lone parent so you can benefit from a higher earnings disregard (see p279);
- for some of the rules for help with housing costs – eg, for your mortgage (see Chapter 20).

Part 2: Main means-tested benefits and tax credits
Chapter 5: Income support
4. The amount of benefit

For who counts as a child, see p220. You do not have to be the child's parent. For when you count as responsible for a child and when s/he counts as living in your household, see pp222–25.

2

4. **The amount of benefit**

Income support (IS) tops up your income to a level that is set by the government. The amount you get depends on your needs (your 'applicable amount') and on how much income and capital you (and your partner) have.[20] There are three steps involved in working out your IS.

Step one: calculate your applicable amount
Your applicable amount consists of:
- a personal allowance (see p230); *plus*
- premiums (see p236) for any special needs; *plus*
- housing costs – eg, for your mortgage or loan for repairs and improvements (see Chapter 20).

Do you have children?

IS does not include allowances and premiums for your children. Instead, you can claim child tax credit (CTC). However, in some cases, if you have not yet been awarded CTC, you can continue to get allowances and premiums for your children until you claim and are awarded CTC (see p230). If you *do* get allowances and premiums for your children, there are special rules for how their income and capital are treated (see p269 and p356).

Step two: calculate your income
This is the amount you (and your partner) have coming in each week from, for instance, other benefits, part-time earnings, working tax credit and maintenance (see Chapter 14). If you have capital over £6,000 (£10,000 if you live in a care home), it also includes your 'tariff income' (see p293).

Step three: deduct income from applicable amount

Example

Mr and Mrs Hughes, aged 27 and 29, have a daughter aged 10. Mr Hughes has been caring for his daughter, who is severely disabled. He gets carer's allowance (CA) of £62.70. Mrs Hughes gets child benefit and CTC, as well as disability living allowance (DLA) for her daughter. The couple live in rented accommodation. Their applicable amount is:

Personal allowance	£114.85
Carer premium	£34.95
Total	£149.80

Their income (CA) to be taken into account is £62.70. Child benefit, CTC and DLA are all ignored.

Their IS is £149.80 (applicable amount) *minus* £62.70 (income) = £87.10

If your income is too high for you to qualify for IS currently, you might qualify once you, your partner or a child included in your claim become entitled to another benefit (a 'qualifying benefit') because you are then entitled to premiums. Make your claim for IS at the same time as your claim for the qualifying benefit (see p1160).

You might get a reduced amount of IS if:
- you (or, in some cases, your partner) were required to take part in a work-focused interview and you failed to do so without good cause (see p1124); *or*
- you are a lone parent without any children under three, you were required to undertake work-related activity and you failed to do so without good cause (see p1128); *or*
- you have committed a benefit offence (see p1265).

Different rules for calculating your benefit can apply if you are in one of the groups to whom special rules apply (see below).

5. Special benefit rules

Special rules may apply to:
- 16/17-year-olds who have been, or are being, looked after by a local authority (see p936);
- people subject to immigration control (see Chapter 65);
- people who have come from or are going abroad (see Chapters 66 and 67);
- people who are studying (see Chapter 40);
- people without accommodation, people involved in a trade dispute, people who (or whose partner or children) are in hospital or living in a care home or other similar accommodation, or people in prison or detention (see Chapter 41).

6. Claims and backdating

The general rules about claims and backdating are covered in Chapter 49. This section explains the specific rules that apply to income support (IS).

Part 2: Main means-tested benefits and tax credits
Chapter 5: Income support
6. Claims and backdating

Making a claim

A claim for IS can be made:

- by phone on 0800 055 6688 (Welsh 0800 012 1888; textphone 0800 023 4888) Monday to Friday, 8am to 6pm.[21] You are sent a written statement of your circumstances for you to approve and sign; *or*
- by completing a paper claim form approved by the DWP.[22] Send your completed form to your local Jobcentre Plus office. You may also be able to claim at an alternative office (see p1148). Return the form within one month of your initial contact or you may lose benefit. Keep a copy in case queries arise.

In practice, the DWP prefers you to start your claim by phone. There is no rule that says you must do so, but it is best to make your claim in this way if you can.

You must provide any information or evidence required (see p111). You can amend or withdraw your claim before a decision is made (see p1149). If there is a delay in making a claim, you may be able to get a short-term advance (see p1177).

Forms

Get Form A1 from a Jobcentre Plus office or download it at www.gov.uk/income-support/how-to-claim. Phone if you need an alternative format – eg, Braille, large print or audio CD. You may also be able to get the form at your local Citizens Advice Bureau, welfare rights service or advice centre.

Note:

- You can make initial contact with the DWP by phone or letter to say you want to claim. The date of your initial contact is important because it usually determines the date on which your claim is treated as made (see p111).
- If you download a form, or get one from, for example, an advice centre, it is important to phone the DWP to ensure your date of claim is the earliest possible date (see p111). You are given your date of initial contact to enter on the form.
- If you are claiming IS within 26 weeks of a previous entitlement, you may be able to claim IS again without having to give as much detail of your circumstances as is usually required. This is known as 'rapid reclaim'.

Housing benefit

If you claim IS by phone, your housing benefit (HB) claim is usually completed at the same time and passed to the local authority on your behalf. Otherwise, you must make a separate claim to your local authority. You can use your postcode to find out how and where to claim at www.gov.uk/apply-housing-benefit-from-council. If you are making a 'rapid reclaim' for IS, you may also be able to make a rapid reclaim for HB.

Who should claim

If you are a single person or a lone parent, you claim on your own behalf. If you are one of a couple, you must choose which one of you claims for you both. See p215 for who counts as a couple. If you have a choice about who can claim and you cannot agree, a decision maker decides.[23]

Can you change who claims?

You can change which partner claims, provided the partner previously claiming agrees.[24]
It can be worth swapping who claims, for example, if one of you:
– is about to go abroad or otherwise lose entitlement – eg, becomes a student;
– fits into one of the groups of people who can claim IS, but the other does not. You should both get advice about how to protect your national insurance record;
– is working less than 16 hours a week and the other is working between 16 and 24 hours a week (see p989). In this case, you and your partner might also be able to claim working tax credit (WTC). Get advice to see how you would be better off financially.

If you are unable to manage your own affairs, another person can claim IS for you as your 'appointee' (see p1149).

Information to support your claim

For the general information requirements that apply to all benefits, see p1150.

It is important that you provide any information required when you claim. This is known as the 'evidence requirement'. Until you do, you may not count as having made a valid claim (see p1152).[25] Correct any defects as soon as possible or your date of claim may be affected.[26] See p1153 for further information about the evidence requirement and to see whether you are exempt.

If you have a mortgage, you are given an additional form for your lender to complete. If it is not possible to assess your housing costs (see Chapter 20) accurately or your entitlement to the severe disability premium (see p242), the decision maker can exclude these from your IS until they can be calculated.[27]

Even if you have provided all that was required when you claimed, you may be asked to provide further information to support your claim (see p1154). You may also be asked to provide information after you are awarded IS and, if you fail to do so, your IS could be suspended or even terminated (see p1185).

The date of your claim

The date of your claim is important as it determines when your entitlement to IS starts.[28] This is not necessarily the date from when you are paid. For information about when payment of IS starts, see p113.

Your date of claim is not necessarily the date it is received by the DWP. It can be an earlier date (see p112).

Part 2: Main means-tested benefits and tax credits
Chapter 5: Income support
6. Claims and backdating

Your **'date of claim'** is usually the earliest of:[29]
- the date you first contact a benefit office (eg, you ask to claim IS by phone or letter or you submit a 'defective' claim) or someone does this on your behalf, so long as a properly completed claim form (if issued) and all the information required (see p111) are provided within one month; *or*
- if you claim by phone, the date of your call, even if you were given more time to provide information, so long as you have done so;[30] *or*
- the date your properly completed claim form (if issued) and all the information required are received by the benefit office (or, if you can claim at an alternative office, that office).

Note: you must make sure your claim is valid. If it is 'defective', you are given a short time to correct the defects (see p1152). If you do, your claim is treated as having been made when you initially claimed.[31]

There are exceptions to the rules above.
- If you claim WTC and are refused because neither you nor your partner are in full-time paid work for WTC purposes (see p196), your date of claim for IS is the date you claimed WTC.[32] However, you must claim IS within 14 days of the decision refusing you WTC. You can ask for your IS claim to start on a later date instead – eg, if your income is currently too high, but is due to decrease.
- If you claim universal credit (UC) and, on the basis of information you provided, you are treated as satisfying the UC 'gateway' conditions or as living in a gateway area, but the DWP later discovers that the information was incorrect, unless you have already been paid UC, the DWP should advise you that you are not entitled to claim UC. If you then claim IS within a month of being told this and if your claim is later than the date of your UC claim (taking into account any backdating you have requested and been allowed), your IS claim is treated as made on the date of your UC claim, or a later date if you would have been entitled from that later date.[33]

In some cases you can claim in advance (see p113) and in some cases your claim can be backdated (see p112). If you want this to be done, make this clear when you claim or the DWP might not consider it. If you claimed IS when you should have claimed carer's allowance (CA) instead of or in addition to IS, see p113.

Backdating your claim

It is very important to claim in time. A claim for IS can normally only be backdated for a maximum of three months and only in limited circumstances. See p1157 for the general rules on when an IS claim can be backdated.

Your claim can be backdated for more than three months if you claim backdated IS after an award of a qualifying benefit and an earlier IS claim had been refused (see p1160).[34] If you claimed WTC or UC when you should have claimed IS, see above to find out if your date of claim can be backdated.

If you might have qualified for IS earlier, but did not claim because you were given the wrong information by the DWP or because you were misled by it, you could ask for compensation (see p1396) or complain to the Ombudsman via your MP (see p1401).

If you claim the wrong benefit

If you claim IS and you should have claimed CA instead of or in addition to IS, a decision maker can treat your IS claim as a claim for CA.[35] This could help you qualify for a backdated carer premium. **Note:** if you claimed WTC or UC when you should have claimed IS, see p112 to see whether your date of claim can be backdated.

Claiming in advance

If you do not qualify for IS from the date of your claim (unless this is because you fail the habitual residence test – see p1537) but will do so within the next three months, you can be awarded IS from the first date on which you qualify.[36] This gives the DWP time to ensure you receive benefit as soon as you are entitled. The date of your claim is the date on which you qualify.[37] Tell the DWP that you want to claim in advance. You might have to persuade the DWP that it can accept a claim in advance.

You might not be entitled to IS currently, but will be once you (or your partner or a child included in your claim) become entitled to another 'qualifying benefit' (eg, disability living allowance, personal independence payment or CA) because you are then entitled to premiums. You should make your claim for IS at the same time as the claim for the qualifying benefit. If you are:

- refused IS, claim again when you get a decision about the qualifying benefit and ask for your IS to be backdated to the date of your first IS claim or to the date of entitlement to the qualifying benefit, if that is later (see p1160);
- awarded IS, you might be entitled to a higher rate once the outcome of the claim for the qualifying benefit is known. Ask for a revision or a supersession if you think this applies to you (see p1300).

7. Getting paid

The general rules on getting paid are covered in Chapter 49. This section explains the specific rules that apply to income support (IS).

When is income support paid?

You are normally paid fortnightly in arrears.[38] The day you are paid depends on your national insurance number (see p1174).

You are paid in advance if you are returning to work after a trade dispute.[39]

IS is a weekly benefit. However, if you are only entitled to IS for part of a week, you are only paid for the part-week.[40]

If you are entitled to less than 10 pence a week (£5 a week if you are getting IS while involved in a trade dispute), you are not paid IS at all, unless you are receiving another social security benefit which can be paid with IS.[41] If you are entitled to less than £1 a week, a decision maker can decide to pay you at 13-week intervals in arrears.[42]

Your entitlement to IS usually starts from the date of your claim (see p111).[43]

Note:

- Deductions can be made from your IS to pay to third parties (see p1187).
- Your IS might be paid at a reduced rate if you have been given a sanction for:
  - failing to take part in a work-focused interview (see p1124) or, if you are a lone parent and do not have any children under three, to undertake work-related activity (see p1128); *or*
  - a benefit offence (see p1265).
- For information on missing payments, see p1174. If you cannot get your IS payments because you have lost your bank or Post Office card or have forgotten your PIN, see p1173. If your 'simple payment' card has been lost or stolen, or if you have forgotten your memorable date, see p1173.
- If payment of your IS is delayed, see p1165. If you are waiting for a decision on your claim, or to be paid, you might be able to get a short-term advance (see p1177). If you wish to complain about how your claim has been dealt with or claim compensation, see Chapter 58.
- If payment of your IS is suspended, see p1185.
- If you are overpaid IS, you might have to repay it (see Chapter 52) and, in some circumstances, you may have to pay a penalty (see p1256). If you have been accused of fraud, see Chapter 53.

Change of circumstances

You must report changes in your circumstances that you have been told you must report, as well as any that you might reasonably be expected to know might affect your right to, the amount of, or the payment of, your benefit. You should do this as soon as possible, preferably in writing. See p1184 for further information.

If you have a mortgage, the DWP can ask your lender about any changes in the amount you owe. If you have this information (eg, from an annual statement you receive from your lender), you must also advise the DWP in case your lender fails to do so. Make sure the DWP takes this information into account so you are not overpaid IS.

When there has been a relevant change of circumstances, a decision maker looks at your claim again and makes a new decision. To see when your IS is then adjusted, see p115.

When your income support is adjusted

As a general rule, if you are paid IS in arrears, your IS is adjusted from the beginning of the week in which the change of circumstances takes effect.[44] There are a number of exceptions, including the following.[45]

- If a decision is to your advantage, but you failed to notify the DWP of a change within the time limit (normally one month, but this can be extended – see p1295), your IS is adjusted:
  - if you are paid in arrears, from the beginning of the week in which you notified the change; *or*
  - if you are paid in advance, from the day on which you notified the change if this is the day you are paid benefit or, if it is not, your IS is adjusted from the next week.

- Your IS is adjusted from the date of the change of circumstances (or the day on which this is expected to take place) if:
  - you are paid IS in arrears and the change of circumstances means you no longer qualify for IS, unless this is because your income is too high;
  - you live in a care home for part of the week and are entitled to disability living allowance or personal independence payment when you are staying elsewhere. This means that you can be paid, for example, the severe disability and enhanced disability premiums (see p242 and p240) when you are staying away from the care home.

8. Tax, other benefits and the benefit cap

Tax

Income support (IS) is not taxable except if you are involved in a trade dispute and you are claiming it for your partner.

Means-tested benefits and tax credits

IS is an automatic passport to maximum housing benefit (HB), but you have to make a separate claim. It is also an automatic passport to maximum child tax credit (CTC) and usually to maximum working tax credit (WTC). WTC is taken into account as income when working out your IS, but CTC is not.

You may be able to choose whether to claim IS, income-based jobseeker's allowance or income-related employment and support allowance. If you have a partner, s/he may be able to claim one of these benefits for you and, if s/he is at least the qualifying age for pension credit (PC – see p147), s/he may be able to claim PC for you, instead of your claiming IS. Get advice about this. You may need to work out how you would be better off financially and the sort of work-focused interviews you may have to attend. See p142 for further information.

Part 2: Main means-tested benefits and tax credits
Chapter 5: Income support
8. Tax, other benefits and the benefit cap

If you work less than 16 hours a week and your partner works at least 16 hours but less than 24 hours a week, you and your partner may also be able to claim WTC. Before deciding whether to claim, get advice to see how you would be better off financially.

If you or your partner have just stopped work or reduced your hours, you might get what is known as 'WTC run-on' for a four-week period (see p202).

Non-means-tested benefits

In some situations, while you are on IS you get national insurance credits (see p965).

Most non-means-tested benefits are taken into account as income when working out the amount of IS you get. However, attendance allowance, disability living allowance, personal independence payment, armed forces independence payment, guardian's allowance and, if you are getting CTC, child benefit are not taken into account. It can still be worth claiming non-means-tested benefits, even if they are taken into account. If you or your partner qualify for certain non-means-tested benefits, you also qualify for certain premiums (see p236) and, therefore, a higher rate of IS.

You might only qualify for IS once you or your partner, or a child included in your claim, are awarded another benefit, known as a 'qualifying benefit'. To make sure you do not lose out while waiting for the outcome of a claim for a qualifying benefit, claim IS at the same time. If your IS claim is refused, once the qualifying benefit is awarded claim IS again and ask for it to be backdated to the date of your first claim (see p1160).

The benefit cap

In some cases, there is a limit on the total amount of specified benefits you can receive (a 'benefit cap'). IS is one of the specified benefits. However, the benefit cap only applies if you are getting HB or UC. See p1180 for further information.

Passports and other sources of help

If you are entitled to IS, you also qualify for health benefits such as free prescriptions (see Chapter 29) and education benefits such as free school lunches (see p860). You may also qualify for social fund payments (see Chapter 36), Healthy Start food and vitamins (see p857) and help from your local welfare assistance scheme (see p856). You may be entitled to a council tax reduction (see p854).

Financial help on starting work

If you stop getting IS because you or your partner start work, or your earnings or hours in your existing job increase, you may be able to get mortgage interest run-on (if you have a home loan – see p474) or extended payments of HB (if you pay rent – see p86). Your local authority may also provide extended help with council tax. See p866 for information about other financial help you might get.

Notes

1. Who can claim income support
1 s124 SSCBA 1992
2 Reg 6(5) UC(TP) Regs
3 Reg 4ZA and Sch 1B IS Regs
4 R(IS) 10/05
5 Sch 1B para 7(c) and (d) IS Regs
6 Sch 1B paras 1-2A, 14, 14A and 14B IS Regs
7 CIS/2260/2002
8 The rules on paternity leave are in Part 2 PAL Regs
9 *JS v SSWP (IS)* [2015] UKUT 306 (AAC)
10 CIS/0542/2001
11 R(IS) 10/05
12 Sch 1B paras 3 and 23 IS Regs
13 CIS/866/2004
14 CIS/4312/2007
15 Sch 1B paras 4-6 IS Regs
16 R(IS) 8/02
17 Sch 1B paras 10-12, 15, 15A and 28 IS Regs
18 Sch 1B paras 9A and 18-22 IS Regs

2. The rules about your age
19 s124(1)(a) SSCBA 1992

4. The amount of benefit
20 s124(4) SSCBA 1992

6. Claims and backdating
21 Reg 4(11A) and (11B) SS(C&P) Regs
22 Reg 4(1A), (5) and (6) SS(C&P) Regs
23 Reg 4(3) SS(C&P) Regs
24 Reg 4(4) SS(C&P) Regs
25 Reg 4(1A), (7A), (9), (12) and (13) SS(C&P) Regs
26 Reg 6(1A) SS(C&P) Regs
27 Reg 13 SS&CS(DA) Regs
28 Reg 19(1) and Sch 4 para 6 SS(C&P) Regs
29 Reg 6(1ZA) and (1A) SS(C&P) Regs; R(IS) 10/06

30 Reg 6(1)(c) and (d) SS(C&P) Regs
31 Reg 6(1A) SS(C&P) Regs
32 Reg 6(28) SS(C&P) Regs
33 Art 3A WRA(No.9)O
34 Reg 6(16)-(18) SS(C&P) Regs
35 Reg 9(1) and Sch 1 SS(C&P) Regs; reg 2(3) ESA(TP) Regs
36 Reg 13(1) and (9) SS(C&P) Regs
37 Reg 13(1) SS(C&P) Regs

7. Getting paid
38 Sch 7 para 1 SS(C&P) Regs
39 Sch 7 paras 2(d) and 6(2) SS(C&P) Regs
40 s124(5) and (6) SSCBA 1992; reg 73 IS Regs
41 Reg 26(4) SS(C&P) Regs
42 Sch 7 para 5 SS(C&P) Regs
43 Sch 7 paras 3 and 6 SS(C&P) Regs
44 Reg 7 and Sch 3A para 1(a) SS&CS(DA) Regs
45 Reg 7 and Sch 3A paras 1(b) and 2-6 SS&CS(DA) Regs

Chapter 6

Income-based jobseeker's allowance

This chapter covers:
1. Who can claim income-based jobseeker's allowance (p119)
2. The rules about your age (p125)
3. People included in the claim (p131)
4. The amount of benefit (p132)
5. Special benefit rules (p133)
6. Claims and backdating (p133)
7. Getting paid (p141)
8. Tax, other benefits and the benefit cap (p141)

Note: unless otherwise stated, references to income-based jobseeker's allowance (JSA) in this chapter also refer to joint-claim JSA.

Key facts

- Jobseeker's allowance (JSA) is a benefit for people who are looking for work.
- There are three types of JSA. **Contribution-based JSA** is a non-means-tested benefit. **Income-based JSA** and **joint-claim JSA** are means-tested benefits that can top up contribution-based JSA.
- You do not have to have paid national insurance contributions to qualify for income-based JSA or joint-claim JSA.
- You cannot qualify for income-based JSA or joint-claim JSA if you or your partner count as being in full-time paid work.
- You must normally be fit for work and satisfy the 'jobseeking conditions'.
- In a number of situations (eg, if you do not take up a job or a place on an employment programme), you may be given a sanction and your JSA may be paid at a reduced rate.
- JSA is administered and paid by the DWP.
- If you disagree with a JSA decision, you can apply for a revision or a supersession, or appeal against it. You must apply for a mandatory reconsideration before you can appeal.

1. Who can claim income-based jobseeker's allowance

You qualify for jobseeker's allowance (JSA) if:[1]

- you do not count as being in full-time paid work (see p124); *and*
- you do not have limited capability for work. However, in certain circumstances, people who are sick or who have gone abroad for NHS hospital treatment can get JSA (see p124); *and*
- you are not in 'relevant education' (see p872). In addition, if you are a full-time student, you usually cannot get JSA (see p874); *and*
- you satisfy 'jobseeking conditions' (see Chapter 45) – ie, you must:
  - be available for work; *and*
  - be actively seeking work; *and*
  - have a current jobseeker's agreement with the DWP. The DWP calls this a 'claimant commitment'; *and*
- you are below pension age (see p771); *and*
- you are in Great Britain. JSA can continue to be paid in limited circumstances while you are temporarily away (see p1599).

The above conditions apply to all types of JSA. To qualify for income-based JSA, you must also satisfy extra rules (see below).

You may qualify for income-based JSA even if you do not qualify for contribution-based JSA. You may qualify for both income-based JSA and contribution-based JSA.

Note: if you come under the universal credit (UC) system (see p20), you cannot make a new claim for income-based JSA and should claim UC instead. If you already get income-based JSA but become entitled to UC (eg, because you become a member of a couple and your partner is getting UC), your income-based JSA may stop.

Extra rules for income-based jobseeker's allowance

You qualify for income-based JSA if, in addition to satisfying the rules that apply to all types of JSA (see above):[2]

Part 2: Main means-tested benefits and tax credits
Chapter 6: Income-based jobseeker's allowance
1. Who can claim income-based jobseeker's allowance

- your income is not more than your applicable amount (see p132); *and*
- your savings and other capital are worth £16,000 or less. Some capital (in particular your home) is ignored (see Chapter 17); *and*
- your partner does not count as being in full-time paid work (see p124); *and*
- you are aged 18 or over. If you are a 16/17-year-old, you might get income-based JSA if you satisfy special rules (see pp125–30); *and*
- if you are a joint-claim couple (see below), at least one of you is aged 18 or over. If one of you is a 16/17-year-old, you can get income-based JSA if the member of the couple who is 16/17 satisfies special rules (see pp125–30); *and*
- neither you nor your partner are claiming and entitled to income support (IS), income-related employment and support allowance (ESA) or pension credit (PC), and, if you are not a joint-claim couple (see p120), your partner is not claiming and entitled to income-based JSA. If you or your partner can qualify for IS, income-related ESA or PC, check whether this would make you better off (see p142). **Note:** if you become a member of a couple and your partner is getting UC, you no longer qualify for income-based JSA; *and*
- you are not included as a child in someone else's IS or income-based JSA claim (see p220). However, you can qualify for JSA in your own right in a number of situations (see p125) and you cannot be included in someone's claim for income-based JSA if you are (or would be) entitled to JSA;[3] *and*
- you satisfy the 'habitual residence' and the 'right to reside' tests. To find out if you are exempt from these tests, see Chapter 66; *and*
- you are not a 'person subject to immigration control' (see p1516). There are exceptions to this rule.

Joint-claim couples

If you are a 'joint-claim couple', both you and your partner must usually make a joint claim for JSA and satisfy all the rules for getting income-based JSA. You are a 'joint-claim couple' if you are a member of a couple (see p215) and:[4]
- at least one of you is 18 or over. If one of you is 16 or 17, special rules apply (see p125); *and*
- neither of you is responsible for children in the circumstances described below.

There are exceptions. For the rules on when one of you does not have to satisfy all the conditions, see p121 and, on what happens if one of you does not qualify for JSA, see p135.

Responsible for children

You do not have to claim joint-claim JSA if you or your partner are responsible for a child (see p220 for who counts). For these purposes, you count as being responsible for a child if:[5]
- you are entitled to child benefit for her/him; *or*

- no one is receiving child benefit for her/him but:
  - you are the only person who has claimed child benefit for her/him and your claim has not yet been decided; *or*
  - s/he usually lives with you; *or*
- someone else is responsible for her/him, but s/he is staying with you so that s/he can attend school; *or*
- you are looking after her/him for the local authority or a voluntary organisation (or, in Scotland only, s/he has been boarded out with you) under specific provisions; *or*
- you are looking after her/him with a view to adoption.

Even if you do not get child benefit for your child and none of the other rules above apply, if you share actual responsibility for the child (eg, with your ex-partner) and are a 'substantial minority carer' (ie, you have the child with you for at least 104 nights a year), you may be able to argue that you should still be regarded as responsible for the child.[6] Get advice and see CPAG's *Welfare Rights Bulletin 185* (pp9–11) and *194* (pp5–6).

If, while you are entitled to JSA, you or your partner become responsible for a child under 16, you no longer qualify for joint-claim JSA. However, your JSA can continue without interruption if you or your partner provide the DWP with evidence of this, if required, and notify the DWP which one of you is to continue claiming income-based JSA for you both.[7]

If, while you are entitled to JSA, you or your partner stop being responsible for any children, or all the children concerned have either died or reached the age of 16 and are not qualifying young people for child benefit purposes (see p572), you and your partner must claim joint-claim JSA.[8] Your JSA can continue without interruption if the DWP has sufficient information to award you joint-claim JSA and you or your partner have told the DWP which one of you has been nominated to receive payment for you both.

When joint-claim couples do not have to satisfy all the conditions

If you are a member of a couple who must make a joint claim for JSA (see p120), provided one of you satisfies all the rules for claiming JSA, the two of you can still qualify for joint-claim JSA even if the other does not satisfy the jobseeking conditions, has limited capability for work, is in relevant education (see p872) or is not in Great Britain. The one who does not satisfy the rules must be below pension age (see p772), not count as being in full-time paid work (see p124) and be in one of the exempt groups below.[9] You must still make a joint claim for JSA and satisfy all the other requirements.

Exempt groups

You are in an exempt group if, for at least one day in a benefit week, you:[10]

- are studying full time. You must be:

Part 2: Main means-tested benefits and tax credits
Chapter 6: Income-based jobseeker's allowance
1. Who can claim income-based jobseeker's allowance

2

- a 'qualifying young person' for child benefit purposes (see p572) or a full-time student (see p874). You must normally be in education at the time you and your partner claim JSA, but there are exceptions; *or*
- someone who can claim IS while in 'relevant education', other than a refugee learning English (see p872).

You can only be in this exempt group for one joint claim, unless another one is made after JSA entitlement ceased when one of you started full-time paid work, was summoned to do jury service or was within a linked period (see p700 – the definition of a linked period is the same as for contribution-based JSA);[11] *or*

- are a carer who could claim IS (see p104). If you cease meeting this condition or stop being a carer, you continue to fit into an exempt group for a further eight weeks; *or*
- are entitled to statutory sick pay; *or*
- are incapable of work but are treated as capable of work because you are disqualified from receiving incapacity benefit – eg, because of misconduct or failure to accept treatment (see p271 of the 2008/09 edition of this *Handbook*); *or*
- have, or are treated as having, limited capability for work or are treated as if you do not have limited capability for work because you are disqualifed from receiving ESA – eg, because of misconduct or failure to accept treatment (see p637). **Note:** you can qualify for contributory ESA and joint-claim JSA at the same time;[12] *or*
- provide medical evidence to show that you have limited capability for work – ie, a self-certificate (for no longer than seven days) or a current medical certificate from your doctor (the DWP may accept other evidence if it is unreasonable to require you to provide this). You are exempt indefinitely on this basis without having to satisfy the work capability assessment; *or*
- are incapable of work, or have limited capability for work, because of your pregnancy. You do not have to show that there is a serious risk to your health or that of your baby;[13] *or*
- are at least the qualifying age for PC (see p147). In practice, this only applies if you are a man at least that age but under 65. In this situation, you might be better off claiming PC rather than JSA; *or*
- are a refugee learning English in order to obtain employment. You must be on a course for more than 15 hours a week and, at the time the course started, you must have been in Great Britain for a year or less. You can only be exempt for nine months on this ground; *or*
- are required to go to court or a tribunal as a JP, juror, witness or party to the proceedings; *or*
- are not a 'qualifying young person' for child benefit purposes (see p572) and are on a training course for people aged 16 to 24 provided by the Secretary of State, the Welsh Ministers or a local enterprise company in Scotland; *or*

- are involved in a trade dispute. **Note:** this does not apply if your partner is also involved in a trade dispute.

If you are in some of the exempt groups above, you should also qualify for IS. If you have limited capability for work, you may also qualify for income-related ESA. If you are at least the qualifying age for PC (see p147), you might qualify for PC. In these cases, you can choose whether to claim IS/income-related ESA/PC or JSA. See p142 for further information before deciding what to do.

Note: before 1 November 2010, there were other groups of sick and disabled people who were also exempt. You may still come into one of these groups. See p398 of the 2012/13 edition of this *Handbook* for further information.

Jobseeking periods

A '**jobseeking period**' is the period during which you:[14]
- meet the conditions that apply to all types of JSA (see p119); *or*
- do not satisfy the jobseeking conditions but receive hardship payments (see Chapter 51).

Note:
- You are not usually entitled to JSA for the first seven days of your 'jobseeking period'. These are known as 'waiting days' (see p705).
- If you are a man of at least the qualifying age for PC (see p147) but under 65, special rules apply which mean that in some circumstances your jobseeking period continues even though you do not satisfy the jobseeking conditions.[15]

Certain days do not count as part of a jobseeking period. The rules are broadly the same as for contribution-based JSA (see p699). However, in addition, days for which you have been refused JSA because you have not provided your partner's national insurance number do not count as part of a jobseeking period. **Note:** periods when you were entitled to contribution-based JSA under the UC system (see p24) are included in your jobseeking period – eg, if you are now entitled to income-based JSA.[16]

In some cases, two or more jobseeking periods can be linked together and treated as if they were one. Also, certain periods in which you satisfy other conditions ('linked periods') can be linked to a jobseeking period (see p700).[17] This means, for example, that:
- if you make a fresh claim for JSA but your jobseeking period links with a previous one, you do not have to serve any waiting days (see p132) to get JSA;
- if the combined jobseeking periods are at least two years, you might be able to get JSA while attending a qualifying course (see p1028).

Part 2: Main means-tested benefits and tax credits
Chapter 6: Income-based jobseeker's allowance
1. Who can claim income-based jobseeker's allowance

Full-time paid work

You cannot usually qualify for income-based JSA if you or your partner are in full-time paid work. If you are the JSA claimant, this means 16 hours or more each week.[18] For your partner, this means 24 hours or more each week. All the rules on work are covered in Chapter 43.

If you are a member of a joint-claim couple, you cannot get joint-claim JSA if either one of you is in full-time paid work. If one of you is not working or is working fewer than 16 hours a week, the other can then work up to 24 hours a week. In this situation, you do not have to make a joint claim.[19] The person working fewer than 16 hours can claim income-based JSA.

In some situations, you are treated as *not* being in full-time work even if you work 16/24 hours or more (see p996). In others, you are treated as being in full-time work when you are not (see p996). See p992 for how your hours are calculated and p991 for what counts as paid work.

Note: if you or your partner have just taken up full-time paid work, you may be able to claim IS for help with your housing costs for the first four weeks. This is known as 'mortgage interest run-on' (see p474).

Would you be better off claiming another benefit instead?
1. You and your partner might be able to qualify for both working tax credit (WTC) and JSA because the rules for what counts as full-time paid work for WTC and JSA are different. This may apply, for example, if:
– your partner normally works 16/24 hours or more but is off sick or on maternity, adoption, paternity or shared parental leave;
– you work less than 16 hours and your partner works at least 16 hours but less than 24 hours each week.
Get advice to see how you would be better off financially.
2. If you or your partner are at least the qualifying age for PC and either of you is working 16/24 hours or more each week, you might be able to claim PC or WTC (or both if your income is low enough). There is no full-time paid work rule for PC, but earnings are taken into account when working out how much you can get.

Limited capability for work

To qualify for JSA you must not have 'limited capability for work'.[20] See Chapter 44 for details about the test that decides this. **Note:** if a decision maker has decided that you have (or do not have) limited capability for work for ESA purposes, you are automatically treated as having (or not having) limited capability for work for JSA.[21] This means that if your health improves and you move onto JSA from ESA, you may be asked to provide medical evidence that you no longer have limited capability for work. In all cases, you must still show that you are available for work if you are ill or have a disability. However, there are some special rules that allow you to restrict your availability (see p1040).

Even if you have limited capability for work, you do not have to stop claiming JSA in some situations – ie:

- for certain short periods of up to 13 weeks; *or*
- if you are temporarily absent from Great Britain to obtain NHS hospital treatment under certain provisions.

See p701 for further information. The rules are the same as for contribution-based JSA.

2. The rules about your age

You cannot usually qualify for:

- **income-based jobseeker's allowance** (JSA) until you are 18. There are special rules that can help you qualify if you are 16 or 17 (see p125). If you do not qualify, check whether you qualify for income support (IS) or employment and support allowance (ESA) instead. Even if you cannot get JSA, IS or ESA, you may qualify for housing benefit (HB);
- **joint-claim JSA** unless you and your partner are both 18. If only one of you is 18 or over, the other must satisfy the conditions for income-based JSA in her/his own right as a 16/17-year-old (see below).[22] If both of you are under 18, you do not count as a joint-claim couple and so one of you may be able to claim income-based JSA for the other.

You cannot claim any type of JSA if you are pension age or over (see p772). In practice, there is usually no point in remaining on income-based JSA if you are a man of at least the qualifying age for pension credit (PC – see p147), which is currently lower than a man's pension age (age 65), as you qualify for PC because of your age without having to satisfy any jobseeking conditions. You may also receive automatic national insurance (NI) credits (see p974). You (and your partner) should be no worse off on PC than on income-based JSA.

16/17-year-olds

If you are aged 16 or 17, you can qualify for:

- **income-based JSA** if you satisfy the basic rules of entitlement and you are entitled to it under the rules described on p126;
- **joint-claim JSA** if you satisfy the basic rules of entitlement, you are a member of a couple and your partner is 18 or over and you would qualify for income-based JSA under the rules described on p126.[23] Usually, you must both satisfy all the conditions for entitlement, but see p121 for the exceptions. If both of

Part 2: Main means-tested benefits and tax credits
Chapter 6: Income-based jobseeker's allowance
2. The rules about your age

you are under 18, you do not count as a joint-claim couple and so one of you may be able to claim income-based JSA for both of you.

You should not have your claim refused or be turned away by the DWP simply because of your age or because you have been included in someone else's claim for benefit or tax credits. Remember the following.

- The usual rules about claims and payments apply. However, there are additional rules (see p134).
- There are special rules for calculating your JSA applicable amount if you are a member of a couple (see p232).
- In general, you are subject to the same jobseeking conditions as people aged 18 or over. However, there are some important differences – eg, you must be actively seek work *and* training (see p1047).
- You can generally be given a sanction in the same way as claimants aged 18 or over. However, some special rules apply for good reason (see p1137), sanction periods are sometimes shorter and the amount by which your benefit can be reduced is sometimes lower than for older claimants (see p1095).

Note: you can qualify for **contribution-based JSA** if you satisfy the contribution conditions (see Chapter 32). However, because you are unlikely to have paid sufficient NI contributions before you are 18, it is unlikely you will qualify.

When you cannot qualify

In addition to the situations that apply to claimants aged 18 or over, you cannot qualify for income-based JSA if you:[24]

- qualify for contribution-based JSA; *or*
- are being, or were previously, looked after by a local authority in the circumstances described on pp936–37. There are exceptions to those rules.

Remember that, in most cases, you cannot qualify for JSA if you are in 'relevant education' (see p872). You may be able to claim JSA during a period after your education ends (during the child benefit 'extension period') if you satisfy the rules on pp127–28.

When you can qualify

You can qualify for income-based JSA while you are 16 or 17 if you are a person who can claim:

- at any time before age 18 (see p127); *or*
- during the child benefit extension period (see p127); *or*
- during other limited periods (see p128); *or*
- on a discretionary basis – ie, you are awarded severe hardship payments (see p129).

Qualifying at any time before age 18

You can qualify for income-based JSA at any time before you are 18 if you satisfy the normal conditions of entitlement and:[25]

- you are in one of the groups of people who can claim IS (see pp102–06). In this case, you can choose whether to claim JSA or IS. It is usually better to claim IS because you do not have to be available for and actively seeking work and training and therefore risk benefit sanctions. You can still look for work. If you claim IS rather than JSA, however, you might not receive NI credits (see Chapter 42); *or*
- you have limited capability for work (see Chapter 44). In this case, you may qualify for ESA or universal credit instead of JSA; *or*
- you are one of a couple and at least one child under 16 can be included in your claim (see p220).

Qualifying during the child benefit extension period

You can qualify for income-based JSA during a period of 20 weeks after leaving education or training (called the child benefit 'extension period' – see p575), if:[26]

- you are married or in a civil partnership and satisfy other conditions (see p128); *or*
- you are an orphan with no one acting as your parent – eg, a foster carer or any other person with parental responsibility for you; *or*
- you are living away from your parents and any person acting as your parent and:
  - immediately before you were 16 you were:
    - in custody; *or*
    - being looked after by a local authority. In England and Wales, you must have been placed with someone other than a close relative. In Scotland, you cannot have been living with your parents or a close relative; *or*
  - you are living at a place you went to:
    - as part of a programme of resettlement or rehabilitation under the supervision of the probation service or a local authority; *or*
    - to avoid physical or sexual abuse; *or*
    - because you need special accommodation because of mental or physical illness or disability; *or*
  - your parents (or the person acting in place of them) are unable to support you financially and they are in custody or unable to enter Great Britain (eg, because of the UK Immigration Rules) or are 'chronically sick or mentally or physically disabled'; *or*
  - this is because you are estranged from them (see p873), you are in physical or moral danger, or there is a serious risk to your physical or mental health.

Part 2: Main means-tested benefits and tax credits
Chapter 6: Income-based jobseeker's allowance
2. The rules about your age

Close relative

'Close relative' means parent, step-parent, parent-in-law, parent of a civil partner, son, stepson, son-in-law, son of a civil partner, daughter, stepdaughter, daughter-in-law, daughter of a civil partner, brother, sister or the partner of any of these.[27]

You can qualify for income-based JSA during the child benefit extension period if you are married or in a civil partnership and your partner is:[28]

- 18 or over; *or*
- under 18. This only applies if s/he does not qualify for contribution-based JSA, s/he was not previously looked after by a local authority in the circumstances described on pp936–37 and s/he:
  – is registered for work and training; *or*
  – is treated as being responsible for a child under 16 who is a member of her/his household (see p220); *or*
  – is laid off or on short-time working and is available for work under the special rules described on p1033; *or*
  – is temporarily absent from Great Britain and is taking a child or qualifying young person for whom s/he is responsible and who lives with her/him (see p220) abroad for treatment (for the first eight weeks of the absence); *or*
  – is incapable of work and training because of a physical or mental condition and a doctor confirms that as a result of the severity of the disease or condition, s/he is likely to be for at least 12 months; *or*
  – fits into one of certain groups of people who can claim IS – ie, people with childcare responsibilities and carers (other than those on parental or paternity leave), pregnant women, pupils, students (other than, in most cases, disabled or deaf students) and people on training courses, refugees learning English, or certain people who are subject to immigration control.

This means that you can claim JSA, although in many of these cases your partner can claim either JSA or IS (or, if s/he has limited capability for work, ESA) instead.

Qualifying during other limited periods

Even if you are not someone who qualifies for income-based JSA at any time before you are 18 (see p127), you may be able to claim it for a limited period.

- You can qualify after the end of the child benefit extension period (see p575) if:[29]
  – you are in one of the groups of people who can claim income-based JSA during that period and you are discharged from custody or detention after it ends (for up to eight weeks from the day of discharge); *or*
  – you have to live away from your parents and anyone acting as your parent following a stay in accommodation provided by a local authority in England under specified provisions (for up to eight weeks from the date of leaving the

accommodation, whether before or after the end of the extension period). If you leave less than eight weeks before the end of the extension period, you first get income-based JSA under the rules on p127, and then your benefit can continue under this rule until the end of the eight-week period. Remember that some people cannot claim JSA when they stop being looked after by a local authority (see p936).

- You can qualify during any period that you are laid off or are on short-time working and are available for work under the special rules described on p1033.[30]
- If you have accepted an offer to enlist in the armed forces within eight weeks of the offer being made and you were not in employment or training when it was made, you can qualify for income-based JSA until you are due to enlist. However, this does not apply if you have ever been sanctioned in certain specified situations – eg, because you failed to accept a place on a training scheme or employment programme, or lost a place (or a job) through misconduct.[31]

Qualifying for severe hardship payments

If you do not qualify for income-based JSA under any of the rules for 16/17-year-olds above, or for IS, you can still be paid income-based JSA on a discretionary basis if severe hardship will result if you are not paid.[32] These are referred to as 'severe hardship payments' in this *Handbook*. You must have registered for training, but you must not be receiving any training.

Remember the following.

- If you are one of a couple and you are only getting income-based JSA at one of the lower couple rates (see p232), you may be eligible for a higher couple rate if a severe hardship direction is made in respect of your partner.
- Severe hardship payments are payments of JSA, so you are automatically eligible for other benefits – eg, HB.
- There are special rules about sanctions that only apply to severe hardship payments (see p1095).

You must have a 'severe hardship direction' to get severe hardship payments. Authorised staff in the Jobcentre Plus office can consider whether to issue one, but must refer your case to the Under Eighteens Support Team (UEST) for a decision, if their decision is likely to be negative.[33] A decision should be made within 24 hours.

All your circumstances should be considered. The factors that should be taken into account include:[34]

- your financial circumstances, including your income, capital and outgoings;
- whether the person with whom you live is on a means-tested benefit;
- whether you are homeless or at risk of eviction if severe hardship payments are not paid;

Part 2: Main means-tested benefits and tax credits
Chapter 6: Income-based jobseeker's allowance
2. The rules about your age

- whether you have any health problems, are pregnant or are vulnerable and at risk for any reason and whether you have access to food and accommodation.

How do you get a severe hardship direction?

1. Provide as much evidence as you can to show that you will experience severe hardship without JSA.

2. Explain fully why your parents are not supporting you or why they should not be expected to continue to do so and, if relevant, why it could be damaging if they were to be contacted. The DWP should accept this and should not refuse a severe hardship direction just because you are living at home.

3. If the DWP wants to contact a responsible third party, such as a relative, social worker, youth worker or recognised voluntary worker, to corroborate what you have said, it must ask your permission.[35] If you refuse this without good reason, your case is referred directly to the UEST. If you have written evidence from, or are accompanied by, a responsible third party, further enquiries of, or contact with, your parents may not be necessary.

4. If there is difficulty in obtaining evidence from your parents or a third party, the interviewing officer should consider a short-term severe hardship direction. You can then receive severe hardship payments while further enquiries are made.

Once a severe hardship direction is issued, the normal rules and procedures for claiming income-based JSA apply. Severe hardship payments are paid in arrears. If you need money urgently, you could apply for a short-term advance (see p1177).

A severe hardship direction normally lasts for eight weeks, but it can be longer or shorter than this – eg, it may be shorter if you are starting work or training soon, or evidence to support your application is not easily available.[36]

When your severe hardship direction ends, you can apply for it to be renewed. A severe hardship direction can also be revoked, which means that you can no longer get severe hardship payments. A direction can (but does not have to) be revoked if:[37]

- your circumstances have changed and you would no longer experience severe hardship if you did not receive severe hardship payments; *or*
- the direction was given in ignorance of, or because of a mistake about, a material fact and, but for this, would not have been given. Any overpayment may be recoverable (see Chapter 52);[38] *or*
- you failed to follow up an opportunity of a place on a training scheme or rejected an offer of a place and cannot show a good reason for having done so. 'Good reason' is not defined in the rules. If your severe hardship direction is revoked on this ground, you can apply for another one straight away, but if one is made, your severe hardship payments are reduced for a two-week period.

You cannot appeal against the decision about whether:[39]
- you would experience severe hardship;
- to issue or revoke a severe hardship direction or how long it should last;
- a certificate of 'good reason' should be issued (see p1138).

However, you can ask for a revision or a supersession of a decision against which you do not have a right of appeal. You do not have to show specific grounds in this situation. Any reasons you give for disagreeing with the decision should be considered. You can also ask for a review of a decision not to issue a severe hardship direction.[40]

In addition, you can complain to your MP. You might be able to apply for a judicial review (see p1378). If, for example, you obtain more evidence of your hardship, you could also make a new claim.

3. **People included in the claim**

If you are single, you claim income-based jobseeker's allowance (JSA) for yourself.

If you are a 'joint-claim couple' (see p120), you and your partner must usually both claim joint-claim JSA. If you are not a joint-claim couple, either you claim income-based JSA for both of you or, if your partner meets the qualifying conditions for income-based JSA, s/he claims for you both. Whichever one of you claims JSA, the other may qualify for national insurance (NI) credits in order to protect her/his NI record. See Chapter 42 for more details about NI credits.

If you are a member of a couple, your applicable amount includes a personal allowance for a couple and can include premiums based on both your and your partner's circumstances. When your benefit is worked out, your partner's income and capital are usually added to yours.

There are some situations in which you must show that you are 'responsible' for a child who is living in your household – eg:
- in order to take advantage of the special rules to help you meet the jobseeking conditions (see Chapter 45);
- to show you are a lone parent so you can benefit from a higher earnings disregard (see p279);
- for some of the rules for help with housing costs – eg, for your mortgage or loan for repairs and improvements (see Chapter 20).

See p220 for who counts as a child. You do not have to be the child's parent. For when you count as responsible for a child and when s/he counts as living in your household, see pp222–25.

Note: there are different rules about children for deciding whether you must claim joint-claim JSA (see p120).

Part 2: Main means-tested benefits and tax credits
Chapter 6: Income-based jobseeker's allowance
4. The amount of benefit

4. The amount of benefit

After any 'waiting days' (see below), income-based jobseeker's allowance (JSA) tops up your income to a level set by the government. The amount you get depends on your needs (your 'applicable amount') and on how much income and capital you (and your partner) have.[41]

Your applicable amount consists of:

- a personal allowance (see p230); *and*
- premiums (see p236) for any special needs; *and*
- housing costs – eg, for your mortgage or loan for repairs and improvements (see Chapter 20). **Note:** in many cases, you can only get help with housing costs for 104 weeks (see p445).

Income-based JSA is calculated in the same way as for income support (IS – see p108).

Do you have children?

Income-based JSA does not include allowances and premiums for your children. Instead, you can claim child tax credit (CTC). However, in some cases, if you have not yet been awarded CTC, you can continue to get allowances and premiums for your children (see p230). If you do get allowances and premiums for your children, there are special rules for the treatment of their income and capital (see p269 and p356).

You might get a reduced amount of JSA if:

- you have been given a sanction (see Chapter 48); *or*
- you are a member of a joint-claim couple and your partner has not made a joint claim with you (see p135); *or*
- you are not a member of a joint-claim couple, you have a partner and s/he has failed to attend a work-focused interview without good cause (see p1124); *or*
- you are receiving a hardship payment of income-based JSA (see Chapter 51); *or*
- you have committed a benefit offence (see p1265).

Different rules for calculating your JSA may apply if you are in one of the groups to whom special rules apply (see p133).

Waiting days

You are not entitled to JSA for the first seven 'waiting days' of any jobseeking period (see p123) unless:[42]

- your claim is linked to a previous claim for JSA so both are treated as part of the same jobseeking period. For joint-claim couples, this includes a previous claim made by either of you separately; *or*
- you (or, for joint-claim couples only, either of you) have been entitled to IS, employment and support allowance (ESA), incapacity benefit or carer's allowance within the 12 weeks before you become entitled to JSA; *or*

- you are the member of a joint-claim couple nominated to be paid JSA and are in receipt of a training allowance; *or*
- you are 16 or 17 and getting JSA under the severe hardship rules (see p129).

In addition, you do not have to serve any waiting days if you swap from claiming IS or ESA to claiming JSA, or you and your partner swap which of you claims IS, ESA or JSA for both of you, and the new claim is for JSA.[43]

If you receive income-based JSA, you are entitled to maximum housing benefit during any waiting days.[44] You may be able to get a short-term advance during your waiting days (see p1177).

5. Special benefit rules

Special rules may apply to:
- 16/17-year-olds (see p125);
- workers who are laid off or working short time (see p1028);
- people subject to immigration control (see Chapter 65);
- people who have come from or are going abroad (see Chapters 66, 67 and 68);
- people who are studying (see Chapter 40);
- people without accommodation, people involved in a trade dispute and people who are (or whose partner or children are) in hospital or living in a care home or other similar accommodation, or people in prison (see Chapter 41).

6. Claims and backdating

The general rules about claims and backdating are covered in Chapter 49. This section explains the specific rules that apply to income-based jobseeker's allowance (JSA).

Making a claim

Information on how to make a claim for JSA is on pp709–11. Remember that income-based and contribution-based JSA are two types of one benefit. If you want the DWP to assess your entitlement to both, it is important to make this clear when you claim and answer all the relevant questions and provide all the necessary information.

Note:
- If you are 16 or 17 years old, you must usually register for work and training (see p134).

Part 2: Main means-tested benefits and tax credits
Chapter 6: Income-based jobseeker's allowance
6. Claims and backdating

- If you are claiming JSA within 26 weeks of a previous claim, you may be able to claim without having to give as much detail of your circumstances as is usually required. This is known as 'rapid reclaim'.

16/17-year-olds

If you are 16 or 17 and are claiming JSA, the usual rules apply. However, if you do not come under the universal credit (UC) system, you must first register for both work and training at the place specified by the DWP. This may be at the Jobcentre Plus office itself or where the local authority provides careers advice (see below).[45] Ask the Jobcentre Plus office where to register if you are in any doubt. **Note:**

- You do not have to register if you are claiming under the special rules for people laid off or on short-time working (see p1028) or if you have accepted an offer to enlist in the armed forces (see p129).[46]
- You must register at the Jobcentre Plus office if you are unable to register at the specified place because there is an emergency affecting it, such as a strike or a fire, or you would experience hardship because of the extra time it would take to register there.[47]

Local authority careers advice

The DWP refers to the places that provide careers advice to young people as 'local authority youth services'. Your local authority may call its service Connexions, Young People's Services or the Careers Service, Careers Wales, Skills Development Scotland or Careers Scotland.

If you are claiming severe hardship payments, remember to state this when you claim JSA and insist on your right to make a claim. You must have a severe hardship direction (see p129).

Who should claim

For income-based JSA, if you are a single person or a lone parent, you claim on your own behalf. Unless you must make a joint claim for JSA (see p135), if you are a member of a couple you must choose which one of you claims for you both. See p215 for who counts as a couple. If you cannot agree who should claim, a decision maker decides.[48] If you are not the person claiming JSA, you may wish to claim national insurance (NI) credits to protect your NI record (see p967). If you claim NI credits, you can also qualify for help from the schemes for assisting people to obtain employment.

If you are unable to manage your own affairs, another person can claim JSA for you as your 'appointee' (see p1149).

Joint claims for jobseeker's allowance

If you are a joint-claim couple (see p120), both you and your partner must usually:[49]

- claim JSA; *and*
- satisfy all the rules for getting income-based JSA (see p119).

There are exceptions. In some cases, one of you does not have to satisfy all the conditions for getting JSA and you can still make a joint claim (see p121). In other cases, you can qualify for income-based JSA even if your partner does not qualify for joint-claim JSA (see below).

If your partner does not qualify for joint-claim jobseeker's allowance

If you are a member of a joint-claim couple and you satisfy all the rules for getting income-based JSA (see p119), in certain circumstances you can qualify for income-based JSA even if your partner does not qualify for joint-claim JSA. This is the case if your partner:[50]

- failed to attend the initial interview (see p136); *or*
- failed to meet the jobseeking conditions (see p1027); *or*
- is subject to immigration control (see p1516); *or*
- is temporarily absent from Great Britain (see p1590); *or*
- does not satisfy the 'habitual residence' or the 'right to reside' tests (see Chapter 66); *or*
- is over pension age (see p772). In this situation, you both might be better off if your partner were to claim pension credit (PC) for you rather than JSA; *or*
- works 16 or more, but less than 24, hours a week. **Note:** in this case, you may be able to qualify for working tax credit; *or*
- has claimed maternity allowance or statutory maternity pay; *or*
- is pregnant and there are 11 weeks or less before the week the baby is due; *or*
- was pregnant and her pregnancy ended not more than 28 weeks ago – ie, when her baby was born or she had a miscarriage; *or*
- is receiving an unemployment benefit from another country under a reciprocal agreement (see p1533); *or*
- is receiving statutory sick pay and was working 16 hours or more a week immediately before s/he became incapable of work.

In the first four cases, JSA entitlement is calculated as if you were a single claimant.[51] In the remaining cases, JSA entitlement is calculated for both of you in the normal way. In all other respects, you are treated as a couple and, therefore, your partner's income and capital are taken into account.

Part 2: Main means-tested benefits and tax credits
Chapter 6: Income-based jobseeker's allowance
6. Claims and backdating

Information to support your claim

For the general information requirements that apply to all benefits, see p1150.

While you are getting income-based JSA, you must satisfy the jobseeking conditions. So, as well as giving all the necessary facts about your circumstances, you are expected to attend and participate in:[52]

- an initial interview when you claim (see below); *and*
- an interview when you sign on (see p1055); *and*
- further interviews as required (see p1057).

It is important that you provide any information required when you claim. This is known as the 'evidence requirement'. Until you do, you may not count as having made a valid claim (see p1152). Correct any defects as soon as possible or your date of claim may be affected. See p1153 for the evidence requirement and to see whether you are exempt.

If you have a mortgage, you are given an additional form to give to your lender.

Even if you have provided all that was required when you claimed, you may be asked to provide further information to support your claim (see p1154). You may also be asked to provide information after you are awarded JSA, and if you fail to do so, your JSA could be suspended, or even terminated (see p1185).

The initial interview

You (or, if you are claiming joint-claim JSA, both you and your partner) must usually attend and participate in an initial interview.[53] If you do not attend the interview at the right time, your date of claim is affected (see p139). If you do not attend the interview at all (and the DWP does not waive the requirement to do so), you have not made a valid claim and so do not qualify for JSA.

If you claim online, the DWP phones or texts you within two working days to arrange your initial interview.

If attending the Jobcentre Plus office would mean that you would have to be away from home for too long, arrangements can be made for your initial interview to be carried out elsewhere.

The DWP says you should bring two forms of identification to the interview (eg, your passport or driving licence), along with your P45 if you have one.[54] If you have been sent a claim form, complete it before your interview. If you do not provide all the evidence and information required, your interview might not go ahead unless you are exempt from the evidence requirement (p1153).

At the interview:

- you are told what is expected from you while you are receiving JSA;
- you and your work coach discuss what work you are looking for and what you intend to do to find it;
- a jobseeker's agreement (see p1049) is drawn up for you to sign;

- you may be referred to a job vacancy immediately. However, a jobseeker's agreement should still be completed to establish entitlement in case you do not get the job.

The interview also covers what you were doing before you became unemployed and, in particular, why you left your previous job. If the person who interviews you thinks that you may have left voluntarily or been dismissed for misconduct, your case is referred to a decision maker who will probably make further enquiries before deciding whether to give you a sanction (see Chapter 48).

The date of your claim

The date of your claim is important as it determines when your entitlement to JSA starts (subject to the rules on waiting days – see p132). This is not necessarily the date from when you are paid. For information about when payment of JSA starts, see p141.

You are not usually entitled to JSA for any day before your date of claim.[55] Your date of claim is not necessarily the date it is received by the DWP; it can be an earlier date.

Your '**date of claim**' depends on whether or not you are required to attend an initial interview (see p136). If you (or you and your partner if you are a joint-claim couple) are required to attend an initial interview, your date of claim is usually:

- the date you first contact the Jobcentre Plus office if you (or both of you) attend the interview at the time specified by the DWP and by that time a properly completed claim is or has been provided (on a form or by phone) with all the information and evidence required. If you (or your partner) fail to attend the interview, see p139;[56] *or*
- if you are a joint-claim couple and only one of you is required to attend an initial interview, the earliest of:[57]
  - the date you or your partner first contacted the Jobcentre Plus office, provided a properly completed claim (on a form or by phone) with all the information and evidence required is provided within one month of your first contact; *or*
  - the date on which a properly completed claim (on a form) with all the information and evidence required is received at the Jobcentre Plus office or a claim made by phone is properly completed, provided the person who is required to attend an interview does so. If you (or your partner) fail to attend the interview, see p139.

Forms

In this section, the term '**form**' refers to a paper form or a claim form completed online.

Part 2: Main means-tested benefits and tax credits
Chapter 6: Income-based jobseeker's allowance
6. Claims and backdating

If you are not required to attend an initial interview and you are not a member of a joint-claim couple, your date of claim is usually the earliest of:[58]

- the date you first contacted the Jobcentre Plus office, so long as a properly completed claim (on a form or by phone) with all the information and evidence required is provided within one month of your first contact; *or*
- the date on which a properly completed claim (on a form) with all the information and evidence required is received at the Jobcentre Plus office or a claim made by phone is properly completed.

Whether or not you (and your partner) are required to attend an initial interview, the DWP can extend the time you have to provide or make a properly completed claim up to the date one month after the date you first contacted the Jobcentre Plus office to claim JSA.[59] This is discretionary, so provide your claim as required wherever possible.

Note: you must make sure your claim is valid. If it is 'defective', you are given a short time to correct the defects (see p1152). If you do, your claim is treated as having been made when you initially claimed.[60]

There are **exceptions** to the above rules.

- If you claim working tax credit (WTC) and are refused because neither you nor your partner are in full-time paid work for WTC purposes (see p196), your date of claim for JSA is the date you claimed WTC.[61] However, you must claim JSA within 14 days of the decision refusing you WTC. You can ask for your JSA claim to start on a later date instead – eg, if your income is currently too high, but is due to decrease.
- If you claim UC and, on the basis of information you provided, you are treated as satisfying the gateway conditions for UC or as living in an area in which those conditions apply, but the DWP discovers that the information was incorrect, unless you have already been paid UC, you should be advised by the DWP that you are not entitled to claim UC. If you then claim JSA and your date of claim is no later than one month after being told that you are not entitled to claim UC, and if (taking into account any backdating you have requested and been allowed) your JSA claim is later than the date of your UC claim, your JSA claim is treated as having been made on the date of your UC claim.[62]

In some cases you may be able to claim in advance (see p140), and in some cases your claim can be backdated (see p139). If you want this to be done, make this clear when you claim or the DWP may not consider it.

Have you or your partner claimed contribution-based jobseeker's allowance?

1. If you are a member of a couple and one of you claims contribution-based JSA but is not entitled to it and a subsequent income-based JSA claim is made by the other member of the couple (or both of you if you are a joint-claim couple), the date of claim for income-based JSA is the date of the earlier claim for contribution-based JSA.[63]

2. If your partner has been claiming contribution-based JSA, this expires and you claim income-based JSA, the date of claim for your income-based JSA is the day after your partner's entitlement expires.[64]

3. If you claim contribution-based JSA as well as joint-claim JSA, you and your partner may be required to attend an initial interview. If you do, but your partner does not, you may be able to argue that your date of claim for contribution-based JSA is the date of your initial contact with Jobcentre Plus.

If you fail to attend the initial interview

If you (or your partner if you are a joint-claim couple) fail to attend your initial interview (see p136) at the time specified by the DWP or fail to provide a properly completed claim by the date of the interview and cannot show 'good cause' for this, the rules above do not apply. Instead, so long as a properly completed claim with all the information and evidence required has by then been provided, your date of claim is:

- if you are not a joint-claim couple, the date you eventually go to the Jobcentre Plus office. Your entitlement to JSA cannot start until that date;[65] *or*
- if you are a joint-claim couple and:[66]
  - you are both required to attend an interview, the date one of you eventually goes to the Jobcentre Plus office. Your entitlement to JSA cannot start until that date. However, in this situation, you can only get the single person's rate of JSA until the other attends an interview;[67] *or*
  - only one of you is required to attend an interview, the date the person who is required to attend eventually goes to the Jobcentre Plus office. Your entitlement to JSA cannot start until that date.

'Good cause' is not defined. All relevant circumstances must be considered. These may relate to your abilities or to external factors. The general test is whether there is some factor that would probably cause a reasonable person of your age and experience to act, or fail to act, as you did.[68]

Backdating your claim

It is very important to claim in time. A claim for JSA can normally only be backdated for a maximum of three months, and only in limited circumstances. The general rules on backdating are covered on p1157. See p1060 for the backdating rules if you make a new claim for JSA when your entitlement ends after you failed to sign on or participate in an interview.

Your claim can be backdated more than three months if you claim backdated JSA after an award of a qualifying benefit and an earlier JSA claim was refused (see p1160). If you claimed WTC or UC when you should have claimed JSA, see p138 to find out whether your date of claim can be backdated.

Part 2: Main means-tested benefits and tax credits
Chapter 6: Income-based jobseeker's allowance
6. Claims and backdating

If you might have qualified for JSA earlier but did not claim because you were given the wrong information or were misled by the DWP, you could ask for compensation (see p1396) or complain to the Ombudsman via your MP (see p1401).

If you want to get your jobseeker's agreement backdated, see p1053.

If you claim the wrong benefit

If you claim WTC or UC when you should have claimed JSA, see p138 to see whether your date of claim can be backdated.

Claiming in advance

If you do not qualify for JSA from the date of your claim (unless this is because you fail the habitual residence test – see p1537), but will do so within the next three months, you can be awarded JSA from the first date on which you qualify.[69] This gives the DWP time to ensure you receive benefit as soon as you are entitled. Let the DWP know you want to claim in advance when you claim and at your initial interview. You might have to persuade the DWP that it can accept a claim in advance.

You might not be entitled to income-based JSA currently, but would be once you (or your partner, or a child included in your claim) become entitled to another 'qualifying benefit' (eg, disability living allowance, personal independence payment or carer's allowance) because you are then entitled to premiums. Make your claim for JSA at the same time as the claim for the qualifying benefit. If you are:

- refused JSA, claim again when you get a decision about the qualifying benefit and ask for your JSA to be backdated to the date of your first JSA claim, or to the date of entitlement to the qualifying benefit, if that is later (see p1160);
- awarded JSA, you might be entitled to a higher rate once the outcome of the claim for the qualifying benefit is known. Apply for a revision or a supersession if you think this applies to you (see p1300).

After you are awarded jobseeker's allowance

Once you have been awarded JSA, in order to continue to receive it you (and if you are a joint-claim couple, you and your partner) must:

- attend and participate in regular interviews; *and*
- confirm that you continue to be entitled to JSA – eg, by signing on.

See p1054 for further information about the requirements after you are awarded JSA. **Note:** you are expected to verify your claim for income-based JSA annually by completing a questionnaire and signing a declaration.

If you fail to participate in interviews, you may be given a sanction (see Chapter 48). If you fail to sign on or to participate in interviews, your entitlement to JSA can end (see p1057).

Note: in some cases, if you fail to provide information when required to do so, your JSA could be suspended or even terminated (see p1185). If you have a partner (and you are not getting joint-claim JSA), s/he might be required to attend a work-focused interview (see p1066). If s/he fails to do so without good cause, your income-based JSA might be paid at a reduced rate.

7. Getting paid

Information about payment of your jobseeker's allowance (JSA) is on p716. The rules are the same as for contribution-based JSA.

If you and your partner are a joint-claim couple, you must nominate which one of you receives payment for both of you. If you cannot agree, a decision maker decides.[70] If your JSA is being paid at a reduced rate because one of you has been given a sanction, it is paid to the other member of the couple.[71] Even if you are not the person nominated to receive the JSA, if you separate from your partner and s/he cannot be traced, you can be paid any arrears of JSA that are due.[72]

Change of circumstances

You must report changes in your circumstances that you have been told you must report, as well as any that you might reasonably be expected to know might affect your right to, the amount of, or the payment of, your benefit, including any that are likely to occur. You should do this as soon as possible, preferably in writing. See p1184 for further information.

If you have a mortgage, the DWP can ask your lender about any changes in the amount you owe during your JSA claim. If you have this information (eg, from an annual statement you receive from your lender), you must also advise the DWP in case your lender fails to do so. Make sure the DWP takes this information into account so you are not overpaid JSA.

If there has been a relevant change of circumstances, a decision maker looks at your claim again and makes a new decision. To see when your JSA is then adjusted, see p717. The rules are the same as for contribution-based JSA.

Note: if you become a member of a couple with someone entitled to universal credit, your entitlement to income-based JSA ends (see p28).

8. Tax, other benefits and the benefit cap

Tax

Jobseeker's allowance (JSA) is taxable.[73] The maximum amount of JSA that is taxable is:

Part 2: Main means-tested benefits and tax credits
Chapter 6: Income-based jobseeker's allowance
8. Tax, other benefits and the benefit cap

- if you are claiming for yourself, an amount equal to the appropriate personal allowance for a person of your age (see p230); *or*
- if you are a member of a couple, an amount equal to the income-based JSA personal allowance for a couple (half this amount if your partner is unable to claim JSA because s/he is involved in a trade dispute – see p940).

The tax is not deducted while JSA is being paid but reduces the refund you would otherwise receive through PAYE (pay as you earn) when you return to work.

Any refunds of PAYE payments are paid to you at the end of the tax year to which they relate. Any other tax refund is paid only when you stop getting JSA.

Means-tested benefits and tax credits

Income-based JSA is an automatic passport to maximum housing benefit (HB), but you have to make a claim. It is also an automatic passport to maximum child tax credit (CTC) and is usually an automatic passport to maximum working tax credit (WTC).

You cannot claim JSA and income support (IS) at the same time. You cannot claim income-based JSA at the same time as pension credit (PC) or income-related employment and support allowance (ESA). If you have a partner, s/he can claim IS, income-related ESA or PC and you might be able to claim contribution-based JSA, but not income-based JSA.

Which benefit should you claim?
In some situations you need to choose whether to claim income-based JSA or IS (or income-related ESA or PC). You should consider the following.

1. The rates of IS, the guarantee credit of PC and income-based JSA are usually the same. The rate of income-related ESA can be higher or lower than the rate of IS, income-based JSA or PC.

2. If you are an owner occupier and need help with housing costs:
- the upper limit for loans can be higher for IS, income-based JSA and income-related ESA than for PC (see p462). If you are entitled to IS, income-based JSA or income-related ESA with a higher upper limit, but you then claim PC, the upper limit can continue to apply in some circumstances (see p463);
- you might only get help with your housing costs for 104 weeks if you claim income-based JSA (see p445). You can get help indefinitely if you claim IS, income-related ESA or PC.

3. You do not have to sign on or look for work if you are claiming IS, ESA or PC (nor does your partner). However, if you claim IS, the only reason you qualify is because you are a lone parent and you do not have any children under three, or you claim ESA and are not in the support group, you may have to undertake work-related activity (see p1068).

4. You may want to claim JSA or ESA instead of IS in order to receive national insurance (NI) credits (see p967). You might not be entitled to NI credits if you claim IS.

5. If you are given a sanction, you or your partner should claim IS, ESA or PC if you are eligible.

6. If you claim PC:

– there is currently no capital limit and the tariff income rules are more generous;

– there is no rule preventing you or your partner from doing full-time paid work, although any earnings are taken into account when working out how much PC you can get.

If your partner works at least 16 hours but less than 24 hours each week, you and your partner might be able to claim WTC as well as, or instead of, income-based JSA. However, before deciding whether to claim, seek advice to see how you would be better off financially (see p124).

If you or your partner have just stopped work or reduced your hours, you might get what is known as 'WTC run-on' for a four-week period (see p202).

WTC is taken into account as income when working out your income-based JSA, but CTC is not.

Non-means-tested benefits

While you are on JSA you are entitled to NI credits (see p967).

Most non-means-tested benefits are taken into account when working out the amount of income-based JSA you can get. However, attendance allowance, disability living allowance, personal independence payment, armed forces independence payment, guardian's allowance and, if you are getting CTC, child benefit, are not taken into account. It can still be worth claiming non-means-tested benefits even if they are taken into account. If you or your partner qualify for certain ones of these, you also qualify for certain premiums (see p236) and, therefore, a higher rate of income-based JSA. You might only qualify for income-based JSA once you (or your partner or a child included in your claim) are awarded another benefit – known as a 'qualifying benefit'. To make sure you do not lose out while waiting for the outcome of a claim for a qualifying benefit, claim JSA at the same time. If your claim for income-based JSA is refused, once the qualifying benefit is awarded claim JSA again and ask for it to be backdated to the date of your first claim (see p1160).

The benefit cap

In some cases, there is a limit on the total amount of specified benefits you can receive (a 'benefit cap'). JSA is one of the specified benefits. However, the benefit cap only applies if you are getting housing benefit (HB) or UC. See p1180 for further information.

Part 2: Main means-tested benefits and tax credits
Chapter 6: Income-based jobseeker's allowance
Notes

Passports and other sources of help

If you are entitled to income-based JSA, you also qualify for health benefits such as free prescriptions (see Chapter 29) and education benefits such as free school lunches (see p860). You may also qualify for social fund payments (see Chapter 36) and help from your local welfare assistance scheme (see p856). You may be entitled to a council tax reduction (see p854).

Financial help on starting work

If you stop getting JSA because you or your partner start work, or your earnings or your hours in your existing job increase, you might be able to get mortgage interest run-on if you have a home loan (see p474) or extended payments of HB if you pay rent (see p86). Your local authority may also provide extended help with council tax. See p866 for information about other financial help you might get.

Notes

1. Who can claim income-based jobseeker's allowance
1   s1 JSA 1995
2   ss3, 3A and 13 JSA 1995
3   Reg 76(2)(b) JSA Regs
4   s1(2B) and (4) JSA 1995; reg 3A(1) JSA Regs; CJSA/2633/2004
5   s1(4) JSA 1995; reg 3A(1) JSA Regs
6   *Hockenjos v Secretary of State for Social Security* [2004] EWCA Civ 1749, reported as R(JSA) 1/05 and R(JSA) 2/05
7   Sch 1 para 9A JSA 1995; reg 3B JSA Regs
8   Sch 1 paras 9B and 9C JSA 1995; reg 3C JSA Regs
9   Reg 3D JSA Regs; Sch 1 para 8A JSA 1995
10 Sch A1 JSA Regs
11 Reg 3D(3) and (4) JSA Regs
12 s1(6A) WRA 2007
13 CIS/0542/2001
14 Reg 47(1) and (2) JSA Regs
15 Reg 49 JSA Regs; reg 40 JSA Regs 2013
16 Art 13 WRA(No.9)O; Art 11(2) WRA(No.11)O
17 Sch 1 para 3 JSA 1995; reg 48 JSA Regs
18 Reg 51 JSA Regs
19 Reg 3E(2)(g) JSA Regs

20 s1(2)(f) JSA 1995
21 Sch 1 para 2 JSA 1995; reg 10 SS&CS(DA) Regs

2. The rules about your age
22 s3A(1)(e) JSA 1995; reg 58 JSA Regs
23 s3A(1)(d) and (e) JSA 1995
24 Reg 57(1), definition of 'young person', JSA Regs
25 ss3(1)(f)(iii) and 3A(1)(e)(ii) JSA 1995; reg 61(1)(b), (c) and (g) and (2)(b) JSA Regs
26 ss3(1)(f)(iii) and 3A(1)(e)(ii) JSA 1995; regs 57 and 59 JSA Regs
27 Reg 1(3) JSA Regs
28 Reg 57(2)(a) and (4) JSA Regs
29 ss3(1)(f)(iii) and 3A(1)(e)(ii) JSA 1995; reg 60 JSA Regs
30 Reg 61(1)(a) and (2)(a) JSA Regs
31 Reg 61(1)(f) and (2)(e) JSA Regs
32 ss3(1)(f)(ii), 3A(1)(e)(i) and 16 JSA 1995
33 DWP guidance, *Making a Severe Hardship Decision*, para 121, www.gov.uk/government/publications/jsa-for-16-to-17-year-olds-guidance-for-dwp-staff-making-a-severe-hardship-decision

Chapter 6

Income-based jobseeker's allowance

34 DWP guidance, *Making a Severe Hardship Decision*, paras 42-68, 106-120 and 209-12
35 DWP guidance, *Making a Severe Hardship Decision*, paras 7-41
36 s16(2) and (4) JSA 1995; DWP guidance, *Making a Severe Hardship Decision*, paras 131-37
37 s16(3) JSA 1995
38 s71A SSAA 1992
39 Sch 2 para 1(a) SSA 1998
40 DWP guidance, *Making a Severe Hardship Decision*, paras 124-25

4. The amount of benefit
41 ss4(3) and (3A) and 13 JSA 1995
42 Sch 1 para 4 JSA 1995; reg 46 JSA Regs; Arts 12 and 13 WRA(No.9)O; Art 11(2) WRA(No.11)O
43 Reg 14A SS&CS(DA) Regs
44 Reg 2(3)(b) HB Regs

6. Claims and backdating
45 Reg 62 JSA Regs
46 Reg 62(1) JSA Regs
47 Reg 62(2) JSA Regs
48 Reg 4(3B)(a) SS(C&P) Regs
49 s1(2B) and (4) JSA 1995; reg 3A(1) JSA Regs; CJSA/2633/2004
50 s1(2C) JSA 1995; reg 3E JSA Regs
51 Sch 5 paras 10, 13A and 17A JSA Regs
52 s8(1) and (1A) JSA 1995; regs 23 and 23A JSA Regs
53 Reg 4(6)(a) SS(C&P) Regs
54 www.gov.uk/jobseekers-allowance/how-to-claim
55 Reg 19(1) and Sch 4 para 1 SS(C&P) Regs
56 Reg 6(4ZA), (4ZB)(a) and (4A)(a)(i) SS(C&P) Regs
57 Reg 6(4ZC)(a) and (b) SS(C&P) Regs
58 Reg 6(4A)(b) SS(C&P) Regs
59 Reg 6(4AB) SS(C&P) Regs
60 Reg 6(4AB) SS(C&P) Regs
61 Reg 6(28) SS(C&P) Regs
62 Art 3A WRA(No.9)O
63 Reg 4(3B)(b) SS(C&P) Regs
64 Reg 4(3B)(c) SS(C&P) Regs
65 Reg 6(4A)(a)(ii) SS(C&P) Regs
66 Reg 6(4ZB)(b) and (4ZC)(c) SS(C&P) Regs
67 Sch 5 para 17A JSA Regs
68 CS/371/1949
69 Reg 13(1) and (9) SS(C&P) Regs

7. Getting paid
70 s3B JSA 1995
71 ss19(7), 19A(10) and 19B(8) JSA 1995
72 Reg 30A SS(C&P) Regs

8. Tax, other benefits and the benefit cap
73 ss671-75 IT(EP)A 2003

Chapter 7

Pension credit

This chapter covers:

Key facts

- Pension credit (PC) is a benefit for people on a low income who are at least the qualifying age.
- Women can claim PC when they reach pension age. Men can claim when they reach what would be the pension age for a woman with the same date of birth.
- There are two types of PC: **guarantee credit** ensures a minimum level of income and **savings credit**, which is intended to 'reward' you for making provision for your retirement, such as via savings or an occupational pension. You can be entitled to either guarantee credit, savings credit or both. Savings credit is being phased out from April 2016.
- PC is a means-tested benefit.
- You do not have to have paid national insurance contributions to qualify.
- You can qualify for PC whether you are in or out of work.
- PC is administered and paid by the Pension Service, which is part of the DWP.
- If you disagree with a PC decision, you can apply for a revision or supersession, or appeal against it. You must apply for a mandatory reconsideration before you can appeal.

1. Who can claim pension credit

Guarantee credit

You qualify for guarantee credit if:[1]
- you have reached the qualifying age (see below);[2]
- you are in Great Britain (with exceptions for periods of temporary absence – see p1601) and satisfy the 'habitual residence' test and the 'right to reside' test (see Chapter 66);[3]
- your partner (if you have one) is not entitled to pension credit (PC);[4]
- you have no income or your income is below the appropriate minimum guarantee (see p148);[5]
- you are not a 'person subject to immigration control' (see p1516), although there are exceptions to this rule (see p1520).[6]

Savings credit

You qualify for savings credit if:[7]
- either:
  - you and your partner (if you have one) reached pension age before 6 April 2016; or
  - either you or your partner reached pension age (see p772) before 6 April 2016, you were awarded savings credit with effect from before 6 April 2016, you were entitled to it immediately before 6 April 2016 and you have remained entitled to it;[8]
- you or your partner are 65 or over;[9]
- you are in Great Britain (except for periods of temporary absence – see p1601) and satisfy the 'habitual residence' test and the 'right to reside' test (see Chapter 66);[10]
- your partner (if you have one) is not entitled to PC;[11]
- you are not a 'person subject to immigration control', although there are exceptions to this rule (see p1520);[12]
- you have 'qualifying income' that exceeds the 'savings credit threshold', but is not so high that it produces a nil award (see p151).[13]

2. The rules about your age

Entitlement to pension credit for both men and women is linked to the minimum qualifying age at which a woman can receive state retirement pension.[14] The qualifying age is rising steadily to 66 (by 2020) and will eventually go up to 68.[15] When you reach the qualifying age depends on your date of birth. **Note:** this applies to both men and women.

Part 2: Main means-tested benefits and tax credits
Chapter 7: Pension credit
4. The amount of pension credit

- If your date of birth is before 6 April 1950, your qualifying age is 60.
- If your date of birth is between 6 April 1950 and 5 December 1953 inclusive, see Appendix 12 to find your qualifying age.
- If your date of birth is after 5 December 1953, your qualifying age is 65 or over. To check your pension age, see www.gov.uk/calculate-state-pension.

In addition, for savings credit, you must meet the rules described p147.

3. People included in the claim

If you are single, you claim pension credit (PC) for yourself. If you are a member of a couple, either you claim PC for both you and your partner or, if your partner also meets the qualifying conditions for PC, s/he can claim for you both. The 'appropriate minimum guarantee' that forms part of the calculation of your benefit includes an allowance for a couple and can include additional amounts based on both your and your partner's circumstances. When your benefit is worked out, your partner's income and capital are usually added to yours. See p215 for who counts as a couple. Whichever one of you claims PC, if the other is not yet pension age, s/he may qualify for national insurance (NI) credits in order to protect her/his NI record. See Chapter 42 for more details about NI credits. If you are a man under age 65, see in particular p974.

Your appropriate minimum guarantee that forms part of the calculation of your benefit cannot include allowances and premiums for your child(ren). Instead, check to see whether you qualify for child tax credit (see Chapter 9).

4. The amount of pension credit

The amount of pension credit (PC) you receive depends on whether you are single or a member of a couple, or have any disabilities, caring responsibilities or eligible housing costs. The maximum amount of guarantee credit you could receive is reduced by your income (subject to any applicable disregards). For savings credit, the rules are slightly more complicated (see p151). For information on income and capital, see Chapters 15 and 18. However, for information on qualifying income for savings credit, see p151.

Guarantee credit

Your maximum guarantee credit is known as the 'appropriate minimum guarantee'[16] and is made up of:
- standard minimum guarantee; *and*
- where applicable, additional amounts.

Standard minimum guarantee

If you do not have any additional needs, you receive an award of PC which ensures that your weekly income is brought up to one of the following standard minimum guarantee levels.

Single person[17]	£159.35
Couple[18]	£243.25
Each additional spouse in a polygamous marriage[19]	£83.90

Additional amounts

If you have additional needs (eg, a disability, caring responsibilities or housing costs), your award brings your income to the level of the standard minimum guarantee plus additional amounts. These broadly correspond to the premiums and housing costs payable with income support (IS), with an additional transitional amount to ensure that you are not worse off as a result of moving onto PC from IS, income-based jobseeker's allowance (JSA) or income-related employment and support allowance (ESA).

Additional amounts

Severe disability[20] The qualifying rules are broadly the same as for the IS severe disability premium (see p242).	£62.45	£124.90 (if both partners qualify)
Carer[21] The rules are the same as those for the IS carer premium (see p246).	£34.95	£34.95 (for each partner who qualifies)
Housing costs[22] These provisions broadly mirror those for IS, but with some exceptions.	See Chapter 20	
Transitional[23]	See below	

Transitional amount

If you are in receipt of IS, income-based JSA or income-related ESA immediately before you first become entitled to PC, in order to ensure you are not worse off by moving onto PC, your appropriate minimum guarantee may include a transitional amount.[24] The transitional amount reduces over time by any increase in your appropriate minimum guarantee and ceases when you or your partner stop being entitled to PC (disregarding any break in entitlement of less than eight weeks).[25]

Part 2: Main means-tested benefits and tax credits
Chapter 7: Pension credit
4. The amount of pension credit

When your appropriate minimum guarantee may be reduced

Your appropriate minimum guarantee may be reduced in certain circumstances. The most important of these are if:[26]

- you are a couple and one of you is a 'person subject to immigration control' (see p1523);
- you are a prisoner (see p928);
- your partner is abroad (see p1602);
- you are a member of a religious order. In this case, your applicable amount is nil.

The guarantee credit calculation

Step one: calculate your appropriate minimum guarantee

This consists of:

- standard minimum guarantee for you and your partner, if you have one; *plus*
- additional amounts for any special needs and/or housing costs.

Step two: calculate your income

This is the amount you have coming in each week – eg, from benefits, private pensions and earnings.[27] Not all income counts (eg, personal independence payment (PIP), disability living allowance, attendance allowance (AA), child tax credit and child benefit are disregarded in full) and some income can be disregarded (see Chapter 15). See also p156 for assessed income periods. If you have capital over £10,000, you are treated as having £1 for every £500 (or part of £500) capital that exceeds £10,000.[28]

Step three: deduct income from appropriate minimum guarantee

The amount of your guarantee credit is your appropriate minimum guarantee less any relevant income you have.[29] If your income is above the appropriate minimum guarantee, you do not qualify for any guarantee credit, but you might qualify for some savings credit. You may qualify for guarantee credit if you or your partner become entitled to a qualifying benefit, like AA, which may increase the amount of your appropriate minimum guarantee.

Examples

Barbara is single and aged 68. She is in receipt of AA. She lives alone and no one gets carer's allowance for looking after her. She lives in rented accommodation.

Her appropriate minimum guarantee is:

Standard minimum guarantee (single person rate)	£159.35
Severe disability additional amount	£62.45
Total	**£221.80**

Her weekly income is her basic state pension of £122.30. AA is ignored as income.

She is therefore entitled to £99.50 guarantee credit to bring her total income up to £221.80.

She is also entitled to maximum housing benefit and any other passported benefits that may apply.

Maria and Geoff are a couple. Maria is 62 and Geoff is 67. Their 24-year-old daughter lives with them and she is in receipt of income-based JSA. They have eligible weekly housing costs of £40. Maria receives the enhanced rate of the daily living component of PIP and Geoff gets AA.

Their appropriate minimum guarantee is:

Standard minimum guarantee (couple rate)	£243.25
Eligible housing costs	£40.00
Total	**£283.25**

Their joint weekly income for calculating PC is £288.60, made up of basic state pension of £195.60 (Maria £73.30, Geoff £122.30), occupational pension of £90 and £3 deemed income from £11,500 savings. PIP and AA are ignored as income.

They are not entitled to any guarantee credit because their income exceeds their appropriate minimum guarantee of £283.25. Their appropriate minimum guarantee does not include a severe disability addition because their 24-year-old daughter lives with them.

Savings credit

Savings credit is being phased out from April 2016. You can now only get savings credit if:

- you and your partner, if you have one, reached pension age (ie, the age at which you can claim your retirement pension – see p772) before 6 April 2016; or
- either you or your partner reached pension age (see p772) before 6 April 2016, you were awarded savings credit with effect from before 6 April 2016, you were entitled to it immediately before 6 April 2016 and you have remained entitled to it.[30]

You or your partner must also be 65 or over.

In addition, the amount of your 'qualifying income' must be above the savings credit threhold of:[31]

Single person	£137.35
Couple	£218.42

'Qualifying income' for this purpose is all income that counts for guarantee credit (see Chapter 15) except:[32]

- working tax credit;
- incapacity benefit;

Part 2: Main means-tested benefits and tax credits
Chapter 7: Pension credit
6. Claims and backdating

- contributory ESA;
- contribution-based JSA;
- severe disablement allowance;
- maternity allowance;
- maintenance payments for you, or your partner, from a spouse or former spouse.

The amount of savings credit to which you are entitled is subject to a maximum figure, known as the '**maximum savings credit**'.[33]

Single person	£13.20
Couple	£14.90

For details of how to calculate the amount of savings credit, see pp138–39 of the 2016/17 edition of this *Handbook*.

5. Special benefit rules

Special rules may apply to:
- people subject to immigration control (see Chapter 65);
- people who have come from or are going abroad (see Chapters 66 and 67);
- people who are in hospital or living in a care home or other similar accommodation, or people in prison or detention (see Chapter 41).

6. Claims and backdating

The general rules about claims and backdating are covered in Chapter 49. This section explains the specific rules that apply to pension credit (PC).

Making a claim

A claim can be made:[34]
- by telephone. Call the Pension Service on 0800 99 1234 (textphone: 0800 169 0133) from 8am to 6pm, Monday to Friday. This is the Pension Service's 'preferred route' for claiming;
- in writing on the approved form (Form PC1). You ask for this by telephoning the number above. Local authority housing benefit offices and some other 'alternative offices' (see p1148) can provide this form but will also encourage you to claim by telephone.

If you want to speak to someone in person about PC, you can go to a 'local service information point'. Find out where your nearest one is at http://pensions-service.direct.gov.uk/en/information-points/home.asp.

You must provide any information or evidence required (see below). In certain circumstances, the DWP may accept a written application not on the approved form (see p1152). You can amend or withdraw your claim before a decision is made (see p1149). If there is a delay in dealing with your claim, you may be able to get a short-term advance of benefit (see p1177).

Who should claim

If you are a single person, you must claim on your own behalf. If you are one of a couple, you must choose which one of you claims for you both (see p215). If you cannot agree who should claim, a decision maker decides.[35]

You can swap who claims as long as the partner previously claiming agrees. It may be worthwhile doing so – eg, if one of you is about to go abroad.

If you are unable to manage your own affairs, another person can claim PC for you as your 'appointee' (see p1149).

Information to support your claim

For the general information requirements that apply to all benefits, see p1150.

It is important that you provide any information required when you claim. Until you do, you may not count as making a valid claim (see p1152). Correct any defects as soon as possible or your date of claim may be affected.

Information and evidence relevant to your PC claim include specific details of any personal pension scheme to which you belong.[36]

When you claim, you are asked about your circumstances, including information about any income or savings and any housing costs you or your partner have. If further information or verification is needed, a letter is sent for you to complete and return with any requested verification within a month (or longer if considered reasonable).

If the claim was made in writing to the local authority or, in England, to the county council, the local authority or county council can accept and obtain information and evidence, and give advice about the PC claim.

If you claim in advance (see p154), the one-month time limit starts from the day after the advance period ends.[37]

Once your claim has been decided, you are sent a statement of details, setting out the information on which the award is based. You are asked to check this and report any omissions or changes.

Even if you have provided all that was required when you claimed, you may be asked to provide further evidence to support your claim (see p1154). You may also be asked to provide information after you are awarded PC and if you fail to do so, your PC could be suspended, or even terminated (see p1185).

Part 2: Main means-tested benefits and tax credits
Chapter 7: Pension credit
6. Claims and backdating

The date of your claim

The date of your claim is important as it determines when your entitlement to PC starts. This is not necessarily the date from when you are paid. For information about when payment of PC starts, see p155.

Your '**date of claim**' (unless the backdating rules apply) is:[38]

- the date your claim, properly completed with all the required information and evidence, is received at the appropriate office (the DWP, local authority housing benefit office or county council); or
- the date you notify the appropriate office of your intention to claim, and you submit a properly completed claim with all the required information and evidence within one month of this date.

Note: you must make sure your claim is valid. If it is 'defective', you are given a short time to correct the defects (see p1152). If you do, your claim is treated as having been made when you initially claimed.[39] If you are making an advance claim for PC before you have reached the qualifying age and your claim is defective, you may correct it at any time before the end of the advance period.[40]

In some cases, you can claim in advance (see below) and in some cases your claim can be backdated (see below). If you want this to be done, make this clear when you claim or the DWP might not consider it.

Backdating your claim

It is important that you claim in time because PC can only be backdated for up to three months. Your claim can be backdated if you satisfy the qualifying conditions over the period for which you require backdating – you do not have to show why your claim was late.[41] If you want your claim to be backdated, it is important that you request this as claims are not automatically backdated. When you make a telephone claim, you should be asked about the date from which you want your claim to start.

If you claim backdated PC within three months of being awarded a qualifying benefit and an earlier PC claim was refused because you did not get a qualifying benefit (see p1160) at that time, your PC can be backdated to the date of your earlier PC claim or the date when the qualifying benefit was first payable, whichever is later.[42]

For general rules on backdating, see p1156.

Claiming in advance

You can make an advance claim for PC to give the DWP time to ensure you receive your benefit as soon as you become entitled. However, you cannot make an advance claim if the reason you do not qualify straight away is because you fail the habitual residence test (see p1538). PC can be claimed up to four months before you qualify, whether this is before you reach the qualifying age and know you will be entitled when you reach that age or after you reach the qualifying age when you know you will have a future entitlement – eg, because of a drop in income.[43] The date of your claim is the date on which you qualify.[44]

7. **Getting paid**

The general rules on getting paid are in Chapter 50. This section explains the specific rules that apply to pension credit (PC).

When is pension credit paid?

	Qualifying age on or after 6 April 2010	Qualifying age before 6 April 2010
When is PC paid?	The day you are paid depends on your national insurance number (see p1174).[45]	Monday, or the same day as your retirement pension is paid.[46]
How often is PC paid?	Weekly, fortnightly or four-weekly in arrears.	Weekly in advance. If you were entitled to income support immediately before 6 October 2003 and paid in arrears, PC is also paid in arrears.[47]

If you are entitled to less than 10 pence a week, you are not paid PC, unless you are receiving another social security benefit that can be paid with PC,[48] although you will still have an underlying entitlement. If your entitlement is less than £1 a week, a decision maker can decide to pay you quarterly in arrears.

There may be a delay between the date of your claim and the date PC becomes payable. This is because payment does not normally start until the first payday following the claim.[49] There are exceptions to this rule.[50]

Note:

- Deductions can be made from your PC to pay to third parties (see p1187).
- Your PC might be paid at a reduced rate if you have been sanctioned for benefit offences (see p1265).
- For information on missing payments, see p1174. If you cannot get your PC payments because you have lost your bank or Post Office card or have forgotten your PIN, see p1173. If your 'simple payment' card has been lost or stolen, or if you have forgotten your memorable date, see p1173.
- If payment of your PC is delayed, see p1165. If you are waiting for a decision on your claim, or to be paid, you might be able to get a short-term advance (see p1177). If you wish to complain about how your claim has been dealt with, or claim compensation, see Chapter 58.

- If payment of your PC is suspended, see p1185.
- If you are overpaid PC, you might have to repay it (see Chapter 52) and, in some circumstances, you may have to pay a penalty (see p1256). If you have been accused of fraud, see Chapter 53.

Change of circumstances

You must report changes in your circumstances that you have been told to report, as well as any that you might reasonably be expected to know might affect your right to, the amount of, or the payment of your benefit. You should do this as soon as possible, preferably in writing. See p1184 for further information.

See below for the circumstances that do not need to be reported during the assessed income period.

If there are any changes to the amount of housing costs you owe or the interest payable, your lender is required to report these to the DWP.[51] If you have this information, also inform the DWP in case your lender fails to do so. To avoid an overpayment, make sure that the DWP takes this information into account.

If there has been a relevant change of circumstances, a decision maker looks at your claim again and makes a new decision. To find out when the new decision takes effect, see p1292.

When your pension credit is adjusted

Generally, your PC is adjusted from the day the change occurs or is expected to occur, if this is the day you are paid benefit. If it is not, your PC is adjusted from the start of the next benefit week.

However, there are a few exceptions to this general rule.[52]

Assessed income period

If you were already getting PC before 6 April 2016, an assessed income period may have been set. From 6 April 2016, no new assessed income periods will be set.

An 'assessed income period is a set period during which you are not required to report any changes in certain types of your income, known as 'retirement provision'.[53] 'Retirement provision' means income from:[54]

- retirement pension (other than state retirement pensions);
- an annuity (other than retirement pension income);
- capital;
- periodic payments from the Pension Protection Fund or the Financial Assistance Scheme.

The effect of this is that if you have an increase in, or subsequently start to receive, retirement provision during your assessed income period, you do not have to report this to the DWP. All other income changes that affect your PC entitlement must be reported to the DWP as soon as they occur. During the assessed income period, your PC entitlement may change as a result of 'deemed increases in retirement provision' – eg, periodic increases in an occupational pension. See the 2015/16 edition of this *Handbook* for details.

When an assessed income period ends

Before 6 April 2016 an assessed income period could be set for a fixed period, usually five years or, if you were 75 or over, for an indefinite period.[55] If your assessed income period was set to end before 1 April 2019, it ends on the date specified on your award letter, or earlier if you have a change of circumstances (see below). If your assessed income period was due to end between 1 April 2019 and 5 April 2021, it now ends on an earlier date.[56] The DWP should write to you about six months before the new end date takes effect. If an assessed income period has been set for an indefinite period, it continues unless you have a change of circumstances (see below). Fixed-term assessed income periods are being shortened by between approximately 24 and 32 months.

Change of circumstances
Your assessed income period comes to an end if:[57]
- you become a member of a couple;
- you cease to be a member of a couple;
- you or your partner reach the age of 65;
- you are no longer entitled to PC;
- you are single and enter a care home on a permanent basis;
- payments of retirement provision due to you stop temporarily or are less than the amount due, and your PC award is superseded as a result.

8. Tax, other benefits and the benefit cap

Tax

Pension credit (PC) is not taxable.

Means-tested benefits and tax credits

The guarantee credit of PC is a passport to maximum housing benefit (HB), but you have to make a separate claim. If you are only entitled to the savings credit, your HB claim is subject to a standard calculation. The Pension Service provides the local authority with the assessed income figure (the figure the DWP used to work out your PC entitlement).

The £16,000 capital limit for HB does not apply if you receive the guarantee credit (with or without the savings credit). It does apply if you only receive the savings credit.

Part 2: Main means-tested benefits and tax credits
Chapter 7: Pension credit
8. Tax, other benefits and the benefit cap

If you are a man aged between the qualifying age for PC (see p147) and 65, you may be able to choose between claiming income-based jobseeker's allowance (JSA) or PC. When deciding which benefit to claim, you should be aware of the different rules for these two benefits to ensure you will be better off. For example, there is no capital limit or 16-hour work rule for PC, but there is for income-based JSA. Similarly, if you are a man aged between the qualifying age for PC (see p147) and 65, you can choose between claiming employment and support allowance (ESA) and PC, or, in some situations, between claiming contributory ESA and PC. However, regardless of age, no one can get income-related ESA and PC at the same time. Also, if you are a member of a couple and you claim PC, your partner cannot be entitled to income-related ESA. You may want to seek advice about any 'better-off' considerations. See p142 for further information.

PC continues after the introduction of universal credit (UC). However, you cannot get both PC and UC at the same time. If you already get PC and then become entitled to UC, your PC stops (see p25).

PC is a passport to maximum working tax credit (WTC) and child tax credit (CTC), but you must make a separate claim.[58] CTC does not count as income when calculating PC, but WTC does.[59]

Non-means-tested benefits

Some non-means-tested benefits are taken into account as income when calculating entitlement to PC. Others have a £10 disregard and some are disregarded entirely. See Chapter 15 for details.

Qualifying for certain non-means-tested benefits can help you qualify for more PC. For example, if you get carer's allowance, you may be entitled to a carer addition with your appropriate minimum guarantee.

The benefit cap

In some cases, there is a limit on the total amount of specified benefits you can receive (a 'benefit cap'). PC is *not* one of the specified benefits. The benefit cap only applies if you are getting HB or UC. If you are getting HB, the benefit cap does not normally apply if you are at least the qualifying age for PC. See p1180 for further information.

Passports and other sources of help

If you are entitled to PC, you may also be eligible for:
- a Christmas bonus (see p863);
- health benefits, if you are getting the guarantee credit of PC (see Chapter 29);
- free school lunches, if you are getting the guarantee credit of PC. This only applies in England and Wales – in Scotland, you can qualify via CTC (see p860);
- social fund payments (see Chapter 36);

- council tax reduction from your local authority (see p854);
- home insulation grants and discretionary grants from the local authority towards the cost of home improvements (see p865).

Notes

1. Who can claim pension credit
1   s2 SPCA 2002
2   s1(6) SPCA 2002
3   s1(2)(a) SPCA 2002; regs 2-4 SPC Regs
4   s4(1) SPCA 2002
5   s2(2) SPCA 2002; reg 6 SPC Regs
6   s4(2) SPCA 2002
7   s3 SPCA 2002
8   s3 SPCA 2002, as amended by PA 2014; reg 7A SPC Regs
9   s3(1) SPCA 2002
10 s1(2)(a) SPCA 2002; regs 2-4 SPC Regs
11 s4(1) SPCA 2002
12 s4(2) SPCA 2002
13 s3(2)-(4) SPCA 2002

2. The rules about your age
14 s1(6) SPCA 2002
15 s126 and Sch 4 PA 1995

4. The amount of pension credit
16 s2(3) SPCA 2002
17 Reg 6(1)(b) SPC Regs
18 Reg 6(1)(a) SPC Regs
19 Reg 6 and Sch 3 para 1(5) SPC Regs
20 Reg 6(4) and (5) SPC Regs
21 Reg 6(6)(a) SPC Regs
22 Reg 6(6)(c) SPC Regs
23 Reg 6(6)(b) SPC Regs
24 Reg 6(6)(b) and Sch 1 para 6 SPC Regs
25 Sch 1 paras (6), (8) and (9) SPC Regs
26 Reg 6(2)(b) and (3) SPC Regs
27 s15 SPCA 2002; regs 14-24 SPC Regs
28 Reg 15(6) SPC Regs
29 s2(2) SPCA 2002
30 s3 SPCA 2002, as amended by PA 2014; reg 7A SPC Regs
31 Reg 7(2) SPC Regs
32 Reg 9 SPC Regs
33 s3(7) SPCA 2002; reg 7(1)(a) SPC Regs

6. Claims and backdating
34 Reg 4D SS(C&P) Regs
35 Reg 4D(7) SS(C&P) Regs
36 Reg 7(4) SS(C&P) Regs
37 Reg 7(1C) SS(C&P) Regs
38 Reg 4F SS(C&P) Regs
39 Reg 4D(6E) SS(C&P) Regs
40 Regs 4D(12) and 4E(3) SS(C&P) Regs
41 Reg 19(2) and (3) SS(C&P) Regs
42 Reg 6(16) and (18) SS(C&P) Regs
43 Regs 4E and 13D(4) SS(C&P) Regs
44 Reg 13D SS(C&P) Regs

7. Getting paid
45 Reg 26BA SS(C&P) Regs
46 Reg 26B SS(C&P) Regs
47 Reg 36(6) SPC(CTMP) Regs
48 Reg 13 SPC Regs
49 Reg 16A(1) and (4) SS(C&P) Regs
50 Reg 16A(2) SS(C&P) Regs
51 Sch 9A para 10 SS(C&P) Regs
52 Reg 7 and Sch 3B SS&CS(DA) Regs
53 ss6-10 SPCA 2002; regs 10-12 SPC Regs
54 s7(6) SPCA 2002
55 s9(1) SPCA 2002
56 Reg 12(d) and Sch IIIA SPC Regs
57 s9(4) SPCA 2002; reg 12 SPC Regs

8. Tax, other benefits and the benefit cap
58 s7(2) TCA 2002; reg 4(1)(d) TC(ITDR) Regs
59 s15(1)(b) SPCA 2002

Chapter 8

2

Universal credit

This chapter covers:
1. Who can claim universal credit (p161)
2. The rules about your age (p162)
3. People included in the claim (p164)
4. The amount of benefit (p164)
5. Special benefit rules (p169)
6. Claims and backdating (p169)
7. Getting paid (p173)
8. Tax, other benefits and the benefit cap (p178)

Key facts
- Universal credit (UC) is a benefit for people on a low income who are in or out of work and who come under the UC system.
- UC replaces income support, income-based jobseeker's allowance, income-related employment and support allowance, housing benefit, child tax credit and working tax credit.
- UC is being introduced gradually for new claimants. Eventually, it will be introduced for all claimants.
- UC is a means-tested benefit.
- You do not have to have paid national insurance contributions to qualify.
- UC can be paid in addition to non-means-tested benefits, but some of these are taken into account as income when calculating your UC.
- A 'benefit cap' may be applied if the total amount of certain benefits you receive exceeds a specified amount and your UC can be reduced.
- UC is administered and paid by the DWP.
- If you disagree with a UC decision, you can apply for a revision or supersession, or appeal against it. You must apply for a mandatory reconsideration before you can appeal.

1. Who can claim universal credit

You qualify for universal credit (UC) if you (and your partner, if you are in a couple):

- come under the UC system (see p20 for an explanation of when you come under the system, and the note below); *and*
- satisfy the **'basic conditions'** – ie:[1]
  - you are aged 18 or over and under the qualifying age for pension credit (PC). **Note:** some 16/17-year-olds can get UC (see p162);
  - you are not 'receiving education', although there are some exceptions (see p162);
  - you satisfy the 'habitual residence' and the 'right to reside' tests (see Chapter 66), and you are in, or treated as in, Great Britain (see Chapters 66 and 67);
  - you are not a 'person subject to immigration control' (see p1515);
  - you have accepted a 'claimant commitment' (see p1071). This is an agreement that you will meet certain requirements.[2] In particular, the claimant commitment includes the work-related requirements you normally must meet, which may include attending work-focused interviews, work preparation, work search and work availability; *and*
- satisfy the **'financial conditions'** – ie:[3]
  - your income is not too high;
  - your savings and other capital are £16,000 or less.

Note: in some areas, the rules on when you come under the UC system include having to satisfy 'gateway' conditions when you make a claim for UC. The gateway conditions include rules about your age, whether you are a member of a couple and whether you have children. In these 'gateway' areas, if you do not satisfy the gateway conditions when you claim UC, you do not come under the UC system and so cannot get UC, even if you satisfy the rules described in this chapter. However, the UC gateway areas are gradually being replaced by 'full service' areas, in which there are no gateway conditions. If you live in a UC full service area, when you claim UC you come under the UC system – the rules described in this chapter determine whether or not you can get UC.

Couples

If you are a member of a couple (see p215), you must usually make a joint claim. Both of you must satisfy the basic conditions and (on a joint basis) the financial conditions for UC.[4]

Both of you do not need to meet all the basic conditions (and you can get UC as a couple in the normal way) if one of you is:[5]

- over the qualifying age for PC; *or*
- 'receiving education' (but see p162 if one of you is 16 or 17).

Part 2: Main means-tested benefits and tax credits
Chapter 8: Universal credit
2. The rules about your age

Even though you are a member of a couple and one of you does not satisfy the conditions for UC, there are limited circumstances in which you can make a claim as a single person. In this situation, your UC amounts are for a single person, but your income and capital are still assessed jointly. You can claim as a single person if your partner is:[6]

- aged 16 or 17 and is not someone who can get UC as an under-18-year-old (see below for who can); *or*
- not in (or treated as in) Great Britain, including if s/he has failed the habitual residence or right to reside test (see Chapter 66); *or*
- a 'person subject to immigration control' (see Chapter 65); *or*
- a prisoner or serving a sentence while detained in hospital, or is a member of a religious order and is fully maintained by the order.

You can also claim as a single person if you are in a polygamous marriage and:[7]
- your spouse is still married to someone else from an earlier marriage; *and*
- the other person in the earlier marriage is still living in the same household as your spouse.

Receiving education

In general, you cannot claim UC if you are 'receiving education'. The basic rule is that if you are a qualifying young person (see p572) or undertaking full-time education, study or training, you are regarded as 'receiving education'.[8] There are exceptions – eg, if you have a child or a disability, are on a traineeship, or are without parental support. For full details, see Chapter 40.

If you are a member of a couple making a joint claim and one of you is receiving education (and not eligible for UC) but the other is not, you may still be entitled to UC as a couple (see p161).

2. The rules about your age

In most cases, you (and your partner, if you are making a joint claim) must be 18 or over to claim universal credit (UC). However, some 16/17-year-olds can claim UC (see below).[9]

You must be under the qualifying age for pension credit (PC – see p147).[10] If you are in a couple, at least one of you must be under the qualifying age for PC. If one of you is at least the qualifying age for PC, this is sometimes called being in a 'mixed age' couple.

16/17-year-olds

You must normally be at least 18 years old to qualify for UC. If you are aged 16 or 17, you can get UC if one of the following applies.[11]

- You have limited capability for work, or you have submitted and are covered by a medical certificate saying you are not fit for work and you are waiting for an assessment of your capability for work.
- You have 'regular and substantial caring responsibilities for a severely disabled person' – ie, you meet the conditions of entitlement to carer's allowance (CA – see Chapter 25), or would do but for the fact that your earnings are too high.[12] This does not apply if you receive earnings from those caring responsiblities. You do not have to claim CA. **Note:** you do not qualify under this rule if you were previously looked after by a local authority (see p937).
- You are responsible for a child aged under 16 (see p222).
- You are a member of a couple and your partner satisfies the basic rules of entitlement for UC and is responsible for a child.
- You are pregnant and there are 11 weeks or less before the week your baby is due. **Note:** you do not qualify under this rule if you were previously looked after by a local authority (see p937).
- You had a baby (or your baby was stillborn) not more than 15 weeks ago. **Note:** you do not qualify under this rule if you were previously looked after by a local authority (see p937).
- You are without parental support (including support from someone acting in place of your parent – eg, a foster parent). For these purposes, you are treated as without parental support if you are not being looked after by a local authority, and:[13]
  - you are an orphan – ie, you do not have any parents; *or*
  - you have to live away from your parents because you are estranged from them (see p873 for the meaning) or there is a serious risk to your physical or mental health or you would experience significant harm if you lived with them; *or*
  - you are living away from your parents and they are unable to support you financially because they have a physical or mental impairment, or they are in custody, or they are prohibited from entering Great Britain – eg, because of the UK Immigration Rules.
  Note: you do not qualify under this rule if you were previously looked after by a local authority (see p937).

Note:
- If you are a member of a couple and one of you is either 18 or over or satisfies the rules above, but the other does not, the one who is 18 or over or who satisfies the above rules can claim UC as a single person, but the other partner's income and capital are taken into account.[14]
- If you qualify for UC and you are without parental support or you were previously looked after by a local authority, you do not have to serve any waiting days before you can be paid UC.[15]

Part 2: Main means-tested benefits and tax credits
Chapter 8: Universal credit
4. The amount of benefit

3. People included in the claim

If you are single, you claim universal credit (UC) for yourself. If you are a member of a couple, you and your partner must usually make a joint claim for UC (see p170).[16] See p215 for who counts as a couple.

Your maximum amount (see Chapter 13), which forms part of the calculation of your benefit, includes elements for a child(ren) for whom you are responsible. **Note:** the number of children included in your maximum amount may be limited to two (see p258).

There are some situations in which you must show that you are 'responsible' for a child – eg:

- in order to take advantage of the special rules to help you meet the claimant responsibilities (see p1073 and p1068);
- so you can benefit from a work allowance when calculating your UC entitlement (see p167);
- for some of the rules for the housing costs element (see Chapter 22).

You can count as responsible for any child under 16 and for any 'qualifying young person' (see p220 for who counts as a child).[17] You do not have to be the child's parent. For when you count as responsible for a child, see p222.

4. The amount of benefit

Universal credit (UC) is a means-tested benefit. The amount of UC you get depends on your family circumstances and:

- your 'maximum amount' of UC. This is made up of a standard allowance and various 'elements'; *and*
- how much capital and income you have.

The amount you get is calculated over a monthly 'assessment period' (see below). As your income increases, your UC award is reduced.

Note: the rules described below vary depending on whether you are in a 'full service' area (see p24) or 'gateway' area (see p22).[18] In particular, there are slightly different rules on reporting childcare costs (see p264), assessment periods when a couple form or split up or when a new award is made within six months of a previous award ending (see p28), and on calculating unearned income (see p352).

Assessment period

The '**assessment period**' is one calendar month, beginning with the first date of entitlement to UC.[19] Each subsequent assessment period (ie, a calendar month) usually begins on the same day of the month except if:

– the first day of entitlement to UC falls on the 31st of the month, in which case each assessment period begins on the last day of the month;

– the first day of entitlement to UC falls on the 29th or 30th of the month, in which case each assessment period begins on the 29th or 30th. In February, it begins on the 27th (or in a leap year, on the 28th);

– your entitlement has started before the actual date of claim because of the backdating rules, in which case the first assessment period begins on the first day of entitlement and ends on the day before the date of claim.

Note: if you have 'waiting days' at the start of your claim when you are not entitled to UC (see below), your assessment period does not begin until these are over. Also, you may be able to keep the same assessment period as in a previous claim (see p169).

Examples

Carmen claims UC on 31 July. She is making a new claim as a single person after having previously claimed as part of a couple, so is not subject to 'waiting days' (see below). Her first monthly assessment period is from 31 July until 30 August inclusive. Her next assessment period begins on 31 August, and the one after that begins on 30 September.

Dave claims on 3 November. He is subject to seven 'waiting days' before his entitlement can begin (see below), so his assessment period does not begin until 10 November, and the one after that begins on 10 December.

Calculating universal credit

Waiting days

When you make a new claim, if you (and/or your partner in a joint claim) are subject to 'all work-related requirements' (see p1080) on the first day of your claim, or if the only reason you are not subject to all work-related requirements is because you have limited capability for work, you are not entitled to any UC for the first seven 'waiting days' of your claim, unless:[20]

- you are making a new claim as a single person following the end of previous UC entitlement as part of a couple, or a new claim as a couple and both you and your partner were previously getting UC as single people; *or*
- your assessment periods (see p164) for your UC award begin on the same day of each month as the assessment periods for a previous award of UC; *or*
- on the first day of your claim you (and/or your partner in a joint claim):
  – are terminally ill; *or*
  – have recently been a victim of domestic violence; *or*
  – are a 'care leaver' (ie, you are aged 16 or 17 and were previously looked after by a local authority – see p162), or are aged under 22 and claiming UC for the first time having been a care leaver before becoming 18; *or*
  – are aged 16 or 17 and have no parental support; *or*

Part 2: Main means-tested benefits and tax credits
Chapter 8: Universal credit
4. The amount of benefit

- have been a prisoner within the last month; *or*
- have been entitled to contribution-based jobseeker's allowance (JSA) or contributory employment and support allowance (ESA) under the UC system within the last three months; *or*
- have been entitled to contribution-based or income-based JSA, contributory or income-related ESA or income support (IS) within the last three months, having lost entitlement because of paid work; *or*
- have been entitled to income-based JSA, income-related ESA, IS, housing benefit, child tax credit or working tax credit within the last month.

Working out your universal credit

Your UC is worked out in the following way.

- **Step one:** calculate your maximum amount. See Chapter 13 for details of this.
- **Step two:** work out your earnings and check whether any can be ignored.
- **Step three:** work out your other income and how much can be ignored.
- **Step four:** calculate your total income.
- **Step five:** calculate your UC entitlement.

Step one: calculate your maximum amount

Your maximum UC is made up of the total (worked out on a monthly basis) of:[21]

- a standard allowance – for a single claimant or a couple (see p258);
- a child element for each child, with an increase for disabled and severely disabled children (see p258). **Note:** from 6 April 2017, the number of children for whom you can get a child element may be limited to two;
- a limited capability for work element (see p260) or a limited capability for work-related activity element (p262) for an adult who is too ill to work. **Note:** the limited capability for work element is abolished for new claims made on or after 3 April 2017 (see p260);
- a carer element for someone looking after a severely disabled person (see p263);
- a housing costs element for renters or owner-occupiers (see Chapter 22);
- a childcare costs element (see p264).

Example

Gail and Joe are a couple both aged over 25. They claim UC in May 2017. They have two children. Gail works; Joe is ill and has limited capability for work and for work-related activity. They do not have housing or childcare costs.

Gail and Joe's maximum amount for UC is calculated as follows:

Standard allowance	£498.89
Child element (first child)	£231.67
Child element (second child)	£231.67
Limited capability for work-related activity element	£318.76
Total	**£1,280.99**

Step two: work out your earnings and how much can be ignored

See Chapter 16 for how to work out your earnings (called 'earned income' for UC).

Once you have established your earnings, check whether any can be ignored when calculating your UC. This is done by comparing your earnings with a set amount, called a 'work allowance' (see below).

If your earnings do not exceed the work allowance, they are all ignored. If your earnings are more than your work allowance, 63 per cent of the excess is taken into account as income.[22] You are only entitled to a work allowance if certain circumstances apply.

The way your earnings reduce the amount of your UC is sometimes called the **'taper'** – ie, the rate at which your UC tapers away as your earnings increase. As your earnings rise above any that are ignored, your UC reduces by 63 pence for every extra pound you earn.

The work allowance

A work allowance only applies if you (or your partner) are responsible for a child or have limited capability for work.

The amount of the allowance depends on whether your UC includes a housing costs element. Only one work allowance can apply.

Amount of the work allowance

UC includes a housing costs element	£192
UC does not include a housing costs element	£397

Examples

Anne is a lone parent with a child aged six. She rents her home and is entitled to the housing costs element in her UC. She has a part-time job from which her earned income for UC over her assessment period is £300.

Because Anne has a child a work allowance applies and so some of her earnings can be ignored. Anne's UC includes a housing costs element, so her work allowance is £192. Anne's earned income exceeds her work allowance by £108 (£300 – £192). Sixty-three per cent of this excess is £68.04. Therefore, £68.04 of Anne's earned income is taken into account when calculating her UC.

Gail and Joe are a couple with two children. They have a mortgage, but are not entitled to a housing costs element in their UC because Gail has earned income from work (see p487). Joe is ill and has limited capability for work and work-related activity. Gail's earned income for UC over their assessment period is £1,200.

Because they have children and also because Joe has limited capability for work, a work allowance applies and some of Gail's earnings can be ignored. Their UC does not include a

Part 2: Main means-tested benefits and tax credits
Chapter 8: Universal credit
4. The amount of benefit

housing costs element, so the work allowance is £397. Gail's earnings exceed the work allowance by £803 (£1,200 – £397). Sixty-three per cent of this excess is £505.89. So £505.89 of Gail and Joe's earned income is taken into account when calculating their UC.

Step three: work out your other income and how much can be ignored

See Chapter 16 for how to work out your other income and how much can be ignored.

If you have other income (eg, other benefits), unless it is ignored it affects your UC by reducing it pound for pound. This is in addition to any reductions from your earnings.

Income from capital

If you and your partner have more than £16,000 capital, you cannot get UC. If you have more than £6,000 but £16,000 or less, you count as having an income of £4.35 a month for every £250, or part of £250, over £6,000.[23] This assumed monthly income is sometimes referred to as 'tariff income'.

For how to calculate your capital, including assumed monthly income, see Chapter 17.

Step four: calculate your total income

Add together the income that is to be taken into account under Steps two and three.

Step five: calculate your universal credit entitlement

Deduct your total income to be taken into account (Step four) from your maximum UC (Step one).

Note: if you are transferred from a means-tested benefit or tax credit to UC, you may also be entitled to transitional protection (see p169). The transfer process is currently not expected to begin before September 2019

Example

Gail and Joe are a couple both aged over 25, with two children. Gail works and earns £1,200 in their monthly assessment period. Joe is ill and has limited capability for work and work-related activity. He gets fortnightly payments of contributory ESA of £219.30. For UC purposes, this is converted to a monthly figure of £475.15. They do not have housing costs or childcare costs included in their UC. They have savings of £5,000.

Their total income to be taken into account under Step four is £505.89 in earned income, plus £475.15 contributory ESA during their monthly assessment period = £981.04

Their maximum UC under Step one = £1,280.99

Their monthly UC entitlement = £1,280.99 – £981.04 = £299.95

Transitional protection

From some point, currently expected to be in September 2019, claimants with existing awards of means-tested benefits and tax credits will begin to have their claims transferred to UC. The DWP calls this 'managed migration'. If you are transferred to UC and your UC maximum amount is less than the amount you were getting on the benefit you were transferred from, your UC includes transitional protection in the form of an additional amount to make up the difference. **Note:** at the time this *Handbook* was written, the date when the transfer of existing claims would begin and the rules on transitional protection had not been finalised. See CPAG's online service and *Welfare Rights Bulletin* for updates.

Transitional protection can only apply if your claim is transferred by the DWP as part of the 'managed migration' process. It does not apply, for example, if you claim UC after a change of circumstances. So you could find that if you claim UC, your UC is worth less than the means-tested benefits or tax credits you were getting previously.

5. Special benefit rules

Special rules may apply to:
* 16/17-year olds (see p162);
* people subject to immigration control (see Chapter 65);
* people who have come from or are going abroad (see Chapters 66 and 67);
* people who are studying (see Chapter 40);
* people in prison or detention (see Chapter 41).

6. Claims and backdating

You can only claim universal credit (UC) if you come under the UC system (see p20).

The general rules about claims and backdating are covered in Chapter 49. This section explains the specific rules that apply to UC.

Making a claim

Claims for UC must be made online at www.gov.uk/apply-universal-credit. If you need help claiming online, call the UC helpline on 0345 600 0723 (textphone: 0345 600 0743). Calls to the helpline are not free of charge. The DWP adviser may complete on online form on your behalf or suggest a local support service (eg, from your council) that may be able to help you.

In theory, a claim can be made by telephone if the DWP has provided a number for this and is willing to accept a claim in this way.[24] However, in practice, if you

Part 2: Main means-tested benefits and tax credits
Chapter 8: Universal credit
6. Claims and backdating

do not have internet access, the DWP says you should access the internet at your local jobcentre or through local support services. In exceptional circumstances, if you are unable to use either a computer or a telephone, the DWP may make a home visit to help you claim, but you should not rely on this.

You can amend or withdraw your claim before a decision is made (see p1149). If you are in financial need while waiting to be paid, you may be able to get a short-term advance of UC (see p1177).

Forms
There are no paper claim forms for UC. The claim form is only available online.

When you do not need to make a claim

If you live in a UC 'gateway' area (see p22), you do not have to make a claim for UC (and you keep the same assessment period as before) if you have previously claimed UC and:[25]

- you were refused UC because your earnings were too high, or lost entitlement because of an increase in your earnings; *and*
- it is not more than six months since your claim, or since your entitlement stopped; *and*
- your circumstances have changed and you provide details of your earnings to the DWP.

You also do not need to make a new claim (and you keep the same assessment period as before) if you have previously claimed UC and:[26]

- you were entitled as a single claimant, are now part of a couple and your partner was also entitled to UC as a single claimant. Although you do not need to make a new joint claim, you must tell the DWP that you are now part of a couple; *or*
- you are now a member of a couple and either you or your partner (but not both of you) was entitled to UC as a single claimant and that award has now been terminated; *or*
- you were a member of a couple making a joint claim but have now ceased to be a couple and your former partner has reported that you have ceased to be a couple. Except if you live in the UC 'full service' area (see p24), if you are the first to tell the DWP that you are no longer a couple, you must make a new claim.

Who should claim

If you are single, you claim on your own behalf as a single person. If you are a member of a couple, you must normally make a joint claim with your partner.[27] For when you count as a couple, see p164. If you are a member of a couple and one of you does not satisfy the conditions for UC, you can claim as a single person (although your income and capital are assessed jointly with your partner) in certain circumstances (see p161). The DWP treats your joint claim as one made by a single person.[28]

If you are unable to manage your own affairs, another person can claim UC for you as your 'appointee' (see p1149).[29]

Information to support your claim

For the general information requirements that apply to all benefits, see p1150.

It is important that you provide any information required when you claim. Until you do, you may not count as having made a valid claim (see p1152). Correct any defects as soon as possible, or your date of claim may be affected (see below).

You may be asked to attend an interview at your local Jobcentre Plus office to supply further information, such as details of your income and savings.

If you are working for an employer, the DWP uses a 'real-time information system' to obtain information about your earnings. Your employer is required to send information to HM Revenue and Customs every time your wages are paid.

Even if you have made a valid claim, you may be asked to provide further evidence (see p1154). You may also be asked to provide information after you are awarded UC and if you fail to do so, your UC could be suspended, or even terminated (see p1185).

The date of your claim

The date of your claim is important as it determines when your entitlement to UC starts (subject the the rules on waiting days – see p165). This is not necessarily the date from when you are paid. For information about when payment of UC starts, see p173.

Your **'date of claim'** is usually the date on which your online claim is received by the DWP.[30] If you received help from the DWP in making the claim before you claimed online, your date of claim is the date you notified the DWP that you intended to make it. If you claim by telephone, your date of claim is the date on which the claim is 'properly completed', or earlier if you previously notified your intention to claim and the claim is made within a month of that.

Note: you must make sure your claim is valid. If it is 'defective', you are given a short time to correct the defects (see p1152). If you do, your claim is treated as having been made when you initially claimed.[31] In practice, the DWP expects relatively few defective claims, as it is not possible to make an online claim without essential information.

In some cases, you can claim in advance (see p172) and in some cases your claim can be backdated (see p172). If you want this to be done, make this clear when you claim or the DWP might not consider it.

Part 2: Main means-tested benefits and tax credits
Chapter 8: Universal credit
6. Claims and backdating

Backdating your claim

A claim for UC can only be backdated for a maximum of one month, and only if one or more circumstances applied that meant you could not reasonably have claimed earlier. If you are making a joint claim, both you and your partner must satisfy this rule. Your claim can be backdated if:[32]

- you were previously getting jobseeker's allowance or employment and support allowance and you were not notified that your entitlement was going to end before it did;
- you have a disability (the rules do not define this);
- you were unwell and this meant you could not claim online or by telephone on time, and you have now supplied medical evidence showing that you were unwell;
- you could not claim online because of a system failure or planned system maintenance, and you have now claimed on the first day that the system was working;
- you had a joint claim for UC but this terminated because you stopped being a couple, you were the first to report that you ceased to be a couple and you have now reclaimed UC as a single person;
- you made a joint claim for UC and this was either turned down or awarded but later terminated because your partner did not accept the claimant commitment, but you have now ceased to be a couple and you have reclaimed UC as a single person.

If you might have qualified for benefit earlier, but did not claim because you were given the wrong information by the DWP or because you were misled by it, you could ask for compensation (see p1396) or complain to the Ombudsman through your MP (see p1401).

If you claim the wrong benefit

There are no rules for when a claim for another benefit can be treated as a claim for UC. You should claim UC as soon as you can and, if necessary, ask for the claim to be backdated.

Claiming in advance

If you claim UC when you are not yet entitled, but the DWP thinks that you will be entitled within one month of the day you claimed, it can make an advance award. If this applies, your claim is treated as made on the first day on which you are entitled to UC.[33] However, the DWP intends to accept advance claims only in very limited circumstances – eg, from prisoners who are to be released within a month. Otherwise, the intention is that a partially completed online claim can be left open for a time until it can be submitted at the appropriate time.[34]

7. **Getting paid**

The general rules on getting paid are covered in Chapter 50. This section explains the specific rules that apply to UC.

When is universal credit paid?

You are normally paid within seven days of the end of an assessment period. UC is usually paid monthly, in arrears. It is expected that if you live in Scotland, from June 2017 you will be able to request that you are paid twice monthly. See CPAG's online serice and *Welfare Rights Bulletin* for updates.[35] Otherwise, if you find being paid monthly difficult to budget for, you may be able to request more frequent payment under an 'alternative payment arrangement' (see p174).

Your award is assessed over an 'assessment period' of one calendar month, beginning from the date your entitlement starts (see p164).[36] UC should normally be paid directly into your account within seven days of the last day of the monthly assessment period or, if this is not possible, 'as soon as reasonably practicable' thereafter.[37]

In practice, you can expect to get your first payment of UC around six weeks after claiming, if your claim is successful. This is because there may be a seven-day 'waiting period' before your entitlement (and, therefore, your assessment period) begins (see p165), and then because UC is paid a month in arrears. If you are in financial need in the meantime, or if there is a delay in subsequent payments, you may be able to get a short-term advance of UC (see p1177). Otherwise, you may be able to get help from your local authority (see p856).

Couples can decide which partner is paid. The DWP can decide that the other partner should be paid instead or can split the payments between you if it considers it to be in your interests, the interests of a child for whom you are responsible (see p222), or the interests of a severely disabled person and your UC includes a carer element (see p263).[38]

If you need a loan for an item you cannot afford, you can ask for a 'budgeting advance' of UC (see p175).

Your UC can be paid in whole or in part to another person on your behalf, if the DWP considers this is necessary to protect your interests, or those of your partner, a child for whom you are responsible (see p222), or a severely disabled person and your UC includes a carer element (p263).[39]

The housing costs element to cover mortgage interest is paid directly to your mortgage lender, but the housing costs element to cover rent is normally paid to you rather than your landlord, unless paying your landlord would be in your interest. Official guidance says that your landlord can request that payment is made to her/him, and that request will be granted automatically if your rent is over two months in arrears.[40] It is expected that if you live in Scotland, from June 2017 you will be able to request that payment is made direct to your landlord. See CPAG's online service and *Welfare Rights Bulletin* for updates. Otherwise, you may be able to request payment to your landlord under an 'alternative payment arrangement' (see below).

Note:

- Deductions can be made from your UC to pay third parties (see p1187).
- Your UC might be paid at a reduced rate if you have been sanctioned (see Chapter 48) or committed a benefit offence (see p1265).
- For information on missing payments, see p1174. If you cannot get your UC payments because you have lost your bank or Post Office card or you have forgotten your PIN, see p1173. If your 'simple payment' card is lost or stolen or if you have forgotten your memorable date, see p1173.
- If payment of your UC is delayed, see p1165. If you are waiting for a decision on your claim, or to be paid, you might be able to get a short-term advance (p1177). If you wish to complain about how your claim has been dealt with, or claim compensation, see Chapter 58.
- If payment of your UC is suspended, see p1185.
- If you are overpaid UC, you might have to repay it (see Chapter 52) and, in some circumstances, you may have to pay a penalty (see p1256). If you have been accused of fraud, see Chapter 53.

Alternative payment arrangements

If you find monthly payments difficult to budget for, or if having your UC housing costs for rent paid to you rather than to your landlord is leading to serious arrears, or if you need payment to be split between you and your partner, it may be possible to have an alternative payment arrangement. This is discretionary and there is no right of appeal. You must show that you cannot manage the usual payment arrangement and, as a result, there is a risk of financial harm to you or to someone in your family. According to government guidance, the following applies.[41]

- The DWP must be satisfied that alternative payment arrangements should apply, based on your inability to cope with usual payment and on your circumstances. For example, are you managing to pay your bills on time? Can you manage a monthly budget? Are you used to managing money with your partner?
- Alternative payment arrangements are considered in the following order of priority:
  - paying rent directly to your landlord to safeguard your home;
  - more frequent payment – ie, two payments a month, rather than just one. Exceptionally, more frequent payments can be considered;

- splitting payment between the partners in a couple in specific situations – eg, if one partner is mismanaging the UC award or if there is domestic violence.

- The DWP splits claimants into those with circumstances with a 'high likely need' for alternative payment arrangements and those with 'less likely need'.

You are in high likely need if you:
- have drug, alcohol and other addiction problems;
- have learning difficulties;
- have severe debt problems;
- are living in temporary or supported accommodation;
- are homeless;
- have experienced domestic violence or abuse;
- have a mental health condition;
- are currently in rent arrears or at threat of eviction or repossession;
- are aged 16 or 17, or have left local authority care;
- are a family with multiple and complex needs.

You are in less likely need if you:
- have third-party deductions in place – eg, for utility arrears;
- are a refugee or asylum seeker;
- have a history of rent arrears;
- were previously homeless or living in supported accommodation;
- have a physical disability;
- have just left prison or hospital;
- are recently beareaved;
- have problems with language skills;
- are an ex-servicewoman/man;
- are not in education, employment or training.

Budgeting advances

Budgeting advances are extra amounts of UC that are intended to help you with expenses – eg, buying essential furniture or household equipment. Budgeting advances must be repaid, usually by deductions from future payments of your UC. They are discretionary. If you are refused a budgeting advance, you do not have a right to appeal against this decision.

If you are awarded a budgeting advance, the DWP must send you notice in writing that you will have it deducted from subsequent payments of your UC and that, if it is not deducted, you must otherwise repay it. The same rules apply to deductions from your UC that apply to the recovery of overpayments on p1239.

To get a budgeting advance:[42]
- you must apply for one; *and*
- you (or your partner if you are a couple) must be getting UC and (unless the expense is 'necessarily related' to employment) have been getting UC (or

income support (IS), income-based jobseeker's allowance (JSA), income-related employment and support allowance (ESA) or pension credit) for a continuous period of at least six months when the claim is made; *and*

* you satisfy the earnings and recovery conditions (see below).

The earnings and recovery conditions
The 'earnings condition'. If you are not a member of a couple, your earnings from work must not exceed £2,600 in the period covered by the previous six complete monthly assessment periods. If you are a member of a couple, your joint earnings from work must not exceed £3,600 in this period. **Note:** if you are self-employed, your actual earned income is taken into account, not any assumed minimum income under the 'minimum income floor' (see p341).

The 'recovery condition'. There must be no outstanding budgeting advance (ie, which has not yet been recovered) paid to you (or your partner) and the DWP is satisfied that the budgeting advance can reasonably be expected to be recovered, taking into account all your debts and other liabilities.

The minimum amount of a budgeting advance is £100. The maximum payable is:
* if you are single and not responsible for a child, £348;
* if you are in a couple and not responsible for a child, £464;
* if you are responsible for a child and either single or in a couple, £812.

For when you are responsible for a child, see p220.

If your capital (or your joint capital if you are a couple) is over £1,000, the budgeting advance is reduced by the amount the capital exceeds £1,000. For how your capital is calculated, see Chapter 17.

Change of circumstances

You must report changes in your circumstances that you have been told you must report, as well as any that you might reasonably be expected to know might affect your right to, the amount of, or the payment of, your benefit. You should do this as soon as possible. Changes can be reported by telephoning the UC helpline on 0345 600 0723 (textphone: 0345 600 0743) – these calls are not free. It is advisable also to report the change in writing if you can. In the UC 'full service' areas (see p22), you are expected to report a change via your online account. See p1184 for further information.

If you become a member of a couple with someone who is not entitled to UC, her/his entitlement to IS, income-based JSA, income-related ESA, housing benefit (except for specified accommodation – see p45), working tax credit or child tax credit ends (see p28).

If you are working and being taxed through PAYE (pay as you earn), the DWP should get information about changes in your earnings automatically from HM

Revenue and Customs through the 'real-time information system'. However, this does not change your responsibilities, and if your employer has not reported your earnings, you must report them yourself.[43] Check with your employer that your earnings are being reported as you are paid. If you are self-employed, you must report your earnings every month.

Note: you cannot get UC and be in the tax-free childcare scheme, which is due to be introduced gradually in 2017 (see p864). If you register for the scheme, your UC award may be terminated. See CPAG's online service and *Welfare Rights Bulletin* for updates.

When you notify the DWP of a change of circumstances, the decision on your UC is changed by a supersession. The general rule is that a supersession takes effect from the first day of the monthly assessment period in which the change occurred or is expected to occur.[44] So a change that occurs part-way through a monthly assessment period can be treated as having occurred on the first day of the period. Exceptions to this may apply. For full details, see p1292.

Note:
- If you are required by the DWP to report your earnings and your earnings decrease, the supersession takes effect from the first day of the assessment period in which the decrease occurred, even if you report it later.[45]
- A change of circumstances which is advantageous to you is only backdated to the start of the assessment period in which it occurred if you report it before the end of that assessment period, unless the time allowed is extended. Otherwise, the change applies from the start of the assessment period in which you reported it. For full details, see p1294.

Examples

Terry, a lone parent with one child, is entitled to maximum UC of £594.90 a month – ie, a standard allowance of £317.82, plus a child element of £277.08. His assessment period begins on 5 October. Halfway through this assessment period, Terry stops being responsible for a child as his son goes to live with his mother, and so Terry is no longer entitled to the child element. His maximum UC entitlement reduces to £317.82 a month. This change is not advantageous to Terry, but is backdated to the start of the assessment period – ie, to 5 October. This includes a period before he lost entitlement to the child element.

However, Terry is not overpaid UC as he does not get paid until seven days after the end of the assessment period on 4 November. So Terry gets paid just £317.82 for the whole of the assessment period in which the change occurred.

Julie is entitled to maximum UC of £317.82 per month (a standard allowance). Towards the end of her monthly assessment period, she has a child and her maximum UC entitlement increases by £277.08 as it now includes a child element. The change is advantageous to Julie. She reports the change before the end of the assessment period and it is backdated to the start of the assessment period – ie, including a period before she

Part 2: Main means-tested benefits and tax credits
Chapter 8: Universal credit
8. Tax, other benefits and the benefit cap

had her child. When Julie gets paid (after the end of the assessment period in which the change occurred), she gets the additional £277.08 for the whole period. If Julie did not report the change until the start of her next assessment period, it may only have applied from the start of that period.

8. Tax, other benefits and the benefit cap

Tax

Universal credit (UC) is not taxable.

Means-tested benefits and tax credits

If you come under the UC system (see p20), you cannot qualify for income support, income-based jobseeker's allowance (JSA), income-related employment and support allowance (ESA), housing benefit (HB) except for specified accommodation (see p45), child tax credit (CTC) or working tax credit (WTC). If your partner is claiming one of these benefits and you come under the UC system, you claim UC as a couple instead (see p27). If you are already getting one of the above benefits when UC is introduced (and, in the case of HB, CTC and WTC, you have not already claimed UC), it is expected that your claim will be transferred to a claim for UC at some point between July 2019 and 2022.

You cannot get pension credit (PC) at the same time as UC because of the rules about your age (see p162). If you are a couple and one of you has reached the qualifying age for PC, and you live in a 'gateway' area, the current rules prevent you from coming under the UC system on a new claim. However, if you live in a 'full service' area and one (but not both) of you has reached the qualifying age for PC, you can come under the UC system (see p20). In this situation, if you get UC, you can no longer get PC.

Non-means-tested benefits

For the rules on entitlement to national insurance credits for people on UC, see p968.

When you come under the UC system (see p20), you can still claim contribution-based JSA or contributory ESA, but they are taken into account in full as income for UC (and so reduce your UC entitlement).

You can also claim other non-means-tested benefits at the same time as UC – eg, carer's allowance (CA), child benefit, personal independence payment, statutory sick pay and statutory maternity, adoption, paternity and shared parental pay.

For how non-means-tested benefits are treated when working out your income for UC, see Chapter 16.

It can be worth claiming non-means-tested benefits. For example, if you get CA, you may be entitled to a carer element in your UC (see p263). If your child gets disability living allowance, you may be entitled to a disabled child addition (see p258).

The benefit cap

In some cases, there is a limit on the total amount of specified benefits you can receive (a 'benefit cap'). UC is one of the specified benefits. The benefit cap only applies if you are getting HB or UC. See p1180 for further information.

Passports and other sources of help

If you are entitled to UC, you may also qualify for health benefits such as free prescriptions and other payments such as free school lunches.[46] See Chapter 29 for details on health benefits, Chapter 39 for other payments including Healthy Start food and vitamins and free school lunches.

If you are entitled to UC, you may be entitled to a Sure Start maternity grant, a funeral expenses payment or cold weather payments from the social fund (see Chapter 36). You may be entitled to a council tax reduction (see p854).

Notes

1. Who can claim universal credit
1   ss3 and 4 WRA 2012; reg 9 UC Regs
2   s14 WRA 2012
3   s5 WRA 2012
4   ss3 and 4 WRA 2012
5   Reg 3(2) UC Regs
6   Reg 3(3) UC Regs
7   Reg 3(4) UC Regs
8   Reg 12 UC Regs

2. The rules about your age
9   s4(3) WRA 2012; reg 8 UC Regs
10 s4(4) WRA 2012
11 Reg 8(1) and (2) UC Regs
12 Reg 30 UC Regs
13 Reg 8(3) and (4) UC Regs
14 Reg 3(3) UC Regs
15 Reg 19A(3)(b)(iii) and (iv) UC Regs

3. People included in the claim
16 s2 WRA 2012
17 s10 WRA 2012

4. The amount of benefit
18 The Universal Credit (Digital Service) Amendment Regulations 2014, No.2887
19 Reg 21 UC Regs
20 Reg 19A UC Regs, as modified by reg 16A UC(TP) Regs
21 s8 WRA 2012
22 Reg 22 UC Regs
23 Regs 18 and 72 UC Regs

6. Claims and backdating
24 Reg 8 UC,PIP,JSA&ESA(C&P) Regs
25 Reg 6 UC,PIP,JSA&ESA(C&P) Regs; reg 21(3) UC Regs

26 Reg 9(6)-(8) UC,PIP,JSA&ESA(C&P)
    Regs; reg 21(3) UC Regs
27 s2 WRA 2012
28 Reg 9 UC,PIP,JSA&ESA(C&P) Regs
29 Reg 51 UC,PIP,JSA&ESA(C&P) Regs
30 Reg 10 UC,PIP,JSA&ESA(C&P) Regs
31 Reg 10(2) UC,PIP,JSA&ESA(C&P) Regs
32 Reg 26 UC,PIP,JSA&ESA(C&P) Regs
33 s98 WRA 2012; reg 32
    UC,PIP,JSA&ESA(C&P) Regs
34 para A2048 ADM

7. Getting paid
35 Reg 47 UC,PIP,JSA&ESA(C&P) Regs; The
    Universal Credit (Claims and Payments)
    (Scotland) Regulations 2017 (draft)
36 s7 WRA 2012; reg 21 UC Regs
37 Reg 47(2) UC,PIP,JSA&ESA(C&P) Regs
38 Reg 47(6) UC,PIP,JSA&ESA(C&P) Regs
39 Reg 58 UC,PIP,JSA&ESA(C&P) Regs
40 HB Circular A13/2013
41 DWP, *Personal Budgeting Support and
    Alternative Payment Arrangements:
    guidance,* April 2016
42 Regs 12-15 SS(PAB) Regs
43 Reg 61 UC Regs
44 Sch 1 para 20 UC,PIP,JSA&ESA(DA) Regs
45 Sch 1 para 22 UC,PIP,JSA&ESA(DA) Regs

8. Tax, other benefits and the benefit cap
46 The basic power for passporting is in Sch
    2 para 39 WRA 2012.

Chapter 9

Child tax credit

This chapter covers:
1. Who can claim child tax credit (p182)
2. The rules about your age (p187)
3. People included in the claim (p188)
4. The amount of child tax credit (p188)
5. Claims and backdating (p189)
6. Getting paid (p191)
7. Tax, other benefits and the benefit cap (p192)

Key facts

- Child tax credit (CTC) is paid to families with children or qualifying young people.
- You do not have to have paid national insurance contributions to qualify.
- CTC is paid whether or not you or your partner are working.
- CTC does not count as income for income support, income-based jobseeker's allowance, income-related employment and support allowance or pension credit (PC) purposes, and can be paid in addition to these benefits.
- CTC is administered and paid by HM Revenue and Customs.
- If you disagree with a CTC decision, you can apply for a mandatory reconsideration and then appeal if you are unhappy with the outcome.

Future changes

At some point before September 2018, depending on where you live, you will no longer be able to make a new claim for CTC unless you have three or more children, or are at least the qualifying age for PC, or you are already entitled to working tax credit.

From 2019, the DWP will begin to transfer exisiting CTC claimants to universal credit. See p20 for further information, and CPAG's online service and *Welfare Rights Bulletin* for updates.

Part 2: Main means-tested benefits and tax credits
Chapter 9: Child tax credit
1. Who can claim child tax credit

1. **Who can claim child tax credit**

You qualify for child tax credit (CTC) if:[1]

- you (or your partner) are 'responsible' for a child or qualifying young person (see below);
- your income is sufficiently low (see Chapter 60);
- you are 'present' and 'ordinarily resident' in the UK. You can be treated as present and ordinarily resident in the UK in some circumstances – eg, if you are temporarily away. You can be treated as not being in the UK if you claim CTC and do not have a 'right to reside'. You must usually have been living in the UK for at least three months, although there are exceptions to this rule. See Chapter 66 for further information;
- you are not a 'person subject to immigration control' (see Chapter 65);
- you are not a universal credit (UC) claimant. If you already get CTC but then become entitled to UC, your CTC stops.

If you live in a UC 'full service' area (see p24), you cannot make a new claim for CTC unless you are already entitled to working tax credit (WTC), or are at least the qualifying age for pension credit.[2] If you live in a UC full service area and need to make a new claim for three or more children, it is expected that you will be directed to claim CTC.[3] **Note:** although full-time paid work does not affect your entitlement to CTC, income from work affects the amount you can be paid.

Children

To qualify for CTC, you must be 'responsible' for at least one child or qualifying young person.[4] The terms 'child' or 'children' in this chapter also refer to qualifying young people. You do not have to be the child's parent. You could, for example, be the grandparent, sister or brother. See p184 for when you count as responsible for a child and p186 for when you do not count as responsible.

If you are entitled to CTC for a child (or would have been had you made a claim) and the child dies, you continue to be entitled to CTC for the child for eight weeks immediately following her/his death (or to the date your child would have turned 20, if this is earlier).[5]

Who counts as a child

Someone counts as a child until her/his 16th birthday.[6] In some circumstances, a young person aged under 20 also counts as a child. HM Revenue and Customs (HMRC) refers to her/him as a **'qualifying young person'**.

A young person counts as a child during any period:[7]

- from her/his 16th birthday until 31 August following that birthday, whether or not s/he is in full-time non-advanced education or 'approved training' (but see p184 for when s/he may not count as a child);

- from 1 September following her/his 16th birthday (or from 31 August if s/he turns 16 on that date), while s/he is under 20 and in:
  - full-time non-advanced education (see p573) or in appropriate full-time education (in England only). This does not apply if s/he is getting the education because of her/his employment. A young person counts as being in full-time education during any gaps between the ending of one course and the start of another, if s/he is enrolled on and commences the other course; *or*
  - approved training (see p575 for what counts) or has been enrolled on or accepted to undertake approved training. This does not apply if s/he is getting the training through a contract of employment.

  The course or approved training must have begun before s/he reached 19, or s/he must have been enrolled on or accepted to undertake the course or approved training before that age. HMRC may accept that a 19-year-old who changes course after turning 19 is covered, provided s/he has been in full-time non-advanced education or approved training continuously. **Note:** there is no equivalent to the child benefit 'terminal date rule' (see p575) so, unless the young person is under 18 and the rule in the next bullet point applies, s/he cannot count as a child once the course or training ends. Therefore, ensure you notify HMRC when the course or training ends;
- from 1 September following her/his 16th birthday (or from 31 August if s/he turns 16 on that date), while s/he is under 18, has ceased full-time education or approved training and it is not more than 20 weeks since s/he did so. S/he must notify HMRC within three months of ceasing full-time education or approved training that s/he has registered for work or training with a qualifying body – eg, the place where the local authority provides careers advice for young people or the Ministry of Defence. This rule can apply again if s/he goes back into full-time education or approved training and ceases again.

What should you do when your child turns 16?

Notify HMRC in the September after your child's 16th birthday if s/he is staying on in non-advanced education, appropriate full-time education (in England only), or approved training. In England, this applies even though the school participation age has risen to 17. To be sure that your CTC continues, you should also notify HMRC in the September after your child's 17th, 18th and 19th birthdays that s/he is continuing in education.

When working out whether a young person counts as being in full-time education or approved training, HMRC ignores:[8]

- an interruption of up to six months, whether it began before or after the young person turned 16; *and*
- an interruption of any length which is due to the young person's illness or disability 'of the mind or body'.

Part 2: Main means-tested benefits and tax credits
Chapter 9: Child tax credit
1. Who can claim child tax credit

The interruption is only ignored if HMRC thinks it is reasonable to do so. You should notify HMRC if the above applies.

When a young person does not count as a child

A young person cannot count as a child during any period following her/his 16th birthday in which:[9]

- having ceased full-time education or approved training, s/he is in full-time paid work. This means work of 24 hours or more per week. For information about:
  - what counts as paid work, see p197;
  - how the hours are calculated, see p197;
  - situations when the young person is not treated as being in full-time paid work, see p203.

  The rules are the same as for WTC.

  Remember that, even if a young person has *not* started full-time paid work, s/he cannot count as a child from 1 September after her/his 16th birthday if s/he has ceased full-time education or 'approved training' and has not registered for work or training with a qualifying body; *or*

- s/he gets income support (IS), income-based jobseeker's allowance (JSA), income-related employment and support allowance (ESA) or UC in her/his own right. **Note:** you do not count as responsible for a child aged 16 or over if s/he gets CTC or contributory ESA in her/his own right (see p186).

Being responsible for a child

For tax credit purposes, a child can only count as the responsibility of one claimant (or joint-claim couple).[10] You are treated as 'responsible' for a child if:[11]

- s/he normally lives with you. HMRC calls this the 'normally living with test'; *or*

- s/he normally lives with you, and also with someone else (ie, a shared care arrangement), but you have the main responsibility for her/him. HMRC calls this the 'main responsibility test'. This test only applies if you and another person (or couple) make competing claims for CTC for the same child.

Note:

- Entitlement to child benefit is not a specific factor in working out who is responsible for a child for CTC purposes.

- If a child for whom you are treated as being responsible has a child of her/his own (eg, your grandchild) who normally lives with her/him, you also count as being responsible for that child, but not if your child is 16 or over and is awarded CTC in her/his own right.[12]

The 'normally living with test'

The rules do not define when a child counts as 'normally living with' you. HMRC says it means that your child 'regularly, usually, typically' lives with you and that this allows for temporary or occasional absences.[13] So if your child counts as normally living with you, s/he should also count as doing so even if s/he is away from home – eg, because s/he is away at school or for a temporary period on holiday or in hospital. You can argue that a child is normally living with you if s/he spends more time with you than with anyone else.[14]

Your child can count as normally living with you even if s/he also lives with someone else, or only lives with you for part of the week and lives for part of the week with someone else – eg, her/his other parent. This means that more than one person could apply for CTC for the same child. However, CTC can only be paid to one claimant (or joint-claim couple). If more than one claims, see the 'main responsibility test' below.

The 'main responsibility test'

If you (and your partner) and at least one other person (or couple) with whom the child also normally lives claim CTC for the same child, you only qualify for CTC for the child if you can show you have the 'main responsibility' for her/him. The main responsibility test applies if:[15]

- your child normally lives with both you and:
  - at least one other person in another household – eg, with you and with the child's other parent from whom you have separated; or
  - someone who is not your partner in the same household – eg, with you and with the child's grandparent where you live together.

  It also applies if it is a combination of these situations. 'Household' is not defined. See p225 for ideas about what might count as a household; and
- you and at least one of the other people with whom your child normally lives claim CTC.

You and the other CTC claimant(s) can decide which of you should count as having main responsibility. If you cannot agree, a decision maker decides.[16] You can challenge the decision (see p187).

'Main responsibility' is not defined in the rules. The tax credit approach is different from that for child benefit, housing benefit or child support maintenance, and does not refer to the legal concept of 'parental responsibility'.[17] The decision maker is likely to consider things like:[18]

- whether any court orders exist that set out where your child is to live or who is to care for her/him (although the terms of a court order are not conclusive – what matters is what is happening in practice[19]);
- who pays for your child's food and clothes and who is responsible for giving her/him pocket money, but financial responsibility is not solely determinative;
- who your child normally lives with, but time spent is not solely determinative;
- where the majority of her/his clothes and belongings are kept and who does her/his laundry;

Part 2: Main means-tested benefits and tax credits
Chapter 9: Child tax credit
1. Who can claim child tax credit

- who is the main contact or registered address for the school or college, nursery or childcare provider, and who takes most responsiblity for your child when s/he is at school;[20]
- who arranges appointments to see a doctor/dentist.

Even though you may be sharing responsibility for a child and s/he normally lives with you for part of the week, HMRC might not treat you as having the main responsibility. There is no provision for allowing CTC to be split between parents if a child divides her/his time between their homes.

Do you share responsibility for a child?
If you share responsibility for your child(ren) equally with other CTC claimant(s), it may be difficult to decide who has the main responsibility. If you and another claimant have more than one child, you can each claim CTC for different children – eg, if you have two children, you could claim for one and the other claimant could claim for the other.

When you do not count as responsible for a child

Even if a child normally lives with you, you do *not* count as responsible for the child and cannot qualify for CTC for her/him during any period when s/he is:[21]
- provided with, or placed in, accommodation and the accommodation or the child's maintenance is funded wholly or partly by the local authority under specified provisions or out of other public funds. This includes children staying with foster carers who get foster payments for them from the local authority. This does not apply if your child is staying in certain forms of residential accommodation and this is only necessary because your child has a disability or because her/his health would be significantly impaired or further impaired if s/he were not staying in the accommodation. You must have been treated as responsible for her/him immediately before s/he went into the accommodation;[22] *or*
- being looked after by a local authority and has been placed with you because you want to adopt her/him. This only applies if the local authority is paying for the child's accommodation or maintenance or both under specified provisions; *or*
- in custody. This only applies if your child:
  - is serving a life or unlimited sentence; *or*
  - is serving a term of more than four months; *or*
  - has been detained 'during Her Majesty's pleasure'; *or*
- at least 16 and:
  - is awarded CTC in her/his own right for a child for whom s/he is responsible; *or*
  - receives WTC in her/his own right (including in a joint claim); *or*
  - is entitled to and receiving contributory ESA in her/his own right; *or*

– is married, in a civil partnership or living with someone as a couple and her/his partner is not in full-time non-advanced education or approved training (see p573 and p575 for what counts); *or*

– is your partner and and you are living with her/him.

Note: a young person does not count as a child if s/he gets IS, income-based JSA, income-related ESA or UC in her/his own right (see p184).

Challenging a decision

HMRC might say that:

- your child does not normally live with you or that you are not the person with main responsibility for her/him, so you are not entitled to CTC;
- someone else has claimed CTC for your child(ren) and now satisfies the main reponsibility test when you have been getting CTC for the same child(ren). In this case, your entitlement to CTC ends and you may have been overpaid, but only from the first date on which the question of main responsibility arose.[23] If HMRC has paid two claimants for the same period for the same child who normally lives with both claimants, this is likely to be an official error and so any overpayment should not be recovered.[24]

If you think a decision is wrong and it affects your tax credits, you can request a mandatory reconsideration and then appeal if you are unhappy with the outcome. In an appeal about the main responsibility test, the First-tier Tribunal should ensure that both competing claimants have an opportunity to put their case.[25] See Chapter 64 for more information about getting a tax credit decision changed. If as a result of a decision or following the outcome of an appeal HMRC says you have been overpaid, you can dispute recovery (see p1477).

It is possible that the DWP, the local authority, the Tax Credit Office and the Child Benefit Office might reach different conclusions about whether your child(ren) can be included in your claims. If so, you should appeal *all* the decisions with which you disagree.

2. The rules about your age

You (and your partner) must be aged at least 16 to qualify for child tax credit (CTC).[26] There is no upper age limit. If you are under 16, someone else (eg, your parent or the adult with whom you normally live) may be able to claim CTC for you *and* your child.

Part 2: Main means-tested benefits and tax credits
Chapter 9: Child tax credit
4. The amount of child tax credit

3. People included in the claim

You can only qualify for child tax credit (CTC) if you are responsible for one or more children. Some qualifying young people continue to count as children until they are 20. See pp182–87 for who counts as a child and when you count as responsible for her/him.

If you are single, you claim CTC yourself.[27] However, if you are a member of a couple, you must claim CTC jointly with your partner.[28] For information about who counts as a couple for tax credit purposes, see p1451. **Note:** if you claim jointly with your partner, but then cease to count as a couple (or you claim as a single person, but then become a member of a couple), your entitlement to CTC ends. You should therefore report this change in your circumstances and claim tax credits as a single person (or a couple) immediately.

If you are a couple:

- when working out how much CTC you get, your partner's income is added to yours (see Chapter 60);
- CTC is paid to the person who is the main carer of your children (see p1460).

4. The amount of child tax credit

The amount of child tax credit (CTC) you get depends on:

- your maximum CTC. This is made up of a combination of 'elements':
  - child element (£2,780 a year) – one for each child. **Note:** a child element is not payable for a child born on or after 6 April 2017 if you already have two or more children included in your award. There are exceptions (see p1409 for more information);
  - disabled child element (£3,175 a year) – one for each child who qualifies;
  - severely disabled child element (£1,290 a year) – one for each child who qualifies;
  - family element (£545 a year) – only if the claim includes a child born before 6 April 2017.

  For details of how you qualify for the above elements, see Chapter 59;
- how much income you have; *and*
- the 'income threshold figure' that applies to you.

If you are on a means-tested benefit

Being on income support (IS), income-based jobseeker's allowance (JSA), income-related employment and support allowance (ESA) or pension credit (PC) is an automatic passport to maximum CTC.[29] You, therefore, do not need to work out your income or capital. In these circumstances, CTC equals maximum CTC.

If you are not on a means-tested benefit

If you are not on IS, income-based JSA, income-related ESA or PC, follow the steps below to calculate your CTC.

- **Step one:** work out your 'relevant period' (see p1407).
- **Step two:** work out your maximum entitlement (your maximum CTC) for the relevant period (see p1408).
- **Step three:** work out your 'relevant income' (see p1429 and p1421).
- **Step four:** compare your income with the 'income threshold figure' for the relevant period. This is £16,105 a year if you are entitled to CTC only, or £6,420 a year if you are entitled to CTC and your maximum amount of tax credits includes working tax credit (WTC) elements.[30] See p1421 for further information.
- **Step five:** calculate your CTC entitlement for the relevant period (see p1422). If your income is less than the income threshold figure, CTC equals your maximum CTC. If your income exceeds the income threshold figure, your maximum CTC is reduced by 41 per cent of the excess.

You may also be entitled to WTC. Full details of both calculations are in Chapter 59.

5. Claims and backdating

The general rules on claiming, backdating and how your claim can be renewed at the end of the year are in Chapter 61. This section gives an outline of the rules on claims for child tax credit (CTC).

Making a claim

Your first claim for CTC must usually be made in writing on Form TC600.[31] You use the same form for CTC and for working tax credit (WTC). See p1453 for how and where to make a claim. Keep a copy of your claim form in case queries arise.

You can amend or withdraw your claim before you are given notice of the decision on it.[32]

Who should claim

If you are a member of a couple, you must make a joint claim with your partner. If you are not a member of a couple, you claim yourself. For information about who counts as a couple for tax credit purposes, see p1451. If you cannot make your claim yourself, an 'appointee' (see p1453) can claim on your behalf.

Part 2: Main means-tested benefits and tax credits
Chapter 9: Child tax credit
5. Claims and backdating

Information to support your claim

When you claim CTC, you must:[33]
- satisfy the national insurance number requirement (see p1455);
- provide proof of your identity, if required;
- supply information to support your claim (see p1455).

It is important that you provide all the information required. If you do not do so, a decision might be delayed, or HM Revenue and Customs (HMRC) may decide to reject your claim as not validly made. Caselaw has established that there is a right of appeal (after mandatory reconsideration) against a decision to reject a tax credits claim that is not made on the correct form or that does not contain all the required information.[34] If HMRC requires further information before it makes a decision on your claim, see p1457 for details of the time you must be given to provide this and what happens if you fail to do so.

When to claim

The general rule is that your claim runs from the date it is received by HMRC.[35] You cannot make a claim in advance of the tax year for which you are claiming. However, you may be able to get your claim backdated. **Note:** if you claimed universal credit when you should have claimed CTC, see p1454.

Is your income too high?

Awards of CTC are always based on annual income. HMRC bases the initial award of CTC on your (and your partner's) *previous* tax year's income. If you think your income may be too high to qualify for CTC currently, you can make a 'protective claim' so that you do not lose out if you expect your income to fall (see p1454).

Backdating your claim

It is important to claim in time. A claim for CTC can usually only be backdated for a maximum of 31 days.[36] See p1459 for further information.

Note: if you are waiting to hear whether your child or qualifying young person is entitled to disability living allowance (DLA), personal independence payment (PIP) or armed forces independence payment, you should claim CTC, even if you will not qualify for CTC until the disabled child element or severely disabled child element can be included. If you do not qualify, you are given a 'nil award'. A special rule then allows your entitlement to these elements to be backdated for more than one month (see p1460). You must notify HMRC within one month of the date the DLA, PIP or armed forces independence payment is awarded.

Renewal awards

After the end of the tax year in which you claimed CTC, you (and your partner), receive an 'annual review' from HMRC asking you to confirm or declare your income and your household circumstances for the previous tax year (see p1468). If required, you must reply within a strict time limit. HMRC then makes a final decision, based on your actual income during the tax year. It decides whether you were entitled to CTC and, if so, the amount of your award. HMRC also uses the information about your income and household circumstances for the previous tax year to renew your award for the next tax year.[37] Some awards are finalised and renewed automatically on the information held by HMRC, as shown on your annual review, but you must check this and report any errors or changes. **Note:** if you have a 'nil award', you may be given notice that your claim will not be renewed unless you specifically request this.

6. Getting paid

This section gives an outline of the rules about payment of child tax credit (CTC). For more information about getting paid, see p1460.

Payment of CTC is normally made into the bank (or similar) account of whomever you nominate on the claim form as the main carer of your children (see p1460). If you are unable to act for yourself, payment can be made to someone else on your behalf – called your 'appointee' (see p1453).[38]

When is child tax credit paid?

You are paid every week or every four weeks, whichever you choose on the claim form, although HM Revenue and Customs (HMRC) can decide how often.[39]

You can be paid by cheque while your account arrangements are finalised.

Note:

- Even if you have been sanctioned for a benefit offence, your CTC cannot be paid at a reduced rate.
- If you have forgotten your PIN, see p1173. The issues are the same as for benefits.
- If payment of your CTC is delayed and this is causing hardship, ask HMRC to make an 'urgent next day/same day payment' (see p1461). If you wish to complain about how your claim has been dealt with, see p1398. You might be able to claim compensation (see p1396).
- If payment of your CTC is suspended or postponed, see p1461.
- If you are overpaid CTC, you might have to repay it (see Chapter 62). In some cases, interest can be added to the overpayment. In some circumstances, you

Part 2: Main means-tested benefits and tax credits
Chapter 9: Child tax credit
7. Tax, other benefits and the benefit cap

may have to pay a penalty (see p1490). If you have been accused of fraud, see Chapter 63.

Change of circumstances

Your initial award of CTC is made on the basis of your (and your partner's) previous year's income and your personal circumstances on the date of your claim. If your current year's income or your personal circumstances change, your award of CTC can be amended. Remember the following.

- There are some changes you *must* report to HMRC (see p1462). If you fail to do so within one month, you might be given a financial penalty. Some changes end your entitlement to CTC and you must make a fresh claim.
- Other changes that affect your maximum entitlement to CTC are not compulsory to report, so you cannot be given a penalty, but should still be reported to avoid an overpayment or underpayment – eg, when you have a baby or if one of your children stops getting disability living allowance (see p1464). Changes that increase your maximum entitlement to CTC can generally only be backdated one month from when you notify HMRC. Changes that decrease your entitlement generally take effect from the date of change so may result in an overpayment.
- It is optional to report an estimated change in your current year income (see p1465). Your actual income is always taken into account at the end of the tax year, but you may want to consider reporting an estimate sooner to avoid an overpayment or underpayment of CTC.
- Report if you become a member of a couple with someone entitled to universal credit. Your entitlement to CTC will end (see p28).

Note: if you apply for, and are entitled to, payments under the new tax-free childcare scheme, your CTC award is terminated, as you cannot get both at the same time. The tax-free childcare scheme is due to be introduced in early 2017. See p864 for more details.

7. Tax, other benefits and the benefit cap

Tax

Child tax credit (CTC) is not taxable.

Means-tested benefits and tax credits

CTC is not taken into account as income for income support (IS), income-based jobseeker's allowance (JSA), income-related employment and support allowance (ESA) or pension credit (PC).

CTC is not counted as income for universal credit (UC), but there are very limited circumstances when you can be entitled to CTC during an assessment period for UC.[40] This can happen if you become the new partner of a UC claimant (see p28), in which case her/his assessment period continues on the same date, so can cover a period during which you were entitled to CTC before becoming a couple.[41]

Unless you are on IS, income-based JSA or income-related ESA or are at least the qualifying age for PC (see p147), the amount of CTC you are paid *is* taken into account in the same way as income for housing benefit (HB).

If you get arrears of CTC, these count as capital for means-tested benefits and can be disregarded in some circumstances (see p367 and p393).

If you are in full-time paid work, you might qualify for working tax credit (WTC) in addition to CTC.

Non-means-tested benefits

CTC can be paid in addition to any non-means-tested benefits to which you (or your partner) are entitled, including child benefit, but see Chapter 60 for which of these benefits may be taken into account as income for CTC. If your child qualifies for disability living allowance (DLA), personal independence payment (PIP) or armed forces independence payment, you qualify for the disabled child or severely disabled child elements of CTC and the income from DLA, PIP or armed forces independence payment is ignored.

The benefit cap

In some cases, there is a limit on the total amount of specified benefits you can receive (a 'benefit cap'). CTC is one of the specified benefits. However, the benefit cap only applies if you are getting HB or UC. See p1180 for further information.

Passports and other sources of help

If you are entitled to CTC, you may also qualify for:
- health benefits such as free prescriptions (see Chapter 29). You do not have to satisfy the means test if you are getting CTC and your gross annual income is below a set amount; *and*
- education benefits such as free school lunches (see p860).

You may also qualify for a Sure Start maternity grant or a social fund funeral expenses payment. If you have a low income, you may be entitled to a council tax reduction (see p854).

Note: if you apply for, and are entitled to, payments under the new tax-free childcare scheme, your CTC award is terminated, as you cannot get both at the same time. See p864 for more details.

Part 2: Main means-tested benefits and tax credits
Chapter 9: Child tax credit
Notes

Notes

2

1. Who can claim child tax credit
1 ss3(3) and (7), 8 and 42 TCA 2002; regs 3-5 CTC Regs; reg 3 TC(R) Regs; reg 3 TC(Imm) Regs
2 Art 7(4) and (5) WRA(No.23)O
3 *Welfare Reform: written statement*, HCWS96, House of Commons, *Hansard*, 20 July 2016
4 s8(1) TCA 2002
5 s8(5) TCA 2002; reg 6 CTC Regs
6 s8(3) TCA 2002; reg 2(1), definition of 'child', CTC Regs
7 s8(4) TCA 2002; regs 2, definition of 'qualifying young person' and 'full-time education', 4 and 5(1)-(3A) CTC Regs
8 Reg 5(7) CTC Regs
9 Regs 2, definition of 'remunerative work', and 5(4) CTC Regs
10 Reg 3(1) rule 2.2 CTC Regs
11 s8(2) TCA 2002; reg 3(1) rules 1 and 2 CTC Regs
12 Reg 3(1) rule 4 Case D and (2) CTC Regs
13 TCTM 02202
14 CFC/1537/1995
15 Reg 3(1) rule 2 CTC Regs
16 Reg 3 rule 3 CTC Regs
17 *PG v HMRC* [2016] UKUT 216 (AAC)
18 TCTM 02204; *PG v HMRC* [2016] UKUT 216 (AAC)
19 *GJ v HHRC (TC)* [2013] UKUT 561 (AAC)
20 *KN v HMRC* [2009] UKUT 79 (AAC)
21 Reg 3(1) rule 4.1 CTC Regs
22 Reg 3(1) rule 4.2 CTC Regs; reg 9 CB Regs
23 *LP v HMRC* [2014] UKUT 533 (AAC)
24 *SH v HMRC and SC* [2013] UKUT 297 (AAC)
25 *CM v HMRC* [2014] UKUT 272 (AAC)

2. The rules about your age
26 s3(3) TCA 2002

3. People included in the claim
27 s3(3)(b) TCA 2002
28 s3(3)(a) and (5A) TCA 2002; reg 2(1) CTC Regs; CTC/3864/2004; R(TC) 1/07

4. The amount of child tax credit
29 ss7(2) and 13 TCA 2002; reg 4 TC(ITDR) Regs
30 Reg 3(2) and (3) TC(ITDR) Regs

5. Claims and backdating
31 Reg 5 TC(CN) Regs
32 Reg 5(7) TC(CN) Regs; R(IS) 3/05
33 Reg 5(3)-(6) TC(CN) Regs
34 *CI v HMRC (TC)* [2014] UKUT 158 (AAC)
35 s5(2) TCA 2002
36 Reg 7 TC(CN) Regs
37 Regs 11 and 12 TC(CN) Regs

6. Getting paid
38 s24(3) TCA 2002; reg 6 TC(PC) Regs
39 Regs 8 and 13 TC(PC) Regs

7. Tax, other benefits and the benefit cap
40 Reg 66 UC Regs
41 Reg 5(2)(b)(iii) UC(TP) Regs; reg 21(3B) UC Regs

Chapter 10

Working tax credit

This chapter covers:
1. Who can claim working tax credit (below)
2. The rules about your age (p205)
3. People included in the claim (p205)
4. The amount of working tax credit (p205)
5. Claims and backdating (p207)
6. Getting paid (p208)
7. Tax, other benefits and the benefit cap (p210)

Key facts
- Working tax credit (WTC) is paid to some low-paid workers. It tops up your wages if you are in full-time paid work (known as 'remunerative work').
- You do not have to have paid national insurance contributions to qualify.
- WTC is administered and paid by HM Revenue and Customs.
- If you disagree with a WTC decision, you can apply for a mandatory reconsideration and then appeal if you are unhappy with the outcome.

Future changes
At some point before September 2018, depending on where you live, you will no longer be able to make a new claim for WTC unless you are at least the qualifying age for pension credit, or are already entitled to child tax credit. From 2019, the DWP will begin to transfer existing WTC claimants to universal credit. See p20 for further information, and CPAG's online service and *Welfare Rights Bulletin* for updates.

1. Who can claim working tax credit

You qualify for working tax credit (WTC) if:[1]
- you (or your partner) are in full-time paid work (see p196);
- your income is sufficiently low (see Chapter 60);
- you are 'present' and 'ordinarily resident' in the UK. You can be treated as present and ordinarily resident in the UK in some circumstances – eg, if you are away temporarily. See Chapter 66 for further information;

Part 2: Main means-tested benefits and tax credits
Chapter 10: Working tax credit
1. Who can claim working tax credit

- you are not a 'person subject to immigration control' (see Chapter 65);
- you are not a universal credit (UC) claimant (see p1450). If you already get WTC but then become entitled to UC, your WTC stops.

If you live in a UC 'full service' area (see p24), you cannot make a new claim for WTC unless you are already entitled to child tax credit, or are at least the qualifying age for pension credit.[2]

Full-time paid work

To qualify for WTC, you or your partner must be in full-time paid work. HM Revenue and Customs (HMRC) calls this 'remunerative work'.[3] The number of hours required to be classed as full-time for tax credits purposes depends on your circumstances. See below for what counts as full-time work and p197 for what counts as paid work and for how your hours are calculated. 'Work' includes self-employment and work which is done from home.

In some circumstances, you may be treated as not being in full-time paid work even if you are (see p203). In others, you may be treated as if you are in full-time paid work when you are not (see p201). If you are unsure whether you are in full-time paid work, see p200.

Income from work affects your entitlement to WTC. This means that, although your (or your partner's) hours of work are high enough for you to qualify, you might not satisfy the means test.

If neither you nor your partner are in full-time paid work, you may be able to claim income support (IS), jobseeker's allowance (JSA) or employment and support allowance (ESA). You may be able to choose whether to claim IS/JSA/ESA or WTC. In some situations, you may be able to claim both IS/JSA/ESA and WTC – eg, if you are a 'term-time only' worker or are off sick and getting statutory sick pay (SSP). This is because different rules on what counts as full-time paid work apply. See p1000 for information about what you should consider.

What counts as full-time work
You count as being in full-time work if any of the following apply.[4]
- You work at least **30 hours** a week and you are 25 or over.
- You work at least **16 hours** a week and:
  - you have a physical or mental disability which puts you at a disadvantage in getting a job and you qualify for a disabled worker element; *or*
  - you are 60 or over; *or*
  - you are a single claimant and are responsible for at least one child or qualifying young person (see p184); *or*
  - you are a member of a couple, you (or your partner) are responsible for at least one child or qualifying young person (see p184) and your partner counts as incapacitated for the purposes of the childcare element (see

p1415), or is entitled to carer's allowance (CA – including an underlying entitlement), or is a hospital inpatient or is in prison.
- You and your partner's combined hours of work are at least **24 hours** a week, and you (or your partner) are responsible for at least one child or qualifying young person (see p184). One of you must do at least 16 hours a week. If only one of you works, that person must work at least 24 hours a week.

If you are under 25, you can only qualify for WTC if you work at least 16 hours a week and qualify for a disabled worker element, or you are responsible for a child in the circumstances above.

If your circumstances change and you are no longer responsible for a child or qualifying young person, or no longer qualify for a disabled worker element, unless you are 60 or over, you may have to increase your weekly hours to at least 30 to continue to qualify for WTC. See Chapter 61 for more information on changes of circumstances and when you must report them.

At the date of your claim, you must be working or have accepted an offer of work which is expected to start within seven days.[5] In the latter case, you only count as being in full-time paid work when the work begins. The work must be expected to continue for at least four weeks after you make your claim (or if you have accepted an offer of work, after the work starts).[6]

Note:
- You can continue to count as being in full-time work for four weeks after you leave work, or your hours reduce to less than the number you (or your partner) need to do. See p202 for information about this 'WTC run-on'.
- If you normally work sufficient hours a week, but are off sick or on maternity, paternity or adoption leave, you may be able to claim WTC as you can be treated as being in full-time paid work (see p201). You may also be able to claim IS, JSA or ESA.

What counts as paid work

'Paid work' includes work for which you are paid or expect to be paid.[7] Payment of a benefit (eg, CA) does not count for these purposes. The information on p991 about what counts as paid work for means-tested benefits also applies to WTC.

How your hours are calculated

How you calculate your hours depends on whether you are employed or self-employed.[8]
- If you are employed, include all the hours:
  - you normally work under your contract, if you are an apprentice or employee; *or*
  - you normally perform in the office in which you are employed, if you are an office holder. This includes if you are in an elective office or are a company director; *or*

Part 2: Main means-tested benefits and tax credits
Chapter 10: Working tax credit
1. Who can claim working tax credit

– for which you are normally paid by the employment agency with whom you have a contract, if you are an agency worker.

- If you are self-employed, include all the hours you normally do for payment or for which you expect to be paid, and on activities which are necessary to the employment.

Paid meal and refreshment breaks count towards the total hours you work.[9] Also included is any time allowed for medical appointments, but only if this is to treat or monitor your disability and if you are paid, or expect to be paid, for the time.[10] Your total hours from more than one job are added together.

Periods when you are on a customary or paid holiday from work are ignored when calculating your hours.[11] Likewise, unpaid meal and refreshment breaks are ignored.

Employed and self-employed[12]

You count as '**employed**' if you are employed under a contract of service or apprenticeship and your earnings are taxable as employment income under certain provisions of the Income Tax (Earnings and Pensions) Act 2003.

You count as '**self-employed**' if you are carrying out a trade, profession or vocation that is organised and regular, on a commercial basis and with a view to making a profit.

Hours you normally work

Whether you are employed or self-employed, the measure for WTC purposes is the number of hours you normally work.[13] 'Normally' is not defined in the WTC rules. HMRC says you should calculate your hours based on what you 'regularly, usually or typically' do and that the number of hours you normally work might not be the number of hours specified in your contract of employment.[14] The hours that are relevant are those you *actually* work. If you routinely do paid overtime, argue that these are hours you normally work and that they should be included. See p199 if your hours fluctuate.

Example

Jen is a cashier in a supermarket. Her partner stays at home to look after their children. She is contracted to work 21 hours a week over a three-day week but she does 3.5 hours overtime almost every week. She gets an unpaid half-hour lunch break. When Jen and her partner claim WTC, she has just returned from two weeks' paid holiday.

Jen normally works 21 + 3.5 = 24.5 hours a week. Unpaid lunch breaks and the time she was on paid holiday are not taken into account. As Jen and her partner are responsible for children, one of them needs to work at least 16 hours a week and, between them, they need to work at least 24 hours a week. Jen therefore counts as being in full-time paid work.

When working out your normal hours if you are self-employed, HMRC says you can include not only the hours you spend providing orders or services but also those that are necessary to your self-employment – eg, trips to wholesalers and retailers, visits to potential clients, advertising or canvassing, cleaning the business or vehicles used as part of the business, bookkeeping and research work.[15]

If your hours fluctuate
Working out the number of hours you normally work is straightforward if:
- you do the same number of hours each and every week; *or*
- your hours vary, but you always do at least enough hours each week to count as being in full-time paid work.

However, if your weekly hours fluctuate, it can be more complicated. Unless you are a term-time only worker (see p200), there is no rule on how to average your hours. There is no requirement to work the necessary number of hours each and every week, and a common sense approach should be applied.[16] If you have a regular pattern of work (a recognised work cycle), HMRC says the hours you normally work are those that reflect an overall view of the pattern of your hours over a representative period, or over a year.[17] For example, if you always work two weeks on and two weeks off, you could argue that your hours should be averaged over a four-week period.

If you are in any doubt about what your normal hours are, contact HMRC and get advice. To avoid a potential overpayment, it is advisable to report your actual hours every four weeks. If you are unsure whether you are in full-time paid work, see p200.

Examples
Shane works in a residential project. He works three weeks on and one week off. When he is on, he works 40 hours a week. His average hours are 40 x 3 ÷ 4 = 30 hours a week. Shane can try to argue that he normally works 30 hours or more a week. As Shane is aged 45, does not have a physical or mental disability and has no children, he must work at least 30 hours a week. He therefore counts as being in full-time paid work.

Jana is contracted to do 15 hours a week. However, she gets regular overtime of three hours every other week. Her average hours are 15 + 18 ÷ 2 = 16.5 hours. Jana can try to argue that she normally works 16 hours or more a week. As Jana is a lone parent, she need only work 16 hours or more a week. She therefore counts as being in full-time paid work.

If you think your average hours have been calculated unfairly, you can request a mandatory reconsideration and then appeal. You should first work out whether you would be better off claiming IS/JSA/ESA/UC rather than WTC (see p1000).

Part 2: Main means-tested benefits and tax credits
Chapter 10: Working tax credit
1. Who can claim working tax credit

Term-time only workers

A term-time only worker rule applies if:[18]

- you work in a school, an educational establishment or other place of employment; *and*
- you have a recognisable 'work cycle' that lasts for a year; *and*
- your 'work cycle' includes periods of school holidays or similar vacations during which you do not work.

If the term-time only worker rule applies, periods when you are not working are ignored when deciding whether you are in full-time paid work. In practice, if the hours of work you do during term time mean you are in full-time paid work during term time, you also count as being in full-time paid work over the holidays. You can claim WTC during this period if your normal hours of work each week are sufficient during term time. Because the way hours are calculated is different for JSA and ESA, if you are not paid for the holidays, you may also be able to claim JSA (or if you have a partner, s/he may also be able to claim income-related ESA) during these periods if you satisfy the other qualifying conditions.

Example

Dee is 35 years old and has no children. She is a cleaner at a local college and works 35 hours a week, 36 weeks of the year. She does not work (and is not paid) when the students are on study leave and on holiday. The periods when Dee does not work are ignored. She is in full-time paid work during term time because she works 30 hours or more a week. She therefore counts as being in full-time paid work throughout the year and can claim WTC.

Note:

- It may not be clear whether you have a work cycle that lasts a year – eg, if you have only started your job recently or have a fixed-term contract that finishes at the end of the school term, or are employed on a casual or relief basis.[19] If you have an indefinite contract to work in term time only, you can argue that you have a yearly work cycle from the start.[20]
- If you work casually or intermittently (eg, you are a seasonal worker who works in the summer but you are unemployed the rest of the year), HMRC might say your work cycle is that part of the year in which you are working and that you do not count as being in full-time work when you are unemployed.[21]

If you are unsure whether you are in full-time paid work

If you are unsure whether the number of hours you normally work are sufficient at the date of your claim, contact HMRC to request a claim form. Bear in mind that a claim for WTC can be backdated for 31 days automatically (see p1459), so there is scope to postpone claiming WTC until you are certain. If time is running out and you are still uncertain, consider making a claim to protect your position.

You must declare how many hours you usually work on the claim form and then report any changes.

If you are refused WTC because neither you nor your partner are in full-time paid work for WTC purposes and within 14 days of that decision you claim IS or JSA, your claim for IS or JSA can be backdated to the date you claimed WTC.[22] This rule does not apply to ESA. However, your ESA claim can be backdated for up to three months.

People treated as being in full-time paid work

You or your partner are treated as being in full-time paid work in a number of situations.

Maternity, adoption, paternity or shared parental leave

You or your partner are treated as being in full-time paid work when:[23]

- you are being paid statutory maternity pay (SMP), statutory adoption pay (SAP), statutory paternity pay (SPP), statutory shared parental pay (SSPP) or maternity allowance (MA); *or*
- you are absent from work during the first 39 weeks of maternity leave, or adoption leave or two weeks of paternity leave; *or*
- you are absent from work during a period of statutory shared parental leave, but only during the period in which you would have been paid SSPP had you qualified.

If you are an employee, you are treated as being in full-time paid work from the start of the period above, provided you are in full-time paid work for WTC purposes immediately before the period begins. However, if this is not the case (eg, you are under 25, or are 25 or over but working less than 30 hours a week, and the child you and your partner are having or adopting is your first), you are treated as being in full-time paid work from the date of birth (or adoption), as long as you would have counted as being in full-time paid work had you been responsible for a child or qualifying young person immediately before the period begins.[24]

If you are self-employed, you count as being in full-time paid work during any period when the above would have applied had the work done in the week before the period began been as an employee.

If you do not return to work when your SMP, SAP, SPP, SSPP or MA ends, or after the allowed number of weeks of leave, you must notify HMRC, as you are no longer treated as being in full-time paid work under this rule. The statutory entitlement to maternity or adoption leave is 52 weeks, but you are only treated as working for tax credits purposes for the first 39 weeks.

Note: you should notify HMRC if you are in any of the above situations and provide an estimate of the current year income. This is because any MA is ignored as income for WTC, as is the first £100 a week of any SMP, SAP, SPP and SSPP.

Part 2: Main means-tested benefits and tax credits
Chapter 10: Working tax credit
1. Who can claim working tax credit

Periods of ill health

You or your partner are treated as being in full-time paid work when:[25]

- you are being paid SSP; *or*
- you are:
  - being paid IS because you are entitled to SSP or because you are incapable of work due to pregnancy; *or*
  - being paid ESA; *or*
  - getting national insurance (NI) credits because you are incapable of work or have limited capability for work.

The period treated as 'in work' while on IS, ESA or credits only applies for 28 weeks.

You must have been in full-time paid work for WTC purposes immediately before the period began.

If you are self-employed, you count as being in full-time paid work during any period when the above would have applied had the work done in the week before the period began been as an employee.

If you do not return to work when your SSP ceases (or after 28 weeks on IS, ESA or NI credits), you no longer count as being in full-time paid work under this rule.

Working tax credit run-on

If you or your partner stop work or reduce your hours, you can get 'WTC run-on'. You are treated as being in full-time paid work for the four weeks immediately after you stop work, or your hours reduce to fewer than the number you (or your partner) must do to count as being in full-time paid work.[26] This means you continue to qualify for:

- WTC for the four-week period, even if you would otherwise no longer count as being in full-time paid work;
- all the elements you were previously getting for that period (eg, the 30-hour element and the childcare element), even if the reduction in hours means you would otherwise lose entitlement to these.

You must report the change in your circumstances to HMRC within one month.

Other situations

You or your partner are treated as being in full-time paid work:

- if you were in full-time paid work within the past seven days.[27] This means you can make a new claim or continue to qualify for WTC – eg, during a short period between jobs or when you are on jury service for no more than one week;
- during any period when you are on strike or are suspended from work while complaints or allegations against you are investigated, provided you were in full-time paid work for WTC purposes immediately before the start of the

period. You must not be on strike for longer than 10 consecutive days when you should be working.[28]

Moving between situations in which you are treated as being in full-time work
The rules allow you to be treated as being in full-time paid work for WTC purposes for certain periods in the situations described on p201. If you move from one situation to another (eg, maternity leave followed by sickness leave), HMRC has confirmed that you can continue to be treated as being in work throughout the second period, provided you were treated as being in work immediately before it began.[29] However, the Upper Tribunal has held that you cannot continue to be treated as being in work if you move from a period on SSP to a period on ESA, or if you move from the four-week 'run-on' period (see p202) to a period on MA.[30]

People treated as not being in full-time paid work
You or your partner are treated as *not* being in full-time paid work during any period during which you are receiving pay in lieu of notice after you stop work, unless you continue to qualify under the four-week 'run-on' rule (see p202).[31] In addition, you or your partner are treated as *not* being in full-time paid work if:[32]
- you are a volunteer, or are working for a charity or voluntary organisation and are giving your services free (except for your expenses);
- you are providing care for someone who is staying with you temporarily but who is not normally a member of your household; *and*
  - the only payment you receive is from a health authority, a local authority, a voluntary organisation, a clinical commissioning group or the person her/himself for caring for her/him; *and*
  - the payment is disregarded as a tax-free payment under HMRC's 'rent-a-room' scheme (see p1442).
  Note: if you are an adult placement carer who has *not* opted for the 'rent-a-room' scheme, you *can* count as being in full-time paid work;[33]
- you are working on a training scheme and are being paid a training allowance (see below), unless the training allowance or the money you are being paid by the DWP is subject to income tax as a profit from work;[34]
- the only payment you receive, or expect to receive, is a sports award from a sports council;
- you are working while you are a sentenced or remand prisoner. This means you cannot qualify for WTC even if the work you do is outside the prison – eg, while you are on temporary release.

Training allowance
A '**training allowance**' is an allowance paid to maintain you or a member of your family:[35]
- by a government department or by or on behalf of the Secretary of State, Scottish Enterprise or the Highlands and Islands Enterprise; *and*

Part 2: Main means-tested benefits and tax credits
Chapter 10: Working tax credit
1. Who can claim working tax credit

– for the period, or part of a period, during which you are on a course provided or approved by, or under arrangements made by, any of the above.

Allowances paid to, or in respect of, you by a government department or by the Scottish government are not included if these are paid because you are a trainee teacher or on a full-time course of education, unless this is under arrangements made under section 2 of the Employment and Training Act 1973.

Students

You are not excluded from claiming WTC simply because you are a student. However, you must do sufficient hours of paid work in addition to your studies or during the holidays and the work must be expected to last for four weeks.

Is the work part of your course?

1. If you are paid in return for the work you do (eg, you are paid by an employer during a work placement), you can argue that you are in full-time paid work.

2. Any work you do in studying for a degree or other qualification does not count as full-time paid work – any grant or loan you receive is not paid in return for work done on the course.

3. You are not considered to be in full-time paid work if you are a student nurse, because the NHS bursary and other grants or loans you get are not payments for work done on the course and do not count as income for tax credit purposes.[36]

When calculating how much WTC you can get, student loans and most other student income are disregarded. See p1439 for what income counts.

Foster carers

If you are working sufficient hours as a foster carer (or approved kinship carer, in Scotland), you can qualify for WTC. HMRC generally accepts that foster carers meet the definition of self-employed (see p197), even if you have no profits and no loss for income tax purposes, and the hours of work you declare on your claim form should be accepted.[37] If you do more than one job, the total hours are added together. So, if you are doing work in addition to foster caring, the hours from the other work can be added to those spent foster caring.

Fostering allowances (and kinship care allowances, in Scotland) that qualify for tax relief are generally ignored when calculating your WTC. See p1444 for further information.

Would you be better off claiming another benefit instead?

If you or your partner are a foster carer (or approved kinship carer, in Scotland) receiving a payment for looking after a child from a local authority or voluntary organisation, you are (or s/he is) treated as *not* being in full-time paid work for IS, JSA and ESA (see p997). Consider how you would be better off financially.

2. The rules about your age

You (and your partner) must be aged at least 16 to make a claim for working tax credit (WTC).[38] There is no upper age limit.

If you are under 25, you can only qualify for WTC if you work at least 16 hours a week and you are a disabled worker or are responsible for a child in the circumstances described on p196.

3. People included in the claim

If you are a single person, you claim working tax credit (WTC) for yourself.[39] However, if you are a member of a couple (see p1451), you must claim WTC jointly with your partner.[40] WTC includes elements for you and your partner and for the special needs of either of you (see Chapter 59). When working out how much WTC you get, your partner's income is added to yours (see Chapter 60). **Note:** if you claim jointly with your partner but then cease to count as a couple (or you claim as a single person but then become a member of a couple), your entitlement to WTC ends. You should therefore report this change in your circumstances and claim tax credits as a single person (or a couple) immediately.

If you are responsible for at least one child or qualifying young person:

- you (or your partner) must work at least 16 hours a week to qualify for WTC (although if you are a member of a couple, in most cases your combined hours must be at least 24 a week);
- and you are a couple and one of you works at least 16 hours a week, your hours of work can be added to those of your partner to enable you to qualify for the 30-hour element (see p1412);
- you (and your partner) might qualify for the childcare element of WTC if you pay for childcare.

See p182 for who counts as a child or qualifying young person. The rules are the same as for child tax credit (CTC).[41] The terms 'child' or 'children' in this chapter include qualifying young people.

For when you count as responsible for a child, see p184. HM Revenue and Customs uses the same test as for CTC.[42]

4. The amount of working tax credit

The amount of working tax credit (WTC) you get depends on:

- your maximum WTC. This is made up of a combination of 'elements' (see Chapter 59 for how you qualify for these):

Part 2: Main means-tested benefits and tax credits
Chapter 10: Working tax credit
4. The amount of working tax credit

- basic element (£1,960 a year);
- disabled worker element (£3,000 a year). More than one can be included if you are a member of a couple and you both qualify;
- lone parent/couple element (£2,010 a year);
- 30-hour element (£810 a year);
- severe disability element (£1,290 a year). More than one can be included if you are a member of a couple and you both qualify;
- childcare element;
- how much income you have (see Chapter 60); *and*
- the 'income threshold figure'.

If you are on a means-tested benefit

Being on income support (IS), income-based jobseeker's allowance (JSA), income-related employment and support allowance (ESA) or pension credit (PC) is an automatic passport to maximum WTC.[43] You therefore do not need to work out your income. In these circumstances, WTC equals maximum WTC. **Note:** this does not apply while you are getting 'WTC run-on' (see p202).

Can you claim a means-tested benefit with working tax credit?

There are not many situations in which you can claim IS, income-based JSA or income-related ESA at the same time as WTC. This is because you cannot claim IS or JSA if you or your partner are in full-time paid work for IS/JSA purposes, and you cannot claim income-related ESA if you do *any* work (unless this is work you may do while claiming (see p1021) or if your partner is in full-time paid work for ESA purposes. However, you might be able to claim both – eg, if you (or your partner) are a 'term-time only' worker or are off sick. It does not matter how many hours you (or your partner) work for PC. However, WTC counts in full as income for IS, income-based JSA, income-related ESA and PC.

If you are not on a means-tested benefit

If you are not on IS, income-based JSA, income-related ESA or PC, follow the steps below to calculate your WTC.

- **Step one:** work out your 'relevant period' (see p1407).
- **Step two:** work out your maximum entitlement (your maximum WTC) for the relevant period (see p1421).
- **Step three:** work out your 'relevant income' (see p1421 and p1429).
- **Step four:** compare your income with the 'income threshold figure' for the relevant period – £6,420 a year for WTC.[44]
- **Step five:** calculate your WTC entitlement for the relevant period (see p1422). If your income is less than the 'income threshold figure', WTC equals your maximum WTC. If your income exceeds the 'income threshold figure', your maximum WTC is reduced by 41 per cent of the excess.

You may also be entitled to child tax credit. Full details of both calculations are in Chapter 59.

5. Claims and backdating

The general rules on claiming, backdating and how your claim can be renewed at the end of the year are in Chapter 61. This section gives an outline of the rules on claims for working tax credit (WTC).

Making a claim

Your first claim for WTC must usually be made in writing on Form TC600. You use the same form for WTC and for child tax credit (CTC). See p1453 for more information about how and where to make a claim. Keep a copy of your claim form in case queries arise.

You can amend or withdraw your claim before you are given notice of the decision on it.[45]

Who should claim

If you are a member of a couple, you must make a joint claim with your partner. If you are not a member of a couple, you claim for yourself. For information about who counts as a couple for tax credit purposes, see p1451. If you cannot make your claim yourself, an 'appointee' (see p1453) can claim on your behalf.

Information to support your claim

When you claim WTC, you must:[46]
- satisfy the national insurance number requirement (see p1455);
- provide proof of your identity, if required;
- supply information to support your claim (see p1455).

It is important that you provide all the information required. If you do not do so, a decision may be delayed, or HMRC may decide to reject your claim as not validly made. Caselaw has established that you have a right of appeal (after a mandatory reconsideration) against a decision to reject a tax credits claim that is not made on the correct form or that does not include all the required information, particularly if you have a reasonable excuse for not supplying the information.[47] If HMRC requires further information, see p1457 for details of the time you must be given to provide this and what happens if you fail to do so.

When to claim

The general rule is that your claim runs from the date it is received by HMRC.[48] You cannot make a claim in advance of the tax year in which you are claiming,

Part 2: Main means-tested benefits and tax credits
Chapter 10: Working tax credit
6. Getting paid

but you *can* claim WTC in advance of starting work, provided you expect to start work within seven days and will be entitled to WTC within seven days of starting work.[49] However, you may be able to get your claim backdated. **Note:** if you claimed universal credit when you should have claimed WTC, see p1454.

Is your income currently too high?

Awards of WTC are always based on annual income. HMRC bases the initial award of WTC on your (and your partner's) *previous* tax year's income. If you think your income may be too high to qualify for WTC currently, you can make a 'protective claim' so you do not lose out if your income is expected to fall (see p1454).

Backdating your claim

It is very important to claim in time. A claim for WTC can usually only be backdated for a maximum of 31 days.[50] See p1459 for further information.

Note: there is a special backdating rule if you claim WTC when you are awarded a qualifying benefit – eg, disability living allowance, personal independence payment or armed forces independence payment (see p1459). Under this rule, your WTC can be backdated more than 31 days.

Renewal awards

At the end of the tax year in which you claimed WTC, you (and your partner if you are a member of a couple) receive an 'annual review' from HMRC asking you to confirm or declare your income and your household circumstances for the previous tax year (see p1468). If required, you must reply within a strict time limit. HMRC then makes a final decision, based on your actual income during the tax year. It decides whether you were entitled to WTC and, if so, the amount of your award. HMRC also uses the information about your income and household circumstances for the previous tax year to renew your award for the next tax year.[51] Some awards are finalised and renewed automatically on the information held by HMRC, as shown on your annual review, but you must check this and report any errors or changes. **Note:** if you have a 'nil award', you may be given notice that your claim will not be renewed unless you specifically request this.

6. Getting paid

This section gives an outline of the rules on payment of working tax credit (WTC). For more information about getting paid, see p1460.

Payment of WTC is normally made into your bank (or similar) account. If you make a joint claim, any WTC to which you are entitled towards your childcare expenses is paid to whomever you nominated on the claim form as the main carer of your child(ren) (see p1460), but cannot be paid directly to the childcare provider. If you are unable to act for yourself, payment can be made to someone on your behalf – called your 'appointee' (see p1453).[52]

When is working tax credit paid?
You are paid every week or every four weeks, whichever you choose on the claim form, although HM Revenue and Customs (HMRC) can decide how often.[53]

You can be paid by cheque while your account arrangements are finalised.
Note:
- You can be disqualified from being paid WTC if you have committed a benefit offence (see p1268).
- If you have forgotten your PIN, see p1173. The issues are the same as for benefits.
- If payment of your WTC is delayed and this is causing hardship, ask HMRC to make a 'next day/same day payment'. If you wish to complain about how your claim has been dealt with, see p1398. You might be able to claim compensation (see p1396).
- If payment of your WTC is suspended or postponed, see p1461.
- If you are overpaid WTC, you might have to repay it (see Chapter 62). In some cases, interest can be added to the overpayment. In some circumstances, you may have to pay a penalty (see p1490). If you have been accused of fraud, see Chapter 63.

Change of circumstances

Your award of WTC is made on the basis of your (and your partner's) previous year's income and your personal circumstances on the date of your claim. If your current year's income or your personal circumstances change, your award of WTC can be amended. Remember the following.
- There are some changes you *must* report to HMRC (see p1462). If you fail to do so within one month, you might be given a financial penalty. Some changes end your entitlement to WTC and you have to make a fresh claim.
- Other changes that affect your maximum entitlement to WTC are not compulsory to report, so you cannot be given a penalty, but should still be reported to avoid an underpayment or overpayment – eg, when your hours increase to 30 or more so you would qualify for a 30-hour element, or the rate of your partner's personal independence payment award is reduced so you no longer qualify for the severe disability element (see p1464). Changes that increase your maximum entitlement to WTC can generally only be backdated one month from when you notify HMRC. Changes that decrease entitlement generally take effect from the date of change, so may result in an overpayment.

Part 2: Main means-tested benefits and tax credits
Chapter 10: Working tax credit
7. Tax, other benefits and the benefit cap

- It is optional to report an estimated change in your current year's income (see p1465). Your actual income is always taken into account at the end of the tax year, but you may want to consider reporting an estimate sooner to avoid an overpayment or underpayment of WTC.

If you are claiming WTC and you only qualify for the lone parent or childcare element because you (or your partner) are responsible for a child and the child dies, you are paid WTC for a further eight weeks (or to the date your child would have turned 20, if this is earlier) as if this had not happened.[54] This is only the case if you would have continued to qualify for the element but for the child's death. After that period, you may continue to qualify for WTC – eg, if you still satisfy the means test and work sufficient hours to count as being in full-time paid work.

Note:
- If you become a member of a couple with someone entitled to universal credit, your entitlement to WTC ends (see p28).
- If you apply for, and are entitled to, payments under the new tax-free childcare scheme, your WTC award is terminated, as you cannot get both at the same time. The tax-free childcare scheme is due to be introduced in early 2017. See p864 for more details.

7. Tax, other benefits and the benefit cap

Tax

Working tax credit (WTC) is not taxable.

Means-tested benefits and tax credits

WTC counts as income for income support (IS), income-based jobseeker's allowance (JSA), income-related employment and support allowance (ESA), pension credit (PC) and housing benefit (HB). **Note:**
- You may be able to claim IS/income-based JSA/income-related ESA or WTC, for example, if your partner works more than 16 but less than 24 hours a week. You may be able to claim both IS/income-based JSA/income-related ESA and WTC at the same time in some circumstances (see p1000).
- There is no rule that prevents you or your partner doing full-time paid work while claiming PC, so you can claim WTC at the same time as PC.
- In some cases, if you are an owner occupier and have to pay housing costs (see Chapter 20), you might be better off financially if you claim IS, income-based JSA, income-related ESA or PC.
- If you qualify for HB, you might get an additional earnings disregard (see p281 and p322).

- WTC does not count as income for universal credit (UC), but there are very limited circumstances when you can be entitled to WTC during an assessment period for UC.[55] This can happen if you become a new partner of a UC claimant (see p28), in which case her/his assessment period continues on the same date, so can cover a period in which you were entitled to WTC before becoming a couple.[56]
- If you get arrears of WTC, these count as capital for means-tested benefits and can be disregarded in some circumstances (see p367 and p393).

If you have dependent children (including a 'qualifying young person'), you might qualify for child tax credit (CTC) in addition to WTC.

Non-means-tested benefits

In some situations, while you are receiving WTC you get national insurance credits (see p975).

WTC can be paid in addition to any non-means-tested benefits to which you (or your partner) are entitled, but see Chapter 60 for which of these benefits may be taken into account as income for WTC. Qualifying for certain non-means-tested benefits means you may also qualify for the disabled worker element or severe disability element of WTC.

The benefit cap

In some cases, there is a limit on the total amount of specified benefits you can receive (a 'benefit cap'). WTC is *not* one of the specified benefits. The benefit cap does *not* apply if you or your partner are entitled to WTC. See p1180 for further information.

Passports and other sources of help

If you are entitled to WTC, you may also qualify for health benefits, such as free prescriptions (see Chapter 30). You do not have to satisfy the means test if your gross annual income is below a set amount and you are getting WTC which includes a disabled worker element or a severe disability element, or CTC with your WTC.

You may qualify for a Sure Start maternity grant or a social fund funeral expenses payment. You may be entitled to a council tax reduction (see p854).

Note: if you apply for, and are entitled to, payments under the new tax-free childcare scheme, your WTC award is terminated, as you cannot get both at the same time. See p864 for more details.

Part 2: Main means-tested benefits and tax credits
Chapter 10: Working tax credit
Notes

Notes

1. Who can claim working tax credit
1 ss3(3) and (7), 10 and 42 TCA 2002; regs 4-8 WTC(EMR) Regs; reg 3 TC(R) Regs; reg 3 TC(Imm) Regs
2 Art 7(4) and (5) WRA(No.23)O
3 s10(1) TCA 2002
4 Reg 4(1) (second condition) WTC(EMR) Regs
5 Reg 4(1) (first condition) WTC(EMR) Regs
6 Reg 4(1) (third condition) WTC(EMR) Regs
7 Reg 4(1) (fourth condition) WTC(EMR) Regs
8 Reg 4(3) WTC(EMR) Regs
9 Reg 4(4)(b) WTC(EMR) Regs
10 Reg 4(5) WTC(EMR) Regs
11 Reg 4(4)(a) WTC(EMR) Regs
12 Reg 2(1) WTC(EMR) Regs
13 Reg 4(3) WTC(EMR) Regs
14 TCTM 02451-52
15 TCTM 02453
16 CTC/2103/2006
17 TCTM 02457
18 Reg 7 WTC(EMR) Regs; *Stafford and Banks v CAO* [2001] UKHL 33 (HL), reported as R(IS) 15/01
19 R(JSA) 8/03; CIS/914/1997; CJSA/2759/1998
20 R(JSA) 5/02
21 R(JSA) 1/07; *Saunderson v SSWP* [2012] ScotCS CSIH 10
22 Reg 6(28) SS(C&P) Regs
23 Reg 5 WTC(EMR) Regs
24 Reg 5A WTC(EMR) Regs
25 Reg 6 WTC(EMR) Regs
26 Reg 7D WTC(EMR) Regs
27 Reg 8 WTC(EMR) Regs
28 Regs 7A and 7B WTC(EMR) Regs
29 HMRC Benefits and Credits Consultation Group email to CPAG, 20 December 2007
30 *TK v HMRC* [2016] UKUT 45 (AAC); *AG v HMRC* [2017] UKUT 67
31 Reg 7C WTC(EMR) Regs
32 Reg 4(2) WTC(EMR) Regs
33 TCTM 02440
34 Reg 4(2)(c) and (d) and (2A) WTC(EMR) Regs
35 Reg 2(1) WTC(EMR) Regs
36 R(FIS) 1/83; R(FIS) 1/86; TCTM 02431
37 TCTM 02440

2. The rules about your age
38 s3(3) TCA 2002

3. People included in the claim
39 s3(3)(b) TCA 2002
40 s3(3)(a) and (5A) TCA 2002; CTC/3864/2004; R(TC) 1/07
41 Reg 2, definition of 'child' and 'qualifying young person', WTC(EMR) Regs
42 Reg 2(2) WTC(EMR) Regs

4. The amount of working tax credit
43 ss7(2) and 13 TCA 2002; reg 4 TC(ITDR) Regs
44 Reg 3(2) TC(ITDR) Regs

5. Claims and backdating
45 Reg 5(7) TC(CN) Regs; R(IS) 5/05
46 Reg 5(3)-(6) TC(CN) Regs
47 *CI v HMRC (TC)* [2014] UKUT 158 (AAC)
48 s5(2) TCA 2002
49 Reg 10 TC(CN) Regs
50 Reg 7 TC(CN) Regs
51 Regs 11 and 12 TC(CN) Regs

6. Getting paid
52 s24(3) TCA 2002; reg 6 TC(PC) Regs
53 Regs 8 and 13 TC(PC) Regs
54 Reg 19 WTC(EMR) Regs; reg 6 CTC Regs

7. Tax, other benefits and the benefit cap
55 Reg 66 UC Regs
56 Reg 5(2)(b)(iii) UC(TP) Regs; reg 21(3B) UC Regs

Part 3

General rules for means-tested benefits

Chapter 11

* *

People included in the claim

This chapter covers:
1. Couples (below)
2. Children (p220)
3. Households (p225)

This chapter covers the rules for means-tested benefits. For child tax credit and working tax credit, see Chapters 9 and 10.

Key facts

- Whether you count as a member of a couple or have children included in your claim can be relevant for all the means-tested benefits.
- You count as a member of a couple if you are married or in a civil partnership and are living in the same household with your partner. You also count as a couple if you are not married or in a civil partnership, but are living with your partner as if you were living together as a married couple.
- A child or 'qualifying young person' can be included as part of your family in your claim if you are responsible for her/him. For all benefits except universal credit (UC), s/he must also live in your household. For UC, s/he must normally live with you.
- You can continue to count as a couple, and children and young people can continue to be included in your claim, while you are living apart temporarily.

---

1. Couples

You and your partner count as a 'couple' for means-tested benefit purposes if you are both 16 or over and you are:[1]
- married or civil partners and members of the same household; *or*
- not married or civil partners but 'living together as a married couple'.

For when you count as living in the same 'household', see p225. **Note:** for pension credit (PC) only, if your partner is a 'person subject to immigration control' (see p1516), you are treated as not being members of the same household and so do not count as a couple.[2]

Part 3: General rules for means-tested benefits
Chapter 11: People included in the claim
1. Couples

Spouse or civil partner

Being married to someone does not necessarily mean that you cannot be treated as part of a couple with someone else instead.[3]

There are special rules if you are polygamously married.[4] You count as 'polygamously married' if you are married to more than one person and your marriages took place in a country that permits polygamy (see also p544).[5] For employment and support allowance (ESA) only, you and all your partners must also be living in the same household (see p225).

You count as someone's **civil partner** if you are both of the same sex and have been registered as her/his civil partner.

Living together as a married couple

You count as a couple if you are 'living together as a married couple'. This is referred to as 'cohabiting' in this *Handbook*. This can apply to you if are in a different or a same-sex relationship.[6]

If you are awarded income support (IS), income-based jobseeker's allowance (JSA) or income-related ESA, usually the local authority should not make a separate decision about whether you are cohabiting when considering your claim for housing benefit (HB).[7] However, if the local authority thinks that the benefit claim on which your HB claim is based is fraudulent, it can decide that you are not entitled to HB.[8] If you have not been awarded IS, income-based JSA, income-related ESA or PC, the local authority must consider whether you are cohabiting and may reach a different conclusion from that of the DWP.[9]

The factors below are used as 'signposts' to determine whether or not you are cohabiting.[10] No one factor, in itself, is conclusive, as it is your overall relationship and your particular circumstances that are looked at.[11] Caselaw says that the 'emotional aspect' of the relationship (your interdependence, devotion, love and affection) should be considered in addition to the factors below.[12] This does not necessarily conflict with the factors below but, like your individual circumstances, should not be regarded as conclusive. For example, if your partner stays with you for three nights or more a week, you should not automatically be treated as living together as a couple.

Are you cohabiting?

1. Do you live in the same household? See p217.

2. Do you have a sexual relationship? See p217.

3. What are your financial arrangements? See p217.

4. Is your relationship stable? See p217.

5. Do you have children? See p217.

6. How do you appear in public? See p218.

Living in the same household

If you live in the same household, you may be treated as cohabiting. For what counts as a 'household', see p225.

Even if you *do* share a household, you may not be cohabiting. It is essential to look at *why* two people are in the same household.[13] For example, if you are living in the same household for 'care, companionship and mutual convenience', you can argue that you are not 'living together as husband and wife'.[14]

Being in a sexual relationship

In practice, a decision maker may not ask you about the existence of a sexual relationship, in which case s/he only has the information if you volunteer it. However, if you are appealing about whether you are a member of a couple, the First-tier Tribunal should consider this and may well ask you about it.[15] If you do not have a sexual relationship, you should make this known (and perhaps offer to show your separate sleeping arrangements).

Having a sexual relationship is not sufficient, by itself, to prove you are cohabiting. If you have never had a sexual relationship, there is a strong (but not necessarily conclusive) presumption that you are not cohabiting.[16] A couple who abstain from a sexual relationship before marriage should not be counted as cohabiting until they are formally married.[17]

Your financial arrangements

If one person is supported by the other or your household expenses are shared, this may be treated as evidence that you are cohabiting. However, it is important to consider how expenses are shared. There is a difference between, on the one hand, paying a fixed weekly contribution or rigidly sharing bills 50/50 (which does *not* suggest cohabitation) and, on the other hand, a common fund for income and expenditure (which might).

A stable relationship

Marriage and civil partnership are expected to be stable and lasting and so an occasional or brief association should not be regarded as cohabitation. However, the fact that your relationship is stable does not make it cohabitation – eg, you can have a stable relationship as a landlord and lodger, but not be cohabiting.

The way you spend your time together, the activities you undertake together and the things you do for each other are relevant, so questions about how you spend your holidays and how you organise the shopping, the laundry and cleaning may be important.

Children

If you have had a child together and live in the same household as the other parent, there is a strong (but not conclusive) presumption of cohabitation.

Part 3: General rules for means-tested benefits
Chapter 11: People included in the claim
1. Couples

Your appearance in public

Decision makers may check the electoral roll and claims for other benefits to see if you present yourselves as a couple. Many couples retain their separate single identities publicly. If you do not have a committed emotional loving relationship that is publicly acknowledged, you can argue that you are not living together as a married couple.[18]

Couples living apart

If you separate permanently (ie, you do not intend to resume living with your partner), you no longer count as a couple.[19] When deciding whether you intend to resume living together or not, your intention must be 'unqualified' – ie, it must not depend on something over which you have no control, such as the right of entry to the UK being granted by the Home Office[20] or the offer of a suitable job.[21]

If you and your partner are living apart temporarily, you continue to count as a couple because you are still treated as members of the same household. However, if you were not living together in the same household before your time apart, you should not be regarded as living apart temporarily.[22] Your former household need not have been in this country.[23] However, there are exceptions to this rule (see below).

Note: if you and your partner continue to count as a couple while you are temporarily living apart, your partner's income and capital continue to be treated as yours. However, in certain situations, except for universal credit (UC), your benefit is calculated in a different way (see p923 and p931).

Exceptions

Even if you and your partner are only living apart temporarily, **you no longer count as a couple if:**

- **for IS, income-based JSA, income-related ESA, PC and HB,** you are likely to be separated for more than 52 weeks. However, you still count as a couple if you are unlikely to be separated for 'substantially' longer than 52 weeks and there are exceptional circumstances, such as a stay in hospital, or having no control over the length of the absence;[24]
- **for UC,** you have been separated (or expect to be separated) for more than six months.[25] If either you or your partner go abroad, see p1605. If your partner is a prisoner, serving a sentence while in hospital or a member of a religious order who is fully maintained by that order, you cannot get UC as a couple, but you can claim as a single person;
- **for IS, income-based JSA, income-related ESA and PC:**[26]
    - either of you are in custody;
    - either of you are released on temporary licence from prison;
    - either of you are detained in a high security psychiatric hospital (in Scotland, a 'state hospital') under the mental health provisions;

- either of you are staying permanently in a care home, an Abbeyfield Home or an independent hospital;
- you are abroad and do not qualify for benefit while temporarily absent from Great Britain. For when you qualify while temporarily absent and for when your partner is abroad, see p1597 (for IS), p1599 (for income-based JSA), p1594 (for income-related ESA) and p1601 (for PC).

Challenging a decision that you are a couple

Your benefit may be stopped or adjusted if the decision maker decides you are a member of a couple.

The decision maker might decide that you are cohabiting if someone regularly stays overnight, even though you might have none of the long-term commitments generally associated with marriage or a civil partnership. Couples with no sexual relationship who live together (eg, as landlord and lodger or as flat sharers) also sometimes fall foul of the rule. People who provide mutual support and share household expenses are not necessarily cohabiting.[27]

If you disagree with a decision that you are a couple, you can apply for a revision or supersession (see Chapter 54), or appeal to the First-tier Tribunal (see Chapter 55). You must apply for a mandatory reconsideration before you can appeal.

How do you show that you are not a couple?

1. Consider carefully what evidence to submit:
- if you are married or in a civil partnership, to show that you are not living in the same household with your spouse or civil partner;
- if you are not married or in a civil partnership, in relation to each of the six questions on p216, the emotional aspect of your relationship and any other matters you consider relevant.

2. Provide evidence if the other person has another address (eg, a rent book and other household bills), receipts for board and lodging, statements from friends and relatives, or evidence of a formal separation, divorce proceedings or a dissolution application or order.

You do not have to prove that you are not a couple when you first claim benefit, but you must provide any information that is reasonably required to decide your claim.[28] Neither party has the burden of proof in this situation – a decision should simply be made on all the evidence available.[29] In contrast, if your benefit as a single person is stopped because it is alleged that you are a couple, the burden of proof is on the decision maker to prove that you are.[30]

If your benefit is stopped because it is decided that you are a couple, challenge the decision and reapply immediately if your circumstances change. Also apply for any other benefits for which you might qualify – eg, HB, as the local authority

Part 3: General rules for means-tested benefits
Chapter 11: People included in the claim
2. Children

may reach a different decision to the DWP.[31] You should apply for other benefits for which you previously automatically qualified – eg, health benefits (see Chapter 29).

If you are still entitled to a means-tested benefit as a couple, you should be paid on that basis.

2. Children

A child (see below for who counts) may count as part of your family and be included in your benefit claim. However, you can only get additional amounts in your benefit for her/him in certain circumstances.

A child is part of your family for benefit purposes and is included in your claim if:

- for income support (IS), income-based jobseeker's allowance (JSA), income-related employment and support allowance (ESA) and housing benefit (HB):
  - you or your partner are 'responsible' for her/him (see p222); *and*
  - s/he is living in your 'household' (see p223);[32]
- for universal credit (UC), you or your partner are 'responsible' for her/him – ie, s/he 'normally lives' with you (see p222).[33]

You do not have to be the child's parent.

A child stops being included in your claim when you no longer fulfil the conditions described above or s/he no longer counts as a child (see below).

Note: children are not included in claims for pension credit (PC). Instead, you must claim child tax credit (CTC) for the child.

If a child is part of your family for benefit purposes and is included in your claim, you can get an additional amount included in your HB and UC. You can only get an additional amount for a child in your IS or income-based JSA if:

- you already have a current claim for IS or income-based JSA that began before 6 April 2004; *and*
- you had a child included in that claim before 6 April 2004 and you have not been awarded CTC.

Note: from 6 April 2017, you only get additional amounts in your benefit for a maximum of two children. For more information, see p234 for HB, IS and income-based JSA and p258 for UC.

ESA does not include additional amounts for children.[34]

Who counts as a child

A person usually counts as a child if:[35]

- s/he is aged under 16; *or*

- s/he is aged 16 or over but under 20 and counts as a 'qualifying young person' for child benefit purposes. This includes, for example, most young people who are at school or college full time studying for GCSEs or A levels (or equivalent), or who are doing approved training. See p572 for who counts as a qualifying young person. A young person can continue to count as a child after s/he has left school or training until the 'terminal date' (see p575) or the end of the child benefit 'extension period' (see p575); *or*
- for UC, s/he is aged 16 or over but under 20 and counts as a 'qualifying young person' under the UC rules. This includes most young people studying for GCSEs or A levels or who are doing approved training. Specifically, it means someone who:[36]
  - is aged 16 but who has not reached 1 September following her/his 16th birthday; *or*
  - is aged 16–19 but who has not yet reached 1 September following her/his 19th birthday, and has been accepted for (or has enrolled on) approved training or non-advanced education at school or college, or another institution approved by the Secretary of State (see below). During term time there must be more than 12 hours on average a week of tuition, practical work, supervised study and examinations. Meal breaks and unsupervised study are not included.

Note: a 19-year-old must have started (or been accepted for or enrolled on) the education or training before reaching 19 in order to count as a qualifying young person.

Approved training and non-advanced education for universal credit
'**Approved training**' is training that is approved by the DWP and provided under section 2(1) of the Employment and Training Act 1973 or section 2(3) of the Enterprise and New Towns (Scotland) Act 1990.
A course is '**non-advanced**' if it is below the level of 'advanced education'. Courses that count as advanced education include university degrees and other courses above GCSE, A level and Scottish National Qualifications above higher or advanced higher level.[37] See p573 for more examples of advanced and non-advanced courses.

Who does not count as a child

A person does *not* count as a child if:[38]
- s/he is getting certain benefits or tax credits in her/his own right and so does not count as a qualifying young person (see p581). For IS and income-based JSA, s/he may not count as a child if s/he is entitled to one of these benefits but is not getting it – eg, because it has been suspended; *or*

Part 3: General rules for means-tested benefits
Chapter 11: People included in the claim
2. Children

- s/he is excluded from entitlement to IS, income-based JSA and HB because s/he is aged 16 or 17, has left local authority care on or after 1 October 2001 and certain other conditions apply (see p936); *or*
- for UC, s/he is receiving UC, ESA or JSA in her/his own right.

Responsibility for a child

For IS, income-based JSA (but not joint-claim JSA), income-related ESA and HB, a child is included in your claim if you are 'responsible' for her/him and s/he is living in your 'household'. For UC, a child is included in your claim if you are 'responsible' for her/him.

- **You are treated as responsible for a child for IS** if you get child benefit for her/him (see Chapter 26).[39] If no one gets child benefit, you are responsible if you are the only one who has applied for it. In all other cases, the person responsible is the person with whom the child usually lives.[40] If a child for whom you are responsible gets child benefit for another child, you are also responsible for that child.[41]
- **You are treated as responsible for a child for JSA** if either you get child benefit for her/him or, if no one gets child benefit for her/him, the child 'usually lives' with you or you are the only person who has applied for child benefit.[42] If you share responsibility for the child, even if you do not get child benefit for her/him, you might be regarded as responsible for her/him if you are the 'substantial minority carer' – ie, you have the child with you for at least 104 nights a year.[43] Get advice if necessary. If a child for whom you are responsible gets child benefit for another child, you are also responsible for that child. **Note:** the rules for when you count as responsible for a child for the purposes of deciding whether you must claim joint-claim JSA are different (see p120).[44]
- **You are treated as responsible for a child for ESA** if s/he 'usually lives' with you. This is not defined in the rules.[45]
- **You are treated as responsible for a child for HB** if the child is 'normally living' with you.[46] This means that s/he spends more time with you than with anyone else.[47] If it is unclear in whose household the child lives, or if s/he spends an equal amount of time with two parents in different homes (this may not mean literally three and a half days with each parent[48]), you are treated as having responsibility if:[49]
  - you get child benefit for her/him (see Chapter 26);
  - no one gets child benefit, but you have applied for it;
  - no one has applied for child benefit, or both of you have applied, but you appear to have the most responsibility.

Note: an argument that a shared carer who does not get child benefit for a child can still be regarded as responsible for her/him for HB has been rejected by the Upper Tribunal. It was also held that 'substantial minority carers' cannot be regarded as responsible for a child for HB.[50]

- **You are treated as responsible for a child for UC** if s/he 'normally lives' with you. Although the UC rules do not say so, this is likely to mean that s/he spends more time with you than with anyone else. If the child normally lives with two (or more) people who are not a couple (eg, if s/he lives in the homes of separated parents), the person who is responsible is whoever has the 'main responsibility'. In this situation, the people concerned can agree who this is. The DWP can decide otherwise or, if there is no agreement, decide which person has the main responsibility.[51] You cannot be treated as responsible for a child during any period in which s/he is:[52]
  - looked after by a local authority, except planned short breaks in local authority care to provide respite care for the person who normally looks after her/him, and except if the child is living with you and you are her/his parent or (unless you are a foster parent) someone with parental responsibility for her/him; *or*
  - a prisoner; *or*
  - temporarily absent from your household (see p225) and has been absent for more than six months, including if this is for medical treatment abroad; *or*
  - (after one month) absent from Great Britain for a reason other than medical treatment.

For HB, it is only necessary to look at who gets child benefit when it is unclear in whose household the child *normally* lives. For IS, it is essential to look first at who gets child benefit, and only if this is not decisive is it relevant to look at where the child *usually* lives. This difference may mean, for example, that in some situations, one parent may be able to claim IS for a child while the other parent can claim HB for the same child at the same time.

A child can only be the responsibility of one person in any week for IS, income-based JSA and HB.[53] The rules for ESA do not expressly say this but, in any case, a person can only be responsible for a child if s/he usually lives with her/him. If benefit is paid for a child, it cannot be split between parents if a child divides her/his time equally between their two homes. The person who has main responsibility for the child has the child included in her/his claim for UC.

Living in the same household

In addition to being responsible for her/him, a child is only included in your claim if s/he is a member of the same household. If you count as responsible for a child, s/he is usually treated as a member of your household, despite any temporary absence. For exceptions to the rule, see p224. For what 'household' means, see p225.

Note: there is no 'household' test for UC. You must simply be 'responsible' for the child.

Part 3: General rules for means-tested benefits
Chapter 11: People included in the claim
2. Children

When a child does not count as a member of your household

A child does *not* count as a member of your household if:[54]

- **for IS, JSA, ESA and HB,** s/he is not living with you and:
  - has no intention of resuming living with you; *or*
  - is likely to be absent for more than 52 weeks, unless there are exceptional circumstances, such as being in hospital, or if you have no control over the length of absence and the absence is unlikely to be substantially longer than 52 weeks;
- **for IS, JSA, ESA and HB:**
  - s/he is being fostered by you or your partner following a formal placement by social services. This does not apply if you are fostering privately or if social services has made a less formal arrangement for the child to live with you;
  - s/he is living with you or your partner prior to adoption and has been placed by social services or an adoption agency;
  - s/he is boarded out with you or your partner, whether or not with a view to adoption (for JSA, ESA and HB only);
  - s/he has been placed with someone else prior to adoption;
  - s/he is in the care of, or being looked after by, the local authority and not living with you. However, s/he counts as a member of your household on the days when s/he comes home – eg, for the weekend or a holiday.[55] Make sure you tell the decision maker in good time. For HB, your child counts as a member of the household for all that week whether s/he returns for all or only part of it;[56]
- **for IS, JSA and ESA,** s/he is not living with you and:
  - has been in hospital or in a local authority home (for non-temporary accommodation) for more than 12 weeks and has not been in regular contact with you or other members of your household. The 12 weeks run from the date s/he went into hospital or the home, or from the date you claim IS/JSA/ESA, if later.[57] However, the 12 weeks run from the date s/he went into the hospital or home if:[58]
    - you were getting income-based JSA immediately before your claim for IS; *or*
    - you were getting IS or income-related ESA immediately before your claim for JSA; *or*
    - you were getting IS or income-based JSA immediately before your claim for ESA;
  - is in custody. Note that a child can still be included in your claim for any periods s/he spends at home;[59]
  - has been abroad for more than four weeks, or for more than eight weeks (26 weeks for ESA) to get medical treatment.[60] The four-/eight-/26-week period runs from the day s/he went abroad, or from the day you claim IS/JSA/ESA, if later. However, the four-/eight-/26-week period is calculated from the day after the child went abroad if:[61]

- you were getting income-based JSA immediately before your claim for IS; *or*
- you were getting IS or income-related ESA immediately before your claim for JSA; *or*
- you were getting IS or income-based JSA immediately before your claim for ESA;
- **for IS and income-based JSA**, s/he is living with you and away from her/his parental or usual home in order to attend school. The child is not included in your claim, but remains a member of her/his parent's household.[62]

---

3. Households

The term **'household'** is not defined. Whether you should be treated as members of the same household is decided on the particular facts of your case. In all cases, you must spend the major part of your time in the same household. **Note:** for pension credit only, if your partner is a 'person subject to immigration control' (see p1516), you are treated as *not* being members of the same household and so do not count as a couple.[63]

A house or flat can contain a number of separate households and if one person has exclusive occupation of separate accommodation from another, s/he is not considered to be living in the same household. Physical presence is not, in itself, conclusive. There must be a 'particular kind of tie' binding two people together in a domestic establishment. So, for example, a husband and wife may be in separate households in the same care or nursing home.[64] A household must also involve two or more people living together as a unit and enjoying a reasonable level of independence and self-sufficiency. In one case, it was held that a married couple sharing a room in a residential home because they needed help organising their personal care and domestic activities were not self-sufficient and did not live in a domestic establishment, and therefore did not share a household.[65]

Is there a separate household?
If you think you should not be treated as a member of the same household as someone, check whether you can show that you maintain separate households. A separate household may exist if there are:
- independent arrangements for storing and cooking food or separate eating arrangements;
- independent financial arrangements or separate commitments for housing costs;
- no evidence of family life.

You cannot be a member of more than one household at the same time.[66] So if you are a member of one couple, you cannot also be treated as part of another. If

Part 3: General rules for means-tested benefits
Chapter 11: People included in the claim
Notes

two people maintain separate homes (ie, they each have a separate address where they usually live), they cannot share the same household.[67] Even if you have the right to occupy only part of a room, you may have your own household.[68]

If you are separated from your partner, but living under the same roof, you should not be treated as a couple if you are maintaining separate households. Any 'mere hope' of a reconciliation is not a 'reasonable expectation' if at least one partner has accepted that the relationship is at an end.[69]

Note: if you are still married or in a civil partnership, a shared attitude that the relationship is at an end may not be enough to show there is no shared household.[70]

Notes

1. **Couples**
1 s137(1) SSCBA 1992; CFC/7/1992
  IS Reg 2(1) IS Regs
  JSA s35(1) JSA 1995; reg 1(3) JSA Regs
  ESA Sch 1 para 6(5) WRA 2007; reg 2(1)
  ESA Regs
  PC s17(1) SPCA 2002; reg 1(2) SPC
  Regs
  HB Reg 2(1) HB Regs; reg 2(1) HB(SPC)
  Regs
  UC s39 WRA 2012
2 Reg 5(1)(h) SPC Regs
3 R(SB) 8/85
4 **IS** Regs 18 and 23 IS Regs
  JSA Regs 84 and 88(4) and (5) JSA Regs
  ESA Regs 68 and 83 ESA Regs
  PC Reg 8 and Sch 3 SPC Regs
  HB Regs 23 and 25 HB Regs; regs 22
  and 23 HB(SPC) Regs
  UC Reg 3(4) and (5) UC Regs
5 **IS** Reg 2(1) IS Regs
  JSA Reg 1(3) JSA Regs
  ESA Reg 2(1) ESA Regs
  PC s12 SPCA 2002
  HB Reg 2(1) HB Regs; reg 2(1) HB(SPC)
  Regs
  UC Reg 3(5) UC Regs

6 **IS** Reg 2(1) IS Regs
  JSA s35(1A) JSA 1995; reg 1(3) JSA Regs
  ESA Sch 1 para 6(6) WRA 2007; reg 2(1)
  ESA Regs
  PC s17(1A) SPCA 2002; reg 1(2) SPC
  Regs
  HB Reg 2(1) HB Regs; reg 2(1) HB(SPC)
  Regs
  IS/HB s137(1A) SSCBA 1992
  UC s39 WRA 2012
7 *R v Penwith DC HBRB ex parte Menear*, 24
  HLR 120, 11 October 1991. However,
  AM v Chelmsford Borough Council (HB)
  [2013] 245 (AAC) suggests that this only
  applies to the assessment of income and
  capital, and not to cohabitation
  questions.
8 *R v South Ribble BC HBRB ex parte
  Hamilton*, 33 HLR 102, 24 January 2000
  (CA)
9 CH/4014/2007
10 *Crake and Butterworth v SBC* [1982] 1 All
  ER 498; [1981] 2 FLR 264 (QBD)
11 R(SB) 17/81; R(G) 3/71; CIS/87/1993
12 *PP v Basildon District Council (HB)* [2013]
  UKUT 505 (AAC)
13 *Crake and Butterworth v SBC* [1982];
  [1981] 2 FLR 264 (QBD), quoted in
  R(SB) 35/85
14 R(SB) 35/85
15 CIS/87/1993; CIS/2559/2002; CIS/
  2074/2008

16 CIS/87/1993
17 CSB/150/1985
18 *JP v SSWP (IS)* [2014] UKUT 17 (AAC)
19 **IS** Reg 16(2)(a) IS Regs
    JSA Reg 78(2)(a) JSA Regs
    ESA Reg 156(3)(a) ESA Regs
    PC Reg 5(1)(a)(i) SPC Regs
    HB Reg 21(2)(a) HB Regs; reg 21(2)(a)
    HB(SPC) Regs
    UC Reg 3(6) UC Regs
20 CIS/508/1992; CIS/13805/1996
21 CIS/484/1993
22 **IS** Reg 16(1) IS Regs
    JSA Reg 78(1) JSA Regs
    ESA Reg 156(2) ESA Regs
    PC Reg 5(2) SPC Regs
    HB Reg 21(1) HB Regs; reg 21(1)
    HB(SPC) Regs
    UC Reg 3(6) UC Regs
    All *Broxtowe Borough Council v CS (HB)*
    [2014] UKUT 186 (AAC)
23 CIS/508/1992
24 **IS** Reg 16(2) IS Regs
    JSA Reg 78(2) JSA Regs
    ESA Reg 156(3) ESA Regs
    PC Reg 5(1)(a) SPC Regs
    HB Reg 21(2) HB Regs; reg 21(2)
    HB(SPC) Regs
25 Reg 3(6) UC Regs
26 **IS** Reg 16(3) IS Regs
    JSA Reg 78(3) JSA Regs
    ESA Reg 156(4) ESA Regs. This wrongly
    refers to Chapter 4, but correctly refers
    to the rules on temporary absence from
    Great Britain.
    PC Reg 5(1)(b)-(d) and (f) SPC Regs
27 CSSB/145/1983
28 **IS/ESA/PC** Reg 7(1) SS(C&P) Regs
    JSA Reg 223 JSA Regs
    HB Reg 86 HB Regs; reg 67 HB(SPC)
    Regs
    UC Reg 37 UC,PIP,JSA&ESA(C&P) Regs
29 CIS/317/1994
30 R(I) 1/71
31 R(H) 9/04

2. Children
32 s137 SSCBA 1992
    JSA s35 JSA 1995; reg 77 JSA Regs
    ESA Reg 2(1), definition of 'family', ESA
    Regs
33 s10 WRA 2012; reg 4(2) UC Regs
34 Reg 1 SS(WTCCTC)(CA) Regs

35 **IS** Reg 14 IS Regs
    JSA s35 JSA 1995; regs 1(3) and 76 JSA
    Regs
    ESA Reg 2(1) ESA Regs
    HB Reg 19 HB Regs; reg 19 HB(SPC)
    Regs
    IS/HB s137 SSCBA 1992
    UC s40 WRA 2012; regs 2 and 5 UC Regs
36 Reg 5 UC Regs
37 Reg 12(3) UC Regs
38 **IS** Reg 14(2) IS Regs
    JSA Reg 76(2) JSA Regs
    ESA Reg 2(1), definition of 'young
    person', ESA Regs
    HB Reg 19(2) HB Regs; reg 19(2)
    HB(SPC) Regs
    UC Reg 5(5) UC Regs
39 Reg 15(1) IS Regs
40 Reg 15(2) IS Regs
41 Reg 15(1A) IS Regs
42 Reg 77(1)-(3) JSA Regs
43 Reg 77 JSA Regs, as applied in *Hockenjos
    v Secretary of State for Social Security*
    [2004] EWCA Civ 1749, reported as
    R(JSA) 2/05. However, see also CJSA/
    2507/2002.
44 Reg 77(2) JSA Regs
45 Reg 156(10) ESA Regs
46 Reg 20(1) HB Regs; reg 20(1) HB(SPC)
    Regs
47 CFC/1537/1995
48 CFC/1537/1995
49 Reg 20(2) HB Regs; reg 20(2) HB(SPC)
    Regs
50 *JD v SSWP and London Borough of
    Richmond upon Thames (HB)* [2013]
    UKUT 642 (AAC); *JB v SSWP and
    Basingstoke and Deane BC (HB)* [2014]
    UKUT 223 (AAC)
51 Reg 4 UC Regs
52 Reg 4(6) and (7) UC Regs
53 **IS** Reg 15(4) IS Regs
    JSA s3(1)(d) JSA 1995; reg 77(5) JSA
    Regs
    HB Reg 20(3) HB Regs; reg 20(3)
    HB(SPC) Regs
54 **IS** Reg 16 IS Regs
    JSA Reg 78 JSA Regs
    ESA Reg 156 ESA Regs
    HB Reg 21 HB Regs; reg 21 HB(SPC)
    Regs
55 **IS** Regs 15(3) and 16(6) IS Regs
    JSA Regs 77(4) and 78(7) JSA Regs
    ESA Reg 156(8) ESA Regs
56 Reg 21(5) HB Regs; reg 21(5) HB(SPC)
    Regs

Part 3: General rules for means-tested benefits
Chapter 11: People included in the claim
Notes

57 **IS** Reg 16(5)(b) IS Regs
   JSA Reg 78(5)(c) JSA Regs
   ESA Reg 156(6)(c) ESA Regs
58 **IS** Reg 16(5A) IS Regs
   JSA Reg 78(6) JSA Regs
   ESA Reg 156(7) ESA Regs
59 **IS** Regs 15(3) and 16(6) IS Regs
   JSA Regs 77(4) and 78(5)(i) and (7) JSA
   Regs
   ESA Reg 156(6)(h) and (8) ESA Regs
60 **IS** Reg 16(5)(a) and (aa) IS Regs
   JSA Reg 78(5)(a) and (b) JSA Regs
   ESA Reg 156(6)(a) and (b) ESA Regs
61 **IS** Reg 16(5A) IS Regs
   JSA Reg 78(6) JSA Regs
   ESA Reg 156(7) ESA Regs
62 **IS** Reg 16(7) IS Regs
   JSA Reg 78(8) JSA Regs

3. **Households**
   63 Reg 5(1)(h) SPC Regs
   64 *Santos v Santos* [1972] 2 All ER 246; CIS/
      671/1992; CIS/81/1993
   65 CIS/4935/1997
   66 R(SB) 8/85
   67 R(SB) 4/83
   68 CSB/463/1986
   69 CIS/72/1994
   70 CIS/2900/1998

Chapter 12

Applicable amounts

Key facts

- Applicable amounts are used in some means-tested benefits to help calculate the amount of benefit to which you are entitled.
- Applicable amounts apply in income support, income-based jobseeker's allowance, income-related employment and support allowance (ESA) and housing benefit (HB). There are additional amounts in the guarantee credit of pension credit for people who are severely disabled or who are carers, which are similar to applicable amounts.
- Applicable amounts differ according to the benefit you are claiming. They are made up of personal allowances, premiums, housing costs and, in some cases, components. You may have one or more of these included.
- In some cases, if you were on a benefit for incapacity for work and have been transferred to ESA, your applicable amount for income-related ESA and HB may also include a transitional addition.

1. What are applicable amounts

Your applicable amount for income support (IS), income-based jobseeker's allowance (JSA) and income-related employment and support allowance (ESA) is the amount you are expected to live on each week. Your applicable amount for housing benefit (HB) is the amount used to see how much help you need with your rent. This chapter explains how to work out your applicable amount for these benefits. For the way your benefit is calculated, see p108 for IS, p704 for income-based JSA, p36 for income-related ESA and p59 for HB.

What is included in your applicable amount

Your applicable amount is made up of:

- **personal allowances:** the amount the law says you need for living expenses (see below);
- **premiums:** the amount given for certain extra needs you, your partner or children may have (see p236);
- **a support or work-related activity component** in income-related ESA and, in some circumstances, in HB (see p250);
- **housing costs** in IS, income-based JSA and income-related ESA only (see Chapter 20);
- **any transitional addition** in income-related ESA and HB only, if you have been transferred to ESA from incapacity benefit (IB), severe disablement allowance (SDA) or IS on the grounds of disability (see p252).

Can you get allowances and premiums for children?

IS and income-based JSA have not included allowances and premiums for children since 6 April 2004. However, you may continue to have these included if:[1]

– you have a claim which began before 6 April 2004; *and*
– you had a child included in the claim before 6 April 2004; *and*
– you have not yet been awarded child tax credit (CTC).

In these circumstances, personal allowances and premiums for children continue to be included in your claim (and amounts for a new child can be added) unless you claim and are awarded CTC.

2. Personal allowances

The amount of your personal allowance in income support (IS), income-based jobseeker's allowance (JSA), income-related employment and support allowance (ESA) and housing benefit (HB) depends on your age and whether you are claiming as a single person or a couple. You also get an allowance for each child included in your HB and, in some circumstances, in IS and income-based JSA.

If you are polygamously married (see p215), you receive an extra amount for each additional spouse in your household.[2] However, unless you are entitled to joint-claim JSA (see p120), if any additional spouse is under the age of 18, you only receive an extra amount for her/him if:[3]

- for IS, income-based JSA and income-related ESA, s/he is either responsible for a child (see p222) or would otherwise meet the special conditions for qualifying for JSA as a 16/17-year-old (see p125); *or*
- for IS and income-related ESA, s/he would qualify for that benefit in her/his own right were s/he not a member of a polygamous marriage.

Rates of personal allowances for people aged 18 or over

Note:
- Some 16/17-year-olds may also be entitled to these rates (see p232).
- Some allowances refer to the qualifying age for pension credit (PC).[4] For this, see p147.

	IS/JSA/ESA/HB	HB only – claimant or partner is at least qualifying age for pension credit
Single claimant:		
Aged 18–24	£57.90	
Aged 25 or over	£73.10	
Aged 18 or over and ESA includes (or would include) a support or work-related activity component (see p250) (ESA/HB only)	£73.10	
Aged between qualifying age for PC and 64 inclusive		£159.35
Aged 65 or over		£172.55
Lone parent:		
Aged 18 or over	£73.10	
Aged between qualifying age for PC and 64 inclusive		£159.35
Aged 65 or over		£172.55
Couple:		
Both aged 18 or over	£114.85	
One or both aged between qualifying age for PC and 64 inclusive		£243.25
One or both aged 65 or over		£258.15
One aged under 18 (some IS/JSA/ESA cases only – see p232 – and all HB cases)	£114.85	
One aged under 18 (other IS/JSA/ESA cases – see p232):		
either	£73.10	
or	£57.90	
Polygamous marriages (each additional qualifying spouse in household):		
Partner aged 18 or over, or under 18 in certain circumstances (see p230)	£41.75	
Claimant and all partners aged under 65		£83.90
One or more aged 65 or over		£85.60

Rates of personal allowances for 16/17-year-olds

- For IS and income-based JSA:
  - if you are single and aged 16 or 17 (including if you are a lone parent), you get the same rate as single 18–24-year-olds – ie, £57.90; *or*
  - if you are in a couple (unless one of the special circumstances below applies) and your partner is also aged under 18, you get £57.90. If your partner is aged 18 or over, see the table on p233.
- For income-related ESA:
  - you get £57.90; *or*
  - if your ESA includes the support or work-related activity component, you get £73.10; *or*
  - if you are in a couple (unless in one of the special circumstances on p232) and your partner is also under 18, the same amounts as above (£57.90 or £73.10) apply.
- For HB:
  - if you are single (including if you are a lone parent), you get the same rate as 18–24-year-olds – ie, £57.90; *or*
  - if you are entitled to ESA and qualify for either the support or work-related activity component (see p250), you get £73.10; *or*
  - if you are in a couple and your partner is also under 18, you get £87.50. If your partner is aged 18 or over, or if you are entitled to ESA including either component, you get £114.85.

  For this purpose, you count as qualifying for an ESA component even if your actual award of ESA is nil – eg, because you are only entitled to national insurance contribution credits.

Note: most 16/17-year-olds who have previously been looked after by a local authority cannot claim IS/JSA or HB (see p936).

Young couples in special circumstances

Note: the following rules apply to IS, income-based JSA and income-related ESA only.[5]

If you are a young couple, the amount of personal allowance paid depends on your ages and whether one or both of you are entitled to IS, income-based JSA (including JSA severe hardship payments – see p129) or income-related ESA, or you would be if you were a single person. The amount of your ESA personal allowance depends on whether you are in the ESA assessment phase or the ESA main phase, and on whether you qualify for the support or work-related activity component (see p250). For some couples, the personal allowance may be no more than that for a single person.

Age	£pw
Both aged 16–17, higher rate:	
ESA assessment phase	87.50
ESA main phase	114.85
IS/JSA	87.50
Both aged 16–17, lower rate:	
ESA assessment phase	57.90
ESA main phase	73.10
IS/JSA	57.90
One aged 16–17, one 18 or over, higher rate:	
ESA assessment phase	114.85
ESA main phase	114.85
IS/JSA	114.85
One aged 16–17, one 18–24, lower rate:	
ESA assessment phase	57.90
ESA main phase	73.10
IS/JSA	57.90
One aged 16–17, one 25 or over, lower rate:	
ESA assessment phase	73.10
ESA main phase	73.10
IS/JSA	73.10

If both of you are aged 16 or 17, you get the higher rate in the following circumstances.
- For IS:
  - one of you is responsible for a child; *or*
  - both of you would qualify for IS or income-related ESA if you were not a couple; *or*
  - the claimant's partner would qualify for income-based JSA or JSA severe hardship payments if s/he were single.
- For JSA:
  - one of you is responsible for a child; *or*
  - both of you would qualify for income-based JSA if you were not a couple; *or*
  - the claimant would qualify for income-based JSA and her/his partner would qualify for IS or income-related ESA if you were not a couple, or you would both qualify for JSA severe hardship payments if you were single; *or*
  - one of you would qualify for JSA severe hardship payments if you were single and the other for income-based JSA, IS or income-related ESA if s/he were single; *or*
  - you are married or civil partners and you both qualify for income-based JSA, or one does and the other is registered for work or training.

- For ESA:
  - one of you is responsible for a child; *or*
  - both of you would qualify for income-related ESA if you were not a couple; *or*
  - the claimant's partner would qualify for IS if s/he were single; *or*
  - the claimant's partner would qualify for income-based JSA or JSA severe hardship payments as a single person.

The higher rate is paid at the main phase rate if the claimant qualifies for a support or work-related activity component (see p641). Otherwise, it is paid at the assessment phase rate.

If one of you is aged 16 or 17 and the other is 18 or over, you get the higher rate personal allowance in the following circumstances.

- For IS, the younger partner qualifies for IS or income-related ESA (or s/he would do so if s/he were not a member of a couple) or income-based JSA or JSA severe hardship payments.
- For JSA, the younger partner is treated as responsible for a child, or qualifies for income-based JSA or JSA severe hardship payments, or either IS (or s/he would do so were s/he not a member of a couple) or income-related ESA (were s/he to make a claim).
- For ESA, the younger partner would either qualify for IS or income-related ESA (were s/he not a member of a couple), or for income-based JSA or JSA severe hardship payments. It is paid at the same rate in the assessment phase and main phase.

Qualifying for jobseeker's allowance

For these purposes, if you are under 18, you qualify for:

– income-based JSA, if you meet the rules for income-based JSA described on p126;

– JSA severe hardship payments, if you are subject to a severe hardship direction (see p129).

Personal allowances for children

Personal allowances for children are included in your HB applicable amount. IS, income-based JSA and income-related ESA do *not* usually include personal allowances for children. However, if you have been claiming IS or income-based JSA since before 6 April 2004, these can sometimes be included (see p230). **Note:** you cannot get personal allowances for children in joint-claim JSA, as you cannot claim this type of JSA if you have children.

For when children are included in your claim and for who counts as a child, see p220.

Note: your child's income and capital do not affect the amount of HB to which you are entitled. However, if you are still entitled to a personal allowance for your child in your IS or income-based JSA, you do not get an allowance for a child in your IS or income-based JSA if s/he has over £3,000 capital. See p269 for how a child's income may affect IS or income-based JSA.

You get one personal allowance for each child. However, you do not get a personal allowance for a third or subsequent child born on or after 6 April 2017, unless an exception applies. Also, for HB only, you do not get a personal allowance for a third or subsequent child who becomes part of your claim (eg, the child of a new partner) on or after 6 April 2017, or in a new claim made on or after that date, unless an exception applies. This is known as the 'two-child limit'. The limit applies to children for whom you or your partner are responsible and who are living in your household (see p220).[6]

If you already had a personal allowance for a third or subsequent child included in your HB on 5 April 2017, you continue to get a personal allowance for her/him while that award continues. Also, if you get a child element of child tax credit (CTC) for a child, you get a personal allowance for that child in your HB.

The personal allowance can become payable for a third child to whom this two-child limit applies who is born on or after 6 April 2017 if an older child leaves the household (so that you are no longer responsible for her/him), or if a young person leaves education (so that s/he no longer qualifies). In these situations, you should report the change as soon as possible so that you continue to get the maximum two personal allowances.

Exceptions to the two-child limit

The two-child limit does not apply in some cases. A personal allowance is payable for a third or subsequent child to whom the rule would apply who is:[7]

- born in a multiple birth, other than the first born if you already have two or more children;
- living with you on a long-term basis because s/he is unable to live with her/his parents, s/he would otherwise be at risk of entering the care system and you are caring for her/him as a family member or friend;
- being adopted by you from local authority care;
- likely to have been conceived as a result of rape or in a controlling or coercive relationship and you are not living with the alleged perpetrator; *or*
- the child of a parent under 16, and you are responsible for that parent.

For an exception to apply for a child in your HB claim, you must be getting a child element in your CTC for her/him because an exception applies.

See Appendix 14 for more details.

Rate of personal allowance for children

For HB (and for IS and income-based JSA if still included), there is one rate of personal allowance for children who are included in your claim – £66.90. You get one personal allowance for each child.

3. Premiums

Premiums are added to your personal allowance and are intended to help with the extra expenses of age or having a disability or, in some circumstances, children. Some premiums are not included in some of the means-tested benefits. Pension credit (PC) does not include premiums, but has allowances, which are very similar to the severe disability premium and the carer's premium.

Note: if you or your partner have reached the qualifying age for PC (see p147) and are not getting income support (IS), income-based jobseeker's allowance (JSA), income-related employment and support allowance (ESA) or universal credit (UC), your housing benefit (HB) can only include the family, disabled child, enhanced disability for a child, severe disability and carer premiums.[8] In these circumstances, your HB cannot include a disability premium.

See p249 for information about backdating premiums. See p248 for the premium rates and for which premiums can be paid in addition to other premiums.

Premiums for children

Certain premiums can be included in your HB applicable amount if you have children included in your claim. These are the family premium, disabled child premium and the child rate of the enhanced disability premium. IS, income-based JSA and income-related ESA do not usually include these premiums. However, if you have been claiming IS or income-based JSA since before 6 April 2004, see p230.

For when children are included in your claim, see p220. See p220 for who counts as a child.

Note: your child's income and capital do not affect the amount of your HB. However, if you are still entitled to premiums for children in your IS or income-based JSA, you do not get a premium (except a family premium) for a child who has over £3,000 capital. See p269 for how a child's income may affect IS or income-based JSA.

Family premium

You cannot get a family premium in any new HB claim made on or after 1 May 2016, or any new IS or income-based JSA claim made on or after 6 April 2004. The family premium cannot be included in any claim for income-related ESA.

Otherwise, you may be entitled to a family premium if at least one child is included in your claim (see p220). Only one family premium can be included no matter how many children you have.[9]

The premium can be paid even if you are not the parent of the child.

For HB, if you had a child included in your claim before 1 May 2016, you continue to get the premium, provided you still have a child included and you do not make a new claim for HB on or after that date.[10]

For IS and **income-based JSA**, you are only entitled to a family premium in certain circumstances (see p230). If you are entitled, a family premium is included even if you do not receive a personal allowance in your IS or income-based JSA for any child because s/he has capital over £3,000.

If a child who is being looked after by a local authority or who is in custody comes home for part of a week, your IS or income-based JSA includes a proportion of the weekly premium, based on the number of days the child is with you.[11] You can be paid the full premium in your HB if your child who is being looked after by a local authority is part of your household for any part of the week, provided the local authority thinks this is reasonable, given how often and for how long the child is at home with you.[12]

Disabled child premium

You are entitled to a disabled child premium in your HB and, if applicable, your IS and income-based JSA (see p230), for each child included in your claim who gets disability living allowance (DLA), personal independence payment (PIP), amed forces independence payment if s/he is at least 16, or extra-statutory payments to compensate for non-payment of DLA or PIP, or who is blind.[13] A disabled child premium can still be included for a third or subsequent child, even if you do not get a personal allowance for her/him because of the 'two-child limit' (see p234). Income-related ESA does not include a disabled child premium.

A child is treated as blind if s/he is certified as severely sight impaired or blind by a consultant ophthalmologist, and for the first 28 weeks after s/he has ceased to be certified as such on regaining her/his sight.[14] If DLA or PIP stops because the child has gone into hospital, see p915.

If your child is looked after by a local authority or is in custody for part of the week, the disabled child premium is affected in the same way as the family premium (see above).

Your child's capital does not affect the amount of your HB.[15] For IS and income-based JSA, if your child has over £3,000 capital or has been in hospital for more than 52 weeks, you do not get this premium.[16]

If your child dies

If your child dies, you may be able to continue receiving the disabled child premium for eight weeks.[17] This applies if:

- you get child benefit for the child following her/his death (see p591); *and*
- you were getting the disabled child premium for that child in your applicable amount immediately before her/his death.

Disability premium

Income-related ESA does not include a disability premium.

You qualify for a disability premium if none of the exclusions (see p239) apply and one of the following qualifying conditions applies.[18] The person who satisfies the qualifying condition must be under the qualifying age for PC (see p147). For IS and income-based JSA, if you or your partner have reached the qualifying age for PC, you may get the higher pensioner premium instead (see p242). There is a single rate and a couple rate, which applies whether one or both of you satisfy the conditions.

- You (or your partner) are getting a qualifying benefit. These are:[19]
  - DLA (see Chapter 27), PIP (see Chapter 34), armed forces independence payment or an equivalent benefit paid to meet attendance needs because of an injury at work (see Chapter 31) or a war injury;[20]
  - attendance allowance (AA), DLA or PIP if you (or your partner) were getting one of these benefits, but payment was suspended when one of you became a hospital patient.[21] In the case of IS and income-based JSA only, you or your partner must previously have qualified for a disability premium;
  - incapacity benefit (IB) paid at the long-term rate;
  - for IS and income-based JSA, your partner or, for joint-claim JSA, you or your partner, were getting IB paid at the long-term rate which stopped at pension age for income-based JSA (including joint-claim JSA)[22] or when retirement pension became payable for IS. For IS, you must have been continuously entitled to IS or income-based JSA since that time.[23] If it was your partner who reached pension age or began receiving a retirement pension, s/he must still be alive.[24] You or your partner must have previously qualified for a disability premium;[25]
  - war pensioner's mobility supplement;
  - the disabled worker element or severe disability element of working tax credit (WTC);
  - severe disablement allowance (SDA). For IS and HB you must be getting SDA; for income-based JSA your partner must be getting it. For joint claim JSA, either you or your partner must be getting it;
  - an NHS invalid trike or private car (for you or your partner) because of a disability;[26]
  - extra-statutory payments to compensate you or your partner for not getting any of the above benefits.[27]

Once you qualify for the disability premium, you or your partner are treated as still getting a qualifying benefit if you no longer receive it because of the overlapping benefit rules (see p1175).[28]

- You (or your partner) are certified as severely sight impaired or blind by a consultant opthalmologist. If you (or your partner) regain your sight, you still qualify for 28 weeks after you stop being certified.
- You have incapacity for work (see p683 of the 2013/14 edition of this *Handbook*) and have had incapacity for work or been treated as having it or (for IS and joint-claim JSA only) entitled to statutory sick pay (SSP) for 364 days (or 196 days if you are terminally ill). Your incapacity for work must have started before 27 October 2008. If you become entitled to benefit on the basis of limited capability for work instead of incapacity for work (see Chapter 44), the premium stops.
- For joint-claim JSA only, either you or your partner have (or are treated as having) 'limited capability for work' (see p1003) for a continuous qualifying period of:
  - 196 days if you or s/he are 'terminally ill'; *or*
  - 364 days in all other cases.

  For this purpose, gaps in your periods of limited capability for work that last no more than 12 weeks are ignored.[29]

If you undertake training

If you go on a government training course or receive a training allowance for any period, you keep the disability premium even though you may stop receiving one of the qualifying benefits, or cease to be entitled to SSP during the course, provided you continue to be entitled to IS, income-based JSA or HB. After the course, the premium continues if you are getting a qualifying benefit, remain entitled to SSP (for IS only), or remain incapable of work.[30]

Exclusions

You may not be entitled to the disability premium in your IS or income-based JSA once you or your partner have been receiving free treatment as a hospital inpatient for more than 52 weeks (see p909).

You cannot get a disability premium in your HB if:

- you have, or are treated as having, limited capability for work.[31] This applies even if you would otherwise qualify for the premium – eg, if you (or your partner) get DLA, PIP or are certified as blind or severely sight impaired. If your partner is the HB claimant and s/he does not have (and is not treated as having) limited capability for work, the disability premium can be included;[32] *or*
- you have reached the qualifying age for PC and neither you nor your partner are getting IS, income-based JSA, or income-related ESA.

> *Do you have limited capability for work?*
> 1. If you claim ESA or national insurance credits on the basis of limited capability for work and you are a member of a couple, it may be beneficial for your partner to be the HB claimant instead of you in order for the disability premium to be be included in your applicable amount. Local authorities are advised to tell you if this is the case.[33]
> 2. If you have (or are treated as having) limited capability for work, although you cannot qualify for a disability premium, you may qualify for either the support or work-related activity component in your applicable amount, although this is not normally until after the ESA 'assessment phase' has ended. **Note:** the work-related activity component has been abolished for new claims from 3 April 2017.
> 3. If your partner has limited capability for work but you do not, you can still qualify for the disability premium, which is paid at the couple rate. However, if the disability premium is awarded, you cannot qualify for a support or work-related activity component in your applicable amount.

Enhanced disability premium

The enhanced disability premium can be paid in respect of disabled adults and disabled children.[34]

You are entitled to an enhanced disability premium for an adult (at the single or couple rate) in your IS, income-based JSA, income-related ESA and HB if:

- you or your partner receive the highest rate care component of DLA, the enhanced rate of the daily living component of PIP or armed forces independence payment. If it is your partner who satisfies this, s/he must be under the qualifying age for PC; *or*
- for income-related ESA, you qualify for the support component (see p641); *or*
- for HB, the decision maker has determined that you have, or can be treated as having, limited capability for work-related activity (see p1010).

This premium can be paid in addition to both the disability and severe disability premiums (see p248). For more details of the premiums with which the enhanced disability premium can be paid, see p248.

Once you or your partner reach the qualifying age for PC (see p147), you are paid the pensioner premium (or the higher personal allowance in HB) instead.

For HB, you qualify for one enhanced disability premium for each child included in your claim who receives the highest rate care component of DLA (or extra-statutory payments to compensate for non-payment of this), the enhanced rate of the daily living component of PIP or armed forces independence payment.

For IS and income-based JSA, you are only entitled to the child rate of this premium in certain circumstances (see p230). If your child dies, the premium continues for eight weeks if you or your partner continue to get child benefit for her/him (see p591).

An enhanced disability premium can still be included for a third or subsequent child, even if you do not get a personal allowance for her/him because of the 'two-child limit' (see p234).

Income-related ESA does not include the child rate of this premium (although you can qualify for the adult rate).

In most cases, you (or your partner or child) are treated as receiving the highest rate of the DLA care component or the enhanced rate of the daily living component of PIP during any period when DLA or PIP is suspended while you are in hospital.

However, the following people cannot qualify:

- for the child rate, for IS and income-based JSA only, children who have been in hospital for more than 52 weeks, or who have more than £3,000 in capital;[35]
- some people who have been in hospital for more than 52 weeks or, in some cases, if their partner has (see p914).

Pensioner premiums

There is a pensioner premium and a higher pensioner premium. They are paid at the same rate.[36]

You qualify for a pensioner premium if:

- your partner has reached the qualifying age for PC (see p147). This applies to IS, income-based JSA and income-related ESA; *or*
- you have reached the qualifying age for PC. This applies to men claiming income-based JSA and income-related ESA. Women of the same age must claim PC instead of income-based JSA or income-related ESA.

You qualify for a higher pensioner premium instead of a pensioner premium in IS or income-based JSA if:

- your partner is aged 80 or over; *or*
- you or your partner are sick or disabled and certain conditions are satisfied (see below).

There are no pensioner premiums in HB. You get a higher personal allowance instead.

Although paid at the same rate as the pensioner premium, qualifying for the higher pensioner premium may be important – eg, because it qualifies you for a £20 earnings disregard (see p279) or because it meets one of the qualifying conditions for the disabled worker element in WTC (see p1412). For joint-claim JSA, there is no pensioner premium or higher pensioner premium on age grounds if your partner is aged 75 or over.

These premiums are paid at a single or couple rate. The couple rate of the premium is included in your applicable amount even if only one partner fulfils the condition. The rate of the pensioner premium in income-related ESA depends on whether or not you are entitled to the work-related activity or support component (see p251) and whether you are a member of a couple.

Higher pensioner premium

You qualify for the higher pensioner premium in IS or income-based JSA if:[37]

- your partner is aged 80 or over;
- for IS, your partner has, or for income-based JSA you or your partner have, reached the qualifying age for PC (see p147) and receive a qualifying benefit (eg, AA, DLA, PIP or SDA), are certified as severely sight impaired or blind, or have an NHS trike or a private car allowance.
  If your AA, DLA or PIP stops because you go into hospital, see p911. If you are getting SDA, see below;
- for income-based JSA, you (or, for joint-claim JSA, you or your partner) were getting a disability premium as part of your IS or income-based JSA before you reached the qualifying age for PC (see p147) and you have continued to claim income-based JSA since then. You must have been getting a disability premium at some time during the eight weeks before you reached the qualifying age for PC and have received IS or JSA continuously since then.[38] You are treated as being continuously entitled to benefit if there is a break in your entitlement of eight weeks or less, which includes the day you reached the qualifying age for PC;
- for IS, you were getting a disability premium as part of your IS or income-based JSA at some time in the eight weeks before your partner reached the qualifying age for PC (see p147) and have continued to get IS since then. You are treated as being continuously entitled to benefit if there is a break in your entitlement of eight weeks or less, including the day your partner reached the qualifying age for PC.[39]

Note: you may not be entitled to the higher pensioner premium once you or your partner have been receiving free treatment as a hospital inpatient for more than 52 weeks (see p914).

In the case of couples, the person who was the benefit claimant before s/he reached the qualifying age for PC must continue to claim after that, but the claimant does not need to have been the person who qualified for the disability premium.

If you get SDA when you reach 65, you are awarded it for life.[40] This also applies even if it ceases to be paid because you get retirement pension at a higher rate.[41]

Severe disability premium and pension credit additional amount

You qualify for a severe disability premium or for the additional amount for severe disability in the guarantee credit of PC if *all* the following apply to you.[42]

- You receive a 'qualifying benefit' (see below). If you are a couple for IS, income-based JSA, income-related ESA or HB, your partner must also be getting a qualifying benefit, or be certified as severely sight impaired or blind by a consultant ophthalmologist (or treated as certified because it is no more than 28 weeks since s/he stopped being certified).[43] For PC, both of you must be getting a qualifying benefit or one must be getting a qualifying benefit and the other certified as severely sight impaired or blind or treated as certified. For PC only, either partner can be the claimant.[44] If you are a member of a couple, you and your partner are treated as getting any of these benefits while one or both of you are in hospital, but only if you are not claiming the premium or additional amount for severe disability on the basis that your partner (or you, for PC) is certified as severely sight impaired or blind or treated as certified.[45] For IS, income-based JSA, income-related ESA and HB, the benefit must be paid for you or your partner. Receipt of benefit for someone else (eg, a child) does not count.[46] It is probably intended that the same rule should apply to PC.
- No non-dependant aged 18 or over (eg, an adult son or daughter) is 'normally residing with you' (see p244). It does not matter whose house it is.[47] Someone is only counted as residing with you if you share accommodation, apart from a bathroom, lavatory or a communal area such as a hall, passageway or a room in common use in sheltered accommodation. If s/he is separately liable to pay for the accommodation, s/he does not count as residing with you.[48]
- No one gets carer's allowance (CA) or the UC carer element for looking after you or, if you are a couple, no one gets CA or the UC carer element for both of you (but see p917 if you and/or your partner go into hospital). If you are a member of a couple and someone gets CA or the carer element for one (but not both) of you, but you are both disabled, you can get the severe disability premium at the single person's rate. Only actual receipt of CA counts (except if it is not paid because of the loss of benefit rules – see p1265).[49] No account is taken of any underlying entitlement to CA if it is awarded but not paid because of the overlapping benefit rules, or of any extra-statutory payments to compensate for its not being paid. Similarly, no account is taken of any backdated payments or arrears of CA or of the carer element.[50] Also argue that no account should be taken of any overpaid CA or carer element of UC and that, if you have been denied the premium because of a CA or carer element overpayment, it should be repaid to you (see p247).

Receiving a qualifying benefit

A 'qualifying benefit' is either AA, the middle or highest rate care component of DLA, the daily living component of PIP, armed forces independence payment, constant attendance allowance or exceptionally severe disablement allowance (or the equivalent war pension). You are 'treated as receiving' a qualifying benefit if you receive an extra-statutory payment to compensate you for not receiving that benefit.[51]

Couples

You get the couple rate if both you and your partner get a qualifying benefit and no one gets CA or the carer element of UC for either of you. If CA or the carer element of UC is paid for one of you, or if your partner does not get a qualifying benefit but is certified as severely sight impaired or blind by a consultant ophthalmologist (or treated as certified), you get the single person's rate. In polygamous marriages, the single rate is awarded for each eligible spouse who gets a qualifying benefit while CA or the carer element of UC is not paid.

Note:

- You and/or your partner are treated as getting a qualifying benefit, even though it has stopped because you/your partner have been in hospital for more than four weeks, but the severe disability premium is paid at the single person's rate only. Similarly, for IS, income-based JSA, income-related ESA and HB, if you are a couple, you are treated as receiving CA or the carer element of UC even though you are no longer getting it because the person for whom you care has been in hospital for more than four weeks.[52]

- For couples on IS, JSA and income-related ESA only, if you or your partner temporarily move into a care home, you still count as a couple but your applicable amount is calculated in a different way (see p923).[53] If your applicable amount is calculated as if you and your partner were single claimants, this means that, if the person who stays at home gets a qualifying benefit, a severe disability premium is included in the applicable amount of that person.

- For PC, if you or your partner temporarily move into a care home, you still count as a couple if you have not been apart for substantially more than 52 weeks (see p922). So, once the partner in the care home loses her/his AA or DLA care component, no severe disability premium can be paid for either of you, even if the partner at home gets a qualifying benefit.

Who is not a non-dependant

Non-dependants are adults living with you who are not included in your benefit claim (eg, adult son or daughter, or a parent), but who are regarded as being able to contribute towards your household costs.

The following people who live with you do *not* count as non-dependants.[54]

For IS, income-based JSA, income-related ESA, HB and PC:

- anyone aged under 18;
- anyone else who receives a qualifying benefit for the severe disability premium (see p242);[55]
- anyone who is certified as severely sight impaired or blind by a consultant ophthalmologist (or treated as certified);[56]
- anyone staying in your home who normally lives elsewhere. In deciding whether someone normally lives with you or elsewhere, it may be relevant to

consider things like why the residence started, how long it has continued and your relationship;[57]
- any person (and, for IS, income-based JSA, income-related ESA and PC only, her/his partner) employed by a charitable or voluntary body as a resident carer for you or your partner if you pay a charge for that service (even if the charge is only nominal).[58] **Note:** these rules do not apply to a live-in carer employed directly by you (even if, for example, you are paying her/him from direct payments made to you by social services for that purpose).

For IS, income-based JSA, income-related ESA and HB:
- any member of your 'family' (see p246 for who counts). This may include any child under the age of 20 (see p220) as well as your partner, although your partner must be getting a qualifying benefit (or would be if s/he were not in hospital) or be certified as severely sight impaired or blind, for you to get the severe disability premium (see p242);
- any child or qualifying young person who is living with you but who is not a member of your household (see p223).[59]

For IS, income-based JSA, income-related ESA and PC:
- any person (or her/his partner) who jointly occupies (see p246) your home and is either the co-owner with you or your partner, or jointly liable with you or your partner, to make payments to a landlord for occupying it. If this person is a close relative (see p246), however, s/he *does* count as a non-dependant *unless* the co-ownership or joint liability to make payments to a landlord existed either before 11 April 1988 or by the time you or your partner first moved in;
- any person (or any member of her/his household) who is liable to pay you or your partner on a commercial basis (see p246) for occupying the dwelling (eg, tenants or licensees), unless s/he is a close relative of you or your partner;
- any person (or any member of her/his household) to whom you or your partner are liable to make payments on a commercial basis for occupying the dwelling, unless s/he is a close relative of you or your partner.

For PC:
- any child or qualifying young person.[60] This is defined in the same way as for UC (see p220).

Note: for IS, income-based JSA, income-related ESA and PC, if someone comes to live with you in order to look after you (or your partner) and has not lived with you before, your severe disability premium or amount for severe disability remains in payment for the first 12 weeks after the carer moves in, even if s/he would otherwise count as a non-dependant.[61] After that, you lose the premium or the amount for severe disability. The carer should then consider claiming CA (see Chapter 25).

For HB:[62]
- any person who jointly occupies your home and is either the co-owner with you or your partner, or liable with you or your partner to make payments for occupying it. A joint occupier who was a non-dependant at any time within the previous eight weeks counts as a non-dependant if the local authority thinks that the change of arrangements was created to take advantage of the HB scheme;
- any person who is liable to pay you or your partner on a commercial basis for occupying the dwelling unless s/he is a close relative of you or your partner, or if the local authority thinks that the rent or other agreement has been created to take advantage of the HB scheme (but this cannot apply if the person was otherwise liable to pay rent for the accommodation at any time during the eight weeks before the agreement was made);
- any person, or any member of her/his household, to whom you or your partner are liable to make payments for your accommodation on a commercial basis unless s/he is a close relative of you or your partner.

Definitions

'**Close relative**' is a parent, parent-in-law (including a civil partner's parent), son, son-in-law (including a son's civil partner), daughter, daughter-in-law (including a daughter's civil partner), brother, sister, step-parent (including a parent's civil partner), stepson (including a civil partner's son), stepdaughter (including a civil partner's daughter), or the partners of any of these.[63]

'**Member of the family**' means your partner and any child who lives in your household and for whom you or your partner count as 'responsible' (see p220).[64]

'**Jointly occupies**' is a legal relationship involving occupation by two or more people (whether as owner-occupiers, tenants or licensees) with one and the same legal right.[65] It does not exist if people merely have equal access to different parts of the premises.

'**Commercial basis**' has no legal meaning, and there is no requirement for there to be an intention to make a profit.[66] It may be sufficient if a 'reasonable' charge is made, even if this does not fully cover the cost of the accommodation and meals being provided.[67] The reasonableness of the charge should be judged just against the cost of occupying the dwelling, not taking account of the additional costs of providing food, clothing and care.[68] A useful, but not conclusive, test to apply is to consider whether the same arrangement *might* have been entered into with a lodger.[69]

'**Liability**' means a legal or contractual liability, although there is no requirement that any arrangements need to be in writing.[70]

Carer premium and pension credit additional amount

You qualify for a carer premium, or an additional amount in PC, if you or your partner are entitled to CA (see Chapter 25).[71]

You are entitled to CA even if you do not receive it because of the overlapping benefit rules (see p1175) – eg, you get contributory ESA or retirement pension instead.

If the person you or your partner are getting CA for dies, or you or your partner stop being entitled to CA for another reason, your entitlement to a carer premium continues for a further eight weeks. The eight-week period runs from the Sunday after the death (or from the date of the death, if the death occurs on a Sunday). In other cases, it runs from the date entitlement to CA stops. If you first claim IS, income-based JSA, income-related ESA or (if you or your partner are below the qualifying age for PC) HB after the CA stops, you continue to qualify for a carer premium for eight weeks after the death or, if it stops for another reason, after entitlement to CA stops.[72]

A double rate premium is awarded if both you and your partner satisfy the conditions for it.

Should you claim carer's allowance?

1. Before claiming CA, consider how your claim might affect the entitlement to the severe disability premium, or the amount for severe disability in the guarantee credit of PC (see p242), of the disabled person for whom you care – particularly if the only financial advantage to you as the carer is the amount of the carer premium, which may be worth considerably less than the severe disability premium (but see p242 for the rules on notional income).

2. Any backdated award of CA does not affect a disabled person's entitlement to the severe disability premium or the amount for severe disability in the guarantee credit of PC.[73] You may be able to take advantage of this rule so that you are paid CA or the carer premium for the same period in which the disabled person has already received a severe disability premium or an amount for severe disability in PC.

3. Although the severe disability premium or amount for severe disability is not payable throughout any period during which a carer is receiving CA, if you are a carer and it is later decided that you have been overpaid CA, the disabled person should ask for the decision refusing her/him the severe disability premium or the amount for severe disability to be revised. You must be both entitled to *and* in receipt of CA for the severe disability premium not to be payable.[74]

4. Other than for HB, if payment of CA stops, the severe disability premium can be backdated to the date the CA stopped.[75]

Rates of premiums

Rates of premiums

The following premiums can be paid in addition to any other premium, except that the enhanced disability premium cannot be paid in addition to the pensioner or higher pensioner premium.[76]

Family premium	£17.45
Disabled child premium	£60.90
(for each qualifying child)	
Severe disability premium	
Single (or one partner qualifies)	£62.45
Couple (both partners qualify)	£124.90
Carer premium	
Single (or one partner qualifies)	£34.95
Couple (both partners qualify)	£69.90
Enhanced disability premium	
Child (for each qualifying child)	£24.78
Single	£15.90
Couple (one or both partners qualify)	£22.85

Only one of the following premiums can be paid. If you qualify for more than one, you get the highest.[77]

Family premium for HB (lone parent increase)	£4.75
Disability premium	
Single	£32.55
Couple	£46.40
Pensioner and higher pensioner premium for IS/income-based JSA	
Single (income-based JSA only; not payable in IS)	£86.25
Couple	£128.40
Pensioner premium for income-related ESA	
Claimant entitled to support component:	
Single	£49.70
Couple	£91.85
Claimant entitled to work-related activity component:	
Single	£57.20
Couple	£99.35
Claimant not entitled to either component:	
Single	£86.25
Couple	£128.40

Note: the lone parent increase to the family premium is only payable in HB if you were entitled to it on 5 April 1998 and certain changes in your circumstances do not occur. For more information, see p793 of the 2011/12 edition of this *Handbook*.[78]

Backdating premiums

To qualify for the disability, enhanced disability, higher pensioner, severe disability, disabled child or carer premium, you or your partner or child must usually have been awarded a 'qualifying benefit' that applies to each premium. The date you can begin to get your premium may, therefore, depend on the date from which your qualifying benefit is awarded. However, because of the time it may take to deal with your claim for the qualifying benefit, or if your claim is backdated (see p1156) or initially refused but awarded some time later after a revision (see p1276), supersession (see p1287) or appeal (see p1309), you may not get your premium straight away and you may have to apply for it to be backdated.

If you are already getting benefit

If you are already getting IS, JSA, ESA, HB or PC, you should ask for your award of this benefit either to be revised or superseded and for your premium to be backdated to the date from which the qualifying benefit is awarded, or to when you first got (or claimed) IS, JSA, ESA, HB or PC, if that is later. There is no limit to the period for which arrears can be paid to you.[79]

If you were refused benefit

If you have previously claimed IS or income-based JSA, but your claim was refused because at the time you or your partner or child did not get the qualifying benefit for the premium (see p1160), you should make another IS or income-based JSA claim once the qualifying benefit is awarded. To get full backdating you should have claimed the qualifying benefit before, or no later than 10 days after, the first IS or income-based JSA claim. You must then make your second claim for IS or income-based JSA within three months of the decision awarding the qualifying benefit. The second claim, including the premium, is backdated to the date of the first IS or income-based JSA claim, or to the date from which the qualifying benefit was awarded if that is later.[80] If the qualifying benefit is initially refused, or awarded at a lower rate than you need for the premium, but is later decided in your favour, to get full backdating you must make your second IS or income-based JSA claim within three months of the date the qualifying benefit is decided in your favour on revision, supersession or appeal.[81]

A new claim for income-related ESA can be backdated for a maximum of three months. You do not need to establish a reason for the backdating.

For HB, you may be limited to one or a maximum of three months' backdating, depending on your age (see p81).

For the backdating rules for PC, see p154.

If you lose entitlement to benefit

If you lose your existing IS or income-based JSA as a result of having your (or your partner or child's) qualifying benefit stopped or reduced, or while you are waiting for a claim for a qualifying benefit to be decided, and that qualifying benefit is then awarded, or reinstated on a revision, supersession or appeal (or you make a later claim for the qualifying benefit), you should make a new claim for IS or income-based JSA. Provided you claim within three months of the favourable decision on the qualifying benefit, your IS or income-based JSA is fully backdated to the date your entitlement previously ended, or to the date from which the qualifying benefit is payable if that is later.[82]

If you lose your HB because you lose entitlement to a qualifying benefit, the decision ending your HB can be revised if the qualifying benefit is reinstated. Your HB can be fully backdated in this situation. You must tell the local authority that you have had your qualifying benefit reinstated, but you do not need to make a fresh claim for HB.[83]

4. Components

Your applicable amount for income-related employment and support allowance (ESA) and, in certain circumstances, housing benefit (HB) may include either:[84]
- a support component (see p251); *or*
- a work-related activity component (see p251). **Note:** the work-related activity component has been abolished for new claims from 3 April 2017.

You cannot be awarded both components at the same time.

You can qualify for one of these components in your HB if either you or your partner meet the conditions for it and have limited capability for work (see p251). If you qualify for one component and your partner qualifies for the other, the component for which *you* qualify is awarded.[85]

To qualify for a component in income-related ESA, you must meet the conditions yourself. If you have a partner and both you and your partner have limited capability for work, you can choose which of you is the claimant. If only one of you qualifies for a component, it may be beneficial for that person to be the claimant. If in doubt, get advice.

Note:
- You cannot qualify for a component in your HB applicable amount if you have reached the qualifying age for pension credit (see p147).
- For HB, provided either you or your partner satisfy the conditions for the component and have limited capability for work, it does not matter if ESA is not paid, or if your entitlement to ESA has stopped because of the rules on how long you can be paid contributory ESA.
- For income-related ESA, if you or your partner have been receiving free treatment as a hospital inpatient for a continuous period of more than 52 weeks, you cannot qualify for either component.[86]

Support component

In order to qualify for a support component in your income-related ESA, you must meet the conditions described on p641. The rules are the same as for contributory ESA.

You qualify for a support component in your HB if:[87]

- you or your partner have claimed ESA and you are entitled to the support component (see p641), or you have been refused ESA but you would have been entitled to the component had you been entitled to ESA; *and*
- you are not entitled to a disability premium (p238); *and*
- either you or your partner have limited capability for work-related activity (see p1010 – the rules are the same as for contributory ESA).

Work-related activity component

The work-related activity component has been abolished for new claims from 3 April 2017. For details of who can still get a work-related activity component in ESA, see p641.

You can still get a work-related activity component in your HB if:[88]

- you or your partner have claimed ESA and are entitled to the work-related activity component (see p641), or you have been refused ESA but you would have been entitled to the component had you been entitled to ESA; *and*
- you are not entitled to a disability premium (p238); *and*
- the decision maker has determined that you or your partner have, or can be treated as having, limited capability for work (see p1003).

Note: you keep the maximum work-related activity component in HB even if you lose it in ESA because of a sanction.[89] The full amount of ESA continues to be taken into account as your income.

Rates of components

There is no higher rate of the support or work-related activity component paid for couples.

Rates of components[90]

Support component	£36.55
Work-related activity component	£29.05

Backdating components

Your entitlement to either the support or work-related activity component in your ESA normally starts once the 'assessment phase' has ended (see p639 – the rules are the same as for contributory ESA). If your assessment phase ends later than 13 weeks after you claim, your entitlement to a component can be backdated to the beginning of the 14th week of your claim.[91] If you make a claim, or request a revision or supersession of your entitlement, expressly on the grounds of being terminally ill (see p643 – the rules are the same as for contributory ESA), you do not have to wait for the assessment phase to end to qualify for the support component, but can qualify either from the date of your claim, or from the date on which you became terminally ill if that is later.[92]

If you are getting HB and you become entitled to a support or work-related activity component, you qualify for that component in your applicable amount from the Monday on or after your entitlement to the component began. However, if your HB entitlement starts after the date your entitlement to the component began, you qualify for the component in your HB applicable amount from the date your entitlement to HB began.[93]

If you only become entitled to HB once a component is awarded to you, you should claim (or reclaim) HB as promptly as you can since you can only get a maximum of one months' backdating (see p78).

5. Transitional addition

All incapacity benefit (IB), severe disablement allowance (SDA) and income support (IS) 'on the grounds of disability', claims have now been (or soon will have been) transferred to employment and support allowance (ESA) and your entitlement reassessed (see p672). When this happens, you may have a transitional addition included in your income-related ESA or housing benefit (HB) applicable amount.

If your claim for IS on grounds of disability is transferred to income-related ESA and your ESA is worth less than your IS, you are entitled to a transitional addition of ESA. For details, see p37.

If your claim for IB or SDA has been transferred to contributory ESA (see p672):
- you may no longer be entitled to the disability premium in your HB applicable amount, as this is not paid if you are the claimant and have limited capability for work;
- if your HB applicable amount would be reduced because of the transfer of your (or your partner's) IB or SDA claim to contributory ESA, it includes a transitional addition to make up the difference and ensure that you do not immediately lose out.[94]

A transitional addition is not necessary if:[95]
- you (or your partner) are transferred to income-related ESA. In this case, you are entitled to maximum HB; or
- you (or your partner) are over the qualifying age for pension credit (p147). In this case, your applicable amount is not affected by the transfer to ESA.

You are entitled to a transitional addition in your HB if:[96]
- you (or your partner) have been transferred to contributory ESA and, on the date of the transfer, your HB applicable amount is reduced as a result; *or*
- on transfer to ESA, you (or your partner) are found not to have limited capability for work, you have appealed against this and you are entitled to contributory ESA pending the appeal (see p1016), and your HB applicable amount is reduced as a result. If you win your appeal, the transitional addition is recalculated (because your contributory ESA applicable amount may now include a component).[97]

The transitional addition is not permanent. It is reduced by the amount of any increases to your HB. It ends on 5 April 2020, or earlier in certain circumstances – eg, if your entitlement to contributory ESA or HB stops. For details, see p238 of the 2016/17 edition of this *Handbook*.

Notes

1. What are applicable amounts
1 Reg 1(3) and (7) SS(WTCCTC)(CA) Regs

2. Personal allowances
2 **IS** Reg 18(1)(b) IS Regs
JSA Regs 84(1)(b) and 86B(b) JSA Regs
ESA Reg 68(1)(b) ESA Regs
HB Reg 23(b) HB Regs; Sch 3 para 1 HB(SPC) Regs
3 **IS** Reg 18(2) IS Regs
JSA Reg 84(2) JSA Regs
ESA Reg 68(2) ESA Regs
4 **IS** Sch 2 Part 1 IS Regs
JSA Sch 1 Part 1 JSA Regs
ESA Sch 4 Part 1 ESA Regs
HB Sch 3 Part 1 HB Regs; Sch 3 Part 1 HB(SPC) Regs
5 **IS** Sch 2 para 1(3) IS Regs
JSA Sch 1 para 1(3) JSA Regs
ESA Sch 4 para 1(3) ESA Regs
6 Regs 5, 6 and 9 The Social Security (Restrictions on Amounts for Children and Qualifying Young Persons) Amendment Regulations 2017, No.376; reg 22 HB Regs; reg 22 HB (SPC) Regs

7 Regs 5, 6 and 9 The Social Security (Restrictions on Amounts for Children and Qualifying Young Persons) Amendment Regulations 2017, No.376; reg 22 HB Regs; reg 22 HB (SPC) Regs

3. Premiums
8 Sch 3 paras 3 and 6-9 HB(SPC) Regs
9 **IS** Sch 2 para 3 IS Regs
JSA Sch 1 para 4 JSA Regs
HB Sch 3 para 3 HB Regs; Sch 3 para 3 HB(SPC) Regs
10 Reg 4 Housing Benefit (Abolition of the Family Premium and Date of Claim) (Amendment) Regulations 2015, No.1857
11 **IS** Regs 15(3) and 16(6) IS Regs
JSA Regs 74(4) and 78(7) JSA Regs
12 Reg 21(4) and (5) HB Regs; reg 21(4) and (5) HB(SPC) Regs
13 **IS** Sch 2 paras 14 and 15(6) IS Regs
JSA Sch 1 para 16 JSA Regs
HB Sch 3 paras 16 and 20(7) HB Regs; Sch 3 paras 8 and 12(3) HB(SPC) Regs

14 **IS** Sch 2 paras 12(1)(a)(iii) and (2) and 14(c) IS Regs
JSA Sch 1 para 14(1)(h) and (2) JSA Regs
HB Sch 3 paras 13(1)(a)(v) and (2) and 16(c) HB Regs; Sch 3 para 8(b) HB(SPC) Regs

15 Reg 25(3) HB Regs; reg 23(3) HB(SPC) Regs

16 **IS** Sch 2 para 14(2)(a) IS Regs
JSA Sch 1 para 16(2)(a) JSA Regs

17 **IS** Sch 2 para 14 IS Regs
JSA Sch 1 para 16 JSA Regs
HB Sch 3 para 16 HB Regs; Sch 3 para 8 HB(SPC) Regs

18 **IS** Sch 2 para 11 IS Regs
JSA Sch 1 paras 13, 14, 20G and 20H JSA Regs
HB Sch 3 para 12 HB Regs

19 **IS** Sch 2 para 12(1)(a)(i) IS Regs
JSA Sch 1 paras 14(1)(a)-(d) and 20H(1)(a)-(d) JSA Regs
HB Sch 3 para 13(1)(a)(i) HB Regs

20 **IS** Reg 2(1) IS Regs
JSA Reg 1(3) JSA Regs
HB Reg 2(1) HB Regs
All Definition of 'attendance allowance'

21 **IS** Sch 2 para 12(1)(d) IS Regs
JSA Sch 1 paras 14(1)(g)(ii) and 20H(1)(h)(ii) JSA Regs
HB Sch 3 para 13(1)(a)(iii) HB Regs

22 R(IS) 7/02

23 **IS** Sch 2 para 12(1)(c)(i) IS Regs
JSA Sch 1 paras 14(1)(g)(i) and 20H(1)(h)(i) JSA Regs
HB Sch 3 para 13(1)(a)(ii) HB Regs

24 **IS** Sch 2 para 12(1)(c)(i) IS Regs
JSA Sch 1 paras 14(1)(g)(i) and 20H(1)(h)(i) JSA Regs

25 **IS** Sch 2 para 12(1)(c) IS Regs
JSA Sch 1 paras 14(1)(g) and 20H(1)(h) JSA Regs

26 **IS** Sch 2 para 12(1)(a)(ii) IS Regs
JSA Sch 1 paras 14(1)(e) and (f) and 20H(1)(f) and (g) JSA Regs
HB Sch 3 para 13(1)(a)(iv) HB Regs

27 **IS** Sch 2 para 14A IS Regs
JSA Sch 1 paras 18 and 20K JSA Regs
HB Sch 3 para 18 HB Regs

28 **IS** Sch 2 para 7(1)(a) IS Regs
JSA Sch 1 paras 8(1)(a) and 20D(1)(a) JSA Regs
HB Sch 3 para 7(1)(a) HB Regs

29 Sch 1 para 20H(1)(ee) JSA Regs

30 **IS** Sch 2 paras 7(1)(b) and 12(5) IS Regs
JSA Sch 1 paras 8(1)(b) and 20D(b) JSA Regs
HB Sch 3 paras 7(1)(b) and 13(5) HB Regs

31 The rules only refer to the 'claimant'.

32 Sch 3 para 13(9) HB Regs

33 HB/CTB Circular A11/2008

34 **IS** Sch 2 para 13A IS Regs
JSA Sch 1 paras 15A and 20IA JSA Regs
ESA Sch 4 para 7 ESA Regs
HB Sch 3 para 15 HB Regs; Sch 3 para 7 HB(SPC) Regs

35 **IS** Sch 2 para 13A IS Regs
JSA Sch 1 para 15A JSA Regs

36 **IS** Sch 2 paras 9 and 9A IS Regs
JSA Sch 1 paras 10, 11, 20E and 20F JSA Regs
ESA Sch 4 para 5 ESA Regs

37 **IS** Sch 2 para 10 IS Regs
JSA Sch 1 paras 12 and 20F JSA Regs

38 Sch 1 paras 12(1)(a)(ii) and (c)(ii) and (2) and 20F(1)(b) and (2) JSA Regs

39 Sch 2 para 10(1)(b)(ii), (3) and (4) IS Regs; reg 32 IS(JSACA) Regs

40 CIS/458/1992

41 **IS** Sch 2 para 7(1)(a) IS Regs
JSA Sch 1 paras 8(1)(a) and 20D(1)(a) JSA Regs

42 **IS** Sch 2 para 13 IS Regs
JSA Sch 1 paras 15 and 20I JSA Regs
ESA Sch 4 para 6 ESA Regs
PC Reg 6(4) and Sch 1 paras 1 and 2 SPC Regs
HB Sch 3 para 14 HB Regs; Sch 3 para 6 HB(SPC) Regs

43 **IS** Sch 2 para 13(2A) IS Regs
JSA Sch 1 paras 15(3) and 20I(2) JSA Regs
ESA Sch 4 para 6(3) and (9) ESA Regs
HB Sch 3 para 14(3) HB Regs; Sch 3 para 6(3) HB(SPC) Regs

44 Sch 1 para 11(b) and (c) SPC Regs

45 **IS** Sch 2 para 13(3A)(a) IS Regs
JSA Sch 1 paras 15(5)(a) and 20I(4)(a) JSA Regs
ESA Sch 4 para 6(5)(a) ESA Regs
PC Sch 1 para 1(2)(b) SPC Regs
HB Sch 3 para 14(5) HB Regs; Sch 3 para 6(7) HB(SPC) Regs

46 **IS** Sch 2 para 14B IS Regs
JSA Sch 1 paras 19 and 20L JSA Regs
ESA Sch 4 para 10 ESA Regs
HB Sch 3 para 19 HB Regs; Sch 3 para 11 HB(SPC) Regs
See also R(IS) 10/94, upheld in *Rider v CAO, The Times,* 30 January 1996 (CA)

47 *Bate v CAO* [1996] 2 All ER 790, reported as R(IS) 12/96

48 **IS** Reg 3(4) and (5) IS Regs
JSA Reg 2(6) and (7) JSA Regs
ESA Reg 71(6) ESA Regs
HB Reg 3(4) HB Regs; Sch 3 para 6(7)
HB(SPC) Regs

49 **IS** Sch 2 para 13(2)(a)(iii) and (b) IS Regs
JSA Sch 1 paras 15(1)(c) and (2)(d) and
20I(1)(d) JSA Regs
ESA Sch 4 para 6(2)(a)(iii) and (b) ESA
Regs
PC Sch 1 para 1(1)(a)(iii) SPC Regs
HB Sch 3 para 14(2)(a)(iii) and (b) HB
Regs; Sch 3 para 6(2)(a)(iii) and (b)
HB(SPC) Regs

50 **IS** Sch 2 para 13(3ZA) IS Regs
JSA Sch 1 paras 15(7) and 20I(6) JSA
Regs
ESA Sch 4 para 6(6) ESA Regs
PC Sch 1 para 2(c) SPC Regs
HB Sch 3 para 14(6) HB Regs; Sch 3 para
6(8) HB(SPC) Regs

51 **IS** Sch 2 para 14A IS Regs
JSA Sch 1 paras 18 and 20K JSA Regs
ESA Sch 4 para 9 ESA Regs
PC Sch 1 para 1(2)(a)(ii) SPC Regs
HB Sch 3 para 18 HB Regs; Sch 3 para
10 HB(SPC) Regs

52 **IS** Sch 2 para 13(3A) IS Regs
JSA Sch 1 paras 15(5) and 20I(4) JSA
Regs
ESA Sch 4 para 6(5) ESA Regs
PC Reg 6(5) and Sch 1 para 1(2)(b) SPC
Regs
HB Sch 3 para 14(5) HB Regs; Sch 3 para
6(7) HB(SPC) Regs

53 **IS** Reg 16(1) and Sch 7 para 9 IS Regs
JSA Reg 78(1) and Sch 5 para 5 JSA Regs
ESA Reg 156 and Sch 5 para 4 ESA Regs

54 **IS** Reg 3 and Sch 2 para 13 IS Regs
JSA Reg 2 and Sch 1 paras 15 and 20I
JSA Regs
ESA Reg 71 and Sch 4 para 6 ESA Regs
PC Sch 1 para 2 SPC Regs
HB Reg 3 HB Regs; reg 3 HB(SPC) Regs

55 **IS** Sch 2 para 13(3)(a) IS Regs
JSA Sch 1 paras 15(4)(a) and 20I(3)(a)
JSA Regs
ESA Sch 4 para 6(4)(a) ESA Regs
PC Sch 1 para 2(2)(a) SPC Regs
HB Sch 3 para 13(4) HB Regs; Sch 3 para
6(6) HB(SPC) Regs

56 **IS** Sch 2 para 13(3)(d) IS Regs
JSA Sch 1 paras 14(1)(h) and (2),
15(4)(c), 20H(1)(i) and (3) and 20I(3)(c)
JSA Regs
ESA Sch 4 para 6(4)(c) and (9) ESA Regs
PC Sch 1 para 2(2)(b) and (c) SPC Regs
HB Sch 3 para 14(4)(b) HB Regs; Sch 3
para 6(6)(b) HB(SPC) Regs

57 CIS/14850/1996, para 10

58 **IS** Reg 3(2)(c) and (d) IS Regs
JSA Reg 2(2)(c) and (d) JSA Regs
ESA Reg 71(2)(c) and (d) ESA Regs
PC Sch 1 para 2(d) and (e) SPC Regs
HB Reg 3(2)(f) HB Regs; reg 3(2)(f)
HB(SPC) Regs

59 **IS** Reg 3(2)(b) IS Regs
JSA Reg 2(2)(b) JSA Regs
ESA Reg 71(2)(b) ESA Regs
HB Reg 3(2)(c) HB Regs; reg 3(2)(c)
HB(SPC) Regs

60 Sch 1 para 2(2)(f) SPC Regs

61 **IS** Sch 2 para 13(3)(c) and (4) IS Regs
JSA Sch 1 paras 15(4)(b) and (6) and
20I(3)(b) and (5) JSA Regs
ESA Sch 4 para 6(4)(b) and (7) ESA Regs
PC Sch 1 para 2(3) and (4) SPC Regs

62 Regs 3 and 9(1) HB Regs; regs 3 and 9(1)
HB(SPC) Regs

63 **IS** Reg 2(1) IS Regs
JSA Reg 1(3) JSA Regs
ESA Reg 2(1) ESA Regs
HB Reg 2(1) HB Regs; reg 2(1) HB(SPC)
Regs
All Definition of 'close relative'

64 **IS/HB** s137(1) SSCBA 1992
JSA s35(1) JSA 1995
ESA Reg 2(1) ESA Regs

65 *Bate v CAO* [1996] 2 All ER 790 (HL)

66 R(IS) 11/98, tribunal of commissioners

67 CSIS/43/1989

68 CIS/754/1991; R(IS) 11/98, para 12

69 R(IS) 11/98, para 8

70 CIS/754/1991

71 **IS** Sch 2 para 14ZA IS Regs
JSA Sch 1 paras 17 and 20J JSA Regs
ESA Sch 4 para 8 ESA Regs
PC Reg 6(6)(a) and Sch 1 para 4 SPC
Regs
HB Sch 3 para 17 HB Regs; Sch 3 para 9
HB(SPC) Regs

72 **IS** Sch 2 paras 7 and 14ZA(3) and (4) IS Regs
JSA Sch 1 paras 8, 17(3) and (4) and 20J(3) and (3A) JSA Regs
ESA Sch 4 para 8(2)-(4) ESA Regs
PC Sch 1 para 4(2) and (3) SPC Regs
HB Sch 3 paras 7 and 17(3) and (4) HB Regs; Sch 3 paras 5 and 9(3) HB(SPC) Regs

73 **IS** Sch 2 para 13(3ZA) IS Regs
JSA Sch 1 paras 15(7) and 201(6) JSA Regs
ESA Sch 4 para 6(6) ESA Regs
PC Sch 1 para 1(2)(c) SPC Regs
HB Sch 3 para 14(6) HB Regs; Sch 3 para 6(8) HB(SPC) Regs

74 **IS** Sch 2 para 13(2)(a)(iii) and (b) IS Regs
JSA Sch 1 paras 15(1)(c) and (2)(d) and 201(1)(d) JSA Regs
ESA Sch 4 para 6(2)(a)(iii) and (b) ESA Regs
PC Sch 1 para 1(1)(ii), (b) and (c)(iv) SPC Regs
HB Sch 3 para 14(2)(a)(iii) and (b) HB Regs; Sch 3 para 6(2)(a)(iii) and (b) HB(SPC) Regs

75 Reg 7(2)(bc) SS&CS(DA) Regs

76 **IS** Sch 2 para 6(2) IS Regs
JSA Sch 1 paras 7(2) and 20C(2) JSA Regs
ESA Sch 4 para 3 ESA Regs
HB Sch 3 para 6 HB Regs

77 **IS** Sch 2 para 5 IS Regs
JSA Sch 1 paras 6 and 20B JSA Regs
HB Sch 3 para 5 HB Regs

78 Sch 3 para 3 HB Regs

79 **IS/JSA/ESA** Regs 3(7) and 6(2)(e) SS&CS(DA) Regs
HB Regs 4(7B) and 7(2)(i) HB&CTB(DA) Regs

80 Reg 6(16)-(18) SS(C&P) Regs

81 Reg 6(26) SS(C&P) Regs

82 Reg 6(19), (20) and (30) SS(C&P) Regs

83 Reg 4(7C) HB&CTB(DA) Regs

4. **Components**

84 **ESA** s4(2), (4) and (5) WRA 2007
HB Reg 22 and Sch 3 paras 21-24 HB Regs

85 Sch 3 para 22(2) HB Regs

86 Reg 69(2) and Sch 5 para 13 ESA Regs

87 Sch 3 paras 22 and 24 HB Regs

88 Sch 3 para 23 HB Regs; Sch 2 Part 1 ESAUC(MA) Regs

89 Because there is no provision to remove it in these circumstances.

90 **ESA** Sch 4 paras 12 and 13 ESA Regs
HB Sch 3 paras 25 and 26 HB Regs

91 Regs 6(2)(r) and 7(38) SS&CS(DA) Regs

92 Reg 7(1)(a) ESA Regs; regs 3(9)(c), 6(2)(a) and 7(2)(be) SS&CS(DA) Regs

93 Regs 4(7B), 7(2)(o) and 8(14D) HB&CTB(DA) Regs

5. **Transitional addition**

94 Sch 3 paras 27 and 30 HB Regs

95 HB/CTB Circular A14/2010, paras 21-23

96 Sch 3 para 27(1) HB Regs

97 HB/CTB Circular A14/2010, para 28 and Annex C

Chapter 13

Universal credit maximum amount

Key facts

- Together with your income and capital, the maximum amount of universal credit (UC) is used to calculate the amount of UC to which you are entitled.
- The maximum amount is made up of a standard allowance plus, where applicable, one or more elements, depending on your circumstances.
- The maximum amount is similar, but not identical, to the applicable amount used to calculate other means-tested benefits, such as income support and income-based jobseeker's allowance.

1. What is the maximum amount

Your maximum universal credit (UC) is made up of the total of:
- a standard allowance, either for a single claimant or a couple making a joint claim (see p258);
- a child element for each child, with an increase for disabled and severely disabled children (see p258). **Note:** there is a 'two-child limit' for new claims or additional children on or after 6 April 2017;
- an element for an adult who is ill and assessed as having limited capability for work (see p260) or an element for an adult who is assessed as having limited capability for work and is also unable to engage in work-related activity (see p262);
- a carer element for someone caring for a severely disabled person (see p263);
- a childcare costs element (see p264);
- a housing costs element for help with your rent or mortgage interest costs (see p266).

Part 3: General rules for means-tested benefits
Chapter 13: Universal credit maximum amount
3. Elements

2. The standard allowance

A standard allowance is always included in your universal credit (UC) maximum amount. The amount depends on your age and whether you are claiming as a single person or making a joint claim with your partner (see p170).[1]

If you are a member of a couple, but one of you is temporarily absent from the household for more than six months, you stop being treated as a couple (see p218).

Even if you do not stop being treated as a couple under this rule, your UC is affected if one of you goes abroad and cannot be treated as in Great Britain while temporarily absent (see p1605).

If you are making a joint claim with your partner and your partner dies, your standard allowance continues at the joint claim rate for the remainder of the monthly UC assessment period (see p164) in which the death occured, and for the next two assessment periods. The rest of your maximum amount is also unaffected by the death during this period.[2]

Note: if one member of a couple does not satisfy the rules of entitlement for UC, the other partner may be able to claim as a single person (see p170). In this case, the standard allowance for a single claimant is used.

Rates of standard allowance

Single claimant	per month
Under 25	£251.77
25 or over	£317.82
Joint claimants	
Both under 25	£395.20
One or both 25 or over	£498.89

3. Elements

Child element

Before 6 April 2017, you got a child element for each child or young person you or your partner were responsible for. You are 'responsible' for a child if s/he is normally living with you (see p220).[3] The child must be aged under 16, or 16–19 and a 'qualifying young person' for universal credit (UC) purposes (see p220).[4]

However, from 6 April 2017, you cannot get an element for a third or subsequent child (unless you are covered by the exceptions – see p260). This is known as the 'two-child limit'.[5] The limit applies to children who you or your partner are responsible for and who normally live with you (see p220). If you already have child elements included in your UC for three or more children born before 6 April 2017, you continue to get them in your current award.

You cannot get a child element for a third or subsequent child born on or after 6 April 2017, unless an exception applies. Between 6 April 2017 and 31 October 2018, if you already have three or more children, you cannot claim UC for the first time (or more than six months after the end of a previous award, or more than one month after the end of a joint claim on becoming single). You will be directed to claim child tax credit (CTC) instead. **Note:** a 'two-child limit' also applies to CTC (see p188). If you get UC and a third or subsequent child born before 6 April 2017 becomes part of your claim (eg, a child of a new partner), you can get a child element for her/him if you have at least two other children born before that date for whom you or your partner are already responsible.[6]

From 1 November 2018, you can get a child element for a third or subsequent child if s/he was born before 1 April 2017 and you got an element for her/him on 31 October 2018 (or in a UC or CTC award that ended within the last six months).

The child element can become payable for a third child to whom the two-child limit would apply if an older child leaves the household (so that you are no longer responsible for her/him), or if a young person leaves education (so that s/he no longer qualifies). In these situations, you should report the change as soon as possible so that you continue to get the maximum two child elements.

There is a higher rate of the child element for the eldest or only child.[7] This is abolished from 6 April 2017, but continues to apply to an eldest or only child born before that date.[8]

If a child is disabled, the child element is increased by a **'disabled child addition'**. You get the lower rate if the child is entitled to disability living allowance (DLA) or personal independence payment (PIP). You get the higher rate if s/he is entitled to DLA care component at the highest rate, the daily living component of PIP at the enhanced rate, or if s/he is certified as severely sight impaired or blind by a consultant ophthalmologist.[9] The disabled child addition is still paid for a child, even if you cannot get a child element for the same child because of the 'two-child limit'.[10]

If your child dies, you continue to get the child element included in your maximum amount for the remainder of the monthly UC assessment period in which the death occurred, and for the next two assessment periods. The rest of your maximum amount is also unaffected by the death during this period.[11]

Rates of child element

	per month
First child (born before 6 April 2017)	£277.08
Second/subsequent child/all children born on or after 6 April 2017, subject to 'two-child limit'	£231.67
Disabled child addition	
Lower rate	£126.11
Higher rate	£372.30

Part 3: General rules for means-tested benefits
Chapter 13: Universal credit maximum amount
3. Elements

Exceptions to the two-child limit

The 'two child limit' does not apply in some cases. A child element is payable for a third or subsequent child to whom the limit would apply but who is:[12]

- born in a multiple birth, other than the first born if you already have two or more children;
- living with you on a long-term basis because s/he is unable to live with her/his parents and would otherwise be at risk of entering the care system and you are caring for her/him as a family member or friend;
- being adopted by you from local authority care;
- likely to have been conceived as a result of rape or in a controlling or coercive relationship;
- the child of a parent under the age of 16, and you are responsible for that parent.

See Appendix 14 for more information.

Limited capability for work element

The limited capability for work element has been abolished for new claimants from 3 April 2017.[13] From this date, you can no longer get the element if you are making a new claim for UC, or if you are already on UC but then start to have limited capability for work, unless you have been getting the limited capability for work-related activity element. You can still get the limited capability for work-related activity element (see p262).

You can still get the limited capability for work element after 3 April 2017 if you (or your partner) are entitled to UC and have limited capability for work (see Chapter 44) and:[14]

- you were getting the element in your current award of UC (or had limited capability for work and were waiting for the element to be included in your UC) immediately before 3 April 2017;
- you were getting the limited capability for work-related activity element in your current award of UC immediately before 3 April 2017 and on a re-assessment it is decided that you are entitled to the limited capability for work element instead;
- it needs to be decided whether you had limited capability for work for UC before 3 April 2017, you have supplied a medical certificate, but the decision that you do have limited capability for work is not made until after this date, including if that decision is made following a revision or an appeal;
- you were entitled to employment and support allowance (ESA) or to national insurance (NI) credits for limited capability for work (see p968) immediately before 3 April 2017, and you are still entitled or you remained entitled from 3 April until you claimed UC;

- you claimed ESA before 3 April 2017, but the initial decision on your claim was changed following a revision or an appeal, and on or after 3 April 2017 your UC award needs to be changed to take account of this;
- you were entitled to incapacity benefit, severe disablement allowance, income support 'on the grounds of disability' (see p105) or NI contribution credits for incapacity for work (see p968) immediately before 3 April 2017, you remained entitled on or after 3 April 2017 until you claimed UC and certain other conditions apply. If you are in this situation, get specialist advice.

Note: if you work and earn an amount at least equal to a certain earnings threshold, you may be treated as *not* having limited capability for work (see p1004).

If you (or your partner in a joint claim) are also entitled to the limited capability for work-related activity element (see p262), you receive that instead – you cannot get both elements.

If you can still get the limited capability for work element, it is not usually included in your UC for the first three months of your claim. After this three-month period, it is included from the start of your next assessment period. The three months usually begins on the day on which you provide a medical certificate. The element can be included straight away if you (or your partner in a joint claim):[15]

- are terminally ill; *or*
- were entitled to the element (or the limited capability for work-related activity element) immediately before your current UC award started and the previous UC award ended because you became a member of a couple or you stopped being a member of a couple; *or*
- were entitled to the element (or the limited capability for work-related activity element) and your previous award of UC ended in the six months before your current award started, because your income was too high; *or*
- are entitled to an award of contributory ESA paid under the UC system that includes the work-related activity component (or you were entitled, but you no longer get ESA because of the rules on the duration of contributory ESA – see p645).

If you are transferring to UC from ESA and were entitled to the work-related activity component in your ESA (see p641), you are treated as having limited capability for work and the limited capability for work element can be included in your UC straight away.

If you were still in the ESA 'assessment phase' (see p639), the time you spent in the assessment phase counts towards the three-month period.[16]

If your award of UC immediately follows an 'extended period of sickness' on jobseeker's allowance (JSA – see p702), the element can be included after 13 weeks beginning with the first day of that period.[17]

Part 3: General rules for means-tested benefits
Chapter 13: Universal credit maximum amount
3. Elements

If you are making a joint claim with your partner, only one limited capability for work element can be included, even if you both meet the conditions.[18]

If you were previously getting UC as a single person but then form a couple with someone who was not entitled to UC, but who was getting ESA that included the work-related activity component (see p641), the limited capability for work element is included in your joint UC award.[19] However, if your partner's ESA assessment phase (see p639) lasted less than 13 weeks, the limited capability for work element is not included in your joint UC award immediately. Instead, you must wait until 13 weeks have passed since your partner's ESA assessment phase began. The element is then included from the start of your next UC assessment period.[20]

If you also satisfy the conditions for the carer element (see p263), usually the carer element is included instead of the limited capability for work element. If you have a joint claim and your partner satisfies the conditions for both the limited capability for work element and the carer element, again only the carer element is included. However, if you only qualify for one of these elements and your partner qualifies for the other, both elements can be included.[21]

Example
Sam and Sharon have a joint claim for UC, made before 6 April 2017. They have a disabled son, George. Sam has limited capability for work. Sharon is George's carer and satisfies the conditions for the carer element. Both the limited capability for work element and the carer element were included in Sam and Sharon's UC award before 6 April 2017, and continue as long as they remain entitled.
Note: if Sam were also a carer for George, they could nominate Sharon as the main carer for George so that both the limited capability for work and carer elements can continue to be paid.

Rate of limited capability for work element

	per month
Limited capability for work	£126.11

Limited capability for work-related activity element

A limited capability for work-related activity element is included in your maximum amount if you (or your partner in a joint claim) have been assessed as having limited capability for work-related activity.[22] For how this is assessed, see p1010 – the rules are very similar to those that apply for ESA.

In general, if you are qualifying for the element for the first time, it is not included in your claim for a period of three months, after which it is included from the start of your next assessment period. The three months usually begins on the day on which you provide a medical certificate. It can be included straight away if you (or your partner in a joint claim):[23]

- are terminally ill; or
- were entitled to the element (or the limited capability for work element) immediately before your current UC award started and your previous award of UC ended because you became a member of a couple or you stopped being a member of a couple; or
- were entitled to the element (or the limited capability for work element) and your previous award of UC ended within the six months before your current award started, because your income was too high; or
- are entitled to the limited capability for work element in your UC, but are then assessed as entitled to the limited capability for work-related activity element; or
- are entitled to an award of ESA that includes the support component.

If you are transferring from ESA to UC and were entitled to the support component in your ESA (see p641), you are treated as having limited capability for work-related activity and the limited capability for work-related activity element is included in your UC straight away. If you were still in the 'assessment phase' for ESA (see p639), the time you spent in the assessment phase counts towards the three-month period.[24]

The rules on including the limited capability for work-related activity element after an extended period of sickness on JSA, if you are making a joint claim with your partner, and if you were previously getting UC as a single person but then form a couple, are the same as those that apply to the limited capability for work element (see p260).

If you (or in a joint claim, your partner) also satisfy the conditions for the carer element (see below), the limited capabililty for work-related activity element is paid instead.[25]

Rate of limited capability for work-related activity element

	per month
Limited capability for work-related activity	£318.76

Carer element

A carer element is included in your maximum amount if you have 'regular and substantial' caring responsibilities for a severely disabled person. This means that you satisfy, or would satisfy were it not for the level of your earnings, the conditions for carer's allowance (CA) – eg, you are caring for at least 35 hours a week (see p556). You do not need to have claimed CA. **Note:** you do not qualify for the carer element if you have any earnings from your caring responsibilities.[26]

Part 3: General rules for means-tested benefits
Chapter 13: Universal credit maximum amount
3. Elements

If you are making a joint claim, you can get two carer elements if both you and your partner satisfy the conditions, provided you are not caring for the same person. If you are both caring for the same person, you get one carer element. You can decide between you which partner should be entitled – eg, if it is necessary for your partner to be entitled to the carer element so that you can also get the limited capability for work or limited capability for work-related activity element. If you do not decide which one of you should be entitled to the carer element, the DWP decides for you.[27] Similarly, if somone other than your partner is caring for the same person, only one of you can get CA or the carer element of UC for that care. You can decide between you who should be entitled.[28]

If the person you care for dies, the carer element continues for the rest of the monthly UC assessment period in which the death occurred, and for the next two assessment periods. The rest of your maximum amount is also unaffected by the death during this period.[29]

Rate of carer element

	per month
Carer	£151.89

Childcare costs element

A childcare costs element is included in your maximum amount if you are working (or have an offer of work) and you have childcare costs for 'relevant childcare' – eg, a registered childminder (see p265).

The amount of the element is 85 per cent of your childcare costs, up to a maximum of £646.35 a month for one child and £1,108.04 a month for two or more children.[30]

Future changes

If you are entitled to UC, you cannot be eligible for tax-free childcare payments, as you cannot get UC and tax-free childcare at the same time. In the future, if you register for the tax-free childcare scheme, all of your UC could be terminated.[31] The scheme is expected to be introduced in early 2017. See p864 for more details, and see CPAG's online service and *Welfare Rights Bulletin* for updates.

To get the childcare costs element you must be in paid work (there are no minimum hours) or have an offer of paid work that is due to start before the end of your next UC monthly assessment period (see p164).[32] If you are a member of a couple, your partner must also be in paid work, unless s/he cannot provide childcare her/himself because s/he has limited capability for work (see Chapter 44), or s/he is caring for a severely disabled person and gets (or would be entitled to) CA (see p555), or s/he is temporarily absent from your household. **Note:** you stop counting as a couple if your partner is (or is expected to be) absent from Great Britain for more than six months.[33] If your partner is temporarily absent abroad, see p1590.

You are treated as still in paid work if you are getting statutory sick pay, statutory maternity pay, statutory adoption pay, statutory paternity pay, statutory shared parental pay or maternity allowance. You are also treated as still in paid work if your work ended during the assessment period concerned or in the previous one – you can continue to get the childcare costs element for one month after your work ends.[34]

In addition, you must meet all the following conditions.[35]

- You pay charges for 'relevant childcare' (see below) for a child for whom you are responsible – ie, s/he normally lives with you.
- The child is aged under 16 or has not reached the 1st September following her/his 16th birthday.
- The childcare charges are to enable you to do paid work (or were to enable you to do paid work but that work has stopped).
- You report the charges to the DWP no later than the end of the monthly UC assessment period following the assessment period in which the charges were paid. In the 'full service' areas (see p21) you must usually report the charges before the end of the assessment period in which the charges were paid, but the DWP may allow you to report them later then this, under the same rules that apply to late notification of a change in circumstances (see p1296).

Relevant childcare

'**Relevant childcare**' means care for a child provided by the following.

In England:[36]

– a registered childcare provider – ie, someone registered with Ofsted under Part 3 of the Childcare Act 2006; *or*

– a school on school premises out of school hours (or at any time if the child has not reached compulsory school age); *or*

– an official domiciliary care provider – ie, one registered with the Care Quality Commission.

In Scotland:[37]

– a registered childminder or similar provider of daycare – ie, registered as such under the Public Services Reform (Scotland) Act 2010; *or*

– a childcare agency under the Public Services Reform (Scotland) Act 2010; *or*

– a local authority registered to provide childminding or daycare under the Public Services Reform (Scotland) Act 2010.

In Wales:[38]

– a registered childminder or daycare provider – ie, registered under Part 2 of the Children and Families (Wales) Measure 2010; *or*

Part 3: General rules for means-tested benefits
Chapter 13: Universal credit maximum amount
Notes

– someone providing daycare that would count for registration, were it not for the fact that it is provided in a care home, hospital, children's home, residential family centre or school; or

– someone providing childcare under a Welsh Assembly scheme for tax credit purposes; or

– out of school hours, a school on school premises or a local authority; or

– an official domiciliary care worker – ie, under the Domiciliary Care Agencies (Wales) Regulations 2004; or

– a foster parent (but not for the child who s/he is fostering) if, were it not for the fact that the child is too old, the childcare would count as registered childcare or daycare – ie, under Part 2 of the Children and Families (Wales) Measure 2010.

The following *does not count* as relevant childcare:[39]

– care provided by a 'close relative' of the child (ie, parent, parent-in-law, son, daughter, son-in-law, daughter-in-law, stepson, stepdaughter, stepbrother, stepsister, and a partner of any of these) wholly or mainly in the child's home;[40]

– care provided by a foster parent, foster carer or kinship carer for a child who the person is fostering or looking after as a kinship carer.

Rates of childcare costs element

	per month
Maximum for one child	£646.35
Maximum for two or more children	£1,108.04

Housing costs element

A housing costs element is included in your maximum amount for qualifying housing costs. Housing costs can be either rent or owner-occupier payments. See Chapter 22 for when you are entitled and the amount of your housing costs element.

Notes

2. The standard allowance
1 Reg 36 UC Regs
2 Reg 37 UC Regs

3. Elements
3 Reg 4 UC Regs
4 Reg 24 UC Regs
5 s10(1A) WRA 2012; reg 24A UC Regs

6 Regs 39–42 UC(TP) Regs
7 Reg 36 UC Regs
8 *Welfare Reform: written statement,* HCWS96, House of Commons, *Hansard,* 20 July 2016
9 Reg 24 UC Regs
10 s10(2) WRA 2012; reg 36 UC Regs
11 Reg 37 UC Regs
12 Sch 12 UC Regs
13 s16 WRWA 2016
14 Sch 1 Part 2 ESAUC(MA) Regs
15 Reg 28 UC Regs
16 Regs 20 and 21 UC(TP) Regs
17 Reg 20A UC(TP) Regs
18 Reg 27(4) UC Regs
19 Reg 19(3) UC(TP) Regs
20 Reg 20(2) UC(TP) Regs
21 Reg 29(4) UC Regs
22 Reg 27 UC Regs
23 Reg 28 UC Regs
24 Regs 19 and 20 UC(TP) Regs
25 Reg 29(4) UC Regs
26 Regs 19 and 20 UC Regs
27 Reg 29(2) and (3) UC Regs
28 Reg 29(3) UC Regs; s70(7) SSCBA 1992
29 Reg 37 UC Regs
30 Regs 34 and 36 UC Regs
31 DWP, *Universal Credit: increasing the childcare offer,* December 2014
32 Reg 32 UC Regs
33 Reg 3(6) UC Regs
34 Reg 32(2) UC Regs
35 Reg 33 UC Regs; reg 2(2) Universal Credit (Digital Service) Amendment Regulations 2014, No.2887
36 Reg 35(2) UC Regs
37 Reg 35(3) UC Regs
38 Reg 35(4) UC Regs
39 Reg 35(7) UC Regs
40 Reg 2, definition of 'close relative', UC Regs

Chapter 14

Income: under pension credit age

This chapter covers:
1. Whose income counts (below)
2. What counts as income (p269)
3. Earnings (p270)
4. Income other than earnings (p284)
5. Notional income (p299)
6. Working out weekly income (p302)

This chapter explains the rules for working out your weekly income for income support, income-based jobseeker's allowance (JSA) and income-related employment and support allowance. It also covers housing benefit (HB) if you and your partner are under the qualifying age for pension credit (PC). For PC and HB for those over the qualifying age for PC, see Chapter 15. For universal credit, see Chapter 16; for tax credits, see Chapter 60; for carer's allowance, see Chapter 25; and for health benefits, see Chapter 29.

Key facts
- Your entitlement to income support (IS), income-based jobseeker's allowance (JSA), income-related employment and support allowance (ESA) and housing benefit (HB) and the amount you get depend on how much income you have.
- Your own income counts and, if you are a member of a couple, your partner's income also counts.
- Some income may be completely or partly ignored, or it may count in full.
- Some income may be treated as capital and some capital treated as income.
- If you get IS, income-based JSA or income-related ESA, you are entitled to maximum HB, so you do not need to work out your income again for HB.

1. Whose income counts

Your income counts and, if you are a member of a couple, your partner's income also counts (see p269). The income of your dependent children may affect your income support (IS) or income-based jobseeker's allowance (JSA) if you have been on benefit since before 6 April 2004 (see below).

Income of a partner

If you are a member of a couple (see p215), your partner's income is added to yours.[1]

Note: if you or your partner are getting IS, income-based JSA or income-related employment and support allowance (ESA), all of your (and your partner's) income is ignored for housing benefit.[2]

If you or your partner are under 18 and so the rate of the IS, income-based JSA or income-related ESA personal allowance for a couple (£114.85) is reduced to £73.10 or £57.90 (see p232), an amount of income equivalent to the reduction is ignored.[3]

Income of a dependent child

Maintenance paid to or for a child is usually disregarded (see p287).

The income of a dependent child does not affect your means-tested benefits. However, for IS and income-based JSA, if you have been getting benefit since before 6 April 2004 with a child included in your claim and you do not yet have an award of child tax credit, her/his income is counted as yours if s/he does not have capital of over £3,000.[4] Some income may be disregarded.

See p903, p927 and p935 of the 2012/13 edition of this *Handbook* for details.[5]

2. What counts as income

All income is taken into account for income support (IS), income-based jobseeker's allowance (JSA) and income-related employment and support allowance (ESA) unless it is specifically disregarded.

If you get IS, income-based JSA or income-related ESA, all your income is ignored for housing benefit (HB). All income is also ignored for HB if you come under the universal credit (UC) system and (in exceptional circumstances) can get both HB and UC. Otherwise, all income is taken into account for HB, other than income that is specifically disregarded.

Income only counts if it is paid to you for your own use. It does not count if you cannot prevent it being paid to a third party (eg, under an attachment of earnings order), although other payments for you made to a third party might count (see p300).[6]

Income is converted into a weekly amount (see p302).

Part 3: General rules for means-tested benefits
Chapter 14: Income: under pension credit age
3. Earnings

Income or capital?

The difference between income and capital is not defined. Payments of income are normally made in respect of a specified period and form part of a regular series of payments.[7] However, sometimes a one-off payment can be income depending on what it is paid for – eg, a settlement for underpaid wages under equal pay legislation.[8] Some income is treated as capital (see p361) and some capital is treated as income (see p293).

3. **Earnings**

How earnings are treated depends on whether you are employed (see below) or self-employed (see p276). In both cases, some of your earnings can be disregarded (see p278).

Employed earnings

This section explains how any earnings received by you or your partner and, in some cases, a dependent child (see p269) are treated. The same rules apply to your (but not your partner's or child's) earnings if you are claiming contribution-based jobseeker's allowance (JSA – see p705).

To work out how earnings are taken into account, do the following.

- Check whether the payments count as earnings (see below). In some cases, payments are treated as capital, as income other than earnings, or ignored altogether.
- Calculate your net earnings (see p272 and p276).
- Work out weekly net earnings (see p302).
- Deduct the appropriate weekly earnings disregard (see p278);
- Work out the date from when earnings are taken into account (see p303). For income support (IS), income-based JSA and income-related employment and support allowance (ESA), also work out the period covered by the earnings (see p302). Normally, a payment counts from the date it is due to be paid and for the length of time it has been paid – eg, a month's wages count for a month, starting from the day they are due, at the weekly rate as calculated.

There are special rules for how payments affect benefit when you leave a job (see p273).

What counts as earnings

'Earnings' means 'any remuneration or profit derived from ... employment'. As well as your wages, this includes:[9]

- any bonus or commission (including tips);
- holiday pay (but see p273 if your job ends or you are off work);

- for HB, any statutory sick pay (SSP) or contractual sick pay.[10] For IS, income-based JSA and income-related ESA, all sick pay is treated as income other than earnings and, therefore, does not attract an earnings disregard and is counted in full less any tax, class 1 national insurance (NI) contributions and half of any pension contributions;[11]
- for HB, any statutory maternity pay (SMP), statutory adoption pay (SAP), statutory paternity pay (SPP) or statutory shared parental pay (SSPP) or any other payment made to you by your employer while you are on maternity, adoption, paternity or shared parental leave.[12] For IS, income-based JSA and income-related ESA, all such pay is treated as income other than earnings and, therefore, does not attract an earnings disregard and is counted in full less any tax that is payable, class 1 NI contributions and half of any pension contributions;[13]
- any payments made by your employer for expenses not 'wholly, exclusively and necessarily' incurred in carrying out your job, including any travel expenses to and from work, and any payments made to you for looking after members of your family. The latter can apply if you are looking after your child, even if s/he cannot be included in your claim;
- a retainer (eg, payments during the school holidays if you work for the school meals service[14]) or a guarantee payment – eg, if you are working short time or laid off;[15]
- certain compensation payments in respect of the termination of your employment, including employment tribunal awards and pay in lieu of notice. See p273 for the way these are treated when you stop work. For IS, JSA and income-related ESA, compensatory refunds of contributions to an occupational scheme[16] are not treated as earnings;
- an equal pay settlement – eg, through a 'single-status agreement';[17]
- any payment of a non-cash voucher which is liable for class 1 NI contributions.[18] Non-cash vouchers that are not liable for contributions are classed as payments in kind (see below).[19]

What does not count as earnings

Examples of payments not counted as earnings include the following.

- Payments in kind (eg, petrol) are ignored,[20] unless you are on IS or income-based JSA and involved in a trade dispute (see p940), although the notional income rules may be applied instead (see p299).[21] Although non-cash vouchers liable for class 1 NI contributions are not treated as payments in kind, vouchers which are not liable for contributions (eg, certain childcare and charitable vouchers) are treated as payments in kind and are disregarded.[22]
- The value of any free accommodation provided as part of your job should be ignored.[23]
- An advance of earnings or a loan from your employer is treated as capital.[24] However, it is treated as earnings for IS or income-based JSA if you or your partner are involved in, or have returned to work after, a trade dispute.

Part 3: General rules for means-tested benefits
Chapter 14: Income: under pension credit age
3. Earnings

- Payments towards expenses that are 'wholly, exclusively and necessarily' incurred during the course of your work, such as travelling expenses, are ignored.[25] For example, deductions could be made for:
  - tools or work equipment;
  - special clothing or uniforms;[26]
  - postage and telephone costs (including rental);[27]
  - fuel costs (including standing charges);
  - secretarial expenses;[28]
  - running a car (including petrol, tax, insurance, repairs and maintenance and rental on a leased car).[29]
  If any expenditure is for both business and private use, it should be apportioned as appropriate (and any determination by HM Revenue and Customs normally followed).[30]
- If you are a local councillor, travelling expenses and subsistence payments are (and basic allowances may be[31]) ignored as expenses 'wholly, exclusively and necessarily' incurred in your work.
- Earnings payable abroad which cannot be brought into Britain (eg, because of exchange control regulations) are ignored.[32] **Note:** if your earnings are paid in another currency, any bank charges for converting them into sterling are deducted before taking them into account.[33]
- Any occupational pension[34] counts as income other than earnings and the net amount is taken into account in full.[35] See p706 (and p643) for the occupational pension rules for contribution-based JSA (and contributory ESA).
- If you are a member of the reserve forces, earnings while on training are disregarded for up to 43 days in your first year of training and 15 days thereafter, to allow you to keep a minimum 10 pence a week IS, JSA or income-related ESA entitlement.[36]

Calculating net earnings from employment

Both your 'gross' earnings and 'net' earnings must be calculated.

Gross and net earnings

'**Gross earnings**' means the amount of earnings received from your employer less deductions for any expenses wholly, necessarily and exclusively incurred by you in order to carry out the duties of your employment.[37] See p270 for what counts as earnings and p271 for examples of expenses that can be deducted.

'**Net earnings**' means your gross earnings less any deductions made for:[38]

- income tax;
- class 1 NI contributions;
- half of any contribution you make towards a personal or occupational pension scheme.

For HB, if your earnings are estimated, the amount of tax and NI contributions you would expect to pay on those earnings is also estimated. This amount, plus half of any pension contribution you are paying, is then deducted.[39]

For HB, the local authority has the discretion to ignore changes in tax or NI contributions for up to 30 benefit weeks. This can be used, for example, if April tax changes are not reflected in your actual income until several months later. When the changes are eventually taken into account and your benefit entitlement is either increased or reduced accordingly, you are not treated as having been underpaid or overpaid benefit during the period of the delay.[40]

Payments when you stop work

When you stop work and claim benefit, your final earnings are usually ignored, with some exceptions. If you were claiming benefit while working, your final earnings are generally taken into account.

Your job ends before benefit starts

If your employment ends before your entitlement to benefit begins, any payments that count as earnings (see p270), including wages, holiday pay (but see p274) and pay in lieu of notice, are ignored as income for that benefit, except for the following payments.[41]

- A retainer counts as earnings.
- If you were in full-time paid work, certain employment tribunal awards (and 'out-of-court' settlements) count as earnings, including:
  - compensation because of unfair dismissal;[42]
  - a 'protective' award when an employer fails to comply with redundancy procedures and, for JSA, a compensatory award in respect of trade union activity;[43]
  - for IS, income-related ESA and HB, pay under a continuation of contract award or for arrears of pay in respect of a reinstatement or re-engagement order.[44]

  If you were in part-time work, the above are all ignored for IS, income-related ESA and HB, but count for JSA.
- Guarantee payments for workless days or while suspended on medical or maternity grounds count as earnings, including when awarded by an employment tribunal.[45]
- Arrears of statutory or contractual sick, maternity, adoption, paternity and shared parental pay and lump-sum advance payments are taken into account for IS, JSA and income-related ESA as income, without any earnings disregard, from when they are paid for the same length of time covered by the arrears. They are ignored for HB.[46]
- Statutory redundancy pay counts as capital.[47]
- Contractual redundancy pay (deducting an amount for statutory entitlement) is ignored completely for JSA.[48] For IS, income-related ESA and HB, it counts as

Part 3: General rules for means-tested benefits
Chapter 14: Income: under pension credit age
3. Earnings

capital unless, for IS and income-related ESA, you work part time and have not been paid all your pay in lieu of notice due, in which case it is ignored.[49]
- Some redundancy schemes make periodic payments after leaving work. These are treated as income other than earnings.[50]
- Ex gratia payments and other kinds of compensation (other than employment tribunal awards) are treated in the same way as contractual redundancy pay.
- Holiday pay is usually ignored. However, if your job ends, it counts as capital if your contract provides for it to be payable more than four weeks after termination of employment – eg, in some cases if you leave without giving notice.[51]

For what counts as 'full-time paid work', see p989. For this rule, the IS definition also applies to income-related ESA (except for term-time workers whose hours are assessed under the JSA rule).[52]

Note: the above only applies to benefits you claim after employment ends. So, for example, if you are already getting HB when you leave your job, but not IS, JSA or income-related ESA, your final earnings are disregarded for IS/JSA/income-related ESA in this way, but not for HB. See p275 for how final payments are treated when you are already getting benefit.

Example
Gina is made redundant from a full-time job on 31 May and leaves with one month's wages, her full four weeks' pay in lieu of notice, contractual redundancy pay of £5,000 and three days' holiday pay. All are due to be paid on 31 May. She claims IS and HB after her job ends. Final wages, pay in lieu of notice and holiday pay are ignored. Redundancy pay is treated as capital. Her capital is below the limit and she is entitled to benefit from 1 June.

You stop work but your job has not ended
If you stop work before your benefit begins but your employment has not ended (eg, you go on sick leave or maternity leave), statutory and contractual sick, maternity, adoption, paternity and shared parental pay are taken into account as income without any earnings disregard for IS, JSA and income-related ESA.[53] For HB, they count as earnings with the usual disregard.[54] If holiday pay is due to be paid more than four weeks after you stopped work, it is treated as capital (unless, for IS/JSA, you are involved in a trade dispute). If it is paid less than four weeks after you stopped work, it is ignored.[55] All other payments that count as earnings are ignored, except for a retainer or guarantee payments for workless days or for medical or maternity suspension.[56] If you are suspended from work, any earnings are taken into account as normal.
    Note: these rules only apply to benefits you claim after you stop work. If, for example, you are already getting HB when you stop work, but not IS/JSA/income-

related ESA, your final earnings are ignored in this way for IS/JSA/income-related ESA, but not for HB.

You were claiming benefit when working

If your job ends and you were claiming benefit while you were in work, any payments made to you when that job ends are taken into account as earnings as follows.[57]

- Final earnings are taken into account as normal (including wages, bonuses and expenses that count as earnings).
- For IS, income-related ESA and HB, pay in lieu of notice is taken into account; for IS and income-related ESA, final earnings are taken into account first, followed by pay in lieu of notice.
- Contractual redundancy pay, ex gratia payments and other types of compensation (other than employment tribunal awards) above the level of entitlement to statutory redundancy pay:
  - are treated as capital for IS and income-related ESA, if you work out your notice or get full pay in lieu of notice. Otherwise, they are taken into account as earnings for one week only;
  - together with pay in lieu of notice, are treated as earnings for JSA, up until the end of the fixed-term contract, if you had one, or until the end of the notice period (sometimes longer if the employer says it covers a longer period). For JSA, if none of the payment covers pay in lieu of notice or early termination of a fixed-term contract, the total of these payments covers a standard number of weeks arrived at by dividing the payment by the weekly maximum statutory redundancy payment (£489) if this is shorter than the notice period;
  - are treated as capital for HB, except any amount representing loss of income, which is taken into account as earnings.

  The week(s) the payments count for start after the period covered by final earnings and any pay in lieu of notice.
- Holiday pay normally counts as earnings. However, it counts as capital if it is payable more than four weeks after employment ends or is interrupted – eg, if you are off sick before your employment ends. For IS, JSA and income-related ESA, it counts for the number of weeks covered by the holiday pay (not the number of working weeks[58]) starting after the period covered by other payments listed in the above three bullet points.
- An employment tribunal award (eg, for unfair dismissal) is taken into account as earnings.
- Arrears of sick, maternity, adoption, paternity and shared parental pay count as earnings for HB, and as income other than earnings for IS, JSA and income-related ESA.[59]
- Statutory redundancy payments are treated as capital.

Part 3: General rules for means-tested benefits
Chapter 14: Income: under pension credit age
3. Earnings

Example

Neelam has been getting HB while working part time. She earned £50 a week. She finishes work on 16 July and on that day is given £60, made up of £30 final wages and £30 holiday pay. The £60 wages and holiday pay are taken into account as normal for HB, deducting the earnings disregard. She claims JSA on 17 July. For JSA, her final wages and holiday pay are ignored, so none of the £60 is taken into account. Her JSA starts on 24 July after the seven waiting days.

Self-employed earnings

This section explains how any earnings from self-employment received by you or your partner and, in some cases, a dependent child (see p269) are treated. The same rules apply to your (but not your partner's or child's) earnings if you are claiming contribution-based JSA (see p705).

To work out how earnings are taken into account, do the following.

- Calculate net earnings (see below).
- Work out your average earnings (see p277).
- Deduct the appropriate weekly earnings disregard (see p278).

Calculating net earnings

Your **'net profit'** must be worked out. This consists of your self-employed earnings minus:[60]

- reasonable expenses (see below); *and*
- income tax and NI contributions; *and*
- half of any premium paid in respect of a personal pension scheme which is eligible for tax relief.

Drawings from capital do not count as income, whether the business is in profit or not.[61] If you receive payments for board and lodging, these do not count as earnings,[62] but as other income (less any disregards, see p291).

If you are getting help with your business under a DWP scheme and this is classed as the 'self-employment route' (eg, New Enterprise Allowance), income and expenses are treated differently (see p294).

Reasonable expenses

Expenses must be reasonable and 'wholly and exclusively' incurred for the purposes of your business.[63] This involves similar considerations to those that apply to the allowances permitted in assessing gross earnings of employed earners. If a car or telephone, for example, is used partly for business and partly for private purposes, the costs of it can be apportioned and the amount attributable to business use can be deducted.[64]

Reasonable expenses include:[65]

- repayments of capital on loans for replacing equipment and machinery;
- repayments of capital on loans for, and income spent on, the repair of a business asset except if this is covered by insurance;
- interest on a loan taken out for the purposes of the business;
- excess of VAT paid over VAT received.

Reasonable expenses do not include:[66]
- any capital expenditure;
- depreciation;[67]
- money for setting up or expanding the business – eg, the cost of adapting the business premises;
- any loss incurred before the beginning of the current assessment period. If the business makes a loss, the net profit is nil. The losses of one business cannot be offset against the profit of any other business in which you are engaged, or against your earnings as an employee[68] (although if two businesses or employments share expenses, these may be apportioned and offset);[69]
- capital repayments on loans taken out for business purposes;
- business entertainment expenses;
- for HB, debts (other than proven bad debts) – but the expenses of recovering a debt can be deducted.

Working out average earnings from self-employment

For IS, income-based JSA and income-related ESA, the weekly amount is the average of earnings:[70]
- over a period of one year (in practice, normally the last year for which accounts are available);[71]
- over a more appropriate period if you have recently taken up self-employment, there has been a change that will affect your business, or for any other reason if a different period may enable any part, or all, of your income and expenditure to be calculated more accurately.

For HB, the amount of your weekly earnings is averaged over an 'appropriate' period (usually based on your last year's trading accounts), which must not be longer than a year.[72]

For all benefits, if your earnings are royalties, copyright payments or payments under the Public Lending Right scheme, the amount of earnings is divided by the weekly amount of benefit that would be payable if you had not received this income plus the amount that would be disregarded from those earnings (for income-related ESA, the amount of benefit that would be payable includes any contributory ESA).[73] For IS, income-based JSA and income-related ESA, you are not entitled to benefit for the resulting number of weeks. For HB, earnings are taken into account for the resulting number of weeks.

Part 3: General rules for means-tested benefits
Chapter 14: Income: under pension credit age
3. Earnings

If you stop doing self-employed work, any earnings from that work are disregarded except for royalties and copyright and Public Lending Right scheme payments.[74]

Childminders

In practice, childminders are always treated as self-employed. Your net profit is deemed to be one-third of your earnings less income tax, your NI contributions and half of personal pension scheme contributions (see p276).[75] The rest of your earnings are completely ignored.

Disregarded earnings

Some of your earnings from employment or self-employment are disregarded and do not affect your benefit. The amount of the disregard depends on your circumstances. For IS, income-based JSA and HB, the three main levels of disregard are £25, £20 or £5/£10. For HB, there is an additional disregard depending on the hours you work, a childcare costs disregard (see p281) and a permitted work disregard.

For income-related ESA, the main level of disregard is £20. However, different rules apply if you are doing 'permitted work' (see below).

For the amount of disregarded earnings for contribution-based JSA, see p1021.

Disregards for income-related employment and support allowance

Permitted work disregard

- All your earnings from 'permitted work' (see p1023) are disregarded up to whichever earnings limit applies: £20 or £120. (Only £20 can be disregarded from self-employed earnings from royalties, copyright payments or Public Lending Right scheme payments.)[76]
- If your earnings are less than the £20 or £120 limit, up to £20 of what is left can be disregarded from your partner's earnings.[77]

Note: earnings for permitted work (for both contributory and income-related ESA) are assessed in the same way as earnings are generally for income-related ESA described in this chapter.[78]

£20 disregard

Twenty pounds of your earnings (including those of your partner) is disregarded if:[79]

- you are doing work you may do while claiming ESA (see p1021), but only if it is:
  - as a councillor; or
  - as a disability member of the First-tier Tribunal. If you are also doing 'permitted work', instead of the £20 disregard, any unused permitted work disregard up to £20 can be deducted from these tribunal earnings; or

- during an emergency to protect someone or to prevent serious damage to property or livestock; *or*
- while receiving assistance in pursuing self-employment under a government scheme;
- your partner is in part-time employment of under 24 hours a week (but if you are doing permitted work, see p278);
- your partner would be treated as not being in full-time paid work for IS purposes, other than if this is because of qualifying for mortgage interest run-on (see p996); *or*
- your partner is working, but does not count as being in full-time paid work because s/he:
  - is childminding in her/his home; *or*
  - is a carer under the rules for who can claim IS (see p104); *or*
  - is receiving assistance under the 'self-employment route' – eg, New Enterprise Allowance; *or*
  - is an auxiliary coastguard, part-time firefighter, part-time member of a lifeboat crew or member of the reserve forces; *or*
  - is working as a councillor; *or*
  - would not qualify for JSA on the grounds that s/he has been involved in a trade dispute (see p940), or it is the first 15 days following her/his return to work after having been involved in a trade dispute.

Disregards for income support, income-based jobseeker's allowance and housing benefit

£25 disregard

Lone parents on HB have £25 of their earnings ignored.[80] **Note:** if you get IS, income-based JSA or income-related ESA, all your earnings are disregarded for HB, so this £25 disregard does not apply.

£20 disregard

Twenty pounds of your earnings (including those of your partner) is disregarded if:

- for IS or income-based JSA, you are a lone parent;[81]
- you or your partner qualify for a disability premium (see p238).[82] For IS and income-based JSA, you are treated as qualifying for the premium if you would do so but for the fact that you are in hospital;
- for HB, you or your partner qualify for a severe disability premium (see p242), the support component or work-related activity component (see p251), or you are in the 'work-related activity group' (see p642);[83]
- you or your partner qualify for a carer premium (see p246). The disregard applies to the carer's earnings. If both partners in a couple get the carer premium, £20 is disregarded from their combined earnings. If you are the carer

Part 3: General rules for means-tested benefits
Chapter 14: Income: under pension credit age
3. Earnings

and the claimant, and your earnings are less than £20, up to £5 (£10 for HB) of the disregard can be used on your partner's earnings (or all of what is left of it if your partner's earnings are from one of the services listed in the next bullet point) – but the total disregard cannot be more than £20;[84]

- you or your partner are an auxiliary coastguard, part-time firefighter, part-time member of a lifeboat crew or member of the reserve forces.[85] If you earn less than £20 for doing any of these services, you can use up to £5 (up to £10 for HB, if you have a partner) of the disregard on another job[86] or on a partner's earnings from another job;[87]
- for IS and income-based JSA only, you are a member of a couple, your benefit would include a disability premium but for the fact that one of you qualifies for the higher pensioner premium (see p242), and one of you is under the qualifying age for pension credit (PC) (see p147) and either of you are in employment;[88]
- for IS and income-based JSA only, you or your partner qualify for the higher pensioner premium (see p242) and, immediately before reaching the qualifying age for PC (see p147), you or your partner were in part-time employment and you were entitled to a £20 disregard because of qualifying for a disability premium. Since reaching the qualifying age for PC, you or your partner must have continued in part-time employment, although breaks of up to eight weeks when you were not getting IS, income-based JSA or income-related ESA are ignored.[89]

If you qualify under more than one category, you still have a maximum of only £20 of your earnings disregarded.

Basic £5 or £10 disregard
If you do not qualify for a £25 or £20 disregard (or, for HB, the permitted work disregard), £5 of your earnings is disregarded if you are single. If you claim as a member of a couple, £10 of your total earnings is disregarded – whether or not you are both working.[90]

Permitted work disregard for housing benefit
If you or your partner are doing 'permitted work' (see p1023 for what this means) and getting contributory ESA, incapacity benefit (IB), severe disablement allowance (SDA) or NI credits for limited capability for work or incapacity, the permitted work earnings limit for that benefit or credit (either £20 or £120) is also disregarded from earnings for HB.[91] This is instead of the usual disregard of £5, £10, £20 or £25.

If earnings from permitted work are less than the limit, you can use up the rest:
- on your partner's earnings, up to a maximum of £20 or up to the limit if s/he is also doing permitted work, but there is only one disregard between you; *or*

- on your own earnings from other work. See p1021 for other work you may do while claiming one of these benefits. If you are a lone parent, you can also top up the disregard on earnings from other work to £25.

Note: there is also an earnings disregard for permitted work for income-related ESA but not for IS.

Additional disregard for housing benefit

For HB only, whichever earnings disregard applies is increased by £17.10 if:[92]

- you or your partner receive the 30-hour element as part of your (or your partner's) working tax credit (WTC – see p1412); *or*
- you or your partner are aged 25 or over and work 30 hours or more a week on average; *or*
- you or your partner work 16 hours or more a week on average and you have a child who is part of your family for benefit purposes (see p220), or your HB includes the family premium (see p236); *or*
- you are a lone parent and work 16 hours or more a week on average; *or*
- you or your partner work 16 hours or more a week on average and your HB includes a disability premium (see p238), the support component or work-related activity component (see p250), or you are in the 'work-related activity group' (see p642). For couples, the partner for whom the premium/component is awarded or who is in the work-related activity group must be working 16 hours or more a week on average.

The additional earnings disregard does not apply if your total earnings are less than the total of £17.10 plus any earnings disregard and childcare costs disregard (see below). In this case, £17.10 is disregarded from any WTC awarded to you or your partner, but the earnings disregard is not increased.

Note: only one additional disregard is allowed from your (or your partner's) earnings.

Example

Owen and Mia are a couple with one child aged eight. Owen gets contributory ESA and HB. Mia works part time for 16 hours a week earning £120.

The amount of Mia's earnings taken into account for HB is £82.90 a week. From her £120 wages, £20 is disregarded because Owen is in the work-related activity group, and £17.10 is disregarded because they have a child and Mia works sufficient hours for the additional disregard.

Childcare costs disregard for housing benefit

For HB, up to £175 a week for one child, or up to £300 a week for two or more children, can be deducted from your (or your partner's) earnings (from employment or self-employment) for childcare costs if you are:[93]

Part 3: General rules for means-tested benefits
Chapter 14: Income: under pension credit age
3. Earnings

- a lone parent working 16 hours or more a week; *or*
- a couple and both of you work 16 hours or more a week, or one of you works 16 hours or more a week and the other is 'incapacitated' (see p283), or is in hospital or prison.

The most that can be deducted for one child is £175, even if you pay more. For more than one child, £300 is the maximum even if you pay more or have to pay for more than two children.

It is not necessary for the childcare to be provided only while you are at work, nor for it to be work-related, and there is no requirement for the charges to be reasonable.

You can still get this disregard for childcare costs if you are off work sick, although for lone parents it stops after 28 weeks (see p283).

If you also get WTC or child tax credit (CTC) and your earnings, once other HB disregards have been allowed, are less than the deduction for childcare costs, your earnings and the WTC/CTC are added together before the deduction for childcare costs is made.[94]

The childcare costs disregard only applies to charges you pay for certain types of childcare provided for any child(ren) in your family under the age of 15 (or 16 if s/he is disabled). A child is not treated as having reached the age of 15/16 until the day before the first Monday in September following her/his 15th/16th birthday.[95] A child is defined as disabled if s/he is:[96]

- in receipt of disability living allowance (DLA), personal independence payment (PIP), armed forces independence payment; *or*
- certified as severely sight-impaired or blind by a consultant ophthalmologist, or stopped being certified before the first Monday in September following her/his 16th birthday, but no more than one year and 28 weeks before then.

The childcare must be provided:[97]

- by a registered childminder or other registered childcare provider (such as a nursery or local authority daycare service); *or*
- out of school hours for children between the ages of eight and 15/16, by a school on school premises or a local authority – eg, an out-of-hours or holiday play scheme; *or*
- by another relevant childcare provider (see p1416 – these are the same as for WTC).

You cannot include charges for care provided by a relative of the child in the child's own home even if s/he is a registered childminder, nor charges paid by you to your partner or by your partner to you for a child in your family. You can include charges for childcare outside the child's home provided by a relative, provided s/he is not your partner and is a registered childminder. The registered childminder could be a former partner who may even be the child's parent. Charges for compulsory education do not count.

If you or your partner are on maternity, adoption, paternity or shared parental leave, you are treated as working, and so can get the childcare disregard if you (or your partner):[98]

- were working in the week immediately before the leave began; *and*
- are entitled to SMP, SAP, SPP, SSPP (see Chapter 37) or maternity allowance (MA) (see Chapter 33), or are getting IS because you are on paternity leave.

You are no longer treated as working and so cannot get the childcare costs disregard when:

- the maternity, adoption, paternity or shared parental leave ends; *or*
- if you are not receiving the childcare element of WTC, you or your partner stop getting SMP, SAP, SPP, SSPP or MA, or IS because you are on paternity leave; *or*
- if you are receiving the childcare element of WTC when you stop getting SMP, SAP, SPP, SSPP or MA or IS because you are on paternity leave, you stop getting the childcare element of WTC.

You can get the childcare costs disregard for the new child in your family while you are still on maternity, adoption, paternity or shared parental leave.

Childcare costs and ill health or disability

Provided you were working at least 16 hours a week immediately before you started getting one of the following benefits, you can still have a childcare costs disregard while off work sick for the first 28 weeks while you are getting SSP, ESA or NI credits for limited capability for work.[99]

After 28 weeks, lone parents who are off work sick can no longer get a childcare costs disregard, but couples can do so (before or after 28 weeks) if one of them works 16 hours or more a week and the other is treated as 'incapacitated'.

Incapacitated

You (or your partner) are treated as **'incapacitated'** if:[100]

– you get ESA which includes a support or work-related activity component; *or*
– you get short-term higher rate or long-term IB or SDA; *or*
– you get attendance allowance, DLA, PIP, armed forces independence payment or constant attendance allowance (or an equivalent award under the war pensions or industrial injuries schemes) or you would receive one of these benefits but for the fact that you (or your partner) are in hospital; *or*
– you have an invalid carriage or similar vehicle; *or*
– your HB includes a disability premium, support component or work-related activity component for the incapacitated person's incapacity or limited capability for work, or that person is in the 'work-related activity group' (see p642); *or*

Part 3: General rules for means-tested benefits
Chapter 14: Income: under pension credit age
4. Income other than earnings

– you (but not your partner) have been treated either as having limited capability for work or as being incapable of work for a continuous period of 196 days or more (disregarding any break of up to 84 or 56 days respectively).

Calculating childcare costs

The costs to be taken into account are estimated over whatever period, not exceeding a year, that will give the best estimate of the average weekly charge based on information provided by the childminder or care provider.

4. Income other than earnings

As well as income from earnings, most other forms of income are taken into account in full, less any tax due. To work out the weekly income to take into account, check whether the payment can be disregarded in part or in full, deduct any tax due and work out the weekly amount (see p302). Where a taxable benefit or other unearned income is not taxed at source and you have not yet had a tax assessment, ask HM Revenue and Customs for a forecast of the tax due on that income; otherwise the DWP calculates how much tax to deduct.[101] For housing benefit (HB), the local authority has discretion to ignore changes in tax rates and in the maximum rate of child tax credit (CTC) and working tax credit (WTC) for up to 30 weeks – eg, where April changes are not reflected in your income until later.[102]

Benefits and tax credits

Benefits and tax credits that are taken into account

The following count in full:
- bereavement allowance, widow's pension and industrial death benefit;
- carer's allowance (CA);
- for HB only, CTC. See p287 if your CTC is reduced to recover a tax credit overpayment;
- child's payment under the Armed Forces Compensation Scheme (but if it is paid for a dependent child, it is usually ignored – see p269);
- contribution-based jobseeker's allowance (JSA);
- contributory employment and support allowance (ESA). If ESA is paid at a reduced rate because of a sanction, it is still the full rate that counts;[103]
- incapacity benefit (IB) and severe disablement allowance;
- industrial injuries benefits, except constant attendance allowance and exceptionally severe disablement allowance, which are disregarded;
- maternity allowance;
- retirement pensions;

- statutory sick pay, statutory maternity pay, statutory adoption pay, statutory paternity pay and statutory shared parental pay count for income support (IS), income-based JSA and income-related ESA only, less any class 1 national insurance contributions and half of any pension contributions and any tax.[104] These are treated as earnings for HB and, therefore, may benefit from an earnings disregard (see p278);[105]
- WTC:
  - for IS, income-based JSA and income-related ESA;
  - for HB, except if earnings are too low to use the whole £17.10 additional full-time earnings disregard (see p281). In this case, £17.10 is disregarded from your WTC instead of your earnings. You must satisfy the conditions for the additional earnings disregard and have earnings of less than £17.10 plus whichever other earnings disregard applies plus any childcare costs disregard.[106] If earnings are too low to use the full childcare costs disregard, see p282.

See p287 if a tax credit overpayment is being deducted.

Benefits and tax credits that are not taken into account

The following are ignored completely:

- armed forces independence payment;
- attendance allowance (AA);[107]
- bereavement support payment;[108]
- child benefit.[109] However, for IS and income-based JSA, it is taken into account if you have been getting IS or income-based JSA since before 6 April 2004 and have an amount for that child in your claim (and do not get CTC);[110]
- Christmas bonus;[111]
- constant attendance allowance, exceptionally severe disablement allowance or severe disablement occupational allowance paid because of an injury at work or a war injury;[112]
- CTC is ignored for IS, income-based JSA and income-related ESA;[113]
- disability living allowance (DLA);[114]
- guardian's allowance;[115]
- HB;[116]
- IS, income-based JSA and income-related ESA are ignored for HB.[117] There are special HB rules for these (see p60);
- mobility supplement under the War Pension Scheme;[118]
- personal independence payment (PIP);[119]
- any extra-statutory payment made to you to compensate for non-payment of IS, income-based JSA, income-related ESA, universal credit (UC), mobility supplement, AA, DLA or PIP;[120]
- social fund payments.[121] They are also disregarded as capital indefinitely;
- any supplementary payments to war widows, widowers or surviving civil partners for pre-1973 service;[122]

Part 3: General rules for means-tested benefits
Chapter 14: Income: under pension credit age
4. Income other than earnings

- any increase for a child dependant is ignored for IS or income-based JSA if you get CTC and for income-related ESA. For all benefits, any increase for adult or child dependants who are not members of your family paid with a benefit (eg, IB or retirement pension) or a service pension is ignored;[123]
- any payment made by the DWP to compensate for the loss of HB;[124]
- any payment in consequence of a reduction in liability for council tax, including from a council tax reduction scheme.[125]

Benefits that are partly taken into account

For HB only, widowed mother's allowance and widowed parent's allowance have £15 ignored.[126]

The following benefits have £10 ignored (or more for HB – see below):[127]

- for IS, income-based JSA and income-related ESA only, widowed mother's allowance and widowed parent's allowance;
- war disablement pension;
- guaranteed income payment and survivor's guaranteed income payment under the Armed Forces Compensation Scheme (or if another pension reduces the payment to below £10, ignore the remainder from the pension);
- war widow's, widower's or surviving civil partner's pension;
- an extra-statutory payment made instead of the above pensions;
- similar payments made by another country;
- a pension from any government paid to the victims of Nazi persecution.[128]

Even if you have more than two payments which attract a £10 disregard, only £20 in all can be ignored.[129] However, the £10 disregard allowed on the above payments is in addition to the total disregard of any mobility supplement or AA (ie, constant attendance allowance, exceptionally severe disablement allowance and severe disablement occupational allowance) paid as part of a war disablement pension.

The £10 disregard may overlap with other disregards, such as on student loans and access funds (see p896 and p900), when a combined maximum of £20 is allowed.

Local authorities may have discretionary local schemes to increase the £10 disregard on war disablement pension, war widow's or widower's pension, and the guaranteed income payment and survivor's guaranteed income payment in your HB. Most increase the disregard or ignore the full amount, so check your local scheme.[130]

Benefit delays

Problems can arise if a decision maker tries to take into account a benefit you are not receiving (such as child benefit) because it has been delayed. In such a case, the benefit should not be treated as income possessed by you. For IS, income-based JSA and income-related ESA, you should get your full benefit and the DWP deducts the difference from the arrears of the delayed benefit when it is eventually awarded.[131]

For the treatment of payments of arrears of certain benefits and tax credits, see p367.

Tax credit overpayments

For HB, if a tax credit overpayment is being recovered, it is the amount of your tax credit award less any reduction to recover the overpayment that is taken into account.[132] Because HB entitlement is based on the amount of tax credits you are actually paid at the time, local authorities do not treat you as having been underpaid HB for the earlier period when tax credits were being overpaid, so your HB award is not revised for that period.[133]

For IS, income-based JSA and income-related ESA, the rules are less clear, but the intention seems to be to take into account the actual award paid – eg, after any overpayment has been deducted.[134]

Maintenance payments

If you get **child maintenance** for a child who is a member of your family, it is all ignored if it is made by the child's parent (who is not your partner) or by another 'liable relative' (see p288).[135] Child maintenance payments include:

- any payment made voluntarily;
- payments under a court order or consent order;
- child support maintenance (assessed by the Child Support Agency or Child Maintenance Service);
- in Scotland, payments under a registered maintenance agreement.

Note: arrears of regular child support maintenance should be treated as income for a past period. Arrears are ignored as income if, for HB, they cover a period since 27 October 2008 or, for other benefits, since 12 April 2010. Before that, arrears may mean that you have been overpaid benefit, although some overpaid benefits can be deducted from arrears before you get them.[136]

Other kinds of maintenance

If you get another kind of maintenance payment from a former partner (eg, maintenance for yourself):[137]

- £15 is ignored for HB if you have a child who is part of your family for benefit purposes (see p220) or a family premium included in your HB. If you get maintenance from more than one person, only £15 of the total is ignored;
- for other benefits, it is regarded as a 'liable relative' payment and usually counts in full (see p288).

Part 3: General rules for means-tested benefits
Chapter 14: Income: under pension credit age
4. Income other than earnings

Liable relative

A 'liable relative' is:[138]

– a spouse, civil partner, former spouse or civil partner; or

– parent of a child who is a member of your family; or

– someone who can reasonably be treated as the child's father because of the financial support he makes.

For IS, income-based JSA and income-related ESA, any payment from a liable relative other than child maintenance is taken into account in full as income, whether it is paid regularly or as a lump sum, with some exceptions as follows.[139]

- Payments made directly to someone else and not to you (ie, to a third party) are taken into account as maintenance if they are for certain normal living expenses (food, clothing, footwear), for certain bills (fuel, council tax, water charges), for rent met by HB or for housing costs met by IS, JSA or ESA (such as mortgage interest payments). Payments for other kinds of expenses, such as mortgage capital repayments paid directly to the mortgage lender or TV licence payments paid directly, are ignored.[140] This means it can be better for you if your ex-partner pays these other kinds of expenses directly rather than to you. If you use your maintenance payments to pay the mortgage yourself, all of it is taken into account as your income, not just the amount for mortgage interest, so you will get less benefit.

- Payments in kind, such as food, holidays and clothing, are ignored (except if you are involved in a trade dispute).

- Gifts (eg, birthday and Christmas presents) of up to £250 in total in any period of 52 weeks are not taken into account as maintenance, but may count as capital.

- If you have already spent a payment before the DWP makes its decision about the effect on your benefit, the payment is ignored provided you did not deliberately get rid of the money in order to claim or increase your benefit. The issues are the same as the deprivation of income/capital rule on p371.

- A payment from a 'disposition of property' because of divorce, separation, nullity or dissolution of a civil partnership is not taken into account as maintenance (so is not treated as income), but usually counts as capital. This applies, for example, if your former partner buys out your interest in a home so you get a lump-sum settlement instead of a share of the property itself.[141]

- Payments for a child who is not a member of your household (eg, a child looked after by a local authority and not living with you, or a child in custody) do not count as maintenance. They should be ignored if you spend the money on the child, but count as income if you keep the money or spend it on yourself.[142]

- A payment made after the liable relative has died no longer counts as maintenance (so is not automatically treated as income), but is still taken into account as income or capital under the normal rules.

If you get payments towards maintenance from someone who is not a liable relative (eg, a grandparent), this normally counts as a voluntary payment and is ignored (see p290).

If you pay maintenance

If you *pay* maintenance to a former partner or a child not living with you, your payments are not disregarded for the purpose of calculating your income for any benefits.[143] See p376 if part of a personal or occupational pension is paid to a former partner.

Student loans and grants

For the special rules on the treatment of student loans, grants and other payments made to students, see Chapter 40.

Adoption, fostering and similar payments

Adoption allowance

An adoption allowance is disregarded in full, except in the following circumstances.[144]

- If the adoption allowance is paid for a child who is not a member of your family (eg, because the adoption order has not yet been granted), it is fully disregarded in England.[145] In Scotland and Wales, any amount you spend on the child is disregarded and any you keep for yourself is taken into account.[146]
- For IS and income-based JSA, if you have been getting benefit since before 6 April 2004 with a child included in your claim and do not have an award of CTC, the adoption allowance is taken into account in full up to the level of the adopted child's personal allowance and any disabled child premium.[147] Above that level it is ignored. If the child has capital over £3,000, you get no benefit for that child and all the adoption allowance is disregarded.[148] Get advice to check whether you would be better off claiming CTC or UC instead.

Fostering allowance

The way a fostering allowance is treated depends on whether the arrangement is official or private. If a child is placed or boarded out with you by a local authority or a voluntary organisation under specific legal provisions,[149] the child is not counted as a member of your family (see p223) and any fostering allowances you receive while the child is placed with you should be ignored altogether.[150] If the fostering arrangement is a private one, any money you receive from the child's parent(s) is counted as maintenance (see p287).

Part 3: General rules for means-tested benefits
Chapter 14: Income: under pension credit age
4. Income other than earnings

Child arrangements order allowance and similar payments

If you are paid a child arrangements order allowance by a local authority (in England and Wales), this is treated in the same way as an adoption allowance (see p289).[151] Any payments made by the biological parents count as maintenance (see p287). In Scotland, kinship care payments can be made under different legal provisions. If made under section 22 of the Children (Scotland) Act 1995 or regulation 33 of the Looked After Children (Scotland) Regulations 2009, they are ignored altogether, but if made under section 50 of the Children Act 1975, they are treated in the same way as an adoption allowance.[152]

Special guardianship allowance

The law treats a special guardianship allowance, payable in England and Wales for a child who is a member of your family, in the same way as an adoption allowance (see p291), but official guidance advises that it should be fully disregarded for IS and income-based JSA.[153]

Charitable, voluntary and personal injury payments

Payments from infected blood payment schemes

Any payments from specified schemes for people infected with HIV or hepatitis C through blood products and NHS treatment are disregarded in full.[154]

Payments can still be disregarded if you give them to certain relatives or they inherit them from you after your death.

Any income or capital that derives from any such payments is also disregarded.

Other payments

Most other charitable or voluntary payments that are made irregularly and are intended to be made irregularly are treated as capital and are unlikely to affect your benefit claim unless they take your capital above the limit.[155] However, if you are on IS or income-based JSA, they count as income if you are involved in a trade dispute and, for IS only, for the first 15 days following your return to work after a dispute (see p940).[156]

Payments made on a regular basis

Charitable and voluntary payments and certain personal injury payments (see below) are ignored if they are made, or are due to be made, regularly.[157]

A 'voluntary payment' is one given without getting anything back in return.[158]

For IS and income-based JSA, these payments are not disregarded where you are involved in a trade dispute and, for IS only, for the first 15 days following your return to work after a trade dispute.

Payments from a former partner, or the parent of your child, are dealt with as maintenance (see p287).

The personal injury payments that qualify under the above rules are:[159]

- payments from a trust fund set up out of money paid because of any personal injury to you; *or*
- payments under an annuity purchased either under an agreement or court order set up because of any personal injury to you, or from money paid because of any personal injury to you; *or*
- payments you get under an agreement or court order because of any personal injury to you. This does not include an occupational pension – eg, if you have retired early because of personal injury.[160]

See also p300 for payments made to someone else on your behalf and p297 for payments disregarded under miscellaneous income.

Concessionary coal to former British Coal workers and their surviving partners is ignored (except to strikers). Cash in lieu of coal counts in full.[161]

Income from tenants and lodgers

How income from tenants is treated depends on whether or not you live in the same property.

Lettings without board

If you let out a room(s) in your home to tenants, sub-tenants or licensees under a formal contractual arrangement, £20 of your weekly charge for each tenant, sub-tenant or licensee (and her/his family) is ignored.[162] The balance counts as income.

If someone shares your home under an informal arrangement, any payment s/he makes to you for living and accommodation costs is ignored,[163] but a non-dependant deduction may be made from any HB or housing costs paid with IS/income-based JSA/income-related ESA (see p67 and p464).

Boarders

If you have a boarder(s) on a commercial basis in your own home, and the boarder or any member of her/his family is not a close relative of yours, the first £20 of the weekly charge is ignored and half of any balance remaining is then taken into account as your income.[164] For HB, this applies even if the boarder is a close relative and it is not a commercial arrangement. However, there might still be a non-dependant deduction for her/him (see p67). This disregard applies for each boarder you have. The charge must normally include at least some meals.[165] If you have a business partner, even though your gross income includes just your share of the weekly charge to boarders, you still get the full disregard of £20 plus half the excess for each boarder.[166]

Note: if you let part of your home, any income left after applying the above disregards which is intended to be used to meet any housing costs of your own which are not met by IS, income-based JSA, income-related ESA or HB, may also be disregarded (see p295).[167]

Part 3: General rules for means-tested benefits
Chapter 14: Income: under pension credit age
4. Income other than earnings

Tenants in other properties

If you have a freehold interest in a property other than your home and you let it out, the rent is normally treated as capital.[168] This rule also applies if you have a leasehold interest in another property which you are sub-letting. The full rent counts initially (as well as the capital value of the property itself) but, if you spend some on a debt that is immediately repayable (eg, a monthly mortgage payment) after a period (eg, a month for monthly paid rent), only what remains continues to count as capital. If you spend it on something else to deliberately increase your benefit, the notional capital rules could treat you as still having the money (see p370).[169]

The rent is treated as income if the property you let is in one of the categories where the capital value is disregarded (see p362). In this case, the expenses listed below are deducted from the income.

Income from capital

In general, actual income generated from capital (eg, interest on savings) is ignored as income.[170] It counts as capital from the date you are due to receive it.[171] However, income derived from the following categories of disregarded capital (see p362) is treated as income:[172]

- your home;
- your former home, if you are estranged, divorced or your civil partnership has ended;
- property which you have acquired for occupation as your home, but into which you have not yet been able to move;
- property which you intend to occupy as your home, but which needs essential repairs or alterations;
- property occupied wholly or partly by a partner or relative of any member of your family who has reached the qualifying age for pension credit (see p147) or is incapacitated;
- property occupied by your former partner, unless you are estranged, divorced or your civil partnership has ended;
- property for sale;
- property which you are taking legal steps to obtain to occupy as your home;
- your business assets;
- a trust of personal injury compensation.

Some expenses are deducted from this income. Income from property (other than your current home) is ignored up to the amount of the total mortgage repayments (ie, capital and interest, and any payments that are a condition of the mortgage, such as insurance or an endowment policy),[173] council tax and water charges paid in respect of the property for the same period over which the income is received.[174]

Tariff income from capital

If your capital is over a certain level, you are treated as having an assumed income from it, called your '**tariff income**'. You are assumed to have an income of £1 a week for every £250, or part of £250, by which your capital exceeds £6,000 but does not exceed £16,000.[175]

If you are in a care home or similar accommodation (see p355), tariff income applies between £10,000 and £16,000.

Capital that counts as income

The following capital is treated as income:
- instalments of capital outstanding when you claim benefit, if they would bring you over the capital limit. For IS, income-based JSA and income-related ESA, the instalments to be counted are any outstanding, either when your benefit claim is decided, or when you are first due to be paid benefit, whichever is earlier, or at the date of any subsequent supersession.[176] For HB, it is any instalments outstanding when your claim is made or treated as made, or when your benefit is revised or superseded.[177] The outstanding instalments count as income by spreading them over the number of weeks between each instalment;[178]
- any payment from an annuity[179] (see p294 for when this is disregarded);
- any professional and career development loan (see p899);[180]
- for IS only, a tax refund if you or your partner have returned to work after a trade dispute (see p940);[181]
- periodic payments made under an agreement or court order for any personal injury to you (see p290 for when these are disregarded);[182]
- some lump sums from liable relatives (see p287).

Note: capital counted as income cannot also be treated as producing a tariff income (see above).[183]

Sometimes, you may find that withdrawals from a capital sum are treated as income.[184] This is most likely if the sum was intended to help cover living expenses over a particular period – eg, a bank loan taken out by a mature student. If this is not the intended use of any capital sum, dispute the decision. Even if the sum is intended for living expenses, argue that, unless it is actually paid in instalments, it should be treated as capital.[185] A loan that you have an obligation to repay immediately should not be treated as your income (or capital), however it is paid.[186]

Income tax refunds

Pay as you earn (PAYE) refunds and self-employment tax refunds are treated as capital.[187]

For IS and JSA, tax refunds paid during a trade dispute are treated as income and taken into account.[188] For IS only, if you or your partner have returned to

Part 3: General rules for means-tested benefits
Chapter 14: Income: under pension credit age
4. Income other than earnings

work after a trade dispute (see p940), tax refunds are treated as income and are taken into account in full.[189]

Income from employment and training programmes

Payments from employment or training programmes under section 2 of the Employment and Training Act 1973 or section 2 of the Enterprise and New Towns (Scotland) Act 1990 are treated as follows.[190]

The following payments are taken into account:
- for ESA, those made as a substitute for ESA or JSA; for other benefits, payments made as a substitute for IS, JSA or ESA – eg, a training allowance;
- those intended for certain living costs while you are participating in a scheme to enhance your employment prospects. Payments for food, ordinary clothing or footwear, fuel, rent met by HB, housing costs met by IS, JSA or income-related ESA, council tax or water charges are all taken into account.

All other payments are disregarded – eg:
- travel expenses;
- training premium;
- childcare expenses;
- special needs payments;
- expenses for participating in a specified scheme for assisting people to obtain employment (see p1103);[191]
- New Enterprise Allowance weekly allowance.

For ESA, any payment for expenses incurred in complying with a requirement to undertake work-related activity (see p1068) is ignored.[192]

If you have been getting help under the 'self-employment route' (eg, for JSA and HB, the New Enterprise Allowance), any payments to meet expenses 'wholly and necessarily' incurred while trading, or used for the repayment of a loan necessary for the business, are also disregarded if they are from a special account set up for this programme.[193] Income built up in your special account while you are getting this help is treated as capital for HB.[194] At the end of the programme, this is treated as income for IS/JSA/ESA and spread over the same number of weeks in the future for which you have been receiving assistance, less any income tax due on the profits and an earnings disregard appropriate to your circumstances (see p278).[195]

Occupational and personal pensions and annuities

Although you can usually choose to take some, or all, of your occupational or personal pension from age 55, your benefit is not affected if you do not – ie, there is no notional income or capital assumed. Any regular withdrawals from your pension pot or pension income you take count in full as income. If you take a lump sum, this counts as capital, and notional capital rules can apply to how you spend it (see p370).[196]

Discretionary payments from a hardship fund are not regarded as an occupational pension, but are treated as charitable or voluntary payments (see p290).[197]

Payments from an annuity count in full unless:

- the annuity is set up with money paid because of personal injury to you, or under an agreement or court order because of personal injury to you (see p290);
- the annuity is set up with money from a home income plan, in which case income from the annuity equal to the interest payable on the loan with which the annuity was bought is ignored if:[198]
  - you used at least 90 per cent of the loan made to you to buy the annuity; *and*
  - the annuity will end when you and your partner die; *and*
  - you or your partner are responsible for paying the interest on the loan; *and*
  - you (if you took out the loan), or your partner (if s/he did), were at least 65 at the time the loan was made; *and*
  - the loan is secured on a property which you or your partner own or in which you have an interest, and the property on which the loan is secured is your home, or that of your partner.

If the interest on the loan is payable after income tax has been deducted, it is an amount equal to the net interest payment that is disregarded; otherwise, it is the gross amount of the interest payment.

Mortgage and insurance payments

For IS, income-based JSA and income-related ESA only, payments you receive under a mortgage protection policy on your home count as income up to the level of the housing costs included in your 'applicable amount'. If the payments are higher than this, disregarded from the excess is whatever you use to pay:[199]

- the interest on a qualifying loan which is not met by the DWP – eg, if the interest on the loan is higher than the DWP's standard interest rate;
- capital repayments on a qualifying loan;
- any premiums on the policy and any buildings insurance policy on your home.

Any amount of the mortgage protection policy payments left over counts as your income.

Example

Samir claims JSA help with his housing costs. His mortgage lender charges £22.42 interest weekly on a £30,000 mortgage. His mortgage interest is higher than the standard rate so he still has £4.42 a week interest to pay as well as £23 capital repayments, £5 a week

Part 3: General rules for means-tested benefits
Chapter 14: Income: under pension credit age
4. Income other than earnings

premiums on his buildings insurance and another £5 a week premiums on a mortgage protection policy, adding up to £37.42. The policy pays him £70 a week, of which £37.42 is ignored and the remaining £32.58 is taken into account as income.

For IS, income-based JSA and income-related ESA only, provided you have not already used insurance payments for the same purpose, any money you receive which is given, and which you use, to make the following payments is ignored:[200]
- payments under a secured loan which do not qualify under the housing costs rules (see Chapter 20);
- interest payments that are not met under the housing costs rules, even though some interest payments under the loan may be met;
- capital repayments on a qualifying loan;
- payments of premiums on an insurance policy which you took out to insure against the risk of not being able to make the payments in the above three categories, and premiums on a buildings insurance policy;
- payment of any rent that is not covered by HB (see Chapter 4);
- payment of the part of your accommodation charge in a care home that exceeds that payable by a local authority.

If you are using maintenance from a former partner or parent of your child (but not child maintenance, which is disregarded whatever you use it for) to pay these costs, it may be taken into account as a 'liable relative payment', unless it is paid directly to someone else – eg, a lender (see p287).

For HB only, payments you receive under an insurance policy to insure against the risk of being unable to maintain payments on a loan secured on your home are ignored. However, anything you get above the total of the following counts as your income:[201]
- the amount you use to maintain your payments; *and*
- any premium you pay for the policy; *and*
- any premium for an insurance policy to insure against loss or damage to your home.

Payments you receive under an insurance policy to insure against the risk of being unable to maintain hire purchase or similar payments or other loan payments (eg, credit card debts) are also ignored. However, anything you get above the amount you use to make your payments and the premium for the policy counts as your income.[202]

Social services, community care and other payments

The following payments are ignored:
- local welfare provision to meet an immediate short-term need or establish or maintain a settled home in certain circumstances (see p856);[203]

- payments from a local authority for children, families and people in need, made under section 17 of the Children Act 1989, section 12 of the Social Work (Scotland) Act 1968 or under section 22 of the Children (Scotland) Act 1995.[204] See p940 if you or your partner are involved in a trade dispute;
- payments from a local authority for young people who were previously looked after by the local authority, paid under sections 23B or 24A of the Children Act 1989 or section 30 of the Children (Scotland) Act 1995. A payment under section 23C is also ignored as the young person's income and as yours if s/he passes it to you, s/he was in your care, is still living with you and is aged 18 or over – eg, under 'staying put' arrangements. In Scotland, this applies to payments under sections 26A and 29 of the Children (Scotland) Act 1995 and includes young people aged 16 or over in 'continuing care'. See p940 if you or your partner are involved in a trade dispute;[205]
- direct payments to you under an education, health and care plan for a child with special educational needs (paid in England);[206]
- any community care or healthcare direct payments. Local authorities or the NHS pay these to disabled people or carers to buy their own services instead of providing services directly. A direct payment is not ignored as the income of the person you pay for services, even if this is your partner;[207]
- any payment you or your partner receive for looking after a person temporarily in your care if it is paid under community care arrangements by the NHS, local authority, voluntary organisation or the person being looked after.[208] Any HB paid to you by a local authority for that person is not ignored, although see p291 for other possible disregards;
- payments under the Supporting People programme for support services to help you live independently are ignored indefinitely.[209] Landlords receiving such payments for providing the services do not benefit from this disregard, although other disregards may apply (see p291);
- if you live in a care home and a local authority arranged your place, local authority payments towards your fees are ignored for IS, JSA and income-related ESA. If a local authority did not arrange your place, any payment intended and used for your maintenance is fully disregarded if it is a voluntary or charitable payment, and partly disregarded if not – up to the difference between the care home fees and your applicable amount;[210]
- a lump-sum payment from a local authority to enable you to make adaptations to your home for a disabled child. This is treated as capital and ignored.[211]

Miscellaneous income

The following income is ignored:
- any discretionary housing payments paid by a local authority;[212]
- education maintenance allowances (paid in Scotland and Wales) and 16 to 19 bursary fund payments (paid in England).[213] These are paid to some young people staying on at school or other non-advanced education;

Part 3: General rules for means-tested benefits
Chapter 14: Income: under pension credit age
4. Income other than earnings

- any payment to cover your expenses if you are working as an unpaid volunteer, or working unpaid for a charity or voluntary organisation;[214]
- payments in kind (except for IS or income-based JSA, if you or your partner are involved in a trade dispute – see p940).[215] These may include food, fuel, cigarettes,[216] clothing, holidays, gifts, accommodation, transport or nursery education vouchers. However, see p299 for the rules on notional income and p270 for the rules on non-cash vouchers paid as earnings. Items for essential living needs provided by the Home Office to an asylum-seeking partner are ignored for IS, income-based JSA and income-related ESA;
- a payment (other than a training allowance) to a disabled person under the Disabled Persons (Employment) Act 1944 to assist her/him to obtain or retain employment;[217]
- any payments, other than for loss of earnings or a benefit, made to jurors or witnesses for attending court;[218]
- Victoria Cross or George Cross payments or similar awards;[219]
- income paid outside the UK which cannot be transferred here;[220]
- if income is paid in another currency, any bank charges for converting the payment into sterling;[221]
- fares to hospital and refunds for prescription or dental charges;[222]
- payments instead of milk tokens and vitamins, or Healthy Start food vouchers;[223]
- payments to assist prison visits;[224]
- for HB, if you make a parental contribution to a student's grant or loan, an equal amount of any 'unearned' income you have for the period the grant or loan is paid. If your 'unearned' income does not cover the contribution, the balance can be disregarded from your earnings. If you are a parent of a student under 25 in advanced education who does not get a grant or loan (or who only gets a smaller discretionary award), up to £57.90 of your contribution to her/his living expenses is ignored from your 'unearned' income (less the weekly amount of any discretionary award the student has). This is only ignored during the student's term. Any balance can be disregarded from your earnings;[225]
- a sports award made by UK Sport from National Lottery funds for living expenses is taken into account. This covers food, ordinary clothing or footwear, fuel, council tax, water charges and rent (less any non-dependant deductions) for which HB could be payable or housing costs that could be met by IS, income-based JSA or income-related ESA. Payments for anything else are ignored – eg, sportswear and dietary supplements to enhance performance;[226]
- any payment for expenses if you are being consulted as a service user by the DWP or a health, care or housing body that provides statutory services (expenses do not count as earnings either).[227]

5. Notional income

In certain circumstances, you may be treated as having income even if you do not possess it or if you have used it up.

Deliberately getting rid of income

If you deliberately get rid of income in order to claim or increase your benefit, you are treated as though you still receive that income.[228] The basic issues involved are the same as those for deliberately getting rid of capital (see p371). **Note:** the rule only applies if the purpose of the deprivation is to gain benefit for yourself (or your family). It should not apply if, for example, you stop claiming carer's allowance (CA) solely so that another person can become entitled to the severe disability premium (see p242).[229] However, if you do not claim a benefit which would clearly be paid if you did, it may be argued that you have failed to apply for income (see below). The rule still applies if you move from one benefit to another in the case of income support (IS), jobseeker's allowance (JSA) and employment and support allowance (ESA). For example, if you got rid of income to increase your ESA and then claim JSA instead, you are still treated as having the income for your JSA claim.

Failing to apply for income

If you fail to apply for income to which you are entitled without having to fulfil further conditions, you are deemed to have received it from the date you could have obtained it.[230]

This does not include, for example, income from:

- a discretionary trust; *or*
- a trust set up from money paid as a result of a personal injury; *or*
- funds administered by a court as a result of a personal injury; *or*
- a rehabilitation allowance made under the Employment and Training Act 1973; *or*
- JSA (for IS, JSA and ESA) or ESA (for ESA only); *or*
- if you are under the qualifying age for pension credit (see p147), a personal or occupational pension scheme or payments from the Pension Protection Fund, so your benefit is not affected if you do not withdraw money from your pension pot. If you withdraw money regularly, it is taken into account as income. However, if you or your partner have reached that age and choose not to take your full pension, you are treated as having an income;[231] *or*
- working tax credit and child tax credit.[232]

For other income or benefits, it must still be certain that it would be paid upon application (and the rule ceases to apply as soon as a claim is made[233]). It may, therefore, be difficult to establish that there is 'no doubt' that CA, for example,

Part 3: General rules for means-tested benefits
Chapter 14: Income: under pension credit age
5. Notional income

would be paid to a carer who does not wish to claim it because of the effect on another person's severe disability premium (see p242).[234]

Income due to you that has not been paid

For IS, income-based JSA and income-related ESA only, you are treated as possessing any income that is owing to you – eg:[235]
- wages that are legally due to you, but are not paid (see below); *or*
- an occupational pension payment that is due but has not been received, unless the pension scheme has insufficient funds.[236]

This rule should not apply if:
- any social security benefit has been delayed; *or*
- you are waiting for a late payment of a government training allowance or a benefit from a European Economic Area country; *or*
- money is due to you from a discretionary trust or a trust set up from money paid as a result of a personal injury; *or*
- you are owed earnings when your job has ended because of redundancy but these have not been paid to you.[237]

The income must be due to *you* (or your family) and for your own benefit.[238]

Unpaid wages

This applies to IS, income-based JSA and income-related ESA only.

If you have wages due to you, but you do not yet know the exact amount or you have no proof of what they will be, you are treated as having a wage similar to that normally paid for that type of work in that area.[239] If your wages cannot be estimated, you might qualify for a short-term advance (see p1177).[240] For how wages are estimated for housing benefit, see p304.

Income paid to someone else on your behalf

If money is paid to someone on your behalf (eg, a landlord for your rent), this can count as notional income.[241] If so, it is still subject to the usual disregards that would apply if it were actual income – eg, a voluntary or charitable payment of income is ignored whether it is paid directly to you or to someone else on your behalf. See p375 for a description of these third-party rules – they are the same as those for notional capital.

Income in kind given to a third party for you is ignored (eg, a food parcel used to prepare meals for you) unless, for IS or income-based JSA, you or your partner are involved in a trade dispute. However, money given to someone who uses it to buy you goods or services counts as notional income under the usual rules.

Income paid to you for someone else

If you or your partner get a payment for somebody not in the 'family' (eg, a relative living with you), it counts as your income if you keep any of it yourself or spend it on yourself or your partner unless it is – eg:[242]

- from a specified infected blood payment scheme (see p290);
- concessionary coal under the Coal Industry Act 1994;
- a payment for an approved employment-related course of education, or specified scheme for assisting people to obtain employment (see p1103);
- income in kind (eg, a food parcel given to you to make meals for someone else), unless, for IS or income-based JSA, you or your partner are involved in a trade dispute.

Cheap or unpaid labour

If you are helping another person or an organisation by doing work that would normally be paid, or be paid a higher wage, you are deemed to receive a wage similar to that normally paid for that kind of job in that area.[243]

The burden of proving that your work is something for which an employer would pay, and what the comparable wages are, lies with the decision maker.[244]

The rule does not apply if:[245]

- you are on an unpaid approved work placement or work experience; *or*
- you are on a government employment or training programme with no training allowance, or only travel or meals expenses; *or*
- you can show that the person (including a limited company[246]) cannot, in fact, afford to pay, or afford to pay more; *or*
- you work for a charitable or voluntary organisation or as a volunteer, and it is accepted that it is reasonable for you to give your services free of charge.[247] A 'volunteer' is someone who, without any legal obligation, performs a service for another person without expecting payment.

Sometimes it may also be reasonable to do a job free of charge from a sense of community duty, particularly if the job would otherwise remain undone and there would be no financial profit to an employer.[248]

If you are caring for a sick or disabled relative, it is usually accepted that it is reasonable to do this free of charge rather than expecting her/him to pay you from benefits. However, if you need to show that it is reasonable, you should take into account, for instance:[249]

- how much care you give and what other care options there are;
- your housing arrangements;
- whether you gave up work to care;
- the risk of your losing entitlement to CA if you were paid, or to a social services assessment of your needs;
- whether your relative would actually pay you.

Part 3: General rules for means-tested benefits
Chapter 14: Income: under pension credit age
6. Working out weekly income

6. **Working out weekly income**

Income support, income-based jobseeker's allowance and income-related employment and support allowance

As well as working out weekly income for income support (IS), income-based jobseeker's allowance (JSA) and income-related employment and support allowance (ESA), you also need to know the period that payments cover. These rules apply to earnings from employment and income other than earnings. See p277 for how self-employed earnings are assessed.

- Work out the period covered by the income (see below).
- Work out the date from when to start taking the income into account (see p303).
- Convert income into a weekly amount if necessary (see p303). There are special rules on variable income, payments for less than a week and overlapping payments.

Period covered by a payment

- If a payment of income is made for an identifiable period, it is taken into account for a period of equal length.[250] For example, a week's part-time earnings are taken into account for a week. If you are paid monthly, the payments are taken into account for the number of weeks between the date you are treated as having been paid and the date you are next due to be paid.
- If the payment does not relate to a particular period, the amount of the payment is divided by the amount of the weekly IS, income-based JSA or income-related ESA to which you would otherwise be entitled. If part of the payment should be disregarded, the amount of IS, income-based JSA or income-related ESA is increased by the appropriate disregard. The result of this calculation is the number of weeks that you are not entitled to IS, income-based JSA or income-related ESA.[251]

Example

Conor receives £950 net earnings for work which cannot be attributed to any specific period of time. He and his partner are both aged 28. Their rent is met by housing benefit (HB). Conor's income-based JSA is £114.85. As a couple, they are entitled to a £10 earnings disregard.

Divide £950 by the weekly JSA (£114.85) plus the disregard (£10). 950 ÷ 124.85 = 7.6091

This is seven whole weeks (7 x £124.85 = £873.95), with £76.05 left over.

This means that Conor is not entitled to income-based JSA for seven weeks and the remaining £76.05 (less a £10 earnings disregard, leaving £66.05) is taken into account in calculating his benefit for the following week.

- Payments made on leaving a job, if not ignored, are taken into account for a forward period (see p273).

Date from when a payment counts

For IS, income-based JSA and income-related ESA, the date from when a payment of earnings and/or other income counts depends on when it was due to be paid. If it was due to be paid before you claimed IS, income-based JSA or income-related ESA, it counts from the date on which it was due to be paid.[252] Otherwise, it is treated as having been paid on the first day of the benefit week in which it is due, or on the first day of the first benefit week after that in which it is practicable to take it into account.[253]

Payments of IS, JSA, ESA, universal credit and maternity allowance (MA) are treated as paid on a daily basis for each day for which they are paid.[254]

Benefit week

The 'benefit week' for JSA, and usually also for IS and ESA although this may vary, is normally the seven days ending with the day allocated to you according to your national insurance number (also your payday).[255] The benefit week for HB is the seven days starting on a Monday.[256]

The date a payment is due may be different from the date of actual payment. Earnings are due on the employee's normal payday. If the contract of employment does not reveal the date of due payment and there is no evidence to indicate otherwise, the date the payment was received should be taken as the date it was due.[257] If your contract of employment is terminated without proper notice, outstanding wages, wages in hand, holiday pay and any pay in lieu of notice are due on the last day of employment and are treated as having been paid on that day, even if this does not happen (although these are usually disregarded).[258]

If you receive compensation (eg, in a sex discrimination equal pay case), there is disagreement as to whether the relevant date is the date when the earnings in question were due to be paid[259] or when the compensation was awarded.[260]

For the treatment of payments at the end of a job, see p273.

Converting income into a weekly amount

To convert income to a weekly amount:
- if the payment is for less than a week, it is treated as the weekly amount;
- if the payment is for a month, multiply by 12 and divide by 52;
- multiply a payment for three months by four and divide by 52;
- divide a payment for a year by 52 (unless it is a working tax credit (WTC) payment, in which case divide by 365 and multiply by seven);
- for any other period, divide the payment by the number of days in the period then multiply by seven.

Part 3: General rules for means-tested benefits
Chapter 14: Income: under pension credit age
6. Working out weekly income

If you work on certain days but are paid monthly, it is necessary to decide whether the payment is for the days worked or for the whole month. This generally depends on the terms of your contract of employment,[261] but may depend on how your employer has arranged to make payments to you.[262]

Variable income

If your income fluctuates or your earnings vary because you do not work every week, your weekly income may be averaged over the cycle, if there is an identifiable one, or, if there is not, over five weeks, or over another period if this would be more accurate.[263] If the cycle involves periods when you do no work, those periods are included in the cycle, but not other absences – eg, holidays or sickness.

Part-weeks

- If income covering a period up to a week is paid before your first 'benefit week' (see p303) and part of it is counted for that week or if, in any case, you are paid for a period of a week or more and only part of it is counted in a particular benefit week, multiply the whole payment by the number of days it covers in the benefit week, then divide the result by the total number of days covered by the payment.[264]
- If any payment of MA falls partly into the benefit week, only the amount paid for those days is taken into account. For any payment of IS, JSA or ESA, that amount is the weekly amount multiplied by the number of days in the part-week and divided by seven.[265]

Overlapping payments

If you have regularly received a certain kind of payment of income from one source and in a particular 'benefit week' (see p303) you receive that payment and another of the same kind from the same source (eg, if your employer first pays you sick pay in arrears and this then overlaps with a payment in advance), the maximum amount to be taken into account is the one paid first.[266]

This does not apply if the second payment was due to be taken into account in another week but the overlapping week is the first in which it could practically be counted (see p303).

Housing benefit

To assess your current normal weekly income for HB, you should do the following.
- Average your earnings over a past period (see p305 for earnings from employment and p277 for self-employed earnings).
- Estimate income other than earnings (see p284 for what income counts) by looking at an appropriate period of up to 52 weeks. The period chosen must give an accurate assessment of your income.[267]

- Convert earnings from employment and income other than earnings into a weekly amount if necessary:
  - count a payment for less than a week as the weekly amount;
  - multiply a monthly payment by 12 and divide by 52;
  - for other periods, divide the payment by the number of days in the period then multiply by seven.
- Deduct the appropriate earnings disregard(s) (see p278).
- Work out the date from when the income is taken into account (see below).

Averaging earnings

For HB, earnings as an employee are usually averaged out over the previous:
- five weeks if you are paid weekly; *or*
- two months if you are paid monthly.[268]

If your earnings vary, or if there is likely to be, or has recently been, a change (eg, you usually do overtime but have not done so recently, or you are about to get a pay rise), the local authority may average them over a different period if this is likely to give a more accurate picture of what you are going to earn.[269]

If you are on strike, the local authority should not take into account your pre-strike earnings and average them out over the strike period.[270]

If you have only just started work and your earnings cannot be averaged over the normal period (ie, five weeks or two months), an estimate is made, based on any earnings you have been paid so far if these are likely to reflect your future average wage. If you have not yet been paid or your initial earnings do not represent what you will normally earn, your employer must provide an estimate of your average weekly earnings.[271] Remember that if you start work after having been on certain benefits, you may get four weeks' extended payments of HB at the same amount (see p86). If your earnings change during your award, your new weekly average figure is estimated on the basis of what you are likely to earn over whatever period (up to 52 weeks) best allows an accurate estimate.[272] If averaging does not result in a weekly figure, the amount is converted (see above).

Date from when a payment counts

The average weekly earnings from employment is taken into account for HB from the start of a new claim or from the first day of the 'benefit week' (see p303) after you start work if you are already getting HB. If average weekly earnings change, the new amount counts from the date of change, even if you are not paid until later.[273]

Child tax credit and WTC are taken into account instalment by instalment – eg, if paid weekly or four-weekly, each instalment counts for the seven or 28 days ending on the day it is due to be paid.[274] Other benefits are taken into account for the period they are paid for.[275]

Part 3: General rules for means-tested benefits
Chapter 14: Income: under pension credit age
Notes

Notes

1. Whose income counts

1 **IS/HB** s136(1) SSCBA 1992
JSA s13(2) JSA 1995
ESA Sch 1 para 6(2) WRA 2007; reg 83
ESA Regs
2 **HB** Schs 4 para 12 and 5 para 4 HB Regs
3 **IS** Reg 23(4) IS Regs
JSA Reg 88(3) JSA Regs
ESA Reg 83(4) ESA Regs
4 **IS** Reg 23(2) IS Regs
JSA Reg 88(2) JSA Regs
ESA Reg 83(2) ESA Regs
HB Reg 25(3) HB Regs
5 **IS** Reg 44(4) and Sch 8 para 15 IS Regs
JSA Reg 106(4) and Sch 6 para 18 JSA
Regs
Both Reg 1 SS(WTCCTC)(CA) Regs

2. What counts as income

6 R(IS) 4/01
7 *R v SBC ex parte Singer* [1973] 1 WLR 713
8 *Minter v Kingston Upon Hull City Council
and Potter v SSWP* [2011] EWCA Civ
1155

3. Earnings

9 **IS** Reg 35(1) IS Regs
JSA Reg 98(1) JSA Regs; reg 58(1) JSA
Regs 2013
ESA Reg 95(1) ESA Regs; reg 80(1) ESA
Regs 2013
HB Reg 35(1) HB Regs
All R(SB) 21/86
10 Reg 35(1)(i)-(j) HB Regs
11 **IS** Regs 35(2)(b) and 40(4) and Sch 9
paras 1, 4 and 4A IS Regs
JSA Regs 98(2)(c) and 103(6) and Sch 7
paras 1, 4 and 5 JSA Regs; reg 58(2)(c)
JSA Regs 2013
ESA Regs 95(2)(b) and 104(8) and Sch
8 paras 1, 4 and 5 ESA Regs; reg
80(2)(b) ESA Regs 2013
12 Reg 35(1)(i)-(j) HB Regs
13 **IS** Regs 35(2)(b) and 40(4) and Sch 9
paras 1 and 4 IS Regs
JSA Regs 98(2)(c) and 103(6) and Sch 7
paras 1 and 4 JSA Regs; reg 58(2)(c) JSA
Regs 2013
ESA Regs 95(2)(b) and 104(8) and Sch
8 paras 1 and 4 ESA Regs; reg 80(2)(b)
ESA Regs 2013

14 **IS** Reg 35(1)(e) IS Regs
JSA Reg 98(1)(d) JSA Regs; reg 58(1)(d)
JSA Regs 2013
ESA Reg 95(1)(e) ESA Regs; reg 80(1)(e)
ESA Regs 2013
HB Reg 35(1)(e) HB Regs
15 R(IS) 9/95
16 **IS** Reg 35(3)(a)(iv) IS Regs
JSA Reg 98(3)(d) JSA Regs; reg 67(4)(d)
JSA Regs 2013
ESA Reg 95(4), definition of
'compensation', ESA Regs; reg 80(4)
ESA Regs 2013
17 *Minter v Kingston Upon Hull City Council
and Potter v SSWP* [2011] EWCA Civ
1155
18 **IS** Reg 35(1)(j) IS Regs
JSA Reg 98(1)(h) JSA Regs; reg 58(1)(i)
JSA Regs 2013
ESA Reg 95(1)(k) ESA Regs; reg 80(1)(k)
ESA Regs 2013
HB Reg 35(1)(k) HB Regs
19 **IS** Reg 35(2A) IS Regs
JSA Reg 98(2A) JSA Regs; reg 58(3) JSA
Regs 2013
ESA Reg 95(3) ESA Regs; reg 80(3) ESA
Regs 2013
HB Reg 35(3) HB Regs
20 **IS** Reg 35(2)(a) and Sch 9 para 21 IS
Regs
JSA Reg 98(2)(a) and Sch 7 para 22 JSA
Regs; reg 58(2)(a) JSA Regs 2013
ESA Reg 95(2)(a) and Sch 8 para 22 ESA
Regs; reg 80(2)(a) ESA Regs 2013
HB Reg 35(2)(a) and Sch 5 para 23 HB
Regs
21 CIS/11482/1995
22 Vol 5 Ch 26, para 26096 DMG
23 **IS** Reg 35(2)(a) IS Regs
JSA Reg 98(2)(a) JSA Regs; reg 58(2)(a)
JSA Regs 2013
ESA Reg 95(2)(a) ESA Regs; reg 80(2)(a)
ESA Regs 2013
HB Reg 35(2)(a) HB Regs
All Vol 5 Ch 26, para 26040 DMG
24 **IS** Reg 48(5) IS Regs
JSA Reg 110(5) JSA Regs
ESA Reg 112(5) ESA Regs
HB Reg 46(5) HB Regs

25 **IS** Reg 35(2)(c) IS Regs
   JSA Reg 98(2)(d) JSA Regs; reg 58(2)(d) JSA Regs 2013
   ESA Reg 95(2)(c) ESA Regs; reg 80(2)(c) ESA Regs 2013
   HB Reg 35(2)(b) HB Regs
26 R(FC) 1/90
27 CFC/26/1989
28 R(FIS) 4/85
29 R(IS) 13/91; R(IS) 16/93; CFC/26/1989
30 R(FIS) 4/85; R(FC) 1/91; R(IS) 13/91
31 CIS/77/1993; CIS/89/1989
32 **IS** Sch 8 para 11 IS Regs
   JSA Sch 6 para 14 JSA Regs; Sch para 9 JSA Regs 2013
   ESA Sch 7 para 9 ESA Regs
   HB Sch 4 para 13 HB Regs
33 **IS** Sch 8 para 12 IS Regs
   JSA Sch 6 para 15 JSA Regs; Sch para 10 JSA Regs 2013
   ESA Sch 7 para 10 ESA Regs
   HB Sch 4 para 14 HB Regs
34 **IS** Reg 35(2)(d) IS Regs
   JSA Reg 98(2)(e) JSA Regs; reg 58(2)(e) JSA Regs 2013
   ESA Reg 95(2)(d) ESA Regs; reg 80(2)(d) ESA Regs 2013
   HB Reg 35(2)(c) HB Regs
35 **IS** Reg 40(4) and Sch 9 para 1 IS Regs
   JSA Reg 103(6) and Sch 7 para 1 JSA Regs
   ESA Reg 104(8) and Sch 8 para 1 ESA Regs
   HB Reg 40(10) and Sch 5 para 1 HB Regs
36 **IS** Sch 8 para 15A IS Regs
   JSA Sch 6 para 19 JSA Regs
   ESA Sch 7 para 11A ESA Regs
37 *Parsons v Hogg* [1985] 2 All ER 897 (CA), appendix to R(FIS) 4/85
38 **IS** Reg 36(3) IS Regs
   JSA Reg 99(1) and (4) JSA Regs; reg 59(1) and (3) JSA Regs 2013
   ESA Reg 96(3) ESA Regs; reg 81(2) ESA Regs 2013
   HB Reg 36(3) HB Regs
39 Regs 29(2) and 36(6) HB Regs
40 Reg 34 HB Regs; para BW2.34 GM
41 **IS** Sch 8 paras 1(1)(a) and (2) and 2 IS Regs
   JSA Sch 6 paras 1(1)(a) and (2) and 2 JSA Regs; Sch paras 1(1)(a) and (2) and 2 JSA Regs 2013
   ESA Sch 7 paras 1(1)(a) and (2) and 2 ESA Regs
   HB Sch 4 paras 1(b) and 2(b)(i) HB Regs

42 **IS** Reg 35(1)(g) IS Regs
   JSA Reg 98(1)(f) JSA Regs; reg 58(1)(f) JSA Regs 2013
   ESA Reg 95(1)(g) ESA Regs
   HB Reg 35(1)(g) HB Regs
43 **IS** Reg 35(1)(h) IS Regs
   JSA Reg 98(1)(g) JSA Regs; reg 58(1)(h) JSA Regs 2013
   ESA Reg 95(1)(i) ESA Regs
   HB Reg 35(1)(h) HB Regs
44 **IS** Reg 35(1)(h) IS Regs
   ESA Reg 95(1)(i) ESA Regs
   HB Reg 35(1)(h) HB Regs
45 **IS** Sch 8 paras 1(1)(a), (2)(a)(ii), (2)(b)(ii) and 2 IS Regs
   JSA Sch 6 paras 1(1)(a), (2)(a)(ii), (2)(b)(ii) and 2 JSA Regs; Sch paras 1(1)(a), (2)(a)(ii), (2)(b)(ii) and 2 JSA Regs 2013
   ESA Sch 7 paras 1(1)(a), (2)(a)(ii), (2)(b)(ii) and 2 ESA Regs
   HB Sch 4 paras 1(b)(i)(bb), (b)(ii)(bb) and 2 HB Regs
46 **IS** Regs 35(2)(b) and 40(4) and Sch 9 paras 4 and 4A IS Regs; R(IS) 8/99
   JSA Regs 98(2)(c) and 103(6) and Sch 7 paras 4 and 5 JSA Regs; reg 58(2)(c) JSA Regs 2013
   ESA Regs 95(2)(b) and 104(8) and Sch 8 paras 4 and 5 ESA Regs
   HB Reg 35(1)(i) to (j) and Sch 4 paras 1(b) and 2(b)(i) HB Regs
47 **IS** Reg 35(3)(a)(iii) IS Regs
   JSA Reg 98(2)(f) JSA Regs; reg 58(2)(f) JSA Regs 2013
   ESA Reg 95(4), definition of 'compensation', ESA Regs
   HB Because not listed as earnings in reg 35 HB Regs
48 Regs 98(1)(b), (3) and 104(4) and Sch 6 para 1(1) JSA Regs
49 **IS** Reg 35(1)(i) and (3) and Sch 8 paras 1(1)(a) and 2 IS Regs
   JSA Reg 98(1)(b) and Sch 6 paras 1(1)(a) and 2 JSA Regs; reg 58(1)(b) and Sch paras 1(1)(a) and 2 JSA Regs 2013
   ESA Reg 95(1)(j) and (4) and Sch 7 paras 1(1)(a) and 2 ESA Regs
   HB Reg 35 HB Regs
   All CJSA/82/98
50 **IS** Reg 35(1)(b) IS Regs
   JSA Regs 98(2)(b) and 103(6)(a) JSA Regs; reg 58(2)(b) JSA Regs 2013
   ESA Reg 95(1)(b) ESA Regs
   HB Reg 35(1)(b) HB Regs

Part 3: General rules for means-tested benefits
Chapter 14: Income: under pension credit age
Notes

51 **IS** Regs 35(1)(d) and 48(3) IS Regs
JSA Regs 98(1)(c) and 110(3) JSA Regs;
reg 58(1)(c) JSA Regs 2013
ESA Regs 95(1)(d) and 112(3) ESA Regs
HB Regs 35(1)(d) and 46(3) HB Regs
52 Sch 7 para 14 ESA Regs
53 **IS** Regs 35(2)(b) and 40(4) IS Regs
JSA Regs 98(2)(c) and 103(6) JSA Regs;
reg 58(2)(c) JSA Regs 2013
ESA Regs 95(2)(b) and 104(8) ESA Regs
54 Reg 35(1)(i)-(j) and Sch 4 paras 1(c) and
2(b)(ii) HB Regs
55 **IS** Regs 35(1)(d) and 48(3) and Sch 8
paras 1(1)(b) and 2 IS Regs
JSA Regs 98(1)(c) and 110(3) and Sch 6
paras 1(1)(b) and 2 JSA Regs; reg
58(1)(c) and Sch paras 1(1)(b) and 2 JSA
Regs 2013
ESA Regs 95(1)(d) and 112(3) and Sch
7 paras 1(1)(b) and 2 ESA Regs
HB Regs 35(1)(d) and 46(3) and Sch 4
paras 1(c) and 2(b)(ii) HB Regs
56 **IS** Sch 8 paras 1(1)(b) and 2 IS Regs
JSA Sch 6 paras 1(1)(b) and 2 JSA Regs;
Sch paras 1(1)(b) and 2 JSA Regs 2013
ESA Sch 7 paras 1(1)(b) and 2 ESA Regs
HB Sch 4 paras 1(c) and 2(b)(ii) HB Regs
57 **IS** Reg 35 IS Regs
JSA Reg 98 JSA Regs; reg 58 JSA Regs
2013
ESA Reg 95 ESA Regs
HB Reg 35 HB Regs
58 R(JSA) 1/06
59 **IS** Regs 35(2)(b) and 40(4) IS Regs
JSA Regs 98(2)(c) and 103(6) JSA Regs;
reg 58(2)(c) JSA Regs 2013
ESA Regs 95(2)(b) and 104(8) ESA Regs
60 **IS** Regs 37(1) and 38(3) IS Regs
JSA Regs 100(1) and 101(4) JSA Regs;
regs 60(1) and 61(3) JSA Regs 2013
ESA Regs 97(1) and 98(3) ESA Regs;
regs 82(1) and 83(2) ESA Regs 2013
HB Regs 37 and 38(3) HB Regs
61 *AR v Bradford Metropolitan District
Council* [2008] UKUT 30 (AAC), reported
as R(H) 6/09
62 **IS** Reg 37(2)(a) IS Regs
JSA Reg 100(2)(a) JSA Regs; reg 60(2)(a)
JSA Regs 2013
ESA Reg 97(2)(a) ESA Regs; reg 82(2)(a)
ESA Regs 2013
HB Sch 5 para 42 HB Regs

63 **IS** Reg 38(3)(a), (4), (7) and (8)(a) IS
Regs
JSA Reg 101(4) and (8) JSA Regs; reg
61(3) and (7) JSA Regs 2013
ESA Reg 98(3)(a), (4), (7) and (8)(a) ESA
Regs; reg 83(2)(a), (3), (6) and (7)(a)
ESA Regs 2013
HB Reg 38(3)(a), (4), (7) and (8)(a) HB
Regs
64 R(IS) 13/91; R(FC) 1/91; CFC/26/1989
65 **IS** Reg 38(6) and (8)(b) IS Regs
JSA Reg 101(7) and (9) JSA Regs; reg
61(6) and (8) JSA Regs 2013
ESA Reg 98(6) and (8)(b) ESA Regs; reg
83(5) and (7)(b) ESA Regs 2013
HB Reg 38(6) and (8)(b) HB Regs
66 **IS** Reg 38(5) IS Regs
JSA Reg 101(6) and (8) JSA Regs; reg
61(5) and (7) JSA Regs 2013
ESA Reg 98(5) ESA Regs; reg 83(4) ESA
Regs 2013
HB Reg 38(5) HB Regs
67 *SSWP v SK (CA)* [2013] UKUT 12 (AAC);
[2014] AACR 24
68 **IS** Reg 38(11) IS Regs
JSA Reg 101(12) JSA Regs; reg 61(11)
JSA Regs 2013
ESA Reg 98(11) ESA Regs; reg 83(10)
ESA Regs 2013
HB Reg 38(10) HB Regs
All R(FC) 1/93
69 CFC/836/1995
70 **IS** Regs 30 and 38(10) IS Regs; R(JSA) 1/
09
JSA Regs 95 and 101(11) JSA Regs; regs
55 and 61(10) JSA Regs 2013
ESA Regs 92 and 98(10) ESA Regs; regs
77 and 83(9) ESA Regs 2013
71 Vol 5 Ch 27, para 27054 DMG, but see
GM v SSWP (JSA) [2010] UKUT 221
(AAC); [2011] AACR 9
72 Regs 30(1) and 33(2) HB Regs
73 **IS** Reg 30(2) IS Regs
JSA Reg 95(2) JSA Regs; reg 55(2) JSA
Regs 2013
ESA Reg 92(2) ESA Regs
HB Reg 37(3) and (4) HB Regs
74 **IS** Sch 8 para 3 IS Regs
JSA Sch 6 para 4 JSA Regs; Sch para 4
JSA Regs 2013
ESA Sch 7 para 4 ESA Regs
HB Sch 4 para 2A HB Regs
75 **IS** Reg 38(9) IS Regs
JSA Reg 101(10) JSA Regs; reg 61(9) JSA
Regs 2013
ESA Reg 98(9) ESA Regs; reg 83(8) ESA
Regs 2013
HB Reg 38(9) HB Regs

76 Sch 7 paras 5 and 5A ESA Regs
77 Sch 7 para 6 ESA Regs
78 Reg 88 ESA Regs; reg 39(5) ESA Regs 2013
79 Sch 7 paras 7 and 14 ESA Regs
80 Sch 4 para 4 HB Regs
81 **IS** Sch 8 para 5 IS Regs
   JSA Sch 6 para 6 JSA Regs
82 **IS** Sch 8 para 4(2) IS Regs
   JSA Schs 6 para 5(1) and (2) and 6A para 1(1) and (2) JSA Regs
   HB Sch 4 para 3(2) HB Regs
83 Sch 4 para 3(2) HB Regs
84 **IS** Sch 8 paras 6A and 6B IS Regs
   JSA Schs 6 paras 7 and 8 and 6A para 2 JSA Regs
   HB Sch 4 paras 5 and 6 HB Regs
85 **IS** Sch 8 para 7(1) IS Regs
   JSA Schs 6 para 9(1) and 6A para 3 JSA Regs
   HB Sch 4 para 8(1) HB Regs
86 **IS** Sch 8 para 8 IS Regs
   JSA Schs 6 para 10 and 6A para 4 JSA Regs
   HB Sch 4 para 9 HB Regs
87 **IS** Sch 8 para 7(2) IS Regs
   JSA Schs 6 paras 9 and 10 and 6A paras 3 and 4 JSA Regs
   HB Sch 4 para 8(2)(b) HB Regs
88 **IS** Sch 8 para 4(3) IS Regs
   JSA Schs 6 para 5(3) and 6A para 1(3) JSA Regs
89 **IS** Sch 8 para 4(4) and (7) IS Regs
   JSA Schs 6 para 5(4) and (7) and 6A para 1(4) and (5) JSA Regs
90 **IS** Sch 8 paras 6 and 9 IS Regs
   JSA Schs 6 paras 11 and 12 and 6A para 6 JSA Regs
   HB Sch 4 paras 7 and 10 HB Regs
91 Sch 4 para 10A HB Regs
92 Sch 4 para 17 HB Regs
93 Regs 27(1)(c) and 28 HB Regs; reg 30(1)(c) HB(SPC) Regs
94 Reg 27(2) HB Regs; reg 30(2) HB(SPC) Regs
95 Reg 28(6) HB Regs; reg 31(6) HB(SPC) Regs
96 Reg 28(13) HB Regs; reg 31(13) HB(SPC) Regs
97 Reg 28(6)-(8) HB Regs; reg 31(6)-(8) HB(SPC) Regs
98 Reg 28(14) HB Regs; reg 31(14) HB(SPC) Regs
99 Reg 28(2)-(4) HB Regs; reg 31(2)-(4) HB(SPC) Regs
100 Reg 28(11), (12) and (12A) HB Regs; reg 31(11), (12) and (12A) HB(SPC) Regs

4. Income other than earnings

101 R(IS) 4/05
102 Reg 34 HB Regs; BW2.34 GM
103 **IS** Reg 40(6) IS Regs
    JSA Reg 103(5B) JSA Regs
    HB Reg 40(5A) HB Regs
104 **IS** Reg 35(2) and Sch 9 para 4 IS Regs
    JSA Sch 7 para 5 JSA Regs
    ESA Reg 95(2) and Sch 8 para 4 ESA Regs
105 Reg 35(1)(i) HB Regs
106 Sch 5 para 56 HB Regs
107 **IS** Sch 9 para 9 IS Regs
    JSA Sch 7 para 10 JSA Regs
    ESA Sch 8 para 11 ESA Regs
    HB Sch 5 para 9 HB Regs
108 **IS** Sch 9 para 5B(2) IS Regs
    JSA Sch 7 para 6B(2) JSA Regs
    ESA Sch 8 para 7(2) ESA Regs
    HB Sch 5 para 65 HB Regs
109 **IS** Reg 7(4)-(6) SS(WTCCTC)(CA) Regs
    JSA Reg 8(3)-(5) SS(WTCCTC)(CA) Regs
110 **IS** Sch 9 para 80 IS Regs
    JSA Sch 7 para 76 JSA Regs
    ESA Sch 8 para 68 ESA Regs
    HB Sch 5 para 67 HB Regs
111 **IS** Sch 9 para 33 IS Regs
    JSA Sch 7 para 35 JSA Regs
    ESA Sch 8 para 37 ESA Regs
    HB Sch 5 para 32 HB Regs
112 **IS** Sch 9 para 9 IS Regs
    JSA Sch 7 para 10 JSA Regs
    ESA Sch 8 para 11 ESA Regs
    HB Sch 5 paras 6 and 9 HB Regs
113 **IS** Sch 9 para 5B(1) IS Regs
    JSA Sch 7 para 6B(1) JSA Regs
    ESA Sch 8 para 7(1) ESA Regs
114 **IS** Sch 9 paras 6 and 9 IS Regs
    JSA Sch 7 paras 7 and 10 JSA Regs
    ESA Sch 8 paras 8 and 11 ESA Regs
    HB Sch 5 para 6 HB Regs
115 **IS** Sch 9 para 5A(1) IS Regs
    JSA Sch 7 para 6A(1) JSA Regs
    ESA Sch 8 para 6 ESA Regs
    HB Sch 5 para 50 HB Regs
116 **IS** Sch 9 paras 5 and 52 IS Regs
    JSA Sch 7 paras 6 and 51 JSA Regs
    ESA Sch 8 paras 64 and 65 ESA Regs
    HB Sch 5 para 51 HB Regs
117 Sch 5 para 4 HB Regs
118 **IS** Sch 9 para 8 IS Regs
    JSA Sch 7 para 9 JSA Regs
    ESA Sch 8 para 10 ESA Regs
    HB Sch 5 para 8 HB Regs
119 **IS** Sch 9 paras 6 and 9 IS Regs
    JSA Sch 7 paras 7 and 10 JSA Regs
    ESA Sch 8 paras 8 and 11 ESA Regs
    HB Sch 5 para 6 HB Regs

Part 3: General rules for means-tested benefits
Chapter 14: Income: under pension credit age
Notes

120 **IS** Sch 9 paras 7 and 8 IS Regs
JSA Sch 7 paras 8 and 9 JSA Regs
ESA Sch 8 paras 9 and 10 ESA Regs
HB Sch 5 paras 7 and 8 HB Regs
121 **IS** Sch 9 para 31 IS Regs
JSA Sch 7 para 33 JSA Regs
ESA Sch 8 para 35 ESA Regs
HB Sch 5 para 31 HB Regs
122 **IS** Sch 9 paras 54-56 IS Regs
JSA Sch 7 paras 53-55 JSA Regs
ESA Sch 8 paras 49, 51 and 52 ESA Regs
HB Sch 5 paras 53-55 HB Regs
123 **IS** Sch 9 paras 5B(3) and 53 IS Regs
JSA Sch 7 paras 6B(3) and 52 JSA Regs
ESA Sch 8 paras 7(3) and 50 ESA Regs
HB Sch 5 para 52 HB Regs
124 **IS** Sch 9 para 40 IS Regs
JSA Sch 7 para 42 JSA Regs
ESA Sch 8 para 42 ESA Regs
HB Sch 5 para 36 HB Regs
125 **IS** Sch 9 para 46 IS Regs
JSA Sch 7 para 45 JSA Regs
ESA Sch 8 para 44 ESA Regs
HB Sch 5 para 41 HB Regs
126 Sch 5 para 16 HB Regs
127 **IS** Sch 9 para 16 IS Regs
JSA Sch 7 para 17 JSA Regs
ESA Sch 8 para 17 ESA Regs
HB Sch 5 para 15 HB Regs; Sch Part 2
HB&CTB(WPD) Regs
128 *MN v (1) Bury Council (2) SSWP (HB)*
[2014] UKUT 187 (AAC)
129 **IS** Sch 9 para 36 IS Regs
ESA Sch 8 para 39 ESA Regs
JSA Sch 7 para 38 JSA Regs
HB Sch 5 para 34 HB Regs
130 s134(8) SSAA 1992; HB&CTB(WPD)
Regs
131 s74(2) SSAA 1992
132 Regs 32 and 40(6) HB Regs; reg 32
HB(SPC) Regs
133 CH/1450/2005
134 CIS/1064/2004 seems to lend weight to
this approach.
135 **IS** Sch 9 para 73 IS Regs
JSA Sch 7 para 70 JSA Regs
ESA Sch 8 para 60 ESA Regs
HB Sch 5 para 47A HB Regs
136 *KW v Lancaster City Council v SSWP (HB)*
[2011] UKUT 266 (AAC); s74A SSAA
1992
137 Sch 5 para 47 HB Regs
138 **IS** Reg 54 IS Regs
JSA Reg 117 JSA Regs
ESA Reg 119 ESA Regs
139 **IS** Regs 54 and 55 IS Regs
JSA Regs 117 and 118 JSA Regs
ESA Regs 119 and 120 ESA Regs

140 **IS** Reg 42(4)(a) IS Regs
JSA Reg 105(10)(a) JSA Regs
ESA Reg 107(3)(c) ESA Regs
141 R(SB) 1/89
142 **IS** Reg 42(4)(b) IS Regs
JSA Reg 105(10)(b) JSA Regs
ESA Reg 107(4) ESA Regs
143 CIS/683/1993
144 **IS** Sch 9 para 25(1)(a) and (1A) IS Regs
JSA Sch 7 para 26(1)(a) and (1A) JSA
Regs
ESA Sch 8 para 26(1)(a) and (2) ESA
Regs
HB Sch 5 para 25(1)(a) and (2) HB Regs
145 **IS** Sch 9 para 25(1A) IS Regs
JSA Sch 7 para 26(1A) JSA Regs
ESA Sch 8 para 26(2) ESA Regs
HB Sch 5 para 25(2) HB Regs
146 **IS** Reg 42(4)(b) IS Regs
JSA Reg 105(10)(b) JSA Regs
ESA Reg 107(4) ESA Regs
HB Reg 42(6)(c) HB Regs
All Vol 5 Ch 28, para 28174 DMG
147 **IS** Sch 9 para 25(1)(a) and (2)(b) IS Regs
JSA Sch 7 para 26(1)(a) and (2)(b) JSA
Regs
148 **IS** Sch 9 para 25(2)(a) IS Regs
JSA Sch 7 para 26(2)(a) JSA Regs
Both Reg 1 and Schs 1 para 23(c) and 2
para 23(c) SS(WTCCTC)(CA) Regs
149 That is, under ss23(2)(a) or 59(1)(a) CA
1989 or (in Scotland) s26 C(S)A 1995 or
regs 33 or 51 Looked After Children
(Scotland) Regulations 2009, No.210
150 **IS** Sch 9 para 26 IS Regs
JSA Sch 7 para 27 JSA Regs
ESA Sch 8 para 28 ESA Regs
HB Sch 5 para 26 HB Regs
151 **IS** Sch 9 para 25(1)(c) and (2) IS Regs
JSA Sch 7 para 26(1)(c) and (2) JSA Regs
ESA Sch 8 para 26(1)(b) ESA Regs
HB Sch 5 para 25(1)(ba) HB Regs
152 **IS** Sch 9 paras 25(1)(ba), 26(a)(iii) and
28(1)(c) IS Regs
JSA Sch 7 paras 26(1)(ba), 27(a)(iii) and
29(1)(c) JSA Regs
ESA Sch 8 paras 26(1)(b), 28(a)(iii) and
30(1)(c) ESA Regs
HB Sch 5 paras 25(1)(ba), 26(a)(iii) and
28 HB Regs
153 **IS** Sch 9 para 25(1)(e) IS Regs; Vol 5 Ch
28, para 28402 DMG
JSA Sch 7 para 26(1)(e) JSA Regs; Vol 5
Ch 28, para 28402 DMG
ESA Sch 8 para 26(1)(d) ESA Regs
HB Sch 5 para 25(1)(d) HB Regs

154 **IS** Sch 9 para 39 IS Regs
  JSA Sch 7 para 41(1) JSA Regs
  ESA Sch 8 para 41 ESA Regs
  HB Sch 5 para 35 HB Regs
155 **IS** Reg 48(9) IS Regs
  JSA Reg 110(9) JSA Regs
  ESA Reg 112(7) ESA Regs
  HB Reg 46(6) HB Regs
156 **IS** Reg 48(10)(a) IS Regs
  JSA Reg 110(10) JSA Regs
157 **IS** Sch 9 para 15 IS Regs
  JSA Sch 7 para 15 JSA Regs
  ESA Sch 8 para 16 ESA Regs
  HB Sch 5 para 14 HB Regs
158 R(H) 5/05 explains the difference
  between a loan and a voluntary
  payment.
159 **IS** Sch 9 para 15(5A) IS Regs
  JSA Sch 7 para 15(5A) JSA Regs
  ESA Sch 8 para 16(3) ESA Regs
  HB Sch 5 para 14 HB Regs
160 *Malekout v SSWP* [2010] EWCA Civ 162;
  [2010] AACR 28
161 Vol 5 Ch 28, para 28102 DMG
162 **IS** Sch 9 para 19 IS Regs
  JSA Sch 7 para 20 JSA Regs
  ESA Sch 8 para 20 ESA Regs
  HB Sch 5 para 22 HB Regs
163 **IS** Sch 9 para 18 IS Regs
  JSA Sch 7 para 19 JSA Regs
  ESA Sch 8 para 19 ESA Regs
  HB Sch 5 para 21 HB Regs
164 **IS** Sch 9 para 20 IS Regs
  JSA Sch 7 para 21 JSA Regs
  ESA Sch 8 para 21 ESA Regs
  HB Sch 5 para 42 HB Regs
165 **IS** Reg 2(1) IS Regs
  JSA Reg 1(3) JSA Regs
  ESA Reg 2(1) ESA Regs
  HB Sch 5 para 42(2) HB Regs
  IS/JSA/HB definition of 'board and
  lodging accommodation'
  ESA definition of 'board and lodging'
166 CIS/521/2002
167 CIS/13059/1996
168 **IS** Reg 48(4) IS Regs
  JSA Reg 110(4) JSA Regs
  ESA Reg 112(4) ESA Regs
  HB Reg 46(4) HB Regs
  All *CAO v Palfrey and Others, The Times,*
  17 February 1995; R(IS) 26/95
169 CIS/563/1991
170 **IS** Sch 9 para 22(1) IS Regs
  JSA Sch 7 para 23 JSA Regs
  ESA Sch 8 para 23(1) ESA Regs
  HB Sch 5 para 17(1) HB Regs

171 **IS** Reg 48(4) IS Regs
  JSA Reg 110(4) JSA Regs
  ESA Reg 112(4) ESA Regs
  HB Reg 46(4) HB Regs
172 **IS** Sch 9 para 22(1) IS Regs
  JSA Sch 7 para 23(2) JSA Regs
  ESA Sch 8 para 23(2) ESA Regs
  HB Sch 5 para 17(1) HB Regs
173 CFC/13/1993
174 **IS** Sch 9 para 22(2) IS Regs
  JSA Sch 7 para 23(2) and (3) JSA Regs
  ESA Sch 8 para 23(2) and (3) ESA Regs
  HB Sch 5 para 17(2) HB Regs
175 **IS** Reg 53 IS Regs
  JSA Reg 116 JSA Regs
  ESA Reg 118 ESA Regs
  HB Reg 52 HB Regs
176 **IS** Reg 41(1) IS Regs
  JSA Reg 104(1) JSA Regs
  ESA Reg 105(1) ESA Regs
177 Reg 41(1) HB Regs
178 **IS** Reg 29(2) IS Regs
  JSA Reg 94(2) JSA Regs
  ESA Reg 91(2) ESA Regs
  HB Reg 33 HB Regs
179 **IS** Reg 41(2) IS Regs
  JSA Reg 104(2) JSA Regs
  ESA Reg 105(2) ESA Regs
  HB Reg 41(2) HB Regs
180 **IS** Reg 41(6) IS Regs
  JSA Reg 104(5) JSA Regs
  ESA Reg 105(4) ESA Regs
  HB Reg 41(4) HB Regs
181 Regs 41(4) and 48(2) IS Regs
182 **IS** Reg 41(7) IS Regs
  JSA Reg 104(6) JSA Regs
  ESA Reg 105(5) ESA Regs
  HB Reg 41(5) HB Regs
183 **IS** Sch 10 para 20 IS Regs
  JSA Sch 8 para 25 JSA Regs
  ESA Sch 9 para 25 ESA Regs
  HB Sch 6 para 22 HB Regs
184 *R v SBC ex parte Singer* [1973] 1 All ER
  931; *R v Oxford County Council ex parte
  Jack* [1984] 17 HLR 419; *R v West Dorset
  DC ex parte Poupard* [1988] 20 HLR 295
185 R(H) 8/08
186 *Leeves v Chief Adjudication Officer* [1998]
  EWCA 1706, reported as R(IS) 5/99; CIS/
  2287/2008
187 **IS** Reg 48(2) IS Regs
  JSA Reg 110(2) JSA Regs
  ESA Reg 112(2) ESA Regs
  HB Reg 46(2) HB Regs
188 **IS** s126(5) SSCBA 1992
  JSA s5(2)(c) JSA 1995
189 Regs 41(4) and 48(2) IS Regs

Part 3: General rules for means-tested benefits
Chapter 14: Income: under pension credit age
Notes

190 **IS** Sch 9 para 13 IS Regs
JSA Sch 7 para 14 JSA Regs
ESA Sch 8 para 15 ESA Regs
HB Sch 5 para 13 HB Regs
191 **IS** Sch 9 para 1A IS Regs
JSA Sch 7 paras A2 and A3 JSA Regs
ESA Sch 8 para 1A ESA Regs
HB Sch 5 paras A2 and A3 HB Regs
192 Sch 8 para 15A ESA Regs
193 **IS** Sch 9 para 64 IS Regs
JSA Sch 7 para 62 JSA Regs
ESA Sch 8 para 55 ESA Regs
HB Sch 5 para 58 HB Regs
194 Reg 46(7) HB Regs
195 **IS** Regs 39C and 39D IS Regs
JSA Regs 102C and 102D JSA Regs
ESA Regs 102 and 103 ESA Regs
196 DMG Memo 12/15
197 Vol 5 Ch 28, para 28090 DMG
198 **IS** Reg 41(2) and Sch 9 para 17 IS Regs
JSA Reg 104(2) and Sch 7 para 18 JSA
Regs
ESA Reg 105(2) and Sch 8 para 18 ESA
Regs
HB Reg 41(2) HB Regs
199 **IS** Sch 9 para 29 IS Regs; Vol 5 Ch 28,
para 28240 DMG
JSA Sch 7 para 30 JSA Regs
ESA Sch 8 para 31 ESA Regs
200 **IS** Sch 9 para 30 IS Regs
JSA Sch 7 para 31 JSA Regs
ESA Sch 8 para 32 ESA Regs
All R(IS) 13/01
201 Sch 5 para 29 HB Regs
202 **IS** Sch 9 para 30ZA IS Regs
JSA Sch 7 para 31A JSA Regs
ESA Sch 8 para 33 ESA Regs
HB Sch 5 para 29 HB Regs
203 **IS** Sch 9 para 31A IS Regs
JSA Sch 7 para 33A JSA Regs
ESA Sch 8 para 35A ESA Regs
HB Sch 5 para 31A HB regs
204 **IS** Sch 9 para 28 IS Regs
JSA Sch 7 para 29 JSA Regs
ESA Sch 8 para 30 ESA Regs
HB Sch 5 para 28 HB Regs
205 **IS** Sch 9 para 28(2) and (5) IS Regs
JSA Sch 7 para 29(2) and (5) JSA Regs
ESA Sch 8 para 30(2) and (3) ESA Regs
HB Sch 5 para 28A HB Regs
206 **IS** Sch 9 para 79 IS Regs
JSA Sch 7 para 75 JSA Regs
ESA Sch 8 para 67 ESA Regs
HB Sch 5 para 66 HB Regs

207 **IS** Sch 9 para 58 IS Regs
JSA Sch 7 para 56 JSA Regs
ESA Sch 8 para 53 ESA Regs
HB Sch 5 para 57 HB Regs
All *Casewell v SSWP* [2008] EWCA Civ
524, reported as R(IS) 7/08
208 **IS** Sch 9 para 27 IS Regs
JSA Sch 7 para 28 JSA Regs
ESA Sch 8 para 29 ESA Regs
HB Sch 5 para 27 HB Regs
209 **IS** Sch 9 para 76 IS Regs
JSA Sch 7 para 72 JSA Regs
ESA Sch 8 para 63 ESA Regs
HB Sch 5 para 63 HB Regs
210 **IS** Sch 9 paras 15, 30A and 66 IS Regs
JSA Sch 7 paras 15, 32 and 64 JSA Regs
ESA Sch 8 paras 16, 34 and 56 ESA Regs
211 **IS** Sch 10 para 8(b) IS Regs
JSA Sch 8 para 13(b) JSA Regs
ESA Sch 9 para 12(b) ESA Regs
HB Sch 6 para 10(b) HB Regs
212 **IS** Sch 9 para 75 IS Regs
JSA Sch 7 para 71 JSA Regs
ESA Sch 8 para 62 ESA Regs
HB Sch 5 para 62 HB Regs
213 **IS** Sch 9 para 11 IS Regs
JSA Sch 7 para 12 JSA Regs
ESA Sch 8 para 13 ESA Regs
HB Sch 5 para 11 HB Regs
214 **IS** Sch 9 para 2 IS Regs
JSA Sch 7 para 2 JSA Regs
ESA Sch 8 para 2 ESA Regs
HB Sch 5 para 2 HB Regs
215 **IS** Sch 9 para 21 IS Regs
JSA Sch 7 para 22 JSA Regs
ESA Sch 8 para 22 ESA Regs
HB Sch 5 para 23 HB Regs
216 para BW2 Annex B para 13 GM
217 **IS** Sch 9 para 51 IS Regs
JSA Sch 7 para 50 JSA Regs
ESA Sch 8 para 48 ESA Regs
HB Sch 5 para 49 HB Regs
218 **IS** Sch 9 para 43 IS Regs
JSA Sch 7 para 43 JSA Regs
ESA Sch 8 para 43 ESA Regs
HB Sch 5 para 39 HB Regs
219 **IS** Sch 9 para 10 IS Regs
JSA Sch 7 para 11 JSA Regs
ESA Sch 8 para 12 ESA Regs
HB Sch 5 para 10 HB Regs
220 **IS** Sch 9 para 23 IS Regs
JSA Sch 7 para 24 JSA Regs
ESA Sch 8 para 24 ESA Regs
HB Sch 5 para 24 HB Regs
221 **IS** Sch 9 para 24 IS Regs
JSA Sch 7 para 25 JSA Regs
ESA Sch 8 para 25 ESA Regs
HB Sch 5 para 33 HB Regs

222 **IS** Sch 9 para 48 IS Regs
JSA Sch 7 para 47 JSA Regs
ESA Sch 8 para 45 ESA Regs
HB Sch 5 para 44 HB Regs
223 **IS** Sch 9 para 49 IS Regs
JSA Sch 7 para 48 JSA Regs
ESA Sch 8 para 46 ESA Regs
HB Sch 5 para 45 HB Regs
224 **IS** Sch 9 para 50 IS Regs
JSA Sch 7 para 49 JSA Regs
ESA Sch 8 para 47 ESA Regs
HB Sch 5 para 46 HB Regs
225 Schs 4 para 11 and 5 paras 19 and 20 HB Regs
226 **IS** Sch 9 para 69 IS Regs
JSA Sch 7 para 67 JSA Regs
ESA Sch 8 para 57 ESA Regs
HB Sch 5 para 59 HB Regs
227 **IS** Sch 9 para 2A IS Regs
JSA Sch 7 para 2A JSA Regs
ESA Sch 8 para 2A ESA Regs
HB Sch 5 para 2A HB Regs

5. Notional income
228 **IS** Reg 42(1) IS Regs
JSA Reg 105(1) JSA Regs
ESA Reg 106(1) ESA Regs
HB Reg 42(1) HB Regs
229 Vol 5 Ch 28, paras 28608-16 DMG; see also CIS/15052/1996
230 **IS** Reg 42(2) IS Regs
JSA Reg 105(2) JSA Regs
ESA Reg 106(2) ESA Regs
HB Reg 42(2) HB Regs
231 **IS** Reg 42(2ZA) and (2A) IS Regs
JSA Reg 105(2B) and (3) JSA Regs
ESA Reg 106(3) and (4) ESA Regs
232 **IS** Reg 42(2)(e) and (f) IS Regs
JSA Reg 105(2)(d) JSA Regs
ESA Reg 106(2)(e) and (f) ESA Regs
HB Reg 42(2)(f) and (g) HB Regs
233 CIS/16271/1996
234 Vol 5 Ch 28, paras 28608-16 DMG
235 **IS** Reg 42(3) IS Regs
JSA Reg 105(6) JSA Regs
ESA Reg 107(1) ESA Regs
236 **IS** Reg 42(3A) and (3B) IS Regs
JSA Reg 105(7)(a), (8) and (9) JSA Regs
ESA Reg 107(2)(a) and (b) ESA Regs
237 **IS** Reg 42(3C) IS Regs
JSA Reg 105(7)(d) JSA Regs
ESA Reg 107(2)(c) ESA Regs
238 CIS/15052/1996, para 10
239 **IS** Reg 42(5) IS Regs
JSA Reg 105(12) JSA Regs
ESA Reg 108(1) ESA Regs
240 Reg 2 SS(PAOR) Regs

241 **IS** Reg 42(4)(a) IS Regs
JSA Reg 105(10)(a) JSA Regs
ESA Reg 107(3) ESA Regs
HB Reg 42(6)(b) HB Regs
242 **IS** Reg 42(4)(b) and (4ZA) IS Regs
JSA Reg 105(10)(b) and (10A) JSA Regs
ESA Reg 107(4) and (5) ESA Regs
HB Reg 42(6)(c) and (7) HB Regs
243 **IS** Reg 42(6) IS Regs; CIS/191/1991
JSA Reg 105(13) JSA Regs
ESA Reg 108(3) ESA Regs
HB Reg 42(9) HB Regs
244 R(SB) 13/86
245 **IS** Reg 42(6A) IS Regs
JSA Reg 105(13A) JSA Regs
ESA Reg 108(4) ESA Regs
HB Reg 42(10) HB Regs
246 R(SB) 13/86
247 **IS** Reg 42(6A)(a) IS Regs
JSA Reg 105(13A)(a) JSA Regs
ESA Reg 108(4)(a) ESA Regs
HB Reg 42(10)(a) HB Regs
248 CIS/147/1993
249 *Sharrock v CAO*, 26 March 1991 (CA); CIS/93/1991; CIS/422/1992; CIS/701/1994

6. Working out weekly income
250 **IS** Reg 29(2) IS Regs
JSA Reg 94(2) JSA Regs; reg 54(2) JSA Regs 2013
ESA Reg 91(2) ESA Regs; reg 76(2) ESA Regs 2013
251 **IS** Reg 29(2)(b) IS Regs
JSA Reg 94(2)(b) JSA Regs; reg 54(2)(c) JSA Regs 2013
ESA Reg 91(2)(c) ESA Regs; reg 76(2)(c) ESA Regs 2013
252 **IS** Reg 31(1)(a) IS Regs
JSA Reg 96(1)(a) JSA Regs; reg 56(a) JSA Regs 2013
ESA Reg 93(1)(a) ESA Regs; reg 78(a) ESA Regs 2013
253 **IS** Reg 31(1)(b) IS Regs
JSA Reg 96(1)(b) JSA Regs; reg 56(b) JSA Regs 2013
ESA Reg 93(1)(b) ESA Regs; reg 78(b) ESA Regs 2013
254 **IS** Reg 31(2) IS Regs
JSA Reg 96(2) JSA Regs
ESA Reg 93(2) ESA Regs
255 **IS** Reg 2(1) IS Regs
JSA Reg 1(3) JSA Regs; reg 2(2) JSA Regs 2013
ESA Reg 2(1) ESA Regs; reg 2 ESA Regs 2013
256 Reg 2 HB Regs
257 R(SB) 33/83

Part 3: General rules for means-tested benefits
Chapter 14: Income: under pension credit age
Notes

258 R(SB) 22/84; R(SB) 11/85
259 CIS/590/1993
260 *SSWP v JP (JSA)* [2010] UKUT 90 (AAC)
261 R(IS) 3/93
262 R(IS) 10/95
263 **IS** Reg 32(6) IS Regs
       JSA Reg 97(6) JSA Regs; reg 57(5) JSA
       Regs 2013
       ESA Reg 94(6) ESA Regs; reg 79(5)(b)
       ESA Regs 2013
264 **IS** Reg 32(2) and (3) IS Regs
       JSA Reg 97(2) and (3) JSA Regs; reg
       57(2) and (3) JSA Regs 2013
       ESA Reg 94(2) and (3) ESA Regs; reg
       79(2) and (3) ESA Regs 2013
265 **IS** Reg 32(4) IS Regs
       JSA Reg 97(4) JSA Regs
       ESA Reg 94(4) ESA Regs
266 **IS** Reg 32(5) and Sch 8 para 10 IS Regs
       JSA Reg 97(5) and Sch 6 para 13 JSA
       Regs; reg 57(4) and Sch para 8 JSA Regs
       2013
       ESA Reg 94(5) and Sch 7 para 8 ESA
       Regs; reg 79(4) ESA Regs 2013
267 Reg 31 HB Regs
268 Reg 29(1)(a) HB Regs
269 Reg 29(1)(b) HB Regs; para BW2/W2.53
       GM
270 *R v HBRB of the London Borough of Ealing
       ex parte Saville* [1986] 18 HLR 349
271 Reg 29(2) HB Regs
272 Reg 29(3) HB Regs
273 Reg 29A HB Regs
274 Reg 32 HB Regs
275 Reg 31(2) HB Regs

Chapter 15

. . . .

Income: over pension credit age

This chapter covers:
1. Whose income counts (below)
2. What counts as income (p316)
3. Earnings (p317)
4. Income other than earnings (p323)
5. Notional income (p330)
6. Working out weekly income (p331)

This chapter explains the rules for working out your weekly income for pension credit (PC) and for housing benefit (HB) if you or your partner are over the qualifying age for PC and neither of you are on income support (IS), income-based jobseeker's allowance (JSA), income-related employment and support allowance (ESA) or universal credit (UC). See Chapter 14 for the rules for IS, income-based JSA and income-related ESA and for HB if you and your partner are under the qualifying age for PC. See Chapter16 for the rules for UC.

Note: whenever HB is referred to in this chapter, this only applies to the rules for people over the qualifying age for PC.

Key facts
- Your entitlement to pension credit (PC) and housing benefit (HB) and the amount you get depends on how much income you have.
- Your own income counts and, if you are a member of a couple, your partner's income also counts.
- Some income may be completely or partly ignored, or it may count in full.
- If you get the guarantee credit of PC, you are entitled to maximum HB, so you do not need to work out your income again for HB.

1. **Whose income counts**

If you are a member of a couple (see p215), your partner's income is added to yours.[1]

. . . . .
315

Part 3: General rules for means-tested benefits
Chapter 15: Income: over pension credit age
2. What counts as income

The income of a dependent child does *not* affect pension credit or housing benefit.[2]

---

2. **What counts as income**

Pension credit

For pension credit (PC), **'income'** means:[3]

- earnings (see p318 and p320);
- certain benefits and tax credits, including state retirement pensions and war pensions (see p323);
- maintenance (see p325);
- income from tenants and lodgers (see p326);
- income from capital (see p326);
- other specified miscellaneous income, including occupational and personal pensions (see p327);
- notional income (see p330);
- any income paid in lieu of the above.

For each type of income, some income is taken into account and some is ignored in the assessment of PC. If the rules do not specify a type of income as being included in the assessment, it is ignored and does not affect your benefit.

For the rules on qualifying income for the savings credit and the 'assessed income period', see Chapter 7.

Housing benefit

How your income affects your entitlement to housing benefit (HB) depends on whether you are getting PC and, if so, which type of PC.

If you get pension credit guarantee credit

If you (or your partner) get the guarantee credit of PC, all your (and your partner's) income is ignored.[4] This is because entitlement to guarantee credit of PC acts as a passport to maximum HB.

If you get pension credit savings credit

If you (or your partner) only get the savings credit of PC, your income for HB purposes is the income (and capital) figure used by the DWP to work out your PC, plus:[5]

- the amount of savings credit of PC;
- any income (and capital) of your partner which was not taken into account in the PC calculation; *and*

- any income of a non-dependant, but only in the very limited circumstances when her/his income can be treated as yours under the HB rules (see p71);[6]

minus:[7]
- an amount disregarded from your earnings for childcare charges (see p323);
- the higher amount disregarded from your earnings if you:
  - are a lone parent (see p321);
  - pay maintenance (see p325);
- any additional full-time earnings disregard (see p322);
- any earnings disregarded from 'permitted work' (see p322);
- any discretionary increase to the £10 disregard for war pensions, and war widow's and widower's pensions (see p325).

If you do not get pension credit

If you or your partner are over the qualifying age for PC (see p147) and do not get the guarantee or savings credit of PC (or income support, income-based jobseeker's allowance, income-related employment and support allowance or universal credit), income is defined in the same way as for PC (see p316).[8] Some income is taken into account and some disregarded, but the rules are not always the same as for PC. The differences are explained in the relevant sections below.

Net weekly income

The income that is taken into account is the amount after deducting any tax or national insurance (NI) contributions.[9]

For HB, the local authority may ignore changes (eg, Budget changes) in tax or NI contributions and the maximum rate of tax credits for up to 30 benefit weeks. When the changes are eventually taken into account, you are not treated as having been underpaid or overpaid benefit during the period of the delay.[10]

Once you have worked out what income should be taken into account, this is converted into a weekly amount (see p331) and the total taken into account in the benefit assessment. See p332 for the date from which a payment is counted. Chapters 4 and 7 explain how income affects the amount of HB or PC you get.

3. Earnings

How earnings are treated depends on whether you are an employed earner (see p318) or are self-employed (see p320). In both cases, some of your earnings can be disregarded (see p320).

Part 3: General rules for means-tested benefits
Chapter 15: Income: over pension credit age
3. Earnings

Employed earnings

What counts as earnings

'**Earnings**' means 'any remuneration or profit derived from... employment'. As well as your wages, this includes:[11]

- any bonus or commission (including tips);
- holiday pay – but this is ignored if your employment ends before your pension credit (PC) or housing benefit (HB) entitlement starts;
- statutory sick pay and contractual sick pay,[12] statutory maternity pay, statutory adoption pay, statutory paternity pay or statutory shared parental pay or any other payment made to you by your employer while you are on maternity leave;[13]
- any payments made by your employer for expenses not wholly, exclusively and necessarily incurred in carrying out your job, such as travel expenses to and from work, and payments made to you for looking after members of your family;
- pay in lieu of notice, or pay in lieu of remuneration except for periodic payments following redundancy. However, all earnings, including pay in lieu, are ignored if your employment ends before your PC or HB entitlement starts;
- a retainer fee (eg, payment during the school holidays if you work for the school meals service[14]) or a guarantee payment;[15]
- an equal pay settlement – eg, through a 'single status agreement';[16]
- any payment of a non-cash voucher which is liable for class 1 national insurance (NI) contributions.[17] Non-cash vouchers that are not liable for contributions (eg, certain childcare and charitable vouchers) are classed as payments in kind and ignored.[18]

What does not count as earnings

Examples of payments not counted as earnings include the following.

- If you become entitled to HB or PC after your employment ends, all earnings are disregarded except certain royalties.[19]
- Payments in kind (eg, petrol) are ignored.[20]
- An advance of earnings or a loan from your employer should be treated as capital.[21]
- The value of free accommodation provided as part of your job should be ignored.[22]
- Payments towards expenses that are wholly, exclusively and necessarily incurred, such as travelling expenses during the course of your work, are ignored.[23]
- If you are a local councillor, travelling expenses and subsistence payments are (and basic allowances may be[24]) ignored as expenses wholly, exclusively and necessarily incurred in your work.
- If your earnings are paid in another currency, any bank charges for converting them into sterling are deducted before taking them into account.[25]

- The net amount of any occupational pension,[26] although not counted as earnings, counts as income other than earnings and is taken into account in full.[27]
- Any compensation payments made by an employment tribunal for unfair dismissal or unlawful discrimination do not count as earnings.[28]

Calculating net earnings from employment

Both your 'gross' earnings and 'net' earnings must be calculated. It is your 'net earnings' that are taken into account in the assessment. See p331 for how earnings are converted into a weekly amount.

Gross and net earnings

'Gross earnings' means the amount of earnings received from your employer less deductions for any expenses wholly, necessarily and exclusively incurred by you in order to carry out the duties of your employment.[29] See p270 for what counts as earnings and p271 for examples of expenses that can be deducted.

'Net earnings' means your gross earnings less any deductions made for:[30]

– income tax;

– class 1 NI contributions;

– half of any contribution you make towards a personal or occupational pension scheme.

If your earnings are estimated for HB, the amount of tax and NI you would expect to pay on those earnings is estimated and deducted, together with half of any pension contributions you are paying.[31]

Payments when you stop work

Redundancy payments are treated as capital.[32]

If you leave a job before you claim HB or PC, any earnings should be disregarded except certain copyright royalties, and payments for patents, trademarks or under the Public Lending Right scheme.[33]

If you are already getting HB or PC when you leave your job, your earnings are not disregarded for that benefit.

For PC, any final payment is treated as having been paid on the date your next regular payment of earnings would have been paid and taken into account for the same period, unless the final payment is higher than the normal amount. If it is higher, work out over how many normal payment periods it counts – eg, if the final payment is between two and three times as much as normal, it counts over three payment periods.[34]

Part 3: General rules for means-tested benefits
Chapter 15: Income: over pension credit age
3. Earnings

Example

Sandra has been getting PC and working part time. She earns £25 a week, paid on a Friday. She finishes work on Wednesday 5 August and on that day is given £35, made up of £15 final wages and £20 holiday pay. This £35 is treated as having been paid on Friday 7 August and taken into account for two benefit weeks: £25 in the first week and the remaining £10 in the second week.

Self-employed earnings

Calculating net earnings

Your '**net profit**' over the period before your claim must be worked out. This consists of your self-employed earnings minus:[35]

- reasonable expenses (see p276 – the rules are the same as those for people under the qualifying age for PC, except that expenses relating to debts are not excluded); *and*
- income tax and NI contributions; *and*
- half of any premium paid in respect of a personal pension scheme which is eligible for tax relief.[36] You must supply certain information about the scheme or annuity contract to the DWP or local authority, if requested.[37]

If you receive payments for board and lodging charges, these do not count as earnings, but as other income (less any disregards – see p326).[38]

Working out average earnings from self-employment

The weekly amount is the average of earnings:[39]

- over a period of one year (in practice, normally the last year for which accounts are available); *or*
- over a more appropriate period if you have recently taken up self-employment or there has been a change which will affect your business.

Childminders

In practice, childminders are always treated as self-employed. Your net profit is deemed to be one-third of your earnings less income tax, NI contributions and half of certain pension contributions.[40] The rest of your earnings are completely ignored.

Disregarded earnings

Some of your earnings from employment or self-employment are disregarded and do not affect your PC or HB. The amount of the disregard depends on your circumstances. The three main levels of disregard are £25, £20 or £5/£10. For HB, there is also an additional disregard depending on the hours you work, a childcare costs disregard and a permitted work disregard.

£25 disregard

Lone parents on HB have £25 of their earnings ignored.[41] This does not apply to PC.

£20 disregard

Pension credit

Twenty pounds of your earnings (including those of your partner) is disregarded if:

- you are a lone parent;[42]
- you or your partner qualify for an additional amount of PC for a carer (see p246). If both of you qualify, only £20 is disregarded in total;[43]
- you or your partner are in receipt of:[44]
  - employment and support allowance (ESA), long-term incapacity benefit (IB), severe disablement allowance (SDA); or
  - attendance allowance (AA), disability living allowance (DLA), personal independence payment (PIP), armed forces independence payment or a mobility supplement; or
  - the disabled worker or severe disability element of working tax credit (WTC);
- you or your partner are certified as severely sight-impaired or blind by a consultant ophthalmologist;[45]
- you or your partner previously had a £20 earnings disregard in your income support, income-based jobseeker's allowance or income-related ESA and that benefit ended no more than eight weeks before PC entitlement began (the disregard ends if you have a break in employment of more than eight weeks) or, immediately before reaching pension age, there was a £20 disregard in your PC because you or your partner were getting IB or SDA. You cannot get this disregard if you have more than an eight-week break in your PC claim;[46]
- you or your partner are an auxiliary coastguard, part-time firefighter, part-time lifeboat crew or in the reserve forces.[47] If earnings are less than £20 a week, what is left over can be disregarded from your, or your partner's, earnings from any other employment.

Note: if you qualify under more than one category, you still have a maximum of only £20 of your earnings disregarded.

Housing benefit

Twenty pounds of your earnings is disregarded if:

- you or your partner qualify for a carer premium. If both of you qualify, only £20 is disregarded in total;[48]
- you or your partner are in receipt of:[49]
  - ESA with a work-related activity or support component, long-term IB or SDA; or

Part 3: General rules for means-tested benefits
Chapter 15: Income: over pension credit age
3. Earnings

- AA, DLA, PIP, armed forces independence payment or a mobility supplement; *or*
  - the disabled worker or severe disability element of WTC;
- you or your partner are certified as severely sight-impaired or blind by a consultant ophthalmologist;[50]
- you or your partner have (or are treated as having) limited capability for work and the assessment phase has ended;[51]
- you or your partner are (or are treated as) incapable of work and have been for a continuous period of 364 days (196 days if you are terminally ill);[52]
- you or your partner had a £20 earnings disregard in your HB or council tax benefit (CTB) in the eight weeks before you or your partner reached the qualifying age for PC. You cannot get this disregard if you have more than an eight-week break in your employment or in your HB claim (or previously, CTB claim);[53]
- you or your partner are an auxiliary coastguard, part-time firefighter, part-time lifeboat crew or in the reserve forces. If earnings are less than £20 a week, what is left can be disregarded from your or your partner's earnings from other employment.[54]

Note: if you qualify under more than one category, you still have a maximum of only £20 of your earnings disregarded.

Permitted work disregard for housing benefit

For HB only, £20 or £120 is disregarded from earnings if you or your partner are doing 'permitted work' in the circumstances described on p280.[55]

Basic £5 or £10 disregard

If you do not qualify for a £25 or £20 disregard (or a permitted work disregard for HB), £5 of your earnings is disregarded if you are single. If you claim as a member of a couple, £10 of your total income is disregarded, whether or not you are both working.[56]

Additional disregard for housing benefit

For HB only, whichever earnings disregard applies is increased by £17.10 if:[57]
- you or your partner receive the 30-hour element as part of your (or your partner's) WTC (see p1412); *or*
- you or your partner work 30 hours or more a week on average; *or*
- you or your partner work 16 hours or more a week on average and you have a child who is part of your family for benefit purposes (see p220) or your HB includes the family premium (see p236); *or*
- you are a lone parent and work 16 hours or more a week on average; *or*
- you or your partner work 16 hours or more a week on average and one or both of you get long-term IB, ESA which includes a support or work-related activity

component, SDA, AA, DLA, PIP, armed forces independence payment, a mobility supplement or the disabled worker or severe disability element in your WTC, or you are certified as severely sight-impaired or blind by a consultant ophthalmologist or have been incapable of work for 364 days (196 days if terminally ill). For couples, the partner who is disabled is the one who must be working 16 hours or more a week on average.

The additional earnings disregard does not apply if your total earnings are less than the total of £17.10, plus any earnings disregard and childcare costs disregard (see below). In this case, £17.10 is disregarded from any WTC awarded to you or your partner, but the earnings disregard is not increased.

Note: only one additional disregard is allowed from your (or your partner's) earnings.

Childcare costs disregard for housing benefit

For HB only, up to £175 a week for one child, or up to £300 a week for two or more children, can be deducted from your (or your partner's) earnings (from employment or self-employment) for childcare costs in certain circumstances.[58] The rules are the same as those for people under the qualifying age for PC (see p281), except you can also have a childcare costs disregard if you are a couple and one of you works 16 hours or more a week and the other is aged 80 or over. There is no childcare costs disregard for PC.

4. Income other than earnings

Benefits and tax credits

Some benefits and tax credits are taken into account as income; others are disregarded, either in full or partly.

Benefits and tax credits that are taken into account

The following benefits and tax credits are taken into account:
- bereavement allowance, widow's pension and industrial death benefit;
- carer's allowance;
- a war orphan's pension, dependant's allowance or payment under the Armed Forces Compensation Scheme for someone whose parent died and who is still eligible as an adult because of disability;[59]
- contribution-based jobseeker's allowance;
- incapacity benefit and severe disablement allowance;
- contributory employment and support allowance (ESA). If ESA is paid at a reduced rate because of a sanction, the full rate still counts;[60]
- industrial injuries benefits, except constant attendance allowance and exceptionally severe disablement allowance, which are disregarded;

Part 3: General rules for means-tested benefits
Chapter 15: Income: over pension credit age
4. Income other than earnings

- maternity allowance;
- retirement pensions;
- statutory sick pay, statutory maternity pay, statutory adoption pay, statutory paternity pay and statutory shared parental pay. These are treated as earnings and may benefit from an earnings disregard (see p320);[61]
- working tax credit (WTC). However, for housing benefit (HB), if your earnings are too low to use the whole £17.10 additional full-time earnings disregard (see p322), £17.10 is disregarded from your WTC instead.[62] If earnings are too low to use the full childcare costs disregard, see p282. If a tax credit overpayment is being recovered from your WTC award, it is the amount of the WTC award less the overpayment that is taken into account for pension credit (PC) and HB;
- foreign social security benefits which are similar to the benefits listed above.[63]

Benefits and tax credits that are not taken into account

The following benefits and tax credits are ignored completely:[64]
- armed forces independence payment;
- attendance allowance (AA);[65]
- bereavement payments. These are taken into account as capital;[66]
- bereavement support payment;
- child benefit;[67]
- child tax credit;[68]
- Christmas bonus (see p863);[69]
- constant attendance allowance, exceptionally severe disablement allowance or severe disablement occupational allowance paid because of an injury at work or a war injury;[70]
- disability living allowance;[71]
- guardian's allowance;[72]
- HB;[73]
- mobility supplement under the War Pension Scheme;[74]
- personal independence payment;[75]
- social fund payments;[76]
- supplementary payments to pre-1973 war widows or widowers;[77]
- increases for child dependants. Increases for adult dependants are only ignored if the dependant is not your partner.[78]

Benefits that are partly taken into account

The following benefits have £15 ignored:
- for HB only, widowed mother's allowance and widowed parent's allowance.[79]

The following benefits have £10 ignored (or more for HB – see p325):
- for PC only, widowed mother's allowance and widowed parent's allowance;[80]
- war disablement pension;[81]

- guaranteed income payment and survivor's guaranteed income payment under the Armed Forces Compensation Scheme (if reduced to under £10 by another pension, the remainder is disregarded from the pension);[82]
- war widow's, widower's or surviving civil partner's pension;[83]
- an extra-statutory payment made instead of the above pensions;[84]
- similar payments made by another country;[85]
- a pension from any government paid to the victims of Nazi persecution.[86]

The £10 disregard allowed on the above war pensions is in addition to the total disregard of any mobility supplement or AA (ie, constant attendance allowance, exceptionally severe disablement allowance and severe disablement occupational allowance) paid as part of a war disablement pension.

Local authorities may have discretionary local schemes to increase the £10 disregard on a war disablement, war widow's, widower's or surviving civil partner's pension and on the guaranteed income payment and survivor's guaranteed income payment in your HB.[87] Most increase the disregard or ignore the full amount, so check your local scheme.

Benefit delays

If you have made a claim for benefit but have not yet been paid, the benefit should not be treated as income possessed by you. For PC, you should get your full benefit and the DWP deducts the difference from arrears of the delayed benefit when it is eventually awarded.[88]

For the treatment of payments of arrears of certain benefits and tax credits, see p393.

Maintenance payments

For PC, any maintenance payments for you or your partner made by your (or your partner's) spouse/civil partner or former spouse/civil partner count in full as income. Maintenance for a child is ignored completely.[89]

For HB, if you have a child who is part of your family for benefit purposes (see p220) or have a family premium included in your HB, £15 of any maintenance payments for you or your partner made by your (or your partner's) spouse/civil partner or former spouse/civil partner is disregarded.[90] If you receive maintenance from more than one person, only £15 of the total is disregarded. Other kinds of maintenance (eg, for a child) do not count as income and are ignored completely.[91]

If you *pay* maintenance to a former partner or a child not living with you, your payments are not disregarded for the purpose of calculating your income for PC or HB.[92] See p331 if part of a personal or occupational pension is paid to a former partner.

Part 3: General rules for means-tested benefits
Chapter 15: Income: over pension credit age
4. Income other than earnings

Income from tenants and lodgers

How income from tenants is treated depends on whether or not you live in the same property.

Lettings without board

If you own or are the tenant of your home, and you rent out a room(s) under an agreement, £20 of your weekly charge for each person is ignored. The balance is taken into account.[93]

If someone shares your home under an informal arrangement and is not paying rent under an agreement, any money s/he pays is ignored,[94] but a non-dependant deduction may be made from any HB or housing costs paid with PC.

Boarders

If you have a boarder in your own home, the first £20 a week of the amount s/he pays you is ignored and half of any balance remaining is taken into account as your income.[95] For PC, this does not apply if the boarder is a close relative (see p454) or the arrangement is not commercial.[96] Instead, the whole payment is ignored but there could be a non-dependant deduction from any housing costs paid with PC.[97] For HB, a non-dependant deduction could apply on top of this disregard if the boarder is a close relative or the arrangement is not commercial.[98]

This disregard applies for each boarder you have. The charge must normally include at least some meals.[99] If you have a business partner, even though your gross income includes just your share of the weekly charge to boarders, you still get the full disregard of £20 plus half the excess for each boarder.[100]

Tenants in other properties

Rent from a property other than your home is not taken into account as income.[101] Instead, the value of the property counts as capital and is treated as producing a 'deemed income' (see p327). If the value of the property can be disregarded (see p390), both the rent and the capital value are ignored (there is no deemed income).[102]

Income from capital

The general rule is that capital (unless it is disregarded) is assumed to provide a set rate of income – called 'deemed income' (see p327). Actual income generated from capital is ignored as income, except from the following types of capital.[103] In these cases, any actual income (but no deemed income) is taken into account.[104]
Note: for HB, it is only taken into account if the total capital listed below is worth more than £10,000.[105]

Actual income from the following capital is taken into account:
- the value of the right to receive a payment in the future of:
  - income under a life interest or liferent;

- rent, unless you only have a reversionary (ie, future) interest in the property. For the way the actual rent is treated, see p326;
- the surrender value or income under an annuity;
- property held in a trust, but not charitable trusts or, for PC, trusts set up out of payments from personal injury to you or your partner or, for HB, from the Independent Living Funds, the London Bombings Relief Charitable Fund or from specified infected blood payment schemes. Income from a discretionary trust can be ignored in some circumstances (see p329).

If deemed income is taken into account, actual income from the same capital is ignored.[106]

There are no rules that treat capital of any kind as though it were income.

Deemed income

For PC, if you have capital above £10,000, you are treated as having an assumed income of £1 a week for every £500, or part of £500, by which your capital exceeds £10,000.[107] There is no upper capital limit.

For HB, the following applies.

- If you or your partner are getting the guarantee credit of PC, all of your (and your partner's) capital is ignored.[108]
- In any other case, there is a capital limit of £16,000.[109] If you have capital above £10,000, you are treated as having an assumed income of £1 a week for every £500, or part of £500, of capital between £10,000.01 and £16,000.[110]

For PC and HB, you are not treated as having any deemed income on capital that is disregarded (see p390).

Example

Samuel, aged 72, has savings of £12,000. Deemed income of £4 a week is taken into account. Any interest from the savings is ignored as income.

Occupational and personal pensions

The following income is taken into account:[111]

- an occupational pension;
- income from a personal pension;
- income from a retirement annuity contract, including an annuity purchased for you or transferred to you on divorce;
- payments from a former employer for early retirement on the grounds of ill health or disability, unless this was under a court order or settlement of a claim;[112]
- an overseas pension;

Part 3: General rules for means-tested benefits
Chapter 15: Income: over pension credit age
4. Income other than earnings

- a Civil List Act pension;[113]
- payment under an equity release scheme.[114] This provides regular payments from a loan secured on your home. For some home income plans where you buy an annuity, interest on the loan can be disregarded (see below);
- payments from the Financial Assistance Scheme and periodic payments from the Pension Protection Fund (these help some people with underfunded occupational schemes whose employer has gone out of business).

Some charitable trusts provide discretionary income to people retired from specific occupations. This is ignored for PC and HB.[115]

Occupational and personal pension options

If you have a defined contribution occupational or personal pension (a 'money purchase' pension), for benefit purposes you are generally expected to buy an annuity or take the equivalent income that would be payable through an annuity. Income from an annuity is taken into account. Income that you draw directly from your pension pot (eg, invested in 'flexi-access drawdown') is compared to the amount you could get from an annuity and whichever amount is higher is taken into account.[116]

If you also take a lump sum, this counts as your capital.[117] **Note:** if you choose to take a lump sum and spend it in the hope of increasing benefit entitlement, you are likely to be caught by the rules on deprivation of capital (see p371).

If you leave some, or all, of the funds in your pension pot, you are treated as having notional income, usually based on the annuity those funds could yield (see p330).

If you are below PC age, the rules are different (see p294).

Specified miscellaneous income

Any income from copyright royalties and payments for patents, trademarks or under the Public Lending Right scheme are counted in full. Add the payments to your earnings (if any), if you are the first owner of the copyright or patent or author of the book, and deduct the appropriate earnings disregards on p320.[118]

The following income is ignored:

- income paid outside the UK which cannot be transferred here;[119]
- if income is paid in another currency, any bank charges for converting the payment into sterling;[120]
- income from an annuity is normally taken into account. However, an amount equal to the interest payable on the loan with which the annuity was bought is ignored if:[121]
  - you used at least 90 per cent of the loan made to you to buy the annuity; *and*
  - the annuity will end when you and your partner die; *and*
  - you or your partner are responsible for paying the interest on the loan; *and*

- you (if you took out the loan) or your partner (if s/he did) were at least 65 at the time the loan was made; *and*
- the loan is secured on a property which you or your partner own or have an interest in, and the property on which the loan is secured is your home or your partner's home.

If the interest on the loan is payable after income tax has been deducted, it is an amount equal to the net interest payment that is disregarded, otherwise it is the gross amount of the interest payment;

- any discretionary payment made to you by trustees is ignored altogether, except if the payment is for the purpose of:
  - obtaining food, ordinary clothing or footwear, or household fuel. School uniforms and sportswear are examples of clothing and footwear that are not ordinary; *or*
  - paying rent, council tax or water charges for which you or your partner (if any) are liable. 'Rent' means eligible rent for HB, less any non-dependant deductions; *or*
  - meeting housing costs which could be met by PC.

  In this case, £20 of the payment is disregarded or, if the payment is less than £20, the whole of the payment is disregarded.[122] If this disregard overlaps with certain other disregards (eg, certain war pensions), a combined maximum of £20 is allowed.[123] **Note:** this is a weekly disregard, so payments spread over different or successive benefit weeks attract a £20 disregard for each week;
- periodic payments made to you or your partner under an agreement entered into in settlement of a claim for any injury to you or your partner;[124]
- any payment ordered by a court to be made to you or your partner because of an accident, injury or disease you or your partner (or, for HB only, your child) have.[125]

Other income

Only income that is specified in the rules can affect your benefit (see p316). Any other kind of income is ignored – eg:

- local welfare payments;
- student loans and grants.[126] For HB only, see p298 if you make a parental contribution to a student's grant or loan or towards your under-25-year-old child's expenses in advanced education;
- adoption allowances, fostering allowances, child arrangements order payments and kinship care payments;[127]
- charitable and voluntary payments are not taken into account as income, so if a charity or a person gives you voluntary payments, these do not reduce your benefit. **Note:** maintenance payments can affect your benefit (see p325);
- payments for expenses if you are being consulted as a service user by certain public bodies. Other payments count as earnings but, if you choose not to take

Part 3: General rules for means-tested benefits
Chapter 15: Income: over pension credit age
5. Notional income

them or have them paid to someone else on your behalf, they do not count as your notional income.[128]

5. **Notional income**

In certain circumstances, you may be treated as having income that you do not possess.

Note: if you are working but earning less than the going rate, you are not treated as though your wages are higher than those you get, as you are for other means-tested benefits (see p301).

Deliberately getting rid of income

If you deliberately get rid of income in order to claim or increase your benefit, you are treated as though you were still in receipt of that income.[129] The basic issues involved are the same as those for deliberately getting rid of capital (see p396). **Note:** this rule can only apply if the purpose of the deprivation is to gain benefit for *yourself* (or your partner). It should not apply if, for example, you stop claiming carer's allowance (CA) solely so that another person (who is not your partner) can become entitled to a severe disability premium (see p242).[130]

If you give up income you get from a small occupational or personal pension to take a lump sum instead, you could be caught by this rule. However, if this is a 'trivial commutation lump sum', you are not treated as still having that income (although the capital counts). There are similar sounding lump sums (eg, 'trivial commutation lump-sum death benefit' which is paid to a dependant), which do not have this protection, so get advice from your pension provider.[131]

Failing to apply for pension income

Sometimes you can be treated as having pension income even though you have not applied for it.[132] There are no rules to treat you as having any other income, such as another benefit, that you could have applied for but did not.

Deferring a state pension

If you defer your state pension, category A or B pension, graduated retirement benefit or any shared additional pension paid on divorce, you are not treated as having that income for housing benefit (HB) before you claim it. However, you are treated as having that income for pension credit (PC).

The amount that counts for PC is the pension to which you would expect to be entitled were you to claim, less any overlapping benefit you get – eg, CA. If you have a choice of taking a lump sum instead of extra pension income, the amount is based on your taking the lump-sum option (there is no lump-sum choice when claiming a deferred post-April 2016 state pension). To take account of the time it can take to process claims, you are only treated as having this income from the date you could expect to get it were you to make a claim.

For both PC and HB, you are treated as having any amount of category C or D pension and age addition to which you might expect to be entitled if you were to claim. For PC, any overlapping benefit you get is deducted.

Leaving funds in an occupational or personal pension

You are treated as having any income from an occupational pension you have elected to defer beyond the scheme's retirement age,[133] as though you had claimed it. For PC, the time it might take to process it is taken into account and any overlapping benefit is deducted. If you have a defined contribution occupational or personal pension, for benefit purposes you are generally expected to buy an annuity or take the equivalent income that would be payable through an annuity.[134]

If you leave funds in your pension pot, you are treated as having notional income based on the annuity those funds could yield. If you take one or more lump sums from your pension pot, these count as capital and notional income is worked out on what is left in your pension pot. See p327 for how pension payments are treated.

Income paid to someone else on your behalf

Any money that counts as income and is paid to someone on your behalf is normally treated as being yours and is then either taken into account or ignored as income under the rules described in this chapter. The exception is for payments of income made under an occupational or personal pension scheme (or, for HB only, from the Pension Protection Fund) if you or your partner are bankrupt (or the subject of a sequestration order). In this case, if the payment is made to the trustee or other person acting on your creditors' behalf and you (and your partner) have no income other than the payment made, it is not treated as being yours.[135] If you have had a judicial separation rather than a divorce so that usual pension splitting arrangements are not available, and a court has ordered you to pay part of your pension to your former partner, you could argue this does not count as yours.[136]

6. Working out weekly income

To assess your weekly income, you should do the following.
- Work out whether income is taken into account, or fully or partly disregarded (see p315).
- If income varies, work out an average income (see p332).
- Convert income into a weekly amount if necessary (see p332).
- Add any deemed weekly income from capital (see p327).

Part 3: General rules for means-tested benefits
Chapter 15: Income: over pension credit age
6. Working out weekly income

Averaging income

If your earnings vary because you do not work the same hours every week, your weekly income may be averaged over the cycle, if there is an identifiable one.[137] If you do not work a recognisable cycle or your income fluctuates, your income is worked out on the basis of:[138]

- the last two payments before your claim was made or treated as made (or, where applicable, before your claim was superseded) if those payments are at least one month apart; *or*
- the last four payments before your claim was made or treated as made (or, where applicable, before your claim was superseded) if the last two payments are less than a month apart; *or*
- calculating (or estimating for housing benefit – HB) any other payments that would give a more accurate figure for your average weekly income.

In all cases, if the cycle involves periods when you do no work, these are included in the cycle, but not other absences – eg, holidays or sickness.

The payment is treated as if made for a period of a year if you are entitled to:[139]

- royalties or other sums for the use of any copyright, patent or trademark; *or*
- payments for any book registered under the Public Lending Right scheme 1982; *or*
- payments made on an occasional basis.

Converting income into a weekly amount

Pension credit (PC) and HB are calculated on a weekly basis, so your earnings and other income have to be converted into a weekly amount if necessary. The following rules apply to income from employment and other income.[140] For income from self-employment, see p320.

- If the payment is for less than a week, it is treated as the weekly amount.
- If the payment is for a month, multiply by 12 and divide by 52.
- Multiply a payment for three months by four and divide by 52.
- Divide a payment for a year by 52.
- Multiply payments for any other periods by seven and divide by the number of days in the period.

Date from when a payment counts

The general rule for PC is that benefits are treated as paid on the last day of the PC 'benefit week' in which the benefit is payable, but on the first day if the benefit is paid in advance.[141] Some benefits are treated slightly differently. Contribution-based jobseeker's allowance, contributory employment and support allowance and maternity allowance are treated as having been paid on the day that benefit is payable. For HB, benefits are taken into account over the period for which they are payable.[142]

For other types of income, for PC the general rule is that income counts from the date it is paid for the length of time it has been paid – eg, a month's occupational pension paid on 10 November counts from 10 November to 9 December.[143]

For HB, weekly earnings are taken into account from the start of a new claim or from the first day of the 'benefit week' after you start work. If average weekly earnings change, the new amount counts from the date of change, even if you are not paid until later.[144]

Benefit week

For PC, a **'benefit week'** is the seven days ending on the day PC is payable if paid in arrears, or starting on that day if paid in advance.[145]

For HB, a 'benefit week' is the seven days starting on a Monday.[146]

Notes

1. Whose income counts
1 **PC** s5 SPCA 2002
  HB s136(1) SSCBA 1992
2 Reg 23(3) HB(SPC) Regs

2. What counts as income
3 s15 SPCA 2002; reg 15 SPC Regs
4 Regs 25 and 26 HB(SPC) Regs
5 Reg 27(4) HB(SPC) Regs
6 Reg 24 HB(SPC) Regs
7 Reg 27(4) HB(SPC) Regs
8 Reg 29 HB(SPC) Regs
9 **PC** Reg 17(10) SPC Regs
  HB Reg 33(12) HB(SPC) Regs
10 Reg 34 HB(SPC) Regs

3. Earnings
11 **PC** Reg 17A(2) SPC Regs
  HB Reg 35(1) HB(SPC) Regs
12 **PC** Reg 17A(h) and (k) SPC Regs
  HB Reg 35(1)(h) and (k) HB(SPC) Regs
13 **PC** Reg 17A(h)-(k) SPC Regs
  HB Reg 35(1)(h)-(k) HB(SPC) Regs
14 **PC** Reg 17A(2)(e) SPC Regs
  HB Reg 35(1)(e) HB(SPC) Regs
15 R(IS) 9/95

16 *Minter v Kingston Upon Hull CC and Potter v SSWP* [2011] EWCA Civ 1155
17 **PC** Reg 17A(2)(g) SPC Regs
  HB Reg 35(1)(g) HB(SPC) Regs
18 **PC** Reg 17A(4) SPC Regs
  HB Reg 35(3) HB(SPC) Regs
19 **PC** Sch 6 para 6 SPC Regs
  HB Sch 4 para 8 HB(SPC) Regs
20 **PC** Reg 17A(3)(a) SPC Regs
  HB Reg 35(2)(a) HB(SPC) Regs
21 Vol 14 Ch 86, para 86058 DMG
22 Vol 14 Ch 86, para 86054 DMG
23 **PC** Reg 17A(3)(b) SPC Regs
  HB Reg 35(2)(b) HB(SPC) Regs
24 CIS/77/1993; CIS/89/1989
25 **PC** Sch 6 para 7 SPC Regs
  HB Sch 4 para 10 HB(SPC) Regs
26 **PC** Reg 17A(3)(c) SPC Regs
  HB Reg 35(2)(c) HB(SPC) Regs
27 **PC** s15(1)(c) SPCA 2002
  HB Reg 29(1)(c) HB(SPC) Regs
28 **PC** Reg 17A(3)(e) SPC Regs
  HB Reg 35(2)(e) HB(SPC) Regs
29 *Parsons v Hogg* [1985] 2 All ER 897 (CA), appendix to R(FIS) 4/85
30 **PC** Regs 17(10) and 17A(4A) SPC Regs
  HB Reg 36(2) and (4) HB(SPC) Regs

Part 3: General rules for means-tested benefits
Chapter 15: Income: over pension credit age
Notes

• •

31 Reg 36(5) HB(SPC) Regs
32 Vol 14 Ch 86, para 86162 DMG
33 **PC** Sch 6 para 6 SPC Regs
    HB Sch 4 para 8 HB(SPC) Regs
34 Reg 17ZA SPC Regs
35 **PC** Reg 17B(5) SPC Regs; reg 13(1) and
    (4) SSB(CE) Regs
    HB Reg 39(1)-(3) HB(SPC) Regs
36 **PC** Reg 17B(1) SPC Regs; regs 2 and
    13(4) SSB(CE) Regs
    HB Regs 2(1) and 39(2) and (11)
    HB(SPC) Regs
37 Reg 32(3) SS(C&P) Regs
    HB Reg 67(5) HB(SPC) Regs
38 **PC** Reg 17B(4)(b) SPC Regs; reg 12(2)
    SSB(CE) Regs
    HB Reg 38(2)(a) HB(SPC) Regs
39 **PC** Reg 17B SPC Regs; reg 11(1)
    SSB(CE) Regs
    HB Reg 37(1) HB(SPC) Regs
40 **PC** Reg 17B(5)(b) SPC Regs; reg 13(10)
    SSB(CE) Regs
    HB Reg 39(8) HB(SPC) Regs
41 Sch 4 para 2 HB(SPC) Regs
42 Sch 6 para 1 SPC Regs
43 Sch 6 paras 3 and 4A SPC Regs
44 Sch 6 para 4(1)(a) SPC Regs
45 Sch 6 para 4(1)(b) SPC Regs
46 Sch 6 para 4(2)-(4) SPC Regs
47 Sch 6 para 2 SPC Regs
48 Sch 4 para 4 HB(SPC) Regs
49 Sch 4 para 5(1)(a) HB(SPC) Regs
50 Sch 4 para 5(1)(b) HB(SPC) Regs
51 Sch 4 para 5(1)(d) HB(SPC) Regs
52 Sch 4 para 5(1)(c) HB(SPC) Regs
53 Sch 4 para 5(2) HB(SPC) Regs
54 Sch 4 para 3 HB(SPC) Regs
55 Sch 4 para 5A HB(SPC) Regs
56 **PC** Sch 6 para 5 SPC Regs
    HB Sch 4 para 7 HB(SPC) Regs
57 Sch 4 para 9 HB(SPC) Regs
58 Reg 30(1)(c) HB(SPC) Regs

4. Income other than earnings
59 **PC** Reg 15(5)(a) and (ab) SPC Regs
    HB Reg 29(1)(h) and (l) HB(SPC) Regs
60 **PC** Reg 15(3) SPC Regs
    HB Reg 29(3) HB(SPC) Regs
61 **PC** Reg 17A(2)(h)-(j) SPC Regs
    HB Reg 35(1)(h)-(j) HB(SPC) Regs
62 **PC** s15(1)(b) SPCA 2002
    HB Sch 5 para 21 HB(SPC) Regs
63 **PC** Reg 15(2) SPC Regs
    HB Reg 29(1)(k) HB(SPC) Regs
64 **PC** Reg 15(1) SPC Regs
    HB Reg 29(1)(j) HB(SPC) Regs
65 **PC** Reg 15(1)(b) SPC Regs
    HB Reg 29(1)(j)(ii) HB(SPC) Regs

66 **PC** Reg 15(1)(n) SPC Regs
    HB Reg 29(1)(j)(xiii) HB(SPC) Regs
67 Reg 15(1)(j) SPC Regs
68 s15 SPCA 2002
69 **PC** Reg 15(1)(k) SPC Regs
    HB Reg 29(1)(j)(x) HB(SPC) Regs
70 **PC** Reg 15(1)(c) and (e) and Sch 4 para
    2 SPC Regs
    HB Reg 29(1)(j)(iii) and (v) and Sch 5
    para 2 HB(SPC) Regs
71 **PC** Reg 15(1)(a) SPC Regs
    HB Reg 29(1)(j)(i) HB(SPC) Regs
72 **PC** Reg 15(1)(g) SPC Regs
    HB Reg 29(1)(j)(vii) HB(SPC) Regs
73 **PC** Reg 15(1)(l) and (m) SPC Regs
    HB Reg 29(1)(j)(xi) and (xii) HB(SPC)
    Regs
74 **PC** Sch 4 para 3 SPC Regs
    HB Sch 5 para 3 HB(SPC) Regs
75 **PC** Reg 15(1)(aa) SPC Regs
    HB Reg 29(ia) HB(SPC) Regs
76 **PC** Reg 15(1)(i) SPC Regs
    HB Reg 29(1)(j)(ix) HB(SPC) Regs
77 **PC** Sch 4 paras 4-6 SPC Regs
    HB Sch 5 paras 4-6 HB(SPC) Regs
78 **PC** Reg 15(1)(h) SPC Regs
    HB Reg 29(1)(j)(viii) HB(SPC) Regs
79 Sch 5 paras 7 and 8 HB(SPC) Regs
80 Sch 4 paras 7 and 7A SPC Regs
81 **PC** Sch 4 para 1(a) SPC Regs
    HB Sch 5 para 1(a) HB(SPC) Regs; Sch
    Part 1 HB&CTB(WPD) Regs
82 **PC** Sch 4 para 1(cc) SPC Regs
    HB Sch 5 para 1(d) HB(SPC) Regs
83 **PC** Sch 4 para 1(b), (ba) and (c) SPC
    Regs
    HB Sch 5 para 1(b) and (c) HB(SPC)
    Regs; Sch Part 1 HB&CTB(WPD) Regs
84 **PC** Sch 4 para 1(d) SPC Regs
    HB Sch 5 para 1(e) HB(SPC) Regs
85 **PC** Sch 4 para 1(e) SPC Regs
    HB Sch 5 para 1(f) HB(SPC) Regs
86 **PC** Sch 4 para 1(f) SPC Regs
    HB Sch 5 para 1(g) HB(SPC) Regs
    Both *MN v (1) Bury Council (2) SSWP
    (HB)* [2014] UKUT 187 (AAC)
87 ss134(8) and 139(6) SSAA 1992; *R v
    South Hams District Council ex parte Ash,
    The Times,* 27 May 1999
88 s74(2) SSAA 1992
89 Reg 15(5)(d) SPC Regs
90 Sch 5 para 20 HB(SPC) Regs
91 Reg 29(1)(o) HB(SPC) Regs
92 CIS/683/1993
93 **PC** Sch 4 para 9 SPC Regs
    HB Sch 5 para 10 HB(SPC) Regs

94 **PC** Income from capital under s15(1)(i) SPCA 2002 would count, but is ignored under regs 15(6) and 17(8), Sch 5 para 1A and Sch 4 para 18 SPC Regs
   HB Reg 29(1)(i) HB(SPC) Regs
95 **PC** Sch 4 para 8 SPC Regs
   HB Sch 5 para 9 HB(SPC) Regs
96 Reg 1(2), definition of 'board and lodging accommodation', SPC Regs
97 Sch 4 para 18 SPC Regs
98 Reg 2(1), definition of 'board and lodging accommodation', HB(SPC) Regs
99 **PC** Reg 1(2) SPC Regs
   HB Reg 2(1) HB(SPC) Regs
   Both Definition of 'board and lodging accommodation'
100 CIS/521/2002
101 **PC** s15(1)(i) SPCA 2002; Sch 4 para 18 SPC Regs
   HB Reg 29(1)(i) and Sch 5 para 22 HB(SPC) Regs
102 **PC** Reg 17(8) SPC Regs
   HB Regs 29(1)(i) and 44(2) HB(SPC) Regs
103 **PC** Sch 4 para 18 SPC Regs
   HB Sch 5 para 22 HB(SPC) Regs
104 **PC** s15(1)(i) SPCA 2002; reg 15(6) and Sch 4 para 18 SPC Regs
   HB Reg 29(1)(i) HB(SPC) Regs
105 Sch 5 para 24 HB(SPC) Regs
106 **PC** Sch 4 para 18 SPC Regs
   HB Sch 5 para 22 HB(SPC) Regs
107 s15(2) SPCA 2002; reg 15(6) SPC Regs
108 Regs 25 and 26 HB(SPC) Regs
109 Reg 43 HB(SPC) Regs
110 Reg 29(2) HB(SPC) Regs
111 **PC** ss15(1)(c) and 16(1) SPCA 2002; reg 16 SPC Regs
   HB Reg 29(1)(c) HB(SPC) Regs
112 **PC** Reg 16 SPC Regs
   HB Reg 29(1)(s) HB(SPC) Regs
113 **PC** Reg 16 SPC Regs
   HB Reg 29(1)(t) HB(SPC) Regs
114 **PC** Reg 16 SPC Regs
   HB Reg 29(1)(w) HB(SPC) Regs
115 Vol 14 Ch 85, para 85136 DMG
116 **PC** Reg 18(2)-(10) SPC Regs
   HB Reg 41(4)-(8) HB(SPC) Regs; HB Circular A7/2015
117 Memo DMG 12/15
118 **PC** Reg 17(9) SPC Regs
   HB Reg 33(8) HB(SPC) Regs
119 **PC** Sch 4 para 15 SPC Regs
   HB Sch 5 para 16 HB(SPC) Regs
120 **PC** Sch 4 para 16 SPC Regs
   HB Sch 5 para 17 HB(SPC) Regs

121 **PC** Sch 4 para 10 SPC Regs
   HB Sch 5 para 11 HB(SPC) Regs
122 **PC** Sch 4 para 11 SPC Regs
   HB Sch 5 para 12 HB(SPC) Regs
123 **PC** Sch 4 para 11(3)(b) SPC Regs
   HB Sch 5 para 12(3) HB(SPC) Regs
124 **PC** Sch 4 para 14 SPC Regs
   HB Sch 5 para 15 HB(SPC) Regs
125 **PC** Sch 4 para 13 SPC Regs
   HB Sch 5 para 14 HB(SPC) Regs
126 The rules do not include grants and loans in the definition of 'income'.
127 **PC** s15 SPCA 2002; regs 15 and 17B(4) SPC Regs
   HB Regs 29 and 38(2) HB(SPC) Regs
128 **PC** Regs 17A(3)(f), 18(7A) and 24(2) SPC Regs
   HB Regs 35(2)(f), 41(8C) and 42(3) HB(SPC) Regs

5. Notional income
129 **PC** Reg 18(6) to (8B) SPC Regs
   HB Reg 41(8) to (8BD) HB(SPC) Regs
130 Vol 5 Ch 28, paras 28608-16 DMG; see also CIS/15052/1996
131 **PC** Reg 18(9) SPC Regs
   HB Reg 41(11) HB(SPC) Regs
132 **PC** Reg 18(1)-(5) SPC Regs
   HB Reg 41(1)-(7) HB(SPC) Regs
133 Vol 14 Ch 85, para 85453 DMG; *BRG v SSWP (SPC)* [2014] UKUT 246 (AAC)
134 **PC** Reg 18(2)-(16) SPC Regs; Memo DMG 12/15
   HB Reg 41(4)-(8) HB(SPC) Regs; HB Circular A7/2015
135 **PC** Reg 24 SPC Regs
   HB Reg 42 HB(SPC) Regs
136 CH/1672/2007

6. Working out weekly income
137 **PC** Reg 17(2)(b)(i) SPC Regs
   HB Reg 33(2)(b)(i) HB(SPC) Regs
138 **PC** Reg 17(2)(b)(ii) SPC Regs
   HB Reg 33(2)(b)(ii) HB(SPC) Regs
139 **PC** Reg 17(4) SPC Regs
   HB Reg 33(4) HB(SPC) Regs
140 **PC** Reg 17(1) SPC Regs
   HB Reg 33(1) HB(SPC) Regs
141 Reg 13B SPC Regs
142 Reg 33(6) HB(SPC) Regs
143 R(PC) 3/08; *PS v SSWP (SPC)* [2016] UKUT 21 (AAC)
144 Reg 33(2A) and (3A) HB(SPC) Regs
145 Reg 1(2) SPC Regs
146 Reg 2 HB(SPC) Regs

Chapter 16

Income: universal credit

3

This chapter covers:
1. Whose income counts (below)
2. What counts as income (p337)
3. Earnings (p338)
4. Income other than earnings (p344)
5. Notional income (p351)
6. Working out monthly income (p351)

Key facts
- Your entitlement to universal credit (UC) and how much you get depends on your income.
- Your own income counts and, if you are a member of a couple, your partner's income also counts.
- Your earnings from employment and self-employment are taken into account on a monthly basis over each 'assessment period'.
- If earnings from self-employment are low, your UC award may be worked out on more earnings than you get, based on the number of hours the DWP expects you to work.
- Certain other kinds of income are also taken into account.

1. **Whose income counts**

Only your own income counts in working out your universal credit (UC) award if you are single.[1]

Couples usually make a joint claim, and your UC award is worked out using both your income and your partner's income.[2]

There are some situations in which one member of a couple qualifies for UC but the other does not – eg, in certain circumstances if your partner is under age 18, does not meet residence tests, is out of the country or is in prison (see p161). In these cases, you make a single claim. You do not get any amount for your partner in the UC award, but your partner's income (and capital) is still added to yours when working out the award.[3]

Children's income is ignored.

2. **What income counts**

The amount of universal credit (UC) you are entitled to depends on how much income you have.

'Income' for UC means:[4]

- earnings from employment (see p338) and self-employment (see p339);[5] *and*
- certain income other than earnings:[6]
  - certain benefits (see p344);
  - maintenance for you or your partner, but not for a child (see p345);
  - student loan and grants. See p888 for how much of the loan counts and which grants are ignored;
  - certain income from employment and training schemes (see p346);
  - occupational and personal pensions (see p346);
  - certain insurance payments (see p346);
  - income from an annuity (see p347);
  - income from a trust (see p347 for which types are ignored);
  - 'assumed' income from savings and other capital (see p348);
  - sports awards from UK Sport (see p349);
  - miscellaneous income (see p349);
  - capital that is treated as income (see p337).

In some situations, you may be treated as having income that you do not actually have. This is called 'notional income' (see p351). If a type of income is not specified in the rules as being included for UC, it is ignored and does not affect your award. See p349 for some examples of income that is ignored.

Income is taken into account month by month for each assessment period (see p164). You can keep a certain amount of earnings from employment and self-employment, known as your 'work allowance', before your award is affected if you are responsible for a child or have limited capability for work. As your earnings increase, the amount of UC you get decreases: 63 per cent of the amount above the work allowance is deducted from the maximum amount of UC or 63 per cent of all your earnings if you have no work allowance (see p167). The whole of income other than earnings, if it is taken into account, is deducted from the maximum amount of UC. See p168 for how your UC award is worked out.

Income or capital?

Any amounts that are paid regularly and that refer to a specific period are treated as income and not as capital.[7] This is so even if payments might otherwise be regarded as capital or as being part capital – eg, payments under an annuity are treated as income.

If you have a lump sum that is payable by instalments, each instalment is treated as income while your capital remains above the £16,000 upper limit for

Part 3: General rules for means-tested benefits
Chapter 16: Income: universal credit
3. Earnings

getting UC. Once what is left of the lump sum, added to any other capital you have, is below this limit, each instalment is treated as capital.[8]

3. Earnings

How earnings are treated depends on whether you are employed (see below) or self-employed (see p339).

Employed earnings

To work out the amount of earnings from employment to take into account, do the following.
- Check whether the payment counts as earnings (see below).
- Work out monthly earnings for the assessment period (see p351).
- Calculate net earnings for the assessment period (see p339).

The amount worked out as above is your monthly earnings from employment used in the universal credit (UC) assessment. If you also have self-employed earnings, these are also worked out (see p339) and added to your monthly employed earnings to give your total earned income. See p167 for how your earnings affect your UC award.

What counts as earnings

'**Earnings**' means 'remuneration or profits derived from... employment'. This includes:[9]
- wages and overtime pay;
- tips, bonuses, and commission;
- fees;
- holiday pay;
- statutory sick pay or other sick pay from your employer;
- statutory maternity pay, statutory adoption pay, statutory paternity pay, statutory shared parental pay or other pay from your employer while you are on maternity, paternity, parental or adoption leave;
- any refund of income tax or national insurance (NI) contributions for a tax year when you were in paid work. This includes tax from unearned income but not from self-employment (see p340).

The DWP usually gets information on your earnings from the records your employer sends to HM Revenue and Customs (HMRC) each time you are paid (see p351). So what counts for earnings for UC is normally what is recorded on PAYE (pay as you earn) records and is defined in terms of what counts as taxable income. However, there are differences, and not all kinds of taxable income count for UC purposes.

What does not count as earnings

Types of income not taken into account as earnings for UC include the following (some of which are taxable):[10]

- expenses incurred 'wholly, exclusively and necessarily' in the course of your employment;[11]
- certain taxable and tax-exempt expenses and allowances – eg, mileage allowance or homeworkers' additional expenses (these are usually listed on HMRC Form P11D which your employer gives you);[12]
- expenses if you are a service user being consulted about provision of services by certain public bodies;[13]
- benefits in kind – eg, a salary sacrifice scheme, non-cash vouchers (eg, for childcare), living accommodation connected with work, cars and car fuel benefits, parking or meals;[14]
- allowances for special types of employment – eg, certain armed forces allowances, free coal to miners or allowances in lieu of coal, offshore oil and gas workers' travel, subsistence and accommodation allowances.[15]

Payments when you stop work

Your final earnings when you stop work are taken into account in the assessment period in which they are paid.[16] This includes arrears of pay, pay in lieu of notice and accrued holiday pay.[17] The following lump-sum payments are taken into account as capital:[18]

- statutory and contractual redundancy pay;
- employment tribunal awards for unfair dismissal;
- pay in lieu of notice for damages for breach of contract.

Working out net earnings

From your monthly earnings for the assessment period, deduct the following payments you make in that period:[19]

- income tax;
- class 1 NI contributions;
- any contribution you make towards a personal or occupational pension scheme. If you pay contributions through your employer, your payslips should show your wages after the contributions have been deducted, so there is no further deduction to make.

Also deduct any charity payments under a payroll giving scheme.

Self-employed earnings

To work out the amount of your self-employed earnings to take into account in the UC assessment, do the following.[20]

- Work out your actual receipts for the assessment period (see p340).

Part 3: General rules for means-tested benefits
Chapter 16: Income: universal credit
3. Earnings

- Deduct permitted expenses from your receipts (see below). This gives your gross profit.
- From the gross profit (or your share of the gross profit if you are in a business partnership), deduct any payment made in the assessment period for:
  - income tax;
  - class 2 and 4 NI contributions;
  - contributions made by you to a personal or occupational pension (but not if these have already been deducted from employed earnings).

Check whether the amount worked out as above (adding earnings from employment if you have any) is above the set minimum level of earnings (see p341).

Receipts from self-employment

The starting point to work out how much self-employed earnings are taken into account is the actual amount of receipts into the business in the assessment period – eg, sales, takings, payment for work.[21] Include:[22]

- any refund of income tax, VAT or NI contributions for the self-employment;
- receipts in kind – ie, the value of the goods or service you provided for which you accepted payment in kind;[23]
- sale of business assets (if previously deducted from earnings for UC as an expense). If you stop using an asset for the business but do not sell it, the market value counts as a receipt.

To work out gross profit, deduct any permitted expenses from these receipts (see below).

Permitted expenses

Expenses must be reasonable and 'wholly and exclusively' incurred for purposes of your business.[24] Reasonable expenses may include:[25]

- regular costs – eg, rent, wages, utilities and insurance;
- stock purchase;
- stationery and advertising;
- repairs of business assets;
- transport (but see below for flat-rate deductions);
- equipment purchase and hire;
- up to £41 repayment of interest on a loan – eg, for an overdraft or credit card;
- VAT.

These are just examples. The deduction allowed is usually the actual amount of permitted expenses paid in the assessment period. However, there are flat-rate deductions for the use of a vehicle that you can choose to include instead of the actual expense of buying and using the vehicle:[26]

- for a motorcycle, 24 pence a mile;
- for a car, van or other vehicle, 45 pence a mile for the first 833 miles, then 25 pence a mile after that (for a car, you must use this rate rather than the actual expense).

If an expense has been incurred partly for business and partly for private purposes, the expense can be apportioned and the part that is identifiably for business deducted.[27] There are set deductions for the following.[28]

- If you use your own home for 'income-generating activities' for the business, instead of deducting actual expenses, there is a flat-rate deduction that depends on the number of hours completed in the assessment period. Activities include providing services to customers, business administration, sales and marketing, but do not include being on call.[29] The deduction is:
  - £10 for work of at least 25 hours, but no more than 50 hours in the month;
  - £18 for work of more than 50 hours, but no more than 100 hours;
  - £26 for more than 100 hours.
- If you live in premises that you use mainly for your business, deduct an amount from the expenses relating to the premises, depending on the number of people living there:
  - £350 if you live alone;
  - £500 if you live with one other person;
  - £650 if you live with two or more other people.

Example

Margo runs a guest house. She and her partner, Jerry, live in the guest house. Margo works out her expenses as £1,500 for the monthly assessment period for the whole house. She finds it difficult to say which expenses are for the business. Instead of apportioning expenses for business and personal use, she deducts £500 from the £1,500 for the whole house. The expenses allowed are £1,000.

Minimum level of earnings

If your main work is self-employment but your earnings are low, your UC may be worked out on higher earnings than you have. This is called the **'minimum income floor'** and is generally at the level of the national minimum wage for the number of hours the DWP expects you to work, usually 35 hours a week. This applies if:[30]

- you are in 'gainful self-employment' (see p343); *and*
- you are not in a 'start-up' period (see p344); *and*
- you must meet all the work-related requirements (see p1080). This is set out in your claimant commitment that the DWP gives you when you claim UC. If you are not subject to any work-related requirements, or just subject to work-

Part 3: General rules for means-tested benefits
Chapter 16: Income: universal credit
3. Earnings

focused interviews or work preparation, your actual earnings from self-employment are taken into account, however low.

If you are single and the minimum income floor applies to you, your earnings are treated as being at the individual earnings threshold in any assessed income period in which earned income from self-employment, together with any earnings from employment, is below this level.[31] This is the same threshold explained on p1084 used to decide work-related requirements, with a notional amount for tax and NI contributions deducted.

> *Example*
> Jake has a window cleaning business. He is single. For the current assessment period he declares earnings of £300. The DWP works out Jake's minimum income floor to be £1,048.18 a month (35 hours a week x £7.50 x 52 ÷ 12, less £89.32 for notional tax and NI contributions). Jake's UC award for the assessment period is worked out on earnings of £1,048.18.

If you are in a couple and the minimum income floor applies to you, normally your combined earnings for the UC assessment are your partner's earnings added to the minimum income floor for you. However, you cannot be treated as having combined earnings of more than a certain amount. This amount is the same as the joint earnings threshold for couples used to decide if there are any work-related requirements to fulfil as explained on p1084, but with a notional amount for tax and NI contributions deducted.[32]

- If your actual combined earnings are above the joint earnings threshold, your actual earnings count in the UC assessment, with no minimum income floor.
- If your actual combined earnings (ie, ignoring the minimum income floor) are below the joint earnings threshold in any assessed income period, your earnings are treated as being the individual earnings threshold (see p1084), less:
  - a notional amount for tax and NI contributions; *and*
  - an amount to ensure that, when added to your partner's earnings, you are not treated as having more than the joint earnings threshold.

> *Example*
> Maja and Jan are a couple. Jan is a self-employed builder and Maja works part time in a shop. They have a two-year-old child and Maja is the 'responsible carer'. Jan declares earnings of £500 and Maja £600. The DWP works out Jan's minimum income floor to be £1,048.18 a month (35 hours a week x £7.50 x 52 ÷ 12, less £89.32 for tax and NI contributions).
> Jan and Maja's actual combined earnings are £1,100 (£500 + £600).

This is below their joint earnings threshold of £1,568.18 (£1,048.18 for Jan plus £520.00 for Maja (16 hours a week x £7.50 x 52 ÷ 12 with no tax or NI contribution deduction at this earnings level)).

Adding Jan's minimum income floor to Maja's actual earnings gives £1,648.18 (£1,048.18 + £600). This is £80 above their joint earnings threshold of £1,568.18, so Jan is treated as having earnings of £968.18 (£1,048.18 – £80).

3

Gainful self-employment

When you claim UC or when you tell the DWP that you are self-employed, you are asked to attend a 'gateway' interview if you are someone who must meet all work-related requirements. You are asked to bring evidence that you are in gainful self-employment. This means that:[33]

- the self-employment is your main employment – ie, it is your only employment or, if you also work for an employer, you normally spend more hours or have more earnings from your self-employment; *and*
- your earnings count as self-employed earnings – ie, they are not employed earnings and are from carrying out a 'trade, profession or vocation'.[34] If it is not clear whether you are employed or self-employed, the DWP may look at a number of factors including whether you pay your own tax, whether your work is supervised and whether you can decide your own hours;[35] *and*
- your self-employment is 'organised, developed, regular and carried on in expectation of profit' – eg, whether you work for financial gain, how many hours you do, whether you have a business plan or have taken steps to get work, what work is arranged, whether you are registered as self-employed with HMRC, and whether you advertise your business.[36]

The DWP may decide that you are in gainful self-employment even though you are off sick and not able to do any work or you have no income at all from your business at present. If you disagree with a decision to apply a minimum income floor, you can ask for a mandatory reconsideration and then appeal. You may argue, for example, that your self-employment is no longer organised or regular and you no longer have an expectation of profit. Bear in mind that business assets can only be disregarded for a limited time (see p365). If you are off sick and your weekly earnings are below 16 times the hourly rate of the minimum wage (see Appendix 10), send in medical certificates so that the DWP can assess whether you have limited capability for work (see p1004 for how your earnings affect this assessment). If so, only your actual earnings should be taken into account – because you should no longer be subject to all work-related requirements (see p341).

If your business is new, but the DWP decides that it counts as gainful self-employment, you have a start-up period before the minimum income floor applies (see p344).

Part 3: General rules for means-tested benefits
Chapter 16: Income: universal credit
4. Income other than earnings

If you are not in gainful self-employment, you must still report your earnings and these are taken into account in your UC award, but no minimum income floor is applied.

Start-up period

If you are self-employed, your UC is worked out on your actual earnings, no matter how low, during a 'start-up period'. The minimum income floor does not apply.

This start-up period of 12 months starts from the beginning of the assessment period in which the DWP decides you are in gainful self-employment, provided you began your self-employment (as your main employment) at some point in the 12 months before that.[37] You must also be taking active steps to increase your earnings to the level of your individual earnings threshold – ie, the level that means you no longer have to meet work-related requirements (see p1084). The DWP can end the start-up period if it decides you are no longer taking active steps to increase your earnings or are no longer in gainful self-employment.

Once you have had one start-up period, you cannot have another one for the same self-employment. However, if you have stopped that work and started new self-employed work, you can have a new start-up period, but only if more than five years have passed since the start of the earlier period.

4. **Income other than earnings**

Only certain specified types of income, other than earnings, are taken into account for universal credit (UC). These are listed on p337 and explained in more detail below. This kind of income reduces your UC pound for pound. Any other kind of income that is not earnings is ignored.

Benefits

Some benefits are taken into account as income, while others are disregarded.

Benefits that are taken into account

The following benefits count in full:[38]

- bereavement allowance;
- carer's allowance;
- employment and support allowance (ESA);
- incapacity benefit;
- industrial injuries benefit, except constant attendance allowance and exceptionally severe disablement allowance which are disregarded;
- jobseeker's allowance (JSA);
- maternity allowance;

- retirement pensions;
- severe disablement allowance;
- statutory sick pay, statutory maternity pay, statutory adoption pay, statutory paternity pay and statutory shared parental pay. These are treated as earnings and so may benefit from the work allowance;
- widow's pension, widowed mother's allowance and widowed parent's allowance;
- foreign social security benefits that are similar to the benefits listed above;
- an overpayment of income support, income-based JSA (not joint-claim JSA), income-related ESA or housing benefit if you are not entitled to that benefit and the overpayment falls within a UC assessment period.[39]

Benefits that are not taken into account

All other benefits are ignored – eg:
- armed forces independence payment;
- attendance allowance;
- bereavement payment (but it counts as capital);
- bereavement support payment;
- child benefit;
- disability living allowance;
- guaranteed income payment and surviving guaranteed income payment under the Armed Forces Compensation Scheme;
- guardian's allowance;
- industrial injuries constant attendance allowance and exceptionally severe disablement allowance;
- personal independence payment;
- war disablement pension;
- war widows', widowers' or surviving civil partners' pensions.

Maintenance payments

Maintenance for a child is ignored completely.

Any maintenance for you or your partner made by your or your partner's spouse/civil partner or former spouse/civil partner under a court order or under a maintenance agreement counts in full as income.

If a former partner makes payments directly to a third party (eg, your mortgage lender), this should not count as your income.[40] However, if there is income available to you which you choose not to access, you could be caught by the 'notional income' rules (see p351).

If you *pay* maintenance to a former partner or a child not living with you, your payments are not disregarded when working out your income for UC.

Part 3: General rules for means-tested benefits
Chapter 16: Income: universal credit
4. Income other than earnings

Student loans and grants

For the special rules on the treatment of student loans, grants and other payments made to students, see Chapter 40.

Employment and training schemes

Payments from employment or training programmes under section 2 of the Employment and Training Act 1973 or section 2 of the Enterprise and New Towns (Scotland) Act 1990 are treated as follows.[41]

The following payments are taken into account:
- those made as a substitute for UC – eg, a training allowance;
- those intended for certain living costs. Payments for food, ordinary clothing or footwear, fuel, rent or other housing costs, including council tax, are all taken into account.

All other payments are disregarded – eg:
- travel expenses;
- training premium;
- childcare expenses;
- special needs payments.

Occupational and personal pensions

The following income is taken into account:[42]
- an occupational pension;
- income from a personal pension;
- income from a retirement annuity contract (including an annuity purchased for you or transferred to you on divorce);
- payments from a former employer for early retirement on the grounds of ill health or disability, unless this was under a court order or settlement of a claim;
- an overseas pension;
- a Civil List Act pension;
- payment under an equity release scheme. This provides regular payments from a loan secured on your home;
- payments from the Financial Assistance Scheme and periodic payments from the Pension Protection Fund (these help some people with underfunded occupational schemes whose employer has gone out of business).

Insurance payments

The following two types of insurance policy payments count as income:[43]
- illness, accident or redundancy insurance. Payments under a policy to insure against these risks are taken into account in full;

- mortgage protection policy and other loan protection policies for a loan secured on the home you live in. Payments under a policy to insure against the risk of being unable to maintain payments on a mortgage or loan secured on your home are taken into account if:
  - the payment is to pay interest on the mortgage or loan. The whole payment for interest counts even if your interest is more than the standard rate included in your UC. Any part of the payment for another purpose is ignored – eg, for capital repayment or policy premium; *and*
  - you have a housing element included in your UC for the mortgage or loan. If you or your partner have some earned income, your UC does not include a housing element, so the whole of any mortgage protection payment you get is ignored.

Income from an annuity

Income from an annuity is taken into account, except income from an annuity bought from personal injury compensation, which is ignored.[44] An annuity is usually when you pay a lump sum to an insurance company, often on retirement, with the capital built up in your personal pension, which then pays you an income for the rest of your life. It may also be through a home income plan where the annuity is bought with a loan secured on the home.

Income from trusts, personal injury payments and special compensation schemes

If you get an amount awarded to you because of a personal injury, it can be disregarded in certain circumstances.[45]

- If you receive the compensation in regular payments, they are disregarded as income.
- If the compensation is in a trust, both the capital value of the trust and any income from it is ignored. For more about trusts, see p357 and about how payments from personal injury trusts or other trusts are treated, see pp358–59.
- If the compensation was used to buy an annuity, payments under the annuity are ignored.
- If the compensation is administered by the court on your behalf or can only be used by direction of the court, the capital is ignored and regular payments are disregarded as income.
- If the compensation is not used in one of the above ways, it is disregarded as capital for 12 months. This gives you a chance to spend some or all of it, or to put it in a trust or buy an annuity.

Income from a trust that is not set up from personal injury compensation is taken into account, whether it is a discretionary trust or other type of trust.

Part 3: General rules for means-tested benefits
Chapter 16: Income: universal credit
4. Income other than earnings

Special compensation schemes

Any payment of income or capital from certain special schemes approved or set up by government are ignored if they are:[46]

- to support people with a disability to live independently;
- for those with variant CJD (Creuzfeldt-Jacob disease) or infected from contaminated blood products;
- compensation for the London bombings in July 2005;
- World War Two compensation (rather than a war pension).

Income from capital

If you have capital over £16,000, you are not entitled to UC. If your capital is below this level, it can affect the amount of income that is taken into account. This is either because you have actual income from the capital, such as income from a trust, or because it is assumed that the capital is giving you a certain amount of income.

Assumed monthly income

If your capital is over £6,000 but not more than £16,000, you are treated as having some income from it. This assumed monthly income is set at the rate of £4.35 a month for every £250, or part of £250, between £6,000.01 and £16,000.[47]

Example
Nuala and Ian have savings of £9,100. They are treated as having an income of £56.55 a month from their savings.
£9,100 – £6,000 = £3,100
£3,100 ÷ £250 = 12.4 (ie, 12 x £250 plus part of £250)
13 x £4.35 = £56.55

In working out how much capital you have, some capital is disregarded (see p362). You are not treated as having an assumed monthly income from disregarded capital.[48]

Note: the lower limit is £6,000 in all circumstances, even if you are in a care home (when the lower capital limit is £10,000 for other means-tested benefits).

Rental or other income from capital

If your capital is treated as giving you an assumed monthly income, any actual income you have from the same capital is treated as part of your capital from the day it is due to be paid to you.[49] For example, if you own a property, other than the home in which you live, rent is taken into account not as income but as capital and added to the capital value of the property itself (see also p350). However, if the value of the property can be disregarded (see p362), there is no assumed income, which means that the rental income is also ignored.[50] If you are running a property business, rental income counts as self-employed earnings (see p339).

Example

Sadiq owns a flat that he rents out for £1,000 a month which he uses to pay the mortgage. He does not live in the flat himself and is not running a property business, so the rent he gets does not count as income for UC but is added to his capital. The flat is valued at £100,000 but only £7,000 counts as capital once his outstanding mortgage and expenses of sale are deducted. For UC, he has an assumed monthly income of £34.80 worked out on capital of £7,000 + £1,000 = £8,000 (8 x £4.35 = £34.80).

Actual income from two types of capital is specifically taken into account. These are income from an annuity and from a trust, unless the income is disregarded because the annuity or trust is from personal injury compensation (see p347). In these two cases, the capital is not also treated as giving you an assumed monthly income.[51] For example, if you have income from a trust (except one set up from a personal injury payment), it counts as your income, but the capital value of the trust is not treated as giving you an assumed monthly income. See p358 for more about how trusts are treated.

Sports awards

A sports award from UK Sport out of National Lottery funds for living expenses is taken into account. This covers food, ordinary clothing and footwear, fuel, rent, housing costs and council tax for you, your partner or dependent child.[52] Amounts for anything else are ignored – eg, sportswear.

Specified miscellaneous income

If a type of income is not listed in the rules as being taken into account (p337), it is ignored for UC. The category of 'miscellaneous income' only includes unearned income that is taxable under the HM Revenue and Customs 'sweep-up' provisions in Part 5 of the Income Tax (Trading and Other Income) Act 2005.[53] This includes copyright royalties if your writing does not amount to a trade or profession, and unusual tax situations – eg, tax avoidance schemes.

Other income

Only income specified in the rules and described above can affect your UC. Any other kind of income is ignored – eg:
- adoption allowances, fostering allowances, child arrangements order payments and kinship care payments;

Part 3: General rules for means-tested benefits
Chapter 16: Income: universal credit
5. Notional income

- support from a charity. However, it may count as income from a trust if the charity's funds are in a trust, although it is not clear that the DWP intends the rules to work this way;
- voluntary payments – eg, if a relative gives you regular money. However, if it is voluntary maintenance for you (rather than for a child, which is always ignored) from a separated or former spouse or civil partner, this is taken into account;
- payments to third parties – eg, if a relative pays your phone bill for you;
- rental income from a room you let in your own home.[54] This is because actual income that comes from capital that is disregarded (the value of the home you live in is disregarded) is not in the list of income that is taken into account. On the other hand, if you rent out a property that you do not live in, the capital value of that property is taken into account and the rent is treated as capital, not as income. This is because actual income that comes from capital that is *not* disregarded is generally treated as capital (see p348).

5. **Notional income**

In some circumstances, you can be treated as having income that you do not actually have.

Deliberately getting rid of income to claim or increase benefit

If your earnings from employment or self-employment are deliberately reduced in order to claim or increase your universal credit (UC), you are treated as though you still have that income.[55] In particular, this applies if you got UC, or more UC, and the DWP believes that this was a foreseeable result and was what you intended. Even if it is your employer who has arranged for you to lose income, you are still caught by this rule if you or your employer intended you to get UC, or more UC, by doing so.

Cheap or unpaid labour

If you are doing work for someone or for an organisation for free or for less than the going rate (eg, you are working for a relative), you are treated as though you had earnings that would be reasonable for that work.[56] The comparison is with what the pay would be for similar work in the same location.

You are not treated as having more income than you receive for that work if:[57]

- the person cannot afford to pay you, or pay you more than s/he does;
- you work for a charitable or voluntary organisation or as a volunteer and it is accepted that it is reasonable for you to give your services free of charge or at less than the going rate;

- you are on a government-approved employment or training programme;
- you are a service user who is being consulted about provision of services by certain public bodies.

Failing to apply for income

If you fail to apply for income that would be available to you if you applied for it, you are treated as having that income.[58]

However, you cannot be treated as having another benefit that you have not applied for, with the exception of retirement pension.

If you are over pension credit (PC) age, you may be treated as having pension income even though you have not applied for it. The rules are the same as those for PC on p330. If you are under PC age, you can choose not to apply for pension income without your UC award being affected.

This rule does not apply to earnings from employment or self-employment.

---

6. **Working out monthly income**

Universal credit (UC) is paid in arrears for the monthly assessment period (see p164) just past. Awards are worked out month by month. Your award is adjusted as your earnings or other income increase or decrease, but always for a whole assessment period.[59] UC awards are not adjusted for income changes part way through the monthly assessment period. See p176 for reporting changes in your earnings and when this affects your award.

Monthly earned income

When you first claim, the DWP can make a decision on whether you qualify for UC based on an estimate of your earnings.[60] At the end of the first assessment period, your award is based on your actual earnings instead.[61]

The amount of earnings used to work out your UC award for each assessment period is based on the actual amount you received in that assessment period.[62] There is no averaging from one month to the next.

If you are employed, your employer is required to report your earnings to HM Revenue and Customs (HMRC) every time you are paid. This is called 'real-time information'. The employed earnings figure used in the UC assessment is taken from the amount in the report(s) received by the DWP in that assessment period.[63]

The DWP is not obliged to use the real-time information report – eg, if:[64]

- your employer is not providing accurate reports on time;
- HMRC fails to pass on a report;
- the information in the report is wrong.

If you think the DWP has used the wrong earnings figure or the real-time information report is wrong, send any evidence you have of the correct amount

Part 3: General rules for means-tested benefits
Chapter 16: Income: universal credit
6. Working out monthly income

and ask for a formal decision. You can then ask for a mandatory reconsideration.[65] However, unless the DWP thinks it is a failure or mistake, if no real-time information report is received, you are simply treated as having no earnings for that assessment period.

If you are self-employed, you must report your earnings every month. Your UC award is based on the actual amount received in the assessment period and the actual amounts paid – eg, tax and expenses. The way you work out your earnings for the assessment period is explained on p339.

If you are asked to self-report, you must act quickly in order for your earnings to be taken into account in the same assessment period as you received them. If you report late, the DWP can treat earnings as received in that later period. If you fail to provide information or evidence, payment of UC may be suspended (see p1185).

Monthly income other than earnings

Each type of income you have that is not earnings is worked out as a monthly amount – eg:[66]

- multiply weekly payments by 52 and divide by 12;
- multiply fortnightly payments by 26 and divide by 12;
- multiply payments for four weeks by 13 and divide by 12;
- multiply payments for three months by four and divide by 12;
- a payment of income for a whole year is divided by 12.

If your income varies and there is a cycle that can be identified, take one cycle and convert this into a monthly amount. If there is no cycle to the income, it is worked out by taking three months of income, or another period if that would give a more accurate picture, and calculating an average monthly amount.

Note: there are different rules for working out student income (see p888).

Example
Dan gets contributory employment and support allowance (ESA) of £204.30 every two weeks. The amount of ESA taken into account in his UC award is £442.65 (£204.30 x 26 ÷ 12).

If you live in a 'full service' area (see p24) and you start or stop getting unearned income, the amount taken into account is worked out over the number of days for which the income is paid in that assessment period. For example, if ESA of £146.20 a fortnight is awarded from 18 November (giving a monthly amount of £316.77) and your assessment period runs from 29 October to 28 November, the amount taken into account for that period is £114.56 (£316.77 x 12 ÷ 365 x 11 days).

Notes

1. Whose income counts
1 s8(4)(a) WRA 2012
2 s8(4)(b) and Sch 1 para 4(5) WRA 2012;
  reg 22(1) UC Regs
3 Regs 3(3) and (6) and 22(3) UC Regs

2. What income counts
4 s8(3) WRA 2012
5 Reg 52 UC Regs
6 Reg 66 UC Regs
7 Reg 46(3) UC Regs
8 Reg 46(4) UC Regs

3. Earnings
9 Reg 55(2), (4) and (4A) UC Regs; HMRC,
  Employment Income Manual, para 00520
10 Reg 55(2) and (3)(a) UC Regs
11 Part 5, ch 2, s336 IT(EP)A 2003
12 Part 4 IT(EP)A 2003
13 Regs 53(2) and 55(3)(b) UC Regs
14 Part 3, chs 2-11 and Part 4, ch 6 IT(EP)A
  2003
15 Part 4, ch 8 IT(EP)A 2003
16 Reg 54(1) UC Regs
17 Reg 55(2) UC Regs. These are 'general
  earnings' under s7(3) IT(EP)A 2003 – see
  HMRC, *Employment Income Manual*,
  para 12850.
18 Reg 55(2) UC Regs. These come under
  s401 IT(EP)A 2003 and are therefore not
  'general earnings' under s7(3) – see
  HMRC, *Employment Income Manual*,
  paras 12960 and 13005.
19 Reg 55(5) UC Regs
20 Reg 57 UC Regs
21 Regs 54 and 57(3) UC Regs
22 Reg 57(4) and (5) UC Regs
23 para H4184 ADM
24 Reg 58(1) UC Regs
25 Reg 58(2) and (3) UC Regs; para H4214
  ADM
26 Reg 59(2) UC Regs
27 Reg 58(1)(b) UC Regs
28 Reg 59(3) and (4) UC Regs
29 para H4241 ADM
30 Reg 62(1) and (5) UC Regs
31 Reg 62(2) and (4) UC Regs
32 Reg 62(3) and (4) UC Regs
33 Reg 64 UC Regs
34 Reg 57(1) UC Regs

35 para H4016 ADM
36 para H4050 ADM
37 Reg 63 UC Regs

4. Income other than earnings
38 Reg 66(1)(a) and (b) UC Regs; reg 28(1)
  UC(TP) Regs
39 Reg 10 UC(TP) Regs
40 Because there is no rule to treat
  payments to a third party as yours; DWP
  email to CPAG, 7 February 2013
41 Reg 66(1)(f) UC Regs
42 Reg 67 UC Regs; reg 16 SPC Regs
43 Reg 66(1)(h) UC Regs
44 Reg 66(1)(i) UC Regs
45 Reg 75 UC Regs
46 Reg 76 UC Regs
47 Reg 72(1) UC Regs
48 Reg 72(2) UC Regs
49 Reg 72(3) UC Regs
50 Regs 66 and 72 UC Regs
51 Reg 72(2) UC Regs
52 Reg 66(1)(g) UC Regs
53 Reg 66(1)(m) UC Regs; Part 5 IT(TOI)A
  2005
54 para H5112 ADM

5. Notional income
55 Reg 60(1) and (2) UC Regs
56 Reg 60(3) UC Regs
57 Reg 60(4) UC Regs
58 Reg 74 UC Regs

6. Working out monthly income
59 Sch 1 paras 20-30 UC,PIP,JSA&ESA(DA)
  Regs
60 Reg 54(2)(a) UC Regs
61 para H3011 ADM
62 Reg 54 UC Regs
63 Reg 61(2)(a) UC Regs
64 Reg 61 UC Regs
65 Reg 41 UC,PIP,JSA&ESA(DA) Regs
66 Reg 73 UC Regs

Chapter 17

Capital: under pension credit age

3

This chapter covers:
1. The capital limits (p355)
2. Whose capital counts (p355)
3. What counts as capital (p356)
4. Disregarded capital (p362)
5. Notional capital (p370)
6. How capital is valued (p377)

This chapter explains how capital affects your entitlement to income support, income-based jobseeker's allowance, income-related employment and support allowance and universal credit. It also applies to housing benefit (HB) if you and your partner are under the qualifying age for pension credit (PC). Chapter 18 explains the rules for PC and for HB if you or your partner are over the qualifying age for PC. For the capital limits for health benefits, see Chapter 29. There are no capital rules for non-means-tested benefits.

Key facts
- If you have more than £16,000 capital, you are not entitled to income support (IS), income-based jobseeker's allowance (JSA), income-related employment and support allowance (ESA), housing benefit (HB) or universal credit (UC).
- If you have capital above a lower limit, your benefit is affected because this is assumed to give you a certain income, often called 'tariff income'.
- Some kinds of capital are ignored when working out your benefit – eg, the value of the home in which you live.
- Getting IS, income-based JSA, income-related ESA or UC means the amount of your HB is automatically the maximum, so there is no need to work out your capital again for HB (although usually you cannot get both UC and HB).

1. The capital limits

There is a lower and upper limit.[1]
- The lower limit is £6,000.
- The upper limit is £16,000.

If you have over £16,000 of capital, you are not entitled to benefit. The first £6,000 is ignored and does not affect your weekly benefit. If you have between £6,000.01 and £16,000, you may be entitled to benefit, but it is assumed that you have some income from your capital. This is known as 'tariff income' or, for universal credit (UC), as 'assumed monthly income'.

This 'tariff income' (see p293) is assumed to be £1 a week for every £250, or part of £250, of your capital within these limits. For UC, this assumed monthly income (see p348) is £4.35 a month for every £250, or part of £250, of your capital within these limits.

If you live in a care home, see below.

Whichever limit applies, some capital is disregarded (see p362). You may also be treated as having some capital which you do not actually have (see p370).

Care homes

If you live permanently in a care home (see p922):
- the lower limit is £10,000, or £6,000 for UC;
- the upper limit is £16,000.

Tariff income starts above £10,000 or, for UC, above £6,000.

For housing benefit (HB), the £10,000 lower limit applies if you live permanently in one of the limited categories of care home for which HB is payable (see p923).[2] Some temporary absences (see p53) are ignored.

Example
Colin gets income-related employment and support allowance (ESA). He has £8,100 in savings. He is assumed to have tariff income of £9 a week. Colin moves permanently into a care home. Because his savings are below the £10,000 limit, they are now disregarded entirely. A few months later he sells his home and gets £80,000. As a result, he is no longer entitled to income-related ESA.

2. Whose capital counts

Your partner's capital

If you are a member of a couple (see p215), your partner's capital is added to yours.[3]

Part 3: General rules for means-tested benefits
Chapter 17: Capital: under pension credit age
3. What counts as capital

If your partner is a 'person subject to immigration control', her/his capital is added to yours even if you are not paid benefit for her/him (see p1523). In the limited circumstances when couples must make a single claim for universal credit rather than a joint claim, your partner's capital is still added to yours (see p161).[4]

Your child's capital

Your child's capital is not added to yours and does not affect your benefit.[5] However, if you still have amounts for children included in your income support or income-based jobseeker's allowance (see p230), although your child's capital is not added to yours, if it is over £3,000, you cannot get benefit included for her/him other than the family premium (see p236).[6] If this applies, any income of the child is not counted as yours.[7]

3. What counts as capital

All your capital is taken into account, unless it is disregarded (see p362) or is treated as income (see p370).

The term 'capital' is not defined. In general, it means lump-sum or one-off payments rather than a series of payments – eg, it includes savings, property and statutory redundancy payments.[8] For how other payments when you stop work are treated, see p273, and for universal credit (UC), see p339.

Capital payments can normally be distinguished from income because they are not payable for any specified period(s) and they are not part of a regular series of payments (although capital can be paid by instalments).[9]

Note: some capital is treated as income (see p293 and p337) and some income is treated as capital (see p361).

Savings

Your savings generally count as capital – eg, cash you have at home, premium bonds, shares, unit trusts and money in a bank account or building society.

There is no provision to disregard money put aside to pay bills.[10] If your savings are just below the capital limit, you could pay bills by monthly direct debit or use a budget account to keep your capital below the limit.

For income support (IS), income-based jobseeker's allowance (JSA), income-related employment and support allowance (ESA) and housing benefit (HB), your savings from past earnings can only be treated as capital when all relevant debts, including tax liabilities, have been deducted.[11] Savings from other past income (including benefits – see p367) are treated as capital after the period for which the income was paid has lapsed – eg, a weekly payment of child benefit becomes capital a week after it is paid and a monthly occupational pension becomes capital after a month.[12]

Fixed-term investments

Capital held in fixed-term investments counts. However, if it is presently unobtainable, it may have little or no value. If you can convert the investment into a form that lets you access it or sell your interest, or raise a loan through a reputable bank using the asset as security, the amount you can get for it counts. If it takes time to produce evidence about the nature and value of the investment, you may be able to get a short-term advance of IS, JSA, ESA or UC (see p1177) or a payment on account of HB (see p89).

Property and land

Any property or land that you own counts as capital. Many types of property are disregarded (see p362). See also 'proprietary estoppel' on p358.

Loans and ownership of capital

A loan to you usually counts as money you possess. In the following situations, you can argue that a loan or money you hold for someone else should not count as your capital:

- a loan granted on condition that you only use the interest, but do not touch the capital because the capital element has never been at your disposal;[13]
- money you have been paid to be used for a particular purpose on condition that the money must be returned if not used in that way;[14]
- property you have bought on behalf of someone else who is paying the mortgage;[15]
- money held in your bank account on behalf of another person, which is to be returned to her/him at a future date;[16]
- savings from someone else's benefit paid to you as an appointee – eg, your child's disability living allowance;[17]
- when you get a loan, you are under an immediate obligation to repay it.[18]

See p293 if you find that a loan is taken into account as income even though it is paid as a lump sum.

If you lend money to someone, it could still count as your 'notional capital' (see p370), depending on your reasons for lending it. You normally have a legal right to be repaid and this, in itself, could have a capital value, although the value would normally be less than the amount loaned, and could be nil if you have no expectation of getting the money back.[19]

Trusts

A trust is a way of owning any asset such as money, a house or shares. A 'trustee' looks after the capital and owns the legal title. The trustee uses the capital for the

Part 3: General rules for means-tested benefits
Chapter 17: Capital: under pension credit age
3. What counts as capital

benefit of someone else (the 'beneficiary'). If you are a trustee, the capital is not yours to use for yourself unless you are also a beneficiary.

The value of the assets held in trust is treated differently depending on the kind of trust. If you are the adult beneficiary of:

- a non-discretionary trust, you can obtain the asset from the trustee at any time. You effectively own the asset and so its market value counts as your capital;
- a discretionary trust, you cannot insist on receiving payments from it. Payments are at the discretion of the trustee within the terms of the trust. The trust asset itself does not normally count as your capital because you cannot demand payment (of either income or capital);[20]
- a trust which gives you the right to receive payments in the future (eg, on reaching 25) has a current capital value, unless disregarded (see p366).

If the beneficiary is under 18, even with a non-discretionary trust, s/he has no right to payment until s/he is 18 (16 in Scotland, or later if that is what the trust stipulates). Her/his interest may nevertheless have a current value.

If you transfer an asset into a trust in order to increase benefit entitlement, it could still count as yours under the 'notional capital' rules (see p371).

Do you hold an asset for someone else?

There may be a trust even without a formal trust deed.[21] If you hold an asset as a trustee, it is not part of your capital.

You are only a trustee if either:

– someone gives you an asset on the express condition that you hold it for someone else (or use it for her/his benefit); *or*

– you have expressed a clear intention that your own asset is for someone else's benefit and renounced its use for yourself.[22]

It is not enough just to intend to give someone an asset; you usually must transfer it in a particular way for there to be a trust. However, if you lead someone to believe that you are transferring your interest in some property or land to her/him, but fail to do so (eg, it is never properly conveyed) and that person acts on the belief that s/he has ownership (eg, s/he improves or repairs it, or takes on a mortgage), it would then be unfair if s/he were to lose out if you insisted that you were still the owner.[23] In this case, you can argue the capital asset has been transferred to her/him and you are like a trustee. So, when claiming benefit, you can insist that it is not your capital asset, but the other person's. This is referred to as **'proprietary estoppel'**.

If money (or another asset) is given to you to be used for a special purpose, it may be possible to argue that it should not count as your capital.[24]

Payments from trust funds

Whether your money is in a discretionary or non-discretionary trust can make a difference to how your benefits are affected.

For IS, income-based JSA, income-related ESA and HB, payments made:
- from a discretionary trust count as income or capital depending on the nature of the payment.[25] Capital payments are taken into account in full, but income from the trust is generally treated as a voluntary payment and is ignored;[26]
- from a non-discretionary trust count in full as capital, whatever the nature of the payment;[27]
- from a trust set up from money for a personal injury to you or your partner are treated more generously (see p359).

Trustees may have a discretion to use such funds to purchase items that would normally be disregarded as capital, such as personal possessions (eg, a wheelchair, car or new furniture) or to arrange payments that would normally be disregarded as income – eg, ineligible housing costs. Similarly, they may have discretion to clear debts or pay for a holiday, leisure items or educational or medical needs. See p290 for the treatment of voluntary payments, and p290 and p300 for the treatment of payments made to third parties.

For UC, there is no difference between a discretionary and non-discretionary trust in the way that payments to you from the trust are treated. In either case, they are taken into account. Generally, regular payments for a particular period are treated as income, and a lump sum is treated as capital.[28] If trustees of a discretionary trust choose to pay your bills directly or buy you something that is disregarded (eg, because it is a personal possession), this should not affect your benefit. If the trust is from money for a personal injury, see below.

Note:
- Putting money in a discretionary trust has the advantage of the value of the trust itself being disregarded. Note, however, that if you transfer money into a trust in order to get more benefit, it can still count as yours under the notional capital rules (see p370).
- Capital in a non-discretionary trust is taken into acount. If this takes you over the £16,000 capital limit, you are not entitled to benefit. However, for UC, you are not treated as having an assumed monthly income from the capital.[29]

Payments of personal injury compensation

A payment that does not come from a trust and is made because of personal injury to you or your partner is disregarded for 52 weeks.[30] This gives you time to spend some or all of the payment, or put it into a trust or annuity, before your benefit is affected. The 52 weeks start from when you receive the payment (for UC, this is defined as when it is paid to you). As you spend it, the disregard reduces to the level of the payment you have left. A subsequent payment for the same injury is not disregarded unless it is put into a trust.

If a trust fund has been set up out of money paid because of a personal injury to yourself or your partner, its value is ignored without a time limit.[31] For the payment to be disregarded, it is not necessary for the trust to be set up by a formal

Part 3: General rules for means-tested benefits
Chapter 17: Capital: under pension credit age
3. What counts as capital

deed. The important point is that the person who is awarded the compensation should not be able to have any direct access to it.

If the personal injury was to your partner and s/he has since died, you cannot carry over the remainder of the 52-week disregard, or if the payment is in a trust fund, it is no longer ignored.[32] If the personal injury was to a child, income or capital belonging to the child does not count as yours, so compensation paid for the child should not affect your benefit. However, if you still get amounts for a child included in your IS or JSA (see p356), the value of a personal injury trust for a child is not ignored.

If you have money in a trust from a personal injury to you or your partner, income from the trust is disregarded.[33] This also means that any regular payment is disregarded if it is paid for a particular period even if, for example, you get it just once a year.[34] However, a lump sum from the trust that is not for a particular period is taken into account as capital. It should not affect your benefit if trustees give you regular payments, pay your bills or, instead of giving you a lump sum, buy you something that would be disregarded because it is a personal possession – eg, furniture or a car.

Personal injury
'Personal injury' includes not only accidental and criminal injuries, but also any disease and injury as a result of a disease.[35]

Trust funds administered by a court

The value of a trust fund is also ignored if damages are awarded for personal injury and the money is paid into a special fund administered by a court – eg, the Court of Protection.[36] As well as ignoring the capital value, income from these funds is also ignored.[37] This also applies if the fund is for children to compensate for the death of a parent (except for UC).

Note: the notional income and capital rules (see p299 and p370) do not apply to trusts or funds administered by a court that have been set up as a result of a personal injury (although there is no specific exclusion for UC).

Money held by your solicitor

Money held by your solicitor normally counts as your capital. This includes compensation payments, other than for personal injury, before a trust fund has been set up.[38] A payment for personal injury to you or your partner is ignored for 52 weeks from when you receive it (see p359). If it is sent to your solicitor first, it is likely the 52 weeks start from when the solicitor receives it. If you have had legal aid and your solicitor is holding money back while working out the statutory charge to be deducted for legal costs, it does not count as your capital, as it is not possible to identify the capital which belongs to you until any statutory charge has been quantified and deducted.[39]

Income treated as capital

Certain payments that appear to be income are treated as capital.

For IS, income-based JSA, income-related ESA and HB, the following payments are treated as capital:[40]

- income from capital (eg, interest on a bank account) and income from property let to tenants (see p291). However, the following count as income, not capital:
  - income from the first five disregarded property bullet points listed on p362;
  - trust funds administered by a court (see p360);
  - income from the home of a partner, former partner or relative in the circumstances described on p364;
  - income from the home in which you normally live;
  - income from business assets or personal injury trusts.
- a lump sum or 'bounty' paid to you not more than once a year as a part-time firefighter, part-time member of a lifeboat crew, auxiliary coastguard or member of the reserve forces. If paid more often, it counts as earnings;
- the following payments:
  - an advance of earnings or loan from your employer;
  - holiday pay which is not payable until more than four weeks after your employment ends or is interrupted;
  - income tax refunds;
  - irregular (one-off) charitable or voluntary payments.
  This does not apply to IS or income-based JSA if you are involved in a trade dispute, or to IS if you are returning to work after a dispute (see p940);
- for IS, income-based JSA and income-related ESA only, a discharge grant paid on release from prison;
- for HB only, any arrears of child tax credit or working tax credit;[41]
- for HB only, the gross receipts from work carried out under New Enterprise Allowance.

For UC, actual income from capital (unless the capital is disregarded – see p362) is treated as capital from the day it is due to be paid – eg, interest on savings or rent from a property that is not your home.[42] This avoids double counting income from capital, which is also treated as giving you an assumed monthly income (see p355).

Example

Gordon has £7,000 savings, which give him interest of £8 a month. His UC assessment takes into account an assumed monthly income from his savings of £17.40 (£4.35 a month for each £250 above the £6,000 lower capital limit) and his actual £8 interest is added to his capital.

Part 3: General rules for means-tested benefits
Chapter 17: Capital: under pension credit age
4. Disregarded capital

4. **Disregarded capital**

Your home

If you own the home in which you normally live, its value is ignored.[43]

This disregard applies to any home in which you are treated as normally living – eg, because you are only temporarily living away from it (see p456). If you own more than one property, only the one that you normally occupy is disregarded under this rule.[44]

Exceptionally, for means-tested benefits other than universal credit (UC), two separate properties can be regarded as a single home as though one was an annexe of the other, if you personally (rather than a member of your family) normally occupy both properties.[45] This is more likely for a large family, but you could argue that it should apply if neither property on its own meets your family's needs – eg, if you are a carer living between two properties.[46] The UC rules are not quite the same, but you could argue that the same should apply.

Your home includes any garage, garden, outbuildings and land belonging to the property, including croft land.[47]

When the value of the property is disregarded

The value of the property can be disregarded, even if you do not normally live in it, in the following circumstances.

- **If you have left your former home following a marriage or relationship breakdown,** the value of the property is ignored for 26 weeks (six months for UC) from the date you left. It may also be disregarded for longer if any of the steps below are taken. If it is occupied by your former partner who is a lone parent, its value is ignored as long as s/he lives there.[48]
- **If you have sought legal advice or have started legal proceedings in order to occupy property as your home,** its value is ignored for 26 weeks (six months for UC) from the date you first took either of these steps.[49] The 26 weeks can be extended if it is reasonable to do so, if you need longer to move in.
- **If you are taking reasonable steps to dispose of a property,** its value is ignored for 26 weeks (six months for UC) from the date you first took such steps (which may be before you claim benefit).[50] The steps you take must be 'reasonable'. Advertising at an unrealistic sale price does not count, but placing the property with an estate agent or contacting a possible buyer should,[51] as might taking ancillary proceedings to resolve financial issues in a divorce.[52] The disregard can continue beyond 26 weeks, even for years if it is reasonable – eg, if a court orders that the former matrimonial home should not be sold until the children are grown up. Taking a property off the market and putting it on again does not necessarily begin a new 26-week period, but it may do if the second attempt to sell is quite separate.[53]

- If you are carrying out essential repairs or alterations which are needed so that you can occupy a property as your home, the value of the property is ignored for UC for six months from the date you began the repairs or, for other benefits, for 26 weeks from the date you first began to take steps to carry them out.[54] 'Steps' may include applying for planning permission or a grant or loan to make the property habitable, employing an architect or finding someone to do the work.[55] If you cannot move into the property within that period because the work is not finished, its value can be disregarded for as long as is necessary to allow the work to be carried out.

- If you have acquired a property and intend to live there as your home but have not yet moved in, its value is ignored for UC for six months from the date you acquired it, or for longer if that is reasonable.[56] For other benefits, it is ignored if you intend to live there within 26 weeks of acquiring it.[57] If you cannot move in by then, the value of the property can be ignored for as long as seems reasonable.

- If you sell your home and intend to use the money from the sale to buy another home, the capital is ignored for 26 weeks from the date of the sale (for UC, six months from the date you received the money).[58] This also applies even if you do not actually own the home but, for a price, you surrender your tenancy rights to a landlord.[59] If you need longer to complete a purchase, your capital can continue to be ignored if it is reasonable to do so. You do not have to have decided within the 26 weeks to buy a particular property. It is sufficient if you intend to use the proceeds to buy some other home within the 26-week (or extended) period,[60] although your 'intention' must involve more than a mere 'hope' or 'aspiration'.[61] There must be an element of 'certainty' which may be shown by evidence of a practical commitment to another purchase, although this need not involve any binding obligation.[62] If you intend to use only part of the proceeds of sale to buy another home, only that part is disregarded even if, for example, you have put the rest of the money aside to renovate your new home.[63]

- If your home is damaged or you lose it altogether, any payment in consequence of that, including compensation, which is to be used for its repair, or for acquiring another home, is ignored for 26 weeks. For UC, an insurance policy payment is ignored for six months from the date it is received, but not other kinds of payments.[64] In either case, it can be ignored for longer if it is reasonable to do so.

- If you have taken out a loan or been given money for the express purpose of essential repairs or alterations (for UC) or repairs or improvements (for other benefits) to your home, it is ignored for 26 weeks (six months for UC), or longer if it is reasonable to do so.[65] If it is a condition of the loan that it must be returned if the improvements are not carried out, you should argue that it should be ignored altogether.[66]

Part 3: General rules for means-tested benefits
Chapter 17: Capital: under pension credit age
4. Disregarded capital

- **If you have deposited money with a housing association as a condition of occupying your home,** this is ignored indefinitely.[67] If money which was deposited for this purpose is now to be used to buy another home, this is ignored for 26 weeks (six months for UC), or longer if reasonable, in order to allow you to complete the purchase.[68]
- **Grants made to buy a home** are ignored for UC for six months, and are ignored for other benefits for up to 26 weeks if made to local authority tenants to buy a home or do repairs or alterations to it. They can be ignored for longer, if reasonable, to allow completion of the purchase or the repairs/alterations. **Note:** the repairs or alterations must be required to make the property fit for occupation as your home.[69]

When considering whether it is reasonable to extend the period of any disregard, all the circumstances should be considered – eg, your personal circumstances, any efforts made by you to use or dispose of the home[70] and the general state of the market. In practice, periods of around 18 months are not considered unusual.

It is possible for property to be ignored under more than one of the above paragraphs in succession.[71]

Some income generated from property which is disregarded is ignored (see p292).

The home of a partner, former partner or relative

The value of a home (see p362) is ignored if it is occupied as her/his home by:[72]
- someone over the qualifying age for pension credit (PC – see p147), or who has limited capability for work or is incapacitated (see p365), who is:
  - a relative of yours or of your partner or dependent child; *or*
  - your spouse or civil partner, provided you are still treated as living in the same household (see p215), or your cohabitee, provided you are still treated as living together as a married couple (see p216);
- for UC (instead of the rule above), a close relative who is over the qualifying age for PC or has limited capability for work;
- your former partner from whom you are not estranged but are living apart (and are, therefore, not treated as still living together or as living in the same household) – eg, if one of you is living in a care home;
- your former partner from whom you are estranged and who is a lone parent. If your former partner is not a lone parent, the value of the home is ignored for 26 weeks (six months for UC) from the date you ceased to live in the home. You are 'estranged' if you are living apart because your relationship has broken down, even if the separation is amicable.[73]

3

Definitions

'**Incapacitated**' is not defined, but guidance suggests it refers to someone who is getting an incapacity or disability benefit, or who is sufficiently incapacitated to qualify for one of those benefits.[74] However, you should argue for a broader interpretation, if necessary.

'**Close relative**' includes: a parent, son, daughter, step-parent, stepson, stepdaughter, parent-in-law, son-in-law, daughter-in-law, brother or sister, or a partner of any of these people.[75] It also includes half-brothers and sisters and adopted children.[76]

'**Relative**' is a close relative or a grandparent or grandchild, uncle, aunt, nephew or niece.[77]

Personal possessions

All personal possessions, including jewellery, furniture or a car, are ignored.[78] A personal possession has been defined as any physical asset not used for business purposes, other than land.[79] For example, in one case, a static caravan on a non-residential site was treated as a personal possession. However, a home that you own but do not live in is not normally a personal possession but counts as capital (see p362). Personal possessions are not ignored if you have bought them in order to be able to claim or get more benefit. In this case, the sale value, rather than the purchase price, is counted as actual capital and the difference is treated as notional capital (see p370).[80]

Compensation (or for UC, an insurance payment) for damage to, or the loss of, any personal possessions, which is to be used for their repair or replacement, is ignored for six months, or longer if reasonable.[81]

Business assets

If you are self-employed, your business assets are ignored for as long as you continue to work in that business.[82]

If you cannot work because of incapacity, the disregard runs for 26 weeks from the date of claim if you intend to work in the business again when you are able, or for longer if reasonable in the circumstances.[83] For UC, the disregard runs for six months from when you stopped work if you can reasonably expect to work in the business again when you recover, or for longer if reasonable in the circumstances.[84]

If you stop working in the business, you are allowed a reasonable time to sell these assets without their value affecting your benefit. For UC, the assets are ignored for six months, provided you are taking reasonable steps to sell them, or longer if reasonable.[85]

For UC, if the purchase value of an asset was deducted as an expense from your earnings and you later sell or stop using the asset for the business, the sale price (or market value if you were to sell) is treated as a receipt when working out your earnings (see p340).[86]

It is sometimes difficult to distinguish between personal and business assets. The test is whether the assets are 'part of the fund employed and risked in the

Part 3: General rules for means-tested benefits
Chapter 17: Capital: under pension credit age
4. Disregarded capital

business'.[87] If the assets of a business partnership (eg, plant and machinery) have been sold but the partnership has not yet been dissolved, the proceeds of sale can still count as business assets.[88] **Note:** letting a single house is not likely to constitute a business.[89]

For the treatment of business assets if you are taking part in the New Enterprise Allowance, see p370.

Personal pension schemes

The value of a fund held in a personal pension scheme is ignored.[90] For UC, it is intended to ignore these funds, although there is no specific rule.[91] The value of the right to receive an occupational or personal pension is also ignored.

Insurance policy and annuity surrender values

The surrender value of a life assurance policy is ignored.[92] Some investments include an element of life insurance – eg, endowment policies. If the policy terms include how the payment on death is calculated, the whole investment is ignored.[93] However, you cannot choose to put money in such an investment in order to increase your benefit entitlement, because you are likely to be caught by the notional capital rule if you do (see p371).

For benefits other than UC, the surrender value of any annuity is also ignored (see p293 and p355),[94] as is the value of the right to receive any payment under an annuity. Any payment under the annuity counts as income[95] (but see p294 for when this is ignored).

Future interest in property

For benefits other than UC, a future interest in most kinds of property is ignored.[96] A **'future interest'** is one which will only revert to you, or become yours for the first time, when some future event occurs – eg, where someone else has a life interest in a fund and you are only entitled to it after that person has died.

However, this does not include a freehold or leasehold interest in property which has been let *by you* to tenants. If you did not let the property to the tenant (eg, because the tenancy was entered into before you bought the property), your interest in the property should be ignored as a future interest in the normal way.

The right to receive a payment in the future

If you know that you will receive a payment in the future, you could sell your right to it at any time so it has a market value and therefore constitutes an actual capital resource. For benefits other than UC, the value of this is ignored if it is a right to receive:

- income under a life interest or, in Scotland, a life rent;[97]
- an occupational or personal pension (this is also ignored for UC);[98]

- any rent if you are not the freeholder or leaseholder.[99] Any actual income which this right generates for you and which is not disregarded as income can be taken into account as income;
- any payment under an annuity (see p297).[100] Any actual income generated by this right and which is not disregarded as income can be taken into account as income;
- any earnings or income that is ignored because it is frozen abroad;[101]
- any outstanding instalments if capital is being paid by instalments;[102]
- any payment under a trust fund set up with money paid because of a personal injury to you or your partner.[103]

Benefits and other payments

Arrears of benefits and tax credits

For income support (IS), income-based jobseeker's allowance (JSA), income-related employment and support allowance (ESA) and housing benefit (HB), arrears of specified benefits and other payments (see p368) are ignored for:[104]

- 52 weeks after they are received by you; *or*
- longer in some cases of official error. If arrears are £5,000 or more and are paid to compensate for an official error (see p1280), they are ignored until the end of your (or your partner's) award. If you or your partner then reclaim the same benefit, or move from IS, income-based JSA or income-related ESA to another of these three benefits, they continue to be ignored for the whole of this next and any subsequent awards if there is no gap between awards.

Arrears of the following benefits are ignored, as above:
- attendance allowance (AA);
- bereavement support payment;
- child tax credit (CTC);
- council tax benefit (CTB);
- disability living allowance (DLA);
- discretionary housing payments;
- income-related ESA;
- HB;
- IS;
- income-based JSA;
- mobility supplement;
- personal independence payment (PIP);
- UC;
- working tax credit (WTC);
- concessionary payments instead of any of the above.

Also ignored for 52 weeks from the date you receive the payment are:
- arrears of certain payments to war widows, widowers and surviving civil partners;[105]

Part 3: General rules for means-tested benefits
Chapter 17: Capital: under pension credit age
4. Disregarded capital

- fares to hospital, payments for prescriptions and dental charges;[106]
- payments in lieu of milk tokens, vitamins or Healthy Start food vouchers;[107]
- payments to assist prison visits.[108]

For **UC**, arrears of the following benefits, and any compensation you get for late payment of these, are ignored for 12 months from when you receive them:[109]
- UC;
- any benefit that is ignored as income for UC – eg, child benefit, PIP and DLA (see p344);
- IS, income-based JSA, income-related ESA, HB, CTB, CTC and WTC.

Other payments

The following payments are ignored. (**Note:** they only apply to UC if specified):
- initial lump sum of bereavement support payment (ignored for 52 weeks from the date you receive it or 12 months for UC);[110]
- social fund payments (for UC these are ignored for 12 months);[111]
- refunds of council tax liability (ignored for 52 weeks from the date you receive the arrears);[112]
- 20 per cent of money in a tax-free childcare account is ignored for UC and, arguably, for other benefits (see p864);[113]
- a payment to a disabled person under the Disabled Persons (Employment) Act 1944 (other than a training allowance or training bonus) to assist with employment, or a local authority payment to assist blind homeworkers;[114]
- any payments made to holders of the Victoria or George Cross (these are also ignored for UC);[115]
- any payments by the Secretary of State to compensate for the loss of entitlement to HB;[116]
- payments under the Supporting People programme.[117]

Charitable and personal injury payments

- **Charitable payments.** For means-tested benefits other than UC, any payment in kind by a charity is ignored.[118]
- **Personal injury payments.** A personal injury payment can be disregarded for 52 weeks after you first receive it and without time limit when it is held in a trust (see p359).
- **Special compensation schemes.** Any payment of capital (or income) from certain special schemes approved or set up by the government are ignored if they are:[119]
  - for UC, to support people with a disability to live independently;
  - for you or your partner who has variant CJD (Creutzfeldt-Jacob disease). If you are the parent of someone with variant CJD, the payment is ignored for two years. For a dependent child of someone with variant CJD, the payment

is ignored for benefits other than UC until s/he reaches 20, finishes full-time education or for two years, whichever is later;

- in respect of someone infected from contaminated blood products. If you give money from the payment to your partner or, for benefits other than UC, to your dependent child, it is ignored for her/his benefit claim indefinitely. If you have no partner or children and you give the money to your parent, it is ignored for two years;
- compensation for the London bombings in July 2005;
- World War Two compensation (rather than a war pension).

Funeral plan payments

The value of any funeral plan contract is ignored indefinitely for UC but not other benefits.[120] A funeral plan contract is a contract under which you make payments to another person to ensure you are provided with a funeral and the sole purpose of the plan is to provide a funeral.

Social services, community care and other payments

The following payments from a local authority are ignored indefinitely (for 12 months for UC):[121]

- payments for children and families made under section 17 of the Children Act 1989, section 12 of the Social Work (Scotland) Act 1968 or, for HB, section 22 of the Children (Scotland) Act 1995;
- payments to young people who have previously been looked after by the local authority made under sections 23B or 24A of the Children Act 1989 or section 30 of the Children (Scotland) Act 1995. A payment under section 23C of the Children Act 1989 is also ignored as the young person's capital, and as yours if s/he passes it to you and s/he was in your care, is still living with you and is aged 18 or over (eg, under 'staying put' arrangements). In Scotland, this applies to payments under sections 26A and 29 of the Children (Scotland) Act 1995 and includes young people aged 16 or over in 'continuing care';
- for UC only, payments to meet welfare needs related to old age or disability, unless it is for certain living expenses (eg, food, fuel, clothing, footwear, rent, housing costs or council tax) for you, your partner or dependent child.

See p940 if you or your partner are involved in a trade dispute.

Also ignored indefinitely for benefits other than UC are:

- local welfare provision to meet an immediate short-term need or establish or maintain a settled home in certain circumstances;[122]
- community care or healthcare direct payments;[123]
- education, health and care plan payments, paid in England for a child with special educational needs;[124]
- special guardianship allowances, payable in England and Wales;[125]
- payments under sections 2, 3 or 4 of the Adoption and Children Act 2002.[126]

Part 3: General rules for means-tested benefits
Chapter 17: Capital: under pension credit age
5. Notional capital

Employment and training programme payments

For benefits other than UC, some payments are ignored for 52 weeks from the date they are received:[127]

- payment for travel or other expenses from a specified scheme for assisting people to obtain employment (see p1103);
- for income-related ESA, payment for travel or other expenses for undertaking required work-related activity;
- payment under section 2 of the Employment and Training Act 1973 or section 2 of the Enterprise and New Towns (Scotland) Act 1990;
- capital acquired for the purpose of participating under the 'self-employment route' – eg, for income-based JSA and HB, New Enterprise Allowance.[128] Any capital acquired is ignored for as long as you are receiving assistance for taking part in the programme and, after you have ceased trading, for as long as is reasonable in order to dispose of the assets.[129]

For when employment and training programme payments are treated as income, notional income and notional capital, see p294, p300 and p375.

Miscellaneous payments

The following payments are disregarded for benefits other than UC:

- a sports award made by the UK Sport National Lottery funds, except for any part of the award which is made for ordinary living expenses (see p298). It is disregarded for 26 weeks;[130]
- an education maintenance allowance or a 16 to 19 bursary fund payment are ignored indefinitely;[131]
- for IS, income-based JSA and income-related ESA, any payments made to jurors or witnesses for attending at court, except for payments for loss of earnings or benefit.[132]

Capital treated as income

Some payments which appear to be capital are treated as income, not as capital (see p293 and p337).[133]

5. Notional capital

In certain circumstances, you are treated as having capital that you do not have. This is called **'notional capital'**.[134] There is a similar rule for notional income (see p299, p350 and p350). Notional capital counts in the same way as the capital you do have.

For benefits other than universal credit (UC), you may be treated as having notional capital if:

- you deliberately deprive yourself of capital in order to claim or increase benefit (see below);
- you fail to apply for capital which is available to you (see p375);
- someone makes a payment of capital to a third party on your behalf or on behalf of a member of your family (see p375);
- you (or a member of your family) receive a payment of capital on behalf of a third party and you (or the member of your family) use or keep the capital (see p377);
- you are a sole trader or a partner in a business which is a limited company (see p377).

For UC only, you may be treated as having notional capital if:
- you deliberately deprive yourself of capital in order to claim or increase the amount of your UC (see below);
- you are a sole trader or a partner in a business (see p377).

Note: if you are treated as having notional capital because you have deliberately deprived yourself of capital in order to claim or increase benefit, a 'diminishing notional capital rule' (see p373) may be applied so that the value of the notional capital you are treated as having is considered to reduce over time.

Deliberately getting rid of capital

If you deliberately get rid of capital in order to claim or increase your benefit, you are treated as still having it.[135] The same applies if your partner got rid of capital, even if s/he did so before you became a couple.[136] You are likely to be affected by this rule if, at the time of using up your money, you knew that you might qualify for benefit (or more benefit), or qualify more quickly as a result. You should not be affected if you knew nothing about the effect of using up your capital (eg, you did not know about the capital limit for claiming benefit)[137] or if you have been using up your capital at a rate which is reasonable in the circumstances. This is because you cannot have the intention if you do not know about the capital rules.[138] Knowledge of capital limits can be inferred from a reasonable familiarity with the benefit system as a claimant,[139] but, if you fail to make enquiries about the capital limit, this does not constitute an intention to secure benefit.

In practice, arguing successfully that you have not deprived yourself of capital to get or increase benefit may depend on whether you can show that you would have spent the money in the way you did (eg, to pay off debts or reduce your mortgage) regardless of the effect on your benefit entitlement. If this is unclear, the burden of proving that you did it to get benefit lies with the decision maker.

Your intentions

Even if you did know about the capital limits, it still has to be shown that you intended to obtain, retain or increase your benefit.[140] For example, in one case, a

Part 3: General rules for means-tested benefits
Chapter 17: Capital: under pension credit age
5. Notional capital

claimant faced repossession of his home and transferred ownership to his daughter (who he feared would otherwise be made homeless), despite having been warned by DWP staff that he would be disqualified from benefit if he did so. It was held that, under the circumstances, he had not disposed of the property with the intention of gaining benefit.[141] The longer the period that has elapsed since the disposal of the capital, the less likely it is for the purpose of obtaining benefit.[142] However, no matter how long it has been since you may have disposed of an asset, there is no set 'safe' period after which benefit can be claimed without the need for further enquiry.[143]

If you use up your resources, you may have more than one motive for doing so. Even if qualifying for benefit is only a lesser motive for your actions and the main motive is something different (eg, ensuring your home is in good condition by spending capital on repairs and improvements), you may still be considered to have deprived yourself of a resource in order to gain benefit.[144]

The test is not what the money has been spent on, but your intention behind the expenditure. However, examples of the kinds of expenditure that could be caught by this rule are expensive holidays and putting money in trust.[145] **Note:** for income support (IS), income-based jobseeker's allowance (JSA) and income-related employment and support allowance (ESA), putting money in trust for yourself does not constitute deprivation if the capital came from compensation paid for a personal injury.[146]

You can deprive yourself of capital, even if you receive another resource in return.[147] For example, if you buy a car so that you can get more benefit, your actual capital includes the value of the car, and the difference between that and the purchase price is treated as notional capital.[148]

For UC, if the reason you used up your capital was to buy goods or services, you must show why this was reasonable in the circumstances. If the expenditure was reasonable, you are not treated as having deprived yourself of capital.[149]

Paying off debts and bankruptcy

For benefits other than UC, if you pay off a debt that you are legally required to repay immediately, you may not be counted as having deprived yourself of capital in order to gain benefit.[150] It is the facts of your case that are important: if you paid off an immediately repayable debt when you thought it would not be recalled for some time, you might be considered to have deprived yourself of money in order to get benefit. However, even if you pay off a debt that you are not legally required to repay immediately, the decision maker must still prove that you did so in order to get benefit.[151]

For UC, you are allowed to repay or reduce a debt. This does not count as depriving yourself of capital.[152]

If you are declared bankrupt, you cannot spend your capital without court approval and cannot usually be held to have deprived yourself of it if you do. Capital you have (but cannot spend) does not count for benefit purposes from the date of the bankruptcy order.[153] However, if you deliberately go bankrupt or do not take reasonable steps to discharge the bankruptcy in order to get benefit, your capital can still count as notional capital.

How notional capital is calculated

Notional capital is generally calculated in the same way as actual capital and the same disregards usually apply (see p362).[154] However, you may not be able to rely on the 26-week (or longer) disregard you would otherwise be allowed to take steps to dispose of a property (see p362), even if the new owner is trying to sell it (but there is conflicting caselaw on this).[155]

If more than one benefit is involved

If you have intentionally deprived yourself of capital in order to get IS, it does not necessarily follow that you also intended to get housing benefit (HB). Similarly, deprivation of capital to get income-based JSA cannot be treated as a deprivation for IS, although deprivation for IS can be treated as deprivation for income-based JSA, and deprivation for IS or income-based JSA can be treated as deprivation for income-related ESA. Each decision maker must reach her/his own decision on each benefit. This may result in different conclusions being drawn for each benefit. Even if intent is found in two different benefits, there may be different views about the amount of capital that has been intentionally disposed of.

However, if you are considered to have deprived yourself of capital for the purposes of claiming HB and you then make a successful claim for IS, income-based JSA or income-related ESA, the local authority should put the notional capital rules for HB on hold for as long as the other benefit remains in payment.[156]

The diminishing notional capital rule

The 'diminishing notional capital rule' provides a way of working out how the value of your notional capital may be treated as reducing over time. It only applies if you have deliberately deprived yourself of capital.[157]

Income support, income-based jobseeker's allowance, income-related employment and support allowance and housing benefit

The diminishing notional capital rule applies from the first week after the week in which it is decided that notional capital is to be taken into account.

- If your benefit has been refused because of notional capital, the amount of notional capital is reduced by the amount of IS, income-based JSA or income-related ESA you would have had if notional capital had not been taken into account for that benefit. In each case, if you would also have had HB, or more HB, without the notional capital, this extra HB also reduces the amount of notional capital for the other means-tested benefit claimed.[158] Notional capital for an HB claim that has been refused is reduced by the amount of HB you would have had, and any IS, income-based JSA or income-related ESA you

Part 3: General rules for means-tested benefits
Chapter 17: Capital: under pension credit age
5. Notional capital

would have had, if notional capital had not been taken into account.[159] Make sure you claim the benefit you would otherwise have got so that the reduction in notional capital is worked out correctly.

- If your benefit is reduced because of tariff income from your notional capital, that capital is diminished by the amount of the reduction each week. For example, if your notional capital is £6,750 (and you have no other capital), giving a tariff income of £3 a week, the reduction is £3 a week until it reaches £6,500, when it will be £2 and so on. For HB, the amount of your notional capital is also reduced by the amount of IS, income-based JSA or income-related ESA you would have had if no notional capital had been taken into account.

- The reduction in your notional capital is calculated on a weekly basis. However, if your benefit has been stopped altogether because of the notional capital rule, the weekly amount by which your notional capital is reduced is fixed for at least 26 weeks. Even if the amount of benefit to which you would have been entitled increases during this period, there is no change in the amount by which the capital is reduced. However, guidance for HB states that, in circumstances not related to capital (eg, if you have had a baby), a new assessment can be made.[160] If you reclaim benefit 26 weeks or more after your previous claim, your benefit entitlement can be recalculated from the week after your second claim. If it is more than it was previously, the weekly amount by which your notional capital is reduced is increased, but the weekly reduction stays the same as in the earlier assessment if your benefit entitlement remains unchanged or is less than it was before. You do not have to reclaim at the end of every 26-week period, but there can be no recalculation unless and until you do. Once the amount of reduction has been recalculated in this way, it is again fixed for the same period. Ask the DWP for a forecast of when your notional capital will reduce to a point when a fresh claim might succeed. The onus is on you to reclaim when it is to your advantage to do so – ie, when you may qualify for an increased assessment or because you have requalified for benefit.[161] If you delay, you may lose out, as new assessments cannot take effect before you reclaim. However, if you reclaim too soon, you must wait until the fixed periods have lapsed before you can apply for a fresh determination.

- If you have both actual and notional capital, you may have to use your actual capital to meet your living expenses. There is no reason why this should affect the amount by which your notional capital is diminished, even if this effectively results in double counting. Any reduction in your actual capital should be taken into account in calculating any tariff income arising from your combined actual and notional capital, unless you have spent it at such a rate and in such a way that it raises questions of intent, when you may find that the notional capital rules are applied all over again.

Universal credit

Notional capital is added to any actual capital you may have. This may reduce your UC award because of the assumed monthly income from capital being included in the assessment (see p348), or end it altogether. The notional capital amount is not fixed, but reduces over time at a set rate, as follows.

If you are treated as having notional capital of:[162]

- over £16,000 and your UC entitlement stops, in the following month the amount of UC you would have received but for the notional capital is deducted from the amount of notional capital;
- between £6,000 and £16,000, in the following month the amount of the assumed monthly income from that notional capital is deducted from the amount of notional capital.

Notional capital is reduced in the same way in each subsequent month. If your UC stops altogether, make a fresh claim when you think you might become entitled. Ask the DWP to tell you how long it will be before a new claim might succeed. If you have both actual and notional capital, you may need to spend your actual capital to meet your living expenses.

Failing to apply for capital

For benefits other than UC, you are expected to apply for any capital that is due to you – eg, if money is held by a court which could be released if you applied, or an unclaimed premium bond win. If you would get capital if you applied for it, you are treated as having that capital. There is no similar rule for UC.[163]

You are only treated as having such capital from the date you could obtain it. This rule does not apply if you do not apply for:

- capital from a discretionary trust; or
- capital from a trust (or fund administered by a court) set up from money paid as a result of a personal injury; or
- capital from a personal pension scheme or, if you are under the qualifying age for pension credit (see p147), from an occupational pension scheme or payment from the Pension Protection Fund; or
- a loan which you could only get if you gave your home or other disregarded capital (see p362) as security; or
- for HB only, child tax credit or working tax credit.[164]

Capital payments made to a third party on your behalf

If someone pays an amount to a third party (eg, a fuel company or a building society) for you or your partner (or a child for HB, or for IS or income-based JSA if children are still included in your claim – see p356), this may count as your capital for benefits other than UC. It counts if the payment is to cover:[165]

Part 3: General rules for means-tested benefits
Chapter 17: Capital: under pension credit age
5. Notional capital

- certain normal living expenses – ie, food, household fuel, council tax, water charges or ordinary clothing or footwear. School uniforms and sportswear are not ordinary clothing,[166] nor are special shoes needed because of a disability.[167] Payments made, for instance, for food or clothes for you or your partner count as yours. However, since a child's capital is not counted as belonging to you, a payment to, for example, a clothes shop for your child should count as the child's notional capital and not yours, and, in most cases, is ignored;
- rent which could be met by HB (less any non-dependant deductions);
- for IS, income-based JSA and income-related ESA only, housing costs which could be met by IS, income-based JSA or income-related ESA.

Payments to a third party do *not* count as yours if they are:[168]
- for other kinds of expenses (eg, a TV licence or mortgage capital repayments), unless they come from a benefit or pension (see below);
- from a specified infected blood payment scheme (see p368);
- for participating in a specified scheme for assisting people to obtain employment (see p1103).

Payments from an occupational or personal pension scheme or from the Pension Protection Fund to a third party count as yours regardless of whether or not the payments are used, or intended to be used, for ordinary living expenses.[169] They are disregarded if:
- you (or your partner) are bankrupt (or the subject of a sequestration order), the payment is made to the trustee or other person acting on your creditors' behalf and you and your partner (or your family for HB, and for IS or income-based JSA if amounts for children are still included in your claim) have no income other than the payment made;[170] *or*
- the payments do nothing to support you financially and, therefore, do not reduce or remove your need to be supported by IS, income-based JSA, income-related ESA or HB – eg, deductions from an occupational pension made under an attachment of earnings order to a former partner.[171] If you have had a judicial separation, rather than divorce, so the usual pension-splitting arrangements are not available, and a court has ordered you to pay part of your pension to your former partner, you could argue that this does not count as yours.[172]

For IS, income-based JSA and income-related ESA only, payments *derived* from certain social security benefits (including war disablement pensions, war widows' pensions and Armed Forces Compensation Scheme payments) and paid to a third party count:[173]
- as yours, if you are entitled to the benefit; *and*
- as your partner's, if s/he is entitled to the benefit.

For IS, income-based JSA and income-related ESA, there are different rules if you could be liable to pay maintenance (see p287).

Capital payments made to you for a third party

For benefits other than UC, if you or your partner get a payment for someone not in your family (eg, a relative who does not have a bank account), it only counts as yours if it is kept or used by you.[174] For HB (and for IS or income-based JSA if amounts for children are still included in your claim – see p356), the same also applies to payments received by a member of your family for someone not in the family. Payments from a specified infected blood payment scheme (see p368), or a specified scheme for assisting people to obtain employment (see p1103), do not count at all. Payments from pension schemes paid for a third party are disregarded in the same circumstances as described on p375.

Companies run by sole traders or a few partners

Normally, if you hold shares in a company, their value is taken into account. If, however, your influence in the company is such that you are like a sole trader or like a partner in a small partnership, you are treated accordingly. For IS, income-based JSA, income-related ESA and UC, the value of your shareholding is ignored but you are treated as having a proportionate share of the capital of the company.[175] However, these company assets are not taken into account while you are doing any work on the company's business,[176] even if you only do a little work for the company – eg, taking messages.[177] It has, however, been held that a 'sleeping partner' in a business managed and worked exclusively by others may not benefit from this disregard. As well as having a financial commitment to the business, you must also be involved or engaged in it in some practical sense as an earner.[178]

For HB, the local authority has discretion about whether to apply the same rules as for IS. If it decides to, it must apply them all.[179]

Note: for UC, income from the company, or your share of it, is regarded as your self-employed earnings. If this is your main employment, it counts as 'gainful employment', so that you can be treated as having a minimum level of earnings from that employment if your actual earnings are low (see p341).[180] You may also have employed earnings as a director or employee.

6. How capital is valued

Market value

Your capital is valued at its current market or surrender value.[181] This means the amount of money you could raise by selling it or raising a loan against it. This is

Part 3: General rules for means-tested benefits
Chapter 17: Capital: under pension credit age
6. How capital is valued

the price that would be paid by a willing buyer to a willing seller on a particular date.[182] So if an asset is difficult or impossible to realise, its market value should be heavily discounted or even nil.[183]

If you cannot legally dispose of capital (eg, because of a restraint order), the market value is nil.[184]

In the case of a house, an estate agent's figure for a quick sale is a more appropriate valuation than the district valuer's figure for a sale within three months.[185]

It is not uncommon for an unrealistic assessment to be made of the value of your capital. If you disagree with the decision, you could ask for a revision or appeal (see Chapters 54 and 55).

Expenses of sale

If there would be expenses involved in selling your capital, 10 per cent is deducted from its value (before any debts are deducted) for the cost of sale.[186]

Debts

Deductions are made from the gross value of your capital for any debt or mortgage secured on it.[187] If a creditor (eg, a bank) holds the land certificate to your property as security for a loan and has registered notice of its deposit at the Land Registry, this counts as a debt secured on your property.[188] If a single mortgage is secured on a house and land, and the value of the house is disregarded for benefit purposes, the whole of the mortgage can be deducted when calculating the value of the land.[189]

If you have debts that are not secured against your capital (eg, tax liabilities), these cannot be offset against the value of your capital.[190] However, once you have repaid your debts, your capital may be reduced. **Note:** you can still be treated as having the capital if you deliberately get rid of it in order to get benefit (see p371).

If you have an overdrawn bank account and have savings in another account with the same bank, the amount of the overdraft should be deducted from your savings if the terms of the accounts allow the bank to make these transfers.[191]

Jointly owned capital

If you own any capital asset (except as a partner in a company – see p377) with someone else under a 'joint tenancy', you are treated as owning an equal share of the asset with the other owner(s) – eg, if you own the asset with one other person, you are each treated as having a 50 per cent share of it.[192] This applies regardless of whether the capital asset is in the UK or abroad. See p380 for the rules that apply to assets abroad.[193] However, for universal credit (UC), if you can show that you own unequal shares, only the value of the share you own is taken into account.[194]

This does not apply if you jointly own the capital asset as 'tenants in common'.[195] In this case, your actual share in the asset is valued.

Joint tenancies and tenancies in common

With a '**joint tenancy**', each co-owner owns the whole of the capital asset 'jointly and severally'. If one of the joint tenants were to die, her/his interest in the asset would pass automatically to the other joint tenant(s).

With a '**tenancy in common**', each co-owner owns a discrete share in the asset. This share can be passed on by the person who has died to whoever s/he wishes.

If you have a joint tenancy, the value of your deemed share is calculated in the same way as your actual capital. However, it is only the value of your deemed share looked at in isolation that counts, and this will usually be worth less than the same proportion of the value of the whole asset. For example, if the asset is a house, the value of any deemed share may be very small or even worthless, particularly if the house is occupied and there is a possibility that the sale of the property cannot be forced. This is because even a willing buyer could not be expected to pay much for an asset s/he would have difficulty making use of.[196] Whether a sale can be forced depends on individual circumstances, and valuations should take into account legal costs and the length of time it could take to gain possession of the property.[197] A valuation should set out details of the valuer's expertise (where relevant), describe the property in sufficient detail to show that all factors relevant to its value have been taken into account, and state any assumptions on which it is based.[198] You may need to challenge any decision (see Chapters 54 and 55) based on an inadequate valuation.

Treatment of assets after a relationship breakdown

When partners separate, assets, such as a former home or bank account, may be in joint or sole names. If, for instance, a bank account is in joint names, you and your former partner are treated as having a 50 per cent share each under the rules on jointly held capital (see p378). This does not apply to UC if you can show that you own a different share. On the other hand, a former partner may have a right to some, or all, of an asset that is in your sole name – eg, s/he may have deposited most of the money in a bank account in your name. If this is established, you may be treated as not entitled to the whole of the account but as holding part of it as trustee for your former partner.[199] If an asset such as the matrimonial home belongs to your former partner and you have no share in it, you cannot be treated as having any interest in it under the Matrimonial Causes Act 1973 unless you take divorce or separation proceedings and get a property order.[200]

Part 3: General rules for means-tested benefits
Chapter 17: Capital: under pension credit age
6. How capital is valued

Shares

Shares are valued at their current market value less 10 per cent for the cost of sale, and after deducting any 'lien' held by brokers for sums owed for purchase or commission.[201] Market value can be worked out from the listed share price. If a more exact value is needed (eg, because your capital is close to the limit), it should be calculated using HM Revenue and Customs guidance, by taking the lowest and highest share prices for the day and using the lowest price plus a quarter of the difference between the two.[202] Fluctuations in price between routine reviews of your award are normally ignored. If you have a minority holding of shares in a company, the value of the shares should be based on what you could realise on them, and not by valuing the entire share capital of the company and attributing to you an amount calculated according to the proportion of shares held.[203] For UC, there are no special rules about valuing shares.

Unit trusts

Unit trusts are valued on the basis of the 'bid' price quoted in newspapers. No deduction is allowed for the cost of sale because this is already included in the 'bid' price.[204]

The right to receive a payment in the future

The value of any such right that is not ignored (see p366) is its market value – what a willing buyer will pay to a willing seller.[205] For something which is not yet realisable, this may be very small.

Overseas assets

If you have assets abroad and there are no exchange controls or other prohibitions to prevent you transferring your capital to the UK, your assets are valued at their current market or surrender value in that country.[206] If there are problems getting benefit because it is difficult to get the assets valued, you may be able to get a short-term advance of UC, income support, income-based jobseeker's allowance or income-related employment and support allowance (see p1177), or a 'payment on account' of housing benefit (see p89).

If you are not allowed to transfer the full value of your capital to this country, you are treated as having capital equal to the amount that a willing buyer in this country would give for those assets.[207] This may bear little relation to the actual value of the assets.

Ten per cent is deducted if there are expenses of sale, and deductions are made for any debts or mortgage secured on the assets abroad. If the capital is realised in a currency other than sterling, charges payable for converting the payment are also deducted.[208]

Notes

1. The capital limits

1 **IS** Regs 45 and 53 IS Regs
JSA Regs 107 and 116 JSA Regs
ESA Regs 110 and 118 ESA Regs
HB Regs 43 and 52 HB Regs
UC Regs 18 and 72 UC Regs
2 Reg 52(3)-(5), (8) and (9) HB Regs

2. Whose capital counts

3 **IS/HB** s136(1) SSCBA 1992
JSA s13(2) JSA 1995
ESA Sch 1 para 6(2) WRA 2007
UC s5(2) WRA 2012
4 Reg 18(2) UC Regs
5 **IS** Reg 23(2) IS Regs
JSA Reg 88(2) JSA Regs
ESA Reg 83(2) ESA Regs
HB Reg 25(3) HB Regs
UC s5 WRA 2012
6 **IS** Reg 17(1)(b) IS Regs
JSA Reg 83(b) JSA Regs
7 **IS** Reg 44(5) IS Regs
JSA Reg 106(5) JSA Regs

3. What counts as capital

8 para BW1.71 GM; Vol 5 Ch 29, para 29020 DMG
9 *R v SBC ex parte Singer* [1973] 1 WLR 713
10 R(IS) 3/93
11 R(SB) 2/83; R(SB) 35/83; R(IS) 3/93
12 R(IS) 3/93 para 22
13 R(SB) 12/86
14 R(SB) 53/83; R(SB) 1/85; *MW v SSWP (JSA)* [2016] UKUT 469 (AAC)
15 R(SB) 49/83
16 R(SB) 12/86; for how this works in Scotland, see *JK v SSWP (JSA)* [2010] UKUT 437 (AAC); [2011] AACR 26; *DF v SSWP* [2015] UKUT 611 (AAC)
17 *MC v SSWP (IS)* [2015] UKUT 600 (AAC)
18 CIS/2287/2008
19 *JC v SSWP* [2009] UKUT 22 (AAC)
20 *Gartside v Inland Revenue Commissioners* [1968] 1 All ER 121; [1968] AC 553
21 R(SB) 1/85; CIS/30/1993; *SB v SSWP (IS)* [2012] UKUT 252 (AAC)
22 R(IS) 1/90; CSIS/639/2006
23 R(SB) 23/85; CSIS/639/2006
24 *Barclays Bank v Quistclose Investments Ltd* [1970] AC 567; R(SB) 49/83; CFC/21/1989

25 CIS/25/1989
26 **IS** Sch 9 para 15 IS Regs
JSA Sch 7 para 15 JSA Regs
ESA Sch 8 para 16 ESA Regs
HB Sch 5 para 14 HB Regs
All Vol 5 Ch 29, para 29239 DMG
27 **IS** Reg 48(4) IS Regs
JSA Reg 110(4) JSA Regs
ESA Reg 112(4) ESA Regs
HB Reg 46(4) HB Regs
28 Regs 46, 48 and 66(1)(j) UC Regs
29 Reg 72(2) UC Regs
30 **IS** Sch 10 para 12A IS Regs
JSA Sch 8 para 17A JSA Regs
ESA Sch 9 para 17 ESA Regs
HB Sch 6 para 14A HB Regs
UC Reg 75(6) UC Regs
31 **IS** Sch 10 para 12 IS Regs
JSA Sch 8 para 18 JSA Regs
ESA Sch 9 para 16 ESA Regs
HB Sch 6 para 14 HB Regs
UC Reg 75(4) UC Regs
32 R(IS) 3/03
33 **IS** Sch 9 para 15 IS Regs
JSA Sch 7 para 15 JSA Regs
ESA Sch 8 para 16 ESA Regs
HB Sch 5 para 14 HB Regs
UC Reg 75(4) UC Regs
34 **UC** Reg 46(3) UC Regs
All *R v ex parte Singer* [1973] 1 WLR 713
35 R(SB) 2/89; *KQ v SSWP (IS)* [2011] UKUT 102 (AAC); [2011] AACR 43
36 **IS** Sch 10 paras 44 and 45 IS Regs
JSA Sch 8 paras 42 and 43 JSA Regs
ESA Sch 9 paras 43 and 44 ESA Regs
HB Sch 6 paras 45 and 46 HB Regs
UC Reg 75(5) UC Regs
All R(IS) 9/04; *CP v SSWP (IS)* [2011] UKUT 157 (AAC)
37 **IS** Sch 9 paras 15 and 22 IS Regs
JSA Sch 7 paras 15 and 23 JSA Regs
ESA Sch 8 paras 16 and 23 ESA Regs
HB Sch 5 paras 14 and 17 HB Regs
UC Reg 75(5) UC Regs
38 *Thomas v CAO*, appendix to R(SB) 17/87
39 CIS/984/2002
40 **IS** Reg 48 IS Regs
JSA Reg 110 JSA Regs
ESA Reg 112 ESA Regs
HB Reg 46 HB Regs

Part 3: General rules for means-tested benefits
Chapter 17: Capital: under pension credit age
Notes

41 Reg 46(9) HB Regs
42 Reg 72(3) UC Regs

4. Disregarded capital

43 **IS** Sch 10 para 1 IS Regs
JSA Sch 8 para 1 JSA Regs
ESA Sch 9 para 1 ESA Regs
HB Sch 6 para 1 HB Regs
UC Sch 10 para 1 UC Regs
44 **IS** Sch 10 para 1 IS Regs
JSA Sch 8 para 1 JSA Regs
ESA Sch 9 para 1 ESA Regs
HB Sch 6 para 1 HB Regs
UC Schs 3 para 1(1) and 10 para 1(2)
UC Regs
45 R(JSA) 9/03; R(SB) 10/89
46 *MM v SSWP (IS)* [2012] UKUT 358 (AAC)
47 **IS** Reg 2(1), definition of 'dwelling
occupied as the home' IS Regs; R(SB) 3/
84; CIS/427/1991 and R(IS) 3/96
JSA Reg 1(3), definition of 'dwelling
occupied as the home', JSA Regs
ESA Reg 2(1), definition of 'dwelling
occupied as the home', ESA Regs
HB Sch 6 para 1 HB Regs
UC Sch 3 paras 1(4) and 2 UC Regs
48 **IS** Sch 10 para 25 IS Regs
JSA Sch 8 para 5 JSA Regs
ESA Sch 9 para 5 ESA Regs
HB Sch 6 para 25 HB Regs
UC Reg 48(2) and Sch 10 para 5 UC
Regs
49 **IS** Sch 10 para 27 IS Regs
JSA Sch 8 para 7 JSA Regs
ESA Sch 9 para 7 ESA Regs
HB Sch 6 para 27 HB Regs
UC Reg 48(2) and Sch 10 para 4(1)(b)
and (2) UC Regs
50 **IS** Sch 10 para 26 IS Regs
JSA Sch 8 para 6 JSA Regs
ESA Sch 9 para 6 ESA Regs
HB Sch 6 para 26 HB Regs
UC Reg 48(2) and Sch 10 para 6 UC
Regs
All CIS/6908/1995; R(IS) 4/97
51 R(SB) 32/83
52 R(IS) 5/05
53 *SP v SSWP* [2009] UKUT 255 (AAC)
54 **IS** Sch 10 para 28 IS Regs
JSA Sch 8 para 8 JSA Regs
ESA Sch 9 para 8 ESA Regs
HB Sch 6 para 28 HB Regs
UC Reg 48(2) and Sch 10 para 4(1)(c)
UC Regs
55 *R v London Borough of Tower Hamlets
Review Board ex parte Kapur*, 12 June
2000, unreported

56 Reg 48(2) and Sch 10 para 4(1)(a) UC
Regs
57 **IS** Sch 10 para 2 IS Regs
JSA Sch 8 para 2 JSA Regs
ESA Sch 9 para 2 ESA Regs
HB Sch 6 para 2 HB Regs
58 **IS** Sch 10 para 3 IS Regs
JSA Sch 8 para 3 JSA Regs
ESA Sch 9 para 3 ESA Regs
HB Sch 6 para 3 HB Regs
UC Reg 48(2) and Sch 10 para 13(a) UC
Regs
59 R(IS) 6/95
60 R(IS) 7/01
61 CIS/685/1992
62 CIS/8475/1995; CIS/15984/1996
63 R(SB) 14/85
64 **IS** Sch 10 para 8(a) IS Regs
JSA Sch 8 para 13(a) JSA Regs
ESA Sch 9 para 12(a) ESA Regs
HB Sch 6 para 10(a) HB Regs
UC Reg 48(2) and Sch 10 para 14 UC
Regs
65 **IS** Sch 10 para 8(b) IS Regs
JSA Sch 8 para 13(b) JSA Regs
ESA Sch 9 para 12(b) ESA Regs
HB Sch 6 para 10(b) HB Regs
UC Reg 48(2) and Sch 10 para 15 UC
Regs
66 *Barclays Bank v Quistclose Investments Ltd*
[1970] AC 567; CSB/975/1985
67 **IS** Sch 10 para 9(a) IS Regs
JSA Sch 8 para 14(a) JSA Regs
ESA Sch 9 para 13(a) ESA Regs
HB Sch 6 para 11(a) HB Regs
UC Sch 10 para 12 UC Regs
68 **IS** Sch 10 para 9(b) IS Regs
JSA Sch 8 para 14(b) JSA Regs
ESA Sch 9 para 13(b) ESA Regs
HB Sch 6 para 11(b) HB Regs
UC Reg 48(2) and Sch 10 para 13(b) UC
Regs
69 **IS** Sch 10 para 37 IS Regs
JSA Sch 8 para 9 JSA Regs
ESA Sch 9 para 36 ESA Regs
HB Sch 6 para 38 HB Regs
UC Reg 48(2) and Sch 10 para 13(c) UC
Regs
70 CIS/4757/2003
71 CIS/6908/1995
72 **IS** Sch 10 paras 4 and 25 IS Regs
JSA Sch 8 paras 4 and 5 JSA Regs
ESA Sch 9 paras 4 and 5 ESA Regs
HB Sch 6 paras 4 and 25 HB Regs
UC Sch 10 paras 2, 3 and 5 UC Regs
73 R(IS) 5/05; CH/3777/2007

74 **HB** BW1/Annex A/A1.01 GM
Other benefits Vol 5 Ch 29, para
29437 DMG
75 Reg 2 UC Regs
76 CSB/209/1986; CSB/1149/1986; R(SB)
22/87
77 **IS** Reg 2(1) IS Regs
JSA Reg 1(3) JSA Regs
ESA Reg 2(1) ESA Regs
HB Reg 2(1) HB Regs
78 **IS** Sch 10 para 10 IS Regs
JSA Sch 8 para 15 JSA Regs
ESA Sch 9 para 14 ESA Regs
HB Sch 6 para 12 HB Regs
UC Reg 46(2) UC Regs
79 R(H) 7/08
80 CIS/494/1990 and R(IS) 8/04
81 **IS** Sch 10 para 8(a) IS Regs
JSA Sch 8 para 13(a) JSA Regs
ESA Sch 9 para 12(a) ESA Regs
HB Sch 6 para 10(a) HB Regs
UC Reg 48(2) and Sch 10 para 14 UC
Regs
82 **IS** Sch 10 para 6(1) IS Regs
JSA Sch 8 para 11(1) JSA Regs
ESA Sch 9 para 10(1) ESA Regs
HB Sch 6 para 8(1) HB Regs
UC Sch 10 para 7 UC Regs
83 **IS** Sch 10 para 6(2) IS Regs
JSA Sch 8 para 11(2) JSA Regs
ESA Sch 9 para 10(2) ESA Regs
HB Sch 6 para 8(2) HB Regs
84 Reg 48(2) and Sch 10 para 8(b) UC Regs
85 Reg 48(2) and Sch 10 para 8(a) UC Regs
86 Reg 57(5) UC Regs
87 R(SB) 4/85
88 CIS/5481/1997
89 CFC/15/1990; R(FC) 2/92; *RM v Sefton
Council (HB)* [2016] UKUT 357 (AAC)
90 **IS** Sch 10 para 23A IS Regs
JSA Sch 8 paras 28 and 29 JSA Regs
ESA Sch 9 paras 28 and 29 ESA Regs
HB Sch 6 para 32 HB Regs
UC Sch 10 para 10 UC Regs – the
disregard for the actual value of the fund
is not in the regulations, but it is
intended to be disregarded.
91 Email from DWP to CPAG, 7 February
2013
92 **IS** Sch 10 para 15 IS Regs
JSA Sch 8 para 20 JSA Regs
ESA Sch 9 para 20 ESA Regs
HB Sch 6 para 17 HB Regs
93 R(IS) 7/98
94 **IS** Sch 10 para 11 IS Regs
JSA Sch 8 para 16 JSA Regs
ESA Sch 9 para 15 ESA Regs
HB Sch 6 para 13 HB Regs

95 **IS** Reg 41(2) IS Regs
JSA Reg 104(2) JSA Regs
ESA Reg 105(2) ESA Regs
HB Reg 41(2) HB Regs
All *Beattie v Secretary of State for Social
Security* [2001] EWCA Civ 498,
upholding CIS/114/1999, reported as
R(IS) 10/01
96 **IS** Sch 10 para 5 IS Regs
JSA Sch 8 para 10 JSA Regs
ESA Sch 9 para 9 ESA Regs
HB Sch 6 para 7 HB Regs
97 **IS** Sch 10 para 13 IS Regs
JSA Sch 8 para 18 JSA Regs
ESA Sch 9 para 18 ESA Regs
HB Sch 6 para 15 HB Regs
98 **IS** Sch 10 para 23 IS Regs
JSA Sch 8 para 28 JSA Regs
ESA Sch 9 para 28 ESA Regs
HB Sch 6 para 31 HB Regs
UC Sch 10 para 10 UC Regs
99 **IS** Sch 10 para 24 IS Regs
JSA Sch 8 para 30 JSA Regs
ESA Sch 9 para 30 ESA Regs
HB Sch 6 para 33 HB Regs
100 **IS** Sch 10 para 11 IS Regs
JSA Sch 8 para 16 JSA Regs
ESA Sch 9 para 15 ESA Regs
HB Sch 6 para 13 HB Regs
101 **IS** Sch 10 para 14 IS Regs
JSA Sch 8 para 19 JSA Regs
ESA Sch 9 para 19 ESA Regs
HB Sch 6 para 16 HB Regs
102 **IS** Sch 10 para 16 IS Regs
JSA Sch 8 para 21 JSA Regs
ESA Sch 9 para 21 ESA Regs
HB Sch 6 para 18 HB Regs
103 **IS** Sch 10 para 12 IS Regs
JSA Sch 8 para 17 JSA Regs
ESA Sch 9 para 16 ESA Regs
HB Sch 6 para 14 HB Regs
104 **IS** Sch 10 para 7 IS Regs
JSA Sch 8 para 12 JSA Regs
ESA Sch 9 para 11 ESA Regs
HB Sch 6 para 9 HB Regs
105 **IS** Sch 10 para 41 IS Regs
JSA Sch 8 para 39 JSA Regs
ESA Sch 9 para 40 ESA Regs
HB Sch 6 para 9 HB Regs
106 **IS** Sch 10 para 38 IS Regs
JSA Sch 8 para 36 JSA Regs
ESA Sch 9 para 37 ESA Regs
HB Sch 6 para 40 HB Regs
107 **IS** Sch 10 para 39 IS Regs
JSA Sch 8 para 37 JSA Regs
ESA Sch 9 para 38 ESA Regs
HB Sch 6 para 41 HB Regs

Part 3: General rules for means-tested benefits
Chapter 17: Capital: under pension credit age
Notes

• •

3

108 **IS** Sch 10 para 40 IS Regs
    JSA Sch 8 para 38 JSA Regs
    ESA Sch 9 para 39 ESA Regs
    HB Sch 6 para 42 HB Regs
109 Sch 10 para 18 UC Regs
110 **IS** Sch 10 para 72 IS Regs
    JSA Sch 8 para 65 JSA Regs
    ESA Sch 9 para 60 ESA Regs
    HB Sch 6 para 62 HB Regs
    UC Sch 10 para 20 UC Regs
111 **IS** Sch 10 para 18 IS Regs
    JSA Sch 8 para 23 JSA Regs
    ESA Sch 9 para 23 ESA Regs
    HB Sch 6 para 20 HB Regs
    UC Sch 10 para 16 UC Regs
112 **IS** Sch 10 para 36 IS Regs
    JSA Sch 8 para 35 JSA Regs
    ESA Sch 9 para 35 ESA Regs
    HB Sch 6 para 37 HB Regs
113 Memo ADM 26/16
114 **IS** Sch 10 paras 42 and 43 IS Regs
    JSA Sch 8 paras 40 and 41 JSA Regs
    ESA Sch 9 paras 41 and 42 ESA Regs
    HB Sch 6 paras 43 and 44 HB Regs
115 **IS** Sch 10 para 46 IS Regs
    JSA Sch 8 para 44 JSA Regs
    ESA Sch 9 para 45 ESA Regs
    HB Sch 6 para 47 HB Regs
    UC Sch 10 para 19 UC Regs
116 **IS** Sch 10 para 31 IS Regs
    JSA Sch 8 para 33 JSA Regs
    ESA Sch 9 para 33 ESA Regs
    HB Sch 6 para 30 HB Regs
117 **IS** Sch 10 para 66 IS Regs
    JSA Sch 8 para 59 JSA Regs
    ESA Sch 9 para 55 ESA Regs
    HB Sch 6 para 57 HB Regs
118 **IS** Sch 10 para 29 IS Regs
    JSA Sch 8 para 31 JSA Regs
    ESA Sch 9 para 31 ESA Regs
    HB Sch 6 para 34 HB Regs
119 **IS** Sch 10 paras 22 and 65 IS Regs
    JSA Sch 8 paras 27 and 58 JSA Regs
    ESA Sch 9 paras 27 and 54 ESA Regs
    HB Sch 6 para 24 HB Regs; Sch 6 paras
    24 and 56 HB Regs
    UC Reg 76 UC Regs
120 Sch 10 para 11 UC Regs
121 **IS** Sch 10 para 17 IS Regs
    JSA Sch 8 para 22 JSA Regs
    ESA Sch 9 para 22 ESA Regs
    HB Sch 6 para 19 HB Regs
    UC Sch 10 para 17 UC Regs
122 **IS** Sch 10 para 18A IS Regs
    JSA Sch 8 para 23A JSA Regs
    ESA Sch 9 para 23A ESA Regs
    HB Sch 6 para 20A HB Regs

123 **IS** Sch 10 para 67 IS Regs
    JSA Sch 8 para 60 JSA Regs
    ESA Sch 9 para 56 ESA Regs
    HB Sch 6 para 58 HB Regs
124 **IS** Sch 10 para 71 IS Regs
    JSA Sch 8 para 64 JSA Regs
    ESA Sch 9 para 59 ESA Regs
    HB Sch 6 para 61 HB Regs
125 **IS** Sch 10 para 68A IS Regs
    JSA Sch 8 para 61A JSA Regs
    ESA Sch 9 para 58 ESA Regs
    HB Sch 6 para 60 HB Regs
126 **IS** Sch 10 para 68 IS Regs
    JSA Sch 8 para 61 JSA Regs
    ESA Sch 9 para 57 ESA Regs
    HB Sch 6 para 59 HB Regs
127 **IS** Sch 10 paras 1A and 30 IS Regs
    JSA Sch 8 paras A2, A3 and 32 JSA Regs
    ESA Sch 9 paras 1A, 32 and 32A ESA
    Regs
    HB Sch 6 paras A2, A3 and 35 HB Regs
128 **IS** Sch 10 para 52 IS Regs
    JSA Sch 8 para 47 JSA Regs
    ESA Sch 9 para 46 ESA Regs
    HB Sch 6 para 49 HB Regs
129 **IS** Sch 10 para 6(3) and (4) IS Regs
    JSA Sch 8 para 11(3) and (4) JSA Regs
    ESA Sch 9 para 10(3) and (4) ESA Regs
    HB Sch 6 para 8(3) and (4) HB Regs
130 **IS** Sch 10 para 56 IS Regs
    JSA Sch 8 para 51 JSA Regs
    ESA Sch 9 para 47 ESA Regs
    HB Sch 6 para 50 HB Regs
131 **IS** Sch 10 para 63 IS Regs
    JSA Sch 8 para 52 JSA Regs
    ESA Sch 9 para 52 ESA Regs
    HB Sch 6 para 51 HB Regs
132 **IS** Sch 10 para 34 IS Regs
    JSA Sch 8 para 34 JSA Regs
    ESA Sch 9 para 34 ESA Regs
133 **IS** Sch 10 para 20 IS Regs
    JSA Sch 8 para 25 JSA Regs
    ESA Sch 9 para 25 ESA Regs
    HB Sch 6 para 22 HB Regs

5. Notional capital
134 **IS** Reg 51(6) IS Regs
    JSA Reg 113(6) JSA Regs
    ESA Reg 115(8) ESA Regs
    HB Reg 49(6) HB Regs
    UC Regs 50(1) and 77(2) UC Regs
135 **IS** Reg 51(1) IS Regs
    JSA Reg 113(1) JSA Regs
    ESA Reg 115(1) ESA Regs
    HB Reg 49(1) HB Regs
    UC Reg 50(1) UC Regs
136 R(IS) 7/07
137 CIS/124/1990; CSB/1198/1989

138 CIS/124/1990
139 R(SB) 9/91
140 CIS/40/1989
141 CIS/621/1991. See also CJSA/3937/ 2002 and *LH v SSWP (IS)* [2014] UKUT 60 (AAC).
142 CIS/264/1989
143 R(IS) 7/98 para 12(3)
144 R(SB) 38/85; R(IS) 1/91; R(H) 1/06
145 para BW1.714 GM
146 **IS** Reg 51(1)(a) IS Regs
JSA Reg 113(1)(a) JSA Regs
ESA Reg 115(1)(a) ESA Regs
147 R(SB) 40/85
148 R(IS) 8/04
149 Reg 50(2)(b) UC Regs
150 R(SB) 12/91; *Verna Jones v SSWP* [2003] EWCA Civ 964, unreported; *VW v SSWP (IS)* [2015] UKUT 51 (AAC); [2015] AACR 39
151 CIS/2627/1995; *Verna Jones v SSWP* [2003] EWCA Civ 964, unreported
152 Reg 50(2)(a) UC Regs
153 *KS v SSWP* [2009] UKUT 122 (AAC); [2010] AACR 3
154 **IS** Reg 51(6) IS Regs
JSA Reg 113(6) JSA Regs
ESA Reg 115(8) ESA Regs
HB Reg 49(7) HB Regs
155 CIS/30/1993, but other commissioners have taken a different view (see for example, CIS/25/1990 and CIS/81/ 1991)
156 para BW1.831 GM
157 **IS** Reg 51A(1) IS Regs
JSA Reg 114(1) JSA Regs
ESA Reg 116(1) ESA Regs
HB Reg 49(1) HB Regs
UC Reg 50(3) UC Regs
158 **IS** Reg 51A IS Regs
JSA Reg 114 JSA Regs
ESA Reg 116 ESA Regs
159 Reg 49 HB Regs
160 para BW1.795 GM
161 R(IS) 9/92
162 Reg 50(3) UC Regs
163 **IS** Reg 51(2) IS Regs
JSA Reg 113(2) JSA Regs
ESA Reg 115(2) ESA Regs
HB Reg 49(2) HB Regs
164 Reg 49(2) HB Regs
165 **IS** Reg 51(3)(a)(ii) and (8) IS Regs
JSA Reg 113(3)(a)(ii) and (8) JSA Regs
ESA Regs 2(1) and 115(3)(c) ESA Regs
HB Reg 49(3)(a) and (7) HB Regs

166 **IS** Reg 51(8) IS Regs
JSA Reg 113(8) JSA Regs
ESA Reg 2(1) ESA Regs
HB Reg 49(7)(b) HB Regs
167 Vol 5 Ch 29, para 29867 DMG
168 **IS** Reg 51(3)(a)(ii), (3A)(a) and (ba) IS Regs
JSA Reg 113(3)(a)(ii), (3A)(a), (bb) and (bc) JSA Regs
ESA Reg 115(3)(c), (5)(a) and (ba) ESA Regs
HB Reg 49(3)(b), (4)(a), (bb) and (bc) HB Regs
169 **IS** Reg 51(3)(a)(ia) IS Regs
JSA Reg 113(3)(a)(ia) JSA Regs
ESA Reg 115(3)(b) ESA Regs
HB Reg 49(3)(a) HB Regs
170 **IS** Reg 51(3A)(c) IS Regs
JSA Reg 113(3A)(c) JSA Regs
ESA Reg 115(5)(c) ESA Regs
HB Reg 49(4)(c) HB Regs
171 R(IS) 4/01
172 CH/1672/2007
173 **IS** Reg 51(3)(a)(i) IS Regs
JSA Reg 113(3)(a)(i) JSA Regs
ESA Reg 115(3)(a) ESA Regs
174 **IS** Reg 51(3)(b) IS Regs
JSA Reg 113(3)(b) JSA Regs
ESA Reg 115(4) ESA Regs
HB Reg 49(3)(c) HB Regs
175 **IS** Reg 51(4) IS Regs
JSA Reg 113(4) JSA Regs
ESA Reg 115(6) ESA Regs
HB Reg 49(5) HB Regs
UC Reg 77(1) and (2) UC Regs
176 **IS** Reg 51(5) IS Regs
JSA Reg 113(5) JSA Regs
ESA Reg 115(7) ESA Regs
HB Reg 49(6) HB Regs
UC Reg 77(3)(a) UC Regs
177 Vol 5 Ch 29, para 29879 DMG; see also R(IS) 13/93
178 R(IS) 14/98
179 Reg 49(5) HB Regs
180 Reg 77(3) UC Regs

6. How capital is valued
181 **IS** Reg 49(a) IS Regs
JSA Reg 111(a) JSA Regs
ESA Reg 113 ESA Regs
HB Reg 47(a) HB Regs
UC Reg 49(1) UC Regs
182 R(SB) 57/83; R(SB) 6/84
183 R(SB) 18/83
184 *CS v SSWP* [2014] UKUT 518 (AAC)
185 R(SB) 6/84

3

Part 3: General rules for means-tested benefits
Chapter 17: Capital: under pension credit age
Notes

186 **IS** Reg 49(a) IS Regs
JSA Reg 111(a) JSA Regs
ESA Reg 113(a) ESA Regs
HB Reg 47(a) HB Regs
UC Reg 49(1) UC Regs
187 **IS** Reg 49(b) IS Regs
JSA Reg 111(b) JSA Regs
ESA Reg 113(b) ESA Regs
HB Reg 47(b) HB Regs
UC Reg 49(1)(b) UC Regs
188 CIS/255/1989
189 R(SB) 27/84
190 R(SB) 2/83; R(SB) 31/83
191 *JRL v SSWP (JSA)* [2011] UKUT 63 (AAC); [2011] AACR 30
192 **IS** Reg 52 IS Regs
JSA Reg 115 JSA Regs
ESA Reg 117 ESA Regs
HB Reg 51 HB Regs
UC Reg 47 UC Regs
193 CIS/2575/1997
194 Reg 47 UC Regs
195 *Hourigan v SSWP* [2002] EWCA 1890, reported as R(IS) 4/03
196 CIS/15936/1996; CIS/263/1997; CIS/3283/1997 (joint decision); R(IS) 26/95
197 R(IS) 3/96
198 R(JSA) 1/02
199 R(IS) 2/93
200 R(IS) 1/03
201 **IS** Reg 49(a) IS Regs
JSA Reg 111(a) JSA Regs
ESA Reg 113 ESA Regs
HB Reg 47(a) HB Regs
202 R(IS) 18/95; Vol 5 Ch 29, paras 29665-70 DMG
203 R(SB) 18/83; R(IS) 2/90
204 **IS/JSA** Vol 5 Ch 29, para 29681 DMG
HB BW1/1.530 GM
205 *Peters v CAO* (appendix to R(SB) 3/89)
206 **IS** Reg 50(a) IS Regs
JSA Reg 112(a) JSA Regs
ESA Reg 114(a) ESA Regs
HB Reg 48(a) HB Regs
UC Reg 49(2)(a) UC Regs
207 **IS** Reg 50(b) IS Regs
JSA Reg 112(b) JSA Regs
ESA Reg 114(b) ESA Regs
HB Reg 48(b) HB Regs
UC Reg 49(2)(b) UC Regs
208 **IS** Sch 10 para 21 IS Regs
JSA Sch 8 para 26 JSA Regs
ESA Sch 9 para 26 ESA Regs
HB Sch 6 para 23 HB Regs
UC Reg 49(3) UC Regs

Chapter 18

Capital: over pension credit age

This chapter explains the rules for working out your capital for pension credit (PC) and for housing benefit (HB) if you or your partner are over the qualifying age for PC and neither of you are on income support (IS), income-based jobseeker's allowance (JSA), income-related employment and support allowance (ESA) or universal credit (UC). If you do get IS, income-based JSA, income-related ESA or UC, your capital is ignored for HB. Chapter 17 explains the rules for IS, income-based JSA, income-related ESA, UC and for HB if you and your partner are under the qualifying age for PC.

Key facts

- There is no capital limit for pension credit (PC).
- Generally, you are not eligible for housing benefit (HB) if your total capital is over £16,000. However, if you get the guarantee credit of PC, there is no capital limit for HB because all your capital is ignored.
- If you have capital over £10,000, this affects the amount of PC or HB you get because it is assumed to give you a certain income, called 'deemed income'.
- Capital includes your and your partner's savings, investments and property. Some kinds of capital are ignored when working out your PC or HB – eg, if you own the home in which you live.
- If you deliberately get rid of capital in order to get more benefit, you are treated as still having it. This is called 'notional capital'.

Part 3: General rules for means-tested benefits
Chapter 18: Capital: over pension credit age
1. The capital limits

1. **The capital limits**

Pension credit

There is no upper capital limit for pension credit (PC), beyond which you are excluded from benefit. The the lower limit is £10,000.

Capital of £10,000 or less is ignored. If you have capital above £10,000, you are treated as having a deemed income of £1 for every £500, or part of £500, by which your capital exceeds £10,000.[1]

Housing benefit

The lower capital limit for housing benefit (HB) is £10,000 and the upper limit is £16,000.[2]

If you have over £16,000, you are not entitled to benefit. The first £10,000 is ignored. If you have capital above £10,000, you are treated as having a deemed income of £1 for every £500, or part of £500, by which your capital exceeds that amount.[3]

However, if you get the guarantee credit of PC, all your and your partner's capital (and income) is ignored for HB.[4] This is because entitlement to PC guarantee credit acts as a passport to maximum HB. Because PC has no upper capital limit, you can get maximum HB even with capital above £16,000.

If you get the savings credit of PC but not the guarantee credit, the following applies.[5]

- Your capital for HB purposes is the capital figure worked out by the DWP for your PC. This is modified to include any capital belonging to your partner which was not taken into account in the PC calculation.
- During an 'assessed income period' (see p156), an increase in capital does not affect your PC savings credit, but may affect HB. If capital rises above £16,000 (worked out by the local authority under the HB rules), you are no longer entitled to HB. If capital increases but is still less than £16,000, the local authority must continue to use the DWP's capital figure.

Example

Amy is 67 and a widow. She has a state pension and a personal pension. She gets HB and the savings credit of PC, but not the guarantee credit. Her PC award letter shows that her assessed income period ends in April 2018. When she inherits £20,000 her HB stops, but her PC is not affected until April 2018.

2. Whose capital counts

Your partner's capital is added to yours.[6]

The capital of any dependent child does not affect your pension credit or housing benefit.

3. What counts as capital

The term 'capital' is not defined. In general, it means lump-sum or one-off payments rather than a series of payments – eg, savings, investments and property.[7]

Savings

Your savings generally count as capital – eg, cash you have at home, premium bonds, stocks and shares, unit trusts and money in a bank account.

Savings from past income (including benefits – see p393) are treated as capital after the period for which the income was paid has lapsed. There is no provision to disregard money put aside to pay bills.[8] If your savings are just below the capital limit, you could pay bills by monthly direct debit or use a budget account to keep your capital below the limit.

Fixed-term investments

Capital held in fixed-term investments counts. However, if it is presently unobtainable, it may have little or no value. If you can convert the investment into a realisable form, sell your interest, or raise a loan through a reputable bank using the asset as security, the amount you can get for it counts. If it takes time to produce evidence about the nature and value of the investment, you may be able to get a short-term advance of pension credit (see p1177) or a payment on account of housing benefit (see p89).[9]

Property and land

Any property or land that you own counts as capital. Many types of property are disregarded (see p391). See also 'proprietary estoppel' on p358.

Loans

A loan to you usually counts as money you possess. However, in some limited circumstances you can argue that a loan should be disregarded (see p357). If you lend someone money, see p357.

Part 3: General rules for means-tested benefits
Chapter 18: Capital: over pension credit age
4. Disregarded capital

Trusts

Money or property held in a trust for you or your partner is ignored when working out deemed income (see p326). You are not assumed to have a fixed income from the trust.[10] This applies to both discretionary and non-discretionary trusts. However, payments actually made from the trust can be taken into account. If made regularly, payments are treated as income. For discretionary trusts, regular payments are either disregarded in full or in part (see p328). If payments are not made regularly, they are taken into account as capital.

The rules are different if the trust is set up from personal injury payments. Payments made from certain charitable trusts are specifically ignored (see p394).

Payments of personal injury compensation

Any money paid because of a personal injury to you or your partner is ignored whether or not it has been placed into a trust.[11] Neither deemed income (see p326) nor actual income from the fund is taken into account. The capital value is not ignored if it was paid in respect of someone who is no longer a member of your family – eg, because s/he has died.[12] 'Personal injury' includes not only accidental and criminal injury but also any disease and injury as a result of a disease.[13]

Trust funds administered by a court

The value of a trust fund is also ignored where damages are awarded in respect of personal injury and the money paid into a special fund to be administered by a court – eg, the Court of Protection. Payments from these funds are ignored completely, both as capital and income.[14]

---

4. **Disregarded capital**

Some kinds of capital are ignored in the assessment of pension credit (PC) and housing benefit (HB).

Your home

If you own the home you normally live in, its value is ignored.[15]

Your home

Your '**home**' includes any garage, garden, outbuildings and land, together with any premises that you do not occupy as your home but which it is impractical or unreasonable to sell separately – eg, croft land.[16]

This disregard applies to any home in which you are treated as normally living – eg, because you are only temporarily living away from it (see p456). However, if you own more than one property, only the value of the one normally occupied is disregarded under this rule.[17] Exceptionally, two separate properties can be regarded as a single home, as though one was an annexe of the other, if you personally (rather than a member of your family) normally occupy both.[18] This is most likely to be the case for a large family, but other situations are possible where neither property on its own caters for a family's needs – eg, if there is a carer living between two properties.[19]

When the value of the property is disregarded

The value of the property can be disregarded, even if you do not normally live in it, in the following circumstances.

- **If you have left your former home following a marriage or relationship breakdown,** the value of the property is ignored for 26 weeks from the date you left. It may also be disregarded for longer if any of the steps below are taken. If it is occupied by your former partner who is a lone parent, its value is ignored as long as s/he lives there.[20]

- **If you have sought legal advice or have started legal proceedings in order to occupy property as your home,** its value is ignored for 26 weeks from the date you first took either of these steps.[21] The 26 weeks can be extended, if it is reasonable to do so, if you need longer to move into the property.

- **If you are taking reasonable steps to dispose of any property,** its value is ignored for 26 weeks from the date you first took such steps (which may start before you claimed benefit).[22] See p362 for more details.

- **If you are carrying out essential repairs or alterations which are needed so that you can occupy a property as your home,** the value of the property is ignored for 26 weeks from the date you first began to take steps to carry them out.[23] See p363 for more details.

- **If you have acquired a property for occupation as your home but have not yet moved in,** its value is ignored if you intend to live there within 26 weeks of acquiring it.[24] If you cannot move in by then, the value of the property can be ignored for as long as seems reasonable.

- **Any amounts paid to you or deposited in your name for the sole purpose of buying a home for you to live in or carrying out essential repairs or alterations to your home or the home you intend to occupy** are ignored for a year from the date you were paid them.[25] This includes money from the sale of a home that you earmark to buy another place to live in. For PC, if there is an assessed income period (p156) that extends beyond the year's disregard, the rules provide for the disregard to last until the end of that period. However, it is not clear how this applies in all cases. For example, it would not apply if your PC entitlement or assessed income period began only after the year's disregard

Part 3: General rules for means-tested benefits
Chapter 18: Capital: over pension credit age
4. Disregarded capital

had expired. Arguably, it should apply in other cases where there is an assessed income period.[26]

- **Any compensation paid under an insurance policy because of loss or damage to your home** is ignored for a year from the date it is paid to you.[27] For PC, if there is an assessed income period, it can be disregarded until the end of that period in the same way as explained in the bullet point above.

When considering whether to increase the period of any disregard, all the circumstances should be considered – eg, your personal circumstances, any efforts made by you to use or dispose of the home[28] and the general state of the market. In practice, periods of around 18 months are not considered unusual.

It is possible for property to be ignored under more than one of the above paragraphs in succession.[29]

The home of a former partner or relative

The value of a home (see p390) is ignored if it is occupied wholly or partly as her/his home by:[30]

- a relative of yours or of your partner (see p365 for who this includes) who is over the qualifying age for PC (see p147) or is incapacitated (see below);[31]
- your former partner from whom you are not estranged, divorced or out of a civil partnership – eg, if one of you is living in a care home;
- your former partner from whom you are estranged, divorced or out of a civil partnership if s/he is a lone parent. If s/he is not a lone parent, the value of the home is ignored for 26 weeks from the date you ceased to live in the home.[32]

Incapacitated
'Incapacitated' is not defined, but guidance suggests it refers to someone who is getting an incapacity or disability benefit, or who is sufficiently incapacitated to qualify for one of those benefits.[33] However, you should argue for a broader interpretation, if necessary.

Personal possessions

All personal possessions, including items such as jewellery, furniture or a car, are ignored.[34]

Compensation paid under an insurance policy for damage to, or loss of, your personal possessions is ignored for a year from the date you were paid the compensation or, for PC only, until the end of the assessed income period (if there is one) if that is longer.[35]

Business assets

If you are self-employed, your business assets are ignored for as long as you continue to work in that business.[36] If you cannot work because of physical or mental illness, but intend to work in the business when you are able, the disregard operates for 26 weeks from the date of claim, or for longer if reasonable in the circumstances.[37] For more about this, see p365.

Insurance policy and annuity surrender values

The surrender value of any life assurance policy is ignored.[38] Some investments include an element of life insurance – eg, endowment policies. If the policy terms include how the payment on death is calculated, the whole investment is ignored.[39] However, you cannot choose to put money into such an investment in order to increase your benefit entitlement, because you are likely to be caught by the notional capital rule if you do (see p395).

The surrender value of any annuity is also ignored for the purposes of the deemed income rule (see p326). Any actual income the surrender value generates for you, and which is not disregarded as income, can be taken into account as income.[40] Any payment under the annuity counts as income (but see p328 for when this is ignored).[41]

Future interests in property

A future interest in most kinds of property is ignored.[42] A **'future interest'** is one which will only revert to you, or become yours for the first time, when some future event occurs. For more about this, see below.

The right to receive a payment in the future

If you know you will receive a payment in the future, you could sell your right to that payment at any time, so it has a market value and therefore constitutes an actual capital resource. The value of this is ignored for some types of payment (see first four bullet points listed on p366).[43]

Benefits and other payments

Arrears of specified benefits (see p394) are ignored:[44]
- for one year after they are received by you; *or*
- for PC, if there is an assessed income period that extends beyond the year's disregard (p156). The rules provide for the disregard to last until the end of that period. However, it is not clear how this applies in all cases. For example, it does not apply if your PC entitlement or assessed income period began only after the year's disregard had expired.[45] Arguably, it should apply in other cases where there is an assessed income period;[46] *or*
- for the remainder of the PC or HB award if the payment is £5,000 or more for arrears or late payment of a specified benefit (see p394), which was made to compensate for an official error, and which you received in full since becoming entitled to PC or HB. If you got the compensation before then, it is still

Part 3: General rules for means-tested benefits
Chapter 18: Capital: over pension credit age
4. Disregarded capital

disregarded if your current award follows immediately from a previous award of income support (IS), income-based jobseeker's allowance (JSA), income-related employment and support allowance (ESA), universal credit (UC), HB or council tax benefit (CTB) (or PC for current awards of HB) in which the compensation was disregarded, or it is still being disregarded in an award of one of those benefits.

Specified benefits
The '**specified benefits**' are:
– attendance allowance, bereavement support payment, disability living allowance, personal independence payment, armed forces independence payment, income-based JSA, income-related ESA, IS, UC, PC, HB, CTB, child tax credit, constant attendance allowance and exceptionally severe disablement allowance;
– for PC only, child benefit and social fund payments;
– for HB only, working tax credit and discretionary housing payments;
– concessionary payments (ie, compensation) made instead of any of the above benefits or payments made in lieu of any of these benefits.

Also ignored for one year (or, for PC, to the end of the assessed income period) from when you get the payments are:
• local welfare provision payments;
• refunds of council tax, including from the council tax reduction scheme;
• payments under the Supporting People programme;
• arrears of a supplementary pension to war widows, widowers or surviving civil partners for pre-1973 service.

The initial lump sum of bereavement support payment is ignored for 52 weeks from when you get the payment.

Ignored indefinitely are:[47]
• the lump-sum state retirement pension if you deferred your pension and chose a lump sum rather than increased income;
• community care or health direct payments;
• payments from a local authority to a young person in Scotland aged 16 or over in 'continuing care' or passed to you by the young person if s/he still lives with you and was in your care;
• for HB, direct payments under an education, health and care plan, paid in England for a child with special educational needs.

Charitable and personal injury payments

• **Personal injury payments.** Any money paid because of a personal injury to you or your partner is ignored (see p390).

- **Special compensation schemes.** Any payment of capital (or income) from certain special schemes approved or set up by government are ignored if they are, for example:[48]
  - for you or your partner who has variant CJD (Creutzfeldt-Jakob disease). If you are the parent of someone with variant CJD, the payment is ignored for two years;
  - from a specified infected blood payment scheme. You can give money from the payment to your partner and it is ignored indefinitely in her/his benefit claim or, if you have no partner or children, to your parent and it is ignored for two years;
  - compensation for the London bombings in July 2005;
  - World War Two compensation (rather than a war pension) if you, your partner or deceased spouse or civil partner were interned as a prisoner of war in Japan, lost a child, suffered injury or forced labour or lost property.

Funeral plan payments

The value of any funeral plan contract is ignored indefinitely.[49]

A funeral plan contract is a contract under which:
- you make at least one payment to another person;
- that person undertakes to ensure you are provided with a funeral; *and*
- the sole purpose of the plan is to ensure you are provided with a funeral.

Payments in other currencies

Any payment in a currency other than sterling is taken into account after disregarding banking charges or commission payable on conversion.[50]

5. Notional capital

In certain circumstances, you are treated as having capital which you do not have. This is called **'notional capital'**.[51] There is a similar rule for notional income (see p330).

You are treated as having notional capital if you:
- deliberately deprive yourself of capital in order to claim or increase benefit (see p396);
- are in a position like a sole trader or a partner in a business (see p396).

Notional capital counts in the same way as capital you do have, except that a 'diminishing notional capital rule' (see p373) may be applied so that the value of the notional capital you are treated as having is considered to reduce over time.

Part 3: General rules for means-tested benefits
Chapter 18: Capital: over pension credit age
6. How capital is valued

Deliberately getting rid of capital

If you deliberately get rid of capital in order to claim or increase your benefit, you are treated as still having it (see p371).[52] You are not treated as having deprived yourself of capital if:

- you pay off or reduce a debt which you owe; *or*
- you pay for goods or services if the purchase of those goods or services was reasonable in the circumstances of your case.

Diminishing notional capital

The diminishing notional capital rule applies if you are treated as having notional capital because of depriving yourself of capital.

If you are getting pension credit (PC), the amount of the notional capital goes down each week by the extra PC you are losing because of the notional capital.[53] For example, if your notional capital is £11,000, you have £2 a week less PC because of 'deemed income' (see p327) so £2 a week is deducted from the notional capital until it reaches £10,500 when it will be £1 a week.

If you are not getting any PC, notional capital goes down, not just by the amount of PC you would have had, but also by any additional housing benefit (HB) you would have had if notional capital had not been taken into account. Ask the DWP for a forecast of when it is worth claiming again. If in doubt, you can claim every 26 weeks (but not more often).

For HB, the same rule applies to reduce your notional capital except that, not only is it reduced by the amount of HB you are losing because of the notional capital, but it is also reduced by any PC you would have been entitled to (or income-based jobseeker's allowance or income-related employment and support allowance), whether or not you are currently getting HB.[54]

Companies run by sole traders or a few partners

The value of shares you hold is normally taken into account, but not if you are treated as a sole owner or partner in the business. Instead, your share of the value of the company itself counts. See p377 – the rules are the same except that local authorities have no discretion but are obliged to follow these rules.[55]

6. **How capital is valued**

There are a number of issues to consider when valuing capital.
- **Market value.** Capital is valued at its current market or surrender value,[56] which could be very low if it is difficult to sell. See p377 for more information.
- **Expenses of sale.** If there would be expenses involved in selling your capital, 10 per cent is deducted from its value for the cost of sale.[57]

- **Debts.** Deductions are made from the 'gross' value of your capital for any debt or mortgage secured on it.[58] For more information, see p378.
- **Capital that is jointly owned under a joint tenancy.** If you jointly own any capital asset (except as a partner in a company, when the rules explained on p396 apply instead) under a joint tenancy, you are treated as owning an equal share of the asset with all other owners.[59] For example, if two of you own the asset, you are each treated as having a 50 per cent share of it. This rule does not apply, however, if you jointly own the capital asset as 'tenants in common'.[60] For more information, see p378.
- **Treatment of assets after a relationship breakdown.** There are no specific rules about this, but there is some guidance and caselaw (see p379).
- **Shares** are valued at their current market value, less 10 per cent for the cost of sale and after deducting any 'lien' held by brokers for sums owed for the cost of their acquisition and any commission.[61] See p380 for more details.
- **Unit trusts** are valued on the basis of the 'bid' price. No deduction is allowed for the cost of sale because this is already included in the 'bid' price.[62]
- **The right to receive a payment in the future.** The value that is not ignored (see p393) is its market value – ie, what a willing buyer would pay to a willing seller.[63] For something which is not yet realisable, this may be very small.
- **Overseas assets.** If you have assets abroad, and there are no exchange controls or other prohibitions that would prevent you transferring your capital to this country, your assets are valued at their current market or surrender value in that country.[64] If you are not allowed to transfer your capital, you are treated as having capital equal to the amount that a willing buyer in this country would give (which might not be very much).[65] Deduct any debts or mortgage secured on the assets, 10 per cent for any expenses of sale and any charges for converting the payment into sterling.[66]

Notes

1. The capital limits
1 s15(2) SPCA 2002; reg 15(6) SPC Regs
2 Reg 43 HB(SPC) Regs
3 Reg 29(2) HB(SPC) Regs
4 Reg 26 HB(SPC) Regs
5 Reg 27 HB(SPC) Regs

2. Whose capital counts
6 **PC** s5 SPCA 2002
   HB s136(1) SSCBA 1992

3. What counts as capital
7 BP1/P1.71 GM
8 R(IS) 3/93
9 **PC** Reg 2 SS(PAOR) Regs
   HB Reg 74(1) HB(SPC) Regs

Part 3: General rules for means-tested benefits
Chapter 18: Capital: over pension credit age
Notes

10 **PC** Sch 5 para 28 SPC Regs
   HB Sch 6 para 30 HB(SPC) Regs
11 **PC** Sch 5 para 16(1) SPC Regs
   HB Sch 6 para 17(1) HB(SPC) Regs
12 R(IS) 3/03
13 R(SB) 2/89
14 **PC** Schs 4 paras 13 and 14, and 5 para
   16(2) SPC Regs
   HB Schs 5 paras 14 and 15, and 6 para
   17(2) HB(SPC) Regs

4. Disregarded capital
15 **PC** Sch 5 para 1A SPC Regs
   HB Sch 6 para 26 HB(SPC) Regs
16 **PC** Reg 1(2) SPC Regs
   HB Reg 2(1) HB(SPC) Regs
   Both Definition of 'dwelling occupied
   as the home'
17 **PC** Sch 5 para 1A SPC Regs
   HB Sch 6 para 26 HB(SPC) Regs
18 R(JSA) 9/03; R(SB) 10/89
19 *MM v SSWP (IS)* [2012] UKUT 358 (AAC)
20 **PC** Sch 5 para 6(1) SPC Regs
   HB Sch 6 para 6(1) HB(SPC) Regs
21 **PC** Sch 5 para 2 SPC Regs
   HB Sch 6 para 2 HB(SPC) Regs
22 **PC** Sch 5 para 7 SPC Regs
   HB Sch 6 para 7 HB(SPC) Regs
   Both CIS/6908/1995; R(IS) 4/97
23 **PC** Sch 5 para 3 SPC Regs
   HB Sch 6 para 3 HB(SPC) Regs
24 **PC** Sch 5 para 1 SPC Regs
   HB Sch 6 para 1 HB(SPC) Regs
25 **PC** Sch 5 paras 17 and 19 SPC Regs
   HB Sch 6 paras 18 and 20 HB(SPC) Regs
26 *DG v SSWP (SPC)* [2010] UKUT 241
   (AAC). But see CPC/206/2005 and CPC/
   1928/2005, which suggest an assessed
   income period could be reduced on
   revision in some cases.
27 **PC** Sch 5 paras 17 and 18 SPC Regs
   HB Sch 6 paras 18 and 19 HB(SPC) Regs
28 CIS/4757/2003
29 CIS/6908/1995
30 **PC** Sch 5 para 4 SPC Regs
   HB Sch 6 para 4 HB(SPC) Regs
31 **PC** Reg 1(2) SPC Regs
   HB Reg 2(1) HB(SPC) Regs
   Both Definition of 'close relative'
32 **PC** Sch 5 para 6 SPC Regs
   HB Sch 6 para 6 HB(SPC) Regs
33 **PC** para 84444 DMG
   HB para BP1, Annex A1.01 GM
34 **PC** Sch 5 para 8 SPC Regs
   HB Sch 6 para 8 HB(SPC) Regs
35 **PC** Sch 5 paras 17 and 18 SPC Regs
   HB Sch 6 paras 18 and 19 HB(SPC) Regs

36 **PC** Sch 5 para 9 SPC Regs
   HB Sch 6 para 9 HB(SPC) Regs
37 **PC** Sch 5 para 9A SPC Regs
   HB Sch 6 para 10 HB(SPC) Regs
38 **PC** Sch 5 para 10 SPC Regs
   HB Sch 6 para 11 HB(SPC) Regs
39 R(IS) 7/98
40 **PC** Sch 5 para 26 SPC Regs
   HB Sch 6 para 29 HB Regs
41 **PC** s15(1)(d) SPCA 2002
   HB Reg 29(1)(d) HB(SPC) Regs
   Both R(IS) 10/01
42 **PC** Sch 5 para 5 SPC Regs
   HB Sch 6 para 5 HB(SPC) Regs
43 **PC** Sch 5 paras 22 and 24-26 SPC Regs
   HB Sch 6 paras 24 and 27-29 HB(SPC)
   Regs
44 **PC** Sch 5 paras 17, 20, 20A and 20B SPC
   Regs
   HB Sch 6 paras 18, 21, 22 and 26B
   HB(SPC) Regs
45 *DG v SSWP(SPC)* [2010] UKUT 241
   (AAC)
46 But see CPC/206/2005 and CPC/1928/
   2005, which suggest that an assessed
   income period could be reduced on
   revision in some cases.
47 **PC** Sch 5 paras 23A, 23AA, 23C and 23D
   SPC Regs
   HB Sch 6 paras 26A, 26AA, 26D, 26F
   and 26G HB(SPC) Regs
48 **PC** Sch 5 paras 12-15 SPC Regs
   HB Sch 6 paras 13-16 HB(SPC) Regs
49 **PC** Sch 5 para 11 SPC Regs
   HB Sch 6 para 12 HB(SPC) Regs
50 **PC** Sch 5 para 21 SPC Regs
   HB Sch 6 para 23 HB(SPC) Regs

5. Notional capital
51 **PC** Reg 21 SPC Regs
   HB Reg 47 HB(SPC) Regs
52 **PC** Reg 21(1) SPC Regs
   HB Reg 47(1) HB(SPC) Regs
53 Reg 22 SPC Regs
54 Reg 48 HB(SPC) Regs
55 **PC** Reg 21(3) and (4) SPC Regs
   HB Reg 47(3) and (4) HB(SPC) Regs

6. How capital is valued
56 **PC** Reg 19(a) SPC Regs
   HB Reg 45(a) HB(SPC) Regs
57 **PC** Reg 19(a) SPC Regs
   HB Reg 45(a) HB(SPC) Regs
58 **PC** Reg 19(b) SPC Regs
   HB Reg 45(b) HB(SPC) Regs
59 **PC** Reg 23 SPC Regs
   HB Reg 49 HB(SPC) Regs
60 R(IS) 4/03

61 **PC** Reg 19(a) SPC Regs
   HB Reg 45(a) HB(SPC) Regs
62 **PC** Vol 14 Ch 84, para 84772 DMG
   HB BP1/P1.530 GM
63 *Peters v CAO* (appendix to R(SB) 3/89)
64 **PC** Reg 20(a) SPC Regs
   HB Reg 46(a) HB(SPC) Regs
65 **PC** Reg 20 SPC Regs
   HB Reg 46(b) HB(SPC) Regs
66 **PC** Sch 5 para 21 SPC Regs
   HB Sch 6 para 23 HB(SPC) Regs

Part 4

Paying for housing

Chapter 19

· ·

Housing benefit rent restrictions

This chapter covers:
1. Which rent restriction rules apply (below)
2. The local housing allowance rules (p407)
3. The social sector rules: the 'bedroom tax' (p415)
4. The local reference rent rules (p420)
5. The pre-January 1996 rules (p428)
6. Common definitions (p433)
7. Delaying a rent restriction (p436)

This chapter covers the rent restriction rules for housing benefit (HB). The rent restriction rules for the universal credit (UC) housing costs element are covered in Chapter 22. However, the rules about local housing allowances for UC are broadly the same as for HB, so these rules are covered in this chapter where relevant.

Key facts

- If you are a private tenant, the rent used to calculate your housing benefit (HB) may be restricted under one of three schemes and your HB may be based on a rent lower than the one you are liable to pay.
- If you are a local authority or housing association tenant and your home has more bedrooms than the rules allow, the rent used to calculate your HB may be restricted under the social sector rules (often called the 'bedroom tax'). In exceptional cases, if you are a housing association tenant, your rent may be restricted under one of the private tenant schemes.
- If your rent is restricted, you may be able to get discretionary housing payments from your local authority to help with any shortfall.

1. Which rent restriction rules apply

There are four rent restriction schemes.
- **The local housing allowance rules** (see p407): your housing benefit (HB) is based on the local housing allowance that is appropriate for you.

Part 4: Paying for housing
Chapter 19: Housing benefit rent restrictions
1. Which rent restriction rules apply

- **The social sector rules, often called the 'bedroom tax'** (see p415): a deduction may be made when calculating your HB if you are considered to have too many bedrooms.
- **The local reference rent rules** (see p420): your HB is based on a rent officer's 'determinations'.
- **The pre-January 1996 rules** (see p428): your HB may be restricted if your home is too large or your rent is too high.

Whether any of the above rent restriction rules apply to you depends on the type of tenancy you have, whether your tenancy is excluded (see p406) and, in some cases, when you claim HB or how long you have lived in your home.

To check whether any of the rent restriction rules apply and, if so, which ones, see below if you are a private tenant, p405 if you are a housing association tenant or p406 if you are a local authority tenant.

Are you thinking of moving home?
If you are getting HB and are considering a move, or there will be a break in your claim, check whether the rules that will apply to you are more or less favourable than at present. If the local reference rent rules will apply, you can find out the rent figure that will be used to calculate your HB from the local authority (see p426). If the local housing allowance rules will apply, you can find out the current rate of the appropriate local housing allowance (see p414).

Private tenants

Work out which rent restriction rules apply if you are a private tenant as follows.
- **Step one:** check whether your tenancy is an excluded tenancy (see p406). If so, none of the rent restriction rules apply.
- **Step two:** if your tenancy is not an excluded tenancy and you make a new claim for HB or move on or after 7 April 2008:
  - if you live in 'exempt accommodation' (see p428), the pre-January 1996 rules apply. In limited cases, they also apply if you are an 'exempt claimant' (see p428);
  - if your rent includes board and attendance, or you live in a hostel, houseboat, mobile home or caravan, the local reference rent rules apply. They may also apply in other situations if the local authority considers your rent to be unreasonably high or your accommodation to be unreasonably large (see p420).

In all other cases, the local housing allowance rules may apply.

Note: if your HB was restricted under any of the rules that applied before 7 April 2008, it continues to be restricted under those rules until there is a break in your claim or you move to a new home. If any of the rent restriction rules apply to you at that point, your HB is restricted under the rules that then apply.

Example

Daniel lives in a private rented flat with his partner and child. He has been getting HB since October 2005. This was being restricted under the local reference rent rules. When his partner had a baby in 2013, they moved to a two-bedroom private rented house. The local authority reassessed Daniel's HB claim using the local housing allowance rules.

Housing association tenants

Work out which rent restriction rules apply if you are a housing association tenant as follows.

- **Step one:** check whether your tenancy is an excluded tenancy (see p406). If so, the local housing allowance rules, the local reference rent rules and the pre-January 1996 rules do not apply. However, the social sector rules (the 'bedroom tax') may apply if neither you nor your partner are at least the qualifying age for pension credit (PC).
- **Step two:** if your tenancy is *not* an excluded tenancy and you make a new claim for HB or move on or after 7 April 2008:
  - if you live in 'exempt accommodation' (see p428), the pre-January 1996 rules apply. In limited cases, they also apply if you are an 'exempt claimant' (see p428);
  - if your rent includes board and attendance, or if you live in a hostel, houseboat, mobile home or caravan, the local reference rent rules apply. They *may* also apply in other situations if the local authority considers your rent to be unreasonably high or your accommodation to be unreasonably large (see p420).

  In all other cases, the local housing allowance rules may apply. **Note:** the local housing allowance rules and the pre-January 1996 rules generally only apply to private tenants.
- **Step three:** if the local housing allowance rules, the local reference rent rules and the pre-January 1996 rules do not apply, and neither you nor your partner are at least the qualifying age for PC, check whether the social sector rules apply.

Note: if your HB was restricted under any of the rules that applied before 7 April 2008, it continues to be restricted under those rules until there is a break in your claim or you move to a new home. If any of the rent restriction rules apply to you at that point, your HB is restricted under the rules that then apply.

Part 4: Paying for housing
Chapter 19: Housing benefit rent restrictions
1. Which rent restriction rules apply

Local authority tenants

If you are a local authority tenant, the social sector rules (the 'bedroom tax') may apply if neither you nor your partner are at least the qualifying age for PC (see p415). If you are at least the qualifying age for PC, the pre-January 1996 rules may, in exceptional cases, apply (see p428). **Note:** before 3 March 2014, the pre-January 1996 rules could apply to claimants of any age.

Excluded tenancies

If you are a private or local authority tenant and have an excluded tenancy, the local housing allowance rules, the local reference rent rules and the pre-January 1996 rules do not apply to you. However, if your landlord is a registered housing association, and neither you nor your partner are at least the qualifying age for PC, the social sector rules may apply to you (see p415).

The following are excluded tenancies:[1]

- a regulated or protected tenancy – ie, a tenancy entered into before 15 January 1989 or, in Scotland, 2 January 1989;
- a tenancy in an approved bail or probation hostel. However, if you are required to live in such a hostel, you cannot qualify for HB towards the rent you pay to the hostel (see p51);
- a housing action trust tenancy;
- a former local authority or new town letting which has been transferred to a new owner. However, your tenancy is not excluded if there has been a rent increase since the transfer and:
  - the local authority considers your rent to be unreasonably high; *or*
  - if the transfer took place before 7 October 2002, the local authority considers your accommodation to be unreasonably large.
  If this is the case, the local reference rent rules apply;
- a shared ownership tenancy – ie, you are buying part of your house or flat and renting the rest. However, your tenancy is not excluded if your shared ownership tenancy is with a private landlord, in which case the local housing allowance rules may apply (see p407);
- a letting by a registered housing association,[2] by a county council (if you live in a caravan or mobile home provided on a travellers' site[3]) or in a caravan, mobile home or houseboat (if you are also liable to make payments to a local authority – eg, for site or mooring fees). However, your tenancy is not excluded if:
  - the local authority considers your rent to be unreasonably high; *or*
  - you or your partner are at least the qualifying age for PC and neither of you are getting income support, income-based jobseeker's allowance or income-related employment and support allowance (or universal credit) and the local authority considers your accommodation to be unreasonably large.
  In both cases, the local reference rent rules apply.

If none of the rent restriction rules apply

If none of the rent restriction rules apply to you, the local authority still has discretion to decrease your eligible rent to an amount it considers 'appropriate'.[4] It should have evidence which justifies doing so and must exercise its discretion properly. All the circumstances should be taken into account, including your health and financial circumstances, the special housing-related needs of anyone occupying your home and whether alternative accommodation is available to HB claimants.[5] Local authorities should rarely use their powers to decrease your HB in this way. If your HB is reduced under this rule, apply for a revision or appeal (see Chapters 54 and 55).

Do the local housing allowance or local reference rent rules apply?

The local authority may say that it can decrease your eligible rent even if the local housing allowance or the local reference rent rules apply.[6] However, you can argue that the local authority can only use its discretion to decrease your eligible rent if it has been determined under the normal HB rules.[7]

2. The local housing allowance rules

If the local housing allowance rules apply, they determine the amount of rent used to calculate your housing benefit (HB) – called your 'maximum rent' in this *Handbook*.

Your maximum rent may be lower than the rent you must pay and can never exceed the local housing allowance that is appropriate for you based on the number of bedrooms the rules allow (see p408).

The local housing allowance rules apply if, on or after 7 April 2008, you:[8]

- claim HB; *or*
- move to a new home while you are entitled to HB; *or*
- live in a former 'pathfinder' area and the pilot local housing allowance rules applied to you before that date. In this case, you may have transitional protection (see p437).

The local housing allowance rules can apply if you are a private tenant, including if you have a shared ownership tenancy with a private landlord. They can also apply if you are a housing association tenant, but not if your landlord is a registered social landlord (in Wales or Scotland) or a non-profit or 'profit-making registered provider of social housing' (in England). If your landlord is a profit-making registered provider of social housing, your accommodation must be available at a rent below the market rate.[9]

Part 4: Paying for housing
Chapter 19: Housing benefit rent restrictions
2. The local housing allowance rules

Note:
- These rules *never* apply if you are a local authority tenant.
- These rules do *not* apply if you have an excluded tenancy (see p406), or if the local reference rent or the pre-January 1996 rules apply.

Maximum rent

Your 'maximum rent' for HB purposes is the appropriate local housing allowance for you (see below) or, if lower, your 'cap rent'.[10] The local authority might call this your 'maximum rent (LHA)'. The 'eligible rent' used to calculate your HB (see p62) is your maximum rent.[11]

Cap rent

Your **'cap rent'** is the rent you are liable, or treated as liable, to pay for your home (including service charges).[12] If you share accommodation with anyone other than your partner and you are jointly liable for the rent with her/him, the local authority apportions the cap rent between you.

The local authority may say it has general discretion to decrease your cap rent to an amount it considers appropriate (but see p407).

Note:
- If you share accommodation and are jointly liable for the rent (eg, you are joint tenants) with someone other than your partner (or a child included in your claim), and you are not members of the same household, your maximum rent is based on the local housing allowance that applies to you (see below), subject to the cap rent rule.
- A rent restriction can be delayed in specified circumstances (see p436).

Examples

Phil, aged 28, shares a privately rented house with four friends. Phil claims HB. The rent for the house is £300 a week. His cap rent is £60 (£300 ÷ 5).

Mary and her partner Jim have a joint tenancy of a private flat with Mary's cousin. Mary claims HB. The rent for the flat is £210 a week. Mary and Jim pay two-thirds of the rent because they have a bigger room. The local authority decides that Mary's cap rent is £140 (£210 ÷ 3 x 2).

Which local housing allowance is appropriate

The local housing allowance that is appropriate for you depends on the area in which you live and the category of dwelling that applies to you. To establish the category of dwelling that applies (see p411), you must first know how many bedrooms you are allowed under what are known as the 'size criteria' (see below).

Note: the rules for the universal credit (UC) housing costs element are also covered in this section. For UC, the rules on the categories of dwelling (see p411) and the local housing allowance rates (see p413) are broadly the same as for HB. These sections and the endnotes, therefore, also refer to UC rules. However, the UC rules for the number of bedrooms allowed are different from those for HB. For these, see p503.

The number of bedrooms you are allowed for housing benefit

For HB, you are allowed (up to a maximum of four bedrooms):[13]

- one bedroom for each of the following 'occupiers', each coming only into the first category for which s/he is eligible:
  - a couple (see p215 for who counts);
  - a 'member of a couple who cannot share a bedroom' (see p433 for who counts);
  - a member of a couple whose partner is a 'member of a couple who cannot share a bedroom';[14]
  - a person aged 16 or over;
  - a 'child who cannot share a bedroom' (see p433 for who counts);
  - two children under 16 of the same sex;
  - two children under 10;
  - a child under 16; *and*
- one or two additional bedrooms in specified situations (see p410).

Note: you are only allowed a bedroom for a 'child who cannot share a bedroom' or a 'member of a couple who cannot share a bedroom' if you have a bedroom in your home that is additional to those you would be allowed if the child or the member of the couple *were* able to share a bedroom. 'Bedroom' is not defined, but see p435 for what may count.

For the local housing allowance rules, an '**occupier**' is:[15]

- you and anyone else living in the dwelling who the local authority is satisfied occupies your dwelling as a home (other than a joint tenant who is not a member of your household). If you are a joint tenant with someone (other than your partner or a child included in your claim) and you are not members of the same household, your maximum rent is based on the local housing allowance that applies to you, subject to the cap rent (see p408);
- your (or your partner's) son, daughter, stepson or stepdaughter who is in the armed forces deployed on operations who was your non-dependant (see p67) before being deployed, provided s/he intends to return home.

'Occupiers' therefore include not only your partner and children, but also other people – eg, a joint tenant who *is* a member of your household, a non-dependant

Part 4: Paying for housing
Chapter 19: Housing benefit rent restrictions
2. The local housing allowance rules

or a live-in carer. However, a foster child or child placed with you for adoption under specified provisions does not count as an occupier, but you may qualify for an additional bedroom if you or your partner are a 'qualifying parent or carer' (see p434).[16]

You can argue that someone is an 'occupier' if s/he normally lives with you, but is temporarily away.[17] However, if you share the care of a child, the child is considered to be occupying the home of the parent with whom s/he normally lives.[18] **Note:** the local authority may use the rules described on p53 to decide whether someone counts as occupying your home.

Examples

Bill and Sarah have two sons, both under age 10. Sarah's nephew, aged 20, lives with them. They claim HB. They are allowed three bedrooms under the size criteria: one for Bill and Sarah, one for the sons and one for the nephew. The appropriate local housing allowance is that for a dwelling with three bedrooms.

Terry, aged 40, lives with his father in the same household. They are joint tenants. The rent for the flat is £300 a week. Terry works part time and earns £200 a week after deductions of tax and national insurance contributions. He claims HB.

The appropriate local housing allowance is that for a two-bedroom dwelling (£250) – see p408. Terry's cap rent is £150 (£300 ÷ 2). His maximum rent (and his eligible rent) is therefore £150, as this figure is lower than the local housing allowance.

Terry has no non-dependants. Therefore, his maximum HB is £150.

His applicable amount is £73.10 (the standard amount for a single person aged 25 or over).

His income to be taken into account is £195 a week (£5 of his earnings are disregarded).

The difference between his income and his applicable amount is £121.90.

65% x £121.90 = £79.24 a week.

Terry's HB is therefore £150 – £79.24 = £70.76 a week.

Additional bedrooms

You are allowed one additional bedroom if you satisfy one of the following conditions. If you satisfy both, you are allowed two additional bedrooms.[19]

- **Non-resident carer.** If you (or your partner), a person who occupies your dwelling as a home (eg, your child or a non-dependant) or a child or young person in respect of whom you or your partner are a 'qualifying parent or carer' (eg, your foster child) are a 'person who requires overnight care' (see p434 for who counts), you are allowed one additional bedroom for a non-resident carer. Even if more than one person requires overnight care, only one additional bedroom is allowed.

- **Adoption, fostering and kinship care.** If you (or your partner) are a 'qualifying parent or carer' (ie, certain foster parents and people with whom a child has been placed for adoption – see p434 for who counts), you are allowed one additional bedroom. Even if you (or your partner) have more than one foster child or child placed with you for adoption, only one additional bedroom is allowed.

Note:
- The rules were amended from 1 April 2017 to allow an additional bedroom for people living with you who require overnight care. If you were already getting HB on that date and had not been allowed an additional bedroom, the local authority should reassess your HB claim and pay you any arrears due. The government says that arrears can only be backdated to 1 April 2017. You should argue this is wrong and get advice.[20]
- There are a number of other situations when you may need more bedrooms than shown above – eg, if you need an additional room to store equipment required because of a severe disability, or if you live in a dwelling adapted for you under a 'sanctuary scheme', or if you share the care of your child, but s/he counts as normally living with her/his other parent. You should appeal if you are affected, but your appeal may be held up while the courts are considering other cases.[21]

See CPAG's online service and *Welfare Rights Bulletin* for updates.

Example
Seamus and Elaine are the foster parents of two children. Their non-dependent son, aged 24, lives with them. They are allowed three bedrooms under the size criteria: one for Seamus and Elaine, one for their son and one additional room because they are each a 'qualifying parent or carer'. The appropriate local housing allowance is that for a dwelling with three bedrooms.

Categories of dwelling

The category of dwelling that applies to you depends on how many bedrooms you are allowed (see p409) and whether or not you are living in shared accommodation.

One-bedroom shared accommodation

The one-bedroom shared accommodation category of dwelling applies if you are only allowed one bedroom under the size criteria (eg, if you do not have any children, you are not a 'person who requires overnight care' (see p434) or a 'qualifying parent or carer' (see p434)) and:[22]
- you are under 35 (even if you do not live in shared accommodation). See p412 for exceptions. **Note:** for UC, this category also applies if you are a member of a couple but are claiming as a single person (see p161); *or*

Part 4: Paying for housing
Chapter 19: Housing benefit rent restrictions
2. The local housing allowance rules

- for HB only, you (and your partner) live in shared accommodation. You count as living in shared accommodation if you do not have the exclusive use of at least two rooms, or the exclusive use of one room as well as the exclusive use of a bathroom, a toilet and a kitchen or facilities for cooking. See below for exceptions.

There are exceptions to the rule. This category of dwelling does not apply (even if you live in shared accommodation) if:[23]

- you have a non-dependant living with you (see p67 for HB and p501 for UC); *or*
- for HB only, you (or your partner) qualify for a severe disability premium; *or*
- for UC only, you are getting attendance allowance, the middle or highest rate of the disability living allowance care component, the daily living component of personal independence payment or armed forces independence payment; *or*
- you are under the age of 22 and:
  - were provided with accommodation by the local authority under specified provisions. For UC only, you must be at least 18 and must have counted as looked after by a local authority before you were 18 (see p937).[24] **Note:** in some cases, you cannot claim HB or get the UC housing costs element if you are being, or were previously, looked after by a local authority (see p937); *or*
  - for HB only:
    - were looked after by (in the care of), or under the supervision of, a local authority under specific legal provisions after you turned 16; *or*
    - ceased to be subject to a compulsory supervision order under section 83 of the Children's Hearings (Scotland) Act 2011 which had continued after you turned 16. **Note:** there are exceptions; *or*
- you are a single claimant aged at least 25 and:
  - have been living in a hostel for homeless people for three months or more (this does not have to be continuous) and while living there you have accepted support services to assist you in being rehabilitated or resettled in the community; *or*
  - are an offender subject to specific multi-agency risk management arrangements. For UC, you do not have to be at least 25.

Note: if the shared accommodation category of dwelling does not apply to you, the DWP says that your HB should be based on the local housing allowance for one-bedroom self-contained accommodation.[25] This applies even if you live in shared accommodation.

One-bedroom self-contained accommodation

The one-bedroom self-contained accommodation category of dwelling applies if you are allowed one bedroom under the size criteria (see p409).[26] For UC only, it must be reasonable for you to occupy this category of accommodation.[27]

For HB only, you must have:

- the exclusive use of at least two rooms; *or*
- the exclusive use of one room as well as the exclusive use of a bathroom, a toilet and a kitchen or facilities for cooking.

You have the 'exclusive use' of a room if you have the legal right to exclude others from the room.[28]

Rooms

'Room' for HB means a bedroom or a 'room suitable for living in', other than one you share with someone who is not a member of your household, a non-dependant or someone who pays rent to you or your partner.[29]

Dwellings with two or more bedrooms

If you are allowed more than one bedroom under the size criteria, the category of dwelling that applies is that for a dwelling with the number of bedrooms you are allowed (see p409 for HB and p503 for UC), up to a maximum of four.[30] So this category applies, for example, if you are a lone parent or a member of a couple with children, you have a non-dependant living with you, you are a 'person who requires overnight care', someone who lives with you is a 'member of a couple who cannot share a bedroom', you are a 'qualifying parent or carer' (see p434 for who counts), or (for HB) you are a joint tenant with someone who is a member of your household. For UC only, it must be reasonable for you to occupy this category of accommodation, taking into account the number of people in your 'extended benefit unit' (see p501 for who counts).[31]

Local housing allowance rates

Local housing allowances for each category of dwelling are set by the rent officer annually on the last working day of January, to take effect the following April. A local housing allowance is usually the lowest of two figures:[32]

- the amount of rent at the 30th percentile point of local market rents for assured tenancies in what is known as a 'broad rental market area'; *or*
- the local housing allowance rate determined on 30 January 2015 (or the rate as amended if the rent officer made an error in specified circumstances).

However, for some categories of dwelling in some specified areas (where rents are known to be higher), a local housing allowance is the rate determined on 30 January 2015 (or the rate as amended if the rent officer made an error in specified circumstances) increased by 3 per cent, up to a set maximum.[33]

Part 4: Paying for housing
Chapter 19: Housing benefit rent restrictions
2. The local housing allowance rules

How long a maximum rent applies

Your maximum rent is based on the local housing allowance that is appropriate at the time your claim is assessed. Your HB is paid on this basis until the next time the local authority assesses your claim.[34] This is usually only annually (on 1 April), even if the amount of the local housing allowance changes. When the local authority reassesses your claim, it uses the local housing allowance that is then appropriate. Some changes of circumstance can lead to an earlier reassessment – ie, if:[35]

- there is a change in the category of dwelling that applies to you (see p411) – ie, you are allowed more or fewer bedrooms because, for instance, someone has moved in with you or has moved out, or your child has reached aged 16 and is allowed her/his own bedroom; *or*
- your partner or a child included in your claim (see p220) (or a relative of yours or your partner who lives in the same accommodation as you without a separate right to do so) dies; *or*
- there is a change that affects the amount of your cap rent – eg, the rent you pay goes up or down; *or*
- you move to a new home.

Your maximum rent is then based on the local housing allowance that is appropriate on the date of the change.[36] However, you may qualify for a protected rate of HB (transitional protection) if you live in a former 'pathfinder' area (see p437).

Example
Cleo rents a three-bedroom house from a private landlord. She pays £170 a week rent. She has one son, aged seven. The appropriate local housing allowance is that for a dwelling with two bedrooms. When she claims income support and HB, this is £105. Cleo's maximum rent (and eligible rent) is £105. Cleo has no non-dependants, so this is also her maximum HB and, therefore, her weekly HB.
Cleo's Aunt Sue comes to live with her. As there has been a change in the category of dwelling that applies to Cleo (this is now a dwelling with three bedrooms), the local authority reassesses her claim. The local housing allowance for a dwelling with three bedrooms is now £158. Cleo's maximum rent (and eligible rent) is £158. Aunt Sue is on incapacity benefit, so a non-dependant deduction of £14.80 must be made. Cleo's maximum HB, and therefore her HB, is £143.20 a week (£158 – £14.80).

If you are considering renting accommodation

If you are considering renting accommodation privately, you are likely to claim benefit and the local housing allowance rules apply, you may want to find out the rent figure that will be used to calculate it. If you are already claiming benefit, you may wish to find out the rent figure that will be used when your claim is reassessed (usually annually).

Check which category of dwelling applies to you (see p411) and work out the appropriate local housing allowance. Then check the amount of the appropriate local housing allowance in your area at http://lha-direct.voa.gov.uk/search.aspx.

Challenging a rent restriction

You cannot appeal against the amount of the local housing allowance. However, you *can* appeal against local authority decisions about your award of HB which involve the local housing allowance – ie, you can challenge the factual basis on which a particular local housing allowance was used, such as whether the local housing allowance for one-bedroom shared accommodation applies to you or whether someone occupies accommodation with you.[37]

3. The social sector rules: the 'bedroom tax'

If you are a social sector tenant (ie, you are a local authority or housing association tenant, not a private tenant), the social sector rules may apply if you are living in accommodation that has more bedrooms than you are allowed under what are known as the 'size criteria' (see p418).[38] If the social sector rules apply, they determine the amount of rent used to calculate your housing benefit (HB) – called your 'maximum rent' in this *Handbook*. These rules are commonly referred to as the 'bedroom tax', or by the DWP as the 'removal of the spare room subsidy' or the 'under-occupation charge'.

The social sector rules do *not* apply if:[39]

- you or your partner are at least the qualifying age for pension credit (see p147);
- the local housing allowance rules, the local reference rent rules or the pre-January 1996 rules apply (see p407, p420 and p428). **Note:** the pre-January 1996 rules can only apply in exceptional cases. The local housing allowance rules and the local reference rent rules *never* apply if you are a local authority tenant;
- your tenancy is one of the excluded tenancies listed on p406 (other than the last one), and your landlord is *not* a registered housing association;
- you have a shared ownership tenancy – ie, you are buying part of your house or flat and renting the rest;
- your rent is for mooring charges for a houseboat or for caravan or for mobile home site fees;
- you live in specified types of temporary accommodation for homeless people provided by a local authority or a registered housing association.

Note: if the pre-January 1996 rules apply to you (ie, you are an 'exempt claimant' or live in 'exempt accommodation'), the social sector rules do *not* apply.

Part 4: Paying for housing
Chapter 19: Housing benefit rent restrictions
3. The social sector rules: the 'bedroom tax'

Maximum rent

If you (and your partner) are the only people liable for the rent for your home, your 'maximum rent' is determined under the following steps.[40] The local authority may call this your 'maximum rent (social sector)'. The 'eligible rent' used to calculate your HB (see p62) is your maximum rent.[41] **Note:** if you are jointly liable for the rent with someone other than your partner (ie, with a joint tenant), see p417.

- **Step one:** establish the number of bedrooms in your home. 'Bedroom' is not defined, but see p435 for what may count.
- **Step two:** work out how many bedrooms you are allowed for all the people who occupy your home (see p418).
- **Step three:** calculate your eligible rent under the normal rules (see p62). This is the contractual rent for the whole dwelling minus any ineligible service charges. If the number of bedrooms in your home is the same as or lower than the number in Step two, this is your maximum rent.
- **Step four:** if you have more bedrooms in your home than the number in Step two, your maximum rent is the amount in Step three, reduced by:
  - 14 per cent, if you have one too many bedrooms; *or*
  - 25 per cent if you have at least two too many bedrooms.

If it appears to the local authority that the amount in Step four is still too high to be met by HB, it has a general discretion to reduce your maximum rent further.[42]

Note: a restriction can be delayed in specified circumstances (see p436).

Have you signed a tenancy agreement after 1 April 2016?

If you sign a new social sector tenancy agreement, or renew your agreement, after 1 April 2016, the government says that, from 1 April 2019, the amount of rent your HB can cover will be capped at the local housing allowance that would apply under the local housing allowence rules (see p408). This cap will also apply to all tenants in supported accommodation from that date. See CPAG's online service and *Welfare Rights Bulletin* for updates.

Examples

Raj and Indira rent a two-bedroom flat from a housing association. Their rent is £140 a week. Raj works part time and earns £200 a week after deductions of tax and national insurance. Indira claims HB. Under the size criteria, they are allowed one bedroom. They therefore have one too many bedrooms.

14% x £140 = £19.60. Therefore, Indira's maximum rent (and her eligible rent) is £120.40 (£140 − £19.60). She has no non-dependants. Therefore, her maximum HB is £120.40. Her applicable amount is £114.85 (the standard amount for a couple).

The income to be taken into account is £190 a week (£10 of Raj's earnings are disregarded). The difference between income and her applicable amount is, therefore, £75.15.
65% x £75.15 = £48.85 a week.
Indira's HB is, therefore, £120.40 – £48.85 = £71.55 a week.

Sally is the lone parent of a child aged two. She rents a four-bedroom council house. Her rent is £170 a week. Sally is on income support (IS). Under the size criteria, Sally is allowed two bedrooms (one for her and one for her child). She therefore has two bedrooms too many.
25% x £170 = £42.50. Therefore, Sally's maximum rent (and her eligible rent) is £127.50 (£170 – £42.50). She has no non-dependants. Therefore, her maximum HB is £127.50. Because she is on IS, this is also the amount of HB she is paid.

If you are a joint tenant

If you (and your partner) are liable for the rent with at least one other person (eg, you are a joint tenant with someone other than your partner), the local authority apportions the amount in Step three or Step four (as the case may be) between you, taking into account all the circumstances, including the number of people and the proportion of rent each pays.[43]

Example

Sue and Dave are joint tenants of a four-bedroom council house. They are not a couple. Their rent is £210 a week. Sue pays £140 and Dave pays £70. Sue is an approved foster parent. Dave loses his job and claims income-based jobseeker's allowance (JSA) and HB. Under the size criteria, he is allowed three bedrooms: one for himself, one for Sue and an additional room because Sue counts as a 'qualifying parent or carer'. He therefore has one too many bedrooms.
14% x £210 = £29.40
£210 – £29.40 = £180.60
Dave pays one-third of the rent, and the local authority apportions the maximum rent accordingly. One-third of £180.60 = £60.20
Therefore, Dave's maximum rent (and his eligible rent) is £60.20. He has no non-dependants. Therefore his maximum HB is £60.20.
Because Dave gets income-based JSA, he is automatically passported to maximum HB. His HB is therefore £60.20.
Note: if Sue were also to claim HB, her maximum rent (and eligible rent and maximum HB) would be two-thirds of £180.60 = £120.40

Part 4: Paying for housing
Chapter 19: Housing benefit rent restrictions
3. The social sector rules: the 'bedroom tax'

The number of bedrooms you are allowed

You are allowed:[44]
- one bedroom for each 'occupier' (see below), each coming only into the first category for which s/he is eligible:
  - a couple (see p215 for who counts);
  - a 'member of a couple who cannot share a bedroom (see p433 for who counts);
  - a member of a couple whose partner is a 'member of a couple who cannot share a bedroom';[45]
  - a person who is aged 16 or over;
  - a 'child who cannot share a bedroom' (see p433 for who counts);
  - two children under 16 of the same sex;
  - two children under 10;
  - a child under 16; *and*
- one or more additional bedrooms in specified circumstances (see p418).

Unlike the local housing allowance rules, there is no maximum number of bedrooms.

For the social sector rules, an **'occupier'** is anyone who the local authority is satisfied occupies your dwelling as a home.[46] 'Occupiers' therefore include not only you and your partner or children included in your claim but also other people – eg, a joint tenant, a non-dependant or a live-in carer. However, a foster child or child placed with you for adoption under specified provisions does not count as an occupier, but you may qualify for an additional bedroom if you or your partner (or another person jointly liable for the rent with you) are a 'qualifying parent or carer' (see p434).[47]

Note:
- The local authority must include a member of the armed forces deployed on operations as an occupier if s/he is your (or your partner's) son, daughter, stepson or stepdaughter who was your non-dependant (see p67) before being deployed and s/he intends to return home.[48]
- You can argue that someone counts as occupying your home if s/he normally lives with you but is temporarily away.[49] However, if you share the care of a child, the child is considered to be occupying the home of only one parent – the parent with whom the child normally lives.[50] **Note:** the local authority may use the rules described on p53 to decide whether someone counts as occupying your home.

Additional bedrooms

You are allowed one additional bedroom if you satisfy one of the following conditions. If you satisfy both, you are allowed two additional bedrooms.[51]
- **Non-resident carer.** If you (or your partner), a person who occupies your dwelling as a home (eg, your child or a non-dependant) or a child or young

person in respect of whom you or your partner are a 'qualifying parent or carer' (eg, your foster child) are a 'person who requires overnight care' (see p434 for who counts), you are entitled to one additional bedroom for a non-resident carer. Even if more than one person requires overnight care, only one additional bedroom is allowed.

- **Fostering, adoption and kinship care.** If you (or your partner) are a 'qualifying parent or carer' (ie, certain foster parents and people with whom a child has been placed for adoption – see p434 for who counts), you are allowed one additional bedroom. Even if, for example, you (or your partner) have more than one foster child, only one bedroom is allowed.

In addition, if you are jointly liable for the rent with someone other than your partner (eg, a joint tenant), you are allowed an additional bedroom for her/him if s/he (or her/his partner) is a 'person who requires overnight care' or a 'qualifying parent or carer'.[52] You are allowed two additional bedrooms if both conditions are satisfied.

Note:

- The rules were amended from 1 April 2017 to allow an additional bedroom for people living with you who require overnight care. If you were already getting HB on that date and had not been allowed an additional bedroom, the local authority should reassess your HB claim and pay you any arrears due. The government says that arrears can only be backdated to 1 April 2017. You should argue this is wrong and get advice.[53]
- There are a number of other situations when you may need additional bedrooms – eg, if you need an additional room to store equipment required because of a severe disability, or you live in a dwelling that was adapted for you under a 'sanctuary scheme', or if you share the care of your child but s/he counts as normally living with her/his other parent. You should appeal if you are affected, but your appeal may be held up while the courts are considering other cases.[54]

See CPAG's online service and *Welfare Rights Bulletin* for updates.

Examples

Angus lives with his wife and child in a four-bedroom council house. He claims HB. Angus gets the daily living component of personal independence payment and needs a carer to stay with him overnight. He is therefore a 'person who requires overnight care'. Under the social sector rules, he is allowed three bedrooms: one for himself and his wife, one for his child and one for a non-resident carer. He therefore has one too many bedrooms and the social sector rules apply.

Bill, an approved foster parent, shares a four-bedroom council house with his mother and father. His foster daughter lives with them. Bill's mother is severely disabled and requires,

Part 4: Paying for housing
Chapter 19: Housing benefit rent restrictions
4. The local reference rent rules

and receives, overnight care. Bill and his father are joint tenants. Bill claims HB. Under the size criteria, Bill is allowed two bedrooms: one for him and one for his mother and father. However, he is allowed one additional bedroom because he is a 'qualifying parent or carer' and one additional bedroom because his mother is a 'person who requires overnight care'. So he is allowed a total of four bedrooms. For the purposes of the social sector rules, he does not have too many bedrooms.

Challenging a rent restriction

If you disagree with the local authority's decision to apply a rent restriction (eg, if you think you do not have too many bedrooms) or with the amount of the restriction (eg, if you think you only have one too many bedrooms, not two), you can ask for a revision or appeal (see Chapters 54 and 55).

4. The local reference rent rules

If the local reference rent rules apply, the local authority uses determinations made by the rent officer (see p422) to establish the amount of rent used to calculate your housing benefit (HB) – called your 'maximum rent' in this *Handbook*.

The local reference rent rules apply to you if:[55]

* you live in a hostel, houseboat, mobile home or caravan; *or*
* your rent includes board and attendance; *or*
* your landlord is a registered housing association or is a county council (if you live in a caravan or mobile home provided on a travellers' site[56]), or you are renting a caravan, mobile home or houseboat (and you are also liable to make payments to a local authority – eg, for the site or mooring fees). However, the local reference rent rules only apply if the local authority considers your rent to be unreasonably high (or, in some cases, your accommodation to be unreasonably large). Otherwise, you have an 'excluded tenancy' (see p406); *or*
* your tenancy was a local authority or new town letting, but it has been transferred to a new owner. However, the local reference rent rules only apply if there has been a rent increase since the transfer; *and*
  – the local authority considers your rent to be unreasonably high; *or*
  – if the transfer took place before 7 October 2002, the local authority considers your accommodation to be unreasonably large.

Otherwise, you have an 'excluded tenancy' (see p406).

Note:
* These rules can also apply to other tenants, but only if you were entitled to HB immediately before 7 April 2008 under the local reference rent rules that then applied. See p421 for further information.

- These rules do *not* apply if you have an 'excluded tenancy' (see p406), or if the local housing allowance or the pre-January 1996 rules apply (see p428).
- These rules *never* apply if you are a local authority tenant.

Even if you are not someone to whom the current local reference rent rules would apply (eg, you rent a private house or flat), if you were entitled to HB immediately before 7 April 2008 and the local reference rent rules applied to you, they continue to do so:

- even following any of the changes of circumstances listed on p422, and when the local authority has to reassess your claim;[57] *and*
- until you make a new claim for HB (ie, after a break in your claim) or you move to a new home.[58] If any rent restriction rules still apply to you at that point, your HB is restricted under the rules that are then applicable.

Maximum rent

If the local reference rent rules apply, your 'maximum rent' for HB purposes and, therefore, your 'eligible rent' (see p62), is usually the lowest of the rent officer's determinations, even if the rent you pay is higher.[59]

Your 'maximum rent' is:[60]

- the lowest of the claim-related rent (see p423) or the local reference rent (see p425); *or*
- if you are a 'young individual' (see p426) and it is relevant, the lowest of the single room rent (see p425) or the claim-related rent (minus any payments for meals); *or*
- if you have been continuously entitled to, and in receipt of, HB for the same property since 5 October 1997, the local reference rent plus half the difference between the local reference rent and the claim-related rent.[61] If you or your partner are a 'welfare-to-work beneficiary', breaks in your claim of up to 52 weeks are ignored. For information about who counts as a welfare-to-work beneficiary, see p686 of the 2013/14 edition of this *Handbook*.

Example

Jo and Louis are a couple who rent a three-bedroom mobile home with a living room and separate dining room. They pay rent of £120 a week. The rent officer decides that the accommodation is too big and that the rent is too high, so makes significantly high and size-related rent determinations. S/he notifies the local authority of a claim-related rent of £90 and a local reference rent of £80. Their maximum rent is therefore £80 a week.

Note:

- Your maximum rent only covers the rent you pay for residential accommodation. If you are in shared accommodation, your maximum rent can be apportioned between you and the people with whom you share.[62]

Part 4: Paying for housing
Chapter 19: Housing benefit rent restrictions
4. The local reference rent rules

- A rent restriction can be delayed in specified circumstances (see p436).
- If you are considering renting accommodation, the local reference rent rules apply and you are likely to claim HB, you can apply to the local authority for a pre-tenancy determination to find out the rent that will be used to calculate it (see p426).

How long a maximum rent applies

Once your maximum rent is set, your HB is paid on the basis of this until the next time the local authority refers your claim to the rent officer (usually annually). However, if you negotiate with your landlord and s/he agrees a new rent which is lower than the maximum rent, your HB is recalculated using your new rent.[63]

The rent officer's determinations

When the local reference rent rules apply, in certain specified situations the local authority must apply to the rent officer and ask her/him to make 'determinations'. The rent officer makes determinations about the rent for your home (see p423), comparing it with the rent for other private sector tenancies in the area. S/he also makes determinations that indicate the average rents for specific types of accommodation (see p425).

When the local authority must apply to the rent officer

The local authority must apply to the rent officer if:[64]

- you make a new claim for HB or move to a new home while you are entitled to HB; *or*
- a previous reference to the rent officer was made in respect of your claim at least 52 weeks ago; *or*
- there has been a specified change of circumstances since a rent officer's determination (see below); *or*
- your HB was being restricted under the local housing allowance rules, but these no longer apply – eg, if the home you rent was sold to a housing association and the local reference rent rules now apply instead.

Specified changes of circumstance

The local authority must apply to the rent officer if there has been one of the following changes in circumstance since a rent officer's determination.[65]

- The number of occupiers has changed (except in a hostel). Argue that this should not apply if someone who normally lives with you is only away temporarily.[66]
- There has been a substantial change in the condition of the dwelling or the terms of the tenancy (other than a rent increase).
- There has been an increase in the rent under a term of the tenancy, unless the previous determination was a significantly high, size-related or exceptionally high rent determination.[67]

- A size-related rent determination was made and there has since been a change in the composition of the household, or a child living with you has reached the age of 10 or 16.
- You or your partner, a person who occupies your dwelling as a home, or or a child or young person in respect of whom you or your partner are a 'qualifying parent or carer' (eg, your foster child) become, or cease to be, a 'person who requires overnight care' (see p434) or you or your partner become or cease to be a 'qualifying parent or carer' (see p434), or a child becomes, or stops being, a 'child who cannot share a bedroom' (see p433) or a person occupying your dwelling as a home becomes, or stops being, a 'member of a couple who cannot share a bedroom' and this affects the size of accommodation you are allowed under the size criteria (see p424).

When the local authority cannot apply to the rent officer
The local authority *cannot* apply to the rent officer for determinations if:

- a rent officer determination has been made for the same tenancy (or a tenancy in the same dwelling) on substantially the same terms within the last 52 weeks.[68] This means that a determination made for a previous tenant may be valid for your HB claim. A new application *is* needed if you are a young individual and no single room rent has yet been determined (see p426);
- you live in a hostel and a rent officer determination has been made for similar accommodation in the hostel, sleeping the same number of people as yours, within the last 12 months and there has been no change of circumstances in respect of that accommodation.[69]

Determinations about the rent for your home
The rent officer makes the following determinations about the rent for your home.

- A **'significantly high rent determination'** if your rent is significantly higher than that paid for similar tenancies and dwellings in the immediate area around your home. This determination is the amount your landlord might reasonably be paid for your tenancy.[70]
- An **'exceptionally high rent determination'** if s/he considers the 'rent payable' for your home to be exceptionally high. This determination is the highest amount your landlord might reasonably be paid for an assured tenancy in the neighbourhood for a home that is the same size as yours (or the size you are allowed under the size criteria).[71]
- A **'size-related rent determination'** if your accommodation is larger than you are allowed under the size criteria (see p424). This determination is the amount your landlord might reasonably be paid for a similar tenancy of an appropriate size for you in the vicinity.[72] **Note:** if you are a single person under 35, the rent officer must also identify a single room rent (see p425).

The **'claim-related rent'** is the lowest of the determinations above or, if no such determination was made, the rent you are supposed to pay.[73]

Part 4: Paying for housing
Chapter 19: Housing benefit rent restrictions
4. The local reference rent rules

The size of accommodation you are allowed

Under the 'size criteria', the rent officer allows you one bedroom or 'room suitable for living in' for each of the following 'occupiers' (see below), each coming only into the first category for which s/he is eligible:[74]

- a couple (see p215 for who counts);
- a 'member of a couple who cannot share a bedroom' (see p433 for who counts);
- a member of a couple whose partner is a 'member of a couple who cannot share a bedroom';[75]
- a person who is aged 16 or over;
- two children under 16 of the same sex;
- a 'child who cannot share a bedroom' (see p433 for who counts);
- two children under 10;
- a child under 16.

Note: you are only allowed a bedroom for a 'child who cannot share a bedroom' or a 'member of a couple who cannot share a bedroom' if you have a bedroom in your home that is additional to those you would be allowed if the child or the member of the couple *were* able to share a bedroom. 'Bedroom' is not defined, but see p435 for what may count.

You are allowed an additional bedroom (or 'room suitable for living in') if you satisfy one of the following conditions. If you satisfy both conditions, you are allowed two additional bedrooms (or rooms suitable for living in).[76]

- **Non-resident carer.** If you (or your partner), a person who occupies your dwelling as a home (eg, your child or a non-dependant) or a child or young person in respect of whom you or your partner are a 'qualifying parent or carer' (eg, your foster child) are a 'person who requires overnight care' (see p434 for who counts), you are allowed one additional room for a non-resident carer. Even if more than one person requires overnight care, only one additional room is allowed.
- **Fostering, adoption and kinship care.** If you (or your partner) are a 'qualifying parent or carer' (see p434 for who counts), you are allowed one additional bedroom. Even if, for example, you (or your partner) have more than one foster child, only one additional room is allowed.

Note: unlike the local housing allowance rules, there is no maximum number of bedrooms.

You are also allowed the following number of 'rooms suitable for living in'.

Number of occupiers	Number of rooms
Fewer than four	One
Four to six	Two
Seven or more	Three

If any of the rooms in your home are not suitable for living in (eg, because of their size or lack of ventilation), argue that they should be ignored.

A person counts as an **'occupier'** if the local authority includes her/him on the form used to refer your tenancy to the rent officer.[77] This can include people in addition to your partner or children included in your claim – eg, a non-dependant or a live-in carer. It does not include a foster child or a child placed with you for adoption under specified provisions, but you may be entitled to an additional bedroom if you (or your partner) are a 'qualifying parent or carer' (see p434).[78]

Note:

- Someone also counts as an occupier if s/he is your (or your partner's) son, daughter, stepson or stepdaughter who lives with you and who is in the armed forces, even when s/he is deployed on operations, provided s/he intends to return home.
- You can argue that someone is an occupier if s/he normally lives with you, but is temporarily away.[79] However, if you share the care of a child, the child is considered to be occupying the home of only one parent – the parent with whom s/he normally lives.[80] **Note:** the local authority may use the rules described on p53 to decide whether someone counts as occupying your home.

Example
Alice and Len have three children: two sons, aged 12 and 14, and a daughter, aged 17. They are allowed one room for themselves, one for their sons and one for their daughter – three bedrooms, as well as two other 'rooms suitable for living in'. They are therefore allowed five rooms, as well as a kitchen, bathroom and toilet.

Determinations that indicate average rents

The rent officer makes determinations that indicate the average rents for specific types of accommodation in a 'broad rental market area'. These are as follows.

- The **'local reference rent'** is the mid-point of 'reasonable market rents' for assured tenancies in the broad rental market area appropriate to the size of property in which you live (or the size you are allowed under the size criteria – see p424).[81] This is only provided if the claim-related rent (see p423) exceeds it.[82]
- The **'single room rent'** is the mid-point of 'reasonable market rents' for assured tenancies in the broad rental market area in which the tenant has exclusive use of one bedroom only, and other than that only shares a living room, kitchen, toilet and bathroom, and makes no payment for board and attendance.[83] It is only used to calculate your HB if you are a 'young individual' (see p426).

Part 4: Paying for housing
Chapter 19: Housing benefit rent restrictions
4. The local reference rent rules

Young individuals

If you are a 'young individual', in most cases the rent officer identifies a single room rent. Your 'maximum rent' (see p421) is based on this figure unless you qualify for a severe disability premium as part of your applicable amount, you have a non-dependant living with you (see p67) or the pre-January 1996 rules apply to you (see p428).[84] In general, you count as a 'young individual' if you are a single claimant under 35. However, you do not count as a 'young individual' if:[85]

- your landlord is a registered housing association; *or*
- you are under the age of 22 and:
  - were looked after by (in the care of), or under the supervision of, a local authority under specific legal provisions after you turned 16 or were provided with accommodation by the local authority under section 20 of the Children Act 1989; *or*
  - ceased to be subject to a compulsory supervision order under section 83 of the Children's Hearings (Scotland) Act 2011 which had continued after you turned 16. **Note:** there are exceptions; *or*
- you are a 'person who requires overnight care' (see p434 for who counts); *or*
- you are a 'qualifying parent or carer' (see p434 for who counts); *or*
- you are at least 25 and:
  - have been living in a hostel for homeless people for three months or more (this does not have to be continuous) and while living in such a hostel have accepted support services to assist you in being rehabilitated or resettled in the community; *or*
  - are an offender subject to specific multi-agency risk management arrangements.

Service charges in rent officer determinations

The local authority notifies the rent officer of the amount of rent you are supposed to pay, whether this includes service charges and the amount of the charges that can and cannot be met by HB (see p64).[86] The claim-related rent (see p423) does not include ineligible charges unless you live in one-room accommodation and the landlord provides substantial board and attendance. In this case, the claim-related rent and local reference rent (though not the single room rent) include charges for meals.[87]

If you are considering renting accommodation

If you are considering renting accommodation privately, the local reference rent rules apply and you are likely to claim HB, you might want to find out the rent figure that will be used to calculate it. In this case, you can apply for a **pre-tenancy determination**.[88] You can also apply if you are already receiving HB and your tenancy is due for renewal, but your tenancy agreement must have started at least 11 months before you apply.[89]

Note:

- You must apply in writing on the form approved by your local authority. Both you and your prospective landlord must sign it.[90]
- A pre-tenancy determination is usually valid for a year.[91] So, if someone else applied for a pre-tenancy determination for your accommodation in the previous 12 months, it also applies to you.
- You cannot appeal against a pre-tenancy determination. However, if you accept the tenancy and claim HB, you can ask for it to be redetermined (see below). If you subsequently negotiate a lower rent with your landlord which is lower than your 'maximum rent', your HB is recalculated using your new rent.[92]

Challenging a rent restriction

You cannot appeal against a rent officer's determination. However, the local authority can ask for it to be redetermined on your behalf.[93]

Do you want a redetermination?

1. You must apply to the local authority in writing no later than one month after the date you are notified of its decision on your HB claim. The local authority must then apply to the rent officer for a redetermination and pass any representations you make or evidence you supply to her/him within seven days.

2. If you ask for a revision or appeal against an HB decision and this relates, in whole or in part, to the rent officer's determinations, the local authority should apply for a redetermination.[94]

3. The rent officer must notify the local authority of her/his decision within 20 working days.[95]

The local authority can ask for a rent officer redetermination even if you have not done so, and must do in some circumstances.[96] If there has been a property-related error, the rent officer can send a substitute determination automatically.[97] You can ask for a redetermination in any of these situations. Otherwise, you are limited to one request for a rent officer determination.[98]

The rent officer's redetermination might reduce your maximum rent, so consider your position carefully before requesting one – you could end up with less HB. If the redetermination:[99]

- reduces your maximum rent (see p421), it only applies from the Monday after the date of redetermination, so you have not been overpaid;
- increases your maximum rent, it applies from the date of the original decision and you should be paid any HB arrears.

Note: you can appeal against local authority decisions about your award of HB which involve rent officer determinations – ie, you can challenge the factual basis

Part 4: Paying for housing
Chapter 19: Housing benefit rent restrictions
5. The pre-January 1996 rules

on which the rent officer made a determination, such as whether you are a 'young individual' or whether someone occupies accommodation with you.[100] If you are in doubt, you may want to appeal *and* ask for a redetermination.

5. **The pre-January 1996 rules**

Before January 1996, the rent restriction rules were less harsh than the rules that replaced them. These rules still apply if you are claiming housing benefit (HB) and you live in 'exempt accommodation' or if you are an 'exempt claimant'. If they apply, they determine the amount of rent that is used to calculate your HB – called your 'maximum rent' in this *Handbook*.

Note: you cannot generally qualify for HB if you come under the universal credit (UC) system (see p20). However, if you live in 'exempt accommodation', the help you get with your rent for this is not provided in UC. Instead you can claim HB for the rent you pay and the pre-January 1996 rules apply.

Exempt accommodation

The pre-January 1996 rules apply to you if you live in 'exempt accommodation' – ie, if it is:[101]

* temporary accommodation (resettlement places) for people without a settled way of life, funded by the government; *or*
* accommodation provided by a housing association, non-metropolitan county council, registered charity or voluntary organisation where that body, or a person acting on its behalf, also provides you with care, support or supervision.[102] You must need the care, support or supervision and it must be more than a token or minimal amount.[103] **Note:** if the person (or body) providing the care, support or supervision has a contract with the local authority to provide these, but is not providing the accommodation, the decision maker is likely to say it is not exempt accommodation.[104]

Exempt claimants

The pre-January 1996 rules also apply to you if you are an 'exempt claimant' – ie, you are a private tenant (or, in exceptional cases, a local authority or housing association tenant) and you:[105]

* have been continuously entitled to and in receipt of HB since 1 January 1996; *and*
* continue to occupy the same property as your home (except if you are forced to move because fire, flood or natural catastrophe makes it uninhabitable).

Even if the above applies, you do *not* count as an exempt claimant if you are a local authority or registered housing association tenant unless:[106]

- you (or your partner) are at least the qualifying age for pension credit (PC – see p147); *or*
- the pre-January 1996 rules applied to you on or before 31 March 2013 – ie, using these rules, the local authority:
  - restricted your rent; *or*
  - decided that your accommodation was too large or your rent was too high, but did not restrict your rent because the rules for those in a protected group applied (see p431), or the restriction was delayed for either of the reasons on p436.

Note: any local authority and registered housing association tenant could count as an exempt claimant before 3 March 2014. Your local authority may have applied the social sector rules to you in error before this date. See p400 of the 2016/17 edition of this *Handbook* for information.

If you are an exempt claimant, provided when you make a new claim you are *not* someone to whom the local housing allowance rules apply (see p407):[107]

- breaks in your HB claim of up to four weeks are ignored (52 weeks if you or your partner are a 'welfare-to-work beneficiary' – see p686 of the 2013/14 edition of this *Handbook* for who counts);
- an exemption can be transferred to you if you claim HB because:
  - an exempt claimant dies and you are a member of her/his family, or a relative (see p437 for who counts) occupying the same accommodation without a separate right to do so. You must continue to occupy the same property and claim within four weeks of the death;
  - your partner (who was exempt) has been detained in custody and is not entitled to HB under the temporary absence rules (see p53). You must continue to occupy the same property and claim within four weeks of her/his detention;
  - your partner (who was exempt) has left the dwelling and you claim within four weeks of the date s/he left.

The exemption can only be transferred if either the exempt claimant was in receipt of HB at the time s/he died (or left the dwelling) or had become a 'welfare-to-work beneficiary' (see above) within the previous 52 weeks.[108] If it cannot be transferred, other rent restriction rules may apply when you make a new claim.

Note: if you are thinking of making *any* changes to your claim, check whether this would mean you are no longer an exempt claimant and, therefore, the local reference rent rules, the local housing allowance rules or the social sector rules apply.

Part 4: Paying for housing
Chapter 19: Housing benefit rent restrictions
5. The pre-January 1996 rules

Maximum rent

Your 'maximum rent' for HB purposes (and your 'eligible rent' – see p62) is:

- your contractual rent minus ineligible services. It only covers the rent you pay for residential accommodation. If you are in shared accommodation, the rent is apportioned between you and the people with whom you share;[109] *or*
- if the local authority decides your 'eligible rent' should be restricted, the amount it considers appropriate.[110]

If the local authority restricts your rent, it must take into account the cost of suitable alternative accommodation and other circumstances that are reasonably relevant to the decision – eg, pregnancy, the difficulty of finding other suitable accommodation and whether it would have to rehouse you if you had to move.[111] It should not be unduly influenced by the amount of subsidy it is paid by the government, but can take this into account when deciding on a reasonable level of rent. Your eligible rent cannot be reduced below what is payable for suitable alternative accommodation.[112]

When your rent can be restricted

The local authority must restrict your eligible rent if it decides your accommodation is unreasonably large or your rent is unreasonably high.[113] However, if you are in a 'protected group' (see p431), your eligible rent can only be restricted if:[114]

- cheaper suitable alternative accommodation is available to you; *and*
- it is reasonable to expect you to move.

Note: a rent restriction can be delayed in some circumstances (see p436).

Is your accommodation unreasonably large?

Your accommodation counts as unreasonably large if it is larger than is reasonably needed for you and anyone else who occupies the accommodation, whether or not they are part of your family. The local authority must take account of suitable alternative accommodation occupied by other households of the same size.[115] The key question is the size of home you need, rather than the size of home you want.[116] However, this should include whether you need additional space – eg, because someone who lives with you has a disability, or someone who lives elsewhere visits you regularly.

Is your rent unreasonably high?

Your rent counts as too high if it is unreasonably high compared with that for suitable alternative accommodation elsewhere.[117] 'Rent' includes, among other things, service charges or licence fees you must pay.[118] In making the comparison, the local authority must consider the full range of rents that could be paid for such accommodation and not just the cheapest.[119] If your rent is within the range or just above it, the local authority may find it difficult to justify finding your rent to be unreasonably high.[120]

Note: when deciding whether your rent is unreasonably high, the local authority may ask a rent officer to assess a reasonable rent for your property, but the figures are not binding. The local authority (not the rent officer) must decide whether your rent is unreasonably high, using different criteria from that used by the rent officer.[121]

Suitable alternative accommodation

The alternative accommodation must be 'suitable' for the age and health of all the people that the local authority must take into account, having regard to the nature of the accommodation and the facilities available.[122] The local authority must consider these factors, even if you do not raise your housing needs yourself.[123]

The local authority must take into account: you, your partner, any child(ren) included in your claim and any of your (or your partner's) relatives (see p437 for who counts) who live in the same dwelling as you without a separate right to do so.[124]

The local authority must compare your home with 'alternative accommodation'.

- It is not sufficient for the local authority simply to show that cheaper or smaller alternative accommodation exists.
- It cannot just compare homes with the same number of bedrooms. Some effort must be made to establish what other facilities are available.[125]
- It must compare your home with other properties offering the same security of tenure – eg, if you have an assured tenancy, the local authority may not rely on comparisons with accommodation that is let on assured shorthold tenancies, or with council or housing association properties.[126]
- It does not have to exclude properties which you cannot take because the landlord wants a deposit that you cannot afford.[127] However, if you are in a 'protected group', you might be able to argue that the accommodation is not available to you (see below).
- It should not make comparisons with other parts of the country where accommodation costs differ widely from local ones, but it may compare your property with one in a less expensive area within a city.[128]

Are you in a protected group?

If the local authority decides that your rent or the size of your accommodation is unreasonable, it must consider whether you are in a 'protected group'.[129] You are in a protected group if any of the people the local authority must take into account:[130]

- are at least the qualifying age for PC (see p147); *or*

Part 4: Paying for housing
Chapter 19: Housing benefit rent restrictions
5. The pre-January 1996 rules

- satisfy any of the tests for being (or treated as being) incapable of work or for having limited capability for work;[131] *or*
- have a child (including a 'qualifying young person') living with them for whom they are responsible (see p222).

If you are in a protected group, the local authority cannot restrict your rent unless:
- cheaper suitable alternative accommodation is available. The local authority must prove that it exists and is available to you. It must:
  - have sufficient evidence to show there is an active housing market with accommodation of a suitable type, rent and location for you, but it does not need to refer to specific properties;[132]
  - take into account personal factors, such as whether you can afford to pay a deposit, in considering whether accommodation is 'available'.[133] If the local authority produces a list of properties that it says are available to you, try to show that they are not available because of your personal circumstances;[134] *and*
- it thinks it is reasonable to expect you to move. It must take into account the effects of a move on:[135]
  - your ability to retain your job; *and*
  - the education of any child or young person living with you. In considering this, the local authority must justify any decision that it is reasonable to make the child travel to, or move, school.[136]

The local authority may say that it does not need to consider any other factors, such as your health.[137] However, if there are good reasons why you cannot move other than those listed above, try to argue that alternative accommodation cannot be suitable.[138]

Rent increases

If your landlord increases your rent, the local authority cannot increase your eligible rent by the full amount if it decides that the increase is:[139]
- unreasonably high compared with increases in suitable alternative accommodation. The local authority must consider the amount of the increase, as well as what your rent was and what your rent will be, and compare it with the rent in the suitable alternative accommodation.[140] It should also consider, for example, the quality of the accommodation, your age and state of health, whether you would have to move if the increase is not met and how a move would affect you;[141] *or*
- unreasonable because there has been an increase within the preceding 12 months.

If the local authority considers a rent increase to be unreasonable, it may refuse to meet all of that increase or meet only so much of it as it considers appropriate. If your rent has been increased for the second time in under 12 months but is still below the market level for suitable alternative accommodation, or the increase reflects improvements made to your accommodation, argue for the full amount to be allowed.

Challenging a rent restriction

If you disagree with the local authority's decision to apply a rent restriction (eg, if you think the rules do not apply in your case) or with the amount of the restriction (eg, if you think you should be allowed a higher number of bedrooms), you can ask for a revision or appeal (see Chapters 54 and 55).

6. Common definitions

There are some terms that are the same for some or all of the rent restriction rules. These are covered in this section and are referred to above where relevant.

Member of a couple who cannot share a bedroom

If you and your partner, or the members of any couple occupying your dwelling as a home (eg, your non-dependants), cannot share a bedroom, you are allowed an additional room under the size criteria for the local housing allowance, social sector and local reference rent rules. To count as a 'couple who cannot share a bedroom':[142]

- the person who cannot share must be getting the higher rate of attendance allowance (AA), the middle or highest rate of disability living allowance (DLA) care component, the daily living component of personal independence payment (PIP) or armed forces independence payment; *and*
- the local authority must be satisfied that because of her/his disability, the person cannot reasonably share a bedroom with the other member of the couple.

Note: before 1 April 2017, a bedroom might not have been allowed (when it should have been) for a disabled member of a couple who cannot share a bedroom. You should apply for a revision on grounds of official error if you were affected and think you should have been allowed an additional bedroom.[143]

Child who cannot share a bedroom

If a child who cannot share a bedroom is living in your home, you are allowed an additional room for her/him under the size criteria for the local housing allowance, social sector and local reference rent rules. To count as a 'child who cannot share a bedroom':[144]

- the child must be under 16 and must be entitled to the middle or highest rate of DLA care component, whether or not it is being paid; *and*

Part 4: Paying for housing
Chapter 19: Housing benefit rent restrictions
6. Common definitions

- the local authority must be satisfied that because of her/his disability, the child cannot reasonably share a bedroom with another child under 16.

Note: before 4 December 2013, a bedroom might not have been allowed (when it should have been) for a severely disabled child who cannot share a bedroom. You should apply for a revision on grounds of official error if you were affected and think you should have been allowed a bedroom for a disabled child.[145]

Person who requires overnight care

If you (or your partner), a person who occupies your dwelling as a home (eg, your child or a non-dependant) or a child or young person in respect of whom you or your partner are a 'qualifying parent or carer' (eg, your foster child) are a 'person who requires overnight care', you are allowed an additional room under the size criteria for the local housing allowance, social sector and local reference rent rules. Under the social sector rules, you are also allowed an additional bedroom for someone who is jointly liable for the rent with you if s/he (or her/his partner) is a 'person who requires overnight care' (see p419).

A person counts as a 'person who requires overnight care' if:[146]
- s/he is getting AA, the middle or highest rate of DLA care component, the daily living component of PIP or armed forces independence payment; or
- s/he has, or if the person is a child you have, provided the local authority with sufficient certificates, documents, information or evidence to satisfy it that overnight care is required.

In addition, arrangements must have been made for one or more people who do not live with you to provide overnight care and to stay overnight regularly in your home for this purpose. You must satisfy the local authority that this care is reasonably required. The carer does not necessarily have to stay overnight on the majority of nights, but the care must be needed often and steadily enough that a bedroom has to be available for the carer.[147] The carer must be provided with the use of a bedroom additional to those used by other people who live with you. 'Bedroom' is not defined, but see p435 for what might count.

Note: a person can count as a 'person who requires overnight care' while away from your home, provided s/he can be treated as occupying it – eg, while temporarily absent.

Qualifying parent or carer

If you (or your partner) are a 'qualifying parent or carer', you are allowed an additional bedroom under the local housing allowance, social sector and local reference rent rules. Under the social sector rules, you are also allowed an additional bedroom for someone who is jointly liable for the rent with you if s/he (or her/his partner) is a 'qualifying parent or carer' (see p419).

You count as a 'qualifying parent or carer' if:[148]

- a child has been placed (or in Scotland boarded out) with you under specified provisions – eg, prior to adoption or as a foster parent; *or*
- you are an approved foster parent (in Scotland this includes foster and kinship carers). This applies even if you do not currently have a child placed with you, provided you have become an approved foster parent, or have fostered a child, within the last 52 weeks.

To come within the definition, you must have a bedroom in your home that is additional to those used by the other people living in your home. 'Bedroom' is not defined, but see below for what might count.

What counts as a bedroom

When working out the number of bedrooms you are allowed under the size criteria for the local housing allowance, social sector and local reference rent rules, you may need to consider what counts as a bedroom. For example:

- if the local authority decides you have too many bedrooms in your home and therefore restricts your rent under the local housing allowance or social sector rules, you can try to argue that a room in your home *is not* a bedroom;
- if you are not allowed a bedroom for a 'member of a couple who cannot share a bedroom' (see p433), a 'child who cannot share a bedroom' (see p433), a 'person who requires overnight care' (see p434) or a 'qualifying parent or carer' (see p434) because the local authority decides you do not have a bedroom in your home that is additional to those used by other people, you can try to argue that a room in your home (eg, a living room) *is* a bedroom.

'Bedroom' is not defined in the rules. It is the ordinary meaning of the word that is relevant. It could be, for example, a lounge or living room, provided it contains a bed or is used for sleeping.[149]

The starting point is whether the room can be used as a bedroom – ie, a room is a bedroom if it is furnished and can be used for sleeping in. How a property is described by the landlord (eg, as a two- or three-bedroom house) or whether a room is designated as a bedroom may be relevant. However, the basis on which your rent is charged (eg, if your flat has two bedrooms but your landlord only charges the rent for a one-bedroom flat) is not relevant.[150]

You can try to argue that the local authority should not count a room in your home as a bedroom and, therefore, that your housing benefit should not be reduced (or reduced as much) under the rent restriction rules. In deciding whether a room is a bedroom, the local authority should, for example, take into account:[151]

- the size of the room (the dimensions and height) – eg, whether it can accommodate a single bed, a bedside table, somewhere to store clothes and

Part 4: Paying for housing
Chapter 19: Housing benefit rent restrictions
7. Delaying a rent restriction

there is space to dress and undress. If a room is too small, provide a measured plan and photographs if you can; *and*

- access to the room and whether it has adequate natural and electric lighting, heating, ventilation and privacy.

Suggest your personal use of the room should also be taken into account (eg, if you use the room to store equipment you need because of a severe disability), as well as whether your home has been converted or adapted – eg, if two small bedrooms have been converted into one big bedroom, or if a bedroom has been redesignated as a living room on professional advice.[152]

7. **Delaying a rent restriction**

In some situations, a reduction in your housing benefit (HB) (a rent restriction) can be delayed. A rent restriction can be delayed:
- in specified circumstances (see below);
- if the local housing allowance rules apply and you qualify for 'transitional protection' (see p437).

Specified circumstances

A rent restriction can be delayed:
- for up to 12 months, if a member of your family (or any of your or your partner's relatives who lived in the same accommodation as you without a separate right to do so) dies and you still live there (temporary absences of up to 13 weeks are allowed);[153]
- for up to 13 weeks, if you, or a member of your family (or any of your or your partner's relatives who live in the same dwelling as you without a separate right to do so) could meet the costs of the dwelling when you took them on (this could include other bills as well as the rent). This only applies if neither you nor your partner were entitled to HB in the 52 weeks before your current award of HB.[154]

Under the local housing allowance and social sector rules, your eligible rent can change before the end of the 12-month/13-week period if, as calculated under these rules, it is now the same or higher, or you move to a new home or another member of your family (or relative) dies.[155] **Note:** if the local housing allowance rules apply and you qualify for transitional protection, different rules may apply after a member of your family or a relative dies.

Family members and relatives[156]

'**Family**' means you, your partner and any child or qualifying young person for whom you or your partner are responsible and who lives in your household.

'**Relative**' means a close relative (see p50 for who counts) or a grandparent, grandchild, uncle, aunt, nephew or niece.

Example

Mr and Mrs Connor and their four-year-old son live in a private three-bedroom flat. They pay rent of £225 a week. Until her recent death, Mr Connor's mother lived with them. Mr Connor's maximum rent (and eligible rent) was being restricted to the local housing allowance for a three-bedroom property (£190).

When he notifies the local authority of the death of his mother, his new maximum rent (and eligible rent) is the local housing allowance for a two-bedroom property (£150). However, the decrease is delayed for 12 months from the date of his mother's death.

Mr Connor gets income support. Before his mother's death, his HB was £175.20 a week (£190 *minus* a non-dependant deduction of £14.80).

For 12 months from his mother's date of death, his HB is £190 a week.

Transitional protection

When HB rules change, you could be entitled to a lower rate of HB than you were before. In some cases, your old (higher) rate of HB can be protected for a period. This is called transitional protection.

The local housing allowance rules were piloted in 18 'pathfinder' areas from late 2003 until 7 April 2008. The pilot rules were more generous than the current local housing allowance rules. If you live in a former pathfinder area, you may still have transitional protection. See pp282–83 of the 2011/12 edition of this *Handbook* for further information.

In the past, there were other situations when you could qualify for transitional protection – ie, if:

* your HB was calculated on the basis of the local housing allowance rules immediately before 1 April 2011; *or*
* you were at least 25 but not yet 35 and your HB was calculated on the basis of the local housing allowance for one-bedroom self-contained accommodation before 1 January 2012.

See pp317–18 of the 2012/13 edition of this *Handbook* for details.

Part 4: Paying for housing
Chapter 19: Housing benefit rent restrictions
Notes

Notes

4

1. Which rent restriction rules apply

1 Regs 13C(5)(a) and (c) and 14(2)(b) and Sch 2 paras 3-13 HB Regs; regs 13C(5)(a) and (c) and 14(2)(b) and Sch 2 paras 3-13 HB(SPC) Regs

2 Reg 2(1) and Sch 2 para 3(1A) HB Regs. Note that in England this means a 'private registered provider of social housing', but if the provider is profit-making, only if the housing is available at a rent below the market rate.

3 The law refers to 'gypsies and travellers' – Sch 2 para 3 HB Regs; Sch 2 para 3 HB(SPC) Regs

4 Reg 12B(6) HB Regs; reg 12B(6) HB(SPC) Regs

5 *R on the application of Laali v Westminster CC* [2002] HLR 179; *R v Macclesfield BC HBRB ex parte Temsamani* [1999] unreported (QBD); A4 Annex B GM

6 Regs 12C(2) and (3) and 13D(12) HB Regs; regs 12C(2) and 13D(12) HB(SPC) Regs

7 *AA v Chesterfield BC* [2011] UKUT 156 (AAC)

2. The local housing allowance rules

8 Reg 13C(1), (2)(a)-(c) and (5) HB Regs; reg 13C(1), (2)(a)-(c) and (5) HB(SPC) Regs

9 Reg 13C(5)(a) HB Regs; reg 13C(5)(a) HB(SPC) Regs

10 Reg 13D(5) HB Regs; reg 13D(5) HB(SPC) Regs

11 Reg 12D(2)(a) HB Regs; reg 12D(2)(a) HB(SPC) Regs

12 Reg 13D(4) and (12) HB Regs; reg 13D(4) and (12) HB(SPC) Regs

13 Reg 13D(2)(c) and (3) HB Regs; reg 13D(2)(c) and (3) HB(SPC) Regs

14 Reg 2(6) HB Regs; reg 2(7) HB(SPC) Regs

15 Reg 13D(12) HB Regs; reg 13D(12) HB(SPC) Regs. Both, definition of 'occupiers'.

16 Reg 21(3) HB Regs; reg 21(3) HB(SPC) Regs; *AA v Chesterfield BC and SSWP (HB)* [2011] UKUT 156 (AAC)

17 *R(H) 8/09*; *SK v South Hams DC (HB)* [2010] UKUT 129 (AAC); [2010] AACR 40

18 *R v Swale BC HBRB ex parte Marchant* [1999] 1 FLR 1087 (QBD); [2000] 1 FLR 246; *R (Cotton and Others) v SSWP and New Forest DC and Others* [2014] EWHC 3437 (Admin), 22 October 2014; *PC v SSWP (HB)* [2014] UKUT 467 (AAC); *MR v North Tyneside Council and SSWP* [2015] UKUT 34 (AAC); *SSWP v MM and Northumberland CC* [2015] UKUT 624 (AAC)

19 Reg 13D(3A) and (3B) HB Regs; reg 13D(3A) and (3B) HB(SPC) Regs

20 *R (Carmichael) v SSWP and R (Rutherford) v SSWP* [2016] UKSC 58

21 *R (MA and Others) v SSWP* [2014] EWCA Civ 13, 21 February 2014; *R (Cotton and Others) v SSWP and New Forest DC and Others* [2014] EWHC 3437 (Admin)

22 **HB** Reg 13D(2)(a) HB Regs; reg 13D(2)(a) HB(SPC) Regs
UC Sch 4 paras 27 and 28 UC Regs

23 **HB** Regs 2(1), definition of 'young individual', (b)-(f) and (i) and (1A)-(1C),and 13D(2)(a) HB Regs; reg 13D(2)(a) and (12) HB(SPC) Regs
UC Sch 4 para 29 UC Regs

24 **HB** Regs 2(1), definition of 'young individual', (c) and (f) and 13D(2)(a) HB Regs; reg 13D(2)(a) and (12) HB(SPC) Regs
UC Sch 4 para 29(2) UC Regs

25 Ch 2 paras 2.060 and 2.080 *Local Housing Allowance Guidance Manual*

26 **HB** Reg 13D(2)(b) HB Regs; reg 13D(2)(b) HB(SPC) Regs
UC Sch 4 paras 8 and 25(2) UC Regs

27 Sch 4 para 8(1) UC Regs

28 *JS v SSWP and Cheshire West and Chester BC (HB)* [2014] UKUT 36 (AAC); [2014] AACR 26

29 Reg 13D(2)(b) HB Regs; reg 13D(2)(b) HB(SPC) Regs

30 **HB** Reg 13D(2)(c) HB Regs; reg 13D(2)(c) HB(SPC) Regs
UC Sch 4 paras 8, 25(2) and 26 UC Regs

31 Sch 4 para 8(1) UC Regs

32 **HB** Reg 13D(1) HB Regs; reg 13D(1)
HB(SPC) Regs; Art 4B(2A) and (2B) and
Sch 3B RO(HBF)O; Art 4B(2A) and (2B)
and Sch 3B RO(HBF)(S)O
UC Sch 4 para 25(2) and (5) UC Regs;
Arts 3 and 4 and Sch 1 RO(UCF)O

33 Sch 3B paras 2(3A) and 5A RO(HBF)O;
Sch 3B para 2(3A) RO(HBF)(S)O; Sch 1
paras 2(3A) and 5A RO(UCF)O

34 Regs 12D(2) and 13C(3) HB Regs; regs
12D(2) and 13C(3) HB(SPC) Regs

35 Regs 2, definition of 'linked person',
12D(2)(b) and 13C(2)(d) HB Regs; regs
2, definition of 'linked person',
12D(2)(b) and 13C(2)(d) HB(SPC) Regs

36 Reg 13D(1) and (12) HB Regs; reg
13D(1) and (12) HB(SPC) Regs. Both,
definition of 'relevant date'.

37 *LB Bexley v LD (HB)* [2010] UKUT 79
(AAC); *SK v South Hams DC (HB)* [2010]
UKUT 129 (AAC); [2010] AACR 40

3. The social sector rules: the 'bedroom tax'

38 Reg A13(1) HB Regs

39 Regs 2(1), definition of 'registered
housing association', and A13(1)-(4) HB
Regs

40 Reg B13(2) HB Regs

41 Reg 12BA HB Regs

42 Reg B13(4) HB Regs

43 Reg B13(2)(c) HB Regs

44 Reg B13(5) and (8) HB Regs

45 Reg 2(6) HB Regs

46 Reg B13(5) HB Regs

47 Reg 21(3) HB Regs; reg 21(3) HB(SPC)
Regs

48 Reg B13(8) HB Regs

49 R(H) 8/09; *SK v South Hams DC (HB)*
[2010] UKUT 129 (AAC); [2010] AACR
40

50 *R v Swale BC HBRB ex parte Marchant*
[1999] 1 FLR 1087 (QBD); [2000] 1 FLR
246; *R (Cotton and Others) v SSWP and
New Forest DC and Others* [2014] EWHC
3437 (Admin); *PC v SSWP (HB)* [2014]
UKUT 467 (AAC); *MR v North Tyneside
Council and SSWP* [2015] UKUT 34
(AAC)

51 Reg B13(6)(a) and (b), (7)(a) and (9)(a),
(b) and (e) HB Regs

52 Reg B13(6)(ab) and (b), (7) and (9)(c)
and (d) HB Regs

53 *R (Carmichael) v SSWP and R (Rutherford)
v SSWP* [2016] UKSC 58, 9 November
2016

54 *R (MA and Others) v SSWP* [2014] EWCA
Civ 13; *R (Cotton and Others) v SSWP and
New Forest DC and Others* [2014] EWHC
3437 (Admin); *PC v SSWP (HB)* [2014]
UKUT 467 (AAC)

4. The local reference rent rules

55 Regs 13(1), 13C(5)(a)-(e) and (6) and
14(1) HB Regs; regs 13(1), 13C(5)(a)-(e)
and (6) and 14(1) HB(SPC) Regs

56 The law refers to 'gypsies and travellers'
– Sch 2 para 3 HB Regs; Sch 2 para 3
HB(SPC) Regs

57 Regs 13(1) and 14(1)(c), (f) and (g) and
(8) HB Regs; regs 13(1) and 14(1)(c), (f)
and (g) and (8) HB(SPC) Regs

58 Reg 13C(2)(a)-(c) HB Regs; reg
13C(2)(a)-(c) HB(SPC) Regs

59 Reg 12C HB Regs; reg 12C HB(SPC)
Regs

60 Reg 13(2), (3) and (5) HB Regs; reg
13(2) and (3) HB(SPC) Regs

61 Reg 13(4) HB Regs; reg 13(4) HB(SPC)
Regs; Sch 3 para 8 HB&CTB(CP) Regs

62 Reg 12C(2) and (3) HB Regs; reg 12C(2)
HB (SPC) Regs

63 Reg 13ZB(1) HB Regs; reg 13ZB(1)
HB(SPC) Regs

64 Reg 14(1) and (8) HB Regs; reg 14(1)
and (8) HB(SPC) Regs

65 Reg 14(1) and (8) and Sch 2 para
2(3)(a)-(d) and (f)-(h) HB Regs; reg
14(1) and (8) and Sch 2 para 2(3)(a)-(d),
(f) and (g) HB(SPC) Regs

66 R(H) 8/09; *SK v South Hams DC (HB)*
[2010] UKUT 129 (AAC); [2010] AACR
40

67 CH/1556/2006; CH/3590/2007

68 Sch 2 para 2(1) and (2) HB Regs; Sch 2
para 2(1) and (2) HB(SPC) Regs

69 Reg 14(2)(a) and (7) HB Regs; reg
14(2)(a) and (7) HB(SPC) Regs

70 Sch 1 para 1 RO(HBF)O; Sch 1 para 1
RO(HBF)(S)O

71 Sch 1 para 3 RO(HBF)O; Sch 1 para 3
RO(HBF)(S)O

72 Sch 1 paras 1(4) and 2 RO(HBF)O; Sch 1
paras 1(4) and 2 RO(HBF)(S)O

73 Sch 1 para 6 RO(HBF)O; Sch 1 para 6
RO(HBF)(S)O

74 Reg 2(6) HB Regs; Sch 2 para 1
RO(HBF)O; Sch 2 para 1 RO(HBF)(S)O

75 Reg 2(6) HB Regs; reg 2(7) HB(SPC)
Regs

Part 4: Paying for housing
Chapter 19: Housing benefit rent restrictions
Notes

76 Sch 2 paras 1A and 1B RO(HBF)O; Sch 2 paras 1A and 1B RO(HBF)(S)O
77 Art 2(1) RO(HBF)O; Art 2(1) RO(HBF)(S)O. Both, definition of 'occupier'.
78 Reg 21(3) HB Regs; reg 21(3) HB(SPC) Regs
79 R(H) 8/09; *SK v South Hams DC (HB)* [2010] UKUT 129 (AAC); [2010] AACR 40
80 *R v Swale BC HBRB ex parte Marchant* [1999] 1 FLR 1087 (QBD); [2000] 1 FLR 246; *R (Cotton and Others) v SSWP and New Forest DC and Others* [2014] EWHC 3437 (Admin); *PC v SSWP (HB)* [2014] UKUT 467 (AAC); *MR v North Tyneside Council and SSWP* [2015] UKUT 34 (AAC); *SSWP v MM and Northumberland CC* [2015] UKUT 624 (AAC)
81 Sch 1 para 4 RO(HBF)O; Sch 1 para 4 RO(HBF)(S)O
82 Sch 1 para 9(2) RO(HBF)O; Sch 1 para 9(2) RO(HBF)(S)O
83 Sch 1 para 5 RO(HBF)O; Sch 1 para 5 RO(HBF)(S)O
84 Reg 13(5) and (6) HB Regs
85 Regs 2(1) and (1A)-(1C), definition of 'young individual', HB Regs
86 Reg 114A(6) and (8)(a) HB Regs
87 Sch 1 paras 5(2)(c) and 7(1) RO(HBF)O; Sch 1 paras 5(2)(c) and 7(1) RO(HBF)(S)O
88 Reg 14(1)(e) and (2) HB Regs; reg 14(1)(e) and (2) HB(SPC) Regs
89 Reg 14(8) HB Regs; reg 14(8) HB(SPC) Regs. Both, definition of 'prospective occupier'.
90 Reg 14(1)(e) and (8) HB Regs; reg 14(1)(e) and (8) HB(SPC) Regs. Both, definition of 'specified matters'.
91 Sch 2 para 2(2)(b) HB Regs; Sch 2 para 2(2)(b) HB(SPC) Regs
92 Reg 13ZB(2)-(4) HB Regs; reg 13ZB(2)-(4) HB(SPC) Regs
93 Reg 16 HB Regs; reg 16 HB(SPC) Regs
94 Reg 16(1)(b) HB Regs; reg 16(1)(b) HB(SPC) Regs
95 Arts 2(1), definition of 'relevant period', and 4 and Sch 3 RO(HBF)O; Arts 2(1), definition of 'relevant period', and 4 and Sch 3 RO(HBF)(S)O
96 Regs 15 and 17 HB Regs; regs 15 and 17 HB(SPC) Regs
97 HB/CTB Circular G5/2005
98 Regs 16(3) and (4) and 18 HB Regs; regs 16(3) and (4) and 18 HB(SPC) Regs

99 Regs 16(5) and 79(1) HB Regs; regs 16(5) and 59(1) HB(SPC) Regs; reg 8(2) and (6) HB&CTB(DA) Regs
100 *SK v South Hams DC (HB)* [2010] UKUT 129 (AAC); [2010] AACR 40; *LB Bexley v LD (HB)* [2010] UKUT 79 (AAC)

5. The pre-January 1996 rules
101 Reg 13C(5)(b) HB Regs; reg 13C(5)(b) HB(SPC) Regs; Sch 3 para 4(1)(b) and (10) HB&CTB(CP) Regs; CH/1289/2007
102 R(H) 7/07; R(H) 4/09; CH/3900/2005; CH/2726/2008; *East Hertfordshire DC v KT* [2009] UKUT 12 (AAC); *Bristol CC v AW* [2009] UKUT 109 (AAC)
103 R(H) 7/07; CH/1289/2007; *Salford CC v PF* [2009] UKUT 150 (AAC)
104 R(H) 2/07
105 Sch 3 para 4(1)(a), (2), (3) and (4) HB&CTB(CP) Regs
106 Reg 2(1), definition of 'registered housing association', HB Regs; Sch 3 para 4(2)(aa) HB&CTB(CP) Regs
107 Reg 13C HB Regs; reg 13C HB(SPC) Regs; Sch 3 para 4(2)(a) and (b), (5), (6), (9) and (10) HB&CTB(CP) Regs
108 Sch 3 para 4(10), definition of 'previous beneficiary', HB&CTB(CP) Regs
109 Reg 12(3)-(5) HB Regs and reg 12(3)-(5) HB(SPC) Regs as set out in Sch 3 para 5(1) HB&CTB(CP) Regs
110 Reg 13(3) HB Regs and reg 13(3) HB(SPC) Regs as set out in Sch 3 para 5(1) HB&CTB(CP) Regs
111 *R v City of Westminster HBRB ex parte Mehanne* [1992] 2 All ER 317
112 *R v Brent LBC HBRB ex parte Connery* [1989] 22 HLR 40 (QBD)
113 Reg 13(3) HB Regs and reg 13(3) HB(SPC) Regs as set out in Sch 3 para 5(2) HB&CTB(CP) Regs
114 Reg 13(4) HB Regs and reg 13(4) HB(SPC) Regs as set out in Sch 3 para 5(2) HB&CTB(CP) Regs
115 Reg 13(3)(a) HB Regs and reg 13(3)(a) HB(SPC) Regs as set out in Sch 3 para 5(2) HB&CTB(CP) Regs
116 *R v Kensington and Chelsea RBC HBRB ex parte Pirie* [1997] 26 March, unreported (QBD)
117 Reg 13(3)(b) HB Regs and reg 13(3)(b) HB(SPC) Regs as set out in Sch 3 para 5(2) HB&CTB(CP) Regs; *R v Kensington and Chelsea RBC ex parte Abou-Jaoude*, 10 May 1996, unreported (QBD); *SS v Birmingham City Council and SSWP (HB)* [2013] UKUT 418 (AAC)

Chapter 20

Help with housing costs: means-tested benefits

4

This chapter covers:
1. When you can get help with housing costs (p443)
2. Which housing costs can be met (p446)
3. Liable to pay housing costs (p454)
4. Costs for the home in which you normally live (p455)
5. Calculating the amount of housing costs (p460)
6. Waiting periods (p468)
7. Linking rules (p470)
8. Mortgage interest run-on (p474)

This chapter covers the housing costs rules for income support, income-based jobseeker's allowance, income-related employment and support allowance and pension credit. It does not cover the rules on housing costs for universal credit (see Chapter 22) or for help with your rent in housing benefit (see Chapter 4).

Key facts

- If you own or are buying your home, or are a long leaseholder, income support (IS), income-based jobseeker's allowance (JSA), income-related employment and support allowance (ESA) and pension credit (PC) can include help with a variety of housing payments. These include mortgage payments and loans for repairs and improvements, and some other housing costs such as ground rent and service charges.
- The amount of help you get for loans is not based on what you pay your lender. It is calculated by applying a standard rate of interest to your outstanding debt.
- The help you get for loans is usually paid directly to your lender.
- You might not get help with your housing costs in IS, JSA and ESA during an initial 'waiting period'.
- In some cases, if you are getting JSA, you can only get help with your housing costs for 104 weeks.

Future changes

The government says that from April 2018, help with 'owner-occupier payments' will be paid as a loan. This will apply to IS, income-based JSA, income-related ESA, PC and universal credit. You will have to repay the loan when the house is sold or when you return to work. You will also have to pay administration costs and interest on the amount of help provided. It is not known if any transitional protection will be provided. See CPAG's online service and *Welfare Rights Bulletin* for updates.

1. When you can get help with housing costs

You may be able to get help with your housing costs included in your income support (IS), income-based jobseeker's allowance (JSA) or income-related employment and support allowance (ESA) applicable amount, or your pension credit (PC) appropriate minimum guarantee.[1] The following steps can help you work out whether you qualify.

- **Step one:** check whether the housing costs are a type that can be met (see p446) – ie, a home loan, a loan for repairs and improvements or certain 'other housing costs' such as ground rent and service charges.
- **Step two:** check whether you or your partner count as liable to pay the housing costs, or can be treated as liable (see p454).
- **Step three:** check whether the housing costs are for the home in which you normally live (see p455).
- **Step four:** calculate the weekly amount you get (see p460). Remember:
  - restrictions might be made if you took out your loan or increased it while entitled to IS, JSA, income-related ESA or PC or in a period between claims (see p448), if your loan is above an upper limit (see p462) or if your housing costs are excessive (see p463);
  - deductions might be made for other people living in your home (known as non-dependants – see p464);
  - for IS, JSA and ESA only, you might not get an amount for housing costs during a 'waiting period' in the early weeks of your claim (see p468);
  - if modified rules apply to you (see p444) and you are claiming JSA, you might only get help with your housing costs for 104 weeks (see p445).

When the rules have changed

The rules for housing costs have changed a number of times in the past. The help you can get with your housing costs may depend on when you first became liable for the costs or when your benefit claim started. In particular, note the following.

Part 4: Paying for housing
Chapter 20: Help with housing costs: means-tested benefits
1. When you can get help with housing costs

- If, after 1 October 1995, you took out a new or increased loan while entitled to benefit, or in a period between claims, you might not get help with it (see p448).
- You might continue to get help with certain types of housing costs that could be paid with IS before 2 October 1995, but which can no longer be paid with IS, JSA or ESA (see p453).
- If you claim IS, JSA or ESA after 4 January 2009, modified rules may apply (see below). In this case, the upper limit for loans is higher than for claims before that date. However, if you are claiming JSA, you may only get help with your housing costs for 104 weeks (see p445).

Modified rules: new claims from January 2009

Modified rules were introduced on 5 January 2009, and are still in place. If the modified rules apply to you:

- the upper limit for your loans is £200,000 (see p462); *and*
- if you are claiming JSA, there is usually a 104-week limit on the time you can get help with housing costs for your mortgage or loan for repairs and improvements (see p445).

The modified rules apply if your claim for IS, or any type of JSA or ESA, is (or was) made after 4 January 2009. If you have to serve a waiting period (see p468), you do not have to be receiving IS, JSA or ESA during that period – ie, if your income is too high for you to qualify for IS, income-based JSA or income-related ESA until help with housing costs is included.

You must meet *at least one* of the following conditions.[2]

- This is your first claim – ie, neither you nor your partner have ever been awarded IS, ESA or JSA in the past, nor have either of you received PC at any time before your claim was made (or treated as made).
  You cannot meet this condition if you are treated as being in continuous receipt of the benefit you are now claiming under the linking rules on pp470–474 for a period beginning on or before 4 January 2009 and ending immediately before the date your claim is made (or treated as made).
- There is a gap between a previous claim and your current claim – ie, you or your partner have been awarded IS, JSA or ESA in the past, but you did not receive IS, JSA, ESA or PC, and your partner did not receive PC, immediately before your current claim was made (or treated as made).
  You cannot meet this condition if you are treated as being in continuous receipt of IS, JSA or ESA under the linking rules on pp470–74 during the gap – ie, during the period beginning when you were last receiving IS, ESA or JSA (whether on your own or as a member of a couple) and ending immediately before the date your current claim is made (or treated as made).
- You (or your partner) were receiving PC before your (or her/his) claim for IS, ESA or JSA was made or treated as made. However, you cannot meet this

condition if you or your partner were getting PC which included help with housing costs in the 12 weeks or less (26 weeks or less in some cases when you have been receiving payments under an employment insurance policy which has since run out) before becoming entitled to IS, income-based JSA or income-related ESA.

- The modified rules have applied to you before on a previous claim.

The modified rules also apply if you were entitled to IS, contribution-based or income-based JSA or contributory or income-related ESA on 4 January 2009 but were still in a waiting period (see p468).

Examples

Julia was claiming and entitled to IS until she returned to work in December 2008. She was made redundant in July 2017 and claimed JSA. The modified rules apply because although she was entitled to IS in the past, she is not treated as receiving IS, JSA or ESA between the end of her IS claim and her claim for JSA. Her upper limit for loans is £200,000, but she can only get help with housing costs for 104 weeks.

Ruth received IS as a lone parent until her youngest child turned 10 on 1 July 2010. She then claimed JSA. Her upper limit for loans is £100,000 and she can get help with her housing costs indefinitely.

Edwina is a lone parent. She claimed IS on 13 June 2017 when she and her partner separated. She had never claimed or been entitled to IS, JSA or ESA before. However, her former partner had claimed IS for her for a few years until they separated. The modified rules do not apply because she is treated as receiving IS immediately before her entitlement began (see p472 – 'Couples and former couples'). Her upper limit for loans is £100,000 and she can get help with her housing costs indefinitely.

Note: different rules applied between 5 January 2009 and 5 January 2010. For full details, see pp833–34 of the 2009/10 edition of this *Handbook*.

104-week limit on the time you can get help with housing costs

If you are claiming income-based JSA and the modified rules apply to you (see p444), you can no longer get help with mortgages, other home loans or loans for repairs and improvements (see p446 and p451) once you have been getting help with either or both of these types of housing costs for 104 weeks.[3] The earliest the 104 weeks can start is 4 January 2009. The DWP only counts the weeks when help with housing costs is included in your applicable amount. The following are ignored:

- weeks in your waiting period;
- weeks in which your upper limit is £100,000 (see p462);

Part 4: Paying for housing
Chapter 20: Help with housing costs: means-tested benefits
2. Which housing costs can be met

- if you have claimed JSA before, weeks when help with housing costs was included in your applicable amount in your previous claim. This only applies if you are *not* treated as receiving JSA continuously during the period between your previous and current claims under the linking rules described on pp470–74.

Example

Jim claims JSA. After he serves his 39-week waiting period, he gets help with his housing costs for 30 weeks. His JSA stops when he takes a temporary job for 10 weeks. When he claims JSA again, help with housing costs can only be included in his applicable amount for a further 74 weeks (104 – 30). Because the gap between his two claims is less than 12 weeks, the linking rules apply and he is treated as receiving JSA during the gap between claims.

This rule does not apply and you can get help with your housing costs indefinitely if:

- you are claiming JSA and the modified rules do not apply to you; *or*
- you or your partner were claiming and entitled to IS or ESA and this was no more than 12 weeks before your entitlement to JSA started. However, any entitlement to IS which is 'mortgage interest run-on' (see p474) is ignored if you or your partner were getting JSA immediately before this;[4] *or*
- you are claiming IS, ESA or PC.

---

2. **Which housing costs can be met**

Your income support (IS), income-based jobseeker's allowance (JSA), income-related employment and support allowance (ESA) or pension credit (PC) can include help with:

- mortgages and other loans for house purchase (see below);
- loans used to pay for certain repairs and improvements or to meet a service charge for these (see p451);
- 'other housing costs' – eg, ground rent, payments under co-ownership schemes and service charges (see p452).

Note: if you are a tenant, rent is covered by housing benefit (HB – see Chapter 4). If you come under the universal credit (UC) system (see p20), rent is usually covered by UC (see Chapter 22).

Mortgages and loans

An amount towards meeting the interest payments on a qualifying home loan can be included in your IS, income-based JSA or income-related ESA applicable amount or in your PC appropriate minimum guarantee. You must have a home loan – eg, a mortgage, a hire purchase agreement or other loan to help you buy your home.[5]

Payment of the amount of your IS, income-based JSA, income-related ESA or PC housing costs for the loan is usually made directly to the lender.

Loans that qualify

The following loans qualify.[6]

- **Loans taken out to buy the home in which you normally live.** Loans taken out to buy an existing property, as well as those to pay for materials and labour to build your own home, are covered.[7] If all or part of your loan was not taken out with the immediate intention of paying for your home (eg, it was to buy a car or set up a business), or is for deferred interest, you cannot get help with the loan (or part of the loan) even if it is secured on your home (but see p453 for the rules about housing costs that are no longer paid).[8]
- **Loans taken out to buy an additional interest in the home in which you normally live** – eg:
  - by buying out your ex-partner's share in your home after you separate. However, if your ex-partner has registered a right to occupy your home (a 'Class F land charge') you cannot get help with a loan to pay her/him to remove it;[9]
  - by purchasing the freehold on a leasehold property;[10]
  - by buying your partner's share from a trustee if s/he is bankrupt;[11]
  - by buying out sitting tenants.[12]
- **Loans taken out to repay a loan, which itself would have qualified.** However, if the second loan includes amounts that do not qualify for help (eg, to pay debts or for a holiday), you only get help with the amount of the original loan.

Example
Alan took out a mortgage of £60,000. £45,000 was to pay off a mortgage to buy his home and £15,000 was to pay off business debts. He gets help with the loan of £45,000.

Note:
- Loans for costs necessary to help you buy your home or an additional interest (eg, search, valuation or legal fees and stamp duty) are covered.[13]
- If your home is used for both business and domestic purposes, you can only get help with the loan for the part where you live.[14]
- Even if a loan qualifies, you cannot get help with it with IS, income-based JSA or income-related ESA if the loan is interest-free. It may be possible to argue that you can get help with an interest free loan with PC.[15]

Part 4: Paying for housing
Chapter 20: Help with housing costs: means-tested benefits
2. Which housing costs can be met

- The rules for help with mortgages and loans changed on 2 October 1995. If you took out your loan before that date, you might still be able to get help under the old, more favourable, rules (see p453).

Taking out or increasing loans while entitled to benefit

Even if your loan qualifies, you cannot usually get help with it if the loan was incurred (eg, it was taken out or increased) during a 'relevant period' (see below) and this was after 1 October 1995.[16] **Note:**

- The rule can also apply if the loan was incurred before specified earlier dates. See p439 of the 2014/15 edition of this *Handbook* for details.
- The rule does not apply to loans taken out for repairs and improvements, or to 'other housing costs'.

The DWP is likely to say that this rule even applies if you are awarded backdated IS, income-based JSA, income-related ESA or PC for the day on which you became liable for, or increased, your loan.[17]

Relevant periods

A 'relevant period' is a period:

- for IS:[18]
  - when you were entitled to IS, income-based JSA or income-related ESA; *or*
  - when you were living as a member of the family (see p449 for who counts) of someone who was entitled to IS, income-based JSA or income-related ESA; *or*
  - of up to 26 weeks between two of either of the types of period above;
- for JSA:[19]
  - when you were entitled to IS, JSA or income-related ESA; *or*
  - when you were living as a member of the family (see p449 for who counts) of someone who was entitled to IS, JSA or income-related ESA; *or*
  - of up to 26 weeks between two of either of the types of period above.

  Note: official guidance suggests that the DWP might only apply this rule if you (or the family member with whom you were living) were entitled to IS, *income-based* JSA or income-related ESA;[20]
- for ESA and PC:[21]
  - when you were entitled to IS, income-based JSA, income-related ESA or PC; *or*
  - when your partner was entitled to IS, income-based JSA, income-related ESA or PC; *or*
  - of up to 26 weeks between two of either of the types of period above.

For these purposes, you and your partner are *not* treated as entitled to IS, JSA or income-related ESA under the linking rules described on pp470–73.[22]

Note: if you become liable for the loan during a period of 26 weeks or more between two relevant periods, you *can* get help with the cost.

Member of the family

'**Member of the family**' means your partner (if you are a member of a couple) and any child or qualifying young person who lives in your household and for whom you or your partner count as responsible (see p222).[23] If you are included in someone else's claim for a relevant benefit (eg, s/he is your mother or father), you are a member of her/his family.

Full help with a new or increased loan

You *can* get help with a loan even if you took it out during a relevant period (see p448), if you:

- took out, or increased, your loan to buy a home which is better suited than your former home to the special needs of a 'disabled person' (see below).[24] There is no rule that says you must buy the home or take out the loan within a certain time before or after the disabled person moves in.[25] However, there must be a link between the purchase of the home, the loan and the move.[26] The person must qualify as disabled at the time the loan is taken out.[27] S/he does not have to be a member of your family or to have previously lived with you;
- increased your loan and moved to a new home because you needed to provide separate sleeping accommodation for a boy and a girl aged 10 or over but under 20 and who live with you and (for IS, ESA or JSA) for whom you or your partner are responsible or (for PC) who you or your partner are looking after.[28] You can argue that this should apply if both children will be 10 or over in the reasonably near future.[29]

A '**disabled person**' is:[30]

- for ESA, someone to whom ESA is paid after the assessment phase has ended;
- for IS, JSA and PC, someone getting ESA that includes a support component. For PC, this only applies if the person is under 20 and you or your partner are responsible for her/him ('responsible is not defined in the rules);
- for IS, JSA and ESA, someone who would get contributory ESA, but her/his entitlement has ended because of the rules on how long ESA can be paid;
- if s/he is someone who can still get a work-related activity component after 3 April 2017 (see p641), for IS, JSA and PC, someone getting ESA that includes this component or (for PC) someone who would get contributory ESA with this component, but her/his entitlement has ended because of the rules on how long ESA can be paid. For PC, this only applies if the person is under 20 and you or your partner are responsible for her/him ('responsible is not defined in the rules);

Part 4: Paying for housing
Chapter 20: Help with housing costs: means-tested benefits
2. Which housing costs can be met

- if s/he is someone who cannot get a work-related activity component after 3 April 2017 (see p641):
  - for IS and PC, someone in the 'work-related activity group' (see p642);
  - for PC, someone who would be in the 'work-related activity group' (see p641), but her/his entitlement to ESA has ended because of the rules on how long ESA can be paid.

  For PC, this only applies if the person is under 20 and you or your partner are responsible for her/him ('responsible is not defined in the rules);
- for IS, JSA and ESA, a child or young person who counts as disabled or severely disabled for the child tax credit disabled child or severely disabled child element;
- for IS and JSA, someone for whom you (or someone living with you) are getting a disabled child, disability, enhanced pensioner or higher pensioner premium (or who would get one of these premiums if s/he were on IS or JSA);
- for ESA and PC:
  - someone who would qualify for a disability premium if s/he were on IS;
  - someone who is 75 or over;
- for PC:
  - someone who would qualify for a higher pensioner premium if s/he were on IS;
  - someone under 20 for whom you or your partner are responsible ('responsible' is not defined in the rules) to whom disability living allowance, personal independence payment or armed forces independence payment is payable (or would be payable were s/he not a patient), or who is certified severely sight-impaired or blind by a consultant ophthalmologist (or is within 28 weeks of ceasing to be certified);
- someone entitled to UC who has limited capability for work or limited capability for work-related activity. For PC, this only applies if the person is under 20 and you or your partner are responsible for her/him ('responsible' is not defined in the rules).

A person continues to count as a disabled person even if, under the incapacity or capability for work rules, s/he is either disqualified from receiving benefit or is treated as capable of work or as not having limited capability for work. For IS, JSA and PC, this includes if s/he is disqualified from receiving ESA while a prisoner or because of her/his absence abroad.

Restricted help with a new or increased loan

You *can* get help with a loan even if you took it out during a relevant period (see p448), but the amount you get might be restricted, in the following situations. You can get help if you:[31]
- took out a loan to pay off an original home loan – eg, you have remortgaged your home; *or*

- paid off an original loan (this can be a home loan, or a loan for repairs or improvements), and have now taken out a new loan for a new property, even if this is some time later – eg, you have moved home.

The original loan must have qualified (see p447 and p452) during the relevant period. Unless the loan is one for which you can get full help (see p449), you can only get help with the amount of the original loan and cannot get help with any increase. So if your original mortgage was £30,000 and you took out a new loan for £35,000, you can only get help with housing costs on £30,000 of the second loan.

Did you divorce or separate from your partner?

If, following divorce or separation, you buy your former partner's share of your home during a relevant period, you cannot get help with the mortgage for that share. Similarly, if you take out a loan or increase an existing loan to buy a home after separation, the restriction, in principle, applies. However, you can argue that each of you should be entitled to help with housing costs up to the amount of the loan you were liable to pay when you were together – eg, if you were liable to pay £50,000 when you were together, you should each be entitled to help with housing costs on a mortgage of up to £50,000 when you separate.[32]

You *can* get help with a loan if you buy a home and the week before:
- you were in rented accommodation and getting HB. To begin with, you only get the amount of HB to which you were entitled plus any 'other housing costs' (see p452) you were already getting;[33]
- you were only getting 'other housing costs' (see p452) paid with your IS, income-based JSA, income-related ESA or PC – eg, for service charges.[34] To begin with, you only get the amount you had been getting for those other costs.

In both cases, you get any subsequent increases in the standard rate of interest (see p461) or the other housing costs and do not lose these if the standard rate or costs go down again.[35]

Loans for repairs and improvements

IS, income-based JSA, income-related ESA and PC do not meet the cost of repairs and improvements to your home or the cost of service charges for these (although service charges for *minor* repairs and maintenance *can* be covered as other housing costs – see p453). However, if you take out a loan to pay for specified types of repairs and improvements (see p452) or a service charge (or to pay off an earlier loan taken out for this purpose), you can get help with this.[36]

Part 4: Paying for housing
Chapter 20: Help with housing costs: means-tested benefits
2. Which housing costs can be met

You must use the loan for the repairs and improvements or service charge within six months (longer if this is reasonable). A bank overdraft that is taken out to pay for the repairs and improvements counts as a loan.[37]

Repairs and improvements that qualify

You can only get help with loans for repairs or improvements undertaken to maintain the fitness of your current home,[38] or any part of the building in which it is contained, for human habitation.[39] This includes loans towards the cost of necessary survey work.[40] In addition, the loan must be for specified repairs and improvements – ie, for:[41]

- providing a bath, shower, toilet, wash basin and the necessary plumbing for these, and the provision of hot water not connected to a central heating system;[42]
- repairs to your heating system;
- damp-proof measures (you can argue this includes repairs to a roof[43]);
- providing:
  - ventilation and natural lighting;
  - drainage facilities;
  - facilities for preparing and cooking food (but not for storing it);[44]
  - home insulation;
  - electric lighting and sockets;
  - storage facilities for fuel or refuse;
- repairing unsafe structural defects;
- adaptations for a disabled person (see p449 for who counts);
- providing separate sleeping accommodation for a boy and a girl aged 10 or over but under 20 for whom you or your partner are responsible and who live with you. For PC, 'responsible' is not defined in the rules. For IS, JSA and ESA, see p222. You can argue that this should apply if both children will be 10 or over in the reasonably near future.[45]

If your loan includes amounts for other repairs and improvements, you can only get help with the proportion which relates to any of the items listed above.
Note:
- The rules for help with loans for repairs and improvements changed on 2 October 1995. If you took out your loan before then, you might still be able to get help under the old, more favourable, rules (see p453).
- Payment of the amount of your IS, income-based JSA, income-related ESA or PC for housing costs for the loan is usually made directly to the lender.

Help with other housing costs

Your IS, income-based JSA, income-related ESA or PC can include some 'other housing costs'.[46] These are:
- service charges (see p453). Note that some service charges are excluded;

- rent or ground rent if you have a lease of more than 21 years. If your lease is of 21 years or less, the rent or ground rent might be met by HB instead (see p45);[47]
- rentcharge payments (payments similar to ground rent);
- payments under a co-ownership scheme;
- rent if you are a Crown tenant (minus any water charges[48]);
- payments for a tent and its pitch if that is your home.

Service charges

Your IS, income-based JSA, income-related ESA or PC can include charges for services. Some service charges are ineligible (see p66 – the rules are the same as for HB).[49] Some service charges can only be met if they relate to the provision of 'adequate accommodation'.[50]

Services

A '**service**' is something that is agreed and arranged on your behalf and for which you are required to pay – eg, if you own a flat and the freeholder arranges for the exterior of the building to be painted, for which you have to pay a share of the cost.

Bear the following in mind.
- Service charges to cover minor repairs and maintenance are eligible. However, those for any of the repairs and improvements on p452 are not.[51] You are expected to take out a loan to pay for these and can claim help with this.
- Payments for support services are not eligible. Instead, you can get help with these through your local authority.
- House insurance paid under the terms of your lease can be a service charge, but insurance required by a bank as a condition of your mortgage is not.[52]
- Services provided by an authority that you arrange yourself are not covered. Thus, charges for water and sewerage paid to a water company are not met.[53]

Old rules: housing costs that are no longer paid

You can continue to get help with certain types of housing costs that could be paid with IS before 2 October 1995, but which can no longer be paid with IS, income-based JSA or income-related ESA. These are accumulated arrears of interest, interest on certain loans for repairs and improvements and interest on certain secured loans that were not for house purchase.[54] See p484 of the 2013/14 edition of this *Handbook* for further information.

Part 4: Paying for housing
Chapter 20: Help with housing costs: means-tested benefits
3. Liable to pay housing costs

3. Liable to pay housing costs

You count as liable to pay housing costs if:[55]
- either you, or your partner, are liable to pay them. However, you do not count as liable to pay housing costs if you pay these to someone who is a member of your household (see p225 for the meaning of 'household'). If you or your partner share liability, you might only get help with your share (see below);
- you share the costs with other members of your household and are treated as liable to pay them (see below). You might only get help with your share;
- someone else is liable to pay them but is not paying, so you have to meet the cost yourself in order to continue to live in your home. You must show that it is reasonable in all the circumstances for you to pay instead – eg, if you have given up your home to live with and care for someone and s/he has now gone into a care home, or if you have separated from your partner (even if you have not lived in the home continuously since your partner left[56]).

Note: if you are not required to pay any housing costs currently (eg, if you do not have to pay under the terms of your mortgage), you cannot receive income support, income-based jobseeker's allowance, income-related employment and support allowance or pension credit for housing costs. For example, this applies to special mortgage schemes for pensioners where the mortgage is repaid from your estate when you die rather than by your making regular monthly payments.[57]

Shared liability

If you or your partner share liability with someone (eg, you have a joint mortgage, or you are treated as liable under the rule described below), you might only get help with your share. However, if the other person is not paying her/his share, you can argue that you should get help with the full amount.[58]

You are treated as liable to pay housing costs (even if you are not legally liable) if:
- you share the costs with other members of your household; *and*
- at least one of those with whom you share is liable.

You can be paid for your share, provided the people with whom you share are not your or your partner's 'close relatives' (see below) and it is reasonable to treat you as sharing responsibility for the costs.[59]

Close relative

'Close relative' means a parent, parent-in-law (including a civil partner's parent), son, son-in-law (including a son's civil partner), daughter, daughter-in-law (including a daughter's civil partner), brother, sister, step-parent (including a parent's civil partner), stepson (including a civil partner's son) or stepdaughter (including a civil partner's daughter), or the partners of any of these. 'Sister' or 'brother' includes a half-sister or half-brother. An adopted child ceases to be related to her/his birth family on adoption and becomes the relative of her/his adoptive family.[60]

4. Costs for the home in which you normally live

4

You can get help with housing costs for the home in which you normally live.[61] You cannot usually be paid for any other home. Even if you are liable to pay the mortgage on a property, if you have no immediate intention of living there, you cannot get help with the cost.[62]

Your home

Your **'home'** is defined as the building, or part of the building, in which you live. This includes any garage, garden, outbuildings and other premises and land which it is not reasonable or practicable to sell separately.[63] You can argue that a home can consist of more than one building if you occupy more than one dwelling – eg, because your family is too large for one.[64]

There are special rules if you:
- have just moved into your home (see below);
- are temporarily absent from home (see p456);
- are liable to pay housing costs on more than one home (see p458).

Moving home

If you have just moved into your home but were liable to pay housing costs before moving in, your income support (IS), income-based jobseeker's allowance (JSA), income-related employment and support allowance (ESA) or pension credit (PC) can include help with these costs for up to four weeks before you moved in if your delay in moving was reasonable, you claimed IS, JSA, income-related ESA or PC before moving in, and:[65]
- you were waiting for adaptations to be finished to meet your or your partner's disability needs or those of:
  - for IS, JSA and ESA, a child or qualifying young person included in your claim (see p220); or
  - for PC, someone under 20 for whom you or your partner are responsible ('responsible' is not defined in the rules).

Part 4: Paying for housing
Chapter 20: Help with housing costs: means-tested benefits
4. Costs for the home in which you normally live

The adaptations do not need to involve a change to the fabric or structure of the dwelling, but must be reasonably required and have a clear connection to the disability;[66] or

- you became responsible for the housing costs while you were in hospital, or were in a care home or an independent hospital (or, for IS, JSA and ESA only, in an Abbeyfield home); or
- you were waiting for 'local welfare provision'[67] or a social fund payment for a need connected with the move – eg, for removal expenses or items to help you set up home. In addition, for IS, JSA and ESA you must:
  - have a child aged five or under living with you, or be getting child tax credit for a child of any age which includes a disabled child or severely disabled child element; or
  - for IS and JSA only, qualify for a disability, severe disability, disabled child or pensioner premium; or
  - for ESA only, be getting main phase ESA (ie, after the assessment phase has ended) or qualify for a severe disability or pensioner premium.

Note: the amount for housing costs is not actually included until you move in. If the earlier IS, JSA, ESA or PC claim you made before you moved was turned down, you must claim again within four weeks of moving in to qualify.

Temporary absence from home

If you are temporarily absent from home but are still entitled to IS, income-based JSA, income-related ESA or PC, have not rented out your home and intend to return, help with your housing costs continues to be paid for a period. You can argue that you count as temporarily absent even if you have not yet stayed there – eg, you move your furniture and belongings in but then have to go into hospital.[68] **Note:** your entitlement may be affected if you are absent from home outside Great Britain (see Chapter 67).

You can get help with housing costs for up to:

- **13 weeks** while you are away, whatever the reason. You must be unlikely to be away for longer than this;[69]
- **52 weeks** if you fit into one of the groups on pp457–58. You must be unlikely to be away for longer than this (or, in exceptional circumstances, unlikely to be away for substantially longer than this).[70]

The 13 and 52 weeks both run from the date you leave home. The day you leave home is included, but not the day you return home.[71] If, for example, you have been away from home for 10 weeks and then have grounds to continue to get help with housing costs for 52 weeks, you only get this for the balance: 42 weeks.

However, a new period of absence starts if you return home even for a short stay – eg, a day or a weekend.[72]

Are you going to be away from home for a period?

1. You must let the DWP know that you are going to be absent from your normal home, preferably before you go away.

2. Make it clear that your absence is going to be temporary and how long you are likely to be away.

3. Your intention to return, and whether or not you are unlikely to be away for longer than 13/52 weeks, is considered initially based on the circumstances on the date you leave your home, unless you are in a care home, independent hospital (or, for IS, JSA or ESA, an Abbeyfield home) for a trial period (see below).[73] If at any time after that date, you no longer intend to return or it becomes likely that you will be away from home for more than the 13/52 weeks, your entitlement can be reconsidered.[74]

Note: if you have someone living with you who is temporarily absent (eg, a student who is away during term time), the DWP may use these rules to decide whether s/he is a non-dependant (see p464).[75]

If you have to live in temporary accommodation while essential repairs are done to your normal home and you only have to pay for housing costs for one of the homes, your IS, income-based JSA, income-related ESA or PC covers these costs.[76] This is not subject to the normal limits on temporary absence from home.[77] If you have to pay housing costs for both homes, you may be able to claim IS, income-based JSA, income-related ESA or PC for both for up to four weeks under the rules on housing costs for more than one home (see p458). However, after the four weeks, you are only paid for one home – your normal home if you are unlikely to be away for more than 13/52 weeks, or your temporary home if you will be away for longer.

Housing costs for up to 52 weeks

You can get help with your housing costs for up to 52 weeks if you are in a care home or an independent hospital (or, for IS, JSA and ESA only, an Abbeyfield home) for a trial period to see if it suits your needs. On the date you enter the accommodation, you must intend to return home if it is not suitable.[78] You can only get your housing costs met for up to 13 weeks.[79] If the accommodation does not suit your needs, you can have further trial periods in other homes, as long as you are not away from home for more than 52 weeks in total.

You can get help with your housing costs for up to 52 weeks if you are unlikely to be away for longer than this (or, in exceptional circumstances, unlikely to be away for substantially longer than this) in the following situations.[80]

- You are resident in a hospital or a similar institution. If you are claiming JSA, this must be during a two-week period of sickness when you are treated as

Part 4: Paying for housing
Chapter 20: Help with housing costs: means-tested benefits
4. Costs for the home in which you normally live

capable of work for JSA purposes (see p702 – the rules are the same as for contribution-based JSA). If you are sick for longer than this, claim IS, income-related ESA or PC. **Note:** you cannot get help with housing costs after you have been resident in hospital for 52 weeks even if this is because you are seriously mentally ill. However, a new period of absence starts if you return home even for a short stay.[81]

- You are receiving care (approved by a doctor) in the UK or abroad, or you, your partner or a dependent child (for PC, a dependant under 20) are receiving medical treatment or convalescing in the UK or abroad (approved by a doctor). This must not be in a care home or an independent hospital (or, for IS, JSA and ESA only, an Abbeyfield home).
- You are attending a specified 'training course' in the UK or abroad.
- You are required to live in an approved hostel or an address away from your normal home as a condition of bail.
- For IS, ESA and PC only, you are in prison on remand pending trial or sentence. You can argue that this applies even if you are simultaneously serving another sentence.[82] If you were claiming JSA before going into prison, you must instead claim IS, income-related ESA or PC to cover your housing costs. Once you are sentenced, you are no longer entitled to IS, ESA or PC.
- You are in a care home or an independent hospital (or, for IS, JSA and ESA only, an Abbeyfield home) for short-term or respite care.
- You are providing care for someone living in the UK or abroad (approved by a doctor).
- You are caring for a child under 16 (or, for PC only, someone under 20) whose parent or guardian is receiving medical treatment or care (approved by a doctor) away from home.
- You are away from home because of a fear of violence (see p459 if you need to claim for two homes and for what counts as violence).
- You are a full-time student (see p874) and:
  - living apart from your partner but cannot get help with housing costs for two homes (see p459); *or*
  - a single claimant or a lone parent who is liable to pay housing costs on both a term-time and a home address.

There must be some causal link between your absence from home and being in one of the situations above.[83]

Housing costs for more than one home

In most cases, you can only get help with the housing costs for one home. If you occupy more than one dwelling as a home (eg, because you have a large family), you can argue that you only have one home.[84]

If you have to pay housing costs for two homes, you *can* get IS, income-based JSA, income-related ESA or PC for both:[85]

- for up to **four weeks** if you have moved into a new home and cannot avoid having to pay for the other one as well;[86]
- **indefinitely** if you left your home because of a fear of violence. Provided you left home because of this and are still away from home because of this, it does not matter if you were away from home for some other reason during this period – eg, because you were in prison.[87] You have to show that it is reasonable for you to get payment for two homes. Thus, if you do not intend to return home or someone else is paying the mortgage, you might not get IS, income-based JSA, income-related ESA or PC for both homes.

  'Violence' means violence against you and not caused by you.[88] For the purpose of these rules, it must be fear of violence:[89]
  - in your home. Fear of a racial attack should be covered, provided the attack would take place in your home. Remember that your garden and garage, for example, count (see p455); *or*
  - from a former partner; *or*
  - for IS, JSA and ESA, from a child or qualifying young person who is no longer included in your claim; *or*
  - for PC, from a close relative (see p454 for who counts);
- **indefinitely** if you are one of a couple and you or your partner are a full-time student or on a training course and living away from your home (see below).

If you have to live in temporary accommodation while essential repairs are done to your normal home and you only have to pay for housing costs for one of the homes, see p457.

If you have to live away from your normal home because you or your partner are a full-time student (see p874) or on a specified training course:[90]
- if you are one of a couple and have to live apart, you can get help with housing costs for both of your homes if it is reasonable for you to get help with both;
- if you are a single person or lone parent and must pay housing costs for *either* your normal home *or* your term-time accommodation but not both, you can get help with housing costs for the home for which you pay.

If neither of the above applies, you may only get help with your usual home for up to 52 weeks during a temporary absence (see p456).[91]

If you have been getting help with housing costs for your term-time accommodation and you stop living there during a vacation, you cannot continue to get this unless you are away because you are in hospital.[92]

Part 4: Paying for housing
Chapter 20: Help with housing costs: means-tested benefits
5. Calculating the amount of housing costs

5. Calculating the amount of housing costs

Once you have worked out which housing costs can be met, you can calculate the amount you get.

- **Step one:** calculate the weekly amount for:
  - home loans (see p461);
  - loans for repairs and improvements (see p461);
  - 'other housing costs' (see p462).

  Remember to deduct any restrictions being made because you took out your home loan or increased it while entitled to income support (IS), jobseeker's allowance (JSA), income-related employment and support allowance (ESA) or pension credit (PC), or in a period between claims (see p448), because your home loan or loan for repairs and improvements is above the upper limit (see p462) or because your housing costs are excessive (see p463).

- **Step two:** add these amounts together.
- **Step three:** deduct any amounts for other people living in your home (known as non-dependants – see p464).

Example

Marvin has a repayment mortgage for a two-bedroom flat that he took out when he was working. His father, who is on contributory ESA, lives with him. He claims JSA for the first time in May 2017. The outstanding loan of £210,000 qualifies. He pays ground rent of £286 a year and a qualifying service charge for caretaker services of £8.50 a week.

Step one: Marvin's loan is higher than the relevant upper limit (£200,000 – see p462).

£200,000 x 3.12% (standard interest rate – see p461) = £6,240

£6,240 ÷ 52 = £120 a week for his loan.

£286 ÷ 52 = £5.50 a week for ground rent + £8.50 a week for service charges = £14 a week for 'other housing costs'.

Step two: Marvin's weekly JSA help with housing costs is therefore:

£120 + £14 = £134

Step three: the weekly non-dependant deduction for Marvin's father is £14.80. £134 – £14.80 = £119.20. Help with housing costs is not included until he has served a 39-week waiting period. Because the modified rules apply to him (see p444), help with housing costs is then only included for up to 104 weeks.

Note:

- For IS, JSA and ESA only, you might not get an amount for housing costs during a 'waiting period' in the early weeks of your claim (see p468).
- You might only get a share of the housing costs if you share liability or are treated as liable because you share the costs with someone (see p454).
- If you are involved in a trade dispute, see Chapter 41 for when your housing costs can be met.

Loans

The amounts included in your benefit for loans for house purchase, and for repairs and improvements, are calculated with a formula, using a standard rate of interest (see below). They do not always cover the whole of your loan payments. You cannot get help with associated insurance premiums – eg, if you have an endowment mortgage, you do not get the insurance element paid.

There can be a limit on the amount that can be paid. If the total of your loans is more than an upper limit (usually £100,000 or £200,000), the amount might only be calculated using this figure (see p462). Whether or not your loans are lower than the upper limit, if your housing costs are still thought to be excessive, they may be restricted (see p463).

The formula

The weekly amount for loans is worked out using a special formula.[93] A **standard rate of interest** is used, not what you must pay, even if this is higher or lower. The standard rate can be varied. At the time of writing the rate was 3.12 per cent.[94] You can find out the current rate at www.gov.uk/support-for-mortgage-interest.

The amount of your loans that qualify (see p447 and p452), less any restrictions that have been made (see p450 and p462), is multiplied by the standard rate of interest. This figure is divided by 52 to reach a weekly amount.

Example

Mr and Mrs Khan have a repayment mortgage and a loan for repairs and improvements. The outstanding loans of £30,000 and £5,000 qualify. They also have a loan for a conservatory. This does not qualify. They pay interest at the rate of 6.1%.

£30,000 x 3.12% = £936

£5,000 x 3.12% = £156

Their weekly IS help with housing costs is (£936 ÷ 52) + (£156 ÷ 52) = £21

When housing costs for loans are recalculated

Even if there is a reduction in the amount of your outstanding loan, your benefit for housing costs is usually only recalculated annually, on the anniversary of the date these were first met.[95] However, if you are getting PC, you or your partner are at least 65, and a non-dependant has come to live with you (or your non-dependant's circumstances have changed) and this means the amount for housing costs to which you are entitled reduces, this is recalculated 26 weeks after the date of the change (or, if there is more than one change in respect of the same non-dependant, the first of these).[96]

If you or your partner were getting (or were treated as getting) IS, income-based JSA, income-related ESA or PC which included help with housing costs in the 12 weeks or less before becoming entitled to another of these benefits, the same

Part 4: Paying for housing
Chapter 20: Help with housing costs: means-tested benefits
5. Calculating the amount of housing costs

amount is met as was met when you were getting the other benefit, unless there has been a change of circumstances affecting the calculation, other than a reduction in the amount of your outstanding loan.[97] For IS, JSA and ESA, the 12 weeks is extended to 26 weeks if you or your partner reclaimed IS, income-based JSA, income-related ESA or PC within 26 weeks of a previous claim during which help with housing costs was included and you have been receiving payments under an employment insurance policy which has since run out.

Other housing costs

You are paid the normal weekly charge for all 'other housing costs' covered by IS, income-based JSA, income-related ESA and PC (see p452).[98] If you pay your 'other housing costs' annually or irregularly, the weekly amount is worked out by dividing what is payable for the year by 52.[99] However, see below for fuel charges that can be deducted.

If your 'other housing costs' have been waived because you or your partner (or, for IS, JSA or ESA only, a child or qualifying young person included in your claim – see p220 for who counts) have paid for repairs or redecoration that are not your responsibility, you can still get IS, income-based JSA, income-related ESA or PC for them for up to eight weeks.[100]

Deductions for fuel charges

The following charges for fuel (if this is included in your 'other housing costs') cannot be met.[101] If the charge for fuel is not specified, set deductions are made.

Heating	£28.80	Lighting	£2.30
Hot water	£3.35	Cooking	£3.35

Restrictions if your housing costs are too high

The amount of benefit you get for housing costs can be restricted if your:
- loans exceed an upper limit (see below); *or*
- total housing costs are considered excessive (see p463).

The upper limit

If the total of your loans is more than an upper limit, your housing costs might not be met in full.[102] This includes all mortgages taken out to buy your home and any loans for repairs and improvements. The restriction is applied proportionately to each loan. If a loan was taken out to adapt your home for a disabled person (see p449 for who counts), it is ignored when working out whether your loans exceed the upper limit. If you are getting help with the housing costs for more than one home (see p458), you can be paid up to the limit for each.[103]

Your upper limit is:
- £200,000 if you are claiming IS, JSA or ESA and the modified rules described on p444 apply to you. See below if you become entitled to PC; *or*
- £100,000 in most other cases.

If you are entitled to IS, JSA or ESA with an upper limit of £200,000, but you then claim PC, this upper limit continues to apply if:[104]
- the modified rules described on p444 applied to you (or your partner); *and*
- you (or your partner) were entitled to IS, JSA or ESA no more than 12 weeks before you became entitled to PC (or, where your claim for PC is backdated, before the date you claimed PC). Make sure you claim PC in time; *and*
- immediately before your (or your partner's) entitlement to IS, JSA or ESA ended, your (or her/his) applicable amount included an amount for a mortgage (or other house purchase loan) or a loan for repairs and improvements.

Note: see pp838–39 of the 2011/12 edition of this *Handbook* for details of the old limits which may still apply to some loans taken out before 10 April 1995.

Excessive housing costs

Whether or not an upper limit applies to you (see above), the amount of benefit you get for housing costs can be restricted in the following situations.[105]
- Your home (excluding any part which you let) is too big for you, your partner and:
  - for IS and JSA, any children or qualifying young people included in your claim, foster children, children placed with you for adoption and any non-dependants (see p464);
  - for ESA and PC, anyone under 20 living with you and any non-dependants (see p464).

  When deciding whether your home is too big, a comparison is made with other suitable accommodation given the size of your household. Everyone's needs must be considered – eg, if someone needs extra space because of a disability, or you have a child or relative in a care home who regularly comes to stay with you, your need for a large home may be justified.
- The area in which you live is more expensive than other areas where there is suitable accommodation. The area should not be chosen on too wide a basis.
- The outgoings on your home which are met by IS, income-based JSA, income-related ESA or PC are higher than those in other suitable accommodation in the area.

The capital value of your home cannot be taken into account.[106] **Note:** in some situations, no restriction should be made or a restriction should be delayed (see p464).

Part 4: Paying for housing
Chapter 20: Help with housing costs: means-tested benefits
5. Calculating the amount of housing costs

If it is appropriate to restrict the amount of benefit you get for your housing costs:

- the amount you get is based on the amount of loan you would need in order to get suitable alternative accommodation.[107] This must be assessed in practical and realistic terms;
- any loans that are repayable on the sale of your home which would leave you with less money to purchase another home should be taken into account;[108]
- if the equity in your property is sufficient to buy a new home outright, without a loan, your housing costs could be nil.[109]

When a restriction is delayed or not made

No restriction can be made, even if suitable accommodation is available, if it is not reasonable for you (and your partner) to look for cheaper accommodation. Account should be taken of:[110]

- the general level of housing costs in the area and whether suitable accommodation is available – ie, whether property is generally available, but not necessarily available to you personally;[111]
- your family circumstances and those of the people who live with you.

A move may not be reasonable if:

- the size of your family would make it difficult to find accommodation;
- you need to be near relatives or friends to provide (or receive) care or support;
- it would be difficult to sell your property, you could not get a mortgage on another property or you have negative equity;[112]
- you have lived in your home for many years and it is now too large because you are separated or divorced, your children have left home or your partner has died;
- before your claim you were advised by the DWP that your housing costs would not be restricted.[113]

Even if it is reasonable for you to move, a restriction can be delayed for 26 weeks if you (or your partner) were able to meet your housing costs when they were first taken on, and for a further 26 weeks if you are trying to find cheaper accommodation.[114] Periods of 12 weeks or less when you stop getting IS, income-based JSA, income-related ESA or PC (and some other specified periods) can be included when calculating the 26 weeks.[115]

Deductions for non-dependants

If other people normally live with you in your home who are not part of your family for benefit purposes (called 'non-dependants'), a set deduction is usually made from the amount of benefit you get for housing costs.[116] This is because it is assumed the non-dependant makes a contribution towards your outgoings, whether or not s/he does so. Examples of non-dependants are adult sons or daughters or elderly relatives who share your home. For who counts as a non-dependant, see p67 (the issues are the same as for housing benefit – HB).

The DWP may use the rules on p456 to work out if someone is only temporarily absent from your home.[117] If you think the DWP has wrongly assumed that a person is normally living with you, ask for a revision or appeal (see Chapters 54 and 55). You must apply for a mandatory reconsideration before you can appeal.

People who are not non-dependants

The following people do not count as non-dependants, even if they normally live with you, and no deduction is made (although any rent or lodging charges s/he pays to you affect the amount of your IS, income-based JSA, income-related ESA or PC – see p291 and p326).[118]

- Your partner and:
  - for IS, JSA and ESA only, any child or qualifying young person included in your claim and any child or qualifying young person living with you who does not count as a member of your household (see p224) – eg, a foster child or a child placed with you prior to adoption;
  - for PC only, anyone under 20 for whom you or your partner are responsible ('responsible' is not defined in the rules).
- Someone who is liable to pay you or your partner on a commercial basis in order to live in your home (eg, a subtenant, licensee or boarder), along with other members of her/his household. This does not apply if the person is your or your partner's close relative (see p454 for who counts). A low charge does not necessarily mean that the arrangement is not commercial. You do not have to make a profit. An arrangement between friends can be commercial.[119]
- For IS, JSA and ESA only, someone other than a close relative (see p454 for who counts) to whom you, or your partner, are liable to make payments on a commercial basis (ie, as a subtenant, licensee or boarder) in order to live in her/his property. Other members of her/his household also do not count as non-dependants.
- Someone who jointly occupies your home and is a co-owner or joint tenant with you or your partner. Your joint occupier's partner is also not a non-dependant. For IS, JSA and ESA only, close relatives (see p454 for who counts) who jointly occupy your home are treated as non-dependants unless they had joint liability before 11 April 1988 or joint liability existed on or before the date you first lived in the property (or your partner did, if s/he is the joint owner/tenant). However, a non-dependant deduction is not made for them even though they are non-dependants (see p466).
- Someone who is employed by a charitable or voluntary organisation as a resident carer for you, or your partner, and who you pay for that service (even if the charge is nominal). If the carer's partner lives in your home, s/he also does not count as a non-dependant.

Part 4: Paying for housing
Chapter 20: Help with housing costs: means-tested benefits
5. Calculating the amount of housing costs

When a deduction is not made

No non-dependant deduction is made for any of your non-dependants if either you or your partner:[120]

- are certified as severely sight-impaired or blind by a consultant ophthalmologist (or are within 28 weeks of ceasing to be certified);
- get attendance allowance (AA) (or equivalent benefits paid because of injury at work or a war injury), the care component of disability living allowance (DLA), the daily living component of personal independence payment (PIP) or armed forces independence payment.

In addition, no deduction is made for a non-dependant:[121]

- who is staying with you but whose normal home is elsewhere;
- for whom a deduction is already being made from your HB;
- who is 16 or 17 years old;
- who is under 25 years old and:
  - getting IS or income-based JSA; *or*
  - if s/he is someone who can still get a work-related activity component after 3 April 2017 (see p641), is getting income-related ESA which does not include a work-related activity or support component; *or*
  - if s/he is someone who cannot get a work-related activity component after 3 April 2017 (see p641), s/he is getting income-related ESA and:
    - for ESA, is still in the assessment phase (see p639);
    - for IS, is not in the 'work-related activity group' (see p642) or the 'support group' (see p641);
    - for JSA and PC, her/his income-related ESA does not include a support component and s/he is not in the 'work-related activity group' (see p642); *or*
    - entitled to universal credit, provided s/he does not have any earned income;
- who is getting PC;
- who gets a training allowance in connection with youth training under specific provisions;[122]
- who is a full-time student during her/his period of study (see p874). This includes those getting JSA who count as full-time students while on a specified government scheme for assisting people to obtain employment (see p1103).[123] **Note:** no deduction is made during the summer vacation but, unless you are getting PC and you or your partner are 65 or over, only if the student is not in full-time paid work (see p989);
- who is not living with you at present because s/he:
  - has been in hospital for more than 52 weeks. Separate stays in hospital which are not more than 28 days apart are added together when calculating the 52 weeks;
  - is a prisoner (see p929 for who counts);

- for IS, JSA and ESA only, who is a close relative (see p454 for who counts) and a co-owner or joint tenant with you, or your partner. For PC, no deduction is made because co-owners and joint tenants do not count as non-dependants, even if they are close relatives.

The amount of the deduction

If you have a non-dependant living with you who is 18 or over and for whom a deduction must be made, a fixed amount is deducted, whatever s/he pays you. Unless your non-dependant is in full-time paid work, a £14.80 deduction is made each week. If your non-dependant is in full-time paid work, the amount of the deduction depends on her/his gross weekly income.[124]

Gross weekly income	Weekly non-dependant deduction
£430 or more	£95.45
£346–£429.99	£86.95
£259–£345.99	£76.35
£200–£258.99	£46.65
£136–£199.99	£34.00
Less than £136	£14.80

The rules on full-time paid work are covered in Chapter 43. **Note:**
- A non-dependant who is not in (or is treated as not in) full-time paid work does not attract the higher level of deduction even if her/his gross weekly income is £136 or more.
- For PC, if someone is getting IS or income-based JSA for more than three days in a benefit week, s/he does not count as being in full-time paid work in that week.[125] This means the lower deduction (£14.80) is made (or, in some cases, no deduction is made).

Gross income includes wages before tax and national insurance are deducted, plus any other income the non-dependant has, but not AA (or equivalent benefits paid because of injury at work or a war injury), DLA, PIP, armed forces independence payment or certain payments from the Macfarlane Trusts and similar funds (see p290), or, for PC only, payments in kind.[126]

Do you know your non-dependant's income?
You should try to provide information to show which deduction applies. However, if you do not know your non-dependant's income, ask the DWP to consider the circumstances – eg, if your non-dependant is doing a job which is normally very poorly paid. **Note:** the DWP should not assume that your non-dependant is earning the highest amount. It should assess the likely level of your non-dependant's earnings on the evidence available.[127]

Part 4: Paying for housing
Chapter 20: Help with housing costs: means-tested benefits
6. Waiting periods

A deduction is made for each non-dependant in your home. However, if you have a non-dependant couple and a non-dependant deduction applies to both members, only one deduction is made – the highest applicable.[128] The couple's joint income counts.

If you are a joint occupier with someone other than your partner, any deductions are shared proportionally between you and the other joint occupier(s).[129]

If your housing costs are not met in full

If you do not have enough money to pay your lender, you may be in danger of losing your home, particularly if you are on benefit for a long time. Inform your lender and discuss how to resolve the situation. Your lender may be prepared to accept interest-only payments for a while. Get independent money advice. **Note:**

- Some housing costs (eg, service charges or ground rent) can be deducted from your benefit and paid on your behalf (see p1190).
- You may be able to increase your income by taking in lodgers (but see p291 and p326).
- Some payments made directly to the lender by relatives, friends or a charity towards your housing costs that are not being met can be ignored when calculating your entitlement to IS, income-based JSA or income-related ESA.[130]
- If you get charitable or voluntary payments, these are ignored as income (see p290 and p329).

Ultimately, you may have to sell your home and buy somewhere cheaper. If you move out and put your house up for sale, the capital value of your property can be disregarded for a period while you take reasonable steps to sell it (see p362 and p391).[131] If you rent it out while trying to sell, see p292 and p326 for how the income is treated.

6. **Waiting periods**

Even if you qualify for help with your housing costs, these are not usually included in your benefit until you have been entitled (or treated as entitled) to income support (IS), jobseeker's allowance (JSA) or employment and support allowance (ESA) for a number of weeks. This is known as a 'waiting period'.[132] In some cases, there is no waiting period and you get help with your housing costs straight away (see p469). **Note:**

- If you are entitled to some IS, JSA or ESA during your waiting period, even though housing costs are not included in your applicable amount, the decision maker should do a supersession when your waiting period ends, and your housing costs are then included from the end of that period.[133]

- If you are *not* entitled to some IS, JSA or ESA during your waiting period, help with your housing costs can still be included when it ends if you are *treated* as entitled to IS, JSA or ESA during the waiting period. In some cases, you have to make a fresh claim for IS, income-based JSA or income-related ESA (when sufficient weeks have passed). For information about when you can be treated as entitled to IS, JSA or ESA, see the linking rules on pp470–74.

In addition, if you (or your partner) reclaim IS, income-based JSA or income-related ESA within 26 weeks of a previous award of benefit which included help with housing costs and you (or s/he) have been receiving payments under an employment insurance policy which has since run out, periods between those claims are ignored when calculating the waiting period.[134] Because the number of weeks in the previous claim can be added to the number of weeks in your current claim for that benefit, this means that you can requalify for help with housing costs sooner.

No waiting period

Help with your housing costs can be included straight away if:[135]
- you claim and are awarded pension credit (PC); *or*
- your partner is at least the qualifying age for PC (see p147) or, for JSA only, you are at least that age; *or*
- you can be treated as entitled to IS, JSA or ESA for sufficient weeks during the period before your claim; *or*
- you have already been entitled to IS, JSA or ESA for sufficient weeks when you agree to pay your loan or other housing costs (but see p448 for the rules restricting the amount you can get if you take out or increase a loan while entitled to benefit or in a period between claims); *or*
- you were getting help with your housing costs when your IS, JSA or ESA ceased because you:
  - became a 'work or training beneficiary' (see p471) or a 'welfare-to-work beneficiary' (see p686 of the 2013/14 edition of this *Handbook*); *or*
  - started full-time paid work or training for work or self-employment, or increased your hours or your pay (provided you qualify for a longer linking period – see p473).

  You must claim IS, income-based JSA or income-related ESA again within 104 weeks (if you are a 'work or training beneficiary' or a 'welfare-to-work beneficiary') or 52 weeks (if you qualify for a longer linking period); *or*
- you are claiming for payments as a Crown tenant, under a co-ownership scheme or for a tent and the site on which it stands.

39-week waiting period

If help with your housing costs cannot be included without a waiting period (see above), a 39-week waiting period applies.[136] No housing costs are included in your

Part 4: Paying for housing
Chapter 20: Help with housing costs: means-tested benefits
7. Linking rules

applicable amount until you have been entitled (or treated as entitled) to IS, JSA or ESA for 39 weeks.

7. Linking rules

You are treated as entitled to, or receiving, income support (IS), income-based jobseeker's allowance (JSA) or income-related employment and support allowance (ESA) for certain periods, even though you were not actually entitled to or receiving it. These are known as 'linking rules'.

- Periods when you are treated as entitled to IS, income-based JSA or income-related ESA can count towards your waiting period (see p468), so you can get full help with housing costs earlier.
- The modified rules on p444 do not apply to you if you are treated as receiving IS, income-based JSA or income-related ESA during the specified period, so for example, the £200,000 upper limit for loans does not apply.
- Periods that count towards the 104-week maximum time for help with housing costs with JSA link, if you are treated as receiving JSA continuously between them (see p445), so the weeks in the linked periods are added together.
- You can sometimes continue to get help with certain types of housing costs that are no longer met (see p453) if there is a break in your claim.

General rules

You are treated as entitled to and receiving:[137]
- IS for any period when you were entitled to or receiving income-based JSA or income-related ESA;
- JSA for any period when you were entitled to or receiving IS or income-related ESA;
- income-related ESA for any period when you were entitled to or receiving IS, income-based JSA or pension credit (PC);
- IS or JSA for any period when you were receiving JSA as a 'joint-claim couple' (see p120);
- IS, JSA or income-related ESA during a period of no more than 12 weeks between two periods when:
  - for IS and JSA, you were entitled to, receiving or treated as receiving, IS, JSA or income-related ESA, or were treated as entitled to one of these while your income or capital was too high in the circumstances described on p471; *or*
  - for ESA, you were entitled to, receiving or treated as receiving, IS, income-based JSA, income-related ESA or PC, or were treated as entitled to one of these while your income or capital was too high in the circumstances described on p471.

The 12 weeks is extended to 104 weeks if you or your partner are a 'work or training beneficiary' (see below), or to 52 weeks if you qualify for a longer linking period (see p473);

- IS or JSA during any period for which you are awarded IS, JSA or income-related ESA after a revision, supersession or appeal;
- income-related ESA during any period for which you are awarded IS, income-based JSA, income-related ESA or PC after a revision, supersession or appeal.

Work or training beneficiary

You count as a work or training beneficiary during a period of up to 104 weeks that links two periods of limited capability for work if:[138]

- you stopped being entitled to benefit or another 'advantage' (eg, national insurance (NI) credits) to which you were entitled on the basis that you had limited capability for work; *and*
- you had limited capability for work for more than 13 weeks in the most recent past period of limited capability for work. If that period started when you were transferred from incapacity benefit (IB)/severe disablement allowance (SDA)/ IS on grounds of disability to ESA (see p672), it does not matter if it was 13 weeks or less; *and*
- within a month of your entitlement to the benefit or advantage ceasing, you start paid work (other than work you may do while claiming – see p1021) or training.

Even if you satisfy these conditions, you are not a work or training beneficiary if your most recent past period of limited capability for work ended because you were found not to have limited capability for work – ie, you failed the work capability assessment.

Note: there were similar linking rules for those claiming IS, SDA or IS on the grounds of disability – 'welfare-to-work beneficiary' rules. See previous editions of this *Handbook* for details.

Income or capital is too high

If, when you claimed, you were not entitled to IS, income-based JSA or income-related ESA (or, for ESA only, to PC) because your income was too high or your capital was over £16,000, you can be treated as entitled to IS, income-based JSA or income-related ESA for a period of up to 39 weeks. This includes if your contribution-based JSA was the same as, or higher than, your income-based JSA applicable amount (or your contributory ESA was the same as or higher than your income-related ESA applicable amount).

This applies if, on all the days in the period, you are:[139]

- entitled to contribution-based JSA, statutory sick pay, IB or contributory ESA (or NI credits for unemployment, incapacity or limited capability for work). A

Part 4: Paying for housing
Chapter 20: Help with housing costs: means-tested benefits
7. Linking rules

previous claim for IS, *income-based* JSA or *income-related* ESA is not required;[140] *or*
- for IS only, treated as receiving IS or income-based JSA.[141]

This also applies if you are a lone parent or a carer (see below for who counts).[142] In this case, you or someone claiming on your behalf must have previously claimed and been refused IS or income-based JSA or (for IS and JSA only) contribution-based JSA or (for JSA and ESA only) income-related ESA or (for ESA only) PC. However, this rule does not apply if, during the 39-week period:
- for IS and JSA, you or your partner count as being in full-time paid work (see p989), or you are a full-time student who cannot claim IS or JSA (see p874); *or*
- for ESA, you count as being in paid work, your partner counts as being in full-time paid work (see p989) or you are in full-time education and are getting disability living allowance, personal independence payment or armed forces independence payment; *or*
- you are temporarily absent from Great Britain other than:
  - for IS and ESA, during the first four weeks of absence in specified circumstances or if you are away solely because you are accompanying a dependent child for medical treatment; *or*
  - for JSA, in circumstances in which you would normally continue to qualify for JSA (see p1599).

Carer

You count as a '**carer**' for IS and ESA if you are someone who would qualify for IS as a carer (see p104). You count as a 'carer' for JSA if you have caring responsibilities and are, therefore, allowed to restrict the hours you are available for work (see p1042).

If these rules apply and you were not entitled to IS, income-based JSA or income-related ESA only because your income was too high and you were getting payments under a mortgage payment protection policy, you are treated as entitled to IS, income-based JSA or income-related ESA for *any* period for which the payments were made.[143] This could be longer than 39 weeks.

Couples and former couples

You are treated as entitled to and receiving IS, income-based JSA or income-related ESA during the time when any of the following apply.[144]
- Your former partner was receiving, or was treated as receiving, IS, income-based JSA (but, for IS and JSA, not joint-claim JSA), income-related ESA or PC for you both, provided you claim IS, income-based JSA or income-related ESA within 12 weeks of separating (104 weeks if you are a 'work or training beneficiary' (see p471), or 52 weeks if you qualify for a longer linking period – see p473).

- Your partner was receiving, or was treated as receiving, IS, income-based JSA or income-related ESA (or, for ESA only, PC) on her/his own, provided you make a claim for IS, income-based JSA or income-related ESA within 12 weeks of becoming a couple (or a 'joint-claim couple' – see p120). Unless you are a joint-claim couple, the time limit is 104 weeks if you or your partner are a 'work or training beneficiary' (see p471), or 52 weeks if you qualify for a longer linking period (see below).
- Your partner was receiving or treated as receiving IS, income-based JSA (but, for IS and JSA, not joint-claim JSA) or income-related ESA (or, for ESA only, PC) for you both, if you take over the claiming role – ie, you swap who claims for both of you.

Employment and training schemes

You are treated as entitled to and receiving IS, income-based JSA or income-related ESA during periods when you stop receiving IS, income-based JSA or income-related ESA (or, for ESA only, PC) because you or your partner are on training under specific provisions or are on an employment training rehabilitation course.[145]

Former claimant's family

You are treated as entitled to and receiving IS, income-based JSA or income-related ESA during the time when someone who was not your partner (the 'former claimant' – eg, your parent or an adult acting as your parent) was entitled to:[146]
- IS or income-based JSA;
- for JSA and ESA only, income-related ESA; *or*
- for ESA only, PC.

In all cases, you and a child or young person must have counted as a member of the former claimant's family and the child or young person must now count as a member of *your* family (see p449 for who counts). You must make a claim for IS, income-based JSA or income-related ESA within 12 weeks of the former claimant's entitlement ceasing. So, for example, this applies if your mother or father was claiming benefit for you and your child, but you are now claiming IS, income-based JSA or income-related ESA. **Note:** the 12 weeks can be extended to 104 weeks if you are a 'work or training beneficiary' (see p471), or 52 weeks if you qualify for a longer linking period (see below).

Longer linking periods

Some of the 12-week periods and time limits above are extended to 52 weeks – referred to in this *Handbook* as 'longer linking periods'. You qualify for a longer linking period if you stop getting IS, JSA or income-related ESA because:[147]
- you or your partner:

Part 4: Paying for housing
Chapter 20: Help with housing costs: means-tested benefits
8. Mortgage interest run-on

- start work or increase your hours; *or*
- are taking steps to get work or self-employment while on a training course funded under specified provisions;[148] *and*
- as a result, your earnings or your income are too high, or (for IS and JSA) you or your partner count as being in full-time paid work, or (for ESA) you count as being in paid work or your partner counts as in full-time paid work (see p989).

You only qualify for a longer linking period if, immediately before the day your entitlement to IS, income-based JSA or income-related ESA ceased, help with housing costs:[149]
- was included in your IS, income-based JSA or income-related ESA; *or*
- would have been included but for a non-dependant deduction (see p464).

8. **Mortgage interest run-on**

When you (or your partner) return to work or increase your hours and so count as being in full-time paid work, you no longer qualify for income support (IS), income-based jobseeker's allowance (JSA) or income-related employment and support allowance (ESA). However, you might qualify for mortgage interest run-on. If you do, you are paid IS for your housing costs for the first four weeks after you go into full-time paid work, even if the benefit you were claiming was income-based JSA or income-related ESA. **Note:**
- You do not have to make a claim to qualify for mortgage interest run-on; it is paid automatically.[150] However, you must let the DWP know you are starting full-time paid work.
- Mortgage interest run-on is not taxable.
- Mortgage interest run-on is included in the 'benefit cap' (see p1180).
- You might get health benefits (see Chapter 29) and education benefits, such as free school lunches (see p860).

Who can claim mortgage interest run-on

You qualify for mortgage interest run-on if:[151]
- you or your partner take up a new job or increase your weekly hours of work and so count as being in full-time paid work for IS purposes (see p989). You must expect the work to last for at least five weeks; *and*
- throughout the 26 weeks before the day you count as being in full-time paid work, you or your partner were receiving IS, income-based JSA or income-related ESA. Periods when you were receiving mortgage interest run-on do not count towards the 26 weeks;[152] *and*
- on the day before you or your partner commenced the work, your IS, income-based JSA or income-related ESA applicable amount included help with any of

the types of housing costs that can be met (see p446) and you or your partner are still liable to pay the housing costs.

If you qualify, you are paid IS for the housing costs for the first four weeks of full-time paid work.[153] Mortgage interest run-on is paid to you, *not* directly to your lender.[154]

The amount of mortgage interest run-on

You are paid the lowest of:[155]

- the weekly amount of IS, income-based JSA or income-related ESA for housing costs that you were getting immediately before you or your partner took up full-time paid work. See p460 for how these costs are calculated; *or*
- your or your partner's IS, income-based JSA or income-related ESA entitlement in the week before you took up full-time paid work (or the amount to which you would have been entitled had you not been getting a training allowance).

Your earnings from the full-time paid work and any other income you get are disregarded.[156] All of your capital is also disregarded.[157]

Your mortgage interest run-on can be adjusted if specified changes occur.[158]

Notes

1. When you can get help with housing costs

1. **IS** Regs 17(1)(e) and 18(1)(f) and Sch 3 para 1 IS Regs
   JSA Regs 83(7), 84(1)(g) and 86A(d) and Sch 2 para 1 JSA Regs
   ESA Regs 67(1)(c) and 69(1)(d) and Sch 6 para 1 ESA Regs
   PC Reg 6(6)(c) and Sch 2 para 1 SPC Regs
2. Regs 1, definition of 'relevant benefit', and 8 SS(HCSA)(A&M) Regs; regs 7 and 8 SS(HCA) Regs
3. Regs 3, 6(a), 8 and 11(b) SS(HCSA)(A&M) Regs; Sch 2 para 4A JSA Regs, as inserted by regs 8 and 11 SS(HCSA)(A&M) Regs; reg 7 SS(HCA) Regs

4. Sch 2 para 4A(3) and (4) JSA Regs, as inserted by reg 6 SS(HCSA)(A&M) Regs; Sch 2 para 4A(6) and (7) JSA Regs, as inserted by reg 11 SS(HCSA)(A&M) Regs

2. Which housing costs can be met

5. CIS/14483/1996
6. **IS** Sch 3 para 15 IS Regs
   JSA Sch 2 para 14 JSA Regs
   ESA Sch 6 para 16 ESA Regs
   PC Sch 2 para 11 SPC Regs
7. R(IS) 11/94
8. R(IS) 14/01; CPC/3322/2007
9. R(IS) 4/95
10. R(IS) 7/93
11. R(IS) 6/94
12. R(IS) 24/95
13. R(IS) 11/94

Part 4: Paying for housing
Chapter 20: Help with housing costs: means-tested benefits
Notes

14 **IS** Sch 3 para 5 IS Regs
   JSA Sch 2 para 5 JSA Regs
   ESA Sch 6 para 7 ESA Regs
   PC Sch 2 para 6 SPC Regs
15 *RV v SSWP (IS)* [2013] UKUT 273 (AAC)
16 **IS** Sch 3 para 4(2)-(4) IS Regs
   JSA Sch 2 para 4(2)-(4) JSA Regs
   ESA Sch 6 para 6(2)-(4) ESA Regs
   PC Sch 2 para 5(2)-(4) SPC Regs
   All *Saleem v Secretary of State for Social
   Security,* reported as R(IS) 5/01; *SSWP v
   Mohammed* [2011] EWCA Civ 1358;
   [2012] AACR 29
17 CPC/3226/2005; CPC/3992/2007; CIS/
   88/2008
18 Sch 3 para 4(4) IS Regs; reg 32 IS(JSACA)
   Regs
19 Sch 2 paras 4(4) and 18(1)(c) JSA Regs
20 Vol 4 Ch 23, para 23466 DMG
21 **ESA** Sch 6 para 6(4) ESA Regs
   PC Sch 2 para 5(2) and (4) SPC Regs
22 **IS** Sch 3 para 4(4B) IS Regs
   JSA Sch 2 para 4(4B) JSA Regs
   ESA Sch 6 para 6(6) ESA Regs
23 **IS** s137 SSCBA 1992
   JSA s35 JSA 1995
24 **IS** Sch 3 paras 1(3) and (4) and 4(9) IS
   Regs
   JSA Sch 2 paras 1(3) and (4) and 4(9)
   JSA Regs
   ESA Sch 6 paras 1(3) and (4) and 6(11)
   ESA Regs
   PC Sch 2 paras 1(2)(a) and (3) and 5(10)
   SPC Regs
   All R(IS) 12/08; *CL v SSWP (IS)* [2015]
   UKUT 259 (AAC)
25 CIS/3295/2003
26 *Ahmed v SSWP* [2011] EWCA Civ 1186;
   [2012] AACR 23
27 R(IS) 20/98
28 **IS** Sch 3 para 4(10) IS Regs
   JSA Sch 2 para 4(10) JSA Regs
   ESA Sch 6 para 6(12) ESA Regs
   PC Sch 2 para 5(11) SPC Regs
   All *Saleem v Secretary of State for Social
   Security,* reported as R(IS) 5/01; CIS/
   1068/2003
29 CIS/14657/1996; *SSWP v CA* [2009]
   UKUT 13 (AAC)
30 **IS** Sch 3 para 1(3) and (4) IS Regs
   JSA Sch 2 para 1(3) and (4) JSA Regs
   ESA Sch 6 para 1(3) and (4) ESA Regs
   PC Sch 2 para 1(2)(a) and (3) SPC Regs
31 **IS** Sch 3 para 4(6) IS Regs
   JSA Sch 2 para 4(6) JSA Regs
   ESA Sch 6 para 6(8) ESA Regs
   PC Sch 2 para 5(7) SPC Regs
   All *AH v SSWP (IS)* [2010] UKUT 353
   (AAC)

32 CIS/11293/1995
33 **IS** Sch 3 para 4(8) IS Regs
   JSA Sch 2 para 4(8) JSA Regs
   ESA Sch 6 para 6(10) ESA Regs
   PC Sch 2 para 5(9) SPC Regs
   All CIS/4712/2002
34 **IS** Sch 3 para 4(11) IS Regs
   JSA Sch 2 para 4(11) JSA Regs
   ESA Sch 6 para 6(13) ESA Regs
   PC Sch 2 para 5(12) SPC Regs
35 R(IS) 8/94
36 **IS** Sch 3 para 16 IS Regs
   JSA Sch 2 para 15 JSA Regs
   ESA Sch 6 para 17 ESA Regs
   PC Sch 2 para 12 SPC Regs
   All CIS/1480/2005
37 R(IS) 22/98
38 R(IS) 5/96
39 *SSWP v AR (IS)* [2012] UKUT 308 (AAC);
   JT v SSWP [2013] UKUT 194 (AAC)
40 CIS/14657/1996
41 **IS** Sch 3 para 16(2) IS Regs
   JSA Sch 2 para 15(2) JSA Regs
   ESA Sch 6 para 17(2) ESA Regs
   PC Sch 2 para 12(2) SPC Regs
42 *KW v SSWP (IS)* [2012] UKUT 180 (AAC)
43 CIS/2132/1998; R(IS) 2/07; *SSWP v AR
   (IS)* [2012] UKUT 308 (AAC)
44 R(IS) 16/98; *DC v SSWP (JSA)* [2010]
   UKUT 459 (AAC)
45 CIS/14657/1996; *SSWP v CA* [2009]
   UKUT 13 (AAC)
46 **IS** Sch 3 para 17(1) IS Regs
   JSA Sch 2 para 16(1) JSA Regs
   ESA Sch 6 para 18(1) ESA Regs
   PC Sch 2 para 13(1) SPC Regs
47 CH/3110/2003; R(H) 3/07
48 **IS** Sch 3 para 17(5) IS Regs
   JSA Sch 2 para 16(5) JSA Regs
   ESA Sch 6 para 18(5) ESA Regs
   PC Sch 2 para 13(5) SPC Regs
49 **IS** Sch 3 para 17(2)(b) IS Regs
   JSA Sch 2 para 16(2)(b) JSA Regs
   ESA Sch 6 para 18(2)(b) ESA Regs
   PC Sch 2 para 13(2)(b) SPC Regs
50 R(IS) 4/91; CIS/1460/1995; CIS/15036/
   1996
51 **IS** Sch 3 para 17(2)(c) IS Regs
   JSA Sch 2 para 16(2)(c) JSA Regs
   ESA Sch 6 para 18(2)(c) ESA Regs
   PC Sch 2 para 13(2)(c) SPC Regs
   All CIS/15036/1996; CIS/488/2008
52 R(IS) 4/92; R(IS) 19/93
53 CIS/4/1988
54 Reg 3 IS(AT) Regs; Sch 6 para 20(2) ESA
   Regs

3. Liable to pay housing costs

55 **IS** Sch 3 para 2 IS Regs
JSA Sch 2 para 2 JSA Regs
ESA Sch 6 para 4 ESA Regs
PC Sch 2 para 3 SPC Regs

56 *Ewens v Secretary of State for Social Security,* reported as R(IS) 8/01

57 CIS/636/1992, confirmed by the Court of Appeal in *Brain v CAO,* 2 December 1993

58 **IS** Sch 3 para 5(5) IS Regs
JSA Sch 2 para 5(5) JSA Regs
ESA Sch 6 para 7(5) ESA Regs
PC Sch 2 para 6(5) SPC Regs
All R(SB) 22/87

59 R(IS) 4/95

60 **IS** Reg 2(1) IS Regs
JSA Reg 1(3) JSA Regs
ESA Reg 2(1) ESA Regs
PC Reg 1(2) SPC Regs
All R(SB) 22/87

4. Costs for the home in which you normally live

61 **IS** Sch 3 para 3(1) IS Regs
JSA Sch 2 para 3(1) JSA Regs
ESA Sch 6 para 5(1) ESA Regs
PC Sch 2 para 4(1) SPC Regs

62 CIS/297/1994; *PJ v SSWP (SPC)* [2014] UKUT 152 (AAC)

63 **IS** Reg 2(1) IS Regs
JSA Reg 1(3) JSA Regs
ESA Reg 2(1) ESA Regs
PC Reg 1(2) SPC Regs
All Definition of 'dwelling occupied as the home'; s137(1) SSCBA 1992 and reg 2(1), definition of 'dwelling', ESA Regs

64 *SSWP v Mohamed Miah,* reported as R(JSA) 9/03; R(H) 5/09

65 **IS** Sch 3 para 3(7) and (13) IS Regs
JSA Sch 2 para 3(7) and (13) JSA Regs
ESA Sch 6 para 5(7) and (13) ESA Regs
PC Sch 2 para 4(7) SPC Regs

66 *R (Mahmoudi) v LB Lewisham and Another* [2014] EWCA Civ 284; [2014] AACR 14

67 **IS** Reg 2(1) IS Regs
JSA Reg 1(3) JSA Regs
ESA Reg 2(1) ESA Regs
PC Reg 1(2) PC Regs

68 R(H) 9/05

69 **IS** Sch 3 para 3(10) IS Regs
JSA Sch 2 para 3(10) JSA Regs
ESA Sch 6 para 5(10) ESA Regs
PC Sch 2 para 4(10) SPC Regs

70 **IS** Sch 3 para 3(11)-(13) IS Regs
JSA Sch 2 para 3(11)-(13) JSA Regs
ESA Sch 6 para 5(11)-(13) ESA Regs
PC Sch 2 para 4(11)-(13) SPC Regs

71 *KdeS v Camden LB (HB)* [2011] UKUT 457 (AAC)

72 *R v Penwith DC ex parte Burt* [1990] 22 HLR 292 (QBD)

73 CH/1237/2004

74 CH/3893/2004

75 R(H) 8/09; *SK v South Hams DC (HB)* [2010] UKUT 129 (AAC); [2010] AACR 40

76 **IS** Sch 3 para 3(5) IS Regs
JSA Sch 2 para 3(5) JSA Regs
ESA Sch 6 para 5(5) ESA Regs
PC Sch 2 para 4(5) SPC Regs

77 CIS/719/1994

78 *SSWP v Selby DC and Bowman* [2006] EWCA Civ 271, reported as R(H) 4/06

79 **IS** Sch 3 para 3(8) and (9) IS Regs
JSA Sch 2 para 3(8) and (9) JSA Regs
ESA Sch 6 para 5(8) and (9) ESA Regs
PC Sch 2 para 4(8) and (9) SPC Regs

80 **IS** Sch 3 para 3(11)-(13) IS Regs
JSA Sch 2 para 3(11)-(13) JSA Regs
ESA Sch 6 para 5(11)-(13) ESA Regs
PC Sch 2 para 4(11)-(13) SPC Regs

81 *Obrey and Others v SSWP* [2013] EWCA Civ 1584

82 *MR v Bournemouth BC (HB)* [2011] UKUT 284 (AAC)

83 *Torbay BC v RF* [2010] UKUT 7 (AAC); [2010] AACR 26

84 R(H) 5/09

85 **IS** Sch 3 para 3(6) IS Regs
JSA Sch 2 para 3(6) JSA Regs
ESA Sch 6 para 5(6) ESA Regs
PC Sch 2 para 4(6) SPC Regs

86 CH/1911/2006

87 CIS/543/1993

88 CIS/339/1993

89 **IS** Sch 3 para 3(6)(a) IS Regs
JSA Sch 2 para 3(6)(a) JSA Regs
ESA Sch 6 para 5(6)(a) ESA Regs
PC Sch 2 para 4(6)(a) SPC Regs

90 **IS** Sch 3 para 3(3), (6)(b) and (13) IS Regs
JSA Sch 2 para 3(3), (6)(b) and (13) JSA Regs
ESA Sch 6 para 5(6)(b) ESA Regs
PC Sch 2 para 4(6)(b) SPC Regs

91 **IS** Sch 3 para 3(11)(c)(viii) IS Regs
JSA Sch 2 para 3(11)(c)(viii) JSA Regs
ESA Sch 6 para 5(11)(c)(viii) ESA Regs
PC Sch 2 para 4(11)(c)(viii) SPC Regs

92 **IS** Sch 3 para 3(4) IS Regs
JSA Sch 2 para 3(4) JSA Regs
ESA Sch 6 para 5(4) ESA Regs
PC Sch 2 para 4(4) SPC Regs

Part 4: Paying for housing
Chapter 20: Help with housing costs: means-tested benefits
Notes

5. Calculating the amount of housing costs

93 **IS** Sch 3 para 10 IS Regs
JSA Sch 2 para 9 JSA Regs
ESA Sch 6 para 11 ESA Regs
PC Sch 2 para 7(1) SPC Regs

94 **IS** Sch 3 para 12 IS Regs
JSA Sch 2 para 11 JSA Regs
ESA Sch 6 para 13 ESA Regs
PC Sch 2 para 9 SPC Regs
All Memo DMG 19/15

95 **IS** Sch 3 para 8(1A) and (1B) IS Regs; reg 7(14) and (23) and Sch 3A paras 12 and 13 SS&CS(DA) Regs
JSA Sch 2 para 7(2)-(2B) JSA Regs; reg 7(18) and (23) and Sch 3A paras 12 and 13 SS&CS(DA) Regs
ESA Sch 6 para 9(2) and (3) ESA Regs; reg 7(17D) and (23) and Sch 3C paras 9 and 10 SS&CS(DA) Regs
PC Sch 2 para 7(2) and (4C) SPC Regs; reg 7(17A) SS&CS(DA) Regs

96 Reg 7(17B) and (17C) SS&CS(DA) Regs

97 **IS** Sch 3 para 1A IS Regs
JSA Sch 2 para 1A JSA Regs
ESA Sch 6 para 3 ESA Regs
PC Sch 2 para 7(4A)-(5) SPC Regs

98 **IS** Sch 3 para 17(1) IS Regs
JSA Sch 2 para 16(1) JSA Regs
ESA Sch 6 para 18(1) ESA Regs
PC Sch 2 para 13(1) SPC Regs

99 **IS** Sch 3 para 17(3) IS Regs
JSA Sch 2 para 16(3) JSA Regs
ESA Sch 6 para 18(3) ESA Regs
PC Sch 2 para 13(3) SPC Regs

100 **IS** Sch 3 para 17(4) IS Regs
JSA Sch 2 para 16(4) JSA Regs
ESA Sch 6 para 18(4) ESA Regs
PC Sch 2 para 13(4) SPC Regs

101 **IS** Sch 3 para 17(2) IS Regs
JSA Sch 2 para 16(2) JSA Regs
ESA Sch 6 para 18(2) ESA Regs
PC Sch 2 para 13(2) SPC Regs

102 **IS** Sch 3 para 11(4) and (5) IS Regs
JSA Sch 2 para 10(3) and (4) JSA Regs
ESA Sch 6 para 12(3) and (4) ESA Regs
PC Sch 2 para 8(1) and (2) SPC Regs
All Regs 3-6 and 8-11 SS(HCSA)(A&M) Regs; reg 7 SS(HCA) Regs

103 **IS** Sch 3 para 11(6) IS Regs
JSA Sch 2 para 10(5) JSA Regs
ESA Sch 6 para 12(5) ESA Regs
PC Sch 2 para 8(3) SPC Regs

104 Reg 12 SS(HCSA)(A&M) Regs; reg 8 SS(HCA) Regs

105 **IS** Sch 3 para 13 IS Regs
JSA Sch 2 para 12 JSA Regs
ESA Sch 6 para 14 ESA Regs
PC Sch 2 para 10 SPC Regs

106 **IS** Sch 3 para 13(2) IS Regs
JSA Sch 2 para 12(2) JSA Regs
ESA Sch 6 para 14(2) ESA Regs
PC Sch 2 para 10(2) SPC Regs

107 **IS** Sch 3 para 13(3) IS Regs
JSA Sch 2 para 12(3) JSA Regs
ESA Sch 6 para 14(3) ESA Regs
PC Sch 2 para 10(3) SPC Regs

108 CJSA/2683/2002

109 R(IS) 9/91; CJSA/2536/2000

110 **IS** Sch 3 para 13(4) and (5) IS Regs
JSA Sch 2 para 12(4) and (5) JSA Regs
ESA Sch 6 para 14(4) and (5) ESA Regs
PC Sch 2 para 10(4) and (5) SPC Regs
All R(SB) 6/89; R(SB) 7/89

111 R(SB) 7/89

112 R(IS) 10/93; CIS/347/1992;

113 CSB/617/1988. This case has been reported as R(SB) 4/89, but the reported version omits the relevant paragraphs.

114 **IS** Sch 3 para 13(6) IS Regs
JSA Sch 2 para 12(6) JSA Regs
ESA Sch 6 para 14(6) and (10) ESA Regs
PC Sch 2 para 10(6) SPC Regs
All *Secretary of State for Social Security v Julien,* reported as R(IS) 13/92; R(SB) 7/89; CIS/104/1991; CJSA/2536/2000

115 **IS** Sch 3 paras 13(7) and (9) and 14(15) IS Regs
JSA Sch 2 paras 12(7) and (9) and 18(1)(c) JSA Regs
ESA Sch 6 paras 14(7), (9) and (10) and 20(1)(c) ESA Regs
PC Sch 2 para 10(7), (9) and (10) SPC Regs

116 **IS** Reg 3 and Sch 3 para 18 IS Regs
JSA Reg 2 and Sch 2 para 17 JSA Regs
ESA Reg 71 and Sch 6 para 19 ESA Regs
PC Sch 2 paras 1(4)-(9) and 14 SPC Regs

117 R(H) 8/09; *SK v South Hams DC (HB)* [2010] UKUT 129 (AAC); [2010] AACR 40

118 **IS** Reg 3 IS Regs
JSA Reg 2 JSA Regs
ESA Reg 71 ESA Regs
PC Sch 2 para 1(4)-(7) SPC Regs

119 CSB/1163/1988

120 **IS** Sch 3 para 18(6) IS Regs
JSA Sch 2 para 17(6) JSA Regs
ESA Sch 6 para 19(6) ESA Regs
PC Sch 2 para 14(6) SPC Regs

121 **IS** Sch 3 para 18(7) IS Regs
JSA Sch 2 para 17(7) JSA Regs
ESA Sch 6 para 19(7) ESA Regs
PC Sch 2 para 14(7) SPC Regs

4

122 Made under s2 ETA 1973 or s2 Enterprise and New Towns (Scotland) Act 1990 or by the Secretary of State for people enlisted in HM Forces for any special term of service specified in regulations made under s2 Armed Forces Act 1966.

123 Reg 3 JSA(SAPOE) Regs

124 **IS** Sch 3 para 18(1) and (2) IS Regs
JSA Sch 2 para 17(1) and (2) JSA Regs
ESA Sch 6 para 19(1) and (2) ESA Regs
PC Sch 2 para 14(1) and (2) SPC Regs

125 Sch 2 para 2(6) SPC Regs

126 **IS** Sch 3 para 18(8) IS Regs
JSA Sch 2 para 17(8) JSA Regs
ESA Sch 6 para 19(8) ESA Regs
PC Sch 2 para 14(8) SPC Regs

127 CH/48/2006

128 **IS** Sch 3 para 18(3) and (4) IS Regs
JSA Sch 2 para 17(3) and (4) JSA Regs
ESA Sch 6 para 19(3) and (4) ESA Regs
PC Sch 2 para 14(3) and (4) SPC Regs

129 **IS** Sch 3 para 18(5) IS Regs
JSA Sch 2 para 17(5) JSA Regs
ESA Sch 6 para 19(5) ESA Regs
PC Sch 2 para 14(5) SPC Regs

130 **IS** Reg 42(4)(a)(ii) IS Regs
JSA Reg 105(10)(a)(ii) JSA Regs
ESA Reg 107(3)(c) ESA Regs

131 **IS** Sch 10 para 26 IS Regs
JSA Sch 8 para 6 JSA Regs
ESA Sch 9 para 6 ESA Regs
PC Sch 5 para 7 SPC Regs

6. Waiting periods

132 **IS** Sch 3 para 8 IS Regs
JSA Sch 2 para 7 JSA Regs
ESA Sch 6 para 9 ESA Regs

133 *SK v SSWP* [2013] UKUT 138 (AAC)

134 **IS** Sch 3 para 14(8) and (9) IS Regs
JSA Sch 2 para 13(10) and (11) JSA Regs
ESA Sch 6 para 15(13) and (14) ESA Regs

135 **IS** Sch 3 para 9 IS Regs
JSA Sch 2 para 8 JSA Regs
ESA Sch 6 para 10 ESA Regs

136 **IS** Sch 3 paras 1(2) and 8 IS Regs
JSA Sch 2 paras 1(2) and 7 JSA Regs
ESA Sch 6 paras 1(2) and 9 ESA Regs
All CJSA/2028/2000

7. Linking rules

137 **IS** Sch 3 para 14(1)(a), (3A) and (15) IS Regs; reg 32 IS(JSACA) Regs
JSA Sch 2 paras 13(1)(a), (2A) and (4) and 18(1)(c) JSA Regs
ESA Sch 6 paras 15 (1)(a), (5), (15) and (16) and 20(1)(c) ESA Regs

138 Sch 6 para 1(3A)-(3C) ESA Regs

139 **IS** Sch 3 para 14(4) and (5) IS Regs; reg 32 IS(JSACA) Regs
JSA Sch 2 paras 13(5) and (6) and 18(1)(c) JSA Regs; reg 32 IS(JSACA) Regs
ESA Sch 6 paras 2(9), 15(8) and (9) and 20(1)(c) ESA Regs
All CIS/621/2004

140 CJSA/4613/2001

141 Sch 3 para 14(5)(c) IS Regs; reg 32 IS(JSACA) Regs

142 **IS** Sch 3 para 14(4), (5A) and (5B) IS Regs; reg 32 IS(JSACA) Regs
JSA Sch 2 paras 13(7) and (8) and 18(1)(c) JSA Regs; reg 32 IS(JSACA) Regs
ESA Sch 6 paras 2(9), 15(8), (10) and (11) and 20(1)(c) ESA Regs
All CIS/621/2004

143 **IS** Sch 3 para 14(6) IS Regs
JSA Sch 2 para 13(9) JSA Regs
ESA Sch 6 para 15(12) ESA Regs

144 **IS** Sch 3 para 14(1)(c), (d) and (e), (3A), (14) and (15) IS Regs
JSA Sch 2 paras 13(1)(c), (d), (dd) and (e), (4) and (16) and 18(1)(c) JSA Regs
ESA Sch 6 paras 15(1)(c), (d) and (e), (15) and (19) and 20(1)(c) ESA Regs

145 **IS** Sch 3 para 14(3), (3A) and (15) IS Regs
JSA Sch 2 paras 13(3), (4) and 18(1)(c) JSA Regs
ESA Sch 6 paras 15(3), (5) and 20(1)(c) ESA Regs

146 **IS** Sch 3 para 14(1)(f) and (3A) IS Regs
JSA Sch 2 para 13(1)(f) and (4) JSA Regs
ESA Sch 6 paras 15(1)(g) and (5) and 20(1)(c) ESA Regs

147 **IS** Sch 3 para 14(11) and (12) IS Regs
JSA Sch 2 para 13(13) and (14) JSA Regs
ESA Sch 6 paras 2(9) and 15(16) and (17) ESA Regs

148 Schemes mentioned in reg 19(1)(r)(i)-(iii) JSA Regs

149 **IS** Sch 3 para 14(13) IS Regs
JSA Sch 2 para 13(15) JSA Regs
ESA Sch 6 para 15(18) ESA Regs

8. Mortgage interest run-on

150 Reg 3(h) SS(C&P) Regs
151 Reg 6(5) and (8) IS Regs
152 Reg 6(7) IS Regs
153 Reg 6(6) IS Regs
154 Sch 9A para 3(9) SS(C&P) Regs
155 Sch 7 para 19A(1) IS Regs
156 Schs 8 para 15C and 9 para 74 IS Regs
157 Sch 10 para 62 IS Regs
158 Sch 7 para 19A(2) and (3) IS Regs

Chapter 21

Discretionary housing payments

This chapter covers:
1. Who can claim discretionary housing payments (below)
2. The rules about your age (p482)
3. People included in the claim (p482)
4. The amount of discretionary housing payments (p482)
5. Claims, decisions and getting paid (p482)
6. Tax, other benefits and the benefit cap (p483)

Key facts

- Discretionary housing payments are extra payments that can be made by your local authority if you need help to meet your housing costs – eg, because you are affected by the benefit cap, or your rent has been restricted.
- You must be entitled to housing benefit or universal credit for your rent payments to get discretionary housing payments.
- You do not have a 'right' to discretionary housing payments. They are paid from a cash-limited budget allocated to your local authority by the government.
- You cannot appeal to the First-tier Tribunal against a discretionary housing payment decision, but you can ask the local authority for a review.

Future changes

From 1 April 2017, the Scottish Parliament has the power to make rules on discretionary housing payments in Scotland. See CPAG's online service and *Welfare Rights Bulletin* for updates.

1. **Who can claim discretionary housing payments**

A local authority can pay you discretionary housing payments if you are entitled to:[1]

- housing benefit (HB); *or*
- universal credit (UC) that includes a housing costs element for rent payments.

You must appear to the local authority to require financial assistance in addition to the benefit to which you are entitled in order to meet your housing costs. For example, if your HB or UC is being paid at a reduced rate because non-dependant deductions are being made, because of the benefit cap, or under any of the rent restriction rules in Chapter 19 or Chapter 22, you may be able to get discretionary housing payments to make up the difference. Housing costs include rent in advance, deposits and removal expenses, so you may be able to get discretionary housing payments for these.

The local authority has discretion on whether to pay you, the amount to pay you (within certain limits) and over what period to pay you, even though your HB or UC housing costs element is being paid in full direct to your landlord on your behalf.[2]

DWP guidance to local authorities is at www.gov.uk/government/publications/discretionary-housing-payments-guidance-manual. Further information about discretionary housing payments is at *Ask CPAG Online* (www.cpag.org.uk/content/ask-cpag-online-discretionary-housing-payments).

When discretionary housing payments cannot be made

Discretionary housing payments cannot be made to you if your need for financial assistance arises as a consequence of:[3]
- ineligible service charges under the HB (see p66) or the UC scheme (p489);
- water and sewerage charges;
- liability for council tax. However, you may be able to get help from your local authority's council tax reduction scheme (see p854);
- your rent payments increasing to cover arrears of rent, service charges or other unpaid charges;
- a reduced benefit decision because you refused to co-operate in pursuing maintenance for your child(ren);
- your benefit (eg, income support or employment support allowance) being reduced because you refused to take part in a work-focused interview;
- your jobseeker's allowance (JSA) or UC being paid at a reduced (or nil) rate because you have been sanctioned under specified rules;
- if you are 16 or 17, your severe hardship payments of JSA (see p129) being reduced because you gave up a place on a training scheme or failed to attend without a good reason;
- your benefit being suspended;
- a reduction in your benefit because an overpayment of HB, UC or council tax benefit is being recovered;
- your benefit being restricted because of a benefit offence (see p1265).

Part 4: Paying for housing
Chapter 21: Discretionary housing payments
4. The amount of discretionary housing payments

2. **The rules about your age**

There are no lower or upper age limits for discretionary housing payments.

3. **People included in the claim**

You claim discretionary housing payments for yourself. However, your circumstances and needs as well as those of your child(ren) and your partner should be taken into account in deciding whether you can be paid.

4. **The amount of discretionary housing payments**

Discretionary housing payments are normally paid in weekly amounts. The local authority can decide how much you can be paid, how long you can be paid and how far your payments can be backdated.[4] However, it can only pay discretionary housing payments for periods during which you are (or were) entitled to housing benefit (HB) or universal credit (UC) that includes a housing costs element for rent payments.

You cannot be paid more than:[5]

- if you are entitled to HB and your discretionary housing payments are calculated as a weekly amount, the amount of your rent and other payments that can be met by HB (see p45), not including any amounts paid for ineligible service charges and rent-free periods; *or*
- if you are entitled to UC and your discretionary housing payments are calculated as a monthly amount, the amount of your housing costs element for rent payments. See Chapter 22 for how this is calculated.

Any HB (or UC) you have already received (or will receive) for the period may be deducted.[6]

There is no restriction on the amount of one-off payments.[7] Larger amounts (eg, for rent in advance or a rent deposit) can therefore be paid by a lump sum.

Note:

- In deciding whether to pay you discretionary housing payments and, if so, how much to pay you, the local authority can look at what income and capital you have. However, it cannot take disability living allowance, attendance allowance or personal independence payment into account.[8]
- If you need additional help with housing costs because there is a shortfall between your HB (or UC) and the rent you are liable to pay, ensure the local

authority knows this, in particular if you are getting UC as it might not already have this information.

5. Claims, decisions and getting paid

Ask your local authority how to make a claim for discretionary housing payments. It may accept a claim from you, or from someone acting on your behalf, provided *you* are entitled to housing benefit (or universal credit that includes a housing costs element for rent payments).[9] Your local authority decides what 'form or manner' your claim should take – eg, in writing or by other means.[10]

You must provide grounds for your claim and provide any other information that the local authority specifies.[11] Provide any evidence that shows why you need discretionary housing payments – eg, a financial statement and evidence of any disability or medical condition affecting you or the people who live with you.

Note:

- If you want your claim to be backdated, tell the local authority.
- You must be given written notice of the local authority's decision on your claim and the reasons for its decision as soon as is 'reasonably practicable'.[12]
- The local authority can pay you or, if reasonable, someone else where appropriate.[13]
- It is your duty to report any change in your circumstances that may be relevant to payment of your discretionary housing payments continuing.[14]

Getting a decision changed

You do not have a right to appeal to the First-tier Tribunal against a discretionary housing payment decision. However, you can ask the local authority for a review of its decision.[15] You are entitled to written notice of, and reasons for, the review decision as soon as is 'reasonably practicable'.[16] You might be able to challenge a review decision by judicial review (see p1378). If the local authority's decision involves maladministration (error or wrongdoing) which results in injustice to you, you can also complain to the Ombudsman (see p1401).

6. Tax, other benefits and the benefit cap

Discretionary housing payments are not taxable.

Discretionary housing payments are disregarded as income and capital for the purposes of all the means-tested benefits and tax credits.[17]

You may quailify for discretionary council tax reduction (see p854) in additon to discretionary housing payments. Ensure you claim both types of payment, if relevant, to avoid missing out.

Part 4: Paying for housing
Chapter 21: Discretionary housing payments
Notes

The benefit cap

In some cases, there is a limit on the total amount of specified benefits you receive (a 'benefit cap'). Discretionary housing payments are *not* among the specified benefits. See p1180 for further information.

Notes

4

1. Who can claim discretionary housing payments
1 s69 CSPSSA 2000; reg 2(1) DFA Regs
2 Reg 2(2) DFA Regs
3 Reg 3 DFA Regs

4. The amount of discretionary housing payments
4 Reg 5 DFA Regs
5 Reg 4 DFA Regs
6 *Gargett, R (on the application of) v Lambeth LB* [2008] EWCA Civ 1450
7 paras 2.9 and 2.10 *Discretionary Housing Payments Guidance Manual*
8 *R (Hardy) v Sandwell MBC* [2015] EWHC 890 (Admin), 30 March 2015

5. Claims, decisions and getting paid
9 Reg 6 DFA Regs
10 Reg 6(1)(a) DFA Regs
11 Reg 7 DFA Regs
12 Reg 6(3) DFA Regs
13 Reg 6(2) DFA Regs
14 Reg 7(b) DFA Regs
15 Reg 8 DFA Regs
16 Reg 6(3) DFA Regs

6. Tax, other benefits and the benefit cap
17 **IS** Schs 9 para 75 and 10 para 7(1)(d) IS Regs
JSA Schs 7 para 71 and 8 para 12(1)(d) JSA Regs
ESA Schs 8 para 62 and 9 para 11(1)(c) ESA Regs
PC Reg 15 SPC Regs
HB Schs 5 para 62 and 6 para 9(1)(d) HB Regs; reg 29 HB(SPC) Regs
UC Reg 66 UC Regs

Chapter 22

Universal credit housing costs

This chapter covers:
1. When you get a housing costs element (p486)
2. Payments that can be met (p487)
3. Liability for payments (p490)
4. Occupying accommodation as a home (p494)
5. The rules about your age (p498)
6. The amount for rented accommodation (p500)
7. The amount for owner-occupiers (p514)

This chapter covers the rules for the universal credit (UC) housing costs element, including the rent restriction rules. However, the rules about local housing allowances for UC are broadly the same as for housing benefit, so these are covered in Chapter 19 where relevant.

Key facts
- Your universal credit (UC) can include a housing costs element if you are renting accommodation, are an owner-occupier or if you pay service charges.
- If you are a private tenant (or you live in certain types of temporary accommodation), the rent used to calculate your housing costs element is based on a local housing allowance for a property with the number of bedrooms the rules allow.
- If you are a social rented sector tenant (eg, your landlord is a local authority or housing association) and your home has more bedrooms than the rules allow, your housing costs element is usually reduced by a percentage.
- You cannot get a housing costs element for owner-occupier payments if you (or your partner) have any earned income, however low your earnings are.
- There is a limit on the amount of help you can get for owner-occupier payments and you might not get a housing costs element during an initial 'waiting period'.
- If your housing costs element is for rent payments and you need extra financial assistance to meet your housing costs, you may be able to get discretionary housing payments from your local authority.

Part 4: Paying for housing
Chapter 22: Universal credit housing costs
1. When you get a housing costs element

Future changes

From 2018, help with 'owner-occupier payments' will be paid as a loan. This will apply to income support, income-based jobseeker's allowance, income-related employment and support allowance, pension credit and UC. You will have to repay the loan when the house is sold or when you return to work. You will also have to pay administration costs and interest on the amount of help provided. It is not known if any transitional protection will be provided.

The government says that from 1 April 2019, the amount of rent your housing costs element can cover will be capped at the local housing allowance that would apply under the local housing allowance rules (see p407). It says that this will apply to all tenants on UC, including those in supported accommodation.

In the future, the rules on UC housing costs may be different in Scotland.

See CPAG's online service and *Welfare Rights Bulletin* for updates.

1. **When you get a housing costs element**

Your universal credit (UC) maximum amount can include a housing costs element to provide help with your rent payments (see p487) or with the costs of buying your home (owner-occupier payments – see p488). It can also include some help with service charges (service charge payments – see p489). Ensure that you let the DWP know that you pay rent or are buying your home, so a housing costs element is included.

You qualify for a housing costs element if:[1]

- your accommodation is in Great Britain; *and*
- your accommodation is residential – ie, not for a business. If your accommodation is partly for a business and partly residential, you can qualify for a housing costs element for the part that is residential; *and*
- you or your partner are liable to make eligible payments for the accommodation that you occupy as your home (see p487, p490 and p494).

The accommodation can comprise the whole of a building or part of a building – eg, a flat in a block, a bedsit in a house or a room in a shared house. You can get a housing costs element whether or not the accommodation comprises separate and self-contained premises.[2]

Note: if you qualify for a work allowance, you live in rented accommodation and a housing costs element is included in your UC maximum amount, you qualify for a lower work allowance and therefore more of your earnings are taken into account (see p167).

When you cannot get a housing costs element

Your UC maximum amount *cannot* include a housing costs element:

- for rent payments, if you are 16 or 17 and are being, or were previously, looked after by a local authority (see p937);[3]
- for rent payments, if you live in a 'full service' area and you are at least 18 but under 22, you are a single person (or a member of a couple claiming as a single person), you are not responsible for any children and you have to meet all the work-related requirements (see p1080). There are a number of exceptions (see p498);[4]
- for owner-occupier payments, during an assessment period in which you (or your partner) have any earned income (see p338), however much your earnings are.[5] This includes earnings from work you can do while claiming contributory employment and support allowance (see p1021) or from work of less than 16 hours a week you can do while claiming contribution-based jobseeker's allowance (see p989). The nature and duration of the work is not relevant – eg, it does not matter if your job is part time or temporary. **Note:** this only applies to the owner-occupier payments you make, so if you have a shared ownership tenancy, you can still get a housing costs element for your rent and your service charge payments;
- if you live in 'specified accommodation' (see p488), for the rent you pay for that accommodation. You *can* get housing benefit for this.

2. Payments that can be met

To qualify for a housing costs element, the payments you make must be eligible. This is called the 'payment condition' in this *Handbook*. There are three types of eligible payments:

- rent payments (see below);
- owner-occupier payments (see p488); *and*
- service charge payments (see p489).

A housing costs element can include any of the eligible payments that you make. **Note:** if you have a shared ownership tenancy (ie, you are buying part of your home and renting the rest), your housing costs element can include rent and owner-occupier payments, as well as the service charge payments you make.[6]

Rent payments

Eligible rent payments (referred to as 'rent payments' in this *Handbook*) include the rent you pay to your landlord, but can also include other types of payment, such as payments as a licensee and for bed and breakfast or hostel accommodation. The eligible payments are:[7]

Part 4: Paying for housing
Chapter 22: Universal credit housing costs
2. Payments that can be met

- rent;
- payments for a licence or permission to occupy accommodation;
- mooring charges payable for a houseboat;
- site rent for a caravan or mobile home (but not for a tent); *and*
- contributions made by a resident of a charity's almshouse towards its maintenance and the essential services in it. The almshouse must be provided by a housing association.

Payments that are not eligible

The following types of payments are not eligible, and cannot be included in your housing costs element:[8]

- ground rent;
- payments for a tent or its pitch;
- payments for approved premises – eg, a bail or probation hostel;
- payments made for 'specified accommodation' (see below). You can get housing benefit (HB) for this (see Chapter 4); *and*
- payments made for a care home (see below).

Definitions

'**Specified accommodation**' is:[9]

– accommodation provided by a relevant body to meet your need for, and where you get, care, support or supervision; *or*

– temporary accommodation (eg, a refuge) provided by a local authority or a relevant body because you have left your home because of domestic violence (see p1035 – the meaning is the same as for jobseeker's allowance); *or*

– a local authority hostel for homeless people where you get care, support or supervision to assist you to be rehabilitated or resettled within the community; *or*

– 'exempt accommodation' (see p428 – the meaning is the same as for HB).

For these purposes, a 'relevant body' is a county council (in England) or a housing association, registered charity or voluntary organisation.

'**Care home**' means a care home (in England and Wales), a care home service (in Scotland) or an independent hospital.[10]

Owner-occupier payments

The eligible payments (referred to as 'owner-occupier payments' in this *Handbook*) are:[11]

- interest payments on a loan that is secured on the accommodation you occupy, or are treated as occupying, as a home (see p494), whatever the purpose of the loan; *and*
- payments made under alternative finance arrangements to enable you to acquire an interest in the accommodation you occupy, or are treated as occupying, as a home (see p494) – eg, for a Sharia-compliant mortgage.

You cannot get help with associated insurance premiums – eg, if you have an endowment mortgage, you do not get the insurance element paid.

Service charge payments

The eligible payments (referred to as 'service charge payments' in this *Handbook*) are payments:[12]

- for the costs of, or charges for, services or facilities for the use or benefit of people occupying the accommodation – eg, window cleaning or garden maintenance; *or*
- fairly attributable to the costs of, or charges for, services or facilities connected with accommodation that are available for the use or benefit of people occupying the accommodation – eg, provision of laundry facilities.

The payments do not have to be separately identified – eg, in your tenancy agreement. It does not matter if they are paid in addition to, or as part of, your rent, or if they are made under the same or a different agreement to that under which you occupy your home.

If you live in social rented sector accommodation (other than temporary accommodation), or you are getting a housing costs element for owner-occupier payments, you must satisfy extra conditions and the rules specify the only categories of payments that are eligible.

Payments that are not eligible

Payments are not eligible and cannot be included in your housing costs element if:[13]

- you have taken out a loan to make the payments and it is secured on the accommodation you occupy, or are treated as occupying, as a home. However, any payments you make on the loan may qualify as owner-occupier payments (see p488); *or*
- the services or facilities to which the payments relate are for someone occupying a tent, approved premises (eg, a bail or probation hostel), a care home (see p488) or 'exempt accommodation' (see p428 – you may qualify for HB).

Extra conditions for service charge payments

If you live in social rented sector accommodation (other than in temporary accommodation – see p507 for what counts), or you are getting a housing costs element for owner-occupier payments, service charge payments are only eligible if you must make them as a condition of occupying your accommodation – eg, as part of your tenancy agreement or lease, not as an optional extra.[14] The costs and charges must be reasonable, must be for services and facilities that are reasonable to provide and must fit into one of the following categories.[15]

- Payments to maintain the general standard of accommodation – ie, for:

Part 4: Paying for housing
Chapter 22: Universal credit housing costs
3. Liability for payments

- cleaning the outside of windows on the upper floors of a multi-storey building; *or*
- if you have a shared ownership tenancy or are getting a housing costs element for owner-occupier payments, internal or external maintenance or repair of the accommodation. The payments must be separately identifiable.

- Payments for the general upkeep of communal areas – ie, for the ongoing maintenance of, and the supply of, water, fuel or any other commodity to internal or external areas – eg, communal gardens, tenant parking facilities, laundry rooms and children's play areas.

- Payments for basic communal services. They must be for the provision, ongoing maintenance, cleaning or repair of basic services generally available to everyone living in the accommodation – eg, refuse collection, communal lifts, secure building access, fire alarm systems or wireless or television aerials to receive a service free of charge. The DWP says it should also include payments for someone employed to provide an eligible service (eg, a concierge, groundskeeper or caretaker), as well as the costs of managing and administering eligible services.[16]

- Accommodation-specific charges. These must be for the use of essential items specific to the particular accommodation you occupy – eg, for furniture or domestic appliances.

However, payments are *not* eligible and cannot be included in your housing costs element if they are:[17]

- for services or facilities for which public funding is available, whether or not you are entitled to such funding;
- connected to the use of an asset which will result in the transfer of that asset, or any interest in it – eg, payments for furniture and equipment that will eventually become yours;
- for food, medical services or personal services (including laundry, cleaning or personal care).

3. **Liability for payments**

To qualify for a housing costs element, you (or your partner) must be liable to make eligible payments on a commercial basis, or you (or s/he) must be treated as liable (see p491).[18] This is called the 'liability condition' in this *Handbook*. **Note:** you (or your partner) can be treated as not liable to make payments, even if you are (see p492).

For what 'liable' may mean in respect of rent payments, see p47. The issues are the same as for housing benefit.

In deciding if your agreement is on a commercial basis, the DWP must look at the whole agreement and take all the circumstances into account. The DWP should consider, among other things, the following.[19]

- Whether your agreement includes terms that are not legally enforceable. This might arise, for example, if you do household chores. However, if you do chores in exchange for a lower rent, it could be considered commercial.
- The rent you have agreed to pay. However, the rent does not have to be a market rent. Your agreement can count as commercial even if your landlord is not collecting the full contractual rent from you – eg, if it is not being met in full because of the way your housing costs element is calculated.
- Your relationship to the person to whom you are liable. However, just because s/he is a relative or close friend, or s/he provides you with care and support does not mean that your agreement is non-commercial.

Note: if you live in rented accommodation and are jointly liable to make payments with someone, the way your housing costs element is calculated takes this into account (see p508 and p511).

People treated as liable to make payments

You (or your partner) are treated as liable to make payments:[20]
- if a child or qualifying young person for whom you (or your partner) are responsible (see p222) is liable to make the payments;
- if you are a member of a couple but you are claiming universal credit (UC) as a single person (other than if you are in a polygamous marriage) and your partner is liable to make the payments. See p162 for when you can claim as a single person;
- if someone else is liable to make the payments but is not doing so (see below);
- if payments are waived by the person to whom you are liable (eg, your landlord) as reasonable compensation for your carrying out reasonable repairs or redecoration which s/he would otherwise have had to carry out; *or*
- during rent-free periods (for rent and service charge payments only).

Another person is liable but is not paying

You (or your partner) are treated as liable to make payments if someone else is liable to make them but is not doing so, and you must make the payments yourself to continue to live in your home.[21] In addition, you must show that:
- it would be unreasonable to expect you to make other arrangements; *and*
- it is reasonable in all the circumstances to treat you as liable. In deciding what is reasonable for owner-occupier payments, the DWP can take into account the fact that the liable person may benefit from your making the payments.

This might apply, for example, if you have given up your home to live with and care for someone and s/he has now gone into a care home, or if you have separated

Part 4: Paying for housing
Chapter 22: Universal credit housing costs
3. Liability for payments

from your partner (even if you have not lived in the home continuously since your partner left).[22]

For rent payments, it does not matter whether or not the landlord is prepared to transfer the tenancy to you or wants to evict you. If the DWP refuses to treat you as liable, point out that the eligibility rules for the housing costs element and the rules for transferring tenancies are separate. If you are refused the housing costs element, ask for a revision or appeal. You must apply for a mandatory reconsideration before you can appeal.

4 People treated as not liable to make payments

You (or your partner) can be treated as though you are *not* liable to make payments. This applies if you are in specified situations (see below and p493) and also if the DWP considers the liability to be 'contrived' (see p493). In addition, you are treated as not liable to make:

- any payments that are for an increase in the amount that you would otherwise be liable to pay, which is as a result of outstanding arrears of any payment or charge for your accommodation, or for accommodation you previously occupied, or for any other unpaid payment or charge;[23]
- service charge payments, if you are liable to make them to someone who lives in your household (see p225 for the meaning) and you are not liable to make either rent or owner-occupier payments.[24]

People treated as not liable to pay rent and service charges

You are treated as not liable to make rent payments if you are liable to make them to:[25]

- someone who also lives in the accommodation, and who is:
  - your partner, or a child or qualifying young person for whom you (or your partner) are responsible (see p222); *or*
  - a close relative of yours or your partner, or of a child or qualifying young person for whom you (or your partner) are responsible (see p222).
  For example, this applies if you are living with, and pay rent to, your parents. If you are liable to pay service charge payments to the person, you are also treated as not liable for those payments;
- a trustee of a trust or a company and the trustees or beneficiaries of that trust, or the owners or directors of the company, include you, your partner or a qualifying young person (or in the case of trusts, a child) for whom you (or your partner) are responsible (see p222), or a close relative of any of these. The close relative must live with you in the accommodation.
  If you are liable to pay service charge payments to a trustee of the same trust (or of another trust whose trustees or beneficiaries include any of the people listed in the above bullet point), or to the same company (or a company whose

owners or directors include any of the people listed in the above bullet point), you are also treated as not liable for those payments.

Close relative
A 'close relative' is a parent, parent-in-law (including a civil partner's parent), son, son-in-law (including a son's civil partner), daughter, daughter-in-law (including a daughter's civil partner), brother, sister, step-parent (including a parent's civil partner), stepson (including a civil partner's son), stepdaughter (including a civil partner's daughter), or the partners of any of these.[26] It also includes half-brothers and sisters.[27] Relations with in-laws or step-relatives are severed by divorce (or dissolution of a civil partnership) but arguably not by death – eg, a stepchild is still a stepchild after the death of her/his mother.

People treated as not liable to pay owner-occupier payments and service charges
You are treated as not liable to make owner-occupier payments if you are liable to make them to someone who lives in your household (see p225 for the meaning).[28] If you are liable to pay service charge payments to the same person, you are also treated as not liable for those payments.

Contrived agreements
Even if none of the specified situations above apply, you may still be treated as not liable to make payments if your liability was 'contrived' to get the housing costs element included in your UC, or to increase the amount of your housing costs element.[29] The DWP says this applies if either you or your landlord, or both of you, contrived the liability.[30] For your agreement to count as contrived, it must amount to an abuse of the UC scheme or take improper advantage of it – ie, that the main reason you entered into the agreement to make payments was to obtain or increase your UC housing costs element.[31] All the circumstances should be taken into account when deciding whether this is the case, including what the person you are liable to pay has to say.[32] An agreement can count as contrived even if it was created from the best of motives.[33]

Does the DWP say your agreement is contrived?
The DWP may say that your agreement is contrived if you are in any of the situations described on pp48–50 for HB. If it does, get advice. 'Contrived' is not defined in the rules. You can argue the following.
1. Your agreement should not count as contrived just because the person you are liable to pay is your parent[34] or because you hope to be able to claim UC to help you with your rent or mortgage – ie, if your main purpose is to get accommodation, not to obtain the UC housing costs element.[35]
2. You should not be regarded as having a contrived agreement just because you try to find out what payments can be covered by UC – eg, before moving in.

Part 4: Paying for housing
Chapter 22: Universal credit housing costs
4. Occupying accommodation as a home

3. Tenants of a landlord who deliberately charges high rents in order to have them paid by UC may be affected by this provision, even though they had no such intention themselves. However, the fact that a landlord sets a high rent does not, in itself, mean that the liability is contrived.[36]

4. If your landlord says s/he will evict you if you cannot get the UC housing costs element, or get it increased, this suggests that the agreement is *not* contrived.[37] If the DWP says your agreement is contrived and does not include a housing costs element in your UC, you can appeal. You must apply for a mandatory reconsideration first.

4. **Occupying accommodation as a home**

To qualify for the universal credit (UC) housing costs element, you must normally occupy the accommodation for which you make eligible payments as your home.[38] This is called the 'occupation condition' in this *Handbook*. You cannot usually get a housing costs element for any other home. However, there are special rules if you:

* have just moved into your home (see below);
* are liable to make payments for more than one dwelling (see p495);
* are temporarily absent from home (see p496);
* are in temporary accommodation while repairs are carried out on your home (see p497);
* have left your previous home because of a fear of domestic violence (see p497).

Moving home

If you have moved into new accommodation, you are treated as occupying it for up to one month before you moved in, provided you met the payment condition (see p487) and the liability condition (see p490) for the accommodation immediately before you moved in, and:[39]

* there was a delay in moving into your accommodation, this was reasonable, and was necessary to enable the accommodation to be adapted to meet needs you, your partner or a child or qualifying young person for whom you (or your partner) are responsible (see p222) have because of a disability. The adaptations do not need to involve a change to the fabric or structure of the dwelling, but must be reasonably required and have a clear connection to the disability needs.[40] The person with the needs must be getting the middle or highest rate of disability living allowance care component, attendance allowance, armed forces independence payment or the daily living component of personal independence payment.

Note: in these circumstances you may also qualify for a housing costs element for your former home (see below), or for housing benefit (HB) for your former home if it was 'specified accommodation' (see p488); or

- you became liable to make payments on your new accommodation while you were a patient or were living in a care home (see p488 for the meaning), or if you make a joint claim, while both of you were.

Patient

For these purposes, you are a '**patient**' if you are undergoing medical or other treatment as an inpatient in any hospital or similar institution.[41] You do not have to be receiving the treatment free of charge.

More than one dwelling

You cannot usually be treated as occupying accommodation which consists of more than one dwelling.[42] If you do, to decide which dwelling you normally occupy as your home, the DWP must consider all the circumstances, including the people who live with you in each dwelling. **Note:** different rules apply if you are living away from your normal home because of a fear of domestic violence (see p497).

You can get a housing costs element for two dwellings for up to **one month**, if there was a delay in moving into your new accommodation, this was reasonable, and was necessary to enable the accommodation to be adapted to meet needs you, your partner or a child or qualifying young person for whom you (or your partner) are responsible (see p222) have because of a disability.[43] The conditions are the same as those for moving home (see p494).

You can get a housing costs element for both your previous and your new accommodation if, immediately before you moved, you qualified for a housing costs element for your previous accommodation and satisfied the payment condition (see p487) and the liability condition (see p490) for your new accommodation. **Note:** if you are only liable to make payments for your new accommodation, you may qualify for a housing costs element for that accommodation (see p494).

You can get a housing costs element for two dwellings **indefinitely**, if you have been housed in two dwellings by a 'provider of social housing' because of the number of children and qualifying young people who live with you.[44] You must normally occupy both dwellings with children or qualifying young people for whom you (or your partner) are responsible (see p222). You must meet the payment condition (see p487) and the liability condition (see p490) for both dwellings.

Part 4: Paying for housing
Chapter 22: Universal credit housing costs
4. Occupying accommodation as a home

> **Provider of social housing**
>
> A **'provider of social housing'** is a local authority, a non-profit registered provider of social housing, a profit-making registered provider of social housing (if you have been housed in social housing) or a registered social landlord.[45]

Temporary absence from home

If you are only temporarily absent from the accommodation you normally occupy as a home, you continue to be treated as occupying it for up to six months, whatever the reason for your absence.[46] **Note:** you can be treated as occupying your normal home for a longer period if you have to live in other accommodation because repairs are being carried out on your normal home (see p497) or you are living away from home because of a fear of domestic violence (see p497).

You can argue that you count as temporarily absent from accommodation even if you have not yet stayed there – eg, you move your furniture and belongings in, but then have to go into hospital.[47] A new period of absence starts if you return home for even a short stay. A stay of at least 24 hours may be enough.[48]

If you are a prisoner or are on temporary release from prison, you can get a housing costs element under this rule while you are temporarily absent from home, but only if you were entitled to UC as a single person immediately before you became a prisoner, your UC included a housing costs element and your prison sentence is not expected to last more than six months.[49] If you are a member of a couple, your partner may instead be able to continue to claim UC with a housing costs element in your absence.

Note:

- You are no longer treated as occupying your normal home when your absence has lasted, or is expected to last, longer than six months. The decision whether or not your absence from home is expected to last longer than six months should initially be based on the circumstances on the date you leave your home.[50] If at any time after that date you no longer intend to return, or it becomes likely that you will be away from home for more than six months, your entitlement can be reconsidered.[51]
- If you are temporarily absent from Great Britain for longer than a set period (from one to six months depending on the circumstances), your entitlement to UC may be affected. See p1605 for further information.
- Separate rules are used to determine how many bedrooms you are allowed if a member of your extended benefit unit (ie you, your partner, your child or qualifying young person, or a non-dependant) is temporarily absent from your home (see p505).

Temporary accommodation while repairs are carried out

If you are required to move into temporary accommodation because essential repairs are being carried out on your normal home, but you intend to return to that home:[52]

- if you meet the payment condition (see p487) and the liability condition (see p490) for only one of the homes, you are treated as occupying that home and you get a housing costs element indefinitely for the payments you make in respect of it; *or*
- if you meet the payment condition (see p487) and the liability condition (see p490) for both homes, you are only treated as occupying one home (your normal home) and you get a housing costs element indefinitely for the payments you make for that home.

'**Essential repairs**' means basic works rather than luxuries, but they need not be necessary to make the house habitable.[53]

Domestic violence

Special rules apply if you are living in accommodation other than your normal home, and it is unreasonable to expect you to return to that home because of a reasonable fear of violence. You must fear violence in the home, or violence from a former partner against you or any child or qualifying young person for whom you are responsible (see p222). You must intend to return to your normal home. If these rules apply:[54]

- you are treated as occupying both the accommodation you are living in *and* the accommodation you normally live in for up to 12 months if:
  - you meet the payment condition (see p487) and the liability condition (see p490) for both your current accommodation and your normal home; *and*
  - it is reasonable to include an amount for the payments for both homes in your housing costs element; *or*
- if you only meet the payment condition and the liability condition for one of the homes, you are treated as occupying that home indefinitely (but see below). It must be reasonable to include an amount for the payments for that accommodation in your housing costs element. **Note:** if one of the homes is 'specified accommodation' (eg, a refuge – see p488), you can qualify for HB for the specified accommodation and can get a housing costs element for the other home.

In both cases, you are no longer treated as occupying your normal home when your absence has lasted, or is expected to last, longer than 12 months.[55] The decision whether or not your absence from home is expected to last longer than 12 months should initially be based on the circumstances on the date you leave your home.[56] If at any time after that date you no longer intend to return, or it

Part 4: Paying for housing
Chapter 22: Universal credit housing costs
5. The rules about your age

becomes likely that you will be away from home for more than 12 months, your entitlement can be reconsidered.[57]

5. **The rules about your age**

You must usually be aged at least 18 and under the qualifying age for pension credit (PC – see p162) to qualify for universal credit (UC). If you are a member of a couple, at least one of you must be under the qualifying age for PC. Some 16/17-year-olds may be able to qualify (see p162). **Note:** if you are:

- 16 or 17 and are being, or were previously, looked after by a local authority (see p937), you cannot qualify for a housing costs element for rent payments;
- 18 to 22, if you live in a 'full service' area and are a single person (or a member of a couple claiming as a single person), in most cases, you cannot qualify for a housing costs element for rent payments. There are a number of exceptions (see below);
- a single claimant under 35 without children, and you are living in private rented or certain types of temporary accommodation, the amount of your housing costs element for rent payments may be restricted to the local housing allowance for one-bedroom shared accommodation, even if you do not live in shared accommodation. See p411 – the rules on the categories of dwelling are the same as for housing benefit (HB).

If you are aged 18 to 22

From 1 April 2017, your UC cannot usually include a housing costs element for rent payments if you live in a 'full service' area (see p24), you are at least 18 but under 22, you are a single person (or a member of a couple claiming as a single person) and you have to meet all the work-related requirements (see p1080).[58] There are a number of exceptions (see below). **Note:** you can continue to qualify for a housing costs element for rent payments if you were getting a UC housing costs element or HB immediately before this rule would otherwise apply, but only until a housing costs element ceases to be included in your UC.[59]

Exceptions

You can get a housing costs element for rent payments if:[60]

- you are responsible for at least one child or qualifying young person (see p223); *or*
- the one-bedroom shared accommodation category of dwelling does *not* apply to you (see p412) because you are getting the middle or highest rate of the disability living allowance care component or the daily living component of personal independence payment, you were looked after by a local authority

after you were 18 or you are an offender subject to specific multi-agency risk management arrangements; *or*

- you are living in temporary accommodation (see p507 for what counts); *or*
- you do not have any parents or you cannot live with your parents because neither of them occupies accommodation as a home in Great Britain; *or*
- the DWP thinks it is inappropriate for you to live with your parents. This includes if there would be a serious risk to your physical or mental health or you would experience significant harm if you lived with them. The government suggests that this should apply if you have told your work coach, someone in the local authority or a trusted medical or other professional that you are estranged from your parents; *or*
- your expected hours of work (see p1075) are less than 35 a week; *or*
- you do not have to meet a work-search requirement for a period because you are temporarily unfit for work (see p1087), because of a bereavement (see p1088) or because of any of the 'other temporary circumstances' on p1089; *or*
- you have experienced or been threatened with domestic violence by your partner or former partner or by a 'family member' (see p1035 for who counts. The rule is the same as for jobseeker's allowance); *or*
- you have sufficient earned income (see below).

Sufficient earned income

Even if you are aged 18 to 22, you can get a housing costs element for rent payments if you have sufficient earned income.[61] 'Earned income' does not include income from self-employment you are treated as having under the rules on the minimum level of earnings (see p341). This applies during any assessment period in which your earned income is at least the normal threshold or, if you are employed as an apprentice on the last day of the assessment period, at least the threshold for apprentices. This also applies for a period of six consecutive months starting on the earliest of:

- the first day of your first assessment period if your earned income was at least the normal threshold (or if you were employed as an apprentice for the duration of the six-month period, the threshold for apprentices) in each of the six calendar months ending before the calendar month in which you claimed UC; *or*
- the first day of an assessment period in which your earned income is less than the threshold. Your earned income must have been at least the normal threshold (or if you were employed as an apprentice for the duration of the six-month period, the threshold for apprentices) in each of the six assessment periods immediately before that day, or if you have not yet been getting UC for six assessment periods, in each of the six months made up of the assessment periods before that day plus the number of calendar months ending before the calendar month in which you claimed UC.

Part 4: Paying for housing
Chapter 22: Universal credit housing costs
6. The amount for rented accommodation

Earned income thresholds
The '**normal threshold**' is 16 times the minimum wage for a person aged 21 or over but under 25, multiplied by 52 and divided by 12.[62] The '**threshold for apprentices**' is 16 times the minimum wage for an apprentice multiplied by 52 and divided by 12.[63] In both cases, the amount is rounded down to the nearest pound.

6. **The amount for rented accommodation**

To calculate the amount of your housing costs element for rented accommodation, see p506 if you live in private rented accommodation (or temporary accommodation) or p509 if you live in social rented sector housing (other than temporary accommodation). For what counts as temporary accommodation, see p507. There are general rules that apply to all types of rented accommodation (see below).

Note:
- If you qualify for a work allowance and a housing costs element is included in your universal credit (UC) maximum amount, you only get a lower work allowance and so more of your earnings are taken into account (see p167).
- If you have a shared ownership tenancy (ie, you are buying part of your home and renting the rest), your housing costs element can include amounts for both the rent and owner-occupier payments you make.[64] Your service charge payments are calculated as for rent payments.
- Your housing costs element is normally paid to you. However, payment can be made to another person (eg, your landlord) if it appears to the DWP to be necessary to protect your interests, or those of your partner or any child or qualifying young person for whom you or your partner are responsible (see p222), or those of a severely disabled person for whom you are caring and in respect of whom you get a carer element.[65]

General rules

In all cases, to calculate your housing costs element for rent payments, you must first work out:
- the monthly equivalent of your rent payments, if these are paid other than calendar monthly;[66]
- who counts as a member of your 'extended benefit unit' (broadly, the people who live with you in your accommodation – see p501); *and*
- the number of bedrooms you are allowed under the size criteria (see p503).

How do you work out monthly equivalents?

If you pay your rent:

– weekly, multiply by 52 and divide by 12;

– two-weekly, multiply by 26 and divide by 12;

– four-weekly, multiply by 13 and divide by 12;

– three-monthly, multiply by four and divide by 12;

– annually, divide by 12.

If you have a regular rent-free period, to work out the monthly equivalent divide the total payments you make over the year by 12 – eg, if you have four rent-free weeks each year and so only pay rent for 48 weeks, divide the total of the 48-week payments by 12.

Note:

- If you are a joint tenant, the housing costs element calculation takes this into account (see p508 and p511).
- Special rules apply if you qualify for a housing costs element for more than one dwelling (see p513).

Extended benefit unit

The members of your 'extended benefit unit' are:[67]

- you;
- your partner;
- any child or qualifying young person for whom you (or your partner) are responsible (see p222);
- any non-dependant (see below for who counts).

Note: people can continue to count as a member of your extended benefit unit while absent from home for a temporary period (see p496 and p505). You can continue to count as responsible for a child or qualifying young person while s/he is absent from your household for a period (see p223).

Who counts as a non-dependant

Other people who normally live in your accommodation with you (other than your partner and your children) are called 'non-dependants'. Examples of non-dependants are adult sons or daughters (and their children), or elderly relatives or friends who share your home.

A person only counts as your non-dependant if s/he normally lives with you (and your partner) in your accommodation.[68] So, for example, if someone is only staying with you temporarily but has a home elsewhere, or is homeless and is only using your address as a postal address, s/he does not count as a non-dependant. If you think the DWP has wrongly assumed that a person is (or is not) your non-dependant, ask for a revision or appeal. **Note:** some people do not count as non-dependants even if they live with you (see p502).

Part 4: Paying for housing
Chapter 22: Universal credit housing costs
6. The amount for rented accommodation

A person is only 'living with you' if s/he has her/his home with you and shares some accommodation with you.[69] This includes sharing the kitchen (unless it is only used by someone else to prepare food for her/him[70]).

A person only counts as 'normally living with you' if s/he has been there long enough to regard your home as her/his normal home.[71]

A number of factors should be taken into account to decide whether a person normally lives with you, including:

- the relationship between you;
- how much time s/he spends at your address;
- where her/his post is sent;
- where s/he keeps her/his clothes and personal belongings;
- whether her/his stay or absence from your address is temporary or permanent and, if s/he is absent temporarily, how long the absence has lasted (see p505);
- whether s/he has another place that could be regarded as home and if, for instance, s/he pays rent there or just travels around.

People who are not non-dependants

Even if they normally live with you, the following people do *not* count as your (and your partner's) non-dependants:[72]

- a child or qualifying young person for whom no one in your extended benefit unit (see p501) is responsible;
- if you (or your partner) are a foster parent, your foster child(ren);
- someone to whom you (or your partner) are liable to make rent or service charge payments, and any member of her/his household – eg, your resident landlord and her/his family;
- someone who has already been treated as the non-dependant of another UC claimant, if the other claimant is also liable to make rent or service charge payments for the accommodation you occupy. This means that you are not allowed a bedroom for her/him, but also that a deduction from your housing costs element for a housing costs contribution (see p512) is not made for her/him. It is only made from the housing costs element of the other claimant;
- someone who is liable to make rent or service charge payments on a commercial basis for the accommodation you occupy, whether this is to you or your partner, or to another person – eg, s/he is your lodger or sub-tenant, or a joint tenant.

You are not allowed bedrooms for any of the above under the size criteria (see p503). However, no deduction for housing costs contributions (see p512) is made for them.

Note: your partner and any child or qualifying young person for whom you (or your partner) are responsible (see p222) do not count as non-dependants.[73] However, you *are* allowed bedrooms for them because they count as members of your extended benefit unit.

The number of bedrooms you are allowed

If you live in rented accommodation, to calculate your housing costs element you need to know how many bedrooms you are allowed under what is known as the '**size criteria**'. This depends on the number, ages and gender of the people who count as members of your 'extended benefit unit' (see p501 for who counts).

You are allowed:[74]

- one bedroom for each of the following members of your 'extended benefit unit':
  - you (and your partner if you are a member of a couple);
  - a qualifying young person for whom you (or your partner) are responsible (see p222);
  - a non-dependant aged at least 16 (see p501 for who counts). **Note:** you are allowed one bedroom for every non-dependant, even if they are members of a couple;
  - two children under 16 of the same sex;
  - two children under 10;
  - any other child under 16.

Note: if a member of your extended benefit unit fits into more than one category, s/he is treated as being in the category that results in the lowest number of bedrooms; *and*

- one or more additional bedrooms in specified situations (see below).

If you are a private tenant (or you live in temporary accommodation – see p507), the maximum number of bedrooms you are allowed, including any additional bedrooms, is four.[75] If you are a social rented sector tenant, there is no maximum number of bedrooms.

Note:

- A bedroom can be included for a person in your extended benefit unit during her/his temporary absence from home (see p505). In some cases, this only applies for a period.
- If your partner or a child or qualifying young person for whom you (or your partner) were responsible (see p222), a non-dependant or a severely disabled person for whom you were caring dies, your UC continues to be calculated as if s/he has not died for the assessment period in which the death occurred and the following two assessment periods. So if you are no longer allowed as many bedrooms under the size criteria, this does not affect your housing costs element until after the three assessment periods.[76]

Additional bedrooms

In addition to the number of bedrooms you are allowed under the rules above, you are allowed one or more additional bedrooms if you satisfy any of the following conditions. If you satisfy more than one of the conditions, you are

Part 4: Paying for housing
Chapter 22: Universal credit housing costs
6. The amount for rented accommodation

allowed the total number of additional bedrooms to which you are entitled under each condition you satisfy.[77]

- **Non-resident carer.** You are allowed one additional bedroom for a non-resident carer if you (or your partner), any other person in your 'extended benefit unit' (see p501 – eg, your child or non-dependant), or a child or young person in respect of whom you meet the 'foster parent condition' (see below) need someone to stay overnight and provide care regularly, and overnight care has been arranged and is provided.[78] The person must get attendance allowance (AA), the middle or highest rate of disability living allowance (DLA) care component, the daily living component of personal independence payment (PIP) or armed forces independence payment. Even if more than one person requires overnight care, only one additional bedroom is allowed.

- **Member of a couple who cannot share a bedroom.** You are allowed one additional bedroom if you and your partner are not reasonably able to share a bedroom because of your (or her/his) disability. The person who cannot share must be getting the higher rate of AA, the middle or highest rate of DLA care component, the daily living component of PIP or armed forces independence payment.

- **Disabled child who cannot share a bedroom.** You are allowed one additional bedroom if you (or your partner) or another member of your extended benefit unit (eg, a non-dependant) are responsible for a child under 16 who would normally be expected to share a bedroom under the size criteria above, but cannot reasonably do so because of her/his disability. The child must be getting the middle or highest rate of DLA care component. If more than one child qualifies, you are allowed as many additional bedrooms as you need to ensure that each has her/his own bedroom. **Note:** before 4 December 2013, an additional bedroom might not have been allowed (when it should have been) for a severely disabled child who could not share a bedroom. You should apply for a revision on grounds of official error if you were affected and think you should have been allowed an additional bedroom for a disabled child.[79]

- **Adoption, fostering and kinship care.** You are allowed one additional bedroom if you (or your partner) have a child placed with you for adoption or you are a foster parent (in Scotland this includes kinship carers). This is called the 'foster parent condition'. If you are a foster parent, you meet this condition even if you do not currently have a child placed with you, provided you have become an approved foster carer, or have fostered a child, within the last 12 months. You are only allowed one bedroom even if, for example, you have more than one foster child, or if both you and your partner are foster parents or adopters.

Examples

Michael and Barbara have two daughters, aged 10 and 13, and two sons, aged 15 and 22. The 10-year-old daughter is severely disabled and is unable to share a bedroom because of this. Michael's parents live with them. They claim UC. Under the size criteria, they are allowed one bedroom for Michael and Barbara, one bedroom for the daughters, one bedroom each for the sons and one bedroom for each of Michael's parents. They are allowed an additional bedroom for their 10-year-old daughter. They are therefore allowed a total of seven bedrooms. They are private tenants, so their housing costs element is calculated based on a four-bedroom property – the maximum allowed. If they had been social sector tenants, their housing costs element would have been calculated based on a seven-bedroom property.

Jim is the foster parent of two sisters aged 10 and 16. He has two sons aged 10 and 12, one of whom is getting the middle rate of DLA care component and cannot share a bedroom because of his disability. Under the size criteria, Jim is allowed one bedroom for himself, and would normally be allowed one bedroom for his two sons. However, he is allowed one additional bedroom for his disabled son, and one additional bedroom because he is a foster parent. He is therefore allowed a total of four bedrooms.

Note:
- The rules were amended from 1 April 2017 to allow an additional bedroom if you and your partner cannot share a bedroom because of a disability, and if people living with you require overnight care. If you were already getting a UC housing costs element on that date and had not been allowed an additional bedroom, the DWP should reassess your UC claim and pay you any arrears due. The government says that arrears can only be backdated to 1 April 2017. You should argue this is wrong and get advice.[80]
- There are a number of other situations when you may need more bedrooms than shown above – eg, if you need an additional room to store equipment required because of a severe disability, or if you live in a dwelling adapted for you under a 'sanctuary scheme', or if you share the care of your child, but s/he counts as normally living with her/his other parent. You should appeal if you are affected, but your appeal may be held up while the courts are considering other cases.[81]

See CPAG's online service and *Welfare Rights Bulletin* for updates.

Temporary absence from home

When determining how many bedrooms you are allowed under the size criteria, a person can continue to be included in your extended benefit unit while temporarily absent from your home.

Part 4: Paying for housing
Chapter 22: Universal credit housing costs
6. The amount for rented accommodation

You (or your partner) are included during:[82]
- the one to six month period you (or your partner) continue to qualify for UC while temporarily absent from Great Britain (see p1605); *or*
- the first six months you are a prisoner, provided immediately before becoming a prisoner you were entitled to UC as a single person, you were getting a housing costs element and your sentence is not expected to last longer than six months.

Note: you (and your partner) can be treated as occupying your home during other periods when you are temporarily away (see pp496–97).

If, immediately before the start of the period of absence, s/he was included in your extended benefit unit and you were getting a housing costs element, **your child or qualifying young person is included:**[83]
- during the first six months of her/his absence if s/he is:
  - being looked after by a local authority; *or*
  - a prisoner, provided her/his sentence is not expected to last longer than six months;
- in any other case, for the period you continue to be treated as responsible for her/him while s/he is absent from your household (see p223).

If, immediately before the start of the period of absence, s/he was included in your extended benefit unit, **your non-dependant is included:**[84]
- indefinitely, if s/he is your (or your partner's) son, daughter, stepson or stepdaughter who is a member of the armed forces deployed on operations;
- during the one- (or two-) month period s/he continues (or would have continued) to qualify for UC while temporarily absent from Great Britain (see p1605);
- during the first six months of her/his absence if s/he is:
  - temporarily absent from Great Britain to receive medical treatment or convalescence or to take her/his partner, child or a qualifying young person for medical treatment or convalescence (see p1605);
  - a prisoner, provided her/his sentence is not expected to last longer than six months;
- in any other case, for up to six months. However, s/he is no longer included if the absence lasts (or is expected to last) longer than six months.

Note: other than if your non-dependant is a member of the armed forces deployed on operations, you must also have been getting a housing costs element immediately before the start of the period of absence.

Private tenancies and temporary accommodation

If you are a private tenant, or you live in temporary accommodation (see p507), your housing costs element is calculated as follows.[85]

- **Step one:** work out your core rent (broadly the amount of rent you pay – see p508) and your cap rent (the maximum housing costs element you can be paid – see p509).
- **Step two:** if your extended benefit unit (see p501) includes any non-dependants, deduct any housing costs contribution that applies (see p512) from the lowest of your core rent or your cap rent. This is the amount of your housing costs element. It can never be lower than nil – ie, no further reduction can be made to your UC award.[86]

Note: if you qualify for a housing costs element for more than one dwelling, special rules apply (see p513).

4

Temporary accommodation
Your accommodation is '**temporary accommodation**' if you live in a specified type of homeless accommodation that does not count as 'exempt accommodation' (see p428) and your rent is payable to a local authority or a provider of social housing (see p496 for the meaning).[87] **Note:** if you live in 'exempt accommodation' you may qualify for housing benefit (HB) for the rent you pay there.

Examples
Hannah, aged 24, is a joint tenant of a four-bedroom private flat with Carol, a friend. Another friend lodges with them. The rent for the flat is £1,000 a month, including services. Hannah claims UC. Her extended benefit unit includes Hannah and the lodger; Carol does not count as a non-dependant.
Step one: Hannah's core rent is £1,000 ÷ 2 x 1 = £500 a month.
Hannah's cap rent is the local housing allowance for two-bedroom accommodation. In her area this is £400 a month. Her cap rent is lower than her core rent.
Step two: Hannah's housing costs element is, therefore, £400 – £70.06 (housing costs contribution) = £329.94
Note: if Carol claims UC after Hannah, her extended benefit unit does not include the lodger as a non-dependant so Carol's cap rent is the local housing allowance for one-bedroom shared accommodation. No housing costs contribution is deducted.

Patrick and Isla rent a four-bedroom private flat. They pay £150 a week. Their rent includes service charge payments for the communal lift. Patrick's uncle Gerald and his partner live with them.
Step one: Patrick and Isla's core rent is £150 x 52 ÷ 12 = £650 a month. Their cap rent is the local housing allowance for three-bedroom accommodation (under the size criteria, they are allowed one bedroom for themselves and one bedroom each for Gerald and his partner). In their area, the local housing allowance rate is £520 a month. Their cap rent is lower than their core rent.

Part 4: Paying for housing
Chapter 22: Universal credit housing costs
6. The amount for rented accommodation

Step two: Patrick and Isla's extended benefit unit includes two non-dependants. Housing costs contributions of £70.06 x 2 = £140.12 are therefore deducted. Their housing costs element is therefore £379.88 (£520 – £140.12).

Core rent

If you are solely liable to make payments, your 'core rent' is the sum of all the eligible rent and service charge payments that you are liable (or treated as liable) to make – ie, the amounts you actually pay using the monthly equivalent.[88]

Jointly liable for payments

If you are jointly liable to make payments with someone, different rules apply. Your core rent is worked out using the following steps.[89]

- **Step one:** work out the sum of all of the eligible rent and service charge payments for which you and your joint tenant(s) are liable, for the whole of the accommodation, using the monthly equivalents.
- **Step two:**
  - if the only people who are jointly liable are in the list of 'relevant family members' below (eg, only you and your partner are liable), your core rent is the amount in Step one; *or*
  - if one or more people in the list of relevant family members below are jointly liable with one or more others who are not relevant family members (eg, you, your partner and a friend are joint tenants), divide the amount in Step one by the total number of people who are liable and multiply by the number of relevant family members who are liable. This is your core rent. However, if the DWP is satisfied that it would be unreasonable to take this amount as your core rent, it must apportion the amount in a manner it considers appropriate, taking into account the number of people who are jointly liable and the amount of the rent and service charge payments for which each is liable.

Relevant family members

The **'relevant family members'** (the DWP may call these 'listed persons') are you, your partner and any child or qualifying young person for whom you (or your partner) are responsible (see p222).[90]

Example

Jan and her partner Lois are joint tenants of a two-bedroom private flat with a friend.
Step one: the rent is £120 a week. The monthly equivalent is £120 x 52 ÷ 12 = £520
Step two: Jan and Lois are jointly liable with a person who is not a 'relevant family member'. Their core rent is therefore £520 ÷ 3 (the number of joint tenants) x 2 (the number of relevant family members) = £346.67 a month.

Cap rent

Your 'cap rent' is normally the local housing allowance for the category of dwelling that applies to you, in the area where you live.[91] This depends on how many bedrooms you are allowed under the size criteria (see p503), to a maximum of four bedrooms. To work out which category of dwelling applies, see p411. For information about the local housing allowance rates, see p413.

Social rented sector tenancies: the 'bedroom tax'

If you are a 'social rented sector' tenant (other than if you live in temporary accommodation – see p507 for the meaning), your housing costs element can include an amount for rent payments and service charge payments. You are a 'social rented sector' tenant if you pay your rent to a 'provider of social housing' (see p496).[92] If these rules apply, a deduction is usually made when your housing costs element is calculated if the number of bedrooms you are allowed under the 'size criteria' (see p503) is lower than the number of bedrooms in your home. This is commonly referred to as the 'bedroom tax' or by the DWP as the 'removal of the spare room subsidy' or the 'under occupation charge'. 'Bedroom' is not defined. See p435 for what may count. The issues are the same as for HB.

How your housing costs element is calculated depends on whether you are solely or jointly liable to make these payments. **Note:**

- If you qualify for a housing costs element for more than one dwelling, special rules apply (see p513).
- Your housing costs element may be lower than as calculated below if the DWP thinks your rent or service charge payments are higher than it is reasonable for a housing costs element to meet.[93] In this case, the DWP can apply to the rent officer. If the rent officer thinks that your landlord could reasonably have expected to get a lower amount of rent than what you pay, the lower amount is used to calculate your housing costs element, unless the DWP is satisfied that this is not appropriate.

Future changes

The government says that from 1 April 2019, the amount of rent your housing costs element can cover will be capped at the local housing allowance that would apply under the local housing allowance rules (see p20). It says that this will apply to all tenants on UC, including those in supported accommodation. This could mean that you will get a lower amount of UC. See CPAG's online service and *Welfare Rights Bulletin* for updates.

Part 4: Paying for housing
Chapter 22: Universal credit housing costs
6. The amount for rented accommodation

Solely liable to make payments

If you are solely liable to make payments, your housing costs element is worked out as follows.[94]

- **Step one:** work out the number of bedrooms in your home and also the number of bedrooms you are allowed under the size criteria (see p503).
- **Step two:** work out the amount of your eligible rent payments (see p487).[95] If you pay your rent other than calendar monthly, work out the monthly equivalent (see p501).
- **Step three:** work out the amount of your eligible service charge payments (see p489).[96] Deduct any amount that relates to the supply of a 'commodity' to your accommodation – eg, for water or fuel. If you pay your service charges other than calendar monthly, work out the monthly equivalent (see p501).
- **Step four:** total the payments in Step two and Step three. Unless Step five or Step six applies, this is your housing costs element.
- **Step five:** unless you have a shared ownership tenancy, if the number of bedrooms in your home is greater than the number of bedrooms you are allowed under the size criteria (see Step one), reduce the amount in Step four by:[97]
  - 14 per cent, if you have one too many bedrooms; *or*
  - 25 per cent if you have two or more too many bedrooms.
  Unless Step six applies, this is your housing costs element.
- **Step six:** if your extended benefit unit includes any non-dependants, deduct any housing costs contributions that apply (see p512) from the amount in Step four or Step five as appropriate.[98] This is your housing costs element.

Your housing costs element can never be lower than nil – ie, no further reduction can be made to your UC award.[99]

Example

Kirsty rents a four-bedroom house from the local authority. She and her partner live there with their 14-year-old daughter. Their rent is £125 a week. They have four rent-free weeks every year. Their 'extended benefit unit' does not include any non-dependants.

Step one: they have four bedrooms in their home. They are allowed two bedrooms under the size criteria: one bedroom for Kirsty and her partner and one bedroom for their daughter.

Step two: the monthly equivalent of their rent payments is £125 x 48 ÷ 12 = £500

Step three: they do not have any service charge payments.

Step four: the total payment is £500 a month.

Step five: they have two bedrooms too many. The amount in Step four must be reduced by 25 per cent. 25% x £500 = £125. £500 – £125 = £375

Their housing costs element is therefore £375 a month.

Jointly liable to make payments

If you are jointly liable to make payments with someone (eg, you are a joint tenant), different rules apply.[100] Work out the total of the monthly equivalent of the eligible rent and service charge payments (see p487 and p489) for which you and your joint tenant(s) are liable, for the whole of the dwelling. Remember to deduct any amount that relates to the supply of a 'commodity' to your accommodation – eg, for water or fuel. Then, if:

- the only people who are jointly liable are in the list of relevant family members on p508 (eg, you and your partner are the only joint tenants), a reduction is made as under Step five on p510 if the number of bedrooms in your home is greater than the number you are allowed under the size criteria (see p503). However, if you have a shared ownership tenancy, no reduction is made; *or*
- one or more people in the list of relevant family members on p508 are jointly liable with one or more others who are not relevant family members (eg, you and a friend are joint tenants), divide the total rent and service charge payments by the total number of people who are liable and multiply by the number of relevant family members who are liable to get the amount that can be included. However, if the DWP is satisfied that it would be unreasonable to take this amount as your rent, it must apportion the amount in a manner it considers appropriate, taking into account the number of jointly liable people and the amount of the rent and service charge payments for which each is liable. **Note:** no reduction is made as under Step five on p510.

If your extended benefit unit includes any non-dependants, deduct any housing costs contribution that applies (see p512).[101]

Note: your housing costs element can never be lower than nil – ie, no further reduction can be made to your UC award.[102]

Example

Len is the joint tenant of a three-bedroom housing association flat with his friend. The rent is £180 a week.

The monthly equivalent of the rent payments is £180 x 52 ÷ 12 = £780 a month.

They do not have any service charge payments.

The total payment is £780 a month.

Len is the only relevant family member. The amount that can be included in his housing costs element is therefore £780 ÷ 2 (the number of joint tenants) x 1 (the number of relevant family members) = £390 a month. No reduction is made as under Step 5 on p510.

Len's 'extended benefit unit' does not include any non-dependants. His housing costs element is therefore £390 a month.

Part 4: Paying for housing
Chapter 22: Universal credit housing costs
6. The amount for rented accommodation

Housing costs contributions

If your extended benefit unit includes a 'non-dependant' (see p501), a set deduction is usually made from your housing costs element.[103] This is because it is assumed that the non-dependant makes a contribution towards your outgoings, whether or not s/he does so. The DWP calls these deductions 'housing costs contributions'. They are also known as 'non-dependant deductions'. In some circumstances, no deductions are made. **Note:**

- No deduction is made from owner-occupier payments.
- A non-dependant can only be a member of the extended benefit unit of one UC claimant (or pair of joint claimants),[104] so a deduction is only made from one UC claimant's (or pair of joint claimants') housing costs element.

No housing costs contributions

No deduction is made for any of your non-dependants if you (or your partner):[105]

- are certified as severely sight impaired or blind by a consultant ophthalmologist; *or*
- receive AA (or equivalent benefits paid because of injury at work or a war injury), the middle or highest rate care component of DLA, the daily living component of PIP or armed forces independence payment, or would receive one of these but for being in hospital.

No deduction is made for any non-dependant who is:[106]

- staying with you but who does not live with you in your accommodation – ie, her/his home is elsewhere;
- receiving AA, the middle or highest rate of DLA care component, the daily living component of PIP or armed forces independence payment, or who would receive it but for being in hospital;
- receiving carer's allowance;
- receiving pension credit;
- a prisoner;
- under 21 years old;
- your (or your partner's) son, daughter, stepson or stepdaughter who is in the armed forces and is deployed on operations. **Note:** this only applies if s/he lived with you immediately before leaving, and intends to live with you at the end of the operations;
- responsible for a child under five.

The amount of the deduction

If a deduction for housing costs contributions must be made, it is made for every non-dependant who is a member of your extended benefit unit (see p501).[107] The deduction is a fixed amount of £70.06 for the assessment period, whether or not s/he is a member of a couple, whatever her/his income and whatever s/he pays you.[108]

Special rules: more than one dwelling

Special rules apply if you qualify for a housing costs element for more than one dwelling.

If you have been housed in two dwellings by a provider of social housing (see p495) because of the number of your children, your housing costs element is calculated using a single calculation.[109] All the eligible payments for both dwellings are taken into account, and the number of bedrooms you are treated as having is the total number in both dwellings. Your housing costs element is calculated as for social rented sector tenancies (see p509) if you pay rent to a social sector landlord for both dwellings and neither is temporary accommodation. Otherwise, your housing costs element is calculated as for private sector tenancies (see p506). **Note:** for private sector tenancies and temporary accommodation, if the cap rents for the two dwellings are different (eg, because they are in different areas), the lowest amount at the time your housing costs element is first calculated is used.[110] Your housing costs element continues to be calculated on the basis of the cap rent for that dwelling until you move to other accommodation.

Example

Phil and Holly have been housed by the local authority in temporary accommodation. They have been housed in two dwellings because they have five children: two girls aged 15 and 17, and three boys aged 12, 14 and 20. Holly's mother lives with them. Under the size criteria, they are allowed six bedrooms: one bedroom for Phil and Holly, one bedroom each for the two girls, one bedroom for the youngest boys, one bedroom for the oldest boy and one bedroom for Holly's mother. Their cap rent is limited to the local housing allowance for a four-bedroom dwelling. For one dwelling, this is £950 a month and for the other, which is in a different area, this is £1,000 a month. Their cap rent is therefore £950. **Note:** their core rent (see p508) is the sum of the eligible payments they make for *both* dwellings.

If there was a delay in moving into your home because of adaptations for a disabled person and you qualify for a housing costs element for both your old and your new accommodation (see p495), amounts are calculated for each home as for social rented sector or private sector tenancies (as appropriate) and your housing costs element is the total of these.[111] However, housing costs contributions for a non-dependant (see p512) are only deducted from the rent payments for your old home.

If you are living away from your normal accommodation because of a fear of domestic violence and qualify for a housing costs element for both your current and your normal home (see p497), amounts are calculated for each home as for social rented sector or private sector tenancies (as appropriate) and your housing costs element is the total of these.[112] However, housing costs contributions from

Part 4: Paying for housing
Chapter 22: Universal credit housing costs
7. The amount for owner-occupiers

non-dependants (see p512) are only deducted from the rent payments for the home you are occupying.

7. **The amount for owner-occupiers**

If you are an owner-occupier, your housing costs element can include an amount for owner-occupier payments and service charge payments. The amount you get for owner-occupier payments is not the amount you pay, but is calculated using a formula.

Once you have worked out which owner-occupier and service charge payments are eligible, the amount of your housing costs element is worked out as follows.[113]

- **Step one:** calculate the amount of eligible owner-occupier payments (see below).
- **Step two:** calculate the amount of eligible service charge payments (see p518).
- **Step three:** add these amounts together. This is the amount of your housing costs element.

Note:

- If you have a shared ownership tenancy (ie, you are buying part of your home and renting the rest), your housing costs element can also include an amount for the rent payments you make (see p500). In this case, your service charge payments are calculated as for rented accommodation.[114]
- You cannot get a housing costs element (other than for rent and service charges if you have a shared ownership tenancy) if you (or your partner) have any earned income, however much your earnings are.[115] This includes earnings from work you can do while claiming contributory employment and support allowance (see p1021) or from work of less than 16 hours a week you can do while claiming contribution-based jobseeker's allowance (see p989).
- You may only qualify for a housing costs element after a 'waiting period' (see p516).
- If your partner or a child or qualifying young person for whom you (or your partner) were responsible (see p222), or a severely disabled person for whom you were caring, dies, your universal credit (UC) continues to be calculated as if s/he has not died for the assessment period in which the death occurred and the following two assessment periods. This means, for example, that her/his absence from your home does not affect your housing costs element until after the three assessment periods.[116]
- Your housing costs element is normally paid directly to your lender.[117]

How your owner-occupier payments are calculated

The amount for owner-occupier payments included in your housing costs element for an assessment period is worked out using a special formula and a standard interest rate.[118] It is not what you are actually liable to pay, even if this is higher or lower.

At the time of writing, the **standard rate** is 3.12 per cent. The standard rate can be varied. You can find out the current rate at www.gov.uk/support-for-mortgage-interest.

There can be a limit on the amount of housing costs that can be paid. If the total of your loans is more than an upper limit, your loan interest payments and alternative finance payments are calculated using your upper limit (see below).

Loan interest payments

For loan interest payments (see p488), the amount of capital outstanding on your loan(s) that qualifies (or, if lower, your upper limit) is multiplied by the standard rate (see above).[119] This figure is divided by 12 to reach a monthly amount. The upper limit for loans is normally £200,000. However, if any loan (or part of a loan) was taken out to make necessary adaptations to your accommodation to meet needs you, your partner or a child or qualifying young person for whom you (or your partner) are responsible have because of a disability:[120]

- the amount of any loan (or part of a loan) for the adaptations is disregarded in working out whether your total loans exceed £200,000; *and*
- your upper limit is £200,000 plus the amount of the loan(s) (or parts of a loan) for the adaptations.

Example

Jim and Ina have a repayment mortgage and a loan for adaptations for their child's disability needs. The total outstanding is £300,000, £5,000 of which is for the adaptations. £5,000 is disregarded when working out whether their loan exceeds £200,000.

£300,000 – £5,000 = £295,000

This amount is restricted to £200,000.

£200,000 + £5,000 = £205,000

£205,000 x 3.12% (standard rate) = £6,396

Their housing costs element for the assessment period is £6,396 ÷ 12 = £533

Alternative finance payments

For alternative finance payments (see p488), the purchase price of the accommodation to which the payments relate (or, if lower, £200,000), is multiplied by the standard rate (see p514).[121] This figure is divided by 12 to reach a monthly amount. **Note:** the 'purchase price' is the price paid by a party (other than you) to acquire an interest in the accommodation, minus the amount of any initial payment made by you in connection with acquiring that interest and any payment made before a housing costs element was included in your UC.

Part 4: Paying for housing
Chapter 22: Universal credit housing costs
7. The amount for owner-occupiers

Example

Imran's home was purchased for £125,000 with the help of a Sharia-compliant mortgage. He made an initial payment of £8,000, and a further payment of £4,000 before he claimed UC.

£125,000 – £8,000 (the initial payment) – £4,000 (further payment) = £113,000

£113,000 x 3.12% (standard rate) = £3,535.60

His housing costs element for the assessment period is £3,525.60 ÷ 12 = £293.80

When your housing costs element is recalculated

Even if there is a change in the amount of your outstanding loan(s) or alternative finance payments, your housing costs element is only recalculated annually, on the anniversary of the date it was first included in your UC.[122]

The waiting period

A housing costs element for owner-occupier payments (and for service charge payments if you also make these) normally cannot be included for a period (called a 'waiting period' in this *Handbook;* the DWP may call it a 'qualifying period'). See below for exceptions.

If:[123]

- you have a new award of UC (ie, you claim for the first time or claim after a break in your entitlement to UC), a housing costs element cannot be included until there have been nine consecutive assessment periods in which you have been receiving UC and, were it not for the waiting period rule, you would otherwise qualify for a housing costs element for owner-occupier payments;
- a housing costs element ceases to be included in your UC award for any reason (eg, because you have earnings from a temporary job), but your entitlement to UC continues, a housing costs element cannot be included again until there have been nine consecutive assessment periods in which, were it not for the waiting period rule, you would otherwise qualify for a housing costs element for owner-occupier payments.

If you cease to qualify for a housing costs element for any reason during a waiting period, the waiting period stops running.[124] A new waiting period starts again from the beginning under whichever of the above rules apply.

Example

Claire makes a claim for UC. She is unemployed at the time and has no income. She is an owner-occupier and (but for having to serve a waiting period) she qualifies for a housing costs element. She waits nine consecutive assessment periods and a housing costs element is included in her UC. Claire gets a part-time temporary job so she no longer qualifies for a housing costs element, although her entitlement to UC continues. When her job ends, a housing costs element will be included again once she has been receiving UC for a further nine consecutive assessment periods.

Note: there are no waiting period rules for rent payments. Thus, if you have a shared ownership tenancy (ie, you are buying part of your home and renting the rest), your housing costs element can include the rent and service charge payments you make during your waiting period for the owner-occupier payments.

Exceptions

There are limited exceptions to the general waiting period rule.

- If you are entitled to contribution-based jobseeker's allowance (JSA) or contributory employment and support allowance (ESA) under the UC system (see p20) immediately before your award of UC starts, any period when you were only receiving one of those benefits may be treated as an assessment period (or part of an assessment period) that counts towards your waiting period.[125]

- If you (or your partner or a former partner) were entitled to income support (IS), income-based JSA or income-related ESA in the one month before the date you claimed (or are treated as claiming) UC (or you would have been entitled but for your entitlement ending because the benefit was abolished):[126]
  - if your (or your partner's or former partner's) IS/JSA/ESA included help with housing costs (see Chapter 20), you do not have to serve a waiting period, and your UC award can include a housing costs element straight away; *or*
  - if your (or your partner's or your former partner's) IS/JSA/ESA did not yet include help with housing costs because you were serving a waiting period (see p468), your UC waiting period is 273 days, minus the number of days you were entitled to IS/JSA/ESA (this includes time in which you were treated as entitled under the linking rules – see p470), as well as any time between the date IS/JSA/ESA ended and the date you are awarded UC.

- If an award of UC made while you were a joint claimant ended because you (and your now former partner) ceased to be a couple, you meet the occupation condition for the same home you occupied with your former partner and you are awarded UC in your own right:[127]
  - if a housing costs element was not yet included in your joint award of UC, any assessment period (or part of an assessment period) in respect of which you had been receiving UC counts towards the waiting period for your new award. For example, if you and your former partner had been receiving UC for 45 days, a housing costs element can be included once you have been receiving UC for nine assessment periods, minus 45 days;
  - if a housing costs element was included in your joint award of UC, you do not have to serve another waiting period; a housing costs element is included straight away.

This can also apply to your former partner – ie, if s/he continues to occupy the same accommodation and also claims, and is awarded, UC.

Part 4: Paying for housing
Chapter 22: Universal credit housing costs
Notes

Service charge payments

If you are an owner-occupier and you make eligible service charge payments (see p489), an amount for these is included in your housing costs element whether or not you also make owner-occupier payments.[128] The amount is calculated as follows.[129]

- **Step one:** work out the amount of each eligible service charge payment.
- **Step two:** work out the period for which each eligible service charge payment is payable, and if payments are made other than calendar monthly, work out the monthly equivalent (see p501 – the rules are the same as for rent payments).
- **Step three:** add all the monthly amounts together. This is the amount of service charge payments that can be included in your housing costs element.

If your housing costs are not met in full

If you do not have enough money to pay your housing costs, you may be in danger of losing your home, particularly if you are on UC for a long time. Discuss how to resolve the situation with your lender; it may be prepared to accept interest-only payments for a while. Get independent money advice.

Ultimately, you may have to sell your home. If you move out and put your home up for sale, the capital value of your property can be disregarded for a period while you take reasonable steps to sell it (see p362). If you rent it while trying to sell, see Chapter 16 for how the income is treated. **Note:** you may be able to qualify for a council tax reduction (see p854).

Notes

1. When you get a housing costs element
1 s11 WRA 2012; regs 25 and 26 UC Regs
2 s11(2)(c) WRA 2012
3 Reg 8 and Sch 4 para 4 UC Regs
4 Sch 4 paras 4A and 4B UC Regs
5 Reg 26(5) and Sch 5 para 4 UC Regs

2. Payments that can be met
6 Reg 26(4)-(6) UC Regs
7 Reg 25(2)(a) and Sch 1 para 2 UC Regs
8 Sch 1 paras 2 and 3 UC Regs
9 Sch 1 para 3A UC Regs
10 Sch 1 para 1 UC Regs
11 Reg 25(2)(b) and Sch 1 paras 4-6 UC Regs

12 Reg 25(2)(c) and Sch 1 para 7(1), (2) and (4) UC Regs
13 Sch 1 para 7(1) and (3) UC Regs
14 Sch 1 para 8(3) UC Regs
15 Sch 1 para 8(4) and (5) UC Regs
16 para F2074 ADM
17 Sch 1 para 8(6) UC Regs

3. Liability for payments
18 Reg 25(3) UC Regs
19 R v Poole BC ex parte Ross [1995] 28 HLR 351 (QBD); CH/1076/2002; CH/296/2004; CH/1097/2004
20 Sch 2 paras 1-4 UC Regs
21 Sch 2 para 2 UC Regs

Part 4: Paying for housing
Chapter 22: Universal credit housing costs
Notes

99 Sch 4 para 14(3) UC Regs
100 Sch 4 paras 3, 6, 30-32, 35 and 36 UC Regs
101 Sch 4 para 33 UC Regs
102 Sch 4 para 14(3) UC Regs
103 Sch 4 paras 13, 22 and 33 UC Regs
104 Sch 4 para 9(2)(f) UC Regs
105 Sch 4 para 15 UC Regs
106 Sch 4 para 16 UC Regs
107 Sch 4 para 13 UC Regs
108 Sch 4 para 14(1) UC Regs
109 Sch 4 para 17 UC Regs
110 Sch 4 para 25(3) and (4) UC Regs
111 Sch 4 para 18 UC Regs
112 Sch 4 para 19 UC Regs

7. The amount for owner-occupiers
113 Reg 26(3) and Sch 5 paras 8-11 and 13 UC Regs
114 Reg 26(4)-(6) UC Regs
115 Sch 5 para 4 UC Regs
116 Reg 37 UC Regs
117 Reg 59 and Sch 5 UC,PIP,JSA&ESA(C&P) Regs
118 Sch 5 para 12 UC Regs
119 Sch 5 para 10 UC Regs
120 Sch 5 para 10(2) and (3) UC Regs
121 Sch 5 paras 1(2) and 11 UC Regs
122 Sch 5 paras 10(4) and 11(4) UC Regs
123 Sch 5 para 5(1) and (2) UC Regs
124 Sch 5 para 5(3) UC Regs
125 Reg 2, definitions of 'JSA' and 'ESA', and Sch 5 para 6 UC Regs
126 Reg 29 UC(TP) Regs 2014
127 Sch 5 paras 1(2) and 7 UC Regs
128 Reg 26(3) UC Regs
129 Sch 5 para 13 UC Regs

Part 5

Other benefits

Chapter 23

Attendance allowance

This chapter covers:

Key facts

- Attendance allowance (AA) is a benefit for people with disabilities who have attention or supervision needs and who are aged 65 or over when they claim.
- AA is a non-means-tested benefit.
- You do not have to have paid national insurance contributions to qualify.
- You can qualify for AA whether or not you work.
- AA can be paid in addition to other benefits and is disregarded as income for means-tested benefits and tax credits.
- AA is administered and paid by the DWP's Disability and Carers Service.
- If you disagree with an AA decision, you can apply for a revision or supersession, or appeal against it. You must apply for a mandatory reconsideration before you can appeal.

Future changes

In the future, the rules on AA may be different in Scotland. See CPAG's online service and *Welfare Rights Bulletin* for updates.

1. **Who can claim attendance allowance**

You qualify for attendance allowance (AA) if:[1]
- you satisfy the residence conditions (see p1574);
- you are not a 'person subject to immigration control', although there are exceptions to this (see p1516);
- you are aged 65 or over when you first claim (see below);
- you satisfy the disability conditions (see below);
- you are not entitled to the care component of disability living allowance (DLA) (see Chapter 27) or personal independence payment (see Chapter 34).

The disability conditions

AA is paid at a lower or higher rate, depending on your care and supervision needs.

You get the lower rate of AA if you satisfy one of the daytime disability conditions *or* one of the night-time disability conditions.[2]

You may also get the lower rate of AA if you undergo renal dialysis (see p526).

You get the higher rate of AA if you satisfy one of the daytime disability conditions *and* one of the night-time disability conditions.[3]

You also get the higher rate of AA if you are terminally ill (see p526).

The daytime disability conditions are that you are so severely disabled, physically or mentally, that throughout the day you need:[4]
- frequent attention from another person in connection with your bodily functions; *or*
- continual supervision in order to avoid substantial danger to yourself or others.

The night-time disability conditions are that you are so severely disabled, physically or mentally, that at night you need:[5]
- prolonged or repeated attention from another person in connection with your bodily functions; *or*
- another person to be awake for a prolonged period or at frequent intervals to watch over you in order to avoid substantial danger to yourself or others.

The daytime and night-time disability conditions are the same as those for the middle and highest rates of the care component of DLA (see p604).

Unless you are terminally ill, you must have satisfied the disability conditions for six months before the first day of entitlement.[6]

2. **The rules about your age**

You can only claim attendance allowance (AA) if you are aged 65 or over. If you are approaching your 65th birthday, it may be better to claim personal independence payment (PIP) if you can rather than AA, since PIP has a mobility component in addition to a daily living component (see Chapter 34). Because the disability tests for PIP are different from those for AA, it may be worth making a claim for AA after you reach 65 if your claim for PIP is refused. Get specialist advice if this applies to you.

Note: your award continues if you are getting:

*   PIP when you turn 65; *or*
*   disability living allowance (DLA) and you turned 65 on or before 8 April 2013.

You can renew your award of either benefit, and cannot claim AA while you still get it. This also means that you can claim, or continue to receive, the mobility component after you reach 65 in certain circumstances if you continue to satisfy the relevant disability conditions (see p611 for DLA and p754 for PIP).

If you are over 65 and need to renew or change a DLA or PIP award, or have received DLA or PIP within the last 12 months, see p611 for DLA and p753 for PIP.

Future changes

From 2018, the minimum age at which you can claim AA is likely to change in line with pension age (see p771).

3. People included in the claim

You claim attendance allowance (AA) for yourself. Your partner may qualify for AA or personal independence payment (see Chapter 34) or may still have an existing award of disability living allowance (DLA – see Chapter 27) in her/his own right. Your child(ren) may qualify for DLA in their own right.

4. The amount of benefit

Attendance allowance is paid at one of two weekly rates:[7]

*   the lower rate is £55.65;
*   the higher rate is £83.10.

5. Special benefit rules

Special rules may apply to:

*   people on renal dialysis (see p526);
*   people who are terminally ill (see p526);

- people subject to immigration control (see Chapter 65);
- people who have come from or are going abroad (see Chapters 66, 67 and 68);
- people who are in hospital or a hospice, living in a care home or other similar accommodation, or people in prison or detention (see Chapter 41).

Renal dialysis

If you are undergoing renal dialysis on a kidney machine, special rules may apply that entitle you to the lower rate of attendance allowance (AA).[8]

To qualify, you must have treatment regularly for two or more sessions a week. The dialysis must normally require the attendance or supervision of another person.

If you dialyse in hospital as an outpatient, you must not have help from any member of the staff. Others who dialyse in hospital do not qualify by this special route but can count these spells of hospital dialysis towards the qualifying period. This can help you get AA more quickly for the times you dialyse at home, if you alternate between dialysis in hospital and at home. Even if you do not qualify under this route, you may qualify under the ordinary conditions.

Terminal illness

You are regarded as 'terminally ill' if you have a progressive disease and can reasonably be expected to die within six months as a result.[9] This does not mean that it must be more likely than not that you will die within this period. It simply means that death within six months would not be unexpected.

If you are terminally ill, you are automatically treated as satisfying the conditions for the higher rate of AA. This is paid straight away without your having to serve the six-month qualifying period.[10] These claims are referred to as 'claims under the special rules'. See p527 for how to make a special rules claim. The special rules only apply if your claim, or a request for a revision or supersession of an existing claim, expressly states that you are terminally ill.[11] The DWP can supersede your award if your condition or prognosis improves so that you are no longer regarded as 'terminally ill'.

6. **Claims and backdating**

The general rules about claims and backdating are covered in Chapter 49. This section explains the specific rules that apply to attendance allowance (AA).

Making a claim

A claim for AA must be in writing. To secure your date of claim (see p528), you should request the approved form (AA1) from the AA Service Centre. It is usually best to send the completed form to the Attendance Allowance Unit (see Appendix 1). You can also take or send it to any other DWP office, and may be able to take or send it to an 'alternative office' (see p1148).

Forms

Form AA1 is available from the AA Service Centre on 0345 605 6055 (textphone: 0345 604 5312).

The form should be date stamped. Keep a record of the date you asked for the form. The DWP may complete a checklist to assess your 'potential benefit entitlement'. This is not part of the claim process and you should always be sent a claim pack.

Claim packs are also available from Citizens Advice Bureaux and other advice agencies. A version of the form that can be filled in online and then printed is available at www.gov.uk. These packs are not date stamped.

Send in the completed form as soon as possible to secure your date of claim (see p528).

Note: the success of an AA claim can often depend on how well you have completed the claim form, so try to include all the relevant information and use extra pages if necessary. Keep a copy of your claim form in case queries arise. There are useful tips on completing the form in the disability living allowance (DLA) chapter (see pp618–23). Although those pages focus on DLA for children, the disability conditions for the middle and highest rate care component of DLA are the same as the conditions for AA. As there is no mobility component for AA, problems you have with walking outdoors may only be relevant to your AA claim if you need attention or supervision while walking.

You must provide any information or evidence required (see p528). In certain circumstances, the DWP may accept a written application which is not on the approved form.[12] You can amend or withdraw your claim before a decision is made (see p1149).

Claims for terminally ill people are made in a different way (see below).

Who should claim

You normally claim AA for yourself. If you are unable to manage your own affairs, another person can claim AA for you as your 'appointee' (see p1149).

Claiming for terminally ill people

To claim under the special rules for terminal illness (see p526), you must provide Form DS1500, completed by your GP or consultant, detailing your medical condition. You do not need to fill in the parts of the AA claim form relating to your need for personal care.

When the decision maker receives Form DS1500, s/he makes an assessment on whether you meet the special rules. If s/he decides you do not, you can claim in the normal way or request a mandatory reconsideration of the decision.

Someone else is allowed to make a claim, to apply for a revision or supersession or to appeal, on behalf of a terminally ill person without her/his knowledge or permission.[13]

Information to support your claim

For the general information requirements that apply to all benefits, see p1150.

It is important that you provide any information required when you claim. Until you do, you may not count as having made a valid claim (see p1152). Correct any defects as soon as possible or your date of claim may be affected. See p621 for the evidence you might want to provide to help support your claim.

Even if you have provided all that was required when you claimed, you may be asked to provide further information to support your claim (see p1154). You may also be asked to provide information after you are awarded AA and if you fail to do so, your AA could be suspended, or even terminated (see p1185).

The date of your claim

The date of your claim is important as it determines when your entitlement to AA starts. This is not necessarily the date from when you are paid. For information about when payment of AA starts, see p530.

The '**date of your claim**' is the date your request for a claim pack is received by the DWP or 'alternative office' (see p1148), provided you return the properly completed form within six weeks of the date of your request.[14] If the DWP has issued a form without date stamping it, write and explain when and where it was issued and ask to be paid from that date or six weeks before you sent it in.[15] There is also some discretion to extend the six-week deadline, so if you return the form late explain why.

If your claim form was issued by an advice agency or downloaded from the internet, it will not have a date stamp on it and your date of claim is the date the completed form is received by the DWP.

Note: you must make sure your claim is valid. If it is 'defective', you are given a short time to correct the defects (see p1152). If you do, your claim is treated as having been made when you initially claimed.[16]

In some cases you can claim in advance (see p529). If you want to do this, make this clear when you claim or the DWP might not consider it. If you claimed DLA or personal independence payment (PIP) when you should have claimed AA, or if you claimed industrial injuries disablement benefit, see p529.

Backdating your claim

It is very important to claim as soon as you think you might qualify. A claim for AA *cannot* be backdated.[17]

If you might have qualified for benefit earlier but did not claim because you were given the wrong information or were misled by the DWP, you could ask for a compensation payment (see p1396) or complain to the Ombudsman (see p1401).

If you claim the wrong benefit

A claim for DLA or PIP can be treated as a claim for AA and vice versa, but only if it appears to the decision maker that you are not entitled to the benefit you claimed (see p1161). A claim for an increase of industrial injuries disablement benefit where constant attendance is needed can be treated as a claim for AA and vice versa (see p1161).[18]

Claiming in advance

A claim for AA can be made before you have satisfied the six-month qualifying period (see p524),[19] or any other qualifying condition. Provided you claim no more than six months before you would qualify for AA, a decision can be made on your claim in advance of your date of entitlement. The date of your claim is the date on which you qualify.

Renewal claims

AA can be awarded for fixed periods (see p530). Renewal claims can be invited up to six months before your old award expires. It is important that you return your completed renewal claim form before your old award expires as no backdating is possible.

Decision makers normally treat your renewal claim as a new claim, beginning on the day after your old award runs out.[20] However, they may use the information you give in the renewal claim to revise or supersede your existing award, in which case your entitlement may be changed earlier.[21] If you think you have a strong case for an increased award, return your renewal form early and ask for a revision or supersession. If this is not the case, it is advisable to return the form nearer the date your current award expires.

If your AA award has ended, you can reclaim the same rate within two years without having to serve the standard six-month qualifying period again.[22]

How your claim is dealt with

A decision maker can award AA on the basis of your claim form alone, but may choose to contact someone you have named on the form for more information. It is a good idea to include details of all the medical professionals and other people who know and understand your needs and, if possible, enclose evidence from them. If the decision maker cannot obtain sufficient information, s/he may also arrange for you to be given a medical examination by a healthcare professional acting on behalf of the DWP, who may visit you at home.

If you refuse a medical examination without good cause, the decision maker must decide your claim against you.[23]

The decision maker may telephone you to ask for further information. If you do not want to be telephoned, state this clearly on the claim form.

The DWP aims to deal with new claims for AA within 40 working days. Claims made under the special rules for terminal illness (see p526) should be decided more quickly.[24]

7. **Getting paid**

The general rules on getting paid are covered in Chapter 50. This section explains the specific rules that apply to attendance allowance (AA).

When is attendance allowance paid?

You are normally paid on a Monday, but the DWP can vary the payday.[25] AA is normally paid every four weeks in arrears. However, AA can be paid:

– at shorter intervals in individual cases;[26]

– weekly in advance.

If you leave hospital or a care home and expect to return within 28 days, AA can be paid at a daily rate for days at home.[27]

Note:

- If you are claiming other DWP benefits, AA may be paid in a single payment with them instead.
- Even if you have been sanctioned for a benefit offence (see p1265), you must be paid your AA.
- For information on missing payments, see p1174. If you cannot get your AA payments because you have lost your bank or Post Office card or have forgotten your PIN, see p1173. If your 'simple payment' card has been lost or stolen, or if you have forgotten your memorable date, see p1173.
- If payment of your AA is delayed, see p1165. If you wish to complain about how your claim has been dealt with, or claim compensation, see Chapter 58.
- If payment of your AA is suspended, see p1185.
- If you have been overpaid AA, you might have to repay it (see Chapter 52) and, in some circumstances, you may have to pay a penalty (see p1256). If you have been accused of fraud, see Chapter 53.

Length of awards

Awards of AA can be made for either fixed or indefinite periods.[28] The length of an award depends on how long a decision maker estimates your current needs may last. If you have an indefinite award, you will not have to make a renewal claim at any stage, but the DWP can reduce or stop your award if it has grounds to revise or supersede it.

There is no legal minimum length for an award.[29] If you think benefit should be awarded for longer, perhaps because your condition is such that your care needs will not decrease, you can consider asking for a revision (see p1276). However, if you challenge the length of your award, the rate of your award may also be reconsidered. If your award is for a fixed period, you are invited to make a renewal claim up to six months before the award ends (see p529).

Awards under the special rules for terminal illness are normally made for a fixed period of three years (see p526).

Change of circumstances

You must report changes in your circumstances that you have been told to report, as well as any that you might reasonably be expected to know might affect your right to, the amount of or payment of your benefit. You should do this as soon as possible, preferably in writing. See p1184 for further information.

If your condition deteriorates so that you become eligible for the higher rate, benefit can be backdated to the day you become eligible, provided you tell the DWP no later than a month after completing the six-month qualifying period. If payment of (but not entitlement to) AA has stopped (eg, while you are in hospital or a care home), still notify the DWP so that the correct rate is paid when payment resumes. If you do not report a change of circumstances within the month, benefit can still be backdated if you do so within 13 months and there were special circumstances that meant it was not practical to report the change earlier.[30]

If your condition improves so that you do not qualify for the higher rate or you lose benefit altogether, the new decision usually takes effect from the date you tell the DWP of the improvement, or from the date of the decision if the DWP changed it without your asking.[31] It only takes effect from an earlier date (and causes an overpayment) if you should have realised earlier that the change should have been reported. It is accepted that it is difficult for claimants to realise when a gradual improvement begins to affect benefit entitlement.[32]

8. Tax, other benefits and the benefit cap

Tax

Attendance allowance (AA) is not taxable.[33]

Means-tested benefits and tax credits

AA is not taken into account as income when calculating any of the means-tested benefits. AA is paid on top of these benefits, and if you or your partner receive AA, this can increase the amount you get (or mean that you qualify for means-tested benefits for the first time, if your income was previously too high). AA is also ignored when calculating child tax credit and working tax credit (WTC).

If you get income support (IS) or income-based jobseeker's allowance (JSA), a higher pensioner premium (see p242) is included in your IS or JSA if you have a partner who receives AA.

If your partner receives AA, a severe disability premium is included in your IS, income-based JSA or income-related employment and support allowance (ESA) if you meet the other conditions for that premium. A severe disability premium is included in your housing benefit (HB), or an addition for severe disability is included in the guarantee credit of pension credit (PC) if you receive AA and meet the other conditions for that premium or addition (see p242).

If you receive AA, a limited capability for work-related activity element (see p262) is included in your universal credit (UC), as you are treated as having limited capability for work-related activity (see p1010).

An award of AA at any rate counts as a qualifying benefit for the disabled worker element of WTC. If you or your partner get the higher rate of AA, a severe disability element is included in WTC (see Chapter 59).

If you or your partner are entitled to AA, non-dependant deductions are not made from your HB (see p67) or from any housing costs included in IS, income-based JSA, income-related ESA and the guarantee credit of PC that either of you get (see p464). No housing costs contributions from a non-dependant are made from your UC housing costs if you, your partner or the non-dependant receive AA (see p512).

Non-means-tested benefits

AA may be paid in addition to any other non-means-tested benefits, except that it 'overlaps' with armed forces independence payment (see p862) and constant attendance allowance under the industrial injuries scheme (see p687) or war pensions scheme.[34] See p1175 for details of the overlapping benefits rules. You cannot claim AA if you are entitled to personal independence payment or the care component of disability living allowance.[35]

If you are receiving AA and someone regularly looks after you, that person may be entitled to carer's allowance (CA – see Chapter 25). However, your entitlement to a severe disability premium (or severe disability additional amount) can be affected if s/he receives CA.

The benefit cap

In some cases, there is a limit on the total amount of specified benefits you can receive (a 'benefit cap'). AA is *not* one of the specified benefits. The benefit cap does *not* apply if you or your partner receive AA, or are entitled to AA but it is not payable because you (or s/he) are in hospital or a care home. In other cases, it only applies if you are getting HB or UC. See p1180 for further information.

Passports and other sources of help

You qualify for a Christmas bonus if you receive AA at any rate (see p863). You may qualify for council tax reduction (see p854).

If any member of your household receives AA at any rate, you may get a grant for help with insulation and other energy efficiency measures in your home (see p865).

Notes

5

1. Who can claim attendance allowance
1 ss64, 65 and 66 SSCBA 1992; reg 2 SS(AA) Regs
2 s65(3) SSCBA 1992
3 s65(3) SSCBA 1992
4 s64(2) SSCBA 1992
5 s64(3) SSCBA 1992
6 ss65(1)(b) and 66(1)(a)(ii) SSCBA 1992

4. The amount of benefit
7 Sch 4 Part III SSCBA 1992

5. Special benefit rules
8 s65(2) SSCBA 1992; reg 5 SS(AA) Regs
9 s66(2)(a) SSCBA 1992
10 s66(1) SSCBA 1992
11 Regs 3(9)(b) and 6(6)(c) SS&CS(DA) Regs

6. Claims and backdating
12 Reg 4(1) SS(C&P) Regs
13 s66(2)(b) SSCBA 1992; regs 3(9)(b), 6(6)(c) and 25(b) SS&CS(DA) Regs
14 Reg 6(8), (8A) and (9) SS(C&P) Regs
15 Reg 6(8A) SS(C&P) Regs
16 Reg 6(1)(b) SS(C&P) Regs
17 s65(4) SSCBA 1992
18 Reg 9(1) and Sch 1 SS(C&P) Regs; reg 25(3) and (4) UC,PIP,JSA&ESA(C&P) Regs
19 s65(6) SSCBA 1992
20 Reg 13C SS(C&P) Regs
21 CDLA/14895/1996

22 s65(1)(b) SSCBA 1992; reg 3 SS(AA) Regs
23 s19(3) SSA 1998
24 www.gov.uk/attendance-allowance/ how-to-claim

7. Getting paid
25 Reg 22(3) and Sch 6 SS(C&P) Regs
26 Reg 22 SS(C&P) Regs
27 Reg 25 SS(C&P) Regs
28 s65(1)(a) SSCBA 1992
29 R(DLA) 11/02
30 Regs 7(9)(b) and 8 SS&CS(DA) Regs
31 s10(5) SSA 1998
32 Reg 7(2)(c) SS&CS(DA) Regs; *RD v SSWP (DLA)* [2011] UKUT 95 (AAC); *DC v SSWP (DLA)* [2011] UKUT 336 (AAC)

8. Tax, other benefits and the benefit cap
33 s677 IT(EP)A 2003
34 Sch 1 paras 5 and 5a SS(OB) Regs
35 s64(1) and (1A) SSCBA 1992

Chapter 24

Bereavement benefits

This chapter covers:

Key facts

- Bereavement benefits are paid to widows, widowers and surviving civil partners.
- If your spouse or civil partner died on or after 6 April 2017, the relevant bereavement benefit is the new **bereavement support payment**. If s/he died before this date, you may be able to get one of the old bereavement benefits: a lump-sum **bereavement payment**, **widowed parent's allowance** for people with dependent children or pregnant women, and **bereavement allowance** for people who were aged at least 45 when their spouse or civil partner died.
- To qualify for all bereavement benefits, your late spouse or civil partner must have either satisfied the national insurance contribution conditions, or been an 'employed earner' and died as a result of an industrial accident or disease.
- Usually, you must be under pension age to qualify for bereavement benefits.
- Bereavement benefits are non-means-tested benefits.
- You can qualify for bereavement benefits whether you are in or out of work.
- Beginning a new relationship may affect your entitlement.
- Bereavement benefits are administered and paid by the DWP.
- If you disagree with a bereavement benefit decision, you can apply for a revision or a supersession, or appeal against it. You must apply for a mandatory reconsideration before you can appeal.

Note: at the time this *Handbook* was published, the regulations introducing bereavement support payment had not been finalised. The bereavement support payment provisions outlined in this chapter are therefore based on draft regulations and the government's stated intentions and are subject to change. See CPAG's online service and *Welfare Rights Bulletin* for updates.

1. Bereavement support payment

Bereavement support payment is a new benefit for people whose spouse or civil partner dies on or after 6 April 2017. It comprises monthly payments, payable for a maximum period of 18 months, and a lump-sum payment in the first month.

Who can claim bereavement support payment

You qualify for bereavement support payment if:[1]
- you are a widow, widower or surviving civil partner;
- your spouse or civil partner died on or after 6 April 2017;
- your late spouse or civil partner either:
  - satisfied the national insurance condition (see p982); *or*
  - was an 'employed earner' and died as a result of an industrial injury or disease (see p545);
- you are under pension age; *and*
- you satisfy the residence condition (see p1572).

Time limits

To be paid bereavement support payment for the maximum 18-month period, you must make a claim within three months of the date your spouse or civil partner died (see p548).

To qualify for the initial lump-sum payment, you must claim within 12 months of your spouse or civil partner's death.[2]

Note: under the old bereavement benefits system, there are exceptions to the time limits if:
- you did not find out straight away that your spouse or civil partner had died; *or*
- you presume that s/he has died, but this has not been established for certain.

See p549 for more information. It is not yet known whether these provisions will also apply to bereavement support payment. See CPAG's online service and *Welfare Rights Bulletin* for updates.

The rules about your age

There is no lower age limit for bereavement support payment. Anyone who is old enough to legally marry or form a civil partnership may qualify.

Bereavement support payment cannot be paid if you are pension age or over, but you may qualify for state pension (see p770) or a survivor's inherited state pension instead (see p775).

People included in the claim

You claim bereavement support payment for yourself. You cannot get an increase for a new partner, or for your child(ren). If you have a dependent child, you are, however, paid the higher rate of bereavement support payment (see below).[3]

The amount of bereavement support payment

There are two rates of bereavement support payment – a standard rate and a higher rate. You qualify for the higher rate if:[4]
- you were pregnant when your spouse or civil partner died; *or*
- you were entitled to child benefit when your spouse or civil partner died; *or*
- since your spouse or civil partner died, you have become entitled to child benefit for a child or qualifying young person who was residing with you or your late spouse/civil partner immediately before s/he died. This applies even if you subsequently cease to be entitled to child benefit for that child or qualifying young person.

Rates of bereavement support payment[5]

	Standard rate	Higher rate
Initial lump sum	£2,500	£3,500
Monthly amount	£100	£350

Starting a new relationship

If you start cohabiting with a new partner, enter into a new civil partnership, or remarry, this does not affect your entitlement to bereavement support payment.[6]

2. Bereavement payment

A bereavement payment is a one-off, lump-sum payment that can be paid if your spouse or civil partner died before 6 April 2017. It can be paid on its own, or in addition to widowed parent's allowance or bereavement allowance.

Note: bereavement payment will be abolished from 6 April 2018.

Who can claim a bereavement payment

You qualify for a bereavement payment if:[7]
- you are a widow, widower or surviving civil partner;
- your spouse or civil partner died before 6 April 2017;
- your late spouse or civil partner either:
  - satisfied the national insurance (NI) contribution conditions (see p982); *or*
  - was an 'employed earner' and died as the result of an industrial injury or disease (see p545); *and*
- when your spouse or civil partner died, you were either:
  - under pension age; *or*
  - over pension age and your spouse or civil partner was not entitled to a category A retirement pension when s/he died; *and*
- you satisfy the residence conditions (see p1572).

Time limit

To qualify for a bereavement payment, you must make a claim within 12 months of your spouse or civil partner's death,[8] unless:
- you were receiving retirement pension on the date s/he died;[9] *or*
- you did not find out straight away that s/he had died; *or*
- you presume that s/he has died, but this has not been established for certain (see p549).

The rules about your age

There is no lower age limit for entitlement to a bereavement payment. Anyone who is legally old enough to marry or form a civil partnership may qualify.

There is, however, an upper age limit (see above).

People included in the claim

You claim a bereavement payment for yourself. You cannot claim any increase for your child(ren).

The amount of bereavement payment

A bereavement payment is a lump sum of £2,000.[10]

Starting a new relationship

A bereavement payment is not paid to you if, at the time of your spouse's or civil partner's death, you were cohabiting with someone else.[11] However, your entitlement is not affected if you marry, form a civil partnership or start cohabiting *after* the death of your late spouse or civil partner.

3. **Widowed parent's allowance**

Widowed parent's allowance can only be paid if your spouse or civil partner died before 6 April 2017.

You cannot receive widowed parent's allowance and bereavement allowance at the same time. However, you may qualify for bereavement allowance if your entitlement to widowed parent's allowance ends within 52 weeks of the death of your spouse or civil partner – eg, if you stop getting child benefit. If you can choose between the two, it is preferable to claim widowed parent's allowance, as it is not time-limited to 52 weeks and there is no reduction if you are aged under 55.

In addition to your widowed parent's allowance, you may also qualify for bereavement payment (see p536).

Who can claim widowed parent's allowance

You qualify for widowed parent's allowance if:[12]
- you are a widow, widower or surviving civil partner;
- your spouse or civil partner died before 6 April 2017;
- your late spouse or civil partner either:
  - satisfied the national insurance (NI) contribution conditions (see p983); *or*
  - was an 'employed earner' and died as the result of an industrial injury or disease (see p545);
- you are under pension age; *and*
- you are:
  - entitled to child benefit for at least one 'eligible child' (see below); *or*
  - a widow and you are pregnant by your late husband; *or*
  - a widow or a surviving civil partner, you were residing with your late spouse or civil partner immediately before her/his death, and you are pregnant as a result of artificial insemination by a donor or *in vitro* fertilisation which was carried out before her/his death.

Eligible child

The term 'child' in this section means both a 'child' and a 'qualifying young person' (see p572 for the definitions).

A child counts as an 'eligible child' if:[13]
- s/he is yours and your late spouse's/civil partner's child; *or*
- you were residing with your late spouse or civil partner immediately before s/he died and *you* were entitled to child benefit for the child at that time – ie, even if the child is not your late spouse's/civil partner's child; *or*
- immediately before s/he died, your late spouse or civil partner was entitled to child benefit for the child – ie, even if the child is not your child.

If you and your spouse or civil partner were living apart at the time of her/his death, you can still be considered to have been residing with her/him if your separation was only intended to be temporary.[14] This depends on the facts of your case.[15]

Note:

- You still count as entitled to child benefit if it has been awarded to you, but you have elected for it not to be paid to avoid the high-income child benefit charge (see p591).
- If you were residing together, you are treated as entitled to any child benefit to which your late spouse or civil partner was entitled, and vice versa.[16]
- You or your late spouse or civil partner can be treated as entitled to child benefit if you would have been entitled to it had you claimed it, and had the child in question not been abroad.[17]
- If you have been widowed before, or survived a previous civil partner, and this meant that you were left to care for a dependent child(ren), you can qualify for widowed parent's allowance on the basis of the death of your most recent spouse or civil partner, even if you were not residing with her/him when s/he died.[18]

Time limit

Provided you meet all the conditions of entitlement on p538, there is no time limit for claiming widowed parent's allowance after the death of your spouse or civil partner's. It then remains payable until you no longer meet one of the above conditions – eg, your child is no longer an eligible child because of her/his age.

The rules about your age

There is no lower age limit for widowed parent's allowance. Anyone who is legally old enough to marry or form a civil partnership may qualify.

Widowed parent's allowance cannot be paid if you are pension age or over, but you may qualify for state pension (see p770) or a survivor's inherited state pension instead (see p775).

People included in the claim

You claim widowed parent's allowance for yourself. You cannot claim widowed parent's allowance if you have a new partner (see p540). New claims do not include an increase for your child(ren), although if you have been in receipt of widowed parent's allowance since 5 April 2003, it may still include an addition for a child.

The amount of widowed parent's allowance

Widowed parent's allowance is made up of:
- a basic allowance. The full weekly rate of this is £113.70, but it may be paid at a reduced rate if your late spouse's or civil partner's NI contribution record was incomplete (see below);
- an additional earnings-related payment based on your late spouse's or civil partner's earnings under the additional state pension scheme, if her/his NI contribution record qualifies you for this (see p983). You may be entitled to this even if her/his contribution record is not sufficient for you to qualify for basic widowed parent's allowance.[19]

Reduction if your late spouse or civil partner had an incomplete contribution record

If your late spouse or civil partner had an incomplete NI contribution record, the amount of widowed parent's allowance you receive is reduced proportionately (see p984).[20] You may be able to increase your entitlement to widowed parent's allowance by paying voluntary NI contributions on your spouse's or civil partner's behalf, even though s/he has died. Contact HM Revenue and Customs' National Insurance Enquiries helpline (tel: 0300 200 3500; textphone: 0300 200 3519) about this. See p963 for further details, and p964 for the time limits for making such payments.

Starting a new relationship

Entitlement to widowed parent's allowance ends if you remarry or enter into a new civil partnership. You cannot requalify for it, even if you subsequently get divorced or if your civil partnership is dissolved. It is suspended if you begin cohabiting (see p545), but can be reinstated if you stop cohabiting.[21]

4. Bereavement allowance

Bereavement allowance can only be paid if your spouse or civil partner died before 6 April 2017. It can be paid for up to 52 weeks from the date of your spouse or civil partner's death. You cannot receive bereavement allowance and widowed parent's allowance at the same time. If you can choose between the two, it is preferable to claim widowed parent's allowance, as it is not time-limited and there is no reduction if you are aged under 55.

In addition to qualifying for bereavement allowance, you may also be entitled to bereavement payment (see p536).

Note: bereavement allowance will be abolished from 6 April 2018.

Who can claim bereavement allowance

You qualify for bereavement allowance if:[22]
- you are a widow, widower or surviving civil partner;
- your spouse or civil partner died before 6 April 2017;
- your late spouse or civil partner either:
  - satisfied the national insurance (NI) contribution conditions (see p983); *or*
  - was an 'employed earner' and died as the result of an industrial injury or disease (see p545);
- you were at least 45 years old when your spouse or civil partner died; *and*
- you are under pension age.

Time limit

As bereavement allowance is only payable for a maximum of 12 months from the date of your spouse or civil partner's death, in practice you must make a claim within 12 months of her/his death, unless:
- you did not find out straight away that s/he had died; *or*
- you presume that s/he has died, but this has not been established for certain (see p549).

The rules about your age

You must have been aged 45 or over at the time your spouse or civil partner died to qualify for bereavement allowance. The allowance is reduced if you were under 55 when s/he died (see p542).

Bereavement allowance cannot be paid if you are pension age or over, but you may qualify for state pension (see p770) or a survivor's inherited state pension (see p775).

People included in the claim

You claim bereavement allowance for yourself. You cannot claim bereavement allowance if you have a new partner (see p542). You cannot get an increase for your child(ren). If you have at least one dependent child, you may be able to get widowed parent's allowance instead. This is preferable, as it is not limited to 52 weeks and there is no reduction if you are aged under 55.

The amount of bereavement allowance

The full weekly rate of bereavement allowance is £113.70.

Your bereavement allowance is reduced if:

- you were aged under 55 when your spouse or civil partner died;[23] *or*
- your late spouse's or civil partner's NI contribution record was incomplete.[24]

Reduction because of your age

Your bereavement allowance is reduced if you were under 55 when your spouse or civil partner died. For each year, or part of a year, you were under 55, the bereavement allowance you would otherwise have received is reduced by 7 per cent. This percentage reduction remains the same for as long as you receive bereavement allowance.

Age when spouse or civil partner died	Rate of bereavement allowance (£pw)
54	105.86
53	97.78
52	89.82
51	81.86
50	73.91
49	65.95
48	57.99
47	50.03
46	42.07
45	34.11

Reduction if your late spouse or civil partner had an incomplete contribution record

If your late spouse or civil partner had an incomplete NI contribution record, the amount you get is reduced proportionately. See p984 for the rate of reduction, and p963 for how to increase your entitlement by paying voluntary NI contributions.

Starting a new relationship

Entitlement to bereavement allowance ends if you remarry or enter into a new civil partnership. You cannot requalify for it even if you subsequently get divorced or your civil partnership is dissolved. It is suspended if you are cohabiting (see p545), but can be reinstated if you stop cohabiting.[25]

5. Definitions

Widows, widowers and surviving civil partners

To qualify for bereavement benefits, you must be a widow, widower or surviving civil partner. For this to apply, you must have been married to your spouse (in either a same-sex or opposite-sex marriage), or in a civil partnership with your partner, at the date of her/his death (but see below). The marriage or civil partnership must have been valid under UK law.

A number of court cases have challenged the lawfulness of refusing bereavement benefits to surviving unmarried partners, particularly where there are children. A recent High Court judgment in Northern Ireland found that the refusal of widowed parent's allowance to a woman who was not married to her late partner amounted to unjustifiable discrimination. However, the Court of Appeal in Northern Ireland went on to rule that the legal relationship between unmarried cohabitees is not analogous with that of spouses or civil partners, including in the context of contributory benefits, and therefore different treatment is justified.[26]

Marriage 'by cohabitation with habit and repute'

In Scotland,[27] you can count as a widow or widower if you were married by 'cohabitation with habit and repute', even if you did not go through a wedding ceremony, provided your cohabitation began before 4 May 2006.[28] For this to apply, your relationship must have been like that of a husband and wife and more than simply living together – there must have been something about it which meant it could be inferred that you and your partner consented to marriage and that nothing existed that would have prevented a valid marriage taking place – eg, one of you being married to someone else.[29] In addition, your relationship must have been such that other people generally believed that you were married.[30]

If you have more than one bereavement

If, following the death of your spouse or civil partner, you remarry or form a new civil partnership and your new spouse or civil partner then dies, your entitlement to bereavement benefits depends on the national insurance contribution record of your most recent spouse or civil partner.

Invalid marriages

A **void** marriage or civil partnership (ie, one in which at least one of the partners was not eligible to marry or form a civil partnership) is invalid. From a legal point of view, it is treated as if it never existed.[31] In England and Wales, a **voidable** marriage or civil partnership is treated as having been valid until a decree absolute of annulment is pronounced.[32] Questions about the validity of marriages or civil partnerships are decided by a special unit at the DWP. If a question arises over the validity of your marriage or civil partnership, get advice from a family law specialist.

Separation, divorce and dissolution

If you were divorced when your former spouse died, or if your civil partnership had been dissolved when your former civil partner died, you are not a widow, widower or surviving civil partner.

A divorce only becomes effective when the decree absolute is pronounced (a decree of divorce, in Scotland), and a civil partnership is dissolved when a final dissolution order is issued (a decree of dissolution, in Scotland). If you were in the process of obtaining a divorce or of dissolving your civil partnership but your spouse or civil partner died before it was finalised, you are still a widow, widower or surviving civil partner (and so may be entitled to bereavement benefits). This is the case even if you were judicially separated.

Polygamous marriages

If your marriage was polygamous, you are not usually entitled to bereavement benefits following the death of your spouse because, generally, the law in England, Wales and Scotland does not treat you as legally married unless your marriage is a monogamous one.[33]

Note:

- If your marriage was *previously* polygamous rather than actually polygamous when your spouse died (eg, if any other spouse had already died), you can qualify.
- A marriage is only considered polygamous if the law of the country where the marriage takes place permits either party to have another wife or husband.[34]
- Whether your marriage is considered polygamous depends on whether you were your spouse's first wife or husband, and on where you and your spouse were 'domiciled' at the time of your marriage and any subsequent marriage. In general terms, 'domicile' means the country in which you have chosen to make your permanent home.[35] In particular, no one who is domiciled in England or Wales is allowed to contract a polygamous marriage anywhere in the world even if the local law allows it.[36]

Example

At the time of their wedding, Shaznaz and her husband were domiciled in Pakistan and were married under Islamic law. After the wedding they came to live in England, made their permanent home here and had no intention of returning to live in Pakistan at any time. Later, Shaznaz's husband returned temporarily to Pakistan and married a second wife. As her husband was domiciled in England rather than Pakistan at the time of the second marriage, English law does not recognise the second marriage and, therefore, regards Shaznaz as her late husband's only wife. Provided she meets the other conditions of entitlement, she is entitled to bereavement benefits.[37] If her husband had re-acquired domicile in Pakistan at the time of his second marriage, and his second wife was still alive, both marriages would be polygamous, and neither wife could claim bereavement benefits.[38]

Cohabitation

'**Cohabiting**' means living with someone as if you are a married couple. Deciding whether or not you are cohabiting may not be straightforward. For futher information, see p216.

If the DWP refuses you a bereavement benefit because it believes you are cohabiting and you do not agree, you can challenge its decision (see Chapters 54 and 55).

Industrial accident or disease

The meaning of 'industrial accident or disease' is discussed on p676 and p680. To qualify for bereavement benefits, the industrial accident or disease must have been a cause of your late spouse or civil partner's death, but it need not have been a direct cause or the only cause.[39] Your late spouse or civil partner must have been an 'employed earner' – ie, an employee, not self-employed (see p958).[40]

6. Special benefit rules

Special rules may apply to:
- widows whose husbands died before 9 April 2001 (see below);
- people who have obtained a gender recognition certificate (see p546);
- people who are going abroad (see Chapter 67);
- people in prison or detention (see Chapter 41).

Widows whose husbands died before 9 April 2001

If you are a widow whose husband died before 9 April 2001, you are not entitled to bereavement benefits, but you may still be getting widowed mother's allowance or widow's pension.

For an explanation of the main qualifying conditions for these widows' benefits, see the 2000/01 edition of this *Handbook*. See pxvii for the current rates of widows' benefits.

If your entitlement to widowed mother's allowance ends because you no longer have an eligible child, you may qualify for a widow's pension. This can be paid until you reach 65, provided you satisfy the qualifying conditions.

Once you reach pension age, you may be entitled to both state pension and either widow's pension or widowed mother's allowance. Because of the overlapping benefit rules, you cannot receive both in full at the same time. It is likely to be preferable to claim a state pension, as you are then free to remarry, cohabit or form a new civil partnership, without losing any entitlement.

People who have obtained a gender recognition certificate

If you annulled or dissolved an existing marriage or civil partnership in order to obtain a full gender recognition certificate (which, before 10 December 2014 in England and Wales and 16 December 2014 in Scotland, you had to do)[41], you are not entitled to bereavement benefits on the basis of your ex-spouse's or ex-civil partner's national insurance contribution record, if s/he subsequently dies.

If you are getting widow's pension when a full gender recognition certificate is issued, any entitlement ends. Widowed mother's allowance also ends, but you can qualify for widowed parent's allowance instead.[42]

7. **Claims and backdating**

The general rules about claims and backdating are covered in Chapter 49. This section explains the specific rules that apply to bereavement benefits.

Making a claim

A claim for **bereavement support payment** can be made:
- by telephoning the DWP's Bereavement Service on 0345 606 0265 (or 0345 606 0275 for Welsh speakers; textphone: 0345 606 0285, or 0345 606 0295 for Welsh speakers). After giving information on the telephone, you are sent a statement to approve, sign and return; *or*
- in writing, normally on the approved form (see p547); *or*
- online at www.gov.uk.

If you were receiving a retirement pension when your spouse or civil partner died, you do not need to make a claim in order to qualify for a **bereavement payment**.[43] However, it is advisable to ensure that the DWP is aware of the death by telephoning the DWP's Bereavement Service (see above). If this does not apply, you must make a claim to qualify for a bereavement payment.

To qualify for **widowed parent's allowance** or **bereavement allowance**, you must always make a claim. Your claim can be made in the same ways as for bereavement support payment (see above).

If there is a delay in dealing with your claim, you may be able to get a short-term advance of benefit (see p1177).

Forms

At the time of writing, the approved form for bereavement support payment was not known. See CPAG's online service and *Welfare Rights Bulletin* for updates.

Form BB1 is the approved form for bereavement payment, widowed parent's allowance and bereavement allowance.

When you register the death you are normally given a Certificate of Registration of Death. If you complete the form on the certificate and send it to the DWP, you should be sent the correct bereavement benefit form. Alternatively, you can get this form by telephoning Jobcentre Plus (tel: 0800 055 6688, or 0800 012 1888 for Welsh speakers; textphone: 0800 023 4888) or online (www.gov.uk).

Who should claim

You must normally claim bereavement benefits yourself. If you are unable to manage your own affairs, another person can claim bereavement benefits for you as your 'appointee' (see p1149).

Information to support your claim

For the general information requirements that apply to all benefits, see p1150.

It is important that you provide any information required when you claim. Until you do, you may not count as having made a valid claim (see p1152). Correct any defects as soon as possible or your date of claim may be affected.

You are normally also expected to provide proof of your spouse's or civil partner's death. If you have reported the death to a local DWP office under the 'Tell Us Once' arrangements (see p1184), you are given a reference number, which you can use as proof of death when you make a claim through the Bereavement Service.

Alternatively, when you register the death you get a death certificate, which can be provided as proof. If you do not have proof that your spouse or civil partner has died, see p549.

You are also usually expected to provide your marriage or civil partnership certificate.[44] Caselaw has provided guidance on assessing evidence from countries where reliable documentary proof of life events, such as marriage, may not be available.[45]

You may be asked for additional information after you have made your claim, or even after benefit has been awarded. You should provide the information promptly, as otherwise your benefit may be suspended or even terminated (see p1185).

The date of your claim

The date of your claim is important as it determines:
- when your entitlement to bereavement support payment, widowed parent's allowance or bereavement allowance starts. This is not necessarily the date from when you are paid. For information about when payment of a bereavement benefit starts, see p550; *and*
- whether you qualify for an initial lump sum of bereavement support payment or bereavement payment.

The **'date of your claim'** is normally the date of your call, if you claim by telephone, or the date your written claim is received.[46]

You must make sure your claim is valid. If it is 'defective', you are given a short time to correct the defects (see p1152). If you do, your claim is treated as having been made when you initially claimed.[47]

Backdating your claim

Bereavement support payment is automatically backdated to the date of your spouse or civil partner's death, provided you claim within three months of the date of her/his death.[48]

Your bereavement support payment award ends 18 months after your spouse or civil partner dies,[49] so you should claim within three months of the date of her/his death to receive the maximum 18-month award. However, if you claim more than three months after the date of her/his death, your claim is automatically backdated for three months.[50]

Because of this, you can a make claim for bereavement support payment up until 21 months after your spouse or civil partner dies, but you will not receive the maximum award.[51]

Examples

John's wife dies on 6 May 2017. He claims bereavement support payment on 10 July 2017. It is paid for the period 6 May 2017 to 6 November 2018 – ie, he receives the maximum 18-month award.

Susan's civil partner dies on 20 August 2017. She claims bereavement support payment on 4 February 2018. It is paid for the period 4 November 2017 to 20 February 2019. The length of her award is therefore limited to approximately 15.5 months.

Sameena's husband dies on 10 July 2017. She claims bereavement support payment on 28 March 2019. It is paid for the period 28 December 2018 to 10 January 2019. The length of her award is therefore limited to two weeks. She also misses out on the intitial lump-sum payment.

Payment of **widowed parent's allowance** and **bereavement allowance** can be backdated for up to three months before the date you make your claim, provided you satisfy the qualifying conditions over that period. You do not need to show reasons why your claim is late.

If you might have qualified for benefit earlier but did not claim because you were given the wrong information or were misled by the DWP, you could make a complaint (see Chapter 58).

If there is a delay in hearing or uncertainty about a death

If you did not find out straight away that your spouse or civil partner had died, but you find out within 12 months of the death, you can:[52]

- apply for a bereavement payment within 12 months of becoming aware of her/his death; *and*
- claim widowed parent's allowance or bereavement allowance, and request that it be backdated to the date of her/his death.

If it is presumed that your spouse or civil partner has died, but this has not been established for certain, you can ask the DWP to make a decision that s/he has died (or is likely to have died) on a particular date. You should provide the information and evidence that has led you to presume s/he has died. If the DWP makes such a decision, you can then:[53]

- apply for a bereavement payment within 12 months of the date of that decision; *and*
- claim widowed parent's allowance or bereavement allowance, and have it backdated to the date the DWP has decided your late spouse or civil partner died.

If you claim the wrong benefit

The decision maker can treat a claim for state pension as a claim for bereavement benefits and vice versa.[54] See p1161 for details of interchanging claims in this way.

Claiming in advance

You can claim bereavement benefits up to three months before you expect to qualify. In most circumstances, you will not know of your need to claim benefit in advance, but this may be relevant if, for example, you know that you will no longer be cohabiting.[55] The date of your claim is the date on which you qualify.

8. **Getting paid**

The general rules on getting paid are covered in Chapter 50. This section explains the specific rules that apply to bereavement benefits.

When are bereavement benefits paid

Bereavement support payment is paid monthly in arrears, on the same day of the month as the date of death of your spouse or civil partner. In months when it cannot be paid on this day because it falls on the 29th, 30th or 31st, it is paid on the last day of the month.[56] Widowed parent's allowance and bereavement allowance are normally paid fortnightly, in arrears.

Bereavement support payment, widowed parent's allowance and bereavement allowance are daily benefits. Payments can be made for part periods at the beginning and end of claims. Part-payments are calculated using the daily rate.

Note:

- Your **widowed parent's allowance** or **bereavement allowance** might be paid at a reduced rate in certain circumstances (see p540 and p542).
- You may not be paid **bereavement support payment, widowed parent's allowance,** or **bereavement allowance** if you have received a sanction for a benefit offence (see p1265).
- For information on missing payments, see p1174. If you cannot get your payments because you have lost your bank or Post Office card or have forgotten your PIN, see p1173. If your 'simple payment' card has been lost or stolen, or if you have forgotten your memorable date, see p1173.
- If payment of your bereavement benefit is delayed, see p1165. If you are waiting for a decision on your claim, or to be paid, you might be able to get a short-term advance (see p1177). If you wish to complain about how your claim has been dealt with, or claim compensation, see Chapter 58.
- If payment of your **bereavement support payment, widowed parent's allowance** or **bereavement allowance** is suspended, see p1185.
- If you are overpaid a bereavement benefit, you might have to repay it (see Chapter 52) and, in some circumstances, you may have to pay a penalty (see p1256). If you have been accused of fraud, see Chapter 53.

Change of circumstances

You must report changes in your circumstances that you have been told to report, as well as any that you might reasonably be expected to know might affect your right to, the amount of, or the payment of, your benefit. You should do this as soon as possible, preferably in writing. See p1184 for further information.

If a change of circumstances affects your entitlement to **widowed parent's allowance** or **bereavement allowance**, before your benefit can be stopped or adjusted, the decision maker should first revise or supersede the earlier decision on your entitlement (see Chapter 54).[57] The date from when a new decision takes effect following a supersession normally depends on whether or not it is advantageous to you and whether you reported the change in time (see p1293).

9. Tax, other benefits and the benefit cap

Tax

Bereavement support payment and **bereavement payment** are not taxable.[58] **Widowed parent's allowance** and **bereavement allowance** are taxable (except for any increase to widowed parent's allowance for children, which you may still receive, if you have been in receipt of it since 5 April 2003).[59]

Means-tested benefits and tax credits

The initial lump-sum of **bereavement support payment** counts as capital for all means-tested benefits, but it is disregarded for up to 52 weeks. The monthly payments count as income, but are disregarded for all means-tested benefits, including universal credit (UC).[60] Bereavement support payment is ignored when calculating your entitlement to tax credits, as it is not taxable.

A **bereavement payment** is counted as capital for all means-tested benefits. It is ignored when calculating your entitlement to tax credits.

Widowed parent's allowance and **bereavement allowance** count as income for means-tested benefits. However:

- £10 of your weekly widowed parent's allowance is disregarded when calculating your entitlement to income support (IS),[61] income-based jobseeker's allowance (JSA),[62] income-related employment and support allowance (ESA)[63] and pension credit (PC);[64]
- an increase in your widowed parent's allowance for a child is disregarded when calculating your entitlement to income-related ESA and PC, and may be ignored when calculating your entitlement to IS and income-based JSA (see p286 and p324); *and*
- £15 of your weekly widowed parent's allowance is disregarded when calculating your entitlement to housing benefit (HB).[65] However, if you are getting the savings credit (and not the guarantee credit) of PC, the income used to calculate your HB is that used by the DWP to calculate your entitlement to PC (which includes only a £10 disregard from your widowed parent's allowance – see p316).

There are no equivalent widowed parent's allowance disregards for UC.[66]

For tax credits, **widowed parent's allowance** counts as pension income and **bereavement allowance** counts as benefit income.

If your partner was entitled to HB when s/he died and you claim HB within a month of her/his death, your HB claim can be treated as having been made on the date your partner died (see p77). In some circumstances, it can be backdated further (see p78).

Non-means-tested benefits

Bereavement support payment does not overlap with contribution-based JSA or contributory ESA – you can be paid bereavement support payment at the same time.[67]

Widowed parent's allowance and **bereavement allowance** are affected by the overlapping benefit rules (see p1175).

If you receive an increase in your **widowed parent's allowance** for a child, the overlapping benefit rules may also affect you. If you receive child benefit or guardian's allowance for the same child, see p1177.

Once you reach pension age, your entitlement to **bereavement support payment**, **widowed parent's allowance** or **bereavement allowance** stops. However, you may qualify for state pension (see p770) or a survivor's inherited state pension instead (see p775).

If your bereavement benefit stops before you reach pension age, you may qualify for national insurance credits following bereavement for contributory ESA and contribution-based JSA (see p974).[68]

The benefit cap

In some cases, there is a limit on the total amount of specified benefits you can receive (a 'benefit cap'). **Bereavement support payment** is not a specified benefit – payments do not count towards the benefit cap.[69] However, **bereavement allowance** and **widowed parent's allowance** are specified benefits.[70] The benefit cap only applies if you are getting HB or UC. £15 of your weekly **widowed parent's allowance** is ignored if the cap is applied through your HB. See p1180 for further information.

Passports and other sources of help

If you are entitled to widowed parent's allowance, you are also entitled to a Christmas bonus (see p863). **Note:** at the time of writing, it was not yet known whether bereavement support payment would entitle you to a Christmas bonus. See CPAG's online service or *Welfare Rights Bulletin* for updates.

In some circumstances, you may qualify for a social fund funeral expenses payment (see p791).

If you have low income and capital, you may be entitled to HB (see p44) and/ or council tax reduction (see p854).

Chapter 24

Bereavement benefits

For advice about what to do after someone dies, see www.gov.uk. In Scotland, see also the Scottish government leaflet, *What to Do After a Death in Scotland* (www.gov.scot/publications/2013/03/9207/0).

Notes

1. **Bereavement support payment**
   1 s30 PA 2014
   2 Reg 3(2) and (5) BSP Regs (draft)
   3 Reg 4 BSP Regs (draft)
   4 Reg 4 BSP Regs (draft)
   5 Reg 3(1)-(6) BSP Regs (draft)
   6 *Bereavement Support Payment Regulations 2017: written statement,* HCWS409, House of Commons, *Hansard,* 12 January 2017, para 5

2. **Bereavement payment**
   7 ss36 and 60(2) and (3) SSCBA 1992
   8 Reg 19(3A) SS(C&P) Regs
   9 Reg 3(da) SS(C&P) Regs
   10 Sch 4 Part II SSCBA 1992
   11 s36(2) SSCBA 1992

3. **Widowed parent's allowance**
   12 ss39A and 60(2) and (3) SSCBA 1992
   13 s39A(3) SSCBA 1992
   14 Reg 2(4) SSB(PRT) Regs
   15 CIS/1059/2014
   16 s122(4) SSCBA 1992
   17 Reg 16ZA(1)(a) SS(WB&RP) Regs
   18 Reg 16ZA(2) SS(WB&RP) Regs
   19 Reg 6(2) SS(WB&RP) Regs
   20 Reg 6 SS(WB&RP) Regs
   21 s39A(4), (4A) and (5) SSCBA 1992

4. **Bereavement allowance**
   22 ss39B and 60(2) and (3) SSCBA 1992
   23 ss39C(5) SSCBA 1992
   24 Reg 6 SS(WB&RP) Regs
   25 s39B(4), (4A) and (5) SSCBA 1992

5. **Definitions**
   26 *McLaughlin* [2016] NICA 53
   27 But see *CAO v Bath* [1999] (CA), reported as R(G) 1/00; R(G) 2/70

28 R(G) 5/83; s3 Family Law (Scotland) Act 2006; The Family Law (Scotland) Act 2006 (Commencement, Transitional Provisions and Savings) Order 2006, No.212
29 R(G) 1/71
30 CSG/7/1995; CSG/681/2003; but see also CSG/648/2007
31 R(G) 2/63
32 R(G) 1/73
33 *Hyde v Hyde* [1866]; reg 2 SSFA(PM) Regs
34 Reg 1(2) SSFA(PM) Regs
35 R(S) 2/92
36 s11(3) MCA 1973
37 R(G) 1/95
38 R(G) 1/93; R(P) 2/06
39 CI/142/1949; R(I) 14/51
40 ss2(a) and 60(2) SSCBA 1992

6. **Special benefit rules**
   41 s4 GRA 2004
   42 Sch 5 paras 3-5 GRA 2004

7. **Claims and backdating**
   43 s1 SSAA 1992
   44 Reg 7(1) SS(C&P) Regs
   45 CP/4062/2004; see also CP/891/2008 and *AR v SSWP* [2012] UKUT 467 (AAC)
   46 Reg 6(1) and (1ZA) SS(C&P) Regs
   47 Regs 4(7), (7ZA), (8), (12) and (13) and 6(1) SS(C&P) Regs
   48 Reg 2(2)(a) BSP Regs (draft)
   49 Reg 2(3) BSP Regs (draft)
   50 Reg 2(2)(b) BSP Regs (draft)
   51 Reg 2(2)(b)(ii) BSP Regs (draft)
   52 ss1(2) and 3(1)(b)(ii), (2)(b) and (3) SSAA 1992; s8 SSA 1998; CG/7235/95, para 13
   53 ss1(2) and 3(1)(b)(i), (2)(a) and (3) SSAA 1992; s8 SSA 1998; CG/7235/95, para 14

54 Reg 9(1) and Sch 1 Part I SS(C&P) Regs
55 Reg 13 SS(C&P) Regs

8. Getting paid
56 Reg 3 BSP Regs (draft)
57 Reg 17 SS(C&P) Regs

9. Tax, other benefits and the benefit cap
58 *Bereavement Support Payment Regulations 2017: written statement*, HCWS409, House of Commons, *Hansard*, 12 January 2017, para 5
59 ss577-79, 661 and 676 IT(EP)A 2003
60 *Bereavement Support Payment Regulations 2017: written statement*, HCWS409, House of Commons, *Hansard*, 12 January 2017, para 5
61 Reg 40 and Sch 9 para 16(h) IS Regs
62 Reg 103 and Sch 7 para 17(e) JSA Regs
63 Sch 8 para 17(i) ESA Regs
64 Sch IV para 7 SPC Regs
65 Reg 40 and Sch 5 para 16 HB Regs; reg 29 and Sch 5 paras 7 and 8 HB(SPC) Regs
66 Regs 22 and 66 UC Regs
67 *Bereavement Support Payment Regulations 2017: written statement*, HCWS409, House of Commons, *Hansard*, 12 January 2017, para 5
68 Reg 8C SS(Cr) Regs
69 *Bereavement Support Payment Regulations 2017: written statement*, HCWS409, House of Commons, *Hansard*, 12 January 2017, para 5
70 Regs 75A, 75C and 75G HB Regs; reg 79 UC Regs

Chapter 25

Carer's allowance

Key facts

- Carer's allowance (CA) is paid to people who care for someone who is severely disabled.
- CA is a non-means-tested benefit.
- You do not have to have paid national insurance contributions to qualify.
- You can qualify for CA whether you are in or out of work, but you must not earn more than £116 a week.
- CA can be paid in addition to other benefits and tax credits, but the overlapping benefit rules may apply. CA counts as income for means-tested benefits.
- CA is administered and paid by the DWP's Carer's Allowance Unit.
- If you disagree with a CA decision, you can apply for a revision or a supersession, or appeal against it. You must apply for a mandatory reconsideration before you can appeal.

Future changes

In the future the rules on CA may be different in Scotland. See CPAG's online service and *Welfare Rights Bulletin* for updates.

Part 5: Other benefits
Chapter 25: Carer's allowance
1. Who can claim carer's allowance

1. **Who can claim carer's allowance**

You qualify for carer's allowance (CA) if:[1]
- you are caring for a 'severely disabled person' (see below). You do not have to be the person's relative, nor do you have to live with her/him;
- the care you give is regular and substantial (see below);
- you are not gainfully employed, which means you earn £116 or less a week (see p557);
- you are not in full-time education (see p890);
- you are aged 16 or over;
- you satisfy the residence conditions (see p1574);
- you are not a 'person subject to immigration control' (see p1516).

Severely disabled person
In this chapter, a '**severely disabled person**' is someone to whom either attendance allowance (AA), the highest or middle rate of disability living allowance (DLA) care component, either rate of the daily living component of personal independence payment (PIP), armed forces independence payment or constant attendance allowance in respect of an industrial or war disablement (see p687) is payable.[2]

Note:[3]
- Only one person can qualify for CA or the carer's element of universal credit for caring for the same disabled person. If you cannot agree on who this should be, the DWP decides.
- Even if you care for two or more disabled people, you can only qualify for one award of CA for the same day.

Regularly and substantially caring

To qualify for CA, you must be 'regularly and substantially' caring for a severely disabled person. You satisfy this requirement during any week in which you are (or are likely to be) engaged and regularly engaged in caring for her/him for 35 hours or more.[4] A week runs from Sunday to Saturday.[5] Caring can include supervision as well as assistance. If some of the time is spent preparing for the disabled person to come to stay with you or clearing up after her/his visit, this can also count towards the 35 hours.[6]

Note:
- You cannot average the hours if you provide care for more than 35 hours in some weeks and fewer than 35 in others.[7] You must be caring for at least 35 hours in each week of your claim.
- If you are caring for two or more disabled people, you can only qualify for CA if you are caring for at least one of them for 35 hours or more a week.[8] You

cannot add together the hours you are caring for both/all of them to make up the 35.

Breaks from caring

Once you have been caring for a severely disabled person for a while, you can take a temporary break from caring and continue to qualify for CA. This applies if you have been providing care for at least 35 hours a week in 22 of the last 26 weeks (or for at least 14 of the last 26 weeks, and the reason you did not provide care for 22 weeks was that either you or the disabled person were in hospital or in a similar institution). Weeks before you claimed CA can be counted. This means you can have a four-week break from caring in any period of six months, or a 12-week break if one of you was in hospital or in a similar institution (see p910 for what counts) for at least eight of those weeks.[9]

CA stops if the AA, DLA, PIP or constant attendance allowance of the person for whom you are caring stops because s/he is in hospital or in a similar institution (see p911).[10]

If the person receiving care dies

If the person you care for dies, you continue to be entitled to CA for a further eight weeks, even though you are no longer providing care, provided you satisfy the other qualifying conditions. The eight weeks run from the Sunday following the death, or from the day of the death if this was a Sunday.[11]

Gainfully employed

You cannot qualify for CA if you are 'gainfully employed'. You count as gainfully employed in a week (and cannot qualify for CA in that week) if your earnings from employment and/or self-employment in the previous week were more than £116.[12] For the way earnings are calculated, see below. Your earnings are ignored if you are working during a period when you are not actually caring for the severely disabled person – eg, because s/he is in hospital or you are on a four-week break from caring (see above).[13]

Earnings from employment

To work out how earnings from employment affect your entitlement to CA:
- check whether the payment counts as earnings (see below) and whether it can be disregarded (see p561);
- work out your weekly net earnings (see p559);
- work out the date from when your earnings count and the period they cover (see p559).

What counts as earnings

For employees, **'earnings'** mean 'any remuneration or profit derived from... employment'. The main type of income which counts as earnings is, therefore, your wages. The following are also included:[14]

Part 5: Other benefits
Chapter 25: Carer's allowance
1. Who can claim carer's allowance

- any bonus or commission (including tips);
- holiday pay (but not if it is payable more than four weeks after a job ends or is interrupted);
- compensation for unfair dismissal and certain other types of compensation under the Employment Rights Act 1996 or under trade union legislation;
- an equal pay settlement;[15]
- any payments made by an employer for expenses not 'wholly, exclusively and necessarily' incurred in carrying out the job, including any travel expenses to and from work, and any payments made to you for the cost of arranging care for members of your family;
- a retainer (eg, paid during the school holidays to people who work for the school meals service) or a guarantee payment;
- statutory and/or contractual sick, maternity, adoption, paternity and shared parental pay;
- certain payments at the end of a job (see below).

This list is not exhaustive and other payments from employment may also count as earnings.[16]

It is the pay you actually receive that is taken into account, rather than what you are legally entitled to,[17] so if you receive less than the minimum wage, it is this lesser amount that counts as 'earnings'.

What does not count as earnings

The following are examples of payments that *do not* count as earnings:
- periodic payments made as part of a redundancy scheme;[18]
- occupational pension payments;[19]
- payments towards expenses that are 'wholly, exclusively and necessarily' incurred in the performance of employment, such as travelling expenses during the course of work;[20]
- payments relating to expenses incurred for participating in a service user consultation.[21]

See p561 for information on earnings disregards.

Payments when you stop work

If you stop work before you claim CA, your final earnings generally do not affect your benefit. Provided your entitlement begins after the employment ends, the following are disregarded:[22]
- final wages, paid or due, including bonuses, commission, tips and expenses that count as earnings;
- holiday pay;
- pay in lieu of notice;
- pay in lieu of remuneration – eg, a loss of earnings payment to a councillor;

- statutory or contractual redundancy pay and other compensation payments (other than from an employment tribunal complaint).

Certain final payments *are* taken into account (unless you are over pension age and they are paid on retirement):[23]
- statutory or contractual maternity, adoption, paternity, shared parental and sick pay;
- an employment tribunal award or settlement of a complaint to a tribunal or court – eg, compensation for unfair dismissal;
- a retainer.

If you are already entitled to CA when a job ends, any final earnings at the end of that employment are not disregarded.

Calculating net earnings from employment

'Earnings' are net earnings. '**Net earnings**' are gross earnings less any deductions made for income tax, class 1 national insurance (NI) contributions (but not class 3 voluntary contributions[24]) and half of any contribution made towards a personal or occupational pension scheme.[25] It is the amount of weekly earnings that is important; monthly earnings are multiplied by 12 and divided by 52 to arrive at a weekly figure.[26] If payment is for a period of less than a week, it is treated as a payment for a week.[27]

If your earnings fluctuate, your weekly earnings may be averaged as follows.[28]
- If you have a regular pattern of work, your weekly earnings are averaged over one complete 'cycle' of work. This includes periods when no work is done if this forms part of your regular pattern of work – eg, if you regularly work three weeks on and one week off, your earnings are averaged over four weeks.
- In any other case, your earnings are averaged over five weeks, or whatever other period enables the average weekly earnings to be assessed more accurately.[29]

The date from when earnings from employment are counted

Earnings are usually treated as having been received on the first day of the benefit week in which they are due to be paid.[30] If the payment is made on a different date to that on which it is due, see p875 of the 2014/15 edition of this *Handbook*.

Benefit week
The '**benefit week**' is the seven days corresponding to the week for which CA is paid.[31]

The period covered by earnings from employment

Earnings count for a future period starting from the above date. The length of that period is worked out as follows.[32]

Part 5: Other benefits
Chapter 25: Carer's allowance
1. Who can claim carer's allowance

- If a payment is made for a particular period, it is taken into account for the number of benefit weeks corresponding to that period. For example, a week's part-time earnings are taken into account for a week. For monthly payments, earnings are taken into account for the number of weeks between the date they are treated as paid and the date the next monthly earnings are treated as paid. If a payment is for a particular period but is a one-off (eg, holiday pay on leaving a job if the final payments count – see p558), it is taken into account for the number of weeks from the date it is due to the date the next normal monthly earnings would be treated as paid.[33]
- One-off payments that are not for a specific period are divided by the relevant earnings limit (£116 in 2017/18) plus one penny and any disregard that applies to your earnings to work out the number of weeks for which you will not get benefit.
- If two payments of different types of earnings are made (eg, wages and holiday pay) and the periods worked out as above overlap, they are taken into account consecutively.[34]

Earnings from self-employment

Weekly earnings from self-employment (including any allowance from a DWP scheme to assist with the business[35]) are averaged over a year unless:[36]
- you have recently become self-employed; *or*
- there has been a change that is likely to affect the normal pattern of the business.

In either case, earnings are averaged over whatever other period the decision maker considers will give the most accurate figure. This means that when you first claim CA, you should provide an up-to-date set of accounts.

For royalties or similar payments (eg, from copyrights), the period for which these payments count is calculated in a similar way to that for payments made for unspecified periods to employees.[37]

See p561 for the way earnings of childminders, members of a partnership or share fishermen are calculated. Otherwise, it is the net profit from self-employment that is used.

'**Net profit**' is calculated by taking the earnings from self-employment over the period and deducting:[38]
- expenses incurred during the period wholly and exclusively for the purposes of the business. If a car or telephone, for example, is used partly for business and partly for private purposes, the costs of it can be apportioned and the amount attributable to business use can be deducted.[39] Certain expenses cannot be deducted, including business entertainment, repayment of capital on a business loan, capital expenditure and depreciation, and providing board and lodging or renting a room in your home;
- income tax and NI contributions;[40] *and*

- half of any contributions made during the period towards a personal pension scheme or retirement annuity contract.

Childminders are always treated as self-employed and your net profit is deemed to be one-third of your earnings from childminding less income tax, NI contributions and half of certain pension contributions.[41] The rest of your earnings are completely ignored.

For members of a partnership or share fishermen, the relevant share of the 'net profit' is used, and expenses incurred wholly and exclusively for the business are deducted before calculating the share of the profits. After that, income tax, NI contributions and half of any premiums paid into a personal pension or under a retirement annuity contract are deducted from the share.[42]

Notional earnings

You are treated as having 'notional earnings' if it is not possible to work out your actual earnings from employment or self-employment when your claim is decided.[43] This may apply if, for example, the job is new and pay depends on performance, or it is a new business and there is no way of calculating what the profits of that business will be. If so, the 'notional earnings' are an amount that is considered reasonable, taking into account the number of hours worked and the earnings paid for comparable work in the area.

Estimates of the appropriate deductions for income tax and NI contributions and half of any occupational or personal pension contributions are deducted from notional earnings, as are any earnings disregards or, where relevant, allowances for childcare or care costs.

Disregarded earnings

Some income, which might otherwise be classed as earnings, is specifically disregarded and does not affect your CA entitlement. The same earnings disregards apply whether the earnings are from employment or self-employment.

When calculating earnings, the cost of looking after the person you care for, up to a maximum amount, can be deducted from your earnings. If you are getting CA and, because of your work, you have to pay for someone (other than a 'close relative') to look after the severely disabled person for whom you care (or to look after a child under 16 for whom you or your partner are getting child benefit), these care costs can be deducted when your earnings are calculated (in addition to any disregarded earnings).[44] The maximum deduction is 50 per cent of the figure which would otherwise be your net earnings. Any disregarded income is deducted from your net earnings before calculating the 50 per cent figure.

Close relative

'**Close relative**' means a parent, son, daughter, brother, sister or partner (see p215) of you or the severely disabled person for whom you care.

Part 5: Other benefits
Chapter 25: Carer's allowance
3. People included in the claim

In addition, the following amounts can be disregarded from your earnings:[45]
- any payment made to you by someone who normally lives with you on an informal or non-contractual basis as part of her/his contribution towards shared living expenses;
- the first £20 a week of any income for renting out room(s) in your home;
- the first £20 of any income you receive each week for providing board and lodging in your home. If you get more than £20 a week, 50 per cent of the excess is also disregarded. This disregard applies to each person who lodges with you;
- payments from a local authority or voluntary organisation for fostering or accommodating a child under formal arrangements;
- payments from a health authority, clinical commissioning group, local authority or voluntary organisation for providing temporary care. There is no set time after which care is no longer temporary;[46]
- income tax refunds;
- if you are an employee, any loan or advance of earnings from your employer;
- certain bounty payments made to part-time firefighters, auxiliary coastguards, members of the territorial or reserve armed forces and part-time lifeboat crews;
- unless you are abroad yourself, earnings payable abroad which cannot be brought into Great Britain and any bank charges for converting earnings paid in another currency into sterling.

2. The rules about your age

You can claim carer's allowance (CA) if you are aged 16 or over.[47] There is no upper age limit. However, because of the overlapping benefit rules, if you receive retirement pension you may not be paid CA, even if you qualify (see p1175). Even if you are not paid CA, you may qualify for a carer premium (in pension credit, a carer addition) in your means-tested benefits (see p246) or a carer element in your universal credit (see p263).

3. People included in the claim

You claim carer's allowance (CA) for yourself. You cannot normally claim any increase in your CA for an adult dependant or a child.

Can you get an increase for an adult or child?
You may continue to qualify for an increase in your CA for:
– your spouse or civil partner, or for someone who cares for your child, if you were entitled to the increase before 6 April 2010 (but see p563 for when it may end);

– a child, if you were entitled to the increase before 6 April 2003 and your entitlement has continued since that date.

If an increase for a child stops being paid for 58 days or less, you may continue to qualify for the increase.[48]

If you are a member of a couple, you may not get an increase for a child if your partner's earnings are at or above the earnings limit. In 2017/18, this is £230 a week for the first child plus £30 for each subsequent child.

If you qualify, you are paid £8 for the eldest child and £11.35 for each subsequent child.

You do not get an increase for an adult dependant if s/he earns more than £36.90 a week. If you do qualify, you are paid £36.90 a week.

See p745 of the 2012/13 edition of this *Handbook* for further details. For other rules relating to entitlement to the increase, see pp746–48 of the 2002/03 edition. See p552 of the 2013/14 edition for when an increase for an adult may end.

4. The amount of benefit

Carer's allowance (CA) is paid at a weekly rate of £62.70.[49]

If you are still entitled to an increase in your CA for an adult or for a child, see pxvii for the amounts.

Note: if you are a member of a couple, your CA might be paid at a reduced rate if your partner fails to take part in a work-focused interview (see p1066).

5. Special benefit rules

Special rules may apply if:
• you are subject to immigration control (see Chapter 65);
• you have come from or are going abroad (see Chapters 66, 67 and 68);
• you, or the person you are caring for, are in hospital or in prison, or the person you are caring for is in a care home or other similar accommodation (see Chapter 41).

6. Claims and backdating

The general rules on claims and backdating are covered in Chapter 49. This section explains the specific rules that apply to carer's allowance (CA).

If you are claiming a means-tested benefit, see p568 before claiming CA. It is not always advisable for you to claim CA because of the effect it has on your other benefits (and possibly those of the person for whom you care).

Part 5: Other benefits
Chapter 25: Carer's allowance
6. Claims and backdating

Making a claim

A claim for CA must be made in writing. You can do this by completing:
- an online application form at www.gov.uk/carers-allowance; *or*
- the approved form. Send it to the Carer's Allowance Unit, Mail Handling Site A, Wolverhampton WV98 2AB. You may also be able to make your claim by taking or sending it to an 'alternative office' (see p1148).

Keep a copy of your claim form in case queries arise.

You must provide any information or evidence required (see below). In certain circumstances, the DWP may accept a written application not on the approved form.[50] You can amend or withdraw your claim before a decision is made (see p1149). If there is a delay in making a claim, you may be able to get a short-term advance of benefit (see p1177).

Forms

Get Form DS700 (DS700SP if you get retirement pension) from your local Jobcentre Plus office, DWP office or telephone contact centre, or from www.gov.uk/government/publications/carers-allowance-claim-form, or the Carer's Allowance Unit by email at cau.customer-services@dwp.gsi.gov.uk or by telephone on 0345 608 4321 (textphone: 0345 604 5312; text relay: 18001 0345 608 4321).

Who should claim

You must normally claim CA on your own behalf. However, if you are unable to manage your own affairs, another person can claim CA for you as your 'appointee' (see p1149).

Before claiming, you should be aware of how CA affects your entitlement to means-tested benefits and the means-tested benefit entitlement of the person for whom you care (see p568).

Information to support your claim

For the general information requirements that apply to all benefits, see p1150.

It is important that you provide any information required when you claim. Until you do, you may not count as having made a valid claim (see p1152). Correct any defects as soon as possible or your date of claim may be affected.

The CA claim forms contain a declaration to be completed by the person for whom you care or the person acting for her/him. This asks for confirmation that you provide 35 hours' care a week and explains that her/his benefit may be affected if your claim is successful. Even if this declaration is not completed, the DWP should still make a decision on your claim, although it is likely to be delayed. If the declaration raises questions about the level of care you provide, the DWP may refuse your claim.

Even if you have provided everthing that was required when you claimed, you may be asked to provide further evidence to support your claim (see p1154). You may also be asked to provide information after you are awarded CA and if you fail to do so, your CA could be suspended, or even terminated (see p1185).

The date of your claim

The date of your claim is important as it determines when your entitlement to CA starts. This is not necessarily the date from when you are paid. For information about when payment of CA starts, see p566.

Your '**date of claim**' is usually the date on which your completed claim form is received by the DWP or a designated 'alternative office' (see p1148).[51] If you submit your claim online, your date of claim is usually the date it is received, although a decision maker has the discretion to treat it as having been received on an earlier or later date than this.[52]

Note: you must make sure your claim is valid. If it is 'defective', you are given a short time to correct the defects (see p1152). If you do, your claim is treated as having been made when you initially claimed.[53]

In some cases, you can claim in advance (see p566) and, in some cases, your claim can be backdated (see below). If you want this to be done, make this clear when you claim or the DWP may not consider it. If you claimed income support (IS) when you should have claimed CA, see p566.

Backdating your claim

It is very important to claim in time. A claim for CA can usually only be backdated for a maximum of three months.[54] You must satisfy the qualifying conditions over that period. You do not have to show any reasons why your claim was late.

Your claim can be backdated for more than three months if:[55]

- you claim CA within three months of a decision to award a 'qualifying benefit' to the person for whom you care (including a decision made by the First-tier Tribunal, the Upper Tribunal or a court). Your CA is backdated to the first day of the benefit week in which the qualifying benefit is payable. However, if the decision awarding the qualifying benefit was made following a renewal claim where a fixed period award has ended or is due to end, your CA is only backdated to the first day of the benefit week in which the renewal award became payable; *or*
- your CA stopped because the 'qualifying benefit' of the person for whom you care was reduced or stopped. This includes if a fixed-term award for the qualifying benefit came to an end or if payment of attendance allowance (AA), disability living allowance (DLA) or personal independence payment (PIP) stopped because the person for whom you care went into hospital, a care home or other similar accommodation. If you make a further claim within three months of the decision to reinstate the qualifying benefit, or of payment

starting again, your CA is backdated to the date your earlier claim ended or the date from when the qualifying benefit was re-awarded or became payable again, whichever is later.

Qualifying benefit

A **'qualifying benefit'** is either AA, the middle or highest rate DLA care component, either rate of the daily living component of PIP, armed forces independence payment or constant attendance allowance.

If you might have qualified for benefit earlier but did not claim because you were given the wrong information by the DWP or because you were misled by it, you could ask for compensation (see p1396) or complain to the Ombudsman via your MP (see p1401).

If you claim the wrong benefit

If you claim IS when you should have claimed CA (either in addition to or instead of IS), a decision maker can treat your IS claim as a claim for CA (see p1161).[56] This applies even if you claim IS 'on the grounds of disability' (see p105). This may enable you to get round the strict time limits on backdating (see p565).

Claiming in advance

You can claim CA up to three months before you qualify.[57] This gives the DWP time to ensure you receive benefit as soon as you are entitled. The date of your claim is the date on which you qualify. The decision maker can award benefit from a future date if s/he believes you will satisfy all the CA qualifying conditions on that date. You may want to consider claiming in advance – eg, if you are currently earning more than £116 a week, but you plan to stop work or reduce your hours.

7. **Getting paid**

The general rules on getting paid are covered in Chapter 50. This section explains the specific rules that apply to carer's allowance (CA).

When is carer's allowance paid?

You are paid on a Monday (or Wednesday if the person for whom you care receives constant attendance allowance with an industrial injuries benefit or war pension).[58] CA is paid weekly in advance or four-weekly in arrears (13-weekly in arrears if you agree).[59]

Payments normally run from the first payday after the date of your claim, unless the date of your claim is on your payday, when they run from that day.

Note:

- CA awards are usually made for an indefinite period, but can be made for a fixed period – eg, if a change of circumstances is expected.[60]
- Deductions can be made from your CA to repay certain loans (see p1196) and, in some cases, to pay child support maintenance (see p1193).
- You may not be paid CA if you have been sanctioned for benefit offences (see p1265).
- For information on missing payments, see p1174. If you cannot get your CA payments because you have lost your bank or Post Office card or you have forgotten your PIN, see p1173. If you have lost your 'simple payment' card, or you have forgotten your memorable date, see p1173.
- If payment of your CA is delayed, see p1165. If you are waiting for a decision on your claim, or to be paid, you may be able to get a short-term advance (see p1177). If you wish to complain about how your claim has been dealt with, or claim compensation, see Chapter 58.
- If payment of your CA is suspended, see p1185.
- If you are overpaid CA, you may have to repay it (see Chapter 52) and, in some circumstances, you may have to pay a penalty (see p1256). If you have been accused of fraud, see Chapter 53.

Change of circumstances

You must report changes in your circumstances that you have been told to report, as well as any that you might reasonably be expected to know might affect your right to, the amount of, or the payment of, your benefit. You should do this as soon as possible, preferably in writing. See p1184 for further information. You can also notify your change of circumstances online at www.gov.uk/carers-allowance.[61]

When there has been a relevant change of circumstances, a decision maker looks at your claim again and makes a new decision. To find out the date from which the new decision takes effect, see p1293.

8. Tax, other benefits and the benefit cap

Tax

Carer's allowance (CA) (including an increase for your spouse, civil partner, or someone who cares for your child, if you still receive this) is taxable.[62] However, increases for children (if you still receive these) are not taxable.

Part 5: Other benefits
Chapter 25: Carer's allowance
8. Tax, other benefits and the benefit cap

Means-tested benefits and tax credits

Before you claim CA, consider how your claim might affect your entitlement to means-tested benefits and tax credits. If in doubt, obtain advice.

If you are awarded CA and the person for whom you care has a severe disability premium/additional amount included in her/his income support (IS), income-based jobseeker's allowance (JSA), income-related employment and support allowance (ESA), pension credit (PC) or housing benefit (HB), her/his entitlement to that premium/additional amount can be affected (see p247). Bear in mind that the severe disability premium/additional amount is worth more than the carer premium/additional amount.

If you receive CA, you come within one of the groups of people who can claim IS.

If you are a member of a 'joint-claim couple' claiming income-based JSA, you are not required to satisfy the jobseeking conditions (see Chapter 45) if you are a carer who could claim IS (see p104). You may wish to consider claiming IS or PC instead of income-based JSA.

If you are claiming universal credit (UC), you do not have to meet any of the work-related requirements (see p1081) if you qualify for CA, or you would do but for the fact that your earnings are higher than £116 a week.

CA counts in full as income for working tax credit (WTC) and child tax credit (CTC). Remember, however, that you cannot get CA if you are in 'gainful employment (see p557).

If you are a member of a couple with at least one child or qualifying young person and one of you is entitled to CA, the other only has to work 16 hours a week to qualify for WTC (see p196). You may also qualify for the childcare element in WTC (see p1414).

Income

CA counts in full as income for all means-tested benefits. However, in some cases an increase in your CA for an adult or child can be ignored. See p324 for PC and HB if you are at least the qualifying age for PC, and p285 for all other means-tested benefits.

CA counts as qualifying income for the savings credit of PC (see p151).

Note:
- For IS, income-based JSA and income-related ESA, and, if you are under the qualifying age for PC, HB, if you choose not to claim CA and the DWP decides that you failed to apply for it deliberately, you may be treated as if you receive it (see p299).
- For all means-tested benefits other than UC, if you give up your claim for CA, you can be treated as if you receive it if the DWP decides that you deliberately deprived yourself of it in order to qualify for, or increase your entitlement to, benefit for yourself or your family (but see p299 and p330).

The amount of means-tested benefits

If you receive CA (or are entitled to it but do not receive it because of the overlapping benefit rules – see p1175), a carer premium/additional amount is included in your IS, income-based JSA, income-related ESA, PC and HB.

If you are claiming UC, and:

- you are a member of a couple, you can get a childcare costs element if one of you is in paid work and the other is not in paid work, is unable to provide childcare and qualifies for CA;
- you (or your partner) qualify for CA, or would do but for the fact that your (or her/his) earnings are higher than £116 a week, a carer element is included in your UC maximum amount. However, if you:
  - have limited capability for work and are a carer, your UC cannot include both a limited capability for work element and a carer element for the same person;
  - are a single claimant with limited capability for work-related activity, your UC includes a limited capability for work-related activity element instead of a carer element;
  - are a member of a couple, your UC includes the limited capability for work-related activity element if one has not already been included for your partner. However, if a limited capability for work-related activity element has been included for you, a carer element can be included for your partner if s/he satisfies the conditions, whether or not s/he would also qualify for a limited capability for work-related activity element.

You may need to work out how you would be better off financially.

Non-means-tested benefits

For each week you receive CA, you can get national insurance credits (see p972).

CA is subject to the overlapping benefit rules, which means that you may not be paid CA in full if another earnings-replacement benefit (eg, retirement pension) is paid to you (see p1175).

The benefit cap

In some cases, there is a limit on the total amount of specified benefits you can receive (a 'benefit cap'). Since 7 November 2016, following a High Court decision, CA is no longer one of these specified benefits.[63] If you receive CA (or you would receive it but for the overlapping benefit rules), you are exempt from the cap. See p1180 for further information.

Passports and other sources of help

If you get CA (or would get it but for the overlapping benefit rules), you are entitled to a Christmas bonus (see p863). You may be able to get help, support and services from your local authority – ask for a carer's assessment. If you have a low income, you may be entitled to council tax reduction (see p854).

Notes

1. Who can claim carer's allowance
1 s70 SSCBA 1992; reg 9(1) SS(ICA) Regs
2 s70(2) SSCBA 1992; reg 3 SS(ICA) Regs
3 s70(7) SSCBA 1992
4 Reg 4(1) SS(ICA) Regs
5 s122 SSCBA 1992
6 CG/6/1990
7 R(G) 3/91
8 Reg 4(1A) SS(ICA) Regs
9 Reg 4(2) SS(ICA) Regs
10 *SSWP v Pridding* [2002] EWCA Civ 306
11 s70(1A) SSCBA 1992
12 Reg 8(1) SS(ICA) Regs
13 Reg 8(2) SS(ICA) Regs
14 Reg 9 SSB(CE) Regs
15 *Minter v Kingston Upon Hull CC and Potter v SSWP* [2011] EWCA Civ 1155
16 R(IS) 9/95; CIS/743/1992
17 R(IB) 7/03
18 Reg 9(1)(b) SSB(CE) Regs
19 Reg 2(1) SSB(CE) Regs
20 Reg 9(3) SSB(CE) Regs; *Parsons v Hogg* [1985] 2 All ER 897 (CA), appendix to R(FIS) 4/85
21 Reg 9(3)(b) SSB(CE) Regs
22 Sch 1 para 12 SSB(CE) Regs
23 Sch 1 para 12(2) SSB(CE) Regs
24 CIS/521/1990
25 Reg 10(4) SSB(CE) Regs
26 Regs 6(1) and 8(1)(b)(i) SSB(CE) Regs
27 Reg 8(1)(a) SSB(CE) Regs
28 Reg 8(3) SSB(CE) Regs
29 CG/4941/2003
30 Reg 7(b) SSB(CE) Regs
31 Reg 2(1) SSB(CE) Regs
32 Reg 6(2) SSB(CE) Regs
33 *Cotton v SSWP* [2009] EWCA Civ 1333; [2010] AACR 17
34 Reg 6(3) SSB(CE) Regs; *Cotton v SSWP* [2009] EWCA Civ 1333; [2010] AACR 17
35 Reg 12(1) SSB(CE) Regs
36 Reg 11(1) SSB(CE) Regs
37 Reg 11(2) SSB(CE) Regs
38 Reg 13(1)(a) and (b), (4) and (5) SSB(CE) Regs
39 R(IS) 13/91; R(FC) 1/91; CTC/26/1989
40 See also reg 14 SSB(CE) Regs
41 Regs 13(10) and 14 SSB(CE) Regs
42 Reg 13(5) SSB(CE) Regs
43 Reg 4(1) and (3) SSB(CE) Regs and R(IB) 7/03, disapplying reg 4(2) of these Regs
44 Regs 10(3) and 13(3) and Sch 3 SSB(CE) Regs
45 Sch 1 SSB(CE) Regs
46 CG/1752/2006

2. The rules about your age
47 s70(3) SSCBA 1992

3. People included in the claim
48 Art 3 TCA(No.3)O

4. The amount of benefit
49 Sch 4 SSCBA 1992

6. Claims and backdating
50 Reg 4(1) SS(C&P) Regs
51 Reg 6(1)(a) and (1ZA) SS(C&P) Regs
52 Reg 4ZC and Sch 9ZC para 4(1) and (2) SS(C&P) Regs
53 Reg 6(1)(b) SS(C&P) Regs
54 Reg 19 SS(C&P) Regs
55 Reg 6(16)-(22), (33) and (34) SS(C&P) Regs
56 Reg 9(1) and Sch 1 SS(C&P) Regs
57 Reg 13 SS(C&P) Regs

7. Getting paid
58 Reg 22(3) and Sch 6 SS(C&P) Regs
59 Reg 22(1) SS(C&P) Regs
60 Reg 17 SS(C&P) Regs
61 Reg 32ZA SS(C&P) Regs

8. Tax, other benefits and the benefit cap
62 ss660, 661 and 676 IT(EP)A 2003
63 Reg 83(1)(i) and (j) UC Regs

Chapter 26

Child benefit and guardian's allowance

This chapter covers:
1. Who can claim child benefit (p572)
2. Who can claim guardian's allowance (p581)
3. The rules about your age (p584)
4. People included in the claim (p584)
5. The amount of benefit (p584)
6. Special benefit rules (p585)
7. Claims and backdating (p587)
8. Getting paid (p589)
9. Tax, other benefits and the benefit cap (p591)

Key facts
- You may be entitled to child benefit if you are responsible for a child or 'qualifying young person'. You do not need to be the child's parent to qualify.
- You may be entitled to guardian's allowance if you are responsible for a child or qualifying young person and one or both of her/his parents have died. Usually, you must not be the child's parent to qualify.
- Child benefit and guardian's allowance are non-means-tested benefits.
- You do not need to have paid national insurance contributions to qualify.
- You can qualify for child benefit and guardian's allowance whether you are in or out of work.
- If your (or your partner's) income is over £50,000 in a tax year, you (or s/he) may be liable to pay tax in respect of child benefit, known as a 'high-income child benefit charge'. Guardian's allowance is not taxable.
- Child benefit and guardian's allowance are administered and paid by HM Revenue and Customs.
- If you disagree with a decision, you can apply for a revision or a supersession, or appeal against it. You must apply for a mandatory reconsideration before you can appeal.

Part 5: Other benefits
Chapter 26: Child benefit and guardian's allowance
1. Who can claim child benefit

1. **Who can claim child benefit**

Note: in this chapter the term 'child' is used to refer to both a child and a 'qualifying young person'.

You qualify for child benefit for a child if:[1]

- s/he counts as a 'child' or 'qualifying young person' (see below); *and*
- you are 'responsible' for the child (see p577); *and*
- you have priority over other claimants (see p578); *and*
- you and the child satisfy the residence conditions (see p1573); *and*
- you are not a 'person subject to immigration control', although there are exceptions to this (see Chapter 65).

In some circumstances, even if you meet the above qualifying conditions, you cannot get child benefit (see p581). If your child has died, see p591.

Note: guardian's allowance is a separate benefit, but to get it you must usually be entitled to child benefit. For who can claim guardian's allowance, see p581.

Who counts as a child

Anyone aged under 16 is a **'child'** for child benefit purposes.[2] Child benefit can continue to be paid for a child after s/he reaches 16 for as long as s/he counts as a 'qualifying young person'.

Who counts as a qualifying young person

A **'qualifying young person'** is someone who is aged 16 or over and under 20 who:[3]

- is either undertaking, enrolled on or accepted on a qualifying course of education (see p573) or 'approved training' (see p575). **Note:** there are some restrictions for 19-year-olds; *or*
- is not undertaking, enrolled on or accepted on a qualifying course of education or approved training, and has not reached 1 September after her/his 16th birthday (or, if s/he was born on 31 August, has not reached 2 September after her/his 16th birthday);[4] *or*
- is 16 or 17 years old, is not in *any* education or training, and is in an 'extension period' (see p575); *or*
- has left a qualifying course of education or approved training, and has not passed the end of the week that includes her/his 'terminal date' (see p575).

If more than one of the above grounds apply to your child, s/he counts as a qualifying young person until the last date that applies.[5] However, see p581 for when you cannot get child benefit for a qualifying young person.

If child benefit for your child stops because s/he no longer counts as a qualifying young person, but s/he later counts as a qualifying young person again, you can make a new claim (but see p576 if there is just a temporary interruption in meeting the conditions).

Education

Someone aged 16 or over but under 20 counts as a qualifying young person if:[6]

- s/he is attending a course of 'full-time non-advanced education' (see p574), which s/he started, or was enrolled or accepted on, before reaching 19; *or*
- s/he is receiving 'appropriate full-time education' in England (see p574), which s/he started, or was enrolled or accepted on, before reaching 19; *or*
- s/he was previously on one of the above courses and is now enrolled or accepted on another such course.

To count as a qualifying young person, the course must not be provided as a result of your child's employment or because of an office s/he holds (but see p576).

See p576 if your child's education is interrupted.

Note:

- If your child leaves one of the above kinds of education before s/he is 20, you may still qualify for child benefit if s/he counts as a qualifying young person on another ground (see p572).
- HM Revenue and Customs (HMRC) says that it will treat a young person who starts a course of full-time non-advanced education while 19 as having begun the course before turning 19 if s/he has been in full-time, non-advanced education *continuously* since before turning 19. This ensures s/he is a qualifying young person while on the new course, even if s/he was not enrolled or accepted on it before turning 19.

Relevant education

In the regulations, the term 'relevant education' is used. **'Relevant education'** is defined as any education which is full time and not advanced. This term is only used in the rules that treat your child as a qualifying young person until 31 August after her/his 16th birthday (see p572) or her/his terminal date (see p575). Any education that counts as 'full-time, non-advanced education' (see p574) also counts as relevant education. HMRC states that 'appropriate full-time education' in England (see p574) is also always treated as relevant education.[7]

Part 5: Other benefits
Chapter 26: Child benefit and guardian's allowance
1. Who can claim child benefit

Examples of non-advanced and advanced courses of education[8]

Non-advanced courses	Advanced courses
GCSEs	A university degree
AS and A levels	NVQ level 4
NVQ and SVQ level 3 and below	Higher National Diploma or Higher
International Baccalaureate	National Certificate
Scottish National Qualifications (up to	Diploma of Higher Education
Higher or Advanced Higher level)	A teaching qualification
BTEC and OCR Nationals	SVQ level 4 and above

Full-time non-advanced education

To count as 'full-time, non-advanced education', your child's course must normally be provided at a school or college.[9] If s/he is educated elsewhere (eg, at home), this also counts if s/he was being educated in this way before the age of 16 and the decision maker approves the education.[10] If s/he started home education after the age of 16 because of additional needs related to a disability, s/he should satisfy this condition.[11]

To count as full time, the course must last for an average of over 12 hours a week during term time, including tuition, supervised study, exams and practical work, but excluding meal breaks and unsupervised study.[12] '**Supervised**' study requires the close proximity of a teacher or tutor to enforce discipline, and provide encouragement and help.[13]

The table above lists examples of advanced and non-advanced courses.

Appropriate full-time education

To count as 'appropriate full-time education', the education must:[14]
- be provided in England and be suitable for the child having regard to her/his age, ability and aptitude and to any special educational needs s/he has; *and*
- not be an advanced course (see above for examples).

It does not matter where the education is provided, as long as it is provided in England.

If the education is provided at home, it is always treated as full time. Education which is not provided at a school is treated as full time if it is:[15]
- a study programme developed by a further education college, higher education institution or training provider to meet an individual student's needs, which is provided over at least 540 hours in any 12-month period; *or*
- a programme of activity provided to enable the child to participate in education or training.

Approved training

Note: in England, there is no 'approved training', so you should check whether your child's training counts as 'appropriate full-time education' (see p574).

A child aged 16 or over but under 20 counts as a qualifying young person if:[16]

- s/he is on a course of approved training, which s/he started, or was enrolled or accepted on, before s/he reached 19; *or*
- s/he was on a course of full-time non-advanced education or approved training and is now enrolled or accepted on a course of approved training.

The course must not be provided under a contract of employment (but see p576). 'Approved training' includes:[17]

- in Scotland, Employability Fund activity;
- in Wales, Traineeships or Foundation Apprenticeships.

See p576 if your child's training is interrupted.

If your child leaves approved training before turning 20, you may still qualify for child benefit for her/him if she counts as a qualifying young person on another basis (see p572).

The extension period

If a child is aged 16 or 17, s/he continues to count as a qualifying young person, and so you can continue to qualify for child benefit for her/him, during an 'extension period' if:[18]

- s/he is not in any kind of education or training; *and*
- s/he is registered as available for work, education or training with the Careers Service or a specified body; *and*
- s/he is not in remunerative work (see p581 for what counts); *and*
- you were entitled to child benefit for her/him immediately before the extension period started; *and*
- you apply in writing (or by another method if HMRC accepts this) within three months of the date your child's education or training finished.

The extension period starts from the Monday after your child's course of education or training ends and lasts for 20 weeks from that date. If your child turns 18 during the extension period, unless s/he counts as a qualifying young person on another ground (see p572), your child benefit for her/him ends from the first child benefit payday on or after her/his 18th birthday.[19]

If your child's ability to satisfy the above conditions is interrupted, see p576.

The 'terminal date rule'

If your child leaves a qualifying course of education (see p573) or approved training (see above) before reaching 20, s/he continues to count as a qualifying young person until either:[20]

Part 5: Other benefits
Chapter 26: Child benefit and guardian's allowance
1. Who can claim child benefit

- her/his 'terminal date' if this falls on a Sunday, or the first Sunday after her/his 'terminal date' (see below); *or*
- if earlier, the Sunday of the week in which s/he turns 20, unless s/he turns 20 on a Monday (in which case child benefit ends the day before the 20th birthday).

A child does not count as a qualifying young person under this rule if s/he is in remunerative work (see p581).

Terminal date

Your child's **'terminal date'** is the first of the following dates that falls after the date s/he left education or training:

– the last day in February; *or*

– 31 May; *or*

– 31 August; *or*

– 30 November.

Note:
- If, after leaving a course of education, a child returns to sit an external examination in connection with the course, s/he is treated as still being in education until the date of the last exam, provided s/he was entered for the exam before leaving the course.[21]
- A child who has completed her/his Highers or Advanced Highers in Scotland is treated as being in education until the date a comparable course in England or Wales ends, if this is later.[22] This is because exams are often taken earlier in Scotland than in England and Wales.
- A child cannot count as a qualifying young person if her/his course of education or training is provided as a result of her/his job. However, provided s/he is under 20, it is arguable that s/he can count as a qualifying young person from the date s/he leaves such a course under the terminal date rule. This is because the rules on terminal dates do not exclude people whose course was provided under an employment contract.

Interruptions

If there is a break in a child's ability to satisfy the conditions for being a qualifying young person, this can be ignored:[23]
- for up to six months (whether or not the interruption began before or after the child was 16) if it is 'reasonable' in the circumstances; *or*
- indefinitely if it is caused by the child's physical or mental illness or disability, and the length of the interruption is 'reasonable' in the circumstances.

This means a child can still count as a qualifying young person during the interruption. HMRC states that this rule only applies if there is an interruption during a child's course of education or training, but arguably it could also apply to 16/17-year-olds during the extension period.

However, an interruption cannot be ignored if, immediately afterwards, a child starts or is likely to start:[24]

- a training course which is not 'approved training'; or
- a course of advanced education; or
- education connected to her/his employment.

Responsible for a child

You are only entitled to child benefit for a child if you are 'responsible' for her/him. You count as responsible for a child in any week in which:[25]

- you have the child living with you (see below); or
- you contribute to the cost of supporting the child (see p578).

A child 'living with' you

To be living with you, the child 'must live in the same house or other residence as [you] and also be carrying on there with [you] a settled course of daily living'.[26] This does not mean the same as 'residing together' or 'presence under the same roof'.[27] A child may be 'living with' you even while away. There are special rules if your child is looked after by a local authority (see p585).

Living apart

If a child lived with you in the past, but you are now living apart, s/he is treated as living with you if you have not lived separately for more than 56 days in the last 16 weeks.[28] When calculating whether a child has been apart from you for 56 days, days of absence are ignored if s/he is away only to:[29]

- receive education or training (HMRC states that this rule only applies to full-time education or approved training); or
- stay in certain types of residential accommodation, if this is necessary only because of the child's disability or because her/his health would be 'significantly impaired or further impaired' were s/he not staying there (but see below); or
- receive inpatient treatment in a hospital or similar institution (but see below).

In the latter two situations above, a maximum of 12 consecutive weeks' absence can be ignored, unless you are regularly incurring expenditure in respect of the child, in which case the period of absence can be ignored indefinitely.[30] If you are making visits, or giving the child pocket money, this condition is likely to be satisfied. Two or more periods in hospital or residential accommodation separated by 28 days or less are treated as one when calculating the 12-week period.

Part 5: Other benefits
Chapter 26: Child benefit and guardian's allowance
1. Who can claim child benefit

However, even if a child is not living with you, you may still qualify for child benefit for her/him if you are contributing to the cost of supporting her/him (see below).

See p1591 if your child is abroad.

Example

Amy's son was in hospital for 18 weeks. She regularly took him food, drinks and comics. On being discharged, he stays with his aunt for a month before returning home. Amy is entitled to child benefit for her son while he is away. He is treated as still living with her while he is in hospital as she regularly incurs expenditure for him. He also counts as still living with her while staying with his aunt, as he is not considered to have been absent from home for more than 56 days in the previous 16 weeks. The period he was in hospital is ignored when calculating the 56-day period.

Contributing to the cost of supporting a child

If a child is not living with you, you can still qualify for child benefit if you contribute to the cost of supporting her/him. To satisfy this condition, you must contribute at least the amount of child benefit that would be payable for the child (see p584).[31]

Note:
- Contributions need not be regular, but must total the amount of child benefit that you would qualify for during the period that is being considered.[32]
- Payments in kind, rather than cash, may be counted.[33]
- If you reside with your spouse or civil partner, any contribution made by one of you may be treated as a contribution by the other.[34]
- If you and another person(s) each contribute less than the amount of child benefit for the child, but your total contributions are at least the amount of child benefit payable, one of you is treated as contributing the whole sum. If you do not agree on who it is to be, HMRC decides.[35] If you qualify for child benefit on this basis, once it has been awarded you alone must contribute at least the amount of child benefit paid for the child to continue to be entitled.

Priority between claimants

It is possible for more than one person to meet the conditions of entitlement for child benefit for the same child – eg, a child may live with one parent and be maintained by the other. However, only one person can be awarded child benefit for a particular child. There is an order of priority for who receives child benefit when two or more people have claimed it and would otherwise be entitled.[36]

You are only entitled to child benefit if you make a claim, so the priority rules only apply if at least two people have claimed child benefit for the same child and both would qualify for it.[37] In this situation, claimants take priority in the following order:[38]

- a person with whom the child lives (who has priority over a person who counts as responsible for a child only because s/he is contributing to the cost of supporting the child);
- a wife, if a husband and wife are residing together (see p580);
- a parent (including a step-parent). A 'parent' means a child's 'legal parent', so can include an adoptive parent or someone who has 'legal parental responsibility';[39]
- the mother (including a stepmother), if the parents are residing together but are not married (see p580);
- in any other case, the person agreed by those entitled;
- if there is no agreement, the person HMRC selects. **Note:** you cannot appeal against this decision[40] – but see p1315.

If a new claim takes priority over an existing claim, child benefit continues to be paid on the existing claim for the three weeks following the week in which the new claim is made, unless the existing claimant withdraws her/his claim earlier, or her/his child benefit entitlement ends for another reason.[41] Even if your claim has priority, you normally cannot receive child benefit for a period before you made your claim during which it has already been paid to someone else for the same child (but see p590).

If you have claimed child benefit and want someone who has equal or lower priority to you to receive it, contact the Child Benefit Office (see Appendix 1).[42]

It may be advisable to concede priority to your partner if you spend time abroad, as child benefit normally ends if you have been abroad for more than eight weeks (or 12 weeks in some circumstances – see p1591).

Separation and the priority rules

Problems can arise if there are competing child benefit claims from recently separated parents. Even if the child only lives with one parent, s/he may also be treated as still living with the other parent for a period (usually 56 days) under the rules described on p577. If you are in this situation and your child lives with you, but is still treated as living with her/his other parent, both of you are potentially entitled to child benefit for the child. If neither of you is willing to withdraw your claim, the priority rules apply (see p578). This means, in practice, that a claim made by the mother normally takes priority for 56 days after you separate permanently, whoever the child lives with. However, if the father got child benefit before you separated, his claim has priority for three weeks after the week in which the mother claims.[43]

Note: if your ex-partner was getting child benefit when you made your competing claim, see p590.

Part 5: Other benefits
Chapter 26: Child benefit and guardian's allowance
1. Who can claim child benefit

Do you share the care of a child?

If you share the care of your child with her/his other parent from whom you have separated, both of you may potentially be entitled to child benefit for her/him. If you cannot agree on who should receive it, HMRC uses its discretion to decide who it is reasonable to pay the child benefit to. This usually involves deciding who has the greater responsibility of care. In deciding how best to present your case to HMRC, consider the following questions.

1. How many hours each week do each of you care for the child?

2. What are the terms of any court orders? Do they reflect the care arrangements in practice?

3. Where are the child's possessions kept?

4. At which address is the child registered with services, such as school and her/his doctor?

5. What contributions do each of you make towards the cost of bringing up the child? (This may not be conclusive if the resources of one parent are greater than the other.)

6. What impact might the decision have on each parent?

7. Are there other children of the same relationship for whom child benefit is paid? For example, in one case, the High Court held that, where two parents had nearly equal responsibility for the care of their two children, it was not unreasonable for the decision maker to decide that each parent should receive child benefit in respect of one child.[44]

These are just examples of the issues HMRC might consider – each case depends on its circumstances.

Residing together

It may be important to decide whether a couple are 'residing together' (or 'residing with' each other)[45] if two people make a claim for child benefit for the same child (see p578) or if child benefit is claimed for a child who is married (see p581).

If you are married, in a civil partnership or are a parent of a child, you and your spouse/civil partner/the other parent of your child are still treated as residing together, even if you are apart, if:[46]

- your absence from each other is not likely to be permanent; *or*
- the absence is solely because one or both of you is an inpatient in a hospital, or a similar institution that caters for people with mental health problems, whether this is likely to be temporary or permanent.

Even if you have not lived together, you can be treated as residing together if your absence from each other is not likely to be permanent.[47]

It is possible to be absent from one another while you are living under the same roof – eg, if you are maintaining separate households.[48]

When you cannot get child benefit

Even if you meet all the entitlement conditions, you cannot get child benefit if:[49]
- you are the child's spouse, civil partner or partner; *or*
- the child is married, in a civil partnership or living with her/his partner as if they were married or civil partners[50] unless:
  - the child's spouse, civil partner or partner is in full-time, non-advanced education or approved training; *or*
  - the child is not residing with her/his spouse or civil partner (see p580); *or*
- in some circumstances, the child is in 'remunerative work' (see below for what counts); *or*
- the child is aged 16 or over and receiving:
  - income support (see Chapter 5);
  - income-based jobseeker's allowance (see Chapter 6);
  - employment and support allowance (see Chapters 3 and 28);
  - working tax credit (see Chapter 10);
  - child tax credit (see Chapter 9);
  - universal credit (see Chapter 8); *or*
- the child has spent more than eight consecutive weeks (but see p585):
  - in prison or other custody; *or*
  - being looked after by a local authority.

16–19-year-olds who work

If your child is under 16, your entitlement to child benefit for her/him is unaffected by any work that s/he does.

If your child is 16 or over and only counts as a qualifying young person under the 'terminal date' rule (see p575) or is in an extension period (see p575), child benefit is not payable for her/him if s/he is in 'remunerative work'. This means that s/he works for 24 hours or more a week and the work is done for payment, or in the expectation of payment. [51]

However, if your child is a qualifying young person on any other ground (see p572), any work s/he does should not affect your entitlement to child benefit.

2. Who can claim guardian's allowance

You qualify for guardian's allowance for a 'child' or 'qualifying young person'(see p572 for who counts – the rules are the same as for child benefit) if:[52]
- you are entitled, or treated as entitled, to child benefit for her/him (see p582); *and*
- s/he is an 'eligible child' (see p582) and either:
  - s/he is living with you, or treated as living with you (see p577); *or*
  - you contribute to the cost of providing for the child (see p583); *and*

Part 5: Other benefits
Chapter 26: Child benefit and guardian's allowance
2. Who can claim guardian's allowance

- the residence conditions are satisfied (see p1574); *and*
- you are not the child's parent (but see p584).

If a child for whom you get guardian's allowance dies, see p591.

Entitled to child benefit

In general, to qualify for guardian's allowance, you must be entitled to child benefit (see p572). If you are not entitled to child benefit, you are treated as being entitled to it if:[53]
- you are residing with your spouse or civil partner and s/he is entitled to child benefit for the child; *or*
- you are living in Great Britain and would have been entitled to child benefit for the child had you (or your spouse or civil partner, if you reside with her/him) not been getting a family benefit from another country.

You can also be treated as entitled to child benefit in the week before your entitlement to child benefit begins. This allows your guardian's allowance to start from the same date as child benefit.[54]

Note: you still count as being entitled to child benefit even if you have chosen not to receive it to avoid the high-income child benefit charge (see p591).

Eligible child

A child is an **'eligible child'** if:[55]
- both her/his parents (or, if s/he has been adopted, adoptive parents) have died; *or*
- one of her/his parents (or adoptive parents) has died and:
  - at the time of the death you did not know where the other parent was and you have not been able to trace her/him (see p583); *or*
  - the other parent is sentenced to a term of imprisonment or is detained in hospital by a court order (but see p583); *or*
- when s/he was born her/his parents were unmarried, her/his mother has died and the child's paternity has not been clearly established (but see below if the child has been adopted); *or*
- s/he was adopted by only one person and that person has died; *or*
- her/his parents (or adoptive parents) are divorced or their civil partnership has been dissolved, one parent has died and:
  - at the time of the death, the surviving parent did not have custody of, and was not maintaining, the child; *and*
  - there is no court order for the child to reside with the surviving parent; *and*
  - the surviving parent is not liable for maintaining the child under a court order or child support maintenance assessment/calculation.

Missing parents

If one of the child's parents is dead, you may qualify for guardian's allowance if, at the date of the death, you did not know the whereabouts of her/his other parent and since then you have been unable to discover her/his whereabouts, despite making reasonable efforts to do so – eg, by asking known relatives and friends and checking old addresses.[56] It may not be necessary to make such efforts if you can show there is a danger that you or the child might experience harm or undue distress if you try to trace the missing parent – eg, if s/he is a threat to your, or the child's, physical safety or emotional wellbeing.[57]

If contact has been made with a surviving parent since the death of the other parent (but before the decision on the claim), guardian's allowance cannot be paid, as the whereabouts of the surviving parent are known.[58] This might apply even if the contact was only fleeting, such as at the funeral, and even if the surviving parent later disappears.

If contact has not been made, but you are able to communicate with the surviving parent in some way, this is likely to be sufficient to show that her/his whereabouts are known.[59] 'Whereabouts' is not the same as an address, so showing that you do not know where the surviving parent lives may not be enough to qualify for guardian's allowance if you have sufficient details of where s/he lives, works or can habitually be found. However, if all that you know is that the surviving parent is in a large urban area, you could argue that her/his whereabouts are unknown.

Prison sentences

If one of the child's parents is dead and the other is in prison, you are only entitled to guardian's allowance if the surviving parent is:[60]

- serving a sentence of imprisonment or detention and, at the date of the death, has at least two years of that sentence remaining; *or*
- detained in hospital by order of a court under specified legislation.

There are detailed rules about what counts as imprisonment or detention, and for calculating whether the length of a sentence amounts to two years, so get advice if you are affected.[61] Guardian's allowance is reduced if the parent in prison contributes to the cost of providing for the child.[62]

Contributing to the cost of providing for a child

To qualify for guardian's allowance for a child who does not live with you, you must contribute at least £16.70 a week to the cost of providing for her/him. This must be in addition to any contribution you make in order to qualify for child benefit for the child (see p578).[63]

When calculating whether you contribute at least £16.70 a week, you can include contributions made by your spouse or civil partner if you reside together. If you are not currently making contributions, you can be treated as doing so if

Part 5: Other benefits
Chapter 26: Child benefit and guardian's allowance
5. The amount of benefit

you provide a written undertaking to do so once you are awarded guardian's allowance. Any decision to pay your guardian's allowance on this basis may be revised if you do not actually make the contributions.[64]

Parents, adoptive parents and step-parents

A child's parent cannot qualify for guardian's allowance for her/him unless one of the following exceptions applies.[65]

- If a child is adopted, her/his adoptive parents count as parents, so one of her/his biological parents can claim guardian's allowance (if the qualifying conditions are met).
- Adoptive parents can continue to receive guardian's allowance if they were entitled to it immediately before the adoption.
- HM Revenue and Customs states that a step-parent does not count as a parent for guardian's allowance and so may be entitled to guardian's allowance for a stepchild.[66]

3. The rules about your age

There is no upper or lower age limit for entitlement to child benefit or guardian's allowance.

4. People included in the claim

You claim child benefit for each child for whom you are responsible. You claim guardian's allowance for each eligible child (see p582).

5. The amount of benefit

Child benefit is paid at the following weekly rates.[67]

	£pw
Eldest eligible child	20.70
Other children (each)	13.70

The higher rate of child benefit is normally paid for the eldest (or only) child in a family.[68] However, if you live with your partner and each of you has children from a previous relationship for whom you receive separate child benefit, the higher rate is only paid to the person who has the eldest child.[69]

Guardian's allowance is paid at a rate of £16.70 a week for each eligible child.[70]

6. Special benefit rules

Special rules may apply to your child benefit or guardian's allowance if:

- your child is being looked after by a local authority, or is in prison or detention (see below);
- you or your child have come from abroad or are going abroad (see Chapters 66, 67 and 68);
- you are in prison or detention (see Chapter 41).

Your child is being looked after by a local authority, or is in prison or detention

Note: the rules in this section prevent you from receiving guardian's allowance for an 'eligible child' (see p582) if your child benefit for that child stops.

Special rules apply if your child is:[71]

- being looked after by a local authority and is provided with, or placed in, accommodation under certain legislation and at least part of the cost of either the accommodation or the child's maintenance is paid from local authority or public funds (but see p586); or
- subject to a compulsory supervision order and living in residential accommodation under certain legislation; *or*
- in prison or another form of detention, such as a detention centre or young offenders' institution, as a result of criminal proceedings or non-payment of a penalty imposed on conviction.

If any of these circumstances apply to your child and have done so for at least one day a week in the last eight consecutive weeks, you cannot be entitled to child benefit for her/him after the eight-week period unless the child 'ordinarily' lives with you throughout at least one whole day each week (even if s/he is not actually at home in that particular week).[72] A 'day' runs from midnight to midnight, so, in practice, s/he ordinarily has to stay with you for two nights during a week for you to qualify.[73] A 'week' means seven days beginning with a Monday.[74]

After the first eight weeks' absence, even if the child does not 'ordinarily' live with you for at least one day a week, you still qualify for child benefit when the child comes to stay with you for a week or more.[75]

Note:

- Even if your child ordinarily lives with you or comes to stay with you for over a week, if the local authority is making certain payments you may still not qualify for child benefit (see p586).

Part 5: Other benefits
Chapter 26: Child benefit and guardian's allowance
6. Special benefit rules

- If your child stops being looked after by a local authority, subject to a supervision order or in prison for at least a week (ie, from Monday to Sunday), but s/he is subsequently in one of those circumstances once more, the eight-week period should start again.
- You are not excluded from entitlement to child benefit for a child on the grounds that s/he is being looked after by a local authority if s/he is placed in residential accommodation by a local authority because s/he has a disability or because her/his health would be significantly impaired or further impaired were s/he not in the accommodation.[76] If your child is living away from you in these circumstances, see p577.
- If the child is detained in a hospital or similar institution because of mental health problems, s/he is only treated as being in prison if s/he was moved there from prison or detention and the expected release date under her/his sentence has not passed. Otherwise, you can continue to get child benefit, provided you meet the normal qualifying conditions.[77]
- If the child has been detained in custody but is not sentenced to a term of imprisonment or detention, you are entitled to child benefit for her/him for the period of her/his earlier detention.[78]

Fostering, adoption and kinship care

- *You* cannot qualify for child benefit for a child if, for any day in a week, a local authority has arranged for her/him to be placed with you under placement, looking after or fostering arrangements and the local authority is paying you an allowance towards the cost of her/his accommodation or maintenance under section 22C(10) of the Children Act 1989, regulation 33 of the Looked After Children (Scotland) Regulations 2009 or under section 81(13) of the Social Services and Well-being (Wales) Act 2014.[79]
- *No one* can qualify for child benefit for a child if s/he has been placed for adoption in the house of her/his prospective adopters and a local authority is making a payment for the child's accommodation or maintenance under the above provisions.[80]

If these circumstances do not apply, the normal rules on entitlement apply, including the rules on children who are being looked after by a local authority described on p585 (and the exceptions to these rules described on p585).

Your entitlement to child benefit is not affected if you are looking after a child under private fostering arrangements.

7. Claims and backdating

The general rules about claims and backdating are covered in Chapter 49. This section explains the specific rules that apply to child benefit and guardian's allowance.

Making a claim

A claim for child benefit should be made in writing to the Child Benefit Office (see Appendix 1).

You must usually get child benefit to be able to claim guardian's allowance, but must make a separate claim. A claim for guardian's allowance should be made in writing to the Guardian's Allowance Unit at the Child Benefit Office (see Appendix 1).

Keep a copy of your claim form in case queries arise. HM Revenue and Customs (HMRC) has the discretion to accept claims made in another way. However, it is unlikely to accept any claim not made in writing.

You must provide any information and evidence required (see p588). You can amend or withdraw your claim before a decision is made (see p1149). If there is a delay in dealing with your claim, you may be able to get an interim payment (see p1179).

Forms

The approved child benefit form is Form CH2, which is available from the Child Benefit Office. The approved guardian's allowance form is Form BG1, which is available from the Guardian's Allowance Unit. Both forms are also available from www.gov.uk. They can be completed online, but must be printed, signed and sent by post.[81]

Note: at the time this *Handbook* was written, HMRC was planning to trial a new online child benefit claims service for people who do not already receive it during 2017. This may be introduced more widely later in 2017. See CPAG's online service and *Welfare Rights Bulletin* for updates.

Who should claim

You must normally make your own claim for child benefit and guardian's allowance. If you are unable to manage your own affairs, another person can claim for you as your 'appointee' (see p1149).

If someone else also makes a claim for child benefit for the same child, you are only entitled to child benefit for that child if you have priority over the other claimant (see p578).

If you are a married woman and you live with your husband, you are entitled to guardian's allowance rather than him.[82] However, it can be paid to either of

Part 5: Other benefits
Chapter 26: Child benefit and guardian's allowance
7. Claims and backdating

you, unless you ask for your husband not to be paid guardian's allowance on the approved form.[83]

Information to support your claim

For the general information requirements that apply to all benefits, see p1150.

It is important that you provide any information required when you claim. Until you do, you may not count as having made a valid claim (see p1152). Correct any defects as soon as possible or your date of claim may be affected.

HMRC needs to see an original copy of your child's birth or adoption certificate when you claim child benefit, except if your child was born on or after 1 July 2009 and you provide the 'system number' from her/his birth certificate, or your claim is verified by a local office under the 'Tell Us Once' scheme.[84]

If you claim guardian's allowance, you must normally provide the child's original birth certificate, together with the original death certificates of her/his parent(s) and an adoption certificate, if relevant to your claim.

You can send any original documents that you must provide to the Child Benefit Office. You should also be able to take them to your local Jobcentre Plus office, where a copy can be made and certified, and the certified copy sent to the Child Benefit Office.[85]

Even if you have provided all that was required when you claimed, you may be asked to provide further evidence to support your claim (see p1154). You may also be asked to provide information after you are awarded benefit. If you fail to do so, your benefit could be suspended, or even terminated (see p1185).

The date of your claim

The date of your claim is important as it determines when your entitlement to child benefit and guardian's allowance starts. This is not necessarily the date from when you are paid. For information about when payment of benefit starts, see p589.

Your '**date of claim**' is normally the date on which your claim form is received at the Child Benefit Office. If HMRC has stated in writing that another office can receive your claim, the date of claim is the date it is received by that office.[86]

Note: you must make sure your claim is valid. If it is 'defective', you are given a short time to correct the defect (see p1152). If you do, your claim is treated as having been made when you initially claimed.[87]

In some cases, you can claim in advance (see p589), and in some cases your claim can be backdated (see below). If you want this to be done, make this clear when you claim or HMRC might not consider it. If you initially claimed the wrong benefit, see p589.

Backdating your claim

It is very important to claim in time. A claim for child benefit or guardian's allowance can normally only be backdated for a maximum of three months.[88]

There are special rules if you are getting benefit and move between Great Britain and Northern Ireland, or if you have been recognised as a refugee (see p1528). You do not have to show any reason why your claim was late. However, if someone else has an award of child benefit for the same child, see p590.

If you might have qualified for child benefit or guardian's allowance earlier but did not claim because you were given the wrong information or misled by the DWP or HMRC, you could ask for compensation (see p1396) or complain to the Ombudsman through your MP (see p1401).

If you claim the wrong benefit

A claim for guardian's allowance can be treated as a claim for child benefit for the same child and vice versa.[89] See p1161 for further information.

Claiming in advance

If you do not qualify for child benefit or guardian's allowance when you claim but will qualify for it within three months of that date, the decision maker has the discretion to award you benefit in advance and treat your date of claim as the date on which you first qualify.[90]

8. Getting paid

The general rules on getting paid are covered in Chapter 50. This section explains the specific rules that apply to child benefit and guardian's allowance.

When is your benefit paid?

You are normally paid on a Monday (or on a Tuesday), although the decision maker has discretion to choose any day of the week as your normal payday. Benefit is usually paid four-weekly for three weeks in arrears and one week in advance. Payment begins from the Monday after the date of your claim (see p588) or, if the date of your claim is a Monday, from that date (but see p590 if someone else has been getting child benefit for the child).[91]

You can choose for child benefit to be paid weekly if:
- you are a lone parent; *or*
- you or your partner get income support, income-based jobseeker's allowance, income-related employment and support allowance, pension credit or universal credit;[92] *or*
- the decision maker is satisfied that a four-weekly payment 'is causing hardship'.[93]

You cannot choose for guardian's allowance to be paid weekly. However, if you are entitled to both benefits, your guardian's allowance is always paid at the same time as your child benefit.[94]

Child benefit and guardian's allowance are weekly benefits, so cannot be paid for periods of less than a week.

If your entitlement ends, payment normally continues up to, but not including, the following Monday. However, if your entitlement ends on a Monday, your benefit is normally paid up to, but not including, that day.

Your benefit is awarded for an indefinite period unless this would be inappropriate – eg, if a change is expected in the near future.[95]

Note:

- Child benefit or guardian's allowance can be paid to someone else if this is needed to protect your interests or the interests of the child.[96]
- Even if you have been sanctioned for a benefit offence, you must be paid child benefit and guardian's allowance.
- If you have forgotten your PIN, see p1173. If a cheque is lost or stolen, see p1174.
- If your payment of child benefit or guardian's allowance is delayed (see p1165), you might be able to get an interim payment (see p1179). If you wish to complain about how your claim has been dealt with, or claim compensation, see Chapter 58.
- If your payment of child benefit or guardian's allowance is suspended, see p1185.
- If you are overpaid benefit, you might have to repay it (see Chapter 52) and, in some circumstances, you may have to pay a penalty (see p1256). If you have been accused of fraud, see Chapter 53.

If someone else has been getting child benefit for the child

If you make a claim for child benefit and someone else is already getting it for that child, you are only entitled if your claim has priority over the claim of the existing claimant (see p578). If so, your benefit starts from the beginning of the fourth week after the week in which you claim, unless the existing claimant withdraws her/his claim before this or stops qualifying for child benefit for another reason.

Even if your claim has priority, if child benefit has already been paid to someone else for the same child for a period before you claimed, you are only entitled to child benefit for that period in the following two situations.[97]

- A decision maker (or, if the decision was made on an appeal, the First-tier or Upper Tribunal) has decided that the child benefit paid to the other claimant is recoverable because s/he failed to disclose, or misrepresented, a material fact (see p1227) and no appeal against that decision has been made within the time limit. Note that if you appeal against a decision refusing your child benefit

claim under this rule, the tribunal cannot decide that the other claimant was not entitled for a period before you claimed.[98]
- A decision has been made that the other claimant was not entitled to child benefit, and s/he has voluntarily repaid the child benefit for that period.

The above rules usually prevent you from becoming entitled to guardian's allowance for a child if someone else is getting child benefit for that child (as you must usually be entitled to child benefit to qualify for guardian's allowance – see p582).

Change of circumstances

You must report any change in your circumstances that you are told to report, as well as any that you might reasonably be expected to know might affect your right to, the amount of, or the payment of your benefit. You should do this as soon as possible, preferably in writing.

You can also report changes of circumstances at www.gov.uk. See p1184 for further information.

When there has been a relevant change of circumstances, a decision maker looks at your claim again and makes a new decision. For the date from which the new decision takes effect, see p1293.

If a child dies

If a child dies and you were entitled to child benefit for her/him when s/he died, your benefit is paid for the following eight weeks, or until the Monday after s/he would have been 20, if that is sooner. If your partner got child benefit for the child and s/he also dies, you are entitled to benefit for the eight-week period if you were living together when s/he died.[99]

If a child dies in the same week s/he was born, you can also qualify for child benefit for this period if you satisfied the other conditions of entitlement during that week.[100]

These rules allow you to also qualify for guardian's allowance for a child during a period after s/he dies, provided s/he continues to count as an 'eligible child'. You do not need to satisfy the conditions about living together or providing for her/his needs (see p581).[101]

9. Tax, other benefits and the benefit cap

Tax

Guardian's allowance is not taxable.[102]

If your income in a tax year is over £50,000, you are liable to pay tax on your 'taxable child benefit' for that year. This is called the 'high-income child benefit

Part 5: Other benefits
Chapter 26: Child benefit and guardian's allowance
9. Tax, other benefits and the benefit cap

charge'. It is only your income that is counted – not the combined income of you and your partner.

Your 'taxable child benefit' includes child benefit for any week that starts in the tax year which is paid to:[103]

- you; *or*
- your partner (but only for weeks when you were partners); *or*
- someone who gets child benefit for a child who lives with you, but not with her/him (but only if neither that person nor her/his partner is liable for the charge themselves).

If both you and your partner have income over £50,000, whoever has the highest income is liable for the charge for the weeks throughout which you were partners. If you are liable for the charge, you must declare this to HM Revenue and Customs (HMRC) by including details of your income on a self-assessment tax form within the time limit for doing so. See p582 of the 2013/14 edition of this *Handbook* for further details.

Note:[104]

- The high-income child benefit charge is 1 per cent of your taxable child benefit for each complete £100 income you have over £50,000 in a tax year. If your income is over £60,000, the charge equals the amount of taxable child benefit.
- Child benefit awarded for the period after a child dies is not included in your taxable child benefit.

Electing not to be paid child benefit

You (or your partner, if s/he is the claimant) can ask HMRC not to pay child benefit, in order to avoid liability for the high-income child benefit charge. HMRC may not agree to this – eg, if deductions are being made from child benefit to collect an overpayment.[105]

If you elect not to be paid (rather than just not claiming child benefit, or ending or withdrawing your claim), your underlying entitlement to child benefit continues and so you (or someone you live with or who cares for your child) may still qualify for national insurance (NI) credits (see p969 and p971). You can also qualify for guardian's allowance if the child is an 'eligible child' (see p582), or other benefits, such as more generous bereavement benefits (see Chapter 24), provided you meet the other entitlement conditions. For these reasons, consider claiming child benefit, even if you do not want it to be paid.

Note: after electing not to receive child benefit, you have up to two years after the end of the tax year to ask for child benefit to be paid for that year, if you realise that your child benefit would have been more than the charge.

Means-tested benefits and tax credits

Means-tested benefits and tax credits can be paid in addition to child benefit and guardian's allowance.

Usually, any child benefit and guardian's allowance you get are ignored when calculating your entitlement to income support and income-based jobseeker's allowance.[106] However, see p285 for when child benefit is taken into account.

Child benefit and guardian's allowance are also ignored when calculating entitlement to employment and support allowance, pension credit, housing benefit (HB), working tax credit, child tax credit and universal credit (UC).[107]

Non-means-tested benefits

Increases in non-means-tested benefits for dependent children were abolished in 2003, but some people still get them. You cannot get both guardian's allowance and an increase for the same child.[108]

If you still get an increase for a child, it is reduced if you also receive the higher rate of child benefit (£20.70) for that child (see p1177).[109]

If you are awarded child benefit for a child aged under 12, you (or, in some circumstances, someone who resides with you or cares for your child) can qualify for NI credits (see p969 and p971).

Your entitlement to any other non-means-tested benefit is not affected by your entitlement to child benefit or guardian's allowance.

The benefit cap

In some cases, there is a limit on the total amount of specified benefits you can receive (a 'benefit cap'). Child benefit is one of the specified benefits. However, the benefit cap only applies if you are getting HB or UC.

You are exempt from the benefit cap if you are entitled to guardian's allowance.[110]

See p1180 for further information.

Passports and other sources of help

If your income is low, you may be entitled to a council tax reduction (see p854). You may be eligible for free school lunches for your child (see p860).

Children and young people under 19 may qualify for health benefits (see Chapter 29). Young people aged 16 to 19 who are in non-advanced education may qualify for financial help with their studies (see p861).

Notes

1. **Who can claim child benefit**
  1 ss141-44 and 146 SSCBA 1992; s115 IAA 1999
  2 s142(1) SSCBA 1992
  3 s142(2) SSCBA 1992; regs 2-7 CB Regs
  4 If a child turns 16 on 31 August, HMRC states s/he is only a qualifying young person up to and including that day but, arguably, this is not correct; para 07030 CBTM; reg 4(3) CB Regs
  5 Reg 2(2) CB Regs
  6 Reg 3 CB Regs
  7 para 07020 CBTM, but see also regs 3 and 1(3) CB Regs. It is not clear that 'appropriate full-time education' always counts as 'full time' for the purpose of the definition of 'relevant education' in the regulations.
  8 Reg 1(3) CB Regs
  9 Reg 3(2)(a)(i) CB Regs
  10 Reg 3(2)(a)(ii) and (3) CB Regs
  11 *JH v HMRC (CHB)* [2015] UKUT 479 (AAC) [2016] AACR 15, although the regulations and guidance are yet to be amended – see para 07020 CBTM
  12 Reg 1(3) CB Regs
  13 R(F) 1/93, but see also *Flemming v SSWP* [2002] EWCA Civ 641 (reported as R(G) 2/02) and *SSWP v Deane* [2010] EWCA Civ 699
  14 Reg 3(2)(ab) CB Regs; s4 Education and Skills Act 2008
  15 s4 Education and Skills Act 2008; reg 3 Duty to Participate in Education or Training (Miscellaneous Provisions) Regulations 2013, No.1205
  16 Reg 3(2)(c), (d) and (4) CB Regs
  17 Reg 1(3) CB Regs; para 07024 CBTM
  18 Reg 5 CB Regs
  19 Reg 14 CB&GA(Admin) Regs; reg 5(3) CB Regs
  20 Reg 7 CB Regs
  21 Reg 7(2)2.1 CB Regs
  22 Reg 7(2)1.3 CB Regs
  23 Reg 6(2) and (3) CB Regs
  24 Reg 6(4) CB Regs
  25 s143 SSCBA 1992
  26 R(F) 2/81
  27 R(F) 2/79
  28 s143(2) SSCBA 1992

  29 s143(3) SSCBA 1992; reg 9 CB Regs; para 06040 CBTM
  30 s143(3)(b) and (c) and (4) SSCBA 1992; reg 10 CB Regs
  31 s143(1)(b) SSCBA 1992
  32 *RK v HMRC (CHB)* [2015] UKUT 357 (AAC); [2016] AACR 4 (note that a different view was taken in R(U) 14/62)
  33 R(U) 3/66
  34 Reg 11(4) CB Regs
  35 Reg 11 CB Regs
  36 s144(3) and Sch 10 SSCBA 1992
  37 s13(1) SSAA 1992
  38 Sch 10 SSCBA 1992
  39 s147(3) SSCBA 1992; R(F) 1/08
  40 Sch 2 para 4 SSA 1998
  41 Sch 10 para 1 SSCBA 1992
  42 Regs 14 and 15 CB Regs
  43 CF/1771/2003
  44 *R (on the application of Ford) v Board of Inland Revenue* [2005] EWHC Admin 1109; see also *R (Chester) v Secretary of State for Social Security* [2001] EWHC Admin 1119
  45 *Grove v Insurance Officer,* reported as an appendix to R(F) 4/85
  46 s147(4) SSCBA 1992; regs 1(3) and 34 CB Regs
  47 R(F) 4/85
  48 R(F) 3/81
  49 Sch 9 paras 1 and 3 SSCBA 1992; regs 8, 12,13 and 16 CB Regs
  50 But see *KW v HMRC (CB)* [2011] UKUT 489 (AAC)
  51 Regs 1(3), 5(2)(c) and 7(3) CB Regs

2. **Who can claim guardian's allowance**
  52 ss77 and 122(5) SSCBA 1992
  53 s122(4) SSCBA 1992; reg 4A SSB(Dep) Regs
  54 Reg 4A(1)(b) and (3) SSB(Dep) Regs
  55 s77(2) and (8)(a) SSCBA 1992; regs 4-7 GA(Gen) Regs
  56 s77(2)(b) SSCBA 1992
  57 para 12090 CBTM
  58 CG/60/1992; R(G) 2/83
  59 CG/60/1992; CF/2735/2003
  60 Reg 7 GA(Gen) Regs
  61 Reg 7 GA(Gen) Regs

62 s77(8)(c) SSCBA 1992; reg 8 GA(Gen) Regs
63 s77(6)(b) SSCBA 1992
64 Reg 5 SSB(Dep) Regs
65 s77(10) and (11) SSCBA 1992; regs 4 and 6(2) GA(Gen) Regs; R(G) 4/83 (appendix)
66 para 12010 CBTM; but see also R(F) 1/08

5. The amount of benefit
67 Reg 2(1) CB(R) Regs
68 Reg 2(1) CB(R) Regs
69 Reg 2(2) CB(R) Regs
70 Sch 4 Part III SSCBA 1992

6. Special benefit rules
71 s147(2) and Sch 9 para 1 SSCBA 1992; regs 16-19 CB Regs
72 Reg 16(1)(b)(iv) and (2) CB Regs
73 R(F) 3/85
74 s147(1) SSCBA 1992
75 Reg 16(1)(b)(i)-(iii) CB Regs
76 Regs 9 and 18(b) CB Regs
77 Reg 17(2)-(5) CB Regs
78 Regs 1(3) and 17(1) CB Regs
79 Reg 16(3) CB Regs
80 Reg 16(4) and (5) CB Regs

7. Claims and backdating
81 Regs 2, definition of 'writing', and 5 CB&GA(Admin) Regs
82 s77(9) SSCBA 1992
83 Reg 10 GA(Gen) Regs; para 12080 CBTM
84 https://www.gov.uk/register-birth. 'Tell Us Once' is not available in all areas.
85 Regs 3(2) and 5(5) CB&GA(AA) Regs
86 Reg 5(3) CB&GA(Admin) Regs
87 Reg 10 CB&GA(Admin) Regs
88 Reg 6 CB&GA(Admin) Regs
89 Reg 11 CB&GA(Admin) Regs
90 Reg 12 CB&GA(Admin) Regs

8. Getting paid
91 Reg 13 CB&GA(Admin) Regs
92 Reg 19 CB&GA(Admin) Regs
93 Reg 18(3) CB&GA(Admin) Regs
94 Reg 18(4) CB&GA(Admin) Regs
95 Reg 15 CB&GA(Admin) Regs
96 Reg 33 CB&GA(Admin) Regs
97 Sch 10 para 1 SSCBA 1992; s13(2) SSAA 1992; reg 38 CB Regs; CF/2826/2007
98 *CB v HMRC and AE (CHB)* [2016] UKUT 506 (AAC)
99 s145A SSCBA 1992; reg 20 CB Regs
100 s145A(3) SSCBA 1992
101 s145A(4) SSCBA 1992

9. Tax, other benefits and the benefit cap
102 s677 IT(EP)A 2003
103 ss681B, 681D and 681H IT(EP)A 2003
104 ss681C, 681E and 681H IT(EP)A 2003
105 s13A SSAA 1992; see also HMRC, *Elections Not to Receive Child Benefit*, 26 October 2012 (directions made under s13A SSAA 1992), available from www.gov.uk/government/uploads/system/uploads/attachment_data/file/365848/cb-directions.pdf
106 Sch 9 para 5B IS Regs; Sch 7 para 6B JSA Regs
107 **ESA** Sch 8 para 7(2) ESA Regs
     PC Regs 9 and 15(1)(j) SPC Regs
     HB Sch 5 para 65 HB Regs; regs 27 and 29 HB(SPC) Regs
     UC Reg 66 UC Regs
     TC Reg 7 TC(DCI) Regs
108 Reg 7(4) SS(OB) Regs
109 Reg 8 SS(OB) Regs
110 **HB** Reg 75F(1)(i) HB Regs
     UC Reg 83(1)(k) UC Regs

Chapter 27

Disability living allowance

This chapter covers:
1. Disability living allowance mobility component (p597)
2. Disability living allowance care component (p604)
3. The rules about your age (p611)
4. People included in the claim (p614)
5. The amount of benefit (p614)
6. Special benefit rules (p614)
7. Claims and backdating (p615)
8. Getting paid (p623)
9. Transfers to personal independence payment (p626)
10. Tax, other benefits and the benefit cap (p628)

New claims for disability living allowance (DLA) can only be made for children under 16. People aged 16 to 64 who have a disability can claim personal independence payment (PIP). See Chapter 34 for details. When a child who gets DLA turns 16, s/he is normally invited to claim PIP (see p626).

Many adults who already receive DLA will continue to receive it for some time (see p611). See Chapter 27 of the 2015/16 edition of this *Handbook* for full details of the DLA rules for adults. If you are 16 or over but were under 65 on 8 April 2013 and were already getting DLA, the government intends that you will be invited to claim PIP by 2018 and your DLA will end. See p626 for how this affects you.

Key facts
- Disability living allowance (DLA) is a benefit for people with disabilities who need help getting around and/or with supervision or attention needs.
- You must be under 16 to make a new claim.
- DLA has a care component and a mobility component. You make one claim for DLA and can qualify for one or both of the components. Each component has different rates.
- DLA is a non-means-tested benefit.
- You can qualify for DLA whether you are in or out of work.
- You do not have to have paid national insurance contributions to qualify.
- DLA can be paid in addition to other benefits and is disregarded as income for means-tested benefits and tax credits.

- DLA is administered and paid by the DWP's Disability and Carers Service.
- If you disagree with a DLA decision, you can apply for a revision or a supersession, or appeal against it. You must apply for a mandatory reconsideration before you can appeal.

Future changes

In the future, the rules on DLA may be different in Scotland. See CPAG's online service and *Welfare Rights Bulletin* for updates.

---

1. **Disability living allowance mobility component**

Disability living allowance (DLA) mobility component is for children under 16 who have difficulties when walking. It can be paid at a lower or higher rate.

See p621 for tips on answering the mobility questions on the DLA claim form.

Who can claim

A child qualifies for DLA mobility component if:[1]
- s/he satisfies the residence conditions (see p1574);
- s/he is not a 'person subject to immigration control', although there are some exceptions (see p1516);
- s/he satisfies the age rules (see p611);
- s/he satisfies the 'disability conditions' for either the higher rate (see p598) or the lower rate (see p602);
- unless s/he is terminally ill (see p614), s/he has satisfied the disability conditions throughout the three months immediately before the award begins (see p617 if you are reclaiming) and is likely to continue to satisfy them for the next six months;
- s/he is likely to be able to 'benefit from enhanced facilities for locomotion'.

To benefit from enhanced facilities for locomotion

To qualify for either rate of the DLA mobility component, a child must be able to '**benefit from enhanced facilities for locomotion**'. This means s/he must be able to make outdoor journeys from time to time. It is not essential that s/he is interested in or enjoys going out, provided it would be beneficial for her/him to do so. For example, s/he can get DLA mobility component even if s/he has to be carried to a car for a ride.[2]

Part 5: Other benefits
Chapter 27: Disability living allowance
1. Disability living allowance mobility component

Disability conditions for the higher rate mobility component

A child qualifies for the higher rate mobility component if:[3]

- s/he has a disability from a physical cause that means s/he is unable, or virtually unable, to walk (see below); *or*
- s/he is both blind and deaf (see p600); *or*
- s/he is blind or severely visually impaired (see p600); *or*
- s/he was born without feet or is a double amputee (see p601); *or*
- s/he has a 'severe mental impairment', has 'severe behavioural problems' and qualifies for the highest rate of DLA care component (see p601).

'Unable or virtually unable to walk'

A child is eligible for the higher rate if:[4]

- s/he is unable to walk; *or*
- her/his ability to walk outdoors is so limited in terms of the distance, speed, length of time, or the manner in which s/he can make progress on foot without severe discomfort that s/he is virtually unable to walk; *or*
- the exertion required to walk would constitute a danger to her/his life or be likely to lead to a serious deterioration in her/his health.

Personal circumstances, such as the location of the child's home, should not be taken into account. It is not, for instance, relevant if s/he lives a long way from the nearest bus stop,[5] or if s/he cannot use public transport.

Physical disability

A child's inability, or virtual inability, to walk must have a physical cause.[6] There can be a physical cause, such as pain or dizziness, even without a medically diagnosed origin. It does not matter if the original cause was mental, provided a current physical impairment affects her/his walking. For example, if a child's walking is impaired by weakness due to anorexia nervosa, the cause is physical.[7] Myalgic encephalomyelitis (ME), or chronic fatigue syndrome, should be accepted as having a physical origin unless there is evidence that any mobility restrictions are purely psychological.[8] A child's discomfort from chronic diarrhoea might make her/him virtually unable to walk.[9] Inability to make any progress on foot because of behavioural problems may qualify if the cause is physical – eg, Down's syndrome or autism are both accepted as physical disorders of development of the brain.[10]

Unable to walk

A child is unable to walk if s/he cannot move her/his body along by alternate, weight-bearing steps of the feet.[11]

Prostheses, aids and medication

A child's ability to walk is considered taking into account any prosthesis or artificial aid s/he uses, or that would be suitable for her/him.[12] S/he may not qualify if s/he is able to walk with crutches. However, if s/he has one leg and no artificial limb suitable to use, s/he is regarded as 'unable to walk', even if s/he can get around on crutches.[13] If s/he has no feet, s/he qualifies automatically (see p601).[14]

Any medication the child normally and reasonably uses is taken into account – eg, it may not be practical to carry a bulky nebuliser.[15] However, s/he should not be expected to undergo surgery. Her/his walking should be assessed as s/he is now, not how s/he might be after any treatment.[16]

Outdoors

The test is how a child copes with the terrain and environment normally encountered outdoors. If s/he has problems with balance on uneven pavements and roads, or has a lung or other condition which is made worse by wind or rain, these should be taken into account.[17] Walking indoors (eg, in a school) is not necessarily an indication of her/his ability to walk outdoors.[18]

Distance

The law does not require a specific distance to be used when determining a child's inability to walk. In practice, s/he may be refused benefit if you state on the claim form that s/he can walk more than 50 metres. However, her/his walking speed, the time it takes to cover the distance and the manner of walking are also relevant, so give details about these on the claim form. Caselaw says that walking speeds of less than 60 metres per minute are slow, so if an older child cannot walk this fast without severe discomfort, you should say so.[19]

Without severe discomfort

Any walking that a child can achieve only with severe discomfort should be ignored when considering whether s/he is virtually unable to walk.[20] This is a lesser test than 'severe pain or distress'.[21] If, when walking, s/he feels severe discomfort (eg, pain or breathlessness brought on by walking), make this clear.[22] S/he may be able to walk a distance without severe discomfort, a further distance that causes severe discomfort, and then have to stop altogether. The test is how far s/he can walk before going any further causes severe discomfort. You should state this distance on the claim form, rather than how far s/he can walk before actually having to stop. If s/he can walk further without severe discomfort after a brief rest, this could be taken into account.[23]

If a child is in severe discomfort before s/he starts to walk, even if the pain gets no worse, s/he should count as being virtually unable to walk, provided her/his disability affects the physical act of walking – eg, if s/he has an injured foot.[24] S/he

Part 5: Other benefits
Chapter 27: Disability living allowance
1. Disability living allowance mobility component

does not count as being virtually unable to walk if something unconnected with walking (eg, a skin condition affected by sunlight) causes the discomfort.[25]

The exertion required to walk

A child can qualify for the higher rate mobility component if the exertion required to walk endangers her/his health. If the deterioration in health is sudden, you must show that s/he would never recover, or recovery would take a significant period of time (eg, 12 months) or would require some form of medical intervention. So, a child with ME who needs a few days' rest after walking would not satisfy this test.[26] The fact that walking may cause a child stress, or lead to a deterioration in mental health, does not count.[27]

5 Blind and deaf

A child qualifies for the higher rate mobility component if:

- the degree of disablement resulting from her/his loss of vision is 100 per cent; *and*
- the degree of disablement resulting from her/his loss of hearing is 80 per cent on a scale where 100 per cent represents absolute deafness;[28] *and*
- the combined effect of the blindness and deafness means that s/he is unable to walk to any intended or required destination while outdoors without the help of another person.[29]

The regulations do not specify how to assess the degree of disablement, but caselaw suggests that the industrial injury provisions should be used (see p682).[30] So 100 per cent disablement through 'loss of vision' means 'loss of sight to such an extent as to render the claimant unable to perform any work for which eyesight is essential'.[31] This is the definition used when someone is registered as severely sight impaired (blind). However, whether or not a person is registered is not conclusive of whether s/he satisfies this condition.[32]

If a child's level of hearing loss, averaged between both ears at 1, 2 and 3 kHz, is at least 87 decibels, s/he satisfies the 80 per cent disablement test.[33] S/he may have to undertake a hearing test. The assessment of hearing ability takes into account any hearing aid s/he uses or could reasonably be expected to use.[34]

Blind or severely visually impaired

A child must have been certified blind or severely sight impaired and have combined visual accuity, in both eyes, on the 'Snellen scale', while using appropriate corrective lenses if necessary, of:[35]

- less than 3/60; *or*
- 3/60 or more, but less than 6/60, if s/he has a complete loss of peripheral vision and a central visual field of no more than 10 degrees.

'Appropriate' corrective lenses are ones that s/he can wear without discomfort.[36] The test has to be met by both eyes – an average cannot be used if her/his level of vision in one eye is worse than the other.[37]

The Snellen test is taken indoors. This may be discriminatory.[38] If a child does not qualify according to the Snellen scale but her/his vision is significantly worse outdoors, seek specialist advice.

People without feet

If a child does not have feet or legs (missing from the ankle or above), s/he is automatically treated as being unable to walk,[39] even if s/he can walk with prostheses.

Severe mental impairment and behavioural problems

A child qualifies for the higher rate mobility component if:[40]

- s/he has a 'severe mental impairment' – ie, arrested development, or incomplete physical development, of the brain, which results in severe impairment of intelligence and social functioning; *and*
- s/he displays severe behavioural problems – ie:
  - s/he exhibits extreme disruptive behaviour; *and*
  - s/he regularly requires someone else to intervene and physically restrain her/him to prevent her/him causing injury to her/himself or others or damage to property; *and*
  - s/he is so unpredictable that another person has to be present and watching over her/him whenever s/he is awake;[41] *and*
- s/he qualifies for the highest rate of the DLA care component (see p604).

If a child does not meet all the above conditions, s/he might still qualify for the higher rate mobility component because a disability prevents her/him from walking effectively, so that s/he is virtually unable to walk (see p598).[42]

Arrested or incomplete development

'Arrested or incomplete development' must occur before the brain reaches its final development. This is during the thirties or early forties for most people, so any condition that affects a child should be accepted as occurring before this.[43] As a result of this arrested or incomplete brain development, s/he must also have a severe impairment of intelligence *and* of social functioning (although these are closely related – see below).[44]

Severe impairment of intelligence

An IQ of 55 or less is generally accepted as a 'severe impairment of intelligence'. However, using a crude measure of intelligence based on IQ alone is not appropriate. Some children may have a higher IQ but be unable to apply it practically.[45] A child's 'useful intelligence' (eg, her/his 'degree of judgement in

Part 5: Other benefits
Chapter 27: Disability living allowance
1. Disability living allowance mobility component

relation to everyday living', including factors such as her/his sense of danger) should also be taken into account.[46] For example, an autistic child with no awareness of danger may have severely impaired intelligence even if her/his IQ is over 55, and an assessment of language and communication skills (rather than other measures of intelligence) may be particularly important in considering a child's social functioning.[47]

Physical restraint

Physical restraint may involve as little as a hand on the arm. You do not need to show that any force is used.[48] If the presence of someone who watches over a child is enough to prevent her/him from being disruptive, or a specially adapted environment allows her/him to be safely left alone, s/he may not pass the test. However, the decision maker should not focus only on how s/he is outdoors or in a structured safe environment, and must consider her/his need for, and the nature of, intervention in all environments.[49] Involuntary behaviour, such as falls due to seizures, can be classed as 'disruptive'.[50]

Disability condition for the lower rate mobility component

A child qualifies for the lower rate mobility component if s/he can walk but is 'so severely disabled physically or mentally' that s/he cannot get around outdoors 'without guidance or supervision from another person most of the time'.[51] S/he must also satisfy the 'additional requirements' test (see below).

Any ability s/he may have to use familar routes without guidance or supervision should be ignored.[52] Entitlement to the lower rate mobility component is based on the child's need for supervision or guidance, rather than any physical difficulty s/he has walking, which might qualify her/him for the higher rate.[53]

The 'additional requirements' test

You must show that a child requires guidance or supervision and also that either:[54]
- s/he requires substantially more guidance or supervision than children of her/his age in 'normal' physical and mental health; *or*
- children of the same age in 'normal' physical and mental health would not require such guidance or supervision.

The fact that all young children require some guidance or supervision outdoors is not the point. If a child needs a substantially greater amount of guidance or supervision, or a different type of guidance or supervision, compared to what is normally needed by children of a similar age, s/he should qualify.[55] For example, a child with a visual impairment or learning disability may need an adult to hold, guide or watch over her/him in situations in which most children of a similar age would only require someone to acccompany them. Similarly, a young deaf child may need someone to stay within touching distance, whereas a hearing child would not.[56]

See p618 for tips on how to describe a child's needs on the claim form.

Supervision

'Supervision' can be precautionary (eg, accompanying and watching over a child) in order to monitor a child's physical, mental or emotional state in case s/he needs more assistance to continue walking. It can also be monitoring the route ahead for obstacles, dangers, places or situations which might upset her/him. Supervision can also be more active, such as encouraging, persuading or cajoling a child, or distracting her/him from fears[57] or possibly alarming situations.[58]

Unlike the 'continual supervision' condition for the DLA care component, the child does not need to require supervision to prevent 'substantial danger'.[59] If s/he qualifies for the care component because s/he requires continual supervision, s/he may also qualify for the lower rate mobility component.[60] However, this is not automatic; her/his eligibility must be assessed on the mobility criteria alone.[61]

The supervision does not need to improve the child's walking ability, but should enable her/him to 'take advantage of the faculty of walking'. It is enough that supervision helps, even if it does not remove risks completely or if s/he may not always respond well to the person providing it.[62] If s/he needs to have supervision (eg, to provide help in the event of seizures or a severe asthma attack),[63] even though s/he has no difficulty getting about, s/he can qualify for the lower rate mobility component.[64]

Guidance

'Guidance' can mean physically leading or directing a child, giving oral suggestions or persuasion, helping to avoid obstacles or places that upset her/him, or leading or persuading a child when s/he becomes disorientated or is anxious. Even if a companion only intervenes occasionally, s/he could still be guiding 'most of the time' if a child would otherwise not know when to change direction. If a child has a visual impairment, s/he may need guidance to follow directions, avoid obstacles or cross roads (even if s/he uses a guide dog or cane). If s/he is deaf and her/his main method of communication is sign language, s/he may require guidance in unfamiliar places if s/he is unable to ask for or follow directions. However, an older child may not qualify if s/he can study maps, read street signs or communicate with passers by.[65]

Fear and anxiety

A child can qualify for the lower rate mobility component on the basis of a mental as well as a physical disablement. If s/he has an anxiety disorder and needs the help of an escort to overcome fear of going outside, s/he is likely to satisfy the 'guidance or supervision' requirement.[66] There is conflicting caselaw, but if no amount of reassurance can persuade her/him to go outside, s/he may not

Part 5: Other benefits
Chapter 27: Disability living allowance
2. Disability living allowance care component

qualify.[67] However, if s/he can just manage a walk into her/his garden, this could be enough to qualify.[68]

Any fear or anxiety that stops a child going out alone must be a symptom of mental disability in order to count. Fear and anxiety arising from a physical disability, such as a rational fear of having to cope with incontinence while alone, is not sufficient, although s/he may still have a physical need for supervision.[69] If her/his physical disability causes such fear or anxiety that s/he can be said to be mentally disabled, s/he may qualify.

2. **Disability living allowance care component**

Disability living allowance (DLA) care component is for children under 16 with attention or supervision needs. It can be paid at a lowest, middle or highest rate.

See p618 for tips on completing the DLA claim form.

Who can claim

A child qualifies for the DLA care component if:[70]
- s/he satisfies the residence conditions (see p1574);
- s/he is not a 'person subject to immigration control', although there are some exceptions (see p1516);
- s/he is under the age of 16 when you first claim (see p611);
- s/he is not in residential care (see p917);
- s/he satisfies the disability conditions for the lowest, middle or highest rate of the care component (see below) and, unless s/he is terminally ill, s/he satisfies the 'additional requirements' test (see p605);
- unless s/he is terminally ill (see p614), the child has satisfied the disability conditions throughout the three months immediately before the award begins (see p617 if you are reclaiming) and s/he is likely to continue to satisfy them for the next six months.

The disability conditions

A child qualifies for the **lowest rate care component** if s/he is so severely disabled, physically or mentally, that s/he requires (see p606) attention from another person for a significant portion of the day (whether during a single period or a number of periods) in connection with her/his bodily functions (see p607 and p609).[71]

A child qualifies for the **middle rate care component** if:
- s/he satisfies one of the daytime disability conditions (see p605) *or* one of the night-time disability conditions (see p605);[72] *or*
- s/he undergoes renal dialysis in certain circumstances (see p614).[73]

A child qualifies for the **highest rate care component** if:
- s/he satisfies one of the daytime disability conditions (see below) *and* one of the night-time disability conditions (see below);[74] *or*
- s/he is terminally ill (see p614).[75]

The daytime disability conditions are that a child is so severely disabled, physically or mentally, that s/he requires (see p606):[76]
- frequent attention from another person throughout the day in connection with her/his bodily functions (see p607); *or*
- continual supervision throughout the day in order to avoid substantial danger to her/himself or others (see p610).

The night-time disability conditions are that a child is so severely disabled, physically or mentally, that s/he requires (see p606):[77]
- prolonged or repeated attention from another person at night (see p610) in connection with her/his bodily functions (see p607); *or*
- another person to be awake at night for a prolonged period or at frequent intervals to watch over her/him (see p611) in order to avoid substantial danger to her/himself or others.

The 'additional requirements' test

You must show not only that a child requires attention or supervision, but also that either:[78]
- the child has attention or supervision requirements 'substantially in excess of the normal requirements' of a child of the same age; *or*
- the child has substantial attention or supervision requirements which younger children in 'normal' physical and mental health may also have, but which children of the same age and in 'normal' physical and mental health would not have. If this is due to 'developmental delay', see below.

This extra test does not apply if you are claiming DLA care component for a child who is terminally ill.[79]

The fact that all young children require assistance throughout the day is not the point. If a child needs more assistance, or assistance of a different type, compared to the assistance normally required by a child of the same age, s/he should qualify.[80] See p618 for tips on how to describe a child's needs on the claim form.

'So severely disabled physically or mentally'

To qualify, a child must be 'so severely disabled physically or mentally' that s/he needs attention or supervision. S/he does not need to have a specific medical condition. What is important is that s/he is so disabled that s/he has care needs.[81]

Part 5: Other benefits
Chapter 27: Disability living allowance
2. Disability living allowance care component

However, medical evidence can still be important to establish that s/he is disabled and what her/his care needs are.[82]

Problems sometimes arise if, for example, a child has behavioural problems or a developmental delay that have not been attributed to a disability. In one case, it was ruled that what is key is whether a child has the physical or mental power to control the behaviour.[83]

Attention and supervision

'Requires'

To satisfy the attention or supervision conditions, you must show that a child 'requires this assistance' from another person. The assistance must be 'reasonably required' rather than 'medically required'.[84] For example, if an incontinent child needs help changing bedding, this help should count as 'reasonably required', even if not actually required to protect her/his skin. Bear in mind that all younger children may be incontinent from time to time, and the attention a child requires must be substantially more than, or different from, the attention normally needed by children of the same age (see p605).

Reasonably requires attention

Attention must be 'reasonably required to enable' a child 'as far as reasonably possible to live a normal life'. Having a social life, recreation and cultural activities are part of normal life. If a child is blind, it is, therefore, reasonable for you to read to her/him, describe television pictures, or guide her/him during social outings. Similarly, if a child has learning disabilities, it is reasonable for her/him to travel to, or take part in, social and recreational pursuits. A child's age and interests should be taken into account when deciding what is reasonable.[85]

Reasonably requires supervision

The requirement for supervision need only be reasonable. A child cannot be expected to avoid every risk of harm in order to avoid the need for supervision. Most risks can be avoided by staying in a chair all day, but that may be totally unreasonable.[86] It is not reasonable to expect a child to avoid all situations in which s/he might fall.[87]

When considering a child's need for continual supervision (see p610), you can argue that the fact that supervision is provided shows it is needed. Bear in mind that the supervision must be substantially more than, or different from, the supervision a child the same age might normally require (see p605).

Refusing medical treatment

Refusing medical treatment for a child may affect whether or not s/he qualifies. If treatment offered by her/his doctor would remove the need for help, the attention or supervision a child gets may not be reasonably required. However, it may not be 'reasonably appropriate' for you to agree to the treatment – eg, because of the risks or side effects.[88] Attention or supervision should be accepted as reasonable if you refuse invasive surgery for a child.[89]

Attention

The attention a child requires must be in connection with 'bodily functions' – ie, the normal action of any organ of the body, or a number of organs acting together.

The attention is in connection with bodily functions if it is a substitute method of providing what the bodily function would provide were it not impaired.[90] For example, guiding a visually impaired child so that s/he is able to walk outside should be treated as attention with the bodily function of 'seeing', rather than of 'walking'. A guide assists with 'seeing' by acting 'as the eyes'. Similarly, help to push a child who uses a wheelchair should be treated as attention.[91]

'Attention' is 'a service of a close and intimate nature... involving personal contact carried out in the presence of the disabled person'.[92] So helping a child to drink counts; carrying the drinks to where s/he is sitting does not.[93] Although attention must usually involve personal contact, it need not be *physical* contact. Contact established by the spoken word may count if, for example, a child is blind.[94] Thus, reading, describing or giving verbal instructions can be attention.

Similarly, if a child would neglect her/himself unless cajoled or stimulated to do routine tasks, s/he may require attention in the form of active stimulation.[95] Spoken reassurance can count if it must be given in the physical presence of a child. Bear in mind that the attention must be substantially more than, or different from, the attention a child the same age might normally require (see p605).

Attention or supervision?

'Attention' involves a service of an 'active nature'.[96] 'Supervision' is passive and 'may be precautionary or anticipatory, yet never result in intervention'.[97] Where supervision does lead to intervention, it becomes attention, so the two categories can overlap. If a child needs to be supervised because s/he is likely to fall and injure her/himself, s/he receives attention when a carer gives her/him a steadying hand or warns of an obstacle.[98] If attention is frequent, a child qualifies for the middle rate care component, even if the supervision is not 'continual' throughout the day. Sometimes an act can be both supervision and attention. It is, therefore, important to emphasise the full extent of a child's needs without trying to fit them neatly into either category at the expense of leaving things out.

Communication

Communication is made up of a 'bundle' of bodily functions, including functions of the brain (such as language processing, or comprehension) or the senses (such as hearing). You need to identify what bodily function is impaired and what attention is needed from another person in connection with that bodily function.[99] If a child is profoundly deaf, s/he may need an interpreter because

Part 5: Other benefits
Chapter 27: Disability living allowance
2. Disability living allowance care component

s/he cannot hear spoken language,[100] or extra effort may be required to initiate a two-way conversation.[101]

Explaining written information to a child with poor literacy skills as a result of deafness[102] or a learning disability may also qualify.[103]

Domestic duties

Although attention must normally be carried out in a child's presence, a period of attention can also include incidental activities that could take place without her/him. For example, if a carer strips a soiled bed at night, the additional tasks of wringing out the sheets or hanging them up to dry could count as attention if done on the spot, as would cleaning a soiled carpet in the event of incontinence.[104] Taking the washing away or doing the cleaning at a different time does not qualify as attention.

Domestic tasks performed by a carer outside a child's presence do not normally count as attention. There is conflicting caselaw on whether helping an older child do domestic tasks that children of the same age might normally do for themselves is attention that is reasonably required.[105] Helping a child who has a visual impairment to tidy up around the house is assistance with the bodily function of 'seeing' and can count as attention.[106] Similarly, helping a child with a learning disability to go shopping for clothes may include attention to help her/him communicate her/his requirements. Argue that if an older child can learn to tidy up at home or shop for her/himself, this is part of what constitutes a 'normal life' (see the definition of 'requires' on p606).[107]

Childcare

If an older child is a parent, help to enable her/him to look after her/his children can also count as attention.[108] For example, lifting or holding a baby for feeding is a sufficiently intimate service.[109] It will help if you can identify the bodily function in connection with which the child needs attention. Similarly, assistance to take part in outdoor activities with her/his children allows a young parent to lead a normal social life.[110] However, while help provided to a young parent with a disability may count as attention, help given directly to her/his child does not.[111]

Special diets

Attention only counts if it needs to be given in a child's physical presence, so it is often difficult to include help with food preparation. Arguably though, this type of help may count as attention if it forms part of a broader sequence of care tasks. For example, the various parts of the process of regulating the blood sugar levels of a younger diabetic child, some of which require personal contact and some of which do not, should all be treated as attention because they are integral elements of an overall regime.[112] A child with a learning disability or an eating disorder might need similar help to eat properly.

Night and day

A child who needs help using the toilet at 3am, when most people are asleep, clearly needs that help at night. Depending on the age of a child and the amount and type of attention required, this may be attention that children of the same age do not normally need. Problems in showing that attention is needed at night can arise when a child needs supervision or attention in the late evening or early morning.

'Night' is 'that period of inactivity' which begins when 'the household, as it were, closes down for the night'.[113] The pattern of activities of each household needs to be taken into account. If a carer stays up into the small hours to help a child but would otherwise go to bed earlier, that should count as night care.[114] Similarly, if a carer gets up early in the morning to help her/him rather than rise later with the rest of the household, that should count as night care.[115] 'Night' is normally assumed to be the period beginning at around 11pm and ending around 7am.[116] The definition of 'night' for a child is the same as for an adult, so that attention given to a child in the evening before the adults have gone to bed counts only towards satisfying the day condition.[117]

'Attention... for a significant portion of the day'

If a child needs attention for a 'significant portion of the day', s/he qualifies for the lowest rate care component.[118] This can be either one period or a number of periods – eg, s/he could need help with activities connected with getting up at the beginning of the day, such as dressing and washing, and with activities connected with going to bed at the end of the day, such as undressing and washing, but otherwise not need extra help. Help at night does not count for the lowest rate.[119]

'A significant portion of the day' is often taken to mean an hour or thereabouts.[120] However, if a child's carer spends less time than that in total but has to give help for a number of short periods, that might qualify.[121]

If a carer does not have much time available or the help s/he gives is in spells of particularly concentrated activity, less than an hour's help may be enough. Factors like the amount, importance or effect of the attention may be taken into account.[122]

Frequent attention throughout the day

To satisfy the day attention condition, you must show that a child needs frequent attention throughout the day.[123] 'Frequency' refers to the number and pattern of times attention is needed over a period of time, and should be considered as a whole.[124] If the spread of times when attention is needed is uneven, this should not necessarily disqualify a child.[125] The aggregate amount of time taken up is not relevant. So it is possible for a child to need help frequently for a short period each time, and so qualify for the middle rate care component, even if the total amount of time may not be regarded as a 'significant portion of the day', and so s/he might not qualify for the lowest rate.[126]

Part 5: Other benefits
Chapter 27: Disability living allowance
2. Disability living allowance care component

If a child only needs help at the beginning and end of the day, this is unlikely to be accepted as frequent. Help with toileting (eg, to reach the toilet, use a commode or deal with zips) or help to walk inside the house are both examples of activities that most children usually engage in frequently. Most children who satisfy this condition do so by virtue of a range of different types of care needs.

Prolonged or repeated attention at night

The help a child needs during the night must be either prolonged or repeated.[127] There is no clear definition of 'prolonged'. An assumption that 20 minutes is prolonged has been accepted as a reasonable starting point, but shorter periods should also be considered.[128] **'Repeated'** simply means twice or more.[129]

Because sleeping is a 'bodily function', soothing a child back to sleep counts as giving attention in connection with a bodily function.[130]

Continual supervision

A child satisfies the daytime supervision condition if s/he requires another person to provide 'continual supervision' throughout the day to avoid the risk of substantial danger to the child or to others.[131] Supervision can be precautionary and anticipatory. It does not necessarily involve direct intervention. The supervision test has four aspects.[132]

- **There must be a substantial danger to a child or someone else as a result of her/his medical condition.** What is a 'substantial danger' must be decided on the facts of each case. For example, if a child falls and loses consciousness (eg, due to seizures), s/he would not be able to do anything to save her/himself from injury and so this is more likely to be a 'substantial danger' than if other children fall but only sustain minor bruises.

- **The substantial danger must be one against which it is reasonable to guard.** This involves weighing the remoteness of the risk and the seriousness of the consequences should it arise. For example, the consequences of allowing a child to run out onto the road could be dire, even though such an incident may be isolated.[133] Thus, it can be argued that the child reasonably requires continual supervision.[134] In assessing the likelihood of danger, the decision maker must look at what has happened in the past as well as what may happen in the future.[135]

- **There must be a need for the supervision.** What counts is the level of supervision a child 'reasonably requires' (see p606). If s/he has mental health problems and is at risk of harming her/himself, it would be wrong to suggest that no amount of supervision would prevent a determined child from doing this and supervision is, therefore, not required. The correct approach is to decide whether supervision would result in 'a real reduction in the risk of harm' to her/him.[136]

- **The supervision must be continual.** This is something less than 'continuous', but supervision which is required only occasionally or spasmodically is insufficient.[137] However, the fact that, for example, a child may need less supervision in a safe structured environment, such as school, does not mean that continual supervision is not required.[138] If it is unavoidable that a child is left alone for a period, s/he can still qualify if you can show that s/he is at risk during this time. A child who is liable to epileptic fits without warning may need continual supervision, although attention for the period between the fits is not required.[139] Even if s/he has warning of the fits so that s/he can prevent her/himself from falling, s/he may require continual supervision if s/he suffers from prolonged periods of confusion, or needs monitoring to make sure s/he comes out of the seizure safely afterwards.[140]

Bear in mind that the supervision a child requires must be substantially more than, or different from, the supervision normally needed by children of the same age (see p605).

Watching over

A child satisfies the night-time supervision condition if s/he needs someone to be awake to watch over her/him at night to avoid the risk of substantial danger to her/him or others.[141] The person watching over must be awake for a 'prolonged period' or 'at frequent intervals'. A 'prolonged period' may mean 20 minutes or more.[142] 'At frequent intervals' means more than twice. The frequent intervals need not be spread throughout the night, but can be concentrated in one part of the night.[143]

3. **The rules about your age**

New claims for disability living allowance (DLA) can only be made for children under 16.

The higher rate mobility component can be paid from age three onwards and the lower rate mobility component from age five.[144] The three months before the child reaches this age can form the qualifying period, enabling payment to be made from her/his birthday.

There is no lower age limit for DLA care component. However, a baby must still meet the qualifying conditions for three months before DLA becomes payable, unless s/he is terminally ill.[145]

See p626 for how the introduction of personal independence payment (PIP) affects a child's DLA when s/he turns 16.

Adults with existing disability living allowance claims

If you are 16 or over and get DLA (including if you turned 65 after 8 April 2013), see p626 for how the introduction of PIP affects you.

Part 5: Other benefits
Chapter 27: Disability living allowance
3. The rules about your age

If you turned 65 on or before 8 April 2013

If you get DLA and turned 65 on or before 8 April 2013, you can continue to receive it and are unaffected by the introduction of PIP.

You can make a renewal claim if your DLA award expires, provided you reclaim within a year of the previous award ending.[146] If you are awarded the same rate, you can be paid without having to serve the standard qualifying period again.

If your condition has changed since you turned 65 so that you need more assistance, your award can be increased to the middle or highest rate of the care component. This applies regardless of which component or rate you previously had. You must show that you have met the qualifying conditions for the increased rate for six months (not three months) before it can be awarded, unless you had already completed a three-month qualifying period before you turned 65.[147] This is because the rules about qualifying periods for people in receipt of DLA care component at the age of 65 or over are the same as for attendance allowance (AA).[148] This applies both when a renewal claim is made and when an award is revised or superseded.

If you have an existing award of DLA that was made before you turned 65 (ie, not an award made on a renewal claim, or on a revision or supersession decision, after you turned 65), you can be awarded any rate of either component if you request a revision or supersession of your award after you are 65, provided you show that you have satisfied the disability conditions for the new rate or component since before you turned 65.[149] Otherwise, you cannot qualify for either rate of the mobility component or the lowest rate of the care component for the first time after you turned 65.

If your award was made after you turned 65 (either on a renewal claim or on a revision or supersession of a decision) and you have an award of the lower rate of the mobility component, it cannot be increased to the higher rate of the mobility component after you have turned 65. If you have an award of either rate of the mobility component, you can be awarded the middle or highest rate of the care component on a renewal claim or a revision or supersession, but not the lowest rate.[150]

Examples

Tom turned 65 in 2008, and is now 73. Tom has MS, and has received the middle rate of the care component and the higher rate of the mobility component of DLA since he was 64. Tom's award expires when he turns 74. Because he was 65 before 8 April 2013, Tom can make a renewal claim for DLA. His mobility has not changed, but the decision maker accepts that he now needs sufficient care at night to qualify for the highest rate care component. An indefinite award of the highest rate of the care component and the higher rate of the mobility component is made on the renewal claim. The decision maker accepts that Tom's night-time needs have existed for six months, and so the new rate is paid from the date his renewal award starts.

Sheila turned 65 on 8 March 2013, and is now 69. Sheila has an indefinite award of the middle rate of the care component, which was made in 2001. Sheila's condition has deteriorated steadily since the award was made, and for several years she has been able to walk only very short distances, and only with severe discomfort. She is advised to request a supersession of her award. The decision maker accepts that Sheila has been virtually unable to walk since before she turned 65. Her award is superseded to include the higher rate of the mobility component from the date of her supersession request.

If it has been over a year since your last DLA award ended, you must claim AA (see Chapter 23) instead of DLA. If you make a renewal claim for DLA in these circumstances, it will be treated as a claim for AA.

Differences in the rules for adults

There are some important differences between the rules for DLA for adults and those for children that are described in this chapter. See Chapter 27 of the 2015/16 edition of this *Handbook* for full details of the rules for adults.

The most important points are the following.

1. Adults can qualify for the lowest rate of the care component on the basis of a 'cooking test'.[151] This rule does not apply to children. Under the cooking test, you qualify if you are so severely disabled, physically or mentally, that you cannot prepare a cooked main meal for yourself if you have the ingredients. This is not about whether, or how, you actually cook. It is a hypothetical test about what you can reasonably do. It looks at whether you can do all the tasks to cook a labour-intensive, freshly cooked main meal for one using a traditional cooker. It should look at your ability to, for example, plan a meal, chop and prepare food, use kitchen equipment, lift pans and tell when food is cooked properly.

2. The additional requirements test that a child must satisfy before s/he can qualify for the care component (see p605) or the lower rate mobility component (see p602) does not apply to adults. So you just need to show that you satisfy the disability conditions to qualify for benefit. You do not need to show that the attention or supervision you need is more, or of a different type, than assistance other adults might need.

3. The types of assistance an adult needs, and the reason for needing the assistance, may be different from those that apply to a child. The examples explained in this chapter focus on the needs and assistance that are most relevant to children. If you need different types of assistance, or assistance for other reasons, make sure you explain those. Do not assume that you will not qualify for DLA. For example, the types of assistance an adult needs to enjoy a normal life (including a reasonable social life), with domestic tasks or to communicate, will be quite different from a child's needs. If you need attention or supervision because of, for example, alcohol or drug dependency, or to prevent risk of harm because of mental health problems, make sure you explain those. If you live alone and do not get all the attention or supervision you need, remember that it is the help you reasonably require that counts, not the help you actually get.

Part 5: Other benefits
Chapter 27: Disability living allowance
6. Special benefit rules

4. **People included in the claim**

You claim disability living allowance for a child under 16.

5. **The amount of benefit**

Disability living allowance (DLA) mobility component is paid at one of two weekly rates:[152]
- the lower rate is £22.00;
- the higher rate is £58.00.

DLA care component is paid at one of three weekly rates:[153]
- the lowest rate is £22.00;
- the middle rate is £55.65;
- the highest rate is £83.10.

6. **Special benefit rules**

Special rules may apply to children:
- on renal dialysis (see below);
- who are terminally ill (see below);
- subject to immigration control (see Chapter 65);
- who have come from or are going abroad (see Chapters 66, 67 and 68);
- in hospital or a hospice or living in a care home or other similar accommodation, or in a young offenders' institution or other form of detention (see Chapter 41).

Renal dialysis

If a child is undergoing renal dialysis on a kidney machine, special rules may apply that entitle her/him to the middle rate of disability living allowance (DLA) care component.[154] The rules are the same as for attendance allowance (AA – see p526).

Terminal illness

If a child is terminally ill, s/he is automatically treated as satisfying the conditions for the highest rate of the DLA care component and does not need to satisfy the three-month qualifying period.[155] Claims for children who are terminally ill are referred to as 'claims under the special rules' (see p616). The rules are the same as for AA (see p526).[156]

S/he does not automatically get DLA mobility component. S/he must satisfy the usual disability conditions (except the three-month qualifying period) and be likely to continue to satisfy them for the next six months (see p597) until the anticipated date of death.[157]

7. Claims and backdating

The general rules about claims and backdating are covered in Chapter 49. This section explains the specific rules that apply to disability living allowance (DLA).

Making a claim

A claim for DLA must be in writing. You should do this by requesting and completing the approved claim form (DLA1A Child). It is best to request a form by phone from the DLA helpline (see below). The DWP may complete a checklist to assess a child's 'potential benefit entitlement'. This is not part of the claim process and you should always be sent a claim pack. It is best to send the completed form to the address on it (the Disability Benefits Centre). You can also take or send it to any other DWP office, and may be able to take or send it to an 'alternative office' (see p1148).

Forms

Form DLA1A Child is available from the DLA helpline on 0345 712 3456 (textphone: 0345 722 4433).

The form should be date stamped. You have six weeks from the date of your request to return it. If you return it within this time, the date you requested it will be treated as your date of claim.[158] Keep a record of the date you asked for the form.

Claim packs are also available from Citizens Advice Bureaux or other advice agencies. A version of the form that can be filled in online and then printed is available at www.gov.uk. These packs are not date stamped. Send in the completed form as soon as possible. Your date of claim is the date your completed form is received by the DWP (see p616 for details).

Note: the success of a DLA claim can often depend on how well you have completed the claim form. Include all the relevant information and use extra pages if necessary. Keep a copy of the form in case queries arise. For tips on completing the form, see p618.

You must provide any information required (see p616). In certain circumstances, the DWP may accept a written application which is not on the

Part 5: Other benefits
Chapter 27: Disability living allowance
7. Claims and backdating

approved form (see p1152).[159] You can amend or withdraw the claim before a decision is made (see p1149).

Claims for terminally ill children are made in a different way (see below).

Who should claim

A claim for a child under 16 is made by an appointee (see p1149). This is usually the child's parent. We use 'you' throughout this chapter to refer to the appointee who is claiming on behalf of a child.

Note: before a child reaches 16, the DWP should ask whether s/he will continue to need an appointee or will be able to handle her/his own benefits affairs. See p626 for how the introduction of personal independence payment (PIP) affects DLA for a child when s/he turns 16.

Claiming for a child who is terminally ill

If you are claiming on the basis of a child's terminal illness (see p614), you must tick the box on the claim form to say you are claiming under the 'special rules'.[160] In addition to the claim form you must provide Form DS1500, completed by the child's GP or consultant, detailing her/his medical condition. However, you do not need to fill in the parts of the claim form relating to her/his need for personal care. If you also wish to claim the mobility component for the child, you must answer all the relevant questions on the claim form. If the decision maker decides that the child does not meet the special rules, you can claim in the normal way or request a mandatory reconsideration of the decision.

Information to support your claim

For the general information requirements that apply to all benefits, see p1150.

It is important that you provide any information required when you claim. Until you do, you may not count as having made a valid claim (see p1152). You should correct any defects in your claim as soon as possible or your date of claim may be affected. **Note:** for DLA, there is no requirement to provide a national insurance number for a child under 16.

For suggestions about evidence you might want to provide when completing the claim form, see p618.

Even if you have provided all that was required when you claimed, you may be asked to provide further information to support the claim (see p1154). You may be asked to provide information after DLA is awarded, and if you fail to do so, DLA could be suspended or even terminated (see p1185).

The date of your claim

The date of your child's claim is important as it determines when her/his entitlement to DLA starts. This is not necessarily the date from when DLA is paid. For information about when payment of DLA starts, see p623.

The date of claim is not necessarily the date it is received by the DWP. The **'date of claim'** is the date your request for a claim pack is received by the DWP or an 'alternative office' (see p1148), provided you return the properly completed form within six weeks of the date of your request.[161]

If the DWP has issued a form without date stamping it, write and explain when and where it was issued and ask to be paid from that date or six weeks before you sent it in.[162] There is also some discretion to extend the six-week deadline, so if you return the form late, explain why.[163]

If you are using a claim form issued by an advice agency or downloaded from the internet, your date of claim is the date the DWP receives your completed form.

Note: you must make sure the claim is valid. If it is 'defective', you are given a short time to correct the defects (see p1152). If you do, the claim is treated as having been made when you initially claimed.[164]

In some cases, a claim can be made in advance (see below). If you want to do this, make this clear when you claim or the DWP might not consider it. If a claim was made for attendance allowance (AA) or PIP instead of DLA, see p566.

Backdating your claim

It is very important to claim in time. A claim for DLA *cannot* be backdated.[165]

If a child might have qualified for benefit earlier but you did not claim because you were given the wrong information or were misled by the DWP, you could ask for a compensation payment (see p1396) or complain to the Ombudsman through your MP (see p1401).

If you claim the wrong benefit

If you claim AA or PIP by mistake for a child under 16 instead of DLA, the claim for AA or PIP can be treated as a claim for DLA, and vice versa (see p1161).[166]

Claiming in advance

A claim for DLA can be made before a child has satisfied the three-month qualifying period,[167] or any other qualifying condition. Provided you claim no more than three months before s/he would qualify for DLA, a decision can be made on the claim in advance of her/his date of entitlement. The date of the claim is the date on which the child qualifies.

Renewal claims

DLA can be awarded for fixed periods (see p624). Renewal claims can be invited up to six months before a child's old award expires. It is important that you send back your completed renewal claim form before her/his old award expires, as no backdating is possible.

Decision makers normally treat a renewal claim as a new claim beginning on the day after an old award runs out.[168] However, they may use the information

Part 5: Other benefits
Chapter 27: Disability living allowance
7. Claims and backdating

you give in the renewal claim to revise or supersede the child's existing award, in which case her/his entitlement may be changed earlier.[169] If you think a child has a strong case for an increased award, return the renewal form early and ask for a revision or supersession. If this is not the case, it is advisable to return the form nearer the date her/his current award runs out, but in time for a decision to be made before it does run out.

On a renewal claim, a child does not have to serve the three-month qualifying period again, provided s/he meets all the other qualifying conditions for the rate s/he previously received. The last three months of the previous award is treated as the qualifying period.[170] However, if s/he qualifies for a different rate when you reclaim, s/he does have to serve the standard qualifying period.

When a child approaches age 16, s/he will normally be required to claim PIP, rather than make a renewal claim for DLA. See p626 for details.

See p626 for how the introduction of PIP affects adults who get DLA (including those who turned 65 after 8 April 2013) and p611 for how adults who receive DLA and turned 65 on or before 8 April 2013 can make a renewal claim for DLA.

Completing the claim form

The DLA claim form is long and asks about different aspects of a child's mobility problems and supervision and attention needs. If you find it difficult to complete the form, the DWP can help you by telephone or, in some circumstances, can send a visiting officer to your home. Most advice agencies can also help. The following advice should help you fill in the form as fully as possible.

- **Give as much detail as you can.** Fill in all the pages that are relevant. If the same difficulties apply on more than one page, repeat the information or refer back to earlier in the form. The same help may count towards both the care component and the mobility component and should be repeated on the form – eg, if a child needs attention to deal safely with seizures, this may help satisfy the conditions for the care component but may also mean that s/he needs guidance and supervision when walking outdoors.[171] Do not feel bound by the size of the boxes. If you need extra space to explain the child's situation, use a separate piece of paper. Do not worry if a lot of the questions do not apply to the child. The information you give in just one section could be enough for her/him to qualify for DLA. There is space to include details of people who know about her/his difficulties – include carers and support workers, as well as medical professionals. There is also a statement to be completed by someone who knows the child. If her/his doctor fills this in, the doctor should not charge for this.[172] If you do not have anyone who can complete it, leave it blank.
- **Frequency, variability and duration.** You are asked throughout the form to estimate how long the child needs help for, and how often. You should explain:

– how long s/he needs help for, to show that s/he needs attention for a 'significant portion of the day' (see p609), or needs 'prolonged' attention at night (see p610);

– how often s/he needs help, to show that s/he needs 'frequent attention throughout the day' (see p609) or 'watching over' repeatedly during the night (see p611);

– how many days a week s/he needs help, to establish her/his overall needs, particularly if s/he has a variable or fluctuating condition. If the child's condition does not vary but s/he only receives all the help s/he needs on certain days, say that s/he needs help seven days a week. It is the help needed, not the help s/he gets, that counts. If s/he only has problems a few days a week, s/he will not necessarily be refused DLA. It is the broad overall picture of needs that counts, not simply comparing the number of 'good' days and 'bad' days.[173] Explain fully the help s/he needs on 'bad' days, but include the help needed on 'good' days as well so that you give an overall picture.

● **Extra attention, supervision or guidance.** When explaining about a child's 'extra' requirements, bear in mind that they must be 'substantially in excess' of those required by a child of the same age who does not have a disability (see p602). It can be difficult to explain what is 'substantially in excess' of the norm. It may be either because of the extra time you devote or the degree of attention, supervision or guidance a child requires.[174] The fact that it may not be unusual for some children of the same age to require similar assistance is the wrong approach. The comparison should be with an 'average child' the same age – ie, a child of average intelligence whose behaviour is neither particularly good nor bad.[175] Children with a disability may need extra help to develop daily living skills, language and social skills. For example, babies with sensory impairments may require more physical stimulation to aid parental bonding and develop communication skills. A child with a disability might require intensive help with eating, whereas children of the same age might be expected to eat unaided or only need certain foods cut up. Similarly, a child with a disability could require supervision to avoid dangers that children would usually be expected to deal with themselves by that particular age. A child with a disability may need help to use toys, or may need to be coaxed to explore her/his environment. A child with a disability may also develop these skills later than other children. Similarly, you may let a non-disabled child play outdoors and instruct her/him not to cross roads. You may be able to supervise the child indirectly without having to watch her/him all the time. However, you may have to supervise directly a child with sensory impairments or behavioural problems, or confine her/him indoors. Consider also whether certain activities are more difficult for the child than usual – eg, if they cause her/him pain, or make her/him dizzy, tired or breathless. If s/he takes a long time to perform particular tasks, explain this. Also say if s/he is not able to

Part 5: Other benefits
Chapter 27: Disability living allowance
7. Claims and backdating

perform a particular activity adequately – eg, if s/he cannot bend to reach her/his feet when washing.

- **About the child's development.** The questions on development are extremely important to show that children who have disabilities need extra care or supervision. You may not know exactly when a child should be crawling, walking, speaking, using the toilet independently and feeding her/himself. If you are not sure, ask your health visitor or paediatrician. For example, most children pick up and eat food by 8–12 months. Therefore, if you are still feeding a child after 12 months, you are providing attention that a non-disabled child of the same age would not need. It often helps to make comparisons with other children you know. When completing renewal forms, always describe all the child's needs. Bear in mind that, if you do not mention something, the decision maker may suppose that the child no longer needs the same help as s/he did when s/he was younger. However, it is wrong for the decision maker to assume that all children with disabilities develop in the same way.

- **Aids and adaptions**. The form asks about aids and adaptations the child uses or has been assessed for. If a decision maker thinks that a child can use a particular aid or adaptation, s/he may decide the child does not need attention or supervision. Therefore, try to explain how useful any equipment actually is, the help the child needs to use the equipment and whether s/he still needs extra help from another person in spite of the equipment. If, for instance, you have had a bath rail fitted, but s/he still finds it very difficult to climb in or out of a bath, explain this. If a child uses picture cards to communicate, explain the amount of help s/he needs to use them, and how long this takes to communicate effectively compared to communication with a non-disabled child.

- **Communicating.** Prelingual deaf children, whose first language is British Sign Language, may need help to understand or communicate in written or spoken English. Blind children will not only need help to understand written information, but may also need help to learn Braille. Children with learning difficulties may need help to express themselves or understand other people.

- **Mental disabilities**. In the sections on help with communication and on supervision during the day, you should mention any problems caused by anxiety, intrusive thoughts or anger, or learning difficulties. The questions throughout the claim pack ask if the child needs encouraging or prompting with bodily functions, as well as physical help with them. If s/he needs assistance to undertake social, leisure and recreational activities, information about that help may also fit in the mobility section of the form. At the end of the form there is a page to 'tell us anything else you think we should know'. It often helps to summarise mental health problems here and explain any other attention or supervision needs the child has.

- **Sensory impairments**. The section on help with communication applies to deaf children who may need an interpreter or other help with communicating or reading, or blind children who need to have books or correspondence read to them. Blind children may need additional help with lots of daily activities. Explain the help required throughout the form. For example, they may need someone to tell them if they have stains on their clothes or if their hands are clean – you should explain these problems in the 'dressing' and 'washing' sections. The help a child with a sensory impairment needs to undertake social and recreational activities should also be explained.
- **School-age children**. Children who have a disability, particularly those with sensory impairments or learning disabilities, usually require extra help with their school work. This should be explained, as well as other help (eg, help going to the toilet) that they may need at school. Extra help in the classroom or with homework due to special educational needs can count towards a child's attention needs, as cognition is a bodily function of the brain (see p607).[176] Straightforward teaching would probably not be sufficiently intimate to qualify,[177] but additional help (eg, because of dyslexia) may count.[178]
- **When the child is in bed at night**. Only the needs the child has after the rest of the household has gone to bed count as night-time needs (see p609).
- **Mobility**. See p598 and p602 and the tactics on p621 for how to describe a child's walking ability or the help s/he needs getting about outdoors. Children can only qualify for DLA mobility component from the age of three, but problems with getting around may also indicate care or supervision needs, so explain these even if the child is younger than three. It can be difficult to explain how a child with a disability requires 'substantially more' guidance or supervision outdoors in order to qualify for the lower rate mobility component (see p602). This is because most young children do not go out, at least in unfamiliar places, on their own. However, a child with a sensory impairment or learning disability may require much more direct or close supervision than a non-disabled child.[179] A child may normally be allowed to walk in the presence of an adult, but a child with a disability may require an adult to hold or guide her/him. Also, even a 'familiar route' may be hazardous to a child whose sight is impaired. It may help to make comparisons with siblings or classmates. A child with attention deficit disorder may need to be accompanied to school or to local shops, whereas other children might be allowed to go alone.[180]

What evidence should you provide?

When making a claim, and especially when preparing for an appeal, ensure that you have as much evidence as possible to support what you say about the child in the claim pack. This can include any of the following.

Part 5: Other benefits
Chapter 27: Disability living allowance
7. Claims and backdating

Evidence that you provide about your knowledge of the child:

About her/his care needs. Often the easiest way for a decision maker or First-tier Tribunal to get a picture of a child's care needs and their pattern is for you to keep a diary for a week or a month. Use this to record variations in her/his condition and the help s/he needs. This can be particularly useful if s/he has unpredictable care needs or experiences irregular events, such as seizures or falls, which mean that s/he needs extra supervision. Usually this is best presented as a table, using a row for each date and three or four columns to record the help s/he needs. The DLA claim form shows an example. You can also ask other carers, friends or other family members to keep a diary, or write letters in support of the claim or appeal.

About her/his walking ability. Walk outdoors with the child to measure the distance s/he can walk without severe discomfort, then write a description of the time it takes to walk this far. It may help to give an example of the distance – eg, 'S/he can walk past five houses – about 40 metres.'

Describe the terrain. Is it rough? Are there steps or slopes which present her/him with problems?

Explain what sort of discomfort s/he experiences (eg, pain or breathlessness) and how it changes as s/he walks.

Describe her/his manner of walking – eg, s/he may have problems with balance, or may walk with a limp, drag her/his feet or shuffle.

Say if the child needs to stop to rest. Try to explain how far s/he can walk before s/he needs to stop, and for how long s/he needs to rest. Bear in mind that if s/he can walk a further distance without severe discomfort after a brief rest, it is the total distance that counts.

It might help to download a map or satellite picture from the internet and measure the distances on it.

Go somewhere unfamiliar with the child and describe all the difficulty s/he has and the guidance s/he needs.

Evidence from third parties:

Doctors' reports. These could be reports which have already been provided by specialists to the child's GP. Often hospital doctors will send copies of reports to the child's parent/ guardian when they write them. The GP can be asked for copies of any reports you do not have from the child's medical records. Alternatively, ask the GP or specialist to write a specific letter for the child's claim or appeal. The doctor may charge for writing reports and providing copies from the child's records. It is not usually worth providing hospital appointment letters and other routine documents which do not comment on the child's diagnosis, treatment or disability. The DWP may request a specific report from the child's GP. It can help to make an appointment to discuss the day-to-day problems s/he has before this is written.

Reports from other medical professionals. Reports from health visitors, physiotherapists, psychiatric and other specialist nurses and occupational therapists can often provide more detailed information about a child's disability and how it affects her/his day-to-day life than reports from doctors, who only discuss symptoms and treatment.

Social services and educational reports. If a child has had a social care needs assessment, this can be very helpful. A statement of special educational needs may provide useful supporting evidence of the extra help s/he needs in school.

DWP medical services assessments. The DWP's decisions can be based on reports prepared by doctors or other healthcare professionals acting on behalf of the DWP to assess your child's entitlement to DLA. These should not necessarily be preferred to your own evidence or to that of your doctor. You should examine any report carefully and explain why any unhelpful findings or assessments are wrong. If, however, the assessment report supports your claim, you should highlight this.

How your claim is dealt with

A decision maker can award DLA on the basis of the claim form alone, but may choose to contact someone you have named on the form for more information. It is a good idea to include details of all the medical professionals and other people who know and understand the child's needs, and, if possible, enclose evidence from them.

The decision maker may telephone you to ask for further information. If you do not want to be telephoned, write this clearly on the claim form.

If the decision maker cannot get sufficient information, s/he may also arrange for the child to be given a medical examination by a healthcare professional acting on behalf of the DWP, who will sometimes visit her/him at home.

If you (or an older child) refuse a medical examination 'without good cause', the decision maker is likely to refuse the claim.[181]

The DWP aims to deal with new claims for DLA within 40 working days. Claims made under the special rules for terminal illness (see p614) should be decided more quickly. If you disagree with the decision, you can ask for a revision and then appeal (see Chapters 54 and 55) on behalf of the child. See p621 for suggestions about the evidence you can use to support a claim, revision or appeal.

8. Getting paid

The general rules on getting paid are covered in Chapter 50. This section explains the specific rules that apply to disability living allowance (DLA).

As DLA is claimed for a child under the age of 16, it is usually paid to an adult with whom s/he is living. The DWP appoints the adult (an 'appointee') to act on the child's behalf. The appointee is normally the child's parent.[182]

DLA can continue to be paid to the appointee in some circumstances when the child and appointee are not living together, including during a temporary separation of up to 12 weeks, or when the child is absent at a boarding school or in residential care (although other rules may mean that payment stops in such circumstances – see Chapter 41). DLA ceases to be paid to the appointee immediately when the child is in the care of a local authority or any similar arrangement, unless the arrangement is not intended to last for more than 12 weeks.[183]

When is disability living allowance paid?

You are normally paid on a Wednesday, but the DWP can vary the payday.[184] DLA is usually paid every four weeks in arrears. However:

– DLA can be paid at shorter intervals in individual cases;[185]
– DLA under the special rules for terminal illness can be paid weekly.

If the child leaves hospital or a care home and expects to return within 28 days, DLA can be paid at a daily rate for days at home.[186]

Note:

- If you are claiming other DWP benefits, DLA may be paid in a single payment with them instead.
- The higher rate of the DLA mobility component can be paid directly to Motability if you are buying a car through the scheme (see p630).
- Even if you have been sanctioned for a benefit offence (see p1265), you must be paid DLA.
- For information on missing payments, see p1174. If you cannot get your DLA payments because you have lost your bank or Post Office card or you have forgotten your PIN, see p1173. If you have lost your 'simple payment' card, or you have forgotten your memorable date, see p1173.
- If payment of DLA is delayed, see p1165. If you wish to complain about how your claim has been dealt with, or claim compensation, see Chapter 58.
- If payment of a child's DLA is suspended, see p1185. If you have been overpaid DLA, you might have to repay it (see Chapter 52) and, in some circumstances, you may have to pay a penalty (see p1256). If you have been accused of fraud, see Chapter 53.

Length of awards

Awards of DLA can be made for either fixed or indefinite periods.[187] The length of an award depends on how long a decision maker estimates the child's current needs may last.

Awards are usually made for at least six months because of the requirement that a child should satisfy the disability conditions for the next six months. However, there is no legal minimum length for an award.[188] If you think benefit should be awarded for longer, perhaps because the child's condition is such that her/his care or mobility needs will not decrease, consider asking for a revision (see p1276). Bear in mind that if you challenge the length of her/his award, the rate of the award may also be reconsidered. Even if a child has a longer term award, the DWP can reduce or stop the award if it has grounds to revise or supersede it.

If an award is for a limited period, you will be invited to make a renewal claim up to six months before the award runs out (see p617). However, see p626 for how the introduction of personal independence payment (PIP) affects a DLA renewal claim when a child reaches 16. The introduction of PIP will affect a child when s/he reaches 16 even if s/he currently has an indefinite award of DLA.

A 'special rules' award (see p614) on the basis of terminal illness is normally made for a fixed period of three years. If there is already a mobility award in place, the length of the special rules award may be adjusted to finish at the same time as the mobility award.

Although DLA has two components, there can only be a single DLA award, consisting of one or both components. If a child has an award of both components, they must be aligned to end on the same day (even if they started at different times).[189]

Change of circumstances

You must report any change in a child's circumstances that you have been told you must report, as well as any that you might reasonably be expected to know might affect her/his right to, the amount of, or payment of DLA. You should do this as soon as possible, preferably in writing. See p1184 for further information.

If a child's condition deteriorates so that s/he becomes eligible for a higher rate or another component, benefit can be backdated to the day s/he becomes eligible, provided you tell the DWP no later than a month after s/he completes the three-month qualifying period. If payment of (but not entitlement to) DLA has stopped (eg, while a child is in a care home), still notify the DWP so that the correct rate is paid when payment resumes.

If you do not report a change of circumstances within the month, benefit can still be backdated if you do so within 13 months and there were 'special circumstances' that meant it was not practical to report the change earlier.[190]

If a child's condition improves so that s/he should drop down a rate, lose a component or lose benefit altogether, the new decision normally takes effect from the date you tell the DWP of the improvement, or from the date of the decision if the DWP changed it without your asking.[191] It only takes effect from an earlier date (and causes an overpayment) if you should have realised earlier that the change should have been reported. It is accepted that it may be difficult to realise when a gradual improvement begins to affect benefit entitlement.[192]

Part 5: Other benefits
Chapter 27: Disability living allowance
9. Transfers to personal independence payment

9. Transfers to personal independence payment

Personal independence payment (PIP – see Chapter 34) is gradually replacing disability living allowance (DLA) for all working-age people.

If you are 16 or over (and were under 65 on 8 April 2013) and already get DLA, you will be invited to claim PIP and your DLA will end (see p628). You do not need to do anything until you are notified in writing by the DWP. You will be invited to claim PIP when your DLA award expires instead of making a renewal claim for DLA. You will also be invited to claim PIP if you report a change in your circumstances relevant to the level of your DLA award (unless the change is that you are leaving Great Britain or, from 29 June 2016, that a child is a patient in hospital and still getting her/his DLA – see p625).[193]

Other people aged 16 or over who get DLA and were under 65 on 8 April 2013 will be invited to claim PIP, probably by late 2017. If you are 65 or over by the time you are invited to claim, you are assessed for PIP as if you were under 65 and so you will have access to all the components and rates of PIP.[194] If you are not awarded any rate of PIP, your claim for PIP should be treated as a claim for attendance allowance (see Chapter 23) and the DWP will consider whether you qualify for it.[195]

If you are claiming DLA for a child, s/he will normally be affected by the transfer to PIP when s/he reaches 16.[196] The transfer to PIP will not affect her/him before then.[197] The DWP will normally write to you when the child is 15 years and 7 months old. However, from 29 June 2016, if your child is entitled to DLA as a patient in hospital, s/he is exempt from the transfer to PIP while s/he remains in hospital.[198]

If your child is about to turn 16 and her/his award of DLA for either component is for a fixed term that is due to end on the day before her/his 16th birthday or within the following six months, the DWP will extend the award if it will expire before a decision can be made on her/his PIP entitlement.[199] The award is extended until the day before s/he turns 17 or, if earlier, the day her/his DLA ends under the rules on transferring to PIP.[200] These extensions are to give her/him time to claim PIP and have a decision made on entitlement.

The DWP says that, if you get DLA under the 'special rules' on the basis of terminal illness (see p614), you will only be invited to claim PIP when your current award expires. This includes children reaching 16 who would otherwise have to claim PIP.[201]

Always check letters about your DLA carefully to see whether you have been asked to claim PIP.

If you are 16 or over (and were under 65 on 8 April 2013) you can choose to claim PIP, even if you are entitled to DLA and have not been sent a letter telling you to claim PIP.[202]

Should you claim personal independence payment?

1. If you have received a letter saying that you must claim PIP, you should do so straight away as your DLA award will end (see p628).

2. If you have *not* been sent a letter telling you to claim PIP, get specialist advice before claiming PIP, to help you decide whether it is a good idea to do so. This is because the entitlement conditions are completely different and you may not qualify for PIP at all. If you claim PIP, your DLA award ends. Once you have claimed PIP, you cannot change your mind.[203]

3. The DWP says that, if you already get the higher rate mobility component and highest rate care component of DLA and have not been sent a letter telling you to claim PIP, it will advise you not to proceed with a claim for PIP unless you report that your condition has improved.[204]

Note: if you get DLA and you turned 65 on or before 8 April 2013, you are not affected by the transfer to PIP and continue to receive DLA for as long as you meet the qualifying conditions.[205] See p611 for how you can make a renewal claim for DLA or seek a different rate.

Claims for personal independence payment

If you are sent a written invitation to claim PIP, this must inform you that you have 28 days to make a claim and tell you how to do so. The 28-day time limit can be extended, if the DWP thinks it is reasonable to do so.[206] The letter must also tell you that, if you do not claim PIP, your DLA award will end and when this will happen.[207]

You should make a claim for PIP, following the instructions in the letter, as soon as possible, because your DLA award will end whether you claim PIP or not.[208] If you do not claim PIP within the time allowed, your DLA award is suspended from your next payment day.[209] You must be sent a letter explaining that your award has been suspended and will be terminated if you do not claim PIP within 28 days of the date on which it was suspended.[210] If you do so, your award of DLA is reinstated. If you still do not claim PIP, your DLA award ends from the date it was suspended.[211] You should make a new claim for PIP if you satisfy the rules of entitlement (see p736).

If you get DLA and have been invited to claim PIP or are in the process of claiming PIP and notify the DWP of a change of circumstances that may affect your entitlement to DLA, this is treated as a change of circumstances affecting your entitlement to PIP.[212]

Part 5: Other benefits
Chapter 27: Disability living allowance
10. Tax, other benefits and the benefit cap

Once you make a claim for PIP, the assessment process is the same as for a new claim (see p757).

If you do not provide information needed to assess your entitlement to PIP (see p759 and p760) and do not have a good reason, your PIP claim will be refused. If this happens, your DLA award ends 14 days after the first DLA payday following the decision refusing your PIP claim.[213] If you are later awarded PIP because you win an appeal against the decision that you do not have good reason, your PIP award starts from the day after your DLA award ended.[214]

These rules apply if you choose to claim PIP as well as if you are notified that your DLA will stop and invited to claim PIP.[215]

When your disability living allowance ends

If you make a claim for PIP, your DLA award continues until a decision is made on your PIP claim. Your DLA award ends:[216]

- if you are terminally ill (see p755) and your payment of PIP is higher than your payment of DLA was, on either the Tuesday after your PIP claim is decided or the day before your next normal DLA payday, whichever is earlier; *or*
- in any other case, four weeks after the next DLA payday after the decision is made on your PIP claim (whether or not you are awarded PIP).

Your entitlement to PIP starts from the day after your DLA award ends. The rules above also apply if your claim for DLA is refused and you then claim PIP, but the refusal is then overturned following a revision or appeal before your PIP claim is decided.[217] If your PIP claim is decided before the decision on your DLA refusal is changed, any DLA award that is later made to you ends on:[218]

- the day before your PIP award started; *or*
- four weeks after the next DLA payday following the decision to refuse you PIP.

If you withdraw your claim, or notify the DWP that you do not wish to claim PIP when invited to do so, your DLA award ends 14 days after the first DLA payday following the date you notified the DWP.[219]

You must be notified in writing of the date your DLA award ends and the start date of any PIP award.[220]

10. **Tax, other benefits and the benefit cap**

Tax

Disability living allowance (DLA) is not taxable.[221]

Means-tested benefits and tax credits

DLA for a child is not taken into account as income when calculating any of the means-tested benefits or tax credits for a person who has responsibility for the child. DLA is paid on top of these benefits and tax credits, and getting DLA can increase the amount of them (or mean that the person qualifies for means-tested benefits or tax credits for the first time, if her/his income was previously too high).

If your child is entitled to DLA, your housing benefit (HB) includes a disabled child premium (see p237). If s/he gets the highest rate care component, your HB also includes an enhanced disability premium (see p240). These premiums are also included in your income support (IS) and income-based jobseeker's allowance (JSA) if you do not yet get child tax credit (CTC). If your child is entitled to DLA and you come under the universal credit (UC) system (see p20), you can be paid a disabled child addition in your UC. This is paid at the higher rate if s/he is entitled to the highest rate of the care component (see p258).

If you or your partner are entitled to DLA, your IS, income-based JSA and, unless you have reached the qualifying age for pension credit (PC), HB include the disability premium (see p238) (or for IS and JSA only, higher pensioner premium – see p242 – if either of you have reached the qualifying age for PC). If you or your partner are entitled to the highest rate of the DLA care component and aged under the qualifying age for PC, you also get an enhanced disability premium (see p240). This is also paid with income-related employment and support allowance (ESA – see p240). A severe disability premium/addition is included in IS, income-based JSA, income-related ESA, the guarantee credit of PC and HB, if you receive the highest or middle rate of the DLA care component and meet the other conditions for that premium/addition (see p242).

A disabled child element is included in CTC for each child who gets DLA (at any rate). If s/he gets the highest rate of the DLA care component, a severely disabled child element is included in CTC. An award of DLA at any rate counts as a qualifying benefit for the disabled worker element in working tax credit (WTC). If you or your partner get the highest rate care component, a severe disability element is included in WTC (two elements are included if you both get the highest rate). See Chapter 59 for futher information.

If you or your partner are entitled to the DLA care component, non-dependant deductions (see p464) are *not* made from any housing costs covered by your HB or IS, income-based JSA, income-related ESA or the guarantee credit of PC. No housing costs contributions from a non-dependant are taken into account when calculating your UC housing costs if you, your partner or the non-dependant receive the DLA middle or highest rate care component (see p512).

If you or your partner have reached the qualifying age for PC but you must claim UC because the other person has not yet reached this age, and the person over the qualifying age for PC is entitled to DLA, you qualify for the limited capability for work element in your UC award (see p260). If the person over the qualifying age for PC is entitled to the highest rate of the DLA care component, you get the limited capability for work-related activity element in your UC award instead (see p262).

5

Part 5: Other benefits
Chapter 27: Disability living allowance
10. Tax, other benefits and the benefit cap

Non-means-tested benefits

DLA may be paid in addition to any other non-means-tested benefits, except that:

- DLA overlaps with armed forces independence payment;[222]
- DLA care component overlaps with attendance allowance and constant attendance allowance under the industrial injuries scheme (see p687) or war pensions scheme (see p862);[223] *and*
- DLA mobility component overlaps with the war pensioners' mobility supplement payable under the war pensions scheme (see p862).[224]

See p1175 for details of the overlapping benefits rules.

You cannot be paid both DLA and personal independence payment (see p735).

A person who regularly looks after a child or adult who gets the highest or middle rate of DLA care component may be entitled to carer's allowance (CA – see Chapter 25). However, if you are an adult and your carer gets CA, it may affect your entitlement to a severe disability premium (or additional amount).

The benefit cap

In some cases, there is a limit on the total amount of specified benefits you can receive (a 'benefit cap'). DLA is *not* one of the specified benefits. The benefit cap does *not* apply if you, your partner or child receive DLA (or are entitled to DLA, but it is not payable because you, or s/he, are in hospital or a care home). In other cases, it only applies if you are getting HB or UC. See p1180 for further information.

Passports and other sources of help

You qualify for a Christmas bonus if you receive DLA at any rate (see p863). If you are on a low income, you may be entitled to council tax reduction (see p854).

If you get the higher rate of DLA mobility component, you or your carer can be exempt from paying road tax on a car used solely by you or for you. Contact the Disability Benefits Centre (see Appendix 1) for an exemption certificate.

If you get the higher rate of the mobility component, you should qualify for the blue badge scheme of parking concessions, which operates throughout Great Britain and the European Economic Area (with certain local variations). Contact your local authority for further information.

If any member of your household receives DLA at any rate, you can get a grant for help with insulation and other energy efficiency measures in your home (see p865) and may be entitled to other benefits, such as concessionary travel.

Motability

Motability is a charity that runs a scheme to help you lease or buy a car if you receive (or a child for whom you are responsible receives) the higher rate of DLA mobility component for a period of 12 months or more (see p597). DLA mobility component is paid directly to Motability.[225] You may also have to make extra payments. For further information, telephone 0300 456 4566 or visit www.motability.co.uk.

Notes

1. Disability living allowance mobility component
1 ss71(6) and 73 SSCBA 1992
2 CM/5/1986; *BP v SSWP* [2009] UKUT 90 (AAC)
3 s73 SSCBA 1992; reg 12(1)(b) SS(DLA) Regs
4 Reg 12(1)(a) SS(DLA) Regs
5 R(M) 3/78
6 Reg 12(1)(a) SS(DLA) Regs; R(M) 2/78; R(DLA) 4/06
7 CDLA/1525/2008
8 CDLA/2822/1999; CDLA/4329/2001
9 *MMF v SSWP (DLA)* [2012] UKUT 312 (AAC)
10 R(M) 3/86; CSDLA/202/2007; CDLA/3839/2007; *DM v SSWP (DLA)* [2010] UKUT 375 (AAC)
11 R(M) 2/89; CDLA/97/2001; *Sandhu v SSWP* [2010] EWCA Civ 962
12 Reg 12(4) SS(DLA) Regs
13 R(M) 2/89
14 Reg 12(1)(b) SS(DLA) Regs
15 CDLA/3188/2002; *HJ v SSWP (DLA)* [2010] UKUT 307 (AAC)
16 R(M) 1/95; CSDLA/171/1998
17 CM/208/1989
18 *JK v SSWP (DLA)* [2010] UKUT 197 (AAC)
19 CDLA/1389/1997; CDLA/2195/2008
20 R(M) 1/81
21 R(M) 2/92
22 R(M) 1/83
23 CM/267/93; CDLA/608/1994; R(DLA) 4/03
24 R(DLA) 4/04
25 *Hewitt and Diment v CAO* 29 June 1998, reported as R(DLA) 6/99
26 R(M) 1/98; CDLA/3941/2005 interpreted 'exertion' to mean the activity of walking 'however slight the exertion'.
27 *KS v SSWP (DLA)* [2013] UKUT 390 (AAC)
28 Reg 12(2) SS(DLA) Regs
29 Reg 12(3) SS(DLA) Regs
30 R(DLA) 3/95
31 Sch 2 SS(GB) Regs
32 *GB v SSWP (DLA)* [2016] UKUT 566 (AAC)
33 Reg 34(2) and Sch 3 Parts II & III SS(IIPD) Regs
34 Reg 12(2)(b) SS(DLA) Regs
35 s73(1AB) SSCBA 1992; reg 12(1A) SS(DLA) Regs
36 *NC v SSWP (DLA)* [2012] UKUT 384 (AAC)
37 *SSWP v IK (DLA)* [2014] UKUT 174 (AAC)
38 *SSWP v YR (DLA)* [2014] UKUT 80 (AAC)
39 Reg 12(1)(b) SS(DLA) Regs
40 s73(3) SSCBA 1992; reg 12(5) and (6) SS(DLA) Regs
41 *JH v SSWP (DLA)* [2010] UKUT 456 (AAC); *AH v SSWP (DLA)* [2012] UKUT 387 (AAC); *SSWP v MG (DLA)* [2012] UKUT 429 (AAC)
42 R(M) 3/86; CSDLA/202/2007
43 *N McM v SSWP (DLA)* [2014] UKUT 312 (AAC)
44 R(DLA) 3/98; *MP v SSWP (DLA)* [2014] UKUT 426 (AAC)
45 *M (a child) v CAO* 29 October 1999, reported as R(DLA) 1/00
46 CDLA/95/1995; *DM v SSWP (DLA)* [2015] UKUT 87 (AAC)
47 CDLA/3215/2001; *CD v SSWP (DLA)* [2013] UKUT 68 (AAC); *MP v SSWP (DLA)* [2014] UKUT 426 (AAC)
48 CDLA/2054/1998
49 R(DLA) 7/02; R(DLA) 9/02; CDLA/3244/2001; CDLA/2955/2008; *SSWP v DM (DLA)* [2010] UKUT 318 (AAC); *SSWP v MG (DLA)* [2012] UKUT 429 (AAC)

5

50 *TV v SSWP (DLA)* [2013] UKUT 364
(AAC)
51 s73(1)(d) SSCBA 1992
52 R(DLA) 6/03
53 CDLA/42/1994
54 s73(4A) SSCBA 1992
55 *BM v SSWP (DLA)* [2015] UKUT 18
(AAC); *KC-M S (by EC) v SSWP (DLA)*
[2015] UKUT 284 (AAC)
56 CDLA/2268/1999
57 R(DLA) 3/04
58 CDLA/42/1994
59 CDLA/42/1994
60 CDLA/42/1994; CDLA/3360/1995;
CSDLA/591/1997; CDLA/2643/1998
61 R(DLA) 4/01
62 *IN v SSWP (DLA)* [2013] UKUT 249 (AAC)
63 R(DLA) 6/05
64 R(DLA) 4/01
65 R(DLA) 4/01
66 CDLA/42/1994; R(DLA) 3/04
67 CDLA/2364/1995 and *KH v SSWP (DLA)*
[2015] UKUT 8 (AAC), but see CDLA/42/
1994
68 CDLA/2142/2005
69 Reg 12(7) and (8) SS(DLA) Regs; R(DLA)
3/04; CDLA/2409/2003; R(DLA) 6/05;
SSWP v DC (DLA) [2011] UKUT 235
(AAC)

**2. Disability living allowance care
component**
70 ss71(6) and 72 SSCBA 1992
71 s72(1)(a) and (4)(c) SSCBA 1992
72 s72(4)(b) SSCBA 1992
73 Reg 7 SS(DLA) Regs
74 s72(4)(a) SSCBA 1992
75 s72(5) SSCBA 1992
76 s72(1)(b) SSCBA 1992
77 s72(1)(c) SSCBA 1992
78 s72(1A)(b) SSCBA 1992
79 s72(5) SSCBA 1992
80 R(DLA) 1/05; *BM v SSWP (DLA)* [2015]
UKUT 18 (AAC); [2015] AACR 29
81 R(DLA) 3/06, tribunal of commissioners
82 CDLA/4475/04
83 R(DLA) 3/06, tribunal of commissioners
84 R(A) 3/86; *Mallinson v Secretary of State
for Social Security*, 21 April 1994 (HL),
reported as R(A) 3/94
85 *Secretary of State for Social Security v
Fairey* (aka *Halliday*), 21 May 1997 (HL),
reported as R(A) 2/98
86 R(A) 3/89
87 R(A) 5/90
88 CDLA/3925/1997; *HJ v SSWP (DLA)*
[2010] UKUT 307 (AAC)
89 R(DLA) 10/02

90 *Mallinson v Secretary of State for Social
Security*, 21 April 1994 (HL), reported as
R(A) 3/94
91 *SJ v SSWP (DLA)* [2014] UKUT 222 (AAC)
92 Reg 10C SS(DLA) Regs; *R v National
Insurance Commissioner ex parte
Secretary of State for Social Services*
[1981] 1 WLR 1017 (CA), also reported
as R(A) 2/80
93 R(A) 1/06
94 *Mallinson v Secretary of State for Social
Security*, 21 April 1994 (HL), reported as
R(A) 3/94
95 CA/177/1988; CDLA/14696/1996;
R(DLA) 1/07, tribunal of commissioners
96 R(A) 3/74
97 R(A) 2/75
98 CA/86/1987
99 R(DLA) 1/07, tribunal of commissioners
100 *R v Social Security Commissioner ex parte
Butler*, February 1984, unreported and
*Secretary of State for Social Security v
Fairey* (aka *Halliday*), 21 May 1997 (HL),
reported as R(A) 2/98
101 *Secretary of State for Social Security v
Fairey* (aka *Halliday*), 21 May 1997 (HL),
reported as R(A) 2/98; R(DLA) 1/02;
R(DLA) 2/02; R(DLA) 3/02; *SSWP v PV
(DLA)* [2010] UKUT 33 (AAC)
102 R(DLA) 2/02
103 CDLA/3607/2001
104 *Cockburn v CAO and Another*, 21 May
1997 (HL), reported as R(DLA) 2/98;
Ramsden v SSWP, 31 January 2003 (CA),
reported as R(DLA) 2/03
105 CDLA/267/1994, CDLA/11652/1995,
CDLA/3711/1995, CDLA/12381/1996,
CDLA/16996/1996, CDLA/16129/1996
and CDLA/4352/1999 are useful, but
conflict with CSDLA/281/1996 and
CSDLA/314/1997
106 CDLA/267/1994
107 *Secretary of State for Social Security v
Fairey* (aka *Halliday*), 21 May 1997 (HL),
reported as R(A) 2/98
108 CDLA/16129/1996, CDLA/16996/1996
and CDLA/4352/1999 are helpful, but
conflict with CSDLA/314/1997
109 CDLA/4352/1999 and CDLA/5216/
1998, the latter being more restrictive
110 CDLA/4352/1999
111 CDLA/5216/1998
112 R(DLA) 1/98
113 *R v National Insurance Commissioner ex
parte Secretary of State for Social Services*
[1974] 1 WLR 1290 (DC), also reported
as R(A) 4/74
114 CDLA/2852/2002

115 CDLA/997/2003
116 R(A) 1/04
117 R(A) 1/78
118 s72(1)(a)(i) SSCBA 1992
119 R(DLA) 8/02
120 CDLA/58/1993
121 CSDLA/29/1994
122 *Ramsden v SSWP*, 31 January 2003 (CA),
    reported as R(DLA) 2/03
123 s72(1)(b)(i) SSCBA 1992
124 R(DLA) 5/05
125 CA/140/1985
126 *AB v SSWP (DLA)* [2015] UKUT 522
    (AAC)
127 s72(1)(c)(i) SSCBA 1992
128 R(DLA) 5/05
129 R(DLA) 5/05
130 R(A) 3/78
131 s72(1)(b)(ii) SSCBA 1992
132 R(A) 1/83
133 CA/15/1979, approved in R(A) 1/83
134 R(A) 2/89
135 CA/33/1984
136 R(A) 3/92
137 R(A) 1/73
138 *CP v SSWP (DLA)* [2013] UKUT 230
    (AAC)
139 *Moran v Secretary of State for Social
    Services, The Times,* 14 March 1987
    (CA), reported as R(A) 1/88
140 R(A) 5/81
141 s72(1)(c)(ii) SSCBA 1992
142 Vol 10 Ch 61, para 61165 DMG
143 Vol 10 Ch 61, para 61164 DMG

3. The rules about your age
144 s73(1A) SSCBA 1992
145 s72(2) and (5) SSCBA 1992
146 Sch 1 paras 3(3), 5(3), 6 and 7 SS(DLA)
    Regs; see also CSDLA/388/2000
147 Reg 6(3) and (4) SS(DLA) Regs
148 Sch 1 para 3(2) SS(DLA) Regs
149 Sch 1 para 1(3) SS(DLA) Regs
150 Sch 1 paras 2, 6 and 7 SS(DLA) Regs; *DB
    v SSWP (DLA)* [2016] 205 (AAC)
151 s72(1A)(a) SSCBA 1992

5. The amount of benefit
152 Reg 4(2) SS(DLA) Regs
153 Reg 4(1) SS(DLA) Regs

6. Special benefit rules
154 Reg 7 SS(DLA) Regs
155 s72(5) SSCBA 1992
156 ss72(5) and 66(1) and (2) SSCBA 1992
157 s73(9)(b)(ii) and (12) SSCBA 1992

7. Claims and backdating
158 Reg 6(8), (8A) and (9) SS(C&P) Regs
159 Reg 4(1) SS(C&P) Regs
160 ss72(5) and 73(12) SSCBA 1992; regs
    3(9)(b) and 6(6)(c) SS&CS(DA) Regs
161 Reg 6(8), (8A) and (9) SS(C&P) Regs
162 Reg 6(8A) SS(C&P) Regs
163 Reg 6(9) SS(C&P) Regs
164 Reg 6(1)(b) SS(C&P) Regs
165 s76(1) SSCBA 1992
166 Reg 9(1) and Sch 1 SS(C&P) Regs; reg
    25(3) and (4) UC,PIP,JSA&ESA (C&P)
    Regs
167 Reg 13A(1) SS(C&P) Regs
168 Reg 13C SS(C&P) Regs
169 CDLA/14895/1996
170 Regs 6 and 11 SS(DLA) Regs
171 R(DLA)4/01; CDLA/333/2005; *DN v
    SSWP (DLA)* [2016] UKUT 233 (AAC)
172 DWP, *DWP Medical (Factual) Reports: a
    guide to completion,* April 2014
173 R(A) 2/74; see also *Moyna v SSWP,* 31
    July 2003 (HL), reported as R(DLA) 7/03;
    DJ v SSWP (DLA) [2016] UKUT 169 (AAC)

174 CSDLA/76/1998
175 CA/92/1992; *DJ v SSWP (DLA)* [2016]
    UKUT 169 (AAC)
176 *SSWP v Hughes (a minor),* reported as
    R(DLA) 1/04
177 CDLA/1983/2006
178 *KM v SSWP (DLA)* [2013] UKUT 159
    (AAC); [2014] AACR 2
179 CDLA/2268/1999
180 CDLA/4806/2002
181 s19(3) SSA 1998

8. Getting paid
182 Reg 43 SS(C&P) Regs
183 Reg 43 SS(C&P) Regs
184 Reg 22(3) and Sch 6 SS(C&P) Regs
185 Reg 22 SS(C&P) Regs
186 Reg 25 SS(C&P) Regs
187 s71(3) SSCBA 1992
188 R(DLA) 11/02
189 s71(3) SSCBA 1992; CDLA/2887/2008
190 Reg 7(9) SS&CS(DA) Regs
191 s10(5) SSA 1998
192 Reg 7(2)(c) SS&CS(DA) Regs; *RD V
    SSWP (DLA)* [2011] UKUT 95 (AAC); *DC v
    SSWP (DLA)* [2011] UKUT 336 (AAC)

**9. Transfers to personal independence
    payment**
193 Reg 3(5) and (6) PIP(TP) Regs
194 Reg 27 PIP(TP) Regs

195 DWP, *Personal Independence Payment Handbook*, April 2016, p18, available at www.gov.uk
196 Reg 3(3) PIP(TP) Regs
197 Reg 5(1) PIP(TP) Regs
198 Reg 3(4A) and (5B) PIP(TP) Regs
199 Reg 19 PIP(TP) Regs
200 Reg 18 PIP(TP) Regs
201 DWP, *Personal Independence Payment Handbook*, April 2016, p37
202 Reg 4 PIP(TP) Regs
203 Regs 12, 13 and 15 PIP(TP) Regs
204 DWP, *Personal Independence Payment Handbook*, April 2016, p18
205 Reg 4(1)(a) PIP(TP) Regs
206 Reg 8(4) PIP(TP) Regs
207 Regs 3 and 7 PIP(TP) Regs
208 Regs 9, 11 and 17 PIP(TP) Regs
209 Reg 9 PIP(TP) Regs
210 Reg 10 PIP(TP) Regs
211 Reg 11 PIP(TP) Regs
212 Reg 20 PIP(TP) Regs
213 Reg 13(1) PIP(TP) Regs
214 Regs 13(2) and 17(2)(b) PIP(TP) Regs
215 Reg 12 PIP(TP) Regs
216 Reg 17 PIP(TP) Regs
217 Reg 30 PIP(TP) Regs
218 Reg 17(4) and (5) PIP(TP) Regs
219 Regs 14 and 15 PIP(TP) Regs
220 Reg 17(1) and (3) PIP(TP) Regs

10. **Tax, other benefits and the benefit cap**
221 s677 IT(EP)A 2003
222 Art 24C Armed Forces and Reserve Forces (Compensation Scheme) Order 2011, No.517
223 Sch 1 para 5 SS(OB) Regs
224 Reg 42(1)(b)(ii) SS(C&P) Regs
225 Regs 44, 45 and 46 SS(C&P) Regs

Chapter 28

Contributory employment and support allowance

This chapter covers:
1. Who can claim employment and support allowance (p636)
2. The rules about your age (p638)
3. People included in the claim (p638)
4. The amount of benefit (p638)
5. Special benefit rules (p646)
6. Claims and backdating (p647)
7. Getting paid (p650)
8. Tax, other benefits and the benefit cap (p652)

Key facts

- Employment and support allowance (ESA) is a benefit for people who have 'limited capability for work' (ie, they are unable to work because of illness or disability) and who are not entitled to statutory sick pay.
- Entitlement to ESA is assessed by a test called the 'work capability assessment'.
- There are two types of ESA: **contributory ESA** (which is not means tested, but you must satisfy a national insurance contributions test) and **income-related ESA** (which is means tested).
- In some cases, contributory ESA is paid for a maximum of 365 days.
- If you qualify for income-related ESA as well as contributory ESA, you may be able to get your contributory ESA topped up with income-related ESA.
- ESA is administered and paid by the DWP.
- If you disagree with an ESA decision, you can apply for a revision or supersession, or appeal against it. You must apply for a mandatory reconsideration before you can appeal. All parts of the decision may be looked at.

Part 5: Other benefits
Chapter 28: Contributory employment and support allowance
1. Who can claim employment and support allowance

1. **Who can claim employment and support allowance**

You qualify for contributory employment and support allowance (ESA) if you satisfy the following basic rules (which apply to both contributory and income-related ESA), and you satisfy the extra rules for contributory ESA below.

You satisfy the basic rules for ESA if you:[1]
- have 'limited capability for work' (see p1003); *and*
- are aged 16 or over, but under pension age (see p772); *and*
- are in Great Britain (see p646 if you go abroad); *and*
- are not entitled in your own right to income support (IS) or jobseeker's allowance (JSA), and are not in a couple entitled to joint-claim JSA (see p120). However, you can get contributory ESA if you are entitled to joint-claim JSA and do not have to satisfy all the JSA conditions (see p121); *and*
- are not entitled to statutory sick pay; *and*
- are not engaged in any work, whether it is paid or unpaid, unless it is work you are allowed to do while claiming (called 'permitted work' – see p1023).

Note: if you come under the universal credit (UC) system (see p20), your contributory ESA is affected, and some different rules apply, even if you are not claiming or getting UC – eg, there are different rules on overpayments (see Chapter 52), claimant responsibilities (Chapter 47) and sanctions (Chapter 48).

You are not usually entitled to ESA for the first seven days of your claim (see p1021). However, you may be able to get a short-term advance of ESA paid to you during this waiting period (p1177). You cannot get ESA and certain other benefits at the same time (see p652).

Most claimants of ESA (except those in the 'support group' – see p641) must take part in work-focused interviews and some can be required to undertake 'work-related activity'. If you come under the UC system, you must also accept a claimant commitment. From summer 2017, it is expected that this will also apply to new claims, even if you do not come under the UC system. See Chapter 47 for details.

Note: in the future it is expected that you must be entitled to work in the UK (and not be prevented from taking up work under immigration provisions) to qualify for contributory ESA.[2] There may be exceptions. See CPAG's online service and *Welfare Rights Bulletin* for updates.

Extra rules for contributory employment and support allowance

As well as satisfying the basic rules for ESA above, you qualify for contributory ESA if:[3]
- you satisfy the national insurance (NI) contribution conditions (see p978); *or*

- you were getting incapacity benefit or severe disablement allowance and you have been transferred to contributory ESA (see p672); *or*
- you satisfied the conditions for ESA in youth and you remain entitled (see below).

Note: you may get income-related ESA if you do not qualify for contributory ESA, or you may be entitled to income-related ESA to top up your contributory ESA. If you come under the UC system (see p20), you cannot get income-related ESA and must claim UC instead.

Employment and support allowance in youth

ESA in youth was abolished for new claimants from 1 May 2012.[4] For details of the rules, see Chapter 10 of the 2012/13 edition of this *Handbook*. If you were already getting ESA in youth when it was abolished, it stops after you have been getting it for a year, beginning on your first day of entitlement. Days when you receive the support component (see p641) are ignored.

If you lose entitlement to ESA in youth because you have received it for a year, but have still got limited capability for work and are put in the 'support group' (see p641) because your condition has worsened, you can requalify for contributory ESA without having to satisfy the NI contribution conditions.[5]

Disqualification from benefit

You can be disqualified from receiving ESA for up to six weeks if you:[6]
- have 'limited capability for work' because of your own misconduct (but not, for example, if this is due to pregnancy or a sexually transmitted disease); *or*
- have failed without 'good cause' to accept medical treatment (excluding vaccination, inoculation or major surgery) recommended by a doctor treating you and which would be likely to overcome your limited capability for work; *or*
- have failed without 'good cause' to stop engaging in behaviour that would 'retard' your recovery; *or*
- are absent from your home without telling the DWP where you may be found without 'good cause'.

'Good cause' is not defined.

You are not disqualified if you inform the DWP of your circumstances and you are considered to be in hardship – ie, if you are:[7]
- pregnant, or a member of your family is pregnant;
- a single claimant aged under 18, or a member of a couple and both of you are under 18;
- responsible (or your partner is responsible) for a child who lives with you. This does not apply to contributory ESA if you come under the UC system (see p20);

Part 5: Other benefits
Chapter 28: Contributory employment and support allowance
4. The amount of benefit

- entitled (or your partner is entitled) to attendance allowance (AA), the middle or highest rate of the care component of disability living allowance (DLA), the daily living component of personal independence payment (PIP) or armed forces independence payment;
- waiting (or your partner is waiting) for a decision on a claim for AA, DLA, PIP or armed forces independence payment;
- caring (or your partner is caring) for someone who is entitled to AA, the middle or highest rate care component of DLA, the daily living component of PIP or armed forces independence payment (or who is waiting for a decision on a claim for AA, DLA, PIP or armed forces independence payment);
- at least the qualifying age for pension credit (see p147), or your partner is;
- at risk of hardship (or a member of your family is at risk) if ESA is not paid to you, including if there is a 'substantial risk' that you will not have sufficient essential items such as food, clothing and heating.

In one of the above situations, your ESA is paid at a reduced rate. You get 80 per cent of your basic allowance in contributory ESA, or 80 per cent of your personal allowance in income-related ESA (see p230).[8]

You can also be disqualified from receiving contributory ESA during any period in which you are:
- absent from Great Britain (see p1594); *or*
- a prisoner or detained in legal custody (see Chapter 41).

2. **The rules about your age**

To satisfy the basic rules for employment and support allowance, you must be aged at least 16 but under pension age (see p772).

3. **People included in the claim**

You claim contributory employment and support allowance (ESA) for yourself. You cannot claim any increases for your partner or children.

4. **The amount of benefit**

You are paid a basic allowance of employment and support allowance (ESA) during an initial 'assessment phase' (see p639). After this, during the 'main phase', you may also get an additional component of ESA. You can get either a 'support component' (see p641) or a 'work-related activity component' (see p641). **Note:**

the work-related activity component has been abolished for new claimants from 3 April 2017. For who can still get the component, see p641. You may also be entitled to a transitional addition because you have been transferred from incapacity benefit (IB) or severe disablement allowance (SDA) (see p672).

There are no increases in contributory ESA for other adults or children.

Your contributory ESA may be reduced if:

- you get a pension or a councillor's allowance (see p643); *or*
- the work-related activity component (see p641) applies to you and you do not comply with requirements to attend work-focused interviews and carry out work-related activity (see Chapter 46 or, if you come under the universal credit (UC) system, Chapter 47); *or*
- you have been given a sanction because you have committed a benefit offence (see p1265).

Note:

- If you are appealing against a decision that you do not have limited capability for work and get ESA pending your appeal being heard (see p1017), you are paid at the assessment phase rate – ie, you get the basic allowance only.
- You may also be entitled to income-related ESA. If you are, your contributory ESA is topped up by your income-related ESA. If you come under the UC system (see p20), you cannot get income-related ESA, but you may be entitled to UC as well as contributory ESA.

Waiting days

You are not entitled to ESA for a period of seven '**waiting days**' at the beginning of your period of limited capability for work (see p1021).[9] This does not apply if:

- your entitlement to ESA starts within 12 weeks of your entitlement to income support (IS), IB, SDA, pension credit, jobseeker's allowance (JSA), carer's allowance, statutory sick pay or maternity allowance (MA) coming to an end; *or*
- you have requalified for contributory ESA on the basis of being put in the support group (see p641), having previously lost entitlement because of the rules on how long you can be paid contributory ESA (see p645); *or*
- you are terminally ill, or you have been discharged from the armed forces and three or more days before the discharge were days of sickness absence.

You may be able to get a short-term advance during your waiting period (see p1177).

The assessment phase

The first weeks of your entitlement to ESA are known as the 'assessment phase'. This applies to both contributory and income-related ESA. During this phase,

Part 5: Other benefits
Chapter 28: Contributory employment and support allowance
4. The amount of benefit

your ESA does not usually include an additional component. You just get a basic allowance of contributory ESA, the amount of which depends on your age. **Note:** in certain circumstances, you can get an additional component even though the assessment phase has not ended (see p643).

The assessment phase ends after 13 weeks, unless the DWP has not yet decided whether you have limited capability for work – eg, because it has not yet completed the work capability assessment (see Chapter 44). If this is the case, the assessment phase does not end until the DWP has made its decision.[10] In practice, delays of longer than 13 weeks in completing assessments are common. If you are claiming immediately after an 'extended period of sickness' on JSA (see p702), the 13-week period starts on the first day of the period of sickness.

If the assessment phase lasts longer than 13 weeks, the additional component is backdated to the 14th week of your claim.[11]

If you are appealing against a decision that you do not have limited capability for work and are getting ESA pending your appeal (see p1017), the assessment phase does not usually end until the First-tier Tribunal has made its decision. However, if you experience a new condition or your condition significantly worsens before your appeal is heard, a new determination on your limited capability for work can be made and it is possible for the assessment phase to end.[12]

It is possible for your assessment phase to begin on the first day of a period of previous entitlement to ESA (of either kind), so that some, or all, of the 13 weeks are treated as already served.[13] This happens if your current period of limited capability for work is linked to a previous one (see p1021) in which you were entitled to ESA for less than 13 weeks. In these circumstances, your assessment phase ends when your combined entitlement from the previous and current ESA awards amounts to 13 weeks, unless the DWP has not yet completed your assessment, in which case it does not end until the DWP has made its decision.

If you were on JSA during an 'extended period of sickness' (see p702), this counts as time when you had a previous entitlement to ESA.

Calculating your contributory employment and support allowance

Contributory ESA is worked out as follows.
- Add together the basic allowance and the amount of any component to which you are entitled, as follows.
  - In the 'assessment phase' (see p639), you are normally only entitled to a basic allowance.[14] This is £57.90 if you are under 25 or £73.10 if you are 25 or over. In some circumstances, such as if you are terminally ill, you may also be entitled to either a support component or a work-related activity component (see p641 and p643).

- After the assessment phase is over, you are entitled to a basic allowance of £73.10, irrespective of your age. If you qualify, you can also get a support component of £36.55 a week (see below) or (if you can still get it) a work-related activity component of £29.05 a week (see below).
- Deduct from this sum an amount for certain pension payments or for a councillor's allowance, if applicable (see p643).
- Add any transitional addition to which you are entitled if you have been transferred to ESA from IB or SDA. See p672 for details of the transfer process and p644 for how the transitional addition is calculated.[15]

Note: when calculating your ESA entitlement after you have been transferred to contributory ESA from IB or SDA (see p672), the assessment phase does not apply and so the support component or (if you can still get it) the work-related activity component is included straight away.

Support component

The support component can be included in your entitlement to both contributory and income-related ESA.[16]

In most cases, you are entitled to the support component if:
- the assessment phase (see p639) has ended (but see p643); *and*
- as well as having limited capability for work, you are also assessed as having 'limited capability for work-related activity' (see p1009).

The support group

If you are assessed as having, or are treated as having, limited capability for work-related activity, the DWP describes you as being in the '**support group**'.

The DWP decides whether or not you have limited capability for work-related activity as part of the work capability assessment (see p1003). You can appeal if you do not agree with the DWP's decision, although you must apply for a mandatory reconsideration first. If you appeal and the First-tier Tribunal finds that you have limited capability for work, it should also consider whether you have limited capability for work-related activity.[17]

If you are in the support group, you do not have to take part in work-focused interviews or associated activity as a condition of getting benefit.[18]

Note: if you are transferred from IB or SDA to contributory ESA, or from IS on the grounds of disability to income-related ESA (see p672), the support component is included straight away, as the assessment phase does not apply.

Work-related activity component

The work-related activity component has been abolished for new claimants of both contributory and income-related ESA from 3 April 2017.[19] From this date,

Part 5: Other benefits
Chapter 28: Contributory employment and support allowance
4. The amount of benefit

you can no longer get the component if you are making a new claim for ESA (but see below). You may still be able to get the support component.

You can still get the work-related activity component after 3 April 2017 if:[20]

- you claimed ESA before 3 April 2017, you were awarded the component and are getting it now, even if it was not decided that you were entitled to the component until after this date;
- you claimed ESA before 3 April 2017 and you are re-assessed and put in the 'work-related activity group' (see below), even if you had previously been entitled to the support component in your ESA;
- you claimed ESA before 3 April 2017 and were found not to be entitled, but this decision is changed following a mandatory reconsideration or an appeal and you are found to have been entitled to ESA before this date;
- you claimed ESA before 3 April 2017 and had limited capability for work (see Chapter 44), you have had a break in your period of limited capability for work, but you have reclaimed ESA within 12 weeks of your previous period ending;
- you were entitled to ESA before 3 April 2017 and then became entitled to MA, and you have reclaimed ESA within 12 weeks of your MA ending;
- your assessment phase (see p639) for a previous ESA claim began before 3 April 2017, but you were entitled to ESA for no more than 13 weeks and you have reclaimed it within 12 weeks of your previous entitlement ending;
- you claimed ESA on or after 3 April 2017, but your claim was backdated to before this date, and it is decided that you are in the 'work-related activity group' (see below);
- you are transferred from IB or SDA to contributory ESA, or from IS to income-related ESA, and placed in the 'work-related activity group' (see below).

The work-related activity group

If you are assessed under the work capability assessment as having limited capability for work, but not for work-related activity (see Chapter 44), the DWP describes you as being in the '**work-related activity group**'. This is the case, even if you cannot get the work-related activity component. The DWP also describes you as being in the work-related activity group if you are treated as having limited capability for work (see p1005), except if you are waiting for your work capability assessment to be carried out or if you are appealing.[21]

If you can get it, the work-related activity component can be included in both contributory and income-related ESA if:[22]

- the assessment phase (see p639) has ended (but see p643); *and*
- you are not assessed as having 'limited capability for work-related activity' (see p1009) – ie, you are not entitled to the support component; *and*
- you comply with the requirement to attend work-focused interviews and associated activity (see p1064). If you do not, your ESA may be reduced.

You may be required to take part in work-focused interviews and undertake work-related activity (see Chapter 46 or, if you come under the UC system, Chapter 47).

Note: if you are being transferred from IB or SDA to contributory ESA, or from IS on the grounds of disability to income-related ESA (see p672), the work-related activity component is included straight away, as the assessment phase does not apply.

Getting a component before the assessment phase has ended

You are entitled to the support component or the work-related activity component (if you can still get it) before the assessment phase has ended if:[23]

- you have requalified for contributory ESA after having previously lost it because of the rules on how long it can be paid (see p645) and now satisfy the conditions for the support component; or
- you are terminally ill (ie, you have a progressive disease, as a result of which your death can reasonably be expected within six months) and have either claimed ESA on these grounds, or asked for a revision or supersession and have said that you are terminally ill. In this case, you qualify for the support component automatically and it is included straight away; or
- your period of limited capability for work is linked under the 12-week linking rule (see p1021) to an earlier period in which you were entitled to ESA, you were entitled to a component in this earlier claim and it did not end because you were found fit for work – ie, you did not fail the work capability assessment. In this case, the component can be included straight away; or
- your period of limited capability for work is linked under the 12-week linking rule (see p1021) to an earlier period in which you were entitled to ESA, you were entitled to a component or that award lasted 13 weeks or longer, and it ended either because you failed the work capability assessment or before you could be assessed. In this case, you can only get the component again once you have been assessed as passing the work capability assessment, although it is dated from the start of your second award; or
- your ESA entitlement started within 12 weeks of your losing entitlement to IS, when your IS ended it included the disability premium and the sole reason for your losing entitlement to IS was that you are a lone parent and your youngest child no longer met the age rules (see p102).

Deductions for pension payments and councillor's allowance

A deduction is made from your contributory ESA if you receive certain pension payments of over £85 a week and/or if you are a local councillor and your net allowances are more than £120 a week.[24]

Part 5: Other benefits
Chapter 28: Contributory employment and support allowance
4. The amount of benefit

Pension payments taken into account for contributory ESA are periodic payments made under:[25]
- any personal, occupational or public service pension scheme;
- any permanent health insurance policy arranged by your employer that provides payments in connection with ill health or disability after your employment ends. However, if you contributed more than 50 per cent of the pension premiums, the amount you receive from this kind of pension is ignored;
- the Pension Protection Fund and the Financial Assistance scheme.

If the total amount of the gross pension payments you receive is more than £85 a week, your contributory ESA is reduced by half the pension payments above £85.

Other types of pension payments (including one-off, lump-sum payments) are ignored. The following types of payment are also ignored:[26]
- any part of your pension paid directly to an ex-spouse or ex-civil partner by the pension scheme trustees under a court order (although the DWP may not accept this);[27]
- any payments you receive as a result of the death of the pension holder;
- any shortfall in your pension if it cannot be paid in full because the pension scheme is in deficit or has insufficient funds;
- payments under a pension scheme for death as a result of military or war service under section 639(2) of the Income Tax (Earnings and Pensions) Act 2003, or a guaranteed income payment.

Note: if you are transferred from IB to ESA (see p672) and your pension payment was ignored immediately before the transfer, it continues to be ignored in your ESA.[28] This includes if your IB was not reduced because you were entitled to the highest rate of disability living allowance care component, if you were transferred from SDA to long-term IB, and if you were transferred from invalidity benefit to long-term IB.

If you are a local councillor and your net allowances are more than £120 a week, your contributory ESA is reduced by the amount by which the net allowances exceed £120.[29] **Note:** this limit usually increases in October.

Transitional addition

If you have transferred to contributory ESA from IB or SDA, you may be entitled to a transitional addition in your ESA.

When deciding whether you qualify for a transitional addition, the decision maker compares the following amounts.[30]
- The amount of IB or SDA to which you were entitled immediately before the 'effective date'. This is the date on which your IB or SDA was converted into an award of ESA (see p672). Any increases you received in your IB or SDA for an adult or child are included in the amount. However, the adult increase is no

longer included if you no longer satisfy the conditons for getting it, and the child increase is no longer included if you stop getting child benefit for the child. Most deductions made from IB or SDA are ignored.

- The amount of contributory ESA to which you are entitled on the effective date. The work-related activity component or support component is included in the amount.

If the amount of ESA is less than the amount of IB or SDA, you get the difference between the two amounts as a transitional addition, added to your contributory ESA. The transitional addition is reduced by the amount of the annual increase in contributory ESA (ignoring any increase in your housing costs) and by increases in your contributory ESA as a result of changes in your circumstances.

If your entitlement to contributory ESA ends but you requalify for it, the transitional addition can be included again if your new period of limited capability for work can be linked to the old one (see p672).[31]

No transitional addition will be paid after 5 April 2020.

For more details, see p638 of the 2013/14 edition of this *Handbook*.

Duration of contributory employment and support allowance

Contributory ESA is only paid for a maximum of 365 days. However, any time when you have limited capability for work-related activity (p1009) is ignored when calculating the 365 days – ie, time spent in the 'support group'. So, once you have received contributory ESA for a year and have not been entitled to the support component, you lose your entitlement to contributory ESA. You may, however, be entitled to income-related ESA. The following applies.[32]

- Time spent in the assessment phase is taken into account when calculating the 365-day period, except if you were assessed as having limited capability for work-related activity (p1009) and put in the support group.
- If you are appealing about not being in the support group, days when you get ESA while you are appealing are taken into account when calculating the one-year period. This time is then ignored if your appeal is successful.
- If you have been transferred from IB or SDA to contributory ESA, your one-year period is calculated from the date your award was converted to contributory ESA.

You can requalify for contributory ESA again if:[33]

- you remain assessed or treated as having limited capability for work, and you are also assessed as having limited capability for work-related activity for the support component (see p1009); or
- the tax years used to decide whether you satisfy the national insurance (NI) contribution conditions (see p978) include at least one year which is later than the last of the relevant tax years which applied to your previous entitlement,

Part 5: Other benefits
Chapter 28: Contributory employment and support allowance
5. Special benefit rules

and you satisfy the NI contribution conditions again. If you continue to have limited capability for work and still get income-related ESA, under the linking rules (p1021) the tax years remain the same as those that applied to your previous entitlement, so you cannot requalify in this way. However, if you have a break in your ESA entitlement altogether (ie, of both contributory and income-related ESA) of more than 12 weeks, you start a new period of limited capability for work and the linking rules do not apply.[34]

Example

Ravi is aged 24. He has worked since leaving school and has a full NI contribution record, but in July 2016 had to leave his job because of ill health. He gets the standard rate of the daily livng component of personal independence payment. He is not assessed as being in the ESA support group. As Ravi's wife works full time, he is not entitled to any income-related ESA.

ESA during assessment phase = £57.90 (basic allowance for someone aged under 25).

ESA during main phase = £102.15 (basic allowance of £73.10 *plus* work-related activity component of £29.05 because Ravi qualified before it was abolished).

Because Ravi is not in the support group, his award of contributory ESA, which began in July 2016, is limited to one year.

The relevant tax years for the NI contribution conditions are 2013/14 and 2014/15.

After a year of payment, Ravi's contributory ESA stops on 1 July 2017. His condition has not changed and he still does not qualify for the support component. He still has limited capability for work. As his ESA has stopped completely (ie, he is not entitled to income-related ESA either), after 12 weeks Ravi may requalify for contributory ESA. This is because when he makes a new claim for ESA he starts a new period of limited capability for work which does not link to his previous one. One of the relevant tax years that applies to the new claim (2015/16) is later than the years that applied to Ravi's previous claim. However, he must still satisfy the NI contribution conditions again using the new relevant tax years.

5. **Special benefit rules**

Special rules may apply to:
- people subject to immigration control (employment and support allowance in youth only) (see Chapter 65);
- people going abroad (see Chapters 67 and 68);
- people in prison or detention (see Chapter 41).

6. Claims and backdating

The general rules about claims and backdating are covered in Chapter 49. This section explains the specific rules that apply to both contributory and income-related employment and support allowance (ESA).

In most cases, you must attend a medical examination to assess whether you have limited capability for work (p1003) or limited capability for work-related activity (p1009). Also, unless you are in the 'support group' (see p641), you are usually required to attend compulsory work-focused interviews and, in some cases, carry out work-related activity (see p1064).

If you are appealing against a decision that you do not have limited capablity for work, you do not need to make a claim for ESA in order to get ESA pending your appeal, although you must submit a medical certificate.[35] For when ESA can be paid pending an appeal, see p1017.

Note: if you are refused contributory ESA because you do not meet the national insurance (NI) contribution conditions, in some cases it may be worth claiming at a later date that falls in a different benefit year (see p978).

Making a claim

Contributory and income-related ESA are two types of the same benefit. When you claim ESA, in order for the DWP to assess your entitlement to both types, it is important to answer all the relevant questions and provide all the necessary information.

A claim for ESA can be made:[36]
- by telephone. This is the way the DWP prefers you to claim. Telephone a Jobcentre Plus contact centre (Monday–Friday, 8am–6pm, tel: 0800 055 6688; Welsh language: 0800 012 1888; textphone: 0800 023 4888); *or*
- in writing by completing the approved claim form. A form can be downloaded from www.gov.uk/government/publications/employment-and-support-allowance-claim-form. Send the completed form to your local Jobcentre Plus office. If the DWP has arranged for a local authority to receive claims for ESA, you can also send it to the local authority housing benefit office.

Note: you do not have to start your claim by telephone, but it is best to make your claim in the way the DWP prefers if you can. If you claim in writing, keep a copy of your claim form in case queries arise. The DWP intends to introduce online claims at some point.

You must provide any information or evidence required (see p649). You can amend or withdraw your claim before a decision is made (see p1149). If there is a delay in deciding your claim, you may be able to get a short-term advance of benefit (see p1177).

Part 5: Other benefits
Chapter 28: Contributory employment and support allowance
6. Claims and backdating

Forms

The approved claim form is Form ESA1. Get this from www.gov.uk/government/
publications/employment-and-support-allowance-claim-form, your local Jobcentre Plus
office or telephone contact centre.

If you come under the universal credit system

If you come under the universal credit (UC) system (see p20), a claim for ESA is a
claim for contributory ESA only. You must claim UC instead of income-related
ESA. You may have difficulty claiming contributory ESA (the DWP sometimes
calls this 'new style' ESA), as the online UC claim form does not specifically refer
to it, and some UC work coaches and jobcentre staff have wrongly said that you
cannot get any sort of ESA under the UC system. The DWP has issued guidance,
setting out how it prefers you to claim.[37]

- Check www.gov.uk/guidance/jobcentres-where-you-can-claim-universal-credit
  to see whether you live in a UC 'full service' area. These are listed with an
  asterisk. If so, telephone 0345 600 4272 (textphone: 0345 600 0743).
- If you do not live in a UC 'full service' area, make your claim by phoning the
  UC service centre on 0345 600 0723 (textphone: 0345 600 0743).
- Say that you wish to claim 'new style' contributory ESA.
- You should be sent Form ESA1(UC), usually by email.
- An appointment should also be arranged for you at your local Jobcentre Plus
  office. Take your completed ESA1(UC) claim form and proof of identity with
  you.

If you cannot claim in this way, tell your UC work coach at the jobcentre that you
want to claim 'new style' ESA and that you need Form ESA1(UC).

Who should claim

You claim contributory ESA on your own behalf. However, if you are unable to
manage your own affairs, another person can claim ESA for you as your
'appointee' (see p1149).

If you are employed

If you are employed, you should normally be paid statutory sick pay (SSP – see
Chapter 38) for the first 28 weeks of your limited capability for work. If your
employer thinks that you are not entitled to SSP, or if your entitlement to SSP has
run out, it should complete and give you Form SSP1 and you should claim ESA.
You are normally expected to include Form SSP1 and a medical certificate with
your claim. If your employer refuses you SSP on the grounds that you are not
entitled to it, your claim for ESA can be backdated to the date of your SSP claim
(see p650). If you disagree with your employer's decision not to pay SSP, you can

refer the matter to HM Revenue and Customs (HMRC – see Chapter 57), but do not delay claiming ESA. If you have asked HMRC to decide whether you are entitled to SSP, tell the DWP this when you claim ESA.

Information to support your claim

For the general information requirements that apply to all benefits, see p1150.

It is important that you provide any information required when you claim. Until you do, you may not count as having made a valid claim (see p1152). Correct any defects as soon as possible or your date of claim may be affected.

For the first seven days of your limited capability for work, the DWP should accept a self-certificate as medical evidence. After seven days, you must provide a medical certificate from your doctor. If it is unreasonable to expect you to provide this, the DWP can accept other evidence if that is sufficient.[38]

You may be referred by the DWP for a medical assessment. If you do not attend the medical without good cause, your claim can be refused.[39]

Even if you have provided all that was required when you claimed, you may be asked to provide further evidence to support your claim (see p1154). You may also be asked to provide information after you are awarded ESA and, if you fail to do so, your ESA could be suspended, or even terminated (see p1185).

The date of your claim

The date of your claim is important as it determines when your entitlement to ESA starts (subject to the rules on waiting days – see p639). This is not necessarily the date from when you are paid. For information about when payment of ESA starts, see p650.

Unless it is backdated (see p650), the 'date of your claim' is usually the date of your telephone call, or the date your claim form is received at a DWP office (or a local authority office – see p647).[40] However, if you notify the DWP that you intend to send a claim form and you send a properly completed form within one month, your date of claim is the date you notified the DWP that you intended to claim.

There is an exception if you claim UC in a UC 'gateway' area and, on the basis of information you provided, you are treated as satisfying the gateway conditions, but the DWP discovers that the information was incorrect. Unless you have already been paid UC, you should be advised by the DWP that you are not entitled to claim UC. If you then claim ESA within a month of being told this and if (taking into account any backdating you have requested and been allowed) your claim is later than the date of your UC claim, your ESA claim is treated as made on the date of your UC claim, or a later date if you would have been entitled from that later date.[41]

Note: you must make sure your claim is valid. If it is 'defective', you are given a short time to correct the defects (see p1152). If you do, your claim is treated as having been made when you initially claimed.[42]

In some cases, you can claim in advance (see below) and in some cases your claim can be backdated (see below). If you want this to be done, make this clear when you claim or the DWP might not consider it. If you claimed SSP or maternity allowance (MA) when you should have claimed ESA, see below.

Backdating your claim

Your claim can be backdated for up to three months before the day you actually claim – ie, for time during this period when you were entitled to ESA. You should state from which date you are claiming in that period and ask for it to be backdated. You do not need special reasons for backdating.[43]

If you claim the wrong benefit

If your employer has decided that you are not entitled to SSP and you claim ESA within three months of being notified in writing of this, your ESA claim is treated as having been made on the date of your SSP claim.[44]

A claim for MA can be treated as a claim for ESA and vice versa.[45] If your MA claim is accepted as a claim for ESA, your ESA can be backdated for up to three months before the date you claimed MA if you satisfy the qualifying conditions during that period (see p1161).

If you claimed UC when you should have claimed ESA, see p649 to see whether your date of claim can be backdated.

Claiming in advance

You can claim ESA up to three months before the date on which you qualify for it.[46] The date of your claim is the date on which you qualify.

Starting work when your claim ends

If you start work, you may be able to benefit from the rules for linking periods of limited capability for work should you fall sick again later (see p1021). If this is the case, provided you claim ESA again within a 12-week linking period, you get the same amount of ESA that you previously received.

---

7. Getting paid

Note: this section applies to both contributory and income-related employment and support allowance (ESA).

The general rules on getting paid are covered in Chapter 50. This section explains the specific rules that apply to ESA.

When is employment and support allowance paid?

The day you are paid depends on your national insurance number (see p1174).[47] ESA is usually paid fortnightly in arrears, although it can be paid at different intervals, including at a daily rate of one-seventh of the weekly amount.[48]

ESA is a weekly benefit, although in some cases it can be paid for a part-week.[49]

Note:
- Your contributory ESA might be paid at a reduced rate in some circumstances (see p639).
- Deductions can be made from your ESA to pay to third parties (see p1187).
- You might not be paid ESA, or it might be paid at a reduced rate, if you have been sanctioned for a benefit offence (see p1265). **Note:** you may also be sanctioned for other reasons (see Chapter 48).
- For information on missing payments, see p1174. If you cannot get your ESA payments because you have lost your bank or Post Office card or you have forgotten your PIN, see p1173. If you have lost your 'simple payment' card, or you have forgotten your memorable date, see p1173.
- If payment of your ESA is delayed, see p1165. If you are waiting for a decision on your claim, or to be paid, you might be able to get a short-term advance (see p1177). If you wish to complain about how your claim has been dealt with, or claim compensation, see Chapter 58.
- If payment of your ESA is suspended, see p1185. This includes if you have failed to supply evidence of your limited capability for work.
- If you are overpaid ESA, you might have to repay it (see Chapter 52) and, in some circumstances, you may have to pay a penalty (see p1256). If you have been accused of fraud, see Chapter 53.

Change of circumstances

You must report changes in your circumstances that you have been told you must report, as well as any that you might reasonably be expected to know might affect your right to, the amount of, or the payment of your benefit. You should do this as soon as possible, preferably in writing. See p1184 for further information.

Your ESA is usually adjusted from the beginning of the week in which the change of circumstances takes effect.[50] However, there are exceptions – eg, if you have notified the DWP that you are terminally ill or if you have failed to notify it of a change about your limited capability for work (see p1292).[51]

Part 5: Other benefits
Chapter 28: Contributory employment and support allowance
8. Tax, other benefits and the benefit cap

8. Tax, other benefits and the benefit cap

Tax

Contributory employment and support allowance (ESA), including ESA in youth, is taxable.[52] If you have been transferred from incapacity benefit (IB) or severe disablement allowance (SDA) to contributory ESA (see p672), your contributory ESA is still taxable, even if your IB/SDA was not. This includes any contributory ESA paid as a transitional addition.[53]

Means-tested benefits and tax credits

Your contributory ESA counts as income for the purposes of means-tested benefits if you do not get income-related ESA. If you are getting contributory ESA, you may also be entitled to income-related ESA to top this up or, if you are at least the qualifying age for pension credit (PC), to PC to top this up. If you come under the universal credit (UC) system (see p20), you may be entitled to UC to top up your contributory ESA.

You cannot claim ESA and income support (IS) in your own right at the same time.[54] If it is possible for you to claim either ESA or IS (eg, if you are also a lone parent or a carer), you must decide which benefit to claim. Get advice about this, as it affects the amount of benefit you get and the sort of work-focused interviews you must attend.

You cannot claim ESA and income-related jobseeker's allowance (JSA) in your own right, including as part of a joint-claim couple, at the same time. However you can get contributory ESA if you are part of a JSA joint-claim couple and you do not have to satisfy all the JSA conditions (see p121).[55] If your partner is entitled in her/his own right to income-based JSA (and it is not joint-claim JSA – eg, because you have a dependent child), you can get contributory ESA at the same time.

You can get ESA and housing benefit (HB) at the same time. You may be entitled to an additional component as part of your HB (see p250). If you are transferred from IB or SDA to contributory ESA (see p672) and do not get income-related ESA, you may get a transitional addition in your HB (see p672).

If you have a partner and s/he works sufficient hours, you and your partner may be able to claim working tax credit (WTC). ESA counts as a 'qualifying benefit' for the disability element of WTC (see p1412). If you have children, you may be able to claim child tax credit.

Non-means-tested benefits

While you are on contributory ESA, you may be entitled to national insurance credits (see p965).

Contributory ESA is affected by the rules on overlapping benefits (see p1175), which means that you may not be paid it in full if another earnings-replacement benefit is paid to you.

You are not entitled to ESA if you are entitled to statutory sick pay.[56] You can still get contributory ESA if you get statutory maternity pay (SMP), statutory adoption pay (SAP) or statutory paternity pay (SPP). You can get contributory ESA and statutory shared parental pay (SSPP) if the amount of the SSPP is less than the amount of ESA. Your ESA is reduced by the amount of the SMP, SAP or SSPP you get.[57]

You cannot claim ESA and contribution-based JSA in your own right at the same time. If your partner is entitled to contribution-based JSA, you can claim ESA.

The benefit cap

In some cases, there is a limit on the total amount of specified benefits you can receive (a 'benefit cap'). ESA is one of the specified benefits. However, the benefit cap does not apply if you or your partner receive ESA which includes a support component. In other cases, it only applies if you are getting HB or UC. See p1180 for further information.

Passports and other sources of help

If you receive contributory ESA, you may be eligible for a Christmas bonus (see p863).

You may also qualify for health benefits such as free prescriptions (see Chapter 29), and education benefits such as free school lunches (see p860).

You may be entitled to council tax reduction (see p854).

Financial help on starting work

If you stop getting contributory ESA because you start work, you may be able to get extended payments of HB if you pay rent (see p86). Your local authority may provide extended help with council tax. See p866 for information about other financial help you may get.

Notes

1. **Who can claim employment and support allowance**
   1 ss1 and 20(1) WRA 2007; reg 40(1) and (7) ESA Regs; reg 37(1) and (8) ESA Regs 2013
   2 s62 WRA 2012 (not yet in force)

   3 Sch 1 paras 1-4 WRA 2007
   4 s53 WRA 2012; s1(3A) WRA 2007
   5 s52 WRA 2012
   6 s18 WRA 2007; reg 157 ESA Regs; reg 93 ESA Regs 2013

7   Regs 157(3) and 158 ESA Regs; reg 94
    ESA Regs 2013
8   Sch 5 para 14 ESA Regs; reg 63 ESA Regs
    2013

4. The amount of benefit

9   Reg 144 ESA Regs; reg 85 ESA Regs
    2013
10 s24(2) WRA 2007; reg 4 ESA Regs; reg 5
    ESA Regs 2013
11 Reg 7(38) SS&CS(DA) Regs; reg 35(7)
    UC,PIP,JSA&ESA(DA) Regs
12 Regs 4, 5 and 147A ESA Regs; regs 5, 6
    and 87 ESA Regs 2013
13 Reg 5 ESA Regs; reg 6 ESA Regs 2013
14 s2(1)(a) WRA 2007; regs 7 and 67(2)
    and Sch 4 para 1(1)(b) and (c) ESA Regs;
    regs 7 and 62(1) ESA Regs 2013
15 s2(2) and (3) WRA 2007; reg 67(2) and
    (3) and Sch 4 paras 1(a), 12 and 13 ESA
    Regs; Sch 2 para 12 ESA(TP)(EA)(No.2)
    Regs
16 ss2(2) and 4(4) WRA 2007
17 *PM v SSWP (ESA)* [2012] UKUT 188
    (AAC)
18 Reg 54 ESA Regs; ss11 and 11D WRA
    2007
19 s15 WRWA 2016
20 Sch 1 Part 1 ESAUC(MA) Regs
21 Reg 2 IS Regs; reg 1 JSA Regs; reg 1 SPC
    Regs; reg 2 HB Regs; reg 2 HB(SPC)
    Regs; reg 1 SFCWP Regs
22 ss2(3) and 4(5) WRA 2007
23 Reg 7 ESA Regs; reg 7 ESA Regs 2013
24 Regs 72-79 ESA Regs; regs 64-72 ESA
    Regs 2013
25 s3 WRA 2007; regs 72, 72A and 74 ESA
    Regs; regs 64, 65 and 67 ESA Regs 2013
26 Reg 75 ESA Regs; reg 68 ESA Regs 2013
27 R(IB) 1/04 applied this to IB, but it is not
    followed by the DWP for ESA
28 Schs 1 para 11 and 2 para 14
    ESA(TP)(EA)(No.2) Regs
29 Regs 76(1), 79 and 94(1) ESA Regs; regs
    69, 72 and 79 ESA Regs 2013
30 Regs 9, 10, 12 and 13
    ESA(TP)(EA)(No.2) Regs
31 Reg 16 ESA(TP)(EA)(No.2) Regs
32 ss51 and 52 WRA 2012; ss1A and 1B
    WRA 2007
33 ss1A and 1B WRA 2007
34 Vol 8 Ch 41, para 41847 DMG

6. Claims and backdating

35 Reg 3(j) SS(C&P) Regs; reg 7 ESA Regs
    2013
36 Regs 4G and 4H SS(C&P) Regs; regs 13
    and 15 ESA Regs 2013

37 www.gov.uk/guidance/new-style-
    employment-and-support-allowance
38 Regs 2 and 5 SS(ME) Regs
39 s19 SSA 1998; reg 23 ESA Regs
40 Reg 6(1F) SS(C&P) Regs; regs 14 and 16
    UC,PIP,JSA&ESA(C&P) Regs
41 Art 3A WRA(No.9)O
42 Regs 4G(5) and 4H(6) and (7) SS(C&P)
    Regs; regs 13(5) and 15(4)
    UC,PIP,JSA&ESA(C&P) Regs
43 Reg 19 and Sch 4 para 16 SS(C&P) Regs;
    reg 28 UC,PIP,JSA&ESA(C&P) Regs
44 Reg 10(1A) SS(C&P) Regs; reg 17
    UC,PIP,JSA&ESA(C&P) Regs
45 Reg 9 and Sch 1 SS(C&P) Regs; reg 25
    UC,PIP,JSA&ESA(C&P) Regs
46 Reg 13(9) SS(C&P) Regs; reg 34
    UC,PIP,JSA&ESA(C&P) Regs

7. Getting paid

47 Reg 26C(2) SS(C&P) Regs; reg 51
    UC,PIP,JSA&ESA(C&P) Regs
48 Reg 26C SS(C&P) Regs; reg 51(5)
    UC,PIP,JSA&ESA(C&P) Regs
49 Vol 8 Ch 46, para 46011 DMG
50 Reg 7(2)(a) and Sch 3C SS&CS(DA)
    Regs; reg 35 and Sch 1 para 1
    UC,PIP,JSA&ESA(C&P) Regs
51 Reg 7(2) and (25) and Sch 3C
    SS&CS(DA) Regs; reg 35 and Sch 1
    paras 6 and 9 UC,PIP,JSA&ESA(C&P)
    Regs

8. Tax, other benefits and the benefit cap

52 ss658(4) and 661(1) IT(EP)A 2003
53 Sch 2 para 6A ESA(TP)(EA)(No.2) Regs
54 s1(3)(e) WRA 2007
55 s1(3)(f) WRA 2007
56 s20 WRA 2007
57 Regs 80-82A ESA Regs; regs 73-75 ESA
    Regs 2013

Chapter 29

Health benefits

This chapter covers:
1. Who can claim health benefits (below)
2. Prescriptions (p661)
3. Dental treatment and dentures (p662)
4. Sight tests and glasses (p662)
5. Wigs and fabric supports (p663)
6. Fares to receive NHS treatment (p664)
7. Claims and refunds (p665)

Key facts
- Health benefits provide help with the costs of NHS prescriptions, dental treatment, sight tests and glasses, and wigs and fabric supports, as well as fares to receive NHS treatment.
- Some people are exempt from charges and can get full help with NHS costs and fares. Others qualify for full or partial help in specific situations or if their income and capital are under a certain amount.
- Health benefits are administered by the NHS Business Services Authority.

1. Who can claim health benefits

Although the NHS generally provides free healthcare, there are fixed charges for some items and services such as prescriptions, dental treatment, sight tests and glasses, and wigs and fabric supports. You may also have fares to pay to get to hospital or another establishment for NHS treatment. However, you may qualify for full help with the charges and fares (ie, you may get the items or services free of charge) or you may get partial help.

In some cases, you must make a claim (see p665). If you pay for an item or service that you could have received free, or at a reduced cost, you can apply for a refund (see p667).

Full help

You qualify for full help with charges and fares if you:
- are in an exempt group (see p656); *or*

- satisfy specific conditions, depending on the item or service. See p661 for prescriptions, p662 for dental treatment and dentures, p662 for sight tests and glasses, p663 for wigs and fabric supports and p664 for fares to receive NHS treatment; *or*
- qualify under the low income scheme (see p657).

Exempt groups

You qualify for full help with charges and fares if you are in an exempt group. You are in an exempt group if:[1]

- you, or a member of your family (see p657 for who counts) receive any of the following qualifying benefits:
  - income support (IS), income-based jobseeker's allowance (JSA), income-related employment and support allowance (ESA) or the guarantee credit of pension credit (PC); *or*
  - child tax credit (CTC), or both CTC and working tax credit (WTC), or WTC that includes a disabled worker or severe disability element. Your gross annual income for tax credits must not exceed £15,276;
  - universal credit (UC). You must either have no earnings or you (in England and Wales, you and your partner) must earn £435 or less a month (if your UC does not include a child, limited capability for work or limited capability for work-related activity element), or £935 a month or less (if your UC includes one or more of these elements). The higher earnings threshold applies if you (or your partner in a joint UC claim) are assessed as having limited capability for work but the limited capability for work element is not included in your UC because it has been abolished (see p260);
- you, or a member of your family, are an asylum seeker who is receiving asylum support (see p1526). Dependants for whom you are claiming asylum support count as members of your family;
- you are aged 16 or 17 and are receiving support from a local authority after being looked after (in Scotland, receiving support under section 29(1) of the Children (Scotland) Act 1995 after leaving care). This does not appear to apply for sight tests in England and Wales or for vouchers for glasses and contact lenses in England.

Even if you are not in one of the exempt groups, note the following.

- If you are a war disablement pensioner, you may qualify for free prescriptions and wigs and fabric supports. You may also be able to claim money back for dental treatment, fares to hospital, sight tests, glasses or contact lenses. You must have a valid war pension exemption certificate, and you must need the items or treatment, or to travel, because of your war disability. See p665 for where to claim.
- If you are a hospital inpatient, all medication and NHS treatment is provided free of charge (including glasses and contact lenses if prescribed through the

Hospital Eye Service). If you are an outpatient or are at a walk-in centre, medication taken and treatment given while you are in the hospital or walk-in centre is also provided without charge (but you may be charged for dentures and bridges).

Member of the family

'**Family**' means you and your partner and any child or qualifying young person included in your claim for the qualifying benefit or tax credit (see p220 for means-tested benefits and p182 for tax credits).

Partial help

If you do not qualify for full help with charges and fares, you may still qualify for partial help under the low income scheme (see below).

The low income scheme

You and members of your family (see above for who counts) may be entitled to full or partial help with NHS charges under the low income scheme, even if you do not qualify on other grounds. You must make a claim (see p665). The low income scheme is administered by the NHS Business Services Authority (see Appendix 1).

You (and members of your family) qualify for full help under the low income scheme if:

- you have capital of less than £16,000 (or if you live permanently in a care home, less than £23,250 in England and Scotland, or £24,000 in Wales).[2] Your capital is calculated as for IS (see Chapter 17); *and*
- your income (see p660) does not exceed your 'requirements' (see p658) by more than 50 per cent of the current cost of an English prescription (currently 50 per cent of £8.20 = £4.10).[3] If your income exceeds your requirements by more than this amount, see below to find out whether you qualify for partial help with charges.

Partial help with items and services

If you do not qualify for full help with NHS charges, you (and members of your family) may qualify for partial help with these under the low income scheme. You may qualify for:[4]

- reduced-cost dental treatment (including check-ups) and appliances (including dentures); *and*

- reduced-cost sight tests. There is no set charge for sight tests, so it is worth shopping around if you are not entitled to a free test; *and*
- vouchers towards the cost of glasses and contact lenses; *and*
- in England, reduced-cost wigs and fabric supports (these are free in Wales and Scotland); *and*
- partial help with fares to receive NHS treatment.

Note: in England, you cannot qualify for reduced-cost prescriptions under the low income scheme, only free prescriptions. If you cannot qualify for free prescriptions, see p661 for information about prepayment certificates. In Wales and Scotland, prescriptions are free of charge.

You are expected to pay up to a set amount towards the charges. The set amount is:[5]

- for dental charges and charges for wigs and fabric supports, three times the amount by which your income exceeds your requirements (your 'excess income');
- for glasses or lenses, twice the amount of your excess income;
- for a sight test or fares to receive NHS treatment, the amount of your excess income.

Example

Martin's income exceeds his requirements by £6 so he cannot qualify for full help under the low income scheme. However, he may get partial help. He has to pay the first £18 of dental charges and charges for wigs and fabric supports, the first £6 of the cost of a sight test, the first £12 towards the cost of glasses and lenses and the first £6 of his fares to receive NHS treatment. If he lives in England, he must pay the full cost of prescriptions.

Calculating your requirements

Your 'requirements' are similar to the IS 'applicable amount' (see Chapter 12). The most significant elements and differences are set out p659. There are no reductions in the applicable amounts of people who are subject to immigration control or who are not habitually resident in the UK, or for students, people engaged in a trade dispute or people without accommodation.

Your requirements are made up of the following elements.[6]

- **Personal allowance(s):**

Single person aged under 25	£57.90
Single person aged under 25, entitled to ESA work-related activity or support component, or incapable of work for at least 28 weeks starting on or after 27 October 2008	£73.10
Single person aged 25–59 or lone parent aged under 60	£73.10
Single person or lone parent aged 60 or over	£155.60
Couples, both partners aged under 60	£114.85
Couples, one or both partners aged 60 or over	£237.55

- **Premiums:** the disability, enhanced disability, severe disability and carer premiums are added to your requirements if you would qualify for them under the IS rules (see p236).

  A disability premium can also be included if you or your partner have been incapable of work for 28 weeks. It can also be included if you (or your partner) have been awarded ESA which includes a work-related activity or support component, or if you (or s/he) have been getting ESA for at least 28 weeks. You (and your partner) must be under 60.

  If you are a single claimant or a lone parent, the amount of the disability premium is increased to £36.20 if you qualify for an ESA support component or if you are getting the middle or highest rate care component of disability living allowance (DLA), either rate of the daily living component of personal independence payment (PIP) or armed forces independence payment, and have been getting ESA or have been incapable of work, for at least 28 weeks.

  An enhanced disability premium can be included if you (or your partner) are getting the DLA highest rate care component, the enhanced rate of the daily living component of PIP, armed forces independence payment or ESA which includes a support component. You (and your partner) must be under 60.

- **Weekly council tax.**
- **Weekly rent** *less* **any housing benefit** (HB) and any non-dependant deductions, applied broadly in the same way as the deductions under the rules on IS housing costs (see p464). Deductions for fuel and ineligible service charges are made in accordance with the HB rules.
- **Weekly mortgage interest and capital payments on loans** secured on a home, to buy a home or to adapt a home for the special needs of a disabled person, and payments on an endowment policy relating to the purchase of a home. Some other housing costs can be included. Deductions are made for non-dependants.

If you live permanently in a care home, your requirements are your weekly accommodation charge, including meals and services, and a personal expenses allowance. If your place is being funded by a local authority (fully or in part), you are exempt from some charges.

Calculating your income

Your income is calculated as for IS (see Chapter 14), with modifications. These include the following.[7]

- Your income is normally taken into account in the week in which it is paid. If you are affected by a trade dispute, your normal earnings are taken into account.

- You are entitled to an earnings disregard of £20 if you would qualify for a disability premium (see p238), or if you or your partner are aged 60 or over.

- If you (or your partner) are doing permitted work while claiming ESA (see p1023), the amount of earnings that can be disregarded is the same as for income-related ESA (see p278). If you *and* your partner are both doing permitted work, the disregard is applied to your joint income.

- The full amount of your (or your partner's) contributory ESA is taken into account, even if it is paid at a reduced rate because you failed to take part in a work-focused interview. This does not appear to apply if you come under the UC system (see p20).

- Regular liable relative payments (see p287) count as weekly income. Irregular payments are averaged over the 13 weeks prior to your claim. Lump-sum payments are treated as capital.

- Student loans and grants are divided by 52, unless you are in your final year or are doing a one-year course, in which case the loan is divided by the number of weeks you are studying. The £10 disregard from student loans only applies if you are eligible for a premium, you receive an allowance because of deafness, or you are not a student but your partner is. In addition, in England and Wales, sums in excess of a specified amount of a maintenance grant and certain loans paid to Scottish students studying in England or Wales are disregarded. Also, if a voluntary payment is taken into account, up to £20 of it is disregarded.

- Insurance policy payments for housing costs that cannot be met by IS count as income, but payments for unsecured loans for repairs and improvements (including premiums) are ignored.

- If you live permanently in residential or nursing care:
  – in Wales, no tariff income from any capital is taken into account;
  – in England and Scotland, the lower threshold for tariff income is £14,250. Remember that if your place is being funded by a local authority (in full or in part), you are exempt from some charges.

- The savings credit of PC is ignored as income.

2. Prescriptions

Prescriptions are free in Scotland and Wales. You qualify for free prescriptions in England (and you can get an English prescription free of charge in Scotland and Wales) if:[8]

- you are in one of the exempt groups listed on p656; *or*
- you qualify under the low income scheme (see p657); *or*
- you are aged 60 or over; *or*
- you are aged under 16, or you are under 19 and in full-time education; *or*
- you are pregnant or have given birth in the last 12 months; *or*
- you are a permanent resident in a care home and your place is being partly or wholly funded by a local authority; *or*
- you have:
  - a continuing physical disability, which prevents you leaving your home except with the help of another person;
  - epilepsy requiring continuous anti-convulsive therapy;
  - a permanent fistula, including a caecostomy, ileostomy, laryngostomy or colostomy, needing continuous surgical dressing or an appliance;
  - diabetes mellitus (except where treatment is by diet alone);
  - diabetes insipidus and other forms of hypopituitarism;
  - myxoedema;
  - hypoparathyroidism;
  - forms of hypoadrenalism (including Addison's disease), for which specific substitution therapy is essential;
  - myasthenia gravis;
  - a sexually transmitted disease; *or*
- you are prescribed or given specific medicines in respect of a pandemic disease; *or*
- you are undergoing treatment for cancer, the effects of cancer or the effects of cancer treatment; *or*
- you are in prison or a young offenders' institution or other secure accommodation (or were given the prescription while you were); *or*
- you are detained under the Immigration Act 1971 or section 62 of the Nationality, Immigration and Asylum Act 2002.

Prepayment certificates

In England, if you are not exempt from charges and you need more than three prescription items in three months or 12 items in a year, you can save money by buying a prepayment certificate.

Apply online, by post, by telephone or at a registered chemist on Form FP95, which you can get from chemists, some surgeries and relevant health bodies. You can also get the form from www.nhsbsa.nhs.uk/HealthCosts/2131.aspxor

telephone: 0300 330 1341. You can pay by credit or debit card or in monthly instalments by direct debit.

A refund can be claimed in certain circumstances – eg, if you buy a prepayment certificate and then qualify for free prescriptions.

3. **Dental treatment and dentures**

NHS dental check-ups are free in Scotland. In England, Wales and Scotland, you qualify for free NHS dental treatment (including check-ups) and appliances (including dentures) if, when your treatment is arranged or charges are made:[9]

- you are in one of the exempt groups listed on p656; *or*
- you qualify under the low income scheme (see p657); *or*
- you are under 18, or you are under 19 and in full-time education; *or*
- in Wales, for free check-ups only, you are under 25 or are 60 or over; *or*
- you are pregnant or have given birth within the last 12 months; *or*
- you are a permanent resident in a care home and your place is being partly or wholly funded by a local authority; *or*
- in England and Wales, you are in prison or a young offenders' institution; *or*
- you are a patient of the Community Dental Service (available if you have difficulty getting treatment because of a disability or for other reasons – contact your health authority for details) or an NHS hospital dental service. **Note:** there may be a charge for dentures and bridges.

4. **Sight tests and glasses**

Free sight tests

NHS sight tests are free in Scotland. In England and Wales you qualify for a free NHS sight test if:[10]

- you are in one of the exempt groups listed on p656; *or*
- you qualify under the low income scheme (see p657); *or*
- you are aged 60 or over; *or*
- you are under 16, or you are under 19 and in full-time education; *or*
- you are registered blind or partially sighted; *or*
- you have been prescribed complex or powerful lenses; *or*
- you have been diagnosed as having diabetes or glaucoma or are at risk of getting glaucoma; *or*
- you are aged 40 or over and are the parent, brother, sister or child of someone with glaucoma; *or*
- you are a patient of the Hospital Eye Service; *or*
- in England, you are on leave from prison or a young offenders' institution.

Vouchers for glasses and contact lenses

If you are given a prescription for glasses following an eye test, you may be entitled to a voucher that you can use to buy glasses or contact lenses if you need these for the first time, or because your previous ones have worn out through fair wear and tear, or your new prescription differs from your old one. You qualify if:[11]
- you are in one of the exempt groups listed on p656; *or*
- you qualify under the low income scheme (see p657); *or*
- you are under 16, or under 19 and in full-time education; *or*
- you are a Hospital Eye Service patient needing frequent changes of glasses or contact lenses; *or*
- in England, you are on leave from prison or a young offenders' institution; *or*
- you have been prescribed complex or powerful lenses.

In addition, you may be entitled to a voucher when your glasses or lenses need to be replaced or repaired if, because of illness (illness or disability in Scotland), you have lost or damaged them and the cost of repair or replacement is not covered by insurance or warranty. This only applies if:[12]
- you are under 16, or under 19 and in full-time education. **Note:** the requirement for the loss or damage to have been caused by illness (illness or disability in Scotland) does not apply to children under 16 and, in England, to young people under 18 who were previously looked after by a local authority);[13] *or*
- you or a member of your family (see p657 for who counts) are covered by the first bullet point listed under 'Exempt groups' on p656; *or*
- you qualify under the low income scheme (see p657); *or*
- you have been prescribed complex or powerful lenses.

You can redeem the voucher at any supplier when you buy your glasses or contact lenses (or have glasses repaired). Vouchers are, however, only valid for two years.[14] Vouchers might not cover the full cost of the glasses or lenses you choose to buy. Prices vary; you may need to shop around if you do not want to pay the extra cost.

5. **Wigs and fabric supports**

Wigs and fabric supports are free in Scotland and Wales. You qualify for free wigs and fabric supports in England if:[15]
- you are in one of the exempt groups listed on p656; *or*
- you qualify under the low income scheme (see p657); *or*
- you are a hospital inpatient; *or*
- you are aged under 16, or under 19 and in full-time education; *or*

- you are a permanent resident in a care home and your place is being partly or wholly funded by a local authority; *or*
- you are in prison or a young offenders' institution or are detained under the Immigration Act 1971 or section 62 of the Nationality, Immigration and Asylum Act 2002.

6. **Fares to receive NHS treatment**

You qualify for full help with your fares to attend a hospital or any other establishment for NHS treatment or services if:[16]
- you are in one of the exempt groups listed on p656; *or*
- you qualify under the low income scheme (see p657); *or*
- you are a permanent resident in a care home and your place is being partly or wholly funded by a local authority; *or*
- you live in the Isles of Scilly or the Scottish Islands or Highlands and have to travel more than a specified distance. Special rules, including maximum costs, apply.[17]

The travel expenses of a companion can also be covered – eg, if your child is attending a hospital and you need to accompany her/him, or if you need to be accompanied for medical reasons. You get help with the cost of travelling by the cheapest means of transport that is reasonable and, in Scotland, if necessary, the cost of overnight accommodation. This usually means standard-class public transport. If you have to travel by car or taxi, you should be paid a mileage allowance and road and toll charges, or taxi fares.

Claim at the place where you receive NHS treatment. You may be able to request payment in advance of travelling if this is necessary.

Travel expenses can be covered if you are travelling abroad to receive NHS treatment if the means and cost of travel, as well as any requirements for a companion, have been agreed in advance with the health service body that has arranged the treatment. In England and Wales, you are entitled to payment for the cost of travel to and from the airport, ferry port or international train station if you are in one of the above groups. You are also entitled to payment or repayment of onward travelling expenses to the treatment centre, whether or not you come into one of the above groups. In Scotland, the rules do not specify what can be covered.

7. **Claims and refunds**

In some situations, you do not have to make a claim for help with charges.

- If you are exempt on the grounds of your age, receipt of a qualifying benefit or because you are a full-time student under 19, complete the back of the prescription form (if required), or complete the appropriate form at your dentist, optician or hospital.
- If you are an asylum seeker receiving asylum support, an HC2 certificate is issued by the Home Office. For further advice, telephone Asylum Help on 0808 800 0630.
- You need an exemption certificate (which you should be sent automatically) if you are exempt because you receive tax credits. This could be up to eight weeks after you are awarded tax credits. If you have not yet received your exemption certificate, sign the prescription form, or other appropriate form, to say you do not have to pay, and use your tax credits award notice as proof.
- If you are exempt because you are pregnant or have given birth in the last 12 months, you need an exemption certificate. Obtain one by completing a form, which you can get from your doctor, midwife or health visitor.
- If you are entitled to free prescriptions because you have one of the conditions listed on p661 or you are undergoing treatment for cancer, the effects of cancer or the effects of cancer treatment, you need an exemption certificate. Apply on Form FP92A, which you can get from your doctor, hospital or pharmacist.

In other cases, you must make a claim. **Note:** if you are a war disablement pensioner, contact the Treatment Group, Veterans UK, Ministry of Defence, Norcross, Thornton Cleveleys FY5 3WP, telephone 0808 191 4218.

Claiming under the low income scheme

To get full or partial help with charges and fares under the low income scheme, you must make a claim. This includes if you are an asylum seeker, but you are not receiving asylum support. If you *are* receiving asylum support, see above. This also includes if you are exempt because you live in a care home or you are aged 16 or 17 and were previously looked after by a local authority.

Claim on Form HC1, available from Jobcentre Plus offices or NHS hospitals, some chemists, GP practices, dentists, opticians or advice centres. At www.nhsbsa.nhs.uk you can request that a form be sent to you (in England only) or, in Scotland, you can download it. You can also get a form by telephoning 0300 330 1343 (England), 0131 275 6386 (Scotland) or 0845 603 1108 (Wales). Another person can apply on your behalf if you are unable to act for yourself.

If you live in a care home or you are aged 16 or 17 and were previously looked after by a local authority, you can use a shorter Form HC1(SC).

Getting a certificate and when it expires

If you qualify for:
- full help, you are sent an HC2 certificate;
- partial help, you are sent an HC3 certificate which tells you the contribution you must make towards the charges.

Certificates are normally valid for 12 months. However, they are usually valid for:[18]
- five years if you are a single person aged 65 or over, or one of a couple, one aged 60 or over and the other aged 65 or over. This only applies if you do not receive earnings, or payments from an occupational pension, a personal pension or an annuity, and you do not have a dependent child or young person as a member of your household; *or*
- six months from the date of claim if you are receiving asylum support; *or*
- until the end of your course or the start of the next academic year if you are a full-time student.

Make a repeat claim on Form HC1 shortly before the expiry date. If you have a five-year certificate, you must notify the issuing authority of any changes in the composition of your family or household. In other cases, changes of circumstances (eg, starting work and increases in income) do not affect the validity of a certificate. However, if the change could result in increased help (eg, your income has *decreased*), you can reapply for a fresh assessment before the certificate expires.

Proof of entitlement

You are normally asked for proof that you are entitled to full or partial help with charges, although you should not be denied an item or service if you are unable to provide the required evidence. If you have an HC2 or HC3 certificate, show this to the dentist, optician, hospital or pharmacist (you may also have to enter details on the appropriate form). In other cases, you may need to show evidence of your date of birth, student status or exemption certificate.

Overpayments and fraud

If you receive help to which you were not entitled, you can be issued with a penalty notice requiring you to pay the charge you should have paid plus a penalty, unless you can show that you did not act 'wrongfully' or with 'any lack of care'. The penalty can be increased if you do not pay it within 28 days, and court proceedings can be taken to recover the debt. Anyone wrongly claiming help with charges on your behalf can be liable to pay a penalty charge. You can also be prosecuted if you obtain help wrongly, on the basis of a false statement or representation.[19]

Delays and complaints

For general queries, telephone 0300 330 1343. You can ask for a formal review of the decision on your claim by writing to the Review Section at the NHS Business Services Authority. See Appendix 1 for the address.

If there are delays in obtaining a certificate, you can complain to the customer services manager. If necessary, you could pay for the treatment or items you need then try to obtain a refund (see below).

Refunds

If you pay for an item or service that you could have got free, or at reduced cost, you can apply for a refund. Do this within three months of paying the charge, although the time limit can, in some cases, be extended if you can show good cause for applying late – eg, you were ill.[20]

Apply for a refund of a prescription charge (in England) on Form FP57, which you must obtain when you pay as one cannot be supplied later. For other items and services, apply on the relevant Form HC5. You can get the forms by telephoning 0300 330 1343, or from a Jobcentre Plus office or NHS hospital. You must submit a receipt or other documents to show that you have paid the charge. If you need an HC2 or HC3 certificate and have not applied for one, send a Form HC1 with your application for a refund.

Notes

1. Who can claim health benefits

1 **E** Regs 2-5 NHS(TERC) Regs; reg 3 POS Regs; reg 8 NHS(OCP) Regs 2013
S Regs 2 and 4 NHS(TERC)(S) Regs; regs 3 and 8 NHS(OCP)(S) Regs
W Regs 2-5 NHS(TERC)(W) Regs; reg 13 NHS(GOS) Regs; regs 3 and 8 NHS(OCP) Regs

2 **E** Sch 1 Table A NHS(TERC) Regs
S Sch Part 1 NHS(TERC)(S) Regs
W Sch 1 Table A NHS(TERC)(W) Regs

3 **E** Reg 5(2)(e) and (f) NHS(TERC) Regs; reg 3(2)(c) and (d) POS Regs; regs 3(2) and 8(3)(b) and (c) NHS(OCP) Regs 2013
S Reg 4(2)(c) and (d) NHS(TERC)(S) Regs; regs 3(2) and 8(3)(e) and (f) NHS(OCP)(S) Regs
W Reg 5(2)(e) NHS(TERC)(W) Regs; reg 13(2)(e) and (f) NHS(GOS) Regs; regs 3(2) and 8(3)(e) and (f) NHS(OCP) Regs

4 **E** Reg 6 NHS(TERC) Regs; regs 3 and 8 NHS(OCP) Regs 2013
S Reg 5 NHS(TERC)(S) Regs; regs 3 and 8 NHS(OCP)(S) Regs
W Reg 6 NHS(TERC)(W) Regs; regs 3 and 8 NHS(OCP) Regs

5 **E** Reg 6 NHS(TERC) Regs; regs 7, 15 and 20 NHS(OCP) Regs 2013
  S Reg 5 NHS(TERC)(S) Regs; regs 14 and 19 NHS(OCP)(S) Regs
  W Reg 6 NHS(TERC)(W) Regs; regs 7, 14 and 19 NHS(OCP) Regs

6 **E** Reg 17 and Sch 1 Table B NHS(TERC) Regs
  S Reg 8 and Sch Part 2 NHS(TERC)(S) Regs
  W Reg 16 and Sch 1 Table B NHS(TERC)(W) Regs

7 **E** Reg 16 and Sch 1 Table A NHS(TERC) Regs
  S Reg 8 and Sch Part 1 NHS(TERC)(S) Regs
  W Reg 15 and Sch 1 Table A NHS(TERC)(W) Regs

2. Prescriptions

8 **E** Reg 10-13 NHS(CDA) Regs; regs 4 and 5 NHS(TERC) Regs
  S Regs 3 and 4 NHS(FP&CDA)(S) Regs
  W Regs 3, 4 and 8 NHS(FP&CDA)(W) Regs; regs 4 and 5 NHS(TERC)(W) Regs

3. Dental treatment and dentures

9 **E** s177 NHSA 2006; regs 3 and 7 and Sch 5 NHS(DC) Regs; regs 4 and 5 NHS(TERC) Regs
  S Sch 11 NHS(S)A 1978; reg 5 and Sch 2 NHS(DC)(S) Regs; regs 3 and 4 NHS(TERC)(S) Regs
  W s126 NHS(W)A 2006; regs 3 and 7 and Sch 5 NHS(DC)(W) Regs; regs 4 and 5 NHS(TERC)(W) Regs

4. Sight tests and glasses

10 **E** Reg 3 POS Regs; regs 3 and 8 NHS(OCP) Regs 2013
   W Reg 13 NHS(GOS) Regs; regs 3 and 8 NHS(OCP) Regs

11 **E** Regs 8 and 9 NHS(OCP) Regs 2013
   S Regs 8 and 9 NHS(OCP)(S) Regs
   W Regs 8 and 9 NHS(OCP) Regs

12 **E** Regs 8 and 16 NHS(OCP) Regs 2013
   S Regs 8 and 15 NHS(OCP)(S) Regs
   W Regs 8 and 15 NHS(OCP) Regs

13 **E** Reg 16(3) NHS(OCP) Regs 2013
   S Reg 15(1) NHS(OCP)(S) Regs
   W Reg 15(1) NHS(OCP) Regs

14 **E** Reg 12(1) NHS(OCP) Regs 2013
   S Reg 12(1) NHS(OCP)(S) Regs
   W Reg 12(1) NHS(OCP) Regs

5. Wigs and fabric supports

15 **E** Regs 10,11 and 12 NHS(CDA) Regs; regs 4 and 5 NHS(TERC) Regs
   S Regs 3 and 4 NHS(FP&CDA)(S) Regs
   W Regs 3, 4 and 8 NHS(FP&CDA)(W) Regs

6. Fares to receive NHS treatment

16 **E** s183(a) NHSA 2006; regs 3 and 5 NHS(TERC) Regs
   S s75A(1)(b) NHS(S)A 1978; regs 3 and 4 NHS(TERC)(S) Regs
   W s131(a) NHS(W)A 2006; regs 3 and 5 NHS(TERC)(W) Regs

17 **E** Reg 9 NHS(TERC) Regs
   S Reg 7 NHS(TERC)(S) Regs

7. Claims and refunds

18 **E** Reg 8 NHS(TERC) Regs
   S Reg 10 NHS(TERC)(S) Regs
   W Reg 8 NHS(TERC)(W) Regs

19 **E** ss193 and 194 NHSA 2006
   S ss99ZA and 99ZB NHS(S)A 1978
   W ss141 and 142 NHS(W)A 2006

20 **E** Reg 11 NHS(TERC) Regs; reg 18 NHS(CDA) Regs; regs 6 and 24 NHS(OCP) Regs 2013
   S Reg 11 NHS(TERC)(S) Regs; reg 5 NHS(FP&CDA)(S) Regs; reg 20 NHS(OCP)(S) Regs
   W Reg 10 NHS(TERC)(W) Regs; regs 3(10) and 11A NHS(FP&CDA)(W) Regs; regs 6 and 20 NHS(OCP) Regs

Chapter 30

....

Incapacity benefit and severe disablement allowance

This chapter covers:
1. Incapacity benefit (below)
2. Severe disablement allowance (p671)
3. Transferring to employment and support allowance (see p672)

Key facts

- Incapacity benefit (IB) and severe disablement allowance (SDA) are benefits for people who are incapable of work.
- IB was abolished for new claims on 27 October 2008. You cannot normally make a new claim for IB, although some people who get income support 'on the grounds of disability' can still do so.
- SDA was abolished for new claims on 6 April 2001. No new claims can be made, but certain people entitled to it before this date can continue to receive it.
- If you cannot work because of sickness or disability, you must usually claim employment and support allowance (ESA). Most existing IB or SDA claims have been transferred to ESA, but some remain to be transferred during 2017/18.

1. Incapacity benefit

Incapacity benefit (IB) was abolished on 27 October 2008. You can only be entitled to IB now if:[1]

- you are already entitled and you continue to meet the qualifying conditions (see p670); or
- you are entitled to income support (IS) 'on the grounds of disability' (see p102), claim IB and meet the qualifying conditions on p670.

Note: if you are already getting IB, you continue to do so until your entitlement is reassessed under the work capability assessment and your claim is transferred to one for employment and support allowance (ESA). A few cases remain to be transferred during 2017/18. You are not reassessed if you reached pension age before 6 April 2014 (see p672).

Who is still entitled

You still qualify for IB if you are already entitled and either you reached pension age before 6 April 2014 or no decision has yet been made on converting your IB award to ESA (see p672).

A few people still on IS 'on the grounds of disability' may still qualify for IB. For more details, see p674 of the 2013/14 edition of this *Handbook*.

The amount of benefit

IB is paid at three rates: a lower rate of short-term IB, a higher rate of short-term IB after 28 weeks of entitlement, then long-term IB after 52 weeks.

	Under pension age £pw	Pension age or over £pw
Long-term IB		
Claimant	106.40	–
Increase for an adult	61.80	–
Short-term IB (higher rate)		
Claimant	95.00	106.40
Increase for an adult	48.15	59.50
Short-term IB (lower rate)		
Claimant	80.25	102.10
Increase for an adult	48.15	59.50

You may be able to claim an increase in your IB for an adult – ie, your spouse or civil partner, or someone who cares for your child. See pp681–83 of the 2013/14 edition of this *Handbook* for details. The increase is not paid if the adult has earnings above a certain amount (£73.10 a week in 2017/18) or, if you are not residing with her/him or the increase is of the lower rate of short-term IB, s/he earns more than the amount of the increase that would apply.

Increases for children and young people were abolished on 6 April 2003, but some people entitled to an increase before then continue to qualify. You do not get the increase for a child if your partner's earnings are above the earnings limit. In 2017/18 this is £230 for the first child, increased by £30 for each subsequent child. If you qualify, you are paid £8 for the eldest child and £11.35 for each other child. For full details of increases for adults and children, see pp680–82 of the 2013/14 edition of this *Handbook*.

Once you are entitled to long-term IB, you are paid an age-related addition if you were under 45 on the first day of your period of incapacity for work. It is paid at two rates, depending on your age on this day. See p677 of the 2013/14 edition of this *Handbook* for full details.

Age	£pw
Under 35	11.25
Under 45	6.25

2. Severe disablement allowance

Future changes

In the future, the rules on severe disablement allowance (SDA) may be different in Scotland. See CPAG's online service and *Welfare Rights Bulletin* for updates.

SDA was abolished on 6 April 2001, but certain people entitled to it before that date can continue to receive it.

Note: if you are already getting SDA, you continue to do so until your entitlement is reassessed under the work capability assessment and your claim is transferred to one for employment and support allowance (ESA). Some cases remain to be transferred during 2017/18. You are not reassessed, and can continue to get SDA, if you reached pension age before 6 April 2014 (see p672).

Who is still entitled

You still qualify for SDA if you reached pension age before 6 April 2014 or no decision has yet been made on converting your SDA to ESA (see p672) and:[2]
- you were getting SDA before 31 January 2011 and there has been no break in your entitlement since then; *and*
- you continue to meet the qualifying conditions, including being incapable of work or treated as incapable of work (see p683 of the 2013/14 edition of this *Handbook* for details).[3]

See Chapter 4 of the 2000/01 edition of this *Handbook* for the qualifying conditions for SDA, and for more information see p679 of the 2013/14 edition of this *Handbook*.

The amount of benefit

The current basic rate of SDA is £75.40 a week. You may also be entitled to an age addition (see pxix for amounts).

Part 5: Other benefits
Chapter 30: Incapacity benefit and severe disablement allowance
3. Transferring to employment and support allowance

You may be able to claim an increase in your SDA for an adult (£37.10). You do not get the increase if s/he earns more than £73.10 or, if you are not residing with her/him, s/he earns more than the amount of the increase – ie, £37.10. Increases for children and young people were abolished on 6 April 2003, but some people entitled to an increase before then continue to qualify. If this applies to you, you are paid £8 for the eldest child and £11.35 for each other child. You do not get the increase for a child if your partner's earnings are above a certain amount (in 2017/18, £230 for the eldest child, plus an additional £30 for each subsequent child). For full details of increases for adults and children, see pp679–82 of the 2013/14 edition of this *Handbook*.

3. **Transferring to employment and support allowance**

If you were claiming incapacity benefit (IB), severe disablement allowance (SDA) or income support (IS) 'on the grounds of disability' on 27 October 2008 and have remained entitled, your claim continues as an 'existing award'. However, unless you reached pension age before 6 April 2014, at some time the decision maker will decide whether your entitlement to IB, SDA or IS can be converted to an award of employment and support allowance (ESA). A few remaining cases will be decided during 2017/18. You do not need to make a claim for ESA.[4] At the end of this process, people claiming national insurance (NI) contribution credits on the grounds of incapacity for work will have their entitlement reassessed to see whether they qualify for NI credits on the grounds of 'limited capability for work'.

You are notified that you will be reassessed for ESA.

During the reassessment, the decision maker considers whether you satisfy the basic rules for ESA, including having limited capability for work under the work capability assessment (see Chapter 44). You are sent a questionnaire (ESA50) about limited capability for work and may be required to attend a medical. Your entitlement to your existing award continues while you are being reassessed.

The decision maker then decides whether your existing award can be converted to ESA. This is known as a 'conversion decision'.

If you are transferred to ESA, the transfer is automatic; you do not need to do anything.

Awards of IB and SDA are converted to awards of contributory ESA (without your needing to satisfy the NI contribution conditions for contributory ESA). Awards of IS are converted to awards of income-related ESA. If you are transferred to contributory ESA, you may also be entitled to income-related ESA.

For more details about transfer to ESA, see Chapter 31 of the 2016/17 edition of this *Handbook*.

Notes

1. **Incapacity benefit**
   1 Reg 2 ESA(TP) Regs

2. **Severe disablement allowance**
   2 Art 4 WRPA(No.9)O; reg 2 ESA(TP) Regs;
   reg 24 ESA(TP)(EA)(No.2) Regs
   3 s68 SSCBA 1992; reg 4 WRPA(No.9)O

3. **Transferring to employment and
   support allowance**
   4 Reg 3(1) SS(C&P) Regs

Chapter 31

Industrial injuries benefits

This chapter covers:
1. Who can claim industrial injuries benefits (below)
2. Industrial injuries disablement benefit (p686)
3. Reduced earnings allowance (p688)
4. Retirement allowance (p690)
5. Special benefit rules (p690)
6. Claims and backdating (p691)
7. Getting paid (p693)
8. Tax, other benefits and the benefit cap (p694)

Key facts

- Industrial injuries benefits are paid if you are disabled as a result of an accident at work or a disease caused by your job (but not if this is self-employment).
- The main industrial injuries benefit is **disablement benefit**, but you may also qualify for **reduced earnings allowance** or **retirement allowance**.
- All industrial injuries benefits are non-means-tested benefits.
- You do not have to have paid national insurance contributions to qualify.
- You can qualify whether you are in or out of work.
- Industrial injuries benefits are administered and paid by the DWP.
- If you disagree with an industrial injuries benefit decision, you can apply for a revision or a supersession, or appeal against it. You must apply for a mandatory reconsideration before you can appeal.

Future changes

In the future, the rules on industrial injuries disablement benefit may be different in Scotland. See CPAG's online service and *Welfare Rights Bulletin* for updates.

1. Who can claim industrial injuries benefits

You qualify for industrial injuries benefits if you satisfy the 'industrial injury condition' – ie:[1]

- you have had a 'personal injury' in an 'industrial accident' (see p676) or you have a 'prescribed industrial disease' (see p680); *and*
- at the time of the injury you were an employed earner (see below); *and*
- as a result of that accident or disease, you have had a 'loss of faculty' (see p681); *and*
- as a result of that 'loss of faculty', you are 'disabled'.

Industrial injuries benefits include industrial injuries disablement benefit (IIDB), reduced earnings allowance (REA) and retirement allowance. You can only qualify for REA or retirement allowance if your accident or disease occurred before October 1990.

If you have been injured by your work, you may also have the right to sue your employer. Legal help may be available and you may be able to get a free consultation with a solicitor. Your right to compensation from your employer is separate from your rights to benefit under the industrial injuries scheme (although your compensation may be reduced if you have received benefits from the DWP – see p1199).

Employed earners

You can only claim industrial injuries benefits if you were an 'employed earner' (see p958) and your accident or disease was caused by your employment.[2] If you are self-employed, you are excluded from the scheme.

If you pay, or ought to pay, class 1 national insurance (NI) contributions (see p959) as an employed earner you can qualify for industrial injuries benefits. This includes if you pay class 1 (and, in the case of volunteer development workers, class 2 – see p959) contributions while abroad.[3]

You can also qualify if your earnings are too low to pay contributions. Certain workers are treated as employed earners – eg, apprentices, agency workers, taxi drivers, office cleaners and various others.[4] You can also be treated as an employed earner if you are participating in a government course or training scheme which forms part of a mandatory work scheme. The person or organisation providing the training is treated as the employer for the purposes of making a claim.[5]

You are treated as *not* being an employed earner if:[6]

- you are employed by your spouse or civil partner and either your employment is not for the purpose of her/his business or profession (eg, if your partner employs you as her/his carer) or your earnings are normally below the lower earnings limit (see p959); *or*
- you are employed by a close relative (parent, step-parent, grandparent, son, daughter, stepchild, grandchild, brother, sister, half-brother or half-sister) in a private house where you both live, and your employment is not for your relative's trade or business carried out there; *or*
- you are a member of, or a civilian employed by, visiting armed forces, unless you are normally resident in the UK.

Part 5: Other benefits
Chapter 31: Industrial injuries benefits
1. Who can claim industrial injuries benefits

Personal injury

Personal injury includes the obvious, such as broken legs or arms, but also covers the less obvious, such as strains and psychological injury.[7] So an assault at work causing slight physical injury may cause a far greater injury to the mind by resulting in agoraphobia or a breakdown. In difficult cases, the question is whether or not you have experienced a physiological or psychological change for the worse. It is not enough just to be in pain if the pain is merely a symptom of an existing condition and does not make that condition substantially worse.[8] The damage must be to you or part of you. Dislocation of an artificial hip joint counts as a personal injury,[9] but damage to a pair of spectacles does not.[10]

Accident

The term **'accident'** has been defined as an unlooked-for mishap or occurrence.[11] However, an accident need only be unexpected from your point of view.[12] It does not matter if it could have been anticipated by an expert. If you do a heavy or dangerous job where accidents are common, a resulting injury is just as much an accident as if your job is sedentary and comparatively safe. A heart attack can be an injury but there needs to be some external event or series of events causing it, such as heavy lifting or work-related stress.[13] Deliberate acts by third parties can be accidents – eg, assaults on security workers or on staff in shops and hospitals.[14]

An accident is 'industrial' if you can show a connection with your work. This connection is established if the accident arose 'out of and in the course of your employment'.[15] Remember that, despite the name, it is not only industrial workers who can have 'industrial accidents'; all employees can. For example, if you are an office worker and a badly loaded filing cabinet tilts and falls on you, this should count as an 'industrial accident'. There need not be a dramatic event; any accident sustained while you are doing your job can qualify – eg, spilling a hot drink and scalding yourself. An illness brought on by conversation could count as being caused by an industrial accident.[16]

Accident or process?

Benefit is payable for an 'accident', but not for a 'process' (unless it causes a 'prescribed disease' – see p680). To fall from a ladder and break your leg is an accident, but to work for many years as a heavy manual worker and have a sore back is a cumulative process, as is breathing in dust over many years.[17] However, sometimes a series of events, over a period of time, can be treated as an accident for benefit purposes.[18] The cumulative effect of a series of incidents can also result in an accident.[19] Furthermore, you should not be excluded from entitlement to benefit simply because you cannot identify which incidents caused the injury.[20]

Example

Cyril's job is trimming excess plastic from electrical cables with a pair of clippers. A particularly rigid batch comes through and each cut requires greater strength. Over two or three days he suffers a strain injury in his hand. The series of cuts constitutes a series of accidents that meets the definition.

It is easier to establish the series of events as an accident if the period of time is fairly short,[21] or if it is noticed at an identifiable moment.[22] An accident is proved if you can establish that an identifiable occurrence must have happened, even if it is impossible to prove when.[23]

In the course of employment

The accident must arise 'in the course of employment'. Difficulties arise when work rules are broken, or when you do something not directly connected with work.

Generally, when you arrive at your employer's workplace and are on her/his private property, you are 'in the course of your employment'. You do not have to have clocked in or have reported to your workplace. If you arrive early (eg, to get ready for work or to have a meal in the canteen),[24] you are covered, although if you arrive early to play games or for your own convenience, you are not.[25] You are probably covered during breaks from working if you remain on the employer's property,[26] but probably not if you go elsewhere. So if, during a tea break, you go to a local shop to buy a snack, you are outside the course of your employment.[27] If you are allowed to have a snack either at home or at work while still on duty, you are covered.[28]

While at work most activities are considered to be in the course of employment.[29] Chatting[30] or attending union meetings,[31] for example, are 'reasonably incidental' to the employment, provided they are not done in breach of instructions.[32] Even if you were doing something in breach of instructions, you may still be covered if:

- the accident would have been taken as arising out of, and in the course of, your employment if you had not been acting in breach of those instructions; *and*
- what you were doing was for the purposes of, or in connection with, your employment.[33]

Example

Clara works in a paper factory where there is an absolute ban on riding on the load of a forklift truck. She is seen riding on the load, falls off and is injured. Usually she would not be covered, but she saw the load was slipping and rode on the truck in order to hold it on. This was done for the purposes of her employment and so on this occasion she is covered.

Part 5: Other benefits
Chapter 31: Industrial injuries benefits
1. Who can claim industrial injuries benefits

Even if you are at home, depending on your contract, you may be covered.[34] You may be covered when you are off on sick leave, if you are engaged in contractual duties.[35]

Example

While on sick leave with stress, John is seen relaxing in the park by a former colleague he had reported for theft. He is assaulted and his jaw is broken. This is an industrial accident arising *out of* his employment (see p679) but not in the course of it, as he was not engaged in any contractual duties, or any activities related to his work, at the time of the assault.

In putting forward your claim (see p691) or arguing your case at an appeal (see Chapter 55), consider all aspects of your employment, including the wording of your contract and the degree of flexibility in the arrangements between you and your employer.[36]

Accidents while travelling

Accidents while travelling have been a source of much dispute. You are not in the course of your employment (see p677) during ordinary journeys to and from work, unless you are travelling on transport operated by or on behalf of your employer, or arranged by your employer, and not being operated in the ordinary course of a public transport service.[37]

Many employees have no set place of work – eg, lorry drivers, local authority home helps, fuel company employees. Obviously, a lorry driver is at work when driving her/his lorry, but gas company workers travelling directly from home to their first job of the day are not always in the course of employment (see p677), even if driving a company van. It depends on the circumstances, including the rules for the use of the van.[38] In one case, a home help was found to be in the course of her employment travelling between jobs, but not going to the first job or from the last. This is because she became engaged in her employment once she started at the first job and remained engaged until the end of the day.[39]

Some employees with no fixed hours of work may be regarded as covered from the moment of leaving home.[40] Some cases have eased the rules on travelling – eg, to conferences or meetings. So, you can be treated as being at your place of work while attending a meeting at a site where you do not work.[41] You must look at all the factors when deciding whether or not you were in the course of your employment. For example, a police officer who had to travel about 40 miles from home to a training course was in the course of his employment while travelling.[42] Provided you go reasonably directly, with no marked deviation from a proper route, and do not embark on activities unrelated to the journey, you may be covered.

One important factor in deciding whether you are in the course of your employment is whether you receive wages for travelling.[43] However, if you receive a flat-rate travelling allowance as compensation for having to work at a workplace other than your normal base, this may not be enough to make your journey to your alternative workplace part of your work.[44]

Out of employment

As well as arising in the course of your employment (see p677), the accident (see p676) must arise 'out of' your employment, so that in some way the employment contributed to it. For example, the fact that you suffered a detached retina at work is not sufficient to show it arose 'out of' the employment, but medical evidence which shows that it was caused by sudden head movements while inspecting a production line enables you to establish that an industrial accident (see p676) took place. An unexplained fracture while walking at work is not an industrial accident,[45] but it is if you slip and the fracture occurs while you are falling onto the ground. You are covered even if you are more susceptible to injury because, for example, your bones are brittle[46] or your eyesight is poor.

Example

Joe, a farm worker, suffers sudden pain in the groin while doing his normal job of digging. It is found that a previous hernia, which had been surgically repaired, has given way again. The decision maker says that this could have happened at any time and so did not arise 'out of' the employment. Joe's doctor says it could have happened at any time but probably did so at that time because of the heavy digging. The First-tier Tribunal awards him benefit.

An accident also arises out of your employment if it arises in the course of employment (see p677) and it is caused by:[47]
* another's misconduct, 'skylarking' or negligence; or
* the behaviour or presence of an animal (including a bird, fish or insect); or
* your being struck by any object or by lightning.

In all cases, you must not have contributed to the accident by your conduct, either outside your employment or by any act 'not incidental to' the employment. (This involves looking at what you are employed to do, then at whether you were discharging a duty when the accident occurred, or whether what you were doing was reasonably incidental to that duty.) If you are skylarking at work and are injured as a result, for example, this is not incidental to your employment. If you act to deter someone else from doing so, however, this does not take you out of the course of your employment.[48]

An accident is deemed to arise out of, and in the course of, your employment if you are helping people in an emergency, or trying to save property at or near where you are employed.[49]

Part 5: Other benefits
Chapter 31: Industrial injuries benefits
1. Who can claim industrial injuries benefits

Prescribed industrial disease

It is necessary for the disease to be a **'prescribed industrial disease'**. This means it is on a list,[50] set out in regulations, of diseases that are known to have a link to a particular 'prescribed' occupation (see below).[51] Each prescribed disease has a statutory definition and you must fit within that. It is not sufficient simply to have a medical diagnosis that you have a particular condition.[52] From time to time new diseases are added to the list. However, you cannot claim for a disease for any period before it was added to the list.[53] Each prescribed industrial disease has a letter and number to identify it – eg, prescribed disease A12 is carpal tunnel syndrome and prescribed disease D1 is pneumoconiosis. The complete list is in Appendix 8.

If the DWP accepts that you have a prescribed industrial disease, other diseases which result from it are included when assessing your 'loss of faculty' and disablement.[54] See p681 for how your disablement is assessed.

Prescribed occupations

Different diseases are 'prescribed' for specific types of jobs because particular jobs have different health risks. To qualify for benefit on grounds of a prescribed industrial disease, you must have a disease which is on the list and prove that:

- you have worked in one or more of the jobs for which that disease is prescribed ('prescribed occupations'); *and*
- your job caused the disease.

If the DWP refuses to accept that you have worked in a prescribed occupation, you should obtain advice, preferably from your trade union, or from an advice agency. An expert's report may help to prove your case.

Time limits

For most prescribed diseases, you do not have to have worked in a prescribed occupation for any minimum length of time. You can also claim at any time, even if it is many years since you worked in that occupation. However, there are exceptions to these general rules. For example, if you have occupational deafness (prescribed disease A10), you must have worked in a prescribed occupation for 10 years and claim within five years of having done so.[55] If you have occupational asthma (prescribed disease D7), you must claim within 10 years of working in a prescribed occupation.[56] If you have cataracts (prescribed disease A2), you must have worked in a prescribed occupation for five years or more in aggregate.[57] Appendix 8 lists relevant time limits or qualifying periods for other prescribed diseases.

Cause

For some diseases, unless the contrary can be proved, it is assumed that, if you have the disease within a particular interval (one, two, six or 12 months, depending on the disease) of working in the prescribed occupation (see p680), the occupation caused it.[58] With other diseases, there is a presumption that a specific type of occupation caused them, regardless of when you last worked in that occupation.[59] There are also diseases where no assumed link exists (eg, dermatitis – prescribed disease D5), and you must establish the link 'on a balance of probabilities' – ie, that it is more likely than not that there is a connection.[60] The DWP investigates the connection issue, and you may need to ask your GP or consultant for a report linking the disease to your occupation. Guidance issued to decision makers tells them that, for some prescribed diseases, barring exceptional circumstances, the presumption that the disease was caused by the occupation should be automatic.[61]

There are different time conditions for carpal tunnel syndrome (prescribed disease A12[62]), in respect of some occupations, tuberculosis (prescribed disease B5), pneumoconiosis (prescribed disease D1), and diseases due to chemical agents.[63]

Example

Fern has been a farm worker for 10 years and has developed osteoarthritis of the hip (prescribed disease A13). She also broke her hip on a climbing holiday three years ago. The climbing accident does not alter the presumption that her prescribed disease was caused by her occupation.

Onset and recrudescence

The **'onset'** (date of starting) of a prescribed disease is taken as the date you first had a relevant 'loss of faculty' (see below). In deafness cases, it is the later of either the date you first experienced the loss of faculty or the date you successfully claimed benefit.[64]

In diseases other than deafness, asthma and respiratory conditions, you can improve and then worsen again. It is important to know whether it is a **'recrudescence'** (fresh outbreak of the existing disease) or a completely new attack. The first is deemed to be a continuation of the existing prescribed disease;[65] with the second, you have to wait 15 weeks before disablement benefit can be claimed. If a further attack starts during a current period of assessment, it is assumed to be a recrudescence unless proved otherwise.

Loss of faculty and disablement

In addition to showing the link between your injury or disease and your occupation, you must also establish that you have had a 'loss of faculty' and are 'disabled'.

'Loss of faculty' is the damage or impairment of part of the body or mind caused by the industrial accident or disease. **'Disability'** is the inability to do

Part 5: Other benefits
Chapter 31: Industrial injuries benefits
1. Who can claim industrial injuries benefits

something as a result of that damage or impairment. The total of all of your disabilities, taken together, amount to a **'disablement'**. This disablement is expressed as a percentage.

In assessing your disablement, the decision maker considers three questions.

- Has the relevant industrial accident (see p676) or prescribed disease (see p680) resulted in a loss of faculty (see below)?
- What is the extent of disablement resulting from a loss of faculty (this is expressed as a percentage – see below)?
- What period is to be taken into account by the assessment (see p685)?

A loss of faculty

A **'loss of faculty'** is an 'impairment of the proper functioning of part of the body or mind'[66] caused by an accident or disease. A 'loss of faculty' is not the same as disablement. It includes disfigurement, even if the disfigurement is not accompanied by a loss of physical faculty.[67] A decision that there has been a personal injury resulting from an industrial accident (see p676) does not prevent a decision maker or the First-tier Tribunal from finding that there is no loss of faculty.[68]

The extent of disablement

The extent of your disablement is assessed on a percentage basis. In order to qualify for disablement benefit (see p686), generally you must reach a threshold of at least 14 per cent disablement. However, a finding of at least 1 per cent may permit a claim for REA (see p688).

Any assessment between 14 and 19 per cent is treated as being 20 per cent.[69] If the total disablement from all industrial accidents and diseases is more than 20 per cent, it is rounded to the nearest multiple of 10 per cent, with multiples of 5 per cent being rounded upwards.[70] For example, an assessment of 22 per cent is rounded down to 20 per cent, an assessment of 25 per cent is rounded up to 30 per cent, as is an assessment of 26 per cent.

Some assessments of disablement are set out in regulations.[71] These are known as 'prescribed degrees of disablement' and include various amputations (eg, loss of a hand or a leg) and degrees of hearing loss (see Appendix 7). However, even in these cases, the decision maker must take into account the real disablement resulting from an injury and increase or decrease the figure to arrive at a reasonable assessment[72] – eg, the loss of a right hand is more disabling for a right-handed person than for a left-handed person. The full extent of your disablement caused by the injury must be taken into account. A further disablement or condition which arises at a later date, but which can be shown to be caused by the industrial accident or disease, must be included in the assessment.[73]

Impaired function of the pleura, pericardium or peritoneum caused by diffuse mesothelioma automatically has an assessment of 100 per cent disablement.[74]

Apart from age, sex and physical and mental condition, your personal circumstances must be ignored, so that particular problems you may have, like the location of your office, or the distance to the nearest bus stop, are not taken into account.

Your disablement should be assessed by comparing you with a person of the same age and sex whose physical and mental condition is 'normal'.[75]

When there is no prescribed degree of disablement, reference may be made to the prescribed percentages to help with the assessment.[76] Although you may suggest that your assessment should be a particular percentage, the decision maker makes her/his own judgement.[77]

What happens at the assessment?

It is important that you are straightforward with the examining healthcare professional. There are checks to establish that your symptoms are consistent with the injury, and that your movements are consistent with the disablement you claim you have. Therefore, how you walk into the room and how you undress are also considered. Make sure that the person examining you is aware of all the things that you now cannot do as a result of your injury or disease.

Offsets if your disability has more than one cause

If a disability is congenital or arose before an industrial one, it is deducted from the total disablement.[78] The reduction is often called the 'offset'. Mistakes are sometimes made because the decision maker incorrectly offsets for medical conditions that have not caused any disability.

Examples

Sam loses a hand, which would normally be 60 per cent, but he had previously lost the index finger. So 14 per cent is deducted, leaving 46 per cent (rounded up to 50 per cent).

Rhian has a back injury as a result of an industrial accident. A decision maker has reduced her assessment by 5 per cent on the grounds of a pre-existing disability of which she knew nothing. Many people have spines that are slightly curved as a result of lifting things. The decision maker may have looked at an x-ray, correctly considered that her curved spine was not due to the relevant accident and then incorrectly reduced her assessment.

In the second example, the decision maker should have considered whether the pre-existing loss of faculty (see p681), the curved spine, really had (or would have) led to disablement that would have occurred regardless of the industrial accident. S/he should have considered, among other things, whether the loss of faculty led to disablement before the industrial accident occurred. There is no physical disablement if you do not have any pain or restriction of movement and it is,

Part 5: Other benefits
Chapter 31: Industrial injuries benefits
1. Who can claim industrial injuries benefits

therefore, wrong to reduce your assessment unless there is a good reason for deciding that disablement would have arisen during the period of assessment even if the industrial accident had not occurred.

In the second example, depending on the medical opinion:

- there may be no offset; *or*
- it may be appropriate to make a life award (see p685) with some uniform offset over the whole period in respect of any future back problems Rhian is likely to have; *or*
- it may be appropriate to make a stepped assessment, making no offset initially but bringing one in at some future date, or applying different levels of offset for different parts of the period covered by the award.[79]

No reduction is made if your injury is one for which the regulations award 100 per cent and this is considered a reasonable assessment for the industrial accident.[80]

The decision maker should also bear in mind that, even if you had a pre-existing problem which caused a disability, the accident may worsen the effects of it, as well as cause a new problem. In such a case, the assessment should reflect the increase in the original problem as well as the new disability.[81]

If another disability arose after an industrial accident, the decision maker first has to assess the disablement arising from the industrial injury. If it is less than 11 per cent, any disability from the other cause is ignored; if it is more than 11 per cent, any extra disablement caused by the effect of the industrial injury on the other disability is added.[82]

Examples
Ali loses a little finger in an industrial accident and is assessed as 7 per cent disabled as a result. He then loses the other fingers of that hand in a non-industrial accident. He continues to be assessed as 7 per cent disabled because of the industrial accident.

Paul loses the middle, ring and little fingers of one hand in an industrial accident and is assessed as 30 per cent disabled as a result. He then loses the index finger of that hand in a non-industrial accident. His total disablement is now 50 per cent. But loss of the index finger only would have been 14 per cent. The disablement resulting from his industrial accident may, therefore, be reassessed at 36 per cent (50 per cent *minus* 14 per cent), which is rounded up to 40 per cent.

Two or more industrial accidents or diseases
If you have more than one industrial accident, the percentages of disablement (see p682 and Appendix 7) can be added together and may entitle you to benefit, even if neither accident would do so on its own. If you have two or more industrial accidents, you may end up in a situation where the second or later accident is

made worse by the interaction with the effect of the previous accident(s). Your most recent assessment should include an increase for any such interaction.[83] This also applies if an industrial disease (see p680) interacts with the effects of an industrial accident.

Example

Steve has a fall at work and seriously injures his left leg. He receives a life assessment of 10 per cent. Years later, he has a further fall and seriously injures the other leg. He is assessed as 10 per cent disabled for that accident, with a further 5 per cent for the extra disability he has as a result of the interaction between the two injuries. The total of 25 per cent is rounded up, resulting in payment of a 30 per cent pension.

There are special rules if you have pneumoconiosis. The rules allow for certain conditions to be taken into account in order to increase the assessment, even though these conditions did not arise from the pneumoconiosis. Any effect of tuberculosis is assessed with the effects of the pneumoconiosis.[84] If your disability is assessed at 50 per cent because of the pneumoconiosis, any additional disability because of chronic obstructive pulmonary disease is added.[85] If you have made such a claim for pneumoconiosis, you cannot then make a separate claim for chronic obstructive pulmonary disease.[86]

The period covered by the assessment

The decision maker or the first-tier tribunal decides how long you are likely to be affected by a relevant loss of faculty and how long you have already been affected (see p682). Percentage assessments are usually made for six months, or for one or two years, or are given for life,[87] but definite dates must be given.

An assessment is either final or provisional.[88] You get a provisional assessment when there is doubt about what will happen in the future, and you are automatically called for another assessment at the end of the period.[89] Life assessments are final.

If you are given a final assessment for a fixed period, this means that the decision maker believes you will no longer be affected by your accident or disease by the end of that period. If you think that the effects of the accident or disease will last for longer, consider an appeal against that assessment (see Chapter 55).

If your condition deteriorates during a period of assessment, or if you still have a disability at the end of a period for which you have been given a final assessment, you should apply for a supersession (see p1287).

An assessment of disablement for occupational deafness is for life.[90]

Part 5: Other benefits
Chapter 31: Industrial injuries benefits
2. Industrial injuries disablement benefit

2. **Industrial injuries disablement benefit**

The main benefit linked to industrial accidents and diseases is industrial injuries disablement benefit (IIDB). You may qualify for additional amounts of benefit paid as increases to IIDB. These are:

- constant attendance allowance (see p687);
- exceptionally severe disablement allowance (see p688);
- reduced earnings allowance (see p688).[91]

Who can claim industrial injuries disablement benefit

You qualify for IIDB if:[92]

- you satisfy the industrial injury condition (see p674) as a result of one or more industrial accidents (see p676) or prescribed diseases (see p680); *and*
- your resulting disablement is assessed as being at least 14 per cent (1 per cent in the case of pneumoconiosis, byssinosis and diffuse mesothelioma) (see p682 and Appendix 7); *and*
- 90 days (excluding Sundays) have elapsed since the date of the accident or of the onset of the prescribed disease or injury (if you have mesothelioma, you can be paid without serving this waiting period).

Disqualification

You may be disqualified for up to six weeks if you do not provide the required information or notify changes in your circumstances, or do not have a medical examination or treatment. You cannot, however, be disqualified for refusing to have an operation, unless it is a minor one.[93]

The rules about your age

There are no specific age rules or requirement to have paid national insurance contributions. You must simply be under a contract of employment. Therefore, a child who is working is covered, as well as a person over pension age. If the contract under which you work is illegal, you must ask the DWP to make a decision that you are covered by the scheme.[94]

People included in the claim

You claim IIDB for yourself. You cannot claim any increases for an adult or your child(ren) unless you are getting unemployability supplement (abolished for new claims after 5 April 1987).

The amount of benefit

The amount of benefit you get depends on the extent of your disablement.[95] See p682 for how this is assessed.

Extent of disablement	£ per week
100%	169.70
90%	152.73
80%	135.76
70%	118.79
60%	101.82
50%	84.85
40%	67.88
30%	50.91
11% – 20%	33.94

Since 1 October 1986, IIDB can be paid if the assessment of your disablement is at least 14 per cent,[96] except in the cases of pneumoconiosis, byssinosis and diffuse mesothelioma, when it must be at least 1 per cent.[97] Before 1 October 1986, IIDB was paid for an assessment of disablement of at least 1 per cent. The old rules are still in force for claims made before this date.[98] If you are getting a payment as a result of such a small percentage assessment, see p176 of the 17th edition of CPAG's *Rights Guide to Non-Means-Tested Benefits*.

You may be able to get an increase of benefit (see below).

Increases of industrial injuries disablement benefit

You get increased IIDB if you qualify for constant attendance allowance or exceptionally severe disablement allowance.

Constant attendance allowance

You qualify for constant attendance allowance if:[99]

- you are entitled to industrial injuries disablement benefit based on a degree of disablement assessed at 100 per cent; *and*
- you require constant attendance as a result of the relevant loss of faculty (see p681).

Disablement as a result of pre-1948 industrial accidents and diseases, war injuries and injuries incurred while on police or fire duty, may be taken into account in considering the degree of your disablement.

Part 5: Other benefits
Chapter 31: Industrial injuries benefits
3. Reduced earnings allowance

The amount you get depends on the extent of your disability and the amount of attendance you need.

Rate	£ per week
Part-time attendance	33.95
Standard maximum	67.90
Intermediate	101.85
Higher	135.80

Exceptionally severe disablement allowance

This is paid at the weekly rate of £67.90 if you are entitled to constant attendance allowance (or would be if you were not in hospital) at the higher or intermediate rate and you are likely to remain so permanently.[100]

3. **Reduced earnings allowance**

Reduced earnings allowance (REA) is available if you had an accident or started to have a disease before 1 October 1990. A successful first claim can still be made now if you had an accident or disease before this date.

The amount of REA you get depends on whether your current earnings, or earnings in a job which it is considered you could do, are less than the current earnings in your previous 'regular occupation'. This involves looking at your work history and the content of your job, rather than at your job title.

See Chapter 31 of the 2015/16 edition of this *Handbook* for the qualifying conditions for REA.

Who is still entitled to reduced earnings allowance

You qualify for REA if:[101]
- you satisfy the industrial injury condition (see p674) because of an industrial accident (see p676) before 1 October 1990 or an industrial disease (see p680) the onset of which was before that date (see p681); *and*
- your resulting disablement is assessed as being at least 1 per cent (see p682 and Appendix 7); *and*
- as a result of a relevant loss of faculty, either:
  - you are incapable and likely to remain permanently incapable of following your regular occupation and are incapable of following employment of an equivalent standard which is suitable in your case; *or*
  - you are, and have been at all times since the end of the 90-day qualifying period for industrial injuries disablement benefit (IIDB), incapable of

following your regular occupation or employment of an equivalent standard which is suitable in your case.

For more details, see p695 of the 2015/16 edition of this *Handbook*.

If you were entitled to REA on 30 October 1990 and you then lost entitlement to it for one or more days, you cannot regain entitlement to it for the same accident or prescribed disease. However, if you were not entitled to REA until after 30 October 1990, breaks in entitlement (eg, because of a temporary improvement in your condition) do not prevent you from re-qualifying.[102]

If you have reached pension age and you gave up regular employment on or after 10 April 1989, and you were entitled to REA on the day before you gave up that employment, this ends your entitlement to REA.[103] If you have given up regular employment, you receive retirement allowance instead (see p690). This is paid to you at a lower rate.

5

Regular employment

'**Regular employment**' means working for an average of 10 hours or more a week within a period of five or more weeks of such employment.[104]

However, some claimants have been successful in claiming REA after pension age and retaining REA rather than moving onto the lower rate of retirement allowance (see p690). This is on the basis that the law allows a person who is over pension age and claiming REA for the first time to be paid REA rather than retirement allowance.[105]

If you were entitled to REA on either 10 April 1988 or 9 April 1989, and on that date you were over pension age and were retired, or were treated as retired, you remain entitled to the allowance for life. For the meaning of 'retired or treated as retired' in this context, see p69 of the 12th edition of CPAG's *Rights Guide to Non-Means-Tested Benefits*.

If you are claiming on the basis of an industrial disease, it (or the extension of an existing category of prescribed diseases) must have been added to the list of prescribed diseases before 10 October 1994.[106]

The amount of benefit

The amount of REA you get is the amount by which your current earnings, or earnings in a job which it is considered you could do, are less than the current earnings in your previous regular occupation (see p697 of the 2015/16 edition of this *Handbook*).[107]

If you are unemployed, the DWP's healthcare professional is asked for your limitations, a DWP disability employment adviser is asked what job s/he thinks you could do and Jobcentre Plus is asked to quote a wage which such a job would pay in your area.

Part 5: Other benefits
Chapter 31: Industrial injuries benefits
5. Special benefit rules

Once the first assessment has been made, the amount is usually increased in line with earnings in that industry or workplace, unless that regular occupation (see p689) has ceased to exist.[108] In this case, it is calculated as rising in line with the nearest 'occupational group' as defined by the DWP. You can ask for a fresh assessment to take into account your prospects of advancement, but you must show that promotion would have happened (eg, at the end of a period of employment or training), not just that it might have happened had you been particularly diligent.[109]

The maximum amount you can receive for any one award is £67.88 a week.[110] The total you can receive from IIDB and REA (whether for one or more awards) is 140 per cent of the standard rate of IIDB.[111] If you were over pension age and retired before 6 April 1987, your allowance is reduced if it would otherwise mean you would be receiving more than 100 per cent of the standard rate of IIDB.[112] If you qualified for REA and were retired or treated as retired on either 10 April 1988 or 9 April 1989, you continue to receive the allowance at the same 'frozen' rate. Its value, therefore, erodes over time.

4. **Retirement allowance**

Retirement allowance is a reduced rate of reduced earnings allowance (REA – see p688) for people over pension age, paid for life.

You qualify for retirement allowance if:[113]

- you are over pension age (see p772);
- you have given up regular employment (see p689);
- you were entitled to REA at a rate of at least £2 a week (in total, if you had more than one award) immediately before you gave up regular employment;
- you are not entitled to REA.

You can only get one award of retirement allowance, even if you had more than one award of REA.[114]

The amount of retirement allowance you get is £16.97 a week or 25 per cent of the amount of REA you were receiving, whichever is the lower. There are no increases for dependants.

5. **Special benefit rules**

Special rules may apply to:

- people who are going abroad (see Chapters 67 and 68);
- people in prison or detention (see Chapter 41).

6. **Claims and backdating**

The general rules about claims and backdating are covered in Chapter 49. This section explains the specific rules that apply to industrial injuries benefits.

Making a claim

Claims for industrial injuries benefits other than retirement allowance (see below) must be made in writing.[115] You can download a claim form from www.gov.uk, or phone (tel: 0345 758 5433; textphone: 0345 608 8551) to request a form. Keep a copy of your claim form in case queries arise. The DWP intends to introduce telephone and online claims at some point.

You must provide any information or evidence required (see p691). In certain circumstances, the DWP may accept a written application not on the approved form.[116] You can amend or withdraw your claim before a decision is made (see p1149). If there is a delay in making a claim, you may be able to get a short-term advance of benefit (see p1177).

Note: you do not have to make a claim for retirement allowance.[117]

Forms

There are different forms depending on the benefit claimed and on whether you are claiming for an accident or a disease. You can download the forms from www.gov.uk.[118]

Who should claim

You claim for yourself. If you are unable to manage your own affairs, another person can claim industrial injuries benefits for you as your 'appointee' (see p1149).

Information to support your claim

For the general information requirements that apply to all benefits, see p1150.

It is important that you provide any information required when you claim. Until you do, you may not count as having made a valid claim (see p1152). Correct any defects as soon as possible or your date of claim may be affected.

Even if you have provided all that was required when you claimed, you may be asked to provide further evidence to support your claim (see p1154). You may also be asked to provide information after you are awarded industrial injuries benefits and if you fail to do so, your benefit could be suspended, or even terminated (see p1185).

Part 5: Other benefits
Chapter 31: Industrial injuries benefits
6. Claims and backdating

The date of your claim

The date of your claim is important as it determines when your entitlement to industrial injuries benefits starts. This is not necessarily the date from when you are paid. For information about when payment of benefit starts, see p693.

The '**date of your claim**' is the date it is received at the industrial injuries disablement benefit (IIDB) centre.

Note: you must make sure your claim is valid. If it is 'defective', you are given a short time to correct the defects (see p1152). If you do, your claim is treated as having been made when you initially claimed.[119]

In some cases, you can claim in advance (see below) and in some cases your claim can be backdated (see below). If you want this to be done, make this clear when you claim or the DWP may not consider it. If you claimed disability living allowance, personal independence payment or attendance allowance instead of constant attendance allowance, see below.

Backdating your claim

It is important to claim in time. Your claim can be backdated for up to three months if you satisfy the qualifying conditions over that period. You do not have to show any reasons why your claim was late. The rules on backdating are covered on p1156.

If you might have qualified for benefit earlier but did not claim because you were given the wrong information or were misled by the DWP, ask for compensation (see p1396) or complain to the Ombudsman via your MP (see p1401).

If you claim the wrong benefit

In some circumstances, it is possible for a claim for one benefit to be treated as a claim for a different benefit (see p1161). However, for industrial injuries benefits it is only possible to 'interchange' constant attendance allowance with disability living allowance, personal independence payment and attendance allowance.

Claiming in advance

An advance claim can be made for IIDB if you have had an accident or have a prescribed disease and you are within the 90-day waiting period. The date of your claim is the date on which you qualify. Otherwise it is not possible to claim industrial injuries benefits in advance.

Renewal claims

Assessments can be provisional or final, and for a limited period or for life. A provisional assessment means that the decision maker considers that your medical condition has not yet settled down, and may get worse or better. At the end of a provisional assessment, you are invited to be re-examined. A final assessment means that the decision maker believes that your condition has settled down and your case is dealt with once and for all. At the end of a period of award, you must therefore apply for a renewal of benefit.

If you are awarded IIDB for a particular disease, you may recover at some point but subsequently have a further attack. If there is a continuation (or recrudescence) of the old disease, you do not have to wait 90 days before becoming entitled to IIDB.

7. Getting paid

The general rules on getting paid are covered in Chapter 50. This section explains the specific rules that apply to industrial injuries benefits.

When are industrial injuries benefits paid?

You are paid on a Wednesday,[120] weekly in advance or four weeks in arrears.[121]

Note:
- You might not be paid your industrial injuries benefit if you have been sanctioned for a benefit offence (see p1265).
- For information on missing payments, see p1174. If you cannot get your payments because you have lost your bank or Post Office card or you have forgotten your PIN, see p1173. If you have lost your 'simple payment' card, or you have forgotten your memorable date, see p1173.
- If payment of your industrial injuries benefit is delayed, see p1165. If you are waiting for a decision on your claim, or to be paid, you may be able to get a short-term advance (see p1177). If you wish to complain about how your claim has been dealt with, or claim compensation, see Chapter 58.
- If payment of your industrial injuries benefit is suspended, see p1185.
- If you are overpaid industrial injuries benefit, you may have to repay it (see Chapter 52) and, in some circumstances, you may have to pay a penalty (see p1256). If you have been accused of fraud, see Chapter 53.

Change of circumstances

You must report any change of circumstances that you have been told you must report, as well as any that you might reasonably be expected to know might affect your right to, the amount of, or the payment of your benefit. You should do this as soon as possible, preferably in writing. See p1184 for further information.

Part 5: Other benefits
Chapter 31: Industrial injuries benefits
8. Tax, other benefits and the benefit cap

8. **Tax, other benefits and the benefit cap**

Tax

Industrial injuries benefits are not taxable.[122]

Means-tested benefits and tax credits

Industrial injuries disablement benefit, reduced earnings allowance and retirement allowance are taken into account in full for all the means-tested benefits. Constant attendance allowance and exceptionally severe disablement allowance are disregarded. Industrial injuries benefits are ignored as income for tax credits.

Non-means-tested benefits

In general, the overlapping benefits rule does not apply to industrial injuries benefits. It is possible, for example, to receive full disablement benefit as well as full employment and support allowance.

Carer's allowance (see Chapter 25) may be paid to someone who is 'regularly and substantially caring' for you while you are receiving constant attendance allowance (see p687).[123]

If your spouse or civil partner died as a result of an industrial accident or disease, you may qualify for a bereavement benefit even though the national insurance contribution conditions are not satisfied (see p541).[124]

The benefit cap

In some cases, there is a limit on the total amount of specified benefits you can receive (a 'benefit cap'). Industrial injuries benefits are *not* specified benefits. The benefit cap only applies if you are getting housing benefit or universal credit. It does *not* apply if you or your partner get industrial injuries disablement benefit, reduced earnings allowance or retirement allowance. See p1180 for further information.

Passports and other sources of help

You qualify for a Christmas bonus if you receive disablement benefit, but only if it includes unemployability supplement or constant attendance allowance (see p863). If you are on a low income, you may be entitled to council tax reduction (see p854).

If you have (or you are a dependant of someone who has died and who had) pneumoconiosis (including asbestosis, silicosis and kaolinosis), byssinosis, diffuse mesothelioma, diffuse pleural thickening, or primary carcinoma of the lung if accompanied by asbestosis or diffuse pleural thickening, and you cannot get compensation from your employer (eg, because s/he has ceased trading), or you do not have a realistic chance of obtaining damages from that employer, you may be able to get a one-off lump-sum payment in addition to any industrial injuries benefit.[125] You can be entitled to a one-off lump-sum payment from the DWP for diffuse mesothelioma (including if you are a dependant of someone who had that condition immediately before they died), without the need to have worked.[126] The time limit for claiming is 12 months (from the date of diagnosis or death) and the time limit may be extended if there is good cause. All these lump-sum payments may be recovered (ie, deducted) from compensation (see p1200).

Notes

1. Who can claim industrial injuries benefits

1 s94(1) SSCBA 1992
2 ss94(1) and 108(1) SSCBA 1992
3 Reg 10C(5) and (6) SSB(PA) Regs
4 Regs 2, 4 and 6 SS(EEEIIP) Regs
5 Regs 2 and 3 IIB(ETSC) Regs; s95A SSCBA 1992
6 Reg 3 SS(EEEIIP) Regs
7 R(I) 49/52
8 R(I) 1/76
9 R(I) 5/81
10 R(I) 1/82
11 *Fenton v Thorley* [1903] AC 443 (HL)
12 CI/123/1949
13 *Jones v Secretary of State for Social Services* [1972] AC 944 (HL), also reported as an appendix to R(I) 3/69; *SSWP v Scullion* [2010] EWCA Civ 310
14 *Trim Joint District School Board of Management v Kelly* [1914] AC 667 (HL)
15 s94(1) SSCBA 1992
16 CI/105/1998; CI/142/2006
17 *Roberts v Dorothea Slate Quarries Co. Ltd* [1948] 2 All ER 201 (HL)
18 R(I) 24/54; R(I) 43/55
19 CI/3370/1999
20 *Mullen v SSWP* [2002] Session Case 251; SLT 149; SCLR 475; *Greens Weekly Digest* 3-121, IH (2DIV)
21 R(I) 43/61; R(I) 4/62
22 R(I) 18/54
23 CI/159/1950

24 *R v National Insurance Commissioner ex parte East* [1976] ICR 206 (DC), also reported as an appendix to R(I) 16/75
25 R(I) 1/59; R(I) 45/55
26 *R v Industrial Injuries Commissioner ex parte AEU* [1966] 2 QB 31 (CA), also reported as an appendix to R(I) 4/66
27 R(I) 10/81
28 *R v National Insurance Commissioner ex parte Reed* (DC), reported as an appendix to R(I) 7/80
29 s94(3) SSCBA 1992
30 R(I) 46/53
31 R(I) 9/57
32 *R v Industrial Injuries Commissioner ex parte AEU* [1966] 2 QB 31 (CA), also reported as an appendix to R(I) 4/66
33 s29(6)(b) SSA 1998; CI/210/1950
34 R(I) 64/51
35 R(I) 1/99
36 *Nancollas v Insurance Officer* [1985] 1 All ER 833 (CA), also reported as an appendix to R(I) 7/85
37 s99 SSCBA 1992
38 R(I) 1/88
39 R(I) 12/75
40 R(I) 4/70
41 R(I) 1/93
42 *Nancollas v Insurance Officer* [1985] 1 All ER 833 (CA); *Ball v Insurance Officer* [1985] 1 All ER 833 (CA); both also reported as an appendix to R(I) 7/85
43 *Smith v Stages* [1989] 2 WLR 529 (HL)

44 R(I) 1/91
45 R(I) 6/82
46 R(I) 12/52
47 s101 SSCBA 1992
48 R(I) 3/67
49 s100 SSCBA 1992
50 Sch 1 SS(IIPD) Regs
51 Reg 2 SS(IIPD) Regs
52 R(I) 3/03
53 R(I) 2/03; R(I) 4/96
54 Reg 3 SS(IIPD) Regs
55 Regs 2(c) and 25 SS(IIPD) Regs
56 Reg 36 SS(IIPD) Regs
57 Reg 2(e) SS(IIPD) Regs
58 Reg 4(1), (4) and (5) SS(IIPD) Regs
59 Reg 4(2) and (6) SS(IIPD) Regs
60 Reg 4(1) SS(IIPD) Regs
61 DMG Memo 26/16
62 Reg 4(5) SS(IIPD) Regs
63 Reg 4(1) SS(IIPD) Regs
64 Reg 6(2)(c) SS(IIPD) Regs
65 Reg 7 SS(IIPD) Regs
66 *Jones v Secretary of State for Social
    Services* [1972] AC 944 (HL), also
    reported as an appendix to R(I) 3/69
67 CI/499/2000; s122(1) SSCBA 1992
68 s30 SSA 1998
69 s103(3) SSCBA 1992
70 s103(2) and (3) SSCBA 1992; regs 15A
    and 15B SS(IIPD) Regs
71 Sch 2 SS(GB) Regs; Sch 3 SS(IIPD) Regs
72 Reg 11(6) SS(GB) Regs
73 *JL and DO v SSWP (II)* [2011] UKUT 294
    (AAC); [2012] AACR 15
74 Reg 20A SS(IIPD) Regs
75 Sch 6 para 1 SSCBA 1992
76 Reg 11(8) SS(GB) Regs; R(I) 5/95; R(I) 1/
    04
77 CI/636/1993. In some cases, it may be
    an error of law to arrive at a different
    figure without giving reasons for this
    (para 10).
78 Reg 11(3) SS(GB) Regs
79 CI/34/1993
80 Reg 11(7) SS(GB) Regs
81 R(I) 3/91
82 Reg 11(4) SS(GB) Regs
83 R(I) 3/91
84 Reg 21 SS(IIPD) Regs
85 Reg 22 SS(IIPD) Regs
86 Reg 2(d) SS(IIPD) Regs
87 Sch 6 para 6 SSCBA 1992
88 Sch 6 para 7 SSCBA 1992
89 Sch 6 para 6(2)(b) SSCBA 1992
90 Reg 29 SS(IIPD) Regs

2. **Industrial injuries disablement benefit**
91 Sch 7, Part VI, para 14(1A) SSCBA 1992
92 ss103 and 108 SSCBA 1992
93 Reg 40 SS(GB) Regs
94 s97 SSCBA 1992
95 Sch 4 SSCBA 1992
96 s103(1) SSCBA 1992
97 Reg 20(1) SS (IIPD) Regs
98 Sch 7 para 9(1)(a) SSCBA 1992; reg 14
    SS(II&D)MP Regs
99 s104 SSCBA 1992
100 s105 SSCBA 1992

3. **Reduced earnings allowance**
101 Sch 7 paras 11 and 12(1), (2) and (7)
    SSCBA 1992
102 Sch 7 para 11(2) SSCBA 1992
103 Sch 7 para 13(1) SSCBA 1992
104 Reg 2 SS(II)(RE) Regs; R(I) 3/93; *SSWP v
    NH (II)* [2010] UKUT 84 (AAC)
105 Sch 7 paras 11 and 13(1) SSCBA 1992;
    SS(II)(RE) Regs
106 Sch 7 para 11(1)(b) SSCBA 1992
107 Sch 7 para 11(10) SSCBA 1992
108 Sch 7 para 11(14) SSCBA 1992
109 Sch 7 para 11(6) SSCBA 1992
110 Regs 2 and 3 Social Security (Industrial
    Injuries) (Reduced Earnings Allowance
    and Transitional) Regulations 1987,
    No.415; Sch 7 para 11(13) SSCBA 1992
111 Sch 7 para 11(10) SSCBA 1992
112 Sch 7 para 11(11) SSCBA 1992

4. **Retirement allowance**
113 Sch 7 para 13 SSCBA 1992
114 *TA v SSWP (II)* [2010] UKUT 101 (AAC)

6. **Claims and backdating**
115 Reg 4(1) SS(C&P) Regs
116 Reg 4(1) SS(C&P) Regs
117 Reg 3(e) SS(C&P) Regs
118 s68(1) WRA 2012
119 Reg 6(1)(b) SS(C&P) Regs

7. **Getting paid**
120 Sch 6 para 3 SS(C&P) Regs
121 Reg 22 SS(C&P) Regs

8. **Tax, other benefits and the benefit cap**
122 s667 IT(EP)A 2003
123 Regs 14, 17 and 21 SS(IB)(T) Regs
124 s60(2) and (3) SSCBA 1992
125 Pneumoconiosis etc (Workers'
    Compensation) Act 1979
126 Part 4 CMOPA 2008

Chapter 32

Contribution-based jobseeker's allowance

This chapter covers:
1. Who can claim contribution-based jobseeker's allowance (p698)
2. The rules about your age (p704)
3. People included in the claim (p704)
4. The amount of benefit (p704)
5. Special benefit rules (p708)
6. Claims and backdating (p708)
7. Getting paid (p716)
8. Tax, other benefts and the benefit cap (p717)

Key facts
- Jobseeker's allowance (JSA) is a benefit for people who are looking for work.
- There are three types of JSA: **contribution-based JSA** (a non-means-tested benefit), **income-based JSA** (a means-tested benefit) and **joint-claim JSA** (a means-tested benefit paid if you must make a joint claim with your partner).
- You may be able to get your contribution-based JSA topped up with income-based JSA or joint-claim JSA, or universal credit (UC).
- To qualify for contribution-based JSA, you must have paid sufficient national insurance contributions.
- You cannot qualify for contribution-based JSA if you count as being in full-time paid work.
- You must normally be fit for work and satisfy the jobseeking conditions (if you do not come under the UC system) or meet work-related requirements (if you come under the UC system).
- In a number of situations (eg, if you do not take up a job or an employment programme or training scheme opportunity), you may be given a sanction and your JSA may be paid at a reduced rate.
- JSA is administered and paid by the DWP.
- If you disagree with a JSA decision, you can apply for a revision or a supersession, or appeal against it. You must apply for a mandatory reconsideration before you can appeal.

Part 5: Other benefits
Chapter 32: Contribution-based jobseeker's allowance
1. Who can claim contribution-based jobseeker's allowance

1. Who can claim contribution-based jobseeker's allowance

You qualify for jobseeker's allowance (JSA) if:[1]

- you do not count as being in full-time paid work (see p700); *and*
- you do not have limited capability for work. However, in certain circumstances, people who are sick or who have gone abroad for NHS hospital treatment can get JSA (see p701); *and*
- you are not in 'relevant education'. In addition, if you are a full-time student you usually cannot get JSA. See p872 and p874 if you do not come under the universal credit (UC) system and p891 if you come under the UC system; *and*
- you are below pension age (see p772); *and*
- you are in Great Britain. JSA can continue to be paid in limited circumstances while you are temporarily away (see p1599). Contribution-based JSA can be paid if you are unemployed and looking for work in a European Economic Area country (see p1601).

You can qualify for contribution-based JSA whether or not you come under the UC system (see p20).

In addition to the rules above, the following apply.

- **If you do not come under the UC system,** you must satisfy 'jobseeking conditions' – ie, you must:
  - be available for work; *and*
  - be actively seeking work; *and*
  - have a current jobseeker's agreement with the DWP (the DWP calls this a 'claimant commitment').

  Your entitlement ends if you fail to do so and, in some cases, you can be given a sanction if you claim again. See Chapter 45 for full details of these conditions.
- **If you come under the UC system,** you must accept a 'claimant commitment'. **Note:** while you are entitled to JSA, you can be required to meet work-related requirements which have been imposed on you, as well as some requirements connected to these – ie:[2]
  - work-focused interviews;
  - work preparation;
  - work search;
  - work availability.

  You can be given a sanction if you fail to do so. See Chapter 47 for full details of these requirements.

In all cases, you must satisfy extra rules (see p699).

Extra rules for contribution-based jobseeker's allowance

To get contribution-based JSA, in addition to satisfying the rules that apply to all types of JSA (see p698), you must:[3]
- satisfy the contribution conditions (see p978). This depends on your record of national insurance (NI) contributions and credits in the two tax years immediately before the benefit year in which your jobseeking period begins (or in which a period linked to a jobseeking period begins, if earlier). For example, if you claim JSA immediately after a period of limited capability for work, the contribution test is applied using the date on which you first had limited capability for work; *and*
- not be claiming and entitled to income support (IS); *and*
- not have earnings above a prescribed amount (see p706).

Jobseeking periods

A '**jobseeking period**' is the period during which you:
- meet the conditions that apply to all types of JSA (see p698); *or*
- do not satisfy the jobseeking conditions but receive JSA hardship payments (see Chapter 51).[4]

Periods to which this definition applies both before and after you come under the UC system (see p20) are included.[5]

Note:
- You are not usually entitled to JSA for the first seven days of your 'jobseeking period'. These are known as 'waiting days' (see p705).
- If you are a man of at least the qualifying age for pension credit (PC – see p147) but under 65, special rules apply which mean that in some circumstances your jobseeking period continues even though you do not satisfy the jobseeking conditions.[6]

What does not count as part of a jobseeking period

The following do not count as part of a jobseeking period:[7]
- days for which you do not claim (or are not treated as claiming) JSA;
- if you do not come under the UC system (see p20), days for which you lost your entitlement to JSA because you failed to participate in an interview when required or to 'sign on';
- a period for which you claimed backdated benefit which has been refused;
- any week (Sunday to Saturday) for which you are not entitled to JSA because you were involved in a trade dispute (see p940) for all or part of that week;
- days on which you are not entitled to JSA because you have not provided your NI number (see p1150).

Part 5: Other benefits
Chapter 32: Contribution-based jobseeker's allowance
1. Who can claim contribution-based jobseeker's allowance

Linked jobseeking periods

In some cases, two or more jobseeking periods can be linked together and treated as if they were one period. Also, certain periods in which you satisfy other conditions ('linked periods' – see below) can be linked to a jobseeking period. This means, for example, that:

- the question of whether you satisfy the NI contribution conditions for contribution-based JSA is decided by looking at your situation at the beginning of the first jobseeking period (or a period linked to a jobseeking period if earlier) and not at the beginning of your current claim;[8]
- if you make a fresh claim for JSA but your jobseeking period links with a previous one, you do not have to serve any waiting days (see p705) to get JSA;
- if the jobseeking periods together are longer than 182 days, you cannot get any more contribution-based JSA (see p707).

Two jobseeking periods are treated as linked if they are separated by one or any combination of the following:[9]

- any period of no more than 12 weeks; *or*
- a period during which you are doing jury service; *or*
- a 'linked period' (see below); *or*
- any period of no more than 12 weeks which comes between two linked periods or between a jobseeking period and a 'linked period'.

Linked periods

A '**linked period**' is any period during which you:[10]

– are entitled to carer's allowance, but only if this allows you to get contribution-based JSA when you would not otherwise satisfy the contribution conditions; *or*

– are incapable of work or treated as incapable of work; *or*

– have, or are treated as having, limited capability for work (see Chapter 44); *or*

– are entitled to maternity allowance; *or*

– are undergoing training for which a training allowance is payable.

You cannot argue that a period spent taking time out of work to look after children is a linked period for these purposes.[11]

Full-time paid work

You cannot usually qualify for contribution-based JSA if you are in full-time paid work. This means 16 hours or more each week.[12] All the rules on work are covered in Chapter 43.

In some situations, you are treated as *not* being in full-time work even if you work 16 hours or more (see p996). In others, you are treated as being in full-time work when you are not (see p996). See p992 for how your hours are calculated and p991 for what counts as paid work.

If your partner is not in full-time paid work, you (or s/he) may qualify for a means-tested benefit to top up your contribution-based JSA. If your partner is in full-time paid work, you (and s/he) may qualify for working tax credit or, if you come under the UC system (see p20), UC.

Note: if you or your partner have just taken up full-time paid work and you do not come under the UC system, you may be able to claim IS for help with your housing costs for the first four weeks. This is known as 'mortgage interest run-on' (see p474).

Limited capability for work

To qualify for JSA you must not have 'limited capability for work'.[13] See Chapter 44 for details about the test that decides this. **Note:** if you do not come under the UC system and a decision maker has decided that you have (or do not have) limited capability for work for employment and support allowance (ESA), you are automatically treated as having (or not having) limited capability for work for JSA.[14]

If your health improves and you move onto JSA from ESA (or UC), you may be asked to provide medical evidence that you no longer have limited capability for work. In all cases, you must still show that you are available for work if you are ill or have a disability. However, there are special rules that allow you to restrict your availability (see p1040). If you come under the UC system, there are special rules to help you meet the work-related requirements (see p1078).

Periods of sickness when you can claim jobseeker's allowance

Even if you have limited capability for work (or are incapable of work), in some situations you do not have to stop claiming JSA. You can be treated as not having limited capability for work (or as being capable of work):

- during a short period of up to two weeks (see p702); *or*
- during an extended period of up to 13 weeks (see p702); *or*
- while you are temporarily absent from Great Britain for the purpose of getting NHS hospital treatment (see p703).

In all cases, you can continue to claim JSA if the *only* reason why you would not otherwise qualify is that you are unable to work because of ill health.[15]

You do not have to continue to claim JSA in these situations and may qualify for ESA, PC or UC instead of JSA. If you are only going to be unable to work for a short time, it may be better to continue to claim JSA. You should obtain advice if you are unsure. Take the following into account.

- Switching from JSA to another benefit and then back again when you are no longer sick means you must make a succession of benefit claims. You could be without income while these are being processed and you may start or cease to come under the UC system. However, switching from JSA allows you to escape the pressure of being fully available for, and looking for, work.

Part 5: Other benefits
Chapter 32: Contribution-based jobseeker's allowance
1. Who can claim contribution-based jobseeker's allowance

- If you qualify for income-based JSA, the amount you get can be higher than the amount you get on income-related ESA – eg, if you qualify for a disability premium in JSA, and do not qualify for a component in ESA. However, the rate of contributory ESA can be higher than the rate of contribution-based JSA.
- If you qualify for contribution-based JSA, you can only receive this for 182 days in any jobseeking period (see p707). Contributory ESA is paid for 365 days (see p645).

Two-week periods of sickness

You are allowed up to two two-week periods of sickness in a jobseeking period (see p700) or, if your jobseeking period has lasted more than 12 months, in any successive 12-month period.[16] The two-week periods do not include any period when you qualify (or go on to qualify) for an 'extended period of sickness' under the rules below.[17]

This applies unless you state in writing that you are going to claim (or have claimed) ESA or UC or, if you do not come under the UC system (see p20), incapacity benefit, severe disablement allowance or income support. If you become ill when you do not come under the UC system, the two-week period continues if you later come under the UC system (see p20).[18] If you are sick more often than this, or for a longer period, you may be able to claim JSA during an 'extended period of sickness' (see below). Otherwise, you must claim ESA or PC (or UC) instead of JSA for the time you are unable to work.

You must make a written declaration that you will be unfit for work from a specific date or for a specific period on a form available at the Jobcentre Plus office.[19]

You are not allowed a two-week period of sickness if you were getting statutory sick pay in the eight weeks before you were sick, or if the period of sickness follows immediately after an 'extended period of sickness' under the rules below.[20] Instead, you can claim benefit on the basis of having limited capability for work without having to serve any 'waiting days' (see p639).

Note: if you do not come under the UC system, you are treated as being available for, and actively seeking, work during the period of sickness.[21] If you come under the UC system, you do not have to meet a work search requirement and a special rule helps you meet the work availability requirement.[22] If you are sick for more than seven days, you must provide a medical certificate from a doctor.

Extended periods of sickness

You are allowed what is known as an 'extended period of sickness' if:[23]

- you state that you have been, or expect to be, unable to work for more than two weeks, but not for more than 13 weeks; or

- you have already been unable to work for two two-week periods of sickness under the rules described above and you have been, or expect to be, unable to work for two weeks or less.

This applies unless you state in writing that you are going to claim (or have claimed) ESA or UC. You must satisfy the DWP that you are unable to work by providing evidence as required. This includes a medical certificate from a doctor.

You are treated as capable of work, or as not having limited capability for work, for up to 13 weeks from the first day you are sick, or until you are no longer sick if this is sooner.[24] You are only allowed one extended period of sickness in the 12 months that start on the first day of sickness.[25] If you are sick for longer than 13 weeks, or more often than once in the 12 months, you must claim ESA or PC (or UC) instead of JSA for the time you are unable to work.

You are not allowed an extended period of sickness if you were getting statutory sick pay in the eight weeks before you were sick.[26] Instead, you can claim benefit on the basis of having limited capability for work without having to serve any waiting days (see p639).

Note: if you do not come under the UC system, you are treated as available for work during the period of sickness.[27] You are treated as actively seeking work in any week in which you are allowed an extended period of sickness, unless it would be reasonable for you to take steps to seek employment, and you have not taken such steps. Whether it is reasonable is at the discretion of your work coach. If you come under the UC system, you do not have to meet a work search requirement if the DWP is satisfied that it would be unreasonable to require you to comply with one, and a special rule helps you meet the work availability requirement.[28]

NHS treatment abroad

You are treated as not having limited capability for work (or as capable of work) if you are temporarily absent from Great Britain for the purpose of getting NHS hospital treatment under certain provisions.[29] You can claim for an indefinite period. This applies unless you have stated in writing before the period of absence begins that you have claimed ESA immediately before the beginning of the period.

You must make a written declaration that you will be unfit for work from a specific date or for a specific period on a form available at the Jobcentre Plus office.[30]

Note: if you do not come under the UC system, you are treated as being available for, and actively seeking, work during the period of sickness.[31] If you come under the UC system, you do not have to meet a work search requirement and a special rule helps you meet the work availability requirement.[32]

Part 5: Other benefits
Chapter 32: Contribution-based jobseeker's allowance
4. The amount of benefit

2. **The rules about your age**

There is no minimum age for entitlement to contribution-based jobseeker's allowance (JSA). However, in practice, because you can only qualify if you satisfy the national insurance contribution conditions, you are unlikely to qualify before you are 18. You cannot claim any type of JSA if you are pension age or over (see p772).

3. **People included in the claim**

You claim contribution-based jobseeker's allowance for yourself. You cannot claim any increases for your partner or child(ren).

4. **The amount of benefit**

After any waiting days (see p705), contribution-based jobseeker's allowance (JSA) is paid at the following weekly rates.[33]

Age of claimant	£pw
Under 25	57.90
25 or over	73.10

These amounts are reduced penny for penny if you receive certain pension payments of more than £50 in any week or any part-time earnings. For more on how these types of income affect contribution-based JSA, see p705. Other types of income and any capital, including any earnings and capital of your partner, do not affect your contribution-based JSA.

Note:
- Contribution-based JSA is only paid for a limited period (see p707).
- You may qualify for income-based JSA (including joint-claim JSA) or, if you come under the universal credit (UC) system, UC, to top up your contribution-based JSA if you satisfy the means test – eg, if you have a partner or (for UC) a child, if you, your partner or child have a disability so you qualify for premiums or elements, or if you have a mortgage or loan for repairs and improvements or (for UC) you pay rent.
- Your JSA might be paid at a reduced (or nil) rate if you are given a sanction (see Chapter 48) or if your JSA has been restricted because you have committed a benefit offence (see p1265).

Waiting days

You are not entitled to JSA for the first seven 'waiting days' of any jobseeking period (see p699) unless:[34]

- your claim is linked to a previous claim for JSA so both are treated as part of the same jobseeking period; *or*
- you have been entitled to income support (IS), employment and support allowance (ESA), incapacity benefit or carer's allowance within the 12 weeks before you become entitled to JSA.

In addition, you do not have to serve any waiting days if you swap from claiming IS or ESA to claiming JSA.[35]

You may be able to get a short-term advance during your waiting period (see p1177).

Income for contribution-based jobseeker's allowance

Earnings and pension payments you receive can affect your entitlement to contribution-based JSA.[36] Any other income you receive does not affect your contribution-based JSA (but see p1175 for the rules on overlapping benefits).

Note:

- You cannot qualify for JSA if you are in full-time paid work, so it is earnings from part-time work that are taken into account.
- Any savings you have and the income and savings of your partner and children do not affect your contribution-based JSA, but do affect income-based JSA, joint-claim JSA and UC.

Earnings

Your earnings from part-time work can affect your entitlement to contribution-based JSA. The rules on the following are the same as for income-based JSA:

- what counts as earnings (p270);
- calculating net earnings from employment (p272);
- payments when you stop work (p273);
- calculating net earnings from self-employment (p276);
- working out average earnings from self-employment (p277);
- childminders (p278);
- how weekly earnings from employment are assessed (p302).

Different rules apply to:

- disregarded earnings. For contribution-based JSA, £5 a week of your earnings is disregarded. However, a different rule applies if you are an auxiliary coastguard, a part-time firefighter, a part-time lifeboat crew member or a member of the reserve forces: £20 a week is disregarded.[37] If you earn less than £20 for doing

Part 5: Other benefits
Chapter 32: Contribution-based jobseeker's allowance
4. The amount of benefit

any of these services, you can use up to £5 of the disregard on earnings from another job;

- how earnings affect your contribution-based JSA (see below).

How earnings affect your contribution-based jobseeker's allowance

Your contribution-based JSA is affected by earnings as follows.

- Your contribution-based JSA is reduced by the full amount of any earnings you receive over the disregarded amount.[38]
- You are not entitled to contribution-based JSA for any week in which your earnings exceed a **prescribed amount**.[39] However, the days in any week when your earnings exceed this amount do not count towards your maximum 182 days of contribution-based JSA (see p707).

The prescribed amount is not the same for everyone. It is calculated by adding together the amount of the relevant earnings disregard and the rate of contribution-based JSA paid to someone your age (see p704), and then deducting one penny.

Example

Maggie, aged 35, is entitled to contribution-based JSA of £73.10 a week. She works part time and her net earnings are £45 a week. Her earnings disregard is £5 a week. Maggie therefore gets £33.10 contribution-based JSA a week (£73.10 – £40). Applying the formula: (£73.10 + £5) – £0.01 = £78.09. If Maggie were to earn more than £78.09 a week, she would not be entitled to contribution-based JSA.

Pension payments

Certain pension payments you receive may also affect your contribution-based JSA.[40] The gross amount of your pension payments is taken into account – ie, the amount before tax is deducted, and this is converted into a weekly amount.[41]

Any pension payments you receive because of the death of a person who was a member of a pension scheme are ignored.[42] For example, if your late partner was a member of a scheme, any payment made to you following her/his death does not affect your contribution-based JSA.

£50 of your weekly pension payments (or if you get more than one pension, of the total of your weekly pensions) is disregarded, and your contribution-based JSA is reduced by the remainder.[43]

Any pension payment you receive is counted from the first day of the benefit week in which the payment is made to you.[44]

Example

Brian claims JSA and is entitled to contribution-based JSA from Wednesday 26 April 2017. His benefit week begins on a Friday. He starts receiving a personal pension of £68 a week from Monday 1 May 2017. £18 a week (£68 – £50) is deducted from his contribution-based JSA from the benefit week starting Friday 28 April 2017.

If your pension is increased when you are on contribution-based JSA, the change should be taken into account from the first day of the benefit week in which the increase is paid.[45] **Note:**

- The amount of your pension payments may mean that you are not paid any JSA. However, unless your earnings also exceed the prescribed amount (see p706), you remain *entitled* to contribution-based JSA (provided you also satisfy the other conditions for getting JSA).
- Any day on which you are entitled to JSA (even if it is not paid) counts towards your 182 days' entitlement to contribution-based JSA (see below).
- A combination of earnings and pension payments may mean that you are not paid any JSA, even though you may remain entitled to it.

Duration of contribution-based jobseeker's allowance

You cannot receive more than 182 days of contribution-based JSA in any jobseeking period (see p699) or in two or more jobseeking periods if your entitlement is based on national insurance (NI) contributions in the same two contribution years.[46] Even if it may take you longer than others to get a job because you have a disability, you are unlikely to be able to argue that the rule discriminates against you.[47]

The 182 days can include days both before and after you come under the UC system (see p20).[48] You can have another 182 days of contribution-based JSA for a later claim if:[49]

- you satisfy the contribution conditions; *and*
- at least one of the two contribution years used to decide whether you satisfy the contribution conditions is later than the second contribution year used to decide your previous entitlement. This can only apply if you are in a later jobseeking period than the one during which you exhausted your entitlement to contribution-based JSA. **Note:** if you are a man aged at least the qualifying age for pension credit (see p147) but under 65, there are special rules that deem your jobseeking period to continue when it would end under the normal rules, so making it difficult for you to requalify for contribution-based JSA.[50]

Days that count towards the 182-day total

Each day for which you are entitled to contribution-based JSA, even if you are not paid, counts, including days when the amount of JSA you are paid has been reduced to nil because you have been given a sanction, or because you are getting a pension or a combination of pension and earnings.

Days on which you are *not* entitled to contribution-based JSA can also count. This applies to days within a jobseeking period (both before and after you come

Part 5: Other benefits
Chapter 32: Contribution-based jobseeker's allowance
6. Claims and backdating

under the UC system) on which you are not entitled to contribution-based JSA because:[51]

- you are entitled to and claiming IS or your earnings are above the prescribed amount (see p706), and your contribution-based JSA is not payable either because you have been given a sanction (see Chapter 48) or because you have committed a benefit offence; *or*
- you do not meet the jobseeking conditions and you are receiving a JSA hardship payment (see p1208).

Days on which you are not entitled to JSA and which do *not* count include:
- waiting days (see p705);
- days in any benefit week in which you are not entitled to JSA because you earn more than the prescribed amount (see p706) – but see above if you have been given a sanction;
- days when you are refused contribution-based JSA because you do not meet the jobseeking conditions and you are *not* getting a JSA hardship payment.

Note: if you are a laid-off or short-time worker (see p1028), days you claim contribution-based JSA count towards your 182 days of entitlement, even if your benefit is reduced to take account of your earnings. So, if you think you are likely to become fully unemployed in the near future and you are not claiming income-based JSA, you might gain more JSA overall by not claiming it until you are fully unemployed. However, if your earnings drop below the lower earnings limit (see Appendix 9), you cease to be treated as paying NI contributions. You may then wish to claim JSA, which entitles you to NI credits.

5. **Special benefit rules**

Special rules may apply to:
- people who have come from or are going abroad (see Chapters 65, 66, 67 and 68);
- people who are are studying (see Chapter 40);
- people involved in a trade dispute (see Chapter 41).

6. **Claims and backdating**

The general rules about claims and backdating are covered in Chapter 49. This section explains the specific rules that apply to jobseeker's allowance (JSA).

Note: in rare cases, it may be beneficial for you to delay your claim for contribution-based JSA so that you can draw on a different year's record of national insurance (NI) contributions.

While you are getting contribution-based JSA, you must satisfy the jobseeking conditions or meet work-related requirements. So, as well as giving all the necessary information, you are expected to attend and participate in an initial interview when you claim (see p711). You are also expected to attend and participate in:

- an interview when you sign on (see p1055) and further interviews as required (see p1057); *or*
- if you come under the universal credit (UC) system (see p20), interviews connected to work-related requirements (see p1080), including when you sign on. You might also be required to attend work-focused interviews (see p1074).

If you fail to participate in an interview, you could be given a sanction (see p1103 and p1121). If you do not come under the UC system and you fail to sign on or participate in an interview, your entitlement to JSA could end (see p1058 and p1058).

For further information about the officers who deal with JSA claims, see p1162 and p1027.

Making a claim

You can start your claim for JSA:

- at www.gov.uk/jobseekers-allowance/how-to-claim (but see below if you come under the UC system);[52] *or*
- by telephone on 0800 055 6688 (Welsh: 0800 012 1888; textphone: 0800 023 4888), Monday to Friday, 8am to 6pm (but see below if you come under the UC system). You are sent a written statement of your circumstances to approve, sign and to return to the DWP;[53] *or*
- by completing a paper claim form approved by the DWP.[54] JSA claim forms are only available from Jobcentre Plus offices. If you do not come under the UC system (see p20), one must be provided free of charge if you notify the DWP of your intention to claim. Keep a copy in case queries arise.[55]

You must normally attend the Jobcentre Plus office to complete your claim at an initial interview (see p711).[56]

In practice, the DWP prefers you to start your claim online, or by telephone if you cannot claim online. There is no rule that says you must start your claim online or by telephone, but it is best to make your claim in the way the DWP prefers if you can. If you cannot do either, you may be asked to attend the Jobcentre Plus office to make your claim in person. Get advice if you are unable to claim online or use a telephone and the Jobcentre Plus office tells you that you cannot start your claim in any other way.

You may be sent or given a form to complete about the work you will be looking for and how you intend to go about getting it. The information you give forms the basis of your jobseeker's agreement (or claimant commitment).

Part 5: Other benefits
Chapter 32: Contribution-based jobseeker's allowance
6. Claims and backdating

You must provide information or evidence as required (see p711). You can amend or withdraw your claim before a decision is made (see p1149). If there is a delay in deciding your claim, you may be able to get a short-term advance (see p1177).

Note:

- You can make initial contact with the DWP by telephone or letter to say you want to claim. The date of your initial contact is important because it usually determines the date on which your claim is treated as made (see p712).
- Income-based and contribution-based JSA are two types of one benefit. If you want the DWP to assess your entitlement to both, answer all the relevant questions and provide all the necessary information when making your claim.
- If you are claiming JSA within 26 weeks of a previous entitlement, you may be able to claim without having to give as much detail of your circumstances as is usually required – known as 'rapid reclaim' for JSA. If you made your previous claim online, you can reopen it online. Information is available at www.gov.uk/jobseekers-allowance/how-to-claim.

If you come under the universal credit system

If you come under the UC system (see p20), you can claim contribution-based JSA as well as UC. The DWP sometimes calls it 'new style' JSA. In practice, it can be difficult to claim contribution-based JSA because the online UC form does not specifically refer to it and some UC work coaches and jobcentre staff have wrongly said you cannot get JSA under the UC system. The DWP has issued guidance, setting out how it prefers you to claim.[57]

- Check www.gov.uk/guidance/jobcentres-where-you-can-claim-universal-credit to see whether you live in a UC 'full service' area. These are listed with an asterisk. If so, phone 0345 600 4272 (textphone: 0345 600 0743).
- If you do not live in a UC 'full service' area, make your claim by phoning the UC service centre on 0345 600 0723 (textphone: 0345 600 0743).
- Say that you want to claim 'new style' contribution-based JSA.
- You should be sent Form UCJSA 1, usually by email.
- An appointment should also be arranged for you at your Jobcentre Plus office. Take your completed UCJSA 1 claim form and proof of identity with you.

If you cannot claim in this way, tell your UC work coach at the jobcentre that you want to claim 'new style' JSA and that you need Form UCJSA 1.

Housing benefit

If you claim JSA online or by telephone, your housing benefit (HB) claim is often completed at the same time and passed to the local authority on your behalf. If this does not happen, you must make a separate claim to your local authority. You can use your postcode to find out how and where to claim at www.gov.uk/

apply-housing-benefit-from-council. If you are making a rapid reclaim for JSA, you may also be able to make a rapid reclaim for HB.

Claiming national insurance credits

If you are claiming national insurance credits but not JSA (see p967), the normal claim procedures for getting JSA apply to you.

Who should claim

You claim contribution-based JSA on your own behalf. If you are unable to manage your own affairs, another person can claim JSA for you as your 'appointee' (see p1149).

Information to support your claim

For the general information requirements that apply to all benefits, see p1150.

It is important that you provide any information required when you claim. Until you do, you may not count as having made a valid claim (see p1152).[58] This is known as the 'evidence requirement'. See p1153 for this and to see if you are exempt. Correct any defects as soon as possible or your date of claim may be affected. **Note:** the evidence requirement does not apply if you come under the UC system.

Even if you have provided all that was required when you claimed, you may be asked to provide further information to support your claim (see p1154). You may also be asked to provide information after you are awarded JSA and if you fail to do so, your JSA could be suspended, or even terminated (see p1185).

The initial interview

You must usually attend and participate in an initial interview.[59] If you do not attend the interview at the right time, your date of claim is affected (see p713). If you do not attend the interview at all (and the DWP does not waive the requirement to do so), you have not made a valid claim and so do not qualify for JSA.

If you claim JSA online, the DWP will telephone or text you within two working days to arrange your initial interview.

If attending the Jobcentre Plus office would mean that you would have to be away from home for too long, arrangements can be made for your interview to be carried out elsewhere.

The DWP says you should take two forms of identification to the interview – eg, your passport or driving licence, along with your P45 if you have one.[60]

If you have been sent a claim form, complete it before your interview. If you do not provide all the evidence and information required, your interview might not go ahead unless you are exempt from the evidence requirement (p1153).

At the interview:

Part 5: Other benefits
Chapter 32: Contribution-based jobseeker's allowance
6. Claims and backdating

- you are told what is expected from you while you are receiving JSA;
- you and your work coach discuss what work you are looking for and what you intend to do to find it;
- a jobseeker's agreement (or claimant commitment) is drawn up for you to sign;
- you may be referred to a job vacancy immediately. However, a jobseeker's agreement (or claimant commitment) should still be completed to establish entitlement in case you do not get the job.

The interview also covers what you were doing before you became unemployed and, in particular, why you left your previous job. If the person who interviews you thinks that you may have left voluntarily or been dismissed for misconduct, your case is referred to a decision maker who will probably make further enquiries before deciding whether to give you a sanction (see Chapter 48).

The date of your claim

The date of your claim is important as it determines when your entitlement to JSA starts (subject to the rules on waiting days – see p705).[61] This is not necessarily the date from when you are paid. For information about when payment of JSA starts, see p716.

Your date of claim is not necessarily the date it is received by the DWP. It can be an earlier date (see below).

Your **'date of claim'** depends on whether or not you are required to attend an initial interview (see p711):

- if you are required to attend an initial interview, your date of claim is the date you first contact the Jobcentre Plus office if you attend your initial interview at the time specified by the DWP and by that time a properly completed claim is, or has been, provided (on a form or by telephone) with all the information and evidence required. The DWP can extend the time you have to provide or make a properly completed claim up to the date one month after the date of first contact. This is discretionary, so provide your claim as required wherever possible. If you fail to attend your initial interview, see p713;[62] *or*
- if you are not required to attend an initial interview, your date of claim is the earliest of:[63]
  - the date you first contact the Jobcentre Plus office, so long as a properly completed claim (on a form or by telephone) with all the information and evidence required is provided within one month of your first contact or, if you come under the UC system (see p20), a longer period that the DWP thinks is reasonable; *or*
  - the date on which a properly completed claim (on a form or by telephone) with all the information and evidence required is received at the Jobcentre Plus office; *or*

– if you come under the UC system (see p20) and you are notified that your claim is defective and you supply all the information required within one month of this, the date your claim is received.

Note: you must make sure your claim is valid. If it is 'defective', you are given a short time to correct the defects (see p1152). If you do, your claim is treated as having been made when you initially claimed.[64]

In some cases, you can claim in advance (see p714) and in some cases your claim can be backdated (see p714). If you want this to be done, make this clear when you claim or the DWP might not consider it.

There are exceptions to the above rules.

- If you claim working tax credit (WTC) and you are refused because neither you nor your partner are in full-time paid work for WTC purposes (see p196), your date of claim for JSA is the date you claimed WTC.[65] However, you must claim JSA within 14 days of the decision refusing you WTC. You can ask for your JSA claim to start on a later date instead – eg, if your earnings are currently too high, but are due to decrease.

- If you claim UC and, on the basis of information you provided, you are treated as satisfying the 'gateway' conditions for a claim for UC or as living in an area where those conditions apply, but the DWP discovers that the information was incorrect, unless you have already been paid UC, you should be advised by the DWP that you are not entitled to claim UC. If you then claim JSA within a month of being told that, and if (taking into account any backdating you have requested and been allowed) your claim is later than the date of your UC claim, your JSA claim is treated as having been made on the date of your UC claim.[66]

Note: if you are a member of a couple and one of you claims contribution-based JSA but is not entitled to it and a subsequent income-based JSA claim is made by the other partner (or you and your partner if you are a joint-claim couple), the date of claim for income-based JSA is the date of the earlier claim for contribution-based JSA.[67] If your partner has been claiming contribution-based JSA, this expires and you claim income-based JSA, the date of claim for your income-based JSA is the day after your partner's entitlement expires.[68]

Forms

In this section, '**form**' refers to a paper form or a claim form completed online.

If you fail to attend the initial interview

If you fail to attend your initial interview at the time specified by the DWP, or you fail to provide a properly completed claim by the date of the interview and cannot show good cause for this, the rules above do not apply. Instead, so long as a properly completed claim with all the information and evidence required is

Part 5: Other benefits
Chapter 32: Contribution-based jobseeker's allowance
6. Claims and backdating

provided, your date of claim is the date you eventually go to the Jobcentre Plus office. Your entitlement to JSA cannot start until that date.[69]

'Good cause' is not defined. All relevant circumstances must be considered. These may relate to your abilities, or to external factors. The general test is whether there is some factor that would probably cause a reasonable person of your age and experience to act, or fail to act, as you did.[70]

Backdating your claim

It is very important to claim in time. A claim for JSA can be backdated for a maximum of three months, but only in exceptional circumstances. The general rules on backdating are covered on p1157. See p1060 for the backdating rules that apply if you do not come under the UC system (see p20) and you make a new claim for JSA after your entitlement ended when you failed to sign on or participate in an interview. **Note:** if you claimed WTC or UC when you should have claimed JSA, see p713 to see whether your date of claim can be backdated.

If you might have qualified for JSA earlier but did not claim because you were given the wrong information or were misled by the DWP, you could ask for compensation (see p1396) or complain to the Ombudsman through your MP (see p1401).

If you want to get your jobseeker's agreement backdated, see p1053. If you want the time limit for accepting your claimant commitment to be extended, see p1072.

If you claim the wrong benefit

If you claim WTC or UC when you should have claimed JSA, see p713 to see whether your date of claim can be backdated.

Claiming in advance

If you do not qualify for JSA from the date of your claim, but will do so within the next three months, you can be awarded JSA from the first date on which you qualify.[71] This gives the DWP time to ensure you receive benefit as soon as you are entitled. Let the DWP know you want to claim in advance when you claim and at your initial interview. You might have to persuade the DWP that it can accept a claim in advance.

You might only qualify for contribution-based JSA currently but would also be entitled to income-based JSA once you or your partner (or a child who can be included in your claim) become entitled to another 'qualifying benefit' (eg, disability living allowance, personal independence payment or carer's allowance) because you are then entitled to premiums. Tell the DWP you want your entitlement to income-based JSA to be considered when you claim the qualifying benefit. See p1300 for further information about revisions and supersessions in this situation.

After you are awarded jobseeker's allowance

Once you have been awarded JSA, in order to continue to receive it you must:
- attend and participate in regular interviews; *and*
- confirm that you continue to qualify for JSA – eg, by signing on.

In some cases, if you fail to participate in interviews, you may be given a sanction (see p1103 and p1121). In other cases, if you do not come under the UC system and you fail to sign on or participate in interviews, your entitlement to JSA can end (see p1057).

If you do not come under the UC system, you are required to meet the jobseeking conditions and your entitlement to JSA ends if you fail to do so. When you claim JSA again, you can be given a sanction. If you come under the UC system, you are required to meet work-related requirements and you can be given a sanction if you fail to do so. See Chapters 45 and 47 for further information about the requirements after you are awarded JSA, and Chapter 48 for information about sanctions.

Note: you may be asked to provide information after you are awarded JSA. If you do not do so, your JSA could be suspended or even terminated (see p1185).

Referral to job, training or employment scheme vacancies

While you are claiming JSA, you may be referred to job vacancies.

You risk being given a sanction if you refuse to apply for a job vacancy without a good reason. Alternatively, you could be issued with a jobseeker's direction or be required to meet a work preparation requirement (eg, to take some action to improve your job prospects), and risk being given a sanction if you refuse or fail to do so. Refusing to apply for a job or vacancy on a scheme or programme may also raise doubts about whether you are available for work.

If you are not considered ready for a job, you are likely to be referred to a place on a training or employment scheme – eg, Work Experience or the Work Programme (see p1103). You can be sanctioned for not attending or for leaving early.

See Chapter 48 for information about sanctions.

If you have a disability

If you have a disability that affects your search for work, you may be eligible for specialist help from the DWP. For further information, see www.gov.uk/specialist-employability-support. Every Jobcentre Plus office has a disability adviser who is responsible for good practice relating to disabled people.

You may want to ask for specialist help if, for example:
- you think the service from the Jobcentre Plus office, or a government programme or scheme, is not meeting your needs; *or*
- your health problem or disability has worsened significantly, or you have a new disability or health problem and need specialist help; *or*

- you need new skills in order to do a job; *or*
- you need practical help with looking for a job – eg, help in getting to interviews or identifying specialist equipment; *or*
- you are not clear about the effect your disability has on the job options open to you.

7. **Getting paid**

The general rules on getting paid are covered in Chapter 50. This section explains the specific rules that apply to jobseeker's allowance (JSA). **Note:** the rules in this section apply to all types of JSA.

When is jobseeker's allowance paid?

JSA is normally paid fortnightly in arrears.[72]

JSA is a weekly benefit, although in some cases it can be paid for part weeks.[73] Most questions about entitlement and payment are decided in relation to a particular 'benefit week' – ie, the period of seven days ending on the day of the week allocated to you according to your national insurance (NI) number.[74]

If you are entitled to less than 10p a week, you are not paid JSA at all,[75] but you are still eligible for NI credits (see p967). If you are entitled to less than £1 a week, a decision maker can decide to pay you at longer intervals of not more than 13 weeks.[76]

Note:
- Deductions can be made from your JSA to pay to third parties (see p1187).
- Your JSA might be paid at a reduced (or nil) rate if you have been sanctioned for a benefit offence (see p1265). **Note:** you may also be given a sanction for other reasons (see Chapter 48).
- For information on missing payments, see p1174. If you cannot get your JSA payments because you have lost your bank or Post Office card or you have forgotten your PIN, see p1173. If you have lost your 'simple payment' card, or you have forgotten your memorable date, see p1173.
- If payment of your JSA is delayed, see p1165. If you are waiting for a decision on your claim, or to be paid, you might be able to get a short-term advance (see p1177). If you wish to complain about how your claim has been dealt with, or claim compensation, see Chapter 58.
- If payment of your JSA is suspended, see p1185.
- If you are overpaid JSA, you might have to repay it (see Chapter 52) and, in some circumstances, you may have to pay a penalty (see p1256). If you have been accused of fraud, see Chapter 53.

Change of circumstances

You must report changes in your circumstances that you have been told you must report, as well as any that you might reasonably be expected to know might affect your right to, the amount of or the payment of your benefit, including any that are likely to occur. You should do this as soon as possible, preferably in writing. See p1184 for further information.

When there has been a relevant change of circumstances, a decision maker looks at your claim again and makes a new decision.

As a general rule, your JSA is adjusted from the first day of the benefit week in which the change occurs or is expected to do so.[77] There are a number of exceptions to this rule.[78] In particular, if a decision is to your advantage, but you failed to notify the DWP of a change within the time limit (normally one month, but this can be extended – see p1295), your JSA is adjusted:

- if you are paid in arrears, from the first day of the benefit week in which you notified the change; *or*
- if you are paid in advance, from the day on which you notified the change, if this is the first day of the benefit week. If it is not, your JSA is adjusted from the next week.

8. Tax, other benefits and the benefit cap

Tax

Jobseeker's allowance (JSA) is taxable.[79] The maximum amount of JSA that is taxable is:

- an amount equal to the weekly rate of JSA for a person of your age (see p704); *or*
- if you are a member of a couple, an amount equal to the income-based JSA applicable amount for a couple which would be included if you were getting income-based JSA.

The tax is not deducted while JSA is being paid, but reduces the refund you would otherwise receive through pay as you earn (PAYE) when you return to work.

Any tax refunds of PAYE payments are paid to you at the end of the tax year to which they relate. Any other tax refund is paid only when you stop getting JSA.

Means-tested benefits and tax credits

If you are getting contribution-based JSA, you may also be entitled to income-based JSA, or if you are at least the qualifying age for pension credit (PC – see p147) to PC, to top this up. If you come under the universal credit (UC) system (see p20), you may be entitled to UC to top up your contribution-based JSA.

Part 5: Other benefits
Chapter 32: Contribution-based jobseeker's allowance
8. Tax, other benefits and the benefit cap

Your contribution-based JSA counts as income for the purposes of means-tested benefits unless you get income-based JSA, PC or UC, in which case it is ignored for housing benefit (HB) purposes.

You cannot claim JSA and income support (IS) at the same time. If you have a partner, s/he can claim IS, income-related employment and support allowance or PC and you can claim contribution-based JSA (but not income-based JSA).

If you have a partner and s/he works sufficient hours, you and your partner might be able to claim working tax credit (WTC). If you have children, you may be able to claim child tax credit.

If you or your partner have just stopped work or reduced your hours, you might get what is known as 'WTC run-on' for a four-week period (see p202).

Non-means-tested benefits

While you are on JSA you are entitled to national insurance credits (see p967). Contribution-based JSA is affected by the overlapping benefit rules (see p1175).

The benefit cap

In some cases, there is a limit on the total amount of specified benefits you can receive (a 'benefit cap'). JSA is one of the specified benefits. However, the benefit cap only applies if you are getting HB or UC. See p1180 for further information.

Passports and other sources of help

If you are entitled to income-based JSA or UC in addition to contribution-based JSA, you may also qualify for health benefits such as free prescriptions (see Chapter 29) and education benefits such as free school lunches (see p860). Even if you are not entitled to one of those benefits, you may qualify for health benefits if your income is low enough (see p657). You may qualify for council tax reduction (see p854). You may also qualify for social fund payments (see Chapter 36) and help from your local welfare assistance scheme (see p856).

Financial help on starting work

If you stop getting income-based JSA because you or your partner start work, or your earnings or hours in your existing job increase, you might be able to get mortgage interest run-on (if you have a home loan – see p474) or extended payments of HB (if you pay rent – see p86). Your local authority may provide extended help with council tax. See p866 for information about other financial help you might get.

Notes

1. Who can claim contribution-based jobseeker's allowance
1 s1 JSA 1995
2 ss6-6I JSA 1995
3 s2 JSA 1995
4 Reg 47(1) and (2) JSA Regs; reg 37(1) JSA Regs 2013
5 Arts 12 and 13 WRA(No.9)O; Arts 10(2) and 11(2) WRA(No.11)O
6 Reg 49 JSA Regs; reg 40 JSA Regs 2013
7 Reg 47(3) JSA Regs; reg 37(2) JSA Regs 2013
8 s2(1) and (4) JSA 1995
9 Reg 48 JSA Regs; reg 39 JSA Regs 2013
10 Reg 48(2) and (3) JSA Regs; reg 39(2) and (4) JSA Regs 2013
11 *LE v SSWP* [2009] UKUT 166 (AAC). The judge decided that the rule indirectly discriminated against women but that the discrimination was justified.
12 Reg 51 JSA Regs; reg 42 JSA Regs 2013
13 s1(2)(f) JSA 1995
14 Sch 1 para 2 JSA 1995; reg 10 SS&CS(DA) Regs
15 Regs 55(1), 55ZA(1) and 55A(1) JSA Regs; regs 46(1), 46A(1) and 47(1) JSA Regs 2013
16 Reg 55(1) and (3) JSA Regs; reg 46(1) and (3) JSA Regs 2013
17 Reg 55(7) JSA Regs; reg 46(7) JSA Regs 2013
18 Arts 12 and 13 WRA(No.9)(O); Arts 10(2) and 11(2) WRA(No.11)O
19 Reg 55(2) JSA Regs; reg 46(2) JSA Regs 2013
20 Reg 55(4) and (6) JSA Regs; reg 46(4) and (6) JSA Regs 2013
21 Regs 14(1)(l) and 19(1)(l) JSA Regs
22 Reg 16(5) JSA Regs 2013
23 Reg 55ZA(1), (3) and (3A) JSA Regs; reg 46A(1), (3) and (3A) JSA Regs 2013
24 Reg 55ZA(4) JSA Regs; reg 46A(4) JSA Regs 2013
25 Reg 55ZA(5) JSA Regs; reg 46A(5) JSA Regs 2013
26 Reg 55ZA(6) JSA Regs; reg 46A(6) JSA Regs 2013
27 Regs 14(1)(l) and 19(1)(lzl) JSA Regs
28 Reg 16A JSA Regs 2013
29 Reg 55A JSA Regs; reg 47 JSA Regs 2013
30 Reg 55A(2) JSA Regs; reg 47(2) JSA Regs 2013
31 Regs 14(1)(l) and 19(1)(ll) JSA Regs
32 Reg 16 JSA Regs 2013

4. The amount of benefit
33 s4(1) and (2) JSA 1995; reg 79 JSA Regs; reg 49 JSA Regs 2013
34 Sch 1 para 4 JSA 1995; reg 46 JSA Regs; reg 36 JSA Regs 2013; Arts 12 and 13 WRA(No.9)(O); Arts 10(2) and 11(2) WRA(No.11)O
35 Reg 14A(4) SS&CS(DA) Regs; reg 48(5) UC,PIP,JSA&ESA(DA) Regs
36 s4(1) JSA 1995
37 Regs 99(3) and 101(3) and Sch 6 JSA Regs; regs 59(2) and 61(2) and Sch JSA Regs 2013
38 s4(1)(b) JSA 1995; reg 80 JSA Regs; reg 50 JSA Regs 2013
39 s2(1)(c) JSA 1995; reg 56(1) and (2) JSA Regs; reg 48 JSA Regs 2013
40 ss4(1) and 35(1) JSA 1995; R(JSA) 1/01
41 Reg 81 JSA Regs; reg 51 JSA Regs 2013; R(U) 8/83
42 Reg 81(2)(c) and (d) JSA Regs; reg 51(4) JSA Regs 2013
43 Reg 81(1) JSA Regs; reg 51(1) JSA Regs 2013
44 Reg 81(1A) JSA Regs; reg 51(2) JSA Regs 2013
45 Reg 81(1B) JSA Regs; reg 51(3) JSA Regs 2013
46 s5(1) JSA 1995
47 *PL v SSWP (JSA)* [2016] UKUT 177 (AAC)
48 Arts 12 and 13 WRA(No.9)(O); Arts 10(2) and 11(2) WRA(No.11)O
49 s5(2) JSA 1995
50 Reg 49 JSA Regs; reg 40 JSA Regs 2013
51 Reg 47(2) and (4) JSA Regs; reg 37(3) JSA Regs 2013; Arts 12 and 13 WRA(No.9)O; Arts 10(2) and 11(2) WRA(No.11)O

6. Claims and backdating
52 Reg 4ZC SS(C&P) Regs; reg 3 and Sch 2 UC,PIP,JSA&ESA(C&P) Regs
53 Reg 4(11A) and (11B) SS(C&P) Regs; reg 23 UC,PIP,JSA&ESA(C&P) Regs

54 Reg 4(1A) SS(C&P) Regs; reg 21
UC,PIP,JSA&ESA(C&P) Regs
55 Reg 4(5) SS(C&P) Regs
56 Reg 4(6)(a) SS(C&P) Regs; reg 19
UC,PIP,JSA&ESA(C&P) Regs
57 www.gov.uk/guidance/new-style-
jobseekers-allowance
58 Reg 4(1A), (7B), (9), (12) and (13)
SS(C&P) Regs; regs 21 and 23
UC,PIP,JSA&ESA(C&P) Regs
59 Reg 4(6)(a) SS(C&P) Regs; reg 19
UC,PIP,JSA&ESA(C&P) Regs
60 www.gov.uk/jobseekers-allowance/
how-to-claim
61 Reg 19(1) and Sch 4 para 1 SS(C&P)
Regs; reg 29(1) UC,PIP,JSA&ESA(C&P)
Regs
62 Reg 6(4A)(a)(i) and (4AB) SS(C&P) Regs;
reg 20 UC,PIP,JSA&ESA(C&P) Regs
63 Reg 6(4A)(b) SS(C&P) Regs; regs 22 and
24 UC,PIP,JSA&ESA(C&P) Regs
64 Reg 6(4AB) SS(C&P) Regs; reg 21
UC,PIP,JSA&ESA(C&P) Regs
65 Reg 6(28) SS(C&P) Regs
66 Art 3A WRA(No.9)O
67 Reg 4(3B)(b) SS(C&P) Regs
68 Reg 4(3B)(c) SS(C&P) Regs
69 Reg 6(4A)(a)(ii) SS(C&P) Regs; reg 20(2)
UC,PIP,JSA&ESA(C&P) Regs
70 CS/371/1949
71 Reg 13(1) and (9) SS(C&P) Regs; reg 34
UC,PIP,JSA&ESA(C&P) Regs

7. Getting paid
72 Reg 26A SS(C&P) Regs; reg 52
UC,PIP,JSA&ESA(C&P) Regs
73 s1(3) and Sch 1 para 5 JSA 1995; reg
150 JSA Regs; reg 64 JSA Regs 2013
74 Reg 1(3) JSA Regs; reg 2(2) JSA Regs
2013
75 Reg 87A JSA Regs; reg 52 JSA Regs 2013
76 Reg 26A(3) SS(C&P) Regs; reg 52(3)
UC,PIP,JSA&ESA(C&P) Regs
77 Reg 7 and Sch 3A para 7 SS&CS(DA)
Regs; reg 35 and Sch 1
UC,PIP,JSA&ESA(DA) Regs
78 Reg 7 and Sch 3A para 8-13 SS&CS(DA)
Regs; reg 35 and Sch 1 Part 1
UC,PIP,JSA&ESA(DA) Regs

8. Tax, other benefits and the benefit cap
79 ss671-75 IT(EP)A 2003

Chapter 33

Maternity allowance

This chapter covers:
1. Who can claim maternity allowance (below)
2. The rules about your age (p728)
3. People included in the claim (p728)
4. The amount of benefit (p728)
5. Special benefit rules (p728)
6. Claims and backdating (p729)
7. Getting paid (p731)
8. Tax, other benefits and the benefit cap (p732)

Key facts
- Maternity allowance (MA) is a benefit for women who are pregnant or have recently given birth and who are not entitled to statutory maternity pay.
- MA is a non-means-tested benefit.
- You do not need to have paid national insurance contributions to qualify.
- MA is affected by the overlapping benefit rules, so you may not be able to get MA and another earnings-replacement benefit at the same time.
- You may be disqualified from MA if you work.
- MA is administered and paid by the DWP.
- If you disagree with a decision on MA, you can apply for a revision or supersession, or appeal against it. You must apply for a mandatory reconsideration before you can appeal.

1. **Who can claim maternity allowance**

You may qualify for maternity allowance (MA) if:
- you are, or have been, employed or self-employed (see p722); *or*
- you have helped your spouse or civil partner with her/his self-employment (see p726).

Future changes

The government intends to abolish class 2 national insurance (NI) contributions from April 2018. Currently, these can determine the amount of MA you receive if you are self-employed, or can enable you to qualify for MA if you help your spouse or civil partner with her/his self-employment (see p723 and p726). The government plans instead to:

– allow women who satisfy the MA employment condition on the basis of self–employment (see p722) to qualify for the maximum rate of MA if they pay three class 3 NI contributions (and to qualify for the lowest rate of MA if they to do not – currently £27 a week); *and*

– remove the requirement that a woman's spouse or civil partner must have paid class 2 NI contributions in order for her to qualify for MA on the basis of having helped with her spouse's or civil partner's self–employment.[1]

At present, your entitlement to MA is not affected by your immigration status (see Chapter 65) but it is expected that, from some point in the future, you will have to be entitled to work in the UK to qualify for MA.[2] There may be exceptions.

See CPAG's online service and *Welfare Rights Bulletin* for updates.

If you have been employed or self-employed

You qualify for MA on the basis of your employment or self-employment if you:[3]

- satisfy the employment condition (see below); *and*
- satisfy the earnings condition (see p723); *and*
- are pregnant or have recently given birth, and you are within your 'maternity allowance period' (MA period – see p724); *and*
- are not entitled to statutory maternity pay (SMP).

In certain circumstances, you may be disqualified from receiving MA (see p727) – eg, if you work during your MA period.

Note: if you get SMP (or if you would have got SMP but for having reduced your maternity pay period in connection with a claim for statutory shared parental pay (SSPP) or shared parental pay), you cannot receive MA for the same week for the same baby, even if you have more than one job or have been self-employed as well as employed.[4] If you are employed, or you have been recently, you may be expected to submit Form SMP1 from your employer to show that you are not entitled to SMP (see p729).

Employment condition

To qualify for MA on the basis of your employment or self-employment, you must have been an employed or self-employed earner for at least 26 weeks in the 66 weeks immediately before your expected week of childbirth (EWC). This 66-week period is called the 'test period'.[5] If you are an employed or self-employed earner for part of a week, the whole of that week counts. The 26 weeks do not need to be consecutive and you do not need to have worked in the same job for the whole period. You need only show that you have been an employed and/or self-employed earner for any part of each of the 26 weeks. For the meaning of employed and self-employed earner, see p958. See p728 if you have worked abroad. For the date on which your test period starts, see Appendix 11 .

Expected week of childbirth
The '**expected week of childbirth**' is the week, starting on a Sunday, in which your baby is due to be born.

Example
Rita's baby is due on Saturday 8 July 2017.
Rita's EWC begins on Sunday 2 July 2017 and her 66-week 'test period' runs from Sunday 27 March 2016 to Saturday 1 July 2017.

Earnings condition

To qualify for MA on the basis of your employment or self-employment, your average weekly earnings in 13 weeks of your test period (or, if you are self-employed, the average weekly earnings you are treated as having) must be at least £30 a week. This is known as the 'MA threshold'. For how earnings are averaged, see p724.[6] For when you count as employed or self–employed, see p958.

Earnings from employment

If you are employed, your gross earnings are used to calculate your average weekly earnings. What counts as earnings for MA purposes is the same as for SMP (see p817).[7] If you get a backdated pay rise for the period over which your earnings are averaged, this is included in the calculation.[8]

Earnings from self-employment

The amount you actually earn from self-employment is not taken into account. Instead, you are treated as earning a certain amount and this figure is used to calculate your average weekly earnings. For each week:[9]

- for which you have paid a class 2 NI contribution, you are treated as having earnings of an amount 90 per cent of which is equal to the maximum amount of MA that can be paid for that week. This means that from 10 April 2017, you are treated as having earnings of £156.64 a week (from 6 April 2015 to 9 April 2017, you are treated as earning £155.09 a week). If this applies for at least 13 weeks in your 66-week test period, you qualify for MA of £140.98 a week;[10]

- for which you could have paid a class 2 contribution but have not done so, you are treated as having earnings of £30 a week – ie, equal to the MA threshold.

Note: if you are self-employed, your liability to pay class 2 contributions is calculated after the end of the tax year through the income tax self–assessment procedure. To help you meet the condition in the first bullet point on p723, you can pay class 2 contributions early, on a voluntary basis, at any time from the week to which the contribution relates until 31 January after the tax year in which the week falls (see p959).[11]

Calculating average earnings

Your average weekly earnings are calculated as follows.[12]

- If you have paid class 2 contributions as a self-employed person (see p959) for at least 13 weeks in your 66-week test period, no calculation is needed – you automatically qualify for MA of £140.98 a week. **Note:** see p704 of the 2016/17 edition of this *Handbook* if this includes weeks prior to 6 April 2015 for which you had an NI small earnings exception certificate.
- Otherwise, add together your earnings (or the earnings you are treated as having from self-employment – see p723) in the 13 weeks in your 66-week test period when your earnings are highest and divide the total by 13. If you have more than one job, the earnings from all your jobs, including earnings you are treated as having from self-employment, are counted.

In both cases, the 13 weeks do not need to be consecutive. If you are not paid weekly, work out your weekly earnings by dividing the payments you receive by the nearest number of weeks in the period for which they are paid.[13]

Maternity allowance period

MA awarded on the basis of your employment or self-employment can only be paid for weeks in the MA period.[14] This is a period of up to 39 consecutive weeks that normally starts on the day your maternity pay period would have begun had you been entitled to SMP (see p821). However:[15]

- if you are not employed or self-employed at the beginning of the 11th week before your EWC (see p723), your MA period starts from the beginning of that week (but if your baby was born before this, it starts from the day after the birth); *and*
- if you are not entitled to MA during the 11th week before your EWC, but you become entitled to it before your baby is born (perhaps because you then meet the earnings or employment condition), provided you have stopped work, the earliest day on which your MA period can start is the day you become entitled to MA, and the latest it can start is the day after the birth.

To calculate the 11th week before your EWC, see Appendix 11.

Reducing your maternity allowance period and statutory shared parental pay

If your MA is awarded on the basis of your employment or self-employment, you can reduce your MA period so that the father of your child or your partner can qualify for SSPP from her/his employer (see p806) and/or shared parental leave from work. If s/he meets the qualifying conditions, s/he can then get SSPP for the number of weeks that would have been remaining in your MA period.

To reduce your MA period, you must give the DWP a 'curtailment notification'. This just means you must inform the DWP that you intend to reduce your MA period. It is always advisable to do this in writing, although the DWP cannot insist on this. Your notification should be given to the DWP office that deals with your MA claim at least eight weeks before the date you have chosen to end your MA period (although the DWP has discretion to accept less notice than this if it considers it appropriate), and must include the date on which you want your MA period to end.[16] This 'curtailment date' must be:[17]

- the last day of a week. For this purpose, a week usually starts on the day of the week on which your MA period began; *and*
- at least two weeks after the birth (or four weeks after it, if you are employed in a factory or workshop) and at least one week before the last day of your MA period.

The father of your baby or your partner may get SSPP even while you get MA, provided you have given a curtailment notification to indicate your intention to reduce your MA period. If you just return to work without doing so, your MA period is not reduced (although you will be disqualified from getting MA once you have worked for more than 10 days – see p727) and, until you give such notification, the child's father or your partner cannot get SSPP. If you give the DWP a curtailment notification after returning to work, the curtailment date is the last day of the week in which you give it.[18] See p812 for how the number of weeks of SSPP are calculated in this situation.

Your MA period (and so your entitlement to MA) ends on the curtailment date if the father of your baby or your partner qualifies for SSPP or shared parental leave. As it is only possible to cancel a curtailment notification in limited circumstances, think carefully about giving up your MA in this way. To revoke a curtailment notification, you must inform the DWP that you want to do so before the curtailment date. This is called a 'revocation notification'. You can only revoke a curtailment notification if:[19]

- you gave the curtailment notification before your child was born. In this situation, you must give the revocation notification within six weeks of the birth, but can subsequently give another curtailment notification; *or*
- your partner dies. In this situation, you must give the revocation notification within a reasonable time after the death and it must include the date of death.

Your spouse's or civil partner's self-employment

If you do not qualify for MA on the basis of your own employment or self-employment, you may qualify if you have helped your spouse or civil partner with her/his self-employment. This applies if:[20]

- you are pregnant (or you have had your baby); *and*
- you are within your 14-week qualifying period (see below); *and*
- your spouse or civil partner was a self-employed earner in at least 26 weeks in the 66 weeks immediately before your EWC and s/he has paid class 2 NI contributions for those 26 weeks (but see below); *and*
- for at least part of each of those 26 weeks you took part in, or assisted, your spouse or civil partner with her/his self-employment, but you were not employed by, or in partnership with, her/him; *and*
- you are not entitled to SMP for the same pregnancy.

Note: although your spouse or civil partner is not liable to pay class 2 contributions until after the end of the tax year, s/he can pay them early, on a voluntary basis, to help you to meet the above condition (see p959).[21]

In certain circumstances, you may be disqualified from receiving MA (see p727).

14-week qualifying period

MA awarded on the basis that you have helped your spouse or civil partner with her/his self-employment can only be paid for weeks in the qualifying period. This is the period of 14 consecutive weeks starting from:[22]

- the beginning of the 11th week before your EWC, if you stopped working with your spouse or civil partner before this date; *or*
- the day after you stop working with your spouse or civil partner, if you stop during the period that runs from the start of the 11th week before your EWC until the day you have your baby. Once you have reached the fourth week before your EWC, this applies even if you just refrain from working with your spouse or civil partner (eg, because you are unwell), if this is at least in part because of your pregnancy or childbirth; *or*
- if neither of the above apply, the day after you have your baby.

'Stopping work' means either stopping permanently or until after the birth. To calculate the 11th week before your EWC, see Appendix 11.

Note: if you are not entitled to MA during the 11th week before your EWC but you become entitled to it before your baby is born, provided you have stopped working with your spouse or civil partner, the earliest day your 14-week qualifying period can start is the day you become entitled to MA and the latest is the day after the birth.[23]

Disqualification from maternity allowance

In some circumstances, you can be disqualified from MA if you work or if you fail to attend a medical examination.

If you work

It is important to tell the DWP of any work that you do. This is because the DWP can disqualify you from receiving MA for as long as is reasonable given the circumstances if:[24]

- you are entitled to MA on the basis of your own employment or self-employment (see p722) and you work for more than 10 days during your MA period. The disqualification must be for at least the number of days you worked in excess of these 10 days. Both employed and self-employed work counts and the 10 days do not need to be consecutive. If you work for part of a day, it counts as a full day. If you work for 10 days or less, your MA is unaffected, even if you are paid for that work;
- you are entitled to MA on the basis of helping with your spouse or civil partner's self-employment (see p726) and you do *any* work during your 14-week qualifying period. This applies if the work is helping your spouse or partner with her/his business or work you do as an employee or as a self-employed earner. The disqualification must be for at least the number of days you worked.

You can challenge the DWP's decision, including its decision on the length of the disqualification period (see Chapters 54 and 55).

Note:
- If you are employed and on maternity leave, working for your employer for more than 10 days may affect your continued entitlement to leave. If you do not want your maternity leave to end, get employment advice before agreeing to such work.
- If you have been disqualified from MA because you have worked for more than 10 days, provided you have not brought your MA period to an end by submitting a curtailment notification (see p725), you may be able to get MA again if you stop work and are still within your MA period. If you are employed and your maternity leave has been brought to an end, this could be during a period when you take shared parental leave. It is not necessary for you to end your MA period in order to qualify for shared parental leave, but it may be necessary to submit a curtailment notification for a partner in the application to qualify for SSPP and/or shared parental leave.

If you fail to attend a medical

You are disqualified from receiving MA if, before the birth of your baby, you fail to attend a medical examination without good cause. For this to apply, you must have been given written notice of the examination at least three days beforehand by the DWP or someone acting on its behalf. The DWP can disqualify you for as long as is reasonable given the circumstances, but the disqualification cannot start until the day of the missed examination and cannot continue once you have given birth.[25]

Whether or not you have good cause for failing to attend depends on your circumstances. You can challenge the DWP's decision on whether you have good cause or on the length of the disqualification period (see Chapters 54 and 55).

2. The rules about your age

There are no upper or lower age limits for receiving maternity allowance.

3. People included in the claim

You claim maternity allowance for yourself. You cannot claim any increase for your partner or child(ren).

4. The amount of benefit

If you qualify for maternity allowance (MA) on the basis of your own employment or self-employment, it can only be paid during the 39-week MA period (see p724). The amount you receive is either 90 per cent of your average weekly earnings or £140.98 a week, whichever is less.[26] See p724 for how your average earnings are calculated. If you qualify because you help with your spouse's or civil partner's self-employment, MA is only payable during the 14-week qualifying period. The amount you receive is £27 a week.

5. Special benefit rules

Special rules may apply to:
- people who are going abroad (see Chapters 67 and 68);
- people in prison or detention (see Chapter 41).

There are also special rules if you have been employed abroad.
- If, following a period of employment abroad, you have returned to Great Britain and you remained ordinarily resident in Great Britain while you were away, you may be able to rely on periods of employment abroad to satisfy the employment and earnings condition for maternity allowance (MA).[27]

- In some circumstances, you may be able to rely on periods you have worked in other European Economic Area countries to qualify for MA (see p1578).

6. Claims and backdating

The general rules about claims and backdating are covered in Chapter 49. This section explains the specific rules that apply to maternity allowance (MA).

If you are (or have recently been) employed, you may be entitled to statutory maternity pay (SMP – see Chapter 37) from your employer (or ex-employer) instead of MA. If you were employed in the 15th week before your expected week of childbirth (EWC), the DWP expects you to have applied for SMP from your employer. If your employer (or ex-employer) has decided you are not entitled to SMP, it should give you Form SMP1 explaining why and you should send this to the DWP to support your claim for MA. If you disagree with your employer's decision, or your employer fails to give you a decision, also ask HM Revenue and Customs to make a decision on your entitlement to SMP (see Chapter 57).

Making a claim

A claim for MA must be made in writing, normally on the approved form. Send your completed form to the DWP office which deals with claims for MA. The relevant address is included on the form. Keep a copy of your claim form in case queries arise. Your claim will not be accepted unless it is received after the 15th week before your EWC.[28]

You must complete the form in accordance with the instructions on it. See p730 for the information and evidence you are expected to provide in connection with your claim. The decision maker at the DWP may accept a written application not on the approved form.[29] You can amend or withdraw your claim before a decision is made (see p1149). If you are waiting for a decision on your claim or you are waiting to be paid, you may be able to get a short-term advance of benefit (see p1177).

Forms

The approved form is Form MA1, which you can get from the Jobcentre Plus national contact centre (tel: 0800 055 6688; textphone: 0800 023 4888) or from www.gov.uk.

Who should claim

You must normally claim MA for yourself. However, if you are unable to manage your own affairs, another person can claim MA for you as your 'appointee' (see p1149).

Information to support your claim

For the general information requirements that apply to all benefits, see p1150.

It is important that you provide any information required when you claim. Until you do, you may not count as having made a valid claim (see p1152). Correct any defects as soon as possible as your date of claim may be affected.

You must also provide evidence, normally a certificate from your doctor or a registered midwife, giving the expected date of birth of your child (Form MAT B1) and, if you are claiming MA after your baby is born, giving the date of the baby's birth.[30] This certificate is not accepted as evidence of your EWC if it is issued before the 20th week before your EWC. If you cannot obtain Form MAT B1, other evidence can be accepted, if it is sufficient in the circumstances.

If you have been employed, the DWP also expects you to provide pay slips or some other written proof of your earnings and Form SMP1 from any employer for whom you worked during the 15th week before your EWC. Do not delay sending your claim for MA because you are waiting for your SMP1 or evidence of your earnings; you can send these in later.

Even if you have provided all that was required when you claimed, you may be asked to provide further evidence to support your claim (see p1154). You may also be asked to provide information after you are awarded MA. If you fail to do so, your MA could be suspended, or even terminated (see p1185).

The date of your claim

The date of your claim is important as it can determine when your entitlement to MA starts. This is not necessarily the date from when you are paid. For information about when payment of MA starts, see p731.

The **'date of your claim'** is normally the date it is received at a DWP office.[31]

Note: you must make sure your claim is valid. If it is 'defective', you are given a short time to correct the defect (see p1152). If you do, your claim is treated as having been made when you initially claimed.[32]

In some cases, you can claim in advance (see p731) and in some cases your claim can be backdated (see below). If you want this done, make this clear when you claim or the DWP may not consider it. If you claimed employment and support allowance (ESA) instead of MA, or if you have been refused SMP, see p731.

Backdating your claim

A claim for MA can be backdated for up to three months if you satisfy the qualifying conditions over that period. You do not have to show any reasons why your claim was late.[33]

If you might have qualified for benefit earlier but did not claim because you were given the wrong information or were misled by the DWP, you could ask for compensation (see p1396) or complain to the Independent Case Examiner or to the Ombudsman through your MP (see p1397 and p1401).

If you claimed ESA instead of MA, or if you have been refused SMP, see p731.

If you claim the wrong benefit

A claim for ESA may also be treated as a claim for MA and vice versa (see p1161).[34] This may allow you to get your claim for MA backdated for more than the usual three months.

If your employer (or former employer) has decided that you are not entitled to SMP and you claim MA within three months of being notified of your employer's decision in writing, your claim for MA is treated as having been made either on the date you gave your employer notice of when you wanted the maternity pay period to start or at the beginning of the 14th week before your EWC, whichever is later.[35]

Claiming in advance

You cannot make a claim for MA until after the 15th week before your EWC (ie, until week 26 of pregnancy), but you should claim as soon as possible after that.[36] However, if you qualify for MA on the basis of your own employment or self-employment, it may be worth waiting a few weeks before claiming if this means you will have higher average earnings, and these would increase the amount of your MA.

7. Getting paid

The general rules on getting paid are covered in Chapter 50. This section explains the specific rules that apply to maternity allowance (MA).

When is maternity allowance paid?
The day you are paid depends on your national insurance number (see p1174). MA is normally paid fortnightly in arrears.[37]

If you have claimed in time and are entitled to MA, payment normally runs from the first day of your MA period (see p724) or 14-week qualifying period (see p726) until that period ends. To calculate the amount of MA due for a period of less than a week, the daily rate of MA is used, which is one-seventh of the weekly amount.[38] Note:

- In some circumstances, you can be disqualified from receiving MA (see p727).
- Even if you have been sanctioned for a benefit offence (see p1265), you must be paid your MA.

- For information on missing payments, see p1174. If you cannot get your MA payments because you have lost your bank or Post Office card or you have forgotten your PIN, see p1173. If you have lost your 'simple payment' card, or you have forgotten your memorable date, see p1173.
- If payment of your MA is delayed, see p1165. If you are waiting for a decision on your claim, or to be paid, you might be able to get a short-term advance (see p1177). If you wish to complain about how your claim has been dealt with, or claim compensation, see Chapter 58.
- If payment of your MA is suspended, see p1185.
- If you are overpaid MA, you might have to repay it (see Chapter 52) and, in some circumstances, you may have to pay a penalty (see p1256). If you have been accused of fraud, see Chapter 53.

5 Change of circumstances

You must report any change in your circumstances that you have been told you must report, as well as any that you might reasonably be expected to know might affect your right to, the amount of, or the payment of, your benefit. You should do this as soon as possible, preferably in writing. See p1184 for further information.

If the change affects your entitlement to MA, a decision maker looks at your claim again and makes a new decision (see p1287). The date from which the new decision takes effect depends on whether or not it is advantageous to you and whether you reported the change in time (see p1293).

8. Tax, other benefits and the benefit cap

Tax

Maternity allowance (MA) is not taxable.[39]

Means-tested benefits and tax credits

Unless you come under the universal credit (UC) system (see p20), being pregnant or on maternity leave may allow you to qualify for income support (IS – see p102). Alternatively, you may qualify for income-related employment and support allowance (ESA – see Chapter 3), as you are treated as having limited capability for work over the period when you get MA or, in certain circumstances, if you are pregnant (see p1006). You cannot qualify for both IS and ESA at the same time, so if you are unsure which you would be better off claiming, get advice.

Although you may not qualify for jobseeker's allowance (JSA) during a period when you get MA, if your partner is not in full-time paid work, s/he may qualify. If you are a member of a couple who would normally have to make a joint claim for JSA and you get MA, you may not need to make a joint claim for your partner to qualify for income-based JSA (see p120 and p135).

You may qualify for for working tax credit (WTC – see Chapter 10) as well as MA, because sometimes you can be treated as being in full-time work for WTC purposes while getting MA (see p201). If you are entitled to WTC, you may be able to get help with the cost of childcare before you resume work (see p1414). Once you are responsible for a child you may also qualify for child tax credit (CTC – see Chapter 9).

If you come under the UC system (see p20), you may qualify for UC (see Chapter 8) instead of IS, income-based JSA, income-related ESA, WTC or CTC (but see p181).

The MA you get is taken into account in full when calculating your entitlement to IS, income-based JSA, income-related ESA, the guarantee credit of pension credit, housing benefit (HB) and UC. MA is ignored when calculating your entitlement to WTC and CTC.

Non-means-tested benefits

MA is affected by the overlapping benefit rules (see p1175).

If you are entitled to MA on the basis of your employment or self-employment, you cannot get statutory sick pay (SSP) during your MA period. However, reducing your MA period may allow the father of your baby or your partner to get statutory shared parental pay and/or shared parental leave (see Chapter 37).

You can get national insurance credits for each week for which you get MA (because you are treated as having limited capability for work in those weeks – see p968).

You may qualify for both MA and contributory ESA (because you can be treated as having limited capability for work during the period when you are entitled to MA) but you cannot receive both benefits in full because of the overlapping benefit rules. In some circumstances, contributory ESA may be more than your MA entitlement. A claim for MA may be treated as a claim for ESA (see p1161).

The benefit cap

In some cases, there is a limit on the total amount of specified benefits you can receive (a 'benefit cap'). MA is one of the specified benefits. However, the benefit cap only applies if you are getting HB or UC. See p1180 for further information.

Passports and other sources of help

For details of whether you may qualify for:
- a Sure Start maternity grant from the social fund, see p789;
- certain health benefits, see Chapter 29;
- Healthy Start food vouchers and vitamins, see p857;
- council tax reduction, see p854;
- tax-free childcare, see p864.

Notes

1. Who can claim maternity allowance
1 HM Government, *Autumn Statement 2016*, para 5.2; *Abolishing Class 2 and Reforming Class 4 National Insurance Contributions: response to the consultation*, December 2016
2 s63 WRA 2012 (not yet in force)
3 s35 SSCBA 1992
4 s35(1)(d) and (3E) SSCBA 1992
5 s35(1)(b) SSCBA 1992
6 ss35(1)(c) and (6A) and 35A(4) SSCBA 1992
7 s35A(4)(a) SSCBA 1992; reg 2 SS(MatA)(E) Regs
8 Reg 6(2) SS(MatA)(E) Regs
9 Reg 3 SS(MatA)(E) Regs
10 s35A(5)(c), (5A) and (5B) SSCBA 1992; reg 5 SS(MatA)(E) Regs
11 Reg 90ZA SS(Con) Regs
12 Regs 4 and 6 SS(MatA)(E) Regs
13 Reg 6(3) SS(MatA)(E) Regs
14 ss35(2) and 165 SSCBA 1992; reg 2(2)SMP Regs
15 ss35(2) and 165 SSCBA 1992; reg 2 SMP Regs; reg 3 SS(MatA) Regs
16 Regs 3-5 MA(C) Regs
17 Reg 5(2) and (4) MA(C) Regs
18 Reg 5(5) MA(C) Regs
19 Reg 6 MA(C) Regs
20 s35B(1) and (2) SSCBA 1992
21 Reg 90ZA SS(Con) Regs
22 s35B(4)-(8) SSCBA 1992
23 Reg 3(2B) and (2C) SS(MatA) Regs
24 Reg 2(1)-(4) SS(MatA) Regs
25 Reg 2(7) and (8) SS(MatA) Regs

4. The amount of benefit
26 ss35(1) and 35A SSCBA 1992

5. Special benefit rules
27 SS(MatA)(WA) Regs

6. Claims and backdating
28 Reg 14(1) SS(C&P) Regs
29 Reg 4(1) SS(C&P) Regs
30 Reg 2(3) SS(ME) Regs
31 Reg 6(1) SS(C&P) Regs
32 Regs 4(7) and (7ZA) and 6(1) SS(C&P) Regs
33 Reg 19(2) SS(C&P) Regs

34 Regs 9 and 11 and Sch 1 Part I SS(C&P) Regs; regs 18 and 25 UC,PIP,JSA&ESA(C&P) Regs
35 Reg 10(3) and (4) SS(C&P) Regs
36 Reg 14 SS(C&P) Regs

7. Getting paid
37 Reg 24 SS(C&P) Regs
38 s35(5) SSCBA 1992

8. Tax, other benefits and the benefit cap
39 s677 IT(EP)A 2003

Chapter 34

Personal independence payment

This chapter covers:
1. Who can claim personal independence payment (p736)
2. The rules about your age (p753)
3. People included in the claim (p754)
4. The amount of benefit (p754)
5. Special benefit rules (p755)
6. Claims and backdating (p755)
7. Getting paid (p761)
8. Tax, other benefits and the benefit cap (p763)

Key facts
- Personal independence payment (PIP) is a benefit for adults with disabilities who have difficulty with getting around and/or with daily living activities.
- PIP has a daily living component and a mobility component. You can qualify for one or both components.
- PIP is a non-means-tested benefit.
- You do not have to have paid national insurance contributions to qualify.
- You can qualify for PIP whether you are in or out of work.
- PIP is administered and paid by the DWP.
- If you disagree with a PIP decision, you can apply for a revision or a supersession, or appeal against it. You must apply for a mandatory reconsideration before you can appeal.

Future changes

In the future the rules on PIP may be different in Scotland. See CPAG's online service and *Welfare Rights Bulletin* for updates.

Part 5: Other benefits
Chapter 34: Personal independence payment
1. Who can claim personal independence payment

1. Who can claim personal independence payment

Note: if you are currently entitled to disability living allowance (DLA), see p627 to help you decide whether or not to claim personal independence payment (PIP).

You qualify for PIP if:

- you are aged 16 or over[1] and, in most cases, under 65 (see p753);[2]
- you are not a 'person subject to immigration control', although there are some exceptions to this (see Chapter 65);[3]
- you satisfy the residence conditions (see p1574);[4]
- you satisfy the disability conditions for the daily living component, the mobility component or both (see below);[5]
- unless you are terminally ill, you satisfy the 'required period' condition. This usually means that your needs must be expected to last at least a year (see p752).

The disability conditions

A points-based test is used to asseses how your physical or mental condition affects your ability to undertake specific daily living activities (see p737) and mobility activities (see p748).[6] Each activity has a list of statements (called 'descriptors'), describing different difficulties or types of help needed. Each descriptor has a points score, and you get points for one descriptor for each activity – the one which best describes the difficulties you have with that activity. See p751 if your difficulties with the activities vary on different days.

Note: your difficulties with the activities can be due to either your physical or mental condition.[7] However, if you have a difficulty that is not caused by a physical or mental condition, this does not allow you to score points for an activity.

Example

Jessie has a learning disability. He needs help to read letters and so he scores points for the reading and understanding signs, symbols and words activity (see p745). James never learned to read at school. This is not due to a physical or mental condition, so he cannot score points for this activity.

The points you score for each activity relevant to a component are then added together. You qualify for a component at:[8]

- the standard rate if you score eight points or more; *or*
- the enhanced rate if you score 12 points or more.

Note: you automatically qualify for the enhanced rate of the daily living component if you are terminally ill (see p755).

The daily living activities

There are 10 daily living activities in the assessment. Remember that your difficulties with the activities must be caused by a physical or mental condition for you to score points. This section does not cover every kind of disability or health problem, so think carefully about how your condition affects your ability to undertake each of the activities.

At the time this *Handbook* was written the law was evolving quickly, as the Upper Tribunal decided cases that affect the interpretation of the descriptors (see p1350). See CPAG's online service or *Welfare Rights Bulletin* for updates.

The assessment of your ability to manage daily living activities distinguishes between different kinds of help you may need. You do not score any points if you can manage an activity 'unaided', which means without the use of an 'aid or appliance', or without 'supervision', 'prompting' or 'assistance'.[9]

These terms have particular definitions (see below). The highest scoring descriptor for most of the activities is awarded if you cannot undertake the activity at all, even with these kinds of help.

Assistance, supervision and prompting[10]

'**Assistance**' means physical help from another person with completing some part of an activity. It could arguably include someone doing the whole activity for you if there is no 'cannot' descriptor for that activity.[11] It does not include giving verbal instructions; this counts as 'prompting'.

'**Supervision**' means the continuous presence of another person throughout the activity to ensure your safety. The question of whether you need supervision is separate to whether you can manage the activity 'safely' (see p750), so you may score points for a supervision descriptor even if you would not come to harm on the majority of days if left unsupervised.[12] The risk does not need to be caused by one of the activities; it is enough that you need continuous supervision to carry out the activity reliably (see p750).[13]

'**Prompting**' means that another person needs to remind or encourage you to carry out an activity, or explain how to do it. You can score points for a prompting descriptor even if you can sometimes manage unaided if there is a specific or urgent impetus to undertake the activity. Whether you can manage the activity on a normal day when there is not such an urgent impetus must also be considered.[14] The person prompting you does not need to be in your presence, so prompting by telephone can arguably allow you to score points in the assessment, if it is needed for you to carry out an activity.

Whether you can undertake activities 'reliably' with these kinds of help must also be considered (see p750).

Part 5: Other benefits
Chapter 34: Personal independence payment
1. Who can claim personal independence payment

Your needs must usually last for at least one year. This is known as the 'required period condition' (see p752).

For how to decide which descriptor you satisfy if your difficulties vary, see p751.

Note: you automatically qualify for the enhanced rate of the daily living component if you are terminally ill (see p755), even if you have no problems with any of the activities.

Aids and appliances

You score points for most of the daily living activities if you do not need help from another person, but can only manage the activity using an 'aid or appliance'. This is defined as something that improves, provides or replaces a mental or physical function (including a prosthetic limb) – eg, a walking stick or wheelchair, modified cutlery or kitchen utensils needed because of your disability, or adaptations to your home such as grab rails in the shower and a shower seat.[15] If you do not normally use an aid or appliance, it is taken into account if you could 'reasonably be expected' to use one to help you with the activity.[16]

Could you use an aid or appliance?

When you could reasonably be expected to use an aid or appliance is not set out in the regulations. Guidance suggests that the factors to be taken into account include:[17]

– whether or not you can afford to buy an aid or appliance;

– whether an aid or appliance is available to you; *and*

– whether it is practical for you to use an aid or appliance – eg, whether you can store it in your home.

If you are assessed as needing an aid or appliance to manage an activity and you think this is not reasonable, you can ask for a mandatory reconsideration of the decision (see p1276). Try to obtain evidence to show that you still need help from someone, despite using the aid or appliance.

An aid or appliance is not necessarily something that only people with a disability or health condition use.[18] However, to be awarded points in the assessment because you can only manage an activity by using an aid or appliance, you must need to use it because of your physical or mental condition. The aid does not have to be designed to help with the task that you need it for, but must improve, provide or replace a function that is vital to managing the activity assessed, not just to managing it in a particular way.[19] For example, many people sit down to dress, so you will not score points for needing to do this because of your condition, if you are otherwise able to dress and undress reliably.

Your ability to use reasonably practicable alternatives may mean that you are assessed as managing an activity 'unaided'. However, any alternatives you must use should not be too restrictive, or they may count as aids to help you manage the activity.[20]

Examples

Bill needs to wear slip-on shoes because it takes him more than twice as long to tie his shoelaces as it used to before he had problems with manual dexterity. He can manage all his other clothing unaided. As slip-on shoes are a reasonable adjustment for Bill to make, he can dress and undress unaided.

Ben has severely restricted motor function following a stroke. He must wear slip-on shoes to manage alone. He must also wear loose-fitting clothing, cardigans without buttons and trousers with elasticated waistbands to be able to dress within a reasonable time. The clothing that Ben must wear in order to dress reliably without help amounts to his using aids to dress and undress, even though other people without Ben's difficulties may also choose to wear them.

Activity one: preparing food

Descriptors	Points
a. Can prepare and cook a simple meal unaided.	0
b. Needs to use an aid or appliance to be able to either prepare or cook a simple meal.	2
c. Cannot cook a simple meal using a conventional cooker but is able to do so using a microwave.	2
d. Needs prompting to be able to either prepare or cook a simple meal.	2
e. Needs supervision or assistance to either prepare or cook a simple meal.	4
f. Cannot prepare and cook food.	8

Definitions[21]

'**Simple meal**' means a cooked one-course meal for one using fresh ingredients.

'**Prepare**' means make food ready for cooking or eating.

'**Cook**' means to heat food at or above waist height. This means that your ability to bend down and get food from a low oven is irrelevant.[22]

See also the definitions common to all the daily living activities on p737.

If you have problems cooking due to the size of your family, this is not relevant, unless you would struggle with the same tasks even if just cooking for yourself. Descriptor 1c only considers whether you can *cook* using a microwave – your ability to *prepare* the ingredients for a simple meal must also be considered.[23] To 'prepare' food, you must be able to peel and chop vegetables.[24] If you must use

Part 5: Other benefits
Chapter 34: Personal independence payment
1. Who can claim personal independence payment

pre-prepared vegetables, you score points for needing assistance to prepare or cook a meal, unless you could prepare them with an aid or appliance. Aids to help you prepare and cook food could include a perching stool,[25] single lever arm taps,[26] specialist cooking utensils or a spiked chopping board.

If you would be at risk of serious harm if you prepared food by yourself, you can satisfy descriptor 1e on the basis that you need supervision, even if that harm would only happen on a minority of days – eg, if you have uncontrolled epilepsy and are having two or three seizures a week.[27] It is arguable that you satisfy descriptor 1f if you are completely unable to either prepare or cook food, no matter how much help you get, even though you can manage the other task unaided.[28]

Activity two: taking nutrition

Descriptors	Points
a. Can take nutrition unaided.	0
b. Needs:	2
(i) to use an aid or appliance to be able to take nutrition; *or*	
(ii) supervision to be able to take nutrition; *or*	
(iii) assistance to be able to cut up food.	
c. Needs a therapeutic source to be able to take nutrition.	2
d. Needs prompting to be able to take nutrition.	4
e. Needs assistance to be able to manage a therapeutic source to take nutrition.	6
f. Cannot convey food and drink to her/his mouth and needs another person to do so.	10

Definitions[29]
'Take nutrition' means to cut food into pieces, convey food and drink to one's mouth and chew and swallow food and drink, or to take nutrition by using a therapeutic source.
'Therapeutic source' means parenteral or enteral tube feeding, using a rate-limiting device such as a delivery system or feed pump.
See also the definitions common to all the daily living activities on p737.

This activity focuses on the mechanical actions involved in eating and drinking (or using a theraputic source); the nutritious quality of what you eat or drink is not relevant.[30] However, if your mental condition means that you would not eat or drink at all without prompting from someone else, you satisfy descriptor 2d.[31]

If you spill so much food that you need to change your clothes after eating, this is arguably not taking nutrition to an acceptable standard. Unless an aid or appliance (eg, adapted cup or cutlery), help to cut up your food, or prompting from someone else, means you can do this reliably, you should satisfy descriptor 2f.

Activity three: managing therapy or monitoring a health condition

Descriptors	*Points*
a. Either:	0
(i) does not receive medication or therapy or need to monitor a health condition; *or*	
(ii) can manage medication or therapy or monitor a health condition unaided.	
b. Needs any one or more of the following:	1
(i) to use an aid or appliance to be able to manage medication;	
(ii) supervision, prompting or assistance to be able to manage medication;	
(iii) supervision, prompting or assistance to be able to monitor a health condition.	
c. Needs supervision, prompting or assistance to be able to manage therapy that takes no more than 3.5 hours a week.	2
d. Needs supervision, prompting or assistance to be able to manage therapy that takes more than 3.5 but no more than seven hours a week.	4
e. Needs supervision, prompting or assistance to be able to manage therapy that takes more than seven but no more than 14 hours a week.	6
f. Needs supervision, prompting or assistance to be able to manage therapy that takes more than 14 hours a week.	8

Definitions[32]

'**Manage medication**' means to take medication, where a failure to do so is likely to result in a deterioration in your health.

'**Medication**' means medication to be taken at home which is prescribed or recommended by a registered doctor, nurse or pharmacist.

'**Monitor a health condition**' means to detect significant changes in your health condition which are likely to lead to a deterioration in your health, and to take action advised by a registered doctor or nurse, or a health professional who is regulated by the Health and Care Professions Council, without which your health is likely to deteriorate.

'**Manage therapy**' means to undertake therapy, where a failure to do so is likely to result in a deterioration in your health.

'**Therapy**' means therapy to be undertaken at home which is prescribed or recommended by a registered doctor, nurse or pharmacist, or a health professional regulated by the Health and Care Professions Council. It does not include taking or administering medication, or any action which, in your case, comes within the definition of 'monitor a health condition'.

See also the definitions common to all the daily living activities on p737.

Part 5: Other benefits
Chapter 34: Personal independence payment
1. Who can claim personal independence payment

Examples of 'therapy' include needing help with dialysis, to use oxygen or undertake specialist massage treatment at home. General supervision provided in supported accommodation is not 'therapy'.[33] Smoking cessation treatment and weight loss counselling do not count as therapy if there is no evidence that smoking or obesity are making your condition worse.[34] From 16 March 2017, help with your medication or monitoring your health condition cannot help you to satisfy descriptors 3c-f, as they are excluded from the definition of 'therapy'.[35]

When deciding which descriptor is satisfied, the amount of time you need help with therapy is relevant, not the length of time the therapy takes.[36] You can count the help you need to set up a machine you use for your therapy (eg, a TENS machine), even if you can manage unaided once it has been set up.[37]

As the descriptors about therapy refer to the length of time you need help for during 'a week', you should not be excluded by the rule on fluctuating conditions (see p751) if you only need help with your therapy on a minority of days.

Monitoring your health condition could include someone helping you to check your blood sugar levels, or someone checking regularly on how your mental health is – eg, if you have schizophrenia which is normally controlled by medication.

Aids and appliances to help you manage medication could include a dosette box to organise pills if you are forgetful, or a specialist device to help you to inject yourself, if you have difficulty with manual dexterity. However, an inhaler or syringe does not count as an aid, as it is a way of delivering medication, as opposed to something you need to use to help you manage your medication independently.[38]

Activity four: washing and bathing

Descriptors	Points
a. Can wash and bathe unaided.	0
b. Needs to use an aid or appliance to be able to wash or bathe.	2
c. Needs supervision or prompting to be able to wash or bathe.	2
d. Needs assistance to be able to wash either her/his hair or body below the waist.	2
e. Needs assistance to be able to get in or out of a bath or shower.	3
f. Needs assistance to be able to wash her/his body between the shoulders and waist.	4
g. Cannot wash and bathe at all and needs another person to wash her/his entire body.	8

Definitions
'Bathe' includes getting into or out of an unadapted bath or shower.[39]
See also the definitions common to all the daily living activities on p737.

If you cannot get into an unadapted bath without help, you satisfy descriptor 4e, even if you have a wet room at home so never need to do this.[40] A bath seat counts as an aid for this activity.[41]

To wash to an acceptable standard, you should be clean when you have finished. If you can manage to wash and bathe yourself but it takes a very long time, you can argue that you need help to do so within a reasonable time period. Which descriptor applies to you depends on what kind of help would allow you to wash safely and within a reasonable time period.

If you can only motivate yourself to have a bath or shower if you have something important to do that day, it is arguable that you still need prompting to wash or bathe if you would not manage this unprompted on a normal day.[42]

Activity five: managing toilet needs or incontinence

Descriptors	Points
a. Can manage toilet needs or incontinence unaided.	0
b. Needs to use an aid or appliance to be able to manage toilet needs or incontinence.	2
c. Needs supervision or prompting to be able to manage toilet needs.	2
d. Needs assistance to be able to manage toilet needs.	4
e. Needs assistance to be able to manage incontinence of either bladder or bowel.	6
f. Needs assistance to be able to manage incontinence of both bladder and bowel.	8

Definitions[43]

'Manage incontinence' means to manage involuntary evacuation of the bowel or bladder, including using a collecting device or self-catheterisation, and cleaning oneself afterwards.

'Toilet needs' means getting on and off an unadapted toilet, evacuating the bladder and bowel, and cleaning oneself afterwards.

See also the definitions common to all the daily living activities on p737.

Even if you only need an aid or appliance or help from someone else to manage any one of the three things included in the definition of 'toilet needs' above, you should still score some points for this activity.[44] Examples of aids and appliances include a stoma and colostomy bag,[45] incontinence pads,[46] or a shower head used to clean yourself.[47] A commode can also count as an aid, but you can only score points for this activity if part of the reason you must use it that your condition means you have difficulty with toilet needs or incontinence (not if you only need to use it because of problems managing the stairs at home, for example).[48] You score more points if you need help from someone else to use one of these things.

Part 5: Other benefits
Chapter 34: Personal independence payment
1. Who can claim personal independence payment

Difficulty dressing and undressing to use the toilet does not allow you to score points for this activity.[49]

Activity six: dressing and undressing

Descriptors	Points
a. Can dress and undress unaided.	0
b. Needs to use an aid or appliance to be able to dress or undress.	2
c. Needs either:	2
(i) prompting to be able to dress, undress or determine appropriate circumstances for remaining clothed; *or*	
(ii) prompting or assistance to be able to select appropriate clothing.	
d. Needs assistance to be able to dress or undress their lower body.	2
e. Needs assistance to be able to dress or undress their upper body.	4
f. Cannot dress or undress at all.	8

Definitions
'Dress and undress' includes putting on and taking off socks and shoes.[50]
See also the definitions common to all the daily living activities on p737.

If you must wear them because of your health problem or disability, clothes that are easier to manage, such as slip-on shoes, cardigans rather than jumpers or zips rather than buttons, may count as aids to help you dress, depending on the extent to which your choices are restricted by your condition(s).[51] If you only need one of these things (eg, your only difficulty is with tying shoelaces), this may, nonetheless, allow you to dress and undress unaided.[52] If you need to sit down to dress or undress, this does not count as needing an aid or appliance.[53]

To score points for this activity it is only necessary that you need help with either dressing or undressing, not both. Similarly, help with either your shoes or socks is sufficient for you to score points.[54]

Activity seven: communicating verbally

Descriptors	Points
a. Can express and understand verbal information unaided.	0
b. Needs to use an aid or appliance to be able to speak or hear.	2
c. Needs communication support to be able to express or understand complex verbal information.	4
d. Needs communication support to be able to express or understand basic verbal information.	8
e. Cannot express or understand verbal information at all even with communication support.	12

Definitions[55]

'**Basic verbal information**' means information in your native language conveyed verbally in a simple sentence.

'**Complex verbal information**' means information in your native language conveyed verbally in either more than one sentence or one complicated sentence.

'**Communication support**' means support from a person trained or experienced in communicating with people with specific communication needs, including interpreting verbal information into a non-verbal form and vice versa.

See also the definitions common to all the daily living activities on p737.

If you have problems speaking English because you have never learned the language, this does not count. If you find it hard to make yourself understood when talking to strangers (and this is due to a physical or mental condition rather than your accent), you can argue that you need help to communicate to an acceptable standard and within a reasonable time period. A hearing aid you use or a voice synthesizer should be accepted as aids to help with this activity. If you manage by writing information down to be understood, this is not communicating verbally at all.

The definition of 'communication support' includes both someone with specialist training, like a British Sign Language interpreter, and also a family member or support worker who is experienced in helping you to communicate.[56] How many points you score depends on whether you need help with even a single simple sentence, or whether you can manage this but need help with anything more complicated. If you have problems speaking or understanding speech because of a mental health problem or cognitive impairment, you can score points for this activity if your problems are with the act of speaking, hearing or understanding verbal communication – ie, not just a reluctance to speak because you are shy in social situations.[57]

Activity eight: reading and understanding signs, symbols and words

Descriptors	Points
a. Can read and understand basic and complex written information either unaided or using spectacles or contact lenses.	0
b. Needs to use an aid or appliance, other than spectacles or contact lenses, to be able to read or understand either basic or complex written information.	2
c. Needs prompting to be able to read or understand complex written information.	2
d. Needs prompting to be able to read or understand basic written information.	4
e. Cannot read or understand signs, symbols or words at all.	8

Part 5: Other benefits
Chapter 34: Personal independence payment
1. Who can claim personal independence payment

Definitions[58]

'**Basic written information**' means signs, symbols and dates written or printed in standard size text in your native language.

'**Complex written information**' means more than one sentence of written or printed standard size text in your native language.

'**Read**' includes reading signs, symbols and words, but does not include Braille. The exclusion of Braille from the definition of 'read' means that if you have no effective sight at all, you are assessed as being unable to read.

See also the definitions common to all the daily living activities on p737.

If your ability to read is affected so that you satisfy a descriptor at certain times of the day, you should score points for this activity, even if you can read unaided at others times of the day.[59] Similarly, it is arguable that you should only be assessed as needing an aid or appliance to read (rather than someone to help) if you can read both outside and inside using aids.

If you have a mental or cognitive impairment, you may need help to understand the meaning of written information, and so should score points for this activity. If you have never learned to read in English, you only score points for this activity if this is because of a physical or mental condition.[60]

Activity nine: engaging with other people face to face

Descriptors	Points
a. Can engage with other people unaided.	0
b. Needs prompting to be able to engage with other people.	2
c. Needs social support to be able to engage with other people.	4
d. Cannot engage with other people due to such engagement causing either:	8
(i) overwhelming psychological distress to the claimant; *or*	
(ii) the claimant to exhibit behaviour which would result in a substantial risk of harm to the claimant or another person.	

Definitions[61]

'**Psychological distress**' means distress related to an enduring mental health condition or an intellectual or cognitive impairment.

'**Social support**' means support from a person trained or experienced in assisting people to engage in social situations.

See also the definitions common to all the daily living activities on p737.

This activity looks at your ability to interact with individuals or small groups.[62] 'Engage with other people' means to interact in a contextually and socially appropriate manner, understand body language and establish relationships.[63] Your ability to interact with strangers, as well as people you know, should be considered. Even if you undertake social activities (eg, going to a pub), you may still score points for this activity if you cannot engage with other people without help during that time.[64]

You can argue that you need social support with this activity, even if the support is not always available, provided you need the support to engage with other people.[65] If you need help from a family member or support worker, this should count as social support.[66] However, as the descriptors distinguish between 'prompting' and 'social support', to satisfy descriptor 9c, you must show that you cannot engage with other people with encouragement from someone you know less well.[67]

Activity 10: making budgeting decisions

Descriptors	Points
a. Can manage complex budgeting decisions unaided.	0
b. Needs prompting or assistance to be able to make complex budgeting decisions.	2
c. Needs prompting or assistance to be able to make simple budgeting decisions.	4
d. Cannot make any budgeting decisions at all.	6

Definitions[68]

'Complex budgeting decisions' means decisions involving calculating household and personal budgets, managing and paying bills and planning future purchases.
'Simple budgeting decisions' means decisions involving calculating the cost of goods and calculating the change required after a purchase.
See also the definitions common to all the daily living activities on p737.

The focus of this activity is on your difficulty in making decisions because of your physical or mental condition, rather than any poor money management skills. If you do not have an intellectual or cognitive impairment, it is unlikley that you will be awarded points for this activity based solely on your physical health problems.[69] However, if you have difficulty making decisions because of a physical condition (eg, you need someone to read information repeatedly to be able to make a decision because you have a visual impairment), you may arguably satisfy descriptor 10b.[70] If your mental health problems mean that you cannot face dealing with your own finances, this arguably means that you should score points for descriptor 10b.[71]

Part 5: Other benefits
Chapter 34: Personal independence payment
1. Who can claim personal independence payment

The mobility activities

There are two mobility activities in the assessment. Remember that your difficulties with the activities must be caused by a physical or mental condition for you to be able to score points. This section does not cover every kind of disability or health problem, so think carefully about how your condition affects your ability to manage each of the activities.

At the time this *Handbook* was written, the law was evolving quickly as the Upper Tribunal decided cases that affect the interpretation of the descriptors (see p1350). See CPAG's online service and *Welfare Rights Bulletin* for updates.

Whether you can undertake the activities 'reliably' must also be considered (see p750).

Your needs must usually last for at least one year. This is known as the 'required period condition' (see p752).

For how to decide which descriptor you satisfy if your difficulties vary, see p751.

Activity one: planning and following journeys

Descriptors	Points
a. Can plan and follow the route of a journey unaided.	0
b. Needs prompting to be able to undertake any journey to avoid overwhelming psychological distress to the claimant.	4
c. For reasons other than psychological distress, cannot plan the route of a journey.	8
d. For reasons other than psychological distress, cannot follow the route of an unfamiliar journey without another person, assistance dog or orientation aid.	10
e. Cannot undertake any journey because it would cause overwhelming psychological distress to the claimant.	10
f. For reasons other than psychological distress, cannot follow the route of a familiar journey without another person, an assistance dog or an orientation aid.	12

Definitions[72]

'Assistance dog' means a dog trained to guide or assist a person with a sensory impairment.

'Orientation aid' means a specialist aid designed to assist disabled people to follow a route safely. A standard satnav does not count as an orientation aid, although one designed or modified for disabled people might.[73]

'Prompting' means reminding, encouraging or explaining by another person.

'Psychological distress' means distress related to an enduring mental health condition or an intellectual or cognitive impairment.

'Unaided' means without the use of an aid or appliance, or without supervision, prompting or assistance.

The use of the words 'follow the route' means that you can satisfy descriptors 1d and 1f if you need someone to help you navigate, accompany you to supervise you and make sure you are safe, or to deal with unexpected diversions, but not if you only need help from another person to communicate with people you meet during a journey.[74] **Note:** from 16 March 2017, if the only reason you need someone with you is because following journeys causes you psychological distress, you cannot satisfy descriptors 1d and 1f (or descriptor 1c if psychological distress prevents you from planning journeys).[75]

If you are unable to go out at all (even if accompanied) because of the level of psychological distress this would cause, you should satisfy descriptor 1e.

If you need prompting from someone else to start any journey, you can potentially satisfy descriptor 1b, even if you do not need to be accompanied on the journey by another person.[76]

Activity two: moving around

Descriptors	Points
a. Can stand and then move more than 200 metres, either aided or unaided.	0
b. Can stand and then move more than 50 metres but no more than 200 metres, either aided or unaided.	4
c. Can stand and then move unaided more than 20 metres but no more than 50 metres.	8
d. Can stand and then move using an aid or appliance more than 20 metres but no more than 50 metres.	10
e. Can stand and then move more than one metre but no more than 20 metres, either aided or unaided.	12
f. Cannot, either aided or unaided:	12
(i) stand; *or*	
(ii) move more than one metre.	

Definitions[77]

'**Aided**' means with the use of an aid or appliance, or with supervision, prompting or assistance.

'**Stand**' means to stand upright with at least one biological foot on the ground.

'**Unaided**' means without the use of an aid or appliance, or without supervision, prompting or assistance.

See also the definitions of 'supervision', 'prompting' and 'assistance' on p737.

The descriptors in this activity look at your ability to 'stand and then move', so any movement you can manage using a wheelchair is ignored. If you are a double amputee, you are treated as unable to stand, even if you can walk with prosthetic

Part 5: Other benefits
Chapter 34: Personal independence payment
1. Who can claim personal independence payment

limbs, and you satisfy descriptor 2f. The descriptors assess your ability outdoors on the usual type of surfaces you might encounter, including your ability to manage kerbs, but not flights of steps or steep slopes.[78]

The number of points you score depends on the distance you can move and whether you can move unaided or need an aid or appliance. If you can manage more than 50 metres reliably using an aid or appliance, you can only satisfy descriptor 2a and 2b, even if you can only manage less than 50 metres unaided.[79]

It is not necessary for you to be able to manage the distance mentioned in a descriptor in one go, as brief stops do not mean that you cannot move this distance.[80]

However, the length and duration of any stops are relevant to whether you can move the distances reliably (see below). If you can manage to move a particular distance 'within a reasonable time period', the fact that you can only move slowly is not relevant to whether you are managing the activity to an acceptable standard.[81] However, pain, dizziness and breathlessness are all relevant to whether you are able to move to an acceptable standard (or safely). If moving around causes you significant pain, its impact on your ability to manage this activity can be considered, even if the pain has no known physical cause.[82]

Managing an activity reliably

You are only assessed as being able to undertake an activity at the level described by a descriptor if you can complete it 'reliably'. Unless you can manage the activity in *all* the following ways, you must be awarded a higher scoring descriptor.[83]

- **Safely.** This is defined as being in a manner that is unlikely to cause harm to you or anyone else, either during or after the activity. The focus is on how likely any harm is to occur, rather than how serious it would be if it did.[84] However, you can still score points for needing 'supervision', even if you would not come to harm on a majority of days if left unsupervised, as the severity of harm must also be considered.[85]
- **To an acceptable standard.** This is not defined in the regulations, and what it means is closely linked to the activity in question. However, official guidance states that this is about whether the standard achieved is 'good enough.' The level of pain you experience when managing an activity is one factor that should be considered.[86]
- **Repeatedly.** This is defined as being as often as it is reasonably required for you to carry out the activity. This means that if you have problems with an activity at some point during a day, you should satisfy a scoring descriptor on that day.[87]
- **Within a reasonable time period.** This is defined as being no more than twice the maximum time normally taken by someone with no health problems or disabilities to complete the activity.

These definitions still leave a lot of discretion to the decision maker, so you may need to ask for a mandatory reconsideration and then appeal, and argue that you cannot undertake the activities reliably.

Fluctuating conditions

If a scoring descriptor applies to you at some point in a day (ie, 24 hours), you should be accepted as satisfying it on that day, unless the amount of help you need is so minimal that it can be ignored.[88]

Example

Archie has a visual impairment, which causes him particular problems in poor light. If it is dark outside, he needs another person to be able to follow the route of an unfamiliar journey reliably. At other times during the day, he can normally follow journeys reliably by himself. He should satisfy descriptor 1(d) in the planning and following journeys activity (see p748).

The assessment also takes into account how your condition affects you on different days. Which descriptor you satisfy in an activity is considered over a 'required period'. This is usually the same one-year period as the 'required period condition' (see p752), or the nine months following your date of claim if you are reclaiming PIP and the 'special rule' on p753 applies.[89]

The descriptor you are awarded is decided as follows.[90]

- If only one descriptor in the activity applies to you on over 50 per cent of the days in the required period, that descriptor is used.
- If two or more descriptors each apply to you on over 50 per cent of the days in the required period, the one that scores the most points is used.
- If neither of the above bullet points apply, but the number of days on which you satisfy two or more scoring descriptors totals more than 50 per cent of the days in the required period, the scoring descriptor that applies most often is used. If two descriptors apply on the same number of days, the highest scoring one is used.

Example

Aisha makes a new claim for PIP. She has arthritis in her hips, which affects her ability to get into the bath. The required period is 365 days. On 104 days (two days a week) she can wash and bathe reliably unaided. On 156 days (three days a week), she manages to get into the bath using the grab rails the local occupational therapy department has fitted to help her remain independent. On a further 105 days (two days a week), she needs assistance from a family member to get into the bath reliably.

The third bullet point above applies, as no single descriptor is satisfied on over half the days in the required period. Aisha is awarded the points in descriptor 4b (see p742) as she

Part 5: Other benefits
Chapter 34: Personal independence payment
1. Who can claim personal independence payment

satisfies one or other of the scoring descriptors on 251 days in the required period, and this descriptor applies most often. She needs to score at least six points for the other daily living activities in order to qualify for the daily living component.

It can be very difficult to decide which descriptors you satisfy if your condition fluctuates. It may be helpful for you to keep a diary over several weeks to help explain how your condition affects you.

When calculating which descriptor you should satisfy under this rule, it is important to think about what your needs are every day, bearing in mind that you may not need to attempt some of the activities every day. For example, if you have a mental health condition and you can only go out or make budgeting decisions on good days, which happen a couple of times a week, this does not mean that you should not score any points for these activities. Similarly, the fact that you can sometimes manage activities if there is a specific reason you must do so does not mean that you do not need prompting to manage them on other days.[91]

If you have more than one fluctuating condition and these affect your ability to manage a particular activity independently of each other, you may be affected on more than half of the days in the required period, even if each condition only affects you on a minority of days.[92]

The required period condition

Usually, you must have met the disability conditions for a certain period of time before you can be awarded PIP and must be expected to continue to meet them for another period of time. This is known as the 'required period condition' and comprises these two separate periods.[93]

To qualify for PIP, you must normally have met the disability conditions for a component at a particular rate for three months (known as the 'past period'). On the date this requirement is satisfied, your needs must be expected to continue for at least a further nine months (known as the 'prospective period').[94] This means that if your needs are not expected to last for at least one year, you do not normally qualify for PIP (but see p753).

If you do not satisfy the required period condition when you claim, the decision maker can make an award starting up to three months afte s/he decides your claim, if you will satisfy the required period condition by then.[95]

Once you have been awarded PIP, you must satisfy the required period condition for every day of your award.[96] This means that if your needs are no longer expected to last for nine months or more, you should report this as a change of circumstances. Get advice if you think your condition may have improved to the extent that your award could be affected.

Note:
- There is no required period condition if you claim PIP on the grounds that you are terminally ill (see p755). This means that you can qualify for PIP as soon as you are accepted as being terminally ill.[97]
- If you claim PIP and you either get disability living allowance (DLA – see p626) or your DLA award ended less than two years ago (one year ago, if you are 65 or over), you do not have to satisfy the past period test. You must still satisfy the prospective period test.[98]
- A special rule applies if:
  - you used to get PIP; *and*
  - your award ended less than two years ago (one year, if you are 65 or over); *and*
  - you are reclaiming on the basis of substantially the same condition(s) or a new condition that developed as a result of your previous one.

In this situation, the past period test relates to the last three months of your previous award. So, if you met the disability conditions for a component at a particular rate during this time, you qualify for the same component from the date of your new claim (provided you satisfy the prospective period test at that date).[99]

---

2. **The rules about your age**

You must be aged 16 or over to claim personal independence payment (PIP).[100] The upper age limit for making a new claim is currently 65.[101] However, there are several exceptions to the upper age limit.
- If you claimed PIP before turning 65, an award can be made to you.[102]
- If you are entitled to PIP when you turn 65, your award continues until its end date, provided you still meet the entitlement conditions.[103]
- Your award of PIP can be revised or superseded (see Chapter 54) after you turn 65, but your entitlement to the mobility component is restricted (see p754).[104]
- If you were previously entitled to PIP, you can reclaim it within one year of your previous award ending, even if you are now 65 or over. This rule also applies to a PIP renewal claim made after you turn 65. Your new claim must be on the basis of the same disability or health condition(s) as your former award, or a new condition that has developed as a result of the original one(s).[105]
- If you were under 65 on 8 April 2013 and you are either entitled to disability living allowance (DLA) or your entitlement to DLA ended less than one year ago, you can claim PIP regardless of your age.[106] See p627 if you still get DLA and are thinking about claiming PIP.

Future changes

The upper age limit for claiming PIP will increase as pension age rises (see p772).

Part 5: Other benefits
Chapter 34: Personal independence payment
4. The amount of benefit

Mobility component for people 65 and over

If you are entitled to the mobility component when you turn 65, you continue to get it, provided you continue to meet the entitlement conditions. However, if you make a PIP claim (including a renewal claim) after turning 65, your entitlement to the mobility component must be due to the same condition(s) as your previous award, or a new condition that has developed as a result of the original one(s).[107] Special rules restrict the rate you can get.

- You only qualify for the enhanced rate of the mobility component if you meet the entitlement conditions for that rate and you got the enhanced rate in an award which ended less than one year before you claim.[108]
- You can qualify for the standard rate if you meet the entitlement conditions and you got either rate of the mobility component in an award which ended less than one year before you claim.[109]

If your existing award of PIP is revised or superseded because of a change that happens after you turn 65, you can only be awarded the mobility component if you currently get it, or it stopped less than a year before the date on which the decision takes effect.[110] Also, to get the mobility component at the same rate, your entitlement must be due to substantially the same condition(s) as your previous award.[111] You can move from the enhanced rate to the standard rate (even if your mobility needs result from a new condition),[112] but you cannot qualify for the mobility component for the first time or move from the standard rate to the enhanced rate.[113]

There are no restrictions on your entitlement to the mobility component because of your age if you were under 65 on 8 April 2013 and either you are entitled to DLA and claiming PIP as part of the transfer process (see p626), or your entitlement to DLA ended less than a year ago.[114]

3. People included in the claim

You claim personal independence payment (PIP) for yourself. Your partner may qualify for PIP or attendance allowance (AA) her/himself, or still get disability living allowance (DLA). Your child may qualify for DLA in her/his own right, or for PIP when s/he turns 16. See Chapter 23 for information about AA and Chapter 27 for information about DLA.

4. The amount of benefit

The daily living component of personal independence payment (PIP) is paid at one of two weekly rates:[115]

- the standard rate is £55.65;
- the enhanced rate is £83.10.

The mobility component of PIP is paid at one of two weekly rates:[116]
- the standard rate is £22;
- the enhanced rate is £58.

5. Special benefit rules

Special rules may apply to:
- people who are terminally ill (see below);
- people subject to immigration control (see Chapter 65);
- people who have come from or are going abroad (see Chapters 66, 67 and 68);
- people who are in hospital or living in a care home or other similar accommodation, or people in prison or detention (see Chapter 41).

Terminal illness

You are regarded as 'terminally ill' if you have a progressive disease from which your death can reasonably be expected within six months.[117] If you claim personal independence payment (PIP) and you are terminally ill, you are treated as satisfying the disability conditions for the enhanced rate of the daily living component.[118] You must satisfy the disability conditions for the mobility component (see p748), but you do not need to satisfy the required period condition (see p752).[119] If you claim PIP and are terminally ill, it does not matter how long you have lived in the UK.[120] However, there are other residence tests that you must satisfy (see p1574).

Claims from terminally ill people are referred to as 'special rules' claims. If you want to claim PIP, or you are requesting a revision or supersession, on the basis of being terminally ill, you should expressly state this.[121] Someone else can claim PIP on behalf of a terminally ill person without her/his knowledge or authority.[122]

Note: the process of claiming PIP is different if you are terminally ill (see p756).

6. Claims and backdating

The general rules about claims and backdating are covered in Chapter 49. This section explains the specific rules that apply to personal independence payment (PIP).

Note: if you currently get disability living allowance (DLA), you should think carefully about whether to claim PIP or not (see p627).

Part 5: Other benefits
Chapter 34: Personal independence payment
6. Claims and backdating

Making a claim

You must normally claim PIP by telephone.[123] If you are unable to claim by phone, you can ask for a paper claim form to be sent to you.[124] Online claims may be introduced in the future.

Forms

The easiest way to make a claim or get a claim form (Form PIP1) sent to you is by phoning 0800 917 2222 (textphone: 0800 917 7777). You *cannot* get a claim form from a local DWP office or advice centre. If you cannot use the phone and there is no one to help you, write asking for a claim form to Personal Independence Payment New Claims, Post Handling Site B, Wolverhampton WV99 1AH. This will delay your date of claim.

You must provide any information or evidence required (see below). You can amend or withdraw your claim before a decision is made (see p1149).

If you get PIP already and your award ends within the next year, see p762.

People who are terminally ill

The PIP claims process is different if you are terminally ill. You should explain that your claim is on the grounds of terminal illness when making it. Your GP or hospital consultant should complete Form DS1500, giving details of your condition and prognosis.

You are asked questions about your mobility needs as part of your claim. If you are accepted as terminally ill, you are not asked to complete a separate questionnaire, or attend a consultation in person.[125]

Someone else can claim PIP on behalf of a terminally ill person without her/his knowledge or authority.[126] If you have claimed PIP on someone else's behalf, you can also ask for a revision or supersession (see p1273), and appeal against the decision without her/his knowedge or authority.[127]

Who should claim

You must normally make a claim for PIP yourself. If you are unable to manage your own affairs, another person can claim PIP for you as your 'appointee' (see p1149). Someone else can also make the claim if the person for whom it is made is terminally ill (see above).

Information to support your claim

For the general information requirements that apply to all benefits, see p1150.

It is important that you provide any information required when you claim. Until you do, you may not count as having made a valid claim (see p1152). Correct any defects as soon as possible or your date of claim may be affected.

Once you have made a valid claim, there is a separate assessment process to help the decision maker decide whether you satisfy the disability conditions (see below).

Even if you have provided all that was required when you claimed, you may be asked to provide further evidence (see p1154). You may also be asked to provide information after you are awarded PIP and if you fail to do so, your PIP could be suspended, or even terminated.

The date of your claim

The date of your claim is important as it determines when your entitlement to PIP starts. For information about when payment of PIP starts, see p761.

If you claim by telephone, your **'date of claim'** is usually the date of your phone call.[128] If you request a paper claim form, your date of claim is the date your request is received by the DWP, provided it receives the properly completed form within one month (or longer if reasonable).[129]

Note: you must make sure your claim is valid. If it is 'defective', you are given a short time to correct the defects (see p1152). If you do, your claim is treated as having been made when you initially claimed.[130]

In some cases, you can claim in advance (see below). If you claimed DLA or attendance allowance (AA) when you should have claimed PIP, see below.

Backdating your claim

You cannot backdate a claim for PIP, even if you would have qualified had you claimed sooner.[131]

If you claim the wrong benefit

A claim for PIP can be treated as a claim for DLA or AA and vice versa.[132] In both cases, this only applies if the decision maker thinks you are not entitled to the benefit you actually claimed. See p1161 for further information.

Claiming in advance

You can claim PIP in advance if you do not satisfy the entitlement conditions, but will do so within three months of the date your claim is decided.[133] This is particularly relevant if you do not satisfy the required period condition (see p752) when you first claim. The date on which you first qualify is treated as your date of claim for the purpose of paying your PIP.

If you already get PIP, you can make a renewal claim up to six months before your award ends (see p762).

The assessment process

If the DWP decides that you meet the basic entitlement conditions for PIP (see p736) when you make a claim, you are then assessed to see whether you meet the

Part 5: Other benefits
Chapter 34: Personal independence payment
6. Claims and backdating

disability conditions. You are also assessed if your existing award is being reviewed (see p762) or you request a supersession because your circumstances have changed (see p762). As part of the assessment process, you may be required to:[134]

- provide information or evidence about your ability to undertake daily living or mobility activities (normally in the form of a questionnaire); *and*
- attend and participate in a consultation with a health professional.

The majority of claims involve a face-to-face consultation with a health professional.

The questionnaire

You are sent a questionnaire, which asks for permission to contact professionals who know how your condition affects you. If you have just claimed PIP, the questionnaire (PIP2) asks for details of all the people who know how your condition affects you, and more information about your condition(s) and any treatment you get. See below for how to complete the questionnaire.

If your award is being reviewed (see p762), you are sent a different questionnaire (AR1 or PIP 1043), which asks whether anything has changed since you were awarded PIP, and when this happened. If your needs have changed, see below for help in completing the questionnaire – the advice also applies if your award is being reviewed.

You are asked questions relating to the 10 daily living activities (see p737) and two mobility activities (see p748).

How should you complete the PIP2 questionnaire?

1. Read the notes on the form before answering the questions. It may help to draft your answers on a separate sheet of paper first. For some things that may be relevant when completing the questionnaire, see pp737–50.

2. Many advice agencies can help you to complete the questionnaire. If you have difficulties with English, reading or writing, you should get help.

3. If someone else has to fill in the questionnaire for you, or you are only able to do so yourself slowly, or with pain, explain this.

4. Compare your answers with the information on pp737–50 to work out your likely score. Your answers should not be exaggerated, but check that you have not underestimated any of your problems and have given all the detail you can.

5. Remember that many of the terms in the assessment have special definitions. For example, 'dressing and undressing' includes how you manage putting on, or taking off, shoes or socks.

6. If you have good and bad days, explain this. You may need different types of help (see p737) with an activity on different days or at different times of day. If so, try to explain how often you need each kind of help, as this is also relevant to the points that you score (see p751).

7. List any aids or appliances (see p738) that you need to help you complete an activity, and any problems you have using them.

8. Explain if an activity takes you a long time or puts you at risk, or if you cannot complete it as often as you need to or only to a low standard (see p750).

9. Your account of the effects of your health problems or disability may be less likely to be believed later if you did not mention them on the questionnaire. It is a good idea to ask someone who knows you well to check that your answers fully explain the help you need.

10. If you have any other information that is relevant to your difficulties with daily living or mobility activities, send this with the questionnaire. This could include a report from an occupational therapist or consultant, information from your doctor or a support worker, or a statement from a friend or family member (although the DWP is likely to give less weight to information from someone who knows you in a personal capacity). If you are unsure whether evidence is helpful, check how closely it relates to the activities in the assessment. Evidence that confirms the severity of the condition that causes your difficulties is also useful – eg, x-rays, test results or a Certificate of Visual Impairment.

11. Make a copy of the completed questionnaire before returning it to the DWP, and keep a copy of any additional information that you send with it.

On receiving your completed questionnaire, the DWP sends it to a health professional who decides what other evidence s/he thinks is needed. This may include asking you to participate in a consultation (see p760).

If you do not return the questionnaire

You have one month from the day it was sent to you to return the questionnaire. You may be allowed longer, if this is considered to be reasonable.[135] If you do not return the questionnaire (or any other information that is requested), your claim is refused, unless you can show that you have a good reason for not returning it.[136] If your existing PIP award is being reviewed and you do not return the questionnaire, your award is stopped unless you can show a good reason.[137]

In deciding whether you have a good reason, the state of your health and the nature of your disability must be taken into account, along with any other reasons.[138] If the DWP knows that you have a mental or cognitive impairment and you do not return the questionnaire, your claim may be referred to a health professional to organise a consulation instead.[139] However, the regulations do not say this, so you should always try to return the questionnaire if you are able to do so.

Is your questionnaire likely to be returned late?

If it looks like you are not going to return your questionnaire on time, contact the DWP immediately to explain why, and ask for an extension of time. You should complete and return it as soon as possible. If the DWP does not accept that you have a good reason and makes a decision that you are not entitled to PIP, write to the DWP stating your reasons and ask for a mandatory reconsideration (see p1284). You should also make a new claim in case your request is unsuccessful.

Part 5: Other benefits
Chapter 34: Personal independence payment
6. Claims and backdating

The consultation

You can be asked to participate in a consultation with a health professional to assess whether you satisfy the disability conditions (even if you already have an award of PIP). Two companies, Atos and Capita, carry out PIP consultations for the DWP[140] and should contact you to explain what you need to do. You can find more information in letters they send to you, or on their websites.[141]

Before deciding whether you need to have a consultation, the health professional decides whether to ask for evidence from someone who knows you. It is possible that a health professional will prepare a report without a consultation.[142]

Most people have a consultation as part of the process of claiming PIP. This is normally face to face in an assessment centre. You can take someone along to support you, and s/he can also give information to the health professional.[143] In order to produce a report for the decision maker, the health professional asks you questions about your condition and how you manage the different daily living and mobility activities.

What should you do at the consultation?

1. Explain as much as possible about how you are affected by your condition(s).

2. Remember that the assessment report can also include informal observations of your behaviour – eg, your ability to walk from the waiting area and whether you have attended the consultation by yourself.

3. If you need to take additional painkillers to attend the consultation, explain this, and also what you can and cannot do taking your normal dose.

4. If you have good and bad days, make sure that you explain this, and how your needs are different on a bad day. This is especially important if you are assessed on a good day.

5. If you are not fluent in English, it is vital that someone who can translate for you attends. Contact the assessment provider as soon as possible if you need an interpreter.

If you are asked to attend an assessment centre but you cannot manage this, you can ask for an assessment at home or a local healthcare centre. However, you should try to provide medical evidence explaining why you cannot attend an assessment centre.[144] If your request is refused and you do not attend, your claim may be refused (see below).

If you do not participate in a consultation

Failure to participate in the consultation (including not attending an assessment centre) without good reason results in your claim being refused.[145] If your existing PIP award is being reviewed and you do not participate in a consultation, your award is stopped unless you have a good reason.[146]

You must have been sent written notice (including by email if you have agreed that the DWP can use it to contact you) of the date and time of the consultation (and, for face-to-face consultations, where it will take place) at least seven days in advance.[147] However, this rule does not apply if you accept less notice or notice by telephone.[148]

In deciding whether you have a good reason for not participating in the consultation, the state of your health and the nature of your disability must be considered, along with any other reasons.[149]

If the DWP decides that you did not participate in a consultation without good reason, write to the DWP and explain why you could not participate, and ask for a mandatory reconsideration (see p1284). You should also make a new claim in case your request is unsuccessful.

7. **Getting paid**

The general rules on getting paid are in Chapter 50. This section explains the specific rules that apply to personal independence payment (PIP).

When is personal independence payment paid?

PIP is usually paid on the same day of the week as the decision was made on your claim, but this can be changed by the DWP.[150] PIP is usually paid every four weeks in arrears, or if you are terminally ill, weekly in advance.[151]

Payment of PIP normally starts from your date of claim (see p757).

Note: the enhanced rate of the mobility component can be paid directly to Motability (see p765) if you are buying or leasing a car through the scheme.[152]

- Payment of PIP may be made to someone else on your behalf, if this is needed to protect your interests.[153]
- Even if you have been sanctioned for a benefit offence (see p1265), you must be paid PIP.
- For information on missing payments, see p1174. If you have lost your bank or Post Office card or you have forgotten your PIN, see p1173. If you have lost your 'simple payment' card, or you have forgotten your memorable date, see p1173.
- If payment of your PIP is delayed, see p1165. If you wish to complain about how your claim has been dealt with, or claim compensation, see Chapter 58.
- If payment of your PIP is suspended, see p1185.
- If you are overpaid PIP, you may have to repay it (see Chapter 52) and, in some circumstances, you may have to pay a penalty (see p1256). If you have been accused of fraud, see Chapter 53.

Length of awards

PIP is normally awarded for a fixed period – eg, one, two or five years. The length of award depends on how likely your needs are to change over time. You are normally awarded PIP for three years if you are terminally ill.[154]

An indefinite award can be made if a fixed-term award would be inappropriate.[155] Most indefinite awards are reviewed every 10 years, to check they are still correct.[156]

If you think that you should have been given a longer award of PIP, you can ask for a mandatory reconsideration (see p1276), and appeal if the decision is not changed.[157] However, if you do this, the amount of benefit that you have been awarded may also be reconsidered.

Note: your entitlement to PIP can be reassessed at any time after it has been awarded.[158] For what happens if your award is coming to an end, see below.

Reviews and renewal claims

PIP is normally awarded for a fixed period (see above). If you already get PIP, you can make a renewal claim up to six months before your award ends.[159] However, you may not need to do this, as your claim may be reviewed by the DWP one year before it ends (see below).[160] If your claim is not reviewed, the DWP may not contact you until three months before your award ends.

Is your personal independence payment award ending?

If you are awarded PIP for a fixed period, you may be referred for a review of your entitlement a year before your award is due to end. The DWP calls this a 'planned review'. The process of reviewing your award is similar to the assessment process for new claims (see p757). It is important that you return the questionnaire and take part in any consultation that is arranged, as otherwise your existing award may be superseded and removed immediately (see p1290). Once the review is completed, a decision maker decides whether to carry out a supersession (see p1287). A supersession decision could extend, change or remove your PIP award.

If your award has less than six months left to run and the DWP has not contacted you, consider either making a renewal claim or requesting a supersession (see p1287) to ensure you get a decision before your award runs out. Get advice about the likely impact on your current award.

Change of circumstances

You must report any changes in your circumstances that you have been told you must report, as well as any that you might reasonably be expected to know might affect your right to, the amount of, or the payment of, PIP. You should do this as soon as possible, preferably in writing. See p1184 for further information.

If payment of (but not entitlement to) PIP has stopped (as you are in hospital, a care home or prison – see Chapter 41), still notify the DWP of any changes so the correct rate is paid when payment resumes.

If there has been a relevant change of circumstances, a decision maker looks at your claim again and makes a new decision. To find out the date from which the new decision takes effect, see p1294.

8. Tax, other benefits and the benefit cap

Tax

Personal independence payment (PIP) is not taxable.[161]

Means-tested benefits and tax credits

PIP is not taken into account as income when calculating means-tested benefits and tax credits. PIP is paid on top of these benefits. Getting PIP can increase the amount you get or can mean that you qualify for means-tested benefits or tax credits for the first time, if your income was previously too high.

If you or your partner are entitled to PIP, you may qualify for one or more of the following extra amounts:

- disability premium in income support (IS), income-based jobseeker's allowance (JSA) or housing benefit (HB) if you are under the qualifying age for pension credit (PC) (see p238);
- higher pensioner premium in IS or income-based JSA if you have a partner and either of you have reached the qualifying age for PC (see p242);
- enhanced disability premium in IS, income-based JSA, income-related employment and support allowance (ESA) or HB if you or your partner are entitled to the enhanced rate of the daily living component and are under the qualifying age for PC (see p240);
- severe disability premium/addition in IS, income-based JSA, income-related ESA, the guarantee credit of PC or HB if you or your partner are entitled to the daily living component and meet other conditions (see p242);
- disabled worker element in working tax credit (WTC) if you or your partner are entitled to PIP, work 16 hours a week or more and meet other conditions (see p1412);
- severe disability element in WTC if you or your partner are entitled to the enhanced rate of the daily living component (see p1414);
- limited capability for work-related activity element in universal credit (UC) if you or your partner are entitled to the enhanced rate of the PIP daily living component and over the qualifying age for PC (see p262). A limited capability for work element is included instead if the person over the qualifying age for

Part 5: Other benefits
Chapter 34: Personal independence payment
8. Tax, other benefits and the benefit cap

PC was entitled to PIP, but not the enhanced rate of the daily living component since before 3 April 2017 and in other circumstances (see p260).

If your child is entitled to PIP and still counts as part of your household, you may qualify for the following extra amounts:

- disabled child premium in HB and (if you do not get child tax credit – CTC) in IS or income-based JSA (see p237);
- enhanced disability premium in HB if s/he is entitled to the enhanced rate of the daily living component and (if you do not get CTC) in IS or income-based JSA (see p240);
- disabled child element in CTC (see p1410);
- severely disabled child element in CTC if s/he is entitled to the enhanced rate of the daily living component (see p1410); *or*
- disabled child addition in UC, which is paid at a higher rate if s/he is entitled to the enhanced rate of the daily living component (see p258).

If you or your partner receive the daily living component, non-dependant deductions are not made from your HB (see p67), or from any housing costs included in your IS, income-based JSA, income-related ESA or the guarantee credit of PC (see p464). No housing cost contributions from a non-dependant are taken into account when calculating your UC housing costs if you, your partner or the non-dependant receive the daily living component (see p512).

Non-means-tested benefits

PIP may be paid in addition to any other non-means-tested benefits, except that:

- if you are entitled to PIP, you cannot claim disability living allowance[162] or attendance allowance;[163]
- PIP overlaps with armed forces independence payment (see p863);[164]
- PIP daily living component overlaps with constant attendance allowance under the industrial injuries scheme (see p687) or war pensions scheme (see p862);[165]
- PIP mobility component is not paid if you get a war pensioners' mobility supplement payable under the war pensions scheme (see p862), or a grant for the use of a vehicle from the NHS.[166]

If you get the daily living component of PIP and someone regularly looks after you, that person may be entitled to carer's allowance (CA – see Chapter 25). However, your entitlement to a severe disability premium/addition can be affected if s/he receives CA, so always seek advice.

The benefit cap

In some cases, there is a limit on the total amount of specified benefits you can receive (a 'benefit cap'). PIP is *not* one of the specified benefits. The benefit cap does *not* apply if you, your partner or child get PIP (even it is not payable because the person entitled is in hospital or a care home). In other cases, it only applies if you are getting HB or UC. See p1180 for further information.

Passports and other sources of help

You qualify for a Christmas bonus if you receive PIP (see p863).

If you get PIP, you may be entitled to other 'passported' benefits such as a 'blue badge' or a concessionary travel card. Contact your local authority for more information.

If you get the enhanced rate of the PIP mobility component and you or your carer have a car used only by you or for you, you are exempt from vehicle excise duty (road tax). If you get the standard rate, you get a 50 per cent reduction to your vehicle excise duty.

If you have a low income, you may be entitled to council tax reduction (see p854).

Motability

Motability is a charity that runs a scheme to help you lease or buy a car if you receive the enhanced rate of PIP mobility component and have 12 months or more left to run on your award.

PIP mobility component is paid directly to Motability.[167] You may also have to make extra payments. For further information, telephone 0300 456 4566 or see www.motability.co.uk.

Notes

1. **Who can claim personal independence payment**
   1 Reg 5 PIP(TP) Regs
   2 s83 WRA 2012; Part 6 SS(PIP) Regs
   3 s115(1), (3) and (4) IAA 1999
   4 ss77(3) and 84 WRA 2012; Part 4 SS(PIP) Regs
   5 s77(2) WRA 2012
   6 ss78-80 WRA 2012; Part 2 and Sch 1 SS(PIP) Regs

   7 *SSWP v LB (PIP)* [2016] UKUT 530 (AAC)
   8 Regs 5 and 6 SS(PIP) Regs
   9 Sch 1 Part 1 SS(PIP) Regs
   10 Sch 1 Part 1 SS(PIP) Regs

11 That assistance can be with just part of an activity appears to be implicitly accepted in *AI v SSWP (PIP)* [2016] UKUT 322 (AAC): the judge suggests that assistance descriptors may *also* apply if a claimant is completely unable to manage an activity, but the point is not explicitly decided.

12 *SB v SSWP (PIP)* [2016] UKUT 219 (AAC). At the time this *Handbook* was written, the relationship between 'supervision' and 'safely' was due to be considered afresh by a three-judge panel of the Upper Tribunal, in cases CSPIP/97/2016 and CSPIP/106/2016. See CPAG's online service and *Welfare Rights Bulletin* for updates.

13 *SSWP v IM (PIP)* [2015] UKUT 680 (AAC)

14 *GG v SSWP (PIP)* [2016] UKUT 194 (AAC)

15 Reg 2 SS(PIP) Regs

16 Reg 4(2) SS(PIP) Regs

17 Ch P2 Appendix 2 ADM

18 *CW v SSWP (PIP)* [2016] UKUT 197 (AAC); [2016] AACR 44; *NA v SSWP (PIP)* [2015] UKUT 572 (AAC)

19 *CW v SSWP (PIP)* [2016] UKUT 197 (AAC); [2016] AACR 44; *AP v SSWP (PIP)* [2016] UKUT 501 (AAC)

20 *PE v SSWP (PIP)* [2015] UKUT 309 (AAC); [2016] AACR 10; *JM v SSWP (PIP)* [2016] UKUT 542 (AAC)

21 Sch 1 Part 1 SS(PIP) Regs

22 *RH v SSWP (PIP)* [2015] UKUT 281 (AAC)

23 *AI v SSWP (PIP)* [2016] UKUT 322 (AAC)

24 *LC v SSWP (PIP)* [2016] UKUT 150 (AAC)

25 *EG v SSWP (PIP)* [2015] UKUT 275 (AAC)

26 *GB v SSWP (PIP)* [2015] UKUT 546 (AAC), although the DWP has suggested that it no longer believes that this decision is correct, so this may not be accepted – see *AP v SSWP (PIP)* [2016] UKUT 501 (AAC)

27 *SB v SSWP (PIP)* [2016] UKUT 219 (AAC). At the time this *Handbook* was written, the relationship between 'supervision' and 'safely' was due to be considered by a three-judge panel of the Upper Tribunal, in cases CSPIP/97/2016 and CSPIP/106/2016. See CPAG's online service and *Welfare Rights Bulletin* for updates.

28 *AI v SSWP (PIP)* [2016] UKUT 322 (AAC)

29 Sch 1 Part 1 SS(PIP) Regs

30 *MM and BJ v SSWP (PIP)* [2016] UKUT 490 (AAC)

31 *SA v SSWP (PIP)* [2015] UKUT 512 (AAC)

32 Sch 1 Part 1 SS(PIP) Regs

33 *DC v SSWP (PIP)* [2016] UKUT 11 (AAC)

34 *AH v SSWP (PIP)* [2016] UKUT 276 (AAC), although note that this case is subject to a further appeal to the Court of Appeal. See CPAG's online services and *Welfare Rights Bulletin* for updates.

35 Until 16 March 2017, when the law was changed, needing help with medication and monitoring your health could potentially allow you to score points for descriptors 3c-f. See *SSWP v LB (PIP)* [2016] UKUT 530 (AAC) and get expert advice if you think that this might affect you.

36 *MF v SSWP (PIP)* [2015] UKUT 554 (AAC); [2016] AACR 20

37 *RH v SSWP (PIP)* [2015] UKUT 281 (AAC)

38 *RB v SSWP (PIP)* [2016] UKUT 556 (AAC)

39 Sch 1 Part 1 SS(PIP) Regs

40 *SP v SSWP (PIP)* [2016] UKUT 190 (AAC); [2016] AACR 43

41 *AP v SSWP (PIP)* [2016] UKUT 501 (AAC)

42 *GG v SSWP (PIP)* [2016] UKUT 194 (AAC)

43 Sch 1 Part 1 SS(PIP) Regs

44 *GW v SSWP (PIP)* [2015] UKUT 570 (AAC)

45 *JM v SSWP (PIP)* [2016] UKUT 296 (AAC)

46 *GW v SSWP (PIP)* [2015] UKUT 570 (AAC)

47 *BS v SSWP (PIP)* [2016] UKUT 456 (AAC)

48 *KW v SSWP (PIP)* [2017] UKUT 54 (AAC)

49 *GP v SSWP (PIP)* [2015] UKUT 498 (AAC)

50 Sch 1 Part 1 SS(PIP) Regs

51 *PE v SSWP (PIP)* [2015] UKUT 309 (AAC); [2016] AACR 10

52 *JM v SSWP (PIP)* [2016] UKUT 542 (AAC)

53 *CW v SSWP (PIP)* [2016] UKUT 197 (AAC); [2016] AACR 44; *AP v SSWP (PIP)* [2016] UKUT 501 (AAC)

54 *JM v SSWP (PIP)* [2016] UKUT 542 (AAC)

55 Sch 1 Part 1 SS(PIP) Regs

56 *TC v SSWP (PIP)* [2016] UKUT 550 (AAC)

57 *SSWP v GJ (PIP)* [2016] UKUT 8 (AAC)

58 Sch 1 Part 1 SS(PIP) Regs

59 *TR v SSWP (PIP)* [2015] UKUT 626 (AAC); [2016] AACR 23

60 *KP v SSWP (PIP)* [2017] UKUT 30 (AAC)

61 Sch 1 Part 1 SS(PIP) Regs

62 *AM v SSWP (PIP)* [2017] UKUT 7 (AAC)

63 *SF v SSWP (PIP)* [2016] UKUT 543 (AAC); *SSWP v AM (PIP)* [2015] UKUT 215 (AAC)

64 *HJ v SSWP (PIP)* [2016 UKUT 487 (AAC)

65 *PR v SSWP (PIP)* [2015] UKUT 584 (AAC), although note that in *AH v SSWP (PIP)* [2016] UKUT 276 (AAC) the DWP has been granted permission to appeal to the Court of Appeal regarding the scope of 'social support'. See CPAG's online services and *Welfare Rights Bulletin* for updates.
66 *MMcK V SSWP (PIP)* [2016] UKUT 191 (AAC), although this case may be subject to a further challenge. See CPAG's online services and *Welfare Rights Bulletin* for updates.
67 *HL v SSWP (PIP)* [2015] UKUT 694 (AAC)
68 Sch 1 Part 1 SS(PIP) Regs
69 *RB v SSWP (PIP)* [2016] UKUT 393 (ACC)
70 *SSWP v LB (PIP)* [2016] UKUT 530 (AAC)
71 *PR v SSWP (PIP)* [2015] UKUT 584 (AAC)
72 Sch 1 Part 1 SS(PIP) Regs
73 *RB v SSWP (PIP)* [2016] UKUT 304 (AAC)
74 *MH v SSWP (PIP)* [2016] UKUT 531 (AAC)
75 Until 16 March 2017, when the law was changed, the effects of psychological distress could potentially allow you to satisfy these descriptors. See *MH v SSWP (PIP)* [2016] UKUT 531 (AAC), and get specialist advice if you think that this may affect you.
76 See *MH v SSWP (PIP)* [2016] UKUT 531 (AAC), and note that the definition of 'prompting' does not say that the other person must be in your physical presence.
77 Sch 1 Part 1 SS(PIP) Regs
78 *DT v SSWP (PIP)* [2016] UKUT 240 (AAC)
79 *AP v SSWP (PIP)* [2016] UKUT 501 (AAC), but note that *KL v SSWP (PIP)* [2015] UKUT 612 (AAC) came to a different conclusion, and interprets the law more generously.
80 *KN v SSWP (PIP)* [2016] UKUT 261 (AAC)
81 *KL v SSWP (PIP)* [2016] UKUT 545 (AAC)
82 *NK v SSWP (PIP)* [2016] UKUT 146 (AAC)
83 Reg 4(2A) and (4) SS(PIP) Regs
84 *CE v SSWP (PIP)* [2015] UKUT 643 (AAC)
85 *SB v SSWP (PIP)* [2016] UKUT 219 (AAC). At the time this *Handbook* was written, the relationship between 'supervision' and 'safely' was due to be considered by a three-judge panel of the Upper Tribunal, in cases CSPIP/97/2016 and CSPIP/106/2016. See CPAG's online service and *Welfare Rights Bulletin* for updates.
86 *PS v SSWP (PIP)* [2016] UKUT 326 (AAC)
87 *TR v SSWP (PIP)* [2015] UKUT 626 (AAC); [2016] AACR 23

88 *TR v SSWP (PIP)* [2015] UKUT 626 (AAC); [2016] AACR 23, which held that this is essentially a question of whether an activity can be undertaken 'repeatedly' (para 34)
89 Reg 7(3) SS(PIP) Regs
90 Reg 7 SS(PIP) Regs
91 *GG v SSWP (PIP)* [2016] UKUT 194 (AAC)
92 *AK v SSWP (PIP)* [2015] UKUT 620 (AAC)
93 *AH v SSWP (PIP)* [2016] UKUT 541 (AAC)
94 s81 WRA 2012; regs 12-14 SS(PIP) Regs
95 Reg 33(1) UC,PIP,JSA&ESA(C&P) Regs
96 Reg 14(b) SS(PIP) Regs
97 s82(2) and (3) WRA 2012
98 Reg 23 PIP(TP) Regs
99 Regs 15 and 26 SS(PIP) Regs

2. The rules about your age
100 Reg 5 PIP(TP) Regs
101 s83(2) WRA 2012
102 Reg 25(b) SS(PIP) Regs
103 Reg 25(a) SS(PIP) Regs
104 Reg 27 SS(PIP) Regs
105 Regs 15 and 26 SS(PIP) Regs
106 Reg 27 PIP(TP) Regs
107 Regs 15 and 26 SS(PIP) Regs
108 Reg 26(2)(c)(i) SS(PIP) Regs
109 Reg 26(2)(c)(ii) and (d) SS(PIP) Regs
110 Reg 27 SS(PIP) Regs
111 Reg 27(3)(a)(ii) and (3)(b) SS(PIP) Regs
112 Reg 27(3) SS(PIP) Regs
113 Reg 27(3)(a)(i) and (4) SS(PIP) Regs
114 Reg 27 PIP(TP) Regs. The definitions of 'previous award' and 'component' in reg 2 SS(PIP) Regs mean that regs 15 and 26 of those regulations only apply to people who have had a previous PIP award.

4. The amount of benefit
115 Reg 24(1) SS(PIP) Regs
116 Reg 24(2) SS(PIP) Regs

5. Special benefit rules
117 s82(4) WRA 2012
118 s82(2) WRA 2012
119 s82(3) WRA 2012
120 Reg 21 SS(PIP) Regs
121 s82(1)(b) WRA 2012; regs 5(2)(c) and 23(2) UC,PIP,JSA&ESA(DA) Regs
122 s82(5) WRA 2012

6. Claims and backdating
123 DWP, *Personal Independence Payment Handbook*, April 2016, p18
124 Reg 11(1) UC,PIP,JSA&ESA(C&P) Regs; DWP, *Personal Independence Payment Handbook*, April 2016, p20

125 DWP, *Personal Independence Payment Handbook*, April 2016, pp34-37
126 s82(5) WRA 2012
127 Reg 49(c) UC,PIP,JSA&ESA(DA) Regs
128 Reg 12(1)(b) UC,PIP,JSA&ESA(C&P) Regs
129 Reg 12(1)(c) UC,PIP,JSA&ESA(C&P) Regs
130 Regs 11(6) and 12 UC,PIP,JSA&ESA(C&P) Regs
131 Reg 27 UC,PIP,JSA&ESA(C&P) Regs
132 Reg 25(3) and (4) UC,PIP,JSA&ESA(C&P) Regs
133 Reg 33(1) UC,PIP,JSA&ESA(C&P) Regs
134 s80(4)-(6) WRA 2012; regs 8 and 9 SS(PIP) Regs
135 Reg 8(1) and (2) SS(PIP) Regs
136 Reg 8(3) SS(PIP) Regs
137 Reg 26(2) UC,PIP,JSA&ESA(DA) Regs; *KB v SSWP (PIP)* [2016] UKUT 537 (AAC)
138 Reg 10 SS(PIP) Regs
139 PIP AG, p15
140 Broadly speaking, if you live in Scotland, Northern England, London, Southern England or East Anglia, the contractor is Atos. If you live in the Midlands or Wales, it is Capita. There is a detailed map showing postcode areas covered by each contractor at www.gov.uk/government/publications/pip-postcode-map-uk.
141 www.capita-pip.co.uk or www.atoshealthcare.com/pip
142 Reg 9(1) SS(PIP) Regs says that you 'may' be asked to attend a consultation.
143 PIP AG, p43
144 PIP AG, pp47-48
145 Reg 9(2) SS(PIP) Regs
146 Reg 26(2) UC,PIP,JSA&ESA(DA) Regs; *KB v SSWP (PIP)* [2016] UKUT 537 (AAC)
147 Reg 9(3)(a) and (4) SS(PIP) Regs
148 Reg 9(3)(b) SS(PIP) Regs
149 Reg 10 SS(PIP) Regs

7. Getting paid
150 Reg 49 UC,PIP,JSA&ESA(C&P) Regs
151 Reg 48(2) UC,PIP,JSA&ESA(C&P) Regs
152 Reg 62 UC,PIP,JSA&ESA(C&P) Regs
153 Reg 58(2) UC,PIP,JSA&ESA(C&P) Regs
154 para P2079 ADM
155 s88(2) and (3) WRA 2012
156 para P2062 ADM
157 *RS v SSWP (PIP)* [2016] UKUT 85 (AAC)
158 Reg 11 SS(PIP) Regs
159 Reg 33(2) UC,PIP,JSA&ESA(C&P) Regs
160 para P2061 ADM

8. Tax, other benefits and the benefit cap
161 s677(1) IT(EP)A 2003
162 Reg 22(1) PIP(TP) Regs
163 s64(1) and (1A) SSCBA 1992
164 Sch 1 para 5a SS(OB) Regs
165 Sch 1 para 5 SS(OB) Regs
166 Reg 61 UC,PIP,JSA&ESA(C&P) Regs
167 Regs 62, 63 and 64 UC,PIP,JSA&ESA(C&P) Regs

Chapter 35

Retirement pensions

This chapter covers:
1. Who can claim state pension (p770)
2. The rules about your age (p771)
3. People included in the claim (p772)
4. The amount of benefit (p772)
5. Special benefit rules (p777)
6. Claims and backdating (p778)
7. Getting paid (p781)
8. Tax, other benefits and the benefit cap (p782)

This chapter covers the rules that apply to people who reach pension age on or after 6 April 2016 and who are eligible for the new state retirement pension, known as 'state pension'. People who reached pension age before 6 April 2016, including those who had already claimed their state retirement pension and those who had deferred claiming it, continue on the previous retirement pension scheme. In this chapter, these pensions are referred to as 'old' retirement pensions. For more details about these, see the 2015/16 edition of this *Handbook*.

Key facts
- State pension is a non-means-tested, contributory benefit, paid to people who reach pension age on or after 6 April 2016.
- State pension is an individual pension based solely on your own national insurance contributions (although there are some limited exceptions).
- You can qualify whether you are in or out of work.
- State pension is affected by the overlapping benefit rules.
- State pension is administered and paid by the Pension Service, which is part of the DWP.
- If you reached pension age before 6 April 2016, you cannot get state pension, but you may be entitled to an 'old' retirement pension instead.
- If you disagree with a decision on your state pension, you can apply for a revision or a supersession, or appeal against it. You must apply for a mandatory reconsideration before you can appeal.

1. **Who can claim state pension**

You can get state pension if you reach pension age (see p772) on or after 6 April 2016. Whether you qualify, and the amount you receive, depends on your national insurance (NI) contribution record. If you do not have any qualifying years (ie, years in which you paid or were credited with sufficient NI contributions) before 6 April 2016, you must have 35 qualifying years to receive a state pension at the full rate. If you have at least 10 qualifying years of contributions, you may receive a reduced rate of state pension.[1] If you have qualifying years from before 6 April 2016, your state pension is paid at the transitional rate (see p774). This may be more or less than, or the same as, the full rate. You normally need at least 10 qualifying years to receive any state pension. See Chapter 42 for full details of the contribution conditions for state pension.

Did you reach pension age before 6 April 2016?

If you reached pension age before 6 April 2016, you cannot claim state pension. However, you may be entitled to an 'old' retirement pension – ie, a category A, category B or category D retirement pension. This applies even if you reached pension age before 6 April 2016 but deferred claiming your retirement pension until after that date.

The rules for old retirement pensions are not explained in detail in this chapter. See Chapter 36 of the 2015/16 edition of this *Handbook* for full details.

From 12 October 2015, existing claimants of old retirement pension, and people who reached pension age before 6 April 2016 but have not yet claimed, may be able to pay class 3A NI contributions. This can increase their entitlement to additional state pension as part of their old retirement pension. See p961 for details.

You do not automatically become entitled to state pension just by reaching pension age. You must claim, unless you come within the exceptions on p779. If you do not claim, you are treated as having deferred your state pension (see below).

You do not have to retire from work if you reach pension age and claim state pension. If you decide to carry on working, your earnings do not reduce the state pension you receive and you no longer pay NI contributions. However, the amount of tax you pay may increase because state pension is taxable.

There are some groups of claimants to whom special rules apply (see p777).

Deferring your state pension

Once you reach pension age, you can choose to defer your entitlement to state pension. In return, you later become entitled to a higher rate of pension. **Note:** you do not have the option of taking a taxable lump-sum payment plus interest.

You can defer your state pension by simply not claiming it when you reach state pension age. If you are already claiming, you can choose to stop getting it in order to get more later on, but you can only do this once. To stop claiming, you must notify the Pension Service by telephone or in writing.[2] You can specify a future date on which you want to stop claiming, provided this is within four weeks of your notifying the Pension Service.[3] You can cancel the deferment at any time by making a claim for state pension, and can backdate that cancellation by up to 12 months.[4]

Your state pension is increased by one-ninth of 1 per cent for each week of deferment.[5] For example, if you defer your pension for one year, it increases by approximately 5.8 per cent, which increases a full state pension by approximately £9 a week. You are not entitled to any increase unless you defer your pension for long enough to earn an increase of at least 1 per cent.[6]

The increase is calculated on the amount you would have received immediately before the end of the deferral period if you had not deferred claiming. If your entitlement changes during the deferral period (eg, because you become entitled to an inherited amount on the death of your spouse or civil partner – see p775), the calculation takes this into account so that it is based on the rates of pension to which you would have been entitled throughout the deferral period.[7]

You do not receive an increase in state pension for any whole week in the period of deferral in which:[8]

- you get severe disablement allowance, incapacity benefit, carer's allowance, widow's pension, widowed mother's allowance or unemployability supplement, or your spouse, civil partner or anyone you are residing with is receiving an increase in any of those benefits for you;
- you would have been disqualified from receiving state pension because you were a prisoner; or
- you are, or your partner is, in receipt of pension credit, universal credit, income support, income-based jobseeker's allowance or income-related employment and support allowance.

If you die either while you are deferring your state pension or after you have started to receive your state pension, your deferral increase is not inheritable.

If you are going to live abroad and have deferred your state pension, see p777.

2. The rules about your age

State pension can be claimed when you reach pension age (see p772) if this is on or after 6 April 2016. If you reached pension age before this date, you may be entitled to an 'old' retirement pension instead (see Chapter 36 of the 2015/16 edition of this *Handbook*).

You can claim state pension if you are:

- a man born on or after 6 April 1951; or
- a woman born on or after 6 April 1953.

Note: under the Gender Recognition Act 2004, if you are a transgender person and have been granted a full gender recognition certificate, your pension is paid on the basis of your acquired gender.[9]

Pension age

Pension age for men and women is being equalised in the period up to November 2018.

If you are a man born before 6 December 1953, your pension age is currently 65.

If you are a woman born before 6 April 1950, your pension age is 60. Women born between 6 April 1950 and 5 July 1953 will reach pension age at an age between 60 and 64 (see Appendix 12 for details). Women born between 6 July 1953 and 5 December 1953 will reach pension age during their 65th year.

From December 2018, the pension age for men and women will rise to 66 by October 2020. Between 2026 and 2028 it will rise to 67.[10] A person born after 5 October 1954 but before 6 April 1960 will reach pension age at 66. A person born between 6 April 1960 and 5 March 1961 will reach pension age at up to 66 years and 11 months, depending on her/his date of birth. Someone born after 5 March 1961 but before 6 April 1977 will reach pension age at 67.[11]

3. People included in the claim

You claim state pension for yourself. You do not get an increase in your state pension for an adult dependant or your child(ren).

If you are entitled to an 'old' retirement pension and already have an increase included for an adult dependant or child, the increase can continue to be paid in certain circumstances. See Chapter 33 of the 2012/13 edition of this *Handbook* for details of those who continue to qualify for an increase. You do not get the increase for your child if your partner's earnings are at or above the earnings limit. In 2017/18, this is £230 a week for the first child, increased by £30 for each subsequent child. If you qualify, you are paid £8 a week for the eldest child for whom child benefit is also paid, and £11.35 a week for each subsequent child. You do not get the increase for an adult dependant if s/he resides with you and earns more than £73.10 a week, or if s/he resides elsewhere and earns more than £66.35 a week. If you qualify, you are paid £66.35 a week.

4. The amount of benefit

The full weekly rate of state pension is £159.55. In addition, you may receive a higher pension if you deferred your entitlement to state pension (see p770). Some people may receive a transitional rate of state pension that is higher than £159.55

(see p774). You can request a statement estimating your state pension entitlement from the Future Pension Centre by telephone on 0345 3000 168 (textphone: 0345 3000 169), or by writing to the Pension Service.

You are not entitled to any increase in state pension for an adult or child dependant.

The amount of 'old' retirement pensions

If you reached pension age before 6 April 2016, you cannot get state pension but may instead be entitled to an 'old' retirement pension.

Category A retirement pension is paid at a weekly rate of £122.30.

Category B retirement pension for a spouse or civil partner is paid at a weekly rate of £73.30.

Category B retirement pension for a widow, widower or surviving civil partner is paid at a weekly rate of £122.30.

Category D retirement pension is paid at a weekly rate of £73.30.

The above amounts are the full rates. If you have not paid or been credited with sufficient national insurance (NI) contributions to qualify for the full rate, you get a reduced rate.

If you receive one of these retirement pensions, you receive an age addition of 25 pence a week if you are over 80.

Depending on which of these pensions you are entitled to, you may also receive:

– graduated retirement benefit, based on earnings between 1961 and 1975;
– an additional state pension, based on earnings after 5 April 1978;
– a higher pension if entitlement was deferred;
– an amount equivalent to the age-related addition to long-term incapacity benefit if you were receiving this within eight weeks of reaching pension age (see p772). If you have an additional state pension, this amount is offset against it;
– an increase for a dependent adult or child (see p772);

See Chapter 36 of the 2015/16 edition of this *Handbook* for full details of when you may be entitled to these additional amounts.

State pension is an individual pension based solely on your own contributions (except in the circumstances described on p774) – ie, there is no entitlement based on the contributions of your spouse or civil partner. State pension is based on NI contributions made wholly for tax years from 2016/17 onwards, has a single rate and is not inheritable. If your spouse or civil partner reached state pension age before 6 April 2016, s/he may be entitled to an 'old' retirement pension based on your NI contributions up to 5 April 2016 (a category B pension, or if your marriage or civil partnership legally ends, a category A pension).

If you do not have the required qualifying years (see p977) for the full rate of state pension, you get a reduced rate. This is calculated by multiplying 1/35th of the full rate by the number of qualifying years (which must be at least 10 to receive any state pension).[12] For example, if you have 17 qualifying years, you receive a state pension of £77.50 a week (17 x £159.55/35). Only people whose qualifying years are all from 2016/17 onwards have their state pension calculated this way.

For many years, people are likely to have a mix of contributions made before and after 6 April 2016. NI contributions and credits for years before 6 April 2016 count towards your state pension. There are transitional rules that aim to ensure anyone reaching pension age after this date receives at least the same level of entitlement as they would have had under the 'old' retirement pension scheme based on their own NI contributions.

There are transitional provisions for:

- people who have paid, been treated as having paid, or been credited with contributions for tax years before the introduction of state pension (see below);
- women who, before 1977, elected to pay a reduced rate of contributions (see p775); *and*
- inheriting entitlement from a late spouse or civil partner who had made contributions for tax years before the introduction of state pension (see p775).

Transitional rate of state pension

If you have qualifying years (see p977) before 6 April 2016, the amount of your state pension is worked out to ensure that your 'starting amount' is at least as much as you would have received using the 'old' retirement pension rules.[13] You must have at least 10 qualifying years to receive a transitional rate of state pension.[14]

Your 'starting amount' is the higher of:

- your entitlement to 'old' retirement pension. This takes account of your entitlement to basic category A retirement pension, additional pension and graduated retirement benefit. See Chapter 36 of the 2015/16 edition of this *Handbook*; *and*
- your entitlement under the new state pension rules as if they had applied throughout your working life.

In each case, a deduction is made if you were contracted out from the additional state pension scheme.

If you were entitled to a substantial amount of additional pension, your starting amount may be higher than the full rate of state pension. If so, the difference between your starting amount and the full rate is called your 'protected payment'. Your protected payment is paid on top of your full state pension and is increased each year in line with inflation. Your transitional rate of state pension up to the level of the full state pension is increased each year at the same rate as the state pension.[15] Any further qualifying years you have do not add more to your state pension.

If your starting amount is lower than the full state pension, you can add additional qualifying years up to the amount needed to qualify for a full-rate state pension or until you reach pension age, whichever is first. You may wish to do this even if you already have more than 35 qualifying years – eg, if, despite having more than 35 qualifying years, you do not qualify for the full rate because a deduction has been applied to reflect contracting out.[16] You may be able to pay NI contributions to fill in gaps in your record (see Chapter 42). Each qualifying year beginning on or after 6 April 2017 adds £159.55/35 (ie, approximately £4.56) a week to your state pension.

Women who paid reduced-rate contributions

Before 1977, married women and widows could opt out of gaining entitlement to retirement pension in their own right by electing to pay reduced-rate NI contributions (see Chapter 42). Their entitlement to retirement pension was based on the contributions of their spouse.

State pension is based on an individual's own contribution record, but there are special transitional rules for women who reach pension age on or after 6 April 2016 and who have paid reduced-rate contributions. These transitional rules apply if you still held the right to pay reduced-rate NI contributions at the start of the period of 35 years ending in the tax year before you reach pension age – ie, if you reach pension age in May 2016, you had a 'reduced-rate election' in force at the beginning of the 1981/82 tax year.

If you have any qualifying years from having paid or been credited with sufficient NI contributions in some tax years before 2016/17, there is an alternative calculation if this would be more beneficial than the transitional rate to which you would otherwise be entitled. This is at least equivalent to the combination of:[17]

- the standard rate of basic 'old' retirement pension for a person claiming on the NI contributions of a spouse or civil partner (£73.30 if you are married or in a civil partnership and your spouse or civil partner has also reached state pension age, or £122.30 if you are widowed, divorced or if your civil partnership is dissolved); *and*
- any additional pension to which you are entitled based on your own contribution record.

If you have no qualifying years from before 6 April 2016, you receive a transitional rate of state pension equivalent to the full category B retirement pension if both you and your spouse have reached pension age, or to the full category A retirement pension if you are no longer married or in a civil partnership.[18]

Widows, widowers and surviving civil partners

If you reach pension age on or after 6 April 2016, there are transitional rules that may allow you to qualify for an amount of state pension (known as a 'survivor's inherited state pension') based on the additional pension that your late spouse or civil partner would have been entitled to under the 'old' retirement pension scheme. This only applies if you were married or in a civil partnership before 6 April 2016 and your spouse or civil partner died while you were married or civil partners. If you were under pension age when s/he died and you remarry or enter a new civil partnership before you reach pension age, you do not qualify.[19]

If your spouse or civil partner reached pension age, or died below pension age, before 6 April 2016, you may be entitled to an inherited amount based on the amount of additional pension you would have been entitled to under the 'old' category B retirement pension rules.[20]

If:

- your spouse or civil partner reached pension age, or died below pension age, on or after 6 April 2016; *and*
- was entitled to the transitional rate of state pension immediately before s/he died (or would have been if s/he had reached pension age before s/he died or on the same day as you reached pension age); *and*
- her/his transitional rate was, or would have been, more than the full rate of state pension,

you may be entitled to an inherited amount of half of the difference between her/his transitional rate and the full rate of state pension.[21]

Your survivor's pension is paid in addition to any state pension or transitional rate of state pension (including one paid to women who elected to pay reduced-rate NI contributions – see p775).

You do not lose this amount if you marry or enter a civil partnership again after reaching pension age. However, as this new marriage or civil partnership takes place after 6 April 2016, you cannot get an inherited amount from your new spouse/civil partner if s/he subsequently dies, even if this would have been a higher amount.

Note: if you reach pension age before 6 April 2016, and your spouse or civil partner dies after this date, you may still be able to qualify for a category B retirement pension based on her/his contributions for tax years before the tax year beginning 6 April 2016. See Chapter 36 of the 2015/16 edition of this *Handbook* for more details. This applies whether s/he reached pension age before 6 April 2016 or not.

For how your entitlement to bereavement benefits affects entitlement to state pension, see Chapter 24.

Inheriting a deferred 'old' retirement pension

You may inherit an amount of state pension equivalent to an inherited deferred amount of 'old' retirement pension if:[22]

- your spouse or civil partner reached pension age before 6 April 2016;
- s/he had either claimed her/his 'old' retirement pension and was receiving a weekly increase from having deferred it, or was still deferring her/his 'old' retirement pension when s/he died; *and*

- at the time of her/his death you were over pension age or, if you were under pension age, you have not remarried or entered a new civil partnership before reaching pension age.

If your spouse or civil partner was deferring her/his 'old' retirement pension when s/he died and had deferred it for at least 12 months, you can choose to claim this amount as a lump sum or as a weekly state pension (a 'widowed person's or surviving civil partner's lump sum or pension'). If you do not make a choice within three months of being notified by the DWP of your right to do so (or such longer period as the DWP may allow), you are paid a lump sum. In certain circumstances, you can change your mind, provided you do so within three months of making a choice.[23] If your spouse or civil partner was already getting her/his 'old' retirement pension or s/he had deferred it for less than 12 months, you receive the inherited deferral payment as an extra weekly amount.

These rules mean that you have the same options as you would have had under the 'old' retirement pension system, so it applies regardless of when you reach pension age.

Inherited graduated retirement benefit

You may be entitled to an amount of inherited survivor's state pension based on the graduated retirement benefit entitlement of your late spouse or civil partner. This is based on graduated contributions s/he may have paid between 1961 and 1975. You have the option of choosing a lump sum or a weekly amount if s/he had deferred her/his entitlement to graduated retirement benefit for at least 12 months at the time of her/his death.[24]

5. Special benefit rules

Special rules may apply to:
- people who have come from or are going abroad (see below);
- people in prison or detention (see Chapter 41).

People coming from or going abroad

If you have lived elsewhere than the UK during your working life, your state pension may be affected – eg, it may be paid at a reduced rate. However, there are reciprocal arrangements with many countries that may help you qualify for a full pension. If you worked in another European Economic Area (EEA) state, you may benefit from the European Union (EU) co-ordination rules (see Chapter 68). Your employment in another EEA state can count towards your national insurance contribution record in determining your entitlement to state pension (see p1617). If you are not covered by the EU co-ordination rules, you may be able to benefit from a reciprocal agreement or an association or co-operation agreement (see p1533).

If you go to live abroad, you can take your pension with you to any other country. However, unless you move to live in another EEA state, Switzerland, Gibraltar or a country with which the UK has a reciprocal agreement for pensions, you are not entitled to uprating increases, so the amount of pension you receive is frozen at the rate at which it was paid when you went abroad. Similarly, if you claim a deferred pension abroad, the uprating increases that occurred while you were abroad are ignored when calculating both the deferral increase and rate payable.[25]

6. **Claims and backdating**

The general rules about claims and backdating are covered in Chapter 50. This section explains the specific rules that apply to state pension.

Making a claim

You must usually make a claim for state pension (unless you come within the exceptions below). A claim for state pension can be made:[26]

- in writing by completing the approved form. Send it to the Pension Service. You may be able to make your claim by taking or sending it to an alternative office (see p1148); *or*
- by telephone on 0800 731 7898 (textphone: 0800 731 7339); *or*
- online at www.gov.uk/claim-state-pension-online.

If you claim in writing, keep a copy of your claim form in case queries arise.

You must provide any information or evidence required (see p779). In certain circumstances, the DWP may accept a written application not on the approved form.[27] You can amend or withdraw your claim before a decision is made (see p1149). If there is a delay in making a claim, you may be able to get a short-term advance of benefit (see p1177).

Forms

The state pension claim form (Form BR1NSP) is normally sent to you by the DWP about four months before you reach pension age. Otherwise, you can get it from the state pension claim line on 0800 731 7898 (textphone: 0800 731 7339) or at www.gov.uk/state-pension/how-to-claim.

If you are a widow

If you are a widow, you do not need to make a claim for state pension if either:[28]
- you are over 65 when you stop getting widowed mother's allowance; *or*
- you are getting a widow's pension immediately before your 65th birthday.

You need to make a claim for state pension if you want to start receiving it before your widow's pension or widowed mother's allowance stops. If your widow's pension or widowed mother's allowance includes additional state pension, you receive this as an extra amount on top of your state pension, provided you do not remarry or form a new civil partnership before you reach pension age. If your state pension, plus any inherited amount, is less than your widow's pension or widowed mother's allowance, you are paid the difference until those benefits come to an end.

If you make a claim for state pension, your pension should be calculated under the rules (including the various transitional rules) as they apply to you. You do not need to identify and claim for the different elements that apply to you.[29]

Who should claim

You must normally claim state pension on your own behalf. However, if you are unable to manage your own affairs, another person can claim state pension for you as your 'appointee' (see p1149).

Information to support your claim

For the general information requirements that apply to all benefits, see p1150.

It is important that you provide any information required when you claim. Until you do, you may not count as having made a valid claim (see p1152). Correct any defects as soon as possible or your date of claim may be affected.

When you claim state pension, you must prove you have reached pension age. For most people, it is sufficient to produce your birth certificate, but problems can occur if you were born in a country which did not have a formal system of registering births. Other evidence that can prove your birth date includes:
- passport or identity card;
- school or health records;
- army records;
- statements from people who know you.

Even if you provide all that was required when you claim, you may be asked to provide further evidence to support your claim (see p1154). You may be asked to provide information after you are awarded state pension and if you fail to do so, your state pension can be suspended, or even terminated (see p1185).

The date of your claim

The date of your claim is important as it determines when your entitlement to state pension starts. This is not necessarily the date from when you are paid. For information about when payment of state pension starts, see p781.

The **'date of your claim'** is the date your written or telephone claim, properly completed with all the required evidence and information, is received at the appropriate office (the DWP, local authority housing benefit office or other designated office). A claim made by telephone is made on the date of the telephone call. **Note:** telephone claims cannot be made at designated offices.[30]

Note: you must make sure your claim is valid. If it is 'defective', you are given a short time to correct the defects (see p1152). If you do, your claim is treated as having been made when you initially claimed.[31]

In some cases, you can claim in advance (see p781) and in some cases your claim can be backdated (see below). If you want this to be done, make this clear when you claim or the DWP might not consider it. If you claimed the wrong benefit when you should have claimed state pension, see below.

Backdating your claim

It is very important to claim in time, because the maximum period for backdating is 12 months. You cannot backdate your claim for any period before the date you would have first become entitled to state pension.[32] You do not have to show any reason why your claim is late. The rules on backdating are covered on p1156.

If you claim more than 12 months after you became entitled to state pension, you are treated as having deferred your entitlement. You may want to consider the impact on your deferral amount when requesting backdating. If you backdate your claim, it reduces the amount of time you deferred claiming your pension, which reduces the amount of your weekly increase. Weigh up the financial implications of your options when considering backdating – if necessary, get advice.

If you might have qualified for state pension earlier but did not claim because you were given the wrong information or were misled by the DWP, you could ask for compensation (see p1396) or complain to the Ombudsman via your MP (see p1401).

If you claim the wrong benefit

If you have claimed the wrong benefit, in certain circumstances it is possible for your claim to be interchanged with another benefit.[33] For state pension, this interchange is only possible with bereavement benefits. If you make a claim for state pension, your pension should be calculated under the rules (including the various transitional rules) as they apply to you. You do not need to identify and claim for the different elements that apply to you. If you claim state pension on the wrong form (eg, you complete a claim form for 'old' retirement pension), it is likely to be treated as a valid claim if the form is properly completed.[34]

Claiming in advance

Claims for state pension (including a claim where you have deferred your entitlement – see p770) can be made up to, but no more than, four months in advance.[35] You should take advantage of this, as it can take a long time to sort out your contribution record. The date of your claim is the date on which you qualify.

7. **Getting paid**

The general rules on getting paid are covered in Chapter 50. This section explains the specific rules that apply to state pension. **Note:** rules on payment of 'old' retirement pension are very similar to rules on payment of state pension. See p781 of the 2015/16 edition of this *Handbook*.

When is state pension paid?

The day you are paid depends on your national insurance number (see p1174).[36] State pension is normally paid weekly, fortnightly or four-weekly in arrears. It can be paid every 13 weeks if you agree, or at longer intervals of up to a year if the DWP directs and you are entitled to less than £5 a week.[37]

State pension is payable from the date on which you reach pension age. If this is a day other than your payday, part-week payments are made.

Note:

- Deductions can be made from your state pension to pay third parties (see p1187).
- Even if you have been sanctioned for benefit offences (see p1265), you must be paid your state pension.
- For information on missing payments, see p1174. If you cannot get your pension payments because you have lost your bank or Post Office card or have forgotten your PIN, see p1173. If your 'simple payment' card has been lost or stolen, or if you have forgotten your memorable date, see p1173.
- If payment of your state pension is delayed, see p1165. If you are waiting for a decision on your claim, or to be paid, you might be able to get a short-term advance (see p1177). If you wish to complain about how your claim has been dealt with, or claim compensation, see Chapter 58.
- If payment of your state pension is suspended, see p1185.
- If you are overpaid state pension, you might have to repay it (see Chapter 52) and, in some circumstances, you may have to pay a penalty (see p1256). If you have been accused of fraud, see Chapter 53.

Change of circumstances

You must report changes in your circumstances that you have been told you must report, as well as any that you might reasonably be expected to know might affect your right to, the amount of, or the payment of, your state pension. You should do this as soon as possible, preferably in writing. See p1184 for further information.

8. **Tax, other benefits and the benefit cap**

Tax

State pension (and 'old' retirement pension) is taxable.[38] This includes inheritable lump-sum payments of deferred 'old' retirement pension and graduated retirement benefit.[39]

Means-tested benefits and tax credits

State pension (and 'old' retirement pension) is taken fully into account for the purposes of means-tested benefits, but pensioners receive a higher rate of some means-tested benefits. They are partially taken into account as income for tax credits (see Chapter 60).

You may qualify for pension credit (PC) to top up your state pension income (see p147).

Non-means-tested benefits

State pension (and 'old' retirement pension) is affected by the overlapping benefit rules (see p1175).

The benefit cap

In some cases, there is a limit on the total amount of specified benefits you can receive (a 'benefit cap'). State pension (and 'old' retirement pension) is *not* a specified benefit.[40] The benefit cap only applies if you are getting housing benefit (HB) or universal credit. If you are getting HB, the benefit cap normally only applies if you are below PC age. See p1180 for further information.

Passports and other sources of help

You qualify for a Christmas bonus (see p863) if you receive state pension (or 'old' retirement pension).[41] People aged 60 or over qualify for free prescriptions and eye tests regardless of their income. If you are on a low income, you may be entitled to council tax reduction (see p854).

Notes

1. Who can claim state pension

1 s2(1)-(3) PA 2014; reg 13(1) SP Regs
2 Reg 7 SP Regs
3 Reg 8 SP Regs
4 Reg 9 SP Regs
5 s17(4) PA 2014; reg 10 SP Regs
6 s17(2) PA 2014
7 Reg 12A SP Regs
8 Regs 11 and 12 SP Regs

2. The rules about your age

9 Sch 5 para 6A GRA 2004
10 s126 and Sch 4 PA 1995; s26 PA 2014
11 Memo DMG 18/14

4. The amount of benefit

12 s3(2) PA 2014
13 s5 and Sch 1 PA 2014
14 s4 PA 2014; reg 13(2) SP Regs
15 Sch 2 PA 2014; ss148AC and 151A SSAA 1992
16 PA 2014 Explanatory Notes, para 61
17 s11 and Sch 6 PA 2014
18 s12 and Sch 7 PA 2014
19 s7 and Schs 3 and 4 PA 2014
20 Sch 3 paras 2-4 PA 2014
21 Sch 3 paras 5-8 PA 2014
22 s8 PA 2014
23 ss8 and 9 PA 2014; regs 4-6 SP Regs
24 s10 PA 2014; regs 15-20 SP Regs

5. Special benefit rules

25 ss18(3) and 20 PA 2014; s179 SSAA 1992; regs 21-23 SP Regs

6. Claims and backdating

26 Regs 4 and 4ZC SS(C&P) Regs
27 Reg 4(1) SS(C&P) Regs
28 Reg 3(d) SS(C&P) Regs
29 Reg 3(ja) SS(C&P) Regs
30 Reg 6 SS(C&P) Regs
31 Reg 6(1)(b) SS(C&P) Regs
32 Reg 19(1) and Sch 4 SS(C&P) Regs
33 Reg 9(1) and Sch 1 SS(C&P) Regs
34 Reg 4(1) SS(C&P) Regs
35 Regs 15 and 15B(2) SS(C&P) Regs

7. Getting paid

36 Reg 22CA(4) SS(C&P) Regs
37 Reg 22CA(2) and (3) SS(C&P) Regs

8. Tax, other benefits and the benefit cap

38 s577(2)(za) IT(EP)A 2003
39 s8(4B) Finance (No.2) Act 2005
40 s96(11)(za) WRA 2012
41 s150(2) SSCBA 1992

5

Chapter 36

Social fund payments

This chapter covers:
1. Budgeting loans (below)
2. Sure Start maternity grants (p789)
3. Funeral expenses payments (p791)
4. Cold weather payments (p797)
5. Winter fuel payments (p798)
6. Tax, other benefits and the benefit cap (p800)

Key facts

- The social fund covers one-off loans and payments for specific expenses or circumstances.
- Budgeting loans are interest-free loans. Sure Start maternity grants, funeral expenses payments, cold weather payments and winter fuel payments are non-repayable.
- Social fund loans and payments are administered and paid by the DWP.
- If you disagree with a budgeting loan decision, there is an internal review system and then a further review to the Independent Case Examiner.
- If you disagree with a decision on a Sure Start maternity grant, funeral expenses payment, cold weather payment or winter fuel payment, you can apply for a revision or appeal against it. You must apply for a mandatory reconsideration before you can appeal.

Future changes

In the future, the rules on Sure Start maternity grants, funeral expenses payments, cold weather payments and winter fuel payments may be different in Scotland. See CPAG's online service and *Welfare Rights Bulletin* for updates.

1. Budgeting loans

To be eligible for a budgeting loan, you must satisfy all the following conditions, which are in legally binding directions. **Note:** if you come under the universal credit (UC) system (see p20), you cannot apply for a budgeting loan and must apply for a budgeting advance of your UC payments instead (see p175).

- **You must be in receipt of a 'qualifying benefit'** when your budgeting loan application is determined.[1] Qualifying benefits are: income support (IS), income-based jobseeker's allowance (JSA), income-related employment and support allowance (ESA) and pension credit (PC) (guarantee or savings credit). Payments on account and hardship payments are included. You are treated as being in receipt of a qualifying benefit if it is being paid to you, or to an appointee on your behalf. You are eligible if you receive a backdated award of a qualifying benefit, covering the date your application is determined. The High Court has held that you are not 'in receipt of' a qualifying benefit if your partner or another member of your family is the claimant.[2] If you are a member of a 'joint-claim couple', you are only eligible for a budgeting loan if you are the partner being paid JSA.

- **You and/or your partner, between you, must have been receiving a qualifying benefit throughout the 26 weeks before the date on which your application is determined**, disregarding any number of breaks of 28 days or less.[3] A period covered by a payment of arrears should count, as should any benefit received while in Northern Ireland. The waiting days at the start of a claim for JSA or ESA (see p705 and p639) do not count. More than one partner could help you satisfy the qualifying period.

- **You must not have too much capital.**[4] Any budgeting loan award is reduced by the amount of capital you have in excess of £1,000 (£2,000 if you or your partner are 61 or over). Capital is calculated as for the qualifying benefit that you are receiving (see Chapters 17 and 18). Payments made from the Family Fund to you, your partner or child, and refugee integration loans are ignored. Capital held by your child(ren) should be disregarded.

- **You, or your partner, must not be involved in a trade dispute** (see p940).[5]

- **You must not be a 'person subject to immigration control'** (there are exceptions to this rule) – see p1516.

- **The loan must be for one or more of the following categories of allowable expenses**, the need for which occurs in the UK:[6]
  - furniture and household equipment;
  - clothing and footwear;
  - maternity expenses;
  - funeral expenses;
  - rent in advance and/or removal expenses to secure fresh accommodation;
  - improvement, maintenance and security of the home;
  - travelling expenses;
  - expenses associated with seeking or re-entering work;
  - hire purchase and other debts for any of the above items.

You are required to tick the category of expense for which you need the loan on the application form. You are not required to specify the particular items you need – eg, a bed or a winter coat.

- **The loan must be a minimum of £100.**[7] You must state how much you are asking for on your application form. In practice, the maximum amount you can be offered will be determined with reference to the baseline figure and the weightings applied to it (see below).
- **You must be likely to be able to repay the loan** (see p788).[8]

The amount

The amount of loan you are offered depends on the following factors.[9]

- The amount you request. You are not offered more than you ask for, but you may be offered less because of the factors below.
- The legal minimum amount and the capital rules. You cannot be offered a loan of less than £100. The amount of your award is reduced if you have too much capital.
- The baseline figure and weighting of your application (see below). In practice, this will determine the maximum amount that you can be offered.
- The amount of any outstanding social fund loan debt you or your partner have. You cannot be liable to repay more than £1,500 in total.
  - If you have no outstanding social fund loans, you are offered the maximum amount appropriate to the weighting of your application, or the amount you have requested, if this is lower.
  - If you have an outstanding social fund loan debt, the maximum amount you can borrow is reduced by this amount.
- The amount you are likely to be able to repay. Generally, this is the amount you can repay within 104 weeks (see p788).

Baseline figure and weightings[10]
The '**baseline figure**' is determined by the Secretary of State and is the maximum loan that a single person can receive. Although, in theory, the baseline figure may change it has been set at £348 for over three years.
The baseline figure is multiplied (or '**weighted**') by one and one-third for couples without children, and by two and one-third for families with children (including lone parents).

Although decisions are legally made by decision makers, decision making is largely an automated process, with weightings and awards automatically calculated by computer.

Applying and getting paid

An application for a budgeting loan should normally be made to your local Jobcentre Plus office. Applications must be made in writing, either on the approved Form SF500, or in some other written form accepted by the Secretary of State. You can get the application forms from your local DWP office, or download them from www.gov.uk. An application can be made on your behalf by another person, provided you give your written consent (this is not necessary, however, if an appointee is acting for you).[11]

Your application is treated as made on the day it is received by the DWP.[12] If your application was incomplete and you comply with a request for additional information, your application is treated as made on the day it was originally received.

Payments are generally made into the account into which your qualifying benefit is paid or, if you do not have an account, in the same way as your qualifying benefit is paid.

Challenging a decision

Decisions are made by decision makers in accordance with the weighting critieria and your ability to repay. The DWP may telephone you to inform you of the decision on your application. If you are offered a loan and you are happy with the offer, you can accept it during the telephone call. However, you should still receive a written decision on your application, with an explanation if it has been refused or partly refused, together with a notification of your right to request a review.

The review is carried out by a different decision maker. However, a decision is only likely to be changed if it was based on incorrect information about your circumstances, or if the amount you are allowed to borrow has increased.

You must apply for a review of a decision by writing to the office where the decision was made within 28 days of the date the decision was issued to you.[13] Your application must include your grounds for requesting a review.[14] If someone is making an application on your behalf, it must be accompanied by your written authority (unless the person is your appointee – see p1149).[15]

Late applications can be accepted for 'special reasons'.[16] Special reasons are not defined but could include, for example, ill health, a domestic crisis or wrong advice.

However, if your application is out of time, it may be quicker to submit a new application.

If a decision is not wholly revised in your favour, the reviewing officer must either telephone or write to you to explain why and ask further questions if necessary.

If you are still unhappy with the decision, you can ask the Independent Case Examiner (see p1397) to undertake a second-tier review.[17] Do this in writing within 28 days, although the time limit may be extended if there are special reasons.

Repayments

All loans must be repaid to the DWP.[18]

The decision maker may give you more than one option for repaying a loan, depending on whether you have any other outstanding social fund loans and your other financial commitments. S/he may offer an option of a higher loan with an increased repayment rate, but you cannot be asked to repay at a rate higher than 20 per cent of your IS, income-based JSA or income-related ESA applicable amount or PC appropriate minimum guarantee plus any child tax credit or child benefit you receive. The loan must be repaid within 104 weeks.

You receive a written decision on your application for a budgeting loan with details of any loan offers and repayment terms. You have 14 days from the date the decision was sent to return the declaration agreeing to one of the offers made to you. This time limit can be extended for 'special reasons'.[19]

Note: the rules for the repayment of budgeting loans also apply to any outstanding crisis loans you may still have.

Methods of repayment

Budgeting loans are nearly always recovered by direct deductions from benefit, although you can make a payment at any time to pay off all or part of the debt. Deductions can only be made from the following benefits:[20]

- IS;
- JSA (contribution-based or income-based);
- ESA (contributory or income-related);
- PC;
- UC;
- incapacity benefit;
- severe disablement allowance;
- carer's allowance;
- disablement benefit, reduced earnings allowance and industrial death benefit;
- bereavement benefits (excluding the lump-sum bereavement payment) and widows' benefits;
- retirement pensions;
- maternity allowance.

Deductions can also be made from increases of benefit for age and dependants, and additional benefit under the additional state pension scheme.

A loan can be legally recovered from:[21]

- you (the applicant) or the person who the loan was for;
- your partner, if you are living together as a couple (as defined for IS purposes – see p215);

- a person who is liable to maintain either the person who made the application or the person on whose behalf it was made.

Rescheduling repayment terms

You cannot request a review of a decision relating to repayment terms or recovery. If you have accepted a loan, however, and the repayment terms are causing hardship (eg, because your financial situation has deteriorated), you can ask the DWP to reschedule the loan by lowering the weekly repayment rate.

2. Sure Start maternity grants

You qualify for a Sure Start maternity grant if you satisfy all of the following rules.

- **You or your partner have been awarded one of the following qualifying benefits** (including payments on account and hardship payments) in respect of the day you claim a maternity grant:[22]
  - income support (IS);
  - income-based jobseeker's allowance;
  - income-related employment and support allowance;
  - child tax credit which includes a child, disabled child or severely disabled child element (see p1409);
  - working tax credit including the disabled worker or severe disability element (see p1412);
  - pension credit (guarantee or savings credit);
  - universal credit.

  You are eligible if you receive a backdated award of a qualifying benefit covering the date you claim a maternity grant. If you are waiting for a decision on a claim for a qualifying benefit, the DWP may defer making a decision on your maternity grant claim until the qualifying benefit claim has been decided. If your maternity grant claim is refused while you are waiting for a decision on a qualifying benefit, you should reclaim a maternity grant within three months of being awarded the qualifying benefit. **Note:** if you do not claim a maternity grant within the time limits (see p790), a backdated award of a qualifying benefit does not qualify you for a grant. If you are not entitled to a qualifying benefit in your own right because you are under 16 (or under 19 and in 'relevant education' – see p872), a member of your family can claim a maternity grant for you if s/he is getting a qualifying benefit in respect of you.

- **One of the following applies:**[23]
  - you or a member of your family are pregnant or have given birth in the last three months (including stillbirth after 24 weeks of pregnancy);
  - you are the parent (but not the mother and not the mother's partner) of a child who is less than 12 months old, or you are responsible for that parent, and you are responsible for the child;

Part 5: Other benefits
Chapter 36: Social fund payments
2. Sure Start maternity grants

- you are the guardian of a child who is less than 12 months old;
- you or your partner have a child who is less than 12 months old placed with you for adoption and you are responsible for the child;
- you have adopted a child who is less than 12 months old under a recognised adoption which takes place outside the UK;
- you or your partner have been granted a child arrangements order, parental order (following a surrogate pregnancy) or adoption order for a child who is less than 12 months old.

In the last six cases, you are entitled to a payment even if one has already been made to the birth mother or a member of her family.[24]

- **There is no other member of your family who is under 16 at the time of claim**. However, a grant can be awarded for each child of a multiple birth, but the number of grants is reduced if there are other children in the family who are under 16. For example, if you give birth to triplets and already have one or more children under 16 in the family (and none of them are multiple births) two grants are awarded, or if you already have twins you are awarded one grant. If you are under 20 and another member of your family claims for you, the grant is payable, provided you do not have other children under 16.[25]
- **You or your partner are not involved in a trade dispute** (see p940), unless specified circumstances apply.[26]
- **You claim within the time limits** (see p790).
- **You have received health and welfare advice from a healthcare professional** (see p791).[27]
- **You are not a 'person subject to immigration control'** (there are exceptions to this rule) – see p1516.

The terms 'partner' and 'family' in the above rules have almost the same meanings as they do for IS purposes (see Chapter 11).[28]

The amount

You are entitled to a grant of £500 for each child or expected child.[29] The payment is not affected by any capital you have and is not repayable.

Claiming and getting paid

Claim on Form SF100, which you can get from your local Jobcentre Plus office or from www.gov.uk, or by telephone (0345 603 6967). There are strict time limits for claiming. You can claim a maternity grant at any time from 11 weeks before the first day of your expected week of childbirth until three months after the actual date of the birth. If you adopt a child, have a child arrangements order for a child or have a child by a surrogate mother, you can claim up to three months following the date of the adoption, child arrangments order or parental order, subject to the child being under 12 months when the claim is made. There is no provision for claiming outside the time limits.[30]

The back of your claim form must be signed by a healthcare professional (ie, midwife, health visitor or doctor) to confirm that you have received health and welfare advice about your baby or your maternal health.

Your date of claim is normally the date your form is received by the DWP.[31] If you make a written claim in some other way, you should be sent the appropriate form to complete. If you return it within one month, or such longer period as the Secretary of State considers reasonable, your date of claim is the date the DWP received your initial application.[32] See p789 for when your claim can be backdated if you are subsequently awarded a qualifying benefit.

If you are overpaid a maternity grant, you may have to repay it (see Chapter 52) and, in some circumstances, you may have to pay a penalty (see p1256).

3. **Funeral expenses payments**

You qualify for a funeral expenses payment if you satisfy all of the following rules.
- **You or your partner have been awarded one of the following qualifying benefits** (including payments on account and hardship payments) in respect of the day you claim a funeral payment:[33]
  - income support (IS);
  - income-based jobseeker's allowance;
  - income-related employment and support allowance;
  - housing benefit (HB);
  - child tax credit which includes a child, disabled child or severely disabled child element (see p1408);
  - working tax credit which includes the disabled worker or severe disability element (see p1411);
  - pension credit (guarantee or savings credit);
  - universal credit.

  You are eligible if you receive a backdated award of a qualifying benefit which covers the date you claim a funeral payment. If you are waiting for a decision on a claim for a qualifying benefit, the DWP may defer making a decision on a claim for a funeral payment until the qualifying benefit claim has been decided. If your claim for a funeral payment is refused while you are waiting for a decision on a qualifying benefit claim, reclaim within three months of being awarded the qualifying benefit. **Note:** if you do not claim a funeral payment within the time limit, a backdated award of a qualifying benefit will not qualify you for a grant.
- **You or your partner are in one of the categories of eligible people** listed below who can be treated as responsible for the funeral expenses.
- **You or your partner accept responsibility for funeral expenses** (see p794).[34] If you are claiming as a 'close relative' or 'close friend', it must also be reasonable for you to accept responsibility.

Part 5: Other benefits
Chapter 36: Social fund payments
3. Funeral expenses payments

- The funeral (ie, burial or cremation) takes place in the UK,[35] unless you or your partner are covered by specified European Union legislation, in which case the funeral can take place in any European Economic Area (EEA) state or Switzerland (see p794).[36]
- A social fund funeral payment has not already been made in respect of the deceased (but the amount of a previous award can be revised up to the maximum allowed under the rules).[37]
- The deceased was 'ordinarily resident' in the UK when s/he died (see p1537).[38]
- You are not a 'person subject to immigration control' (there are exceptions to this rule) – see p1516.
- You claim within the time limits (see p796).

5 Eligible people

You are only eligible for a funeral payment if you or your partner fall into one of the following categories of people who can be treated as responsible for the funeral costs.[39]

- You were the 'partner' of the deceased when s/he died.
- The deceased was a 'child' for whom you were responsible when s/he died and there is no 'absent parent', or there is an absent parent but s/he (or her/his partner) was getting a qualifying benefit (see p791) when the child died. If there is an absent parent who was not getting a qualifying benefit when the child died, you may qualify for a payment as a close relative of the deceased. If the deceased was a stillborn child, you are eligible for a funeral payment if you were the parent or the parent's partner, and it does not matter whether there is an absent parent.
- You were a parent, son or daughter of the deceased and it is reasonable for you to accept responsibility for the funeral expenses (see p794).
- You were a 'close relative' or a 'close friend' of the deceased and it is reasonable for you to accept responsibility for the funeral expenses (see p794), and you are not excluded by the rules below.

Definitions[40]
'Child' is defined as for IS purposes (see p220). You are 'responsible' for a child if you get, or could get, child benefit for her/him (see p222).
'Stillborn child' means a child born dead after 24 weeks of pregnancy.
'Absent parent' means a parent of a deceased child, where the child:
– was not living in that parent's household at the date of death; *and*
– was living with another person who was responsible for her/him.
'Close relative' means parent, parent-in-law, son, son-in-law, daughter, daughter-in-law, step-parent, stepson, stepson-in-law, stepdaughter, stepdaughter-in-law, brother, brother-in-law, sister, sister-in-law.

'**Close friend**' is not defined in the law. It can include a relative who is not a close relative – eg, a grandparent or grandchild.[41]

'**Partner**' has the same meaning as for IS (see p215). You also count as a partner, however, if you were living in a care home when the deceased died and:[42]

– you and your spouse or civil partner were living in the same home; *or*

– you were a member of a couple before one or both of you moved into such a home.

This rule is designed to enable a surviving partner to claim a funeral payment if one or both partners were in a home at the date of death.

Exclusion of certain close relatives and friends

If you claim as a close relative or close friend of the deceased (see p794), you cannot get a payment if:

- the deceased had a partner (unless that partner died before the funeral without making a claim for a funeral payment);[43]
- the deceased was a child or stillborn child and a responsible person or parent is able to claim a funeral payment under the rules set out above;[44]
- there is a parent, son or daughter of the deceased, apart from:[45]
  - anyone under the age of 18;
  - anyone aged 18 or 19 who counts as a qualifying young person for child benefit purposes (see p572);
  - anyone who (or whose partner) has been awarded a qualifying benefit (see p791);
  - anyone estranged from the deceased when s/he died ('estranged' is not defined, but has connotations of emotional disharmony);[46]
  - students aged 18 on a full-time course of advanced education (see p874), or aged 19 to pension age on any full-time course;
  - members of a religious order which fully maintains them;
  - prisoners (including those in youth custody or a remand centre) who (or whose partners) were getting a qualifying benefit immediately before being detained;
  - inpatients receiving free treatment in a hospital or similar institution, who (or whose partners) were getting a qualifying benefit immediately before becoming a patient;
  - asylum seekers receiving asylum support from the Home Office or a local authority (see p1526);
  - anyone who is ordinarily resident (see p1537) outside the UK;
- there is a close relative of the deceased who was in *closer contact* with the deceased than you were, taking into account the nature and extent of such contact;[47]
- there is a close relative of the deceased who was in *equally close contact* with the deceased as you were and who (or whose partner) is not getting a qualifying benefit (see p791).[48]

Part 5: Other benefits
Chapter 36: Social fund payments
3. Funeral expenses payments

Note: the last two bullet points do not apply if the close relative was under the age of 18 when the deceased died, or was a student, member of a religious order, prisoner, inpatient or asylum seeker as set out above, or was ordinarily resident outside the UK.[49]

If you are refused a payment on this ground, the DWP (not you) must establish whether there is another close relative who is not getting a qualifying benefit.[50]

Examples

Jane is not entitled to a funeral payment because, although she looked after her brother for many years before he died, he had a son who is not getting a qualifying benefit (see p791). Although the son rarely saw his father, they were not estranged.

Yuri is entitled to a funeral payment when his close friend Robert dies because, although Robert had two surviving close relatives, a son and a sister-in-law, the son is getting HB and Yuri was in closer contact with Robert than either of them were.

Accepting responsibility for funeral costs

To qualify for a funeral payment, you or your partner must 'accept responsibility' for funeral expenses.[51] The key factor is whether you are liable to pay the costs of a funeral, rather than whether you have made the arrangements.[52]

If the funeral director's account or contract is in your name, you should normally be treated as having accepted responsibility. If the account or contract is in someone else's name (or another person has paid the bill), you can still be 'responsible' if:

- s/he is acting as your agent – eg, because you are too distressed to act on your own behalf;[53] *or*
- s/he transfers liability to you, prior to full payment, with the consent of the funeral director.[54]

If you are a close relative (see p792) or close friend of the deceased, it must also be 'reasonable' for you to accept responsibility for the funeral expenses, in the light of the nature and extent of your contact with the deceased.[55] In one case, it was held reasonable for a person to have accepted responsibility for his father's funeral even though he had not seen him for 24 years. This did not erase the contact they had had in the previous 30 years.[56]

European Economic Area nationals

You can get a funeral payment for a funeral that takes place in any member state of the EEA or Switzerland (see p1609) if:[57]

- you are a 'worker' or self-employed, or you retain that status; *or*
- you are a member of the family of a worker – ie:

- her/his spouse or civil partner;
- the worker's/spouse's/civil partner's child, grandchild or other descendant who is either under 21 or dependent;
- a dependent relative of the worker, spouse or civil partner in the ascending line – eg, a parent or grandparent; *or*
- you have a permanent right to reside in the UK.

For more details on the benefit rights of EEA nationals, see Chapter 68.

If you have ever been refused a payment for a funeral that took place in an EEA state and you satisfied the above rules, you should ask for a revision (see p1279).

The amount

You are entitled to a payment that is sufficient to cover:[58]
- the necessary costs of purchasing a new burial plot with the exclusive right of burial in it and necessary burial fees. The burial of ashes following cremation is not, however, covered;
- the necessary cremation fees, including medical references, certificates and removing a pacemaker (restricted to £20 if not carried out by a doctor);
- the costs of documentation necessary for the release of the deceased's assets;
- the reasonable cost of transport for the portion of journeys in excess of 80 kilometres (50 miles), undertaken to:
  - transport the body within the UK to a funeral director's premises or to a place of rest;
  - transport the coffin and bearers in a hearse and the mourners in another vehicle from the funeral director's premises or place of rest to the funeral. The cost of this plus burial in an existing plot cannot exceed the cost of such transport plus the purchase and burial costs of a new plot;[59]
- the necessary expenses of one return journey for the responsible person to arrange or attend the funeral. The maximum allowed is the cost of a return journey from home to the place where the burial or cremation costs are incurred;
- up to £700 for any other funeral expenses – eg, funeral director's fees, religious costs, flowers and other transport costs.

Note:
- The cost of any items or services provided under a pre-paid funeral plan or equivalent arrangement cannot be met. Expenses not covered by the plan can be met if they fall into the above categories, but the maximum allowed under the last category is restricted to £120.[60]
- Costs relating to religious requirements cannot be included in the amount allowed for burial and transport.[61]

Part 5: Other benefits
Chapter 36: Social fund payments
3. Funeral expenses payments

If the amount awarded does not cover your funeral expenses, you may be able to claim a budgeting loan (see p784).

Deductions from awards

The following are deducted from an award of a funeral payment.[62]

- The deceased's assets available to you or a member of your family (defined as for IS purposes) without probate or letters of administration. However, if you have a joint account with the deceased, those assets become yours at the point of death and cannot be deducted.[63] Assets at the date of death count, even if you have spent or distributed them before your claim for a funeral payment.[64] However, arrears of most benefits and tax credits payable to the deceased at the date of death are excluded from the assets.[65]
- A lump sum legally due to you or a member of your family from an insurance policy, occupational pension scheme, burial club or equivalent source on the death of the deceased.
- Any contribution towards funeral expenses made to you or a member of your family by a charity, or a relative of yours or of the deceased.
- A funeral grant paid by the government for a war disablement pensioner.
- An amount paid or payable under a pre-paid funeral plan or equivalent arrangement (whether or not the plan was fully paid).

Any capital you have apart from the above has no effect on the amount of the funeral payment. Any payments from the Macfarlane Trust, the Macfarlane (Special Payments) Trusts, MFET Ltd, the Fund, the Eileen Trust, the CJD Trusts, the Skipton Fund, the Caxton Foundation or the London Bombings Relief Charitable Fund are not deducted from an award of a funeral payment.[66]

Claiming and getting paid

Claim on Form SF200, which you can get from your local Jobcentre Plus office or from www.gov.uk or by telephone (via the Bereavement Service on 0345 606 0265; textphone 0345 606 0285). There are strict time limits for claiming. You can claim at any time from the date of death to up to three months after the date of the funeral.[67] There is no provision for late claims.

When completing the form, bear in mind the rules about accepting responsibility for the funeral expenses and your contact with the deceased.

Your date of claim is normally the date the form is received by the DWP or the date you make your phone claim.[68] If you do not complete Form SF200 properly or apply in writing but not on the form, you should be sent the form to complete or correct. If you submit it within one month, or a longer period if the Secretary of State considers this reasonable, your claim is treated as being made on the date you originally applied.[69] See p791 for when your claim can be backdated if you are subsequently awarded a qualifying benefit.

Payment is normally made directly to the funeral director, unless you have already paid the bill.[70]

If you are overpaid a funeral payment, you may have to repay it (see Chapter 52) and, in some circumstances, you may have to pay a penalty (see p1256). However, see below for recovery from the deceased's estate.

Recovery from the deceased's estate

The Secretary of State is entitled to recover funeral expenses payments from the deceased's estate and normally seeks to do so.[71] Funeral expenses are a first charge on the estate and have priority over anything else (although there may be insufficient assets for full repayment).[72]

4. Cold weather payments

You qualify for a cold weather payment if you satisfy all the following rules.
- **There is a period of cold weather** in the area where you have your usual home. This is defined as seven consecutive days during which your designated local weather station either forecasts or records a temperature at or below zero degrees celsius.[73]
- **You have been awarded pension credit** (guarantee or savings credit) for at least one day during the period of cold weather. **You also qualify if you have been awarded income support (IS), income-based jobseeker's allowance (JSA), income-related employment and support allowance (ESA) or universal credit (UC)** for at least one day during the period of cold weather[74] and:
  - your IS or income-based JSA applicable amount includes a disability, severe disability, enhanced disability, disabled child, pensioner or higher pensioner premium (see p236); *or*
  - your income-related ESA applicable amount includes the pensioner premium, severe disability premium or enhanced disability premium, or you have been assessed as having, or are treated as having, limited capability for work or limited capability for work-related activity; *or*
  - your UC includes an increase for a disabled or severely disabled child, or you have been assessed as having, or are treated as having, limited capability for work or limited capability for work-related activity, and you are not in employment or gainful self-employment during the period of cold weather or on the day it is forecast; *or*
  - you are responsible for a child under five; *or*
  - you are getting child tax credit which includes a disabled child or severely disabled child element (see p1408).

Part 5: Other benefits
Chapter 36: Social fund payments
5. Winter fuel payments

- You are not living in a care home, independent hospital, Abbeyfield Society establishment, or accommodation provided under the Polish Resettlement Act (unless you are responsible for a child under five or getting child tax credit which includes a disabled child or severely disabled child element).[75]
- You are not a 'person subject to immigration control' (there are exceptions to this rule) – see p1516.

The amount

The sum of £25 is paid for each week of cold weather.[76]

Claiming and getting paid

You do not need to make a claim for a cold weather payment. The DWP should automatically pay you if you qualify. Your district DWP should publicise when there are periods of cold weather in your area. If you do not receive payment and you think you are entitled, submit a written claim and ask for a written decision. A payment cannot be made more than 26 weeks from the last day of the winter period (1 November to 31 March) in which the cold weather period fell.[77] If you are overpaid a cold weather payment, you might have to repay it (see Chapter 52) and, in some circumstances, you may have to pay a penalty (see p1256).

---

5. **Winter fuel payments**

You qualify for a winter fuel payment if you satisfy all the following rules.[78]
- **You are at least the qualifying age for pension credit** (PC – see p147) in the 'qualifying week'.
- **You are ordinarily resident in Great Britain** (see p1579) **or you are habitually resident in another European Economic Area country with an average winter temperature that is not higher than that of the warmest part of the UK or in Switzerland.**
- **You claim in time** (see p799), if a claim is required.
- **You are not excluded from a payment under the rules below.**

The qualifying week
The **'qualifying week'** is the week beginning on the third Monday in September.

Who cannot get a winter fuel payment

You are excluded from entitlement to a payment if, throughout the qualifying week (see above):[79]
- you are serving a custodial sentence;

- you have been receiving free inpatient treatment for more than 52 weeks in a hospital or similar institution (see p910);
- you are receiving PC, income-based jobseeker's allowance (JSA) or income-related employment and support allowance (ESA) and you are living in residential care;[80]
- you are a 'person subject to immigration control' (there are exceptions to this rule) – see p1516.

Residential care

You count as **'living in residential care'** if you are living in a care home (ie, an independent home which is registered or exempt from registration, or a local authority home which provides board), independent hospital or accommodation provided under the Polish Resettlement Act throughout the qualifying week and the 12 preceding weeks, disregarding temporary absences.

The amount

Subject to the rules below, you are entitled to a winter fuel payment of:[81]
- £200 if you are aged between the qualifying age for PC and 79 (inclusive) in the qualifying week (see p798); *or*
- £300 if you are aged 80 or over in the qualifying week.

If you do not get PC, income-based JSA or income-related ESA and you share your accommodation with another qualifying person (whether as a partner or friend), you get £100 if you are both aged between the qualifying age for PC and 79 or £150 if you are both aged 80 or over. If only one of you is aged 80 or over, s/he gets £200 and the other person gets £100.

If you get PC, income-based JSA or income-related ESA, you (and your partner if you have one) get £200 if one or both of you is aged between the qualifying age for PC and 79, or £300 if one or both of you is aged 80 or over, regardless of whether there is anyone else in your household who qualifies.

If you are living in residential care (see p798) in the qualifying week and are not getting PC, income-based JSA or income-related ESA, you are entitled to a payment of £100 if you are aged between the qualifying age for PC and 79, or £150 if you are aged 80 or over.

Claiming and getting paid

You should automatically receive a payment without having to make a claim if you received a payment the previous year, or if you are getting retirement pension or any other social security benefit (apart from child benefit, universal credit, council tax reduction and housing benefit) in the qualifying week.[82]

Part 5: Other benefits
Chapter 36: Social fund payments
6. Tax, other benefits and the benefit cap

Otherwise, you must claim a winter fuel payment on or before 31 March following the qualifying week.[83] To ensure you receive your payment before Christmas, submit your claim before the qualifying week. You can claim via the winter fuel payments helpline on 0345 915 1515 (local rate) (textphone: 0345 606 0285), or you can download a claim form from www.gov.uk/winter-fuel-payment.

You should get a written decision.

If you are a member of a couple and your partner is receiving income support, the payment can be made to either of you (even though your partner is under the qualifying age for PC – see p147).[84]

The government aims to make payments between mid-November and Christmas.

6. **Tax, other benefits and the benefit cap**

Social fund loans and payments are not taxable.

They are disregarded as income and capital for the purposes of means-tested benefits and tax credits, and do not affect entitlement to any non-means-tested benefits.

In some cases, there is a limit on the total amount of specified benefits you can receive (a 'benefit cap'). Social fund loans and payments are *not* one of the specified benefits. The benefit cap only applies if you are getting housing benefit or universal credit.

Notes

1. Budgeting loans
1　Dir 8 BLG
2　*R v SFI ex parte Davey*, 19 October 1998 (HC), unreported
3　Dir 8 BLG
4　Dir 9 BLG
5　Dir 8 BLG
6　Dir 2 BLG
7　Dir 53 BLG
8　Dir 11 BLG
9　Dir 53 BLG
10　Dir 52 BLG
11　Reg 4 SF(AM) Regs
12　Reg 5 SF(AM) Regs
13　Reg 2(1)(a) and (2)(a) SF(AR) Regs
14　Reg 2(4) SF(AR) Regs
15　Reg 2(6) SF(AR) Regs
16　Reg 2(3) SF(AR) Regs
17　para 60 Part 4 BLG
18　s78(1) SSAA 1992
19　Reg 6(3) and (4) SF(AM) Regs
20　Reg 3 SF(RDB) Regs
21　s78(3) SSAA 1992

2. Sure Start maternity grants
22　Reg 5(2) SFM&FE Regs
23　Reg 5(3) SFM&FE Regs
24　Reg 3A SFM&FE Regs
25　Reg 5A SFM&FE Regs
26　Reg 6 SFM&FE Regs
27　Reg 5(4) SFM&FE Regs
28　Reg 3(1) and (2) SFM&FE Regs
29　Reg 5(1) SFM&FE Regs
30　Reg 19 and Sch 4 para 8 SS(C&P) Regs
31　Reg 6(1)(a) SS(C&P) Regs
32　Regs 4(7) and 6(1)(b) SS(C&P) Regs

3. Funeral expenses payments
33　Reg 7(3) and (4) SFM&FE Regs
34　Reg 7(7) SFM&FE Regs
35　Reg 7(9)(b) SFM&FE Regs
36　Reg 7(9)(a) SFM&FE Regs
37　Reg 4(1) and (2) SFM&FE Regs
38　Reg 7(5) SFM&FE Regs
39　Reg 7(8)(a)-(e) SFM&FE Regs
40　Reg 3(1) SFM&FE Regs
41　CIS/788/2003
42　Reg 3(2) SFM&FE Regs
43　Regs 7(8)(e) and 8(4) SFM&FE Regs
44　Reg 7(8)(e) SFM&FE Regs; R(IS) 7/04

45　Reg 8(1) and (2) SFM&FE Regs
46　R(SB) 2/87
47　Reg 8(7)(a) SFM&FE Regs
48　Reg 8(7)(b) SFM&FE Regs
49　Reg 8(8) SFM&FE Regs
50　*Kerr v Department for Social Development (NI)* [2004] All ER(D) 65; [2004] UKHL 23
51　Reg 7(7) SFM&FE Regs
52　CSB/488/1982
53　CIS/12344/1996; R(IS) 6/98
54　CIS/85/1991
55　Reg 7(8)(e) SFM&FE Regs
56　CIS/12783/1996
57　Reg 7(10) SFM&FE Regs
58　Reg 9(1), (2) and (3) SFM&FE Regs
59　Reg 9(8) SFM&FE Regs
60　Reg 9(10) SFM&FE Regs
61　Reg 9(7) SFM&FE Regs
62　Reg 10(1) SFM&FE Regs
63　Vol 7 Ch 39, para 39404 DMG
64　R(IS) 14/91
65　Reg 10(1A) SFM&FE Regs
66　Reg 10(2) SFM&FE Regs
67　Sch 4 para 9 SS(C&P) Regs
68　Reg 6(1)(a) SS(C&P) Regs
69　Regs 4(7) and 6(1)(b) SS(C&P) Regs
70　Reg 35(2) SS(C&P) Regs
71　s78(4) SSAA 1992; CIS/616/1990
72　R(SB) 18/84

4. Cold weather payments
73　Reg 2(1) and (2) SFCWP Regs
74　Regs 1A(2) and (3) and 6 SFCWP Regs
75　Reg 1A(4) SFCWP Regs
76　Reg 3 SFCWP Regs
77　Reg 2(6) SFCWP Regs

5. Winter fuel payments
78　Reg 2 SFWFP Regs
79　Reg 3 SFWFP Regs
80　Reg 1(2) and (3) SFWFP Regs
81　Reg 2 SFWFP Regs
82　Reg 4 SFWFP Regs
83　Reg 3(1)(b) and (2) SFWFP Regs
84　Reg 36(2) SS(C&P) Regs

Chapter 37

Statutory maternity, adoption, paternity and shared parental pay

5

This chapter covers:

Key facts

- Statutory maternity pay (SMP), statutory adoption pay (SAP), statutory paternity pay (SPP) and statutory shared parental pay (SSPP) are payments made to certain employees by their employers in connection with the birth or adoption of a child.
- SMP, SAP, SPP and SSPP are not means tested, although they have employment and earnings conditions.
- You do not have to have paid national insurance contributions to qualify.
- You do not need to intend to return to work to qualify for SMP, SAP, SPP or SSPP. You do not have to repay SMP, SAP, SPP or SSPP, even if you do not return to work.
- You may be entitled to more maternity, adoption, paternity or shared parental pay under your employment contract.
- If you disagree with your employer's decision on your entitlement, or if your employer has failed to make a decision, you can challenge this.

Future changes

In 2015 the government announced plans to change the rules for SSPP, possibly from 2018, to enable a child's grandparent to claim SSPP and shared parental leave from her/his employer if the child's mother or adopter chooses to reduce her/his maternity, maternity allowance or adoption pay period to allow this.[1] See CPAG's online service and *Welfare Rights Bulletin* for updates.

1. **Introduction**

This chapter describes the rules on the statutory payments your employer may be liable to pay you for a birth or adoption of a child. These are statutory maternity pay (SMP), statutory adoption pay (SAP), statutory paternity pay (SPP) and statutory shared parental pay (SSPP).

Note: SPP and SSPP can be awarded for a birth or an adoption. In this *Handbook*, payments for a birth are referred to as SPP (birth) or SSPP (birth), and payments for an adoption are referred to as SPP (adoption) or SSPP (adoption). When SPP or SSPP is used, the rules described apply to both types of SPP or SSPP.

Definitions

In this chapter, the term **'mother'** is used only in relation to statutory payments for a birth and so does not include an adoptive mother.

'Adopter' means an adoptive parent, but also includes a local authority foster parent in the situation described on p805.

You count as the **'partner'** of the child's mother or adopter (whether or not you have jointly adopted the child) if either:

– you are her/his spouse or civil partner; *or*

– you live with her/him and the child in an 'enduring family relationship'. In this situation, a parent, grandparent, sister, brother, aunt, uncle, half-sister or half-brother cannot count as your partner and, if you are adopted, neither can your adoptive parents. For SSPP, a child, grandchild, niece or nephew also cannot count as your partner.

Payments for a birth of a child

Circumstance	You may qualify for
You are the baby's mother	SMP and SSPP (birth); *or* Maternity allowance (MA)
You are the baby's father or the mother's partner	SPP (birth) and SSPP (birth)

If you are pregnant or have recently given birth, you may qualify for:

- SMP from your employer during the 39-week maternity pay period. See p807 for the qualifying conditions. If you do not qualify for SMP, you may be entitled to MA instead (see Chapter 34);
- SSPP (birth) from your employer, provided you share the care of your baby with the baby's father or your partner, you both meet the qualifying conditions, you get SMP and you choose to end your maternity pay period early. Swapping from SMP to SSPP allows you greater flexibility in when you take paid leave. See p806 and p810 for the qualifying conditions.

If you are the father of a baby or if your partner (see p803) **has recently given birth**, you may qualify for:

- up to two weeks' SPP from your employer. This can usually only be paid within eight weeks of the birth. Both men and women can qualify for SPP. See p807 and p809 for the qualifying conditions;
- SSPP (birth), provided you share the care of the baby with the mother, she gets either SMP or gets MA on the basis of her employment or self-employment and she is willing to end her maternity pay or MA period early. For the qualifying conditions, see p806 and p810.

See p805 for factors to consider when deciding whether to swap SMP or MA for SSPP and p806 for the interaction between SSP and SSPP.

See p824 if your baby was born with the help of a surrogate.

Expected week of childbirth

The '**expected week of childbirth**' is the week, starting on a Sunday, in which your baby is due to be born.

Payments for an adoption of a child

Circumstances	You may qualify for
You have adopted a child	SAP and SSPP (adoption)
You and your partner have jointly adopted a child	SAP or SPP (adoption) and SSPP (adoption)
Your partner has adopted a child	SPP (adoption) and SSPP (adoption)

If you are adopting a child, you may qualify for SAP from your employer during the 39-week adoption pay period. See p807 and p808 for the qualifying conditions for SAP. See p805 if you are jointly adopting a child.

If your partner (see p803) **has recently adopted a child**, you may qualify for up to two weeks' SPP from your employer. This can usually only be paid within eight weeks of the adoption placement. Both men and women can qualify for SPP. See p807 and p809 for the qualifying conditions.

If you share the care of the child with your partner, you both meet certain conditions relating to work and earnings and you get SAP, you may choose to end your adoption pay period early so that:
- you may qualify for SSPP (adoption). Swapping from SAP to SSPP can offer greater flexibility in when you take paid leave; *and/or*
- your partner may qualify for SSPP (adoption) and/or shared parental leave.

If you are jointly adopting a child with your partner, only one of you can get SAP in respect of the adoption, and neither of you can get both SAP and SPP for the same adoption. Your partner may qualify for SPP while you get SAP, or vice versa.[2] To decide who should apply for SAP, it may be useful to calculate what your overall household income would be over the adoption pay period in the two scenarios. For the amount of SAP and SPP that is paid, see p821. If in doubt, get advice.

See below for the factors to consider when deciding whether to swap SAP for SSPP (adoption).

See p824 if you are adopting a child who was born with the help of a surrogate.

Foster parents approved as adopters

If you are a local authority foster parent who, in England, has been approved as a prospective adopter, you count as an adopter of a child when s/he has been placed with you by an adoption agency as her/his prospective adopter (this is also known as a 'fostering for adoption' placement). You may therefore qualify for SAP, SPP (adoption) or SSPP (adoption) while the child is fostered by you, before the actual adoption.[3] It is intended that this also applies to foster carers approved as prospective adopters in Wales but, at the time of writing, the regulations had not been amended.[4]

Choosing whether to apply for statutory shared parental pay

If you qualify for SMP or SAP, or for MA on the basis of your own employment or self-employment (see p722), and you want your child's father or your partner to have paid leave from work to look after your child, you can choose to end your maternity pay, adoption pay or MA period early to allow her/him to get SSPP (provided s/he meets the other entitlement conditions). Even if s/he does not intend to claim or is not entitled to SSPP, if you get SMP or SAP you may choose to reduce your maternity or adoption pay period to claim SSPP yourself (if you qualify for it), as it can offer greater flexibility in when you take paid leave. For either of you to qualify, you must share the main care of the child, and you must both meet certain conditions relating to work and earnings.

In effect, the unused weeks of your maternity pay, adoption pay or MA period are converted into weeks of SSPP (although there can never be more than 37

Part 5: Other benefits
Chapter 37: Statutory maternity, adoption, paternity and shared parental pay
2. Who is entitled

available weeks of SSPP). If both you and your partner qualify for SSPP, and you both intend to claim it, you share the available weeks of SSPP between you in whatever proportion you choose. You can get SSPP for the same or different weeks. Alternatively, either one of you can get all the available weeks of SSPP. The weeks of SSPP can be paid over one continuous period or over more than one separate period, provided the weeks fall within a year of the birth or adoption placement.

If you get SMP or SAP, you can only qualify for SSPP once you have ended your maternity or adoption pay period. However, the child's father or your partner may qualify for SSPP while you are still getting MA, SMP or SAP, provided you have given proper notice of your intention to reduce your MA, maternity pay or adoption pay period (see p725 and p813).[5]

What should you consider before applying for statutory shared parental pay?

1. Think carefully about giving notice that you want to end your maternity, adoption or MA pay period. Once you have done so, you can only retract that notice and continue to get SMP, SAP or MA in very limited circumstances (see p814 and p725).

2. For some weeks, the amount of your SMP or SAP may be higher than the amount of SSPP, because neither SMP nor SAP is capped at a maximum amount for the first six weeks of payment (see p821).

3. The amount of SMP, SAP or SSPP you receive may be different from the amount of SSPP the child's father or your partner would receive, because the amount you get is related to your respective average earnings (see p821).

4. If you are entitled to contractual maternity or adoption pay to top up your SMP or SAP, check whether this differs from the amount of any contractual shared parental pay to which you or your partner may be entitled to top up your SSPP entitlement.

5. Swapping from SMP, SAP or MA to SSPP may affect your entitlement to other benefits (see p832 and p732).

6. If you are the child's father or the partner of the child's mother/adopter, although you can be entitled to both SPP and SSPP following a birth or adoption, you cannot get SPP for any week for which you either get SSPP or you are on shared parental leave, or for any subsequent week. If you want to get your full entitlement to both SPP and SSPP, you must take your SPP before you start your SSPP or shared parental leave.[6]

2. Who is entitled

You qualify for statutory maternity pay (SMP), statutory adoption pay (SAP), statutory paternity pay (SPP) or statutory shared paternity pay (SSPP) from your employer if:

- you satisfy the conditions specific to SMP (see p807), SAP (see p808), SPP (see p809) or SSPP (see p810); *and*

- you meet the common qualifying conditions – ie:[7]
  - you satisfy the continuous employment rule (see p814); *and*
  - you satisfy the earnings condition (see p817); *and*
  - you have given the appropriate notice and information (see p825); *and*
  - you are not carrying out work for the employer paying you SMP, SAP, SPP or SSPP (but see p818).

Note:
- SMP, SAP, SPP and SSPP may not be payable if you work for other employers during your maternity, adoption or paternity pay period or during the period(s) for which you claim SSPP (see p820).
- Your employer cannot restrict your right to SMP, SAP, SPP or SSPP by its own rules or contract with you and cannot require you to contribute towards the cost of SMP, SAP, SPP or SSPP.[8]

To help you work out whether you meet the entitlement conditions for SMP, SPP (birth) and SSPP (birth), there is a list of relevant dates for 2017/18 in Appendix 11.

There are some groups of people to whom special rules apply (see p821).

Statutory maternity pay

You qualify for SMP if you satisfy the common conditions (see above) and you are within your maternity pay period.[9]

The maternity pay period

SMP can only be paid during the 'maternity pay period'.[10] This is a period of 39 consecutive weeks which starts from, at the earliest, the beginning of the 11th week before the expected week of childbirth (EWC – see p804), unless your baby is born before this, and at the latest, the day after your baby is born. Within these limits, you can normally choose when your maternity pay period begins by notifying your employer of when you want your SMP to start. However, if you have to stop work earlier than planned, your maternity pay period may begin earlier.

- If your baby is born before the 11th week before the EWC, or before the date you had arranged to start your SMP, your maternity pay period begins on the day after the birth.
- If you are off work because of your pregnancy on or after the start of the fourth week before your EWC but not later than the day after you have your baby, your SMP starts on the day after the first day of such absence in that period. This does not apply if your absence is not related to your pregnancy.
- If you leave your job, see p822.

Part 5: Other benefits
Chapter 37: Statutory maternity, adoption, paternity and shared parental pay
2. Who is entitled

If your baby is born earlier or later than expected, but after your maternity pay period has begun, your maternity pay period is not extended or reduced. If your maternity pay period starts earlier than you intended because of an early birth, the 39 weeks run from the date your SMP starts.

Note: you may choose to reduce the period for which you are paid SMP if you and/or the father of your child/your partner are entitled to SSPP or if s/he is entitled to shared parental leave (see p813). See p805 for information on the relationship between SSPP and SMP.

Statutory adoption pay

You qualify for SAP if you satisfy the common conditions listed on p806 and:[11]
- a child has been, or is expected to be, placed with you for adoption under UK law (see p824 if the child is adopted from abroad); *and*
- you are within the adoption pay period (see below); *and*
- you have not elected to receive SPP; *and*
- if you have jointly adopted a child, your co-adopter is not claiming SAP.

If you are a local authority foster parent in the situation described on p805, you may qualify for SAP when a child is placed with you.

See p805 for the relationship between SAP and SPP and p805 for the relationship between SAP and SSPP. See p832 if you are entitled to statutory sick pay (SSP).

The adoption pay period

SAP can only be paid during the 'adoption pay period'.[12] This is a period of 39 consecutive weeks which normally begins, at the earliest, 14 days before the day you expect the child to be placed with you and, at the latest, on the date of placement. Provided you request that your SAP starts within these time limits and give your employer the required period of notice (see p826), you can choose whether you want your adoption pay period to begin either:[13]
- on a particular date, although if the child is placed with you before that date, the adoption pay period begins on the date of placement; *or*
- on the day of placement (without specifying an actual date). If you are working on that day, your adoption pay period begins on the next day.

Your adoption pay period may end early if the child:[14]
- is returned to the adoption agency or society after being placed with you; *or*
- dies after being placed with you for adoption; *or*
- is not placed with you, but your adoption pay period has already begun.

In these circumstances, your adoption pay period ends eight weeks after the end of the week in which the child is returned or dies, or in which you are notified that the placement is not to take place, if this is earlier than it would have otherwise ended. In this situation, a week runs from Sunday to Saturday.

Note: you may choose to reduce the period for which you are paid SAP if you and/or your partner are entitled to SSPP or if s/he is entitled to shared parental leave (see p813). See p805 for information on the relationship between SAP and SSPP.

Statutory paternity pay

You qualify for SPP during the paternity pay period (see p810) if you meet the common conditions listed on p806 and:[15]

- **for SPP (birth):**
  - while receiving SPP, you intend to care for the child or to support the child's mother; *and*
  - you are the child's father and you have (or you expect to have) responsibility for her/his upbringing, or you are the partner of the child's mother (see p803) and together with her you have (or you expect to have) the main responsibility for the child's upbringing;
- **for SPP (adoption):**
  - while receiving SPP, you intend to care for the child or to support the adopter or your co-adopter; *and*
  - your partner (see p803), or both you and your partner, have been matched with a child for adoption under UK law (see below). If the child is adopted from abroad, see p824; *and*
  - you have (or you expect to have), together with the adopter or your co-adopter, the main responsibility for the child's upbringing; *and*
  - you have not elected to receive SAP.

If you and/or your partner are a local authority foster parent in the situation described on p805, you may qualify for SPP (adoption).

Matched for adoption

You are '**matched for adoption**' when an adoption agency or adoption society decides that you would be a suitable adoptive parent for a particular child. It should be able to provide you with a '**matching certificate**' to verify this. If you are a local authority foster parent in the situation described on p805, you are also matched for adoption when an adoption agency decides to place a child with you as her/his prospective adopter.

In either case, the date you are notified of a match is the date you receive the adoption agency's/society's notification, rather than the date it is sent.[16]

See p805 for the relationship between SPP and SAP, and p806 for the relationship between SPP and SSPP. See p832 if you are entitled to SSP.

Part 5: Other benefits
Chapter 37: Statutory maternity, adoption, paternity and shared parental pay
2. Who is entitled

The paternity pay period

SPP can be paid for a maximum of two consecutive weeks, called the 'paternity pay period', although you can choose to receive it for just one week.[17] The earliest SPP can be paid is from the child's date of birth or the date of the child's placement for adoption, and the latest is eight weeks after this date. If the child is born before the EWC (see p804), the latest SPP (birth) can be paid is eight weeks after the first day of the EWC (but see p818 if you work during your paternity pay period).[18]

Provided you request that your SPP be paid within this period and you give your employer sufficient notice of when you want it to be paid (see p827), you can choose to start your paternity pay period on:[19]

- a particular date; *or*
- the day of the baby's birth, or the day of the child's placement for adoption (without specifying an actual date). If you are at work on that day, your paternity pay period begins on the next day; *or*
- a day falling a certain number of days after that (without specifying an actual date).

Statutory shared parental pay

You qualify for SSPP if you satisfy the common conditions listed on p806 and:[20]

- you intend to care for the child during each week for which you get SSPP; *and*
- you have a partner in the application (see below) who consents to your SSPP claim; *and*
- your partner in the application meets the employment and earnings test (see p811); *and*
- you meet the particular conditions for SSPP (birth) or SSPP (adoption) described below.

For **SSPP (birth)** you must be either:

- the mother of the child and:
  - at the date of the birth, you and the father of the child, or you and your partner, have the main responsibility for the care of the child. See p803 for the meaning of 'partner'. In these circumstances, the father or your partner is '**your partner in the application**'; *and*
  - you were entitled to SMP as result of the birth and you have reduced your maternity pay period (see p813); *or*
- the father of the child, or the partner of the mother and:
  - at the date of birth you and the child's mother have the main responsibility for the care of the child. In these circumstances, the mother is '**your partner in the application**'; *and*
  - the mother is, or has been, entitled to maternity allowance (MA) (based on her own employment or self-employment – see p722) or SMP and she reduces her MA or maternity pay period (see p725 and p813).

For SSPP (adoption) you must be either:
- an adopter who has been getting SAP as a result of the adoption placement (**Note:** for SSPP, the term '**adopter**' refers to the person who has been entitled to SAP and not, if the child has been jointly adopted by two people, to the other co-adopter) and:
  - you have reduced your adoption pay period (see p813); *and*
  - at the date of the placement, you and your partner have the main responsibility for the care of the child. See p803 for the meaning of 'partner'. In these circumstances, your partner is '**your partner in the application**'; *or*
- the partner of the adopter (whether or not you are a joint adopter) and:
  - at the date of the adoption placement you and the child's adopter have the main responsibility for the care of the child. In these circumstances, the adopter is '**your partner in the application**'; *and*
  - your partner in the application is, or has been, entitled to SAP as a result of the adoption placement and reduces her/his adoption pay period (see p813).

If you are a local authority foster parent in the situation described on p805, you may qualify for SSPP (adoption), see p805.

See p812 for the period(s) over which SSPP may be paid. See p805 for the relationship between SMP, SAP and SSPP and p806 for the relationship between SPP and SSPP.

Note:
- If you get SMP or SAP, you cannot qualify for SSPP until your maternity or adoption pay period has ended. However, your partner in the application can qualify for SSPP before your MA, maternity or adoption pay period has ended, provided you have given your employer(s) a curtailment notification or notice confirming your intention to reduce the period (see p725 and p813).
- If the child's mother or adopter dies or if the child has been adopted from abroad, the qualifying conditions for SSPP are modified (see p823 and p824).

The employment and earnings test

To qualify for SSPP, you must meet the continuous employment rule and the earnings condition described on p814 and p817 and your partner in the application must satisfy the employment and earnings test.

Your partner satisfies the employment and earnings test if:[21]
- s/he has been an employed or self-employed earner (see p958) for any 26 weeks in the 66-week period that runs up to and includes the week before:
  - the EWC, for SSPP (birth); *or*
  - the week in which the adopter was notified of the adoption match, for SSPP (adoption).

  If s/he has been employed or self-employed for part of a week, it counts as a whole week; *and*

Part 5: Other benefits
Chapter 37: Statutory maternity, adoption, paternity and shared parental pay
2. Who is entitled

- s/he had average earnings of at least £30 a week in 13 weeks of that 66-week period. The average is calculated by adding her/his earnings in the 13 weeks when her/his earnings were highest and dividing the total by 13. The 13 weeks do not need to be consecutive. If s/he is self-employed, her/his actual earnings from self-employment are not counted. Instead, s/he is treated as having earnings of £30 in any week for which s/he has paid a class 2 national insurance (NI) contribution or, for weeks before 6 April 2015, for which s/he had a certificate of exception from paying class 2 contributions.

What counts as earnings for employed earners is the same as for the earnings condition for SMP, SPP, SAP and SSPP (see p817). Any backdated pay (including a backdated pay rise) which is received after the end of the 66-week period, but which is paid for any week in that period, can be included in the calculation of the average weekly earnings.[22] To calculate the weekly amount if earnings are not paid weekly, the total sum paid is divided by the nearest whole number of weeks for which it is paid.

When statutory shared parental pay can be paid

If you qualify for SSPP, the maximum number of weeks over which it can be paid to you is calculated as follows. This calculation applies in the same way whether you are the mother/adopter of the child or the child's father/partner of the mother or adopter.[23]

Step one:
- If the mother or adopter's MA, maternity pay or adoption pay period is being reduced because s/he has given her employer a curtailment notification or notice (see p725 and p813), deduct from 39 the number of weeks in the MA, maternity pay or adoption pay period up until the curtailment date.
- If the mother or adopter's entitlement to MA, SMP or SAP has stopped because s/he has returned to work (see p818 and p727) without giving a curtailment notification or notice, deduct from 39 the number of weeks for which MA, SMP or SAP was payable up until it stopped because of her/his return to work.

The resulting amount is the total number of weeks' SSPP available.

Step two:
- If your partner in the application (see p810) is entitled to SSPP, deduct the number of weeks s/he notifies her/his employer that s/he intends to claim SSPP from the total number of weeks' SSPP available. If s/he is entitled to SSPP from more than one employer, all the weeks of SSPP are counted, although if s/he gets SSPP from more than one employer for the same week, that week is only counted once.

The resulting amount is the number of weeks for which *you* can claim SSPP.

If you are the mother or adopter and you have been getting SMP or SAP, you cannot get SSPP until your maternity or adoption pay period has ended – ie, until after the curtailment date in your curtailment notice. See p813 for the earliest date this can be. However, your partner in the application can get SSPP for weeks before the curtailment date, even while you are getting MA, SMP or SAP, provided the weeks fall after the birth or adoption placement and you have given the DWP a curtailment notification (for MA) or your employer a curtailment notice (for SMP or SAP). See p806 if your partner in the application also intends to apply for SPP.[24]

You cannot be paid SSPP for any day falling on or after the child's first birthday (for SSPP (birth)) or on or after the first anniversary of her/his placement for adoption (for SSPP (adoption)).[25] You can choose to claim SSPP over a continuous period or over any number of shorter periods, provided your employer agrees to your taking shared parental leave over those periods. If both you and your partner in the application intend to claim SSPP, you can request that it be paid for the same, or different, weeks.

Note:

- Although your employer must agree if you ask to take your shared parental leave over one continuous period (provided you are entitled), it does not have to agree to your taking your shared parental leave over two or more discontinuous periods.
- If SMP or SAP is paid by more than one employer, the number of weeks deducted from 39 in Step one is the number of weeks from the start of the first maternity or adoption pay period to begin until the last day of the last of those periods to end or, if it is later, until the last day on which the mother or adopter returned to work in any of those jobs, if s/he did so without giving a curtailment notice.[26]

See p818 if you work in the period for which your SSPP is paid. See p822 if you give up or lose your job.

Reducing your maternity or adoption pay period

If you are entitled to SMP or SAP, you can reduce your maternity or adoption pay period to allow you and/or the father of the child or your partner to qualify for SSPP (see p810) or to allow her/him to get shared parental leave.[27] To reduce your maternity or adoption pay period, you must give your employer a '**curtailment notice**'. This is simply written notification that you intend to reduce your maternity or adoption pay period. You must give this to your employer at least eight weeks before the date you have chosen to end your maternity or adoption pay period.[28] If you send it to your employer in a properly addressed and pre-paid envelope, it is treated as given to your employer on the date you post it. Alternatively, if your employer has agreed, the notice can be sent electronically.[29]

Part 5: Other benefits
Chapter 37: Statutory maternity, adoption, paternity and shared parental pay
2. Who is entitled

In the notice you must state the date on which you want your maternity or adoption pay period to end.

This '**curtailment date**' must be on the last day of a week (for this purpose, a week starts on the day of the week on which your maternity or adoption pay period began), be at least one week before the last day of your maternity or adoption pay period and either:[30]

- for SMP, be at least two weeks after the birth (or four weeks after it if you are employed in a factory); or
- for SAP, be at least two weeks after the day your adoption pay period started.

If you get SMP or SAP from more than one employer, before you and/or your partner in the application (see p810) can qualify for SSPP, you must give each employer a curtailment notice, and the curtailment date you give to each employer must fall in the same week (for this purpose a week starts on a Sunday).[31]

If you give your employer a curtailment notice after returning to work, the curtailment date is the last day of the week in which you give it.[32] See p812 for how to calculate the number of weeks for which SSPP can be awarded in this situation.

You can only cancel a curtailment notice before the date your maternity or adoption pay period is due to end. To do so you must give notice to your employer, in writing. This is called a '**revocation notice**'. You can only do this:[33]

- for SMP, if you gave the curtailment notice before your child was born. In this situation, you must give the revocation notice within six weeks of the birth, but can subsequently give another curtailment notice; or
- for SMP or SAP, if your partner in the application dies. In this situation, you must give the revocation notice within a reasonable time after the death and it must include the date of death.

The continuous employment rule

To qualify for SMP, SAP, SPP or, if you are the claimant, SSPP, you must satisfy the continuous employment rule. To do so:[34]

- you must have been employed by your employer (see p815) for a continuous period of at least 26 weeks ending with:
  - **for SMP, SPP (birth) and SSPP (birth)**, the 15th week before the EWC (see p804); or
  - **for SAP, SPP (adoption) and SSPP (adoption)**, the week in which you are notified that you have (or, for SPP and SSPP, the adopter has) been matched with a child for adoption (see p809).

For SMP, SPP and SSPP, if you are employed for only part of the first of those 26 weeks, it still counts as a full week (HMRC's intention is that this also applies to SAP);[35] and

- **for SPP**, you must have been continuously employed by that same employer from the end of:

- the 15th week before the EWC, until the day that the child is born (for SPP (birth)); *or*
- the week in which the adopter was notified of being matched with a child until the day of the adoption placement (for SPP (adoption)); *and*

- **for SSPP**, you must have been continuously employed by that same employer from the 15th week before the EWC (for SSPP (birth)) or the week in which you were notified of being matched with a child (for SSPP (adoption)), until the week before your first period of SSPP begins (see p812).

See p822 if your employer has dismissed you 'solely or mainly' to avoid paying you SMP, SAP, SPP or SSPP.

See p816 if there have been breaks in your employment.

Appendix 11 contains a table of relevant dates for SMP, SPP (birth) and SSPP (birth) for all the weeks in 2017/18.

Note:

- If the baby is born in or before the 15th week before the EWC, you satisfy the continuous employment rule if you would have done so for SMP and SPP (birth) had the baby been born on the expected date or, for SSPP (birth), had the baby been born after the 15th week before the EWC. In this situation, to qualify for SSPP, you must also be continuously employed by the same employer from the date of the baby's birth until the week before your first period of SSPP begins.[36]

- For SMP, if you are employed for only part of the 15th week before your EWC, the whole week still counts towards your period of continuous employment.[37]

- For SAP, if you are employed for only part of the week in which you receive the notification of a match, the whole week still counts.[38]

- For SSPP, you must have been entitled to be in the employment at the end of the 15th week before the EWC or the week the adopter is notified of the adoption match. At the time of writing, 'entitled to be in employment' is not defined in the legislation, but it appears to be intended to mean that you are not prevented from working under immigration provisions.[39]

- It is expected that from some point in the future you will also have to be entitled to be in employment in the UK (and not prevented from working under immigration provisions) at the end of the 15th week before the EWC or the week the adopter is notified of the adoption match to qualify for SMP, SPP or SAP.[40] There may be exceptions. See CPAG's online service and *Welfare Rights Bulletin* for updates.

Employed by an employer

To satisfy the continuous employment rule, you must have been continuously employed by an employer who was liable to pay secondary class 1 NI contributions for you, or who would have been liable to pay them had your earnings been high enough (see p959), or had you been older (if you are under 16).[41]

Part 5: Other benefits
Chapter 37: Statutory maternity, adoption, paternity and shared parental pay
2. Who is entitled

If you count as an 'employed earner' for NI purposes (see p958), you normally count as an employee for SMP, SAP, SPP and SSPP.[42] If you are employed under a contract of apprenticeship, you count as an employee.[43]

You do not need to have a written contract of employment to count as an employee. Periods of employment for the same employer in another European Economic Area state may count towards your period of continuous employment.[44] However, even if you are an employee you may not be entitled to SMP, SAP, SPP or SSPP if your employer is based outside Great Britain (see p1603).[45] See p1603 if you are employed abroad.

Breaks in employment

For SMP, SAP, SPP and, if you are the claimant, SSPP, if you return to work for the same employer following a break in your employment, certain weeks when you were not employed can still count towards your 26 weeks' continuous employment. These include weeks in which, for all or part of the week, you were:[46]

- incapable of work because of sickness or injury, unless your incapacity lasted for more than 26 consecutive weeks;
- absent because your employer temporarily had no work to offer you – eg, you are an agency worker and the agency is unable to find you work in any particular week;
- absent from work, but because of an arrangement or custom, you are regarded as continuing in employment – eg, on public holidays or an annual shutdown, or if you are a teacher employed on a term-by-term contract;
- for SMP only, absent from work wholly or partly because of pregnancy or childbirth if there were no more than 26 weeks between your contracts with your employer, and you were employed by your employer both before and after you had your baby but not during the period of your absence;
- for SMP only, absent from work while on paternity, adoption, shared parental or parental leave.

If it is your employer's practice to offer work for separate periods of six months or less, at least twice a year, to people who have worked for it before, in some circumstances if you are off work because of illness or pregnancy, you do not have to have returned to work in order to benefit from the above rules.[47]

Note: the above rules are only relevant when there is a *break* in your employment with your employer. So, for example, more than 26 weeks' sickness absence should count towards your continuous employment if you remain employed by your employer while off sick.

If your employment is legally transferred from one employer to another, your employment is unbroken.[48] If you have been reinstated or re-engaged following an unfair dismissal claim, any period between your dismissal and reinstatement or re-engagement counts towards your 26 weeks' continuous employment.[49]

See p944 if your continuity of employment is affected by a strike and p822 if you have been dismissed by your employer.

The earnings condition

To qualify for SMP, SAP, SPP or, if you are the claimant, SSPP, your average gross weekly earnings during the 'relevant period' (see below) must be at least equal to the lower earnings limit for NI contributions.[50] The lower earnings limit used is the one in force at the end of:

- the 15th week before the EWC (see p804) (unless your baby is born before or during the 15th week before the EWC), for **SMP, SPP (birth) and SSPP (birth)**;[51]
- the week in which you or the adopter are notified of being matched with the child for adoption (see p809), for **SAP, SPP (adoption) and SSPP (adoption)**.

For the tax year 2017/18, the lower earnings limit is £113 a week (see Appendix 9 for the amounts for other years). If your average weekly earnings during the relevant period fall below the lower earnings limit (eg, because you are sick and receiving just SSP), you do not qualify for SMP, SAP, SPP or SSPP.

See p822 if you have been dismissed. See Appendix 11 for relevant dates for SMP, SPP (birth) and SSPP (birth) for weeks in 2017/18.

Relevant period[52]

For SMP, SPP (birth) and SSPP (birth), the '**relevant period**' is the period between:
– your last normal payday that falls either in or before the 15th week before the EWC or before the week in which the baby is born, if that is earlier; *and*
– the day after your last normal payday falling at least eight weeks before that.

For SAP, SPP (adoption) and SSPP (adoption), the '**relevant period**' is the period between:
– your last normal payday that falls in or before the week in which you or the adopter are notified of being matched with a child for adoption; *and*
– the day after your last normal payday falling at least eight weeks before that.

For this purpose, a week runs from Sunday to Saturday. If you are paid at intervals of one or more calendar months, your average earnings are calculated by dividing your earnings by the number of calendar months in the relevant period (to the nearest whole number), multiplying by 12 and dividing by 52.

What counts as earnings

As well as your gross wages, bonuses and any overtime pay you receive during the relevant period, your earnings include payments such as:[53]

- SSP, SMP, SAP and SPP. For SMP and SSPP, they also include SSPP;

Part 5: Other benefits
Chapter 37: Statutory maternity, adoption, paternity and shared parental pay
2. Who is entitled

- arrears of pay following reinstatement or re-engagement in your job or a continuation of your contract of employment under the Employment Rights Act 1996.

Certain payments (eg, some payments in kind) are ignored.[54]

Pay rises

For SMP, if you are awarded a pay rise that affects your wages for any part of the period running from the first day of your relevant period (see p817) until the last day of your statutory maternity leave, your employer should reassess your average earnings over the relevant period to take account of this increase (even if the pay rise did not actually increase your wages for any week in the relevant period). If you would have been awarded a pay rise but for being on maternity leave, you are still treated as receiving it. For these purposes, 'statutory maternity leave' includes both ordinary and additional maternity leave under the Employment Rights Act 1996. Your employer should recalculate your average weekly earnings as if your earnings in each of the weeks of your relevant period included the increase, and pay any arrears of SMP due to you.[55] If you become entitled to SMP as a result of the pay rise, your employer should deduct any payments of MA that you have received for the same period from the SMP you are owed.[56]

For SAP, SPP and SSPP, only a backdated pay rise that is paid in respect of the relevant period is included in the calculation of your average earnings. Your employer should recalculate your average weekly earnings following the rise and pay any arrears of SAP, SPP or SSPP due to you.[57]

Work

Your entitlement to SMP, SAP, SPP or SSPP is not affected by work you do on a self-employed basis during your maternity, paternity or adoption pay period, or during the period(s) for which you are paid SSPP (provided no class 1 NI contributions are payable on your earnings from that work and, for SPP and SSPP, you continue to meet the caring conditions – see pp809–10). However, your entitlement may be affected if you work for an employer.

Working for the employer who is paying you

You can do up to 10 days' work for the employer who pays you **SMP** or **SAP** during your maternity or adoption pay period without your entitlement to these payments being affected. These 10 days (called 'keeping in touch days') do not have to be consecutive, but if you work for only part of a day, it still counts as a full day of work. The same rules apply for **SSPP**, except you may work for up to 20 days (called 'shared parental leave in touch days') in the weeks for which you are claiming SSPP without your SSPP from that employer being affected.

However, if you do any work for that employer (even if is just for part of a week) in excess of:[58]

- your 10 keeping in touch days, you lose a week's SMP or SAP for every week in which you do that further work;
- your 20 shared parental leave in touch days, you cannot get SSPP for any subsequent week for which you have claimed it if you do any work in that week.

If you do *any* work during the paternity pay period for an employer who is paying you SPP, that employer is not liable to pay you SPP for the week in which you work.[59]

The above rules apply even if you are working for the employer under a new contract which did not exist before your maternity, paternity or adoption pay period began.

Note:

- If you intend to work for more than 10 days for the employer who is paying you SMP or SAP, this may affect your continued entitlement to maternity or adoption leave (and so may also affect your entitlement to SMP or SAP for the remainder of the maternity or adoption pay period). If you do not want to bring your period of leave to an end, get employment advice before agreeing to such work.
- If, because you work for your employer for more than 20 days, you lose SSPP for some of the weeks you had arranged to get it, it may be possible to make up for the loss, provided you can give the necessary notice to your employer that you wish to vary the weeks over which SSPP is paid (see p829). Alternatively, it may be possible for the SSPP to be paid to your partner in the application (see p810), provided s/he can give her/his employer the necessary notice, or notice of the variation, of the periods over which s/he wants to be paid SSPP. However be aware that the notice conditions for varying shared parental leave are more stringent.
- For SMP, if you return to work for your employer but you are subsequently off work sick during the maternity pay period, you are not entitled to SSP. Instead, you can get SMP for each week in which you are off work for a whole week. This does not apply if you have curtailed your maternity pay period and are past the curtailment date (see p813), but if you had returned to work before giving a curtailment notice (see p813), any additional weeks' SMP you are paid while off work sick are ignored when calculating the number of weeks for which SSPP can be paid.[60]

Payment from more than one employer

If more than one employer is liable to pay you SMP, SAP or SPP, unless the payments are just one award apportioned between them (see p821), any work you do for one employer does not affect your entitlement to SMP, SAP or SPP from the other.

Part 5: Other benefits
Chapter 37: Statutory maternity, adoption, paternity and shared parental pay
3. The rules about your age

If more than one employer is liable to pay you SSPP, you must usually be on shared parental leave from all such jobs in order to qualify for SSPP from any of them. You cannot continue to work for one employer while getting SSPP from another unless the day on which you work is a shared parental leave in touch day. The number of weeks' SSPP you can get from each employer is calculated without reference to any weeks of SSPP you receive from another. However, if you plan to claim SSPP from each employer for different weeks, all the weeks for which you receive SSPP are counted when calculating the number of weeks' SSPP your partner in the application (see p810) can claim. Therefore, you may be better off claiming SSPP from your employers for the same weeks if your partner intends to claim SSPP as well.[61]

Working for another employer

The general rule is that, if you work for another employer not liable to pay you SMP, SAP, SPP or SSPP, you cannot get SMP, SAP, SPP or SSPP for the week in which you work. You also cannot get SMP, SAP and SPP for the remainder of your maternity, paternity or adoption pay period.[62]

However, there are two exceptions.

- For SMP, if the work is done while you are on maternity leave but before your baby is born, your entitlement to SMP is unaffected.[63]
- Your SMP, SAP, SPP or SSPP is not affected by any work you do for an employer who is not liable to pay you SMP, SAP, SPP or SSPP if you also worked for that employer in the:
  - 15th week before the EWC, for SMP, SPP (birth) and SSPP (birth); *or*
  - week in which you or the adopter were notified that you had been matched with a child for adoption, for SAP and SPP (adoption); *or*
  - 15th week before the expected week of the child's placement for adoption, for SSPP (adoption).[64]

Unless it is work that does not affect your SMP, SAP, SPP or SSPP, you must notify the employer who is paying you SMP, SAP, SPP or SSPP of any work that you do for another employer. For SMP, SAP or SPP, you must do so within seven days of the first day in your maternity, adoption or paternity pay period on which you do such work. For SSPP, you must do so within seven days of the first day on which you do the work. It is advisable to inform your employer in writing. For SAP, SPP and SSPP, your employer has the right to request this information in writing.[65]

3. **The rules about your age**

There are no upper or lower age limits for statutory maternity pay, statutory adoption pay, statutory paternity pay and statutory shared parental pay.

4. People included in the claim

You claim statutory maternity pay, statutory adoption pay, statutory paternity pay and statutory shared parental pay for yourself. You cannot claim any increase for your partner or child(ren).

5. The amount of benefit

	Maximum period of payment	Gross amount[66]
Statutory maternity pay (SMP) and statutory adoption pay (SAP)	39 weeks	First six weeks: 90% of average weekly earnings Remaining 33 weeks: Lesser of £140.98 or 90% of average weekly earnings
Statutory paternity pay (SPP)	Two weeks	Lesser of £140.98 or 90% of average weekly earnings
Statutory shared parental pay (SSPP)	37 weeks	Lesser of £140.98 or 90% of average weekly earnings

If you satisfy the conditions of entitlement to SMP, SAP, SPP or SSPP with more than one employer (or under two or more contracts with the same employer), you can get SMP, SAP, SPP or SSPP from each job. However, if your earnings from any of your jobs are aggregated when calculating your liability to pay national insurance contributions, the jobs are counted as one and the amount of SMP, SAP, SPP or SSPP your employers must pay is apportioned between them.[67]

6. Special benefit rules

Special rules may apply to:
- you if your baby is stillborn, you have had a multiple birth or adopted more than one child (see p823);
- people applying for statutory shared parental pay (SSPP) if their partner in the application dies (see p823);
- people who have adopted a child from abroad (see p824);
- people whose baby is born with the help of a surrogate (see p824);
- people in prison or detention (see p925);
- people who give up their job or who have been dismissed (see p822);

Part 5: Other benefits
Chapter 37: Statutory maternity, adoption, paternity and shared parental pay
6. Special benefit rules

- people who are abroad or going abroad (see Chapter 67);
- people involved in a trade dispute (see p944).

If you give up your job or are dismissed

Your employer is still liable to pay you statutory maternity pay (SMP), statutory adoption pay (SAP), statutory paternity pay (SPP) or SSPP if:

- after your maternity, adoption or paternity pay period has started, or after you have started your first period of SSPP, you give up your job, you are dismissed or your job ends (but see p1392 if your employer is insolvent);[68] *or*
- your employer dismisses you at any time, provided this was 'solely or mainly' to avoid paying SMP, SAP, SPP or SSPP and you had been employed by that employer for at least eight continuous weeks. In this situation, the amount of your SMP, SAP or SPP is calculated using your average earnings for the eight-week period ending with the last day for which you were paid. The amount of your SSPP is calculated using your average earnings over the period which ends on the last day you were paid and starts on the day after your last payday which falls at least eight weeks before that;[69] *or*
- you satisfy the qualifying conditions for SMP, SAP, SPP or SSPP and your job ends for any reason at any time after:[70]
  - the beginning of the 15th week before your expected week of childbirth (EWC), for SMP; *or*
  - the beginning of the week in which you were notified of being matched with a child for adoption (see p809), for SAP; *or*
  - the day on which the child is born, for SPP (birth); *or*
  - the day on which the child is placed for adoption, for SPP (adoption); *or*
  - for SSPP, the beginning of the week in which your first period of SSPP starts.

For SMP, if your job ends at any time after the start of the 15th week before your EWC or, for SAP, if it ends before the adoption pay period is due to start, you are not required to have given your employer notice of your intention to take maternity or adoption leave, although you must still give your employer information to support your entitlement to SMP or SAP, as described on p825 and p826 – eg, evidence of the expected date of birth for SMP.[71]

If you qualify for SMP but your job ends before your maternity pay period was due to start, your SMP starts at the beginning of the 11th week before your EWC or, if your job ends after this, on the day after you finish work, unless your baby is born before these dates.[72] If you qualify for SAP but your job ends before your adoption pay period was due to start, it starts 14 days before the expected date of placement or, if your job ends after this, on the day after you finish work, unless your child is placed with you before this.[73]

If you are dismissed while pregnant or on maternity, adoption, paternity or shared parental leave, get advice about your employment rights urgently.

If you start work for another employer after giving up your job or being dismissed, see p820.

Stillbirths, multiple births and adoptions

If your baby is stillborn after 24 weeks' pregnancy, SMP and SPP (birth) are payable in the same way as for a live birth, so if you have a stillbirth certificate, you can qualify.[74] If the baby is stillborn before you have completed 24 weeks' pregnancy, this is treated as a miscarriage, and SMP and SPP (birth) are not payable. You may qualify for statutory sick pay (SSP) or employment and support allowance (ESA) if you are unfit for work. If you come under the universal credit system (UC – see p20), although you cannot get income–related ESA, you may qualify for UC as well as SSP or contributory ESA (see Chapter 28). If the baby is born alive but then dies (even after only a moment), this is a live birth and you can get SMP or SPP (birth) even if it happens before 24 weeks' pregnancy. Even if SMP has been awarded in respect of the birth, SSPP (birth) can only be paid if the child's death occurs after you have given notice to your employer of your intention to claim SSPP (see p828).[75]

No additional SMP, SAP, SPP or SSPP is payable if you or your partner give birth to more than one baby, or have more than one child placed with you for adoption, unless this happens as part of a different adoption arrangement.[76]

Statutory shared parental pay if your partner in the application dies

If the mother of the child (for SSPP (birth)) or the adopter (for SSPP (adoption)) died before the end of her/his maternity allowance (MA) period, maternity pay period or adoption pay period, you may still qualify for SSPP if you would have done so had s/he not died. In this situation, the normal rules for SSPP apply, with modifications.[77]

- If the mother or adopter died before s/he gave a curtailment notification or notice indicating that s/he intended to reduce her/his MA, maternity or adoption pay period (see p725 and p813), the number of weeks for which you can get SSPP is 39, minus any weeks for which MA, SMP or SAP was paid. If s/he had given a curtailment notification or notice before s/he died, any weeks' SSPP she had taken are also deducted.
- If s/he died before her MA, maternity pay or adoption pay period started, s/he is taken to have qualified for MA (on the basis of her own employment or self-employment), SMP or SAP if s/he would have done had s/he not died, and you are entitled to 39 weeks' SSPP.

If you are the mother or adopter of the child and the child's father (for SSPP (birth)) or your partner (for SSPP (birth)) or (adoption)) died before you have given the DWP or your employer a curtailment notification or notice, you are not entitled

Part 5: Other benefits
Chapter 37: Statutory maternity, adoption, paternity and shared parental pay
6. Special benefit rules

to SSPP, but can continue to receive MA, SMP or SAP instead. If your partner in the application for SSPP (see p810) dies after you have given your employer a curtailment notice, you can either revoke the notice if the curtailment date has not passed (in this situation your MA, maternity pay or adoption pay period is not reduced even if your partner in the application had received some SSPP from her/his employer), or you can still claim SSPP. If you qualify, the number of weeks' SSPP you can get is equal to the unused portion of your maternity pay or adoption pay period minus the number of weeks' SSPP that your partner in the application claimed up to the date s/he died.[78]

In either situation, if the death occurred before you gave your employer notice of your intention to claim SSPP, the notice and information you must give your employer should be given eight weeks before the start of the first period for which you want to claim SSPP or, if this is not reasonably practicable, as soon as reasonably practicable after the death, but in all cases before the first day for which you want to claim.[79]

If you are adopting a child from abroad

If you are adopting a child from abroad, you may be entitled to SAP or SPP (adoption) and SSPP (adoption). To qualify, you must satisfy the normal rules of entitlement for SAP, SPP (adoption), or SSPP (adoption) described in this chapter, but with certain modifications. Although you must have 'official notification' that you have been approved for adoption from UK authorities (see below), you will not have been matched with a child for adoption by UK authorities under UK law, and it is primarily the rules that refer to the date of placement and the date of notification of being matched for adoption (both of which do not apply to overseas adoptions) that are modified.[80] Use Form SC6 (for SAP) or Form SC5 (for SPP), available from www.gov.uk, to apply for SAP or SPP from your employer for an overseas adoption. At the time of writing, there is no official form for SSPP. If a placement is made under UK law, the normal rules of entitlement to SAP, SPP and SSPP apply.

Official notification

'Official notification' for an overseas adoption is a written notification issued by, or on behalf of, a relevant UK authority stating that it has issued, or is going to issue, a certificate to the overseas authority confirming that you are approved for adoption. It is sometimes called a Certificate of Eligibility and Suitability to Adopt.

If your baby is born with the help of a surrogate

If you have had a child with the help of a surrogate mother, you may qualify for SAP, SPP (adoption) or SSPP (adoption) if:[81]
- you have obtained a parental order from the court; *or*

- on the date of the child's birth you intend to apply for a parental order from the court within six months of the baby's birth, and you expect your application to be successful.

To obtain a parental order in this situation, your court application must be made jointly with the 'other parent' (ie, your spouse, civil partner or partner), and at least one of you must be a biological parent of the child.

If this applies, your entitlement to SAP, SPP (adoption) and SSPP (adoption) can stem from the birth of the child rather than adoption. The rules are modified to ensure that entitlement relates to the child's EWC or date of birth instead of the date of the adoption match or adoption placement.

If both you and the person with whom you have obtained (or intend to apply for) a parental order qualify, only one of you can elect to receive SAP – the other may apply for SPP (adoption). You must decide who applies for which payment. You must be each other's partner in the SSPP application.

7. Claims

Making a claim

It is not necessary for you to complete a claim form to qualify for statutory maternity pay (SMP), statutory adoption pay (SAP), statutory paternity pay (SPP) or statutory shared parental pay (SSPP), but you must give your employer certain notice and information.

Notification sent to your employer in a properly addressed and pre-paid letter is treated as having been given on the day it is posted.[82] For SSPP, you can send notice and information to your employer electronically, if your employer has agreed to this.[83]

There are different notice requirements for statutory maternity, adoption, paternity and shared parental leave. If your employer offers its own maternity, adoption, paternity or shared parental pay scheme as well as SMP, SAP, SPP or SSPP, the notice requirements for this scheme may also be different. Check this with your employer.

Notice and information for statutory maternity pay

To qualify for SMP, you must give your employer:

- notice (in writing, if your employer requests this) of the date from when you want to get SMP. This must be given at least 28 days before you expect payment to start or, if this is not practicable, as soon as reasonably practicable after that.[84] See p807 for when it is possible for your SMP to start; *and*
- evidence of the expected date of birth (normally Form MAT B1 issued by your doctor or registered midwife). You must provide this evidence no more than

three weeks after the start of your maternity pay period. This time limit can be extended to the end of the 13th week of the maternity pay period if you have good cause for the delay.[85]

The terms 'as soon as reasonably practicable' and 'good cause' are not defined in the regulations – you must show that any delay was reasonable, given your circumstances.

If you give your employer less notice than this or you do not provide the above evidence within the time limit, your employer may not pay you SMP. If you think your employer's decision is wrong, you can challenge it (see Chapter 57).

The earliest you can be issued with Form MAT B1 is the start of the 20th week before your expected week of childbirth (EWC). If you do not have Form MAT B1, your employer can accept other medical evidence, but it must be substantially like it.[86]

If your employment ends in or after the 15th week before your baby is due, see p822.

If your baby is born early

If your baby is born before your maternity leave has started, your maternity pay period normally begins on the day after you had your baby rather than the day you planned.

To qualify for SMP, you must inform your employer (in writing, if your employer requests this) of the date your baby was born if either:

- s/he is born during or before the 15th week before your EWC; *or*
- you informed your employer of the date from when you wanted your SMP to start, but s/he was born before then.

You must do this within four weeks of the birth or, if this is not practicable, as soon as reasonably practicable after that.[87]

In addition, if your baby is born before you intended to start your maternity pay period, you must give your employer evidence of the week in which you had the baby (eg, a birth certificate, or Form MAT B1 if the child's date of birth is given on this) and of the expected date of birth, within three weeks of the start of your maternity pay period. This time limit can be extended to the end of the 13th week of the maternity pay period if you have good cause for the delay.[88]

Notice and information for statutory adoption pay

To qualify for SAP, you must give your employer:[89]

- notice (in writing, if your employer requests this) of:
  - when you want your SAP to start (see p808 for when it can start); *and*
  - the date on which you expect the child to be placed with you for adoption; *and*
- a written declaration that you want to receive SAP rather than SPP; *and*

- documents from the adoption agency giving certain information, including the date on which the child is expected to be (or was) placed with you and the date on which it informed you of this. The 'matching certificate' provided by the adoption agency or adoption society gives this information.

This notice and information must be given at least 28 days before your adoption pay period is due to start or, if this is not practicable, as soon as is reasonably practicable after that date (see p826), otherwise your employer may not pay you SAP. In this situation, it may be possible to argue that your SAP should start later, once the necessary time limit for providing the notice or information has passed, as long as payment would still fall within the adoption pay period (see p808). This may mean, however, that you might not be entitled to SAP for a full 39 weeks. If you are in this position, get advice. If you think your employer's decision is wrong, you can challenge it (see Chapter 57).

In addition to the above notice, if you choose to start your adoption pay period on the day the child is placed with you, you must give your employer further notice of the date on which the placement occurs as soon as is reasonably practicable.[90]

If your employment ends before your adoption pay period begins, see p822.

Notice and information for statutory paternity pay
To qualify for SPP, you must give your employer written notice of the weeks for which you want your employer to award you SPP, including the date you want it to start (see p810 for when it can be paid) and whether you want to get it for one or two weeks, and:[91]

- for SPP (birth):
  - the EWC and, if the child has already been born, the date of birth; *and*
  - a declaration stating that you meet each of the conditions for SPP (birth) described on p809 – eg, that you are the partner of the child's mother and, with her, will have main responsibility for the child's upbringing; *or*
- for SPP (adoption):
  - the date you expect the child to be placed for adoption, or the date s/he was placed if the placement has already happened; *and*
  - the date on which the adopter was notified of the adoption match (see p809); *and*
  - a declaration stating that you meet each of the conditions for SPP (adoption) described on p809.

You must give your employer this notice and information no later than the last day of the 15th week before the EWC (for SPP (birth)) or no later than seven days after the date the adopter was notified of the adoption match (for SPP (adoption) – see p809). If this is not reasonably practicable, you must give it as soon as is reasonably practicable after that date (see p826). If you do not, your SPP can start later, once the necessary notice has been given, provided payment would still fall within the period for which SPP can be paid.

To provide the above notice and information to your employer, you may use Form SC3 for SPP (birth) or Form SC4 for SPP (adoption), available from www.gov.uk/paternity-pay-leave.

In addition, if you notified your employer that you want to start your paternity pay period:[92]

- on the day the child is born or is placed with you for adoption, or on a day falling a certain number of days after that, you must tell your employer the actual date of birth or placement, as soon as is reasonably practicable (see p826) after that date;
- on a specific date, but the child is not born or placed with you until after that date, you must give your employer notice of the new date on which you want your paternity pay period to start, as soon as is reasonably practicable.

Notice and information for statutory shared parental pay

To qualify for SSPP, you must give your employer:[93]

- notice of:
  - the maximum number of weeks for which you would be entitled to SSPP if your partner in the application (see p810) does not claim it; *and*
  - the number of weeks you and your partner in the application each intend to claim SSPP; *and*
  - the period(s) that you intend to claim SSPP from your employer; *and*
  - the EWC and the date of birth (for SSPP (birth)) or the date on which the adopter was notified of the adoption match and the date of the adoption placement (for SSPP (adoption)); *and*
- a written declaration from your partner in the application stating:
  - her/his name, address and national insurance (NI) number (if s/he does not have one, s/he must state this); *and*
  - s/he consents to your claim for SSPP; *and*
  - s/he will share the main responsibility for the care of the child with you; *and*
  - s/he meets the employment and earnings test (see p811); *and*
  - if s/he is the person entitled to maternity allowance (MA), SMP or SAP in respect of the child, the date on which her/his MA, maternity pay or adoption pay period began, that s/he has (or will) reduced the MA, maternity pay or adoption pay period (see p724 and p813), the number of weeks by which it is to be reduced and that s/he will inform you if it is no longer going to be reduced; *and*
- a written declaration from you stating:
  - the information you have given is correct; *and*
  - you meet the qualifying conditions for SSPP (see p807 and p810) *and either:*

- if you are the child's father or partner of the mother or adopter, that you will inform your employer if the mother or adopter's MA, maternity pay or adoption pay period is no longer going to be reduced; *or*
- if you are entitled to SMP or SAP in respect of the child, the date on which your maternity pay or adoption pay period began, the number of weeks by which it is to be reduced (see p813) and that you will inform your employer if it is no longer going to be reduced.

This notice and information must be given at least eight weeks before the start of the first period for which you want to claim SSPP from that employer. If you are unable to provide your employer with the child's date of birth (for SSPP (birth)) or date of the adoption placement (for SSPP (adoption)), because s/he was not born or placed by that time, you must provide this information as soon as is reasonably practicable after the birth or placement (see p826), but at least before the start of your first period of SSPP.[94] Forms to request SSPP and leave are available through a link on www.gov.uk/shared-parental-leave-and-pay.

If within 14 days of receiving the above notice and information your employer requests the following information from you, you must provide this within 14 days of your employer's request:[95]

- the name and address of your partner's employer. If s/he does not have one, you must give your employer written confirmation of this, signed by both you and your partner *and either:*
- for SSPP (birth), a copy of the child's birth certificate, or a declaration from you confirming that a certificate has not been issued; *or*
- for SSPP (adoption), documentation from the adoption agency or society giving its name and address, the date the adopter was notified of the adoption match and the expected date of the child's placement for adoption.

You can change the period(s) over which you claim SSPP, provided you give your employer notice of the change, in writing, at least eight weeks before the date the first of the new periods is due to start.[96] You can also change the number of weeks for which you claim SSPP if you give your employer written notice of the change and include details of the number of weeks you and your partner in the application have claimed SSPP (or intend to do so) and a written declaration from your partner in the application stating s/he agrees with the change.[97]

If the baby is born early

If you are claiming SSPP (birth) and the baby is born more than eight weeks before the start of the EWC (see p804) and before you have given your employer the above notice and information, you do not have to give your employer the notice and information eight weeks before you want your SSPP to start, provided you give it as soon as reasonably practicable after the birth and at least before the start of your first period of SSPP. You do not have to provide the baby's birth certificate.[98]

If you have given your employer the notice and information detailed above but you want to change the period(s) over which you claim SSPP (birth) because the baby was born before the start of the EWC, you can do so without giving your employer eight weeks' notice of the change, provided:[99]

- at least one of the periods for which you had previously intended to claim SSPP started in the eight weeks falling after the first day of the EWC; *and*
- you give your employer notice of the change as soon as reasonably practicable after the birth; *and*
- the new period(s) starts the same length of time after the birth as it would have done had the baby been born on the first day of the EWC.

Who should claim

If you are entitled to SMP, SAP, SPP or SSPP but are not well enough to deal with your own affairs, HM Revenue and Customs (HMRC) can appoint someone else to act for you.[100] This person must apply in writing to be your 'appointee' (see p1149). For further information, contact HMRC's general enquiry line (tel: 0300 200 3500; textphone: 0300 200 3519).

If you claim the wrong benefit

If you are sick with a pregnancy-related illness in the four weeks before the week your baby is due, your employer can start your maternity leave (even if it is sooner than you had planned) and pay you SMP rather than statutory sick pay. It cannot do this if your illness is *not* pregnancy related.[101]

You may get a claim for MA backdated if your employer has informed you that you are not entitled to SMP (see p731).

8. **Getting paid**

Statutory maternity pay (SMP), statutory adoption pay (SAP), statutory paternity pay (SPP) and statutory shared parental pay (SSPP) are usually paid by your employer in the same way and at the same intervals as your normal wages or salary.[102]

Note:

- If you are also entitled to contractual maternity, adoption, paternity or shared parental pay from your employer, SMP, SAP, SPP or SSPP forms part of your payments. Your employer can offset any payment of SMP, SAP, SPP or SSPP from its contractual liability to pay you for the same period.[103]

- Your employer cannot pay you SMP, SAP, SPP or SSPP by making a payment in kind, or by providing board and lodging, or for SMP, SAP or SPP, by providing a service or some other facility.[104]
- If you become entitled to SMP because of a pay rise, your employer can deduct any maternity allowance (MA) you received for the same period from the SMP you are owed.[105]
- If your entitlement has been decided by a decision maker from HM Revenue and Customs (HMRC), or by the First-tier or Upper Tribunal, your employer may be required to pay you within a certain time limit (see p1392). If your employer cannot or will not pay you, see p1392 for when payment can be made by HMRC.
- The rules on overpayments described in Chapter 52 do not apply to SMP, SAP, SPP or SSPP. If your employer thinks it has overpaid you SMP, SAP, SPP or SSPP, it may attempt to recover the sum by making a deduction from your wages. If this happens, get advice. If your employer decides you have been paid SMP in error, consider claiming MA. You may be able to get this backdated (see p731).
- If your employer becomes insolvent, see p1392.
- For SAP and SSPP, HMRC, not your employer, pays you if you are entitled for a period after you were imprisoned or detained (see p926), if you were subsequently released without charge, found not guilty or given a non-custodial sentence.[106]

Change of circumstances

You must keep your employer informed of any change of circumstances that may affect your entitlement, such as starting work for someone else during the maternity, adoption or paternity pay period or in any week for which you get SSPP (see p820). For SSPP, you must inform your employer if the person getting MA, SMP or SAP decides to revoke the arrangement to reduce her/his MA, maternity pay or adoption pay period (see p813).

If your employment ends for any reason, see p822. If you qualify for SMP, SAP, SPP or SSPP, your entitlement is not affected if you go abroad.

9. **Tax, other benefits and the benefit cap**

Tax

Statutory maternity pay (SMP), statutory adoption pay (SAP), statutory paternity pay (SPP) and statutory shared parental pay (SSPP) are treated as earnings, and you pay tax and national insurance (NI) contributions as appropriate.[107]

Part 5: Other benefits
Chapter 37: Statutory maternity, adoption, paternity and shared parental pay
9. Tax, other benefits and the benefit cap

Means-tested benefits and tax credits

Unless you come under the universal credit system (UC – see p20), in some circumstances, being pregnant or on maternity, adoption, or paternity leave may allow you to qualify for income support (IS – see p102). In certain situations, you can be treated as having limited capability for work while you are pregnant (see p1006) and so may qualify for income-related employment and support allowance (ESA). You cannot qualify for income-based jobseeker's allowance (JSA) if you are getting SMP or if you are on adoption, paternity or shared parental leave, because you are treated as unavailable for work. However, your partner may qualify for JSA.[108] If you are a member of a 'joint-claim couple' for JSA (see p120) and you are pregnant, in some circumstances you do not need to meet all the conditions to qualify (see p121) and, in some circumstances (including if you get SMP), only your partner needs to claim.

If you are unsure whether you would be better off if you claim IS or income-related ESA, or if your partner claims income-based JSA, get advice.

If you get SMP, SAP, SPP or SSPP, you may be entitled to working tax credit (WTC – see Chapter 10) as, in some circumstances, you can be treated as being in full-time work when getting one of these payments (or for some periods when you are on maternity, adoption, paternity or shared parental leave – see p201). You may also qualify for child tax credit (CTC – see Chapter 9). If you are entitled to WTC, you may be able to get help with the cost of childcare, even before you return to work (see p1414).

If you are getting SMP, SAP, SPP or SSPP, you may be able to get an allowance for childcare costs deducted from your earnings when calculating your entitlement to housing benefit (HB – see p281).

If you come under the UC system, you usually cannot make a new claim for the above means-tested benefits and tax credits. For both UC and ESA, in some circumstances you can be treated as having limited capability for work-related activity while pregnant (see p1010).

Your SMP, SAP, SPP or SSPP is taken into account for IS, income-related ESA and income-based JSA (see p284). SMP, SAP, SPP and SSPP are treated as earnings for pension credit and HB (see p270 and p318). The first £100 of your weekly SMP, SAP, SPP or SSPP is ignored when calculating your entitlement to WTC and CTC, and any amount you receive over £100 is counted as employment income. SMP, SAP, SPP and SSPP are treated as earnings for UC and your net earnings are taken into account (see p338 and, for deductions that are made from earnings, p339).

Non-means-tested benefits

Unless you come under the UC system, you cannot get contribution-based JSA if you are receiving SMP or if you are on adoption, paternity or shared parental leave, as you are treated as being unavailable for work (see p1037). At the time of writing, if you come under the UC system, provided you do not have limited capability for work and are not treated as having limited capability for work (but see p698), you may qualify for contribution-based JSA while getting SMP, SAP, SPP or SSPP. As you must accept a claimant commitment to qualify for JSA (see p1071), get advice before claiming if you are still employed – the DWP may contact your employer and this may jeopardise your employment.

You cannot get statutory sick pay (SSP) when you are receiving SMP. See p847 for how your SSP entitlement is affected if you are pregnant. You cannot receive SAP, SPP or SSPP for any week in which you are entitled to SSP.[109]

If you get SMP, you cannot also get MA for the same period in respect of the same pregnancy.[110]

If you are getting SMP, SAP or SSPP, you may qualify for NI credits (see p973). It may be important to claim credits in order to protect your future entitlement to contributory benefits, such as state pension.

Contributory employment and support allowance

You can qualify for contributory ESA as well as SPP if you satisfy the conditions for contributory ESA during your paternity pay period.

You can qualify for contributory ESA while you are getting SMP, SAP or SSPP if you have limited capability for work (or you can be treated as having limited capability for work – see p1005) and if, on the day before your maternity or adoption pay period began, or on the day immediately before the first period of SSPP began:[111]

- you had (or could be treated as having) limited capability for work; *and*
- you satisfied the NI contribution conditions for contributory ESA.

However, if you are entitled to contributory ESA and either SMP, SAP or SSPP, your contributory ESA is reduced by the amount of SMP, SAP or SSPP you receive for the same week.

In some circumstances, you can be treated as having limited capability for work if you are pregnant or have recently given birth or as having limited capability for work–related activity if you are pregnant (see p1005 and p1010).

The benefit cap

In some cases, there is a limit on the total amount of specified benefits you can receive (a 'benefit cap'). SMP, SAP, SPP and SSPP are *not* specified benefits. The benefit cap only applies if you are getting HB or UC. See p1180 for further information.

Passports and other sources of help

For details of:
- Sure Start maternity grants from the social fund, see p789. In some circumstances, you may qualify for a maternity grant even if you are not the mother of the child;

- free prescriptions and free NHS dental treatment, see Chapter 29;
- Healthy Start food vouchers and vitamins, see p857;
- council tax reduction, see p854;
- tax-free childcare, see p864.

Notes

5

1 Treasury announcement, 5 October 2015

1. Introduction

2 **SAP** s171ZL(4) and (4A) SSCBA 1992
  SPP s171ZB(4) SSCBA 1992
3 Reg 2(2)(c) and (d), (3) and (4) SPPSAP(G) Regs; reg 2 SSPP(G) Regs
4 **SAP** s171ZL(11) and (12) SSCBA 1992
  SPP s171ZB(10) and (11) SSCBA 1992
  SSPP s171ZV(17) and (18) SSCBA 1992
5 Regs 11(2) and 23(2) SSPP(G) Regs
6 s171ZE(3A) SSCBA 1992

2. Who is entitled

7 **SMP** ss164(2)-(5) and 165(4), (5) and (8) SSCBA 1992
  SAP s171ZL(2)(b)-(d), (3), (6) and (7) SSCBA 1992
  SPP ss171ZA(2) and (3), 171ZB(2) and (3), 171ZC and 171ZE(5) and (6) SSCBA 1992
  SSPP ss171ZU(2) and (4) and 171ZV(2) and (4) SSCBA 1992
8 **SMP** s164(6) and (7) SSCBA 1992
  SAP s171ZO SSCBA 1992
  SPP s171ZF SSCBA 1992
  SSPP s171ZZ SSCBA 1992
9 s164(2) SSCBA 1992
10 s165 SSCBA 1992; reg 2 SMP Regs; reg 1(2) SMPSS(MA) Regs
11 s171ZL(2) and (4) SSCBA 1992
12 Reg 21 SPPSAP(G) Regs
13 s171ZN(2) SSCBA 1992; reg 21 SPPSAP(G) Regs
14 Reg 22 SPPSAP(G) Regs
15 ss171ZA(2), 171ZB(2) and (4) and 171ZE(4) SSCBA 1992; regs 4 and 11 SPPSAP(G) Regs; reg 4(2)(b) and (c) PAL Regs

16 **SAP&SPP** Reg 2(2)(b) SPPSAP(G) Regs
  SSPP Reg 2(4) SSPP(G) Regs
17 s171ZE(2) SSCBA 1992; reg 12(3) SPPSAP(G) Regs
18 s171ZE(3) SSCBA 1992; regs 8 and 14 SPPSAP(G) Regs
19 Regs 6 and 12 SPPSAP(G) Regs
20 ss171ZU and 171ZV SSCBA 1992; regs 3, 4, 5, 17 and 18 SSPP(G) Regs
21 Reg 29 SSPP(G) Regs
22 Reg 29(3) SSPP(G) Regs
23 Regs 10 and 22 SSPP(G) Regs
24 Regs 11(2) and 23(2) SSPP(G) Regs
25 Regs 11(1) and 23(1) SSPP(G) Regs
26 Regs 10(4)-(6) and 22(2)-(4) SSPP(G) Regs
27 Regs 4-6 and 8-11 SMP&SAP(C) Regs
28 Regs 7 and 12 SMP&SAP(C) Regs
29 Reg 3 SMP&SAP(C) Regs
30 Regs 7(2), (3) and (6) and 12(2) and (5) SMP&SAP(C) Regs
31 Regs 2, 7(4) and 12(3) SMP&SAP(C) Regs
32 Regs 7(5) and 12(4) SMP&SAP(C) Regs
33 Regs 8 and 13 SMP&SAP(C) Regs
34 **SMP** s164(2)(a) SSCBA 1992
  SAP s171ZL(2)(b) and (3) SSCBA 1992
  SPP ss171ZA(2)(b) and (d) and (3) and 171ZB(2)(b) and (d) and (3) SSCBA 1992
  SSPP ss171ZU(2)(c) and (f) and (4)(d) and (g) and 171ZV(2)(c) and (f) and (4)(d) and (g) SSCBA 1992; regs 30 and 31 SSPP(G) Regs
35 **SMP** Reg 16A SMP Regs
  SAP&SPP Reg 35A SPPSAP(G) Regs
  SSPP Regs 30(1A) and (1B) and 31 (1A) and (1B) SSPP(G) Regs

36 **SMP** Reg 4(2)(a) SMP Regs
SPP Reg 5(a) SPPSAP(G) Regs
SSPP Reg 30(2) and (3) SSPP(G) Regs

37 Reg 11(4) SMP Regs

38 Reg 33(4) SPPSAP(G) Regs

39 ss171ZU(2)(d) and (4)(e) and
171ZV(2)(g) and (4)(e) SSCBA 1992.
The definition in s173A is to be inserted
by s63(9) Welfare Reform Act 2012
which, at the time of writing, was not
yet in force.

40 s63 WRA 2012

41 **SMP** s171(1) SSCBA 1992; reg 17 SMP
Regs
SAP&SPP ss171ZJ(1) and (2) and
171ZS(1) and (2) SSCBA 1992; reg 32
SPPSAP(G) Regs
SSPP s171ZZ4(1) SSCBA 1992; reg 33
SSPP(G) Regs

42 **SMP** Reg 17 SMP Regs
SAP&SPP Reg 32 SPPSAP(G) Regs
SSPP Reg 33 SSPP(G) Regs

43 **SMP** Reg 17(2) SMP Regs
SAP&SPP Reg 32(2) SPPSAP(G) Regs
SSPP Reg 33(4) SSPP(G) Regs

44 **SMP** Regs 2 and 5 SMP(PAM) Regs
SAP&SPP Regs 3, 5 and 6
SPPSAP(PAM) Regs
SSPP Regs 5 and 7 SSPP(PAM) Regs

45 **SMP** Reg 17(3) SMP Regs
SAP&SPP Reg 32(3) SPPSAP(G) Regs
SSPP Reg 33(5) SSPP(G) Regs

46 **SMP** Reg 11(1) SMP Regs
SAP&SPP Reg 33 SPPSAP(G) Regs
SSPP Reg 34 SSPP(G) Regs

47 **SMP** Reg 11(3A) SMP Regs
SAP&SPP Reg 33(3) SPPSAP(G) Regs
SSPP Reg 34(4) SSPP(G) Regs

48 **SMP** Reg 14 SMP Regs
SAP&SPP Reg 36 SPPSAP(G) Regs
SSPP Reg 37 SSPP(G) Regs

49 **SMP** Reg 12 SMP Regs
SAP&SPP Reg 34 SPPSAP(G) Regs
SSPP Reg 35 SSPP(G) Regs

50 **SMP** ss164(2)(b) and 171(4) SSCBA
1992
SAP ss171ZL(2)(d) and 171ZS(6)-(8)
SSCBA 1992
SPP ss171ZA(2)(c), 171ZB(2)(c), and
171ZJ(6)-(8) SSCBA 1992
SSPP ss171ZU(2)(e) and (4)(f),
171ZV(2)(e) and (4)(f) and 171ZZ4(6)-
(8) SSCBA 1992; regs 30 and 31
SSPP(G) Regs

51 **SMP** s164(2)(b) SSCBA 1992; reg
4(2)(b) SMP Regs
SPP s171ZA(2)(c) and (3) SSCBA 1992;
reg 5(b) SPPSAP(G) Regs
SSPP s171ZU(2)(e) and (4)(f) SSCBA
1992; reg 30(2)(b) SSPP(G) Regs

52 **SMP** Reg 21 SMP Regs
SPP s171ZA(2)(c) and (3) SSCBA 1992;
SSPP Reg 32 SSPP(G) Regs

53 **SMP** Reg 20 SMP Regs
SAP&SPP Reg 39 SPPSAP(G) Regs
SSPP Reg 32(7) and (8) SSPP(G) Regs

54 **SMP** Reg 20(2)(a) SMP Regs
SAP&SPP Reg 39(2)(a) SPPSAP(G) Regs
SSPP Reg 32(7)(a) SSPP(G) Regs

55 Reg 21(7) SMP Regs

56 Reg 21B SMP Regs

57 **SAP&SPP** Reg 40(7) SPPSAP(G) Regs
SSPP Reg 32(6) SSPP(G) Regs

58 **SMP** s165(4) and (5) SSCBA 1992; reg
9A SMP Regs
SAP s171ZN(3) and (4) SSCBA 1992;
reg 27A SPPSAP(G) Regs
SSPP Regs 4(2)(g), 5(2)(e), 12, 15,
17(2)(g), 18(2)(e), 24 and 27 SSPP(G)
Regs

59 s171ZE(5) and (6) SSCBA 1992

60 Regs 10(1)(a)(i) and 22(1)(a)(i) SSPP(G)
Regs

61 ss171ZU(2)(n) and (o) and (4)(o) and
(p) and 171ZV(2)(n) and (o) and (4)(o)
and (p) SSCBA 1992; regs 10(7) and (8)
and 22(5) and (6) SSPP(G) Regs

62 **SMP** s165(6) SSCBA 1992; reg 8(2)
SMP Regs
SAP s171ZN(5) SSCBA 1992; reg 26(1)
SPPSAP(G) Regs
SPP s171ZE(7) SSCBA 1992; reg 17(1)
SPPSAP(G) Regs
SSPP ss171ZU(2)(n) and (4)(o),
171ZV(2)(n) and (4)(o) and 171ZY(4)
SSCBA 1992; regs 12, 15, 24 and 27
SSPP(G) Regs

63 s165(6) SSCBA 1992

64 **SMP** Reg 8(1) SMP Regs
SAP Reg 25 SPPSAP(G) Regs
SPP Regs 10 and 16 SPPSAP(G) Regs
SSPP Regs 12, 15, 24 and 27 SSPP(G)
Regs

65 **SMP** Reg 24 SMP Regs
SAP Reg 26(2) and (3) SPPSAP(G) Regs
SPP Reg 17(2) and (3) SPPSAP(G) Regs
SSPP Regs 12(2) and (3) and 24(2) and
(3) SSPP(G) Regs

5. **The amount of benefit**
66 **SMP** s166 SSCBA 1992
   SAP Reg 3 SPPSAP(WR) Regs
   SPP Reg 2 SPPSAP(WR) Regs
   SSPP Reg 40 SSPP(G) Regs
67 **SMP** s164(3) SSCBA 1992; reg 18 SMP
   Regs
   SAP&SPP ss171ZD(1) and 171ZM(1)
   SSCBA 1992; reg 38 SPPSAP(G) Regs
   SSPP s171ZX(1) SSCBA 1992; reg 39
   SSPP(G) Regs

6. **Special benefit rules**
68 **SMP** s164(2)(a) and (3) SSCBA 1992
   SAP s171ZM SSCBA 1992
   SPP s171ZD SSCBA 1992
   SSPP s171ZX SSCBA 1992
69 **SMP** s164(8) SSCBA 1992; reg 3(1)
   SMP Regs
   SAP s171ZM(2) SSCBA 1992; reg 30
   SPPSAP(G) Regs
   SPP s171ZD(2) SSCBA 1992; reg 20
   SPPSAP(G) Regs
   SSPP s171ZX(2) SSCBA 1992; reg 42
   SSPP(G) Regs
70 **SMP** s164(2)(a) SSCBA 1992
   SAP s171ZL(2)(b) and (3) SSCBA 1992
   SPP ss171ZA(2)(b) and (d) and
   171ZB(2)(b) and (d) SSCBA 1992
   SSPP Regs 30(2)(a) and (c) and 31(2)(a)
   and (c) SSPP(G) Regs
71 **SMP** Regs 22 and 23(4) and (5) SMP
   Regs
   SAP Regs 24 and 29 SPPSAP(G) Regs
72 s165(2) SSCBA 1992; reg 2(5) SMP Regs
73 Reg 29 SPPSAP(G) Regs
74 **SMP** s171(1) SSCBA 1992
   SPP s171ZA(5) SSCBA 1992
75 s171ZY(3) SSCBA 1992; reg 13 and Sch
   para 6 SSPP(G) Regs
76 **SMP** s171(1) SSCBA 1992
   SAP s171ZL(5) SSCBA 1992
   SPP ss171ZA(4) and 171ZB(6) SSCBA
   1992
   SSPP ss171ZU(16) and 171ZV(16)
   SSCBA 1992
77 Sch, paras 1, 4, 5, 7, 10 and 11 SSPP(G)
   Regs
78 Sch, paras 2, 3, 8 and 9 SSPP(G) Regs
79 Sch SSPP(G) Regs

80 SSCBA(AAO) Regs;
   SPP(A)&SAP(AO)(No.2) Regs; Statutory
   Paternity Pay (Adoption) and Statutory
   Adoption Pay (Adoptions from
   Overseas) (Administration) Regulations
   2003, No.1192; Statutory Shared
   Parental Pay (Adoption from Overseas)
   Regulations 2014, No.3093
81 **SSP** ss171ZA, 171ZB and 171ZE SSCBA
   1992, as modified by Sch 1
   SSCBA(APOC) Regs; SPPSAP(G) Regs, as
   modified by regs 6-16 and 24
   SPPSAP(POPA) Regs
   SAP ss171ZL and 171ZN SSCBA 1992,
   as modified by Sch 2 SSCBA(APOC)
   Regs; SPPSAP(G) Regs, as modified by
   regs 17-24 SPPSAP(POPA) Regs
   SSPP s171ZV SSCBA 1992, as modified
   by Sch 3 SSCBA(APOC) Regs; SSPP(G)
   Regs, as modified by SSPP(POC) Regs

7. **Claims**
82 **SMP** Regs 22(4) and 23(3) SMP Regs
   SAP&SPP Reg 47 SPPSAP(G) Regs
   SSPP Reg 49(3)(b) SSPP(G) Regs
83 Reg 49 SSPP(G) Regs
84 s164(4) and (5) SSCBA 1992
85 Reg 22 SMP Regs
86 Reg 2 SMP(ME) Regs
87 Reg 23 SMP Regs
88 Reg 22 SMP Regs
89 s171ZL(6) and (7) SSCBA 1992; regs 23
   and 24 SPPSAP(G) Regs
90 Reg 23 SPPSAP(G) Regs
91 s171ZC(1) and (3)(c) SSCBA 1992; regs
   9 and 15 SPPSAP(G) Regs
92 Regs 7 and 13 SPPSAP(G) Regs
93 ss171ZU(2)(i)-(k) and (4)(j)-(l),
   171ZV(2)(i)-(k) and (4)(j)-(l) and
   171ZW(1)(b) SSCBA 1992; regs 6, 7, 19
   and 20 SSPP(G) Regs
94 Regs 6(1)(a) and (b), 7(1)(a) and (b),
   19(1)(a) and (b) and 20(1)(a) and (b)
   SSPP(G) Regs
95 Regs 6(1)(c) and (4), 7(1)(c) and (4),
   19(1)(c) and (4) and 20(1)(c) and (4)
   SSPP(G) Regs
96 ss171ZU(14) and (15) and 171ZV(14)
   and (15) SSCBA 1992; regs 8(1) and
   21(1) SSPP(G) Regs
97 Regs 8(2) and (3) and 21(2) and (3)
   SSPP(G) Regs
98 Reg 9(3) and (4) SSPP(G) Regs
99 Reg 9(1) and (2) SSPP(G) Regs

100 **SMP** Reg 31 SMP Regs
SAP&SPP Reg 46 SPPSAP(G) Regs
SSPP Reg 48 SSPP(G) Regs
101 Sch 11 para 2(h) SSCBA 1992; reg 2(4)
SMP Regs

8. Getting paid
102 **SMP** Reg 27 SMP Regs
SAP&SPP Reg 41 SPPSAP(G) Regs
SSPP Reg 43 SSPP(G) Regs
103 **SMP** Sch 13 para 3 SSCBA 1992
SAP s171ZP(5) SSCBA 1992
SPP s171ZG(2) SSCBA 1992
SSPP s171ZZ1 SSCBA 1992
104 **SMP** Reg 27 SMP Regs
SAP&SPP Reg 41 SPPSAP(G) Regs
SSPP Reg 43 SSPP(G) Regs
105 Reg 21B SMP Regs
106 **SAP** Reg 44 SPPSAP(G) Regs
SSPP Reg 46 SSPP(G) Regs

9. Tax, other benefits and the benefit cap
107 s4(1)(a)(ii)-(v) SSCBA 1992
108 Reg 15(bc) and (c) JSA Regs
109 **SAP** Reg 27(1)(a) SPPSAP(G) Regs
SPP Reg 18(a) SPPSAP(G) Regs
SSPP Regs 14(1)(a) and 26(1)(a)
SSPP(G) Regs
110 s35(1)(d) SSCBA 1992
111 s20(2)-(5), (6) and (7) WRA 2007; regs
80, 81 and 82A ESA Regs; regs 73, 74
and 75A ESA Regs 2013

5

Chapter 38

Statutory sick pay

This chapter covers:
1. Who is entitled to statutory sick pay (below)
2. The rules about your age (p845)
3. People included in the claim (p846)
4. The amount of benefit (p846)
5. Special benefit rules (p847)
6. Claims and backdating (p848)
7. Getting paid (p850)
8. Tax, other benefits and the benefit cap (p851)

Key facts
- Statutory sick pay (SSP) is paid by employers to certain employees who are unfit for work.
- SSP can be paid for up to 28 weeks.
- SSP is a non-means-tested benefit.
- Your entitlement to SSP is not based on your national insurance contribution record, but your usual earnings must be above a certain amount to qualify.
- If you qualify, SSP is the minimum amount your employer should pay while you are sick. You may be entitled to more under your contract.
- In some circumstances, you may qualify for SSP even if you have been dismissed by your employer.
- If you disagree with your employer's decision on your entitlement to SSP, or if your employer has failed to make a decision, you can challenge this.

1. Who is entitled to statutory sick pay

You qualify for statutory sick pay (SSP) if:[1]
- you are an employee (see p839); *and*
- you are incapable of work (see p839); *and*
- you are within a period of incapacity for work (see p842); *and*
- you are within your period of entitlement to SSP (see p842); *and*
- the day is a qualifying day (see p845); *and*

- your normal earnings are at least the lower earnings limit for national insurance (NI) contributions (see p844).

There are some groups of people to whom special rules apply (see p847). Certain people do not qualify for SSP (see p843). See below if your employer has dismissed you solely or mainly to avoid paying SSP.

Note: it is expected that from some point in the future, you will have to be entitled to work in the UK (and not be prevented from taking up work under immigration provisions) to qualify for SSP.[2] See CPAG's online service and *Welfare Rights Bulletin* for updates.

Employees

To be entitled to SSP you must be an employee. If you count as an 'employed earner' for NI purposes (see p958), or you would do so but for being under 16, you normally count as an employee for SSP purposes – eg, you may count as an employee if you are an agency worker.

You do not have to have a written contract of employment. It is the fact that you are employed that matters. Your right to SSP cannot be taken away by any document, whether you sign it or not. If your employer dismisses you to avoid paying SSP, see below.[3]

Even if you are an employee, you are treated as if you are not (and so your employer does not have to pay you SSP) if your employer is:

- not resident and not present in Great Britain, and does not have a place of business in Great Britain (and is not treated as having one); *or*
- exempt from social security legislation because of an international treaty.[4]

Dismissal from work

If your employer dismisses you during your period of entitlement to SSP solely or mainly to avoid paying you SSP, it is still liable to pay you SSP. In these circumstances, your employer should continue to pay you SSP until either your period of entitlement to SSP ends or until your contract would have ended had you not been dismissed, whichever occurs first.[5] If your employer dismisses you for another reason (ie, not solely or mainly to avoid paying you SSP), you are not normally entitled to SSP from that employer once your contract ends.

Incapable of work

To qualify for SSP, you must be 'incapable of work'. This has a meaning specific to SSP. Other tests, such as that of 'limited capability for work' described in Chapter 44, do not apply to SSP.

To be **'incapable of work'** for SSP purposes, you must be:[6]

- incapable of doing work that you could reasonably be expected to do under the terms of your contract because you have a specific disease, or a physical or mental disablement; *or*
- treated as incapable of such work (see p841).

Part 5: Other benefits
Chapter 38: Statutory sick pay
1. Who is entitled to statutory sick pay

Usually, after seven days of absence your employer expects you to provide a medical certificate from a doctor as evidence of your incapacity for work. This is also known as a 'fit note' or 'statement of fitness to work'.

On the medical certificate your doctor can state either that you are not fit for work, or that you 'may be fit for work taking account of the following advice'. These statements are not related to your specific job. If your doctor thinks you may be fit for some work, s/he can include a description of the effects of your condition on your ability to work and specify whether s/he thinks you may benefit from a phased return to work, altered hours, amended duties or workplace adaptations to facilitate your return to work.[7]

If you have been, or are likely to be, incapable of work for four weeks or more, your GP may, if s/he thinks it is appropriate, refer you to Fit for Work for an occupational health assessment (a Fit for Work assessment), which involves drafting a return to work plan. If you have been off work for four weeks and your GP has not referred you for a Fit for Work assessment, your employer can refer you for one. Your participation is voluntary – you should not be referred unless you agree, and you should only be referred if you have a reasonable prospect of being able to return to work and if you have not had a previous referral in the last 12 months (and were given a return to work plan).

Fit for Work

'**Fit for Work**' is a government-funded independent service run by Health Management Ltd in England and Wales (http://fitforwork.org) and by NHS Scotland in Scotland (http://.fitforworkscotland.scot).

A Fit for Work assessment takes account of your work, health and home situation and is normally carried out by telephone. If you agree, the assessor may contact your employer and/or your GP. The assessor draws up a 'return to work plan' which may give 'advice and recommendations' 'to support you back to work' or may state that you are not fit for work or that there are no limitations to your return to work – ie, that you are not incapable of work. The assessor should discuss the plan with you and you can decide whether a copy of it should be sent to your GP and your employer. You can choose to have some parts of the plan omitted from any copy that is sent. You may be contacted again by Fit for Work if you have not returned to work as anticipated.

If you agree to your employer seeing your return to work plan, it can accept it as evidence of your incapacity for work without you needing to submit further medical certificates.

Note:
- If your GP wants to refer you for a Fit for Work assessment, but you are unsure, discuss your concerns with her/him. If you refuse, you still require medical evidence of your incapacity for work and may need your GP to provide this.

- A return to work plan can help your GP support your return to work and may help you to negotiate with your employer about adjustments needed to allow you to return to work.
- If adjustments to facilitate your return to work are recommended on your medical certificate or your return to work plan and your employer does not agree to these, it can accept the certificate or plan as evidence of your incapacity for work.
- If the return to work plan indicates there is no limitation to your return to work, or the plan or your medical certificate states your return would be possible with certain adjustments which your employer is able to make, you may be expected to return to work within the time indicated and your employer may decide to stop your SSP if you do not do so.
- If you are only fit for work if your duties are changed to such an extent that it would not be reasonable to expect you to do them given the terms of your contract (whether these are written down or not), you may be able to argue that you still qualify for SSP. However, get independent advice on your employment situation before refusing to accept a change in your duties.

Does your employer doubt your incapacity for work?

1. It is up to your employer to decide whether it accepts that you are incapable of work. If it does not, it does not pay you SSP, although you can challenge its decision.

2. If your employer doubts your incapacity for work, it can get further advice. It may consult its own medical officer (if it has one), your doctor (with your permission), Fit for Work or HM Revenue and Customs (HMRC).

3. If you have been incapable of work for four weeks or more, your employer may suggest referring you for a Fit for Work assessment. You do not have to agree, but your employer may draw an adverse inference if you refuse, or if it knows that you have been assessed and it has not received a copy of the return to work plan.

4. If the matter is not resolved and your employer consults HMRC, HMRC may involve its Medical Service (MS) and, with your permission, the MS may contact your doctor to arrange for you to have a medical examination with an MS doctor (or other healthcare professional). Your employer is then given only the MS's view on whether you are fit for work in the job you do. It is still your employer's decision whether or not to pay you SSP.

5. If your employer refuses to pay you SSP, you can ask HMRC to make a decision on your entitlement (see Chapter 57).

Treated as incapable of work

Even if you are not actually incapable of work, your employer may treat you as incapable of work if:[8]
- you have been officially excluded or prevented from working because you have (or it is suspected that you have) an infection, disease or contamination

Part 5: Other benefits
Chapter 38: Statutory sick pay
1. Who is entitled to statutory sick pay

detailed under public health legislation, or you have been in contact with a case of such an infection, disease or contamination; *or*
- you are under medical care in connection with a specific disease or physical or mental disablement; *and*
  - a doctor has stated that you should not work as a precautionary measure or in order to convalesce; *and*
  - you do not go in to work for your employer.

If you are incapable of work for just part of a day, you must be treated as incapable of work for the whole day provided you do not do any work on that day. If you are a shift worker and you are incapable of work for part of a day but you do some work on that day, you should still be treated as incapable of work for the whole day if you only finish a shift that began the day before and you do not do any work on a shift that starts on that day and ends the next.

Period of incapacity for work

For SSP to be paid, you must be within a 'period of incapacity for work'. This is defined as four or more consecutive days of incapacity for work (see p839). This means that you can only qualify for SSP if you are incapable of work for at least four days in a row. Every day of the week (including Sunday) counts, even if it is not a day on which you would normally work. Days of incapacity for work that fall before or after the period covered by your contract can still be included in your period of incapacity for work (but see p844 if you have not yet started work).[9]

Two or more periods of incapacity for work are 'linked' and treated as a single period if they are separated by eight weeks or less.[10]

Period of entitlement to statutory sick pay

You only qualify for SSP if you are within 'a period of entitlement'. In certain circumstances, a period of entitlement cannot arise and so you do not qualify for SSP (see p843).

When entitlement to statutory sick pay starts

A period of entitlement normally starts on the first day of your period of incapacity for work, unless your contract of employment starts either during your period of incapacity for work or between two linked periods of incapacity for work (see p844).[11]

When entitlement to statutory sick pay ends

A period of entitlement to SSP ends (and so your SSP stops) if:[12]
- your period of incapacity for work ends (see above); *or*
- you reach your maximum 28 weeks' entitlement to SSP from a particular employer (see p847); *or*

- your contract of employment ends (unless it has been brought to an end by your employer solely or mainly to avoid paying SSP – see p839); or
- in certain circumstances, you are pregnant or have just had a baby (see p847); or
- you reach the third anniversary of the start of the period of entitlement; or
- you are imprisoned or detained in legal custody (see p926).

Two or more periods of incapacity for work that are separated by eight weeks or less are linked and treated as a single period.[13] This is why it may be possible for you to have a period of entitlement which lasts for three years and not to have exhausted your 28 weeks' entitlement to SSP over that period.

If you have received your maximum 28 weeks' entitlement to SSP from a particular employer and you are still incapable of work, see p847.

If your employer stops paying you SSP because it decides your period of entitlement has ended, see p850.

When statutory sick pay is not paid

In certain circumstances a period of entitlement to SSP cannot arise. As a result, you do not qualify for any SSP during your period of incapacity for work.

A period of entitlement cannot arise if:[14]

- your normal weekly earnings are below the lower earnings limit (see p844); or
- at some time in the 85 days before the date on which your period of entitlement would have begun you were entitled to employment and support allowance (ESA) or, in some circumstances, you would have been entitled. For this to apply, you must have claimed ESA (or made a claim for another benefit that was treated as a claim for ESA). If you have limited capability for work, you may qualify for ESA instead of SSP; or
- at the time when your period of entitlement would have begun there is a strike at your workplace (but see p944); or
- you have not yet started work under your contract of employment (but see p844 if you had an earlier contract with the same employer); or
- you are in prison or legal custody (see p926); or
- at the time when your period of entitlement would have begun, you were entitled to statutory maternity pay (SMP) or, in some circumstances, maternity allowance (see p847); or
- you are within the period immediately before or after you give birth (see p847).

If your employer decides not to pay you SSP on any of the above grounds, see p850.

Note:

- If you qualified for either incapacity benefit or severe disablement allowance in the 57 days before your period of entitlement to SSP would have started, you may not qualify for SSP. Instead, if you have limited capability for work, you

Part 5: Other benefits
Chapter 38: Statutory sick pay
1. Who is entitled to statutory sick pay

may qualify for ESA. See p619 of the 2012/13 edition of this *Handbook* for details.

- If you are not entitled to work in the UK, see p839.

People with low earnings

You cannot get SSP if your 'normal weekly earnings' are less than the lower earnings limit for NI contributions (£113 a week in the tax year 2017/18 – see p959).

Your **'normal weekly earnings'** are calculated by averaging your gross earnings from your employer (ie, before tax and NI contributions are deducted) over the period between:[15]

- your last normal payday before your period of entitlement to SSP began (see below); *and*
- the day after the last normal payday that falls at least eight weeks before this.

Only payments actually made in this period count, even if, in theory, you should have been paid more.[16] However, if your employer has unlawfully withheld *all* of your wages for the period over which your earnings are averaged, you should not be excluded from entitlement to SSP on the basis you have low earnings if you otherwise would have qualified.[17]

If you are paid every one or more calendar months, your average earnings are calculated by dividing your earnings over the above period by the number of calendar months in the period (to the nearest whole number), multiplying by 12 and dividing by 52. If you are paid at other intervals and the period is not an exact number of weeks, the average is calculated by dividing your earnings by the number of days in the above period and multiplying by seven.

As well as your wages, your gross earnings include payments such as:[18]

- SSP, SMP, statutory adoption pay, statutory paternity pay and statutory shared parental pay;
- maternity pay;
- arrears of pay following reinstatement or re-engagement in your job or a continuation of a contract of employment under particular legislation.

Certain payments (eg, some payments in kind) are ignored.[19]

There are special rules to calculate your earnings if you have not been employed sufficiently long to have been paid wages over this eight-week period.[20]

See p846 if you have more than one job.

People who have not yet started work

If you have agreed to work for an employer but have not started work when your period of incapacity for work begins, you are not entitled to SSP from that employer for any day during your period of incapacity for work, unless your current contract of employment can be linked to a previous one with the same employer. Your employment is linked if there are eight weeks or less between the date your new contract starts and the date your last contract with the employer ended.[21] You do not have to have written contracts for this to apply.

Qualifying days

You can only be entitled to SSP for 'qualifying days'. SSP is not paid for your first three qualifying days, which are known as 'waiting days' (see below).[22]

Qualifying days are usually those days of the week on which you normally work. However, other days may be selected as qualifying days by agreement between you and your employer if they would better reflect your contract of employment – eg, if you work a complicated shift pattern. For this purpose, a week begins on Sunday and there must be a minimum of one qualifying day in each week.[23]

Any agreement to choose days that relate to the days you are incapable of work, or to the period of entitlement to SSP, is ignored. If you and your employer cannot agree which days are qualifying days, they are presumed to be:[24]

- the days on which it is agreed that you are required to work; *or*
- Wednesday, if it is agreed that you are not required to work on any day in that week – eg, offshore oil workers, who may work two weeks 'on' and then two weeks 'off'; *or*
- if you cannot agree about which days you are or are not required to work, every day in the week, except days on which you and your employer agree that no employee works (if you can agree at least to that extent).

Required to work
'Required to work' means required by the terms of your contract of employment.[25] Days when you can choose whether or not to work do not count – eg, voluntary overtime shifts.

Waiting days

SSP is not paid for the first three qualifying days in a period of entitlement.[26] These are called **'waiting days'** and, as they must be qualifying days, they are not necessarily the first three days of your sickness.

If your period of incapacity for work can be linked to an earlier one in your period of entitlement with the same employer (see p842), any waiting days you served in the earlier linked period(s) do not have to be served again and you can get SSP from your first qualifying day in your present one.

2. The rules about your age

There are no lower or upper age limits for entitlement to statutory sick pay.

Part 5: Other benefits
Chapter 38: Statutory sick pay
4. The amount of benefit

3. **People included in the claim**

You claim statutory sick pay for yourself. You cannot claim any increases for your partner or child(ren).

4. **The amount of benefit**

Statutory sick pay (SSP) is not paid for the first three qualifying days in a period of entitlement (see p845). After that, it is payable at a rate of £89.35 a week. If you qualify, the weekly amount of SSP is the same irrespective of the number of hours you normally work for your employer each week when you are not sick.[27]

SSP is a daily benefit so it can be paid for periods of less than a week. The daily rate is calculated by dividing the weekly amount of SSP by the number of qualifying days you have in that week. A week for these purposes runs from Sunday to Saturday.[28]

Example
Zofia is employed in a shop and works four days a week (Wednesday to Saturday). These are her qualifying days. After injuring her hand, she is incapable of work for just over two weeks. In the week of her injury, she works on Wednesday and is off sick for the rest of the week. Her period of entitlement to SSP begins on Thursday, the first day of her absence, but she is not entitled to SSP for that week as the first three qualifying days in her period of entitlement (Thursday to Saturday) are waiting days. As she is incapable of work for all her qualifying days in the next week she gets £89.35 SSP. In the following week she is off sick on Wednesday, Thursday and Friday and returns to work on Saturday. She receives £67.01 SSP (£89.35 divided by her four qualifying days to give a daily rate paid for three days).

People with more than one job

If you cannot work, you are entitled to SSP from any job for which you fulfil the qualifying conditions. So, you can get payments of SSP for each of two contracts with the same employer (eg, if you are both a daytime teacher and an evening tutor with a local authority) or payments from two separate employers. However, if the earnings from any of your different jobs are added together when calculating your liability to pay class one national insurance contributions (which usually means you contribute less than if they had been treated separately), you can only receive a total of £89.35 a week from those jobs. Your employers' liability to pay you SSP is apportioned by agreement between them or, if they cannot agree, in proportion to their share of your combined earnings.[29]

It is possible for you to be unable to work on one contract and be entitled to SSP, but be able to work on a different contract – eg, if you perform different tasks for each.

Maximum entitlement to statutory sick pay

You are entitled to a maximum of 28 weeks of SSP from a particular employer in any one period of entitlement (see p842) – ie, 28 times the weekly rate of SSP.[30]

Once you have reached your maximum 28 weeks' entitlement with a particular employer, you cannot qualify for SSP again from that employer for the same contract until your current period of incapacity for work ends and a new one arises. Previous periods of incapacity for work are linked to your current one if they are separated by eight weeks or less.[31] However, see p843 if you got employment and support allowance (ESA) in the intervening period.

If you are still incapable of work after you have received your 28-week entitlement to SSP, consider claiming ESA (see Chapters 3 and 28).

5. Special benefit rules

Special rules may apply to:
- people who are going abroad (see p1603);
- women who are pregnant or who have recently given birth (see below);
- people involved in a trade dispute or people in prison or detention (see Chapter 41).

Women who are pregnant or who have recently given birth

If you are entitled to statutory maternity pay (SMP – see p807), you cannot get statutory sick pay (SSP) during the maternity pay period. If you are entitled to maternity allowance (MA) on the basis of your own employment or self–employment (see p721), you cannot get SSP during the MA period.[32] Within the limits set out on p724 and p807 (and unless your baby is born early), you can choose when your maternity pay or MA period begins. So, for example, your employer cannot insist that you claim SMP or MA at the earliest possible date in order to limit the period for which it has to pay SSP.

Even if you are not entitled to SMP or MA, or if you are entitled to MA on the basis that you have helped your spouse or civil partner with her/his self-employment (see p726):[33]
- you cannot get SSP (because a period of entitlement cannot arise) if your period of incapacity for work started at some time during the 18 weeks which run from the first of the following dates:
  – the beginning of the week in which you had your baby (but see p848); *or*

Part 5: Other benefits
Chapter 38: Statutory sick pay
6. Claims and backdating

- if you are incapable of work either wholly or partly because of your pregnancy on a day that falls in the four weeks before your 'expected week of childbirth' (see p804), the beginning of the week that contains the first such day;
- if SSP is already being paid to you (because your period of entitlement started before the above period, or because your incapacity for work was not initially linked to your pregnancy), it stops from the first of the following dates:[34]
  - the first day falling on or after the beginning of the fourth week before your expected week of childbirth when you are incapable of work wholly or partly because of your pregnancy; *or*
  - the date on which you have your baby.

In this situation, a week begins on a Sunday. If your baby is stillborn before you have completed 24 weeks of pregnancy, you qualify for SSP if you satisfy the other conditions of entitlement.

6. **Claims and backdating**

To qualify for statutory sick pay (SSP), you must notify your employer of your incapacity for work, rather than notifying the DWP or HM Revenue and Customs (HMRC).

Making a claim

You do not need to complete a claim form to qualify for SSP, just inform your employer that you are sick (see below). Your employer should then decide whether you are entitled to SSP.

Telling your employer that you are sick

Your employer can decide both the time within which it wants to be notified of your sickness absence and the way that it should be told. Your employer must take reasonable steps to inform you of how and when it wants to be notified of your absence.[35] However, for SSP purposes, your employer cannot insist that you notify it of your sickness:[36]

- earlier than the first qualifying day (which is not necessarily your first day of sickness – see p845), or by a specific time on the first qualifying day;
- personally;
- by providing medical evidence;
- more than once a week;
- on a printed form or other document it provides.

Time limits

The following time limits apply for notifying your employer.[37]

- You must notify your employer of your incapacity for work within the time limit set by your employer, if it has taken reasonable steps to inform you of this (unless it requires you to give notice earlier than the first qualifying day).
- If your employer has not taken reasonable steps to inform you, or if it has made no arrangements about the notification it requires, you must notify your employer of your incapacity for work in writing on or before the seventh day after your first qualifying day (see p845).
- This seven-day time limit, or your employer's time limit, can be extended by one month if you have good cause for the delay. What is 'good cause' is not defined in the regulations, but you must show that your delay was reasonable given the circumstances.
- If it is not practical for you to inform your employer within that time, the time limit can be extended further, provided you have notified it as soon as is reasonably practicable and you have notified it on or before the 91st day after your first qualifying day.

Notice sent in a properly addressed pre-paid letter is treated as having been given on the day it was posted. If you do not notify your employer of your absence within the above time limits, you can still be entitled to SSP (and qualify for a total of 28 weeks' payment in your period of entitlement if you are off work for that long), but your entitlement starts from a later date.[38]

Information to support your claim

Your employer can require you to provide 'such information as may reasonably be required' to determine your claim for SSP.[39]

Medical evidence

For the first seven days of your incapacity for work you are only required to provide a self-certificate as evidence of your incapacity for work. Your employer cannot insist on your obtaining a medical certificate.[40] After the first seven days, an employer usually expects you to provide a medical certificate from a doctor. If you provide a certificate from someone else, such as an osteopath or chiropractor, this can be accepted if your employer considers it sufficient.[41] Whatever type of medical evidence you provide, it is up to your employer to decide whether or not to accept it. See Chapter 57 if you want to challenge your employer's decision. See p840 for information on evidence of your incapacity for work.

Who should claim

As your employer cannot insist that you personally notify it of your incapacity for work, someone else can notify your employer on your behalf.

If you are not well enough to be able to deal with your own affairs, HMRC can appoint someone else to act for you (an 'appointee' – see p1149). For further information contact HMRC's National Insurance Enquiries helpline (tel: 0300 200 3500; textphone: 0300 200 3519).

If you claim the wrong benefit

A claim for another benefit cannot be treated as a claim for SSP. However, if you have notified your employer of your sickness, but you are not entitled to SSP, you may be able to get a claim for employment and support allowance (ESA) backdated more than the usual three months (see p650).

Backdating your entitlement

To qualify for SSP, you must notify your employer of your sickness (see p848). Even if you have not notified your employer promptly, your entitlement can still be backdated if you do so within the time limits on p849.

If statutory sick pay ends or is refused

If your employer decides that you are not entitled to SSP or stops paying you, it should provide you with a statement (usually on Form SSP1) within certain time limits, giving you the reasons for its decision.[42] If you do not agree with your employer's decision, see Chapter 57 for how to challenge it.

Whether or not you agree with your employer's decision, you should consider claiming other benefits. If you are not well enough to work, consider claiming ESA (see Chapters 3 and 28). The DWP usually asks HMRC to make a decision on your entitlement to SSP before it makes a decision on your claim for ESA.

7. Getting paid

Statutory sick pay (SSP) is usually paid in the same way and at the same intervals as your wages or salary.

SSP is a daily benefit, so if you qualify for it, it can be paid for periods of less than a week. See p846 for the way the daily rate is calculated.

Note:

- If you are entitled to contractual sick pay from your employer, SSP forms part of your pay. Your employer can deduct the amount of SSP you are entitled to from the contractual sick pay it is liable to pay you for the same period.[43]
- Your employer cannot pay you SSP by making a payment in kind or by providing board and lodging, a service or other facilities.[44]
- Deductions that can be made from your wages (eg, union subscriptions) can also be made from your SSP.[45]

- If your entitlement to SSP has been decided by HM Revenue and Customs (HMRC) or by the First-tier Tribunal or Upper Tribunal, your employer may be required to pay your SSP within a certain time limit (see p1392).
- If your employer cannot or will not pay you, see p1392 for details of when payment of SSP can be made by HMRC.
- The rules on overpayments and recovery of overpaid benefit described in Chapter 52 do not apply to SSP. If your employer pays you SSP and later decides that you were not entitled to it, it may attempt to recover the sum it considers overpaid by making a deduction from your wages. If this happens, get advice. If your employer decides that you have been overpaid SSP in error, consider claiming employment and support allowance (ESA). You may be able to get your claim backdated (see p650).

Change of circumstances

Notify your employer of any change in your circumstances that may affect your entitlement to SSP.

8. Tax, other benefits and the benefit cap

Tax

Statutory sick pay (SSP) is treated like any other earnings. You pay tax and, depending on the amount of your earnings in the same week, national insurance (NI) contributions by pay as you earn (PAYE) in the normal way.[46]

Means-tested benefits and tax credits

You cannot qualify for employment and support allowance (ESA) during your period of entitlement to SSP.[47] However, in some circumstances you may be *treated* as getting ESA (or income support (IS) or income-based jobseeker's allowance (JSA)) while you are entitled to SSP. This may help you get an amount for certain housing costs in these benefits earlier. See p471 for more details.

Entitlement to SSP may allow you to qualify for IS (see p102). Alternatively, if your partner is not in full-time paid work, s/he may qualify for JSA. If you are a member of a 'joint-claim couple' for JSA and you get SSP, you may not need to make a joint claim for your partner to qualify for income-based JSA for you both (see p135). If you have to make a joint claim, you do not need to satisfy all the usual conditions for joint-claim JSA if you get SSP (see p121).

In some circumstances, you can be treated as being in full-time work for working tax credit (WTC – see Chapter 10) while you are getting SSP (see p201). It is not necessary for you to have claimed WTC before you became ill, so if you are not getting WTC, perhaps because your income was too high before you went on

Part 5: Other benefits
Chapter 38: Statutory sick pay
8. Tax, other benefits and the benefit cap

SSP, check whether you can qualify for it now. Also, in some circumstances, entitlement to SSP can help you to qualify for the disabled worker element and/or a childcare element in your WTC (see p1412 and p1414).[48]

SSP is taken into account when calculating your entitlement to IS and income-based JSA (see p284). It is treated as earnings for pension credit (PC) and housing benefit (HB). See Chapters 14 or 15 for details. For WTC and child tax credit, any SSP you receive during the course of the tax year is taken into account as employment income (see p1436).

If you get SSP, an allowance for certain childcare charges may be deducted from your earnings when calculating your entitlement to HB (see p281).

If you come under the universal credit (UC) system (see p20), you may qualify for UC as well as SSP. SSP is treated as employed earnings for UC. When calculating your entitlement to UC, it is your net earnings that are taken into account, so certain amounts may be deducted before applying the work allowance (see p339 and p167). For the purpose of qualifying for help with the cost of childcare in your UC, you can be treated as still in paid work while getting SSP (see p264).

Non-means-tested benefits

You cannot get ESA, statutory adoption pay (SAP), statutory paternity pay (SPP) or statutory shared parental pay (SSPP) while you are getting SSP.[49]

You cannot qualify for SSP during your maternity pay period or, if your entitlement is based on your own employment or self–employment, during your maternity allowance (MA) period (see p722).[50] If you get MA on the basis of your spouse's or partner's employment or self–employment, see p847. SSP counts towards the earnings condition for MA, statutory maternity pay, SAP, SPP and SSPP, and counts as earnings for carer's allowance, increases in non-means-tested benefits for dependants and reduced earnings allowance, and so may affect your entitlement to these benefits.

SSP does not affect your entitlement to other non-means-tested benefits.

Unless you have other earnings, such as occupational sick pay, you do not have to pay NI contributions while on SSP as the weekly rate of SSP is below the NI lower earnings limit. Instead, you are entitled to class one NI credits (see p968).[51]

The benefit cap

In some cases, there is a limit on the total amount of specified benefits you can receive (a 'benefit cap'). SSP is *not* a specified benefit. The benefit cap only applies if you are getting HB or UC. The benefit cap may not apply if you or your partner have worked recently and you may count as in work while receiving SSP. See p1180 for further information.

Passports and other sources of help

If you are on a low income, you may be entitled to certain health benefits (see Chapter 29). You may be entitled to council tax reduction (see p854).

Notes

1. Who is entitled to statutory sick pay

1 ss151-155 and Schs 11 and 12 SSCBA 1992
2 s63 WRA 2012
3 ss151 and 163(1) SSCBA 1992; regs 4 and 16 SSP Regs
4 Reg 16(2) SSP Regs
5 Reg 4 SSP Regs
6 s151(4) SSCBA 1992
7 Sch 1 SSP(ME) Regs
8 Reg 2 SSP Regs
9 s152 SSCBA 1992
10 s152(3) SSCBA 1992
11 s153(2), (7) and (8) SSCBA 1992
12 ss153(2) and (12) and 155 SSCBA 1992; reg 3(1), (3) and (4) SSP Regs
13 s152(3) SSCBA 1992
14 s153(3) and Sch 11 SSCBA 1992; reg 3 SSP Regs
15 s163(2) SSCBA 1992; regs 17 and 19 SSP Regs
16 CSSP/2/1984; CSSP/3/1984
17 *Seaton v HMRC* [2011] UKUT 297 (TCC)
18 Reg 17 SSP Regs
19 Reg 17(2) SSP Regs
20 Reg 19(7) and (8) SSP Regs
21 Sch 11 para 6 SSCBA 1992
22 ss154 and 155(1) SSCBA 1992
23 s154(3) SSCBA 1992
24 Reg 5(2) and (3) SSP Regs
25 R(SSP) 1/85
26 s155(1) SSCBA 1992

4. The amount of benefit

27 s157 SSCBA 1992
28 s157(3) SSCBA 1992
29 Regs 20 and 21 SSP Regs
30 s155(2)-(4) SSCBA 1992
31 s152(3) SSCBA 1992

5. Special benefit rules

32 s153(2)(d) and (12) SSCBA 1992
33 Reg 3(5) SSP Regs
34 Reg 3(4) SSP Regs

6. Claims and backdating

35 Reg 7(1) and (4) SSP Regs
36 Reg 7(1), (4) and (5) SSP Regs
37 Reg 7(1)-(3) SSP Regs
38 s156(3) SSCBA 1992
39 s14(1) SSAA 1992
40 Reg 2(2) SSP(ME) Regs
41 Reg 2(1) SSP(ME) Regs
42 Reg 15 SSP Regs

7. Getting paid

43 Sch 12 para 2 SSCBA 1992
44 Reg 8 SSP Regs
45 s151(3) SSCBA 1992

8. Tax, other benefits and the benefit cap

46 s4(1) SSCBA 1992
47 s20(1) WRA 2007
48 Regs 6, 9 and 13 WTC(EMR) Regs
49 s20(1) WRA 2007; regs 18 and 27 SPPSAP(G) Regs; regs 14(1)(a) and 26(1)(a) SSPP(G) Regs
50 s153(2)(d) and (12) SSCBA 1992
51 Reg 8B(2)(iii) SS(Cr) Regs

Chapter 39

Other payments

This chapter covers:
1. Council tax reduction (below)
2. Local welfare assistance schemes (p856)
3. Healthy Start food and vitamins (p857)
4. Education benefits (p860)
5. Free milk for children (p862)
6. Payments for former members of the armed forces (p862)
7. Christmas bonus (p863)
8. Other financial help (p864)

Key facts
- There are a number of payments you may be able to get in addition to your benefits. For some of these you must be receiving a 'qualifying benefit'.
- You may be able to get financial help from your local authority – eg, your council tax may be reduced, you may qualify for help under its welfare assistance scheme or your child may be able to get help with certain costs of education, such as free school lunches.
- Under the Healthy Start scheme, you can get vouchers for milk, fruit and vegetables, and coupons for free vitamins. Free milk is also available to children in daycare under the welfare food scheme.
- You can get a £10 Christmas bonus if you are entitled to a qualifying benefit in the relevant week.
- Other sources of financial help are available – eg, if you are on a low income, starting work, have children, are an older person, have an illness or disability, need help with home improvements or have other special needs.

1. Council tax reduction

If you need help to pay your council tax, you might be able to get a reduction under your local authority's council tax reduction scheme. **Note:** a council tax reduction is *not* a social security benefit or a tax credit and the rules for benefits and tax credits in this *Handbook* do not apply.

In:[1]
- England and Wales, local authorities may devise their own local schemes which must meet minimum requirements. In Wales, if a local authority does not adopt its own scheme, a default scheme applies. Check with your local authority whether it has its own local scheme or whether the default scheme applies;
- Scotland, there is a national scheme, administered by local authorities.

The rules for all the schemes, along with some commentary, are in CPAG's *Housing Benefit and Council Tax Reduction Legislation 2016/17*.

Some of the minimum requirements that must be met in all the local schemes for people who are at least the qualifying age for pension credit (PC), the default scheme in Wales and in the national scheme in Scotland are as follows. Unless indicated, these are *not* minimum requirements for the local schemes in England and Wales for people under the qualifying age for PC.

- To qualify for a council tax reduction, you:
  - must be liable for council tax on the dwelling in which you are a resident. Some temporary absences from home are allowed;
  - must make an application for a council tax reduction;
  - must not be subject to immigration control (see p1516) and you must satisfy the habitual residence test (see p1537).

  Note: the above are also minimum requirements for the local schemes in England and Wales for people under the qualifying age for PC.
- Some students are excluded from getting a council tax reduction.
- Council tax reduction is means tested – ie, the amount you get depends on your income. However, if you or your partner are getting the guarantee credit of PC, all your income is ignored. If you are under the qualifying age for PC and you or your partner are getting income support, income-based jobseeker's allowance or income-related employment and support allowance, all your income is ignored. **Note:** this is also a minimum requirement for local schemes in Wales for people under the qualifying age for PC.
- There is a capital limit (currently £16,000). However, if you or your partner are getting the guarantee credit of PC, all your capital is ignored. **Note:** this is also a minimum requirement for local schemes in Wales for people under the qualifying age for PC.
- You may be able to get extended help for a period if you take up paid work, more paid work or better paid work.
- In England and Scotland, but not in Wales, there is an alternative maximum council tax (known as 'second adult rebate') designed to help you if you share your home with anyone on a low income.
- Applications for a council tax reduction can be backdated in some circumstances. **Note:** this is also a minimum requirement for local schemes in England and Wales for people under the qualifying age for PC.

- If you disagree with a council tax reduction decision, you can appeal, initially to the local authority. Appeals must be in writing and made within one month of your being sent the decision in Wales or within two months in Scotland. There are no formal time limits for appeals in England.
- If you are not satisfied with the outcome of the appeal, you can make a further appeal to a valuation tribunal (in England and Wales) or the council tax reduction review panel (in Scotland). In England and Wales, you must appeal within two months of the date of the local authority's response. In Scotland, you must appeal within 42 days of the date of the response.

Check with your local authority whether you qualify for a council tax reduction. Ensure the rules are being applied correctly in your case. If your local authority has adopted its own scheme, check that it meets the minimum requirements. If you think your local scheme may be unlawful, irrational or discriminatory, get specialist advice.

In England and Wales, you may apply to your local authority for a discretionary reduction of your council tax bill. If the local authority refuses, you can appeal against its decision to a valuation tribunal.[2]

2. Local welfare assistance schemes

Help may be available under local welfare assistance schemes set up by your local authority (in England) or by the devolved administrations (in Wales and Scotland). The DWP may refer to this as 'local welfare provision'.

You may qualify if you need help, for example:
- with immediate short-term needs in a crisis – eg, if you do not have sufficient resources, or you need help with expenses in an emergency or as a result of a disaster, such as a fire or flood in your home;
- to establish yourself in the community following a stay in institutional or residential accommodation, or to help you remain in the community;
- to set up a home in the community as part of a planned resettlement programme;
- to ease exceptional pressure on your family;
- to enable you to care for a prisoner or young offender on temporary release;
- with certain travel expenses – eg, to visit someone in hospital, to attend a funeral, to ease a domestic crisis, to visit a child living with her/his other parent or to move to suitable accommodation.

In England, the local scheme is entirely at your local authority's discretion. Check with your local authority to find out what help is available, whether you qualify and how to apply.

In Wales, the Discretionary Assistance Fund for Wales offers non-repayable emergency assistance payments and individual assistance payments.

In Scotland the Scottish Welfare Fund provides community care grants and crisis grants. The basic rules for the scheme are set by the Scottish government, with each local authority having some discretion. You should apply to your local authority.[3]

For more information on local welfare assistance schemes, see www.cpag.org.uk/lwas.

3. Healthy Start food and vitamins

If you qualify for Healthy Start food and vitamins, you get free vitamins as well as vouchers that can be used to buy specified types of food.

Healthy Start food

If you qualify for Healthy Start food, you:[4]
- get fixed-value vouchers (worth £3.10 each) that can be exchanged for 'Healthy Start food' at registered food outlets; *or*
- are paid an amount equal to the value of the vouchers to which you are entitled, if there is no registered food outlet within a reasonable distance of your home.

Healthy Start food
'Healthy Start food' means liquid cow's milk and cow's milk-based infant formula, fresh or frozen fruit and vegetables including loose, pre-packed, whole, sliced, chopped or mixed fruit or vegetables (but not fruit or vegetables to which fat, salt, sugar, flavouring or any other ingredients have been added).[5]

Who can claim Healthy Start food
You qualify for Healthy Start food vouchers:[6]
- **if you are pregnant** and have been for more than 10 weeks, and you are:
  - 18 or over and are entitled to (or are a member of the family of someone who is entitled to) a 'qualifying benefit' (see p858);
  - under 18, whether or not you are entitled to a qualifying benefit (but not if you are excluded from these because you are a 'person subject to immigration control' – see p1516); *or*
- **if you are a mother** who has 'parental responsibility' for a child and:
  - you are 16 or over and entitled to (or you are a member of the family of someone who is entitled to) a qualifying benefit other than income-related employment and support allowance (ESA). If you are entitled to universal

credit (UC), your child must be under one year old. For other benefits, your child must be under one or it is less than a year since her/his expected date of birth. This means you can continue to qualify for vouchers for a period after your child is one – ie, if s/he was born prematurely; *or*

– it is less than four months since your baby's expected date of birth and you have not yet notified Healthy Start that s/he was born. You must have been entitled to a qualifying benefit before your baby was born. This allows your entitlement to vouchers to continue until you notify the birth. Once you do, you can then qualify under the rule above (if you are 18 or over). **Note:** as long as you provided the notification within the four-month period, you can also get extra vouchers for your child from her/his date of birth.

If you qualify for vouchers for more than one child under this rule (eg, you have twins), you get a voucher for each. If you do not have 'parental responsibility' but would otherwise qualify for vouchers, your child qualifies instead of you;[7]

• **for a child under four** who is a member of your family. You or a member of the family must be entitled to a qualifying benefit (see below) other than income-related ESA.

In practical terms, this means that each week you get one voucher for each of your children aged between one and four, two vouchers for each of your children under one (or within one year of their expected date of birth), plus one voucher if you are pregnant.

Example
Vera is 17 weeks pregnant. She has three children: twin girls aged two and a boy aged seven. She is getting income support (IS). She qualifies for a voucher because she is more than 10 weeks pregnant. Her twins each qualify for a voucher as they are under four. Her son does not qualify for a voucher. Vera gets three vouchers each week totaling £9.30. When the baby is born, Vera will still be entitled to a voucher because she will be a mother of a child under one. The baby will also be entitled to a voucher. She will then get four vouchers each week, totalling £12.40.

Definitions
The **'qualifying benefits'** are IS, income-based jobseeker's allowance and, in some cases, income-related ESA. Child tax credit (CTC) is also a qualifying benefit, provided that gross income for CTC purposes does not exceed £16,190 and there is no entitlement to working tax credit (WTC), other than if this is during the four-week WTC run-on period (see p202). UC is a qualifying benefit if during the last complete assessment period or the assessment period before that you (and your partner) earned £408 or less. If you subsequently cease to be entitled to UC or your earnings exceed the £408 threshold, you continue to qualify for Healthy Start food for a further eight weeks after the last complete assessment period.

'**Parental responsibility**' means parental responsibility as defined in section 3(1) of the Children Act 1989 (in England or Wales) or section 1(1) of the Children (Scotland) Act 1995 (in Scotland).[8]

'**Family**' means a person and her/his partner and any child or qualifying young person who is a member of her/his household and for whom s/he or her/his partner counts as responsible.[9] So, for example, if you are not entitled to a qualifying benefit but are included in your mother's or father's claim for one of these, you can qualify for Healthy Start food vouchers.

To count as the member of a family of someone entitled to UC, s/he must be 'responsible' for you under the UC rules (see p222) and must also satisfy the £408 earnings rule described in the definition of 'qualifying benefits' p858.

If you are an asylum seeker receiving asylum support, you receive an extra amount to help you buy healthy food if you are pregnant or have a child under three.

Claims

You must make an initial claim for Healthy Start food vouchers in writing and must provide specified information and evidence.[10] You can:

- complete the form in the Healthy Start leaflet (HS01), available from midwives, health visitors, maternity clinics and some doctors' surgeries or from 0345 607 6823;
- download a form or complete it online and print it off, or email yourself a form at www.healthystart.nhs.uk.

The form must be countersigned by a health professional (eg, a midwife or health visitor) who certifies when your baby is due (if you are pregnant) and that you have been given appropriate advice about healthy eating and breastfeeding. If you are under 16, your claim must also be signed by your parent or carer. Send the completed form to: Healthy Start Issuing Unit, Freepost RRTR-SYAE-JKCR, PO Box 1067, Warrington WA55 1EG.

If you are getting Healthy Start food vouchers while you are pregnant and then inform Healthy Start of your baby's birth by telephone while s/he is under four months old, you can get extra vouchers for her/him from her/his date of birth.[11] You may need to make a claim for CTC for her/him (or add her/him to your existing claim) to ensure that you continue to get the vouchers.

If you do not get vouchers to which you think you are entitled, or have any other problems with these, contact the Healthy Start Issuing Unit on 0345 607 6823.

Healthy Start vitamins

If you qualify for Healthy Start food vouchers, you also qualify for Healthy Start vitamins.[12] Mothers and pregnant women are entitled to 56 vitamin tablets and children under four to 10 millilitres of vitamin drops every eight weeks. Ask your local health professional what the local arrangements are for getting your free vitamins.

You do not have to make a separate claim for Healthy Start vitamins; you are sent Healthy Start vitamin coupons with your Healthy Start food vouchers. However, you must show evidence to the vitamin supplier that you are entitled (ie, the letter to which your most recent Healthy Start vouchers were attached) and, if requested, proof of your child's age.[13]

4. Education benefits

Financial help is available from your local authority if you are in school or are a student, or if you have children in school or college.

Free school lunches

School children are entitled to free school lunches if their families receive:[14]
- income support (IS), income-based jobseeker's allowance or income-related employment and support allowance (ESA);
- child tax credit and have annual taxable income of £16,190 (in England and Wales) or £16,105 (in Scotland), or less. However, this does not apply if the family is entitled to working tax credit (WTC) unless:
  - this is during the four-week 'WTC run-on' period (see p202); or
  - in Scotland only, the WTC award is based on annual taxable income of £6,420 or less – ie, the family gets maximum WTC;
- universal credit (UC). **Note:** the government may introduce an earnings threshold, but at the time this *Handbook* was written no rules had been made, and it was not clear whether this would apply in Scotland and Wales. See CPAG's online service and *Welfare Rights Bulletin* for updates;
- in England and Wales only, guarantee credit of pension credit (PC).

Also entitled are:
- 16–18-year-olds receiving the above benefits or tax credits in their own right;[15]
- asylum seekers in receipt of support provided under Part VI of the Immigration and Asylum Act 1999;
- in Scotland, a child attending pre-school nursery (or similar) who is entitled under any of the four bullet points above, or if her/his family receives PC, incapacity benefit or severe disablement allowance, or if since the age of two the child is being, or has been, looked after by a local authority or is the subject of a kinship care or guardianship order.[16]

Note: in England and Scotland, free school lunches are provided to all children during the first three years of primary school. In Wales, free school breakfasts are provided to all children in primary schools maintained by the local authority.[17]

School transport and school clothes

Local authorities must provide **free transport to school** for pupils aged five to 16 if it is considered necessary to enable that pupil to get to the 'nearest suitable school'. This applies if the pupil lives more than a set distance from that school. However, if there is no safe walking route, a pupil must be given free transport no matter how far away s/he lives from the nearest suitable school. Free school transport must also be be provided to pupils with special educational needs and to those whose parents are on a low income – ie, if they qualify for free school lunches or their parents are on the maximum rate of WTC.

Local authorities can give **grants for school uniforms and other school clothes**. Each authority determines its own eligibility rules. Some school governing bodies or parents' associations also provide help with school clothing.

Education maintenance allowance and 16 to 19 bursaries

Education maintenance allowance is a means-tested payment for young people aged 16 to 19 who stay on in further education and are ordinarily resident in Wales or Scotland. Payments are made directly to the young person and are conditional on regular course attendance. The young person receives a weekly allowance during term time. The amount depends on the household income. For further details, see www.studentfinancewales.co.uk or www.emascotland.com.

16 to 19 bursaries are payments for young people aged 16 to 19 who stay on in further education or training in England. These are available through the school, college or training provider. Certain young people in need (eg, young people in care, care leavers, young people who get IS or UC, or who get ESA and either disability living allowance or personal independence payment) can get the maximum bursary. Discretionary bursaries are available to those in financial difficulty. See www.gov.uk/1619-bursary-fund for further information.

Neither payment counts as income for any benefits or tax credits the parent may be getting. They are also not affected by any income the young person has from part-time work.

Note: if you are a student, to find out what help is available to finance your studies contact your local authority or college or university, or see www.gov.uk/student-finance. Also see CPAG's *Student Support and Benefits Handbook* and *Benefits for Students in Scotland Handbook*.

5. **Free milk for children**

Children under five are entitled to 189–200 millilitres of free milk on each day they are looked after for two hours or more:[18]
- by a registered childminder or daycare provider; *or*
- in a school, playcentre or workplace nursery which is exempt from registration; *or*
- in local authority daycare.

Children under one are allowed fresh or dried milk. This is provided by the welfare food scheme.

6. **Payments for former members of the armed forces**

If you are a former member of the armed forces, you can claim under the following schemes, administered by the Ministry of Defence.

You can qualify for **war pension disablement benefits** if you have ill health or a disablement caused by service before 6 April 2005. The degree of your disablement is assessed on a percentage scale, with 100 per cent being the level of disablement that qualifies for the maximum award. If you are assessed at 20 per cent or more, you receive a pension and if you are assessed at under 20 per cent you receive a lump sum (gratuity). You can also qualify for a number of supplementary allowances. Two of these are particularly important.

- **Constant attendance allowance.** You qualify for this if your disablement is assessed at 80 per cent or more, and because of your disablement you require 'constant attendance'. This has the same meaning as either 'attention' or 'supervision' for attendance allowance (AA) or disability living allowance (DLA) care component (see p606). The allowance is paid at four different rates depending on the number of hours for which you require constant attendance and whether this is in the daytime or at night. If you claim AA, DLA care component or the daily living component of personal independence payment (PIP), any constant attendance allowance to which you are entitled is deducted from these benefits. **Note:** the top two rates of constant attendance allowance are considerably more than the highest rates of AA, DLA care component or PIP daily living component.
- **Mobility supplement.** You qualify for this if your disablement is assessed at 40 per cent or more, and because of your disablement your ability to walk is 'of little or no practical use'. This is, in effect, the same test as for the higher rate of the mobility component of DLA. There is a single rate of benefit, which is the same as for the DLA higher rate mobility component and PIP enhanced

mobility component. If you claim DLA mobility component or PIP mobility component, any mobility supplement to which you are entitled is deducted. **Note:** unlike DLA and PIP, there is no upper age limit for claiming mobility supplement.

You can qualify for help under the **Armed Forces Compensation Scheme** if you have ill health or a disablement caused by service on or after 6 April 2005. The main benefit is a lump-sum payment. To qualify, you must have had an injury or ill health that comes within one of the specified 'descriptors'. Each descriptor is assigned to a 'tariff level', running from one (the most severe) to 15, which determines the amount payable. If you receive an award of at least tariff level 11, you also qualify for a 'guaranteed income payment', calculated as a percentage of your salary on the day your service in the armed forces ended. Awards are at 30, 50, 75 or 100 per cent, depending on your tariff level.

Armed forces independence payment is payable to those entitled to a guaranteed income payment under the Armed Forces Compensation Scheme at the 50 per cent rate or more. It is payable at a rate equivalent to the total of the enhanced rates of both the daily living and mobility components of PIP.

For more information, see www.gov.uk/government/organisations/veterans-uk or call Veterans UK on 0808 1914 218.

7. **Christmas bonus**

You qualify for a Christmas bonus of £10 if you are entitled (or treated as being entitled) to any of the qualifying benefits for at least part of the 'relevant week' (even if the benefit is paid later).[19] The relevant week is usually the week beginning with the first Monday in December.[20]

Qualifying benefits[21]

Armed forces independence payment; attendance allowance; disability living allowance; carer's allowance; disablement benefit (if it includes unemployability supplement or constant attendance allowance); contributory employment and support allowance which includes either the support or the work-related activity component; long-term incapacity benefit; industrial death benefit for widows or widowers; mobility supplement; retirement pensions; pension credit (PC); personal independence payment, severe disablement allowance, war disablement pension (if you are at least pension age – see p772),[22] war widow's or surviving civil partner's pension; widowed mother's allowance; widowed parent's allowance; and widow's pension.

You may also qualify for an extra bonus for your partner (a further £10) if s/he has not received a bonus in her/his own right, and:[23]

- you are both at least pension age (see p772) and you are entitled, or may be treated as entitled, to an increase of one of the qualifying benefits in respect of her/him; *or*
- you are both at least the qualifying age for PC (see p147) and the only qualifying benefit you get is PC.

The bonus is not taxable and has no effect on other benefits or tax credits.

It is paid automatically. However, you should contact the DWP if you have not obtained your bonus within a year. Otherwise, your right is lost.[24]

8. **Other financial help**

This *Handbook* is mainly concerned with information about social security benefits and tax credits. However, there is other financial help to which you may be entitled, especially if you are on a low income, have children, have an illness, disability or other special needs, or are an older person.

See the *Disability Rights Handbook*, published by Disability Rights UK, for help for those with care needs.

Food banks

If you are experiencing severe financial hardship (eg, caused by debt or benefit delays), you may be able to get vouchers for food which can be redeemed at a food bank. Vouchers are available from frontline care professionals such as doctors and social workers. Jobcentre Plus staff may also give out vouchers. Further information and contact details for many food banks can be found at www.trusselltrust.org or by contacting your local authority.

You may be able to get help with food or meals through local community groups which are part of the FareShare network. Further information is available at www.fareshare.org.uk.

Tax-free childcare

Tax-free childcare is a government scheme: you pay money into a childcare account, which is then topped up by the government. It is due to be introduced in early 2017 and available to all qualifying parents by the end of 2017,[25] at which point the existing childcare vouchers scheme will close to new applicants.[26]

The government tops up each payment of 80p you make into an online childcare account by 20p. The maximum annual top-up for each child in qualifying childcare is £2,000 a year (the government intends the maximum amount to be £4,000 for each disabled child).

Payments can be made up until 1 September after the child's 11th birthday (16th birthday if s/he is disabled). There is no limit on the number of children for whom you can make payments.[27]

The government has indicated that you (and your partner) must be working and have a maximum annual income of £100,000 and a minimum weekly income of £120 (the minimum wage for people over 25 multiplied by 16) to join the scheme.[28]

Note: you cannot be in the tax-free childcare scheme and still get tax credits or universal credit (UC).[29] If you are entitled to UC, you are not eligible for the scheme. Your tax credit award stops once you register for tax-free childcare – ie, you lose all your entitlement, not just the childcare element. The government may introduce rules that mean you lose all your UC entitlement if you register for the scheme.

If you are considering tax-free childcare, you should therefore check whether or not you will be better off. In most cases, you will be better off continuing to claim tax credits or UC.

See Chapters 9 and 10 for how to calculate your tax credit entitlement and Chapter 8 for how to calculate UC. If you are any doubt, get advice.

Note:
- The maximum amount of top-up payments in the tax-free childcare scheme is £2,000 a year per qualifying child (£4,000 a year for a disabled child).
- Tax-free childcare does not include any other amounts, and must be spent on childcare. Tax credits and UC include amounts for adults, children and disability as well as a childcare element (in working tax credit and UC), and UC includes an amount for your housing costs.
- You must reconfirm your circumstances with the tax-free childcare scheme every three months, whereas tax credits are assessed on annual income and finalised annually, and UC uses a monthly assessment period.
- The government says that you will be able to leave the tax-free childcare scheme (and possibly get tax credits or UC again), but can only do so a limited number of times, unless there has been a relevant change of circumstances – eg, a change in the make-up of your household or a change in your work.

See CPAG's online service and *Welfare Rights Bulletin* for updates.

Repairs, improvements and energy efficiency

Your local authority may be able to provide you with a grant to help with the cost of improving your home. The main types of grant available are:
- home improvement grants; *and*
- disabled facilities grants.

You may also be able to get:
- assistance from a home improvement agency (a local not-for-profit organisation) to repair, improve, maintain or adapt your home, sometimes called 'care and repair' or 'staying put' schemes, or with small repairs, safety checks and odd jobs from a handyperson service.

For information see, in England, www.foundations.uk.com, in Wales, www.careandrepair.org.uk and in Scotland, www.careandrepairscotland.co.uk.

- a grant for help with insulation and other energy efficiency measures in your home. Help with fuel bills may also be available. Different schemes operate in England, Wales and Scotland. For further information, contact the Energy Saving Advice Service on 0300 123 1234 (England, Northern Ireland and Wales), 0808 808 2282 (Scotland) or at www.energysavingtrust.org.uk. For more details, see CPAG's *Fuel Rights Handbook*.

Special funds for sick or disabled people

A range of help is available for people with an illness or disability to assist with things like paying for care services in their own home, equipment, holidays, furniture and transport needs, and for people with haemophilia or HIV contracted via haemophilia treatment. Grants are also available for practical support to help people do their jobs – eg, to pay for specialist equipment and travel. For more information, see the *Disability Rights Handbook*, published by Disability Rights UK.

Help from social services

Local authority social services departments have statutory duties to provide a range of practical and financial help to families, children, young people, older people, people with disabilities, carers and asylum seekers.

Charities

There are many charities that provide various types of help to people in need. Your local authority social services department or local advice centre may know of appropriate charities that could assist you, or you can consult publications, such as *A Guide to Grants for Individuals in Need* and the *Charities Digest*, in your local library. The organisation Turn2us has a website (www.turn2us.org.uk) with details of the charities that can provide financial help. In many cases, applications for support can be made directly from the website. Information on grants available for individuals can also be found on the website www.grantsforindividuals.org.uk.

Financial help when starting work

If you or your partner start working full time, you might be entitled to some financial support, administered by Jobcentre Plus, to help your transition into work after a period of time on benefit. Check with your Jobcentre Plus office or employment scheme or programme provider to see what is available. Do this before you start work, because you may have to apply before your job starts or within a short period of it starting. Some information is available at www.gov.uk/moving-from-benefits-to-work.

Notes

1. Council tax reduction
1 s13A Local Government Finance Act 1992
   E CTRS(DS)E Regs; CTRS(PR)E Regs
   W CTRS(DS)W Regs; CTRSPR(W) Regs
   S CTR(S) Regs; CTR(SPC)S Regs
2 s13A(1)(c) Local Government Finance Act 1992

2. Local welfare assistance schemes
3 Welfare Funds (Scotland) Act 2015; The Welfare Funds (Scotland) Regulations 2016, No.107

3. Healthy Start food and vitamins
4 Regs 5(2) and 8 HSS&WF(A) Regs
5 Regs 2(1) and 5(1) and Sch 3 HSS&WF(A) Regs; HSS(DHSF)(W) Regs
6 Reg 3 HSS&WF(A) Regs
7 Reg 3(5) HSS&WF(A) Regs
8 Reg 2(1) HSS&WF(A) Regs
9 Reg 2(1) HSS&WF(A) Regs
10 Reg 4 and Sch 2 HSS&WF(A) Regs
11 Reg 4(2) HSS&WF(A) Regs
12 Reg 3 HSS&WF(A) Regs
13 Reg 8A HSS&WF(A) Regs

4. Education benefits
14 **E** s512ZB Education Act 1996; The Education (Free School Lunches) (Prescribed Tax Credits)(England) Order 2003, No.383; The Free School Lunches and Milk (Universal Credit) Order 2013, No.650
   W s512ZB Education Act 1996; The Education (Free School Lunches) (Prescribed Tax Credits) (Wales) Order 2003, No.879 (W.110); The Free School Lunches and Milk (Universal Credit) (Wales) Order 2013, No.2021 (W.199)
   S s53(3) Education (Scotland) Act 1980; The Education (School Lunches) (Scotland) Regulations 2015, No. 269
15 For CTC, the legislation only provides for this in Scotland.
16 The Education (School Lunches) (Scotland) Regulations 2015, No.269
17 s88 School Standards and Organisation (Wales) Act 2013

5. Free milk for children
18 Reg 18 WF Regs

7. Christmas bonus
19 ss148(1) and 149(1) SSCBA 1992
20 s150(4) SSCBA 1992
21 s150(1) SSCBA 1992
22 s149(4) SSCBA 1992
23 ss148(2) and (5) and 150(2) SSCBA 1992
24 Reg 38 SS(C&P) Regs

8. Other financial help
25 www.gov.uk/government/news/tax-free-childcare-10-things-parents-should-know
26 The Childcare Payments (Eligibility) Regulations 2015, No.448; The Childcare Payments Regulations 2015, No.522
27 The Childcare Payments Regulations 2015, No.522 and The Childcare Payments (Eligibility) Regulations 2015, No.448
28 Reg 15 Childcare Payments (Eligibility) Regulations 2015, No.448
29 ss30 and 31 Childcare Payments Act 2014

5

Part 6

Special benefit rules

Chapter 40

Benefits for students

This chapter covers:

England, Scotland and Wales have separate education systems. The same terms (eg, further, higher and advanced education) are often used within the education systems of all three countries, but they can have different technical meanings. Terms are used in the benefit rules to define different levels of education (eg, relevant, non-advanced and advanced) for benefit purposes. However, these terms are not generally used by educational institutions.

This chapter covers only those benefits which are potentially affected if you are studying.

Key facts

- If you are a part-time student, your benefits are not usually affected by your studying, although there are extra conditions to meet for jobseeker's allowance.
- Most full-time students are excluded from claiming means-tested benefits. There are some exceptions, including for parents, disabled students and some young people on further education courses.
- Even if you can claim means-tested benefits, most student funding counts as income and reduces or stops your benefit.
- If you are a full-time student and are taking time off your course but have not abandoned it completely, you still count as a student and cannot usually claim benefits.
- Child tax credit, working tax credit and certain benefits, including maternity allowance, statutory sick pay, child benefit, disability living allowance and personal independence payment, have no special eligibility rules for full-time students, so you can claim these in the same way as anyone else, although your student income may affect your entitlement in some cases.

Part 6: Special benefit rules
Chapter 40: Benefits for students
1. Income support and jobseeker's allowance

1. **Income support and jobseeker's allowance**

If you are studying, you may count as being in 'relevant education' (see below), or as a 'full-time student' (see p874). You cannot usually qualify for income support (IS) or jobseeker's allowance (JSA) (either contribution-based or income-based). There are some exceptions, however, which are outlined in this section. You may also be able to qualify if you are studying part time (see p878).

Note: this section deals with the rules for income-based JSA, and for contribution-based JSA if claiming under the current system. The rules are different for contribution-based JSA if you come under the universal credit system (see p891).

Relevant education

If you are in relevant education, you can only qualify for IS in some circumstances and you cannot usually qualify for JSA.[1] However, note that for JSA a young person on a traineeship does not count as being in relevant education. In these rules, a traineeship is a course of up to six months which helps 16–24-year-olds to prepare for work and is funded or arranged by the Secretary of State under section 14 of the Education Act 2002.[2]

You count as being in **'relevant education'** if you are a 'qualifying young person' for child benefit purposes (see p572) – ie, you are under 20 and in full-time, non-advanced education or approved training on which you were accepted, enrolled or started when you were under 19.[3] For these purposes, 'full time' means more than 12 hours a week in term time, not including meal breaks and unsupervised study. 'Non-advanced' means anything below degree, HNC or HND level.

You can continue to count as being in relevant education for a period after your education or training ends – eg, if you have enrolled on another course or during what is known as the child benefit 'extension period' (see p572).

Entitlement to income support while in relevant education
You can qualify for IS while in relevant education if:[4]
- you are the parent of a child for whom you are treated as responsible and who is a member of your household (see p222); *or*
- you are a refugee who is learning English to obtain employment (see p105); *or*
- you are an orphan and have no one acting in place of your parents; *or*
- you have left local authority care and you have to live away from your parents and any person acting in their place (see p873). **Note:** if you are a care leaver aged 16 or 17 (see p937), you can only qualify for IS while you are in relevant education if you are a lone parent and treated as responsible for a child;[5] *or*
- you have to live away from your parents and any person acting in their place (see p873) because:

- you are estranged from them; *or*
- you are in physical or moral danger; *or*
- there is a serious risk to your physical or mental health.

The physical or moral danger does not have to be caused by your parents. Therefore, a young person who is a refugee and cannot rejoin her/his parents can claim IS while at school;[6] *or*

- you live apart from your parents and any person acting in their place, they are unable to support you and:
  - they are in prison; *or*
  - they are unable to come to Britain because they do not have leave to enter under the UK Immigration Rules;[7] *or*
  - they are chronically sick, or are mentally or physically disabled. This covers people who could get a disability premium or higher pensioner premium, get employment and support allowance (ESA) including a work-related or support component (or who would be entitled to contributory ESA including a work-related component but this has stopped being paid after 52 weeks), have an armed forces grant for car costs because of disability, or who are substantially and permanently disabled.

You may be able to claim IS under some of the above rules beyond age 20 if you are in one of the groups of full-time students who can claim (see p877).

Definitions
A **'person acting in place of your parents'** can include a local authority or voluntary organisation if you are being cared for by them, or foster carers, but only until you leave care.[8] It does not include a person who is your sponsor under the Immigration Rules.[9] In the last bullet point above, however, a person acting in place of your parents includes the person with whom you are placed, but does not expressly include the local authority.[10]

'Estrangement' implies emotional disharmony,[11] where you have no desire to have any prolonged contact with your parents or they feel similarly towards you. It is possible to be estranged even though your parents are providing some financial support or you still have some contact with them. If you are being cared for by a local authority, it is also possible to be estranged from the local authority. If you are, you could qualify for IS if you have to live away from accommodation provided by a local authority.[12]

Entitlement to jobseeker's allowance while in relevant education
You cannot qualify for JSA while in relevant education unless you are someone who can qualify for IS while in relevant education (see p872),[13] or you are treated as not being in relevant education. If you *can* qualify for IS while in relevant education, it may be better for you to claim IS.

In some cases, if you were previously on certain benefits and are now on a non-advanced course, which would be part time according to the rules for full-time

Part 6: Special benefit rules
Chapter 40: Benefits for students
1. Income support and jobseeker's allowance

students (ie, over 12 but not over 16 hours), you do not count as being in relevant education and can claim JSA.[14]

When someone else is entitled to benefits for you

If you cannot qualify for IS or JSA because you are in relevant education, someone else may be able to get child benefit, child tax credit (CTC) and working tax credit if s/he is treated as 'responsible' for you. In some circumstances, you may count as both a person who can qualify for IS while in relevant education and as a person for whom someone else can qualify for child benefit and CTC. Get advice on how you would be better off financially.

When you leave relevant education

Once you have left relevant education, you may be able to qualify for IS or JSA if you satisfy the rules for getting those benefits (see Chapters 5 and 6). Remember, you can continue to count as being in relevant education for a period after your education or training ends – eg, if you have enrolled on another course or during the child benefit 'extension period' (see p575). While you continue to be treated as in relevant education, you are only entitled to IS in the circumstances on p872.

Full-time students

If you are a full-time student, you cannot usually qualify for IS or JSA for the duration of your course, including vacations.[15] See p877 for exceptions to this rule. See p901 if you give up, change or take time out of your course and p878 if you are studying part time.

You count as a full-time student if you are not in relevant education (p872), you are not getting a training allowance, and:[16]

- you are under 19 and attending or undertaking a full-time course of 'advanced education'. '**Advanced education**' means degree- or postgraduate-level qualifications, teaching courses, diplomas of higher education, HND or HNC and all other courses above advanced GNVQ or equivalent, OND, A levels or a Scottish national qualification (higher or advanced level). See p875 for what counts as a full-time course; or
- you are 19 or over but under pension age (see p772) and attending or undertaking a full-time course of study. If your course is full time, you are treated as a full-time student regardless of the level of the course, unless you are aged under 20 and can still be treated as being in 'relevant education' (see p872). See p875 for what counts as a full-time course; or
- you are on a sandwich course (see p875).

You are treated as a student until either the last day of your course or until you abandon or are dismissed from it.[17] The '**last day of the course**' is the date on which the last day of the final academic year is officially scheduled to fall.[18]

For JSA, the period of study includes periods during which you are doing work connected to the course, even if this is after the normal end of your study.[19]

Full-time courses

In England and Wales, your course counts as full time and you are treated as a full-time student if:[20]

- it is totally or partly funded by the Secretary of State under section 14 of the Education Act 2002, section 100 of the Apprenticeships, Skills, Children and Learning Act 2009 or the Welsh government and your personal 'learning agreement' involves more than 16 hours of 'guided learning' each week. Courses include academic or vocational courses leading to a recognised qualification. The Secretary of State and the Welsh government also fund basic literacy and numeracy courses, English as a Second or Other Language (ESOL) programmes, Access and similar courses that prepare you to move on to qualification-bearing courses, and courses developing independent living skills for people with learning difficulties. The number of guided learning hours you do each week is set out in your learning agreement. This is signed by you and the college. The DWP uses this agreement to decide whether or not you are on a full-time course;[21] *or*
- it is not funded by the Secretary of State under section 14 of the Education Act 2002, section 100 of the Apprenticeships, Skills, Children and Learning Act 2009 or the Welsh government and is a 'full-time course of study'.

In Scotland, your course counts as full time and you are treated as being a full-time student if:[22]

- it is totally or partly funded by the Scottish Ministers at a college of further education, is not higher education *and* your personal learning document states that your course:
  - involves more than 16 hours a week of classroom-based or workshop-based programmed learning under the guidance of a teacher; *or*
  - involves more than 21 hours' study a week, 16 hours or less of which involve classroom-based or workshop-based programmed learning, and the rest of which involve using structured learning packages with the help of a teacher. The number of hours of 'learning' you do each week is set out in your learning document. This is signed by you and the college. The DWP uses this document to decide whether or not you are on a full-time course; *or*
- it is a course of higher education which is funded wholly or in part by the Scottish Ministers and is a full-time course of study; *or*
- it is not funded by the Scottish Ministers and is a full-time course of study.

Sandwich courses

A course is a 'sandwich course' if it consists of alternate periods of full-time study at your educational institution and periods of industrial, professional or work

Part 6: Special benefit rules
Chapter 40: Benefits for students
1. Income support and jobseeker's allowance

experience organised so that, taking the course as a whole, you attend the periods of full-time study for an average of at least 18 weeks in each year.[23] This does not apply if it is a course of initial teacher training. If your periods of full-time study and work experience alternate within any week of your course, the days of full-time study are aggregated with each other and with any weeks of full-time study to determine the number of weeks of full-time study in each year.

Work experience includes periods of employment abroad for modern language students whose course is at least half composed of modern language study.

Health-related courses

If you attend a health-related course for which you are entitled to receive an NHS bursary, you are treated as a full-time or part-time student as appropriate, and not an employee.[24]

Modular courses

A modular course is one that consists of two or more modules and your college or university requires you to complete successfully a specific number of modules before it considers you to have completed the course.[25] You are treated as a full-time student if you are currently attending part of a modular course that would be classed as a full-time course.[26] You are treated as a full-time student for the period beginning on the day your course is defined as a full-time course and ending on the last day on which you are registered with your college or university as attending or undertaking that part of your course. This includes any vacations, unless that vacation follows the last day on which you are required to attend or undertake your course, or on such earlier date that you finally abandon or are dismissed from that part of the course.[27]

If you have failed examinations or failed to complete a module, any period in which you attend or undertake the course in order to retake those examinations or modules is classed as part of the full-time course and you are treated as a full-time student (even if your college or university registers you as a part-time student during your re-sit period).[28]

Because the rules do not define what is a full-time course, unless funded by the Secretary of State under section 14 of the Education Act 2002, section 100 of the Apprenticeships, Skills, Children and Learning Act 2009 or Scottish Ministers (see p875), you may be able to argue that you are not attending a full-time course, regardless of your attendance, if your course is not defined as full time or part time by your college or university.[29]

Other courses

If your course does not automatically count as full time under the rules above, whether it counts as a 'full-time course of study' depends on the college or university. Definitions are often based on local custom and practice within education institutions. The college or university's definition is not absolutely final, but if you want to challenge it, you will have to produce a good argument showing why it should not be accepted.[30] If your course is only for a few hours each week, argue that it is not full time. However, a course could be full time even though you only have to attend a few lectures a week.[31]

Full-time students entitled to income support

Even if you are a full-time student, you can qualify for IS (although most student funding counts as income) if you are:[32]

- a lone parent under age 18 (regardless of the age of your child/ren), or a lone parent of a child under five; *or*
- a lone foster carer of a child under 16; *or*
- single, or are one of a couple and both of you are full-time students and:
  - you fit into one of the groups of people who can claim IS (see Chapter 5); *and*
  - you (or, if you are one of a couple, either one or both of you) are responsible for a child or young person (see p577); *and*
  - it is the summer vacation;
- a refugee who is learning English to obtain employment (see p105); *or*
- in, enrolled on or accepted for full-time non-advanced education and you are aged under 21, or you are 21 and you reached that age while in such education. In addition, you must:
  - have no parents (or anyone acting in their place); *or*
  - have to live away from your parents (or anyone acting in their place) because you are estranged from them, or are in physical or moral danger or there is a serious risk to your physical or mental health; *or*
  - be living away from your parents (or anyone acting in their place) and they cannot support you financially and they are:
    - chronically sick or mentally or physically disabled; *or*
    - in prison; *or*
    - prohibited from entering or re-entering Great Britain.

Full-time students entitled to jobseeker's allowance

Even if you are a full-time student, you can qualify for JSA (although most student funding counts as income) if you are:

- single and responsible for a child or, if you are one of a couple, both of you are full-time students and either one or both of you is responsible for a child (see p577). This exception only applies during the summer vacation and if you are actually available for work, or treated as available because you are on either of the courses in the next bullet point;[33] *or*
- on an employment-related course of up to two weeks that has been approved in advance by the DWP,[34] or a Venture Trust training programme of up to four weeks.[35] In either case, only one course is allowed in any 12-month period; *or*

Part 6: Special benefit rules
Chapter 40: Benefits for students
1. Income support and jobseeker's allowance

- participating in a scheme for assisting people to obtain employment (eg, Skills Conditionality – see p1103) – ie, you have been required to attend full-time training under it;[36] *or*
- aged 25 or over and on a qualifying course (see p1028);[37] *or*
- waiting to go back to your course, having taken approved time out because of an illness or caring responsibility and that has now come to an end (see p901).

Maintaining two homes

In some cases, if you qualify for IS, income-based JSA or housing benefit, you may be entitled to help with the costs of more than one home if you have to live away from your normal home to attend a course. For further details, see p57 and p458.

Part-time students

If you are studying but are not in relevant education (see p872) or attending a full-time course (see p875), you are treated as attending a part-time course and classed as a part-time student.

Entitlement to income support while studying part time

You can get IS while studying part time if you are not on a full-time course and you satisfy the other rules for getting IS (see Chapter 5).

If you are currently studying part time on a course you previously attended full time, the DWP may argue that you are attending a full-time course and should, therefore, be treated as a full-time student. It may be possible to challenge this interpretation.[38] Seek specialist advice if you are in this situation.

Entitlement to jobseeker's allowance while studying part time

You count as a part-time student if your course is not full time.[39] You can qualify for JSA while studying part time if you meet the jobseeking conditions – ie, you are available for work, actively seeking work and you have a valid jobseeker's agreement (see Chapter 45) or claimant commitment (see Chapter 47). If you have agreed restrictions with the DWP on the hours that you are available for work, there are special rules that can help you claim JSA and study part time (see p879).

When you claim JSA, you may be asked to fill in a 'student questionnaire'. Your answers are taken into account when deciding whether you are available for and actively seeking work. The DWP needs to be satisfied that you are genuinely available for and actively seeking work while you are studying part time.

Availability for work and part-time study

Your availability for work should not be affected by your part-time course if your hours of study or training are at times outside your agreed pattern of availability (see p1042) – ie, they do not clash with the times you are willing and able to work. If the hours of your course *do* clash with the times you say you are available for work (as set out in your jobseeker's agreement or claimant commitment – see p1049), you are only accepted as available for work if either:[40]

- you are able to rearrange the hours of the course or study to fit around your job; *or*
- you are willing and able to give up the course should a job become available.

Deciding whether you are available for work

A number of factors should be considered when deciding whether you are available for work while you are studying part time. If, for example, it appears you are not willing or able to give up your course or that you cannot confine your study to times that would fit in with employment, you are treated as not being available for work. The factors that may be relevant include:[41]

- where you are studying or training away from home, whether you can be contacted if a job becomes available;
- the extent of your efforts to find employment;
- how important the successful completion of the course is to your future career, including whether it will enhance your chances of finding employment;
- whether you gave up a job or training to do the course;
- the days and hours you are required to attend the course;
- whether the times of attendance could be altered to fit in with any job you might obtain or whether successful completion of the course is possible if you miss some of the scheduled attendances;
- the duration of the study or training;
- whether a fee was paid and, if so, the amount and whether any of the fee could be refunded or transferred if you abandoned or interrupted your studies. If you have paid a fee, it may be more difficult (depending on the amount) to convince the DWP that you are prepared to abandon the course;
- whether you received a grant and, if so, the source, the amount and whether you would have to repay any or all of it if you interrupted or abandoned the course.

The guidance for decision makers states that where a number of claimants are following the same course, some may be able to show that they are available, but others may not.[42] The DWP should consider each claim individually and not operate a blanket policy. The DWP assumes that you may be less willing to leave a course if you are near its end or as the chance of obtaining a qualification approaches.[43]

Restricted availability for work and part-time study

There are special rules that can help you qualify for JSA if you are a part-time student. These say that, in certain circumstances, the fact that you are on your course is ignored when deciding whether you are available for work if the hours of your course fall wholly or partly within the times you say you are available for

Part 6: Special benefit rules
Chapter 40: Benefits for students
1. Income support and jobseeker's allowance

work. However, you still have to be available for and actively seeking work during the rest of the week when you are not on your course.

These rules apply to you if you are a part-time student, and you are willing and able to rearrange the hours of your course to take up a job and the restrictions on your hours of availability have been agreed with the DWP because:[44]

- of your physical or mental condition (see p1040); *or*
- of your caring responsibilities (see p1042); *or*
- you are working 'short time' (see p1028); *or*
- they leave you available for work for at least 40 hours a week (see p1042).

You must also satisfy one of two conditions.

- For the three months immediately before the date you started the course, you were unemployed and getting JSA, or incapable of work and getting IS, incapacity benefit (IB) or ESA, or you were on a course of 'training'.
- In the six months immediately before you started the course, you were unemployed and getting JSA, or incapable of work and getting IS, IB or ESA, or you were on a course of training for a total of at least three months and, for any remaining part of the six months, you were working full time or earning too much to qualify for benefit.

The three-month and six-month periods can only begin after you have reached your terminal date (see p575) and are treated as having ceased to be in relevant education (see p575).

Training

'**Training**' means training for which young people aged under 18 are eligible, or for which a person aged 18–24 may be eligible, provided or arranged by the Secretary of State under section 14 of the Education Act 2002, the Welsh government or Skills Development Scotland.[45]

Calculating income and capital

The normal rules for assessing your income and capital apply if you are a student (see Chapters 14 and 17). However, there are special rules for assessing the amount of money available from grants, loans and other types of financial support that apply to students (see p891), including people claiming IS while in 'relevant education'.[46] These rules do not apply if you are receiving a training allowance. For which student grants or loans do not count as income, see p894 and p896.

2. Employment and support allowance

Whether you can qualify for employment and support allowance (ESA) while studying full time depends on the type of ESA you want to claim. You can qualify for contributory ESA as a full-time student (see p636). You cannot qualify for income-related ESA if you are 'receiving education' unless you are getting disability living allowance (DLA), personal independence payment (PIP) or armed forces independence payment (see below). You may be able to qualify if you are studying part time (see p882).

Note: in certain circumstances, if you are attending a training course and are paid a training allowance, you cannot qualify for ESA because you do not count as having limited capability for work (see p1004).[47]

Income-related employment and support allowance

If you are 'receiving education' you can only qualify for income-related ESA if you are getting DLA, PIP or armed forces independence payment.[48] This usually applies for the duration of your course, including vacations. See p882 if you have finished studying and p901 if you give up, change or take time out from your course.

For income-related ESA purposes, you count as 'receiving education' if you are:
- a 'qualifying young person' for child benefit purposes (see p572);[49] *or*
- undertaking a 'course of study'.[50] The DWP may refer to you as a 'full-time student'. The definition is the same as the definition of full-time student for income support (IS) and jobseeker's allowance (JSA) (see p874). A course of study is the same as a full-time course for IS and JSA, and, for ESA, also includes a sandwich course (see p875).

Note:
- The term 'full-time student' is used in the rest of this section to refer to someone who is receiving education for income-related ESA purposes.
- Unless you are a 'qualifying young person' for child benefit purposes, if you qualify for income-related ESA as a full-time student because you are getting DLA, PIP or armed forces independence payment, you automatically count as having limited capability for work (see p1005).[51]

Maintaining two homes

In some cases, if you are a full-time student and you qualify for income-related ESA or housing benefit, you may be entitled to help with the costs of more than one home if you have to live away from your normal home to attend a course. For further details, see p57 and p458.

Part 6: Special benefit rules
Chapter 40: Benefits for students
3. Housing benefit

When you stop being a full-time student

Once you stop being a full-time student, you may be able to claim income-related ESA (see Chapter 3). However, bear the following in mind.

- If you were a 'qualifying young person' for child benefit purposes (eg, you were under 20 and on a full-time course of non-advanced education – see p572), you continue to count as a qualifying young person for a period after your education or training ends – eg, if you have enrolled on another course or during the child benefit 'extension period' (see p575). While you continue to be treated as a qualifying young person, you can only qualify for income-related ESA if you are receiving DLA, PIP or armed forces independence payment. If you cannot qualify for ESA in your own right, your parents may be able to continue to claim child benefit and tax credits for you.

- If you counted as a full-time student other than because you were a 'qualifying young person' for child benefit purposes (see p572), you continue to be treated as a full-time student until the last day of your course, or until you abandon the course or are dismissed from it (see p901).

Studying part time

You can qualify for ESA if you are studying part time. The definition of part-time study is different for contributory ESA and for income-related ESA.

You can qualify for contributory ESA if you are studying part time *or* full time.

You can qualify for income-related ESA if you do not count as a full-time student under the rules described on p881.

When someone else is entitled to benefits for you

If you are under 20, a 'qualifying young person' for child benefit purposes (see p572) and cannot qualify for ESA because you are 'receiving full-time education' (see p881) or are a full-time student (see p881), someone else may be able to qualify for child benefit, child tax credit (CTC) and working tax credit if s/he is treated as 'responsible' for you. In some circumstances, you may count as both a person who can qualify for ESA and a person for whom someone else can qualify for child benefit and CTC. Get advice on how you would be better off financially.

3. **Housing benefit**

Note: if you have reached the qualifying age for pension credit (PC – see p147) and neither you nor your partner are in receipt of income support (IS), income-based jobseeker's allowance (JSA) or income-related employment and support allowance (ESA), the student rules for housing benefit (HB) do not apply and there are no restrictions on your studying and qualifying for HB.[52]

Whether you can claim HB (see Chapter 4) depends on whether you are classed as a full-time or a part-time student.

Full-time students

If you are a full-time student (see p874), you cannot usually qualify for HB, but there are some exceptions – eg, students with children and young people in non-advanced education (see below).

The rules for deciding whether you are a full-time student are similar to the rules for IS and JSA (see p874), except that there is no separate rule in HB if you are in 'relevant education' (see p872).

Part-time students

You may be able to qualify for HB if you are studying part time. The rules for deciding whether you are a part-time student are similar to the rules for IS and JSA (see p878), except that there is no separate rule in HB if you are in 'relevant education' (see p872).

Partners of students

If your partner is not a student, s/he can qualify for HB if s/he meets the qualifying conditions.[53] The claim is assessed in the normal way, except that the rules about being away from term-time accommodation (see p884) apply to your partner's claim.[54] Additionally, the special rules for assessing any income you receive from grants, loans and other types of financial support for students apply (see p891).

Full-time students entitled to housing benefit

You can qualify for HB (although most student funding counts as income) if:[55]
- you are on IS, income-based JSA or income-related ESA or universal credit (UC) except if your UC includes an amount for housing costs (see Chapter 22); *or*
- you are under 21, not following a course of higher education (higher education includes degree courses, teacher training, HND, HNC and postgraduate courses), or are aged 21 and you reached that age while on such a course and are still on it, or you are a child or a 'qualifying young person' for child benefit purposes (see p572); *or*
- you and your partner are both full-time students and either or both of you are responsible for a child or qualifying young person (see p572). **Note:** unlike for IS and JSA, this provision applies throughout the year; *or*
- you are a lone parent responsible for a dependent child or qualifying young person aged under 20 (see p572); *or*
- you are a lone foster carer and the child has been formally placed with you; *or*
- you meet the conditions for the disability premium (see p238). **Note:** you cannot qualify for a disability premium if you have limited capability for work; *or*

Part 6: Special benefit rules
Chapter 40: Benefits for students
3. Housing benefit

- you have been (or have been treated as) incapable of work (see p683 of the 2013/14 edition of this *Handbook*) for 196 days (28 weeks); *or*
- you have had (or have been treated as having) limited capability for work (see p1003) for 196 days (28 weeks) and you continue to have it. Two or more periods are joined to form a single period if they are separated by 12 weeks or less. **Note:** claims from 27 October 2008 are assessed under these rules rather than the incapacity for work rules in the bullet point above, unless, broadly, you already get incapacity benefit or IS because of incapacity for work; *or*
- you meet the conditions for the severe disability premium (see p242); *or*
- you qualify for a disabled students' allowance because you are deaf; *or*
- you are waiting to go back to your course, having taken approved time out because of an illness or caring responsibility and this has now come to an end (see p902).

Note: even if you are a full-time student who comes into one of the exception categories listed above, you still cannot qualify for HB if the circumstances under the two headings below apply to you.

Being away from your term-time accommodation

Even if you are a full-time student who can qualify for HB (see p883), if your main reason for occupying your home is to enable you to attend your course, you cannot qualify for HB on that home for any full week when you are absent from it outside your period of study (see p893).[56]

This rule does not apply if:

- you are away from home because you are in hospital;[57]
- the main reason for occupying your home is *not* to enable you to attend your course but for some other purpose – eg, to provide a home for your children or for yourself because you do not have a home elsewhere to live when you are not attending your course. If this applies, any absences outside your period of study are dealt with under the temporary absence rules (see p53).

Accommodation rented from an educational establishment

If you are a full-time student who can qualify for HB (see p883), you can usually get HB even if you rent your accommodation from your educational establishment.[58] If you are a part-time student, this rule applies if you would be able to qualify for HB if you were treated as a full-time student.

You cannot, however, get HB if you are a:

- full-time student waiting to go back to your course, having taken approved time out because of illness or caring responsibilities (see p902) and your illness or caring responsibilities have not yet ended; *or*
- part-time student whose only basis of entitlement to HB if you were a full-time student would be that you are receiving IS, income-based JSA or income-related ESA.

These two exceptions do not apply if:

- your educational establishment itself rents the accommodation from a third party other than on a long lease or where the third party is an education authority providing the accommodation as part of its functions; *or*
- the accommodation is owned by a separate legal body – eg, a company established to build halls of residence.

You cannot get HB if the local authority decides that your educational establishment has arranged for your accommodation to be provided by a person or body other than itself in order to take advantage of the HB scheme.

Living in different accommodation during term time

The rules about claiming HB for two homes are explained on p57. If you are one of a couple and receive HB for two homes, the assessment of HB for each home is based on your joint income and your applicable amount as a couple.

Calculating housing benefit

If you or your partner are on IS, income-based JSA, income-related ESA, UC or the guarantee credit of PC, you are entitled to maximum HB (see Chapter 4).

If you are not on IS, income-based JSA, income-related ESA, UC or the guarantee credit of PC but you or your partner are eligible for HB, your entitlement is calculated in the same way as for other claimants (see Chapters 14 and 17), except that there are special rules for assessing the amount of money available from grants, loans and other types of financial support for students (see p891). **Note:** for courses lasting more than one year, in many cases loans and grants are not counted as income over the summer vacation. You may find, therefore, that your HB entitlement is higher over this period, or that you are only entitled to HB during the summer vacation, and that you need to make a new claim or check that your entitlement is reviewed at that time.

Payments

Students are covered by all the normal rules on the administration and payment of HB (see Chapter 4). However, there is a provision that can apply specifically to students. The local authority may decide to pay a rent allowance once each term, although students have the same right as other claimants to insist on fortnightly payments if their entitlement is more than £2 a week.[59]

4. Universal credit

Universal credit (UC) is being introduced gradually over the next few years. For more information about when you come under the UC system, see p20.

Part 6: Special benefit rules
Chapter 40: Benefits for students
4. Universal credit

Undertaking a course of study (the law refers to this as 'receiving education') may mean that you are not eligible for UC, unless you are in one of the groups of people for whom an exception is made (see below). In general, these are students with children, some disabled students and young students in non-advanced education who have no parental support.

Receiving education

If you are 'receiving education', in most cases you are not eligible for UC.[60] There are exceptions (see below).

You are 'receiving education' if you are:[61]

- a 'qualifying young person'. You must be on, or accepted on, a course of non-advanced education or approved training of at least 12 hours a week, and you must have been enrolled on, accepted on or have started the course before you turned 19. You can continue to be a qualifying young person until 31 August after your 19th birthday (see p220).[62] You are not a qualifying young person if you are on a traineeship (see p872); *or*
- on a full-time course of advanced education. This is education above the level of advanced GNVQ, AS/A level or a Scottish national qualification (higher or advanced higher), and includes degree-level or postgraduate-level courses, and HNDs; *or*
- on another full-time course of study or training for which a loan or grant is provided for your maintenance.

Note: if none of the above apply, but you are on a course that is not compatible with your work-related requirements (see p887), you are treated as if you are receiving education.[63]

You count as receiving education from the start to the end of your course, or sooner if you abandon it or are dismissed from it.[64] The rules for when you count as a student if you are on a modular course are the same as those for income support (see p876).

Entitlement to universal credit while receiving education

You are eligible for UC while receiving education (although at least some of your student funding may count as income) if you are:[65]

- under 21 on a non-advanced course (or you are aged 21 and turned 21 on the course) and are 'without parental support' (see p887);
- responsible for a child or qualifying young person (p220);
- a single foster parent;
- a member of a couple, both of you are full-time students and one of you is responsible for a child or is a foster parent;

- assessed as having limited capability for work (see p1003) and you also get attendance allowance, disability living allowance or personal independence payment;
- over the qualifying age for pension credit (see p147);
- a student with a partner who is not a student, or who is a student but would be entitled to UC her/himself while receiving education;[66]
- waiting to return to your course after taking time out because of illness or caring responsibilities (see p890).[67]

Without parental support

'Without parental support' means you are not looked after by a local authority and you:[68]

– have no parent; *or*

– cannot live with your parents because you are estranged from them, or because there is a serious risk to your physical or mental health, or you would suffer significant harm if you lived with them; *or*

– are living away from your parents, and they cannot support you financially because they are ill or disabled, in prison or not allowed to enter Britain.

'Parent' includes someone acting in place of a parent.

When someone else can claim for you

If you cannot get UC yourself, someone may be able to claim for you if you are a 'qualifying young person' – ie, generally, if you are under 20 and in non-advanced education (see p220).

Work-related requirements

Most people claiming UC have work-related requirements as a condition of getting benefit, which may involve undertaking work-related activity or looking for work (see p1073). However, you have no work-related requirements if you are receiving education and are eligible for UC under one of the first six bullet points above and you are:[69]

- under 21 (or 21 and you turned 21 on your course) in non-advanced education and 'without parental support' (see above); *or*
- in receipt of student income which is taken into account for UC – ie, a student loan or a grant for maintenance (see p888).

Note: even if you do not fit into one of the above groups, you may have no work-related requirements under the general rules – eg, if you are responsible for a child under one, or if you are severely disabled (see p1081).

If you are on a full-time course but do not get a loan or grant, you may therefore be subject to all work-related requirements, and must be available for and actively seeking work (see p1080). This is more likely to be the case if you are in non-

Part 6: Special benefit rules
Chapter 40: Benefits for students
4. Universal credit

advanced education or on a postgraduate course, as there may be no student loan available, and grants for maintenance are limited.

Studying part time

If you are on a part-time course, you may still be treated as 'receiving education' if the course is not compatible with your work-related requirements.[70] So if you are subject to all work-related requirements, you must show that you meet these despite being on a part-time course. In some cases, it may be possible to argue that the course should be seen as 'voluntary work preparation', and therefore reduce your work search requirements (see p1075).[71]

If you are on a part-time course that is accepted as being compatible with your work-related requirements, you can get UC.

Student income and universal credit

If you (or your partner) have student income, it may count as income for UC. The rules below set out what student income counts, and how it is assessed.[72]

You are counted as having student income if you are undertaking a course and have a student loan or grant in respect of that course.[73]

Student loans

Student loans for maintenance[74] count as income if you could get a loan by taking 'reasonable steps', even if you choose not to apply for one. The maximum loan you could be entitled to (for a postgraduate master's degree loan, 30 per cent of the maximum) is taken into account as income.

This is the case even if the loan is reduced because of an assessed parental (or partner) contribution, or if part of the loan is replaced by a grant. However, if you are eligible for a special support element as part of your maintenance loan in England, this loan should be disregarded. You many need to get a statement from Student Finance England explaining your entitlement. In Scotland, a student loan includes a young student's bursary.[75]

A grant paid for the same period as the loan is disregarded unless it is for the maintenance of someone who is part of your UC claim (eg, a partner or a child) or for rent payments that are met by UC.[76]

Grants

If you do not get a loan but receive a grant, the grant income is taken into account for UC (subject to the disregards p889). If you get a loan, see above for what grant income is taken into account. The term 'grant' means an educational grant or award. It does not include a student loan or a grant paid to someone under 21 in non-advanced education to enable them to finish a course.[77]

This means that education maintenance allowance payments and 16 to 19 bursary fund payments do not count as student income.

Access or discretionary fund payments are likely to count as student income (as an 'educational grant'), unless they can be disregarded under the rules below. Grant income is completely disregarded if you do not get a loan and it is a payment:[78]

- for tuition fees or exams;
- in respect of your disability;
- for extra costs for residential study away from your usual place of study during term time;
- to pay for the costs of your normal home (if you live somewhere else during your course), unless these are met by your UC;
- for the maintenance of someone who is not included in your UC claim;
- for books, equipment, course travel costs or childcare costs.

Calculating student income

UC is paid for an 'assessment period' of one month (see p173). Student income counts as income in assessment periods that fall during the course, as well as in the assessment period in which the course, and any subsequent year of the course, begins.[79] Student income is ignored in the assessment period in which the last week of the course or the start of the long vacation falls. The long vacation is the longest holiday, lasting at least a month, in a course which is at least two years long. Student income is also ignored in any other assessment period that falls completely within the long vacation.[80]

In each assessment period, £110 of student income is disregarded.

To work out how much of your student income is taken into account:

Step one: calculate your annual loan or grant or, if the course lasts for less than a year, the amount of loan or grant for the course.

Step two: work out how many assessment periods apply for that year, or for the course if it is less than a year long.

Step three: divide the amount from Step one by the number of assessment periods in Step two.

Step four: deduct £110.

Example

Susan gets a student loan of £8,200 in total. This includes a special support element of £3,469, which is disregarded, leaving £5,878. Year one of her course runs from 3 October 2016 to 19 May 2017. Her assessment periods run from the third of the month to the second of the following month. Her loan counts as income for seven assessment periods.

£5,878 ÷ 7 = £839.71

£839.71 – £110 = £729.71

Susan's UC is calculated on student income of £729.71 a month from 3 October 2016 to 2 May 2017.

Part 6: Special benefit rules
Chapter 40: Benefits for students
5. Other benefits

Taking time out from your course

During a period of temporary absence from your course, you usually still count as receiving education, so the student rules apply. Therefore, if you take time out because you have to re-sit exams or because you are ill, you still count as receiving education and are only eligible for UC if you are in one of the groups that is exempt – eg, you are a parent.

You do not count as 'receiving education' and can claim UC if you have taken time out from your course because of illness or caring responsibilities, you have now recovered or your caring responsibilities have ended, you are not eligible for a grant or student loan, and you are waiting to return to your course.[81] Your institution must have agreed to your taking time out, and you must have recovered from your illness or your caring responsibilities must have ended within the last year.

If you leave your course completely, you no longer count as receiving education, so the normal UC rules apply. Student income is taken into account up to the end of the assessment period before the one in which you leave the course.

5. **Other benefits**

Carer's allowance

You cannot qualify for carer's allowance (CA – see Chapter 25) if you are in full-time education.[82] Usually, if the course you are attending is described by the university, college or school as full time, you are regarded as being in full-time education, although there may be exceptions – eg, if you are exempted from parts of the course.[83] So the actual hours you attend may not be crucial; but if you are attending for 21 hours a week or more (as specified by the institution), you are treated as being in full-time education. When calculating the 21 hours, you include only hours spent in 'supervised study' (see below). You ignore any time spent on meal breaks or unsupervised study undertaken on or off the premises of the educational establishment.[84]

You are treated as still being in full-time education during vacations and any temporary interruption of the course, but not if you have abandoned the course or been dismissed from it. If an interruption is not temporary (eg, if you have agreed with your institution to take a whole year out of your course), you may be able to claim CA.[85]

Supervised study

'**Supervised study**' does not depend on whether your supervisor (ie, teacher, tutor, lecturer) is present with you.[86] If your study is directed to your course of education and the curriculum of your course and it is undertaken to meet the reasonable requirements of your course, it normally counts as supervised study. It counts regardless of whether that study is undertaken on or off the premises of the educational institution you attend.

'Unsupervised study' means work beyond the reasonable requirements of your course. In assessing your hours of attendance, evidence from your educational institution about the amount of time you are expected to study to complete your course is important.

Contribution-based jobseeker's allowance

If you come under the universal credit (UC) system (see p20) and are claiming contribution-based jobseeker's allowance (JSA), the rules in this section apply, not the rules on p874.

Students who are in 'relevant education' cannot claim contribution-based JSA. You are in relevant education in the same way that you count as 'receiving education' for UC.

You are in relevant education if you are:[87]
- a qualifying young person (see p572);
- on a full-time course of advanced education;
- on another full-time course for which a loan or grant is provided for your maintenance;
- on a course which is not compatible with your work-related requirements.

Note: you can claim contribution-based JSA, even if you are in relevant education, if you took time out because of illness or caring responsibilities, you have now recovered or the caring responsibilities have ended, and you are waiting to rejoin your course.

National insurance credits

You may be able to receive national insurance credits (see Chapter 42) for a tax year in which you were on a full-time course.

6. Calculating income from grants and loans

Note: the rules in this section apply to the calculation of income support (IS), income-based jobseeker's allowance (JSA), income-related employment and support allowance (ESA) and housing benefit (HB). They apply if you are a part-time or a full-time student. For the rules on *entitlement* to these benefits if you are studying, see the relevant section in this chapter. If you are claiming universal credit, the rules are different (see p888).

If you (or your partner) are a student, some of your (or your partner's) income from a grant, a loan and certain other forms of financial support for students are taken into account when calculating the amount of your benefit under the special

Part 6: Special benefit rules
Chapter 40: Benefits for students
6. Calculating income from grants and loans

rules set out below.[88] Your other income and capital are dealt with under the normal rules (see Chapter 14 and 17).

The DWP has issued guidance to decision makers concerning the treatment of various types of financial support to students. Often this guidance only covers some of the benefits to which this section refers. For example, guidance may have been issued for HB purposes, but no equivalent guidance has been issued for IS, JSA or ESA. In addition, the legislation and guidance may not cover all sources of student support across the UK, particularly as new sources of support are introduced. You should, therefore, check the current position.

- The information in this section applies to support available to new students for the academic year 2016/17. For the treatment of grant and loan income for students who started their course in previous academic years, see the relevant edition of this *Handbook*.
- Grant and loan income does not affect your contribution-based JSA or contributory ESA.
- Any student income you have from a grant or loan is not taken into account as income if you are claiming HB and you:
  - are getting IS, income-based JSA, income-related ESA or the guarantee credit of pension credit (PC); *or*
  - have reached the qualifying age for PC (see p147) and you (or your partner) are not getting IS, income-based JSA or income-related ESA.[89]

Student support

There are many types of financial support available. These are paid in the form of either a grant or a loan. Some types of grant or loan are available to all students who meet the conditions of entitlement; others are available on a discretionary basis. The support varies depending on whether you live in England, Wales or Scotland. For more information, see www.gov.uk/student-finance or CPAG's *Student Support and Benefits Handbook*, or, for Scottish students studying in Scotland, see CPAG's *Benefits for Students in Scotland Handbook*.

Grants

The term 'grant'[90] includes any kind of educational grant or award, bursary (such as those paid by the NHS for certain health-related courses), scholarship, studentship, exhibition or supplementary allowance. It does not include payments from access funds (see p899), education maintenance allowances or similar payments.

Some grants are ignored as income (see p894) and others are taken into account. When calculating income from a grant, special rules and disregards apply.

If you are assessed as entitled to a parental or partner's contribution to your grant, it counts as income whether or not it has been paid to you.[91] However, only the amount of contribution you actually receive counts if:

- for IS, you are a lone parent, a lone foster carer or a disabled student (see p877); *or*
- for JSA, you qualify for a disability premium (see p238); *or*
- for ESA, you are a lone parent or a full-time student who gets disability living allowance (DLA) or personal independence payment (PIP).

General rules on calculating grant income

Your grant income is apportioned:[92]

- if it is payable for your period of study (unless you are attending a sandwich course), over the number of benefit weeks in your period of study;
- if it is payable for a period other than your period of study, over the number of benefit weeks in the period for which the grant is payable.

In most cases, the former applies and your grant income is assessed over a period starting from the 'benefit week' which coincides with (or immediately follows) the first day of your 'period of study' (see below) and ending with the benefit week, the last day of which coincides with (or immediately precedes) the last day of your period of study. In this context, 'benefit week' means the week for which benefit is paid.[93]

This means your grant income is apportioned over the number of complete benefit weeks in your period of study. Any part weeks at the beginning or end of that period are ignored. **Note:** this rule does not apply to an NHS bursary (see p894).

Period of study

'Period of study' means:[94]

– for a course of one year or less, from the start of the course to the last day of the course;
– for a course of more than one year, in the first and subsequent years (but not the final year), from the start of the course, or the start of the year of the course to:
  – if the grant is payable for a period of 12 months, the day before the start of the next year of the course; *or*
  – in any other case, the day before the start of your normal summer vacation;
– in the final year of a course lasting more than one year, from the start of the final year of the course and ending with the last day of the course.

If you are attending a **sandwich course**, your grant income is taken into account over a different period. Any periods spent on placement or work experience in your period of study are excluded and your grant is apportioned over the remaining benefit weeks in your period of study. **Note:** this only applies if your

Part 6: Special benefit rules
Chapter 40: Benefits for students
6. Calculating income from grants and loans

grant is payable for your period of study. If your grant is payable for a different period, it is taken into account over the number of benefit weeks in the period for which it is payable.

Specific types of grant income

Postgraduate awards made by research councils and the British Academy are apportioned over the number of benefit weeks in the period for which they are payable (usually a calendar year).

NHS bursaries are paid in monthly instalments. They should be taken into account over 52 or 53 weeks (if there are 53 benefit weeks, including part weeks, in the year).[95] If you are studying for an undergraduate diploma or degree or postgraduate qualification in **social work**, you may be eligible for a non-means-tested bursary administered by the NHS in England, the Care Council for Wales or the Scottish Social Services Council. The bursary or grant counts in full as grant income and is apportioned according to the rules above.

If you receive a **supplementary allowance** for an adult dependant as part of a student loan (or you could have received one had you taken reasonable steps to apply for one), the allowance is apportioned over the same period as a student loan (see p896).

If you receive a supplementary allowance from any other source, but you do not receive a student loan (or could not have received one even if you had taken reasonable steps to apply for one), it is apportioned over the same period as 'basic' grant income (see p892).[96] If you receive a supplementary allowance for an adult dependant as part of an NHS bursary, this is apportioned over 52 or 53 weeks.[97]

Note: students on health-related courses, except nursing and midwifery diploma courses, may be eligible for supplementary allowances for an adult dependant under both an NHS bursary and (reduced-rate) student loan. These separate allowances for an adult dependant are, therefore, taken into account over different periods.

In Scotland, a **care leavers' grant** of up to £105 a week towards accommodation, which is paid during the long vacation only, is taken fully into account as income for each week in which it is paid.

The **Scottish young person's bursary** is apportioned in the same way as the student loan (see p896).

Grant income that is ignored

The following grant income is ignored:[98]

- any allowance for tuition and examination fees;
- disabled students' allowance;
- any allowance to meet the cost of residential study away from your normal educational establishment during term time;
- any allowance for the cost of your normal home (away from college) but, for IS, JSA and ESA, only to the extent that your rent is not met by HB;

- any amount for a partner or child living abroad;
- for IS/JSA/ESA only, any amount intended to maintain a dependent child (unless you still have amounts for children included in your IS/JSA and do not get child tax credit);
- any amount intended for the childcare costs of a dependent child;
- any amount intended for the cost of books and equipment;
- any amount intended for travel costs related to course attendance;
- parents' learning allowance;
- special support grant;[99]
- if you have been required to make a contribution to your own grant (eg, because you have other income, such as maintenance), an amount equivalent to that contribution is disregarded.[100] In the case of a couple, the amount of any contribution that one member has been assessed to pay to her/his partner who is a student is disregarded from the non-student's income;[101]
- an education maintenance allowance, 16 to 19 bursary or similar payments, including a Care to Learn payment, a further education Welsh government learning grant or Passport to Study grant;[102]
- higher education bursary for care leavers.

In addition to the amounts ignored under the rules above, the following fixed sums are ignored.[103] These disregards apply only to the grant you receive for your period of study and not to any supplementary allowances you may be paid during the long vacation.[104]

- A fixed amount of £390 for books and equipment (2016/17 academic year). If your grant includes a specific amount to cover the cost of books and equipment, that amount is ignored in addition to this fixed amount.
- A fixed amount of £303 for the cost of travel (2016/17 academic year). If your grant includes a specific amount to cover the cost of travel expenses for attendance on your course, that amount is ignored in addition to this fixed amount. If your actual travel costs are higher than any sum specified in your grant for travel (which is ignored under the rules above) plus this fixed amount, the additional costs are not ignored and are taken into account.[105]

Note:
- If you also receive a student loan, the above two fixed sums are not disregarded when calculating your grant income, but are disregarded from your loan income instead (see p896).
- For the purpose of these fixed amounts, the 2016/17 academic year began on 1 August 2016 if your period of study (see p893) began in August 2016. If your period of study began on or after 1 September 2016, the fixed sums apply from that date. At the time of writing, the amounts for 2017/18 were not available. See CPAG's online service and *Welfare Rights Bulletin* for updates.

Part 6: Special benefit rules
Chapter 40: Benefits for students
6. Calculating income from grants and loans

Loans

A loan is treated as income but is subject to special rules and disregards. Note that some supplementary allowances paid under the student loan provisions are paid as non-repayable grants and are treated as grant income (see p892).

Calculating income from a student loan

How your, or your partner's, student loan is treated depends on whether your course lasts for one year or less, or for a longer period.[106] The maximum amount of available loan (for a postgraduate master's degree loan, 30 per cent of the maximum) is taken into account even if you do not apply for a loan or for the maximum amount,[107] unless, for ESA only, you are taking time out for ill health and are not receiving a student loan.[108] The special support element in a maintenance loan is ignored as income[109] – you may need to get a statement from Student Finance England showing the breakdown of your loan entitlement.

You are treated as having a parental or partner's contribution to your loan whether or not it has been paid to you. However, only the amount of contribution you actually receive counts if:[110]

- for IS, you are a lone parent, a lone foster carer or a disabled student (see p877); *or*
- for JSA, you qualify for a disability premium (see p238); *or*
- for ESA, you are a full-time student who gets DLA or PIP (see p881).

A student loan for maintenance or supplementary allowance paid to a student on a Postgraduate Certificate in Education course is treated in the same way as student loans and supplementary allowances for undergraduate students.

Dependants' grants are taken into account over the same period as the student loan if you have a student loan or you are eligible for one.[111]

If you are on a health-related course funded by the NHS, only the lower maximum loan rate should be taken into account.

Loan income that is ignored

The following are ignored.

- Loans paid for tuition fees (known as a 'fee loan' or a 'fee contribution loan').[112]
- If you have been required to make a contribution to your own loan (eg, because you have other income, such as maintenance), an amount equivalent to that contribution is disregarded as income.[113] In the case of a couple, the amount of any contribution that one member has been assessed to pay to her/his partner who is a student is disregarded from the non-student's income.[114]

Once any of the above income has been deducted from your loan income, also ignored is a fixed amount of:[115]

- £390 for the cost of books and equipment (2016/17 academic year); *and*
- £303 for the cost of travel (2016/17 academic year).

If your actual costs are higher than the amounts for books and equipment and travel, any additional costs cannot be ignored.[116]

Note:
- If you also receive a grant, the two fixed sums above are ignored from your loan income rather than your grant income (see p894).
- For the purpose of the above fixed amounts, the 2016/17 academic year began on 1 August 2016 if your period of study (see p893) began in August 2016. If your period of study began on or after 1 September 2016, the fixed sums apply from that date.

At the time of writing, the amounts for 2017/18 were not available. See CPAG's online service and *Welfare Rights Bulletin* for updates.

Ten pounds a week is ignored for each week in the period over which your loan income is taken into account (see below). This amount may overlap with other disregards applied to certain war pensions (see p286) and access funds (see p899). A combined maximum sum of £20 a week can be ignored.

The period over which loan income is taken into account

Academic year

The rules give a definition of an 'academic year' for the purposes of calculating student loan income. This definition may be different from the actual academic year of the educational institution you attend.

> **Academic year**
>
> 'Academic year' means a period of 12 months beginning on 1 January, 1 April, 1 July or 1 September according to whether your course begins in the winter, the spring, the summer or the autumn respectively. If you are required to begin attending your course during August or September and to continue attending through the autumn, the academic year of your course is treated as beginning in the autumn rather than summer – ie, from 1 September.[117]

Benefit weeks

Loan income is apportioned over a period of 'benefit weeks'.

The first benefit week may fall before the start of your actual academic year and the last benefit week may fall either before or after the last day of your academic year (academic years vary between educational institutions). This may mean your benefit is recalculated several times depending on when your actual academic year falls in relation to the relevant benefit weeks. You need to make a new claim or check that your entitlement is revised at these times.

If you are required to start attending your course in August, or your course is for less than one academic year, the period begins with the benefit week, the first day of which coincides with, or immediately follows, the first day of the course.[118]

Part 6: Special benefit rules
Chapter 40: Benefits for students
6. Calculating income from grants and loans

If your academic year does not start on 1 September, your loan payable for that academic year is apportioned equally between the benefit weeks in the period beginning with the benefit week, the first day of which coincides with, or immediately follows, the first day of that academic year and ending with the benefit week, the last day of which coincides with, or immediately precedes, the last day of that academic year. Excluded from that are any benefit weeks falling entirely within the quarter during which, in the opinion of the decision maker, your longest vacation falls.[119]

Quarters
'Quarter' means one of the periods from 1 January to 31 March, 1 April to 30 June, 1 July to 31 August, or 1 September to 31 December.[120]

In the first, or only, year of your course, your loan income (calculated under the rules below) is ignored for each benefit week that falls before the start of your 'period of study' (the first day of the first term). This is because you cannot be treated as a student until you actually start your course.[121]

A course lasting for one academic year or less
Your loan is apportioned over the benefit weeks beginning with the benefit week, the first day of which coincides with, or immediately follows, the first day of the 'academic year' (or, if a course begins in August, from the first day of the first benefit week on or after the first day of the course) and ending with the benefit week, the last day of which coincides with, or immediately follows, the last day of the course.

A course lasting for more than one academic year
Unless it is your final year (see below), your loan is apportioned over the period from the earlier of:
- the first day of the first benefit week in September; *or*
- the first benefit week, the first day of which coincides with, or immediately follows, the first day of the autumn term.

It is taken into account until the last day of the benefit week that coincides with, or immediately precedes, the last day of June.

Final year of a course
Your loan is taken into account over the period beginning with either:
- if the final academic year starts on 1 September, the benefit week, the first day of which coincides with, or immediately follows, the earlier of 1 September or the first day of the autumn term; *or*

- the benefit week, the first day of which coincides with, or immediately follows, the first day of the academic year.

It is taken into account until the benefit week, the last day of which coincides with, or immediately precedes, the last day of the course.

Calculating income from other types of loan

Professional and career development loans paid under section 2 of the Employment and Training Act 1973 are treated as income.[122] However, this income is ignored except where it is intended to meet 'daily living expenses' and your course or education has not been completed.[123]

Any financial support you receive that is paid in the form of a loan (other than a student loan or a professional and career development loan), including a loan received from an overseas source, does not count as a student loan or a grant.[124] It is taken into account as 'other income' (see p284).

Payments from access funds

Access funds (which include the discretionary learner support funds available to some students in further education, the Financial Contingency Fund in Wales, any hardship funds offered by higher education institutions in England, the 16 to 19 bursary fund in England and discretionary funds in Scotland) are administered by colleges and universities.[125] Individual educational institutions may call all or part of these funds by other names – eg, access bursary, mature students' bursary and childcare support. Payments from access funds should be distinguished from payments with similar names from other sources – eg, hardship loans.

How a payment from access funds is treated depends on whether it is paid as a single lump sum, in instalments or to bridge the period before you start your course or receive a student loan payment.

A single lump-sum payment

A single lump-sum payment is treated as capital but is disregarded for 52 weeks if the payment is intended for, and used for, any items, expenses or charges which you or your partner may incur (other than 'daily living expenses').[126] However, if the payment is intended for but not used for these items, expenses or charges, it is taken into account as capital immediately. A single lump-sum payment made for 'daily living expenses' counts as capital immediately.

Daily living expenses
'Daily living expenses' are:
- food;
- ordinary clothing or footwear – ie, for normal daily use, but not including school uniforms or that are used solely for sporting activities;
- household fuel;

Part 6: Special benefit rules
Chapter 40: Benefits for students
6. Calculating income from grants and loans

- for IS/JSA/ESA only, rent for which HB is payable;
- for HB, your 'eligible rent', minus any non-dependant deductions;
- for IS/JSA/ESA only, housing costs met by IS, income-based JSA or income-related ESA;
- council tax;
- water charges.

Payments made in instalments

Payments made in instalments are treated as income, but are disregarded in full.[127] However, if the payment is intended and used for daily living expenses, it is taken into account as income for each week it is intended to cover, except for the first £20 a week, which is disregarded. This amount may overlap with other disregards applied to certain war pensions (see p286) and student loans (see p896). A combined maximum sum of £20 a week can be ignored.

Payments before course starts or student loan received

A payment (whether paid as a single payment or in instalments) is ignored, even if it is for 'daily living expenses', if it is made:[128]
- on or after whichever is the earlier of 1 September or the first day of your course, if it is intended to bridge the period before you receive your student loan; or
- before the first day of your course, if it is made in anticipation of your becoming a student.

Other sources of income intended to cover study costs

If you receive a payment from any source other than a grant or student loan, which is intended to cover items or expenses that would be ignored when calculating grant income, the payment made from that other source for those items or expenses is also ignored.[129] You must show that the payment is necessary for you to be able to attend the course. Any sum paid, which is not necessary (or is likely to exceed the sum necessary) for you to attend the course, counts as income. For example, if your grant or student loan does not cover all your tuition fees, any money received from another source such as a parent, intended to make up the difference, is ignored as income. However, if the amount you receive is greater than is likely to be necessary to pay the difference, the amount above that sum counts as income.

Student support once you have completed your course

For IS/JSA/ESA only, any grant income, student loan, assessed contribution made by a parent or spouse/civil partner as part of the loan or grant, or a professional and career development loan that you received no longer counts as income once you have completed the course.[130] However, as most (but not all) types of student support are not taken into account for a period after your course is due to end, it should also be ignored as income for HB once you have completed the course.

Presumably, any student financial support you have left once you have completed your course counts as capital (see Chapter 17), as there are no provisions to disregard it under the rules about capital.

7. Giving up, changing or taking time out from your course

Note: this section only applies to income support (IS), jobseeker's allowance (JSA), income-related employment and support allowance (ESA) and housing benefit (HB). However, this section does *not* apply if (for IS and JSA) you are (or were) in 'relevant education' (see p872 and p874 instead), or (for ESA) you are (or were) a 'qualifying young person' for child benefit purposes (see p881 and p882 instead). There is no equivalent rule for HB. For universal credit rules if you are taking time out, see p890.

If you abandon your course or are dismissed from it, you can qualify for IS, JSA or income-related ESA from the day after that date so long as you satisfy the other rules for getting these benefits (see Chapters 5, 6 and 3). If you are on a sandwich course (see p875), or your course includes a compulsory or optional period on placement, you count as a full-time student during the sandwich or placement period, even if you have been unable to find a placement or your placement comes to an end prematurely.[131]

If you attend a course at an educational institution that provides training or instruction to enable you to take examinations set and marked by an entirely different and unconnected body (ie, a professional institution) and you abandon or take time out from it because you fail the examinations set by the other body (or you finish the course at the educational institution but fail the exams), you may be able to argue that you are not a student from the date you left the course at your educational institution, even if you intend to re-sit the examinations set by the other body at a later date.[132]

If you are taking time out of your course for any other reason and for however long a period, you cannot qualify for IS, JSA or income-related ESA during your period of absence,[133] except in the limited circumstances set out below (but if you are taking time out from a modular or similar course, see also p876).

You may retain entitlement to some student support on a statutory or discretionary basis – eg, through student loans or hardship funds. You should seek specialist advice.

If you complete one course and start a different course, you are not treated as a student in any period between the courses.[134]

Part 6: Special benefit rules
Chapter 40: Benefits for students
7. Giving up, changing or taking time out from your course

Changing from full-time to part-time attendance

If, for personal reasons, you have to change from full-time to part-time attendance on a 'traditional' full-time course, you may be able to argue that you have abandoned your full-time course and are registered on a part-time course and, therefore, that you are not a full-time student.[135]

If, because of exam failure or any other reason, you change to a different course, or your college requires you to change the level of course (eg, from A level to GCSE) and this involves a change from full-time to part-time study, argue that you are a part-time student.[136]

However, changing your attendance may affect your entitlement to any student support you may be receiving. Seek advice on this before acting.

Time out to be a carer

If you are a full-time student and you have taken time out from your course to care for someone, you cannot qualify for IS, JSA or income-related ESA unless you are someone who can qualify while studying (see p877 and p881). In some cases, you may be able to get carer's allowance (see p890).

You can qualify for JSA and HB, but not IS or income-related ESA, when your caring responsibilities have come to an end.[137] **Note:** the rules do not provide a definition of caring responsibilities or when they come to an end. You can then qualify for a maximum period of one year, provided you are not eligible for a student grant or loan during the period, until whichever is the earlier of:

- the day you rejoin your course; *or*
- the first day from which your educational institution has agreed you can rejoin your course.

Time out because of illness

If you are a full-time student and you have taken time out from your course because you are ill, you cannot qualify for income-related ESA unless you get disability living allowance, personal independence payment or armed forces independence payment.

Once your illness has ended, you can qualify for JSA and HB. The rules are the same as for when caring responsibilities have ended (see above).

Time out because you are pregnant

If you are a full-time student and you have taken time out from your course because you are pregnant, you cannot qualify for IS, JSA or income-related ESA, unless you are someone who can qualify while studying (see p877 and p881). It has been decided that, for JSA, this provision does not *directly* discriminate against women under European Union (EU) law.[138] It was also subsequently decided that it does not *indirectly* discriminate against women under EU law, and that it is not incompatible with the Human Rights Act.[139] **Note:**

- Check to see whether you qualify for statutory maternity pay or maternity allowance.
- Once your baby is born, you may then qualify for IS (eg, if you are a lone parent) or you or your partner may qualify for HB.

Calculating income from grants and loans

Grants

For IS, income-based JSA and income-related ESA, if you cease to be a full-time student before your course finishes, any grant you have received is taken into account as if you were still a student (see p892) until the earliest of:[140]

- the date you repay the grant; *or*
- the last date of the academic term or vacation in which you ceased to be a full-time student; *or*
- if the grant is paid in instalments, the day before the date the next instalment would have been paid had you still been a full-time student.

For HB, it is not taken into account as if you were still a student.[141] Instead, it is taken into account until the grant provider asks you to repay it. Until then, it should be calculated over an appropriate period.[142] It could be argued that your grant should be taken into account as income only to the end of the period which your last instalment was meant to cover.

Loans

For income-related ESA, if you suspend attendance on your course because of illness or disability and this is confirmed in writing by the educational institution, you are not treated as having any part of a student loan which has not been paid to you.

If you abandon or are dismissed from your course before it finishes, there are special rules on how your student loan is treated for IS, income-based JSA, income-related ESA and HB.

If you abandon your course before you have received the final instalment of your student loan, it is taken into account using the formula:[143]

$$\frac{A - (B \times C)}{D}$$

A = the maximum amount of student loan available to you (see p896), including any amount paid as a grant intended to maintain your dependants, that you would have received had you remained a student until *the last day of the academic term* in which you abandoned or were dismissed from your course, less any disregards that apply (see p896). This amount is the 'relevant payment'. If, however, you were paid in two or more instalments in a quarter (eg, monthly, as is currently the case for Scottish students studying in Scotland), A = the relevant payment that you would have received, calculated in the same way except that it

Part 6: Special benefit rules
Chapter 40: Benefits for students
7. Giving up, changing or taking time out from your course

is the amount that you would have received had you remained a student up until *the day you abandoned or were dismissed from your course.*

B = the number of benefit weeks immediately following the benefit week which includes the first day of your academic year to the benefit week immediately before that which includes the day on which you abandoned or were dismissed from your course (for HB, calculate up until the week that includes the one in which you left the course).

C = the weekly amount of student loan for the academic year which would have been taken into account to calculate your benefit under the normal rules (see p896) but without applying the £10 a week disregard (see p896). This applies regardless of whether you were actually entitled to benefit before you abandoned or were dismissed from your course.

D = the number of benefit weeks beginning with the benefit week which includes the day on which you abandoned or were dismissed from your course and ending with the benefit week which includes the last day of the last 'quarter' (see p899) for which your relevant payment (see A) would have been payable to you had you remained on your course, or to the day before which you would have been due your next loan payment, if earlier.

Example

Bhavna abandons her three-year degree course at a university outside London on 28 October 2016 during the first term of her second year. Her benefit week starts on a Tuesday. Her assumed maximum loan income (ignoring any special support element) would have been taken into account for 42 weeks (first complete benefit week in September to last complete benefit week in June).

Step one: calculate the relevant payment

Loan instalment paid for first term (33% x £5,878)	£1,939.74
less deduction for books and travel	£693.00
Total taken into account	**£1,246.74**

Step two: calculate the benefit weeks prior to leaving the course

6 September 2016 to 24 October 2016	=	**7 weeks**

Step three: calculate maximum loan for the academic year

Maximum loan	£5,878
less deduction for books and travel	£693
Total loan	£5,185
Weekly amount	
(£5,185 ÷ 42 weeks)	=	**£123.45**

Step four: calculate complete benefit weeks from the benefit week including the date of abandonment to the end of the benefit week including the end of the quarter

25 October 2016 to 2 January 2017	=	**10 weeks**

$$\frac{1{,}246.74 - (7 \times 123.45)}{10} = £38.25$$

Therefore, £38.25 a week is taken into account from 25 October 2016 to 2 January 2017 (10 weeks) and nothing thereafter.

Note: this formula can result in a nil loan income figure depending on the exact date in your term that you abandon, or are dismissed from, your course.

If you voluntarily repay your student loan, for IS, income-based JSA and income-related ESA you are treated as still having that loan income calculated under the above rules.[144] However, for all the benefits, guidance to decision makers says you should not be treated as having any loan income if the Student Loans Company demands you repay the loan instalment immediately.[145]

Notes

1. **Income support and jobseeker's allowance**
   1 s124(1)(d) SSCBA 1992; s1(2)(g) JSA 1995
   2 Reg 54(4A) JSA Regs
   3 **IS** Reg 12 IS Regs
     JSA Reg 54 JSA Regs
   4 Regs 4ZA and 13(2)(a)-(e) IS Regs
   5 Reg 2(1)(b)(i)&(ii) C(LC)SSB Regs; reg 13(2)(a) and (b) IS Regs; Vol 6 Ch 30, para 30525 DMG
   6 R(IS) 9/94
   7 R(IS) 9/94
   8 CIS/11766/1996
   9 R(IS) 9/94
   10 Reg 13(3)(a)(ii) IS Regs
   11 R(SB) 2/87
   12 CIS/11441/1995
   13 s1(2)(g) JSA 1995; regs 54, 57(2) and (4)(a) and 61(1)(c) JSA Regs
   14 Reg 54(3) and (4) JSA Regs
   15 **IS** Reg 4ZA(2) IS Regs
     JSA Reg 15(a) JSA Regs
   16 **IS** Reg 61(1) IS Regs
     JSA Reg 1(3) JSA Regs
     Both Definition of 'full-time student'
   17 **IS** Reg 2(1), definition of 'period of study', IS Regs
     JSA Reg 1(3A) JSA Regs
     HB Reg 53(2)(b) HB Regs
   18 **IS** Reg 61(1), definition of 'last day of the course', IS Regs
     JSA Reg 130, definition of 'last day of the course', JSA Regs
     HB Reg 53(1), definition of 'last day of the course', HB Regs

   19 Reg 4, definition of 'period of study', JSA Regs
   20 **IS** Reg 61(1), definitions of 'full-time course of advanced education' and 'full-time course of study', IS Regs; Vol 6 Ch 30, para 30148 DMG
     JSA Reg 1(3), definition of 'full-time student', JSA Regs
     HB Reg 53(1), definition of 'full-time course of study', HB Regs
   21 Vol 6 Ch 30, paras 30197-98 DMG
   22 **IS** Reg 61, definitions of 'full-time course of advanced education' and 'full-time course of study', IS Regs; Vol 6 Ch 30, para 30149 DMG
     JSA Reg 1(3), definition of 'full-time student', JSA Regs
     HB Reg 53(1), definitions of 'full-time course of study' and 'higher education', HB Regs
   23 **IS** Reg 61(1) IS Regs
     JSA Reg 1(3) JSA Regs
     HB Reg 53(1) HB Regs
     All Definition of 'sandwich course'
   24 R(IS) 19/98
   25 **IS** Reg 61(4) IS Regs
     JSA Reg 1(3C) JSA Regs
     HB Reg 53(4) HB Regs
   26 **IS** Reg 61(2)(a) IS Regs
     JSA Reg 1(3A)(a) JSA Regs
     HB Reg 53(2)(a) HB Regs
   27 **IS** Reg 61(3)(b) IS Regs
     JSA Reg 1(3B)(b) JSA Regs
     HB Reg 53(3)(b) HB Regs
   28 **IS** Reg 61(3)(a) IS Regs
     JSA Reg 1(3B)(a) JSA Regs
     HB Reg 53(3)(a) HB Regs

6

Part 6: Special benefit rules
Chapter 40: Benefits for students
Notes

29 R(IS) 15/98; R(IS) 7/99; CJSA/836/1998; R(IS)1/00; *Chief Adjudication Officer v Webber* [1997] 4 All ER 274
30 R(SB) 40/83; R(SB) 41/83
31 **IS** Reg 61, definitions of 'full-time course of advanced education' and 'full-time course of study', IS Regs
JSA Reg 1(3), definition of 'full-time student', JSA Regs
32 Reg 4ZA and Sch 1B IS Regs
33 Reg 15(2) and (3) JSA Regs
34 Reg 14(1)(a) JSA Regs
35 Reg 14(1)(k) JSA Regs
36 Reg 7(2) JSA(SAPOE) Regs
37 Regs 17A and 21A JSA Regs
38 CIS/152/1994; R(IS) 15/98; CJSA/836/1998; R(IS) 1/00
39 Reg 1(3), definition of 'part-time student', JSA Regs
40 Vol 4 Ch 21, para 21241 DMG
41 Vol 4 Ch 21, para 21242 DMG
42 Vol 4 Ch 21, para 21243 DMG
43 Vol 4 Ch 21, para 21244 DMG
44 Reg 11 JSA Regs
45 Reg 11(3) JSA Regs
46 Regs 2(1) and 61(1), definitions of 'student' and 'course of study', IS Regs

2. **Employment and support allowance**
47 Reg 32(2) and (3) ESA Regs
48 Sch 1 para 6(1)(g) WRA 2007; reg 18 ESA Regs
49 Reg 15 ESA Regs
50 Reg 14 ESA Regs
51 Regs 14 and 33(2) ESA Regs

3. **Housing benefit**
52 There are no student rules in the HB(SPC) Regs.
53 Reg 8(1)(e) HB Regs
54 Reg 58 HB Regs
55 Reg 56(2) HB Regs
56 Reg 55(1) HB Regs
57 Reg 55(2) HB Regs
58 Reg 57 HB Regs
59 Reg 92(7) HB Regs

4. **Universal credit**
60 s4(1)(d) WRA 2012
61 Reg 12 UC Regs
62 Reg 5 UC Regs
63 Reg 12(4) UC Regs
64 Reg 13 UC Regs
65 Reg 14 UC Regs
66 Reg 3(2)(b) UC Regs
67 Reg 13(4) UC Regs
68 Reg 8(3) UC Regs
69 Reg 89 UC Regs

70 Reg 12(4) UC Regs
71 Reg 95(4) UC Regs
72 Regs 68-71 UC Regs
73 Reg 68(1) UC Regs
74 Reg 68(7) UC Regs
75 Reg 68(7) UC Regs
76 Reg 68(3) UC Regs
77 Reg 68(7) UC Regs
78 Reg 70 UC Regs
79 Reg 68(1) UC Regs
80 Reg 68(7) UC Regs
81 Reg 13(4) UC Regs

5. **Other benefits**
82 Reg 5 SS(ICA) Regs
83 *SSWP v Deane* [2010] EWCA Civ 699
84 Reg 5(2) SS(ICA) Regs
85 *SM v SSWP* [2016] UKUT 406 (AAC)
86 R(G) 2/02
87 Reg 45 JSA Regs 2013

6. **Calculating income from grants and loans**
88 **IS** Regs 2(1), definition of 'student', and 61(1), definition of 'course of study', IS Regs
JSA Regs 1(3), definition of 'full-time student', and 130, definition of 'course of study', JSA Regs
ESA Reg 131, definition of 'full-time student', ESA Regs
HB Reg 53(1), definition of 'student' and 'course of study', HB Regs
89 Reg 29 HB(SPC) Regs
90 **IS** Reg 61(1) IS Regs
JSA Reg 130 JSA Regs
ESA Reg 131(1) ESA Regs
HB Reg 53(1) HB Regs
All Definition of 'grant'
91 **IS** Reg 61(1) IS Regs
JSA Reg 130 JSA Regs
ESA Reg 131(1) ESA Regs
HB Reg 53(1) HB Regs
All Definition of 'grant income'
92 **IS** Reg 62(3) IS Regs
JSA Reg 131(4) JSA Regs
ESA Reg 132(4) ESA Regs
HB Reg 59(5) HB Regs
93 Sch 7 para 4 SS(C&P) Regs
94 **IS** Reg 61(1) IS Regs
JSA Reg 1(3) JSA Regs
ESA Reg 131(1) ESA Regs
HB Reg 53 HB Regs
All Definition of 'period of study'
95 **IS** Reg 62(3A) IS Regs
JSA Reg 131(5) JSA Regs
ESA Reg 132(5) ESA Regs
HB Reg 59(6) HB Regs

96 **IS** Reg 62(3) IS Regs
JSA Reg 131(4) JSA Regs
ESA Reg 132(4) ESA Regs
HB Reg 59(5) HB Regs
97 **IS** Reg 62(3A) IS Regs; R(IS) 15/95
JSA Reg 131(5) JSA Regs
ESA Reg 132(5) ESA Regs
HB Reg 59(6) HB Regs
98 **IS** Reg 62(2) and (2A) IS Regs
JSA Reg 131(2) and (3) JSA Regs
ESA Reg 132(2) and (3) ESA Regs
HB Reg 59(2) and (3) HB Regs
99 **IS/JSA** Vol 6 Ch 30, para 30329 DMG
ESA Vol 9 Ch 51, paras 51919-20 DMG
HB paras C2/2.170-73 GM
100 **IS** Reg 67A IS Regs
JSA Reg 137A JSA Regs
ESA Reg 141 ESA Regs
HB Reg 67 HB Regs
101 **IS** Reg 67 IS Regs
JSA Reg 137 JSA Regs
ESA Reg 140 ESA Regs
HB Reg 66 HB Regs
102 **IS** Schs 9 para 11 and 10 para 63 IS Regs
JSA Schs 7 para 12 and 8 para 52 JSA Regs
ESA Schs 8 para 13 and 9 para 52 ESA Regs
HB Schs 5 para 11 and 6 para 51 HB Regs
103 **IS** Reg 62(2A) IS Regs
JSA Reg 131(3) JSA Regs
ESA Reg 132(3) ESA Regs
HB Reg 59(3) HB Regs
104 CIS/91/1994
105 R(IS) 7/95
106 **IS** Reg 61(1) IS Regs
JSA Reg 130 JSA Regs
ESA Reg 131(1) ESA Regs
HB Reg 53(1) HB Regs
All definition of 'student loan'
107 **IS** Reg 66A(3) and (4) IS Regs
JSA Reg 136(3) and (4) JSA Regs
ESA Reg 137(4) and (5) ESA Regs
HB Reg 64(3) and (4) HB Regs
108 Reg 137(4A) ESA Regs
109 **IS** Reg 66D IS Regs
ESA Reg 139A ESA Regs
JSA Reg 136C JSA Regs
HB Reg 64B HB Regs
110 **IS** Reg 66A(4) IS Regs
ESA Reg 137(5) ESA Regs
JSA Reg 136(4) JSA Regs
111 **IS** Reg 62(3B) IS Regs
ESA Reg 132(6) ESA Regs
HB Reg 59(7) HB Regs

112 **IS** Reg 66C IS Regs
JSA Reg 136B JSA Regs
ESA Reg 139 ESA Regs
HB Reg 64A HB Regs
113 **IS** Reg 67A IS Regs
JSA Reg 137A JSA Regs
ESA Reg 141 ESA Regs
HB Reg 67 HB Regs
114 **IS** Reg 67 IS Regs
JSA Reg 137 JSA Regs
ESA Reg 140 ESA Regs
HB Reg 66 HB Regs
115 **IS** Reg 66A(2) and (5) IS Regs
JSA Reg 136(2) and (5) JSA Regs
ESA Reg 137(3) and (6) ESA Regs
HB Reg 64(2) and (5) HB Regs
116 R(IS) 7/95
117 **IS** Reg 61(1) IS Regs
JSA Reg 130 JSA Regs
ESA Reg 131(1) ESA Regs
HB Reg 53(1) HB Regs
All Definition of 'academic year'
118 **IS** Reg 66A(2)(a) IS Regs
JSA Reg 136(2)(a) JSA Regs
ESA Reg 137(3)(a) ESA Regs
HB Reg 64(2)(a) HB Regs
119 **IS** Reg 66A(2)(aa) IS Regs
JSA Reg 136(2)(aa) JSA Regs
ESA Reg 137(3)(b) ESA Regs
HB Reg 64(2)(b) HB Regs
120 **IS** Reg 66A(2)(aa) IS Regs
JSA Reg 136(2)(aa) JSA Regs
ESA Regs 104(6) and 137(3)(c) ESA Regs
HB Reg 64(2)(b) HB Regs
All The Education (Student Support) (No.2) Regulations 2008, No.1582
121 CIS/3734/2004
122 **IS** Reg 41(6) IS Regs
JSA Reg 104(5) JSA Regs
ESA Reg 105(4) ESA Regs
HB Reg 41(4) HB Regs
123 **IS** Sch 9 para 13 IS Regs
JSA Sch 7 para 14 JSA Regs
ESA Sch 8 para 15 ESA Regs
HB Sch 5 para 13 HB Regs
124 R(IS) 16/95
125 **IS** Reg 61(1) IS Regs
JSA Reg 130 JSA Regs
ESA Reg 131(1) ESA Regs
HB Reg 53(1) HB Regs
All Definition of 'access funds'
126 **IS** Reg 68(3) and (4) IS Regs
JSA Reg 138(3) and (4) JSA Regs
ESA Regs 2(1) and 142(3) ESA Regs
HB Regs 2(1) and 68(3) and (4) HB Regs

6

Part 6: Special benefit rules
Chapter 40: Benefits for students
Notes

127 **IS** Reg 66B IS Regs
JSA Reg 136A JSA Regs
ESA Regs 2(1) and 138 ESA Regs
HB Regs 2(1) and 65 HB Regs
128 **IS** Reg 66B(4) IS Regs
JSA Reg 136A(4) JSA Regs
ESA Reg 138(4) ESA Regs
HB Reg 65(5) HB Regs
129 **IS** Reg 66(1) IS Regs
JSA Reg 135(1) JSA Regs
ESA Reg 136(1) ESA Regs
HB Reg 63 HB Regs
130 **IS** Sch 9 paras 13 and 61 IS Regs
JSA Sch 7 paras 14 and 59 JSA Regs
ESA Sch 8 paras 15 and 54 ESA Regs

7. Giving up, changing or taking time out from your course

131 CIS/368/1992; R(IS) 6/97
132 R(JSA) 2/02; CJSA/1965/2008
133 R(IS) 7/99
134 R(IS) 1/96
135 Vol 6 Ch 30, paras 30230-33 DMG;
paras C2/2.41-42 GM
136 CIS/152/1994; R(IS) 15/98
137 **JSA** Reg 1(3D) and (3E) JSA Regs
HB Reg 56(6) and (7) HB Regs
138 R(JSA) 3/02
139 *CM v SSWP* [2009] UKUT 43 (AAC); R(IS)
7/09
140 **IS** Regs 29(2B) and 32(6A) IS Regs
JSA Regs 94(2B) and 97(7) JSA Regs
ESA Regs 91(4) and 94(7) ESA Regs
141 para C2/2.425 GM
142 *Leeves v Chief Adjudication Officer*,
reported as R(IS) 5/99; reg 31(1) HB
Regs
143 **IS** Reg 40(3A), (3AA), (3AAA) and (3AB)
IS Regs
JSA Reg 103(5), (5ZA), (5AZA) and
(5ZB) JSA Regs
ESA Reg 104(4)-(6) ESA Regs
HB Reg 40(7)-(9) HB Regs
144 Reg 6(6)(a) SS&CS(DA) Regs; CJSA/
549/03
145 Vol 6 Ch 30, para 30470 DMG; para C2/
2.421 GM

Chapter 41

Benefits in hospital, care homes, prison and in other special circumstances

This chapter covers:
1. Hospital patients (below)
2. People in care homes and similar accommodation (p917)
3. Prisoners (p925)
4. Paying for your normal home (p933)
5. 16/17-year-old care leavers (p936)
6. People without accommodation (p938)
7. People involved in a trade dispute (p940)

Key facts

- Your benefit entitlement may be affected if you (or your partner, child or non-dependant) go into hospital, a care home or prison. It may also be affected if you are without accommodation, if you are aged 16 or 17 and were previously looked after by a local authority, or if you or your partner are involved in a trade dispute.
- Some benefits are not payable, or are payable at a reduced rate, either immediately or after a specified period.
- You should always notify the relevant benefit authority as soon as possible if any of the above circumstances apply, or cease to apply, to avoid being overpaid or underpaid.

1. Hospital patients

Many benefits are affected after you, your partner or child have been a patient in a hospital, or in a similar institution to a hospital, for a period of time. In some cases, benefit is no longer paid. In other cases, it is paid at a reduced rate.

See p933 for information on paying for your normal home while you are a patient.

Part 6: Special benefit rules
Chapter 41: Benefits in hospital, care homes, prison and in other special circumstances
1. Hospital patients

You can arrange for someone else to collect your benefit while you are a patient (see p1173). If you are unable to manage your affairs, someone else can act as your appointee (see p1149).

Always inform the relevant benefit authority as soon as you can if your benefits may be affected by the rules described below to avoid being overpaid or underpaid.

Who counts as a patient

You count as a 'patient' if you are being maintained free of charge while undergoing medical or other treatment as an inpatient in a hospital or 'similar institution'. The treatment must be provided and funded under NHS legislation, or in a hospital or similar institution which is maintained or administered by the Defence Council.[1] You do *not* count as a patient if you are getting treatment as a private patient, you are meeting the cost of your treatment in a private hospital, or your placement is funded by a local authority.[2]

Note: the universal credit (UC) rules do not refer to 'patients', but your UC may be affected if you (or your partner or child) have been in hospital or a similar institution for a period of time (see p917).

Definitions
'Hospitals' include all NHS hospitals, armed forces hospitals and special hospitals such as Broadmoor and Rampton. Prison hospital wings do not count as hospitals.[3]
A **'similar institution'** to a hospital is not defined in the law, but can include some care homes (see below), hospices and rehabilitation units that provide medical or nursing care.[4]
'Medical or other treatment' is treatment by a doctor, dentist or professionally qualified or trained nurse, or by someone under the supervision of such a person.[5]

If you are in a care home, you do not count as a patient merely because the NHS is contributing to the cost of your nursing care. However, if your nursing needs are more than incidental and ancillary to any other care needs you may have, the NHS is responsible for meeting your care home costs in full. In this case, you count as a patient. The NHS must carry out an assessment to decide whether it is responsible for your continuing care. If it decides it is, you should only be treated as a patient for benefit purposes from the day of the decision.[6] If you are *not* getting medical or other treatment at the care home, but get this elsewhere (eg, at an out patient clinic), you should not count as a patient, but you may be affected by the rules for care homes (see p918).[7]

Note: if you are detained in hospital serving a sentence of imprisonment under certain provisions, you may be treated as a prisoner rather than a patient for benefit purposes (see p930).

The days on which you count as a patient

You count as a patient from the day after the day you enter hospital (or a similar institution) up to and including:

- for attendance allowance (AA), disability living allowance (DLA) and personal independence payment (PIP), the day before the day you leave (unless, for PIP only, you go straight into a care home or prison, in which case you count as a patient until the day you leave hospital);[8] *or*
- for other benefits, the day you leave.[9]

Example

Hilda is claiming PIP and employment and support allowance (ESA). She is taken ill and admitted to hospital on 1 January. After successful treatment, she is discharged on 21 January.

For PIP purposes, she counts as a patient from 2 January up to and including 20 January = 19 days.

For ESA purposes, she counts as a patient from 2 January up to and including 21 January = 20 days.

Jobseeker's allowance

You cannot qualify for contribution-based jobseeker's allowance (JSA) if you have limited capability for work (see p1003). You must also be available for, and actively seeking, work (see p1027). If you cannot satisfy these conditions because you are in hospital, you may need to claim ESA, pension credit (PC) or UC (if you come under the UC system – see p20) instead. Alternatively, your partner may be able to claim income support (IS), JSA, ESA or PC instead of you. However, you can continue to get JSA:

- for up to 13 weeks during a period of sickness; *or*
- indefinitely, if you are absent from Great Britain for NHS hospital treatment.

In these circumstances, you are treated as not having limited capability for work and as satisfying the jobseeking requirements for JSA. See p701 for further information.

Disability benefits and carer's allowance

After you have been a patient for 28 days, you are not paid AA, DLA or PIP.[10]

However, if you were under 18 when you went into hospital, you continue to be paid DLA or PIP regardless of how long you are in hospital. This applies whether or not you were entitled to DLA or PIP when you went into hospital. If you are under 16 and were entitled to DLA when you went into hospital, you can continue to get DLA after the age of 16 (and have your DLA renewed) while you remain in hospital – you do not have to claim PIP.[11]

Part 6: Special benefit rules
Chapter 41: Benefits in hospital, care homes, prison and in other special circumstances
1. Hospital patients

Your *entitlement* to AA, DLA or PIP continues even though payment stops under the above rules. This means that payment can begin again following your discharge from hospital without your having to make a new claim. Payment can be at a daily rate if you are expected to be readmitted within 28 days.[12]

There is a 28-day 'linking rule'.[13]

- Different periods spent as a patient that are separated by 28 days or less are linked together and treated as one period.
- Periods spent as a resident in a care home (or, for PIP only, as a prisoner) link with periods spent as a patient if they are 28 days or less apart.

Example

Horace is claiming AA. He goes into hospital for an operation on 16 July and is discharged on 30 July. He counts as a patient from 17 July up to and including 29 July = 13 days. His AA is not affected by his stay in hospital.

Horace has to go back into hospital for further treatment on 10 August. He counts as a patient again from 11 August. As there are less than 28 days between his discharge and readmission, the two spells in hospital are linked. When he has been a patient for a further 15 days, he cannot be paid AA.

Note:
- If you are awarded AA, DLA or PIP while you are a patient aged 18 or over, payment cannot begin until you are discharged.[14]
- You can continue to be paid the mobility component of DLA while you are a patient if you have been a patient since 31 July 1995 (other than if you are detained under the Mental Health Act). You are paid at the lower rate (even if you would otherwise qualify for the higher rate). This transitional protection ends if you cease to be a patient for more than 28 consecutive days.[15]
- If you are terminally ill, you can be paid AA, DLA or PIP while you are in a hospice, provided the DWP has been informed that you are terminally ill.[16] In most cases, the DWP must be informed in writing.
- You continue to be exempt from the 'benefit cap' (see p1180) even if you or your partner are no longer receiving AA, DLA or PIP after being a patient for 28 days.[17]

You no longer qualify for carer's allowance (CA) if the person you care for no longer receives AA, DLA or PIP – ie, after s/he has been a patient for 28 (or 84, if a child) days. If the person you care for is discharged and payment of AA, the DLA care component or the daily living component of PIP resumes, you should reclaim CA if you satisfy the rules for entitlement. Your claim can be backdated to the date from when AA or DLA is payable again, provided you reclaim CA within three months of that date.[18] This should also apply when PIP becomes payable again, but at the time of writing the rules had not been amended to cover this situation.

Once you have been caring for a disabled person for a period, a temporary break in caring does not affect your CA (see p557), including if you (or the person you care for) are a hospital patient. You can remain entitled to CA for up to 12 weeks in any period of 26 weeks. This can be useful if you (or the person you care for) are in and out of hospital. However, if the person you care for has been a patient for 28 days and is no longer receiving AA, DLA or PIP (see p911), your entitlement to CA ends, even though you have not yet had a break of 12 weeks.

Means-tested benefits

See p917 for how UC is affected.

If your, or your partner's, disability benefit stops

When payment of your (or your partner's) AA, DLA or PIP stops after being in hospital for 28 days, the severe disability premium included in your IS, income-based JSA, income-related ESA or housing benefit (HB) or the severe disability addition in your PC is affected.[19]

- If you are a single claimant, you are no longer entitled to the severe disability premium in your IS, income-based JSA, income-related ESA or HB, or to the PC severe disability addition.

- If you are a member of a couple, you (or your partner) are treated as getting AA, DLA or PIP if the only reason it is not being paid is because you (or s/he) are a patient. This means that you continue to get the severe disability premium/addition in your means-tested benefit. However, it is paid at the single rate instead of the couple rate. For the purposes of entitlement to the severe disability premium/addition, your carer is also treated as getting CA if s/he would be entitled to and receiving it, but for the fact that you (or your partner) have been a patient for longer than 28 days.[20]

Entitlement to the disability premium in IS, income-based JSA and HB, the enhanced disability premium in IS, income-based JSA, income-related ESA and HB, and the higher pensioner premium in IS and income-based JSA, are not affected when payment of AA, DLA or PIP stops after 28 days.[21] However, these premiums can be affected if you (or your partner) are a patient for 52 weeks (see p914).

Note: for IS only, if you are only in hospital for part of the week and are entitled to PIP when you are staying elsewhere, you can be paid the severe disability and enhanced disability premiums when you are staying away from the hospital from the date the change occurs (or is expected to occur).[22]

If your carer's allowance stops

You no longer qualify for CA when the AA, DLA or PIP of the person you are caring for stops. In this situation, the carer premium in your IS, income-based JSA, income-related ESA and HB or the carer addition in PC can continue to be paid for

Part 6: Special benefit rules
Chapter 41: Benefits in hospital, care homes, prison and in other special circumstances
1. Hospital patients

up to eight weeks after your entitlement to CA stops (see p246). After this, you are no longer entitled to a carer premium or addition. If your CA stops because *you* are a patient, the person you were caring for may become entitled to the severe disability premium or addition.

If you have been in hospital for 52 weeks

You still count as a couple for IS, JSA, ESA, PC and HB while you and your partner are temporarily apart. However, you no longer count as a couple if you are likely to be separated for more than 52 weeks or, in exceptional circumstances (including a stay in hospital), substantially more than 52 weeks.[23] If you no longer count as a couple, your means-tested benefits are assessed as if you were a single claimant (or lone parent).

If your child has been in hospital for more than 52 weeks, s/he may no longer count as living with you (see p224) and no longer be included in your claim.

Note:
- HB and help with your housing costs may no longer be payable once you have been away from home for a period. For information about paying for your normal home while you are a patient, see p933.
- If you have a non-dependant living with you and s/he has been a patient for 52 weeks, non-dependant deductions made for her/him stop (see p935).
- For HB, if you are a member of a couple, a deduction for childcare charges can be made from earnings if one of you is in full-time paid work and the other is in hospital (see p281 and p323).

The rate of IS, income-based JSA or income-related ESA may be lower if you (or your partner) have been a patient for a continuous period of more than 52 weeks, because you are no longer entitled to certain premiums (see below). You may have already lost the severe disability and carer premiums after 28 days (see p913). HB is likewise affected, if you are not (or are no longer) entitled to IS, income-based JSA or income-related ESA.

There are no 'linking rules' with these provisions. This means that if you are discharged from hospital and are then re-admitted, a new period as a patient starts and you can again be entitled to IS, income-based JSA, income-related ESA or HB premiums at the rate you were getting before your admission to hospital.

Premiums and components: single claimants and lone parents

If you are a single claimant or a lone parent and you have been a patient for more than 52 weeks:[24]
- the disability premium is not included in your IS or income-based JSA;
- the higher pensioner premium is not included in your income-based JSA (the pensioner premium is still included);
- the enhanced disability premium is not included in your IS, income-based JSA or income-related ESA;

- the work-related activity component and the support component are not included in your income-related ESA;
- the enhanced disability premium is not included in your HB (the disability premium and the work-related activity and support component are still included).[25]

Premiums and components: couples

If you are a member of a couple and:

- both you and your partner have been a patient for more than 52 weeks:
  - the pensioner premium and enhanced disability premium are not included in your IS, income-based JSA or income-related ESA. **Note:** the pensioner premium is included in your IS if your partner qualifies, or in your income-based JSA or income-related ESA if you or your partner qualify;[26]
  - the disability premium is not included in your IS or income-based JSA;
  - the work-related activity component and the support component are not included in your income-related ESA;
- both you and your partner have been a patient for more than 52 weeks, the enhanced disability premium is not included in your HB (the disability premium, the work-related activity component and the support component can still be included);[27]
- one of you has been a patient for more than 52 weeks:
  - you are paid the normal rate of IS and income-based JSA, but without any premiums for the patient, other than the pensioner premium;[28]
  - you are paid the normal rate of income-related ESA if you are the patient. If your partner is the patient, you are paid the normal rate including any work-related activity or support component, but without any premiums for your partner, other than the pensioner premium.[29]

Premiums: children

If you have a child and s/he is (or you are) a patient, s/he may no longer be included in your claim if s/he no longer counts as living with you (see p220). If this happens, you can no longer get allowances and premiums for her/him in your HB (and in your IS or income-based JSA, if still included). If s/he is still included in your claim:

- you continue to be entitled to the normal HB premiums, including the disabled child and enhanced disability premiums – these are not affected if you or your child have been a patient for more than 52 weeks;[30]
- if your child is the patient, you are no longer entitled to the disabled child premium and enhanced disability premium for her/him in IS and income-based JSA.[31]

Part 6: Special benefit rules
Chapter 41: Benefits in hospital, care homes, prison and in other special circumstances
1. Hospital patients

Other benefits

Child benefit

Your entitlement to child benefit can be affected if your child is not living with you. However, periods of up to 84 days when your child is receiving inpatient treatment in a hospital or similar institution are ignored. If your child has been in hospital for at least 84 days, you remain entitled to child benefit if:

- you are regularly incurring expenditure in respect of the child; *or*
- you are contributing at least the amount of child benefit to the cost of supporting the child.

See p577 for details of these rules.

Child tax credit

Child tax credit (CTC) remains payable for a child, provided s/he normally lives with you.[32] Guidance from HM Revenue and Customs says this means that the child 'regularly, usually, typically' lives with you, and that this allows for temporary absences.[33] You remain entitled to CTC if your child is in hospital on a temporary basis.

Contributory employment and support allowance

You are not entitled to a work-related activity or support component in your contributory ESA once you have been a patient for a continuous period of more than 52 weeks.[34]

Increases for an adult or a child in non-means-tested benefits

If you are still entitled to an increase in a non-means-tested benefit for an adult or child (eg, with CA or incapacity benefit), this is no longer payable once you (or both you and the adult or child) have been a patient for 52 weeks, unless you apply to the DWP to pay the increase on your behalf to:[35]

- the person for whom the increase is paid; *or*
- someone else approved by the DWP. The DWP must be satisfied that the payment will be used for the benefit of:
  - the person for whom the increase is paid, if you are a patient; *or*
  - at least one of your children, if both you and the person are patients.

There are no 'linking rules' with this provision. This means that if you (or the person for whom you are paid the increase) are discharged from hospital and are then readmitted, a new period as a patient starts and you can be paid the increase again. **Note:** if you cease to satisfy the conditions for an increase for an adult, or an increase for a child stops being paid for more than 58 days, you lose your entitlement to it.

Winter fuel payments

You are not entitled to a winter fuel payment if you have been a patient for more than 52 weeks.[36]

Universal credit

Your UC is normally unaffected until you (or your partner or child) have been in hospital for more than six months. However, you are no longer entitled to a carer element once the AA, DLA or PIP of the person you care for stops because s/he has been in hospital for more than 28 days.[37]

Couples

You and your partner continue to count as a couple for UC while one of you is temporarily absent from the household, including when one of you is in hospital. You must continue to make a joint claim with your partner and UC is paid as usual. If the partner who is not in hospital is working, you may qualify for a childcare costs element (see p264). However, if the absence exceeds (or is expected to exceed) six months, you no longer count as a couple.[38] If you no longer count as a couple:

- you can no longer make a joint claim for UC;
- the calculation of your benefit no longer includes amounts for your partner;
- you should notify the DWP as you may have to reclaim UC as a single person.

Children

A child continues to be included in your claim while s/he is temporarily absent from your household because s/he is in hospital. However, s/he is no longer included in your claim if the absence exceeds (or is expected to exceed) six months.[39] If your child is no longer included in your claim:

- the calculation of your benefit no longer includes amounts for her/him;
- your work allowance (see p1670) and the work-related requirements you must meet may change (see Chapter 47).

---

2. People in care homes and similar accommodation

Most benefits are paid as normal if you live in a care home or similar type of accommodation. However, some benefits are no longer payable and some may be paid at a reduced rate. The benefits affected are covered on pp918–25, but see p577 for how your child benefit could be affected if you or your child are resident in a care home.

Part 6: Special benefit rules
Chapter 41: Benefits in hospital, care homes, prison and in other special circumstances
2. People in care homes and similar accommodation

Always inform the DWP (and local authority) promptly if your benefits may be affected by the rules described on pp918–25, to avoid being overpaid or underpaid.

Care homes and similar accommodation

There is not sufficient space in this *Handbook* to cover all the different kinds of care homes and similar accommodation, and the funding arrangements for people living in them. The rules covered below mainly apply to homes which provide you with accommodation and personal and/or nursing care. They do not apply to other types of supported or sheltered accommodation, even if you are receiving personal care services from your local authority social services department (social work department in Scotland). Some homes are run by the NHS, some by local authorities, and some are independent. If your place is funded by the NHS, you may count as a 'patient' in a hospital or similar institution, in which case the rules on p909 apply to you. If you are in a local authority-funded or independent home, you may have to contribute part of the cost.

Attendance allowance, disability living allowance and personal independence payment

You cannot usually be paid attendance allowance (AA), the disability living allowance (DLA) care component or the personal independence payment (PIP) daily living component once you have been a resident in a care home for 28 days if any of the 'costs of any qualifying services' provided for you are met out of public or local funds under specified provisions (see below).[40] Until then, AA, the DLA care component and the PIP daily living component are paid as normal. See p920 for exceptions to these rules.

Care homes, qualifying services and specified provisions

For these purposes a '**care home**' is an establishment that provides you with accommodation as well as nursing or personal care.[41]

'**Qualifying services**' are the costs of accommodation, board and personal care.[42] For AA and DLA, the 'costs of any qualifying services' do *not* include the cost of:[43]

– domiciliary services (including personal care) provided in a private dwelling;
– improvements to, or furniture or equipment provided for, a private dwelling because of the needs of a disabled person, or for a care home, for which a grant or payment was made out of public funds, except if the grant or payment is of a regular or repeated nature;
– social and recreational activities outside the care home;
– buying or running a motor vehicle used in connection with any qualifying service provided in the care home.

The 'specified provisions' are:[44]

- Part III of the National Assistance Act 1948, sections 59 and 59A of the Social Work (Scotland) Act 1968, the Mental Health (Care and Treatment) (Scotland) Act 2003, the Community Care and Health (Scotland) Act 2002, the Mental Health Act 1983, section 57 of the Health and Social Care Act 2001 and Part 1 of the Care Act 2014; or
- any other Acts relating to people with disabilities or (in the case of DLA and PIP only) young people, education or training – eg, in some special residential schools.

In most cases, a local authority pays for the services in a care home under one of these provisions, but it is always worth checking. Local authorities also have powers to provide accommodation under housing legislation and the Local Government Act 1972, in which case AA, DLA and PIP are not affected.[45] **Note:** the First-tier Tribunal can decide that your placement is being funded under a different legal power than the one the local authority has stated.[46]

Note:

- DLA mobility component, PIP mobility component and armed forces independence payment are paid as normal however long you are a resident in a care home.
- If your entitlement to AA, DLA care component or PIP daily living component begins while you are in a care home, you cannot be paid for days when you count as resident in the care home (including the first 28 days).[47]
- Entitlement to AA, DLA or PIP continues while you are in a care home, even after payment stops. This means that payment can begin again when you are no longer resident in a care home. If you expect to return within 28 days, you can be paid at a daily rate from when you leave.[48]
- You continue to be exempt from the 'benefit cap' (see p1180), even if you or your partner or child are no longer receiving AA, DLA or PIP after being resident in a care home for 28 days.[49]
- If the NHS provides nursing services in a care home and your nursing needs are more than merely incidental and ancillary to other care needs, you may be treated as a 'patient' for AA, DLA and PIP purposes (see p910).[50]
- If the local authority is funding your place, it assesses what you must pay towards the costs, using a means test that takes account of your capital and income (including your AA, DLA care component and PIP daily living component if you are a permanent resident). However, your AA, DLA care component or PIP daily living component normally stops after 28 days, even if you are meeting some of the costs yourself, unless one of the exceptions applies (see p920). If you are 'self-funding', see p920.
- If you think the DWP has refused payment of AA, DLA or PIP wrongly, you can appeal (see Chapter 55). You must apply for a mandatory reconsideration first.

Part 6: Special benefit rules
Chapter 41: Benefits in hospital, care homes, prison and in other special circumstances
2. People in care homes and similar accommodation

Exceptions to the rules

There are exceptions to the rules. You can continue to be paid AA, DLA care component and PIP daily living component after you have been resident in a care home for 28 days if:

- you are terminally ill and are in a hospice, provided the DWP has been informed that you are terminally ill. In most cases, the DWP must be informed in writing;[51] *or*
- for DLA and PIP only, you are a student and the cost of your accommodation is wholly or partly met from a student grant or loan, or from a grant made to educational institutions under specified legislation;[52] *or*
- you are under 16 (for DLA) and being looked after by a local authority, or under 18 (for DLA and PIP) and receiving services from your local authority because of your disability or health, but only if you have been placed by the local authority in a private dwelling with a family, a relative or some other suitable person;[53] *or*
- for DLA and PIP, your accommodation is outside the UK and the costs of any qualifying services are being met by a local authority under specified legislation relating to education – eg, at the Higashi School;[54] *or*
- you are 'self-funding' (see below).

If you are self-funding

You can continue to be paid AA, DLA care component and PIP daily living component if you are meeting the whole cost of all the 'qualifying services' from your own resources, or with the help of another person or a charity – known as 'self-funding'.[55] This applies whether you are in an independent or local authority home. You count as self-funding even if:

- you are claiming benefits, such as income support (IS), employment and support allowance (ESA), pension credit (PC), universal credit (UC), AA, DLA or PIP; *or*
- a local authority has arranged and contracted to pay for your placement, provided you are paying the whole cost of all the 'qualifying services'; *or*
- a local authority is temporarily funding your placement while you sell a property (eg, your former home), or where you have entered into what is known as a 'deferred payment agreement'. You must be liable and able to repay the local authority in full when the property is sold, or when payment under the deferred agreement falls due. This is known as 'retrospective self-funding'.[56]

Are you likely to become self-funding?

If you move into a care home and are initially receiving help with the fees from the local authority, the DWP should suspend payment of your AA, DLA or PIP if you are likely to become self-funding in the future – eg, if you are only getting local authority help while you sell your former home, or your capital is likely to increase above the limit of the local authority's means test. When you repay the local authority and become self-funding, payment can resume and any arrears can be paid to you. If the DWP terminated payment of your AA, DLA or PIP and refuses to pay you arrears when you become self-funding, you can argue that the decision to terminate payment should be revised on the grounds of 'official error'.[57]

Days on which you count as being resident in a care home

The general rule is that you do not count as resident in a care home on the day you enter and the day you leave.[58] However, if you:[59]

- are a patient in a hospital or similar institution (or, for PIP only, a prisoner) and enter a care home, you count as a resident in the care home from:
  - for benefits other than PIP, the day you enter;
  - for PIP, the day after the day you enter; *and*
- leave a care home and enter a hospital or similar institution as a patient (or, for PIP only, become a prisoner), you cease to count as a resident in the care home on the day after you leave.

There is a 28-day 'linking rule'. This means that different periods as a resident in a care home separated by 28 days or less link together for the purpose of calculating the 28 days when you can continue to be paid AA, DLA care component or PIP daily living component. Periods spent as a patient in a hospital or similar institution (or, for PIP only, as a prisoner) also count towards the 28-day limit on payment if they are separated by 28 days or less from periods when you are resident in a care home in the circumstances described above.[60]

It can be important to plan periods of respite care in the light of the linking rules so that you can continue to be paid AA, DLA care component and PIP daily living component for as long as possible. This also enables your carer to keep her/his carer's allowance (CA).

How other benefits are affected

If payment of AA, DLA care component or PIP daily living component stops, CA is affected in the same way as for hospital patients (see p911). The carer premium, paid with IS, income-based jobseeker's allowance (JSA), income-related ESA and housing benefit (HB), and the carer addition paid with PC can continue to be paid for up to eight weeks after CA stops (see p246), but the UC carer element stops as soon as the relevant disability benefit stops.[61]

Once payment of AA, DLA care component or PIP daily living component stops because you have been resident in a care home for 28 days, you are no longer entitled to the severe disability premium or addition paid with IS, income-based JSA, income-related ESA, HB and PC. In addition, you may no longer be entitled to the disability, enhanced disability or higher pensioner premium if the only reason you qualified was because you were receiving AA, DLA care component or PIP daily living component.

Part 6: Special benefit rules
Chapter 41: Benefits in hospital, care homes, prison and in other special circumstances
2. People in care homes and similar accommodation

Note:
- For IS and ESA only, if you only live in a care home part of the week and are entitled to DLA when you are staying elsewhere, you can be paid, for example, the severe disability and enhanced disability premiums when you are staying away from the care home from the date the change occurs (or is expected to occur).[62] For ESA, this also applies if you are entitled to PIP when you are staying elsewhere.
- For ESA only, you qualify for the enhanced disability premium if you are getting the ESA support component, even if you are not receiving the DLA care component or PIP daily living component.
- If you are still being paid AA, DLA care component or PIP daily living component (eg, because you have not yet been in a care home for 28 days), you may be entitled to a severe disability premium, even if you were not before – eg, if you are no longer treated as living with a non-dependant or a partner.

Means-tested benefits

See p924 for how your UC is affected.

How your IS, income-based JSA, income-related ESA, PC and HB are affected depends on whether you (or your partner or child) are temporarily or permanently living in a care home. If you are in a care home (on either basis), these benefits are generally calculated in the usual way. If payment of your AA, DLA care component or PIP daily living component stops, you may no longer be entitled to certain premiums (see p921). For information about paying for your normal home, see p933.

Care homes

For IS, JSA, ESA, PC and HB, '**care home**' means:[63]
- a care home (a care home service in Scotland) as defined in section 3 of the Care Standards Act 2000 or paragraph 2 of Schedule 12 to the Public Services Reform (Scotland) Act 2010. If the home comes within the definition, it counts as a care home even if it also has some other function, such as an educational institution;[64]
- an Abbeyfield home run by the Abbeyfield Society or its affiliates;
- an independent hospital (an independent healthcare service in Scotland) as defined in section 275 of the National Health Service Act 2006 (in England) other than a health service hospital, section 2 of the Care Standards Act 2000 (in Wales) or section 10F(1)(a) and (b) of the National Health Service (Scotland) Act 1978 (in Scotland).

If you are not sure whether you live in a relevant home, get advice.

Note:
- If you have a partner, you may no longer count as a couple if you (or your partner) are resident in a care home. If your child is resident in a care home, s/he may no longer be included in your claim (see p923).

- For PC, if you have an 'assessed income period' (see p156), it comes to an end if you do not have a partner and are provided with accommodation in a care home (other than in an Abbeyfield home) on a permanent basis. This means your income may be reassessed.[65]

Housing benefit for your care home

You cannot usually get HB for the rent you pay to your care home.[66] For these purposes, a care home does *not* include an Abbeyfield home. There are exceptions if you were entitled to HB for your care home when the rules changed at various times in the past and you have transitional protection.[67]

Note: if you are on a placement under the adult placement scheme (a scheme similar to fostering, but for adults) living with an approved carer, the normal conditions of entitlement to HB apply.[68] You *can* get HB for the rent you pay.

Tariff income from savings

For IS, income-based JSA, income-related ESA, and if you and your partner are under the qualifying age for PC (see p147), for HB, if you are permanently resident in a care home, the threshold for calculating your tariff income from any capital is increased to £10,000 (see p355). This also applies if you live in Polish resettlement accommodation (certain care homes for Polish people who came to the UK as refugees after the Second World War). Some temporary absences from the care home or resettlement accommodation are ignored.[69] For HB, the £10,000 threshold is only relevant (and only applies) in the limited situations in which you can get HB while living in a care home. For PC (and for HB, if you or your partner are at least the qualifying age for PC), the threshold is always £10,000 (see p388).

Partners and children

- If you or your partner move into a care home permanently (for PC only, other than to an Abbeyfield home), you no longer count as a couple.[70] This also applies if you and your partner are both in care homes permanently, even if you are in the same home and the same room.[71] If you do not count as a couple, your benefit, and that of your partner, is calculated as if you were single claimants.
- If you or your partner move into a care home temporarily, you still count as a couple if you intend to live together again. This only applies if you are unlikely to be apart for more than 52 weeks or your time apart is longer than 52 weeks, but there are exceptional circumstances and the time apart is unlikely to be substantially longer than 52 weeks.[72] If you still count as a couple:
  - your PC and HB continue to be assessed under the normal rules. This means that, once the person in the care home stops getting AA, DLA care component or PIP daily living component, no severe disability premium (or

Part 6: Special benefit rules
Chapter 41: Benefits in hospital, care homes, prison and in other special circumstances
2. People in care homes and similar accommodation

additional amount) for either of you can be included in your applicable amount;

– your applicable amount for for IS, income-based JSA and income-related ESA is calculated in a special way. You receive the amount for two single claimants if this is higher than the amount you receive as a couple. This can include the severe disability premium in respect of either or both of you, as if you were single claimants, even if you are not normally entitled to it at home.[73]

If child benefit stops because your child lives in a care home or is being looked after by a local authority, this may affect whether s/he is included in your claim (see p220). If your child is no longer included, you can no longer get a personal allowance and premiums for her/him in your HB (or your IS or income-based JSA, if still included – see p230). Entitlement to premiums for your child is also affected if s/he is no longer paid DLA or PIP.

Universal credit

How your UC is affected depends on whether you (or your partner or child) are temporarily or permanently living in a care home and, if only temporarily, the length of time you (or s/he) have been absent from your household. If the absence is temporary, your UC is generally calculated in the usual way until you (or your partner or child) have been (or are expected to be) living in a care home for more than six months. UC may also be affected if a non-dependant has been living in a care home for more than six months (see p935).

For the definition of 'care home', see p922. The meaning is the same as for other means-tested benefits, but it does not include an Abbeyfield home.[74]

Note:
• You cannot get the UC housing costs element for the rent you pay to your care home.[75]
• The lower capital threshold for the tariff income rule remains £6,000.

Couples

You and your partner continue to count as a couple while one of you is temporarily absent from the household, including when one of you is in a care home. You must continue to make a joint claim and UC is paid as normal. If the person who is not living in a care home is working, you may qualify for the childcare costs element (see p264). However, if the absence is permanent or it exceeds (or is likely to exceed) six months, you no longer count as a couple.[76] If you no longer count as a couple:
• you can no longer make a joint claim for UC;
• the calculation of your benefit no longer includes amounts for your partner;
• you may need to reclaim UC as a single claimant.

Children

A child continues to be included in your claim while s/he is temporarily absent from your household because s/he is in a care home. However, s/he is no longer included in your claim if the absence exceeds (or is expected to exceed) six months.[77] If your child is no longer included in your claim:

- the calculation of your benefit no longer includes amounts for her/him;
- the work-related requirements you must meet may change (see Chapter 47).

Social fund payments

Some social fund payments are affected if you are in a care home. You cannot get:

- a cold weather payment if you are in a care home (see p922 for the meaning) or Polish resettlement accommodation, unless you are responsible for a child under five or you are getting child tax credit which includes a disabled child or severely disabled child element. Note: you are *not* exempt from this rule simply because you are getting UC which includes an increase for a disabled or severely disabled child. It is not known whether this is an error or the intention;[78]
- a winter fuel payment if you are getting income-based JSA, income-related ESA or PC and are (and for a period have been) in a care home or Polish resettlement accommodation (see p798). If you are not getting one of these benefits, you are entitled to a winter fuel payment of £100–£300.[79]

3. Prisoners

Most benefits are affected if you are a prisoner. Some are not payable, some are suspended and some are only payable for a temporary period. There are also issues to consider if you are given an alternative sentence to prison.

Always inform the DWP (and local authority) as soon as you, or a member of your family, enter or leave prison to avoid any underpayment or overpayment of benefit. If you are being held on remand and are then sentenced, notify the benefit authorities as soon as this happens. Do not assume that the prison will do this for you.

Non-means-tested benefits

You are disqualified from getting most non-means-tested benefits while you are a prisoner. For statutory sick pay (SSP), statutory maternity pay (SMP), statutory adoption pay (SAP), statutory paternity pay (SPP) and statutory shared parental pay (SSPP), see p926. For other non-means-tested benefits, see p926. In some

Part 6: Special benefit rules
Chapter 41: Benefits in hospital, care homes, prison and in other special circumstances
3. Prisoners

cases, payment of your benefit is only suspended pending the outcome of your trial or sentence (see p927). For benefits that are payable, see p927.

Prisoners

You count as a **'prisoner'** for non-means-tested benefits if you are in prison or detained in legal custody.[80] You do *not* count as a prisoner if you are on bail or living in approved premises (eg, a bail or probation hostel), or if you are released on parole, temporary licence or under a home detention curfew (electronic tagging).

See p930 if you are detained in a hospital or similar institution as a person with a mental disorder.

Statutory sick, maternity, adoption, paternity and shared parental pay

If you are a prisoner (see above) you:[81]
- are not entitled to SSP. Your current entitlement ends and a new period of entitlement cannot begin;
- cannot be paid SMP or SPP for the whole of your maternity or paternity pay period, even if you are released from prison during it. If you cannot be paid SMP, check whether you can be paid maternity allowance (MA) instead on your release from prison;
- cannot be paid SAP or SSPP, unless you are subsequently released without charge or after being found not guilty, or you are convicted but do not receive a custodial sentence. If these exceptions apply, you should receive arrears for the period you were detained and payment should also resume for any period of entitlement after your release.

Other non-means-tested benefits

If you are a prisoner (see above) you cannot be paid attendance allowance (AA), bereavement benefits, disability living allowance (DLA), carer's allowance (CA), contributory employment and support allowance (ESA), incapacity benefit (IB), MA, reduced earnings allowance (REA), retirement allowance, retirement pensions or severe disablement allowance (SDA).[82] Pending trial or sentencing, these benefits are only suspended, which means that you may be owed arrears if you do not receive a prison sentence (see p927).

You are paid **personal independence payment** (PIP) for the first 28 days that you count as a prisoner, whatever the outcome of the proceedings against you.[83] However, this does not apply if you are awarded PIP while you are a prisoner, in which case you are not paid PIP until your release from prison.[84] There is a 'linking rule' that means that different periods spent as a prisoner separated by one year or less are linked together and treated as one period.[85] Periods spent in a care home or hospital are also linked with periods spent as a prisoner (see p911 and p921).

You cannot be paid an **increase in CA, IB, retirement pensions or SDA for your spouse or civil partner** if s/he is a prisoner.[86] Your entitlement to an increase in these benefits for an adult looking after a child ends if the adult is a prisoner.[87] If your entitlement ends, you might not be able to claim it again. This rule is not relevant for the other benefits listed above as there are no increases for a spouse/civil partner/adult caring for a child.

For non-means-tested benefits that are payable, see below.

If you do not come under the universal credit (UC) system (see p20), you are unable to satisfy the jobseeking conditions for **jobseeker's allowance** (JSA) while you are in prison. In addition, you are treated as being unavailable for work if you are a prisoner on temporary release. This means that you cannot qualify for (and therefore cannot be paid) JSA. However, unless you count as a prisoner, you are treated as available for and actively seeking work during temporary police detention (legal custody in Scotland) of up to 96 hours (see Chapter 45).

If you come under the UC system, you are unable to meet the work-related requirements while you are in prison. In addition, you are treated as not having met the work availability requirement if you are a prisoner on temporary release under specified provisions.[88] However, you may be able to satisfy the DWP that you should not have to meet a work search requirement during temporary police detention (legal custody in Scotland) (see p1090).

Benefits that are suspended

If you are a remand prisoner awaiting trial or sentence, payment of contributory ESA, IB, SDA, AA, DLA, CA, MA, REA, retirement pensions, retirement allowance and bereavement benefits is suspended pending the outcome. An increase of CA, IB, retirement pension or SDA for your spouse or civil partner is suspended if s/he is a remand prisoner. If you (or s/he) subsequently receive a sentence of imprisonment or detention (including a suspended sentence), you are not paid the benefits for the whole period you are (or s/he is) in prison.[89]

If you (or your spouse or civil partner) do not receive a sentence of imprisonment or detention, or your conviction is quashed, full arrears of any of the benefits that have been withheld are payable when you are released.[90] Arrears are only payable if the normal conditions of entitlement for benefit were met while you (or your spouse/civil partner) were a remand prisoner. For the purpose of entitlement to an increase in your benefit for a spouse or civil partner, you should be treated as still 'residing with' her/him while s/he is in prison, unless your marriage/partnership has broken down and your separation is likely to be permanent.[91]

Benefits payable

You are entitled to **industrial injuries disablement benefit** (but not any of the increases on p687) for periods when you are a prisoner. However, you are not paid until you are released and you can only get a maximum of 12 months' arrears.[92] If

Part 6: Special benefit rules
Chapter 41: Benefits in hospital, care homes, prison and in other special circumstances
3. Prisoners

you are in prison for more than a year, you should be paid for the 12-month period which gives you the most benefit.[93] You are entitled to full arrears for any period you were on remand, provided you are not subsequently sentenced to imprisonment or detention.[94]

You are entitled to **child benefit** and **guardian's allowance:**[95]

- while you are a prisoner. You must continue to be 'responsible' for the child (see p577). If you are in prison for some time, you may want to arrange for child benefit to be paid to the person looking after your child;
- while your child is a prisoner, but entitlement to child benefit usually ends after eight weeks.[96] There are exceptions to the rules (see p585). Full arrears are payable at the end of any period of remand if your child is not sentenced to imprisonment or detention. Once entitlement to child benefit ends, entitlement to guardian's allowance in respect of the child also ends.

Note: if child benefit stops because your child is a prisoner, this may affect whether you can get an increase for her/him with your non-means-tested benefits, and personal allowances and premiums for her/him with your housing benefit (HB) (and income support (IS) or income-based JSA if still included). If you lose the increase (or the allowance and premiums), you may no longer qualify for this. For increases for a child, see the chapter in this *Handbook* about the benefit you are claiming. For IS and JSA, see p230.

Means-tested benefits

If you are a prisoner (see p929):

- you cannot qualify for income-based JSA as you are unable to satisfy the jobseeking conditions. If you need help with your housing costs for your home, you must claim IS, income-related ESA or pension credit (PC) for this (see p934);
- you can qualify for IS, income-related ESA and the PC guarantee credit for up to 52 weeks while you are detained in custody awaiting trial or sentence, but you only get your housing costs paid (see p934). These stop once you have been sentenced;[97]
- you can qualify for HB for a limited period (see p934);
- you cannot get any savings credit of PC;[98]
- you may be entitled to the PC severe disability additional amount if you do not receive a sentence of imprisonment and you are given arrears of AA or DLA on your release.[99]

If you have a non-dependant who is a prisoner, no non-dependant deduction is made for her/him.[100] However, for HB you may no longer qualify for a bedroom for her/him after a period. See p67 and p464 for further information about non-dependant deductions.

For information about UC if you (or your partner or child) are a prisoner, see below.

Prisoners

For IS, JSA, ESA, PC and HB, you count as a '**prisoner**' if you are:[101]

– detained in custody (eg, in prison or a young offenders' institution) awaiting trial or sentence (on remand) or following a sentence of imprisonment; *or*

– on temporary release under specific provisions (this does not include parole licence).

You do not count as a prisoner if you are detained in hospital under specific mental health provisions (but see p930 if you received a prison sentence as a result of a criminal conviction). Check to see whether your benefit is affected by the special rules for hospital patients instead (see p913). In addition, you do not count as a prisoner if you are:

• released on licence or parole; *or*
• on bail or living in approved premises – eg, a bail or probation hostel; *or*
• released under a home detention curfew (electronic tagging).

Partners and children

If you have a partner and one of you is a prisoner:

• you no longer count as a couple for IS, income-based JSA, income-related ESA or PC;[102]
• you continue to count as a couple for HB, provided you intend to live together again and the prisoner is unlikely to be away for substantially longer than 52 weeks.[103] If the partner who is not a prisoner is working, s/he may be able to have childcare costs deducted from her/his earnings (see p281 and p323).[104]

If you no longer count as a couple, the partner who is *not* a prisoner can claim benefit as a single person (or lone parent).

If child benefit stops because your child is a prisoner, s/he may no longer be included in your claim for HB, IS or income-based JSA, in which case your entitlement to a personal allowance and premiums for her/him might be affected.

Child tax credit (CTC) continues to be paid for your child, unless s/he has been sentenced to more than four months in prison, in which case CTC stops and s/he no longer counts as a dependant for working tax credit (WTC).[105]

Universal credit

If you are a prisoner (see above – the definition is the same as for means-tested benefits), you can get the UC housing costs element for up to six months. To be entitled, you must have been getting the housing costs element immediately before you were a prisoner.[106] You do not get any other element. See p934 for details.

Part 6: Special benefit rules
Chapter 41: Benefits in hospital, care homes, prison and in other special circumstances
3. Prisoners

If your partner or a child included in your claim is a prisoner, see below. If you have a non-dependant who is a prisoner, no deduction is made from your housing costs element for housing costs contributions (see p512), but you may no longer qualify for a bedroom for her/him after a period (see p505).[107]

Couples

If you are a member of a couple and one of you is a prisoner, or is serving a prison sentence while detained in hospital, the other partner can claim UC as a single claimant, however long the term of imprisonment.[108] Provided you still count as a couple, your and your partner's income and capital are still assessed jointly, but the amount of your UC is that for a single person.[109] If the partner who is not a prisoner is working, you may qualify for a childcare costs element (see p264). In any case, if the absence from the household exceeds (or is expected to exceed) six months, you no longer count as a couple.[110] The amount of your housing costs element for rent payments may be affected (see p933).

Children

If your child is a prisoner, s/he can no longer be included in your claim (see p223).[111] If your child is no longer included in your claim:
- the calculation of your benefit no longer includes amounts for her/him;
- the amount of your housing costs element for rent payments may be affected (see p933);
- the work allowance which applies to you and work-related requirements you must meet may change (see Chapter 47).

Social fund payments

You cannot get a winter fuel payment if you are serving a custodial sentence (see p798). You cannot get other social fund payments if you are not getting a qualifying benefit (see Chapter 36).[112]

If you are detained under mental health legislation

Special rules apply for non-means-tested benefits (other than contribution-based JSA, SSP, SMP, SAP, SPP and SSPP) and for IS, income-related ESA, PC and UC, if, although you received a prison sentence as a result of a criminal conviction, you are currently detained in a hospital or similar institution as a person with a mental disorder under sections 45A or 47 of the Mental Health Act 1983, section 59A of the Criminal Procedure (Scotland) Act 1995 or section 136 of the Mental Health (Care and Treatment) (Scotland) Act 2003. This applies if you are:[113]
- ordered to be detained in hospital by a court after you are convicted, where the court specifies a length of sentence; *or*
- sent to prison, but later transferred to hospital by order.

If this applies, although you are a hospital patient, you are treated as a prisoner for the above benefits, but only until you would have been entitled to be released under your original sentence or, if you are held under an indeterminate sentence (eg, you are a life prisoner), until your release is authorised.[114] After that, if you are still in hospital, your benefit might be affected under the rules that apply to hospital patients (see p909).

Note:

- The rules do not apply to JSA, but in this situation you are unable to satisfy the jobseeking conditions (or, if you come under the UC system, the work-related requirements).
- If you are detained in a hospital or similar institution under provisions other than those listed above (eg, you were convicted of a criminal offence but were ordered to be detained in hospital and were not given a prison sentence), you might be paid non-means-tested benefits, or you may qualify for IS, income-related ESA, PC or UC. Check whether your benefit is affected under the rules that apply to hospital patients.

Community sentences

If you have been given a community sentence that involves punishment or supervision in the community, you do not count as a prisoner. However, you should bear the following in mind.

- There might be a question about whether you satisfy the jobseeking conditions for JSA (or the work-related requirements for UC or JSA if you come under the UC system – see p20). Guidance suggests that Jobcentre Plus should liaise with the Probation Service (in Scotland, Criminal Justice Social Work Services) to avoid any problems.[115]
- If you undertake basic skills training and are treated as a full-time student, this may affect your entitlement to benefits (see Chapter 40).
- You should be able to argue that the notional income rules for means-tested benefits should not apply if you participate in unpaid work as part of your sentence (see p301).

If you are on bail or living in approved premises

Your non-means-tested benefits are paid as normal if you are on bail or living in approved premises (eg, a bail or probation hostel) or other accommodation as a condition of bail. However, special rules can apply for means-tested benefits.

For IS, income-based JSA, income-related ESA, PC and HB, if you have a partner and you are temporarily separated because one of you is living away from home, you still count as a couple if you intend to live together again, but only if you are unlikely to be apart for more than 52 weeks or, in exceptional circumstances, substantially longer than 52 weeks.[116] For IS, income-based JSA and income-related ESA only, if one of you is living in an approved bail or

Part 6: Special benefit rules
Chapter 41: Benefits in hospital, care homes, prison and in other special circumstances
3. Prisoners

probation hostel, your applicable amount is calculated in a special way – at either the single rate for each of you added together, or the couple rate, whichever is the greater.[117]

For UC, you and your partner continue to count as a couple while one of you is temporarily absent from the household. You must continue to make a joint claim and UC is paid as normal. However, if the absence exceeds (or is expected to exceed) six months, you no longer count as a couple.[118] If you no longer count as a couple, you can no longer make a joint claim for UC and the calculation of your benefit no longer includes amounts for your partner.

If you are required to live away from home in an approved bail or probation hostel:

- you cannot get HB for the rent you pay for the hostel;[119]
- you can continue to get HB and help with your housing costs in IS, income-based JSA, income-related ESA or PC for your normal home (see p933). These are paid for up to 52 weeks, provided you intend to return home and you are unlikely to be away for longer than this (or, in exceptional circumstances, substantially longer than this);[120]
- you cannot get the UC housing costs element for the hostel.[121] You can get the housing costs element for your normal home for up to six months, provided you are not expected to be away for longer.[122]

If you are no longer entitled to help with housing costs paid with IS, income-based JSA, income-related ESA or PC, to HB for your normal home, or to the UC housing costs element, these can be paid to another person if s/he is (or can be treated as) liable (see p490, p454 and p47).

Benefits on release

If you are **temporarily released** (on temporary licence), you no longer count as a prisoner for non-means-tested benefits. You still count as a prisoner for means-tested benefits (unless you are released on parole licence).

When you are **permanently released** from prison, you should claim any benefits to which you are entitled as soon as possible. The prison gives you a discharge form that can help you prove your identity. You may also be interviewed by a DWP liaison officer before you leave prison, who should point out which benefits you might be able to claim.

- As IS, income-based JSA, income-related ESA and UC are generally paid in arrears, you may need to apply for a budgeting advance (see p175) or a short-term advance (see p1177).
- For JSA, you are treated as satisfying the jobseeking conditions for the first seven days after your release.[123] **Note:** this does not apply if you come under the UC system (see p20).

- If you are at least 25 and are an offender who is subject to multi-agency risk management arrangements, you are exempt from the private sector rent restriction rules for single claimants under 35 (see p426).
- You may receive a discharge grant from the Prison Service, which counts as capital for IS, income-based JSA and income-related ESA purposes.[124] The rules do not say how it should be treated for HB, PC or UC.
- If you are released without being sentenced to imprisonment or detention, you should receive any arrears of your non-means-tested benefits that were suspended (see p927).
- If you are released following the quashing of a conviction, you are entitled to national insurance credits for the period you were imprisoned or detained (see p976).

Help with travelling expenses

The Prison Service can help you with travelling expenses when you are temporarily or permanently released from prison.

The Assisted Prison Visits Unit can help a partner or close relative (or another person if s/he is your only visitor) with the cost of visiting you in prison, or the cost of someone bringing your children to visit you. S/he must be getting 'qualifying income'.

Application forms are available at www.gov.uk, from the prison and from the Assisted Prison Visits Unit, PO Box 2152, Birmingham B15 1SD (tel: 0300 063 2100). You can also email assisted.prison.visits@noms.gsi.gov.uk.

Qualifying income

'Qualifying income' is IS, income-based JSA, income-related ESA, PC and UC, and health benefits on low-income grounds, as well as CTC or WTC. The WTC must include a disabled worker element, or you must be getting CTC and WTC.

4. Paying for your normal home

The benefit you can get to help pay for your normal home may be affected while you, or your partner, child or non-dependant, are temporarily in hospital (whether as an NHS or private patient), a care home or prison. **Note:** if you leave your home permanently (eg, you become a permanent resident in a care home), you are no longer entitled to benefit for it.

If you are temporarily in hospital or a care home

You may no longer qualify for:
- housing benefit (HB), or help with your housing costs in your income support (IS), income-based jobseeker's allowance (JSA), income-related employment

Part 6: Special benefit rules
Chapter 41: Benefits in hospital, care homes, prison and in other special circumstances
4. Paying for your normal home

and support allowance (ESA) or pension credit (PC) once you have been absent (or are likely to be absent) from home for more than 52 weeks or, in exceptional circumstances, substantially longer than 52 weeks (see p53 and p456);
- universal credit (UC) housing costs element if your absence from home exceeds (or is expected to exceed) six months (see p496).

Note:
- Another person (eg, your partner) might be able to qualify for these benefits instead of you if s/he is (or can be treated as) liable to pay the rent or housing costs (see p47, p454 and p496).
- There are no 'linking rules' with these provisions. This means that, if a new period as a patient or in a care home starts, you can again be entitled to HB or an amount in your IS, income-based JSA, income-related ESA or PC or UC – eg, if you are discharged from hospital and then are readmitted.
- You can be treated as occupying, but temporarily absent from, a new dwelling, even if you have not yet stayed there, if you move your furniture and belongings in but cannot move in yourself – eg, because you have to go into hospital.[125]
- For HB and help with your housing costs paid with IS, income-based JSA, income-related ESA or PC, there are special rules if you are a temporary resident in a care home for a trial period. If you intend to return home, you can get these benefits for up to 13 weeks for each trial period (in different care homes) subject to an overall maximum of 52 weeks (see p54 and p457).[126] This rule does not apply to the UC housing costs element.

If you are in prison

While you are detained in custody awaiting trial or sentence, you can get HB and help with your housing costs paid with IS, income-related ESA or PC for your normal home for up to 52 weeks, provided you intend to return home and you are unlikely to be away for longer than this (or, in exceptional circumstances, unlikely to be away for substantially longer than this) and you do not sub-let your home.[127] See p935 for the UC rules. You cannot qualify for income-based JSA while you are in prison because you are unable to meet the jobseeking conditions and must claim IS, income-related ESA or PC to get help with your housing costs. **Note:** you can qualify for IS while you are awaiting trial or sentence (see p105).

If you are serving a custodial sentence, you can get HB for up to 13 weeks, provided you are unlikely to be away from your normal home for longer than this – ie, you are serving a short sentence.[128] The 13 weeks run from the date you were first in prison.[129] So any time you spend in prison awaiting trial or sentence counts towards the 13 weeks. If you are serving a sentence of more than 13 weeks, you may still be entitled to HB, as prisoners serving short sentences are often released early under a home detention curfew (electronic tagging).

If you are a prisoner, whether you are awaiting trial or sentence or are serving a custodial sentence, you can continue to qualify for a UC housing costs element for your normal home for up to six months. However, you can only qualify *following* a sentence of imprisonment if you have not been sentenced to a term that is expected to go beyond the six-month period from when you first went into prison. You can only get the housing costs element if you were entitled to it immediately before becoming a prisoner.[130]

If you are on temporary release under specific provisions, you continue to be treated as a prisoner.[131] This means that, even if you return home, you are still treated as if you are away from home.

If you are a convicted prisoner, you are not entitled to IS, income-based JSA, income-related ESA or PC and cannot get help with your housing costs.

For HB, you are still treated as if you are away from home and these periods count towards the 13/52 weeks for which HB may be payable.[132]

These periods also count towards the six months for which the UC housing costs element may be payable.

Note:

- You should report any change in your circumstances as soon as possible – ie, when you are remanded in custody, are serving a custodial sentence or are being released from custody.
- If you do not qualify for HB for 52 or 13 weeks under the rules described above, you can continue to get HB for a former home for up to four benefit weeks if you are still liable to pay rent for it, and you could not reasonably have avoided this liability – eg, because your tenancy agreement required you to give notice.[133]
- HB, housing costs paid with IS, income-based JSA, income-related ESA or PC, and the UC housing costs element can be paid to another person (eg, your partner), if s/he is (or can be treated as) liable to pay the rent or housing costs (see p47, p454 and p490).

If you are not already getting IS, income-related ESA, PC or HB when you go into prison, you should make a claim to protect your position. These benefits can only be backdated for a limited period. See the chapter in this *Handbook* about the benefit you want to claim for details.

Partners, children and non-dependants

If your partner, child or non-dependant is away from home because s/he is in hospital, a care home or prison, this could affect the amount of your HB or housing costs paid with your IS, income-based JSA, income-related ESA, PC or UC. This could apply, for example, if s/he no longer counts as living with you or, for UC, s/he no longer counts as a member of your extended benefit unit (see p501). Bear the following in mind.

Part 6: Special benefit rules
Chapter 41: Benefits in hospital, care homes, prison and in other special circumstances
5. 16/17-year-old care leavers

- If you live in rented accommodation, you may no longer be allowed the same number of bedrooms under the size criteria (see p409, p418, p424 and p503) and your HB or UC housing costs element may be reduced. For UC, this only applies if your partner, child or non-dependant is absent (or expected to be absent) from home for more than six months.[134]
- For IS, JSA, ESA and PC, help with housing costs might be restricted if your costs are considered to be excessive because your home is too large (see p463).
- If your non-dependant is absent, check whether a deduction for housing costs contributions or a non-dependant deduction should still be made for her/him (see p67, p464 and p512).

---

5. **16/17-year-old care leavers**

You cannot qualify for income support (IS), income-based jobseeker's allowance (JSA), housing benefit (HB) or universal credit (UC) if you are aged 16 or 17 and count as having previously been 'looked after' by a local authority (although there are exceptions – see p937[135]). This is usually described as being a 'care leaver'. Your local authority must assess and meet your needs for maintenance, accommodation and support. In addition, you cannot be treated as a child member of the family of a person claiming IS, income-based JSA, income-related employment and support allowance (ESA) or HB. So, for example, s/he cannot get allowances and premiums for you with her/his HB.[136]

Being looked after

Being '**looked after**' means, for example, that you were subject to a care, supervision or permanence order, or provided with accommodation by the local authority under specified legal provisions.

If you count as previously looked after by a local authority, you *can* qualify for ESA and, in limited cases, for UC (see p162).[137] However, no housing costs element for rent payments can be included in your UC.[138] If you qualify for UC, you do not have to serve any waiting days (see p165) before you can be paid.[139]

Note:

- If you are *currently* being looked after by a local authority:
  - you cannot be included as a child in another person's claim for IS, income-based JSA, income-related ESA or HB if you are not living with her/him (see Chapter 11);
  - for UC purposes, you generally cannot be treated as the responsibility of a person, so, for example, s/he cannot get child elements for you in her/his UC. However there are exceptions to this (see p223);[140]

- a person cannot usually qualify for child benefit or child tax credit for you (see p186 and p581).
- In England and Wales, if you are *currently* being looked after by a local authority and have been looked after for at least 13 weeks starting after your 14th birthday, you cannot qualify for IS, income-based JSA or HB unless any of the exceptions below apply.[141] Similar rules apply to UC, including (from 26 May 2016) in Scotland.[142]
- Local DWP and social services offices should liaise to ensure any disputes about who is responsible for supporting you are quickly resolved. If you are refused both benefit and social services support, get specialist advice.

When you count as previously looked after

You count as previously looked after by a local authority if you are no longer looked after, you are aged 16 or 17 and:[143]

- you were looked after by a local authority (and, in Scotland, were provided with accommodation) for at least 13 weeks. The 13-week period must have started after your 14th birthday and, in England and Wales, ended after you turn 16. In Scotland, the rules refer to being looked after at or beyond your 16th birthday and, for UC from 26 May 2016, to a three-month period, rather than a 13-week period.[144] The local authority must be obliged to provide you with aftercare services;[145] *or*
- in England or Wales, you are not subject to a care order, but you were in hospital, or detained in a remand centre or a young offenders' or similar institution when you became 16 and, immediately before you were in hospital or detained, you were looked after by a local authority (in Wales, accommodated) for at least 13 weeks since your 14th birthday.[146]

The 13 weeks do not have to be continuous. Some pre-planned short-term placements, after which you return to the care of your parent, or person acting as your parent, do not count towards the 13 weeks.[147] For UC, in Scotland, any period where you have been placed with a member of your family does not count towards the three months.[148]

Note: in England and Wales, you are not excluded from IS, income-based JSA or HB or UC if you have been in a family placement (ie, living with your parent, someone with parental responsibility for you or someone who had a child arrangements order for you before you were looked after) for at least six months (unless the placement has broken down).[149]

When you are not excluded from benefit

Even if you were previously looked after by a local authority, you can qualify for IS or income-based JSA (but not HB) if you are a lone parent, a lone foster parent

Part 6: Special benefit rules
Chapter 41: Benefits in hospital, care homes, prison and in other special circumstances
6. People without accommodation

or getting statutory sick pay.[150] Care leavers are not excluded from ESA, so if you are not able to work due to ill health you may be able to claim ESA.

Note: in England and Wales, these exceptions also apply if you are currently being looked after by a local authority and have been looked after for at least 13 weeks starting after your 14th birthday.

In Scotland, you are also not excluded from benefit if you are living with your family or another person who has parental responsibility for you (unless you are receiving regular financial assistance from the local authority under section 29(1) of the Children (Scotland) Act 1995).[151]

You can get UC even though you count as a care leaver, if you (or your partner if you have one) is responsible for a dependent child or if you have limited capability for work. However, you cannot get the housing costs element for your rent.[152]

---

6. **People without accommodation**

Entitlement to non-means-tested benefits, universal credit (UC) and pension credit (PC) is unaffected if you do not have accommodation. However, income support (IS), income-based jobseeker's allowance (JSA) and income-related employment and support allowance (ESA) may be paid at a reduced rate (see p939). If you do not have accommodation, you may have problems satisfying the jobseeking conditions for JSA (or the claimant responsibilities if you come under UC system – see p20) (see p939).

If you become homeless and have no money, you can apply for a budgeting advance or a short-term advance (see p175 and p1177). It is possible to get help at any time in an emergency. You may also be able to claim local welfare assistance (see p856).

If you are homeless, the local authority may have a duty to assist you with accommodation or advice. A child or young person may be entitled to help from social services.

Note:
- If you are at least 25, have been living in a homeless hostel for at least three months and have accepted rehabilitation or resettlement support, you are exempt from the private sector UC and housing benefit rent restriction rules for single people under 35.
- You can qualify for help with payments for a tent and its pitch (if that is your home) with IS, income-based JSA, income-related ESA and PC (see p452). You cannot get a UC housing costs element for rent payments you make for a tent or the site on which a tent stands.[153]

Jobseeking conditions and claimant responsibilities

Even if you are homeless, to qualify for JSA you must satisfy jobseeking conditions (see Chapter 45). If you come under the UC system (see p20), to qualify for contribution-based JSA, contributory ESA or UC, you must accept a claimant commitment and, to avoid being sanctioned, meet any work-related requirements that have been imposed on you (see Chapter 47).

Being homeless may reduce your prospects of finding work, but personal circumstances that reduce your chances of being employed should not prevent you getting JSA or UC. You can be available for work even if you do not have accommodation. However, it must be possible for you to be contacted at short notice in order to satisfy the requirement that you are willing and able to take up any job immediately, or after the amount of notice allowed (see p1078 and p1031). You may satisfy this requirement by daily visits to the Jobcentre Plus office, or a drop-in centre or support group where a message can be left for you – eg, to notify you of vacancies.

Note:
- The fact that you are homeless should be taken into account when deciding whether you are actively seeking work or satisfy the work search requirement. For JSA, when deciding what steps it is reasonable for you to take to find work, the DWP is specifically required to take into account the fact that you have no accommodation and the steps you need to take (and took) to find a home.[154]
- If you come under the UC system, the DWP can agree deductions from your expected hours of work search for time you spend dealing with a domestic emergency or other temporary circumstances, which can include homelessness.[155] See p1076 for further information.

Income support, income-based jobseeker's allowance and income-related employment and support allowance

The amount of your IS, income-based JSA and income-related ESA may be lower than normal if you are a person 'without accommodation'.[156] You get the personal allowance for you (and your partner), but do not get any premiums.[157] In addition, you do not get either the work-related activity or support component in your income-related ESA. Note: there are no special rules about the amount of UC payable if you do not have accommodation.

Having no fixed address is *not* the same as being 'without accommodation'. If you have accommodation, but are staying in different places on different nights (eg, with different friends or relatives), your IS, income-based JSA or income-related ESA should be paid as normal.[158]

Part 6: Special benefit rules
Chapter 41: Benefits in hospital, care homes, prison and in other special circumstances
7. People involved in a trade dispute

* *

Accommodation

'**Accommodation**' is not defined in the rules and should be interpreted widely and flexibly. The DWP says that, to count as having accommodation, you must have 'an effective shelter from the elements which is capable of being heated, in which occupants can sit, lie down, cook and eat, and which is reasonably suited for continuous occupation. The site of the accommodation may alter from day to day, but it is still accommodation if the structure is habitable.'[159]

Examples include tents, caravans and other substantial shelters. However, the DWP is likely to say that cardboard boxes, bus shelters, sleeping bags and cars do not qualify.[160]

* *

Note: if you are temporarily absent from the accommodation you normally occupy as your home, even if you are living a lifestyle as though you have no accommodation (eg, you are sleeping rough), you should be treated as having accommodation.[161]

7. **People involved in a trade dispute**

If you (or your partner) are involved in a trade dispute, income support (IS), jobseeker's allowance (JSA) and universal credit (UC) are affected, as well as benefits paid to you by your employer, increases for an adult paid with non-means-tested benefits and some social fund payments. You can still qualify for housing benefit (HB), income-related employment and support allowance (ESA) and pension credit (PC), but there are issues to consider (see p946).

Note:
- Trade dispute law is complex. If there is any doubt about whether you are involved in a trade dispute, get specialist employment advice.
- If you need financial help when you return to work after a trade dispute, you may qualify for an IS loan for the first 15 days (see p946).

Income support and jobseeker's allowance

You can qualify for **IS** while you are involved in a trade dispute, and for the first 15 days after you return to work (see p105).[162] This may be the case even if you do not normally qualify for IS.[163]

You are not entitled to **JSA** (including hardship payments) for the whole of any week (seven days from Sunday) if you (or if you are a joint-claim couple, both of you) are involved in a trade dispute for one or more days during that week.[164] Weeks when you are not entitled to JSA do not count as part of your 'jobseeking period' (see p699).[165] This means, for instance, that they do not count towards your 26-week entitlement to contribution-based JSA. If you have a partner and only one of you is involved in a trade dispute, unless you are a joint-claim couple (see p120), the partner who is not involved can claim income-based JSA. If you are a joint-claim couple, you can both claim income-based JSA.[166] The partner involved in the trade dispute does not have to satisfy the jobseeking conditions.

For IS, you are (and, for IS and income-based JSA, your partner is) treated as being in full-time paid work for the first seven days you are involved in a trade dispute.

You (and your partner) cannot qualify for IS or income-based JSA for this period.[167] This does not apply if your partner was already entitled to IS or income-based JSA, or you were already entitled to IS, when you became involved in the dispute. If the trade dispute causes a series of stoppages, this only applies for seven days from the start of the first stoppage.[168] After the seven-day period, you are not treated as being in full-time paid work, but your IS or your partner's IS or income-based JSA is calculated under special rules (see p943).[169]

Trade disputes

A 'trade dispute' is any dispute between employers and employees or between employees and employees connected with terms or conditions of employment, or the employment or non-employment of anyone.[170] Note: this definition is wider than that of 'lawful industrial action' for employment law purposes.

You count as being involved in a trade dispute if:[171]

- you are not working because of a 'stoppage of work' caused by a trade dispute at your 'place of work' (see below). This applies until the stoppage ends, even if you are not a party to the dispute or your contract has been terminated as part of the dispute (but see p942);[172] or
- you withdraw your labour to further a trade dispute, whether or not there is a stoppage of work at your place of work.

For IS and income-based JSA, you can be awarded benefit at a reduced rate, pending a decision on whether you are involved in a trade dispute.[173] You cannot appeal to the First-tier Tribunal against this decision.[174] However, the decision maker should then carry out a revision of the decision once full information and evidence is available and you can appeal against the new decision.

Stoppage of work and place of work

A 'stoppage of work' could be due to a strike, lock-out or any other stoppage caused by a trade dispute. The stoppage does not have to involve everyone, or to stop all work.[175] The DWP says that there is no 'stoppage' if normal work continues through the employment of replacement workers or reorganisation.[176]

'Place of work' means the place or premises where you are employed, but it does not include a separate department carrying out a different branch of work, which is commonly undertaken as a separate business elsewhere. For example, a colliery canteen worker laid off during a miners' strike was not 'involved in a trade dispute at her place of work'.[177] It can be difficult to establish that separate branches are separate businesses.[178]

Part 6: Special benefit rules
Chapter 41: Benefits in hospital, care homes, prison and in other special circumstances
7. People involved in a trade dispute

You do *not* count as being involved in a trade dispute if:

- you can prove you are not directly interested in the dispute – ie, you will not be affected by its outcome.[179] This could apply if your terms and conditions will not be affected by the outcome of the dispute, or your employment has permanently ended and you will not gain anything from the dispute, but it may be difficult to convince the DWP that your employment has permanently ended, as when a dispute is settled it is common for the employer to agree to re-employ those who were dismissed during it;[180] *or*
- you can prove that during a stoppage of work:[181]
  - you have been made redundant; *or*
  - you have become genuinely employed elsewhere – ie, not just to avoid the trade dispute rules;[182] *or*
  - you genuinely resume employment with your employer and then leave for a reason other than the trade dispute. **Note:** if you claim JSA, your benefit may be sanctioned if you leave (see p1097 and p1117).

For income-based JSA (if your partner is the claimant) and IS, even if you are (or count as) involved in a trade dispute, the special rules for those involved in a trade dispute do not apply:[183]

- while you have limited capability for work or are incapable of work; *or*
- from the sixth week before the week you are due to have a baby to the end of the seventh week after the week the baby is born; *or*
- from the day you return to work with the same employer, even if the dispute is continuing or you are doing a different job.

Amount of income support or income-based jobseeker's allowance

Even if you can qualify for IS or income-based JSA while you (or your partner) are involved in a trade dispute, the amount that is payable is reduced and may mean that you are not actually entitled to any IS or income-based JSA. Your applicable amount is calculated in a special way and it is assumed that you have a set level of strike pay. Certain income is taken into account, even if this would be disregarded were you (or your partner) not involved in a trade dispute. **Note:** if you are entitled to IS of less than £5 a week, you are only paid if you are receiving another benefit that can be paid together with IS as a single payment.[184]

Applicable amount

Your IS or income-based JSA applicable amount is calculated as follows.

If you are a single claimant, or a member of a couple (without children) both involved in a trade dispute:

- your applicable amount for IS is reduced to nil;[185]
- you are not entitled to any JSA.[186]

If you are a lone parent, or a member of a couple (with children) both involved in a trade dispute:

- your IS applicable amount only includes:[187]
  - personal allowances for your children, the family premium and any premiums for your children (if still included); *and*
  - housing costs;
- you are not entitled to any JSA.[188]

If you are a member of a couple (with or without children) and only one of you is involved in a trade dispute, your applicable amount only includes:[189]
- half the normal personal allowance for a couple and half of any premiums paid at the couple rate;
- any premiums payable solely in respect of the person *not* involved in the trade dispute;
- personal allowances for your children, the family premium and premiums for your children (if still included); *and*
- housing costs.

Actual and assumed strike pay

If you (or your partner) are involved in a trade dispute, £40.50 a week is deducted from your IS or income-based JSA as 'assumed strike pay', whether or not you or your partner receive any payments.[190] Any payments you or your partner do receive from a trade union in excess of £40.50 a week count as income (actual payments of up to £40.50 are ignored). If you and your partner are both involved in a trade dispute, only £40.50 in total is ignored.[191]

Example

Cliff is on strike. His partner is not involved in the dispute. Their only income is £45.50 a week strike pay.

Applicable amount	£57.40	(half normal amount)
less income	£5.00	(strike pay over £40.50)
	= £52.40	
less	£40.50	(assumed strike pay)
IS payable =	**£11.90**	

Other income and capital

Other income and capital are treated as normal for IS and income-based JSA, except that the following payments are taken into account in full as income:[192]
- any refunds of income tax paid or due under the PAYE (pay as you earn) rules;
- any payment received or due because you are not working – eg, a loan or grant from your local authority social services department (social work department in Scotland), if this is made to help with a need that has arisen since you stopped work;[193]

Part 6: Special benefit rules
Chapter 41: Benefits in hospital, care homes, prison and in other special circumstances
7. People involved in a trade dispute

- if you still get allowances and premiums for your children in your IS or JSA, payments made under the Children Act 1989 or Children (Scotland) Act 1995 to promote the welfare of children. Otherwise they count in full as capital;
- charitable or voluntary payments and certain personal injury payments (see p290), except any payments from the Independent Living Fund (2006) or a specified infected blood payment scheme;
- payments in kind (except payments from the Independent Living Fund (2006) or a specified infected blood payment scheme) paid to the person involved in the trade dispute or to a third party (unless for items allowable under the notional income and capital rules – see p300 and p375);
- holiday pay payable more than four weeks after your employment is terminated or interrupted (subject to any earnings disregard);
- an advance of earnings or a loan from an employer (subject to any earnings disregard).

Universal credit

You remain entitled to UC if you are involved in a trade dispute. However, if you (or your partner) have withdrawn your labour in support of a trade dispute, you are treated as having the same earnings you would have received were it not for the trade dispute, even if you are not getting these. This does not apply if your contract of service has been terminated. The definiton of 'trade dispute' is wider than for IS and JSA and refers directly to employment law.[194] **Note:** any strike pay you receive (eg, from your trade union) does not count as income.[195]

Benefits paid to you by your employer

Statutory sick pay

You cannot qualify for statutory sick pay (SSP) unless you are within a 'period of entitlement'. A period of entitlement cannot arise if, on the date it would begin, there is a stoppage of work because of a trade dispute at your place of work (ie, you became incapable of work during the trade dispute), unless you can prove that you did not have a direct interest in the dispute on or before that date.[196] You are not entitled to SSP throughout your period of sickness, even if the trade dispute ends. You might, however, qualify for IS or ESA. **Note:** you can continue to qualify for SSP if you were already entitled to SSP when the trade dispute began.

'Stoppage of work' and 'trade dispute' are not defined in the SSP rules. However, an overtime ban or working to grade does not count as a stoppage of work.[197] For what might count as a stoppage of work and place of work, see p941.

Statutory maternity, adoption, paternity and shared parental pay

To qualify for statutory maternity pay (SMP), statutory adoption pay (SAP), statutory paternity pay (SPP) or statutory shared parental pay (SSPP), you must have been employed for a continuous period of at least 26 weeks ending on a specified date (see p814). For this purpose, any week in which you are not working because of a stoppage of work because of a trade dispute at your place of work does not break your continuity of employment.[198] However, unless you can prove that at no time you had a direct interest in the trade dispute:

- any such week does *not* count towards the total of 26 weeks' employment you need to qualify for SMP, SAP, SPP or SSPP; *and*
- if you are dismissed during the stoppage of work, your continuity of employment ends on the day you stopped work.

This could mean that you cannot qualify for SMP, SAP, SPP or SSPP.

For information about the meaning of 'trade dispute', 'stoppage of work' and 'place of work', see p941. The rules are the same as for JSA.[199]

Increases for an adult in non-means-tested benefits

You are not entitled to an increase of incapacity benefit (IB), severe disablement allowance (SDA), carer's allowance (CA) or category A retirement pension for an adult who is involved in a trade dispute.[200] For information about what counts as being involved in a trade dispute, see p941. The rules are the same as for JSA. If the adult returns to work, you can only reclaim an increase for her/him with IB and SDA. **Note:** you cannot make a new claim for an increase for an adult with CA or category A retirement pension. If you are getting an increase in one of those benefits and lose your entitlement to it, you cannot claim it again.

Social fund payments

Involvement in a trade dispute has no effect on entitlement to a funeral expenses, cold weather or winter fuel payment. You cannot, however, qualify for a budgeting loan if you or your partner are involved in a trade dispute.[201] For Sure Start maternity grants, see below.

For information about when you count as being involved in a trade dispute, see p941. The rules are the same as for JSA.

You do not count as being involved in a trade dispute during a period when you are incapable of work, or from the sixth week before the week you are due to have a baby to the end of the seventh week after the week the baby is born.[202]

Sure Start maternity grant

If you or your partner are involved in a trade dispute, your entitlement to a Sure Start maternity grant is not affected if your qualifying benefit is income-related ESA, PC or UC. However, you can only qualify for a Sure Start maternity grant if your qualifying benefit is:[203]

- IS or income-based JSA, if the trade dispute has been going on for at least six weeks when you claim a maternity grant; *or*

Part 6: Special benefit rules
Chapter 41: Benefits in hospital, care homes, prison and in other special circumstances
7. People involved in a trade dispute

- CTC or working tax credit, if you claimed the relevant tax credit before the trade dispute began.

Housing benefit, income-related employment and support allowance and pension credit

There are no rules that reduce the amount of your HB, income-related ESA and PC if you or your partner are involved in a trade dispute. However, bear the following in mind.

- For income-related ESA, your partner is treated as not being in full-time paid work if s/he is involved in a trade dispute, and for the first 15 days following her/his return to work after having been involved in a trade dispute.[204]
- For HB and PC, it does not matter if you or your partner are treated as being in full-time paid work. See Chapter 43 for further information.
- You may become entitled to HB, income-related ESA or PC (or an increased amount of these) if your (or your partner's) income drops because of a trade dispute.
- For HB, if your earnings are reduced due to a trade dispute, the local authority should take this into account and not just consider your pre-strike earnings.[205] Your earnings can be averaged over a different period than normal if this results in a more accurate estimate (see p305 and p331).
- For income-related ESA and PC, you can apply to have your award reassessed under the rules on variable earnings (see p304 and p332).

Non-dependants

Non-dependant deductions made from your IS, JSA, ESA or PC housing costs and from HB are usually higher if your non-dependant is in full-time paid work. However, if your non-dependant is involved in a trade dispute, this may mean that the non-dependant deduction should be reduced. See p69, p467 and p996 for further information.

Income support loans on return to work

If you return to work with the same employer, whether or not the trade dispute has ended, you can qualify for IS in the form of a loan for the first 15 days back at work.[206] You fit into one of the groups of people who can claim IS and are not treated as being in full-time paid work for this period.[207] However, if you are a member of a couple, you are not entitled to IS if your partner is in full-time paid work.[208] See Chapter 43 for what counts as full-time paid work.

Your income and capital are calculated as if you were still involved in the trade dispute, except that the rules about actual and assumed strike pay, and other payments received because you or your partner are not working (see p943), do not apply.[209]

Repayment of the loan

Any IS paid during your first 15 days back at work can be recovered through deductions from your earnings.[210] If this is not practical (eg, because you are currently unemployed), it can be recovered directly from you.[211] The rules specify the amount of earnings you must be left with after deductions are made to repay your IS loan and the calculations your employer must make if your earnings come above that level on a particular payday.[212]

Your employer normally starts to make deductions from your earnings from the first payday after receiving a deduction notice from the DWP.[213] Your employer *cannot* make a deduction if you satisfy her/him that you did not receive the IS loan. Your employer has to report this development to the DWP.[214] The deduction notice expires automatically after 26 weeks.

You must tell the DWP within 10 working days if you leave a job or start another while part of your IS loan remains unpaid.[215] It is a criminal offence to fail to do so.[216] It is also a criminal offence for your employer to fail to keep records of deductions and supply the DWP with these.[217] If your employer fails to make a deduction (or makes too low a deduction) which should have been made from your pay, the DWP can recover the amount from your employer instead.[218]

Notes

1. Hospital patients
1 **PIP** s86 WRA 2012; reg 29(2) SS(PIP) Regs
Other benefits Reg 2(4) SS(HIP) Regs; reg 6 SS(AA) Regs; regs 8 and 12A SS(DLA) Regs; NHSA 2006; NHS(W)A 2006; NHS(S)A 1978; NHSCCA 1990
All *SSWP v TR (DLA)* [2013] UKUT 622 (AAC)
2 Vol 3 Ch 18, paras 18021 and 18059 DMG; R(DLA) 2/06
3 Vol 3 Ch 18, paras 18028-33 and 18041 DMG
4 *White v CAO, The Times,* 2 August 1993, reported as R(IS) 18/94; *Botchett v CAO, The Times,* 8 May 1996, 2 CCLR 121 (CA); *R v North and East Devon Health Authority ex parte Coughlan* [1999] 2 CCLR 285; R(DLA) 2/06
5 *SSWP v Slavin* [2011] EWCA Civ 1515; [2012] AACR 30
6 Vol 3 Ch 18, para 18067 DMG

7 R(DLA) 2/06; *SSWP v Slavin* [2011] EWCA Civ 1515; [2012] AACR 30; *JP v SSWP* [2013] UKUT 524 (AAC)
8 **AA** Reg 6(2A) SS(AA) Regs
DLA Regs 8(2A) and 12A(2A) SS(DLA) Regs
PIP Reg 32(2) SS(PIP) Regs
9 Reg 2(5) SS(HIP) Regs
10 **AA** Regs 6 and 8(1) SS(AA) Regs
DLA Regs 8, 10(1), 12A and 12B(1) SS(DLA) Regs
PIP Regs 29 and 30(1) SS(PIP) Regs
11 Regs 3(4A) and (5B) and 19 PIP(TP)Regs
12 **AA/DLA** Reg 25 SS(C&P) Regs
PIP Reg 50 UC,PIP,JSA&ESA(C&P) Regs
13 **AA** Reg 8(2) SS(AA) Regs
DLA Regs 10(5) and 12B(3) SS(DLA) Regs
PIP Reg 32(4) and (5) SS(PIP) Regs

Part 6: Special benefit rules
Chapter 41: Benefits in hospital, care homes, prison and in other special circumstances
Notes

14 **AA** Reg 8(3) SS(AA) Regs
DLA Regs 10(3) and 12B(2) SS(DLA) Regs
PIP Reg 30(2) SS(PIP) Regs
15 Regs 12B(3)-(6) and 12C(1) and (2) SS(DLA) Regs
16 **AA** Reg 8(4) and (5) SS(AA) Regs
DLA Regs 10(6) and (7) and 12B(9A) and (12) SS(DLA) Regs
PIP Reg 30(3) and (4) SS(PIP) Regs
17 **HB** Reg 75F(1)(f) HB Regs
UC Reg 83(1)(h) UC Regs
18 Reg 6(19)-(21) SS(C&P) Regs
19 **IS** Sch 2 paras 13(3A) and 15(5)(b)(i) IS Regs
JSA Sch 1 paras 15(5) and 20(6)(b)(i) JSA Regs
ESA Sch 4 paras 6(5) and 11(2)(b)(i) ESA Regs
PC Reg 6(5) and Sch 1 para 1(2)(b) SPC Regs
HB Sch 3 paras 14(5) and 20(6)(b)(i) HB Regs; Sch 3 paras 6(7) and 12(1)(b)(i) HB(SPC) Regs
20 There is no such deeming rule in the SPC Regs. It is not needed because the SPC Regs set out the beneft rates in a different way than for other benefits.
21 **IS** Sch 2 paras 12(1)(d) and 13A(1) IS Regs
JSA Sch 1 paras 14(1)(g)(ii) and 15A(1) JSA Regs
ESA Sch 4 para 7 ESA Regs
HB Sch 3 paras 13(1)(a)(iii) and 15(1) HB Regs; Sch 3 para 7 HB(SPC) Regs
22 Sch 3A para 3(i) SS&CS(DA) Regs
23 **IS** Reg 16(1) and (2) IS Regs
JSA Reg 78(1)-(2) JSA Regs
ESA Reg 156(1)-(3) ESA Regs
PC Reg 5(1)(a) SPC Regs
HB Reg 21(1) and (2) HB Regs; reg 21(1) and (2) HB(SPC) Regs
24 **IS** Reg 2(1), definition of 'long-term patient', and Sch 2 paras 11(2)(a) and 13A(2)(b) IS Regs
JSA Reg 1(3), definition of 'long-term patient', and Sch 1 paras 12(5)(a), 13(2)(a) and 15A(2)(b) JSA Regs
ESA Schs 4 para 7(2)(a) and 5 para 13 ESA Regs
HB Sch 3 para 15(2) HB Regs
25 Sch 3 para 15(2) HB Regs

26 **IS** Reg 2(1), definition of 'long-term patient', and Sch 2 paras 10(6), 11(2)(b) and 13A(2)(c) IS Regs
JSA Reg 1(3), definition of 'long-term patient', and Sch 1 paras 12(5)(b), 13(2)(b), 15A(2)(c), 20F(5), 20G(2)(b) and 20IA(2)(b) JSA Regs
ESA Schs 4 para 7(2)(b) and 5 para 13 ESA Regs
27 Sch 3 para 15(2) HB Regs
28 **IS** Reg 2(1), definition of 'long-term patient', and Sch 2 paras 10(6), 11(2)(c) and 13A(2)(d) IS Regs
JSA Reg 1(3), definition of 'long-term patient', and Sch 1 paras 12(5)(c), 13(2)(c), 15A(2)(c), 20F(5), 20(G)(a) and 20IA(2)(a) JSA Regs
29 Sch 3 paras 5, 6, 7, and Sch 5 para 13 ESA Regs
30 Sch 3 paras 15(1) and 16(a) HB Regs; Sch 3 paras 7 and 8(a) HB(SPC) Regs
31 **IS** Reg 2(1), definition of 'long-term patient', and Sch 2 paras 13A(2)(a) and 14(2) IS Regs
JSA Reg 1(3), definition of 'long-term patient', and Sch 1 paras 15A(2)(a) and 16(2) JSA Regs
32 Reg 3 CTC Regs
33 TCTM 02202
34 Sch 5 para 13 ESA Regs; reg 63(1) ESA Regs 2013
35 Reg 2(2) and (3) SS(HIP) Regs
36 Reg 3 SFWFP Regs
37 Regs 29(1) and 30 UC Regs
38 s39 WRA 2012; reg 3(6) UC Regs
39 s10 WRA 2012; reg 4(7) UC Regs

2. **People in care homes and similar accommodation**
40 **AA/DLA** ss67(2) and 72(8) SSCBA 1992; regs 7 and 8(1) SS(AA) Regs; regs 9 and 10(1) SS(DLA) Regs
PIP s85 WRA 2012; regs 28 and 30(1) SS(PIP) Regs
41 ss67(3) and 72(9) SSCBA 1992; s85(3) WRA 2012
42 **AA/DLA** ss67(4) and 72(10) SSCBA 1992
PIP s85(4) WRA 2012
43 Reg 7(3) SS(AA) Regs; reg 9(6) SS(DLA) Regs
44 **AA** Reg 7(2) SS(AA) Regs
DLA Reg 9(2) SS(DLA) Regs
PIP Reg 28(2)-(4) SS(PIP) Regs
45 CDLA/1465/1998; CDLA/2127/2000
46 CA/2985/1997

47 **AA** Reg 8(3) SS(AA) Regs
DLA Reg 10(3) SS(DLA) Regs
PIP Reg 30(2) SS(PIP) Regs

48 **AA/DLA** Reg 25 SS(C&P) Regs
PIP Reg 50 UC,PIP,JSA&ESA(C&P) Regs

49 **UC** Reg 83(1)(h) UC Regs
HB Reg 75F(1)(f) HB Regs

50 R(DLA) 2/06

51 **AA** Reg 8(4) and (5) SS(AA) Regs
DLA Reg 10(6) and (7) SS(DLA) Regs
PIP Reg 30(3) SS(PIP) Regs

52 **DLA** Reg 9(3) SS(DLA) Regs
PIP Reg 28(2)(f) SS(PIP) Regs

53 **DLA** Reg 9(4)(a) and (b) and (5)
SS(DLA) Regs
PIP Reg 28(3)(a) and (4) SS(PIP) Regs

54 **DLA** Reg 9(4)(c) SS(DLA) Regs
PIP Reg 28(3)(b) SS(PIP) Regs

55 **AA** Reg 8(6) SS(AA) Regs
DLA Reg 10(8) SS(DLA) Regs
PIP Reg 30(5) SS(PIP) Regs
Steane v CAO and Secretary of State, 24
July 1996, reported as R(A) 3/96

56 R(A) 1/02; CA/3800/2006; *CAO v
Creighton and Others*, 15 December
1999 (NICA), reported as R 1/00 (AA);
SSWP v DA [2009] UKUT 214 (AAC)

57 *SSWP v JL (DLA)* [2011] UKUT 293 (AAC)

58 **AA** Reg 7(4) SS(AA) Regs
DLA Reg 9(7) SS(DLA) Regs
PIP Reg 32(1) and (2) SS(PIP) Regs

59 **AA** Reg 7(5) and (6) SS(AA) Regs
DLA Reg 9(8) and (9) SS(DLA) Regs
PIP Reg 32(3) SS(PIP) Regs

60 **AA** Reg 8(2) SS(AA) Regs
DLA Reg 10(5) SS(DLA) Regs
PIP Reg 32(4) SS(PIP) Regs

61 Regs 29(1) and 30 UC Regs

62 **IS** Sch 3A para 3(h) and (i) SS&CS(DA)
Regs
ESA Sch 3C para 3(f) and (g)
SS&CS(DA) Regs

63 **IS** Reg 2(1) IS Regs
JSA Reg 1(3) JSA Regs
ESA Reg 2(1) ESA Regs
PC Reg 1(2) SPC Regs
HB Reg 2(1) HB Regs; reg 2(1) HB(SPC)
Regs

64 *SA v SSWP (IS)* [2010] UKUT 345 (AAC);
[2011] AACR 16

65 Reg 12(c) SPC Regs

66 Reg 9(1)(k) HB Regs; reg 9(1)(k)
HB(SPC) Regs

67 Sch 3 para 9 HB&CTB(CP) Regs

68 HB/CTB Circular A20/05

69 **IS** Reg 53(1A), (1B) and (1C) IS Regs
JSA Reg 116(1A), (1B) and (1C) JSA Regs
ESA Reg 118(2), (3) and (4) ESA Regs
HB Reg 52(3)-(5), (8) and (9) HB Regs

70 **IS** Reg 16(3)(e) IS Regs
JSA Reg 78(3)(d) JSA Regs
ESA Reg 156(4)(d) ESA Regs
PC Reg 5(1)(b) SPC Regs
HB Reg 21(2) HB Regs; reg 21(2)
HB(SPC) Regs

71 Appendix to CIS/4934/1997; CIS/4965/
1997; CIS/5232/1997; CIS/3767/1997

72 **IS** Reg 16(1) and (2) IS Regs
JSA Reg 78(1)-(2) JSA Regs
ESA Reg 156(1)-(3) ESA Regs
PC Reg 5(1)(a) SPC Regs
HB Reg 21(1) and (2) HB Regs; reg
21(1) and (2) HB(SPC) Regs

73 **IS** Sch 7 paras 9 and 10 IS Regs
JSA Schs 5 paras 5 and 6 and 5A paras 4
and 5 JSA Regs
ESA Sch 5 paras 4 and 5 ESA Regs
All CIS/1544/2001

74 Sch 1 para 1 UC Regs

75 Sch 1 para 3(d) UC Regs

76 s39 WRA 2012; reg 3(6) UC Regs

77 s10 WRA 2012; reg 4(7) UC Regs

78 Reg 1A(4) and (5) SFCWP Regs

79 Regs 1 and 2 SFWFP Regs

3. **Prisoners**

80 **ESA** s18(4)(b) WRA 2007
PIP s87 WRA 2012
SSP/SMP/SAP/SPP/SSPP Reg 3(1)
and (2) SSP Regs; reg 9 SMP Regs; regs
18(c) and 27(1)(c) SPPSAP(G) Regs; regs
14 and 26 SSPP(G) Regs
Other benefits s113(1)(b) and Sch 9
para 1 SSCBA 1992; reg 2(9) and (10)
SS(GB) Regs; reg 10(2)(d) and Sch 2
para 7(b)(ii) SSB(Dep) Regs; R(S) 8/79

81 Reg 3(1) and (2) SSP Regs; reg 9 SMP
Regs; regs 18(c) and 27(1)(c) SPPSAP(G)
Regs; regs 14 and 26 SSPP(G) Regs

82 **ESA** s18(4)(b) WRA 2007; reg 160 ESA
Regs; reg 96 ESA Regs 2013
Other benefits s113(1)(b) SSCBA
1992; reg 2 SS(GB) Regs; s19 PA 2014;
regs 2 and 3 SP Regs

83 s87 WRA 2012; reg 31(1) SS(PIP) Regs

84 Reg 31(2) SS(PIP) Regs

85 Reg 32(1) and (5) SS(PIP) Regs

86 s113(1)(b) SSCBA 1992

87 Regs 10(2)(d) and 12 and Sch 2 para
7(b)(ii) SSB(Dep) Regs; reg 14 SS(IB-ID)
Regs

88 Reg 13(1)(b) JSA Regs 2013

Part 6: Special benefit rules
Chapter 41: Benefits in hospital, care homes, prison and in other special circumstances
Notes

89 **ESA** Reg 160(1), (2) and (5)(c) ESA
Regs; reg 96(1), (2) and (6)(c) ESA Regs
2013
Other benefits Reg 2(2) and (8)(c)
SS(GB) Regs; reg 14 SS(ICA) Regs; s19
PA 2014; regs 2 and 3 SP Regs
All R(S) 1/71

90 **ESA** Reg 161 ESA Regs; reg 97 ESA Regs
2013
Other benefits Reg 3 SS(GB) Regs; reg
14 SS(ICA) Regs

91 CS/541/1950

92 Regs 2(6) and (7) and 3(1) SS(GB) Regs

93 Reg 2(7) SS(GB) Regs; Vol 3 Ch 12, para
12091 DMG

94 Reg 2(2) and (7) SS(GB) Regs

95 **CB** s113(1)(b) SSCBA 1992. Child
benefit is not in Parts 2-5 of that Act.
GA Reg 2(5) SS(GB) Regs

96 Sch 9 para 1(a) SSCBA 1992; regs 16
and 17 CB Regs

97 **IS** Sch 1B para 22, Sch 3 para 3(11) and
(12) and Sch 7 para 8 IS Regs
ESA Schs 5 para 3 and 6 para 5(11) and
(12) ESA Regs
PC Reg 6(2)(a), (3), (6)(c), (7), (9) and
(10) SPC Regs

98 Reg 7(3) SPC Regs

99 Reg 6(3)(b) and (4) SPC Regs

100 **IS** Sch 3 para 18(7)(g) IS Regs
JSA Sch 2 para 17(7)(g) JSA Regs
ESA Sch 6 para 19(7)(g) ESA Regs
PC Sch 2 para 14(7)(e) SPC Regs
HB Reg 74(7)(f) HB Regs; reg 55(7)(f)
HB(SPC) Regs

101 **IS** Reg 21(3) IS Regs
JSA Reg 85(4) JSA Regs
ESA Reg 69(2) ESA Regs
PC Reg 1(2) SPC Regs
HB Reg 7(14) and (16)(c)(i) HB Regs;
reg 7(14) and (16)(c)(i) HB(SPC) Regs

102 **IS** Reg 16(3)(b) IS Regs
JSA Reg 78(3)(b) JSA Regs
ESA Reg 156(4) ESA Regs
PC Reg 5(1)(c)(ii) and (iii) SPC Regs

103 Reg 21(2) HB Regs; reg 21(2) HB(SPC)
Regs

104 Reg 28 HB Regs; reg 31 HB(SPC) Regs

105 Reg 3, Rule 4.1 Case C, CTC Regs; reg
2(2) WTC(EMR) Regs

106 Reg 19 UC Regs

107 Sch 4 paras 11 and 16(2)(h) UC Regs

108 Reg 3(3)(c) UC Regs

109 Regs 18, 22(3) and 36(3) UC Regs

110 s39 WRA 2012; reg 3(6) UC Regs

111 Reg 4(6)(b) UC Regs

112 *Stewart v SSWP* [2011] EWCA Civ 907
decided that the exclusion of prisoners
from entitlement to a funeral expenses
payment did not breach the HRA 1998.

113 **IS** Reg 21(3ZA)-(3ZC) and Sch 7 para 2A
IS Regs
ESA Regs 69(3)-(5), 160(3)-(4A) and
Sch 5 para 12 ESA Regs; reg 96(3)-(5)
ESA Regs 2013
PC Reg 8 and Sch 3 para 2 SPC Regs
PIP Reg 31(3) and (4) SS(PIP) Regs
UC Reg 19(1)(c) and (4) UC Regs
Other benefits Reg 2(3), (4) and (4A)
SS(GB) Regs
All CSS/239/2007; *JB v SSWP (IS)* [2010]
UKUT 263 (AAC)

114 **IS** Reg 21(3ZA)-(3ZC) and Sch 7 para 2A
IS Regs
ESA Regs 69(3)-(5), 160(3)-(4A) and
Sch 5 para 12 ESA Regs; reg 96(3)-(5)
ESA Regs 2013
PC Reg 8 and Sch 3 para 2 SPC Regs
PIP Reg 31(3) and (4) SS(PIP) Regs
UC Reg 19(1)(c) and (4) UC Regs
Other benefits Reg 2(3)-(4A) SS(GB)
Regs
All CSS/239/2007; *JB v SSWP (IS)* [2010]
UKUT 263 (AAC)

115 paras 21198-02 DMG

116 **IS** Reg 16(2) IS Regs
JSA Reg 78(2) JSA Regs
ESA Reg 156(3) ESA Regs
PC Reg 5(1)(a) SPC Regs
HB Reg 21(1) and (2) HB Regs; reg
21(1) and (2) HB(SPC) Regs

117 **IS** Sch 7 para 9(a)(v) IS Regs
JSA Schs 5 para 5(a)(vi) and 5A para
4(a)(vi) JSA Regs
ESA Sch 5 para 4(a)(v) ESA Regs

118 s39 WRA 2012; reg 3(6) UC Regs

119 Reg 7(5) HB Regs; reg 7(5) HB(SPC)
Regs

120 **IS** Sch 3 para 3(11)(c)(i) and (12) IS Regs
JSA Sch 2 para 2(11)(c)(i) and (12) JSA
Regs
ESA Sch 6 para 5(11)(c)(i) and (12) ESA
Regs
PC Sch 2 para 4(11)(c)(i) and (12) SPC
Regs
HB Reg 7(16)(c)(i) and (17) HB Regs;
reg 7(16)(c)(i) and (17) HB(SPC) Regs

121 Schs 1 paras 1 and 3(c) and 3 para 1(1)
UC Regs

122 Sch 3 para 9 UC Regs

123 Regs 14(1)(h) and 19(1)(h) JSA Regs
124 **IS** Reg 48(7) IS Regs
    JSA Reg 110(7) JSA Regs
    ESA Reg 112(6) ESA Regs

4. Paying for your normal home
125 R(H) 9/05
126 **IS** Sch 3 para 3(8)-(12) IS Regs
    JSA Sch 2 para 3(8)-(12) JSA Regs
    ESA Sch 6 para 5(8)-(12) ESA Regs
    PC Sch 2 para 4(8)-(12) SPC Regs
    HB Reg 7(11)-(13), (16) and (17) HB
    Regs; reg 7(11)-(13), (16) and (17)
    HB(SPC) Regs
127 **IS** Sch 1B para 22, Sch 3 para 3(11) and
    (12) and Sch 7 para 8 IS Regs
    ESA Sch 5 para 3 and Sch 6 para 5(11)
    and (12) ESA Regs
    PC Reg 6(2)(a), (3), (6)(c), (7), (9) and
    (10) and Sch 2 para 4(11) and (12) SPC
    Regs
    HB Reg 7(16)(c)(i) and (17) HB Regs;
    reg 7(16)(c)(i) and (17) HB(SPC) Regs
128 Reg 7(13) HB Regs; reg 7(13) HB(SPC)
    Regs
129 CSH/499/2006
130 Reg 19 UC Regs
131 **IS** Reg 21(3) and Sch 7 para 8(a) IS Regs
    JSA Reg 85(4) JSA Regs
    ESA Reg 69(2) and Sch 5 para 3(a) ESA
    Regs
    PC Regs 1(2) and 6 SPC Regs
    UC Reg 2(1) UC Regs
132 Reg 7(14) and (15) HB Regs; reg 7(14)
    and (15) HB(SPC) Regs; R(IS) 17/93
133 Reg 7(7) HB Regs; reg 7(7) HB(SPC)
    Regs; Ch A3, paras 3.430-32 GM
134 Sch 4 para 11 UC Regs

5. 16/17-year-old care leavers
135 **IS** Reg 4ZA(3A) IS Regs
    JSA Reg 57, definition of 'young
    person', JSA Regs
    IS/JSA/HB ss6 and 8(6) C(LC)A 2000;
    C(LC)SSB(S) Regs
    UC Reg 8(1), (2) and (4) UC Regs
136 **IS** Reg 14(2)(c) IS Regs
    JSA Reg 76(2)(d) JSA Regs
    ESA Reg 2(1), definition of 'young
    person', ESA Regs
    HB Reg 19(2)(c) HB Regs; reg 19(2)(c)
    HB(SPC) Regs
137 The C(LC)A 2000 was not amended to
    exclude previously looked-after young
    people from entitlement to ESA or UC.
138 Reg 8(4) and Sch 4 para 4 UC Regs
139 Reg 19A(3)(b)(iii) UC Regs
140 Regs 4(6)(a) and 4A UC Regs

141 s6 C(LC)A 2000
142 Reg 8(1) and (4) UC Regs
143 **IS** Reg 4ZA(3A) IS Regs
    JSA Reg 57, definition of 'young
    person', JSA Regs
    IS/JSA/HB ss6 and 8(6) C(LC)A 2000;
    C(LC)SSB(S) Regs
    UC Reg 8(4) UC Regs
144 Reg 2(2)(b) C(LC)SSB(S) Regs; reg
    8(4)(b) UC Regs
145 s6 C(LC)A 2000; reg 3 CL(E) Regs; reg
    40(1) CPP&CR(E) Regs; regs 3 and 4
    C(LC)(W) Regs; C(LC)SSB(S) Regs
146 Reg 3 CL(E) Regs; reg 4(1) and (2)
    C(LC)(W) Regs
147 ss6 and 8(6) C(LC)A 2000; regs 40(2)
    and 48 CPP&CR(E) Regs; reg 3(3) CL(E)
    Regs; regs 3(2) and 4(2A) C(LC)(W)
    Regs; reg 2(4)(a) C(LC)SSB(S) Regs
148 Reg 8(4)(b) UC Regs
149 Reg 3(5) and (6) CL(E) Regs; reg 4(4)-(6)
    C(LC)(W) Regs
150 Reg 2 C(LC)SSB Regs; reg 2(3)
    C(LC)SSB(S) Regs. The C(LC)SSB Regs
    have been amended to include
    entitlement to income-related ESA, but
    this is not needed because the C(LC)A
    2000 was not amended.
151 Reg 2(2) C(LC)SSB(S) Regs
152 Sch 4 para 4 UC Regs

6. People without accommodation
153 Sch 1 paras 1 and 3(b) UC Regs
154 Reg 18(3)(j) JSA Regs
155 **JSA** Reg 12(2) and (3) JSA Regs 2013
    UC Reg 95(2) UC Regs
156 This rule was challenged under the HRA
    1998, but the court decided the rules
    did not conflict with it: *R(RJM) v SSWP*
    [2008] UKHL 63
157 **IS** Sch 7 para 6 IS Regs
    JSA Schs 5 para 3 and 5A para 2 JSA
    Regs
    ESA Sch 5 para 1 ESA Regs
158 Vol 4 Ch 24, para 24157 and Vol 9 Ch
    54, para 54157 DMG
159 Vol 4 Ch 24, paras 24158-59 and Vol 9
    Ch 54, paras 54158-59 DMG
160 Vol 4 Ch 24, paras 24159-60 and Vol 9
    Ch 54, paras 54159-60 DMG; R(IS) 23/
    98
161 Vol 4 Ch 24, paras 24162 and Vol 9 Ch
    54, para 54162 DMG

7. People involved in a trade dispute
162 Sch 1B para 20 IS Regs
163 Sch 1B para 20 IS Regs

Part 6: Special benefit rules
Chapter 41: Benefits in hospital, care homes, prison and in other special circumstances
Notes

164 ss14, 15A and 35(1), definition of 'week', JSA 1995

165 Reg 47(3)(e) JSA Regs; reg 37(2)(d) JSA Regs 2013

166 ss15 and 15A JSA 1995; reg 3D and Sch A1 para 17 JSA Regs

167 **IS** Reg 5(4) IS Regs
JSA Reg 52(2) and (2A) JSA Regs

168 Vol 6 Ch 32, paras 32678-79 DMG

169 **IS** Reg 6(4)(b) IS Regs
JSA Reg 53(g) and (gg) JSA Regs

170 s126 SSCBA 1992; ss14 and 35(1), definition of 'trade dispute', JSA 1995

171 s14(1) and (2) JSA 1995; s126 SSCBA 1992

172 R(U) 1/65; Vol 6 Ch 32, paras 32121-25 and 32160-61 DMG

173 Regs 13(2)(a)(i) and 15(a)(i) SS&CS(DA) Regs

174 Sch 2 paras 13 and 19 SS&CS(DA) Regs

175 R(U) 7/58; R(U) 1/87

176 Vol 6 Ch 32, para 32107 DMG

177 s14(4) and (5) JSA 1995; CU/66/1986(T)

178 R(U) 4/62; R(U) 1/70

179 s14(1)(b) JSA 1995

180 *Presho v Insurance Officer* [1984] (see R(U) 1/84); *Cartlidge v CAO* [1986] 2 All ER 1; R(U) 1/87

181 s14(3) JSA 1995

182 R(U) 6/74

183 **IS** ss126(1) and (2) and 127(a) SSCBA 1992
JSA s15(4) JSA 1995; reg 171 JSA Regs

184 Reg 26(4) SS(C&P) Regs

185 s126(3)(a) and (d)(i) SSCBA 1992

186 ss14 and 15A JSA 1995

187 s126(3)(b) and (d)(ii) SSCBA 1992

188 s14 JSA 1995

189 **IS** s126(3)(c) SSCBA 1992
JSA ss15(2)(a) and (b) and 15A(4) and (5) JSA 1995

190 **IS** s126(5)(b) and (7) SSCBA 1992
JSA ss15(2)(d) and 15A(5) JSA 1995; reg 172 JSA Regs

191 **IS** Sch 9 para 34 IS Regs
JSA Sch 7 para 36 JSA Regs

192 **IS** s126(5)(a) SSCBA 1992; regs 35(1)(d), 41(3), 42(4) and 48(2), (5), (6), (9), (10)(a) and (c), and Sch 9 paras 15(3)(b), 21, 28 and 39, and Sch 10 paras 17 and 22 IS Regs
JSA ss15(2)(c) and 15A(5) JSA 1995; regs 98(1)(c), 104(3), 105(10) and 110(2), (5), (6), (9) and (10)(a) and (c), and Sch 7 paras 15(3)(b), 22, 29 and 41, and Sch 8 paras 22 and 27 JSA Regs

193 R(SB) 29/85

194 Regs 2, definition of trade dispute, and 56 UC Regs

195 Reg 66 UC Regs

196 Sch 11 paras 2(g) and 7 SSCBA 1992

197 R(SSP) 1/86

198 **SMP** Reg 13 SMP Regs
SAP/SPP Reg 35 SPPSAP(G) Regs
SSPP Reg 36 SSPP(G) Regs

199 Reg 13 SMP Regs was not amended when the JSA 1995 came into force.

200 s91 SSCBA 1992; s14 JSA 1995

201 SF Dir 8(1)(b); s14 JSA 1995

202 s126(1) and (2) SSCBA 1992; s14 JSA 1995; reg 171 JSA Regs; reg 3 SFM&FE Regs; SF Dir 8

203 Regs 3(1) and 6 SFM&FE Regs; s126 SSCBA 1992; s14 JSA 1995

204 Reg 43(2)(b) ESA Regs

205 *R v HBRB London Borough of Ealing ex parte Saville* [1986] HLR 349

206 s127 SSCBA 1992

207 Reg 6(4)(b) and Sch 1B para 20 IS Regs

208 s127(b) SSCBA 1992

209 s127(a) SSCBA 1992; regs 35(1)(d), 41(3) and (4), 42(4) and 48(6) and (10) and Sch 9 paras 15, 21, 28 and 39 and Sch 10 para 17 IS Regs

210 s127(c) SSCBA 1992; reg 18 SS(PAOR) Regs

211 Regs 19(3)-(5) and 26 SS(PAOR) Regs

212 Reg 19(3)-(5) SS(PAOR) Regs

213 Regs 20, 21 and 22(5) and (6) SS(PAOR) Regs

214 Reg 27(3) SS(PAOR) Regs

215 Reg 28 SS(PAOR) Regs

216 Reg 29 SS(PAOR) Regs

217 Regs 27 and 29 SS(PAOR) Regs

218 Reg 27(5) SS(PAOR) Regs

Part 7

Work and work-related rules

Chapter 42

National insurance contributions

This chapter covers:
1. Contributions and contributory benefits (p956)
2. Paid contributions (p957)
3. National insurance credits (p965)
4. Contribution conditions for benefits (p977)

This chapter explains the national insurance (NI) contribution rules relevant to contributory benefits. For details of the NI number requirement that applies to most benefits, see p1150.

Key facts

- Entitlement to contributory benefits, and sometimes the amount paid, depends on your national insurance (NI) contribution record. For some benefits, it depends on the contribution record of your spouse or civil partner, or your late spouse or civil partner.
- If you are employed or self-employed, you may be liable to pay NI contributions. If you are not liable to pay contributions, in some circumstances you can be awarded NI 'credits', or you may be able to pay contributions voluntarily.
- There are different types of NI contributions (called 'classes'). Not all classes of NI contributions or all types of NI credits count for all contributory benefits.
- NI contributions are collected by HM Revenue and Customs.

Future changes

The government plans to abolish class 2 NI contributions from April 2018, replacing them with changed class 4 contributions. Under the proposals, class 4 contributions will count towards the contribution conditions for state pension, bereavement support payment and contributory employment and support allowance (ESA). If you are self-employed, you will be liable to pay the new class 4 contributions if your annual profits are above a certain amount. If your annual profits are below this amount, provided they are at least equivalent to 52 x lower earnings limit for that year (see p959) – called the 'small profits limit' – you

Part 7: Work and work-related rules
Chapter 42: National insurance contributions
1. Contributions and contributory benefits

will be treated as having paid class 4 contributions in that year. If your profits are below the small profits limit:

– transitional arrangements are planned, so that you may be able to qualify for contributory ESA on the basis of earlier years' class 2 contributions;

– payment of class 3 contributions will count towards contributory ESA as well as state pension.

It is also planned that NI credits for foster carers (see p969) will count towards the contribution conditions for contributory ESA and contribution-based jobseeker's allowance.[1]

See CPAG's online service and *Welfare Rights Bulletin* for updates.

1. Contributions and contributory benefits

Benefits that have national insurance (NI) contribution conditions are:
- contribution-based jobseeker's allowance (JSA);
- contributory employment and support allowance (ESA);
- bereavement support payment, bereavement payment, widowed parent's allowance and bereavement allowance;
- category A and B retirement pensions;
- incapacity benefit (IB – but see p669);
- widows' benefits (but see p545).

These are known as **'contributory benefits'**.

Entitlement to contributory benefits normally depends on NI contribution conditions being met. For the detailed rules on the contribution conditions for these benefits, see pp977–84.

In some circumstances, you may be liable to pay NI contributions. If you are not, in order to help you meet the contribution conditions for some contributory benefits, you may either be credited with earnings or with contributions, or you can choose to pay contributions. For details of NI 'credits', see p965.

Note:
- It may be possible for you to rely on the contributions you have paid in other European Economic Area states to qualify for contributory benefits (see p1617).
- Your NI contribution record is based on the NI contributions you have paid, or the NI credits you have received, for each tax year – ie, 6 April to 5 April.
- If you are self-employed, your entitlement to maternity allowance (MA) and the amount you receive may be affected by whether you have paid class 2 NI contributions (see p723). For you to qualify for MA on the basis that you help your spouse or civil partner with her/his self-employment, s/he must meet conditions relating to class 2 NI contributions (see p726).

How decisions are made

Most decisions on NI contributions are made by an officer of HM Revenue and Customs (HMRC). Appeals against such decisions can be decided by an HMRC review or by the First-tier Tribunal (Tax).[2] The process is similar to appealing against an HMRC decision on your entitlement to a statutory payment (see p1386).

Decisions relating to entitlement to NI credits are made either by HMRC or the DWP, depending on the type of NI credit.

If you disagree with a decision on your entitlement to NI credits, you can apply for a revision or supersession (see Chapter 54), or you can appeal against it. You must apply for a mandatory reconsideration before you can appeal. Your appeal is decided by the First-tier Tribunal (Social Security and Child Support) (see Chapter 55).[3]

---

2. Paid contributions

There are seven different types ('classes') of paid national insurance (NI) contribution.[4] Three of these (classes 1, 2 and 3) can help you to qualify for contributory benefits, but only class 1 contributions count for *all* contributory benefits. Class 3A contributions, which could only be paid if you reached pension age before 6 April 2016, count towards entitlement to additional state pension. See p782 of the 2015/16 edition of this *Handbook* for details of additional state pension.

If you are an 'employed earner', you may be liable for class 1 contributions depending on the amount you earn. If you are a 'self-employed earner', you are normally liable to pay class 2 contributions unless your profits are low or you are exempt from payment (and you may also be liable for class 4 contributions). If you are not liable to pay contributions, you may choose to pay class 2 (if you are self-employed) or class 3 contributions voluntarily. These are known as 'voluntary contributions'.

Class of contribution	Payable by	Giving entitlement to
Class 1	Employed earners and their employers	All benefits with contribution conditions
Class 1A and 1B	Employers of employed earners	No benefits
Class 2	Self-employed earners	All benefits with contribution conditions, except contribution-based jobseeker's allowance (JSA)

Part 7: Work and work-related rules
Chapter 42: National insurance contributions
2. Paid contributions

Class 3	Voluntary contributors	State pension, category A and B retirement pensions, bereavement payment, widowed parent's allowance and bereavement allowance
Class 3A	Voluntary contributors	An amount (a 'unit') of additional state pension
Class 4	Self-employed earners	No benefits

The rules about your age

- You are not liable for class 1 or 2 contributions if you are under 16 or over pension age (see p772).[5]
- You cannot pay class 3 contributions if you are under 16 (and sometimes if you are 17 or 18) or for the tax year in which you reach pension age or any subsequent tax year.[6]

Employed earners and self-employed earners

Your liability to pay class 1, 2 or 4 NI contributions depends on whether you are an employed or self-employed earner.[7] It is normally clear whether you are employed or self-employed. If there is a dispute, it usually concerns whether you are employed under a *contract of service* (in which case you are an employee) or a *contract for services* (in which case you are self-employed).[8] **Note:**

- To be an employed or self-employed earner, you must be 'gainfully employed'.
- Office holders, including people in elective office, who receive earnings are classed as employed earners. Office holders include judges, registrars of births, marriages and deaths and most company directors.
- Certain people are deemed to be employed earners. These include office cleaners, many agency workers and people employed by their spouse or civil partner for the purposes of their spouse's or civil partner's employment.[9]
- Examiners, moderators and invigilators are deemed to be self-employed.[10]
- If you have two or more jobs, it is possible to be both employed and self-employed.
- You do not have to pay NI contributions on earnings from certain kinds of employment – eg, if you are employed by your spouse or civil partner and it is not for the purpose of her/his employment, or if you are employed in your home by a close relative who lives with you and the job is not for a trade or business that is carried out there.[11]

More than one job

If you are employed as an employed earner in more than one job, the basic rule is that your liability to pay class 1 contributions is calculated for each job as if the other(s) did not exist, although the total you pay is subject to a maximum.[12] There are some exceptions – eg, if you have two different jobs for the same employer or employers who carry on business in association with each other. In this situation, to stop employers avoiding liability, earnings from these jobs are normally added together and your NI contributions are based on your total earnings.[13]

If you are self-employed and also have a job as an employed earner, you may be liable to pay both class 1 and class 2 contributions, subject to a maximum.[14]

Class 1 contributions

Class 1 contributions have two elements: primary contributions (paid by employed earners) and secondary contributions (paid by employers).[15]

The amount of primary class 1 contributions you pay depends on the amount you earn in relation to the upper and lower earnings limit for the tax year, and to the amount of that year's 'primary threshold'. See Appendix 9 for details of the earnings limits and the primary threshold.

If your earnings are equal to or below the primary threshold (£157 a week in 2017/18), you do not have to pay NI contributions on them. If they are between the lower earnings limit (£113 a week in 2017/18) and the primary threshold, you are treated as if you had paid class 1 NI contributions on those earnings.[16]

If you earn more than the primary threshold, you are liable to pay class 1 contributions of 12 per cent of your earnings between the primary threshold and upper earnings limit (£866 a week in 2017/18), plus 2 per cent of the earnings you have above the upper earnings limit.[17] If you are a married woman or widow with reduced liability for contributions (see p962), you pay lower class 1 contributions.[18]

Note: it is your employer's responsibility to deduct your contributions from your earnings and pay them with its own contributions to HM Revenue and Customs (HMRC).[19] If your employer has failed to pay your contributions to HMRC, you are treated as though they had been paid, unless you have been negligent, or consented to or connived in that arrangement.[20]

Class 2 contributions

You must pay class 2 contributions for each week in a tax year in which you are a self-employed earner (see p958), unless your taxable profits in that year are below the 'small profits threshold' or you are exempt from payment. The small profits threshold for 2017/18 is £6,025. The main grounds for being exempt from payment of class 2 contributions are that you receive certain benefits – eg, maternity allowance (MA) or employment and support allowance (ESA) for the week to which the contribution relates, or carer's allowance for at least part of that week.[21]

Your liability for class 2 contributions is calculated annually after the end of the tax year using the income tax self-assessment procedure. They are payable

Part 7: Work and work-related rules
Chapter 42: National insurance contributions
2. Paid contributions

with any income tax and class 4 contributions for which you are liable in the same year (but see below if you are claiming MA).[22]

Even if you are not liable to pay class 2 contributions, provided you are a self-employed earner, you may still choose to pay voluntary class 2 contributions to protect your NI contribution record (see p963).[23]

Class 2 contributions are payable at a flat rate.[24] The current and previous year's rates are:

2017/18	£2.85 a week
2016/17	£2.80 a week

Note:
- For tax years before 2015/16, the self-assessment procedure was not used to collect class 2 contributions. For details, see the 2014/15 edition of this *Handbook*.
- Married women and widows with reduced liability for contributions (see p962) are not liable for class 2 contributions and cannot pay them voluntarily.[25]
- Volunteer development workers employed abroad and share fishermen pay class 2 contributions at special rates, which count towards contribution-based JSA, unlike other class 2 contributions.[26]

Class 2 contributions and maternity allowance

Payment of class 2 contributions becomes due on 31 January after the end of the tax year for which they are paid. You can pay class 2 contributions early, on a voluntary basis, in order to increase your entitlement to MA (see p724), or your spouse or civil partner can pay them early to enable you to qualify for MA on the basis that you help with her/his self-employment (see p726). In either situation, the contributions may be paid at any time from the week to which they relate. If you (or your spouse or civil partner) pay them early and are later assessed as liable to pay class 2 contributions for the same weeks under the self-assessment procedure, these voluntary contributions are converted to cover that liability, so you do not pay twice.[27]

Class 3 contributions

Payments of class 3 contributions are voluntary.[28] They only give entitlement to state pension, category A and B retirement pensions, bereavement payment, widowed parent's allowance and bereavement allowance and are not payable if your earnings factor is otherwise sufficient in that tax year to meet the contribution condition for those benefits (see p978).[29] To help you decide whether to pay class 3 contributions, see p963. **Note:** you cannot qualify for bereavement payment, widowed parent's allowance or bereavement allowance if your spouse or civil partner died on or after 6 April 2017, but you may qualify for bereavement support payment instead. Class 3 contributions do not count towards the contribution condition for bereavement support payment.

Class 3 contributions are paid at a flat rate. The current and previous year's rates are:[30]

2017/18	£14.25 a week
2016/17	£14.10 a week

Class 3A contributions

If you reached pension age before 6 April 2016 and you were entitled to, or had deferred your entitlement to, a category A, B or D retirement pension or graduated retirement benefit (see Chapter 36 of the 2015/16 edition of this *Handbook*), you could pay up to 25 class 3A contributions. Each class 3A contribution 'bought' a unit of additional state pension, worth £1.01 a week in 2017/18.[31] Class 3A contributions do not count for any other purpose. Any additional state pension you qualify for may also increase your spouse's or civil partner's state pension if you die (see p775), or a proportion of it can be paid in a category B retirement pension if s/he reached pension age before 6 April 2016. If your spouse or civil partner died before 6 April 2017 and you qualify for widowed parent's allowance, any class 3A contributions s/he paid (or you paid in her/his name, after his death) may increase the amount of widowed parent's allowance you get (see p540). See p782 of the 2015/16 edition of this *Handbook* for details of the additional state pension scheme.

The deadline for payment of class 3A contributions was 5 April 2017. However, if you requested information about them from HMRC before 6 April 2017, you can pay later than this, provided you pay within the 30-day period, beginning on the day on which HMRC sends you the information.[32]

You can request a repayment of any class 3A contributions that have been paid if:[33]

- you apply for repayment within 90 days of paying the contribution; *or*
- the person who paid the contribution died within 90 days of the payment.

Any additional state pension already paid as a result of the class 3A contribution is deducted from the repayment. For more information on class 3A contributions, see the 2016/17 edition of this *Handbook*.

Pre-1975 contributions

The present contribution system was introduced on 6 April 1975. Between 5 July 1948 and 5 April 1975, class 1 contributions were paid by a 'flat-rate stamp' in the same way as class 2 and class 3 contributions.

Part 7: Work and work-related rules
Chapter 42: National insurance contributions
2. Paid contributions

Before 6 April 1975, contribution years were not the same as tax years, as they are now. Transitional arrangements in both 1948 and 1975 may have resulted in your having a contribution year that was not 12 months long, which may explain what would otherwise be anomalies in your contribution record.

Reduced liability for married women and widows

Women who were married or widowed on 6 April 1977 could choose to pay reduced class 1 or no class 2 contributions, provided they applied to do so before 12 May 1977.[34]

If you 'elected' to pay at this reduced rate, you can continue to do so until you either apply to pay the full rate again (called 'revoking an election') or until the right to pay reduced contributions is automatically lost.[35] These reduced-rate contributions do not help you build up entitlement to contributory benefits.

If you have paid reduced-rate NI contributions and reach pension age on or after 6 April 2016, see p775 for how your state pension may be calculated. If you reached pension age before 6 April 2016 and you do not qualify for a retirement pension based on your own contributions, you may qualify for a category B retirement pension instead. See Chapter 36 of the 2015/16 edition of this *Handbook* for details.

To revoke your election, complete the form in HMRC leaflet CF9 for married women or CF9A for widows (available from www.gov.uk/topic/personal-tax/national-insurance).

Coming from abroad and going abroad

The rules on liability for NI contributions when you have come to the UK from abroad, or if you go abroad, are complex. In particular, the rules described below may not apply if you are covered by the European Union co-ordination rules (see p1611) or if you move from or to a country which has a reciprocal agreement with the UK (see p1533). In some circumstances, contributions paid in other countries count towards British benefits. In particular, this may apply if you have paid contributions in the European Economic Area (see p1608). You may also be entitled to benefits from other countries while you are in this country.

If you have come from abroad and are employed or self-employed in Great Britain, you may be liable for class 1 or 2 (and 4) contributions.[36] If you are self-employed but not liable to pay contributions, you may be able to pay class 2 contributions voluntarily. If you are not liable to pay contributions, you can choose to pay class 3 contributions if you are resident (see p1536) in Great Britain throughout the course of the tax year in respect of which you wish to pay contributions and, in some circumstances, even if you have not been resident for the whole tax year.[37]

If you are abroad working as an employee and your employer has a place of business in Britain, in some circumstances for the first year you must still pay class

1 contributions. If you are not liable, or are no longer liable, to pay class 1 contributions, it may be worth paying class 3 contributions (see below).[38]

If you are self-employed outside Great Britain, you may pay class 2 contributions if you wish, provided you were employed or self-employed immediately before you left Britain and either:

- you have been resident in Great Britain for a continuous period of at least three years at some time in the past; *or*
- you have paid contributions producing an earnings factor of at least 52 times the lower earnings limit in each of three years in the past (see p978 and Appendix 9 for the meaning of these terms). Each set of 52 flat-rate contributions paid before April 1975 counts as satisfying that condition in respect of one year.[39]

Certain volunteer development workers who are employed abroad may also be allowed to pay class 2 contributions.[40]

Normally, class 3 contributions may be paid while you are abroad if you satisfy either of the conditions which would allow you to pay class 2 contributions (but you do not need to have been employed or self-employed before you left Britain or while abroad). You may also pay them if you paid class 1 contributions for the first year you were employed abroad.[41]

For information on payment of NI contributions while abroad, see www.gov.uk or telephone HMRC's NI helpline (tel: 0300 200 3500, or from abroad: +44 191 203 7010; textphone: 0300 200 3519).

Northern Ireland and Isle of Man contributions count towards British benefits.

Improving your contribution record

If there are years for which you do not have a full contribution record, it may be beneficial to pay voluntary class 2 contributions (if you are self-employed but not liable to pay class 2 contributions – see p959) or class 3 contributions (see p960). These are called 'voluntary contributions'. Before paying voluntary contributions in respect of a tax year, check whether you qualify for NI credits in that year. (In any event, you are not entitled to pay class 3 contributions if you would instead be entitled to class 3 credits – see p965.[42]). You can request a national insurance statement to check whether there are gaps in your contribution record by completing an online form (www.gov.uk), or by telephoning or writing to HMRC's NI Contributions and Employer Office (see Appendix 1).

If it is more than 30 days before you reach pension age, you can also request a state pension statement to help you decide whether to pay voluntary contributions. You can do this online (www.gov.uk), by telephoning the Future Pension Centre (tel: 0345 300 0168; textphone: 0345 300 0169) or by post using Form BR19 (available at www.gov.uk). If you are within 30 days of pension age,

Part 7: Work and work-related rules
Chapter 42: National insurance contributions
2. Paid contributions

contact the Pension Service for details of your state pension (tel: 0800 731 7898; textphone: 0800 731 7339).

Should you make voluntary contributions?

1. Both class 2 and 3 contributions may help you qualify for state pension, or qualify for a higher rate of state pension. Class 2 contributions also count for contributory ESA.

2. Class 2 contributions count for bereavement support payment; class 3 contributions and NI credits do not.

3. Both class 2 and 3 contributions count for bereavement payment, widowed parent's allowance and bereavement allowance. You can only qualify for these benefits if your spouse or civil partner died before 6 April 2017, but contributions can be paid on your late spouse's or civil partner's behalf after this date (see below).

4. Voluntary contributions may be paid on behalf of a contributor after her/his death, provided they are paid no later than s/he would have been allowed to pay them.[43]

5. Consider the cost of paying voluntary contributions and compare this to the additional amount of benefit that might be awarded.

6. Class 2 and 3 contributions paid late do not always count for benefit purposes (see p964).

7. If you have overpaid contributions for a particular year, or have paid voluntary contributions in error, you may be able to get a refund.[44]

8. Get advice before paying voluntary contributions for years in which you have paid contributions abroad. In some cases, these can count towards British benefits (see p961).

9. If in doubt about paying the contributions, get advice.

Late payment of contributions

Payments of class 1, 2 or 3 NI contributions are considered late if they are paid after the date on which they are due to be paid.

If you are liable for class 1 contributions, your employer is responsible for paying them to HMRC. If your employer failed to pay these or has paid them late, you are treated as if the contributions had been paid (usually on the date they were due to be paid), unless you have been negligent or consented to, or connived in, the failure to pay.[45]

Class 2 contributions (including voluntary class 2 contributions) are due on the 31st January after the end of the tax year for which they are paid. Class 3 contributions are due 42 days after the end of the tax year for which they are paid.[46]

Contributions paid after these dates normally cannot help you to qualify for contributory benefits for any period before you pay them and they can usually only count towards your benefit entitlement for the period from the date they have been paid if:[47]

- for class 1 contributions, they were paid by the end of the second tax year after the tax year for which the contributions are paid; *or*
- for class 2 or 3 contributions, they are paid by the end of the sixth tax year after the tax year in which you are liable to pay them or, if they are voluntary contributions, in which you are entitled to pay them (although special rules apply if you make late payments of class 2 contributions through PAYE (pay as you earn)); *or*
- for class 3 contributions (for any tax year in which, for at least six months, you were a full-time apprentice, in full-time education or training or a prisoner, and for the year before and after such a year in which you met this condition but for less than six months), they are paid by the end of the sixth complete tax year after the end of a period of education, apprenticeship or imprisonment.

Even if paid within these time limits, class 2 contributions paid late cannot count for the second contribution condition for contribution-based JSA and contributory ESA, until six weeks after they have been paid.[48] This also applies to class 1 contributions which are paid after the start of the relevant benefit year (see p978) unless they can be treated as paid earlier in the circumstances described above.

In limited circumstances, contributions paid after the above time limits can still count for benefit purposes.[49] For example:

- If you reached pension age between 6 April 2008 and 5 April 2015, you can pay additional class 3 contributions for any six tax years (but not tax years before 1975/76), provided you already have at least 20 years that count as qualifying years for retirement pension. If you reached pension age before 6 April 2010, years of home responsibilities protection can count towards the 20 years (see p970), but at least one of those 20 years must comprise paid (not just credited) contributions. You must pay the additional contributions within six years of reaching pension age. Any additional contributions paid on or after 6 April 2011 count for benefit purposes from the date they are paid.[50]
- If you reach pension age on or after 6 April 2016, you have until 5 April 2023 to pay voluntary contributions for any of the tax years from 2006/07 to 2015/16.[51]

3. National insurance credits

In some circumstances, you can be 'credited' with earnings (sometimes known as class 1 credits) or with class 3 contributions. 'Credits' can help you satisfy:

- the second contribution condition for benefits with two contribution conditions – ie, contribution-based jobseeker's allowance (JSA), contributory employment and support allowance (ESA), and if your spouse or civil partner died before 6 April 2017, widowed parent's allowance and bereavement allowance; *and*
- the contribution conditions for retirement pensions (see p966).

Part 7: Work and work-related rules
Chapter 42: National insurance contributions
3. National insurance credits

Not all types of credits count for all these contributory benefits, although many class 1 credits do. Class 3 credits count for widowed parent's allowance, bereavement allowance and state pension. They also count for category A and B retirement pensions.

Note:

- You can only receive sufficient credits in any tax year to meet the contribution condition for that year.[52]
- Some credits are awarded automatically; others you must claim. To help you decide whether to claim credits or to see whether you have been awarded credits, you can check your NI contribution record at www.gov.uk or you can apply for a statement of your NI record using the online form available at www.gov.uk or by telephoning the number below.
- Credits cannot help you to satisfy the first contribution condition for benefits with two contribution conditions, or to qualify for bereavement support payment or bereavement payment, which have a single contribution condition.
- If you are a married woman with reduced liability for contributions (see p962), you can only qualify for credits for universal credit (UC – see p968), for certain parents and carers (see p969), for family members providing childcare (see p971), for official error (see below), starting credits (but see p972) or credits following bereavement (see p974). You are not entitled to other types of credits.
- Some people were credited with earnings for the tax years from 1993/94 to 2007/08 following an official error arising from discrepancies between the DWP and HM Revenue and Customs (HMRC) computer systems.[53] These credits were awarded automatically. See the 2009/10 edition of this *Handbook* for details.

Enquiries about credits can be made to the national insurance (NI) Helpline (tel: 0300 200 3500; textphone: 0300 200 3519).

Retirement pensions and credits

If you reach pension age on or after 6 April 2016, you may qualify for state pension. If you reached pension age before this date, you may qualify for category A or B retirement pension.

Most types of credits (including class 3 credits) can help you meet the contribution conditions for these benefits, and help determine the amount you receive.

For transitional rate state pension (see p774), most kinds of credits for tax years before 6 April 2016 can be taken into account when calculating your 'starting amount'.

Credits for unemployment

These credits can help you meet the contribution conditions for all contributory benefits (see p956), except bereavement support payment and bereavement payment.

You can be credited with earnings equal to the lower earnings limit for either:[54]

- each complete week (ie, the seven days from Sunday to Saturday) for which you receive JSA (or for which you would have received JSA but for the loss of benefit for benefit offences rules – see p1265); *or*
- each complete week in which you are not entitled to UC (to be entitled, you normally must have claimed it) but for which you satisfy or can be treated as satisfying the following qualifying conditions for JSA – ie, you:
  - are not engaged in full-time paid work (see p989); *and*
  - are not in relevant education (see p872); *and*
  - do not have limited capability for work (see Chapter 44); *and*
  - are under pension age; *and*
  - are either available for and actively seeking work (see p1030 and p1044) or, if you come under the UC system, satisfy the work search and work availability requirements (see p1075 and p1077), or you would have satisfied the availability and actively seeking work requirements or the work search and work availability requirements in that week but for having limited capability for work (see p701) or being incapable of work for part of the week.

You may also qualify for credits for weeks before 29 October 2013 in which you would have satisfied the above conditions for JSA but were treated as being in full-time paid work because you received a compensation payment. See p885–86 of the 2013/14 edition of this *Handbook* for details.

Credits for unemployment are awarded automatically if you get JSA. Otherwise, you must apply in writing to Jobcentre Plus, either on the first day for which you are claiming them or within a reasonable period of time after that. You must provide the DWP with the evidence it requires to show that you satisfy the conditions.

Even if you are not entitled to JSA, it may be important to continue to 'sign on' at the Jobcentre Plus office in order to get credits for unemployment and protect your right to contributory benefits.

However, you do not get credits for weeks in which:[55]

- you would not have been entitled to JSA (whether or not you actually claimed it) because you are involved in a trade dispute; *or*
- your JSA is reduced (or not paid) because you have been sanctioned. See p1094 and p1109 for the circumstances when this may apply; *or*

Part 7: Work and work-related rules
Chapter 42: National insurance contributions
3. National insurance credits

- you are receiving hardship payments of income-based or joint-claim JSA (see p1207); *or*
- you are a 16/17-year-old receiving JSA severe hardship payments (see p129).

Credits for limited capability for work or incapacity for work

These credits can help you meet the contribution conditions for all contributory benefits, except bereavement support payment and bereavement payment.

You can be credited with earnings equal to the lower earnings limit for each complete week during which you either:[56]

- were entitled to statutory sick pay (SSP); *or*
- had limited capability for work; *or*
- would have had limited capability for work had you been entitled to contributory ESA (even if the reason you are not entitled to contributory ESA is because of the 365-day limit – see p645) or had you claimed ESA or maternity allowance (MA); *or*
- were incapable of work or could be treated as incapable of work, or you would have been had you made a claim for incapacity benefit (IB) or MA. For information on incapacity for work, see p683 of the 2013/14 edition of this *Handbook*.

You cannot qualify for these credits for weeks in which you are entitled to UC, unless you are also entitled to ESA, SSP, MA, IB or severe disablement allowance in those weeks (to be entitled to UC, you normally must claim it). You also cannot qualify for these credits for days on which you were treated as not having limited capability for work (see p1004) or not being incapable of work (or on which you would have been, had you otherwise been entitled to ESA or IB).

These credits are awarded automatically if you get ESA or MA. To apply for credits on the basis you get SSP, write to HMRC's NI Contributions and Employer Office (see Appendix 1). In other circumstances, you must apply to Jobcentre Plus. Unless the credits are awarded automatically, you must apply for them before the end of the benefit year (ie, by the first Saturday in January – see p978) following the tax year in which you are entitled to the credit. This time limit can be extended if it is considered reasonable to do so, given your circumstances.[57]

Credits for universal credit

These credits can help you meet the contribution conditions for widowed parent's allowance, bereavement allowance and state pension. They also count for category A and B retirement pensions. They are awarded automatically.

If you are entitled to UC for at least part of a week, you can be credited with a class 3 contribution for that week.[58]

Credits for certain parents and carers

These credits can help you meet the contribution conditions for widowed parent's allowance, bereavement allowance and state pension. They also count for category A and B retirement pensions.

You can be credited with a class 3 contribution for each week which falls after 6 April 2010 if:

- for any part of the week, you are awarded child benefit for a child under the age of 12;[59] *or*
- you reside with someone who, for any part of the week, is awarded child benefit for a child aged under 12 and:
  - you share responsibility with that person for a child under 12; *and*
  - in the tax year to which the credit relates, the person awarded child benefit has paid or been credited with NI contributions with an earnings factor of more than 52 times that year's lower earnings limit (see Appendix 9 and p978). In calculating this, any credits s/he gets on the basis of the child benefit award are ignored.[60]

Note: in this situation, for weeks from 6 April 2016, the rules on when you qualify for a class 3 credit for state pension are different and indicate only that you must be the partner of someone who gets child benefit for a child, you must reside with your partner and you both must share the responsibility for the child. The rules do not expressly state that the child must be under 12 (although your partner still must have paid or been credited with sufficient NI contributions, as described above);[61] *or*

- in that week you are caring for someone for at least 20 hours, or for more than one person for a total of at least 20 hours and:[62]
  - the person(s) for whom you care is entitled to a qualifying benefit (see p970); *or*
  - the decision maker considers that the level of care provided is appropriate.

  You can continue to qualify for these credits for 12 weeks after the week in which you stop satisfying this condition – this allows you to have breaks in caring of up to 12 weeks without losing credits; *or*
- in that week you satisfy the conditions for carers who may qualify for income support (IS) described on p104 (the rules do not state that you must get IS to qualify for credits in this situation);[63] *or*
- for any part of the week, you are an approved foster parent or foster carer (including a kinship carer in Scotland);[64] *or*
- the week falls in the 12 weeks:[65]
  - before the date you become entitled to carer's allowance (CA); *or*
  - following the week in which you stop being entitled to CA (unless you already qualify for credits for CA for that week – see p972).

Part 7: Work and work-related rules
Chapter 42: National insurance contributions
3. National insurance credits

Qualifying benefit

A **'qualifying benefit'** includes the daily living component of personal independence payment, attendance allowance, the middle or highest rate of disability living allowance care component, armed forces independence payment, constant attendance allowance in respect of an industrial or war disablement and certain payments under the Pneumoconiosis, Byssinosis and Miscellaneous Diseases Benefits Scheme or Workmen's Compensation (Supplementation) Scheme.[66]

Unless you are entitled on the basis that you are awarded child benefit for a child under 12, in most circumstances you must be ordinarily resident in Great Britain and not in prison or in legal custody to qualify for these credits.[67]

If you get child benefit, IS or CA, the credits are awarded automatically. If you qualify because you are caring for someone for at least 20 hours, apply to the DWP using a carer's credit application form (Form CC1). Otherwise apply to HMRC on Form CF411A. Both forms are available at www.gov.uk. Your application must be received before the end of the tax year following the tax year to which the credits relate. This time limit can be extended if the DWP or HMRC considers it reasonable in the circumstances.[68]

Note: you can qualify for these credits on the basis of an award of child benefit even if you (or the person with whom you reside) have elected not to receive the child benefit because of the high-income child benefit charge (see p592).

Credits for home responsibilities protection

Home responsibilities protection, which helped a contributor satisfy the contribution conditions for bereavement allowance, widowed parent's allowance and category A or B retirement pension, was abolished on 6 April 2010 and was replaced with NI credits for certain parents and carers (see p969).

Any year of home responsibilities protection awarded up to and including 2009/10 is converted into 52 class 3 NI contributions:

- for widowed parent's allowance and bereavement allowance, if the contributor died on or after 6 April 2010;
- for category A retirement pension, if you reached pension age on or after that date;
- for calculating your entitlement to the transitional rate of state pension, if you qualify for it.

However, for widowed parent's allowance and bereavement allowance, this conversion can only be done for half the requisite number of years needed to qualify for a full basic widowed parent's allowance or bereavement allowance (see p983). For category A retirement pension and for calculating the transitional rate of state pension, it can be done for a maximum of 22 years.[69]

If the contributor reached pension age or died before 6 April 2010, see the 2009/10 edition of this *Handbook* for how years of home responsibilities protection affect the contribution conditions for category B retirement pension.

Credits for family members providing childcare

If you do not qualify for credits as a parent or a carer (see p969), these credits can help you meet the contribution conditions for widowed parent's allowance, bereavement allowance and state pension. They also count for category A retirement pension if you reached pension age on or after 6 April 2012 and for category B retirement pension in certain circumstances. See the 2015/16 edition of this *Handbook* for details.

From 6 April 2011, you can be credited with a class 3 contribution for each week during which you provide childcare for a child aged under 12, if:[70]

- you are a specified 'family member' of the child (you do not need to be a blood relative and many ex-family members count – see below); *and*
- someone has been awarded child benefit for the child for that week and, in the tax year in which the week falls, her/his contribution record is sufficient for the year to count as a qualifying year for state pension (see p985). In calculating this, any credits s/he gets on the grounds of receiving child benefit for a child under 12 are ignored; *and*
- you are ordinarily resident in Great Britain (see p1537).

There is no set number of hours for which you must care for the child to qualify. Only one person can qualify for these credits for a particular week for the same child. However, if childcare is shared, it may be possible for someone else to get credits for different weeks in a tax year or, if you look after more than one child, for you each to get credits for the same week in respect of one of the children.

You must apply to HMRC for these credits after the end of the tax year in question. There is no time limit for claiming.[71] Use Form CA9176 (for specified adult childcare credits), available at www.gov.uk.

Note: if you satisfy the qualifying conditions, you can still get these credits, even if the person entitled to child benefit elects not to receive it because of the high-income child benefit charge (see p592).

Family member

You count as a **'family member'** if you are:[72]

– the child's parent (from 6 April 2016 for state pension only, if you are her/his non-resident parent, but see p969 if you reside together), grandparent, great or great-great-grandparent, sibling, aunt or uncle (including if you are an adopted, step- or half-sibling of the child or of the child's parent);

Part 7: Work and work-related rules
Chapter 42: National insurance contributions
3. National insurance credits

– a spouse or civil partner, or former spouse or civil partner, of any of the above relatives, or her/his son or daughter;
– a partner or former partner of any of the above (including, for instance, a former partner of a former spouse of one of the above relatives), or her/his son or daughter;
– the child's niece, nephew or first cousin;
– a spouse, civil partner or partner (or former spouse, civil partner or partner) of the child's first cousin.

A '**partner**' is someone with whom the relative lives as if they were married.

Credits for carer's allowance

These credits can help you meet the contribution conditions for all contributory benefits, except bereavement support payment and bereavement payment. They are awarded automatically.

You can be credited with earnings equal to the lower earnings limit for each week in which you receive CA (see Chapter 25), or would receive it but for the loss of benefit for benefit offences rules (see p1265).[73] You also receive credits if the only reason why you do not receive CA is because you are receiving widowed parent's allowance, bereavement allowance or a widow's benefit instead. **Note:** this does not apply to bereavement support payment, as you can receive both CA and bereavement support payment at the same time.

If you are caring for someone but are not entitled to these credits, you may qualify for credits for certain carers (see p969).

Starting credits

These credits can help you meet the contribution conditions for widowed parent's allowance and bereavement allowance. They also count for category A and B retirement pensions and for calculating the transitional rate of state pension (see p986). They are awarded automatically.

You can receive class 3 credits for the tax years in which you reach the age of 16, 17 and 18 if you would otherwise have had an insufficient contribution record for those years to count towards the contribution conditions for the above benefits.[74]

However, for category A and B retirement pensions (and for calculating the transitional rate of state pension), you could only qualify for these credits:
- for tax years falling before 6 April 2010; *and*
- if you had to make an application for an NI number to be allocated to you, if your application for an NI number was made before 6 April 2010.

No credits were made under this provision for years before 6 April 1975.

Education and training credits

For the purpose of qualifying for contribution-based JSA and contributory ESA, you can be credited with earnings equal to the lower earnings limit for either one of the two complete tax years that fall before the relevant benefit year (see p978) if:

- for any part of those tax years you were on:[75]
  - a course of full-time training, including training to acquire occupational or vocational skills (or, if you are disabled, a part-time course of at least 15 hours a week); or
  - a course of full-time education; or
  - an apprenticeship; and
- in the other tax year in which you must satisfy the second contribution condition for the benefit (see p980), you have an earnings factor of 50 times the lower earnings limit without relying on this provision; and
- you were at least 18 (or you reached 18) in the tax year in question; and
- you were under 21 when the course or apprenticeship started; and
- your course of education, training or apprenticeship has finished.

You can receive credits which count for all contributory benefits (except bereavement support payment and bereavement payment) for each week in which you are undertaking a training course approved by a DWP decision maker if:[76]

- in that week you were not entitled to UC – but see p968 for credits if you were entitled to UC. To be entitled to UC, you normally must have claimed it; and
- the training is full time (or at least 15 hours a week if you are disabled) or it is an introductory course; and
- the training is not part of your job; and
- the training is intended to last for one year or less (except in certain circumstances, if it is a course for disabled people); and
- you were 18 or over at the beginning of the tax year in which the week falls.

If the course was arranged by Jobcentre Plus, you get the credits automatically. Otherwise, you must apply to HMRC's NI Contributions and Employer Office (see Appendix 1).

Credits for statutory maternity, adoption, additional paternity and shared parental pay

These credits can help you meet the contribution conditions for all contributory benefits, except bereavement support payment and bereavement payment.

You can be credited with earnings equal to the lower earnings limit for each week for which you receive statutory maternity pay, statutory adoption pay or

Part 7: Work and work-related rules
Chapter 42: National insurance contributions
3. National insurance credits

statutory shared parental pay, or for which you received additional statutory paternity pay.[77]

To apply for these credits, write to HMRC's NI Contributions and Employer Office (see Appendix 1). Your application must be received before the end of the benefit year (see p978) following the tax year in which the week falls, but this time limit may be extended if it is reasonable to do so.

Credits for jury service

These credits can help you meet the contribution conditions for all contributory benefits, except bereavement support payment and bereavement payment.

You are entitled to be credited with earnings equal to the lower earnings limit for each week after 6 April 1988 during which you spend at least part of the week on jury service, unless you are self-employed in that week.[78]

To apply for these credits, write to HMRC's NI Contributions and Employer Office (see Appendix 1). Your application must be received before the end of the benefit year (see p978) following the tax year in which the week falls (or such further period as is reasonable).

Credits following bereavement

These credits help you meet the contribution conditions for contribution-based JSA and contributory ESA. They are awarded automatically.

If you were entitled to bereavement payment, widowed parent's allowance or bereavement allowance, you can be credited with sufficient earnings for each year up to and including the one in which your entitlement to any of those benefits stopped, to enable you to satisfy the second contribution condition for contribution-based JSA or contributory ESA (but see the note below).[79]

For the purpose of satisfying the second contribution condition for contributory ESA, you are also entitled to credits for each year up to and including the one in which your entitlement to widow's allowance (abolished in April 1988) or widowed mother's allowance ended (but see the note below).[80]

Note: you cannot qualify for credits following bereavement if your entitlement to widowed parent's allowance, bereavement allowance, widow's allowance or widowed mother's allowance stopped because you married or entered into a civil partnership, or if payment stopped because you started cohabiting (see p545).

Credits for men approaching pension age

These credits can help you meet the contribution conditions for all contributory benefits, except bereavement support payment and bereavement payment. They are awarded automatically but you cannot qualify for these credits in any tax year in which you were abroad for more than 182 days.

If you are a man who was born before 6 October 1954, you can be credited with earnings (known as 'autocredits') from the tax year in which you would have reached pension age had you been a woman (see Appendix 12) up to, but not including, the tax year in which you reach the age of 65.[81] If you are self-employed, to qualify for credits for weeks in the above tax years (for which you are not liable to pay a class 2 contribution), you must either:

- be liable for at least one class 2 contribution in any of the above tax years; *or*
- not be liable to pay class 2 contributions because your profits are below the small profits threshold (see p959) or because you have had a small earnings exception for at least one week in any of the above tax years.

It is not possible to have a small earnings exception for tax years from 2015/16. See the 2014/15 edition of this *Handbook* for further details.

When calculating your entitlement to state pension, credits awarded on the above grounds only count for tax years before the 2016/17 tax year. For state pension for tax years from 6 April 2016, if you are a man born before 6 October 1953, you can be credited with earnings equal to the lower earnings limit (see Appendix 9) for weeks in the tax year in which you would have reached pension age had you been a woman and in any subsequent tax year up to but not including the tax year in which you reach the age of 65.[82] If you are self-employed, you can only qualify for these credits if:

- you would have been liable to pay class 2 contributions had your profits not been below the small profits threshold; *or*
- you are exempt from paying class 2 contributions for at least one week in the tax year because you were getting a particular benefit (see p959).

Credits for tax credits

These credits are awarded automatically.

For each week for which you receive, for any part of the week, the disabled worker element or severe disability element in working tax credit (WTC), you are entitled to be credited with earnings equal to the lower earnings limit. These credits count for all contributory benefits, except bereavement support payment and bereavement payment.[83]

Alternatively, for each week for which you are paid WTC (without the disabled worker element or the severe disability element), you are credited with earnings equal to the lower earnings limit to help you satisfy the contribution conditions for widowed parent's allowance, bereavement allowance and state pension. They also count for category A and B retirement pensions. In this case, if WTC was paid to you as a member of a couple but only one of you has earnings, the credits are awarded to that person. If you both have earnings, they are awarded to the person to whom WTC is paid.[84]

Part 7: Work and work-related rules
Chapter 42: National insurance contributions
3. National insurance credits

You can only qualify for either of these credits during any week in which you were:[85]

- employed and earning less than the lower earnings limit (see p959); *or*
- self-employed but not liable to pay class 2 contributions because your profits were below the small profits threshold (see p959) or you had a small earnings exception. (It is not possible to have a small earnings exception for tax years from 2015/16. See the 2014/15 edition of this *Handbook* for further details); *or*
- self-employed but exempt from paying class 2 contributions because you were getting a particular benefit (see p959). However, this does not apply for category A and B retirement pensions and only applies for state pension for weeks which fall in a tax year from 6 April 2016 (provided you did not qualify for the disabled worker or severe disability element in your WTC), otherwise it applies for state pension and the other benefits for weeks from 1 January 2017.

If you used to get working families' tax credit, disabled person's tax credit, family credit or disability working allowance, see the 1999/00 and 2002/03 editions of this *Handbook* for details of similar credits.

Credits for a quashed conviction

These credits can help you meet the contribution conditions for all contributory benefits, except bereavement support payment and bereavement payment.

If you were imprisoned or detained in legal custody after being convicted of an offence, and that conviction has subsequently been quashed by the courts, you can be credited with earnings for each week during at least part of which you were imprisoned or detained.[86]

To apply for these credits, write to HMRC's NI Contributions and Employer Office (see Appendix 1). Application by email may also be accepted.

Credits for service families

These credits can help you meet the contribution conditions for all contributory benefits, except bereavement support payment and bereavement payment.

From 6 April 2010, you can be credited with earnings equal to that year's lower earnings limit for each week during any part of which you were:[87]

- the spouse or civil partner of a member of the armed forces (or someone treated as such for the purpose of occupying accommodation); *and*
- accompanying, or were treated as accompanying, her/him on an assignment outside the UK.

You must usually apply for these 'class 1' credits on the approved form (Form MODCA1, available at www.gov.uk), once you have a confirmed date for the end of the overseas posting and before the end of the tax year following the tax year in which the overseas assignment ended. This time limit can be extended if it is reasonable, given your circumstances.

The decision maker has discretion to accept an application made before you receive confirmation of the end date of the overseas assignment. If your application is accepted, you can be awarded credits for the period before your application, but you must make a further application under these rules for credits for any subsequent period.

Alternatively, to help you meet the contribution conditions for state pension only, you can be credited with a class 3 contribution for each week in any tax year from 6 April 1975 in which, for at least part of the week, you meet the above conditions, provided the member of the armed forces you were accompanying had paid or been credited with sufficient NI contributions for that year to count as a qualifying year (see p985).[88] In this situation, you must normally apply for the credits on an approved form. There is an online form at www.gov.uk. Applications can only be made for a past period.

Note: in respect of years from 6 April 2010, claim the class 1 credits if you satisfy the conditions for them, as they count towards the contribution conditions for more benefits – the class 3 credits only count for state pension.

4. Contribution conditions for benefits

Entitlement to contributory benefits normally depends on the national insurance (NI) contribution conditions being met.

- **For state pension**, your entitlement is based on your own NI contribution record. However, in some cases, for the transitional rate of state pension, the amount you receive depends on the contribution record of your spouse or civil partner (or your late or former spouse or civil partner) (see p774).
- **For contribution-based jobseeker's allowance (JSA) and contributory employment and support allowance (ESA)**, your entitlement is based on your own NI contribution record (unless you qualify for contributory ESA without needing to satisfy the contribution conditions).
- **For bereavement support payment, bereavement payment, widowed parent's allowance or bereavement allowance**, the relevant 'contributor' is your late spouse or civil partner.

You may be credited with earnings or contributions to fill gaps in your contribution record (see p965 for further details).

NI contributions normally cannot count for benefit purposes until after they have been paid (if they are paid late, see p964). However, in some circumstances, your entitlement to benefit, or the amount of benefit you are entitled to, may depend on class 2 or 3 contributions which you have not yet paid because the due date for their payment has not been reached (see p964). In this situation, provided

Part 7: Work and work-related rules
Chapter 42: National insurance contributions
4. Contribution conditions for benefits

you pay the contributions by the due date, they can be treated as paid earlier.[89] If you claimed benefit before paying the contributions, once you have paid them the earlier decision on your claim can be revised to take account of the contributions.[90] See p982 for details of this rule in relation to contribution-based JSA and contributory ESA. For other benefits, this may not apply if you are late in notifying HM Revenue and Customs (HMRC) of your self-employment.

If you reached pension age before 6 April 2016, see the 2015/16 edition of this *Handbook* for the contribution conditions for category A and B retirement pensions. The contribution conditions for incapacity benefit and widow's pensions are covered in previous editions of this *Handbook*.

It may be possible for you to rely on the contributions you have paid in other European Economic Area states to qualify for contributory benefits (see p1608).

If you are a woman who has paid reduced-rate NI contributions, see p775 for how your state pension is calculated.

Earnings factors

Payment of class 1, 2 and 3 contributions gives rise to an 'earnings factor', which is used to calculate your entitlement to contributory benefits.

The earnings factor for class 1 contributions is the amount of earnings, excluding those above the upper earnings limit, on which those contributions have been paid. Each class 2 or 3 contribution gives rise to an earnings factor equal to that year's lower earnings limit (see Appendix 9).[91]

If you (or, for benefits that do not rely on your own contribution record, the contributor) have been credited with earnings or class 3 contributions, these NI credits count towards the earnings factor to help you meet the contribution conditions for certain contributory benefits (see p965).[92]

Jobseeker's allowance and employment and support allowance

Contribution-based JSA and contributory ESA have two contribution conditions. These conditions relate to particular tax years falling before the 'relevant benefit year'. In some situations, you can qualify for contributory ESA without having to satisfy the contribution conditions (see p979). In other situations, the first contribution condition is modified to make it easier to meet (see p980).

Relevant benefit year

A '**benefit year**' is almost the same as a calendar year and runs from the first Sunday in January.[93]

The '**relevant benefit year**' for contribution-based JSA is the benefit year in which the jobseeking period began or, if earlier, the benefit year in which a period that is linked to the jobseeking period began (see p699).[94]

The 'relevant benefit year' for contributory ESA is the benefit year in which your current period of limited capability for work started. However, if you otherwise would not meet the contribution conditions for contributory ESA, your relevant benefit year can instead be any benefit year which includes any part of your current period of limited capability for work (or any part of any period(s) of limited capability for work that can be linked to your current period – see p1021). **Note:** a period of limited capability for work cannot include a period that falls before the three-month time limit for backdating an ESA claim.[95]

When the contribution conditions do not apply

You can qualify for contributory ESA without having to satisfy the contribution conditions if:[96]

- your contributory ESA ended because you had received it for 365 days in the circumstances described on p645, you continued to have (or be treated as having) limited capability for work after your entitlement ended and you now have, or are treated as having, limited capability for work-related activity (see p1009). In this situation, you can qualify for contributory ESA again without having to satisfy the contribution conditions; *or*
- you are transferred to contributory ESA, having previously received incapacity benefit (IB) or severe disablement allowance (SDA) (see p672). In this situation, when you are transferred, the contribution conditions for contributory ESA are waived (but, if your contributory ESA is subsequently stopped because of the 365-day limit and you want to reclaim it, you must meet the usual contribution conditions to get contributory ESA again unless the previous bullet point applies); *or*
- you were getting IB or SDA but, following a determination that you do not have limited capability for work, your IB or SDA is not converted into contributory ESA and you have appealed against the decision. In this situation, you are treated as satisfying the contribution conditions for contributory ESA while you are pursuing your appeal (see p1017).

The first condition

To satisfy the first contribution condition for contribution-based JSA and contributory ESA, in one of the last two complete tax years before the relevant benefit year (see p978), you must have paid contributions on earnings (in respect of class 1 contributions), or have paid contributions producing an earnings factor (in respect of class 2 contributions), of at least 26 times that year's lower earnings limit – eg, £2,938 in 2017/18: 26 x £113. For contribution-based JSA, only class 1 contributions count towards meeting this condition (unless you are a share fisherman or volunteer development worker, when special class 2 contributions also count). For ESA, both class 1 and class 2 contributions count.[97]

When calculating the earnings on which you paid class 1 contributions, you cannot include any earnings above the lower earnings limit, so you must have

Part 7: Work and work-related rules
Chapter 42: National insurance contributions
4. Contribution conditions for benefits

worked for at least 26 weeks in one of the last two tax years before your relevant benefit year to meet this condition. The 26 weeks do not need to be consecutive but must fall in a single tax year.

Note:
- The first contribution condition can be relaxed in some circumstances (see below).
- The contributions must be paid, or treated as paid (see p982), before the week for which contribution-based JSA or contributory ESA is claimed.
- A widow can be treated as satisfying the first NI contribution condition for contributory ESA if she was entitled to widowed mother's allowance but her entitlement has ended (this does not apply if her entitlement ended because she married or entered into a civil partnership, or if payment stopped because she started cohabiting).[98] She may also be credited with contributions to satisfy the second condition (see p974).

When the first condition is relaxed

In some situations, the first contribution condition is relaxed, so that sufficient contributions paid in *any* one tax year are enough to satisfy the condition, provided they were paid, or treated as paid (see p982), before the week for which you are claiming the benefit.

For contribution-based JSA and contributory ESA, this applies if you were entitled to credits for service families (see p976) in at least one week in the tax year before the relevant benefit year (see p978).[99]

For contributory ESA, it also applies if you:[100]
- were entitled to carer's allowance (CA) in the last complete tax year before the relevant benefit year (even if it was not paid because of the overlapping benefit rules – see p1175); *or*
- were entitled to NI credits for a quashed conviction at some time in any tax year before the relevant benefit year (or you would have been entitled to such credits had you claimed them); *or*
- were in full-time paid work (see p196) for more than two years immediately before your period of limited capability for work began and you were entitled to working tax credit which included a disabled worker or severe disability element (see p1412 and p1414).

The second condition

To satisfy the second contribution condition for contribution–based JSA and contributory ESA, in each of the last two complete tax years ending before the relevant benefit year (see p978), you must have paid contributions, or received NI credits, which produced an earnings factor of at least 50 times the lower earnings limit (£5,650 in 2017/18: 50 x £113). Only certain NI credits count towards meeting this condition – eg, credited class 3 contributions do not (see pp965–76). To count, any paid contributions must be class 1 contributions (or special class 2 contributions) for contribution-based JSA, or class 1 or 2 contributions for contributory ESA.[101]

If you want to claim contributory ESA again after a previous award ended because of the 365-day limit, you may be able to requalify without having to satisfy the contribution conditions (see p979). If these circumstances do not apply, normally you can only requalify if you satisfy the contribution conditions and if one of the tax years in which you satisfy the second contribution condition falls after the last tax year you relied on to meet the condition for your earlier claim (see p645). The only exception to this is if you did not have to meet the contribution conditions when you were previously awarded contributory ESA because either you were transferred from IB or SDA, or you were getting ESA in youth. In this situation, the usual contribution conditions apply to your new claim for contributory ESA.[102]

The timing of your claim

In rare cases, it may be beneficial for you to delay a claim for contribution-based JSA so that you can draw on a different year's contribution record. This is because the years in which you must meet the contribution conditions depend on the benefit year in which your jobseeking period starts. So, for example, if your current jobseeking period is not linked to an earlier one (see p700) and you claim before 1 January 2017, you must meet the contribution conditions in the tax years 2013/14 and 2014/15, whereas if you claim on 1 January 2017, you must meet them in 2014/15 and 2015/16.

Any day for which you do not claim does not count as part of your jobseeking period (see p699),[103] so it is easy to postpone when that period begins. However, if you claim and are refused benefit because the contribution conditions are not satisfied, your jobseeking period will have started. You must then normally wait for more than 12 weeks to make a fresh claim. The 12-week gap breaks the jobseeking period.

The situation is different for contributory ESA. If your claim for contributory ESA is refused only on the grounds that you do not meet the contribution conditions, in some cases it can be worth making a later claim that falls in a different benefit year (see p978). However, if a previous award of contributory ESA ended because of the 365-day limit and you are making a new claim, see above.

Example

Shanti lives with her partner who works full time. Shanti was self-employed and paid class 2 NI contributions throughout the tax years 2014/15 and 2015/16 (in the tax year 2013/14 she did not pay NI contributions or get NI credits). In December 2016, she became ill and claimed contributory ESA for the first time. The relevant benefit year (see p978) was 2016 and the two complete tax years falling before that are 2013/14 and 2014/15. Having no contributions or credits for 2013/14 , Shanti was refused contributory ESA. If she claims

Part 7: Work and work-related rules
Chapter 42: National insurance contributions
4. Contribution conditions for benefits

again in the 2017 benefit year (which started on 1 January 2017), the contributions she paid in 2014/15 and 2015/16 are counted and she may qualify for contributory ESA. The rules allow 2017 to count as her relevant benefit year because part of her period of limited capability for work falls in that year.

Class 2 contributions treated as paid earlier

Since 6 April 2015, because the deadline for payment of class 2 contributions for a tax year is the 31st January after the end of that year, your entitlement to contributory ESA (or contribution–based JSA on the basis of special class 2 contributions) may depend on class 2 contributions that are not yet due to be paid. If you claim benefit before paying the contributions, your claim may be refused because you do not meet the contribution conditions. You can choose to pay class 2 contributions early to try to avoid this problem – if you do, write to HMRC to ensure it knows the payment you are making is intended to be an early payment of class 2 contributions. Alternatively, provided you pay the contributions by the 31st January, they can be treated as paid on an earlier date to enable you to qualify for contribution–based JSA or contributory ESA from a date before they were actually paid.[104]

Example
Sonja is self-employed and lives with her partner who works full time. Sonja becomes ill and unable to work on 4 January 2017 and claims ESA on the same day. Her relevant benefit year is 2017. The tax years in which she must have met the contribution conditions for contributory ESA are 2014/15 and 2015/16. Although she paid class 2 contributions for each week in 2014/15, her claim for contributory ESA is refused because she has not yet submitted her self–assessment tax return for 2015/16 and has not paid class 2 contributions for that tax year. On 29 January 2017 she submits her self-assessment return and pays class 2 contributions for 2015/16. She asks the DWP to reconsider the decision to refuse her contributory ESA. As Sonja paid her class 2 contributions by the due date (31 January 2017), they can be treated as paid before 4 January 2016. The earlier decision to refuse her claim is revised and she is awarded contributory ESA from 11 January 2017 (she is not entitled for the first seven days of her period of limited capability for work – see p636).

Bereavement support payment and bereavement payment

If your late spouse or civil partner dies on or after 6 April 2017, you may qualify for bereavement support payment. If s/he died before this date, you may qualify for bereavement payment (see Chapter 24). To satisfy the contribution condition for these benefits, your late spouse or civil partner must have paid NI contributions in any one tax year which produced an earnings factor (see p978) of at least 25 times that year's lower earnings limit – eg, £2,825 in 2017/18: 25 x £113.

For bereavement support payment, this condition must be met in any one tax year in your late spouse's or civil partner's working life, but only class 1 or 2 NI contributions count (see p984 for the meaning of 'working life').[105]

For bereavement payment, this condition must be met in any one tax year before your late spouse or civil partner reached pension age (or before s/he died, if s/he died before reaching pension age) and class 1, 2 or 3 contributions count. If your late spouse or civil partner only became liable to pay contributions in either the last complete tax year before the benefit year in which s/he reached pension age or in which s/he died (if s/he died before reaching pension age), or in the tax year before that, the sum of any class 1, 2 or 3 contributions paid in *any* year can count.[106]

In certain circumstances, the contribution condition for bereavement payment is treated as satisfied if your late spouse or civil partner had previously successfully claimed and met the first contribution condition for maternity allowance (MA) or IB. **Note:** MA no longer has contribution conditions, although it did for women whose expected week of childbirth was before 20 August 2000.[107]

Widowed parent's allowance and bereavement allowance

There are two contribution conditions for widowed parent's allowance and bereavement allowance. **Note:** you can only qualify for these benefits if your late spouse or civil partner died before 6 April 2017.

The first condition

In any one tax year before s/he died or reached pension age, your late spouse or civil partner must have paid class 1, 2 or 3 NI contributions which produced an earnings factor (see p978) of at least 52 times that year's lower earnings limit – eg, £5,824 in 2016/17: 52 x £112.[108] The payment of 50 flat-rate contributions for any time before 6 April 1975 also satisfies this condition.[109]

The first condition is deemed to be satisfied if the contributor was receiving the support or work-related activity component of ESA (see p641) or long-term IB either:[110]

- in the year in which s/he died (if s/he died before reaching pension age) or in which s/he reached pension age; *or*
- in the preceding year.

The second condition

To qualify for the maximum basic rate of widowed parent's allowance or bereavement allowance, in the required number of tax years during your late spouse's or civil partner's working life s/he must have paid class 1, 2 or 3 NI contributions, or received NI credits, which produced an earnings factor of at least 52 times that year's lower earnings limit – eg, £5,824 in 2016/17: 52 x

Part 7: Work and work-related rules
Chapter 42: National insurance contributions
4. Contribution conditions for benefits

£112.[111] Most, but not all, NI credits count towards meeting this condition (see pp965–76).

Working life

The contributor's **'working life'** is the period from the beginning of the tax year in which s/he reached the age of 16 up to, but excluding, the year in which s/he reached pension age or in which s/he died (if s/he died before reaching pension age).[112] If s/he was over 16 on 5 July 1948, her/his working life may have started on a different date.[113]

The required number of years needed to satisfy this condition depends on the length of your late spouse or civil partner's 'working life', and is calculated as follows.[114]

Length of working life	Required number of years
1–10 years	Length of working life minus one
11–20 years	Length of working life minus two
21–30 years	Length of working life minus three
31–40 years	Length of working life minus four
41–50 years	Length of working life minus five

Note:
- A reduced rate of benefit may be paid if you have not met the second contribution condition for the required number of years (see below).
- If your spouse or civil partner died before 6 April 2010, past years of home responsibilities protection may reduce the required number of years over which you must meet the second contribution condition. See the 2009/10 edition of this *Handbook* for details.
- To calculate the number of years before 6 April 1975 in which you satisfied the contribution condition, add together all the contributions paid or credited before 6 April 1975, and divide the answer by 50, rounding up if the result is not a whole number, provided that does not produce a number greater than the number of years of your working life before 6 April 1975.

Reduced benefit because of insufficient contributions

Benefit can be paid at a reduced rate if the second contribution condition is not satisfied for the required number of years, provided it is satisfied in at least 25 per cent of the required number. The benefit is paid at a percentage of the amount which would otherwise be paid. The percentage is calculated by expressing the number of years in which the condition is satisfied as a percentage of the required number of years and rounding it up to the nearest whole number.[115] Thus, if you are a widow and your husband's working life was 12 years, so that the required number of years is 10, and he only satisfied the condition in eight years, you receive 80 per cent of the basic rate of widowed parent's allowance or bereavement allowance.

If you still qualify for them, increases for children are paid in full.[116]

It may be possible for you to pay class 3 contributions to increase the number of years in which the second contribution condition is satisfied, but see p963 for what to consider before doing so.

Retirement pensions

If you reached pension age before 6 April 2016, you are not entitled to state pension but may be entitled to category A or B retirement pension instead.[117] For the NI contribution conditions for category A and B retirement pensions, see the 2015/16 edition of this *Handbook*.

State pension

If you reach pension age on or after 6 April 2016 (ie, if you are a woman born on or after 6 April 1953 or a man born on or after 6 April 1951), you may be entitled to state pension (see Chapter 35).

Your entitlement to state pension and the amount you receive depends on the number of NI 'qualifying years' you have.

Qualifying years[118]

A '**qualifying year**' is a tax year in your working life in which you have paid class 1, 2 or 3 NI contributions or received NI credits which, in total, produced an earnings factor of at least 52 times that year's lower earnings limit – eg, £5,876 in 2017/18: 52 x £113. For the meaning of 'earnings factor', see p978, and for the meaning of 'working life', see p984. Most, but not all, kinds of NI credits can be counted. For tax years before 6 April 1978, the earnings factor must be at least 50 times that year's lower earnings limit for the year to count as a qualifying year.[119]

To qualify for state pension, you must have at least 10 qualifying years (but see below if you paid a reduced rate of NI contribution as a married woman).[120]

If one of your qualifying years is a tax year before 6 April 2016, your entitlement to state pension is calculated at the transitional rate (see p986).[121]

Note:

- If you have paid reduced-rate NI contributions as a married woman or widow and your election to pay at a reduced rate was in force at the start of the 35-year period which ends in the tax year before you reach pension age, you do not need to have 10 qualifying years to qualify for state pension.[122] See p775 for how your entitlement is calculated.
- If your spouse or civil partner has died, you may qualify for an amount of state pension based on her/his contribution record. See p775 for details.

Part 7: Work and work-related rules
Chapter 42: National insurance contributions
4. Contribution conditions for benefits

The transitional rate of state pension

If at least one of your qualifying years (see p987) falls before 6 April 2016, your entitlement to state pension is assessed at the transitional rate. The amount you receive depends on your 'starting amount'. Your starting amount is based on your contribution record up to 6 April 2016. Your starting amount is the greater of either:[123]

- the weekly amount of basic category A retirement pension, additional state pension and graduated retirement benefit you would have qualified for had you reached pension age on 6 April 2016 and had the new state pension scheme not been introduced. See below for how your basic category A retirement pension is calculated and the 2015/16 edition of this *Handbook* for details of additional state pension and graduated retirement benefit; *or*
- the weekly amount of state pension you would be entitled to on 6 April 2016 if you reached pension age on that date, using the number of qualifying years you had up to that date (see p985). You are entitled to the full rate of state pension if you have at least 35 qualifying years in your working life. If you have less than 35 qualifying years (but at least 10), you build up one thirty-fifth of the full weekly rate of state pension for each of your qualifying years.

If you have been contracted out of the state second pension scheme, the above amounts are adjusted to reflect this.

See p774 for further details of how the transitional rate of state pension is calculated. If your starting amount is less than the full rate of state pension, it can be increased if you have further qualifying years falling after 5 April 2016. Each further qualifying year adds one thirty-fifth of the full weekly rate of state pension to your starting amount up to the maximum of the full weekly rate of state pension. You may be able to increase your number of qualifying years by claiming NI credits and/or making voluntary NI contributions (see p963).

You can get an estimate of your starting amount by applying for a state pension statement (see p963).

Note: if your spouse or civil partner has died, you may qualify for an inherited amount of state pension based on her/his contribution record (see p775).

The basic category A retirement pension figure used[124]

If, before 6 April 2016, you have at least 30 qualifying years, the amount of basic category A retirement pension used in the calculation of your starting amount is the full weekly rate of that pension (see p773). If you have less than 30 qualifying years, it is one-thirtieth of the full weekly rate of the basic category A retirement pension for each of your qualifying years up to 6 April 2016. In certain circumstances, you can substitute your contributions with those of your late or former spouse or civil partner when calculating the amount of category A retirement pension.

Notes

1 HM Government, *Abolishing Class 2 and Reforming Class 4 National Insurance Contributions: response to the consultation,* December 2016

1. Contributions and contributory benefits

2 s11 SSC(TF)A 1999; Part III SSC(DA) Regs; Arts 6(c)(i) and 7 First-tier Tribunal and Upper Tribunal (Chambers) Order 2010, No.2655

3 Sch 3 para 17 SSA 1998; s17 SSC(TF)A 1999; Arts 2-4 National Insurance Contribution Credits (Transfer of Functions) Order 2009, No.1377

2. Paid contributions

4 s1(2) SSCBA 1992

5 ss6(1) and (3) and 11(7) SSCBA 1992

6 s13 SSCBA 1992; regs 48(1) and 49(1)(f) and (2A)-(2C) SS(Con) Regs

7 s2(1) SSCBA 1992

8 *Ready Mix Concrete South East Ltd v Ministry of Pensions and National Insurance* [1968] 2 QB 497 (QBD); *Global Plant v Secretary of State for Health and Social Security* [1971] 3 All ER 385 (QBD)

9 Sch 1 paras 1-5A SS(CatE) Regs; *ITV Services Ltd v HMRC* [2012] UKUT 47 (TCC)

10 Sch 1 paras 6 SS(CatE) Regs

11 Sch 1 paras 7-12 SS(CatE) Regs

12 Regs 13, 14, 15 and 21 SS(Con) Regs

13 Sch 1 para 1 SSCBA 1992; regs 13, 14, 15 and 21 SS(Con) Regs

14 Reg 21 SS(Con) Regs

15 ss6 and 7 SSCBA 1992

16 ss6 and 6A SSCBA 1992

17 s8 SSCBA 1992

18 Reg 131 SS(Con) Regs

19 Sch 1 para 3 SSCBA 1992

20 Reg 60 SS(Con) Regs

21 s11 SSCBA 1992; reg 43 SS(Con) Regs

22 s11(5) SSCBA 1992

23 s11(6) SSCBA 1992; reg 43 SS(Con) Regs

24 s11(2) SSCBA 1992

25 Reg 127(1) SS(Con) Regs

26 Regs 125, 149, 151 and 152 SS(Con) Regs

27 Regs 1(2) and 90ZA SS(Con) Regs

28 s13 SSCBA 1992

29 s14 SSCBA 1992; reg 49 SS(Con) Regs

30 s13(1) SSCBA 1992

31 s14A SSCBA 1992; regs 3 and 4 SSC3AC(UAP) Regs

32 s14A(1) and (1A) SSCBA 1992

33 Reg 56A SS(Con) Regs

34 Reg 127 SS(Con) Regs

35 Regs 128(1) and 130 SS(Con) Regs

36 ss2(1), 6 and 11 SSCBA 1992; reg 145(1)(a), (c), (d) and (2) SS(Con) Regs

37 Reg 145(1)(c) and (e) SS(Con) Regs

38 Reg 146 SS(Con) Regs

39 Regs 147 and 148 SS(Con) Regs

40 Regs 149 and 151 SS(Con) Regs

41 Regs 146(2)(b), 147 and 148 SS(Con) Regs

42 s11(6) SSCBA 1992; regs 43(3), 48 and 49 SS(Con) Regs

43 Reg 62 SS(Con) Regs

44 Regs 52, 52A, 56 and, from 12 October 2015, 56A SS(Con) Regs; *Clifford Bonner and Others v HMRC* [2010] UKUT 450 (TCC)

45 Reg 60 SS(Con) Regs; reg 5 SS(CTCNIN) Regs

46 Reg 1(2) SS(CTCNIN) Regs

47 Reg 4 SS(CTCNIN) Regs; reg 48(3)(b) SS(Con) Regs

48 Reg 4(7) and (8) SS(CTCNIN) Regs

49 Regs 50 and 61 SS(Con) Regs; regs 4(11), 5A, 6, 6A and 6B SS(CTCNIN) Regs

50 s13A SSCBA 1992; reg 3(8D) SS&CS(DA) Regs; reg 6C SS(CTCNIN) Regs

51 Regs 50C and 61B SS(Con) Regs

3. National insurance credits

52 Reg 3 SS(Cr) Regs; reg 25(2) SP Regs

53 Regs 8D, 8E and 8F SS(Cr) Regs

54 Reg 8A SS(Cr) Regs; regs 26 and 29 SP Regs

55 Reg 8A(5) SS(Cr) Regs; regs 26 and 29 SP Regs

56 Reg 8B SS(Cr) Regs; regs 26 and 29 SP Regs

Part 7: Work and work-related rules
Chapter 42: National insurance contributions
Notes

57 Reg 8B(4) SS(Cr) Regs; regs 26 and 29 SP Regs
58 Reg 8G SS(Cr) Regs; regs 26 and 31 SP Regs
59 s23A(2) and (3)(a) SSCBA 1992; regs 27 and 34(1)(a) SP Regs
60 s23A(2) and (3)(c) SSCBA 1992; regs 2, 5(1)(a), 6 and 9 SS(CCPC) Regs; reg 27 SP Regs
61 Reg 34(1)(b) and (2)-(4) SP Regs
62 s23A(2) and (3)(c) SSCBA 1992; regs 5(1)(b) and 7(1)(c) SS(CCPC) Regs; regs 27, 37(1) and (2)(a) and 38(1)(c) SP Regs
63 s23A(2) and (3)(c) SSCBA 1992; reg 5(1)(c) SS(CCPC) Regs; reg 37(1) and (2)(b) SP Regs
64 s23A(2) and (3)(b) SSCBA 1992; reg 4 SS(CCPC) Regs; reg 36 SP Regs
65 Reg 7 SS(CCPC) Regs; reg 38(1)(a) and (b) and (2) SP Regs
66 Reg 2 SS(CCPC) Regs; reg 37(4) SP Regs
67 Reg 8 SS(CCPC) Regs; regs 34(2), 36(1) and 37(3) SP Regs
68 Regs 9-12 SS(CCPC) Regs; regs 34(2)(e), 36(3), 37(5) and (6) and 39(a) SP Regs
69 s23A(5)-(7) SSCBA 1992; reg 27 SP Regs
70 Reg 9F SS(Cr) Regs; reg 26 and 35 SP Regs
71 Reg 9F(8) SS(Cr) Regs; reg 39(b) SP Regs
72 Sch SS(Cr) Regs; reg 35(6)-(8) SP Regs
73 Reg 7A SS(Cr) Regs; regs 26 and 29 SP Regs
74 Reg 4 SS(Cr) Regs; reg 26 SP Regs
75 Reg 8 SS(Cr) Regs
76 Reg 7 SS(Cr) Regs; regs 26 and 29 SP Regs
77 Reg 9C SS(Cr) Regs; regs 26 and 29 SP Regs
78 Reg 9B SS(Cr) Regs; regs 26 and 29 SP Regs
79 Reg 8C SS(Cr) Regs
80 Reg 3(1)(b) SSB(MW&WSP) Regs
81 Reg 9A SS(Cr) Regs; reg 26 SP Regs
82 Reg 32 SP Regs
83 Reg 7B SS(Cr) Regs; regs 26 and 29 SP Regs
84 Reg 7C SS(Cr) Regs; regs 26 and 30 SP Regs
85 Regs 7B(2) and 7C(1) SS(Cr) Regs; regs 26, 29 and 30(1) SP Regs
86 Reg 9D SS(Cr) Regs; regs 26 and 29 SP Regs
87 Reg 9E SS(Cr) Regs; regs 26 and 29 SP Regs
88 Regs 28 and 33 SP Regs

4. Contribution conditions for benefits

89 Regs 7(1) and 7A SS(CTCNIN) Regs
90 Reg 3(8J) and (8K) SS&CS(DA) Regs
91 s22 SSCBA 1992; Sch 1 SS(EF) Regs
92 s22(5) (5A), (5ZA) and (5ZB) SSCBA 1992
93 s21(6) SSCBA 1992; s2(4) JSA 1995; Sch 1 para 3 WRA 2007
94 s2(4) JSA 1995
95 Sch 1 para 3(1)(f) WRA 2007; regs 2(1) and 13 ESA Regs; reg 2 and 14 ESA Regs 2013
96 s1B WRA 2007; Sch 2 paras 2 and 15 ESA(TP)(EA)(No.2) Regs
97 **JSA** ss1(2)(d) and 2 JSA 1995; regs 45A, 158 and 167 JSA Regs; regs 34, 69 and 75 JSA Regs 2013
     ESA Sch 1 para 1 WRA 2007; reg 7A ESA Regs; reg 8 ESA Regs 2013
98 Reg 3(1) SSB(MW&WSP) Regs
99 Reg 45B JSA Regs; reg 8(2)(ca) ESA Regs; reg 35 JSA Regs 2013; reg 9(2)(d) ESA Regs 2013
100 Reg 8 ESA Regs; reg 9 ESA Regs 2013
101 s2 JSA 1995; Sch 1 para 2 WRA 2007; regs 158 and 167 JSA Regs; regs 69 and 75 JSA Regs 2013
102 s1A WRA 2007
103 Reg 47(3)(a) JSA Regs; reg 37(2)(a) JSA Regs 2013
104 Reg 7A SS(CTCNIN) Regs; reg 3(8E) SS&CS(DA) Regs; reg 17(3) UC,PIP,JSA&ESA(DA) Regs
105 s31 PA 2014
106 s21 and Sch 3 para 4 SSCBA 1992
107 Sch 3 paras 7 and 9 SSCBA 1992
108 Sch 3 para 5 SSCBA 1992
109 Reg 6 SS(WBRP&OB)(T) Regs
110 Sch 3 para 5(6) and (6A) SSCBA 1992
111 Sch 3 para 5(3) SSCBA 1992
112 Sch 3 para 5(8) SSCBA 1992
113 Reg 7(7) SS(WBRP&OB)(T) Regs; s20 and Sch 3 para 5(5) SSCBA 1992
114 Sch 3 para 5(5) SSCBA 1992
115 Reg 6 SS(WB&RP) Regs
116 s60(4)-(6) SSCBA 1992; reg 6(3) SS(WB&RP) Regs
117 s1 PA 2014
118 s2(4) PA 2014
119 s4(4) and (5) PA 2014
120 Reg 13 SP Regs
121 s4(1)(c) PA 2014
122 s11(1) PA 2014
123 s5 and Sch 1 PA 2014
124 Sch 1 paras 2 and 3 PA 2014

Chapter 43

Work and benefits

This chapter covers:
1. The full-time paid work rule (below)
2. People treated as in full-time paid work (p996)
3. People treated as not in full-time paid work (p996)
4. Self-employed people (p998)
5. Universal credit (p999)
6. Non-means-tested benefits (p999)
7. Working tax credit and means-tested benefits (p1000)

Key facts
- You cannot usually qualify for income support (IS) or income-based jobseeker's allowance (JSA) if you or your partner are in full-time paid work, or for income-related employment and support allowance (ESA) if your partner is in full-time paid work. You cannot qualify for contribution-based JSA if you are in full-time paid work.
- You cannot qualify for IS on the basis that you are incapable of work or for any type of ESA if you do any work, unless it is work you are permitted to do while claiming.
- Your eligibility for housing benefit and pension credit is not affected if you or your partner are in full-time paid work.
- Your eligibility for universal credit is not affected if you or your partner are in full-time paid work. However, you cannot get a housing costs element for owner-occupier payments if you or your partner have any earnings, no matter how low these are, or whatever hours you work.
- Earnings affect the amount of all of your means-tested benefits.
- Entitlement to some non-means-tested benefits and tax credits is affected by issues to do with work and employment.

1. The full-time paid work rule

Paid work affects income support (IS), jobseeker's allowance (JSA), employment and support allowance (ESA), housing benefit (HB) and pension credit (PC) in

Part 7: Work and work-related rules
Chapter 43: Work and benefits
1. The full-time paid work rule

different ways. If you or your partner (or a non-dependant) work full time for payment and are paid for the work, you count as being in what the DWP calls 'remunerative work'. This is called 'full-time paid work' in this *Handbook*. The number of hours that count as being 'full time' depends on the benefit concerned and whether the person working is you (the claimant) or your partner.

- If you do any paid work (unless it is work that you can do while claiming – see p1021), you are not entitled to ESA.[1]
- If your partner is in full-time paid work, you cannot usually qualify for IS, income-based JSA or income-related ESA.[2] Your partner's working hours do not affect your entitlement to contribution-based JSA or contributory ESA.
- Your eligibility for universal credit (UC), HB and PC is not affected if you or your partner are in full-time paid work. For HB, however, work can affect the way your income is calculated – eg, whether you can get an additional earnings disregard (see p281 and p322) or a childcare costs disregard (see p281 and p323). You will not receive a UC housing costs element for owner-occupied payments if you or your partner have any earnings, regardless of your hours of work or the amount you earn.
- In some situations, a child who is aged 16 or over who does paid work for 24 hours a week or more does not count as a qualifying young person who can be included in your claim (see p220 and p572). In this case, you might not be able to get an allowance or premiums in your HB for her/him (or, if still included, in your IS or income-based JSA).
- If you have a non-dependant living with you, the amount of the non-dependant deduction made from your IS, income-based JSA, income-related ESA or PC housing costs, and from your HB, can be higher if your non-dependant is in full-time paid work (see p467 and p69).

See p991 for what counts as paid work and p992 for how the hours are calculated. 'Work' includes self-employment and work which is done from home. In some circumstances, you may be treated as not in full-time paid work even if you are (see p996). In others, you may be treated as if you are in full-time paid work when you are not (see p996).

Note: income from work is taken into account for all the means-tested benefits and you may not satisfy the means test if your earnings are too high.

If you or your partner are in full-time paid work, you may be able to claim working tax credit (WTC). The definition of full-time paid work for WTC can differ from those for IS, JSA and ESA. So you may be able to choose whether to claim IS/JSA/ESA or WTC. You may be able to claim both IS/JSA/ESA/PC and WTC. For IS and JSA, if you are a single claimant, this only applies in limited situations – eg, if you are a 'term-time only' worker or you are off sick and getting statutory sick pay. For ESA, this usually only applies if your partner counts as in full-time paid work for WTC purposes. You cannot qualify for ESA if *you* work, unless it is work you can do while claiming (see p1021). See p1000 for factors to consider.

What counts as full-time work

For IS, JSA and HB, **you** count as in 'full-time work' if you work 16 hours or more a week.[3] See p992 for how the hours are calculated. You cannot qualify for ESA if you do *any* number of hours of work, unless it is work you can do while claiming (see p1021). **Your partner** counts as in 'full-time work':

- for IS, income-based JSA (but not joint-claim JSA) and income-related ESA, if s/he works 24 hours or more a week;[4]
- for HB, if s/he works 16 hours or more a week.[5]

For IS, JSA, ESA, PC and HB, **your non-dependant** counts as in full-time paid work if s/he works 16 hours or more a week.[6]

Note:

- For PC, there is no rule for when you or your partner count as in full-time work because the number of hours worked do not matter.
- For joint-claim JSA, you do not have to make a joint claim with your partner if s/he works 16 or more hours a week.[7]
- For HB, you and your partner may have to work more than 16 hours to benefit from an additional earnings disregard (see p281 and p322).

Example

Della works 15 hours a week. She can claim income-based JSA, provided her earnings are not too high. If she works an additional five hours, she would be in full-time work and would no longer be able to claim JSA. She would still be able to get HB, but her income could affect the amount she could receive.

What counts as paid work

'**Paid work**' is work for which you are paid, or for which it is expected that you will be paid – ie, there is an expectation that you get payment, now or at some date in the future, even if no payment is finally made.[8] Whether or not you are paid or are working in expectation of payment should be decided at the time the work is done, not, for example, at the end of the year or accounting period.[9]

Note:

- You must have a real prospect of payment, not just a hope or desire to make money – eg, a self-employed writer who has never sold a manuscript and has no publisher's contract may have no real expectation of payment and so is not in paid work even if s/he spends a lot of time writing.[10]
- Some of the initial work necessary to set up a business may not count as paid work if it is unpaid preparatory work done in the hope of further paid work.[11]

Part 7: Work and work-related rules
Chapter 43: Work and benefits
1. The full-time paid work rule

- If your business is not yet making money or has ceased to make a profit, you may count as working in expectation of payment if you are taking drawings against future profit or if the business is likely to yield profit in the future. Ultimately, it depends on how viable your business is. With no prospect of a profit, the decision maker is likely to want to know why you are working for nothing.[12]
- Paid work includes work for which you receive payment in kind – eg, free meals or accommodation or free produce for farm workers.[13]

How your hours are calculated

Include all hours actually worked for which payment is made or which you work in expectation of payment. If you do more than one job, add the hours from each together. If routine paid overtime is done, include those hours. If work is casual or intermittent (eg, you are a seasonal worker who works in the summer, but you are unemployed for the rest of the year), you can argue that only the hours when you are in work are relevant (but see p994 for 'term-time' workers).[14] Your word should be accepted unless there is reason for doubt.

Note:
- If your hours fluctuate, there are rules on how they should be averaged (see p993).
- For IS, JSA and income-related ESA only, paid lunch hours and breaks count towards the total hours.[15]
- For PC and HB, the rules do not say how to calculate the hours of work unless these fluctuate. However, for PC, the DWP says that you should only count the hours for which payment is made or which are worked in expectation of payment, including overtime, but not including paid breaks – eg, lunch or tea breaks.[16]
- For JSA only, any hours spent caring for someone for whom it would be possible to qualify for IS as a carer (see p104) are ignored, unless the carer is employed and paid to act as a carer.[17] For IS and ESA, although hours spent caring are not ignored, you and your partner (for IS), and your partner (for ESA), are treated as not in full-time paid work in this situation (see p997).

If you are unsure whether you (or your partner) are in full-time paid work, see p995. If you think the average hours have been calculated wrongly so you cannot claim the benefit you want, you can appeal. Work out first whether you are better off claiming IS/JSA/ESA or WTC (see p1000). Likewise, appeal if your non-dependant's hours have been calculated unfairly and the DWP or local authority is making a non-dependant deduction that is too high. **Note:** except for HB, you must apply for a mandatory reconsideration before you can appeal (see Chapters 54 and 55).

If your hours fluctuate

If your (or your partner's or your non-dependant's) hours fluctuate, an average of the weekly hours is calculated as follows.

Regular pattern of work

If there is a regular pattern of work (a 'work cycle'), the average hours worked throughout each cycle are used – eg, if you regularly work three weeks on and one week off, your hours are the average over the four-week period (the 'work cycle').[18] Weeks when you are on paid holiday, off sick, or on maternity, paternity, shared parental or adoption leave, or are absent from work without a good reason, are disregarded – ie, the hours you would have worked are included when calculating the average hours.[19]

Note:

- If you work casually or intermittently (eg, you are a seasonal worker and work in the summer but you are unemployed during the rest of the year), you can argue that your work cycle is that part of the year in which you are in work and that you do not count as in work when you are unemployed.[20]
- If you (or your partner or non-dependant) have a work cycle that lasts a year with periods in which you do not work (eg, in a school):
  - for JSA and ESA, if the average hours of work you (or your partner) do over the whole cycle means you (or your partner) are not in full-time paid work, you can claim JSA or income-related ESA. However, you may only qualify during periods when your income is sufficiently low – eg, during unpaid summer holidays. You could also claim WTC if you (or your partner) work sufficient hours each week during term time (see Chapter 10);
  - for IS, PC and HB, the 'term-time only' worker rule applies (see p994).

Example

Eduardo, a shop worker, works two seven-and-half hour shifts each week, on Monday and Wednesday. Every three weeks he works two additional weekend shifts. These are also seven-and-half hours each.

Over his work cycle of three weeks, Eduardo works a total of 60 hours. So his average working week is 20 hours.

Eduardo's partner can claim income-related ESA because Eduardo is not in full-time paid work for this purpose (although his earnings would be included in the ESA calculation). However, Eduardo cannot claim JSA himself, even though he is available for and actively seeking more work, because the JSA regulations regard his work as full time.

No regular pattern of work

If there is no regular pattern of work (no recognisable work cycle), an average of your hours is used. This is the average over the five weeks immediately before the date of your claim (or of a supersession decision), or the average over a longer or a

Part 7: Work and work-related rules
Chapter 43: Work and benefits
1. The full-time paid work rule

shorter period if this would give a more accurate figure.[21] The five-week period may not be appropriate if the average is distorted – eg, if you have done a short period of overtime that is not typical.[22]

No work pattern yet established

If you (or your partner or non-dependant) have not yet established a recognisable work cycle, the number of hours or average number of hours you are expected to work each week is used.[23] This may apply, for example, if you have just started work or if your working arrangements have changed and your previous work cycle no longer applies. Once there is sufficient evidence to calculate your average hours, the decision can be revised or superseded.

'Term-time only' workers

For IS, PC and HB, if you have a recognisable work cycle, with periods when you do not work, that lasts for a year, the 'term-time only' worker rule applies. The average number of hours in the periods when you are actually working (eg, during term time) determines whether you are in full-time paid work throughout the year.[24] People who work in schools, colleges or similar institutions are affected by this rule, hence its name, but it could apply in any other seasonal job. In practice, if your average hours of work during term-time mean you are in full-time paid work during term time, you also count as being in full-time paid work over the school holidays, even if you do no work and are not paid. This means:

- if you or your partner count as in full-time paid work, you cannot claim IS during the school holidays. You might be able to claim JSA or ESA. You can claim WTC if you normally work sufficient hours each week (see p196);
- if a non-dependant counts as in full-time paid work, higher rate non-dependant deductions may continue to be made from your HB or your IS, JSA or ESA housing costs (see p69 and p467) throughout the year.

Although this rule may apply to other seasonal workers, if you work casually or intermittently and are unemployed the rest of the year, you can argue that it does not.[25] If your contract comes to an end before a period of absence from work, you should not count as a term-time only worker, unless there is an understanding with your employer that you are expected to start work again.[26]

Sometimes it might not be clear whether you have a work cycle that lasts a year – eg, if you have only started your job recently or have a fixed-term contract that finishes at the end of the school term, or you are employed on a casual or relief basis.[27] It takes time before it can be said that you have a yearly work cycle.[28] However, if you have an indefinite contract to work in term time only, the decision maker may say that you have a yearly work cycle from the start.[29]

Example

Sheila is a school meals worker. She works 20 hours a week, 38 weeks of the year. She gets four weeks' paid holiday, but otherwise is not paid when she is not working at the school. Her average hours are calculated as follows:

20 hours x 38 weeks = 760 hours. 52 weeks – 4 weeks' paid holiday = 48 weeks.

760 hours divided by 48 weeks = 15.84 average hours a week.

Sheila can claim JSA if her income is low enough as she is not in full-time paid work for JSA purposes. She might also qualify for WTC. She cannot qualify for IS as the term-time only worker rule applies and her hours during term time are too high.

If you are unsure whether you are in full-time paid work

If you are unsure whether you or your partner are working for 16/24 hours or more a week, you should make a claim in any event. If your situation then changes or it becomes clearer that your hours are sufficiently low, provide details of the hours you (or your partner) have worked since you claimed. Provided you do this before the decision maker makes a decision, s/he should take the new information into account. If you are refused benefit because your hours were too high, but later your circumstances change, make a fresh claim.

Alternatively, if you are refused WTC because you or your partner do not count as in full-time paid work for WTC purposes and within 14 days of that decision you claim IS (or, if you do not come under the UC system, JSA), your claim for IS or JSA can be backdated to the date you claimed WTC.[30] This rule does not apply to ESA. However, your ESA claim can be backdated for up to three months.

If your (or your partner's) circumstances change while you are claiming:

- IS, JSA or ESA, you may be uncertain about whether the paid work is now full time – eg, if your average weekly hours change or your partner now gets regular overtime. If it appears that you (or your partner) are now working 16/24 hours or more a week, report this to the DWP to avoid an overpayment. Also check to see whether you qualify for WTC. Remember, you cannot qualify for ESA if *you* do *any* paid work, unless it is work you can do while claiming (see p1021);
- HB, report this to the local authority. A change in your hours of work may affect your entitlement to an additional earnings, or a childcare costs, disregard (see p281).

In all cases, increases or decreases in your earnings can affect the amount of benefit to which you are entitled.

If your non-dependant's circumstances change while you are claiming HB (or help with housing costs in IS, JSA, ESA or PC), report this to the local authority (or DWP) to enable your non-dependant deduction to be adjusted.

Part 7: Work and work-related rules
Chapter 43: Work and benefits
3. People treated as not in full-time paid work

2. **People treated as in full-time paid work**

You or your partner can be treated as being in full-time paid work, even if you are not, if:

- for income support (IS), jobseeker's allowance (JSA) and housing benefit (HB), you or your partner (or for employment and support allowance (ESA), your partner) normally work full time, but are **on holiday** and there is a common intention that the employment will be resumed once the holiday is over.[31] Whether you count as on holiday depends on your contractual or legal entitlement to holiday. You can argue that you only count as on holiday if you are paid for it.[32] However, for JSA, even if you do not count as in full-time paid work because you are on unpaid leave, you are likely to have difficulty persuading the DWP that you are available for and actively seeking work (see Chapter 46). For IS and HB, in some cases, if you are a full-time 'term-time only' worker and your cycle of work lasts a year, you are treated as in full-time work during the school holidays (see p994);

- for IS, JSA and HB, you or your partner (or, for ESA, your partner) are **absent from full-time paid work without a good reason**.[33] All your circumstances should be taken into account. Whether or not your employer has authorised the absence is not conclusive, although if it is authorised, it is likely that you have a good reason;

- for IS and JSA, you or your partner stopped full-time paid work, but you are still **within the period covered by payment in lieu of earnings or wages, or certain holiday pay** (unless they can be disregarded). For ESA, this rule applies if you stopped paid work or if your partner stopped full-time paid work.[34]
Note: most earnings and payments *are* disregarded if the employment ends before entitlement to IS, JSA or ESA starts. You (or your partner) are *not* treated as in full-time paid work and you can claim IS, JSA or ESA as soon as the work finishes. See p273 for details on payments when you stop work.

For IS, JSA, PC and HB, **your non-dependant** can also be treated as in full-time paid work under the rules above. For ESA, your non-dependant can also be treated as in full-time paid work if s/he normally works full time but is on holiday, or is away from work 'without good cause'.

You or your partner can be treated as in full-time paid work for the first seven days you (or s/he) are **involved in a trade dispute**. See p940 for information about entitlement to, and the amount of, IS or JSA during a trade dispute.

3. **People treated as not in full-time paid work**

There are situations when you (or your partner or non-dependant) are treated as not in full-time paid work, even if you actually are. For income support (IS), jobseeker's allowance (JSA) and employment and support allowance (ESA), see below. For housing benefit (HB) and pension credit (PC), see p998.

Income support, jobseeker's allowance and employment and support allowance

You (and your partner and your non-dependant) are treated as not being in full-time paid work in the following circumstances. Unless indicated, this applies to you for IS and JSA, and to your partner for IS, income-based JSA and income-related ESA, if you (or s/he):[35]

- are working on a training scheme and are being paid a training allowance under specific provisions;
- for JSA only, are on Work Experience or, if you do not come under the universal credit system, are participating in a specified scheme for assisting people to obtain employment – eg, the Work Programme (see p1103);
- are a volunteer (other than for a relative) or are working for a charity or voluntary organisation and are giving your services free (except for your expenses);
- are providing care for someone:
  - who is staying with you but who is not normally a member of your household and you receive payments from a health authority, local authority or voluntary organisation, or from the person concerned under section 26(3A) of the National Assistance Act 1948 for caring for her/him;
  - for IS and ESA, in the circumstances described on p104. This means that any hours of work you do are ignored, not just the hours you spend caring. For JSA, the hours you spend caring are ignored in this situation (see p992);
- are a foster carer (or, in Scotland only, a kinship carer) receiving a payment from a local authority or voluntary organisation for a child you are looking after. For working tax credit purposes, you can count as being in full-time paid work (see p204);
- work as a part-time firefighter, auxiliary coastguard, member of the Territorial Army or reserve forces, or member of a lifeboat crew;
- are performing duties as a local authority councillor;
- for IS and ESA only, are working as a childminder in your (or her/his) home;
- are engaged in an activity for which you (or s/he) receive, or expect to receive, a sports award from UK Sport and no other payment is made;
- for IS only, qualify for mortgage interest run-on (see p474);
- are doing work in connection with your course of education as a student;[36]
- are on maternity, adoption, paternity or shared parental leave or are absent from work because you are sick, even if when you are not on leave or off sick you normally work 16/24 hours or more each week.[37]

Part 7: Work and work-related rules
Chapter 43: Work and benefits
4. Self-employed people

Note:
- For ESA, *you* do not count as in paid work if you are doing work you can do while claiming (see p1021).
- You, your partner or your non-dependant can also be treated as not in full-time paid work if you (or s/he) are involved in a trade dispute or, for IS or ESA, have recently returned to work following one. See p940 for more about IS or JSA during a trade dispute.

Housing benefit and pension credit

You (or your partner or non-dependant) are treated as *not* being in full-time paid work if:[38]
- you (or s/he) are on maternity, adoption, paternity or shared parental leave or are absent from work because you are sick, even if when you are not on leave or off sick you normally work 16 hours or more each week. However, for HB, you and your partner *can* count as in full-time paid work on such leave to enable you to get an earnings disregard for childcare costs (see p281 and p323);
- the only payment you (or s/he) receive is a sports award from UK Sport.

In addition, you (or your partner or non-dependant) are treated as *not* being in full-time paid work in a benefit week, if in that week you (or s/he) are on IS or income-based JSA (or for HB only, income-related ESA) for more than three days.[39]

---

4. **Self-employed people**

Self-employed people may work long hours for little income, or even make a loss. Nevertheless, all work in expectation of payment counts as paid work. The DWP counts payments from the business to meet living expenses (in cash or in kind) as payment for work unless the drawings are from the business capital.[40] If you simply invest in a business and do not help to run it, you are not treated as self-employed.[41]

Note:
- If you work sufficient hours, you count as in full-time paid work.
- It may be difficult to establish whether or not you are in full-time paid work – eg, if there are periods when you have no work, or if you only work part of the year (eg, seasonally) on a regular basis. Whether or not you are in work depends on whether you are carrying out activities in connection with self-employment. Whether or not you are in full-time paid work depends on how many hours you are doing in expectation of payment (using the rules described earlier in this chapter). During periods when you are not in work, or if you have ceased trading, you should not count as in paid work.[42]

- When calculating the number of hours you work each week, the decision maker counts all those necessary to run your business, including time spent visiting potential customers, providing estimates, advertising, bookkeeping, visiting wholesalers and retailers, cleaning the premises and doing research work – eg, if you are a writer.[43] The hours spent on services for which you are paid count, as well as other time which is essential for your business – eg, preparation time or unsuccessfully soliciting new customers.[44] The decision maker should accept your statement unless there is a reason for doubt.[45]

5. Universal credit

You can qualify for universal credit (UC) whether or not you or your partner are in paid work. Bear the following in mind.

- Income from work is taken into account in working out how much UC you get.
- You may not have to satisfy any work-related requirements if you have sufficient earnings (see p1084).
- You (and your partner) must satisfy a work condition to get a childcare costs element (see p264).
- You cannot get a UC housing costs element for owner-occupier payments if you have any earnings, no matter how low or how few hours you work (see Chapter 22). You *can* get a housing costs element for rent payments.
- If you are getting UC and have earnings above a set amount, you are exempt from the benefit cap (see p1181).

6. Non-means-tested benefits

Entitlement to some non-means-tested benefits is affected by issues to do with work and employment. For the rules for a specific benefit, see the relevant chapter in this *Handbook*.

- You cannot qualify for:
  - carer's allowance if you are 'gainfully employed' – ie, you earn more than £116 each week (see p557 for how this is calculated);
  - benefits based on your incapacity for work or limited capability for work (eg, contributory employment and support allowance) in any week you do any work unless this is work you can do while claiming – called 'permitted work';
  - contribution-based jobseeker's allowance if you are in full-time paid work. The rules described in this chapter apply.
- To qualify for:
  - industrial injuries benefits, you must have been an employed earner when you had an accident or contracted a disease;

Part 7: Work and work-related rules
Chapter 43: Work and benefits
7. Working tax credit and means-tested benefits

- maternity allowance, you must satisfy an employment condition.
- Statutory sick pay, statutory maternity pay, statutory adoption pay, statutory paternity pay and statutory shared parental pay are linked to your being employed (not self-employed) and in some cases you can get them even if your employment ends.
- Whether you are an employed earner or self-employed affects your national insurance contributions (see Chapter 42).

7. **Working tax credit and means-tested benefits**

The work rules for working tax credit (WTC) are outlined in Chapter 10. Differences between the work rules for WTC and those for income support (IS), income-based jobseeker's allowance (JSA), and income-related employment and support allowance (ESA) mean that you can qualify for WTC and a means-tested 'income' benefit at the same time – eg, if you:

- are off work sick, and are receiving statutory sick pay, or within 28 weeks of claiming ESA (see p202);
- are a term-time only worker, during the school holidays (see p994); *or*
- have a partner, s/he counts as a 'disabled worker' for WTC, and s/he works between 16 and 24 hours per week (see p196).

If you qualify for both, note:

- WTC counts in full as income for IS, income-based JSA and income-related ESA;
- only taxable contributory ESA and contribution-based JSA count as income for WTC (see p652 and p717) – means-tested benefits are disregarded.

Which means-tested benefit or tax credit should you claim?

1. If you can choose between claiming IS, JSA or ESA and WTC, check which passported benefits you lose or gain (see p12).

2. You get free school lunches for your child(ren) if you are getting IS, income-based JSA or income-related ESA, but (generally) not if you are getting WTC (see p860).

3. If you claim IS, JSA or ESA, you can get help with your housing costs (see Chapter 20). You cannot get help with housing costs with WTC.

4. There is a capital limit for IS, income-based JSA and income-related ESA, but not for WTC.

5. You can get help with your childcare costs if you claim WTC, but not with IS, JSA or ESA.

Notes

1. The full-time paid work rule

1 Sch1 para 6 (1)(e) WRA 2007; regs 40 and 41 ESA Regs; reg 37 ESA Regs 2013
2 s124(1)(c) SSCBA 1992; s3(1)(e) JSA 1995; Sch 1 para 6(1)(f) WRA 2007
3 **IS** Reg 5 IS Regs
JSA Reg 51 JSA Regs; reg 42 JSA Regs 2013
HB Reg 6(1) HB Regs; reg 6(1) HB(SPC) Regs
4 **IS** Reg 5(1A) IS Regs
JSA Reg 51(1)(b) JSA Regs
ESA Reg 42(1) ESA Regs
5 Reg 6(1) HB Regs; reg 6(1) HB(SPC) Regs
6 **IS** Regs 2(1) and 5 IS Regs
JSA Reg 51(1)(c) JSA Regs
ESA Sch 6 para 2(1) ESA Regs
PC Sch 2 para 2(1) SPC Regs
HB Reg 6(1) HB Regs; reg 6(1) HB(SPC) Regs
7 Reg 3E(2)(g) JSA Regs
8 R(IS) 5/95; *Fiore v CAO*, 20 June 1995
9 *CAO v Ellis* [1995] (CA), reported as R(IS) 22/95; CTC/626/2001
10 R(IS) 1/93
11 *Kevin Smith v CAO* [1994] (CA), reported as R(IS) 21/95
12 *CAO v Ellis* [1995] (CA), reported as R(IS) 22/95; CIS/434/1994
13 CFC/33/1993; R(FIS) 1/83
14 R(JSA) 1/07; *Saunderson v SSWP* [2012] ScotCS CSIH 10
15 **IS** Reg 5(7) IS Regs
JSA Reg 51(3)(a) JSA Regs; reg 42(3)(a) JSA Regs 2013
ESA Regs 42(2) and 45(9) and Sch 6 para 2(7) ESA Regs
16 Ch78 App5, paras 21, 23, 30 and 47 DMG
17 Reg 51(3)(c) JSA Regs; reg 42(3)(c) JSA Regs 2013
18 **IS** Reg 5(2)(b)(i) IS Regs
JSA Reg 51(2)(b)(i) JSA Regs; reg 43(2)(b)(i) JSA Regs 2013
ESA Regs 42(2) and 45(8)(b)(i) and Sch 6 para 2(2)(a) ESA Regs
PC Sch 2 para 2(4) SPC Regs
HB Reg 6(2)(a) HB Regs; reg 6(2)(a) HB(SPC) Regs

19 R(JSA) 5/03
20 R(JSA) 1/07; *Saunderson v SSWP* [2012] ScotCS CSIH 10
21 para 20322 DMG
IS Reg 5(2)(b)(ii) IS Regs
JSA Reg 51(2)(b)(ii) JSA Regs; reg 42(2)(b)(ii) JSA Regs 2013
ESA Regs 42(2) and 45(8)(b)(ii) and Sch 6 para 2(2)(b) ESA Regs
PC Sch 2 para 2(2)(b) SPC Regs
HB Reg 6(2)(b) HB Regs; reg 6(2)(b) HB(SPC) Regs
22 CFC/2963/2001; *NS v SSWP (IS)* [2015] UKUT 423 (AAC)
23 **IS** Reg 5(2)(a) IS Regs
JSA Reg 51(2)(a) JSA Regs; reg 42(2)(a) JSA Regs 2013
ESA Regs 42(2) and 45(8)(a) and Sch 6 para 2(3) ESA Regs
PC Sch 2 para 2(4) SPC Regs
HB Reg 6(4) HB Regs; reg 6(4) HB(SPC) Regs
All R(IS) 8/95
24 **IS** Regs 2(2)(b)(i) and 5(3B) IS Regs
PC Sch 2 para 2(3) SPC Regs
HB Reg 6(3) HB Regs; reg 6(3) HB(SPC) Regs
All *Stafford and Banks v CAO* [2001] UKHL 33, reported as R(IS) 15/01
25 R(JSA) 1/07; *Saunderson v SSWP* [2012] ScotCS CSIH 10; *MC v SSWP (IS)* [2013] UKUT 384 (AAC) (provides a useful summary of the equivalent rules on earnings)
26 CJSA/3832/2006
27 R(JSA) 8/03
28 CIS/914/1997; CJSA/2759/1998
29 R(JSA) 5/02
30 Reg 6(28) SS(C&P) Regs

Part 7: Work and work-related rules
Chapter 43: Work and benefits
Notes

2. People treated as in full-time paid work

31 **IS** Reg 5(3) IS Regs
JSA Reg 52(1) JSA Regs; reg 43(1) JSA
Regs 2013
ESA Reg 42(3) and Sch 6 para 2(4) ESA
Regs
PC Sch 2 para 2(5) SPC Regs
HB Reg 6(5) HB Regs; reg 6(5) HB(SPC)
Regs
All R(U) 1/62

32 R(JSA) 5/03; Vol 4 Ch 20, para 20309
DMG

33 **IS** Reg 5(3) IS Regs
JSA Reg 52(1) JSA Regs; reg 43(1) JSA
Regs 2013
ESA Reg 42(3) and Sch 6 para 2(4) ESA
Regs
PC Sch 2 para 2(5) SPC Regs
HB Reg 6(5) HB Regs; reg 6(5) HB(SPC)
Regs

34 **IS** Reg 5(5) and (5A) IS Regs
JSA Reg 52(3) and (3A) JSA Regs; reg
43(2) and (3) JSA Regs 2013
ESA Regs 41(2) and (3) and 42(4) and
(5) ESA Regs

3. People treated as not in full-time paid work

35 **IS** Reg 6(1) and (5) IS Regs
JSA Reg 53(a)-(f) and (i)-(m) JSA Regs;
reg 44 JSA Regs 2013
ESA Reg 43 and Sch 6 para 2(6) and (8)
ESA Regs

36 R(FIS) 1/86; CDWA/1/1992

37 **IS** Reg 5(3A) IS Regs
JSA Reg 52(1) JSA Regs; reg 43(1) JSA
Regs 2013
ESA Reg 43(3) and Sch 6 para 2(5) ESA
Regs
All CIS/621/2004

38 **PC** Sch 2 para 2(7) and (8) SPC Regs
HB Reg 6(7) and (8) HB Regs; reg 6(7)
and (8) HB(SPC) Regs

39 **PC** Sch 2 para 2(6) SPC Regs
HB Reg 6(6) HB Regs; reg 6(6) HB(SPC)
Regs

4. Self-employed people

40 Vol 4 Ch 20, para 20238 DMG

41 CIS/649/1992

42 R(JSA) 1/09; *GM v SSWP (JSA)* [2010]
UKUT 221 (AAC); [2012] AACR 9;
Saunderson v SSWP [2012] ScotCS CSIH
10

43 Vol 4 Ch 20, para 20265 DMG

44 R(FIS) 6/85; *Kazantzis v CAO* [1999],
reported as R(IS) 13/99

45 Vol 4 Ch 20, para 20267 DMG

Chapter 44

•••

Limited capability for work

This chapter covers:
1. The work capability assessment (below)
2. Challenging a decision (p1015)
3. Periods of limited capability for work (p1021)
4. Work you can do while claiming (p1021)

Key facts

- If you are too disabled or ill to work and are assessed as having 'limited capability for work', you may be entitled to employment and support allowance (ESA), national insurance credits and, in some circumstances, to an additional amount in your housing benefit (HB).
- Your capability for work is assessed by a test called the 'work capability assessment'.
- The work capability assessment also tests whether you have 'limited capability for work-related activity'. If so, you are placed in the 'support group' for ESA and may be entitled to an additional amount of HB.
- If you come under the universal credit (UC) system, the work capability assessment tests whether you have limited capability for work and limited capability for work-related activity, and so are entitled to an extra amount of UC.
- In general, you cannot work and have limited capability for work at the same time, although certain kinds of work are allowed.
- If you disagree with the decision about your limited capability for work or work-related activity, you can apply for a revision or supersession, or appeal against it. You must apply for a mandatory reconsideration before you can appeal.

1. **The work capability assessment**

The work capability assessment is used to decide whether you have 'limited capability for work' – ie, whether your physical and mental health is such that you cannot be expected to work. It is used as part of the test for entitlement to

Part 7: Work and work-related rules
Chapter 44: Limited capability for work
1. The work capability assessment

income-related and contributory employment and support allowance (ESA). It is also used to decide whether you can get extra amounts included in universal credit (UC) and what sort of claimant responsibilities apply to you if you come under the UC system.

The work capability assessment is also used to decide whether you are entitled to national insurance (NI) credits for limited capability for work (see Chapter 42) and, if you have claimed ESA and housing benefit (HB), whether you are entitled to a work-related activity component in your HB (see p250). **Note:** this component is abolished for new claims from 3 April 2017. In all these cases, whether you have limited capability for work is decided under the rules for ESA.

The work capability assessment also determines whether you have 'limited capability for work-related activity' (see p1010). This is a different test, used to decide whether your health condition is so severe that you cannot be expected to work or to engage in activity such as attending interviews about looking for work or retraining. If you have limited capability for work-related activity, you are placed in the 'support group' for ESA (see p641). If you have claimed both ESA and HB, you are entitled to a support component as part of your HB (see p251). In both cases, whether you have limited capability for work-related activity is decided under the rules for ESA.

The work capability assessment is 'an assessment of the extent to which [a person] who has some specific disease or bodily or mental disablement' is capable of performing specified activities, or is incapable of performing them.[1] If you have certain limitations in performing these activities, you score points in the assessment. The activities, limitations and points are in Appendix 4.

You satisfy the work capability assessment if you score sufficient points (see p1008), or you do not score sufficient points but you have exceptional circumstances (see p1009). You also satisfy the work capability assessment if you are treated as having limited capability for work (see p1005).

Treated as not having limited capability for work

For ESA, you are treated as not having limited capability for work (ie, to have failed the work capability assessment, even if you have been assessed as satisfying it) if you:

- do not return the ESA50 questionnaire (see p1011) or attend the medical (see p1013) while the work capability assessment applies to you, and you do not have good cause (see p1011 and p1013); *or*
- do any work, except certain work you can do while claiming (see p1021);[2] *or*
- are disqualified from receiving contributory ESA for more than six weeks because you are a prisoner. If this applies, but you are entitled to income-related ESA (ie, pending trial or sentence pending conviction), you are only treated as not having limited capability for work after your entitlement has ended;[3] *or*

- attend a training course and receive a training allowance or premium, unless your ESA claim is for a period beginning after you stopped attending the course, or if the training allowance or premium was only for travelling or meal expenses;[4] *or*
- are (or were) a member of the armed forces and the day in question is a day of sickness absence from duty.[5]

For UC, you are treated as not having limited capability for work if:[6]
- you have previously failed the work capability assessment, either for UC or for contributory ESA under the UC system. The DWP does not reassess you unless the decision was made in ignorance of, or based on a mistake about, a material fact, or there has been a relevant change in your condition; *or*
- you do not return the UC50 questionnaire, or you do not attend the medical and do not have good reason for this.

In addition for UC, if you work, you are automatically treated as not having limited capability for work if your monthly earnings are at least the level of earnings you would receive for 16 hours' work a week paid at the rate of the national minimum wage for people aged 25 and over, converted to a monthly amount – ie, in 2017/18 earnings at or above £520 a month.[7] However, you can work and earn above this threshold without automatically being treated as not having limited capability for work if you are:
- entitled to attendance allowance (AA), disability living allowance (DLA) or personal independence payment (PIP), or you have already been assessed as having limited capability for work (although the DWP may still reassess you); *or*
- automatically treated as having limited capability for work because of a specific circumstance (eg, you are terminally ill – see below), or you are treated as having limited capability for work-related activity (see p1010).

Treated as having limited capability for work

You are automatically treated as having limited capability for work if a specific circumstance (sometimes called an 'exemption') applies to you.[8]

Employment and support allowance and universal credit
For both ESA and UC, you are treated as having limited capability for work if:
- you are terminally ill – ie, your death can reasonably be expected within six months;
- you are receiving chemotherapy or radiotherapy treatment for cancer, recovering from such treatment or are likely to receive such treament within six months from the date the DWP determines whether or not you pass the work capability assessment;

Part 7: Work and work-related rules
Chapter 44: Limited capability for work
1. The work capability assessment

- you have been given official notice not to work because of being in contact with an infectious disease;
- you are an inpatient in hospital where you have been medically advised to stay for at least 24 hours, or are recovering from treatment as an inpatient (and the DWP is satisfied that your condition remains sufficiently serious), including if you are attending a residential programme of rehabilitation for drug or alcohol addiction;
- you are receiving plasmapheresis, regular weekly treatment for haemodialysis for chronic renal failure, or regular weekly treatment for total parenteral nutrition for gross impairment of enteric function, or are recovering from such treatment (and, for ESA only, the DWP is satisfied that you should continue to be treated as having limited capability for work). For ESA in the first week of such treatment, you must be receiving it or recovering from it for at least two days. You continue to be treated as having limited capability for work if your treatment later goes down to one day a week. However, you cannot get income-related ESA in any week in which you work (apart from work you can do while claiming – see p1021), although you can claim contributory ESA for the days of treatment and recovery;[9]
- you are pregnant and there is a serious risk to your health or your baby's health if you do not refrain from work.

Employment and support allowance only

For ESA only, you also are treated as having limited capability for work if:

- you are entitled to the support component on the basis that you meet one of the eating and drinking descriptors in the test for limited capability for work-related activity (see p1009);
- you are entitled to statutory sick pay for the purpose of the 196-day qualifying period (see p637) for ESA in youth;
- you are pregnant or have recently given birth, you are not entitled to maternity allowance (MA) or statutory maternity pay, you have a medical certificate giving the expected or actual date of birth, and you are within the period beginning with the first day of the sixth week before the expected week of childbirth (or the actual day of childbirth if earlier) and ending on the 14th day after you have the baby;
- you are pregnant, in the MA period and entitled to MA;
- you are waiting for an assessment or you are appealing and you satisfy certain conditions (see p1007);
- **for income-related ESA only**, you are in education, you are not a 'qualifying young person' (see p572) and you are eligible for income-related ESA because you receive DLA, PIP or armed forces independent payment;
- **for contributory ESA only**, you come under the UC system (see p20) and have already been assessed as having limited capability for work for UC.[10]

If you are waiting for an assessment or you are appealing

For ESA only, you are treated as having limited capability for work if:[11]

- you are applying for ESA and have provided a current medical certificate, but the work capability assessment has not yet been carried out. You can get ESA while waiting for your assessment. However, this does not apply if you are reclaiming ESA after having failed the work capability assessment, unless your condition has significantly worsened or you have a new health condition. Your condition has significantly worsened if it is considered that you would now be likely to pass the work capability assessment;[12]

- you are appealing against a decision that you have failed the work capability assessment (ie, you were found not to have limited capability for work) and you have submitted a medical certificate. However, unless your current claim for ESA was made before 30 March 2015, this only applies if:
  - this is the first time you have failed the work capability assessment; *or*
  - this the first time you have failed the work capability assessment since a previous decision that you satisfied it (see p1017); *or*
  - your condition has significantly worsened. Your condition has significantly worsened if it is considered that you would now be likely to pass the work capability assessment;[13] *or*
  - you have a new health condition;

- you are reclaiming ESA and have provided a current medical certificate, after being treated as failing the work capability assessment because you failed to return the ESA50 questionnaire or failed to attend the medical. You can get ESA while waiting for your assessment. However, this only applies if:
  - you have now returned the questionnaire; *or*
  - it is more than six months since the decision treating you as not having limited capability for work; *or*
  - your condition has significantly worsened. Your condition has significantly worsened if it is considered that you would now be likely to pass the work capability assessment;[14] *or*
  - you have a new health condition.

Examples

Julie had back pain and so applied for ESA, but failed the work capability assessment. Later, she develops depression and reclaims ESA. The decision maker accepts that Julie has a new condition, and so treats her as having limited capability for work and pays her ESA while a new work capability assessement is arranged.

Dom claims ESA, but fails the work capability assessment. He requests a mandatory reconsideration of the decision, but it is not changed, so Dom appeals. As this is the first time Dom has failed the work capability assessment and he has supplied a current medical certificate, he is treated as having limited capability for work and so can get ESA while his appeal is pending.

Part 7: Work and work-related rules
Chapter 44: Limited capability for work
1. The work capability assessment

Universal credit only

For UC only, you are treated as having limited capability for work if:[15]

- you have already been assessed as having limited capability for work for contributory ESA paid under the UC system; *or*
- you are at least the qualifying age for pension credit (PC – see p147) and entitled to DLA or PIP.

If you are transferring to UC from ESA, you are treated as having limited capability for work if you were entitled to the work-related activity component in your ESA (see p641).[16]

Note: unlike for ESA, there is no UC rule that treats you as having limited capability for work while you are waiting for the work capability assessment to be carried out.

Scoring points

The assessment does not take into account actual jobs, your education or training, or any language or literacy problems. It is a test of your ability to perform certain activities, taking account of a 'specific bodily disease or disablement' or a 'specific mental illness or disablement', and the direct results of medical treatment (from a registered doctor) for these.[17] There are two lists of activities: one physical, one mental. Under each activity, there is a further list of statements, called 'descriptors', which describe different levels of difficulty in carrying out the activity. Attached to each descriptor is a points score. You are awarded the highest scoring descriptor in each activity that applies to you, taking into account your ability when wearing or using any aid, appliance or prosthesis that you normally wear or use, or any aid or appliance that you could reasonably be expected to wear or use.[18] For the full list of activities, descriptors and points, see Appendix 4.

To satisfy the test, you must score a total of 15 points or more. The points can be scored in one or more activities, and scores from the physical and mental activities can be combined. For example, you can score nine points in the physical test and six points in the mental test. To score points in the physical test, your incapacity must arise from a 'specific bodily disease or disablement', and to score points in the mental test, your incapacity must arise from a 'specific mental illness or disablement'.[19]

Good days and bad days, pain and tiredness

Generally, what counts is your capability as it is 'most of the time'. If you cannot repeat an activity without a reasonable degree of regularity, you should be considered unable to perform it. The following points should apply.

- Your ability to perform an activity with some degree of repetition should be considered and a 'broad-brush' approach applied, rather than just a day-by-day approach.[20]

- A descriptor should apply to you if you cannot perform the activity most of the time. The severity of your condition, the frequency of your good and bad days and the unpredictability of the bad days are all relevant.[21]
- If you have long periods of remission, you may be considered capable of work during these periods. This depends on the severity of your condition and on the length of your periods of ill health and your periods of remission.[22]
- Pain, fatigue and the increasing difficulty you may have in performing an activity on a repeated basis compared with someone in good health should be taken into account.[23] 'Pain' may include nausea and dizziness.[24]
- Any risk to your health in performing an activity should be considered, particularly if carrying it out is against medical advice. If the risk is sufficiently serious, you may be considered incapable of the activity.[25]

Exceptional circumstances

If you do not score sufficient points to satisfy the work capability assessment, you are treated as doing so if:[26]
- you have an uncontrolled or uncontrollable life-threatening disease, and there is medical evidence to show this. There must be reasonable cause for the disease not to be controllable by a recognised therapeutic procedure; or
- because of your illness, there would be a substantial risk to the mental or physical health of any person were you to be found not to have limited capability for work. The 'substantial risk' is one that could arise from the sort of work you may be expected to do, or from the journey to or from work, although it is not necessary to go into the detail of individual job descriptions or potential jobseeker's agreements.[27] However, this exceptional circumstance does not apply to you if the risk could be significantly reduced by reasonable adjustments in your workplace, or by your taking medication prescribed by your doctor.

Limited capability for work-related activity

The work capability assessment includes an assessment of whether you have limited capability for work-related activity. This is to decide whether your health is such that you cannot be expected to do things like attend work-focused interviews or retraining. In effect, the test decides whether you come into the support group for ESA (see p641) and whether you are entitled to a limited capability for work-related activity element in your UC (see p262). If you have claimed HB as well as ESA, it is used to decide whether you are entitled to a support component in your HB (see p251). See p1010 for details of the assessment.

You may automatically count as having limited capability for work-related activity, or you may be required to complete a questionnaire and/or attend a medical. If you do not return the questionnaire or take part in the medical and do

Part 7: Work and work-related rules
Chapter 44: Limited capability for work
1. The work capability assessment

not have 'good cause' ('good reason' for UC), you are treated as not having limited capability for work-related activity.

When deciding whether you have good cause (and, in practice, whether you have good reason for UC), the decision maker must take into account:[28]
- whether you were outside Great Britain at the time you were notified;
- your state of health;
- the nature of any disability you have;
- any other matter s/he thinks appropriate.

Assessing limited capability for work-related activity

To have limited capability for work-related activity, your mental or physical condition must be such that one or more statements (or 'descriptors') describing a severe limitation in certain activities could be applied to you. For the activities and descriptors, see Appendix 5.

A descriptor applies if it applies to you for the majority of the time(s) you try to do the activity described. You are assessed wearing any prosthesis that you are normally fitted with or wear, and/or using any aid or appliance that you normally wear or use, or could reasonably be expected to wear or use.[29]

Some descriptors in Appendix 5 are about physical incapacity. To have them applied to you, your incapacity must arise from 'a specific bodily disease or disablement'. Other descriptors are about mental incapacity. To have them applied to you, your incapacity must arise from 'a specific mental illness or disablement'.[30]

The DWP may retest you to find out whether there has been a relevant change of circumstances, to see whether a previous finding was wrong or mistaken, or (for ESA only) if it is three months or more since your last test.[31]

You may be required to complete a questionnaire and/or attend a medical examination.

Treated as having limited capability for work-related activity

You are treated as having limited capability for work-related activity if:[32]
- you have a terminal illness – ie, your death can reasonably be expected within six months; *or*
- you are receiving chemotherapy or radiotherapy treatment for cancer, or are recovering from that treatment, or you are likely to receive such treatment within six months from the date the DWP determines whether or not you have limited capability for work-related activity. In any of these circumstances, the DWP must be satisfied that you have limited capability for work-related activity. When deciding this, the decision maker should take into account the medical evidence to see if your cancer treatment has side effects which are likely to limit your ability to do work-related activity;[33] *or*
- because of a specific disease or disablement, there would be a substantial risk to your mental or physical health or to the mental or physical health of

someone else if you were found not to have limited capability for work-related activity; *or*

- you are pregnant and there would be a serious risk of damage to your health or to your baby's health if you do not refrain from work-related activity and, for UC only, from work; *or*
- for UC only, you have reached the qualifying age for PC (see p147) and are entitled to AA, the highest rate of the DLA care component or the enhanced rate of the PIP daily living component.

If you are transferring to UC from ESA and were in the support group for ESA, you are treated as having limited capability for work-related activity if you were entitled to the support component in your ESA (see p641).[34]

The work capability assessment process

Information is sought from your doctor and, unless you are treated as having limited capability for work (see p1005), you are sent a questionnaire (ESA50 or UC50) to complete. In most cases, you are required to attend a medical examination at an assessment centre with a doctor (or other approved healthcare professional) from the DWP medical service. Assessments are carried out on behalf of the DWP medical service by the Health Assessment Advisory Service. For official information about the assessment, such as having an audio recording of your medical, using an interpreter and the location of assessment centres, see www.chdauk.co.uk. For advice about the questionnaire and medical, see below and p1013.

As part of the assessment, the doctor (or other approved healthcare professional) also carries out an assessment of whether you have limited capability for work-related activity.

There are no rules on how often you are reassessed. Usually, this is decided by the DWP medical service. **Note:** the government has announced that the DWP will stop reassessing people with 'the most severe conditions and disabilities' who have already been assessed as having limited capability for work-related activity.[35] This change is expected to be introduced during 2017.

The questionnaire

Unless it is already accepted that you have limited capability for work, or you are treated as having limited capability for work, you are sent a questionnaire (ESA50 or UC50) to complete.

How do you complete the questionnaire?

1. Read the notes on the form before answering the questions. It may be helpful to draft your answers on a separate sheet of paper first.

2. If someone has to complete the questionnaire for you, or if you can only do so yourself slowly or with pain, explain this.

Part 7: Work and work-related rules
Chapter 44: Limited capability for work
1. The work capability assessment

3. Make sure to list all your symptoms. If you have to appeal, the First-tier Tribunal may be less likely to believe you have symptoms if you did not mention them on the questionnaire. Ask someone who knows you well to check your answers.

4. If you have good and bad days, explain this. If possible, give a rough estimate of how often you could perform the activity and how often you could not.

5. Compare the draft of your answers with the list in Appendix 4 and work out your score. Your answers should not be exaggerated, but check that you have not underestimated any of your problems and that you have given all the detail you can.

6. If you have any difficulties with English or with reading and writing, get independent help before you submit the form.

7. If someone has helped you fill out the form, include her/his details at the end where the form asks about this.

8. Always make a copy of your questionnaire with your answers before returning it.

You have four weeks from the date the questionnaire is sent to complete and return it. A reminder must be sent to you at least three weeks after the questionnaire was sent. You must then be given a further week from the date the reminder was sent to return the questionnaire. If you still do not return it in time, you are treated as not having limited capability for work, unless you can show that you had good cause (for UC, good reason) for not returning it on time.[36]

Good cause and good reason

When deciding whether you have '**good cause**', the decision maker must consider all the circumstances, including whether you were outside Great Britain at the relevant time, your state of health and the nature of your disability. In practice, the same sort of issues should be taken into account when deciding whether you have '**good reason**' for UC.[37]

If you are late in completing and returning the questionnaire, do so as soon as you can and explain why you were late. If your benefit stops because you are considered not to have had good cause/reason, but you think you did, consider challenging the decision (see p1015). It is understood that 'safeguarding' procedures apply if you are considered to be 'vulnerable' – eg, if you have a serious mental health condition. The safeguarding procedures are not a legal requirement, but involve extra checks before treating you has not having limited capability for work. If you think you are vulnerable, ask whether the safeguarding procedures were applied to you. You should also make a fresh claim for benefit. If the decision maker decides that you did not have good cause/reason, you can appeal (see Chapter 55). You must apply for a mandatory reconsideration first.

On receiving your completed questionnaire, the decision maker considers whether you should be treated as having limited capability for work or if you clearly score enough points to satisfy the test. If neither of these apply, a medical examination is arranged.

Medical examinations

You may be required to attend a medical examination as part of the work capability assessment. Bear in mind the following.

- If you fail to attend a medical examination without good cause (for UC, good reason), you are treated as not having limited capability for work.
- If you cannot attend the medical, contact your assessment centre immediately to explain why and ask for another appointment.
- If you are too ill to travel, ask to be examined at home.
- You can claim your travel expenses for going to the medical. If you have to attend by taxi or minicab, you cannot claim for your fares unless your assessment centre agrees to this before you travel.
- You can take a friend or adviser to the medical with you.
- The medical examiner takes into account the information on your questionnaire, what you tell her/him, and your appearance and behaviour during the assessment.

In order to complete the medical report, the medical examiner asks about your condition and assesses whether, in her/his opinion, you have limited capability for work. S/he considers your abilities in each of the specific areas of activity set out in Appendix 4.

The medical examiner asks about your typical day and uses the information to assess your ability to perform the activities in the work capability assessment. Make sure to tell the examiner about things like good and bad days and what medication you are taking. S/he then completes a report (an ESA85 or UC85), indicating which descriptors s/he thinks apply to you and sends it to the decision maker.

Failing to attend a medical examination

If you do not attend a medical examination without good cause (good reason for UC), you are treated as not having limited capability for work – ie, you fail the work capability assessment. You must have been sent notice of the date and time of the medical at least seven days beforehand, unless you agreed to accept less than this.[38]

Good cause and good reason

When deciding whether you have '**good cause**' for ESA, the decision maker must consider all the circumstances, including those that apply to the questionnaire (see p1011). 'Good cause' may also include being too ill or distressed on the day of the medical, or wishing to be examined by someone of the same sex and this was not possible. You may also be able to show that you had good cause if your refusal to attend was based on a firm religious conviction.[39] In practice, the same sort of things should be taken into account when deciding whether you have '**good reason**' for UC.

Part 7: Work and work-related rules
Chapter 44: Limited capability for work
1. The work capability assessment

If your benefit stops because you are considered not to have good cause/reason for failing to attend the medical, but you think you did, consider challenging the decision (see p1015). It is understood that 'safeguarding' procedures apply if you are considered to be 'vulnerable' – eg, if you have a serious mental health condition. The safeguarding procedures are not a legal requirement, but involve extra checks before treating you as not having limited capability for work. If you think you are vulnerable, ask whether the safeguarding procedures were applied to you. You should also make a fresh claim for benefit. If the decision maker does not accept that you had good cause/reason, consider appealing (see Chapter 55). You must apply for a mandatory reconsideration first.

The decision

The decision on whether or not you have limited capability for work is made by a DWP decision maker. The decision maker can disagree with the medical report, although in practice this is unusual. The medical examiner includes in the medical report a suggested date when the work capability assessment should be applied to you again in order to retest your capability. You cannot appeal about how often you are retested.

If the decision maker does not consider that you have limited capability for work, you are not entitled to ESA and your claim is refused. If you have been getting ESA, your award is revised or superseded (see Chapter 54) and your benefit is stopped. For UC, depending on your circumstances, you might still be able to get some UC, although you are not entitled to the elements for limited capability for work or work-related activity.

What should you do next?

1. If you have been refused ESA (but do not want to challenge the decision) and do not have a job to return to, you can sign on and claim jobseeker's allowance (JSA). Claim as soon as possible, as backdating is only possible in limited circumstances (see p1157). If you come under the UC system (see p20), you cannot get income-based JSA and must claim UC instead. You may still be able to get contribution-based JSA.

2. Remember that if you want to claim ESA again, there are special rules on when you can be treated as having limited capability for work (see p1005). However, if you can satisfy these rules and your new period of limited capability for work is not more than 12 weeks after the end of a previous one, the periods are linked so that, for example, you can be entitled to your former rate of ESA straight away (see p1021).

3. If you think you are not well enough to work, you may be able to challenge the decision by appealing to the First-tier Tribunal (see Chapter 55). You must apply for a mandatory reconsideration first.

4. If you challenge the decision, you cannot get ESA while your request for a mandatory reconsideration is being considered. You may be entitled to another benefit, such as JSA or income support (IS), instead – but note that if you make a new claim for JSA this may result in your coming under the UC system and having to claim UC instead (see p20). Once you

have appealed, if this is the first time you have been found not to have limited capability for work because you have failed the work capability assessment, or the first time since a previous decision that you pass it, and you have also submitted a medical certificate, you can get ESA again (instead of JSA or IS) pending the appeal. However, if this is the second or subsequent time that you have failed the work capability assessment, see p1016. **Note:** there is no similar rule for UC, as you may still be able to get some UC, even though you do not have limited capability for work.

2. **Challenging a decision**

You can challenge a decision by applying for a revision or supersession (see Chapter 54), or by making an appeal (see Chapter 55). You must apply for a mandatory reconsideration before you can appeal.

Initially, the DWP makes a 'determination' on your limited capability for work.[40] The determination should then be incorporated into a decision about your entitlement to benefit or national insurance (NI) credits for limited capability for work. You only have a right of appeal (after a mandatory reconsideration) once this is included in a decision.[41]

Appeals are considered by the First-tier Tribunal, which must include a medically qualified person (see p1338). The tribunal does not have to follow either the ESA85 or UC85 medical report or the decision maker's decision.

Note: when you appeal against a decision, the whole decision can be looked at again if it is considered right to do so. For example, you may be appealing about limited capability for work, but the tribunal may go on to look at whether or not you should be in the support group for employment and support allowance (ESA). Or you may be appealing about whether you should be in the support group, but the tribunal may want to reconsider whether you have limited capability for work. This could result in your losing some, or even all, of your entitlement.

Are you appealing?

1. Get advice from one of the organisations listed in Appendix 2.

2. Remember that there are only certain circumstances in which you can work and still be regarded as having limited capability for work (see p1003). If you work while you are appealing, you may lose entitlement to benefit, even if you eventually win your appeal.

3. Request a copy of the medical evidence that the DWP holds on your file. If you appeal, a copy of the medical report should be included in the appeal papers that the DWP sends to you and HM Courts and Tribunals Service.

4. Request an oral hearing of your appeal. This will give the tribunal the opportunity to hear from you first hand about how your condition affects you, and what happened at the medical examination.

Part 7: Work and work-related rules
Chapter 44: Limited capability for work
2. Challenging a decision

5. Discuss your limited capability for work with your own doctor. In practice, it can be very difficult to win an appeal if your GP or consultant does not support you.

6. Get medical evidence to support your appeal, if you can. This could be from your GP or your consultant, or from both. It is more helpful if this comments on the things at issue in your appeal rather than just setting out your diagnosis and treatment. Check whether your doctor insists on charging you.

7. If you cannot get medical evidence yourself, consider using previous medical reports if you passed the work capability assessment and getting evidence from other sources – eg, a community nurse or an occupational therapist. You could ask the tribunal to obtain further medical evidence, although in practice, it may refuse.[42]

8. The tribunal should make a decision based on all the evidence – medical and non-medical. If necessary, point out that it can prefer your own or your doctor's evidence to that of the medical examiner.[43]

9. DWP medical reports are in electronic form. These may have inconsistencies or errors in them. The tribunal must deal with any discrepancies and take these into account when considering the weight to be given to different sources of evidence.[44]

10. The tribunal cannot carry out its own examination of you.[45] However, be aware that it may observe your conduct in the room – eg, how you walk or sit.

11. Consider asking a person who lives with you or who knows you well to attend the hearing to describe the day-to-day problems you have.

12. Take a list of any medication you are taking to the hearing.

Getting benefit while challenging a decision

You can continue to get UC while your request for a mandatory reconsideration is being considered and while your appeal is pending.

If you have been refused ESA because you have failed the work capability assessment, you cannot get ESA while your request for a mandatory reconsideration is being considered. You may be entitled to one of the following instead:

- jobseeker's allowance (JSA) (see p1019) – but see the note below; *or*
- income support (IS) (see p1019); *or*
- if you come under the universal credit (UC) system (see p20), UC (see p1020) – but see the note below.

Once you have appealed, you may be able to get ESA while your appeal is pending (see p1017). This is usually the best option, if you are able to get ESA. Alternatively, you may be able to get JSA, IS or UC pending the appeal instead.

Note: claiming JSA or UC, or making a new claim for ESA, at any point may bring you under the UC system. If you live in UC 'gateway' area (see p22), you will *not* come under the UC system if, when you claim, you are waiting for the outcome of a mandatory reconsideration or of an appeal against a decision that you are not entitled to ESA. You are most likely to come unde the UC system if you live in a UC 'full service' area (see p24) – eg, if you make a new claim for JSA while your request for a mandatory reconsideration is being considered, or if you cannot get ESA while you are waiting for your appeal to be heard but later try making a new claim for ESA. Getting ESA pending your appeal does *not* mean that you come under the UC system, as it does not require a new claim to be made.

Once you come under the UC system, you cannot get income-based JSA or income-related ESA from that point on, including if you are waiting for your appeal to be heard (see below). You can get UC instead. This remains the case, even if your appeal against the decision about your limited capability for work is successful.

Example

Jim lives in a UC 'full service' area. He was getting income-related ESA, but this stops when he fails the work capability assessment. Jim requests a mandatory reconsideration of the decision, and decides to claim JSA in the meantime. As Jim has made a new claim for JSA, he now comes under the UC system and must claim UC instead.

Jim then appeals and gets UC while his ESA appeal is pending. Jim's appeal against the work capability assessment is eventually successful, but he remains on UC and does not go back to income-related ESA. If Jim had decided not to claim JSA, once he appealed he may have been able to get income-related ESA pending his appeal instead of having to claim UC.

Employment and support allowance

If you appeal against a decision that you do not have limited capability for work and it is the first such decision you have had, or the first since a previous decision that you have limited capability for work, and you have submitted a medical certificate, you are entitled to ESA until the First-tier Tribunal makes its decision.[46] In this chapter, this is referred to as 'ESA pending an appeal'. You cannot get ESA pending an appeal if you are being *treated as* not having limited capability because you did not return the questionnaire or attend the medical (see p1011 and p1013).

Once you have appealed, the government has said that your ESA pending an appeal can cover the period when your request for a mandatory reconsideration was being considered.[47]

However, you cannot get ESA pending an appeal if the decision that you do not have limited capability for work is the second, or a subsequent, such decision you have had in a row, unless your condition has significantly worsened or you have a new condition. This applies if a decision you are appealing against is about a claim made on or after 30 March 2015. Your condition has significantly worsened if it is considered that you might now pass the work capability assessment.[48]

Part 7: Work and work-related rules
Chapter 44: Limited capability for work
2. Challenging a decision

Examples

Megan claims ESA in June 2017. She is found not to have limited capability for work – ie, she fails the work capability assessment. Megan challenges this by asking for a mandatory reconsideration, but the decision is not changed. She appeals and sends in a medical certificate. Megan is entitled to ESA pending the appeal as this is the first time she has failed the work capability assessment.

Alex claimed ESA in June 2016. He was found not to have limited capability for work (ie, he failed the work capability assessment), but he appealed and successfully challenged this. The tribunal decided that he had limited capability for work and he was paid ESA. In May 2017, Alex has another work capability assessment, and fails it. After a mandatory reconsideration, Alex appeals again and sends in a medical certificate. Alex is entitled to ESA pending the appeal: although he has failed the work capability assessment for a second time, it is the first time that he has done so since a prevous decision (ie, that of the tribunal) that he does have limited capability for work.

Jill claimed ESA in December 2016, but failed the work capability assessment and so was not entitled. She tries claiming JSA for a while instead. However, although her condition has not changed, she feels too ill and so, in May 2017, decides to try reclaiming ESA. It is decided that Jill fails the work capability assessment again and so her second claim is also refused. Jill appeals against the decision. As this is a second such decision Jill has had in a row, and her condition has not changed, she cannot get ESA pending her appeal.

If you have limited capability for work, but are appealing about whether or not you should be put in the support group, you remain entitled to ESA while your request for a mandatory reconsideration is being considered and while your appeal is pending. However, the amount you are paid does not include the support component.

Note:
- To get ESA pending an appeal, you must continue to submit medical certificates. You do not need to make a new claim for ESA.[49]
- ESA pending an appeal does not include the work-related component or support component, although it can include any premiums and housing costs to which you are entitled.[50]
- You are treated as having limited capability for work while you are appealing, so usually the DWP does not assess you in this period. However, if you develop a new condition or your condition significantly worsens, the DWP can assess you again. If it determines that you have limited capability for work, you can get ESA in the normal way (including either of the additional components) from that point on. The First-tier Tribunal still considers your appeal for the

period up until then. Even if the DWP determines that you do not have limited capability for work, you remain entitled to ESA pending the appeal.[51]

- If your appeal is successful, the original decision about your limited capability for work is changed so that you are entitled to ESA. Your ESA continues in the normal way, and you can qualify for an additional component.
- If your appeal is successful but the DWP considers that your condition improved while the appeal was pending, it might decide that you do not have limited capability for work now.[52] You can appeal against this decision, and should be able to get ESA pending the appeal again.[53]
- If you lose your appeal, the original decision that you do not have limited capability for work is not changed. From the week after the week in which the First-tier Tribunal notifies the DWP of its decision, the DWP treats you as not having had limited capability for work while you were getting ESA pending your appeal.[54] Your entitlement to ESA therefore stops, although you keep the ESA that was paid to you pending the appeal. Although you can appeal against the decision to treat you as not having limited capability for work, the prospect of success is likely to be limited, as the rules allow the DWP to do this when you have lost your appeal. To continue to get ESA in this situation, whether you appeal or not, you must make a fresh claim.[55]
- If you lose your appeal and make a new claim for ESA, you cannot be treated as having limited capability for work (and so get ESA while waiting for a work capability assessment) unless your condition has significantly worsened or you have a new health condition.

Jobseeker's allowance

You may be able to claim JSA while you are waiting for your request for a mandatory reconsideration to be considered.

Once you have appealed, instead of claiming ESA pending an appeal, you may be able to claim (or continue to claim if you have already done so) JSA, at least until the First-tier Tribunal makes its decision. This may be an attractive option if you cannot get ESA pending the appeal.

To get JSA, you must 'sign on' as being available for and actively seeking work (see p1030 and p1044), and must be prepared to accept any reasonable work within your limitations, even while your appeal is pending. You can place restrictions on your availability if these are reasonable in light of your condition (see p1038). If you win your appeal and you are entitled to ESA, your JSA award is removed and you should get arrears of ESA if they are worth more than the JSA you received.[56] If you lose your appeal, you can remain on JSA, provided you continue to satisfy the rules.

Income support

You may be able to claim IS (see Chapter 5) while you are waiting for your request for a mandatory reconsideration to be considered.

Part 7: Work and work-related rules
Chapter 44: Limited capability for work
2. Challenging a decision

Once you have appealed, instead of getting ESA pending an appeal or JSA, in limited circumstances you may be entitled to claim IS – eg, as a lone parent or carer (see p101).

You do not have to 'sign on' as available for and actively seeking work in order to get IS. However, unless you win your appeal, you are not entitled to NI credits for limited capability for work. Therefore, you should check to see how to protect your NI contribution record while on IS (see Chapter 42). Get advice if necessary. If you win your appeal, you cannot remain entitled to both ESA and to IS at the same time. Normally, your award of IS is removed and you should get arrears of ESA if they are worth more than the IS you received. If you lose your appeal, you can remain on IS, provided you continue to satisfy the rules.

Universal credit

If you come under the UC system (see p20), you can get UC instead of income-related ESA, income-based JSA or IS. This applies while you are waiting for your request for a mandatory reconsideration to be considered and once you have appealed, even if the decision was about your claim for ESA. You may still be able to get contributory ESA or contribution-based JSA. If your challenge is successful and you are regarded as having limited capability for work, you remain on UC even if the decision you challenged was about ESA. Your UC then includes a limited capability for work (or limited capability for work-related activity) element.[57] If your challenge is unsuccessful, you may still be able to get UC, but will not be entitled to a limited capability for work or limited capability for work-related activity element.

If your condition worsens

If your condition has significantly worsened since the decision, or you have a new condition, and you are not already getting ESA pending the appeal (see p1017), you could make a new claim for ESA. In this situation, you should be treated as having limited capability for work until a new work capability assessment is carried out (see p1005).

Note: if you make a new claim for ESA and you come under the UC system (see p20), you cannot get income-related ESA. You can get UC instead. You may still be able to get contributory ESA.

If you are already getting ESA pending the appeal, you could inform the DWP and ask it to make a determination on your limited capability for work. If the DWP thinks that you still fail the work capability assessment, your entitlement to ESA after the appeal has been decided could be affected, even if you win your appeal.

For **UC**, these rules are slightly different. Once there has been a decision that you do not have limited capability for work, there is no further work capability assessment, unless there is evidence to suggest that the decision was made in ignorance of, or based on a mistake about, a material fact, or there has been a relevant change in circumstances regarding your condition.[58]

3. **Periods of limited capability for work**

A 'period of limited capability for work' for employment and support allowance (ESA) generally means a period in which you have, or are treated as having, limited capability for work. It does not include any period not covered by your claim for ESA.[59] However, see the linking rules below. For universal credit (UC), there are no rules on periods of limited capability for work.

Linking rules

Different periods of limited capability for work can be joined or 'linked' to form one continuous period for ESA. The effect is that you are treated as having had limited capability for work throughout the whole of the linked period. Different periods are linked if they are not more than 12 weeks apart.[60] **Note:** a 104-week linking rule applies to housing costs for 'work or training beneficiaries' (see p471).

If periods of limited capability for work are linked, it means that:
- the question of whether or not you satisfy the national insurance contribution conditions for ESA may be decided at the beginning of the first period (see p978);[61]
- you do not have to serve further 'waiting days' (see p639) before becoming entitled to ESA because you have already served them;
- you may be entitled to one of the additional ESA components straight away, or once you have been reassessed as passing the work capability assessment;
- for the purposes of the rules on housing costs, certain linking rules apply (see p470).

4. **Work you can do while claiming**

The general rule is that you cannot work and be entitled to employment and support allowance (ESA) at the same time.[62] With certain exceptions (see p1022), in any week in which you work (paid or unpaid), you are not entitled to ESA and you are automatically treated as not having limited capability for work, even if it has previously been decided that you do.[63]

However, you are only treated as not entitled to ESA on the actual days that you work, rather than the whole week, if you work:
- during the first week of your claim; *or*
- during the last week in which you had limited capability for work or were treated as having limited capability for work.[64]

Part 7: Work and work-related rules
Chapter 44: Limited capability for work
4. Work you can do while claiming

It is arguable that work that is so minimal that it can be regarded as trivial or negligible[65] should be ignored.

You can do certain work without automatically being treated as not having limited capability for work. For how earnings from this may affect income-related ESA, see Chapter 14. **Note:** earnings under the 'permitted work' rules (see p1023) under the relevant earnings limit are ignored.

You can do the following:[66]
- work as a local councillor;
- work (for a maximum of one day or two half days a week) as a member of the First-tier Tribunal if you have been appointed because of your experience of disability issues;
- domestic work (eg, cooking and cleaning) in your own home;
- caring for a relative (see below);
- caring for another person living with you under specific legislation relating to accommodating children or temporarily caring for someone else if you are paid for this;
- work you do to protect someone or prevent serious damage to property or livestock during an emergency;
- work done while receiving assistance in pursuing self-employment under section 2 of the Employment and Training Act 1973 or section 2 of the Enterprise and New Towns (Scotland) Act 1990 (test-trading);
- voluntary work that is not for a relative (see below), provided the only payment you receive is to cover your reasonable expenses and it is considered reasonable for you to work free of charge;
- work done in the course of a work placement (unpaid work experience with an employer) approved in writing by the DWP before the placement starts;
- for contributory ESA, any work you do in a week in which you are treated as having limited capability for work because you are having certain regular treatment (eg, haemodialysis for chronic renal failure) or are recovering from that treatment (see p1005);[67]
- 'permitted work' (see p1023).

Relatives

A **'relative'** is a grandparent, grandchild, uncle, aunt, nephew, niece, and includes **'close relatives'** – ie, parent, parent-in-law, son, son-in-law, daughter, daughter-in-law, step-parent, stepson, stepdaughter, brother, sister, or the partner of any of these.

There is no general rule that you cannot work and be entitled to universal credit (UC) at the same time. However, if you earn more than a set monthly amount from work, you may be treated as not having limited capability for work – ie, even if you have passed the work capability assessment. See p1004.

Permitted work

'Permitted work' (sometimes called 'exempt' work) is work of any kind, which you can do:[68]

- as part of a treatment programme done under medical supervision while you are in hospital or regularly attending hospital as an outpatient, provided you do not earn more than £120 a week; *or*
- for an unlimited period, provided you do not earn more than £20 a week. This is called the 'permitted work lower limit'; *or*
- for an unlimited period, provided you do not earn more than £120 a week and you are in 'supported (sometimes called 'supervised') work' (see below); *or*
- on average, for less than 16 hours a week and in any week you do not earn more than £120 a week. This is called the 'permitted work higher limit'. For how your hours are calculated, see p992.

Supported work

'**Supported work**' is work which is supervised by someone employed by a public or local authority, or by a voluntary organisation or community interest company, whose job it is to find work for people with disabilities. This could include work in a sheltered workshop or with help from social services. The DWP usually says that you need not have the person working alongside you, although the support should be ongoing and regular. Where possible, check in advance that the DWP agrees that the work counts as supported work.

If your earnings in any week are higher than the relevant limit, you are not entitled to ESA for that week.[69] Your earnings are worked out for this purpose in the same way as for income-related ESA (see p270), except that only your own earnings count, not those of your partner. Only your earnings count, not any other kind of income.

Although there are no special rules, you should inform the DWP as soon as possible about any permitted work you do. If the particular activities you carry out in your work suggest that your limited capability might have changed, the DWP might reassess this.

Note: the amounts referred to in the first, third and fourth bullet points above are usually increased in October. See CPAG's online service and *Welfare Rights Bulletin* for updates.

Part 7: Work and work-related rules
Chapter 44: Limited capability for work
Notes

Notes

1. The work capability assessment

1 **ESA** Reg 19 ESA Regs; reg 15 ESA Regs 2013
   UC Reg 39 UC Regs
2 Reg 44 ESA Regs; reg 37 ESA Regs 2013
3 Reg 159 ESA Regs; reg 95 ESA Regs 2013
4 Reg 32(2) ESA Regs; reg 27 ESA Regs 2013
5 Reg 32(1) ESA Regs; reg 27(1) ESA Regs 2013
6 Regs 41, 43 and 44 UC Regs
7 Reg 41(2) and (3) UC Regs
8 **ESA** Regs 20, 25 and 26 ESA Regs; regs 16, 22 and 26 ESA Regs 2013
   UC Reg 39(6) and Schs 8 and 9 UC Regs
9 Regs 26, 44 and 46 ESA Regs; regs 22, 38 and 40 ESA Regs 2013; Vol 8 Ch42, paras 42049-58 DMG
10 Reg 16(1)(h) ESA Regs 2013
11 Reg 30 ESA Regs; reg 26 ESA Regs 2013
12 *EI v SSWP (ESA)* [2016] UKUT 397 (AAC)
13 *EI v SSWP (ESA)* [2016] UKUT 397 (AAC)
14 *EI v SSWP (ESA)* [2016] UKUT 397 (AAC)
15 Reg 39 and Sch 8 UC Regs
16 Reg 19(2) UC(TP) Regs
17 **ESA** Reg 19 ESA Regs; reg 15 ESA Regs 2013
   UC Regs 39 and 42 UC Regs
18 **ESA** Reg 19(4) ESA Regs; reg 15(4) ESA Regs 2013
   UC Reg 42(2) UC Regs
19 **ESA** Reg 19(5) ESA Regs; reg 15(5) ESA Regs 2013
   UC Reg 39(4) UC Regs
20 *AF v SSWP (ESA)* [2011] UKUT 61 (AAC); *SAG v Department for Social Development (ESA)* [2011] NICom 171
21 CIB/14534/1996
22 CIB/2620/2000
23 CIB/14587/1996; CIB/14722/1996; CIB/13161/1996; CIB/13508/1996
24 CIB/14722/1996
25 CSIB/12/1996
26 **ESA** Reg 29 ESA Regs; reg 25 ESA Regs 2013
   UC Sch 8 paras 4 and 5 UC Regs
27 *Charlton v SSWP* [2009] EWCA Civ 42; *JW v SSWP* [2011] UKUT 416 (AAC)
28 Regs 36-39 ESA Regs; regs 34-36 ESA Regs 2013
29 **ESA** Reg 34(3) ESA Regs; reg 30(3) ESA Regs 2013
   UC Reg 42(2) UC Regs
30 **ESA** Reg 34(6) ESA Regs; reg 30(6) ESA Regs 2013
   UC Reg 40(3) UC Regs
31 **ESA** Reg 34 ESA Regs; reg 30 ESA Regs 2013
   UC Reg 41 UC Regs
32 **ESA** Reg 35 ESA Regs; reg 31 ESA Regs 2013
   UC Sch 9 UC Regs
33 paras 42057 and 42365 DMG
34 Reg 19(4) UC(TP) Regs
35 *Employment and Support Allowance: written statement*, HCWS174, House of Commons, *Hansard*, 10 October 2016
36 **ESA** Reg 22 ESA Regs; reg 18 ESA Regs 2013
   UC Reg 43 UC Regs
37 Reg 24 ESA Regs; reg 18 ESA Regs 2013
38 **ESA** Reg 23 ESA Regs; reg 19 ESA Regs 2013
   UC Reg 44 UC Regs
39 R(IS) 9/51

2. Challenging a decision

40 **ESA** Reg 19 ESA Regs; reg 15 ESA Regs 2013
   UC Reg 39 UC Regs
41 Vol 1 Ch 6, para 06041 DMG
42 s20 SSA 1998; R(S) 3/84
43 CIB/407/1998; CIB/1149/1998; R(M) 1/93; CIB/3074/2003
44 CIB/511/2005
45 s20(3) SSA 1998
46 Reg 30(1) and (3) ESA Regs; reg 26(1) and (3) ESA Regs 2013
47 House of Commons, *Hansard*, Written Answers, 16 December 2013, col 486W
48 Memo DMG 10/15
49 Reg 30(3) ESA Regs; reg 26(3) ESA Regs 2013 ; reg 3(j) SS(C&P) Regs; reg 7 UC,PIP,JSA&ESA(C&P) Regs
50 Reg 5(4) ESA Regs; reg 6(5) ESA Regs 2013 provides that the assessment phase applies pending the First-tier Tribunal's decision

51 Reg 147A(2) and (4) ESA Regs; reg 87(2) and (4) ESA Regs 2013
52 Reg 147A(6) and (7) ESA Regs; reg 87(7) and (8) ESA Regs 2013
53 This is because the DWP will have made a determination that you do not have limited capability for work, and not merely treated you as not having limited capability for work, so reg 30(3) ESA Regs and reg 26(3) ESA Regs 2013 should apply.
54 Reg 147A(5) ESA Regs; reg 87(5) ESA Regs 2013
55 Reg 3(j) SS(C&P) Regs; reg 7 UC,PIP,JSA&ESA(C&P) Regs; Memo DMG 33/10, para 52
56 Memo DMG 51/10; reg 3(5G) and (5H) SS&CS(DA) Regs; reg 16(3) UC,PIP,JSA&ESA(DA) Regs
57 Art 24 WRA(No.9)O
58 Reg 41(4) UC Regs

3. Periods of limited capability for work
59 Reg 2, definition of 'period of limited capability for work', ESA Regs
60 Regs 2 and 145 ESA Regs; regs 2 and 86 ESA Regs 2013
61 Paras 1-3 Sch 1 WRA 2007

4. Work you can do while claiming
62 Reg 40 ESA Regs; reg 37 ESA Regs 2013
63 Regs 40 and 44 ESA Regs; regs 37 and 38 ESA Regs 2013
64 Reg 40(4) ESA Regs; reg 37(4) ESA Regs 2013
65 CIB/5298/1997; CIB/6777/1999
66 Regs 40 and 45 ESA Regs; regs 37 and 39 ESA Regs 2013
67 Reg 46 ESA Regs; reg 40 ESA Regs 2013
68 Reg 45 ESA Regs; reg 39 ESA Regs 2013
69 Regs 40(1) and (2)(f) and 45 ESA Regs; regs 37(2)(f) and 39 ESA Regs 2013

7

Chapter 45

. . . .

Jobseeking and other conditions

This chapter covers:

If you come under the universal credit system (see p20), the rules in this chapter do not apply to you. See Chapter 47 instead.

Key facts

- To qualify for jobseeker's allowance (JSA), you must usually satisfy jobseeking conditions – ie, you must be available for work, actively seek work and have a current jobseeker's agreement (the DWP calls this a 'claimant commitment').

- In some cases, there are special rules to help you satisfy the jobseeking conditions, including if you are a lone parent, have a disability or have experienced or been threatened with domestic violence.

- You may be able to place some restrictions on the work you are available to do, but you must usually still have a reasonable prospect of getting a job.

- If your entitlement to JSA ends because you were found not to be available for or to actively seek work, you can be given a sanction when you make a new claim for JSA and your JSA may be paid at a reduced (or nil) rate.

- There are a number of things you must do after you have been awarded JSA. These include 'signing on', and attending and participating in regular interviews.

- If you disagree with a decision on whether you are available for or actively seeking work, or about your jobseeker's agreement, you can apply for a revision or a supersession, or appeal against it. You must apply for a mandatory reconsideration before you can appeal.

1. The jobseeking conditions

To qualify for jobseeker's allowance (JSA) if you do not come under the universal credit (UC) system, you must usually satisfy three jobseeking conditions. You must:
- be (or be treated as) available for work; *and*
- be (or be treated as) actively seeking work; *and*
- have (or be treated as having) a current jobseeker's agreement with the DWP.

There are special rules if:
- you are a laid-off or short-time worker (see p1028);
- you are in full-time training or study (see p1028);
- in limited cases, you are participating in a specified scheme for assisting people to obtain employment (see p1029);
- you are a lone parent (see p1031);
- you have experienced or been threatened with domestic violence (see p1035);
- you have a disability (see p1040);
- you are 16 or 17 (see p1039, p1047 and p1051).

Note: the DWP calls your jobseeker's agreement a 'claimant commitment'. However, it is the rules about jobseeker's agreements that must be satisfied. These are *not* the same as for claimant commitments under the UC system.

If you do not satisfy the jobseeking conditions, or there is doubt about whether you do, you may be able to get hardship payments (see Chapter 51).

Note: the government says that from April 2017, if you are aged 18 to 21 and on UC, you will have to participate in intensive support from the date you claim – called the 'youth obligation'. It is not clear if this will also apply if you do not come under the UC system. See CPAG's online service and *Welfare Rights Bulletin* for updates.

Employment officers

Employment officers (EOs) are officers of the Secretary of State for Work and Pensions, or any other person officially designated as an EO by her/him.[1] The officers who work in Jobcentre Plus offices are EOs. They are sometimes called personal advisers or work coaches. Their job is to agree with you the steps you will take to get back to work, keep a check on those steps, offer practical help and advice, and notify you of job vacancies. You cannot apply for a revision or supersession of, or appeal against, their decisions.

At the time this *Handbook* was written, the Secretary of State had designated specified providers of the Work Programme and two schemes that have now ended (Community Work Placements and the Supervised Jobsearch Pilot Scheme) as EOs.[2] However, this is *only* for the purpose of informing you of job vacancies

Part 7: Work and work-related rules
Chapter 45: Jobseeking and other conditions
1. The jobseeking conditions

and requiring you to attend a job interview. **Note:** you can be given a high level sanction if you are informed of a vacancy by an EO (including those designated as EOs) and you do not apply for it or accept it if offered to you (see p1098).

Laid-off and short-time workers

Special rules allow you to be treated as available for and actively seeking work for up to 13 weeks if you have been laid off or put on short-time working, even though you are still subject to your normal employment contract and so have a duty to return to work or to working full time as soon as your employer wants you to do so. See p1033 and p1048 for information.

Laid-off and short-time worker[3]
You count as '**a person who is laid off**' if you have a job, but your work and wages have been suspended because of temporary adverse industrial conditions – eg, you are a farm worker whose work is suspended because of a food safety scare.
You count as '**a person who is kept on short-time**' if you have a job, but your hours of work have been reduced because of temporary adverse industrial conditions – eg, you are a secretary in a solicitor's office whose hours are reduced because the property market is flat and there is no conveyancing to be done.

Full-time training and study

If you are studying full time, you are treated as unavailable for work and therefore cannot qualify for JSA. However, there are exceptions. You are *not* treated as unavailable for work if you are:[4]
- on a 'qualifying course' (see p1029); *or*
- on an employment-related course or a residential training programme run by the Venture Trust (see p1034); *or*
- participating in a 'traineeship' – ie, a course for people aged 16 to 24 funded by the Secretary of State under section 14 of the Education Act 2002 that lasts no more than six months and includes a work experience placement and training to help you prepare for work; *or*
- a lone parent, or a member of a couple who are both students, you (or your partner) are responsible for a child (see p222) and it is the summer vacation. You must satisfy all the normal rules on being available for work or be treated as being available for work because you are on an employment-related course or a residential training programme run by the Venture Trust (see p1034).

Note: you do not have to be available for work if you are participating in a specified scheme for assisting people to obtain employment (see p1029) while you are a full-time student.

You can get JSA while attending a **'qualifying course'** if:[5]
- you are aged 25 or over; *and*
- you had been 'receiving benefit' (see below) during a jobseeking period (see p123 and p699) for at least two years at the time the course starts. When working out whether you have been receiving benefit for two years, the rules for linking jobseeking periods apply (see p123 and p700); *and*
- an EO (see p1027) approves your attendance; *and*
- you satisfy the special conditions for being treated as available for and actively seeking work (see p1034 and p1048).

Once you have started the course, it becomes compulsory. This means that if you abandon it without a good reason or are dismissed because of misconduct, you could be given a sanction (see Chapter 48).

Qualifying courses and receiving benefit

A **'qualifying course'** is a course of further education (or of a higher standard if your EO agrees) which is employment related and lasts no more than 12 consecutive months.[6]
'Receiving benefit' means getting benefit as an unemployed person (eg, JSA), or national insurance credits for unemployment or under the rules that apply to men born before 6 October 1954 who are not yet 65 (known as 'autocredits' – see p974).[7]

You might be able to get JSA while studying part time, or while waiting to go back on your course having taken approved time out because of an illness or caring responsibilities that have now ended (see p878 and p902).

Getting a training allowance

Provided you are not a child or qualifying young person for child benefit purposes (see p572), if you are receiving training and getting a specified type of training allowance, you can get income-based JSA without having to satisfy the jobseeking conditions.[8] For these purposes, 'training' does not include training for some people aged 16 to 24 provided by the Secretary of State, the Welsh Ministers or by Skills Development Scotland, Scottish Enterprise or Highlands and Islands Enterprise. However, if you are receiving this type of training, you might qualify for income support (see p105).

Schemes for assisting people to obtain employment

If you are participating in a specified scheme for assisting people to obtain employment (eg, the Work Programme – see p1104), you do not have to be available for work or to actively seek work if:[9]
- you count as a full-time student; *or*
- it is the first week after you are released from detention in prison, a remand centre or youth custody.

Part 7: Work and work-related rules
Chapter 45: Jobseeking and other conditions
2. Available for work

However, you are likely to be required to take specific steps to improve your chances of getting work while participating.

You do not have to actively seek work if you are participating in New Enterprise Allowance.[10]

2. **Available for work**

To qualify for jobseeker's allowance (JSA), you must be available for work. The general rule is that to be available for work you must be:[11]

- 'willing and able' to take up work 'immediately' (see p1031); *and*
- available at any time of the day and on any day of the week; *and*
- prepared to take a job that would involve working for *at least* 40 hours a week; *and*
- prepared to work for *less than* 40 hours a week if required to do so. In practice, this means that you must be prepared to work part time.

However, you may be able to place restrictions on your availability for work (see p1038), such as the type of work or the days and times you are available.

In some circumstances:

- you do not have to be available for work if you are getting a training allowance (see p1029) or if you are participating in a specified scheme for assisting people to obtain employment (see p1029);
- you can be treated as being available for work even if you are not (see p1033);
- you can qualify for joint-claim JSA even if you or your partner (but not both of you) are not available for work (see p121).

Your availability for work is considered at an initial interview when you first claim JSA (see p136 and p711). Your jobseeker's agreement contains details of the particular days and times that you are available for work (your 'pattern of availability') as well as any other restrictions you may place on your availability.

Note:

- The DWP can decide that you are not available for work without having to show that you have turned down a job.[12] However, the fact that you turn down a job does not necessarily mean that you are not available.
- If your entitlement to JSA ends because you have not complied with the requirement to be available for work, you may be given a sanction when you claim JSA again (see p1107).
- If you are not available or treated as available for work, you cannot get JSA under the normal rules, but you may be able to get hardship payments (see Chapter 51).

If you are a lone parent

If you are a lone parent and have childcare responsibilities, you must be available for work to qualify for JSA. However, some special rules can apply.

- You only need to be able to take up a job on one week's (or, in some cases, 28 days') notice (see p1032).
- You may be treated as available for work if:
  - you have a five-year-old child who is not at school full time (see p1033); *or*
  - you are looking after a child under 16:
    - when s/he is sick. This can count as a domestic emergency (see p1036); *or*
    - because the person who normally looks after her/him is ill, away from home or looking after someone else (see p1033); *or*
    - during the school holidays or at times when s/he is excluded from school and not receiving education provided by the local authority (see p1033).
- You may be able to restrict your availability for work:
  - to your child's normal school hours, if you have a child under 13 (see p1042); *or*
  - to less than 40 hours a week (see p1042); *or*
  - in any way, if you are the subject of a parenting order or have entered into a parenting contract in respect of a child under 16 (see p1040).

Note: some of these rules can also apply if you are a member of a couple.

Willing and able to take up work immediately

Being **willing** to work is essentially a test of your attitude – your desire and willingness to work. What you do in practice to display this willingness is usually dealt with under the rules for actively seeking work.

You must be prepared to take up work as an employed person – being only available for self-employment is not sufficient.[13] However, this means that you do not count as being unavailable for work if you refuse to work as a self-employed person.

In order to be **able** to work, it must be lawful for you to work in Great Britain.[14] Your immigration status may affect this – eg, if a condition of your entry is that you do not work. In addition, there must be nothing to prevent you from receiving job offers (eg, because you are away from home for more than a short time) and nothing to prevent you from acting on them straight away – eg, because you have other commitments that you cannot easily abandon.

Being able to take up work **immediately** means that you must usually be able to start work without any delay, with little more than the time needed to get washed and dressed and have breakfast.[15] You can be allowed more time than this in some situations (see p1032).

Part 7: Work and work-related rules
Chapter 45: Jobseeking and other conditions
2. Available for work

When you are allowed more time

You do not have to be available for work immediately in the following situations. You only need to be available for work:

- **on one week's notice** if you are doing voluntary work or have caring responsibilities (see below for what counts).[16] You must be willing and able to attend a job interview on 48 hours' notice. However, if you have caring responsibilities for a child under 16 and you can show these make it unreasonable for you to take up a job or attend an interview within these periods, you only have to be available on **28 days' notice** and be willing and able to attend an interview on seven days' notice;

- **on 24 hours' notice** if you are providing a paid or unpaid service (other than if you are doing voluntary work or have caring responsibilities).[17] This includes services you provide for family or friends on a non-commercial basis, such as giving someone a regular lift to work in your car.[18] It could also include activities that are of service to the community in general (eg, offenders working in the community as part of their punishment) and tribunal members;

- **after your notice period** has passed if you are working part time. This applies if you have a duty to give your employer notice that you are leaving work under employment law.[19] If under the terms of your contract you must give longer notice, argue that the longer notice period should apply.

Note: if the DWP agrees that you are only available to work at certain times (see p1042), you are not required to be able to take up employment at times when you are not available.[20] However, you must be willing and able to take up the offer as soon as you reach the next period in your pattern of availability (the days and times you are available).

Definitions[21]

'Voluntary work' is work which is done for a charity or other not-for-profit organisation or for anyone other than your partner or a child who is included in your claim, for which you receive no payment other than for your reasonable expenses.

'Caring responsibilities' means responsibility for looking after a member of your 'household' (see p225 for the meaning of household) or a close relative who is a child under 16, someone over pension age or someone who needs care because of her/his mental or physical condition. This applies even if you share the responsibilities with someone – eg, with your partner.

'Close relative' means partner, parent, step-parent, parent-in-law, parent of a civil partner, grandparent, son, stepson, son-in-law, son of a civil partner, daughter, stepdaughter, daughter-in-law, daughter of a civil partner, brother, sister, grandchild or the partner of any of these.

Treated as available for work

Even if you are not actually available for work, you can be treated as if you are for periods during your claim. You must still satisfy the other conditions of entitlement to JSA.

Lone parents

You are treated as available for work in any week in which you are the lone parent of a five-year-old child who is included in your claim (see p220) and is not in full-time education.[22] This only applies if s/he is not required by law to be in full-time education and it would be unreasonable for you to make other arrangements for her/his care.

Looking after a child under 16

You are treated as available for work if you are looking after a child under 16, and:[23]

- you are a member of a couple and are looking after the child while your partner is temporarily absent from the UK (for a maximum of eight weeks). The child must be included in your claim (see p220); or
- the person who normally looks after the child is ill, temporarily away from home or looking after her/his partner or another child who is ill (for a maximum of eight weeks). You must be looking after the child full time; or
- you have caring responsibilities for the child (see p1032 for what counts) and you are looking after her/him:
  - during the school holidays or other similar vacation. This only applies if it would be unreasonable to make other arrangements; or
  - at a time when s/he is excluded from school and is not receiving education provided by the local authority. This only applies if there are no other arrangements it would be reasonable for you to make.

Laid-off and short-time workers

You are treated as available for work for the first 13 weeks of a period of being laid off or of short-time working (see p1028), provided:[24]

- you are willing and able to:
  - return immediately to your job; and
  - take up immediately (subject to the rules on p1032) any 'casual employment' that is within daily travelling distance of your home. If you are a short-time worker, this only has to be during the hours when you are not working in your normal job; and
- in the case of short-time working only, the weekly total of the number of hours during which you are working and the number of hours during which you are available for casual employment is at least 40 hours (unless you are restricting

Part 7: Work and work-related rules
Chapter 45: Jobseeking and other conditions
2. Available for work

your hours of availability to less than 40 because of a physical or mental condition or because of caring responsibilities – see p1040 and p1042).

Definitions

A **'week'** is any period of seven consecutive days.[25]

'Casual employment' is work that the employer is prepared for you to leave without giving any notice.[26]

Studying and training

Special rules apply in some situations when you would not normally count as being available for work while studying. You are treated as available:[27]

- for one period of up to two weeks in any 12 months when you are a full-time student (see p874) on an employment-related course which has been approved in advance by your employment officer (EO). See below for more generous rules if you are on a 'qualifying course';
- if you are participating in a 'traineeship' – ie, a course for people aged 16 to 24 funded by the Secretary of State under section 14 of the Education Act 2002 that lasts no more than six months and includes a work experience placement and training to help you prepare for work;
- if you are attending a compulsory residential course as part of an Open University course (for up to one week for each course);
- if you are attending a residential training programme run by the Venture Trust under arrangments made by the Scottish Ministers (for one programme for a maximum of four weeks in any 12 months).

If you are on a 'qualifying course' (see p1029), you are treated as being available for work in any week:[28]

- which falls entirely or partly in term time, so long as you provide written evidence within five days of its being requested, confirming that you are attending and making satisfactory progress on the course. This must be signed by you and by the college or educational establishment; *or*
- in which you are taking exams relating to the course; *or*
- which falls entirely in a vacation, if you are willing and able to take up any casual employment (see p1048) immediately.

Note: some people getting a training allowance do not have to satisfy the jobseeking conditions (see p1029). If you are a full-time student participating in a specified scheme for assisting people to obtain employment, you do not have to be available for work (see p1029).

Temporary absence from Great Britain

You are treated as available for work when you are temporarily absent from Great Britain and you are:[29]

- taking a child who is included in your claim (see p220) abroad temporarily for specified medical treatment (for a maximum of eight weeks);[30] *or*
- attending a job interview (for a maximum of seven days). You must tell your EO in advance and confirm it in writing if required to do so; *or*
- a member of a couple and the pensioner, enhanced pensioner, higher pensioner, disability or severe disability premium is being paid for your partner (see Chapter 12) and you are both away from Great Britain (for a maximum of four weeks); *or*
- abroad for the purpose of getting NHS hospital treatment (see p703); *or*
- a member of a joint-claim couple on the date of your claim and, on the day your partner makes the claim for JSA, you are:
  - in Northern Ireland (for a maximum of four weeks) but only if you are unlikely to be away for more than 52 weeks; *or*
  - attending a job interview (for a maximum of seven days).

If you are looking after a child because your partner is temporarily absent from the UK, see p1033.

Domestic violence

If you notify the DWP that you have experienced, or been threatened with, domestic violence from your partner, your former partner or a family member (see below for who counts), you are treated as available for work for four weeks from the date of notification.[31] This only applies if you are not living at the same address as the person and if the domestic violence (or threat of domestic violence) took place within the 26 weeks before you notified the DWP.

The four-week period is extended to 13 weeks if you provide 'relevant evidence' during the four weeks from a person acting in an official capacity. You are only treated as available for work under this rule once in any 12-month period. The four and 13 weeks run on whether or not you are entitled to JSA for the whole period. However, you can ask for the 13-week period to be suspended, but the 13 weeks must then be used up within 12 months of the date you notified the DWP about the domestic violence.

Definitions

'**Domestic violence**' means any incident or pattern of incidents of controlling behaviour, coercive behaviour, violence or abuse, including physical, sexual, psychological, financial or emotional abuse, regardless of your gender or sexuality.[32]

A '**family member**' for these purposes means the following members of your family, or of the family of your partner or your former partner: grandparent, grandchild, parent, parent-in-law, son, son-in-law, daughter, daughter-in-law, step-parent, stepson, stepdaughter, brother, brother-in-law, sister, sister-in-law, or the partner of any of these.[33]

A '**person acting in an official capacity**' means a healthcare professional, a police officer, a registered social worker, your employer or your trade union representative. It also means

Part 7: Work and work-related rules
Chapter 45: Jobseeking and other conditions
2. Available for work

any public, voluntary or charitable body with which you have had direct contact in connection with domestic violence.[34]

'Relevant evidence' is written evidence from a 'person acting in an official capacity' that shows that your circumstances are consistent with those of a person who has experienced or been threatened with domestic violence in the 26 weeks before you notified the DWP, or that shows you have made contact with the person about an incident that occurred in those 26 weeks.[35]

Community activities

You are treated as available for work:[36]

- if you are required to attend a court or tribunal as a justice of the peace, juror, witness or party to any proceedings (but not if you come within the definition of 'prisoner' – see p929) (for a maximum of eight weeks). You must have notified your EO beforehand.[37]
  Note: if you are selected as a juror, you must attend court when asked to do so. However, if this is for more than eight weeks, you may be able to claim income support (IS) instead of JSA (see p105);
- if you are engaged in crewing or launching a lifeboat, are carrying out duties as a part-time firefighter or are engaged during an emergency as a member of an organised group which is helping to save lives, prevent injury or a serious threat to the health of others or protect property;[38]
- if you are on training as a member of a reserve force. If you are in your first year of training, this applies for a maximum of 43 days in that year. If you are engaged in annual continuous training, this applies for a maximum of 15 days in any calendar year;
- for one period of up to two weeks in any 12 months when you are attending a residential work camp in Great Britain organised by a charity, local authority or voluntary organisation for the benefit of the community or the environment.[39]

Bereavement and domestic emergencies

You are treated as available for work if you are dealing with circumstances arising from:[40]

- a domestic emergency affecting you or a close friend or close relative (see p1032 for who counts) – eg, if you have recently become homeless (but only if you take reasonable steps to find accommodation) or if you are looking after one of your children who is ill; *or*
- the death or serious illness of a close friend or close relative; *or*
- the death of someone for whom you had caring responsibilities (see p1032); *or*
- the funeral of a close friend or close relative.

You are usually treated as being available during the time it takes to deal with the matter and for up to a week at a time, but on no more than four occasions in any 12-month period. There are exceptions.

- You are allowed longer periods, on more occasions, if the domestic emergency is that you have recently become homeless.[41]
- If you have caring responsibilities for a child under 16, you can be treated as available for up to eight weeks in one or other of the first two situations (or a combination of these) on one occasion in any 12-month period. If this applies, you can then only be treated as being available for up to a week on three more occasions in the 12-month period.[42]

Other

You are treated as available for work:[43]

- if you have been discharged from detention in prison, a remand centre or a youth custody institution, but only if you have not been required to participate in a specified scheme for assisting people to obtain employment (see p1104) (for one week from the date of discharge). If you have been required to participate in a scheme, you are instead exempt from being available for work (see p1029);
- during temporary police detention (legal custody in Scotland) of up to 96 hours, but not if you come within the definition of 'prisoner' (see p929);[44]
- during a two-week or extended period of sickness under the rules described on p702, or if you are temporarily absent from Great Britain for the purpose of getting NHS hospital treatment (see p703);
- if you were recently found not to have limited capability for work, and your time limit for claiming JSA is extended because you were not told promptly enough that your entitlement to IS, employment and support allowance (ESA) or incapacity benefit had ended so you could not claim JSA in time (during the period for which the time limit is extended);
- during any part of a week at the beginning of your claim if, in respect of all the days concerned, you satisfy some specified rules for being available for work;[45]
- during any part week at the end of your claim.

Treated as unavailable for work

Even if you are (or can be treated as) available for work, you are nevertheless treated as unavailable for work if:[46]

- you are a full-time student (see p874). **Note:** there are exceptions (see p1028);
- you are on temporary release from prison;
- you are receiving maternity allowance or statutory maternity pay;
- you are on adoption, paternity or shared parental leave;
- it is during any part of a week at the beginning of your claim. You are treated as being unavailable for work unless you satisfy specified rules for being treated as available for that period.

Part 7: Work and work-related rules
Chapter 45: Jobseeking and other conditions
2. Available for work

Unavailable for part of a week

On occasion, you might be unavailable for work for a short period during a benefit week – eg, because you are away from home. If this happens and you have:

- put restrictions on the times that you are available (see p1042):[47]
  - your JSA is not affected if the period during which you are *not* available comes entirely outside the particular days and times that you are available for work (your 'pattern of availability'); *or*
  - you lose JSA for the whole of that benefit week if all or part of the period during which you are not available comes within your pattern of availability;
- *not* put any restrictions on the times you are available, you may lose benefit for that week because you are not available to take up work immediately.[48] For this reason, it is best to avoid signing a jobseeker's agreement with totally unrestricted times that you are available.

If you are arrested and held by the police for a short time but then released, you can be treated as available for work for up to 96 hours while you are detained.

If you are doing voluntary work and have placed restrictions on the total number of hours you are available to work (see p1042), any voluntary work you do (see p1032 for what counts) within your pattern of availability must be ignored when deciding if you are available, provided you are willing and able to rearrange the voluntary work within:[49]

- one week's notice, in order to take up any job whose hours fall within your pattern of availability;
- 48 hours' notice, to attend an interview in connection with an opportunity for work at a time that falls within your pattern of availability.

There is a similar rule in certain cases if you are a part-time student (see p878).

Restrictions on availability for work

You can restrict your availability for work *in any way* if the restrictions are reasonable in light of your physical or mental condition and, in some cases, if you have specified caring responsibilities for a child under 16 (see p1040). Otherwise, if you can prove that you still have a reasonable prospect of securing employment (see p1039), you can place some restrictions on the work you are available to do. These are:[50]

- the type of work for which you are available (see p1040);
- the number of hours, days and times you are available (see p1042);
- the terms and conditions of employment for which you are available, including the rate of pay (see p1043);
- the location of the job (see p1043).

Any restrictions are entered in your jobseeker's agreement. If you and the DWP have not agreed in advance that there are certain types of work which you cannot, or are unwilling to, do, it may prove difficult to justify turning down such a job if it is offered to you later.

If you are 16 or 17

If you are 16 or 17, in general you are subject to the same rules about availability for work as people aged 18 or over. However, you can usually restrict your availability to jobs where the employer provides 'suitable training'.[51] You do not have to show that you have a reasonable prospect of securing employment (see below) despite this restriction.

You *cannot* restrict your availability to jobs offering suitable training if:

- you have been given a sanction in specified circumstances either under the normal JSA rules or under the special rules for severe hardship payments; *or*
- you are claiming JSA under the special rules for people laid off or on short-time working (see p1033); *or*
- you are claiming under the special rules for people waiting to enlist in the armed forces (see p129).

Suitable training

Deciding whether training is '**suitable training**' involves considering factors such as your personal abilities and skills, your preference and the preference of your training provider, the level of qualification you are aiming for, the length of the training, how easily you can travel to the training and how soon the training will begin.[52]

If you have only worked for a short time but you received training for that type of work or obtained relevant qualifications, you could argue that you have a usual occupation and so should be given a 'permitted period' (see p1041).

A 'reasonable prospect' of securing employment

You must usually show that you have a 'reasonable prospect' of securing employment, despite any restrictions you are allowed to place on your availability. This does not apply if you can restrict your availability in any way (see p1040) or if, because you are a lone parent, you can restrict your availability to your child's normal school hours (see p1042), or if you are 16 or 17 and restrict your availability to jobs offering suitable training (see above).[53] The DWP must consider all the evidence and, in particular:[54]

- your skills, qualifications and experience; *and*
- the type and number of job vacancies within daily travelling distance of your home; *and*
- the length of time you have been unemployed; *and*
- the job applications that you have made and their outcome; *and*

Part 7: Work and work-related rules
Chapter 45: Jobseeking and other conditions
2. Available for work

- whether you are willing to move home to take up a job, but only where you are placing restrictions on the type of job you are prepared to do.

Should you put restrictions on the work you will take?

Your job prospects may be poor. However, if you do not put any restrictions on the work you will take, you are accepted as being available for work. If you impose more than one type of restriction, the cumulative effect on your job prospects is considered. Therefore, think carefully about whether it is sensible to apply restrictions, and if so how many.

Restricting your availability in any way

You can restrict your availability for work in any way if:[55]

- the restrictions are reasonable in light of your physical or mental condition (see below); *or*
- you have caring responsibilities (see p1032) for a child under 16 and you are the subject of a parenting order or have entered into a parenting contract in respect of the child under specific provisions. The restrictions must be reasonable in light of the terms of the order or contract.

This means that you can restrict the type of work for which you are available, as well as the number of hours, the days and times, the terms and conditions of employment, the location of the job, and any other matter whatsoever. If the restrictions you impose are reasonable in light of your physical or mental condition, or the terms of the order or contract, you do not have to show that you have reasonable prospects of securing employment.

Your physical or mental condition

If you want to restrict your availability for work because of your physical or mental condition, you are normally expected to provide medical evidence. However, if your prospects of work are poor, you should consider whether you are capable of work. If not, it may be in your interest to claim ESA or pension credit (PC) (or universal credit – UC) instead of JSA.

If you also place restrictions on your availability that are not connected with your physical or mental condition, you must show that you have a reasonable prospect of securing employment (see p1039) with all your restrictions.[56] Therefore, think carefully before placing additional restrictions on your availability.

The type of work

The general rule is that you must be available for any type of employment, but you are allowed to place restrictions on the sort of jobs for which you are available, provided you have a reasonable prospect of securing employment (see p1039).[57] In addition, special rules allow you to make restrictions:

- during your 'permitted period' if you have one (see below);
- if you are a laid-off or short-time worker (see p1033);
- because of a sincerely held religious belief or conscientious objection (see below).

Permitted periods

If you have previously done work of a particular type (a 'usual occupation'), you can be allowed a 'permitted period' of between one and 13 weeks from the date you claim JSA during which you are allowed to be available only for vacancies in your usual occupation or which pay at least what you would normally receive, or both.[58] Any other restrictions you place on your availability must be consistent with the conditions of work that are normal in your usual occupation.

> ### Usual occupation
> The term **'usual occupation'** is not defined in the rules. The DWP says that if you have followed an occupation for a long time, this can count as your usual occupation, and also that a new occupation may count as your usual occupation if you intend to follow that type of work in future.[59]

Not everyone is allowed a permitted period. Whether you are and, if so, how long it lasts, are matters that are discussed at your initial interview. It should be entered in your jobseeker's agreement.[60] The DWP must consider:[61]

- your usual occupation and any relevant skills or qualifications you may have; *and*
- the length of time you have spent training for or have worked in that occupation, and the length of time since you have worked in the occupation; *and*
- the availability and location of jobs in that area of work.

Note: if you are a laid-off or short-time worker (see p1028), you are not entitled to a permitted period unless you lose your job completely during the first 13 weeks of being laid off or working short time.[62] In this case, you may be allowed a permitted period, but it must end no more than 13 weeks after the start of your JSA claim.

Religious belief or conscientious objection

You do not have to be available for work that offends a sincerely held religious belief or a sincere conscientious objection – eg, a job in a company associated with live animal exports if you have a conscientious objection to these.[63] You must still have reasonable prospects of securing employment despite those restrictions and any other restrictions you may have imposed (see p1039).[64]

Part 7: Work and work-related rules
Chapter 45: Jobseeking and other conditions
2. Available for work

The number of hours, days and times

You can restrict the total number of hours you are available, provided you are available for at least 40 hours a week and:[65]

- you have agreed with the DWP the particular days and times that you are available for work (a 'pattern of availability') and this has been recorded in your jobseeker's agreement;[66] *and*
- you still have reasonable prospects of securing employment despite the restrictions (see p1039) and they do not *considerably* reduce your prospects of securing employment.

You are allowed to restrict the total number of hours you are available to less than 40 in some situations if you are a lone parent (see below) or if you have caring responsibilities (see below). If you are a short-time or laid-off worker, see p1033.

Note: you must be prepared to work for the maximum number of hours for which you are available, but you must also be prepared to accept jobs that offer fewer hours than you would wish.

If you are a lone parent

If you are a lone parent and a child who is included in your claim (see p220) is under 13, you only need to be available for work during your child's normal school hours.[67] This means that you can restrict the total number of hours, days and times you are available. You do not have to show that you still have reasonable prospects of securing employment. **Note:**

- You also count as a person with caring responsibilities in this situation, so you may be able to restrict the total number of hours further.
- The DWP might say that 'normal school hours' does not include the time it takes you to travel to and from the school to drop your child off or to collect her/him. Seek advice and argue that this is wrong.

Caring responsibilities

If you have caring responsibilities (see p1032), you can restrict the total hours you are available to less than 40 hours a week if:[68]

- you are available for employment for at least 16 hours a week and for as many hours as your caring responsibilities permit, taking into account relevant factors, including the particular hours and days you spend caring, whether your caring responsibilities are shared with someone else, and the age and physical and mental condition of the person for whom you care; *and*
- you have a reasonable chance of securing employment (see p1039) despite the restricted hours. You do not have to show this if you have caring responsibilities for a child under 16 and an EO decides that you would not satisfy this condition because of the type and number of job vacancies within daily travelling distance of your home.

If you are a carer and you cannot make yourself available for work for at least 16 hours a week, you might be able to claim IS (or UC) or, if you are at least the qualifying age (see p147), PC rather than JSA.

The terms and conditions of employment

You can make restrictions on the terms and conditions of employment for which you are available (including the rate of pay – but see below), provided you can show that you still have reasonable prospects of securing employment despite those restrictions and any other restrictions you may have imposed (see p1039).[69]

The rules about minimum working conditions (see Appendix 10) can affect your claim for JSA. The DWP should not object to your placing a restriction on your availability for work – ie, that you will not accept a job if the terms do not comply with the legal requirements, such as if an employer is offering a job at less than the national minimum wage. You can try to argue that the rule that says you must still have reasonable prospects of finding work despite the restriction (see p1039) does not apply, as the DWP should assume that all employers will obey the law.

Note: the DWP says you should *not* be told to apply for jobs that include a 'zero-hour contract' or an 'employee shareholder contract' and that you should not be given a sanction if you refuse or fail to apply for or to accept such a vacancy.[70] So you should argue that you should not have to be available for this type of job.

The rate of pay

You can restrict the rate of pay:

- during your permitted period (see p1041), if you have one, to the rate you are accustomed to receiving in your usual occupation;[71]
- for six months from the date you claimed JSA, provided you still have reasonable prospects of securing employment (see p1039).[72]

Any restrictions you may place on the rate of pay should be agreed at your initial interview. These should be recorded in your jobseeker's agreement.

What should you remember?
1. It is *vital* that the wage or salary you say you are willing to accept should not be higher than the going rate for the jobs you have said you are looking for.
2. You should not be expected to work for a rate of pay below the national minimum wage (see p1662).

The location of the job

You can make restrictions on the localities within which you are available for work, provided you can show that you still have reasonable prospects of securing employment in the selected areas (see p1039).[73]

Part 7: Work and work-related rules
Chapter 45: Jobseeking and other conditions
3. Actively seeking work

3. **Actively seeking work**

To qualify for jobseeker's allowance (JSA), you must actively seek work. Special rules apply if you have been allowed a 'permitted period' (see p1047). In some cases you:

- do not have to actively seek work if you are participating in a specified scheme to obtain employment (see p1029) or you are getting a training allowance (see p1029);
- can be treated as if you are actively seeking work even if you are not (see p1048);
- can qualify for joint-claim JSA even if you or your partner (but not both of you) are not actively seeking work (see p121).

Note: if your entitlement to JSA ends because you failed to comply with the requirement to actively seek work, you may be given a sanction when you claim JSA again (see p1107).

What you must do

To count as actively seeking work:

- in each benefit week (and part week at the beginning of your claim) you must take such 'steps' as you can reasonably be expected to have to take in order to have the best prospects of securing employment in Great Britain;[74]
- you are expected to take a minimum of three steps unless taking fewer steps is all that it is reasonable for you to do.[75] **Note:** it is possible that, in some weeks, there may be no steps that you could reasonably be expected to take.[76]

For information about how you prove that you are actively seeking work, see p1046.

Your jobseeker's agreement (the DWP calls this a 'claimant commitment') says what steps you have agreed to take to find work. The DWP is likely to suggest that you take considerably more than three steps each week. Bear in mind that by signing the agreement you are accepting that it is reasonable for you to take the number of steps specified. However, in the event of a dispute, point out if you felt you had no option but to agree to what was proposed.

The DWP is likely to look at whether or not you have kept to your jobseeker's agreement in deciding whether you are actively seeking work.[77] You do not necessarily have to take all the steps in your agreement each week to prove you are actively seeking work: the test is what you *did*, not what you did not do.[78] However, if there is a dispute, the DWP is likely to say that what is in your jobseeker's agreement is a good indication of what you could reasonably have been expected to do. Bear in mind that the DWP says that looking for work should be a full-time job and may expect you to take a large number of steps and to spend a considerable amount of time actively seeking work.

If your chances of getting work are poor, there may only be a limited number of steps you can take each week, but it may be reasonable for the DWP to expect you to take all of them. If they are good, there may be many steps you could take each week, but it might not be reasonable for the DWP to expect you to take all of them.[79]

Note:

- You may be asked at an interview to change the steps you will take to find work. Your adviser may propose a change in your jobseeker's agreement (see p1053).
- At your regular interview, the steps you have taken are reviewed. You might not count as actively seeking work if it is considered that you should be taking more steps or ones that give you a better chance of finding work.
- If the DWP decides that you are not actively seeking work, your entitlement to JSA ends. If you then claim JSA again, you can be given a sanction (see p1107).

What counts as a 'step'

Steps are not limited to applying for job vacancies. Anything you do that might lead to your applying for, or being offered, employment should count as a step. Steps include:[80]

- applying for jobs in writing, personally or by phone, as well as seeking information from advertisements, advertisers, agencies or employers;
- calling or visiting employers to see if they are recruiting;
- registering with an agency or appointing someone else to help you find work – eg, an agent if you are looking for work in the entertainment field;
- preparing a CV;
- asking a previous employer for a reference;
- preparing a list of, or looking for information about, employers who may be able to offer you a job, as well as looking for information about an occupation with a view to finding a job in that occupation;
- getting specialist advice following referral by an employment officer (EO) on how to improve your chances of finding a job – eg, from a disability employment adviser.

There are many other things that could count as steps – eg, searching for jobs using the government's 'universal jobmatch' and making enquiries about jobs via the internet or by email. Remember to keep a record as proof.

You must take steps to find work in Great Britain.[81] This applies even if you are also seeking work in another country.

When the DWP decides whether you have been actively seeking work, it must disregard a step if (unless there are reasons beyond your control) you:[82]

- act in a violent or abusive manner; *or*

Part 7: Work and work-related rules
Chapter 45: Jobseeking and other conditions
3. Actively seeking work

- spoil an application if the step is completing a job application; *or*
- undermine your prospects of getting a job by your behaviour or appearance.

Deciding what steps are reasonable

When the DWP decides whether the steps you took in a particular week were reasonable, all the circumstances must be considered, including:[83]

- your skills, qualifications and abilities;
- any physical or mental limitations you may have;
- the length of time you have been unemployed, and your work experience;
- the steps you have taken in previous weeks and how they have improved your chances of finding a job;
- the availability and location of job vacancies;
- any time you have spent:
  - launching or crewing a lifeboat or acting as a part-time firefighter, undertaking duties as a member of any reserve forces, attending an Outward Bound course or taking part in an organised group helping in an emergency;
  - undertaking voluntary work and the extent to which it may have improved your chances of finding a paid job;
  - improving your chances of finding a job by training to use aids to overcome any physical or mental disabilities you may have or, if you are blind, training to use a guide dog;
  - as a part-time student on an employment-related course or that you have spent on a government-sponsored employment or training programme for which no training allowance is paid, if this is for less than three days a week. **Note:** if the course is for three days or more, you are treated as actively seeking work (see p1048);
- any circumstances that have resulted in your being treated as being available for work (see p1033);
- whether you have applied for, taken part in or accepted a place on a course funded by the government or European Union, which is designed to help you select, train for, obtain or retain employment or self-employment;
- if you are homeless, the steps which you needed to take and did take to find a home. It should be accepted that being homeless may limit the steps you can take to look for work and that you need time to look for somewhere to live.

Proving you are actively seeking work

Always keep careful records of the steps you take to get a job. The DWP may give you a form on which to do this, or you may be asked to keep an online record.

How do you prove you are actively seeking work?

1. Check your jobseeker's agreement carefully to ensure you understand what the DWP expects you to do each week. You must be able to give details of the steps you have taken, so it is extremely important that you keep records of your attempts to get a job. Make a

note every time you do anything that might count as a 'step' towards actively seeking work. Include the dates and times, who you spoke to and what was said.

2. Keep copies of any letters or emails you send, and of any advertisements to which you reply. If you deliver your CV or a job application by hand, ask for a receipt as proof.

3. Tell the EO if you have difficulty using a computer, or reading or writing, or with the English language. You can get a friend or relative to help you compile your record (and to help you look for jobs). The DWP may be prepared to accept an oral report.

4. Sometimes your activities to seek work may be looked at more intensively than normal, so ensure that they are always sufficient. Do not rely on the fact that they have not been challenged up to now.

5. The government's 'universal jobmatch' shows the jobs that have been suggested for you and the jobs for which you have applied. The DWP may ask you to allow it to access your account to check up on what you have been doing.

6. If there are jobs that have been suggested but which you have not applied for, your EO may question whether you are actively seeking work. It is therefore best to follow up enough suggestions and apply for jobs, even if you think they are not appropriate.

If you are 16 or 17

If you are 16 or 17, in general you are subject to the same rules about actively seeking work as people aged 18 or over. However, unless you are claiming under the special rules for people laid off or on short-time working or for people waiting to enlist in the armed forces (see p1028 and p129), extra rules apply. To qualify for JSA you are:[84]

- required to actively seek both work *and* 'suitable training' (see p1039); *and*
- expected to take at least one step to find work and one step to find suitable training, unless taking one step is all that it is reasonable for you to do.

This does not apply if you have been given a sanction under specified provisions either under the normal JSA rules or under the special rules for severe hardship payments.

In addition to the usual list of activities that count as a step (see p1045), the activities of seeking training and seeking full-time education also count.

Actively seeking work during your permitted period

If you have been allowed a permitted period (see p1041), you count as actively seeking work during that period even if you are only looking for jobs in your normal line of work or at your normal level of pay, or both.[85] If you have been self-employed in your usual occupation at any time within the 12 months before you claim JSA, you count as actively seeking work if you are seeking self-employment in that occupation.

Part 7: Work and work-related rules
Chapter 45: Jobseeking and other conditions
3. Actively seeking work

Treated as actively seeking work

Even if you are not actively seeking work, you can be treated as if you are.

- If you are a laid-off or short-time worker (see p1028), you are treated as actively seeking work during any benefit week (see p303) in which you are subject to the special rules on availability described on p1033 for at least three days. You must take all the steps that you can reasonably be expected to take which give you the best prospects of finding casual employment.[86]
- If you are attending a 'qualifying course' with the approval of an EO (see p1029) and are treated as being available for work (see p1034), you are also treated as actively seeking work.[87] If this is in any week that falls entirely in a vacation, you must take such steps as can reasonably be expected in order to have the best prospects of securing 'casual employment' – ie, employment that you can leave without giving notice or, if you must give notice, that you can leave before the end of the vacation.
- You are allowed two weeks (longer in some circumstances) during which time you are regarded as actively seeking work while away from home (see p1049).

Other situations in which you can be treated as actively seeking work generally mirror those where you are treated as available for work and have the same maximum lengths (see pp1033–37).[88] However, in most cases, you are only considered to be actively seeking work if the situation affects you for at least three days in the 'benefit week' (see p303 for the definition). There are differences. You are treated as actively seeking work in any week:[89]

- in which you are allowed an extended period of sickness under the rules described on p702. However, this does not apply if it would be reasonable for you to take steps to seek employment in that week, and you have not taken such steps;
- which is part of a period in which you are taking active steps to set yourself up as self-employed under a scheme to assist people to do so (for up to eight weeks). This can only apply once in any period of entitlement to JSA. The scheme must be provided or funded by a specified government agency. **Note:** if you are participating in New Enterprise Allowance, you do not have to actively seek work;[90]
- in which you spend at least three days on a government-sponsored employment or training course or programme for which you are not paid a training allowance. This does not apply if you are on Work Experience, or on any of the schemes for assisting people to obtain employment listed on p1104.

You are *not* treated as actively seeking work just because you have caring responsibilities for a child under 16 and are looking after her/him during the school holidays or at a time when s/he is excluded from school (see p1033).

Absence from home

While you are on JSA, you can be treated as actively seeking work while away from home – eg, on holiday.[91] You still have to be available for work, so you are expected to give an assurance that you are willing and able to cut your absence short if notified of a job. In any 12-month period, you can be away from home for up to:[92]

- three weeks, if during each week you spend at least three days on an Outward Bound course; or
- if you are blind, two weeks, plus up to four other weeks spent attending training in the use of guide dogs for at least three days a week; or
- two weeks, in any other case.

If you are away for longer than this and so cannot be treated as actively seeking work, you must show that you are looking for work while you are away.

You must usually be in Great Britain to qualify for JSA. To check whether you can get JSA while temporarily away, see p1599, and whether you can be treated as available for work, see p1034. If you are unemployed and want to look for work in another European Economic Area country, see p1601 to see whether you can be paid your contribution-based JSA. Even if you cannot get JSA while you are away, you might be able to get national insurance credits (see p967).

What should you do before you go away?

1. Inform the DWP before you go away. You can be required to give notice in writing.[93]

2. You must be available for work and be able to receive information about job offers. You must, therefore, provide details of how you can be contacted or how you plan to contact the DWP while you are away.[94]

3. Check with your Jobcentre Plus office when you must sign on when you return home (see p1055). This could be a day that is not your usual signing day. If you do not sign on when you are supposed to, you may lose benefit for the whole of the period you were away unless you can show you had a good reason for failing to sign on (see p1058).

4. The jobseeker's agreement

To qualify for jobseeker's allowance (JSA), you must agree and sign a 'jobseeker's agreement'.[95] This enables the DWP to monitor and direct your search for a job and gives you a chance to put any agreed restrictions on your availability for work

Part 7: Work and work-related rules
Chapter 45: Jobseeking and other conditions
4. The jobseeker's agreement

on record. It is discussed with you during your initial interview (see p136 and p711).

Claimant commitment

The DWP calls your jobseeker's agreement a **'claimant commitment'** and you are asked to confirm that you understand that it acts as your jobseeker's agreement. However, all the rules about jobseeker's agreements described in this section continue to apply. If you claim contribution-based JSA under the universal credit system (see p20), the rules for claimant commitments are different (see p1071). If you are in any doubt about which rules apply to you, ask the DWP and seek advice – eg, from your local welfare rights service, law centre or Citizens Advice Bureau.

Until you have agreed the contents of the jobseeker's agreement with your employment officer (EO), your claim for JSA is not passed to a decision maker to decide whether you are entitled to JSA. However, see p1052 for situations when you can be treated as having signed an agreement. If a decision on your claim is delayed or JSA is refused because you have not entered into a jobseeker's agreement, you may be able to get hardship payments (see Chapter 51).

The agreement is not valid until it has been signed by you and the EO.[96] It can be in electronic form and can be signed by an electronic signature.[97] You must be given a copy.[98] To find out when your agreement can be backdated, see p1053. For what happens if you cannot agree, see p1052.

Note: some people getting a training allowance do not have to have a current jobseeker's agreement (see p1029). In some cases, you can qualify for joint-claim JSA even if you or your partner (but not both of you) do not have a current jobseeker's agreement (see p135).

What is in the jobseeker's agreement

A jobseeker's agreement must contain specific information, such as your name and the date of the agreement. It must also include:[99]

- the type of job you are going to actively seek. If you are allowed to place restrictions on the type of work for which you are available, these are entered in a separate box;[100]
- the total number of hours that you are available for work each week (unless you say that you are prepared to work at any time), with a breakdown of what hours you are available on each day. This is known as your 'pattern of availability'. For information on restricting the number of hours and the times for which you are available, see p1042;
- how quickly you must be available for work (see p1031), and other restrictions you are placing on the work for which you are available – eg, the level of pay or the distance you are prepared to travel;

- the steps you are to take to seek work or to improve your chances of work – eg, preparing a CV and attending relevant courses;
- if you have been allowed a 'permitted period' (see p1041), the dates on which it starts and ends;
- a statement of your rights if you and the EO cannot agree on what should be in the agreement. These are your rights:
  - to have a proposed jobseeker's agreement referred to a decision maker (see p1052 and p1053); *and*
  - to seek a revision or a supersession of, or to appeal against any determination or direction of the decision maker. You must apply for a mandatory reconsideration before you can appeal.

  Note: the jobseeker's agreement you are asked to sign might not set out these rights very clearly, but insist on making use of them where necessary.

It also advises you to keep a record of what you do to find work and states that if you do not do enough, your JSA might be affected.

Your jobseeker's agreement is not binding on you or the DWP; there is no automatic penalty if you fail to keep it.[101] However, the contents of the agreement and whether you have abided by it are important evidence if there is ever a dispute about whether you are available for or actively seeking work, and also if you are ever accused of refusing a suitable job offer.[102] If you have done everything in your jobseeker's agreement, try to argue that you should not be accused of not being available for or actively seeking work.[103]

Do you think your jobseeker's agreement is unreasonable?

You may think that what your jobseeker's agreement says you are expected to do to find work is unreasonable – eg, you are expected to take too many steps, or you are expected to be available for work for too many hours or at unreasonable times. You can ask for your jobseeker's agreement to be referred to a decision maker. However, you risk losing benefit if you refuse to sign the jobseeker's agreement.

Rather than refusing to sign the jobseeker's agreement proposed by your EO, it may be better to sign it and then write to the DWP saying that you would like to change it (see p1053). You should not lose JSA, provided you comply with the original agreement while the variation is being considered. It is important to make it clear that you intend to do so.

If you are 16 or 17

If you are 16 or 17, in general, your jobseeker's agreement is the same as that for someone aged 18 or over, although it places an emphasis on training. However, it must explain the rules about sanctions for claimants under 18 (including when JSA is payable at a reduced rate), unless you are claiming JSA because you are laid off or are on short-time working (see p1028) or you have accepted an offer to enlist in the armed forces.[104]

Part 7: Work and work-related rules
Chapter 45: Jobseeking and other conditions
4. The jobseeker's agreement

Treated as signing a jobseeker's agreement

The rules that treat you as signing a jobseeker's agreement are mainly to deal with situations where there is an unavoidable delay between the date you claim JSA and the date of your initial interview (see p136 and p711), and so enable JSA to be put into payment before the interview. Other situations in which you can be treated as signing a jobseeker's agreement include:[105]

- for as long as you are treated as being available for work because of circumstances that arose between your date of claim and your initial interview;
- if there are circumstances affecting the normal procedures for claiming, awarding or paying JSA (eg, a computer failure at the DWP, a strike by staff or severe weather), which make it impracticable or unduly difficult for you to comply with them;[106]
- during the period of up to 13 weeks during which you are treated as available for work because you have experienced, or been threatened with, domestic violence (see p1035), if you have not signed a jobseeker's agreement before the period begins.

Disputes about a jobseeker's agreement

You and your EO may disagree about what should be in your jobseeker's agreement. Your EO is not allowed to sign your jobseeker's agreement unless s/he is satisfied that you will qualify as being available for and actively seeking work if you comply with its terms.[107] If s/he thinks you are placing unreasonable restrictions on your availability for work, or that the steps you propose to take to actively seek work are not sufficient, s/he will not sign an agreement based on your proposals. In this situation:[108]

- the EO may refer a proposed jobseeker's agreement (including one proposed by you) to a decision maker; *or*
- if you ask your EO to do so, s/he *must* refer a proposed agreement to a decision maker immediately.

You should apply for hardship payments immediately (see Chapter 51).

What happens when a referral to a decision maker is made

When a proposed jobseeker's agreement is referred to a decision maker, s/he:[109]

- decides whether you would qualify as being available for and actively seeking work if you were to comply with the agreement and whether it is reasonable to expect you to comply with it;
- may direct the EO to enter into a jobseeker's agreement on whatever terms the decision maker considers appropriate – those either you or the EO propose, or terms prepared by the decision maker her/himself;
- may order that, if the agreement is entered into, it should be backdated (see p1053).

The decision maker must make a decision within 14 days of the agreement being referred, unless to do so would be impracticable, and must notify you of the decision.[110] If you are happy with the decision, you must see your EO and sign the agreement. If you are unhappy with it, you can ask for the decision to be revised or superseded, or appeal (see Chapters 54 and 55). You must apply for a mandatory reconsideration before you can appeal.

If the decision maker decides in your favour, your jobseeker's agreement can be backdated (see below) and, if so, you are paid arrears of JSA from the date of your claim. However, if the decision maker decides against you, you are unlikely to get any backdating. You therefore risk losing benefit if you refuse to sign the jobseeker's agreement while it is being considered by the decision maker.

Backdating the jobseeker's agreement

A jobseeker's agreement is automatically backdated to the first day you claimed JSA, provided you and your EO can agree about what it should contain but not always if it is referred to a decision maker.[111] This includes any date to which your claim has been backdated (see p1157).

If the agreement is referred to a decision maker, it is only backdated if s/he makes a direction ordering this.[112] S/he must consider all the relevant circumstances including:[113]

- whether it was reasonable for you to refuse to accept the agreement proposed by the EO; *and*
- whether the terms of any alternative agreement that you may have proposed are reasonable; *and*
- whether you have subsequently said that you would be prepared to accept the agreement proposed by the EO; *and*
- the date on which you were first prepared to enter into an agreement that the decision maker considers to be reasonable; *and*
- the fact that the first opportunity you had to sign a jobseeker's agreement was later than the date of your claim for JSA.

Changing your jobseeker's agreement

The terms of your jobseeker's agreement can be changed by agreement between you and your EO. Any change must be in writing and signed by you and the EO.[114] This can be in electronic form and can be signed by an electronic signature.[115]

Both you and the EO can propose changes at any time. Put your proposals in writing, giving full details of the changes you want to make and your reasons. Explain how your proposals give you a reasonable chance of finding a job.

An EO cannot agree to a change unless s/he considers that the terms mean that you satisfy the jobseeking conditions.[116] If you and the EO:

- agree the proposed changes, you must be given a copy of the new jobseeker's agreement;[117]

Part 7: Work and work-related rules
Chapter 45: Jobseeking and other conditions
5. Interviews and signing on

- do not agree the proposed changes, these can be referred to a decision maker.[118] They *must* be referred to a decision maker if you request this.

What happens when a referral to a decision maker is made

When a proposed change to a jobseeker's agreement is referred to a decision maker, your existing agreement remains in force until a decision is made. Payment of your JSA might be suspended, or even terminated, if you do not stick to the terms of the agreement if this causes a doubt about whether you are available for or actively seeking work. **Note:**

- If the decision maker believes that both your and the EO's proposals are reasonable and you would qualify as being available for and actively seeking work, s/he should change the agreement along the lines you propose.[119]
- The decision maker can direct a change of the jobseeker's agreement, the terms and when the new agreement takes effect.[120] The terms can be those that either you or the EO have proposed, or terms prepared by the decision maker her/himself. If a change you proposed is accepted and it makes the terms of the agreement less restrictive, argue that the new agreement should take effect from the date on which you proposed the change.[121]

If you do not sign the new agreement within 21 days of the date a change in your jobseeker's agreement is directed, the decision maker can bring the agreement to an end.[122] If this happens, your entitlement to JSA is terminated, including during any revision, mandatory reconsideration or appeal period, unless you qualify for hardship payments (see Chapter 51).

If you are unhappy with the decision maker's decision, you can request a revision or appeal (see Chapters 54 and 55). You must apply for a mandatory reconsideration before you can appeal. If your appeal is allowed, the original jobseeker's agreement revives and you are owed arrears, even if the tribunal directs another change in the agreement.[123]

5. **Interviews and signing on**

While you are getting jobseeker's allowance (JSA), you (or both of you if you are a joint-claim couple) must normally participate in regular interviews and sign a declaration ('sign on') regularly, usually at the Jobcentre Plus office.[124] This is to enable the DWP to check that you have satisfied the jobseeking conditions and that you continue to qualify for JSA. You can be required to provide information and evidence about your circumstances, your availability for work and how you have been actively seeking work.[125] You can be notified of the manner, time and place of an interview by phone, post or electronic means.[126] If you:

- fail to sign on, your entitlement to JSA may end (see p1058);

- fail to participate in an interview, your entitlement to JSA may end or you may be given a sanction (see p1057 and p1060).

Note: when you first claim JSA, you must attend an initial interview (see p136 and p711). If you do not attend the interview at the right time, your date of claim is affected (see p139 and p713). If you do not attend the interview at all (and the DWP does not waive the requirement to do so), you have not made a valid claim and so do not qualify for JSA.

Travel expenses

Your travel expenses to and from the Jobcentre Plus office to participate in interviews and to sign on are generally not reimbursed. If travelling to sign on is causing you hardship, ask whether you can sign on by post (see p1056).

You may be able to have your travel expenses reimbursed if you are given an appointment for an interview on a day other than the day you normally sign on, or if you have to attend a different office on your normal signing-on day and you incur additional costs. If you are signing on by post but are required to attend for an interview, you may also be entitled to a refund of travel costs.

Regular interviews

While you are getting JSA, you (or both of you, if you are a joint-claim couple) must normally attend the Jobcentre Plus office to participate in a regular interview (generally every fortnight). At the interview, you must 'sign on' (see below). Take your records and proof of your attempts to find work with you. The interview aims to:

- keep a regular check on what you are doing to find work and make sure that your jobseeker's agreement remains up to date and relevant;
- discuss any difficulties you are experiencing and identify any help and support that the DWP can give you;
- check whether there have been any relevant changes in your circumstances;
- decide whether you should be sent for a job vacancy, or required to attend a course or participate in a training or employment scheme.

You may be referred to an employment officer (EO) for a more in-depth interview if what you say raises a doubt about whether you remain entitled to JSA. If the EO thinks your job search activities have been inadequate, payment of your JSA may be suspended while a decision maker considers your entitlement to JSA.

Signing on

At your regular interview, you must sign a declaration (known as 'signing on') that:[127]

Part 7: Work and work-related rules
Chapter 45: Jobseeking and other conditions
5. Interviews and signing on

- you have been available for and actively seeking work or could be treated as if you were and, for most 16/17-year-olds, that you have been actively seeking suitable training (see p1047). See p1046 for information about proving you are actively seeking work; *and*
- there has been no change in your circumstances that might affect the amount of, or your right to, JSA (other than those you may have already notified to the DWP).

If you fail to sign on, your entitlement to JSA can end (see p1058) or you may be given a sanction under the rules that apply to interviews (see p1060).

You are normally told your regular signing-on day and time at the start of your claim. Generally, you must sign on every fortnight. This is the case even if you are paid weekly. **Note:** the government says that from some point in future, you will be required to sign on weekly for the first three months of your JSA claim. See CPAG's online service and *Welfare Rights Bulletin* for updates.

You may be required to sign on and participate in interviews more frequently – eg, if the Jobcentre Plus office thinks you need more help to find work, if you are suspected of fraud or if you have no fixed abode. Because decisions about how often you have to sign on are made by EOs, you do not have a right of appeal. However, you can ask for the frequency to be altered – eg, if your circumstances change or the cost of travel causes hardship.

Have you been told that you are not entitled to jobseeker's allowance?

If you are told that you are not entitled to JSA, you can argue that you no longer have to sign on – eg, while you are appealing against the decision.[128] However, if your appeal is successful, in order to be paid arrears you must show that you have satisfied the jobseeking conditions since the last time that you signed on, which can often be difficult. So it is always best to continue to sign on to protect your position.

Signing on by post

The DWP might allow you to sign on by post – eg, if you live a long way from the Jobcentre Plus office, or the cost of travel to the jobcentre causes you hardship, or you have a mental or physical disability which restricts your mobility. Even so:

- you must attend, and participate in, any further interviews required. You could try to get an interview arranged nearer your home, if attending at the Jobcentre Plus office would result in your being away from home for a long time;
- you must send a signed declaration and show that you are available for and actively seeking work. If this is not received at the time specified by the DWP, your entitlement to JSA ends, unless you can show a good reason for the delay (see p1058). If you cannot show this, you must make a fresh claim for JSA.

Further interviews

If you remain unemployed for a period of time, you must participate in a number of additional interviews. If you fail to do so, your entitlement to JSA can end (see p1058) or you can be given a sanction (see p1060).

Some interviews take place at set intervals. However, you can be required to participate in an interview at any time – eg, if the DWP thinks you need more help with your search for work or there is a question about whether you fulfil the jobseeking conditions.

At the interview, an EO reviews your situation, the type of work you are looking for and the steps you are taking to find it. You may be asked to agree to a change of your jobseeker's agreement (see p1053) to record any change in the type of work for which you are looking or the steps you will take to find it.

When your entitlement to jobseeker's allowance ends

Your entitlement to JSA can end if:
- you fail to 'sign on' on the day you were notified to do so (see p1058). However, it does not end if you contact the Jobcentre Plus office within five working days of your failure and show you had a 'good reason'; *or*
- you fail to participate in an interview when you are required to do so (see p1058). However, it does not end if you contact the Jobcentre Plus office within five working days of your failure. You may, instead be given a sanction if you cannot show you had a 'good reason' (see p1060).

Ensure that you go to the Jobcentre Plus office within five working days of your failure to participate in an interview or to sign on. Explain why you have a good reason – eg, if you did not receive notice that you were supposed to attend, or genuinely misunderstood when you were supposed to attend.

What should you do if your entitlement ends?

1. If a decision is made to stop your entitlement, ask for the decision to be revised, or appeal against it. You must apply for a mandatory reconsideration before you can appeal.

2. To protect your position, make a new claim for JSA as soon as possible. Ask for it to be backdated under the normal rules, or if you are allowed to sign on by post under the special rule on p1060.

3. If you have missed signing on, ask the Jobcentre Plus office to accept the information about your search for work that is available on your universal jobmatch account, or any other information that you would have provided on your signing-on day. If this is accepted, the decision maker should revise the decision that stopped your benefit so that you are at least paid up to the date you did not sign on.[129]

Part 7: Work and work-related rules
Chapter 45: Jobseeking and other conditions
5. Interviews and signing on

Failure to sign on

Your entitlement to JSA can end if you do not provide a signed declaration on the day you were notified to do so, unless you can show a good reason within five working days of your failure.[130] You must be given five days before a decision is made to end your entitlement.[131] 'Good reason' is not defined in the rules, but for information about what may count, see p1133. See p1057 for how you can minimise your loss. **Note:** your signing-on day is usually the day of your regular interview. You therefore may instead lose your entitlement or be given a sanction under the rules about participating in interviews (see below and p1060) – ie, if you failed to sign on because you did not show up at the Jobcentre Plus office for your regular interview.[132]

If your entitlement to JSA ends, you must make a fresh claim. You lose JSA for the whole period between the date on which your entitlement ends and the date on which you are treated as having claimed again. If you failed to sign on, the date on which your entitlement to JSA ends is the earliest of:[133]

- the day after the last day for which you have provided information or evidence that shows you continue to be entitled to JSA – eg, at your regular fortnightly interview. In many cases, this is the day after the last day on which you signed on. Ask the Jobcentre Plus office to accept the information that you would have provided on your signing-on day. If this is accepted, you can be paid up to the day you did not sign on;[134]
- the day on which you should have signed on.

The date on which you are treated as having claimed JSA again is normally the first day on which you contact the Jobcentre Plus office again. See p1060 to see if your new claim can be backdated.

The effect of this is that, if you fail to sign on, you may lose JSA for the full period for which you would have been paid had you signed on at the right time. In addition, you lose JSA for the days between the day you missed signing on and the day you next contact the Jobcentre Plus office.

Failure to participate in an interview

Your entitlement to JSA can end if you do not participate in an interview when you are notified by an EO that you are required to do so – eg, you are late for or miss the appointment, or you turn up but refuse to answer questions. Notification of your regular interviews is normally given when you first claim JSA. Notification of these, and of further interviews, can be sent or given in writing, by telephone or by electronic means.[135]

Did you not receive notification?

If you can show that you did not receive notification to attend an interview, this means that you have not failed to participate and, therefore, your entitlement to JSA should not end (nor should you be given a sanction).

1. If you are told that you failed to participate in an interview that was arranged face to face without any written confirmation being sent or given to you, argue that this is not a valid way of notifying an appointment.

2. If you did not receive notification of an interview, ask for proof that the appointment was made.

3. The law usually assumes that when a letter has been sent correctly addressed and with the full postage paid, it will be received. So if notification was sent to you, you must put forward a good case to show why this assumption should not be made – eg, you have always responded properly to other notifications when these were received from the Jobcentre Plus office or there are problems with your postal address.[136]

If you are notified by an EO that you must participate in an interview on a specified date, unless you contact the EO within five working days (see below), your entitlement to JSA ends if you fail to participate in the interview:[137]

- at the right time – eg, you attend on the right day, but are late. This only applies if, when you failed to participate in an interview on a previous occasion, the DWP gave or sent you a written notice warning you that, if you fail to participate the next time you are required to do so, your entitlement to JSA could cease or you could be given a sanction. **Note:** if you failed to sign on because you were late for the interview, you may instead lose your entitlement under the rules about failing to sign on (see p1058). Under those rules, you do not have to have been given a warning; *or*

- on the right day. You do not have to have been given a warning.

Your entitlement to JSA can only end if you do not contact the EO within five working days of the date you failed to participate in an interview.[138] You must be given five days before a decision is made to end your entitlement.[139] **Note:** you may be given a sanction if you cannot show a good reason (see p1060).

If you contact the EO more than five days from the date you failed to participate in an interview, your entitlement to JSA ends and you must make a fresh claim. You lose JSA for the whole period between the date on which your entitlement ends and the date on which you are treated as having claimed again. The date on which your entitlement to JSA ends can never be earlier than the day after the last time you participated in an interview. Otherwise, it is the earliest of:[140]

- the day after the last day for which you have provided information that shows you continue to be entitled to JSA – eg, at your regular fortnightly interview. In many cases, this means the day after the last day on which you signed on. Ask the Jobcentre Plus office to accept the information that you would have provided at the interview. If this is accepted, you can be paid up to the day you did not participate in the interview;[141]

- the day on which you should have participated in an interview.

Part 7: Work and work-related rules
Chapter 45: Jobseeking and other conditions
5. Interviews and signing on

The date on which you are treated as having claimed JSA again is usually the first day on which you contact the Jobcentre Plus office again. However, if this was the same day as the failure to participate in an interview, you are treated as having made your fresh claim on the *following* day.[142] See below to see whether your new claim can be backdated.

Note:
- If you fail to attend and participate in your initial interview (ie, when you claim JSA), you might not be awarded JSA or your date of claim might be affected.
- If the requirement to attend or participate in an interview is for a training or employment scheme or programme, your entitlement does not end, but you can be given a sanction under other rules (see Chapter 48).[143]

Backdating your new claim

If your entitlement to JSA has ceased because you failed to participate in an interview or to sign on and you have to make a new claim, in limited cases it may be possible to get your new claim backdated and so avoid some, or all, of the loss of JSA. Your claim can be backdated:
- under any of the normal rules (see p1157); *or*
- to the day after your entitlement to JSA ended, provided you make a new claim for JSA immediately after you are informed that your entitlement ended.[144] This only applies if you are not normally required to attend the Jobcentre Plus office (eg, you sign on by post) and you did not receive the notice to attend.

When you are given a sanction

Your entitlement to JSA does not end if you fail to participate in an interview when required, but you contact the EO within five working days. However, you may be given a sanction unless you can show a 'good reason'. See p1103 for the sanction rules if you fail to participate in an interview and p1133 for what may count as a good reason. You may be able to get hardship payments (see Chapter 51).

Notes

1. The jobseeking conditions

1 ss9(13), 35(1) and 36(1A) and (2) and (4) JSA 1995
2 The Jobseeker's Allowance (Work Programme) (Employment Officers) Designation Order 2014; Memo DMG 29/14; Memo DMG 30/14
3 Reg 4 JSA Regs
4 Regs 1(3), 14(1)(a), (aa) and (k), 15(1)(a), (2) and (3) and 17A(1) JSA Regs
5 Reg 17A(2), (3) and (5) JSA Regs
6 Reg 17A(7) and (8) JSA Regs
7 Reg 17A(7) and (8) JSA Regs
8 Regs 1(3) and 170 JSA Regs
9 Reg 7 JSA(SAPOE) Regs
10 Reg 7 JSA(SAPOE) Regs

2. Available for work

11 s6(1) JSA 1995; reg 6 JSA Regs
12 R(U) 44/53
13 s6(1) and (9) JSA 1995
14 *Shaukat Ali v CAO*, appendix to R(U) 1/85
15 *Secretary of State for Social Security v David,* 15 December 2000, reported as R(JSA) 3/01
16 Regs 4 and 5(1)-(1B) and (6) JSA Regs
17 Reg 5(2) JSA Regs
18 CU 96/1994
19 Reg 5(3) JSA Regs
20 Reg 5(4) JSA Regs
21 Reg 4 JSA Regs
22 Reg 17B JSA Regs
23 Reg 14(1)(e), (g), (t) or (u) JSA Regs
24 Reg 17(1)-(3) JSA Regs
25 Reg 17(5) JSA Regs
26 Reg 4 JSA Regs
27 Reg 14(1)(a), (aa) (f) and (k) JSA Regs
28 Reg 17A(3) and (7) JSA Regs
29 Reg 14(1)(c), (m), (n), (nn), (p) and (q) JSA Regs
30 Reg 14(4) JSA Regs
31 Reg 14A JSA Regs
32 Reg 14A(10) JSA Regs
33 Reg 14A(10) JSA Regs
34 Reg 14A(10) JSA Regs
35 Reg 14A(10) JSA Regs
36 Reg 14(1)(b), (d), (r) and (v) JSA Regs
37 Reg 14(2B) JSA Regs
38 Reg 14(5) JSA Regs
39 Reg 4 JSA Regs
40 Reg 14(2) and (2ZC) JSA Regs
41 Reg 14(2ZD) JSA Regs
42 Reg 14(2ZA) and (2ZB) JSA Regs
43 Reg 14(1)(h), (i), (j), (l), (o) and (s) JSA Regs
44 CJSA/5944/1999
45 Reg 14(2A) JSA Regs; R(JSA) 2/07
46 Reg 15 JSA Regs
47 Reg 7(3) JSA Regs
48 *Secretary of State for Social Security v David,* 15 December 2000, reported as R(JSA) 3/01
49 Reg 12 JSA Regs
50 s6(2) and (3) JSA 1995; regs 6, 7, 8, 13 and 13A JSA Regs
51 Reg 64(2) and (3) JSA Regs
52 Reg 57(1) JSA Regs
53 Regs 10 and 64(3) JSA Regs
54 Reg 10(1) JSA Regs
55 Reg 13(3) and (3A) JSA Regs
56 Reg 8 JSA Regs
57 Reg 8 JSA Regs
58 s6(5), (7) and (8) JSA 1995; reg 16 JSA Regs
59 Vol 4 Ch 21, paras 21399 and 21403-04 DMG
60 Reg 31(f) JSA Regs
61 Reg 16(2) JSA Regs
62 Reg 17(4) JSA Regs
63 Vol 4 Ch 21, para 21451 DMG
64 Reg 13(2) JSA Regs
65 Reg 7(2) JSA Regs
66 R(JSA) 2/07
67 Reg 13A JSA Regs
68 Regs 4 and 13(4)-(7) JSA Regs
69 Reg 8 JSA Regs
70 Vol 6 Ch 34, paras 34415-18, 34335-38 and 34743 DMG
71 Reg 16(1) JSA Regs
72 Regs 8 and 9 JSA Regs
73 Reg 8 JSA Regs

3. Actively seeking work

74 s7(1) JSA 1995; reg 18A JSA Regs; *GP v SSWP (JSA)* [2015] UKUT 476 (AAC); [2016] AACR 14
75 Reg 18(1) JSA Regs
76 CJSA/2162/2001

Part 7: Work and work-related rules
Chapter 45: Jobseeking and other conditions
Notes

77 *R (Smith) v SSWP* [2015] EWHC 2284 (Admin)
78 CJSA/1814/2007
79 Vol 4 Ch 21, paras 21616-20 DMG
80 Reg 18(2) JSA Regs
81 *GP v SSWP (JSA)* [2015] UKUT 476 (AAC); [2016] AACR 14
82 Reg 18(4) JSA Regs
83 Reg 18(3) JSA Regs
84 Regs 65 and 65A JSA Regs
85 Reg 20 JSA Regs
86 Reg 21 JSA Regs
87 Reg 21A JSA Regs
88 Regs 19 and 21B JSA Regs
89 Regs 1(3) and 19(1)(lzl), (q), (r) and (3) JSA Regs
90 Reg 7 JSA(SAPOE) Regs
91 Reg 19(1)(p) JSA Regs
92 Reg 19(2) JSA Regs
93 Reg 19(1)(p) JSA Regs
94 R(U) 4/66

4. The jobseeker's agreement

95 s1(2)(b) JSA 1995
96 s9(3) JSA 1995
97 s9(3A) JSA 1995
98 s9(4) JSA 1995
99 s9(1) JSA 1995; reg 31 JSA Regs
100 *HS v SSWP* [2009] UKUT 177 (AAC); [2010] AACR 10
101 CJSA/1814/2007
102 *R (Smith) v SSWP* [2015] EWHC 2284 (Admin)
103 CJSA/2162/2001
104 Reg 66 JSA Regs
105 Reg 34 JSA Regs
106 CJSA/935/1999
107 s9(5) JSA 1995
108 s9(6) JSA 1995
109 ss9(6)(a) and (b) and (7)(b) and (c) JSA 1995
110 s9(7)(a) and (8)(b) JSA 1995; reg 33 JSA Regs
111 Reg 35 JSA Regs
112 s9(7)(c) JSA 1995
113 s9(8)(a) JSA 1995; reg 32 JSA Regs
114 s10(1) and (2) JSA 1995
115 s10(2A) JSA 1995
116 s10(4) JSA 1995
117 s10(3) JSA 1995
118 s10(5) JSA 1995
119 s10(7)(a) JSA 1995; reg 39 JSA Regs; Vol 4 Ch 21, para 21951 DMG
120 s10(6)(b) and (d) JSA 1995
121 R(JSA) 2/07
122 s10(6)(c) JSA 1995; reg 38 JSA Regs; *GM v SSWP (JSA)* [2014] UKUT 57 (AAC)
123 CJSA/4435/1998

5. Interviews and signing on

124 s8 JSA 1995; regs 23 and 23A JSA Regs
125 Reg 24(1)-(5A) JSA Regs
126 Regs 23 and 23A JSA Regs
127 s8 JSA 1995; regs 24(6) and (10) and 65A JSA Regs
128 CJSA/1080/2002; *GM v SSWP (JSA)* [2014] UKUT 57 (AAC)
129 R(JSA) 2/04
130 Regs 25(1)(c) and (1A) and 27 JSA Regs; *SSWP v Michael Ferguson* [2003] EWCA Civ 536, reported as R(JSA) 6/03
131 *DL v SSWP (JSA)* [2013] UKUT 295 (AAC)
132 R(JSA) 2/04
133 Reg 26 JSA Regs; *SSWP v Michael Ferguson* [2003] EWCA Civ 536, reported as R(JSA) 6/03; R(JSA) 2/04
134 R(JSA) 2/04
135 Regs 23 and 23A JSA Regs
136 Regs 23 and 23A JSA Regs; s7 Interpretation Act 1978; R(JSA) 1/04
137 s8(2) JSA 1995; reg 25(1)(a) and (b) and (1A) JSA Regs
138 Reg 25(1)(a) and (b)(iii) JSA Regs
139 *DL v SSWP (JSA)* [2013] UKUT 295 (AAC)
140 Reg 26 JSA Regs; *SSWP v Michael Ferguson* [2003] EWCA Civ 536, reported as R(JSA) 6/03; R(JSA) 2/04
141 R(JSA) 2/04
142 Reg 6(4C) SS(C&P) Regs
143 Reg 25(1A) JSA Regs
144 Reg 6(4B) SS(C&P) Regs

Chapter 46

Claimant responsibilities

This chapter covers:
1. Work-focused interviews (below)
2. Taking part in an interview (p1067)
3. Work-related activity (p1068)

This chapter covers the work-related responsibilities you may have in order to get certain benefits. For the jobseeking conditions for jobseeker's allowance, see Chapter 45. If you come under the universal credit system, see Chapter 47.

Key facts
- You and your partner may have to take part in work-focused interviews for income support (IS), jobseeker's allowance, employment and support allowance (ESA), incapacity benefit, severe disablement allowance and carer's allowance. In some cases, if you fail to take part in an interview when you claim IS, you are not entitled to benefit.
- If you only qualify for IS because you are a lone parent and you do not have any children under three, or you are entitled to ESA and you are not in the support group, you may be required to undertake some work-related activity.
- If you do not take part in work-focused interviews or undertake work-related activity and you cannot show good cause, you may be given a sanction. Your benefit is then paid at a reduced rate. However, you may qualify for hardship payments.

1. Work-focused interviews

If you are getting specified benefits, you (or, in some cases, your partner) can be required to take part in work-focused interviews. Claimants who are not required to attend an interview can still take part in the schemes on a voluntary basis.

At the interview, job opportunities, training and rehabilitation are discussed. The nature of your interview depends on the state of your health and your caring commitments. In some cases, it is assumed that you will not be returning to work for some time and the focus is therefore on helping you to keep in contact with

Part 7: Work and work-related rules
Chapter 46: Claimant responsibilities
1. Work-focused interviews

the employment market. In other cases, it is assumed that you will return to work soon and the focus is on taking steps towards full-time paid work.

There are currently a number of rules under which you can be required to take part in work-focused interviews:

- interviews for employment and support allowance (ESA) and benefits for incapacity (see below);
- interviews for lone parents entitled to income support (IS – see p1065);
- Jobcentre Plus interviews for certain IS claimants (see p1066);
- interviews for the partners of people entitled to specified benefits (see p1066).

You (or your partner) may be required to take part in interviews by decision makers at the DWP. You (or your partner) can also be required to take part in interviews by advisers contracted by the DWP – eg, in the Work Programme (see p1104).[1] If you (or your partner) do not take part, you could be given a sanction and your benefit could then be paid at a reduced rate (see p1124). Under the Jobcentre Plus rules, if you fail to take part when you claim IS, you may be treated as not having made a claim (see p1066) and therefore cannot qualify for IS.

There have been many changes to the rules on work-focused interviews since they were introduced. See previous editions of this *Handbook* for details.

Interviews for employment and support allowance and benefits for incapacity

Unless you are exempt (see p1065), you come under these rules if you are entitled to ESA or you have been given an 'advance award' of ESA (see p37).[2] These rules also apply if you are entitled to IS on the grounds of incapacity for work (see p102), incapacity benefit (IB) or severe disablement allowance (SDA), and can apply if you make a new claim for one of those benefits. **Note:** if you have been getting IB or SDA since 14 December 2008, you may be required to take part in work-focused interviews under the Jobcentre Plus scheme instead.

If these rules apply, you can be required to take part in work-focused interviews in order to continue to receive the full rate of your benefit.[3] For ESA, you may be required to take part in an interview at around week four of your claim – called a 'health and work conversation'.

Note:

- There are no limits on the frequency or timing of interviews.
- The requirement to take part in an interview can be deferred to another date if it is considered that an interview would not be of assistance or appropriate.[4] There is no right of appeal about this.
- If you fail to take part in a work-focused interview without good cause, you may be given a sanction and your benefit is then paid at a reduced rate.

Exemptions

You are not required to take part in work-focused interviews if:[5]
- you are at least the qualifying age for pension credit (PC – see p147); *or*
- you are a lone parent and responsible for a child under one who is a member of your household (see p222 and p223); *or*
- for IB, IS and SDA, you are treated as incapable of work because you have a severe condition. See p703 of the 2010/11 edition of this *Handbook* for what counts as a severe condition; *or*
- the decision maker thinks that an interview would not be (or would not have been) of assistance because you are (or were likely to be) starting or returning to work; *or*
- for ESA:
  - the decision maker has decided that you have, or are treated as having, limited capability for work-related activity – ie, you are in the support group (see p641); *or*
  - you are only entitled to contributory ESA at a nil rate – eg, because of your pension income.

Work-focused interviews for lone parents

Unless you are exempt, you must take part in work-focused interviews under the rules described in this section if you are entitled to IS and you are a lone parent responsible for and living in the same household as a child (see p222).[6] This can apply even if your youngest child is aged five or over, or if you are someone who can claim IS as a lone parent and also on another basis – eg, if you are also a carer on carer's allowance (CA). **Note:** some lone parents whose youngest child is aged one or over must take part in work-focused interviews under the Jobcentre Plus rules for IS claimants instead of under these rules (see p1066).

Note:
- The requirement to take part in an interview can be deferred to another date (and in some cases waived) if it is considered that it would not be of assistance or appropriate.[7] There is no right of appeal about this.
- The frequency and timing of the interviews depends on whether you are claiming IS solely as a lone parent or if you are claiming on another basis.[8]
- If you fail to take part in a work-focused interview and cannot show good cause, you may be given a sanction and your IS is then paid at a reduced rate (see p1124).

Exemptions

You are not required to take part in work-focused interviews if you are:[9]
- under 18; *or*
- responsible for a child aged under one who is a member of your household; *or*
- already subject to the Jobcentre Plus rules for other IS claimants (see p1066) or the rules for ESA and benefits for incapacity (see p1064).

Part 7: Work and work-related rules
Chapter 46: Claimant responsibilities
1. Work-focused interviews

Jobcentre Plus interviews for income support

Unless the rules for ESA and benefits for incapacity apply to you (see p1064), or you are exempt, the Jobcentre Plus rules apply to most claims for IS (including claims from some lone parents and those claiming on the grounds of incapacity for work). You are required to take part in a work-focused interview:

- when you make a new claim for IS. However, this does not apply if you are a lone parent responsible for a child under five or a lone parent under 18, or someone claiming on the grounds of incapacity for work;[10]
- as a condition of continuing to receive the full rate of IS. In this case, the frequency and timing of interviews depends on whether you are claiming IS solely as a lone parent or if you are claiming on another basis.[11]

Note:
- The requirement to take part in an interview can be deferred to another date (and, in some cases, waived) if it is considered that an interview would not be of assistance or appropriate.[12] There is no right of appeal about this.
- If you fail to take part in an interview when you claim IS, you are treated as not having made a claim and are therefore not entitled to benefit.[13] If, when you claim IS, your interview is deferred to another date, you are paid IS in the meantime and, if you fail to take part in the interview, your entitlement to IS is terminated.[14]
- Otherwise, if you are entitled to IS and you fail to take part in a work-focused interview and cannot show good cause, you may be given a sanction and your IS is then paid at a reduced rate (see p1124).
- If you are a lone parent on IS, whether you come under this scheme or the lone parents' scheme on p1065 depends on when you first claimed IS.
- If you have been getting IB or SDA since 14 December 2008, you may be required to take part in work-focused interviews under this scheme, instead of under the scheme for ESA and benefits for incapacity. The rules are broadly the same as for IS.

Exemptions

You are not required to take part in work-focused interviews if you are a lone parent responsible for a child under one.[15]

Work-focused interviews for partners

If you are a member of a couple and you are entitled to a specified benefit (see p1067), unless s/he is exempt, your partner may be required to take part in work-focused interviews if:[16]
- you and your partner are both aged 18 or over but under the qualifying age for PC (see p147); *and*

- you have been continuously entitled to a specified benefit for 26 weeks or more; *and*
- the benefit is paid to you at a higher rate because of your partner – eg, you get the couple rate of income-based jobseeker's allowance (JSA) or get an increase for an adult with CA.

Specified benefits

The '**specified benefits**' are IS, income-based JSA (but not joint-claim JSA), ESA, IB, SDA and CA.[17]

Note:
- Your partner must take part in one work-focused interview as a condition of your receiving the full amount of your benefit. However, if you are claiming income-based JSA and you or your partner are responsible for a child aged one or over who is a member of your household, your partner must take part in further interviews every six months.[18]
- The requirement to take part in an interview can be waived or deferred to another date if it is considered that it would not be of assistance or appropriate.[19] There is no right of appeal about this.
- If your partner fails to take part in a work-focused interview and cannot show good cause, you may be given a sanction and your benefit is then paid at a reduced rate (see p1124).

Exemptions

Your partner is not required to take part in a work-focused interview under these rules if:[20]
- s/he is entitled to one of the specified benefits in her/his own right. However, in this case, your partner may be required to take part in a work-focused interview under one of the other sets of rules described in this chapter; *or*
- you or your partner are responsible for a child under one who is a member of your household.

2. Taking part in an interview

Work-focused interviews normally take place at the local DWP or Jobcentre Plus office or, for employment and support allowance (ESA), by telephone. An interview can take place in your home if the DWP considers that going to the office would cause undue inconvenience or endanger your health.[21] There is no right of appeal against this decision.

'**Taking part**' in an interview means that you must:[22]
- turn up at the time and place notified. For ESA, if you are not required to attend an interview in person, you must be available (eg, by telephone) on the date and at the time notified and respond to any contact made;

Part 7: Work and work-related rules
Chapter 46: Claimant responsibilities
3. Work-related activity

- 'participate in discussions' with your work coach about your employability and about any reasonable activity you are willing to do (or have done) which may enhance your employment prospects. **Note:** this does not apply if it is your partner who is required to take part in an interview. If you are on income support (IS) and are required to take part under the Jobcentre Plus rules, this only applies if you are a lone parent or are claiming on the grounds of incapacity for work;
- answer questions about your educational qualifications, employment history, any current work and your future hopes for working, vocational training, employment skills and abilities and medical conditions that affect your chances of getting a job, and your caring or childcare responsibilities;
- discuss and assist in completing an 'action plan'. The action plan includes any action you and the work coach agree is reasonable and you are willing to take. There is nothing to say you must take the steps in the action plan. **Note:**
  - This does not apply for ESA (where an action plan is only drawn up if it is decided that you must undertake 'work-related activity' – see below) or for work-focused interviews for partners.
  - If you are on IS and are required to take part under the Jobcentre Plus rules, this only applies if you are a lone parent or are claiming on the grounds of incapacity for work;
- in further interviews, discuss your progress, how the action plan might be amended and any further support that might be available to you.

Under the Jobcentre Plus rules (see p1066), if you are under 18, 'taking part' also requires you to attend an interview with a person specified by the DWP – eg, someone at the place where the local authority provides careers advice.[23]

---

3. **Work-related activity**

Unless you are exempt, you may be required to undertake some 'work-related activity'. If the DWP decides that you are required to do so, you must be notified properly.[24] Any requirement must be reasonable, taking into account your circumstances.[25] You may be required to undertake work-related activity if you are required to take part in work-focused interviews *and* you are entitled to:[26]
- income support (IS), the only reason you are entitled is because you are a lone parent and you do not have any children under three; *or*
- employment and support allowance (ESA). **Note:** you are exempt from the requirement to take part in work-focused interviews if you have, or are treated as having, limited capability for work-related activity – ie, you are in the support group (see p641).

You may be required to undertake the work-related activity by decision makers at the DWP as well as by advisers contracted by the DWP – eg, in the Work Programme (see p1104).[27] If the DWP refers you to a scheme, the scheme manager decides what, if any, work-related activity you are required to undertake. If you fail to take part in work-related activity without good cause, you may be given a sanction (see p1128).

The main features are as follows.

- 'Work-related activity' is activity that makes it more likely that you will get a job or remain in work.[28] The exact activity is at the discretion of your adviser. For ESA, it specifically includes work experience and work placements. However, the DWP says you cannot be required to undertake work experience; this is voluntary.[29] So if you do not undertake work experience, you should *not* be given a sanction.
- You cannot be required to apply for a job or undertake work (as an employee or otherwise).[30] If you are put under pressure to do so, get advice.
- For ESA, you cannot be required to undergo medical treatment.[31]
- All work-related activity must be recorded in an '**action plan**', which must be in writing and specify the activity you are required to undertake.[32] You must be given a copy. An action plan must be reconsidered if you request it, and a written decision issued following the request.[33]
- A requirement about the time at, or by which, you must undertake work-related activity can be lifted if the decision maker (or adviser) considers it would be (or would have been) unreasonable.[34]

For IS, you can restrict the times you are required to be available to undertake work-related activity, but you must be available during your child's normal school hours, or during periods in which you have entrusted someone over 18 to supervise your child on a temporary basis (other than for healthcare) – eg, a babysitter or member of your family.[35] For ESA, if you are the lone parent of a child under 13, you can only be required to undertake work-related activity during your child's normal school hours.[36]

Exemptions

You cannot be required to undertake work-related activity if:[37]
- you are a lone parent who is responsible for a child under three who is a member of your household (see p222 and p223); *or*
- you are exempt from the requirement to take part in work-focused interviews; *or*
- for IS, as well as being a lone parent, you come within any of the other groups of people who can claim IS (see p102); *or*
- for ESA, you are entitled to carer's allowance, or your ESA includes a carer premium (p246).

Notes

1. Work-focused interviews

1 **ESA** Reg 62 ESA Regs
Other benefits Reg 2(1) SS(JPI) Regs; reg 2(1) SS(WFILP) Regs; reg 2(1) SS(JPIP) Regs; reg 11 SS(IBWFI) Regs
2 Reg 54(2)(a) ESA Regs
3 **ESA** Regs 54-62 ESA Regs
Other benefits SS(IBWFI) Regs
4 **ESA** Reg 59 ESA Regs
Other benefits Reg 5 SS(IBWFI) Regs
5 **ESA** Regs 54(2) and 60 ESA Regs
Other benefits Regs 3(4)-(6) and 5(2) SS(IBWFI) Regs; reg 10 SS(IFW) Regs
6 Regs 2-2ZB SS(WFILP) Regs
7 Regs 5 and 6 SS(WFILP) Regs
8 Regs 2(4), (2ZA)(2) and 2ZB(5) and (6) SS(WFILP) Regs
9 Reg 4 SS(WFILP) Regs
10 Regs 2(1) and 3(1)(a)(i) and (d) SS(JPI) Regs
11 Regs 4, 4ZA and 4A SS(JPI) Regs
12 Regs 6 and 7 SS(JPI) Regs
13 Reg 12(2)(a) SS(JPI) Regs
14 Regs 7(3) and 12(2)(b) SS(JPI) Regs
15 s2A(2A)(b) SSAA 1992; reg 8 SS(JPI) Regs
16 s2AA SSAA 1992; regs 2, 'definition of partner', and 3 SS(JPIP) Regs
17 s2AA(2) SSAA 1992
18 Reg 3A SS(JPIP) Regs
19 Regs 5 and 6 SS(JPIP) Regs
20 Reg 7 SS(JPIP) Regs

2. Taking part in an interview

21 Reg 10(2) SS(JPI) Regs; reg 2C(3) SS(WFILP) Regs; reg 6(2) SS(IBWFI) Regs; reg 56(2) ESA Regs; reg 9(2) SS(JPIP) Regs
22 Reg 11(2)-(2B) SS(JPI) Regs; reg 3 SS(WFILP) Regs; regs 6 and 7 SS(IBWFI) Regs; reg 57 ESA Regs; reg 10(1) and (2) SS(JPIP) Regs
23 Regs 3(3) and 11(3) SS(JPI) Regs

3. Work-related activity

24 **IS** Reg 3 IS(WRA) Regs
ESA Reg 5 ESA(WRA) Regs
25 **IS** Reg 2(3)(a) IS(WRA) Regs
ESA Reg 3(4)(a) ESA(WRA) Regs

26 **IS** s2D SSAA 1992; reg 2 IS(WRA) Regs
ESA s13 WRA 2007; reg 3 ESA(WRA) Regs
27 **IS** Reg 11 IS(WRA) Regs
ESA Reg 9 ESA(WRA) Regs
28 **IS** s2D(9)(d) SSAA 1992
ESA s13(7) and (8) WRA 2007
29 para 4 Memo DMG 41/12
30 **IS** Reg 2(3)(b) IS(WRA) Regs
ESA Reg 3(4)(b)(i) ESA(WRA) Regs
31 Reg 3(4)(b)(ii) ESA(WRA) Regs
32 **IS** Reg 3 IS(WRA) Regs
ESA Reg 5 ESA(WRA) Regs
33 **IS** Reg 5 IS(WRA) Regs
ESA Reg 7 ESA(WRA) Regs
34 **IS** Reg 4 IS(WRA) Regs
ESA Reg 6 ESA(WRA) Regs
35 Reg 10 IS(WRA) Regs
36 Reg 3(5) ESA(WRA) Regs
37 **IS** Reg 2(2) IS(WRA) Regs
ESA Reg 3(2) ESA(WRA) Regs

Chapter 47

Claimant responsibilities: the universal credit system

This chapter covers:
1. The claimant commitment (below)
2. The work-related requirements (p1073)
3. Which requirements apply (p1080)

This chapter covers your responsibilities if you come under the universal credit (UC) system. If you do not come under the UC system, see Chapters 45 and 46.

Key facts
- If you come under the universal credit (UC) system, to qualify for UC, contribution-based jobseeker's allowance or contributory employment and support allowance, you must usually accept a 'claimant commitment'.
- There are work-related requirements, some or all of which you may have to meet. These are: **work-focused interviews, work preparation, work search** and **work availability**.
- If you do not meet the work-related requirements, you may be given a sanction. Your benefit is then paid at a reduced (or nil) rate. However, you may qualify for UC hardship payments.

1. **The claimant commitment**

If you come under the universal credit (UC) system (see p20), you must usually accept a claimant commitment to qualify for UC, contribution-based jobseeker's allowance (JSA) and contributory employment and support allowance (ESA).[1] If you are claiming UC jointly with your partner, both of you must usually accept a claimant commitment.[2] If you are required to accept one and do not do so, you are not entitled to UC, JSA or ESA.

You *can* qualify for UC, contribution-based JSA or contributory ESA without accepting a claimant commitment if the DWP considers that you cannot accept one because you lack the capacity to do so, or there are exceptional circumstances in which it would be unreasonable to expect you to accept one – eg, you are likely

Part 7: Work and work-related rules
Chapter 47: Claimant responsibilities: the universal credit system
1. The claimant commitment

to be in hospital for weeks, there is a domestic emergency or the Jobcentre Plus office is closed because of an emergency.[3]

The claimant commitment is a record of your responsibilities while you are receiving benefit.[4] It is prepared by the DWP following discussions with you and is in such form as it thinks fit. It must include:[5]

- the work-related requirements you must meet (see p1080); *and*
- any other information the DWP thinks is appropriate to include.

Note: even if you do not have to meet any work-related requirements, your claimant commitment explains your other responsibilities – eg, to report changes in your circumstances.

Accepting your claimant commitment

You must accept the most up-to-date version of your claimant commitment using the method specified by the DWP. This could be electronically (eg, online), by telephone or in writing.[6] Be sure to use the method specified or you may not count as accepting the claimant commitment.

If no, or not all, work-related requirements are to be imposed on you, your first claimant commitment is usually accepted as part of the normal claims process. Otherwise, your claimant commitment is drawn up for you to accept by your personal adviser (sometimes called a 'work coach') during a face-to-face discussion. Ensure that you inform your adviser of any problems you may have in meeting the work-related requirements and that any limitations you are allowed (see p1078) are put on record.

Note:
- The DWP says you should be given a 'cooling-off' period of up to seven days if you refuse to accept a claimant commitment, to give you the chance to reconsider.[7]
- If you are not happy with your claimant commitment, you may be able to get it reviewed (see p1073).

The DWP specifies a time within which you must accept your claimant commitment. If you accept it within that time, you are usually treated as accepting it on the date of your claim (or any date to which your claim has been backdated).[8] However, if you are awarded UC or ESA without making a claim, you are treated as accepting it on the first day of the first assessment period (for UC) or the first benefit week (for ESA) of your benefit award.

The time within which you must accept your claimant commitment (including one that has been updated) can be extended, if:
- for UC and JSA, you ask the DWP to review any action that it has been proposed you take as a work search or work availability requirement, or whether there should be any limitations on these requirements;[9]
- for ESA, you ask for an extension.[10]

In both cases, the DWP must be satisfied that your request is reasonable.

What happens if you miss the time limit?

If you miss the time limit specified by the DWP (including any extension allowed), your entitlement to benefit can only start from the date you actually accept your claimant commitment. It is therefore vital that you accept your claimant commitment in time.

Reviewing your claimant commitment

Your claimant commitment can be reviewed and updated as the DWP thinks fit.[11] This is done on an ongoing basis to record the expectations placed on you when these have changed and the consequences for failing to comply with them. See p1072 for when the time for accepting your claimant committment can be extended if you ask for a review.

There is nothing to prevent you from asking for your claimant commitment to be reviewed and updated at any time. If the DWP agrees to review it, comply with the work-related requirements that have been imposed on you while a review is being considered. It is important to make it clear that you intend to do so.

2. The work-related requirements

If you come under the universal credit (UC) system (see p20) and you are entitled to UC, contribution-based jobseeker's allowance (JSA) or contributory employment and support allowance (ESA), you may have to meet work-related requirements, even if you are in paid work.[12] However, there are some situations when no work-related requirements can be imposed on you (see p1081). See pp1080–90 for which (if any) requirements may apply.

If you do not meet the requirements, you continue to be entitled to benefit, but you may be given a sanction and your benefit may be paid at a reduced (or nil) rate (see Chapter 48). **Note:** if you are entitled to UC and also to contribution-based JSA or contributory ESA, you only need to meet one set of work-related requirements – those for UC.[13]

The work-related requirements are:
- work-focused interviews (see p1074);
- work preparation (see p1074);
- work search (UC and JSA only – see p1075); *and*
- work availability (UC and JSA only – see p1077).

Note: you may also have to attend other interviews connected to the work-related requirements while you are entitled to contribution-based JSA, contributory ESA or UC (see p1080).

Part 7: Work and work-related rules
Chapter 47: Claimant responsibilities: the universal credit system
2. The work-related requirements

Your claimant commitment sets out the work-related requirements you must meet and the specific actions you must take to satisfy these requirements. The requirements can be adjusted to reflect your personal circumstances – eg, if you are a lone parent, a carer or have an illness or disability.

The work-focused interview requirement

If a work-focused interview requirement is imposed on you, you must take part in one or more work-focused interviews – ie, interviews relating to work or work preparation.[14] You may also have to participate in other interviews for any purpose connected to the work-related requirements (see p1080). For ESA, you may be required to take part in an interview at around week four of your claim – called a 'health and work conversation'

The DWP tells you how, when and where a work-focused interview is to take place. A work-focused interview may:[15]

- assess your prospects for obtaining or remaining in work (paid work, more paid work or better paid work for UC);
- assist or encourage you to obtain or remain in work (paid work, more paid work or better paid work for UC);
- identify activities you can undertake and opportunities for training, education or rehabilitation that will make it more likely that you will obtain or remain in work (paid work, more paid work or better paid work for UC);
- for UC, determine whether you are in gainful self-employment (see p343) or whether you are in a 'start-up period' (see p344);
- identify current or future work opportunities that are relevant to you.

The work preparation requirement

If a work preparation requirement is imposed on you, you must take 'particular action' specified by the DWP that makes it more likely that you will obtain paid work, more paid work or better paid work.[16] The DWP can specify the amount of time you must spend doing any particular action.

For these purposes, **'particular action'** includes attending a skills assessment, improving personal presentation, participating in training or in an employment programme (eg, the Work Programme – see p1104), undertaking work experience or a work placement and developing a business plan.[17] If you have limited capability for work (see Chapter 44), it also includes taking part in a work-focused health-related assessment – ie, an assessment by a healthcare professional, including how far your capability for work can be improved by taking steps in respect of your physical or mental condition.

If you are aged 18 to 21

The government intends to introduce a 'youth obligation' for new claims for UC from April 2017 if you are 18 to 21 years old, are unemployed, must meet all the work-related requirements (see p1080) and are claiming UC in a 'full service' area.

If this applies, you receive intensive support from day one of your claim. Once you have been getting UC for six months, you must apply for an apprenticeship or traineeship, gain work-based skills or go on a mandatory community work placement. See CPAG's online services and *Welfare Rights Bulletin* for updates.

The work search requirement

If a work search requirement is imposed on you, you are expected to take 'all reasonable action' (see below) to obtain paid work, more paid work or better paid work. You must also take any 'particular action' specified by the DWP.[18]

Particular action

For these purposes, '**particular action**' includes carrying out work searches, applying for jobs, creating and maintaining an online profile, registering with an employment agency and seeking references.[19] The DWP can specify the amount of time you must spend doing any 'particular action'.

Note: if you are told to apply for a particular job vacancy, you are treated as failing to meet the work search requirement if you do not participate in an interview for the vacancy.[20]

All reasonable action

In general, you are expected to look for work, regardless of its type or the salary. However, certain limitations can apply to the work you are available for and seeking to do (see p1078).

To count as taking 'all reasonable action' to find paid work, more paid work or better paid work, you must take action that gives you the best prospects of obtaining work. You must normally spend a specified number of hours in each week seeking work – ie:[21]

- at least the weekly number of hours you are expected to work (your 'expected hours' – see below), minus any deductions the DWP allows (see p1076); *or*
- fewer hours than your 'expected hours', provided the DWP is satisfied that you have taken all reasonable action despite the lower number of hours.

If you have been unemployed for any length of time, the DWP may only be satisfied that you are taking all reasonable action if you are making job applications. If you are not, the DWP may ask if you were really spending the number of hours you are meant to spend seeking work.

Your expected hours

You are normally expected to work 35 hours a week (your 'expected hours'). However, a lower number of expected hours applies in some cases. This is the number that the DWP thinks is:[22]

Part 7: Work and work-related rules
Chapter 47: Claimant responsibilities: the universal credit system
2. The work-related requirements

- compatible with your caring responsibilities, if you are a 'relevant carer', a 'responsible carer' (for UC your child must have reached compulsory school age) or a 'responsible foster parent' (see p1083 for the definitions) and the DWP is satisfied that you have reasonable prospects of obtaining paid work, more paid work or better paid work;
- for UC, compatible with your caring responsibilities, if you are a 'responsible carer' of a child who has not yet reached compulsory school age;
- compatible with your child's normal school hours (including travelling time to and from school), if you are a 'responsible carer' (or, for JSA only, a 'responsible foster carer') for a child under 13. For UC, your child must have reached compulsory school age. 'Responsible foster carer' is not defined, but it is presumed this is meant to apply if you are a 'responsible foster parent' (see p1083);
- reasonable in the light of your impairment, if you have a 'physical or mental impairment'.

The DWP can agree **deductions** from your expected hours of work search for time you spend:[23]

- carrying out paid work; *or*
- carrying out voluntary work. This must not be for more than 50 per cent of your expected hours; *or*
- carrying out a work preparation requirement or 'voluntary work preparation' – ie, action that is agreed with the DWP that you take on a voluntary basis to make it more likely you will obtain paid work, more work or better paid work; *or*
- dealing with temporary childcare responsibilities, a domestic emergency, funeral arrangements or other temporary circumstances.

Examples

Kathy is claiming contribution-based JSA. She is looking for shop work. To get relevant experience, she volunteers in a charity shop for 10 hours a week. Her 'expected hours' are 35 hours a week. However, she need only spend 25 hours a week looking for work because the DWP agrees to deduct the 10 hours during which she is doing voluntary work.

Jim and Bill are joint UC claimants. Jim spends a lot of time caring for Bill who is on long-term sick leave. All of the work-related requirements are imposed on Jim. No work-related requirements are imposed on Bill because he has limited capability for work-related activity. Jim counts as a 'relevant carer' and his 'expected hours' are 16 hours a week (the hours the DWP is satisfied are compatible with his caring responsibilities). He is therefore meant to look for work for 16 hours a week. Jim only looked for work for 10 hours this week because he was offered and accepted a job working 18 hours a week, starting next week. The DWP agrees that he has taken all reasonable action despite the lower hours.

Proving you are searching for work

Always keep careful records of the steps you take to get a job. The DWP may give you a form on which to do this, or you may be asked to keep an online record.

How do you prove you are searching for work?

1. Check your claimant commitment to ensure you understand what the DWP expects you to do each week. You must be able to give details of the action you have taken (eg, at your interview when you sign on), so it is extremely important that you keep records of your attempts to get a job.

2. Make a note every time you do anything that may count as work search. Include the dates and times, who you spoke to and what was said.

3. Keep copies of any letters or emails you send, of any advertisements to which you reply and of any job applications you make. If you deliver your CV or a job application by hand, ask for a receipt as proof.

4. Tell the DWP if you have difficulty using a computer, or reading or writing, or with the English language. You can get a friend or relative to help you compile your record (and to help you look for jobs). The DWP may be prepared to accept an oral report.

5. Sometimes your activities to seek work may be looked at more intensively than normal, possibly going back over several past weeks, so ensure that they are always sufficient. Do not rely on the fact that they have not been challenged by the jobcentre up to now.

6. The government's 'universal jobmatch' shows what jobs have been suggested for you and the jobs for which you have applied. The DWP may ask you to allow it to access your account to check up on what you have been doing.

7. If there are jobs that have been suggested that you have not applied for, your adviser may question whether you meet the work search requirement. It is therefore best to follow up enough suggestions and apply for jobs even if you feel they are not appropriate.

The work availability requirement

If a work availability requirement is imposed on you, you must be able and willing immediately to:[24]

- take up paid work, more paid work or better paid work; *and*
- attend an interview in connection with obtaining paid work, more paid work or better paid work.

Certain limitations can apply to the work you are available for and seeking to do. See p1078 for further information.

Note: for JSA, you are treated as *not* having met the work availability requirement if you are a prisoner on temporary release under specified provisions.[25]

Part 7: Work and work-related rules
Chapter 47: Claimant responsibilities: the universal credit system
2. The work-related requirements

Able and willing to take up work or attend an interview immediately

For information about what may count as being able and willing to take up work immediately, see p1031. The issues are similar to those for the jobseeking conditions for JSA.

Although the rules normally permit no delay, you can in some situations be allowed more time. You must be given:[26]

- **up to one week** to take up work if you are doing voluntary work, if the DWP is satisfied you need longer;
- **up to one month** to take up work if you are a 'responsible carer' or a 'relevant carer' (see p1083 for the definitions), if the DWP is satisfied you need longer, taking into account alternative care arrangements;
- **until after your notice period** has passed if you are working and you have a duty under employment law, or under the terms of your contract, to give your employer notice that you are leaving work.

In all the situations above, you can also be given **up to 48 hours' notice to attend an interview** in connection with obtaining work.

In some cases even if no work search requirement can be imposed on you for a period, you must still be able and willing to take up paid work or attend an interview immediately, once the circumstances that exempt you from the requirement no longer apply. In other cases, you must be able and willing to attend an interview *before* the circumstances that exempt you no longer apply. See pp1087–90 for further information.

Limitations on availability and search for work

You must be allowed to place limitations on the work you are available for and seeking to do, provided the DWP is satisfied that certain conditions apply. Limitations can be applied to:[27]

- the type of work;
- the number of hours a week, or the times, you can work;
- the rate of pay;
- the location of the work.

In addition, the DWP, at its discretion, can allow you to place additional limitations. For example, the DWP may agree that you should not have to seek work of a particular type if it offends a sincerely held religious belief or a sincere conscientious objection – eg, a job in a slaughterhouse if you are a vegetarian.

Limitations may be either indefinite or for a limited period.

The type of work

Limitations can be placed on the type of work in the following circumstances.[28]

- If you have previously done work of a particular type, you can limit your work search and availability to work of a similar type for up to three months from your date of claim (or if you were exempt from work-related requirements while getting UC because you had sufficient earnings, from the date you cease paid work if this is later), if the DWP is satisfied that you still have a reasonable prospect of getting work despite the limitation. Ensure you understand when the period starts and ends.

- If you have a 'physical or mental impairment' that has a substantial adverse effect on your ability to do work of a particular type, you do not have to be available for or look for work of that type.

The number of hours

You are normally expected to search for work for at least 35 hours a week (see p1075 for the rules about your 'expected hours') but it is understood that the DWP may expect you to be *available* for work of up to 48 hours a week. However, if you are a 'relevant carer' or a 'responsible carer' (see p1083 for the definitions), or you have a 'physical or mental impairment', your 'expected hours' are lower, and in this situation the hours you are expected to search for work and to be available for work are the same.[29]

The rate of pay

If you have previously done work at a particular rate of pay, you can limit your work search and availability to work for a similar rate of pay for up to three months from your date of claim (or if you were exempt from work-related requirements while getting UC because you had sufficient earnings, from the date you cease paid work if this is later), if the DWP is satisfied that you still have a reasonable prospect of getting work despite the limitation.[30] Ensure you understand when the period starts and ends.

The location of the work

There are limitations on the location of the work you must search for and be available to do.[31]

- You need only be available for and look for work in locations that are no more than 90 minutes travel time from your home in either direction.
- If you have a 'physical or mental impairment' that has a substantial adverse effect on your ability to do work in particular locations (eg, you cannot manage stairs), you do not have to be available for work or to look for work in such places.

The effect of the rules on minimum working conditions

The rules about minimum working conditions (see Appendix 10) can affect your claim for UC or JSA if you are looking for work. It should be possible for you to claim that a limitation should apply to the work you are available to do – ie, that you will not accept a job if the terms do not comply with the legal requirements –

Part 7: Work and work-related rules
Chapter 47: Claimant responsibilities: the universal credit system
3. Which requirements apply

eg, if an employer is offering a job at less than the minimum wage (the government calls this the 'national living wage' if you are 25 or over).

Other interviews

The DWP can require you to participate in an interview for any purpose connected to any of the work-related requirements (called 'connected requirements') – ie, to:[32]

- impose a work-related requirement on you; *or*
- verify that you have complied with a work-related requirement; *or*
- assist you to comply with a work-related requirement.

At the interviews, you may be asked to provide evidence and information. You may also be asked to report any changes in your circumstances that are relevant to the imposition of work-related requirements on you and your compliance with them.

Note:
- If you fail to participate in an interview, you may be given a low level sanction (see p1121) and your benefit may be paid at a reduced (or nil) rate.
- For UC and JSA, it is under these rules that you are likely to be required to take part in regular interviews and to 'sign on'.

3. **Which requirements apply**

Many people must meet *all* the work-related requirements (see below). However:
- in some cases, work-related requirements cannot be imposed on you (see p1081); *or*
- you may only have to meet a work-focused interview requirement (see p1085); *or*
- you may only have to meet a work-focused interview and a work preparation requirement (see p1087); *or*
- you may not have to meet a work search or a work availability requirement for a period (see p1087).

Note: if you are entitled to universal credit (UC) and also to contribution-based jobseeker's allowance (JSA) or contributory employment and support allowance (ESA), you only need to meet one set of work-related requirements – those for UC.[33]

All work-related requirements

Unless you are covered by any of the exceptions described on pp1081–90, for UC and JSA the DWP *must* impose a work search requirement and a work availability requirement on you. It can also impose a work-focused interview requirement or a work preparation requirement, or both, and is likely to do so.[34] **Note:** if you are getting ESA, a work search and work availability requirement can *never* be imposed on you.

Get advice if you think you should have been covered by any of the exceptions, but have been required to meet all the requirements. You may be able to apply for judicial review. If you are given a sanction for failing to meet a requirement, you can appeal. You must apply for a mandatory reconsideration first.

No work-related requirements

No work-related requirements *at all* can be imposed on you in some situations. These are generally when the DWP cannot reasonably expect you to work or prepare for work over a sustained period, or if you are already earning all that it is reasonable to expect you to earn. No work-related requirements can be imposed on you if:

- you are a recent victim of domestic violence (see below). **Note:** if you are *only* getting contribution-based JSA, this is the *only* situation when no work-related requirements can be imposed on you; *or*
- for UC and contributory ESA (or if you are getting *both* contribution-based JSA *and* UC), you fit into a specified group – ie, you are:
  - looking after children or have other responsibilities (see p1082);
  - sick or disabled (see p1083);
  - for UC only, in work (see p1084);
  - in other specified situations (see p1085).

In addition, any requirements that have already been imposed cease to have effect.[35]

Domestic violence

All work-related requirements that have been imposed on you cease to have effect for 13 consecutive weeks from the date you notify the DWP that you have experienced, or been threatened with, domestic violence from your partner, your former partner or a family member and you satisfy specified conditions (see below).[36] In addition, no new work-related requirements can be imposed on you during this period. If you are getting UC, if you normally have to meet all the work-related requirements and you are the 'responsible carer' of a child under 16 (see p1083), no work availability or work search requirements can be imposed for a further 13 consecutive weeks – ie, for 26 weeks in total.

You must satisfy all the following conditions.
- This rule must *not* have applied to you in the 12 months before you notify the DWP.
- The domestic violence (or threat of domestic violence) must have taken place within the six months before you notify the DWP.

Part 7: Work and work-related rules
Chapter 47: Claimant responsibilities: the universal credit system
3. Which requirements apply

- When you notify the DWP, you must *not* be living at the same address as the person who was violent or threatened violence.
- As soon as possible, and no later than one month after you notify the DWP, you must provide evidence from a person acting in an official capacity that shows that your circumstances are consistent with those of a person who has experienced, or been threatened with, domestic violence in the six months before you notified the DWP, and that you have made contact with the person acting in an official capacity about an incident that occured in that six-month period.

See p1035 for who counts as a 'family member' and a 'person acting in an official capacity' and for what counts as domestic violence. The rules are the same as for the JSA jobseeking conditions.

Looking after children and other caring responsibilities

If you are getting UC or contributory ESA, no work-related requirements can be imposed on you if:[37]

- you have 'regular and substantial caring responsibilities for a severely disabled person' (see below); *or*
- you have caring responsibilities for one or more severely disabled people for at least 35 hours a week, but do not satisfy the qualifying conditions for carer's allowance (CA). For UC, this only applies if the decision maker is satisfied that it would be unreasonable for you to meet a work search requirement and a work availability requirement, even if these were limited.

For these purposes, a person is **'severely disabled'** if s/he is someone to whom attendance allowance, the highest or middle rate of disability living allowance care component, the daily living component of personal independence payment, armed forces independence payment or constant attendance allowance under the industrial or war disablement schemes (see p687) is payable.[38] You have **'regular and substantial caring responsibilities for a severely disabled person'** if you satisfy the qualifying conditions for CA (see Chapter 25), or you would do but for the fact that your earnings are higher than allowed (currently £116 a week – see p557).[39] This does not apply if you receive earnings from those caring responsibilities. You do not have to be getting CA.

If you are getting UC or contributory ESA, no work-related requirements can be imposed on you if:[40]

- for UC, you are the 'responsible carer' (see p1083) of a child under one; *or*
- for ESA, you are not a member of a couple and you are responsible for a child under one – eg, you are a lone parent. The rules do not define when you count as responsible for a child; *or*
- you are the 'responsible foster parent' (see p1083) of a child under one; *or*

- you are an 'adopter' (see below) and it is not more than 12 months (for UC) or 52 weeks (for ESA) since your child was placed with you for adoption. You can elect for the 12 months (or 52 weeks) to start in the 14 days before your child was expected to be placed with you;
- you are pregnant and there are 11 weeks or less before the week your baby is due; *or*
- you had a baby not more than 15 weeks ago (including if this was a stillbirth).

Definitions

You are an **'adopter'** if you have been matched with a child by an adoption agency and you are, or are intended to be, the 'responsible carer' of the child.[41] This does not apply if you are the foster parent or a close relative of the child.

You are a **'relevant carer'** if:[42]

– you are the parent of a child, have caring responsibilites for her/him but are not the 'responsible carer'; *or*

– you have caring responsibilities for someone who has a 'physical or mental impairment' (and for JSA only, which means s/he needs such care).

You are a **'responsible carer'**:[43]

– for UC, if you are a single person who is responsible for a child under 16 (see p220) – eg, you are a lone parent;

– for JSA and ESA, if you are the only person responsible for a child under 16.

If you are a member of a couple, you are a 'responsible carer' for UC if you or your partner (for JSA and ESA, you and your partner) are responsible for a child under 16 and you and your partner have nominated you as responsible for the child. Only one of you can be nominated. The nomination applies to all your children. It can only be changed once in the 12 months after the nomination or if there has been a relevant change of circumstances.

You are a **'responsible foster parent'** if you are the child's only foster parent, or if you are a member of a couple who are foster parents and you and your partner have nominated you as the 'responsible foster parent'.[44] Only one of you can be nominated. The nomination applies to all your children. It can only be changed once in the 12 months after the nomination or if there has been a relevant change of circumstances.

Sick and disabled people

If you are getting UC or contributory ESA, no work-related requirements can be imposed on you if:[45]

- you have both limited capability for work and limited capability for work-related activity – ie, you are in the support group (see Chapter 44); *or*
- for ESA, you are entitled to ESA, but it is paid at a nil rate – eg, because you are getting an occupational pension.

Part 7: Work and work-related rules
Chapter 47: Claimant responsibilities: the universal credit system
3. Which requirements apply

You are in work

If you are getting UC, no work-related requirements can be imposed on you if you are working and you are:[46]

- a single claimant and your average monthly earnings are at least your individual earnings threshold (see below); *or*
- a member of a couple and your combined average monthly earnings are at least your joint earnings threshold (see below); *or*
- self-employed and are treated as having a minimum earnings level (see p341); *or*
- an apprentice and your average monthly earnings are at least the amount you would be paid at the rate of the national minimum wage (see Appendix 10) for 30 hours work (or, if lower, for your weekly 'expected hours' – see p1075).

Your monthly earnings are calculated using your gross actual or estimated earned income – ie, before income tax, national insurance contributions and pension contributions have been deducted.[47] If your earnings fluctuate, these are averaged over one cycle of work or, if there is no cycle, over three months or the period that enables the average to be worked out more accurately. The DWP can disregard earnings from employment that has ended if this enables it to determine your monthly earnings more accurately.

Earnings thresholds

To work out your:

- **individual earnings threshold**, multiply the amount you would earn at the hourly rate of the national minimum wage (see Appendix 10) by the relevant number of hours for you (see below). Multiply this amount by 52 and divide it by 12;[48]
- **joint earnings threshold** if you are a member of a couple, work out the sum of your and your partner's individual earnings thresholds and add these together.[49] However, if you are claiming as a single person (see p162), your joint earnings threshold is the sum of your individual threshold and the amount someone would be paid at the rate of the minimum wage for 35 hours work (multiplied by 52 and divided by 12).

Fractions of a pound are ignored.[50]

For your individual threshold, the **relevant hours** are:[51]

- 16 hours a week, but only if (even though you are exempt from any work-related requirements under this rule) you would otherwise be someone who only has to meet a work-focused interview requirement (see p1085) or a work-focused interview requirement and a work preparation requirement (see p1087); *or*

- the hours you are expected to work each week (your 'expected hours') – usually 35 a week. A lower number of hours can apply (see p1075).

Examples

James is a lone parent aged 24 and his son is one year old. He is a UC claimant who would otherwise be someone who only has to meet a work-focused interview requirement. He works 10 hours a week and is paid £520 a month. 16 hours x £6.95 = £111.20. £111.20 x 52 ÷ 12 = £481.87. His individual earnings threshold is therefore £481. His earnings therefore exceed his individual earnings threshold. No work-related requirements can be imposed on him.

Raj and Sunita are joint UC claimants aged 40. They have three children, one of whom is under 13. They agree that Sunita should be the 'responsible carer'. Raj's 'expected hours' are 35 a week. The decision maker has agreed that Sunita's 'expected hours' are 21 a week as these are compatible with their children's school hours (see p1075). Raj works 30 hours a week and earns £1,200 a month. 35 hours x £7.50 = £262.50. £262.50 x 52 ÷ 12 = £1,137.50. His individual earnings threshold is therefore £1,137. Sunita works 15 hours a week and earns £700 a month. 21 hours x £7.50 = £157.50. £157.50 x 52 ÷ 12 = £682.25. Her individual earnings threshold is therefore £682. Their joint earnings threshold is therefore £1,137 + £682 = £1,819. Their joint earnings (£1,900) therefore exceed their joint earnings threshold. No work-related requirements can be imposed on either of them.

Other situations

If you are getting UC or contributory ESA, no work-related requirements can be imposed on you if:[52]

- for UC, you are at least the qualifying age for pension credit (see p147). This is only relevant if you are a member of a couple and your partner is not yet that age; *or*
- you are in full-time non-advanced education or training and you have no parental support (see p163). For ESA, this also applies if you have been enrolled or accepted for the education or training. For both UC and ESA, you must be under 21, or be aged 21 and have reached that age while on the course; *or*
- for UC, you are eligible for UC while receiving education (see p886) and you have student income (see p888) for your course which is taken into account when calculating your UC. If your student income is a postgraduate master's degree loan, this only applies if your course is full time.

Work-focused interview requirement only

A work-focused interview requirement, and no other work-related requirements, can be imposed on you if you are getting UC or contributory ESA and you are someone who is only expected to stay in touch with the labour market and to

Part 7: Work and work-related rules
Chapter 47: Claimant responsibilities: the universal credit system
3. Which requirements apply

begin to think about going back to work, or taking up more or better paid work. This applies if:[53]

- for UC, you are the 'responsible carer' (see p1083) of a child aged one; *or*
- for ESA, you are a a single person who is responsible for a child aged at least one but under three; *or*
- you are a foster parent, and you:
  - are the 'responsible foster parent' (see p1083) of a:
    - child aged at least one but under 16; *or*
    - qualifying young person (see p220). The decision maker must be satisfied that s/he has care needs which make it unreasonable for you to have to meet a work search requirement or a work availability requirement even if these were limited (for UC), or a work preparation requirement (for ESA); *or*
  - are *not* the 'responsible foster parent' (see p1083) of a child under 16 or a qualifying young person, but the decision maker is satisfied that the child or young person has care needs which make it unreasonable for you to have to meet a work search requirement or a work availability requirement even if these were limited (for UC), or a work preparation requirement (for ESA); *or*
  - do not have a child or qualifying young person placed with you currently, but intend to have one placed with you and within the past eight weeks:
    - for UC, you have been in any of the situations described above applying to foster parents; *or*
    - for ESA, you have been the 'responsible foster parent' of a child aged at least one but under 16; *or*
- you have become a 'friend or family carer' (see below) for a child under 16 in the past 12 months, and you are her/his 'responsible carer' (see p1083).

Note: if your child is under one, if you are the 'responsible foster parent', or for UC, the 'responsible carer', or for ESA a single person who is responsible for the child, no work-related requirements can be imposed on you (see p1082).

Friend or family carer[54]
You are a **'friend or family carer'** if you are responsible for a child under 16 but are not her/his parent or step-parent. You must be taking care of the child because:

– s/he has no parents, or has parents who are unable to care for her/him. For when you count as responsible for a child for UC, see p223. 'Responsible for a child' is not defined in the ESA rules; *or*

– it is likely that s/he would otherwise be looked after by a local authority because there are concerns about her/his welfare.

If you have been getting UC or ESA on the basis that you have to meet additional work-related requirements but you now fit into one of the groups above, any requirements previously imposed on you cease to apply.[55]

Work-focused interview and work preparation requirement only

A work-focused interview requirement *and* a work preparation requirement (but no other work-related requirements) can be imposed on you if you are someone who can only be expected to prepare for a move into paid work, more paid work or better paid work – eg, by participating in a training or employment scheme. For UC this applies if you are the 'responsible carer' (see p1083) of a child aged two. This also applies if you are entitled to contributory ESA or UC and you have limited capability for work (see Chapter 44).[56] If you are only entitled to UC, in most cases, you do not automatically count as having limited capability for work until you have had a work capability assessment (see p1005 for some exceptions). Make sure your work coach knows how your illness affects what you can do and ask her/him to use her/his discretion in deciding what requirements to impose on you.

Note:
- In some situations (eg, if you are in the support group), no work-related requirements at all can be imposed on you (see p1081).
- If you have been getting UC on the basis that you have to meet other work-related requirements, any requirements previously imposed cease to apply.[57]

No work search or work availability requirement for a period

If you are getting contribution-based JSA or UC or both, a work search and a work availability requirement cannot be imposed on you for a period (but you may have to meet other work-related requirements) in a number of situations. **Note:** for ESA, a work search or work availability requirement can *never* be imposed on you.

Sick and disabled people

If you are getting contribution-based JSA or UC, a work search requirement cannot be imposed on you for certain specified periods if you are unfit for work. This usually applies for a maximum of 14 days and no more than twice in any 12-month period.[58] For the first seven days, you must provide a declaration that you are unfit for work. For any further days, you must provide a fit note from your doctor (for UC only, this only applies if requested by the DWP). For the purposes of the work availability requirement, you only need to be willing and able to take up work and attend an interview when the period of sickness has ended.[59]

In some other situations, the DWP has a discretion whether or not to impose a work search requirement. This applies:[60]

Part 7: Work and work-related rules
Chapter 47: Claimant responsibilities: the universal credit system
3. Which requirements apply

- for UC, if you are unfit more than twice, or for longer than 14 days if the DWP thinks it would be unreasonable to require you to meet a work search requirement even if it were limited;
- for JSA, if you are allowed an 'extended period of sickness' of up to 13 weeks under the rules described on p702 and the DWP thinks it would be unreasonable to require you to meet a work search requirement.

You must provide a fit note from your doctor. For UC only, this only applies if requested by the DWP.

For the purposes of the work availability requirement, you only need to be willing and able to take up work and attend an interview for UC when those circumstances no longer apply or, for JSA, when the period of sickness has ended.[61] However, if the DWP thinks it is reasonable to require you to attend an interview, you must be able and willing to attend one before the period of sickness has ended.

Bereavement and domestic violence

If you are getting contribution-based JSA or UC, a work search requirement cannot be imposed on you if it is less than six months since the death of your partner or a child under 16 (or, for UC only, a 'qualifying young person').[62] You or your partner must have been responsible for the child or qualifying young person, or you must have been the child's parent. For when you count as responsible for a child for UC, see p223. 'Responsible for a child' is not defined in the JSA rules.

For UC only, a work search requirement cannot be imposed on you if you are the 'responsible carer' of a child under 16 (see p1083 for who counts), and there has been a 'significant disruption' in your normal childcare responsibilities because in the last 24 months:[63]

- a parent, sister or brother, or a person who was the previous responsible carer, of the child has died; *or*
- any person who normally lived in the same accommodation as the child has died. The person does not have to have been a relative or carer. S/he must have being living in the accommodation at the time of her/his death, and must not be liable to make payments for the accommodation on a commercial basis; *or*
- the child has been a victim of, or witness to, an incident of violence or abuse. This does not apply if you are the perpetrator of that violence or abuse.

This can apply for one month in each of the four consecutive six-month periods after the event occurs, beginning on a date specified by the DWP after you have notified it of the circumstances, so long as the DWP is satisfied that the circumstances apply.[64] However, if the death affecting the child is that of your partner or another child or of a qualifying young person and the rules described above apply, or if *you* are the victim of the domestic violence and the rules on p1081 apply, the month runs concurrently with any period you have been allowed under those rules.

For the purposes of the work availability requirement, you only need to be willing and able to take up work and attend an interview once the circumstances no longer apply.[65]

You are in work

If you are getting UC, a work search requirement cannot be imposed on you, but you may have to meet other work-related requirements, if:[66]

- you are a single claimant and your employed earnings (see p338) are at least £338 a month; or
- you are a member of a couple and your joint employed earnings (see p338) are at least £541 a month.

However, this rule does not apply if you are selected to participate in the In Work Pilot Scheme (a scheme testing what work-related requirements are appropriate to impose if you have a job), and a work search requirement can be imposed on you, even if your monthly employed earning are at least £338 or £541.[67]

Note: if your monthly earnings are above your individual or joint earnings threshold, no work-related requirements can be imposed on you (see p1084), so this rule only applies if your monthly employed earnings are at least £338 or £541, but lower than your earnings threshold.

Example

Nicola, aged 23, is working part time. Her gross pay is £870 a month. Under the UC rules, she is expected to work 35 hours a week. 35 x £6.95 = £243.25. £243.25 x 52 ÷ 12 = £1,054.08. Her individual earnings threshold is therefore £1,054. Although she is not exempt from all the work-related requirements, because her take-home pay is more than £338 a month, no work-search requirement can be imposed on her unless she is selected to participate in the In Work Pilot Scheme.

For the purposes of the work availability requirement, you only need to be willing and able to take up work and attend an interview once the circumstances no longer apply – ie, once your earnings reduce to below the relevant limit.[68]

Other temporary circumstances

If you are getting contribution-based JSA or UC, a work search requirement cannot be imposed on you if:[69]

- you are attending a court or tribunal as a witness or party to the proceedings; or
- you qualify for JSA or UC while you are temporarily absent from Great Britain (see p1599 and p1605) because you are:

Part 7: Work and work-related rules
Chapter 47: Claimant responsibilities: the universal credit system
3. Which requirements apply

- for JSA only, attending a job interview; *or*
- for JSA only, receiving, or taking your child under 16, for medical treatment; *or*
- for UC only, receiving, or taking your child under 16 (or your partner or a qualifying young person) for, medical treatment or convalescence or care; *or*
- you are receiving and participating in a structured recovery-orientated course of treatment for alcohol or drug addiction and have been for no more than six months; *or*
- you are subject to protection arrangements under section 82 of the Serious Organised Crime and Police Act 2005 and have been for no more than three months – ie, if you are under protection while involved as a witness in a criminal investigation or proceedings; *or*
- for UC only, you are a prisoner (see p929); *or*
- for UC, you are engaged in an activity that the DWP approves as being a public duty. This is not defined, but should include, for example, being on jury service, crewing a lifeboat or carrying out duties as a volunteer firefighter or special constable.[70] For JSA, see below.

For the purposes of the work availability requirement, you only need to be willing and able to take up work and attend an interview once the circumstances no longer apply.[71]

If the DWP is satisfied that it would be unreasonable for you to have to meet a work search requirement even if this were limited, a work search requirement cannot be imposed on you if:[72]

- for JSA only, you are carrying out a public duty; *or*
- you are carrying out a work preparation requirement (see p1074) or 'voluntary work preparation' (ie, action agreed with the DWP that makes it more likely that you will get paid work); *or*
- you have temporary childcare responsibilities; *or*
- there are other temporary circumstances. Temporary circumstances could include anything that makes it unreasonable for you to have to seek work – eg, becoming homeless, caring for a relative, or a flood, fire or other disaster at your home. For UC, dealing with domestic emergencies and funeral arrangements are specifically included.

For the purposes of the work availability requirement, you only need to be willing and able to take up work and attend an interview when the circumstances no longer apply.[73] However, for UC, if the DWP thinks it is reasonable to require you to attend an interview, you must be able and willing to attend one before the circumstances cease to apply.

Notes

1. The claimant commitment
1 **UC** s4(1)(e) WRA 2012
   JSA s1(2)(b) JSA 1995
   ESA s1(3)(aa) WRA 2007
2 s3(2) WRA 2012
3 **UC** Reg 16 UC Regs
   JSA Reg 8 JSA Regs 2013
   ESA Reg 45 ESA Regs 2013
   All para J1026 ADM
4 **UC** s14(1) WRA 2012
   JSA s6A(1) JSA 1995
   ESA s11A(1) WRA 2007
5 **UC** s14(1)-(4) WRA 2012
   JSA s6A(1)-(4) JSA 1995
   ESA s11A(1)-(4) WRA 2007
6 **UC** s14(5) WRA 2012; reg 15 UC Regs
   JSA s6A(5) JSA 1995; reg 7 JSA Regs 2013
   ESA s11A(5) WRA 2007; reg 44 ESA Regs 2013
7 para J1010 ADM
8 **UC** Reg 15(1) and (2) UC Regs
   JSA Reg 7(1) JSA Regs 2013
   ESA Reg 44(1) and (2) ESA Regs 2013
9 **UC** Reg 15(3) UC Regs
   JSA Reg 7(2) JSA Regs 2013
10 Reg 44(3) ESA Regs 2013
11 **UC** s14(2) WRA 2012
   JSA s6A(2) JSA 1995
   ESA s11A(2) WRA 2007

2. The work-related requirements
12 **UC** s13 WRA 2012
   JSA ss6 and 6F JSA 1995
   ESA s11 WRA 2007
13 **JSA** Reg 5(2) JSA Regs 2013
   ESA Reg 42(2) ESA Regs 2013
14 **UC** s15 WRA 2012
   JSA s6B JSA 1995
   ESA s11B WRA 2007
15 **UC** Regs 87 and 93 UC Regs
   JSA Reg 10 JSA Regs 2013
   ESA Reg 46 ESA Regs 2013
16 **UC** s16(1) and (2) WRA 2012
   JSA s6C(1) and (2) JSA 1995
   ESA s11C(1) and (2) WRA 2007
17 **UC** s16(3)-(6) WRA 2012
   JSA s6C(3) JSA 1995
   ESA s11C(3)-(6) WRA 2007

18 **UC** s17(1) WRA 2012
   JSA s6D(1) JSA 1995
19 **UC** s17(2) and (3) WRA 2012
   JSA s6D(2) and (3) JSA 1995
20 **UC** Reg 94 UC Regs
   JSA Reg 11 JSA Regs 2013
21 **UC** Reg 95(1) UC Regs
   JSA Reg 12(1) JSA Regs 2013
22 **UC** Reg 88 UC Regs
   JSA Reg 9 JSA Regs 2013
23 **UC** Reg 95(2)-(4) UC Regs
   JSA Regs 4(1) and 12(2) and (3) JSA Regs 2013
24 **UC** s18(1) and (2) WRA 2012; regs 87 and 96(1) UC Regs
   JSA s6E(1) and (2) JSA 1995; regs 3(7) and 13(1) JSA Regs 2013
25 Reg 13(1)(b) JSA Regs 2013
26 **UC** Reg 96(2)-(5) UC Regs
   JSA Regs 2 and 13(2)-(5) JSA Regs 2013
27 **UC** s17(4) and (5) WRA 2012
   JSA s6D(4) and (5) JSA 1995
28 **UC** Reg 97(4)-(6) UC Regs
   JSA Reg 14(3) and (4) JSA Regs 2013
29 **UC** Reg 97(2) UC Regs
   JSA Reg 14(5) JSA Regs 2013
30 **UC** Reg 97(4) and (5) UC Regs
   JSA Reg 14(3) JSA Regs 2013
31 **UC** Reg 97(3) and (6) UC Regs
   JSA Reg 14(2) and (4) JSA Regs 2013
32 **UC** s23 WRA 2012
   JSA s6G JSA 1995
   ESA s11G WRA 2007

3. Which requirements apply
33 **JSA** Reg 5(2) JSA Regs 2013
   ESA Reg 42(2) ESA Regs 2013
34 **UC** s22 WRA 2012
   JSA s6F JSA 1995
35 **UC** s19(5) WRA 2012
   JSA Reg 15(1)(a) JSA Regs 2013
   ESA s11D(3) WRA 2007
36 **UC** Reg 98 UC Regs
   JSA Regs 5 and 15 JSA Regs 2013
   ESA Reg 49 ESA Regs 2013
37 **UC** s19(2)(b) WRA 2012; reg 89(1)(b) UC Regs
   JSA Reg 5 JSA Regs 2013
   ESA s11D(2)(b) WRA 2007; reg 47(1)(a) ESA Regs 2013

Part 7: Work and work-related rules
Chapter 47: Claimant responsibilities: the universal credit system
Notes

38 **UC** Reg 89(2) UC Regs
   ESA Reg 47(5) ESA Regs 2013
39 **UC** Reg 30 UC Regs
   ESA Reg 47(2) and (3) ESA Regs 2013
40 **UC** s19(2)(c) WRA 2012; reg 89(1)(c),
   (d) and (f) UC Regs
   JSA Reg 5 JSA Regs 2013
   ESA s11D(2)(c) WRA 2007; reg
   47(1)(b), (c), (f) and (g) ESA Regs 2013
41 **UC** Reg 89(3) UC Regs
   ESA Reg 47(5) ESA Regs 2013
42 **UC** Reg 85 UC Regs
   JSA Reg 4(1) JSA Regs 2013
43 **UC** s19(6) WRA 2012; reg 86 UC Regs
   JSA Reg 4 JSA Regs 2013
   ESA Reg 41 ESA Regs 2013
44 **UC** Regs 85 and 86 UC Regs
   JSA Reg 4 JSA Regs 2013
   ESA Reg 41 ESA Regs 2013
45 **UC** s19(2)(a) WRA 2012
   ESA s11D(2)(a) WRA 2007; reg 47(1)(e)
   ESA Regs 2013
46 Reg 90 UC Regs
47 Reg 90(6) UC Regs
48 Reg 90(2) UC Regs
49 Reg 90(3) UC Regs
50 Reg 6(1A) UC Regs
51 Regs 88 and 90(2) UC Regs
52 **UC** s19 WRA 2012; reg 89(1)(a) and (e)
   UC Regs
   ESA s11D WRA 2007; reg 47(1)(d) ESA
   Regs 2013
53 **UC** s20 WRA 2012; reg 91 UC Regs
   JSA Reg 5 JSA Regs 2013
   ESA s11E WRA 2007; reg 48 ESA Regs
   2013
54 **UC** Reg 91(3) UC Regs
   ESA Reg 48(3) ESA Regs 2013
55 **UC** s20(3) WRA 2012
   ESA s11E(3) WRA 2007
56 **UC** s21 WRA 2012
   JSA Reg 5 JSA Regs 2013
   ESA s11F WRA 2007
57 s21(4) WRA 2012
58 **UC** Reg 99(1)(a) and (4) UC Regs
   JSA Reg 16(1)(a) and (5) JSA Regs 2013
59 **UC** Reg 99(1)(b) and (4) UC Regs
   JSA Reg 16(1)(b) and (5) JSA Regs 2013
60 **UC** Reg 99 and (5)(c) UC Regs
   JSA Reg 16A(1) and (2) JSA Regs 2013
61 **UC** Reg 99 (2B), (2C), (5A) and (5B) UC
   Regs
   JSA Reg 16A(4)-(6) JSA Regs 2013
62 **UC** Reg 99(1) and (3)(d) UC Regs
   JSA Reg 16(3)(c) JSA Regs 2013
63 Reg 99(1) and (4A) UC Regs
64 Reg 99(4B) and (4C) UC Regs

65 **UC** Reg 99(1)(b) UC Regs
   JSA Regs 16(1)(b) JSA Regs 2013
66 Regs 6(1A) and 99(1), (6) and (6A) UC
   Regs
67 The Universal Credit (Work-Related
   Requirements) (In Work Pilot Scheme)
   Amendment Regulations 2015, No.89
68 Reg 99(1)(b) UC Regs
69 **UC** Reg 99(1) and (3)(a)-(c) and (e)-(g)
   UC Regs
   JSA Regs 4(1) and 16(1) and (3)(a), (b),
   (d) and (e) JSA Regs 2013
70 para J3208 ADM
71 **UC** Reg 99(1)(b) UC Regs
   JSA Reg 16(1)(b) JSA Regs 2013
72 **UC** Reg 99(2A) and (5)(a) and (b) UC
   Regs
   JSA Reg 16(1) and (4) JSA Regs 2013
73 **UC** Reg 99 (2B), (2C), (5A) and (5B) UC
   Regs
   JSA Reg 16(1)(b) JSA Regs 2013

Chapter 48

Sanctions

This chapter covers:
1. Jobseeker's allowance sanctions (below)
2. Universal credit system sanctions (p1108)
3. Other benefit sanctions (p1124)
4. Common rules (p1129)
5. Deciding whether you should be sanctioned (p1139)
6. Challenging a sanction decision (p1140)

Key facts

- If you are getting jobseeker's allowance or universal credit you can be given a sanction if you do not meet certain requirements – eg, if you fail to participate in interviews, if you leave work voluntarily or because of misconduct, if you do not accept a job or a place on a training scheme or employment programme, or you are found not to be available for work or actively seeking work.
- You can be given a sanction if you are getting some other benefits and you do not take part in work-focused interviews or, in some cases, work-related activity.
- You may be able to avoid a sanction if you can show that you have a good cause or a good reason for your actions.
- If you are given a sanction, your benefit is paid at a reduced (or nil) rate for a period.
- You may qualify for hardship payments if you have been given a sanction.
- You can apply for a revision or supersession, or appeal against a sanction decision. You must apply for a mandatory reconsideration before you can appeal.

1. Jobseeker's allowance sanctions

If you are entitled to any type of jobseeker's allowance (JSA) and you do not come under the universal credit (UC) system (see p20), you can be given a sanction under the rules described in this section. There are high level sanctions (see p1097) and low level sanctions (see p1102) and sanctions if you are found not to

Part 7: Work and work-related rules
Chapter 48: Sanctions
1. Jobseeker's allowance sanctions

be available for work or to be actively seeking work (see p1107). If you come under the UC system and are getting contribution-based JSA, different rules apply (see p1108).

Note: we refer to things that can lead to your being given a sanction as 'sanctionable actions'. The DWP may call these 'sanctionable failures'.[1]

High level sanctions	Sanction period: 13, 26 or 156 weeks
Losing a job because of misconduct (p1097)	
Leaving a job voluntarily (p1097)	
Refusing or failing to apply for or accept a job (p1098)	
'Neglecting to avail' yourself of a job opportunity (p1099)	
Low level sanctions	Sanction period: four or 13 weeks
Failing to participate in interviews (p1103)	
Failing to participate in a specified scheme for assisting people to obtain employment (p1103)	
Other training scheme or employment programme sanctions (p1105)	
Failing to carry out a jobseeker's direction (p1106)	
Found not to be available for or actively seeking work (p1107)	Sanction period: four or 13 weeks

If you are given a sanction, JSA is paid at a reduced (or nil) rate during a fixed period. For information about the amount of JSA payable, see p1095. You might be able to get hardship payments (see p1207).

Note:
- The days in your sanction period count towards your 182 days of entitlement to contribution-based JSA, even if you are not actually paid any benefit.
- If you are 16 or 17, there are some special rules for the benefit reduction and sanction periods (see p1095), and to help you show you have a good reason for what you did or did not do (see p1137).
- Special rules apply if you were given a sanction while you came under the UC system, but you no longer do so (see p1114).
- If you disagree that you should be given a sanction or disagree with the sanction period, you can challenge the decision (see p1140).
- For housing benefit (HB) purposes, if you satisfy the conditions for entitlement to income-based JSA, you are treated as being on it even if you are not being paid it because of a sanction.[2] In this situation, the local authority should *not* end your entitlement to HB. You remain entitled to maximum HB.

Different rules apply if you have been given a sanction because of a benefit offence (see p1265).

The benefit reduction

JSA is paid at a reduced (or nil) rate during the sanction period.[3] **Note:** special rules apply if you are aged 16 or 17 (see below).

If you are a:
- single person, a member of a couple (other than a joint-claim couple) or a member of a joint-claim couple and both of you are given a sanction, your JSA is reduced by 100 per cent of the amount of JSA that is payable to you – ie, you are not paid any JSA during the sanction period;
- member of a joint-claim couple and only one of you is given a sanction, your JSA is paid at the rate of:
  - contribution-based JSA, if the person who has not been given a sanction qualifies for it; *or*
  - hardship payments, if you and your partner qualify (see p1207); *or*
  - in any other case, income-based JSA calculated as if the person who has not been given the sanction is a single person. However, any income or capital either of you have is taken into account in the calculation.

In this situation, the joint-claim JSA is paid to the person who has not been given a sanction.[4]

If your JSA is paid at a reduced (or nil) rate, you might be able to get hardship payments (see p1207). Check to see whether you (or your partner) qualify for income support, income-related employment and support allowance (ESA) or pension credit instead of JSA. If you are a member of a couple (other than a joint-claim couple), your partner might be able to claim JSA instead of you.

If you are given more than one sanction

No benefit reduction can be made for a new sanction for any days when your JSA is already being paid at a reduced (or nil rate) because of a previous sanction.[5] If you are a member of a joint-claim couple, this only applies if both the new and the previous sanctions are as a result of a sanctionable action by the same member of the couple. Because of the rules for when a sanction period starts, this means that if you are given more than one sanction for the same period, the sanctions effectively overlap.[6]

Special rules if you are 16 or 17

If you are receiving income-based JSA, your benefit reduction is lower than for older claimants during a fixed sanction period of two weeks if:[7]
- you lost a place on a training scheme or employment programme because of misconduct; *or*

Part 7: Work and work-related rules
Chapter 48: Sanctions
1. Jobseeker's allowance sanctions

- without a good reason, you:
  - refused or failed to carry out a jobseeker's direction; *or*
  - gave up a place on a training scheme or employment programme or refused or failed to apply for or to accept, or neglected to avail yourself of, a place on one; *or*
  - refused or failed to apply for or to accept a job, or neglected to avail yourself of a job opportunity; *or*
  - failed to participate in an interview as required.

If you reach the age of 18 before the end of your two-week sanction, the sanction ends and you are paid the full rate of JSA for an 18-year-old. If you stop claiming JSA before the two weeks is over and then claim again, you are paid JSA at the reduced rate for the remainder of the two-week period.

If you are getting a training scheme sanction under the special system for severe hardship payments (see p1138), the benefit reduction is also lower than for older claimants during the two-week sanction period.[8] If your severe hardship direction is revoked (see p130), you can apply for severe hardship payments again immediately, but they are paid at a reduced rate for two weeks.

If you are given a sanction under the rules described above, your JSA is reduced by 40 per cent of the single person's (or lone parent's) personal allowance, even if you are a member of a couple, or by 20 per cent if you are pregnant or seriously ill.[9] Your JSA is also only reduced by 20 per cent if you are sanctioned under the normal rules (not the severe hardship rules) and your partner (or a child in your claim) is pregnant or seriously ill. 'Seriously ill' is not defined.

Note: if you are given a sanction for any other reason, the ordinary sanction periods and amounts of JSA apply and you might qualify for hardship payments (see p1207).

If you stop claiming jobseeker's allowance

If you stop claiming JSA before the end of your sanction period, the sanction can be applied if you claim JSA again. Unless you have been in employment for at least 26 weeks, your JSA is paid at a reduced (or nil) rate for the amount of the sanction period that is still outstanding.[10] If you are a member of a joint-claim couple, this rule only applies if the sanction on the previous award was imposed because of a 'sanctionable action' of yours (or your current partner's) – eg, the sanction was not imposed on a former partner.[11]

If the DWP is satisfied that since the date of your most recent sanctionable action, you have been in employment for a period of at least 26 weeks, or for more than one period totalling at least 26 weeks, the sanction is not applied if you claim JSA again.[12] 'Employment' for these purposes includes self-employment, provided your income is more than your applicable amount (see Chapter 12).[13]

High level sanctions

For when you can be given a high level sanction, see below. For the length of the sanction period, see p1100. For when the sanction period starts, see p1102.

When you can be given a high level sanction

You can be given a high level sanction if you:[14]
- lose a job because of 'misconduct' (see below); *or*
- leave a job voluntarily without a good reason (see below); *or*
- refuse or fail to apply for or accept a job without a good reason (see p1098); *or*
- 'neglect to avail' yourself of a job without a good reason (see p1099).

A **'job'** for these purposes does not include employment while participating in an employment programme (see p1105) or self-employment.[15] When considering whether you should be given a sanction, the decision maker should only look at your last employment preceding your claim and your subsequent actions.[16]

Note: before 2 March 2016, you could be referred to a scheme called Mandatory Work Activity and be given a high level sanction if you failed to participate in it on or before 27 April 2016. For further information, see p1087 of the 2016/17 edition of this *Handbook*.

Losing a job because of misconduct

You can be given a high level sanction if you lose your job because of misconduct.[17] This includes if you are suspended from work for misconduct or if you resigned rather than being dismissed.[18] You cannot be sanctioned for misconduct in self-employment. For information about what may count as misconduct, see p1131, and for whether misconduct caused the loss of employment, see p1132. **Note:** the DWP says you should *not* be given a sanction if you leave a job that includes a 'zero-hour contract'.[19]

Leaving your job voluntarily

You can be given a high level sanction if you leave your job 'voluntarily' without a 'good reason' (see p1133).[20] A sanction can only be imposed if:
- you were in employment (not self-employment); *and*
- you were not in a 'trial period' (see p1099).

The decision maker is the one who has to show that you left your employment voluntarily. However, to avoid a sanction, *you* must then show that you had a good reason for leaving. For information about whether you left voluntarily, see p1130, and for information about what may happen if you take retirement, see p1131. **Note:** the DWP says you should *not* be given a sanction if you leave a job that includes a 'zero-hour contract'.[21]

Part 7: Work and work-related rules
Chapter 48: Sanctions
1. Jobseeker's allowance sanctions

Refusing or failing to apply for, or to accept, a job

You can be given a high level sanction if you are informed of a job vacancy by an employment officer (EO – see p1027 for who counts for these purposes) and you refuse or fail to apply for it or to accept it when it is offered to you.[22] This does not apply if you can show you have a good reason (see p1133).

To be sanctioned, you must have been informed of a job vacancy by an EO. You can try to argue that this does not include an appointment with a recruitment agency.[23] You may be informed orally, in writing or by other means – eg, by text or email. No sanction should be imposed if you did not receive the notification. Your reading a job advert that is displayed in a Jobcentre Plus office or on the Jobcentre Plus website 'universal jobmatch' does not, by itself, amount to being informed by the EO.

'Informed' is not defined in the rules. The DWP says it means 'to provide information about something in particular in a formal manner' and that some obligation should be attached to it.[24] It says you should be clearly informed of the specific vacancy, what you are expected to do and by when, and the consequence of failing to comply. You should be given sufficient information to enable you to pursue the vacancy.

If you are informed of a vacancy and are unsure about what your financial situation would be, seek advice about the amount of financial help you would get if you took the job, including in-work benefits, passported benefits and free childcare. However, it may be difficult to show you have a good reason for refusing a job because of your income or the rate of pay.

Have you been informed of a job that is not appropriate?

1. In some cases, you may be informed by an EO of a vacancy for a job that you think is unsuitable for you or for which you think you are not qualified. In this situation, to avoid the risk of being sanctioned, it is best to apply for the job and let the employer be the one to say you are not suitable.

2. 'Universal jobmatch' shows what jobs have been suggested for you and the jobs for which you have applied. If there are jobs that have been suggested that you have not applied for, at your regular interview your adviser may question whether you are actively seeking work. In this case, to ensure you are not sanctioned or your entitlement to JSA is not terminated, it is best to follow up suggestions and apply for jobs, even if you feel they are not appropriate.

Note:

- The decision maker cannot give this sanction if the job was vacant because of a stoppage of work caused by a trade dispute.[25]
- The DWP says you should *not* be told to apply for jobs that include a 'zero-hour contract' or an 'employee shareholder contract' and that you should *not* be given a sanction if you refuse or fail to apply for or to accept such a vacancy.[26]

- You can be expected to apply for and accept temporary work. You cannot escape a sanction on the grounds that a job is temporary.
- If you repeatedly fail to take jobs that are offered to you, a decision maker may also decide that you are not available for or actively seeking work and end your entitlement to JSA altogether. You may then be sanctioned when you claim JSA again (see p1107).

The DWP may treat you as having refused to apply for or accept a job if you:[27]
- do not complete the job application form properly or you give inappropriate answers to questions on the form. However, if you submit your application to the DWP and it does not pass this on to a potential employer, you can argue that you did not fail to apply for the job; *or*
- do not attend or are late for a job interview, or you go to the wrong place through your own negligence; *or*
- behave in such a way that you lose the chance of getting the job. This should only apply to things you actually said or did (or refused to do) and should not apply just because a prospective employer disliked your appearance or manner; *or*
- accept a job but fail to start it or impose unreasonable conditions so that the offer is withdrawn.

'Neglecting to avail' yourself of a job

You can be given a high level sanction if you fail to take up a reasonable opportunity of employment without a good reason (see p1133).[28] This is called 'neglecting to avail' yourself of a job. You do not have to be informed of a vacancy by an EO for this sanction to apply.

In practice, this sanction usually only applies where the opportunity for employment is with your current or former employer – eg, if you do not return to work with a former employer after what was originally intended to be a temporary break such as maternity leave, or you refuse an offer of alternative employment in a redundancy situation. However, it may be applied more generally.[29]

The DWP is likely to give a sanction if, for example, you knew you had a reasonable chance of getting the job and did not take the necessary steps to get it. However, it cannot give a sanction if:
- the job was vacant because of a stoppage of work caused by a trade dispute;[30] *or*
- the 'opportunity' is for further work with an employer you have been working for during a trial period (see below).

Trial periods

In certain circumstances, you may take a job for a trial period and leave it without the risk of being sanctioned for leaving voluntarily or for 'neglecting to avail' yourself of a reasonable opportunity of employment.[31] The rules lay down both a minimum and a maximum length for the trial period. You *must* leave the

Part 7: Work and work-related rules
Chapter 48: Sanctions
1. Jobseeker's allowance sanctions

employment within the specified times to avoid being given a sanction. You do not have to have agreed with the DWP that you were taking it up on a trial basis.

Trial period

A **'trial period'** is the period of eight weeks, starting with the beginning of your fifth week and ending at the end of your 12th week in a job. Weeks in which you work for fewer than 16 hours are ignored.[32] The DWP includes periods when you are not actually working but you are required by your contract to be in a certain place in order to carry out a job.[33] Periods when you are off work sick or on holiday, even if you are paid, do not count when calculating the number of hours. To be sure you are covered by this rule, you must work at least some of the fifth week and leave before you have worked all of the 12th. In calculating the fifth and the 12th weeks, the 'week' starts on the day you begin work and ends at midnight seven days later.[34]

The trial period rule applies if, for at least 13 weeks before the day you begin employment, you have not:[35]
- worked (including as a self-employed person); *or*
- been a full-time student (see p874) or in 'relevant education' (see p872). You do not count as a full-time student if you were in receipt of a training allowance.[36]

If you are dismissed or you leave the job as an alternative to being dismissed, you might still be given a sanction if this was because of misconduct.

Note: if you do not claim JSA for more than 12 consecutive weeks (ie, until after the trial period), a new 'jobseeking period' (see p123 and p699) begins when you next claim. This means:
- you have to serve a further seven waiting days (see p132 and p705) before getting JSA; *and*
- you may not qualify for contribution-based JSA if you no longer satisfy the contribution conditions.

Length of the sanction period

If you are given a high level sanction, it is usually imposed for 13 weeks. However, it can be imposed for:[37]
- 26 weeks, if you have been given a high level sanction once previously (but see below) for a sanctionable action of yours (not your partner's); *or*
- 156 weeks (three years), if you have been given a high level sanction at least twice previously (but see below) for a sanctionable action of yours (not your partner's), the most recent of which was for 26 or 156 weeks.

For the longer sanction periods to apply, the most recent previous sanctionable action must have taken place at least two weeks, but less than 52 weeks, before your current sanctionable action. The 52 weeks run from the date of the previous sanctionable action, not from the date of the decision imposing the previous sanction, which could be some time later. If the most recent previous sanctionable action was within two weeks of the current one, the length of the new sanction is the same as the previous one. If it was 52 weeks or more before the current one, the length of the new sanction period is the same as if you were given a sanction for the first time.

Losing a job because of misconduct (see p1097), leaving a job voluntarily (see p1097) and 'neglecting to avail' yourself of a job (see p1099) *before* your date of claim (see p137 and p712) do not count as sanctionable actions for the purpose of working out whether a 26- or 156-week sanction period should be applied.[38]

For when your sanction period could be reduced, see below. For what happens if you stop claiming JSA, see p1096.

Note: if you are given a 26- or 156-week sanction but later a previous sanction is removed (eg, by the First-tier Tribunal), ask a decision maker to reduce the sanction period if relevant.[39] If s/he fails to do so, appeal. If you have already appealed against the later sanction, the tribunal should take the removal of the previous sanction into account.[40]

Reduced sanction periods

If you are sanctioned because, before the day you claim JSA, you lost a job due to misconduct (see p1097), you left a job voluntarily (see p1097) or you 'neglected to avail' yourself of a job (see p1099):[41]

- if the job was only due to last for a 'limited period' that ends on or before the end of the sanction period that would normally apply, the sanction period is the number of days starting with the day after the date of the sanctionable action and ending on the day the job would have ended, minus the number of days between the date of the sanctionable action and your date of claim (see p137 and p712). A 'limited period' is a specific length of time that is either fixed or which can be ascertained before it begins by reference to some relevant circumstance;[42] *or*
- in other cases, the sanction period that would normally apply is reduced to take account of days on which you did not claim JSA – ie, by the number of days between the date of the sanctionable action and your date of claim (see p137 and p712).

In practical terms, this means that if you claim JSA after the job would have ended, your benefit is not paid at a reduced (or nil) rate.[43]

Part 7: Work and work-related rules
Chapter 48: Sanctions
1. Jobseeker's allowance sanctions

Examples
Rita quits her job on 4 May. It was only due to last until 6 July. She claims JSA on 11 May. She cannot show a good reason for leaving her job so is given a high level sanction. This is the first time she has been sanctioned, so a 13-week sanction period would normally apply.

The period starting on 5 May (the day after the date of the sanctionable action) and ending on 6 July (the day the job would have ended) is 63 days.

The number of days between 4 May (the date of the sanctionable action) and 11 May (her date of claim) is six days.

63 days – 6 days = 57 days. Rita is therefore sanctioned for 57 days (eight weeks and one day).

Tom is dismissed from a permanent job because of misconduct on 2 September. He claims JSA on 8 October. He failed to apply for a job six months ago, and was then given a 13-week high level sanction. He is now given a sanction for losing his job because of misconduct. This time a 26-week sanction period would normally apply.

26 weeks x 7 days = 182 days.

The number of days between 2 September (the date of the sanctionable action) and 8 October (his date of claim) is 35 days.

182 days – 35 days = 147 days. Tom is therefore sanctioned for 147 days (21 weeks).

When the sanction period starts

The sanction period normally starts on the first day of the benefit week (see p303) after the last benefit week for which you were paid JSA.[44] However, if you have not been paid any JSA since the sanctionable action, the sanction period starts on the first day of the benefit week in which it took place.

Low level sanctions

For when you can be given a low level sanction, see below. For the length of the sanction period, see p1106. For when the sanction period starts, see p1107.

When you can be given a low level sanction

You can be given a low level sanction if you:[45]
- fail to participate in an interview without a good reason (see p1103); *or*
- fail to participate in a specified scheme for assisting people to obtain employment without a good reason (see p1103); *or*
- refuse or fail to apply for or to accept, give up, fail to attend or 'neglect to avail' yourself of a place on a training scheme or employment programme without a good reason (see p1105); *or*
- lose a place on a training scheme or employment programme through misconduct (see p1105); *or*

- refuse or fail to carry out a jobseeker's direction without a good reason (see p1106).

Failure to participate in an interview

You can be given a low level sanction if you are given a notice by an EO that you must participate in an interview on a specified date and you fail to participate in the interview without a good reason (see p1133). Notice can be given in writing, by telephone or by electronic means.[46] This applies if you fail to participate:[47]

- at the right time – eg, you attend on the right day but are late. There must have been a previous occasion in which you failed to participate in an interview at the right time and the EO must have given or sent you a written notice warning you that, if you failed to participate at the right time the next time you were required to do so, your entitlement to JSA could cease or you could be sanctioned; *or*
- on the right day.

To avoid being given a sanction on this ground, you must contact the EO within five working days and show you had a good reason for your failure.

Note:

- In some cases, if you fail to participate in an interview, your entitlement to JSA could instead end (see p1058) – ie, if you do not contact the EO within five working days.
- If you attend and participate in an interview but do not sign on, your entitlement to JSA could end (see p1058).
- If the requirement to attend and participate is for a training or employment scheme or programme (including schemes for assisting people to obtain employment), your entitlement does not end, and these sanction rules do not apply. However, you can be given a sanction under other rules.

Schemes for assisting people to obtain employment

You can be given a low level sanction if you fail to participate in a specified scheme for assisting people to obtain employment (see p1104 for which schemes) without a good reason (see p1133).[48] For other training scheme and employment programme low level sanctions, see p1105.

What information should you be given about a scheme?

1. You must be given notice in writing.[49] The notice must give you specified information, including the day on which your participation will begin, what you must do to participate and the consequences of failing to do so. The hours, where you are to participate and the likely nature of the tasks you will be expected to do should be included. You cannot simply be told that you must carry out any activities required by the scheme provider.

2. You may be able to argue that before a notice requiring you to participate is given, you should be provided with enough information about the scheme and the criteria for being

Part 7: Work and work-related rules
Chapter 48: Sanctions
1. Jobseeker's allowance sanctions

placed on it to enable you to make informed and meaningful representations on why you should not be required to participate.[50] You should also be able to make such representations about any activity you are required to undertake once you have been required to participate.[51] See CPAG's online service and *Welfare Rights Bulletin* for updates.

3. If you were not given proper notice, including if you did not receive notice (eg, because it was sent to the wrong address), you can argue that you cannot be given a sanction if you failed to participate in the scheme.[52] **Note:** scheme providers can notify you that you are required to participate in a particular scheme, but they cannot decide to give you a sanction if you do not do so. Only a DWP decision maker can do this.[53]

The following are the **current specified schemes.**[54]

- **The Work Programme:** up to two years of back-to-work support to assist those at risk of becoming long-term unemployed. **Note:** the government says that this scheme is to be replaced by the Work and Health Programme from the end of 2017. See CPAG's online service and *Welfare Rights Bulletin* for updates.
- **Skills Conditionality:** skills training.
- **The sector-based work academy:** up to six weeks of pre-employment training, a work experience placement for an agreed period and a guaranteed job interview or support in the application process. **Note:** the DWP says that it is voluntary to agree to participate in this scheme, but if you agree, it can be compulsory to attend the training element and job interview and you can be given a sanction if you fail to do so.[55] However, sanctions should not be given for failing to take part in the work experience except in cases of misconduct.
- **New Enterprise Allowance:** self-employment support. **Note:** if you are claiming JSA or ESA, your partner can also join this scheme.
- **Full-time Training Flexibility:** training for 16 to 30 hours a week for those on JSA continuously for at least 26 weeks.
- **Day One Support for Young People:** 13 weeks of a work placement for the benefit of the community for up to 30 hours a week and up to 10 hours a week supported work search for those aged 18 to 24 with less than six months' work history since leaving full-time education. 'Work history' includes employment, voluntary work, internships and work experience.
- **Derbyshire Mandatory Youth Activity Programme.**

Schemes may be added to or deleted from the above list, so get advice if you are in doubt about whether a scheme is specified. Remember that even if a scheme is not specified, other sanction rules may apply (see p1105).

You may be told to participate in **Help to Work** if you are still without a job after two years on the Work Programme. Although referred to as a 'scheme', it appears that Help to Work is actually a package of measures under which you can be given a low level sanction for failing to participate in an interview (see p1103) or failing to carry out a jobseeker's direction (see p1106). If you are told to participate in Help to Work, you may be expected to attend jobcentre interviews every day, do unpaid community work placements or attend for intensive jobcentre support or training.

Note: before 31 March 2016, you could be required to participate in Community Work Placements. See p1090 of the 2016/17 edition of this *Handbook* for further information.

Other training scheme and employment programme sanctions

You can be given a low level sanction in connection with 'training schemes' or 'employment programmes' if you:[56]

- lose your place because of 'misconduct'. See the information on p1131 – references to an employer should be read as references to your scheme or programme provider; *or*
- give up or fail to attend without a good reason (see p1133). You might be treated as failing to attend if you have been absent without authorisation, even if the absence is only for one day, or if you arrive late and are not allowed to attend;[57] *or*
- are informed by an EO of a place and refuse or fail to apply for or accept it without a good reason (see p1133). See the information in the section about refusing or failing to apply for or accept a job on p1098. References to an employer should be read as references to your scheme or programme provider; *or*
- 'neglect to avail' yourself of a reasonable opportunity of a place without a good reason (see p1133).

Training schemes and employment programmes

A **'training scheme'** is any scheme or course designed to help you gain skills, knowledge or experience that will make it more likely that you will obtain work, or be able to do so.[58]

An **'employment programme'** is any programme or scheme designed to assist you to prepare for, or move into, work.[59]

If you refuse to start a scheme or programme or if you fail to attend or leave a scheme or programme without a good reason, you can be given a sanction under these rules. If it is a specified scheme for assisting people to obtain employment, once you have begun, you may be given a sanction if you fail to participate in it (see p1103).

Note: the government says it is voluntary to agree to join Work Experience (work placements of two to eight weeks, or 12 weeks if you are offered an apprenticeship). However, if you agree, the rules above can apply, although the government says that sanctions should only be given if you leave as a result of misconduct.

Part 7: Work and work-related rules
Chapter 48: Sanctions
1. Jobseeker's allowance sanctions

Jobseeker's direction sanctions

You can be given a low level sanction if you refuse or fail to carry out a reasonable jobseeker's direction, without a good reason (see p1133).[60] A jobseeker's direction must be reasonable. It would not be reasonable, for example, if it would not help you find a job or increase your chances of being employed, was at odds with your sincere conscientious or religious beliefs or if it might unlawfully discriminate against you on grounds such as gender, disability, religion or nationality.

Any jobseeker's direction must be relevant to *your* needs and to the circumstances of the local labour market. If the EO (sometimes called your work coach) accepts that a jobseeker's direction was unreasonable, or could not be carried out in the time required, s/he cancels it.

Jobseeker's direction

A **'jobseeker's direction'** is a direction given by your EO aimed at assisting you to find a job or increase your chances of employment.[61]

A jobseeker's direction might, for example, direct you to apply for a specific job vacancy, to use the DWP job-posting and job-matching service ('universal jobmatch'), to attend a training or employment scheme, or to improve your appearance or behaviour in order to present yourself better to potential employers. You can be given an opportunity to take the action voluntarily before any direction is given. It must be clear that you are being given a jobseeker's direction.[62]

A jobseeker's direction can be given at any time and more than once. It states the time within which you are expected to comply with it, and checks are made to ensure that you have done so. Each refusal to carry out a direction could result in your being sanctioned.

Note: you cannot appeal against an EO's decision to issue a jobseeker's direction. However, if you are sanctioned for failing to carry one out, you can challenge this on the basis that the direction that led to the sanction was not given to you, was not reasonable, or that you did not fail to carry it out or you have a good reason for not carrying it out.[63]

Length of the sanction period

If you are given a low level sanction, it is imposed for:[64]

- four weeks; *or*
- 13 weeks, if you have been given one or more of this type of low level sanction for a sanctionable action of yours (not your partner's), the most recent of which took place at least two weeks, but less than 52 weeks, before your current sanctionable action. If the most recent previous sanctionable action was within two weeks of the current one, the length of the new sanction is the same as the previous one. If it was 52 weeks or more before the current one, the

length of the new sanction period is the same as if you were given a sanction for the first time.

The 52 weeks run from the date of the previous sanctionable action, not from the date of the decision imposing the previous sanction, which could be some time later.

Note: if you are 16 or 17 and are given a sanction for failing to participate in an interview as required, or for giving up a place on, or failing to attend, a training scheme or employment programme or failing to apply for or to accept, or neglecting to avail yourself of, a place on one, or for losing a place on a training scheme or employment programme because of misconduct, or for refusing or failing to carry out a jobseeker's direction, a lower two-week sanction period can instead apply (see p1095).

For what happens if you stop claiming JSA, see p1096.

If you are given a 13-week sanction but later the previous sanction is removed (eg, by the First-tier Tribunal), ask a decision maker to reduce the sanction period if relevant.[65] If s/he fails to do so, appeal. If you have already appealed against the later sanction, the tribunal should take the removal of the previous sanction into account.[66]

When the sanction period starts

The sanction period normally starts on the first day of the benefit week after the last benefit week (see p303) for which you were paid JSA.[67] However, if you have not been paid any JSA since the sanctionable action, the sanction period starts on the first day of the benefit week in which it took place.

Found not to be available for or actively seeking work

If you were previously entitled to JSA and that entitlement ended because you (or if you are a member of a joint-claim couple, your partner or both of you) did not comply with the requirement to be available for or to be actively seeking work, you can be given a sanction when you make a new claim for JSA.[68] The DWP may refer to this as an 'intermediate level sanction'. **Note:** the DWP suggests that this sanction cannot be given if you are under 18 and are claiming income-based JSA.[69]

Even if a previous entitlement to JSA ended in the circumstances above, you cannot be given a sanction for this reason if:[70]

- you were treated as being available for work (see p1033) or as actively seeking work (p1048) but the reason for this no longer applied; *and*
- you then failed to comply with the requirement to be available for or to actively seek work and as a result your entitlement to JSA ended; *and*
- the DWP considers that, in your circumstances, it is not appropriate to sanction you.

Part 7: Work and work-related rules
Chapter 48: Sanctions
2. Universal credit system sanctions

Length of the sanction period

If you are given a sanction because a previous entitlement to JSA ended when you (or if you are a member of a joint-claim couple, your partner) were found not to be available for work or to be actively seeking work, a sanction is normally imposed for:[71]

- four weeks, if entitlement has only ended once for this reason; *or*
- 13 weeks, if entitlement has ended two or more times for this reason and the most recent time is at least two weeks, but less than 52 weeks, since the time before. If the most recent previous sanctionable action was within two weeks of the current one, the length of the new sanction is the same as the previous one. If it was 52 weeks or more before the current one, the length of the new sanction period is the same as if you were given a sanction for the first time.

Any period that is more than 13 weeks since your (or your partner's) entitlement to JSA ended cannot be included in the sanction period.[72] For when your sanction period could be reduced, see below. For what happens if you stop claiming JSA, see p1096.

Note: if you are given a 13-week sanction but later the previous sanction is removed (eg, by the First-tier Tribunal), ask a decision maker to reduce the sanction period if relevant.[73] If s/he fails to do so, appeal. If you have already appealed against the later sanction, the tribunal should take the removal of the previous sanction into account.[74]

Reduced sanction periods

The four- or 13-week sanction period is reduced by the number days on which you were not paid JSA. This is the number of days starting on the first day of the benefit week (see p303) following the benefit week in which you were last paid JSA on your previous claim and ending with the day before your date of claim (see p137 and p712), or if your JSA was suspended because there was a question about whether you were available for or actively seeking work, the date the suspension ends.[75]

When the sanction period starts

The sanction period starts on your date of claim (see p137 and p712) or, if your JSA was suspended because there was a question about whether you were available for or actively seeking work, on the date the suspension ends.[76]

2. **Universal credit system sanctions**

If you come under the universal credit (UC) system (see p20) and you are entitled to UC, contribution-based jobseeker's allowance (JSA) or contributory employment and support allowance (ESA), you can be given a sanction under the rules described in this section. There are different rules if you do not come under the UC system and are getting any type of JSA or ESA (see p1093 and p1124).

Note: we refer to things that can lead to your being given a sanction as 'sanctionable actions'. The DWP may call these 'sanctionable failures'.[77]

High level sanctions (UC and JSA only) (p1116) Failing to apply for or to accept paid work Ceasing paid work or losing pay for specified reasons	Sanction period: 91, 182 or 1,095 days
Medium level sanctions (UC and JSA only) (p1120) Failing to be available for paid work or to take all reasonable action to get paid work	Sanction period: 28 or 91 days
Low level sanctions (UC, JSA and ESA) (p1121) Failing to meet a work-focused interview requirement Failing to meet a requirement connected to a work-related requirement Failing to meet a work preparation requirement Failing to take a particular action to get paid work (UC and JSA only)	Sanction period: until compliance with a requirement, plus a fixed period of seven, 14 or 28 days
Lowest level sanctions (UC and ESA only) (p1123) Failing to meet a work-focused interview requirement	Sanction period: until compliance with a requirement

If you are given a sanction, your UC, JSA or ESA is paid at a reduced (or nil) rate during a 'sanction period'. In some cases, you cannot be given a sanction if you can show you had a good reason for your actions. For what may count as a 'good reason', see p1133. For information about the amount of benefit payable, see p1110. You might be able to get UC hardship payments (see p1211). Some special rules apply if you are aged 16 or 17. See p1140 for information about challenging a sanction decision.

Part 7: Work and work-related rules
Chapter 48: Sanctions
2. Universal credit system sanctions

Note:
- If you are entitled to UC, the reduction is applied to UC, even if the sanction was in respect of your JSA or ESA claim. See p1114 for information about applying a sanction to another benefit.
- The days in your sanction period count towards your days of entitlement to contribution-based JSA or contributory ESA, even if you are not actually paid any benefit.
- If you disagree that you should be sanctioned, or with the sanction period, you can challenge the decision (see p1140).

If you are given more than one sanction

The number of days your benefit is reduced (the 'sanction period') is worked out for each sanction you are given. If you are given more than one sanction, the sanction periods run consecutively. The total number of days outstanding for all the sanctions cannot be more than 1,095 days. So if a new sanction is imposed, the sanction period is adjusted if it would otherwise go over the 1,095-day limit.[78] If your benefit is already being paid at a reduced rate because of a previous sanction, it is not reduced for a new sanction until the previous reduction ends.[79]

The benefit reduction

If you are given a sanction, your benefit is paid at a reduced (or nil) rate until the sanction period ends. The reduction for each assessment period (or, for JSA and ESA, each benefit week) is calculated as follows.[80]
- **Step one:** take the number of days in the assessment period (or, for JSA and ESA, the benefit week) or, if lower, the total number of outstanding days in the sanction period. Deduct any days in the assessment period (or benefit week) for which the sanction period has been suspended because you have also been given a sanction for a benefit offence (see p1114).
- **Step two:** multiply the number of days in Step one by the relevant daily reduction rate. See below for UC, and p1112 for JSA and ESA.

For UC, the amount in Step two is adjusted so that it is not more than your standard allowance (see p258) or, if you are a joint claimant and only one of you has been sanctioned, so that it is not more than 50 per cent of your standard allowance. The reduction in your UC is made after the benefit cap has been applied, if relevant (see p1180).

Universal credit

For UC, the daily reduction rate is normally the amount of standard allowance that applies to you multiplied by 12 and divided by 365 (the 'high rate').[81] However, the daily reduction is 40 per cent of this amount (the 'low rate') if, at the end of the assessment period for which the reduction is being calculated:[82]

- you do not have to meet any work-related requirements (see p1081) because you:
  - are the responsible carer or responsible foster parent of a child under one;
  - are pregnant and there are 11 weeks or less before the week your baby is due;
  - had a baby not more than 15 weeks ago (including if the baby was stillborn);
  - are adopting a child and it is no more than 52 weeks since the child was placed with you; or
- you can only be required to meet a work-focused interview requirement (see p1085); or
- you are 16 or 17 years old.

If you are a member of a couple and are a joint claimant, the daily rate that applies to you is divided by two.[83] If your partner is also given a sanction, the daily reduction rate that applies to her/him is also divided by two.

The daily reduction rate is nil if, at the end of the assessment period for which the reduction is being calculated, you are someone who does not have to meet any work-related requirements because you have limited capability for work and work-related activity (see p1083).[84]

The daily reduction rates are rounded down to the nearest 10 pence.[85]

Daily reduction rates

	High rate £ per day	Low rate £ per day
Single		
Under 25	8.20	3.30
25 or over	10.40	4.10
Couple		
Both under 25	6.40	2.50
Either 25 or over	8.20	3.20

Note: you may still be entitled to some UC during the assessment period – ie, if you qualify for elements for children or any other elements, such as for childcare or housing costs.

Example

Jim is aged 35 and so is his partner. He and his partner are getting UC as joint claimants. They live in rented accommodation. Jim was given a 182-day high level sanction. There are 150 days outstanding in Jim's sanction period. It is a 30-day assessment period. His partner was not given a sanction.

Step one: the relevant number of days is 30, as this is lower than the number of outstanding days in Jim's sanction period.

Step two: the daily rate is £8.20. The reduction is therefore 30 x £8.20 = £246

Part 7: Work and work-related rules
Chapter 48: Sanctions
2. Universal credit system sanctions

50 per cent of Jim's standard allowance is £249.44 (£498.89 ÷ 2). This is higher than the reduction.

Jim and his partner's UC is therefore reduced by £246 over the assessment period. They continue to get the amount to which they are entitled that exceeds £246, including the help they get with their rent.

Jobseeker's allowance

For JSA, the daily reduction rate is the weekly amount of JSA to which you are entitled multiplied by 52 and divided by 365, rounded down to the nearest 10 pence.[86] The daily reduction rates are therefore as follows. If you are:

- under 25: £8.20;
- 25 or over: £10.40.

Example
Mary is a JSA claimant aged 24. She was given a seven-day low level sanction.
Step one: the relevant number of days is seven.
Step two: 7 x £8.20 = £57.40
Mary's JSA for the benefit week is reduced by £57.40. She is paid the remainder (£0.50). The following benefit week, she is paid the full rate of JSA (£57.90) because the sanction period has ended.

Employment and support allowance

For ESA, the daily reduction rate is normally the weekly amount of ESA to which you are entitled (not including any component) multiplied by 52 and divided by 365, rounded down to the nearest 10 pence (the 'high rate').[87]

The daily reduction rate is 40 per cent of the amount as calculated above (the 'low rate') if, at the end of the benefit week for which the reduction is being calculated:[88]

- you are a lone parent responsible for a child under one or the responsible foster parent of a child under one (see p1083);
- you are pregnant and there are 11 weeks or less before the week your baby is due;
- you had a baby not more than 15 weeks ago (including if the baby was stillborn);
- you are adopting a child and it is no more than 52 weeks since the child was placed with you (see p1083);
- you can only be required to meet a work-focused interview requirement (see p1085).

The daily reduction rate is nil if, at the end of the benefit week for which the reduction is being calculated, you do not have to meet any work-related requirements because you have limited capability for work and for work-related activity (see p1083).[89]

Note:

- The ESA work-related activity component has been abolished for new claims from 3 April 2017. It is not yet known if the rules for the ESA daily reduction rate will therefore be amended. See CPAG's online service and *Welfare Rights Bulletin* for updates.
- If you are getting a reduced rate of ESA because you have been disqualified from receiving ESA for any of the reasons on p637 (eg, because of failure to accept treatment), the daily reduction rates are also reduced.

Daily reduction rates

	High rate £ per day	Low rate £ per day
Entitled to main phase ESA	10.40	4.16
Under 25, not entitled to main phase ESA	8.20	3.28
25 or over	10.40	4.16
Reduced rate ESA due to disqualification:		
Entitled to main phase ESA	8.30	3.32
Under 25, not entitled to main phase ESA	6.50	2.60
25 or over	8.30	3.32

Example

Julie, aged 30, claimed ESA recently. She is getting £73.10 a week ESA. She fails to participate in a work-focused interview but participates three days later. She is given a low level sanction. The indefinite sanction period is two days and the fixed sanction period is seven days. Her sanction period is therefore 2 + 7 = 9 days.

For the first benefit week, the reduction is calculated as follows.

Step one: the relevant number of days is seven (the number of days in the benefit week).

Step two: 7 x £10.40 = £72.80

Julie's ESA is reduced by £72.80 for one benefit week. She is paid the remainder (£0.30).

For the second benefit week, the reduction is calculated as follows.

Step one: the relevant number of days is two (the number of days in the sanction period still outstanding).

Step two: 2 x £10.40 = £20.80

Julie's ESA for the week is reduced by £20.80. She is paid the remainder (£52.30). For the following weeks, she is paid as normal.

Part 7: Work and work-related rules
Chapter 48: Sanctions
2. Universal credit system sanctions

When the sanction period starts and ends

For all levels of sanction, the sanction period starts for:[90]

- UC, on the first day of the assessment period in which the decision is made to give you a sanction or, if your UC was not reduced for the sanction during that period, from the first day of the next assessment period;
- JSA, if you have not been paid any JSA for the benefit week in which the sanctionable action took place, on the first day of that benefit week, or if you have been paid for that week, the first day of the benefit week after the last benefit week for which you were paid JSA;
- ESA, if you have not been paid any ESA for the benefit week in which the decision maker decides you should be sanctioned, on the first day of that benefit week, or if you have been paid for that week, the first day of the benefit week after the last benefit week for which you were paid ESA.

However, if your benefit is already being paid at a reduced rate because of a previous sanction, it is not reduced for a new sanction until the previous reduction ends.

Once a sanction period has begun, it continues unbroken until the sanction period comes to an end.[91] This means, for example, that if you take a job for a short period but then claim UC (or JSA or ESA) again during the period of the sanction, although you are still caught by the sanction, this is only for any days still outstanding in the sanction period. If your UC (or JSA or ESA) entitlement ends before the decision maker has decided to give you a sanction, but the decision to do so is made when you are again entitled to the benefit, the decision is treated as having been made on the day before your previous entitlement ended.[92] So, in practice, the number of days between the two awards of benefit are deducted from the sanction period. See below for special rules if you no longer come under the UC system.

A sanction is **suspended** for any period during which you are sanctioned for a benefit offence (see p1265).[93]

If you no longer come under the universal credit system

Special rules apply if you are given a sanction under the UC system and you subsequently no longer come under that system – eg, your entitlement to UC ends and when you claim benefit again, you no longer satisfy the gateway conditions in the area where you live (see p22). In this case, the sanction period ends on the first day of entitlement to income support, JSA or ESA.[94]

Applying a sanction to another benefit

If you are given a:

- JSA or ESA sanction under the UC system and you become entitled to UC, the reduction is made to your UC instead of your JSA or ESA.[95] It is calculated as for

UC – see p1110 and is made for the remainder of the JSA or ESA sanction period. Any days between the day your entitlement to JSA or ESA ends and the day your entitlement to UC starts are deducted from the period;

- UC sanction, your UC is being paid at a reduced rate when your entitlement ends, you still come under the UC system and you are entitled to JSA or ESA, the reduction is then made to your JSA or ESA.[96] The reduction is calculated as for JSA or ESA – see p1112 and is made for the remainder of the UC sanction period. Any days between the day entitlement to UC ends and the day your entitlement to JSA or ESA starts are deducted from the period.

Special rules apply if you were given a sanction while entitled to JSA (or ESA) before you came under the UC system. In this case, if you are now entitled to:

- JSA (or ESA) under the UC system, but not UC, you are treated as if you were given a JSA (or ESA) sanction under the UC system;[97]
- UC, you are treated as if you were given a UC sanction.[98]

In both cases, the reduction is made for the remainder of the former JSA (or ESA) sanction period, minus any days between the day your former JSA (or ESA) entitlement ended (if relevant) and your current UC, JSA or ESA entitlement starts.

When a sanction is terminated

All sanctions terminate and your benefit is no longer paid at a reduced (or nil) rate if, since the date of the most recent sanctionable action, you have been in paid work for (or for periods that total) at least six months (for UC) or 26 weeks (for JSA or ESA).[99] You count as being in paid work if:

- for UC, your monthly earnings during the six months are at least the amount of your individual earnings threshold (see p1084). This includes if you are treated as having a minimum level of self-employed earnings under the rules described on p341;
- for UC, you are someone who does not have to satisfy any work-related requirements for any of the reasons listed on p1081 and p1085 (other situations) and your monthly earnings during the six months are at least 16 times the minimum wage for a person of your age multiplied by 52 and divided by 12;
- for JSA, your weekly earnings are at least what you would earn for the number of hours you are expected to work (see p1075) at the minimum wage for a person of your age;
- for ESA, your weekly earnings are at least 16 times the minimum wage for a person of your age.

Part 7: Work and work-related rules
Chapter 48: Sanctions
2. Universal credit system sanctions

High level sanctions

For when you can be given a high level sanction, see below. For the length of the sanction period, see p1118. **Note:** you cannot be given a high level sanction if you are entitled to ESA.

When you can be given a high level sanction

If you are entitled to UC or JSA, you can be given a high level sanction if you:[100]

- fail to apply for a particular vacancy or accept an offer of paid work without a good reason (see below); *or*
- cease paid work or lose pay voluntarily without a good reason or because of 'misconduct' (see p1117).

Note: before 2 March 2016, you could be referred to a scheme called Mandatory Work Activity. You could be given a high level sanction if you failed to participate on or before 27 April 2016. For further information, see p1102 of the 2016/17 edition of this *Handbook*.

Failing to apply for or to accept paid work

You can be given a high level UC or JSA sanction if, without a good reason:[101]

- you are told to apply for a particular vacancy for paid work (under a work search requirement) and do not do so, or you fail to take up paid work when it is offered to you (under a work availability requirement). **Note:** if the vacancy was available because of a strike, you cannot be given a sanction;[102] *or*
- you failed to take up an offer of paid work before your claim for UC (or JSA). For UC, you must be subject to all the work-related requirements (see p1080) when you are awarded UC. For both UC and JSA, no reduction in your benefit can be made if the number of days between the date you failed to take up the offer and your date of claim for UC (or JSA) is more than the sanction period that would otherwise apply.

Paid work

'Paid work' for these purposes means work done for payment or for which you expect to be paid.[103]

For when the DWP might treat you as having refused to apply for or accept paid work, see p1099.[104] The issues are similar to those for JSA sanctions that are not under the UC system. **Note:**

- You only have to be available for work and to look for work in locations that are no more than 90 minutes from your home.[105] So you may find it difficult to show you have a good reason if your travel time is shorter than this.
- You may be able to show that you have a good reason for refusing a job if you have previously done work of a particular type or at a particular rate of pay,

you have been allowed to limit your work search to looking for work of a similar type or rate of pay (see p1078), and you refuse a job that does not meet these conditions.

- The DWP says if you are getting UC and you refuse to accept a job under a zero-hour contract without a good reason, you can be given a sanction if the contract allows you to take up work with other employers that will lift your earnings above your individual earnings threshold (see p1084). However, you should not be given a sanction if the zero-hour contract has an exclusivity clause – ie, if you are prevented by the employer from working for any other employer, business or self-employment.[106]

Ceasing paid work or losing pay

Unless any of the exceptions below apply, you can be given a high level UC or JSA sanction if you cease paid work (see p1116) or lose pay:[107]

- 'voluntarily' without a good reason; *or*
- because of misconduct. You can be sanctioned if you are suspended from work for misconduct or if you resigned rather than be dismissed.[108]

For UC, you can be given a sanction on this ground even if no work-related requirements were being imposed on you at the time the event occurred because you were earning a sufficient amount (see p1084 for the earnings thresholds), so long as your ceasing work or losing pay means you are now subject to all the work-related requirements.

For both UC and JSA, you can be given a sanction on this ground if you ceased the paid work or you lost pay before your claim for UC (or JSA). For UC, you must be subject to all the work-related requirements when you are awarded UC. However, for both UC and JSA, no reduction in your benefit can be made if the number of days between the date you ceased work or lost pay and your date of claim for UC (or JSA) is more than the sanction period that would otherwise apply.

For information about whether you left work or lost pay voluntarily, see p1130. For what may happen if you take retirement, see p1131. For what may count as misconduct, see p1131. For whether misconduct caused the loss of work or pay, see p1132.

When you cannot be given a sanction for ceasing paid work or losing pay

For UC only, you cannot be given a sanction on this ground (even if you cease paid work or lose pay voluntarily or because of misconduct) if your monthly earnings (or, if you are a joint claimant, your joint monthly earnings) have not fallen below the amount that means a work search requirement cannot be imposed on you at the present time (see p1089), unless you have been selected to take part in the In Work Pilot Scheme.[109]

Part 7: Work and work-related rules
Chapter 48: Sanctions
2. Universal credit system sanctions

For both UC and JSA, you cannot be given a sanction (even if you cease paid work or lose pay voluntarily) if:[110]

- you volunteer or accept your employer's proposal for redundancy (see p1130); or
- you are allowed to limit the number of hours you are available for work and are looking for work (see p1075), you take up paid work (or more hours of paid work) for more hours than that limit and you cease that paid work (or doing the higher hours) or lose pay within a trial period. 'Trial period' is not defined in the rules, but the DWP says it is a period of 56 days starting on the 29th day and ending on the 84th day on which you took up paid work (or more hours).[111] You can argue that anything that can reasonably be described as a trial period should count; or
- you ceased paid work or lost pay because of a strike; or
- you ceased paid work as a member of the regular or reserve armed forces, or lost pay in that capacity; or
- you have been laid off or kept on short-time work by your employer for at least four consecutive weeks (or for six weeks in a 13-week period). You must have applied for redundancy pay within a specified time.[112]

Length of the sanction period

If you are given a high level JSA sanction or, if you are 18 or over, a UC sanction, it is usually imposed for 91 days. However, it is imposed for:[113]

- 182 days if you have been given a 91-day high level sanction previously (but see below); or
- 1,095 days (three years) if you have been given a 182- or a 1,095-day high level sanction previously (but see below).

If you are given a high level UC sanction and you are 16 or 17 years old, a fixed sanction period is imposed for:[114]

- 14 days; or
- 28 days, if you have been given a 14- or 28-day high level sanction previously (but see below).

For the longer sanction periods to apply, the most recent sanctionable action must have taken place at least 14 days, but less than 365 days, before your current sanctionable action. The 365 days runs from the date of the previous sanctionable action, not from the date of the decision imposing the previous sanction, which could be some time later. If the most recent previous sanctionable action was within 14 days of the current one, the length of the new sanction period is the same as the previous one. If it was 365 days or more before the current one, the length of the new sanction period is the same as if you were given a sanction for the first time. For JSA, a high level UC sanction, and for UC, a high level JSA sanction which has been applied to your UC, also counts for these purposes.[115]

Failing to accept an offer of paid work or ceasing paid work, or losing pay voluntarily or because of misconduct *before* your current date of claim do not count as sanctionable actions for the purpose of working out whether a 182- or 1,095-day (or if you are 16 or 17, a 28-day) sanction period should be applied.[116] Your sanction period may be reduced in the same circumstances (see below).

Note:

- If, when you did not come under the UC system, you were given a JSA sanction and you are then given another sanction under the UC system, the previous sanctionable action can count when the new sanction period is determined.[117]
- If you are given a sanction but later a previous sanction is removed (eg, by the First-tier Tribunal), ask a decision maker to reduce the sanction period if relevant.[118] Appeal if s/he fails to do so. If you have already appealed against the later sanction, the tribunal should take this into account.[119]

Reduced sanction periods

If you are given a high level sanction because, before the date of your claim, you failed to accept paid work, ceased paid work or lost pay voluntarily or because of misconduct, your sanction period is reduced to take account of days when you did not claim UC (or JSA). It is calculated as follows and is the shorter of the following.[120]

- **Step one:** if the job was only due to last for a limited period, work out the number of days starting with the day after the date of your current sanctionable action and ending on the day the paid work would have ended. 'Limited period' is not defined.
- **Step two:** in any other case, work out the sanction period that would normally apply.
- **Step three:** reduce the amount in Step one or Step two as relevant by the number of days between the date of your current sanctionable action and your date of claim (see p171 and p712).

In practical terms, this means that if you claim UC (or JSA) after the job would have ended, or you delay your claim for UC (or JSA) long enough, your benefit is not paid at a reduced (or nil) rate.[121]

Example

Glynis quits her job on 7 October. It was only due to last until 1 November. She claims JSA on 16 November. She is given a high level sanction for the second time in 365 days, so a 182-day sanction period would normally apply. However, her job was only due to last for a limited period.

Part 7: Work and work-related rules
Chapter 48: Sanctions
2. Universal credit system sanctions

> The number of days from 8 October to 1 November is 25 days. The number of days
> between 7 October and 16 November is 39 days. Glynis's sanction period is therefore
> reduced to nil and her JSA is not paid at a reduced rate.

Medium level sanctions

If you are entitled to UC or JSA, you can be given a medium level sanction if,
without a good reason, you:[122]

- do not take all reasonable action to get paid work, more paid work or better
  paid work (under a work search requirement – see p1075); *or*
- are not available for work (under a work availability requirement – see p1077).

Length of the sanction period

If you are given a medium level JSA sanction or, if you are 18 or over, a UC
sanction, it is usually imposed for 28 days. However, it is imposed for 91 days if
you have previously been given a 28-day or 91-day medium level sanction (but
see below).[123]

If you are given a medium level UC sanction and you are 16 or 17 years old, a
fixed sanction period applies of:[124]

- seven days; *or*
- 14 days, if you have been given a seven- or 14-day medium level sanction
  previously (but see below).

For the longer sanction periods to apply, the most recent sanctionable action
must have taken place at least 14 days, but less than 365 days, before your current
sanctionable action. The 365 days runs from the date of the previous sanctionable
action, not from the date of the decision imposing the previous sanction, which
could be some time later. If the most recent previous sanctionable action was
within 14 days of the current one, the length of the new sanction period is the
same as the previous one. If it was 365 days or more before the current one, the
length of the new sanction period is the same as if you were given a sanction for
the first time. For JSA, a medium level UC sanction, and for UC, a medium level
JSA sanction which has been applied to your UC, also counts for these purposes.[125]

Note:
- If, when you did not come under the UC system, you were given a JSA sanction
  and you are then given another sanction under the UC system, the previous
  sanctionable action can count when the new sanction period is determined.[126]
- If you are given a sanction but later a previous sanction is removed (eg, by the
  First-tier Tribunal), ask a decision maker to reduce the sanction period if
  relevant.[127] Appeal if s/he fails to do so. If you have already appealed against
  the later sanction, the tribunal should take the removal of the previous
  sanction into account.[128]

Low level sanctions

If you are entitled to UC, JSA or ESA, you can be given a low level sanction if, without a good reason, you:[129]

- fail to meet a work-focused interview requirement (see p1074). **Note:** for UC and ESA, this does not apply if you are *only* required to meet a work-focused interview requirement. In this case, you can instead be given a lowest level sanction (see p1123); *or*

- fail to meet a requirement (connected to a work-related requirement) to participate in interviews, provide information or evidence, confirm compliance (eg, by signing on) or report a change in your circumstances that is relevant to whether work-related requirements can be imposed on you or to your compliance with a work-related requirement; *or*

- fail to meet a work preparation requirement (see p1074) – eg, you refuse to do a community work placement or to go on a training scheme or employment programme; *or*

- for UC and JSA only, fail to take any particular action specified by the DWP to get paid work, more paid work or better paid work (under a work search requirement – see p1075).

For ESA, to be given a sanction, you must be someone who can be required to meet a work preparation requirement *and* a work-focused interview requirement (see p1087). For UC, you must be someone who can be required to meet all the work-related requirements, or to only meet a work preparation requirement and a work-focused interview requirement.

* *

How quickly do you have to contact the DWP?

The rules do not specify a time within which you must contact the DWP to explain your reasons if you failed to do any of the above. However, to avoid a sanction decision being made, you should contact the DWP as soon possible and provide as much information as you can to show you had a good reason.

* *

Length of the sanction period

If you are given a low level UC, JSA or ESA sanction, it is imposed for both an indefinite period and a fixed period as follows.

Step one: work out the number of days, starting on the date your sanctionable action took place and ending on the earliest of the following:[130]

- the day before the date you meet a 'compliance condition' specified by the DWP; *or*

- for UC and ESA only, the day before the date you come into a category in which you no longer have to meet any work-related requirements (see p1081); *or*

Part 7: Work and work-related rules
Chapter 48: Sanctions
2. Universal credit system sanctions

- the day before the date you are no longer required to take particular action specified in a work preparation requirement; *or*
- the date your entitlement to UC (or JSA or ESA) ends. For UC, this does not apply if this is because you cease to be, or become, a member of a couple.

Compliance condition

A '**compliance condition**' is:[131]

– a condition that you stop a sanctionable action – eg, if you failed to participate in an employment programme, a condition that you must participate; *or*

– a condition relating to your future compliance with a work-related requirement (or a requirement connected to one) – eg, if you failed to attend a training scheme, a condition that you must attend and participate in an interview to discuss what training may be suitable.

Note: if the DWP does not make a decision to give you a sanction until some time after your sanctionable action, you might not have a compliance condition to meet until you are given the sanction. The DWP is still likely to say that your indefinite sanction period runs from the assessment period in which it decides to give you the sanction and lasts for the relevant number of days, starting from the date your sanctionable action took place. Try to argue that you have already complied with the condition before you were given the sanction – eg, if you are given a sanction because you failed to provide your CV on a specified date, but you provided one later. Provide any relevant information and evidence to prove you have already complied. You could also make a complaint about the time the DWP took to decide to give you a sanction (see Chapter 58).

Step two: work out the fixed sanction period.
- For UC if you are at least 18 years old, JSA or ESA, this is usually for seven days. However the period is:[132]
  – 14 days, if you have been given a seven-day low level sanction previously (but see below); *or*
  – 28 days, if you have been given a 14-day or 28-day low level sanction previously (but see below).
- For UC if you are 16 or 17 years old, this is for seven days, but only if you have been given a low level sanction previously (but see below).[133]

For the longer sanction periods to apply, the most recent sanctionable action must have taken place at least 14 days, but less than 365 days, before your current sanctionable action. The 365 days runs from the date of the previous sanctionable action, not from the date of the decision imposing the previous sanction, which could be some time later. If the most recent previous sanctionable action was within 14 days of the current one, the length of the new sanction period is the same as the previous one. If it was 365 days or more before the current one, the length of the new sanction period is the same as if you were given a sanction for the first time. For UC, a low level JSA or ESA sanction that has been applied to your UC, and for JSA, a low level UC or ESA sanction, and for ESA, a low level UC or JSA sanction, also count for these purposes.[134]

Step three: add the number of days in Steps one and two together. This is your low level sanction period.

Note:

- If you were given a JSA or ESA sanction when you did not come under the UC system and you are then given another sanction under the UC system, the previous sanctionable action can count when the new sanction period is determined.[135]
- If you are given a sanction but later a previous sanction is removed (eg, by the First-tier Tribunal), ask a decision maker to reduce the sanction period if relevant.[136] Appeal if s/he fails to do so. If you have already appealed against the later sanction, the tribunal should take the removal of the previous sanction into account.[137]

Lowest level sanctions

For UC and ESA only, you can be given a lowest level sanction if you can only be required to meet a work-focused interview requirement (see p1085) and you fail to participate in a work-focused interview without a good reason.[138]

How quickly do you have to contact the DWP?

The rules do not specify a time within which you must contact the DWP to explain your reasons if you failed to participate in a work-focused interview. However, to avoid a sanction, you should contact the DWP as soon as possible and provide as much information as you can to show you had a good reason.

Length of the sanction period

If you are given a lowest level sanction, it can be imposed indefinitely. It is imposed for the number of days starting on the date your sanctionable action took place and only ends on the earliest of the following:[139]

- the day before the date you meet a 'compliance condition' specified by the DWP (see p1122 for the meaning); *or*
- the day before the date you come into a category in which you no longer have to meet any work-related requirements (see p1081); *or*
- the date your entitlement to UC (or ESA) ends. For UC, this does not apply if this is because you cease to be, or become, a member of a couple.

Part 7: Work and work-related rules
Chapter 48: Sanctions
3. Other benefit sanctions

3. **Other benefit sanctions**

If you do not come under the universal credit (UC) system (see p20), you can be given a sanction if, without 'good cause':
- you (or in some cases, your partner) fail to take part in a work-focused interview while you are entitled to a specified benefit (see below);
- you fail to take part in work-related activity when required to do so while entitled to employment and support allowance (ESA) or income support (IS) (see p1128). For IS, this only applies if the only reason you are on IS is because you are a lone parent and if you do not have any children under three.

If you come under the UC system and are getting contributory ESA, different rules apply (see p1108).

Work-focused interview sanctions

There are currently a number of rules under which you can be required to take part in work-focused interviews while you are entitled to benefit – ie, if you:
- are incapable of work and are entitled to IS, incapacity benefit (IB), severe disablement allowance (SDA) or ESA (see p1064); *or*
- are entitled to IS and are a lone parent (see p1065); *or*
- come under the Jobcentre Plus rules (see p1066); *or*
- are the partner of someone entitled to IS, income-based jobseeker's allowance (JSA) (but not joint-claim JSA), income-related ESA, IB, SDA or carer's allowance (CA) (see p1066).

If you (or your partner) fail to take part without 'good cause', you are given a sanction and your benefit is paid at a reduced rate. For what may count as good cause, see p1125. **Note:**
- What the benefit reduction is, and how long it lasts, depends on the benefit you are getting and the rules under which you are required to take part.
- If you are getting ESA and you experience hardship as a result of a sanction, you may qualify for hardship payments (see p1210).
- If you are getting housing benefit (HB), your entitlement should continue. However, let the local authority know about the change in your circumstances to ensure it has all the information it requires.

For ESA, you have a right of appeal against a decision imposing a sanction.[140] For other benefits, you can appeal against a decision that you did not take part in an interview and a decision that you have not shown good cause for your failure within five working days.[141] If you are given a sanction because your partner fails to take part in an interview, both of you are notified of the decision and both of you have the right to appeal.[142]

Good cause for failing to take part

To avoid a sanction, you (or your partner) must show 'good cause' for failing to take part in a work-focused interview within five working days of:

- the date on which the interview was to take place (for a partner of someone on a specified benefit);[143]
- the date you are notified by the DWP that you failed to participate in the interview (in all other cases). For the rules for those incapable of work, this is the date the notice is sent or given. For the other rules, you can argue this is the date you receive the notice.[144]

How quickly should you contact the DWP?

It is always best to contact the DWP as soon as possible, but you must be given at least five days to show good cause before any decision to impose a sanction is made.[145] However, for benefits other than ESA, you can demonstrate good cause up to a month after the decision that you did not participate was notified to you, if the facts you rely on could not reasonably have been brought to the DWP's attention within five days.[146] There is no equivalent rule for ESA. However, it is understood that in the past the DWP has viewed it as unnecessary to have attempted to show good cause within five days.[147]

When deciding whether you have good cause for benefits other than ESA, the decision maker considers all the circumstances, but in particular must take into account:[148]

- any misunderstanding on your part because of learning, literacy or language difficulties, or misleading information given by the DWP;
- attending a doctor or dentist appointment or accompanying a person for whom you are caring, where the appointment could not reasonably have been rearranged;
- difficulties with transport where no reasonable alternative was available;
- the customs and practices of your religion that prevented you attending at the fixed time;
- attending a job interview;
- the need to pursue employment opportunities for your self-employment;
- whether you or a dependent child or a person for whom you are caring had an accident, sudden illness or relapse;
- attending the funeral of a close friend or relative;
- a disability that makes attendance impracticable;
- any other relevant matter. This depends on the facts in your case, but might include things like emergencies and problems with caring arrangements.

'Good cause' is not defined in the ESA rules. However, the decision maker should consider factors that are broadly the same as above.[149]

Part 7: Work and work-related rules
Chapter 48: Sanctions
3. Other benefit sanctions

The benefit reduction

The amount by which your benefit is reduced depends on the benefit you are claiming and the rules that apply to you. For ESA, see below. For incapacity benefits, see p1126. For other benefits, see below.

Employment and support allowance

If you are entitled to ESA and you are given a sanction, the benefit reduction is 100 per cent of the personal allowance that applies for a single person who qualifies for ESA that includes a support component (ie, the personal allowance for main phase ESA) – currently £73.10 a week.[150] Your weekly benefit cannot be reduced by more than this amount and you must be left with at least 10 pence a week. This means that you are paid any remaining ESA to which you are entitled – ie, if a component, amounts for a partner, premiums or housing costs are included in your applicable amount.

Note: if you experience hardship as a result of the reduction, you may qualify for hardship payments (see Chapter 51).

Examples

Bernie is getting ESA of £114.85 a week for himself and his partner. When he is sanctioned, his benefit is reduced by £73.10 a week and he is paid £41.75 a week for the duration of the sanction period.

Lisa is a single claimant aged 23 living in rented accommodation. She has only been claiming income-related ESA for 10 weeks, so is getting £57.90 a week. When she is sanctioned, her benefit is reduced to 10 pence a week for the duration of the sanction period.

Benefits for incapacity

If you are entitled to IB, SDA or IS on the grounds of disability and are given a sanction, the benefit reduction is 50 per cent of the equivalent of the value of the ESA work-related activity component for the first four weeks of the reduction (currently £14.52 a week), then 100 per cent of the value (currently £29.05 a week) for each following week.[151] Your weekly benefit cannot be reduced by more than these amounts and you must be left with at least 10 pence a week. **Note:** this rule was not amended when the work-related activity component was abolished for new claims from 3 April 2017.

Other benefits

Unless you are getting ESA, IB, SDA or IS on the grounds of disability, if you are given a sanction, the benefit reduction is £14.62 a week.[152] This also applies if it is your partner who fails to take part in an interview.[153] You must be left with at least 10 pence a week. If your benefit is reduced because your partner fails to take part in an interview and you are getting more than one of the specified benefits (see p1067), income-based JSA is the first benefit to be reduced, followed by income-related ESA, IS, IB, SDA and then CA.[154]

Note: your IS cannot be reduced under these rules if it is already being reduced because you failed to take part in a work-focused interview or in work-related activity, and the last reduction was made in the two weeks before your current failure to take part in a work-focused interview.[155]

Length of the sanction period

The length of the sanction period depends on the benefit you are claiming and the rules you come under. For ESA, see below. For other benefits, see p1128.

Employment and support allowance

For ESA, the sanction period is worked out as follows.[156]

- **Step one:** an indefinite-length sanction period is given. This is normally one week for each seven-day period during which you fail to take part in an interview or agree a date when you will do so with the DWP – ie, it lasts until you comply. However, if within one week after you fail to take part in an interview, you take part in one, or agree a date when you will do so, your ESA is only reduced for the relevant fixed period under Step two below. **Note:** if you agree a date with a training scheme or employment programme provider, it passes this information to the DWP. Ensure that the provider has given the correct date (ie, the date you *agreed* to take part in an interview), if this is earlier than the date you took part.
- **Step two:** an additional fixed-period sanction is given as follows:
  - one week, if it is the first time you have been sanctioned; *or*
  - two weeks, if you failed to take part in an interview at least two weeks, but less than 52 weeks, before a previous failure to take part that resulted in a sanction; *or*
  - four weeks, if you failed to take part in an interview at least two weeks, but less than 52 weeks, before a previous failure to take part that resulted in a two- or four-week sanction.

Note: if the most recent sanctionable action was within two weeks of the current one, the length of the new sanction is the same as the previous one. If it was 52 weeks or more before the current one, the length of the new sanction period is the same as if you were given a sanction for the first time. Note also that a sanction ceases to apply if you are no longer someone required to take part in work-focused interviews.[157]

Examples

Sandra does not take part in a work-focused interview with her employment scheme provider and is given a sanction by the DWP. This is the first time she has failed to take part

Part 7: Work and work-related rules
Chapter 48: Sanctions
3. Other benefit sanctions

in an interview. After two days, she agrees to take part in an interview with her scheme provider. She takes part in the interview 10 days later. Her benefit is only paid at a reduced rate for a fixed period of one week because she agreed to take part in an interview within one week of her failure.

Alison does not take part in a work-focused interview. This is the second time she has been given a sanction: she failed to take part in an interview 15 weeks ago. Her ESA starts to be paid at a reduced rate. Three weeks later, she agrees to take part in an interview. The ongoing sanction ends, but her ESA continues to be paid at a reduced rate for a further fixed period of two weeks.

If you are given a sanction but later the previous sanction is removed (eg, by the First-tier Tribunal), ask a decision maker to reduce the fixed sanction period if relevant.[158] If s/he fails to do so, appeal. If you have already appealed against the later sanction, the tribunal should take the removal of the previous sanction into account.[159]

Other benefits

For benefits other than ESA, you are sanctioned for an indefinite period. However, the sanction ceases to apply if:[160]

- you (or your partner) take part in a work-focused interview; *or*
- for IS only, you take part in work-related activity; *or*
- you (or your partner) are no longer required to take part in work-focused interviews under the relevant scheme or you reach the qualifying age for pension credit (see p147).

In addition, if you are given a sanction because your partner failed to take part in a work-focused interview, the sanction ceases to apply if you cease to be partners, or you cease to get additional benefit for her/him.[161]

Work-related activity sanctions

If you are entitled to IS or ESA, you can be required to undertake work-related activity (see p1068). However, for IS, you can only be required to do so if the only reason you are on IS is because you are a lone parent and if you do not have any children under three.

If you fail to undertake work-related activity without good cause, you are given a sanction and your benefit is paid at a reduced rate. You must be given at least five days to show good cause – ie, you must show good cause within five working days of the date you are notified by the DWP that you failed to take part.[162] For IS only, you may still be able to demonstrate good cause up to a month after you are notified that you did not take part, if the facts you rely on could not reasonably have been brought to the DWP's attention within five days.[163] **Note:** if you do not contact the DWP in time to show you have good cause, you can still try to argue that you should not be given a sanction if the requirement to undertake work-related activity was unreasonable.[164]

For IS, the rules for what might count as 'good cause' are the same as for work-focused interview sanctions (see p1125).[165] Good cause is not defined in the ESA rules, but the DWP should consider factors that are broadly the same. For IS and ESA, the rules for the amount of the benefit reduction are the same as for work-focused interview sanctions (see p1126).

Note:

- For IS, when deciding whether you have good cause, the circumstances listed on p1125 must be taken into account, as well as the availability of childcare.[166]
- Your IS cannot be reduced under these rules if it is already being reduced because you failed to take part in a work-focused interview or to undertake work-related activity, and the last reduction was made in the two weeks before your current failure.[167]
- For ESA, if you experience hardship as a result of a sanction, you may qualify for hardship payments (see p1210).
- If you are getting HB, your entitlement should continue. However, let the local authority know about the change in your circumstances to ensure it has all the information required.

You have a right of appeal against a decision imposing a sanction.

Length of the sanction period

For **ESA**, the sanction period is normally one week for each seven-day period during which you fail to:[168]

- undertake the work-related activity set out in your 'action plan' (see p1069); or
- undertake alternative work-related activity notified by the DWP; or
- make an agreement with the DWP to undertake the work-related activity set out in your action plan or alternative work-related activity on an agreed date.

A further fixed period is added (see p1127 – the rules are the same as for ESA work-focused interview sanctions). Your ESA cannot be paid at a reduced rate if you are no longer required to undertake work-related activity or the DWP decides it is no longer appropriate to require you to undertake it at that time.[169]

For **IS**, the sanction period lasts until either you meet a requirement to undertake work-related activity or take part in a work-focused interview, or you are no longer required to undertake work-related activity.[170]

4. Common rules

There are a number of rules and issues that are common to some or all of the benefits and types of sanction. These are covered in this section.

Employment-related sanctions

If you are getting jobseeker's allowance (JSA) or universal credit (UC), you can be given a sanction in a number of situations that relate to employment – eg, you can be given a sanction if you leave a job voluntarily, lose a job because of misconduct or, if you come under the UC system (see p20), if you lose pay voluntarily or because of misconduct.

Leaving a job or losing pay voluntarily

If you are getting JSA or UC, you can be given a high level sanction if you leave your job 'voluntarily' without a good reason (see p1097 and p1117). If you come under the UC system (see p20), you can also be given a high level sanction if you lose pay voluntarily (see p1117).

Voluntarily

'**Voluntarily**' is not defined in the rules, but the DWP says it means that you have brought the situation about by your own acts and of your own free will.[171] You have not left your employment (or lost pay) voluntarily if you had no choice in the matter or there is convincing evidence (eg, medical evidence from your GP) that you were not responsible for your actions.

If you are thinking of reducing your hours for a good reason (eg, because of your caring responsibilities or health), speak to your work coach or personal adviser first and make a written record of your conversations. It is not clear if you would be seen to have lost pay voluntarily in this situation. You may be expected to explore other options.

You are likely to be treated as giving up your job voluntarily if:

- you resign giving notice. If you genuinely believed that your employer was about to end your employment or you were given the 'choice' of resignation or dismissal, you have not left your job voluntarily, but the DWP may then consider whether you lost your job through misconduct (see p1097 and p1117);
- your employer gives you notice to end your employment but then cancels or suspends it, but you decide not to continue in the employment, if it is clear that you have a genuine choice to remain.[172] However, the circumstances may be such as to amount to a 'good reason'.

You have *not* left your job voluntarily if:

- you volunteer, or accept your employer's proposal, for **redundancy**, even if you were offered, or could have applied for, alternative jobs with the same employer.[173] This only applies if there is a redundancy situation at your workplace – eg, if a whole factory or department is closing down or if there is a cut in the number of people needed to carry out certain tasks. **Note:** if you

refuse other work, you might be sanctioned for another reason – eg, refusing employment or 'neglecting to avail' yourself of an opportunity of employment;
- your employer ends your contract of employment.[174] **Note:** if you left your job because your employer imposed a change in your terms or conditions without your agreement and the new terms are less favourable than before, try to argue that you have not left your job voluntarily but have been dismissed, or that you had a good reason for leaving.

Taking retirement

If you take retirement, you might be treated as having left your job voluntarily.[175] Under employment law, your employer cannot usually make you retire at any particular age, so taking retirement is something you do of your own choice. However, you might be able to show you have a good reason – eg, if you can show that the work was getting too much for you because of your age or your health.

Employers sometimes have special early retirement schemes allowing you to take your occupational pension at an earlier age than normal, often in order to deal with a redundancy situation. In this case, you come under the special rules about redundancy (see p1130). Employers often try to avoid using the word 'redundancy' and you may have to prove to the decision maker that a redundancy situation existed.

If you take early retirement under some other special scheme, you cannot show you have a good reason merely because your action was in your employer's interest.[176]

Misconduct

If you are getting JSA or UC, you can be given a high level sanction if you lose your job because of your misconduct (see p1097 and p1117). If you come under the UC system (see p20), you can also be given a high level sanction if lose pay because of misconduct (see p1117).

'**Misconduct**' is not defined in the rules. However, bear the following in mind.
- You are guilty of misconduct only if your actions or omissions are 'blameworthy'. You do not have to have done anything dishonest or deliberately wrong; serious carelessness or negligence may be enough.[177]
- Everyone makes mistakes or is inefficient from time to time. So, for example, if you are a naturally slow worker who, despite making every effort, cannot produce the output required by your employer, you are not guilty of misconduct even if the poor performance may justify your dismissal.
- The misconduct must have some connection with your employment but it does not have to take place during working hours to count. However, a sanction cannot be imposed if the actions or omissions took place before your employment began – eg, you gave inaccurate information about yourself when applying for the job.[178]

Some behaviour is clearly misconduct – eg, dishonesty (whether or not connected with your work) if it causes your employer to dismiss you because s/he no longer trusts you.[179] However, some behaviour is not necessarily misconduct – eg:

- A refusal to carry out a reasonable instruction by an employer is not misconduct if you had a good reason or refused because of a genuine misunderstanding.[180]
- You should not be treated as losing a job because of misconduct if you are dismissed for 'whistleblowing' – ie, for disclosing wrongful behaviour which it was in the public interest to disclose. However, if you have not reported the matter through the proper channels, you might be guilty of misconduct.[181]
- Bad timekeeping and failing to report in time that you are sick might amount to misconduct – eg, if you were persistently late or failed to report that you were sick on a number of occasions.
- Breaking rules covering personal conduct might amount to misconduct, depending on the seriousness of the breach. A breach of a trivial rule might not be misconduct.[182]
- Refusing to work overtime is misconduct if you were under a duty to work overtime when required and the request to do it was reasonable.

Although evidence from your employer is taken into account, the fact that s/he did not describe your actions as 'misconduct' does not guarantee that you can escape a sanction. However, this should go heavily in your favour.

Whether misconduct caused the loss of employment or pay

Your misconduct need not be the only cause of the loss of your employment or pay, but it must be an immediate and substantial reason.[183] If your misconduct was not the real reason for your dismissal (eg, your employer used this as an excuse but really only wanted to reduce staff numbers), you should not be sanctioned.

It is not relevant that your dismissal was unreasonable or an overreaction on your employer's part. However, seek advice to see whether you might have a case for unfair dismissal at an employment tribunal.

If there was misconduct, the exact way in which you lost your employment is not important. You may be summarily dismissed, be dismissed with notice or resign as an alternative to possible dismissal.[184]

Relationship with unfair dismissal and other proceedings

Sometimes the same facts have to be considered by other bodies – eg, employment tribunals and the criminal courts. The questions and legal tests that other bodies use may not be the same as those which apply to benefits.

DWP decision makers, the First-tier Tribunal and employment tribunals are independent of each other; decisions by one are not binding on the other. This means:

- a finding by an employment tribunal that a dismissal was fair does not prevent a decision maker or the First-tier Tribunal from concluding that you did not lose your job through misconduct;[185]
- although the First-tier Tribunal normally accepts a criminal conviction as proof that you have done what is alleged, it must go on to consider whether this was connected with your employment, whether it amounts to misconduct and whether the misconduct was the reason why you lost your employment;
- the decision maker or the tribunal does not have to wait for the outcome of other proceedings before making a decision, but it is more likely to do so if there is a conflict of evidence.[186]

Good reasons

In a number of situations, a sanction cannot be imposed if you have a good reason for your actions. '**Good reason**' is not defined in the rules, but what may count is set out in guidance.[187] If you appeal against the sanction decision, the guidance is not binding on the First-tier Tribunal; it must make up its own mind about what counts as a good reason.

It is up to you to show you have a good reason, but the decision maker should take all the circumstances into account. The factors that may mean you have a good reason depend on the sanction.

How much time are you given to explain your good reasons?

You should be given sufficient time to explain your reasons and to provide relevant evidence. If you do not come under the UC system and you fail to participate in an interview (see p1103), you must be given at least five days. In other cases, the DWP says you should be given at least five days, but you may be given less time than this if you can be contacted by telephone or electronic means. The DWP says that you should be given more time if you have to get information or evidence from someone else, you have a representative, or you have a health condition or there are other temporary circumstances (eg, caring responsibilities) that prevent you from replying.[188]

For ideas about what might count as a good reason, see below. **Note:** for JSA (if you do not come under the UC system), there are some special rules for 16/17-year-olds (see p1137).

What is not a good reason

For JSA (if you do not come under the UC system), if you are sanctioned for refusing or failing to apply for or accept a job (see p1098), neglecting to avail yourself of a job (see p1099) or not carrying out a jobseeker's direction (see p1106), you are *not* treated as having a good reason where your reason relates to the time it took (or would normally take) to travel from your home to your place of employment or a place mentioned in a jobseeker's direction, and back home again, if this was (or is normally) less than one hour and 30 minutes either way by a route or means appropriate to your circumstances – eg, by public transport.[189] This does not apply if the time is unreasonable in the light of your health or your caring responsibilities (see p1032 for the meaning).

For JSA and UC (if you come under the UC system), you may find it difficult to show you have a good reason for failing to apply for, or accept, paid work if your travel time is shorter than 90 minutes. This is because you have to be available for work and to look for work in locations that are up to 90 minutes from your home.[190]

Circumstances that should be taken into account

The decision maker should take all of your circumstances into account when deciding whether you have a 'good reason'. This should include the following.

- Any restrictions or limitations you have been allowed to place on your availability for work, having regard to any discrepancy between these and the requirements of the job. Minor differences might not count. You do not necessarily have a good reason for refusing to apply for a job covered by your restrictions or limitations, but it is a very significant factor to take into account.[191]
- Any condition of yours or personal circumstances that suggest that a particular job, or scheme or programme, or carrying out a jobseeker's direction, would be likely to cause you unreasonable physical or mental stress or significant harm to your health.
- A disease or physical/mental disability that meant you were unable to attend a scheme or programme, or that your health (or that of others) would have been at risk if you had done so.
- You misunderstood what you had to do because of language, learning or literacy difficulties, or because you were misled by the DWP.
- You (or someone for whom you care) were attending a medical, dental or other important appointment which would have been unreasonable to rearrange.
- You are the victim of domestic violence or of bullying or harassment.
- A sincerely held religious or conscientious objection.[192]
- Caring responsibilities that make it unreasonable for you to do the job, attend an interview, participate in the scheme or programme or carry out a jobseeker's direction, including whether suitable childcare would have been (or was) reasonably available.
- You are homeless.
- Any transport difficulties.
- Excessive travelling time involved between your home and the place of work or the scheme or programme or a place mentioned in a jobseeker's direction (but see p1133 for when this does not count as a good reason).

- Unreasonably high expenses (eg, for childcare or travel) that were (or would be) unavoidable if you had taken the job or carried out the jobseeker's direction.

Account should also be taken of any other factor that appears relevant. See, in particular, p1137 for when the terms of a job on offer break the law on minimum working conditions.

Leaving a job

You may be able to show you have a good reason for leaving a job in the following situations.

- Your chances of getting other employment, including self-employment, were good, there were strong reasons for leaving your job and you acted reasonably in doing so.[193]
- You genuinely did not know or were mistaken about the conditions of the job (eg, it was beyond your physical or mental capacity, or was harmful to your health), you gave it a fair trial before leaving and it was reasonable for you to leave when you did.[194]
- You left your job for personal or domestic reasons – eg, to look after a sick relative.[195] Explain why you left your job before looking for, or getting, alternative employment. It could be helpful to show that you tried to negotiate an arrangement with your employer to resolve the problem – eg, for a reduction in your hours or time off work.
- You left your job to move with your partner who has taken a job elsewhere.[196] Relevant factors may include how important it was to your partner's career to make the move and how good your chances are of finding work in the new area.
- Your employer made a change in the terms and conditions of your employment that does not amount to your contract of employment ending. You are expected to use any grievance procedure first.
  If you leave your job because your employer cuts your wages unilaterally, you might not be able to show you have a good reason. However, a cut in pay can mean your existing contract of employment has ended and, therefore, you have been dismissed rather than having left your job.
- You left your job because of a firm offer of alternative employment, but claimed benefit because the offer fell through. However, the DWP may say you do not have a good reason if the offer was cancelled before you left your previous employment or you changed your mind and did not take the new job and you could have stayed in the existing employment, or did not ask your employer if you could stay.

The decision maker should take into account:

- any caring responsibilities you have which made it unreasonable for you to stay in your job and whether suitable childcare was (or could have been) available; *and*
- any childcare expenses you had to pay as a result of being in the job, if they amounted to an unreasonably high proportion of the income you received.

What should you do before you give up a job?

1. Do everything possible to resolve problems before you give up your job. If the conditions of a job are poor, try to sort out any problems (eg, by raising them with your employer, or using any grievance procedure) rather than leaving immediately, and to look for another job seriously before giving one up. You may have difficulty showing you have a good reason if you do not do so.

2. If all else fails or if you think that the hours you are expected to work or the amount of pay you receive is intolerable, you might decide to give up work.

Employers are required to provide certain minimum working conditions and pay the minimum wage (see Appendix 10). These could help to show that you have a good reason for giving up work. Point out that the intention of the Working Time Regulations is to protect the health and safety of workers, so conditions that do not comply with them should be regarded as unacceptable.

3. You are likely to have difficulty showing you have a good reason for leaving a job just because the pay is low. However, you can argue that this does not apply if you left your job because your employer refused to pay the national minimum wage.[197]

Leaving or failing to participate in a training scheme or employment programme

You may be able to show you have a good reason for leaving or failing to participate in a training scheme or employment programme in the following situations.

- Your continued participation would have put your health and safety at risk.
- The travelling time to or from the scheme or programme was excessive.
- You had caring responsibilities, no one else was available to provide the care, and it was not practical to make other arrangements.
- You were attending court as a party to the proceedings, a witness or a juror.
- You were arranging or attending the funeral of a close relative or a close friend.
- You had to deal with a domestic emergency.
- You were engaged in activities of benefit to the community – eg, crewing or launching a lifeboat, working as a part-time firefighter or doing work as part of an organised group for the benefit of others in an emergency.

Refusing a job

You may be able to show you have a good reason for refusing a job – eg:

- if the travelling time to or from the job was more than one hour and 30 minutes;
- if you are within your 'permitted period' (see p1041) and have restricted the type of work for which you are available to your usual occupation or to at least your usual rate of pay, or both, and you refuse a job that does not meet these conditions;
- if you have been laid off or are on short-time working, have been accepted as available only for casual employment and you refuse to take some other type of work;[198]
- if you come under the rules that exempt you from having to be able to start work immediately, and you refuse to take a job which you would have to start immediately (see p1031).

Note: you cannot be given a sanction if you refuse a job because it is vacant because of a trade dispute.[199]

What should you do before refusing a job?

Employers are required to provide certain minimum working conditions and pay the minimum wage (see Appendix 10). Try to argue that you have a good reason for not applying for any job where the terms do not comply with the legal requirements. Make sure that this is the case, particularly where the Working Time Regulations 1998 are concerned, as there are many exceptions and opt-outs that might apply. If the terms offered break the rules about the limit on the number of hours in the average working week, it is possible that the DWP might suggest that you agree to an 'individual opt-out'. Argue that this would be unreasonable, as the working time rules are intended to protect the health and safety of workers. The DWP accepts that you have a good reason for refusing a job if you do so because it does not pay at least the national minimum wage that applies to you.[200]

Special rules for 16/17-year-olds

When deciding whether you have a good reason, if you are getting JSA and you do not come under the UC system, there are special rules for 16/17-year-olds that apply to some training schemes and employment programmes, and to employment-related sanctions.

Training scheme and employment programme sanctions

If you are 16 or 17 and fail to attend, or give up a place on, a training scheme or employment programme or if you do not apply for, do not accept or 'neglect to avail' yourself of a place on one, in addition to any other ground on which you can argue you have a good reason, you have this automatically if:[201]

- it is the first time that you have acted or failed to act in a way that could lead to this type of sanction (under the normal or severe hardship payment rules); *and*
- while claiming JSA, you have never failed to pursue a training opportunity without a good reason, or to complete a training course; *and*
- you were a 'new jobseeker':
  - when you first started the scheme or programme, if a sanction is being considered because you gave up a place; *or*
  - at the time of the act or omission, if the sanction is for another reason.

New jobseeker

You are a '**new jobseeker**' if, since you left full-time education, you have:[202]

- never worked for 16 hours or more a week or done a complete training course; *or*
- never lost a place on a training scheme or employment programme because of misconduct, or (unless you had a good reason) failed to complete a training course or given up a place on a scheme or programme.

A different system of training-related sanctions applies if you are getting severe hardship payments (see p129).[203] In practice, this system adopts the same approach as above – ie, you are only given a sanction if it is the second time you have done something connected with a training scheme or employment programme that deserves a sanction, unless you lost a place on a course because of misconduct or you were not a new jobseeker at the relevant time.

Under the severe hardship sanction rules, if you fail to attend or give up a place on a training scheme, but you had a good reason for this, explain the circumstances fully to the DWP. If it is satisfied that you had a good reason, it must issue a '**certificate of good reason**' and give you a copy as proof.[204] This means that if you start getting severe hardship payments again, you are not subject to a sanction.

Employment-related sanctions

If you are 16 or 17 and have 'neglected to avail' yourself of a reasonable opportunity of a job (see p1099), or refused or failed to apply for or accept a job vacancy (see p1098), in addition to any other ground on which you can argue you have a good reason, you have an automatic good reason if your employer did not offer you suitable training (see p1039 for what counts).[205] This rule does not apply if:

- your JSA has been reduced in the past for the same reason or because you were given a training or employment scheme sanction (under the normal or the severe hardship payments rules); *or*
- your JSA has been stopped in the past because you lost a job because of misconduct (see p1097) or left a job voluntarily without a good reason (see p1097); *or*

- you are claiming under the special rules for 16/17-year-olds who are on short-time working, have been laid off or have accepted a firm offer to join the armed forces (see p129).

5. **Deciding whether you should be sanctioned**

A decision maker decides whether you should be given a sanction, often some time after the 'sanctionable action' took place. Do not presume that because you have not yet been informed of any sanction, your previous action has been excused. You should be issued with notice that you have been given a sanction automatically. This means that you should know you have been given a sanction before your benefit is paid at a reduced (or nil) rate and have a chance to contact the DWP urgently if a mistake has been made.

It is understood that 'safeguarding' procedures apply if you are considered to be 'vulnerable'. This may apply particularly where you have a serious mental health condition. The safeguarding procedures are not a legal requirement, but involve extra checks before you are given a sanction. If you think that you are vulnerable because of your condition but have been given a sanction, ask whether the safeguarding procedures were applied to you.

Note: since March 2016, the DWP has been piloting (in Scotland only) a procedure under which it warns you that it is considering whether to give you a sanction to allow you time to provide further information and evidence that you had a good reason for your actions or failure to do what was required. The DWP will review this information before deciding whether a sanction is appropriate. It is not yet known if or when this procedure will be rolled out nationally. See CPAG's online service and *Welfare Rights Bulletin* for updates.

What can you do to avoid a sanction?

1. If there is a possibility that you will be given a sanction, make sure you give full details of your side of the story. Check all the relevant sections in this chapter to work out what information and evidence you should provide.

2. If, to avoid being given a sanction, you must show you had a good reason or good cause for what you did or did not do, make sure you explain your reasons fully, and provide these in time. See p1125 and pp1133–39 for what may (or may not) count.

3. If you left or were dismissed from a job and it appears there may have been misconduct or that you left voluntarily without a good reason, your former employer is asked for a statement. You should be given an adequate chance to comment on what s/he says. Your remarks may be passed to her/him for further comments. Make sure you explain why you disagree with an allegation of misconduct or why you had a good reason for leaving your job. If you are going to an employment tribunal (eg, to claim unfair dismissal), say so. Discuss your reply with whoever is advising you on this, as you may be asked questions at the employment tribunal hearing by your former employer about what you have said.

Part 7: Work and work-related rules
Chapter 48: Sanctions
6. Challenging a sanction decision

4. If you refused to apply for or accept a job, what the potential employer says might be taken into account. Make sure you explain what enquiries you made about the nature of the job, and your reasons for not applying for or accepting it.

5. If you are taking part in a training scheme or employment programme, your scheme or programme provider must refer your case to a decision maker. Before a sanction is imposed, you should be given an adequate chance to comment on any statements made against you. Bear in mind that even if the scheme or programme provider is satisfied that you have done what was required of you, or that you had a good reason for failing to do so, the decision maker may reach a different conclusion.

6. **Challenging a sanction decision**

If you are given a sanction, your benefit is paid at a reduced rate, often for a lengthy period. It is, therefore, always worth challenging a sanction decision. You can apply for a revision or appeal against it in the usual way. However, if you do not come under the universal credit (UC) system, see p1124 for special rules about work-focused interview sanctions.

You must apply for a mandatory reconsideration before you can appeal. What you are *actually* doing is applying for a revision. You should apply within the very strict time limit for an 'any grounds' revision if you can (see p1312). Ask for the time limit to be extended if your application is late. In some cases, there is no time limit for applying for a mandatory reconsideration – ie, if you can show grounds for an 'any time' revision (see p1279). See p1281 for the specific situations in which a sanction decision can be revised at any time.

You *must* be given written notice of any decision that you can appeal, setting out your right to dispute the decision.[206] Although notification of sanction decisions is meant to happen automatically, this does not always happen. If you were given a sanction but did not receive written notice of the decision, seek advice. You may still be able to seek a mandatory reconsideration and then appeal, even if the decision was made a long time ago. You should hand in your application for a revision to the jobcentre office to ensure it is received as soon as possible. Keep a copy of your application.

Is it worth appealing?

1. An appeal to the First-tier Tribunal gives you a chance to challenge your former employer's (or the scheme or programme provider's) version of events.

2. Attend the appeal hearing if you can. Explain your case fully and, if relevant, the good reasons for what you did or failed to do (see pp1133–39).

3. Provide as much evidence as you can to support your case – eg, medical evidence or evidence about your caring responsibilities. The tribunal can allow witnesses (eg, family members or former work colleagues) to give evidence on your behalf.

Note: if you do not attend the appeal hearing and fresh allegations are made against you, the tribunal should consider an adjournment to allow you to attend or to answer the allegations in writing.

Sanction decisions you can challenge

You can challenge:
- the decision to give you a sanction – eg:
  - whether you failed to do something or did what it is alleged you did;
  - whether you have been properly notified of any requirements – eg, to attend an interview or participate in a scheme;
  - for jobseeker's allowance if you do not come under the UC system and you are given a sanction for failing to carry out a jobseeker's direction, whether the jobseeker's direction was reasonable;
  - whether you have a good reason (see p1133) or good cause (see p1125) for what you did or did not do;
- the length of the sanction period – eg, if there is a dispute about the number of times you have been sanctioned, or you are challenging a previous decision to give you a sanction.

If you have been given a sanction more than once, you should challenge *all* the decisions if possible. Apply for a mandatory reconsideration of all the sanction decisions, asking for the time limit for doing so to be extended if relevant.

If a previous sanction is removed (eg, by a decision maker or the First-tier Tribunal), the sanction period for a later sanction should be reduced.[207] If you have appealed against the later sanction, the tribunal should take the removal of the previous sanction into account.[208]

Further information about challenging sanction decisions is on *Ask CPAG Online* at www.cpag.org.uk/askcpag.

Notes

1. Jobseeker's allowance sanctions
1 Reg 75(5) JSA Regs
2 Reg 2(3)(a) HB Regs; reg 2(3)(a) HB(SPC) Regs
3 ss19(1), 19A(1) and 19B(1-(3) JSA 1995; reg 70 JSA Regs
4 ss19(7), 19A(10) and 19B(8) JSA 1995
5 Reg 70(2) JSA Regs
6 Regs 69(6), 69A(3) and 69B(8) JSA Regs
7 Reg 68 JSA Regs
8 ss16(3)(b), 17(3) and 20(2)(b) JSA 1995; reg 63 JSA Regs

9 Regs 63(1) and (3) and 68(1) and (2) JSA Regs
10 Reg 70C JSA Regs
11 Reg 70C(1)(e) JSA Regs
12 Reg 70C(4) JSA Regs
13 Reg 75(4) JSA Regs
14 s19(2) JSA 1995; reg 70B JSA Regs
15 Reg 75(4) JSA Regs
16 CJSA/3304/1999
17 s19(2)(a) JSA 1995
18 R(U) 10/71; R(U) 2/76
19 Vol 6 Ch 34, paras 34415-18 and 34743 DMG
20 s19(2)(b) JSA 1995
21 Vol 6 Ch 34, paras 34415-18 and 34743 DMG
22 s19(2)(c) JSA 1995
23 *MT v SSWP (JSA)* [2016] UKUT 72 (AAC)
24 Vol 6 Ch 34, paras 34728-29 DMG
25 s20(1) JSA 1995
26 Vol 6 Ch 34, paras 34415-18, 34335-38 and 34743 DMG
27 Vol 6 Ch 34, para 34732 DMG; CJSA/ 2082/2002; CJSA/2692/1999
28 s19(2)(d) JSA 1995
29 *MT v SSWP (JSA)* [2016] UKUT 72 (AAC)
30 s20(1) JSA 1995
31 s20(3) JSA 1995
32 Reg 74(4) JSA Regs
33 Vol 6 Ch 34, para 34704 DMG
34 Reg 75(3) JSA Regs
35 Reg 74 JSA Regs
36 Reg 1(3), definition of 'full-time student', JSA Regs
37 Reg 69(1) and (2) JSA Regs
38 Reg 69(3) JSA Regs
39 Reg 3(6) SS&CS(DA) Regs
40 CJSA/2375/2000
41 Reg 69(4) JSA Regs
42 Reg 69(5) JSA Regs
43 Reg 70A(1) JSA Regs
44 Reg 69(6) JSA Regs
45 s19A(2) JSA 1995
46 Regs 23 and 23A JSA Regs
47 s19A(2)(a) JSA 1995; reg 70A(2)-(4) JSA Regs
48 s19A(2)(b) JSA 1995
49 Reg 5 JSA(SAPOE) Regs
50 *R (Reilly and Another) v SSWP* [2013] UKSC 68; [2014] AACR 9; *SSWP v TJ (JSA)* [2015] UKUT 56 (AAC). *SSWP v TJ* was appealed in *Reilly and Hewstone and Jeffrey & Bevan v SSWP* [2016] EWCA Civ 413 and the court upheld this aspect of the decision.
51 *Reilly and Hewstone and Jeffrey & Bevan v Secretary of State for Work and Pensions* [2016] EWCA Civ 413

52 *PL v SSWP (JSA)* [2013] UKUT 227 (AAC); *DD v SSWP (JSA)* [2015] UKUT 318 (AAC)
53 Reg 17 JSA(SAPOE) Regs
54 Reg 3 JSA(SAPOE) Regs
55 Vol 6 Ch 34, para 34852 DMG
56 s19A(2)(d)-(g) JSA 1995
57 R(JSA) 2/06
58 Reg 75(1)(b) JSA Regs
59 Reg 75(1)(a) JSA Regs
60 s19A(2)(c) JSA 1995
61 s19A(11) JSA 1995
62 *DM v SSWP (JSA)* [2015] UKUT 67 (AAC)
63 *SA v SSWP (JSA)* [2015] UKUT 454 (AAC)
64 Reg 69A(1) and (2) JSA Regs
65 Reg 3(6) SS&CS(DA) Regs
66 CJSA/2375/2000
67 Reg 69A(3) JSA Regs
68 s19B JSA 1995; reg 69B JSA Regs
69 Vol 6 Ch 34, paras 34121 and 34186 DMG
70 Reg 69B(5) JSA Regs
71 Reg 69B(6) JSA Regs
72 s19B(5) JSA 1995
73 Reg 3(6) SS&CS(DA) Regs
74 CJSA/2375/2000
75 Reg 69B(7) JSA Regs
76 Reg 69B(8) JSA Regs

2. Universal credit system sanctions

77 **UC** Reg 100(1) UC Regs
    JSA Reg 17 JSA Regs 2013
    ESA Reg 50 ESA Regs 2013
78 **UC** Reg 101(1)-(3) UC Regs
    JSA Reg 18(1)-(3) JSA Regs 2013
    ESA Reg 51(1)-(3) ESA Regs 2013
79 **UC** Reg 106(c) UC Regs
    JSA Reg 22(c() JSA Regs 2013
    ESA Reg 54(c) ESA Regs 2013
80 **UC** Regs 101(5) and 110 UC Regs
    JSA Regs 17 and 26 JSA Regs 2013
    ESA Regs 50 and 58 ESA Regs 2013
81 Reg 111(1) UC Regs
82 Reg 111(2) UC Regs
83 Reg 111(5) UC Regs
84 Reg 111(3) UC Regs
85 Reg 111(4) UC Regs
86 Reg 27 JSA Regs 2013
87 Reg 59 ESA Regs 2013
88 Reg 60(1) ESA Regs 2013
89 Reg 60(2) ESA Regs 2013
90 **UC** Reg 106 UC Regs
    JSA Reg 22 JSA Regs 2013
    ESA Reg 54 ESA Regs 2013
91 **UC** Reg 107(1) UC Regs
    JSA Reg 23(1) JSA Regs 2013
    ESA Reg 55(1) ESA Regs 2013

92 **UC** Reg 107(2) UC Regs
JSA Reg 23(2) and (3) JSA Regs 2013
ESA Reg 55(2) and (3) ESA Regs 2013

93 **UC** Reg 108 UC Regs
JSA Reg 24 JSA Regs 2013
ESA Reg 56 ESA Regs 2013

94 Art 20 WRA(No.9)O; reg 34 UC(TP) Regs

95 **UC** Reg 112 and Sch 11 paras 1 and 2 UC Regs
JSA Reg 6 JSA Regs 2013
ESA Reg 43 ESA Regs 2013

96 **JSA** Reg 30 JSA Regs 2013
ESA Reg 61 ESA Regs 2013

97 Arts 14, 15, 17 and 18 WRA(No.9)O

98 Regs 30 and 32 UC(TP) Regs

99 **UC** Reg 109 UC Regs
JSA Reg 25 JSA Regs 2013
ESA Reg 57 ESA Regs 2013

100 **UC** s26 WRA 2012; reg 114 UC Regs
JSA s6J JSA 1995; reg 29 JSA Regs 2013

101 **UC** s26(2)(b) and (c) and (4)(a) WRA 2012; reg 113(1)(e) UC Regs
JSA s6J(2)(b) and (c) and (3)(a) JSA 1995; reg 28(1)(c) JSA Regs 2013

102 **UC** Reg 113(1)(a) UC Regs
JSA Reg 28(1)(a) JSA Regs 2013

103 R(IS) 5/95; *Fiory v CAO*, 20 June 1995

104 para K3057 ADM

105 **UC** Reg 97(3) UC Regs
JSA Reg 14(2) JSA Regs 2013

106 paras K3271-K3275 ADM

107 **UC** s26(2)(d), (3) and (4) WRA 2012; reg 113(1)(e) UC Regs
JSA s6J(2)(d) and (3) JSA 1995; reg 28(1)(c) JSA Regs 2013

108 R(U) 10/71; R(U) 2/76

109 Reg 113(1)(g) UC Regs

110 **UC** Reg 113(1)(b)-(d) and (f) and (2) UC Regs
JSA Reg 28(1)(b) and (d)-(f) and (2) JSA Regs 2013

111 para K3213 ADM

112 s148 Employment Rights Act 1996

113 **UC** Regs 102(2)(a) and 112 and Sch 11 para 3 UC Regs
JSA Reg 19 JSA Regs 2013

114 Reg 102(2)(b) UC Regs

115 **UC** Sch 11 para 3 UC Regs
JSA Reg 19 JSA Regs 2013

116 **UC** Reg 102(3) and (5) UC Regs
JSA Regs 17 and 19(2) JSA Regs 2013

117 Reg 33 UC(TP) Regs; Arts 17-19 WRA(No.9)O

118 Reg 14 UC,PIP,JSA&ESA(DA) Regs

119 CJSA/2375/2000

120 **UC** Reg 102(4) and (5) UC Regs
JSA Regs 17 and 19(3) JSA Regs 2013

121 **UC** Reg 113(1)(e) UC Regs
JSA Reg 28(1)(c) JSA Regs 2013

122 **UC** s27 WRA 2012; reg 103(1) UC Regs
JSA s6K JSA 1995; reg 17 JSA Regs 2013

123 **UC** Regs 103(2)(a) and 112 and Sch 11 para 3 UC Regs
JSA Reg 20 JSA Regs 2013

124 Reg 103(2)(b) UC Regs

125 **UC** Sch 11 para 3 UC Regs
JSA Reg 20 JSA Regs 2013

126 Reg 33 UC(TP) Regs; Arts 17-19 WRA(No.9)O

127 Reg 14 UC,PIP,JSA&ESA(DA) Regs

128 CJSA/2375/2000

129 **UC** s27 WRA 2012; reg 104(1) UC Regs
JSA s6K JSA 1995; reg 17 JSA Regs 2013
ESA s11J WRA 2007; reg 50 ESA Regs 2013

130 **UC** Reg 104(2)(a) and (3)(a) UC Regs
JSA Reg 21(2) JSA Regs 2013
ESA Reg 52(a) ESA Regs 2013

131 **UC** s27(6) and (7) WRA 2012
JSA s6K(6) and (7) JSA 1995
ESA s11J(5) and (6) WRA 2007

132 **UC** Regs 104(2)(b) and 112 and Sch 11 para 3 UC Regs
JSA Reg 21(3) JSA Regs 2013
ESA Reg 52(b) ESA Regs 2013

133 Reg 104(3)(b) UC Regs

134 **UC** Sch 11 para 3 UC Regs
JSA Reg 21 JSA Regs 2013
ESA Regs 50 and 52 ESA Regs 2013

135 Regs 31 and 33 UC(TP) Regs; Arts 16-19 WRA(No.9)O

136 Reg 14 UC,PIP,JSA&ESA(DA) Regs

137 CJSA/2375/2000

138 **UC** s27 WRA 2012; reg 105 UC Regs
ESA s11J WRA 2007; reg 50 ESA Regs 2013

139 **UC** Reg 105(2) UC Regs
ESA Reg 53 ESA Regs 2013

3. Other benefit sanctions

140 There is no specific appeal provision, but the DWP confirmed there is a normal right of appeal against such a decision in an email to CPAG, 21 January 2008.

141 s2B SSAA 1992; Sch 2 para 5A SSA 1998; reg 15 SS(JPI) Regs; reg 9 SS(WFLIP) Regs; reg 10 SS(IBWFI) Regs; reg 14 SS(JPIP) Regs

142 Reg 14 SS(JPIP) Regs

143 Reg 10(3) SS(JPIP) Regs

144 Reg 61(1) ESA Regs; reg 8(1) SS(IBWFI) Regs; reg 11(4) SS(JPI) Regs; reg 7(1)(b) SS(WFILP) Regs

145 *DL v SSWP (JSA)* [2013] UKUT 295 (AAC)

146 Reg 12(12) SS(JPI) Regs; reg 7(2) SS(WFILP) Regs; reg 9(11) SS(IBWFI) Regs; reg 11(11) SS(JPIP) Regs
147 Email from DWP to CPAG, 21 January 2008
148 Reg 8 SS(IBWFI) Regs; reg 13 SS(JPIP) Regs; reg 7(5) SS(WFILP) Regs; reg 14 SS(JPI) Regs
149 Vol 9 Ch 53, paras 53029 and 53052-53 DMG
150 Reg 63 ESA Regs
151 Reg 9 SS(IBWFI) Regs
152 Reg 12(2)(c)-(7) SS(JPI) Regs; reg 8 SS(WFILP) Regs
153 Reg 11 SS(JPIP) Regs
154 Reg 11(4) SS(JPIP) Regs
155 Reg 12A SS(JPI) Regs; reg 7(5A) and (5B) SS(WFILP) Regs
156 Reg 63(6)-(11) ESA Regs
157 Reg 64(2) ESA Regs
158 Reg 3(5C) and (6A) SS&CS(DA) Regs
159 CJSA/2375/2000
160 Regs 12(9), (9A) and (12) and 13 SS(JPI) Regs; reg 9(8) and (11) SS(IBWFI) Regs; regs 7(2) and 8(3) and (4) SS(WFILP) Regs; regs 11(9) and (11) and 12 SS(JPIP) Regs
161 Reg 12 SS(JPIP) Regs
162 Reg 8(1) ESA(WRA) Regs; reg 6(1) IS(WRA) Regs; *DL v SSWP (JSA)* [2013] UKUT 295 (AAC)
163 Reg 6(3) IS(WRA) Regs
164 **IS** Regs 2(3)(a) and 4 IS(WRA) Regs
ESA Regs 3(4)(a) and 6 ESA(WRA) Regs
All *LM v SSWP (ESA)* [2016] UKUT 360 (AAC)
165 **IS** Reg 8 IS(WRA) Regs
ESA Reg 8 ESA(WRA) Regs; regs 63 and 64 ESA Regs
166 Reg 7 IS(WRA) Regs
167 Reg 8(4) IS(WRA) Regs
168 Reg 63(6)-(11) ESA Regs
169 Reg 64(1)(b) and (c) ESA Regs
170 Reg 9 IS(WRA) Regs

4. Common rules
171 Vol 6 Ch 34, para 34653 DMG; para K3203 ADM
172 Vol 6 Ch 34, para 34676 DMG; para K3236 ADM
173 **JSA** s19(3) JSA 1995; reg 71 JSA Regs; R(U) 3/91
UC/JSA under UC Reg 113(1)(f) UC Regs; reg 28(1)(f) and (2) JSA Regs 2013
174 R(U) 25/52
175 R(U) 26/51; R(U) 20/64; R(U) 4/70; R(U) 1/81
176 R(U) 3/81

177 R(U) 8/57, para 6
178 R(U) 26/56; R(U) 1/58
179 R(U) 10/53
180 R(U) 14/56
181 *AA v SSWP (JSA)* [2012] UKUT 100 (AAC); [2012] AACR 42
182 R(U) 24/56
183 R(U) 1/57; R(U) 14/57; CU/34/1992
184 R(U) 2/76
185 R(U) 2/74
186 R(U) 10/54
187 Vol 6 Ch 34, paras 34200-506 DMG; Ch K2 ADM
188 paras K2011-14 ADM
189 Reg 72 JSA Regs
190 **UC** Reg 97(3) UC Regs
JSA Reg 14(2) JSA Regs 2013
191 *HS v SSWP* [2009] UKUT 177 (AAC); [2010] AACR 10
192 R(JSA) 7/03 discusses the meaning of 'conscientious objection' in this context.
193 R(U) 4/73
194 R(U) 3/73
195 R(U) 14/52
196 R(U) 19/52; R(U) 4/87; CJSA/2507/2005
197 Vol 6 Ch 34, para 34443 DMG; para K2238 ADM
198 paras K2175-76 ADM
199 **JSA** s21(1) JSA 1995
UC/JSA under UC Reg 113(1)(a) UC Regs; reg 28(1)(a) JSA Regs 2013
200 Vol 6 Ch 34, para 34423 DMG; para K2213 ADM
201 Reg 67(1) JSA Regs
202 Reg 67(3) JSA Regs
203 ss16(3)(b), 17(1), (1A) and (3) and 20(2)(b) JSA 1995; reg 63 JSA Regs
204 s17(4) JSA 1995
205 Reg 67(2) JSA Regs

6. Challenging a sanction decision
206 **UC/JSA&ESA under UC** Reg 51 UC, PIP, JSA&ESA(DA) Regs
Other benefits Regs 3ZA and 28 SS&CS(DA) Regs
207 Reg 3(6) SS&CS(DA) Regs
208 CJSA/2375/2000

Part 8

Claiming benefits and getting paid

Chapter 49

Claims and decisions

This chapter covers:
1. Making a claim (below)
2. Who should claim (p1149)
3. Information to support your claim (p1150)
4. The date of your claim (p1155)
5. Decisions (p1162)

This chapter covers the general rules on claims, backdating and decisions. See the chapter about the benefit you are claiming for the specific rules about that benefit. This chapter does not cover the rules for tax credits (see Chapter 61), statutory sick pay (see Chapter 38), statutory maternity, adoption, paternity and shared parental pay (see Chapter 37), social fund budgeting loans (see p784), health benefits (see Chapter 29), the other payments in Chapter 39, or discretionary housing payments (see Chapter 21). Generally, the rules for housing benefit (HB) are not covered (see Chapter 4), although the national insurance number requirement described in this chapter also applies to HB.

Key facts
- To be entitled to a benefit, you must usually make a claim for it.
- Depending on the benefit, you may be able to claim by telephone, online, on a paper claim form or in person.
- You must usually provide your national insurance number and any other evidence considered reasonable.
- Once you have made a valid claim, a decision must be made by a decision maker at the DWP or HM Revenue and Customs.
- If you want more information about a decision, you can ask for an explanation.

1. Making a claim

In most cases, to be entitled to benefit, you must make a claim for it.[1] If you cannot claim for yourself, an 'appointee' can claim on your behalf (see p1149).

Part 8: Claiming benefits and getting paid
Chapter 49: Claims and decisions
1. Making a claim

How to make a claim

Each benefit has its own rules for how to make a claim and the ways you can do so. See the chapter in this *Handbook* about the benefit you want to claim. In general, you may be able to claim in writing, including online, or by telephone. You may also have to attend an interview to complete your claim, or be sent a written statement to sign and return.

The DWP may encourage you to start your claim online or by telephone. Universal credit (UC) must normally be claimed online, but you may be able to get help if claiming online is difficult for you (see p169).

Child benefit and guardian's allowance are normally claimed in writing. If you need help with the form, you can ask for a visit from HM Revenue and Customs (HMRC), usually by contacting the helpline (see Appendix 1).[2]

Is a telephone or online claim impractical or impossible for you?

If starting a claim by telephone or online is difficult for you, explain this and ask to claim in a different way. For example:
– if speaking in English is difficult, an interpreter can be arranged;
– another person may be able to phone on your behalf, especially if you are there to help;
– if you cannot claim by telephone, you may be able to claim online;
– if you cannot claim by telephone or online, a face-to-face interview could take place at a local Jobcentre Plus office;
– a home visit could be arranged;
– you may be able to claim in person at an 'alternative office' (see below);
– except for UC, a claim form could be completed and sent.

Alternative offices

The DWP has made arrangements to enable you to get help to claim some benefits from an 'alternative office'. You can claim carer's allowance, disability living allowance, income support, employment and support allowance (ESA), pension credit (PC) and retirement pension at an alternative office. If you are over the qualifying age for PC (see p147), you can also claim attendance allowance, bereavement benefits and winter fuel payment at these offices.[3] **Note:** you cannot claim contributory ESA in this way if you come under the UC system (see p20).

Alternative offices[4]

'**Alternative offices**' may include designated DWP offices, designated local authority housing benefit offices and some English county councils. Also included are some local advice centres. If you want to claim at an alternative office, ask whether it has been designated to accept your claim.

Amending or withdrawing your claim

You can amend your claim at any time before a decision is made by writing to the office handling it.[5] In some circumstances, your claim may be treated as having been amended from the date it was originally made. For example, if you claimed ESA but did not request that it be backdated, you can amend your claim to include this and your request should be treated as having been made at the date of your claim. However, if you amend your claim to say that since you claimed, a partner has moved in with you, this amendment only takes effect from the date s/he moved in.

You can withdraw your claim at any time before a decision is made by writing to the office handling it.[6] Notice to withdraw your claim takes effect from the day it is received.

You can also amend or withdraw your claim online if you do so in an approved way.[7]

For benefits other than child benefit and guardian's allowance, you can also amend or withdraw your claim by phoning the DWP office handling it or by any other method of notification that is accepted in your particular case.

In practice, you should also be able to withdraw a claim for a benefit you have already been awarded and your award will be superseded (see p1287), as you should not be forced to continue receiving benefit when you have indicated that you no longer wish to do so.[8]

2. Who should claim

The general rule is that a claim must be made by you, the claimant. For most means-tested benefits, although you usually receive an extra amount because you have a partner, your partner is not a claimant and does not have to make the claim with you. The chapters on individual benefits explain who must make the claim for each benefit.

Appointees

Someone else (eg, a friend or relative) can be authorised to act on your behalf if s/he is aged at least 18 and you cannot claim for yourself – eg, if you have a mental illness or a learning disability.[9] S/he is called an 'appointee'. The appointee takes on your rights and responsibilities as a claimant – eg, s/he must notify changes in your circumstances. Normally, this applies from the date of the appointment, but if someone acts on your behalf and later becomes your appointee, these actions can be validated in retrospect.[10] Someone must normally apply to be an appointee in writing. If you are an appointee for a claimant who dies, you should reapply for appointee status to settle any outstanding benefit matters.[11] An executor of a will

Part 8: Claiming benefits and getting paid
Chapter 49: Claims and decisions
3. Information to support your claim

can pursue an outstanding claim or appeal on behalf of a claimant who has died, even if the decision was made before probate is granted.[12]

Note: if someone is your appointee for housing benefit purposes, the DWP can make her/him an appointee without a written application if s/he agrees to this.[13]

3. **Information to support your claim**

When you claim benefit, you must:
- satisfy the national insurance (NI) number requirement (see below);
- prove your identity, if required (see p1151); *and*
- provide sufficient information to ensure your claim is valid (see p1152).

If you claim in the right way (see p1148) and satisfy the above criteria, you have made a 'valid claim'. It is important that you make a valid claim as it affects your 'date of claim' (see p1155).

If your claim is accepted as valid, it is then referred to a decision maker to decide whether you are entitled to benefit (see p1162).

Note: even if your claim is accepted as valid, you can be asked for additional information and evidence before a decision is made on it (see p1154).

If your claim is not accepted as valid, you should be given a decision saying so. You can appeal against this.[14] You must apply for a mandatory reconsideration first (see p1311).

The national insurance number requirement

You must usually satisfy the NI number requirement by:[15]
- providing an NI number and information or evidence showing it is yours; *or*
- providing evidence or information to enable your NI number to be traced, if you do not know it; *or*
- applying for an NI number if you do not have one and providing sufficient information and evidence to allow one to be allocated. This does not necessarily mean that you must be allocated an NI number. In general, you have done enough if you have supplied all the information that you could reasonably have been expected to with your application.[16]

If you are claiming a means-tested benefit, your partner must usually also satisfy the NI number requirement (but see p1151).[17] This also applies if you are getting benefit and your partner has started living with you and so your benefit award must be superseded.[18]

Note:
- If you do not need to make a claim for the benefit (eg, in some circumstances for retirement pension or bereavement payment), the NI number requirement should not apply.

- If you cannot satisfy the NI number requirement straight away, you may be able to ask for a short-term advance of benefit (see p1177).
- If you are refused benefit because you do not satisfy the NI number requirement, you can ask for a mandatory reconsideration of the decision, and then appeal if the decision is not changed.[19]

Who is exempt

You are exempt from the NI number requirement if the benefit is:
- disability living allowance and you are under 16;[20]
- housing benefit (HB) and you live in a hostel.[21]

If a child (including a qualifying young person – see p572) is included in your claim for universal credit (UC) or HB, or can still be included in your award of income support (IS) or income-based jobseeker's allowance (JSA – see p220), s/he is exempt from the NI number requirement.[22] If you are claiming a means-tested benefit as a couple (see p215) and your partner is a 'person subject to immigration control', s/he could be exempt from the NI number requirement in some situations (see p1525).

Proof of identity

You may be asked to produce further documents or evidence that prove your identity. If you are claiming for your partner, you must also prove her/his identity.

You can prove your identity with a passport, an identity card issued by a European Economic Area state, or a letter from the Home Office. You could also produce your birth certificate, driving licence, a travel pass with a photograph, a local council rent card or tenancy agreement, or even paid fuel or telephone bills.

Note:
- Provide details of any other people who can confirm what you have stated – eg, your solicitor or other legal representative or official organisation.
- You should not be refused benefit simply because you do not have a document, especially if it is unreasonable for you to have or obtain it. Ask the decision maker to make a decision on your claim. You can then appeal (you must apply for a mandatory reconsideration first – see p1311).

In some cases, the available evidence that you are who you say you are may not be accepted. Some claimants may have particular difficulty getting evidence. Ask for an explanation of exactly what is required and why. Complain if you consider any requests for information are unreasonable (see Chapter 58). If you think you have experienced discrimination, get advice – eg, from the Equality Advisory and Support Service.[23]

Part 8: Claiming benefits and getting paid
Chapter 49: Claims and decisions
3. Information to support your claim

Providing sufficient information

Before making a decision on whether you are entitled to benefit, the decision maker can ask you to provide further information or evidence to support your claim, including proof of your identity (see p1151). You must provide sufficient information to ensure your claim is valid.

You must normally attend an interview for a JSA claim to be valid (see below).

For other benefits, or for JSA if you do not have to attend an interview, if you claimed by telephone, see below. If you claimed in writing, see below.

Note: if you claim UC, you may be required to agree your claimant commitment at an interview (see p1071).

Claims for jobseeker's allowance if you must attend an interview

In order for your JSA claim to be valid, you must usually attend an interview at a Jobcentre Plus office. Your claim is then treated as having been made on the date you first notified your intention to claim, or the first date you are claiming for if this is later.[24]

If you fail to attend the interview without good cause or do not submit a properly completed form at or before the interview, you are treated as not having made a valid claim until the date you do so. The DWP has the discretion to allow you up to one month from the date you first notified your intention to claim to rectify the situation.[25]

Claims by telephone

A claim made by telephone is valid if you provide all the information needed during the phone call. If you do not do this, your claim is 'defective'. You are given a chance to remedy the defect.[26] For employment and support allowance (ESA) and pension credit only, you must also approve a written statement of your circumstances if asked to.[27]

For IS, and JSA if you do not come under the UC system (see p20) and do not have to attend an interview to complete your claim, you must supply the necessary information within a month of first notifying your intention to make a claim.[28]

For other benefits (and contribution-based JSA if you come under the UC system), if you supply the necessary information within a month of the date you are first notified of the defect, your claim is treated as having been made when you first notified your intention to claim. The decision maker can extend this one-month period if s/he thinks it is reasonable.[29]

Claims in writing or online

Note: different rules apply to IS claims, and to JSA claims if you do not come under the UC system (see p1153).

For other benefits, if you initially made your claim in writing on the approved form (this includes claiming online if you are able to do so for the particular benefit), it is valid if it is completed in accordance with the instructions on the form. If you do not do this, your claim is defective. You should be given a chance to remedy the defect.[30] If you supply the necessary information within one month of the date you are first notified of the defect, your claim is treated as having been made when it was first received. The decision maker can extend this one-month period if s/he thinks it is reasonable.[31]

Note: if you claim online, the system may not allow you to submit a claim if essential information is not entered. If your claim is not accepted, you should try to claim in another way as soon as you can, otherwise you may lose benefit.[32]

To be valid, written claims for UC, JSA, ESA, IS and personal independence payment (PIP) *must* be made on an approved form (there is no paper claim form for UC, so claims must be made online).[33] For other benefits, any letter or other written communication may be treated as being a valid claim for benefit.[34] In practice, if you make a written claim that is not on the approved form, you are likely to be sent it to complete. If you properly complete and return the form within one month (or longer, if the decision maker considers it reasonable) of its being sent to you, you count as having made a valid claim on the date of your first letter or other written communication.[35]

Written claims for income support and jobseeker's allowance

Unless you come under the UC system (see p20) or you are exempt (see below), a written claim for IS or JSA is not valid unless you:[36]

- claim on the approved form;
- complete the claim form according to the instructions; *and*
- produce all the information and evidence required by the claim form.

This is known as the **evidence requirement** or 'onus of proof' rule.

If you do not meet the evidence requirement, the DWP must notify you that your claim is defective and contact you to put things right. If you complete the form and return it within one month, along with any necessary information or evidence, your claim is treated as having been made on the date you first notified your intention to claim.[37]

You are exempt from the evidence requirement if the information or evidence required does not exist, or it is not reasonably practicable for you to meet the requirement because:[38]

- you have a disability, and you cannot find someone to help you complete the form or get the proof. You can argue that someone else is not expected to proactively offer you help;[39]
- you cannot get evidence without serious risk of harm;
- you can only get evidence from a third party;
- there is sufficient evidence that you are not entitled (eg, because your capital or income is too high), so it is inappropriate to require further information.

Part 8: Claiming benefits and getting paid
Chapter 49: Claims and decisions
3. Information to support your claim

If you cannot complete the form or provide the required information or evidence for one of the reasons listed above, tell the office handling your claim as soon as possible. Ideally, explain your circumstances on the claim form or by telephoning the office. You can provide supporting letters – eg, from a social worker or a solicitor. If the DWP exempts you from the evidence requirement, it might:

- help you to fill in the form or give you longer to complete it; *or*
- collect evidence or information on your behalf; *or*
- tell you that you do not have to provide the information.

The decision maker can ask you for further information or evidence even after s/he has accepted your claim as valid (see below).

Further information to support your claim

Even if your claim has been accepted as valid, you may still be required to provide additional documentation and evidence.[40] Provided you have made a valid claim, your date of claim should not be affected if you fail to do so.[41]

If you must travel to provide the evidence, you may be able to claim your travelling expenses.[42]

You must provide the information or evidence within one month of the request, or within seven days of the request for JSA. A decision maker can allow you longer than this if it is reasonable. If you do not provide the information, adverse conclusions are likely to be drawn and your claim decided on that basis. In some circumstances, decisions must be made in a certain way if the required information is not available (see p1163).

It is best to send evidence and documents to the office handling your claim. For some benefits, a designated local authority, English county council or other 'alternative office' (see p1148) may also be able to accept evidence and documents. If a local authority has used information on your claim for HB and has passed it to the DWP because it is relevant to your claim for another benefit, in most cases the DWP must use that information without checking it further.[43]

If you are asked to provide evidence which you do not have, ask what other evidence would be acceptable. Ask what is required and why, and complain (see Chapter 58) if you think any requests for information are unreasonable. Ask for a decision to be made on your claim. You can appeal against this decision.[44] You must apply for a mandatory reconsideration first (see p1311).

Contacting the benefit office

1. Writing to the DWP or HMRC is the best way to have your case dealt with. It ensures there is a record of what you said and enables you to cover all the points you want to make.

2. Always keep a copy of the letters, forms and other documents you send, as well as copies of those sent to you. This may help you or your adviser to challenge decisions.

3. It is often necessary to telephone the DWP or HMRC. If you do this, make a note of the date and what is said. If the information is important, follow up the phone call with a letter confirming what was said.

4. If you need to visit an office (eg, because your case cannot be dealt with by telephone) and you cannot get there (eg, because of your age, health or a disability), an officer may be able to make a home visit. If you are refused a visit and are not satisfied with the reason you are given, ask to speak to a supervisor or the customer services manager.

Note:

- If your claim involves medical issues, you may have to provide evidence in the form of a questionnaire. In most cases, the decision maker can refer you to a 'healthcare professional' or, for PIP only, a 'health professional' (see below) for an examination and/or a report. If you fail to have an examination and are not accepted as having 'good cause' or 'good reason', your claim will be decided against you.[45] See the chapter in this *Handbook* about the benefit that you have claimed for more details.
- NI contribution issues can be referred to HMRC.

Healthcare professionals and health professionals

A **'healthcare professional'** is a registered medical practitioner (eg, a doctor), registered nurse, or registered occupational therapist or physiotherapist, or for disability living allowance mobility component for a severe visual impairment only, a registered optometrist or orthoptist.[46]

The rules for who counts as a **'health professional'** for PIP are not set out in regulations. Guidance states that paramedics are included, along with doctors, registered nurses, occupational therapists and physiotherapists.[47]

4. The date of your claim

Usually, your date of claim is the date on which a valid claim (see p1150) is received by the DWP, HM Revenue and Customs (HMRC) or local authority. Once a decision is made that you are entitled to benefit, the date from when it is awarded, and the date from when you are paid, is determined by the date of claim. Check the relevant chapter for the specific rules about the date of claim for that benefit and the date from when you are paid.

The date of claim is earlier than the date a valid claim is made if:

- your claim is 'backdated' (see p1156);
- the claim you made for one benefit is treated as a claim for a different benefit instead (see p1161).

Part 8: Claiming benefits and getting paid
Chapter 49: Claims and decisions
4. The date of your claim

In some situations, you may be able to claim a benefit in advance. See the relevant chapter for the specific rules on on the benefit you want to claim.

Backdating your claim

In general, you should claim benefit as soon as you think you qualify. There are strict time limits for making a claim.[48] If you miss the time limit, you may be able to have your claim backdated. If you want your claim to be backdated, you must ask for this to happen, otherwise, except for bereavement support payment, it is not considered.[49]

If you have not asked for backdating, you can ask for your claim to be amended to include backdating before a decision on it is made (see p1149). If a decision has been made on your claim, in order to have a request for backdating considered, you must make a new claim for the past period – your request for backdating runs from when you make this new claim.

The rules for backdating are different, depending on your circumstances and the benefit you have claimed.

- Claims for attendance allowance (AA), disability living allowance (DLA) and personal independence payment (PIP) can never be backdated.[50]
- Claims for some benefits can be backdated without special reasons (see below).
- Claims for income support (IS) and jobseeker's allowance (JSA) can only be backdated in limited circumstances (see p1157).
- For the universal credit (UC) backdating rules, see p172.
- The backdating period is longer for some benefits if you are reclaiming following an award of a 'qualifying benefit' (see p1160).
- Special rules apply if you are reclaiming backdated JSA after your JSA stopped when you failed to attend an interview or sign on (see p1058).

If you are prevented from receiving backdated benefit because of an error of the DWP or, in child benefit and guardian's allowance cases, HMRC, write and request compensation (see p1396). The intervention of an MP or the Ombudsman (see p1401) may help. If you satisfy the conditions for getting benefit, it should be paid from your date of claim, even if backdating is refused. If backdating is refused, you can appeal. You must apply for a mandatory reconsideration first (see p1311). Payment should not be held up because you are challenging a decision on backdating.

Benefits that can be backdated without special reasons

Claims for some benefits can be backdated for up to three months, regardless of the reason why you did not claim earlier. State pension and bereavement payment (but see p548 if you are over pension age) can be backdated for up to 12 months without needing to have special reasons.[51] If you want benefit for a period before the date you make your claim, you must show that you would have qualified for the benefit had you claimed at the time. The benefits that can be backdated without special reasons are:

- bereavement benefits (see p548);
- carer's allowance (CA – see p565);
- child benefit (see p588);
- contributory and income-related (employment and support allowance (ESA – see p650);
- guardian's allowance (see p588);
- industrial injuries benefits (see p692);
- maternity allowance (MA – see p730);
- pension credit (PC – see p154);
- retirement pension (see p780).

Note: also included are incapacity benefit (IB), and increases to IB and severe disablement allowance for an adult. See Chapter 31 of the 2013/14 edition of this *Handbook* for details of the very limited circumstances in which claims for these can still be made.

There are exceptions to the rules.

- The time limit for claiming a bereavement payment can be extended in some cases – eg, when you did not know your partner had died (see p549).
- If you are claiming backdated child benefit or guardian's allowance after being awarded refugee status, see p1528.
- If you miss the time limit to claim disablement benefit for occupational deafness or occupational asthma (see p680) or, if you must claim to qualify, bereavement payment (see p537), you may lose your right to benefit altogether.

Backdating income support and jobseeker's allowance

Your IS or JSA claim can be backdated for up to one or three months in some circumstances, if these circumstances mean you could not reasonably claim sooner. It is important to explain why you are claiming late. In some cases, your claim can be backdated for longer periods after an award of a qualifying benefit (see p1160).

Why are you claiming late?

1. If you can, provide evidence or information that backs up why you are making a late claim – eg, a copy of the letter from your adviser or information from your employer which misled you (see p1159).

2. If you have been misled, misinformed or given insufficient advice by an officer of the DWP, explain how and when this happened and, where possible, give the name and a description of the officer concerned.

3. If relevant, explain why there was no one else who could have helped you to claim.

Part 8: Claiming benefits and getting paid
Chapter 49: Claims and decisions
4. The date of your claim

If a person has been formally appointed by a court or the DWP to act on your behalf, your appointee (see p1149), not you, must show that it was not reasonable to expect her/him to claim sooner than s/he did.[52]

If someone is informally acting on your behalf, you must show that s/he was acting for you. You must also show that it was reasonable for you to delegate responsibility for your claim and that you took care to ensure that the person helping you claimed properly.[53]

One month's backdating

The decision maker must backdate your claim for up to one month if one or more of the following applies (or has applied), and because of this you could not reasonably have been expected to make your claim any earlier.[54]

- The office where you were supposed to claim was closed (eg, because of a strike) and there were no other arrangements for claims to be made.
- You could not get to the DWP office because there were difficulties with the type of transport you normally use and there was no reasonable alternative.
- There were adverse postal conditions – eg, bad weather, a postal strike, or the Post Office failed to act under its agreement to deliver under-stamped mail to the DWP.[55]
- You (or your partner) stopped getting another benefit, but were not informed before your entitlement ceased, so you could not claim IS or JSA in time. **Note:** if you come under the UC system (see p20), this only applies if you stopped getting contributory ESA but were not informed before your entitlement ceased.
- For joint-claim JSA, your partner failed to attend her/his initial interview at Jobcentre Plus.
- You claimed IS or JSA in your own right within one month of separating from your partner.
- A close relative of yours died in the month before your claim. 'Close relative' means your partner, parent, son, daughter, brother or sister.
- You were unable to notify the DWP of your intention to claim because the telephone lines to the office were busy or not working.
- If you come under the UC system, you could not make an online claim for contribution-based JSA because the DWP's computer system was not working.

Three months' backdating

Your claim can be backdated for up to three months if you can show it was not reasonable to expect you to claim earlier than you did for one of the following reasons.[56] If more than one reason applies, the combined effect of all of them must be considered in deciding whether it was reasonable for you to claim earlier.[57]

- You were given information by an officer of the DWP or HMRC and, as a result, thought your claim would not succeed. 'Information' includes general information produced by the DWP or HMRC staff and placed on government websites. It does not have to be the tailored to your circumstances or involve personal communication between you and an officer.[58] **Note:** once you come under the UC system (see p20), the information must be from a DWP officer to allow your JSA claim to be backdated for this reason. The information that is relevant includes if:

- you were given incorrect information or the wrong claim form and this led you to claim the wrong benefit;
- someone with authority to act on your behalf was given incorrect information;[59]
- you were told your claim would not be accepted;[60]
- you were told you did not have to fill in a claim form;[61]
- the refusal of, or failure to respond to,[62] an earlier claim for the same[63] or a different[64] benefit led you to believe that you were not entitled;
- the information was incomplete and had not included advice on claiming when it should have done.[65]

'**Officer**' includes anyone carrying out public functions at the benefit office – eg, a security guard.[66] It does not matter if the information you received was correct or reasonable on the basis of any information that you gave to the officer about your circumstances, provided the officer's advice caused you to think that a claim would fail.[67]

- You were given advice in writing by a Citizens Advice Bureau or other advice worker, a solicitor or other professional adviser (eg, an accountant), a doctor or a local authority and, as a result, thought your claim would not succeed. 'Advice in writing' includes leaflets, emails[68] or information on a website, provided it is directed at claimants in your position. Your claim should be backdated if you are given written confirmation of advice that was originally given to you orally,[69] provided this is done before the decision maker decides whether you are entitled to backdating.[70] The written advice must also be given to you. It is not enough for your adviser to record a note of oral advice unless you are provided with a copy.[71]
- You or your partner were given written information about your income or capital by your employer or former employer, or a bank or building society, and, as a result, you thought your claim would not succeed. **Note:** this does not apply once you come under the UC system.
- You could not get to the DWP office because of bad weather.

In addition, your claim can be backdated for up to three months if:
- you have learning, language or literacy difficulties, or you are deaf or blind; *or*
- you were sick or disabled (but not if you are claiming JSA); *or*
- you were caring for someone who is sick or disabled; *or*
- you were dealing with a domestic emergency that affected you.

Part 8: Claiming benefits and getting paid
Chapter 49: Claims and decisions
4. The date of your claim

In addition, it must have not been 'reasonably practicable' for you to seek help from anyone else to make your claim.[72] If you are mentally ill, this does not necessarily mean you cannot be expected to seek assistance.[73] However, another person is not expected to proactively offer help.[74]

Backdating after an award of a qualifying benefit

If your claim for benefit is refused, it can be backdated if you reclaim it after an award of a 'qualifying benefit'.

Note:

- More generous rules apply for CA (see p565).
- Different rules apply for Sure Start maternity grants (see p789) and funeral expenses payments (see p791).
- This rule does not apply to backdating claims for JSA if you come under the UC system (see p20), or to claims for UC and ESA.

Qualifying benefit

A **'qualifying benefit'** is any benefit (except PIP) awarded to you or someone else, which gives you entitlement to another benefit, or makes another benefit payable at a higher rate. PIP is only a qualifying benefit in relation to backdating entitlement to CA.[75] If you will *only* qualify for a means-tested benefit if you are awarded PIP, you should claim it immediately and ask the DWP not to decide your claim until your PIP claim has been decided. You should also seek specialist advice.

You can get backdating if:[76]

- your original claim (eg, for PC) is refused; *and*
- you, or your partner or dependent child, claimed a qualifying benefit (eg, AA for your partner) no later than 10 working days after your original claim; *and*
- the qualifying benefit is awarded; *and*
- you make a further claim (eg, for PC) within three months of the decision awarding the qualifying benefit and are now entitled due to the award of the qualifying benefit.

In these circumstances, benefit is backdated to the date of your original claim or the date on which the qualifying benefit was first paid, whichever is later.

An additional rule applies if your IS or income-based JSA is terminated. A further claim can be backdated either to the date of the termination, or the date when a qualifying benefit was awarded (whichever date is later) if:[77]

- you, a family member or a person being cared for claim a qualifying benefit; *and*
- you claim IS or income-based JSA within three months of the qualifying benefit being awarded.

Note:

- The qualifying benefit rule also applies if the claim for the qualifying benefit was originally refused, but later awarded after a revision, supersession or appeal.[78]
- If you lost entitlement to benefit (eg, CA), or payment of it stopped because the award of a qualifying benefit (eg, DLA) was terminated or reduced, your benefit is backdated if you reclaim within three months of the reinstatement of the qualifying benefit. This also applies if you lost entitlement to a benefit (eg, you lost your IS because your income increased) but a claim for a qualifying benefit had not yet been decided and, had it been awarded, you would have been entitled again. In this case, your benefit is backdated if you claim within three months of the date the qualifying benefit is awarded.[79]
- If you lost entitlement to your benefit because AA or DLA stopped being paid because the person entitled was in hospital, a care home or other special accommodation, your benefit is backdated if you reclaim it within three months of payment of AA or DLA restarting.[80] **Note:** this rule does not apply when PIP stops in these circumstances.

If you are already entitled to IS, JSA, ESA, PC or UC, you might get a higher rate once you, a family member or a non-dependant qualifies for another benefit. See p1300 for backdating additional benefit in this situation.

If you claim the wrong benefit

If you claim one benefit when you are entitled to another benefit, your claim can sometimes be treated as a claim for that other benefit. This can be a way round the strict rules about your date of claim and backdating, as your claim for the benefit you should have claimed is treated as having been made on the date you claimed the wrong benefit.

A claim for:[81]

- ESA can be treated as a claim for MA and vice versa;
- bereavement benefits can be treated as a claim for state pension and vice versa;
- IS can be treated as a claim for CA;
- AA, DLA or an increase in disablement pension for constant attendance (see p687) can be treated as a claim for any of the others;
- PIP can be treated as a claim for either DLA or AA and vice versa, but only if it appears that you are not entitled to the benefit that you actually claimed;
- child benefit can be treated as a claim for guardian's allowance and vice versa.

Note:

- The decision maker does not have to accept your claim for one benefit as a claim for another. You cannot appeal if this is refused. You can request a revision (see p1276) but your only remedy if the decision maker refuses to change the decision is to seek a judicial review (see p1378).[82]

Part 8: Claiming benefits and getting paid
Chapter 49: Claims and decisions
5. Decisions

- For all benefits, except UC, IS , JSA, ESA and PIP, there is a general power to treat any written document as a claim for benefit, which could arguably include if you filled in the wrong claim form.[83]
- For some benefits, although you cannot be treated as having claimed the right benefit, there are special rules about the date your claim is treated as having been made if you first claimed the wrong benefit and later claim the right one when your claim is refused. For example, if you claim UC but your claim is refused because you do not meet the 'gateway' conditions (see p22) and within one month of the refusal you claim one or more of the benefits that are being replaced by UC (see p19), your claim is treated as having been made on the date you claimed UC. For more details, see 'The date of your claim' in the chapter of this *Handbook* about the benefit you should have claimed.
- If you claimed the wrong benefit as a result of incorrect information given to you by an employee of the DWP or HMRC and the above rules cannot help you, see p1396 for information about how to ask for compensation.

5. **Decisions**

Decisions about benefit entitlement are made by 'decision makers' (see below). A decision must be made once you have made a valid claim (see p1152).
   Note:
- If it is taking too long for a decision to be made, see p1165.
- You can ask for an explanation of a decision, or sometimes for written reasons for the decision (see p1165).
- If there is an accidental error in a decision, it can be corrected (see p1165).
- If you disagree with a decision, you may be able to apply for a revision or a supersession (see Chapter 54), or appeal against it. You must apply for a mandatory reconsideration before you can appeal (see p1311).

Who decides your claim

Decisions about benefits (other than child benefit and guardian's allowance) are made by officers of the DWP. Decisions about child benefit and guardian's allowance are made by officers of HM Revenue and Customs (HMRC). In this *Handbook*, we refer to these officers as 'decision makers'.
   Note: the DWP refers to personal independence payment (PIP) decision makers as 'case managers', although their role is the same.
   Decisions about whether you have limited capability for work or are terminally ill for benefit purposes are made by the DWP, even if the main benefit decision is made by another authority – eg, the local authority.[84]
   You may have to meet someone at your local Jobcentre Plus office to discuss your jobseeking conditions (see Chapter 45) or claimant responsibilities (see

Chapters 46 and 47). In practice, the person you meet is extremely unlikely to be a decision maker, although s/he may make recommendations to the decision maker – eg, about whether you should be given a sanction.

Making a decision

Once you have made a valid claim for benefit (see p1152), your claim is referred to a decision maker to decide whether you are entitled. A decision maker must normally make a decision on the claim,[85] but may sometimes withhold making a decision if there is a 'test case' pending (see p1303).

Before making a decision, the decision maker may request further information (see p1154). If there is a question about the facts of your claim that needs special expertise, the decision maker can get assistance from experts.[86]

Decisions may also be made after you are awarded benefit (eg, if there was a mistake about the facts or your circumstances change) by a revision or a supersession (see Chapter 54). You can be required to supply information or evidence if the decision maker needs this to make her/his decision, and payment of your benefit could be suspended or your award terminated if you fail to do so (see p1185). The same points apply as when providing further information about a claim (see p1154).

If you think a decision is wrong, see p1167.

Decisions made with limited information

The decision maker can make a decision in certain circumstances, even if s/he is waiting for you to provide more evidence or information.

A decision is always made on the basis that the evidence or information needed is adverse to you if:[87]

- for income support (IS) and jobseeker's allowance (JSA) only, it is needed to decide:
  - whether you should be paid benefit (or less benefit) because you (or a member of your family) are involved in a trade dispute (see p940). This does not apply to JSA if you come under the universal credit (UC) system (see p20); or
  - whether you are in relevant education (see p872);
- for IS, employment and support allowance (ESA), social fund payments and pension credit (PC) only, it is needed to decide whether you are entitled to a severe disability premium (additional amount for PC).

Special rules apply if when you claim your retirement pension you have not yet elected whether to take a lump sum or an increased pension (for state pension, this must be because your late partner deferred claiming her/his pension). The decision maker can choose whether or not to decide your claim immediately. If s/he does make a decision on your claim, for state pension s/he *may* revise it when

Part 8: Claiming benefits and getting paid
Chapter 49: Claims and decisions
5. Decisions

you make the election, and for category A or B retirement pension, s/he *must* revise it when you make the election (see p1284).[88]

For PIP, if you are in a care home and evidence or information is required to decide whether the cost of your accommodation will be met from local or public funds, if the decision maker makes 'reasonable enquiries', s/he can make a decision on the evidence or information s/he has.[89]

If further evidence or information is needed to decide what housing costs are paid in your IS, ESA or PC (see Chapter 20), a decision is made on the basis of the evidence or information the decision maker already has.[90] A similar rule for UC housing costs (see Chapter 22) gives the decision maker the discretion to make a decision if further evidence or information is needed.[91]

Special procedure

Certain questions are dealt with by a special procedure. These are to do with national insurance contributions and a person's employment – eg:[92]
- whether you were an 'employed earner' for the purposes of paying contributions or entitlement to industrial injuries disablement benefit; *or*
- whether you were liable to pay a particular class of contributions or have paid contributions for a particular period; *or*
- the amount of contributions you were liable to pay.

These matters are referred to HMRC for a decision, which is then binding on the decision maker.[93] The decision maker can continue to deal with other aspects of your claim, but can defer making a decision on it. The decision maker should also refer matters to HMRC if s/he decides your claim on the basis of facts which do not appear to be disputed (eg, if it appears you do not satisfy the contribution conditions for a benefit), but you apply for a revision or supersession, or appeal against the decision because you dispute the facts – eg, you think your contribution record is wrong.

When HMRC makes a decision, you can appeal against it.[94] The appeals process is similar to appealing against an HMRC decision on your entitlement to statutory payments (see Chapter 57).

The First-tier Tribunal can also require the DWP to refer matters that are HMRC's responsibility, but which are relevant to a benefit appeal, to HMRC for a decision.[95] The DWP may revise the decision on your claim as a result. If not, the matter goes back to the tribunal.

Note: the decision maker can make arrangements for some issues concerning whether you can be credited with earnings or contributions to be decided by HMRC.[96] You can appeal against these decisions in the same way as against DWP decisions. You must first request a mandatory reconsideration of the decision (see p1311).

Delays

HMRC has a 22-day target for dealing with child benefit claims (92 days for claimants from abroad).[97] The DWP no longer publishes official targets, although a suggestion of how long claims should take to be processed can be found in the *DWP Single Department Plan: 2015 to 2020 headline indicators technical detail*. For instance, the 'agreed time' for processing IS claims is five days, JSA is 10 days and ESA is 16 days. All claims should be dealt with as soon as is reasonably practicable, and the published guidelines can be taken into account when determining this.

Is there a delay?

1. If you have been waiting a long time for a decision, check that your claim has been received. If it has not, if possible let the office have a copy, or claim again, and refer to the claim you made earlier.

2. If the DWP or HMRC denies receiving your claim and you must claim again, ask for backdating and refer to your previous claim.

3. If your claim has been received but not dealt with, ask why. If you are not satisfied with the explanation for the delay, complain (see Chapter 58). In extreme cases, it might be possible to apply for judicial review (see p1378).

4. If a decision cannot be made on your claim straight away, ask the office to make a short-term advance of benefit if these are payable for the benefit you have claimed (see p1177), or an interim payment of child benefit or guardian's allowance (see p1179).

5. You may be able to claim a means-tested benefit while a decision is being made on your claim for a non-means-tested benefit. The amount paid may be deducted from arrears of the other benefit(s) you subsequently receive, or you may be asked to repay the amount (see p1223).

6. You may be able to get help from your local authority for any short-term needs in a crisis (see p856).

Correcting a decision

Unless the benefit is child benefit or guardian's allowance, if the decision maker makes an accidental error in her/his decision (eg, a typing error or a miscalculation in the arithmetic), this can be corrected.[98] You must be sent or given written notice of the correction as soon as practicable. To see how the time limit for applying for an 'any grounds' revision of the decision can be extended when a decision has been corrected, see p1277.

Information about decisions

You must be given written notice of a decision against which you can appeal (see p1314 for which decisions). This is usually called a **'decision notice'**. You must be informed of:[99]

Part 8: Claiming benefits and getting paid
Chapter 49: Claims and decisions
5. Decisions

- your right to appeal against the decision; *and*
- your right to a written statement of reasons for the decision, if this is not already included (see below).

You are also told that you must apply for a mandatory reconsideration before you can appeal against the decision (see p1311).

Explanations

You can ask for an explanation of any decision maker's decision. Contact the office that made the decision.

Note: you do not have to ask for an explanation or a written statement of reasons in order to apply for a revision or a supersession, or to appeal.

At the end of the explanation, you should be asked whether you are happy with the decision. If you are not happy, say so. The decision maker should then advise you about your right to apply for a revision (see p1276). S/he may refer to this as a dispute or a mandatory reconsideration.

Explanations are usually given orally. You may also have the right to request a written statement of reasons for a decision (see below) if it is one against which you can appeal.

The time limit for applying for a revision is very strict. It runs from the date you are sent or given the decision with which you disagree (*not* the date of the explanation) and can only be extended in limited circumstances (see p1277). Therefore, ensure you apply for a revision within the time limit, even if the decision has not yet been explained to you.

Written reasons

You may want to see the reasons for a decision in writing. You *only* have a right to a written statement of reasons for a decision if this has not already been provided with the decision *and* it is a decision against which you can appeal. You must ask for the written statement of reasons within one month of the date of the notification of the decision. The decision maker must then provide the statement within 14 days, or as soon as practicable afterwards.[100]

Note: the time limit to apply for a revision is extended if you ask for a written statement of reasons, but *only* if this has not already been provided. See p1277 for further information.

Month

'Month' means a complete calendar month running from the day after the day you were sent or given a decision.[101] For example, a decision sent on 24 July has a time limit that expires at the end of 24 August.

The DWP says that a written statement of reasons is provided automatically with decisions about PIP, bereavement benefits, ESA, maternity allowance, retirement pension, UC and social fund payments. Even for other benefits that are not listed here, if you are in any doubt about whether there is a statement of reasons for the decision, apply for a revision within the time limit.

You may believe that a written statement of reasons has not been included with your decision or is inadequate, but the DWP or HMRC could disagree. In these cases, the decision maker is likely to argue that your time limit for applying for a revision cannot be extended.

If you are in any doubt, you should assume that the time limit for applying for a revision has *not* been extended. If you miss the time limit in this situation, argue that the rules that allow a late application for a revision apply (see p1278). You may also be able to apply for an 'any time' revision (see p1279).

If you disagree with a decision maker's decision

If you think a decision maker's decision is wrong, you may be able to:
- apply for a revision of the decision (see p1276); *or*
- apply for a supersession of the decision (see p1287).

In most cases, you also have the right to appeal to the First-tier Tribunal (see Chapter 55). You must apply for a mandatory reconsideration first (see p1311).

The time limit for applying for what is known as an 'any grounds' revision is strict – normally only one month from the date on the decision letter (see p1277).

Notes

1. Making a claim
1 s1(1) SSAA 1992
2 For details, see www.gov.uk/dealing-hmrc-additional-needs
3 Regs 4(6A)-(6CC), 4D and 4H SS(C&P) Regs
4 Regs 4(6B), 4D(3A) and (4) and 4H(3) SS(C&P) Regs
5 **CB/GA** Reg 8 CB&GA(Admin) Regs
UC/PIP/JSA&ESA under UC Reg 30 UC,PIP,JSA&ESA(C&P) Regs
Other benefits Reg 5(1) and (1A) SS(C&P) Regs

6 **CB/GA** Reg 9 CB&GA(Admin) Regs
UC/PIP/JSA&ESA under UC Reg 31 UC,PIP,JSA&ESA(C&P) Regs
Other benefits Reg 5(2) SS(C&P) Regs
7 **CB/GA** Reg 2 and Sch 2 CB&GA(Admin) Regs
UC/PIP/JSA&ESA under UC Reg 2 and Sch 2 UC,PIP,JSA&ESA(C&P) Regs
Other benefits Reg 4ZC and Sch 9ZC SS(C&P) Regs
8 CJSA/3979/1999; CJSA/1332/2001; CDLA/1589/2005

Part 8: Claiming benefits and getting paid
Chapter 49: Claims and decisions
Notes

2. Who should claim

9 **CB/GA** Reg 28 CB&GA(Admin) Regs
UC/PIP/JSA&ESA under UC Reg 57
UC,PIP,JSA&ESA(C&P) Regs
Other benefits Reg 33 SS(C&P) Regs
10 R(SB) 5/90
11 CIS/642/1994
12 CIS/379/1992
13 **UC/PIP/JSA&ESA under UC** Reg
57(6) UC,PIP,JSA&ESA(C&P) Regs
Other benefits Reg 33(1A) SS(C&P)
Regs

3. Information to support your claim

14 Sch 2 SS&CS(DA) Regs, Sch 3
UC,PIP,JSA&ESA(DA) Regs and Sch 2
CB&GA(DA) Regs do not include such
decisions in the list of decisions against
which there is no right of appeal.
15 **CB/GA** s13(1A) and (1B) SSAA 1992
Other benefits s1(1A) and (1B) SSA
1992
16 CH/4085/2007
17 s1(1A) SSAA 1992
18 *SSWP v Wilson* [2006] EWCA Civ 882
(reported as R(H) 7/06)
19 CH/1231/2004; CH/4085/2007
20 Reg 1A SS(DLA) Regs
21 Reg 4(a) HB Regs; reg 4(a) HB(SPC) Regs
22 **HB** Reg 4(b) HB Regs; reg 4(b) HB(SPC)
Regs
UC Reg 5 UC,PIP,JSA&ESA(C&P) Regs
IS and JSA Reg 2A(a) IS Regs and reg
2A(a) JSA Regs, which still apply in these
cases because of the transitional
protection in reg 1 SS(WTCCTC)(CA)
Regs
23 www.equalityadvisoryservice.com or
phone 0808 800 0082 (textphone:
0808 800 0084)
24 **JSA under UC** Regs 19 and 20
UC,PIP,JSA&ESA(C&P) Regs
JSA Regs 4(6)(a) and 6(4ZB), (4ZC),
(4A)(a) and (4AA) SS(C&P) Regs
25 **JSA under UC** Reg 20(3)
UC,PIP,JSA&ESA(C&P) Regs
JSA Reg 6(4AB) SS(C&P) Regs
26 **UC/PIP/JSA&ESA under UC** Regs 8(4)
and (5), 11(4) and (5), 13 and 23
UC,PIP,JSA&ESA(C&P) Regs
Other benefits Regs 4(11)-(13),
4D(6A)-(6E) and 4G SS(C&P) Regs
27 **ESA under UC** Reg 13(2)
UC,PIP,JSA&ESA(C&P) Regs
Other benefits Regs 4D(6B) and 4G(2)
SS(C&P) Regs
28 Regs 4(7A) and (7B) and 6(1A) and
(4A)(b) SS(C&P) Regs

29 **UC/PIP/JSA&ESA under UC** Regs 8(5)
and (6), 11(5) and (6), 13(4) and (5)
and 23(3) and (4)
UC,PIP,JSA&ESA(C&P) Regs
Other benefits Regs 4(7) and (13),
4D(6D) and (6E) and 4G(4) and (5)
SS(C&P) Regs
30 **CB/GA** Reg 10 CB&GA(Admin) Regs
UC/PIP/JSA&ESA under UC Regs
8(3), 11(3), 15(2) and 21(3)
UC,PIP,JSA&ESA(C&P) Regs
Other benefits Regs 4 (7) and (8),
4D(2) and 4H(2) SS(C&P) Regs
31 **CB/GA** Reg 10 CB&GA(Admin) Regs
UC/PIP/JSA&ESA under UC Regs 8(5)
and (6), 11(5) and (6), 15(3) and (4)
and 21(4) and (5)
UC,PIP,JSA&ESA(C&P) Regs
Other benefits Regs 4(7)(b), 4D (10)
and (11) and 4H(6) and (7) SS(C&P)
Regs
32 *CW v SSWP (JSA)* [2016] UKUT 114
(AAC)
33 **UC/PIP/JSA&ESA under UC** Regs
8(1), 11(1)(a), 15(1) and 21(1)
UC,PIP,JSA&ESA(C&P) Regs
Other benefits Reg 4H(2)
SS(C&P)Regs
34 **CB/GA** Reg 5 CB&GA(Admin) Regs
Other benefits Regs 4(1) and 4D(2)
SS(C&P) Regs
35 **CB/GA** Reg 10 CB&GA(Admin) Regs
Other benefits Reg 4(7ZA) SS(C&P)
Regs
36 Reg 4(1A) SS(C&P) Regs
37 Regs 4(7A) and (7B) and 6(1A) and
(4AB) SS(C&P) Regs
38 Reg 4(1B) SS(C&P) Regs
39 CIS/2057/1998
40 **JSA** Reg 24 JSA Regs; reg 31 JSA Regs
2013
CB/GA Reg 7 CB&GA(Admin) Regs
UC/PIP&ESA under UC Reg 37
UC,PIP,JSA&ESA(C&P) Regs
Other benefits Reg 7 SS(C&P) Regs
41 R(IS) 4/93; CIS/51/2007; *MS v SSWP
(JSA)* [2016] UKUT 206 (AAC)
42 ss180 and 180A SSAA 1992
43 The Social Security (Claims and
Information) Regulations 2007,
No.2911
44 CIS/51/2007
45 **PIP** s80 WRA 2012
ESA ss8-9 WRA 2007
IIDB Reg 12 SS&CA(DA) Regs
Other benefits s19 SSA 1998
46 s39(1) SSA 1998; reg 3 SS(DLA)A Regs
47 PIP AG, p122

4. The date of your claim

48 **CB/GA** Reg 6 CB&GA(Admin) Regs
UC/PIP/JSA&ESA under UC Regs 26-29 UC,PIP,JSA&ESA(C&P) Regs
Other benefits Reg 19 and Sch 4 SS(C&P) Regs

49 R(SB) 9/84

50 ss65(4) and 76 SSCBA 1992; reg 27 UC,PIP,JSA&ESA(C&P) Regs

51 **CB/GA** Reg 6 CB&GA(Admin) Regs
ESA under UC Reg 28 UC,PIP,JSA&ESA(C&P) Regs
Other benefits Reg 19(1)-(3B) and Sch 4 SS(C&P) Regs

52 R(SB) 17/83; R(IS) 5/91; CIS/812/1992

53 R(P) 2/85

54 **JSA under UC** Reg 29(4) and (5) UC,PIP,JSA&ESA(C&P) Regs
Other benefits Reg 19(6) and (7) SS(C&P) Regs

55 CIS/4901/2002

56 **JSA under UC** Reg 29(2) and (3) UC,PIP,JSA&ESA(C&P) Regs
Other benefits Reg 19(4) and (5) SS(C&P) Regs

57 CIS/2484/1999

58 *SSWP v PG (JSA)* [2015] UKUT 616 (AAC), but see also *S K-G v SSWP (JSA)* [2014] UKUT 430 (AAC), which earlier came to the opposite conclusion, holding that 'information' must be tailored to your circumstances in some way.

59 CJSA/4573/1999

60 CJSA/4066/1998

61 CIS/610/1998

62 CJSA/3084/2004

63 R(IS) 3/01

64 CIS/4490/1998

65 CJSA/0580/2003

66 CIS/610/1998

67 CIS/3994/1998; CSIS/815/2004

68 CIS/5430/1999

69 CJSA/1136/1998

70 CIS/5430/1999

71 CIS/5430/1999

72 **JSA under UC** Reg 29(3) UC,PIP,JSA&ESA(C&P) Regs
Other benefits Reg 19(5) SS(C&P) Regs; C12/98 (IS)

73 C12/98 (IS)

74 CIS/2057/1998

75 Reg 6(22) SS(C&P) Regs. PIP does not count for the general rule, as it is not defined as a 'relevant benefit' for the purpose of this regulation.

76 Reg 6(16)-(26) SS(C&P) Regs

77 Reg 6(30) SS(C&P) Regs

78 Reg 6(26) SS(C&P) Regs

79 Reg 6(19) SS(C&P) Regs

80 Reg 6(19)-(21A) SS(C&P) Regs

81 **CB/GA** Reg 11 CB&GA(Admin) Regs
UC/PIP/JSA&ESA under UC Reg 25 UC,PIP,JSA&ESA(C&P) Regs
Other benefits Reg 9 and Sch 1 SS(C&P) Regs

82 **CB/GA** Sch 2 para 6(d) CB&GA(DA) Regs
UC/PIP/JSA&ESA under UC Sch 3 para 1(b) UC,PIP,JSA&ESA(DA) Regs
Other benefits Sch 2 para 5(g) SS&CS(DA) Regs
See also R(A) 3/81

83 **CB/GA** Reg 5(1)(b) CB&GA(Admin) Regs
Other benefits Regs 4(1) and 4D(2) SS(C&P) Regs

5. Decisions

84 **UC/PIP/JSA&ESA under UC** Reg 40 UC,PIP,JSA&ESA(DA) Regs
Other benefits Reg 11 SS&CS(DA) Regs

85 R(SB) 29/83; CIS/807/1992; R(H) 3/05

86 s11(2) SSA 1998

87 **UC/PIP/JSA&ESA under UC** Reg 39 UC,PIP,JSA&ESA(DA) Regs
Other benefits Regs 13(2) and (3) and 15 SS&CS(DA) Regs

88 Regs 13A and 13B SS&CS(DA) Regs

89 Reg 39(5) UC,PIP,JSA&ESA(DA) Regs

90 Reg 13(1) SS&CS(DA) Regs

91 Reg 39(4) UC,PIP,JSA&ESA(DA) Regs

92 s8 SSC(TF)A 1999

93 s10A SSA 1998; Reg 42 UC,PIP,JSA&ESA(DA) Regs; reg 11A SS&CS(DA) Regs

94 s11 SSC(TF)A 1999

95 s24A SSA 1998; Reg 43 UC,PIP,JSA&ESA(DA) Regs; reg 38A SS&CS(DA) Regs

96 s17 SSC(TF)A 1999; Sch 3 para 17 SSA 1998; the National Insurance Contribution Credits (Transfer of Functions) Order 2009, No.1377

97 See www.gov.uk/government/collections/briefings

98 **UC/PIP/JSA&ESA under UC** Reg 38 UC,PIP,JSA&ESA(DA) Regs
Other benefits Reg 9A SS&CS(DA) Regs

99 **CB/GA** Reg 26(1) CB&GA(DA) Regs
UC/PIP/JSA&ESA under UC Reg 51 UC,PIP,JSA&ESA(DA) Regs
Other benefits Reg 28(1) SS&CS(DA) Regs

Part 8: Claiming benefits and getting paid
Chapter 49: Claims and decisions
Notes

• •

100 **CB/GA** Regs 3 and 26(1)(b) and (2)
CB&GA(DA) Regs
UC/PIP/JSA&ESA under UC Regs 3
and 51 UC,PIP,JSA&ESA(DA) Regs
Other benefits Regs 2 and 28(1)(b)
and (2) SS&CS(DA) Regs
101 R(IB) 4/02

Chapter 50

. . . .

Getting paid

This chapter covers:
1. Who is paid (p1172)
2. How and when you are paid (p1172)
3. Overlapping benefits (p1175)
4. Short-term advances (p1177)
5. The benefit cap (p1180)
6. Change of circumstances after you claim (p1184)
7. When payments can be suspended (p1185)
8. When your entitlement is terminated (p1187)
9. Deductions and payments to third parties (p1187)
10. Recovery of benefits from compensation payments (p1199)

This chapter covers the general rules for benefits. See the chapter about the benefit you are claiming for the specific rules about that benefit. This chapter does *not* cover the rules for statutory sick pay (see Chapter 38), statutory maternity, adoption, paternity and shared parental pay (see Chapter 37), payments from the social fund (see Chapter 36), the health benefits in Chapter 29, the other types of financial help in Chapter 39, or discretionary housing payments (see Chapter 21).

For information about payment of tax credits, see Chapter 61.

Key facts
- The DWP, local authority or HM Revenue and Customs (HMRC) decides how benefit is paid to you. There is no right of appeal.
- The DWP and HMRC usually pay your benefit by direct credit transfer into a bank or similar account.
- If your claim or payment of your benefit is delayed, you may be able to get a short-term advance or an interim payment.
- A 'benefit cap' may restrict the total amount of benefit you receive if it is above a certain level.
- You must report certain changes in your circumstances.
- Deductions can be made from your benefit. In certain circumstances, payment of your benefit can be suspended. In addition, your benefit might not be paid, or might be paid at a reduced rate, as a result of a sanction or a penalty.

Part 8: Claiming benefits and getting paid
Chapter 50: Getting paid
2. How and when you are paid

1. **Who is paid**

Payment is usually made directly to you, but there are some circumstances when payments can be made to other people or organisations on your behalf.

- If you are unable to manage your own money or if you die, your benefit is paid to a person appointed to act on your behalf – called an 'appointee' (see p1149).[1]
- You can choose to have child benefit, guardian's allowance, joint-claim jobseeker's allowance (JSA) or universal credit (UC) paid to your partner.
- Your benefit (except housing benefit – HB) can be paid to someone else if it is in the interests of you or your partner, or any of your children for whom you are getting benefit.[2] This includes paying your UC housing costs for rent to someone who then makes payments to your landlord.
- If you are claiming income support (IS), income-based JSA, income-related employment and support allowance (ESA), pension credit (PC) or UC and are getting help with your housing costs for a mortgage (see Chapter 20), these are usually paid directly to your lender on your behalf (see p1190).
- Your HB can be paid directly to your landlord (or the person to whom you pay rent) on your behalf in certain circumstances (see p84). Your UC housing costs for rent are not paid directly to your landlord, unless the DWP thinks the 'alternative payment arrangements' should apply (see p173).
- Deductions can be made from certain benefits (usually IS, JSA, ESA, PC or UC) for certain payments to be made to someone else on your behalf (see p1188).[3]

2. **How and when you are paid**

The DWP or HM Revenue and Customs (HMRC) decides how and when your benefit is paid. There is no right of appeal about this. For how and when housing benefit is paid, see p83.

Note:

- You are usually paid your benefit by direct credit transfer into a bank or similar account (see below).
- If you cannot open or manage an acount, payment can sometimes be made by 'simple payment' (see p1173). Child benefit and guardian's allowance can be paid by cheque (see p1173).
- You can check your universal credit (UC) payments online. If you are unable to do this, ask the DWP for help in accessing your online account. It may be possible to do this by telephone, or possibly in person at a Jobcentre Plus office.

Direct payment

You are usually paid by direct credit transfer into a bank account, building society account or similar account (including a Post Office card account and some credit union accounts). This is called 'direct payment'. If this is not suitable for you, you may be able to get your benefit paid by 'simple payment' (see below), or your child benefit or guardian's allowance paid by cheque (see below). **Note:** the government is writing to people with Post Office card accounts about switching to a bank, building society or credit union account, but Post Office card accounts remain available for the time being.

Your benefit is paid into an account nominated by you or by your appointee.[4]

If you experience difficulty accessing your money as a result of these arrangements, complain to the DWP or HMRC. You could contact your MP.

If someone collects your benefit for you

It should be possible, if necessary, to arrange for someone else to be able to access your account in order to collect your benefit for you. If you already have a bank or building society account, ask the bank or building society about this. If you use a Post Office card account, a second card can be issued to the person who collects your benefit.

If you lose your card or forget your PIN

If you lose your bank card or forget your PIN, contact the bank and ask for a replacement card or new PIN to be issued as soon as possible.

If you use a Post Office card account and you lose your card or forget your PIN, call the customer service helpline number on 0345 722 3344 (typetalk: 0345 722 3355). You should get a replacement card or PIN within four working days.

If you cannot access your benefit while waiting for a new card or PIN, contact the office that pays your benefit for advice.

If all else fails, you may be able to get a payment from your local authority while the problem is sorted out. A payment can be paid if there is a crisis (see p856). If you cannot get access to your benefit, and the DWP or HMRC refuses to remedy the situation, get advice (see Appendix 2).

Payment by 'simple payment' or cheque

If you cannot open or manage an account, your DWP benefits are paid by 'simple payment' at a PayPoint outlet. The DWP sends you a letter and information pack about simple payment, and identifies two PayPoint outlets near your home which you could use. You must produce your simple payment card, a memorable date agreed with the DWP and proof of your identity to get your benefit at the PayPoint outlet. If someone regularly gets your benefit for you, s/he can be issued with her/his own simple payment card. For more information, see www.gov.uk/simple-payment.

If you lose your simple payment card, telephone 0800 032 5872 (open 24 hours). There is also a simple payment telephone helpline on 0845 600 0046 (textphone: 0800 032 5864). Use this if you forget your memorable date.

Part 8: Claiming benefits and getting paid
Chapter 50: Getting paid
2. How and when you are paid

If you cannot open or manage an account, the local authority (for housing benefit) or HMRC (for child benefit and guardian's allowance) may arrange to pay you by another method, including by cheque.

When you are paid

When and how often your benefit is paid depends on the benefit you have claimed.[5] You are sometimes paid in advance and sometimes in arrears. Some benefits have specific paydays; for others, the day you are paid depends on your national insurance (NI) number. See the chapter for the benefit you are claiming.

Last two numbers of your NI number	Day of payment
00–19	Monday
20–39	Tuesday
40–59	Wednesday
60–79	Thursday
80–89	Friday

Missing payments

If you are entitled to benefit, you must be paid it.[6] If your benefit is not paid into your account, your simple payment card does not allow you to collect your benefit or you are not issued with a cheque, the DWP or HMRC must rectify this.

If there is a long delay, the DWP or HMRC may say that your entitlement to payment is lost 12 months after the date it was due to be paid into your account. However, this should not apply if you have not been paid.[7] If necessary, get advice (see Appendix 2).

Emergencies

If you have lost all your money or there has been a crisis, it is possible to get help at any time. Your local police station should have a contact number for DWP staff on call outside normal office hours.

If you are unable to contact the DWP, or it does not help, you may be able to get a payment from your local authority in a crisis (see p856). The police station should have a contact number.

If you need money urgently, you should provide as much information as you can to support your claim. It may help if you can get an advice agency or third party (eg, a health visitor, social worker, doctor or MP) to support you.

3. **Overlapping benefits**

Sometimes, you cannot be paid more than one non-means-tested benefit in full at the same time. This is because of the 'overlapping benefit' rules. These may also apply if:

- more than one person is claiming an increase for the same child or adult (see p1177);
- you are getting child benefit, guardian's allowance or an increase in your non-means-tested benefit for your child (see p1177);
- you are entitled to an increase in your non-means-tested benefit for an adult who is getting one or more of certain benefits her/himself (see p1177).

Disability living allowance (DLA) care component, the daily living component of personal independence payment (PIP), attendance allowance (AA) and armed forces independence payment overlap with each other and with constant attendance allowance.[8] Otherwise AA, DLA, PIP, disablement benefit (see p686), reduced earnings allowance (see p688) and retirement allowance (see p690) can be received in addition to any of the other benefits described in this *Handbook* – eg, you can receive employment and support allowance (ESA), both components of DLA or of PIP and disablement benefit at the same time.

Earnings-replacement benefits

Some benefits compensate you for your inability to work because of unemployment, sickness, pregnancy or old age. These are 'earnings-replacement' benefits. You cannot usually receive more than one of the following earnings-replacement benefits at the same time.

- Contributory benefits:
  - contribution-based jobseeker's allowance;
  - incapacity benefit;
  - contributory ESA;
  - maternity allowance (which counts as contributory for the purposes of this rule);
  - retirement pension;
  - bereavement allowance or widow's pension;
  - widowed parent's allowance or widowed mother's allowance.
- Non-contributory benefits:
  - severe disablement allowance;
  - carer's allowance (CA).

If more than one of the earnings-replacement benefits listed above is payable to you, the following applies.[9]

- A contributory benefit is paid in preference to a non-contributory benefit. This is then topped up by any balance of a non-contributory benefit due.
- If the above does not apply, weekly benefits are paid and topped up by any balance of a daily benefit (unless you make an application to receive the daily benefit in full). See the chapter in this *Handbook* about the benefit you are claiming to see if it is a daily or a weekly benefit.
- If neither of the above bullet points apply, the highest rate benefit is paid or, if the rates are the same, one benefit is paid.

Retirement pensions

You cannot usually get more than one retirement pension at a time.[10] However, there are special rules if you are married or in a civil partnership and at least one of you reached pension age after 6 April 1979, or you are a surviving spouse or civil partner entitled to both a category A and a category B retirement pension (see Chapter 36 of the 2015/16 edition of this *Handbook*), and your category A pension would be paid at a reduced rate because you have not paid sufficient contributions (see p983). In this situation, your basic category A pension is increased by whichever is less of either:[11]

- the amount of the shortfall between your category A pension and the full category A pension of £122.30; *or*
- the amount of your category B pension.

You are also entitled to an additional pension on your own contribution record and one on that of your spouse or civil partner up to the maximum additional pension a person could theoretically receive on one contribution record.[12]

Additional pensions under the old additional state pension scheme and graduated retirement benefit do not overlap with non-means-tested benefits. However, if two or more such benefits are payable with an additional pension and graduated retirement benefit, the benefits are calculated as if the additional pension or graduated retirement benefit is part of the benefit, and the overlapping benefit rule is then applied to the benefits.[13] For more information about additional state pension and graduated retirement benefit, see Chapter 36 of the 2015/16 edition of this *Handbook*.

There are exceptions to this rule if you are a category B retirement pensioner whose own contribution record would entitle you to a category A retirement pension. See p278 of the 2008/09 edition of this *Handbook*. Also, an additional pension paid with widow's pension or widowed mother's allowance (see p545) overlaps with the new state pension (see p770).[14]

An age addition paid with retirement pension overlaps with another age addition.[15]

Increases in non-means-tested benefits for adults

An increase in a non-means-tested benefit for an adult overlaps with certain earnings-replacement benefits (see p1175) or training allowances which are payable to that adult – eg, an increase of retirement pension for your partner is not paid if s/he is being paid CA in her/his own right.[16] If the increase is less than or equal to the benefit payable to the adult, the increase is not paid. If the increase is greater than the basic benefit, you get the difference. This does not apply if the adult is not residing with you and is employed by you to care for a child.

Increases in non-means-tested benefits for children

Only one person can receive child benefit or an increase in a non-means-tested benefit for the same child.

The standard rate of child benefit (see p584) does not overlap with any other benefit. However, if you receive the higher amount payable for your eldest child (see p584), any other non-means-tested benefit (except DLA, PIP and guardian's allowance) or increase paid for the same child is reduced by £3.35.[17] All increases for children overlap with guardian's allowance and are reduced by the amount of guardian's allowance you get for the child.[18]

4. Short-term advances

If you are waiting for a decision on your claim or you are waiting to be paid and you are in 'financial need' (see below for what this means), you may be able to get an advance loan of your benefit.[19] This is called a 'short-term advance' of benefit or, for universal credit (UC), a 'universal credit advance'. We refer to all these payments as short-term advances in this *Handbook*. You must repay the advance by deductions from future payments of your benefit, but you are not charged interest.

Financial need

'**Financial need**' means that because you have not received your benefit, there is a serious risk of damage to the health or safety of you or a member of your family. '**Family**' means your partner and any children for whom you or your partner are responsible (see p577).[20]

You may be in financial need in various circumstances – eg, if you have no money for food or for your gas or electricity meter, or during a 'waiting period' that applies before you are entitled to benefit.

You can get a short-term advance of most benefits. See p1179 for the exceptions. For more information about short-term advances, see *Ask CPAG Online* at www.cpag.org.uk/askcpag.

Part 8: Claiming benefits and getting paid
Chapter 50: Getting paid
4. Short-term advances

If you are in financial need because you are waiting for a decision on your claim, you may be able to get a short-term advance if the decision maker considers it likely that you are entitled to the benefit and:

- you have made a claim, but the claim has not yet been decided; *or*
- you are not required to make a claim for the benefit, but you have not yet been awarded it.

If you are in financial need because you are waiting to be paid, you may be able to get a short-term advance if you have been awarded the benefit and:

- you are waiting for your first payment; *or*
- you have received your first payment, but it was for a shorter period than subsequent payments will be paid for, and you are waiting for your next payment; *or*
- you have had a change of circumstances which increases your entitlement, but your benefit has not yet been increased and paid to you; *or*
- you are entitled to a payment but it is 'impracticable' to pay all or some of it on the date on which it is due.

Note:

- You can request a short-term advance at your local Jobcentre Plus office, or use the telephone number for the specific benefit at www.gov.uk/short-term-benefit-advance. For UC, the DWP encourages you to phone the UC helpline on 0345 600 0723 (textphone: 0345 600 0743), but you could also ask at your intial UC interview. The phone calls are not free – ask the DWP to call you back.
- There are no rules on how much a short-term advance should be. The DWP considers how much you have asked for, how much you can afford to repay and what your benefit entitlement will be. For UC, the DWP usually offers a maximum of 50 per cent of your estimated award.
- The DWP says that you must ask for a UC advance no later than three working days before the end of your monthly assessment period (see p164), unless you are claiming within a month of coming off another means-tested benefit or tax credit.
- You are usually contacted about your application on the day you apply or early the next day. If you are to be offered a short-term advance, you are asked to accept the amount and the repayment terms. You should explain any problems with this: if you do not accept the offer, you are not given the advance.
- There is no right of appeal against a refusal to award a short-term advance.[21] You can ask the DWP to reconsider the decision, but after that the only legal remedy is judicial review (see p1378). You could contact your MP to see whether s/he can help to get the decision reconsidered. You may be able to get help in a crisis from your local authority (see p856). You could also try using the emergency service (see p1174).

- You must be notified of your liability to repay the advance.[22] It is recovered by deductions from subsequent payments of your benefit. Usually, the DWP will want to recover the advance within 12 weeks, at no more than 25 per cent of your benefit. A UC advance is usually recovered within six months, at up to 40 per cent of your monthly UC standard allowance. If you need longer, tell the decision maker and explain why. You can appeal the decision about the repayment from subsequent payments of your benefit, including the rate of the deductions.[23]

Benefits for which you cannot get a short-term advance

You cannot get a short-term advance of:[24]
- housing benefit (HB). If your HB is delayed and you are a private or housing association tenant, you might be able to get an interim payment known as a 'payment on account' (see p89);
- attendance allowance;
- disability living allowance;
- personal independence payment;
- child benefit (see below);
- guardian's allowance (see below);
- statutory sick, maternity, adoption, paternity or shared parental pay.

Interim payments of child benefit and guardian's allowance

If your claim for child benefit or guardian's allowance is delayed, instead of a short-term advance you can ask HM Revenue and Customs (HMRC) for an interim payment. HMRC does not make an interim payment if you have an appeal pending. An interim payment can be made if it seems that you may be entitled to benefit and:[25]
- there is a delay in your making a claim; or
- you have claimed, but not in the correct way – eg, you have filled in the form incorrectly; or
- you have claimed correctly, but it is not possible for the claim to be dealt with immediately; or
- you have been awarded benefit, but it is not possible to pay you immediately, other than by an interim payment.

Note:
- There is no right of appeal against a refusal to award you an interim payment. See the note on p1177 – the same advice applies, except that it is HMRC that must change the decision, not the DWP.
- An interim payment can be deducted from any later payment of the benefit. If it is more than your actual entitlement, the overpayment can be recovered. You should be notified of this in advance.[26]

Part 8: Claiming benefits and getting paid
Chapter 50: Getting paid
5. The benefit cap

5. **The benefit cap**

A 'benefit cap' may limit the total amount of benefit you can be paid.[27] If the total amount of your benefits is capped, the cap is applied:
- by reducing the amount of your housing benefit (HB – see below); *or*
- by reducing the amount of your universal credit (UC – see p1181).

See p1181 and p1182 for the 'specified' benefits that are taken into account when deciding whether the cap applies.

Note: there are a number of situations when the benefit cap does not apply, or when it is not applied immediately (see p1182).

You can appeal (see Chapter 55) against having the benefit cap applied through your HB.[28] There is no right of appeal against a decision to apply the benefit cap through UC. Instead, you must ask for a revision or a supersession (see Chapter 54).

When the benefit cap applies

The benefit cap only applies if:
- you get HB for people below the qualifying age for pension credit (PC), or you get UC; *and*
- none of the exceptions apply (see p1182); *and*
- the total amount of certain specified benefits you (and your partner, if you are a member of a couple) receive is above a certain level (see below for HB and p1181 for UC).

When calculating the amount of benefit you receive, the general rule is that your full benefit entitlement is taken into account. Deductions for repayment of overpayments, payments to third parties, council tax debts, fines and sanctions are generally ignored (but see p1182 for some exceptions if the cap is applied through your HB and you get child tax credit (CTC), widowed mother's allowance or widowed parent's allowance).[29]

If you get housing benefit

The cap applies once your (and, if you are in a couple, your partner's) weekly entitlement to specified benefits exceeds a certain amount. The amount is:
- if you live outside Greater London: £257.69 a week if you are single, or £384.62 a week if you are a couple or a lone parent; *or*
- if you live in Greater London: £296.35 a week if you are single, or £442.31 a week if you are a couple or a lone parent.

Specified benefits

If you get HB, the **'specified benefits'** taken into account for the benefit cap are:[30]
- income support (IS);
- jobseeker's allowance (JSA);
- employment and support allowance (ESA), if neither you nor your partner are in the support group (ESA is not taken into account while you are disqualified from receiving it);
- HB, except for 'specified accommodation'. This means: 'exempt accommodation' (see p428) or accommodation provided by a housing association, charity, voluntary organisation or English county council to meet your need for care, support or supervision; temporary accommodation provided by one of these bodies or a local authority because you have left home because of domestic violence; or a local authority hostel where you get care, support or supervision;
- bereavement allowance;
- child benefit;
- incapacity benefit;
- maternity allowance (MA);
- severe disablement allowance;
- widowed mother's/parent's allowance (after the £15 disregard);
- widow's pension;
- CTC (but if you are repaying an overpayment from the previous tax year, the amount of CTC taken into account is reduced by the amount deducted for the repayment).

Note: bereavement allowance and widowed parent's allowance are being replaced by a single benefit, bereavement support payment. See Chapter 24 for details. It is understood that bereavement support payment will not be a 'specified benefit'.

The local authority does not have to decide whether or not to apply the cap, unless it is told by the DWP that it may apply in your case or that you have had a change in your benefit entitlement. However, it can decide to apply the cap on the basis of information or evidence suggesting that it should do so.[31]

If you get universal credit

The cap applies once your (and, if you are in a couple, your partner's) monthly entitlement to specified benefits exceeds a certain amount. The amount is:
- if you live outside Greater London: £1,116.66 a month (£257.69 a week) if you are single, or £1,666.66 a month (£386.62 a week) if you are a couple or a lone parent; *or*
- if you live in Greater London: £1,284.16 a month (£296.35 a week) if you are single, £1,916.66 a month (£442.31 a week) if you are a couple or a lone parent.

Your benefit payments are converted into monthly amounts for this calculation.

Part 8: Claiming benefits and getting paid
Chapter 50: Getting paid
5. The benefit cap

Specified benefits

If you get UC, the **'specified benefits'** taken into account for the benefit cap are:[32]

– UC;
– JSA;
– ESA, if neither you nor your partner are in the support group (ESA is not taken into account while you are disqualified from receiving it);
– bereavement allowance;
– child benefit;
– MA;
– widowed mother's/parent's allowance;
– widow's pension.

When the benefit cap does not apply

The benefit cap does not apply if:

- you are not getting HB for people below the qualifying age for PC or not getting UC;
- you or your partner are working and get working tax credit (WTC – see below);
- you or your partner (or, in some cases, your child and arguably any other member of your family) are entitled to one of the disability or carer benefits listed on p1183;
- it would be applied through your UC and you and/or your partner work, provided your combined earnings are high enough (see p1183).

In addition, if you or your partner have been working recently, there may be a 'grace period' during which the cap does not apply (see below).

If you get a relatively high amount of HB, the cap is especially likely to apply. If the amount of your HB decreases (eg, because you move to cheaper accommodation), this may mean that the cap no longer applies.

Work-related exceptions

If the benefit cap should be applied through your HB, it is not applied if:[33]

- you (or your partner) are entitled to WTC. This includes if you have claimed WTC but have a nil award because of your income (see p1454); *or*
- you are within a 'grace period' after finishing work (see below).

The benefit cap is not applied for a 'grace period' of 39 weeks if:[34]

- you or your partner were previously in work (either employed or self-employed) for at least 50 weeks out of the 52 weeks before the last day of work; *and*
- in that 50 weeks, the person in work was not entitled to IS, JSA or ESA.

The grace period begins on the day after the last day of work.

You count as still in work while on maternity, adoption, paternity or shared parental leave, or while receiving statutory sick pay (SSP).[35]

If the benefit cap should be applied through your UC, it is not applied if:[36]

- you or your partner are working (either employed or self-employed) and have net monthly earnings of at least £520 in your UC monthly assessment period. Your partner's earnings are added to yours; *or*
- you are within a nine-month 'grace period' (see below).

The benefit cap is not applied for a 'grace period' of nine consecutive months, if:[37]

- your earnings (or your and your partner's combined earnings) from employed or self-employed work are now less than £520 a month but, immediately before the first day on which this applies, they had been at least £520 a month in each of the preceding 12 months; *or*
- before your current period of entitlement to UC, you stopped paid employed or self-employed work and, before you stopped work, your earnings (or your and your partner's combined earnings) had been at least £520 a month in each of the preceding 12 months.

The grace period begins on the most recent day on which either condition applies.

For how earnings from work are calculated for UC, see Chapter 16.

Although not explicitly stated in the UC rules, it is arguable that you count as still in work while on maternity, adoption, paternity or shared parental leave, or while receiving SSP. If you are in this position, get advice.

Benefits for disabled people and carers

The benefit cap does not apply if you or your partner get:

- ESA that includes the support component;
- UC that includes the limited capability for work-related activity component;
- carer's allowance, guardian's allowance, or UC that includes the carer element;
- attendance allowance (or you are entitled to it, but are not paid while you are in hospital or a care home);
- disability living allowance, personal independence payment or armed forces independence payment. This exemption also applies if the person entitled is a child for whom you or your partner are responsible. The exemption continues while the person entitled is not paid benefit while s/he is in hospital or a care home;
- industrial injuries disablement benefit, reduced earnings allowance or retirement allowance;
- a war pension (or you are entitled to it but are not paid while you are in hospital or a care home).

Part 8: Claiming benefits and getting paid
Chapter 50: Getting paid
6. Change of circumstances after you claim

How the benefit cap is applied

If the cap is applied through your HB, the local authority reduces your HB by the amount by which the total amount of the specified benefits you receive exceeds the cap. You must be left with at least 50 pence a week HB, so that you can still access discretionary housing payments and other passported payments.[38]

If the cap is applied through your UC, the DWP reduces your UC by the amount by which the total amount of the specified benefits you receive exceeds the cap. However, if you are entitled to the childcare costs element in your UC (see p264) and this is more than the amount by which your specified benefits exceeds the cap (the 'excess'), your UC is not reduced. If it is not more than the excess, your UC is reduced, but the excess is reduced by your childcare costs element before the reduction is applied.[39]

---

6. Change of circumstances after you claim

You have a duty to report certain changes in your circumstances. The DWP or HM Revenue and Customs (HMRC) should inform you of the main kinds of changes that you must report, but might not list them all. It is also your duty to report *any* change in your circumstances that you might reasonably be expected to know might affect your right to, the amount of, or the payment of, your benefit.[40] For the rules on changes of circumstances that apply to housing benefit, see pp90–93.

You must notify changes promptly to the DWP or HMRC office handling your claim. Check the information sent to you about your benefit award, but get advice if you are in doubt. The rules say that the office handling your claim for child benefit or guardian's allowance includes the HMRC child benefit office (see Appendix 1), or any office specified by HMRC.

You must notify the changes in writing or by telephone.[41] It is best to notify changes in writing so that you have a record of what you have reported. If you report a change by telephone, note the time and date of your call and confirm what was said in writing. Keep a copy of any letters you send. If you give the original to an officer, ask her/him to stamp your copy to confirm s/he has received the original.

There are additional ways you can report a change of circumstances.
- For child benefit and guardian's allowance, you may be able to report the change in person,[42] either at the HMRC child benefit office or another office specified by HMRC. However, it is always better to do so in writing.
- Except for child benefit and guardian's allowance, if the change is a birth or a death, there is a special rule (sometimes called 'Tell Us Once'). You can report such a change in person at a local authority (and, in England, a county council) office specified for that purpose. If the change is a death, you can notify it by telephone to the DWP if a number has been specified for that purpose.[43] Check

with your local authority for the 'Tell Us Once' arrangements in your area – eg, at the registry office.

Note:
- If you do not promptly report a change which you have a duty to notify, any resulting overpayment may be recoverable from you (see Chapter 52).
- If you are considered to have acted 'knowingly' or dishonestly, you may also be guilty of an offence, which may lead to prosecution or a benefit penalty. Even if you have not committed an offence, a civil penalty may be applied (see Chapter 53).

7. When payments can be suspended

Payment of part or all of your benefit can be suspended in certain circumstances. This means that the suspended benefit is not paid to you.

Suspension while an appeal is pending

Your benefit can be suspended if the DWP, the local authority or HM Revenue and Customs (HMRC) is appealing (or considering an appeal) against:[44]
- a decision of the First-tier Tribunal, Upper Tribunal or court to award you benefit; *or*
- a decision of the Upper Tribunal or court about someone else's case if the issue in the appeal could affect your claim. For housing benefit (HB) only, the other case must also be about an HB issue.

The DWP, the local authority or HMRC must give you written notice that it intends to request the statement of reasons from the First-tier Tribunal, or that it intends to apply for leave to appeal, or to appeal. It must do this as soon as is 'reasonably practicable'.[45]

The decision maker must then do one of these things within the usual time limits for doing so (see Chapter 55 and 56).

If s/he does not, the suspended benefit must be paid to you.[46] The suspended benefit must also be paid to you if the decision maker withdraws an application for leave to appeal, withdraws the appeal or is refused leave to appeal and cannot renew the application for leave to appeal.

Suspension for not providing information and evidence

You can be required to supply information or evidence if the decision maker needs this to determine whether your award of benefit should be revised or superseded (see p1276 and p1287).[47]

Part 8: Claiming benefits and getting paid
Chapter 50: Getting paid
7. When payments can be suspended

Payment of your benefit can be suspended if you do not provide the information and evidence, and:[48]
- your benefit has been suspended in the circumstances described p1185; *or*
- you apply for a revision or supersession (see p1276 and p1287); *or*
- you do not provide certificates, documents, evidence and other information about the facts of your case as required;[49] *or*
- your entitlement to benefit is conditional on your being incapable of work or having limited capability for work.

You must be notified in writing if the decision maker wants you to provide information or evidence. Within 14 days, or one month for child benefit, guardian's allowance and housing benefit (HB), or seven days for contribution-based jobseeker's allowance (JSA) if you come under the universal credit (UC) system (see p20) of being sent the request, you must:
- supply the information or evidence.[50] You can be given more time than this if you satisfy the decision maker that this is necessary; *or*
- satisfy the decision maker that the information does not exist or you cannot obtain it.[51]

If the decision maker has not already done so, your benefit can be suspended if you do not provide the information or evidence within the relevant time limit.[52] See p1187 for whether your entitlement to benefit can be terminated.

Suspension for not taking part in a medical examination

Most benefits can be suspended if you do not take part in a medical examination on two consecutive occasions without 'good cause'.[53] This applies if:
- the decision maker is looking at whether you should still be getting a benefit (or whether you are getting it at the correct rate); *or*
- you apply for a revision or a supersession and the decision maker thinks a medical examination is necessary in order to make a decision.

This rule does not apply if the issue is whether you have limited capability for work. For information on these medicals and the consequences of failing to take part in them, see p1013. It also does not apply to personal independence payment. However, if you do not take part in a medical, the DWP may still suspend your benefit because of a doubt about your entitlement (see below).
See p1187 for whether your entitlement to benefit can be terminated.

Suspension in other circumstances

Your benefit can also be suspended in various other circumstances, including if:[54]
- a question has arisen about your entitlement, or if the DWP, HMRC or (for HB) the local authority thinks you are being or have been overpaid;[55]

- you have been getting JSA and a question has arisen about whether you are meeting your jobseeking conditions. Your JSA must be suspended until this matter is resolved. **Note:** this does not apply to contribution-based JSA if you come under the UC system (see p20).[56]

Challenging decisions to suspend benefit

You cannot appeal to the First-tier Tribunal against the decision to suspend your benefit. The only ways to change the decision are to negotiate to get your benefit reinstated or to challenge the decision in the courts by judicial review (see p1378). You could also ask for a short-term advance of benefit (see p1177). Get advice.

The decision maker may be willing to continue to pay your benefit, or at least some of it, if you can show that you will experience hardship otherwise. If you receive a letter telling you that your benefit has been suspended, reply and explain how the suspension affects you and ask for it to be reconsidered. It may be wise to get advice first (see Appendix 2).

8. When your entitlement is terminated

Your entitlement to benefit can be terminated if:
- your benefit was suspended in full, you are then required to provide information or evidence to determine whether the decision awarding you benefit should be revised or superseded, and you fail to do so within one month of the request;[57] *or*
- your benefit was suspended in full because you did not provide information or evidence required to determine whether the decision awarding you benefit should be revised or superseded and it is more than one month since your benefit was suspended.[58]

The termination of your entitlement to benefit takes effect from the date payment was suspended (or an earlier date if you ceased to be entitled for another reason).[59]

Your entitlement to most benefits can also be terminated if you do not take part in a medical examination and it is more than one month since your benefit was suspended on this ground.[60] The decision to do so is discretionary.

If you disagree with a decision to terminate your benefit, you can ask for a revision (see p1276) and then appeal (see Chapter 55).

9. Deductions and payments to third parties

Your benefits are usually paid directly to you, but there are some circumstances when money can be deducted and paid to another person (a third party) on your behalf.

Part 8: Claiming benefits and getting paid
Chapter 50: Getting paid
9. Deductions and payments to third parties

What deductions can be made

Amounts can be deducted from your benefit to pay for:[61]
- housing costs paid to your lender under the mortgage payment scheme (see p1190);
- other housing costs (see p1190);
- rent arrears (see p1191);
- fuel (see p1192);
- water charges (p1193);
- council tax arrears (see p1193);
- child support maintenance (see p1193); *and*
- other payments – eg, loan repayments, fines and other charges (see p1195).

Note: in addition to the above deductions, you may also have deductions made to recover budgeting loans from the social fund (see p788) and overpayments (see p1235) and for penalties for fraud (Chapter 53). Your benefit may also be reduced because the DWP has applied a sanction (see Chapter 48) or because it is recovering a hardship payment (see Chapter 51).

From which benefits can deductions be made

Deductions are usually made from income support (IS), income-based jobseeker's allowance (JSA), income-related employment and support allowance (ESA), pension credit (PC) and universal credit (UC). In some circumstances, they can also be made from contribution-based JSA and contributory ESA (see below).

Deductions can only be made from other benefits to repay eligible loans (see p1195) and child support maintenance that you owe (see p1193).

Deductions from contribution-based jobseeker's allowance and contributory employment and support allowance

Deductions can be made from your contribution-based JSA or your contributory ESA for the payments listed above if you have an 'underlying entitlement' to income-based JSA or income-related ESA – ie, if you were not entitled to contribution-based JSA or contributory ESA, you would be entitled to income-based JSA or income-related ESA at the same rate.[62]

Deductions can also be made from contribution-based JSA and contributory ESA even if you have no underlying entitlement to income-based JSA or income-related ESA for council tax arrears, fines and child support maintenance arrears.

If you come under the UC system (see p20), these rules do not apply. However, deductions for child support maintenance can be made from your contribution-based JSA or contributory ESA (see p1194).

Deductions can also be made from your contribution-based JSA or contributory ESA for mortgage payments if your income-based JSA, income-related ESA or your UC is insufficient to cover the deductions (see p1190).

When deductions can be made

Deductions and direct payments to third parties can only be made if you or your partner are liable to make the payments.[63] Deductions should only be made if there is evidence that you are liable – eg, the bill is in your or your partner's name.

Your written consent is required before deductions for tax credit overpayments and self-assessment tax debts can be made from your **IS**, **income-based JSA**, **income-related ESA** or **PC**. Your consent is also required before deductions are made for arrears of housing costs paid to your lender, rent arrears, service charges for fuel and water, fuel costs (including arrears), water charges (including arrears) and repayment of integration loans if:[64]

- you (or your partner) do not get child tax credit (CTC) and the total to be deducted for these payments exceeds 25 per cent of your family's applicable amount (see Chapter 12) or, in the case of PC, 25 per cent of your minimum guarantee (see p149). Housing costs included in your applicable amount should not be taken into account when calculating the 25 per cent;
- you (or your partner) get CTC, and the total to be deducted for these payments exceeds 25 per cent of your CTC and child benefit and your family's applicable amount (see Chapter 12) or, in the case of PC, your minimum guarantee (see p149). Housing costs included in your applicable amount should not be taken into account when calculating the 25 per cent.

The DWP can make deductions without your agreement if they are made for:
- council tax arrears;
- fines;
- child support maintenance;
- current housing costs;
- nursing home charges or hostel charges not included in housing benefit (HB).

Consent is not needed for these deductions even if the total amount deducted exceeds the 25 per cent referred to above.[65]

Your consent is required before direct payments (including for arrears) are made for fuel costs and water charges from your **UC** if the total amount deducted for these payments exceeds five times 5 per cent of your UC standard allowance and child elements (see Chapter 13).[66]

Otherwise, the DWP can make deductions from your UC without your consent.

The deductions

Deductions are made before you receive your regular benefit payment. If you want to have deductions made to help you clear any arrears or debts, ask the DWP office dealing with your claim. If you disagree with a decision about deductions, you can challenge it by applying for a mandatory reconsideration (see p1311) and then by appealing (see Chapter 55).

Part 8: Claiming benefits and getting paid
Chapter 50: Getting paid
9. Deductions and payments to third parties

The mortgage payment scheme

When you claim IS, income-based JSA, income-related ESA, PC or UC, you may get help with your housing costs. This can include help with mortgage interest payments or interest on loans for repairs and improvements (see Chapters 20 and 22). **Note:** these loans are included in UC as 'owner-occupier' payments. The general rules for payment of housing costs are as follows.

- Housing costs are usually paid direct to your lender four weeks in arrears (monthly in arrears for UC).[67]
- Payment is not made direct to your lender if your lender is not covered by, or has opted out of, the mortgage payment scheme.[68] The DWP should tell you if this is the case and you must then pay your own mortgage.
- If you receive PC and you are only entitled to the savings credit, not to the guarantee credit, direct payments are only made if a written request has been made by you, or the DWP considers that it is in the best interests of you or your family.[69]

The amount paid to your lender is deducted from your total IS, income-based JSA, income-related ESA, PC or UC entitlement.[70] If you are on JSA or ESA and the amount of your income-based JSA or income-related ESA is insufficient to cover the deduction, deductions can be made from your contribution-based JSA or contributory ESA. If you are on UC but the amount is insufficient to cover the deduction, deductions can also be made from your contribution-based JSA or contributory ESA.

You must make up any difference between what the DWP pays to your lender and the amount you owe. If you do not have enough benefit to meet the full cost, all but 10 pence of your benefit (1 pence for UC) is paid and you must pay the rest yourself.[71]

If you are in mortgage arrears, no amount towards the arrears can be deducted from your benefit if deductions are made under the mortgage payment scheme.

Except in the case of PC, if you have a mortgage protection policy, the amount deducted and paid to your lender is reduced by the amount of payment from the policy.[72]

If an overpayment of mortgage interest is paid to your lender, see p1223.

Other housing costs

The amount in your IS, income-based JSA, income-related ESA, PC or UC for your mortgage interest is usually paid directly to your lender under the mortgage payment scheme (see p1190).[73] If this applies to you (or would apply had your lender not opted out of the scheme), the deductions described here only cover payments for debts of other types of housing costs – eg, service charges and, in some cases, rent. For IS, income-based JSA, income-related ESA and PC, see p452, and for UC, see p488. **Note:** rent payments covered by UC are not included in these rules.[74] For the amount of the deductions, see p1196.

If your current IS, income-based JSA, income-related ESA or PC includes money for these other housing costs and you are in debt for such costs (excluding payments for ground rent or rent charge payments, unless paid with your service charges or for a tent[75]), deductions can be made from your IS, JSA, ESA or PC to clear the debt and to meet current payments. Deductions are made if it would be 'in the interests' of you or your family to do so.

You only qualify for direct deductions from IS, income-based JSA, income-related ESA and PC, if you owe more than half of the annual total of the relevant housing cost. This condition can be waived if it is in the 'overriding interests' of you or your family that deductions start as soon as possible – eg, repossession of your home is imminent.[76]

In the case of mortgage payments, the decision maker must be satisfied that there are arrears.[77] You must have paid less than eight weeks' full payments in the last 12 weeks.[78] The amount of mortgage interest taken into account is the amount after deductions for non-dependants (see p464).

To have deductions for other housing costs (in practice, this usually means service charges) from your **UC**, you must be in debt with your other housing costs. Your earnings (or your combined earnings with your partner) must also be below the UC work allowance that applies to you (see p167). If your earnings (or combined earnings) equal or exceed the work allowance for three monthly assessment periods, the deduction must stop.[79]

Rent arrears

If you are in arrears with your rent while on HB, or are £100 or more in arrears of hostel payments, an amount can be deducted from your IS, income-based JSA, income-related ESA or PC and paid directly to your landlord. This can also apply if you are in approved premises under section 13 of the Offender Management Act 2007 and have built up arrears of service charges rather than rent arrears.[80] For the amount of the deductions, see p1196.

Rent arrears do not include the amount of any non-dependant deductions (see p67), but can cover any water charges or service charges payable with your rent and not met by HB. Fuel charges included in your rent cannot be covered by direct deductions if they change more than twice a year.

To qualify for direct deductions, your rent arrears must be equal to at least four times your full weekly rent. If you have not paid your full rent for eight weeks or more, direct deductions can be made automatically if your landlord asks the DWP to make them.[81] If your arrears relate to a shorter period, deductions can only be made if it is in the overriding interests of your family to do so.[82] In either case, the decision maker must be satisfied that you are in rent arrears. Even if you are, you can ask her/him not to make direct deductions – eg, if you are claiming compensation from your landlord because of the state of repair of your home.[83] Once your arrears are paid off, direct payments can continue for any fuel and water charges included in your rent.[84]

Part 8: Claiming benefits and getting paid
Chapter 50: Getting paid
9. Deductions and payments to third parties

Deductions can be made from your UC if you are in debt with your rent (including water, service and other charges included in it) if:[85]

- you are entitled to UC housing costs for rent payments or occupy 'specified accommodation' and get HB for that (p45); *and*
- you occupy the accommodation to which the rent applies; *and*
- your earnings (or if you make a joint claim with your partner, your combined earnings) for the previous UC monthly assessment period (see p164) are below the level of the work allowance that applies to you (see p167). If your earnings (or joint earnings) equal or exceed the work allowance for three monthly assessment periods, the deduction must stop.

The DWP can make a monthly deduction from your UC equivalent to between 10 per cent and 20 per cent of the standard allowance (see p258) that applies in your case and pay it to your landlord. The DWP should take your circumstances into account in deciding how much the deduction will be.

Fuel

If you are in debt with your mains gas or electricity, an amount can be deducted from your IS, income-based JSA, income-related ESA and PC each week and paid to the fuel company in instalments – usually once a quarter.[86] This is called 'fuel direct'. In return, the fuel company agrees not to disconnect you. For the amount of the deduction, see p1196. Deductions can be made if:[87]

- the amount you owe is £73.10 or more (including reconnection or disconnection charges if you have been disconnected); *and*
- you continue to need the fuel supply; *and*
- it is in your, or your family's, interests to have deductions made.

An amount is deducted for the fuel you use each week (your current consumption) as well as for the arrears you owe. The amount deducted for current consumption is whatever is necessary to meet your current weekly fuel costs. This is adjusted if the cost increases or decreases. Deductions for current consumption can be continued after the debt has been cleared.[88]

If you are in debt for any mains gas or mains electricity (including reconnection or disconnection charges), deductions can be made from your UC if your earnings (or, if you are claiming jointly with your partner, your combined earnings) for the previous monthly UC assessment period (see p164) are below the level of the work allowance that applies in your case (see p167).[89] If your earnings equal or exceed the work allowance for three monthly assessment periods, the deduction must stop.

The DWP can make deductions from your UC and pay it to the fuel company. It can deduct a monthly amount equal to 5 per cent of your standard allowance (see p258), plus an additional amount that the DWP considers to be equal to the average monthly fuel costs, except if you are paying for that by other means – eg, a prepayment meter.

Water charges

If you get into debt with charges for water and sewerage, direct deductions can be made from your IS, income-based JSA, income-related ESA and PC.[90] Debt includes any disconnection, reconnection and legal charges. For the amount of the deductions, see p1196. If you pay your landlord for water with your rent, deductions are made under the arrangements for rent arrears (see p1191).[91]

Deductions can be made if you failed to budget and it is in the interests of you or your family to make deductions.[92] If you are in debt to two water companies, you can only have a deduction for arrears made to one at a time. Your debts for water charges should be cleared before your debts for sewerage costs, but the amount paid for current consumption can include both water and sewerage charges.[93]

If you are in debt with charges for water and sewerage (including reconnection charges), deductions may be made from your UC if your earnings (or, if you are claiming jointly with your partner, your combined earnings) for the previous monthly UC assessment period (see p164) are below the level of the work allowance that applies in your case (see p167).[94] If your earnings equal or exceed the work allowance for three monthly assessment periods, the deduction must stop.

The DWP can make a deduction from your UC and pay it to the water company. It can deduct a monthly amount equal to 5 per cent of your standard allowance (see p258), plus an additional amount that the DWP considers necessary to meet your continuing monthly water costs.

Council tax arrears

Deductions for council tax arrears can be made from IS, JSA, ESA, PC or UC if the local authority gets a liability order from a magistrates' court (in Scotland, a summary warrant or decree from a sheriff court) and applies to the DWP for recovery to be made in this way.[95] Deductions can be made for arrears and any unpaid costs or penalties imposed. For the amount of the deductions, see p1196.

Child support maintenance

The rules that apply to deductions depend on which child support rules the child maintenance is payable under. Child support cases are dealt with under:

- the 2012 rules, if a new application for child support is made on or after 25 November 2013. **Note:** the government intends to transfer existing cases to these rules, and to complete this process by some point in 2017;
- the 2003 rules, if child support was applied for on or after 3 March 2003 and the 2012 rules do not apply;

Part 8: Claiming benefits and getting paid
Chapter 50: Getting paid
9. Deductions and payments to third parties

• the 1993 rules, if child support was applied for between 1993 and 3 March 2003.

For full details of which set of rules apply, including on conversion from one set to another, see CPAG's *Child Support Handbook*.

2012 and 2003 rules

If you are liable to pay child support maintenance at the flat rate, a deduction of £5 a week under the 2003 rules, or £7 a week under the 2012 rules, can be made from your:[96]

• IS, income-based JSA, income-related ESA, PC or UC, including if your partner is liable;
• bereavement allowance;
• carer's allowance (CA);
• contributory ESA;
• industrial injuries benefit;
• contribution-based JSA;
• retirement pension;
• war widow's or war disablement pension;
• widowed mother's allowance and widowed parent's allowance;
• widow's pension;
• training allowance (other than Work-Based Learning for Young People or Skillseekers).

The whole of the child support may be deducted from the above benefits.[97] If more than one partner in a couple or polygamous marriage is liable to pay maintenance at the flat rate, it is deducted from any IS, income-based JSA, income-related ESA, PC or UC they jointly receive, with the deduction paid equally. So for example, if both partners in a couple are liable for child support at a flat rate of £5, they each pay £2.50.[98]

Deductions can also be made for any arrears of child support from any of the above benefits, except if IS, income-based JSA, income-related ESA or PC is received by the non-resident parent or her/his partner.

If you come under the UC system (see p20) but have not been awarded UC, deductions for arrears can only be made from your contribution-based JSA or contributory ESA. The deduction for arrears in all cases is £1.20 a week.[99]

Deductions can also be made to recover the collection fee for the Child Maintenance Service's 'collect and pay service' under the 2012 rules.[100]

1993 rules

Under the 1993 rules, deductions can be made from your IS, income-based JSA, income-related ESA, PC or UC as a contribution towards the maintenance of your child(ren). The deduction is a standard amount of £7.40 a week or, for UC, a monthly amount equal to 5 per cent of the non-resident parent's standard allowance (see p258).

If you have children from two or more different relationships, only one deduction can be made and the deduction is apportioned between the people who care for them.[101]

Deductions cannot be made if you:[102]

- are aged under 18; *or*
- would qualify for a family premium (see p236) or have 'day-to-day care' of any child (see CPAG's *Child Support Handbook* for what this means); *or*
- receive:
  - maternity allowance;
  - statutory sick pay or statutory maternity pay;
  - attendance allowance, disability living allowance, personal independence payment or armed forces independence payment;
  - CA;
  - industrial injuries disablement benefit or a war disablement pension;
  - an Armed Forces Compensation Scheme payment or a payment from the Independent Living Funds.

If one of the above benefits is not paid solely because of overlapping benefit rules or an inadequate contribution record, you are still exempt from deductions.

A deduction of half the above standard amount may be made if deductions are also being made for debts of other payments (see p1197).[103] **Note:** at the time this *Handbook* was written, this did not apply to UC.

Deductions may also be made from your contribution-based JSA or contributory ESA for arrears of child support maintenance (unless you come under the UC system – see p20).[104]

Other deductions

Other deductions can be made from your benefit for the following.

- **Residential accommodation charges.** Deductions can be made from your IS, JSA, ESA or PC (not UC) to meet your accommodation charges if you have failed to budget for them and it is considered to be in your interests for deductions to be made.[105]
- **Hostel payments.** If you (or your partner) live in a hostel or approved premises under section 13 of the Offender Management Act 2007, you have claimed HB to meet your accommodation costs and your payments cover fuel, meals, water charges, laundry and/or cleaning of your room, part of your IS, JSA, ESA or PC (not UC) can be paid directly to the hostel for these items.[106]
- **Court fines.** Magistrates' courts (any court in Scotland) can apply to the DWP for a fine, costs or compensation order to be deducted from your IS, JSA, ESA, PC or UC.[107]

Part 8: Claiming benefits and getting paid
Chapter 50: Getting paid
9. Deductions and payments to third parties

- **Eligible loans.** Deductions can be made from your IS, JSA, ESA, PC or UC and (if necessary) your retirement pension or CA towards repaying 'eligible' loans if you have not kept up with the repayments.[108] 'Eligible loans' are loans made by certain not-for-profit lenders, such as community development financial institutions, credit unions and charities, but do not include business loans.
- **Integration loans.** Deductions can be made to repay an integration loan – ie, loans paid to refugees and people granted humanitarian protection and their dependants. Deductions can be made from your IS, JSA, ESA, PC or UC.[109]
- **Tax credit overpayments and self-assessment tax debts.** Deductions can be made from your IS, JSA, ESA or PC (not UC) to repay these. The deduction is paid to HM Revenue and Customs. Your written consent is required.[110] Although deductions cannot be made from your UC, if your entitlement to tax credits has stopped and you are entitled to UC in the same tax year, the DWP can recover the overpayment by making deductions from your UC.[111]

How much can be deducted

If deductions are being made under the rules described in this chapter from your IS, income-based JSA, income-related ESA or PC, the maximum deductions are shown below.

If deductions are made from your UC, in most cases they are made at a fixed rate of 5 per cent of your standard allowance (see p258). In the case of rent arrears, they are made at a rate of at least 10 per cent but not more than 20 per cent of your standard allowance.

Type of arrears	Deduction for arrears	Deduction for ongoing cost
Mortgage payments scheme*	Nil	Current weekly cost
Other housing costs*	£3.70 each housing debt (maximum of £11.10)	Current weekly cost
Rent arrears and hostel payments	£3.70	Nil (met by HB)
Residential accommodation charges	Nil	The accommodation allowance (for those in local authority homes); all but £24.25 of your IS, JSA, ESA or PC (for those in private or voluntary homes)
Hostel payments	Nil	Weekly amount assessed by local authority
Fuel	£3.70 each fuel debt (maximum of £7.40 payable)	Estimated amount of current consumption

Water charges	£3.70 (adjusted every 26 weeks)	Estimated costs
Council tax arrears	£3.70	Nil
Fines	Nil	£5 (lower amount £3.70)
Repayment of eligible loans	Nil	£3.70
Repayment of integration loans	Nil	£3.70
Child support maintenance	£1.20 (2003 and 2012 rules)	£7 (2012 rules); £5 (2003 rules); £7.40 (1993 rules)
Repayment of tax credit overpayments and self-assessment tax debts	Nil	Maximum £11.10

*If you have more than one type of housing cost (ie, one under the mortgage payment scheme and one under other housing costs) and these are not met in full because of a restriction on the amount that can be covered (see p462) or a non-dependant deduction (see p464), the direct payment to meet the current weekly costs is reduced by multiplying the amount of the restriction and/or deduction by the amount of the item of housing costs to be paid directly and then dividing by the amount of total housing costs.[112] This ensures that the deductions are shared proportionately between different housing costs.

More than one deduction

More than one deduction can be made from your IS, income-based JSA, income-related ESA and PC. You must be left with at least 10 pence of benefit.[113] If you are also having an overpayment recovered from your benefit, having agreed to pay a penalty, admitted fraud or been found guilty of fraud (see p1239), the total amount of the deductions cannot exceed £29.60 a week.[114]

Note:
- The maximum amount that can be deducted for arrears and for current child support maintenance under the 1993 rules is £10.96 a week.[115]
- If the combined cost of deductions for arrears and current consumption for fuel, rent, water charges, housing costs arrears and repayment of certain loans is more than 25 per cent of your total applicable amount (see p230) or, for PC, more than 25 per cent of your minimum guarantee (see p149) before housing costs, the deductions cannot be made without your consent.[116]
- Most deductions are taken into account when calculating the total amount of deductions, including all those mentioned in the priority rules (see p1198), as well as those for sanctions (see Chapter 48), benefit offences (p1265) and to recover overpayments of JSA, ESA or UC. Deductions for ongoing costs (as opposed to arrears) of fuel or water charges are ignored. Deductions of more than the limit may still be made for other housing costs (ie, those not covered

Part 8: Claiming benefits and getting paid
Chapter 50: Getting paid
9. Deductions and payments to third parties

by the mortgage payment scheme), rent arrears or fuel debts, if the DWP considers it would be in your best interests.
- If more than one deduction is to be made from your benefit, there is an order of priority (see below).

More than one deduction can be made from your UC, provided you are left with at least one pence of UC. There is a limit to the total number of certain deductions that can be made. No more than three of the following deductions from UC may be made at any one time:[117]
- housing costs not covered by the mortgage payment scheme;
- rent arrears;
- fuel debts;
- water charges;
- child support maintenance under the 1993 rules;
- repayment of eligible loans;
- repayment of integration loans;
- council tax arrears;
- fines, costs and compensation orders.

The total amount payable for fuel debts and water charges combined cannot exceed an amount equal to five times 5 per cent of your standard allowance plus any child elements to which you are entitled (see Chapter 13) without your consent.[118]

Also, the total amount of deductions from UC cannot usually exceed eight times 5 per cent of the standard allowance that applies in your case (p258). However this maximum can be exceeded to allow deductions for housing costs not covered by the mortgage payment scheme, fuel costs and the minimum amount for rent arrears.[119]

Priority between deductions

If you have more debts or current charges than can be met from your benefit (see p1196), they are paid in the following order of priority from your IS, income-based JSA, income-related ESA and PC:[120]
- housing costs not covered by the mortgage payment scheme;
- rent arrears (and related charges);
- fuel charges;
- water charges;
- council tax arrears;
- unpaid fines, costs and compensation orders;
- payments for child support maintenance under the 1993 rules (payments due under the 2003 and 2012 rules are always payable);
- repayment of integration loans;
- repayment of eligible loans;
- repayment of tax credit overpayments and self-assessment tax debts.

If you owe both gas and electricity arrears, the DWP chooses which one to pay first, depending on your circumstances.[121]

If you have been overpaid benefit or given a social fund loan, you may have to repay these through deductions from your benefit.[122] You should argue that these deductions should take a lower priority.

For UC, an order of priority applies if your UC is 'insufficient' to meet all the deductions that apply to it. Your award of UC is 'insufficient' if the total amount of certain deductions would be more than eight times 5 per cent of the standard allowance that applies to you (see p258). The deductions are paid in the following order of priority:[123]

- housing costs not covered by the mortgage payment scheme;
- rent arrears (and related charges), if the amount of the deduction is 10 per cent of your standard allowance;
- fuel;
- council tax arrears;
- fines, if the amount of the deduction is 5 per cent of the standard allowance;
- water charges;
- child support maintenance under the 1993 rules;
- child support maintenance under the 2003 or 2012 rules;
- repayment of social fund payments;
- recovery of hardship payments;
- penalties instead of prosecution for benefit offences;
- recovery of overpayments of benefits or tax credits caused by fraud;
- loss of benefit for benefit offences;
- recovery of overpayments of benefits or tax credits not caused by fraud;
- repayment of integration loans;
- repayment of eligible loans;
- rent arrears (and related charges), if the amount of the deduction is more than 10 per cent of your standard allowance;
- fines, costs and compensation orders, if the amount of the deduction is more than 5 per cent of the standard allowance.

10. Recovery of benefits from compensation payments

If you are seeking compensation from someone (the 'defendant') through the courts (eg, because you have been unfairly dismissed or because you have had a personal injury), you might be awarded damages to compensate you for your loss. However, if, as the result of a defendant's action, you have had to claim benefit, the amount of damages awarded is reduced by the amount of benefit you received.

Part 8: Claiming benefits and getting paid
Chapter 50: Getting paid
10. Recovery of benefits from compensation payments

Employment cases

In an employment case such as wrongful or unfair dismissal, your claim for compensation for loss of earnings may be reduced by the amount of benefit (eg, jobseeker's allowance – JSA) you received.[124] Seek specialist employment law advice. Also, the DWP is able to recover payments of JSA, income support or income-related employment and support allowance from your employer by deductions from your compensation if it is an unfair dismissal or protective award case dealt with in an employment tribunal. In such cases, the DWP sends a 'recoupment notice' to the employer, and a copy to you, setting out the benefit to be deducted before the compensation is paid to you. You may give notice to the DWP that you do not accept the amount recouped within 21 days of the recoupment notice (or longer if allowed), and can appeal to the First-tier Tribunal against the decision that the DWP makes in response.[125]

Personal injury cases

If you are paid compensation for an accident, injury or disease after 6 October 1997, those compensating you can reduce the amount paid to you when you have received benefit in respect of the same loss. They must then pay the money back to the Compensation Recovery Unit (CRU), which is part of the DWP. It does not matter whether the payment is voluntary, with or without legal proceedings, or by order of a court. A reduction is not made if the compensation is paid for pain and suffering, because benefits are not paid for this.

The CRU can only recover the benefit in the right-hand column of the table on p1201, and only if you were paid it as a consequence of the accident, injury or disease.

Note: the CRU can also recover, under a similar scheme with its own rules, certain lump-sum payments made by the DWP to you or a dependant.[126] The lump-sum payments that can be recovered are those made by the DWP for lung diseases under the Pneumoconiosis etc. (Workers' Compensation) Act 1979 (or as compensation if you have had a claim under that Act rejected) or payments under the Diffuse Mesothelioma Payment Scheme.

Details of the procedures to be followed and other advice can be obtained from the CRU (see Appendix 1). A guide to the procedures, *Recovery of Benefits, Lump Sum Payments and NHS Charges: technical guidance*, is available at www.gov.uk/government/collections/cru.

Which benefits can be recovered

All benefits paid to you 'in consequence' of the injury or disease from which you have suffered during the 'relevant period' are recoverable.

The relevant period

The 'relevant period' is usually the period of five years from the date:[127]

– of your accident or injury if you are claiming compensation for an accident or injury; *or*

– you first claimed a recoverable benefit because of the disease if you are claiming compensation in respect of a disease.

The relevant period ends if those compensating you make a final payment of compensation or an agreement is made under which compensation already paid is accepted as being in final payment.[128]

Before you are paid compensation, those compensating you must apply to the DWP for a 'certificate of recoverable benefits'.[129] This tells them which benefits are recoverable.

Those compensating you become liable to pay the DWP for the total amount of recoverable benefit 14 days after the certificate is issued.[130] It is the compensator's obligation, not yours, and so if the compensator fails to pay, the CRU cannot pursue you for the money. The compensator remains liable even if it fails to apply for a certificate.[131]

Offsetting against your compensation

Before the compensator pays your compensation, it can deduct the recoverable benefits paid during the relevant period from certain types of compensation.[132]

Compensation	Recoverable benefits
Loss of earnings	Disability working allowance, disablement benefit, employment and support allowance (ESA), incapacity benefit, income support, invalidity allowance, invalidity pension, JSA, reduced earnings allowance, severe disablement allowance, sickness benefit, statutory sick pay (paid before 6 April 1994), unemployment benefit, unemployability supplement, universal credit
Cost of care	Attendance allowance, disability living allowance (DLA) care component, disablement benefit paid for constant attendance (see p687) or exceptionally severe disablement (see p688), personal independence payment (PIP) daily living component
Loss of mobility	Mobility allowance, DLA mobility component, PIP mobility component

Example

Gary receives a £30,000 compensation payment consisting of £15,000 for loss of earnings, £5,000 for pain and suffering, and £10,000 for the cost of care. By the time the award is made he has received £20,000 of ESA and £5,000 of PIP daily living component. The award for loss of earnings is reduced to nil. Gary receives the full award for pain and suffering, but his award for the cost of care is reduced by £5,000. The compensator is

Part 8: Claiming benefits and getting paid
Chapter 50: Getting paid
10. Recovery of benefits from compensation payments

liable to pay the DWP recoverable benefits of £25,000, and pays Gary a net award of £10,000 (£5,000 pain and suffering plus £5,000 care).

Any compensation reduced by this method is treated as being paid to you. Those compensating you must give you a statement showing how the payment has been calculated, even if the recovery of benefits reduces a particular type of compensation to nil. If the recoverable benefit exceeds the compensation paid to you for a particular loss, those compensating you still have to pay the balance to the DWP.

Exempt payments

The recovery rules apply to all claims, no matter how small. However, certain compensation payments are exempt.[133] These include:

- payments under the Fatal Accidents Act 1996, the Vaccine Damage Payments Act 1979 and the NHS industrial injury scheme;
- payments under the Pneumoconiosis Compensation Scheme and certain payments for loss of hearing;
- criminal injuries compensation;
- contractual sick pay and redundancy payments;
- payments from insurance companies from policies agreed before the accident; *and*
- payments from certain trusts – eg, the Macfarlane Trust, Eileen Trust, MFET Ltd, The Caxton Foundation, UK Asbestos Trust, the Skipton Fund and the EL Scheme Trust.

Challenging a recovery decision

A decision maker may look at a certificate of recoverable benefit again (this is called a review) if s/he is satisfied that there was an error in its preparation, or that it recovers too much benefit, or that the person who applied for the certificate supplied incorrect or insufficient information, as a result of which the amount of benefit recovered is less than it should be.[134] You and those compensating you can both appeal to the First-tier Tribunal (see Chapter 55) against the certificate, but not until the compensation payment has been made and the benefit paid back to the DWP.[135] Also, the person appealing must apply for a review before s/he can appeal. The government says that the review should be applied for within a month of the money being paid back, although the law does not refer to such a time period, and in any case a late application can be accepted.[136] Further appeals can be made to the Upper Tribunal in the usual way (see Chapter 56).[137]

Notes

1. **Who is paid**
1 **HB** Reg 94(2) HB Regs; reg 75(2)
    HB(SPC) Regs
    CB/GA Regs 27 and 28 CB&GA(Admin)
    Regs
    UC/PIP/JSA&ESA under UC Regs 57
    and 58 UC,PIP,JSA&ESA(C&P) Regs
    Other benefits Regs 30 and 33
    SS(C&P) Regs
2 **CB/GA** Reg 34 CB&GA(Admin) Regs
    UC/PIP/JSA&ESA under UC Reg 58
    UC,PIP,JSA&ESA(C&P) Regs
    Other benefits Reg 34(1) and (2)
    SS(C&P) Regs
3 Reg 35 SS(C&P) Regs; reg 60
    UC,PIP,JSA&ESA(C&P) Regs

2. **How and when you are paid**
4 **CB/GA** Reg 16 CB&GA(Admin) Regs
    UC/PIP/JSA&ESA under UC Reg 46
    UC,PIP,JSA&ESA(C&P) Regs
    Other benefits Reg 21 SS(C&P) Regs
5 **CB/GA** Regs 16-20 CB&GA(Admin)
    Regs
    UC/PIP/JSA&ESA under UC Reg 51
    UC,PIP,JSA&ESA(C&P) Regs
    Other benefits Regs 22-26C SS(C&P)
    Regs
6 **HB** Reg 91 HB regs; reg 72 HB(SPC)
    Regs
    CB/GA Reg 18 CB&GA(Admin) Regs
    UC/PIP/JSA&ESA under UC Reg 45
    UC,PIP,JSA&ESA(C&P) Regs
    Other benefits Reg 20 SS(C&P) Regs
7 **CB/GA** Reg 25 CB&GA(Admin) Regs
    UC/PIP/JSA&ESA under UC Reg 55
    UC,PIP,JSA&ESA(C&P) Regs
    Other benefits Reg 38(1)(bb)
    SS(C&P) Regs
    CDLA/2609/2002 commented on the
    way a similar rule applied to payment by
    giro/order book.

3. **Overlapping benefits**
8 Reg 6 SS(OB) Regs
9 Reg 4(5) SS(OB) Regs
10 s43(1) SSCBA 1992; s1 PA 2014; reg
    4(5) SS(OB) Regs
11 ss 51A and 52(2) SSCBA 1992

12 s16(1), (2) and (6) SSCBA 1992; reg 2
    SS(MAP) Regs
13 Reg 4 (2)(f) and (4) SS(OB) Regs
14 Reg 4(4A) SS(OB) Regs
15 Reg 4(3) SS(OB) Regs
16 Reg 10 SS(OB) Regs
17 Reg 8 SS(OB) Regs
18 Reg 7 SS(OB) Regs

4. **Short-term advances**
19 Regs 5 and 6 SS(PAB) Regs
20 Reg 7 SS(PAB) Regs
21 Sch 2 para 20A SS&CS(DA) Regs
22 Reg 8 SS(PAB) Regs
23 Sch 2 para 20A SS&CS(DA) Regs allows
    a right of appeal against decisions on
    deductions under reg 10 SS(PAB) Regs.
24 Reg 3, definition of 'benefit', SS(PAB)
    Regs
25 Reg 22 CB&GA(Admin) Regs
26 Regs 22(3), 41 and 42 CB&GA(Admin)
    Regs

5. **The benefit cap**
27 ss96 and 97 WRA 2012
28 Under Sch 2 para 8A SSA 1998 there is
    no right of appeal for UC, but at the time
    of writing the relevant rule for HB
    appeals at Sch 7 para 6 CSPSSA 2000
    had not been amended.
29 Reg 75C HB Regs; reg 80 UC Regs
30 s96(5A) WRA 2012; regs 75A, 75C and
    75G HB Regs
31 Reg 75B HB Regs
32 s96(5A) WRA 2012; reg 79 UC Regs
33 Reg 75E HB Regs; HB Circular A15/2013
34 Reg 75E(3) HB Regs
35 Reg 75E(4) HB Regs
36 Reg 82(1) UC Regs
37 Reg 82(2) UC Regs
38 Reg 75D HB Regs
39 Reg 81 UC Regs

8

6. **Change of circumstances after you claim**

40 **JSA** Reg 24 JSA Regs
CB/GA Reg 23 CB&GA(Admin) Regs
UC/PIP/JSA&ESA under UC Reg 38 UC,PIP,JSA&ESA(C&P) Regs
Other benefits Reg 32 SS(C&P) Regs

41 **JSA** Reg 24(7) JSA Regs
UC/PIP/JSA&ESA under UC Reg 38(5) UC,PIP,JSA&ESA(C&P) Regs Regs 2, 3 and 5 SS(NCC) Regs, which apply for fraud, allow notification by telephone (unless it is specifically required to be in writing).
Other benefits Reg 32(1B) SS(C&P) Regs

42 Reg 23(5) CB&GA(Admin) Regs

43 Reg 32ZZA SS(C&P) Regs; reg 24 JSA Regs
UC/PIP/JSA&ESA under UC Reg 39 UC,PIP,JSA&ESA(C&P) Regs

7. **When payments can be suspended**

44 **HB** Reg 11(2)(b) HB&CTB(DA) Regs
CB/GA Sch 7 para 13(2) CSPSSA 2000
UC/PIP/JSA&ESA under UC Reg 44(2)(b) and (c) UC,PIP,JSA&ESA(DA) Regs
Other benefits s21(2)(c) and (d) SSA 1998; reg 16(3)(b) SS&CS(DA) Regs

45 **HB** Reg 11(3) HB&CTB(DA) Regs
CB/GA Reg 18(4) and (5) CB&GA(DA) Regs
UC/PIP/JSA&ESA under UC Reg 44(5) UC,PIP,JSA&ESA(DA) Regs
Other benefits Reg 16(4) SS&CS(DA) Regs

46 **HB** Reg 12(1)(b) HB&CTB(DA) Regs
CB/GA Reg 21 CB&GA(DA) Regs
UC/PIP/JSA&ESA under UC Reg 46(c) UC,PIP,JSA&ESA(DA) Regs
Other benefits Reg 20(2) and (3) SS&CS(DA) Regs

47 **HB** Reg 86(1) HB Regs; reg 67(1) HB(SPC) Regs
CB/GA Reg 23 CB&GA(Admin) Regs
UC/PIP/JSA&ESA under UC Reg 38(2) UC,PIP,JSA&ESA(C&P) Regs; reg 45 UC,PIP,JSA&ESA(DA) Regs
Other benefits Reg 32(1) SS(C&P) Regs

48 **HB** Reg 13 HB&CTB(DA) Regs
CB/GA Reg 19 CB&GA(DA) Regs
UC/PIP/JSA&ESA under UC Reg 45(6) UC,PIP,JSA&ESA(DA) Regs
Other benefits Reg 17(2) SS&CS(DA) Regs

49 **HB** Reg 86(1) HB Regs; reg 67(1) HB(SPC) Regs
CB/GA Reg 23 CB&GA(Admin) Regs
UC/PIP/JSA&ESA under UC Reg 38(2) UC,PIP,JSA&ESA(C&P) Regs
Other benefits Reg 32(1) SS(C&P) Regs

50 **HB** Reg 13(4)(a) HB&CTB(DA) Regs
CB/GA Reg 19(2) CB&GA(DA) Regs
UC/PIP/JSA&ESA under UC Reg 45(4)(a) UC,PIP,JSA&ESA(DA) Regs
Other benefits Reg 17(4)(a) SS&CS(DA) Regs

51 **HB** Reg 13(4)(b) HB&CTB(DA) Regs
CB/GA Reg 19(2)(b) CB&GA(DA) Regs
UC/PIP/JSA&ESA under UC Reg 45(4)(b) UC,PIP,JSA&ESA(DA) Regs
Other benefits Reg 17(4)(b) SS&CS(DA) Regs

52 **HB** Reg 13(4) HB&CTB(DA) Regs
CB/GA Reg 19(5) CB&GA(DA) Regs
UC/PIP/JSA&ESA under UC Reg 45(6) UC,PIP,JSA&ESA(DA) Regs
Other benefits Reg 17(5) SS&CS(DA) Regs

53 s24 SSA 1998; reg 19(2) SS&CS(DA) Regs

54 **HB** Sch 7 para 13(2)(a) CSPSSA 2000
CB/GA Reg 18(2) CB&GA(DA) Regs
Other benefits ss21(2)(a) and (b), 22 and 24 SSA 1998

55 **HB** Reg 11(2)(a)(i) and (c) HB&CTB(DA) Regs
CB/GA Reg 18(2)(a) and (c) CB&GA(DA) Regs
UC/PIP/JSA&ESA under UC Reg 44(2)(a)(i) and (iii) UC,PIP,JSA&ESA(DA) Regs
Other benefits Reg 16(3)(a)(i) and (iii) SS&CS(DA) Regs

56 Reg 16(2) SS&CS(DA) Regs; reg 44(2) UC,PIP,JSA&ESA(C&P) Regs does not include this provision.

8. **When your entitlement is terminated**

57 **HB** Reg 14(1)(a) HB&CTB(DA) Regs
CB/GA Reg 20(1)(a) CB&GA(DA) Regs
UC/PIP/JSA&ESA under UC Reg 47(1)(a) UC,PIP,JSA&ESA(DA) Regs
Other benefits Reg 18(1)(a), (2) and (4) SS&CS(DA) Regs

58 **HB** Reg 14(1)(b) HB&CTB(DA) Regs
CB/GA Reg 20(1)(b) CB&GA(DA) Regs
UC/PIP/JSA&ESA under UC Reg 47(1)(b) UC,PIP,JSA&ESA(DA) Regs
Other benefits Reg 18(1)(b), (3) and (4) SS&CS(DA) Regs

8

59 **HB** Reg 14(1) HB&CTB(DA) Regs
  CB/GA Reg 20(2) CB&GA(DA) Regs
  UC/PIP/JSA&ESA under UC Reg
  47(2) UC,PIP,JSA&ESA(DA) Regs
  Other benefits Reg 18(1) SS&CS(DA)
  Regs
60 Reg 19(3) and (4) SS&CS(DA) Regs

9. **Deductions and payments to third
  parties**
61 **UC/PIP/JSA&ESA under UC** Regs 59
  and 60 and Schs 6 and 7
  UC,PIP,JSA&ESA(C&P) Regs
  Other benefits Regs 34A and 35 and
  Sch 9 SS(C&P) Regs; CC(DIS) Regs;
  CT(DIS) Regs; F(DIS) Regs
62 Sch 9 para 1(2) and (3) SS(C&P) Regs
63 Sch 9 para 2(1) SS(C&P) Regs; Sch 6
  para 2(1) UC,PIP,JSA&ESA(C&P) Regs
64 Sch 9 para 8(2) and (4) SS(C&P) Regs
65 Sch 9 para 8 SS(C&P) Regs
66 Sch 6 para 3(3) UC,PIP,JSA&ESA(C&P)
  Regs
67 **UC/PIP/JSA&ESA under UC** Sch 5
  paras 3 and 8 UC,PIP,JSA&ESA(C&P)
  Regs
  Other benefits Reg 34A and Sch 9A
  paras 2 and 6 SS(C&P) Regs
68 **UC/PIP/JSA&ESA under UC** Sch 5
  para 10 UC,PIP,JSA&ESA(C&P) Regs
  Other benefits Sch 9A paras 8 and 9
  SS(C&P) Regs
69 Regs 34A(1A) and 34B and Sch 9A para
  2A SS(C&P) Regs
70 **UC/PIP/JSA&ESA under UC** Sch 5
  para 4 UC,PIP,JSA&ESA(C&P) Regs
  Other benefits Sch 9A para 3 SS(C&P)
  Regs
71 **UC/PIP/JSA&ESA under UC** Sch 5
  para 4(3) UC,PIP,JSA&ESA(C&P) Regs
  Other benefits Sch 9A paras 1 and 3
  SS(C&P) Regs
72 **UC/PIP/JSA&ESA under UC** Sch 5
  para 4(1) UC,PIP,JSA&ESA(C&P) Regs
  Other benefits Sch 9A para 3(4)
  SS(C&P) Regs
73 **UC/PIP/JSA&ESA under UC** Sch 5
  para 3 UC,PIP,JSA&ESA(C&P) Regs
  Other benefits Sch 9A para 6 SS(C&P)
  Regs
74 **UC/PIP/JSA&ESA under UC** Sch 6
  para 6(6) UC,PIP,JSA&ESA(C&P) Regs
  Other benefits Sch 9 para 3(5)
  SS(C&P) Regs
75 **UC/PIP/JSA&ESA under UC** Sch 5
  para 5(7) UC,PIP,JSA&ESA(C&P) Regs
  Other benefits Sch 9 para 1, definition
  of 'housing costs', SS(C&P) Regs

76 Sch 9 para 3(4) SS(C&P) Regs
77 CIS/15146/1996
78 Sch 9 para 3(4) SS(C&P) Regs
79 Sch 6 para 6 UC,PIP,JSA&ESA(C&P)
  Regs
80 Sch 9 para 5 SS(C&P) Regs
81 Sch 9 para 5(1)(c)(i) SS(C&P) Regs
82 Sch 9 para 5(1)(c)(ii) SS(C&P) Regs
83 Sch 9 para 5(6) SS(C&P) Regs;
  R(IS) 14/95
84 Sch 9 para 5(7) SS(C&P) Regs
85 Sch 6 para 7 UC,PIP,JSA&ESA(C&P)
  Regs
86 Sch 9 para 6 SS(C&P) Regs
87 Sch 9 para 6(1) SS(C&P) Regs
88 Sch 9 para 6(4)(b) SS(C&P) Regs
89 Sch 6 para 8 UC,PIP,JSA&ESA(C&P)
  Regs
90 Sch 9 paras 1 and 7 SS(C&P) Regs
91 Sch 9 para 7(1) SS(C&P) Regs
92 Sch 9 para 7(2) SS(C&P) Regs
93 Sch 9 para 7(7) SS(C&P) Regs
94 Sch 6 para 9 UC,PIP,JSA&ESA(C&P)
  Regs
95 CC(DIS) Regs; CT(DIS) Regs; CIS/
  11861/1996
96 **UC/PIP/JSA&ESA under UC** Sch 7
  paras 1 and 2 UC,PIP,JSA&ESA(C&P)
  Regs;
  Other benefits Sch 9B para 2 SS(C&P)
  Regs; Sch 1 para 4(I)(b) and (c) CSA
  1991; reg 4(1) and (2) CS(MCSC) Regs
97 **UC/PIP/JSA&ESA under UC** Sch 7
  para 2 UC,PIP,JSA&ESA(C&P) Regs
  Other benefits Sch 9B para 2 SS(C&P)
  Regs
98 **UC/PIP/JSA&ESA under UC** Sch 7
  para 5 UC,PIP,JSA&ESA(C&P) Regs
  Other benefits Sch 9B paras 4-6
  SS(C&P) Regs
99 **UC/PIP/JSA&ESA under UC** Sch 7
  para 3 UC,PIP,JSA&ESA(C&P) Regs;
  Memo ADM 13/14
  Other benefits Sch 9B para 3 SS(C&P)
  Regs; Memo DMG 17/14
100 Memo DMG 17/14; Memo ADM 14/14,
  on the changes introduced by the Child
  Support Fees Regulations 2014, No.612
101 **UC/PIP/JSA&ESA under UC** Sch 7
  para 2 UC,PIP,JSA&ESA(C&P) Regs
  Other benefits Sch 9 para 7A SS(C&P)
  Regs; reg 28(3) CS(MASC) Regs
102 Reg 28(1) and Sch 4 CS(MASC) Regs
103 s43 CSA 1991; Sch 9 paras 7A and 7B
  SS(C&P) Regs
104 Sch 9 para 7B SS(C&P) Regs
105 Sch 9 para 4 SS(C&P) Regs
106 Sch 9 para 4A SS(C&P) Regs

8

107 F(DIS) Regs
108 **UC/PIP/JSA&ESA under UC** Sch 6
     para 11 UC,PIP,JSA&ESA(C&P) Regs
     Other benefits Sch 9 para 7C SS(C&P)
     Regs
109 **UC/PIP/JSA&ESA under UC** Sch 5
     para 12 UC,PIP,JSA&ESA(C&P) Regs
     Other benefits Sch 9 para 7D SS(C&P)
     Regs; reg 9 The Integration Loans for
     Refugees and Others Regulations 2007,
     No.1598
110 Sch 9 para 7E SS(C&P) Regs
111 Reg 12 UC(TP) Regs
112 Sch 9 para 3(2A) SS(C&P) Regs
113 Sch 9 para 2(2) SS(C&P) Regs
114 Reg 16(5ZA) SS(PAOR) Regs
115 Sch 9 para 8 SS(C&P) Regs
116 Sch 9 paras 5(5), 6(6), 7(8) and 8(2)
     SS(C&P) Regs
117 Sch 6 para 3(1) and (2)
     UC,PIP,JSA&ESA(C&P) Regs
118 Sch 6 para 3(3) UC,PIP,JSA&ESA(C&P)
     Regs
119 Sch 6 para 4 UC,PIP,JSA&ESA(C&P)
     Regs
120 Sch 9 para 9 SS(C&P) Regs
121 Reg 4 CC(DIS) Regs; reg 8 CT(DIS) Regs
122 Regs 15 and 16 SS(PAOR) Regs; reg 3
     SF(RDB) Regs
123 Sch 6 para 5 UC,PIP,JSA&ESA(C&P)
     Regs

10. **Recovery of benefits from
    compensation payments**
124 *Nabi v British Leyland (UK) Ltd* [1980] 1
     WLR 529 (CA)
125 The Employment Protection
     (Recoupment of Jobseeker's Allowance
     and Income Support) Regulations 1996,
     No.2349
126 The Social Security (Recovery of
     Benefits) (Lump Sum Payments)
     Regulations 2008, No.1596
127 s3 SS(RB)A 1997
128 s3(4) SS(RB)A 1997
129 s4 SS(RB)A 1997
130 s6(4) SS(RB)A 1997
131 s7 SS(RB)A 1997
132 s8 and Sch 2 SS(RB)A 1997

133 s1 and Sch 1 SS(RB)A 1997; reg 2 SS(RB)
     Regs
134 s10 SS(RB)A 1997; reg 9 SS&CS(DA)
     Regs
135 ss11 and 12 SS(RB)A 1997
136 s11(2A) SS(RB)(A) 1997; reg 9ZB
     SS&CS(DA) Regs. Neither provide a
     time limit for review. See the official
     guidance at www.gov.uk/government/
     publications/repaying-compensation-
     to-dwp-what-to-do-if-you-think-our-
     decision-is-wrong.
137 s13 SS(RB)A 1997; reg 13 SS(RB)App
     Regs

Chapter 51

. . . .

Hardship payments

This chapter covers:

Key facts

- Hardship payments are reduced-rate payments of jobseeker's allowance (JSA), employment and support allowance (ESA) and universal credit (UC) that are made in limited circumstances, including if you have been sanctioned.
- You or your partner or children must be experiencing hardship. In some cases for JSA, you must be in a 'vulnerable group'.
- You must apply for hardship payments and demonstrate on a regular basis that you are experiencing hardship.
- You do not have to pay back hardship payments of JSA or ESA. You must pay back hardship payments of UC.

1. Hardship payments of jobseeker's allowance

If you do not come under the universal credit (UC) system (see p20), you may be able to get hardship payments of income-based jobseeker's allowance (JSA) – eg, if your JSA is being paid at a reduced (or nil) rate or has been suspended. You do not have to pay them back.[1] Hardship payments of JSA are not made automatically. You must apply for them (see p1218).

When you can get hardship payments

You can qualify for hardship payments of income-based JSA in a number of situations. You cannot qualify for hardship payments if you (or your partner) are

Part 8: Claiming benefits and getting paid
Chapter 51: Hardship payments
1. Hardship payments of jobseeker's allowance

entitled to income support (IS) or income-related employment and support allowance (ESA), or come within one of the groups of people who can claim IS (see Chapter 5).[2] In this case, you or your partner can claim IS or income-related ESA instead of hardship payments. If you or your partner are at least the qualifying age for pension credit (PC – see p147), you (or your partner) might qualify for PC instead of hardship payments.

If, after receiving hardship payments, you are awarded full income-based JSA, IS, income-related ESA or PC for the same period, the income-based JSA, IS, income-related ESA or PC is reduced by the amount of hardship payments you were paid.[3]

Whether you satisfy the jobseeking conditions

You can qualify for hardship payments:
- at the beginning of a claim for JSA if you are waiting for a decision about whether you (or, if you are a member of a joint-claim couple, you or your partner) satisfy the 'jobseeking conditions' (see p1027).[4] If there is any other reason for the delay in deciding your claim, you are not eligible under this rule. You get hardship payments until the decision maker makes a decision on your claim, provided you (or, if you are a member of a joint-claim couple, both of you) continue to satisfy the other conditions for getting income-based JSA;
- if your JSA is suspended because there is doubt about whether you (or, if you are a member of a joint-claim couple, you or your partner) satisfy the 'jobseeking conditions' (see p1027).[5] You get them until the decision maker makes a decision, provided you satisfy the other conditions for getting income-based JSA. If you are a member of a joint-claim couple, both of you must satisfy these conditions (or one of you if the other is in an exempt group – see p121 for who counts);
- if the decision maker decides that you do not satisfy the jobseeking conditions, but only if you are in a vulnerable group. However, you cannot qualify if you (or, if you are a joint-claim couple, either of you) are treated as unavailable for work for one of the reasons listed on p1037.[6]

You normally cannot start receiving hardship payments until the 15th day after your date of claim (not including any waiting days – see p132 and p705) or the 15th day of the suspension, but if you are in a vulnerable group (see p1215), they start sooner (see below).[7] If you are subject to successive 14-day suspensions (eg, at each signing day the employment officer doubts that you took sufficient steps to find work) and so never reach the 15th day of any suspension period, get advice as this may be unlawful.

If you are in a vulnerable group

If you are in a vulnerable group (see p1215), you get hardship payments:[8]
- from the beginning of a claim, subject to the waiting days rules on p132, or if later, the date the DWP decides you are in a vulnerable group;

- if your JSA is suspended, from the date that the suspension begins; *or*
- from the date the decision maker decides that you do not satisfy the 'jobseeking conditions'. You (or if you are a member of a joint-claim couple, both of you) must continue to satisfy the other conditions for getting income-based JSA.

Jobseeker's allowance is reduced because of a sanction

If you are given a sanction (see p1093), you can qualify for hardship payments.[9] **Note:** if you have also committed a benefit offence, see p1265.

If you are in a vulnerable group (see p1215), you get hardship payments from the first day of the period when JSA is not paid. If you are not in a vulnerable group, you cannot get hardship payments until the 15th day of the period. The DWP says that if during a sanction period another sanction is imposed for a different reason, you cannot get hardship payments for the first 14 days of the period of the new sanction.[10] If this happens, you should appeal and argue this is wrong. **Note:** you must apply for a mandatory reconsideration before you can appeal.

Hardship payments continue until the end of the sanction period, provided you satisfy the other conditions for getting income-based JSA. If you are a member of a joint-claim couple, both of you must satisfy these conditions (or one of you if the other is in an exempt group – see p121 for who counts).

The rules about your age

You cannot usually qualify for hardship payments until you are 18. However, if you are 16 or 17, you can qualify if you come within any of the categories of 16/17-year-olds who can qualify for income-based JSA (see p125). **Note:** if you are 16 or 17 and have been sanctioned on specified grounds, you do not need to claim hardship payments because you continue to get income-based JSA, although at a reduced rate (see p1095).

The amount of hardship payments

The weekly amount of hardship payments you get depends on your needs. Your personal allowance, premiums and housing costs are calculated as for income-based JSA. The usual disregards for capital and income are applied. However, your applicable amount is normally reduced by 40 per cent of:[11]

- if you are not a member of a couple, the appropriate personal allowance for a single person of your age;
- if you are a member of a couple (other than a joint-claim couple), the appropriate personal allowance for a single person:
  – aged under 25, if both of you are aged 16 or 17, or if one of you is between 18 and 25 years old and the other is a 16/17-year-old who would not be eligible for income-based JSA in her/his own right;
  – aged 25 or over in all other cases, provided one of you is 18 or over;

Part 8: Claiming benefits and getting paid
Chapter 51: Hardship payments
2. Hardship payments of employment and support allowance

- if you are a member of a joint-claim couple, the appropriate personal allowance for a single person aged 25 or over.

The reduction is only 20 per cent if you or your partner, or a child included in your claim (see p220), are pregnant or 'seriously ill' (not defined). In all cases, the reduction is rounded to the nearest five pence.

2. Hardship payments of employment and support allowance

If you do not come under the universal credit (UC) system (see p20), you may be able to get hardship payments of income-related employment and support allowance (ESA) if your ESA is being paid at a reduced (or nil) rate because you have been given a sanction or because you have committed a benefit offence. You do not have to pay them back.

Note:
- Hardship payments of ESA are not made automatically. You must apply for them (see p1218).
- Different hardship rules apply if you could be disqualified from receiving ESA (eg, because you have limited capability for work through your own misconduct, or you have failed to accept treatment without 'good cause' – see p637), but you are experiencing hardship.

When you can get hardship payments

You can qualify for hardship payments of income-related ESA if:[12]
- your ESA is being paid at a reduced (or nil) rate:
  - because you have been given a sanction for failing to take part in a work-focused interview (see p1124) or for failing to undertake work-related activity (see p1128); or
  - because you have committed a benefit offence (see p1265); and
- you, your partner or a child for whom you or your partner are responsible (see p222) would experience hardship if payments were not made. See p1217 for what is taken into account in deciding whether you would experience hardship.

You must satisfy the rules for entitlement to income-related ESA (see Chapter 3).

The amount of hardship payments

The weekly amount of hardship payments is a percentage of the ESA personal allowance that applies for a single person whose ESA includes a support component (ie, the personal allowance for main-phase ESA), rounded to the nearest five pence. The percentage is:[13]

- 80 per cent, if your ESA does not include a work-related activity component and you or your partner, or a child or qualifying young person for whom you or your partner are responsible and who lives in your household, are pregnant or seriously ill. This is currently 80 per cent of £73.10 = £58.50 a week. **Note:** this does *not* apply if your ESA is being paid at a reduced (or nil) rate because you have committed a benefit offence; *or*
- 60 per cent in all other cases. This is currently 60 per cent of £73.10 = £43.85 a week.

This is paid in addition to any amounts of ESA you are still being paid despite the reduction for the sanction (eg, a component if you qualify), as well as premiums and housing costs, if relevant.

3. Hardship payments of universal credit

If you come under the universal credit (UC) system (see p20), you may be able to get hardship payments of UC if your UC is being paid at a reduced (or nil) rate because you have been given a sanction or because you have committed a benefit offence. You must pay back hardship payments of UC (see p1213). Hardship payments of UC are not made automatically. You must apply for them (see p1218).

If you come under the UC system (see p20) and your contribution-based jobseeker's allowance (JSA) or contributory employment and support allowance (ESA) is paid at a reduced (or nil) rate and you experience hardship, you might qualify for hardship payments of UC.

When you can get hardship payments

If you (or your partner) are given a sanction, you can qualify for hardship payments of UC if:[14]

- you are 18 or over and are given a sanction (or your partner is 18 or over and has been given a sanction) and, as a result, your UC has been paid at a reduced (or nil) rate using the 'high rate' daily reduction (see p1110). **Note:** if you are aged 16 or 17, or your partner is given a sanction and s/he is 16 or 17, you cannot qualify for hardship payments because your UC is paid at a reduced rate using the 'low rate' daily deduction (see p1110); *and*
- for low level sanctions only, you (or your partner, or both of you if both of you have been given a sanction) have complied with any condition specified by the DWP – eg, you have now taken part in a work-focused interview or have agreed to attend training; *and*

Part 8: Claiming benefits and getting paid
Chapter 51: Hardship payments
3. Hardship payments of universal credit

- you (or your partner) apply for hardship payments in the approved manner, or in a way that the DWP accepts is sufficient, and provide any information or evidence required by the DWP; *and*
- you (and your partner) accept that the hardship payments are recoverable; *and*
- the DWP is satisfied that:
  - you (and your partner) have met all the work-related requirements that were in force in the seven days before you applied for hardship payments; *and*
  - you (and your partner) are experiencing hardship (see p1217).

If your UC has been reduced because of a benefit offence (see p1265), you can qualify for hardship payments of UC if:[15]

- you (and your partner) meet all the conditions of entitlement to UC; *and*
- you (and your partner) apply for hardship payments in the approved manner, or in a way that the DWP accepts is sufficient, and provide any information or evidence required by the DWP; *and*
- you (and your partner) accept that the hardship payments are recoverable; *and*
- the DWP is satisfied that you (and your partner) are experiencing hardship (see p1217).

Note: you can qualify under the benefit offences rules even if you (or your partner) are aged 16 or 17.

Hardship payment periods

Each hardship payment is made for the period starting on the date you satisfy all the conditions for getting one including making an application (for sanctions) or the date of your application (for benefit offences) and ending on the day before your next normal UC payday.[16] If the period is seven days or less, a hardship payment is made until the next normal payday for the following assessment period or, if sooner, the last day in respect of which your UC is paid at a reduced (or nil) rate.

How do you ensure you get maximum hardship payments?

Because of the way the rules operate, you must apply for hardship payments of UC in each assessment period in which you need one – ie, in which your UC is paid at a reduced rate. Because the hardship payment period starts when you apply for one and ends on the day before your UC payday, to ensure you get the maximum amount, apply for hardship payments on every UC payday you are paid a reduced rate of UC.

The amount of hardship payments

The amount of hardship payments is worked out as follows.[17]

- **Step one:** determine the amount of the reduction made from your UC for the sanction (see p1110) or the benefit offence (see p1267) in the assessment period before the one in which you apply for hardship payments.
- **Step two:** multiply the amount in Step one by 12 and divide by 365. Take 60 per cent of this amount, rounding to the nearest penny.
- **Step three:** multiply the amount in Step two by the number of days for which hardship payments can be made to you (see p1212).

Example

Dan is a single claimant aged 40. He was given a 91-day medium level sanction in the previous (30-day) assessment period. His normal UC payday is the 3rd of the month. When his UC starts to be paid at a reduced rate, he applies and qualifies for hardship payments. This is on the 7th day of a 31-day month. He therefore gets hardship payments for the period starting on the 7th of the month and ending on the 2nd of the next month (27 days).

Step one: the relevant amount is £312 (£10.40 daily reduction x 30 days).

Step two: £312 x 12 ÷ 365 x 60% = £6.15

Step three: Dan can be paid hardship payments for 27 days.

£6.15 x 27 days = £166.05

Dan's hardship payments for that assessment period are £166.05. He gets these in addition to any UC he can be paid – eg, if he qualifies for a housing costs element.

If Dan is still experiencing hardship, he should apply for hardship payments on the day he receives his next payment of UC (ie, the next 3rd of the month) to ensure he gets maximum hardship payments.

Recovery of hardship payments

You must usually pay back hardship payments of UC.[18] However, hardship payments:

- are *not* recoverable during any assessment period in which you have sufficient monthly earnings (see below); *and*
- *stop* being recoverable (ie, are 'written off'), if, for at least six months since the last day on which your UC was paid at a reduced (or nil) rate (or for two or more periods that total at least six months), you (and your partner, if you are a joint claimant) have had sufficient monthly earnings (see below).

You have sufficient monthly earnings if you (or if you are a joint claimant, you and your partner) are someone who does not have to meet any work-related requirements:

- because your earnings (your combined earnings if you are a joint claimant) are the same as, or above, your earnings threshold (see p1084); *or*
- for any of the other reasons listed on p1081 and p1085 (other situations). If you are a joint claimant you must both be someone who does not have to meet any work-related requirements for one of these reasons.

  In this case, your monthly earnings (your combined monthly earnings if you are a joint claimant) must be at least 16 times the minimum wage for a person of your age (or your partner's age if s/he is younger than you) multiplied by 52 and divided by 12.

Hardship payments can normally only be recovered from the person to whom they were paid. However, if you are a joint claimant, an amount paid to your partner is treated as paid to you, and vice versa.[19]

All the methods used to recover overpayments described on p1239 can be used to recover hardship payments.[20]

4. **Deciding hardship**

When you apply for hardship payments, explain anything that is causing you hardship, or which makes it more likely that you will experience hardship. This includes health, disability, pregnancy, and any special needs you and your partner and children have.

> *Hardship*
> 'Hardship' is not defined in the rules. The DWP says that it means 'severe suffering or privation' (meaning 'a lack of the necessities of life').[21]

When deciding whether or not you are experiencing hardship, there are things the decision maker must consider. For jobseeker's allowance (JSA) see p1215, for employment and support allowance (ESA) see p1217, and for universal credit (UC) see p1217. If your claim is refused, consider applying for a revision or appealing (see Chapters 54 and 55). **Note:** you must apply for a mandatory reconsideration before you can appeal.

In all cases, the decision maker looks at the resources available to you.
- The decision maker normally takes into account income and capital that is disregarded when calculating your benefit – eg, disability living allowance (DLA) and savings below £6,000.
- You should only be treated as having resources that are likely to be actually available to you. For example, if you have savings in a bank account but they are subject to a notice period for withdrawal, you should not be treated as having this capital until you can access it.

- You should not be treated as having resources if these are only available on credit, or you would have to sell any of your possessions.

Jobseeker's allowance

For JSA, even if you are in one of the situations when hardship payments can be made, you cannot get them unless the decision maker is satisfied that you are in a vulnerable group or that you or your partner would experience hardship if payments were not made.[22]

Hardship payments can be made sooner if you are in a vulnerable group. In some situations, you can only get hardship payments if you are in a vulnerable group.

When deciding whether or not you would experience hardship, the decision maker must consider:[23]

- whether you or your partner, or a child included in your claim (see p220), qualify for a disability premium (or a disabled child premium if still included) or the disabled child or severely disabled child element of child tax credit (CTC);
- the resources likely to be available to you or your partner, or a child included in your claim (see p220), if no hardship payments are made, how far these fall short of your reduced applicable amount (see p1209) and the length of time this is likely to be the case. Also included are any resources that may be available from others in your household – eg, your parents. The decision maker cannot take into account any CTC or child benefit.[24] See p1214 for what resources might be taken into account;
- whether there is a 'substantial risk' that you or your partner, or a child included in your claim (see p220), would be without essential items (eg, food, clothes, heating or accommodation) or whether they would be available at considerably reduced levels and, if so, for how long.

Vulnerable groups

You are in a vulnerable group if:[25]

- you or your partner are **pregnant** and would experience hardship if no payment were made;
- you or your partner are **responsible for a child** who would experience hardship if no payment were made. See p222 for when you count as responsible for a child. **Note:** if you are a lone parent and are responsible for a child under five, or you are a lone parent under 18, you can claim income support and cannot claim hardship payments;
- your income-based JSA includes a **disability premium** or would include one if your claim were to succeed and the person for whom the premium is paid would experience hardship if no payment were made;
- you or your partner have a **chronic medical condition** and as a result your (or your partner's) functional capacity is 'limited or restricted by physical impairment', and the decision maker is satisfied that:

8

- it has lasted or is likely to last for at least 26 weeks; *and*
- if no payment were made, the health of the person with the condition would decline further than that of a 'normal healthy adult' within the next two weeks and the person would experience hardship;
- you or your partner:
  - are, for a considerable portion of the week, **caring for someone** who:
    - is getting attendance allowance (AA), the highest or middle rate of the care component of disability living allowance (DLA), either rate of the daily living component of personal independence payment (PIP) or armed forces independence payment. If the person has claimed one of these benefits, you count as being in a vulnerable group for up to 26 weeks from the date of the claim or until the claim is decided, whichever is first; *or*
    - has been awarded AA, the highest or middle rate of DLA care component, the daily living component of PIP or armed forces independence payment but it is not yet in payment; *and*
  - would not be able to continue caring if no hardship payment were made. You do not have to show that the person you are caring for would experience hardship.
  This rule does not apply if the person who is being cared for lives in a care home, an Abbeyfield home or an independent hospital (see p922 for what counts);[26]
- you or your partner are a **16/17-year-old** who can claim income-based JSA (see p125) and would experience hardship if no payment were made (or if you are a joint-claim couple, you both would experience hardship);
- you or your partner are a 16/17-year-old claiming JSA on the basis of a **severe hardship direction** (see p129). You do not have to show that you would experience hardship. However, you do not count as being in a vulnerable group if the person subject to the direction does not satisfy the jobseeking conditions; *or*
- you (or if you are a joint-claim couple, at least one of you) are under 21 at the date of your hardship statement (see p1218) and within the last three years were **being looked after by the local authority** under the Children Act 1989 in England or Wales, were someone the local authority had a duty to keep in touch with under that Act, or you qualified for advice and assistance from the local authority under that Act. Remember that if you are 16 or 17 and were being looked after by a local authority when you reached 16, you usually cannot claim income-based JSA. Instead, your local authority should support and accommodate you. See p936 for further information and exceptions to the rule. **Note:** the Children Act 1989 ceased to apply in Wales from 6 April 2016.

Note: the government intends to amend the rules to allow homeless people and people with certain mental health conditions to count as being in a vulnerable group. See CPAG's online service and *Welfare Rights Bulletin* for updates.

Employment and support allowance

For ESA, when deciding whether or not you would experience hardship, the decision maker must consider:[27]

- whether you or your partner, or a child included in your claim (see p220) qualify for a severe disability premium or an enhanced disability premium, or the disabled child or severely disabled child element of CTC;
- the resources likely to be available to your household if no hardship payments were to be made, and how far these fall short of the amount of hardship payments to which you would be entitled. Also included are any resources that may be available from people who are not members of your household. For ESA sanctions, the decision maker cannot take into account any CTC or child benefit paid to you or your partner for a child who is included in your claim (see p220) or who is a member of your household.[28] See p1214 for information about what resources might be taken into account;
- whether there is a 'substantial risk' that your household would be without essential items (eg, food, clothes, heating or accommodation) or whether they would be available at considerably reduced levels.

The decision maker must also consider the length of time any of the above factors are likely to continue.[29]

Households

For the meaning of **'household'**, see p225. Members of your household can include not just you and your partner and children included in your claim. It can include others who live with you – eg, your parents or a non-dependent young person.

Universal credit

The decision maker only considers you to be in hardship if:[30]

- because your UC has been reduced as a result of a sanction using the 'high rate' daily reduction (see p1110) or because you have committed a benefit offence (see p1267), you (and your partner) cannot meet your immediate and most basic and essential needs, or those of a child for whom you (or your partner) are responsible (see p223). **'Needs'** means accommodation, heating, food and hygiene – eg, products to keep you and your home clean, or nappies for your baby; *and*
- you (and your partner) have made every effort to get alternative sources of support (eg, from your family or a charity) to meet (or partly meet) the needs and to stop incurring any expenditure not relating to basic and essential needs. The DWP says that this should not include expenditure on things you need to help you look for work, such as a telephone and access to the internet, or to maintain your child(ren)'s access to education.[31] The DWP must consider what

Part 8: Claiming benefits and getting paid
Chapter 51: Hardship payments
6. Challenging a hardship payment decision

is reasonable in your case, but you should not be required to sell or pawn anything (other than stocks and shares).[32]

See p1214 for information about what resources might be taken into account.

5. Applying for hardship payments

Hardship payments are not made automatically. You must apply for them in the approved manner, or in such other form as the DWP accepts is sufficient. Check with the Jobcentre Plus office about how you should apply. You must provide information and evidence if required.[33] For jobseeker's allowance (JSA), the DWP calls this a **'hardship statement'**.

Although you cannot receive JSA or employment and support allowance (ESA) hardship payments until you have made your application, there is no general rule to prevent you from receiving these for a period before the date on which you made it.

The likelihood of being able to convince the decision maker that you are experiencing hardship increases over time. Apply for hardship payments at any time you are without the normal payment of JSA, ESA or universal credit (UC). Note, however, that for UC, you cannot qualify for hardship payments (see p1212) in the first assessment period in which you are given a sanction – ie, before you have actually been paid UC at a reduced rate. You have to wait until the beginning of the next assessment period before you can apply.

Note:
- For JSA, while you are receiving hardship payments, you (or, if you are a joint-claim couple, one of you) must normally make a 'hardship declaration' at the Jobcentre Plus office each time you sign on, to confirm that you are still in hardship.[34]
- For UC, you must make a fresh application for hardship payments in each assessment period. See p1212 for how to ensure maximum payments.

6. Challenging a hardship payment decision

If you are refused hardship payments, you can appeal to the First-tier Tribunal (see Chapter 55). You must apply for a mandatory reconsideration before you can appeal. Ask for a written statement of reasons for the decision if this has not already been provided (see p1166).

Remember to tell the DWP if your circumstances worsen while you are applying for a revision or appealing. Ask it to consider whether hardship payments can now be paid based on your new circumstances.

7. Tax, other benefits and the benefit cap

Hardship payments of jobseeker's allowance (JSA) are taxable in the same way as income-based JSA (see p141). Hardship payments of employment and support allowance (ESA) and universal credit (UC) are not taxable.

Claiming other benefits or tax credits

If you have a partner, consider whether s/he could claim income support, income-based JSA, income-related ESA or pension credit instead of you. If so, continue to claim JSA or ESA hardship payments until her/his claim has been decided (to cover the period while the claim is being processed). However, let the DWP know that this is what you are doing so there is no overpayment. If your partner's claim for benefit is accepted, your entitlement to hardship payments ends. You may wish to claim national insurance (NI) credits (see p965), but you cannot be awarded NI credits for any week in which the only income-based JSA you are paid comprises hardship payments.[35]

If your partner counts as being in full-time paid work for working tax credit (WTC) purposes (see p196), check whether you might be better off claiming WTC.

Passported benefits

JSA and ESA (and UC) hardship payments are a type of income-based JSA and income-related ESA (and UC) and so you are still entitled to full housing benefit (HB) and other passported benefits in the usual way. You can also get HB on the basis of having no income. So, whether or not you are getting hardship payments, payment of your HB should not be affected. If it is, contact the local authority immediately. You may also be entitled to a council tax reduction from your local authority (see p854).

Notes

1. Hardship payments of jobseeker's allowance

1 s71ZH(1)(b)-(d) SSAA 1992; s46 WRA 2012; s19C(2)(f) JSA 1995 is not yet in force.
2 Regs 140(3) and 146A(3) JSA Regs
3 Regs 146 and 146H JSA Regs; reg 5(2) Cases 1 and 2 SS(PAOR) Regs
4 Regs 141(2), 142(2), 146C(2) and 146D(2) JSA Regs
5 Regs 141(5), 142(3), 146C(5) and 146D(3) JSA Regs
6 Regs 141(4) and 146C(4) JSA Regs
7 Regs 141(3), 142(2) and (4), 146C(3), and 146D(2) and (4) JSA Regs
8 Regs 141 and 146C JSA Regs
9 Regs 141(6), 142(5), 146C(6) and 146D(5) JSA Regs
10 Vol 6 Ch 35, para 35304 DMG
11 Regs 145 and 146G JSA Regs

2. Hardship payments of employment and support allowance

12 Regs 2(1), definition of 'hardship payment', 64A(a)-(c) and 64B ESA Regs; reg 16A(1) SS(LB) Regs
13 Reg 64D ESA Regs; reg 16C SS(LB) Regs

3. Hardship payments of universal credit

14 Reg 116(1) UC Regs
15 Regs 16D(1) and (2)(a) and 16E(a)-(c) SS(LB) Regs
16 Reg 117 UC Regs; reg 16F SS(LB) Regs
17 Regs 6 and 118 UC Regs; reg 16G SS(LB) Regs
18 s71ZH(1)(a) and (e) SSAA 1992; s28(2)(f) WRA 2012; reg 119 UC Regs; reg 16H SS(LB) Regs
19 s71ZH(4) SSAA 1992
20 s71ZH(5) SSAA 1992

4. Deciding hardship

21 Vol 6 Ch 35, para 35155 DMG
22 Regs 140(1) and (2) and 146A(1) and (2) JSA Regs
23 Regs 140(5) and 146A(6) JSA Regs
24 Reg 140(6) JSA Regs
25 Regs 140(1) and 146A(1) JSA Regs
26 Regs 140(4) and 146A(4) JSA Regs
27 Reg 64C ESA Regs; reg 16A(2) SS(LB) Regs

28 Reg 64C(2) ESA Regs
29 Reg 64C(1)(e) ESA Regs; reg 16A(2)(e) SS(LB) Regs
30 Reg 116(2) and (3) UC Regs; reg 16D(2)(b)-(d) and (3) SS(LB) Regs; Ch L1 ADM
31 paras L1099 and L1100 ADM
32 paras L1084-93 ADM

5. Applying for hardship payments

33 **JSA** Regs 143 and 146E JSA Regs
ESA Reg 64A(d) and (e) ESA Regs; reg 16B SS(LB) Regs
UC Reg 116(1)(c) and (d) UC Regs; reg 16E(a) and (b) SS(LB) Regs
34 Regs 144 and 146F JSA Regs

7. Tax, other benefits and the benefit cap

35 Reg 8A(5)(d) and (dd) SS(Cr) Regs

Chapter 52

....

Overpayments

This chapter covers :
1. Introduction (below)
2. Overpayments that are always recoverable (p1222)
3. Overpayments that are sometimes recoverable (p1226)
4. Recovery of overpaid benefit (p1235)
5. Overpayments of housing benefit (p1241)

For overpayments of tax credits, see Chapter 62.

References in this chapter to HM Revenue and Customs apply to overpayments of child benefit and guardian's allowance.

Key facts

- If you are paid more benefit than you are entitled to, this is called an overpayment.
- There are some situations when overpaid benefit must be repaid, regardless of how it was caused.
- In other situations, except for housing benefit (HB), the general rule is that you must repay the overpayment if it arose because you did not disclose something or you misrepresented something, regardless of whether this was your fault.
- All overpayments of HB must be repaid, except those caused by official error and which you could not have reasonably known were overpayments.
- The DWP, HM Revenue and Customs and local authorities have the discretion not to recover an overpayment in certain situations.

---

1. **Introduction**

An 'overpayment' occurs when you are paid more benefit than you should have been paid. If you are told that you must repay an overpayment, do the following.

- Use the relevant chapters in this *Handbook* to check whether or not you were entitled to some, or all, of the amount that the DWP, HM Revenue and Customs or local authority says is an overpayment. If you were entitled to some, or all, of the amount, you should challenge the decision about your entitlement.

Part 8: Claiming benefits and getting paid
Chapter 52: Overpayments
2. Overpayments that are always recoverable

- If some, or all, of the amount should not have been paid, check whether:
  - for benefits other than housing benefit (HB), the overpayment is is always recoverable (see below);
  - for benefits other than HB, the overpayment is sometimes recoverable, depending on the circumstances. Check whether all three conditions that allow the overpayment to be recovered are met (see p1227 and p1231), and also whether the overpayment can be reduced under the rules described on p1232;
  - the overpayment of HB is recoverable (see p1241). If so, check whether it can be recovered from you (p1245) and whether any amount can be offset against the sum claimed (see p1244).
- If you are not the person whose benefit was overpaid, check whether the overpayment can be recovered from you (see p1234 and p1245).
- Consider whether it is worth asking for the overpayment not to be recovered. For overpayments of HB, see p1245, and for other benefits, see p1235.
- If you must repay an overpayment , check that the method of recovery used is correct and whether you should ask for the money to be recovered in a different way. For overpayments of HB, see p1245, and for other benefits, see p1235.

Note:
- For benefits other than HB, if you are overpaid and this was because you made an incorrect statement or failed to provide information, you may also have to pay a penalty (p1256). If it is considered that an overpayment was made because of fraud, in addition to the overpayment being recovered, you may be prosecuted or given the option of paying a penalty instead of going to court. See Chapter 53 for further information.
- If an overpayment was included in a debt relief order, it cannot be recovered.[1] Similarly, if you are subject to a bankruptcy order, any overpayment that is notified to you as recoverable before the order was made is not recoverable. However, once the order ceases to have effect, any overpayment caused by fraud becomes recoverable.

2. Overpayments that are always recoverable

Except for overpayments of housing benefit (HB – see p1241), the DWP or HM Revenue and Customs (HMRC) can always recover the following overpayments.
- You have been paid too much income support (IS), income-based jobseeker's allowance (JSA), income-related employment and support allowance (ESA) or pension credit (PC) because you were owed income that you have now received (see p1223).
- Too much mortgage interest has been paid directly to your lender (see p1223).

- Too much benefit has been paid into your bank account by mistake (see p1224).
- You come under the universal credit (UC) system (see p20) and you have been paid too much UC, contribution-based JSA or contributory ESA (see p1225).

Although the above overpayments are always recoverable, you may still be able to argue that you were entitled to some, or all, of the amount, or that some or all of the overpayment does not fall into one of the above categories. The decision maker in the DWP, HMRC or local authority also has the discretion not to recover in certain circumstances (see p1235).

You were owed income that you have now received

If you are owed money while you are getting IS, income-based JSA, income-related ESA or PC, this may result in your being overpaid benefit. This is because when you receive the money you are owed, your income for benefit purposes is calculated afresh and you must repay any IS, income-based JSA, income-related ESA or PC to which you would not have been entitled had the money been paid on time.[2]

This rule applies to any income that affects the amount of IS, income-based JSA, income-related ESA or PC you get, including:[3]
- earnings;
- other social security benefits. **Note:** arrears of some benefits are treated as capital and ignored for 52 weeks (see Chapters 17 and 18);
- benefits paid by other European Economic Area member states.[4]

Note: you can appeal about whether an overpayment has occurred and how it has been calculated.[5] You must apply for a mandatory reconsideration before you can appeal (see p1311). You cannot appeal against the decision to recover any overpayment that has occurred, but you can ask the DWP to use its discretion not to recover it (see p1235).

See p1235 for how the overpayment can be recovered.

Too much mortgage interest has been paid to your lender

If you are getting help with your housing costs in your IS, income-based JSA, income-related ESA or PC (see Chapter 20), your mortgage interest is usually paid directly to your lender. Any overpayment of mortgage interest paid must be returned to the DWP by your lender if it arose because:[6]
- you ceased to be entitled to IS, income-based JSA, income-related ESA or PC and the DWP asks for repayment within four weeks of your entitlement ceasing; *or*
- the DWP did not reduce your mortgage interest payments, even though you were entitled to less money because there was a reduction in the amount of

Part 8: Claiming benefits and getting paid
Chapter 52: Overpayments
2. Overpayments that are always recoverable

your outstanding loan, the standard interest rate (see p461) or your actual mortgage interest rate. If you have a deferred interest mortgage, the relevant interest rate is the one you are liable to pay, not the one charged by your lender. If the DWP pays the latter rate by mistake, any resulting overpayment cannot be recovered.[7]

In this case, your mortgage account should simply be corrected. However, if you come off IS, income-based JSA, income-related ESA or PC and the interest is recovered, your account will be in arrears unless you have started to make payments yourself.

In practice, the DWP often stops paying your lender your ongoing mortgage interest until it has recovered the overpayment, rather than asking it to return what was overpaid. The DWP should not do this if you are put into arrears as a result.[8] If you go into arrears, get advice immediately to avoid losing your home.

You can appeal to the First-tier Tribunal (see p1310) if, for example, you dispute the amount of the overpayment, or you do not believe your situation comes into this category.[9] You must apply for a mandatory reconsideration before you can appeal (see p1311). You can ask the DWP to use its discretion not to ask your lender to repay the overpayment.

Note: if your mortgage interest has been overpaid, but not in the above circumstances, the DWP may be able to recover it under the rules described on p1226.[10]

Too much benefit has been credited to your account

Your benefit may be paid by direct credit transfer into a bank or building society account. If you are credited with too much money because of the direct credit transfer system itself, the excess can be recovered in certain circumstances.[11]

The overpayment can only be recovered if it was caused by the direct credit transfer system and:[12]

- you were notified in writing before you agreed to your benefit being paid into a bank or other account that any excess benefit could be recovered; *and*
- it has been certified that you were paid excess benefit because of the direct credit transfer system.

If the excess benefit cannot be recovered under the rules described above, it may be recoverable under the rules described on p1226, or those for recovery following late payment of income (see p1223).

You can appeal to the First-tier Tribunal against a decision to recover excess benefit credited to your bank or other account.[13] You must apply for a mandatory reconsideration before you can appeal (see p1311).

Even if the overpayment is recoverable, you can ask the DWP or HMRC to use its discretion not to recover it (see p1235).

Overpayments if you come under the universal credit system

If you come under the UC system (see p20) and you are overpaid UC, contribution-based JSA or contributory ESA, the DWP can recover any amount of overpaid benefit, regardless of the cause of the overpayment.[14] See p1235 for how the overpayment can be recovered.

Note:
- If you are overpaid, the amount recovered can be reduced (see below).
- In general, the DWP must first change the decision awarding you benefit before it can decide whether the overpayment can be recovered (see p1231).[15]
- The overpayment is usually recovered from the person to whom it is paid, but see p1226 for more details.
- You can appeal against a decision that you have been overpaid. You must request a mandatory reconsideration before you can appeal (see p1310).
- You can ask the DWP to use its discretion not to recover the overpayment (see p1235).

The amount recovered

The amount recovered is the difference between what you received and the amount to which you were entitled after the decision awarding you benefit has been changed.[16] This amount can be reduced in the following circumstances.

Offsetting universal credit

If you were overpaid JSA or ESA, the amount that can be recovered may be reduced by the amount of any UC you could have received. For this to happen, you must have made a claim for UC. The overpaid amount is reduced by the amount of UC you would have got:[17]
- had you notified any change of circumstances that affected your JSA or ESA entitlement (other than a change of dwelling) to the DWP at the time it occurred; or
- had you not misrepresented or failed to disclose something before the award of JSA or ESA; or
- had a mistake by the decision maker not occurred.

You are overpaid universal credit because of a mistake about your capital

If you are overpaid UC because of a mistake about your savings for a period of more than three months, the amount that can be recovered is reduced to take into account the fact that you would have been spending your capital had you not been receiving UC.

At the end of each three-month period for which you have been overpaid, the amount of capital you are regarded as having is reduced by the amount of UC that you were overpaid in these three months.[18] The overpayment for the next three months is then calculated as if you had this reduced amount of capital.

Part 8: Claiming benefits and getting paid
Chapter 52: Overpayments
3. Overpayments that are sometimes recoverable

You are overpaid because you moved home

If you are overpaid the housing element of UC because you moved home, but payments continued being made for your previous home, the decision maker may reduce the amount to be recovered by an amount equal to what you would have received in respect of your new home.[19]

S/he can only do this if the payments for your previous home are made to the same person as those for your new home.[20] If the decision maker reduces the amount to be recovered in this way, the reduction in the overpaid amount is treated as if it were paid in respect of your new home.[21]

From whom can an overpayment be recovered

If you come under the UC system, an overpayment of UC, contribution-based JSA or contributory ESA is usually recoverable from the person to whom it was paid. However, it can be recovered from someone else in the following circumstances.[22]

- If the overpaid amount was paid to an appointee or to someone other than you because it was not in your interest to pay you directly (see p1172), the overpayment can also be recovered from you, the claimant.
- If an overpaid amount was paid to a third party under the rules about deductions and payments to third parties (see p1187), the amount is recoverable from you, the claimant. However, amounts paid to the third party in excess of the amounts allowed by those rules are only recoverable from the third party.
- If the overpaid amount includes an amount for housing costs paid to another person (eg, your landlord) and:
  - the overpayment occurred because someone failed to disclose or misrepresented a material fact (see p1227 and p1231), it is recoverable from that person, not the person to whom it was paid;
  - the overpayment occurred because you moved home, it is recoverable from you, as well as from the person to whom it was paid;
  - the overpayment did not occur for either of the above two reasons, it is recoverable from you, the claimant, not the person to whom it was paid.

3. **Overpayments that are sometimes recoverable**

Except for the overpayments described on p1222 and overpayments of housing benefit (HB – see p1241), some overpayments can only be recovered if:[23]
- you failed to disclose, or you misrepresented, a 'relevant material fact' (see p1227) and this caused the overpayment (see p1227); *and*
- the decision awarding you benefit has been changed (see p1231).

If you have been overpaid and all the above conditions do not apply to the whole of the overpayment, only that part of the overpayment to which they all apply is recoverable from you. For example, if you were paid too much benefit over a two-year period, but you told the DWP about all the relevant facts after the first year, the overpayment made after this was not caused by your failure to disclose and is, therefore, not recoverable from you.

> ### Example
> Seamus was receiving income support (IS) as a carer. The person he was caring for stopped getting personal independence payment (PIP) in 2014. Seamus informed the DWP of this in 2015, but the DWP continued to pay Seamus his IS until 2016. This overpayment from 2015 onwards is not recoverable.

Note:
- The DWP has sometimes claimed that it can recover overpayments outside these rules (ie, even when all the above conditions are not met) under 'common law', but it is not allowed to do so (see p1239).
- Even if an overpayment can be recovered, in some situations amounts must be deducted from the recoverable sum (see p1232).
- This type of overpayment can sometimes be recovered from you, even if you are not the claimant (see p1234).
- You can appeal against a decision that the overpayment is recoverable from you (see p1234). You must apply for a mandatory reconsideration first (see p1311).
- Even if an overpayment is recoverable under these rules, you can ask the DWP or HM Revenue and Customs HMRC) to use its discretion not to recover it (see p1235).

You failed to disclose, or you misrepresented, a material fact

For an overpayment to be recoverable, you must have:
- failed to disclose a relevant 'material fact' (see below); *or*
- misrepresented a relevant 'material fact' (see p1230).

A material fact

A **'material fact'** is one which influences how much benefit you should be paid.[24] Sometimes there can be a difference between your honest opinion and a material fact.[25] For example, a statement about the distance you can walk should be taken as your honest opinion of your ability, rather than as a statement of fact.[26] If the decision maker comes to a different conclusion about the facts, you can argue that an overpayment should not be recovered.[27]

Part 8: Claiming benefits and getting paid
Chapter 52: Overpayments
3. Overpayments that are sometimes recoverable

Facts	Conclusions about the facts
You have arthritis	You have limited capability for work
A friend is sharing your flat	You are living together as husband and wife or civil partners
You have a bad back	Your mobility is severely restricted most of the time

Failure to disclose

You count as having failed to disclose a relevant material fact if:[28]

- you knew about a fact (see below);
- you had a legal duty to disclose that fact (see below); *and*
- you did not comply with that legal duty (see p1229).

Knowledge of a fact

If you did not know about a fact, including if it was a change in your circumstances, you have not 'failed' to disclose it.[29] You cannot fail to disclose something you did not know about unless:

- there was a reason why you should have been aware of it;[30] *or*
- it was reasonable for you to make enquiries, which would have revealed the information to you;[31] *or*
- you had been aware of it, but simply forgot.[32]

Legal duty to disclose

You have two different legal duties to disclose facts: a specific duty and a general duty.

You have a specific duty to disclose a fact that you know about (see above) and you have clearly been told by the DWP or HMRC that you must disclose this type of fact – eg, in your benefit award letter or in the notes which accompanied it.[33]

You do not have a specific legal duty to disclose something unless the instruction is clear and there is no room for doubt about whether or not you are required to report it.[34]

If you were not clearly told that you must report a certain fact, this specific duty to disclose does not apply. If, despite there being a clear instruction to disclose a particular fact in a letter or accompanying notes, you are subsequently told by an officer of the DWP that you do not need to disclose this type of fact, this can mean that you no longer have a duty to disclose it.[35]

You also have a general duty to disclose any change in your circumstances since the decision awarding you benefit was made if you could reasonably be expected to know that your benefit may be affected.[36]

What you can reasonably be expected to know depends on the details of your case. For example, if you were told by the DWP or a lawyer that your benefit would not be affected, or if you were too ill to have realised that it might be, it is arguable that you could not reasonably have been expected to have known that your benefit could be affected.[37] If there is no obvious connection between the fact and the overpaid benefit, argue that it was not reasonable for you to have known that your benefit might be affected.

Complying with your duty to disclose

Generally, to make a valid disclosure, you must tell the 'relevant office' in sufficiently clear terms so that the effect on your claim can be examined.

If you have a specific duty to disclose (see p1228), the 'relevant office' is the one that handles the benefit you are claiming.[38] This may be a benefit delivery centre (eg, for IS) or a central office – eg, for PIP. For special rules on reporting a birth or death (sometimes called 'Tell Us Once'), see p1184.

If you have a general duty to disclose (see p1228), the 'relevant office' is any DWP office or, in jobseeker's allowance (JSA) cases, a specified DWP office. However, it is always best to tell the office handling your claim if you can. For child benefit and guardian's allowance, you can disclose changes in your circumstances to the Child Benefit Office, or any office specified to you by HMRC.[39] Again, it is best to ensure that you tell the Child Benefit Office, as it administers your claim. You only count as having failed to disclose once the time by when it was reasonably practicable for you to have done so has passed – eg, if it was impossible for you to make the disclosure earlier than you did, you have not failed to comply with the general duty to disclose.

If the office already knew about the fact and you were aware of this, it is arguable that you have not failed to disclose. Even if you were not aware that the office already knew, it may be possible to argue that its knowledge means that any failure on your part did not actually cause the overpayment (see p1231). This is especially so if the office would not have acted any differently, even if you had reported the fact to it.[40]

You can usually notify changes in writing or by telephone, but it is best to do so in writing.[41]

If you completed a form while giving information, whether you count as having failed to disclose depends not just on what you said on the form, but also on whether you gave the necessary information in another way.[42] If you do not complete a form correctly and give the relevant information in the wrong place, you have disclosed the facts.[43]

If you made a statement in person or by telephone, but the decision maker says there is no record of this, you should appeal and give as much information as possible about the circumstances in which the disclosure was made – eg, when you called, who you spoke to and what was said.

You should usually make the disclosure yourself, unless you have an appointee acting for you (see p1149).[44] If someone else discloses the fact on your behalf, it must be made to the correct office with your knowledge and you must believe that there is no need to repeat it yourself. If someone else makes the disclosure to an office not handling your claim, but s/he reasonably believes that the information will be passed to the correct office, this may count as disclosure.[45]

Part 8: Claiming benefits and getting paid
Chapter 52: Overpayments
3. Overpayments that are sometimes recoverable

Once you have made a proper disclosure to the office handling your claim, you are not expected to repeat it.[46] However, if you give the information to a different office and subsequently become aware that it has not been acted on, you must take further steps to make a proper disclosure.[47] A short time may elapse before you can reasonably be expected to realise that the original information has not been acted on.[48]

Misrepresentation

Misrepresentation occurs if you have provided information that is inaccurate – eg, you gave a wrong answer to a specific question on the claim form. It does not apply if you have not given information, unless this was deliberately intended to mislead.[49] The following apply.

- It does not matter whether a reasonable person would also have given innaccurate information. No 'failure' on your part needs to be shown.[50]
- It does not matter if you honestly believed that the information you gave was correct – once it is shown to be incorrect, you have misrepresented it. However, you have not misrepresented if you added the phrase 'not to my knowledge' to your statement.[51]
- A written statement may be qualified by an oral one. If you fill in a form incorrectly but explain the situation to an officer when handing in the form, your explanation must be taken into account when deciding whether what is stated on the form is misrepresentation.[52] Similarly, if you give incorrect information in one document but correct information in another, there may not be a misrepresentation.[53] However, if you have declared a fact on a previous claim, but inadvertently give incorrect information on a later claim, you have misrepresented it. The decision maker is not required to check the information you gave on the earlier claim for you.[54]
- If you are incapable of managing your affairs, but nevertheless sign a claim form which is incorrectly completed, you cannot argue later that you were not capable of making a true representation of your circumstances.[55] However, it is arguable that benefit cannot be recovered from you if you:[56]
  - have a disability or you cannot read or write English very well; *and*
  - thought you were signing something different from what you were, or you did not understand the effect of your signature; *and*
  - took precautions to understand what you were signing – eg, you checked the form for accuracy before you signed it.[57]
- If you sign a declaration on a claim form that states, 'I declare that the information I have given is correct and complete', but you left out relevant information because you were unaware of it, this is not misrepresentation unless you knew (or ought reasonably to have known) the information was incomplete.[58]

Note:
- If you did not declare a fact because you were unaware of it, signing the declaration does not amount to a misrepresentation because all you are declaring is that you have correctly disclosed those facts *which were known to you*.[59]
- If you were told by the DWP or HMRC that certain facts are irrelevant to your claim, signing the declaration cannot be a misrepresentation if you fail to disclose these facts.[60]
- If someone else disclosed a fact to an office not handling your claim but s/he reasonably believed it would be passed to the correct office, it may be that disclosure has been made, and therefore your signing the declaration does not amount to a misrepresentation.[61]

Your failure to disclose, or your misrepresentation, has caused the overpayment

An overpayment is only recoverable if it was caused by your failure to disclose (see p1228), or your misrepresenting (see p1230), a material fact (see p1227). **Note:** it is possible that if you have a duty to disclose a fact in respect of one benefit and you fail to do so, this could be regarded as the cause of an overpayment of another benefit.[62]

You may be able to argue that the overpayment was not caused by your failure to disclose or your misrepresentation.
- If the relevant office has been given the correct information to decide your claim by someone else, but does not act on it, you could argue that the overpayment did not arise because of your failure.[63] However, if one DWP office does not inform another about *other* changes in your circumstances (eg, an increase in your earnings), this does not prevent the overpayment resulting from your failure to disclose the information yourself to the second office.[64]
- If the relevant office has obtained information from another source that leads it to think you may be being overpaid but it does not suspend your benefit while it makes enquiries to establish this for certain, it is still possible that the cause of the overpayment is your failure to disclose or your misrepresentation.[65]
- If you have not disclosed a relevant fact to the relevant office and you then sign a declaration that you have reported the relevant facts (eg, when you sign on), this is a misrepresentation.
- If what you say on your claim form is obviously incorrect and the decision maker does not check this, the overpayment will have been caused by official error, not your misrepresentation, and it is not recoverable.[66]

The decision awarding you benefit has been changed

If the decision to award you benefit is considered to be incorrect, it must be changed before any overpayment can be recovered.[67] The only exception to this

Part 8: Claiming benefits and getting paid
Chapter 52: Overpayments
3. Overpayments that are sometimes recoverable

rule is when the circumstances of the overpayment mean that there is no decision that needs to be revised in order for an overpayment to exist – ie, if you were actually paid more than the amount the original decision awarded to you.[68]

A decision to change your benefit award is made by a decision maker, who then carries out a revision or a supersession (see p1276 and p1287). The new decision should state the new amount payable (if any).[69]

During the period when you were overpaid, there may have been more than one decision on your benefit award. Unless *all* these decisions are changed, *all* of the overpayment cannot be recovered.[70]

Note: in practice, there are therefore two decisions that must be made before an overpayment can be recovered from you: the decision that changes a previous decision about your benefit, and the decision that the overpayment is recoverable.[71] Both decisions may be included in one decision letter, but it must be clear that both have been made.[72] It is also possible that your benefit award has been changed, but you are not notified about this until you are also notified that the overpayment is recoverable.[73]

If the decision(s) about your benefit has not been changed and/or the new decision(s) has not been notified to you (or it appears that it may not have been), appeal to the First-tier Tribunal (see p1309) against the decision that the overpayment is recoverable. You must apply for a mandatory reconsideration first (see p1311).

8. The amount that is recovered

The amount of the overpayment is the difference between what you were paid and what you should have been paid.[74] Check that the amount of the overpayment is correct by:

- checking the period of the overpayment;
- working out the total amount of benefit you were paid over the period;
- establishing the correct amount of benefit you should have received during the period;
- deducting this from the total amount of benefit you were paid.

No interest charges may be added to the amount of the overpayment.

The decision maker works out what you should have been paid using the information you originally gave her/him, plus any facts you misrepresented or did not disclose.

If you have been overpaid, the decision maker should deduct from the overpayment any IS, income-based JSA, income-related employment and support allowance (ESA), pension credit (PC) or universal credit (UC) to which you or your partner would have been entitled had benefit been paid correctly.[75]

If additional facts are needed to prove you were underpaid IS, income-based JSA, ESA, PC or UC, you cannot offset the underpayment of these benefits against the overpayment.[76] However, if you have been getting one of these benefits, you can ask the DWP to revise or supersede your award (see p1276 and p1287). It could then withhold any arrears owed to you to reduce the overpayment.

If you were overpaid IS, income-based JSA, income-related ESA or PC because you had too much capital, the overpayment is calculated taking account of the fact that, had you received no benefit, you would have had to use your capital to meet everyday expenses. For each 13-week period, the DWP assumes your capital is reduced by the amount of overpaid benefit.[77] This is known as the 'diminishing capital' rule. If your capital goes below the capital limit, any subsequent overpayment is not recoverable. However, if there are any increases or decreases in your actual capital during the overpayment period, these are also taken into account.[78]

Example

Nina received IS of £100 a week for a period of 30 weeks. She has capital of £20,000. After 13 weeks, the diminishing capital rule means that she is treated as having spent 13 x £100 = £1,300 and her capital is deemed to be £18,700. After a further 13 weeks, her capital is deemed to be £17,400.

After 26 weeks, Nina has paid £5,000 towards her credit card arrears after the credit card company threatened her with court proceedings. As long as obtaining benefit was not the significant purpose for making this payment (see p370), her capital is now deemed to be £12,400.

In addition to checking that the overpayment has been calculated correctly, you should claim any other benefits or tax credits to which you may be entitled and ask for these to be backdated (see p1156 for benefits and p1459 for tax credits) so you can repay the overpayment. Do not delay making the claims or you could lose out.

If you were overpaid a benefit which overlaps with another benefit you claimed but were not paid (see p1175), ask for a revision or supersession of that benefit and ask for it to be paid instead (see p1276).

If you were overpaid a benefit but, in fact, were entitled to another, check whether the claim for the benefit you were overpaid can be treated as a claim for the other (see p1161).

Example

Maxine should not have been receiving IS because her partner is in full-time paid work. However, she is caring for her aunt who is disabled and receiving attendance allowance. Maxine should ask the DWP to treat her claim for IS as a claim for carer's allowance (CA) and offset arrears of CA against the IS she has been overpaid.

Part 8: Claiming benefits and getting paid
Chapter 52: Overpayments
3. Overpayments that are sometimes recoverable

From whom can an overpayment be recovered

An overpayment can be recovered from you if it was caused by your failing to disclose or your misrepresenting a material fact (see p1227).[79] The DWP or HMRC may argue that it can recover the overpayment from you, even if you are not the claimant or you were not paid the benefit. However, it is arguable that only a claimant, an 'appointee', or a person with power of attorney to whom the benefit was paid can fail to disclose a material fact.[80]

If you are an appointee (see p1149), the overpayment can be recovered from you or the claimant (or both of you), depending on your circumstances and the facts of the case – ie, which one of you misrepresented or failed to disclose a material fact. The DWP or HMRC should issue a decision that deals with both your liability.[81] However:

- if the overpaid benefit has not been given to the claimant, the overpayment cannot be recovered from her/him, unless s/he contributed to the misrepresentation or s/he did not disclose a material fact;
- the overpayment cannot be recovered from you if you used 'due care and diligence' in making any statements that led to the overpayment.

Whether the overpayment can be recovered from you if you have **power of attorney** depends on whether the benefit was paid to you. If benefit was paid to you on behalf of the claimant, the overpayment is recoverable from you in the same way as from appointees.[82] If benefit was not paid to you, it cannot be recovered from you.[83]

An overpayment can be recovered from a claimant's estate if s/he dies.[84] Recovery can only begin after either probate or letters of administration have been granted.[85]

Challenging an overpayment decision

If you disagree that an overpayment has been made, or that an overpayment can be recovered (ie, because the required conditions are not met) or with the amount to be recovered (ie, because you were entitled to some, or all, of the payments), you can appeal. You must ask for a mandatory reconsideration first.

If you have missed the time limit for a mandatory reconsideration (see p1312), you can apply for a supersession and then appeal against any refusal to supersede.[86]

The First-tier Tribunal can consider whether you were entitled to some, or all, of the money (the amount of the overpayment), as well as whether the overpayment is recoverable from you on the basis that it was caused by your failure to disclose or misrepresentation. Both issues can also be considered, even if you have only challenged the decision about whether the overpayment is recoverable (and not the decision about your entitlement to benefit during the period of overpayment).[87]

Do not pay back any of the money until your appeal has been decided. If you do so and then successfully appeal, the DWP or HMRC should reimburse you. If it does not, you may be entitled to recover the money in court proceedings because you repaid the money on the basis of a mistake. Write to the DWP or HMRC and explain that you do not intend to repay any of the money until your appeal has been decided. If the DWP or HMRC is already making deductions from your benefit (see p788), ask it to stop doing so straight away.

Note: even if the final decision is that an overpayment of a particular amount is recoverable, the decision maker has the discretion not to recover, so it is sometimes still worth asking that nothing be recovered (see below).

4. **Recovery of overpaid benefit**

Note: this section does *not* apply to recovery of overpayments of housing benefit (HB – see p1241).

If an overpayment can be recovered (see p1222 and p1226), the DWP or HM Revenue and Customs (HMRC) must decide whether to recover it (see below) and, if so, the method to use. The recovery method depends on the type of overpayment. If you come under the universal credit (UC) system and have been overpaid UC, contribution-based jobseeker's allowance (JSA) or contributory employment and support allowance (ESA), see p1239. For all other overpayments, see p1236.

Note: except when seeking to recover overpaid benefit through the courts, there is no time limit within which the DWP or HMRC must begin recovery action.

The discretion not to recover

Even if an overpayment is recoverable, the DWP and HMRC have the discretion not to recover all, or part, of it. The DWP has two policies that set out the situations when recovery is not made.

- Guidance for overpayments of UC, contribution-based JSA and contributory ESA if you come under the UC system (see p1225) states that the DWP can use its discretion not to recover an overpayment if it would cause you hardship.[88] You can also ask the DWP not to recover if the reason why you were overpaid was because of a mistake on the part of the DWP.[89]
- Guidance for all other overpayments emphasises that it is only in exceptional cases that recovery is not pursued.[90] However, the DWP and HMRC can use their discretion to decide not to recover the overpayment, particularly if you acted in good faith and recovery would cause you hardship or be detrimental to your health or the health of your family.

Part 8: Claiming benefits and getting paid
Chapter 52: Overpayments
4. Recovery of overpaid benefit

If you agree to repay the overpayment or you do not ask for recovery not to be made, in almost all cases the DWP or HMRC recovers the overpayment from you. If an overpayment is recoverable from you, but repaying it is difficult, or you think there is a reason why recovery should not take place, contact the DWP/HMRC debt management section. The details should be on the letters you receive about the overpayment. Each case is decided on its merits. You should emphasise that you acted in good faith, point out any misleading advice you received (particularly from the DWP or HMRC) and how repaying would cause you hardship. To demonstrate hardship on financial grounds, you must usually provide full income and expenditure details for you and your family.

If the DWP or HMRC refuses to use its discretion not to recover, you cannot appeal against this decision. Your only possible legal recourse is judicial review (see p1378), but it may also help to involve your MP. The First-tier Tribunal cannot 'write off' part of the overpayment, even if there are mitigating circumstances. It can only decide whether it is recoverable and, if so, how much is repayable.

If you have been underpaid in the past but cannot now get arrears (eg, because of the rules on backdating – see p1156), ask the DWP or HMRC to reduce the amount to be recovered by this sum if it will not write it off altogether.

Methods of recovery

This section applies to all recoverable overpayments, except overpayments of UC, and contribution-based JSA or contributory ESA if you come under the UC system. For these, see p1239.

Deductions from benefit

Recoverable overpayments can usually be repaid through deductions from most of the benefits in this *Handbook*. There are some exceptions.
- Overpayments of child benefit and guardian's allowance can be recovered by deductions from either of these benefits,[91] but overpayments of other benefits cannot be deducted from them.[92]
- No deductions can be made from housing benefit (HB), except for HB or council tax benefit overpayments.[93]

Deductions can only be made from the benefit of the person who must repay the overpayment. However, if you are a member of a couple, overpayments of income support (IS), income-based JSA, income-related ESA and pension credit (PC) can be recovered from benefits either of you receive, provided you are married or living together as if you were married.[94]

Overpayments can also be recovered from arrears of benefit you are owed, except arrears of a benefit that has been suspended (see p1185).[95]

If an overpayment of IS, income-based JSA, income-related ESA or PC occurred because of a duplication of payment, the DWP usually deducts it from the arrears owing to you.[96] However, if it does not do so, you can still be asked to repay it even if you have spent the money.

Note: overpaid benefit cannot be recovered by making deductions from tax credits.

Maximum deductions

The maximum weekly amounts that can be deducted from **IS, income-based JSA, contribution-based JSA** (if you would be entitled to income-based JSA at the same rate), **income-related ESA, contributory ESA** (if you would be entitled to income-related ESA at the same rate) **and PC** are:[97]

- £29.60 if you have agreed to pay a penalty (see p1263), admitted fraud or been found guilty of fraud; *or*
- £11.10 in any other case.

The deduction can be increased by half of any:[98]

- £5, £10 or £20 earnings disregard (see p278); *or*
- charitable income paid on a regular basis subject to a disregard (see p290); *or*
- benefit subject to a £10 disregard (see p278).

If you have been overpaid contribution-based JSA but are not entitled to income-based JSA, the maximum deduction is one-third of the personal allowance for someone of your age (see p231).[99]

The above amounts are maximum amounts. You might be able to persuade the DWP to deduct less. If other deductions are also being made from your benefit, see p1197 for the total maximum amount that can be deducted.

If an overpayment is being recovered from a benefit other than IS, income-based JSA, income-related ESA or PC, the rules limiting the maximum payment that can be deducted do not apply. See p1239 if the overpayment is being recovered from your UC.[100] The DWP usually wants to deduct one-third of your weekly benefit. However, you can argue that your rate of repayment should be less than this.

Deductions from earnings

If you work for an organisation with 10 or more employees, an overpayment can be recovered by your employer deducting amounts from your earnings.[101] If this happens, you and your employer should be sent a notice setting out that deductions from your earnings are to be made and the rules for calculating how much to deduct.[102] You must inform the DWP if you leave your employment and you must give the DWP details of any new employment.[103] Failure to notify the DWP of these issues is a criminal offence.[104] Your employer should inform you, in writing, of how much the deductions are and how they were calculated no later than the day on which you are given a payment which has had a deduction made from it (or, if that is impractical, no later than the following payday).[105]

Part 8: Claiming benefits and getting paid
Chapter 52: Overpayments
4. Recovery of overpaid benefit

The maximum that can be deducted each week is worked out as a percentage of your net earnings – ie, earnings after income tax, class 1 national insurance contributions and pension contributions have been deducted.[106] The maximum is higher if you have been found guilty of an offence.[107]

Maximum deductions from earnings

Net monthly earnings (if paid monthly)	Net weekly earnings (if paid weekly)	Deduction	Deduction if found guilty of an offence
Less than £430	£100 or less	Nil	5%
£430.01 to £690	£100.01 to £160	3%	6%
£690.01 to £950	£160.01 to £220	5%	10%
£950.01 to £1,160	£220.01 to £270	7%	14%
£1,600.01 to £1,615	£270.01 to £375	11%	22%
£1,615.01 to £2,240	£375.01 to £520	15%	30%
£2,240.01 or over	£520.01 or over	20%	40%

If you would be left with less than 60 per cent of your net earnings after the deductions (eg, because amounts are being deducted from your wages or salary for other things), the deduction should be reduced so that you are left with 60 per cent of your net earnings.[108] There are rules on the order of priority in which deductions should be made (see p1198).[109] **Note:** the decision maker can reduce the amount to be deducted below the above percentages by issuing a new notice to your employer with the reduced amount.[110]

Recovery through the courts

Recoverable overpayments of benefit may be recovered by enforcement proceedings in the county court in England or Wales or the sheriff court in Scotland.[111] The DWP or HMRC may use these proceedings if you are no longer claiming benefit.

Once there is a decision from a decision maker, the First-tier Tribunal or Upper Tribunal, the court must enforce it, unless you persuade it to delay enforcement (known as a 'stay of execution') while you appeal against the relevant decision. If you are in this situation, get advice.

Note: recovery action through the courts in England and Wales must be taken within six years of the decision to recover or, if later, any written acknowledgement of the overpayment or voluntary repayment.[112] In Scotland, the DWP regards the time limit as being 20 years from the date of the decision to recover (or, if there was no such decision, five years from the decision that there was an overpayment).[113] Get advice about how these limits apply to you.

· ·

Can the DWP rely on common law?

In the past, the DWP has claimed to be entitled to recover overpayments of benefit under 'common law', even if the overpayment was entirely caused by official error. However, it is now clear that it cannot recover in this way. This means that if the DWP cannot recover an overpayment under the rules described in this chapter (see p1226) because, for example, it was not caused by misrepresentation or a failure to disclose, it cannot reclaim it through the courts.[114]

· ·

Methods of recovery: universal credit, contribution-based jobseeker's allowance and contributory employment and support allowance

This section applies to the recovery of overpayments of UC, and contribution-based JSA or contributory ESA if you come under the UC system (see p1225).

Note: the methods of recovery described in this section can also be used to collect or recover court costs incurred in recovering overpayments, short-term advances (see p1177), budgeting advances of UC (see p175), hardship payments of UC (see p1207), financial penalties for benefit offences (see p1263), civil penalties for incorrect statements (see p1256) and overpayments of tax credits if you are now receiving UC (see p1483).

Deductions from benefit

Overpayments of UC, and contribution-based JSA or contributory ESA if you come under the UC system, can be recovered through deductions from all the benefits in this *Handbook* except IS, HB, social fund payments, child benefit and guardian's allowance.[115]

Maximum deductions from universal credit

Note: the maximum amounts below apply to *all* overpayments being recovered by deductions from your UC – eg, an overpayment of IS that occurred before you came under the UC system.[116]

If an overpayment is being recovered from your UC, the maximum amount that can be deducted each month is the highest of:[117]

- if you or your partner are found guilty of an offence, or have accepted a caution or agreed to pay a penalty in connection with the overpayment (see p1255), or if UC hardship payments are being recovered:
  - £100.71 if you are single and under 25;
  - £127.13 if you are single and 25 or over;
  - £158.08 if you and your partner are both under 25;
  - £199.56 if you or your partner are 25 or over;
- if you have some earned income:
  - £62.94 if you are single and under 25;

Part 8: Claiming benefits and getting paid
Chapter 52: Overpayments
4. Recovery of overpaid benefit

- – £79.46 if you are single and 25 or over;
- – £98.80 if you and your partner are both under 25;
- – £124.72 if you or your partner are 25 or over;
- in all other cases:
  - – £37.77 if you are single and under 25;
  - – £47.67 if you are single and 25 or over;
  - – £59.28 if you and your partner are both under 25;
  - – £74.83 if you or your partner are 25 or over.

You must be left with at least one pence of UC each month after the deduction.[118] The above maximum amounts do not apply if:

- you are being paid arrears of UC (other than if they are as a result of payments being restored following a suspension of your benefit), so the whole of the arrears can be used to recover an overpayment;[119] *or*
- the overpayment is of UC housing costs to cover rent and it is being recovered from someone else – eg, your landlord.[120]

Maximum deductions from jobseeker's allowance or employment and support allowance

The maximum weekly deduction that can be made to recover an overpayment from your JSA is an amount equal to 40 per cent of your JSA.[121]

The maximum weekly deduction that can be made to recover an overpayment from your ESA is 40 per cent of the basic allowance that applies to you (see p638).[122]

In both cases, if the 40 per cent figure is not a multiple of five pence, the amount is rounded up to the next highest multiple of five pence.

Maximum deductions from pension credit

The maximum weekly amount that can be deducted from PC to repay an overpayment under these rules is:[123]

- £18.50 if the overpayment is one for which you were found guilty of an offence, you were cautioned or you agreed to pay a penalty as an alternative to prosecution; *or*
- £11.10 in all other cases.

You must be left with at least 10 pence of PC after any deductions.

Deductions from earnings

Overpayments can be recovered by your employer deducting amounts from your wages or salary.[124] The rules are the same as those outlined on p1237.

Recovery through the courts

The rules for recovering overpayments through the courts are similar to those for the recovery of HB (see p1248).[125]

5. Overpayments of housing benefit

Note: council tax benefit (CTB) was abolished on 1 April 2013. However, it is possible that there may be decisions after this date about CTB overpayments made before this date. You may also still be repaying an overpayment of CTB. The rules on calculating the amount and the recoverability of overpayments of CTB were similar to those for housing benefit (HB). For further details, see p1094 of the 2012/13 edition of this *Handbook*.

If you have been overpaid income support (IS), income-based jobseeker's allowance (JSA) or income-related employment and support allowance (ESA), you may also have been overpaid HB. This is because your automatic passport to maximum HB ceases when you are no longer entitled to these benefits. If you are in this situation, inform the local authority dealing with your HB claim.

What is an overpayment

An 'overpayment' is an amount of HB which has been paid and to which the local authority decides you were not entitled under the HB rules.[126] Being 'paid' includes payment to you, your landlord or someone else, including HB credited to your local authority rent account (see p83).[127]

Overpayments that are always recoverable

An overpayment of HB is always recoverable if:
- it is the result of the local authority's overestimating your HB when making a payment on account (see p89). When the local authority decides how much HB you should get, it must recover any excess you were paid from future HB payments.[128] However, if you stop getting HB before the local authority decides, the overpayment can only be recovered under the other rules (see below); *or*
- it is a future payment that has been credited to your rent account. In this case, the overpayment can be recovered even if it was made as a result of an 'official error'.[129] If an overpayment of HB caused by an official error has been credited to your account for a *past* period, see p1242.

Overpayments that are not recoverable

An overpayment that is not covered by either of the bullet points above is not recoverable if you can show that:[130]
- it was caused by an 'official error' (see p1242); *and*
- no 'relevant person' contributed to making the official error (see p1243); *and*
- no 'relevant person' could reasonably have been expected to realise that an overpayment was being made (see p1243).

Part 8: Claiming benefits and getting paid
Chapter 52: Overpayments
5. Overpayments of housing benefit

Overpayments to which all these criteria apply are sometimes referred to as 'official error' overpayment.

Was the overpayment caused by an official error?

For the overpayment not to be recoverable, it must have been caused by an 'official error'. **Note:** the official error does not have to be the sole cause of the overpayment, but if the substantial cause of the overpayment was something that you did or failed to do, the overpayment is likely to be recoverable.[131]

An 'official error' is a mistake (either an act or omission) by:[132]

- the local authority responsible for HB; *or*
- an officer of the authority; *or*
- a person acting for that authority – eg, an employee of a contractor providing HB services; *or*
- an officer of the DWP or HM Revenue and Customs (HMRC) acting as such.

Examples of 'official error' include the following.

- A mistake made by the local authority in calculating your entitlement.
- A failure by the local authority to reduce your HB when you inform it of a change of circumstances. It is always best to notify changes in writing to the office you have been told to report changes to, and keep a copy. If you have reported a move into work to the DWP by telephone under the arrangements where it passes this on to the local authority (see p90) and have provided all the information and evidence needed, any overpayment that occurs is due to official error. However, if you did not provide all that was needed, the local authority does not treat any overpayment as official error.[133]
- Using a claim form that does not ask a question relevant to your entitlement. Whether or not this counts as an official error depends on the particular facts of your case. Leaving out a particular question is more likely to be an official error if the information omitted is likely to be relevant in a large number of cases, and if it is reasonable for the question to have been asked.[134]
- A failure by another department of the local authority to pass on details of a change of circumstances when it promised to do so. This is an official error because the definition does not require the mistake to be made by the HB office. If you have not been given a particular office to report a change to, you may have fulfilled your duty by reporting the change to any local authority office, and there may be an official error if that office fails to pass it to the HB office.[135]
- A mistake made by the DWP in calculating your entitlement to IS, income-based JSA or income-related ESA which results in an incorrect calculation of your entitlement to HB. However, it is not an official error if the local authority failed to check your entitlement with the DWP, unless it has information that shows the award is wrong or fraudulent.[136]
- A failure by the DWP to pass on information to the local authority.[137]

- Incorrect advice given to you by an officer of the local authority, the DWP or HMRC, provided s/he is acting as an officer at the time (rather than as a friend giving you informal advice).

The list above is not exhaustive.

Did a relevant person contribute to making the offical error?

Even if the overpayment was caused by an official error, if a 'relevant person' contributed to that mistake being made, the overpayment can still be recovered.

Relevant person

A **'relevant person'** is:
- the HB claimant; or
- a person acting on the claimant's behalf, either because the claimant is unable to deal with her/his affairs or because the claimant has asked the authority in writing to deal with the other person on her/his behalf; or
- a person to whom the payment was made, including a different person acting on the claimant's behalf or a landlord.

The relevant person must have caused the *error*, not the overpayment.[138]

The local authority might say that it only needs to show that *any* relevant person caused the official error, but it does not have to pursue that person for the overpayment.[139] If a relevant person caused the official error, the overpayment is recoverable. However, you may still be able to argue that it is not recoverable from you – eg, it was caused by a failure to disclose a relevant fact, but it was not you who failed to disclose. See p1245 for information about from whom overpayments can be recovered.

Did a relevant person realise that an overpayment was being made?

Even if the official error was not caused by a relevant person, an overpayment is still recoverable if any relevant person knew, or ought reasonably to have known, that an overpayment had been made. The test is whether or not you could reasonably have been be expected to *know* (not merely suspect) that an overpayment had occurred. Much depends on what could reasonably have been expected of you given the information available to you, in particular the extent to which the local authority advised you about the scheme, your duties and obligations (especially your duty to notify changes of circumstances).[140]

If you or another relevant person could only have realised that there was an overpayment at some point during the period of the overpayment, the overpayment is only recoverable from that date.

Part 8: Claiming benefits and getting paid
Chapter 52: Overpayments
5. Overpayments of housing benefit

The amount that is recovered

Check the amount of an overpayment to ensure the local authority has calculated it correctly. The local authority should distinguish between parts of an overpayment that are recoverable and those that are not. To calculate the amount of the overpayment, it should:

- determine the period over which you have been paid too much benefit;
- identify the period(s) over which it is entitled to recover;
- work out the total amount of HB you were paid over the period(s) during which it can recover;
- work out the correct amount of HB you should have received during the period(s) of the overpayment. The local authority must award you the amount of HB you (or your partner) would have received if it had been aware of your true circumstances (even if the overpayment occurred before the rules were changed in October 2000). If necessary, it should ask you for any required information or evidence to do this. However, the local authority does not include a change of your address when doing this;[141]
- deduct the HB you should have been paid from what you were paid.[142]

The local authority must not add any interest charges to the amount of the overpayment.[143]

Deductions from the overpayment

As well as any amount of HB which you should have been paid, the local authority must consider deducting other amounts from the overpayment (this is known as 'offsetting'). These are:

- if you are a council tenant, extra rent paid into your rent account. If you have been getting HB during the overpayment period and, for some reason, have paid more into your rent account than you should have paid according to your original (incorrect) benefit assessment, the extra rent you have paid can be deducted from any overpayment made during that period. The local authority might not apply this rule if you paid extra rent to repay rent arrears;[144]
- reductions under the 'diminishing capital rule' (see below).

No other amounts can be deducted.

If you were overpaid HB because you had too much capital, the overpayment is calculated taking into account the fact that, had you received no HB, you would have used your capital. This is known as the **'diminishing capital rule'**. It only applies if you were overpaid for more than 13 weeks and either:[145]

- the overpayment was caused by a misrepresentation of, or a failure to disclose, the amount of your capital (see p1227); *or*
- the overpayment was caused by an error (other than an 'official error' – see p1242) about your capital (or that of a member of your family).

For each 13-week period, the local authority assumes that your capital is reduced by the amount of overpaid HB.[146]

From whom can an overpayment be recovered

The general rule is that a recoverable overpayment can be recovered from the person to whom it was paid – eg, a landlord.[147] However, this does not apply if someone else misrepresented or failed to disclose a material fact, or if someone else should have realised that there was an overpayment at the time.

An overpayment can be recovered from someone other than the person to whom it was paid, including the claimant, if:[148]

- the overpayment was caused by misrepresentation or failure to disclose a material fact (see p1226). In this case, it can be recovered from the person who misrepresented or failed to disclose the fact, but not the person to whom the payment was made; or
- the overpayment was caused by an official error (see p1241) and the claimant (or someone acting on the claimant's behalf) or any other person to whom the HB was paid could reasonably have been expected to realise that there was an overpayment at the time. In this case, it can be recovered from whoever should have realised, but not the person to whom it was paid; or
- neither of the above two bullet points apply, in which case the overpayment is also recoverable from the claimant. Therefore, if you are the claimant, the overpayment may be recovered from you, as well as the person to whom it was paid.

If you are the claimant and the overpayment is recoverable from you, no matter how it was caused, the local authority can also recover the overpayment by deducting any HB paid to your partner, provided you were a couple both at the time of the overpayment and when the deduction is made.[149]

If you think you have been wrongly chosen under these rules (eg, because you did not fail to disclose a material fact), you can appeal to the First-tier Tribunal. However, if the overpayment can be recovered from you under these rules, you cannot appeal simply because you think the local authority should recover from another person instead.[150]

In the event of the death of the person from whom recovery is being sought, the local authority may consider recovering any outstanding overpayment from her/his estate.[151]

Methods of recovery

A local authority can decide how much, if any, of a recoverable overpayment it will recover (but see p89 if the overpayment was of a payment on account).[152] This is similar to the discretion that the DWP and HMRC have to recover overpayments (see p1235).

Part 8: Claiming benefits and getting paid
Chapter 52: Overpayments
5. Overpayments of housing benefit

If the local authority decides to recover, it can ask for the whole amount or recover it by instalments. When an overpayment is recovered from your landlord, note how this affects your liability to pay rent (see p1250). Overpayments of HB can be recovered:

- from payments of HB (see below);
- from other benefits (see p1247);
- by adjusting your rent account if you are a local authority tenant (see p1248);
- by your employer deducting amounts from your wages or salary (see p1248);
- through the courts (see p1248).

The methods used and the rates of recovery should be consistent between groups of claimants. For example, council tenants should not be required to repay an overpayment in a lump sum if private tenants can repay by instalments.

Note: except when seeking to recover overpaid benefit through the courts, there is no time limit within which a local authority must begin recovery action.

Deductions from housing benefit

A local authority can recover an overpayment by deducting amounts from HB payable to any person from whom an overpayment can be recovered (see p1234).[153] As well as yourself, this could be your partner (see below) or your landlord (see below). Deductions can be made from both future payments of HB and any arrears that are owing.

If you have moved home, the local authority may be able to recover an overpayment of HB from your previous home by adjusting the HB paid at your new home. It can decide to do this if:[154]

- the overpayment occurred after you moved, and occurred because you were no longer living at your previous home; *and*
- the same local authority that paid you the overpayment is paying your HB at your new home.

In these circumstances, the local authority can deduct all the weekly HB owing to you for your new home to recover the overpayment, for however many weeks you were overpaid at your previous home.

Deductions from your partner's housing benefit

If you were the claimant and the overpayment, no matter how it was caused, is recoverable from you, the local authority can also recover it by deductions from any HB later awarded to your partner, provided you were a couple at both the time of the overpayment and when the deduction is made.[155]

Deductions from your landlord's housing benefit

The local authority may recover the overpayment from:

- HB paid to your landlord if s/he is claiming HB her/himself;[156]

- HB paid directly to your landlord on your behalf.[157] The notification of the overpayment (see p1249) should make it clear from whom the authority is recovering;
- HB paid directly to your landlord on behalf of other claimants.[158]

When HB is recovered from a landlord in this way, there are special rules on how this affects your liability to pay rent (see p1250).

Maximum deductions

The maximum weekly amount that can be deducted is £18.50 if you have agreed to pay a penalty (see p1263), admitted fraud or been found guilty of fraud, or £11.10 in any other case.[159]

The rate of recovery can be increased by up to half of any amount of earned income which is disregarded as income in the calcualtion of your HB (see p278 and p320).[160] Amounts of income disregarded for childcare costs cannot be used to increase the rate of recovery in this way.

However, you can argue that the rate will cause you hardship and a lesser amount should be recovered instead. You must be left with at least 50p of HB per week.[161]

Deductions from other benefits

The local authority can ask the DWP to recover an overpayment of HB by making deductions from most of the benefits in this *Handbook* (except guardian's allowance and, arguably, child benefit).[162] If the overpayment is recoverable from your partner (see p1245), it can be recovered by deductions from her/his IS, income-based JSA, income-related ESA, pension credit, universal credit or personal independence payment.

An overpayment can also be recovered from any benefits paid to your landlord in her/his own right.[163]

Deductions can only be made if:[164]

- a [recoverable] overpayment has been made as a result of a misrepresentation of, or failure to disclose (see p1227), a material fact by you, on your behalf or by or on behalf of another person to whom HB has been paid; *and*
- the local authority is unable to recover that overpayment from any HB; *and*
- the person who is to repay the overpayment is receiving a sufficient amount of at least one of the relevant benefits to allow deductions to be made.

There are no rules limiting the maximum amount that can be deducted. However, you can argue that your rate of repayment should be reasonable. If you are on IS, income-based JSA or income-related ESA, argue that the weekly maximums for these benefits should apply (see p1237). Ask the DWP to use its discretion to reduce the amounts if the deductions will cause you hardship.

Part 8: Claiming benefits and getting paid
Chapter 52: Overpayments
5. Overpayments of housing benefit

If deductions stop because you are no longer entitled to a particular benefit, or the amount to which you are entitled is insufficient for deductions to be made, the DWP notifies the local authority which, once again, becomes responsible for any further recovery action.

Adjusting your rent account

If you are a local authority tenant, the local authority can recover an overpayment by adding it as a debt to your rent account. If a local authority recovers overpaid HB in this way, the overpayment should be separately identified and you should be informed that the amount being recovered does not represent rent arrears.[165]

If the local authority is seeking to evict you because you have rent arrears, you should get advice. It cannot argue you owe it rent arrears if you have only been overpaid HB. Local authorities are reminded in DWP guidance that overpayments of HB paid to their own tenants are not rent arrears and should not be treated as such.[166]

An overpayment cannot be recovered in this way if you have a private or housing association landlord. However, an overpayment can be recovered from your landlord (see p1246). If the local authority recovers from your landlord, you might count as being in rent arrears (see p1230).

Deductions from earnings

The local authority can order your employer to deduct amounts from your wages or salary in order to recover the overpayment.[167] The rules for this are explained on p1237.

Court action

If a local authority cannot use any of the methods of recovery listed on p1245 and you cannot agree on repayments, it can try to recover the money you owe through the county court (sheriff court in Scotland) if it thinks you can afford to make repayments. It should not start proceedings until your time for challenging the decision has passed.

A local authority should not use court proceedings to recover an overpayment if it has not followed the correct procedure (see p1238) – eg, if it has not issued the correct notification.[168]

A local authority can:

- sue you for the debt created by the overpayment. If the correct procedure has not been followed, you can use this as a defence.[169] You may also be able to claim compensation in certain circumstances. However, you cannot say that you should have received more HB;[170] *or*
- use the special rules to register the overpayment as a debt which can then be recovered using a court procedure.[171] Get advice if you think the local authority is not entitled to do this.

Note: recovery action through the courts in England and Wales must be taken within six years of the decision to recover or, if later, any written acknowledgement of the overpayment or voluntary repayment.[172] In Scotland, the DWP regards the time limit as being 20 years from the date of the decision to recover (or, if there was no such decision, five years from the decision that there was an overpayment). Get advice about how these limits apply to your case.[173]

If the local authority is successful in its court proceedings against you, you may have to pay legal costs and interest, as well as the overpayment. Remember that court procedures often require you to take action within a very short period of time. If the local authority is threatening to use court proceedings, get advice.

Notification of an overpayment

If the local authority decides that a recoverable overpayment has occurred, it must write to the person from whom repayment is being sought (see p1245) within 14 days if possible, notifying her/him of this.[174]

This notification must state:[175]

- that there is an overpayment which is legally recoverable;
- the reason why there is a recoverable overpayment;
- the amount of the recoverable overpayment;
- how the amount of the overpayment was calculated;
- the benefit weeks to which the overpayment relates;
- if recovery is to be made from future benefit, the amount of the deductions;
- if recovery is to be made from your landlord by deductions from someone else's HB, your identity and the claimant from whose HB the deduction will be made;[176]
- your right to ask for a further written explanation of any of the decisions the local authority has made about the overpayment, how you can do this and the time limit for doing so;
- that you have a right to ask the local authority to reconsider any of the decisions it has made about the overpayment, how you can do this and the time limit for doing so.

It may also include any other relevant matters.

Guidance states that the local authority should issue a single notification to all relevant parties (eg, landlord and tenant), saying from whom the overpayment is recoverable and from whom it is not.[177]

If you write and ask the local authority for a more detailed written explanation of any of the decisions it has made about an overpayment, it must send you this within 14 days or, if this is not reasonably practicable, as soon as possible.[178]

If a notification sent to you is a clear decision that there is an overpayment which is recoverable from you, but does not contain all the matters above, it is only valid if the omissions do not put you at a disadvantage.[179] If, for example, it

8

Part 8: Claiming benefits and getting paid
Chapter 52: Overpayments
5. Overpayments of housing benefit

does not set out your right to apply for a revision so that you do not do so until it is too late, you have been put at a disadvantage and so can argue that the overpayment is not recoverable. However, if the decision is not about recoverability and is only about the fact that you have been overpaid, you can argue that there is no decision saying that you must repay the overpayment.[180]

No recovery should be sought until after you have been notified and the one-month time period for asking for a revision or appealing has passed.[181]

The effect of recovery from your landlord

If you are a private or housing association tenant, an overpayment of HB recovered from your landlord (see p1246) could mean that s/he tries to obtain money from you. The landlord could argue that you are in rent arrears as a result and could seek possession of your home.

Whether or not HB was paid directly to your landlord, s/he may still try to argue that, even if you owe no rent, you nevertheless owe a debt under common law. This is probably not correct. If s/he threatens to sue you, get advice straight away.

If you are a local authority tenant, these rules do not apply. However, the local authority can recover an overpayment of HB by making deductions from your rent account (see p1247).

If you were overpaid HB and HB was paid directly to your landlord, the following rules apply.

- If you are overpaid and the local authority recovers the overpayment from your landlord by making deductions from direct payments of other tenants' HB (see p1246), the other tenants are treated as having paid the amount of the deduction towards their rent.[182]
- If you are overpaid and the local authority recovers the overpayment from your landlord by making deductions from direct payments of your HB, you are treated as having paid the amount of the deduction towards your rent if your landlord is convicted of an offence or agrees to pay a penalty (see p1263) in relation to that overpayment.[183] If the local authority decides to recover under this rule, it must notify both your landlord and you that you are to be treated as having paid your rent.[184]

In these situations, your landlord cannot argue that you are in arrears of rent. It is also much easier to argue that your landlord cannot sue you under common law for a debt.

Note: if you were overpaid HB before 4 November 1997, see the different rules on pp1119–20 of the *Welfare Benefits Handbook* 2000/01 and get advice.

Challenging an overpayment decision

You can apply for a revision or appeal (see Chapters 54 and 55) if you want to dispute:

- the decision that you have been overpaid HB;
- the amount of the overpayment;
- the decision that it can be recovered;
- that the overpayment is to be recovered from you under the rules set out on p1245.

Do not pay back any of the money until your challenge has been dealt with. Local authority guidance states that overpayments should not be recovered while under appeal.[185] If the local authority is already making deductions from your HB (see p1244) or deductions are being made from your other benefits (see p1247), ask it to stop this straight away.

Notes

1. Introduction
1 *SSWP v Payne and Anr* [2011] UKSC 60

2. Overpayments that are always recoverable
2 s74 SSAA 1992
3 Reg 7(1) SS(PAOR) Regs
4 R(SB) 3/91
5 See, for example, the appeals in R(SB) 28/85 and R(IS) 6/02
6 Sch 9A para 11 SS(C&P) Regs
7 *R v Secretary of State for Social Security ex parte Craigie* [2000] EWCA Civ 329
8 *R v Secretary of State for Social Security ex parte Golding* 1 July 1996, unreported (CA)
9 CIS/5206/1995
10 CIS/5206/1995
11 s71(4) SSAA 1992; reg 11 SS(PAOR) Regs; reg 35 CB&GA(Admin) Regs
12 Reg 11 SS(PAOR) Regs; reg 35 CB&GA(Admin) Regs
13 Sch 2 para 20(d) SS&CS(DA) Regs
14 s71ZB(1) WRA 2012; Art 5(3A) WRA(No. 8)O
15 s71ZB(3) SSAA 1992
16 Reg 16 SS(OR) Regs
17 Reg 8(3) SS(OR) Regs
18 Reg 7 SS(OR) Regs
19 Reg 9(1)(a) and (b) and (2) SS(OR) Regs
20 Reg 9(1)(c) SS(OR) Regs
21 Reg 9(3) SS(OR) Regs
22 Reg 4 SS(OR) Regs

3. Overpayments that are sometimes recoverable
23 s71(1) and (5A) SSAA 1992; R(SB) 34/83
24 R(SB) 2/92
25 CDLA/5803/1999
26 CDLA/1823/2004
27 R(S) 4/86; R(I) 3/75
28 *B v SSWP* [2005] EWCA Civ 929, reported as R(IS) 9/06. The effect of the decision is that recovery is under reg 32 SS(C&P) Regs and, presumably, under the equivalent rules in reg 24 JSA Regs and reg 23 CB&GA(Admin) Regs.
29 R(SB) 21/82
30 R(SB) 54/83; CSB/296/1985
31 CG/160/1999
32 R(SB) 21/82
33 Reg 32(1A) SS(C&P) Regs
   Reg 24(1)-(5A) JSA Regs
   Reg 38(3) UC,PIP,JSA&ESA(C&P) Regs

34 *Hooper v SSWP* [2007] EWCA Civ 495, reported as R(IB) 4/07. See also official guidance in Memo DMG 26/07.
35 R(A) 2/06
36 Reg 32(1B) SS(C&P) Regs
Reg 24(7) JSA Regs
Reg 38(4) UC,PIP,JSA&ESA(C&P) Regs
37 CSB/510/1987; CIS/545/1992; CIS/1769/1999. These decisions arose from the old test of failure to disclose and it is not clear they apply now. However, the point seems to have been adopted in *DG v SSWP* [2009] UKUT 120 (AAC).
38 R(SB) 15/87; *Hinchy v SSWP* [2005] UKHL 16, reported as R(IS) 7/05
39 Reg 23(5) CB&GA(Admin) Regs
40 CG/5631/1999; CIS/1887/2002; *WA v SSWP* [2009] UKUT 132 (AAC); *GJ v SSWP (IS)* [2010] UKUT 107 (AAC)
41 Reg 32(1B) SS(C&P) Regs requires notification in writing or by telephone, unless the DWP specifically requires otherwise.
42 R(SB) 18/85
43 CWSB/2/1985
44 R(SB) 15/87
45 CDLA/6336/1999
46 R(SB) 15/87; CIS/3529/2008
47 R(SB) 54/83
48 CSB/393/1985
49 CIS/5117/1998
50 R(SB) 9/85
51 *Jones and Sharples v CAO* [1994] 1 All ER 225 (CA); R(SB) 9/85
52 R(SB) 18/85
53 R(SB) 2/91
54 R(SB) 3/90
55 *Sheriff v CAO* [1995] (CA), reported as R(IS) 14/96
56 CG/4494/1999 suggests the principle may apply in social security; R(IS) 4/06 is more doubtful, but does not rule it out.
57 CIS/3846/2001
58 *Jones and Sharples v CAO* [1994] 1 All ER 225 (CA); *Franklin v CAO* [1995] (CA); CIS/674/1994; CIS/583/1994; CIS/674/1994
59 *Franklin v CAO* [1995] (CA)
60 CIS/583/1994
61 CDLA/6336/1999
62 *TM v SSWP (ESA)* [2015] UKUT 109 (AAC)
63 CIS/159/1990; CS/11700/1996; CSIS/7/1994; CG/5631/1999; *GJ v SSWP (IS)* [2010] UKUT 107 (AAC)
64 *Duggan v CAO* [1989] (CA); CG/662/1998; CG/4494/1999; *Hinchy v SSWP* [2003] EWCA Civ 138

65 *JM v SSWP (IS)* [2011] UKUT 15 (AAC)
66 CIS/222/1991
67 s71(5A) SSAA 1992; CIS/3228/2003; R(IS) 13/05. See CPC/3743/2006 for when not all the overpayment period has been covered by the change of the award.
68 Reg 12 SS(PAOR) Regs
69 CIS/3228/2003
70 CSIS/45/1990
71 R(SB) 7/91
72 *LL v SSWP* [2013] UKUT 208 (AAC)
73 This was the case in *Hamilton v Department for Social Development* [2010] NICA 46, but it is clear from *SSWP v AD (IS)* [2011] UKUT 184 (AAC) that whether this is the case depends on the specific decision-making history in your case.
74 R(SB) 20/84; R(SB) 24/87
75 Reg 13(1)(b) and (1A) SS(PAOR) Regs
76 *Commock v CAO*, reported as an appendix to R(SB) 6/90; CSIS/8/1995
77 Reg 14 SS(PAOR) Regs
78 CIS/5825/1999
79 s71(3) SSAA 1992
80 *B v SSWP* [2005] EWCA Civ 929, reported as R(IS) 9/06, which says that overpayments for failure to disclose are recoverable because of a breach of duty by a claimant of reg 32 SS(C&P) Regs; CIS/1996/2006; CIS/2125/2006 ; *PA v SSWP (DLA)* [2016] UKUT 428 (AAC)
81 R(IS) 5/03. This tribunal of commissioners' decision was intended to resolve the conflict between the earlier CIS/332/1993 and R(IS) 5/00, and preferred the latter.
82 *PA v SSWP (DLA)* [2016] UKUT 428 (AAC)
83 CA/1014/1999; CSDLA/1282/2001
84 *Secretary of State for Social Services v Solly* [1974] 3 All ER 922; R(SB) 21/82
85 CIS/1423/1997
86 *PA v SSWP (DLA)* [2016] UKUT 428 (AAC)
87 *MC v SSWP (IS)* [2015] UKUT 600 (AAC)

4. Recovery of overpaid benefit
88 www.gov.uk/government/publications/what-happens-if-you-are-overpaid-universal-credit-jobseekers-allowance-or-employment-and-support-allowance

89 When the Welfare Reform Bill (which introduced these rules) was being debated, the minister said it was the intention not to recover many overpayments which had been caused by official error – see House of Commons, *Hansard*, 19 May 2011, col 1019

90 *Guidance on the Application of Secretary of State Discretion* at www.cpag.org.uk/overpayments-adviser-tools

91 Reg 42A CB&GA(Admin) Regs

92 Reg 16(1) and (2) SS(PAOR) Regs

93 Regs 15 and 16 SS(PAOR) Regs

94 Reg 17 SS(PAOR) Regs

95 Reg 16(3) SS(PAOR) Regs

96 s74(2)(b) SSAA 1992

97 Reg 16(4), (4A), (5) and (6) SS(PAOR) Regs

98 Reg 16(6) SS(PAOR) Regs

99 Reg 16(5A) SS(PAOR) Regs

100 Reg 16(7A) and (7B) SS(PAOR) Regs

101 Reg 18 SS(OR) Regs

102 Reg 19 SS(OR) Regs

103 Reg 23 SS(OR) Regs

104 Reg 30 SS(OR) Regs

105 Reg 21 SS(OR) Regs

106 Reg 20(3) SS(OR) Regs

107 Reg 20(3A)-(3B) SS(OR) Regs

108 Regs 17(1) and 20(7) SS(OR) Regs

109 Reg 29 SS(OR) Regs

110 Reg 25 SS(OR) Regs

111 s71(10) SSAA 1992

112 s9(1) Limitation Act 1980

113 DWP, *Benefit Overpayment Recovery Guide*, based on the provisions of the Prescription and Limitation (Scotland) Act 1973

114 *CPAG v SSWP* [2010] UKSC 54, upholding the decision of the Court of Appeal in *CPAG, R (on the application of) v SSWP* [2009] EWCA Civ 1058

115 Reg 10 SS(OR) Regs

116 Reg 16(7A) and (7B) SS(PAOR) Regs

117 Reg 11 SS(OR) Regs

118 Reg 11(7) SS(OR) Regs

119 Reg 11(8) SS(OR) Regs

120 Reg 11(9) SS(OR) Regs

121 Reg 12 SS(OR) Regs

122 Reg 13 SS(OR) Regs

123 Reg 14 SS(OR) Regs. The maximum recoverable weekly amounts stated in this rule are calculated as percentages of a monthly figure of UC. It is assumed that these are converted to weekly figures.

124 Reg 29A SS(PAOR) Regs

125 s71ZE SSAA 1992

5. Overpayments of housing benefit

126 Reg 99 HB Regs; reg 80 HB(SPC) Regs

127 Reg 99 HB Regs; reg 80 HB(SPC) Regs

128 Reg 93(3) HB Regs; reg 74(3) HB(SPC) Regs

129 Reg 100(4) HB Regs; reg 81(4) HB(SPC) Regs

130 Reg 100(2) HB Regs; reg 81(2) HB(SPC) Regs

131 *Duggan v CAO* [1989] (CA); *R on the application of Sier v Cambridge CC* [2001] EWCA Civ 1523; CH/571/2003; CH/3761/2005

132 Reg 100(3) HB Regs; reg 81(3) HB(SPC) Regs

133 HB/CTB Circular A23/2009

134 *MB v Christchurch BC (HB)* [2014] UKUT 201 (AAC); [2014] AACR 39

135 CH/2567/2007; HB/CTB Circular A15/2009

136 CH/571/2003; CH/5485/2002

137 CH/939/2004; see also *R on the application of Sier v Cambridge CC* [2001] EWCA Civ 1523; CH/3761/2005

138 *R on the application of Sier v Cambridge CC* [2001] EWCA Civ 1523

139 *Warwick DC v Freeman* [1994] 27 HLR 616 (CA); CH/4918/2003

140 *R v Liverpool City Council ex parte Griffiths* [1990] 22 HLR 312; CH/2554/2002; CH/2567/2007

141 Reg 104 HB Regs; reg 85 HB(SPC) Regs; *Adan v London Borough of Hounslow and SSWP* [2004] EWCA Civ 101, reported as R(H) 5/04; CH/4943/2001; HB/CTB Circular A13/2006; *JM v London Borough of Tower Hamlets* [2015] UKUT 460 (AAC)

142 Reg 104(1) HB Regs; reg 85 HB(SPC) Regs

143 *R v Kensington and Chelsea RBC ex parte Brandt* [1995] 28 HLR 528 (QBD), at 537

144 Reg 104(3) HB Regs; reg 85(3) HB(SPC) Regs

145 Reg 103 HB Regs; reg 84 HB(SPC) Regs

146 Reg 103(1)(a) and (b) HB Regs; reg 84(1)(a) and (b) HB(SPC) Regs

147 s75(3)(a) SSAA 1992

148 Reg 101(2) HB Regs; reg 82(2) HB(SPC) Regs

149 Reg 102(1ZA) HB Regs; reg 83(1ZA) HB(SPC) Regs

150 R(H) 6/06

151 DWP, *Housing Benefit Overpayments Guide,* paras 4.43(k) and 4.210-4.289

152 s75(1) SSAA 1992

153 Reg 102 HB Regs; reg 83 HB(SPC) Regs; s75 SSAA 1992

154 Reg 104A HB Regs; reg 85A HB(SPC) Regs
155 Reg 102(1ZA) HB Regs; reg 83(1ZA) HB(SPC) Regs
156 s75(5)(a) SSAA 1992; reg 106 HB Regs; reg 87 HB(SPC) Regs
157 s75(5)(b) SSAA 1992; reg 106 HB Regs; reg 87 HB(SPC) Regs
158 s75(5)(c) SSAA 1992; reg 106 HB Regs; reg 87 HB(SPC) Regs
159 Reg 102 HB Regs; reg 83 HB(SPC) Regs; HB/CTB Circular A42/00
160 Reg 102(4) HB Regs; reg 83(4) HB(SPC) Regs
161 Reg 102(5) HB Regs; reg 83(5) HB(SPC) Regs
162 Reg 105(1)(a) HB Regs
163 s75(5)(a) SSAA 1992; reg 106 HB Regs; reg 87 HB(SPC) Regs
164 Regs 102 and 105 HB Regs; regs 83 and 86 HB(SPC) Regs
165 *R v Haringey LBC ex parte Azad Ayub* [1992] 25 HLR 566 (QBD)
166 DWP, *Housing Benefit Overpayments Guide*, para 4.90
167 Reg 106A HB Regs; reg 87A HB(SPC) Regs
168 *Warwick DC v Freeman* [1994] 27 HLR 616 (CA)
169 *Warwick DC v Freeman* [1994] 27 HLR 616 (CA)
170 *Plymouth CC v Gigg* [1997] 30 HLR 284 (CA)
171 s75(7) SSAA 1992
172 s9(1) Limitation Act 1980
173 DWP, *Benefit Overpayment Recovery Guide*, based on the provisions of the Prescription and Limitation (Scotland) Act 1973
174 Reg 90(1)(b) HB Regs; reg 71(1)(b) HB(SPC) Regs
175 Sch 9 paras 2, 3, 6 and 15 HB Regs; Sch 8 paras 2, 3, 6 and 15 HB(SPC) Regs; para A7.222 GM
176 Sch 9 para 15(2) HB Regs; Sch 8 para 15(2) HB(SPC) Regs
177 HB/CTB Circular A13/2006
178 Reg 90(4) HB Regs; reg 71(4) HB(SPC) Regs
179 *Haringey LBC v Awaritefe* [1999] 32 HLR 517 (CA)
180 CH/1395/2006
181 DWP, *Housing Benefit Overpayments Guide*, Part 4, paras 4.240-4.242
182 s75(6) SSAA 1992
183 s75(6) SSAA 1992; reg 107 HB Regs; reg 88 HB(SPC) Regs

184 Reg 107(3) HB Regs; reg 88(3) HB(SPC) Regs
185 DWP, *Housing Benefit Overpayments Guide*, Part 4, paras 4.240-4.242

Chapter 53

Fraud and penalties

This chapter covers:
1. Civil penalties (p1256)
2. Investigating benefit claims (p1257)
3. Prosecution of offences (p1260)
4. Financial penalties for benefit offences (p1263)
5. Sanctions for benefit offences (p1265)

This chapter covers the rules on fraud for benefits administered by the DWP, housing benefit, child benefit and guardian's allowance. For tax credits and fraud, see Chapter 63. This chapter does not cover the rules for statutory sick, maternity, adoption, paternity and shared parental pay.

Key facts
- When you claim benefit, you must give correct and complete information to the DWP, HM Revenue and Customs (HMRC) or the local authority. You might commit an offence if you deliberately mislead the agency dealing with your claim.
- You must report changes in your circumstances that could affect your entitlement. You may commit an offence if you do not notify the relevant office of changes promptly.
- Even if you are not suspected of fraud, you may receive a fine (known as a 'civil penalty') if you provide incorrect information and you are considered to have acted negligently, or if you have not notified a change of circumstances promptly and do not have a reasonable excuse.
- If the DWP, HMRC or local authority believes you have committed fraud, you may be prosecuted. Alternatively, you may be given the option of paying a financial penalty. Your benefit could be stopped or reduced ('sanctioned'), even if you are not prosecuted.
- If you are suspected or accused of fraud, get advice before taking any action or making any statements.

Part 8: Claiming benefits and getting paid
Chapter 53: Fraud and penalties
1. Civil penalties

1. Civil penalties

You can be given a civil penalty if you or someone acting on your behalf have acted carelessly in relation to your claim but are not considered to have committed fraud.

Civil penalties are different from the financial penalties imposed for benefit offences (see p1263). You cannot be given a civil penalty if you have been charged in connection with or sent a notice about a penalty for a benefit offence, or accepted a formal caution for a benefit offence.

A civil penalty of £50 may given if:[1]

- you 'negligently' make an incorrect statement or representation, or negligently give incorrect information or evidence, about a claim for or an award of a benefit, and you do not take 'reasonable steps' to correct the error; *or*
- you do not provide information or evidence, or you fail to notify a 'relevant change of circumstances', and you do not have a 'reasonable excuse'; *and*
- your negligence or failure results in your being overpaid benefit of more than £65.[2] The overpayment period must start on or after 1 October 2012.

Definitions

A **'relevant change of circumstances'** is one that affects entitlement to benefit.[3]

'Reasonable excuse' has been held to mean something that would have caused a reasonable person of a similar age and experience to act as you did.[4] Your state of health and the information which you received or might have obtained may be relevant.

Other terms used are not defined in the legislation but the DWP has produced guidance on the meaning of the following.[5]

'Negligently' is acting carelessly, not paying attention to or disregarding the importance of anything that needs to be done in relation to your claim.

'Reasonable steps' is doing something which is sensible or practicable to correct an error.

The penalty is added to the overpayment and recovered in the same way (see p1236).[6] If you are claiming jointly with your partner and the penalty is for negligently making or giving incorrect statements, representations, information or evidence, it can be recovered from your partner instead of you, unless s/he was not (and could not reasonably be expected to be) aware of the error.

You can appeal against the imposition of a civil penalty[7] – eg, you can argue that you did not behave negligently or that you had a 'reasonable excuse' for not declaring a change in your circumstances. You must request a mandatory reconsideration before you can appeal (see Chapter 55). **Note:** you may also want to consider appealing against the overpayment decision (see Chapter 52).

2. **Investigating benefit claims**

Investigation of suspected benefit fraud covered by this chapter is carried out by the DWP's Fraud and Error Service. The Fraud and Error Service does not have to tell you straight away about any enquiries it is making. It usually waits until it has collected more information and then asks you to attend an interview to explain matters.

Collecting information

There are special rules allowing the release of information to the DWP from:
- HM Revenue and Customs (HMRC);[8]
- government departments – eg, on issues about passports, immigration, emigration, nationality and prisoners;[9]
- the Registration Service, which is under an additional duty to report particulars of deaths to the DWP for social security purposes and to HMRC;[10]
- local authorities.[11]

Local authorities may also be supplied with information held by the DWP or HMRC, and may share information with other local authorities.[12]

Local authorities, HMRC and the DWP can require information about redirected post and have undelivered social security post returned to them.[13]

All information acquired is confidential to the bodies concerned with the administration of benefit, including private companies contracted to carry out such functions. Unauthorised disclosure of this information is a criminal offence.[14]

Are you unhappy about the use of your personal information?
The Data Protection Act 1998 restricts the use of personal data held about you. If a local authority, the DWP or HMRC makes a request for information which you think is inappropriate or unreasonable, refer the matter to the Information Commissioner (see Appendix 1).

Powers of investigation

As 'authorised officers', fraud investigators have certain powers to obtain information.[15] **'Authorised officers'** can be:
- officials of any government department (not just the DWP);
- employees of local authorities carrying out housing benefit (HB) functions; *or*
- employees of organisations that perform contracted-out HB functions.

Part 8: Claiming benefits and getting paid
Chapter 53: Fraud and penalties
2. Investigating benefit claims

Authorised officers should use a code of practice when obtaining information.[16] Information that is the subject of 'legal privilege' (ie, confidential communication between a legal adviser and her/his client) cannot be requested.[17]

Authorised officers have powers to enter, at a reasonable time, premises which they have reasonable grounds for suspecting are:[18]

- a person's place of employment;
- where a trade or business is carried out or documents relating to it are kept;
- where a personal or occupational pension scheme is administered or documents relating to it are kept;
- where someone operating a compensatory scheme for an industrial accident or disease may be found;
- where a person on whose behalf a compensatory payment for an industrial accident or disease has been made may be found.

This may include someone's home. The authorised officer must show a certificate of appointment if asked for it. S/he can question anyone on the premises, and require, if reasonable, any documents or copies of documents.

Authorised officers cannot come into your home without your permission (except if you run a business from your home) and they cannot detain you. They cannot make you give information or answer questions in such a way as to confess that you, or your partner, are guilty of an offence.[19]

All fraud investigators can use surveillance to investigate social security fraud – eg, observing people entering or leaving premises. Any surveillance must be authorised by an officer of the appropriate level.

Fraud investigators in England and Wales are bound by codes of practice under the Police and Criminal Evidence Act 1984.[20] In Scotland, fraud investigators must work to the common law principle of the 'test of fairness'. If these are breached, this may restrict the use of evidence they have obtained.[21] If you think the officers have acted unfairly, get advice.

Interviews under caution

Fraud investigators may carry out interviews to get information. If you are suspected of fraud, officers should carry out a formal interview, known as an 'interview under caution'. You should receive notification of the interview in writing no more than 10 days in advance.[22]

You should always be cautioned before the interview. If the fraud officer fails to do so, the interview may not be admissible in court. If you do not understand the caution, its meaning should be explained to you. If you appear unable to understand the significance of the interview or what is happening (eg, due to incapacity or a learning disability), you should not be interviewed.[23]

You do not have to answer any questions put to you, but if you do not answer questions, this might be taken as a sign of guilt. If you decide not to answer questions, you could instead prepare a written statement to give to the investigators.

You might not be told why the interview is happening. If you have not been informed of the purpose of the interview, it may be inadmissible as evidence in court.

A formal interview is normally recorded and you can request a copy. A transcript is produced for use at any trial or appeal hearing.

If you have extra travel costs to attend a formal interview, these should be reimbursed. If you need someone to accompany you because you are vulnerable (eg, under 18, have a learning disability or other complex need), her/his travel expenses can also be reimbursed.

Are you suspected of fraud?

1. If you think fraud officers may interview you, get advice before you attend the interview. Free legal advice may be available from a solicitor.

2. Take someone (eg, a solicitor, adviser or friend) to the interview with you. Although s/he cannot speak for you, s/he can support you and take notes. A solicitor is also allowed to advise you during the interview, ask for clarification of questions and challenge improper questioning.

3. Try to remain calm and listen carefully to the questions you are asked. If you do not understand anything, ask for clarification. You must answer the questions yourself. Think carefully about the implications of the answers you give.

4. If you think you can explain why the situation has arisen, you should mention it at the interview, as any explanation you give later is less likely to be believed if you are prosecuted.[24] If you can explain matters, your benefit is less likely to be taken away.

5. Do not confess to something that you did not do just to finish the interview or to prevent your benefit from being stopped.

6. Consider making a complaint (see Chapter 58) if you feel the interview was not conducted fairly or you were treated in a way which failed to take into account issues such as disability.

The effect of a fraud investigation on your benefit

If the DWP, HMRC or local authority have doubts about your entitlement to benefit, other procedures may also be applied at the same time as a fraud investigation.

- In some circumstances, your benefit may be suspended (see p1185) – eg, if there are doubts about your entitlement or if there is a possibility that you are being overpaid.
- You may be asked to provide additional information and evidence. If you do not do so within a specified time limit, your award can be terminated (see p1187). If you still believe that you are entitled to benefit, make a new claim.

Part 8: Claiming benefits and getting paid
Chapter 53: Fraud and penalties
3. Prosecution of offences

If a fraud investigation is taking a long time to complete, your benefit may be suspended for a long time. However, the DWP, HMRC or local authority should not withhold your benefit indefinitely without making a decision on whether or not you are entitled to it. Complain if you think an investigation is taking too long (see p1396). If that brings no results, seek legal advice about forcing the DWP, HMRC or local authority to make a decision.

The decision on whether you should be prosecuted is separate from a decision to recover an overpayment of benefit (see Chapter 52). The two processes are independent and have different tests. Therefore:

- a decision or appeal on your claim does not have to be delayed while you wait for the outcome of a criminal prosecution;[25]
- a court fine does not prevent recovery of an overpayment. If you have to make payments under a compensation order made by a court to the DWP, HMRC or local authority, it cannot also recover that amount as an overpayment.[26]

Acquittal in a fraud case does not necessarily mean that the decision on your benefit entitlement was wrong. Whatever the result of an investigation or prosecution, it may take longer to assess your future claims because your circumstances may be checked more thoroughly. Complain if it takes too long (see p1396). You should not be prevented from making a fresh claim during a fraud investigation if your circumstances change. You can also apply for a short-term advance of benefit (see p1177) or help from a local welfare assistance scheme (see p856).

3. **Prosecution of offences**

Benefit offences can broadly be divided into two categories, based on the severity of the penalty you can potentially be given:

- making false representations in order to claim benefit is the less serious of the benefit offences, see p1261; *and*
- making dishonest representations in order to claim benefit is the more serious benefit offence, see p1262.

In the most serious cases in England and Wales, you may be charged with the criminal offences of theft or fraud, and in Scotland with common law offences.[27] These offences carry more severe penalties.

If found guilty, you can be fined or imprisoned, or both. Any fine that you have to pay is in addition to any recoverable overpayment (see Chapter 52). Your benefits can also be sanctioned for a period (see p1265).

In England and Wales, DWP and HM Revenue and Customs (HMRC) prosecutions are carried out by the Crown Prosecution Service, which also conducts prosecutions on behalf of many local authorities. In Scotland, prosecutions are conducted by the Procurator Fiscal.

False representations

You commit the offence of making false representations if you:
- make a statement which you know to be false or give information or produce documents that you know to be false (or knowingly cause or allow someone else to do so) in order to claim a benefit or payment for yourself or someone else, or for any other purpose relating to the benefit rules.[28] It does not have to be shown that you intended to obtain benefit to which you were not entitled;[29]
- fail to notify the DWP, HMRC or local authority promptly of a change of circumstances which you know affects your entitlement to benefit or another payment. This also applies to appointees and other third parties receiving benefit on your behalf, and landlords receiving direct payments of housing benefit. You count as notifying a change promptly if you do so as soon as reasonably practicable after the change occurs;[30]
- cause or allow another person to fail to notify a change of circumstances to the DWP, HMRC or local authority promptly which you know affects her/his entitlement to benefit or other payment.[31]

You do not 'know' something if you are merely careless about whether or not something is true, or if you fail to find out.[32] You have not committed an offence if you do not notify a change of circumstances that did not affect your entitlement to benefit or if there was already no entitlement to benefit.[33]

The maximum penalty for these offences is a £5,000 fine or three months in prison, or both.[34]

Duty to report a change in circumstances

The rules on fraud and your duty to report a change of circumstances are different to those outlined on p1184. For fraud purposes, you only commit an offence if you do not report promptly a change that you know affects your benefit. However, to avoid potential allegations of fraud or prosecution, you should report *all* changes promptly. It is always advisable to report the change in a way that allows you to show that you have done so – eg, in writing, dated and retain a copy or get a receipt. For more information about reporting changes of circumstances, see p1184.

For an offence to have been committed, you must have acted 'knowingly'. To have acted 'knowingly', you must have been aware of where the change must be reported and the manner in which it must be reported.[35]

Duties of advisers and other third parties

If you are an adviser, you are not under a duty to notify the DWP, HMRC or local authority about a claimant's change of circumstances, provided you have fully

Part 8: Claiming benefits and getting paid
Chapter 53: Fraud and penalties
3. Prosecution of offences

advised her/him of the law and her/his requirement to notify changes in her/his circumstances and provide truthful information. In order to commit an offence of allowing or causing someone to fail to notify a change of circumstances, or knowingly allowing or causing someone to give false information, there must be some sort of implied permission given to the person to not report the change or give false information.[36] You do not 'allow' someone to do something unless you can stop them doing it.[37] You should do nothing to help facilitate a misrepresentation or failure to notify a change of circumstances – eg, help to complete a claim or review form which you know is inaccurate.

Dishonest representations

You commit the offence of making dishonest representations if you make any of the false representations on p1261 in order to claim benefit and you act dishonestly ('knowingly' in Scotland) in doing so.[38] This means that you did something that most people would consider dishonest and that you must have known it was dishonest.[39]

The maximum penalty if you are convicted in a magistrates' court (sheriff court in Scotland) is a £5,000 fine or six months in prison (12 months in Scotland[40]), or both. If you are convicted in the Crown Court (High Court in Scotland), you can receive an unlimited fine or seven years in prison, or both.[41]

Prosecutions

Not all cases in which there is evidence to justify a prosecution are taken to court. Instead, you may be given the chance to pay a penalty (see p1263). In some cases, no fraud action is taken at all. The factors taken into account include the strength of the evidence, the amount of benefit involved, whether an offence was planned and your personal circumstances. The decision about whether or not to prosecute is normally taken by the Crown Prosecution Service or Procurator Fiscal, which can also recommend an administrative caution instead.[42] **Note:** you may have sanctions imposed on certain benefits, even if you are not prosecuted (see p1263).

There are time limits for bringing a prosecution for making false representations in order to claim benefit (see p1261). A prosecution must be started either within three months of the date the DWP, HMRC or local authority (or, in Scotland, the Procurator Fiscal) thinks it has sufficient evidence to prosecute you, or within 12 months of the date you committed the offence, whichever is later.[43]

There are no time limits for bringing a prosecution for making dishonest representations in order to claim benefit (see above).

Are you being prosecuted?

If you are being prosecuted, get advice. You may be entitled to free legal help from a solicitor and representation in court. Check carefully that the Fraud and Error Service is able to prove all the parts of the offence with which you are charged. Do not plead guilty until you have obtained advice.

4. Financial penalties for benefit offences

The Fraud and Error Service may offer you the option of paying a financial penalty under civil law instead of being prosecuted under criminal law. These financial penalties are not the same as the civil penalties described on p1256. Your benefit can still be sanctioned if you accept a financial penalty (see p1265).

The amount of the penalty depends on when the offence was committed.

- For offences committed wholly after 7 May 2012, the penalty is 50 per cent of any amount overpaid, subject to a minimum of £350 even if you were not actually overpaid, and:[44]
  - a maximum of £2,000 if committed partly or wholly before 1 April 2015; *or*
  - a maximum of £5,000 if committed wholly after 31 March 2015.
- For offences committed partly or wholly before 8 May 2012, the amount of the penalty is 30 per cent of the overpayment.

The overpayment must have been caused by an offence you committed on or after 18 December 1997.[45]

The penalty is added to the overpayment of benefit and is recoverable in the same way (see p1236 and p1245).[46]

Note: the DWP no longer offers cautions for offences committed wholly or partly after 1 April 2012. Penalties may be offered instead.[47] For more details about formal cautions, see the 2012/13 edition of this *Handbook*.

The option of paying a penalty

You can be offered the option of paying a penalty if:[48]

- an overpayment has been found to be recoverable from you, or, for offences committed wholly after 7 May 2012, would have been if an award had been made. The DWP, HMRC or local authority must have revised or superseded your award of benefit and issued a decision that an overpayment is recoverable (see Chapter 52); *and*
- the overpayment was due to an act or omission on your part. This must have occurred on or after 18 December 1997;[49] *and*
- there are grounds for prosecuting you for an offence relating to the overpayment.

Part 8: Claiming benefits and getting paid
Chapter 53: Fraud and penalties
4. Financial penalties for benefit offences

The Fraud and Error Service issues you with a notice setting out how the scheme works and giving you information about how to agree to pay a penalty and how to notify your withdrawal of your agreement.[50] If you are not issued with a proper notice, it may not be possible to enforce the penalty.

The notice is sent with an invitation to an interview to discuss accepting the penalty. The interview is only about whether to offer you a penalty. The interview should not be carried out by the same officer who interviewed you under caution (see p1258).[51] You cannot use it to add to or alter any statement you made about the alleged offence in an interview under caution. If you are unable to decide whether or not to accept the penalty at the interview, you should be allowed five days to make up your mind.[52]

What happens if you accept a penalty?[53]

1. If you agree to pay a penalty, you cannot be prosecuted for any offence relating to the overpayment. However, you can still be prosecuted in the future if you commit another offence or one relating to a different overpayment.

2. If it is found on revision, supersession or appeal that the overpayment is not due or not recoverable, any penalty you have paid must be repaid to you. This does not change the fact that you have agreed to pay a penalty in exchange for immunity from prosecution, so you still cannot be prosecuted for the offence.

3. If the amount of the overpayment is changed following a revision, supersession or appeal, the agreement is cancelled, so you lose your immunity from prosecution, and any penalty you have paid must be repaid to you. However, if you make a fresh agreement to accept a penalty, you are again immune from prosecution and the amount of penalty you have already paid can be offset against the new penalty rather than being repaid to you.

If you do not accept the penalty, the Fraud and Error Service *may* pass the case to the Crown Prosecution Service or Procurator Fiscal to consider whether to prosecute you.

Changing your mind

If you agree to pay a penalty, you can change your mind, provided you notify the Fraud and Error Service within 14 days (28 days for offences committed partly or wholly before 8 May 2012) in the manner it specifies.[54] If you decide not to accept the penalty, you lose your immunity from prosecution. If you have already paid any part of it, this must be refunded to you.

Should you agree to pay a penalty?

1. Get advice and consider your options carefully.

2. If you are not prosecuted, your case does not go to court and you cannot get a prison sentence.

3. If you accept a penalty, your benefit may still be sanctioned (see p1265).

4. You may be invited to pay a penalty when there is insufficient evidence to prosecute you. The fraud officer can only recommend that your case be considered for prosecution. The Crown Prosecution Service, Procurator Fiscal or local authority legal department decides whether or not to prosecute (see p1260). You are not automatically prosecuted if you refuse to accept a penalty.

5. If you are prosecuted and found guilty, the court might offer you a caution or community service rather than a fine. On the other hand, you could get a large fine or even a prison sentence.

6. A penalty may be a substantial amount of money. For minor offences, the amount of a fine imposed by the court could be less.

5. Sanctions for benefit offences

Sanctions can be imposed on certain benefits, known as 'sanctionable benefits' (see p1266), if:[55]
- you are convicted of one or more benefit offences in a set of proceedings; *or*
- you agree to pay a financial penalty for a benefit offence instead of being prosecuted (see p1263).

Note: these sanctions are different to those imposed for failing to comply with work-related requirements described in Chapter 48.

Under what is sometimes referred to as the 'one-strike rule' (because it can apply after just one offence), a conviction is not always required as you can be sanctioned by just agreeing to pay a financial penalty for an offence.

If you are convicted of a benefit offence and have already committed an earlier offence(s), a longer sanction may be imposed under the 'two-strikes rule' instead. This applies if:[56]
- you are convicted of one or more benefit offences in the current set of proceedings; *and*
- within five years of the date you committed any of the current offences, you committed an earlier benefit offence, including an offence for which you accepted a financial penalty or formal caution; *and*
- the current offence has not been previously treated as a current offence, and the earlier offence has not been previously treated as an earlier offence, under the two strikes rules in relation to a reduction of your benefits, a joint claim for jobseeker's allowance (JSA) or a family member's benefit under these sanction rules.

The benefit offence(s) must have been committed after 1 April 2010 (for the one-strike rule) or on or after 1 April 2002 (for the two-strikes rule) and be:[57]

Part 8: Claiming benefits and getting paid
Chapter 53: Fraud and penalties
5. Sanctions for benefit offences

- in connection with a 'disqualifying' benefit (see below); *or*
- to attempt, conspire or aid the committing of a benefit offence.

Disqualifying benefits[58]

All social security benefits and tax credits are **'disqualifying' benefits'** for the purposes listed above, except statutory sick pay, statutory maternity pay, statutory adoption pay, statutory paternity pay and maternity allowance.

See below for details of the sanctions that can be applied.

Which benefits can be sanctioned

Sanctions can be imposed on 'sanctionable benefits'. These are all the disqualifying benefits above *except:*[59]
- attendance allowance;
- bereavement payment;
- child benefit;
- child tax credit (CTC);
- Christmas bonus;
- disability living allowance;
- guardian's allowance;
- industrial injuries constant attendance and exceptionally severe disablement allowances;
- joint-claim JSA, but note that it can still be removed or reduced;[60]
- personal independence payment;
- retirement pensions;
- social fund payments;
- war pensions constant attendance allowance, exceptionaly severe disablement allowance and mobility supplement;
- working tax credit (WTC). However, under separate rules, you lose your WTC if you have committed a benefit offence on or after 5 April 2012 (see p1268).

The above benefits cannot therefore be sanctioned.

The sanctions

Usually, sanctionable benefits are not paid during a sanction period (see p1267). In some cases, however, your benefit may be paid at a reduced rate.
- **Income support (IS), income-based JSA, joint-claim JSA, pension credit (PC) and housing benefit (HB)** are usually reduced by 40 per cent of the appropriate personal allowance for a single person of the offender's age (see p231), or 20 per cent if you or a member of your family are pregnant or seriously ill.[61] However:

- if you are a member of a joint-claim JSA couple (see p120), one of you is sanctioned for a benefit offence and the other is not subject to *any* type of sanction (including the sanctions described in Chapter 48), JSA is paid at the rate of:[62]
    - contribution-based JSA, if the person who has not been sanctioned qualifies for it; *or*
    - hardship payments, if you and your partner qualify (see p1209);[63] *or*
    - in any other case, income-based JSA calculated as if the partner who has not been sanctioned were a single person. However, any income or capital of either of you is taken into account;
- if you are a member of a joint-claim JSA couple, one or both of you are sanctioned for a benefit offence and both are also sanctioned under the rules described in Chapter 48, or one of you would qualify for IS, JSA is not paid. However, you may still qualify for hardship payments under the rules described on p1209;[64]
- if you are claiming income-based JSA in any circumstances other than those of a joint-claim couple as described in the bullet points above, you are not paid at the reduced rate unless you qualify under rules which are the same as those that apply for JSA hardship payments as described on p1215.[65] If you are also sanctioned under the rules described in Chapter 48, you do not qualify for a reduced rate of JSA but can still qualify under the rules in Chapter 51;
- HB is unaffected if you or a member of your family are entitled to IS, income-based JSA, income-related employment and support allowance (ESA) or PC during the sanction period.
- **Income-related ESA** is reduced by 100 per cent of the appropriate personal allowance for a single person of the offender's age (see p230), or 40 per cent if you or a member of your family are subject to no work-related requirements (see p1083), or 20 per cent if you or a member of your family are pregnant or seriously ill.[66] You may be able to get hardship payments if your income-related ESA is reduced in this way (see p1210).
- **Universal credit (UC)** is reduced by the same amount as when a sanction for failing to meet your work-related requirements applies (see p1110).[67] However, 16/17-year-olds and those getting a limited capability for work-related activity element are still subject to a full reduction equivalent to the applicable daily standard allowance (50 per cent for a joint claimant).

  If your UC is reduced, you may be able to get hardship payments in the same way as when you are sanctioned for not meeting your claimant responsibilities, except that there are no restrictions for 16/17-year-olds (see p1211).[68]

The sanction period

The sanction period under the one-strike rule (see p1265) is **three years** if:[69]
- you are convicted for serious fraud or conspiracy to defraud; *or*

Part 8: Claiming benefits and getting paid
Chapter 53: Fraud and penalties
5. Sanctions for benefit offences

- the overpayment is at least £50,000; *or*
- you are given a sentence of at least a year; *or*
- the offence is committed over a period of at least two years.

The sanction period under the one-strike rule is **13 weeks** if you are convicted in less serious cases and **four weeks** if you pay a penalty as an alternative to prosecution (see p1263).[70]

Sanction periods under the two-strikes rule are **26 weeks** (except for serious fraud, for which the sanction period is three years) or **three years** if the earlier offence is within five years of a previous one.[71]

The sanction period starts at least 28 days after the determination that a restriction on payment of benefits should apply.[72]

Note: while benefits are sanctioned, an underlying entitlement remains in place to ensure the link between benefits and other entitlements (eg, free school lunches and free prescriptions) remains.

Loss of working tax credit for a benefit offence

You are disqualified from being paid WTC for a set period of time if you have committed a benefit offence.[73] You do not need to have been convicted.

You are disqualified from WTC if:

- you commit a benefit offence concerning a 'disqualifying benefit' (see p1266) on or after 5 April 2012; *and*
- you would be entitled to WTC if it were not for this rule, either as a single person or as part of a joint claim. If you have a joint claim, but only one of you is disqualified from WTC, WTC remains payable, but the amount is reduced by 50 per cent.[74]

The 'one-strike' and 'two-strikes' rules and the definition of a sanctionable offence that apply to sanctionable benefits (see p1265) apply. The sanction periods are also the same (see p1266).

You are not disqualified from receiving CTC under this rule.

Notes

1. Civil penalties

1 ss115C-115D SSAA 1992; SS(CP) Regs
2 Vol 3 Ch 9, para 09420 DMG
3 s115D(6) SSAA 1992
4 *VT v SSWP (IS)* [2016] UKUT 178 (AAC)
5 Vol 3 Ch 9, paras 09425-29 and 09436 DMG
6 Reg 3 SS(OR) Regs
7 *VT v SSWP (IS)* [2016] UKUT 178 (AAC)

2. Investigating benefit claims

8 s127 WRA 2012
9 s122B SSAA 1992
10 ss124, 124A, 124B and 125 SSAA 1992
11 ss122D and 122E SSAA 1992
12 ss122C and 122E SSAA 1992
13 ss182A and 182B SSAA 1992
14 s123 and Sch 4 SSAA 1992
15 ss109A, 109B and 109C SSAA 1992
16 DWP, *Code of Practice on Obtaining Information*, November 2016, available at www.gov.uk
17 s109B(5)(b) SSAA 1992; DWP, *Code of Practice on Obtaining Information*, November 2016, s2.11
18 s109C SSAA 1992
19 ss109B(5) and 109C(6) SSAA 1992
20 s67(9) PACEA 1984
21 s78(1) PACEA 1984; *DHSS v McKee* [1995] 6 *Bulletin of NI Law* 17 (NI Crown Court)
22 DWP, *Fraud Guide: staff guide*, 'Interviews Under Caution, 01 Planning and Preparation', para 82, available at www.gov.uk
23 DWP, *Fraud Guide: staff guide*, 'Interviews Under Caution, 04 Interviewing people at risk', para 18, available at www.gov.uk
24 s34 CJPOA 1994
25 *Mote v SSWP and Chichester District Council* [2007] EWCA Civ 1324, reported as R(IS) 4/08
26 CIS/683/1994; *KP v RB of Kensington and Chelsea* [2014] UKUT 393 (AAC)

3. Prosecution of offences

27 *Osinuga v Director of Public Prosecution* [1997] 30 HLR 853
28 s112(1) SSAA 1992

29 *Clear v Smith* [1981] 1 WLR 399
30 s112(1A)-(1F) SSAA 1992
31 s112(1B) and (1D) SSAA 1992
32 *Taylor's Central Garages v Roper* [1951] 115 JPR 445
33 *R v Passmore* [2007] EWCA Crim 2053; *R v Laku* [2008] EWCA Crim 1745
34 s112(2) SSAA 1992
35 *Coventry City Council v Vassell* [2011] EWHC 1542 (Admin)
36 *R v Chainey* [1914] 1 KB 137 at 142 (DC)
37 *R v Tilley* [2009] EWCA Crim 1426
38 s111A SSAA 1992
39 *R v Ghosh* [1982] EWCA Crim 2
40 s45 Criminal Proceedings etc (Reform) (Scotland) Act 2007
41 s111A(3) SSAA 1992
42 DWP, *Penalties Policy: in respect of social security fraud and error*, January 2015, paras 4.5.2 and 4.5.3, available at www.gov.uk
43 s116(2), (2A) and (7) SSAA 1992; *Bennett v SSWP* [2012] EWHC 371 (Admin)

4. Financial penalties for benefit offences

44 s115A(3)-(3A) SSAA 1992
45 s25(7) SSA(F)A 1997; Art 2(1)(b) SSA(F)AO No.5
46 s115A(4)(a) SSAA 1992
47 DWP, *Fraud Guide: staff guide*, 'Cautions', available at www.gov.uk
48 s115A(1)-(1A) SSAA 1992
49 s25(7) SSA(F)A 1997; Art 2(1)(b) SSA(F)AO No.5
50 s115A(2) SSAA 1992
51 DWP, *Fraud Guide: staff guide*, 'Administrative Penalties: offences committed on or after 8 May 2012', March 2014, available at www.gov.uk
52 DWP, *Fraud Guide: staff guide*, 'Administrative Penalties: offences committed on or after 8 May 2012', March 2014, available at www.gov.uk
53 s115A(4)(b), (6) and (7) SSAA 1992
54 s115A(5) SSAA 1992

5. Sanctions for benefit offences

55 s6B(1) SSFA 2001
56 s7(1) SSFA 2001

Part 8: Claiming benefits and getting paid
Chapter 53: Fraud and penalties
Notes

57 ss6B(13) and 7(8), definition of 'benefit offence', SSFA 2001
58 s6A(1), definition of 'disqualifying benefit', SSFA 2001; reg 19A, definition of 'disqualifying benefit', SS(LB) Regs
59 s6A(1), definition of 'sanctionable benefit', SSFA 2001; reg 19 SS(LB) Regs
60 s8 SSFA 2001
61 ss6B, 7, 8 and 9 SSFA 2001; regs 3, 3A, 5-10, 17 and 18 SS(LB) Regs
62 Reg 4 and 11-13 SS(LB) Regs
63 These are hardship payments under the loss of benefit rules but the qualifying conditions are the same are those described in Chapter 51.
64 Reg 11(4) SS(LB) Regs excludes joint-claim JSA couples both sanctioned under the rules described in Chapter 48, or where one is entitled to IS, from hardship payments under the loss of benefit rules but that does not prevent them from qualifying under the hardship payment rules in Chapter 51.
65 ss7(2) and (4), 8(2) and (4) SSFA 2001; regs 5-8 and 10 SS(LB) Regs
66 Reg 3ZA SS(LB) Regs
67 Reg 3ZB SS(LB) Regs
68 Regs 16D-16H SS(LB) Regs
69 s6B(11A)(a) and (14) SSFA 2001
70 s6B(11A)(b) and (c) SSFA 2001
71 s7(6A) SSFA 2001
72 s6B(11) SSFA 2001; reg 1A SS(LB) Regs
73 ss36A-B TCA 2002
74 Reg 3 The Loss of Tax Credits Regulations 2013, No.715

Part 9

Getting a benefit decision changed

Chapter 54

Revisions and supersessions

Revisions and supersessions

This chapter covers:
1. Getting a decision changed (below)
2. Revisions (p1276)
3. Supersessions (p1287)
4. Revisions and supersessions after a 'qualifying benefit' award (p1300)
5. The 'anti-test case rule' (p1302)

This chapter covers the rules for benefits and the social fund payments in Chapter 36, except budgeting loans. It does *not* cover the rules for statutory sick pay and statutory maternity, adoption, paternity and shared parental pay (see Chapter 57) or the health benefits in Chapter 29.

References in this chapter to HM Revenue and Customs (HMRC) only apply to decisions about child benefit and guardian's allowance. HMRC also makes decisions about tax credits. For these, see Chapter 64.

Key facts
- If you think a decision is wrong, or is no longer correct, you can ask the decision maker to change it by applying for a revision or a supersession.
- In some cases, you must show grounds for a revision or a supersession.
- In some cases, you do not need to show grounds for a revision, but you must ask for one within a set time limit.
- A revision or a supersession takes effect from the date when you are paid arrears if you are entitled to more benefit, or the date when you have been overpaid if you are entitled to less benefit.
- You can also challenge a decision by appealing to the First-tier Tribunal. Unless the benefit is housing benefit, you must apply for a mandatory reconsideration first and the decision maker considers whether to do a revision.

1. Getting a decision changed

If you are getting benefit but you cease to satisfy the conditions of entitlement or if the amount of benefit to which you are entitled should be reduced or increased,

Part 9: Getting a benefit decision changed
Chapter 54: Revisions and supersessions
1. Getting a decision changed

the decision awarding you benefit can be changed. Likewise, if a decision maker's decision is wrong (eg, because s/he got the facts or the law wrong), it can be changed. Decisions can be changed either by:

- a revision (see pp1276–87); *or*
- a supersession (see pp1287–1300).

In some cases, this can only be done if one of the grounds for a revision applies (see p1279). You must always show that one of the grounds for a supersession applies (see p1287). You can apply for a revision or a supersession, or the decision maker can decide to do one.

For information about how to apply for a revision or a supersession, see p1284 and p1291. There is a time limit for applying for what is known as an 'any grounds' revision (normally only one month – see p1277).

Note: in many cases, you also have a right of appeal to the First-tier Tribunal (see Chapter 55). However, unless the benefit is housing benefit (HB), you must apply for a mandatory reconsideration before you can appeal (see p1311). Under the mandatory reconsideration rules, the decision maker must consider whether to carry out a revision before you can appeal.

You can apply for a revision or a supersession of a decision that you cannot appeal (see p1315 for some examples). If you are still dissatisfied, get advice about whether you can apply for a judicial review (see p1378).

> *Getting a decision changed: checklist*
> 1. To get more information about a decision, ask for an explanation or a written statement of reasons if this has not already been provided (see p1166).
> 2. Decide whether to apply for a revision or a supersession, or to appeal. Get advice as soon as possible (see Appendix 2).
> 3. If you decide to appeal, unless the benefit is HB, apply for a mandatory reconsideration first, and obtain a mandatory reconsideration notice (see p1313).
> 4. Ensure you keep within the time limit (see p1277 for revisions and p1318 for appeals).

If a decision is changed in your favour, you usually get more arrears of benefit with a revision than a supersession (see p1286 and p1292 for when a decision takes effect). For this reason, it is best to apply for a revision if you can. If you are in any doubt about how you would be better off, get advice.

For information about challenging a revision or a supersession, see p1286 and p1299. If the decision maker refuses to consider a supersession, see p1299.

> *Revision, supersession or appeal?*
> 1. Unless the benefit is HB, you must apply for a mandatory reconsideration before you can appeal (see p1311). For HB, you can still apply for a revision before you appeal; if your application for a revision is turned down, you can still appeal against the original decision.

2. You can apply for a revision without having to show specific grounds (an 'any grounds' revision) but there is a time limit for doing so. There is no time limit for applying for an 'any time' revision, but you must show there are grounds. However, you cannot appeal against a refusal to do an 'any time' revision (see p1286).

3. In most cases, there is no time limit for applying for a supersession – eg, if there has been a mistake about the facts or if a test case is decided in your favour but you do not become aware of this until some time later. However, you generally get less arrears of benefit if you apply for a supersession rather than a revision or by appealing, even if you are successful. See pp1292–99 for information about when a supersession takes effect.

4. If you apply for a revision or a supersession instead of appealing and the 'anti-test case' rule applies to you (see p1302), the arrears of benefit you get could be limited.

The risks of revision and supersession

Following a revision or a supersession, the original decision may remain the same or be changed to either increase *or* decrease the amount of your benefit, or take away your entitlement altogether. There are particular issues if you apply for a revision or supersession of a disability living allowance (DLA) or a personal independence payment (PIP) decision (see below).

Note:

- Although s/he does not have to do so, the decision maker can consider issues that are not raised in your application for a revision or supersession.[1] So, you may apply for a revision or supersession in the hope that your benefit will be increased, but the outcome could be that you get less benefit. Seek advice before you apply for a revision or supersession if you are concerned about what could happen in your case.

- If a revision or supersession reduces the amount of benefit to which you are entitled, it may mean that you have been overpaid. See Chapter 52 for information about overpayments and when they can be recovered.

Disability living allowance and personal independence payment

Get advice if you want to apply for a revision or supersession because you have not been awarded one component of DLA or PIP when you are already in receipt of the other, or if you are not happy with the rate of a component of DLA or PIP that you have been awarded. In these circumstances, although s/he does not have to do so, the decision maker may consider:

- the component which is not the subject of the revision or supersession;
- whether to reduce the rate of a component, or end your entitlement to it, even if you asked for a higher rate;
- whether to reduce the length of the period for which you have been awarded a component, even if it was originally awarded for an indefinite period.

Part 9: Getting a benefit decision changed
Chapter 54: Revisions and supersessions
2. Revisions

If you report a change of circumstances that is relevant to the rate of DLA to which you are entitled, you are likely to be invited to claim PIP (see p626). Your entitlement to DLA will then end, even if you do not claim PIP.

2. **Revisions**

If you think a decision maker's decision is wrong, you can apply for a revision.[2] The decision maker must then look at the decision again to see whether it can be changed. The DWP, the local authority and HM Revenue and Customs (HMRC) often refer to your request as a dispute or a request for a reconsideration.

Mandatory reconsideration

Unless the benefit is housing benefit (HB), you must apply for a mandatory reconsideration of a decision before you can appeal against it (see p1311). When the DWP or HMRC deals with your application, it looks at its decision again – ie, it considers whether to carry out a revision. The rules and advice on revisions in this chapter therefore apply in full when you apply for a mandatory reconsideration.

When a decision can be revised

You can ask for a decision to be revised or the decision maker can decide to do this.[3] There are two types of revision:
- 'any grounds' revisions: you do not have to show that specific grounds apply (see below), but you must apply within a strict time limit; *and*
- 'any time' revisions: you must show specific grounds (see p1279), but you can apply even if the decision was made a long time ago. This could, therefore, be a way around the strict time limit for appealing to the First-tier Tribunal (see p1318).

The decision maker may decide to revise a decision after you appeal against it, even if s/he did not do so when you applied for a mandatory reconsideration. Your appeal could lapse if s/he revises the decision, even if you do not get everything you want and you have to appeal again (see p1326).

Note: a First-tier (or Upper) Tribunal's decision cannot be revised. In some cases, you can apply for a supersession. Otherwise you must appeal to the Upper Tribunal or a court (see Chapter 56).

'Any grounds' revisions

Note: if you want to appeal against a decision, you must first apply for a mandatory reconsideration. As a matter of law, this is an application for a revision.

You can apply for a revision on any grounds if you do so within a strict time limit, normally one month (see below).[4] You do not have to show specific grounds; it is enough if you simply think a decision is wrong. However, you should still explain why you disagree with the decision and provide information and evidence to support this.

If the decision maker commences action to consider a revision within one month of the date you are sent or given a decision, for benefits other than HB, s/he can decide to revise it her/himself, on any grounds.[5] For HB, a decision maker can also decide to revise a decision her/himself but only if, within one month of the date you are sent or given it, s/he has information which shows that there was a mistake about the facts of your case or the decision was made in ignorance of relevant facts.[6]

A decision maker can only revise a decision on any grounds on the basis of your circumstances at the time:[7]

- the decision took effect; *or*
- in the case of advance awards for benefits other than HB, the decision was made.

If your circumstances have since changed, make a fresh claim or ask for a supersession (see p1287) instead.

Note: if you want to apply for an any grounds revision of a decision about employment and support allowance (ESA), attendance allowance (AA), disability living allowance (DLA) or personal independence payment (PIP) because you (or the person on whose behalf you are claiming) are terminally ill, you must state this explicitly.[8] If you do not do so, the decision maker cannot revise the decision on this ground.

Time limit

You must apply for an 'any grounds' revision:

- **in the case of a Sure Start maternity grant** or a **social fund funeral expenses payment**, within one month of the date you were sent or given the decision, or if later, within the time limit for claiming the payment (see p790 and p796);[9]
- **in the case of a cold weather payment** or a **winter fuel payment**, within one month of the date you were notified of the decision. For these purposes, you are generally assumed to have been notified seven days after the decision was made, but there are exceptions;[10]
- **in the case of HB**, within one month of the date you were sent or given the decision.[11] If a written statement of reasons has not already been included with the decision, days from the date your request for the statement is received by the local authority to the date on which it is provided to you are ignored when calculating the one month;[12]
- **in all other cases:**[13]
  - within one month of the date you were sent or given the decision; *or*

Part 9: Getting a benefit decision changed
Chapter 54: Revisions and supersessions
2. Revisions

– within one month and 14 days of the date you were sent or given the decision, if you requested a written statement of reasons (see p1166) and it is provided within the month; *or*
– within 14 days of a written statement of reasons being provided, if you requested one within one month of the date you were sent or given the decision, but it is not provided within that one-month period.

For benefits (other than a Sure Start maternity grant or a social fund funeral expenses payment, child benefit or guardian's allowance), if an accidental error in a decision has been corrected (see p1165), any day falling before the day on which the correction is notified to you is ignored when calculating the one-month period.[14]

Late requests for an any grounds revision

You can apply for an 'any grounds' revision outside the time limit in limited circumstances, provided this is within an absolute time limit.

The absolute time limit

In most cases, you must apply for an 'any grounds' revision within 13 months of the date you were notified of the decision.[15]

For PIP and universal credit (UC), and, if you come under the UC system (see p20), contribution-based jobseeker's allowance (JSA) and contributory ESA, you must apply within 13 months of the latest date by when your application for a revision should have been received.[16]

If you requested a written statement of reasons (see p1166):

– for HB, days from the date you requested the statement to the date on which it was provided are ignored when calculating the 13 months; *or*
– for other benefits, if the statement of reasons is provided within one month of the date you were notified of the decision, the 13 months are extended by 14 days. If it is provided during a period later than one month after the date you were notified of the decision, the 13 months are extended by 14 days, plus the number of days in that period.

In all cases, your application outside the time limit must contain:[17]
- sufficient details about the decision with which you disagree for it to be identified. Say which benefit you are disagreeing about and the date the DWP, the local authority or HMRC sent you the decision; *and*
- a summary of your reasons for applying late. You must show that:
  – it is reasonable to grant your application; *and*
  – there are special circumstances which mean that it was not practicable for you to apply for a revision within the time limit. Any special circumstances can count. The longer you have delayed applying for a revision, the more compelling these must be.

In addition, for child benefit, guardian's allowance and HB:[18]
- you must show that your application has merit; *and*
- when deciding whether it is reasonable to grant your application, the decision maker cannot take account of the fact that:
  - a court or the Upper Tribunal has interpreted the law in a different way than previously understood and applied;
  - you (or anyone acting for you) misunderstood or were unaware of the relevant law, including the time limits for applying for a revision.

This also applies for benefits other than PIP if you do not come under the UC system and you do not have to apply for a mandatory reconsideration before you can appeal.

Note: you cannot appeal against the decision maker's refusal to let you apply for a revision outside the time limit.[19] The only remedy is judicial review. However, check whether you can make a late appeal against the original decision. For benefits other than HB, the DWP or HMRC may argue that, because of the rules on mandatory reconsideration, you only have a right of appeal against that decision if it has considered a revision of the decision. If you are told this, get advice.

'Any time' revisions

Note: if you want to appeal against a decision, you must first apply for a mandatory reconsideration. As a matter of law, this is an application for a revision.

If you can show there are specific grounds, you can apply for a revision at any time. There is no time limit for applying for an 'any time' revision. If a decision maker refuses to consider an 'any time' revision, see p1286.

In practice, if you apply for a revision (or a mandatory reconsideration) and it is within one month of your being sent or given the decision, the DWP, the local authority or HMRC treats your application as one for an 'any grounds' revision (see p1276). If your application is late and is not accepted by the DWP, the local authority or HMRC, it should go on to consider whether there are grounds for an 'any time' revision.

There are a number of grounds for an 'any time' revision. The main ones are where there has been:
- an official error (see p1280);
- a mistake about or ignorance of facts (see p1280);
- a sanction decision (see p1281);
- an award of a 'qualifying benefit' (see p1282);
- an appeal against a decision (see p1283).

Other grounds for revision are summarised on p1283.

Part 9: Getting a benefit decision changed
Chapter 54: Revisions and supersessions
2. Revisions

Official error

A decision can be revised at any time if there was an official error.[20] **For benefits, other than child benefit and guardian's allowance**, this means:[21]

- an error made by an officer of the DWP or HMRC; *or*
- for HB only, errors made by the local authority or by a person authorised to carry out any function of the local authority or provide services relating to HB; *or*
- other than for HB, errors made by a person employed by someone providing services to the DWP; *or*
- other than for HB, PIP, UC and, if you come under the UC system (see p20), contribution-based JSA and contributory ESA, errors made by an employee of a local authority (or an employee of a person acting on behalf of, or providing services to, a local authority).

For child benefit and guardian's allowance, it means an error made by an officer of HMRC or a person employed by someone providing services to HMRC.[22]

What counts as an official error

The following can count as official errors.

- The decision maker made an error of law – ie, s/he got the law wrong. If the decision maker was only shown to have made an error of law after a later decision of the Upper Tribunal or a court, this ground does not apply.[23] In this case, you could make a fresh claim (or apply for a supersession), and the 'anti-test case rule' could apply (see p1302).
- The decision maker (or local authority) had specific evidence which s/he failed to take into account even though it was relevant. You should argue this applies even if the evidence does not conclusively prove your entitlement, so long as it raised a strong possibility that you were entitled.
- There is documentary or other written evidence of your entitlement that the DWP, the local authority or HMRC had, but failed to give to the decision maker dealing with your claim when the earlier decision was made.
- The decision maker failed to ask you about something that was relevant to your claim. However, the decision maker is likely to say that it is *not* an official error if s/he fails to keep your claim constantly under review or to raise issues that you should have raised, or if s/he fails to make enquiries into things that do not appear to be at issue.[24]

Note: if someone else (eg, you, your partner or your representative) caused or materially contributed to the error, it does not count as an official error.[25] This includes if the way your claim form was completed contributed to the error.[26]

Mistake about or ignorance of facts

A decision can be revised at any time if there was a mistake about the facts of your case or the decision was made in ignorance of relevant facts, but only if, as a result of the mistake or ignorance about the facts, the decision was more favourable to you than it would have been – eg, you were awarded too much benefit.[27] If you have been overpaid, the decision maker may seek to recover the overpayment (see Chapter 52). **Note:** there must have been a mistake about or ignorance of facts, not conclusions or opinions about the facts. See p1228 for some examples.

The rules are different if there was a mistake about, or ignorance of, facts relating to a 'disability determination', a 'limited capability for work determination' or an 'incapacity determination'.[28] In this case, it must be shown that, at the time the decision that you were entitled to a benefit was made (eg, DLA or ESA), you (or the person being paid the benefit) knew, or could reasonably have been expected to know, about the fact and that it was relevant to your benefit. Otherwise, a decision cannot be revised on this ground and you will not have been overpaid benefit, although there may be grounds for a supersession.

***

Disability, limited capability for work and incapacity determinations[29]

A **'disability determination'** is a decision about whether you satisfy the disability conditions for AA or DLA, are disabled for the purposes of severe disablement allowance (SDA), or whether the existence or extent of your disablement is sufficient for you to be entitled to industrial injuries disablement benefit or to be paid at the same rate as that paid immediately before the decision that you were entitled to benefit. It does *not* include decisions about PIP.

A **'limited capability for work determination'** is a decision about whether you have limited capability for work (see Chapter 44) or can be treated as having limited capability for work under specified rules. This does *not* apply if you come under the UC system.

An **'incapacity determination'** is a decision about your incapacity for work under the personal capability assessment, whether you can be treated as incapable of work, or whether there are exceptional circumstances – eg, for incapacity benefit or SDA purposes. See p683 of the 2013/14 edition of this *Handbook*.

***

Note: if the mistake about or ignorance of facts means you should be entitled to *more* benefit:
- a decision can be superseded on this ground (see p1289);
- a decision can be revised on any ground if you satisfy the rules for an 'any grounds' revision (see p1276).

Sanction decisions

A decision can be revised at any time if:[30]
- you do not come under the UC system and it is a decision to give you a sanction because:
  - you (or in some cases your partner) failed to take part in a work-focused interview without good cause (see p1124). This only applies if the decision

Part 9: Getting a benefit decision changed
Chapter 54: Revisions and supersessions
2. Revisions

contained an error and, for ESA only, if you did not materially contribute to the error; *or*

– for ESA and income support (IS) only, you failed to undertake work-related activity without good cause (see p1128). This only applies if the decision contained an error to which you did not materially contribute; *or*

• for JSA and UC, and, if you come under the UC system, ESA, it is a decision to give you a sanction for any reason (see p1093 and p1108).

This means that you can apply for a revision (or a mandatory reconsideration) even if the decision to give you a sanction was made a long time ago. This is useful if you did not realise you could challenge the decision at the time it was made and, for example, you can show you had good cause or a good reason for your actions, or you did not do (or fail to do) what is alleged. If you have been given a sanction more than once, you should apply for a revision (or a mandatory reconsideration) of all the decisions if possible and then appeal if you do not get all that you want. If you are applying for a mandatory reconsideration before you can appeal (see p1311), make this clear in your application. See p1140 for further information about challenging a sanction decision.

Note: for JSA if you do not come under the UC system, a decision can also be revised at any time if the DWP gives you a sanction because you were previously entitled to JSA and that entitlement ended because you were found not to be available for or not to be actively seeking work (see p1107).[31] In practice, this means that if you are awarded and paid JSA while a decision maker considers whether you should be sanctioned, the sanction applies from the date you were awarded JSA.

Awards of a 'qualifying benefit'

A decision can be revised at any time if:

• you are awarded a benefit (eg, IS, income-based JSA, income-related ESA or HB) and, for a period which includes the date that award took effect, you (or your partner, or a child included in your claim – see p220) are awarded another benefit or that other benefit is increased. This can work to your advantage if the other benefit is a 'qualifying benefit' (eg, DLA or carer's allowance – see p1300);[32] *or*

• for IS, JSA, ESA and pension credit (PC) only, if you have a non-dependant living with you (see p464) and since you were awarded IS, income-based JSA, income-related ESA or PC, your non-dependant has been awarded a qualifying benefit (see p1300) for a period that includes the date your award took effect and this means that you are now entitled to a severe disability premium (for IS, JSA or ESA) or a severe disability additional amount (for PC).[33]

A decision to end your entitlement to HB because your (or your partner's or child's) qualifying benefit ceases can also be revised at any time. This only applies if the qualifying benefit is later reinstated following a revision, supersession or appeal.[34] See p1300 for further information. If you are only entitled to a benefit once a qualifying benefit is awarded, see p81 and p1160.

A decision that has been appealed

If you appealed against a decision, and you:

- appealed within the time limit or were allowed a late appeal (see p1318 and p1319) and the appeal has not yet been determined, a decision maker can look at the decision again and revise it.[35] This includes if the First-tier Tribunal has adjourned the hearing or if the Upper Tribunal has sent a case back to the First-tier Tribunal to make a new decision. This enables the decision maker to take new information that has come to light in the appeal process into account; *or*
- make a fresh claim or seek a supersession when your circumstances change (eg, because the First-tier Tribunal cannot, in general, take changes into account – see p1343) and, as a result, a new decision about your entitlement is made, a decision maker can revise the new decision once the appeal has been determined. This only applies if you appealed against a decision to the First-tier Tribunal (or, for HB only, to the Upper Tribunal or a court) and:[36]
  - a fresh claim is decided or the decision is superseded before your appeal is determined; *and*
  - the appeal is then determined; *and*
  - the decision maker would have made her/his decision differently had s/he been aware of the appeal decision at the time her/his decision was made.

Note: if you have appealed against a decision, your appeal could lapse if a decision maker revises the decision, even if you do not get everything you want (see p1326).

Other grounds for revision

There are many other situations when a decision maker can carry out an 'any time' revision. This includes if the decision is one against which you have no right of appeal (see p1315 for which decisions).[37]

Other decisions that can be revised at any time include those:

- to reduce your HB or your UC under the 'benefit cap' rules (see p1180);[38]
- to award you ESA if, when you first claimed ESA, you were not entitled because you were not treated as having limited capability for work (eg, because you had been found to be capable of work and could not show you had a new or worsened medical condition), you were then awarded ESA from a later date and it is now accepted that you did have limited capability for work for the earlier period;[39]
- to end your entitlement to contributory ESA because you have been receiving it for 365 days, but it is subsequently found that you had, or can be treated as having had, limited capability for work-related activity before the decision;[40]

Part 9: Getting a benefit decision changed
Chapter 54: Revisions and supersessions
2. Revisions

- to refuse you PIP because you are resident in a care home and the costs of any qualifying services (see p918) provided for you are met by public funds, the decision was made with incomplete evidence (see p1163) and, after the decision, any of the costs of the qualifying services are recovered from you;[41]
- that are made in consequence of a determination containing an error to which you did not contribute that, because you did not return your questionnaire or you failed to participate in your assessment consultation (see p759 and p760), you do not satisfy the disability conditions for the daily living component or the mobility component of PIP;[42]
- where your maximum rent (for HB) or the amount of rent for the purposes of the housing costs element (for UC) increases because of a rent officer's redetermination, or because a local housing allowance rate or broad rental market area has been amended because of a rent officer's error, or, for HB only, if (in Scotland) an order or notice that your landlord is not entitled to charge rent for your property is revoked following an appeal;[43]
- about state pension (or an 'old' retirement pension), PC or HB, where you or your partner deferred claiming a pension, then changed your option from a higher pension to a lump sum (or, for retirement pension only, vice versa).[44]

Note: the list above is not exhaustive. There are a number of other decisions that can be revised at any time.[45]

How to apply for a revision

For HB, you must apply for a revision (including a late application) in writing.[46]

For benefits other than HB, you do not have to apply for a revision in writing, although it is always best to do so. This ensures that the decision maker understands that you are asking for one, not just seeking an explanation or complaining about the rules. You must apply to the 'appropriate office' (see below).[47] **Note:** if you are applying for a mandatory reconsideration before you can appeal (see p1311), make this clear in your application.

Example
Stan is awarded IS, but the DWP says he is not entitled to help with his housing costs. He telephones the benefit office and complains that he has not got enough money to live on. The benefit office takes no action because it thinks Stan is simply letting off steam, not seeking a revision. Stan should have made it clear he wanted a revision. He can still ask for one, but only if he is within the time limit for an 'any grounds' revision (see p1277) or if there are grounds for an 'any time' revision.

The appropriate office
The **'appropriate office'** is the office specified on the notice of the decision with which you disagree or, for JSA if you do not come under the UC system (see p20), the office where you have to sign on.[48] For benefits (other than child benefit, guardian's allowance,

HB and, if you come under the UC system, contribution-based JSA, contributory ESA and UC), if you are a person who is, or would be, required to attend a work-focused interview as a condition of getting benefit, the Jobcentre Plus office is also an appropriate office.

In all cases, check that your application has been received – eg, to ensure that you do not miss a time limit or, if relevant, to ensure your right of appeal is not affected. Include any information and evidence that supports your case and that may enable the decision maker to revise the decision in your favour. This may mean you can avoid an appeal.

The DWP, the local authority or HMRC can treat an application for a supersession as an application for a revision and an application for a revision as an application for a supersession.[49] In addition, a claim for benefit or a question about your entitlement can be treated as an application for a revision.[50]

Do you need evidence to support your application?

1. If you are the one who wants the revision, the onus is on you to show that there are grounds.

2. If the decision you are trying to get changed was made a long time ago, it can be difficult to identify the grounds. You can obtain information held by the DWP, the local authority or HMRC by making a 'subject access request' under the Data Protection Act 1998. See the Information Commissioner's website at www.ico.org.uk for details.

3. In some cases, the DWP, the local authority or HMRC may say it has destroyed old papers relating to your claim. Ask whether your papers have simply been stored (archived), rather than actually destroyed. You can try to argue that missing papers should be presumed to contain information that is favourable to your case. However, this is unlikely to be accepted unless you can show that the papers should have been retained because they could have been relevant to any potential appeal, or that they were destroyed deliberately to thwart your case.[51]

What the decision maker considers

A decision maker does not have to consider any issues other than those raised in your application for a revision, or which caused her/him to act on her/his own initiative.[52] To ensure s/he considers everthing you want her/him to, you should:

- tell the decision maker all the points about the decision with which you disagree;
- provide any information or evidence that supports your case. This includes, for example, medical evidence from a GP, consultant or other health worker if this is relevant. If the benefit is AA, DLA or PIP, evidence or information from your carer or a diary of your walking, supervision or care needs over a period may be useful. The decision maker may ask you for further information or evidence (see p1286).

Part 9: Getting a benefit decision changed
Chapter 54: Revisions and supersessions
2. Revisions

Providing further evidence and information

The decision maker can ask you for more evidence or information if s/he thinks this is needed to consider all the issues raised by your application for a revision.[53] You must provide this within one month of the request. The decision maker can allow longer. If you do not provide the information, your application is decided on the basis of the information and evidence the decision maker already has. **Note:** the DWP can also ask you to have a medical examination.

Remember, in some cases if you fail to provide information in a specified time period or have a medical examination, payment of your benefit could be suspended, which may lead to your entitlement being terminated (see p1185).

When a revision takes effect

The date a revision takes effect is important. This is the date from when you are paid arrears if you are entitled to more benefit, or have been overpaid if you are entitled to less benefit. In all cases, a revision takes effect from:

- the date the decision being revised took (or would have taken) effect[54] – eg, your date of claim or the date a supersession took effect; *or*
- the correct date, if the date on which the decision being revised took effect was found to be wrong.[55]

It is important to make it clear that you want payment for the past period. You may get less backdating if the 'anti-test case rule' applies (see p1302).

Note: if a decision is revised on the grounds that there was a mistake about, or ignorance of, facts relating to a 'disability determination', a 'limited capability for work determination' or an 'incapacity determination' in the circumstances described on p1281, if the benefit is a qualifying benefit for another benefit (see p1300) and revision of the decision means your entitlement to the other benefit is affected, the decision about the other benefit takes effect on the same date.[56]

Challenging a revision

If a decision is revised or the decision maker refuses to revise a decision, you are notified of this in writing. If you applied for a mandatory reconsideration, this is called a 'mandatory reconsideration notice' (see p1313). If the original decision is one against which you have a right of appeal (see p1314 for which decisions), you can appeal to the First-tier Tribunal against the revised decision (or, in the case of a refusal to do an 'any grounds' revision, against the original decision). Your time limit for appealing (see p1318) runs from the date you are sent or given notification of the result of your application.[57]

If a decision maker refuses to do an 'any time' revision (see p1279) (eg, because s/he does not accept that an official error was made), you cannot appeal against the refusal.[58] However, you could make a late request for an 'any grounds' revision of the original decision, if you are still within the absolute time limit for this. If you want to appeal against the original decision, you could argue that you should be given a mandatory reconsideration notice (see p1313) and then appeal.

3. **Supersessions**

If your circumstances have changed since a decision was made, you can apply for a supersession.[59] You can also apply for a supersession if you think a decision is wrong, but you must show there are grounds.

You can apply for a supersession even if the decision was made a long time ago, but the arrears of benefit you are paid can be limited (see p1292 for when a supersession takes effect). It is usually better to try for a revision or appeal.

When a decision can be superseded

You can ask for a decision maker's decision (and in some cases a First-tier Tribunal's or an Upper Tribunal's decision) to be superseded or the decision maker can decide to do this her/himself.[60] There must be grounds for a supersession. There are many grounds for supersession. The main grounds are:
- a change of circumstances (see below);
- mistakes about or ignorance of facts (see p1289);
- where a decision is legally wrong (see p1289);
- capability for work and disability conditions (see p1290);
- where a qualifying benefit has been awarded (see p1290).

Other grounds for supersession are summarised on p1291.

Note: if a decision could be revised, it cannot be superseded unless there are also grounds for supersession that are not covered by the revision rules.[61]

Change of circumstances

A decision maker's or a tribunal's decision can be superseded if:[62]
- your circumstances have changed since it had effect; *or*
- in the case of advance awards (other than for housing benefit – HB), your circumstances have changed since it was made; *or*
- it is anticipated that your circumstances will change.

There must be a relevant change of circumstances (see p1288).
Note:
- The decision maker may say that a change of circumstances you have reported is a change that could not possibly result in a supersession and so refuse to consider a supersession. If this happens, see p1299.
- If there is doubt about whether a change of circumstances has occurred (eg, whether your medical condition has improved or worsened), it is necessary to

Part 9: Getting a benefit decision changed
Chapter 54: Revisions and supersessions
3. Supersessions

compare the circumstances as they were at the time the decision took effect, and as they were at the time the supersession would take effect.[63]

Note: some changes in your capability for work or the effects of your disability are dealt with under different rules (see p1290).

Relevant changes of circumstances

The change must be what is known as a 'relevant change of circumstances' – ie, it must mean that the original decision (eg, to award you benefit) may no longer be correct. What is relevant can depend on the benefit. Examples include changes in your medical or physical condition, moving home or being absent from home, becoming or ceasing to be a member of a couple, or having a child or a child leaving home. Bear the following in mind.

- An amendment to the law counts, but a decision of a court or the Upper Tribunal that the law has been wrongly interpreted does not.[64]
- Although a new medical opinion does not count, a new medical report following an examination may provide evidence of a relevant change.[65]
- Becoming terminally ill counts for employment and support allowance (ESA), incapacity benefit, attendance allowance (AA), disability living allowance (DLA), personal independence payment (PIP) and universal credit (UC), but you or the person claiming on your behalf must state explicitly that you are terminally ill in the supersession application.[66]
- In respect of your assessed income period for pension credit (PC), the only change of circumstances that counts is that the period has ended for one of the reasons listed on p157.[67] **Note:** assessment periods are being phased out, so may end sooner than expected.
- For income support (IS) and, if you do not come under the UC system, jobseeker's allowance (JSA) and ESA, the repayment of a student loan does not count.[68] This means the loan continues to be treated as income for the period it was intended to cover.

Change of circumstances after benefit is refused

If you were correctly refused benefit but your circumstances are now different, you *cannot* seek a supersession on the grounds of a change of circumstances. You must instead make a fresh claim (unless you are seeking a supersession because there has been a 'recrudescence' of a prescribed disease – see p681).[69] Even if you are appealing against the decision refusing or stopping your benefit, make a fresh claim when your circumstances change, and appeal if you are still refused. Unless the benefit is HB, you must apply for a mandatory reconsideration first. You could lose out if you do not do so, because the tribunal cannot take a change of circumstances into account if it happens after the decision with which you disagree (see p1343).

Mistake about or ignorance of facts

A decision maker's or a tribunal's decision can be superseded if there was a mistake about the facts of your case or if it was made in ignorance of relevant facts. However, in the case of a decision maker's decision, this only applies if:[70]

- for HB, a revision on the same ground cannot be done. Note that the local authority can revise a decision if, within one month of your being sent or given it, it has information that shows that there was a mistake about the facts of your case or the decision was made in ignorance of relevant facts;[71] *or*
- for other benefits, the time limit for applying for an 'any grounds' revision (or any longer period allowed) has passed (see p1277) or, if the decision maker decides to do a supersession her/himself, it is more than one month since you were sent or given the decision.

In practice, this ground for supersession generally only applies if, as a result of a mistake or ignorance about the facts, a decision was less favourable to you than it would have been (eg, you were awarded too little benefit) and you have missed the time limit for seeking an 'any grounds' revision. If a decision is more favourable to you than it would have been (ie, you were being overpaid), a decision maker can instead do an 'any time' revision (see p1280).

Note:
- There must have been a mistake about the facts or the decision maker (or the tribunal) must not have had all the facts, but it does not matter how the mistake came about or whether you could have produced evidence sooner than you did or failed to give the information on your claim form.
- The mistake or ignorance must be in respect of facts, not conclusions or opinions about the facts. See p1228 for some examples.
- Sometimes it is possible to argue that the decision maker's mistake was an error of law. If so, an 'any time' revision on the grounds of official error may be possible (see p1280). This is the better option, as full arrears of benefit are payable.

Decisions that are legally wrong

A decision maker's decision can be superseded if it was legally wrong (known as an error of law)[72] and:

- for HB, a revision on the same ground cannot be done; *or*
- for other benefits, the time limit for seeking an 'any grounds' revision (or any longer period allowed) has passed (see p1277) or, if the decision maker decides to carry out a supersession her/himself, it is more than one month since you were sent or given the decision.

In many cases, if there has been an error of law, an 'any time' revision on the grounds of official error is also possible (see p1280). If the new decision is to your advantage, revision is the better option, as full arrears of benefit are payable.

Part 9: Getting a benefit decision changed
Chapter 54: Revisions and supersessions
3. Supersessions

Note: if you think a decision of the First-tier or Upper Tribunal is legally wrong, you must appeal against it.

Capability for work and disability conditions

A decision maker's or a tribunal's decision can be superseded if it is a decision to award you ESA, UC or national insurance (NI) credits on the basis that you have, or are treated as having, limited capability for work (see Chapter 44), or it is a decision to award you PIP on the basis that you satisfy one of the disability conditions. The decision can be superseded if:

- since the decision was made:[73]
  - a healthcare professional (see p1155 for who counts) or, for PIP and if you come under the UC system ESA, an 'other person' approved by the Secretary of State, has provided medical evidence – eg, on your capability for work (or on whether you satisfy the disability conditions for PIP); *or*
  - the decision maker has decided that you can be treated as having limited capability for work (or, for UC, for work and work-related activity) under specified provisions.

  The rules, therefore, allow the decision maker to consider your entitlement to ESA, UC, NI credits or PIP without identifying a specific change of circumstances (see p1287).[74] The rate of benefit may be increased or reduced, or your entitlement may end. However, entitlement should *only* end if s/he decides on the basis of the evidence that you no longer have limited capability for work, or no longer satisfy the conditions for PIP.[75]

  If you have told the decision maker that your condition has not improved since your last assessment or you have a variable condition, you can argue that reference should be made to earlier assessments and decisions on your claim;[76] *or*

- it is a decision to award you PIP and there has been a determination that, because you did not return your questionnaire or you failed to participate in your assessment consultation (see p759 and p760), you do not satisfy the disability conditions for the daily living component or the mobility component.[77]

Awards of qualifying benefits

A decision maker's or a tribunal's decision awarding you benefit can be superseded if:

- you are awarded the benefit (eg, IS, ESA or HB) but, from a later date than the entitlement began, you or your partner (or a child included in your claim – see p220) become entitled to another benefit or that other benefit is increased. This can work to your advantage if the other benefit is a 'qualifying benefit' (eg, DLA, PIP or carer's allowance – CA) (see p1300);[78] *or*

- for IS, income-based JSA, income-related ESA and PC only, if you have a non-dependant living with you (see p244) and since you were awarded the benefit, your non-dependant has been awarded a qualifying benefit (see p1300) for a period beginning after the date your award took effect, and this means that you are now entitled to a severe disability premium (for IS, JSA or ESA) or a severe disability additional amount (for PC).[79]

See p1300 for further information. If you are only entitled to a benefit once a qualifying benefit is awarded, see p81 and p1160.

Other grounds for supersession

There are other situations when a decision can be superseded, including if the decision is one against which you have no right of appeal (see p1315).[80]

Other decisions that can be superseded include those:

- where your maximum rent (for HB) or the amount of rent for the purposes of the housing costs element (for UC) decreases because of a rent officer's redetermination. **Note:** for HB, a decrease in your maximum rent because a local housing allowance rate or a broad rental market area has been amended due to a rent officer's error, is a change of circumstances;[81]
- which reduced your HB under the 'benefit cap' rules (see p1180), or increased or reduced the reduction;[82]
- about PC and HB, where you or your partner deferred claiming a pension and you are paid a lump sum or repay it because you change your option to a pension increase;[83]
- of the First-tier or Upper Tribunal made while a test case was pending, where the test case is eventually decided in your favour (see p1334).[84]

The list above is not exhaustive. Other decisions can be superseded.[85]

How to apply for a supersession

For HB, you must apply for a supersession in writing.[86] For **benefits other than HB**, you do not have to apply for a supersession in writing, although it is always best to do so. This ensures that the decision maker understands that you are asking for one, not just seeking an explanation or complaining about the rules. Apply to the appropriate office. This is the same as for revisions (see p1284).

A notification of a change in circumstances can be treated as an application for a supersession, so if you are reporting a change of circumstances, check that your application is received to ensure you do not miss the time limit.

When you apply for a supersession, include any information and evidence that supports your case and that may enable the decision maker to change the decision in your favour. For what the decision maker considers, see p1285 and providing further information, see p1286. The issues are the same as for revisions.

Part 9: Getting a benefit decision changed
Chapter 54: Revisions and supersessions
3. Supersessions

Do you need evidence to support your application?

1. If you are the one who wants the supersession, you are the one who must show that there are grounds.

2. If the decision you are trying to get changed was made a long time ago, it can be difficult to identify the grounds. You can obtain information held by the DWP, the local authority or HMRC by making a 'subject access request' under the Data Protection Act 1998. See the Information Commissioner's website at www.ico.org.uk for details.

3. In some cases the DWP, the local authority or HMRC may say it has destroyed old papers relating to your claim. Ask whether your papers have simply been stored (archived), rather than destroyed. You can try to argue that missing papers should be presumed to contain information that is favourable to your case. However, this is unlikely to be accepted unless you can show that the papers should have been retained because they could have been relevant to any potential appeal, or that they were destroyed deliberately to thwart your case.[89]

Note:

- The DWP, the local authority or HMRC can treat an application for a supersession as an application for a revision and an application for a revision as an application for a supersession.[87]

- A claim for benefit or a question about your entitlement, can be treated as an application for a supersession.[88]

Example

The local authority terminates Kate's award of HB because it says she is no longer living in her home. She claims HB again and asks for her claim to be backdated. When her new claim is refused, she appeals. The tribunal treats her appeal as an application for a supersession of the decision to terminate her HB award. Because it is satisfied that she is, and was, living in her home, it supersedes the decision to terminate her HB and her award is re-instated.

When a supersession takes effect

If a decision is superseded, the date the new decision (the supersession) takes effect is important. This is the date from when you are paid arrears if you are entitled to more benefit, or the date from when you have been overpaid if you are entitled to less benefit. It is important to make it clear that you want payment for a past period. **Note:** for how the 'anti-test case rule' may affect the amount of backdated benefit you can receive, see p1302.

The general rule

There is a general rule that applies in many cases. This is that if a decision is superseded, the new decision takes effect from:[90]

- the date you applied for the supersession; *or*

- if the decision maker decides to do a supersession on her/his own, the date the decision is made.

Note: there are many exceptions when the general rule does not apply. For these, the date a supersession takes effect depends on the ground for the supersession. For the exceptions, see below and the chapter in this *Handbook* about the benefit you are claiming.

Changes in your circumstances

If the ground for supersession is a change in your circumstances, when the supersession takes effect usually depends on whether or not it is advantageous to you. For HB, see below and for AA, DLA and PIP, see p1294. For UC and contribution-based JSA and contributory ESA under the UC system, see p1295. For other benefits, see p1295. For certain decisions about disability, incapacity and limited capability for work, see p1296. **Note:**

- If a supersession is advantageous to you, you must usually notify the decision maker of the change within one month or you could lose out. For UC, you must notify her/him before the end of the assessment period in which the change takes place.
- If a supersession is not advantageous to you, you may have been overpaid. The DWP, the local authority or HMRC may seek to recover the overpayment.

There are also some special rules that apply in particular situations, including the following.

- For benefits other than child benefit and guardian's allowance, if there has been a change in the legislation that affects your benefit, the supersession takes effect from the date the legislation takes effect.[91]
- For IS, income-based JSA, income-related ESA and PC, if your carer (or your partner's carer) has stopped being paid CA, the supersession takes effect from the day after the last day for which CA was paid, provided this was to someone other than you or your partner. This means that if you are now entitled to the severe disability premium with your IS, income-based JSA or income-related ESA or the severe disability additional amount with PC, this can be backdated to when the carer stopped getting CA for looking after you (or your partner).[92]
- For ESA and UC, if the change is that you are terminally ill (you must state this in the application for a supersession), the supersession takes effect from the date you became terminally ill.[93]

Housing benefit

For HB, the supersession usually takes effect from the Monday after the week in which the change occurs.[94] There are a number of exceptions to this rule. **Note:** if the change is one you are required to notify to the local authority (other than, if you get PC, one of the types of change covered by the exceptions to the rules

Part 9: Getting a benefit decision changed
Chapter 54: Revisions and supersessions
3. Supersessions

described on p93) and the supersession is *advantageous* to you, the change must be notified within one month of its taking place.[95] The one-month period can be extended in certain circumstances (see p1296). If your application for an extension is refused, see p1297 for when the supersession takes effect.

For further information on when changes in circumstances take effect and exceptions to this rule, see p92.

Attendance allowance, disability living allowance and personal independence payment

For AA, DLA and PIP, the supersession usually takes effect as follows.

- If the decision maker decides to do a supersession her/himself or you apply for a supersession and it is *not advantageous* to you, the supersession usually takes effect from the date on which the change takes place or is expected to take place.[96] There is an exception if the change is one you were required to notify and relates to a disability determination or the disability conditions for PIP (see p1296).

- If the decision maker decides to do a supersession her/himself and the decision is *advantageous* to you, it usually takes effect from the date on which s/he first took action with a view to carrying out a supersession.[97]

- If you apply for the supersession and it is *advantageous* to you:
  - if the decision is about PIP, it usually takes effect on the date the change takes place, or is expected to take place. You must notify the DWP within one month of the change.[98] However, if the change means you are now entitled to a particular rate of benefit, the supersession takes effect from the day you satisfy the conditions of entitlement for that rate (this includes the 'required period condition' – see p752).[99] In this case, you must notify the DWP within one month of satisfying the conditions of entitlement.
  - if the decision is about AA or DLA and the change:[100]
    - means you are now entitled to a particular rate of benefit, the supersession takes effect from the day you satisfy the conditions of entitlement to that rate (this includes the qualifying period condition – see p524, p597 and p604). You must notify the DWP of the change within one month of doing so;
    - makes a difference to whether benefit is payable to you (eg, you leave hospital or a care home), the supersession takes effect from the day of the change. You must notify the DWP of the change within one month of the change.

The one-month periods can be extended (see p1296). If your application for an extension is refused, see p1297 for when the supersession takes effect.

Universal credit, and contribution-based jobseeker's allowance and contributory employment and support allowance under the universal credit system

If you come under the UC system (see p20), for contribution-based JSA, contributory ESA and UC, the supersession usually takes effect as follows.

- If the decision maker decides to do a supersession her/himself or you apply for a supersession and it is *not advantageous* to you, the supersession usually takes effect from the start of the assessment period in which (for UC), or the start of the benefit week in which (for JSA and ESA), the change takes place or is expected to take place.[101] There is an exception if the decision is one you were required to notify and is about limited capability for work (see p1296).
- If the decision maker decides to do a supersession her/himself and the decision is *advantageous* to you, it usually takes effect from the start of the assessment period (for UC) or the start of the benefit week (for JSA and ESA) in which s/he first took action with a view to carrying out a supersession.[102]
- If you apply for the supersession and it is *advantageous* to you, it usually takes effect from:
    - for UC, the start of the assessment period in which the change takes place or is expected to take place, provided the DWP is notified of the change within that assessment period;[103]
    - for JSA and ESA, the start of the benefit week in which the change takes place or is expected to take place, provided the DWP is notified of the change within one month.[104]

The period in which you must report a change can be extended (see p1296). If your application for an extension is refused, see p1297 for when the supersession takes effect.

Other benefits

For other benefits, the supersession takes effect as follows.

- If the decision maker decides to do a supersession her/himself or you apply for a supersession and it is *not advantageous* to you, the supersession usually takes effect from the date of the change of circumstances.[105] There is an exception if the change is one you were required to notify and relates to a disability, limited capability or incapacity for work determination (see p1296).
- If the decision maker decides to do a supersession her/himself and it is *advantageous* to you, it usually takes effect from the start of the benefit week in which s/he first took action with a view to carrying out a supersession.[106]
- If you apply for the supersession and it is *advantageous* to you, the supersession usually takes effect from the date of the change, provided the DWP or HMRC is notified of the change within one month.[107] There are exceptions to this rule for IS, JSA, ESA and PC.[108]

The one-month periods can be extended (see p1296). If your application for an extension is refused, see p1297 for when the supersession takes effect.

Part 9: Getting a benefit decision changed
Chapter 54: Revisions and supersessions
3. Supersessions

Disability, incapacity and limited capability for work

Different rules apply if the decision is *not advantageous* to you, it concerns a change you were required to notify and it related to:

- the disability conditions for PIP; *or*
- if you do not come under the UC system, a disability, limited capability for work or incapacity for work determination (see p1281 for what counts); *or*
- if you come under the UC system, limited capability for work.

In this case, if you (or the person being paid the benefit) failed to notify the change when you knew that you should have, or could reasonably be expected to have known that you should have, the supersession takes effect from the date you (or the person being paid the benefit) ought to have notified the change.[109] However, if you (or the person being paid) could not have been reasonably expected to know that you should have reported the change, the supersession takes effect from:[110]

- for UC, the start of the assessment period in which the DWP makes the decision; *or*
- for other benefits, the date you applied for the supersession, or if the decision maker decides to do a supersession on her/his own, the date the decision is made.

So if your condition is found to have improved in the past, and you could not have been expected to report this, you will not have been overpaid.

Note: if the benefit is a qualifying benefit (see p1300 for what counts) and the supersession means your entitlement to another benefit is affected, the decision about the other benefit takes effect on the same date.[111] This does not apply for UC and, if you come under the UC system, ESA.

Late notification of a change of circumstances

If the supersession is *advantageous* to you and you fail to notify a change within the one-month periods above (or, for UC, within the assessment period), you can apply for an extension of time in limited circumstances, to a **maximum of 13 months**.[112] Your application must contain:[113]

- details of the relevant change of circumstances; *and*
- the reasons why you failed to notify the change in time. You must show that:
  - it is reasonable to grant your request; *and*
  - the change of circumstances is relevant to the decision you want changed; *and*
  - there are special circumstances that mean it was not practicable for you to notify the change within the time limit. The longer you have delayed, the more compelling the special circumstances have to be.

When deciding whether it is reasonable to grant your application, the decision maker cannot take account of the fact that:[114]

- a court or the Upper Tribunal has interpreted the law in a different way than was previously understood and applied;
- you (or anyone acting for you) misunderstood or were unaware of the relevant law, including the time limits for applying for a supersession.

If your application for an extension of time is refused, or your application was made outside the maximum time limit (see p1296), arrears are limited. The supersession takes effect:
- for AA or DLA, from the date you applied for the supersession;[115] *or*
- for IS, JSA, ESA and PC:[116]
  - if you are paid in arrears, from the start of the benefit week in which you notified the change; *or*
  - if you are paid in advance and you notified the change on the first day of the benefit week, from that day. Otherwise it takes effect from the start of the benefit week following the week in which you notified the change; *or*
- for HB, usually from the Monday after the date when you notified the change (see p92);[117] *or*
- for UC, from the start of the assessment period in which you notified the change;[118]
- for other benefits, from the date you notified the change.[119]

Mistake about or ignorance of facts

If there has been a mistake about or ignorance of facts, the general rule on p1292 usually applies. So even if you are entitled to more benefit, arrears are limited. There are exceptions, including the following.

If the First-tier or Upper Tribunal made the original decision in ignorance of relevant facts or made a mistake about the facts and, as a result, it was more *advantageous* to you than it would otherwise have been, the supersession takes effect:[120]
- for ESA if you come under the UC system (see p20) and UC, from the start of the benefit week (for ESA) or the start of the assessment period (for UC) in which the tribunal's decision took effect; *or*
- for other benefits, from the date the tribunal's decision took effect.

If this means that you have been overpaid, the decision maker may seek to recover the overpayment. However, this only happens if you (or the person being paid the benefit) knew, or could reasonably have been expected to know, the fact in question and that it was relevant to the decision:[121] *and*
- the decision related to a disability determination or an incapacity determination (see p1281 for the definitions); *or*
- for UC or contributory ESA if you come under the UC system, it is a decision about your limited capability for work under the work capability assessment or whether you can be treated as having limited capability for work.

Part 9: Getting a benefit decision changed
Chapter 54: Revisions and supersessions
3. Supersessions

If you (or the person being paid) did not know (or could not be expected to know), the general rule on p1292 applies.

For HB, if a decision maker's decision was made in ignorance of facts or there was a mistake about the facts and the new decision is *advantageous* to you, the supersession takes effect from the start of the benefit week in which:[122]

- you applied for the supersession; *or*
- if you did not apply for a supersession, the local authority first had sufficient information to show that the original decision was made in ignorance of, or based on a mistake about, the facts.

The list above is not exhaustive. There are other exceptions to the general rule.[123]

Awards of qualifying benefits

If you are entitled to a benefit at a higher rate because you or your partner (or a child included in your claim) or a non-dependant were awarded a qualifying benefit (see p1300 for what counts), the supersession takes effect on the date of entitlement to the qualifying benefit or to an increase in its rate. For IS, JSA, ESA and PC only, if you had a non-dependant living with you while you were waiting for a decision on your claim for a qualifying benefit, your IS, JSA, ESA or PC award can be superseded to include a severe disability premium (additional amount with PC) from the date the non-dependant can be ignored (or ceased to live with you). See pp1300–02 for further information.

Test cases

If a decision about your benefit is being superseded because of a decision by the Upper Tribunal or a court in another case (a test case), the supersession is effective from the date of the tribunal's or court's decision, even if you did not realise it was relevant to your case until some time later.[124] This could help you get considerable arrears of benefit. For the special rule for the period before the date the test case is decided, see p1302 for the 'anti-test case rule'.

If, while an appeal against the initial decision in a test case was pending:

- for benefits other than HB, a decision was made on your claim for benefit or to make a revision or a supersession, but your benefit was suspended and the test case is eventually decided against you (in whole or in part), the supersession takes effect from the date the earlier decision took effect;[125]
- you appealed to the First-tier or Upper Tribunal, it determined your appeal as if the test case had been decided in the way most unfavourable to you and the test case eventually goes in your favour (see p1334), the supersession takes effect from the date it would have taken effect had the tribunal made its decision in accordance with the decision in the test case.[126] For IS, JSA, ESA and PC, the date is the start of the benefit week (for UC, the start of the assessment period) in which it would have taken effect had the tribunal made its decision in accordance with the decision in the test case.[127]

Other grounds for supersession

There are a large number of other exceptions to the general rule. These include if:

- your maximum rent (for HB) or your rent for the purposes of the housing costs element (for UC) has decreased because of a rent officer's redetermination;[128]
- for ESA (and UC), a healthcare professional (see p1155 for who counts) approved by the Secretary of State has provided medical evidence on your capability for work or a decision maker has decided that you can be treated as having limited capability for work or work-related activity;[129]
- for PC and HB, you or your partner deferred claiming a pension and you are paid a lump sum or change your option to a pension increase;[130]
- entitlement to a benefit depends on your NI contribution record, and the decision needed to be changed because additional contributions have been added to the record.[131]

The list above is *not* exhaustive. There are many other exceptions to the general rule.[132]

Challenging a supersession

Following your application for a supersession, or a decision maker deciding to do a supersession on her/his own, a new decision is issued in writing. If you do not get all that you wanted, you can seek a revision of the new decision. If the decision is one against which you have a right of appeal (see p1314), you can appeal to the First-tier Tribunal, but, unless the benefit is HB, you must apply for a mandatory reconsideration first (see p1311). If you have a right of appeal against the decision, you must be told about this.

If the decision maker has said there are no grounds for a supersession, you must show why there are, and say what you think the new decision should be. If the decision maker has done a supersession, but you do not agree that s/he had grounds for this, you should explain why.

If a decision maker refuses to consider a supersession

When you apply for a supersession, a decision maker must make a decision if your application contains a ground for supersession that is potentially relevant to the amount of benefit you can be paid or the length of time you can be paid it. There are two possibilities.

- The decision maker agrees that there is a reason to change your award. For example, you are claiming HB and notify the decision maker that your non-dependant has moved out and so are entitled to more benefit. In this situation, the decision maker does a supersession.
- The decision maker does not think there is a reason to change your award. For example, you are getting the standard rate of the PIP daily living component, feel your condition has deteriorated and want to claim the enhanced rate instead. However, the decision maker thinks you do not qualify for the

Part 9: Getting a benefit decision changed
Chapter 54: Revisions and supersessions
4. Revisions and supersessions after a 'qualifying benefit' award

enhanced rate. In this situation, the decision maker issues a decision refusing to do a supersession.

In either situation, you can seek a revision of the decision maker's decision or appeal against it.[133] Unless the benefit is HB, you must apply for a mandatory reconsideration before you can appeal (see p1311).

The only situations in which a decision maker does not have to make a decision are if an application has not been made properly and, therefore, cannot possibly lead to a supersession, or if an application is transparently not on a potentially relevant ground for supersession or is otherwise misconceived. In these cases, there is no decision against which you can seek a revision or appeal, but you may be able to apply for a judicial review (see p1378).

4. **Revisions and supersessions after a 'qualifying benefit' award**

Some of the rules for revisions and supersessions can help you if you (or your partner, your child or a non-dependant) become entitled to a 'qualifying benefit'.

Qualifying benefits
A **'qualifying benefit'** is, in general, any benefit which gives you entitlement to another benefit, or makes another benefit payable at a higher rate.

For example, the rules can help if there was a delay in assessing your entitlement to a qualifying benefit (eg, attendance allowance (AA), disability living allowance (DLA), personal independence payment (PIP), carer's allowance (CA) or child benefit) and so:
- you did not get a disability- or carer-related premium in your means-tested benefit, an additional amount in your pension credit (PC) or an element in your universal credit (UC), or allowances for your children. For income support (IS), jobseeker's allowance (JSA), employment and support allowance (ESA) and PC only, this includes where there are delays in assessing your non-dependant's entitlement to a qualifying benefit (see p1301); *or*
- a non-dependant deduction was made from your means-tested benefit.

Note: these rules can help you get arrears of benefit, even if the qualifying benefit was awarded some time ago, and you did not report the change in your circumstances at the time.[134]

You can only apply for a revision or supersession on this ground if you are already entitled to IS, JSA, ESA, PC, housing benefit (HB) or UC.[135] It is, therefore, essential to make a claim for these at the same time as the claim for a qualifying benefit. If you only qualify for one of these when the qualifying benefit is awarded, see p1302.

You or a family member are awarded a qualifying benefit or an increased rate

If you, or your partner or a child included in your claim (see p220), are awarded a qualifying benefit or an increase in its rate, and arrears of the qualifying benefit are payable, your award of IS, JSA, ESA, PC, HB or UC can be increased on revision or supersession and arrears paid for the same length of time.[136] This applies if:

- you are now entitled to premiums/components/elements/additional amounts or, if the qualifying benefit is child benefit, to allowances or premiums for your children paid with your benefit; *or*
- no non-dependant deduction (or for UC, a deduction for housing costs contributions) should now be made from your means-tested benefit because you or your partner are now entitled to AA, the care component of DLA or the daily living component of PIP.

Note: for IS, JSA, ESA and PC only, if you had a non-dependant living with you while you were waiting for a decision on your claim for a qualifying benefit, your IS, JSA, ESA or PC award can be superseded to include the severe disability premium (additional amount), from the date s/he can be ignored (or from the date s/he ceased to reside with you) if this is after the date from which the qualifying benefit is payable.[137]

Example
Gus has been getting income-related ESA and HB for two months. His ESA does not include any premiums and, because his uncle lives with him and his partner, Tanya, a non-dependant deduction is being made from his HB. He claims PIP and Tanya claims CA on 15 July. Six months later, Gus is awarded the enhanced rate of the daily living component of PIP and Tanya is awarded CA, both payable from 15 July. Gus is now entitled to the enhanced disability and carer premiums with his ESA and a non-dependant deduction should not be made from his HB. His ESA and HB awards are superseded and he is paid arrears, backdated to 15 July.

Your non-dependant is awarded a qualifying benefit or an increased rate

For IS, JSA, ESA and PC only, if you have a non-dependant living with you and, but for this, a severe disability premium (additional amount for PC) would be

Part 9: Getting a benefit decision changed
Chapter 54: Revisions and supersessions
5. The 'anti-test case rule'

paid, your award of IS, income-based JSA, income-related ESA or PC can be increased on revision or supersession to include this premium (additional amount) from the date the non-dependant is awarded a qualifying benefit.[138]

If you only qualify when the qualifying benefit is awarded

If you make an unsuccessful claim for a benefit, and only qualify when the qualifying benefit is awarded, you should make a second claim as soon as you hear about the qualifying benefit. See p1160 for further information.

If you only qualify for HB when the qualifying benefit is awarded, see p81. If you lose benefit because of the way the rules operate, ask the local authority for compensation.

Remember, if you only claim for the first time *after* you hear about the qualifying benefit:

- for IS, JSA or UC, you can only get arrears if you satisfy the backdating rules;
- for ESA and PC your claim can only be backdated for up to three months;
- for HB, if you are:
  - at least the qualifying age for PC (see p147) and not getting IS, income-based JSA, income-related ESA or UC, your claim can only be backdated for up to three months; *or*
  - under the qualifying age for PC or either you or your partner are getting IS, income-based JSA, income-related ESA or UC, your claim can only be backdated for up to one month, and only if you can show 'good cause' for your late claim (see p79).

See p565 for a similar rule that helps you get extra backdated CA when the person for whom you care becomes entitled to a qualifying benefit.

5. **The 'anti-test case rule'**

Special rules apply when a case is going through the appeals system that will determine a point of social security law (a test case). The 'anti-test case rule' says that some court and Upper Tribunal decisions should be ignored when decision makers are considering your entitlement to benefit for periods before these decisions were given. If this rule applies, you get arrears of benefit backdated only to the date of the decision in the test case.

How the anti-test case rule operates

The rule applies if the Upper Tribunal or a court decides in an appeal that a decision maker in a totally different case (the test case) has made an error of law (see p1363 for what counts), and you make a claim, or apply for a revision or a supersession (whether before or after the test case decision). In this situation, your decision maker must decide any part of *your* claim (or revision or supersession) which relates to the period *before* the test case decision as if the decision that was under appeal in the test case had been found by the tribunal or court in question not to have been wrong.[139] **Note:**

- The anti-test case rule only applies if the test case is the first authoritative decision on the issue, and not merely a later decision confirming an earlier decision.[140]
- The test case decision only has to be disregarded for the period before it was made if it found the decision maker to have been wrong, not if it found her/him to be right.

You can avoid the anti-test case rule by appealing rather than seeking a revision or supersession if the rules allow you to do so. Unless the benefit is HB, you must apply for a mandatory reconsideration before you can appeal (see p1311).

What happens while a test case is pending

If an appeal (a test case) is pending against a decision of the Upper Tribunal or a court, the decision maker can postpone making a decision on your claim or request for a supersession or revision.[141] This prevents you appealing until a decision is made in the test case. If the decision is postponed, once a decision has been made in the test case, the decision maker makes the decision in your case.[142]

If you would be entitled to benefit even if the test case were decided against you, the decision maker can make a decision on the assumption that the test case has been decided in the way that is most unfavourable to you.[143] However, this does mean that you may at least be paid something while you wait for the result of the test case. Then, if the decision in the test case is in your favour, the decision maker revises her/his decision. **Note:**

- If you already have a decision in your favour, the decision maker can suspend payment of your benefit (see p1185).
- If you have already appealed to the First-tier Tribunal, see p1334.

Part 9: Getting a benefit decision changed
Chapter 54: Revisions and supersessions
Notes

Notes

1. **Getting a decision changed**
   1 **HB** Sch 7 paras 3(2) and 4(3) CSPSSA 2000
   Other benefits ss9(2) and 10(2) SSA 1998

2. **Revisions**
   2 **HB** Sch 7 para 3 CSPSSA 2000
   Other benefits s9 SSA 1998
   3 **HB** Sch 7 para 3(1) CSPSSA 2000; reg 4 HB&CTB(DA) Regs
   CB/GA s9(1) SSA 1998; regs 5, 8, 10 and 11 CB&GA(DA) Regs
   UC/PIP/JSA&ESA under UC s9(1) SSA 1998; regs 5 and 8 UC,PIP,JSA&ESA(DA) Regs
   Other benefits s9(1) SSA 1998; reg 3 SS&CS(DA) Regs
   4 **HB** Reg 4(1)(a) HB&CTB(DA) Regs
   CB/GA Reg 5(2)(b) CB&GA(DA) Regs
   UC/PIP/JSA&ESA under UC Reg 5(1)(b) UC,PIP,JSA&ESA(DA) Regs
   Other benefits Reg 3(1)(b) SS&CS(DA) Regs
   5 **CB/GA** Reg 5(2)(a) CB&GA(DA) Regs
   UC/PIP/JSA&ESA under UC Reg 5(1)(a) UC,PIP,JSA&ESA(DA) Regs
   Other benefits Reg 3(1)(a) SS&CS(DA) Regs
   6 Reg 4(1)(b) HB&CTB(DA) Regs
   7 **HB** Reg 4(10) HB&CTB(DA) Regs
   CB/GA Reg 5(3) CB&GA(DA) Regs
   UC/PIP/JSA&ESA under UC Reg 5(2)(a) UC,PIP,JSA&ESA(DA) Regs
   Other benefits Reg 3(9)(a) SS&CS(DA) Regs; Sch 2 para 25A(1)(b) and (c) ESA(TP)(EA)(No.2) Regs
   8 Reg 3(9)(b) and (c) SS&CS(DA) Regs; reg 5(2)(c) UC,PIP,JSA&ESA(DA) Regs
   9 Reg 3(3) SS&CS(DA) Regs
   10 Regs 1(3), definition of 'date of notification', and 3(1)(b) SS&CS(DA) Regs
   11 Regs 2 and 4(1)(a) HB&CTB(DA) Regs
   12 Reg 4(4) HB&CTB(DA) Regs
   13 **CB/GA** Regs 3 and 5(2)(b) CB&GA(DA) Regs
   UC/PIP/JSA&ESA under UC Regs 2, 3(2) and 5(1)(b) UC,PIP,JSA&ESA(DA) Regs
   Other benefits Regs 1(3), 2(b) and 3(1)(b) SS&CS(DA) Regs
   14 **HB** Reg 10A(3) HB&CTB(DA) Regs
   UC/PIP/JSA&ESA under UC Reg 38(4) UC,PIP,JSA&ESA(DA) Regs
   Other benefits Reg 9A(3) SS&CS(DA) Regs
   15 **HB** Regs 4(4) and 5(3)(b) HB&CTB(DA) Regs
   CB/GA Reg 6(3)(c) CB&GA(DA) Regs
   Other benefits Reg 4 SS&CS(DA) Regs
   16 Reg 6 UC,PIP,JSA&ESA(DA) Regs
   17 **HB** Reg 5(3)(a), (4) and (6) HB&CTB(DA) Regs
   CB/GA Reg 6(3)(a) and (b), (4) and (5) CB&GA(DA) Regs
   UC/PIP/JSA&ESA under UC Reg 6(3)-(6) UC,PIP,JSA&ESA(DA) Regs
   Other benefits Reg 4(3)(a), (4) and (5) SS&CS(DA) Regs
   18 **HB** Reg 5(4)(b) and (5) HB&CTB(DA) Regs
   CB/GA Reg 6(4)(b) and (6) CB&GA(DA) Regs
   Other benefits Reg 4(4)(b) and (6) SS&CS(DA) Regs
   19 R(TC) 1/05
   20 **HB** Reg 4(2)(a) HB&CTB(DA) Regs
   CB/GA Reg 10(2)(a) CB&GA(DA) Regs
   UC/PIP/JSA&ESA under UC Regs 8 and 9(a) UC,PIP,JSA&ESA(DA) Regs
   Other benefits Reg 3(5)(a) SS&CS(DA) Regs
   21 **HB** Reg 1(2) HB&CTB(DA) Regs
   UC/PIP/JSA&ESA under UC Reg 2 UC,PIP,JSA&ESA(DA) Regs
   Other benefits Reg 1(3) SS&CS(DA) Regs
   22 Reg 10(3) CB&GA(DA) Regs
   23 **HB** Reg 1(2) HB&CTB(DA) Regs
   CB/GA Reg 10(3) CB&GA(DA) Regs
   UC/PIP/JSA&ESA under UC Reg 2 UC,PIP,JSA&ESA(DA) Regs
   Other benefits Reg 1(3) SS&CS(DA) Regs

24 CIS/34/2006
25 **HB** Reg 1(2) HB&CTB(DA) Regs
   CB/GA Reg 10(3) CB&GA(DA) Regs
   UC/PIP/JSA&ESA under UC Reg 2
   UC,PIP,JSA&ESA(DA) Regs
   Other benefits Reg 1(3) SS&CS(DA)
   Regs
26 CDLA/393/2006
27 **HB** Reg 4(2)(b) HB&CTB(DA) Regs
   CB/GA Reg 10(2)(b) CB&GA(DA) Regs
   UC/PIP/JSA&ESA under UC Regs 8
   and 9(b) UC,PIP,JSA&ESA(DA) Regs
   Other benefits Reg 3(5)(b) and (d)
   SS&CS(DA) Regs
28 Regs 3(5)(c)and 7A(1) SS&CS(DA) Regs
29 Reg 7A SS&CS(DA) Regs
30 **UC/JSA&ESA under UC** Reg 14(a)-(c)
   UC,PIP,JSA&ESA(DA) Regs
   Other benefits Reg 3(5C), (6), (6A)
   and (7CD) SS&CS(DA) Regs
31 Reg 3(6B) SS&CS(DA) Regs
32 **HB** Reg 4(7B) HB&CTB(DA) Regs
   CB/GA Reg 11 CB&GA(DA) Regs
   UC/PIP/JSA&ESA under UC Regs 8
   and 12 UC,PIP,JSA&ESA(DA) Regs
   Other benefits Reg 3(7) SS&CS(DA)
   Regs
33 Reg 3(7ZA) SS&CS(DA) Regs
34 Reg 4(7C) HB&CTB(DA) Regs
35 **HB** Reg 4(1)(c) HB&CTB(DA) Regs
   CB/GA Reg 8(2) CB&GA(DA) Regs
   UC/PIP/JSA&ESA under UC Regs 8
   and 11(1) UC,PIP,JSA&ESA(DA) Regs
   Other benefits Reg 3(4A) SS&CS(DA)
   Regs
36 **HB** Reg 4(7) HB&CTB(DA) Regs
   CB/GA Reg 8(3) CB&GA(DA) Regs
   UC/PIP/JSA&ESA under UC Regs 8
   and 11(2) UC,PIP,JSA&ESA(DA) Regs
   Other benefits Reg 3(5A) SS&CS(DA)
   Regs
37 **HB** Reg 4(6) HB&CTB(DA) Regs
   CB/GA Reg 9 CB&GA(DA) Regs
   UC/PIP/JSA&ESA under UC Regs 8
   and 10 UC,PIP,JSA&ESA(DA) Regs
   Other benefits Reg 3(8) SS&CS(DA)
   Regs
38 **HB** Reg 4(7H) HB&CTB(DA) Regs
   UC/PIP/JSA&ESA under UC Regs 8
   and 19(1) UC,PIP,JSA&ESA(DA) Regs
39 Reg 3(5D) SS&CS(DA) Regs; regs 8 and
   15(3) UC,PIP,JSA&ESA(DA) Regs
40 Reg 3(5I) SS&CS(DA) Regs; reg 15(5)
   UC,PIP,JSA&ESA(DA) Regs
41 Regs 8 and 18(2) UC,PIP,JSA&ESA(DA)
   Regs
42 Regs 8 and 18(3) UC,PIP,JSA&ESA(DA)
   Regs

43 **HB** Reg 4(3), (7E) and (7F)
   HB&CTB(DA) Regs; reg 18A(1) and (3)
   HB Regs; reg 18A(1) and (3) HB(SPC)
   Regs
   UC/PIP/JSA&ESA under UC Regs 8
   and 19(2) UC,PIP,JSA&ESA(DA) Regs
44 **HB** Reg 4(7D) and (7DA) HB&CTB(DA)
   Regs
   PC Reg 3(7D), (7DA) and (7DB)
   SS&CS(DA) Regs
   Retirement pensions Reg 3(7E)
   SS&CS(DA) Regs
45 **HB** Reg 4(7A) and (7DB) HB&CTB(DA)
   Regs
   UC/PIP/JSA&ESA under UC Regs 8,
   13, 15(2), (4) and (4A), 16, 17 and 18
   UC,PIP,JSA&ESA(DA) Regs
   Other benefits Reg 3(5E)-(5H), (5J),
   (7A), (7CC), (7EA), (7EB), (8B)-(8K)
   SS&CS(DA) Regs
46 Regs 4(8) and 5(2) HB&CTB(DA) Regs
47 **CB/GA** Reg 5(1)(b) CB&GA(DA) Regs
   UC/PIP/JSA&ESA under UC Reg
   5(1)(b) UC,PIP,JSA&ESA(DA) Regs
   Other benefits Reg 3(1)(b)
   SS&CS(DA) Regs
48 **HB** Reg 4(8) HB&CTB(DA) Regs
   CB/GA Reg 2(1), definition of
   'appropriate office', CB&GA(DA) Regs
   UC/PIP/JSA&ESA under UC Reg 2
   UC,PIP,JSA&ESA(DA) Regs
   Other benefits Reg 3(11) SS&CS(DA)
   Regs
49 **HB** Regs 4(9) and 7(6) HB&CTB(DA)
   Regs
   CB/GA Regs 7(1) and 14(1)
   CB&GA(DA) Regs
   UC/PIP/JSA&ESA under UC Regs
   20(1) and 33(1) UC,PIP,JSA&ESA(DA)
   Regs
   Other benefits Regs 3(10) and 6(5)
   SS&CS(DA) Regs
50 R(I) 50/56
51 R(IS) 11/92; *SSWP v TJ (JSA)* [2015]
   UKUT 56 (AAC), paras 213-15
52 **HB** Sch 7 paras 3(2) and 4(3) CSPSSA
   2000
   Other benefits ss9(2) and 10(2) SSA
   1998
53 **HB** Regs 4(5) and 7(5) HB&CTB(DA)
   Regs
   CB/GA Regs 7(2) and (3) and 14(3)
   CB&GA(DA) Regs
   UC/PIP/JSA&ESA under UC Regs
   20(2) and (3) and 33(2) and (3)
   UC,PIP,JSA&ESA(DA) Regs
   Other benefits Regs 3(2) and 6(4)
   SS&CS(DA) Regs

9

Part 9: Getting a benefit decision changed
Chapter 54: Revisions and supersessions
Notes

54 **HB** Sch 7 para 3(3) CSPSSA 2000
Other benefits s9(3) SSA 1998
55 **HB** Reg 6 HB&CTB(DA) Regs
CB/GA Reg 12 CB&GA(DA) Regs
UC/PIP and JSA/ESA under UC Reg
21 UC,PIP,JSA&ESA(DA) Regs
Other benefits Reg 5(1) SS&CS(DA)
Regs
56 Reg 7A(2) SS&CS(DA) Regs
57 s9(5) SSA 1998; Sch 7 para 3(5) CSPSSA
2000; rr22(2)(d)(I) and 23 TP(FT) Rules
58 R(IS) 15/04; *Beltekian v Westminster City
Council and Another* [2004] EWCA Civ
1784, reported as R(H) 8/05; *AS v SSWP
(CSM)* [2012] UKUT 448 (AAC); [2013]
AACR 18

3. **Supersessions**
59 **HB** Sch 7 para 4 CSPSSA 2000
Other benefits s10 SSA 1998
60 **HB** Reg 7(2) HB&CTB(DA) Regs
CB/GA Reg 13(1) CB&GA(DA) Regs
UC/PIP/JSA&ESA under UC Reg 22
UC,PIP,JSA&ESA(DA) Regs
Other benefits Reg 6(2) SS&CS(DA)
Regs
61 **HB** Reg 7(4) HB&CTB(DA) Regs
CB/GA Reg 15 CB&GA(DA) Regs
UC/PIP/JSA&ESA under UC Reg 32
UC,PIP,JSA&ESA(DA) Regs
Other benefits Reg 6(3) SS&CS(DA)
Regs
62 **HB** Regs 7(2)(a) and 7A(4)
HB&CTB(DA) Regs
CB/GA Reg 13(2)(a) CB&GA(DA) Regs
UC/PIP/JSA&ESA under UC Reg 23
UC,PIP,JSA&ESA(DA) Regs
Other benefits Reg 6(2)(a)
SS&CS(DA) Regs; Sch 2 para 25A(2)
ESA(TP)(EA) No.2 Regs
All *Wood v SSWP* [2003] EWCA Civ 53,
reported as R(DLA) 1/03
63 CSDLA/637/2006; CSDLA/822/2006
64 *CAO v McKiernon*, 8 July 1993 (CA),
reported as an attachment to R(I) 2/94
65 *Cooke v Secretary of State for Social
Security* [2001] reported as R(DLA) 6/01;
R(S) 4/86; R(IS) 2/98; CIB/7899/1996;
CIS/856/1994
66 Reg 6(6)(c) SS&CS(DA) Regs; reg 23(2)
UC,PIP,JSA&ESA(DA) Regs
67 Reg 6(8) SS&CS(DA) Regs
68 Reg 6(6)(a) SS&CS(DA) Regs
69 **HB** Sch 7 para 2 CSPSSA 2000
Other benefits s8(2) SSA 1998; reg
12A SS&CS(DA) Regs

70 **HB** Reg 7(2)(b) and (d) HB&CTB(DA)
Regs
CB/GA Reg 13(2)(b) and (c)(i)
CB&GA(DA) Regs
UC/PIP/JSA&ESA under UC Regs 24
and 31(a) UC,PIP,JSA&ESA(DA) Regs
Other benefits Reg 6(2)(b) and (c)
SS&CS(DA) Regs
71 Reg 4(1)(b) HB&CTB(DA) Regs
72 **HB** Reg 7(2)(b) HB&CTB(DA) Regs
CB/GA Reg 13(2)(b) CB&GA(DA) Regs
UC/PIP/JSA&ESA under UC Reg 24
UC,PIP,JSA&ESA(DA) Regs
Other benefits Reg 6(2)(b)
SS&CS(DA) Regs
73 Regs 6(2)(r) and 7A(1) SS&CS(DA) Regs;
reg 26(1) UC,PIP,JSA&ESA(DA) Regs;
CIB/4033/2003; R(IB) 2/05
74 *SF v SSWP (PIP)* [2016] UKUT 481 (AAC);
DS v SSWP (PIP) [2016] UKUT 538 (AAC)
75 CSIB/377/2003; CIB/1509/2004; R(IB)
5/05; *JB v SSWP (IB)* [2010] UKUT 246
(AAC); *ST v SSWP (ESA)* [2012] UKUT
469 (AAC)
76 CIB/1972/2000; CIB/3179/2000; CIB/
3985/2001; *ST v SSWP (ESA)* [2012]
UKUT 469 (AAC); *FN v SSWP (ESA)*
[2015] UKUT 670 (AAC)
77 s80(5) and (6) WRA 2012; reg 26(2)
UC,PIP,JSA&ESA(DA) Regs
78 **HB** Reg 7(2)(i) HB&CTB(DA) Regs
CB/GA Reg 13(2)(e) CB&GA(DA) Regs
UC/PIP/JSA&ESA under UC Reg 23
UC,PIP,JSA&ESA(DA) Regs. Note: for
these benefits, this is dealt with as a
change of circumstances.
Other benefits Reg 6(2)(e)
SS&CS(DA) Regs
79 Reg 6(2)(ee) SS&CS(DA) Regs
80 **HB** Reg 7(2)(e) HB&CTB(DA) Regs
CB/GA Reg 13(2)(d) CB&GA(DA) Regs
UC/PIP/JSA&ESA under UC Reg 25
UC,PIP,JSA&ESA(DA) Regs
Other benefits Reg 6(2)(d)
SS&CS(DA) Regs
81 **HB** Reg 7(2)(c) HB&CTB(DA) Regs; reg
18A(2) HB Regs; reg 18A(2) HB(SPC)
Regs
UC Reg 30 UC,PIP,JSA&ESA(DA) Regs
82 Reg 7(2)(r) HB&CTB(DA) Regs
83 **HB** Reg 7(2)(j), (ja) and (jb)
HB&CTB(DA) Regs
PC Reg 6(2)(o) and (oa) SS&CS(DA)
Regs

84 **HB** Reg 7(2)(d)(ii) HB&CTB(DA) Regs
CB/GA Reg 13(2)(c)(ii) CB&GA(DA) Regs
UC/PIP/JSA &ESA under UC Reg 31(b) UC,PIP,JSA&ESA(DA) Regs
Other benefits Reg 6(2)(c)(ii) SS&CS(DA) Regs

85 **HB** Regs 7(2)(g), (h), (q), (r) and (s) and 7A(2) and (3) HB&CTB(DA) Regs
UC/PIP/JSA&ESA under UC Regs 27, 28 and 29 UC,PIP,JSA&ESA(DA) Regs
Other benefits Reg 6(2)(f), (fa), (h), (j), (k), (l), (m), (n), (p), (q), (s), (sa), (t) and (u) SS&CS(DA) Regs

86 Reg 7(7) HB&CTB(DA) Regs

87 **HB** Regs 4(9) and 7(6) HB&CTB(DA) Regs
CB/GA Regs 7(1) and 14(1) CB&GA(DA) Regs
UC/PIP/JSA&ESA under UC Regs 20(1) and 33(1) UC,PIP,JSA&ESA(DA) Regs
Other benefits Regs 3(10) and 6(5) SS&CS(DA) Regs

88 R(I) 50/56

89 R(IS) 11/92; *SSWP v TJ (JSA)* [2015] UKUT 56 (AAC), paras 213-215

90 **HB** Sch 7 para 4(5) CSPSSA 2000
Other benefits s10(5) SSA 1998

91 **HB** Reg 8(10) HB&CTB(DA) Regs
UC/PIP/JSA&ESA under UC Reg 35(1) and Sch 1 paras 32 and 33 UC,PIP,JSA&ESA(DA) Regs
Other benefits Reg 7(9)(a)(ii), (30) and (30A) SS&CS(DA) Regs

92 Reg 7(2)(bc) SS&CS(DA) Regs

93 Reg 7(2)(be) SS&CS(DA) Regs; reg 35(1) and Sch 1 paras 9 and 28 UC,PIP,JSA&ESA(DA) Regs

94 Reg 8(2) HB&CTB(DA) Regs

95 Reg 8(3) HB&CTB(DA) Regs

96 **AA/DLA** Reg 7(2)(c)(iv) SS&CS(DA) Regs
PIP Sch 1 para 12 UC,PIP,JSA&ESA(DA) Regs

97 **AA/DLA** Reg 7(9)(a) SS&CS(DA) Regs
PIP Sch 1 para 18 UC,PIP,JSA&ESA(DA) Regs

98 Sch 1 paras 12-14 UC,PIP,JSA&ESA(DA) Regs

99 Sch 1 para 15 UC,PIP,JSA&ESA(DA) Regs

100 Reg 7(9) SS&CS(DA) Regs; *SSWP v DA* [2009] UKUT 214 (AAC)

101 Sch 1 paras 1 and 20 UC,PIP,JSA&ESA(DA) Regs

102 Sch 1 paras 10 and 29 UC,PIP,JSA&ESA(DA) Regs

103 Sch 1 para 20 UC,PIP,JSA&ESA(DA) Regs

104 Sch 1 para 1 UC,PIP,JSA&ESA(DA) Regs

105 **CB/GA** Reg 16(5) CB&GA(DA) Regs
Other benefits Reg 7(2)(c)(v) SS&CS(DA) Regs

106 **CB/GA** Reg 16(4) CB&GA(DA) Regs
Other benefits Reg 7(2)(bb) SS&CS(DA) Regs

107 **CB/GA** Reg 16(3)(a) CB&GA(DA) Regs
Other benefits Reg 7(2)(a) SS&CS(DA) Regs

108 Schs 3A, 3B and 3C SS&CS(DA) Regs

109 **UC/PIP/JSA/ESA under UC** Sch 1 paras 7, 8, 11, 16, 17, 19, 23, 24 and 30 UC,PIP,JSA&ESA(DA) Regs
Other benefits Regs 7(2)(c)(ii) and 7A(1) SS&CS(DA) Regs

110 **UC/PIP/JSA&ESA under the UC system** s10(5) SSA 1998; Sch 1 paras 2, 13 and 25 UC,PIP,JSA&ESA(DA) Regs
Other benefits s10(5) SSA 1998; reg 7(2)(c)(v) SS&CS(DA) Regs

111 Reg 7A(2) SS&CS(DA) Regs

112 **HB** Reg 9 HB&CTB(DA) Regs
CB/GA Reg 17 CB&GA(DA) Regs
UC/PIP/JSA&ESA under UC Reg 36 UC,PIP,JSA&ESA(DA) Regs
Other benefits Reg 8 SS&CS(DA) Regs

113 **HB** Reg 9(2)-(4) HB&CTB(DA) Regs
CB/GA Reg 17(3)-(5) CB&GA(DA) Regs
UC/PIP/JSA&ESA under UC Reg 36(3)-(7) UC,PIP,JSA&ESA(DA) Regs
Other benefits Reg 8(3)-(5) SS&CS(DA) Regs

114 **HB** Reg 9(5) HB&CTB(DA) Regs
CB/GA Reg 17(6) CB&GA(DA) Regs
UC/PIP/JSA&ESA under UC Reg 36(7) UC,PIP,JSA&ESA(DA) Regs
Other benefits Reg 8(6) SS&CS(DA) Regs

115 Reg 7(9)(d) SS&CS(DA) Regs

116 Reg 7(2)(b)(i) and (ii) SS&CS(DA) Regs; Sch 1 para 6 UC,PIP,JSA&ESA(DA) Regs

117 Reg 8(3) HB&CTB(DA) Regs; reg 79(1) HB Regs; reg 59(1) HB(SPC) Regs

118 Sch 1 para 21 UC,PIP,JSA&ESA(DA) Regs

119 **CB/GA** Reg 16(3)(b) CB&GA(DA) Regs
UC/PIP/JSA&ESA under UC Sch 1 para 14 UC,PIP,JSA&ESA(DA) Regs
Other benefits Reg 7(2)(b)(iii) SS&CS(DA) Regs

120 **HB** Reg 8(7) HB&CTB(DA) Regs
CB/GA Reg 16(7) CB&GA(DA) Regs
UC/PIP/JSA&ESA under UC Reg 37(1)-(3) UC,PIP,JSA&ESA(DA) Regs
Other benefits Reg 7(5) SS&CS(DA) Regs

9

Part 9: Getting a benefit decision changed
Chapter 54: Revisions and supersessions
Notes

121 **UC/ESA** Regs 2 and 37 (1) and (3)
UC,PIP,JSA&ESA(DA) Regs
Other benefits Reg 7(5) SS&CS(DA)
Regs
122 Reg 8(4) HB&CTB(DA) Regs
123 Sch 3A para 12, Sch 3B para 7 and Sch
3C para 8 SS&CS(DA) Regs; reg 35(2)-
(4) UC,PIP,JSA&ESA(DA) Regs
124 **HB** Reg 8(8) HB&CTB(DA) Regs
CB/GA Reg 16(9) CB&GA(DA) Regs
UC/PIP/JSA&ESA under UC Reg
35(5) UC,PIP,JSA&ESA(DA) Regs
Other benefits Reg 7(6) SS&CS(DA)
Regs
All *MP v SSWP (DLA)* [2010] UKUT 130
(AAC)
125 **CB/GA** Reg 16(9A) CB&GA(DA) Regs
UC/PIP/JSA&ESA under UC Reg
37(5) and (6) UC,PIP,JSA&ESA(DA) Regs
Other benefits Reg 7(6A) SS&CS(DA)
Regs
126 **HB** Reg 8(11) HB&CTB(DA) Regs
CB/GA Reg 16(8) CB&GA(DA) Regs
PIP Reg 37(4)(a) UC,PIP,JSA&ESA(DA)
Regs
Other benefits Reg 7(33) SS&CS(DA)
Regs
127 Sch 3A para 12, Sch 3B para 7 and Sch
3C para 8 SS&CS(DA) Regs; reg
37(4)(b) and (c) UC,PIP,JSA&ESA(DA)
Regs
128 Reg 8(2) and (6) HB&CTB(DA) Regs; reg
35(14) UC,PIP,JSA&ESA(DA) Regs
129 Reg 7(38)-(40) SS&CS(DA) Regs; reg
35(6)-(9) UC,PIP,JSA&ESA(DA) Regs
130 **HB** Reg 8(14A) HB&CTB(DA) Regs
PC Reg 7(7A) SS&CS(DA) Regs
131 Reg 7(8A) SS&CS(DA) Regs; reg 35(13)
UC,PIP,JSA&ESA(DA) Regs
132 **HB** Reg 8(6A), (9), (14D), (14E), (14F),
(14G) and (15) HB&CTB(DA) Regs
UC/PIP/JSA&ESA under UC Reg
35(10)-(12) UC,PIP,JSA&ESA(DA) Regs
Other benefits Reg 7(8), (8ZA), (8ZB),
(10)-(13), (24), (25), (28), (29), (29A)-
(29C), (34)-(37) and (41)-(43)
SS&CS(DA) Regs
133 *Wood v SSWP* [2003] EWCA Civ 53,
reported as R(DLA) 1/03

4. Revisions and supersessions after a 'qualifying benefit' award

134 *HR v Wakefield DC* [2009] UKUT 72
(AAC)
135 **IS/JSA/ESA/PC/UC** s8(2) SSA 1998
HB Sch 7 para 2 CSPSSA 2000

136 **IS/JSA/ESA/PC** Regs 3(7), 6(2)(e) and
7(7) SS&CS(DA) Regs
HB Regs 4(7B) and (7C), 7(2)(i) and
8(14) HB&CTB(DA) Regs; CIS/1178/
2001
UC/PIP/JSA&ESA under UC Regs 12
and 23 and Sch 1 para 31
UC,PIP,JSA&ESA(DA) Regs
137 Reg 7(7)(b) SS&CS(DA) Regs
138 Regs 3(7ZA), 6(2)(ee) and 7(7)
SS&CS(DA) Regs

5. The 'anti-test case rule'

139 **HB** Sch 7 para 18 CSPSSA 2000
Other benefits s27 SSA 1998
All *CAO and Another v Bate* [1996] 2 All
ER 790 (HL)
140 R(FC) 3/98; R(I) 1/03
141 **HB** Sch 7 para 16 CSPSSA 2000
Other benefits s25 SSA 1998
142 **HB** Sch 7 para 18(2) CSPSSA 2000
Other benefits s27(2) SSA 1998
143 **HB** Sch 7 para 16(3) and (4) CSPSSA
2000; reg 15 HB&CTB(DA) Regs
CB/GA s25(3) and (4) SSA 1998; reg 22
CB&GA(DA) Regs
UC/PIP/JSA&ESA under UC s25(3)
and (4) SSA 1998; reg 53
UC,PIP,JSA&ESA(DA) Regs
Other benefits s25(3) and (4) SSA
1998; reg 21 SS&CS(DA) Regs

9

Chapter 55

Appealing to the First-tier Tribunal

This chapter covers:
1. Appealing to the First-tier Tribunal (p1310)
2. How to appeal (p1317)
3. After you send or deliver your appeal (p1323)
4. Hearings (p1335)
5. Proving your case (p1344)
6. The tribunal's decision (p1353)

This chapter covers the rules for appeals to the First-tier Tribunal about benefits, the social fund payments in Chapter 36 (except budgeting loans) and national insurance credits. It does *not* cover the rules for statutory payments (see Chapter 57) or the health benefits in Chapter 29.

References in this chapter to HM Revenue and Customs (HMRC) only apply to decisions about child benefit and guardian's allowance. HMRC also makes decisions about tax credits. For information about these, see Chapter 64.

Key facts
- If you disagree with certain decisions made by the DWP, the local authority or HM Revenue and Customs, you can appeal to the First-tier Tribunal.
- For benefits other than housing benefit, you must apply for a mandatory reconsideration before you can appeal.
- The time limits for appealing are very strict.
- Appeals can take time. If your circumstances change while you are waiting for your appeal to be heard, you may need to make a fresh claim for benefit or seek a supersession.
- The tribunal can allow or reject your appeal, and replace the decision about which you appealed with any decision it thinks is right. This could be more or less favourable to you.
- If your appeal is unsuccessful, you may be able to appeal to the Upper Tribunal.

Part 9: Getting a benefit decision changed
Chapter 55: Appealing to the First-tier Tribunal
1. Appealing to the First-tier Tribunal

Future changes

The government says it wants to change the tribunal system and make all tribunals digital by default. It will pilot online dispute resolution starting some time before April 2018. Appeals will be made online and there will be online hearings, and hearings at telephone or video conferences. The government also says that, in future, there will no longer be an automatic right to an oral hearing. See CPAG's online service and *Welfare Rights Bulletin* for updates.

1. **Appealing to the First-tier Tribunal**

You can appeal against some decisions of the DWP, the local authority or HM Revenue and Customs (HMRC). Appeals are dealt with in the Social Entitlement Chamber of the First-tier Tribunal (Social Security and Child Support) – referred to as the First-tier Tribunal in this *Handbook* (except in Chapter 57). For information about who deals with your appeal, see p1316.

Before you appeal

Before you appeal, you should do the following.
- Make sure you have sufficient information about the decision you are unhappy about. Ask for a written statement of reasons if this has not already been provided (see p1166).
- Check whether you must apply for a mandatory reconsideration before you can appeal and apply within the time limit if relevant. See p1311 for further information.
- Check whether you would be better off applying for a revision or supersession instead of appealing (see below).
- In some cases, you should get advice before you appeal. Because the First-tier Tribunal looks at your case afresh, there is a risk you could lose benefit. For example, if your appeal is about a benefit that can be paid at different rates (eg, personal independence payment (PIP) or industrial injuries disablement benefit), the rate could go down. If you are appealing about an overpayment, the amount could increase.

Revision, supersession or appeal?

1. Unless the benefit is housing benefit (HB), you must apply for a mandatory reconsideration before you can appeal (see p1311).

2. If you are not yet sure if you want to appeal, for all benefits, you can apply for a revision; you get two bites at the cherry, because if your application for a revision is turned down, you can still appeal against the original decision.

3. There is no time limit for applying for certain revisions (known as 'any time' revisions – see p1279), but you must show specific grounds. You can ask for an any time revision even if the time limit for applying for what is known as an 'any grounds' revision or appealing has expired. However, you cannot appeal against a refusal to do an any time revision (see p1286).

4. In most cases, there is no time limit for applying for a supersession – eg, if there has been a mistake about the facts or if a test case is decided in your favour but you do not become aware of this until some time later. However, you generally get less arrears of benefit if you apply for a supersession. See pp1292–99 for information about when a supersession takes effect.

5. If you apply for a revision or a supersession instead of appealing and the 'anti-test case' rule applies to you (see p1302), the arrears of benefit you get could be limited.

Mandatory reconsideration

Unless the benefit is HB, before you can appeal you must ask for the decision you are unhappy with to be looked at again – ie, you must ask for a mandatory reconsideration. The decision maker must then consider whether to revise the decision.

In addition, you can only appeal if:

- for child benefit and guardian's allowance, HMRC has decided not to revise the decision. **Note:** if it revises the decision, you can appeal against the original decision, as revised;[1] *or*
- for other benefits, you have been notified properly, in writing, that you must apply for a revision before you can appeal (the DWP may use the term 'mandatory reconsideration') and the DWP has considered whether to revise the decision.[2]

Except for child benefit and guardian's allowance, you do *not* have to apply for a mandatory reconsideration unless the decision notice (see p1165) includes a statement that you only have a right of appeal if the DWP has considered an application for a revision of the decision. The notice must also inform you of the time limit for applying for an 'any grounds' revision (see p1277) and that you can ask for a statement of reasons for the decision (if one has not been included), within one month of being notified of the decision (see p1166).

If the DWP does not notify you that you only have a right of appeal if it has considered an application for a revision (this is only likely to happen in limited cases), you do *not* have to apply for a mandatory reconsideration before you can appeal. Make this clear on your appeal form and provide proof if you can.

Note: there is further information about mandatory reconsiderations at *Ask CPAG Online* at www.cpag.org.uk/askcpag.

Part 9: Getting a benefit decision changed
Chapter 55: Appealing to the First-tier Tribunal
1. Appealing to the First-tier Tribunal

Applying for a mandatory reconsideration

When you apply for a mandatory reconsideration, you are applying for a revision. There are two types of revision: 'any grounds' revisions (p1276) and 'any time' revisions (see p1279).

It is always best to apply for an any grounds revision, but you must do so within a strict time limit. There is no time limit for applying for an any time revision, but you must show grounds.

It is always best to apply for a mandatory reconsideration in writing, although you can make a verbal application. Make it clear that you are applying for a mandatory reconsideration. For child benefit and guardian's allowance, you can use form CH24A available at www.gov.uk/government/publications/child-benefit-and-guardians-allowance-appeal-form. If you apply by telephone, all calls should be noted, but this may not always happen.

Explain why you disagree with the decision and provide any additional information and evidence that supports your case. It is important to follow up your application to ensure that it has been received.

Have you missed the time limit for an 'any grounds' revision?

You must usually apply for an 'any grounds' revision within one month of the decision with which you disagree. Although the time limit can be extended in exceptional cases (see p1278), there is an absolute time limit. If the decision maker refuses to accept your application for a mandatory reconsideration because you missed the time limit for an 'any grounds' revision , the DWP and HMRC say that you do not have a right of appeal against the decision.[3] However, if you applied to the DWP, argue that it *has* considered whether to revise the decision and that you *can* appeal.

Note: if the decision maker:[4]

– refuses to consider your application for an 'any grounds' revision because it was made outside the time limit for doing so (see p1277), s/he should go on to consider whether there are grounds for an 'any time' revision;

– decides there are no grounds for a revision, s/he should consider whether to do a supersession.

In both cases, you should argue that the decision maker*has*considered whether to revise the decision and that you now have a right of appeal.

If you appeal before first applying for a mandatory reconsideration, the DWP can (but does not have to) treat your appeal as an application for a mandatory reconsideration.[5] If the DWP does not do this, apply for a mandatory reconsideration as soon as possible, explaining why your application is late if relevant. Although there is no equivalent rule for child benefit and guardian's allowance, there is nothing to prevent HMRC from treating an appeal as an application for a mandatory reconsideration.

If you sent or delivered your appeal to the First-tier Tribunal when you should have applied for a mandatory reconsideration first, the tribunal may say your appeal is not valid and return it to you to resolve the issue. If you do not do so, it may 'strike out' your appeal (see p1330).

The mandatory reconsideration notice

The DWP (or HMRC) gives or sends you a mandatory reconsideration notice telling you the result of your application. This notice is proof that the DWP or HMRC has accepted and considered your application for a revision. If you are still unhappy with the decision, you can then appeal to the First-tier Tribunal. You must send a copy of the notice to the tribunal when you appeal (see p1321). Although the tribunal can waive this requirement, this is discretionary and it may instead 'strike out' your appeal (see p1330).[6]

If the DWP (or HMRC) only provides a mandatory reconsideration notice after a long delay, this may put you at a disadvantage – eg, if it is now difficult to obtain evidence to support your appeal. Tell the First-tier Tribunal if you think this improves the DWP's (or HMRC's) chances, or reduces your chances, of winning your appeal.[7]

What should you do if you do not have a mandatory reconsideration notice?

If you have applied for a mandatory reconsideration, but have not been sent or given a mandatory reconsideration notice, try to provide the tribunal with as much evidence as you can that you did apply, and that the DWP (or HMRC) has considered your application. Provide a copy of your application along with proof you posted or delivered it, if possible. Also provide copies of any correspondence with the DWP (or HMRC) and any notes of telephone calls or personal contact with the DWP (or HMRC) since you made the application.

Bear in mind that it is the First-tier Tribunal that decides whether you have a right of appeal, not the DWP or HMRC. However, the only way to be sure you have a right of appeal is to apply for a mandatory reconsideration if you are required to do so.

Who can appeal

You can appeal to the First-tier Tribunal if you are the claimant. However, certain other people can also appeal.
- **If you are appealing about a benefit other than HB**, you have a right to appeal if you are:[8]
  - a claimant;
  - an appointee claiming on someone's behalf (see p1149);
  - claiming attendance allowance, disability living allowance or PIP on behalf of someone who is terminally ill, even if this is without her/his knowledge;

Part 9: Getting a benefit decision changed
Chapter 55: Appealing to the First-tier Tribunal
1. Appealing to the First-tier Tribunal

- a person from whom an overpayment of a benefit or a regulated social fund payment or a duplication of payment of income support, income-based jobseeker's allowance, income-related employment and support allowance (ESA), pension credit or universal credit can be recovered (see Chapter 52). This is the case even if you were not the person who claimed the benefit that was overpaid;[9]
- someone from whom a short-term or budgeting advance, or hardship payments, can be recovered;
- the partner of a claimant, if the decision concerns whether *you* failed to take part in a work-focused interview without good cause;[10]
- a person appointed by the DWP or HMRC to proceed with a claim for benefit made by someone who has since died or to make a claim for (and who has now claimed) benefit for someone who has died.[11]

- **If you are appealing about HB**, you have a right to appeal if you are a person affected by the decision – ie, your rights, duties or obligations are affected by the decision, and you are:[12]
  - a claimant;
  - someone acting for a claimant who is unable to act for her/himself – eg, an appointee (see p75);
  - someone from whom the local authority decides an overpayment can be recovered (including a landlord or agent);[13] *or*
  - a landlord or agent, if the decision concerns whether or not to make a direct payment of HB to you.

In all cases, if the person who appealed dies, the DWP, the local authority or HMRC can appoint someone else to proceed with the appeal.[14]

Decisions you can appeal

You can appeal to the First-tier Tribunal against most decisions taken by the Secretary of State for Work and Pensions (the DWP), a local authority officer or an officer of HMRC (known as decision makers – see p1162).[15] You can appeal against an original decision (even if you have first applied for a revision) or a decision made after a supersession.

You must be given a written notice of any decision that you can appeal.[16] This:
- must give you information about your right to appeal and your right to request a written statement of reasons for it if this has not been included; *and*
- for benefits other than HB, child benefit and guardian's allowance, must include information about applying for a mandatory reconsideration before you can appeal.

Has the decision maker refused to make a decision?

If a decision maker refuses to make a decision on your claim, this effectively prevents your having the right to appeal. You should remind the decision maker that s/he *must* make a decision on every valid claim.[17] Even if the decision maker does not accept that a claim made on the correct claim form is valid, you should be given a decision saying so. You can then appeal and ask the tribunal to decide if your claim is valid.[18]

Note: a decision maker can sometimes postpone making a decision if there is a test case pending (see p1303).

Examples of decisions you can appeal

Whether you are entitled to a benefit.

Whether an overpayment is recoverable (unless it is an overpayment that is always recoverable – see p1222), and the amount of an overpayment.

Whether to impose a civil penalty (see p1256).[19]

Whether your claim has been validly made or can be backdated.

Whether benefit is payable under the overlapping benefit rules.[20]

Whether you should be given a sanction, and whether you had good cause or a good reason for your actions or your failure to take action.

Whether you have limited capability for work or limited capability for work-related activity.

Whether you satisfy the habitual residence test.

Whether you satisfy the disability conditions for benefit.

Whether you can be paid hardship payments.

Whether your award of contributory ESA should end because you have been paid it for 365 days (see p645).[21]

Whether you are available for or actively seeking work.

Whether a jobseeker's agreement is reasonable or you had a good reason for refusing or failing to carry out a jobseeker's direction.

Decisions you cannot appeal

You cannot appeal against some decisions.[22] You *can* ask for an 'any time' revision or a supersession of a decision about which you do not have a right of appeal, whatever your reason for thinking it is wrong.[23] However, if the decision maker refuses to revise or supersede the decision, your only legal remedy is to apply for a judicial review (see p1378).

Examples of decisions you cannot appeal

Who should be the claimant when a couple is unable to decide.

Who should be entitled to child benefit when two people whose claims have equal priority cannot agree.

Part 9: Getting a benefit decision changed
Chapter 55: Appealing to the First-tier Tribunal
1. Appealing to the First-tier Tribunal

Whether a claim for one benefit can be treated as a claim for (or in addition to) another benefit.

Whether to demand recovery of an overpayment, and the amount of weekly deductions.

Whether to suspend payment of benefit.

Whether to appoint a person as an appointee (see p1149).

Whether to make a short-term advance, a budgeting advance or a payment on account.

Who deals with your appeal

Appeals are dealt with by a judge (and in some cases, members) assigned to the First-tier Tribunal. The administration of the work of all tribunals is the responsibility of HM Courts and Tribunals Service (HMCTS), part of the Ministry of Justice. HMCTS officials deal with the day-to-day work of the First-tier Tribunal through a network of regional offices. Any of the following may be be involved with your appeal at some time.

- **A judge**. S/he is always legally qualified. As well as hearing and making the decision on your appeal, s/he carries out various other functions – eg, s/he decides whether you have made your appeal in time, and whether to extend a time limit or to issue directions. See pp1326–31 for some of the functions the judge carries out.
- **A member of the First-tier Tribunal**. S/he could be a doctor, a person with experience of disability or an accountant. S/he hears and makes the decision on your appeal with the judge. To see which members hear and decide your appeal, see p1338.
- **An expert**. If your appeal involves issues that require specialist expertise, an expert (the tribunal may call her/him an 'assessor') may be used.[24] If s/he provides a written report, it should be sent to every party involved in the appeal. The expert cannot take part in making the decision on your appeal.
- **A registrar** (s/he must be legally qualified) or a **tribunal caseworker** (s/he must be appropriately trained). A registrar or a tribunal caseworker can carry out any of the functions of the First-tier Tribunal, under the supervision of a judge. S/he can make all the decisions a judge can make other than the final decision on your appeal.[25]
- **A clerk to the First-tier Tribunal**. S/he can carry out specified functions, including waiving a requirement for you to provide information with your notice of appeal, requiring you to provide information and striking out your appeal (see p1330). S/he attends the appeal hearing in an administrative capacity – eg, to pay expenses. S/he cannot take part in making the decision on your appeal and should not express any views on the case.[26]

You can ask a judge to reconsider a registrar's, a tribunal caseworker's or a clerk's decision. You must apply in writing within 14 days after the date you are sent notice of the decision.[27] The tribunal can give you longer, but there is no guarantee of this, so keep within the time limit wherever possible.

2. **How to appeal**

You must appeal in writing. This is known as a 'notice of appeal'. **Note:** unless it is an appeal about housing benefit (HB), you must usually apply for a mandatory reconsideration before you can appeal (see p1311).

You must appeal within a strict time limit (see p1318). See p1321 to find out what information your notice of appeal must contain to ensure your appeal is valid.

You should use the appropriate form wherever possible. If you do not use the appropriate form, your appeal can be accepted as valid provided it is in writing and includes all the information required (see p1321).

Appeal forms

For HB, use the form approved by your local authority.[28]

For benefits other than child benefit and guardian's allowance, use the appeal form (SSCS1) in the leaflet *Notice of Appeal Against a Decision of the Department for Work and Pensions.*

For child benefit and guardian's allowance, use the appeal form (SSCS5) in the leaflet *Notice of Appeal Against a Decision of HM Revenue and Customs.*

Both forms are available from www.gov.uk/social-security-child-support-tribunal/appeal-tribunal.

Note: if you want the First-tier Tribunal to deal with your appeal quickly, make this clear when you appeal, explaining why. For HB, because you have to send or deliver your notice of appeal to the decision maker (see below), you could write to the tribunal, asking it to intervene.

Where to send your appeal

You must send or deliver your notice of appeal:
- for HB, to the local authority office that sent you the decision.[29] Your appeal is then passed to the First-tier Tribunal;
- for other benefits, direct to the First-tier Tribunal at the appeal centre in Bradford (if you live in England or Wales) or in Glasgow (if you live in Scotland).[30] This is sometimes called 'direct lodgement'. The address to use is on the appeal form. The appeal centre checks if your appeal is valid and if so, passes it to the appropriate regional office.

Part 9: Getting a benefit decision changed
Chapter 55: Appealing to the First-tier Tribunal
2. How to appeal

The time limit for appealing

The time limit for appealing depends on whether or not you had to apply for a rmandatory reconsideration before you could appeal. If you miss the time limit, it can be extended (see p1319), but there is an absolute time limit within which you must appeal (see p1319).

If you had to apply for a mandatory reconsideration

If you had to apply for a mandatory reconsideration before you could appeal (see p1311), your appeal, including all the information described on p1321, must arrive at the First-tier Tribunal within one month after you are sent the mandatory reconsideration notice (see p1313).[31]

Month
'Month' means a complete calendar month running from the day after the day you have been sent or given a decision.[32] For example, a decision sent on 24 July has an appeal time limit that expires at the end of 24 August.
When calculating time, if something has to be done by a certain day, it must be done by 5pm that day. If a time limit ends on a day other than a working day, you have until the next working day to meet the time limit.[33]

If you did not have to apply for a mandatory reconsideration

If you did not have to apply for a mandatory reconsideration, your appeal including all the information described on p1321, must arrive at the relevant office (for HB, this is the office that sent you the decision and for other benefits, this is the First-tier Tribunal) by the latest of the following:[34]
- one month after the date the written decision was sent to you; or
- if you ask for a written statement of reasons for the decision (if one has not already been given to you – see p1166), 14 days after the latest of:
  - the end of that month – ie, if the written statement of reasons is provided within the one-month period, you get one month plus 14 days to appeal; *or*
  - the date the written statement of reasons is provided.

Remember, you must ask for a written statement of reasons within one month of being given notice of a decision.

If you applied for a revision before you appealed and the decision maker revises the decision, but you still want to appeal because you did not get all you want, the one-month time limit runs from the date you are sent the new decision.[35] If you applied for an 'any grounds' revision and the decision maker refused to do a revision, you must appeal within one month of the date you are sent notice of the refusal.[36]

If the decision maker refuses to do an 'any time' revision and says you cannot appeal, you should appeal against the original decision within the time limit (if this has not already passed). If this is not possible, get advice.

If you miss the time limit

If you miss the time limit for appealing, your appeal is still treated as made in time if neither the decision maker nor any other person with a right of appeal against the decision (or anyone who has been added as a party to the appeal – eg, the other parent if you are disputing who counts as responsible for your child) does not object.[37] However, for benefits other than HB, the tribunal can look at the issue of lateness even if the decision maker (or party to the appeal) has not raised an objection. **Note:** for HB appeals only, there are special rules that set out when the decision maker can treat your appeal as made in time and so should not object (see p1320).

If the decision maker (or other person) *does* object, the tribunal can still extend your time limit.[38] There is no guarantee that it will do so, so keep within the time limit wherever possible. There is an absolute time limit for appealing after which you cannot appeal (see below).

In addition to the information you must provide on your appeal form (see p1321), you must include the reasons why your appeal is late.[39] The tribunal can extend the time limit for appealing if this will enable it to deal with your appeal fairly and justly, so give details of any special circumstances that mean this would be the case. See p1320 for some ideas about what may be relevant.

Note:

- The First-tier Tribunal decides whether your appeal has been made within the time limit, *not* the DWP, the local authority or HM Revenue and Customs (HMRC). If you think your appeal has been made within the time limit, explain why when you appeal.
- If you miss the time limit and the First-tier Tribunal does not extend it, you can appeal to the Upper Tribunal against its decision.[40]
- The tribunal can also shorten time limits, but should only do this if this will enable it to deal with your appeal fairly and justly.
- If you are appealing a decision about HB and are required to provide information you did not include with your appeal, your time limit can be extended under separate rules (see p1322).

The absolute time limit for appealing

You cannot appeal if it is more than 12 months after the date your time limit for appealing expired.[41] **Note:** in very exceptional circumstances (eg, if you did not receive notice of the decision you want to appeal), you can argue that the tribunal should waive the absolute time limit and allow you to appeal if this is absolutely necessary to protect your right to a fair hearing.[42] However, this is unlikely to apply unless you have done all that you could to appeal in time.

Part 9: Getting a benefit decision changed
Chapter 55: Appealing to the First-tier Tribunal
2. How to appeal

For HB, if the decision maker thinks your appeal has been made outside the absolute time limit, s/he must refer it to the First-tier Tribunal immediately.[43] The tribunal decides whether your appeal has been made in time, not the local authority.

Note: if the First-tier Tribunal decides that you cannot appeal because your appeal was made outside the absolute time limit, but you think it was made in time, or it refuses to waive the absolute time limit, you can appeal to the Upper Tribunal against the decision.[44]

Housing benefit appeals

A decision maker can treat your HB appeal as made in time if it is in the 'interests of justice'.[45] For these purposes, it is *not* in the interests of justice unless it was not practicable for you to appeal in time because:[46]

- you, your partner or a dependant died or had a serious illness;
- you are not resident in the UK;
- normal postal services were disrupted; *or*
- there are other special circumstances that are 'wholly exceptional'. The longer you have delayed appealing, the more compelling the special circumstances must be.[47]

When deciding whether it is in the interests of justice, account cannot be taken of the fact that:[48]

- a court or the Upper Tribunal has interpreted the law in a different way than was previously understood and applied;
- you (or anyone acting for you) misunderstood or were unaware of the relevant law, including the time limits for appealing.

If the decision maker objects to your appeal being treated as made within the time limit, s/he must refer it to the First-tier Tribunal immediately.[49] The tribunal then decides whether your time limit can be extended.

Why your time limit should be extended

Your reasons and circumstances need to show it would be fair and just to extend your time limit for appealing. What may or may not be such a reason or circumstance cannot be defined in advance, but the following are all relevant.

- **The reasons for the delay.** Explain these as clearly and as fully as possible. Do not worry if some or all of the delay is your fault. Any explanation is better than none at all. Even if you knew the time limit, but simply ignored it, it may be possible to say something favourable. Say if things have been difficult at home or you were confused by the rules or just assumed that the DWP (or the local authority or HMRC) was the expert and had got it right until, for example, you were advised otherwise or read an article in a newspaper. Reasons for the delay could include the fact that:

- you did not receive the decision;
- you made a reasonable mistake in calculating the time limit;
- you posted your appeal in time, but it went astray in the post;
- you were ill;
- a mistake was made by your advisers. It should not make any difference that you might be able to sue them for negligence;
- you were given wrong advice or otherwise misled by the DWP (or the local authority or HMRC) – eg, you were discouraged from appealing by a decision maker who advised you incorrectly that an appeal would be doomed to fail. If you lose money because you are refused a late appeal, consider claiming compensation (see p1396).

- **The length of the delay.** The usual approach is that time limits have to be kept to, and there has to be good reason for not doing so. Short delays are likely to be easier to justify than long delays, but a good reason is still needed.

- **The merits of your appeal.** The more likely your appeal is to succeed, the greater the injustice in refusing to extend the time limit. A strong case is particularly useful if there has been a very long delay and a time limit is usually extended where there has been a 'clear error', which would have long-term continuing effects unless corrected.[50]

- **The amount of money at stake.** Even if there has been no clear error, a time limit may be extended if there is a lot of money at stake.[51]

- **A decision in a test case.** A decision in a test case, establishing that an earlier decision was incorrect, can amount to a reason to extend a time limit, in some circumstances.[52] Such appeals often involve large sums of money and (given the test case) a clear error in the decision which is being appealed against.

Making sure your appeal is valid

The First-tier Tribunal decides whether your appeal is valid, *not* the DWP, the local authority or HMRC. For your appeal to be valid:

- you must provide all the information required (see below). **Note:** even if you do not use the correct appeal form, your appeal can still be valid; *and*
- you must sign your notice of appeal.[53] However, if you have provided written notice that you have appointed a representative, s/he can sign it on your behalf. If your solicitor signs your notice of appeal on your behalf, it should be accepted that s/he is authorised to do so;[54] *and*
- your notice of appeal must be in English or Welsh.

The information you must provide

You must provide:[55]

- your name and address and that of your representative, if you have one;
- the address where documents can be sent or delivered – eg, to you or your representative;

Part 9: Getting a benefit decision changed
Chapter 55: Appealing to the First-tier Tribunal
2. How to appeal

- if you are appealing about HB, details about the decision with which you disagree, sufficient for it to be identified;
- if you are appealing about other benefits:
  - the name and address of any person who had a right of appeal against the decision (see p1313);
  - a copy of the mandatory reconsideration notice (see p1313) or, if you did not have to apply for a mandatory reconsideration before the appeal, a copy of the decision you want to appeal. **Note:** if you were not given written notice that you had to apply for a mandatory reconsideration before you could appeal, state this clearly on the appeal form;
  - any statement of reasons for the decision that you have;
  - any documents in support of your appeal that you have not already supplied to the decision maker;
- a summary of your reasons for believing the decision is wrong (your grounds for appeal). Do not simply say you think the decision is wrong, but explain why.

For HB appeals, it is also helpful to include information and evidence that supports your appeal because a decision maker may look at the decision again before the appeal hearing and might revise it.

Examples

'The decision says I have been overpaid housing benefit because I failed to disclose that my wife had started working part time, but I wrote to the council as soon as she started work and told it what her take-home pay would be.'

'HMRC says I should not get child benefit for my son because he left school in June. This decision is wrong because my son stayed on at school to do his A levels.'

'You say I cannot get disability living allowance care component. This decision is wrong because you have not taken into account the amount of help I need because of my incontinence problems.'

If you had to apply for a mandatory reconsideration before you could appeal and the DWP (or HMRC) only provided a mandatory reconsideration notice after a long delay, this may put you at a disadvantage – eg, if it is now difficult to obtain evidence to support your appeal. Point out if you think this improves the DWP's (or HMRC's) chances, or reduces your chances, of winning your appeal.[56]

What happens if you do not provide sufficient information

If you are appealing about HB and you do not include the information required on your appeal form or in your appeal letter, the local authority can ask you to provide the information you left out.[57] If you used an appeal form, this is returned to you to complete. Be sure to provide the information within the time allowed, otherwise you may not have made your appeal within the time limit.

Your time limit for appealing (see p1318) is extended by:[58]

- 14 days from the date your appeal form is returned to you for completion, if the completed form is received back within 14 days;
- 14 days from the date you are asked for further information, if you provide this within 14 days of the request;
- the length of time you are given to complete the form or provide information, if this is longer than 14 days.

If you do not complete the form properly or provide the information required in time, your appeal, along with any relevant documents and evidence, is forwarded to the First-tier Tribunal by the local authority. It then considers whether your appeal is valid and can go ahead.[59] **Note:** if you complete and return the form or provide the information:

- after the expiry of the time limit, but before your appeal is forwarded to the tribunal, the decision maker should accept that your appeal is valid and then consider whether to object to it being treated as made in time (see p1319);[60]
- before the tribunal makes a decision, any further details you provide must be taken into account.[61]

If your appeal is not accepted as valid, try to make a late appeal (see p1319).

If you are appealing about other benefits and you do not include the information or documents (including the mandatory reconsideration notice) required on the appeal form, the tribunal clerk can waive the requirement, or require you to provide what you left out and then 'strike out' your appeal (see p1330) if you fail to do so.[62] You can ask the tribunal to reconsider the clerk's decision. You must apply in writing within 14 days after the date you are sent notice of the decision.[63] The tribunal can give you longer, but there is no guarantee of this, so keep within the time limit wherever possible. **Note:** if your appeal is struck out, it can be reinstated by the clerk – eg, if you later provide the mandatory reconsideration notice (see p1330).

Note: if you had to (and did) apply for a mandatory reconsideration before you could appeal, but you have not been sent or given a mandatory reconsideration notice, see p1313.

3. After you send or deliver your appeal

If you sent your appeal direct to the First-tier Tribunal, it sends a copy to the DWP or HM Revenue and Customs (HMRC). In all cases, the DWP, the local authority or HMRC prepares its case – known as the 'decision maker's response' (see p1324). For housing benefit (HB) appeals, you are sent an enquiry form (see p1324) to

Part 9: Getting a benefit decision changed
Chapter 55: Appealing to the First-tier Tribunal
3. After you send or deliver your appeal

complete and return to the tribunal. **Note:** you may find that your appeal is not dealt with if there is a test case or a lead case pending that deals with the same issues (see p1334).

The enquiry form

For HB appeals only, when the First-tier Tribunal receives your appeal papers from the local authority, it sends you a questionnaire (called an enquiry form). This asks you whether you want an oral hearing and, if so, when you and your representative (if you have one) are available to attend, if you have not already provided this information – eg, on your appeal form. If you want an oral hearing, you must state this. You should always consult your representative before completing and returning the enquiry form. **Note:** if you have sent your appeal about a benefit other than HB directly to the First-tier Tribunal, you are unlikely to be sent an enquiry form if you have already provided this information on your appeal form.

You should return the enquiry form within 14 days. If you do not return it in time, the tribunal can 'strike out' your appeal (see p1330) or automatically deal with your appeal at a paper hearing. However, you are entitled to receive a ruling on the merits of your appeal, so it should only be struck out on this ground in exceptional cases.[64] For further information about oral and paper hearings, see p1335.

The decision maker's response

The DWP, the local authority or HMRC must prepare a bundle of papers relevant to your appeal (called the 'decision maker's response') and forward this to the First-tier Tribunal:

- for HB, as soon as reasonably practicable. You are entitled to have your appeal heard within a reasonable period of time, so the decision maker should prepare the response and send it to the tribunal without delay. Following a complaint, an Ombudsman said the local authority should forward an appeal to the First-tier Tribunal within 28 days;[65]
- for other benefits, within 28 days of receiving the notice of appeal.[66] The tribunal clerk can bar the decision maker from taking further part in the appeal if the response is late (see p1331), but can lift the bar when the response is eventually received.

Both you and your representative (if any) are normally sent a copy.[67] However, check with your representative as this might not always happen.[68]

If the decision maker opposes your appeal, the response must include any reasons that are not in the documents the First-tier Tribunal has already been given.[69] The decision maker must also provide:[70]

- a copy of any written record of, and statement of reasons for, the decision with which you disagree, if you did not send these with your appeal form;
- copies of all documents s/he has that may be relevant, unless the tribunal directs otherwise. The decision maker must use her/his judgement to decide what is relevant, but the tribunal decides whether s/he may have other relevant evidence and, if so, can direct the decision maker to produce this. If your appeal involves a medical issue or one about your disability, a record of medical examinations you have had in connection with your claim is usually included; *and*
- for HB appeals only, a copy of your appeal form (or letter) along with all the documents you provided with it, and unless already provided to the First-tier Tribunal, the name and address of your representative.

Read through the whole response carefully to find out the case being made against you. Be sure to take it with you to the hearing.

Has your appeal been held up by the decision maker?

You cannot usually bypass the normal procedures. However, note the following.

1. Although you cannot usually expect the First-tier Tribunal to deal with your appeal before the decision maker has had a chance to prepare her/his response, it is free to allow matters to be handled differently if circumstances require it.[71]

2. Ask the tribunal to make a direction (see p1328) requiring the decision maker to provide documents, information and evidence by a specified date, or a direction setting a hearing date.[72]

3. If you are appealing about HB and the decision maker does not forward your appeal within a reasonable period, forward a copy of it to the First-tier Tribunal yourself and follow Steps one and two above.

Note: in some circumstances, the tribunal can bar the decision maker from taking any further part in the appeal (see p1331), in which case your appeal could be decided without a response being made.

Providing other information

Make sure that everything you want to say in support of your appeal has been put in writing and that there are no other documents and evidence that you would like the tribunal to see. **Note:**

- It is always good to provide a written submission and additional evidence or information to support your appeal (known as a 'reply') – eg, independent medical evidence or supporting statements from witnesses.
- You (or your representative) must provide your reply within one month after the date you are sent the decision maker's response.[73] The tribunal can give you longer (or shorter) than one month.[74] There is no guarantee that you will be given longer, so keep within the time limit wherever possible.

Part 9: Getting a benefit decision changed
Chapter 55: Appealing to the First-tier Tribunal
3. After you send or deliver your appeal

Note: the tribunal may issue directions (see p1328) requiring you (or the DWP, the local authority or HMRC) to provide a submission, further information or documents within a specific period. You (or the decision maker) can also ask it to issue directions. If you are given a direction, it is important that you comply with it. If you do not, your appeal can be struck out (see p1330).

When your appeal can lapse

After you appeal, a decision maker may look at the decision you are appealing about again and revise it – eg, on the basis of any facts, information or evidence you provided with your appeal form. This is the case, even though the decision maker had already considered a revision when you applied for a mandatory reconsideration. If the decision maker revises the decision, your appeal could lapse, even if you do not get everything you want, and you have to appeal again.[75]

Your appeal lapses if the revised decision is more advantageous to you than the original decision – eg, the decision:[76]

- awards you benefit at a higher rate or for a longer period;
- lifts a refusal or disqualification of benefit or a sanction (in whole or in part);
- reverses a decision to pay benefit to a third party (see p1187);
- means you gain financially from the revised decision;
- says an overpayment of benefit is not recoverable or that less should be recovered.

If the revised decision is not more advantageous to you, your appeal must go ahead, but against the revised decision.[77] You have one month from the date the decision is sent or given to you to make further representations.[78] At the end of that period (or earlier if you agree in writing), your appeal proceeds unless the decision is revised again and is now more advantageous to you.[79]

If your appeal lapses, you must make a fresh appeal. The DWP says you should not have to apply for another mandatory reconsideration before you can appeal in this situation.[80] Your time limit for appealing (see p1318) runs from the date the revised decision is sent to you.[81]

Note: if the First-tier Tribunal decides that your appeal has lapsed, you can appeal against that decision to the Upper Tribunal. However, it is better if you make a fresh appeal against the original decision.

What the First-tier Tribunal can do

There are procedural rules that the First-tier Tribunal must follow when dealing with your appeal. The aim (known as the 'overriding objective') is to enable it to deal with cases fairly and justly.[82] This includes avoiding delay (provided the issues can be considered properly), avoiding unnecessary formality, seeking flexibility in the proceedings and ensuring that all the parties can participate fully. You, the DWP, the local authority and HMRC must help the First-tier

Tribunal further this objective and co-operate with it. This involves ensuring, as far as possible, that your case is ready by the time of the hearing.[83]

The First-tier Tribunal can:[84]

* extend or shorten any time limits (see below);
* issue directions (see p1328);
* postpone or adjourn your appeal hearing (see p1328);
* 'strike out' your appeal (see p1330) or bar the decision maker or another party to the appeal from taking part (see p1331);
* summon witnesses to attend a hearing, answer questions or produce documents. If someone fails to comply, the First-tier Tribunal can refer the matter to the Upper Tribunal. The Upper Tribunal can punish the person for contempt of court.[85] **Note:** you cannot be required to give evidence or produce any document that you could not be compelled to give by a court;[86]
* suspend the effect of its decision while any application for permission to appeal, or any appeal against or review of that decision, is outstanding.[87]

Note: the rules for what the Upper Tribunal can do are generally the same as for the First-tier Tribunal. The endnotes in this section therefore also refer to Upper Tribunal rules where relevant.

Extending or shortening time limits

Any of the time limits given to you by the First-tier Tribunal can be extended or shortened.[88] The rules do not specify when this should (or must) be done, but the overriding objective of all the tribunal rules is to enable the tribunal to deal with appeals fairly and justly (see p1326).[89]

The tribunal may shorten your and the DWP's, the local authority's or HMRC's time limits if it thinks that delay should be avoided, provided the issues can be considered properly.[90] You might want to ask for the DWP's (or the local authority's or HMRC's) time limits (eg, to comply with a direction) to be shortened if your situation is urgent or your circumstances are exceptional.

If you know that you are going to miss (or have missed) a time limit, you should ask for it to be extended by the tribunal. It does not have to extend any particular time limit, so there is no guarantee that you will be given more time. So you should keep within the time limits wherever possible.

Always ask in writing for a time limit to be extended and apply in advance if you can. Give the reasons why you are going to be (or are) late in meeting the time limit, as well as any special circumstances which mean your time limit should be extended so that your appeal can be dealt with fairly and justly. What may or may not be such a reason or circumstance cannot be defined in advance, but the reasons for, and the length of, the delay are relevant.

Note: for the rules about extending your time limit for appealing, see p1319. For some ideas about what may count as a good reason for a late appeal, see p1320.

Part 9: Getting a benefit decision changed
Chapter 55: Appealing to the First-tier Tribunal
3. After you send or deliver your appeal

Directions

In the course of your appeal, the First-tier Tribunal might issue directions – eg, requiring you (or the DWP, the local authority or HMRC) to provide a submission, further information or documents, or requiring you or a presenting officer (see p1338) to attend a hearing.[91] It must send you and the decision maker (and anyone affected by the direction) notice of any direction it issues, unless it thinks there is a good reason not to do so.[92] You can challenge a direction (eg, if you think insufficient time has been given to comply with it) by applying for another direction to amend, suspend or set aside the first one.[93]

If you are given a direction, it is important that you comply with it. If you fail to comply with a requirement or a direction, the tribunal can take any action it thinks is 'just' – eg, it can:[94]

- waive the requirement;
- require you to remedy the failure;
- strike out your appeal (see p1330); *or*
- conclude that any information or evidence required was adverse to you.[95] However, it should not use this as a way to punish you. It should only decide information or evidence was adverse to you if it is probable that the reason it was not provided was that it did not exist or would harm your case.[96]

Note: the tribunal can also take the above action if it is the DWP, the local authority or HMRC that is given a direction. The tribunal can also bar the DWP, the local authority or HMRC from taking further part in your appeal (see p1331).

If you miss the deadline in a direction, try to provide what has been requested as soon as possible. The tribunal may still consider the information or evidence – eg, if you provide it at the hearing.[97] However, remember that it can decide *not* to consider evidence if it is late or if it would otherwise be unfair to do so.[98]

You or the decision maker can also apply to the First-tier Tribunal to ask it to issue directions. This can be useful, for example, if you are having trouble getting documents or information from the decision maker. You can apply in writing, or orally at the hearing.[99] In either case, you must give reasons for your application.

Postponements and adjournments

The First-tier Tribunal can postpone or adjourn a hearing.[100] The decision can be made by the judge. However, if the issue arises at a hearing and the panel comprises more than one member, the judge should consult the other member(s).[101] The decision must be recorded properly.

Remember that if you do not attend a hearing, the tribunal can hear the appeal without you (see p1337).[102] Your appeal is less likely to succeed if you do not attend.

Your case might be postponed or adjourned if there is a test case or lead case pending which deals with the same issues as your appeal (see p1334).

Getting a hearing postponed

If the hearing date is inconvenient or you want more time to prepare your case, you can ask for the hearing to be postponed to another date. You should apply in writing to the First-tier Tribunal before the hearing date, saying why you want your appeal to be postponed. Make it clear that you do not want the hearing to go ahead in your absence. You should apply as soon as you decide that you want a postponement. Bear the following in mind.

- Do not presume that a postponement will be granted. Telephone before the hearing is due to take place to check if it has been agreed. Be ready to attend the hearing if it goes ahead. If you have a representative, s/he should warn you that your application might not be successful.[103]
- If you do not attend the hearing, the judge conducting the hearing should consider whether it should be adjourned, even if you have been refused a postponement.[104]

The tribunal can postpone your oral hearing even if this is not requested.

Getting a hearing adjourned

If a hearing (either oral or paper) is underway, it can be adjourned – eg, if you or the DWP (or the local authority or HMRC) asks for an adjournment, or if the First-tier Tribunal thinks this is the best course – eg, if more evidence is required or you need time to consider the law. You should consider asking for an adjournment if the tribunal says it is going to consider whether you should get a lower rate of benefit than you are getting currently, to allow you to prepare your case and make representations. If you no longer want to pursue your appeal, you may be able to withdraw it (see p1332).

The tribunal should consider the benefit of an adjournment, why you (or the DWP, the local authority or HMRC) are not ready to go ahead and what the impact would be on the other party and the tribunal system.[105] It should adjourn a hearing:

- if you are not there and there is doubt about whether you received notice of the oral hearing;[106] or
- if you have advised it that you cannot attend, have a good reason for not attending and have asked for another hearing date;[107] or
- if you are unable to attend the hearing (eg, you are in prison or hospital), but your evidence could play an important part in its reaching a decision;[108] or
- if you want to be represented at the oral hearing, but your representative is not available on the date it has been listed and has made a reasonable request for a postponement. Your representative should explain why s/he cannot attend and why no one else can represent you in her/his place;[109] or
- if you need to get a representative – eg, because it is difficult for you to represent yourself, you have mental health problems or the decision with which you disagree concerns a large overpayment;[110] or

Part 9: Getting a benefit decision changed
Chapter 55: Appealing to the First-tier Tribunal
3. After you send or deliver your appeal

- to enable you to get additional evidence which you could not until then have reasonably been expected to realise was needed.[111]

If a hearing is not postponed or adjourned

If the hearing is not postponed or adjourned and the First-tier Tribunal makes a decision with which you disagree, in limited circumstances, you can apply for the decision to be 'set aside' (see p1355). Alternatively, you may be able to appeal to the Upper Tribunal against the First-tier Tribunal's final decision in your appeal on the grounds that its refusal to postpone or adjourn the hearing was an error of law.

When your appeal can be struck out

If you fail to comply with a direction, or in a limited number of other circumstances, your appeal can be 'struck out', in whole or in part. This cancels your appeal, or part of your appeal, and it does not go ahead. If your appeal is struck out because you failed to comply with a direction, see below for when you can get your appeal reinstated.

If you fail to comply with a direction

If you fail to comply with a direction given to you by the First-tier Tribunal (eg, you do not provide the required information or documents):[112]

- your appeal is struck out automatically if you were notified in the direction that a failure to comply *would* lead to your appeal being struck out;
- there is discretion to strike out your appeal if you were notified in the direction that a failure to comply with it *could* lead to your appeal being struck out. Before deciding to do so, the tribunal should consider carefully why the direction was given and whether it can still make a fair and just decision – eg, without the information you were supposed to provide.[113]

In both cases, you can apply for your appeal to be reinstated.[114] You must apply in writing. Your application must be received by the tribunal within one month of your being sent notice that your appeal was struck out. It can give you longer (or shorter) than one month. There is no guarantee that you will be given longer, so keep within the time limit wherever possible. You should explain why you think your appeal should not have been struck out – eg, why you think you *did* comply with the direction, or why you were unable to do so or to comply in time.

Other circumstances

Your appeal *must* be struck out if the First-tier Tribunal does not have 'jurisdiction' to deal with it – eg, you do not have a right to appeal against the decision or you have appealed to the wrong tribunal.[115]

There is *discretion* to strike out your appeal if:[116]

- you failed to co-operate with the First-tier Tribunal to such an extent that it cannot deal with your appeal fairly and justly; *or*

- the First-tier Tribunal considers your appeal has no reasonable prospect of success. It should only strike out your appeal if the result of the appeal is clear and incontestable. It should generally not do so if the facts of the case are in dispute.[117]

In all cases:
- you must be given an opportunity to comment. You should always take this opportunity and explain why you think your appeal should not be struck out – eg, why you had a good reason for failing to co-operate or why you think you have a chance of winning your appeal;
- you cannot apply for your appeal to be reinstated, but may be able to challenge the decision to strike it out.

Challenging a decision to strike out your appeal

If the First-tier Tribunal strikes out your appeal or refuses to reinstate your appeal after it has been struck out, you may be able to make a fresh appeal against the decision maker's decision.[118] See p1318 for the time limit for doing so. Otherwise, you can appeal to the Upper Tribunal against the decision to strike out your appeal or to refuse to reinstate it.[119]

Being barred from taking part in an appeal

The decision maker and any person (other than you) who is taking part in the appeal because s/he has a right of appeal against the decision you are challenging (see p1313) or s/he has been added as a party to the appeal by the tribunal (eg, the other parent if you are disputing who counts as responsible for your child) can be barred from taking further part in the appeal in the same circumstances in which your appeal can be struck out.[120] In practice, this is likely to apply mainly if the decision maker (or other person with a right of appeal):
- fails to comply with a direction; *or*
- fails to co-operate with the tribunal to such an extent that it cannot deal with your appeal fairly and justly.

The decision maker (or other person) can apply for the bar to be lifted in the same circumstances in which you can apply for an appeal to be reinstated (see p1330). If the bar is not lifted, the tribunal does not have to consider any response or other submission made by her/him.[121] It can decide any or all of the issues against her/him and can deal with her/his case more briefly than would otherwise be required. However, the decision maker (or person) still has a right of appeal against the tribunal's decision and a right to apply for a statement of reasons for the decision.[122]

Representatives

You can have a representative to help you with your appeal and to be with you at the hearing.[123] S/he can explain the procedures, present your case to the tribunal

Part 9: Getting a benefit decision changed
Chapter 55: Appealing to the First-tier Tribunal
3. After you send or deliver your appeal

and ensure it is aware of all the relevant issues and the law. You must send or give the tribunal written notice of your representative's name and address or s/he must do this on your behalf. This does not apply for HB if you provide this notice to the local authority before your appeal is forwarded to the tribunal. If your representative is providing the notice, s/he should also provide an authorisation signed by you.

Even if you have not previously notified the tribunal that you have a representative, someone can attend the hearing with you (eg, a friend or relative) and act as one, or assist you at the hearing, if the tribunal agrees.

Once you have given notice that you have a representative, s/he is presumed to be acting for you unless you (or your representative) give notice in writing that this is no longer the case.[124] Your representative must be sent any documents required to be sent to you; these then do not have to be sent to you.[125] However, do not presume this always happens. If you receive documents, check that your representative has also received them.

Meeting the costs

Free legal help is only available in limited cases.
- In England, you cannot get free legal help to cover preparatory work, such as obtaining medical reports and writing submissions. However, if you have a solicitor acting for you in an industrial injury or personal injury claim, s/he may have medical and other reports and evidence which you can use for your benefit appeal. In Scotland, you may be able to get free legal help for preparatory work.
- You cannot *normally* get free legal help from a lawyer to cover representation. You may be able to get this in very exceptional cases, if it is necessary to make these services available to you because a failure to do so would be a breach of your human rights or your rights under European Union law.[126]

If you are not eligible for free advice and assistance, or you want to be represented by a lawyer at an oral hearing, you are likely to have to pay. However, you may be able to get free help from a Citizens Advice Bureau, law centre or advice centre. There are a number of agencies that can advise you and help you prepare your case for the hearing, and even represent you (see Appendix 2). Remember that many non-lawyer advisers know more about social security law than lawyers, and their advice and representation is usually free. See p1331 for the notice you must provide if you have a representative.

Withdrawing an appeal

If you change your mind about appealing, you can withdraw your appeal.[127]
- If you are appealing about HB and your appeal has not yet been passed to the First-tier Tribunal, write to that office, saying that you do not wish your appeal to go ahead. Your authorised representative can write on your behalf.

- In any other case (ie, once your appeal is lodged with the First-tier Tribunal), you can withdraw your appeal:
  - by sending or giving written notice to the tribunal. You can withdraw your appeal before the hearing, and also if a hearing has taken place but was adjourned part-heard. The withdrawal takes effect immediately. Normally, you do not need the tribunal's agreement to withdraw your appeal in this way, but in some cases it may notify you that you can only do so if it agrees; *or*
  - at an oral hearing, but only if the tribunal agrees. The withdrawal takes effect when it agrees.

The tribunal must notify you that the withdrawal of your appeal has taken effect. It must also notify any other party to the appeal (ie, the DWP, the local authority or HMRC), anyone taking part in the appeal because s/he has a right of appeal against the decision you are challenging (see p1313) and anyone added as a party to the appeal by the tribunal – eg, the other parent if you are disputing who counts as responsible for your child.

If you tell the tribunal that you want to withdraw your appeal before the hearing (eg, you telephone the tribunal office), but then you fail to confirm this in writing, the tribunal clerk can waive the requirement to provide written notice.[128] You can ask the tribunal to reconsider the clerk's decision – eg, if you did not send written notice because you changed your mind and no longer wanted to withdraw your appeal. You must apply in writing within 14 days after the date you are sent notice of the decision.[129] The tribunal can give you longer (or shorter) than this. There is no guarantee you will be given longer, so keep within the time limit wherever possible.

If you withdraw your appeal but then decide that you want it to go ahead, you can apply for it to be reinstated.[130] The other parties can also apply for your appeal to be reinstated. You must apply in writing and it must be received by the tribunal within one month after the earliest of the following:

- the date you were sent notice that the withdrawal of your appeal has taken effect; *or*
- if your appeal was withdrawn at an oral hearing and you were present at the hearing when this happened, the date of the hearing.

The tribunal can give you longer (or shorter) than one month. There is no guarantee that you will be given longer, so keep within the time limit wherever possible.

Consent orders

If all the parties (eg, you and the DWP, the local authority or HMRC) agree what the solution to your dispute should be, you can ask the tribunal judge to make a 'consent order' and to make any other appropriate provision you have agreed.[131]

Part 9: Getting a benefit decision changed
Chapter 55: Appealing to the First-tier Tribunal
3. After you send or deliver your appeal

This procedure is unlikely to be relevant in most cases and is only likely to be of use if you are effectively giving up your appeal, but the DWP (or the local authority or HMRC) promises you something in return for this. The First-tier Tribunal only deals with your appeal in this way if it considers it appropriate. It may simply make a decision on your appeal in the usual way.

If a consent order is made, there does not have to be a hearing and no reasons for the order need to be given. Get independent advice *before* agreeing to a consent order.

Test cases and lead cases

Sometimes appeals to the First-tier Tribunal are made by more than one person about the same issues of fact or law. When this happens, there are procedural rules that can mean appeals dealing with the same issues may be delayed until a decision has been made in a test case or a lead case.

Test cases

If a case is pending against a decision of the Upper Tribunal or a court that deals with issues raised in your case (a 'test case'), the DWP (or the local authority or HMRC) can suspend payment of your benefit (see p1185) or even postpone making a decision about your claim (see p1303), pending the outcome of the appeal in the test case. In addition, for benefits other than HB, if a test case is pending and you have already appealed to the First-tier Tribunal (your appeal is then known as a 'look-alike' case), the decision maker can serve notice requiring the First-tier Tribunal in *your* appeal:[132]

- not to make a decision and to refer your case back to her/him; *or*
- to deal with your appeal by either:
  - postponing making a decision until the test case is decided; *or*
  - deciding your appeal as if the test case had been decided in the way most unfavourable to you, but only if this is in your interests. If this happens, and the test case eventually goes in your favour, the decision maker has to make a new decision superseding the tribunal's decision in the light of the decision in the test case.[133]

If the decision on your appeal has been postponed, once a decision has been made in the test case, the decision is made on your appeal.

Lead cases

If appeals are made to the First-tier Tribunal by more than one person about the same issues of fact or law (eg, a number of appeals about service charges from tenants in the same block of flats), the tribunal can specify one or more of the appeals as a 'lead case' and postpone making a decision on all the other related appeals.[134] When it makes its decision in the lead cases(s), the decision can apply to (and be binding on) all the other related appeals. You must be sent a copy of the decision.

If your appeal is not the lead case, you can apply to the tribunal for a direction that the decision does not apply to, and is not binding on, your appeal. You must apply in writing within one month after the date you are sent a copy of the decision. The tribunal can give you longer (or shorter) than this. There is no guarantee that you will be given longer, so keep within the time limit wherever possible.

4. Hearings

Appeals can be dealt with either at a paper or an oral hearing. Your appeal *must* be dealt with at an oral hearing, unless:[135]

- both you and the DWP or the local authority or HM Revenue and Customs (HMRC) have consented (or both of you have not objected) to the appeal being dealt with at a paper hearing; *and*
- the First-tier Tribunal considers that it can decide the matter without an oral hearing. It should explain this in its statement of reasons if you ask for one.

If there is not an oral hearing, the tribunal makes its decision by looking at what you said on your appeal form, any evidence or other information you provided to support your appeal and the decision maker's response. This is known as a paper hearing.

If either you or the DWP (or the local authority or HMRC) have stated that you want an oral hearing, there must be one. If you want an oral hearing, state this on the appeal form or the enquiry form (see p1324). Otherwise, the tribunal presumes that you do not object to a paper hearing.

Why should you choose an oral hearing?

You may not want to attend an oral hearing – eg, because you are worried about speaking for yourself or about the cost or difficulty in attending. Get advice before you decide what to do. Bear the following in mind.

1. You are more likely to win your appeal if you attend an oral hearing, particularly if it concerns a medical issue or your disability, or if the facts of your case are in dispute.

2. If you attend an oral hearing, you can explain your side of the story.

3. You can ask someone to represent you at the hearing (see p1331) and your chances of winning are likely to be higher if you do.[136] You can also take a friend, relative or adviser with you for support.

4. The First-tier Tribunal aims to provide a qualified interpreter if you need one.

5. You, an interpreter and any witnesses may be able to get expenses paid. You can claim for travel (including the extra costs involved for disabled people), meals, loss of earnings and childcare costs.[137]

Part 9: Getting a benefit decision changed
Chapter 55: Appealing to the First-tier Tribunal
4. Hearings

6. If you or your representative cannot attend an oral hearing at a venue (eg, because of a disability), one might be arranged at a venue where you can, or you might be able to be present via a video link or telephone (see p1337).[138]

Paper hearings

You are not sent notice of a paper hearing. The tribunal makes its decision in your absence and you are then notified of its decision.

If you opt for a paper hearing, send the tribunal your arguments about your appeal in writing and any information and evidence you can get to support it (called a 'reply'). Write to the tribunal to let it know you intend to send a reply and state how long it may take to do so.

You must provide your reply within one month after the date you were sent the decision maker's response.[139] If you need longer than this, ask for an extension. If your paper hearing takes place before the month is up and you could (and would) have provided further evidence within that period, you can challenge the tribunal's decision on the ground that it made an error of law.[140]

Have you opted for a paper hearing?
1. If you opt for a paper hearing, your appeal could still be dealt with at an oral hearing if the DWP (or the local authority or HMRC) wants one or the tribunal decides there should be an oral hearing because it can only deal with your appeal fairly and justly by doing so (eg, it needs to ask you questions about the facts of your case), or if during a paper hearing it is uncertain whether or not anyone asked for an oral hearing.[141]
2. If you get unexpected notice of an oral hearing, contact the tribunal to check the reasons for this. You should attend the hearing.
3. If you opt for a paper hearing but then decide you want an oral hearing, you may be able to change your mind. You must tell the tribunal before it makes its decision.

Oral hearings

You must be given reasonable notice of an oral hearing – at least 14 days' notice, unless you agree to less notice than this or there are urgent or exceptional circumstances.[142] The hearing normally takes place at an appeal venue in your area. You can see where the appeal venues are at http://sscs.venues.tribunals.gov.uk//Venues/venues.htm. If you are unable to attend a hearing at the venue, see p1337.

If you have not been given the correct notice (you can argue that this includes the decision maker's response as well as the time and date of the hearing[143]), you can object to the hearing going ahead. If the tribunal decides to proceed with the hearing, attend and explain why your case will be prejudiced (eg, you did not have an adequate time to prepare it) and ask for an adjournment (see p1328).

The tribunal can go ahead with an the oral hearing even if you are not there if:[144]

- it is satisfied that you were notified of the hearing, or that reasonable steps have been taken to notify you; *and*
- it thinks that it is in the interests of justice. The tribunal should always consider the alternative of adjourning the hearing to give you another opportunity to attend (see p1329).

If you turn up late for the hearing, after the tribunal has decided to proceed in your absence, it should still consider whether to allow you to participate, and whether it should adjourn the hearing to give you another opportunity to attend.[145]

An appeal is heard in public unless the tribunal thinks it should be in private.[146] The tribunal can exclude people from hearings in some circumstances. If you want your hearing to be in private, ask for this to be considered. In practice, it is extremely rare for members of the public to attend.

The tribunal can postpone or adjourn a hearing (see p1328).

Alternative venues

Most appeal venues have access for disabled people, and the First-tier Tribunal may meet the cost of special transport to get there. It may also arrange the hearing at another venue – eg, a hotel meeting room near where you live. However, if you are unable to attend a hearing at any of the venues, in rare cases it is possible to hold the hearing in your home (known as a 'domiciliary hearing'), although the tribunal may say this is not necessary if you can use special transport.[147] Include a letter from your doctor with your request for a domiciliary hearing, confirming that you are unable to travel at all – eg, even by private ambulance. You can argue that you can appeal against a decision to refuse you a domiciliary hearing.[148] Alternatively, if the refusal meant that the way your appeal was dealt with was unfair, you may be able to appeal against the decision on your appeal to the Upper Tribunal.[149]

If you are unable to attend a hearing at a venue, you may be able to be present via a video link, telephone or other means of instantaneous two-way electronic communication.[150] Contact the tribunal to see whether this can be arranged.

Note: the First-tier Tribunal must consider how to assist any children under 18, vulnerable adults (eg, severely physically or mentally disabled people 18 or over) and sensitive witnesses to give evidence.[151] This includes allowing them to give evidence by telephone, video link or other means, or appointing someone with special expertise to help the person give evidence. You are a **'sensitive witness'** if the quality of evidence you give is likely to be diminished because of your fear or distress in connection with giving evidence.

Part 9: Getting a benefit decision changed
Chapter 55: Appealing to the First-tier Tribunal
4. Hearings

At the hearing

The following may be present at your appeal hearing.

A **judge** and up to two other **members** (see p1316) hear and decide your appeal. The judge makes a note of what is said by everyone at the hearing. To see which members decide your appeal, see below.

An **expert** (see p1316) may be present if your appeal involves issues that require expertise not available to the tribunal.[152] If s/he provides a written report, it should be sent to every party involved in the appeal. The expert cannot take part in making the decision.

The **tribunal clerk** is there in an administrative capacity – eg, to pay expenses. The clerk cannot take part in making the decision and should not express any views on the case.

A **presenting officer** may be present to represent the decision maker. S/he explains the reasons for the decision, but is not there to defend it at all costs and may provide information which helps your case. Presenting officers often only attend if an appeal is considered complicated. The tribunal can issue a direction requiring a presenting officer to attend the hearing.

You can have a **representative** with you at the hearing.[153] S/he can explain the procedures, present your case and ensure the tribunal is aware of all the relevant issues and the law. If you have one, see p1331 for information about the notice you must send or give the tribunal. You can also be accompanied by someone at the hearing – eg, a friend or relative. The tribunal can give permission for her/him to act as your representative or assist you in presenting your case.[154]

The First-tier Tribunal aims to provide a qualified **interpreter** if you need one. If you do, tell it in advance of the hearing. If a qualified interpreter is not available, it might allow a relative to act as your interpreter if s/he understands that s/he should simply translate accurately and tell your answers in your own words, without comment or explanation.[155]

The judge and members

Those who decide a particular kind of appeal are as follows.[156]

- A judge, a doctor and a person with experience of disability decide attendance allowance (AA), disability living allowance (DLA) and personal independence payment (PIP) appeals. If your appeal only raises issues of law, so a doctor and a person with experience of disability are not needed, a judge can hear your appeal (or a judge and a member whose experience and qualifications are needed to make the decision).
- A judge and a doctor decide appeals about:
  - whether you have limited capability for work under the work capability assessment or have limited capability for work-related activity;
  - industrial injuries benefits or severe disablement allowance (SDA).

  However, if your appeal only raises issues of law, so a doctor is not needed, a

judge can hear your appeal (or a judge and a member whose experience and qualifications are needed to make the decision).[157]
- A judge decides all other appeals on her/his own.

The judge must be legally qualified. S/he always acts as the chair of the hearing.

Unless your appeal is about AA, DLA or PIP, an additional judge can be included in specified cases, an accountant may be included (if the examination of financial accounts is required) or there can be an additional doctor (if there are complex medical issues). However, there can never be more than three deciding an appeal.

If the group deciding your appeal is comprised incorrectly, you can appeal to the Upper Tribunal and argue that this was an error of law.[158]

Note:
- If your appeal is meant to be heard by two or more members but some of these are absent, the hearing can still go ahead, but only if you and the DWP, or the local authority or HMRC agree.[159]
- If you have both a DLA (or PIP) and an employment and support allowance appeal, they should not be heard together or consecutively by the same members. They should be heard completely separately, by entirely different members.[160]
- If your appeal is only partly heard by a judge and at least one member, the group deciding your appeal at a new hearing should generally be the same, or completely different.[161]
- You cannot argue that a doctor should not decide your appeal even if s/he regularly provides medical reports about benefit claimants to the DWP.[162]
- You can argue that the tribunal should not rely on evidence from a DWP doctor with whom any of the members hearing your appeal sit at other times. This depends on how often and how recently this has happened.[163]

Procedure at an oral hearing

When the tribunal is ready to hear your case, you (and your representative) are taken in with any presenting officer. There are no strict rules of procedure. The judge decides how the hearing is conducted.[164] The tribunal's overriding objective is that your appeal is dealt with fairly and justly.[165] This includes ensuring that you are able to participate fully.

What happens at an oral hearing?

1. The judge should introduce everyone present.

2. The judge (and members) often starts by asking you (and the presenting officer) questions. Even if you have a representative, you are usually expected to give your own evidence (see p1345). Be prepared for some searching questions.

3. The presenting officer may be asked to summarise the decision maker's case.

Part 9: Getting a benefit decision changed
Chapter 55: Appealing to the First-tier Tribunal
4. Hearings

4. You should be given the opportunity to explain your case. It is the tribunal's job to help you to say everything you want by putting you at your ease and asking the right questions. If you think there are mistakes in the papers, point them out. You can call witnesses and ask questions of the presenting officer's witnesses. If you forget to say something when it is your turn to speak, do not hesitate to add it at the end of the hearing. See p1344 for help with preparing for your appeal and presenting your case.

5. The tribunal considers all the facts, evidence and law before it makes a decision. It should not bargain with you by 'offering' to allow part of your appeal if you agree to drop other parts – eg, by offering you one component of DLA if you agree not to argue for the other.[166]

Medical examination at the oral hearing

The First-tier Tribunal cannot usually carry out physical examinations.[167] Studying x-ray evidence does not count as a physical examination, so you can ask the tribunal to consider this.[168]

It *can* carry out a physical examination if your appeal relates to the assessment of your disablement for SDA or industrial injuries disablement benefit, or whether you have a prescribed disease or injury.[169] It should let you know during the hearing if it thinks a physical examination is not necessary so you can make representations.[170]

You are examined by the medical member(s) of the tribunal.[171] You can have someone with you as a chaperone or if, for instance, you need help undressing. Make sure you tell the medical member(s) if you are in pain or discomfort. It is also a good idea to provide a full list of any medicines you are taking. After the examination, you should be invited to make further representations to the tribunal if you wish.

Can the tribunal take its observations of you into account?

The tribunal may observe your abilities and behaviour at the hearing and take these into account when making its decision – eg, if your appeal concerns your ability to walk.[172] However, it should not attach undue weight to its observations[173] and you should be given the opportunity to comment on them.[174] Remind the tribunal that what it sees may only be relevant to your physical or mental condition on that day and not in general.[175] Tell it, for instance, whether you have just taken medication or have been resting for some time in the waiting area. **Note:** the tribunal can use information about walking distances it obtains itself – eg, from Google maps. However, the evidence should be presented to you so that you can comment on, or refute, it.[176]

Appeals about disability, incapacity or limited capability for work

If your appeal concerns your disability or your incapacity or limited capability for work, the tribunal considers all the medical and other relevant evidence, and tries to draw out the evidence about your disabilities, listening to all you have to say with the help of questioning from the doctor member(s). This may confirm the opinions expressed in medical reports with which you disagree, or it may support your view. See p1347 for information about medical evidence. Consider the following.

- Tell the tribunal how your disability or limited capability for work affects you at work or in your daily life at home. You should be completely straightforward, neither underplaying nor overplaying your symptoms. If you feel better on some days than others, explain how and how often, and say whether you are being seen on a good day or a bad day.

- The tribunal should not restrict itself to accepting the medical evidence about you given in written reports.[177] If there is conflict between what is said in a report and what you have said in writing (eg, on your claim form), it should not accept the evidence in the report without first listening to what you have to say about how your condition affects you.[178] Ensure that you explain any inconsistencies. It should be particularly careful not to accept automatically the findings in medical reports produced with the assistance of a computer programme.[179]

Referral for a medical report

The tribunal can adjourn the hearing and refer you to a healthcare professional approved by the DWP (see p1155) for a medical examination and report if your appeal concerns:[180]

- whether you are entitled to AA, DLA or PIP, the appropriate rate of benefit or the period for which you are entitled; *or*
- whether you are entitled to SDA; *or*
- whether you are incapable of work or have limited capability for work or for work-related activity; *or*
- the extent of your disablement for SDA or industrial injuries disablement benefit purposes; *or*
- whether you have a loss of faculty as a result of an industrial accident (see p681).

The tribunal can specify the type of healthcare professional to whom you should be referred.[181] The medical examination may take place in your home or at a DWP medical examination centre.

A report may also be requested from your GP or other medical adviser.

The written decision to adjourn for a report should make clear why the tribunal adjourned and what sort of medical evidence is being sought.

Note: athough you cannot be compelled to undergo a medical examination, the tribunal may draw negative conclusions if you refuse.

Part 9: Getting a benefit decision changed
Chapter 55: Appealing to the First-tier Tribunal
4. Hearings

What the tribunal considers

The tribunal's job is to decide whether the decision you are appealing about was correct. It must look at the law and issues afresh, taking into account any new evidence or information you (and the DWP, the local authority or HMRC) provide.

Note:

- The tribunal considers all the evidence.[182] It decides what weight the evidence should be given, taking into account any possible deficiencies when deciding whether the facts are proved.[183] It should decide your appeal in an investigative way, but the members should generally not make their own enquiries into the facts of your case before the hearing.[184]

- You (or the DWP, the local authority or HMRC) can raise an issue at the hearing.[185] However, the tribunal might then adjourn to give the other side a chance to address the point.

- The tribunal should consider an issue if it is in the appeal papers or in any representations you make, or if the evidence should lead it to believe it is relevant to your appeal.[186] It does not have to consider issues that are 'not raised by' your appeal.[187] **Note:**
  - You do not necessarily have to raise an issue with the tribunal for it to be something it should consider, even if you have a representative, but the issue must be one which in some way obviously demands attention.[188] If you have a representative, the tribunal may decide not to investigate matters that s/he does not raise on your behalf.[189]
  - The tribunal can consider issues even if no one has raised them.[190] It should use its discretion fairly.

If you are appealing about not being awarded one component of DLA or PIP when you are already in receipt of the other, or you ask for a higher rate of DLA, PIP or AA than you are already getting, the tribunal does not have to consider issues which are not the subject of your appeal. However, it may decide to consider both components of DLA or PIP, or to consider whether you should get a lower rate of DLA, PIP or AA than you are already getting. You should be given notice of this, and a chance to prepare your case properly and make representations or to consider withdrawing your appeal.[191] Ask for the hearing to be adjourned if you need time or want someone to advise or represent you. If your appeal is being dealt with at a paper hearing, you should be given the opportunity to attend an oral hearing or to withdraw your appeal.[192] You should be given an explanation of why the tribunal decided to use its discretion in this way in the statement of reasons for its decision.[193]

If you are concerned about what might happen in your appeal, you may be able to withdraw it (see p1332). You need permission if you ask to withdraw your appeal at the hearing, or if you are notified that you can only withdraw your appeal if the tribunal agrees. **Note:** the DWP (or the local authority or HMRC) can apply for your appeal to be re-instated (see p1333).

Faulty revisions and supersessions

If your appeal involves a revision or a supersession decision which is faulty, the tribunal can remedy any defect and make any decision that the decision maker could have taken.[194] This includes where the decision maker:

- carried out a supersession but failed to state the grounds or to identify the correct grounds for doing so; *or*
- carried out a supersession when s/he should have conducted a revision (and, in some cases, vice versa).

In addition, the tribunal can decide that an 'any time' revision should be done where no decision has been made on the matter by a decision maker (either to revise the decision or refuse to do so) – ie, if you are appealing because the decision maker refused to carry out a supersession.[195]

If errors in the decision making are extensive, try to argue that the tribunal should correct the decision. However, it can adjourn the hearing, point out the errors to the decision maker and invite the decision maker to reconsider, rather than making any corrections itself.[196]

Changes of circumstances after you appeal

When the tribunal hears your appeal, it considers whether the decision with which you disagree was correct for the period up to and including the date it was made. If your circumstances change after the decision, it cannot take this into account.[197]

Any evidence you get after the decision with which you disagree could still be relevant to your appeal. If the evidence relates to the period before the decision you are disputing was made, or to a past event that was relevant to the decision, it must be taken into account.[198] In some situations, events that happen after the date of the decision can throw light on the situation at or before that date, in which case evidence of such events may also be taken into account – eg, if the tribunal needs to decide if an improvement in your health was likely to happen.

What you should do if your circumstances change

As a general rule, you should consider making a fresh claim (or seeking a supersession) every time your circumstances change, and appeal if you are unhappy with the subsequent decision, particularly if your appeal is about:

- whether you have limited capability for work, have limited capability for work-related activity or qualify for AA, DLA or PIP, or the rate of AA, DLA or PIP to which you are entitled and your condition has worsened;
- whether you satisfy the 'habitual residence test' (see Chapter 66); *or*
- how much income or capital you have, and this changes.

Part 9: Getting a benefit decision changed
Chapter 55: Appealing to the First-tier Tribunal
5. Proving your case

If you wait until the tribunal makes its decision and this goes against you, you could lose out. You can only get arrears from the date your circumstances changed if a fresh claim (or the effect of a supersession) can be backdated. This is only possible in limited circumstances.

Example

Ravi has been getting PIP mobility component. A decision maker decides his condition has improved, so stops his PIP. He appeals. While waiting for his appeal hearing, his condition deteriorates, he makes a fresh claim and is awarded PIP mobility component. When the tribunal hears his appeal against the original decision, it upholds the decision maker's decision. However, because Ravi made a fresh claim when his circumstances changed, he has not lost out.

If you make a fresh claim (or seek a supersession), you can ask the decision maker to wait until your appeal has been determined before making a decision. However, if the decision maker decides the fresh claim (or supersession) and you disagree with the decision:

- you can appeal against the new decision. All the appeals may be heard together by the tribunal, but it may be better for them to be heard separately;[199] *or*
- whether or not you appeal against the new decision, you can ask the decision maker to revise it once your first appeal is determined (see p1283).

Example

Henry claims pension credit (PC) but the decision maker says he does not satisfy the habitual residence test and refuses his claim. He appeals against the decision and makes a fresh claim for PC on 11 May 2017. The new claim is refused. Henry wins his appeal. Because he did not appeal the new decision, the tribunal can only award PC up to 11 May 2017. However, the decision maker does an 'any time' revision and awards PC from that date.

5. **Proving your case**

Appeals to the First-tier Tribunal are taken on many issues – disputes about facts or the law, or both – so the advice given here can only be general. You usually need to think about both the facts and the law because they are connected.

Sorting out the facts

You are likely to know more than anyone else about the facts of your case. Your key task is to pass your knowledge on to the tribunal. It rehears your case completely, so fresh facts and arguments can be put by either side.

How do you ensure the tribunal has all the facts?

1. Check through the appeal papers carefully to work out what evidence the decision maker used in support of the decision. This helps you decide what evidence you need to win your case.

2. Study the decision maker's evidence and think about your arguments – eg, to show how the decision maker may have got the wrong impression.

3. Gather evidence and information to back up your arguments. Send it to the tribunal as soon as possible before your oral hearing. Otherwise, it might decide to adjourn your appeal (see p1328) or even decide not to take the evidence or information into account.[200] The tribunal sends a copy to the DWP, the local authority or HM Revenue and Customs (HMRC), which might then decide to support your appeal.

4. Ask any witnesses who support your case to attend the hearing. The tribunal can refuse to hear witnesses who are not relevant, but it should always be fair to you and generally allow witnesses to speak, even if it looks like they may have nothing useful to say.[201] The tribunal can summon witnesses.[202]

The tribunal can issue directions (see p1328) on how you (or the DWP, the local authority or HMRC) should provide evidence and submissions or on how witnesses should give evidence – eg, orally at a hearing, or by making a written submission or a witness statement within a set period of time.[203] It can accept evidence from you (or the DWP, the local authority or HMRC) even if it was not available to a previous decision maker.[204]

Evidence includes:

- oral evidence – what you (and any witnesses or others) actually say at the hearing. The tribunal cannot dismiss oral evidence without a proper explanation of why it has done so;[205] *and*
- written evidence – any documents you (or the DWP, the local authority or HMRC) provide, including medical evidence.

It can also include video evidence (see p1346).

Oral evidence

You, the presenting officer and witnesses can give your oral evidence at the hearing. You or the DWP (or the local authority or HMRC) can call witnesses, although the tribunal can limit the number.[206]

You are usually expected to give your own oral evidence at the hearing, if you can. Your representative is generally not allowed to give this for you. However,

Part 9: Getting a benefit decision changed
Chapter 55: Appealing to the First-tier Tribunal
5. Proving your case

s/he can assist the tribunal in gathering evidence from you (eg, by asking you questions)[207] and can give her/his *own* evidence based on her/his observations, or factual evidence within her/his own knowledge.[208]

You, your representative and the presenting officer can report what other people have said (called 'hearsay evidence'). The tribunal must carefully weigh up its value, given that the person who originally made the statement is not present at the hearing.[209]

If s/he is at the hearing, the presenting officer puts the DWP's (or the local authority's or HMRC's) case but is not necessarily the person who actually made the decision on your claim. Unless the presenting officer is giving her/his own evidence (eg, because s/he was directly involved in the decision on your claim), any factual statements s/he makes are hearsay evidence, but the tribunal might not doubt the accuracy of the evidence.[210]

Written evidence

Written evidence includes letters, medical and other reports, wage slips, bank statements, birth certificates and anything else that helps prove the facts. If, for example, the DWP (or the local authority or HMRC) says you failed to disclose an increase in your earnings and you have been overpaid, you could explain how and when you did so. It is even better to produce a copy of the letter you sent informing the decision maker of the change, or a letter you received confirming you reported the change. It is not unknown for the DWP (or the local authority or HMRC) to fail to include copies of relevant documents in the decision maker's response. Check the response carefully and submit copies of any missing documents to the tribunal as soon as you can. If you do not have copies, insist that the decision maker provides these. The tribunal can issue a direction requiring the decision maker to do so (see p1328).

Do you disagree with the written evidence?

1. Point out that you have not had the opportunity of questioning the witnesses. You are not entitled to insist on the presence of any particular witness,[211] but you can ask the tribunal to issue a direction for her/him to attend a hearing.

2. Argue that the tribunal should not place any weight on the written evidence of, for instance, an interviewing officer if you are disputing the interview, or an investigating officer if you are disputing what s/he heard or saw.

3. You and the DWP (or the local authority or HMRC) cannot rely on the evidence of an anonymous witness without the consent of the tribunal, and consent should only be given in exceptional circumstances.[212]

Video evidence

The DWP (or the local authority or HMRC) might use video evidence – eg, if you are appealing about entitlement to employment and support allowance or disability living allowance. You cannot prevent it doing so.[213] The tribunal should always find out if the surveillance was properly authorised. You must be given time to view and consider the evidence in advance of the hearing. If relevant, insist that the person who made the video is called as a witness. If the filming was only intermittent and if filming in the intervening periods would have provided evidence favourable to you, point this out to the tribunal.

Medical evidence

You can ask your doctor to provide medical evidence, or ask an advice agency to write to your doctor. Your doctor may charge for such evidence, but an advice agency or solicitor might be able to get a report free. Your medical evidence should deal with the points in dispute and also with the dates relevant to the decision with which you disagree. If your doctor does not know about the effect of your disability on your everyday life, tell her/him about it and ask her/him to confirm that this is consistent with the degree of your disability. Your evidence, or that of a friend or relative, may also be of use.

If you obtain a medical report, send it to the tribunal in advance of the hearing, with a copy of the letter to your doctor as this helps to show that s/he is expressing her/his own opinion about your case. You could also ask your doctor to supply a copy of her/his notes about you over the last few years.

Note: the tribunal can refer you for an examination and obtain a report if it thinks this is necessary (see p1341). If the lack of a report is causing you difficulties at the hearing, remind the tribunal of its power to obtain one.

Do you disagree with the medical evidence?

1. If the medical evidence is adverse to you and is provided by a doctor you do not usually see, point out how long the doctor has known you and what s/he knows about your day-to-day living activities or walking ability. If a doctor does not know you (or know you well) or know how you are affected by your condition, this should be taken into account.

2. If a medical report is provided by a healthcare professional, tell the tribunal about any relevant issues with the examination – eg, if you were not examined or were only given a very short examination, if you were not allowed to explain how you are affected by your condition properly, or if the person examining you has not recorded your answers to her/his questions correctly.

3. Argue that the tribunal should not rely on evidence from a DWP doctor with whom any of the members hearing your appeal sit at other times. This depends on how often and on how recently this has happened.[214]

Checking the law

If you know what the law says, you know what facts you have to prove. The primary sources of social security law are statute law and caselaw decided by the

Part 9: Getting a benefit decision changed
Chapter 55: Appealing to the First-tier Tribunal
5. Proving your case

Upper Tribunal and courts. It is easy to find both, once you know what you are looking for. The footnotes in this *Handbook* point you in the right direction. There are also a number of books that explain the law and refer you to relevant legislation and cases (see Appendix 3).

Look carefully at the decision maker's response (see p1324), as this refers to the statute law and caselaw which s/he thinks is relevant. The DWP (or the local authority or HMRC) does not always get the law right and you should emphasise a point that it has overlooked or got wrong.

Statute law

Statute law comprises Acts of Parliament and regulations (and rules for procedure in the First-tier Tribunal and Upper Tribunal). The Acts set out the main framework and allow regulations and rules covering the details to be made. These regulations and rules are known as statutory instruments. The legislation is often amended, so you must confirm that the ones you are referring to are up to date.

The best way to look up the relevant statute law is in one of the annotated volumes of legislation listed in Appendix 3. Remember that, in rare cases, the books do not contain all the regulations and rules that are relevant. Acts, regulations and rules are also available at www.legislation.gov.uk and amended versions are often available.

Note: benefit law is complicated and the staff who administer benefits are issued with guidance manuals and circulars. The DWP (or the local authority or HMRC) and the First-tier and Upper Tribunals are only bound by what the law says, not by the guidance. Nevertheless, it is sometimes useful to check the guidance. See Appendix 3 for a list of what is available.

If the statute law is ambiguous

If the statute law is ambiguous, the First-tier Tribunal, the Upper Tribunal and the courts can look at statements made to Parliament by ministers when the law was first made.[215] You can check the House of Commons' and House of Lords' official reports (known as *Hansard*) to see what was said in Parliament when the law was first introduced, and the transcripts of debates in the Delegated Legislation Committee at https://hansard.parliament.uk/. You can also check the Explanatory Memorandum that accompanies most statutory instruments. Another source of information is the Social Security Advisory Committee (www.gov.uk/government/organisations/social-security-advisory-committee).

European legislation

Social security benefits are not governed by British law alone. Regulations and Directives made by the European Union (EU) apply in the UK and throughout the European Economic Area (EEA) – eg, to ensure that benefits are received on an equal basis by both men and women.[216] Other EU rules may apply if you move to another EEA state or if you are an EEA national or the family member of an EEA national living in the UK (see Chapters 66, 67 and 68).

Human rights

The Human Rights Act 1998 incorporates into UK law most of the Articles of the European Convention on Human Rights. All legislation must be applied, *so far as it is possible to do so*, in a way which is compatible with this Convention.[217] The First-tier Tribunal must take into account any relevant caselaw of the European Court of Human Rights (ECtHR), but if there is a conflict between a UK court and the ECtHR, the decision of the UK court should generally be followed.[218] The articles of the Convention most likely to be relevant in social security cases are:

- Article 6(1): right to a fair hearing before an independent and impartial tribunal;
- Article 8: right to respect for private and family life;
- Article 1 of the First Protocol: right to peaceful enjoyment of possessions; *and*
- Article 14: prohibition of discrimination.

Note: if your case is one in which a Human Rights Act argument arises, get specialist advice. Challenges in social security cases using the Human Rights Act and the Convention are difficult and need specialist input.

Caselaw

The decision maker's response often refers to decisions of the Upper Tribunal and the courts (known as 'caselaw'). You should also use caselaw to support your appeal if possible. To help you decide which cases to use, see p1351.

Note: before 3 November 2008, decisions now made by the Upper Tribunal were made by social security commissioners.

Identifying Upper Tribunal and commissioners' decisions

All Upper Tribunal decisions have file numbers – eg, CDLA/2195/2008.

- The last numbers indicate the year in which the appeal was lodged.
- The letters after the 'C' indicate the benefit involved in the decision. An extra 'S' after the 'C' denotes a Scottish case, as in CSIB/721/2004.

Upper Tribunal decisions that are published on the official websites (see p1351) are given a 'citation number' (sometimes called a 'neutral citation') – eg, *SW v SSWP (IB)* [2010] UKUT 73 (AAC).

- First, the parties to the appeal are identified. The benefit claimant is identified by initials. The first name (or initials) is the party who appealed and the second, the other party. **Note:** 'SSWP' stands for Secretary of State for Work and Pensions – ie, the DWP.
- Next is the year the decision was given (in square brackets) and the letters 'UKUT' (meaning United Kingdom Upper Tribunal).

Part 9: Getting a benefit decision changed
Chapter 55: Appealing to the First-tier Tribunal
5. Proving your case

- The final number is the appeal number.
- Since 2010, letters to indicate the type of benefit involved in the decision are included.

The most important Upper Tribunal decision are chosen to be reported and are given a new number. All reported decisions:

- from 1951 to 2010 begin with an 'R' – eg, CU/255/1984 became R(U) 3/86. The following letter(s) denote(s) the type of benefit. The last numbers indicate the year in which the decision was published;
- from 2010 begin with the citation number. This is followed by the year the decision is reported (in square brackets), then the letters AACR (meaning Administrative Appeals Chamber Reports) and the reported decision number – eg, *Torbay BC v RF (HB)* [2010] UKUT 7 (AAC); [2010] AACR 26.

Identifying court decisions

Court decisions are identified by the names of the parties involved in the appeal. The first name is usually the party who has appealed and the second name is the other party. In judicial review cases, the case citation begins with 'R'.

Examples of court decisions

Hockenjos v Secretary of State for Social Security [2004] EWCA Civ 1749, 21 December 2004 is a decision of the England and Wales Court of Appeal Civil Division.

R v South Tyneside MBC ex parte Tooley [1997] QBD and *R (Reynolds) v Secretary of State for Work and Pensions* [2002] EWHC Admin 426 are decisions of the England and Wales High Court, formerly known as the Queen's Bench Division and now as the Administrative Court, following applications for judicial review.

Precedent

When the Upper Tribunal or a court decides an appeal, the decision sets a precedent, which a decision maker or the First-tier Tribunal deciding a similar case must follow.[219] Unreported decisions must be followed in the same way as reported ones.[220] **Note:** commissioners' decisions also set a precedent.

If there is an irreconcilable conflict between two or more decisions, the First-tier Tribunal has to choose which decision to follow.[221]

- It normally follows a reported decision of the Upper Tribunal (or a commissioner) in preference to an unreported one.
- It must follow an Upper Tribunal decision made by a three-judge panel (or the decision of a tribunal of commissioners) in preference to a decision of a single judge (or commissioner).
- Decisions of the Supreme Court, House of Lords, the Court of Appeal, the Court of Session or the Court of Justice of the European Union take precedence over all decisions of the Upper Tribunal (and commissioners).[222]

The Upper Tribunal has more freedom than the First-tier Tribunal.

- It does not have to follow an Upper Tribunal decision made by a single judge (or the decision of a single commissioner) if satisfied that the earlier decision was wrong.[223]
- It follows an Upper Tribunal decision made by a three-judge panel (and the decision of a tribunal of commissioners) unless there are compelling reasons not to. If the judge thinks it may be wrong, s/he can ask the President of the Administrative Appeals Chamber for the case to be transferred to another three-judge panel in the Upper Tribunal to reconsider the point.
- If an appeal is heard by a three-judge panel in the Upper Tribunal, the panel does not have to follow the decision of another similarly comprised panel (or tribunal of commissioners), but usually does so.[224]

Which cases to use

Caselaw can seem less precise than statute law, and frequently cases seem to contradict each other. Very often there are small differences in the facts of the cases, which justify the different results. To find cases relevant to your own, use the footnotes in this *Handbook* or any of the publications listed in Appendix 3. Bear the following in mind.

- Find cases where the facts are similar to yours. If cases appear to be against you, look at the facts of those cases and see whether any differences justify a different decision in your case (known as 'distinguishing' cases). One distinction may simply be that what seemed reasonable in the 1950s does not seem fair in the 2010s.[225]
- Most appeals before April 1987 were decided when there was a right of appeal to commissioners on questions of fact as well as law, so the First-tier Tribunal may not necessarily be erring in law if it takes a different view from a commissioner in a pre-April 1987 decision.
- Ensure that the caselaw is still relevant to the decision you are appealing – ie, whether there have been amendments to the statute law since it was decided.
- Check the decisions referred to in the decision maker's response (see p1324) as sometimes they rely on only part of a decision and fail to mention another part which is more favourable to you.

Obtaining Upper Tribunal, commissioners' and court decisions

Many of the Upper Tribunal and commissioners' decisions made before January 2016 are available at www.administrativeappeals.tribunals.gov.uk/Decisions/decisions.htm. Many Upper Tribunal decisions made from January 2016 are available at www.gov.uk/administrative-appeals-tribunal-decisions. Some decisions are also available at www.bailii.org and on the Rightsnet website at www.rightsnet.org.uk. Decisions may also be obtained from the Upper Tribunal Office (see Appendix 1).

Part 9: Getting a benefit decision changed
Chapter 55: Appealing to the First-tier Tribunal
5. Proving your case

Reported decisions are published from time to time in bound volumes, which are sometimes available in law libraries. The bound volumes of decisions from 2010 onwards are called Administrative Appeal Chamber Reports and contain reports of social security cases as well as those from other jurisdictions.

Summaries of reported Upper Tribunal and commissioners' decisions, most highlighted decisions and important court decisions are published in CPAG's *Welfare Rights Bulletin*. However, it is important to use the full decision, not just the summary, at the appeal hearing.

If an unreported decision is to be used at a hearing in the First-tier Tribunal by the DWP (or the local authority or HMRC), a copy should be supplied to you. Similarly, if you wish to use one, you should supply copies to everyone, preferably by sending one to the tribunal in advance of the hearing.

Many court decisions are available online. A useful link to these is at www.bailii.org.

Presenting your case at the hearing

Each case is different and hearings are informal, so there is no set pattern for presenting cases. If you want to make a presentation on your appeal, make this clear to the First-tier Tribunal as soon as possible – eg, before the hearing starts. **Note:** send any detailed submissions, medical reports and other evidence *before* the hearing.

How should you present your case?

1. You can use a written submission at the hearing and read directly from it. However, the tribunal usually asks questions, so be prepared to talk about your case without the script.

2. Make it clear at the start what you think the outcome of the appeal should be – eg, what rate of disability living allowance you think you qualify for, or which employment and support allowance descriptors you think you satisfy, or that your claim for housing benefit should be backdated.

3. Tell the tribunal which parts of the decision maker's response you dispute and the parts with which you agree.

4. It is usually best to set out the facts and call any witnesses before turning to legal arguments.

5. It is the tribunal's job to help you to say everything you want by putting you at your ease and asking the right questions. However, you must also be prepared for some searching questions. If you forget to say something when it is your turn to speak, do not hesitate to add it at the end of the hearing.

6. **The tribunal's decision**

You may be told the tribunal's decision at the hearing and you are given a decision notice confirming it. If it is not given at the hearing or you opted for a paper hearing, the decision notice is sent to you later. It may include a summary of the tribunal's reasons for its decision. You *must* be informed of:[226]

- your right to request a statement of reasons for the decision (see below); *and*
- the conditions for appealing to the Upper Tribunal, including the time limit for doing so.

Note:

- If the tribunal is unable to come to a unanimous decision, it makes a majority decision. The judge has the casting vote.[227]
- A decision can be corrected, superseded, reviewed or set aside (see p1355). You, or the DWP, the local authority or HM Revenue and Customs (HMRC) can also appeal against it to the Upper Tribunal.

Record of proceedings

A record of the tribunal proceedings is made by the judge that indicates the evidence taken and submissions made, as well as any procedural applications.[228] This could be a recording of the hearing or a written record.[229] If you are considering an appeal to the Upper Tribunal, it is a good idea to get a copy. If you foresee disputes about what happened at the hearing, keep your own notes.

The record is kept by the tribunal for six months from the date of its decision or for six months from various other specific dates, including the date you are sent written reasons for its decision. So, if you applied for a statement of reasons for the decision, the record of proceedings should not be destroyed until six months after the statement has been provided.[230]

You can apply for a copy of the record of proceedings. You must do so in writing within the relevant six-month period. The tribunal can give you longer (or shorter) than this. There is no guarantee that you will be given longer, so keep within the time limit wherever possible. Bear in mind that if you apply after the six-month period, the record may have been destroyed. You can apply for a typed copy of a written record – eg, if the written copy is difficult to read. If you are appealing to the Upper Tribunal and are having difficulty getting a record of the proceedings, ask the Upper Tribunal to make an order that one should be provided.

The statement of reasons

The First-tier Tribunal may give the reasons for its decision at the oral hearing, or give or send you a written statement of reasons, prepared by the judge.[231] If you are not provided with a written statement of reasons, you have a right to apply for

Part 9: Getting a benefit decision changed
Chapter 55: Appealing to the First-tier Tribunal
6. The tribunal's decision

one.[232] **Note:** the judge may say that the decision notice is to stand as the written statement of reasons, so check it carefully.

You must generally have a statement of reasons if you want to appeal to the Upper Tribunal. You must show that the First-tier Tribunal made an error of law (see p1363) and it may be difficult to do so without a statement of reasons.

Your request for a statement of reasons must be:[233]

- in writing; *and*
- received by the First-tier Tribunal within one month (see p1318) of your being sent or given its decision notice. It can give you longer (or shorter) than this.[234] There is no guarantee that you will be given longer, so keep within the time limit wherever possible.

The written statement of reasons must be sent to you within one month or as soon as it is reasonably practicable after that.[235] There are however often long delays.

Note:
- If you mistakenly ask the First-tier Tribunal for permission to appeal to the Upper Tribunal instead of asking for a statement of reasons, it should treat this as a request for a statement of reasons.[236]
- If the judge refuses wrongly to provide a statement of reasons, you may have grounds for appeal to the Upper Tribunal.[237]
- If there is a long delay in getting a statement of reasons, you could apply for permission to appeal to the Upper Tribunal. The Upper Tribunal can require the First-tier Tribunal to provide reasons for its decision.[238]

The DWP (or the local authority or HMRC) can also ask for a statement of reasons. If this happens, it usually means it is considering appealing to the Upper Tribunal.

If you win your appeal

If you win your appeal, the DWP (or the local authority or HMRC) should carry out the First-tier Tribunal's decision straight away. It can do this on the basis of the decision notice (see p1353). However, if the DWP, the local authority or HMRC:

- disagrees with the decision, it might consider appealing against it to the Upper Tribunal. In this case, you are not normally paid while it decides what to do. See p1185 for what the DWP (or the local authority or HMRC) must do before it can suspend your benefit. If the DWP/local authority/HMRC decides to appeal, you are not normally paid until the Upper Tribunal decides the case.[239] However, you can ask to be paid if you are left in financial hardship;
- applies for permission to appeal to the Upper Tribunal, the First-tier Tribunal may be able to suspend the effect of its decision until the application is determined (by either tribunal), and then until any review of, or appeal against, the decision is determined.[240]

The First-tier Tribunal can also suspend the effect of its decision if you apply for permission to appeal to the Upper Tribunal.

If you disagree with the tribunal's decision

If you disagree with the First-tier Tribunal's decision, you cannot simply ask it to look at the decision again – eg, if you have additional evidence. However, note the following.

- If the decision contains a clerical mistake or other accidental slip or omission, this can be corrected by the tribunal. This only applies if it is a genuine error such as a typing or spelling mistake or a mathematical miscalculation, not an error of law on an important issue in your appeal – eg, a change of the date of onset of an industrial disease. **Note:** the tribunal cannot use this rule to amend or add to its reasons for the decision, but can amend these if it reviews its decision (see p1367).[241]
- The decision can be superseded by the DWP (or the local authority or HMRC), if there are grounds (see p1287), though arrears can be limited. However, if the tribunal made a mistake about the law, you must appeal to the Upper Tribunal.
- You (or the DWP, the local authority or HMRC) can appeal to the Upper Tribunal against the decision (see Chapter 56).
- If you (or the DWP, the local authority or HMRC) seek permission to appeal to the Upper Tribunal against a decision, the First-tier Tribunal can review it (see p1367).
- The decision can be set aside, which means the decision is cancelled and your appeal is heard again (see below).

If you are considering an appeal to the Upper Tribunal, ask for the First-tier Tribunal's statement of reasons (if one has not yet been provided) within the one-month time limit (see p1353), even if you are first going to apply for the decision to be set aside.

Setting aside a decision on procedural grounds

A First-tier Tribunal decision can only be set aside on procedural grounds if the judge thinks it is 'in the interests of justice' to do so and:[242]

- you, your representative or the DWP (or the local authority or HMRC):
  - were not sent or did not receive appeal papers or other relevant documents, at an appropriate time – eg, in sufficient time before the hearing; *or*
  - were not present at the oral hearing. However, if you (or they) chose not to attend, it might not be 'in the interests of justice' to set the decision aside; *or*
- the tribunal was not sent appeal papers or other documents relating to the proceedings at an appropriate time – eg, in sufficient time before the hearing; *or*
- there was some other procedural irregularity.

Part 9: Getting a benefit decision changed
Chapter 55: Appealing to the First-tier Tribunal
6. The tribunal's decision

You must apply in writing to the First-tier Tribunal. The application must be received no later than one month after the date you are sent the decision notice (see p1353).[243] The tribunal can give you longer (or shorter) than this.[244] There is no guarantee that you will be given longer, so keep within the time limit wherever possible. The rules do not say what the time limit is if you are given the decision notice at the hearing.

Note:
- Applications are normally decided without a hearing.[245] Make sure you give a full explanation of your reasons when you apply. If you could not attend the hearing (eg, because you were ill), provide evidence of this – eg, a note from your doctor. If your application is late, explain the reasons for this.
- If the decision is set aside, your appeal is heard again and a new decision is made. You should be given the opportunity to ask for an oral hearing, even if your appeal was originally decided at a paper hearing.[246]
- If a decision is wrongly set aside, any subsequent rehearing by the First-tier Tribunal is invalid.[247]

In some circumstances, a decision can also be set aside by agreement – ie, when you, the DWP, the local authority or HMRC seek the permission of the First-tier Tribunal to appeal to the Upper Tribunal and you agree the First-tier Tribunal made an 'error of law' (see below).

If the decision is not set aside

If the First-tier Tribunal refuses to set aside a decision, you can appeal to the Upper Tribunal against the refusal.[248] It might be better to try to appeal to the Upper Tribunal against the original decision *and* the refusal. If your application for the First-tier Tribunal's decision to be set aside is refused, the time limit for appealing to the Upper Tribunal can run from the date you are sent notice of this.[249] However, this only applies if you applied for the decision to be set aside within the one-month time limit (or any longer period allowed by the First-tier Tribunal).

Note: the First-tier Tribunal can treat your application for a decision to be set aside as an application for permission to appeal to the Upper Tribunal, or as an application for a correction of the decision.[250]

Setting aside a decision by agreement

The First-tier Tribunal's decision must be set aside if an application is made for permission to appeal to the Upper Tribunal, and you and the DWP (or the local authority or HMRC) agree that the First-tier Tribunal made an 'error of law' (see p1363).[251] Bear in mind that the First-tier Tribunal does not send copies of applications for permission to appeal to the other party. If you think that the DWP (or the local authority or HMRC) might agree that the tribunal made an error of law, you should send it a copy of your application. However, there is no guarantee that it will take any action on this.

Notes

1. Appealing to the First-tier Tribunal

1 s12(1), (2) and (3D) SSA 1998
2 s12(2)(b) and (3A)-(3C) SSA 1998
3 para A3015 ADM
4 paras A3026-29 and 3047 ADM
5 **UC/PIP/JSA&ESA under UC** Reg 7(5)
UC,PIP,JSA&ESA(DA) Regs
Other benefits Reg 3ZA(5)
SS&CS(DA) Regs
6 r7 TP(FT) Rules
7 *MM v SSWP (PIP)* [2016] UKUT 36 (AAC)
8 **CB/GA** Reg 24 CB&GA(DA) Regs
UC/PIP/JSA&ESA under UC reg 49
UC,PIP,JSA&ESA(DA) Regs
Other benefits reg 25 SS&CS(DA)
Regs
All s12 SSA 1998
9 s12(4) SSA 1998
10 Reg 14 SS(JPIP) Regs
11 **CB/GA** Regs 29 and 31 CB&GA(Admin)
Regs
UC/PIP/JSA&ESA under UC Reg 56
UC,PIP,JSA&ESA(C&P) Regs; reg 49(a)
UC,PIP,JSA&ESA(DA) Regs
Other benefits Reg 30(1), (5) and (6)-
(6B) SS(C&P) Regs
12 Sch 7 para 6(3) and (6) CSPSSA 2000;
reg 3 HB&CTB(DA) Regs; *Wirral MBC v
Salisbury Independent Living Ltd* [2012]
EWCA Civ 84; [2012] AACR 37
13 R(H) 3/04; R(H) 10/07
14 **HB/CTB** Reg 21 HB&CTB(DA) Regs
CB/GA Reg 33 CB&GA(DA) Regs
UC/PIP/JSA&ESA under UC Reg
56(1) UC,PIP,JSA&ESA(C&P) Regs
Other benefits Reg 30(1) SS&CS(DA)
Regs
15 **HB** Sch 7 para 6 CSPSSA 2000
CB/GA s12 and Schs 2 and 3 SSA 1998;
reg 25(2) CB&GA(DA) Regs
UC/PIP/JSA&ESA under UC s12 and
Schs 2 and 3 SSA 1998; reg 50(1) and
Sch 2 UC,PIP,JSA&ESA(DA) Regs
Other benefits s12 and Schs 2 and 3
SSA 1998; reg 26 SS&CS(DA) Regs

16 **HB** Reg 10 HB&CTB(DA) Regs
CB/GA Reg 26 CB&GA(DA) Regs
UC/PIP/JSA&ESA under UC Regs 7(3)
and 51 UC,PIP,JSA&ESA(DA) Regs
Other benefits Regs 3ZA and 28
SS&CS(DA) Regs
17 R(SB) 29/83; R(SB) 12/89; CIS/807/
1992; R(H) 3/05
18 R(IS) 6/04
19 *VT v SSWP (IS)* UKUT 178 (AAC); [2016]
AACR 42
20 *SSWP v Adams* [2003] EWCA Civ 796,
reported as R(G) 1/03
21 *MC and JH v SSWP (ESA)* [2014] UKUT
125 (AAC); [2014] AACR 35
22 **HB** Sch 7 para 6(2) CSPSSA 2000; reg
16 and Sch HB&CTB(DA) Regs
CB/GA Sch 2 SSA 1998; reg 25 and Sch
2 CB&GA(DA) Regs
UC/PIP/JSA&ESA under UC Sch 2
SSA 1998; reg 50(2) and Sch 3
UC,PIP,JSA&ESA(DA) Regs
Other benefits Sch 2 SSA 1998; reg 27
and Sch 2 SS&CS(DA) Regs
23 **HB** Regs 4(6) and 7(2)(e) HB&CTB(DA)
Regs
CA/GA Regs 9 and 13(2)(d)
CB&GA(DA) Regs
UC/PIP/JSA&ESA under UC Regs 10
and 25 UC,PIP,JSA&ESA(DA) Regs
Other benefits Regs 3(8) and 6(2)(d)
SS&CG(DA) Regs
24 s28 TCEA 2007
25 Practice Statement: *Delegation of
Functions to Registrars First-tier Tribunal
(Social Entitlement Chamber)*, 1
December 2016; Practice Statement:
*Delegation of Functions to Tribunal
Caseworkers First-tier Tribunal (Social
Entitlement Chamber)*, 20 April 2016;
Practice Statement: *Delegation of
Functions to Tribunal Caseworkers First-
tier Tribunal (Social Entitlement
Chamber)*, 19 October 2016
26 Practice Statement: *Delegation of
Functions to Staff in Relation to the Social
Entitlement Chamber of the First-tier
Tribunal on or after 1 October 2014*, 25
September 2014
27 r4(3) TP(FT) Rules

Part 9: Getting a benefit decision changed
Chapter 55: Appealing to the First-tier Tribunal
Notes

● ●

2. **How to appeal**

28 Reg 20(1) HB&CTB(DA) Regs
29 Reg 20(1) HB&CTB(DA) Regs; r23
    TP(FT) Rules
30 r22 TP(FT) Rules
31 r22(2)(d)(i) TP(FT) Rules
32 CIB/3937/2000; *SSWP v SC (SF)* [2013]
    UKUT 607 (AAC)
33 r12 TP(FT) Rules
34 **HB** r23(2)(a)(i) and (ii) TP(FT) Rules
    Other benefits r22(2)(d)(ii) and Sch 1
    para 5(a) and (b) TP(FT) Rules
    All rr12 TP(FT) Rules
35 s9(5) SSA 1998; Sch 7 para 3(5) CSPSSA
    2000
36 r23(2)(a)(iii) and Sch 1 para 5(c) TP(FT)
    Rules
37 rr22(8)(a) and 23(4) and (5) TP(FT)
    Rules
38 r5(3)(a) TP(FT) Rules
39 rr22(6) and 23(3) TP(FT) Rules
40 *LS v Lambeth LB (HB)* [2010] UKUT 461
    (AAC); [2011] AACR 27
41 rr22(8) and 23(5) and (8) TP(FT) Rules
42 *KK v Sheffield City Council (CTB)* [2015]
    UKUT 367 (AAC); *PM v SSD (AFCS)*
    [2015] UKUT 647 (AAC)
43 r23(7)(b) TP(FT) Rules
44 *LS v Lambeth LB (HB)* [2010] UKUT 461
    (AAC); [2011] AACR 27
45 Reg 19(5A) HB&CTB(DA) Regs
46 Reg 19(6) and (7) HB&CTB(DA) Regs
47 Reg 19(8) HB&CTB(DA) Regs
48 Reg 19(9) HB&CTB(DA) Regs
49 r23(7)(a) TP(FT) Rules
50 R(M) 1/87; R(I) 5/91
51 R(M) 1/87
52 CIS/147/1995
53 rr22(3) and 23(6) TP(FT) Rules
54 r11(5) TP(FT) Rules; *CO v LB Havering
    (CH)* [2015] UKUT 28 (AAC)
55 rr22(3), (4) and (9) and 23(6) TP(FT)
    Rules
56 *MM v SSWP (PIP)* [2016] UKUT 36 (AAC)
57 Reg 20(2)-(6) HB&CTB(DA) Regs
58 Reg 20(6) HB&CTB(DA) Regs
59 Reg 20(7) HB&CTB(DA) Regs
60 para C7/7.128-29 GM
61 Reg 20(8) HB&CTB(DA) Regs
62 rr4 and 7(2) TP(FT) Rules; Practice
    Statement: *Delegation of Functions to
    Staff in Relation to the Social Entitlement
    Chamber of the First-tier Tribunal on or
    after 1 October 2014,* 25 September
    2014, paras 5-7
63 r4(3) TP(FT) Rules

3. **After you send or deliver your appeal**

64 *DTM v Kettering BC (CTB)* [2013] UKUT
    625 (AAC)
65 r24(1A) TP(FT) Rules; Art 6 European
    Convention on Human Rights; s6 HRA
    1998; CH/3497/2005; *MB v Wychavon
    DC* [2013] UKUT 67 (AAC); Complaint
    01/C/13400 against Scarborough BC
66 r24(1)(c) TP(FT) Rules
67 r24(5) TP(FT) Rules
68 r11(6)(a) TP(FT) Rules
69 r24(2) TP(FT) Rules
70 r24(4) TP(FT) Rules; *ST v SSWP (ESA)*
    [2012] UKUT 469 (AAC); *FN v SSWP
    (ESA)* [2015] UKUT 670 (AAC)
71 R(H) 1/07
72 rr5 and 6(1)-(3) TP(FT) Rules
73 r24(6) and (7) TP(FT) Rules
74 r5(3)(a) TP(FT) Rules
75 **HB** Sch 7 para 3(6) CSPSSA 2000
    Other benefits s9(6) SSA 1998
76 **HB** Reg 17(1) and (2) HB&CTB(DA)
    Regs
    CB/GA Reg 27(1) and (5) CB&GA(DA)
    Regs
    UC/PIP/JSA&ESA under UC Reg
    52(1) and (5) UC,PIP,JSA&ESA(DA) Regs
    Other benefits Reg 30(1) and (2)
    SS&CS(DA) Regs
77 **HB** Reg 17(3) HB&CTB(DA) Regs
    CB/GA Reg 27(2) CB&GA(DA) Regs
    UC/PIP/JSA&ESA under UC Reg
    52(2) UC,PIP,JSA&ESA(DA) Regs
    Other benefits Reg 30(3) SS&CS(DA)
    Regs
78 **HB** Reg 17(4) HB&CTB(DA) Regs
    CB/GA Reg 27(3) CB&GA(DA) Regs
    UC/PIP/JSA&ESA under UC Reg
    52(3) UC,PIP,JSA&ESA(DA) Regs
    Other benefits Reg 30(4) SS&CS(DA)
    Regs
79 **HB** Reg 17(5) HB&CTB(DA) Regs
    CB/GA Reg 27(4) CB&GA(DA) Regs
    UC/PIP/JSA&ESA under UC Reg
    52(4) UC,PIP,JSA&ESA(DA) Regs
    Other benefits Reg 30(5) SS&CS(DA)
    Regs
80 para 4 Memo DMG 20/13
81 **HB** Sch 7 para 3(5) CSPSSA 2000;
    r23(2) TP(FT) Rules
    Other benefits s9(5) SSA 1998; Sch 1
    para 5 TP(FT) Rules
82 r2 TP(FT) Rules; r2 TP(UT) Rules
83 *MA v SSWP* [2009] UKUT 211 (AAC)
84 rr5, 6, 8, 15 and 16 TP(FT) Rules; rr5-7,
    8, 15 and 16 TP(UT) Rules

85 s25 TCEA 2007; r7(3) TP(FT) Rules; r7(3) and (4) TP(UT) Rules; *MD v SSWP (Enforcement Reference)* [2010] UKUT 202 (AAC); [2011] AACR 5; *CB v Suffolk CC (Enforcement Reference)* [2010] UKUT 413 (AAC); [2011] AACR 22

86 r16(3) TP(FT) Rules; r16(3) TP(UT) Rules

87 r5(3)(l) TP(FT) Rules; r5(3)(l) and (m) TP(UT) Rules

88 r5(3)(a) TP(FT) Rules; r5(3)(a) TP(UT) Rules

89 r2 TP(FT) Rules; r2 TP(UT) Rules

90 r2(2)(e) TP(FT) Rules; r2(2)(e) TP(UT) Rules

91 rr5, 6 and 15 TP(FT) Rules; rr5, 6 and 15 TP(UT) Rules; *SR v Bristol CC* [2008] UKUT 7 (AAC)

92 r6(4) TP(FT) Rules; r5(4) TP(UT) Rules

93 r6(5) TP(FT) Rules; r6(5) TP(UT) Rules

94 r7 TP(FT) Rules; r7 TP(UT) Rules

95 R(H) 3/05; CCS/3757/2004

96 *SSWP v HS (JSA)* [2016] UKUT 272 (AAC)

97 CIB/4253/2004

98 r15(2)(b) TP(FT) Rules; r15(2)(b) TP(UT) Rules

99 r6(2) and (3) TP(FT) Rules; r6(2) and (3) TP(UT) Rules

100 r5(3)(h) TP(FT) Rules; r5(3)(h) TP(UT) Rules; *MA v SSWP* [2009] UKUT 211 (AAC)

101 *GC v SSWP (ESA)* [2012] UKUT 60 (AAC)

102 r31 TP(FT) Rules; r38 TP(UT) Rules

103 CDLA/1290/2004

104 CDLA/3680/1997

105 *MA v SSWP* [2009] UKUT 211 (AAC)

106 CDLA/5413/1999

107 CIS/566/1991; CS/99/1993

108 CIS/2292/2000; *DC v SSWP (ESA)* [2015] UKUT 150 (AAC)

109 CIS/6002/1997; *R v Social Security Commissioner ex parte Angora Bibi* [2000] unreported (HC); CIB/1009/2004; CIB/2058/2004

110 CIS/3338/2001; *DC v SSWP* [2014] UKUT 218 (AAC)

111 *MH v Pembrokeshire (HB)* [2010] UKUT 28 (AAC)

112 r8(1), (3)(a) and (5) TP(FT) Rules; r8(1), (3)(a) and (5) TP(UT) Rules

113 *DTM v Kettering BC (CTB)* [2013] UKUT 625 (AAC)

114 r8(5) and (6) TP(FT) Rules; r8(5) and (6) TP(UT) Rules

115 r8(2) and (4) TP(FT) Rules; r8(2) and (4) TP(UT) Rules

116 r8(3)(b) and (c) and (4) TP(FT) Rules; r8(3)(b) TP(UT) Rules

117 *AW v IC and Blackpool CC* [2013] UKUT 30 (AAC)

118 R(IS) 5/94

119 *LS v Lambeth LB (HB)* [2010] UKUT 461 (AAC); [2011] AACR 27

120 rr1(3), definition of 'respondent', and 8(7) TP(FT) Rules; rr1(3), definition of 'respondent', and 8(7) TP(UT) Rules

121 r8(8) TP(FT) Rules; r8(8) TP(UT) Rules

122 *ZB v SSWP (CSM)* [2013] UKUT 367 (AAC); *SL v SSWP and KL (CSM)* [2014] UKUT 128 (AAC); *CW v SSWP and Another (CSM)* [2014] UKUT 290 (AAC)

123 r11 TP(FT) Rules; r11 TP(UT) Rules; CIB/1009/2004; CIB/2058/2004

124 r11(6)(b) TP(FT) Rules; r11(4)(b) TP(UT) Rules

125 r11(6)(a) TP(FT) Rules; r11(4)(a) TP(UT) Rules; *MP v SSWP (DLA)* [2010] UKUT 103 (AAC)

126 s10 Legal Aid, Sentencing and Punishment of Offenders Act 2012

127 **HB** Reg 20(9) HB&CTB(DA) Regs; r17 TP(FT) Rules
Other benefits r17 TP(FT) Rules
All *WM v SSWP (DLA)* [2015] UKUT 642 (AAC)

128 rr4 and 7(2)(a) TP(FT) Rules; Practice Statement: *Delegation of Functions to Staff in Relation to the Social Entitlement Chamber of the First-tier Tribunal on or after 1 October 2014*, paras 3 and 4

129 r4(3) TP(FT) Rules

130 r17(4) and (5) TP(FT) Rules

131 r32 TP(FT) Rules; r39 TP(UT) Rules

132 s26 SSA 1998

133 s26(5) SSA 1998

134 rr5(3)(b) and 18 TP(FT) Rules

4. Hearings

135 r27(1) TP(FT) Rules; *MH v Pembrokeshire CC (HB)* [2010] UKUT 28 (AAC); *AT v SSWP (ESA)* [2010] UKUT 430 (AAC); *MM v SSWP (ESA)* [2011] UKUT 334 (AAC)

136 r11 TP(FT) Rules

137 r21 TP(FT) Rules

138 r1 TP(FT) Rules, definition of 'hearing'

139 r24(6) and (7) TP(FT) Rules

140 *MP v SSWP (DLA)* [2010] UKUT 103 (AAC)

141 r5(3)(f) TP(FT) Rules

142 r29 TP (FT) Rules

143 CH/3594/2002

144 r31 TP(FT) Rules; *WT v SSWP (DLA)* [2011] UKUT 93 (AAC)

145 *AK v HMRC (TC)* [2016] UKUT 98 (AAC)

146 r30 TP(FT) Rules

Part 9: Getting a benefit decision changed
Chapter 55: Appealing to the First-tier Tribunal
Notes

147 *KO v SSWP (ESA)* [2013] UKUT 544
(AAC); *LS v SSWP (DLA)* [2015] UKUT
638 (AAC); *DB v SSWP (DLA)* [2016]
UKUT 205 (AAC)
148 *LS v Lambeth LB (HB)* [2010] UKUT 461
(AAC); [2011] AACR 27
149 CIB/2751/2002; CDLA/1350/2004
150 r1(3) TP(FT) Rules, definition of 'hearing'
151 Practice Direction: *Child, Vulnerable
Adult and Sensitive Witnesses*, 30
October 2008; *SW v SSWP (DLA)* [2015]
UKUT 319 (AAC); *LO'L v SSWP (ESA)*
[2016] UKUT 10 (AAC)
152 s28 TCEA 2007
153 r11 TP(FT) Rules; CIB/1009/2004; CIB/
2058/2004
154 r11(7) and (8) TP(FT) Rules
155 *ZO v SSWP(IB)* [2010] UKUT 143 (AAC)
156 Practice Statement: *Composition of
Tribunals in Social Security and Child
Support Cases in the Social Entitlement
Chamber on or after 1 August 2013*, 31
July 2013
157 *CH v SSWP (ESA)* [2017] UKUT 6 (AAC)
158 *MB and Others v SSWP (ESA & DLA)*
[2013] UKUT 111 (AAC); [2014] AACR 1
159 Sch 4 para 15(6) TCEA 2007; *SB v SSWP
(DLA)* [2013] UKUT 531 (AAC); *PF v
SSWP (ESA)* [2015] UKUT 553 (AAC)
160 *PJ v SSWP (ESA)* [2011] UKUT 224 (AAC);
MB and Others v SSWP (ESA & DLA)
[2013] UKUT 111 (AAC); [2014] AACR 1
161 R(U) 3/88; *JH v SSWP and MH* [2016]
UKUT 158 (AAC)
162 *Gillies v SSWP* [2006] UKHL 2, reported
as R(DLA) 5/06
163 *SSWP v Cunningham* [2004] 211,
ScotCS, reported as R(DLA) 7/04;
R(DLA) 3/07
164 Practice Statement: *Composition of
Tribunals in Social Security and Child
Support Cases in the Social Entitlement
Chamber on or after 1 August 2013*, 31
July 2013, para 12
165 r2 TP(FT) Rules
166 CSDLA/606/2003
167 s20(3) SSA 1998
168 R(IB) 2/06
169 s20(3) SSA 1998; r25(2) TP(FT) Rules;
R(DLA) 5/03
170 CI/3384/2006
171 Practice Statement: *Composition of
Tribunals in Social Security and Child
Support Cases in the Social Entitlement
Chamber on or after 1 August 2013*, 31
July 2013, para 14
172 r25(4) TP(FT) Rules

173 R(DLA) 1/95, qualified by CM/2/1994;
GL v SSWP [2008] UKUT 36 (AAC)
174 *ID v SSWP (PIP)* [2015] UKUT 692 (AAC)
175 R(DLA) 8/06
176 *HI v SSWP* [2014] UKUT 238 (AAC)
177 CM/527/1992; CIB/3074/2003
178 CIB/5586/1999
179 CIB/476/2005; CIB/511/2005
180 ss20(2) and 39 SSA 1998; r25(3) and
Sch 2 TP(FT) Rules; *SSWP v DB (PIP)*
[2016] UKUT 212 (AAC)
181 s20(2A) SSA 1998
182 CDLA/2014/2004
183 *Walsall MBC v PL* [2009] UKUT 27 (AAC)
184 *GL v SSWP* [2008] UKUT 36 (AAC); *HI v
SSWP* [2014] UKUT 238 (AAC)
185 CH/1229/2002
186 *Mongan v Department for Social
Development* [2005] NICA 16, reported
as R3/05 (DLA)
187 **HB** Sch 7 para 6(9)(a) CSPSSA 2000
Other benefits s12(8)(a) SSA 1998
188 *Mooney v SSWP* [2004] SLT 1141,
reported as R(DLA) 5/04; *Mongan v
Department for Social Development*
[2005] NICA 16, reported as R3/05
(DLA); *SSWP v Hooper* [2007] EWCA Civ
495, reported as R(IB) 4/07
189 CSDLA/336/2000; CSIB/160/2000;
R(H) 1/02
190 CH/1229/2002; R(IB) 2/04; *AP-H v SSWP
(DLA)* [2010] UKUT 183 (AAC)
191 CI/531/2000; CDLA/1000/2001; CH/
1229/2002; R(IB) 2/04; CDLA/884/
2008
192 CDLA/4184/2004
193 R(IB) 2/04
194 R(IB) 2/04; CH/3009/2002
195 CDLA/1707/2005
196 R(IB) 2/04; R(IB) 7/04; CIS/1675/2004
197 **HB** Sch 7 para 6(9)(b) CSPSSA 2000
Other benefits s12(8)(b) SSA 1998;
R(DLA) 4/05
198 R(DLA) 2/01; R(DLA) 3/01; CJSA/2375/
2000
199 R(SB) 4/85

5. **Proving your case**
200 r15(2) TP(FT) Rules
201 R(SB) 6/82
202 r16 TP(FT) Rules
203 r15(1)(e) and (f) TP(FT) Rules
204 r15(2) TP(FT) Rules
205 R(SB) 33/85; R(SB) 12/89
206 r15(1)(d) TP(FT) Rules; CDLA/2014/
2004
207 CIB/2058/2004

208 r11(5) TP(FT) Rules; CDLA/1138/2003; CDLA/2462/2003; *SK v SSWP (ESA)* [2014] UKUT 141 (AAC)
209 CIS/4901/2002
210 *Walsall MBC v PL* [2009] UKUT 27 (AAC)
211 R(SB) 1/81
212 *JM v SSWP* [2012] UKUT 472 (AAC)
213 R(DLA) 4/02; CIS/1481/2006; *DG v SSWP (DLA)* [2011] UKUT 14 (AAC); *BS v SSWP (DLA)* [2016] UKUT 73 (AAC)
214 *SSWP v Cunningham* [2004] ScotCS 211, reported as R(DLA) 7/04; R(DLA) 3/07
215 *Pepper v Hart* [1992] UKHL 3, 26 November 1992, 3 WLR 1032, *The Times,* 30 November 1992
216 European Equal Treatment Directive (Directive 79/7)
217 s3(1) HRA 1998
218 *Leeds CC v Price* [2006] UKHL 10
219 R(I) 12/75; *Dorset Healthcare Trust v MH* [2009] UKUT 4 (AAC)
220 R(SB) 22/86
221 R(I) 12/75; *Dorset Healthcare Trust v MH* [2009] UKUT 4 (AAC)
222 *CSBO v Leary*, reported as R(SB) 6/85; see generally CS/140/1991
223 R(G) 3/62; R(U) 4/88
224 R(U) 4/88
225 *Nancollas v Insurance Officer* [1985] 1 All ER 833 (CA), reported as R(I) 7/85

6. The tribunal's decision
226 r33 TP(FT) Rules
227 Art 8 First-tier Tribunal and Upper Tribunal (Composition of Tribunal) Order 2008, No.2835
228 Practice Statement, *Record of Proceedings in Social Security and Child Support Cases in the Social Entitlement Chamber on or after 3 November 2008*, 30 October 2008
229 *MK v SSWP (CI)* [2014] UKUT 323 (AAC)
230 *DT v SSWP* [2015] UKUT 509 (AAC)
231 r34(2) TP(FT) Rules
232 r34(3) TP(FT) Rules; CCS/1664/2001
233 r34(4) TP(FT) Rules; CIB/3937/2000
234 r5(3)(a) TP(FT) Rules
235 r34(5) TP(FT) Rules
236 r38(7)(a) TP(FT) Rules
237 *RU v SSWP (ESA)* [2014] UKUT 532 (AAC)
238 r5(3)(n) TP(UT) Rules

239 **HB** Sch 7 para 13 CSPSSA 2000; reg 11 HB&CTB(DA) Regs
CB/GA s21 SSA 1998; reg 18 CB&GA(DA) Regs
UC/PIP/JSA&ESA under UC s21 SSA 1998; reg 44 UC,PIP,JSA&ESA(DA) Regs
Other benefits s21 SSA 1998; reg 16 SS&CS(DA) Regs
240 r5(3)(l) TP(FT) Rules
241 r36 TP(FT) Rules; CI/3887/1999; CSDLA/168/2008; *AS v SSWP (ESA)* [2011] UKUT 159 (AAC)
242 r37(1) and (2) TP(FT) Rules
243 r37(3) TP(FT) Rules
244 r5(3)(a) TP(FT) Rules
245 r27(2) TP(FT) Rules; CSB/172/1990
246 CIB/4193/2003
247 CI/79/1990; CIS/373/1994
248 *LS v Lambeth LB (HB)* [2010] UKUT 461 (AAC); [2011] AACR 27
249 r38(3) and (4) TP(FT) Rules
250 r41 TP(FT) Rules
251 **HB** Sch 7 para 7(3) and (4) CSPSSA 2000
Other benefits s13(3) and (4) SSA 1998

Chapter 56

Appealing to the Upper Tribunal and the courts

This chapter covers:
1. Appealing to the Upper Tribunal (below)
2. How to appeal (p1365)
3. After you get permission to appeal (p1369)
4. The hearing (p1372)
5. The decision (p1374)
6. Appealing to the Court of Appeal or Court of Session (p1375)
7. Applying for judicial review (p1378)

Key facts
- If your appeal to the First-tier Tribunal is unsuccessful, you may be able to appeal to the Upper Tribunal.
- If your Upper Tribunal appeal is unsuccessful, you may be able to appeal to the Court of Appeal or Court of Session.
- Occasionally, if you cannot appeal, you may be able to challenge a decision by a judicial review in the Upper Tribunal or in the High Court or Court of Session.
- There are strict time limits for appealing and for applying for judicial review. They can sometimes be extended.
- Appeals can take time. If your circumstances change while you are waiting for your appeal to be heard, you may need to make a fresh claim for benefit or seek a supersession.

1. Appealing to the Upper Tribunal

You have a right of appeal against any First-tier Tribunal decision (other than an excluded decision) to the Administrative Appeals Chamber of the Upper Tribunal (called the Upper Tribunal in this *Handbook*).[1] Your appeal is dealt with by a judge (or judges). HM Courts and Tribunals Service (HMCTS) is responsible for the administration of the tribunal's work.

There is only one possible ground for appeal to the Upper Tribunal: that the First-tier Tribunal made an 'error of law' (see below).[2] You must first apply for, and obtain, permission to appeal and there is a strict time limit for applying (see p1367). The DWP, the local authority and HM Revenue and Customs (HMRC) have the same appeal rights as you.

Excluded decisions[3]

'Excluded decisions' are certain decisions taken by the First-tier Tribunal when it considers a review (see p1367) – ie, decisions:
– to review, or not to review, an earlier decision;
– to take no action, or not to take any particular action, in the light of a review of an earlier decision;
– to set aside an earlier decision on review (the decision that is set aside is also excluded);
– to refer, or not to refer, a matter to the Upper Tribunal.

If you have evidence not known by the First-tier Tribunal, it might enable you to ask the DWP (or the local authority or HMRC) for a supersession of the tribunal's decision (see p1289) – and you can do so while your appeal is pending. Bear in mind that the amount of arrears you can get with a supersession is usually limited, so you need to continue with your appeal at the same time.

Note:
- If a test case is pending that deals with issues raised in your appeal, you may find that your appeal is delayed. See p1334 – the rules are the same as for the First-tier Tribunal.
- Some Upper Tribunal decisions can be made by approved legally qualified HMCTS staff (called 'registrars').[4] You can ask an Upper Tribunal judge to reconsider a registrar's decision. You must apply in writing within 14 days after the date you are sent notice of the decision. The tribunal can give you longer (or shorter) than this. There is no guarantee you will be given longer, so keep within the time limit wherever possible.
- You can also apply for a judicial review by the Upper Tribunal of a First-tier Tribunal decision against which you do not have a right of appeal. If you are unsure whether you should apply to appeal against a decision or for a judicial review, you can apply for both. The Upper Tribunal decides which is the proper route.

Error of law

The First-tier Tribunal made an error of law in the following situations.[5]
- It got the law wrong or misinterpreted it – eg, it misunderstood the particular benefit rule concerned. **Note:** if the tribunal gives the reasons for its decision in its decision notice (see p1353) and these indicate that it did not apply the

Part 9: Getting a benefit decision changed
Chapter 56: Appealing to the Upper Tribunal and the courts
1. Appealing to the Upper Tribunal

law correctly, the decision notice is likely to be a more reliable statement of its reasons than a later conflicting explanation in a statement of reasons.[6]

- There is no evidence to support its decision.
- It gave you a physical examination when it was not permitted to do so (see p1340) and based its decision on evidence obtained from this.[7]
- The facts are inconsistent with the decision – eg, the tribunal finds that a man and a woman live in separate households, but decides they are living together as husband and wife.[8]
- It took things into account which it should not have, or refused or failed to take things into account which it should have. However, the tribunal has not necessarily made an error of law if it fails to take account of evidence that was not before it at the hearing – ie, evidence only produced when your appeal is before the Upper Tribunal.
- There is a breach of the rules of natural justice. This includes where:
  - the procedure followed by the tribunal leads to unfairness. However, the judge may say that this is not an error of law if it had no effect on the outcome of the case. Examples of procedural unfairness include if:
    - the person presenting the DWP (or local authority or HMRC) case (the presenting officer) is allowed to be in the room with the tribunal members without you;[9] *or*
    - you are not allowed to call witnesses who are likely to be able to give relevant evidence to support you; *or*
    - the tribunal has unreasonably refused to postpone or adjourn a hearing (see p1328), even though you notified it that you could not attend and had a good reason; *or*
    - the tribunal failed to act on a request for an interpreter and, as a result, it was unable to understand your evidence correctly;[10] *or*
    - the standard of interpretation is not adequate and the tribunal does not take appropriate action;[11] *or*
    - the tribunal pressures you into giving up your right to a fair hearing – eg, it bargains with you by 'offering' you one component of disability living allowance if you agree not to argue for the other;[12]
  - you did not get notice of the hearing through no fault of your own and so you lost without having a chance to put your case properly, even if you could have applied for the tribunal's decision to be set aside instead;[13]
  - you (or the DWP, the local authority or HMRC) asked for an oral hearing but one did not take place;[14]
  - you did not receive the decision maker's response or receive it in sufficient time before the hearing, or advance notice of documentary evidence that you had not seen before, and were not given an opportunity to read it properly;[15]
  - the tribunal made a decision at a paper hearing that was more unfavourable to you than the one you had appealed – eg, it removed your entitlement to

benefit without warning you or giving you the chance to make representations.[16]

- It does not give proper findings of fact. The tribunal must find sufficient facts to support its decision.[17] It can rely on the summary of the facts given in the decision maker's response (see p1324), but only if these are not in dispute and s/he has covered all relevant issues.[18] If you and the DWP (or the local authority or HMRC) disagree about the facts, the tribunal must explain which version it prefers and why.

- It does not provide adequate reasons for its decision.[19] The tribunal must not simply say what its decision is; it must give sufficient reasons so that you can see why it reached the conclusion it did. It should refer to the main evidence on which it has relied. However, it is not necessarily an error of law if it does not mention every item of evidence put forward. If the summary of the reasons given in the decision notice are inconsistent with those given in its written statement of reasons, this is an error of law.[20] If a delay in writing the reasons indicates that they are unreliable as an accurate statement of the tribunal's reasoning, you can argue that the reasons are inadequate.[21] **Note:** the tribunal does not have to give its reasons for refusing to adjourn an appeal hearing.[22] However, a refusal to adjourn may be so obviously unfair as to constitute an error of law.

Note: the tribunal has not made an error of law simply because a different judge (and members) or the Upper Tribunal might have reached a different conclusion.[23] An appeal to the Upper Tribunal is *not* another opportunity to argue about the facts of the case.[24]

2. How to appeal

You must first obtain permission to appeal to the Upper Tribunal.[25] This means you must show that the First-tier Tribunal has possibly made an error of law (see p1363) and you have the beginnings of a case. There is a strict time limit for applying for permission to appeal. You must first apply to the First-tier Tribunal for permission. If it refuses (or rejects) your application, you can then apply for permission directly to the Upper Tribunal.

Applying to the First-tier Tribunal

You must apply for permission to appeal, in the first instance, to the First-tier Tribunal.[26] You must usually have a statement of reasons for its decision (see p1353). You may find it difficult to show that it made an error of law without one.
    Your application for permission to appeal must:[27]
- be in writing; *and*

Part 9: Getting a benefit decision changed
Chapter 56: Appealing to the Upper Tribunal and the courts
2. How to appeal

- contain details of your grounds for appeal (ie, the error(s) of law you think the tribunal made) and sufficient information about the decision for it to be identified. If you are making a late application, you must also give your reasons for this; *and*
- state the result you are seeking – eg, say what you think the tribunal's decision should have been, or how it should have dealt with your appeal.

Bear in mind that the person considering your application is often the same judge who decided your appeal, although this is not always the case.[28] Applications for permission to appeal are normally decided without a hearing, so make sure you give a full explanation of your grounds for appeal when you apply.[29]

If you do not have a statement of reasons for the tribunal's decision – eg, because you did not apply for one, or one has not been provided:[30]

- the First-tier Tribunal must treat your application for permission to appeal as an application for a statement of reasons. Unless it decides to give you permission to appeal, you must then seek permission to appeal again once the statement of reasons is provided; *and*
- if your application for a statement of reasons is (or has been) refused because of a delay in making the application (ie, you missed the time limit), the First-tier Tribunal can only allow your application for permission to appeal to go ahead ('admit' it) if it thinks it is in the interests of justice.[31] It then decides whether or not to give you permission. If it refuses to admit your application or to give you permission, you can still apply directly to the Upper Tribunal for permission.

The First-tier Tribunal must send you a record of its decision on your application as soon as practicable.[32] If your application (or a ground for appeal) is refused, you must also be sent a statement of reasons for the refusal and notice of your right to make a fresh application to the Upper Tribunal for permission to appeal, along with information about how to apply, and the time limit for doing so. You should study the First-tier Tribunal's reasons for refusal carefully; be prepared to rethink your arguments before applying to the Upper Tribunal.

Note:

- If you, or the DWP, the local authority or HM Revenue and Customs (HMRC) apply for permission to appeal to the Upper Tribunal, the First-tier Tribunal can:
  - review its decision (see p1367); *or*
  - treat the application for permission to appeal as an application for the decision to be corrected or set aside.[33]
- If you and the DWP (or the local authority or HMRC) agree that the First-tier Tribunal made an error of law, its decision *must* be set aside (see p1356).

Time limit for applying

Your application for permission to appeal must be received by the First-tier Tribunal no later than one month (see p1318) after the latest of the following dates – ie, the date you were sent:[34]

- the decision notice; *or*
- a written statement of reasons (see p1353) for the tribunal's decision. See p1366 if you do not have a statement of reasons; *or*
- notice that, following a review (see below), the reasons for the tribunal's decision were amended, or the decision was corrected; *or*
- notice that an application for the tribunal's decision to be set aside (see p1355) was unsuccessful, but only if you applied for the decision to be set aside within the time limit.

The First-tier Tribunal can extend (or shorten) your time limit.[35] However, there is no guarantee that you will be given longer, so keep within the one-month time limit wherever possible. There is no absolute time limit for applying. See p1320 for when it might be fair and just to extend your time limit. The issues are the same as for appeals to the First-tier Tribunal.

If your time limit is not extended, the First-tier Tribunal must reject your application.[36] If your application is rejected, you can still apply directly to the Upper Tribunal for permission (see p1368). However, it can only allow your application if it considers it is in the interests of justice to do so.[37]

When the First-tier Tribunal can review its decision

When the First-tier Tribunal receives an application for permission to appeal to the Upper Tribunal, it must first consider whether to review its decision.[38] You do not have a right to apply for a review yourself, but if you do, your application can be treated as an application for permission to appeal.[39]

The First-tier Tribunal can only review a decision if it is satisfied that there is an error of law in it (see p1363).[40] This means that if the DWP (or the local authority or HMRC) has applied for permission to appeal, you have the chance to say why the decision should not be changed. If it *does* review the decision, it can:[41]

- correct any accidental errors in the decision or the record of the decision; *and*
- amend the reasons given for the decision – eg, if it considered matters, but inadvertently did not include them in the statement of reasons. However, the tribunal should not add reasons which were not part of its thinking at the time it made its decision;[42] *and*
- 'set aside' the decision. This means the decision is cancelled. The tribunal must then either make a new decision or refer your appeal to the Upper Tribunal to make a decision.

You must be notified in writing of the outcome of the review and your right of appeal (if any).[43] If the First-tier Tribunal has taken any action and you were not

Part 9: Getting a benefit decision changed
Chapter 56: Appealing to the Upper Tribunal and the courts
2. How to appeal

given an opportunity to comment before the review, you must also be notified that you can apply for the action to be cancelled and for the decision to be reviewed again.[44]

If the First-tier Tribunal decides not to review its decision, or reviews it but takes no action, it must consider whether to give you permission to appeal to the Upper Tribunal against the decision.[45]

Applying to the Upper Tribunal

Before you can apply to the Upper Tribunal for permission to appeal, you must first apply to the First-tier Tribunal.[46] If the First-tier Tribunal refuses you permission or rejects your application (eg, because it was late), you may make a fresh application to the Upper Tribunal. You must apply in writing.

Forms

Use Form UT1 (Social Entitlement), available from the regional office of HM Courts and Tribunals Servive (HMCTS), the Upper Tribunal Office (see Appendix 1) or at http://hmctsformfinder.justice.gov.uk/HMCTS/FormFinder.do.

Your application must include:[47]
- your name and address and the name and address of your representative (if any). You must also give the address where documents can be sent or delivered;
- details of the decision you want to appeal;
- the grounds for your appeal – ie, the error(s) of law you think the First-tier Tribunal made;
- if your application is late, a request for your time limit to be extended and the reasons why you are applying late;
- whether you want your application to be dealt with at an oral hearing;
- copies of the First-tier Tribunal's decision, its statement of reasons (if you have one – see p1369) and the notice of its refusal or rejection of your application for permission. If your application to the First-tier Tribunal was rejected because it (or your application for a statement of reasons) was late, you must also include the reasons for the lateness.

The Upper Tribunal can waive any irregularities in your application that concern a failure to comply with the rules.[48] If your application to the First-tier Tribunal for permission to appeal was rejected, either because it was late or your application for a statement of reasons was late, the Upper Tribunal can only allow your application if it thinks it is in the interests of justice to do so.[49]

If you do not have a statement of reasons for the First-tier Tribunal's decision, you are not prevented from applying to the Upper Tribunal for permission to appeal. However, you must still show that the First-tier Tribunal made an error of law (see p1363) without it – eg, if what is said in the decision notice is sufficient to do so.[50] It is an error of law if the First-tier Tribunal fails to provide a statement of reasons where it has a duty to do so – eg, you apply for one in time, but the tribunal says your application was late and refuses to provide one.[51]

You can send your application to the Upper Tribunal office by post, fax or document exchange, or deliver it in person. You can also send it by other methods (eg, email) if you have been given permission by the tribunal.[52]

The Upper Tribunal Office obtains the file of your appeal papers from the regional office of HMCTS. The tribunal considers these as well as what you say in your application before reaching a decision. The DWP (or the local authority or HMRC) normally plays no part in the procedure at this stage. However, the tribunal sometimes asks the DWP (or the local authority or HMRC) to make a submission in cases of particular difficulty. If this happens, you are given an opportunity to reply.

You are sent a written notice of the tribunal's decision on your application, including the reasons for the decision.[53] You cannot appeal against a refusal to grant you permission to appeal, but you might be able to apply for the decision to be set aside (see p1374) or to a court for judicial review (see p1379).[54]

Time limit for applying

Your application for permission to appeal must be received by the Upper Tribunal no later than one month (see p1318) after the date the First-tier Tribunal's refusal (or rejection) was sent to you.[55] The Upper Tribunal can extend (or shorten) your time limit.[56] However, there is no guarantee that you will be given longer, so keep within the one-month time limit wherever possible. The decision whether or not to allow a late appeal to the Upper Tribunal must be made bearing in mind the merits of the appeal and the consequences for you (and the DWP, the local authority or HMRC).[57]

3. After you get permission to appeal

If you have been given permission to appeal by the First-tier Tribunal, you must send the Upper Tribunal:[58]

- a 'notice of appeal', so that it is received within one month after you are sent notice of the permission. You are sent a form on which to do this; *and*
- if you are sending the notice of appeal late, a request for an extension of time and the reasons why your notice is late; *and*

Part 9: Getting a benefit decision changed
Chapter 56: Appealing to the Upper Tribunal and the courts
3. After you get permission to appeal

- a copy of the notice that you have been given permission to appeal; *and*
- a copy of the First-tier Tribunal's decision and its statement of reasons (if you have one); *and*
- your details; *and*
- your reasons for appealing against the decision.

The Upper Tribunal can extend (or shorten) the time limit for receipt of your notice of appeal.[59] There is no guarantee that you will be given longer, so keep within the time limit wherever possible. See p1320 for when it might be fair and just to extend your time limit. The issues are the same as for appeals to the First-tier Tribunal. If your time limit is not extended, the Upper Tribunal rejects your appeal and it does not go ahead.

Note: if you have applied for permission to appeal directly to the Upper Tribunal on Form UT1, unless you are told otherwise, your application is treated as a notice of appeal. In this case, you do not need to send in another.[60]

What the Upper Tribunal can do

There are procedural rules that the Upper Tribunal must follow when dealing with your appeal. The 'overriding objective' of these is to enable the tribunal to deal with cases fairly and justly.[61] This includes avoiding delay (provided the issues can be considered properly), avoiding unnecessary formality, seeking flexibility in the proceedings and ensuring that all the parties can participate fully. You, the DWP, the local authority and HM Revenue and Customs (HMRC) must help the tribunal further the objective and co-operate with it. This involves ensuring, as far as possible, that your case is ready by the time of any hearing.[62] The rules are generally the same as for the First-tier Tribunal, so where relevant, we refer to those rules below.

The Upper Tribunal can:[63]
- extend or shorten any time limits (see p1327). For the rules about extending your time limit for applying for permission to appeal, see p1367 and p1369;
- issue directions (see p1328);
- postpone or adjourn your appeal hearing (see p1328);
- strike out an appeal (see p1330). **Note:** the Upper Tribunal does *not* have the discretion to strike out your appeal on the grounds that there is no reasonable prospect of success;
- bar people from taking part in an appeal (see p1331). **Note:** *you* can be barred from taking part in an appeal if the DWP (or the local authority or HMRC) appealed;
- require the First-tier Tribunal to provide reasons for its decision, or other information or documents relating to its decision or the proceedings;[64]
- summons witnesses to attend a hearing, answer questions and produce documents. If someone fails to comply, the tribunal can punish her/him for

contempt of court.[65] **Note:** you cannot be required to give evidence or produce any document that you could not be compelled to give by a court;[66]

- suspend the effect of its decision while considering any appeal against or review of that decision. It can also suspend the effect of a First-tier Tribunal decision while an application for permission to appeal against the decision is being considered, and pending the appeal being determined.[67]

Representatives

You can have a representative to help you with your appeal.[68] S/he can explain the procedures, present your case and produce a written submission to ensure the Upper Tribunal is aware of all the relevant issues and the law. You must send or give the tribunal written notice of your representative's name and address, or s/he must do this on your behalf. Unless s/he is a solicitor or barrister, if your representative is providing the notice, s/he should also provide an authorisation signed by you. **Note:** even if your representative acted for you in your appeal to the First-tier Tribunal, you must still authorise her/him to act for you in your appeal to the Upper Tribunal.

Even if you have not previously notified the tribunal that you have a representative, someone can attend the hearing with (or for) you and act as your representative, if the tribunal agrees.[69]

Once you have given notice that you have a representative, s/he is presumed to be acting for you unless you give (or s/he gives) notice in writing that this is no longer the case.[70] Your representative must be sent any documents required to be sent to you; these then do not have to be sent to you.[71] However, do not presume this always happens. If you receive documents, check that your representative has also received them.

Meeting the costs

Free legal help from a solicitor is available in limited cases. This is means tested. If you cannot qualify, you may be able to get free help from a Citizens Advice Bureau, law centre or advice centre.

If you are resident in Scotland, free legal help is currently available for Upper Tribunal appeals, including for help preparing for paper, as well as oral, hearings. **Note:** this may change in the future.

If you are resident in England or Wales, free legal help is available for advice and assistance with appealing to the Upper Tribunal, including applications for permission to appeal that are made direct to the Upper Tribunal (but not applications for permission made to the First-tier Tribunal). You may qualify for help from a lawyer to cover representation at an oral hearing before the Upper Tribunal in very exceptional cases. This only applies if it is necessary to make these services available to you because a failure to do so would be a breach of your human rights or your rights under European Union law.[72]

Part 9: Getting a benefit decision changed
Chapter 56: Appealing to the Upper Tribunal and the courts
4. The hearing

If you are granted funding for legal help, you must send a copy of the funding notice (in Scotland, the legal aid certificate) to the Upper Tribunal Office as soon as practicable.[73] You must also let the other parties involved in your appeal know that you have been granted funding.

Withdrawing an appeal

If you change your mind about appealing, you can withdraw your appeal.[74] However, once you have been given permission to appeal, you must have the Upper Tribunal's consent. You must give notice to the tribunal that you want to withdraw your appeal in writing or at an oral hearing.

If you withdraw your appeal but then decide that you want it to go ahead, you can apply for it to be reinstated.[75] You must apply in writing. Your application must be received by the Upper Tribunal within one month after the date it received written notice that you wanted to withdraw your appeal, or, if you withdraw your appeal at an oral hearing, within one month after the date of the hearing. The tribunal can give you longer (or shorter) than one month.[76] There is no guarantee that you will be given longer, so keep within the time limit wherever possible.

The written procedure

When permission to appeal has been given, the Upper Tribunal Office sends you a copy of the appeal file. You and the DWP (or the local authority or HMRC) are asked for responses and are told the timetable for providing them.[77]

The decision maker is usually asked to provide a response first. You are given the chance to reply. You are usually given one month in which to do so, although the tribunal may extend (or shorten) the time limit.[78] There is no guarantee that you will be given longer, so keep within the time limit wherever possible. If you have nothing to add and do not want to reply at any stage, tell the Upper Tribunal Office.

You may find the decision maker supports your appeal. In this case, the tribunal may give its decision without reasons if you consent to this.[79]

Note: because of the length of time you usually have to wait before your case is dealt with, you should make a fresh claim for benefit (or seek a supersession) – eg, if your circumstances change. However, see p1343 (the issues are similar to those for First-tier Tribunal appeals).

4. The hearing

The Upper Tribunal decides whether or not there should be an oral hearing of the appeal.[80] It must take your views, and those of the DWP, the local authority and HM Revenue and Customs (HMRC) into account. The form you are sent on which to provide your submissions asks you whether you want an oral hearing and, if so, why. The tribunal can decide to hold an oral hearing, even if you have not asked for one. However, it normally only holds one if the case involves complicated issues of law that cannot easily be resolved by written argument. If there is no oral hearing, the tribunal reaches a decision on the basis of the written responses and other documents you (and the DWP, local authority or HMRC) have provided.

If the tribunal decides there should be an oral hearing, you must be given at least 14 days' notice, although you may get less notice than this if you agree, or your appeal is urgent or there are exceptional circumstances.[81]

Oral hearings are usually held in Cardiff, Edinburgh, London or Manchester but can be held in other locations, subject to the needs of the case. Your fares are paid in advance. If you live in Wales, you can give your evidence in Welsh.[82]

A hearing closer to your home can exceptionally be held if you have difficulty travelling because of a disability. A judge decides whether or not to hold a local hearing based on, for example, medical evidence and why a local hearing is needed.

You and your representative may be able to participate in the oral hearing via a video link – eg, if your disability makes it difficult for you to travel, or to avoid travel costs and time.[83] You may also be able to participate in the hearing by telephone or other means of instantaneous two-way electronic communication.

What happens at an oral hearing

Usually, one judge hears your appeal. However, if there is a 'question of law of special difficulty', an important point of principle or practice, or it is otherwise appropriate, two or three judges may hear your appeal,[84] but the procedure is the same. **Note:**

- The tribunal may ask you to provide a summary of the arguments you are going to make (a 'skeleton argument') in advance of the hearing. If it does, you must provide one.[85]
- The hearing is more formal than First-tier Tribunal hearings, but the judge lets you say everything you want to. Judges usually intervene a lot and ask questions, so be prepared to argue your case without your script.
- A full set of Upper Tribunal (and commissioners') decisions and the statute law (see p1347) are available for your use.
- The DWP (or the local authority or HMRC) is usually represented by a lawyer, so you should also consider obtaining representation – eg, from a solicitor, your local Citizens Advice Bureau or advice centre. See p1371 for meeting the costs.

Part 9: Getting a benefit decision changed
Chapter 56: Appealing to the Upper Tribunal and the courts
5. The decision

5. **The decision**

There are two stages to an Upper Tribunal decision.[86]
- **Stage one:** the tribunal decides whether the First-tier Tribunal made an error of law. If it decides that it did, the First-tier Tribunal's decision is normally set aside and no longer has any effect. In a few cases, the Upper Tribunal may decide that the error of law had no practical effect on the outcome of your appeal and so the decision does not have to be set aside.
- **Stage two:** if the First-tier Tribunal's decision is set aside, the Upper Tribunal decides how to deal with the case.
  - If the Upper Tribunal agrees that the First-tier Tribunal's decision was wrong, the case is often sent back to the First-tier Tribunal to hear your appeal again and make a new decision. The Upper Tribunal gives directions on how to reconsider the issues. **Note:** although, in this case, your appeal to the Upper Tribunal is successful, the First-tier Tribunal will not necessarily decide your appeal in your favour. However, you may be able to appeal to the Upper Tribunal again if there is another error of law.
  - If the Upper Tribunal thinks the First-tier Tribunal's statement of reasons for its decision contains all the material facts, or it has been able to make any necessary extra findings of fact, it may make the final decision, which might, or might not, be in your favour.

The Upper Tribunal's decision is usually given in writing, but may be given orally at the hearing.[87] Detailed reasons are given. You must be sent a decision notice as soon as is reasonably practicable, as well as notice of your right of appeal, how to appeal and the time limit for doing so.

If you disagree with the Upper Tribunal's decision

If you disagree with the Upper Tribunal's decision, you cannot simply ask it to look at the decision again – eg, if you have additional points to make. However, the following may be done.
- The tribunal may correct any clerical mistake or an accidental slip or omission in a decision or record of a decision.[88]
- The tribunal may set aside its decision on procedural grounds.[89] This means the decision is cancelled. A decision can be set aside if the tribunal thinks it is in the interests of justice and:
  - you, your representative or the DWP, the local authority or HM Revenue and Customs (HMRC) were not sent papers or other documents relating to the proceedings, or did not receive them at an appropriate time, or the tribunal was not sent them at an appropriate time; *or*
  - you, your representative or the DWP (or the local authority or HMRC) were not present at a hearing; *or*

– there has been some other procedural irregularity.

You must apply in writing for a decision to be set aside. Your application must be received by the tribunal no later than one month after you were sent notice of the decision. The tribunal can extend (or shorten) this time limit. However, there is no guarantee that you will be given longer, so keep within the time limit wherever possible.[90]

- The decision can be superseded by the DWP (or the local authority or HMRC) if there are grounds – eg, if there was a mistake about, or ignorance of, the facts (see p1287). However, if the tribunal made a mistake about the law, you must appeal to a court.
- You or the DWP (or the local authority or HMRC) can appeal to the Court of Appeal (in Scotland, the Court of Session) – see below.
- If you (or the DWP, the local authority or HMRC) seek permission to appeal to the Court of Appeal or Court of Session, the tribunal can review its decision (see p1377).

Note: the Upper Tribunal can treat an application for a decision to be corrected, set aside or reviewed, or for permission to appeal against a decision, as an application for any other of these.[91]

6. **Appealing to the Court of Appeal or Court of Session**

You may appeal against an Upper Tribunal decision (other than an excluded decision) to the Court of Appeal (or in Scotland, the Court of Session). You can only do this if the tribunal made an error of law (see p1363 for what may count) and you must first obtain permission to appeal.[92] The DWP, the local authority and HM Revenue and Customs (HMRC) have the same appeal rights as you.

Excluded decisions

'Excluded decisions'[93] are decisions taken by the Upper Tribunal refusing to grant permission to appeal against a First-tier Tribunal decision and certain decisions taken when it considers a review (see p1377) – ie, decisions:

– to review, or not to review, an earlier decision;

– to take no action, or not to take any particular action, in the light of a review of an earlier decision;

– to set aside an earlier decision on review (the decision that is set aside is also excluded).

Part 9: Getting a benefit decision changed
Chapter 56: Appealing to the Upper Tribunal and the courts
6. Appealing to the Court of Appeal or Court of Session

Permission to appeal to the Court of Appeal or the Court of Session cannot be given unless the Upper Tribunal or the Court of Appeal/Court of Session considers that:[94]

- the appeal would raise some important point of principle (or, in England and Wales, practice); *or*
- there is some other compelling reason for it to hear the appeal.

You should obtain advice before appealing. See p1378 for information about meeting the cost of going to court. Before making any application, get advice about whether you could be liable for the other side's costs.

The procedure in the Court of Appeal/Court of Session is strict, formal and far less flexible than the procedure before the tribunals. The DWP (or the local authority or HMRC) is represented by a solicitor and a barrister.

Note: in England and Wales, if the Upper Tribunal decision involves a point of law of general public importance, in exceptional cases, it can allow you to appeal directly to the Supreme Court, rather than appealing to the Court of Appeal first.[95]

How to appeal

You apply for permission to appeal, in the first instance, to the Upper Tribunal. Your application must:[96]

- be in writing; *and*
- contain sufficient information about the tribunal's decision for it to be identified; *and*
- state the error(s) of law you think the tribunal made. This must be identified clearly;[97] *and*
- if your application is late, include a request for an extension of time and the reasons why the application was not made in time; *and*
- state the result you are seeking – eg, what you think the tribunal's decision should have been.

Your application must be received by the Upper Tribunal within three months after the date you were sent:[98]

- written notice of the decision; *or*
- notice that the reasons for the decision have been amended, or the decision has been corrected, following a review; *or*
- notice that an application for a set-aside has been refused. This only applies if the application for a set-aside was made within the time limit (or any longer period allowed).

The tribunal can extend (or shorten) your time limit for applying for permission to appeal to the Court of Appeal/Court of Session.[99] However, there is no guarantee that you will be given longer, so keep within the time limit wherever possible. If your time limit is not extended, the tribunal must refuse your application.[100]

You must be sent a record of the decision on your application as soon as practicable.[101] If your application (or a ground for appeal) is refused, you must also be sent a statement of reasons for the refusal and notice of your right to apply to the Court of Appeal/Court of Session for permission, along with information about how to apply and the time limit for doing so.

When the Upper Tribunal can review its decision

When the Upper Tribunal receives an application for permission to appeal to the Court of Appeal or Court of Session, it can review its decision if:[102]

- when it made the decision, it overlooked a legal provision, or a court or tribunal decision it was required to follow, which could have had a 'material effect' on the decision; or
- since the decision, a court has made a decision which the tribunal must follow. This only applies if the court's decision could have had a 'material effect' on the tribunal's decision had it been made at the time.

If the tribunal *does* review the decision, it can:[103]

- correct accidental errors in the decision or the record of the decision; *and*
- amend the reasons given for the decision; *and*
- set aside the decision. If it does this, it must make a new decision.

You must be notified in writing of the outcome of the review and your right of appeal (if any).[104] If the tribunal has taken any action and you were not given an opportunity to comment before the review, you must also be notified that you can apply for the outcome to be set aside and for the decision to be reviewed again.

If the tribunal does not review its decision, or reviews it but takes no action, it must consider whether to give you permission to appeal to the Court of Appeal/Court of Session.[105]

If the Upper Tribunal refuses permission to appeal

If the Upper Tribunal refuses you permission to appeal, you can make a fresh application to the Court of Appeal or Court of Session.[106] The tribunal's statement of reasons for the refusal must tell you the relevant court.[107] It tells you the time limit for applying: this is very short, so you should lodge your application as soon as possible.

In England and Wales, the Court of Appeal considers your application for permission to appeal without an oral hearing unless it thinks the application cannot be determined fairly without one.[108] If it refuses you permission to appeal, you cannot appeal further or apply for a judicial review.

Part 9: Getting a benefit decision changed
Chapter 56: Appealing to the Upper Tribunal and the courts
7. Applying for judicial review

In Scotland, the procedures for appealing to the Court of Session are similar to those for England and Wales, but there are a number of differences. The Court of Session hears applications for permission to appeal in open court rather than making the decision simply by reading the papers. The application for permission and the appeal itself can be heard at the same time.

If you get permission to appeal

If you are given permission to appeal by the Upper Tribunal or the Court of Appeal/Court of Session, you must serve a notice of appeal on the relevant parties. There are strict time limits for doing this. Get advice immediately if you are in this position. The DWP solicitor accepts the notice of appeal on behalf of the DWP. The solicitor to HMRC accepts on behalf of HMRC (see Appendix 1 for the addresses). Ask your local authority who accepts the notice of appeal on its behalf.

Meeting the cost of going to court

Free legal help from a solicitor is currently available for appeals on a point of law in the Supreme Court, the Court of Appeal, the High Court and the Court of Session, and you should consider obtaining legal advice and representation for these. Free legal help is means tested. You usually have to pay court fees unless you are eligible for free legal help or you are exempt from paying court fees – eg, because of your financial circumstances. If you want to be represented by a lawyer and do not have free legal help, you also have to pay her/his fees and, if you lose your case, your opponent's costs. Before making *any* application to a court, seek advice about whether you could be liable for your opponent's costs.

7. **Applying for judicial review**

It is possible to challenge decisions by a judicial review in:
- the Upper Tribunal (see below); *or*
- the High Court in England and Wales, or the Court of Session in Scotland (see p1379).

Judicial review in the Upper Tribunal

Occasionally, you can challenge a First-tier Tribunal decision by applying for a judicial review by the Upper Tribunal. You cannot usually apply for a judicial review if you have a right of appeal to the Upper Tribunal against the decision. You may need the services of a solicitor or legal advice centre to apply for a judicial review. Check whether you qualify for free legal help. Before making *any* application, get advice about what you might have to pay.

Note: if you are in any doubt about whether you have a right of appeal against a decision you want to challenge, you can apply for both permission to appeal and for a judicial review. The Upper Tribunal decides which is the proper route.

In England and Wales, you can apply for a judicial review of a First-tier Tribunal decision if it is a decision against which you have no right of appeal to the Upper Tribunal and it is a decision:[109]

- made under any of the First-tier Tribunal procedural rules; *or*
- to review (or not to review) a decision following an application for permission to appeal to the Upper Tribunal (see p1367) or a decision as to what action to take in the light of the review.

You must first apply for permission in writing and must include specified information.[110] You can use Form JR1 which is available from the Upper Tribunal Office or at http://hmctsformfinder.justice.gov.uk/HMCTS/FormFinder.do. You must apply promptly and your application must be received by the Upper Tribunal no later than three months after the date of the decision you are seeking to challenge.[111] Provided you apply promptly, the time limit can be extended to:

- one month after the date you were sent written reasons for the First-tier Tribunal's decision; *or*
- one month after the date you were sent notice that an application to set aside the decision (see p1355) was unsuccessful, provided the application was made within the time limit (or longer period allowed).

In Scotland, you can challenge a First-tier Tribunal decision by a judicial review if it is a procedural decision or ruling, including procedural omissions or oversights.[112] You cannot apply directly to the Upper Tribunal; you must first apply to the Court of Session. If specified conditions are satisfied, your case is then transferred to the Upper Tribunal.[113] The Upper Tribunal then decides whether to give you permission. You must apply within three months of the decision you want to challenge, or such longer period as the Court of Session considers equitable.[114]

Judicial review in the High Court or Court of Session

Judicial review in the High Court or Court of Session is a means of challenging the decisions of any form of tribunal, government department or local authority. For example, you can apply for a judicial review of a decision made by:

- a decision maker, if it is a decision against which you do not have a right of appeal (see p1315); *or*
- the DWP refusing you payment of a budgeting loan; *or*
- a local authority about discretionary housing payments.

You cannot usually go to the High Court/Court of Session for a judicial review if you have another independent means of appeal, such as to the First-tier or Upper

Part 9: Getting a benefit decision changed
Chapter 56: Appealing to the Upper Tribunal and the courts
Notes

Tribunal. You should consider obtaining the services of a solicitor or legal advice centre to apply for judicial review. Check whether you qualify for free legal help (see p1378). **Note:**

- In England and Wales, you must apply to the High Court promptly and you must apply within three months of the decision you want to challenge.[115]
- In Scotland, you must apply to the Court of Session within three months of the decision you want to challenge, or such longer period as it thinks equitable.[116]

You can apply for judicial review of Upper Tribunal decisions. Permission is not normally given if you can appeal the decision to a court.

If the application is for judicial review of a decision refusing you permission to appeal against a First-tier Tribunal decision, you must apply no more than 16 days after you were notified of the Upper Tribunal's decision.[117] Your application is decided on the papers. Permission to apply for judicial review is only given if the case would raise some important point of principle or practice, or if there is some other compelling reason for the High Court/Court of Session to hear it. If it is refused, you cannot ask for it to be reconsidered at an oral hearing.

Notes

1. Appealing to the Upper Tribunal
1 s11 TCEA 2007; *LS v Lambeth LB (HB)* [2010] UKUT 461 (AAC); [2011] AACR 27
2 s11 TCEA 2007
3 s11(5)(d) and (e) TCEA 2007
4 r4 TP(UT) Rules; Practice Statement: *Delegation of Functions to Staff on or after 3 November 2008*, 30 October 2008
5 R(A) 1/72; R(SB) 11/83; R(IS) 11/99; R(I) 2/06
6 CIS/2345/2001; CH/4065/2001
7 CDLA/433/1999
8 CDLA/7980/1995; CH/5221/2001; CH/396/2002; CIB/2977/2002
9 *TA v LB of Islington (HB)* [2014] UKUT 71 (AAC)
10 *DS v SSWP (ESA)* [2013] UKUT 572 (AAC)
11 CDLA/2748/2002
12 CSDLA/606/2003
13 CS/1939/1995; CDLA/5413/1999; CIB/303/1999
14 CDLA/3224/2001
15 CH/3594/2002; *RC (Dec'd) v Maldon DC (HB)* [2012] UKUT 333 (AAC)
16 CDLA/1480/2006
17 *ES v SSWP* [2009] UKUT 6 (AAC)
18 R(IS) 4/93
19 R(DLA) 3/08; *SP v SSWP* [2009] UKUT 97 (AAC)
20 *LA v SSWP (ESA)* [2014] UKUT 482 (AAC)
21 CJSA/322/2001; R(IS) 5/04
22 *Carpenter v SSWP* [2003] EWCA Civ 33, reported as R(IB) 6/03
23 CDLA/1456/2002; R(H) 1/03
24 *Basildon DC v AM* [2009] UKUT 113 (AAC)

Chapter 56

Appealing to the Upper Tribunal and the courts

9

Part 9: Getting a benefit decision changed
Chapter 56: Appealing to the Upper Tribunal and the courts
Notes

100 r44(6) TP(UT) Rules
101 r45(3)-(5) TP(UT) Rules
102 s10 TCEA 2007; r45(1) TP(UT) Rules
103 s10(4) and (5) TCEA 2007
104 r46(2) and (3) TP(UT) Rules
105 r45(2) TP(UT) Rules
106 s13(3)-(5) TCEA 2007
107 s13(11)-(13) TCEA 2007; r45(4)(b)
    TP(UT) Rules
108 r52.5 CPR

7. Applying for judicial review

109 s18 TCEA 2007; Practice Direction by
    the Lord Chief Justice, *Classes of Cases
    Specified Under Section 18(6) of the
    Tribunals, Courts and Enforcement Act
    2007*, 29 October 2008
110 r28 TP(UT) Rules
111 r28(2) and (3) TP(UT) Rules; *CICA v First-
    tier Tribunal and CB (CIC)* [2015] UKUT
    371 (AAC)
112 ss20, 20A and 21 TCEA 2007; Act of
    Sederunt (Transfer of Judicial Review
    Applications from the Court of Session)
    2008, SSI No.357; *Currie, Petitioner*
    [2009] CSOH 145; [2010] AACR 8
113 *EF v SSWP* [2009] UKUT 92 (AAC),
    reported as R(IB) 3/09
114 s27A Court of Session Act 1988
115 r54.5 CPR
116 s27A Court of Session Act 1988
117 r54.7A CPR

9

Chapter 57

Challenging decisions on statutory payments

This chapter covers:
1. Information your employer should provide (p1384)
2. Involving HM Revenue and Customs (p1384)
3. Appealing against the decision (p1386)
4. Appeals to the Upper Tribunal (p1391)
5. Appeals to the courts (p1392)
6. Payment if your challenge is successful (p1392)

This chapter explains the rules for challenging decisions on entitlement to statutory payments. These rules do not apply to challenging decisions on other benefits (except some decisions on national insurance contributions – see p957).

In this chapter, when the term First-tier Tribunal is used, it means the First-tier Tribunal (Tax) and when the term Upper Tribunal is used, it means the Upper Tribunal (Tax and Chancery).

Key facts

- Statutory sick pay, statutory maternity pay, statutory adoption pay, statutory paternity pay and statutory shared parental pay are normally paid by your employer (in some cases, your ex-employer). Your employer should make the initial decision on your entitlement.
- If you disagree with your employer's decision, or your employer has failed to make a decision, you can ask HM Revenue and Customs (HMRC) to decide whether you are entitled.
- You and your employer can appeal against an HMRC decision. You can request that your appeal be decided either by an HMRC review or by the First-tier Tribunal. If you disagree with the HMRC review decision, you can still ask the tribunal to consider your appeal.
- If you disagree with the First-tier Tribunal's decision, you may be able to appeal to the Upper Tribunal. If you disagree with the Upper Tribunal's decision, you may be able to appeal to a court.

Part 9: Getting a benefit decision changed
Chapter 57: Challenging decisions on statutory payments
2. Involving HM Revenue and Customs

Future changes

At the time of writing, the government was consulting on plans for significant changes in the way tribunals consider cases.[1]

1. Information your employer should provide

If you have taken the necessary steps to request statutory sick pay (SSP), statutory maternity pay (SMP), statutory adoption pay (SAP), statutory paternity pay (SPP) or statutory shared parental pay (SSPP) from your employer (see p825 and p848), but your employer decides it is not liable to pay you (or your employer has been paying you SSP, but it decides your period of entitlement has, or is due to, come to an end), it should provide you with details of its decision and its reasons within certain time limits.[2] This also applies to a former employer for SMP, SAP, SPP and SSPP.

For SSP, your employer should normally provide this information on Form SSP1 or on its own computerised form if it contains the same information. For SMP, SAP and SPP, it is normally given on Form SMP1, SAP1 or SPP1 respectively. There is no official form for SSPP. If you have given your employer certain evidence to establish your entitlement, it should be returned to you – eg, Form MAT B1 for SMP (see p825).

For SSP and SMP, you can also request a written statement from your employer detailing, in respect of the period before your request:[3]

- the dates it thinks you are entitled to SSP or SMP, and why it thinks SSP is not payable for other days or SMP for other weeks;
- the daily rate of SSP, or the weekly rate of SMP, to which you are entitled.

For SMP, you also have the right to request this information from a former employer. If your request is reasonable, your employer (or former employer) should provide this information within a reasonable time.

2. Involving HM Revenue and Customs

If you disagree with your employer's decision on your entitlement to statutory sick pay (SSP), statutory maternity pay (SMP), statutory adoption pay (SAP), statutory paternity pay (SPP) or statutory shared parental pay (SSPP), or if your employer has failed to make a decision, you can request that HM Revenue and Customs (HMRC) makes a formal decision on your entitlement.[4] There are time limits for doing so (see p1385).

It can take some time to get a final decision on your entitlement, so consider whether there are other benefits or tax credits which you can claim in the interim (see Chapter 1). However, if you claim employment and support allowance (ESA) while waiting for a decision on your SSP, or maternity allowance (MA) while waiting for an SMP decision, the DWP does not normally make a decision on your claim until HMRC has made a decision on your entitlement to SSP or SMP (because you do not qualify for ESA if you are entitled to SSP, nor for MA if you are entitled to SMP). For this reason, the DWP can request that HMRC makes a formal decision on your entitlement to SSP or SMP, if you have not already done so. If you would qualify for ESA or MA, do not delay claiming or you may lose out financially if the final decision is that you do not qualify for SSP or SMP.

Note: if you are thinking of challenging your employer's decision on your entitlement to a statutory payment, consider how this might affect your employment. You may wish to consult an employment adviser to discuss this.

Applying to HM Revenue and Customs for a decision

Forms

You should normally apply on Form SSP14 (for SSP), SMP14 (for SMP), SAP14 (for SAP), SPP14 (for SPP) or ShPP14 (for SSPP), which can be obtained from, and should be returned to, HMRC's Statutory Payments Disputes Team (see Appendix 1).

Your application to HMRC must be made within six months of the earliest date for which your entitlement to SSP, SMP, SAP, SPP or SSPP is in dispute.[5] If obtaining the correct form means you might miss the six-month deadline, apply for a decision by letter. Your letter *must* contain details of the period in respect of which your entitlement to SSP, SMP, SAP, SPP or SSPP is at issue and the grounds on which your employer is refusing payment if you know them.[6]

If possible, send a copy of Form SSP1, SMP1, SAP1 or SPP1 your employer has given you, or the information your employer has given you about its decision on your entitlement to SSPP, and evidence of your entitlement – eg, a medical certificate (if you have been sick for more than seven days), Form MAT B1, or the 'matching certificate' from the adoption agency. However, do not delay your application if you do not have this information.

Requests for further information

HMRC may contact you for further information and is likely to send a form to your employer to complete.

HMRC can require your employer to provide information relating to your entitlement to SSP, SMP, SAP, SPP or SSPP – eg, your employer's decision on your entitlement and the reasons for the decision. HMRC can impose financial penalties on your employer if your employer fails to provide the information. If your employer fails to comply with requests for information, press HMRC to make its own decision on your entitlement.

Part 9: Getting a benefit decision changed
Chapter 57: Challenging decisions on statutory payments
3. Appealing against the decision

HMRC can request information from you if it is making a decision on your entitlement to SSP or SMP, or from you or your spouse, civil partner or partner if it is making a decision on your entitlement to SAP, SPP or SSPP.[7]

HMRC can impose a financial penalty on you for not providing information or documents that you have been reasonably required to provide to decide your entitlement.[8] However, this is only likely to happen if HMRC believes that you have acted fraudulently or have been negligent.

HM Revenue and Customs' decision

In order to resolve your dispute, HMRC may send both you and your employer a written opinion on your entitlement before it issues a formal decision on your application. If you disagree with this, write to HMRC, explaining why. HMRC may give you a deadline to object to its written opinion before it issues a formal decision. HMRC considers any new information you or your employer have provided and should then issue a formal decision on your entitlement.

In some cases, HMRC sends the formal decision without first issuing a written opinion. The formal decision is legally binding on the employer (see p1392 for the time limits for complying). However, both you and your employer have a right to appeal against it (see below).

Varying or superseding a decision

HMRC can change its own decision by varying or superseding it.[9] It can **vary** its decision if it believes that the decision was wrong at the time it was made. It must tell you and your employer of the new decision in writing. The new decision takes effect from the date that the original decision would have had effect if the reason for the variation had been known. If you or your employer have appealed against a decision, HMRC may vary that decision at any time before the appeal is determined.

HMRC can **supersede** an earlier decision if it has become incorrect for any reason – eg, if your circumstances have changed. The new decision takes effect from the date of your change of circumstances.

If HMRC varies or supersedes an earlier decision, either you or your employer can appeal against the new decision.

3. **Appealing against the decision**

Both you and your employer can appeal against an HM Revenue and Customs' (HMRC) decision.[10] This section assumes that you are appealing, but the same rules apply if your employer has appealed.

Your appeal should be made in writing to HMRC and should include your reasons for appealing.[11] Send your appeal to the Statutory Payments Disputes

Team (see Appendix 1). You have a choice about how your appeal is dealt with (see below).

Time limit for appealing

Your appeal should reach HMRC within the 30 days after the date on which HMRC's decision was issued.[12] This time limit can be extended by HMRC, provided you request this in writing, you have a reasonable excuse for not having made your appeal within the time limit and your appeal was made without unreasonable delay.[13] If HMRC does not accept your late appeal, you can apply to the First-tier Tribunal for permission to appeal late (see p1390). If the tribunal refuses the application, you can appeal to the Upper Tribunal.

Choosing how your appeal is dealt with

You can choose whether you would like your appeal to be decided by the First-tier Tribunal or by HMRC conducting a review. To make this choice, in addition to sending your written appeal to HMRC, you should notify:[14]
- the tribunal in writing that you want it to consider your appeal (see p1389); *or*
- HMRC in writing that you want it to conduct a review. (If HMRC conducts a review and you disagree with its decision you can still apply to the tribunal for a decision on your appeal, provided you apply within the time limits on p1388.)

If, having made your appeal, you do not ask either the tribunal to consider your appeal or HMRC to review its decision, HMRC should write to you, offering to review its decision (called an 'HMRC-initiated review' in this chapter). Before HMRC initiates a review, it may try to settle the appeal (see below). However, until HMRC has issued a notification offering you a review, you can still notify the tribunal that you want it to decide your appeal or inform HMRC yourself that you want it to conduct a review.

Settling or withdrawing your appeal

HMRC can try to settle your appeal at any time before the determination of the appeal. If, before the appeal is decided, an agreement is reached between HMRC and you (if you have appealed) or your employer (if your employer has appealed), the matter is treated as settled by agreement and the appeal lapses.[15]

You can withdraw your appeal at any time before it is decided by notifying HMRC and your employer that you wish to do so. Your employer and HMRC have 30 days to object and, if no objection is made, your appeal will lapse.[16]

Part 9: Getting a benefit decision changed
Chapter 57: Challenging decisions on statutory payments
3. Appealing against the decision

Review by HM Revenue and Customs

Initial view on entitlement

If you have asked for your appeal to be decided by an HMRC review, or if HMRC has initiated a review, HMRC first informs you of its 'initial view on your entitlement'.

If you have requested an HMRC review, HMRC should send you its initial view on your entitlement within 30 days, beginning with the date it receives your written request for a review, although it can send it later than this if this is reasonable.[17] The same rules apply if it is your employer who has initiated the review.

If HMRC has initiated the review, HMRC should send its initial view on your entitlement with its offer of a review.[18] You then have 30 days starting on the date of HMRC's letter to inform in writing:[19]

- HMRC, that you want it to conduct the review (see below); *or*
- the First-tier Tribunal, that you want it to decide your appeal (see p1389). In some circumstances, the tribunal can consider your appeal even if you apply after the 30-day time limit (see p1390).

If HMRC has initiated the review but you neither accept the offer of a review nor notify the tribunal that you want it to consider your appeal within the above time limit, HMRC proceeds as if you have agreed to its initial view on your entitlement and treats the matter as settled by agreement. Notification of this should be sent to you and your employer, and your appeal lapses.[20]

The review

After HMRC has issued its initial view on your entitlement (and, for HMRC-initiated reviews, provided you have accepted HMRC's offer of a review), a review is carried out by an HMRC decision maker who was not involved in making the original decision.

If you disagree with HMRC's initial view, it is important to write to explain why. The decision maker must consider any information you provide, if you provide it at a stage that gives her/him a reasonable opportunity to do so.[21]

HMRC should notify you of its review decision and the reasons for it within 45 days beginning with the date it:[22]

- notified you of its initial view of the matter, if you requested the review; *or*
- received your acceptance of its offer of a review, if HMRC initiated the review.

In either case, these time limits can be changed if you agree.

If HMRC does not notify you of its review decision within this time limit, its decision is taken to be the same as its initial view on your entitlement and HMRC must inform you of this.[23]

If you do not agree with the review decision

If you or your employer do not agree with HMRC's review decision, you may notify the First-tier Tribunal that you want it to consider your appeal. The time limit for doing so is 30 days, beginning with the date of either:[24]

- HMRC's letter notifying you of its review decision; *or*
- if HMRC did not notify you of its review decision within the time limit, the date of its letter telling you it has adopted its initial view on your entitlement as its decision.

In the latter situation, you can appeal before receiving HMRC's letter, provided your appeal is made after the expiry of the time limit for making the review decision.

If you do not notify the tribunal within the time limit, your appeal can only be considered if the tribunal gives permission (see p1391).[25]

Alternative dispute resolution

HMRC states that if either you or your employer have notified the First-tier Tribunal that you want it to consider your appeal, HMRC may invite you to apply for alternative dispute resolution. If alternative dispute resolution is suggested before this, do not delay notifying the tribunal of your appeal as the time limits for notifying the tribunal are not put on hold while you consider or take part in alternative dispute resolution. If alternative dispute resolution is used, an HMRC officer who has not been involved in the decision on your entitlement to SSP, SMP, SAP, SPP or SSPP acts as a mediator to try to resolve the dispute. If you reach an agreement, you and your employer are sent written confirmation and, if it is different from HMRC's earlier decision on your entitlement, HMRC may vary its earlier decision (see p1386). For alternative dispute resolution to be used, both you and your employer must agree to it. If you are offered alternative dispute resolution, get advice.

Appeals to the First-tier Tribunal

You can request that the First-tier Tribunal considers your appeal if:[26]

- you have appealed against HMRC's original decision on your entitlement and want your appeal to be decided by the tribunal, rather than by an HMRC review (see p1386);
- you have appealed and HMRC has initiated a review (see p1388). Rather than accept the offer of a review, you can notify the tribunal that you want it to decide your appeal. See p1388 for the time limits for notifying the tribunal, and p1390 if you miss the time limit;
- your appeal against HMRC's original decision has been decided by an HMRC review and you disagree with the decision or if HMRC has not notified you of its review decision within the time limits. See p1388 for the time limits for

Part 9: Getting a benefit decision changed
Chapter 57: Challenging decisions on statutory payments
3. Appealing against the decision

notifying the tribunal that you want it to decide your appeal and below if you miss the time limit;
- you missed the time limit for appealing against HMRC's original decision on your entitlement and HMRC does not agree to accept your late appeal (but see below).

Notifying the First-tier Tribunal

If you want the First-tier Tribunal to consider your appeal, you must notify it in writing. For details of where to find the time limit for doing so, see above. Your written notice must contain certain information, including the details of the decision you are appealing against, the result you want and your grounds for appealing. If you miss the time limit, you must also ask for permission to make a late application and explain why your request is late.[27]

Use Form T240 'Notice of Appeal (tax)', available from www.gov.uk (search for First-tier Tribunal (Tax) and click on 'forms and further guidance') or telephone 0300 123 1024. Your notice should be sent to the First-tier Tribunal (Tax) (see Appendix 1) either by post or electronically. You must include a copy of the written record of the decision you are appealing against and any statement giving the reasons for that decision (eg, the notification HMRC sent informing you of its decision), unless you do not have this information and cannot reasonably obtain it.

Note: when completing Form T240, be aware that statutory payments are described as 'direct taxes' by HMRC.

Missed time limits

If you miss the relevant time limit for notifying the First-tier Tribunal that you want it to determine your appeal or the time limit for appealing against HMRC's original decision on your entitlement (and HMRC does not agree to accept your late appeal), you can still ask the First-tier Tribunal to consider your appeal. It must give its permission for the time limit to be extended. Although there are no specific rules about when the time limit can be extended,[28] the overriding objective of the rules is to enable tribunals to deal with cases fairly and justly.[29] Whether the First-tier Tribunal extends the time limit depends on the circumstances so give detailed reasons why your appeal is late. As you cannot be certain of success, it is essential to keep within the time limits if you can.

How the First-tier Tribunal decides your case

The First-tier Tribunal allocates your case to be considered in one of four ways.[30] Further details of the procedures can be obtained from the First-tier Tribunal (Tax) leaflet T242 *Making an Appeal Explanatory Leaflet*, available from www.gov.uk (search for First-tier Tribunal (Tax) and click on 'forms and further guidance').

The tribunal can confirm HMRC's decision or change it.[31] It must send you a notice informing you of its decision, which may include its full written findings and the reasons for its decision.[32] If you disagree with the tribunal's decision, you may be able to appeal against it to the Upper Tribunal (see below).

In certain circumstances, you can apply for the First-tier Tribunal's decision to be 'set aside' (there is a time limit for doing so), or the tribunal can correct its own decision.[33] The tribunal can also review its decision if you have applied for permission to appeal to the Upper Tribunal and it considers there was an error of law in the decision.[34]

4. Appeals to the Upper Tribunal

You and your employer can appeal to the Upper Tribunal (Tax and Chancery Chamber) against a decision of the First-tier Tribunal, but only on the grounds that the First-tier Tribunal has made an 'error of law' (see p1363).[35] The rules for making an appeal are almost the same as those for making an appeal to the Upper Tribunal (Administrative Appeals Chamber) described in Chapter 56, although there are differences in the procedure for lodging an appeal and in the time limit for applying. You must first apply to the First-tier Tribunal (Tax) for permission to appeal. Your application must normally be received no later than 56 days after the latest of the dates listed on p1367 (usually the date the tribunal sent you its full written reasons for the decision). In some circumstances, the First-tier Tribunal can give permission for you to appeal later than this.[36] Use Form T247 to apply to the First-tier Tribunal for permission to appeal to the Upper Tribunal (available from www.gov.uk – search for 'First-tier Tribunal (Tax)' and click on 'forms and further guidance').

If you have not been sent the First-tier Tribunal's full written findings and reasons, you must obtain these before applying for permission to appeal. Write to the First-tier Tribunal to request these – your request must be received within 28 days of the date it sent you its decision notice. In some circumstances, this time limit can be extended.[37] If the First-tier Tribunal gives permission for you to appeal, you must submit a 'notice of appeal' and certain other information to the Upper Tribunal within the time limit. For further details, see p1369. Use Form FTC1 available from www.gov.uk (search for 'Upper Tribunal (Tax and Chancery Chamber)' and click on 'forms and further guidance').

If the First-tier Tribunal refuses permission for you to appeal or only gives permission on limited grounds, you can apply to the Upper Tribunal for permission (see Appendix 1). Use Form FTC1. See p1369 for the time limits for applying.[38] If, without a hearing, the Upper Tribunal refuses you permission to appeal or to appeal late, or gives permission to appeal subject to conditions or on limited grounds, you can apply for this decision to be reconsidered at a hearing. An application to do so must be made in writing and be received by the Upper Tribunal within 14 days of the date it sent you notice of its decision, although the Upper Tribunal has discretion to extend this time limit.[39] The Upper Tribunal has

Part 9: Getting a benefit decision changed
Chapter 57: Challenging decisions on statutory payments
6. Payment if your challenge is successful

the power to make an order for costs (expenses in Scotland), so before making any application get advice about whether you could be liable for costs if you lose your case.

See Chapter 56 for further information on Upper Tribunal procedures.

5. **Appeals to the courts**

You and your employer can appeal against the decision of the Upper Tribunal to the Court of Appeal (the Court of Session in Scotland) if the tribunal made an 'error of law' – ie, it interpreted the law incorrectly.[40]

You must apply for permission to appeal, which is only granted if certain conditions are met (see p1376). Your application should normally be made to the Upper Tribunal within one month of the date it sent you written reasons for its decision. This time limit can be extended with the tribunal's permission.[41] See p1375 for further details on appealing to the courts.

6. **Payment if your challenge is successful**

If it is decided that your employer should pay you a statutory payment, your employer should pay you within a certain time limit. If your employer has appealed or is within the time limit for doing so, it does not have to pay you until a final decision is given on appeal, or until the time limit for the appeal or a further appeal has passed. If no appeal against the decision has been made (or if the matter has been finally determined), your employer should pay you on or before the first payday after:[42]

- the day the employer is notified that the appeal has been finally disposed of; *or*
- the day the employer receives notification that leave to appeal has been refused, and there is no further opportunity to apply for leave; *or*
- in any other case, the day the time limit for appeal expires.

If, because of your employer's payroll methods, it is not practical for you to be paid at this time, your employer should pay you on or before your next payday after this date.

If your employer does not pay

If your employer does not pay you within the above time limit, HM Revenue and Customs (HMRC) should pay you (although HMRC states it will first contact your employer to try to get it to pay).[43] Write to HMRC's Statutory Payments Disputes Team (see Appendix 1) asking for payment. This applies even if your employer is insolvent, but only for payment owed for the period before the date of insolvency.

For any period that falls after the date of insolvency, HMRC, rather than your employer, is automatically liable to pay you any statutory payment for which you are eligible.[44]

Notes

1 *Transforming Our Justice System*, Ministry of Justice consultation, 15 September 2016

1. **Information your employer should provide**
   2 **SSP** s130 SSAA 1992; reg 15 SSP Regs
     SMP s132 SSAA 1992; reg 25A SMP Regs
     SPP&SAP Reg 11 SPPSAP(A) Regs
     SSPP Regs 2(2) and 11 SSPP(A) Regs
   3 **SSP** s14(3) SSAA 1992
     SMP s15(2) SSAA 1992

2. **Involving HM Revenue and Customs**
   4 s8 SSC(TF)A 1999
   5 **SSP&SMP** Reg 3 SSP&SMP(D) Regs
     SPP&SAP Reg 13 SPPSAP(A) Regs
     SSPP Reg 13 SSPP(A) Regs
   6 **SSP&SMP** Reg 3 SSP&SMP(D) Regs
     SPP&SAP Reg 13 SPPSAP(A) Regs
     SSPP Reg 13 SSPP(A) Regs
   7 **SSP** Reg 14 SSP Regs
     SMP Reg 25 SMP Regs
     SPP&SAP Reg 14 SPPSAP(A) Regs
     SSPP Reg 14 SSPP(A) Regs
   8 **SSP&SMP** s113A SSAA 1992
     SPP/SAP/SSPP s11(1) and (2) Employment Act 2002
   9 s10 SSC(TF)A 1999; regs 5 and 6 SSC(DA) Regs

3. **Appealing against the decision**
   10 s11(2)(a) SSC(TF)A 1999
   11 s12 SSC(TF)A 1999
   12 s12(1) SSC(TF)A 1999
   13 s49 TMA 1970; reg 9 SSC(DA) Regs
   14 ss49A, 49B, 49D and 49I TMA 1970; reg 7 SSC(DA) Regs
   15 s49A(4) TMA 1970; regs 7(2) and 11 SSC(DA) Regs
   16 Reg 11(5) SSC(DA) Regs

17 s49B(2) and (5) TMA 1970
18 s49C(2) TMA 1970
19 ss49C(3) and (8) and 49H TMA 1970
20 s49C(4) TMA 1970; reg 11 SSC(DA) Regs
21 s49E(4) TMA 1970
22 s49E(6) and (7) TMA 1970
23 s49E(8) and (9) TMA 1970
24 s49G TMA 1970
25 s49G(3) TMA 1970
26 ss49D, 49G and 49H TMA 1970
27 r20 TP(FT)(TC) Rules
28 s49(2)(b) TMA 1970; r20(4) TP(FT)(TC) Rules
29 r2 TP(FT)(TC) Rules
30 r23 TP(FT)(TC) Rules
31 Reg 10 SSC(DA) Regs
32 r35 TP(FT)(TC) Rules
33 rr37 and 38 TP(FT)(TC) Rules
34 r41 TP(FT)(TC) Rules

4. **Appeals to the Upper Tribunal**
   35 s11 TCEA 2007; reg 12(2) SSC(DA) Regs
   36 r39 TP(FT)(TC) Rules
   37 rr5(3)(a) and 35(4) and (5) TP(FT)(TC) Rules
   38 r21(3)(b) TP(UT) Rules
   39 rr5(3)(a) and 22(3)-(5) TP(UT) Rules

5. **Appeals to the courts**
   40 s13(2) TCEA 2007; reg 12(2) SSC(DA) Regs
   41 r44 TP(UT) Rules

6. **Payment if your challenge is successful**
   42 **SSP** Reg 9 SSP Regs
     SMP Reg 29 SMP Regs
     SPP&SAP Reg 42 SPPSAP(G) Regs
     SSPP Reg 44 SSPP(G) Regs

Part 9: Getting a benefit decision changed
Chapter 57: Challenging decisions on statutory payments
Notes

43 **SSP** s151(6) SSCBA 1992; reg 9A SSP
Regs
SMP s164(9)(b) SSCBA 1992; reg 7
SMP Regs
SPP&SAP ss171ZD(3) and 171ZM(3)
SSCBA 1992; reg 43 SPPSAP(G) Regs
SSPP s171ZX(3) SSCBA 1992; reg 45
SSPP(G) Regs
44 **SSP** Reg 9B SSP Regs
SMP Reg 7(3) and (4) SMP Regs
SPP&SAP Reg 43(2) and (3) SPPSAP(G)
Regs
SSPP Reg 45(3)-(5) SSPP(G) Regs

Chapter 58

Complaints

This chapter covers:
1. Grounds for a complaint (below)
2. Compensation payments (p1396)
3. Complaining about the DWP (p1396)
4. Complaining about HM Revenue and Customs (p1398)
5. Complaining about a local authority (p1399)
6. Complaining about HM Courts and Tribunals Service (p1400)
7. Using your MP (p1401)
8. Complaining to the Ombudsman (p1401)
9. Legal action (p1403)

Key facts

- A complaint can be made about any government or local authority department, and anyone contracted to provide a service on its behalf.
- You can complain about a delay in dealing with your claim, poor administration, the behaviour of staff, or the way in which a particular policy or practice has impacted on you.
- It is always best to put your complaint in writing, even if you have to start the process by telephone.
- If your complaint is not resolved, you may be able to complain to an Ombudsman or Adjudicator.

1. Grounds for a complaint

If you are dissatisfied with how you have been treated by a government or local authority department, or someone providing a service on its behalf, you can complain.

You can complain about matters such as delays, discourtesy, poor administration, the behaviour of staff, bad advice, or the way in which a particular department's policy or practice impacts on you. You may be able to complain about other issues if you are unhappy about how your claim has been handled or how you have been treated. You can also ask for compensation for any loss you incur related to your complaint (see p1396).

Part 9: Getting a benefit decision changed
Chapter 58: Complaints
3. Complaining about the DWP

If you disagree with a decision about your benefit or tax credit entitlement, you can usually apply for a revision (review, for tax credits) or appeal (see Chapters 54, 55 and 64).

2. **Compensation payments**

You should expect prompt, courteous and efficient service from staff dealing with your claim. If you are dissatisfied with the way your claim has been administered, you can seek compensation. Compensation payments are discretionary.

The DWP, HM Revenue and Customs (HMRC) and local authorities sometimes pay compensation if you can show that you have lost out through their error or delay and the loss cannot be made good by a revision, supersession or appeal (see Chapters 54, 55 and 64) or by backdating your claim. For instance, if you did not claim carer's allowance because you were misled by the DWP and you could not have the benefit backdated for more than three months, you can claim compensation.

The DWP should automatically consider whether compensation should be paid if you are owed arrears of benefit, but you should still write to your local DWP office and ask. If you do not get a sympathetic response, ask your MP (see p1401) to write on your behalf or to take up your case with the social security minister.

The DWP uses a guide, *Financial Redress for Maladministration: staff guide*, to help it decide when and how much compensation (known as 'extra-statutory' or ex gratia payments) should be paid. The guide is available from the DWP website (see Appendix 1). HMRC has a code of practice, *Complaints* (C/FS), which sets out when it makes compensatory payments.

You should ask for a payment equal to the money you have lost. You can also ask for additional amounts to cover interest on arrears and any extra expenses you had, and to compensate you for any hardship or distress experienced because of the mistake. If your loss was as a clear result of incorrect advice or negligence on the part of the agency, you may be able to bring a court action for damages. Get legal advice promptly if this is the case.

3. **Complaining about the DWP**

The DWP has a complaints procedure that applies to the following agencies:
* the Pension Service;
* Jobcentre Plus;
* the Disability and Carers Service;
* DWP Debt Management.

The Child Maintenance Service and Child Support Agency have their own separate complaints procedures (see CPAG's *Child Support Handbook*).

The DWP does not deal with complaints about contracted providers – eg, Work Programme providers and those carrying out medical assessments on behalf of the DWP. To complain about a provider, use the internal complaints procedure which it is required to have. If you are still not satisfied, you can complain to the Independent Case Examiner (see below) and the Parliamentary and Health Service Ombudsman (see p1402).

If you are thinking about complaining, you can ask your local office for any written information on the standards and levels of service that you can expect, including targets for the time it should take to deal with your claim. The DWP website also has information about standards and complaints. All DWP agencies should also be able to provide you with written details about how to complain.

The DWP's preferred method of dealing with complaints is by telephone. If the DWP cannot contact you by phone, it should respond in writing. You can also request that any response is made in writing. All 'tier two' complaints (see below) should receive a written response.

The DWP has an online complaints service for jobseeker's allowance and universal credit claimants. Complaints concerning these benefits can be made at jsacomplaints.itsshared.net/start.

The DWP has a three-stage internal complaints procedure for its agencies.

- **Stage one.** Normally you should first contact the office that dealt with your claim.
- **Stage two.** If you are still dissatisfied, you can make a 'tier one' complaint and have your complaint passed to a complaints resolution manager. S/he should contact you by telephone within 48 hours of receiving the complaint and update you as it progresses. Your complaint should normally be dealt with within 15 working days.
- **Stage three.** If you remain dissatisfied, you can make a 'tier two' complaint and have your complaint passed to a senior DWP manager who should normally deal with your complaint within 15 working days.

If you are still not satisfied, you can complain to the Independent Case Examiner (see below). You may also have grounds to make a complaint to the Ombudsman.

Further details on the complaints procedure for each agency can be found on the DWP website (see Appendix 1).

Complaining to the Independent Case Examiner

The Independent Case Examiner (ICE) deals with complaints about DWP agencies and its contracted providers. ICE also carries out second-tier reviews of budgeting loan decisions (see p787).

Part 9: Getting a benefit decision changed
Chapter 58: Complaints
4. Complaining about HM Revenue and Customs

ICE's role is to consider whether there has been maladministration. It cannot deal with matters of law or cases that are subject to judicial review or other legal procedures, or cases subject to appeal.

You can only make a complaint to ICE if you have already completed the complaints procedure of the particular agency concerned. This usually means that you have had a response to a tier-two complaint. A complaint should be made to ICE no later than six months after the final response from the agency you are complaining about.

Complaints to ICE can be made in writing or by telephone (see Appendix 1). An appointed representative can act on your behalf. You must provide all relevant information, including the final response to your complaint from the agency you are complaining about.

ICE first considers whether it can accept your complaint and should tell you this within two weeks.

If ICE accepts the complaint, it attempts to resolve it by suggesting ways in which you and the agency concerned can come to an agreement. It aims to resolve complaints in this way within eight weeks. If this fails, ICE can ask for all the relevant information from the parties involved and attempt to settle the complaint. If this is not possible, an investigation is carried out and a formal report prepared, setting out how the complaint arose and how it believes it should be settled. ICE aims to do this within 15 weeks. If you remain unhappy, ask your MP to consider referring your complaint to the Parliamentary and Health Service Ombudsman (see p1402).

If you are unhappy with the way ICE dealt with your case, use its own complaints process.

4. **Complaining about HM Revenue and Customs**

If you want to complain about how HM Revenue and Customs (HMRC) has dealt with your tax credit, child benefit or guardian's allowance claim, or with your national insurance credits or contributions, first raise the complaint with the office dealing with your case, or the named contact person on the letters you have received.

If you are not happy with the response, ask for it to be passed to an HMRC customer service adviser. If you are dissatisfied with her/his response, you can ask that your complaint be reviewed by another customer service adviser.

If you are not happy with HMRC's reply, you can ask the Adjudicator to look into it (see p1399).

HMRC's complaints procedure is set out in its factsheet, *Complaints* (C/FS), available on its website (see Appendix 1).

Complaining to the Adjudicator

The Adjudicator deals with complaints about HMRC and is similar in nature to the Independent Case Examiner (see p1397). The Adjudicator only investigates a complaint if you have already completed the HMRC internal complaints procedure. You cannot complain directly to the Adjudicator about an HMRC-contracted service provider; you must complain via HMRC first. A complaint should be made within six months of the final response from HMRC.[1]

A complaint to the Adjudicator should be made in writing, but can be made by telephone (see Appendix 1). You can appoint someone to act on your behalf by completing a form available from the Adjudicator's Office website. You must provide the final response to your complaint from HMRC.

The Adjudicator first considers whether or not it can accept the complaint. Complaints can be made about delays, inappropriate staff behaviour, misleading advice, the use of discretion or any other form of maladministration. The Adjudicator cannot investigate disputes about matters of law. If it can accept the complaint, the Adjudicator starts an investigation and attempts to resolve the issue by mediating an agreement between you and HMRC. If this fails, it can make recommendations, including that compensation be paid. HMRC has undertaken to follow the Adjudicator's recommendations in all but exceptional circumstances.

Is it worth complaining?

The Adjudicator's *Annual Report* 2016 shows that 80.8 per cent (four out of five) of complaints received about tax credits were upheld in 2015/16. This means that where cases are not resolved using HMRC's internal complaints procedure, a referral to the Adjudicator is more likley to have a successful outcome than not. In all the complaints about HMRC in 2015/16, just under £1 million of write-offs and compensation were recommended.

If you are unhappy with the Adjudicator's response, ask your MP to put your complaint to the Parliamentary and Health Service Ombudsman (see p1402). As well as looking at your complaint about HMRC, the Ombudsman may also look into the way in which the Adjudicator has investigated your complaint. Further information about the Adjudicator can be found on the Adjudicator's Office website (see Appendix 1).

5. Complaining about a local authority

If you are unhappy about the actions of your local authority or someone providing services on its behalf and wish to make a complaint, ask for a copy of its complaints policy. Local authorities are required to have an effective complaints

Part 9: Getting a benefit decision changed
Chapter 58: Complaints
6. Complaining about HM Courts and Tribunals Service

procedure, which should be made available to the public. If you are unable to obtain the policy, write to the supervisor of the person dealing with your claim, making it clear why you are dissatisfied. If you do not receive a satisfactory reply, complain to the principal officer. Send a copy of the letter to your ward councillor and to the councillor who chairs the relevant local authority committee – local authority officers are always accountable to the councillors. If this does not produce results, or if the delay is causing you severe hardship, consider a complaint to the Ombudsman (see p1403) or court action.

Government departments also monitor local authorities, so you could contact your MP or write to the relevant minister – eg, the Secretary of State for Work and Pensions.

If you want to make a complaint about an elected member of a council, you must write to the local authority. In England, the Localism Act 2011 requires all local authorities to promote and maintain high standards of conduct by elected members. How they choose to do this may vary depending on the local authority's policy, and you should ask for its procedure for complaining about members. In Wales and Scotland, elected members of a council are subject to a code of conduct. Complaints about Scottish councillors can be made to the Commissioner for Ethical Standards in Public Life in Scotland who can refer cases to the Standards Commission for Scotland (see Appendix 1). Complaints about Welsh councillors can be made to the Public Services Ombudsman for Wales (see Appendix 1).

6. **Complaining about HM Courts and Tribunals Service**

Complaints about the administration of your appeal

HM Courts and Tribunals Service (HMCTS) provides administrative support to the First-tier Tribunal and Upper Tribunal. If you are dissatisfied with the administration of your appeal, complain to HMCTS. Raise your complaint initially with the person who has been dealing with your appeal. Her/his name and telephone number should be on all the correspondence you have received. Alternatively, you can download a complaint form from the HMCTS website (see Appendix 1). You should receive a response to your complaint within 10 working days. If you are not happy with the response, write to the senior manager at the same office and ask for a review. You should receive a response within 10 working days.

If you think the matter has still not been resolved satisfactorily, appeal to the Communications and Customer Service Team (CCST) at HMCTS (the senior manager who dealt with your complaint should give you contact details). This is not an independent appeal, but an internal review of how the complaint has been handled. It is the final stage of the internal complaints procedure. CCST aims to respond within 15 days.

If you are dissatisfied with the CCST response, you can complain to the Parliamentary and Health Service Ombudsman (see p1402).

The leaflet *Unhappy With Our Service: what can you do?* (EX343) is available from the HMCTS website (see Appendix 1).

Complaints about the conduct of tribunal members

If you are unhappy about the way in which you were treated by a tribunal judge or member (eg, because s/he was rude, discourteous or racist), raise the matter initially by writing to the relevant tribunal president within three months of the incident. The name of the appropriate president is on the Judicial Conduct Investigations Office (JCIO) website (see Appendix 1). You should receive an acknowledgement of your complaint within five working days of its being received. The president then investigates the complaint.

If your complaint is about the tribunal president, it should be made to the Senior President of Tribunals. If it is about the Senior President of Tribunals, it should be made to the Lord Chancellor.

The leaflet *The Tribunal Complaints Procedure* (JCI03) is available at the JCIO website (see Appendix 1).

7. **Using your MP**

If you are not satisfied with the reply from the officers to whom you have written, you may wish to take up the matter with your MP.

Most MPs have 'surgeries' in their areas where they meet constituents to discuss problems. You can get the details from your MP's website or local library. You can either go to the surgery or write to your MP with details of your complaint. To find out who your MP is, contact the House of Commons Enquiry Service on 020 7219 4272 or go to www.parliament.uk.

Your MP will probably want to write to the benefit authority for an explanation of what has happened. If you wish to make a complaint to the relevant ombudsman, you must usually do so through your MP. This does not apply if you are complaining to the Ombudsman about a local authority.

8. **Complaining to the Ombudsman**

The role of the Ombudsman is to investigate complaints of maladministration by government departments, including avoidable delays, failure to advise about appeal rights or refusal to answer reasonable questions or respond to

Part 9: Getting a benefit decision changed
Chapter 58: Complaints
8. Complaining to the Ombudsman

correspondence, discourteousness, racism or sexism. The Parliamentary and Health Service Ombudsman deals with complaints about central government departments and the Local Government Ombudsman (in England) or the Public Services Ombudsman (in Scotland and Wales) hears complaints about local government.

Should you ask for compensation first?

It is probably better to pursue a compensation payment before making a complaint to the Ombudsman. This is because, if the Ombudsman does not uphold your complaint, the benefit authority is unlikely to compensate you. Wherever possible, get and keep receipts for expenses such as postage, phone calls, travel and professional advice to help prove the cost of any delay or maladministration.

The Ombudsman does not usually investigate a complaint unless you have exhausted the internal complaints procedure. However, if the authority is not acting on your complaint, or there are unreasonable delays, this delay may also form part of your complaint. The time limit for lodging a complaint with the Ombudsman is normally 12 months from the date you were notified of the matter complained about. However, a delay in bringing a complaint does not necessarily prevent a complaint being heard if there are good reasons for the delay.

The Ombudsman can look at documents on your claim held by benefit authorities. You may be interviewed to check any facts. The Ombudsman can recommend financial redress if you have been unfairly treated or experienced a loss as a result of the maladministration.

A public body, such as the DWP or a local authority, is required to follow the recommendations of a complaints panel unless there are good reasons not to. If it has failed to do so, you may have grounds to complain to the Ombudsman and, in some circumstances, may have grounds for a judicial review (see p1378).

The Parliamentary and Health Service Ombudsman

The Parliamentary and Health Service Ombudsman deals with complaints about all central government departments. This includes the DWP, HM Revenue and Customs, HM Courts and Tribunals Service (HMCTS) and any agencies carrying out functions on behalf of these departments. Complain for Change is a website launched by The Parliamentary and Health Service Ombudsman to encourage and help people to complain about government departments. In order to make a complaint, you must write to your MP, who then refers the complaint to the Ombudsman. See p1401 for how to contact your MP. Remember, the Ombudsman can only investigate complaints of maladministration and not complaints about entitlement, which should be dealt with by the First-tier Tribunal.

The Local Government Ombudsman/Public Services Ombudsman

If you have tried to sort out your complaint with the local authority but you are still not satisfied with the outcome, you can apply to the Local Government Ombudsman (in England) or the Public Services Ombudsman (in Wales and Scotland). The Ombudsman can investigate any cases of maladministration by local authorities, but not matters of entitlement, which are dealt with by the First-tier Tribunal.

You can complain to the Ombudsman either by completing an online form, by post or by telephone (see Appendix 1). Straightforward cases can be dealt with in about three months. A complaint may make the authority review its procedures, which could benefit other claimants.

One outcome of your complaint may be a 'local settlement'. This is where the local authority agrees to take some action that the Ombudsman considers is a satisfactory response to your complaint and the investigation is discontinued. If you are unhappy with the way in which the Ombudsman has dealt with your complaint, seek legal advice as quickly as possible.

9. Legal action

It is not possible to sue a benefit authority for negligence in the way it decides your claim.[2] However, you can seek compensation through the courts if there has been:

- 'misadvice' – ie, if an employee of a benefit authority or HM Courts and Tribunals Service gives wrong advice which leads to some financial loss for you;
- unpaid benefit – ie, if your benefit claim has been determined, but you have not been paid;
- discrimination, victimisation or harassment under the Equality Act 2010;
- a breach of human rights (see p1349).

Although it is possible to seek compensation through the courts, it should never be your first course of action and should only ever be considered after seeking legal advice.

If a benefit authority refuses to process your claim, you may have grounds for a judicial review. Seek legal advice.

Notes

4. Complaining about HM Revenue and Customs
1 For further details, see CPAG's *Tax Credits and Complaints* factsheet at www.cpag.org.uk/content/tax-credits-and-complaints.

9. Legal action
2 *Jones v Department of Employment* [1989] QB 1

Part 10

General rules for tax credits

Chapter 59

Tax credit amounts

This chapter covers:
1. The relevant period (below)
2. The maximum amount of child tax credit (p1408)
3. The maximum amount of working tax credit (p1411)
4. How to calculate the amount of tax credit (p1420)
5. Change of circumstances (p1425)

Key facts

- The amount of tax credits to which you are entitled depends on your family circumstances and your income.
- There are no limits on the amount of savings or other capital that you can have.
- If you are entitled to income support (IS), income-based jobseeker's allowance (JSA), income-related employment and support allowance (ESA) or pension credit (PC), you are automatically entitled to the maximum amount of tax credits that you could receive.
- If you are not entitled to IS, income-based JSA, income-related ESA or PC, you may receive less than your maximum amount of tax credits, depending on the level of your income.
- Your maximum amount of child tax credit depends on how many children you have, and whether any child in your family has a disability.
- The amount of working tax credit depends on whether you are single with no dependants, a lone parent, or a member of a couple, the hours you work, whether you (or your partner) are disabled, and whether you have eligible childcare costs.

---

1. The relevant period

The amount of tax credits you can receive is based on your entitlement during a 'relevant period'. Tax credit awards are calculated using a maximum *annual* amount that you could receive.

- **If you claim at the beginning of the new tax year,** your award is usually calculated on the basis that you will be entitled to tax credits for the whole of

Part 10: General rules for tax credits
Chapter 59: Tax credit amounts
2. The maximum amount of child tax credit

that tax year (6 April to 5 April), and your relevant period is therefore one year.[1] Your annual entitlement is calculated and then paid to you over the course of that year.

- **If you claim tax credits after the beginning of a tax year**, your award is calculated for a period beginning with the date on which you make your claim and ending at the end of that tax year, unless you can have your claim backdated to an earlier period (see p1459). Similarly, if your circumstances change in the course of the year, and your award is amended, a new relevant period begins. The new relevant period is calculated on the basis that it will end at the end of the tax year.[2] In both cases, you are entitled to tax credits for less than a year, and so only a proportion of the annual amount can be paid.

In order to work out your maximum amount of tax credits exactly, therefore, you must know the length of your relevant period.

Relevant period

A '**relevant period**' for child tax credit (CTC) is the number of days in a period of an award during which your maximum amount remains the same.[3]

A '**relevant period**' for working tax credit (WTC) is the number of days in a period during which the elements making up your maximum amount of tax credit (apart from the childcare element) remain the same and your average weekly childcare charge does not change by £10 or more or reduce to nil.[4]

If you are entitled to both CTC and WTC, a '**relevant period**' is one during which both of the above conditions are satisfied.[5]

---

2. **The maximum amount of child tax credit**

The maximum amount of child tax credit (CTC) you can get is calculated by adding together the 'elements' that apply to you.[6] The amount of each element is set at an annual rate. The annual rate is converted to a daily rate by dividing by the number of days in the tax year (365 in 2017/18) and rounding *up* to the nearest penny. To calculate entitlement, the daily rate of each element is then multiplied by the number of days in the relevant period. The effect of this is that entitlement in a whole year is always slightly higher than the annual rates listed below – eg, the family element (£1.50 x 365) works out as £547.50 in 2017/18. If you are entitled to CTC for a period of less than a year, or if your entitlement changes part way through the year, the amount of each of these elements is adjusted so that the correct proportion of your annual maximum amount is paid to you.[7] How entitlement is calculated when entitlement changes part way through a tax year is explained on p1425.

Element	Annual rate	Daily rate
Family element	£545	£1.50
Child element	£2,780	£7.62
Disabled child element	£3,175	£8.70
Severely disabled child element	£1,290	£3.54

Family element

One family element is payable if you are responsible for a child or young person born before 6 April 2017.[8] The family element is not payable in claims that only include children born on or after 6 April 2017. If you are getting CTC for a child born on or after 6 April 2017, without the family element, and then become responsible for another child born before 6 April 2017, the family element is added from the date you became responsible for the older child. If you are responsible for a child born before 6 April 2017, the family element is still payable, even if you are making a new claim for CTC on or after 6 April 2017. Only one family element is payable, regardless of how many children you have.

Child element

You get a child element for each child or young person you are responsible for (see p184). However, a child element is not payable for a child born on or after 6 April 2017, if you already have two or more children included in your CTC award (unless s/he is covered by the exceptions).[9] This is known as the 'two-child limit'. The limit applies to children who you or your partner are responsible for and who normally live with you (see p184). You get a child element for each child born before 6 April 2017, even if you are making a new claim for CTC on or after 6 April 2017.

The child element can become payable for a third child born on or after 6 April 2017 if an older child leaves the household (so that you are no longer responsible for her/him), or if a young person leaves education (so that s/he no longer qualifies). In these situations, you should report the change as soon as possible so that you continue to get the maximum two child elements. You should always notify the Tax Credit Office of the birth of a third or subsequent child so that the child element can become payable if there is a change, and because other elements for disabled children (see p1410) and childcare costs in working tax credit (see p1414) remain payable.

10

Part 10: General rules for tax credits
Chapter 59: Tax credit amounts
2. The maximum amount of child tax credit

Exceptions to the two-child limit

The two-child limit does not apply in some cases. A child element is payable for a third or subsequent child to whom the limit would apply but who is:[10]

- born in a multiple birth, other than the first born if you already have two or more children in your CTC award;
- living with you on a long-term basis because s/he is unable to live with her/his parents, s/he would otherwise be at risk of entering the care system and you are caring for her/him as a family member or friend;
- being adopted by you from local authority care;
- likely to have been conceived as a result of rape or in a controlling or coercive relationship and you are not living with the alleged perpetrator; *or*
- the child of a parent who is a child or 'qualifying, young person' for whom you are responsible.

See Appendix 14 for more details.

Disabled child element

You get a disabled child element for each child you are responsible for who gets disability living allowance (DLA), or young person who gets personal independence payment (PIP) or armed forces independence payment, or who is certified as blind or severely sight impaired by a consultant ophthalmologist, or was certified in the last 28 weeks. The element still applies if DLA or PIP has stopped because your child or young person is in hospital.[11] It is paid in addition to the child element for that child. You still get the disabled child element for a third or subsequent child born on or after 6 April 2017 who is disabled, but not the child element.[12]

Severely disabled child element

You get a severely disabled child element for each child you are responsible for who gets the highest rate of the care component of DLA, or young person who gets the enhanced rate for daily living of PIP, or armed forces independence payment. The element still applies if DLA or PIP has stopped because your child or young person is in hospital.[13] It is paid in addition to the child element and disabled child element for that child. You still get the severely disabled child element for a third or subsequent child born on or after 6 April 2017, but not the child element.

3. **The maximum amount of working tax credit**

The maximum amount of working tax credit (WTC) you get is calculated by adding together the 'elements' that apply to you.[14] The amount of each element, except the childcare element, is set at an annual rate. The annual rate is converted to a daily rate by dividing by the number of days in the tax year (365 in 2017/18) and rounding up to the nearest penny. To calculate entitlement, the daily rate of each element is then multiplied by the number of days in the relevant period. The effect of this is that entitlement in a whole year is always slightly higher than the annual rates listed below – eg, the lone parent or couple element works out as £2,011.15 in 2017/18 (£5.51 x 365). The amount of the childcare element is set using your average *weekly* childcare costs.[15] See p1414 for how your childcare element is calculated.

If you are entitled to WTC for a period of less than a year, or if your entitlement changes part way through the year, the amount of the elements is adjusted so that the correct proportion of your annual maximum amount is paid.[16] See p1425 for how your entitlement is calculated when it changes part way through a tax year.

Element	Annual rate	Daily rate
Basic element	£1,960	£5.37
Lone parent element	£2,010	£5.51
Couple element	£2,010	£5.51
30-hour element	£810	£2.22
Disabled worker element	£3,000	£8.22
Severe disability element	£1,290	£3.54
Childcare element. For this, see p1414.		

10

Basic element

One basic element is paid with each award of WTC. To be entitled to this element, you must be engaged in 'qualifying remunerative work'. In this *Handbook* we call this 'full-time paid work' (see p196).[17] Unless you qualify for the basic element of WTC, you cannot qualify for any of the other elements.[18]

Lone parent element

You get the lone parent element if you claim as a single person and are responsible for a child or qualifying young person.[19]

Part 10: General rules for tax credits
Chapter 59: Tax credit amounts
3. The maximum amount of working tax credit

Couple element

You get the couple element if you are a couple making a joint claim (see p1450).[20] If you are not responsible for a child or qualifying young person, you cannot get the couple element if your partner is serving a prison sentence of more than 12 months or is a 'person subject to immigration control' (see p1516), but you must still make a joint claim.[21] You can only have one couple element included in your maximum amount.[22] For when you count as a couple, see p1451.

30-hour element

You get a 30-hour element if you are:[23]
- a single claimant who works for at least 30 hours a week; *or*
- making a joint claim and either or both of you work for at least 30 hours a week; *or*
- making a joint claim, responsible for a child or qualifying young person, and:
  - you are both working; *and*
  - one of you works at least 16 hours a week; *and*
  - your joint hours of work total at least 30 hours a week.

You can only have one 30-hour element included in your maximum amount.[24]

Disabled worker element

You get a disabled worker element if you:[25]
- work at least 16 hours a week; *and*
- have a disability which puts you at a disadvantage in getting a job; *and*
- receive, or have recently received, a qualifying benefit for sickness or disability.

If you are claiming as a couple, at least one of you must satisfy all these conditions – ie, the element is not payable if only you are working and your partner is disabled.

If both you and your partner meet all these conditions, two disabled worker elements can be paid.[26]

Having 'a disability which puts you at a disadvantage in getting a job' means you must meet any one of the conditions listed in Appendix 6.[27] For initial claims only (where there has been no entitlement to the disabled worker element in the preceding two years), this can include undergoing a period of rehabilitation as a result of an illness or accident, but only for the remainder of the tax year in which you claim.

In order to count as receiving a 'qualifying benefit', you must satisfy one of the following conditions. A disabled worker element can be included in your maximum amount in a new claim or added to an existing tax credit award at any time during the tax year if you report a change (see p1425). You must:

- for at least one day in the 182 days immediately preceding your claim, have been in receipt of:
  - incapacity benefit (IB) at the long-term or short-term higher rate; *or*
  - severe disablement allowance (SDA); *or*
  - employment and support allowance (ESA) for at least 28 weeks (including linked periods); *or*
  - credits for limited capability for work following time limiting of contributory ESA, for at least 28 weeks (including periods on ESA and linked periods); *or*
  - ESA or credits (as above), together with IB, SDA or statutory sick pay (SSP) for at least 28 weeks (including linked periods); *or*
- for at least one day in the 182 days immediately preceding your claim, have been in receipt of a disability premium paid for you with income support (IS), income-based jobseeker's allowance (JSA) or housing benefit (HB), or a higher pensioner premium with IS or JSA; *or*
- have received for at least 140 days forming a single period of incapacity for work (see p842) or limited capability for work (see Chapter 44) (the last of which must have fallen within 56 days of the date of the claim) SSP, occupational sick pay, ESA, or credits for limited capability for work for a period of 20 weeks; *and*
  - have a disability at the date of the claim which is likely to last for at least six months (or for the rest of your life if your death is expected within that time); *and*
  - have gross earnings that are less than they were before the disability began by at least the greater of 20 per cent and £15 a week; *or*
- have undertaken 'training for work' for at least one day in the 56 days immediately preceding the claim *and* were receiving one of the benefits or credits listed in the first bullet point within the 56 days before that training started. 'Training for work' means training provided under the Employment and Training Act 1973, or, in Scotland, the Enterprise and New Towns (Scotland) Act 1990, or training which you attend for 16 hours or more a week if its primary purpose is teaching occupational or vocational skills;[28] *or*
- receive disability living allowance (DLA), personal independence payment (PIP), attendance allowance (AA), armed forces independence payment or a mobility supplement or constant attendance allowance payable with a war pension or industrial injuries disablement benefit. If your qualifying benefit stops or is not payable (eg, because you are in hospital), you are no longer entitled to the disability element on these grounds;[29] *or*
- have an invalid carriage or similar vehicle; *or*
- have been entitled to WTC with the disabled worker element under one of the above first four bullet points within the last 56 days. This can allow you to remain entitled even though the qualifying benefit stopped some time ago, as long as you still have a disability which puts you at a disadvantage in getting a job. Note that this does not apply if you previously only qualified through DLA

10

Part 10: General rules for tax credits
Chapter 59: Tax credit amounts
3. The maximum amount of working tax credit

or PIP, but if you were getting housing benefit with a disability premium, you can remain entitled even though DLA or PIP has stopped.

Renewals or linked claims

If you make a further claim for WTC within 56 days of the day your previous award ended, *and* in that earlier claim you qualified for the disabled worker element under any of the first four bullet points on p1413, you are treated as though you still meet those conditions and can continue to receive the disabled worker element in your new award. You must also still have a disability which puts you at a disadvantage in getting a job (see Appendix 6 – for renewals and new claims within two years of a previous entitlement to the disabled worker element, this must be under Part 1[30]).

You can still benefit from this linking rule if your income was too high for you to receive any WTC within the previous 56 days, provided your maximum amount of WTC would have included the disabled worker element on one of the above grounds.[31]

Severe disability element

You get a severe disability element if you receive the highest rate of the care component of DLA, the enhanced rate of the daily living component of PIP, the higher rate of AA, or armed forces independence payment (including if payment of these has been suspended because you are in hospital).[32] If you have a partner who meets this condition, a severe disability element can be included for her/him, whether or not s/he is in work.

If both you and your partner meet the condition, two severe disability elements can be paid.[33]

10 Childcare element

Your maximum amount of WTC can include a childcare element to help meet the cost of 'relevant childcare' (see p1416).[34] This element is 70 per cent of your actual childcare costs of up to £175 a week for one child or £300 a week for two or more children – ie, up to £122.50 or £210 a week.[35]

To get the childcare element of WTC, you or your partner must be 'responsible for' at least one child.[36] You can include childcare costs for a third or subsequent child born on or after 6 April 2017, even if you do not get the child element for her/him because of the two-child limit. You do not have to be the child's parent. 'Responsible for' has the same meaning for WTC as it does for child tax credit (CTC) (see p184).[37]

The childcare element is part of the maximum WTC calculation and cannot be claimed on its own or as part of CTC.[38]

You must be:[39]

- a lone parent working at least 16 hours a week; *or*

- a member of a couple; *and*
  - you are both working at least 16 hours a week; *or*
  - one of you is working at least 16 hours a week and the other is incapacitated (see below); *or*
  - one of you is working at least 16 hours a week and the other is entitled to carer's allowance (including an underlying entitlement); *or*
  - one of you is working at least 16 hours a week and the other is in hospital or in prison (serving a sentence or remanded in custody).

You are still entitled to the childcare element during periods throughout which you are treated as being in work for WTC purposes – eg, during the first 39 weeks of maternity leave or the four-week run-on period (see p201).[40]

Incapacitated

You or your partner are treated as '**incapacitated**' if you (or your partner, if s/he is the one who is not working):[41]

– get IB or SDA; *or*
– have been getting contributory ESA for at least 28 weeks; *or*
– get contributory ESA after a period on SSP, which adds up to at least 28 weeks, provided you satisfied the national insurance contribution conditions for contributory ESA (the 28 weeks can have been in one period or in periods that can be linked together); *or*
– get contributory ESA after being transferred from IB or SDA; *or*
– are entitled to credits for limited capability for work only because your contributory ESA has stopped after 52 weeks; *or*
– get AA, DLA, PIP or armed forces independence payment (or an equivalent award paid as an increase under the war pensions or industrial injuries disablement scheme), or would get it but for the fact that you are in hospital; *or*
– get industrial injuries disablement benefit with constant attendance allowance; *or*
– have an award of HB which includes a disability premium or a childcare earnings disregard, because the non-working member of the couple is incapacitated; *or*
– were treated as incapacitated solely on the basis of being paid council tax benefit on 31 March 2013 that included a disability premium because the non-working member of the couple was incapacitated, but only if your entitlement to WTC remains continuous from 1 April 2013); *or*
– have an invalid carriage or similar vehicle.

10

You can claim the childcare element for a new baby as well as for any other children for whom you are responsible while you are on statutory maternity, adoption, paternity or shared parental leave (for the first 39 weeks only), or while you are paid maternity allowance. See p201 for these and other situations when you are treated as being in full-time work.

Part 10: General rules for tax credits
Chapter 59: Tax credit amounts
3. The maximum amount of working tax credit

Relevant childcare charges can be for any child in your family up to the last day of the week in which 1 September falls, following the child's 15th birthday or her/his 16th birthday if s/he is disabled.[42]

Disabled child

'**Disabled child**' means a child or qualifying young person who:[43]

– receives DLA, PIP or armed forces independence payment, including if payment has been suspended because s/he is in hospital; *or*

– is certified as blind or severely sight impaired by a consultant ophthalmologist; *or*

– has ceased to be so certified in the 28 weeks immediately preceding the WTC claim.

Relevant childcare

In England, in order to be 'relevant childcare' the childcare must be:[44]

- provided by a childcare provider correctly registered by Ofsted; *or*
- provided by a childminder who is registered with a childminder agency registered with Ofsted; *or*
- provided to a child who is three or four years old by a school under the direction of the school's governing body (or equivalent) on school premises or premises that may be inspected as part of an inspection of the school by the Chief Inspector; *or*
- out-of-school-hours childcare or supervised activity-based childcare provided for a child aged between five and 15 years (16 if disabled) by a school on the school premises or premises that may be inspected as part of an inspection of the school by the Chief Inspector; *or*
- provided for a child by a person registered with the Care Quality Commission as a service provider in relation to the regulated activity of personal care; *or*
- provided by a foster parent who is also registered with Ofsted, but not in respect of the child who is being fostered by that foster parent.

In Wales, in order to be 'relevant childcare', the childcare must be:[45]

- provided by a childcare provider registered by the Care and Social Services Inspectorate Wales; *or*
- provided by an approved foster parent, who is providing daycare or childminding for a child aged eight or over, but not for a child who is being fostered by that foster parent. If the child is under eight, the foster parent must also be registered by the Care and Social Services Inspectorate Wales; *or*
- out-of-school-hours childcare provided by a school on the school premises or by a local authority; *or*
- provided in the child's home by a person approved under the Tax Credits (Approval of Child Care Providers) (Wales) Scheme 2007 or, if several children are being looked after, in one of the children's homes; *or*

- provided by a domiciliary worker or nurse from an agency registered under the Domiciliary Care Agencies (Wales) Regulations 2004 in the child's home.

In Scotland, in order to be 'relevant childcare', the childcare must be:[46]
- provided by a childcare provider registered by the Care Inspectorate; *or*
- in an out-of-school-hours childcare club registered by the Care Inspectorate; *or*
- provided in the child's home by, or introduced through, a childcare agency, sitter service or nanny agency registered by the Care Inspectorate.

If you use a childcare provider in another European Economics Area country, you can include childcare costs approved under that country's equivalent registration scheme.[47] For Crown servants working abroad, HM Revenue and Customs (HMRC) allows relevant childcare provided by a childcare provider approved under a Ministry of Defence accreditation scheme abroad.

You cannot claim help with the costs of childcare provided in your own home if that care is provided by a relative of your child.

'**Relative**' means parent, grandparent, aunt or uncle, brother or sister, whether related by blood, marriage, civil partnership or 'affinity'.[48] By 'affinity', we understand that HMRC means people who are related through a partner, rather than a spouse or civil partner. For example, if childcare is provided in your home by your partner's mother, she is related to the child by affinity, even if your partner is not the child's parent, and so you cannot claim for the cost of paying her.

You can claim help with the costs of childcare provided by a relative away from your home, but s/he must also be a registered or approved childminder. In practice, it is unlikely that a childminder would be able to remain registered for long if only looking after a child to whom s/he was related – contact the relevant agency for advice in this situation. If approved under the Tax Credits (Approval of Child Care Providers) (Wales) Scheme 2007, s/he must also care for at least one other child who is not related to her/him.[49]

You can only claim for charges that you pay. Some employers offer childcare vouchers of up to £55 a week as a salary sacrifice. If you receive childcare vouchers from your employer, you cannot claim the childcare element of WTC for the amount covered by the voucher, so seek advice on whether you are better off accepting vouchers in exchange for part of your salary. If you do accept vouchers, you may still be entitled to WTC, including the childcare element for any remaining childcare costs not covered by the voucher, and your income for tax credits purposes is the lower amount after the vouchers have been deducted from your salary. HMRC has an online calculator (www.gov.uk/childcare-vouchers-better-off-calculator) to help you work out whether you will be better off. From early 2017, a new 'tax-free childcare' scheme is being introduced as an alternative way of supporting working people on middle and higher incomes with childcare costs (see p854), and employer vouchers will no longer be available to new

10

Part 10: General rules for tax credits
Chapter 59: Tax credit amounts
3. The maximum amount of working tax credit

applicants. If you already get childcare vouchers from your employer, you will have the option of applying for tax-free childcare instead, and an online calculator will be available to assist you. However, you cannot get tax-free childcare and tax credits at the same time, and your entire tax credit claim will end if you apply for and are awarded tax-free childcare payments.[50]

You cannot claim the childcare element for free early years' entitlement or for charges in respect of the child's compulsory education or, in England, for childcare during school hours for a child of compulsory school age. If you will not be making payments for childcare until some time after you have claimed WTC, you cannot receive a childcare element for these until you start making the payments. If you have made an arrangement with a childcare provider to pay childcare costs, you can notify HMRC of these up to a week before the childcare is provided.[51]

The amount of the childcare element

Step one: work out your relevant period

Add up the number of days in your relevant period (see p1407). If you are making a claim for tax credits before the beginning of a new tax year, your award is usually based on entitlement at the same rate for a whole tax year, and your relevant period is one year. The tax year 2017/18 has 365 days.

Step two: calculate your relevant childcare charge

Your '**relevant childcare charge**' is your average weekly charge. The way in which your average weekly charge is calculated depends on whether you pay for childcare weekly, monthly or at some other interval, and on whether the amount you pay varies over time.[52]

- If you pay for childcare on a weekly basis and the charge is a fixed weekly amount, add together the charges in the most recent four weeks before the claim and divide by four.
- If you pay for childcare on a weekly basis, have paid for childcare for at least 52 weeks and the charge varies over time, add together the charges in the 52 weeks before the claim and divide by 52.
- If you pay on a monthly basis and the charge is a fixed monthly amount, multiply that monthly amount by 12 and divide the total by 52.
- If you pay on a monthly basis and the charge varies from month to month, add together the charges for the last 12 months and divide the total by 52.
- If there is insufficient information for HMRC to establish your average weekly charge by any of the above methods, the charge is calculated on the basis of information you provide about your childcare costs, using any method which, in its opinion, is reasonable.
- If you have entered into an agreement to pay for childcare that will be provided during the period of your award, your average weekly childcare costs are

calculated on the basis of your own written estimate of these. In practice, you provide this estimate on your tax credit claim form.

- If you are only paying childcare costs for a fixed period (eg, over the summer holidays), your relevant childcare charge can be averaged and paid over that period rather than over the whole year.

When you have calculated your average weekly childcare charges by one of these methods, round the figure up to the nearest whole pound. This is the figure that you should enter on the claim form or notify to HMRC. If this weekly amount is less than the maximum of £175 a week for one child, or £300 a week for two or more children, your actual childcare costs are used, as in Step three. If your actual childcare costs are more than these limits, the maximum amounts are used, as in Step four. There is no minimum amount of childcare charges that can be included.

Step three: calculate your actual childcare costs for the relevant period

The weekly amount from Step two is converted to an amount covering your relevant period. Multiply the weekly charge by 52 to calculate the annual amount. Divide this figure by the number of days in the current tax year to find the daily rate, and then multiply this daily rate by the number of days in your relevant period. This gives your childcare costs for the relevant period. There is no rounding up or down for actual childcare costs at this stage.[53]

Step four: calculate your maximum eligible childcare costs for the relevant period

The maximum eligible weekly amounts are divided by seven and rounded up to the nearest penny to find the daily rate. This daily rate is then multiplied by the number of days in the relevant period.

Maximum childcare costs	Weekly rate	Daily rate
One child	£175	£25.00
Two or more children	£300	£42.86

Step five: calculate the childcare element for the relevant period

Take the lower of the two figures from Steps three and four, and calculate 70 per cent of that figure. Round the amount up to the nearest penny. This gives your childcare element for the relevant period.

Example

Tracy pays a fixed amount of £200 every week in eligible childcare costs for her two children. Her childcare element for the whole of the tax year is calculated as follows.

Step one: work out her relevant period

Tracy's relevant period is one year (365 days).

Step two: calculate her relevant childcare charge

Part 10: General rules for tax credits
Chapter 59: Tax credit amounts
4. How to calculate the amount of tax credit

Her relevant childcare charge is £200 a week for two children. This is below the maximum of £300 a week, so her actual childcare costs are used.

Step three: calculate her actual childcare costs for the relevant period

£200 x 52 = £10,400

(£10,400 ÷ 365) x 365 = £10,400

Step four is not necessary because actual childcare costs are below the maximum.

Step five: calculate the childcare element for the relevant period

Childcare element is 70% x £10,400 = £7,280

Tracy's childcare element for the relevant period (in this case, one whole tax year) is £7,280.

4. **How to calculate the amount of tax credit**

If you are receiving certain benefits

If you or your partner are entitled to income support (IS), income-based jobseeker's allowance (JSA), income-related employment and support allowance (ESA) or pension credit (PC), you are automatically entitled to the maximum amount of child tax credit (CTC) or working tax credit (WTC). **Note:** this does not apply to WTC during the four-week 'run-on' period after stopping work (see p202).[54] You calculate the maximum amount by adding together the elements of each tax credit for which you qualify over your relevant period, as described on pp1408–19. Your maximum amount is not subject to any reduction during the period you are receiving IS, income-based JSA, income-related ESA or PC, regardless of your income in the rest of the current or previous tax year (but see Chapter 62 if an overpayment is being recovered from your award).

If you are not receiving certain benefits

If you or your partner are *not* receiving IS, income-based JSA, income-related ESA or PC, your entitlement is worked out as described below. **Note:** the rates, taper, disregard and thresholds apply to entitlement in 2017/18. To calculate tax credits entitlement for earlier years, see previous editions of this *Handbook*.

Step one: work out your relevant period

Add up the number of days in your relevant period (see p1407). If you are making a claim for tax credit at the beginning of a new tax year, your award is based on entitlement at the same rate for a whole tax year, and your relevant period is one year. The tax year 2017/18 has 365 days.

Step two: calculate your maximum entitlement for the relevant period

First, identify the different elements of each tax credit for which you are eligible. Take the daily rate (see p20) of each element, apart from the childcare element of WTC.

Multiply this daily rate by the number of days in the relevant period. Add the adjusted amounts of each element together. Next, calculate your childcare element for the relevant period as described on p1418.

Add the childcare element for the relevant period to the other elements for the relevant period to find your maximum entitlement for the relevant period.

Step three: work out your relevant income

The income used in the tax credit calculation is your 'relevant income' (see Chapter 60).

HM Revenue and Customs (HMRC) begins by using your previous tax year's income to calculate your award for the current year. To finalise your entitlement at the end of the tax year, it requires details of your income in the year that has just ended (current year income) and compares this with the previous year's income. If your income has not changed, the current year's income is used. If your income has changed by a disregarded amount or less, your entitlement is still based on the previous year's income. If your income has changed by more than a disregarded amount, your entitlement is based on the current year's income after the disregard. Your relevant income is calculated as follows.[55]

- If your current year's income is more than your previous year's income and the difference is not more than the disregarded amount, your previous year's income is used.
- If your current year's income is more than your previous year's income and the difference is more than the disregarded amount, your current year's income minus the disregarded amount is used.
- If your current year's income is less than your previous year's income and the difference is not more than £2,500, your previous year's income is used.
- If your current year's income is less than your previous year's income and the difference is more than £2,500, your current year's income plus £2,500 is used.

Divide this income by the number of days in the tax year to which your claim for tax credits relates (365 in 2017/18) to find the daily rate, then multiply this by the number of days in the relevant period. Round this amount down to the nearest penny. This is your relevant income. See p1429 for more on relevant income, including if your tax credit award is finalised during the year because you become entitled to universal credit.

Step four: compare your income with the threshold

Find the annual threshold that applies to you.

- If you are entitled to WTC only, the annual threshold is £6,420.

10

Part 10: General rules for tax credits
Chapter 59: Tax credit amounts
4. How to calculate the amount of tax credit

- If you are entitled to WTC *and* CTC, the annual threshold is £6,420.
- If you are entitled to CTC only, and not to WTC, the annual threshold is £16,105.

Divide the threshold that applies to you by the number of days in the current tax year, then multiply this figure by the number of days in the relevant period. Round this amount up to the nearest penny. This figure is your threshold for the relevant period.

Step five: calculate tax credit entitlement for the relevant period

- If your income is less than the threshold that applies to you, you are entitled to receive the maximum amount of tax credit(s).
- If your income is greater than the threshold that applies to you, subtract the threshold figure from your relevant income to find your excess income. Calculate 41 per cent of this excess income and round this figure down to the nearest penny. Finally, reduce your maximum amount of tax credit(s) by this amount.
- The different elements of your maximum tax credit are tapered away in a set order.
  - First, the elements of WTC, except for the childcare element, are reduced.
  - Second, the childcare element is reduced.
  - Third, the child elements of CTC plus any disabled or severely disabled child elements for your children are reduced.
  - Finally, the family element is reduced.

10

If you are entitled to CTC only, or to WTC only, and the calculation results in entitlement of less than £26, no tax credit award is made. If you are entitled to both CTC and WTC and the total entitlement is less than £26, no award is made.[56]

To find out the amount of your weekly payment, divide the above total by the number of days in your relevant period to find the daily rate and then multiply this daily rate by seven. If your tax credit is paid four-weekly, multiply the daily rate by 28 to calculate the amount of your payments.

Example
Tracy claims tax credits at the beginning of the tax year 2016/17. During the tax year 2016/17, she worked 20 hours a week and earned £8 an hour gross. During the tax year 2017/18, she continues to work the same hours, with a small rise in pay.
Step one: work out the relevant period
Tracy's relevant period is 365 days.

Step two: calculate her maximum entitlement for the relevant period

		Daily rate	x 365
CTC	Family element	£1.50	£547.50
	Child element for two-year-old child	£7.62	£2,781.30
	Child element for four-year-old child	£7.62	£2,781.30
WTC	Basic element	£5.37	£1,960.05
	Lone parent element	£5.51	£2,011.15
	Childcare element		£7,280.00
Total maximum amount of tax credit			**£17,361.30**

Step three: work out her relevant income

Tracy earned £8,365.71 during the tax year 2016/17. (She is paid £8 an hour gross and works 20 hours a week.)

((£8 x 20) ÷ 7) x 366 = £8,365.71 (rounded down to the nearest penny)

She continues at the same hours, with a small rise in pay during the tax year 2017/18.

((£8.10 x 20) ÷ 7) x 365 = £8,447.14 (rounded down to the nearest penny)

During the year in which tax credits are paid (2017/18), as the increase is below the disregard, her income for the year 2016/17 is used.

Tracy's income for the relevant period is therefore:

(£8,365.71 ÷ 365) x 365 = £8,365.71 (rounded down to the nearest penny)

Step four: compare her income with the threshold for the relevant period

As Tracy will receive both WTC and CTC, her annual threshold figure is £6,420.

The threshold for the relevant period is therefore:

(£6,420 ÷ 365) x 365 = £6,420 (rounded up to the nearest penny)

Step five: calculate tax credit entitlement for the relevant period

Tracy has excess income of £1,945.71 (income of £8,365.71 minus the threshold figure of £6,420).

Apply the taper of 41 per cent to this excess income:

41% x £1,945.71 = £797.75 (rounded up to the nearest penny)

Tracy's maximum tax credit (£17,361.30) is reduced by this amount. Her total tax credit entitlement is:

£17,361.30 – £797.75 = £16,563.55

The reduction is first applied to the elements of her WTC, apart from the childcare element. Tracy's tax credit entitlement for the tax year 2017/18 is:

WTC (not including childcare element)	£3,173.45
Childcare element	£7,280.00
CTC	£6,110.10
Total tax credits	**£16,563.55**

Tax credits are paid weekly or four-weekly. To find the approximate weekly rate of payment, this figure is divided by 365 (the number of days in Tracy's relevant period) and multiplied by 7.

(£16,563.55 ÷ 365) x 7 = £317.65

Part 10: General rules for tax credits
Chapter 59: Tax credit amounts
4. How to calculate the amount of tax credit

Calculating the amount of tax credits: a quick way

For a rough projection of an award, you can use the annual rates as follows.

Step one: calculate maximum tax credits

Add together the annual rates of CTC and WTC elements to which you are entitled. For the childcare element, multiply 70 per cent of the weekly cost by 52 to give an annual amount.

Step two: work out relevant income

This is either your income in the previous tax year, or an estimate of your current year's income after a disregard, if it has increased or decreased by more than the disregarded amounts (see p1421).

Step three: compare income with threshold

The threshold is £6,420 if you are eligible for WTC only, or to WTC and CTC. The threshold is £16,105 if you are eligible for CTC only – ie, you are not working sufficient hours to qualify for WTC.

If your income is below the threshold, the maximum tax credit in Step one is payable.

If your income is above the threshold, the difference is used for Step four.

Step four: work out tax credits payable

The maximum amount of tax credits in Step one is reduced by 41 per cent of your income above the threshold in Step three. This gives an annual figure for a complete tax year, which can be misleading as circumstances may change. It may be more helpful to divide by 52 to give a weekly income figure.

Note: a new calculation must be made if your circumstances change or if your income goes up or down by more than you estimated.

Example

As in the previous examples, Tracy is a lone parent with two children, working 20 hours a week, earning £8.10 an hour, paying £200 a week for childcare.

Step one: calculate maximum tax credits

Maximum CTC = £545 (family element) + £5,560 (2 x child elements £2,780) = £6,105

Maximum WTC = £1,960 (basic element) + £2,010 (lone parent element) + £7,280 (childcare element £200 x 70% x 52 weeks) = £11,250

Total = £17,355

Step two: work out relevant income

Relevant income = £8,320 (£8 x 20 x 52 weeks in 2015/16)

Step three: compare income with threshold

£8,320 (income) − £6,420 (threshold) = £1,900

Step four: work out tax credits payable

£17,355 (maximum tax credits) − £779 (£1,900 x 41%) = £16,576 tax credits payable for complete tax year = £318.77 a week.

5. **Change of circumstances**

There are different ways in which a change in your circumstances can affect your entitlement to tax credits.

- If your circumstances change in a way that affects your maximum entitlement, a new relevant period begins. For example, if a disability benefit which gives entitlement to a disability element is awarded to you or someone included in your claim, this changes your maximum amount of tax credit and starts a new relevant period.
- Other changes, such as becoming single or part of a couple, bring your award to an end. You must make a fresh claim for tax credits, if you remain entitled. This also starts a new relevant period.
- Changes in income do not affect your maximum entitlement and do not bring your existing award to an end, but can affect the amount of tax credit which is payable to you. For example, if your existing award has been based on your current tax year's income and you have a significant rise in your income during that tax year, you may be overpaid tax credit unless you report the change at once, enabling your award to be recalculated.

See p1462 for more information about how these changes affect your award.

In any of these circumstances, your tax credit award must be recalculated. Work through Steps one to five on pp1420–22, for each relevant period.

Example

Tracy claims disability living allowance (DLA) for her four-year-old child and the middle rate of the care component is awarded from day 201 of the tax year 2017/18. She therefore has two relevant periods during this tax year. The first is 200 days long, and the second, from the date her daughter is awarded DLA, is 165 days long. Two calculations must be done.

The first calculation

Step one: work out the relevant period

Tracy's relevant period is 200 days without the disabled child element.

Part 10: General rules for tax credits
Chapter 59: Tax credit amounts
5. Change of circumstances

Step two: calculate maximum entitlement for the relevant period

		Daily rate	x 200
CTC	Family element	£1.50	£300.00
	Child element for two-year-old child	£7.62	£1,524.00
	Child element for four-year-old child	£7.62	£1,524.00
WTC	Basic element	£5.37	£1,074.00
	Lone parent element	£5.51	£1,102.00
	Childcare element		£3,989.05
Maximum tax credit			**£9,513.05**

Step three: work out her relevant income
Relevant income is (£8,365.71 ÷ 365) x 200 = £4,583.95 (rounded down to the nearest penny)
Step four: compare her income with the threshold for the relevant period
Threshold for the relevant period is (£6,420 ÷ 365) x 200 = £3,517.81 (rounded up to the nearest penny)
Step five: calculate tax credit entitlement for the relevant period
Tracy has excess income of £1,066.14 (income £4,583.95 minus threshold £3,517.81).
41% x £1,066.14 = £437.11 (rounded down to the nearest penny)
Maximum tax credit £9,513.05 reduced by £437.11 = £9,075.94
Tracy's tax credit entitlement for the first relevant period of 200 days is £9,075.94.

The second calculation
Step one: work out the relevant period
Tracy's relevant period is 165 days with the disabled child element.
Step two: calculate maximum entitlement for the relevant period

		Daily rate	x 165
CTC	Family element	£1.50	£247.50
	Child element for two-year-old child	£7.62	£1,257.30
	Child element for four-year-old child	£7.62	£1,257.30
	Disabled child element	£8.70	£1,435.50
WTC	Basic element	£5.37	£886.05
	Lone parent element	£5.51	£909.15
	Childcare element		£3,290.96
Maximum tax credit			**£9,283.76**

Step three: work out her relevant income
Relevant income is (£8,365.71 ÷ 365) x 165 = £3,781.75 (rounded down to the nearest penny)
Step four: compare her income with the threshold for the relevant period
Threshold for the relevant period is (£6,420 ÷ 365) x 165 = £2,902.20 (rounded up to the nearest penny)

Step five: calculate tax credit entitlement for the relevant period
Tracy has excess income of £879.55 (income £3,781.75 minus threshold £2,902.20).
41% x £879.55 = £360.61 (rounded down to the nearest penny)
Maximum tax credit £9,283.76 reduced by £360.61 = £8,923.15
Tracy's tax credit entitlement for the second relevant period of 165 days is £8,923.15.

The final amount of tax credits if you claim universal credit

If your tax credits claim is finalised during the year (see p1471) because you become entitled to universal credit (UC), your income is treated differently. During 2017/18, this may happen if you become part of a couple with someone who is already getting UC, or if you come under the UC system (see p20) and make a claim for it. In this situation, your part-year income up to the date you become entitled to UC is required. Your income in the part year is divided by the number of days in that part year, and then multiplied by the number of days in the tax year (365) to find your 'notional current year income'. This figure is then compared with your income in the previous year, to see if it has increased or decreased by more than £2,500. If your notional current year income in 2017/18 has increased or decreased compared to 2016/17 by more than £2,500, your notional current year income is used, after applying the disregard. Your notional current year income is divided by 365 and then multiplied by the number of days in the relevant period and rounded down to the nearest penny to find your relevant income in the relevant period.[57] See p1431 for more information.

Notes

10

1. The relevant period
1 s5(1) TCA 2002
2 s5(2) TCA 2002
3 Reg 8(2) TC(ITDR) Regs
4 Reg 7(2) TC(ITDR) Regs
5 Reg 8(2) TC(ITDR) Regs

2. The maximum amount of child tax credit
6 Reg 7 CTC Regs
7 Regs 7 and 8 TC(ITDR) Regs
8 s13 WRWA 2016
9 s13 WRWA 2016

10 *Exceptions to the Limiting of the Individual Child Element of Child Tax Credit and the Child Element of Universal Credit to a Maximum of Two Children*, HM Government consultation response, January 2017
11 Reg 8(1) and (2) CTC Regs
12 s13(3) WRWA 2016
13 Reg 8(1) and (3) CTC Regs

3. The maximum amount of working tax credit
14 Reg 20 WTC(EMR) Regs
15 Reg 15 WTC(EMR) Regs
16 Regs 7 and 8 TC(ITDR) Regs

Part 10: General rules for tax credits
Chapter 59: Tax credit amounts
Notes

17 Reg 4 WTC(EMR) Regs
18 Reg 3(2) WTC(EMR) Regs
19 Reg 12 WTC(EMR) Regs
20 Reg 11(1) WTC(EMR) Regs
21 Reg 11 WTC(EMR) Regs
22 Reg 3 WTC(EMR) Regs
23 Reg 10 WTC(EMR) Regs
24 Reg 3 WTC(EMR) Regs
25 Reg 9 WTC(EMR) Regs
26 Reg 3(3) WTC(EMR) Regs
27 For further guidance on the terms used,
    see TCM 0122060
28 Reg 9B WTC(EMR) Regs
29 R(TC) 1/06
30 Reg 9A WTC(EMR) Regs
31 Reg 9(8) WTC(EMR) Regs
32 Reg 17 WTC(EMR) Regs
33 Reg 3(3) WTC(EMR) Regs
34 Regs 3 and 13 WTC(EMR) Regs
35 Reg 20(3) WTC(EMR)Regs
36 Reg 14(1) WTC(EMR) Regs
37 Reg 14(1) WTC(EMR) Regs
38 Reg 20 WTC(EMR) Regs
39 Reg 13(1) WTC(EMR) Regs
40 Regs 5-8 WTC(EMR) Regs; Explanatory
    Memorandum to The Working Tax
    Credit (Entitlement and Maximum Rate)
    (Amendment) Regulations 2009,
    No.1829
41 Reg 13(4) WTC(EMR) Regs
42 Reg 14(3) WTC(EMR) Regs
43 Reg 14(4) WTC(EMR) Regs
44 Reg 14(2) WTC(EMR) Regs; see also
    HMRC leaflet WTC5, *Working Tax Credit:*
    help with the costs of childcare
45 Reg 14(2)(f) WTC(EMR) Regs
46 Reg 14(2)(b) WTC(EMR) Regs
47 *NB v HMRC (TC)* [2016] NICom 47
48 Reg 14(1A)(a) and (1B)(a) WTC(EMR)
    Regs
49 Reg 14(1A)(d) WTC(EMR) Regs
50 s30 Childcare Payments Act 2014
51 Reg 27(2A) and (5B) TC(CN) Regs
52 Reg 15 WTC(EMR) Regs
53 Reg 7(3) TC(ITDR) Regs, steps 7-10

4. **How to calculate the amount of tax**
   credit
54 ss7(2) and 13 TCA 2002; reg 4 TC(ITDR)
    Regs
55 s7(3) TCA 2002; reg 5 TC(ITDR) Regs
56 Reg 9 TC(ITDR) Regs

5. **Change of circumstances**
57 Reg 12A and Sch UC(TP) Regs, as
    amended by UC(TP)(A) Regs

Chapter 60

....

Income: tax credits

This chapter covers:
1. Relevant income (below)
2. Whose income counts (p1433)
3. What income counts (p1433)
4. Notional income (p1446)

Key facts
- The amount of tax credits to which you are entitled depends on how much income you have.
- In general, most taxable income is taken into account and non-taxable income is ignored, but there are exceptions.
- The assessment is based on income for a full tax year, 6 April to 5 April.
- The amount to which you are entitled changes if your income increases or decreases by more than £2,500 in the current year compared with the previous year.
- Your savings or other capital are not taken into account, and you are eligible for tax credits whatever the level of your capital. However, interest and other income earned from savings or capital do count.

1. Relevant income

Tax credits are calculated using your 'relevant income'. The assessment is based on income over a full tax year (6 April to 5 April) except during a time when you are getting income support (IS), income-based jobseeker's allowance (JSA), income-related employment and support allowance (ESA) or pension credit (PC). If the tax credit award only runs for part of the year, the full year's income is reduced on a pro rata basis (see p1421), unless your tax credits claim has been ended because you are entitled to universal credit (UC). Your relevant income is either:

- your income in the complete tax year before your claim (previous year's income); *or*
- your income in the complete tax year of your claim (current year's income) after a disregard; *or*

Part 10: General rules for tax credits
Chapter 60: Income: tax credits
1. Relevant income

- your income in the part of the year up to the date you become entitled to UC, (part-year income) spread over the full year, after a disregard has been applied to it.

Note: while you are on IS, income-based JSA, income-related ESA or PC, you are entitled to maximum tax credits without any income test, so the level of your income in the previous or current year does not matter. When your benefit stops, the tax credit award is again based on relevant income.

Previous year's income

Tax credit awards are initially based on your income in the tax year before the year for which you are claiming. This is referred to as the 'previous year's income'. So, for a tax credits claim made from 6 April 2017, the previous year is 2016/17. The claim form only asks for your income in the previous tax year. Your tax credit entitlement is finalised at the end of the year by comparing this figure with your income in the year of the award (current year's income – see below). Your income can increase or decrease by up to a disregarded amount compared with the previous year without it affecting your final entitlement in the current year. If your income has not changed by more than the disregarded amount, your final tax credit entitlement is still based on the previous year's income. Changes of less than the disregarded amounts do not affect your award until the following year.

If HM Revenue and Customs (HMRC) does not receive any information about a change in your income, your award continues to be based on the previous year's income until the end of the tax year.

Current year's income

Your final tax credit entitlement is based on a comparison of the previous year's income with your income in the year for which you are claiming, known as the 'current year's income'. So, for a tax credits claim made from 6 April 2017, the current year is 2017/18. An annual amount for a complete tax year is required, which you may not know for certain until the end of the tax year, but you can provide an estimate during the year. At the end of the tax year, HMRC finalises your entitlement by comparing your previous year's income with your current year's income, and applying a disregard of £2,500 for an increase or decrease in income. This process is called the 'annual review'.

If your income in the current year (2017/18):[1]
- has not changed since the previous year, the current year's income is used;
- has decreased by £2,500 or less, the previous year's income is used;
- has decreased by more than £2,500, the current year's income plus £2,500 is used;
- has increased by £2,500 or less, the previous year's income is used;

- has increased by more than £2,500, the current year's income minus £2,500 is used.

If you tell HMRC during the year about an increase in income of more than £2,500 compared with the previous year, your award can be revised based on an estimate of the current year's income less a disregard of £2,500. This is advisable if you want to reduce the risk of overpayments at the end of the year.

If you expect your income in the current year to decrease by more than £2,500 compared with the previous year, tell HMRC. It may adjust your award, basing it on your estimate plus £2,500. Tell HMRC quickly if you later think your estimate was too low so it can readjust your award. If you do not, you could end up with an overpayment. HMRC may also use a figure for your earnings it obtains via real-time information from your employer for PAYE (pay as you earn) tax purposes.

You can phone the Tax Credit Helpline or write to the Tax Credit Office with details of your current year's income. There is no special form to fill in so make sure you provide full details of *all* your (and your partner's) relevant income for the current year. At the end of the year, HMRC carries out an annual review and you are usually required to declare your income for the year that has just ended.

Examples

From 6 April 2016 to 5 April 2017, Izzy worked part time and earned a total of £8,000. Since then she has worked full time and expects to earn £12,500 in the current year of the award, from 6 April 2017 to 5 April 2018. Her tax credit award is initially based on income of £8,000. Because her income is expected to increase by £4,500 in the current year (ie, above the £2,500 disregard), her final entitlement is based on an income of £10,000 (£12,500 minus £2,500). She should report this change during the year to avoid an overpayment.

From 6 April 2016 to 5 April 2017, Marsha and Bill, who are claiming as a couple, had a total income of £27,000. In the current year of the award, from 6 April 2017 to 5 April 2018, Marsha stops work and they expect to earn £11,000 between them. Their tax credit award is initially based on the previous year's income of £27,000. Because their income is expected to decrease by £16,000 in the current year (£27,000 – £11,000), their final entitlement is based on income of £13,500 (£11,000 + £2,500). For the next year, 6 April 2018 to 5 April 2019, their award will initially be based on an income of £11,000.

Part-year income

Part-year income is only used if your tax credits claim has ended because you are entitled to UC. This allows your tax credits claim to be finalised during the year, so that you will not get an annual review at the end of the tax year (see p1471). During 2017/18, this can happen if you form a couple with someone who is

Part 10: General rules for tax credits
Chapter 60: Income: tax credits
1. Relevant income

entitled to UC or if you come under the UC system and make a claim for UC (see p20). HMRC may decide to wait until the end of the year to finalise an award, if it decides it is not practical to do so during the year.[2]

If your tax credit award is finalised during the tax year because you become entitled to UC, you are asked to provide your income in the part of the year up to the date you become entitled to UC. HMRC then compares this figure with your previous year's income. Your income from 6 April to the date your tax credit award ends is divided by the number of days in that part of the year, and multiplied by the number of days in the tax year (365 in 2017/18), then rounded down to the nearest pound. This is referred to as 'notional current year income' in the legislation.[3] The result is compared with your 2017/18 income, applying the disregard of £2,500 for an increase or decrease.

Example

From 6 April 2016 to 5 April 2017, Jo claimed tax credits as a lone parent working 16 hours a week at £12 an hour, with an income of £9,984. From 6 April 2017 to 12 October 2017, she continues to claim tax credits as a lone parent in the same job, although she takes on extra shifts, working 28 hours a week. On 13 October 2017, she moves in with her partner, Sam, who is already entitled to UC. Jo's tax credit claim is ended and the UC claim becomes a joint claim as a couple. HMRC asks Jo to provide details of her actual earnings from 6 April 2017 to 12 October 2017, a period of 190 days. She calculates the gross taxable amount she has earned in this period, including extra shifts, which she works out as £9,072. HMRC takes this figure, divides it by 190 and multiplies it by 365, then rounds down to the nearest pound, which works out as £17,427. As this exceeds the 2016/17 income by more than £2,500, the notional current year income after applying the disregard is £14,927, and this is the relevant income for the final decision. It does not matter that she is going back to working 16 hours a week in the latter part of the year, so her actual income in 2017/18 will be less than the notional figure used, and her entitlement will not be revised at the end of the year.

Estimating income

There are no special rules for how to estimate income. Using, for instance, payslips and benefit award letters, work out how much income you have already received in the current year and estimate how much you will receive for the remainder of the year. Tax credits are always worked out using annual income (unless you claim UC and in-year finalisation applies – see p1471), so you must include all income received or estimated for the whole tax year, 6 April to 5 April, even if you are asking for an award to be adjusted part way through the year.

If you are self-employed, HMRC's self-assessment helpline (tel: 0300 200 3310; textphone: 0300 200 3319) can advise you how to work out your business profits. You need to estimate your profits for the accounting period that ends in the current tax year. This might be different from your current earnings, particularly if your accounting year end is early in the tax year.

You should always make it clear that you are using an estimate; there is a box to tick on the claim form and annual declaration to do this. If you provide an estimate in response to an annual declaration, you must be notified that this is to be treated as your actual income unless you rectify your estimate by a specified date, which must be at least 30 days after the notice and no later than 31 January.[4]

2. **Whose income counts**

If you are a member of a couple (see p1451), your partner's income is added to yours.[5] Otherwise, only your own income counts.

If you were previously part of a couple, but have separated and are now a single claimant, only your individual income in the previous and current year counts in your new single award, not that of your former partner. In your old award as a couple, your joint income in the previous and current year counts – ie, including the remainder of the tax year after you separated.[6] The income in the complete tax year is used and then apportioned on a pro rata basis for the period of the claim (see p1421).

If you were a single claimant but are now in a couple, your joint income in the previous and current year counts in the new joint claim, even if you were not in a couple in the previous year.[7]

Children's income

Children's income is ignored. However, if you have transferred money under a trust to your child and tax rules treat that income as still belonging to you, it may also be treated as yours for tax credits.[8]

10

3. **What income counts**

In general, taxable social security benefits are taken into account, and gross earnings (before tax and national insurance (NI)) and business profits are taken into account less your pension contributions. Most other income, such as pensions and interest on savings, is added together and taken into account only if the total is more than £300 a year. The rules specify what income must be taken into account and what is disregarded.

If you have a special exemption from income tax, your income is calculated as though you were liable for tax.[9] People such as foreign military personnel, officials of international organisations or consular staff may have such an exemption.

Part 10: General rules for tax credits
Chapter 60: Income: tax credits
3. What income counts

Types of income

Income taken into account falls into certain categories and within each category certain amounts may be disregarded. There is also a general list of income that is disregarded (see p1444).

The income taken into account in the assessment is worked out as follows.[10]

Add together your income, or your joint income if you are a couple, from:

- social security benefits (see below);
- income from employment (see p1436);
- taxable profits from self-employment (see p1439);
- student income (see p1439);
- miscellaneous income (see p1440).

Add together your income, or your joint income if you are a couple, from:

- pension income (see p1440);
- income from investments (see p1441);
- income from property (see p1442);
- foreign income (see p1443);
- notional income (see p1446).

If the total income in the last group of five categories is £300 or less, it is ignored completely; otherwise, deduct £300 and add the remainder to your income from the first group of five categories. **Note:** couples share one £300 disregard.[11]

This gives you the total income that is taken into account – subject to any disregards described later in this chapter.

Example

Mr and Mrs Killean renew their claim for child tax credit (CTC) and working tax credit (WTC) from April 2017. HM Revenue and Customs (HMRC) assesses their claim on their joint income for the year 6 April 2016 to 5 April 2017. In 2016/17, Mrs Killean earned £13,500 before tax and NI contributions. Mr Killean received contributory employment and support allowance (ESA) totalling £4,700 and an occupational pension of £500. Income taken into account is:

Employment income = £13,500

ESA = £4,700

Occupational pension = £200 (ie, £500 less £300 disregard)

Total income = £18,400

Benefits

Generally, benefits are taken into account if they are taxable, and ignored if they are not.

Disregarded benefits

The following benefits are disregarded:[12]
- armed forces independence payment;
- attendance allowance;
- bereavement payment;
- bereavement support payment;[13]
- child benefit;
- Christmas bonus;
- council tax reduction;
- disability living allowance;
- discretionary housing payment;
- guardian's allowance;
- housing benefit (HB);
- income support (IS), except to strikers;
- income-based jobseeker's allowance (JSA) (even though this is taxable);
- income-related ESA, including a transitional addition;[14]
- industrial injuries benefit (except industrial death benefit);
- maternity allowance;
- pension credit (guarantee and savings credit);[15]
- personal independence payment;
- severe disablement allowance;
- short-term lower rate incapacity benefit (IB);
- social fund payments;
- transitional long-term IB (paid if you transferred from invalidity benefit in 1995) but no longer disregarded when converted to ESA;
- any payment to compensate for the loss of IS, JSA or HB;
- any payment in lieu of milk tokens or vitamins;
- increases for a child[16] or adult[17] paid with any of the above.

Tax credits themselves are disregarded. Statutory sick pay (SSP), statutory maternity pay (SMP), statutory adoption pay (SAP), statutory paternity pay (SPP) and statutory shared parental pay (SSPP) are treated as employment income (see p1436). Retirement pensions, widowed mother's allowance, widowed parent's allowance, widow's pension, industrial death benefit and war pensions are treated as pension income (see p1440). Universal credit (UC) is not included as income, but the intention is that once you have started to receive UC, you cannot claim tax credits.[18]

Benefits taken into account

Any benefits not in the list above are taken into account in full. These include:
- bereavement allowance;
- carer's allowance (CA);
- contribution-based JSA;[19]

Part 10: General rules for tax credits
Chapter 60: Income: tax credits
3. What income counts

- contributory ESA, including a transitional addition;
- long-term IB (except the non-taxable transitional long-term IB – see p1435);
- increases for a child or adult (even if not taxable) paid with any of the above.

It is the amount of benefit payable that is taken into account. Arrears of benefit or any ex gratia payment in connection with a benefit are taken into account as income for the year in which the payment of arrears is made.[20]

Each year the DWP should give you a statement of the taxable benefits you received in the previous tax year. You can ask the local benefit office for a replacement if you did not get one. If you get any increase for a child paid with CA or IB (or widowed mother's or widowed parent's allowance), this is not included in the statement but is taken into account as income, so you should include it when completing your tax credit claim form.

Employment income

For tax credits, it is your 'gross' taxable pay that is taken into account.[21] This means your pay before any income tax or NI contributions are deducted, but after pension contributions are deducted.

Income counts whether received in the UK or elsewhere, unless it has been classed as not taxable because it cannot be transferred to or realised in the UK.[22]

What counts as employment income

'Employment income' means the following income received in the tax year:[23]
- any earnings from an office or employment, including:[24]
  - wages and overtime pay;
  - holiday pay and occupational sick pay;
  - bonuses and commission (including tips or gratuities);
  - goods or assets that can be converted into money – eg, gifts of drink, clothes and fuel;
  - payments made on your behalf – eg, rent paid by your employer directly to your landlord;
  - earnings from 'permitted work' (see p1023). **Note:** there is no income test while you are receiving income-related ESA, but this does not mean the earnings are disregarded when applying the income test for other periods;
- taxable expenses (see p1437 for expenses that do not count as earnings);[25]
- any taxable cash voucher, non-cash voucher or credit token – eg, company credit card.[26] Vouchers spent on allowable expenses are ignored;[27]
- taxable payments in connection with the termination of your employment or with a change in your duties or wages, including non-statutory and statutory redundancy payments, pay in lieu of notice and employment tribunal awards for unfair dismissal. With the exception of pay in lieu of notice (except in some cases involving damages for breach of contract or practice),[28] the first £30,000 of the total of such payments is ignored;[29]

- SSP;[30]
- SMP, SAP, SPP and SSPP above £100 a week. The first £100 a week is ignored;[31]
- strike pay from your trade union (even though this is non-taxable);[32]
- the cash equivalent of the benefit of a company car for private use and car fuel benefits if you earn £8,500 or more or you are a company director.[33] Other expenses in connection with the car are ignored.[34] However, if you are a disabled employee with an adapted or automatic company car, the car is exempt from income tax and ignored for tax credits;[35]
- payments for agreeing to restrict your future conduct or activities;[36]
- taxable income from an employee share scheme;[37]
- payment for work done while sentenced or on remand in prison (but note, this does not count as remunerative work).[38]

The taxable value of goods and vouchers is shown on Form P9D or P11D, given to you by your employer at the end of the tax year.

Payments not counted as earnings

Some payments do not count as earnings and are disregarded in the tax credits assessment. Payments from your employer that are not taxable generally do not count as income for tax credits. **Note:** in the autumn statement 2016, the government announced that the tax advantages of salary sacrifice schemes will be removed from April 2017, except for arrangements relating to pensions (including advice), childcare, Cyclescheme and ultra-low emission cars. Arrangements in place before April 2017 will be protected until April 2018, and arrangements for cars, accommodation and school fees will be protected until April 2021. It also announced a review of how benefits in kind are valued for tax purposes and on the use of tax relief for employees' business expenses. Insofar as they are exempt from income tax, ignore the following:[39]

- expenses incurred 'wholly, exclusively and necessarily' in the course of your employment.[40] **Note:** if you are a volunteer with a charity or voluntary organisation, all your expenses are ignored.[41] However, any that are taxable are taken into account – eg, 'round-sum' expense allowances payable irrespective of how you might spend it;[42]
- certain other expenses – eg, for removal benefits, cars or transport for disabled employees, travel and subsistence, mileage allowance, car parking expenses, fixed deductions for work tools and tax-free mobile phone;[43]
- non-taxable vouchers, benefits or credit tokens, such as for recreational facilities, subsidised meals, transport, entertainment or hospitality;[44]
- small gifts or vouchers from third parties, not made in recognition of particular services (not exceeding £250 in total);[45]
- tax-free cycles and cyclist's safety equipment under Cyclescheme;[46]
- homeworkers' additional household expenses;[47]

10

Part 10: General rules for tax credits
Chapter 60: Income: tax credits
3. What income counts

- childcare vouchers or credit tokens for 'relevant childcare' (see p1416) (but any childcare element in your WTC is based on the amount you pay after using the voucher or tokens);[48]
- tax-free award under a staff suggestion scheme and certain other vouchers – eg, for staff canteens, sports and recreation facilities and small gifts;[49]
- certain professional fees – eg, to approved professional bodies, for indemnity insurance or registration under the Protecting Vulnerable Groups Scheme;[50]
- any charity payments under a Payroll Giving scheme[51] (deduct from earnings or from a benefit or pension);[52]
- payment for work-related training, individual learning account training and retraining expenses when leaving employment;[53]
- In-Work Emergency Discretion Fund and Up-front Childcare Fund payments made by the DWP (but in-work payments made by a Work Programme provider, including non-cash items such as clothing or travelcards, are not exempt from income tax and are likely to be treated as employment income);[54]
- tax-exempt bonus payments of up to £3,600 paid to employees or former employees by an employee ownership trust.[55]

Some groups of workers have special income tax exemptions. The following are ignored as earnings for tax credits:
- certain armed forces' allowances – eg, for travel to and from leave, food, certain operational allowances, council tax relief, continuity of education and reserve forces' training;[56]
- free coal to miners, or former miners, or cash in lieu;[57]
- if you are an actor or performer, the tax-free amount of agents' fees;[58]
- expenses for mainland transfers for offshore oil and gas workers;[59]
- Crown employees' foreign service allowance;[60]
- expenses of a minister of religion, including a rent deduction;[61]
- European Commission daily subsistence allowance to seconded national experts.[62]

Deduct pension contributions

Deduct any contributions you make to a personal or occupational pension approved by HMRC.[63]

If you pay contributions through your employer, your P60 or P45 should show your wages after the contributions have been deducted, so there is no further deduction to make.

If you pay the pension contributions directly, deduct the gross annual contributions. Because tax relief is given on personal pension contributions, your actual contributions are less than the gross amount included in the pension plan. It is the higher gross amount that you should deduct from your employment income. Your pension provider should supply you with annual statements of contributions received.

10

If you have no income from employment but are still making pension contributions, deduct the contributions from any other income you may have.

Income from self-employment

Your taxable profits from any 'trade', 'profession' or 'vocation' are taken into account for the relevant year.[64] If you have a business partner, it is taxable profits from your share of the business income that count.[65] This includes trading outside the UK. It also includes profits from renting out property if this is conducted as a business. (If property income comes from a 'trade', income counts without the £300 disregard that would otherwise apply to such income.) If renting property is not conducted as a business, see p1442. You might be asked to provide evidence that your self-emplement is organised and regular, on a commericial basis, with a view to making a profit.

Payments under the New Enterprise Allowance scheme to help you start a new business are not counted as income for working out your trading profits.[66] Taxable profits are shown on your tax return for the relevant year. If you have not yet submitted a tax return, the notes that accompany the tax credit claim form (TC600) explain how to work out your profit. You should deduct allowable business expenses from annual turnover to arrive at a profit figure. HMRC's self-assessment helpline (tel: 0300 200 3310; textphone: 0300 200 3319) should be able to give advice. See also p1432. **Note:** the provision allowing artists, farmers and market gardeners to average out fluctuating profits across two tax years does not apply; it is the actual taxable profit in the relevant year that counts.[67]

Business losses

If your business is run on a commercial basis and has made a loss, your income is nil for that tax year unless you have other income that counts in the assessment. If you do have other income, you should deduct the amount of the loss from that income (from joint income if you are claiming as a couple).[68] If you do not have enough income to offset the full amount, any left over can be carried forward and deducted from profits of the same trade in the next and later tax years.

Deductions from self-employment

Deduct the gross amount of personal pension contributions (see p1438) and any gift aid donation to charity (see p1445).

Student income

The following income is taken into account:[69]
- adult dependants' grant;
- in Scotland, lone parents' grant;
- professional and career development loan, but only any amount applied for or paid in respect of living expenses for the period supported by the loan.[70]

Part 10: General rules for tax credits
Chapter 60: Income: tax credits
3. What income counts

All other kinds of student support are disregarded, including student loans, childcare grants, discretionary grants and hardship funds.

Note: unlike means-tested benefits, students are not excluded from WTC and CTC. Provided you satisfy the eligibility rules, you can qualify.

Miscellaneous income

Any income that does not fit into any of the other nine categories on p1434 is taken into account if it is taxable under the HMRC 'sweep-up' provisions in Part 5 of the Income Tax (Trading and Other Income) Act 2005.[71] This includes copyright royalties if your writing does not amount to a trade or profession.

Pension income

Pension income taken into account

The following pension income is taken into account. The first £300 a year is ignored from the total of your pension and any income from savings, investments, property or foreign or notional income.

- **State retirement pensions and graduated retirement benefit.**[72] (The Christmas bonus and winter fuel payment are ignored.) HMRC says that, as well as your pension, it takes into account any additional state pension, and any increase for an adult or child paid with your pension.[73] Include as income any lump sum to which you become entitled through deferring your state pension.
- **Personal and occupational pensions.**[74] It is the gross amount before tax is deducted that counts. Your pension provider should give you a certificate each year showing how much pension was paid and how much tax deducted. If you retired because of work-related illness or disability caused by injury on duty, only count the amount of pension that you would have been paid if you had retired on non-work-related ill-health grounds. Any extra amount paid is ignored.[75] Tax-free lump sums paid under a personal pension scheme, retirement annuity contract or tax-exempt pension scheme are ignored completely.[76] If you have the option of taking a lump sum from a pension under the new flexibilities for people aged 55 and over, the tax-free amount (usually up to 25 per cent of the total value of the pension pot) is ignored, but other payments count as income. If you choose not to take an income or lump sum from a personal or occupational pension, regardless of your age, this cannot be counted as notional income (see p1446). If you cash in a small pension or the fund is too small to pay a pension (within the 'trivial commutation' limit – your pension provider can advise on this), the lump sum you get counts. If you get a winding-up lump sum when your occupational pension scheme winds up, this counts.
- **Widow's pension, widowed mother's and widowed parent's allowance,** including any increases for a child or adult dependant.[77]

- Industrial death benefit.[78]
- Survivor's guaranteed income payment and child's payment under the Armed Forces Compensation Scheme.[79]

Pension income disregarded

Ignore the following **war pensions**:[80]

- war disablement pension, including constant attendance allowance and mobility supplement;
- annuity or additional pension to holders of the Victoria Cross, George Cross and certain other medals;
- wounds, injury or disablement pensions to members of the armed forces – eg, guaranteed income payment;
- death in service pensions for service in the armed forces or war injuries. If the death in service pension is overlapped by another pension, ignore an equivalent amount from the other pension.

Investment income

There is no capital limit in the tax credit assessment as there is with means-tested benefits. The value of your savings is ignored completely. However, taxable *income* from savings and investments is taken into account. For example, the amount of savings in a bank account is ignored, but the interest on those savings is taken into account.

Investment income is taken into account as described below. The first £300 a year is ignored from the total of your investment income and any income from pensions or property, or foreign or notional income.

Investment income taken into account

Take into account the following amounts before tax is deducted:[81]

- interest on invested money, including outside the UK – eg, interest on savings in a bank account;
- dividends from shares of a company resident in the UK (including the tax credit payable by the company with the dividend);
- income from government stocks and bonds;
- taxable payments from a life assurance policy, life annuity contract or capital redemption policy;
- discounts on securities – ie, the profit from trading in securities such as government stocks and bonds;
- interest, annuity or other annual payment payable as a charge on a property or as a reservation out of it;
- payments from the estate of a deceased person;
- interest arising from a debt owed to you.

Part 10: General rules for tax credits
Chapter 60: Income: tax credits
3. What income counts

Investment income disregarded

Certain investment income is disregarded:

- interest, dividend or bonus from an individual savings account (ISA);[82]
- government bonus payments into a lifetime ISA;
- interest under a certified save as you earn (SAYE) scheme;[83]
- income from savings certificates and tax reserve certificates;[84]
- tax-exempt annual payments made by an individual in the UK not for commercial reasons – eg, from a covenant;[85]
- winnings from betting, pools, lotteries and games with prizes;[86]
- certain compensation payments to Second World War victims;[87]
- tax-free periodical payments of damages for personal injury, disease or death awarded through a court, out-of-court settlement or agreement, and interest on such damages;[88]
- periodical payments from the Thalidomide Trust;[89]
- annuity payments under a Criminal Injuries Compensation Scheme award;[90]
- interest on the first £30,000 of a home income plan loan taken out before 9 March 1999 to buy a life annuity;[91]
- interest on compensation to a child under 18 for the loss of a parent;[92]
- payments from the variant Creutzfeldt-Jakob disease government-funded trust, the Macfarlane Trusts, Independent Living Funds and the Eileen Trust. These are disregarded for the lifetime of the disabled person or a partner who receives the payment or inherits from the estate, or for two years if paid to or inherited by a parent;[93]
- tax-exempt capital element of a purchased life annuity;[94]
- tax-exempt health and employment insurance payments (eg, permanent health insurance or employment protection policies) or immediate-needs annuity payments.[95]

Property income

The capital value of property is ignored but rental income is taken into account unless this is exempt from tax under the 'rent-a-room' scheme.[96] This scheme allows you to rent furnished accommodation in your own home earning up to £7,500 a year tax free.[97]

If you are not within the 'rent-a-room' scheme (eg, you rent out a property that you do not live in yourself), the amount of rent taken into account differs from the new restrictions applied for income tax purposes. You can deduct expenses wholly and exclusively incurred in running the property – eg, repairs, council tax (if you, rather than your tenant, are liable to pay), water charges, insurance premiums and mortgage interest (but not capital repayments of a mortgage).[98] You can offset any losses against property income in the following tax year.

The first £300 a year is ignored from the total of your property income and any pensions, investment income, foreign or notional income.

If you rent out property as a business (eg, you run a hotel or guesthouse), count this as income from self-employment (see p1439).[99]

Income from property outside the UK counts as 'foreign income' (see below).

Income from outside the UK

Although earnings from abroad are taken into account in the same way as UK earnings, other 'foreign income' (eg, from pensions, property or investments) is taken into account subject to the following rules.[100]

The following are disregarded:[101]

- a banking charge or commission for converting currency to sterling;[102]
- social security payments from outside the UK that are equivalent to tax-free UK benefits (see p1434);
- certain pensions or compensation for victims of persecution during World War Two;
- one-tenth of the amount of any overseas pension or of a pension payable in the UK by the governments of certain countries;
- tax-free lump-sum payments under an overseas pension scheme;
- personal injury damages from a court outside the UK;
- certain education allowances payable to workers in the public sector of some countries outside the UK;
- property losses in one tax year that can be offset against property income in the following year;[103]
- maintenance payments;
- income that you are prevented from transferring to the UK by law or by the government of the country where the income arises or because you cannot get foreign currency in that country. Other income that remains abroad is counted.[104]

The first £300 a year is disregarded from the total of your foreign income and any pensions, investment, property or notional income.

Income from outside the UK is still taken into account even if you would normally have tax relief on that income in the UK to avoid double taxation in both countries (such income is treated as though it were taxable in the UK in the normal way).[105]

Converting currency

If your income is in another currency, HMRC expects you to convert it to sterling using an average of the exchange rates over 12 months ending on 31 March for the tax year in which the income is paid.[106] These rates are published on www.gov.uk/government/collections/exchange-rates-for-customs-and-vat. If your tax credit award is based on an estimate of current year's income, the rate of conversion will be adjusted once the exchange rate average is available at the end of the tax year.

Part 10: General rules for tax credits
Chapter 60: Income: tax credits
3. What income counts

General income disregards

All of the following income is disregarded in the tax credit assessment.[107]

Employment and training programmes

Ignore the following income:
- travelling expenses, a living-away-from-home allowance and a training grant if you are participating in training under section 2 of the Employment and Training Act 1973 or, in Scotland, under section 2 of the Enterprise and New Towns (Scotland) Act 1990, or attending a course at an employment rehabilitation centre (where these are not taxable as profits);[108]
- if you are aged 25 or over and getting JSA while on a 'qualifying course', a discretionary payment to help meet your special needs;[109]
- a payment to a disabled person under section 2 of the Employment and Training Act 1973 or section 15 of the Disabled Persons (Employment) Act 1944 to assist disabled people to get or keep employment;[110]
- education maintenance allowance;[111]
- certain DWP payments from former employment programmes. Payments from Work Programme providers are not specifically disregarded and are likely to be treated as employment income.[112]

See also p1438 for other disregarded payments.

Maintenance and children

Any maintenance you receive from an ex-partner, or that your partner receives from her/his ex-partner, is ignored, whether it is paid under a court order or not. Any maintenance for a child or qualifying young person which you receive from her/his parent (if the parent is not currently your partner) is also ignored.[113]

If you *pay* maintenance, you cannot deduct this from income.

If you foster a child placed with you by a local authority or independent fostering provider, all your income from foster care (eg, the fostering allowance) is ignored, provided the annual amount is no more than £10,000 plus £200 a week for each child under 11 and £250 a week for each child aged 11 or over. If your fostering income is over this limit, only the taxable amount is taken into account – ie, the amount above this limit or the actual net profit.[114] There is a similar disregard for local authority payments if a child or adult is placed with you under an adult placement scheme or 'staying put' care for care leavers, or you are a kinship carer of a looked-after child.[115] **Note:** a foster child or looked-after child may not count as a member of your family for tax credits, so you may not get CTC for her/him (see p186).

An adoption allowance,[116] or special guardianship payment for a child who is a member of your household is ignored completely. For a child who lives with you under a residence order, a residence order allowance and any payments made by a local authority under section 17 of the Children Act 1989 or, in Scotland, under section 22 of the Children (Scotland) Act 1995 or section 50 of the Children Act 1975 are ignored.[117]

Other income

The following is ignored from your income:
- any contribution you make to an approved personal or occupational pension scheme (see p1438);[118]
- payments for fares to hospital or to assist prison visits;[119]
- community care direct payments;[120]
- payments under the Supporting People programme;[121]
- asylum support payments or vouchers for a former asylum seeker or dependant;[122]
- trade union provident benefits – eg, sickness or accident benefit or funeral payment;[123]
- payment for expenses incurred if you are an unpaid volunteer with a charity or voluntary organisation;[124]
- jury or witness payments, if this is not compensation for loss of earnings or loss of benefit;[125]
- a payment for someone you are caring for temporarily made to you by a health authority, local authority, voluntary organisation, clinical commissioning group, NHS England, or by the person her/himself under the local authority's financial assessment. This disregard only applies if the payment would be tax free under HMRC's 'rent-a-room' scheme (see p1442);[126]
- any payment under an insurance policy taken out to insure against the risk of being unable to maintain mortgage repayments or other payments on a loan secured on your home. However, any payment you get above the amount you use to maintain the repayments, plus the premiums on that policy or buildings insurance premiums required as a condition of the mortgage, count as your income;[127]
- any payment under an insurance policy taken out to insure against the risk of being unable to maintain repayments under a hire purchase, regulated or conditional sale agreement. However, any payment above the amount you use to maintain the repayments and the premiums on that policy counts as your income;[128]
- the gross amount of any 'gift aid' donation to charity;[129]
- a sports award for anything other than living expenses. Living expenses count as your income. Ignore parts of the award for dietary supplements and living-away-from-home accommodation costs.[130]

10

Part 10: General rules for tax credits
Chapter 60: Income: tax credits
4. Notional income

4. **Notional income**

Sometimes you are treated as though you have income that you do not actually have. This is called '**notional income**'.[131] There are four kinds of notional income.

- **Income you have deprived yourself of to get, or increase, tax credits.**[132] See p371 for details of when this rule might affect you (the basic rules are similar to those that apply to deprivation of capital for benefits).
- **Income that you have failed to apply for.** You are treated as having income that would become available to you if you applied for it.[133] This does not include:
  - income under a trust set up from a personal injury payment;
  - income from a personal pension scheme, regardless of your age;
  - interest on damages awarded through the courts for personal injury;
  - a rehabilitation allowance;
  - state pension;
  - category A or B retirement pension;
  - graduated retirement benefit;
  - shared additional pension.
- **Cheap or unpaid labour.** If you work or provide a service for less than the going rate, you are treated as getting a reasonable rate for the job if the person has the means to pay.[134]

  This does not affect you if you are a volunteer and it is reasonable for you to provide your services free of charge. Nor does it apply if you are on an approved employment or training programme.

  Sometimes carers looking after disabled people have been expected to charge the person they care for under a similar provision affecting means-tested benefits. If you are in this position, see p301 for more details.
- **Income treated as yours under certain tax avoidance provisions or where tax law treats capital as income.** It also counts as your income for tax credits.[135]

10

Notes

1. Relevant income

1 s7(3)(a), (b) and (e) TCA 2002; reg 5 TC(ITDR) Regs
2 Reg 12A(3) UC(TP) Regs
3 s7(4A) TCA 2002; as added by reg 12A and Sch UC(TP) Regs
4 s17(8) TCA 2002; reg 33 TC(CN) Regs

2. Whose income counts

5 s7(5) TCA 2002
6 *PD v HMRC* [2010] UKUT 159 (AAC)
7 R(TC) 1/08
8 Reg 14(2)(b)(vii) TC(DCI) Regs

3. What income counts

9 Reg 3(6) TC(DCI) Regs
10 Reg 3(1) TC(DCI) Regs
11 Reg 3(1) Step 1 TC(DCI) Regs
12 Reg 7(3) TC(DCI) Regs
13 Reg 7(1) TC(DCI) Regs (bereavement support payment is paid under PA 2014 and not taxable under Sch 16)
14 A transitional addition is part of the ESA applicable amount under reg 67(1)(d) ESA Regs, inserted by Sch 2 para 52 ESA(TP)(EA)(No.2) Regs
15 PC paid under SPCA 2002 is, by definition, not counted as social security income under reg 7(1) TC(DCI) Regs.
16 Reg 7(4) TC(DCI) Regs
17 The regulations do not mention the treatment of increases for adults. However, these are non-taxable if paid with a non-taxable benefit and the intention is that tax credits follow suit. See HMRC, *Employment Income Manual,* para 76102.
18 Reg 7(1) TC(DCI) Regs (UC is paid under the WRA 2012)
19 s674 IT(EP)A 2003
20 Reg 7(1)(c) and (d) TC(DCI) Regs; TCM 0120040
21 Reg 4 TC(DCI) Regs
22 Reg 3(3)-(5) TC(DCI) Regs
23 Reg 4 TC(DCI) Regs
24 Regs 2(2) and 4(1)(a) TC(DCI) Regs; HMRC, *Employment Income Manual,* para 00520
25 Reg 4(1)(b) TC(DCI) Regs
26 Reg 4(1)(c)-(e) TC(DCI) Regs

27 ss362-63 IT(EP)A 2003; reg 4(4) Table 1 para 11D and (5) TC(DCI) Regs
28 HMRC, *Employment Income Manual,* paras 12975-79
29 Reg 4(1)(f) TC(DCI) Regs; see also TCTM 04111
30 Reg 4(1)(g) TC(DCI) Regs
31 Reg 4(1)(h) TC(DCI) Regs
32 Reg 4(1)(k) TC(DCI) Regs
33 Reg 4(1)(i) TC(DCI) Regs; s216 IT(EP)A 2003
34 Reg 4(4) Table 1 paras 14B, 14C and 14D TC(DCI) Regs
35 Reg 4(4) Table 1 para 2B TC(DCI) Regs
36 Reg 4(1)(j) TC(DCI) Regs
37 Reg 4(1)(l) TC(DCI) Regs
38 Reg 4(1)(m) TC(DCI) Regs; reg 4(2)(g) WTC(EMR) Regs
39 Reg 4(4) TC(DCI) Regs; for a full list, see TCTM 04200
40 Reg 4(5) TC(DCI) Regs; s336 IT(EP)A 2003
41 Reg 19 Table 7 para 1 TC(DCI) Regs
42 Reg 4(1)(b) TC(DCI) Regs; HMRC, *Employment Income Manual,* para 05100
43 Regs 4(4) Table 1 paras 1, 2A, 2C, 4, 6, 11F, 13, and 20, and 4(5) TC(DCI) Regs
44 Reg 4(4) Table 1 paras 5, 11D and 11E TC(DCI) Regs
45 Reg 4(4) Table 1 para 14 TC(DCI) Regs
46 Reg 4(4) Table 1 para 11D TC(DCI) Regs; ss244 and 266 IT(EP)A 2003
47 Reg 4(4) Table 1 paras 17 and 19 TC(DCI) Regs
48 Reg 4(4) Table 1 para 15 TC(DCI) Regs
49 Reg 4(4) Table 1 paras 5, 8, 11E 12 and 14 TC(DCI) Regs
50 Regs 4(4) Table 1 para 21 and 4(5) TC(DCI) Regs; ss343 and 346 IT(EP)A 2003
51 Reg 4(5) TC(DCI) Regs; s713 IT(EP)A 2003
52 Regs 5(3) and 7(5A) TC(DCI) Regs
53 Reg 4(4) Table 1 paras 11C and 18 TC(DCI) Regs
54 Reg 4(4) Table 1 para 16 TC(DCI) Regs; DWP, *Provider Guidance,* Chapter 13
55 Reg 4 (4) Table 1 para 22 TC(DCI) Regs
56 Reg 4(4) Table 1 paras 3, 3A, 3B, 3C and 7 TC(DCI) Regs

Part 10: General rules for tax credits
Chapter 60: Income: tax credits
Notes

57 Regs 4(4) Table 1 para 9 and 5(2) Table 2 para 11 TC(DCI) Regs
58 Reg 4(5) TC(DCI) Regs; s352 IT(EP)A 2003
59 Reg 4(4) Table 1 para 11A TC(DCI) Regs
60 Reg 4(4) Table 1 para 11B TC(DCI) Regs
61 Reg 4(5) TC(DCI) Regs; s351 IT(EP)A 2003
62 Reg 4(4) Table 1 para 11 TC(DCI) Regs
63 Reg 3(7)(c) TC(DCI) Regs
64 Reg 6(a) TC(DCI) Regs
65 Reg 6(b) TC(DCI) Regs
66 HMRC, *Business Income Manual*, para 40401
67 Reg 6 TC(DCI) Regs
68 Reg 3(1) Step 4 TC(DCI) Regs
69 Reg 8 TC(DCI) Regs
70 Reg 19(c) Table 8 para 2 TC(DCI) Regs
71 Reg 18 TC(DCI) Regs
72 Reg 5(1)(a) TC(DCI) Regs
73 TCTM 04301; HMRC, *Employment Income Manual*, para 76102
74 Reg 5(1)(b)-(o) TC(DCI) Regs
75 Reg 5(2) Table 2 para 9 TC(DCI) Regs
76 Reg 5(2) Table 2 para 10 TC(DCI) Regs
77 Reg 5(1)(a) TC(DCI) Regs
78 Reg 5(1)(a) TC(DCI) Regs
79 Reg 5(1)(b) TC(DCI) Regs; HMRC, *Employment Income Manual*, para 74306
80 Reg 5(2) Table 2 paras 1-8 TC(DCI) Regs
81 Reg 10(1) TC(DCI) Regs
82 Reg 10(2)(a) Table 4 paras 1(a) and (b) TC(DCI) Regs
83 Reg 10(2)(a) Table 4 para 3 TC(DCI) Regs
84 Reg 10(2)(c) TC(DCI) Regs
85 Reg 10(2)(e) TC(DCI) Regs
86 Reg 10(2)(a) Table 4 para 4 TC(DCI) Regs
87 Reg 10(2)(a) Table 4 paras 5-7 TC(DCI) Regs
88 Reg 10(2)(a) Table 4 para 8 TC(DCI) Regs (a lump-sum payment of personal injury compensation or damages is not taxable under s51(2) Taxation of Chargeable Gains Act 1992)
89 TCTM 04608
90 Reg 10(2)(a) Table 4 para 9 TC(DCI) Regs
91 Reg 10(2)(a) Table 4 para 10 TC(DCI) Regs
92 Reg 10(2)(a) Table 4 para 11 TC(DCI) Regs
93 Reg 10(2)(b) Table 5 TC(DCI) Regs
94 Reg 10(2)(a) Table 4 para 12 TC(DCI) Regs
95 Reg 10(2)(a) Table 4 para 13 TC(DCI) Regs; TCTM 04612

96 Reg 11 TC(DCI) Regs
97 Income Tax (Limit for Rent-a-Room Relief) Order 2015, No.1539; see HMRC, Helpsheet HS 223, *Rent a Room Scheme*
98 TCTM 04006; HMRC, *Property Income Manual*, paras 2020-40 and 2105
99 TCTM 04006
100 Reg 12(1) TC(DCI) Regs
101 Reg 12(3) TC(DCI) Regs
102 Reg 3(7)(a) TC(DCI) Regs
103 Reg 12(4) TC(DCI) Regs
104 Reg 3(3) TC(DCI) Regs
105 Reg 3(5A) TC(DCI) Regs
106 Reg 3(6A) TC(DCI) Regs
107 Reg 19 TC(DCI) Regs
108 Reg 19 Table 7 para 2(a)-(c) TC(DCI) Regs
109 Reg 19 Table 8 para 1 TC(DCI) Regs
110 Reg 19 Table 6 para 2 TC(DCI) Regs
111 Reg 19 Table 6 para 5 TC(DCI) Regs
112 Reg 19 Table 6 para 3 TC(DCI) Regs; DWP, *Provider Guidance*, Chapter 13
113 Reg 19 Table 6 para 10 TC(DCI) Regs
114 Reg 19 Table 6 para 9 TC(DCI) Regs
115 Reg 19 Table 6 para 9 TC(DCI) Regs; The Qualifying Care Relief (Specified Social Care Schemes) Order 2011, No.712; s806A ITTOIA 2005
116 Reg 19 Table 6 para 11(a) TC(DCI) Regs
117 Reg 19 Table 6 para 11(a) and (b) TC(DCI) Regs
118 Reg 3(7)(c) TC(DCI) Regs
119 Reg 19 Table 6 paras 12 and 13 TC(DCI) Regs
120 Reg 19 Table 6 para 14 TC(DCI) Regs
121 Reg 19 Table 6 para 14A TC(DCI) Regs
122 Reg 19 Table 6 para 15 TC(DCI) Regs
123 Reg 19 Table 6 para 16 TC(DCI) Regs
124 Reg 19 Table 7 para 1 TC(DCI) Regs
125 Reg 19 Table 8 para 6 TC(DCI) Regs
126 Reg 19 Table 8 paras 3 and 4 TC(DCI) Regs
127 Reg 19 Table 8 para 5(a) TC(DCI) Regs
128 Reg 19 Table 8 para 5(b) TC(DCI) Regs
129 Reg 3(7)(b) TC(DCI) Regs
130 Reg 19 Table 8 para 7 TC(DCI) Regs

4. Notional income
131 Reg 13 TC(DCI) Regs
132 Reg 15 TC(DCI) Regs
133 Reg 16 TC(DCI) Regs
134 Reg 17 TC(DCI) Regs
135 Reg 14 TC(DCI) Regs

Chapter 61

Claims, decisions and getting paid: tax credits

This chapter covers:
1. Who should claim (p1450)
2. How and when to make a claim (p1453)
3. How your claim is dealt with (p1458)
4. Backdating your claim (p1459)
5. Getting paid (p1460)
6. Change of circumstances (p1462)
7. Annual reviews (p1468)
8. Contacting HM Revenue and Customs (p1472)

Key facts

- Tax credits are administered and paid by HM Revenue and Customs. Claims are dealt with by the Tax Credit Office.
- Tax credit claims are dealt with differently from social security benefits. Tax credits are dealt with over a tax year, using annual income, and entitlement is finalised at the end of the tax year.
- Tax credit claims can usually only be backdated for 31 days.
- Your tax credits may be affected by changes in your circumstances or income.
- Tax credit claims are finalised between April and July each year. This annual review also acts as a renewal claim for the new tax year.

Future changes

At some point before September 2018, depending on where you live, you will no longer be able to make a new claim for tax credits. From 2019, the DWP will begin to transfer existing tax credits claimants to universal credit (UC). See p20 for further information and CPAG's online service and *Welfare Rights Bulletin* for updates. If you do not come under the UC system, you can still make a new claim for tax credits. If you are already getting tax credits, you can renew your tax credits claim.

Part 10: General rules for tax credits
Chapter 61: Claims, decisions and getting paid: tax credits
1. Who should claim

1. **Who should claim**

You must be at least 16 years old to claim tax credits.[1]

If you are a member of a married couple or registered civil partnership, or live with someone as if you were married or civil partners, you must claim jointly with your partner. This is known as a 'joint claim'.[2] Both partners must claim the tax credits jointly. HM Revenue and Customs (HMRC) has the discretion to treat a claim by one member of a couple as having also been made by the other member, but usually only uses this power to accept renewal claims by telephone.[3] See p1451 for when you are treated as part of a couple.

If you are a single person, you make a single claim.

If you made a joint claim and are no longer part of a couple, or if you made a single claim and are now part of a couple, your entitlement ends. You must make a new claim.[4] You should tell the Tax Credit Office (TCO) as soon as possible. If you do not, you could be overpaid. You could also incur a financial penalty if you fail to notify the change within one month.[5] When you contact the TCO to report that your joint claim has ended, your new single claim can be made in the same telephone call without the need to fill in a new claim form.[6] If you report that a single claim has ended and you are now part of a couple, HMRC has announced that, as part of a new service from April 2017, details of your new joint claim can be taken by phone without the need to complete a new claim form with your partner. In either case, you should request backdating or you may lose out on tax credits as your new claim can only be backdated for 31 days.

When you cannot claim tax credits

You cannot claim tax credits if you or your partner are a universal credit (UC) claimant. This includes if you are entitled to UC, or have claimed it and are waiting to hear, or are awaiting the outcome of a revision or appeal of a decision that you are not entitled to UC.[7] You are excluded from claiming tax credits within six months of a UC claim or of your last day of entitlement if you are not entitled to UC because your earned income is too high.[8] If you live in a 'full service' area (see p24), you cannot make a new claim for tax credits unless you or your partner are over pension credit qualifying age (see p147).[9] If you live in a UC 'full service' area, you can make a new claim for working tax credit (WTC) if you already get child tax credit (CTC), or a new claim for CTC if you already get WTC.[10]

If you claim tax credits during an entitlement period for payments under the new tax-free childcare scheme, which is being introduced in 2017 (see p864), you cannot get both at the same time. Your tax credits claim is treated as having been made from the date your tax-free childcare account is closed or restricted, or from the date a child ceases to be a qualifying child for tax-free childcare, or after the last day of that three-month entitlement period.[11] You may then be disqualified from applying for tax-free childcare again unless there is a change in your circumstances.[12] Get advice to see whether you are better off with tax credits or tax-free childcare.

Couples

You and your partner count as a 'couple' if you are:[13]
- married or registered civil partners, unless you are separated and this is under a court order or is likely to be permanent; *or*
- not married or registered civil partners, but are living together as if you are.[14]

If you are entitled to tax credits and become part of a couple with someone who is entitled to UC (see p20), your tax credit award ends and you are treated as making a joint UC claim.[15]

Married couples and civil partners

You must claim tax credits jointly with your partner if you are married to her/him or you are registered as civil partners. You still count as a couple for tax credits purposes if you are married or are registered civil partners, and are still in a relationship but are not living together – eg, because of work or housing reasons. You continue to count as a couple while you and your partner are temporarily separated. It does not matter how long the temporary separation lasts (but see p1452 if you or your partner go abroad).

If you and your partner are permanently separated or are separated under a court order, claim tax credits as a single person immediately. This is the case even if you are still living under the same roof and whether or not you are taking steps to divorce your partner or dissolve your civil partnership.[16] The test is whether you are 'separated in circumstances in which the separation is likely to be permanent' and this depends on your (and your partner's) intentions.[17] The focus is on the state of the relationship, not exclusively whether you are living in the 'same household', which differs from the rule for means-tested benefits (see p215).[18] If you are having a trial separation and there is at least a 50 per cent chance of reconciliation, HMRC is likely to say you still count as a couple.[19]

Special rules apply if you are a member of a polygamous unit.[20]

Living together as a couple

You must claim tax credits jointly with your partner if you are living together as if you are married or civil partners. In determining whether or not you count as living together as a couple, HMRC is likely to consider the same factors the DWP does for means-tested benefits.[21] See p216 and p219 for more information.

If you and your partner stop living together, claim tax credits as a single person immediately. However, if you and your partner are only temporarily living apart (eg, one of you is in hospital or in respite care), you may still be treated as a couple.

Part 10: General rules for tax credits
Chapter 61: Claims, decisions and getting paid: tax credits
1. Who should claim

Note: decision makers often apply too narrow an interpretation of the test. For example, there is no rule that says that if your partner stays with you for three nights or more a week you are *automatically* to be treated as a couple living together.

Couples and residence rules

If you or your partner go abroad, either permanently or for more than a set period of time and cannot be treated as being in the UK (see p1604), you cease to satisfy the residence conditions. In this case, you must terminate your joint claim. Failure to do this may result in a penalty (see p1490). The person still in the UK may be able to make a new claim as a single person.

If your partner does not have a right to reside in the UK (see p1542), or has not been living in the UK for three months before the claim (with some exceptions, see p1536), s/he is treated as not being present in the UK for CTC.[22] This means you can claim CTC as a single person. However, these rules do not apply to WTC, so it must still be a joint claim for WTC only. It is advisable to ensure that HMRC is fully aware of these circumstances when you claim.

If your partner is a person subject to immigration control (see p1516) and you have no such restrictions, you make a joint claim for tax credits as a couple (see p1524).[23]

Challenging a decision

If you have claimed tax credits as a single person, HMRC may investigate your claim if it suspects that you are living with a partner. HMRC may ask you for information or evidence and may suspend payments if you have not responded by the specified date (you must be given at least 30 days). If it has evidence to change a decision, HMRC may decide that you are not entitled to claim as a single person. You have the right to request a mandatory reconsideration and, if you are unhappy with the outcome, appeal against such a decision (but not against a suspension of payments) (see Chapter 64). HMRC often relies on information it obtains from credit reference agencies, but in the event of an appeal, it must usually produce all the evidence it used to make the decision, and such information on its own is unlikely to be sufficient to justify a 'living together' decision.[24] No adverse inference can be drawn if you fail to provide information or evidence that you cannot reasonably be expected to provide, or if you have not been adequately notified what is appropriate.[25] HMRC must set out its evidence for having reasonable grounds to change a decision during the year.[26]

If you think a decision about whether or not you count as a couple is wrong and it affects your tax credits, consider requesting a mandatory reconsideration and then appealing. It is possible that the DWP, the local authority and HMRC might reach different conclusions about whether you are a couple. If so, appeal *all* the decisions with which you disagree.

Appointees

The following people can make a claim on your behalf if you are unable to make the claim yourself:[27]

- a receiver appointed by the Court of Protection with power to make a claim for tax credits on your behalf;
- in Scotland, a tutor, curator or other guardian acting or appointed in terms of the law who is administering your estate;
- a person who is your 'appointee' (see p1149) for social security purposes; *or*
- if none of the above applies, a person aged 18 or over who applies to HMRC in writing to act on your behalf and is appointed by HMRC in that capacity.

---

2. How and when to make a claim

You must usually claim tax credits in writing on Form TC600. You have no entitlement to tax credits unless you make a claim.[28] You claim both child tax credit (CTC) and working tax credit (WTC) on one claim form. HM Revenue and Customs (HMRC) has discretion to accept an application not made on the correct claim form, but in practice this rarely happens.[29] There are specific circumstances where a claim may be accepted by other means.

- If you have been getting additional amounts for your children in your income support (IS) and your entitlement to IS ends (eg, because you are a lone parent and have been moved onto jobseeker's allowance (JSA) when your youngest child reached the age of five), the DWP can pass the required information to HMRC to allow a 'deemed claim' for CTC and you do not have to fill in a separate claim form.[30]
- If you are starting work after being on JSA, employment and support allowance (ESA) or IS, your local Jobcentre Plus office can take details of your claim and send it electronically to HMRC as part of the 'In and Out of Work Project'.[31]
- If you were claiming tax credits as a couple and notify the Tax Credit Office (TCO) that you are no longer a couple, your new single claim can be accepted by telephone.
- If you were claiming tax credits as a single person and become part of a couple, HMRC has announced that, as part of a new service from April 2017, your single claim can be converted to a joint claim by telephone without a new claim form.
- If you are renewing a claim, this may be done by telephone, online or automatically in specific cases (see p1457).

You can get a claim form by contacting the Tax Credit Helpline on 0345 300 3900 (textphone: 0345 300 3909), which may also ask you questions about your identity and eligibility for tax credits. Once you have passed the identification

Part 10: General rules for tax credits
Chapter 61: Claims, decisions and getting paid: tax credits
2. How and when to make a claim

process, the Helpline must send a claim form if you request one, even if entitlement is in doubt.[32] If you cannot prove your identity over the telephone, you may be required to attend an interview. Some Citizens Advice Bureaux may also have a supply of claim forms. Even if you are advised by the Helpline that you are not entitled to tax credits, still request a claim form and make a claim if you think you are eligible. There will then be a decision on which to base a mandatory reconsideration and then appeal.

You can also make an online request for a claim form to be sent to you in the post at www.gov.uk/qualify-tax-credits. HMRC expects you to wait up to two weeks for a claim form to arrive. Note that the date of your claim is the date that the completed form is received by HMRC, subject to backdating rules.

Send the completed claim form directly to the TCO in the pre-paid envelope provided (Comben House, Farriers Way, Netherton, Merseyside L75 1AX).[33] Keep a copy of your claim form in case queries arise.

If you have sent your claim form to the TCO and you later realise that the details on it need to be amended, contact the TCO as soon as possible. You can amend or withdraw your claim at any time before it has been decided.[34]

When to claim

You should claim tax credits as soon as you think you are eligible. You cannot make a claim for tax credits in advance of the tax year for which you are claiming.[35] The general rule is that a claim for tax credits runs from the date it is received by the TCO until the end of the tax year in which the claim is made.[36] There is an exception if you claim universal credit (UC) and, on the basis of information you provided, you are treated as living in an area in which UC has been introduced, or as satisfying the gateway conditions for a claim for UC, but the DWP discovers that the information was incorrect. Unless you have already been paid UC, you should be advised by the DWP that you are not entitled to claim UC. If you then claim tax credits within a month of being told that, your tax credits claim is treated as made on the date of your UC claim, or a later date if you would have been entitled from a later date.[37]

If you were entitled to tax credits before the date your claim is received by the TCO, your claim can be backdated for up to 31 days. Backdating of WTC is possible for a longer period if you are a disabled worker and only become entitled to WTC following an award of a qualifying benefit (see p1459).

Once a claim for tax credits has been made, it can be renewed at the end of that tax year (see p1457).

You cannot make a new claim for tax credits if you or your partner are entitled to UC, even if your claim could be backdated to a date before you were entitled to UC.[38]

Should you protect your claim?[39]

Tax credits are always based on annual income. HMRC bases the initial award on your (and your partner's) *previous* tax year's income (see p1430). If your income in the previous year was too high to qualify for tax credits, but you think your income in the current year may be substantially lower and you will qualify (eg, if you are self-employed with a fluctuating income, or your income is going to fall because your work is seasonal, you are going on maternity leave or you might be made redundant), you may wish to consider making a claim, including a request for it to be backdated if relevant.

This is known as a 'protective claim' and you are given a 'nil award'.[40] This means that you are eligible for tax credits and your claim is in the system, but you are currently not paid anything because your previous year's income was too high. This protects your position because once your current year's income is known, HMRC can amend the nil award to make a payment for the whole period of your claim, rather than requiring you to make a new claim, which can only be backdated 31 days. The nil award can be amended during the year or at the end of the tax year, and the new award runs from your original date of claim (or the date to which your claim was backdated).

Information to support your claim

Your claim must usually contain all the information requested on the claim form, unless HMRC decides otherwise.[41] If you do not supply all the requested information, a decision may be delayed, or HMRC may decide to 'reject' your claim as not validly made. Caselaw has found that you have the right of appeal (after a mandatory reconsideration) against a decision to reject a claim that is not made on the correct form or does not contain all the required information.[42] If you need advice about the information required, contact the Helpline (see p1472).

National insurance number requirement

Your claim must include the following for each person:[43]

- your (and your partner's if you are claiming as a couple) national insurance (NI) number plus information or evidence establishing that the number is yours (or your partner's); *or*
- information or evidence to enable HMRC to find your (and your partner's) NI number; *or*
- an application for an NI number, with the necessary evidence or information to allow one to be allocated (this does not necessarily mean that you must actually be allocated an NI number).

You do not need to meet the above NI number requirement if HMRC believes you have a 'reasonable excuse'.[44] 'Reasonable excuse' is not defined, but HMRC says it varies from case to case and discretion must be used fairly.[45] Caselaw has found that you have a right of appeal (after a mandatory reconsideration) against a

Part 10: General rules for tax credits
Chapter 61: Claims, decisions and getting paid: tax credits
2. How and when to make a claim

decision that you do not have a reasonable excuse for not meeting the NI number requirement.[46] If someone has not been given an NI number, you can argue this is a reasonable excuse.

If you or your partner are a 'person subject to immigration control', see p1526 the for NI number requirement and p1519 for how tax credits are affected by your immigration status.

Child benefit reference number

The tax credit claim form asks for the child benefit reference number for any child(ren) for whom you are claiming. You should leave the box blank if you do not know it. There is no legal requirement to claim child benefit in order to be entitled to CTC. If you do not have a child benefit reference number (eg, because you are waiting for your child benefit claim to be processed), do not delay claiming CTC. Child benefit can be backdated three months, but CTC can only be backdated 31 days, and it usually takes longer than this for a child benefit claim to be made and processed. HMRC has confirmed that tax credit claims will not be rejected because the child benefit reference number is missing.[47] It may take longer to confirm the identity of the child, and that you are responsible for the child. However, the tax credit award will still be made from the date of claim, with up to 31 days' backdating. As long as your tax credit claim is received within 31 days of the date of birth of a new baby, or the date you became responsible for a child, it will be awarded from that date, even if it takes longer than this to process.

Income

If you are receiving IS, income-based JSA, income-related ESA or pension credit (PC) when you claim tax credits, you must tick a box to confirm this on the claim form. You do not need to provide any other income details.[48] HMRC expects you to know which type of JSA or ESA you are getting.[49]

Otherwise, when you make a claim for tax credits, you must provide a figure for your income during the previous tax year. If you are part of a couple and making a joint claim, your award is based on your joint income during the previous tax year. This applies even in situations in which you may not have been living as a couple in the previous year, so income before the relationship began still counts as joint income.[50] The notes that accompany the claim form include a working sheet to help you calculate your income. For what counts as income, see Chapter 60.

If you think that your current tax year's income is going to be substantially different to the previous tax year's income, you must still complete the claim form with details of your previous tax year's income. When HMRC makes a decision on your claim, you will be sent an award notice informing you how to notify it of your estimated income for the current year. You can also request that your award be adjusted at any time during the year of the award. Where appropriate, HMRC will adjust your award of tax credits, using your estimated figure of your current year's income (see p1465).

If you worked as an employee throughout the previous tax year, your P60 for that year has details of your taxable income. If you received any payments in kind from your employer, you should have details of these on Form P9D or P11D, which your employer should give you. If you were self-employed throughout the previous tax year, you can use your tax return as the basis for your taxable income. If you were in receipt of taxable social security benefits, you should be able to get a statement of taxable benefit income from the DWP.

Note: if your previous year's income was too high to receive tax credits, but you think your current year's income may be less, you should make a protective claim for tax credits if you meet the qualifying conditions (see p1455).

Bank account details

You are required to provide details of a bank, building society or Post Office card account into which the tax credits can be paid. This is because entitlement depends on having a bank or other account.[51] See p1460 if you do not have an account.

Further information and evidence

HMRC might need further information or evidence before making a decision on a claim, renewal or revision. The information or evidence can be required from you or from your employer or childcare provider. If material is required, HMRC gives notice to provide it within a specified time limit. In all cases, this must be at least 30 days.[52] The basic rule is that you can be required to provide any further information or evidence that HMRC considers necessary. If you do not provide the material requested, your claim should be decided on the information available and you might be refused tax credits. If you provide incorrect information or fail to comply with requirements to provide information or evidence, you may be given a financial penalty or, if you are considered to have acted fraudulently, a fine or imprisonment, or both (see Chapter 63).

Renewing your claim

From 6 April each year, HMRC reviews all tax credit awards (see p1468). This annual review, and your response, is also your renewal claim for the new tax year. Tax credits continue to be paid on a provisional basis during the annual review (see p1462). **Note:** your claim can be renewed until you become entitled to UC, even if you live in a UC full service area (see p24).

Withdrawing your claim

If you no longer wish to claim tax credits, you can withdraw your claim during the annual review (see p1468). However, if you have been receiving 'provisional

Part 10: General rules for tax credits
Chapter 61: Claims, decisions and getting paid: tax credits
3. How your claim is dealt with

payments' (see p1462) since the start of the new tax year, these become overpayments if there is no renewal claim. If you have a nil award because your income is too high for an award to be made, HMRC seeks to withdraw your claim. HMRC writes to you at least 35 days before the annual review to notify you that your claim will not be renewed unless you respond within 30 days that you want your claim to continue.[53] Renewing a nil award protects your future entitlement and may prove valuable if income drops unexpectedly later in the year.[54]

3. **How your claim is dealt with**

Once you have made a valid claim for tax credits (see p1453), HM Revenue and Customs (HMRC) must make a decision on whether you are entitled to either of the tax credits and, if so, at what rate.[55] HMRC may first require you, or your partner if you are making a joint claim, to provide any information or evidence that it needs to make a decision.[56]

You can amend, either verbally or in writing, the details you provided when making your claim at any time until HMRC makes its initial decision and your date of claim will remain the same.[57]

An **'initial decision'** (see p1459) is made at the start of your claim and is based on an estimate of your tax credit award for the whole year (6 April to 5 April) or the remainder of the year if you claim during the year. You are notified of the initial decision in an award notice (TC602). You are asked to check the details on your award notice using a checklist (TC602(SN)). Contact the Tax Credit Office if any of the details shown on the award notice are wrong or have changed. If you do not and an overpayment results, HMRC may expect you to pay it back (see p1478).

A **'revised decision'** may be made during the tax year – eg, following certain changes of circumstances (see p1462). Decisions can be revised at any time during the tax year, and as many times as is required. Each revised decision is notified on a tax credits award notice, Form TC602.

A **'final decision'** is made after the end of the tax year in which your claim was made, as part of the annual review (see p1470). It is based on your circumstances during the year and is the decision that confirms what your entitlement actually was. You are sent a tax credits award notice, Form TC602. A final decision can only be changed in limited circumstances (see p1500).

Unless the decision on your award is changed on revision, mandatory reconsideration or appeal, the initial decision and the final decision are the only decisions on your claim that you will receive.

If you think an initial decision, revised decision or final decision is wrong, you can request a mandatory reconsideration and then appeal (see Chapter 64).

Initial decisions

On receiving your application, HMRC must make an initial decision on whether you are entitled to tax credits and, if so, the amount. The claim form does not distinguish between child tax credit and working tax credit, so HMRC must decide your entitlement for both.

The main evidence normally used relates to your income in the *previous* tax year to the one in which you make your claim and to your circumstances (eg, if you have children or if you are working) in the *current* tax year – ie, the one in which you make your claim. So, for an initial decision for 2017/18, the current year is 2017/18 and the previous year is 2016/17. See Chapter 60 for more details about income.

You must be notified of the initial decision. The notice must include the date on which it is given and your right to request a mandatory reconsideration, and subsequent right to appeal.[58] If you had already claimed tax credits in the previous year, your initial decision for the coming year may be included in the annual review (see p1468).[59] The initial decision sets out the amount of tax credits you are due to receive until the final decision is made, unless it is changed on revision, mandatory reconsideration or appeal.

4. Backdating your claim

In general, your claim for tax credits can be backdated for up to 31 days (but see below), provided you would have satisfied the rules of entitlement throughout the 31-day period.[60] You do not need any reason for backdating. Although HM Revenue and Customs looks at your claim form for evidence of possible backdating, it is best to ask for your claim to be backdated to when you think your entitlement began (subject to the 31-day limit). However, your tax credits claim cannot be backdated to overlap with any period during which you are or were entitled to tax-free childcare (see p864). The claim form does not ask about backdating, so request it separately in writing and follow up by telephone.

A renewal claim can be backdated for longer periods, depending on when you make your annual declaration (see p1469).

If you were entitled to tax credits but no payment was made because you failed to provide sufficient details of an account into which tax credits could be paid and you subsequently provide the necessary details, your payment can be backdated for up to three months from the date you supply the information.[61]

A new claim for working tax credit (WTC) can be backdated for more than 31 days if you have a disability and you have been waiting to hear about a disability benefit. If your claim includes the disabled worker element (see p1412) and you claim within 31 days of being awarded a qualifying disability benefit, usually disability living allowance (DLA) or personal independence payment (PIP), your

10

Part 10: General rules for tax credits
Chapter 61: Claims, decisions and getting paid: tax credits
5. Getting paid

WTC claim can be backdated to the date your DLA or PIP was awarded, provided you were working at least 16 hours throughout the period and did not qualify for WTC without the award of the disability benefit, including where your income was too high.[62]

A new claim for child tax credit (CTC) cannot be backdated for more than 31 days, even if a disability benefit has been awarded for the child. If your income is too high to receive CTC unless a disability element is included, you should make a 'protective claim' (see p1455). If you have an existing award of WTC or CTC and want to be awarded the disability or severe disability elements following an award of a qualifying disability benefit, see p1465.

See p1528 for backdating if you are granted refugee status.

5. **Getting paid**

Who is paid

If you make a joint claim, child tax credit (CTC) and the childcare element of working tax credit (WTC) are paid into the account of the 'main carer' of the child(ren), as nominated on the claim form.[63] The **'main carer'** can be either you or your partner, depending on who you both agree should be paid. If both live at the same address and either you do not identify who should be paid, or you cannot agree, HM Revenue and Customs (HMRC) decides. If you and your partner are not currently living at the same address or one of you is temporarily absent, HMRC decides which of you will be paid. If the main carer changes following an award of tax credits, HMRC can make the payments to that person instead if it considers it reasonable.

If you claim WTC as part of a joint claim and one of you is working, the payment (apart from any amount for childcare) is made to the person who is in full-time paid work (see p196). If you are both in full-time paid work, you can decide who will receive the payment. If you cannot agree, HMRC decides. If you both agree who should be paid, write to the Tax Credit Office (TCO) requesting that payment be made to that person.[64]

If you make a joint claim and your partner dies, you receive any outstanding amount of tax credits that would have been paid to your partner up to the date of death, after which you must make a new claim as a single person.[65]

If an appointee (see p1149) has claimed tax credits on your behalf, payment is normally made to the appointee.[66]

How and when payments are made

HMRC makes payments of tax credits by direct credit transfer into a bank, building society (or similar) or Post Office card account.[67] The government is writing to people with Post Office card accounts about switching to a bank, building society or credit union account, but Post Office card accounts will remain available for the time being. You can request that the payments be made into your account every week or every four weeks, but HMRC has the discretion to make payments weekly or four-weekly as it sees fit. CTC and the childcare element of WTC must be paid at the same time and at the same intervals.[68] Generally, tax credits payments are made in arrears.[69]

If you are entitled to less than £2 tax credits a week, your award may be paid as a lump sum.[70]

If it is not considered appropriate for payments to be made into an account, HMRC can decide on the manner and timing of payment by other means (but it no longer issues cheques).[71] If you do not provide account details, HMRC should write to you, requesting that you supply the information within four weeks, after which your payments may be postponed.[72] If you then require an authority from HMRC to open an account, you have three weeks from the date it supplies you with this to provide details of your account. If you do not provide details of an account within three months of your payments being postponed (or by the end of the relevant tax year if this is earlier), your entitlement may cease from the date payments were postponed. These periods can be extended if there are exceptional circumstances or you have a 'reasonable excuse' for not being able to provide the details within the time limits.[73] If you lose or forget your PIN, see p1173.

Payments of tax credits may be reduced if an overpayment is being recovered. See Chapter 62 for more information.

Urgent payments

There is no provision in the tax credits legislation for payments to be made before a decision has been made on entitlement. However, once a decision has been made to award tax credits, there is detailed staff guidance on making payments urgently when requested by you or via the MP Hotline. Urgent payments should be made where you or your children are experiencing hardship, especially in cases of domestic violence, identity fraud, immediate risk of eviction or other individual circumstances. These payments are variously referred to in the *Tax Credits Manual* as 'manual payments', 'interim payments' and 'user-requested payments'. Payment can be made by the next day into an account.[74]

When payment is postponed or suspended

Payment of tax credits may be postponed or suspended if:[75]

- there is an appeal pending against a decision of the First-tier Tribunal, Upper Tribunal or a court either in your case or in another case that might affect your award (including if HMRC is considering whether to make a further appeal or request a statement of reasons); *or*
- you have failed to provide correct account details; *or*

Part 10: General rules for tax credits
Chapter 61: Claims, decisions and getting paid: tax credits
6. Change of circumstances

- you have failed to respond to a request for information or evidence by a specified date; *or*
- you are receiving 'provisional payments' (see below).

If your income drops during the year, your tax credits may be increased and you may appear to be due some arrears of tax credits for the earlier part of the year. HMRC refers to this as a 'potential payment', and it may be held back until the end of the year when your final income is known. If the underpayment is confirmed at the end of the tax year, it must be paid to you.[76]

Provisional payments

Your claim is renewed by the annual review process from April to July, during which time your tax credits may continue to be paid on a provisional basis.[77]

Provisional payments continue while you are waiting to renew your claim and have not had a final decision on the previous year, or, if you have renewed your claim but not yet received an initial decision, on the new tax year. Provisional payments are discretionary and can be made, adjusted or suspended without a formal decision being made, but you may receive a letter which is referred to as a 'statement like an award notice' (TC602(J)).[78]

If HMRC does not have up-to-date income details, these payments are based on the assumption that your income for the tax year just ended increased in line with average earnings.[79] If your income increased by more than this, you may be overpaid until the review is complete. Therefore, it is best to provide income details as soon as possible and not wait for the annual review. If you withdraw or fail to renew your claim, any provisional payments since the start of the year will become an overpayment because there is no claim for the new tax year.

6. **Change of circumstances**

Changes in your family circumstances, childcare charges or income during your award may lead to changes in your entitlement. If changes do affect your entitlement, this can be altered either soon after the change has occurred, or at the end of the year when the final decision is made and HM Revenue and Customs (HMRC) makes a final check on your details. However, certain changes must be notified to the Tax Credit Office (TCO) within one month or you may incur a penalty. Some other changes which increase your entitlement should be notified within one month if your increased award is to be backdated in full.

Changes that must be notified

Following any change of circumstances that must be notified or that affects your maximum entitlement, the way your tax credits are calculated changes.[80] The changes mean that either your entitlement to tax credits has ceased or that a new 'relevant period' is started from the time the change is treated as taking effect. A new relevant period means that a new calculation of your entitlement is made. See p1407 for more on the relevant period and details of the calculation. Some changes must be notified to the TCO within one month of the date of the change or the date you became aware of the change, if this was later. The notification must be 'given' to the appropriate office (see p1467).[81] If you do not do this, HMRC may impose a financial penalty on you (see p1490). You must notify the TCO within one month if:[82]

- you were claiming as a single person but are now part of a couple. Your tax credit entitlement comes to an end from the time the change occurred, and you must make a new claim;
- you were claiming as a couple but are no longer part of that couple. Your entitlement comes to an end from the date the change occurred, and you must make a new claim;
- you or your partner leave the UK permanently or for more than eight weeks (12 if due to illness or bereavement) and cannot be treated as being in the UK (see p1604). Entitlement comes to an end and you must make a new claim as a single person (and, when s/he comes back, claim again as a couple);
- for child tax credit (CTC) only, you lose your right to reside in the UK (see p1542);
- there has been a decrease of £10 a week or more over four consecutive weeks in your or your partner's average weekly childcare charge (as calculated on p1418) or the childcare costs have stopped. This change takes effect on the day after the four consecutive weeks. If you have been awarded childcare costs for a fixed period that was known when the costs were awarded, the change takes effect from the week following the end of the period of the award, instead of the usual four-week period;[83]
- you or your partner stop normally working at least 16 or 30 hours a week (see p196 for rules about work). You can still count as being in work in some situations – eg, in some cases of illness or maternity and during the four-week run-on of working tax credit (WTC – see p202). For a couple, you do not need to report a change in which partner is working, as long as this does not affect your entitlement or maximum rate;[84]
- you are a couple with children, and you and your partner stop normally working a combined total of 24 or 30 hours a week;
- you or your partner cease to be responsible for one or more of your children (see p184 for when you count as responsible);
- a child for whom you or your partner are responsible dies (see p182 for who counts as a child);
- a child for whom you or your partner are responsible stops counting as a child or qualifying young person, other than by reaching age 20 (see p182 for who counts as a child). You must notify the TCO within one month of the date the change actually occurred, rather than when you became aware of the change.

10

Part 10: General rules for tax credits
Chapter 61: Claims, decisions and getting paid: tax credits
6. Change of circumstances

Changes that terminate your tax credits award

Your tax credit award automatically terminates if:

- you become a universal credit (UC) claimant. This may happen if you become part of a couple with someone who is already entitled to UC, or if you come under the UC system and make a claim for it (see p161). The DWP should inform HMRC that you have claimed and meet the basic conditions for UC. Your tax credit award is terminated, even if you do not receive any UC because your income or capital is too high. If you are not entitled to UC because your earnings are too high, you are excluded from claiming tax credits again for six months from the date of claim or last day of entitlement to UC.[85] Your tax credits claim usually ends on the day before your entitlement to UC begins. However, if you become part of a couple with a UC claimant, your new joint UC claim begins from the start of your new partner's assessment period in which you became a couple.[86] In this case, you are still entitled to tax credits up to the actual date you became a couple;[87]
- you apply for, and are entitled to, tax-free childcare payments. This is a new HMRC-administered scheme to be introduced from early 2017 (see p864). Check whether you will be better off on tax-free childcare before applying. This is only likely to be the case if you are entitled to a small amount of tax credits. Your entire tax credits claim, not just the childcare element, ends on the day before your entitlement period for tax-free childcare begins.[88]

Changes that affect your maximum entitlement

In addition to the changes outlined above, there are other changes in your circumstances that affect your maximum entitlement to tax credits – ie, they affect the tax credit elements to which you are entitled (see Chapter 59).

You do not have to notify the TCO of these changes when they occur. Some changes can be notified up to a week in advance (see p1467). However, most changes which *increase* your entitlement are only backdated for a maximum of one month from the time that you notify the TCO of the change.[89] The only exception concerns one of the disability elements (see below). Changes that *decrease* your entitlement always take effect from the date of change, irrespective of when you notify the TCO. Delaying notifying these changes can lead to an underpayment or overpayment. Overpayments are usually recovered from you (see Chapter 62).

The changes to which these rules apply include:

- you have a new baby, or another child joins your family;
- your child is staying on in full-time non-advanced education after 31 August following his/her 16th birthday (HMRC considers this to be a change, as the default position is that CTC will stop unless you notify it of this);
- you or your partner start normally working at least 16, 24 or 30 hours a week;

- your childcare costs increase by £10 or more a week for at least four weeks in a row. The change takes effect from the first week in which your costs increase.[90] You can report an increase of £10 or more a week as soon as one occurs, provided you expect it to last for at least four weeks. For how your childcare costs are calculated, see p1418.

Changes in entitlement to one of the disability elements

The disabled worker and severe disability elements of WTC can be backdated for more than one month if you notify the TCO that you have been awarded a qualifying disability benefit, usually disability living allowance (DLA) or personal independence payment (PIP), within one month of that award being made.[91] The elements can be backdated to the date the disability benefit was awarded. This includes after an appeal or supersession from a previous tax year. If the award means that you become entitled to WTC for the first time, see p1459.

A similar rule applies to CTC entitlement. If a child for whom you are responsible is awarded DLA or a young person is awarded PIP, you are entitled to the disabled child element. If the child is awarded DLA care component at the highest rate or PIP at the enhanced rate for daily living, you are entitled to the severely disabled child element in your CTC award. The elements can be backdated for more than one month, to the date DLA or PIP was awarded, if you notify the TCO of the award of DLA or PIP within one month of the DLA or PIP decision.[92] This includes after an appeal or supersession from a previous tax year. However, it is not possible to backdate a new claim for CTC in this way, because you would have been eligible anyway provided you were responsible for the child. If your income is too high to receive CTC unless the disabled child or severely disabled child element is awarded, make a 'protective claim' (see p1455). You should report changes to a qualifying disability benefit, as failure to do so may result in an underpayment or overpayment, but a penalty cannot be imposed on you for failing to report a change to a disability benefit.

Changes in income

The initial decision on your award of tax credit is usually based on your previous year's income. Your award can be changed to reflect:
- an expected fall in your annual income of more than £2,500 compared with the previous year (see p1466); *and*
- an expected rise in your annual income of more than £2,500 compared with the previous year (see p1466).

You are not required to report a change in income during the year and a penalty cannot be imposed on you if you fail to do so, unless it is a formal request for information (see p1489). However, it is often worth reporting a change when it occurs to avoid overpayments or underpayments. HMRC may use real-time information on wages obtained from your employer for tax purposes. Remember

Part 10: General rules for tax credits
Chapter 61: Claims, decisions and getting paid: tax credits
6. Change of circumstances

that HMRC always requires a figure for your annual income in the complete tax year, so be careful to keep an in-year estimate accurate and up to date.

If you expect your annual income to fall by more than £2,500

- If you notify the TCO of an estimated decrease in your annual income of more than £2,500 during the year, your tax credit payments may be increased. However, the first £2,500 of the decrease is disregarded, so it is only any decrease over that amount that makes a difference. HMRC adds £2,500 onto the current year's income and bases your award on the result. For example, if your 2016/17 income was £10,000 and your 2017/18 income is £6,000, your tax credits award is based on £8,500.[93]

- An increase in tax credits means that if you get housing benefit (HB), the amount could be reduced because tax credits count as income.

- At the end of the year, it may be that your income did not fall as you predicted and, as a result, you have been overpaid tax credits, which you may have to repay. For example, if your 2016/17 income was £9,000 and you ask for your tax credits to be based on an estimate that your 2017/18 income will be £6,000 but, at the end of 2017/18, your actual income is £8,000, your tax credit award should not have been increased and you will have been overpaid.

- HB takes into account the amount of tax credits you actually *receive*. If you have been overpaid tax credits, HB is *not* increased for the period during which you should have received a lower amount of tax credits. Not only will you usually have to repay the overpaid tax credits, you may have lost out on the additional HB which you would have been able to claim had you been receiving a lower award of tax credits.

- If the TCO is not aware of a fall in income of more than £2,500 during the year, your tax credit entitlement is not adjusted until the final decision at the end of the year. In this instance, you will have been underpaid tax credits for the year, and this should be paid to you as a lump sum. This lump sum counts as capital for HB and is ignored for 52 weeks after you have received it.[94] You will not, therefore, have been overpaid HB as a result of receiving these arrears and you will not have been overpaid or lost out on tax credits.

If you expect your annual income to rise by more than £2,500

- If you notify the TCO that you expect your income to increase by more than £2,500 during the year, your tax credit award is decreased. This may mean that you prevent an overpayment of tax credits building up further during the year (see Chapter 62). Your HB (if you are entitled to any) can then be increased to take account of the lower award of tax credits.

- If the TCO is not aware of an expected rise in your income during the year, you keep being paid the 'extra' tax credits during the year and will incur an overpayment. The overpaid tax credits are usually recoverable from you by a reduction in the tax credits you are paid in the following year, in which case your HB in that year is likely to increase.

- There is no penalty for incurring an overpayment of tax credits on the basis of an increase in income.
- If you have overestimated your income, and it does not rise as expected, you may have been underpaid tax credits and you can receive a lump sum at the end of the year.

Notifying changes of circumstances

You can notify any changes in your circumstances either orally, in writing or online through a government gateway account. The notification must be given to an 'appropriate office', defined as Comben House, Farriers Way, Netherton, Merseyside L75 1AX or any other office specified in writing by HMRC – eg, the TCO address on your award notice (see Appendix 1).[95] This could include the government 'Tell Us Once' service following a death, or the Jobcentre Plus office dealing with your tax credits claim as part of the 'In and Out of Work Project'.

If you did notify the DWP or another part of HMRC of a change which affects your tax credit entitlement and this was not passed on and resulted in an underpayment or overpayment, you should raise this in **any** dispute (see p1477). In practice, to be safe, you should ensure that the TCO has been informed. HMRC encourages claimants to telephone the Helpline with queries or to report a change. However, it is advisable to confirm the notification in writing to the TCO and to keep a copy so you have a record of what you have said and when you said it.

Notification must be given by the person who claimed the tax credit. In joint claim cases, it can be given by either member of the couple.[96]

Some changes of circumstances can be notified up to a week in advance. These are if:[97]

- you have accepted an offer of work and expect to start work within seven days;
- you have arranged childcare and will incur childcare costs during the current tax year;
- your weekly childcare costs are going to change by £10 a week or more.

You can also notify in advance if you expect your child to stay on in full-time, non-advanced education or approved training from 1 September after her/his 16th birthday.[98]

You can amend the notification at any time before the initial award is revised, in which case the amended notification is taken as being notified at the time that your original notification was sent.[99]

If you notify a change of circumstances, HMRC should send you a new award notice (if the change affected your award) within 30 days.[100] If you do not receive one within 30 days, HMRC's leaflet asks you to call the Helpline again. However,

Part 10: General rules for tax credits
Chapter 61: Claims, decisions and getting paid: tax credits
7. Annual reviews

provided you can prove the original notification was made, it is HMRC's responsibility to act on the information provided (see p1478).

7. **Annual reviews**

The annual review is the process by which HM Revenue and Customs (HMRC) finalises your entitlement for the year that has just ended, and makes an initial decision on your award for the year that has just begun. Responding to the annual review is how you renew your claim for tax credits for the new tax year.

If you claimed tax credits for the tax year 2016/17, HMRC should write to you between April and July 2017 enclosing an annual review form (TC603R). This is referred to in the legislation as the 'final notice'.[101] If you have been receiving income support (IS), income-based jobseeker's allowance (JSA), income-related employment and support allowance (ESA) or pension credit (PC) throughout 2016/17 and are still getting one of those benefits, the annual review may tell you that your award will be renewed automatically on the information shown on the notice unless you report a change or error. This automatic renewal process may also apply if HMRC uses real-time information on earnings provided by your employer for pay as you earn (PAYE) purposes, but you must still check that this is correct. In other cases, you may also receive an annual declaration (Form TC603D – see p1469).

If you made more than one claim for tax credits during the previous tax year (eg, because you separated from your partner and made a new claim as a single person), you receive a separate annual review form and annual declaration form, if required, for each claim. If you are sent more than one set of forms covering different claims, check and reply to each separately, even if they ask for the same information.

If you are sent an annual review form, but not an annual declaration form, you are asked to check that all the details about your claim for the previous year are correct and to notify the Tax Credit Office (TCO) of any changes in your circumstances. You are then deemed to have confirmed that all the details in the form are correct.[102] The final decision on the award for 2016/17 and an initial decision on the award for 2017/18 are as set out on the annual review form and you do not receive another notice of the final decision when it is made on or after 31 July. However, always check the form and the notes accompanying it carefully to see whether you need to return the forms or report a change or error.

If the details on the forms sent to you about your claim and income are not correct and you fail to reply within the time allowed, you may not receive the correct amount of tax credit. If you are overpaid as a result, you may have to repay the overpayment. If you fail to notify certain changes of circumstances promptly, you may be given a penalty (see p1490).

If your tax credit award ends because you become entitled to universal credit (UC), see p1471.

The annual declaration

You may receive an annual declaration form (TC603D) that asks for details of your income in the previous tax year.

Responses must usually be on a form provided by HMRC (Form TC603RD). Alternatively, you can call the Helpline or renew your claim online (www.gov.uk). If you are unable to respond to the annual declaration (eg, because of illness), responses can be accepted from receivers and people who are appointees for tax credit or benefit purposes.[103]

If you are sent an annual declaration form, you must always respond to it on or before the date specified – usually 31 July, unless it was issued after 1 July, in which case you must be given at least 30 days to respond. If you are returning the annual declaration form by post, this is the date by which it must be received by the TCO. If you respond in writing but do not use the annual declaration form, HMRC has discretion whether to accept it.[104] Alternatively, you can make your annual declaration by telephone or online on or before the deadline.

If you do not respond to the annual declaration, your tax credit payments will stop, you may have to repay any tax credits paid since 6 April and you may have to pay a penalty.

You must also tell the TCO of any changes in your personal circumstances different from those set out in the annual review form.

For a joint claim, one member of a couple can make the declaration by telephone or online on behalf of her/his partner; if it is in writing, both partners must sign it.[105] If a couple separate during the renewal period, a declaration by one partner allows the claim to be renewed up to the date of separation.[106] Both members of a separated couple are expected to make signed declarations for the previous year to allow the award for that year to be finalised. However, if only one signs the declaration, the award can be finalised, based on the information held by HMRC about the other member.[107]

If you do not know your total income for the period in question, do not delay making your annual declaration. Instead, provide an estimate and send details of your actual income as soon as you can. The annual declaration form allows for this, and there is a box to tick to show that you have given an estimate. You must provide your actual income figure on or before a second deadline, usually 31 January at the latest. The annual declaration form notifies you that if you do not do so, you are treated as having declared that your final income was as estimated, and your estimate is used to finalise your entitlement.[108] Responding to the annual declaration, if required, is how your claim is renewed for the new tax year, and failure to meet the deadline can mean that you lose out on tax credits.

- If you make your annual declaration on or before the 31 July deadline, your renewal claim is backdated to 6 April 2017.[109]

Part 10: General rules for tax credits
Chapter 61: Claims, decisions and getting paid: tax credits
7. Annual reviews

- If you do not make your annual declaration on or before 31 July, HMRC sends you a notice that your payments of tax credits have ceased. If you make your annual declaration within 30 days following the date on the notice, your renewal claim is backdated to 6 April 2017.[110]
- If neither of the above apply, but you make your annual declaration on or before 31 January 2018 and have 'good cause' for making a late declaration, your renewal claim is backdated to 6 April 2017.[111] 'Good cause' is not defined, but HMRC says it will look at each case on its individual merits. It will consider whether you were not able to complete the form because of exceptional circumstances and could not make arrangements for someone else to handle your affairs.[112]
- If you make your annual declaration late without good cause, or after 31 January in any case, this should be treated as a new claim and it can only be backdated for 31 days.[113]

Note: if you are not accepted as having good cause for making a late declaration, you should request a mandatory reconsideration, and then appeal to the First-tier Tribunal if you are unhappy with the outcome.[114] Remember that your late declaration should be treated as a new claim in any case.

The above rules allowing a late declaration to serve as a renewal do not apply if your previous claim was on the basis that you were:[115]

- single and you are now a member of a couple; *or*
- a member of a couple and you are now single.

The final decision

After the annual review has been completed, HMRC must make a final decision on whether you were entitled to tax credits for the tax year in question and, if so, the amount of your entitlement for that year.[116] The final decision can therefore establish that:

- the initial decision was correct and you received the right amount;
- you were underpaid tax credits;
- you were overpaid tax credits.

If you are underpaid tax credits, HMRC must pay you, usually in a lump sum.[117] If you are overpaid, HMRC asks you to pay back the overpayment (see Chapter 62).

If you do not agree that you have been overpaid, it is important that you request a mandatory reconsideration of the lower award notified to you in the final decision.

The final decision is made in two main stages.

- The annual review forms are issued to gather information and evidence about what your income and circumstances were in the year.
- The information from the annual review is used to make a final decision on your entitlement for the year.

HMRC aims to deal with your review within eight weeks of receiving your declaration.[118] If you did not have an annual declaration form to complete, the final decision is as set out in your annual review form (unless, having read your annual review form, you find that you have a change of circumstances to report, in which case HMRC sends you details of your new award after it has dealt with the reported change). If your annual review told you what the final decision will be, and when it will be made, and you do not report any changes, the final decision can be made without further notification.[119] Any other decision must be notified to you in writing, stating the date on which it is made and including details of your right to request a mandatory reconsideration and your subsequent right of appeal.[120] If a decision does not include these details it is defective, and the time limit for requesting a mandatory reconsideration does not start to run.[121]

A final decision must not be made before you have been given the chance to respond to the annual review and make your annual declaration on or before the deadline (usually 31 July). Once you have made your annual declaration, HMRC may make a final decision before the deadline. However, you can still change your declaration on or before the deadline, in which case HMRC may revise the final decision.[122] If you do not make your annual declaration on or before the deadline, the final decision can be made after that date, based on the information held by HMRC at that time.[123] If you have given an estimate, HMRC may make a final decision, but can revise it if you give details of your actual income on or before the second deadline (usually 31 January).

HMRC also sends you an initial decision notice (TC602), setting out your award for the tax year 2017/18.

If your tax credit award ends because you become entitled to UC, the final decision may be made during the tax year (see below).

In-year finalisation

If your tax credits claim ends because you become entitled to UC, your tax credits award is finalised during the year, rather than at the end of the tax year.[124] This may happen if you become part of a couple with someone who is already entitled to UC, or if you come under the UC system (see p20) and make a claim for UC. HMRC may decide to wait until the end of the tax year to finalise an award if it decides it is not practical to do so during the year. If in-year finalisation applies, you do not get another annual review at the end of the year. You are asked to confirm or declare your income up to the date that your tax credits award ended, and your award is based on part-year income (see p1431). If you do not know your exact income, you can provide an estimate within 30 days. However, your estimated part-year income is used to finalise your award and you are not given an opportunity to rectify the estimate later.[125] If you disagree with the final decision following in-year finalisation for any reason, including the income figure used, you can request a mandatory reconsideration and, if you are unhappy with the outcome, appeal (see Chapter 64).

10

Part 10: General rules for tax credits
Chapter 61: Claims, decisions and getting paid: tax credits
8. Contacting HM Revenue and Customs

8. **Contacting HM Revenue and Customs**

You can telephone the Tax Credit Helpline (tel: 0345 300 3900; textphone: 0345 300 3909). Be ready to give your name, address and national insurance (NI) number. Always keep a note of the date and time of your call, with a brief note of what is said and, if possible, the name and title of the person you speak to. HM Revenue and Customs (HMRC) aims to record all calls made to the Helpline, but a small number may not be recorded because of technical difficulties.[126] In the event of a dispute, you can request the recording of your call. If the recording is not available, and you can show that you made a call on a certain date, HMRC has agreed that you should be given the benefit of the doubt about what was said.[127] It is best to follow up your call with a letter confirming the information you have provided and the advice given by the Helpline. Write to the Tax Credit Office at the address on the award notice and include your name, address, NI number and the date. Always keep a copy of your letter. If you are requesting a mandatory reconsideration, appealing, disputing recovery of an overpayment or making a complaint, it is best to use the relevant form or put it in writing. HMRC has introduced a new online service (www.gov.uk/manage-your-tax-credits) to check details of your claim and report changes of circumstances. HMRC's policy is to retain images of claim forms, documents and recordings of telephone calls for five years plus the tax year or from the date of the last decision on that claim.[128]

If things go wrong

It is not possible to sue HMRC for negligence in the way your claim is decided.[129] If a decision is wrong, you can request a mandatory reconsideration and if you are unhappy with the outcome, appeal against it (see Chapter 64). If you are given wrong advice by an employee of HMRC, you may be able to seek compensation either through the courts or through the internal complaints procedure (see p1398). If you are given wrong information by HMRC or the DWP which led to an overpayment, this may be grounds for recovery to be waived (see p1477).

If your claim has been received but not dealt with, ask why. If you are not satisfied with the explanation, make a complaint to HMRC (see Chapter 58). You can also complain if, for example, you have been treated badly or your case has been mishandled. In some cases, you can seek a judicial review (see p1378). If you are unhappy with the way HMRC handles your complaint, you can take it to the Adjudicator's Office and, if still unhappy, to the Parliamentary and Health Service Ombudsman (see p1399).

Notes

1. Who should claim

1 s3(3) TCA 2002
2 s3(3)(a) and (8) TCA 2002
3 Reg 13(3) TC(CN) Regs
4 s3(4) TCA 2002
5 s32(3) TCA 2002; reg 21(2)(a) TC(CN) Regs
6 HMRC, *Departmental Report 2008,* p38
7 Reg 6 UC(TP) Regs
8 Reg 6(2)(ba) UC(TP) Regs
9 See, for example, Art 7 WRA(No.23)O (different orders apply to different 'full service' areas)
10 WRA(No.23)O
11 Reg 7A (4) TC(CN) Regs
12 s32 Childcare Payments Act 2014; reg 18 Childcare Payments (Eligibility) Regs 2015, No.448
13 s3(5A) TCA 2002
14 s48(2) TCA 2002. Tax credits legislation has not been amended to reflect same-sex marriage. HMRC says this is not necessary because the legal interpretation of a married couple is changed via Sch 3 M(SSC)A 2013 and s4 Marriage and Civil Partnership (Scotland) Act 2014.
15 Regs 5 and 6 UC(TP) Regs; reg 9(8) UC,PIP,JSA&ESA(C&P) Regs
16 *HMRC v PD (TC)* [2012] UKUT 230 (AAC)
17 s3(5A)(a)(ii) and (c)(ii) TCA 2002
18 *DG v HMRC (TC)* [2013] UKUT 631 (AAC)
19 R(TC) 2/06
20 TC(PM) Regs
21 *Crake and Butterworth v SBC* [1982] 1 All ER 498; R(SB) 17/81; CTC/3864/2004
22 Reg 3(5) and (6) TC(R) Regs
23 Reg 3(2) TC(Imm) Regs; reg 11(4) WTC(EMR) Regs
24 *TM v HMRC (TC)* [2013] UKUT 444 (AAC); *NI v HMRC (TC)* [2015] UKUT 490 (AAC)
25 *SS v HMRC (TC)* [2014] UKUT 383 (AAC)
26 *SB v HMRC (TC)* [2014] UKUT 543 (AAC)
27 Regs 17 and 18 TC(CN) Regs

2. How and when to make a claim

28 s3(1) TCA 2002
29 Reg 5(2) TC(CN) Regs

30 Reg 4 TCA(TP)O
31 TCM 0136175
32 HMRC Benefits and Credits Consultation Group minutes, 30 May 2012, www.gov.uk/government/groups/benefits-credits-consultation-group-bccg
33 Reg 2 TC(CN) Regs
34 Reg 5(7) TC(CN) Regs
35 Reg 9 TC(CN) Regs
36 s5(2) TCA 2002; reg 4 TC(CN) Regs
37 Art 3A(2)(d) WRA(No.9)O
38 Reg 6 UC(TP) Regs
39 See 'If you know your income will go down' at www.gov.uk/claim-tax-credits/when-to-claim
40 s14(3) TCA 2002
41 Reg 5(3) TC(CN) Regs
42 *CI v HMRC (TC)* [2014] UKUT 158 (AAC), which rejects the decision saying there is no such right in *ZM and AB v HMRC (TC)* [2013] UKUT 547 (AAC)
43 Reg 5(4) TC(CN) Regs
44 Reg 5(6) TC(CN) Regs
45 TCTM 06110
46 *CI v HMRC (TC)* [2014] UKUT 158 (AAC), which rejects the decision saying there is no such right in *ZM and AB v HMRC (TC)* [2013] UKUT 547 (AAC)
47 HMRC reply to CPAG email, 11 April 2012
48 s7(2) TCA 2002; Form TC600, Part 5; reg 4 TC(ITDR) Regs
49 HMRC leaflet WTC8, *Why Overpayments Happen,* pp4-5
50 s7(5)(a) TCA 2002; R(TC) 1/08
51 Reg 14 TC(PC) Regs
52 ss14, 15, 16, 17,18,19 and 22 TCA 2002; regs 30-33 TC(CN) Regs
53 Reg 12(8) TC(CN) Regs
54 s14(3) TCA 2002

3. How your claim is dealt with

55 s14(1) TCA 2002
56 s14(2) TCA 2002
57 Regs 5 and 6 TC(CN) Regs
58 s23 TCA 2002
59 s23(3) TCA 2002

10

Part 10: General rules for tax credits
Chapter 61: Claims, decisions and getting paid: tax credits
Notes

• •

4. **Backdating your claim**
60 Reg 7 TC(CN) Regs
61 Reg 14(2) TC(PC) Regs
62 Reg 8 TC(CN) Regs; *MMB v HMRC (TC)*
    [2014] UKUT 221 (AAC)

5. **Getting paid**
63 Reg 3 TC(PC) Regs
64 Reg 4 TC(PC) Regs
65 Reg 5 TC(PC) Regs
66 Reg 6 TC(PC) Regs
67 Reg 13(1) TC(PC) Regs
68 Reg 8(2), (2A) and (2B) TC(PC) Regs
69 TCTM 08102
70 Reg 10 TC(PC) Regs
71 Regs 9 and 13 TC(PC) Regs
72 Reg 11(2A) TC(PC) Regs
73 Reg 14(3) and (4A)-(4E) TC(PC) Regs;
    TCM 0212200
74 TCM 0212160
75 Reg 11 TC(PC) Regs; HMRC leaflet
    WTC/FS9, *Tax Credits: suspension of
    payments*
76 Reg 12(3) TC(PC) Regs; s30 TCA 2002
77 s24(4) TCA 2002; reg 7 TC(PC) Regs
78 TCTM 09490
79 Reg 12(4) TC(PC) Regs

6. **Change of circumstances**
80 Regs 7(2) and 8(2) TC(ITDR) Regs
81 ss6(3) and 32(3) TCA 2002; regs 2, 21
    and 22 TC(CN) Regs
82 Reg 21(2) TC(CN) Regs
83 Reg 16(5) WTC(EMR) Regs
84 *JL v HMRC (TC)* [2013] UKUT 325 (AAC)
85 Reg 6 (2)(ba) UC(TP) Regs
86 Reg 21(3B) UC Regs
87 Regs 5, 7 and 12A UC(TP) Regs
88 s30 Childcare Payments Act 2014
89 Regs 20 and 25 TC(CN) Regs
90 Reg 16(5)(a) WTC(EMR) Regs
91 Reg 26 TC(CN) Regs
92 Reg 26A TC(CN) Regs
93 s7(3)(d) TCA 2002; reg 5(b) TC(ITDR)
    Regs
94 Sch 6(9) HB Regs
95 Regs 2 and 22 TC(CN) Regs
96 Reg 23 TC(CN) Regs
97 Reg 27 TC(CN) Regs
98 Reg 27(2B) TC(CN) Regs
99 Reg 24 TC (CN) Regs
100 HMRC leaflet COP26, *What Happens If
    We've Paid You Too Much Tax Credits?*

7. **Annual reviews**
101 s17(1) TCA 2002
102 s17(2)(b) and (6)(b) TCA 2002
103 Regs 34-36 TC(CN) Regs

104 *SG v HMRC (TC)* [2011] UKUT 199 (AAC)
105 Reg 34 TC(CN) Regs
106 Reg 13 TC (CN) Regs
107 s18(3) TCA 2002
108 s17(8) TCA 2002; reg 33(b) TC(CN)
    Regs
109 Reg 11(3)(a) TC(CN) Regs
110 Reg 11(3)(b) TC(CN) Regs
111 Reg 11(3)(c) TC(CN) Regs
112 TCM 0136160
113 Reg 11(3)(d) TC(CN) Regs
114 *SG v HMRC (TC)* [2011] UKUT 199
    (AAC), in particular para 84
115 Reg 11(4) TC(CN) Regs
116 s18 TCA 2002
117 s30 TCA 2002
118 HMRC leaflet TC603RD, *Renewing Your
    Tax Credits: getting it right*
119 s23(3) TCA 2002
120 s23(2) TCA 2002
121 *NA v HMRC* [2016] UKUT 404 (AAC),
    para 11
122 s18(5) TCA 2002
123 s18(8) TCA 2002
124 Reg 12A UC(TP) Regs, as amended by
    UC(TP)(A) Regs
125 Sch para 2 UC(TP) Regs, as amended by
    UC(TP)(A) Regs; HMRC leaflet
    TC603URD, *Ending Your Tax Credits
    Award Because of a Claim for Universal
    Credit*

8. **Contacting HM Revenue and Customs**
126 Response to Freedom of Information
    request, 12 January 2009
127 HMRC Benefits and Credits Consultation
    Group minutes, 4 December 2008
128 *AG v HMRC (TC)* [2013] UKUT 530 (AAC)
129 *Jones v Department of Employment*
    [1989] QB 1 (CA)

Chapter 62

· ·

Overpayments of tax credits

This chapter covers:
1. What is an overpayment of tax credits (below)
2. Disputing recovery (p1477)
3. Recovery of overpayments (p1481)
4. Interest on overpayments (p1485)

Key facts

- The rules on the recovery of tax credit overpayments are different from those that apply to most social security benefits.
- All tax credit overpayments are recoverable, however they are caused, but HM Revenue and Customs (HMRC) has the discretion to decide whether or not to recover.
- There are rules on the amount that may be recovered and guidance on the way in which HMRC should recover an overpayment.
- There is no right to request a mandatory reconsideration by HMRC or appeal to an independent tribunal about a decision on whether or not to recover an overpayment of tax credits. However, you can ask HMRC to look at it again and use its discretion not to recover (known as a 'dispute').
- If you do not agree that you were overpaid, you can request a mandatory reconsideration by HMRC of the decision on your entitlement and appeal to an independent tribunal.

1. What is an overpayment of tax credits

The main rules on overpayments are the same for child tax credit (CTC) and working tax credit (WTC).[1] If you (and your partner if you are making a joint claim) are paid more tax credits for a tax year than you are entitled to, the extra amount is regarded as an overpayment.

HM Revenue and Customs (HMRC) can decide to adjust your award during the year of your current tax credit award to prevent an overpayment building up (an **'in-year overpayment'**) and/or recover all or some of the overpayment from you after the end of the tax year (an **'end-of-year overpayment'**).

Part 10: General rules for tax credits
Chapter 62: Overpayments of tax credits
1. What is an overpayment of tax credits

Note: you cannot request a mandatory reconsideration by HMRC or appeal to the First-tier Tribunal against the decision to recover the overpayment. However, you can ask HMRC to use its discretion not to recover. This is referred to as a 'dispute'.

If you do not accept that you received more tax credits than you should have (ie, you were not overpaid because you were correctly entitled to some or all of the amount that HMRC says was an overpayment), you can request a mandatory reconsideration of the decision on your entitlement by HMRC. If you are unhappy with the outcome, you can appeal to the tribunal. See Chapter 64 for more information. If your challenge is successful and the decision on your tax credit entitlement is changed, there is no overpayment (or a lower amount of overpayment) to be recovered.

When an overpayment occurs

The most likely causes of an overpayment are the following.
- Your income falls or rises by more than £2,500 (see p1465) in the current year, compared with the previous tax year.[2]
- You did not tell the Tax Credit Office (TCO) in time about a change of circumstances, or the change was not acted on (see p1462).
- The information you gave the TCO was incorrect, or inaccurately recorded.
- None of the above applies, but an overpayment occurred anyway because of the way the rules on income and changes in circumstances work.

In-year overpayments

In-year overpayments arise during the year of your current tax credit award. Decisions on in-year overpayments can be made during the course of the tax year concerned in the following circumstances.[3]
- If HMRC thinks there is likely to be an overpayment, it can adjust the award (or an award of another tax credit) to reduce or wipe out the overpayment. This may mean that your award is reduced for the rest of the year.
- If an award is terminated on the grounds that you did not satisfy the basic conditions for entitlement, HMRC may decide that the amount already paid to you, or some of it, is to be regarded as an overpayment. The basic conditions of entitlement are, for CTC, that you are responsible for a child (see p182) and, for WTC, that you are engaged in full-time work (see p196).

End-of-year overpayments

End-of-year overpayments are overpayments that are identified after the end of the tax year concerned – ie, after your award for that year has been finalised. HMRC can decide that there has been an end-of-year overpayment when it makes:[4]
- a final decision (see p1470);

- an enquiry decision (see p1501);
- a decision on discovery (see p1501).

Notification of overpayments

HMRC must change the decision on your entitlement and notify you of the new decision.[5] **Note:** you have the right to request a mandatory reconsideration by HMRC and then appeal against any decision about your entitlement (see p1503). If you think that the new decision is wrong and that, therefore, you have not been overpaid as much as HMRC says, or that you have not been overpaid at all, request a mandatory reconsideration. If you are unhappy with the outcome, appeal to the First-tier Tribunal.

You may only find out about an in-year overpayment when HMRC writes to you to say that your entitlement has changed and your payment has been adjusted. If HMRC intends to recover an end-of-year overpayment from you, it must also give you notice of that, how much it is and how it is to be recovered from you. It usually does this at the same time as it writes to you about the final decision on your entitlement for the tax year. **Note:** you cannot request a mandatory reconsideration or appeal against the decision to recover an overpayment.[6]

2. **Disputing recovery**

You cannot request a mandatory reconsideration by HM Revenue and Customs (HMRC) or appeal to the First-tier Tribunal against the decision to recover the overpayment. However, you can ask HMRC to look again at its decision to use its discretion to recover. This is referred to as a 'dispute'.

You should dispute recovery if you accept that you received more tax credits than you were correctly entitled to, but you do not think you should have to pay it back. To dispute recovery, complete Form TC846 (available at www.gov.uk or by contacting the helpline) or write to the Tax Credit Office (TCO). Recovery of the overpayment usually begins immediately and is not suspended during the dispute, although if your dispute is found in your favour, the amount already recovered is refunded to you.[7] There is no legal time limit for disputing recovery, but HMRC expects you to do so within three months of notification of the overpayment or of the outcome of a mandatory reconsideration or an appeal on the decision that gave rise to the overpayment.[8] HMRC says it will consider exceptions to this if you could not reasonably have been expected to act within three months – eg, if you were in hospital. It is arguable that a late dispute should also be allowed if you have been waiting for an explanation of the overpayment.

Part 10: General rules for tax credits
Chapter 62: Overpayments of tax credits
2. Disputing recovery

HMRC has discretion on this, but if it applies the time limit too rigidly, this may be unlawful.

What should you do?

1. If you do not agree that you have been overpaid and you think you were entitled to all, or part, of the amount of tax credit you received, request a mandatory reconsideration by HMRC of the decision on your entitlement that gave rise to the alleged overpayment, using Form WTC/AP. If you are unhappy with the outcome, you can appeal to the First-tier Tribunal on Form SSCS5. Recovery of the overpayment is suspended during the mandatory reconsideration and appeal process.

2. If you have been overpaid because your claim should have ended, but you would have been entitled to some, or all, of the amount you received if you had claimed correctly, ask for the overpayment to be reduced by offsetting your notional entitlement (see p1479).

3. If you accept that you were overpaid, but you do not think you should have to repay some, or all, of the money because you met your responsibilities and some (or all) of the overpayment was caused by HMRC's mistake or failure, dispute the decision to recover, using Form TC846. If there were exceptional circumstances that meant you were unable to meet your responsibilities, tell HMRC about this on the form. The dispute is an internal HMRC process and recovery continues during the dispute. HMRC says that you can only dispute recovery once, unless you provide new information within 30 days of being notified of the outcome of the dispute (or later, in exceptional circumstances).

4. If you cannot afford to repay, ask for the rate of recovery to be reduced, or for recovery to be written off altogether on hardship grounds. Form TC846 does not allow you to raise this in the dispute, so raise this separately via the Tax Credit Payment Helpline or in writing to the address on your notice to pay.

5. If you have mental health problems and recovery may cause you distress, supply evidence in writing and ask for the overpayment to be written off in line with HMRC guidance.

6. If you are still unhappy with the decision to recover, consider applying for judicial review or making a complaint.

The responsibilities test

The way in which HMRC uses its discretion whether or not to recover tax credit overpayments is set out in its leaflet *What Happens If We've Paid You Too Much Tax Credits?* (COP26), which is used if you dispute recovery. If an overpayment has been caused by a mistake or failure to act by HMRC (referred to as failing to meet its 'responsibilities' – see p1479), it may decide not to recover all or part of the overpayment.

However, for the overpayment not to be recovered, you must also show that you have acted correctly in relation to your claim for tax credits – ie, you have met your responsibilities. Your 'responsibilities' are not defined in the law, only in guidance.

If HMRC thinks it has met all its responsibilities but you have not met all of yours, it normally recovers the overpayment. If it thinks that both itself and you have failed to meet responsibilities, it looks at the circumstances and may write off part of the overpayment. An overpayment can still occur even though both you and HMRC have met these responsibilities, in which case HMRC is still likely to seek recovery.

HMRC regards its responsibilities as:
- giving you correct advice based on your information;
- accurately recording your information and paying the correct amount;
- putting right mistakes you tell it about and sending you a corrected award notice;
- accurately recording your notification of changes in your circumstances;
- sending you a new award notice within 30 days of having all the necessary information.

HMRC regards your responsibilities as:
- providing accurate, complete and up-to-date information;
- reporting changes of circumstances throughout the year;
- using the checklist (TC602(SN)) sent with your award notice to tell it if anything is wrong or incomplete;
- checking that your payments match the amount given on the award notice;
- reporting any errors on your award notice, normally within one month.

Note: if there were exceptional circumstances (eg, illness) which meant that you were unable to meet your responsibilities at the time, explain this and HMRC may write off the overpayment. HMRC must take into account your circumstances and your ability to comply.[9] Remember that it is best to dispute the decision to recover the overpayment on Form TC846, and attach additional pages if necessary.

Reducing the overpayment

HMRC may reduce ('offset') the amount of the overpayment by the amount of any tax credit to which you would have been entitled had you claimed correctly – ie, by your 'notional entitlement'. This is to reflect the true loss to the public purse. This process is referred to in HMRC guidance as 'offsetting notional entitlement' and is applied if the overpayment was caused by:[10]
- your ceasing to count as a single claimant and becoming part of a couple (you need details of your partner's income); *or*
- your ceasing to count as part of a couple and claiming instead as a single claimant.

In either case, you should make a new claim and have some tax credit entitlement following the change in your status. HMRC says that offsetting notional

Part 10: General rules for tax credits
Chapter 62: Overpayments of tax credits
2. Disputing recovery

entitlement will be applied to any overpayment which has occurred due to a change in the adult composition of the household in the current year, regardless of why you did not notify the change.[11]

HMRC says that it will proactively identify such cases but, as this cannot be guaranteed, you should contact it yourself if you think you may benefit from offsetting. Offsetting can also be applied to end-of-year overpayments. Because it is a way of HMRC using its discretion not to recover, there is no limit on how far it can go back. Offsetting might not be applied if your claim was incorrect from the start, or if you made a deliberate or repeated error or false statement. In such cases, HMRC may also consider imposing a penalty.

If HMRC refuses to offset your overpayment, ask it to consider any factors you think are relevant, including if there has been no actual loss to the public purse, the stability of the relationship and whether you made a 'genuine error' or not. Although the guidance only refers to single/couple claims, you should request offsetting notional entitlement in other circumstances – eg, if you were overpaid because you left the UK for more than the permitted period but you would have been entitled to tax credits on your return. In some cases, refusals by HMRC to offset may be challenged by judicial review in the courts. Get further advice.[12]

Hardship and mental health

Hardship is not defined, but HMRC leaflet *What Happens If We've Paid You Too Much Tax Credits?* (COP26) refers to financial hardship in terms of family circumstances that lead to extra living costs, such as looking after someone who is chronically ill or disabled, and inability to pay for essential living expenses such as rent, gas or electricity. In cases of hardship, HMRC may put recovery on hold, extend the period over which the overpayment is repaid, partially remit or, in exceptional circumstances, write off the overpayment altogether. Other guidance suggests that consideration is also given to reducing or writing off your overpayment if you have no means to repay, no assets and recovery would cause hardship.[13]

The guidance also states that if you have a mental health problem, HMRC will deal with your case carefully and sympathetically to avoid causing you distress. It may require a letter from a healthcare professional or mental health social worker explaining the nature of your illness, prognosis and prospects for recovery. If your mental health problem existed at the time the overpayment occurred, this may be considered to be exceptional circumstances and so HMRC should consider writing off the overpayment. If you have a mental health problem at the time the overpayment is being recovered, HMRC may decide not to continue with the recovery.[14]

The guidance on hardship and mental health applies whether you are repaying directly or by deductions from an ongoing award, but it may not be commonly known to all helpline staff.

There is a special payment helpline on 0345 302 1429 to discuss hardship. You may also write, with a financial statement, to the HMRC office dealing with repayment. You should *not* use Form TC846 (see p1484) if you want more time to repay. If you remain unhappy with the decision, see p1478 for what you can do.

Taking your dispute further

If HMRC has considered your dispute and you still think you should not have to pay back an overpayment, you can ask HMRC to review its decision, provided you give new information within 30 days (or later in exceptional circumstances). HMRC says that you can only do this once.[15]

The only legal challenge to a decision on recovering an overpayment (ie, either after a dispute or an attempt to negotiate repayment) is by judicial review in the courts. Usually, this is only possible in extreme cases – eg, if HMRC insists on your repaying an overpayment that was clearly caused by an error or failure on its part, you met all your responsibilities and it is urgent that HMRC changes its decision. For more about judicial review, see p1378.

The only other way of persuading HMRC to change its mind is by making a complaint. You first need to use HMRC's own complaints procedure. If you remain dissatisfied, you can complain to the Adjudicator's Office and then to the Parliamentary Ombudsman via your MP. See Appendix 1 for the addresses and Chapter 58 for details about making a complaint. Both can recommend action and order financial compensation, but are likely to take time to complete their investigations. You may wish to involve your MP at an earlier stage of your complaint, as this can produce quicker results.

3. **Recovery of overpayments**

HM Revenue and Customs (HMRC) can recover all or part of any overpayment.[16] It usually recovers the overpayment by:
- adjusting (ie, reducing) your current award; *or*
- requiring you to repay the overpayment.

However, it does not have to recover an overpayment and should exercise discretion. The official policy is in the HMRC leaflet *What Happens If We've Paid You Too Much Tax Credits?* (COP26), which can be obtained from the Tax Credit Helpline on 0345 300 3900 or from www.gov.uk. An overpayment may be written off, in whole or in part, if HMRC has made a mistake or failed to act, and you have acted correctly in connection with your claim.[17] The guidance also allows for recovery to be waived in exceptional circumstances or if it would cause hardship (see p1478).

Part 10: General rules for tax credits
Chapter 62: Overpayments of tax credits
3. Recovery of overpayments

You must be given notice that you must repay an end-of-year overpayment. The notice must also say how much the overpayment is, and how it is to be recovered from you.[18]

HMRC usually begins recovery immediately after it notifies you of the overpayment. It does not ask you whether recovering an overpayment will cause you hardship or if you think it should not be recovered from you. It is, therefore, important to contact the Tax Credit Office (TCO) if you do not think the overpayment should be recovered. HMRC refers to this as a 'dispute' (see p1477). Recovery is not suspended during the dispute process, but if the dispute is found in your favour, the amount already recovered is refunded to you.[19]

Note: if you do not agree that you have been overpaid, request a mandatory reconsideration by HMRC of the decision about your entitlement and, if you are unhappy with the outcome, appeal to the First-tier Tribunal (see Chapter 64). Recovery is suspended during the mandatory reconsideration and appeal process.[20]

Overpayments and award notices

For every overpayment, there should be a revised decision on your entitlement, which is sent as an award notice. The tax credit award notices can be very complicated. You should be sent a checklist (Form TC602(SN)) with your award notice with information used in the calculation for you to check. You can request an award calculation notice (Form TC647) from HMRC, which gives more details about how your payment has been worked out. If it is still unclear, write to the TCO (its address is at the top of the award notice) requesting an individual explanation. However, you should not delay sending in your dispute form while you are waiting for the explanation, as a dispute should usually be made within three months. You can send further details once you have received the full explanation.

If you still do not receive a satisfactory response, consider taking up the matter with your MP or making a complaint (see Chapter 58).

From whom can an overpayment be recovered

In-year overpayments are recovered from you by reducing the ongoing tax credit award. An end-of-year overpayment can be recovered from the person(s) to whom the tax credit award was made. This means:[21]

- if you made a claim as a single person, the overpayment can be recovered from you;
- if you made a joint claim with your partner, the overpayment can be recovered from one or both of you. If you have separated from your partner, HMRC's practice is first to ask you both to repay the overpayment equally. If you wish, you and your ex-partner may agree to pay different amounts. Although HMRC has the power to ask one person to repay the whole amount, guidance states

that usually each person is asked to repay a maximum of half the overpayment, unless one partner has acted fraudulently or negligently and the other is seen to be an 'innocent partner'.[22]

How the overpayment is recovered

You must be notified of the new decision on your entitlement that gave rise to the overpayment.[23] For end-of-year overpayments, HMRC must notify you (and your partner, if it is a joint overpayment) of the amount to be repaid, and how the overpayment is to be repaid.[24] Tax credit overpayments are treated as unpaid tax debts.

HMRC can require you to repay:[25]

- by deductions from ongoing payments of any tax credit (see below). This is HMRC's preferred method of repayment. The amount that is deducted is usually limited;
- directly to HMRC. You should receive a notice showing the full amount to be repaid. You are offered a standard repayment period of 12 monthly instalments, although up to 10 years may be negotiated;
- with your agreement, by deductions from certain benefits paid by the DWP (see p1195);[26]
- with your agreement, via pay as you earn (PAYE) by altering your tax code to allow deductions from your wages;[27]
- by deduction from your bank account, in some cases, or court action (see p1484).[28]

If your tax credit entitlement has ended and you are entitled to universal credit (UC), an outstanding tax credit overpayment may be treated as an overpayment of UC (see p1239).[29] In this case, deductions can be made from your UC or other benefits without your agreement.

Deductions from ongoing awards

HMRC can adjust your tax credit payments so that you receive less money and so, in effect, repay the overpayment. It only does this if you or your partner have previously been overpaid either as single claimants or as part of the same couple. It does not recover an overpayment in this way if you or your partner have previously been overpaid in a joint claim with a different partner. You should be notified of the amount being deducted. There is a maximum amount by which HMRC can reduce your tax credit award to recover an end-of-year overpayment:[30]

- 10 per cent of the award if you are receiving the maximum tax credits to which you could be entitled – ie, with no reduction for income;
- 100 per cent of the award if you receive only the family element of child tax credit (CTC);
- 50 per cent of the award if your income is over £20,000 (this is the figure being treated at the time as your actual current year's income);
- 25 per cent of the award if none of the above apply.

Part 10: General rules for tax credits
Chapter 62: Overpayments of tax credits
3. Recovery of overpayments

Note: these are maximum amounts, although HMRC applies them automatically. If you accept that you should repay but cannot afford to repay at the above rates, ask HMRC to accept repayment at a lower rate. You may need to show why it would cause you hardship (see p1478) to pay at the maximum rate.

The maximum amounts only apply to end-of-year overpayments, but HMRC now takes a different approach with in-year overpayments.[31] It may stop or reduce your ongoing payments by more than the above limits, so that you only receive your estimated remaining entitlement (if any) for the rest of the year.[32] HMRC says that this is to prevent a further overpayment building up, but you can request hardship payments if this leaves you unable to meet your basic living expenses.

HMRC considers adjusting recovery or making payments on hardship grounds if requested.[33] In-year recovery is adjusted to the limits used for end-of-year recovery if you are accepted as being in hardship, or the amount you get may be increased further in exceptional cases.[34] You may be asked to provide details of your income and expenditure. In urgent cases, HMRC says a decision on adjusting payments due to hardship should be made within two working days.[35]

Revised notices of overpayments, changing the method of recovery, can be issued at any time.[36]

Direct payment to HM Revenue and Customs

If you are no longer entitled to tax credits, or you were overpaid as part of a couple and you have now separated, you must repay your overpayment by direct payment to HMRC. HMRC suspends direct recovery if you are already repaying another overpayment (at the 10, 25 or 50 per cent rate described on p1483) through your current tax credit award – but you may need to ask for this.[37] The notice to pay (TC610) asks you to contact HMRC to pay in full or negotiate repayment. If the overpayment has not been repaid and you have not contacted HMRC within 42 days, a reminder letter is sent, followed by a more strongly worded warning letter. If you fail to respond to this letter, HMRC may use a debt collection agency or start legal proceedings to recover the debt.

Other methods of recovery

HMRC may recover tax credit overpayments by deduction from specified benefits with your written consent (see p1195).[38] If you are getting UC, a tax credit overpayment may be treated as an overpayment of UC and can be recovered through deductions from UC without your consent (see p1239).[39] HMRC may recover tax credit from your wages via PAYE, but only with your agreement.[40]

HMRC may recover tax credit debts directly from bank and building society accounts and ISAs. In England and Wales, it can only do so where the debt is £1,000 or more, and you must usually be left with a minimum of £5,000 in your account or accounts.[41] HMRC guidance includes safeguards, including a guaranteed face-to-face visit, before this method is used and there is a right of appeal to the county court.[42] In Scotland, it can apply for bank arrestment under a 'summary warrant'.

If HMRC cannot recover by any other methods, or you do not respond to requests for recovery, it may consider taking legal action. Further action will follow if HMRC considers that you are refusing to repay, or neglecting to keep to an agreement to repay. All the circumstances are taken into account before taking such action, but HMRC may:

- take enforcement proceedings to take control of your goods (England and Wales) or seize and sell your possessions (Scotland). Unless you let HMRC officials or agents into your property, they cannot enter your home and take control of/seize your personal possessions without a warrant from the court; *or*
- take court action against you, including bankruptcy proceedings.

Note: recovery action through the courts in England and Wales must be taken within six years of the decision that there has been an overpayment, or, if later, any written acknowledgement of the overpayment or voluntary repayment.[43] In Scotland, HMRC regards the time limit for court action as being five years from the last effective action.[44]

Negotiating repayment

If you have difficulty repaying, HMRC may agree to your repaying the overpayment over a longer period than normal by making an instalment plan. In cases of hardship, or if your mental health is a factor (see p1478), the overpayment may be written off. Contact the Tax Credit Payment Helpline on 0345 302 1429 (textphone: 0345 300 3909), or write to HMRC at the address on the notice to pay. Usually, you are asked to pay something straight away, and the rest over a later period. HMRC takes into account all the relevant circumstances, including your income, savings, other debts and outgoings. Usually, you must show how the repayments will cause you hardship by providing evidence of your income and expenditure and showing, for example, how you will be unable to meet your essential living expenses, or providing evidence of your mental health problems.

4. Interest on overpayments

Interest may be added to an overpayment being recovered from you (and/or your partner, if you have a joint claim) if HM Revenue and Customs (HMRC) considers that the overpayment is due to 'fraud or neglect' on the part of you (and/or your partner).[45]

Interest is added 30 days after whichever of the following dates apply:[46]

- if you (or your partner) were treated during the tax year concerned as being overpaid as a result of your award being terminated because you did not satisfy

Part 10: General rules for tax credits
Chapter 62: Overpayments of tax credits
Notes

the basic conditions of entitlement (see p1476), the date of the decision terminating the award; *or*

• if the above did not apply, the date in the final notice that you were given to confirm your actual income for the tax year.

When added to the overpayment, the interest is treated as if it were part of the overpayment. This means that it is subject to the same rules as the overpayment itself.[47]

The amount of interest added to the penalty is 6.5 per cent a year or, if it is different from the average lending rate of the main banks, the bank lending rate plus 2.5 per cent.[48]

You can request a mandatory reconsideration of the decision to add interest to an overpayment and, if you are still unhappy, appeal (see Chapter 64). For example, you might wish to argue that you did not act fraudulently or negligently, or that the amount of the interest is wrong. You (and/or your partner, if s/he is subject to the decision) must be given notice of a decision adding interest to an overpayment. The notice must be dated and include details of your right to request a mandatory reconsideration of the decision.[49]

Notes

1. What is an overpayment of tax credits
1 s28 TCA 2002
2 Reg 5 TC(ITDR) Regs
3 s28(5) and (6) TCA 2002
4 s28(1) TCA 2002
5 s23 TCA 2002
6 ss29(1) and (2) and 38 TCA 2002

2. Disputing recovery
7 HMRC leaflet COP26, *What Happens If We've Paid You Too Much Tax Credits?*, p10
8 HMRC leaflet COP26, *What Happens If We've Paid You Too Much Tax Credits?*
9 Adjudicator's Office, *Annual Report 2014*, p20
10 *Pre-Budget Report 2009*; TCM page 0228220; HMRC leaflet COP26, *What Happens If We've Paid You Too Much Tax Credits?*, p4

11 Benefits and Credits Consultation Group email, 16 February 2017
12 For the pre-January 2010 position, see CPAG's *Welfare Rights Bulletin 211*, p4
13 HMRC, *Debt Management and Banking Manual*, 555090
14 HMRC, *Debt Management and Banking Manual*, 555600
15 HMRC leaflet COP26, *What Happens If We've Paid You Too Much Tax Credits?*, p12

3. Recovery of overpayments
16 s28(1) TCA 2002
17 HMRC leaflet COP26, *What Happens If We've Paid You Too Much Tax Credits?*
18 ss28(1) and 29 TCA 2002
19 HMRC leaflet COP26, *What Happens If We've Paid You Too Much Tax Credits?*, p10

20 HMRC leaflet COP26, *What Happens If We've Paid You Too Much Tax Credits?*
21 s28(3) and (4) TCA 2002
22 HMRC leaflet COP 26, *What Happens If We've Paid You Too Much Tax Credits?*, p5; CCM p8290
23 s23 TCA 2002
24 s29 TCA 2002
25 s29(3)-(5) TCA 2002
26 Sch 9(7E) SS(C&P) Regs
27 s29(5) TCA 2002
28 Sch 8 Finance (No.2) Act 2015
29 Reg 12 UC(TP) Regs
30 Reg 12A TC(PC) Regs; HMRC leaflet COP26, *What Happens If We've Paid You Too Much Tax Credits?*
31 Benefits and Credits Consultation Group minutes, 17 July 2007
32 Autumn Statement 2013, para 1.317
33 TCM 0216120; HMRC leaflet COP26, *What Happens If We've Paid You Too Much Tax Credits?*
34 TCM 0214120
35 Benefits and Credits Consultation Group, email 27 November 2016
36 s29(2) TCA 2002
37 HMRC leaflets, *How HMRC Handle Tax Credits Overpayments* and *What Happens If We've Paid You Too Much Tax Credits?* (COP26), p15
38 Sch 9(7E)(3) SS(C&P) Regs
39 Reg 12 UC(TP) Regs
40 Reg 4 Income Tax (Amendment No.4) Regs 2014, No.2689
41 Sch 8 Finance (No.2) Act 2015
42 Autumn Statement 2014, para 2.165
43 s9(1) Limitation Act 1980
44 HMRC, *Debt Management and Banking Manual*, 595080

4. Interest on overpayments

45 s37(1) TCA 2002
46 s37(2)-(3) TCA 2002
47 s37(6) TCA 2002
48 Reg 4 TC(IR) Regs
49 ss37(4) and 38(1)(d) TCA 2002

10

Chapter 63

Investigations, penalties and
fraud: tax credits

This chapter covers:
1. Investigating claims (below)
2. Penalties (p1490)
3. Prosecution for fraud (p1494)

Key facts
- HM Revenue and Customs has wide powers to investigate your tax credits claim and require information from you.
- In certain circumstances, including if you supply incorrect information or do not comply with other requirements, a financial penalty may be imposed.
- If you are considered to have acted fraudulently, you may be prosecuted and fined or imprisoned, or both.

1. Investigating claims

HM Revenue and Customs (HMRC) can require you to supply information and evidence to help it check whether your claim is correct. HMRC refers to investigations into the accuracy of awards as 'examinations' and 'enquiries'. Examinations are carried out on some claims *during* the year in order to check that they are correct. Enquiries may be carried out *after* the year concerned to check that you were paid the correct amount. More serious investigations into fraud may also be carried out.

HMRC might ask you to provide things like bank statements or your rent book. It must give you at least 30 days to provide information. You can appoint someone else to deal with HMRC on your behalf – eg, an adviser, accountant or a relative. HMRC requires a signed letter from you confirming this is what you want (or use Form TC689). However, you are still treated as responsible for the information provided.

HMRC does not currently undertake face-to-face meetings with tax credit claimants as part of a routine examination or enquiry.

Not all examinations or enquiries are fraud investigations. Fraud investigations tend only to happen in the more serious cases and, in such cases, HMRC has additional powers (see p1490).

Examinations

During the tax year of your award, or sometimes before your claim is decided, HMRC may telephone or write to you requiring information or evidence.[1] Normally, it writes to you to say that it is examining your claim, but this is not a legal requirement. There is no limit on the number of examinations that can take place during the same tax year. If the examination is started before your claim is decided, usually you are not paid until it is completed, and an initial decision is made on your claim (see p1459). If it starts while you are already receiving tax credits, usually you continue to be paid while the examination is being carried out. Payments can only be suspended in specific circumstances (see p1461). If an award has already been made, an examination may end without a new decision on your claim but you should be notified that it has been completed.[2] See p1498 for more information on decisions made following an examination.

You cannot stop an examination taking place, but if you are unhappy with the way you are being treated, you can make a complaint (see Chapter 58).

Enquiries

After your tax credit award is finalised at the end of the tax year, HMRC may carry out an enquiry into the award. It may request further information or evidence in connection with your claim. An enquiry can only be opened within one year of the final decision, and only once in respect of a tax year. HMRC must notify you in writing that it is opening an enquiry. When it has completed the enquiry, it must make a decision on your entitlement.[3] See p1501 for more details about decisions made following an enquiry.

You can apply to HMRC to complete its enquiry by making a decision on your tax credit entitlement for the year in question. If HMRC wishes to continue with the enquiry, it passes your request to the First-tier Tribunal, which must give a direction that the enquiry is completed unless it is is satisfied that there are reasonable grounds for it to continue.[4] If you are unhappy with the decision following the enquiry, you can request a mandatory reconsideration and then appeal.

Powers to seek information

HMRC can require you (and/or your partner if you have a joint claim) to provide information or evidence during the course of your award if it believes your award may be wrong (for an examination). It can also require information or evidence after your award has been finalised (for an enquiry).

Part 10: General rules for tax credits
Chapter 63: Investigations, penalties and fraud: tax credits
2. Penalties

It can also do this if it is necessary for a decision on an initial claim, a revision during an award, or a final notice and final decision (see Chapter 61).[5] You must be given at least 30 days to provide the information.[6] HMRC does not have to suspect you of fraud in order to require information or evidence from you.

It is important that you co-operate with requests for information or evidence as far as you can. Even though you may not be the subject of a fraud investigation, HMRC might refuse your claim, suspend your payments or apply for a financial penalty if you refuse to supply information and evidence (see below). If the information or evidence is not available, explain why.

HMRC can also require your employer or childcare provider to provide information. They must be given at least 30 days to do so. If they are subject to these requirements, they can also be subject to penalties (see below). They can be required to provide information and evidence relating to your claim or, for the purpose of a revision during an award or an enquiry (see p1497), your award.[7]

If fraud is suspected

If you are suspected of fraud, HMRC may undertake a civil investigation with a view to imposing a financial penalty (see below). In serious cases, it undertakes a criminal investigation with a view to referring you to the Crown Prosecution Service (or Procurator Fiscal in Scotland) for prosecution (see p1494). Fraud investigations in serious cases may be carried out by an HMRC criminal investigation officer and may be linked to investigations by other sections of HMRC, or by the DWP and local authorities. It is usually explained to you why your claim is being investigated and that you can seek professional advice from someone who can attend any interview with you. It is advisable to seek professional advice as quickly as possible (eg, from a solicitor) if you are being investigated. You are likely to be interviewed under caution (see p1258).

In addition to the powers described above and in Chapter 53, HMRC has specific powers when investigating fraud in connection with tax credits, as it does for tax fraud investigations.[8] If HMRC has 'reasonable grounds' for suspecting serious fraud, a court can make an order requiring that documents containing relevant evidence be delivered by you (or any other person who has them) to HMRC within the time specified in the court order. Falsifying, concealing or destroying or disposing of the documents is also an offence.[9]

2. **Penalties**

A financial penalty may be imposed on you if you have:[10]
* fraudulently or negligently made an incorrect statement or declaration, or supplied incorrect information or evidence; *or*
* failed to comply with requirements.

Despite the use of the word 'fraudulently', these penalties are civil penalties. You do not have to be prosecuted for a criminal offence. If you do not think a penalty should be imposed (eg, because you had a reasonable excuse for not declaring a change in circumstances or you could not obtain the information asked for), tell HM Revenue and Customs (HMRC). You must be notified of the penalty, including the date of the decision and your right to request a mandatory reconsideration and subsequent appeal (see p1505).[11]

In certain circumstances, these rules can also apply in the same way to your employer or your childcare provider (see p1489).

Incorrect statements and information

HMRC can impose a penalty of up to £3,000 (it does not have to impose the maximum) on you if you have acted fraudulently or negligently and you have:[12]
- made an incorrect statement or declaration in connection with a claim, a notification of a change of circumstances (see p1462) or in a response to a final notice (see p1470); *or*
- given incorrect information or evidence in connection with an initial decision (see p1459), a requirement to provide information or evidence during the course of your award, a revision during an award (see p1498), a final decision (see p1470) or an enquiry (see p1501).

There is no definition of 'negligence' but, in practice, HMRC considers what you could reasonably be expected to have known and how careful you were.[13]

Penalties for incorrect statements and information

The maximum penalty is £3,000, although HMRC need not impose the maximum. For a deliberate and wrong new claim, the penalties are set at £600 for the first time, £1,000 for a second wrong new claim and £1,500 for further claims. For a deliberate and wrong declaration in the course of a claim, HMRC sets penalties at 30 per cent of the amount over-claimed, 50 per cent for a second incorrect declaration, or 100 per cent for a third, subject to the £3,000 maximum.[14] The decision must consider whether there are any aggravating or mitigating factors, and that the maximum penalty is reserved for the worst offences.[15] The penalty is payable 30 days after the date you were notified of it.[16] The amount of the penalty may be increased by the addition of interest (see p1493).

If you are a member of a joint-claim couple (see p1450), a penalty may be imposed on you and your partner. However, a penalty cannot be imposed on you if you are an 'innocent partner' – ie, where you were not, and could not reasonably have been expected to have been, aware that your partner had fraudulently or negligently made an incorrect statement or provided incorrect information or evidence.[17] In this case, the penalty is imposed solely on your partner. However, even if a penalty is imposed, or partly imposed, on you and your partner, the total penalty for the same incorrect statement cannot amount to more than £3,000.

10

Part 10: General rules for tax credits
Chapter 63: Investigations, penalties and fraud: tax credits
2. Penalties

If you are acting for someone else and you fraudulently or negligently make an incorrect statement, the penalty applies to you.[18]

Failing to comply

A financial penalty of up to £300 (it does not have to be the maximum) may be imposed for:[19]

* failing to provide information or evidence formally requested by HMRC by a specified date in connection with an initial claim (see p1459), a revision during an award (see p1498), a final decision (see p1470) or for an enquiry (see p1501). HMRC cannot impose such a penalty itself, but may start proceedings to the First-tier Tribunal to impose a penalty;[20] *or*
* failing to comply with a requirement to declare your circumstances or income by a specified date in your annual review (see p1468). HMRC can impose such a penalty itself, but you have the right to request a mandatory reconsideration and then appeal;[21] *or*
* failing to notify a specified change of circumstances within one month of the change or of the date you became aware of the change, if that is later.[22] HMRC can impose such a penalty itself, but you have the right to request a mandatory reconsideration and then appeal. The specified changes are listed on p1462.

A penalty is not imposed if you had a 'reasonable excuse' for not telling HMRC about the change. Tell HMRC if you think this applies. However, HMRC does not accept the fact that you did not know you had to inform it as a reasonable excuse.[23]

Penalties for failing to comply

The maximum penalty for failing to comply is £300. If the penalty is for failing to comply with a request to provide information or evidence, or for failing to comply with a requirement to declare circumstances or income by the date specified in the annual review, there may be a further daily penalty of up to £60 a day for each day you continue to fail to comply. You must be notified of the penalty, including the date on which it is given, and your right to a mandatory reconsideration. The penalty is payable 30 days after the date you were notified of it.[24] The amount of the penalty may be increased by the addition of interest (see p1493).

However, if the penalty is for failing to comply with a request to provide information or evidence, HMRC cannot apply the penalty itself. Instead, it must write to the HM Courts and Tribunals Service, which then summons you to the First-tier Tribunal to decide whether the penalty should be applied.[25] You can appeal against the First-tier Tribunal's decision to the Upper Tribunal (see p1510).

Once you have provided the information or evidence, a penalty cannot be imposed on you. You have not failed to provide information or evidence if you did so within any time that HMRC has allowed you to, or if you had a 'reasonable excuse' for the failure, or if, having had a reasonable excuse, you later provided the information or evidence without unreasonable delay.[26]

If you are a member of a couple and a £300 penalty has been imposed for failing to comply with a requirement about a final notice or for failing to report the specified change of circumstances, the total of that penalty applied to either or both of you is a maximum of £300.[27]

Interest added to penalties

If a penalty is imposed on you, HMRC can apply interest to it. Although it does not have to apply interest, it can do so even if you are not considered to have acted fraudulently or negligently – ie, if the penalty is for failing to comply. The amount of the interest becomes part of the penalty and is recoverable in the same way as the penalty itself.[28]

The amount of interest added to the penalty is 6.5 per cent a year or, if that is different from the average lending rate of the main banks, the bank lending rate plus 2.5 per cent.[29]

You can appeal against the penalty itself and the amount of the penalty. However, there is no right of appeal about the addition of interest.[30]

In addition to the above rules, if HMRC considers that an overpayment has arisen because of 'fraud or neglect' on your part (or, if you are a member of a couple, on the part of one or both of you), it can decide to apply interest to all or some of the overpayment (see p1485).

Recovery of penalties

HMRC has discretion about whether to impose a penalty and, subject to the maximum amounts, the amount. Also, although the penalty itself can only be altered on appeal, HMRC has discretion about whether to insist that you pay all or some of the penalty.[31] If you tried your best to fulfil all your obligations, or if the penalty would cause you hardship, tell HMRC and ask it to exercise its discretion not to recover all or some of the amount.

If HMRC uses its legal powers to recover a penalty, it can:
- take enforcement proceedings to take control of your goods (England and Wales) or seize and sell your personal possessions (Scotland). However, unless you let them into your property, authorised officers cannot enter your home and take control of or seize your goods or possessions unless they have a warrant from the court; or
- take court action against you, including bankruptcy proceedings.[32]

Challenging a penalty

You can tell HMRC that you disagree with the penalty and/or the addition of interest to it – eg, when it contacts you to tell you that you are liable for a penalty.

10

Part 10: General rules for tax credits
Chapter 63: Investigations, penalties and fraud: tax credits
3. Prosecution for fraud

In some cases, it may warn you about a possible penalty before a formal decision is made. It can remove the penalty and/or the interest.

Once a formal decision has been made, you can request a mandatory reconsideration and then appeal, including against the amount of the penalty, but not against any addition of interest (see Chapter 64).

Note: subject to the maximum, the tribunal considering your appeal can increase, as well as decrease, the amount.

For more information on mandatory reconsiderations and appeals, see p1503 and for more on penalty appeals, see p1505.

Have you been given a penalty?

1. Explain to HMRC why you think a penalty should not be imposed – eg, if you acted with reasonable care or had a reasonable excuse for failing to report a change in circumstances.

2. If you get a decision imposing a penalty, you can request a mandatory reconsideration and then appeal. Remember that if the penalty is for failing to provide information requested by HMRC, it can only be imposed by a First-tier Tribunal and you have a right of appeal to the Upper Tribunal against this decision.

3. If you accept that a penalty can be imposed, you can still negotiate with HMRC about the amount. You could argue that the maximum amount should not be imposed in your case – eg, because you acted innocently and to the best of your knowledge or abilities.

4. You can come to an agreement with HMRC about repaying a penalty, but check whether this means that a new decision on the penalty will be issued. If a decision is not issued, you may lose your right to challenge the penalty.

---

3. **Prosecution for fraud**

You are regarded as having committed the offence of fraud if you knowingly take part in fraudulent activity in order to get a tax credit for you or anyone else.[33] If you are prosecuted and then convicted by a court, you are liable to be fined or imprisoned, or both.

Fines and imprisonment

If a court convicts you of fraud in connection with tax credits and:[34]
- you are convicted in a moderately serious case, usually in a magistrates' court (sheriff court in Scotland), you are liable to a maximum of six months' imprisonment or a maximum fine of £5,000, or both; *or*
- you are convicted in a very serious case, usually in the Crown Court (High Court in Scotland), you are liable to a maximum of seven years' imprisonment or a fine of an unlimited amount, or both.

Note: at some point the above rules will change. See CPAG's online service and *Welfare Rights Bulletin* for updates. The planned changes are as follows.[35]

- If your offence is in connection with no more than £20,000 of tax credits, you may be tried only in the magistrates' court (sheriff court in Scotland). If you are convicted, you are liable to a maximum of 51 weeks' (England and Wales) or six months' (Scotland) imprisonment, or a maximum fine of £5,000.
- If the offence is in connection with more than £20,000 of tax credits, you may be tried in either the magistrates' court (sheriff court in Scotland) or the Crown Court (High Court in Scotland). If you are convicted in the magistrates' court/ sheriff court, you are liable to a maximum of 12 months' imprisonment or a maximum fine of £5,000, or both. If you are convicted in the Crown Court/ High Court, you are liable to a maximum of seven years' imprisonment or a fine of an unlimited amount, or both.

Will you be prosecuted?

Whether or not you will be prosecuted is a discretionary decision. Not all cases of fraud end in prosecution. HM Revenue and Customs (HMRC) may investigate your claim under civil investigation procedures – ie, without a view to prosecuting you, but with a view to charging a penalty (see p1490). If you are being investigated *without* a view to prosecuting you, you are usually told about this. However, this does not mean that HMRC cannot change its mind and decide to refer you to the Crown Prosecution Service (the Procurator Fiscal in Scotland) for prosecution.

The factors that it may take into account are likely to include the strength of the evidence, the amount of tax credits involved, whether an offence was planned and your personal circumstances.

Official HMRC policy indicates that criminal investigations are more likely if:[36]

- there is organised or systematic fraud, including conspiracy;
- false statements are made or false documents given during a civil investigation;
- deliberate concealment, deception, conspiracy or corruption is suspected;
- false or forged documents have been used;
- the person involved has committed previous offences or there is a repeated course of unlawful conduct or previous civil action;
- there is a link to suspected wider criminality.

This is not a complete list and, ultimately, everything depends on the circumstances of your case.

What should you do if you are prosecuted?

1. The most important thing to do is to get advice. You may be entitled to legal help and have a solicitor or barrister represent you in court.

2. Check carefully that HMRC can prove all the parts of the offence with which you are charged. Do not plead guilty until you have obtained advice.

Part 10: General rules for tax credits
Chapter 63: Investigations, penalties and fraud: tax credits
Notes

Loss of benefit

If you have committed an offence in connection with working tax credit (WTC) or child tax credit, you can be sanctioned or disqualified from certain other benefits (see p1266). If you have committed an offence in connection with tax credits or other benefits, you can be disqualified from receiving WTC (see p1268).

Notes

1. Investigating claims

1 ss14(2) and 16(3) TCA 2002
2 Sch 2 TCA 2002; HMRC leaflet WTC7, *Tax Credits Penalties,* available at www.gov.uk
3 s19(3) and (8) TCA 2002
4 ss19(9) and (10) and 63(3) TCA 2002
5 ss14(2),15(2),16(3), 18(10), 19(2) and 22 TCA 2002
6 Reg 32 TC(CN) Regs
7 ss14(2)(b),15(2)(b),16(3)(b) and 19(2)(b) TCA 2002; regs 30 and 31 TC(CN) Regs
8 s36 TCA 2002
9 s20BB TMA 1970, as applied by s36 TCA 2002

2. Penalties

10 ss31 and 32 TCA 2002
11 Sch 2 TCA 2002; HMRC leaflet WTC7, *Tax Credits Penalties,* available at www.gov.uk
12 s31 TCA 2002
13 HMRC leaflet WTC7, *Tax Credits Penalties*
14 HMRC leaflet WTC7, *Tax Credits Penalties*
15 *SP v HMRC* [2016] UKUT 238 (AAC)
16 Sch 2 para 1 TCA 2002; HMRC leaflet WTC7, *Tax Credits Penalties*
17 s31(3) TCA 2002
18 s31(5) TCA 2002
19 s32 TCA 2002
20 s32(1)(a) and Sch 2 paras 1 and 3 TCA 2002
21 s32(1)(b) TCA 2002
22 ss3(4) and (7), 6(3) and 32(3) TCA 2002; reg 21(2) TC(CN) Regs
23 s32(5)(b) TCA 2002; CCM 10170

24 Sch 2 para 1 TCA 2002
25 Sch 2 paras 1 and 3 TCA 2002; CCM 10220
26 s32(5) TCA 2002
27 s32(6) TCA 2002
28 s37(5) and (6) TCA 2002
29 Reg 4 TC(IR) Regs
30 ss37(5)-(6) and 38 TCA 2002
31 Sch 2 paras 1 and 5 TCA 2002
32 Sch 2 para 7 TCA 2002

3. Prosecution for fraud

33 s35(1) TCA 2002
34 s35(2) TCA 2002
35 s124 WRA 2012. At the time this *Handbook* was written, there was no commencement order.
36 HMRC criminal investigation policy, available at www.gov.uk

Chapter 64

Getting a tax credit decision changed

This chapter covers:
1. Revisions (below)
2. Mandatory reconsiderations (p1503)
3. Appealing to the First-tier Tribunal (p1507)
4. Appealing to the Upper Tribunal (p1510)
5. Appealing to the Court of Appeal or Court of Session (p1510)

Tax credit appeals are heard by the First-tier Tribunal Social Entitlement Chamber, which also deals with social security benefits. Chapters 55 and 56 cover appeals about benefit decisions. This chapter refers you to these when the tax credit rules are the same as the benefit rules.

Key facts
- Decisions on your tax credit entitlement can be changed by a revision by HM Revenue and Customs, provided certain grounds are met.
- If you think a decision is wrong, you can ask for it to be reviewed. This is called a mandatory reconsideration.
- If you are unhappy with the outcome of a mandatory reconsideration, you can appeal to an independent tribunal – the First-tier Tribunal.
- There are strict time limits for carrying out a revision, applying for a mandatory reconsideration and appealing.

10

1. Revisions

A decision may be revised by HM Revenue and Customs (HMRC). How a revision is made depends on whether the decision with which you disagree is:
- an 'initial decision' on a claim (see p1498); *or*
- a 'final decision' after the tax year has ended following an annual review (see p1500); *or*
- a decision of the First-tier Tribunal (see p1510).

Part 10: General rules for tax credits
Chapter 64: Getting a tax credit decision changed
1. Revisions

The process of revision is used when HMRC uses its power to change a decision – eg, after notification of a change of circumstances. If *you* disagree with a decision, including a revised decision, you should request a mandatory reconsideration and then appeal.

Revising an initial decision during an award

When you claim a tax credit, HMRC must decide whether to make an award and the rate at which to award it.[1] This is called an 'initial decision'. If you disagree with it, you can request a mandatory reconsideration and then appeal (see p1503).

The initial decision can be revised if:

- your circumstances have changed so that you should get an additional or higher element (see below); *or*
- HMRC has reasonable grounds for believing that you are entitled to a different rate of tax credit or that you are not entitled to a tax credit at all (see p1499); *or*
- there has been an official error (see p1500).

If your claim has been turned down altogether or your award has been terminated, you cannot ask for the decision to be revised, unless it is on grounds of official error. You should usually request a mandatory reconsideration within 30 days if you want the decision to be changed. If you do not request a mandatory reconsideration, you must make a fresh claim to get any further tax credits in that tax year.[2]

If your income in the previous year is too high to qualify for a tax credit, but you satisfy the other qualifying conditions, you are awarded a tax credit at a nil rate. This nil-rate award can be revised if your income is estimated to be lower in the current year.[3]

There is a change in your circumstances

If you notify the Tax Credit Office (TCO) that your circumstances have changed so that you should now get an element that you were not previously getting, HMRC must decide whether to amend your award and, if so, how.[4] For example, if you report that you have started to pay childcare costs, your working tax credit (WTC) award can be revised to include the childcare element. HMRC may request further information or evidence before making a revised decision.

If you notify the TCO of the change within one month, the increase in the award can be fully backdated.[5] There are specific rules dealing with the date from when an award is recalculated if there is a change in childcare charges or childcare provided (see p1464).

The increase in your award cannot be backdated for more than one month before the date you provide notification of the change, except in the following cases relating to the disabled and severely disabled child elements of child tax credit (CTC) and the disabled worker and severe disability elements of WTC.

- If you claim and are awarded disability living allowance (DLA) for a child, or personal independence payment (PIP) for a qualifying young person, tell the TCO within one month of the DLA/PIP decision so that the disabled child element or severely disabled child element of CTC is fully backdated.[6] The same should apply if you get DLA or PIP on appeal, or the highest rate of the DLA care component or the enhanced rate of the PIP daily living component following a supersession, mandatory reconsideration or appeal.[7]
- If you are already getting WTC when you claim one of the benefits that would entitle you to a disabled worker or severe disability element in your WTC (eg, DLA or PIP – see p1412), notify the TCO within one month of being awarded the benefit, so that the element can be fully backdated.[8]

If you disagree with a revised decision, you can request a mandatory reconsideration and then appeal to the First-tier Tribunal (see p1503). A revised decision may be revised as many times as necessary, either following another change, on 'reasonable grounds' (see below) or because of official error (see p1502).

Reasonable grounds

HMRC can amend or terminate an award if it has 'reasonable grounds' for believing that you are:[9]
- entitled to a different rate of tax credit; *or*
- not entitled to WTC or not entitled to CTC.

This could happen, for example, because you tell the TCO about an income change or wrong information is used in deciding your claim. It could also happen following an examination into your claim (see p1489).

If the rate of tax credit is changed, HMRC revises your award, taking into account any change in circumstances from the date it arose unless:
- it is a change that increases entitlement to tax credit elements, which can only be backdated for up to one month (see p1498);
- childcare charges decrease by £10 a week or more. In this case, there is a four-week 'run-on' at the same rate before the award is reduced (see p1462);[10]
- there is a four-week 'run-on' because you stop work or reduce your hours below 16, 24 or 30 a week (see p202).

Decisions can only be revised in this way during the period of the award, not after an award has been terminated, nor after a final decision has been made.[11]

Example
Pauline provides an estimate of her income for the current year. This has decreased by more than £2,500 compared with the previous year's income on which her award was based. The initial decision can be revised and her award recalculated based on the current year's income plus £2,500. The estimate she provides must be sufficient to give HMRC reasonable grounds for believing that her entitlement should change.

Part 10: General rules for tax credits
Chapter 64: Getting a tax credit decision changed
1. Revisions

HMRC is not obliged to revise, even when there are grounds. It could leave the changes to be dealt with at the annual review – eg, if it is late in the year and the change is minor.[12]

If you disagree with the revised decision, you can request a mandatory reconsideration and then appeal (see p1503). The burden of proof is on HMRC to set out the reasonable grounds for its decision and the evidence used to support it. If it fails to do so, the decision may be set aside.[13]

Official error

An initial decision can be revised in your favour if it is incorrect because of an official error (see p1502).[14]

Revising a final decision

After 5 April, HMRC carries out the annual review (see p1468) for the year just ended and makes a final decision on your entitlement for that year. It sends you an annual review form which details the circumstances on which the award was based and usually an annual declaration form, giving your income for the tax year just passed.

If HMRC sends you an annual declaration form, you must complete and return it by the deadline given (31 July in most cases). HMRC finalises your entitlement for the year just passed. A final decision is conclusive unless it is changed on mandatory reconsideration or appeal, or in the following circumstances.

- If you change your statement about your income or circumstances before the deadline, the final decision can be changed (see below).
- Once a final decision is made, there is a period during which HMRC can open an enquiry into your entitlement (see p1501). This is known as a 'revision on enquiry'.
- Outside the period of enquiry, a final decision can be revised on 'discovery' of certain information about your tax liability or in relation to fraud or neglect (see p1501). This is known as a 'revision on discovery'.
- A final decision can be revised in your favour because of official error (see p1502).

Changing your statement

If you reply to the annual review notice but then wish to change your statement, you may do so. If it is on or before the deadline given in the notice for replying (31 July in most cases), but HMRC has already made a final decision, the final decision may be revised.[15]

If HMRC only had an estimate of your income for the current year (eg, because you are self-employed and have not yet finalised your accounts), you have a later deadline (usually 31 January) by which to give details of your actual income for that year. If you do so, HMRC must make a new final decision.[16] It can revise the new decision if you change your statement on or before the later deadline.[17] If you do not give further details of actual income, HMRC must nevertheless make a new final decision once the later deadline is passed.

'Revision on enquiry'

HMRC does not need any particular grounds to open an enquiry into your entitlement, and some claims are selected for enquiry at random.[18] It must begin its enquiry by giving you written notice. An enquiry can only be opened for a particular tax year after the final decision for that year has been made, and within a limited period of time. This is known as the 'enquiry window'. It begins immediately after the final decision and ends a year after the deadline by which you had to reply to the annual review notice, or a year after the later deadline for self-employed people and others to supply actual income details if only an estimate was provided.[19] If you are required to submit an income tax return, the enquiry must begin by the day your tax return becomes final.

When the enquiry is completed, HMRC makes a fresh decision on whether you are entitled and how much the award should be. There is no time limit in which HMRC should conclude an enquiry, but you can apply to the First-tier Tribunal for a direction to bring the enquiry to an end.[20]

Only one enquiry into entitlement can be conducted for any one tax year.[21] For more details, see p1489.

If you disagree with the decision, you can ask for a mandatory reconsideration and then appeal (see p1503). It can also be revised if it is incorrect because of an official error (see p1502).[22] HMRC can also revise an enquiry decision by a 'revision on discovery' (see below).

'Revision on discovery'

'Discovery' is a power to revise entitlement in earlier years. If it is too late to 'enquire' into your entitlement, HMRC can still revise a final decision in specific circumstances. A final decision or an enquiry decision may be revised within five years if HMRC has 'reasonable grounds' for believing that your tax credit entitlement is wrong:

- because of a revision of your income tax liability. The revision of your tax credit entitlement must take place within a year of your income tax liability being revised;[23] or
- because of fraud or neglect.[24] The fraud or neglect may be on your part, or your partner's if it is a joint claim, or on the part of anyone acting for you (see p1453). Your tax credit entitlement in a tax year cannot be revised on this ground after five years from the end of the tax year – eg, a tax credit award for 2011/12 (or earlier) cannot be revised after 5 April 2017.[25]

There is nothing to stop HMRC going through this process more than once.[26] If a final decision, enquiry decision or discovery decision has been revised because of official error, this can be further revised in this way.[27]

Part 10: General rules for tax credits
Chapter 64: Getting a tax credit decision changed
1. Revisions

If you disagree with a discovery decision, or do not think HMRC has shown grounds to revise using this power, you can request a mandatory reconsideration and then appeal (see p1503). Alternatively, the decision may be revised if it is incorrect because of an official error.

Official error

An initial decision, final decision, enquiry decision or discovery decision can be revised in your favour if it is incorrect because of an official error.[28] The decision can be revised at any time up to five years after the date of the decision. An official error can include opening an enquiry (see p1501) without notice, and it is arguable that there is an official error if you have not been given the opportunity to contribute to an enquiry.[29]

Official error

'Official error' means an error relating to a tax credit made by an HMRC or DWP officer or a person providing tax credit services for them. If you, or someone acting for you, contributed to the error, it is *not* an official error. An error of law can be an official error, but not if it is only shown to be an error of law because of a later Upper Tribunal or court decision.

How to request a revision

If your circumstances change, there are rules on how HMRC should be notified (see p1467). In other cases, there are no set rules to follow. If you disagree with a decision, you should usually request a mandatory reconsideration, then appeal if you are unhappy with the outcome (see p1503) rather than ask HMRC to use one of its powers to revise a decision. If you are outside the absolute time limit for a mandatory reconsideration or appeal and want a decision to be revised on grounds of official error, you should request this in writing. If HMRC refuses to revise a decision on official error grounds, it is arguable that there is a right of appeal against this decision.[30]

Keep a copy of any letter you send to HMRC. If you call the Tax Credit Helpline, keep a log of your calls: the date and time you made the call, the information provided and what was agreed.

What happens after you request a revision

Before making its decision, HMRC may ask you to provide more information or evidence if it needs this to help with the decision.[31] HMRC may contact your employer or childcare provider if it also needs information from them.[32]

It is important that you respond to a request for information by the date given in the letter. If you do not provide the required information, HMRC may take proceedings to the First-Tier Tribunal to impose a penalty of up to £300, and if you still do not comply, a further daily penalty of up to £60 a day could be imposed. See p1490 for how these penalties are applied.

HMRC must give notice of the decision to you, and to your partner if it is a joint claim. This must include details of your right to appeal.[33]

2. Mandatory reconsiderations

HM Revenue and Customs (HMRC) must carry out a review if you have made a valid request for one, and it must notify you of the outcome. You must be notified of the outcome of the review before you can appeal. A review is known as a mandatory reconsideration, and applies to all tax credit decisions made on or after 6 April 2014.[34]

Who can request a mandatory reconsideration

The following people can request a mandatory reconsideration:[35]
- you, the tax credit claimant. For joint claimants, only one partner needs to make the request;
- for decisions about penalties, the person subject to the penalty;
- an appointee, if you are unable to make the request yourself (see p1453). If you do not have an appointee, the person (who must be 18 or over) who is to act on your behalf should write to HMRC asking to be appointed;
- another person with the power to make a tax credit claim for you – ie, a receiver appointed by the Court of Protection, a judicial factor or guardian.

The law does not specify who can request a mandatory reconsideration, but Form WTC/AP (see p1505) requires a signature from the tax credits claimant or appointee. It also asks whether you are getting help from a representative, and requires your signature to authorise that person to act for you. You may argue that your representative has the right to request a mandatory reconsideration on your behalf with your prior signed authority, but it may be simpler to ensure you sign the request where possible. HMRC does not accept photocopied signatures.

Which decisions can be reconsidered

You can request a mandatory reconsideration of:[36]
- an initial decision;
- a final decision;
- a revised decision (after a change in circumstances, on reasonable grounds or for official error);
- an enquiry decision;
- a discovery decision;
- a decision imposing a penalty;
- a decision charging interest on an overpayment.

Part 10: General rules for tax credits
Chapter 64: Getting a tax credit decision changed
2. Mandatory reconsiderations

Caselaw has found that there is a right to have a mandatory reconsideration and then appeal against the following but, in practice, HMRC may not accept this:

- a decision to reject a claim that is not made on the approved form, or that does not contain all the information requested on the form, including the national insurance (NI) number requirement (see p1455);[37]
- a decision that you do not have good cause for making a late annual declaration (see p1469);[38]
- a refusal to revise a decision on the grounds of official error (see p1502);[39]
- a decision contained in a 'Statement Like an Award Notice' (see p1462).[40]

In these situations, you should request a mandatory reconsideration, quoting the relevant caselaw. If HMRC refuses to carry out a mandatory reconsideration, you should ask for confirmation of this in writing and then appeal to the First-tier Tribunal on Form SSCS5, asking it to decide whether you have a right of appeal.

Which decisions cannot be reconsidered

You cannot request a mandatory reconsideration or appeal against:

- a decision to recover all or part of an overpayment (see below);
- a decision about the rate or method of recovery of an overpayment;
- a decision to postpone payments (see p1461);
- a decision not to accept a late request for a mandatory reconsideration;
- a decision to open an enquiry into your entitlement (but you can apply to the tribunal for a direction to bring an enquiry to an end – see p1489);
- a decision to terminate your tax credit award because you are a universal credit claimant (see p1464);
- a decision to terminate your tax credit award because you have successfully applied for and are entitled to payments under the new tax-free childcare scheme, due to be introduced from early 2017 (see p864).

Decisions to recover overpayments

There is a different process if you want to dispute a decision to recover an overpayment – ie, if you accept that you were overpaid, but do not think you should have to repay any money. If HMRC decides you have been overpaid tax credits, it can recover all or part of them at its discretion, and you cannot request a mandatory reconsideration or appeal against this decision. You can, however, request a mandatory reconsideration of the decision on your entitlement – ie, if you do not agree that you were overpaid, or disagree with the amount. In some cases, HMRC may use its discretion not to recover an overpayment, or to reduce the amount – eg, if recovery would cause hardship (see p1480). Complain to HMRC if you are unhappy with the way your claim has been handled. If your complaint is not resolved to your satisfaction, you can ask the Adjudicator to look into it (see p1398). See Chapter 62 for more information on tax credit overpayments.

How to request a mandatory reconsideration

A mandatory reconsideration must be requested in writing and must identify you (eg, your name and NI number) and the decision in question. It is advisable (but not essential) to use Form WTC/AP, *What To Do If You Think Your Child Tax Credit Or Working Tax Credit Is Wrong,* available at www.gov.uk. If you telephone HMRC to ask for a decision to be reconsidered, this is not a formal request for a mandatory reconsideration. You must still put your request in writing. If your representative requests the mandatory reconsideration on your behalf, your signed authority should be included.

Send your request to HMRC at the address given on the decision notice.

Time limits

Your request for a mandatory reconsideration must be received by HMRC within 30 days of the date given on the decision letter.[41]

You may not get a separate initial or final decision notice if the annual review notice states what the decision will be and the date on which it will be made – usually 31 July. This may apply if your claim has been automatically renewed. In this case, your request for a mandatory reconsideration must be received within 30 days of the date specified as the date on which the decision is made on the annual review notice – eg, by 30 August if the decision date is given as 31 July.

Late requests

If your request for a mandatory reconsideration is received by HMRC outside the 30-day time limit, you must explain why it is late. HMRC may accept a late request within 13 months of the original decision if it is satisfied that there were special circumstances that meant it was not practical for you to meet the time limit. HMRC must also be satisfied that it is reasonable, given all the circumstances, to accept the late request. The longer the delay, the more compelling the reasons must be.[42] Reasons listed as acceptable in the HMRC guidance are if:[43]

- you, your partner or dependant had a serious illness, or have died;
- you are not resident in the UK;
- there has been a disruption in normal postal services.

This list is not exhaustive and other reasons for lateness may be accepted.

If an application to extend the time limit is refused, you cannot ask for this decision to be reconsidered. You do not have a right of appeal against this or the original decision.

Penalty decisions

You can request a mandatory reconsideration of most decisions to impose a penalty. HMRC can impose a penalty for making incorrect statements, failing to report a required change of circumstances, or failing to comply with the annual

Part 10: General rules for tax credits
Chapter 64: Getting a tax credit decision changed
2. Mandatory reconsiderations

review. You can request a mandatory reconsideration in the normal way, then appeal to the First-tier Tribunal with any further appeal to the Upper Tribunal under the usual rules.[44]

However, if you fail to comply with a request for information or evidence, HMRC cannot decide to impose a penalty of up to £300 itself, but must take 'proceedings' to the First-tier Tribunal. You have an opportunity to attend a hearing where the First-tier Tribunal decides whether or not you should be given a penalty. You can then appeal to the Upper Tribunal.[45] The First-tier or Upper Tribunal can also increase a penalty, within the maximum amount allowed. In these penalty appeals to the Upper Tribunal (ie, where the decision was made by the First-tier Tribunal under penalty proceedings), you can appeal against the decision to impose a penalty or the amount; there does not have to be an error of law.[46] The usual time limits and procedures for applying for permission to appeal apply. For information on penalties, see p1490.

After you request a mandatory reconsideration

If a written request is received within the time limit, or a late request is accepted, HMRC must carry out a mandatory reconsideration of the decision in question. The mandatory reconsideration must be carried out as soon as is reasonably practical, and HMRC's stated target is 42 days.[47] If you are still waiting for the outcome of a mandatory reconsideration by the time the final decision is made (usually 31 July) (see p1470), you should also request a mandatory reconsideration against the final decision. If your annual review told you what the final decision would be and when it would be made, you may not get another notice, but you should still request a mandatory reconsideration within 30 days of the date you were told it would be made (usually 31 July).

HMRC may request further information or evidence from you. This must be in writing and specify a date by which it should be provided. If you do not provide the information or evidence by the date specified, HMRC may proceed with the mandatory reconsideration. New information or evidence does not have to be provided as a pre-condition for a mandatory reconsideration.

A penalty cannot be imposed on you for failing to provide information or evidence requested in connection with a mandatory reconsideration.

HMRC must issue a '**mandatory reconsideration notice**', containing sufficient information for you to understand the outcome, details of any change to the decision and the reasons for its conclusion. The outcome must be one of the following.[48]

- The decision is upheld. There is no change to the original decision with which you disagree, and you have the right of appeal.
- The decision is varied. In this case, the original decision is changed. If the decision is changed in your favour but you still disagree with part of it, you can appeal against the decision as varied. You do not have to go through the mandatory reconsideration process again.

• The decision is cancelled. You are left in the position you were in before the decision was made. There does not appear to be a right of appeal in this situation, as this would be against a decision that has been cancelled.

3. **Appealing to the First-tier Tribunal**

You can only appeal against a tax credits decision after a mandatory reconsideration has been carried out and the outcome has been notified to you in writing. Tax credit appeals are heard by the same First-tier Tribunal that deals with social security benefits, which is administered by HM Courts and Tribunals Service (HMCTS).[49] Many of the rules are the same as those for social security benefits (see Chapter 55). This chapter refers you to Chapter 55 where the tax credit rules are the same as the benefit rules.

Who can appeal

The following people have the right of appeal:[50]
• you, the tax credit claimant. For joint claimants, both or either of you can make the appeal. If only one appeals, the First-tier Tribunal decision still applies to both, provided you are both given the right to a hearing;[51]
• for appeals about penalties, the person subject to the penalty;
• an appointee, if you are unable to appeal yourself (see p1453). If you do not have an appointee, the person (who must be 18 or over) who is to act on your behalf in the appeal should write to HM Revenue and Customs (HMRC) asking to be appointed;
• another person with the power to make a tax credit claim for you – ie, a receiver appointed by the Court of Protection, a judicial factor or guardian.[52]

The tribunal rules state that you must sign the appeal, but also state that you can appoint a representative who can do anything that you are required to do, except sign a witness statement. Your representative may sign the appeal on your behalf with your signed consent, but it may be simpler to ensure you sign the appeal yourself if possible.[53]

How to appeal

You must lodge your appeal directly with the tribunal, not with the decision maker. You should appeal on the appropriate form – Form SSCS5 (*Notice Of Appeal Against A Decision Made By HM Revenue and Customs*), which must be signed by you, or by your representative. If your representative signs the appeal, s/he must send your signed authority to act on your behalf. Enclose a copy of the mandatory reconsideration notice, and send Form SSCS5 to HMCTS. Alternatively, you can write a letter. You must include:

10

Part 10: General rules for tax credits
Chapter 64: Getting a tax credit decision changed
3. Appealing to the First-tier Tribunal

- your signature (on the appeal request itself, or on a signed authority for your representative to act on your behalf);
- your name and address;
- the name and address of your representative, if you have one;
- the grounds for appeal – ie, the reasons why you disagree with the decision;
- a copy of the mandatory reconsideration notice.

Time limits

Your appeal must be received by HMCTS within one month of the date on the mandatory reconsideration notice.[54]

Late appeals

If your appeal is received outside the one-month time limit but within the absolute time limit of 13 months, it is accepted provided HMRC does not object and unless the tribunal directs otherwise. If HMRC objects, the tribunal can still accept your appeal if the overriding objective to deal with cases fairly and justly is met.[55] Note that in very exceptional circumstances (eg, if you did not receive notice of the decision you want to appeal), you can argue that the tribunal has discretion to allow you to appeal outside the absolute time limit.[56] However, this is unlikely to apply unless you have done all that you could to appeal in time.

What happens after you appeal

HMRC must prepare its response to your appeal within 28 days of receiving notice of your appeal from the tribunal.[57] Its response (also known as a submission) should include the law used to make its decision, and all relevant information and evidence.[58] You may receive correspondence from HMRC headed 'Solicitor's Office and Legal Services' about your appeal, but this does not mean that HMRC is commencing any form of legal proceedings.

10

Settling the appeal

HMRC may want to settle the appeal without going to the tribunal. You can point out to HMRC where you think its decision is wrong and supply information or arguments you want it to consider. Even though HMRC has already had the opportunity to reconsider its decision, once you have lodged your appeal it may offer you terms on which to settle the appeal. Your appeal can only be settled with your consent. If you do not agree, the appeal must proceed to the tribunal.

If you are asked to settle the appeal, check first whether the proposed agreement gives you everything to which you think you are entitled. Get advice if you are not sure whether or not to agree. If in doubt, continue with the appeal. If you agree to settle, HMRC must write to you setting out the terms of the agreement – eg, giving you a new amount. Your appeal then lapses unless you write to HMRC within 30 days of the date of the written notice of agreement saying you have changed your mind and wish to proceed with your appeal.[59]

If your appeal has not been heard by the end of the year

If your appeal has not been heard by the time you get HMRC's final decision on your entitlement after the end of the year, request another mandatory reconsideration and appeal against the final decision.[60] This is because an in-year decision becomes redundant once a final decision is made, and HMRC is not bound to change the final decision if you won your appeal against the in-year decision. If you have not appealed against the final decision, your appeal against the in-year decision does not automatically lapse, but it becomes academic and will only be worthwhile continuing with in limited circumstances, such as if it is in the public interest, or if it concludes that HMRC made an official error.[61]

Withdrawing an appeal

You can ask to withdraw the appeal if you decide not to go ahead with it. See p1332 for details of withdrawing and reinstating an appeal if you change your mind.

When your appeal can be struck out

Your appeal may be 'struck out' before the hearing in certain circumstances. The rules are the same as those for benefits (see p1330).

The hearing

The tribunal holds an oral hearing if you have asked for one. Otherwise, there is a paper hearing in your absence (see p1335). For information on asking for the hearing to be postponed or adjourned to a later date, see p1328. The tax credit rules are the same as those for benefits, except that there are no special 'test case' provisions for tax credits that can block your appeal or affect its outcome (although payment can be postponed while there is an appeal pending in another case that could affect your own award).[62] The rules on 'lead cases' described on p1334 do apply to tax credits.

Procedures for tax credit appeals

There are procedural rules that the tribunal must follow when dealing with your appeal. See pp1326–33 and pp1338–56 for details. The tax credit rules are the same, with the following exceptions.

- **Medical examinations.** The tribunal cannot refer you to a doctor for a medical examination.[63] However, if your appeal concerns a disability question, it may be important to get your own medical evidence (see p1347).
- **Change in circumstances after you appeal.** The rules apply to tax credits in the same way as they do to benefits except:
    - wherever Chapter 55 refers to 'supersession', read 'revision' for tax credits;
    - if you reclaim or ask for a revision because of a change in circumstances after you appeal, there is no specific provision for a decision maker to revisit

Part 10: General rules for tax credits
Chapter 64: Getting a tax credit decision changed
5. Appealing to the Court of Appeal or Court of Session

her/his decision on that claim or revision once the appeal has been heard on the grounds that s/he would have made a different decision had s/he known what the tribunal's decision would be.

- **After the hearing.** If HMRC is considering an appeal to the Upper Tribunal or has decided to appeal, you are normally not paid until the Upper Tribunal decides the case. HMRC can postpone payment in these circumstances, without notifying you of its intention.[64]
- **If you disagree with the First-tier Tribunal's decision.** The decision cannot be superseded (because supersessions do not apply to tax credits), but it can be revised in any of the ways described in this chapter except for official error (see p1497).

  If the First-tier Tribunal made an error of law, you can appeal to the Upper Tribunal as you can in benefit appeals. For tax credits, HMRC is not prevented from revising the First-tier Tribunal's decision on 'reasonable grounds', which could also include an error of law (if it is still within the tax year of the award).
- **When a decision can be set aside.** If you appeal to the Upper Tribunal, there is no provision obliging the First-tier Tribunal to set aside the decision if both you and HMRC agree that the First-tier Tribunal made an error of law.[65]

4. **Appealing to the Upper Tribunal**

You can appeal to the Upper Tribunal against a decision of the First-tier Tribunal if the First-tier Tribunal made an error of law. In some penalty appeals, you can also appeal about the amount of the penalty (see p1505).

Chapter 56 explains what an error of law is and how to appeal (see p1363). The rules for tax credits are the same as those for benefits, except that if you disagree with the Upper Tribunal decision it cannot be superseded, but it can be revised in any of the ways described on p1497, except because of an official error.

5. **Appealing to the Court of Appeal or Court of Session**

You can appeal to the Court of Appeal (in England and Wales) or to the Court of Session (in Scotland) against a decision of the Upper Tribunal, but only if there has been an error of law (see Chapter 56).

Notes

1. **Revisions**
1 s14(1) TCA 2002
2 s3(2) TCA 2002
3 s14(3) TCA 2002
4 s15(1) TCA 2002
5 Reg 25 TC(CN) Regs; reg 16(5)(a) WTC(EMR) Regs
6 Reg 26A TC(CN) Regs
7 Email from HMRC to CPAG, 8 February 2010
8 Reg 26(3) TC(CN) Regs
9 s16(1) TCA 2002
10 Reg 16(5)(b) WTC(EMR) Regs
11 s16(1) TCA 2002
12 CTC/2662/2005; CTC/3981/2005
13 *SB v HMRC (TC)* [2014] UKUT 543 (AAC); *NI v HMRC (TC)* [2015] UKUT 490 (AAC)
14 s21 TCA 2002
15 s18(5) TCA 2002
16 s18(6) TCA 2002
17 s18(9) TCA 2002
18 s19(1) TCA 2002
19 s19(4) TCA 2002
20 s19(9) TCA 2002
21 s19(11) TCA 2002
22 s21 TCA 2002
23 s20(1) and (3) TCA 2002
24 s20(4) TCA 2002
25 s20(5) TCA 2002
26 s20(6)(a) TCA 2002
27 s20(6)(b) TCA 2002
28 s21 TCA 2002; reg 3 TC(OE) Regs
29 *JI v HMRC (TC)* [2013] UKUT 199 (AAC), para 53
30 *JI v HMRC (TC)* [2013] UKUT 199 (AAC), para 50
31 ss15(2)(b),16(3)(b) and 19(2)(b) TCA 2002
32 Regs 30 and 31 TC(CN) Regs
33 s23 TCA 2002

2. **Mandatory reconsiderations**
34 Footnote to Art 2 Tax Credits, Child Benefit and Guardian's Allowance Reviews and Appeals Order 2014, No.886
35 See HMRC leaflet WTC/AP, *What To Do If You Think Your Child Tax Credit Or Working Tax Credit Is Wrong*
36 s38 TCA 2002

37 *CI v HMRC (TC)* [2014] UKUT 158 (AAC) held that there is a right of appeal, but this disagrees with the earlier *ZM and AB v HMRC (TC)* [2013] UKUT 547 (AAC), which held there there is no such right.
38 *SG v HMRC (TC)* [2011] UKUT 199 (AAC)
39 *JI v HMRC (TC)* [2013] UKUT 199 (AAC), para 50
40 *TM v HMRC (TC)* [2016] UKUT 512 (AAC), but see also *DG v HMRC (TC)* [2016] UKUT 505 (AAC)
41 ss23(2) and 39(1) TCA 2002
42 s21A TCA 2002
43 TCM 0014020
44 s38 TCA 2002
45 s63 and Sch 2 para 4(1) TCA 2002
46 Sch 2 para 4(1) TCA 2002
47 David Gauke MP, Exchequer Secretary to the Treasury, Eighth Delegated Legislation Committee, 26 March 2014
48 s21A(3) TCA 2002

3. **Appealing to the First-tier Tribunal**
49 s63(2) TCA 2002
50 s12 SSA 1998, as applied by reg 4 TC(A) Regs under the power in s63(8) TCA 2001
51 CTC/2612/2005
52 Reg 3 TC(A)(No.2) Regs
53 rr11 and 22 TP(FT) Rules
54 r22(2)(d)(i) TP(FT) Rules
55 rr2 and 5(3)(a) TP(FT) Rules
56 *KK v Sheffield City Council (CTB)* [2015] UKUT 367 (AAC)
57 r24(1)(c) TP(FT) Rules
58 *CS v HMRC (TC)* [2015] UKUT 407 (AAC)
59 s54 TMA 1970, as applied by Tax Credits (Settlement of Appeals) Regulations 2014, No.1933
60 CTC/2662/2005; CTC/3981/2005
61 *RF v HMRC* [2016] UKUT 399 (AAC); *JY v HMRC* [2016] UKUT 407 (AAC)
62 Reg 11 TC(PC) Regs
63 The power to refer to a doctor in s20 SSA 1998 does not apply to tax credits.
64 Reg 11 TC(PC) Regs
65 s13(3) SSA 1998, as applied by reg 5(2) TC(A) Regs under the power in s63(8) TCA 2002

10

Part 11

Immigration and residence
rules for benefits and tax
credits

Chapter 65

. . . .

Coming from abroad: immigration status

This chapter covers:
1. Immigration status (below)
2. Benefits and tax credits affected by immigration status (p1519)
3. Partners and children (p1523)
4. National insurance numbers and contributions (p1525)
5. Asylum seekers and refugees (p1526)

You should check this chapter if you, your partner and child are not all European Economic Area (EEA) nationals. If you are all EEA nationals, the rules in this chapter do not apply to you. In either case, you must satisfy the residence requirements in Chapter 66.

Key facts
- Your immigration status may mean that you are not entitled to some benefits and tax credits, although there are limited exceptions.
- The immigration status of your partner can affect the amount you are paid. If your partner's or child's leave in the UK is on condition that s/he does not have recourse to public funds, your claim could affect her/his right to remain in the UK.

11

1. Immigration status

It is important to know your immigration status, and that of anyone included in your claim, before making a claim for a benefit or tax credit. This is because it affects your right to benefits and tax credits and also because being paid an increased amount for someone included in your claim can affect her/his right to remain in the UK if her/his leave is subject to the condition that s/he has 'no recourse to public funds'. If you are unsure about your immigration status, you should obtain specialist advice from your local law centre, Citizens Advice Bureau or other advice agency that gives immigration advice.

Part 11: Immigration and residence rules for benefits and tax credits
Chapter 65: Coming from abroad: immigration status
1. Immigration status

Who is a 'person subject to immigration control'

Most people, apart from British citizens, are subject to immigration control. However, for benefit and tax credit purposes, the term 'person subject to immigration control' has a specific meaning. It is this meaning that is referred to when the phrase 'person subject to immigration control' is used in this *Handbook*.

You are defined as a **'person subject to immigration control'** if you are not a European Economic Area (EEA) national and you:[1]

- require leave to enter or remain in the UK, but do not have it (see below);
- have leave to enter or remain subject to the condition that you do not have recourse to public funds (see p1517);
- have leave to enter or remain given as a result of a maintenance undertaking (see p1518); *or*
- (arguably) have leave to enter or remain solely because you are appealing a decision to refuse to vary your previous leave (see p1519).

If you are defined as a person subject to immigration control, you are excluded from many benefits and tax credits (see p1519). There are, however, some limited exceptions (see p1520, p1521 and p1522).

Note:

- You cannot be a person subject to immigration control if you are an EEA national (this includes British citizens), as the definition only applies to non-EEA nationals. See p1609 for a list of EEA states.
- If you are not an EEA national but you have a right to reside under European Union (EU) law (eg, as a family member of an EEA worker – see p1560), you do not require leave to enter or remain.[2] If this applies to you, you cannot be refused benefit on the basis of your immigration status even if, for example, your leave is subject to a condition that you do not have recourse to public funds, or subject to a maintenance undertaking. Conditions attached to any leave you have been given do not have any effect while you have a right to reside under the EEA Regulations (see p1545).[3]

You require leave to enter or remain, but do not have it

You are a 'person subject to immigration control' if you require leave to enter or remain but do not have it.[4]

If you are not an EEA national, you require leave to enter or remain in the UK unless you are:

- a person with the right of abode;
- a person with a right of residence in EU law – eg, if you are:
  - a family member of an EEA or Swiss national who has a right to reside in the UK (see p1560);[5]
  - a Swiss national with a right to reside. Swiss nationals, in general, have the same residence rights as EEA nationals and do not require leave to enter or, if they have a right to reside, leave to remain in the UK;[6]

– the primary carer of a British citizen who is in the UK, and it is necessary for you to have a right to reside in the UK so that s/he can continue to reside within the EU.[7] **Note:** having a right to reside on this basis does not entitle you to any benefits that require a right to reside (see p1543), but you can still be entitled to other benefits that do not require a right to reside, such as personal independence payment (PIP) and carer's allowance (CA).

Examples of when you require leave to enter or remain but do not have it include if you:

- are an asylum seeker with temporary admission;
- have overstayed your limited leave to enter or remain;
- have entered the UK without immigration leave and since then have not obtained leave to remain;
- are subject to a deportation order.

Note: there are close links between the benefit authorities and the Home Office. Making a claim for benefit could alert the immigration authorities to your presence and status in the UK. Get specialist immigration advice before claiming if you are unsure about your immigration status.

Your leave has a no recourse to public funds condition

You are a 'person subject to immigration control' if you have leave to enter or remain in the UK that is subject to the condition that you do not have recourse to 'public funds'.[8]

Most people admitted to the UK with time-limited leave, such as spouses/civil partners, students or visitors, are given limited leave to stay which is subject to the condition they do not have recourse to public funds.

Public funds

'Public funds' are defined in the Immigration Rules as:[9]

– attendance allowance;
– CA;
– child benefit;
– child tax credit;
– council tax benefit (now abolished);
– council tax reduction;
– disability living allowance;
– income-related employment and support allowance;
– homelessness assistance and housing provided under specific provisions;
– housing benefit (HB);
– income support;
– income-based jobseeker's allowance;
– local welfare assistance (except the Discretionary Assistance Fund for Wales);

Part 11: Immigration and residence rules for benefits and tax credits
Chapter 65: Coming from abroad: immigration status
1. Immigration status

- pension credit;
- PIP;
- severe disablement allowance;
- social fund payments;
- universal credit;
- working tax credit.

Only the benefits, tax credits and assistance listed in the Immigration Rules are public funds. Therefore, if you get any other benefit or other assistance, you are not in breach of the 'no recourse to public funds' condition.

If you have recourse to public funds when your leave prohibits you from doing so, you have breached a condition of your leave. This may affect your right to remain in the UK: you could be liable to be deported, have further leave refused and/or be prosecuted for committing a criminal offence.[10]

If your leave is subject to a 'no recourse to public funds' condition, you are defined as a 'person subject to immigration control' and (unless you are covered by one of the exceptions – see pp1520–22) you are not entitled to the benefits and tax credits defined as public funds. However, if you *are* covered by one of the exceptions, there is no problem with your claiming and receiving that public fund benefit, as you are not regarded as having recourse to public funds under the Immigration Rules.[11]

Note: you *are* regarded as having recourse to public funds if someone else's benefit is increased because of your presence – eg, if the amount of your partner's HB is greater because you are included in her/his claim. If this happens, you have breached the condition not to have recourse to public funds. Obtain specialist immigration advice before making a claim.

Your leave was given as a result of a maintenance undertaking

If your leave to enter or remain was given as a result of a maintenance undertaking, you are a 'person subject to immigration control'.[12] For example, if an elderly relative is seeking to join family in the UK, it is usual to require a maintenance undertaking.

Maintenance undertaking

A '**maintenance undertaking**' means a written undertaking given by another person under the Immigration Rules to be responsible for your maintenance and accommodation.[13]

There are specific Home Office forms on which an undertaking can be given. However, no official form need be used, provided the undertaking is sufficiently formal and definite.[14] The document must contain a promise or agreement that the other person will maintain and accommodate you in the future. If it merely contains a statement about her/his present abilities and intentions, it does not amount to an undertaking.[15]

Your leave is considered to be 'as a result of a maintenance undertaking' if this was a factor in granting it. It does not need to have been the only, or even a major, factor.[16] However, if the maintenance undertaking was not relevant to your being granted leave, its existence does not make you a person subject to immigration control. If you are in doubt about whether you have leave given as a result of an undertaking, get specialist immigration advice.

You are appealing a refusal to vary your previous leave

If you have leave solely because you have appealed against (or requested an administrative review of) a decision to refuse an application to vary the leave you previously had, you can be considered to be a 'person subject to immigration control'. It is arguable that this does not apply in all cases.[17] If you are refused benefit in these circumstances, you should obtain specialist advice.

Example

Sayf is granted two and a half years' discretionary leave. Just before this expires, he applies for a further period of discretionary leave. His application is refused and he immediately appeals against this decision. His previous discretionary leave is extended while the appeal is pending. It may be argued that he is now a 'person subject to immigration control'.

2. **Benefits and tax credits affected by immigration status**

The general rule is that if you are defined as a 'person subject to immigration control' (see p1516), you are excluded from council tax reduction[18] and the following benefits and tax credits:[19]

- attendance allowance (AA);
- carer's allowance (CA);
- child benefit;
- child tax credit (CTC);
- disability living allowance (DLA);
- income-related employment and support allowance (ESA);
- ESA in youth;[20]
- housing benefit (HB);
- incapacity benefit (IB) for incapacity in youth;[21]
- income support (IS);
- income-based jobseeker's allowance (JSA);
- pension credit (PC);
- personal independence payment (PIP);
- severe disablement allowance (SDA);

11

Part 11: Immigration and residence rules for benefits and tax credits
Chapter 65: Coming from abroad: immigration status
2. Benefits and tax credits affected by immigration status

- social fund payments;
- universal credit (UC);
- working tax credit (WTC).

However, there are limited exceptions when some people subject to immigration control can claim means-tested benefits (see below), some can claim non-means-tested benefits (see p1521) and some can claim tax credits (see p1522).

A person subject to immigration control is only excluded from the above benefits and tax credits and can therefore claim any other benefit. For example, if you have paid sufficient national insurance (NI) contributions, you can claim any of the contributory benefits – eg, retirement pensions, contribution-based JSA and contributory ESA. You can also claim benefits that depend on previous employment – eg, maternity allowance (MA) or industrial injuries benefits. **Note:** the government intends to make it a condition of entitlement to contributory ESA, contribution-based JSA, MA, and statutory sick, maternity, adoption, paternity and shared parental pay that you be entitled to work in the UK.[22] See CPAG's online service and *Welfare Rights Bulletin* for updates.

Exceptions

Means-tested benefits

The relevant benefits are:
- IS;
- income-based JSA;
- income-related ESA;
- PC;
- HB;
- UC.

If you are a 'person subject to immigration control' (see p1516), this does not exclude you from entitlement to the means-tested benefits listed above in the following circumstances.[23]

- You are a national of Macedonia or Turkey[24] and you are lawfully present in the UK – eg, during a period in which you have leave to enter or remain in the UK. (This provision is unlikely to assist if you are an asylum seeker with temporary admission, because although you are lawfully present,[25] your temporary admission does not give you a right to reside, which these benefits require (see p1542), so you would need a right to reside on another basis[26]). You are also not excluded from council tax reduction, although receiving it counts as having recourse to public funds and so breaches any 'no recourse to public funds' condition attached to your leave.[27]
- You have leave to enter or remain given as a result of a maintenance undertaking and have been resident in the UK for at least five years (beginning on either the date you entered the UK or when the maintenance undertaking

was signed, whichever is later). If there are gaps in your residence as a result of your going to live for a period in another country, the periods of residence in the UK can be added together to make the five years.[28] However, depending on your circumstances, you may not have ceased to be resident during the short periods of absence, and each absence must be considered individually (see p1536).[29]

- You have leave to enter or remain given as a result of a maintenance undertaking and the person (or, if more than one, all the people) who gave the undertaking has died.
- You applied for asylum before 3 April 2000, have not had a decision on that application, and are covered by the transitional protection rules.[30] See Chapter 58 of the 2011/12 edition of this *Handbook* for these.

Social fund payments

If you are defined as a 'person subject to immigration control', this does not exclude you from entitlement to social fund payments if you are in any of the exempt categories for means-tested (listed on p1520) or non-means-tested benefits (listed below).[31] However, you must meet the other conditions of entitlement, including (except for winter fuel payments) being in receipt of a qualifying benefit.

Non-means-tested benefits

The relevant benefits are:
- AA;
- CA;
- child benefit;
- DLA;
- ESA in youth;
- IB for incapacity in youth;
- PIP;
- SDA.

If you are a 'person subject to immigration control', this does not exclude you from the non-contributory benefits listed above in the following circumstances.[32]
- You have leave to enter or remain given as a result of a maintenance undertaking.
- You are a member of a European Economic Area national's (see p1609) (including a British citizen's) family.[33] For further information on when this exemption should apply, see CPAG's *Benefits for Migrants Handbook*.
- You are a national of Algeria, Morocco, San Marino, Tunisia or Turkey and either you are currently lawfully working (see p1522) in Great Britain, or you have ceased to be lawfully working in Great Britain for a reason such as

11

Part 11: Immigration and residence rules for benefits and tax credits
Chapter 65: Coming from abroad: immigration status
2. Benefits and tax credits affected by immigration status

pregnancy, childcare, illness or accident, or because you have reached retirement age.[34]
- You are living with a family member (see p1611) who is covered by the above bullet point.
- For DLA, PIP, AA and child benefit only, you are covered by a reciprocal agreement. In practice, this is most helpful for child benefit and, in particular, if you are covered by the agreement with former the Yugoslavia which applies to Bosnia-Herzegovina, Kosovo, Macedonia, Montenegro and Serbia.[35] See p1533 for more information about reciprocal agreements.

Lawfully working

You should be accepted as '**lawfully working**' if you have been insured (by paying, or being credited with, NI contributions),[36] and any work you have done has not breached any conditions attached to your leave. If you are an asylum seeker, you should be accepted as lawfully working if you have permission to work from the Home Office.

Tax credits

If you are a 'person subject to immigration control', this does not exclude you from getting CTC or WTC in the following circumstances.[37]
- You have leave to enter or remain given as a result of a maintenance undertaking and you have been resident in the UK for at least five years (beginning on either the date you entered the UK or when the maintenance undertaking was signed, whichever is later).
- You have leave to enter or remain given as a result of a maintenance undertaking and the person (or, if more than one, all the people) who gave the undertaking has died.
- For CTC only, you are a national of Algeria, Morocco, San Marino, Tunisia or Turkey and either you are lawfully working (see above) in the UK, or you have ceased lawfully working for a reason such as pregnancy, childcare, illness or accident, or because you have reached retirement age.[38]
- For WTC only, you are a national of Macedonia or Turkey and you are lawfully present in the UK – eg, during a period in which you have leave to enter or remain in the UK.
- For CTC only, you are transferring to CTC from an IS or income-based JSA claim that included amounts for a child and you were entitled to that IS or JSA because you came into either the group in the first or last bullet points on p1520.[39]

Note: if you are a person subject to immigration control, but your partner is not (or s/he comes into one of the above groups), you can make a joint claim for tax credits (see p1524).

3. Partners and children

Some benefits and tax credits have special rules that apply if any partner or child who lives with you is subject to immigration control. These rules vary, so check the rules for the benefit or tax credit you want to claim.

Means-tested benefits

Income support, income-based jobseeker's allowance and income-related employment and support allowance

If your partner is a 'person subject to immigration control' (see p1516), s/he is included in your claim for income support (IS), income-based jobseeker's allowance (JSA), including if you are a joint-claim couple, or income-related employment and support allowance (ESA). However, you are only paid a personal allowance at the single person's rate, unless s/he comes into one of the groups that can get the means-tested benefits listed on p1520, in which case, you are paid at the couple rate.[40]

In all cases, your partner is still treated as part of your household and part of your claim. Therefore, her/his work, income and capital can all affect your benefit entitlement. Her/his presence means you cannot claim IS as a lone parent (see p102) and may mean you are not entitled to a severe disability premium (see p242).

Premiums are payable if either you or your partner satisfy the qualifying conditions (see p236) and should be paid at the couple rate.

Note: if your partner's leave to enter or remain in the UK is subject to a 'no recourse to public funds' condition, receiving an additional (or a couple rate of a) premium for her/him could be regarded as having recourse to public funds and affect her/his right to remain in the UK. Obtain specialist immigration advice before making a claim.

Pension credit

If your partner is a 'person subject to immigration control' (whether or not s/he is in one of the exempt groups listed on p1520), s/he is treated as not being part of your household.[41] This means that you are paid as a single person and your partner's income and capital do not affect your claim. If you would otherwise be entitled to the additional amount for severe disability, your partner's presence may mean you are not entitled to it as the DWP may count her/him as 'normally residing with' you for this purpose (see p242).[42]

Housing benefit

If your partner and/or child for whom you are responsible is a 'person subject to immigration control', this does not affect the amount you are paid. Your partner is included in your claim and your applicable amount includes the couple rate of

Part 11: Immigration and residence rules for benefits and tax credits
Chapter 65: Coming from abroad: immigration status
3. Partners and children

the personal allowance and any premiums to which either of you are entitled. Similarly, your child is included in your claim and your applicable amount includes a personal allowance for each child, together with any premiums for which s/he qualifies.

Note: if your partner's and/or child's leave is subject to a 'no recourse to public funds' condition, a claim for housing benefit could result in additional public funds being paid as a result of her/his presence. This could affect her/his right to remain in the UK (see p1517). Obtain specialist immigration advice before making a claim.

Universal credit

If your partner is a 'person subject to immigration control', and is not in one of the groups who can get universal credit (UC) listed on p1519, you must claim UC as a single person.[43] Your award is based on the maximum amount for a single person, but your partner's income and capital are taken into account (see p161).[44]

Non-means-tested benefits

Contributory benefits are not affected by your immigration status, or that of your partner or child. **Note:** the government intends to make it a condition of entitlement to contributory ESA, contribution-based JSA, maternity allowance, and statutory sick, maternity, adoption, paternity and shared parental pay that you be entitled to work in the UK.[45] See CPAG's online service and *Welfare Rights Bulletin* for updates.

Only the claimant's immigration status affects entitlement to non-contributory benefits. Therefore, for **child benefit,** if you are not a 'person subject to immigration control', or you are but you are in one of the exempt groups (see p1521), you can claim for any child for whom you are responsible, regardless of the child's immigration status. However, if the child's leave is subject to a 'no recourse to public funds' condition, receipt of child benefit for her/him may be regarded as recourse and could affect her/his right to remain in the UK. Obtain specialist immigration advice before making a claim.

Similarly, if your child is not a person subject to immigration control, or s/he is but is in one of the exempt groups on p1521, s/he can claim **disability living allowance** even if you are a person subject to immigration control.

Tax credits

If your partner is a 'person subject to immigration control' and you are not (or you are but are in one of the exempt groups on p1522), your joint claim for tax credits (see p1450) is treated as if your partner were not subject to immigration control. You are therefore entitled to working tax credit (WTC) and child tax credit (CTC).[46] However, unless you or your partner are responsible for a child, or your partner is a national of Macedonia or Turkey and lawfully present in the UK, your WTC does not include the couple element.[47]

There are no immigration status conditions for children for tax credits. Consequently, any child for whom you are responsible is included in your claim, and your CTC and/or WTC includes amounts for her/him.

If your partner's leave is on condition that s/he does not have recourse to public funds, s/he is not regarded as having recourse by making a joint tax credits claim with you. This means that you and your partner can make the joint claim without it affecting her/his right to remain in the UK. If such a joint claim includes a child whose leave is on condition that s/he does not have recourse to public funds, any tax credits awarded in respect of that child are also not regarded as recourse.[48]

If your claim for CTC or WTC is *not* a joint claim as described above (ie, in which one partner is a person subject to immigration control) and it includes an amount for a child whose leave is subject to a 'no recourse to public funds' condition, this may be regarded as recourse and could affect her/his right to remain in the UK. Get specialist immigration advice before making a claim.

4. **National insurance numbers and contributions**

Exemption from the national insurance number requirement

In general, the national insurance (NI) number requirement (see p1150) applies, regardless of immigration status, to you and any partner included in your claim (even if you are not going to receive any extra benefit for her/him because s/he is a 'person subject to immigration control' – see p1516). For the rules on when a partner who is a 'person subject to immigration control' is included in your claim, see p1523.

However, if you are the benefit claimant, your partner does not have to satisfy the NI number requirement if:[49]

- s/he is a 'person subject to immigration control' because s/he requires leave to enter or remain in the UK, but does not have it (see p1516); *and*
- s/he has not previously been given an NI number; *and*
- if you are claiming income support, income-based jobseeker's allowance, income-related employment and support allowance or pension credit and your partner is not entitled to that benefit her/himself, or you are claiming housing benefit and your partner fails the habitual residence test (see p1537). However, in practice, it is difficult to see who could satisfy the first bullet point and not satisfy this.

Part 11: Immigration and residence rules for benefits and tax credits
Chapter 65: Coming from abroad: immigration status
5. Asylum seekers and refugees

You are still asked for information about an NI number application for your partner, even though s/he is exempt. An NI number will be refused, but this does not prevent you from being entitled to benefits or tax credits, or council tax reduction.

Note: this exemption does not apply to universal credit (UC). If your partner is a 'person subject to immigration control' because s/he requires leave, you must claim UC as a single person (see p161) and your partner is not required to have an NI number.

Tax credits

The NI number requirement for tax credits is similar to the requirement for benefits (and includes the above exemption for partners who require leave but do not have it). In addition, the NI number requirement does not apply if the Tax Credit Office is satisfied that you (and/or your partner if it is a joint claim) have 'reasonable excuse' for not complying with the requirement – eg, if you are unable to prove your identity because the Home Office has all your documents and you can prove this, for instance, with a letter from your solicitor.[50] **Note:** if your claim is refused because you have not satisfied the NI number requirement, you can appeal on the grounds that either your partner is exempt or you had 'reasonable excuse'.[51] You must apply for a mandatory reconsideration before you can appeal.

National insurance contributions

If you have worked and paid contributions in another European Economic Area country and you are covered by the European Union co-ordination rules (see p1611), these can be taken into account when working out your entitlement to UK contributory benefits (see p1617). Similar rules apply if you have worked and paid contributions in a country with which the UK has a reciprocal agreement (see p1533).[52] You may also be able to make up a shortfall in your contribution record by making voluntary contributions (see p960). Get advice to check whether this is worth doing.

5. **Asylum seekers and refugees**

Asylum seekers

You are referred to as an **'asylum seeker'** while you are waiting for a Home Office decision on an application for refugee status. If you are a non-European Economic Area (EEA) national seeking asylum in the UK, unless you have leave on some other basis or you do not require it (eg, because you are joining your family member who is an EEA national with a right to reside in the UK as a worker), you come within the definition of a 'person subject to immigration control'. This is because you are someone who requires leave, but does not have it (see p1516).

You are therefore excluded from the social security benefits listed on p1519 unless you are in one of the exempt groups on p1520–22.

If benefit can be paid for you either because you are in an exempt group or because your partner can include you in her/his claim, this does not affect your asylum application. You can receive any benefit defined as a 'public fund' (see p1517) because asylum seekers are not subject to any condition not to have recourse to public funds.

If you are excluded from claiming social security benefits because you are a 'person subject to immigration control', you may be entitled to alternative forms of state support. If you are destitute, you may be eligible for asylum support from the Home Office. **Note:** asylum support is taken into account as income when calculating any housing benefit your partner claims. It is not taken into account for universal credit (UC) and, if it is 'income in kind', is disregarded for income support (IS), income-based jobseeker's allowance (JSA) and income-related employment and support allowance (ESA).[53]

However, any IS, income-based JSA, income-related ESA or UC your partner receives is taken into account as income when calculating your asylum support.

If you are not eligible for asylum support or benefits, you may be able to get assistance from your local authority under one or more of the community care provisions, particularly if you have additional needs as a result of your age, sickness or disability. If you have children, or you are a child, you may be eligible for support under the Children Act 1989 or Children (Scotland) Act 1995. Get independent legal advice about what you are entitled to, if possible before you apply, but always if you are refused.

For more information about asylum support, see CPAG's *Benefits for Migrants Handbook*.

Refugees and other leave granted after an asylum application

If you are granted refugee leave, humanitarian protection or discretionary leave (unless it is subject to the condition that you do not have 'recourse to public funds'), you are no longer a 'person subject to immigration control'. Therefore, during this period of leave, your immigration status does not affect your entitlement to benefit and you can claim all benefits, provided you meet the usual rules of entitlement. If you are granted another form of leave that is subject to the condition that you do not have recourse to public funds, you are defined as a 'person subject to immigration control' and excluded from the benefits and tax credits listed on p1519, unless you come within an exempt group (see p1520–22).

If you are granted refugee leave or humanitarian protection, you can be joined by certain family members under the family reunion provisions. A family member who comes to the UK under these provisions is not a 'person subject to immigration control' during her/his period of leave and can claim all benefits, provided s/he meets the usual rules of entitlement.

Part 11: Immigration and residence rules for benefits and tax credits
Chapter 65: Coming from abroad: immigration status
5. Asylum seekers and refugees

If you, or the family member you have joined, have refugee leave or humanitarian protection, you do not need to satisfy the past presence test for the disability and carers benefits (see p1575).

If you are granted refugee status, humanitarian protection or discretionary leave, you are exempt from the habitual residence test (see p1537).

Income support for refugees studying English

Refugees who are studying English are entitled to IS (see p105). If you have been granted refugee leave (not humanitarian protection or discretionary leave), you can claim IS for up to nine months while you are studying if you:[54]

- attend, for more than 15 hours a week, a course for the purpose of learning English so you may obtain employment; *and*
- have been in Great Britain for not more than 12 months on the date the course began.

Backdating tax credits, child benefit and guardian's allowance

If you have been granted refugee leave (not humanitarian protection or discretionary leave), you can claim tax credits, child benefit and guardian's allowance and have them backdated to the date of your asylum application.[55]

You must claim backdated tax credits within one month, and child benefit and guardian's allowance within three months, of receiving the Home Office letter granting you leave as a refugee.[56] If the Home Office letter is sent to a solicitor acting for you, the three- or one-month period starts from the date your solicitor receives the letter.[57]

Your tax credit claim is treated as having been both made on the date you claimed asylum and renewed each subsequent April and, therefore, even if you are not currently entitled to tax credits, you can claim for a past period. This applies, for example, if you come under the UC system (see p20) now, but you did not do so at the date you claimed asylum. You will need to explain this to HM Revenue and Customs and that your claim may need to be processed clerically.

The amount of tax credits paid is reduced by the amount of asylum support you received for your essential living needs over the period.[58]

In many cases, the amount of asylum support is greater than the rate of tax credits and therefore cancels out any entitlement to tax credits over the backdated period. However, if you did not receive asylum support or your tax credit entitlement exceeds the amount of asylum support paid (eg, if you worked sufficient hours to qualify for working tax credit), you can be entitled to an amount of backdated tax credits.

The amount of child benefit and guardian's allowance paid is not reduced by any asylum support you may have received.

Integration loans

If you (or someone upon whom you are dependent) are granted refugee leave or humanitarian protection and you are aged 18 or over, you may be eligible for an integration loan.[59] This is a discretionary loan of at least £100, paid for expenses associated with your integration into UK society, including for employment, education and housing. Claims are decided by the Home Office and so these loans are not covered in this *Handbook*. The application form and guidance notes are available at www.gov.uk.

Notes

1. Immigration status
1 s115(9) IAA 1999
2 s7 IA 1988
3 Sch 3 para 1 I(EEA) Regs
4 s115(9)(a) IAA 1999
5 s7 IA 1988; regs 11 and 14(2) I(EEA) Regs
6 *The Agreement Between the European Community and its Member States, of the one part, and the Swiss Confederation, of the other, on the Free Movement of Persons*, Luxembourg, 21 June 1999, Cm 5639; reg 2 I(EEA) Regs defines Switzerland as an EEA state; reg 11 provides that no EEA national requires leave to enter the UK and Part 2 of I(EEA) Regs provides residence rights.
7 *Zambrano*, C-34/09 [2011] ECR I-01177; *Dereci and Others*, C-256/11 [2011] ECR I-11315; also in UK law: reg 16 I(EEA) Regs
8 s115(9)(b) IAA 1999
9 para 6 Immigration Rules, HC395
10 s24(1)(b)(ii) IA 1971
11 para 6B Immigration Rules, HC395
12 s115(9)(c) IAA 1999
13 s115(10) IAA 1999
14 *R (Begum) v Social Security Commissioner* [2003] EWHC 3380 (Admin)
15 *Ahmed v SSWP* [2005] EWCA Civ 535

16 CIS/3508/2001; see also *SJ v SSWP (SPC)* [2015] UKUT 505 (AAC); [2016] AACR 17
17 s115(9)(d) IAA 1999 referred to Sch 4 para 17 IAA 1999, which was repealed by Sch 9 para 1 NIAA 2002. It may be that the reference should be read as if to s3C(2) IA 1971 (s17(2) Interpretation Act 1978).

2. Benefits and tax credits affected by immigration status
18 Reg 13 CTRS(PR)E Regs; reg 19 CTR(SPC)S Regs; reg 19 CTR(S) Regs; reg 29 CTRSPR(W) Regs; Sch para 20 CTRS(DS)W Regs
19 s115 IAA 1999; s42 TCA 2002; reg 3 TC(Imm) Regs
20 Reg 11(1)(b) ESA Regs; reg 12(1)(b) ESA Regs 2013
21 Reg 16(1)(b) SS(IB) Regs
22 ss61-63 WRA 2012
23 Reg 2(1) and Part 1 of Sch SS(IA)CA Regs
24 Confirmed in *OD v SSWP (JSA)* [2015] UKUT 438 (AAC)
25 *Szoma v SSWP* [2005] UKHL 64
26 *Yesiloz v London Borough of Camden and Another* [2009] EWCA Civ 415

11

Part 11: Immigration and residence rules for benefits and tax credits
Chapter 65: Coming from abroad: immigration status
Notes

27 Reg 13(1A) CTRS(PR)E Regs; reg 19(2)
CTR(S) Regs; reg 19(2) CTR(SPC)S Regs;
reg 29(2) CTRSPR(W) Regs; Sch para
20(2) CTRS(DS)W Regs; para 6A
Immigration Rules. Council tax
reduction is not included in the
regulations referred to in para 6B
Immigration Rules, which disregards
claims made as a result of exemptions.
28 R(IS) 2/02
29 CPC/1005/2005
30 Reg 12 SS(IA)CA Regs; reg 12
SS(PFA)MA Regs
31 Reg 2 SS(IA)CA Regs
32 **AA** Reg 2(1)(a)(ib) SS(AA) Regs
CA Reg 9(1)(ia) SS(ICA) Regs
DLA Reg 2(1)(a)(ib) SS(DLA) Regs
ESA Reg 11(1)(b) and (3) ESA Regs; reg
12(1)(b) and (3) ESA Regs 2013
IB Reg 16(1)(b) and (5) SS(IB) Regs
PIP Reg 16(d)(ii) SS(PIP) Regs
SDA Reg 3(a)(ib) SS(SDA) Regs
All Reg 2(2), (3) and (4)(b) and Sch Part
II SS(IA)CA Regs
33 *JFP v DSD (DLA)* [2012] NICom 267,
which declined to follow the more
restrictive approach of CDLA/708/2007.
However, see also *MS v SSWP (DLA)*
[2016] UKUT 42 (AAC)
34 *Krid v Caisse Nationale d'Assurance
Vieillesse des Travailleurs Salariés
(CNAVTS),* C-103/94 [1995] ECR I-
00719, para 26
35 The Family Allowances, National
Insurance and Industrial Injuries
(Yugoslavia) Order 1958, No.1263
36 *Sürül v Bundesanstalt für Arbeit,* C-262/
96 [1999] ECR I-02685
37 Reg 3 TC(Imm) Regs
38 *Krid v Caisse Nationale d'Assurance
Vieillesse des Travailleurs Salariés
(CNAVTS),* C-103/94 [1995] ECR I-
00719, para 26
39 Regs 3 and 5 TC(Imm) Regs

3. Partners and children
40 **IS** Reg 21(3) and Sch 7 para 16A IS Regs
JSA Reg 85(4) and Sch 5 para 13A JSA
Regs
ESA Reg 69 and Sch 5 para 10 ESA Regs
41 Reg 5(1)(h) SPC Regs
42 Vol 13 para 78946 DMG
43 Reg 3(3) UC Regs
44 Regs 18(2), 22(3) and 36(3) UC Regs
45 ss61-63 WRA 2012
46 Reg 3(2) TC(Imm) Regs

47 Reg 11(4) and (5) WTC(EMR) Regs
48 para 6B Immigration Rules, HC395. The
TC(Imm) Regs are made under s42 TCA
2002.

4. National insurance numbers and contributions
49 **IS** Reg 2A IS Regs
JSA Reg 2A JSA Regs
ESA Reg 2A ESA Regs
PC Reg 1A SPC Regs
HB Reg 4(c) HB Regs; reg 4(c) HB(SPC)
Regs
**Bereavement benefits and
retirement pensions** Reg 1A(c)
SS(WB&RP) Regs
TC Reg 5(8) TC(CN) Regs
50 Reg 5(6) TC(CN) Regs
51 *ZM and AB v HMRC (TC)* [2013] UKUT
547 (AAC); *CI v HMRC (TC)* [2014] UKUT
158 (AAC)
52 Under orders made in powers conferred
by s179 SSAA 1992

5. Asylum seekers and refugees
53 **IS** Sch 9 para 21 IS Regs
JSA Sch 7 para 22 JSA Regs
ESA Sch 8 para 22 ESA Regs
HB Sch 5 para 23 HB Regs
UC Reg 66 UC Regs
54 Reg 4ZA(3)(b) and Sch 1B para 18 IS
Regs
55 **CB/GA** Reg 6(2)(d) CB&GA(Admin)
Regs
TC Regs 3(4)-(9) and 4 TC(Imm) Regs
56 **CB/GA** Reg 6(2)(d) CB and GA(Admin)
Regs
TC Reg 3(5) TC(Imm) Regs
57 *Tkachuk v SSWP* [2007] EWCA Civ 515;
CIS/3797/2003
58 Reg 3(9) TC(Imm) Regs; CTC/3692/
2008
59 s13 Asylum and Immigration
(Treatment of Claimants, etc) Act 2004;
The Integration Loans for Refugees and
Others Regulations 2007, No.1598

11

Chapter 66

Coming from abroad: residence rules

This chapter covers:
1. Introduction (p1532)
2. The different residence and presence tests (p1534)
3. Habitual residence (p1537)
4. Right to reside (p1542)
5. Who has a right to reside (p1544)
6. Rules for specific benefits and tax credits (p1570)

This chapter describes the residence and presence rules that affect your entitlement while you are in Great Britain. If you go abroad, see Chapter 67.

If you or your partner are not a European Economic Area (EEA) national, before using this chapter check Chapter 65 for information on how your immigration status can affect your entitlement to benefits and tax credits.

If you are an EEA national, the European Union co-ordination rules may help you to satisfy the residence and presence tests when you are in the UK. These rules are outlined in Chapter 68.

Key facts

- Different types of residence conditions apply to many benefits and tax credits. These are: **residence**, **ordinary residence**, **right to reside** and **habitual residence**.
- Entitlement to some benefits and tax credits also depends on your being **present** in Great Britain and/or having been present for a certain period of time (known as **'past presence'**). Some require you to have been **'living in'** the UK or common travel area for three months prior to your claim.
- The rules on residence and presence vary between different benefits and tax credits. If you satisfy the conditions for one benefit or tax credit, it does not mean you necessarily satisfy the conditions for another.

Part 11: Immigration and residence rules for benefits and tax credits
Chapter 66: Coming from abroad: residence rules
1. Introduction

1. **Introduction**

Many benefits have residence and/or presence conditions. The rules vary between different benefits and tax credits. Whether you meet the conditions depends on how long you have been in Great Britain, your nationality, your immigration status and whether you are covered by the provisions of European law.

Although many presence and residence rules refer to Great Britain rather than the UK, there is a reciprocal agreement between Britain and Northern Ireland, which means that, generally, you can satisfy the residence conditions if you move between Great Britain and Northern Ireland.

There are residence conditions for the following benefits and tax credits:
- attendance allowance (see p1574);
- bereavement support payment (see p1572);
- carer's allowance (see p1574);
- child benefit (see p1573);
- child tax credit (see p1580);
- disability living allowance (see p1574);
- contributory employment and support allowance (ESA) in youth (see p1574);
- income-related ESA (see p1570);
- guardian's allowance (see p1574);
- housing benefit (see p1570);
- incapacity benefit in youth (see p1574);
- income support (see p1570);
- income-based jobseeker's allowance (JSA – see p1570);
- pension credit (see p1570);
- personal independence payment (see p1574);
- category D retirement pension (see p1578);
- severe disablement allowance (see p1574);
- universal credit (see p1570);
- working tax credit (see p1580).

Council tax reduction also has residence conditions.

Contributory benefits, such as contribution-based JSA, contributory ESA and retirement pensions (except category D), as well as the employment-related benefits (maternity allowance and industrial injuries benefits) do not have residence conditions. However, they have presence requirements, which mean that if you go abroad, some benefits cease and others are not increased unless exceptions apply (see Chapter 67). Industrial injuries benefits also have conditions related to your presence in Great Britain at the time you had your accident or contracted your disease. There are no residence or presence requirements for statutory sick pay, statutory maternity pay, statutory adoption pay, statutory paternity pay and statutory shared parental pay paid by your employer.

Which rules apply

If you are covered by European Union (EU) law, these generally more generous provisions apply. If they do not apply, but you are covered by a reciprocal agreement, the reciprocal agreement provisions apply. If you are not covered by either EU law or a reciprocal agreement, UK law applies.

The UK benefits and tax credits legislation contains rules about the residence and presence conditions that you must satisfy to be entitled to certain benefits. These rules are set out in this chapter.

EU law (legislation and caselaw) applies in the UK and throughout the European Economic Area (EEA). In general, for EU law to apply you must be an EEA national (see p1609) or the family member of an EEA national, and your circumstances must involve more than one EEA state – eg, you are a French national living in the UK. **Note:** the EU law in this *Handbook* has not changed as a result of the vote to leave the EU and continues to apply until the UK formally leaves the EU.

There are two main areas of EU law which affect benefit and tax credit entitlement that are covered in this *Handbook*.

- If you or your family member are an EEA national, EU law may give you a right of residence that enables you to satisfy the right to reside requirement (see p1542).
- If you are covered by the co-ordination rules (see p1611), these can help you get benefits or tax credits in the UK – eg, by enabling you to count periods of residence in any EEA state to satisfy the past presence requirements (see p1534) for UK benefits.

Note: it is not usually necessary to understand how the co-ordination rules may affect you in order to know whether you have a right of residence in EU law, or vice versa. However, it can be helpful to know whether you are covered by the co-ordination rules (see p1611) if you would not otherwise satisfy a requirement to be present, have been present, to have been 'living in' for a past period or be ordinarily resident.

Reciprocal agreements exist between the UK and some other countries that can assist in similar ways to EU law.

Reciprocal agreements with the UK

EEA member states: Austria, Belgium, Croatia, Cyprus, Denmark, Finland, France, Germany, Iceland, Ireland, Italy, Luxembourg, Malta, Netherlands, Norway, Portugal, Slovenia, Spain and Sweden. In general, the reciprocal agreement applies if the EU co-ordination rules do not apply.

Non-EEA member states: Barbados, Bermuda, Bosnia-Herzegovina, Canada, Chile (from 1 June 2015), Guernsey, Isle of Man, Israel, Jamaica, Jersey, Kosova, Macedonia, Mauritius, Montenegro, New Zealand, Philippines, Serbia, Turkey and the United States of America.

Part 11: Immigration and residence rules for benefits and tax credits
Chapter 66: Coming from abroad: residence rules
2. The different residence and presence tests

There are 'association' and 'co-operation' agreements with Algeria, Morocco, San Marino, Slovenia, Tunisia and Turkey.
There are also reciprocal agreements between Great Britain and Northern Ireland.

The scope of the reciprocal agreements differs greatly, in terms of the people covered, the benefits covered and the provisions made. It is therefore crucial to check the individual agreement. You can find the agreements in *The Law Relating to Social Security* at http://lawvolumes.dwp.gov.uk – go to the 'List of Statutory Instruments' and search under the relevant country to find the number and year of the statutory instrument.

2. The different residence and presence tests

The presence and residence conditions you are required to satisfy vary between the different benefits and tax credits. You may be required to satisfy tests for your:
- presence (see below);
- past presence (see below);
- 'living in' for three months (see p1535);
- residence (see p1536);
- ordinary residence (see p1537);
- habitual residence (see p1537);
- right to reside (see p1542).

Presence

You must usually be present in Great Britain at the time you make your benefit or tax credit claim, and continue to be present. There are specific rules that allow you to be treated as present during temporary absences (see Chapter 67). The European Union (EU) co-ordination rules can also mean that you do not need to be present. See the rules for the relevant benefits and tax credits starting on p1570 and p1590.

Being present means being physically present in Great Britain. If the DWP, HM Revenue and Customs or the local authority wants to disqualify you from benefit because you were absent from Great Britain, it must show that you were absent throughout that day. This means that on the day you leave Great Britain and the day you arrive in Great Britain you count as present.

Past presence

For some benefits, in addition to being present at the time you make your claim, you must also have been present in Great Britain for a period of time before you become entitled (see p1574).

If you are covered by the EU co-ordination rules (see p1611), these may exempt you from the requirement or enable you to add certain periods of residence in another European Economic Area (EEA) state to periods of presence in Great Britain (see p1617 and p1575).

Benefits that have a past presence requirement are:

- attendance allowance;
- carer's allowance;
- disability living allowance;
- employment and support allowance (ESA) in youth;
- incapacity benefit (IB) in youth;
- personal independence payment;
- severe disablement allowance (SDA).

Living in for three months

There is a requirement to have been living for the past three months in:

- the common travel area (the UK, Ireland, Channel Islands and the Isle of Man) in order to satisfy the habitual residence test for income-based jobseeker's allowance (JSA – see below); or
- the UK, for child benefit and child tax credit (CTC – see p1536).

The phrase 'living in' is not defined in the regulations and should therefore be given its ordinary, everyday meaning.

You may satisfy this condition even if you have had one or more temporary absences during the three months.[1] When deciding whether you ceased living in the common travel area/UK, the following factors are relevant: the reasons for, and the intended and actual length of, your absence; the duration and connectedness of your *previous* residence in the common travel area/UK; and whether you maintained your accommodation while you were gone and the nature of your accommodation abroad.[2] See p1590 for more information about temporary absences. For child benefit and CTC only, also check whether you are exempt from this requirement (see p1536).

If you are covered by the EU co-ordination rules (see p1611) and have moved to the UK from another EEA state, you may be able to use certain periods of residence there to satisfy this condition (see p1617).

Income-based jobseeker's allowance

To satisfy the habitual residence test (see p1537) for income-based JSA, in addition to having a right to reside and being 'habitually resident in fact', you must have been living in the common travel area for the past three months unless:[3]

- you are exempt from the habitual residence test (see p1540);
- at any time during the last three months you have worked abroad and paid class 1 or 2 national insurance (NI) contributions, or been posted abroad as a Crown servant or while a member of the armed forces;
- your claim began before 1 January 2014.[4]

Part 11: Immigration and residence rules for benefits and tax credits
Chapter 66: Coming from abroad: residence rules
2. The different residence and presence tests

If you are an EEA national moving from another EEA state, you may be able to argue that you can show a link to the UK labour market in other ways and that either this three-month requirement should be interpreted broadly enough to take these other ways into account or be overridden by them.[5] If you are covered by the EU co-ordination rules (see p1611), it may also be possible to argue that you cannot be refused benefit solely because you have lived here less than three months.[6] See CPAG's *Benefits for Migrants Handbook* for more details on these arguments.

Child benefit and child tax credit

To be treated as present in Great Britain for child benefit and present in the UK for CTC, you must have been living in the UK for three months, ending on the first day of your entitlement.[7] This requirement does not apply if you:[8]

- are an EEA national and a 'worker' in the UK (see p1554), including if you have retained that status;
- are an EEA national and a 'self-employed person' in the UK (see p1558), including if you have retained that status;
- are a non-EEA national who would be classed as a 'worker' or 'self-employed person' if you were an EEA national;
- are a Croatian national working in accordance with your worker authorisation document (see p1546);
- are a family member (see p1560), other than an 'extended family member', of someone in any of the four groups above;
- are a refugee;
- have humanitarian protection;
- have leave granted outside the Immigration Rules with no restriction on accessing public funds, or leave to remain in the UK pending an application for indefinite leave to remain as a victim of domestic violence, or leave under the displaced persons provisions;
- have been deported or otherwise legally removed from another country to the UK;[9]
- are returning to the UK after a period working abroad and, other than for last three months of your absence, you were paying UK class 1 or class 2 NI contributions;
- are returning to the UK after an absence of less than 52 weeks, and either:
  - before departing the UK you were ordinarily resident for three months; *or*
  - you were covered by the rules that treat you as present during a temporary absence for eight or 12 weeks during payment of child benefit (see p1591) or CTC (see p1604).

Residence

The requirement to be simply 'resident', rather than 'ordinarily resident' or 'habitually resident', is only a condition for the old category D retirement pension. However, it is a necessary part of being ordinarily resident (see below) or habitually resident (see below). Residence is more than mere physical presence in a country and you can be resident without being present – eg, if you are away for a short holiday. You are usually resident in the country in which you have your home for the time being.[10] You can remain resident during a temporary absence, depending on your circumstances, including the length of your absence, your intentions to return, your accommodation, and where your family and your personal belongings are.

Ordinary residence

The benefits and tax credits that have an ordinary residence requirement are:
- bereavement support payment;
- child benefit;
- CTC;
- ESA in youth;
- IB in youth;
- category D retirement pension;
- SDA;
- social fund funeral payment and winter fuel payment;
- working tax credit.

The term 'ordinary residence' is not defined in the legislation, and caselaw has confirmed that the words should have their natural and ordinary meaning.[11] You are ordinarily resident in a country if you are living there for a settled purpose for the time being (whether for a short or long duration).[12] The Upper Tribunal recently held that the residence must be lawful.[13] There are some exceptions to the requirement to be ordinarily resident, and if you are covered by the EU co-ordination rules, these may assist you in satisfying it (see pp1570–81). In practice, claims are rarely refused on the basis of ordinary residence.

3. Habitual residence

The requirement to be habitually resident applies to:[14]
- attendance allowance (AA);
- carer's allowance (CA);
- disability living allowance (DLA);
- housing benefit (HB);
- income support (IS);
- income-based jobseeker's allowance (JSA);
- income-related employment and support allowance (ESA);
- pension credit (PC);

11

Part 11: Immigration and residence rules for benefits and tax credits
Chapter 66: Coming from abroad: residence rules
3. Habitual residence

- personal independence payment (PIP);
- universal credit (UC).

To be entitled to one of the above benefits, you must be habitually resident in the **'common travel area'** (ie, the UK, the Republic of Ireland, the Channel Islands and the Isle of Man) or be exempt from the test (see p1540).

Note:

- You are also excluded from council tax reduction if you do not satisfy (and are not exempt from) the habitual residence test.[15] See CPAG's *Benefits for Migrants Handbook* for details.
- You may be entitled to a winter fuel payment from the social fund if, instead of being ordinarily resident in Great Britain, you are habitually resident in another European Economic Area (EEA) country or Switzerland (see p1579).
- For AA, CA and DLA, the habitual residence test applies to new claims made, or awards that are revised or superseded, on or after 8 April 2013.[16] If your claim began before this date, the previous requirement to be ordinarily resident continues to apply until your award is revised or superseded.

The habitual residence test

To satisfy the habitual residence test, you must:

- be 'habitually resident in fact' (see p1541);
- for IS, income-based JSA, income-related ESA, PC, HB and UC, have a right to reside (see p1542); *and*
- for income-based JSA only, have been living in the common travel area for the past three months (see p1535).

Some groups of people are exempt from the habitual residence test (see p1540). If you are in one of these groups, you are treated as satisfying the test. Your residence is not examined further and, provided you meet the other conditions of entitlement, you are eligible for benefit. Whether or not you are exempt is not always considered, so if you come into one of these groups, make it clear to the DWP or local authority that you are exempt, particularly if you might not otherwise be accepted as habitually resident.

In practice, for means-tested benefits, the DWP or local authority first considers your right to reside. If you satisfy this requirement, it then considers whether you have been living in the common travel area for the past three months for income-based JSA, and then whether you are 'habitually resident in fact'.

The habitual residence test applies to the benefit claimant. If you are making a joint claim for UC, both partners must satisfy it. If your partner fails the test, you must claim UC as a single person. Your award is based on the maximum amount for a single person, but your partner's income and capital are taken into account (see p170).[17] For other means-tested benefits, if you are the claimant and you satisfy (or are exempt from) the habitual residence test, whether or not your partner satisfies it does not affect your entitlement, unless you are a joint-claim couple for JSA. In this case, if you satisfy the test, but your partner does not, you are entitled to JSA without your partner making a joint claim with you and you are paid as a couple (see p120).

If you fail the habitual residence test

If you fail the habitual residence test, you are not paid any benefit.

- For IS, income-based JSA, income-related ESA and HB, you are classed as a 'person from abroad'. This means for IS, income-based JSA and income-related ESA, you have an applicable amount of nil,[18] and for HB, you are treated as not liable for rent.[19]
- For PC and UC, you are treated as not present in Great Britain.[20]
- For AA, CA, DLA and PIP, you have failed to meet the prescribed residence requirements.[21]

Have you failed the habitual residence test?

1. If you are refused benefit because you have failed the habitual residence test, consider challenging this decision (see Chapters 54 and 55). You may want to contact a local advice agency for help with this.

2. While challenging the decision, you should make a further claim. If this is refused, also challenge that decision and claim again and so on. This is because when the decision refusing your initial claim is looked at again, the decision maker (or First-tier Tribunal) cannot take account of things that have changed since the decision was made. So, if the decision maker considers that you were not habitually resident at the time benefit was originally refused, but you are now (because you have been resident for an appreciable period of time, or, for income-based JSA, you have been living here for three months), s/he cannot take this into account when looking again at the decision in your case. However, s/he can take it into account if sufficient residence had been completed by the date of the decision on your second, or subsequent, claim. Sometimes, the benefit authorities say that you cannot make another claim while your appeal (or request to have the first decision looked at again) is pending. This is wrong and you should, with the help of an adviser if possible, insist on making your claim.

3. Check whether you come into one of the exempt categories (see p1540).

4. Establish which part of the test the decision maker considers you have failed.

5. If the decision maker considers you do not have a right to reside, use the section in this chapter (see p1544) to see which factors are relevant to demonstrating your right to reside.

6. Remember that the habitual residence test applies to the claimant, so (except for UC) even if you have been found not to be habitually resident, your partner may satisfy the test and should make a claim. You can still challenge the refusal of your claim.

7. The local authority must make its own decision for HB and not just follow the DWP's decision that you have failed the habitual residence test. Similarly, if the DWP decides you are entitled to income-based JSA on the basis of your right to reside as a jobseeker, the

Part 11: Immigration and residence rules for benefits and tax credits
Chapter 66: Coming from abroad: residence rules
3. Habitual residence

local authority must determine whether you have *another,* non-excluded, right to reside (see p1542), which would mean you are exempt from the habitual residence test for HB (see below).[22]

8. Although the onus of proof is on the benefit authorities to establish that you are *not* habitually resident,[23] produce as much evidence as possible to show that you *are.*

Who is exempt from the habitual residence test

You are exempt from the habitual residence test for **means-tested benefits** if you:[24]

- are a EEA national and are a 'worker' (see p1554), including if you have retained this status;
- are an EEA national and a 'self-employed person' (see p1558), including if you have retained this status;
- are a family member (see p1560), other than an 'extended family member', of someone in either of the above two groups;
- are an EEA national with a permanent right of residence as a retired or permanently incapacitated worker or self-employed person, or you are a family member of such a person (see p1568);
- are a refugee;
- have discretionary leave, leave granted under the 'destitution domestic violence' concession or temporary protection granted under the displaced persons' provisions;
- have humanitarian protection;
- have been deported, expelled or legally removed from another country to the UK and you are not a 'person subject to immigration control' (see p1516);
- (for income-related ESA only) are being transferred from an award of IS which was transitionally protected from the requirement to have a right to reside (see p1542);
- (for HB only) receive IS, income-related ESA or PC;
- (for HB only) receive income-based JSA and either:
  - you have a right to reside other than one that is excluded for HB (see p1542); *or*
  - you have been receiving both HB and income-based JSA since 31 March 2014. Entitlement on this basis ends when either that entitlement to income-based JSA ceases or you make a new claim for HB.[25]

For **AA, CA, DLA and PIP** the above exemptions do not apply, but you are treated as being habitually resident (as well as treated as present – see p1592) if you are abroad in your capacity as a serving member of the forces, or you are living with someone who is and s/he is your spouse, civil partner, son, stepson, daughter, stepdaughter, father, stepfather, father-in-law, mother, stepmother or mother-in-law.[26]

Establishing you are 'habitually resident in fact'

You must be habitually resident in the 'common travel area' – ie, the UK, Channel Islands, the Isle of Man and the Republic of Ireland.

There is no definition of 'habitual residence' in the legislation. However, there is a considerable amount of caselaw on its meaning, and from this certain principles have emerged.

- There is no comprehensive list of factors that are relevant, so all the facts of your situation should be considered.[27]
- To be habitually resident, you must be resident (see p1536). It is not enough merely to intend to reside in the future.[28]
- You must have a settled intention to reside in the common travel area. It does not need to be permanent; it is enough if you intend to make the common travel area your home for the time being.[29] You must provide evidence of your intention, including your reasons for coming to the common travel area, the strength of your ties (or your 'centre of interest') and the viability of your residence here. Factors that could be relevant include arranging or seeking employment, education or training, joining and/or bringing your family, arranging accommodation, bringing possessions, registering with a doctor, joining clubs and associations, and breaking ties with the place of your previous residence. The viability of your continued residence, although a relevant factor, is not an additional requirement.[30]
- In most cases, you must have an 'appreciable period' of actual residence. How long this period must be is not fixed and depends on your circumstances.[31] The DWP or local authority must not set a standard period of time for which all claimants must be resident before they can become habitually resident, and any such policy should be challenged by judicial review (see p1378). There is an extensive body of caselaw on what constitutes an appreciable period of residence. Periods of between one and three months are frequently cited,[32] but too much weight should not be put on any one decision, nor should any general rule about a specific time period be derived from it.[33] The stronger your settled intention to make your home in the common travel area for the time being, the shorter your period of actual residence needs to be before you can be accepted as habitually resident (and vice versa).[34]

You may not need an appreciable period of actual residence, or the period may be very short, if you are:

- a returning resident. This applies if you have been habitually resident in the common travel area previously, you left in circumstances which meant you ceased to be habitually resident and you then return to live in the common travel area again. The decision on how long a period of residence you need to have in order to resume your previous habitual residence depends on the circumstances in which you left, your links with the common travel area while you were away and the circumstances of your return.[35] You can be found to be habitually resident on the day of your return;

11

Part 11: Immigration and residence rules for benefits and tax credits
Chapter 66: Coming from abroad: residence rules
4. Right to reside

– covered by the European Union co-ordination rules (see p1611) and are claiming income-based JSA, income-related ESA or PC (since these are listed as special non-contributory benefits – see p1614). If this applies, you cannot be denied benefit solely because your period of residence is considered to be too short. Your period of residence is one of the factors that should be taken into account in assessing habitual residence, but it is not an absolute requirement and may be outweighed by other factors.[36]

- A temporary absence, such as a holiday, should not mean that you cease to be habitually resident. This should be accepted if you have a definite date of return[37] or you are abroad for a temporary reason such as a Voluntary Service Overseas placement.[38]
- When deciding whether you are habitually resident, the DWP or local authority must consider the whole period up to the date the decision is made, since the time between the date of your claim and the decision may mean you have been resident for an appreciable period.[39]

4. **Right to reside**

The right to reside requirement applies to:
- income support (IS);
- income-based jobseeker's allowance (JSA);
- income-related employment and support allowance (ESA);
- pension credit (PC);
- housing benefit (HB);
- child benefit;
- child tax credit (CTC);
- universal credit (UC).

Note: you are also excluded from council tax reduction if you do not have a right to reside.[40] See CPAG's *Benefits for Migrants Handbook* for details.

Means-tested benefits

You must have a right to reside in order to satisfy the habitual residence test for IS, income-based JSA, income-related ESA, PC, HB and UC. If you (or your partner, for UC) do not satisfy the habitual residence test because you do not have a right to reside, see p1539.

The right to reside requirement was introduced as part of the habitual residence test for means-tested benefits on 1 May 2004. If you have been receiving IS, income-based JSA, PC, HB (or council tax benefit) since 30 April 2004, you do not need a right to reside in order to continue to receive that benefit or to make a new claim for one of these benefits, provided the periods of entitlement have been continuous since 30 April 2004.[41] Income-related ESA was only included in this list from 31 October 2011, but from that date the same rules apply. You can also make a new claim for income-related ESA without needing a right to reside if it is linked by the 12-week linking rule (see p1021) to a previous period of income-related ESA that was part of a continuous period of entitlement to the above benefits going back to 30 April 2004.

Example

Delphine is French. She came to the UK in 2003 with her baby and claimed IS as a lone parent while living with friends. In 2008, she had another child, moved into a rented flat and made a new claim for HB. In 2012, she started work and so her IS stopped, but she continued to get HB as she had a low income. In 2013, she left her job because her child was seriously ill and she claimed IS as a carer. In April 2017, Delphine became sick and claimed income-related ESA instead of IS.

Delphine does not need to pass the right to reside test for any of these new benefit claims because she has been receiving one of the five benefits for each day since 30 April 2004.

If you received transitionally protected IS on the grounds of incapacity and are then transferred to income-related ESA, you are exempt from the habitual residence test from the date you are transferred to ESA (see p672).[42]

The type of residence right you need

Any right of residence in the common travel area (see p1537) enables you to satisfy the right to reside requirement for each of the means-tested benefits, unless your only right of residence is as:[43]

- a European Economic Area (EEA) national with an initial right of residence during your first three months in the UK (see p1551);
- a family member of the above;
- the primary carer of a British citizen who is dependent on you and would have to leave the European Union (EU) if you left the UK (see p1565). **Note:** this exclusion is arguably unlawful and although legal challenges have not yet been successful, future ones may be.[44] See CPAG's online service and *Welfare Rights Bulletin* for updates;
- (except for income-based JSA) an EEA jobseeker;
- (except for income-based JSA) a family member of an EEA jobseeker. **Note:** this exclusion does not apply if you are a former family member of a jobseeker and have retained your right to reside – eg, following the departure of the jobseeker from the UK (see p1563).[45]

These restrictions mean that if your only right to reside is as an EEA jobseeker, you do not satisfy the right to reside test for any of the means-tested benefits *except* for income-based JSA.

Part 11: Immigration and residence rules for benefits and tax credits
Chapter 66: Coming from abroad: residence rules
5. Who has a right to reside

Child benefit and child tax credit

If you do not have a right to reside for child benefit and CTC, you are treated as not present in Great Britain and, therefore, are not entitled to these benefits.[46] If you are making a joint claim for CTC, you and your partner must both have a right to reside. If only one of you has a right to reside, s/he can make a claim as a single person.

The right to reside requirement was introduced on 1 May 2004. You do not need a right to reside to continue to receive child benefit or CTC if you have been receiving it since before this date.

If you are claiming CTC and you (or your partner if it is a joint claim) lose your right to reside, this is a change of circumstances that you must notify to HM Revenue and Customs within one month (see p1462). The other partner may be able to claim as a single person.

The type of residence right you need

Any right of residence in the UK enables you to satisfy the requirement for child benefit and CTC *except* a right to reside as the primary carer of a British citizen who is dependent on you and would have to leave the EU if you left the UK (see p1565).[47] This exclusion is arguably unlawful and although legal challenges have not yet been successful, future ones may be.[48] See CPAG's online service and *Welfare Rights Bulletin* for updates.

If this rule excludes you from child benefit for a child living with you, someone else who contributes to the cost of that child may be able to claim child benefit instead (see p578).

5. **Who has a right to reside**

Whether or not you have a right to reside can depend on your nationality, immigration status, and the circumstances of you and your family members. You may have a right of residence under UK law or one from European Union (EU) law. You may have more than one right of residence, or you may not have any.

Any residence right is sufficient to satisfy the right to reside requirement, unless it is specifically excluded (see p1542).

You have a right to reside if you are:
- a British citizen;
- an Irish citizen. Irish citizens have a right to reside in Ireland, which is part of the common travel area;
- a Commonwealth citizen with a right of abode;
- a person with leave to enter or remain. You have a right to reside during your period of leave. Any form of immigration leave counts. **Note:** if you have leave which is subject to a condition that you do not have recourse to public funds,

or indefinite leave granted as the result of a maintenance undertaking, you are a 'person subject to immigration control' (see p1516) and, therefore, excluded from benefits on that basis unless you are in an exempt group (see p1519).

The above are examples of some people whose right to reside is clear. It is not an exhaustive list.

If you are a European Economic Area (EEA) national, or the family member or primary carer of an EEA national, your residence rights are more complex and so the rest of this section focuses on this group.

European Economic Area nationals, their family members and carers

In practice, the right to reside requirement mainly affects EEA nationals. The residence rights of EEA nationals, their family members and carers can be complex, as both EU law and UK law must be considered, and both are subject to a considerable amount of interpretation through caselaw.

European Union and UK legislation

EU Directive 2004/38 sets out most of the situations in which an EEA national or her/his family member has a right to reside in the UK. This has been in force since 30 April 2006 and was extended to cover nationals of Norway, Iceland and Liechtenstein from 1 March 2009.[49] Swiss nationals and their family members are covered by a separate agreement which provides similar rights.[50]

The Immigration (European Economic Area) Regulations 2016 (called 'the EEA Regulations' in this *Handbook*) apply to all EEA nationals (except British citizens – see p1546) and Swiss nationals.[51] These give similar rights of residence to those contained in the Directive. Where these rules conflict with, or do not completely incorporate, Directive 2004/38, you can rely on whichever is more favourable to you. The current EEA Regulations replace the the previous, very similar, EEA Regulations 2006, from 1 February 2017.[52]

If you are a family member of a British citizen, see p1562.

If you are an **Irish citizen**, you have a right to reside in Ireland (which is part of the common travel area) and so you satisfy the right to reside requirement for means-tested benefits. If you are the family member of an Irish citizen in the UK, your residence rights as a family member require the Irish citizen to have a relevant right to reside in the same way as family members of other EEA nationals (see p1560).

European Economic Area residence rights: checklist

As EEA resident rights can be affected by many things, it can be helpful to work through the following steps.

Part 11: Immigration and residence rules for benefits and tax credits
Chapter 66: Coming from abroad: residence rules
5. Who has a right to reside

Step one: are you an EEA national with a right to reside based on your current or previous employment or self-employment, or current jobseeking or self-sufficiency (including while a student)? You have a right to reside if you are a 'qualified person'[53] – ie, an EEA national in the UK as a:

- jobseeker (see p1551);
- worker (see p1554), including if you have retained this status (see p1555);
- self-employed person (see p1558), including if you have retained this status (see p1559);
- self-sufficient person (see p1559);
- student (see p1560).

Step two: are you a 'family member' (see p1560) of someone covered in Step one? You have a right to reside even if you are not an EEA national yourself.

Step three: do you have a permanent right of residence (see p1566)? This is normally after five years of 'legal residence' (see p1567).

Step four: do you have a 'derivative' right to reside through someone else's right to reside, but not as her/his family member? This covers certain childrena and carers (see p1565).

Note:
- If you are a Croatian, A2 or A8 national, or a family member of a Croatian, A2 or A8 national, additional restrictions may apply (see below).
- You can have more than one right to reside at a time.[54] For example, you may be both a self-employed person and also the family member of someone with a permanent right of residence.

British citizens

If you are a British citizen, including if you also hold another nationality, you have an automatic right to reside in the UK. If you are the family member of a British citizen, see p1562. If you are the primary carer of a British citizen, see p1565.

Croatian, A2 and A8 nationals

Croatia, A2 and A8 states
Croatia joined the EU on 1 July 2013.
Restrictions are currently in force until 30 June 2018.
The A2 states are: Bulgaria and Romania.
These states joined the EU on 1 January 2007.
Restrictions applied until 31 December 2013.
The A8 states are: Czech Republic, Estonia, Hungary, Latvia, Lithuania, Poland, Slovakia and Slovenia.
These states joined the EU on 1 May 2004.
Rrestrictions applied until 30 April 2009 (see p1547).

The treaties under which the above 'accession' states joined the EU allowed existing member states to restrict accession state nationals' access to their labour markets and their residence rights as workers and jobseekers. The duration of these restrictions was limited to five years from the date the states joined the EU, but could be extended for a further two years if certain conditions were met. The UK government imposed the restrictions for five years and then extended the A8 and A2 restrictions for the additional two-year period. However, this extension of the A8 restrictions from 1 May 2009 to 30 April 2011 was held to be unlawful.[55] This means that A8 nationals were not subject to restrictions during that two-year period. **Note:** the DWP's appeal against this decision is currently waiting to be heard in the Court of Appeal.[56] See CPAG's online service and *Welfare Rights Bulletin* for updates.

Most Croatian nationals have, and A2 and A8 nationals had, certain restrictions on their residence rights as jobseekers, workers or people who retain worker status. **Note:** although the restrictions on A2 and A8 nationals have now ended, they remain relevant if your current or future residence rights are affected by the residence rights you or your family member had during the period of restriction – eg, when establishing permanent residence.

While in force, the restrictions apply, unless you are exempt (see p1548).

If you are a Croatian national and not exempt, you must obtain an 'accession worker authorisation document' (in most cases, an accession worker registration certificate, specifying the employer you can work for) before taking up employment, and then work in accordance with it.[57]

If you are an A2 national and not exempt, during the period of restrictions you were required to obtain an accession worker authorisation document (in most cases, an accession worker card specifying the employer you could work for) before taking up employment, and work in accordance with it.[58]

If you are an A8 national and not exempt, during the period of restrictions you had to work for an 'authorised employer'.[59] Broadly speaking, this meant you had to register each job you took with the Worker Registration Scheme (but see p1550 for the precise meaning, as it can affect your residence rights).

Restrictions on residence rights

If you are a **Croatian national**, unless you are in one of the groups listed below, you are 'subject to worker authorisation' and your residence rights are restricted until 30 June 2018 as follows.[60]

- You do not have a right to reside as a jobseeker.
- You are only defined as a 'worker' if you have an accession worker authorisation document and are working in accordance with it.
- You cannot retain your worker status when you stop work in the ways other workers can (see p1555).

Part 11: Immigration and residence rules for benefits and tax credits
Chapter 66: Coming from abroad: residence rules
5. Who has a right to reside

If you are an **A2 national** who was subject to restrictions (see below for exemptions), your residence rights were restricted between 1 January 2007 and 31 December 2013 in the same way as Croatian nationals.[61]

If you are an **A8 national** who was subject to restrictions (see p1549 for exemptions), your residence rights were restricted between 1 May 2004 and the end of the restrictions (see p1547) as follows.[62]

- You did not have a right to reside as a jobseeker.
- You were only defined as a 'worker' if you were working for an 'authorised employer' (see p1550).
- You could not retain your worker status when you stopped work in the ways other workers can (see p1555). However, if you lost your job within the first month of employment, you could retain your status in those ways, but only until the end of the month. **Note:** questions concerning the legality of excluding A8 nationals from retaining worker status have recently been referred to the Court of Justice of the European Union (CJEU).[63]

The restrictions do not affect other residence rights you may have as an EEA national (eg, as a self-employed or self-sufficient person)[64] or other rights you may have under EU law.

Croatian and A2 nationals not subject to worker authorisation

If you are a Croatian national, or an A2 national before 31 December 2013, you are not subject to worker authorisation if you:[65]

- have (or had on 30 June 2013 (Croatian) or 31 December 2006 (A2)) leave to enter or remain with no restriction on employment;
- were legally working (see p1550) in the UK for 12 months, without breaks of more than 30 days (in total), up to and including 31 December 2006 (A2) or 30 June 2013 (Croatian);
- have legally worked for 12 months (beginning before or after 31 December 2006 (A2) or 30 June 2013 (Croatian), disregarding any breaks of less than 30 days (in total);
- are a 'posted worker' – ie, you are working in the UK for an employer who is not established in the UK;
- are a member of a diplomatic mission (or the family member of such a person) or someone otherwise entitled to diplomatic immunity;
- have dual nationality with the UK or another (non-A2/Croatian) EEA state;
- are the spouse/civil partner (or, Croatian only, unmarried or same-sex partner) of a UK national or of a person settled in the UK;
- are the spouse/civil partner (or, Croatian only, unmarried or same-sex partner) or child under 18 of a person with leave to enter or remain in the UK that allows employment;
- have a permanent right of residence (see p1566);

11

- are a student with a registration certificate, which states that you cannot work more than 20 hours a week (unless it is part of vocational training, during vacations or, for Croatians only, for up to two years as a student union sabbatical officer) and you comply with this. If the certificate confirms you can work during the four months after the course ends, the exemption continues for this period;
- are a family member of an EEA national who has a right to reside, unless the EEA national is an A2 (or, Croatian only, a Croatian) national subject to worker authorisation (or, A2 only, the only reason s/he is not an A2 national subject to worker authorisation is because s/he is covered by the group below);
- are a family member of an A2 (or, if you are Croatian, a Croatian) national subject to worker authorisation who has a right to reside (for an A2 national only, as a worker, student, self-employed or self-sufficient person). If you are a Croatian national (or an A2 national relying on an A2 worker), you are a 'family member' if you are the descendant and either under 21 or dependent, or the spouse/civil partner or (Croatians only) the unmarried or same-sex partner; *or*
- are a 'highly skilled person' – ie, you:[66]
  - met the points-based criteria set out in the Immigration Rules for entering the UK on this basis; *or*
  - have a qualification at degree level or higher in the UK, or Higher National Diploma in Scotland and, within 12 months of this award, you apply for a registration certificate confirming your unconditional access to the labour market.

A8 nationals who were not required to register

If you are an A8 national, you were not required to register your work with the Worker Registration Scheme if you:[67]

- had leave to enter or remain on 30 April 2004 which had no restriction on employment;
- were legally working (see p1550) in the UK for 12 months, without breaks of more than 30 days (in total), up to and including 30 April 2004;
- had legally worked for 12 months (beginning before or after 30 April 2004), disregarding any breaks of less than 30 days (in total);
- were the spouse/civil partner or child under 18 of a person with leave to enter or remain in the UK that allowed employment;
- had dual nationality with the UK or another (non-A8/A2) EEA state or Switzerland;
- were a family member of another EEA or Swiss national who had a right to reside under the EEA Regulations (other than an A8/A2 national subject to registration/authorisation if her/his only right to reside was for the first three months in the UK);

11

Part 11: Immigration and residence rules for benefits and tax credits
Chapter 66: Coming from abroad: residence rules
5. Who has a right to reside

- were the member of a diplomatic mission (or the family member of such a person) or someone otherwise entitled to diplomatic immunity;
- were a 'posted worker' – ie, you were working in the UK for an employer who is not established in the UK.

Legally working

The phrase 'legally working' has a specific meaning and only refers to employment, not self-employment. It is relevant for determining whether you have completed 12 months of legal work in order to be exempt from the restrictions, and whether at a particular time you are, or were, a 'worker'.

If you are a Croatian national (or an A2 national before 1 January 2014), you are 'legally working' if:[68]

- you are/were working in accordance with your worker authorisation document; or
- you are/were working during a period when you are/were in one of the exempt groups on p1548 (other than posted workers); or
- the work was done before 1 July 2013 (for Croatian nationals) or before 1 January 2007 (for A2 nationals), either in accordance with any leave you had under the Immigration Act 1971 or when you did not require leave. This does not apply to work done with permission from the Home Office while you were an asylum seeker.[69]

If you are an A8 national, you were 'legally working' before the restrictions ended (see p1547) if:[70]

- you were working for an authorised employer (see below); or
- you were working during a period when you were in one of the exempt groups on p1549 (other than if you were the spouse/civil partner or child of a person whose leave to enter or remain in the UK allowed employment); or
- the work was done before 1 May 2004 either in accordance with any leave you had under the Immigration Act 1971 or when you did not require leave. This does not apply to work done with permission from the Home Office while you were an asylum seeker.[71]

Authorised employer

If you were an A8 national subject to restrictions, you were defined as working for an 'authorised employer' if you:[72]

– were working within the first month of employment;
– applied for a worker's registration certificate within the first month of work, but did not yet have a certificate or refusal;
– had a valid worker's registration certificate for that employer;
– had been legally working (see above) for that employer since 30 April 2004;

– began work at an agricultural camp between 1 May 2004 and 31 December 2004, and before 1 May 2004 you had been issued with leave under the Immigration Act 1971 as a seasonal worker at such a camp.

If you only applied for a registration certificate after the first month of work, you only count as working for an authorised employer from the date it was issued. It does not apply retrospectively.[73]

If you are a Croatian national subject to restrictions and your employment ends, you stop legally working, stop being a 'worker' and, unless you are in an exempt group, you cannot retain your worker status. However, if you are still under a contract of employment, you continue to be legally working and a worker – eg, if you are on maternity leave, holiday leave, sick leave or compassionate leave (including if the leave is unpaid).[74]

The same applied to A2 and A8 nationals during the relevant periods of restrictions (see p1547).

Initial right of residence

If you are an EEA national, you generally have an initial right of residence for the first three months of your stay in the UK, provided you have a valid identity card or passport and are not an unreasonable burden on the social assistance system of the UK.[75]

You also have a right of residence if you are a family member of an EEA national who has an initial right of residence (even if you are not an EEA national), provided you have a valid passport and are not an unreasonable burden on the social assistance system of the UK.[76]

If this is your only right of residence:
- it does not satisfy the right to reside requirement for income support (IS), income-based jobseeker's allowance (JSA), income-related employment and support allowance (ESA), pension credit (PC), housing benefit (HB) or universal credit (UC). To be entitled to these benefits you need another residence right (see p1542);
- it can count towards meeting the five years' residence required for permanent residency (see p1566).

Jobseekers

If you are an EEA national, you have a right to reside as a jobseeker if:[77]
- you are in the UK and you provide evidence that you are seeking employment and have a 'genuine chance of being engaged'; *and*
- you entered the UK in order to seek employment, or (EEA Regulations only) you are present in the UK seeking employment immediately after having a right to reside as a worker (except if you retained worker status while

11

Part 11: Immigration and residence rules for benefits and tax credits
Chapter 66: Coming from abroad: residence rules
5. Who has a right to reside

involuntarily unemployed – see p1556), a student, a self-employed or self-sufficient person; *and*

- (EEA Regulations only) either you have not already had a right to reside as a jobseeker for 91 days or, if you have, the evidence you provide to show that you are seeking employment and have a genuine chance of being engaged is 'compelling' (see below).[78] This is known as the 'genuine prospects of work test' (see below).

There is no time limit on how long you can have a right to reside as a jobseeker. It continues for as long as you continue to satisfy the above requirements.[79]

If you are a Croatian national subject to worker authorisation, you do not have a right to reside as a jobseeker. Similarly, during the periods of restrictions, if you were an A2 national subject to worker authorisation, or an A8 national required to register your work, you did not have a right to reside as a jobseeker.[80]

Evidence requirements

To have a right to reside as a jobseeker, you must provide evidence that you are seeking employment and have a genuine chance of being engaged.[81] **Note:** you must also provide this evidence under the EEA Regulations to retain your worker status while involuntarily unemployed.

You should be accepted as seeking employment and having a genuine chance of being engaged if you are 'signing on' and are available for work and actively seeking work (see p1030 and p1044) or if you satisfy the work-related requirements (see p1080) if you come under the UC system (see p20). There would only be a few unusual circumstances in which you would satisfy these conditions and not be accepted as having a genuine chance of being engaged.[82]

Under the EEA Regulations (see p1545), the evidence that you are looking for work and have a genuine chance of being engaged must be 'compelling':[83]

- to continue to have a right to reside as a jobseeker for more than 91 days;
- to continue to retain worker status on the basis of being involuntarily unemployed for more than six months (see p1556);
- from the *start* of your period of residence as a jobseeker (unless you have since been absent from the UK for a period of at least 12 months) if you previously:
  - had a right to reside as a jobseeker for a total of 91 days; *or*
  - retained worker status while involuntarily unemployed (see p1556) for at least six months.

Note: the EEA Regulations require that before you can have a right to reside as a jobseeker, you must have been absent from the UK since either of the above applied.[84] However, the DWP and HMRC have not, to date, enforced this.

The requirement for your evidence to be compelling is known as the the 'genuine prospects of work test'.

Do you have genuine prospects of work?

If you are asked to provide compelling evidence to show that you have 'genuine prospects of work', or you are told that you have failed to do so, note the following.

1. The 'genuine prospects of work test' does not apply to you if you have a right to reside *other than* as a jobseeker or as someone retaining worker status on the basis of being involuntarily unemployed.[85] Make sure the DWP or HMRC is aware if you have an alternative right to reside.

2. Check that the requirement has not been incorrectly applied after 91 days when it should, in your circumstances, be applied later. If you have retained worker status on the basis that you are involuntarily unemployed, it should not be applied before six months. Guidance lists examples of periods that can be disregarded when counting either the 91 days or six months, including periods of sickness, periods of temporary absence when you are treated as being in Great Britain (see p1599), and up to 13 weeks where you are treated as being available for work due to domestic violence.[86]

3. The term 'compelling' is not defined in the legislation and so should have its ordinary, everyday meaning. Your evidence must show, on the balance of probabilities, that you are seeking employment and have a genuine chance of being engaged. To require a higher standard of proof would be contrary to EU law:[87] under EU law, although you must be able to provide evidence that you are continuing to seek work and have a genuine chance of being engaged, there is no requirement for the quality of this evidence to change after a particular period of time.[88]

4. If you have been looking unsuccessfully for work for six months or more, this is relevant when considering whether you have a genuine chance of being engaged, but it is only one factor.[89] The decision maker should consider your *chances* of being engaged within a reasonable period and so changes in your circumstances in that future period are relevant.[90]

5. Refer to the guidance to decision makers if it is helpful.[91] However, the examples it includes are not exhaustive and, as guidance, it is not legally binding.

6. Ensure that your evidence is as strong and extensive as possible. Include details of all your qualifications (including those you are expected to obtain shortly), work history (paid and unpaid, both in and out of the UK), and all your skills and abilities that make you employable.

7. If your income-based JSA has been stopped because the DWP decided you failed the 'genuine prospects of work test' and you have a partner, s/he may be able to claim income-based JSA for you both.[92] This does not prevent you challenging the DWP's or HMRC's decision.

Benefit entitlement

If you have a right to reside as a jobseeker, you satisfy the right to reside requirement for income-based JSA, child benefit and child tax credit (CTC). You do not satisfy the right to reside requirement for IS, income-related ESA, PC, HB or UC, and you must have some other right to reside for these. Remember that in

Part 11: Immigration and residence rules for benefits and tax credits
Chapter 66: Coming from abroad: residence rules
5. Who has a right to reside

order to get income-based JSA, child benefit or CTC, unless you are in an exempt group, you must have been living here for the past three months (see p1535) and, for income-based JSA, be 'habitually resident in fact' (see p1538).

Workers

If you are an EEA national and a 'worker' in the UK, you have a right to reside.[93] You satisfy the right to reside requirement for all the benefits that have this requirement and you are exempt from the habitual residence test (see p1540).

You are a 'worker' if:

- you are in an employment relationship. This means you must:[94]
  - provide services;
  - work in return for remuneration;
  - work under the direction of another person;
- the work you do entails activities that are 'genuine and effective', rather than 'marginal and ancillary'.

Is your work genuine and effective?

All the relevant factors must be taken into account when deciding whether your work is genuine and effective, including the following.

1. The duration of the employment. The longer the period of time your employment lasts, the more likely it is that you have established worker status. However, someone working as a steward at Wimbledon for two weeks was held to be a worker.[95]

2. The number of hours worked. There is no minimum threshold. Someone working 10 hours a week was held to be a worker,[96] as was an au pair working 13 hours a week for a modest wage plus and lodging.[97] The European Court of Justice (ECJ) has held that 5.5 hours' work is potentially capable of making someone a worker.[98]

3. The level of your earnings. There must be some remuneration (although it can be in kind, such as board and lodgings[99]), and voluntary work does not result in worker status.[100] The work can be low paid. Provided the work done is genuine and effective, even if your earnings are so low that you need to subsidise your wages with benefits, this is irrelevant to the question of whether or not you are a worker.[101]

4. The regularity of the work. The more regular and less erratic the work, the more likely it is that worker status will be established. It is possible to be a worker while undertaking work through an agency,[102] or while working 'cash in hand' without tax and national insurance (NI) being deducted.[103]

Although guidance to decision makers advises that someone is automatically a worker if s/he has been earning, on average, a threshold income (£157 per week or £680 per month) for three months, it confirms that, in *all* other cases, an individual assessment must be made, taking the above factors into account.[104]

Note: if you are a Croatian national who is subject to worker authorisation, you only count as a 'worker' if you have an accession worker authorisation document and are working in accordance with it. Similarly, during the previous periods of restrictions, if you were an A2 national subject to worker authorisation, you only counted as a 'worker' if you had a worker authorisation document and were working in accordance with it. If you were an A8 national required to register, you only counted as a 'worker' if you were working for an 'authorised employer' (see p1550). For details of these restrcitions and who is affected, see p1546.

You only cease to be a worker when the employment relationship ends. While you are still under a contract of employment, you continue to be a worker. Consequently, you are still a worker if you are a woman on maternity leave (including unpaid maternity leave),[105] or if you are on holiday leave or sick leave (including if it is unpaid).[106]

If you have ceased to be a worker, you may retain your worker status in certain circumstances (see below).

Retaining worker status

You can retain the status of 'worker', even though you are no longer working, if:[107]

- you are involuntarily unemployed and registered as a jobseeker (see p1556);
- you are temporarily unable to work because of an illness or accident (see p1556);
- you are undertaking vocational training (see p1557);
- you have given up work because of the physical constraints of pregnancy or childbirth (see p1557).[108]

Before arguing that you have retained your worker status, check whether you have ceased to be a worker (see above). For example, if you are off work on unpaid sick leave but you can return to your job when you are better, you are still a worker and so you do not need to argue that you have retained your worker status.

Note: if you are a Croatian national subject to worker authorisation, you cannot retain your worker status in the ways described in this section. Similarly, during the previous periods of restrictions, if you were an A2 national subject to worker authorisation or an A8 national required to register, you could not retain your worker status in the ways described in this section. However, if you were an A8 national required to register and you stopped working during the first month of employment, you could retain your worker status in the ways described in this section for the remainder of that month.[109] For details of these restrictions and who they affect see p1546.

11

Part 11: Immigration and residence rules for benefits and tax credits
Chapter 66: Coming from abroad: residence rules
5. Who has a right to reside

You are involuntarily unemployed and registered as a jobseeker

To retain worker status on this basis you must:[110]

- be recorded as involuntarily unemployed;
- have registered as a jobseeker with Jobcentre Plus;
- provide evidence that you are seeking employment and have a genuine chance of being engaged; *and*
- (EEA Regulations only – see p1545) have entered the UK in order to seek employment or be present in the UK seeking employment immediately after having a right to reside as a worker (except if you retained your worker status under this category), a student, or a self-employed or self-sufficient person. **Note:** if you are refused benefit on this basis, you should challenge the decision on the basis that this is not a requirement under EU law.[111]

You are '**involuntarily unemployed**' if you are seeking, and are available to take up, a job. This depends on your remaining in the labour market. The circumstances in which you left your last job are just one factor in determining this, and your actions and circumstances since leaving work are taken into account.[112]

The best way to register as a jobseeker is to claim JSA and/or UC if you come under the UC system, and keep signing on, even if you are not entitled to benefit. If you are looking for work and claim IS, income-related ESA or PC, you should be accepted as having registered as a jobseeker if you declared that you are looking for work before your claim is determined – eg, on your claim form or habitual residence questionnaire.[113]

If you were employed (not necessarily in one continuous job) for more than a year, you can retain your worker status on this basis indefinitely, in the absence of an event that indicates you have withdrawn from the labour market entirely.[114] However after six months, the EEA Regulations (see p1545) require evidence that you are continuing to seek employment and have a genuine chance of being engaged to be 'compelling' (see p1552).[115]

If you were employed for less than a year, the EEA Regulations limit the period during which you can retain your worker status while registered as a jobseeker to a maximum of six months.[116] The EU Directive allows you to retain worker status for no less than six months.[117]

Once you have ceased to retain worker status on this basis, you may be able to have a right to reside as a jobseeker (see p1551).

You are temporarily unable to work because of an illness or accident

To retain your worker status, your inability to work must be temporary. This simply means not permanent.[118] This can apply if you have a permanent health condition that fluctuates and causes temporary periods when you are unable to work.[119] You are considered to be temporarily unable to work if there is a realistic prospect of your being able to work again in the forseeable future.[120] You do not need to have claimed ESA or another benefit on the grounds of inability to work, nor do you need to pass the test of limited capability for work. The test is whether you are unable to do the work you were doing or, if it follows a period in which you were seeking work, the sort of work you were seeking.[121] Your inability to work must be caused by an illness or accident which *you* have – eg, you are not covered if you are unable to work because you are looking after a child who is ill.[122]

If you are unable to work because of pregnancy, see below.

You are undertaking vocational training

You retain your worker status if you are undertaking a vocational training course. Unless you are involuntarily unemployed, the training must be related to your previous employment. If it is not, you must be accepted as being 'involuntarily unemployed'. You should be accepted as 'involuntarily unemployed' if there is no employment available to you that is equivalent to your last employment.[123]

Pregnancy and childbirth

If you have established worker (or self-employed) status and you are now not working because of pregnancy or childbirth, you may still count as a worker (or self-employed person), or you may be able to retain your worker (or self-employed) status.

You do not cease to be a worker while you are still under a contract of employment, so you are still a worker while on maternity leave, whether or not it is paid. This also applies to Croatian nationals from 1 July 2013, and A2 and A8 nationals (including during the periods of restrictions – see p1547) who have established worker status.[124]

You can continue to be a self-employed person if you stop work for a period of maternity leave, but intend to resume your self-employment.[125]

You can retain your worker or self-employed status if you have a pregnancy-related illness that prevents you from working (see p1555).[126]

You can also retain worker status if you gave up work (or seeking work) because of the physical constraints of the late stages of pregnancy or the aftermath of childbirth, provided you start work again (or re-enter the labour market and thereby retain your worker status while involuntarily unemployed – see p1556) within a 'reasonable period' after giving birth.[127] Other than in unusual cases, 52 weeks is a 'reasonable period' and the period will usually start 11 weeks before the due date.[128]

Moving between groups and gaps

You can retain your worker status if you are in one of the groups on p1555 and continue to do so if you move into another category.[129] For example, you may have been involuntarily unemployed and registered as a jobseeker, then you became ill and were temporarily unable to work, and then you got better and embarked on vocational training. You retain your worker status throughout.

Part 11: Immigration and residence rules for benefits and tax credits
Chapter 66: Coming from abroad: residence rules
5. Who has a right to reside

You may be able to retain your worker status if there is a gap between your ceasing work and registering as a jobseeker by claiming JSA.[130] If the delay is more than a few days, all your circumstances, including the reasons for the gap and what you did during it, should be considered to establish whether there was undue delay[131] and whether you withdrew from the labour market during that period.[132] Arguably, you should also be able to retain your worker status if there is a gap between your ceasing work and being temporarily unable to work because of illness or an accident, since there is no requirement that the illness or accident be the reason for your ceasing work. You should also still retain your worker status during a short gap between two different circumstances applying, provided you remain in the labour market during that time.

Self-employed people

If you are an EEA national and a 'self-employed person' in the UK, you have a right to reside[133] and therefore satisfy the right to reside requirement for all the benefits that have this requirement (see p1542). You are also exempt from the habitual residence test (see p1540).

You are a self-employed person if you provide services in return for remuneration, but not under the direction of another person. The work you do must entail activities that are 'genuine and effective' rather than 'marginal and ancillary' (see p1554).[134]

You count as being self-employed when you are established in the UK in order to pursue self-employed activity.[135] You must provide evidence of the steps you have taken or the ways in which you have set yourself up as self-employed. It helps if you have registered with HMRC as self-employed. However, if you have not registered, this does not necessarily mean you cannot be accepted as self-employed.[136]

If you are a Croatian national and you are self-employed, you have the same rights as other EEA nationals; there are no additional restrictions. This was also true of A2 and A8 nationals who were self-employed during the periods of restrictions (see p1547).

If you stop working, you do not necessarily cease to be self-employed. You may be in a temporary lull, and it is accepted that you can continue to be self-employed during such times, depending on your particular circumstances and the evidence you provide – eg, the amount of work you have, any steps you are taking to develop your business or find new work, and your marketing and business administration. Account must also be taken of your motives and intentions.[137]

You can continue to be self-employed if you stop work for a period of maternity leave, but intend to return to self-employment afterwards (see p1557).[138]

If you have ceased to be self-employed, you may be able to retain your self-employed status in certain circumstances (see p1559).

Retaining self-employed status

Like workers, if you have established self-employed status, you can retain it when you have stopped working if you are temporarily unable to work as the result of an illness or accident (see p1555).[139] **Note:** unlike retaining worker status, there are no restrictions on retaining your self-employed status if you are a Croatian national (or an A2 or A8 national during the periods of restrictions – see p1547).

If you have ceased self-employment because of pregnancy, you may be able to retain your self-employed status (see p1557).

You do not retain self-employed status if you are involuntarily unemployed and registered as a jobseeker (although questions have been referred to the CJEU on this[140]) or if you are doing vocational training.[141]

Before arguing that you have retained your self-employed status, check whether you can still count as self-employed (see p1558). If this applies, the question of whether you retain that status does not arise.

Remember that, even if you cannot retain your status as a self-employed person, unless you are a Croatian national subject to worker authorisation, you may have a right to reside as a jobseeker and be able to get income-based JSA, child benefit and CTC on that basis (see p1551).

Self-sufficient people

You have a right of residence as a self-sufficient person if you are an EEA national and you, and any family members who do not have an independent right to reside, have:[142]

- sufficient resources not to become an unreasonable burden on the social assistance system of the UK;[143] *and*
- comprehensive sickness insurance.

The UK government cannot set a fixed amount that is regarded as 'sufficient resources' and must take account of your personal situation.[144] You have 'sufficient resources' if they:[145]

- exceed the maximum level you (and your family) can have to be eligible for 'social assistance' (see below); *or*
- do not exceed that level, but the decision maker considers that you still have sufficient resources, taking into account your (and your family's) personal situation.

The 'maximum level' is the equivalent of your means-tested benefit applicable amount, including any premiums. Your resources also include your accommodation, so if your resources are more than your applicable amount plus your rent, or if friends or family provide you with free and stable accommodation, they should be 'sufficient'.[146]

11

Part 11: Immigration and residence rules for benefits and tax credits
Chapter 66: Coming from abroad: residence rules
5. Who has a right to reside

You cannot automatically be regarded as not self-sufficient just because you make a claim for a means-tested benefit. All your circumstances, including the likely duration of your claim, must be assessed to determine whether or not your benefit claim makes you an unreasonable burden on the social assistance system of the UK.[147]

The source of the resources does not matter.[148] However, you cannot rely on your earnings from employment in the UK to give you self-sufficient status.[149] Check instead whether the employment gives you 'worker' status (see p1554). You can, however, rely on the earnings of your non-EEA national spouse/civil partner.[150]

The requirement to have **comprehensive sickness insurance** cover is satisfied if you have private health insurance.[151] It is also satisfied if the UK can be reimbursed by another state for any NHS costs you incur while in the UK. This usually applies if you are covered by the EU co-ordination rules (see p1611) and another state continues to be your 'competent state' (see p1615).[152] For further information, see CPAG's *Benefits for Migrants Handbook*.

Students

You have a right to reside as a student if you are an EEA national and you:[153]
- are enrolled as a student in a government-accredited college;
- provide an assurance that you have sufficient resources for yourself, and any family members who do not have an independent right to reside, not to become a burden on the UK social assistance system during your intended period of residence (see above); *and*
- together with any family members who do not have an independent right to reside, have comprehensive sickness insurance (see above).

Family members

You have a right to reside if you are a 'family member' (see below) of an EEA national who has either a right to reside as a 'qualified person' (see p1546) or a permanent right to reside. This applies whether or not you are an EEA national yourself. You have a right to reside for as long as the EEA national has a right to reside and for as long as you remain her/his family member.

Family members[154]

You are a **'family member'** if you are the:
– spouse or civil partner of the EEA national;
– child, grandchild or great-grandchild of the EEA national, or of the EEA national's spouse/ civil partner, and you are under 21;
– child, grandchild or great-grandchild of the EEA national, or of the EEA national's spouse/ civil partner, and you are her/his dependant;

– parent, grandparent or great-grandparent of the EEA national, or of the EEA national's spouse/civil partner, and you are her/his dependant.

You remain a spouse or civil partner even if you are separated. You only cease to be a spouse or civil partner on divorce or termination of the civil partnership.[155]

'**Dependence**' is not defined in the legislation, but caselaw has established a number of principles.[156] To be dependent, you must receive support from the other person. The support must be 'material', although not necessarily financial, and must contribute towards your basic necessities. It is irrelevant if there are alternative sources of support, including employment, available.[157]

If you only became dependent on the EEA national in the UK, this does not prevent you from being classed as a family member, unless you are an 'extended family member' (see below), in which case you must have already been dependent in the country from where you have come.[158]

Note:
- If your only right to reside is as the family member of an EEA national who only has a right to reside for her/his initial three months (see p1551), this does not enable you to satisfy the right to reside requirement for IS, income-based JSA, income-related ESA, PC, HB and UC (see p1543).
- If your only right to reside is as the family member of an EEA national who has a right to reside as a jobseeker, this does not enable you to satisfy the right to reside requirement for IS, income-related ESA, PC, UC and HB (see p1542).

Are you unable to prove your right to reside?

If you are relying on your family member for your right to reside and you cannot prove what s/he is doing (eg, if you have separated from your spouse and have no evidence that s/he is a worker), you should ask the DWP, HMRC or local authority to investigate this – eg, by using the database of NI contributions to establish that your spouse is a worker. Provide information about your spouse to enable it to do so. If it refused and you appeal, you can ask the tribunal to direct the DWP, HMRC or local authority to make these investigations and argue that otherwise it has not shown that you do not have a right to reside.[159]

Extended family members

If you do not count as a family member under the above rules, but you have a relative in the UK who is an EEA national, you may be treated as her/his family member if you are her/his 'extended family member' and you have been issued with an EEA family permit, a registration certificate or a residence card (see p1569).[160]

Part 11: Immigration and residence rules for benefits and tax credits
Chapter 66: Coming from abroad: residence rules
5. Who has a right to reside

Extended family member

You are an **'extended family member'** if you are the:[161]

– partner of an EEA national and you are in a durable relationship with her/him; *or*

– relative of an EEA national; *and*

– you satisfy the requirements of the Immigration Rules (other than those relating to entry clearance) for indefinite leave as her/his dependent relative; *or*

– you have serious health problems that require her/his care; *or*

– you previously were dependent on, or a member of the household of, the EEA national in a country other than the UK and either you are accompanying her/him to, or wish to join her/him in, the UK, or you have joined her/him in the UK and continue to be dependent on her/him or to be a member of her/his household.[162]

Family members of British citizens

British citizens do not automatically give residence rights to their family members.

If you are a family member of a British citizen, you have a right to reside on the basis of EU law as her/his family member if s/he has 'genuinely' resided (which requires more than just physical presence) with a right to reside as a worker, self-employed person, self-sufficient person or self-sufficient student, or having acquired a right of permanent residence, in *another* EEA state. On her/his return to the UK, s/he has the same rights as other EEA nationals and can confer rights on you.[163]

The EEA Regulations (see p1545) contain these rights if you are a family member (other than an extended family member) of a British citizen, but interpret them more restrictively than the ECJ has done.[164]

- The EEA Regulations list the following as relevant to whether your residence is or was genuine:[165]
  - whether the British citizen transferred her/his 'centre of life' there;
  - the length of joint residence;
  - the nature and quality of the joint accommodation and whether it was her/his principal residence;
  - the degree of integration;
  - whether it was your first lawful residence in the EU.

  These factors go beyond the findings of the ECJ which, when considering whether residence is 'genuine' has focused on whether the conditions for the relevant residence rights were satisfied.[166]

- The EEA Regulations only give you a right to reside if the British citizen currently has a right to reside under these Regulations (with certain mitigations – eg, if s/he is a self-sufficient person, she need not be covered by comprehensive sickness cover). However, the ECJ has held that it is not necessary for a person who had been a worker in another EEA state to carry out economic activity on

11

her/his return in order for her/his family memeber to have a right of residence.[167]

- If you are a non-EEA national, the EEA Regulations exclude you from having a right to reside on this basis if the purpose of your residence in the other EEA state was to circumvent the immigration laws.[168]

Get specialist advice if any of these restrictions affect you.

If you are the family member of someone with both British and another EEA nationality, note the following.

- Before 16 October 2012, you had the same rights as family members of other EEA nationals.[169] If you already acquired such a right before this date, it continues in limited circumstances.[170] See the 2013/14 edition of this *Handbook* for more details.
- A dual British/other EEA national does not have rights under EU law if s/he has lived all her/his life in the UK. Consequently, you cannot derive any rights from her/him.[171]
- The EEA Regulations exclude EEA nationals who are also British citizens from the definition of 'EEA national'.[172]
- Questions have been referred to the CJEU regarding the residence rights of family members of dual British/other EEA nationals who moved between member states before acquiring dual citizenship.[173] See CPAG's online service and *Welfare Rights Bulletin* for updates.

Former family members who retain their right to reside

In general, if you are the family member of an EEA national who has a right to reside, you lose your right to reside if s/he ceases to be your family member or to have a right to reside. However, there are some exceptions which mean you can retain your right to reside if the EEA national dies or leaves the UK, or if your marriage or civil partnership ends. These rights are in EU Directive 2004/38, but they are not exactly reproduced in the UK EEA Regulations. The benefit authorities accept the rights set out in the EEA Regulations (listed below), but do not always accept those in the Directive (listed on p1564). If you only have a right to reside under the Directive and are refused benefit, you should challenge the decision and get specialist advice.

You retain your right to reside under the EEA Regulations if you are a family member of a 'qualified person' (see p1545) or a person with a permanent right to reside (see p1566) and:[174]

- that person dies and you are:
  - not an EEA national, but if you were, you would be a worker, or a self-employed or self-sufficient person (or you are the family member of such a non-EEA national), and you resided in the UK with a right to reside under the Regulations for at least a year immediately before s/he died; *or*

Part 11: Immigration and residence rules for benefits and tax credits
Chapter 66: Coming from abroad: residence rules
5. Who has a right to reside

- the child or grandchild of the qualified person (or her/his spouse or civil partner) and in education (see p1566) immediately before the death and you remain in education; *or*
- a parent with custody of a child in the previous bullet point; *or*
- that person leaves the UK and you are:
  - the child or grandchild of the qualified person (or her/his spouse or civil partner) and in education (see p1566) immediately before s/he left the UK and you remain in education; *or*
  - a parent with custody of a child in the previous bullet point; *or*
- your marriage or civil partnership to that person is terminated and you are not an EEA national, but if you were, you would be a worker, or a self-employed or self-sufficient person (or you are the family member of such a non-EEA national), and you were residing in the UK with a right to reside under the regulations at the date of the termination and:
  - prior to the termination, the marriage/civil partnership had lasted for at least three years with you both residing in the UK for at least one of those years; *or*
  - you have custody of the qualified person's child; *or*
  - you have a right of access to the qualified person's child, which a court has said must take place in the UK; *or*
  - your continued right of residence in the UK is warranted by particularly difficult circumstances, such as your (or another family member's) being subject to domestic violence during the period of the marriage/civil partnership.

You have a right to reside on this basis for as long as the conditions apply to you,[175] until you can acquire a permanent right of residence (see p1566).[176]

You should retain your right to reside under EU Directive 2004/38 if you are a family member of an EEA national who has a right to reside as a worker, or as a self-employed or self-sufficient person or a student and:

- the EEA national dies and you:[177]
  - are an EEA national; *or*
  - have lived in the UK as her/his family member for at least a year before her/his death and you are a non-EEA national; *or*
- the EEA national leaves the UK and you are:[178]
  - an EEA national; *or*
  - the child or grandchild of the EEA national and in education; *or*
  - the parent with custody of a child in education; *or*
- your marriage or civil partnership to the EEA national is terminated and:[179]
  - you are an EEA national; *or*
  - prior to the commencement of the termination (which must occur while the EEA national is in the UK[180]), the marriage/civil partnership had lasted for at

least three years with you both residing in the UK for at least one of those years; *or*

- you have custody of the EEA national's child; *or*
- you have a right of access to the EEA national's child, which a court has said must take place in the UK; *or*
- your continued right of residence in the UK is warranted by particularly difficult circumstances, such as your being subject to domestic violence during the period of the marriage/civil partnership. Your rights are not retained in this way if your spouse or civil partner left the UK before the termination proceedings began.[181]

Note: periods when you have retained your right to reside under the EU Directive in one of the ways above are not sufficient on their own to enable you to acquire permanent residence after five years (see p1566), because you are also required to show that you are a worker, or a self-employed or self-sufficient person, or you are the family member of such a person.[182]

Derivative right to reside

Some people have a right to reside based on someone else's right to reside, except by being her/his family member.

You have a 'derivative' right to reside on this basis if you are:[183]

- the child (or stepchild[184]) of an EEA national who was a 'worker' in the UK (see p1554) while you were living in the UK, and you are currently in education;[185] *or*
- the primary carer of a child in the above bullet point and the child would be unable to continue her/his education in the UK if you left the UK (see below);[186] *or*
- the primary carer of a self-sufficient child who is an EEA national, who would be unable to remain in the UK if you left the UK;[187] *or*
- the primary carer of a British citizen residing in the UK who would be unable to reside in the UK or another EEA state if you left the UK (see below);[188]
- aged under 18 and your primary carer is covered by either the second, third or fourth bullet points above and s/he would be prevented from residing in the UK if you left the UK, and you do not have leave to enter or remain in the UK.

You may be accepted as having a right to reside as the primary carer even if you share that responsibility with someone else who does not already have a right to reside. If this applies, the consequences of your being required to leave are considered on the basis that both you and the other carer are required to leave.[189]

Note:

- If your only right of residence is as the primary carer of a dependent British citizen who would otherwise have to leave the whole of the EEA, you do not satisfy the right to reside requirement for any benefits or CTC (see p1543 and

Part 11: Immigration and residence rules for benefits and tax credits
Chapter 66: Coming from abroad: residence rules
5. Who has a right to reside

p1544). This is arguably unlawful, and although legal challenges have not yet been successful, future ones may be.[190] See CPAG's online service and *Welfare Rights Bulletin* for updates.

- Periods with a right to reside under any of the above bullet points do not count towards the period of residence required for acquiring a permanent right to reside (see below).

Child in education

To have a right to reside as a worker's child in education and as a primary carer of a child in education, the child must have been in the UK while the parent (or step-parent[191]) was a worker in the UK. The child need not have entered education while the parent (or step-parent) was a worker.[192]

These rights also apply if the worker was an A8 national working during the period of restrictions (see p1546) for an authorised employer (see p1547), even if it was for less than 12 months.[193] As the first month of work an A8 national did was always for an authorised employer, her/his child who was in the UK during that first month of work and who is now in education can also have these rights.[194] These rights also apply in the same way if the worker was a Croatian or (before 1 January 2014) an A2 national working in accordance with her/his worker authorisation document.

Your right to reside as a primary carer of a worker's child in education ends when the child reaches 18, unless s/he continues to need your presence and care in order to be able to pursue and complete her/his education.[195]

Education

'**Education**' excludes nursery education, but includes education before the compulsory school age if it is equivalent to that received at or after compulsory school age – eg, education received by a child under five in a school reception class.[196]

If you are the primary carer of a child of a self-employed EEA national, you are not currently accepted as deriving a right to reside from that child.[197] However, further caselaw is pending.[198] See CPAG's online service and *Welfare Rights Bulletin* for updates.

People with a permanent right of residence

From 30 April 2006, you have a permanent right of residence if you have 'resided legally' (see p1567) in the UK for a 'continuous period of five years' (see below).[199] Once you have this permanent right of residence, you satisfy the right to reside requirement for all benefits that have that requirement.

Once acquired, you only lose your permanent right of residence if you are absent from the UK for more than two consecutive years.[200]

A continuous period of five years

When calculating whether you have **'five years' continuous residence'**, temporary absences from the UK do not affect the continuity of your residence (and you can count the time spent abroad as part of your five years[201]) if:[202]

– they are not more than a total of six months a year; *or*
– they comprise one absence of up to 12 consecutive months for important reasons, such as pregnancy and childbirth, serious illness, study or vocational training, or a posting abroad; *or*
– they are for compulsory military service.

The Court of Appeal has rejected an argument that temporary gaps between periods of legal residence when you remain in the UK should also not affect the continuity of your residence.[203] However, this argument may succeed in a future case.

Guidance to decision makers states that cumulative gaps of up to 30 days in any one year do not break your continuity of residence if they are between two periods when you have different residence rights, but not if they separate two periods when you have the same residence right.[204] Refer to this guidance if it is helpful, but remember it is not legally binding.

If you spend time in prison[205] or if you are removed from the UK under the EEA Regulations or subject to a deportation or expulsion order,[206] this interrupts the continuity of your residence and you cannot count this time towards your five years.

What counts as 'resided legally'

You have 'resided legally' in any period during which you had a right of residence as a:

- worker (see p1554) (including if you retain your worker status – see p1555);
- self-employed person (see p1558) (including if you retain your self-employed status – see p1559);
- self-sufficient person (see p1559);
- student (see p1560);
- jobseeker (see p1551) from 30 April 2006 (but see below);
- family member (see p1560) of any of the above.

If you have a continuous period of five years' residence on the basis of one or more of the above, you have a right of permanent residence under the UK EEA Regulations and (other than as a jobseeker or family member of a jobseeker) EU Directive 2004/38. However, if you need to rely on periods when you were a jobseeker or not in one of these groups, the specific provisions of the EEA Regulations and EU Directive can be relevant.

Part 11: Immigration and residence rules for benefits and tax credits
Chapter 66: Coming from abroad: residence rules
5. Who has a right to reside

Under the EEA Regulations, you must have resided continuously 'in accordance with these regulations', or in accordance with previous regulations,[207] other than with a 'derivative right to reside' (see p1565).[208]

Jobseekers were not listed as having residence rights in the EEA Regulations before 30 April 2006 and, therefore, periods of residence as a jobseeker can only be used towards your five years from 30 April 2006.

Under EU Directive 2004/38, you must have 'resided legally for a continuous period of five years'.[209] This means that you had a residence right under the Directive or under any of the earlier EU legislation that the Directive replaced.[210] This covers all the groups listed above, except for jobseekers and their family members. You are not counted as having 'resided legally' during periods when your right to reside was as the primary carer of either a worker's child in education or a self-sufficient child,[211] or when your right of residence was only in accordance with UK law – eg, a period during which you had leave to remain under the Immigration Rules.[212]

If you are an A8, A2 or a Croatian national, you count as having 'resided legally' during periods before your state joined the EU if you would have come into one of the groups above (other than a jobseeker), or you would have resided in accordance with the EEA Regulations were it not for the fact that you were not an EU national at that time.[213] Once your state joined the EU, the periods when you count as having resided legally are as above, except they are subject to the additional restrictions for A8, A2 and Croatian nationals (see p1547).

Family members

If you are the family member (see p1560) of a person with a permanent right of residence, you have a right to reside for as long as you remain a family member.[214] After five years of being the family member of an EEA national with a permanent right of residence, you acquire a permanent right of residence yourself. You can also add periods as a family member of a person with a permanent right of residence to other periods when you count as 'residing legally' (see p1567) to make up your five years, and so acquire a permanent right of residence.[215]

Permanent residence in less than five years

If you were a worker (see p1554) or self-employed person (see p1558) and the circumstances listed below apply (or if these apply to your family member), you can acquire a permanent right of residence before five years. If so, you are exempt from the habitual residence test (see p1540).

You have a permanent right to reside if you:[216]

- were a worker or self-employed person and:
  - you have stopped working and you have reached retirement age or (workers only) taken early retirement and:
    - your spouse or civil partner is a British citizen (or s/he lost that nationality by marrying you); or

- you worked in the UK for the preceding year and resided in the UK continuously for more than three years; *or*
- you stopped working in the UK because of a permanent incapacity and:
  - your spouse or civil partner is a British citizen (or s/he lost that nationality by marrying you); *or*
  - you have resided in the UK continuously for more than two years; *or*
  - the incapacity was because of an accident at work or occupational disease that resulted in benefit entitlement; *or*
- you previously worked and resided in the UK continuously for three years until you began working in another member state while retaining a place of residence in the UK and returning, as a rule, at least once a week; *or*
- are the family member of a worker or self-employed person in any of the above bullet points and you are both residing in the UK;[217] *or*
- are the family member of a worker or self-employed person who died while still working and who did not acquire a permanent right of residence in one of the above ways and:
  - s/he had lived in the UK for two years; *or*
  - the death resulted from an accident at work or an occupational disease; *or*
  - you lost your UK nationality as a result of marrying her/him.

You can count as periods of employment any period in which you were not working because of illness or accident, or some reason not of your own making, or (workers only) periods of involuntary unemployment (subject to the same limitations as those retaining worker status this way – see p1556).[218]

Other rights of residence under European Union law

If none of the usual ways in which you may have a right of residence under EU law in the UK (see pp1544–69) apply to you, it may be possible to argue that you should still have a right of residence despite not meeting any of the specific conditions.

If you are an EU national, you may be able to argue that you have a right to reside under Article 21 of the Treaty on the Functioning of the European Union. Arguments that you have a right of residence despite not meeting the usual conditions are complex and have, to date, been held not to apply except possibly in exceptional circumstances.[219] You should therefore get specialist advice and always check whether you have a right of residence under one of the other routes first.

Residence documents

To have a right of residence as an 'extended family member' (see p1561), you must have a residence document. If you have some other right of residence, you can also obtain a residence document, but it is not necessary. **Note:** a residence

Part 11: Immigration and residence rules for benefits and tax credits
Chapter 66: Coming from abroad: residence rules
6. Rules for specific benefits and tax credits

document does not, in itself, give you a right to reside – eg, if your right to reside has ended.[220]

You can be issued with the following residence documents.

- **A registration certificate** if you are an EEA national with a right of residence provided under the EEA Regulations.[221]
- **A residence card** if you are a non-EEA national and you have a right to reside as the family member of an EEA 'qualified person' (see p1545) or an EEA national with a permanent right of residence.[222]
- **A derivative residence card** if you have a derivative right to reside – eg, as the primary carer of a worker's child in education.[223]
- **A document certifying permanent right of residence** if you are an EEA national with a permanent right of residence, or a **permanent residence card** if you are a non-EEA national with a permanent right of residence.[224]
- **A residence document** issued, or treated as issued, under previous regulations. These are treated as if they were issued under the current EEA Regulations.[225]
- **A family permit** for entry to the UK if you are a non-EEA family member of an EEA national and do not have any of the other residence documentation.[226]

Forms and further information, including about application fees, are available on the Home Office website.

6. **Rules for specific benefits and tax credits**

This section explains the residence and presence rules for each benefit. It includes which residence and presence tests apply and how you may be assisted by the European Union (EU) co-ordination rules.

For the rules on being paid while you are abroad, see Chapter 67.

Means-tested benefits

To be entitled to **income support (IS), income-based jobseeker's allowance (JSA), income-related employment and support allowance (ESA), pension credit and universal credit (UC)**, you (and your, partner for UC) must:
- be present in Great Britain (see p1534);[227] *and*
- be habitually resident (see p1537), including having a right to reside (see p1542) and, for income-based JSA only, have been living for the past three months (see p1535) in the 'common travel area' – ie, the UK, Republic of Ireland, Channel Islands and the Isle of Man (unless you are exempt – see p1540).[228]

In certain circumstances, the rules treat you as being present in Great Britain during a temporary absence, so you can continue to receive these benefits while you are abroad for limited periods (see Chapter 67).

For UC, if your partner fails the habitual residence test, you must claim UC as a single person. Your award is based on the maximum amount for a single person, but your partner's income and capital are taken into account.[229]

If you come under the UC system, unless you are in a 'full service' area (see p22), you must meet the 'gateway' conditions. These include satisfying additional residence and presence rules. These are that you (and your partner) must:[230]

- be a British citizen; *and*
- have resided in the UK throughout the two years before the date of your claim; *and*
- not have left the UK for a continuous period of more than four weeks during the above period.

To be entitled to **housing benefit (HB)**, you must be habitually resident (see p1537), including having a right to reside (see p1542), in the common travel area (unless you are exempt).[231] Although being present in Great Britain is not a condition of entitlement, going abroad can still affect your entitlement (see p1595).

Note: if you are are moving, or have moved, to Great Britain from Northern Ireland or vice versa and are claiming income-related ESA, see p1576.

If your partner is abroad

If you have a partner who is abroad, you may continue to receive benefit that includes an amount for her/him for a limited period if you are only temporarily living apart. The rules vary between the benefits (see Chapter 67).

If these rules do not apply or at the end of the limited period:

- your applicable amount for IS, income-based JSA and income-related ESA no longer includes an amount for your partner;
- you cease to be entitled to UC as joint claimants. You must claim as a single person. Your award is based on the maximum amount for a single person, but your partner's income and capital are taken into account until you have been, or you expect to be, apart for six months (as then you cease to be treated as a couple).[232]

Your partner's capital, income and work are still taken into account when working out how much of the above benefits you get. This is because s/he is still treated as being part of your household, despite temporarily living away from you, unless you are in any of the situations listed on p218.[233]

Where questions of 'intention' are involved (eg, when deciding whether you or your partner intend to resume living with your family), the intention must be 'unqualified'. This means it must not depend on a factor over which you have no control – eg, the right of entry to the UK being granted by the Home Office,[234] or the offer of a suitable job.[235]

11

Part 11: Immigration and residence rules for benefits and tax credits
Chapter 66: Coming from abroad: residence rules
6. Rules for specific benefits and tax credits

If your child is abroad

If you have a child who is abroad, your benefit entitlement could be affected if s/he ceases to be treated as part of your household (see p223).[236]

If your child is abroad, s/he is only included in your applicable amount for IS, income-based JSA and UC for a limited period, and her absence can also affect your HB (see Chapter 67).

Bereavement benefits

You must be ordinarily resident in Great Britain on the date your spouse or civil partner died to be entitled to bereavement support payment.

You do not need to satisfy any residence or presence rules to be entitled to the 'old' bereavement benefits, except for bereavement payment.

If you are absent from Great Britain when you claim bereavement payment, you are only entitled if:[237]

- your late spouse/civil partner was in Great Britain when s/he died; *or*
- you were in Great Britain on the date of her/his death; *or*
- neither of the above two bullets apply, but you returned to Great Britain within four weeks of her/his death; *or*
- your late spouse's/civil partner's national insurance (NI) contribution record is sufficient for you to satisfy the contribution conditions for widowed parent's allowance and bereavement allowance; *or*
- your spouse/civil partner died while abroad in another European Economic Area (EEA) state and the EU co-ordination rules apply to you (see p1611);
- your spouse/civil partner died while abroad in a state which has a reciprocal agreement with the UK that covers your entitlement to a bereavement payment.

DWP guidance states that if you and your late spouse/civil partner were outside Great Britain when s/he died and you do not return to Great Britain within four weeks of the death (and none of the last three bullets above apply), you are disqualified from a bereavement payment, even if you claim within the time limit (see p536) when you are back in Great Britain.[238] It is arguable that this approach is incorrect and you should only be disqualified if you are absent from Great Britain when you make your claim (and none of the above bullets apply). Get advice if this affects you.

European Union co-ordination rules

If the EU co-ordination rules apply to you (see p1611) and the UK is your 'competent state' (see p1615):[239]

- you can rely on NI contributions paid by your late spouse/civil partner in other EEA states to calculate your entitlement to bereavement benefits (see p1617);

- if your late spouse/civil partner died in another EEA state, s/he can be treated as having died in the UK for the purposes of entitlement to bereavement payment; *and*
- you can be entitled to bereavement support payment or bereavement payment if you reside in another EEA state.

Reciprocal agreements

If you are covered by a reciprocal agreement (see p1533), these can assist in similar ways to the EU co-ordination rules in respect of the relevant country.

Child benefit and guardian's allowance

Child benefit

To be entitled to child benefit, you and your child(ren) must be present in Great Britain (see p1534).[240]

To be treated as present, you (but not your child/ren) must also:[241]

- be ordinarily resident in the UK (see p1537);
- have a right to reside in the UK (see p1544), unless your current claim began before 1 May 2004; *and*
- have been living in the UK for the three months prior to your date of claim (unless you are exempt – see p1536).

You are treated as present if you are:[242]

- a Crown servant posted overseas and:
  - you are, or immediately before your posting abroad you were, ordinarily resident in the UK; *or*
  - immediately before your posting, you were in the UK in connection with that posting; *or*
- the partner of a Crown servant posted overseas and in the same country as her/him or temporarily absent from that country under the same exceptions that enable child benefit to continue during a temporary absence from Great Britain (see p1591);
- a person who is in the UK as a result of your being deported or legally removed from another country.

You and/or your child can be treated as present for limited periods during a temporary absence (see p1591).

While you are treated as present, you continue to satisfy that condition of entitlement. This means that you can continue to receive child benefit if it is already being paid and you can also make a fresh claim during your, or your child's, absence. If you, or your child, spend longer abroad than the permitted periods (see p1591), you (or s/he) cease to satisfy the presence condition and your entitlement to child benefit ends. **Note:** if you or your child are treated as being

11

Part 11: Immigration and residence rules for benefits and tax credits
Chapter 66: Coming from abroad: residence rules
6. Rules for specific benefits and tax credits

present, you must satisfy all the other conditions of entitlement including, if your child is not living with you, contributing to the costs of that child (see p578).

Guardian's allowance

Entitlement to guardian's allowance depends on entitlement to child benefit, so you must meet the conditions for child benefit on p1573.

In addition, at least one of the child's parents must have:[243]

- been born in the UK; *or*
- at some time after reaching the age of 16, spent a total of 52 weeks in any two-year period in Great Britain.

In order to satisfy the second condition above, you are treated as being present in Great Britain during any absence abroad which is due to your employment as a serving member of the forces, an airman or airwoman, mariner or continental shelf worker.

European Union co-ordination rules

If the EU co-ordination rules apply to you (see p1611), you may be able to:

- use certain periods of residence in another EEA country to satisfy the child benefit requirement to have been living in the UK for the past three months (see p1617);
- be paid child benefit and guardian's allowance for a child who is resident in another EEA country without her/him needing to satisfy the rules on temporary absences, provided you satisfy all the other conditions of entitlement, including contributing to the costs of the child (see p578).[244] See p1618 for more details;
- use time spent in another EEA state to satisfy the requirement for guardian's allowance to have spent 52 weeks in any two-year period in Great Britain (see p1617). It may also be arguable that this condition should not apply if you have a 'genuine and sufficient link to the UK ' (see p1575).[245]

Disability benefits and carer's allowance

For attendance allowance (AA), disability living allowance (DLA), **personal independence payment (PIP) and carer's allowance (CA),** you must:[246]

- be present in Great Britain at the time of your claim;
- have been present in Great Britain for at least 104 weeks in the last 156 weeks (the 'past presence test'). See p1534, but see also the exceptions on p1575;
- be habitually resident in the common travel area (see p1537).

For **ESA in youth, incapacity benefit (IB) in youth and severe disablement allowance (SDA),** you must:[247]

- be present in Great Britain at the time of claim (see p1534);

- have been present in Great Britain for not less than 26 weeks in the last 52 weeks (the 'past presence' test). See p1534, but see also below;
- be ordinarily resident in Great Britain (see p1537).

For ESA in youth, IB in youth and SDA, once you satisfy the above, you do not need to do so again during the same period of limited capability for work or incapacity for work.[248]

When you can be treated as present

You are treated as being present during certain absences (see p1590). Any period when you are treated as present can be counted to satisfy both the presence and the past presence tests.

Exceptions to the past presence test

If you are claiming the DLA care component for a baby under six months old, there is a shorter 13-week past presence test. If covered by this, it continues to apply until your child's first birthday. If your child becomes entitled to DLA at between six and 36 months, the past presence test is 26 weeks in the last 156 weeks.

For AA, DLA and PIP, the 104-week (or 26-week or 13-week) past presence test does not apply if you are terminally ill.[249]

If you have (or a family member who you have joined under family reunion provisions has) refugee leave or humanitarian protection, you are exempt from the past presence test.[250]

European Union co-ordination rules

The EU co-ordination rules can make it easier to claim AA, DLA, PIP and CA in the UK and can also enable you to make a new claim if you live in another EEA state.

The past presence test does not apply to AA, DLA, PIP and CA if:[251]

- you are habitually resident in Great Britain; *and*
- you are covered by the co-ordination rules (see p1611); *and*
- you can demonstrate 'a genuine and sufficient link to the UK' (see below).

If you are covered by the co-ordination rules (see p1611), but are not exempt from the past presence test because you are not accepted as having 'a genuine and sufficient link to the UK', you may be able to count certain periods of residence in another EEA state to satisfy the past presence test for these benefits (and also for ESA in youth) (see p1617).[252]

If you are covered by the co-ordination rules (see p1611), you can only be entitled to AA, DLA care component, the daily living component of PIP and CA if the UK is your 'competent state'.[253] This might not be the case if you (or your family member who brings you within the co-ordination rules) receive a pension

11

Part 11: Immigration and residence rules for benefits and tax credits
Chapter 66: Coming from abroad: residence rules
6. Rules for specific benefits and tax credits

from another member state.[254] For further details, see p1615 and CPAG's *Benefits for Migrants Handbook*.

Do you have a genuine and sufficient link to the UK?

Factors that are relevant when demonstrating that you have a 'genuine and sufficient link to the UK' can include:[255]

– whether you have worked in the UK;
– whether you have spent a significant part of your life in the UK;
– whether you have been present in the UK for a reasonable period;
– whether you are receiving a UK contributory benefit;
– whether you are dependent on a family member who has worked in the UK and/or who receives a UK contributory benefit. 'Family member' in this context is not limited to people covered by the definition of 'member of the family' in the co-ordination rules (see p1611), and can, for example, include your sister.[256]

Other factors may be equally or more relevant in your case and may also be affected by the benefit you are claiming.[257]

Contributory employment and support allowance

To be entitled to contributory ESA, you must be in Great Britain.[258] The rules on when you can be paid during a temporary absence are covered in Chapter 67. There are no residence conditions, unless you are claiming contributory ESA in youth (see p1574).

European Union co-ordination rules

If the EU co-ordination rules apply to you (see p1611) and the UK is your 'competent state' (see p1615), you can, if necessary, rely on NI contributions paid in another EEA state to entitle you to contributory ESA in the UK. You may also be able to continue to receive a sickness or invalidity benefit from another EEA state.

Reciprocal agreements

If you have lived and worked in a country with which the UK has a reciprocal agreement (see p1533), you may be able to count periods of insurance paid in that country towards your entitlement to contributory ESA in the UK.

If you have moved from Northern Ireland to Great Britain (or vice versa), reciprocal arrangements in force since 6 April 2016 mean your ESA (both income-related and contributory) should be paid at the same rate.[259] If you moved before this date, DWP policy was to make extra-statutory payments to make up the loss.[260] If you were receiving these payments up to 27 November 2016 and do not satisfy the contribution conditions for contributory ESA, you are *treated as* satisfying these and as having made a claim for ESA from 27 November 2016 and your period of limited capability for work is treated as continuous.[261]

Industrial injuries benefits

To be entitled to any of the industrial injuries benefits, you must have:
- been in Great Britain when the accident at work happened;[262] *or*
- been engaged in Great Britain in the employment that caused the disease (even if you have also been engaged outside Great Britain in that employment);[263] *or*
- been paying UK class 1 or class 2 NI contributions when the accident at work happened or you contracted the disease. Benefit is not payable until you return to Great Britain.[264]

There are exceptions, which mean that you can qualify for benefit in respect of an accident which happens, or a disease which is contracted, outside Great Britain while you are:[265]
- employed as a mariner or airman or airwoman;
- employed as an apprentice pilot on board a ship or vessel;
- on board an aircraft on a test flight starting in Great Britain in the course of your employment.

In these cases, there are also more generous rules for defining when accidents arise 'out of and in the course of' your employment, and for complying with time limits under benefit rules.[266]

European Union co-ordination rules

If the EU co-ordination rules apply to you (see p1611) and the UK is your 'competent state' (see p1615), you can, if necessary, rely on periods of employment and NI paid in other EEA states in order to qualify for industrial injuries benefits in the UK (see p1617).

If you have an accident while travelling abroad in another member state, this can be deemed to have occurred in the state liable to pay industrial injuries benefits.[267] If you have worked in two or more EEA states in a job that gave you a prescribed industrial disease, you get benefit from the state in which you last did work that, by its nature, is likely to cause that disease and which recognises that disease under its industrial injuries scheme.[268]

Contribution-based jobseeker's allowance

To be entitled to contribution-based JSA, you must be in Great Britain.[269] The rules on when you can be paid during a temporary absence are covered in Chapter 67. There are no residence conditions.

European Union co-ordination rules

In most cases, if the EU co-ordination rules apply to you (see p1611), you may be able to count NI contributions paid in another EEA state to entitle you to contribution-based JSA in the UK. However, this is usually only possible if your

Part 11: Immigration and residence rules for benefits and tax credits
Chapter 66: Coming from abroad: residence rules
6. Rules for specific benefits and tax credits

most recent period of paying, or being credited with, contributions was in the UK (see p1617).[270]

If you are coming to, or returning to, the UK to look for work and have been insured in another EEA member state, you may be able to continue to receive that other state's unemployment benefit for up to three months if:[271]

- you were getting it immediately before coming to the UK;
- you have been registered as available for work for four weeks (or less, if that state's rules allow) in that member state;
- you claim JSA within seven days after you were last registered in the other member state; *and*
- you satisfy the JSA jobseeking conditions (if you do not come under the UC system – see p20), or you accept a claimant commitment and you meet your work-related requirements (if you come under the UC system – see p1071).

The three months can be extended to a maximum of six months if the state from which you are claiming the unemployment benefit agrees.[272]

Reciprocal agreements

If you have lived and worked in a country with which the UK has a reciprocal agreement (see p1533), you may be able to count periods of insurance paid in that country towards your entitlement to contribution-based JSA.

Maternity allowance

Entitlement to maternity allowance (MA) is based on past employment. There are no residence requirements, but you are disqualified if you are absent from Great Britain.[273] See p1596 for the rules allowing you to be paid during a temporary absence.

European Union co-ordination rules

If the EU co-ordination rules apply to you (see p1611) and the UK is your 'competent state' (see p1615), you can, if necessary, rely on periods of employment in other EEA states in order to qualify for MA in the UK. See p1617 for more details.

Retirement pensions

Retirement pensions, other than category D retirement pension, do not have any residence or presence entitlement conditions. They can be paid without time limit, whether or not you are present in Great Britain. However, going abroad can mean you are not paid the annual uprating, can be relevant to decisions on deferring your retirement and can prevent you from 'de-retiring' while you are abroad (see p1602).[274]

To be entitled to category D retirement pension, you must have been:[275]

- resident in Great Britain for at least 10 years in any continuous period of 20 years ending on or after your 80th birthday; *and*
- ordinarily resident (see p1537) in Great Britain on either:
  - your 80th birthday; *or*
  - the date on which you claimed category D pension, if later.

European Union co-ordination rules

If the co-ordination rules apply to you (see p1611) and the UK is your 'competent state' (see p1615), you can, if necessary, rely on NI contributions paid, or for category D retirement pension, certain periods of residence completed, in other EEA states to calculate your entitlement to retirement pensions in the UK (see p1617). However, your award may be reduced to reflect the proportion of years of contributions paid, or periods of residence completed, in the UK out of the total years of contributions paid or periods of residence completed in all states.[276] The requirement to be ordinarily resident for category D retirement pension may not apply to you if you can show that you have a 'genuine and sufficient link to the UK' (see p1575).[277]

Reciprocal agreements

If you have lived and worked in a country with which the UK has a reciprocal agreement (see p1533), you may be able to count periods of residence or insurance paid in that country towards your UK retirement pension entitlement.

Social fund funeral and winter fuel payments

Funeral expenses payment

To qualify for a funeral payment:
- the person who has died must have been ordinarily resident (see p1537) in the UK;[278]
- the funeral must usually take place in the UK. However, it can take place in any EEA state if you or your partner are:[279]
  - an EEA national and a worker, including if you have retained this status (see p1554);
  - an EEA national and a self-employed person, including if you have retained this status (see p1558);
  - a family member of one of the above (see p1560);
  - an EEA national with a permanent right of residence acquired in less than five years (see p1568);
  - arguably, a person with any other right of residence in the UK under EU law. For further details, see CPAG's *Benefits for Migrants Handbook*.[280]

Winter fuel payments

To qualify for a winter fuel payment, you must be ordinarily resident (see p1537) in Great Britain on any day in the qualifying week (see p798).[281]

11

Part 11: Immigration and residence rules for benefits and tax credits
Chapter 66: Coming from abroad: residence rules
6. Rules for specific benefits and tax credits

European Union co-ordination rules

You are not required to be ordinarily resident in Great Britain in order to be entitled to a winter fuel payment if, on any day in the qualifying week, you are:[282]

- covered by the EU co-ordination rules (see p1611);
- habitually resident in Switzerland or an EEA country (other than Cyprus, France, Gibraltar, Greece, Malta, Portugal, Spain or the UK); *and*
- can demonstrate a 'genuine and sufficient link to the UK' (see p1575).

Tax credits

To be entitled to **child tax credit** (CTC), you (and your partner if you are making a joint claim) must:[283]

- be present in the UK (see p1534);
- be ordinarily resident in the UK (see p1537);
- have a right to reside in the UK (see p1544), unless you have been receiving CTC since before 1 May 2004; *and*
- have been living in the UK for the three months prior to your date of claim (unless you are exempt – see p1536).

To be entitled to **working tax credit** (WTC), you (and your partner if you are making a joint claim) must be:[284]

- present in the UK (see p1534); *and*
- ordinarily resident in the UK (see p1537).

There are limited exceptions for Crown servants posted overseas, and from the requirement to be ordinarily resident (although in practice, claims are rarely refused on the latter basis).[285]

For the rules on when you can be treated as present, and can therefore either continue to receive tax credits or make a fresh or renewal claim, see p1604.

Being absent (except when when you are treated as being present), ceasing to be ordinarily resident or losing your right to reside are all changes that you must notify to HM Revenue and Customs (HMRC) within one month. If you do not, HMRC may recover any overpaid tax credits (see Chapter 62) and impose a penalty (see Chapter 63).

Couples

If you are a member of a couple and make a joint tax credit claim, you must both satisfy the residence requirements. Your entitlement to tax credits as a couple ends if HMRC considers that you and your partner have separated and this is likely to be permanent,[286] or if either you or your partner:

- are abroad for longer than a permitted temporary absence (see p1604);
- (for CTC only) lose the right to reside;
- cease to be ordinarily resident.

The person who continues to satisfy the residence rules can make a fresh claim for CTC and/or WTC as a single person if s/he is entitled on that basis.

If the partner returns to the UK, or becomes ordinarily resident or acquires a right to reside, you must terminate the single person claim and claim again as a couple.

If you or your partner are abroad (even during a period while treated as present) and you (or s/he) were the only partner in full-time work, you may lose entitlement to WTC if the requirement to be in full-time work is no longer satisfied (see p196).

You have a duty to notify HMRC of any of the above changes within one month (see p1462). If you fail to do so, HMRC may recover any overpaid tax credits (see Chapter 64) and impose a penalty (see Chapter 65).

European Union co-ordination rules

If the EU co-ordination rules apply to you (see p1611), you may be able to be paid CTC for a partner or child resident in another EEA country. See p1618 for more details.

Notes

2. The different residence and presence tests

1 Confirmed in Vol 2 para 072996 DMG
2 *AEKM v Department for Communities (JSA)* [2016] NICom 80, paras 21, 46-48 and 61
3 Reg 85A(2) JSA Regs
4 Reg 3 JSA(HR)A Regs
5 *AEKM v Department for Communities (JSA)* [2016] NICom 80, paras 50-62 and caselaw cited
6 *Swaddling v Chief Adjudication Officer*, C-90/97 [1999] ECR I-01075
7 **CB** Reg 23(5) CB Regs
   CTC Reg 3(6) TC(R) Regs
8 **CB** Reg 23(6) CB Regs
   CTC Reg 3(7) TC(R) Regs
9 **CB** Reg 23(3) CB Regs
   CTC Reg 3(3) TC(R) Regs
10 R(IS) 6/96, para 19; R(P) 2/67
11 R(M) 1/85

12 *R v Barnet London Borough Council ex parte Shah* [1983] 2 AC 309; *GC v HMRC (TC)* [2014] UKUT 251 (AAC)
13 *MS v SSWP (DLA)* [2016] UKUT 42 (AAC)

3. Habitual residence

14 **IS** Regs 21 and 21AA IS Regs
   JSA Regs 85 and 85A JSA Regs
   ESA Regs 69 and 70 ESA Regs
   PC Reg 2 SPC Regs
   HB Reg 10 HB Regs; reg 10 HB(SPC) Regs
   UC Reg 9 UC Regs
   AA Reg 2(1)(a)(i) SS(AA) Regs
   DLA Reg 2(1)(a)(i) SS(DLA) Regs
   PIP Reg 16(c) SS(PIP) Regs
   CA Reg 9(1)(a) SS(ICA) Regs
15 Reg 12 CTRS(PR)E Regs; reg 16 CTR(SPC)S Regs; reg 16 CTR(S) Regs; reg 28 CTRSPR(W) Regs; Sch para 19 CTRS(DS)W Regs
16 Reg 1(2),(3) and (4) SS(DLA,AA&CA)(A) Regs

11

Part 11: Immigration and residence rules for benefits and tax credits
Chapter 66: Coming from abroad: residence rules
Notes

17 Regs 3(3), 18(2), 22(3) and 36(3) UC Regs
18 **IS** Regs 21 and 21AA and Sch 7 para 17 IS Regs
JSA Regs 85 and 85A and Sch 5 para 14 JSA Regs
ESA Regs 69 and 70 and Sch 5 para 11 ESA Regs
19 Reg 10(1) HB Regs; reg 10(1) HB(SPC) Regs
20 **PC** Reg 2 SPC Regs
UC Reg 9 UC Regs
21 **AA** s35(1) SSA 1975; reg 2(1) SS(AA) Regs
DLA s71(6) SSCBA 1992; reg 2(1) SS(DLA) Regs
PIP s77(3) WRA 2012; reg 16 SS(PIP) Regs
CA s70(4) SSCBA 1992; reg 9(1) SS(ICA) Regs
22 Confirmed in *EP v SSWP (JSA)* [2016] UKUT 445 (AAC), paras 24-25
23 R(IS) 6/96
24 **IS** Reg 21AA(4) IS Regs
JSA Reg 85A(4) JSA Regs
ESA Reg 70(4) ESA Regs
PC Reg 2(4) SPC Regs
HB Reg 10(3B) HB Regs; reg 10(4A) HB(SPC) Regs
UC Reg 9(4) UC Regs
25 Reg 3 HB(HR)A Regs
26 **AA** Reg 2(3A) SS(AA) Regs
DLA Reg 2(3A) SS(DLA) Regs
PIP Reg 20 SS(PIP) Regs
CA Reg 9(3) SS(ICA) Regs
27 R(IS) 6/96, paras 17 and 20; CIS/13498/96, para 17
28 CIS/15927/1996
29 *R v Barnet London Borough Council ex parte Shah* [1983] 2 AC 309, para 344; CIS/13498/1996
30 R(IS) 2/00; CIS/4474/2003
31 *Nessa v Chief Adjudication Officer* [1999] UKHL 41
32 CIS/4474/2003
33 CIS/1972/2003
34 CIS/1304/97; CJSA/5394/98
35 CIS/1304/1997; CJSA/5394/1998
36 Art 70 EU Reg 883/04; Art 10a EU Reg 1408/71; *Swaddling v Adjudication Officer*, C-90/97 [1999] ECR I-01075
37 CIS/12703/1996
38 *KS v SSWP (SPC)* [2010] UKUT 156 (AAC)
39 R(IS) 2/00; CIS/11481/1995

4. Right to reside

40 Reg 12 CTRS(PR)E Regs; reg 16 CTR(SPC)S Regs; reg 16 CTR(S) Regs; reg 28 CTRSPR(W) Regs; Sch para 19 CTRS(DS)W Regs
41 Reg 6 SS(HR)A Regs; reg 11 SS(PA)A Regs
42 Reg 70(4)(l) ESA Regs
43 **IS** Reg 21AA(2) and (3) IS Regs
JSA Reg 85A(2) and (3) JSA Regs
ESA Reg 70(2) and (3) ESA Regs
PC Reg 2(2) and (3) SPC Regs
HB Reg 10(3) and (3A) HB Regs; reg 10(3) and (4) HB(SPC) Regs
UC Reg 9(3) UC Regs
44 *Sanneh and Others v SSWP* [2015] EWCA Civ 49. The appeal to the Supreme Court in the joined case of *HC* is due to be heard on 21 and 22 July 2017: *R (on the application of HC) v SSWP* UKSC 2015/0215
45 *Slezak v SSWP* [2017] CSIH 4
46 **CB** Reg 23(4) CB Regs
TC Reg 3(5) TC(R) Regs
47 **CB** Reg 23(4) CB Regs
TC Reg 3(5) TC(R) Regs
48 *Sanneh and Others v SSWP* [2015] EWCA Civ 49. The appeal to the Supreme Court in the joined case of *HC* is due to be heard on 21 and 22 July 2017: *R (on the application of HC) v SSWP* UKSC 2015/0215

5. Who has a right to reside

49 Decision of the EEA Joint Committee No.158/2007
50 Swiss nationals: *Agreement between the European Community and its Member States, of the one part, and the Swiss Confederation, of the other, on the Free Movement of Persons*, 21 June 1999, Cmd 5639. In force from 1 June 2002.
51 Reg 2(1) I(EEA) Regs
52 Reg 1 I(EEA) Regs – except reg 9, which was replaced from 25 November 2016
53 Regs 6 and 14(1) I(EEA) Regs. The same groups are covered in Arts 7 and 14 EU Dir 2004/38 but the term 'qualified person' is not used in the Directive.
54 *SSWP v JB (JSA)* [2011] UKUT 96 (AAC)
55 *TG v SSWP (PC)* [2015] UKUT 50 (AAC)
56 *SSWP v Gubeladze*, C3/2015/1796
57 Reg 8 AC(IWA) Regs
58 Reg 9 A(IWA) Regs
59 Reg 7 A(IWR) Regs
60 Regs 4 and 5 AC(IWA) Regs
61 Reg 6 A(IWA) Regs; reg 7B I(EEA) Regs
62 Reg 5 A(IWR) Regs; reg 7A I(EEA) Regs

11

63 *RP v SSWP (ESA)* (interim decision) [2016] UKUT 422 (AAC), case ref: *Prefata*, C-618/16

64 CIS/1042/2008; *SSWP v JB* [2011] UKUT 96 (AAC)

65 Reg 2 AC(IWA) Regs; reg 2 A(IWA) Regs

66 Reg 4 A(IWA) Regs; reg 3 AC(IWA) Regs

67 Reg 2 A(IWR) Regs

68 Reg 2(5) AC(IWA) Regs; reg 2(12) A(IWA) Regs

70 Reg 2(7) A(IWR) Regs

71 *Miskovic and Another v SSWP* [2011] EWCA Civ 16

72 Reg 7 A(IWR) Regs

73 *SSWP v ZA* [2009] UKUT 294 (AAC); *Szpak v SSWP* [2013] EWCA Civ 46

74 *BS v SSWP* [2009] UKUT 16 (AAC)

75 Reg 13(1) and (3) I(EEA) Regs; Arts 6(1) and 14(1) EU Dir 2004/38

76 Reg 13(2) and (3) I(EEA) Regs; Art 6(2) EU Dir 2004/38

77 Art 45 TFEU; Arts 14 and 24 EU Dir 2004/38; reg 6 I(EEA) Regs

78 Reg 6(1) and (7) I(EEA) Regs; Sch 3 para 1 I(EEA)A Regs; reg 4 Immigration (European Economic Area) (Amendment) (No.3) Regulations 2014, No.2761

79 *The Queen v Immigration Appeal Tribunal, ex parte Antonissen*, C-292/89 [1991] ECR I-00745

80 R(IS) 8/08

81 *The Queen v Immigration Appeal Tribunal, ex parte Antonissen*, C-292/89 [1991] ECR I-00745

82 R(IS) 8/08

83 Reg 6 I(EEA) Regs

84 Reg 6(1), (8) and (9) I(EEA) Regs

85 Confirmed in Vol 2 para 073080 DMG and C1403 ADM

86 Vol 2 para 073108 DMG; DMG Memo 18/15

87 *KS v SSWP* [2016] UKUT 269 (AAC) and ECJ caselaw cited

88 *The Queen v Immigration Appeal Tribunal, ex parte Antonissen*, C-292/89 [1991] ECR I-00745, para 21

89 *SSWP v MB (JSA) (and linked cases)* [2016] UKUT 372 (AAC), para 51

90 *SSWP v MB (JSA) (and linked cases)* [2016] UKUT 372 (AAC), paras 47-48

91 Vol 2 paras 073080-140 DMG; paras C1403-35 ADM

92 Confirmed in Vol 2 paras 073122 and 073160 DMG

93 Regs 6(1) and 14 I(EEA) Regs; Arts 7(1) and 14 EU Dir 2004/38

94 *Lawrie-Blum v Land Baden-Württemberg*, C-66/85 [1986] ECR 02121

95 *Barry v LB Southwark* [2008] EWCA Civ 1440

96 *Rinner-Kühn v FWW Spezial-Gebäudereinigung GmbH and Co. KG*, 171/88 [1989] ECR 02743

97 R(IS) 12/98

98 *Genc v Land Berlin*, C-14/09 [2010] ECR I-00931

99 *Steymann v Staatssecretaris van Justitie*, 196/87 [1988] ECR 06159

100 CIS/1837/2006; CIS/868/2008

101 *I Bettray v Staatssecretaris van Justitie*, C-344/87 [1989] ECR 01621; *Genc v Land Berlin*, C-14/09 [2010] ECR I-00931

102 CIS/1502/2007

103 *JA v SSWP (ESA)* [2012] UKUT 122 (AAC), cited with approval in *EP v SSWP (JSA)* [2016] UKUT 445 (AAC) para 21

104 Vol 2 para 073040 DMG; para C1489 ADM; HB A3/2014, para 15; 'CB and CTC: right to reside establishing whether an EEA national is/was a worker or a self-employed person under EU law', para 7

105 CIS/4237/2007

106 *BS v SSWP* [2009] UKUT 16 (AAC)

107 Art 7(3) EU Dir 2004/38; reg 6(1), (2) and (3) and (5)-(7) I(EEA) Regs

108 *Saint Prix v SSWP*, C-507/12 [2014] ECR, not yet reported

109 Reg 5(4) A(IWR) Regs; reg 7A(4) I(EEA) Regs

110 Art 7(3)(b) and (c) EU Dir 2004/38; reg 6 I(EEA) Regs

111 Art 7(3)(b) and (c) EU Dir 2004/38

112 CH/3314/2005, para 11; *SSWP v MK* [2013] UKUT 163 (AAC)

113 *SSWP v Elmi* [2011] EWCA Civ 1403

114 Art 7(3)(b) EU Dir 2004/38; reg 6(2)(b), (5) and (6) I(EEA) Regs; *SSWP v MM* [2015] UKUT 128 (AAC), para 54

115 Reg 6(1) and (7) I(EEA) Regs

116 Reg 6(2)(c), (3), (5) and (6) I(EEA) Regs

117 Art 7(3)(c) EU Dir 2004/38

118 *SSHD v FB* [2010] UKUT 447 (IAC); *LM v HMRC (CHB)* [2016] UKUT 389 (AAC)

119 CIS/3890/2005

120 *De Brito v SSHD* [2012] EWCA Civ 709; *Konodyba v RB of K&C* [2012] EWCA Civ 982; *Samin v SSHD* [2012] EWCA Civ 1468

121 CIS/4304/2007

122 CIS/3182/2005

123 *SSWP v EM* [2009] UKUT 146 (AAC)

124 CIS/4237/2007

11

Part 11: Immigration and residence rules for benefits and tax credits
Chapter 66: Coming from abroad: residence rules
Notes

125 CIS/1042/2008; *HMRC v GP* [2017] UKUT 11 (AAC)

126 CIS/731/2007

127 *Saint Prix v SSWP*, C-507/12 CR, not yet reported

128 *SSWP v SFF and Others* [2015] UKUT 502 (AAC); *Weldemichael and Another v SSHD* [2015] UKUT 540 (IAC)

129 CIS/4304/2007; *SSWP v IR* [2009] UKUT 11 (AAC); *SSWP v SFF and Others* [2015] UKUT 502 (AAC), para 40

130 CIS/1934/2006

131 *SSWP v MK* [2013] UKUT 163 (AAC); *VP v SSWP (JSA)* [2014] UKUT 32 (AAC), paras 56-61; *SSWP v MM* [2015] UKUT 128 (AAC), paras 47-52

132 *SSWP v IR* [2009] UKUT 11 (AAC)

133 Regs 6(1) and 14 I(EEA) Regs; Arts 7(1) and 14 EU Dir 2004/38

134 *Jany and Others v Staatssecretaris van Justitie*, C-268/99 [2001] ECR I-08615

135 Reg 4(1)(b) I(EEA) Regs

136 *TG v SSWP* [2009] UKUT 58 (AAC)

137 *SSWP v JS (IS)* [2010] UKUT 240 (AAC)

138 CIS/1042/2008; *HMRC v GP* [2017] UKUT 11 (AAC)

139 Art 7(3) EU Dir 2004/38; reg 6(4) I(EEA) Regs

140 *Gusa*, C-442/16, not yet decided

141 *R (Tilianu) v SSWP* [2010] EWCA Civ 1397

142 Art 7(1) EU Dir 2004/38; regs 4(1)(c) and (2)-(4), 6(1) and 14(1) I(EEA) Regs

143 *Pensionsversicherungsanstalt v Brey*, C-140/12 [2013] ECR, not yet reported, paras 54-57

144 Art 8(4) EU Dir 2004/38

145 Reg 4(4) I(EEA) Regs

146 *SG v Tameside MBC (HB)* [2010] UKUT 243 (AAC)

147 *Pensionsversicherungsanstalt v Brey*, C-140/12 [2013] ECR, not yet reported; see also *AMS v SSWP (PC)* [2017] UKUT 48 (AAC)

148 *Commission of the European Communities v Kingdom Belgium*, C-408/03 [2006] ECR I-02647; *Zhu and Chen v SSHD*, C-200/02 [2004] ECR I-09925

149 *VP v SSWP (JSA)* [2014] UKUT 32 (AAC), paras 88-97

150 *Singh and Others v Minister of Justice and Equality* C-218/14 [2015] ECR, not yet reported

151 *W (China) and Another v SSHD* [2006] EWCA Civ 1494

152 *SG v Tameside MBC (HB)* [2010] UKUT 243 (AAC); *SSWP v GS (PC)* [2016] UKUT 394 (AAC)

153 Art 7(1) EU Dir 2004/38; regs 4(1)(d) and (2)-(4), 6(1) and 14(1) I(EEA) Regs

154 Art 2(2) EU Dir 2004/38; reg 7(1) I(EEA) Regs

155 *Diatta v Land Berlin*, 267/83 [1985] ECR 00567

156 CIS/2100/2007, which considers the findings of *Centre Public d'Aide Sociale de Courcelles v Lebon*, 316/85 [1987] ECR 02811; *Zhu and Chen v SSHD*, C-200/02 [2004] ECR I-09925; and *Jia v Migrationsverket*, C-1/05 [2007] ECR I-00001

157 *Reyes v Migrationsverket* C-423/12 [2014] ECR, not yet reported; *Centre Public d'Aide Social de Courcelles v Lebon* C-316/85 [1987] ECR 02811; *ECO v Lim (EEA dependency)* [2013] UKUT 437 (IAC)

158 *Pedro v SSWP* [2009] EWCA Civ 1358; *Jia v Migrationsverket*, C-1/05 [2007] ECR I-00001; *SSHD v Rahman and Others*, C-83/11 [2012] ECR, not yet reported; *Oboh and Others v SSHD* [2013] EWCA Civ 1525

159 *Kerr v DSDNI* [2004] UKHL 23, paras 62-69

160 Reg 7(3) I(EEA) Regs; CPC/3588/2006; *SS v SSWP (ESA)* [2010] UKUT 8 (AAC); *SSWP v LZ (SPC)* [2014] UKUT 147 (AAC)

161 Reg 8 I(EEA) Regs. Most of these groups are covered in Art 3 EU Dir 2004/38, but the term is not used.

162 See also *AA (Algeria) v SSHD* [2014] EWCA Civ 1741; *Dauhoo (EEA Regs – Reg 8(2)) v SSHD* [2012] UKUT 79 (IAC)

163 *R v IAT et Surinder Singh ex parte SSHD*, C-370/90 [1992] ECR I-4265; *O and B v Minister voor Immigratie, Integratie en Asiel*, C-456/12 [2014] ECR, not yet reported; *VW v SSWP (PC)* [2014] UKUT 573 (AAC)

164 Regs 1, 7(4) and 9 I(EEA) Regs since 1 February 2017 and reg 4 and Sch 5 I(EEA) Regs for the earlier period

165 Reg 9(4) I(EEA) Regs

166 *O and B v Minister voor Immigratie, Intergratie en Asiel*, C-456/12 [2014] ERC, not yet reported

167 *Minister voor Vreemdelingenzaken en Integratie v Eind*, C-291/05 [2007] ECR I-10719

168 Reg 9(4) I(EEA) Regs

169 *AA v SSWP* [2009] UKUT 249 (AAC); *HG v SSWP (SPC)* [2011] UKUT 382 (AAC)

170 Sch 3 I(EEA)A Regs 2012 up to 1 February 2017, and Sch 6 para 9 I(EEA) Regs since 1 February 2017

171 *McCarthy v SSHD*, C-434-09 [2011] ECR I-03375

172 Reg 2(1) I(EEA) Regs

173 *Lounes v SSHD* [2016] EWHC 436 (Admin)

174 Reg 10 I(EEA) Regs

175 Reg 14(3) I(EEA) Regs

176 Reg 10(9) I(EEA) Regs

177 Art 12 EU Dir 2004/38

178 Art 12 EU Dir 2004/38

179 Art 13 EU Dir 2004/38

180 *Singh and Others v Minister of Justice and Equality,* C- 218/14 [2015] ECR, not yet reported

181 *SSHD v NA,* C-115/15 [2016] ECR, not yet reported

182 Arts 12, 13 and 18 EU Dir 2004/38

183 Reg 16 I(EEA) Regs

184 *Baumbast and R v SSHD*, C-413/99 [2002] ECR I-07091, para 57; *IP v SSWP (IS)* [2015] UKUT 691 (AAC)

185 See also *London Borough of Harrow v Ibrahim and SSHD*, C-310/08 [2010] ECR I-01065; *Teixeira v London Borough of Lambeth and SSHD*, C-480/08 [2010] ECR I-01107; *GBC Echternach and A Moritz v Minister van Onderwijs en Wetenschappen,* joined cases C-389/87 and C-390/87 [1989] ECR 00723; *Baumbast and R v SSHD*, C-413/99 [2002] ECR I-07091

186 See also *London Borough of Harrow v Ibrahim and SSHD*, C-310/08 [2010] ECR I-01065; *Teixeira v London Borough of Lambeth and SSHD*, C-480/08 [2010] ECR I-01107; *GBC Echternach and A Moritz v Minister van Onderwijs en Wetenschappen,* joined cases C-389/87 and C-390/87 [1989] ECR 00723; *Baumbast and R v SSHD*, C-413/99 [2002] ECR I-07091

187 See also *Zhu and Chen v SSHD*, C-200/02 [2004] ECR I-09925; *SSHD v NA*, C-115/15 [2016] not yet reported

188 See also *Zambrano v ONEm*, C-34/09 [2011] ECR I-01177; *Dereci and Others v Bundesministerium für Inneres*, C-256/11 [2011] ECR I-11315

189 Reg 16(8)-(11) I(EEA) Regs. See also *MA v DSD (JSA)* [2011] NICom 205; *SSWP v MH (IS)* [2016] UKUT 526 (AAC)

190 *Sanneh and Others v SSWP* [2015] EWCA Civ 49. The appeal to the Supreme Court in the joined case of *HC* is due to be heard on 21 and 22 July 2017: *R (on the application of HC) v SSWP* UKSC 2015/0215

191 *Baumbast and R v SSHD*, C-413/99 [2002] ECR I-07091, para 57; *IP v SSWP (IS)* [2015] UKUT 691 (AAC)

192 *Teixeira v London Borough of Lambeth and SSHD*, C-480/08 [2010] ECR I-01107, para 74

193 *SSWP v JS (IS)* [2010] UKUT 347 (AAC)

194 *DJ v SSWP* [2013] UKUT 113 (AAC)

195 *Teixeira v London Borough of Lambeth and SSHD*, C-480/08 [2010] ECR I-01107, para 87; see also *Alarape and Tijani v SSHD*, C-529/11 [2013] ECR, not yet reported

196 Reg 16(7(a) I(EEA) Regs; DMG Memo 24/16, para 15; see also CIS/3960/2007; *Shabani v SSHD* [2013] UKUT 315 (IAC)

197 Joined cases of *Czop* (C-147/11) and *Punakova* (C-148/11) [2012] ECR, not yet reported; *RM v SSWP (IS)* [2014] UKUT 401 (AAC)

198 *Hrabkova v SSWP* C3/2015/2886, heard in the Court of Appeal, awaiting judgment

199 Art 16 EU Dir 2004/38; reg 15 I(EEA) Regs

200 Art 16(4) EU Dir 2004/38; reg 15(3) I(EEA) Regs

201 *Idezuna v SSHD* [2011] UKUT 474 (IAC); *Babajanov v SSHD* [2013] UKUT 513 (IAC)

202 Art 16(3) EU Dir 2004/38; reg 3 I(EEA) Regs

203 *SSHD v Ojo* [2015] EWCA Civ 1301 argument applied: *SSWP v Dias,* C-325/09 [2011] ECR I-06387

204 Vol 2 paras 073433-35 DMG; paras C1812-14 ADM

205 *Nnamdi Onuekwere v SSHD*, C-378/12 [2014] ECR, not yet reported; reg 3(3) I(EEA) Regs

206 Reg 3(3) I(EEA) Regs

207 Sch 6 para 8 I(EEA) Regs

208 Reg 15(1) and (2) I(EEA) Regs

209 Art 16(1) EU Dir 2004/38

210 *SSWP v Taous Lassal*, C-162/09 [2010] ECR I-09217; *SSWP v Dias*, C-325-09 [2011] ECR I-06387

211 *Oakafor and Others v SSHD* [2011] EWCA Civ 499; *Alarape and Tijani v SSHD*, C-529/11 [2013] ECR, not yet reported; *Bee and Another v SSHD* [2013] UKUT 83 (IAC)

212 *Ziolkowski* (C-425/10) and *Szeja* (C-425/10) *v Land Berlin* [2011] ECR I-14035

213 *Ziolkowski* (C-425/10) and *Szeja* (C-425/10) *v Land Berlin* [2011] ECR I-14035; Sch 6 para 8(3) I(EEA) Regs

11

Part 11: Immigration and residence rules for benefits and tax credits
Chapter 66: Coming from abroad: residence rules
Notes

• •

214 Reg 14(2) I(EEA) Regs
215 Regs 14(2) and 15(1)(a) and (b) I(EEA) Regs
216 Regs 5 and 15 I(EEA) Regs; Art 17 EU Dir 2004/38
217 *PM (EEA – spouse - 'residing with') Turkey* [2011] UKUT 89 (IAC)
218 Regs 5(7) and 6(2), and Sch 4 para 2 I(EEA) Regs; regs 7A(3) and 7B(4) I(EEA) Regs; Art 17(1) EU Dir 2004/38
219 See, for example, *Mirga v SSWP* [2016] UKSC 1
220 *SSWP v Dias*, C-325/09 [2011] ECR I006387; *EM and KN v SSWP* [2009] UKUT 44 (AAC); *MD v SSWP (SPC)* [2016] UKUT 319 (AAC)
221 Reg 17 I(EEA) Regs
222 Reg 18 I(EEA) Regs
223 Reg 20 I(EEA) Regs
224 Reg 19 I(EEA) Regs
225 Reg 45 and Sch 6 para 2 I(EEA) Regs
226 Reg 12 I(EEA) Regs

6. Rules for specific benefits and tax credits

227 **IS** s124(1) SSCBA 1992
   JSA s1(2)(i) JSA 1995
   ESA s1(3)(d) WRA 2007
   PC s1(2)(a) SPCA 2002
   UC s4(1)(c) WRA 2012
228 **IS** Regs 21-21AA IS Regs
   JSA Regs 85-85A JSA Regs
   ESA Regs 69-70 ESA Regs
   PC Reg 2 SPC Regs
   UC Reg 9 UC Regs
229 Regs 3(3), 9, 18(2), 22(3) and 36(3) UC Regs
230 Sch 5 WRA(No.9)O, as applied in UC areas by subsequent commencement orders
231 Reg 10 HB Regs; reg 10 HB(SPC) Regs
232 Regs 3, 18(2), 22(3) and 36(3) UC Regs
233 **IS** Reg 16 IS Regs
   JSA Reg 78 JSA Regs
   ESA Reg 156 ESA Regs
   PC Reg 5 SPC Regs
   HB Reg 21 HB Regs; reg 21 HB(SPC) Regs
   UC Regs 3(3) and (6), 18(2), 22(3) and 36(3) UC Regs
234 CIS/508/1992; CIS/13805/1996
235 CIS/484/1993

236 **IS** Reg 16 IS Regs
   JSA Reg 78 JSA Regs
   ESA Reg 156 ESA Regs
   PC Reg 5 SPC Regs
   HB Reg 21 HB Regs; reg 21 HB(SPC) Regs
   UC Reg 4(7) UC Regs
237 s113 SSCBA 1992; reg 4(1) and (2B) SSB(PA) Regs
238 Vol 2 para 077081 DMG, Example 2
239 Arts 5, 6, 7, 42 and 43 EU Reg 883/04
240 s146 SSCBA 1992
241 Reg 23 CB Regs
242 Regs 23, 30 and 31 CB Regs
243 Reg 9 GA(Gen) Regs
244 *RK v HMRC (CHB)* [2015] UKUT 357 (AAC)
245 *Stewart v SSWP*, C-503/09 [2011] ECR I-06497
246 **AA** Reg 2 SS(AA) Regs
   DLA Reg 2 SS(DLA) Regs
   PIP Reg 16 SS(PIP) Regs
   CA Reg 9 SS(ICA) Regs
247 **ESA** Reg 11 ESA Regs; reg 12 ESA Regs 2013
   AA Reg 2 SS(AA) Regs
   DLA Reg 2 SS(DLA) Regs
   CA Reg 9 SS(ICA) Regs
   IB Reg 16 SS(IB) Regs
   SDA Reg 3 SS(SDA) Regs
248 **ESA** Reg 11(4) ESA Regs; reg 12(4) ESA Regs 2013
   IB Reg 16(6) SS(IB) Regs
   SDA Reg 3(3) SS(SDA) Regs
249 **AA** Reg 2(3) SS(AA) Regs
   DLA Reg 2(4) SS(DLA) Regs
   PIP Reg 21 SS(PIP) Regs
250 *MM and IS v SSWP (DLA)* [2016] UKUT 149 (AAC), confirmed in DMG Memo 20/16 and ADM Memo 21/16
251 **AA** Reg 2A SS(AA) Regs
   DLA Reg 2A SS(DLA) Regs
   PIP Reg 22 SS(PIP) Regs
   CA Reg 9A SS(ICA) Regs
252 Art 6 and Annex XI UK entry para 2 EU Reg 883/04; *SSWP v MM and BK v SSWP* [2016] UKUT 547 (AAC)
253 ss65(7), 70(4A) and 72(7B) SSCBA; s84 WRA 2012
254 Arts 23-32 EU Reg 883/04
255 *Stewart v SSWP*, C-503/09 [2011] ECR I-06497; *SSWP v MM and BK v SSWP* [2016] UKUT 547 (AAC) held that the link must be to the UK, not to the UK social security system as specified in the Regulations (paras 28-31). Leave to appeal to the Court of Appeal is being sought.

11

256 *PB v SSWP (DLA)* [2016] UKUT 280 (AAC)
257 *SSWP v JG (IS)* [2013] UKUT 298 (AAC);
     SSWP v Garland [2014] EWCA Civ 1550
258 ss1(3)(d) and 18(4)(a) WRA 2007
259 SS(NIRA) Regs; SS(GBRA)NI Regs
260 DWP guidance, *Extra-statutory Payments
     for Claimants Moving From Northern
     Ireland to Great Britain*, available at
     www.cpag.org.uk/content/dwp-
     guidance-extra-statutory-payments-esa
261 Sch Art 2A-2B SS(NIRA) Regs; Sch Art
     2A-2B SS(GBRA)NI Regs
262 s94(5) SSCBA 1992
263 Reg 14 SS(IIPD) Regs
264 Reg 10C(5) and (6) SSB(PA) Regs
265 Reg 2 SS(II)(AB) Regs; reg 2 SS(II)(MB)
     Regs
266 Regs 3, 4, 6 and 8 SS(II)(MB) Regs; regs
     3 and 6 SS(II)(AB) Regs
267 Art 5 EU Reg 883/04
268 Art 38 EU Reg 883/04; Art 36 EU Reg
     987/09; *SSWP v OF (by MF) (II)* UKUT
     [2011] 448 (AAC)
269 s1(2)(i) JSA 1995
270 Art 61(2) EU Reg 883/04
271 Art 64 EU Reg 883/04
272 Art 64(3) EU Reg 883/04
273 s113(1) SSCBA 1992
274 s113 SSCBA 1992; reg 4(1) SSB(PA)
     Regs
275 Reg 10 SS(WB&RP) Regs
276 Art 52 EU Reg 883/04
277 *Stewart v SSWP*, C-503/09 [2011] ECR, I-
     06497; *SSWP v Garland* [2014] EWCA
     Civ 1550, paras 14 and 28
278 Reg 7(5) SFM&FE Regs
279 Reg 7(9) and (10) SFM&FE Regs
280 *John O'Flynn v Adjudication Officer*, C-
     237/94 [1996] ECR I-02617 (R(IS) 4/
     98); Art 24 EU Dir 2004/38
281 Reg 2 SFWFP Regs
282 Reg 2 SFWFP Regs
283 s3(3) TCA 2002; reg 3(1) and (5) TC(R)
     Regs
284 s3(3) TCA 2002; reg 3(1) TC(R) Regs; *GC
     v HMRC (TC)* [2014] UKUT 251 (AAC)
     contains useful discussion of these
     requirements
285 Reg 3 TC(R) Regs
286 s3(5A) TCA 2002

11

Chapter 67

Going abroad

This chapter covers:
1. The rules on getting paid abroad (below)
2. Rules for specific benefits and tax credits (see p1590)

Key facts

- Most benefits and tax credits are affected if you, or your partner or child, go abroad.
- In certain circumstances, you can continue to receive benefit for a set number of weeks while you are away for a temporary period.
- You may be entitled to receive UK benefits for a longer (or indefinite) period if you go to another European Economic Area state.

1. The rules on getting paid abroad

Most benefits and tax credits are affected if you, or your partner or child, go abroad. Some can always be paid abroad, some can only be paid in certain circumstances and for limited periods, and some have rules affecting the amount that can be paid if you are abroad.

Your entitlement abroad depends on:
- the benefit or tax credit you are claiming (see p1590);
- the reason why you are going abroad;
- whether your absence is temporary or permanent;
- the length of time you are going abroad for;
- the country you are going to;
- whether you are covered by the European Union (EU) co-ordination rules;
- whether you are covered by a reciprocal agreement.

Which rules apply

The **UK benefit and tax credit legislation** contains rules about how your absence affects your entitlement (see p1589). If these allow your entitlement to continue when you are abroad, you do not need to check the other rules.

The **EU co-ordination rules** can be more generous. If you are a European Economic Area (EEA) national (see p1609) (including a British citizen) or a family member of an EEA national and you are going to another EEA state, you may benefit from these. They can help you to be paid your benefits or tax credits when you go abroad for longer than would be the case under UK law. They can also enable you to be paid benefit for a family member living in another EEA state. See pp1590–1606 for information on individual benefits and tax credits and see Chapter 68 for further information on the co-ordination rules.

Reciprocal agreements exist between the UK and some other countries, and can assist in similar ways to the EU co-ordination rules (see p1533). In general, these only apply if the EU coordination rules do not assist you. Great Britain and Northern Ireland also have reciprocal agreements. See p1533 for the countries with agreements.

UK law

Ordinary residence

In order to receive some benefits and tax credits (listed on p1537), you must be 'ordinarily resident' in Great Britain (see p1537). If, by going abroad, you cease to be ordinarily resident, your entitlement also ceases. However, if your absence abroad is temporary and you intend to return to the UK, your ordinary residence is not usually affected.[1] In practice, it is very rare that ceasing to be ordinarily resident is the reason why your entitlement ends when you go abroad. It is more likely that your entitlement ends simply because you are absent (see below). If you receive a decision that your entitlement to a benefit or tax credit has ended because you have ceased to be ordinarily resident, ask for the decision to be looked at again and get specialist advice.

Presence and absence

Most benefits require you to be **present** in Great Britain (the UK, for tax credits). There are rules that allow you to be treated as present and therefore still entitled to the benefit or tax credit in specified circumstances during a temporary absence. Some benefits also have a rule that disqualifies you from entitlement if you are **absent** from Great Britain. There are specified exemptions to this rule for each benefit.

'**Presence**' means being physically present in Great Britain and '**absence**' means not physically present in Great Britain. If the DWP, HM Revenue and Customs or a local authority wants to disqualify you from benefit because you were absent from Great Britain, it must show you were absent throughout that day. This means that, on the day you leave Great Britain and the day you arrive in Great Britain, you count as present.

11

Part 11: Immigration and residence rules for benefits and tax credits
Chapter 67: Going abroad
2. Rules for specific benefits and tax credits

Temporary absence

In specified circumstances, you can be treated as present, and therefore entitled to benefit, during a temporary absence.

For tax credits, child benefit (for your, not the child's, absence), attendance allowance (AA), disability living allowance (DLA) and personal independence payment (PIP), you are defined as being temporarily absent from the UK if, at the beginning of the period of absence, you are unlikely to be absent for more than 52 weeks.[2]

For all other benefits, temporary absence is not defined and you must demonstrate that your absence will be temporary.[3] Provide full details of why you are going abroad, how long you intend to be away, and what you intend to do while abroad. **Note:** although your intentions are relevant, they are not decisive.[4] If your circumstances change while you are abroad (eg, you go abroad for one reason and decide to stay abroad for a different purpose), your absence may no longer be regarded as temporary.[5] Although there is no set period for a temporary absence (except for tax credits, child benefit, AA, DLA and PIP), as a general rule absences of more than 12 months are not considered to be temporary unless there are exceptional circumstances.[6] If the purpose of the trip abroad is obviously temporary (eg, for a holiday, to visit friends or relatives or for a particular course of medical treatment) and you buy a return ticket, your absence should be viewed as temporary.

2. **Rules for specific benefits and tax credits**

Bereavement benefits

In general, bereavement benefits are payable while you are abroad (but see below). However, your benefit is not uprated each year if you have ceased to be ordinarily resident in Great Britain on the day before the annual uprating takes place,[7] unless you have gone to another European Economic Area (EEA) state and you are covered by the European Union (EU) co-ordination rules (see p1611) or can rely on a reciprocal agreement.

If you are absent from Great Britain when (for bereavement support payment) your spouse or civil partner dies, or (for bereavement payment) you make your claim, you are only entitled in limited circumstances. See p1572 for further details.

European Union co-ordination rules

If you are covered by the EU co-ordination rules (see p1613) and you go to stay or live in another EEA state, you can be paid your bereavement support payment, bereavement allowance or widowed parent's allowance for as long as you would receive them if you remained in Great Britain, including any annual uprating.

11

If the EU co-ordination rules apply to you and the UK is your 'competent state' (see p1615):[8]

- for bereavement support payment, the requirement to be ordinarily resident in Great Britain on the date your spouse or civil partner died does not apply if you were resident in another EEA state on that date;
- for bereavement payment, if your spouse or civil partner died in another EEA state, s/he can be treated as having died in the UK.

Child benefit and guardian's allowance

Child benefit

You and your child can be treated as being present in Great Britain during a temporary absence (see p1590).

Provided you are ordinarily resident, you continue to be entitled to child benefit for:[9]

- the first eight weeks; *or*
- the first 12 weeks of any period of absence, or any extension to that period, which is in connection with:
  - the treatment of an illness or disability of you, your partner, a child for whom you are responsible, or another relative of you or your partner; *or*
  - the death of your partner, a child or qualifying young person for whom you or your partner are responsible, or another relative of you or your partner.

Relative

'**Relative**' means brother, sister, parent, grandparent, great-grandparent, child, grandchild or great-grandchild.[10]

Your child is treated as being present during a temporary absence for:[11]

- the first 12 weeks; *or*
- any period during which s/he is absent for the specific purpose of being treated for an illness or disability which began before her/his absence began; *or*
- any period when s/he is in Northern Ireland; *or*
- any period during which s/he is absent because s/he is:
  - receiving full-time education at a school or college in another EEA member state or in Switzerland; *or*
  - engaged in an educational exchange or visit made with the written approval of the school or college which s/he normally attends; *or*
  - a child who normally lives with a Crown servant posted overseas who is either in the same country as her/him or is absent from that country for one of the reasons in the above two bullet points.[12]

11

Part 11: Immigration and residence rules for benefits and tax credits
Chapter 67: Going abroad
2. Rules for specific benefits and tax credits

If a child is born outside the UK during the eight- or 12-week period in which you could be treated as being present in Great Britain, s/he is treated as being in the UK for up to 12 weeks from the start of your absence.[13]

While you and your child are present, or treated as present, you can continue to receive child benefit that was already in payment and can also make a fresh claim during your, or her/his, absence.

Guardian's allowance

Entitlement to guardian's allowance depends on entitlement to child benefit, so you can be paid guardian's allowance abroad for the same period as child benefit.

However, your guardian's allowance is not uprated each year if you have ceased to be ordinarily resident in Great Britain on the day before the annual uprating takes place,[14] unless you have gone to another EEA state and you are covered by the EU co-ordination rules (see below) or you can rely on a reciprocal agreement.

European Union co-ordination rules

Child benefit and guardian's allowance are classed as 'family benefits' under the EU co-ordination rules. If you are covered by these (see p1611):
- you can be paid child benefit and guardian's allowance for a child resident in another EEA country. S/he does not have to be in education; *and/or*
- you can be paid child benefit and guardian's allowance if you are an EEA national and you go to stay or live in another EEA country. Your benefit is uprated in the normal way.

See p1618 for more information.

Disability benefits and carer's allowance

You can be treated as present in Great Britain, and therefore continue to be entitled to attendance allowance (AA), disability living allowance (DLA), personal independence payment (PIP) or carer's allowance (CA), during an absence abroad:[15]
- (for AA, DLA and PIP only) for the first 13 weeks of a 'temporary absence' (see p1590);
- (for AA, DLA and PIP only) for the first 26 weeks of a 'temporary absence' (see p1590) if the absence is solely in connection with medical treatment for your illness or disability that began before you left Great Britain;
- (for CA only) for up to four weeks if your absence is, and was when it began, for a temporary purpose and does not exceed four weeks. If you are not accompanied by the disabled person for whom you are caring, you must satisfy the rules that entitle you to CA during a break from caring (see p557);

- (for CA only) if your absence is temporary and is for the specific purpose of caring for a disabled person who is also absent from Great Britain and who continues to receive AA, DLA care component paid at the highest or middle rate, the daily living component of PIP, armed forces independence payment or constant attendance allowance;
- if you were already abroad on 8 April 2013 but continued to be entitled to AA or DLA because your absence was temporary and for the specific purpose of being treated for an illness or disability that began before you left Great Britain, and the DWP has agreed you should be treated as present. You continue to be treated as being present in Great Britain until either you return or your award is revised or superseded;[16]
- if you are an airman or airwoman, mariner or continental shelf worker;
- while you are a serving member of the armed forces, or you are living with your spouse, civil partner, son, daughter, stepson, stepdaughter, father, father-in-law, stepfather, mother, mother-in-law or stepmother who is a serving member of the armed forces.

You must also continue to be habitually resident (see p1537), unless your current award of AA, DLA or CA began before 8 April 2013, in which case you must continue to be ordinarily resident (see p1537) until that award is terminated, revised or superseded.[17] You are treated as being habitually resident if you are covered by the last bullet point above.

You can continue to be paid an increase in your CA for your spouse/civil partner or dependent adult while s/he is abroad, provided you continue to be entitled to CA and reside with her/him. **Note:** you can be treated as residing together during a temporary absence from each other.[18]

European Union co-ordination rules

If you move to another EEA member state and are covered by the EU co-ordination rules (see p1611), you can continue to be paid (or make a new claim for) AA, the care component of DLA, the PIP daily living component and CA without having to satisfy the presence, past presence and habitual residence tests (see p1574) if:[19]

- you are habitually resident in another EEA state or Switzerland; *and*
- you can demonstrate a 'genuine and sufficient link to the UK' (see p1575).

Note: you can continue to be paid for as long as the UK continues to be your 'competent state' (see p1615).[20]

The above rule has only been in force since April 2013. For the circumstances in which you could be paid in another EEA state before this date, see CPAG's *Benefits for Migrants Handbook*.

DLA mobility component and PIP mobility component are classed as 'special non-contributory benefits' and so can only be paid when you are resident in the UK.[21]

11

Part 11: Immigration and residence rules for benefits and tax credits
Chapter 67: Going abroad
2. Rules for specific benefits and tax credits

If you receive CA while in the UK and the EU co-ordination rules apply to you (see p1611), you may be able to continue to be paid an addition for an adult or child who goes to stay or live in another EEA state. See p1618 for more information.

Employment and support allowance

You cannot normally get employment and support allowance (ESA) if you are not in Great Britain.[22] However, provided you meet the other conditions of entitlement, if you were entitled to ESA immediately before leaving Great Britain and are temporarily absent, you can continue to be entitled:[23]

- **indefinitely** if:
  - your absence is for NHS treatment at a hospital or other institution outside Great Britain; *or*
  - you are living with your spouse, civil partner, son, daughter, stepson, stepdaughter, father, father-in-law, stepfather, mother, mother-in-law or stepmother who is a serving member of the armed forces;
- for the first **four weeks**, if your absence is unlikely to exceed 52 weeks;
- for the first **26 weeks**, if your absence is unlikely to exceed 52 weeks and is solely in connection with arrangements made to treat:
  - your disease or disablement which is directly related to your limited capability for work which began before you left Great Britain; *or*
  - the disease or disablement of a dependent child who you are accompanying.

The treatment must be carried out by, or under the supervision of, a person qualified to provide medical treatment, physiotherapy or similar treatment.

If you are going to Northern Ireland from Great Britain (or vice versa), see p1576.

Note: there are also rules on when you can receive housing costs in your income-related ESA if you are temporarily absent from your home (see p456).

If your partner is abroad

If you are the claimant and you stay in Great Britain, your income-related ESA includes an amount for your partner for:[24]

- the first four weeks s/he is abroad; *or*
- the first 26 weeks if s/he is accompanying a child abroad for treatment in line with the 26-week rule above.

If both you and your partner are abroad, your income-related ESA includes an amount for your partner for the first 26 weeks if both of you are accompanying a child abroad for treatment in line with the 26-week rule above.[25]

After this four- or 26-week period, your benefit is reduced because your applicable amount is calculated as if you have no partner. However, your partner is still treated as being part of your household, and therefore her/his work, income and capital affect your income-related ESA entitlement, unless you are no longer treated as a couple (see p218).[26]

European Union co-ordination rules

If you are covered by the co-ordination rules (see p1611) and the UK is your 'competent state' (see p1615), you can, if you go to live in another EEA state, continue to be paid contributory ESA after the assessment phase, when it is classed as an 'invalidity benefit' (and, in most cases, also during the assessment phase – see p1613).

If the UK continues to pay your contributory ESA while you are resident in another EEA state, the DWP continues to assess your limited capability for work and work-related activity. However, any checks and medicals take place in the state in which you live and the reports are sent to the DWP.[27]

Income-related ESA is listed as a 'special non-contributory benefit' (see p1614) and the EU co-ordination rules cannot help you to be paid abroad. You can only be paid income-related ESA abroad under the UK rules on p1599.

Housing benefit

Although there is no requirement to be present in Great Britain to be entitled to housing benefit (HB), the rules that require you to occupy your home, except during certain temporary absences, can mean that you cease to be entitled if you go abroad.[28] If you are temporarily absent from your home and are outside Great Britain, your entitlement generally only continues during an absence of up to four weeks, unless you come into a limited number of exceptions. For the rules on temporary absence and when you can remain entitled to HB while outside Great Britain for four weeks or longer, see p53.

Note:

- The rules on absences abroad were introduced on 28 July 2016. If you were already temporarily absent abroad on this date, the previous, more generous, rules apply to you until you return to Great Britain.[29] See the 2015/16 edition of this *Handbook* for details.
- If you have an EEA right to reside in the UK (see p1545) and go abroad to another EEA state, it is arguable that the shorter period for which you can be entitled while abroad is discriminatory under EU law and should not apply (see p1616).[30]

11

If your partner or child is abroad

Whether or not you have amounts included in your HB for your partner or child who is abroad depends on whether s/he is treated as part of your household (see p218 and p223). The amount of HB you are entitled to may also depend on whether s/he is treated as occupying the home (see p53).[31]

Part 11: Immigration and residence rules for benefits and tax credits
Chapter 67: Going abroad
2. Rules for specific benefits and tax credits

Incapacity benefit, severe disablement allowance and maternity allowance

If you are temporarily absent from Great Britain, you can continue to be paid incapacity benefit (IB), severe disablement allowance (SDA) and maternity allowance (MA) if:[32]

- you are receiving AA, DLA, PIP or armed forces independence payment (see p1592); or
- the DWP agrees. You can then receive the benefit for the first 26 weeks of your temporary absence; or
- you are the spouse, civil partner, son, stepson, daughter, stepdaughter, father, stepfather, father-in-law, mother, stepmother or mother-in-law of a serving member of the armed forces, and you are abroad only because you are living with her/him.

In addition:

- when you left Great Britain, you must have been continuously incapable of work for six months and have been continuously incapable since your departure; or
- your absence from Great Britain must be for the specific purpose of being treated for an incapacity which began before you left Great Britain; or
- for IB only, the incapacity for work is the result of a personal injury caused by an accident at work (see p676) and your absence from Great Britain is for the specific purpose of receiving treatment for it.

If you are due to have a medical examination, this can be arranged abroad.

Note: most IB and SDA claims have been transferred to ESA (see p669). If you lose entitlement to IB or SDA by going abroad, you are not entitled to contributory ESA on your return if you do not satisfy the contribution conditions at that time.

You can continue to be paid an increase for your spouse/civil partner or dependent adult in your IB or SDA while s/he is abroad if you are entitled to IB/SDA and you are residing with her/him. **Note:** you can be treated as residing together during a temporary absence from each other.[33]

European Union co-ordination rules

If you are covered by the EU co-ordination rules (see p1611) and the UK is your 'competent state' (see p1615):

- you can continue to be paid your IB and SDA if you go to live in another EEA state, as both are classed as 'invalidity benefits' under the EU co-ordination rules (see p1613). Provided you continue to satisfy the rules of entitlement, benefit is paid without any time limit and at the same rate as if you were still in the UK, including your annual uprating. The state from which you claim benefit is the one that determines your degree of invalidity, but any checks and medicals take place in the state in which you are living. The reports are then sent to the paying state;[34]

- **if** you remain in the UK, you may be able to continue to be paid an increase in your IB or SDA for an adult or child if s/he goes to stay or live in another EEA state (see p1618);
- you can be paid MA if you go to stay or live in another EEA country, as MA is classed as a 'maternity benefit' under the EU co-ordination rules (see p1613).[35]

See p1618 for more details.

Income support

You cannot normally get income support (IS) if you are not in Great Britain.[36] However, IS can be paid when you are temporarily absent from Great Britain, provided you meet the other conditions of entitlement:[37]

- **indefinitely** if your absence is for NHS treatment at a hospital or other institution outside Great Britain;
- during the first **four weeks** of your absence, if it is unlikely to exceed 52 weeks and:
  - you are in Northern Ireland; *or*
  - you and your partner are both abroad and s/he satisfies the conditions for one of the pensioner premiums, the disability premium or the severe disability premium (see p236); *or*
  - you are claiming IS on the grounds of being incapable of work and are abroad for the sole purpose of receiving treatment for that incapacity; *or*
  - you are incapable of work; *and*
    - you have been continuously incapable for the previous 28 weeks and you are terminally ill or receiving the highest rate of DLA care component, the enhanced rate of the daily living component of PIP or armed forces independence payment; *or*
    - you have been continuously incapable for 364 days; *or*
  - you are not in one of the following groups of people who can claim IS (see p102):
    - a person in 'relevant education'; *or*
    - involved in a trade dispute, or have returned to work for 15 days or less following the dispute; *or*
    - entitled to statutory sick pay (SSP); *or*
    - appealing a decision that you are not incapable of work; *or*
- during the first **eight weeks** of your absence, if it is unlikely to exceed 52 weeks and is solely in connection with arrangements made to treat a disease or disablement of a child or qualifying young person. The child or young person must be a member of your family (see p220).

11

Part 11: Immigration and residence rules for benefits and tax credits
Chapter 67: Going abroad
2. Rules for specific benefits and tax credits

The treatment must be carried out by, or under the supervision of, a person qualified to provide medical treatment, physiotherapy or similar treatment.

Note: there are also rules on when you can receive housing costs within your IS if you are temporarily absent from your home (see 456).

If your partner is abroad

If you are the IS claimant and you stay in Great Britain, your IS applicable amount includes an amount for your partner who is abroad for:[38]
- the first four weeks; *or*
- the first eight weeks if s/he meets the conditions of the eight-week rule on p1597.

If both you and your partner are abroad, your IS includes amounts for your partner for the first eight weeks if you both meet the conditions of the eight-week rule above.[39]

After this four- or eight-week period, your benefit is reduced because your applicable amount is calculated as if you have no partner. However, your partner is still treated as being part of your household and therefore her/his work, income and capital affect your IS entitlement, unless you are no longer treated as a couple (see p218).[40]

If your child is abroad

If you were getting an amount in your IS for your child before s/he went abroad, you can continue to be paid for her/him for:[41]
- the first four weeks; *or*
- the first eight weeks, if your child meets the conditions of the eight-week rule above.

Industrial injuries benefits

Disablement benefit and retirement allowance are not affected if you go abroad.[42]

Constant attendance allowance and exceptionally severe disablement allowance are payable for the first six months of a temporary absence, or a longer period that the DWP may allow.[43]

Reduced earnings allowance (REA) can be paid while you are temporarily absent abroad for the first three months, or longer if the DWP allows, if:[44]
- your absence from Great Britain is *not* in connection with employment, trade or business; *and*
- your claim was made before you left Great Britain; *and*
- you were entitled to REA before going abroad.

Note: REA has now been abolished. If you break your claim, you may no longer be eligible for benefit.

European Union co-ordination rules

Industrial injuries benefits, except retirement allowance, are classed as 'benefits for accidents at work and occupational diseases' under the EU co-ordination rules (see p1613). If you are covered by these rules (see p1611) and you go to stay or live in another EEA state, you can be paid industrial injuries benefits (except retirement allowance) without any time limit and they are fully uprated each year. See p1618 for more details.

Jobseeker's allowance

You cannot normally get jobseeker's allowance (JSA) if you are not in Great Britain.[45] However, provided you meet the other conditions of entitlement, JSA can be paid when you are temporarily absent:[46]

- **indefinitely**, if you are entitled to JSA immediately before leaving Great Britain and your absence is for NHS treatment at a hospital or other institution outside Great Britain;
- for up to **four weeks**, if you are entitled to JSA immediately before leaving Great Britain and:
  - your absence is unlikely to exceed 52 weeks, you continue to satisfy the conditions of entitlement and you are in Northern Ireland; *or*
  - (except if you come under the universal credit (UC) system – see p20) the absence is unlikely to exceed 52 weeks, you continue to satisfy the conditions of entitlement and your partner is also abroad with you and satisfies the conditions for one of the pensioner premiums, the disability premium or the severe disability premium (see p236); *or*
  - (except if you come under the UC system) you are in receipt of a training allowance in the circumstances set out on p1029;[47]
- for up to **eight weeks**, if you are entitled to JSA immediately before leaving Great Britain and your absence is unlikely to exceed 52 weeks and is solely in connection with arrangements made to treat a disease or disablement of a child or qualifying young person. The treatment must be carried out by, or under the supervision of, a person qualified to provide medical treatment, physiotherapy or similar treatment and the child or young person must be a member of your family (see p220);
- for an absence of up to **seven days**, if you are attending a job interview and you notified the employment officer (EO) before you left (in writing if required). On your return, you must satisfy the EO that you attended the interview as stated;
- for an absence of up to **15 days**, to train as a member of the reserve forces.

You can be treated as being available for work and actively seeking work or, if you come under the UC system (see p20), you are exempt from the work search requirement and are treated as 'able and willing immediately to take up work'

Part 11: Immigration and residence rules for benefits and tax credits
Chapter 67: Going abroad
2. Rules for specific benefits and tax credits

during certain temporary absences abroad. These are similar to, but more limited than, those listed above (see p1034, p1049 and p1089).[48]

Note: there are also rules on when you can receive housing costs in your income-based JSA if you are temporarily absent from your home (see p456).

Joint-claim jobseeker's allowance if your partner is abroad

If you are a joint-claim couple (see p120) and your partner is temporarily absent from Great Britain **on the date you make your claim**, you are paid as a couple for:[49]

- an absence of up to **seven days**, if your partner is attending a job interview;
- up to **four weeks**, if your partner is:
  - in Northern Ireland and the absence is unlikely to exceed 52 weeks; *or*
  - getting a training allowance in the circumstances on p1029.

After this period, your JSA is reduced because your applicable amount is calculated as if you have no partner.[50] However, your partner is still treated as being part of your household, and her/his work, income and capital affect your income-based JSA entitlement unless you are no longer treated as a couple (see p218).[51]

If you are a joint-claim couple and your partner goes abroad **after you claimed** JSA, you continue to be paid as a joint-claim couple:[52]

- for up to **four** weeks, if you are entitled to joint-claim JSA immediately before s/he leaves Great Britain and either:
  - her/his absence is unlikely to exceed 52 weeks, you continue to satisfy the conditions of entitlement, and your partner satisfies the conditions for one of the pensioner premiums, the disability premium or the severe disability premium (see p236); *or*
  - her/his absence is unlikely to exceed 52 weeks, you both continue to satisfy the conditions of entitlement, and your partner is in Northern Ireland; *or*
  - your partner is getting a training allowance in the circumstances on p1029;[53]
- for an absence of up to **seven days**, if your partner is attending a job interview and has notified the EO before leaving (in writing if required). On her/his return, s/he must satisfy the EO that s/he attended the interview as stated.

Income-based jobseeker's allowance if your partner is abroad

If you are the income-based JSA claimant and you stay in Great Britain, your applicable amount includes an amount for your partner while s/he is abroad for:[54]

- the first **four weeks** of a temporary absence; *or*
- the first **eight weeks** if your partner meets the conditions of the eight-week rule on p1599.

If both you and your partner are abroad, your applicable amount includes an amount for your partner for the first eight weeks if both of you meet the conditions of the eight-week rule on p1599.[55]

After this four- or eight-week period, your benefit is reduced because your applicable amount is calculated as if you have no partner. However, your partner is still treated as being part of your household, and therefore her/his work, income and capital affect your income-based JSA entitlement unless you are no longer treated as a couple (see p218).[56]

Income-based jobseeker's allowance if your child is abroad

If you were getting JSA for your child before s/he went abroad, you can continue to be paid for her/him for:[57]

- the **first four weeks**; *or*
- the **first eight weeks** if your child meets the conditions of the eight-week rule on p1599.

European Union co-ordination rules

Contribution-based JSA is classed as an 'unemployment benefit' under the EU co-ordination rules (see p1613). If you are covered by these rules (see p1611) and the UK is your 'competent state' (see p1615), you can continue to be paid contribution-based JSA for up to three months if:[58]

- you satisfied the conditions for contribution-based JSA for at least four weeks before you left the UK, unless before then the DWP authorised you to go abroad; *and*
- you register as unemployed in the EEA state you go to within seven days and comply with its procedures.

Income-based JSA is classed as a 'special non-contributory benefit' under the EU co-ordination rules (see p1614) and therefore these rules cannot assist you to be paid income-based JSA abroad. You can only be paid income-based JSA abroad under the UK rules on p1599.

Pension credit

You cannot normally get pension credit (PC) if you are not in Great Britain.[59] However, provided you meet the other conditions of entitlement, PC can be paid when you are temporarily absent from Great Britain:[60]

- **for up to 26 weeks**, if your absence is not expected to exceed this and it is in connection with your (or your partner's or a child's or qualifying young person's) medical treatment, or medically approved convalescence; *or*
- **for up to four weeks**, if your absence is not expected to exceed this. The four-week period can be extended by a further four weeks if your absence is in connection with the death of your partner or child or qualifying young person, or your (or her/his) close relative, the DWP considers that it would be unreasonable for you to return to Great Britain within the first four weeks, and the absence is not expected to exceed eight weeks.

11

Part 11: Immigration and residence rules for benefits and tax credits
Chapter 67: Going abroad
2. Rules for specific benefits and tax credits

'Qualifying young person' is defined as it is for UC (see p220), but someone receiving JSA, ESA, IS or UC is not a qualifying young person.[61]

'Close relative' is defined as it is for UC (see p493).

Note:

- These rules were made more restrictive on 28 July 2016. If you were already temporarily absent abroad on this date, the previous, more generous, rules apply to you until you return to Great Britain.[62] See the 2015/16 edition of this *Handbook* for details.
- There are also rules on when you can receive housing costs in your PC if you are temporarily absent from your home (see p456).

If your partner is abroad

If you are entitled to PC and your partner is abroad, your PC only includes an amount for her/him if s/he is covered by the rules above.[63] After this, s/he is not treated as being part of your household and you are paid as a single person. Your partner can also stop being treated as part of your household in the circumstances on p218.[64]

European Union co-ordination rules

PC is classed as a 'special non-contributory benefit' under the EU co-ordination rules (see p1614) and therefore these rules cannot assist you to be paid PC abroad. You can only be paid PC abroad under the UK rules on p1601.

Retirement pension

All retirement pensions are payable without time limit while you are abroad.[65] However, unless you have gone to another EEA state and you are covered by the EU co-ordination rules or you can rely on a reciprocal agreement (see p1603), if you are not ordinarily resident (see p1537) in Great Britain:[66]

- on the day before the annual uprating takes place, your benefit is not uprated each year;
- (state pension only – ie, if you reach pension age on or after 6 April 2016), when you claim a pension that you have deferred, the upratings that occurred while you were abroad are ignored when calculating both the deferral increase and rate payable;
- ('old' retirement pensions only – ie, if you reached pension age before 6 April 2016), you cannot stop claiming your pension ('de-retire') in order to accrue a deferral payment,[67]

Although category D retirement pension is payable if you are abroad, you must meet the residence requirements at the date you claim, see p1578.

You can continue to be paid an increase in your category A retirement pension for your spouse/civil partner or dependent adult while s/he is abroad if you are entitled to the pension and residing with her/him.[68] You can be treated as residing together during a temporary absence from each other.[69]

European Union co-ordination rules

Retirement pensions are classed as 'old age benefits' under the EU co-ordination rules (see p1613). If you are covered by these rules (see p1611) and the UK is your 'competent state' (see p1615):

- if you go to stay or live in another EEA state, you can continue to paid your retirement pension without time limit as retirement pensions are classed as 'old age benefits' under the EU co-ordination rules (see p1613). Your retirement pension is paid at the same rate as if you were still in the UK, including your annual uprating;
- you can opt to stop claiming your pension ('de-retire') in order to accrue a deferral payment while living in another EEA state;
- if you remain in the UK, you may be able to continue to be paid an increase for an adult or child if s/he goes to stay or live in another EEA state (see p1618).

Reciprocal agreements

If you are covered by a reciprocal agreement (see p1533) that provides for uprating, you can be paid your pension at the same rate as if you were still in the UK, including your annual uprating. **Note:** the agreements with Canada and New Zealand, and the former agreement with Australia, do not provide for uprating.

Statutory payments

There are no presence or residence rules for SSP, statutory maternity pay (SMP), statutory adoption pay (SAP), statutory paternity pay (SPP) and statutory shared parental pay (SSPP). You remain entitled to these benefits if you go abroad, provided you meet the normal rules of entitlement, including those relating to being an employee (see Chapters 37 and 38).[70]

Although you are generally required to be employed in Great Britain to count as an 'employee', you count as an employee even while employed abroad, in certain circumstances, including if:[71]

- your employer is required to pay secondary class 1 national insurance (NI) contributions for you; *or*
- you are a continental shelf worker or, in certain circumstances, an airman or airwoman or mariner; *or*
- you are employed in another EEA state and, had you been employed in Great Britain, you would have been considered an employee, and the UK is the competent state under the EU co-ordination rules (see p1615).

Your employer is not required to pay you SSP, SMP, SAP, SPP or SSPP if:[72]

- your employer is not required by law to pay employer's class 1 NI contributions (even if those contributions are in fact made) because, at the time they become payable, your employer:
  - is not resident or present in Great Britain; *and*

Part 11: Immigration and residence rules for benefits and tax credits
Chapter 67: Going abroad
2. Rules for specific benefits and tax credits

- has (or is treated as having) no place of business in Great Britain; *or*
- because of an international treaty or convention, your employer is exempt from the Social Security Acts or those Acts are not enforceable against your employer.

European Union co-ordination rules

It is arguable that SSP is a 'sickness benefit' and SMP, SAP, SPP and SSPP are 'maternity/paternity benefits' under the co-ordination rules (see p1613). However, given the generosity of the above UK rules, it is unlikely that you will need to rely on the EU co-ordination rules.

Tax credits

Provided you are ordinarily resident, you can be treated as present and, therefore, entitled to child tax credit (CTC) and working tax credit (WTC) during a 'temporary absence' (see p1590) for:[73]
- the first **eight weeks**; *or*
- the first **12 weeks** of any period of absence, or any extension to that period of absence, which is in connection with:
    - treating an illness or disability of you, your partner, a child for whom you are responsible, or another relative (see below) of either you or your partner; *or*
    - the death of your partner, a child or qualifying young person for whom you or your partner are responsible, or another relative (see below) of you or your partner.

Relative
'**Relative**' means brother, sister, parent, grandparent, grandchild, or great-grandparent or child.[74]

You are also treated as present if you are:[75]
- a Crown servant posted overseas and:
    - you are, or immediately before your posting abroad you were, ordinarily resident in the UK; *or*
    - immediately before your posting you were in the UK in connection with that posting; *or*
- the partner of a Crown servant posted overseas and in the same country as her/him or temporarily absent from that country under the same exceptions that enable tax credits to continue during a temporary absence from Great Britain.

While you are treated as present in any of the above ways, you can continue to receive any tax credits that are already in payment and can make a fresh or renewal claim during your absence.

If you (or your partner, if you are making a joint claim) spend longer abroad than the permitted periods, you cease to satisfy the presence condition and therefore your tax credit entitlement ends. If you do not notify this to HM Revenue and Customs within one month (see p1462), you may be overpaid (see Chapter 62) and could be given a penalty (see Chapter 63).

See p1580 for considerations if you are making a joint claim as a couple.

European Union co-ordination rules

CTC is classed as a 'family benefit' under the EU co-ordination rules. If you are covered by these rules (see p1611), you can be paid CTC:

- for a child resident in another EEA country; *and/or*
- if you are an EEA national and you go to stay or live in another EEA country.

See p1618 for more details.

Universal credit

You cannot normally be paid UC if you (and your partner, if it is a joint claim) are not in Great Britain.[76] However, provided you meet the other conditions of entitlement, UC can be paid when you are temporarily absent from Great Britain for:[77]

- **one month**, if your absence is not expected to exceed, and does not exceed, one month; *or*
- **two months**, if your absence is in connection with the death of your partner or child, or a close relative of yours or of your partner or child, and it would be unreasonable for you to return to Great Britain within the first month; *or*
- **six months**, if your absence is not expected to exceed, and does not exceed, six months and you are a mariner or continental shelf worker; *or*
- **six months**, if your absence is not expected to exceed, and does not exceed, six months and is solely in connection with the medically approved care, convalescence or treatment of you, your partner or child. If this applies to you, you are automatically exempt from the work search requirement and also treated as 'able and willing immediately to take up work' during your absence (see p1087).[78]

If your partner is abroad

If you have a joint claim for UC and you both go abroad, UC continues to be paid while both of you meet one of the conditions listed above. If you both remain abroad for longer than the relevant period, your entitlement ends.

If you stay in Great Britain while your partner is abroad, her/his absence does not affect your entitlement during the one-, two- or six-month period if one of the circumstances listed above applies to her/him. After this time, you cease to be entitled as joint claimants. If your partner has been, or is expected to be, apart from you for six months, you stop being treated as a couple and you may then be entitled as a single person.[79] If you have been apart for less than six months, you must claim as a single person. However, although your award is then based on the maximum amount for a single person, your partner's income and capital are taken into account until you have been apart (or expect to be apart) for six months (as you then cease to be treated as a couple).[80]

If your child is abroad

If your child is abroad, you cease to be entitled for her/him if her/his absence abroad is, or is expected to be, longer than the one-, two- or six-month period allowed in the circumstances above (the circumstances must apply to your child).[81]

European Union co-ordination rules

The DWP considers UC not to be a social security benefit under the EU co-ordination rules (see p1613). This means that the EU co-ordination rules cannot assist you and, if you go to another EEA state, you can only be paid under the UK rules above.

Notes

1. **The rules on getting paid abroad**
   1 *R v Barnet LBC ex parte Shah* [1983] 2 AC 309 (HL), Lord Scarman at p342D; see also *GC v HMRC (TC)* [2014] UKUT 251 (AAC)
   2 **CB** Reg 24(2) CB Regs
     AA Reg 2(3C) SS(AA) Regs
     DLA Reg 2(3C) SS(DLA) Regs
     PIP Reg 17(2) SS(PIP) Regs
     TC Reg 4(2) TC(R) Regs
   3 *Chief Adjudication Officer v Ahmed and Others*, 16 March 1994 (CA), reported as R(S) 1/96
   4 *Chief Adjudication Officer v Ahmed and Others*, 16 March 1994 (CA), reported as R(S) 1/96
   5 R(S) 1/85
   6 R(U) 16/62

2. **Rules for specific benefits and tax credits**
   7 Reg 5 SSB(PA) Regs
   8 Arts 5, 7, 42 and 43 EU Reg 883/04

   9 Reg 24 CB Regs
   10 Reg 24(1) CB Regs
   11 Reg 21 CB Regs
   12 Reg 32 CB Regs
   13 Reg 21(2) CB Regs
   14 Reg 5 SSB(PA) Regs
   15 **AA** Reg 2(2), (3B) and (3C) SS(AA) Regs
      DLA Reg 2(2), (3B) and (3C) SS(DLA) Regs
      PIP Regs 17-20 SS(PIP) Regs
      CA Reg 9(2) and (3) SS(ICA) Regs
   16 Reg 5 SS(DLA,AA&CA)(A) Regs
   17 Reg 1(2), (3) and (4) SS(DLA,AA&CA)(A) Regs
   18 Reg 13 SSB(PA) Regs; Sch 2 para 7 SSB(Dep) Regs; reg 2(4) SSB(PRT)Regs
   19 **AA** Reg 2B SS(AA) Regs
      DLA Reg 2B SS(DLA) Regs
      PIP Reg 23 SS(PIP) Regs
      CA Reg 9B SS(ICA) Regs

11

20 **AA** s65(7) SSCBA 1992
   DLA s72(7B) SSCBA 1992
   PIP s84 WRA 2012
   CA s70(4A) SSCBA 1992
21 *Bartlett and Others v SSWP*, C-537/09 [2011] ECR I-03417; Art 70 EU Reg 883/04; *Swaddling v AO*, C-90/97 [1999] ECR I-01075
22 ss1(3)(d) and 18(4)(a) WRA 2007
23 Regs 151-55 ESA Regs; regs 88-92 ESA Regs 2013
24 Reg 156 and Sch 5 paras 6 and 7 ESA Regs
25 Reg 156 and Sch 5 para 7 ESA Regs
26 Reg 156 ESA Regs
27 Arts 5, 46 and 82 EU Reg 883/04; Arts 27 and 46 EU Reg 987/2009
28 s130(1)(a) SSCBA 1992; reg 7 HB Regs; reg 7 HB(SPC) Regs
29 Reg 5 HB&SPC(TA)(A) Regs; reg 5 HB&SPC(TA)(A) Regs 2016
30 Art 18 TFEU; Art 24 EU Dir 2004/38; *O'Flynn v Adjudication Officer*, C-237/94 [1996] ECR I-02617; R(IS) 4/98
31 Regs 7 and 21 HB Regs; regs 7 and 21 HB(SPC) Regs
32 Reg 2 SSB(PA) Regs
33 Reg 13 SSB(PA) Regs; reg 14 SS(IB-ID) Regs; reg 2(4) SSB(PRT) Regs
34 Arts 5 and 46 EU Reg 883/04; Art 87 EU Reg 987/2009
35 Arts 7 and 21 EU Reg 883/04
36 s124(1) SSCBA 1992
37 Reg 4 IS Regs
38 Reg 21 and Sch 7 paras 11 and 11A IS Regs
39 Reg 21 and Sch 7 para 11A IS Regs
40 Reg 16 IS Regs
41 Reg 16(5) IS Regs
42 Reg 9(3) SSB(PA) Regs
43 Reg 9(4) SSB(PA) Regs
44 Reg 9(5) SSB(PA) Regs
45 s1(2)(i) JSA 1995
46 s21 and Sch 1 para 11 JSA 1995; reg 50 JSA Regs; reg 41 JSA Regs 2013
47 Regs 50(4) and 170 JSA Regs
48 Regs 14 and 19 JSA Regs; reg 16 JSA Regs 2013
49 Regs 50(6B), 86C and 170 and Sch 5A para 7 JSA Regs
50 Sch 5A para 7 JSA Regs
51 Reg 78 JSA Regs
52 Reg 50(3) and (6C) and Sch 5A para 7 JSA Regs
53 Regs 50(4) and 170 JSA Regs
54 Reg 85 and Sch 5 paras 10 and 11 JSA Regs
55 Reg 85 and Sch 5 para 11 JSA Regs
56 Reg 78 JSA Regs
57 Reg 78(5) JSA Regs
58 Art 64 EU Reg 883/04
59 s1(2)(a) SPCA 2002
60 Reg 3 SPC Regs
61 Reg 4A SPC Regs
62 Reg 5 HB&SPC(TA)(A) Regs
63 Reg 5 SPC Regs
64 Reg 5 SPC Regs
65 s113 SSCBA 1992; reg 4(1) SSB(PA) Regs
66 Regs 4(3) and 5 SSB(PA) Regs; ss18 and 20 PA 2014; regs 21-23 SP Regs
67 Reg 6 SSB(PA) Regs
68 Reg 2(4) SSB(PRT) Regs
69 Reg 13 SSB(PA) Regs; reg 10 SSB(Dep) Regs
70 **SSP** Reg 10 SSP(MAPA) Regs
   SMP Reg 2A SMP(PAM) Regs
   SAP/SPP Reg 4 SPPSAP(PAM) Regs
   SSPP Reg 6 SSPP(PAM) Regs
71 Art 6 EU Reg 883/04
   SSP s163(1) SSCBA 1992; reg 16 SSP Regs; regs 5-10 SSP(MAPA) Regs
   SMP s171(1) SSCBA 1992; regs 2, 2A, 5, 7 and 8 SMP(PAM) Regs
   SAP/SPP ss171ZJ(2)-(3) and 171ZS(2)-(3) SSCBA 1992; regs 3, 4, 8 and 9 SPPSAP(PAM) Regs
   SSPP s171ZZ4(2) SSCBA; regs 5, 6, 7, 9, 10 SSPP(PAM) Regs
72 **SSP** Reg 16(2) SSP Regs
   SMP Reg 3 SMP(PAM) Regs; reg 17(3) SMP Regs
   SAP/SPP Reg 2 SPPSAP(PAM) Regs; reg 32(3) SPPSAP(G) Regs; reg 24(4) ASPP(G) Regs
   SSPP Reg 33(5) SSPP(G) Regs; reg 4 SSPP(PAM) Regs
73 Reg 4 TC(R) Regs
74 Reg 2(1) TC(R) Regs
75 Reg 3, 5 and 6 TC(R) Regs
76 ss3 and 4(1)(c) WRA 2012
77 Reg 11 UC Regs
78 Reg 99(1)-(3) UC Regs
79 Reg 3(6) UC Regs
80 Regs 3, 18, 22 and 36 UC Regs
81 Reg 4(7) UC Regs

11

Chapter 68

European Union co-ordination rules

This chapter covers:
1. Introduction (below)
2. Who is covered (p1611)
3. Which benefits are covered (p1612)
4. Principles of co-ordination (p1615)

Key facts
- If you are a European Economic Area (EEA) national, or the family member of an EEA national, and your circumstances involve more than one EEA state, you may be able to benefit from the European Union co-ordination rules.
- The co-ordination rules can help you qualify for benefits in the UK. You can count periods of residence and employment in another EEA state, and insurance contributions paid in another EEA state, to help you meet the conditions of entitlement to the UK benefit you want to claim.
- The co-ordination rules also allow you to be paid a UK benefit in another EEA state for longer than the UK rules allow, and to be paid a benefit by another EEA state while you are in the UK.

11

1. Introduction

If you are a European Economic Area (EEA) national (see p1609) or a family member of an EEA national, you may be able to benefit from European Union (EU) law.

There are two main areas of EU law affecting benefit and tax credit entitlement that are covered in this *Handbook*: the residence rights that enable you to satisfy the right to reside requirement outlined in Chapter 66 and the social security co-ordination rules, which are summarised in this chapter. In general, you do not need to know whether you have a right to reside in order to understand how the co-ordination rules affect you.

The co-ordination rules can help you qualify for benefits in the UK – eg, by enabling you to count periods of residence, insurance and employment in any EEA state to meet the conditions of entitlement. They can also help you to be paid a UK benefit in another EEA state for longer than you would be able to do under UK law alone.

European Union law

EU legislation and caselaw apply in the UK and throughout the EEA. In general, for EU law to apply, you must be an EEA national or the family member of an EEA national and your circumstances must involve more than one EEA state – eg, if you have moved between states, you live in one and work in another, or you live in one but are the national of another.[1]

Member states of the European Union

Austria	Estonia	Italy	Portugal
Belgium	Finland	Latvia	Romania
Bulgaria	France	Lithuania	Slovakia
Croatia	Germany	Luxembourg	Slovenia
Cyprus	Greece	Malta	Spain
Czech Republic	Hungary	The Netherlands	Sweden
Denmark	Ireland	Poland	United Kingdom

Member states of the European Economic Area

The EEA consists of the EU countries plus Iceland, Liechtenstein and Norway.

From 1 June 2002, an agreement with Switzerland means that, in general, Swiss nationals are treated the same as EEA nationals. Any references to EEA nationals, therefore, also include Swiss nationals.[2]

EU law has been extended to the three EEA countries outside the EU so that, in general, EEA nationals are covered by EU law to the same extent as nationals of EU states.

EU law applies beyond the actual territory of the EEA states to countries 'for whose external relations a member state is responsible' – eg, EU law applies to Gibraltar because the UK is responsible for Gibraltar's external relations.[3]

The co-ordination rules

EU law co-ordinates all the social security systems within the EEA. The intention is that people should not lose out on social security protection simply because they move to another member state. **Note:** the co-ordination rules have not

Part 11: Immigration and residence rules for benefits and tax credits
Chapter 68: European Union co-ordination rules
1. Introduction

changed as a result of the UK vote to leave the EU. They continue to apply until the UK formally leaves the EU.

The co-ordination rules contain the following principles.

- **The single state principle.** You can generally only claim benefit from one member state, referred to as the 'competent state' (see p1615).
- **Equal treatment of people.** Discrimination on nationality grounds in terms of access to, the rate of and payment of the benefits covered is prohibited (see p1616).
- **Equal treatment of benefits, income, facts or events.** If receipt of a benefit or a fact or an event has a legal consequence in one member state, this must be recognised in the same way by other member states (see p1616).
- **Aggregation.** Periods of residence, insurance and employment in any EEA state can be used towards entitlement to benefit in another (see p1617).
- **Exportability of certain benefits.** You can continue to be paid certain benefits if you go to another member state (see p1618).
- **Administrative co-operation.** Member states undertake to co-operate in the administration of the co-ordination rules.

The current co-ordination rules succeed, but do not repeal, the previous set of rules (referred to in this *Handbook* as the 'old co-ordination rules'). See p1612 for who is covered by the old rules.

Using the co-ordination rules

In order to rely on the co-ordination rules, check:

- whether you are covered by the current or the old co-ordination rules (see p1612);
- whether you are personally covered (see p1611);
- whether the benefit you want to claim is covered and into which category it falls (see p1612);
- which state is the 'competent state' (see p1615);
- the individual benefit and tax credit rules in Chapter 66 for your entitlement in the UK, or in Chapter 67 if you want to be paid when you or your family are in another EEA state.

The co-ordination rules are complex and this chapter only provides an overview. For more information, see CPAG's *Benefits for Migrants Handbook*.

2. **Who is covered**

In order to be covered by the co-ordination rules, you must come within their **'personal scope'**.

You are within the personal scope of the co-ordination rules if:[4]

- you have been 'subject to the legislation of one or more member states' (see below) and you are:
  - a European Economic Area (EEA) national; *or*
  - a refugee; *or*
  - a stateless person; *or*
- a family member (see below) or a 'survivor' of one of the above (in the UK, a widow, widower or surviving civil partner).

In addition, for the co-ordination rules to apply, your situation must involve more than one member state. This usually means that you must have moved between EEA states, or you live in one and work in another, or you live in one and are the national of another.[5]

Subject to the legislation of a member state

You have been **'subject to the legislation of a member state'** if you have worked in and paid (or should have paid) national insurance (NI) contributions to, or received any social security or special non-contributory benefit (see p1612) from, that state. You may also be subject to the legislation if you are potentially eligible for any social security benefit or special non-contributory benefit.

'Legislation' is defined as 'in respect of each member state, laws, regulations and other statutory provisions and all other implementing measures relating to the social security branches covered by Article 3(1) of the Regulation'.[6]

The **'social security branches'** referred to in this definition include UK benefits that are intended to assist you in the event of one of the risks on p1613.

Family members

Family members of someone covered by the co-ordination rules can also rely on the rules that cover that person (which can vary depending on the type of benefit claimed).

Family members

You are a **'member of the family'** of a person covered by the co-ordination rules if you are:[7]

- someone defined or recognised as a member of the family, or designated as a member of the household, by the legislation under which benefits are provided; *or*

11

Part 11: Immigration and residence rules for benefits and tax credits
Chapter 68: European Union co-ordination rules
3. Which benefits are covered

– if the legislation under which benefits are provided does not distinguish between members of the family and other people to whom the legislation applies, the person's spouse or child either under the age of 'majority' (18 in England and Wales; 16 in Scotland) or older but dependent on the person covered.

If under the legislation you are only considered to be a member of the family or member of the household if you are living in the same household as the person, this condition is considered satisfied if you are mainly dependent on her/him.

When the old co-ordination rules apply

There are two sets of co-ordination rules, as the current rules did not repeal the previous ones. The current rules[8] apply to the majority of benefit claimants. However, the old co-ordination rules[9] apply to you if:

- you are receiving a benefit because you claimed it before the current rules came into force.[10] This depends on your nationality (see below). However, if you claimed benefit before the current rules came into force but did not need to rely on the co-ordination rules (eg, when moving between states) until after that date, the current rules apply.[11] The old rules continue to apply to you for up to 10 years, provided your circumstances do not change. However, you can ask to be transferred and considered under the new rules if this would be better for you. If so, the new rules take effect from the start of the following month;[12] *or*
- you are a national of a non-EEA state (other than a refugee), you are legally resident in the UK or any other EEA state,[13] and you have been employed or self-employed and you have paid (or should have paid) NI contributions, or you have been a student.

When did the current co-ordination rules take effect?
The current co-ordination rules apply to nationals (and their family members) of:
– the European Union member states, refugees and stateless people from 1 May 2010;
– Switzerland from 1 April 2012;
– Iceland, Liechtenstein and Norway from 1 June 2012.

11

Note: as most claims are now covered by the current co-ordination rules, this *Handbook* does not include the old ones. For information on these, see the 2012/13 edition.

3. **Which benefits are covered**

The benefits to which the co-ordination rules apply are referred to as being within the **'material scope'** of the rules.

Individual benefits are not directly referred to. Instead, the rules have broad categories of benefits (eg, 'old age' or 'maternity') designed to cover certain 'risks'. Any social security benefit designed to provide assistance in the event of a particular risk comes into that particular category. Each state must list the benefits it considers to be designed to assist with that risk.

Benefits are also divided into the following types, depending on the conditions of eligibility:

- social security benefits (see below);
- special non-contributory benefits (see p1614);
- social and medical assistance (see p1615).

Those benefits deemed to be social security benefits have the most rights, and special non-contributory benefits provide fewer rights. Social and medical assistance is not covered by the co-ordination rules.

Social security benefits

Risk	UK benefit
Sickness	Attendance allowance (AA) (but see p1614)
	Carer's allowance (CA) (but see p1614)
	Disability living allowance (DLA) care component (but see p1614)
	Personal independence payment (PIP) daily living component
	Statutory sick pay
	Contributory employment and support allowance (ESA) in the assessment phase (but see p1614)
Maternity and paternity	Maternity allowance
	Statutory maternity, adoption, paternity and shared parental pay (but see p1614)
Invalidity	AA, DLA care and mobility component and CA if you were in receipt of benefit before 1 June 1992. If you claimed after this date, see the note on p1614.
	Long-term incapacity benefit
	Severe disablement allowance
	Contributory ESA after the assessment phase
	Arguably, contributory ESA during the assessment phase (see p1614)
	State pension
Old age	Category A, B and D retirement pensions
	Additional pension
	Graduated retirement benefit
	Winter fuel payments
	Increments – eg, to pensions
	Increases of retirement pension for an adult
	Age addition in pensions

11

Part 11: Immigration and residence rules for benefits and tax credits
Chapter 68: European Union co-ordination rules
3. Which benefits are covered

Pre-retirement	None
Survivors	Bereavement benefits
Death grants	Bereavement support payment
	Bereavement payment
Accidents at work	Industrial injuries disablement benefit
and occupational	Constant attendance allowance
diseases	Exceptionally severe disablement allowance
	Reduced earnings allowance
Unemployment	Contribution-based jobseeker's allowance (JSA)
Family benefits (see	Child benefit
p1618)	Child tax credit
	Increases in other benefits for an adult or a child
	Guardian's allowance

Note: AA, CA and DLA care component have been categorised as assisting with different risks at different times. Until 1 June 1992 they were categorised as invalidity benefits. They were then categorised as special non-contributory benefits until this was held to be wrong and they were then re-categorised as sickness benefits.[14] For the relevance of these changing categories for when these benefits could be paid in another EEA state before April 2013, see CPAG's *Benefits for Migrants Handbook*.

The mobility component of DLA has been listed as, and the mobility component of PIP is treated by the DWP as, a special non-contributory benefit.

Note:

- If you have a long-term or permanent disability, it is arguable that contributory ESA during the assessment phase, as well as after, should be regarded as an invalidity benefit.[15] However, in most cases it makes no difference to when it can be paid.
- For rules on 'exporting' family benefits, see p1618.
- The DWP considers that statutory maternity, adoption, paternity and shared parental pay should be treated as pay, rather than as social security or special non-contributory benefits.[16]
- The DWP considers universal credit to be neither a social security benefit nor a special non-contributory benefit.[17]

Special non-contributory benefits

The UK government has only listed pension credit, income-related ESA, income-based JSA and DLA mobility component as special non-contributory benefits.[18] However, it is expected that the mobility component of PIP will also be listed as a special non-contributory benefit and the DWP is currently treating it as such.

Special non-contributory benefits can only be paid in the state where you are resident.[19] See below for details of how residence is determined. However, although you cannot 'export' special non-contributory benefits, all the other co-ordination principles apply.[20]

Social and medical assistance

Benefits that are neither social security nor special non-contributory benefits are considered to be social assistance and are excluded from the co-ordination rules.[21] The UK does not specify which benefits it considers to be social assistance.

4. Principles of co-ordination

The single competent state

In general, under the co-ordination rules, you can only claim a particular type of benefit from one member state and are only liable to pay national insurance (NI) contributions to one member state. This is expressed as the general principle that you can only be subject to the legislation of a single member state.[22]

The '**competent state**' is the one responsible for paying your benefit and to which you are liable to pay NI contributions.[23] In general, it is the state in which you are:[24]

- employed or self-employed, or you are receiving cash benefits as a result of either (except for invalidity, sickness, old age, being a survivor or for an accident at work);
- resident, and from which you receive an unemployment benefit;
- a conscripted member of the armed forces or doing compulsory civilian service;
- a civil servant.

If none of the above apply, the competent state is the state in which you are 'resident' (see below).[25]

There are exceptions to this general rule – eg, in the payment of 'sickness benefits' if you (or your family member who brings you within the co-ordination rules) receive a 'pension' (which can include state benefits other than retirement pensions) from a European Economic (EEA) state other than the one in which you live.[26]

'**Residence**' means habitual residence.[27] If there is a difference of views between two states or institutions about where you are 'resident', they must agree where your centre of interest is, taking into account all your circumstances, including:[28]

- the duration and continuity of your presence in the states concerned;
- your personal situation, including:

Part 11: Immigration and residence rules for benefits and tax credits
Chapter 68: European Union co-ordination rules
4. Principles of co-ordination

- the nature and specific characteristics of any activity pursued – in particular, the place where such activity is habitually pursued, its stability and the duration of any work contract;
- your family status and family ties;
- any unpaid activity, such as voluntary work;
- if you are a student, the source of your income;
- your housing situation – in particular, how permanent it is;
- the state in which you are deemed to reside for tax purposes.

If there is still a dispute, consideration must be given to your intentions, especially the reasons why you moved. This is decisive in establishing your actual place of residence.

If the state in which you claim benefit decides it is not competent, it must pass your claim to the state it considers competent without delay.[29]

If two or more states take a different view on which should pay a benefit, you can get provisional payments from your state of residence or, if you are not resident in any, the state to which you first applied, while the issue is resolved.[30]

For further information on how the competent state is determined, including when exceptions apply, see CPAG's *Benefits for Migrants Handbook*.

When the UK remains the competent state

If you are subject to the legislation of the UK, either because you last worked in the UK or you are resident in the UK, you remain subject to this until:[31]

- you start to work in another EEA state;
- (unless you last worked in the UK) you receive a pension from another EEA state and request that the UK cease to be your competent state;[32]
- in some circumstances, you move to another EEA state and become resident there (see below).

Note: these general rules can be supplemented by other rules specific to the category of benefit being paid.[33]

The point at which the UK stops being responsible for paying your benefit if you move to another state is not always clear and most of the caselaw has considered the old co-ordination rules, which differ in some respects from the current ones. However, in general, if you continue to be entitled to a UK benefit when you move to another state, the UK remains the competent state for paying that benefit until either you become employed/self-employed in the other state or, in certain circumstances, you start to receive a benefit from it.[34]

Equal treatment

If you are covered by the co-ordination rules, you are entitled to the same benefits under the legislation of the competent state (see p1615) as a national of that state.[35] Both direct discrimination based on your nationality and, if it cannot be justified as proportionate and in pursuit of a legitimate aim, indirect discrimination based on your nationality are prohibited.

The co-ordination rules also provide for the legal effects of facts or events, including receipt of a particular benefit or income, to be treated equally.[36] For example, if receipt of attendance allowance (AA) entitles you to have a disability premium included in your housing benefit applicable amount, you should also be entitled to that premium if you are resident in the UK but receive a benefit equivalent to AA from another state.

See CPAG's *Benefits for Migrants Handbook* for further information on equal treatment.

Aggregation

The principle of **'aggregation'** enables you to add together periods of insurance (such as NI contributions in the UK), residence or employment/self-employment completed under the legislation of other EEA states to satisfy the requirements of a benefit.[37] This may be necessary if your entitlement to benefit depends on your fulfilling a certain period of residence, employment or insurance. For example, if you want to claim a UK contribution-based benefit, such as contributory employment and support allowance, but you have not paid sufficient NI contributions, you can rely on contributions paid in other EEA states to satisfy the UK contribution rules. The competent institution (eg, in the UK, the DWP and HM Revenue and Customs) must contact the institutions in the other relevant state(s) to determine the periods completed under their legislation.[38] What constitutes a period of residence, employment or insurance is determined by the legislation of the state under which it took place.[39] However the Upper Tribunal has held that mere residence in another EEA state cannot be used to satisfy the past presence test in disability and carers' benefits (see p1575).[40]

Example

Sancha is a Portuguese national who worked for many years in Portugal. She leaves her job in Portugal and moves to the UK. She works for two weeks before being made redundant. Sancha is expecting a baby in two months' time and claims maternity allowance (MA). She is entitled to MA because she can add her periods of employment in Portugal to her employment in the UK to satisfy the condition of having worked for 26 out of the last 66 weeks.

Note: for unemployment benefits, your periods of insurance or employment or self-employment can only be aggregated if you were last insured or worked in the state from which you claim, unless during your last period of work you resided in a state other than your competent state and you claim in that state where you still reside or have returned to.[41]

Part 11: Immigration and residence rules for benefits and tax credits
Chapter 68: European Union co-ordination rules
4. Principles of co-ordination

Exporting benefits

The co-ordination rules allow you to 'export' certain benefits to another state if you cease to be resident in the member state in which your entitlement arose.

This means that certain benefits may not be reduced, modified, suspended, withdrawn or confiscated just because you go to live in a different state.[42] The rules for exporting vary according to the benefit concerned: some are fully exportable, some may be exportable on a temporary basis, and some are not exportable at all.

Check the individual benefit rules in Chapter 67 to see whether the benefit can be exported. If it can, you should contact the office that pays your benefit well in advance, so that arrangements can be made to pay you in the other state.

Under the co-ordination rules, all benefits categorised as social security benefits are exportable. See p1613 for a list of the UK benefits covered.

The following benefits are fully exportable and can be exported indefinitely:
- invalidity benefits;
- old age benefits;
- survivors' cash benefits;
- pensions for accidents at work or occupational diseases;
- death grants.

The following benefits can be exported for a limited period or subject to certain restrictions:
- unemployment benefits;
- sickness, maternity and paternity benefits (although, in most cases, these are exportable in a similar way to the fully exportable benefits).[43]

Special non-contributory benefits (see p1614) cannot be exported. They are paid only in the state in which you are resident.[44]

Family benefits

Under the co-ordination rules, family benefits in the UK include child benefit, child tax credit (CTC), guardian's allowance and child dependants' additions in other benefits.

You can export family benefits without any time limit, provided there is no change in the competent state.[45] Exported family benefits are uprated in the normal way. You can also be paid for family members (see p1611) living in another member state.[46]

Generally, you are entitled to receive family benefits from your competent state, determined in the usual way. However, if you are receiving a pension, you claim family benefits from the state which is the competent state for paying your pension.[47]

If there is entitlement (which, in most cases, requires a claim to have been made) to family benefits in separate states, there are detailed rules to determine which state has priority to pay. These rules prevent family benefits being claimed from more than one state for the same person for the same period.[48] If the state with priority pays family benefits at a lower rate than a state with lower priority, the latter pays a 'top-up' to supplement the amount paid by the priority state. However, this top-up need not be paid for children residing in another state where entitlement to the family benefit is based on residence only (rather than on employment or receipt of a pension).[49] For further information on family benefits, including the priority rules, see CPAG's *Benefits for Migrants Handbook*.

Overlapping benefit rules

A general principle of the co-ordination rules is that you should not use one period of compulsory insurance to obtain more than one benefit.[50] In general, you are only insured in one EEA member state for any one period, so you cannot use insurance from that period to obtain entitlement to benefits of the same kind from two states. Usually, benefits are adjusted to ensure that either only one state pays the benefit, taking into account periods of insurance in other states, or that the benefit is paid pro rata according to the lengths of the periods of insurance in different member states.

In certain cases, however, you may be paid both the full level of a UK benefit and a proportion of a benefit from another member state, accrued as a result of having paid insurance contributions there. Member states are not allowed to apply provisions preventing the overlapping of their own benefits with those of other member states if it would reduce what you would have received from your years of contributions in the first state alone.[51]

Notes

11

1. Introduction

1 *Petit,* C-153/91 [1992] ECR I-04973; Art 3(1) EU Dir 2004/38
2 *The Agreement between the European Community and its Member States, of the one part, and the Swiss Confederation, of the other, on the Free Movement of Persons,* Luxembourg, 21 June 1999, Cmd 5639 (in force 1 June 2002). Note also that reg 2 I(EEA) Regs defines Switzerland as an EEA state.
3 Art 355(3) TFEU

2. Who is covered

4 Art 2 EU Reg 883/04
5 *Petit,* C-153/91 [1992] ECR I-04973
6 Art 1(l) EU Reg 883/04
7 Arts 1(i) and 2 EU Reg 883/04; *PB v SSWP (DLA)* [2016] UKUT 280 (AAC), paras 8-10
8 EU Reg 883/04
9 EU Reg 1408/71

Part 11: Immigration and residence rules for benefits and tax credits
Chapter 68: European Union co-ordination rules
Notes

• •

10 Art 87(8) EU Reg 883/04; Recital (2), Decision H1 of 12 June 2009 of the Administrative Commission for the Co-ordination of Social Security Systems [2010] OJ C-106/13; *SSWP v PW (CA)* [2013] UKUT 296 (AAC)

11 *KG v SSWP (DLA)* [2015] UKUT 146 (AAC)

12 Art 87(8) EU Reg 883/04

13 Art 1 EU Reg 859/2003

3. Which benefits are covered

14 *Commission of the European Communities v European Parliament and Council of the European Union,* C-299/05 [2007] ECR I-08695; *SSWP v Tolley,* C-430/15 [2017] ECR (not yet reported) recently confirmed that DLA care component is a sickness benefit

15 *Stewart v SSWP,* C-503/09 [2011] ECR I-06497

16 Vol 2 para 070153 DMG

17 SSAC, *Universal Credit and Related Regulations Report and Government Response,* December 2012

18 Art 70 and Annex X EU Reg 883/04

19 Art 70 EU Reg 883/04

20 Art 3(3) EU Reg 883/04; *Dano v Jobcenter Leipzig,* C-333/13 [2014] ECR, not yet reported, paras 46-55

21 Art 3(5) EU Reg 883/04

4. Principles of co-ordination

22 Art 11 EU Reg 883/04

23 Art 1(q) and (s) EU Reg 883/04

24 Art 11 EU Reg 883/04

25 Art 11(3)(e) EU Reg 883/04

26 Arts 23-32 EU Reg 883/04; DMG Memo 26/15; ADM Memo 20/15

27 Art 1(j) EU Reg 883/04

28 Art 11 EU Reg 987/2009

29 Art 81 EU Reg 883/04; Art 2 EU Reg 987/2009; *SSWP v AK (AA)* [2015] UKUT 110 (AAC); DMG Memo 27/15

30 Art 6(2) and (3) EU Reg 987/2009; *SSWP v HR (AA)* [2014] UKUT 571 (AAC); *SSWP v FF* [2015] UKUT 488 (AAC). This decision is being appealed to the Court of Appeal, with the hearing due in May 2017: *Feliccia v SSWP,* C3/2016/358; DMG Memo 27/15; ADM Memo 21/15

31 Arts 11-16 EU Reg 883/04

32 Art 16(2) EU Reg 883/04

33 Title III EU Reg 883/04

34 See for example, *Kuusijärvi v Riksförsäkringsverket,* C-275/96 [1998] ECR I-03419; *HB v HMRC (CHB)* [2014] UKUT 554 (AAC); *SSWP v Tolley* C-430/15 [2017] ECR, not yet reported

35 Art 4 EU Reg 883/04

36 Art 5 EU Reg 883/04

37 Art 6 EU Reg 883/04

38 Art 12 EU Reg 987/2009

39 Arts 1(t)(u) and (v) and 6 EU Reg 883/04; *Decision H6 of 16 December 2010 of the Administrative Commission for the Co-ordination of Social Security Systems* [2011] OJ C-45/04

40 *SSWP v MM and BK v SSWP* [2016] UKUT 547 (AAC). Leave to appeal to the Court of Appeal is being sought.

41 Arts 61 and 65(5)(a) EU Reg 883/04

42 Art 7 EU Reg 883/04

43 Art 7 EU Reg 883/04

44 Art 70 EU Reg 883/04

45 Art 67 EU Reg 883/04; *HB v HMRC (CHB)* [2014] UKUT 554 (AAC)

46 Art 67 EU Reg 883/04; *HMRC v Ruas* [2010] EWCA Civ 291

47 Art 67 EU Reg 883/04, second sentence

48 Art 68 EU Reg 883/04

49 Art 68(2) EU Reg 833/04

50 Art 10 EU Reg 883/04

51 *Teresa and Silvana Petroni v Office National des Pensions Pour Travailleurs Salariés (ONPTS), Bruxelles* 24-75 [1975] ECR 01149

11

Appendices

Appendices

Appendix 1

Useful addresses

HM Courts and Tribunals Service

The President of the Social Entitlement Chamber
5th Floor
Fox Court
14 Gray's Inn Road
London WC1X 8HN
presidentsoffice-
sec@hmcts.gsi.gov.uk
www.gov.uk/government/
organisations/hm-courts-and-
tribunals-service

The President of Appeals Tribunals (Northern Ireland)
1st Floor Headline Building
10–14 Victoria Street
Belfast BT1 3GG
Tel: 028 9056 9131
www.dsdni.gov.uk/contacts/
president-appeals-tribunals

Direct lodgement of appeals

England and Wales
HMCTS SSCS Appeals Centre
PO Box 1203
Bradford BD1 9WP

Scotland
HMCTS SSCS Appeals Centre
PO Box 27080
Glasgow G2 9HQ

Social security and child support tribunal areas

Birmingham (Midlands and South East)
Administrative Support Centre
PO Box 14620
Birmingham B16 6FR
Tel: 0300 123 1142
ASCBirmingham@hmcts.gsi.gov.uk

Cardiff (South West and Wales)
Eastgate House
35–43 Newport Road
Cardiff CF24 0AB
Tel: 0300 123 1142
SSCSA-Cardiff@hmcts.gsi.gov.uk

Glasgow (Scotland)
Wellington House
134–136 Wellington Street
Glasgow G2 2XL
Tel: 0141 354 8400
SSCSA-Glasgow@hmcts.gsi.gov.uk

Leeds (North East)
York House
31–36 York Place
Leeds LS1 2ED
Tel: 0300 123 1142
SSCSA-Leeds@hmcts.gsi.gov.uk

A

Liverpool (North West)
36 Dale Street
Liverpool L2 5UZ
Tel: 0300 123 1142
SSCSA-Liverpool@hmcts.gsi.gov.uk

Newcastle (North East)
Manorview House
Newcastle upon Tyne NE1 6PA
Tel: 0300 123 1142
SSCSA-Newcastle@hmcts.gsi.gov.uk

Sutton (London)
Copthall House
9 The Pavement
Grove Road
Sutton SM1 1DA
Tel: 0300 123 1142
SSCSA-Sutton@hmcts.gsi.gov.uk

First-Tier Tribunal (Tax Chamber)
PO Box 16972
Birmingham B16 6TZ
Tel: 0300 123 1024
www.gov.uk/tax-tribunal
taxappeals@hmcts.gsi.gov.uk

The Upper Tribunal (Administrative Appeals Chamber)

England and Wales
5th Floor
7 Rolls Buildings
Fetter Lane
London EC4A 1NL
Tel: 020 7071 5662
adminappeals@hmcts.gsi.gov.uk
www.gov.uk/administrative-appeals-tribunal

Scotland
George House
126 George Street
Edinburgh EH2 4HH
Tel: 0131 271 4310
utaacmailbox@scotland.gsi.gov.uk

Northern Ireland
Tribunal Hearing Centre
2nd Floor, Royal Courts of Justice
Chichester Street
Belfast BT1 3JF
Tel: 028 9072 4848
tribunalsunit@courtsni.gov.uk

The Upper Tribunal (Tax and Chancery Chamber)

England, Wales and Scotland
5th Floor
7 Rolls Buildings
Fetter Lane
London EC4A 1NL
Tel: 020 7612 9730
uttc@hmcts.gsi.gov.uk
www.gov.uk/tax-upper-tribunal

HM Revenue and Customs
www.gov.uk/government/organisations/hm-revenue-customs

Tax Credit Office
www.gov.uk/child-tax-credit
www.gov.uk/working-tax-credit

Tax credit renewal forms:
HM Revenue and Customs
Tax Credit Office
Comben House
Farriers Way
Netherton L75 1AX

A

Complaints or change of circumstances:
HM Revenue and Customs
Tax Credit Office
BX9 1ER

New claims:
HM Revenue and Customs
Tax Credit Office
Liverpool L75 1AZ

Tax Credit Helplines
Tel: 0345 300 3900
Textphone: 0345 300 3909
Intermediaries helpline:
0345 300 3946

Child benefit
Child Benefit Office
PO Box 1
Newcastle upon Tyne NE88 1AA
Tel: 0300 200 3100
Textphone: 0300 200 3103
Intermediaries helpline:
0300 200 3102
www.gov.uk/child-benefit

Guardian's allowance
Guardian's Allowance Unit
PO Box 1
Newcastle upon Tyne NE88 1AA
Tel: 0300 200 3101
Textphone: 0300 200 3103
www.gov.uk/guardians-allowance

Solicitor's Office
South West Wing
Bush House
Strand
London WC2B 4RD

National insurance
National Insurance Contributions
and Employer Office
HM Revenue and Customs
BX9 1AN
Tel: 0300 200 3500
Textphone: 0300 200 3519
www.gov.uk/personal-tax/national-insurance

Statutory Payments Disputes Team
HM Revenue and Customs
PT Operations NE England
BX9 1AN

Department for Work and Pensions
Caxton House
Tothill Street
London SW1H 9NA
www.gov.uk/dwp

Government Legal Department
Litigation Group, Team B6
General Public Law Litigation
One Kemble Street
London WC2B 4TS
Tel: 020 7210 3000
thetreasurysolicitor@
governmentlegal.gov.uk
www.gov.uk/government/
organisations/government-legal-department

DWP Litigation Division
Caxton House
Tothill Street
London SW1H 9NA

Disability and Carers Service

Attendance Allowance Unit

Mail Handling Site A
Wolverhampton WV98 2AD
Tel: 0345 605 6055
Textphone: 0345 604 5312
www.gov.uk/attendance-allowance

Disability Living Allowance Unit

Claimants born on or before 8 April 1948:
Disability Living Allowance DLA65+
Mail Handling Site A
Wolverhampton WV98 2AH
Tel: 0345 605 6055
Textphone: 0345 604 5312
www.gov.uk/dla-disability-living-allowance-benefit

Claimants born after 8 April 1948, aged 16 years and over:
Disability Living Allowance
Mail Handling Site A
Wolverhampton WV98 2AH
Tel: 0345 712 3456
Textphone: 0345 722 4433
www.gov.uk/dla-disability-living-allowance-benefit

Claimants aged under 16 years:
Disability Benefits Centre 4
Post Handling Site B
Wolverhampton WV99 1BY
Tel: 0345 712 3456
Textphone: 0345 722 4433
www.gov.uk/disability-living-allowance-children

Personal Independence Payment Unit

PIP New Claims
Post Handling Site B
Wolverhampton WV99 1AH
Claims: 0800 917 2222
(textphone 0800 917 7777)
Helpline: 0345 850 3322
(textphone 0345 601 6677)
www.gov.uk/pip

Carer's Allowance Unit

Mail Handling Site A
Wolverhampton WV98 2AB
Tel: 0345 608 4321
Textphone: 0345 604 5312
cau.customer-services@dwp.gsi.gov.uk
www.gov.uk/carers-allowance

Exporting benefits overseas

Exportability Team
Room B201
Pension, Disability and Carers Service
Warbreck House
Warbreck Hill Road
Blackpool FY2 0YE
www.gov.uk/exportability-team

Jobcentre Plus

New benefit claims

Tel: 0800 055 6688
Tel: 0800 012 1888 (Welsh speakers)
Textphone: 0800 023 4888
www.gov.uk/contact-jobcentre-plus

National jobcentre enquiry line
To cancel or change a universal credit appointment:
Tel: 0345 600 0723
Tel: 0345 600 3018 (Welsh speakers)
Textphone: 0345 600 0743
To cancel or change other appointments:
Tel: 0345 604 3719
Tel: 0345 604 4248 (Welsh speakers)
Textphone: 0345 608 8551

Enquiries about ongoing claims and to report bereavement
Jobseeker's allowance, income support, employment and support allowance and incapacity benefit
Tel: 0345 608 8545
Tel: 0345 600 3018 (Welsh speakers)
Textphone: 0345 608 8551
Maternity allowance
Tel: 0345 608 8610
Tel: 0345 608 8674 (Welsh speakers)
Textphone: 0345 608 8553
Bereavement benefits
Tel: 0345 608 8601
Tel: 0345 608 8772 (Welsh speakers)
Textphone: 0345 608 8551
Social fund
Tel: 0345 603 6967
Tel: 0345 608 8756 (Welsh speakers)
Textphone: 0345 608 8553

www.gov.uk/contact-jobcentre-plus

Universal credit
Universal credit helpline
Tel: 0345 600 0723
Tel: 0800 012 1888
(Welsh speakers: to make a claim)
Tel: 0345 600 3018
(Welsh speakers: to report a change)
Textphone: 0345 600 0743
www.gov.uk/universal-credit

The Pension Service
Pension credit
Tel: 0800 991 234
Textphone: 0800 169 0133
www.gov.uk/pension-credit

State retirement pension
Tel: 0800 731 7898 (new claims)
Textphone: 0800 731 7339
Tel: 0345 606 0265
(to report a change of circumstances)
Textphone: 0345 606 0285
Welsh speakers: 0800 731 7936
www.gov.uk/contact-pension-service

International Pension Centre
The Pension Service 11
Mail Handling Site A
Wolverhampton WV98 1LW
Tel: 0191 218 7777
Textphone: 0191 218 7280
www.gov.uk/international-pension-centre

Winter fuel payment
Winter Fuel Payment Centre
Mail Handling Site A
Wolverhampton WV98 1LR
Tel: 0345 915 1515
Textphone: 0345 606 0285
www.gov.uk/winter-fuel-payment

A

NHS Business Services Authority

NHS Help with Health Costs
Bridge House
152 Pilgrim Street
Newcastle upon Tyne NE1 6SN
Tel: 0300 330 1343
(low income scheme)
Tel: 0300 330 1341
(medical and maternity exemption
certificates)
Tel: 0300 330 1347
(NHS tax credit exemption
certificates)
Tel: 0300 330 1341
(prescription pre-payment
certificates)
Textphone: dial 18001,
then the relevant number
www.nhsbsa.nhs.uk/healthcosts

Compensation Recovery Unit

England, Scotland and Wales

Post Handling Site B
Wolverhampton WV99 2FR
www.gov.uk/government/
collections/cru

Northern Ireland

Debt Management
Department for Communities
PO Box 2136
Belfast BT1 9RW
Tel: 0300 123 1030
crsteam.belfast@nissa.gsi.gov.uk
www.nidirect.gov.uk/
compensation-recovery

Local Government Ombudsman

England

PO Box 4771
Coventry CV4 0EH
Tel: 0300 061 0614
www.lgo.org.uk

Scottish Public Services Ombudsman

4 Melville Street
Edinburgh EH3 7NS
Tel: 0800 377 7330
www.spso.org.uk

Public Services Ombudsman for Wales

1 Ffordd yr Hen Gae
Pencoed CF35 5LJ
Tel: 0300 790 0203
www.ombudsman-wales.org.uk

The Parliamentary and Health Service Ombudsman

Millbank Tower
30 Millbank
London SW1P 4QP
Tel: 0345 015 4033
phso.enquiries@ombudsman.org.uk
www.ombudsman.org.uk

The Adjudicator

Helen Megarry
Adjudicator's Office
PO Box 10280
Nottingham NG2 9PF
Tel: 0300 057 1111
www.adjudicatorsoffice.gov.uk

Independent Case Examiner

PO Box 209
Bootle L20 7WA
Tel: 0345 606 0777
ice@dwp.gsi.gov.uk
www.gov.uk/government/
organisations/independent-case-
examiner

Judicial Conduct Investigations Office

81–82 Queens Building
Royal Courts of Justice
Strand
London WC2A 2LL
Tel: 020 7073 4719
inbox@jcio.gsi.gov.uk
http://judicialconduct.judiciary.
gov.uk

Standards Commission for Scotland

Room T2.21 Scottish Parliament
Edinburgh EH99 1SP
Tel: 0131 348 6666
enquiries@standardscommission.
org.uk
www.standardscommissions
cotland.org.uk

Commissioner for Ethical Standards in Public Life in Scotland

Thistle House
91 Haymarket Terrace
Edinburgh EH12 5HE
Tel: 0300 011 0550
info@ethicalstandards.org.uk
www.ethicalstandards.org.uk

Information Commissioner's Office

Wycliffe House
Water Lane
Wilmslow SK9 5AF
Tel: 0303 123 1113

Appendix 2

Information and advice

Independent advice and representation

If you want advice or information on a benefit or tax credit issue, the following may be able to assist.

- Citizens Advice Bureaux (CABx). You can find out where your local CAB is from the Citizens Advice website at www.citizensadvice.org.uk (England and Wales) or www.cas.org.uk (Scotland).
- Law centres. You can find your nearest law centre at www.lawcentres.org.uk.
- Other independent advice centres.
- Local authority welfare rights services.
- Local organisations for particular groups of claimants may offer help. For instance, there are unemployed centres, pensioners' groups and centres for people with disabilities.
- In England and Wales, Civil Legal Advice (tel: 0345 345 4345 or www.gov.uk/civil-legal-advice). In Scotland, Scottish Legal Aid Board (tel: 0845 122 8686 or www.slab.org.uk). **Note:** help with welfare benefits in England and Wales is limited to appeals in the Upper Tribunal and higher courts.

Advice from CPAG

Unfortunately, CPAG is unable to deal with enquiries directly from members of the public, but if you are an adviser you can phone or email for help with advising your client.

Advisers in England, Wales and Northern Ireland can call from 10am to 12pm and from 2pm to 4pm (Monday to Friday) on 020 7812 5231. Email advice is now limited to enquiries that are specifically about universal credit, child benefit and tax credits. Our email address is advice@cpag.org.uk.

Organisations based in Scotland can contact CPAG in Scotland at Unit 9, Ladywell, 94 Duke Street, Glasgow G4 0UW or email advice@cpagscotland.org.uk. A phone line is open for advisers in Scotland from 10am to 4pm (Monday to Thursday) and from 10am to 12pm (Friday) on 0141 552 0552.

Ask CPAG Online is an online resource, answering some frequently asked questions about common problem areas in the benefit and tax credit system. We also offer an email advice service on the topics covered. See www.cpag.org.uk/askcpag.

For more information, see www.cpag.org.uk/advisers.

CPAG takes on a small number of test cases each year. We focus on cases that have the potential to improve the lives of families with children in poverty. If you are an adviser and would like to refer a test case to us please see www.cpag.org.uk/test-case-referrals.

Advice from the DWP

See Appendix 1 of this *Handbook* for contact details for the DWP and HM Revenue and Customs.

Finding help online

Information about benefits and tax credits, including a selection of leaflets and forms, is available on the www.gov.uk website.

CPAG's website (www.cpag.org.uk) has articles, briefings and factsheets on benefit issues.

The Rightsnet website (aimed at advisers) at www.rightsnet.org.uk provides information on new welfare rights legislation, caselaw and guidance. It also provides updates on developments in other areas of social welfare law and has a discussion forum where advisers can discuss particular cases.

Most Acts and regulations can be found at www.legislation.gov.uk.

You can find commissioners' and Upper Tribunal decisions at www.gov.uk/administrative-appeals-tribunal-decisions.

Appendix 3

Useful publications

Many of the books listed here will be in your local public library. Stationery Office books are available from Stationery Office bookshops or ordered by post, telephone, email or online from from TSO Orders, PO Box 29, Norwich NR3 1GN (tel: 0333 202 5070; email: customer.services@tso.co.uk; web: www.tsoshop.co.uk). Many publications listed are available from CPAG; see below for order details, or order from www.shop.cpag.org.uk.

1. Caselaw and legislation

The Law Relating to Social Security
All the legislation but without any commentary. Known as the 'Blue Book'.
Available at http://lawvolumes.dwp.gov.uk and updated up until October 2015.
Check also www.legislation.gov.uk.

Social Security Legislation, Volume I: Non-Means-Tested Benefits and Employment and Support Allowance
D Bonner, I Hooker and R White (Sweet & Maxwell)
Legislation with commentary. 2017/18 edition (September 2017): £113 for the main volume.

Social Security Legislation, Volume II: Income Support, Jobseeker's Allowance, State Pension Credit and the Social Fund
J Mesher, P Wood, R Poynter, N Wikeley and D Bonner (Sweet & Maxwell)
Legislation with commentary. 2017/18 edition (September 2017): £113 for the main volume.

Social Security Legislation, Volume III: Administration, Adjudication and the European Dimension
M Rowland and R White (Sweet & Maxwell)
Legislation with commentary. 2017/18 edition (September 2017): £113 for the main volume.

Social Security Legislation, Volume IV: Tax Credits and HMRC-administered Social Security Benefits
N Wikeley and D Williams (Sweet & Maxwell)
Legislation with commentary. 2017/18 edition (September 2017): £113 for the main volume.

Social Security Legislation, Volume V: Universal Credit
P Wood, R Poynter and N Wikeley (Sweet & Maxwell)
Legislation with commentary. (November 2016): £90 for the main volume.

Social Security Legislation – updating supplement to Volumes I – IV
(Sweet & Maxwell)
The spring 2017 update to the 2016/17 main volumes: £70.

Making Appeals Work Caselaw Pack
(MNP Training)
1st edition (November 2016). £58.50 (printed book), £48.50 (USB), £82.50
(printed book and USB).

PIP Caselaw Pack
(MNP Training)
1st edition (October 2017). £58.50 (printed book), £48.50 (USB), £82.50 (printed
book and USB).

Work Capability Assessment Caselaw Pack
(MNP Training)
3rd edition (June 2017). £58.50 (printed book), £48.50 (USB), £82.50 (printed
book and USB).

Child Support: The Legislation
E Jacobs (CPAG)
Legislation with detailed commentary. 13th edition main volume (autumn
2017): £99 (£84.15 members and CABx).

Housing Benefit and Council Tax Reduction Legislation
L Findlay, R Poynter, S Wright, C George, M Williams, S Mitchell and M Brough
(CPAG)
Legislation with detailed commentary. 2017/18, 30th edition (winter 2017):
£125 including Supplement (£106.24 members and CABx). The 29th edition
(2016/17) is still available, £125 per set (£106.25 members and CABx).

Official guidance

Decision Makers' Guide
Available at www.gov.uk/government/collections/decision-makers-guide-staff-
guide.

Advice for Decision Making: staff guide
Available at www.gov.uk/government/publications/advice-for-decision-making-
staff-guide.

Housing Benefit Guidance Manual
Available at www.gov.uk/government/collections/housing-benefit-claims-
processing-and-good-practice-for-local-authority-staff.

Discretionary Housing Payments Guidance Manual
Available at www.gov.uk/government/publications/discretionary-housing-
payments-guidance-manual.

DWP Health and Work Guidance
Available at www.gov.uk/government/collections/healthcare-practitioners-
guidance-and-information-from-dwp.

Work Capability Assessment (WCA) Handbook: for healthcare professionals
Available at www.gov.uk/government/publications/work-capability-assessment-
handbook-for-healthcare-professionals.

Tax Credits Technical Manual
Available at www.hmrc.gov.uk/manuals/tctmanual.

Budgeting Loan Guide
Available at www.gov.uk/government/publications/budgeting-loan-guide-for-
decision-makers-reviewing-officers-and-further-reviewing-officers.

Personal Independence Payment Assessment Guide for Assessment Providers
Available at www.gov.uk/government/publications/personal-independence-
payment-assessment-guide-for-assessment-providers.

3. Leaflets

The DWP publishes many leaflets, available free from your local DWP or
Jobcentre Plus office. To order DWP leaflets, or receive information about new
leaflets, contact iON, 2nd Floor, One City West, Gelderd Road, Leeds LS12 6NJ,
email: ion-pass@xerox.com or complete the order form at www.gov.uk/
government/publications/dwp-leaflets-order-form. Leaflets on housing benefit
are available from your local council.

4. Periodicals

Welfare Rights Bulletin (CPAG, bi-monthly)
Covers developments in social security law, including Upper Tribunal decisions,
and updates this *Handbook* between editions. The annual subscription is £40 (£34
for members and CABx) but it is sent automatically to CPAG members and
welfare rights subscribers (more information at www.cpag.org.uk/membership).

Articles on social security can also be found in *Legal Action* (Legal Action Group), *Adviser* (Citizens Advice) and the *Journal of Social Security Law* (Sweet & Maxwell).

5. Other publications

CPAG's Welfare Benefits and Tax Credits Online
Includes the full text of the *Welfare Benefits and Tax Credits Handbook* updated throughout the year. Annual subscription £61 per user (£51.85 members and CABx). Bulk discounts are available.
More information at www.shop.cpag.org.uk.

Universal Credit: what you need to know
4th edition, summer: 2017 £15 (£12.75 members and CABx)

Financial Help for Families: what you need to know
1st edition, winter 2017: £15 (£12.75 members and CABx)

Personal Independence Payment: what you need to know
2nd edition, August 2016: £15 (£12.75 members and CABx)

Winning Your Benefit Appeal: what you need to know
2nd edition, December 2016: £15 (£12.75 members and CABx)

Child Support Handbook
25th edition, summer 2017: £36 (£30.60 members and CABx)

Debt Advice Handbook
12th edition, summer 2017: £26 (£22.10 members and CABx)

Fuel Rights Handbook
18th edition, November 2016: £26 (£22.10 members and CABx)

Benefits for Students in Scotland Handbook
15th edition, autumn 2017: £20 (£17 members and CABx)
Available free online at: http://onlinepublications.cpag.org.uk.

Council Tax Handbook
11th edition, February 2016: £22 (£18.70 members and CABx)

Benefits for Migrants Handbook
9th edition, autumn 2017: £36 (£30.60 members and CABx)

Children's Handbook Scotland: a benefits guide for children living away from their parents
10th edition, autumn 2017: £20 (£17 members and CABx)
Available free online at: http://onlinepublications.cpag.org.uk

Help with Housing Costs Vol 1: Guide to universal credit and council tax rebates 2017/18
£39.99 (June 2017)

Help with Housing Costs Vol 2: Guide to housing benefit 2017/18
£39.99 (June 2017)

Disability Rights Handbook 2017/18
£33.99 (May 2017)

Tribunal Practice and Procedure
£65 (4th edition, May 2016)

Big Book of Benefits and Mental Health
£25 (17th edition, April 2017)

Big Book of Benefits and Money for Older People
£35 (1st edition, May 2017)

For CPAG publications and most of those in Sections 1 and 5 contact:
CPAG, 30 Micawber St, London N1 7TB tel: 020 7837 7979. Discounts on CPAG
publications are available to CPAG members and Citizens Advice Bureaux.
Enquiries: email: bookorders@cpag.org.uk. Order forms are available at
www.shop.cpag.org.uk. Postage and packing: free for online subscriptions and
orders up to £10 in value; for order value £10.01–£100, add a flat rate charge of
£3.99; for order value £100.01–£400, add £7.49; for order value over £400, add
£11.49.

Appendix 4

Limited capability for work assessment

Schedule 2 Employment and Support Allowance Regulations 2008 and Schedule 6 Universal Credit Regulations 2013

Activity	Descriptors	Points
Part 1: Physical disabilities		

1. Mobilising unaided by another person with or without a walking stick, manual wheelchair or other aid if such aid is normally or could reasonably be worn or used.	(a) Cannot, unaided by another person, either:
	  (i) mobilise more than 50 metres on level ground without stopping in order to avoid significant discomfort orexhaustion; *or*
	  (ii) repeatedly mobilise 50 metres within a reasonable timescale because of significant discomfort or exhaustion.
		15

	(b) Cannot, unaided by another person, mount or descend two steps even with the support of a handrail.	9

	(c) Cannot, unaided by another person, either:
	  (i) mobilise more than 100 metres on level ground without stopping in order to avoid significant discomfort or exhaustion; *or*
	  (ii) repeatedly mobilise 100 metres within a reasonable timescale because of significant discomfort or exhaustion.
		9

	(d) Cannot, unaided by another person, either:
	  (i) mobilise more than 200 metres on level ground without stopping in order to avoid significant discomfort or exhaustion; *or*
	  (ii) repeatedly mobilise 200 metres within a reasonable timescale because of significant discomfort or exhaustion.
		6

	(e) None of the above applies.	0

Activity	Descriptors	Points
2. Standing and sitting.	(a) Cannot move between one seated position and another seated position which are located next to one another without receiving physical assistance from another person.	15
	(b) Cannot, for the majority of the time, remain at a work station:	9
	(i) standing unassisted by another person (even if free to move around);	
	(ii) sitting (even in an adjustable chair); *or*	
	(iii) a combination of paragraphs (i) and (ii), for more than 30 minutes, before needing to move away in order to avoid significant discomfort or exhaustion.	
	(c) Cannot, for the majority of the time, remain at a work station	6
	(i) standing unassisted by another person (even if free to move around);	
	(ii) sitting (even in an adjustable chair); *or*	
	(iii) a combination of paragraphs (i) and (ii), for more than an hour before needing to move away in order to avoid significant discomfort or exhaustion.	
	(d) None of the above applies.	0
3. Reaching.	(a) Cannot raise either arm as if to put something in the top pocket of a coat or jacket.	15
	(b) Cannot raise either arm to top of head as if to put on a hat.	9
	(c) Cannot raise either arm above head height as if to reach for something.	6
	(d) None of the above applies.	0
4. Picking up and moving or transferring by the use of the upper body and arms.	(a) Cannot pick up and move a 0.5 litre carton full of liquid.	15
	(b) Cannot pick up and move a one litre carton full of liquid.	9
	(c) Cannot transfer a light but bulky object such as an empty cardboard box.	6
	(d) None of the above applies.	0
5. Manual dexterity.	(a) Cannot press a button (such as a telephone keypad) with either hand or cannot turn the pages of a book with either hand.	15
	(b) Cannot pick up a £1 coin or equivalent with either hand.	15
	(c) Cannot use a pen or pencil to make a meaningful mark with either hand.	9
	(d) Cannot single-handedly use a suitable keyboard or mouse.	9
	(e) None of the above applies.	0

A

Activity	Descriptors	Points
6. Making self understood through speaking, writing, typing, or other means which are normally or could reasonably be used, unaided by another person.	(a) Cannot convey a simple message, such as the presence of a hazard.	15
	(b) Has significant difficulty conveying a simple message to strangers.	15
	(c) Has some difficulty conveying a simple message to strangers.	6
	(d) None of the above applies.	0

7. Understanding communication by:
  (i) verbal means (such as hearing or lip reading) alone;
  (ii) non-verbal means (such as reading 16 point print or Braille) alone; *or*
  (iii) a combination of sub-paragraphs (i) and (ii), using any aid that is normally or could reasonably be used, unaided by another person.
	(a) Cannot understand a simple message, such as the location of a fire escape, due to sensory impairment.	15

	(b) Has significant difficulty understanding a simple message from a stranger due to sensory impairment.	15
	(c) Has some difficulty understanding a simple message from a stranger due to sensory impairment.	6
	(d) None of the above applies.	0
8. Navigation and maintaining safety using a guide dog or other aid if either or both are normally used or could reasonably be used.	(a) Unable to navigate around familiar surroundings, without being accompanied by another person, due to sensory impairment.	15
	(b) Cannot safely complete a potentially hazardous task such as crossing the road, without being accompanied by another person, due to sensory impairment.	15
	(c) Unable to navigate around unfamiliar surroundings, without being accompanied by another person, due to sensory impairment.	9
	(d) None of the above applies.	0

9. Absence or loss of control whilst conscious leading to extensive evacuation of the bowel and/or bladder, other than enuresis (bed-wetting), despite the wearing or use of any aids or adaptations which are normally or could reasonably be worn or used.	(a) At least once a month experiences:
	  (i) loss of control leading to extensive evacuation of the bowel and/or voiding of the bladder; *or*
	  (ii) substantial leakage of the contents of a collecting device,
	sufficient to require cleaning and a change in clothing.
		15

	(b) The majority of the time is at risk of loss of control leading to extensive evacuation of the bowel and/or voiding of the bladder, sufficient to require cleaning and a change in clothing, if not able to reach a toilet quickly.	6
	(c) Neither of the above applies.	0

Activity	Descriptors	Points
10. Consciousness during waking moments	(a) At least once a week, has an involuntary episode of lost or altered consciousness resulting in significantly disrupted awareness or concentration.	15
	(b) At least once a month, has an involuntary episode of lost or altered consciousness resulting in significantly disrupted awareness or concentration.	6
	(c) Neither of the above applies.	0

Part 2: Mental, cognitive and intellectual function assessment

Activity	Descriptors	Points
11. Learning tasks.	(a) Cannot learn how to complete a simple task, such as setting an alarm clock.	15
	(b) Cannot learn anything beyond a simple task, such as setting an alarm clock.	9
	(c) Cannot learn anything beyond a moderately complex task, such as the steps involved in operating a washing machine to clean clothes.	6
	(d) None of the above applies.	0
12. Awareness of everyday hazards (such as boiling water or sharp objects).	(a) Reduced awareness of everyday hazards leads to a significant risk of:	15
	(i) injury to self or others; *or*	
	(ii) damage to property or possessions,	
	such that the claimant requires supervision for the majority of the time to maintain safety.	
	(b) Reduced awareness of everyday hazards leads to a significant risk of:	9
	(i) injury to self or others; *or*	
	(ii) damage to property or possessions,	
	such that the claimant frequently requires supervision to maintain safety.	
	(c) Reduced awareness of everyday hazards leads to a significant risk of:	6
	(i) injury to self or others; *or*	
	(ii) damage to property or possessions,	
	such that the claimant occasionally requires supervision to maintain safety.	
	(d) None of the above applies.	0
13. Initiating and completing personal action (which means planning, organisation, problem solving, prioritising or switching tasks).	(a) Cannot, due to impaired mental function, reliably initiate or complete at least two sequential personal actions.	15
	(b) Cannot, due to impaired mental function, reliably initiate or complete at least two sequential personal actions for the majority of the time.	9
	(c) Frequently cannot, due to impaired mental function, reliably initiate or complete at least two sequential personal actions.	6
	(d) None of the above applies.	0

Activity		Descriptors	Points
14. Coping with change.	(a)	Cannot cope with any change to the extent that day to day life cannot be managed.	15
	(b)	Cannot cope with minor planned change (such as a pre-arranged change to the routine time scheduled for a lunch break), to the extent that, overall, day to day life is made significantly more difficult.	9
	(c)	Cannot cope with minor unplanned change (such as the timing of an appointment on the day it is due to occur), to the extent that, overall, day to day life is made significantly more difficult.	6
	(d)	None of the above applies.	0
15. Getting about.	(a)	Cannot get to any place outside the claimant's home with which the claimant is familiar.	15
	(b)	Is unable to get to a specified place with which the claimant is familiar, without being accompanied by another person.	9
	(c)	Is unable to get to a specified place with which the claimant is unfamiliar without being accompanied by another person.	6
	(d)	None of the above applies.	0
16. Coping with social engagement due to cognitive impairment or mental disorder.	(a)	Engagement in social contact is always precluded due to difficulty relating to others or significant distress experienced by the claimant.	15
	(b)	Engagement in social contact with someone unfamiliar to the claimant is always precluded due to difficulty relating to others or significant distress experienced by the claimant.	9
	(c)	Engagement in social contact with someone unfamiliar to the claimant is not possible for the majority of the time due to difficulty relating to others or significant distress experienced by the claimant.	6
	(d)	None of the above applies.	0
17. Appropriateness of behaviour with other people, due to cognitive impairment or mental disorder.	(a)	Has, on a daily basis, uncontrollable episodes of aggressive or disinhibited behaviour that would be unreasonable in any workplace.	15
	(b)	Frequently has uncontrollable episodes of aggressive or disinhibited behaviour that would be unreasonable in any workplace.	15
	(c)	Occasionally has uncontrollable episodes of aggressive or disinhibited behaviour that would be unreasonable in any workplace.	9
	(d)	None of the above applies.	0

A

Appendix 5

Limited capability for work-related activity assessment

Schedule 3 Employment and Support Allowance Regulations 2008 and Schedule 7 Universal Credit Regulations 2013

Activity	Descriptors
1. Mobilising unaided by another person with or without a walking stick, manual wheelchair or other aid if such aid is normally or could reasonably be worn or used.	Cannot either: (a) mobilise more than 50 metres on level ground without stopping in order to avoid significant discomfort or exhaustion; or (b) repeatedly mobilise 50 metres within a reasonable timescale because of significant discomfort or exhaustion.
2. Transferring from one seated position to another.	Cannot move between one seated position and another seated position located next to one another without receiving physical assistance from another person.
3. Reaching.	Cannot raise either arm as if to put something in the top pocket of a coat or jacket.
4. Picking up and moving or transferring by the use of the upper body and arms (excluding standing, sitting, bending or kneeling and all other activities specified in this Schedule).	Cannot pick up and move a 0.5 litre carton full of liquid.
5. Manual dexterity.	Cannot press a button (such as a telephone keypad) with either hand or cannot turn the pages of a book with either hand.
6. Making self understood through speaking, writing, typing, or other means which are normally, or could reasonably be, used unaided by another person.	Cannot convey a simple message, such as the presence of a hazard.

A

Activity	Descriptors

7. Understanding communication by:
   (i) verbal means (such as hearing or lip reading) alone;
   (ii) non-verbal means (such as reading 16 point print or Braille) alone; or
   (iii) a combination of sub-paragraphs (i) and (ii),
using any aid that is normally, or could reasonably, be used unaided by another person.
	Cannot understand a simple message, such as the location of a fire escape, due to sensory impairment.

8. Absence or loss of control whilst conscious leading to extensive evacuation of the bowel and/or voiding of the bladder, other than enuresis (bed-wetting), despite the wearing or use of any aids or adaptations which are normally or could reasonably be worn or used.	At least once a week experiences: (a) loss of control leading to extensive evacuation of the bowel and/or voiding of the bladder; *or* (b) substantial leakage of the contents of a collecting device sufficient to require the individual to clean themselves and change clothing.
9. Learning tasks.	Cannot learn how to complete a simple task, such as setting an alarm clock, due to cognitive impairment or mental disorder.
10. Awareness of hazard.	Reduced awareness of everyday hazards, due to cognitive impairment or mental disorder, leads to a significant risk of: (a) injury to self or others; *or* (b) damage to property or possessions, such that the claimant requires supervision for the majority of the time to maintain safety.
11. Initiating and completing personal action (which means planning, organisation, problem solving, prioritising or switching tasks).	Cannot, due to impaired mental function, reliably initiate or complete at least two sequential personal actions.
12. Coping with change.	Cannot cope with any change, due to cognitive impairment or mental disorder, to the extent that day to day life cannot be managed.
13. Coping with social engagement, due to cognitive impairment or mental disorder.	Engagement in social contact is always precluded due to difficulty relating to others or significant distress experienced by the claimant.
14. Appropriateness of behaviour with other people, due to cognitive impairment or mental disorder.	Has, on a daily basis, uncontrollable episodes of aggressive or disinhibited behaviour that would be unreasonable in any workplace.

Activity	Descriptors

15. Conveying food or drink to the mouth.	(a) Cannot convey food or drink to the claimant's own mouth without receiving physical assistance from someone else;
	(b) Cannot convey food or drink to the claimant's own mouth without repeatedly stopping or experiencing breathlessness or severe discomfort;
	(c) Cannot convey food or drink to the claimant's own mouth without receiving regular prompting given by someone else in the claimant's presence; *or*
	(d) Owing to a severe disorder of mood or behaviour, fails to convey food or drink to the claimant's own mouth without receiving:
	  (i) physical assistance from someone else; *or*
	  (ii) regular prompting given by someone else in the claimant's presence.

16. Chewing or swallowing food or drink.	(a) Cannot chew or swallow food or drink;
	(b) Cannot chew or swallow food or drink without repeatedly stopping or experiencing breathlessness or severe discomfort;
	(c) Cannot chew or swallow food or drink without repeatedly receiving regular prompting given by someone else in the claimant's presence; *or*
	(d) Owing to a severe disorder of mood or behaviour, fails to:
	  (i) chew or swallow food or drink; *or*
	  (ii) chew or swallow food or drink without regular prompting given by someone else in the claimant's presence.

A

Appendix 6

Disability which puts a person at a disadvantage in getting a job

Schedule 1 Regulation 9(1) to the Working Tax Credit (Entitlement and Maximum Rate) Regulations 2002

PART 1

1. When standing he cannot keep his balance unless he continually holds onto something.

2. Using any crutches, walking frame, walking stick, prosthesis or similar walking aid which he habitually uses, he cannot walk a continuous distance of 100 metres along level ground without stopping or without suffering severe pain.

3. He can use neither of his hands behind his back as in the process of putting on a jacket or of tucking a shirt into trousers.

4. He can extend neither of his arms in front of him so as to shake hands with another person without difficulty.

5. He can put neither of his hands up to his head without difficulty so as to put on a hat.

6. Due to lack of manual dexterity he cannot, with one hand, pick up a coin which is not more than $2\frac{1}{2}$ centimetres in diameter.

7. He is not able to use his hands or arms to pick up a full jug of 1 litre capacity and pour from it into a cup, without difficulty.

8. He can turn neither of his hands sideways through 180 degrees.

9. He is certified as severely sight impaired or blind by a consultant ophthalmologist.

10. He cannot see to read 16 point print at a distance greater than 20 centimetres, if appropriate, wearing the glasses he normally uses.

11. He cannot hear a telephone ring when he is in the same room as the telephone, if appropriate, using a hearing aid he normally uses.

12. In a quiet room he has difficulty in hearing what someone talking in a loud voice at a distance of 2 metres says, if appropriate, using a hearing aid he normally uses.

13. People who know him well have difficulty in understanding what he says.

14. When a person he knows well speaks to him, he has difficulty in understanding what that person says.

15. At least once a year during waking hours he is in a coma or has a fit in which he loses consciousness.

16. He has a mental illness for which he receives regular treatment under the supervision of a medically qualified person.

17. Due to mental disability he is often confused or forgetful.

18. He cannot do the simplest addition and subtraction.

19. Due to mental disability he strikes people or damages property or is unable to form normal social relationships.

20. He cannot normally sustain an 8 hour working day or a five day working week due to a medical condition or intermittent or continuous severe pain.

PART 2 (INITIAL CLAIMS ONLY)

21. As a result of an illness or accident he is undergoing a period of habilitation or rehabilitation.

A

Appendix 7

Prescribed degrees of disablement

Schedule 2 to the Social Security (General Benefit) Regulations 1982 SI No.1408

Description of injury	Degree of disablement %
1 Loss of both hands or amputation at higher sites	100
2 Loss of a hand and a foot	100
3 Double amputation through leg or thigh, or amputation through leg or thigh on one side and loss of other foot	100
4 Loss of sight to such an extent as to render the claimant unable to perform any work for which eyesight is essential	100
5 Very severe facial disfigurement	100
6 Absolute deafness	100
7 Forequarter or hindquarter amputation	100
Amputation cases – upper limbs (either arm)	
8 Amputation through shoulder joint	90
9 Amputation below shoulder with stump less than 20.5 cms from tip of acromion	80
10 Amputation from 20.5 cms from tip of acromion to less than 11.5 cms below tip of olecranon	70
11 Loss of a hand or of the thumb and 4 fingers of 1 hand or amputation from 11.5 cms below tip of olecranon	60
12 Loss of thumb	30
13 Loss of thumb and its metacarpal bone	40
14 Loss of 4 fingers of 1 hand	50
15 Loss of 3 fingers of 1 hand	30
16 Loss of 2 fingers of 1 hand	20
17 Loss of terminal phalanx of thumb	20
Amputation cases – lower limbs	
18 Amputation of both feet resulting in end-bearing stumps	90
19 Amputation through both feet proximal to the metatarso-phalangeal joint	80
20 Loss of all toes to both feet through the metatarso-phalangeal joint	40
21 Loss of all toes of both feet proximal to the proximal inter-phalangeal joint	30
22 Loss of all toes of both feet distal to the proximal inter-phalangeal joint	20
23 Amputation at hip	90
24 Amputation below hip with stump not exceeding 13 cms in length measured from tip of great trochanter	80

A

Description of injury	Degree of disablement %	Description of injury	Degree of disablement %
25 Amputation below hip and above knee with stump exceeding 13 cms in length measured from tip of great trochanter, or at knee not resulting in end-bearing stump	70	37 Guillotine amputation of tip without loss of bone	5
		Middle finger:	
		38 Whole	12
		39 2 phalanges	9
26 Amputation at knee resulting in end-bearing stump or below knee with stump not exceeding 9 cms	60	40 1 phalanx	7
		41 Guillotine amputation of tip without loss of bone	4
27 Amputation below knee with stump exceeding 9 cms but not exceeding 13 cms	50	Ring or little finger:	
		42 Whole	7
		43 2 phalanges	6
28 Amputation below knee with stump exceeding 13 cms	40	44 1 phalanx	5
		45 Guillotine amputation of tip without loss of bone	2
29 Amputation of 1 foot resulting in end-bearing stump	30	**Loss of toes of right or left foot**	
30 Amputation through 1 foot proximal to the metatarso-phalangeal joint	30	Great toe:	
		46 Through metatarso-phalangeal joint	14
31 Loss of all toes of 1 foot through the metatarso-phalangeal joint	20	47 Part, with some loss of bone	3
		Any other toe:	
Other injuries		48 Through metatarso-phalangeal joint	3
32 Loss of 1 eye, without complications, the other being normal	40	49 Part, with some loss of bone	1
		2 toes of 1 foot, excluding great toe:	
33 Loss of vision of 1 eye, without complications or disfigurement of the eyeball, the other being normal	30	50 Through metatarso-phalangeal joint	5
		51 Part, with some loss of bone	2
		3 toes of 1 foot, excluding great toe:	
Loss of fingers of right or left hand		52 Through metatarso-phalangeal joint	6
Index finger:		53 Part, with some loss of bone	3
		4 toes of 1 foot, excluding great toe:	
34 Whole	14	54 Through metatarso-phalangeal joint	9
35 2 phalanges	11	55 Part, with some loss of bone	3
36 1 phalanx	9		

The degree of disablement due to occupational deafness is assessed using tables and a formula to be found in reg 34 and Sch 3 Social Security (Industrial Injuries) (Prescribed Diseases) Regulations 1985, as amended.

Appendix 8

Prescribed industrial diseases

Part I of Schedule 1 to the Social Security (Industrial Injuries) (Prescribed Diseases) Regulations 1985 as amended

Prescribed disease or injury	Occupation
A – Conditions due to physical agents	Any occupation involving:
A1 Leukaemia (other than chronic lymphatic leukaemia) or primary cancer of the bone, bladder, breast, colon, liver, lung, ovary, stomach, testis, or thyroid.	Exposure to ionising radiation where the dose is sufficient to double the condition.
A2 Cataract.	Frequent or prolonged exposure to radiation from red-hot or white-hot material.
A3 (a) Dysbarism, including decompression sickness and barotrauma; (b) Osteonecrosis	Subjection to compressed or rarified air or from molten or red-hot material.
A4 Task-specific focal dystonia of the hand or forearm.	Prolonged periods of handwriting, typing or other repetitive movements of the fingers, hand or arm.
A5 Subcutaneous cellulitis of the hand.	Manual labour causing severe or prolonged friction or pressure on the hand.
A6 Bursitis or subcutaneous cellulites arising at or about the knee due to severe or prolonged external friction or pressure at or about the knee.	Manual labour causing severe or prolonged external friction or pressure at or about the knee.
A7 Bursitis or subcutaneous cellulites arising at or about the elbow due to severe or prolonged external friction or pressure at or about the elbow (beat elbow).	Manual labour causing severe or prolonged external friction or pressure at or about the elbow.
A8 Traumatic inflammation of the tendons of the hand or forearm, or of the associated tendon sheaths.	Manual labour, or frequent or repeated movements of the hand or wrist.

Prescribed disease or injury	Occupation
A10 Sensorineural hearing loss amounting to at least 50dB in each ear, being the average of hearing losses at 1, 2 and 3 kHz frequencies, and being due in the case of at least one ear to occupational noise (occupational deafness).	Any occupation involving the use of, or work wholly or mainly in the immediate vicinity of the use of, a:

(a) band saw, circular saw or cutting disc to cut metal in the metal founding or forging industries, circular saw to cut products in the manufacture of steel, powered (other than hand powered) grinding tool on metal (other than sheet metal or plate metal), pneumatic percussive tool on metal, pressurised air arc tool to gouge metal, burner or torch to cut or dress steel based products, skid transfer bank, knock out and shake out grid in a foundry, machine (other than a power press machine) to forge metal including a machine used to drop stamp metal by means of closed or open dies or drop hammers, machine to cut or shape or clean metal nails, or plasma spray gun to spray molten metal;

(b) pneumatic percussive tool to drill rock in a quarry, on stone in a quarry works, used underground, for mining coal, for sinking a shaft, or for tunnelling in civil engineering works;

(c) vibrating metal moulding box in the concrete products industry, or circular saw to cut concrete masonry blocks;

(d) machine in the manufacture of textiles for weaving man-made or natural fibres (including mineral fibres), high speed false twisting of fibres, or the mechanical cleaning of bobbins;

(e) multi-cutter moulding machine on wood, planing machine on wood, automatic or semi-automatic lathe on wood, multiple cross-cut machine on wood, automatic shaping machine on wood, double-end tenoning machine on wood, vertical spindle moulding machine (including a high speed routing machine) on wood, edge banding machine on wood, bandsawing machine (with a blade width of not less than 75 millimetres) on wood including one operated by moving the blade towards the material being cut, or chain saw on wood;

(f) jet of water (or a mixture of water and abrasive material) at a pressure above 680 bar, or jet channelling process to burn stone in a quarry;

Prescribed disease or injury	Occupation
	(g) machine in a ship's engine room, or gas turbine for performance testing on a test bed, installation testing of a replacement engine in an aircraft, or acceptance testing of an Armed Service fixed wing combat aircraft;
	(h) machine in the manufacture of glass containers or hollow ware for automatic moulding, automatic blow moulding, or automatic glass pressing and forming;
	(i) spinning machine using compressed air to produce glass wool or mineral wool;
	(j) continuous glass toughening furnace;
	(k) firearm by a police firearms training officer;
	(l) shot-blaster to carry abrasives in air for cleaning.

A11(a) Intense blanching of the skin, with a sharp demarcation line between affected and non-affected skin, where the blanching is cold-induced, episodic, occurs throughout the year and affects the skin of the distal with the middle and proximal phalanges, or distal with the middle phalanx (or in the case of a thumb the distal with the proximal phalanx), of–

(i) in the case of a person with 5 fingers (including thumb) on one hand, any 3 of those fingers, or

(ii) in the case of a person with only 4 such fingers, any 2 of those fingers, or

(iii) in the case of a person with less than 4 such fingers, any one of them or, as the case may be, the one remaining finger, where none of the person's fingers was subject to any degree of cold-induced, episodic blanching of the skin prior to the person's employment in an occupation described in the second column in relation to this paragraph, or

Prescribed disease or injury	Occupation
(b) significant, demonstrable reduction in both sensory perception and manipulative dexterity with continuous numbness or continuous tingling all present at the same time in the distal phalanx of any finger (including thumb) where none of the person's fingers was subject to any degree of reduction in sensory perception, manipulative dexterity, numbness or tingling prior to the person's employment in an occupation described in the second column in relation to this paragraph, where the symptoms in paragraph (a) or paragraph (b) were caused by vibration.	(a) The use of hand-held chain saws on wood; or (b) the use of hand-held rotary tools in grinding or in the sanding or polishing of metal, or the holding of material being ground, or metal being sanded or polished by rotary tools; or (c) the use of hand-held percussive metal-working tools, or the holding of metal being worked upon by percussive tools, in riveting, caulking, chipping, hammering, fettling or swaging; or (d) the use of hand-held powered percussive drills or hand-held powered percussive hammers in mining, quarrying, demolition, or on roads or footpaths, including road construction; or (e) the holding of material being worked upon by pounding machines in shoe manufacture.
A12 Carpal tunnel syndrome.	(a) The use, at the time the symptoms first develop, of hand-held powered tools whose internal parts vibrate so as to transmit that vibration to the hand; or (b) repeated palmar flexion and dorsiflexion of the wrist for at least 20 hours per week for a period or periods amounting in aggregate to at least 12 months in the 24 months prior to the onset of the symptoms, where 'repeated' means once or more often in every 30 seconds.
A13 Osteoarthritis of the hip.	Work in agriculture as a farmer or farm worker for a period of, or periods which amount in aggregate to, 10 years or more.
A14 Osteoarthritis of the knee.	Work underground in a coal mine for a period of, or periods which amount in aggregate to, at least 10 years in any one or more of the following occupations: (a) before 1 Januray 1986 as a coal miner; or (b) on or after 1 Januray 1986 as a– (i) face worker working on a non-mechanised coal face;* (ii) development worker; (iii) face-salvage worker; (iv) conveyor belt cleaner; or (v) conveyor belt attendant. *"A non-mechanised coal face' means a coal face without either powered roof supports or a power loader machine which simultaneously cuts and loads the coal or without both. Work wholly or mainly fitting or laying carpets or other floors (other than concrete floors) for a period of, or periods which amount in aggregate to, 20 years or more.

A

Prescribed disease or injury	Occupation
B – Conditions due to biological agents	Any occupation involving:
B1 (a) Cutaneous anthrax; (b) Pulmonary anthrax.	(a) Contact with anthrax spores, including contact with animals infected by anthrax; *or* (b) handling, loading, unloading or transport of animals of a type susceptible to infection with anthrax or of the products or residues of such animals.
B2 Glanders.	Contact with equine animals or their carcasses.
B3 Infection by leptospira.	(a) Work in places which are, or are liable to be, infested by rats, field mice or voles, or other small mammals; *or* (b) work at dog kennels or the care or handling of dogs; *or* (c) contact with bovine animals or pigs or their meat products.
B4 (a) Cutaneous larva migrans; (b) Iron deficiency anaemia caused by gastrointestinal infection by hookwork.	Contact with a source of ankylostomiasis.
B5 Tuberculosis.	Contact with a source of tuberculous infection.
B6 Extrinsic allergic alveolitis.	Exposure to moulds or fungal spores or heterologous proteins or any other biological substance that causes extrinsic allergic alveolitis by reason of employment in: (a) agriculture, horticulture, forestry, cultivation of edible fungi or malt-working; *or* (b) loading or unloading or handling in storage mouldy vegetable matter or edible fungi; *or* (c) caring for or handling birds; *or* (d) handling bagasse; *or* (e) work involving exposure to metalworking fluids mist; *or* (f) any other workplace.
B7 Infection by organisms of the genus brucella.	Contact with: (a) animals infected by brucella, or their carcasses or parts thereof, or their untreated products; *or* (b) laboratory specimens or vaccines of, or containing, brucella.
B8 (a) Infection by hepatitis A virus.	Contact with raw sewage.
(b) Infection by hepatitis B or C virus.	Contact with: (a) human blood or human blood products; *or* (b) any other source of hepatitis B or C virus.
B9 Infection by Streptococcus suis.	Contact with pigs infected by Streptococcus suis, or with the carcasses, products or residues of pigs so infected.
B10 (a) Avian chlamydiosis.	Contact with birds infected with chlamydia psittaci, or with the remains or untreated products of such birds.

Prescribed disease or injury	Occupation
(b) Ovine chlamydiosis.	Contact with sheep infected with chlamydia psittaci, or with the remains or untreated products of such sheep.
B11 Q fever.	Contact with animals, their remains or their untreated products.
B12 Orf.	Contact with sheep, goats or with the carcasses of sheep or goats.
B13 Hydatidosis.	Contact with dogs.
B14 Lyme disease.	Exposure to deer or other mammals of a type liable to harbour ticks harbouring Borrelia bacteria.
B15 Anaphylaxis.	Employment as a healthcare worker having contact with products made with natural rubber latex.
C – Conditions due to chemical agents	Any occupation involving:
C1 (a) Anaemia with a haemoglobin concentration of 9g/dl or less, and a blood film showing punctate basophilia. (b) Peripheral neuropathy. (c) Central nervous system toxicity.	The use or handling of, or exposure to the fumes, dust or vapour of, lead or a compound of lead, or a substance containing lead.
C2 Central nervous system toxicity characterised by parkinsonism.	The use or handling of, or exposure to the fumes, dust or vapour of, manganese or a compound of manganese, or a substance containing manganese.
C3 (a) Phossy Jaw.	Work involving the use or handling of, or exposure to, white phosphorus.
(b) Peripheral polyneuropathy with pyramidal involvement of the central nervous system, caused by organic compounds of phosphorus which inhibit the enzyme neuropathy target esterase.	Work involving the use or handling of, or exposure to, organic compounds of phosphorus.
C4 Primary carcinoma of the bronchus or lung.	Exposure to the fumes, dust or vapour of arsenic, a compound of arsenic or a substance containing arsenic.
C5 (a) Central nervous system toxicity characterised by tremor and neuropsychiatric disease.	Exposure to mercury or inorganic compounds of mercury for a period of, or periods which amount in aggregate to, 10 years or more.
(b) Central nervous system toxicity characterised by combined cerebellar and cortical degeneration.	Exposure to methylmercury.
C6 Peripheral neuropathy.	The use or handling of, or exposure to carbon disulphide (also called carbon disulfide).
C7 Acute non-lymphatic leukaemia.	Exposure to benzene.
C12 (a) Peripheral neuropathy. (b) Central nervous system toxicity.	Exposure to methyl bromide (also called bromomethane).
C13 Cirrhosis of the liver.	Exposure to chlorinated naphthalene.
C16 (a) Neurotoxicity. (b) Cardiotoxicity.	Exposure to the dust of gonioma kamassi.
C17 Chronic beryllium disease.	Inhalation of beryllium or a compound of beryllium.

A

Prescribed disease or injury	Occupation
C18 Emphysema.	Inhalation of cadmium fumes for a period of, or periods which amount in aggregate to, 20 years or more.
C19 (a) Peripheral neuropath. (b) Central nervous system toxicity.	Exposure to acrylamide.
C20 Dystrophy of the cornea (including ulceration of the corneal surface) of the eye.	Exposure to quinone or hydroquinone.
C21 Primary carcinoma of the skin.	Exposure to arsenic or arsenic compounds, tar, pitch, bitumen, mineral oil (including paraffin) or soot.
C22 (a) Primary carcinoma of the mucous membrane of the nose or paranasal sinuses. (b) Primary carcinoma of a bronchus or lung.	Work before 1950 in the refining of nickel involving exposure to oxides, sulphides or water-soluble compounds of nickel.
C23 Primary neoplasm of the epithelial lining of the urinary tract (renal pelvis, ureter, bladder and urethra), including papilloma carcinoma-in-situ and invasive carcinoma.	(a) The manufacture of 1-naphtylamine, 2-naphthylamine, benzidine, auramine, magenta or 4 aminobiphenyl (also called biphenyl-4-ylamine); (b) work in the process of manufacturing methylenebis-orthochloroanile (also called MbOCA) for a period of, or periods which amount in aggregate to, 12 months or more; (c) exposure to 2-naphtylamine, benzidine, 4-aminobiphenyl (also called MbOCA) for a period of, or periods which amount in aggregate to, 12 months or more; (d) exposure to orthotoluidine, 4-chloro-2-methylaniline or salts of those compounds; or (e) exposure for a period of, or periods which amount in aggregate to, 5 years or more, to coal tar pitch volatiles produced in aluminium smelting involving the Sodeberg process (that is to say, the method of producing aluminium by electrolysis in which the anode consists of a paste of petroleum coke and mineral oil which is baked in situ).
C24 (a) Angiosarcoma of the liver. (b) Osteolysis of the terminal phalanges of the fingers. (c) Sclerodermatous thickening of the skin of the hand. (d) Liver fibrosis, due to exposure to vinyl chloride monomer.	Exposure to vinyl chloride monomer in the manufacture of polyvinyl chloride.
C24A Raynaud's phenomenon due to exposure to vinyl chloride monomer.	Exposure to vinyl chloride monomer in the manufacture of polyvinyl chloride before 1st January 1984.

Prescribed disease or injury	Occupation
C25 Vitiligo.	The use or handling of, or exposure to, para-tertiary-butylphenol (also called 4-tert-butylphenol), para-tertiary-butylcatechol (also called 4-tert-butylcatechol), para-amyl-phenol (also called p-pentyl phenol isomers), hydroquinone monobenzyl ether of hydroquinone (also called 4-benzyloxyphenol), mono-benzyl ether of hydroquinone (also called 4-benzyloxyphenol) or mono-butyl ether of hydroquinone (also called 4-butoxyphenol).
C26 (a) Liver toxicity. (b) Kidney toxicity.	The use of or handling of, or exposure to, carbon tetrachloride (also called tetrachloromethane).
C27 Liver toxicity.	The use of or handling of, or exposure to the fumes of, or vapour containing, trichloromethane (also called chloroform).
C29 Peripheral neuropathy.	The use of or handling of, or exposure to, n-hexane or n-butyl methyl ketone.
C30 (a) Dermatitis. (b) Ulceration of the mucous membrane or the epidermis.	The use or handling of, or exposure to, chromic acid, chromates or dichromates.
C31 Bronchiolitis obliterans.	The use or handling of, or exposure to, diacetyl (also called butanedione or 2,3-butanedione) in the manufacture of– (a) diacetyl; or (b) food favouring containing diacetyl; or (c) food to which food flavouring containing diacetyl is added.
C32 Carcinoma of the nasal cavity or associated air sinuses (nasal carcinoma).	(a) The manufacture of inorganic chromates; or (b) work in hexavalent chrome plating.
C33 Chloracne	Exposure to substances known as chloracnegans.
C34 Extrinsic allergic alveolitis	Exposure to airborne isocyanates; or to another chemical substance that causes extrinsic allergic alveolitis.
D – Miscellaneous conditions	occupation involving:
D1 Pneumoconiosis.	[Occupations specified in reg 2(b) of, and Part II of Schedule 1 to, the Social Security (Industrial Injuries) (Prescribed Diseases) Regulations 1985 which are too numerous to set out here. They are all occupations involving exposure to dust, such as mining, quarrying, sand blasting, grinding, making china or earthenware, boiler-sealing and other work involving the use of stone, asbestos, etc.]
D2 Byssinosis.	Work in any room where any process up to and including the weaving process is performed in a factory in which the spinning or manipulation of raw or waste cotton or of flax, or the weaving of cotton or flax, is carried on.

A

Prescribed disease or injury	Occupation
D3 Diffuse mesothelioma (primary neoplasm of the mesothelium of the pleura or of the pericardium or of the peritoneum).	Exposure to asbestos, asbestos dust or any admixture of asbestos at a level above that commonly found in the environment at large.
D4 Allergic rhinitis which is due to exposure to any of the following agents: (a) isocyanates; (b) platinum salts; (c) fumes or dusts arising from the manufacture, transport or use of hardening agents (including epoxy resin curing agents) based on phthalic anhydride, tetrachlorophthalic anhydride, trimellitic anhydride or triethylenetetramine; (d) fumes arising from the use of rosin as a soldering flux; (e) proteolytic enzymes; (f) animals including insects and other anthropods used for the purposes of research or education or in laboratories; (g) dusts arising from the sowing, cultivation, harvesting, drying, handling, milling, transport or storage of barley, oats, rye, wheat or maize, or the handling, milling, transport or storage of meal or flour made therefrom; (h) antibiotics; (i) cimetidine; (j) wood dust; (k) ispaghula; (l) castor bean dust; (m) ipecacuanha; (n) azodice-bonamide; (o) animals including insects and other anthropods or their larval forms, used for the purposes of pest control or fruit cultivation, or the larval forms of animals used for the purposes of research, education or in laboratories; (p) glutaraldehyde; (q) persulphate salts or henna; (r) crustaceans or fish or products arising from these in the food processing industry; (s) reactive dyes; (t) soya bean; (u) tea dust; (v) green coffee bean dust; (w) fumes from stainless steel welding; (x) products made with natural rubber latex.	Exposure to any of the agents set out in column 1 of this paragraph.
D5 Non-infective dermatitis of external origin (excluding dermatitis due to ionising particles or electro-magnetic radiant heat).	Exposure to dust, liquid or vapour or any other external agent except chromic acid, chromates or bi-chromates capable of irritating the skin (including friction or heat but excluding ionising particles or electromagnetic radiations other than radiant heat).

Prescribed disease or injury	Occupation
D6 Carcinoma of the nasal cavity or associated air sinuses (nasal carcinoma).	(a) Attendance for work in or about a building where wooden goods are; *or* (b) attendance for work in a building used for the manufacture of footwear or components of footwear made wholly or partly of leather or fibre board; *or* (c) attendance for work at a place used wholly or mainly for the repair of footwear made wholly or partly of leather or fibre board.
D7 Asthma which is due to exposure to any of the following agents: (a) isocyanates; (b) platinum salts; (c) fumes or dusts arising from the manufacture, transport or use of hardening agents (including epoxy resin curing agents) based on phthalic anhydride, tetrachlorophthalic anhydride, trimellitic anhydride or triethylenetetramine; (d) fumes arising from the use of rosin as a soldering flux; (e) proteolytic enzymes; (f) animals including insects and other arthropods used for the purposes of research or education or in laboratories; (g) dusts arising from the sowing, cultivation, harvesting, drying, handling, milling, transport or storage of barley, oats, rye, wheat or maize, or the handling, milling, transport or storage of meal or flour made therefrom; (h) antibiotics; (i) cimetidine; (j) wood dust; (k) ispaghula; (l) castor bean dust; (m) ipecacuanha; (n) azodicarbonamide; (o) animals including insects and other arthropods or their larval forms, used for the purposes of pest control or fruit cultivation, or the larval forms of animals used for the purposes of research, education or in laboratories; (p) glutaraldehyde; (q) persulphate salts or henna; (r) rustaceans or fish or products arising from these in the food processing industry; (s) reactive dyes; (t) soya bean; (u) tea dust; (v) green coffee bean dust; (w) fumes from stainless steel welding; (wa) products made with natural rubber latex; (x) any other sensitising agent (occupational asthma).	Exposure to any of the agents set out in column 1 of this paragraph.

A

Prescribed disease or injury	Occupation
D8 Primary carcinoma of the lung where there is accompanying evidence of asbestosis.	(a) The working or handling of asbestos or any admixture of asbestos; *or* (b) the manufacture or repair of asbestos textiles or other articles containing or composed of asbestos; *or* (c) the cleaning of any machinery or plant used in any of the foregoing operations and of any chambers, fixtures and appliances for the collection of asbestos dust; *or* (d) substantial exposure to the dust arising from any of the foregoing operations.
D8A Primary carcinoma of the lung.	Exposure to asbestos in the course of– (a) the manufacture of asbestos textiles; *or* (b) spraying asbestos; *or* (c) asbestos insulation work; *or* (d) applying or removing materials containing asbestos in the course of shipbuilding, where all or any of the exposure occurs before 1st January 1975, for a period of, or periods which amount in aggregate to, five years or more, or otherwise, for a period of, or periods which amount in aggregate to, ten years or more.
D9 Unilateral or bilateral diffuse pleural thickening.	(a) The working or handling of asbestos; or any admixture of asbestos; *or* (b) the manufacture or repair of asbestos textiles or other articles containing or composed of asbestos; *or* (c) the cleaning of any machinery or plant used in any of the foregoing operations and appliances for the collection of asbestos dust; *or* (d) substantial exposure to the dust arising from any of the foregoing operations.

D10 Primary carcinoma of the lung.	(a) Work underground in a tin mine; *or*
	(b) exposure to bis(chloromethyl) ether produced during the manufacture of chloromethyl methyl ether; *or*
	(c) exposure to zinc chromate, calcium chromate or strontium chromate in their pure forms; *or*
	
	(d) employment wholly or mainly as a coke oven worker–
	  (i) for a period of, or periods which amount in aggregate to, 15 years or more;
	  (ii) in top oven work, for a period of, or periods which amount in aggregate to, 5 years or more; *or*
	  (iii) in a combination of top oven work and other coke oven work for a total aggregate period of 15 years or more, where one year working in top oven work is treated as equivalent to 3 years in other coke oven work.

Prescribed disease or injury	Occupation
D11 Primary carcinoma of the lung where there is accompanying evidence of silicosis.	Exposure to silica dust in the course of: (a) the manufacture of glass or pottery; (b) tunnelling in or quarrying sandstone or granite; (c) mining metal ores; (d) slate quarrying or the manufacture of artefacts from slate; (e) mining clay; (f) using silicous materials as abrasives; (g) cutting stone; (h) stone masonry; *or* (i) work in a foundry.
D12 Except in the circumstances specified in regulation 2(d): (a) chronic bronchitis; *or* (b) emphysema; *or* (c) both, where there is evidence of a forced expiratory volume in one second (measured from the position of maximum inspiration with the claimant making maximum effort) which is: (i) at least one litre below the appropriate mean value predicted, obtained from the following prediction formulae which give the mean values predicted in litres: For a man, where the measurement is made without back-extrapolation, (3.62 x Height in metres) – (0.031 x Age in years) – 1.41; or, where the measurement is made with back-extrapolation, (3.71 x Height in metres) – (0.032 x Age in years) – 1.44. For a woman, where the measurement is made without back-extrapolation, (3.29 x Height in metres) – (0.029 x Age in years) – 1.42; or where the measurement is made with back-extrapolation, (3.37 x Height in metres) – (0.030 x Age in years) – 1.46; *or* (ii) less than one litre.	Exposure to coal dust (whether before or after 5th July 1948) by reason of working– (a) underground in a coal mine for a period or periods amounting in aggregate to at least 20 years; (b) on the surface of a coal mine as a screen worker for a period or periods amounting in aggregate to at least 40 years before 1st January 1983; *or* (c) both underground in a coal mine, and on the surface as a screen worker before 1st January 1983, where 2 years working as a surface screen worker is equivalent to 1 year working underground, amounting in aggregate to at least the equivalent of 20 years underground. Any such period or periods shall include a period or periods of incapacity while engaged in such an occupation.
D13 Primary cacinoma of the nasopharynx	Exposure to wood dust in the course of the processing of wood or the manufacture or repair of wood products, for a period or periods which amount in aggregate to at least 10 years.

Appendix 9

Upper and lower earnings limits

Year	Lower earnings limit (£)	Primary threshold (£)	Upper earnings limit (£)
1990/91	46		350
1991/92	52		390
1992/93	54		405
1993/94	56		420
1994/95	57		430
1995/96	58		440
1996/97	61		455
1997/98	62		465
1998/99	64		485
1999/00	66		500
2000/01	67	76	535
2001/02	72	87	575
2002/03	75	89	585
2003/04	77	89	595
2004/05	79	91	610
2005/06	82	94	630
2006/07	84	97	645
2007/08	87	100	670
2008/09	90	105	770
2009/10	95	110	844
2010/11	97	110	844
2011/12	102	139	817
2012/13	107	146	817
2013/14	109	149	797
2014/15	111	153	805
2015/16	112	155	815
2016/17	112	155	827
2017/18	113	157	866

A

Appendix 10

Minimum working conditions

Employers are required to provide certain minimum working conditions. These rules are relevant to the universal credit and jobseeker's allowance rules about sanctions and being available for and looking for work. A brief summary of the rules follows.

The Working Time Regulations

These regulations are designed to protect the health and safety of workers. The main rules are:

- a limit on the hours in the average working week;
- minimum annual holiday entitlement;
- entitlement to breaks from work (both daily breaks and a longer break once a week) and to rest periods while at work;
- special protection for night workers.

This *Handbook* cannot cover the detailed rules nor the complicated system of exceptions to them. Seek specialist advice if you think your employer is breaking these rules.

The National Minimum Wage Act

This Act provides that the minimum hourly rate of pay in any job should be:

- if you are aged 25 or over, £7.50. The government calls this the 'national living wage';
- if you are aged 21–24, £7.05;
- if you are aged 18–20, £5.60;
- if you are under age 18 and not of compulsory school age, £4.05;
- if you are in the first year of employment or are under 19, and you are employed under a contract of apprenticeship (or treated as if you are), £3.50.

Appendix 11

Statutory payments for a birth and maternity allowance

Baby is expected during the week beginning Sunday	Latest start date of employment for SMP	15th week before the EWC begins Sunday+	Earliest week for SMP or MA begins Sunday++	66-week test period for MA begins Sunday
2.4.17	2.7.16	18.12.16	15.1.17	27.12.15
9.4.17	9.7.16	25.12.16	22.1.17	3.1.16
16.4.17	16.7.16	1.1.17	29.1.17	10.1.16
23.4.17	23.7.16	8.1.17	5.2.17	17.1.16
30.4.17	30.7.16	15.1.17	12.2.17	24.1.16
7.5.17	6.8.16	22.1.17	19.2.17	31.1.16
14.5.17	13.8.16	29.1.17	26.2.17	7.2.16
21.5.17	20.8.16	5.2.17	5.3.17	14.2.16
28.5.17	27.8.16	12.2.17	12.3.17	21.2.16
4.6.17	3.9.16	19.2.17	19.3.17	28.2.16
11.6.17	10.9.16	26.2.17	26.3.17	6.3.16
18.6.17	17.9.16	5.3.17	2.4.17	13.3.16
25.6.17	24.9.16	12.3.17	9.4.17	20.3.16
2.7.17	1.10.16	19.3.17	16.4.17	27.3.16
9.7.17	8.10.16	26.3.17	23.4.17	3.4.16
16.7.17	15.10.16	2.4.17	30.4.17	10.4.16
23.7.17	22.10.16	9.4.17	7.5.17	17.4.16
30.7.17	29.10.16	16.4.17	14.5.17	24.4.16
6.8.17	5.11.16	23.4.17	21.5.17	1.5.16
13.8.17	12.11.16	30.4.17	28.5.17	8.5.16
20.8.17	19.11.16	7.5.17	4.6.17	15.5.16
27.8.17	26.11.16	14.5.17	11.6.17	22.5.16
3.9.17	3.12.16	21.5.17	18.6.17	29.5.16
10.9.17	10.12.16	28.5.17	25.6.17	5.6.16
17.9.17	17.12.16	4.6.17	2.7.17	12.6.16
24.9.17	24.12.16	11.6.17	9.7.17	19.6.16
1.10.17	31.12.16	18.6.17	16.7.17	26.6.16

Appendix 11: Statutory payments for a birth and maternity allowance

Baby is expected during the week beginning Sunday	Latest start date of employment for SMP	15th week before the EWC begins Sunday+	Earliest week for SMP or MA begins Sunday++	66-week test period for MA begins Sunday
8.10.17	7.1.17	25.6.17	23.7.17	3.7.16
15.10.17	14.1.17	2.7.17	30.7.17	10.7.16
22.10.17	21.1.17	9.7.17	6.8.17	17.7.16
29.10.17	28.1.17	16.7.17	13.8.17	24.7.16
5.11.17	4.2.17	23.7.17	20.8.17	31.7.16
12.11.17	11.2.17	30.7.17	27.8.17	7.8.16
19.11.17	18.2.17	6.8.17	3.9.17	14.8.16
26.11.17	25.2.17	13.8.17	10.9.17	21.8.16
3.12.17	4.3.17	20.8.17	17.9.17	28.8.16
10.12.17	11.3.17	27.8.17	24.9.17	4.9.16
17.12.17	18.3.17	3.9.17	1.10.17	11.9.16
24.12.17	25.3.17	10.9.17	8.10.17	18.9.16
31.12.17	1.4.17	17.9.17	15.10.17	25.9.16
7.1.18	8.4.17	24.9.17	22.10.17	2.10.16
14.1.18	15.4.17	1.10.17	29.10.17	9.10.16
21.1.18	22.4.17	8.10.17	5.11.17	16.10.16
28.1.18	29.4.17	15.10.17	12.11.17	23.10.16
4.2.18	6.5.17	22.10.17	19.11.17	30.10.16
11.2.18	13.5.17	29.10.17	26.11.17	6.11.16
18.2.18	20.5.17	5.11.17	3.12.17	13.11.16
25.2.18	27.5.17	12.11.17	10.12.17	20.11.16
4.3.18	3.6.17	19.11.17	17.12.17	27.11.16
11.3.18	10.6.17	26.11.17	24.12.17	4.12.16
18.3.18	17.6.17	3.12.17	31.12.17	11.12.16
25.3.18	24.6.17	10.12.17	7.1.18	18.12.16
1.4.18	1.7.17	17.12.17	14.1.18	25.12.16
8.4.18	8.7.17	24.12.17	21.1.18	1.1.17
15.4.18	15.7.17	31.12.17	28.1.18	8.1.17
22.4.18	22.7.17	7.1.18	4.2.18	15.1.17
29.4.18	29.7.17	14.1.18	11.2.18	22.1.17
6.5.18	5.8.17	21.1.18	18.2.18	29.1.17
13.5.18	12.8.17	28.1.18	25.2.18	5.2.17
20.5.18	19.8.17	4.2.18	4.3.18	12.2.17
27.5.18	26.8.17	11.2.18	11.3.18	19.2.17
3.6.18	2.9.17	18.2.18	18.3.18	26.2.17
10.6.18	9.9.17	25.2.18	25.3.18	5.3.17
17.6.18	16.9.17	4.3.18	1.4.18	12.3.17
24.6.18	23.9.17	11.3.18	8.4.18	19.3.17
1.7.18	30.9.17	18.3.18	15.4.18	26.3.17

Baby is expected during the week beginning Sunday	Latest start date of employment for SMP	15th week before the EWC begins Sunday+	Earliest week for SMP or MA begins Sunday++	66-week test period for MA begins Sunday
8.7.18	7.10.17	25.3.18	22.4.18	2.4.17
15.7.18	14.10.17	1.4.18	29.4.18	9.4.17
22.7.18	21.10.17	8.4.18	6.5.18	16.4.17
29.7.18	28.10.17	15.4.18	13.5.18	23.4.17
5.8.18	4.11.17	22.4.18	20.5.18	30.4.17
12.8.18	11.11.17	29.4.18	27.5.18	7.5.17
19.8.18	18.11.17	6.5.18	3.6.18	14.5.17
26.8.18	25.11.17	13.5.18	10.6.18	21.5.17
2.9.18	2.12.17	20.5.18	17.6.18	28.5.17
9.9.18	9.12.17	27.5.18	24.6.18	4.6.17
16.9.18	16.12.17	3.6.18	1.7.18	11.6.17
23.9.18	23.12.17	10.6.18	8.7.18	18.6.17
30.9.18	30.12.17	17.6.18	15.7.18	25.6.17
7.10.18	6.1.18	24.6.18	22.7.18	2.7.17
14.10.18	13.1.18	1.7.18	29.7.18	9.7.17
21.10.18	20.1.18	8.7.18	5.8.18	16.7.17
28.10.18	27.1.18	15.7.18	12.8.18	23.7.17
4.11.18	3.2.18	22.7.18	19.8.18	30.7.17
11.11.18	10.2.18	29.7.18	26.8.18	6.8.17
18.11.18	17.2.18	5.8.18	2.9.18	13.8.17
25.11.18	24.2.18	12.8.18	9.9.18	20.8.17
2.12.18	3.3.18	19.8.18	16.9.18	27.8.17
9.12.18	10.3.18	26.8.18	23.9.18	3.9.17
16.12.18	17.3.18	2.9.18	30.9.18	10.9.17
23.12.18	24.3.18	9.9.18	7.10.18	17.9.17
30.12.18	31.3.18	16.9.18	14.10.18	24.9.17

+ EWC is the expected week of childbirth. The 15th week before the EWC is relevant to the continuous employment rule and the earnings condition for SMP, SPP (birth) and SSPP (birth). See Chapter 37.

++ This is the 11th week before the baby is due (unless your baby is born earlier. See Chapters 33 and 37 for possible exceptions).

Appendix 12

Pension age for women born between 6 April 1950 and 5 December 1953

Date of birth	Pension age (in years/months)*	Date pension age reached
06.04.50 – 05.05.50	60.1 – 60.0	06.05.2010
06.05.50 – 05.06.50	60.2 – 60.1	06.07.2010
06.06.50 – 05.07.50	60.3 – 60.2	06.09.2010
06.07.50 – 05.08.50	60.4 – 60.3	06.11.2010
06.08.50 – 05.09.50	60.5 – 60.4	06.01.2011
06.09.50 – 05.10.50	60.6 – 60.5	06.03.2011
06.10.50 – 05.11.50	60.7 – 60.6	06.05.2011
06.11.50 – 05.12.50	60.8 – 60.7	06.07.2011
06.12.50 – 05.01.51	60.9 – 60.8	06.09.2011
06.01.51 – 05.02.51	60.10 – 60.9	06.11.2011
06.02.51 – 05.03.51	60.11 – 60.10	06.01.2012
06.03.51 – 05.04.51	61.0 – 60.11	06.03.2012
06.04.51 – 05.05.51	61.1 – 61.0	06.05.2012
06.05.51 – 05.06.51	61.2 – 61.1	06.07.2012
06.06.51 – 05.07.51	61.3 – 61.2	06.09.2012
06.07.51 – 05.08.51	61.4 – 61.3	06.11.2012
06.08.51 – 05.09.51	61.5 – 61.4	06.01.2013
06.09.51 – 05.10.51	61.6 – 61.5	06.03.2013
06.10.51 – 05.11.51	61.7 – 61.6	06.05.2013
06.11.51 – 05.12.51	61.8 – 61.7	06.07.2013
06.12.51 – 05.01.52	61.9 – 61.8	06.09.2013
06.01.52 – 05.02.52	61.10 – 61.9	06.11.2013
06.02.52 – 05.03.52	61.11 – 61.10	06.01.2014
06.03.52 – 05.04.52	62.0 – 61.11	06.03.2014
06.04.52 – 05.05.52	62.1 – 62.0	06.05.2014

A

Date of birth	Pension age (in years/months)*	Date pension age reached
06.05.52 – 05.06.52	62.2 – 62.1	06.07.2014
06.06.52 – 05.07.52	62.3 – 62.2	06.09.2014
06.07.52 – 05.08.52	62.4 – 62.3	06.11.2014
06.08.52 – 05.09.52	62.5 – 62.4	06.01.2015
06.09.52 – 05.10.52	62.6 – 62.5	06.03.2015
06.10.52 – 05.11.52	62.7 – 62.6	06.05.2015
06.11.52 – 05.12.52	62.8 – 62.7	06.07.2015
06.12.52 – 05.01.53	62.9 – 62.8	06.09.2015
06.01.53 – 05.02.53	62.10 – 62.9	06.11.2015
06.02.53 – 05.03.53	62.11 – 62.10	06.01.2016
06.03.53 – 05.04.53	63.0 – 62.11	06.03.2016
06.04.53 – 05.05.53	63.3 – 63.2	06.07.2016
06.05.53 – 05.06.53	63.6 – 63.5	06.11.2016
06.06.53 – 05.07.53	63.9 – 63.8	06.03.2017
06.07.53 – 05.08.53	64.0 – 63.11	06.07.2017
06.08.53 – 05.09.53	64.3 – 64.2	06.11.2017
06.09.53 – 05.10.53	64.6 – 64.5	06.03.2018
06.10.53 – 05.11.53	64.9 – 64.8	06.07.2018
06.11.53 – 05.12.53	65.0 – 64.11	06.11.2018

* For example, '60.1–60.0' means you would be aged between 60 and 60 years and one month, depending on your date of birth, when you reach pension age.

Appendix 13

Abbreviations used in the notes

AAC	Administrative Appeals Chamber	EWCA Crim	England and Wales Court of Appeal (Criminal Division)
AACR	Administrative Appeals Chamber Reports	EWHC	England and Wales High Court
AC	Appeal Cases	FLR	Family Law Reports
All ER	All England Law Reports	HC	High Court
Art(s)	Article(s)	HL	House of Lords
CA	Court of Appeal	HLR	Housing Law Reports
CC	County Council	IAC	Immigration and Asylum Chamber
CCLR	Community Care Law Reports	ICR	Industrial Cases Reports
Ch	chapter	JPR	Justice of the Peace Reports
CJEU	Court of Justice of the European Union	KB	King's Bench
CLY	Current Law Year Book	LB	London Borough
col	column	MBC	Metropolitan Borough Council
CPR	Civil Procedure Rules	NICA	Northern Ireland Court of Appeal
CS	Court of Session	NICom	Northern Ireland Social Security Commissioner
CSIH	Court of Session, Inner House	OJ	Official Journal of the European Union
CSOH	Court of Session, Outer House	para(s)	paragraph(s)
DC	Divisional Court	QB	Queen's Bench Reports
Dir	Directive	QBD	Queen's Bench Division
E	England	r(r)	rule(s)
ECJ	European Court of Justice	Reg(s)	Regulation(s)
ECR	European Court Reports	s(s)	section(s)
ECtHR	European Court of Human Rights	SC	Supreme Court
EEA	European Economic Area	Sch(s)	Schedule(s)
EEC	European Economic Community	SCLR	Scottish Civil Law Reports
EU	European Union	ScotCS	Scottish Court of Session
EWCA Civ	England and Wales Court of Appeal (Civil Division)	SLT	Scots Law Times
		SSAC	Social Security Advisory Committee

SSWP	Secretary of State for Work and Pensions	UKSC	United Kingdom Supreme Court
TCC	Tax and Chancery Chamber	UKUT	United Kingdom Upper Tribunal
TFEU	The Treaty on the Functioning of the European Union	Vol	volume
		W	Wales
UKHL	United Kingdom House of Lords	WLR	Weekly Law Reports

Acts of Parliament

CA 1989	Children Act 1989
C(LC)A 2000	Children (Leaving Care) Act 2000
C(S)A 1995	Children (Scotland) Act 1995
CJPOA 1994	Criminal Justice and Public Order Act 1994
CMOPA 2008	Child Maintenance and Other Payments Act 2008
CPA 2004	Civil Partnership Act 2004
CSA 1991	Child Support Act 1991
CSA 1995	Child Support Act 1995
CSPSSA 2000	Child Support, Pensions and Social Security Act 2000
ECA 1972	European Communities Act 1972
ETA 1973	Employment and Training Act 1973
GRA 2004	Gender Recognition Act 2004
HRA 1998	Human Rights Act 1998
IA 1971	Immigration Act 1971
IA 1988	Immigration Act 1988
IAA 1999	Immigration and Asylum Act 1999
IT(EP)A 2003	Income Tax (Earnings and Pensions) Act 2003
ITTOIA 2005	Income Tax (Trading and Other Income) Act 2005
JSA 1995	Jobseekers Act 1995
M(SSC)A 2013	Marriage (Same Sex Couples) Act 2013
MCA 1973	Matrimonial Causes Act 1973
NHSA 2006	National Health Service Act 2006
NHS(S)A 1978	National Health Service (Scotland) Act 1978
NHS(W)A 2006	National Health Service (Wales) Act 2006
NHSCCA 1990	National Health Service and Community Care Act 1990
NIA 1965	National Insurance Act 1965
NIAA 2002	Nationality, Immigration and Asylum Act 2002
NICA 2015	National Insurance Contributions Act 2015
PA 1995	Pensions Act 1995
PA 2007	Pensions Act 2007
PA 2014	Pensions Act 2014
PACEA 1984	Police and Criminal Evidence Act 1984
PSA 1993	Pension Schemes Act 1993
SPCA 2002	State Pension Credit Act 2002
SSA 1975	Social Security Act 1975

SSA 1998	Social Security Act 1998
SSA(F)A 1997	Social Security Administration (Fraud) Act 1997
SSAA 1992	Social Security Administration Act 1992
SSCBA 1992	Social Security Contributions and Benefits Act 1992
SSC(TF)A 1999	Social Security Contributions (Transfer of Functions etc) Act 1999
SSFA 2001	Social Security Fraud Act 2001
SS(RB)A 1997	Social Security (Recovery of Benefits) Act 1997
TCA 2002	Tax Credits Act 2002
TCEA 2007	Tribunals, Courts and Enforcement Act 2007
TMA 1970	Taxes Management Act 1970
WRA 2007	Welfare Reform Act 2007
WRA 2009	Welfare Reform Act 2009
WRA 2012	Welfare Reform Act 2012
WRPA 1999	Welfare Reform and Pensions Act 1999
WRWA 2016	Welfare Reform and Work Act 2016

Regulations and other statutory instruments

Each set of regulations has a statutory instrument (SI) number and a date. You can find them all at www.legislation.gov.uk.

A(IWA) Regs	The Accession (Immigration and Worker Authorisation) Regulations 2006 No.3317
A(IWR) Regs	The Accession (Immigration and Worker Registration) Regulations 2004 No.1219
AC(IWA) Regs	The Accession of Croatia (Immigration and Worker Authorisation) Regulations 2013 No.1460
ASPP(G) Regs	The Additional Statutory Paternity Pay (General) Regulations 2010 No.1056
BSP Regs	The Bereavement Support Payment Regulations 2017 (draft)
C(LC)SSB Regs	The Children (Leaving Care) Social Security Benefits Regulations 2001 No.3074
C(LC)SSB(S) Regs	The Children (Leaving Care) Social Security Benefits (Scotland) Regulations 2004 No.747
C(LC)(W) Regs	The Children (Leaving Care) (Wales) Regulations 2001 No.2189 (W151)
CB Regs	The Child Benefit (General) Regulations 2006 No.223
CB(R) Regs	The Child Benefit (Rates) Regulations 2006 No.965
CB&GA(AA) Regs	The Child Benefit and Guardian's Allowance (Administrative Arrangements) Regulations 2003 No.494
CB&GA(Admin) Regs	The Child Benefit and Guardian's Allowance (Administration) Regulations 2003 No.492
CB&GA(DA) Regs	The Child Benefit and Guardian's Allowance (Decisions and Appeals) Regulations 2003 No.916

A

CC(DIS) Regs	The Community Charges (Deductions from Income Support) (No.2) Regulations 1990 No.545
CL(E) Regs	The Care Leavers (England) Regulations 2010 No.2571
CPP&CR(E) Regs	The Care Planning, Placement and Case Review (England) Regulations 2010 No.959
CS(MASC) Regs	The Child Support (Maintenance Assessments and Special Cases) Regulations 1992 No.1815
CS(MCSC) Regs	The Child Support (Maintenance Calculations and Special Cases) Regulations 2000 No.2001/155
CT(DIS) Regs	The Council Tax (Deductions from Income Support) Regulations 1993 No.494
CTC Regs	The Child Tax Credit Regulations 2002 No.2007
CTR(S) Regs	The Council Tax Reduction (Scotland) Regulations 2012 No.303
CTR(SPC)S Regs	The Council Tax Reduction (State Pension Credit) (Scotland) Regulations 2012 No.319
CTRS(DS)E Regs	The Council Tax Reduction Schemes (Default Scheme) (England) Regulations 2012 No.2886
CTRS(DS)W Regs	The Council Tax Reduction Schemes (Default Scheme) (Wales) Regulations 2013 No.3035 (W303)
CTRS(PR)E Regs	The Council Tax Reduction Schemes (Prescribed Requirements) (England) Regulations 2012 No.2885
CTRSPR(W) Regs	The Council Tax Reduction Schemes and Prescribed Requirements (Wales) Regulations 2013 No.3029 (W316)
DFA Regs	Discretionary Financial Assistance Regulations 2001 No.1167
ESA Regs	The Employment and Support Allowance Regulations 2008 No.794
ESA Regs 2013	The Employment and Support Allowance Regulations 2013 No.379
ESA(TP) Regs	The Employment and Support Allowance (Transitional Provisions) Regulations 2008 No.795
ESA(TP)(EA)(No.2) Regs	The Employment and Support Allowance (Transitional Provisions, Housing Benefit and Council Tax Benefit) (Existing Awards) (No.2) Regulations 2010 No.1907
ESA(WRA) Regs	The Employment and Support Allowance (Work-Related Activity) Regulations 2011 No.1349
ESAUC(MA) Regs	The Employment and Support Allowance and Universal Credit (Miscellaneous Amendments and Transitional and Savings Provisions) Regulations 2017 No.204
F(DIS) Regs	The Fines (Deductions from Income Support) Regulations 1992 No.2182
GA(Gen) Regs	The Guardian's Allowance (General) Regulations 2003 No.495
HB Regs	The Housing Benefit Regulations 2006 No.213
HB(HR)A Regs	The Housing Benefit (Habitual Residence) Amendment Regulations 2014 No.539

A

HB(SPC) Regs	The Housing Benefit (Persons who have Attained the Qualifying Age for State Pension Credit) Regulations 2006 No.214
HB&CTB(CP) Regs	The Housing Benefit and Council Tax Benefit (Consquential Provisions) Regulations 2006 No.217
HB&CTB(DA) Regs	The Housing Benefit and Council Tax Benefit (Decisions and Appeals) Regulations 2001 No.1002
HB&CTB(WPD) Regs	The Housing Benefit and Council Tax Benefit (War Pension Disregards) Regulations 2007 No.1619
HB&SPC(TA)(A) Regs	The Housing Benefit and State Pension Credit (Temporary Absence) (Amendment) Regulations 2016 No.624
HSS(DHSF)(W) Regs	The Healthy Start Scheme (Description of Healthy Start Food) (Wales) Regulations 2006 No.3108
HSS&WF(A) Regs	The Healthy Start Scheme and Welfare Food (Amendment) Regulations 2005 No.3262
I(EEA) Regs	The Immigration (European Economic Area) Regulations 2016 No.1052
I(EEA) Regs 2006	The Immigration (European Economic Area) Regulations 2006 No.1003
I(EEA)A Regs 2012	The Immigration (European Economic Area) (Amendment) Regulations 2012 No.1547
I(EEA)A Regs 2013	The Immigration (European Economic Area) (Amendment) (No.2) Regulations 2013 No.3032
IIB(ETSC) Regs	The Industrial Injuries Benefit (Employment Training Schemes and Courses) Regulations 2013 No.2540
IS Regs	The Income Support (General) Regulations 1987 No.1967
IS(AT) Regs	The Income Support (General) Amendment and Transitional Regulations 1995 No.2287
IS(JSACA) Regs	The Income Support (General)(Jobseeker's Allowance Consequential Amendments) Regulations 1996 No.206
IS(WRA) Regs	The Income Support (Work-Related Activity) and Miscellaneous Amendments Regulations 2014 No.1097
JSA Regs	The Jobseeker's Allowance Regulations 1996 No.207
JSA Regs 2013	The Jobseeker's Allowance Regulations 2013 No.378
JSA(HR)A Regs	The Jobseeker's Allowance (Habitual Residence) Amendment Regulations 2013 No.3196
JSA(MWAS) Regs	The Jobseeker's Allowance (Mandatory Work Activity Scheme) Regulations 2011 No.688
JSA(SAPOE) Regs	The Jobseeker's Allowance (Schemes for Assisting Persons to Obtain Employment) Regulations 2013 No.276
MA(C) Regs	The Maternity Allowance (Curtailment) Regulations 2014 No.3053
NHS(CDA) Regs	The National Health Service (Charges for Drugs and Appliances) Regulations 2015 No.570

NHS(DC) Regs	The National Health Service (Dental Charges) Regulations 2005 No.3477
NHS(DC)(S) Regs	The National Health Service (Dental Charges) (Scotland) Regulations 2003 No.158
NHS(DC)(W) Regs	The National Health Service (Dental Charges) (Wales) Regulations 2006 No.491
NHS(FP&CDA)(S) Regs	The National Health Service (Free Prescriptions and Charges for Drugs and Appliances) (Scotland) Regulations 2011 No.55
NHS(FP&CDA)(W) Regs	The National Health Service (Free Prescriptions and Charges for Drugs and Appliances) (Wales) Regulations 2007 No.121
NHS(GOS) Regs	The National Health Service (General Ophthalmic Services) Regulations 1986 No.975
NHS(OCP) Regs	The National Health Service (Optical Charges and Payments) Regulations 1997 No.818
NHS(OCP) Regs 2013	The National Health Service (Optical Charges and Payments) Regulations 2013 No.461
NHS(OCP)(S) Regs	The National Health Service (Optical Charges and Payments) (Scotland) Regulations 1998 No.642
NHS(TERC) Regs	The National Health Service (Travelling Expenses and Remission of Charges) Regulations 2003 No.2382
NHS(TERC)(S) Regs	The National Health Service (Travelling Expenses and Remission of Charges) (Scotland) (No.2) Regulations 2003 No.460
NHS(TERC)(W) Regs	The National Health Service (Travelling Expenses and Remission of Charges Regulations) (Wales) 2007 No.1104
OSPP(A)ASPP(A)& SAP(AO)(PAM) Regs	The Ordinary Statutory Paternity Pay (Adoption), Additional Statutory Paternity Pay (Adoption) and Statutory Adoption Pay (Adoptions from Overseas) (Persons Abroad and Mariners) Regulations 2010 No.150
PAL Regs	The Paternity and Adoption Leave Regulations 2002 No.2788
PIP(TP) Regs	The Personal Independence Payment (Transitional Provisions) Regulations 2013 No.387
POS Regs	The Primary Ophthalmic Services Regulations 2008 No.1186
RO(HBF)O	The Rent Officers (Housing Benefit Functions) Order 1997 No.1984
RO(HBF)(S)O	The Rent Officers (Housing Benefit Functions) (Scotland) Order 1997 No.144
RO(UCF)O	The Rent Officers (Universal Credit Functions) Order 2013 No.382
SF(AM) Regs	The Social Fund (Budgeting Loans) (Applications and Miscellaneous Provisions) Regulations 2015 No.1411

A

SF(AR) Regs	The Social Fund (Application for Review) Regulations 1988 No.34
SF(RDB) Regs	The Social Fund (Recovery by Deductions from Benefits) Regulations 1988 No.35
SFCWP Regs	The Social Fund Cold Weather Payments (General) Regulations 1988 No.1724
SFM&FE Regs	The Social Fund Maternity and Funeral Expenses (General) Regulations 2005 No.3061
SFWFP Regs	The Social Fund Winter Fuel Payment Regulations 2000 No.729
SMP Regs	The Statutory Maternity Pay (General) Regulations 1986 No.1960
SMP(ME) Regs	The Statutory Maternity Pay (Medical Evidence) Regulations 1987 No.235
SMP(PAM) Regs	The Statutory Maternity Pay (Persons Abroad and Mariners) Regulations 1987 No.418
SMP&SAP(C) Regs	The Statutory Maternity Pay and Statutory Adoption Pay (Curtailment) Regulations 2014 No.3054
SMPSS(MA) Regs	The Statutory Maternity Pay, Social Security (Maternity Allowance) and Social Security (Overlapping Benefits) (Amendment) Regulations 2006 No.2379
SP Regs	The State Pension Regulations 2015 No.173
SPC Regs	The State Pension Credit Regulations 2002 No.1792
SPC(CTMP) Regs	The State Pension Credit (Consequential, Transitional and Miscellaneous Provisions) Regulations 2002 No.3019
SPP(A)&SAP(AO)(No.2) Regs	The Statutory Paternity Pay (Adoption) and Statutory Adoption Pay (Adoptions from Overseas) (No.2) Regulations 2003 No.1194
SPPSAP(A) Regs	The Statutory Paternity Pay and Statutory Adoption Pay (Administration) Regulations 2002 No.2820
SPPSAP(G) Regs	The Statutory Paternity Pay and Statutory Adoption Pay (General) Regulations 2002 No.2822
SPPSAP(PAM) Regs	The Statutory Paternity Pay and Statutory Adoption Pay (Persons Abroad and Mariners) Regulations 2002 No.2821
SPPSAP(POPA) Regs	The Statutory Paternity Pay and Statutory Adoption Pay (Parental Orders and Prospective Adopters) Regulations 2014 No.2934
SPPSAP(WR) Regs	The Statutory Paternity Pay and Statutory Adoption Pay (Weekly Rates) Regulations 2002 No.2818
SS(AA) Regs	The Social Security (Attendance Allowance) Regulations 1991 No.2740
SS(CatE) Regs	The Social Security (Categorisation of Earners) Regulations 1978 No.1689
SS(CCPC) Regs	Social Security (Contribution Credits for Parents and Carers) Regulations 2010 No.19

SS(Con) Regs	The Social Security (Contributions) Regulations 2001 No.1004
SS(C&P) Regs	The Social Security (Claims and Payments) Regulations 1987 No.1968
SS(CP)Regs	The Social Security (Civil Penalties) Regulations 2012 No.1990
SS(Cr) Regs	The Social Security (Credits) Regulations 1975 No.556
SS(CTCNIN)Regs	The Social Security (Crediting and Treatment of Contributions, and National Insurance Numbers) Regulations 2001 No.769
SS(DLA) Regs	The Social Security (Disability Living Allowance) Regulations 1991 No.2890
SS(DLA,AA&CA)(A) Regs	The Social Security (Disability Living Allowance, Attendance Allowance and Carer's Allowance) (Amendment) Regulations 2013 No.389
SS(DLA)A Regs	Social Security (Disability Living Allowance) (Amendment) Regulations 2010 No.1651
SS(DRPSAPGRB)(MP) Regs	The Social Security (Deferral of Retirement Pension, Shared Additional Pension and Graduated Retirement Benefit)(Miscellaneous Provisions) Regulations 2005 No.2677
SS(EEEIIP) Regs	The Social Security (Employed Earners' Employment for Industrial Injuries Purposes) Regulations 1975 No.467
SS(EF) Regs	The Social Security (Earnings Factor) Regulations 1979 No.676
SS(GB) Regs	The Social Security (General Benefits) Regulations 1982 No.1408
SS(GRB)(No.2) Regs	The Social Security (Graduated Retirement Benefit) (No.2) Regulations 1978 No.393
SS(HCA) Regs	The Social Security (Housing Costs Amendments) Regulations 2015 No.1647
SS(HCSA)(A&M) Regs	The Social Security (Housing Costs Special Arrangements) (Amendment and Modification) Regulations 2008 No.3195
SS(HIP) Regs	The Social Security (Hospital In-Patients) Regulations 2005 No.3360
SS(HR)A Regs	The Social Security (Habitual Residence) Amendment Regulations 2004 No.1232
SS(IA)CA Regs	The Social Security (Immigration and Asylum) Consequential Amendments Regulations 2000 No.636
SS(IB) Regs	The Social Security (Incapacity Benefit) Regulations 1994 No.2946
SS(GBRA)NI Regs	The Social Security (Great Britain Reciprocal Arrangements) Regulations (Northern Ireland) 2016 No.149
SS(IB)MA Regs	The Social Security (Incapacity Benefit) Miscellaneous Amendments Regulations 2000 No.3120

A

SS(IB)(T) Regs	The Social Security (Incapacity Benefit) (Transitional) Regulations 1995 No.310
SS(IB-ID) Regs	The Social Security (Incapacity Benefit – Increases for Dependants) Regulations 1994 No.2945
SS(IBWFI) Regs	The Social Security (Incapacity Benefit Work-focused Interviews) Regulations 2008 No.2928
SS(ICA) Regs	The Social Security (Invalid Care Allowance) Regulations 1976 No.409
SS(IFW) Regs	The Social Security (Incapacity for Work) (General) Regulations 1995 No.311
SS(II)(AB) Regs	The Social Security (Industrial Injuries) (Airmen's Benefits) Regulations 1975 No.469
SS(II)(MB) Regs	The Social Security (Industrial Injuries) (Mariners' Benefits) Regulations 1975 No.470
SS(II&D)MP Regs	The Social Security (Industrial Injuries and Diseases) Miscellaneous Provisions Regulations 1986 No.1561
SS(II)(PD) Regs	The Social Security (Industrial Injuries) (Prescribed Diseases) Regulations 1985 No.967
SS(II)(RE) Regs	The Social Security (Industrial Injuries) (Regular Employment) Regulations 1990 No.256
SS(JPI) Regs	The Social Security (Jobcentre Plus Interviews) Regulations 2002 No.1703
SS(JPIP) Regs	Social Security (Jobcentre Plus Interviews for Partners) Regulations 2003 No.1886
SS(JSA&ESA)(WD)A Regs	The Social Security (Jobseeker's Allowance and Employment and Support Allowance) (Waiting Days) Amendment Regulations 2014 No.2309
SS(LAIP) Regs	The Social Security (Local Authority Investigations and Prosecutions) Regulations 2008 No.463
SS(LB) Regs	The Social Security (Loss of Benefit) Regulations 2001 No.4022
SS(LP) Regs	The Social Security (Lone Parents and Miscellaneous Amendments) Regulations 2012 No.874
SS(LPMA) Regs	The Social Security (Lone Parents and Miscellaneous Amendments) Regulations 2008 No.3051
SS(MA)(No.5) Regs 2009	The Social Security (Miscellaneous Amendments) (No.5) Regulations 2009 No.3228
SS(MA)(No.5) Regs 2010	The Social Security (Miscellaneous Amendments) (No.5) Regulations 2010 No.2429
SS(MAP) Regs	The Social Security (Maximum Additional Pension) Regulations 1978 No.949
SS(MatA) Regs	The Social Security (Maternity Allowance) Regulations 1987 No.416
SS(MatA)(E) Regs	The Social Security (Maternity Allowance) (Earnings) Regulations 2000 No.688
SS(MatA)(WA) Regs	The Social Security (Maternity Allowance) (Work Abroad) Regulations 1987 No.417

A

SS(ME) Regs	The Social Security (Medical Evidence) Regulations 1976 No.615
SS(NCC) Regs	The Social Security (Notification of Change of Circumstances) Regulations 2001 No.3252
SS(NIRA) Regs	The Social Security (Northern Ireland Reciprocal Arrangements) Regulations 2016 No.287
SS(OB) Regs	The Social Security (Overlapping Benefits) Regulations 1979 No.597
SS(OR) Regs	The Social Security (Overpayments and Recovery) Regulations 2013 No.384
SS(PA)A Regs	Social Security (Persons from Abroad) Amendment Regulations 2006 No.1026
SS(PAB) Regs	The Social Security (Payments on Account of Benefit) Regulations 2013 No.383
SS(PAOR) Regs	The Social Security (Payments on Account, Overpayments and Recovery) Regulations 1988 No.664
SS(PFA)MA Regs	The Social Security (Persons From Abroad) Miscellaneous Amendment Regulations 1996 No.30
SS(PIP) Regs	The Social Security (Personal Independence Payment) Regulations 2013 No.377
SS(RB) Regs	The Social Security (Recovery of Benefits) Regulations 1997 No.2205
SS(RB)App Regs	The Social Security (Recovery of Benefits) (Appeals) Regulations 1997 No.2237
SS(SDA) Regs	The Social Security (Severe Disablement Allowances) Regulations 1984 No.1303
SS(STB)(T) Regs	The Social Security (Short-term Benefits) (Transitional) Regulations 1974 No.2192
SS(WB&RP) Regs	The Social Security (Widow's Benefit and Retirement Pensions) Regulations 1979 No.642
SS(WBRP&OB)(T) Regs	The Social Security (Widow's Benefit, Retirement Pensions and Other Benefits) (Transitional) Regulations 1979 No.643
SS(WFILP) Regs	The Social Security (Work-focused Interviews for Lone Parents) and Miscellaneous Amendments Regulations 2000 No.1926
SS(WTCCTC)(CA) Regs	The Social Security (Working Tax Credit and Child Tax Credit) (Consequential Amendments) Regulations 2003 No.455
SSA(F)AO No.5	The Social Security Administration (Fraud) Act 1997 (Commencement No.5) Order 1997 No.2766
SSB(CE) Regs	The Social Security Benefit (Computation of Earnings) Regulations 1996 No.2745
SSB(Dep) Regs	The Social Security Benefit (Dependency) Regulations 1977 No.343
SSB(MW&WSP) Regs	The Social Security (Benefit) (Married Women and Widows Special Provisions) Regulations 1974 No.2010

SSB(PA) Regs	The Social Security Benefit (Persons Abroad) Regulations 1975 No.563
SSB(PRT) Regs	The Social Security Benefit (Persons Residing Together) Regulations 1977 No.956
SSC(DA) Regs	The Social Security Contributions (Decisions and Appeals) Regulations 1999 No.1027
SSC3AC(UAP) Regs	The Social Security Class 3A Contributions (Units of Additional Pension) Regulations 2014 No.3240
SSCBA(AAO) Regs	The Social Security Contributions and Benefits Act 1992 (Application of Parts 12ZA and 12ZB to Adoptions from Overseas) Regulations 2003 No.499
SSCBA(APOC) Regs	The Social Security Contributions and Benefits Act 1992 (Application of Parts 12ZA, 12ZB and 12ZC to Parental Order Cases) Regulations 2014 No.2866
SSCBA(MHMFIB) Regs	The Social Security Contributions and Benefits Act 1992 (Modifications for Her Majesty's Forces and Incapacity Benefit) Regulations 2003 No.737
SSCP(TCA) Regs	The Social Security Commissioners (Procedure) (Tax Credit Appeals) Regulations 2002 No.3237
SS&CS(DA) Regs	The Social Security and Child Support (Decisions and Appeals) Regulations 1999 No.991
SSCSVDOP(DA)(A) Regs	The Social Security, Child Support, Vaccine Damage and Other Payments (Decisions and Appeals) (Amendment) Regulations 2013 SI No.2380
SSFA(PM) Regs	The Social Security and Family Allowances (Polygamous Marriages) Regulations 1975 No.561
SSP Regs	The Statutory Sick Pay (General) Regulations 1982 No.894
SSP(MAPA) Regs	The Statutory Sick Pay (Mariners, Airmen and Persons Abroad) Regulations 1982 No.1349
SSP(ME) Regs	The Statutory Sick Pay (Medical Evidence) Regulations 1985 No.1604
SSP&SMP(D) Regs	The Statutory Sick Pay and Statutory Maternity Pay (Decisions) Regulations 1999 No.776
SSPP(A) Regs	The Statutory Shared Parental Pay (Administration) Regulations 2014 No.2929
SSPP(G) Regs	The Statutory Shared Parental Pay (General) Regulations 2014 No.3051
SSPP(PAM) Regs	The Statutory Shared Parental Pay (Persons Abroad and Mariners) Regulations 2014 No.3134
SSPP(POC) Regs	The Statutory Shared Parental Pay (Parental Order Cases) Regulations 2014 No.3097
TC(A) Regs	The Tax Credits (Appeals) Regulations 2002 No.2926
TC(A)(No.2) Regs	The Tax Credits (Appeals) (No.2) Regulations 2002 No.3196
TC(CN) Regs	The Tax Credits (Claims and Notifications) Regulations 2002 No.2014

TC(DCI) Regs	The Tax Credits (Definition and Calculation of Income) Regulations 2002 No.2006
TC(Imm) Regs	The Tax Credits (Immigration) Regulations 2003 No.653
TC(IR) Regs	The Tax Credits (Interest Rate) Regulations 2003 No.123
TC(ITDR) Regs	The Tax Credits (Income Thresholds and Determination of Rates) Regulations 2002 No.2008
TC(NA)Regs	The Tax Credits (Notice of Appeal) Regulations 2002 No.3119
TC(OE) Regs	The Tax Credits (Official Error) Regulations 2003 No.692
TC(PC) Regs	The Tax Credits (Payments by the Commissioners) Regulations 2002 No.2173
TC(PM) Regs	The Tax Credits (Polygamous Marriages) Regulations 2003 No.742
TC(R) Regs	The Tax Credits (Residence) Regulations 2003 No.654
TCA(No.3)O	The Tax Credits Act 2002 (Commencement No.3 and Transitional Provisions and Savings) Order 2003 No.938
TCA(TP)O	The Tax Credits Act 2002 (Transitional Provisions) Order 2010 No.644
TP(FT) Rules	The Tribunal Procedure (First-tier Tribunal) (Social Entitlement Chamber) Rules 2008 No.2685
TP(FT)(TC) Rules	The Tribunal Procedure (First-tier Tribunal) (Tax Chamber) Rules 2009 No.273
TP(UT) Rules	The Tribunal Procedure (Upper Tribunal) Rules 2008 No.2698
UC Regs	The Universal Credit Regulations 2013 No.376
UC,PIP,JSA&ESA(C&P) Regs	The Universal Credit, Personal Independence Payment, Jobseeker's Allowance and Employment and Support Allowance (Claims and Payments) Regulations 2013 No.380
UC,PIP,JSA&ESA(DA) Regs	The Universal Credit, Personal Independence Payment, Jobseeker's Allowance and Employment and Support Allowance (Decisions and Appeals) Regulations 2013 No.381
UC(TP) Regs	The Universal Credit (Transitional Provisions) Regulations 2014 No.1230
UC(TP)(A) Regs	The Universal Credit (Transitional Provisions) (Amendment) Regulations 2014 No.1626
WF Regs	The Welfare Food Regulations 1996 No.1434
WRA(No.8)O	The Welfare Reform Act 2012 (Commencement No.8 and Savings and Transitional Provisions) Order 2013 No.358
WRA(No.9)O	The Welfare Reform Act 2012 (Commencement No.9 and Transitional and Transitory Provisions and Commencement No.8 and Savings and Transitional Provisions (Amendment)) Order 2013 No.983

A

WRA(No.11)O	The Welfare Reform Act 2012 (Commencement No.11 and Transitional and Transitory Provisions and Commencement No.9 and Transitional and Transitory Provisions (Amendment)) Order 2013 No.1511
WRA(No.13)O	The Welfare Reform Act 2012 (Commencement No.13 and Transitional and Transitory Provisions) Order 2013 No.2657
WRA(No.14)O	The Welfare Reform Act 2012 (Commencement No.14 and Transitional and Transitory Provisions) Order 2013 No.2846
WRA(No.16)O	The Welfare Reform Act 2012 (Commencement No.16 and Transitional and Transitory Provisions) Order 2014 No.209
WRA(No.23)O	The Welfare Reform Act 2012 (Commencement No.23 and Transitional and Transitory Provisions) Order 2015 No.634
WRA(C)(A)O	The Welfare Reform Act 2012 (Commencement No.9, 11, 13, 14 and 16 and Transitional and Transitory Provisions (Amendment)) Order 2014 No.1452
WRPA(No.9)O	The Welfare Reform and Pensions Act 1999 (Commencement No.9, Transitional Provisions and Savings) Order 2000 No.2958
WTC(EMR) Regs	The Working Tax Credit (Entitlement and Maximum Rate) Regulations 2002 No.2005

Other information

ADM	*Advice for Decision Making*, vols A1-V8
BLG	*Social Fund Budgeting Loan Guide*
CBTM	*Child Benefit Technical Manual*
CCM	*Claimant Compliance Manual* (HMRC guidance on investigation of tax credit claims)
DMG	*Decision Makers' Guide*, vols 1-14
GM	*Housing Benefit/Council Tax Benefit Guidance Manual*
PIP AG	*PIP Assessment Guide*
SF Dir	*Social Fund Directive*
TCM	*Tax Credits Manual*
TCTM	*Tax Credits Technical Manual*

A

Appendix 14

'Two-child limit' exceptions

A child element is payable for a third or subsequent child to whom the 'two-child limit' would apply but who is one of the following.

- A child born in a multiple birth, other than the first born if you already have two or more children, So, if you have:
  - no older children, you get the child element for all children in a multiple birth;
  - one older child, you get the child element for all children in a multiple birth;
  - two or more older children, you get the child element for all but one of the children in a multiple birth.
- A child living with you on a long-term basis because s/he is unable to live with her/his parents and you are caring for her/him as a family member or friend. You or your partner must not be the child's parent or step-parent and you must:
  - be named in a child arrangements order under section 8 of the Children Act 1989 or a residence order under article 8 of the Children (Northern Ireland) Order 1995 as a person with whom the child is to live; *or*
  - be the appointed or special guardian, or be entitled to guardian's allowance, for the child; *or*
  - have a kinship care order under section 72(1) of the Children and Young People (Scotland) Act 2014, or parental responsibilities or rights under section 80 of the Adoption and Children (Scotland) Act 2007 for the child; *or*
  - continue to be responsible for the child if any of the above bullet points applied immediately before the child's 16th birthday; *or*
  - have taken care of the child in circumstances in which it is likely that s/he would otherwise have been looked after by a local authority.
- A child who is being adopted by you from local authority care or who has been placed with you for adoption. This exception does *not* apply if:
  - you or your partner were the child's step-parent immediately before the adoption;
  - you or your partner have been the child's parent (other than by adoption) at any other time;
  - the child is being adopted directly from abroad.

A

- A child who is likely to have been conceived as a result of rape, or in a controlling or coercive relationship. You must not be living at the same address as the alleged perpetrator at the time for the exception to apply. A controlling or coercive relationship includes behaviour that causes you to fear, on at least two occasions, that violence will be used against you, or that causes you serious alarm or distress which has a substantial adverse effect on your day-to-day activities. You must provide evidence from an 'approved person' that you have had contact with her/him or another approved person about the rape or relationship. A list of 'approved persons' will be set out in guidance, but is expected to include healthcare professionals, police officers, social workers, registered counsellors, independent sexual violence advisers and approved organisations such as specialist rape charities. Third-party evidence is not required if there has been a conviction for rape or coercive, controlling behaviour in the UK, or for a similar offence abroad, or if you have been awarded criminal injuries compensation in respect of a sexual offence, physical abuse or mental injury, and it is likely that the offence or injury resulted in the conception. For child tax credit (CTC), you can be treated as having provided evidence if you have already provided it to the DWP for universal credit (UC), income support (IS) or jobseeker's allowance (JSA) purposes. For UC, you can be treated as having provided evidence if you have already provided it to HM Revenue and Customs in relation to CTC.
- For CTC, a child whose parent is a child or qualifying young person for whom you are responsible. For UC, a child whose parent is a child under 16 for whom you are responsible.

Third or subsequent child

The order of children (ie, whether a child is the first, second, third or subsequent child) is determined by allocating each child a date:
- if you or your partner are the child's parent, the child's date of birth; or
- in any other case, the date you or your partner became responsible for the child.

The order of children is usually decided according to the earliest of these dates – ie, the child with the earliest allocated date is the 'first child', and so on. However, the order of children must be decided in order to ensure you receive the highest number of child elements if:
- the date for two or more children is the same; or
- you give birth to a child less than 10 months after you became responsible for another child under a 'non-parental caring arrangement'. In this situation, the child under a non-parental caring arrangement is deemed to be the 'third or subsequent child', so that the exception can apply.

Index

How to use this Index

Because the *Handbook* is divided into separate sections covering the different benefits, many entries in the index have several references, each to a different section. Where this occurs, we use the following abbreviations to show to which benefit each reference relates.

AA	Attendance allowance	I-JSA	Income-based jobseeker's allowance
CA	Carer's allowance		
C-ESA	Contributory employment and support allowance	JSA	Jobseeker's allowance
		MA	Maternity allowance
C-JSA	Contribution-based jobseeker's allowance	NI	National insurance
		PC	Pension credit
CTC	Child tax credit	PIP	Personal independence payment
DLA	Disability living allowance	SAP	Statutory adoption pay
ESA	Employment and support allowance	SDA	Severe disablement allowance
HB	Housing benefit	SMP	Statutory maternity pay
IB	Incapacity benefit	SPP	Statutory paternity pay
IIDB	Industrial injuries disablement benefit	SSP	Statutory sick pay
		SSPP	Statutory shared parental pay
IS	Income support	UC	Universal credit
I-ESA	Income-related employment and support allowance	WTC	Working tax credit

Entries against the bold headings direct you to the general information on the subject, or where the subject is covered most fully. Sub-entries are listed alphabetically and direct you to specific aspects of the subject.

Court of Appeal
appealing Upper Tribunal decisions
benefits 1375
WTC/CTC 1510
SSP/SMP/SAP/SPP/SSPP 1392
Court of Session
appealing Upper Tribunal decisions
benefits 1375
WTC/CTC 1510
SSP/SMP/SAP/SSP/SSPP 1392
courts
appealing Upper Tribunal decisions
benefits 1375
WTC/CTC 1510
compensation 1403
recovery of overpayments 1238
HB 1248
UC system 1240
credit sale agreements
HB 47
Creutzfeld-Jakob disease
payments disregarded
over PC age 395
UC 348
under PC age 368
WTC/CTC 1442
Croatia 1546
jobseekers 1547
legally working 1550
not subject to worker authorisation 1548
pregnancy 1557
resided legally 1568
residence rights 1546
restrictions 1547
retaining worker status 1547
self-employment 1558
workers 1547
croft land 362, 390
HB 46
Crown servants
child benefit 1573
WTC/CTC 1604
Crown tenants
HB 46
rent met by IS/I-JSA/I-ESA/PC 453
currency
payments in non-UK currencies
CA 562
means-tested benefits over PC age 328
means-tested benefits under PC age 298
WTC/CTC 1443
custody
see: prisoner
Czech Republic 1546

D
daily living activities
PIP 737
Data Protection Act
access to personal information 1257

date of claim
AA 528
bereavement benefits 548
CA 565
child benefit 588
CTC 190
DLA 616
ESA
C-ESA 649
I-ESA 39
funeral expenses payments 796
guardian's allowance 588
HB 76
industrial injuries benefits 692
IS 111
JSA
C-JSA 712
I-JSA 137
MA 730
PC 154
PIP 757
state pension 780
Sure Start maternity grant 791
UC 171
WTC 207
Day One Support for Young People 1104
daytime attention/supervision 609
deafness
DLA care component 607
DLA mobility component 600
occupational 680, 685
students
HB 884
death
claimant's death
HB 84
delayed claims for bereavement benefits 549
funeral expenses payments 791
of child
child benefit 591
CTC 182
disabled child premium 237
guardian's allowance 591
UC 259
of friend/relative, available for work rule
JSA 1036
of person receiving care
CA 557
parents
guardian's allowance 583
presumption of death for bereavement benefits 549
recovery of funeral expenses payments 797
recovery of overpayments from estate 1234
HB 1245
rent restriction delayed
HB 436
UC 503
reporting 1184